Winter 2016 Volume 21, Number 2

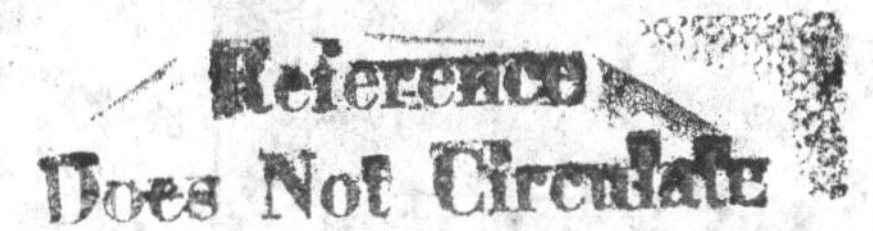

Judicial
YELLOW BOOK

who's who in
federal and
state courts

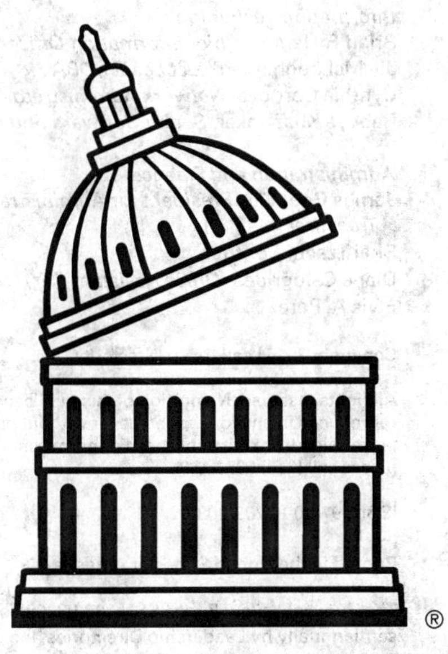

LEADERSHIP DIRECTORIES, INC.

Web Site: www.leadershipdirectories.com
E-mail: info@leadershipdirectories.com

New York Office
1407 Broadway, Suite 318
New York, NY 10018
(212) 627-4140
Fax (212) 645-0931

Washington, DC Office
1667 K Street, NW, Suite 801
Washington, DC 20006
(202) 347-7757
Fax (202) 628-3430

Congressional
YELLOW BOOK
who's who in congress,
including committees and key staff

Federal
YELLOW BOOK
who's who in federal departments and agencies

State
YELLOW BOOK
who's who in the executive and legislative branches of the 50 state governments

Municipal
YELLOW BOOK
who's who in the leading city and county governments and local authorities

Federal Regional
YELLOW BOOK
who's who in the federal government's departments, agencies, diplomatic missions, military installations and service academies outside of Washington, DC

Judicial
YELLOW BOOK
who's who in federal and state courts

Corporate
YELLOW BOOK
who's who at the leading U.S. companies

Financial
YELLOW BOOK
who's who at the leading U.S. financial institutions

News Media
YELLOW BOOK
who's who among reporters, writers, editors and producers in the leading national news media

Associations
YELLOW BOOK
who's who at the leading U.S. trade and professional associations

Law Firms
YELLOW BOOK
who's who in the management of the leading U.S. law firms

Government Affairs
YELLOW BOOK
who's who in government affairs

Foreign Representatives
YELLOW BOOK
who's who in the U.S. offices of foreign corporations, foreign nations, the foreign press and intergovernmental organizations

Nonprofit Sector
YELLOW BOOK
who's who in the management of the leading foundations, universities, museums, and other nonprofit organizations

The Leadership Library®
who's who in the leadership of the United States

Leadership Directories, Inc.
JUDICIAL YELLOW BOOK

Winter 2016, Volume 21, Number 2

Brian C. Beth, *Content Manager*

William W. Cressey, *Chairman of the Board*
Gretchen Teichgraeber, *President and Chief Executive Officer*
James M. Petrie, *Secretary*

Sales, Marketing, and Customer Service
Tom Silver, *Senior Vice President, Sales and Marketing*
Imogene Akins Hutchinson, *Vice President, Brand Development*
Jacqueline Johnson, *Fulfillment Manager*
Michele Anderson; Laurie Consoli;
Anne Marie Del Vecchio; Heather Donegal; Ed Faas;
Alan Fan; Melissa Kaus; Jack Levengard; Jim Marcus;
William Schneider; Nancy Scholem; Judy Smith;
Wanda Speight-Bridgers

Products and Content
Sue Healy, *Senior Vice President, Products and Content*
Tom Zurla, *Assistant Vice President, Content*
Carmela Makabali, *Senior Director, Content and Database Management*
Harris Beringer, *Product Manager*
Dave Marmon, *Senior Product Specialist*
Gareth Sparks, *Manager, Content Development and Quality*
Brendan Timmons, *Product Specialist*

Information Technology
Brian F. Hanley, *Chief Information Officer*
Jill McLoughlin, *Project Leader/DBA*
Cynthia Cordova, *Network Administrator*
Rabeya Khandaker, *Senior Software Engineer*

Administration and Finance
James Gee, *Vice President for Administration and Treasurer*
Shai Tzach, *Controller*
Diane Calogrides, *Office Assistant (NY)*
Elvis A. Perez

ISBN: 978-0-87289-288-0

Printed in the United States of America.

The *Judicial Yellow Book* (ISSN 1082-3298) is published semiannually by Leadership Directories, Inc., 1407 Broadway, Suite 318, New York, NY 10018. Annual subscription: $485. Additional subscriptions delivered to the same individual and address: $364. For airmail postage: Canada and Mexico add $75 per subscription. Outside North America add $100 per subscription.

POSTMASTER: Send address changes to *Judicial Yellow Book*, Leadership Directories, Inc., 1407 Broadway, Suite 318, New York, NY 10018.

For additional information, including details about other Leadership Directories, Inc. publications, please call (212) 627-4140.

Judicial
YELLOW BOOK

Winter 2016

Table of Contents

(continued on next page)

For The Record

By Brian C. Beth
Content Manager, *Judicial Yellow Book* November 16, 2015

This column highlights changes that have taken place in the federal and state judiciaries since publication of the Summer 2015 edition of the *Judicial Yellow Book*.

At the federal level, the Winter 2016 edition provides information on more than 200 courts, 2,300 judges, and 8,500 judicial staff. At the state level, this edition includes information on more than 200 courts, 1,400 judges, and 4,200 judicial personnel. Within the United States Department of Justice, this edition includes information on more than 1,100 DOJ staff in DC area offices, as well as 3,300 United States Attorneys and 1,300 United States Marshals at regional offices.

The Leadership® Content Commitment

Leadership Directories provides high quality, accurate and up to date information on the key leaders in government, business, legal, media and nonprofit organizations in the United States. Every item of information on more than 750,000 people and 150,000 organizations has been verified at the source.

Judicial Yellow Book on the Internet

Leadership® Law Premium is the online version of the *Judicial Yellow Book.* It is available as an annual subscription and includes daily updates and additional content not available in the print directory, plus searching, list-building, and exporting capabilities. For more information, please contact us at (212) 627-4140.

Federal Courts

The following judges have been confirmed and sworn in since the Summer 2015 edition of the *Judicial Yellow Book*. Their chambers are now included for the first time in the *Judicial Yellow Book.*

United States District Courts

Judge	Court	Sworn in
Jill Parrish	District of Utah	8/17/2015
Rolando Olvera	Southern District of Texas	8/31/2015
Ann M. Donnelly	Eastern District of New York	10/21/2015
Lawrence Joseph Vilardo	Western District of New York	10/29/2015
Dale Drozd	Eastern District of California	11/2/2015

For a current list of Presidential judicial nominations please visit:
www.leadershipdirectories.com/About/judicialnominations.aspx

State Courts

The following judges were appointed or elected to their positions by state judicial commissions and governors since the Summer 2015 edition of the *Judicial Yellow Book*.

Judge	Court
Christopher Staring	Arizona Court of Appeals, Division Two
Richard L. Gabriel	Colorado Supreme Court
Elizabeth Harris	Colorado Court of Appeals
Susan L. Kelsey	Florida Court of Appeals, First District
Thomas D. Winokur	Florida Court of Appeals, First District
Robert Altice Jr.	Indiana Court of Appeals, Second District
Samuel T. Wright	Kentucky Supreme Court
D. Kent Savoie	Louisana Court of Appeals Third Circuit
Thomas E. Humphrey	Supreme Judicial Court of Maine
Joan Larsen	Michigan Supreme Court
Natalie E. Hudson	Minnesota Supreme Court
Jack Wilson	Court of Appeals of the State of Mississippi
James M. Dowd	Missouri Court of Appeals, Eastern District
Stephanie Stacy	Nebraska Supreme Court
David Wecht	Supreme Court of Pennsylvania
Kevin M. Dougherty	Supreme Court of Pennsylvania
Christine Donohue	Supreme Court of Pennsylvania
Jane Marum Roush	Supreme Court of Virginia
Rebecca Bradley	Wisconsin Supreme Court
Keith Kautz	Wyoming Supreme Court

The Summer 2016 edition of the *Judicial Yellow Book* will be published in June 2016. As always, the editors of the *Judicial Yellow Book* extend our sincere thanks to the hundreds of government employees who have consistently taken time out of their busy schedules to provide us with accurate and timely information, enabling the *Judicial Yellow Book* to remain as current as possible. We always welcome your comments and suggestions on improving the *Judicial Yellow Book*. We can be reached by phone at (202) 347-7757, by fax at (202) 628-3430, and by email at info@leadershipdirectories.com.

User's Guide

The *Judicial Yellow Book* is divided into five sections: Federal Courts, State Courts, the Department of Justice, Regional Offices, and Indexes. The Federal Courts section lists courts in the following order: The Supreme Court of the United States, United States Courts of Appeals, United States District Courts (arranged alphabetically by state), United States Courts of Limited Jurisdiction, Judicial Conference of the United States, Administrative Office of the United States Courts, Federal Judicial Center, and United States Sentencing Commission. State courts are arranged by state. The State Courts section includes all appellate courts for the 50 states, the District of Columbia, and the four US territories. Within each court, judges are listed hierarchically and in order of seniority. The Department of Justice section lists the DC-based operations and high-ranking officials of the DOJ. The Regional Offices section lists the regional operations of the Executive Office for United States Attorneys and United States Marshals Service.

The following elements are common to most Court entries:

1 Each Listing begins with the court's name, address and communications information (telephone, facsimile, PACER and VCIS numbers, and e-mail and Internet addresses). Courts and offices should be contacted before faxing documents. PACER (Public Access to Court Electronic Records) allows people with a PC to call a district or bankruptcy court database to procure official electronic case information and court dockets. There are fees for PACER usage, and all users must first register with the PACER Service Center (from outside the San Antonio, Texas area, call 1-800-676-6856; in the San Antonio area, call 210-308-3810). This number also may be used to obtain additional information on computer system requirements. VCIS (Voice Case Information System) utilizes an automated voice response system to read case information from a bankruptcy court computer in answer to touch-tone telephone inquiries. VCIS service is free of charge.

2 The **General Information** section may contain a description of the court, the number of judgeships, and the geographic jurisdiction of the court.

3 The **Court Staff** section provides names, titles, communications information (telephone and facsimile numbers, and e-mail addresses), addresses, and educational background.

4 Judges' Listings may include both physical and mailing addresses, communications information, appointment and election information, a short biographical sketch, and judge's staff. The following are elements of the biographical sketch: (a) Date of Birth (b) Education (c) Academic positions the judge may have held (d) Clerkships in a judge's chambers (e) Corporate positions (f) Government positions (g) Judicial positions (h) Legal Practice (i) Military Service (j) Nonprofit positions (k) Current Memberships.

5 Education and Communications Information is provided for each judge's staff immediately following the biographical sketch.

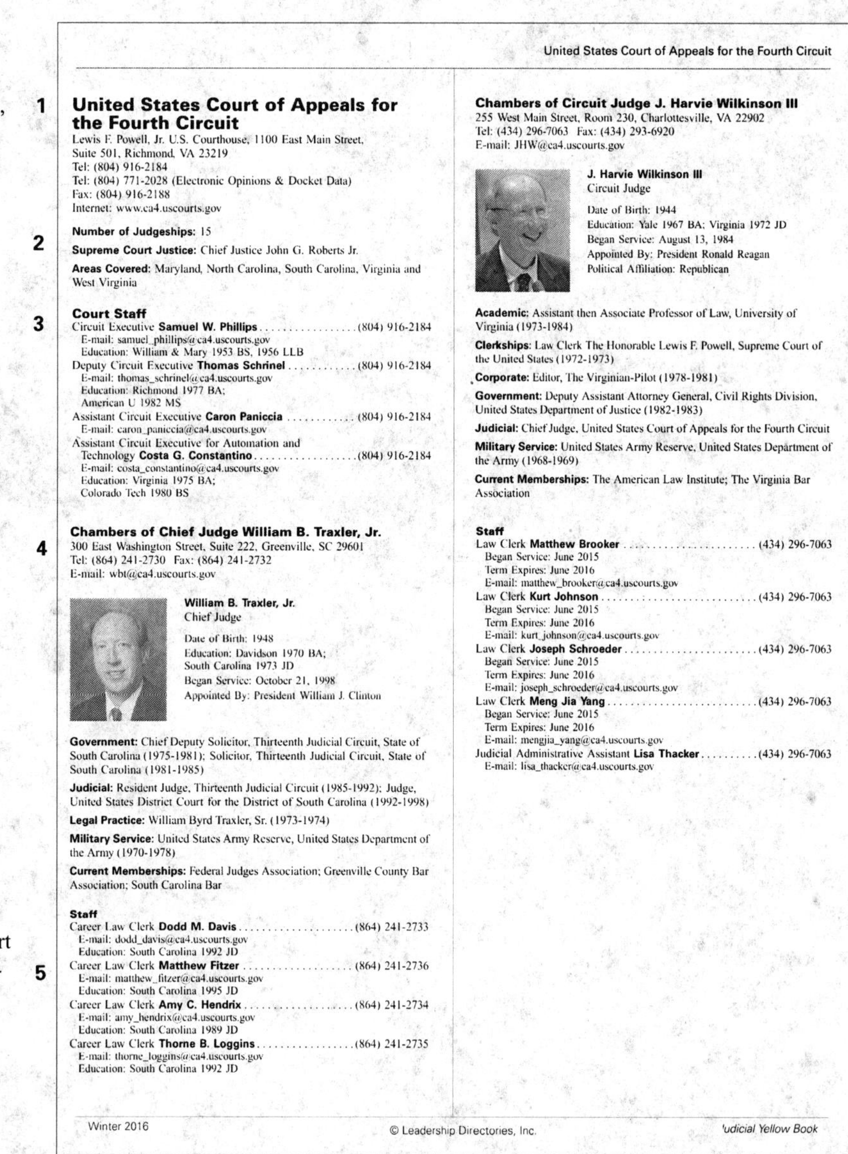

United States Court of Appeals for the Fourth Circuit

1 **United States Court of Appeals for the Fourth Circuit**
Lewis F. Powell, Jr. U.S. Courthouse, 1100 East Main Street, Suite 501, Richmond, VA 23219
Tel: (804) 916-2184
Tel: (804) 771-2028 (Electronic Opinions & Docket Data)
Fax: (804) 916-2188
Internet: www.ca4.uscourts.gov

Number of Judgeships: 15
2 **Supreme Court Justice:** Chief Justice John G. Roberts Jr.
Areas Covered: Maryland, North Carolina, South Carolina, Virginia and West Virginia

Court Staff
3 Circuit Executive **Samuel W. Phillips** . . . . . (804) 916-2184
E-mail: samuel_phillips@ca4.uscourts.gov
Education: William & Mary 1953 BS, 1956 LLB
Deputy Circuit Executive **Thomas Schrinel** . . . . . (804) 916-2184
E-mail: thomas_schrinel@ca4.uscourts.gov
Education: Richmond 1977 BA; American U 1982 MS
Assistant Circuit Executive **Caron Paniccia** . . . . . (804) 916-2184
E-mail: caron_paniccia@ca4.uscourts.gov
Assistant Circuit Executive for Automation and Technology **Costa G. Constantino** . . . . . (804) 916-2184
E-mail: costa_constantino@ca4.uscourts.gov
Education: Virginia 1975 BA; Colorado Tech 1980 BS

Chambers of Chief Judge William B. Traxler, Jr.
4 300 East Washington Street, Suite 222, Greenville, SC 29601
Tel: (864) 241-2730 Fax: (864) 241-2732
E-mail: wbt@ca4.uscourts.gov

William B. Traxler, Jr.
Chief Judge
Date of Birth: 1948
Education: Davidson 1970 BA; South Carolina 1973 JD
Began Service: October 21, 1998
Appointed By: President William J. Clinton

Government: Chief Deputy Solicitor, Thirteenth Judicial Circuit, State of South Carolina (1975-1981); Solicitor, Thirteenth Judicial Circuit, State of South Carolina (1981-1985)

Judicial: Resident Judge, Thirteenth Judicial Circuit (1985-1992); Judge, United States District Court for the District of South Carolina (1992-1998)

Legal Practice: William Byrd Traxler, Sr. (1973-1974)

Military Service: United States Army Reserve, United States Department of the Army (1970-1978)

Current Memberships: Federal Judges Association; Greenville County Bar Association; South Carolina Bar

Staff
Career Law Clerk **Dodd M. Davis** . . . . . (864) 241-2733
E-mail: dodd_davis@ca4.uscourts.gov
Education: South Carolina 1992 JD
5 Career Law Clerk **Matthew Fitzer** . . . . . (864) 241-2736
E-mail: matthew_fitzer@ca4.uscourts.gov
Education: South Carolina 1995 JD
Career Law Clerk **Amy C. Hendrix** . . . . . (864) 241-2734
E-mail: amy_hendrix@ca4.uscourts.gov
Education: South Carolina 1989 JD
Career Law Clerk **Thorne B. Loggins** . . . . . (864) 241-2735
E-mail: thorne_loggins@ca4.uscourts.gov
Education: South Carolina 1992 JD

Chambers of Circuit Judge J. Harvie Wilkinson III
255 West Main Street, Room 230, Charlottesville, VA 22902
Tel: (434) 296-7063 Fax: (434) 293-6920
E-mail: JHW@ca4.uscourts.gov

J. Harvie Wilkinson III
Circuit Judge
Date of Birth: 1944
Education: Yale 1967 BA; Virginia 1972 JD
Began Service: August 13, 1984
Appointed By: President Ronald Reagan
Political Affiliation: Republican

Academic: Assistant then Associate Professor of Law, University of Virginia (1973-1984)

Clerkships: Law Clerk The Honorable Lewis F. Powell, Supreme Court of the United States (1972-1973)

Corporate: Editor, The Virginian-Pilot (1978-1981)

Government: Deputy Assistant Attorney General, Civil Rights Division, United States Department of Justice (1982-1983)

Judicial: Chief Judge, United States Court of Appeals for the Fourth Circuit

Military Service: United States Army Reserve, United States Department of the Army (1968-1969)

Current Memberships: The American Law Institute; The Virginia Bar Association

Staff
Law Clerk **Matthew Brooker** . . . . . (434) 296-7063
Began Service: June 2015
Term Expires: June 2016
E-mail: matthew_brooker@ca4.uscourts.gov
Law Clerk **Kurt Johnson** . . . . . (434) 296-7063
Began Service: June 2015
Term Expires: June 2016
E-mail: kurt_johnson@ca4.uscourts.gov
Law Clerk **Joseph Schroeder** . . . . . (434) 296-7063
Began Service: June 2015
Term Expires: June 2016
E-mail: joseph_schroeder@ca4.uscourts.gov
Law Clerk **Meng Jia Yang** . . . . . (434) 296-7063
Began Service: June 2015
Term Expires: June 2016
E-mail: mengjia_yang@ca4.uscourts.gov
Judicial Administrative Assistant **Lisa Thacker** . . . . . (434) 296-7063
E-mail: lisa_thacker@ca4.uscourts.gov

Winter 2016 © Leadership Directories, Inc. Judicial Yellow Book

Indexes

To assist our subscribers, three indexes have been included in the *Judicial Yellow Book.*

▶Law School Index
Lists Federal and State Court judges and law clerks by their law schools and years of graduation.

▶Name Index
Lists all individuals who appear in the book alphabetically.

▶Organization Index
Lists all organizations that appear in the book alphabetically.

Federal Courts

Supreme Court of the United States [SCOTUS]

U.S. Supreme Court Building, One First Street, NE,
Washington, DC 20543
Tel: (202) 479-3000 Tel: (202) 479-3211 (Public Information)
Tel: (202) 479-3175 (Library)
Tel: (202) 479-3360 (Opinion Announcements)
Tel: (202) 479-3030 (Visitor Information) Fax: (202) 479-2962
Internet: www.supremecourt.gov

Number of Judgeships: 9

The Supreme Court of the United States is the only court mandated by the Constitution and is the court of last resort. The Supreme Court has original jurisdiction over all disputes involving foreign ministers and interstate disputes, and disputes between the federal and state governments. The Court has jurisdiction of cases originating from any other court if the case involves constitutional issues, federal laws or maritime treaties and laws. The Supreme Court may affirm, modify, reverse or remand a decision of a lower court. The Supreme Court is comprised of the Chief Justice and eight associate justices, who are appointed for life by the President and confirmed by the Senate. Among his or her responsibilities, each Justice is assigned to serve as "Circuit Justice" for one or more of the United States Judicial Circuits. The Court holds one term annually, commencing on the first Monday in October.

Court Staff

Clerk of the Court **Scott S. Harris** .... (202) 479-3011
Education: Yale 1988 BS; Virginia 1993 JD

Chief Deputy Clerk **Christopher W. Vasil** .... (202) 479-3027
E-mail: cvasil@supremecourt.gov
Education: Cleveland State 1970; Cleveland-Marshall 1975 JD

Reporter of Decisions **Christine Fallon** .... (202) 479-3000
E-mail: cfallon@supremecourt.gov
Education: West Virginia 1974; Columbus Law 1977 JD

Librarian **Linda Maslow** .... (202) 479-3000
E-mail: lmaslow@supremecourt.gov
Education: Queens Col (NY) 1977 BA; Harvard 1980 JD; Michigan 1984 MALS

Marshal **Pamela Talkin** .... (202) 479-3000
E-mail: ptalkin@supremecourt.gov
Education: Brooklyn 1968 BA, 1971 MA

Counsel **Ethan V. Torrey** .... (202) 479-3000
E-mail: etorrey@supremecourt.gov
Education: Pennsylvania 1992 BA; Columbia 1996 MA, 1999 JD

Curator **Catherine E. Fitts** .... (202) 479-3000
E-mail: cfitts@supremecourt.gov
Education: North Carolina 1987 BA; George Mason 2001 MS

Director of Information Technology **Robert J. Hawkins** .... (202) 479-3000
E-mail: rhawkins@supremecourt.gov

Public Information Officer **Kathleen Landin Arberg** ..... (202) 479-3211
E-mail: karberg@supremecourt.gov
Education: Virginia 1977 BA

Deputy Clerk, Case Management **Cynthia J. Rapp** ...... (202) 479-3031
E-mail: cjrapp@scus.gov

Chambers of Chief Justice John G. Roberts, Jr.

U.S. Supreme Court Building, One First Street, NE,
Washington, DC 20543
Tel: (202) 479-3000

John G. Roberts, Jr.
Chief Justice

Date of Birth: January 27, 1955
Education: Harvard 1976 AB, 1979 JD
Began Service: October 3, 2005
Appointed By: President George W. Bush
State Appointed From: Maryland
Circuit Assignment: District of Columbia Circuit; Fourth Judicial Circuit; Federal Judicial Circuit

Affiliation: Ex Officio Trustee, Board of Trustees, National Gallery of Art; Ex Officio Trustee, Board of Trustees, Hirshhorn Museum and Sculpture Garden, Smithsonian Institution; Ex Officio Member, Board of Regents, Smithsonian Institution; Ex Officio Commission Member, Commission, National Portrait Gallery, Smithsonian Institution

Clerkships: Law Clerk, Circuit Judge Henry J. Friendly, United States Court of Appeals for the Second Circuit (1979-1980); Law Clerk, Associate Justice William H. Rehnquist, Supreme Court of the United States (1980-1981)

Government: Special Assistant, Office of the Attorney General, United States Department of Justice, Ronald Reagan Administration (1981-1982); Associate Counsel to the President, The White House Office, Executive Office of the President, Ronald Reagan Administration (1982-1986); Principal Deputy Solicitor General, United States Department of Justice, George H.W. Bush Administration (1989-1993)

Judicial: Circuit Judge, United States Court of Appeals for the District of Columbia Circuit (2003-2005)

Legal Practice: Associate, Hogan & Hartson LLP (1986-1987); Partner, Hogan & Hartson LLP (1988-1989); Partner, Hogan & Hartson LLP (1993-2003)

Current Memberships: American Academy of Appellate Lawyers; The Edward Coke Appellate American Inn of Court, The American Inns of Court; The American Law Institute

Staff

Law Clerk **Jacob T. "Jake" Brege** .... (202) 479-3000
Began Service: October 2015
E-mail: jbrege@supremecourt.gov
Education: Michigan 2012 JD

Law Clerk **Daniel J. Feith** .... (202) 479-3000
Began Service: October 2015
E-mail: dfeith@supremecourt.gov
Education: Yale 2012 JD

Law Clerk **Joseph B. "Ben" Tyson III** .... (202) 479-3000
Began Service: October 2015
E-mail: btyson@supremecourt.gov
Education: Virginia 2014 JD

Law Clerk **Katherine Booth Wellington** .... (202) 479-3000
Began Service: October 2015
E-mail: kwellington@supremecourt.gov
Education: Yale 2008 BA; Harvard 2013 JD

Counselor to the Chief Justice **Jeffrey P. Minear** .... (202) 479-3000
E-mail: jminear@supremecourt.gov
Education: Utah 1977 BSChE; Michigan 1982 MS, 1982 JD

Chambers of Associate Justice Antonin Scalia

U.S. Supreme Court Building, One First Street, NE,
Washington, DC 20543
Tel: (202) 479-3000

Antonin Scalia
Associate Justice

Date of Birth: 1936
Education: Georgetown 1957 AB; U Fribourg (Switzerland) 1957; Harvard 1960 LLB
Began Service: September 26, 1986
Appointed By: President Ronald Reagan
State Appointed From: Virginia
Circuit Assignment: Fifth Judicial Circuit

Academic: Professor, University of Virginia (1967-1971); Visiting Professor, Georgetown University (1977); Professor, University of Chicago (1977-1982); Visiting Professor, Stanford University (1980-1981)

Corporate: Editor, Regulation Magazine (1979-1982)

Government: General Counsel, Office of Telecommunications Policy, Executive Office of the President, Richard M. Nixon Administration (1971-1972); Chairman, Administrative Conference of the United States (1972-1974); Assistant Attorney General, Office of Legal Counsel, United States Department of Justice (1974-1977)

Judicial: Circuit Judge, United States Court of Appeals for the District of Columbia Circuit (1982-1986)

Legal Practice: Jones, Day, Cockley & Reavis (1961-1967)

Nonprofit: Resident Scholar, American Enterprise Institute (1977)

Current Memberships: Ohio State Bar Association; The Virginia Bar Association

Staff

Law Clerk **Sopan Joshi** .... (202) 479-3000
Began Service: October 2015
E-mail: sjoshi@supremecourt.gov
Education: Northwestern 2013 JD

Law Clerk **Michael E. Kenneally, Jr.** .... (202) 479-3000
Began Service: October 2015
E-mail: mkenneally@supremecourt.gov
Education: Princeton 2006 AB; Harvard 2011 JD, 2014 PhD

Law Clerk **Taylor A.R. Meehan** .... (202) 479-3000
Began Service: October 2015
E-mail: tmeehan@supremecourt.gov

Law Clerk **Jonathan D. Urick** .... (202) 479-3000
Began Service: October 2015
E-mail: jurick@supremecourt.gov
Education: Virginia 2013 JD

Chambers of Associate Justice Anthony M. Kennedy

U.S. Supreme Court Building, One First Street, NE,
Washington, DC 20543
Tel: (202) 479-3000

Anthony M. Kennedy
Associate Justice

Date of Birth: 1936
Education: Stanford 1958 AB; Harvard 1961 LLB
Began Service: February 18, 1988
Appointed By: President Ronald Reagan
State Appointed From: California
Circuit Assignment: Ninth Judicial Circuit

Academic: Professor, McGeorge School of Law, University of the Pacific (1965-1988)

Judicial: Circuit Judge, United States Court of Appeals for the Ninth Circuit (1975-1988)

Chambers of Associate Justice Anthony M. Kennedy *continued*

Legal Practice: Associate, Thelen, Marrin, John & Bridges (1961-1963); Sole Practitioner (1963-1967); Partner, Evans, Jackson & Kennedy (1967-1975)

Military Service: California Army National Guard (1961)

Current Memberships: American Bar Association; Sacramento County Bar Assocaition; State Bar of California

Staff

Law Clerk **Elana Nightingale Dawson** .... (202) 479-3000
Began Service: October 2015
E-mail: edawson@supremecourt.gov
Education: Northwestern 2011 JD

Law Clerk **Samir Deger-Sen** .... (202) 479-3000
Began Service: October 2015
E-mail: sdeger-sen@supremecourt.gov
Education: Yale 2013 JD

Law Clerk **Andrew Kilberg** .... (202) 479-3000
Began Service: October 2015
E-mail: akilberg@supremecourt.gov
Education: Virginia 2014 JD

Law Clerk **C. Harker Rhodes** .... (202) 479-3000
Began Service: October 2015
E-mail: crhodes@supremecourt.gov
Education: Stanford 2012 JD

Chambers of Associate Justice Clarence Thomas

U.S. Supreme Court Building, One First Street, NE,
Washington, DC 20543
Tel: (202) 479-3000

Clarence Thomas
Associate Justice

Date of Birth: 1948
Education: Holy Cross Col 1971; Yale 1974 JD
Began Service: October 23, 1991
Appointed By: President George H.W. Bush
State Appointed From: Georgia
Circuit Assignment: Eleventh Judicial Circuit

Corporate: Attorney, Monsanto Company (1977-1979)

Government: Assistant Attorney General, Office of the Attorney General, State of Missouri (1974-1977); Legislative Assistant (R-MO), Office of Senator John C. Danforth, United States Senate (1979-1981); Assistant Secretary for Civil Rights, United States Department of Education (1981-1982); Chairman, United States Equal Employment Opportunity Commission (1982-1990)

Judicial: Circuit Judge, United States Court of Appeals for the District of Columbia Circuit (1990-1991)

Current Memberships: The Missouri Bar

Staff

Law Clerk **Sarah M. Harris** .... (202) 479-3000
Began Service: October 2015
Education: Harvard 2009 JD

Law Clerk **Robert J. Leider** .... (202) 479-3000
Began Service: October 2015
E-mail: rleider@supremecourt.gov
Education: George Washington 2003 BA, 2009 PhD; Yale 2012 JD

Law Clerk **Marisa C. Maleck** .... (202) 479-3000
Began Service: October 2015
E-mail: mmaleck@supremecourt.gov
Education: Chicago 2011 JD

Law Clerk **Scott G. Stewart** .... (202) 479-3000
Began Service: October 2015
E-mail: sstewart@supremecourt.gov
Education: Stanford 2008 JD

Chambers of Associate Justice Ruth Bader Ginsburg

U.S. Supreme Court Building, One First Street, NE,
Washington, DC 20543
Tel: (202) 479-3000

Ruth Bader Ginsburg
Associate Justice

Date of Birth: 1933
Education: Cornell 1954 BA; Columbia 1959 LLB
Began Service: August 10, 1993
Appointed By: President William J. Clinton
State Appointed From: New York
Circuit Assignment: Second Judicial Circuit

Academic: Research Associate, Project on International Procedure, Columbia Law School (1961-1962); Associate Director, Project on International Procedure, Columbia Law School (1962-1963); Professor of Law, Rutgers, The State University of New Jersey (1963-1972); Professor, Columbia University (1972-1980)

Clerkships: Law Clerk The Honorable Edmund L. Palmieri, United States District Court for the Southern District of New York (1959-1961)

Judicial: Circuit Judge, United States Court of Appeals for the District of Columbia Circuit (1980-1993)

Nonprofit: Founder and Counsel, Women's Rights Project, American Civil Liberties Union (1972-1973); Fellow, Center for Advanced Study in the Behavioral Sciences (1977-1978)

Current Memberships: American Academy of Arts and Sciences; American Bar Association; The American Law Institute; The Association of the Bar of the City of New York; Council on Foreign Relations; The District of Columbia Bar

Staff

Law Clerk **Payvand Ahdout** .... (202) 479-3000
Began Service: October 2015
E-mail: pahdout@supremecourt.gov
Education: Columbia 2013 JD

Law Clerk **Joshua "Josh" Bone** ....(202) 479-3000
Began Service: October 2015
E-mail: jbone@supremecourt.gov
Education: Yale 2013 JD

Law Clerk **Samuel "Sam" Harbourt** .... (202) 479-3000
Began Service: October 2015
E-mail: sharbourt@supremecourt.gov
Education: Harvard JD

Law Clerk **Amy Marshak** .... (202) 479-3000
Began Service: October 2015
E-mail: amarshak@supremecourt.gov
Education: Cornell 2007 BA; NYU 2011 JD

Chambers of Associate Justice Stephen G. Breyer

U.S. Supreme Court Building, One First Street, NE,
Washington, DC 20543
Tel: (202) 479-3000

Stephen G. Breyer
Associate Justice

Date of Birth: 1938
Education: Stanford 1959 AB; Oxford (UK) 1961 BA; Harvard 1964 LLB
Began Service: August 3, 1994
Appointed By: President William J. Clinton
State Appointed From: Massachusetts
Circuit Assignment: First Judicial Circuit

Academic: Assistant Professor, Professor of Law and Lecturer, Harvard Law School (1967-1995); Professor, John F. Kennedy School of Government, Harvard University (1977-1980); Visiting Professor, College of Law, Sydney, Australia; Visiting Professor, University of Rome

Clerkships: Law Clerk The Honorable Arthur Goldberg, United States Court of Appeals for the First Circuit

Chambers of Associate Justice Stephen G. Breyer *continued*

Government: Special Assistant to the Assistant Attorney General, Antitrust Division, Office of the Associate Attorney General, United States Department of Justice (1965-1967); Assistant Special Prosecutor, Watergate Special Prosecution Force (1973); Special Counsel, Committee on the Judiciary, United States Senate (1974-1975); Chief Counsel, Committee on the Judiciary, United States Senate (1979-1980)

Judicial: Circuit Judge, United States Court of Appeals for the First Circuit (1980-1994); Member, United States Sentencing Commission (1985-1989); Member, Judicial Conference of the United States (1990-1994)

Current Memberships: American Academy of Arts and Sciences; American Bar Association; The American Law Institute

Staff

Law Clerk **Galen B. Bascom** .... (202) 479-3000
Began Service: October 2015
E-mail: gbascom@supremecourt.gov
Education: Virginia 2013 JD

Law Clerk **Tejas N. Narechania** .... (202) 479-3000
Began Service: October 2015
E-mail: tnarechania@supremecourt.gov
Education: UC Berkeley 2005 BA, 2005 BS; Columbia 2011 JD

Law Clerk **Aaron D. Pennekamp** .... (202) 479-3000
Began Service: October 2015
E-mail: apennekamp@supremecourt.gov
Education: Georgetown 2013 JD

Law Clerk **Farah F. Peterson** .... (202) 479-3000
Began Service: October 2015
E-mail: fpeterson@supremecourt.gov
Education: Yale 2012 JD

Chambers of Associate Justice Samuel A. Alito, Jr.

U.S. Supreme Court Building, One First Street, NE,
Washington, DC 20543
Tel: (202) 479-3000

Samuel A. Alito, Jr.
Associate Justice

Date of Birth: 1950
Education: Princeton 1972 AB; Yale 1975 JD
Began Service: January 31, 2006
Appointed By: President George W. Bush
State Appointed From: New Jersey
Circuit Assignment: Third Judicial Circuit; Eighth Judicial Circuit

Clerkships: Law Clerk The Honorable Leonard I. Garth, United States Court of Appeals for the Third Circuit (1976-1977)

Government: Assistant United States Attorney, Office of the United States Attorney, United States Department of Justice (1977-1981); Assistant to the Solicitor General, Office of the Solicitor General, United States Department of Justice (1981-1985); Deputy Assistant Attorney General, Office of Legal Counsel, United States Department of Justice (1985-1987); United States Attorney, United States Department of Justice (1987-1990)

Judicial: Circuit Judge, United States Court of Appeals for the Third Circuit (1990-2006)

Staff

Law Clerk **Jonathan A. Berry** .... (202) 479-3000
Began Service: October 2015
E-mail: jberry@supremecourt.gov
Education: Columbia 2011 JD

Law Clerk **James A. "Jim" Ligtenberg** .... (202) 479-3000
Began Service: October 2015
E-mail: jligtenberg@supremecourt.gov
Education: Yale 2010 JD

(continued on next page)

Chambers of Associate Justice Samuel A. Alito, Jr. *continued*

Law Clerk **Barbara Smith Grieco** .... (202) 479-3000
Began Service: October 2015
E-mail: bsmithgrieco@supremecourt.gov
Education: Stanford 2012 JD

Law Clerk **Lucas M. Walker** .... (202) 479-3000
Began Service: October 2015
E-mail: lwalker@supremecourt.gov
Education: Harvard 2009 JD

Chambers of Associate Justice Sonia Sotomayor

U.S. Supreme Court Building, One First Street, NE,
Washington, DC 20543
Tel: (202) 479-3000

Sonia Sotomayor
Associate Justice

Date of Birth: June 25, 1954
Education: Princeton 1976 BA; Yale 1979 JD
Began Service: August 8, 2009
Appointed By: President Barack Obama
State Appointed From: New York
Circuit Assignment: Tenth Judicial Circuit

Government: Assistant District Attorney, City of New York, New York (1979-1984)

Judicial: District Judge, Chambers of District Judge Sonia Sotomayor, United States District Court for the Southern District of New York (1992-1998); Circuit Judge, Chambers of Circuit Judge Sonia Sotomayor, United States Court of Appeals for the Second Circuit (1998-2009)

Legal Practice: Summer Associate, Paul, Weiss, Rifkind, Wharton & Garrison LLP (1978); Owner, Sotomayor and Associates (1983-1986); Partner, Pavia & Harcourt LLP (1988-1992)

Current Memberships: American Philosophical Society; American Bar Association; Association of Judges of Hispanic Heritage; Hispanic National Bar Association; National Association of Women Judges; Puerto Rican Bar Association; Women's Bar Association of the State of New York

Staff

Law Clerk **Easha Anand** .... (202) 479-3000
Began Service: October 2015
E-mail: eanand@supremecourt.gov
Education: Berkeley Law 2014 JD

Law Clerk **Nikolas "Niko" Bowie** .... (202) 479-3000
Began Service: October 2015
E-mail: nbowie@supremecourt.gov
Education: Harvard 2014 JD

Law Clerk **Bridget Fahey** .... (202) 479-3000
Began Service: October 2015
E-mail: bfahey@supremecourt.gov
Education: Yale 2014 JD

Law Clerk **Matthew R. Shahabian** .... (202) 479-3000
Began Service: October 2015
E-mail: mshahabian@supremecourt.gov
Education: NYU 2011 JD

Chambers of Associate Justice Elena Kagan

One First Street, NE, Washington, DC 20543
Tel: (202) 479-3000

Elena Kagan
Associate Justice

Date of Birth: April 28, 1960
Education: Princeton 1981 AB; Oxford (UK) 1983 MPhil; Harvard 1986 JD
Began Service: August 7, 2010
Appointed By: President Barack Obama
State Appointed From: Massachusetts
Circuit Assignment: Sixth Judicial Circuit; Seventh Judicial Circuit

Academic: Professor, Law School, University of Chicago (1995-1997); Visiting Professor, Harvard Law School, Harvard University (1999-2001); Professor, Harvard Law School, Harvard University (2001-2003); Dean, Harvard Law School, Harvard University (2003-2009)

Government: Associate Counsel to the President, Office of the White House Counsel, Executive Office of the President, William J. Clinton Administration (1995-1996); Deputy Assistant to the President for Domestic Policy, Staff, Domestic Policy Council, Executive Office of the President, William J. Clinton Administration (1997-1999)

Staff

Law Clerk **Yaira S. Dubin** .... (202) 479-3000
Began Service: October 2015
E-mail: ydubin@supremecourt.gov
Education: Harvard 2013 JD

Law Clerk **Jeremy M. Feigenbaum** .... (202) 479-3000
Began Service: October 2015
E-mail: jfeigenbaum@supremecourt.gov
Education: Harvard 2014 JD

Law Clerk **Thomas K. Fu** .... (202) 479-3000
Began Service: October 2015
E-mail: tfu@supremecourt.gov
Education: Stanford 2014 JD

Law Clerk **Jonathan S. Meltzer** .... (202) 479-3000
Began Service: October 2015
E-mail: jmeltzer@supremecourt.gov
Education: Yale 2013 JD

United States Courts of Limited Jurisdiction

The United States Courts of Limited Jurisdiction are a special set of federal courts that hear cases based on specific subject matters the court is charged with by jurisdiction as outlined by the U.S constitution or provided by the U.S. Congress. Each court has authority over any case that involves subject matter in its charged jurisdiction. Most cases heard by these courts involve taxes, patents, international trade, members of the armed forces, and money claims against the U.S. government.

United States Court of Federal Claims [COFC]

National Courts Building, 717 Madison Place, NW,
Washington, DC 20439
Tel: (202) 357-6400
Internet: www.uscfc.uscourts.gov

Number of Judgeships: 16

Number of Vacancies: 5

The United States Court of Federal Claims, formerly known as the United States Claims Court, has jurisdiction over claims seeking money judgments against the United States. A claim must be founded upon the United States Constitution; an act of Congress; the regulation of an executive department; an express or implied-in-fact contract with the United States, or damages, liquidated or unliquidated, in cases not sounding in tort. Appeals are to the United States Court of Appeals for the Federal Circuit. All judges on the court are appointed by the President, with Senate consent, for 15-year terms. The chief judge is selected by the President to serve until the age of seventy or until another chief judge is chosen. Retirees may serve as senior judges on assigned cases.

Court Staff

Clerk of Court **Hazel C. Keahey** .... (202) 357-6400 ext. 6411
E-mail: hazel_keahey@ao.uscourts.gov

Chief Deputy Clerk **Lisa Reyes** .... (202) 357-6418
E-mail: lisa_defade@ao.uscourts.gov
Education: Carnegie Mellon 1989 BS; Pittsburgh 1992 JD

Director of IT **Chris Warner** .... (202) 357-6445
E-mail: chris_warner@ao.uscourts.gov

Chief Special Master **Col Denise K. Vowell** .... (202) 357-6354
1440 New York Avenue, NW, Fax: (202) 357-6381
Washington, DC 20005
E-mail: denise_vowell@ao.uscourts.gov

Special Master **Brian H. Corcoran** .... (202) 357-6354
1440 New York Avenue, NW, Fax: (202) 357-6381
Washington, DC 20005

Special Master **Nora Beth Dorsey** .... (202) 357-6354
1440 New York Avenue, NW, Second Floor,
Washington, DC 20005

Special Master **Thomas L. Gowen** .... (202) 357-6359
1440 New York Avenue, NW, Fax: (202) 357-6381
Washington, DC 20005

Special Master **Lisa Hamilton-Fieldman** .... (202) 357-6345
1440 New York Avenue, NW, Fax: (202) 357-6381
Washington, DC 20005

Special Master **George Leo Hastings, Jr.** .... (202) 357-6345
1440 New York Avenue, NW, Fax: (202) 357-6381
Washington, DC 20005
E-mail: george_hastings@ao.uscourts.gov
Education: Michigan 1974 BA, 1977 JD

Special Master **Laura D. Millman** .... (202) 357-6350
1440 New York Avenue, NW, Fax: (202) 357-6381
Washington, DC 20005
E-mail: laura_millman@ao.uscourts.gov
Education: CCNY 1966 BA; Fordham 1976 JD

Special Master **Christian Moran** .... (202) 357-6359
1440 New York Avenue, NW, Fax: (202) 357-6381
Washington, DC 20005
E-mail: christian_moran@ao.uscourts.gov

Chambers of Chief Judge Patricia E. Campbell-Smith

717 Madison Place, NW, Washington, DC 20439
Tel: (202) 357-6400
E-mail: patricia_campbell-smith@ao.uscourts.gov

Patricia E. Campbell-Smith
Chief Judge

Education: Duke 1987 BS; Tulane 1992 JD
Began Service: September 19, 2013
Appointed By: President Barack Obama

Clerkships: Law Clerk, Chambers of Chief Judge Emily Clark Hewitt, United States Court of Federal Claims (1998-2005)

Government: Chief Special Master, United States Court of Federal Claims (2011-2013); Special Master, United States Court of Federal Claims, United States Courts of Limited Jurisdiction (2005-2010)

Judicial: Judge, Chambers of Judge Patricia E. Campbell-Smith, United States Court of Federal Claims (2013)

Chambers of Judge Marian Blank Horn

National Courts Building, 717 Madison Place, NW,
Washington, DC 20005
Tel: (202) 357-6580
E-mail: Marian_Horn@ao.uscourts.gov

Marian Blank Horn
Judge

Date of Birth: 1943
Education: Barnard 1962 AB; Fordham 1969 JD
Began Service: April 14, 1986
Appointed By: President Ronald Reagan
Term Expires: March 2018

Academic: Adjunct Professor of Law, American University (1973-1976)

Government: Assistant District Attorney, Deputy Chief Appeals Bureau, County of Bronx, New York (1969-1972); Litigation Attorney, Federal Energy Administration (1975-1976); Senior Attorney, Strategic Petroleum Reserve Branch, Office of General Counsel, United States Department of Energy (1976-1979); Deputy Assistant Counsel, Procurement and Financial Incentives, United States Department of Energy (1979-1981); Deputy Associate Solicitor, Division of Surface Mining, United States Department of the Interior (1981-1983); Associate Solicitor, Division of General Law, United States Department of the Interior (1983-1985); Principal Deputy Solicitor and Acting Solicitor, United States Department of the Interior (1985)

Legal Practice: Arent, Fox, Kitner, Plotkin & Kahn (1972-1973)

Staff

Law Clerk **Kasia Doulney** .... (202) 357-6580
Career Law Clerk **Jason Matson** .... (202) 357-6580
E-mail: jason_matson@ao.uscourts.gov

Chambers of Judge Lawrence J. Block

National Courts Building, 717 Madison Place, NW,
Washington, DC 20005
Tel: (202) 357-6508 Fax: (202) 357-6514
E-mail: larry_block@ao.uscourts.gov

Lawrence J. Block
Judge

Date of Birth: March 15, 1951
Education: NYU 1973 BS; John Marshall 1981 JD
Began Service: October 2, 2002
Appointed By: President George W. Bush
Term Expires: October 2017

Academic: Adjunct Professor, George Mason University School of Law (1990-1991)

(continued on next page)

Chambers of Judge Lawrence J. Block *continued*

Clerkships: Law Clerk The Honorable Roger J. Miner, United States District Court for the Northern District of New York (1981-1983)

Government: Litigation Attorney, Commercial Litigation Branch, Civil Division, United States Department of Justice Civil Division (1986-1987); Senior Attorney Advisor, Office of Legal Policy and Policy Development, United States Department of Justice (1987-1990); Deputy Assistant General Counsel for Legal Policy, Office of General Counsel, United States Department of Energy (1990-1994)

Legal Practice: Associate, Skadden, Arps, Slate, Meagher & Flom LLP (1983-1986)

Staff
Judicial Assistant **Susan M. Mack** .... (202) 357-6508

Chambers of Judge Susan G. Braden

717 Madison Place, NW, Suite 702, Washington, DC 20439
Tel: (202) 357-6516 Fax: (202) 357-6522
E-mail: susan_braden@ao.uscourts.gov

Susan G. Braden
Judge

Date of Birth: November 8, 1948
Education: Case Western 1970 BA, 1973 JD
Began Service: July 14, 2003
Appointed By: President George W. Bush
Term Expires: July 4, 2018

Legal Practice: Senior Trial Attorney, AntitrustDivision, Department of Justice (1973-1980); Senior Counsel, Office of the Chairman, Federal Trade Commission (1980-1985)

Staff
Law Clerk **Erika A. James** .... (202) 357-6516
Began Service: September 2015
Term Expires: September 1, 2016
Law Clerk **Michelle M. Sohn** .... (202) 357-6516
Began Service: September 2015
Term Expires: September 1, 2016
Judicial Assistant **Karen Glanden** .... (202) 357-6517
E-mail: karen_glanden@ao.uscourts.gov

Chambers of Judge Mary Ellen Coster Williams

717 Madison Place, NW, Washington, DC 20439
Tel: (202) 357-6660 Fax: (202) 357-6666
E-mail: williams_chambers@ao.uscourts.gov
E-mail: maryellen_williams@ao.uscourts.gov

Mary Ellen Coster Williams
Judge

Date of Birth: April 3, 1953
Education: Catholic U 1974 BA, 1974 MA; Duke 1977 JD
Began Service: July 21, 2003
Appointed By: President George W. Bush
Term Expires: July 21, 2018
Political Affiliation: Democrat

Government: Assistant U.S. Attorney, Civil Division (1983-1987)

Judicial: Administrative Judge, General Service Administration Board of Contract Appeals (1989-2003)

Legal Practice: Associate, Fulbright & Jaworski L.L.P. (1977-1979); Associate, Schnader Harrison Segal & Lewis LLP (1979-1983); Partner, Janis, Schuelke & Wechsler (1987-1989)

Current Memberships: American Bar Association; The District of Columbia Bar

Chambers of Judge Mary Ellen Coster Williams *continued*

Staff
Law Clerk **Diane Ghrist** .... (202) 357-6663
Began Service: August 2015
Term Expires: August 2016
E-mail: diane_ghrist@ao.uscourts.gov
Law Clerk **Julia Horwitz** .... (202) 357-6663
Began Service: August 2015
Term Expires: August 2016
E-mail: julia_horwitz@ao.uscourts.gov
Career Law Clerk **Taryn Fry** .... (202) 357-6660
E-mail: taryn_fry@ao.uscourts.gov

Chambers of Judge Charles F. Lettow

717 Madison Place, NW, Washington, DC 20439
Tel: (202) 357-6588 Fax: (202) 357-6594
E-mail: charles_lettow@ao.uscourts.gov

Charles F. Lettow
Judge

Date of Birth: 1941
Education: Iowa State 1962 BSChE; Stanford 1968 LLB; Brown U 2001 MA
Began Service: July 22, 2003
Appointed By: President George W. Bush
Term Expires: July 13, 2018

Clerkships: Law Clerk Ben C. Duniway, United States Court of Appeals for the Ninth Circuit (1968-1969); Law Clerk Warren E. Burger, Supreme Court of the United States (1969-1970)

Government: Counsel, Council on Environmental Quality, Executive Office of the President (1970-1973)

Legal Practice: Associate, Cleary Gottlieb Steen & Hamilton LLP (1973-1976); Partner, Cleary Gottlieb Steen & Hamilton LLP (1976-2003)

Military Service: Second Lieutenant, First Lieutenant United States Army (1963-1965); CPT, United States Army Reserve (1965-1972)

Current Memberships: American Bar Association; The American Law Institute; The District of Columbia Bar; Iowa State Bar Association; Maryland State Bar Association, Inc.; State Bar of California

Staff
Law Clerk **Amy Josselyn** .... (202) 357-6591
Began Service: August 2015
Term Expires: August 2016
E-mail: amy_josselyn@ao.uscourts.gov
Law Clerk **Evan Sherwood** .... (202) 357-6591
Began Service: August 2015
Term Expires: August 2016
E-mail: evan_sherwood@ao.uscourts.gov
Judicial Assistant **Rita Sanderson** .... (202) 357-6589
E-mail: rita_sanderson@ao.uscourts.gov

Chambers of Judge Victor J. Wolski

717 Madison Place, NW, Washington, DC 20439
Tel: (202) 357-6668
E-mail: victor_wolski@ao.uscourts.gov

Victor J. Wolski
Judge

Education: Pennsylvania 1984 BA, 1984 BS; Virginia 1991 JD
Began Service: July 24, 2003
Appointed By: President George W. Bush
Term Expires: July 13, 2018
Political Affiliation: Republican

Academic: Research Associate, Center for Strategic and International Studies, Institute for Political Economy (1984-1988)

Clerkships: Law Clerk, United States District Court for the Northern District of California (1991-1992)

Chambers of Judge Victor J. Wolski *continued*

Government: Speech Writer, Secretary of Agriculture Richard Lyng, United States Department of Agriculture, Ronald Reagan Administration (1988); Counsel, Joint Economic Committee, United States Congress (1997-1998); General Counsel and Chief Tax Advisor, Joint Economic Committee, United States Congress; General Counsel and Chief Tax Advisor, Joint Economic Committee, United States Congress (2000)

Legal Practice: Attorney, Pacific Legal Foundation (1992-1997); Attorney, Cooper, Carvin & Rosenthal (2000-2003)

Current Memberships: The Federalist Society for Law and Public Policy Studies; The John Carroll Society of Washington, DC; Oregon State Bar; State Bar of California; The Supreme Court Historical Society; Washington State Bar Association

Staff
Law Clerk **Sarah Lafreniere** .... (202) 357-6668
Law Clerk **Jarrett Diterle** .... (202) 357-6668
E-mail: jarrett_diterle@ao.uscourts.gov

Chambers of Judge Thomas Craig Wheeler
717 Madison Place, NW, Washington, DC 20439
Tel: (202) 357-6596
E-mail: thomas_wheeler@ao.uscourts.gov

Thomas Craig Wheeler
Judge

Education: Gettysburg 1970 BA; Georgetown 1973 JD
Began Service: November 28, 2005
Appointed By: President George W. Bush

Legal Practice: Associate and Partner, Pettit & Martin (1995); Partner, Piper & Marbury

Current Memberships: Section on Litigation, American Bar Association; The District of Columbia Bar

Chambers of Judge Margaret Mary Sweeney
717 Madison Place, NW, Washington, DC 20439
Tel: (202) 357-6644
E-mail: margaret_sweeney@ao.uscourts.gov

Margaret Mary Sweeney
Judge

Education: Notre Dame 1977 BA; Delaware 1981 JD
Began Service: December 14, 2005
Appointed By: President George W. Bush

Clerkships: Law Clerk, Chief Judge Loren A. Smith, United States Court of Federal Claims (1985-1987)

Government: Trial Attorney, Environment and Natural Resources Division, United States Department of Justice (1987-1999); Attorney Advisor, Office of Intelligence Policy and Review, United States Department of Justice; Special Master, United States Court of Federal Claims, United States Courts of Limited Jurisdiction

Judicial: Court Master, Delaware Family Court (1981-1983); President, United States Court of Federal Claims Bar Association (1999)

Legal Practice: Litigation Associate, Fedorko, Gilbert & Lanctot (1983-1985)

Current Memberships: United States Court of Federal Claims Bar

Chambers of Judge Elaine D. Kaplan
717 Madison Place, NW, Washington, DC 20439
Tel: (202) 357-6400
E-mail: elaine_kaplan@ao.uscourts.gov

Elaine D. Kaplan
Judge

Education: SUNY (Binghamton) 1976 BA; Georgetown 1979 JD
Began Service: November 1, 2013
Appointed By: President Barack Obama

Chambers of Judge Lydia Kay Griggsby
717 Madison Place, NW, Washington, DC 20439
Tel: (202) 357-6400

Lydia Kay Griggsby
Judge

Education: Pennsylvania 1990 BA; Georgetown 1993 JD
Began Service: 2014
Appointed By: President Barack Obama

Chambers of Senior Judge James F. Merow
National Courts Building, 717 Madison Place, NW, Suite 601, Washington, DC 20005
Tel: (202) 357-6612
E-mail: james_merow@ao.uscourts.gov

James F. Merow
Senior Judge

Date of Birth: 1932
Education: George Washington 1953 AB, 1956 JD
Began Service: October 1, 1982
Appointed By: President Ronald Reagan

Government: Trial Attorney, Civil Division, United States Department of Justice (1956); Trial Attorney, Branch Director, Civil Division, United States Department of Justice (1959-1978)

Judicial: Trial Commissioner, United States Court of Claims (1978-1982)

Military Service: United States Army, Judge Advocate General Corps (1956-1959)

Current Memberships: American Bar Association; The District of Columbia Bar; Federal Bar Association; Virginia State Bar

Staff
Career Law Clerk **(Vacant)** .... (202) 357-6612

Chambers of Senior Judge Eric G. Bruggink
National Courts Building, 717 Madison Place, NW, Washington, DC 20005
Tel: (202) 357-6524
E-mail: eric_bruggink@ao.uscourts.gov

Eric G. Bruggink
Senior Judge

Date of Birth: 1949
Education: Auburn 1971 BA, 1972 MA; Alabama 1975 JD
Began Service: April 15, 1986
Appointed By: President Ronald Reagan

Academic: Assistant Director, Alabama Law Institute

Clerkships: Law Clerk The Honorable Frank H. McFadden, United States District Court for the Northern District of Alabama (1975-1976)

Government: Director, Office of Appeals Counsel, Merit Systems Protection Board (1982-1986)

(continued on next page)

Chambers of Senior Judge Eric G. Bruggink *continued*

Legal Practice: Hardwick, Hause & Segrest (1976-1977); Steiner, Crum & Baker (1979-1982)

Current Memberships: Alabama State Bar; The District of Columbia Bar; Federal Circuit Bar Association

Staff

Law Clerk **Brita Zacek** .... (202) 357-6524
Began Service: September 2015
Term Expires: September 2017
E-mail: brita_zacek@ao.uscourts.gov

Career Law Clerk/Administrative Secretary
Jeremy Kehr .... (202) 357-6524
E-mail: jeremy_kehr@ao.uscourts.gov
Education: Regent U 2005 JD

Judicial Assistant **Shera Fitzsimmons** .... (202) 357-6524
E-mail: shera_fitzsimmons@ao.uscourts.gov

Chambers of Senior Judge John P. Wiese

National Courts Building, 717 Madison Place, NW,
Washington, DC 20005
Tel: (202) 357-6652
E-mail: john_wiese@ao.uscourts.gov

John P. Wiese
Senior Judge

Date of Birth: 1934
Education: Hobart 1962 BA; Virginia 1965 LLB
Began Service: October 14, 1986
Appointed By: President Ronald Reagan

Clerkships: Law Clerk, Trial Division, United States Court of Claims (1965-1966); Law Clerk The Honorable Linton M. Collins, United States Court of Claims (1966-1967)

Judicial: Trial Commissioner, United States Court of Claims (1974-1986)

Legal Practice: Cox, Langford & Brown (1967-1969); Hudson & Creyke (1969-1974)

Military Service: United States Army (1957-1959)

Current Memberships: American Bar Association; The District of Columbia Bar

Chambers of Senior Judge Lynn J. Bush

National Courts Building, 717 Madison Place, NW,
Washington, DC 20005
Tel: (202) 357-6532 Fax: (202) 357-6538
E-mail: lynn_bush@ao.uscourts.gov

Lynn J. Bush
Senior Judge

Date of Birth: 1948
Education: Antioch U 1970 BA; Georgetown 1976 JD
Began Service: October 26, 1998
Appointed By: President William J. Clinton

Current Memberships: Board of Contract Appeals Judges Association; Boards of Contract Appeals Bar Association; National Association of Women Judges; National Bar Association

Staff

Law Clerk **(Vacant)** .... (202) 357-6534

Career Law Clerk **John G. Bean** .... (202) 357-6535
E-mail: john_bean@ao.uscourts.gov
Education: Yale 1978 BA;
Southern Maine 1998 MA; Maine 2003 JD

Judicial Assistant **Terri Quintos** .... (202) 357-6533
E-mail: terri_quintos@ao.uscourts.gov

Chambers of Senior Judge Edward J. Damich

National Courts Building, 717 Madison Place, NW,
Washington, DC 20005
Tel: (202) 357-6483 Fax: (202) 357-6490
E-mail: Damich_Chambers@ao.uscourts.gov

Edward J. Damich
Senior Judge

Date of Birth: 1948
Education: Columbus Law 1976 JD; Columbia 1983 LLM, 1991 JSD
Began Service: October 22, 1998
Appointed By: President William J. Clinton

Current Memberships: American Bar Association; The Bar Association of the District of Columbia; The District of Columbia Bar; Federal Circuit Bar Association; Pennsylvania Bar Association; Washington Area Lawyers for the Arts

Staff

Career Law Clerk **Laura M. Barbour** .... (202) 357-6412
E-mail: laura_barbour@ao.uscourts.gov
Education: Columbus Law 1989 JD

Judicial Assistant **Ellan Jackson** .... (202) 357-6484
E-mail: Damich_Chambers@ao.uscourts.gov

Chambers of Senior Judge Nancy B. Firestone

National Courts Building, 717 Madison Place, NW,
Washington, DC 20005
Tel: (202) 357-6540 Fax: (202) 357-6546
E-mail: nancy_firestone@ao.uscourts.gov

Nancy B. Firestone
Senior Judge

Note: On January 7, 2015, President Obama nominated Nancy Firestone to be Judge for another term on the United States Court of Federal Claims.
Date of Birth: 1951
Education: Washington U (MO) 1973 BA; Missouri (Kansas City) 1977 JD
Began Service: December 4, 1998
Appointed By: President William J. Clinton

Current Memberships: American Bar Association; The Missouri Bar

Staff

Judicial Assistant **Diana Pérez-Kidwell** .... (202) 357-6541
E-mail: diana_perez-kidwell@ao.uscourts.gov

United States Court of International Trade

One Federal Plaza, New York, NY 10278-0001
Tel: (212) 264-2800 Tel: (212) 264-2814 (General Info)
Fax: (212) 264-1085
E-mail: webmaster@cit.uscourts.gov
Internet: www.cit.uscourts.gov

Number of Judgeships: 9

Number of Vacancies: 4

The United States Court of International Trade is an Article III court with exclusive nationwide jurisdiction over civil actions against the United States, its agencies and officers. Its jurisdiction also includes certain civil actions brought by the United States, arising out of import transactions and the administration and enforcement of the federal customs and international trade laws. The Court reviews administrative decisions of the Bureau of Customs and Border Protection involving the tariff laws of the United States, including the classification and valuation of imported merchandise. The Court hears judicial challenges to determinations by the United States Department of Commerce and the United States International Trade Commission pertaining to the antidumping and countervailing duty laws. In addition, the Court reviews decisions by the Secretary of Labor, Commerce or Agriculture certifying workers, businesses or agricultural commodity procedures respectively eligible for assistance due to economic injury caused by import competition. The Court also possesses exclusive jurisdiction of actions brought by the United States to: (1) recover civil penalties for fraud, gross negligence or negligence in the entry of imported merchandise; (2) recover upon a bond relating to the importation of merchandise; or (3) recover customs duties. Judges are appointed by the President and confirmed by the Senate. These are Article III judgeships to which members are appointed for life, pending good behavior. Cases are determined by a single judge. Cases raising a constitutional issue or cases with broad significant implications may be assigned by the chief judge to a three-judge panel. Appeals from the Court of International Trade are heard by the United States Court of Appeals for the Federal Circuit. The Court is located in New York City, but sessions may be held anywhere within the United States. The Court is also authorized to hold hearings in foreign countries.

Court Staff

Clerk of Court **Tina Potuto Kimble** .... (212) 264-2908
E-mail: tina_kimble@cit.uscourts.gov Fax: (212) 264-4138
Education: Boston Col 1992 BA; Washington College of Law 1995 JD

Chief Deputy Clerk **Mario Toscano** .... (212) 264-2826
E-mail: mario_toscano@cit.uscourts.gov

Fiscal and Property Operations Manager **(Vacant)** .... (212) 264-2812
Fax: (212) 264-2803

Administrative Manager **Brian Young** .... (212) 264-2831
E-mail: brian_young@cit.uscourts.gov Fax: (212) 264-0441

Operations Manager **Scott Warner** .... (212) 264-2031
E-mail: scott_warner@cit.uscourts.gov

Systems Manager **Bienvenido Burgos** .... (212) 264-2811
E-mail: bienvenido_burgos@cit.uscourts.gov

Training Specialist **Glenn M Johnston** .... (212) 264-2835
E-mail: Glenn_Johnston@cit.uscourts.gov

Library and Attorney Services Director **Daniel R. Campbell** .... (212) 264-2804
E-mail: Daniel_campbell@cit.uscourts.gov Fax: (212) 264-3242
Education: Seton Hall JD; Rutgers MLIS

Chambers of Chief Judge Timothy C. Stanceu

One Federal Plaza, New York, NY 10278-0001
Tel: (212) 264-2923 Fax: (212) 264-7568

Timothy C. Stanceu
Chief Judge

Date of Birth: July 31, 1951
Education: Colgate 1973 AB; Georgetown 1979 JD
Began Service: April 15, 2003
Appointed By: President George W. Bush
Political Affiliation: Republican

Staff

Law Clerk **Valerie Ann Sorenson** .... (212) 264-2880
Law Clerk **Elisa Solomon** .... (212) 264-2880
Case Manager **Cynthia Love** .... (212) 264-2923

Chambers of Judge Delissa A. Ridgway

One Federal Plaza, New York, NY 10278-0001
Tel: (212) 264-5480 Fax: (212) 264-5471

Delissa A. Ridgway
Judge

Date of Birth: 1955
Education: Missouri 1975 BA; Northeastern 1979 JD
Began Service: May 29, 1998
Appointed By: President William J. Clinton

Academic: Adjunct Professor, Washington College of Law, American University (1992-1994); Adjunct Professor/Lecturer, Law School, Cornell University (1999-2006)

Government: Chairperson, Foreign Claims Settlement Commission of the U.S., Office of the Attorney General, United States Department of Justice (1994-1998)

Legal Practice: Shaw, Pittman, Potts & Trowbridge (1979-1994)

Current Memberships: American Bar Foundation; American Bar Association; The American Law Institute; The Association of the Bar of the City of New York; Federal Bar Association; The Foundation of the Federal Bar Association, Federal Bar Association; Women's Bar Association of the District of Columbia

Staff

Law Clerk **Antonia Pereira** .... (212) 264-5480
E-mail: antonia_pereira@cit.uscourts.gov
Law Clerk **Sam Permutt** .... (212) 264-5480
Case Manager **Casey A. Cheevers** .... (212) 264-1615
E-mail: casey_cheevers@cit.uscourts.gov

Chambers of Judge Leo M. Gordon

One Federal Plaza, New York, NY 10278-0001
Tel: (212) 264-1611

Leo M. Gordon
Judge

Education: North Carolina 1973 BA; Emory 1977 JD
Began Service: March 16, 2006
Appointed By: President George W. Bush

Government: Clerk of Court, United States Court of International Trade

Staff

Law Clerk **John P. Healy** .... (212) 264-7960
Began Service: 2009
E-mail: john_healy@cit.uscourts.gov
Law Clerk **Ryan Pratt** .... (212) 264-7566
E-mail: ryan_pratt@cit.uscourts.gov

(continued on next page)

Chambers of Judge Leo M. Gordon *continued*

Case Manager **Steve Taronji** .... (212) 264-2923
Judicial Executive Assistant **Sarah Gonzalez** .... (212) 264-2018
E-mail: sarah_mallo@cit.uscourts.gov
Education: St John's U (NY) 1997 BA, 1999 MA

Chambers of Judge Mark A. Barnett

One Federal Plaza, New York, NY 10278-0001
Tel: (212) 264-1628

Mark A. Barnett
Judge

Education: Dickinson Col 1985 BA; Michigan 1988 JD
Began Service: 2013
Appointed By: President Barack Obama

Staff

Law Clerk **Hayden Windrow** .... (212) 264-1628
Term Expires: August 2016
E-mail: hayden_windrow@cit.uscourts.gov
Education: NYU 2005 JD
Law Clerk **Caroline Wolkoff** .... (212) 264-1628
Term Expires: August 2016
E-mail: caroline_wolkoff@cit.uscourts.gov
Case Manager **Rebecca Demb** .... (212) 264-1628
Executive Assistant **Fidelis Basile** .... (212) 264-1628
E-mail: fidelis_basile@cit.uscourts.gov

Chambers of Judge Claire R. Kelly

One Federal Plaza, New York, NY 10278-0001
Tel: (212) 264-1611

Claire R. Kelly
Judge

Education: Barnard 1987 BA; Brooklyn Law 1993 JD
Began Service: 2013
Appointed By: President Barack Obama

Staff

Law Clerk **Saad Younus** .... (212) 264-1611
Term Expires: August 2016
E-mail: saad_younus@cit.uscourts.gov
Law Clerk **Kenneth Hammer** .... (212) 264-1611
Term Expires: August 2016
E-mail: kenneth_hammer@cit.uscourts.gov
Case Manager **Steve Taronji** .... (212) 264-1611
Executive Assistant **Golda Lawrence** .... (212) 264-1611
E-mail: golda_lawrence@cit.uscourts.gov

Chambers of Senior Judge Gregory W. Carman

One Federal Plaza, New York, NY 10278-0001
Tel: (212) 264-2842 Fax: (212) 264-2017

Gregory W. Carman
Senior Judge

Date of Birth: January 31, 1937
Education: St Lawrence 1958 BA; St John's U (NY) 1961 JD; Judge Advocate Gen 1962
Began Service: March 1983
Appointed By: President Ronald Reagan
Political Affiliation: Republican

Current Memberships: American Bar Foundation; American Bar Association; New York State Bar Association

Staff

Law Clerk **Daniel O. Bodah** .... (212) 264-2842
Began Service: September 2009
E-mail: daniel_bodah@cit.uscourts.gov
Education: Brooklyn Law 2007 JD

Chambers of Senior Judge Gregory W. Carman *continued*

Law Clerk **Catherine Miller** .... (212) 264-2842
Case Manager **Cynthia Love** .... (212) 264-2923
Administrative Assistant **Phyllis Simon** .... (212) 264-2842
E-mail: phyllis_simon@cit.uscourts.gov

Chambers of Senior Judge Jane A. Restani

One Federal Plaza, New York, NY 10278-0001
Tel: (212) 264-3668 Fax: (212) 264-3200

Jane A. Restani
Senior Judge

Date of Birth: 1948
Education: UC Berkeley 1969 BA; UC Davis 1973 JD
Began Service: 1983
Appointed By: President Ronald Reagan

Staff

Law Clerk **Alyssa A. Hill** .... (212) 264-3668
Began Service: September 2014
Term Expires: September 2016
E-mail: alyssa_hill@cit.uscourts.gov
Education: Boston Col 2014 JD
Law Clerk **Rishi R. Gupta** .... (212) 264-3668
Began Service: September 2015
Term Expires: September 2017
E-mail: rishi_gupta@cit.uscourts.gov
Education: American U 2014 JD
Case Manager **Rebecca Demb** .... (212) 264-1628

Chambers of Senior Judge Thomas J. Aquilino, Jr.

One Federal Plaza, New York, NY 10278-0001
Tel: (212) 264-1611 Fax: (212) 264-4638

Thomas J. Aquilino, Jr.
Senior Judge

Date of Birth: 1939
Education: Drew 1962 BA; Rutgers (Newark) 1969 JD
Began Service: May 2, 1985
Appointed By: President Ronald Reagan

Academic: Adjunct Professor, Benjamin N. Cardozo School of Law, Yeshiva University (1984-1995)

Clerkships: Law Clerk The Honorable John M. Cannella, United States District Court for the Southern District of New York (1969-1971)

Legal Practice: Davis Polk & Wardwell (1971-1985)

Military Service: United States Army (1962-1965)

Staff

Case Manager **Steve Taronji** .... (212) 264-1611

Chambers of Senior Judge Nicholas Tsoucalas

One Federal Plaza, Suite 660, New York, NY 10278-0001
Tel: (212) 264-2918 Fax: (212) 264-3202

Nicholas Tsoucalas
Senior Judge

Date of Birth: 1926
Education: Kent State 1949 BS; New York Law 1951 LLB
Began Service: June 6, 1986
Appointed By: President Ronald Reagan
Political Affiliation: Republican

Government: Assistant United States Attorney, Southern District of New York, United States Department of Justice (1955-1959); Supervisor, 1960 Census, 17th and 18th Congressional Districts, United States Department of Commerce (1959-1960)

Chambers of Senior Judge Nicholas Tsoucalas *continued*

Judicial: Judge, Criminal Court of the City of New York (1968-1975); Acting Judge, New York Supreme Court, Kings and Queens Counties (1975-1982); Judge, Criminal Court of the City of New York (1982-1986)

Legal Practice: Private Practice (1953-1955); Private Practice (1959-1968)

Military Service: United States Navy (1944-1946); United States Navy (1951-1952)

Current Memberships: American Bar Association; Eastern Orthodox Lawyers Society; Federal Bar Association; Greek-American Lawyers Association; New York County Lawyers' Association

Staff
Case Manager **Cynthia Love** . . . . (212) 264-2923

Chambers of Senior Judge R. Kenton Musgrave
One Federal Plaza, New York, NY 10278-0001
Tel: (212) 264-2819 Fax: (212) 264-3203

R. Kenton Musgrave
Senior Judge

Date of Birth: 1927
Education: U Washington 1948 BA; Emory 1953 JD
Began Service: November 13, 1987
Appointed By: President Ronald Reagan

Corporate: Vice President and General Counsel, Mattel, Inc. (1963-1971); Director, Ringling Brothers and Barnum and Bailey Combined Shows, Inc. (1968-1972); Director, Orlando Bank & Trust (1970-1973); Assistant General Counsel, Pacific Enterprises Corporation (1975-1981); Vice President, General Counsel and Secretary, Vivitar Corporation (1981-1985); Vice President and Director, Santa Barbara Applied Research, Inc. (1982-1987)

Government: Commissioner, Boy Scouts of America (1952-1955)

Legal Practice: Assistant General Counsel, Lockheed Aircraft and Lockheed International, Inc. (1953-1962); Partner, Musgrave, Welbourn and Fertman (1972-1975)

Current Memberships: International Bar Association; Los Angeles County Bar Association; State Bar of California; State Bar of Georgia

Staff
Law Clerk **Heather Doherty** . . . . (212) 264-2899
Career Law Clerk **Daniel R. Holland** . . . . (212) 264-1773
E-mail: daniel_holland@cit.uscourts.gov
Education: Boston U 1984 BA, 1987 JD, 1988 MBA
Case Manager **(Vacant)** . . . . (212) 264-1628
Executive Assistant **Aurora Medina-Ng** . . . . (212) 264-2819
E-mail: aurora_medina-ng@cit.uscourts.gov
Education: NYU 1979 BS; New School 1996 MS

Chambers of Senior Judge Richard W. Goldberg
One Federal Plaza, New York, NY 10278-0001
Tel: (212) 264-9741 Fax: (212) 264-3243

Richard W. Goldberg
Senior Judge

Date of Birth: 1927
Education: Miami 1952 JD
Began Service: March 23, 1991
Appointed By: President George H.W. Bush

Corporate: Owner and Operator, Regional Grain Processing Firm (1958-1983); Vice Chairman, Minneapolis Grain Exchange

Government: State Senator Richard W. Goldberg (R-ND), North Dakota State Senate (1966-1974); Deputy Under Secretary then Acting Under Secretary, International Affairs and Commodity Programs, United States Department of Agriculture (1983-1989)

Legal Practice: Practicing Attorney, Anderson, Hibey & Blair (1989-1991)

Chambers of Senior Judge Richard W. Goldberg *continued*

Military Service: United States Air Force (1953-1956)

Staff
Law Clerk **Alfred Jensen** . . . . (212) 264-9741
Term Expires: September 2016
E-mail: alfred_jensen@cit.uscourts.gov
Law Clerk **Robert Koneck** . . . . (212) 264-9741
Began Service: August 2015
Term Expires: August 2017
E-mail: robert_koneck@cit.uscourts.gov
Case Manager **Casey A. Cheevers** . . . . (212) 264-1615
Secretary **Maryann Keegan** . . . . (212) 264-9741
E-mail: maryann_keegan@cit.uscourts.gov

Chambers of Senior Judge Donald C. Pogue
One Federal Plaza, New York, NY 10278-0001
Tel: (212) 264-2126 Fax: (212) 264-3201

Donald C. Pogue
Senior Judge

Date of Birth: 1947
Education: Dartmouth BA; Yale 1973 JD, 1974 MA, 1974 JD
Began Service: August 1995
Appointed By: President William J. Clinton

Staff
Law Clerk **Alexandra Khrebtukova** . . . . (212) 264-3184
Began Service: September 2013
E-mail: alexandra_khrebtukova@cit.uscourts.gov
Case Manager **Geoffrey Goell** . . . . (212) 264-1628
Executive Assistant **Janice Blake** . . . . (212) 264-2126
E-mail: janice_blake@cit.uscourts.gov

Chambers of Senior Judge Judith M. Barzilay
One Federal Plaza, New York, NY 10278-0001
Tel: (212) 264-5420 Fax: (212) 264-5487

Judith M. Barzilay
Senior Judge

Date of Birth: 1944
Education: Wichita State 1965 BA; Rutgers 1971 MLS; Rutgers (Newark) 1981 JD
Began Service: June 3, 1998
Appointed By: President William J. Clinton
Political Affiliation: Independent

Staff
Law Clerk **(Vacant)** . . . . (212) 264-5420
Permanent Law Clerk **Matthew Leviton** . . . . (212) 264-5420
E-mail: matthew_leviton@cit.uscourts.gov
Education: Washington College of Law 2006 JD
Case Manager **Steve Taronji** . . . . (212) 264-1611
Administration Manager **Marguerite Raimo-Terlizzi** . . . . (212) 264-5420
E-mail: marguerite_raimo@cit.uscourts.gov

Chambers of Senior Judge Richard K. Eaton
One Federal Plaza, New York, NY 10278-0001
Tel: (212) 264-2900

Richard K. Eaton
Senior Judge

Date of Birth: 1948
Education: Ithaca 1970 BA; Albany Law 1974 JD
Began Service: January 3, 2000
Appointed By: President William J. Clinton

(continued on next page)

Chambers of Senior Judge Richard K. Eaton *continued*

Staff

Law Clerk **Brynne Grady** . . . . (212) 264-2900
Began Service: 2014
Term Expires: September 2016
E-mail: brynne_grady@cit.uscourts.gov

Case Manager **Casey A. Cheevers** . . . . (212) 264-1615

Executive Assistant **E. D. Francis** . . . . (212) 261-2900
E-mail: enid_francis@cit.uscourts.gov

United States Court of Appeals for the Armed Forces [USCAAF]

450 E Street, NW, Washington, DC 20442-0001
Tel: (202) 761-1448 Tel: (202) 761-1452 (Docket Room Phone)
Fax: (202) 761-4672
Internet: www.armfor.uscourts.gov

Number of Judgeships: 5

The United States Court of Appeals for the Armed Forces, formerly known as the Court of Military Appeals, hears matters of law under the Uniform Code of Military Justice involving an officer, the death penalty, a sentence of one year or more imprisonment or dismissal, a dishonorable discharge or bad conduct discharge certified by the service's Judge Advocate General or the General Counsel of the Department of Transportation acting for the Coast Guard. The court's jurisdiction is worldwide. Appeals to this court come in response to court-martials in the Army, Navy-Marine Corps, Air Force and Coast Guard Courts of Criminal Appeals. Its decisions prior to 1984 were final, however now rulings can be appealed to the Supreme Court of the United States for review. The Washington, DC-based court is exclusively an appellate criminal court consisting of five civilian judges appointed to 15-year terms by the President with Senate confirmation.

Court Staff

Clerk **William A. "Bill" DeCicco** . . . . (202) 761-1448
E-mail: Bill.DeCicco@armfor.uscourts.gov Fax: (202) 761-4672
Education: St Mary's Col (CA) 1971 BA;
U San Francisco 1975 JD;
George Washington 1985 LLM

Chief Deputy Clerk of Court **David A. Anderson** . . . . (202) 761-1448
E-mail: David.Anderson@armfor.uscourts.gov Fax: (202) 761-7005
Education: Amherst 1975 BA;
George Washington 1978 JD, 1986 LLM;
Judge Advocate Gen 1989 LLM

Deputy Clerk [Opinions] **Patricia Mariani** . . . . (202) 761-1448
E-mail: patricia.mariani@armfor.uscourts.gov Fax: (202) 761-4672
Education: Smith 1977 AB; Georgetown 1990 JD

Court Executive **Keith L. Roberts** . . . . (202) 761-1448
E-mail: keith.roberts@armfor.uscourts.gov Fax: (202) 761-4672
Education: Washburn 1977 BA, 1980 JD

Security & Operations Officer **Mike Pinette** . . . . (202) 761-1448
E-mail: mike.pinette@armfor.uscourts.gov Fax: (202) 761-7009
Education: Norfolk State 1996 BS

Personnel Administrator **Gail Bissi** . . . . (202) 761-1451
E-mail: Gail.Bissi@armfor.uscourts.gov Fax: (202) 761-7009

Librarian **Agnes Kiang** . . . . (202) 761-1466
E-mail: agnes.kiang@armfor.uscourts.gov
Education: Maryland 1987 MLS

Chambers of Chief Judge Charles E. Erdmann II

450 E Street, NW, Washington, DC 20442-0001
Tel: (202) 761-1458 Fax: (202) 761-7000
E-mail: chip.erdmann@armfor.uscourts.gov

Charles E. "Chip" Erdmann II
Chief Judge

Education: Montana 1975 JD
Began Service: October 15, 2002
Appointed By: President George W. Bush
Term Expires: October 30, 2017

Staff

Secretary **Tracy Taracatac** . . . . (202) 761-1458
E-mail: tracy.taractac@armfor.uscourts.gov

Chambers of Associate Judge Scott Wallace Stucky

450 E Street, NW, Washington, DC 20442-0001
Tel: (202) 761-1461
E-mail: scott.stucky@armfor.uscourts.gov

Scott W. Stucky
Associate Judge

Date of Birth: January 11, 1948
Education: Wichita State 1970 BA; Harvard 1973 JD; Trinity U 1980 MA; George Washington 1983 LLM
Began Service: December 20, 2006
Appointed By: President George W. Bush
Term Expires: September 30, 2021
Political Affiliation: Republican

Affiliation: Member, Federal Bar Association; Member, Sons of Union Veterans of the Civil War; Member, National Society Sons of the American Revolution; Member, The International Legal Fraternity of Phi Delta Phi; Member, Sigma Phi Epsilon Fraternity; Member, Saint Andrew's Society of Washington, D.C.; Member, Army and Navy of the United States of America; Member, Military Order of Foreign Wars of the United States; Member, Military Order of the World Wars; Member, Judge Advocates Association; Member, Sovereign Military Hospitaller Order of St. John of Jerusalem of Rhodes and of Malta

Government: Chief, Docketing and Service Branch, Office of the Secretary, United States Nuclear Regulatory Commission (1982-1983); Legislative Counsel, United States Department of the Air Force, United States Department of Defense (1983-1987); Principal Legislative Counsel, United States Department of the Air Force, United States Department of Defense (1987-1996); General Counsel, Committee on Armed Services, United States Senate (1996-2001); Majority General Counsel, Committee on Armed Services, United States Senate (2003-2006)

Legal Practice: Associate, Ginsburg, Feldman, and Bress (1978-1982)

Military Service: Col, United States Air Force (1973-1978); Judge Advocate United States Air Force, United States Department of Defense (1973-1978); Reserve Judge Advocate United States Air Force, United States Department of Defense (1982-2003)

Staff

Senior Law Clerk **James A. Young** . . . . (202) 761-1461
Secretary **Peter Craig** . . . . (202) 761-1461
Administrative Assistant **Edward McGugin** . . . . (202) 761-1461

Chambers of Associate Judge Margaret A. Ryan

450 E Street, NW, Washington, DC 20442-0001
Tel: (202) 761-5214
E-mail: margaret.ryan@armfor.uscourts.gov

Margaret A. Ryan
Associate Judge

Education: Notre Dame JD
Began Service: December 20, 2006
Appointed By: President George W. Bush

Clerkships: Law Clerk The Honorable J. Michael Luttig, United States Court of Appeals for the Fourth Circuit; Law Clerk The Honorable Clarence Thomas, The Supreme Court of the United States

Chambers of Associate Judge Kevin A. Ohlson

450 E Street, NW, Washington, DC 20442-0001
Tel: (202) 761-1448

Kevin A. Ohlson
Associate Judge

Education: Washington & Jefferson 1982 BA; Virginia 1985 JD
Began Service: November 1, 2013
Appointed By: President Barack Obama

Chambers of Senior Judge H. F. Gierke

450 E Street, NW, Washington, DC 20442-0001
Tel: (202) 761-5207 Fax: (202) 761-7009

H. F. "Sparky" Gierke
Senior Judge

Date of Birth: 1943
Education: North Dakota 1964 BA, 1966 JD
Began Service: November 20, 1991
Appointed By: President George H.W. Bush

Academic: Adjunct Professor, George Washington University Law School; Adjunct Professor, Catholic University of America Columbus School of Law; Adjunct Professor, Barry University of Orlando School of Law

Government: State's Attorney, Office of the State's Attorney, County of McKenzie, North Dakota (1974-1982); City Attorney, Office of the City Attorney, City of Watford, North Dakota (1974-1983)

Judicial: Justice, North Dakota Supreme Court (1983-1991); Chief Judge, United States Court of Appeals for the Armed Forces; Associate Judge, United States Court of Appeals for the Armed Forces (1991-2006)

Legal Practice: Private Practice (1971-1983)

Military Service: United States Army (1967-1971)

Current Memberships: American Association for Justice; American Bar Association; Inter-University Seminar on Armed Forces and Society; National District Attorneys Association; North Dakota State's Attorneys Association; State Bar Association of North Dakota

Chambers of Senior Judge Susan J. Crawford

450 E Street, NW, Washington, DC 20747
Tel: (202) 761-5207 Fax: (202) 761-7009

Susan Jean Crawford
Senior Judge

Date of Birth: 1947
Education: Bucknell 1969 BA; New England 1977 JD
Began Service: November 19, 1991
Appointed By: President George H.W. Bush
Political Affiliation: Republican

Academic: Instructor, Garrett College (1979-1981)

Chambers of Senior Judge Susan J. Crawford *continued*

Government: Assistant State's Attorney, Office of the State's Attorney, Garrett County, Maryland (1978-1980); Principal Deputy General Counsel, United States Department of the Army, United States Department of Defense (1981-1983); General Counsel, United States Department of the Army, United States Department of Defense (1983-1989); Special Counsel to the Secretary, United States Department of Defense (1989); Inspector General, United States Department of Defense (1989-1991)

Judicial: United States Court of Military Appeals (1991)

Legal Practice: Associate, Burnett & Eiswert (1977-1979); Partner, Burnett, Eiswert & Crawford (1979-1981)

Current Memberships: The Edward Bennett Williams American Inn of Court, The American Inns of Court; The District of Columbia Bar; Federal Bar Association; Maryland State Bar Association, Inc.

Chambers of Senior Judge Eugene R. Sullivan

6307 Massachusetts Avenue, Bethesda, MD 20816
Tel: (301) 320-5964 Fax: (301) 320-6835

Eugene R. Sullivan
Senior Judge

Date of Birth: 1941
Education: West Point 1964 BS; Georgetown 1971 JD
Began Service: October 1, 1986
Appointed By: President Ronald Reagan
Political Affiliation: Republican

Clerkships: Law Clerk The Honorable M. C. Mathes, United States Court of Appeals for the Eighth Circuit (1971-1972)

Government: Assistant Special Counsel, Executive Office of the President, Gerald Ford Administration (1974); Trial Attorney, United States Department of Justice (1974-1982); Chief Legal Advisor, National Reconnaissance Office, Ronald Reagan Administration (1982-1986); Deputy General Counsel, General Counsel, United States Department of the Air Force (1982-1984); General Counsel, United States Department of the Air Force, United States Department of Defense, Ronald Reagan Administration (1984-1986); Governor, Wake Island Territory (1984-1986)

Legal Practice: Associate, Patton, Boggs & Blow (1972-1974)

Military Service: United States Army (1964-1969)

Current Memberships: The District of Columbia Bar; The Missouri Bar

Chambers of Senior Judge Walter T. Cox III

450 E Street, NW, Washington, DC 20442-0001
Tel: (202) 761-5207 Fax: (202) 761-7009

Walter T. Cox III
Senior Judge

Date of Birth: 1942
Education: Clemson 1964 BS; South Carolina 1967 JD
Began Service: September 6, 1984
Appointed By: President Ronald Reagan
Political Affiliation: Democrat

Judicial: Resident Judge, South Carolina Circuit Court, 10th Judicial Circuit (1978-1984)

Legal Practice: Partner, Jones, McIntosh, Threlkeld, Newman and Cox (1973-1978)

Military Service: United States Army (1964-1973)

Current Memberships: American Bar Association; Anderson County Bar Association; Anderson County Young Lawyers; The Bar Association of the District of Columbia; Blue Key Honor Society; Federal Bar Association; Judge Advocates Association; South Carolina Bar; South Carolina Trial Lawyers Association

Chambers of Senior Judge Andrew S. Effron

450 E Street, NW, Washington, DC 20442-0001
Tel: (202) 761-5207 Fax: (202) 761-7009
E-mail: andrew.effron@armfor.uscourts.gov

Andrew S. Effron
Senior Judge

Date of Birth: 1948
Education: Harvard 1970 AB, 1975 JD; Judge Advocate Gen 1976, 1984
Began Service: 1996
Appointed By: President William J. Clinton

Chambers of Senior Judge James E. Baker

450 E Street, NW, Washington, DC 20442-0001
Tel: (202) 761-1459 Fax: (202) 761-7001

James E. Baker
Senior Judge

Education: Yale 1982 BA, 1990 JD
Began Service: September 19, 2000
Appointed By: President William J. Clinton

Staff
Personal and Confidential Assistant
Sheila K. L. Moretz . . . . (202) 761-1459
E-mail: sheila.moretz@armfor.uscourts.gov

United States Court of Appeals for Veterans Claims

625 Indiana Avenue, NW, Suite 900, Washington, DC 20004-2950
Tel: (202) 501-5970 Fax: (202) 501-5848

Number of Judgeships: 9

Created in 1988, this Court consisting of a chief judge and eight associate judges has exclusive jurisdiction to review final decisions of the Board of Veterans Appeals, an administrative arm of the Department of Veterans Affairs. Cases involve reviewing the Board's determination of entitlement or disability benefits. The rulings can be appealed to the United States Court of Appeals for the Federal Circuit. The Court of Appeals for Veterans Claims is independent and does not come under the purview of the Judicial Conference of the United States or the Administrative Office of the United States Courts. The President appoints a chief judge and between two and six judges. The appointments are for 15-year terms and subject to Senate confirmation.

Court Staff

Clerk of Court and Executive Officer
COL Gregory O. Block . . . . (202) 501-5980
Affiliation: USA
E-mail: gblock@uscourts.cavc.gov
Education: Washington State BA; Seton Hall JD

Deputy Executive Officer **Patrick Barnwell** . . . . (202) 501-5970 ext. 1050
Began Service: 2007
E-mail: pbarnwell@uscourts.cavc.gov

Counsel to the Court **Cary P. Sklar** . . . . (202) 501-5970 ext. 1037
E-mail: CSklar@uscourts.cavc.gov
Education: Cornell 1978 BS; Georgetown 1981 JD

Senior Staff Attorney **Cynthia Brandon-Arnold** . . . . (202) 501-5902
Education: Syracuse 1982 BA; George Washington 1985 JD

Staff Attorney **Nicole Degraffenreed** . . . . (202) 501-5902 ext. 1167
E-mail: ndegraffenreed@uscourts.cavc.gov

Staff Attorney **Jennifer Dowd** . . . . (202) 501-5902 ext. 1161
E-mail: jdowd@uscourts.cavc.gov
Education: Catholic U 1991 BA; Columbus Law 1995 JD

United States Court of Appeals for Veterans Claims *continued*

Staff Attorney **Diane O'Brien-Holcomb** . . . . (202) 501-5902 ext. 1165
E-mail: dobrien@uscourts.cavc.gov
Education: Villanova 1985 BS; Brooklyn Law 1989 JD

Staff Attorney **Elizabeth Hessman-Talbot** . . . . . (202) 501-5902 ext. 1160
Education: Pittsburgh 1981 BA; Georgetown 1986 JD

Staff Attorney **Alice Szynklewski Hoover** . . . . . (202) 501-5902 ext. 1168
Began Service: 2007
E-mail: ahoover@uscourts.cavc.gov

Staff Attorney **John C. Huebl** . . . . (202) 501-5902 ext. 1159
E-mail: jhuebl@uscourts.cavc.gov
Education: Notre Dame 1986 BA; Columbia 1990 MFA; Northwestern 1998 JD

Staff Attorney **Jeremy Bedford** . . . . (202) 501-5902 ext. 1156

Staff Attorney **Andrew P. Reynolds** . . . . (202) 501-5902 ext. 1158
E-mail: areynolds@uscourts.cavc.gov

Staff Attorney **Sonia Mezei** . . . . (202) 501-5902 ext. 1164
E-mail: smezei@uscourts.cavc.gov

Staff Attorney **Amy Gordon** . . . . (202) 501-5902 ext. 1157

Director, Office of Information Technology
Kendyll Benson . . . . (202) 501-5869

Budget Officer **Eva Armah** . . . . (202) 501-5970 ext. 1040
E-mail: earmah@uscourts.cavc.gov

Personnel Officer **Rebecca Alexander** . . . . (202) 501-5991 ext. 1026
E-mail: ralexander@uscourts.cavc.gov

Public Office Chief Deputy Clerk **Anne P. Stygles** . . . . . . (202) 501-5970
E-mail: astygles@uscourts.cavc.gov

Librarian **Allison Mays-Fentress** . . . . (202) 501-5861

Supervisory Paralegal Specialist
Bernard Woodruff . . . . (202) 501-5902 ext. 1166
E-mail: bwoodruff@uscourts.cavc.gov

Chambers of Chief Judge Lawrence B. Hagel

625 Indiana Avenue, NW, Suite 900, Washington, DC 20004-2950
Tel: (202) 501-5862 Fax: (202) 501-5848
E-mail: lhagel@uscourts.cavc.gov

Lawrence B. Hagel
Chief Judge

Date of Birth: March 27, 1947
Education: Naval Acad 1969 BS; McGeorge 1976 JD; George Washington 1983 LLM
Began Service: December 2003
Appointed By: President George W. Bush
Term Expires: December 15, 2016

Current Memberships: The District of Columbia Bar; Federal Bar Association; Iowa State Bar Association; State Bar of California

Staff

Law Clerk **Amanda Blair** . . . . (202) 501-5862
Began Service: September 2011
E-mail: ablair@uscourts.cavc.gov
Education: Buffalo 2008 BA; Detroit Mercy 2011 JD

Law Clerk **Shannon Beydler** . . . . (202) 501-5862
Began Service: September 2015
Term Expires: September 2016
E-mail: mengler@uscourts.cavc.gov

Law Clerk **Melanie Jasinski** . . . . (202) 501-5862
Began Service: 2007
E-mail: mjasinski@uscourts.cavc.gov
Education: Goucher 1998 BA; Hofstra 2007 JD

Judicial Assistant **Dawn Braquet** . . . . (202) 501-5862
E-mail: dbraquet@uscourts.cavc.gov
Education: Maryland University Col 2013 BS

Chambers of Judge Bruce E. Kasold

625 Indiana Avenue, NW, Suite 900, Washington, DC 20004-2950
Tel: (202) 501-5870
E-mail: bkasold@uscourts.cavc.gov

Bruce E. Kasold
Judge

Education: West Point BS; Florida JD; Georgetown LLM
Began Service: December 31, 2003
Appointed By: President George W. Bush

Staff

Law Clerk **Giovanni DiMaggio** . . . . (202) 501-5870
Began Service: 2013
Term Expires: 2015
E-mail: gdimaggio@uscourts.cavc.gov
Law Clerk **Thomas "Tom" Duncombe** . . . . (202) 501-5870
Began Service: 2010
E-mail: tduncombe@uscourts.cavc.gov
Education: Boston U 2006 BA; Georgetown 2009 JD
Law Clerk **Ryan Eletto** . . . . (202) 501-5870
Began Service: 2014
Term Expires: 2015
Law Clerk **Joshua Hansen-King** . . . . (202) 501-5870
Began Service: 2014
Term Expires: 2015
E-mail: jhansen@uscourts.cavc.gov
Law Clerk **Daniel Hinson** . . . . (202) 501-5870
Began Service: August 2015
Term Expires: August 2017
E-mail: dhinson@uscourts.cavc.gov
Administrative Assistant **Dorothy A. McKinney** . . . . (202) 501-5870
E-mail: dmckinney@uscourts.cavc.gov

Chambers of Judge Alan G. Lance, Sr.

625 Indiana Avenue, NW, Suite 900, Washington, DC 20004-2950
Tel: (202) 501-5887
E-mail: alance@uscourts.cavc.gov

Alan G. Lance, Sr.
Judge

Education: South Dakota 1971; Toledo 1973 JD
Began Service: 2004
Appointed By: President George W. Bush

Academic: Member, Law Review, College of Law, The University of Toledo

Government: Representative, Idaho House of Representatives; Majority Caucus Chairman, Idaho House of Representatives; Attorney General, State of Idaho (1995-2003); Chairman, Conference of Western Attorneys General; Assistant Prosecuting Attorney, Fulton County, Ohio

Military Service: United States Army, The Judge Advocate General (1974-1978)

Profession: Private Practice

Membership: Member, Executive Committee, National Association of Attorneys General; National Commander, The American Legion (1999-2000)

Staff

Law Clerk **Jon Gaffney** . . . . (202) 501-5887
Began Service: August 2011
Term Expires: August 2016
Law Clerk **Victor Pereyra** . . . . (202) 501-5887
Began Service: August 2013
Term Expires: August 2016
E-mail: vpereyra@uscourts.cavc.gov
Law Clerk **Lindsay Luken** . . . . (202) 501-5887
Began Service: August 2013
Term Expires: August 2016
Senior Law Clerk **Anthony Scire** . . . . (202) 501-5887
Secretary **Kia Ore** . . . . (202) 501-5887
E-mail: kore@uscourts.cavc.gov

Chambers of Judge Robert N. Davis

625 Indiana Avenue, NW, Suite 900, Washington, DC 20004-2950
Tel: (202) 501-5863 Fax: (202) 501-5848
E-mail: rdavis@uscourts.cavc.gov

Robert N. Davis
Judge

Education: Hartford 1975; Georgetown 1978 JD
Began Service: 2004
Appointed By: President George W. Bush

Academic: Professor, School of Law, The University of Mississippi; Professor, College of Law, Stetson University; Founder, Journal of National Security Law

Government: Mississippi Commissioner, National Conference of Commissioners on Uniform State Laws; Mediator, United States Postal Service; Appellate Attorney, Commodity Futures Trading Commission; Special Assistant U.S. Attorney, District of Columbia District, United States Department of Justice

Military Service: Member United States Navy Reserve; United States Navy, MacDill Air Force Base, United States Department of Defense

Current Memberships: American Bar Association

Membership: Arbitrator and Mediator, American Arbitration Association; Arbitration Panel Member, United States Olympic Committee

Staff

Law Clerk **Liisa Vehik** . . . . (202) 501-5863
Education: Washington U (MO) 2003 JD
Law Clerk **Jessica Grunberg** . . . . (202) 501-5863
Law Clerk **Angel Caracciolo** . . . . (202) 501-5863
Began Service: 2007
E-mail: acaracciolo@uscourts.cavc.gov
Education: Stetson 2003 JD
Senior Law Clerk **(Vacant)** . . . . (202) 501-5863
Secretary **Sherry Tobe-Williams** . . . . (202) 501-5863
E-mail: stobe@vetapp.gov

Chambers of Judge Mary J. Schoelen

625 Indiana Avenue, NW, Suite 900, Washington, DC 20004-2950
Tel: (202) 501-5867 Fax: (202) 501-5848
E-mail: mschoelen@uscourts.cavc.gov

Mary J. Schoelen
Judge

Education: UC Irvine 1990 BA; George Washington 1993 JD
Began Service: 2004
Appointed By: President George W. Bush

Clerkships: Law Clerk, National Veterans Legal Services Project

Government: Intern, Committee on Veterans' Affairs, United States Senate (1994); Staff Attorney, Vietnam Veterans of America (1994-1997); Minority Counsel, Committee on Veterans' Affairs, United States Senate (1997-2001); Minority General Counsel, Committee on Veterans' Affairs, United States Senate (2001); Deputy Staff Director, Benefits and Programs/General Counsel, Committee on Veterans' Affairs, United States Senate (2001-2004)

Staff

Law Clerk **Linda B. Draghici** . . . . (202) 501-5867
E-mail: ldraghici@uscourts.cavc.gov
Law Clerk **Christen Gallagher** . . . . (202) 501-5867
E-mail: cgallagher@uscourts.cavc.gov
Law Clerk **Dayna K. Ingrassia** . . . . (202) 501-5867
Began Service: July 2011
Senior Law Clerk **Stephanie Forester** . . . . (202) 501-5867
E-mail: sforester@uscourts.cavc.gov
Confidential Assistant **Lorraine Swisher** . . . . (202) 501-5867
E-mail: lswisher@uscourts.cavc.gov

Chambers of Judge Coral Wong Pietsch

625 Indiana Avenue, NW, Washington, DC 20004-2950
Tel: (202) 501-5970 Fax: (202) 501-5848

BG Coral Wong Pietsch
Judge

Education: St Teresa BA; Marquette MA; Columbus Law JD
Began Service: 2012
Appointed By: President Barack Obama
Military: USA (Ret)

Staff
Law Clerk **Emily M. Mills** .... (202) 501-5970
Education: Georgia 2000 BS, 2004 JD
Law Clerk **Lauren Holmsley** .... (202) 501-5970
Law Clerk **James "Rob" Brannon** .... (202) 501-5970
Senior Law Clerk **Andrew Steinberg** .... (202) 501-5970
Confidential Assistant **Lori M. Jackson** .... (202) 501-5970

Chambers of Judge Margaret Bartley

625 Indiana Avenue, NW, Washington, DC 20004-2950
Tel: (202) 501-5970 Fax: (202) 501-5848
E-mail: mbartley@uscourts.cavc.gov

Margaret "Meg" Bartley
Judge

Education: Penn State 1981 BA; Washington College of Law 1993 JD
Began Service: 2012
Appointed By: President Barack Obama

Staff
Law Clerk **Matt Albanese** .... (202) 501-5835
E-mail: malbanese@uscourts.cavc.gov
Education: St John's Col (MD) 2002 BA; George Washington 2010 JD
Law Clerk **Victoria Moshiashwili** .... (202) 501-5835
E-mail: vmoshiashwili@uscourts.cavc.gov
Education: Toronto 1996 BA; UMass (Boston) 2001 MA; Cornell 2004 JD, 2004 LLM
Law Clerk **Shannon Noble** .... (202) 501-5835
E-mail: snoble@uscourts.cavc.gov
Senior Law Clerk **Daniel "Dan" Diluccia** .... (202) 501-5835
E-mail: ddiluccia@uscourts.cavc.gov
Education: Georgetown 2005 BA; Washington College of Law 2010 JD
Confidential Assistant **Suzanne Byrnes** .... (202) 501-5835

Chambers of Judge William S. Greenberg

625 Indiana Avenue, NW, Washington, DC 20004-2950
Tel: (202) 501-5970

William S. Greenberg
Judge

Education: Johns Hopkins 1964 BA; Rutgers 1967 JD
Began Service: December 28, 2012
Appointed By: President Barack Obama
Military: ANG (Ret)

Government: Chairman, Reserve Forces Policy Board, Office of the Assistant Secretary of Defense for Reserve Affairs, United States Department of Defense (2009-2011)

Legal Practice: Partner, Business Litigation, McCarter & English, LLP (1993-2012)

Staff
Senior Law Clerk **Eric Ottenheimer** .... (202) 501-5970
Law Clerk **Thomas Ashton** .... (202) 501-5970
Law Clerk **Samuel Lewis** .... (202) 501-5970
Law Clerk **Leonard Moffa** .... (202) 501-5970

Chambers of Judge William S. Greenberg *continued*

Confidential Assistant **Rose Bennett** .... (202) 501-5970

Alien Terrorist Removal Court

E. Barrett Prettyman U.S. Courthouse, 333 Constitution Avenue, NW, Washington, DC 20001
Tel: (202) 354-3050 Fax: (202) 354-3023

Number of Judgeships: 5

The Alien Terrorist Removal Court was created by the Antiterrorism and Effective Death Penalty Act of 1996. The court has the authority to conduct all proceedings to determine whether an alien should be removed from the United States on the grounds of being a terrorist. Applications for removal proceedings are brought by the Attorney General of the United States after being initiated and investigated by the Department of Justice. Decisions made by this court can be appealed to the United States Court of Appeals for the District of Columbia. The court is made up of five district court judges from five judicial circuits. The judges are appointed for five year terms by the Chief Justice of the United States. Judges may be redesignated by the Chief Justice.

Court Staff

Clerk of Court **Angela D. Caesar** .... (202) 354-3050
Assistant to the Clerk of Court **Denise Watson** .... (202) 354-3051

Chambers of Chief Judge James C. Cacheris

Albert V. Bryan, Sr. U.S. Courthouse, 401 Courthouse Square, Alexandria, VA 22314-5704
Tel: (703) 299-2110 Fax: (703) 299-2249

James C. Cacheris
Chief Judge

Date of Birth: 1933
Education: Pennsylvania 1955 BS; George Washington 1960 JD
Began Service: 1981
Appointed By: President Ronald Reagan

Affiliation: Senior Judge, Chambers of Senior Judge James C. Cacheris, United States District Court for the Eastern District of Virginia

Staff
Law Clerk **(Vacant)** .... (703) 299-2110
Law Clerk **(Vacant)** .... (703) 299-2110
Courtroom Deputy **Janice Allen** .... (703) 299-2110
Secretary **Amy Giannetti-Gillespie** .... (703) 299-2110

Chambers of Senior Judge David D. Dowd, Jr.

John F. Seiberling Federal Building and U.S. Courthouse, Two South Main Street, Akron, OH 44308
Tel: (330) 252-6034

David Dudley Dowd, Jr.
Senior Judge

Date of Birth: 1929
Education: Wooster 1951 BA; Michigan 1954 JD
Began Service: October 8, 1982
Appointed By: President Ronald Reagan

Government: Assistant Prosecuting Attorney, State of Ohio (1961-1967); Prosecuting Attorney, State of Ohio (1967-1975)

Judicial: Judge, Ohio Court of Appeals, Fifth District (1975-1980); Justice, Ohio Supreme Court (1980)

Legal Practice: Partner, Dowd & Dowd, Ltd. (1954-1955); Partner, Dowd & Dowd, Ltd. (1958-1975); Black, McCuskey, Souers & Arbaugh (1981-1982)

Military Service: United States Army (1955-1957)

Chambers of Senior Judge William C. O'Kelley
1942 U.S. Courthouse, 75 Spring Street, SW, Atlanta, GA 30303-3309
Tel: (404) 215-1530 Fax: (404) 215-1538

William C. O'Kelley
Senior Judge

Date of Birth: 1930
Education: Emory 1951 AB, 1953 LLB
Began Service: October 23, 1970
Appointed By: President Richard M. Nixon
Political Affiliation: Republican

Affiliation: Senior Judge (R), Chambers of Senior Judge William C. O'Kelley, United States District Court for the Northern District of Georgia

Government: Assistant United States Attorney, Northern District of Georgia, United States Department of Justice (1959-1961); Special Hearing Officer, United States Department of Justice (1962-1968)

Judicial: Judge, United States Foreign Intelligence Surveillance Court (1980-1987)

Legal Practice: Partner, O'Kelley, Hopkins & Van Gerpen (1961-1970); General Counsel, Georgia Republican Party (1968-1970)

Military Service: United States Air Force (1953-1957); United States Air Force Reserve (1957-1966)

Current Memberships: American Bar Association; Atlanta Bar Association; Federal Bar Association; Gainsville Northeastern Bar Association; Lawyers Club of Atlanta, Inc.; Old War Horse Lawyers' Club; State Bar of Georgia

Staff
Law Clerk **Elliott A. Foote** .... (404) 215-1530
Began Service: September 3, 2015
Term Expires: August 2017
Career Law Clerk **Seunhee Pike** .... (404) 215-1530
E-mail: seunhee_pike@gand.uscourts.gov
Education: Oberlin 1983 BA; Georgia 1988 JD
Secretary **Geri Graham** .... (404) 215-1530
E-mail: geri_graham@gand.uscourts.gov

Chambers of Senior Judge Michael A. Telesca
272 U.S. Courthouse, 100 State Street, Rochester, NY 14614
Tel: (585) 613-4060 Fax: (585) 613-4065

Michael A. Telesca
Senior Judge

Date of Birth: 1929
Education: Rochester 1952 AB; SUNY (Buffalo) 1955 JD
Began Service: 1982
Appointed By: President Ronald Reagan
Political Affiliation: Republican

Affiliation: Senior Judge (R), Chambers of Senior Judge Michael A. Telesca, United States District Court for the Western District of New York

Judicial: Judge, Surrogate Court, Monroe County (1973-1982)

Legal Practice: Partner, Lamb, Webster, Walz & Telesca (1957-1973)

Military Service: United States Marine Corps (1955-1957)

Current Memberships: American Bar Association; The American Inns of Court; The Justinian Society of Jurists; Monroe County Bar Association (NY); New York State Bar Association

Chambers of Senior Judge Harold A. Baker
338 U.S. Courthouse, 201 South Vine Street, Urbana, IL 61801
Tel: (202) 354-3050

Harold Albert Baker
Senior Judge

Date of Birth: 1929
Education: Illinois 1951 BA, 1956 LLB
Appointed By: President Jimmy Carter
Political Affiliation: Democrat

Academic: Adjunct Instructor, College of Law, University of Illinois (1972-1978)

Government: Senior Counsel, Presidential Commission on the Central Intelligence Agency Activities in the United States, Executive Office of the President, Gerald Ford Administration (1974-1975)

Legal Practice: Partner, Wheat, Hatch, Corazza & Baker (1960-1978)

Military Service: United States Navy (1951-1953)

Current Memberships: American Bar Association; American College of Trial Lawyers; Champaign County Bar Association; Illinois State Bar Association

United States Tax Court
400 Second Street, NW, Washington, DC 20217
Tel: (202) 521-0700
Internet: www.ustaxcourt.gov

Number of Judgeships: 15

The United States Tax Court exercises jurisdiction as provided in title 26 of the U.S. code over matters involving Federal taxation, providing a forum in which taxpayers may dispute determinations made by the Internal Revenue Service. Upon receiving a notice of deficiency in tax from the IRS, taxpayers have a choice of three federal forums in which they can obtain a judicial determination of their rights. They may pay the tax and file a claim with the IRS for a refund. If the claim is disallowed, they may then file suit for a refund in a U.S. District Court or the U.S Court of Federal Claims. If they do not wish to pay the tax beforehand, they may litigate the matter in the U.S. Tax Court. The court is composed of 19 judges appointed to 15-year terms by the President with the advice and consent of the Senate; senior judges; and special trial judges (appointed by the Chief Judge and authorized by statute to decide particular categories of cases). Court proceedings take place on the record and are open to the public. Decisions by the court, except those issued in small tax cases, are generally appealable to the United States Courts of Appeals serving the geographic area in which the individual taxpayer resides or the corporate taxpayer has its principle place of business.

Court Staff
Clerk of Court **Robert Di Trolio** .... (202) 521-4600
E-mail: rditrolio@ustaxcourt.gov
General Counsel **Douglas Snoeyenbos** .... (202) 521-3390
Deputy General Counsel **Fig Ruggieri** .... (202) 521-3390
E-mail: fruggieri@ustaxcourt.gov
Director of Human Resources **Ellene Footer** .... (202) 521-4700
E-mail: efooter@ustaxcourt.gov
Librarian **Nancy Ciliberti** .... (202) 521-4585
Fax: (202) 521-4574
Director, Office of Information Systems
Scott Goodrick .... (202) 521-4550
E-mail: sgoodrick@ustaxcourt.gov Tel: (202) 521-4569

Chambers of Chief Judge Michael B. Thornton
400 Second Street, NW, Washington, DC 20217
Tel: (202) 521-0777

Michael B. Thornton
Chief Judge

Date of Birth: 1954
Education: Southern Mississippi 1976 BS, 1977 MS; Tennessee 1979 MA; Duke 1982 JD
Began Service: March 8, 1998
Appointed By: President William J. Clinton
Term Expires: August 6, 2028

Chambers of Judge John O. Colvin
400 Second Street, NW, Washington, DC 20217
Tel: (202) 521-0662
E-mail: jcolvin@ustaxcourt.gov

John O. Colvin
Judge

Date of Birth: 1946
Education: Missouri 1968 AB; Georgetown 1971 JD, 1978 LLM
Began Service: 1988
Appointed By: President Ronald Reagan
Term Expires: August 11, 2019

Current Memberships: Federal Bar Association

Staff
Law Clerk **L. Madeline Obler-Grill** .... (202) 521-3390
Chambers Administrator **Betty Scott Boom** .... (202) 521-0777
Education: High Point 1973 BA

Chambers of Judge Maurice B. Foley
400 Second Street, NW, Washington, DC 20217
Tel: (202) 521-0681
E-mail: jfoley@ustaxcourt.gov

Maurice B. Foley
Judge

Date of Birth: March 28, 1960
Education: Swarthmore 1982 BA; Boalt Hall 1985 JD; Georgetown 1988 LLM
Began Service: April 9, 1995
Appointed By: President William J. Clinton
Term Expires: November 24, 2026

Government: Attorney, Office of the Chief Counsel, Internal Revenue Service, United States Department of the Treasury (1985-1988); Tax Counsel, United States Senate (1988-1993); Deputy Tax Legislative Counsel, United States Department of the Treasury (1993-1995)

Current Memberships: State Bar of California

Staff
Law Clerk **Joshua R. Lake** .... (202) 521-0681
E-mail: jrlake@ustaxcourt.gov
Law Clerk **Vlad Frants** .... (202) 521-0681
E-mail: vfrants@ustaxcourt.gov
Chambers Administrator **Nancy Ciccarello** .... (202) 521-0681
E-mail: nciccarello@ustaxcourt.gov
Secretary **Genia M. Stith** .... (202) 521-0681

Chambers of Judge Joseph H. Gale
400 Second Street, NW, Washington, DC 20217
Tel: (202) 521-0688
E-mail: jgale@ustaxcourt.gov

Joseph H. Gale
Judge

Date of Birth: 1953
Education: Princeton 1976 AB; Virginia 1980 JD
Began Service: February 6, 1996
Appointed By: President William J. Clinton
Term Expires: October 17, 2026

Staff
Law Clerk **Robert Randolph** .... (202) 521-0685
E-mail: rrandolph@ustaxcourt.gov
Law Clerk **Matthew Carruth** .... (202) 521-0685
E-mail: mcarruth@ustaxcourt.gov
Law Clerk **Ross Sharkey** .... (202) 521-0684
E-mail: rsharkey@ustaxcourt.gov
Chambers Administrator **Judith Sebold** .... (202) 521-0686
E-mail: jesebold@ustaxcourt.gov

Chambers of Judge Joseph Robert Goeke
400 Second Street, NW, Room 410, Washington, DC 20217
Tel: (202) 521-0690 Fax: (202) 521-0879
E-mail: jgoeke@ustaxcourt.gov

Joseph Robert Goeke
Judge

Date of Birth: June 22, 1950
Education: Xavier (OH) 1972 BS; Kentucky 1975 JD
Began Service: April 22, 2003
Appointed By: President George W. Bush
Term Expires: April 21, 2018

Government: Office of the Chief Counsel, Internal Revenue Service, United States Department of the Treasury (1980-1988)

Legal Practice: Partner, Mayer, Brown, Rowe & Maw LLP (1988-2003)

Staff
Law Clerk **Eric Biscopink** .... (202) 521-0690
Term Expires: June 2016
Law Clerk **Annie Wurtzebach** .... (202) 521-0690
Term Expires: July 2017
Chambers Administrator **Danielle Vonada** .... (202) 521-0690
E-mail: dvonada@ustaxcourt.gov

Chambers of Judge David D. Gustafson
400 Second Street, NW, Washington, DC 20217
Tel: (202) 521-0850

David D. Gustafson
Judge

Education: Bob Jones U 1978 BA; Duke 1981 JD
Began Service: July 29, 2008
Appointed By: President George W. Bush
Term Expires: July 28, 2023

Government: Court of Federal Claims Section Chief, Tax Division, Office of the Associate Attorney General, United States Department of Justice (2005-2008)

Current Memberships: The District of Columbia Bar

Staff
Law Clerk **Devan Patrick** .... (202) 521-0848
Law Clerk **Nicole Provo** .... (202) 521-0848
Chambers Administrator **Susanne Catlett** .... (202) 521-0850
E-mail: scatlett@ustaxcourt.gov

Chambers of Judge James S. Halpern

400 Second Street, NW, Washington, DC 20217
Tel: (202) 521-0707
E-mail: jhalpern@ustaxcourt.gov

James S. Halpern
Judge

Date of Birth: 1945
Education: Wharton 1967 BS; Pennsylvania 1972 JD; NYU 1975 LLM
Began Service: July 3, 1990
Appointed By: President George H.W. Bush
Term Expires: November 1, 2020

Academic: Assistant Professor, Washington and Lee University (1975-1976); Assistant Professor, St. John's University (1976-1979); Visiting Professor, New York University (1979-1980)

Government: Principal Technical Advisor, Assistant Commissioner and Associate Chief Counsel, Internal Revenue Service, United States Department of the Treasury (1980-1983)

Legal Practice: Associate, Mudge, Rose, Guthrie, Alexander & Ferdon (1972-1974); Associate, Roberts & Holland LLP (1979-1980); Partner, Baker & Hostetler LLP (1983-1990)

Military Service: United States Army (1967-1969); United States Army Reserve, United States Department of the Army (1968-1997)

Staff
Law Clerk **Derek B. Wagner** .... (202) 521-0707
E-mail: dwagner@ustaxcourt.gov
Law Clerk **Frederick E. Wallach** .... (202) 521-0707
E-mail: fwallach@ustaxcourt.gov
Education: Williams 1959 BA; Harvard 1962 JD; George Washington 1970 LLM
Chambers Administrator **Velinda Morton** .... (202) 521-0707
E-mail: vmorton@ustaxcourt.gov
Secretary **Shelia Perry** .... (202) 521-0707
E-mail: sperry@ustaxcourt.gov

Chambers of Judge Mark van Dyke Holmes

400 Second Street, NW, Washington, DC 20217
Tel: (202) 521-0714
E-mail: jholmes@ustaxcourt.gov

Mark van Dyke Holmes
Judge

Date of Birth: July 6, 1960
Education: Harvard 1979 BA; Chicago 1983 JD
Began Service: June 30, 2003
Appointed By: President George W. Bush
Term Expires: June 29, 2018
Political Affiliation: Republican

Clerkships: Law Clerk Alex Kozinski, United States Court of Appeals for the Ninth Circuit (1985-1987)

Government: Counsel to Commissioners, United States International Trade Commission (1991-1996); Deputy Assistant Attorney General, Tax Division (2001-2003)

Legal Practice: Associate, Cahill Gordon & Reindel LLP (1983-1985); Associate, Sullivan & Cromwell LLP (1987-1991); Counsel, Miller & Chevalier (1996-2001)

Current Memberships: Section on Litigation, American Bar Association; Section on Taxation, American Bar Association

Staff
Law Clerk **Zachary Froelich** .... (202) 521-0714
E-mail: zfroehlich@ustaxcourt.gov
Law Clerk **Amber Gorski** .... (202) 521-0714
E-mail: agorski@ustaxcourt.gov
Chambers Administrator **Michelle M. Alvarez** .... (202) 521-0714
E-mail: malvarez@ustaxcourt.gov

Chambers of Judge Kathleen Kerrigan

400 Second Street, NW, Washington, DC 20217
Tel: (202) 521-0750

Kathleen M. "Kathy" Kerrigan
Judge

Education: Boston Col 1985 BS; Notre Dame 1990 JD
Began Service: May 8, 2012
Appointed By: President Barack Obama

Staff
Law Clerk **Catherine Karayan** .... (202) 521-0750
Law Clerk **Michael Lobie** .... (202) 521-0750
Chambers Administrator **Patricia Hodge** .... (202) 521-0750

Chambers of Judge Richard T. Morrison

400 Second Street, NW, Washington, DC 20217
Tel: (202) 521-0853

Richard T. Morrison
Judge

Education: Kansas BS, BA; Chicago MA, JD
Began Service: August 29, 2008
Appointed By: President George W. Bush
Term Expires: August 28, 2023

Clerkships: Law Clerk, Judge Jerry E. Smith, United States Court of Appeals for the Fifth Circuit

Government: Deputy Assistant Attorney General for Appellate and Review, Tax Division, Office of the Associate Attorney General, United States Department of Justice; Acting Assistant Attorney General, Tax Division, Office of the Associate Attorney General, United States Department of Justice (2007)

Legal Practice: Attorney, Tax Law, Baker & McKenzie; Attorney, Tax Controversy Practice Group, Mayer, Brown & Platt LLP

Chambers of Judge Elizabeth Crewson Paris

400 Second Street, NW, Washington, DC 20217
Tel: (202) 521-0839

Elizabeth Crewson Paris
Judge

Date of Birth: January 14, 1958
Education: Tulsa 1980 BS, 1987 JD; Denver 1993 LLM
Began Service: July 30, 2008
Appointed By: President George W. Bush
Term Expires: July 29, 2023
Political Affiliation: Republican

Government: Tax Counsel, Committee on Finance, United States Senate (2000-2008)

Legal Practice: Partner, Brumley Bishop & Paris (1987-1994); Senior Associate, McKenna & Cuneo L.L.P. (1994-1998); Tax Partner, Reinhart, Boerner, Van Deuren, Norris & Rieselbach, s.c. (1998-2000)

Chambers of Judge Juan F. Vasquez

400 Second Street, NW, Room 406, Washington, DC 20217
Tel: (202) 521-0778 Fax: (202) 273-4978
E-mail: jvasquez@ustaxcourt.gov

Juan F. Vasquez
Judge

Date of Birth: 1948
Education: Texas 1972 BBA; Houston 1977 JD; NYU 1978 LLM
Began Service: May 1, 1995
Appointed By: President William J. Clinton
Term Expires: October 12, 2026
Political Affiliation: Democrat

Corporate: Accountant, Coopers & Lybrand LLP (1972-1974)

Government: Attorney, Office of Chief Counsel, Internal Revenue Service, United States Department of the Treasury (1978-1982)

Legal Practice: Attorney, Leighton, Hood & Vasquez (1982-1985); Partner, Leighton & Vasquez (1985-1987); Partner, Juan F. Vasquez, PC (1987-1995)

Current Memberships: Texas Bar Foundation; Section on Taxation, American Bar Association; College of the State Bar of Texas; The Hispanic Bar Association of the District of Columbia; Hispanic National Bar Association; Mexican American Bar Association of San Antonio; Mexican American Bar Association of Texas; National Judicial College; San Antonio Bar Association; San Antonio Bar Foundation; State Bar of Texas

Staff

Law Clerk **Ben Friedman** .... (202) 521-0778
E-mail: bfriedman@ustaxcourt.gov
Law Clerk **James Yu** .... (202) 521-0778
E-mail: jzyu@ustaxcourt.gov
Chambers Administrator **Jean Douglas** .... (202) 521-0778
Secretary **Tammy Staples** .... (202) 521-0778
E-mail: tstaples@ustaxcourt.gov

Chambers of Judge Albert Lauber

400 Second Street, NW, Washington, DC 20217
Tel: (202) 521-0785

Albert G. Lauber
Judge

Education: Yale BA; Cambridge (UK) MA; Yale JD
Began Service: January 31, 2013
Appointed By: President Barack Obama
Term Expires: January 30, 2028

Clerkships: Law Clerk, Chambers of Associate Justice Harry A. Blackmun, Supreme Court of the United States

Government: Tax Assistant to the Solicitor General, Office of the Attorney General, United States Department of Justice; Deputy Solicitor General, Office of the Attorney General, United States Department of Justice (1983-1988)

Legal Practice: Partner, Caplin & Drysdale, Chartered

Chambers of Judge Ronald Buch

400 Second Street, NW, Washington, DC 20217
Tel: (202) 521-0810

Ronald Lee Buch
Judge

Education: Northwood BBA; Michigan State JD; Capital U LLM
Began Service: January 14, 2013
Appointed By: President Barack Obama
Term Expires: January 13, 2028

Legal Practice: Partner, Bingham McCutchen LLP (2001-2011)

Chambers of Judge Joseph W. Nega

400 Second Street, NW, Washington, DC 20217
Tel: (202) 521-0640

Joseph W. Nega
Judge

Education: DePaul BSAcc, JD; Georgetown Col MLT
Began Service: 2013
Appointed By: President Barack Obama

Chambers of Judge L. Paige Marvel

400 Second Street, NW, Washington, DC 20217
Tel: (202) 521-0740
E-mail: jmarvel@ustaxcourt.gov

L. Paige Marvel
Judge

Note: On November 20, 2014, the Senate confirmed L. Paige Marvel for another term as Judge on the United States Tax Court.
Date of Birth: 1949
Education: Notre Dame 1971 BA; Maryland 1974 JD
Began Service: April 6, 1998
Appointed By: President Barack Obama
Term Expires: April 5, 2029
Political Affiliation: Democrat

Current Memberships: American Bar Foundation; American Bar Association; American College of Tax Counsel; The American Law Institute; Maryland State Bar Association, Inc.; Maryland Bar Foundation, Maryland State Bar Association, Inc.

Staff

Law Clerk **Douglas Longhofer** .... (202) 521-0740
E-mail: dlonghofer@ustaxcourt.gov
Law Clerk **Chaim Gordon** .... (202) 521-0740
Began Service: August 2008
E-mail: cgordon@ustaxcourt.gov
Chambers Administrator **Angela Frith** .... (202) 521-0740
E-mail: afrith@ustaxcourt.gov

Chambers of Judge Tamara W. Ashford

400 Second Street, NW, Washington, DC 20217
Tel: (202) 521-0700

Tamara W. Ashford
Judge

Education: Duke AB; Vanderbilt JD; Miami LLM
Began Service: 2014
Appointed By: President Barack Obama

Chambers of Judge Cary Douglas Pugh

400 Second Street, NW, Washington, DC 20217
Tel: (202) 521-0824

Cary Douglas Pugh
Judge

Education: Duke 1987 AB; Stanford 1988 MA; Virginia 1994 JD
Began Service: 2014
Appointed By: President Barack Obama

Chambers of Senior Judge (recalled) Harry Allen Haines

400 Second Street, NW, Washington, DC 20217
Tel: (202) 521-0699

Harry Allen Haines
Senior Judge (recalled)

Date of Birth: May 30, 1939
Education: St Olaf 1961 BA; Montana 1964 LLB; NYU 1966 LLM
Began Service: April 22, 2003
Appointed By: President George W. Bush
Term Expires: April 21, 2018

Academic: Adjunct Professor, School of Law, The Montana University System (1965); Teaching Fellow, New York University Law School (1966); Lecturer-in-Law, University of Montana (1967); Lecturer-in-Law, University of Montana (1970); Lecturer-in-Law, University of Montana (1974); Lecturer-in-Law, University of Montana (1981-1991); Fellow, American College of Trust and Estate Counsel

Legal Practice: Partner, Worden Thane & Haines, PC (1966-2003)

Current Memberships: American Bar Association; State Bar of Montana

Chambers of Senior Judge (recalled) Herbert L. Chabot

400 Second Street, NW, Washington, DC 20217
Tel: (202) 521-0644

Herbert L. Chabot
Senior Judge

Date of Birth: 1931
Education: CCNY 1952 BA; Columbia 1957 LLB; Georgetown 1964 LLM
Began Service: April 3, 1978
Appointed By: President Jimmy Carter

Academic: Adjunct Professor, The George Washington University (1974-1984)

Clerkships: Law Clerk The Honorable Russell E. Train, United States Tax Court (1961-1965)

Government: Associate, Joint Committee on Taxation, United States Congress (1965-1978)

Military Service: United States Army (1953-1955); United States Army Reserve, United States Department of the Army (1955-1963)

Nonprofit: Legal Staff, American Jewish Congress (1957-1961)

Current Memberships: American Bar Association; Federal Bar Association

Staff
Chambers Administrator **(Vacant)** .... (202) 521-0644

Chambers of Senior Judge (recalled) Howard A. Dawson, Jr.

400 Second Street, NW, Washington, DC 20217
Tel: (202) 521-0670 Fax: (202) 521-0875

Howard A. Dawson, Jr.
Senior Judge (recalled)

Date of Birth: 1922
Education: North Carolina 1946 BS; George Washington 1949 JD
Began Service: August 21, 1962
Appointed By: President John F. Kennedy
Political Affiliation: Democrat

Academic: David L. Brennan Distinguished Visiting Professor of Law, School of Law, The University of Akron (1986); Director, Tax Graduate Program and Professor, School of Law, University of Baltimore (1986-1989); Distinguished Visiting Professor of Law, School of Law, University of San Diego (1991)

Chambers of Senior Judge (recalled) Howard A. Dawson, Jr. *continued*

Government: Attorney, Civil Division, Office of Chief Counsel, Internal Revenue Service, United States Department of the Treasury (1950-1953); Civil Advisory Counsel, Atlanta District Office, Internal Revenue Service, United States Department of the Treasury (1953-1957); Regional Counsel, Atlanta Region, Internal Revenue Service, United States Department of the Treasury (1958); Personal Assistant to the Chief Counsel and Assistant Chief Counsel, Office of the Chief Counsel, Internal Revenue Service, United States Department of the Treasury (1958-1962)

Legal Practice: Private Practice (1949-1950)

Military Service: United States Army, Finance Corps (1944-1945); Captain United States Army Reserve, United States Department of the Army

Current Memberships: American Bar Association; The District of Columbia Bar; Federal Bar Association; State Bar of Georgia

Staff
Law Clerk **Daphne Halpern** .... (202) 521-0670

Chambers of Senior Judge (recalled) Julian I. Jacobs

400 Second Street, NW, Washington, DC 20217
Tel: (202) 521-0720
E-mail: jjacobs@ustaxcourt.gov

Julian I. Jacobs
Senior Judge (recalled)

Date of Birth: 1937
Education: Maryland 1958 BA, 1960 LLB; Georgetown 1965 LLM
Began Service: March 30, 1984
Appointed By: President Ronald Reagan

Academic: Adjunct Professor, Graduate Tax Program, University of Baltimore (1991-1994); Adjunct Professor, School of Law, University of San Diego (2001); Adjunct Professor, College of Law, University of Denver (2001)

Government: Attorney, Legislation and Regulations Division, Office of the Chief Counsel, Internal Revenue Service, United States Department of the Treasury (1961-1965); Trial Attorney, Office of the Regional Counsel, Internal Revenue Service, United States Department of the Treasury (1965-1967)

Legal Practice: Associate, Weinberg & Green (1967-1969); Hoffberger & Hollander (1969-1972); Partner, Gordon, Feinblatt, Rothman, Hoffberger & Hollander, LLC (1972-1984)

Chambers of Senior Judge (recalled) Robert P. Ruwe

400 Second Street, NW, Washington, DC 20217
Tel: (202) 521-0751

Robert P. Ruwe
Senior Judge

Date of Birth: 1941
Education: Xavier (OH) 1963 BSBA; Salmon P Chase 1970 JD
Began Service: November 20, 1987
Appointed By: President Ronald Reagan

Government: Special Agent, Intelligence Division (Criminal Investigation), Internal Revenue Service, United States Department of the Treasury (1963-1970); Trial Attorney, District Counsel, Internal Revenue Service, United States Department of the Treasury (1970-1977); Technical Assistant to Deputy Chief Counsel, Office of the Chief Counsel, Internal Revenue Service, United States Department of the Treasury (1977-1979); Director, Criminal Tax Division, Office of the Chief Counsel, Internal Revenue Service, United States Department of the Treasury (1979-1982); Deputy Associate Chief Counsel (Litigation), Office of the Chief Counsel, Internal Revenue Service, United States Department of the Treasury (1982-1984); Director, Tax Litigation Division, Office of the Chief Counsel, Internal Revenue Service, United States Department of the Treasury (1984-1987)

(continued on next page)

Chambers of Senior Judge (recalled) Robert P. Ruwe *continued*

Staff

Law Clerk **Tyler Moser** . . . . (202) 521-0751
Began Service: June 2014
Term Expires: June 2017
Chambers Administrator **Kathy Trenary** . . . . (202) 521-0751
E-mail: ktrenary@ustaxcourt.gov

Chambers of Senior Judge (recalled) Laurence J. Whalen

400 Second Street, NW, Room 331, Washington, DC 20217
Tel: (202) 521-0792

Laurence J. Whalen
Senior Judge

Date of Birth: 1944
Education: Georgetown 1967 BA, 1970 JD, 1971 LLM
Began Service: November 23, 1987
Appointed By: President Ronald Reagan

Government: Trial Attorney, Tax Division, United States Department of Justice (1971-1975)

Legal Practice: Partner, Hamel & Park (1977-1984); Director, Crowe & Dunlevy (1984-1987)

Military Service: United States Army Reserve, United States Department of the Army (1971)

Current Memberships: American Bar Association; Federal Bar Association

Staff

Law Clerk **(Vacant)** . . . . (202) 521-0792
Chambers Administrator **Julie Daniels** . . . . (202) 521-0792

Chambers of Senior Judge (recalled) Joel Gerber

400 Second Street, NW, Washington, DC 20217-0001
Tel: (202) 521-0699
E-mail: jgerber@ustaxcourt.gov

Joel Gerber
Senior Judge (recalled)

Date of Birth: 1940
Education: Roosevelt 1962 BS; DePaul 1965 JD; Boston U 1968 LLM
Began Service: June 18, 1984
Appointed By: President Ronald Reagan
Term Expires: December 14, 2015

Academic: Lecturer, Vanderbilt University (1976-1980); Lecturer, University of Miami (1986-1990)

Government: Trial Attorney, Internal Revenue Service, United States Department of the Treasury (1965-1972); Staff Assistant to Regional Counsel and Senior Trial Attorney, Internal Revenue Service, United States Department of the Treasury (1972-1976); District Counsel, Internal Revenue Service, United States Department of the Treasury (1976-1980); Deputy Chief Counsel, Internal Revenue Service, United States Department of the Treasury (1980-1984); Acting Chief Counsel, Internal Revenue Service, United States Department of the Treasury (1983-1984)

Judicial: Chief Judge, United States Tax Court (2004-2006)

Current Memberships: American Bar Association

Chambers of Senior Judge (recalled) David Laro

400 Second Street, NW, Washington, DC 20217
Tel: (202) 521-0738
E-mail: jlaro@ustaxcourt.gov

David Laro
Senior Judge (recalled)

Date of Birth: 1942
Education: Michigan 1964 BA; Illinois 1967 JD; NYU 1970 LLM
Began Service: November 2, 1992
Appointed By: President George H.W. Bush

Academic: Adjunct Faculty, Georgetown University; Visiting Professor, School of Law, University of San Diego

Corporate: Chairman, Republic Bank (1986-1992); President and Chief Executive Officer, Durakon Industries, Inc. (1989-1991)

Legal Practice: Winegarden, Booth, Shedd and Laro (1970-1975); Laro & Borgeson (1975-1986); David Laro, Attorney at Law (1986-1992); Of Counsel, Dykema Gossett PLLC (1989-1990)

Current Memberships: State Bar of Michigan

Staff

Law Clerk **Helen Trac** . . . . (202) 521-0738
Chambers Administrator **Rebecca Styles** . . . . (202) 521-0738
E-mail: rstyles@ustaxcourt.gov

Chambers of Senior Judge (recalled) Carolyn P. Chiechi

400 Second Street, NW, Washington, DC 20217-0002
Tel: (202) 521-0650

Carolyn P. Chiechi
Senior Judge (recalled)

Date of Birth: 1943
Education: Georgetown 1965 BS, 1969 JD, 1971 LLM
Began Service: October 1, 1992
Appointed By: President George H.W. Bush

Government: Attorney-Advisor, The Honorable Leo H. Irwin, United States Tax Court (1969-1971)

Legal Practice: Associate, Sutherland Asbill & Brennan LLP (1971-1976); Partner, Sutherland Asbill & Brennan LLP (1976-1992)

Current Memberships: American Bar Foundation; American Bar Association; American College of Tax Counsel; The District of Columbia Bar; Federal Bar Association; Women's Bar Association of the District of Columbia

Staff

Law Clerk **(Vacant)** . . . . (202) 521-0650
Attorney-Advisor **Mireille Alfano** . . . . (202) 521-0648
Chambers Administrator **Candace Marshall** . . . . . . (202) 521-0652
E-mail: cmarshall@ustaxcourt.gov

Chambers of Senior Judge (recalled) Stephen J. Swift

400 Second Street, NW, Washington, DC 20217
Tel: (202) 521-0700

Stephen J. Swift
Senior Judge (recalled)

Date of Birth: September 7, 1943
Education: BYU 1967 BS; George Washington 1970 JD
Began Service: August 16, 1983
Appointed By: President Ronald Reagan
Political Affiliation: Republican

Current Memberships: American Bar Association; The District of Columbia Bar; State Bar of California

Chambers of Senior Judge (recalled) Thomas B. Wells

400 Second Street, NW, Washington, DC 20217
Tel: (202) 521-0790

Thomas B. Wells
Senior Judge (recalled)

Date of Birth: 1945
Education: Miami 1967 BS; Emory 1973 JD; NYU 1978 LLM
Began Service: October 13, 1986
Appointed By: President Ronald Reagan
Term Expires: October 9, 2016

Current Memberships: American Bar Association; State Bar of Georgia

Chambers of Senior Judge (recalled) Mary Ann Cohen

400 Second Street, NW, Washington, DC 20217
Tel: (202) 521-0655

Mary Ann Cohen
Senior Judge (recalled)

Date of Birth: 1943
Education: UCLA 1964 BS; USC 1967 JD
Began Service: September 24, 1982
Appointed By: President Ronald Reagan

Current Memberships: American Bar Association; State Bar of California

Staff
Chambers Administrator **Shirley Allison** . . . . (202) 521-0655
E-mail: sallison@ustaxcourt.gov

Chambers of Senior Judge (recalled) Robert A. Wherry, Jr.

400 Second Street, NW, Room 413, Washington, DC 20217
Tel: (202) 521-0800 Fax: (202) 521-0894
E-mail: jwherry@ustaxcourt.gov

Robert A. Wherry, Jr.
Senior Judge (recalled)

Date of Birth: April 7, 1944
Education: Colorado 1966 BS, 1969 JD; NYU 1972 LLM
Began Service: April 23, 2003
Appointed By: President George W. Bush
Term Expires: April 22, 2018

Staff
Law Clerk **Elizabeth Stevens** . . . . (202) 521-0800
E-mail: esteve001@ustaxcourt.gov
Law Clerk **Joseph P. Malca** . . . . (202) 521-0800
E-mail: jpmalca@ustaxcourt.gov
Chambers Administrator **Marisa J. Nickerson** . . . . (202) 521-0800
E-mail: mnickerson@ustaxcourt.gov

Chambers of Chief Special Trial Judge Peter J. Panuthos

400 Second Street, NW, Washington, DC 20217
Tel: (202) 521-4707

Peter J. Panuthos
Chief Special Trial Judge

Date of Birth: 1943
Education: Bryant Col 1966 BS; Suffolk 1969 JD; Boston U 1973 LLM
Began Service: June 13, 1983

Academic: Adjunct Professor of Graduate Tax, Bentley College (1975-1983); Adjunct Professor, Columbus School of Law, The Catholic University of America (2001)

Chambers of Chief Special Trial Judge Peter J. Panuthos *continued*

Government: Attorney, Office of the General Counsel, United States Department of Agriculture (1969-1970); Attorney, Office of the Chief Counsel, Internal Revenue Service, United States Department of the Treasury (1970-1975); Assistant District Counsel, Internal Revenue Service, United States Department of the Treasury (1975-1983)

Current Memberships: American Bar Association; American College of Tax Counsel; Federal Bar Association

Staff
Judicial Assistant **Kathy Lovett** . . . . (202) 521-4707

Chambers of Special Trial Judge Robert N. Armen, Jr.

400 Second Street, NW, Washington, DC 20217
Tel: (202) 521-4711

Robert N. Armen, Jr.
Special Trial Judge

Date of Birth: 1945
Education: Cleveland-Marshall 1979 LLM; Duquesne 1969 BA; Georgetown 1973 JD, 1974 MLT
Began Service: 1993

Academic: Adjunct Faculty, Northern Virginia Community College (1981-1989); Adjunct Faculty, School of Law, University of Baltimore (1988-1990)

Clerkships: Law Clerk The Honorable Howard A. Dawson, Jr. (1981-1983)

Government: Associate, Office of the Chief Counsel, Internal Revenue Service, United States Department of the Treasury (1973-1981)

Staff
Law Clerk **Maggie Stehn** . . . . (202) 521-4711
Judicial Assistant **Meggan Barker** . . . . (202) 521-4711

Chambers of Special Trial Judge Lewis R. Carluzzo

400 Second Street, NW, Washington, DC 20217
Tel: (202) 521-3339

Lewis R. Carluzzo
Special Trial Judge

Date of Birth: 1949
Education: Villanova 1971, 1974 JD
Began Service: 1994

Government: Associate, Office of Chief Counsel, Internal Revenue Service, United States Department of the Treasury (1977-1994)

Legal Practice: Private Practice (1975)

Staff
Law Clerk **Zachary Fried** . . . . (202) 521-3339
Education: George Washington 2006 JD
Judicial Assistant **Carolynn Battle** . . . . (202) 521-3339
E-mail: cbattle@ustaxcourt.gov

Chambers of Special Trial Judge Daniel A. Guy Jr.

400 Second Street, NW, Washington, DC 20217
Tel: (202) 521-3370

Daniel A. Guy, Jr.
Special Trial Judge

Began Service: May 31, 2012

Judicial Panel on Multidistrict Litigation

Thurgood Marshall Federal Judiciary Building, One Columbus Circle, NE, Room G-255 North Lobby, Washington, DC 20002-8004
Tel: (202) 502-2800 Fax: (202) 502-2888
Internet: www.jpml.uscourts.gov

Number of Judgeships: 7

The panel of seven federal circuit and district judges has the power to temporarily transfer to a single district court civil actions pending in different districts that involve one or more common questions of fact. The Chief Justice of the United States Supreme Court appoints the judges from different circuits to serve seven-year terms.

Court Staff

Clerk of the Panel **Jeffery N. Lüthi** .... (202) 502-2800
Panel Executive **Thomasenia P. "Tommie" Duncan** ..... (202) 502-2800
Began Service: September 13, 2010
Education: Brown U 1986 AB; Pennsylvania 1989 JD

Chambers of Chair Sarah S. Vance

500 Poydras Street, Room C255, New Orleans, LA 00000
Tel: (504) 589-7595

Sarah S. Vance
Chair

Date of Birth: 1950
Education: LSU 1971 BA; Tulane 1978 JD

Chambers of Judge Marjorie O. Rendell

601 Market Street, Room 21613, Philadelphia, PA 19106-1598
Tel: (215) 597-3015 Fax: (215) 580-2393

Marjorie O. Rendell
Judge

Date of Birth: 1947
Education: Pennsylvania 1969 BA; Villanova 1973 JD

Current Memberships: American Bankruptcy Institute; American College of Bankruptcy; The J. Willard O'Brien Inn of Court, The American Inns of Court; The American Law Institute; Federal Judges Association; National Association of Women Judges

Chambers of Judge Charles R. Breyer

450 Golden Gate Avenue, San Francisco, CA 94102
Tel: (415) 522-2062

Charles R. Breyer
Judge

Date of Birth: 1941
Education: Harvard 1963 AB; Boalt Hall 1966 LLB

Current Memberships: American Bar Association; San Francisco Bar Association

Chambers of Judge Lewis A. Kaplan

500 Pearl Street, New York, NY 10007-1312
Tel: (212) 805-0216

Lewis A. Kaplan
Judge

Date of Birth: 1944
Education: Rochester 1966 AB; Harvard 1969 JD

Current Memberships: American Bar Association; American College of Trial Lawyers; The American Law Institute; The Association of the Bar of the City of New York; Federal Bar Council; Federal Judges Association; New York State Bar Association

Chambers of Judge Ellen Segal Huvelle

333 Constitution Avenue, NW, Washington, DC 20001
Tel: (202) 354-3230

Ellen Segal Huvelle
Judge

Date of Birth: 1948
Education: Wellesley 1970 BA; Yale 1972 MCP; Boston Col 1975 JD

Current Memberships: American Bar Foundation; American Association for Justice; American Bar Association; The Edward Bennett Williams American Inn of Court, The American Inns of Court; The Bar Association of the District of Columbia; The District of Columbia Bar; Massachusetts Bar Association; National Association of Women Judges; Women's Bar Association of Massachusetts

Chambers of Judge R. David Proctor

1729 Fifth Avenue, Birmingham, AL 35203
Tel: (205) 278-1980

R. David Proctor
Judge

Date of Birth: December 5, 1960
Education: Carson-Newman 1983 BA; Tennessee 1986 JD

Current Memberships: Alabama State Bar; Birmingham Bar Association

Chambers of Judge Catherine D. Perry

111 South Tenth, Room 14.182, St. Louis, MO 63102
Tel: (314) 244-7520

Catherine D. Perry
Judge

Date of Birth: 1952
Education: Oklahoma 1977 BA; Washington U (MO) 1980 JD

Current Memberships: American Bar Association; The Bar Association of Metropolitan St. Louis; Federal Judges Association; Federal Magistrate Judges Association; The Missouri Bar; National Association of Women Judges; Women Lawyers' Association of Greater St. Louis

United States Courts of Appeals

The intermediate appellate courts in the federal judicial system are the courts of appeals. There are eleven circuit courts of appeals plus the District of Columbia Circuit and the Federal Circuit. The Court of Appeals for the Federal Circuit is a specialized appellate court with national jurisdiction, hearing certain appeals (mainly patent appeals) from all of the U.S. district courts. The Federal Circuit also has jurisdiction over appeals from the U.S. Court of Federal Claims, the U.S. Court of International Trade, the U.S. Court of Appeals for Veterans Claims, United States Trademark Trial and Appeal Board, United States Board of Patent Appeals and Interferences, Boards of Contract Appeals, and the U.S. Merit Systems Protection Board. The eleven circuit courts plus the District of Columbia Circuit have appellate jurisdiction over U.S. district courts within its federal circuit (excluding patents) and selected federal agencies. A disappointed party in a district court usually has the right to have the case reviewed in the court of appeals for the circuit. Appeals court judges are appointed for life by the President with the advice and consent of the Senate. Each court of appeals consists of six or more judges, depending on the caseload of the court. The judge who has served on the court the longest and who is under 65 years of age is designated as the chief judge and performs administrative duties in addition to hearing cases.

United States Court of Appeals for the Federal Circuit

Howard T. Markey National Courts Building, 717 Madison Place, NW, Washington, DC 20439
Tel: (202) 275-8000 Tel: (202) 275-8031 (Electronic Opinions Data)
Tel: (202) 275-8030 (Electronic Opinions Voice) Fax: (202) 275-9678
Internet: http://www.cafc.uscourts.gov

Number of Judgeships: 12

Supreme Court Justice: Chief Justice John G. Roberts Jr.

The United States Court of Appeals for the Federal Circuit handles cases by subject matter without regard to the region. The Court hears all appeals for the United States Court of Federal Claims, the United States Court of International Trade and the United States Court of Veterans Appeals. The Federal Circuit hears appeals from United States District Courts in patent cases, cases involving energy regulation and economic stabilization as well as appeals from a variety of administrative proceedings. Established in 1982, the Washington, DC-based Federal Circuit possesses national jurisdiction as a result of the merger between the Appellate Division of the former United States Court of Claims and the United States Court of Customs and Patent Appeals.

Court Staff

Circuit Executive/Clerk of the Court **Daniel O'Toole** ..... (202) 275-8001
Fax: (202) 275-9380
Chief Deputy Clerk **(Vacant)** ..... (202) 275-2021
Deputy Circuit Executive & Operations Officer
Dale Bosley ..... (202) 275-8141
E-mail: bosleyd@cafc.uscourts.gov Fax: (202) 275-9772
Administrative Assistant **Annette Young** ..... (202) 275-8003
E-mail: younga@cafc.uscourts.gov
General Counsel and Senior Staff Attorney
J. Douglas Steere ..... (202) 275-8080
Fax: (202) 275-9561
Senior Deputy Clerk **James Benjamin** ..... (202) 275-8031
E-mail: benjaminj@cafc.uscourts.gov
Senior Deputy Clerk **Karen Smagala Hendrick** ..... (202) 275-8036
Education: George Mason 1974 BA
Senior Deputy Clerk **Linda R. Purdie** ..... (202) 275-8026
E-mail: purdiel@cafc.uscourts.gov
Senior Deputy Clerk **Anne Tomlinson** ..... (202) 275-8024
Deputy Clerk **Cassandra Smith** ..... (202) 275-8032
E-mail: smithc@cafc.uscourts.gov
Deputy Clerk **Laura Whittaker** ..... (202) 275-8033
Deputy Clerk **Christy Thomas** ..... (202) 275-8033
E-mail: thomasc@cafc.uscourts.gov

United States Court of Appeals for the Federal Circuit *continued*

Chief Circuit Mediator **James Amend** ..... (202) 275-8121
E-mail: amendj@cafc.uscourts.gov Fax: (202) 275-9677
Meeting and Training Administrator **Shannon Savage** ... (202) 275-8042
E-mail: savages@cafc.uscourts.gov Fax: (202) 275-9679
STA Senior Counsel **Marilyn Wennes** ..... (202) 275-8061
Fax: (202) 633-5885
Librarian **Patricia M. McDermott** ..... (202) 275-8400
E-mail: mcdermottp@cafc.uscourts.gov Fax: (202) 275-9730
Education: St Joseph Col 1975 AB; Drexel 1980 MLS; George Mason 1991 JD
Mailroom **Reginald C. Walker** ..... (202) 275-8043
E-mail: walkerr@cafc.uscourts.gov Fax: (202) 275-9678

Chambers of Chief Judge Sharon Prost

Howard T. Markey National Courts Building, 717 Madison Place, NW, Washington, DC 20439
Tel: (202) 275-8700

Sharon Prost
Chief Judge

Date of Birth: 1951
Education: Cornell 1973 BS; George Washington 1975 MBA; Washington College of Law 1979 JD; George Washington 1984 LLM
Began Service: October 2001
Appointed By: President George W. Bush

Staff
Law Clerk **Cora Holt** ..... (202) 275-8700
Began Service: January 2015
Term Expires: January 2016
E-mail: holtc@cafc.uscourts.gov
Education: Wisconsin 2011 JD
Judicial Assistant **Charity Dahl** ..... (202) 275-8700
E-mail: dahlc@cafc.uscourts.gov
Administrative Assistant **Patricia J. Grob** ..... (202) 275-8700
E-mail: grobp@cafc.uscourts.gov

Chambers of Circuit Judge Pauline Newman

Howard T. Markey National Courts Building, 717 Madison Place, NW, Washington, DC 20439
Tel: (202) 275-8540
E-mail: newmanp@cafc.uscourts.gov

Pauline Newman
Circuit Judge

Date of Birth: 1927
Education: Vassar 1947 BA; Columbia 1948 MA; Yale 1952 PhD; NYU 1958 LLB
Began Service: May 7, 1984
Appointed By: President Ronald Reagan

Corporate: Research Chemist, American Cyanamid Company (1951-1954); Patent Attorney and House Counsel, FMC Corporation (1954-1984)

Current Memberships: American Bar Association; American Intellectual Property Law Association; Council on Foreign Relations

Staff
Law Clerk **(Vacant)** ..... (202) 275-8540
Judicial Assistant **Wilma Kelly** ..... (202) 275-8540
E-mail: kellyw@cafc.uscourts.gov

Chambers of Circuit Judge Alan D. Lourie

Howard T. Markey National Courts Building, 717 Madison Place, NW, Washington, DC 20439
Tel: (202) 275-8580

Alan D. Lourie
Circuit Judge

Date of Birth: 1935
Education: Harvard 1956 AB; Wisconsin 1957 MS; Pennsylvania 1965 PhD; Temple 1970 JD
Began Service: April 11, 1990
Appointed By: President George H.W. Bush

Corporate: Chemist, Monsanto Company (1957-1959); Chemist, Literature Scientist and Patent Liaison Specialist, Wyeth Laboratories (1959-1964); Vice President, Corporate Patents, SmithKline Beecham Corporation (1964-1990)

Current Memberships: American Bar Association; American Intellectual Property Law Association; Philadelphia Patent Law Association

Staff

Law Clerk **Sydney R. Kestle** . . . . (202) 275-8580
Began Service: September 2014
Term Expires: September 2016
E-mail: kestles@cafc.uscourts.gov
Education: Pennsylvania 2011 BSE; Washington College of Law 2014 JD

Law Clerk **Jihong Lou** . . . . (202) 275-8580
Began Service: August 2013
Term Expires: August 31, 2016
E-mail: louj@cafc.uscourts.gov
Education: San Diego 2012 JD

Law Clerk **Kevin Richards** . . . . (202) 275-8580
Began Service: August 2015
Term Expires: August 31, 2016
E-mail: richardsk@cafc.uscourts.gov

Law Clerk **Grace L. St. Vincent** . . . . (202) 275-8580
Began Service: August 2014
Term Expires: August 31, 2016
Education: Michigan 2011 JD

Judicial Assistant **Charlotte A. Suniega** . . . . (202) 275-8580
E-mail: suniegac@cafc.uscourts.gov

Chambers of Circuit Judge Timothy B. Dyk

Howard T. Markey National Courts Building, 717 Madison Place, NW, Washington, DC 20439
Tel: (202) 275-8680 Fax: (202) 275-9215

Timothy B. Dyk
Circuit Judge

Date of Birth: 1937
Education: Harvard 1958 AB, 1961 LLB
Began Service: June 9, 2000
Appointed By: President William J. Clinton

Academic: Adjunct Professor, The Law Center, Georgetown University; Adjunct Professor, School of Law, University of Virginia; Adjunct Professor, Law School, Yale University

Clerkships: Law Clerk The Honorable Stanley Reed, Supreme Court of the United States (1961-1962); Law Clerk The Honorable Harold H. Burton, Supreme Court of the United States (1961-1962); Law Clerk The Honorable Earl Warren, Supreme Court of the United States (1962-1963)

Government: Special Assistant to the Assistant Attorney General, Tax Division, United States Department of Justice (1963-1964)

Legal Practice: Associate and Partner, Wilmer Cutler Pickering LLP (1964-1990); Partner and Chair, Issues and Appeals Practice, Jones, Day, Reavis & Pogue (1990-2000)

Chambers of Circuit Judge Timothy B. Dyk *continued*

Staff

Judicial Assistant **Henrietta Jessie** . . . . (202) 275-8682
E-mail: jessieh@cafc.uscourts.gov

Chambers of Circuit Judge Kimberly Ann Moore

Howard T. Markey National Courts Building, 717 Madison Place, NW, Washington, DC 20439
Tel: (202) 275-8720

Kimberly Ann Moore
Circuit Judge

Date of Birth: 1968
Education: MIT 1990 BS, 1991 MS; Georgetown 1994 JD
Began Service: September 2006
Appointed By: President George W. Bush

Academic: Assistant Professor Law/Associate Director, Intellectual Property Law Program, Chicago-Kent College of Law (1997-1999); Assistant Professor, School of Law, University of Maryland (1999-2000); Professor of Law, George Mason University (2004-2006)

Clerkships: Law Clerk, Chief Judge Glenn L. Archer, Jr., United States Court of Appeals for the Federal Circuit (1995-1997)

Government: Electrical Engineer, Naval Surface Warfare Center, United States Department of the Navy

Legal Practice: Associate, Kirkland & Ellis LLP (1994-1995)

Chambers of Circuit Judge Kathleen M. O'Malley

717 Madison Place, NW, Washington, DC 20439
Tel: (202) 275-8740 Fax: (202) 275-9033

Kathleen M. O'Malley
Circuit Judge

Date of Birth: 1956
Education: Kenyon 1979 AB; Case Western 1982 JD
Began Service: December 27, 2010
Appointed By: President Barack Obama

Clerkships: Law Clerk The Honorable Nathaniel Jones, United States Court of Appeals for the Sixth Circuit (1982-1983)

Government: Chief of Staff, Office of the Attorney General, State of Ohio (1991-1993)

Judicial: District Judge, Chambers of District Judge Kathleen M. O'Malley, United States District Court for the Northern District of Ohio (1994-2010)

Legal Practice: Associate, Jones, Day, Reavis & Pogue (1983-1984); Partner, Porter, Wright, Morris & Arthur (1985-1991)

Current Memberships: American Bar Association; The Judge Anthony J. Celebrezze Inn of Court, The American Inns of Court; Federal Bar Association; Ohio State Bar Association

Staff

Law Clerk **Stephen Elkind** . . . . (202) 275-8000
Began Service: 2015
Term Expires: August 2016

Law Clerk **Dorothy Du** . . . . (202) 275-8000
Term Expires: August 2016

Law Clerk **Glen Cheng** . . . . (202) 275-8000
Began Service: 2015
Term Expires: August 2016

Career Law Clerk **Lana Guthrie** . . . . (202) 275-8000
E-mail: guthriel@cafc.uscourts.gov
Education: Ohio State 2006 JD

Chambers of Circuit Judge Jimmie V. Reyna
717 Madison Place, NW, Washington, DC 20439
Tel: (202) 275-8000

Jimmie V. Reyna
Circuit Judge

Date of Birth: 1952
Education: Rochester 1975 BA; New Mexico 1978 JD
Began Service: April 7, 2011
Appointed By: President Barack Obama

Legal Practice: Associate, Stewart and Stewart (1986-1993); Partner, Stewart and Stewart (1993-1998)

Nonprofit: President, Hispanic National Bar Association (2006-2007)

Chambers of Circuit Judge Evan J. Wallach
717 Madison Place, NW, Washington, DC 20439
Tel: (202) 275-8640

Evan Jonathan Wallach
Circuit Judge

Date of Birth: 1949
Education: Arizona 1971 BA; Boalt Hall 1976 JD; Cambridge (UK) 1981 LLB
Began Service: November 18, 2011
Appointed By: President Barack Obama

Academic: Part-time Instructor, University of Nevada, Las Vegas (1981-1982)

Government: General Counsel and Public Policy Advisor (D-NV), Office of Senator Harry Reid, United States Senate (1986-1987)

Judicial: Judge, Chambers of Judge Evan J. Wallach, United States Court of International Trade (1995-2011)

Legal Practice: Associate, Lionel Sawyer & Collins (1976-1983); Partner, Lionel Sawyer & Collins (1983-1995)

Military Service: United States Army (1969-1971)

Chambers of Circuit Judge Richard Gary Taranto
Howard T. Markey National Courts Building, 717 Madison Place, NW, Washington, DC 20439
Tel: (202) 275-8800 Fax: (202) 275-9678

Richard Gary Taranto
Circuit Judge

Education: Pomona 1977 BA; Yale 1981 JD
Began Service: March 15, 2013
Appointed By: President Barack Obama

Clerkships: Law Clerk, Chambers of Circuit Judge Robert H. Bork, United States Court of Appeals for the District of Columbia Circuit (1982-1983); Law Clerk, Chambers of Associate Justice Sandra Day O'Connor, Supreme Court of the United States (1983-1984)

Government: Assistant to the Solicitor General, Office of the Solicitor General, United States Department of Justice (1986-1989)

Legal Practice: Associate, Onek, Klein & Farr (1984-1986); Partner, Onek, Klein & Farr (1989-1994); Partner, Farr & Taranto (1994-2013)

Nonprofit: Article and Book Editor, Yale Law Journal

Staff

Law Clerk **Meg Fasulo** . . . . (202) 275-8800
Began Service: September 2015
Term Expires: September 2016
E-mail: fasulom@cafc.uscourts.gov

Law Clerk **Jeffrey Kane** . . . . (202) 275-8800
Began Service: September 2015
Term Expires: September 2016
E-mail: kanej@cafc.uscourts.gov

Chambers of Circuit Judge Richard Gary Taranto *continued*

Law Clerk **Alex Shank** . . . . (202) 275-8800
Began Service: September 2015
Term Expires: September 2016
E-mail: shanka@cafc.uscourts.gov

Law Clerk **Brian Springer** . . . . (202) 275-8800
Began Service: September 2015
Term Expires: September 2016

Chambers of Circuit Judge Raymond T. Chen
717 Madison Place, NW, Washington, DC 20439
Tel: (202) 275-8000

Raymond T. "Ray" Chen
Circuit Judge

Education: UCLA 1990 BS; NYU 1994 JD
Began Service: August 5, 2013
Appointed By: President Barack Obama

Government: Associate Solicitor, Office of the Deputy General Counsel for Intellectual Property Law and Solicitor, U.S. Patent and Trademark Office, United States Department of Commerce (1998-2008)

Chambers of Circuit Judge Todd M. Hughes
717 Madison Place, NW, Washington, DC 20439
Tel: (202) 275-8000

Todd M. Hughes
Circuit Judge

Education: Harvard 1989 AB; Duke 1992 JD, 1992 MA
Began Service: September 30, 2013
Appointed By: President Barack Obama

Chambers of Circuit Judge Kara Farnandez Stoll
717 Madison Place, NW, Washington, DC 20439
Tel: (202) 275-8000
E-mail: stollk@cafc.uscourts.gov

Kara Farnandez Stoll
Circuit Judge

Education: Michigan State 1991 BSEE; Georgetown 1997 JD
Began Service: July 17, 2015
Appointed By: President Barack Obama

Chambers of Senior Judge S. Jay Plager
Howard T. Markey National Courts Building, 717 Madison Place, NW, Washington, DC 20439
Tel: (202) 275-8940

S. Jay Plager
Senior Judge

Date of Birth: 1931
Education: North Carolina 1952 AB; Florida 1958 JD; Columbia 1961 LLM
Began Service: November 11, 1989
Appointed By: President George H.W. Bush

Academic: Law Professor, University of Florida (1958-1964); Law Professor, University of Illinois (1964-1977); Visiting Professor, Law School, University of Wisconsin-Madison (1967-1968); Dean and Professor, School of Law, Indiana University Bloomington (1977-1989); Visiting Fellow, Cambridge University and Rockefeller Foundation Research Center (1980); Visiting Scholar, Stanford University (1984-1985)

(continued on next page)

Chambers of Senior Judge S. Jay Plager *continued*

Government: Counselor to the Under Secretary, United States Department of Health and Human Services (1986-1987); Associate Director, Office of Management and Budget, Executive Office of the President, Ronald Reagan Administration (1987-1988); Administrator, Office of Information and Regulatory Affairs, Executive Office of the President, Ronald Reagan Administration (1988-1989)

Military Service: United States Navy (1948-1970)

Current Memberships: The Florida Bar; Illinois State Bar Association; Indiana State Bar Association

Staff
Law Clerk **Noah Priluck** .... (202) 275-8940
Term Expires: December 2015
E-mail: priluckn@cafc.uscourts.gov
Education: Indiana JD
Administrative Assistant **Donna Sisson** .... (202) 275-8940
E-mail: sissond@cafc.uscourts.gov

Chambers of Senior Judge Raymond C. Clevenger III

Howard T. Markey National Courts Building, 717 Madison Place, NW, Washington, DC 20439
Tel: (202) 275-8950

Raymond C. Clevenger III
Senior Judge

Education: Yale 1959 BA, 1966 JD
Began Service: May 3, 1990
Appointed By: President George H.W. Bush

Academic: Instructor in European History, Yale University (1959-1960)

Clerkships: Law Clerk The Honorable Byron R. White, Supreme Court of the United States (1966-1967)

Government: Special Assistant to the General Counsel, Office of the General Counsel, United States Department of Transportation (1971-1972)

Legal Practice: Wilmer, Cutler & Pickering (1967-1971); Wilmer, Cutler & Pickering (1972-1990)

Current Memberships: American Bar Association; The District of Columbia Bar

Staff
Law Clerk **Michelle Wallace** .... (202) 275-8950
Began Service: September 2015
Term Expires: September 2016

Chambers of Senior Judge Alvin Anthony Schall

Howard T. Markey National Courts Building, 717 Madison Place, NW, Washington, DC 20439
Tel: (202) 275-8960

Alvin Anthony Schall
Senior Judge

Date of Birth: 1944
Education: Princeton 1966 BA; Tulane 1969 JD
Began Service: August 1992
Appointed By: President George H.W. Bush

Government: Assistant United States Attorney, Eastern District of New York, United States Department of Justice (1973-1978); Trial Attorney and Senior Trial Counsel, Civil Division, Commercial Litigation Branch, United States Department of Justice (1978-1987); Assistant to the Attorney General, Office of the Attorney General, United States Department of Justice (1988-1992)

Legal Practice: Associate, Shearman & Sterling LLP (1969-1973); Partner, Perlman & Partners (1987-1988)

Chambers of Senior Judge Alvin Anthony Schall *continued*

Current Memberships: The District of Columbia Bar; New York State Bar Association

Staff
Judicial Assistant **Dollie Lovett** .... (202) 275-8960
E-mail: lovettd@cafc.uscourts.gov

Chambers of Senior Judge Haldane Robert Mayer

Howard T. Markey National Courts Building, 717 Madison Place, NW, Washington, DC 20439
Tel: (202) 275-8560

Haldane Robert Mayer
Senior Judge

Date of Birth: 1941
Education: West Point 1963 BS; William & Mary 1971 JD
Began Service: June 19, 1987
Appointed By: President Ronald Reagan

Academic: Adjunct Professor, University of Virginia (1975-1977)

Clerkships: Law Clerk The Honorable John D. Butzner, Jr., United States Court of Appeals for the Fourth Circuit (1971-1972)

Government: Deputy Special Counsel and Acting Special Counsel, Office of the General Counsel, United States Merit Systems Protection Board, Ronald Reagan Administration (1981-1982)

Judicial: Special Assistant, Supreme Court of the United States (1977-1980); Judge, United States Court of Federal Claims (1982-1987); Chief Judge, United States Court of Appeals for the Federal Circuit (1997-2004); Circuit Judge, Chambers of Circuit Judge Haldane Robert Mayer, United States Court of Appeals for the Federal Circuit (1987-2010)

Military Service: Infantry and Judge Advocates General's Corp, United States Army (1963-1975)

Current Memberships: The District of Columbia Bar; Virginia State Bar

Staff
Career Law Clerk **Lisa Kennedy** .... (202) 275-8568
E-mail: kennedyl@cafc.uscourts.gov
Education: Notre Dame 1983 BA; Duke 1986 JD
Administrative Assistant **Bonnie Ballenger** .... (202) 275-8562

Chambers of Senior Judge Richard Linn

Howard T. Markey National Courts Building, 717 Madison Place, NW, Washington, DC 20439
Tel: (202) 275-8660

Richard Linn
Senior Judge

Education: Rensselaer Poly 1965 BEE; Georgetown 1969 JD
Began Service: 2000
Appointed By: President William J. Clinton

Current Memberships: The Giles S. Rich American Inn of Court, The American Inns of Court

Staff
Judicial Assistant **Mary Ellen Koelz** .... (202) 275-8660

Chambers of Senior Judge William C. Bryson
Howard T. Markey National Courts Building, 717 Madison Place, NW, Washington, DC 20439
Tel: (202) 275-8620

William C. Bryson
Senior Judge

Date of Birth: 1945
Education: Harvard 1969 AB; Texas 1973 JD
Began Service: October 7, 1994
Appointed By: President William J. Clinton

Staff
Secretary **Suzanne Bowden** . . . . (202) 275-8620
E-mail: bowdens@cafc.uscourts.gov

United States Court of Appeals for the First Circuit
John Joseph Moakley U.S. Courthouse, 1 Courthouse Way, Boston, MA 02210-3945
Tel: (617) 748-9057 (General Info)
Tel: (617) 748-4640 (Electronic Opinions & Dockets Data)
Tel: (617) 748-9567 (Records Room) Fax: (617) 748-4081
Internet: www.ca1.uscourts.gov

Number of Judgeships: 6

Supreme Court Justice: Associate Justice Stephen G. Breyer

Areas Covered: Maine, Massachusetts, New Hampshire, Rhode Island and Puerto Rico

Court Staff
Circuit Executive **Susan Goldberg** . . . . (617) 748-9614
E-mail: susan_goldberg@ca1.uscourts.gov Fax: (617) 748-9587
Deputy Circuit Executive **Stacy Anderson** . . . . (617) 748-9370
E-mail: stacy_anderson@ca1.uscourts.gov Fax: (617) 748-9587
Clerk of Court **Margaret Carter** . . . . (617) 748-9057
E-mail: margaret_carter@ca1.uscourts.gov Fax: (617) 748-4081
Education: Harvard 2001 JD
Chief Deputy Clerk **Maria Raia Hamilton** . . . . (617) 748-9053
E-mail: maria_hamilton@ca1.uscourts.gov Fax: (617) 748-4081
Education: Harvard 1989 JD
Senior Staff Attorney **Kathy McGill Lanza** . . . . (617) 748-9608
E-mail: kathy_lanza@ca1.uscourts.gov Fax: (617) 748-9793
Education: Smith 1973 AB; Boston U 1976 JD
Circuit Librarian **Susan C. Sullivan** . . . . (617) 748-9343
E-mail: susan_sullivan@ca1.uscourts.gov Fax: (617) 748-9358
Education: Webster 1970 BA; Case Western 1975 MLS; Boston Col 1993 JD
Settlement Counsel **Patrick King** . . . . (617) 748-9339

Chambers of Chief Judge Jeffrey R. Howard
55 Pleasant Street, Concord, NH 03301
Tel: (603) 225-1525 Fax: (603) 225-1625

Jeffrey R. Howard
Chief Judge

Date of Birth: 1955
Education: Plymouth State Col 1978 BA; Georgetown 1981 JD
Began Service: May 3, 2002
Appointed By: President George W. Bush

Staff
Law Clerk **Ryland Li** . . . . (603) 225-1525
Began Service: September 2015
Term Expires: September 2016
Law Clerk **Christopher Minue** . . . . (603) 225-1525
Began Service: September 2015
Term Expires: September 2016
E-mail: christopher_minue@ca1.uscourts.gov

Chambers of Chief Judge Jeffrey R. Howard *continued*

Law Clerk **Daniel Swartz** . . . . (603) 225-1525
Began Service: September 2015
Term Expires: September 2016
E-mail: daniel_swartz@ca1.uscourts.gov
Judicial Assistant **Lynn Woodward** . . . . (603) 225-1525
E-mail: lynn_woodward@ca1.uscourts.gov

Chambers of Circuit Judge Sandra L. Lynch
John Joseph Moakley U.S. Courthouse, One Courthouse Way, Suite 8710, Boston, MA 02210
Tel: (617) 748-9014
E-mail: sandra_lynch@ca1.uscourts.gov

Sandra L. Lynch
Circuit Judge

Date of Birth: 1946
Education: Wellesley 1968 AB; Boston U 1971 JD
Began Service: May 1, 1995
Appointed By: President William J. Clinton

Current Memberships: American Bar Association; The American Law Institute; Boston Bar Association; International Women's Forum; Massachusetts Bar Association; Massachusetts Women's Forum; National Association of Women Judges; Women's Bar Association of Massachusetts

Staff
Law Clerk **Deena Greenberg** . . . . (617) 748-9016
Began Service: July 2015
Term Expires: July 2016
E-mail: deena_greenberg@ca1.uscourts.gov
Law Clerk **Elizabeth Hadaway** . . . . (617) 748-9016
Began Service: July 2015
Term Expires: July 2016
E-mail: elizabeth_hadaway@ca1.uscourts.gov
Law Clerk **Tsuki Hoshijima** . . . . (617) 748-9016
Began Service: July 2015
Term Expires: July 2016
E-mail: tsuki_hoshijima@ca1.uscourts.gov
Law Clerk **Tyler Runge** . . . . (617) 748-9016
Began Service: July 2015
Term Expires: July 2016
E-mail: tyler_runge@ca1.uscourts.gov
Chambers Administrator **Selena A. Valeriani** . . . . (617) 748-9014
E-mail: selena_valeriani@ca1.uscourts.gov

Chambers of Circuit Judge Juan R. Torruella
José V. Toledo U.S. Courthouse, 300 Recinto Sur Street, San Juan, PR 00901
Tel: (787) 977-6146 Fax: (787) 729-6660

Juan R. Torruella
Circuit Judge

Date of Birth: 1933
Education: Wharton 1954 BS; Boston U 1957 LLB; Puerto Rico 1984 MPA; Virginia 1984 LLM
Began Service: 1984
Appointed By: President Ronald Reagan

Academic: Lecturer, University of Puerto Rico

Government: Attorney, 24th Region, National Labor Relations Board (1958-1960)

Judicial: Judge, United States District Court for the District of Puerto Rico (1974-1982); Member, Judicial Conference of the United States (1994-2001)

Legal Practice: Attorney, Fiddler Gonzalez & Rodriguez, P.S.C. (1960-1967); Private Practice (1967-1974)

(continued on next page)

Chambers of Circuit Judge Juan R. Torruella *continued*

Current Memberships: American Bar Association; The District of Columbia Bar; Federal Bar Association; La Academia Puertorriqueña De Jurisprudencia y Legislación

Staff

Law Clerk **Rebecca Buckwalter-Poza** . . . . (787) 729-6724
Began Service: August 2015
Term Expires: August 2016
E-mail: rebecca_buckwalter@ca1.uscourts.gov

Law Clerk **Jackie Iwata** . . . . (787) 729-6724
Began Service: October 2015
Term Expires: October 2016

Law Clerk **Michelle Pascucci** . . . . (787) 729-6724
Began Service: August 2015
Term Expires: August 2016
E-mail: michelle_pascucci@ca1.uscourts.gov

Law Clerk **Alejandro Salicrup** . . . . (787) 729-6724
Began Service: August 2015
Term Expires: August 2016
E-mail: alejandro_salicrup@ca1.uscourts.gov
Education: Pennsylvania 2010 JD

Judicial Assistant **Nydia E. Feliciano** . . . . (787) 977-6147
Education: Puerto Rico 1972 BA

Chambers of Circuit Judge Ojetta Rogeriee Thompson

John Joseph Moakley United States Courthouse, One Courthouse Way, Suite 6612, Boston, MA 02210
Federal Building and U.S. Courthouse, One Exchange Terrace, Providence, RI 02903-1755
Tel: (401) 272-2960 Fax: (401) 331-2386

Ojetta Rogeriee Thompson
Circuit Judge

Education: Brown U 1973 AB; Boston U 1976 JD
Began Service: April 1, 2010
Appointed By: President Barack Obama

Judicial: Associate Justice, Chambers of Judge O. Rogeriee Thompson, Rhode Island Superior Court (1997-2010)

Staff

Law Clerk **Shamis Beckley** . . . . (401) 272-2960
Began Service: August 2015
Term Expires: August 2016
E-mail: shamis_beckley@ca1.uscourts.gov

Law Clerk **Michael "Mike" Jusczyk** . . . . (401) 272-2960
Term Expires: August 2016
E-mail: mike_jusczyk@ca1.uscourts.gov
Education: Northeastern 2007 JD

Law Clerk **Gina Plata-Nino** . . . . (401) 272-2960
Began Service: August 2015
Term Expires: August 2016
E-mail: gina_plata_nino@ca5.uscourts.gov

Career Law Clerk **Mark LaBollita** . . . . (401) 272-2960
Began Service: April 2010
E-mail: mark_labollita@ca1.uscourts.gov

Chambers of Circuit Judge William J. Kayatta, Jr.

156 Federal Street, Portland, ME 04101
Tel: (207) 699-3600
E-mail: william_kayatta@ca1.uscourts.gov

William J. Kayatta, Jr.
Circuit Judge

Education: Amherst 1976 BA; Harvard 1979 JD
Began Service: March 8, 2013
Appointed By: President Barack Obama

Legal Practice: Partner, Litigation Practice, Pierce Atwood LLP

Nonprofit: Editor, Harvard Law Review; First Circuit Member, Standing Committee on the Federal Judiciary, American Bar Association

Chambers of Circuit Judge William J. Kayatta, Jr. *continued*

Staff

Judicial Assistant **Elizabeth Umland** . . . . (207) 699-3600
E-mail: elizabeth_umland@ca1.uscourts.gov

Chambers of Circuit Judge David Jeremiah Barron

1 Courthouse Way, Boston, MA 02210-3945
Tel: (617) 749-9057

David Jeremiah Barron
Circuit Judge

Education: Harvard 1989 AB, 1994 JD
Began Service: May 23, 2014
Appointed By: President Barack Obama

Academic: Assistant Professor of Law, Harvard Law School, Harvard University (1999-2004); Professor of Law, Harvard Law School, Harvard University (2004-2009)

Government: Team Member, Department of Justice Review Team, President-Elect Obama Transition Team, Executive Office of the President (2008-2009); Acting Assistant Attorney General, Office of Legal Counsel, Office of the Attorney General, United States Department of Justice (2009-2010); Principal Deputy Assistant Attorney General, Office of Legal Counsel, Office of the Attorney General, United States Department of Justice (2009-2010)

Chambers of Senior Judge Norman H. Stahl

John Joseph Moakley U.S. Courthouse, One Courthouse Way, Suite 8730, Boston, MA 02210
Tel: (617) 748-4596
E-mail: norman_stahl@ca1.uscourts.gov

Norman H. Stahl
Senior Judge

Date of Birth: 1931
Education: Tufts 1952 BA; Harvard 1955 LLB
Began Service: August 3, 1992
Appointed By: President George H.W. Bush
Political Affiliation: Republican

Clerkships: Law Clerk The Honorable John V. Spalding, Supreme Judicial Court (1955-1956)

Judicial: District Judge, United States District Court for the District of New Hampshire (1990-1992)

Legal Practice: Partner, Devine, Millimet, Stahl & Branch (1956-1990)

Current Memberships: New Hampshire Bar Association

Staff

Law Clerk **Noah Kaufman** . . . . (617) 748-4588
Began Service: August 2015
Term Expires: August 2016
E-mail: noah_kaufman@ca1.uscourts.gov

Law Clerk **Michael Parsons** . . . . (617) 748-4588
Began Service: August 2015
Term Expires: August 2016
E-mail: michael_parsons@ca1.uscourts.gov

Chambers of Senior Judge Bruce M. Selya

316 U.S. Courthouse, One Exchange Terrace, Providence, RI 02903-1755
Tel: (401) 752-7140 Fax: (401) 752-7150
E-mail: bruce_selya@ca1.uscourts.gov

Bruce M. Selya
Senior Judge

Date of Birth: 1934
Education: Harvard 1955 AB, 1958 LLB
Began Service: November 24, 1986
Appointed By: President Ronald Reagan
Political Affiliation: Republican

Academic: Adjunct Professor of Law, Boston College; Adjunct Professor of Law, Boston University

Clerkships: Law Clerk The Honorable Edward W. Day, United States District Court for the District of Rhode Island (1958-1960)

Government: Member, Judicial Council, Office of the Secretary of State, State of Rhode Island (1964-1972)

Judicial: Judge, Lincoln Probate Court (1965-1972); Judge, United States District Court for the District of Rhode Island (1982-1986); Circuit Judge, Judicial Panel on Multidistrict Litigation

Legal Practice: Partner, Gunning, LaFazia, Gnys & Selya (1960-1974); Partner, Selya & Iannuccillo (1974-1982)

Current Memberships: American Bar Association; Federal Bar Association; Federal Judges Association; Rhode Island Bar Association; Rhode Island Bar Foundation, Rhode Island Bar Association

Staff
Law Clerk **Bradley Hinshelwood** .... (401) 752-7140
Began Service: August 2015
Term Expires: August 2016
E-mail: bradley_hinshelwood@ca1.uscourts.gov
Law Clerk **Nandini Singh** .... (401) 752-7140
Began Service: August 2015
Term Expires: August 2016
E-mail: nandini_singh@ca1.uscourts.gov
Law Clerk **Sara A. Slavin** .... (401) 752-7140
Began Service: August 2015
Term Expires: August 2016
E-mail: sara_slavin@ca1.uscourts.gov
Judicial Assistant **Mary Sampson** .... (401) 752-7140
E-mail: mary_sampson@ca1.uscourts.gov
Personal Assistant **Maria Branco** .... (401) 752-7140
E-mail: maria_branco@ca1.uscourts.gov
Secretary **Judith LoBianco** .... (401) 752-7140
E-mail: judith_lobianco@ca1.uscourts.gov

Chambers of Senior Judge Kermit V. Lipez

156 Federal Street, Portland, ME 04101
Tel: (207) 822-0455 Fax: (207) 822-0467
E-mail: kermit_lipez@ca1.uscourts.gov

Kermit V. Lipez
Senior Judge

Date of Birth: 1941
Education: Haverford 1963 BA; Yale 1967 LLB; Virginia 1990 LLM
Began Service: July 1, 1998
Appointed By: President William J. Clinton
Political Affiliation: Democrat

Government: Staff Attorney, Civil Rights Division, United States Department of Justice (1967-1968); Special Assistant and Legal Counsel, Governor Kenneth M. Curtis (D-ME), Office of the Governor, State of Maine (1968-1971); Legislative Aide (D-ME), Office of Senator Edmund S. Muskie, United States Senate (1971-1972)

Judicial: Justice, Maine Superior Court (1985-1994); Justice, Supreme Judicial Court of Maine (1994-1998); Circuit Judge, Chambers of Circuit Judge Kermit V. Lipez, United States Court of Appeals for the First Circuit (1998-2011)

Chambers of Senior Judge Kermit V. Lipez *continued*

Legal Practice: Private Practice (1973-1975); Partner, Curtis, Thaxter, Lipez, Stevens, Broder & Micoleau (1975-1985)

Current Memberships: The American Law Institute; Cumberland County Bar Association; Maine State Bar Association

Staff
Law Clerk **Claire Chung** .... (207) 822-0455
Began Service: August 2015
Term Expires: August 2016
E-mail: claire_chung@ca1.uscourts.gov
Law Clerk **Anna Fodor** .... (207) 822-0455
Began Service: August 2015
Term Expires: August 2016
E-mail: anna_fodor@ca1.uscourts.gov
Law Clerk **Benjamin Margo** .... (207) 822-0455
Began Service: August 2015
Term Expires: August 2016
Career Law Clerk **Barbara Riegelhaupt** .... (207) 822-0455
E-mail: barbara_riegelhaupt@ca1.uscourts.gov
Education: UCLA 1984 JD
Judicial Assistant **Anita Germani** .... (207) 822-0455
E-mail: anita_germani@ca1.uscourts.gov

Chambers of Senior Judge Michael Boudin

John Joseph Moakley U.S. Courthouse, One Courthouse Way, Suite 8612, Boston, MA 02210
Tel: (617) 748-4431 Fax: (617) 748-4466
E-mail: michael_boudin@ca1.uscourts.gov

Michael Boudin
Senior Judge

Date of Birth: 1939
Education: Harvard 1961 AB, 1964 LLB
Began Service: May 26, 1992
Appointed By: President George H.W. Bush

Current Memberships: American Bar Association; The American Law Institute; The District of Columbia Bar; New York State Bar Association

Staff
Judicial Assistant **Donna DeFreitas** .... (617) 748-4718
E-mail: donna_defreitas@ca1.uscourts.gov

United States Bankruptcy Appellate Panel for the First Circuit

1 Courthouse Way, Suite 910, Boston, MA 02210-3945
Tel: (617) 748-9650 Fax: (617) 748-9659
Internet: www.bap1.uscourts.gov

Number of Judgeships: 12

Court Staff
Clerk **Mary P. Sharon** .... (617) 748-9650
Education: Tufts; Suffolk 1991 JD
Career Law Clerk **Gwen May** .... (617) 748-9650
Staff Attorney **Leslie Storm** .... (617) 748-9650
Case Administrator **Ann M. Williams** .... (617) 748-9650

Chambers of Chief Bankruptcy Judge Joan N. Feeney

5 Post Office Square, Boston, MA 02109-3945
Tel: (617) 748-6631 Fax: (617) 748-6635

Joan N. Feeney
Chief Bankruptcy Judge

Date of Birth: 1953
Education: Connecticut Col 1975 BA; Suffolk 1978 JD
Began Service: 1992
Term Expires: 2020

Current Memberships: American Bankruptcy Institute; Boston Bar Association; Massachusetts Bar Association; National Conference of Bankruptcy Judges

Staff
Career Law Clerk **Margaret M. Crouch** . . . . (617) 748-6631
E-mail: marnie_crouch@mab.uscourts.gov
Education: Duquesne 1984 JD
Career Law Clerk **Ann Fox** . . . . (617) 748-6631

Chambers of Bankruptcy Judge Enrique S. Lamoutte

U.S. Post Office and Courthouse Building, 300 Recinto Sur Street, Suite 251, Old San Juan, PR 00901
Tel: (787) 977-6030 Fax: (787) 977-6035
E-mail: Enrique_S._Lamoutte@prb.uscourts.gov

Enrique S. Lamoutte
Bankruptcy Judge

Date of Birth: 1948
Education: Boston Col 1969 BA; Puerto Rico 1976 JD
Began Service: November 1986
Term Expires: November 6, 2028

Affiliation: Chief Bankruptcy Judge, Chambers of Chief Bankruptcy Judge Enrique S. Lamoutte, United States Bankruptcy Court for the District of Puerto Rico

Clerkships: Law Clerk, United States District Court for the District of Puerto Rico (1977-1979); Law Clerk, United States Bankruptcy Court for the District of Puerto Rico (1979-1983)

Government: Assistant U.S. Attorney, Puerto Rico District, Executive Office for United States Attorneys, United States Department of Justice (1983-1986)

Judicial: Chief Bankruptcy Judge, United States Bankruptcy Appellate Panel for the First Circuit

Military Service: Air National Guard (1969)

Current Memberships: American Bar Association; The District of Columbia Bar; Federal Bar Association; Puerto Rico Chapter, Federal Bar Association

Staff
Career Law Clerk **Madeline Mas** . . . . (787) 977-6034
Began Service: February 2009
Education: Puerto Rico JD
Team Coordinator **Darhma Zayas** . . . . (787) 977-6030
E-mail: evangelina_mendez@prb.uscourts.gov

Chambers of Bankruptcy Judge Henry Jack Boroff

United States Bankruptcy Court, 300 State Street, 2nd Floor, Springfield, MA 01105
Tel: (413) 785-6860 Fax: (413) 781-9478
E-mail: judge_henry_boroff@mab.uscourts.gov
E-mail: henry.boroff@mab.uscourts.gov

Henry Jack Boroff
Bankruptcy Judge

Date of Birth: 1951
Education: Boston U 1975 JD
Began Service: 1993
Term Expires: December 10, 2021

Affiliation: Adjunct Professor, Secured Transactions and Bankruptcy Law, School of Law, Western New England College

Academic: Adjunct Professor, School of Law, Northeastern University (1998-2000)

Legal Practice: Friedman & Atherton (1976-1981); Boroff & Associates (1981-1993)

Staff
Career Law Clerk **Elizabeth Royalty** . . . . (413) 785-6860
E-mail: elizabeth_royalty@mab.uscourts.gov
Education: Cincinnati 2004 JD

Chambers of Bankruptcy Judge J. Michael Deasy

1000 Elm Street, Suite 1001, Manchester, NH 03101
Tel: (603) 222-2640 Fax: (603) 222-2696

J. Michael Deasy
Bankruptcy Judge

Date of Birth: 1945
Education: Rensselaer Poly 1967 BS; Boston Col 1973 JD

Current Memberships: American Bankruptcy Institute; American Bar Association; New Hampshire Bar Association

Chambers of Bankruptcy Judge Brian K. Tester

Jose V. Toledo Federal Building and U.S. Courthouse, 300 Recinto Sur Street, Suite 245, San Juan, PR 00901
Tel: (787) 977-6040 Fax: (787) 977-6045

Brian K. Tester
Bankruptcy Judge

Began Service: 2006

Affiliation: Bankruptcy Judge, Chambers of Bankruptcy Judge Brian K. Tester, United States Bankruptcy Court for the District of Puerto Rico

Chambers of Bankruptcy Judge Frank J. Bailey

Five Post Office Square, Boston, MA 02109
Tel: (617) 748-9650

Frank J. Bailey
Bankruptcy Judge

Education: Georgetown 1977 BSFS; Suffolk 1980 JD
Began Service: 2010

Chambers of Bankruptcy Judge Mildred Caban Flores

Jose V. Toledo Federal Building and U.S. Courthouse, 300 Recinto Sur Street, Courtroom 3, Old San Juan, PR 00901
Tel: (787) 977-6020 Fax: (787) 977-6026

Mildred Caban Flores
Bankruptcy Judge

Chambers of Bankruptcy Judge Melvin S. Hoffman
595 Main Street, Worcester, MA 01608
Tel: (508) 770-8927

Melvin S. Hoffman
Bankruptcy Judge

Chambers of Bankruptcy Judge Edward A. Godoy
MCS Building, 880 Tito Castro Avenue, Ponce, PR 00716
Tel: (787) 977-6074

Edward A. Godoy
Bankruptcy Judge

Chambers of Bankruptcy Judge Diane Finkle
380 Westminster Mall, Room 619, Providence, RI 02903
Tel: (401) 626-3060 Fax: (401) 626-3080

Diane Finkle
Bankruptcy Judge

Chambers of Bankruptcy Judge Bruce A. Harwood
1000 Elm Street, Manchester, NH 03101
Tel: (866) 222-8029

Bruce A. Harwood
Bankruptcy Judge

Education: Northwestern 1978 BA; Washington U (MO) 1981 JD

Chambers of Bankruptcy Judge Peter G. Cary
537 Congress Street, Portland, ME 04101
Tel: (207) 780-3482

Peter G. Cary
Bankruptcy Judge

Education: UMass (Amherst) BA; Boston Col JD

United States Court of Appeals for the Second Circuit
Thurgood Marshall Courthouse, 40 Foley Square, New York, NY 10007
Tel: (212) 857-8500 Tel: (212) 857-8585 (Clerk's Office)
Tel: (212) 857-8544 (Agency Appeals)
Tel: (212) 851-8603 (Admissions) Tel: (212) 857-8595 (Calendar)
Tel: (212) 857-8560 (Case Closing) Tel: (212) 857-8551 (Case Initiation)
Tel: (212) 857-8576 (Civil Appeals)
Tel: (212) 857-8515 (Criminal Appeals)
Tel: (212) 857-8620 (Records) Fax: (212) 857-8710
Internet: www.ca2.uscourts.gov

Number of Judgeships: 13

Supreme Court Justice: Associate Justice Ruth Bader Ginsburg

Areas Covered: Connecticut, New York and Vermont

Court Staff
Circuit Executive **Karen Greve Milton** . . . . (212) 857-8700
E-mail: karen_milton@ca2.uscourts.gov Fax: (212) 857-8680
Education: Pennsylvania 1978 BA;
Case Western 1981 JD
Deputy Circuit Executive **(Vacant)** . . . . (212) 857-8700
Fax: (212) 857-8680
Clerk of the Court **Catherine O'Hagan Wolfe** . . . . (212) 857-8585
E-mail: catherine_wolfe@ca2.uscourts.gov
Education: Fordham 1980 JD

United States Court of Appeals for the Second Circuit *continued*

Deputy Clerk (Interim) **Lucille Carr** . . . . (212) 857-8500
E-mail: lucille_carr@ca2.uscourts.gov
Assistant Circuit Executive for Administration
Janice Kish . . . . (212) 857-8700
E-mail: janice_kish@ca2.uscourts.gov Fax: (212) 857-8680
Assistant Circuit Executive for Automation
Kurt O'Lander . . . . (212) 857-8694
E-mail: kurt_olander@ca2.uscourts.gov Fax: (212) 857-8683
Assistant Circuit Executive for Space and Facilities
Scott Teman . . . . (212) 857-8790
E-mail: scott_teman@ca2.uscourts.gov Fax: (212) 857-8725
Legal Affairs Director **(Vacant)** . . . . (212) 857-8800
Fax: (212) 857-8899
Chief Deputy of Operations **Lucille Carr** . . . . (212) 857-8599
E-mail: lucille_carr@ca2.uscourts.gov Fax: (212) 857-8579
Circuit Librarian **Luis Lopez** . . . . (212) 857-8990
E-mail: luis_lopez@ca2.uscourts.gov Fax: (212) 857-8926
Emerging Technologies Librarian **Evan Pappas** . . . . (212) 857-8990
E-mail: evan_pappas@ca2.uscourts.gov Fax: (212) 857-8928
Human Resources Director **Evelyn Ortiz** . . . . (212) 857-8705
E-mail: evelyn_ortiz@ca2.uscourts.gov Fax: (212) 857-8710

Chambers of Chief Judge Robert A. Katzmann
40 Foley Square, Room 301, New York, NY 10007
Tel: (212) 857-2180 Fax: (212) 857-2189
E-mail: robert_katzmann@ca2.uscourts.gov

Robert Allen Katzmann
Chief Judge

Date of Birth: 1953
Education: Columbia Col (IL) 1973 AB; Harvard 1977 AM, 1978 PhD; Yale 1980 JD
Began Service: July 14, 1999
Appointed By: President William J. Clinton

Staff
Law Clerk **Elizabeth Bentley** . . . . (212) 857-2180
Began Service: September 2015
Term Expires: September 2016
E-mail: liz_bentley@ca2.uscourts.gov
Law Clerk **Celia Choy** . . . . (212) 857-2180
Began Service: August 2015
Term Expires: August 2016
E-mail: celia_choy@ca2.uscourts.gov
Law Clerk **Robert Friedman** . . . . (212) 857-2180
Began Service: September 2015
Term Expires: September 2016
E-mail: robert_friedman@ca2.uscourts.gov
Law Clerk **Donald Gibson** . . . . (212) 857-2180
Began Service: August 2015
Term Expires: August 2016
E-mail: don_gibson@ca2.uscourts.gov
Law Clerk **Sonia Steinway** . . . . (212) 857-2180
Began Service: September 2015
Term Expires: September 2016
Judicial Assistant **Dominique Welch** . . . . (212) 857-2180
E-mail: dominique_welch@ca2.uscourts.gov

Chambers of Circuit Judge Dennis Jacobs
500 Pearl Street, New York, NY 10007
Tel: (212) 857-2150 Fax: (212) 857-2160
E-mail: dennis_jacobs@ca2.uscourts.gov

Dennis Jacobs
Circuit Judge

Date of Birth: 1944
Education: Queens Col (NY) 1964 BA; NYU 1965 MA, 1973 JD
Began Service: December 8, 1992
Appointed By: President George H.W. Bush

(continued on next page)

Chambers of Circuit Judge Dennis Jacobs *continued*

Staff

Judicial Assistant **Terry Papineau** .... (212) 857-2150
E-mail: maria_papineau@ca2.uscourts.gov

Chambers of Circuit Judge José A. Cabranes

U.S. Courthouse, 141 Church Street, New Haven, CT 06510-2030
Tel: (203) 867-8782 Tel: (347) 394-1890 (New York Office Contact)
Fax: (347) 394-1896 Fax: (203) 867-8790
E-mail: jose_cabranes@ca2.uscourts.gov

José A. Cabranes
Circuit Judge

Date of Birth: 1940
Education: Columbia 1961 AB; Yale 1965 JD; Cambridge (UK) 1967 MLitt
Began Service: August 12, 1994
Appointed By: President William J. Clinton
Political Affiliation: Independent

Academic: Instructor, Colegio San Ignacio de Loyola (1961); Supervisor in International Law, Queens' College Cambridge (1966-1967); Associate Professor of Law, Rutgers, The State University of New Jersey (1971-1973); General Counsel and Director of Government Relations, Yale University (1975-1979); Lecturer in Law, Yale University (1976-1982); Trustee, Colgate University (1981-1990); Trustee, Yale University (1987-1999)

Government: Consultant, Commission on Local Government Efficiency and Competitiveness, State of New York (1971); Special Counsel, Governor Rafael Hernández Colón (PDP-PR), Commonwealth of Puerto Rico (1973-1975); Head, Office of the Commonwealth of Puerto Rico (1973-1975); Commissioner, President's Commission on Mental Health, Executive Office of the President, Jimmy Carter Administration (1977-1978); Delegate, Conference on Security and Cooperation in Europe (1977-1978); Consultant to the Secretary, United States Department of State (1978); Commissioner, President's Commission on White House Fellowships, Executive Office of the President, William J. Clinton Administration (1993-1996)

Judicial: District Judge, United States District Court for the District of Connecticut (1979-1994); Chief Judge, United States District Court for the District of Connecticut (1992-1994)

Legal Practice: Casey, Lane & Mittendorf (1967-1971)

Current Memberships: American Bar Foundation; American Academy of Arts and Sciences; Connecticut Bar Association, Inc.; Hispanic National Bar Association

Staff

Law Clerk **Christian Burset** .... (203) 867-8782
Began Service: September 2015
Term Expires: September 2016
E-mail: christian_burset@ca2.uscourts.gov

Law Clerk **Michael Dearington** .... (203) 867-8782
Began Service: September 2015
Term Expires: September 2016

Law Clerk **Conor Reardon** .... (203) 867-8782
Began Service: August 2015
Term Expires: August 2016

Law Clerk **Benjamin "Ben" Schrier** .... (203) 867-8782
Began Service: August 2015
Term Expires: August 2016
E-mail: benjamin_schrier@ca2.uscourts.gov

Judicial Assistant **Janet F. Hansen** .... (203) 867-8782
E-mail: janet_hansen@ca2.uscourts.gov

Chambers of Circuit Judge Rosemary S. Pooler

Federal Building, 100 South Clinton Street, Syracuse, NY 13261
P.O. Box 7395, Syracuse, NY 13261-7395
Tel: (315) 448-0420 Fax: (315) 448-0582
E-mail: rosemary_pooler@ca2.uscourts.gov

Rosemary Shankman Pooler
Circuit Judge

Date of Birth: 1938
Education: Brooklyn 1959 BA; Connecticut 1961 MA; Michigan 1965 JD
Began Service: June 9, 1998
Appointed By: President William J. Clinton

Academic: Visiting Professor, College of Law, Syracuse University (1987-1988)

Government: Director, Consumer Affairs Unit and Assistant Corporation Counsel, City of Syracuse, New York (1971-1973); Common Counsel, City of Syracuse, New York (1974-1975); Chair and Executive Director, Consumer Protection Board, State of New York (1976-1981); Commissioner, State Public Service Commission, State of New York (1981-1986); Staff Director, Subcommittee on Utility Structure and Management of Regulated Utilities, Committee on Corporations, Authorities and Commissions, New York State Assembly (1987)

Judicial: Justice, New York Supreme Court, Fifth Judicial District (1991-1994); Judge, United States District Court for the Northern District of New York (1994-1998)

Legal Practice: Associate Attorney, Rifken, Frankel & Greenman, P.C. (1966-1969); Associate Attorney, Michaels and Michaels (1969-1971)

Nonprofit: Upstate Regional Coordinator, New York Public Interest Research Group (1974-1975); Vice President for Legal Affairs, Atlantic States Legal Foundation, Inc. (1989-1990)

Current Memberships: Association of Justices of the Supreme Court of the State of New York; Federal Judges Association; Onondaga County Bar Association; Women's Bar Association of the State of New York

Staff

Law Clerk **Jan Messerschmidt** .... (315) 448-0420
Began Service: August 2015
Term Expires: August 2016
E-mail: jan_messerschmidt@ca2.uscourts.gov

Law Clerk **John Robinson** .... (315) 448-0420
Began Service: August 2015
Term Expires: August 2016
E-mail: john_robinson@ca2.uscourts.gov

Law Clerk **Ruth Vinson** .... (315) 448-0420
Began Service: August 2015
Term Expires: August 2016
E-mail: ruth_vinson@ca2.uscourts.gov

Career Law Clerk **Lillian Abbott Pfohl** .... (315) 448-0420
E-mail: lillian_pfohl@ca2.uscourts.gov
Education: Syracuse 1999 JD

Judicial Secretary **Christine Marascalchi** .... (315) 448-0420
E-mail: marascal@ca2.uscourts.gov
Education: St Lawrence 1978 BA

Chambers of Circuit Judge Reena Raggi

225 Cadman Plaza East, Brooklyn, NY 11201
Tel: (718) 613-2490 Fax: (718) 613-2497
E-mail: reena_raggi@ca2.uscourts.gov

Reena Raggi
Circuit Judge

Date of Birth: 1951
Education: Wellesley 1973 BA; Harvard 1976 JD
Began Service: October 7, 2002
Appointed By: President George W. Bush

Clerkships: Law Clerk The Honorable Thomas E. Fairchild, United States Court of Appeals for the Seventh Circuit (1976-1977)

Chambers of Circuit Judge Reena Raggi *continued*

Government: Assistant United States Attorney, Eastern District of New York, Office of the United States Attorney, United States Department of Justice (1979-1986); United States Attorney, Eastern District of New York, United States Department of Justice (1986)

Judicial: District Judge, United States District Court for the Eastern District of New York (1987-2002)

Legal Practice: Associate, Cahill Gordon & Reindel LLP (1977-1979); Partner, Windels, Marx, Davies & Ives (1986-1987)

Staff

Law Clerk **Laura Cramer-Babycz** . . . . (718) 613-2490
Began Service: July 2015
Term Expires: July 2016
Education: Harvard 2012 JD

Law Clerk **Lucas Issacharoff** . . . . (718) 613-2490
Began Service: August 2015
Term Expires: August 2016
E-mail: lucas_issacharoff@ca2.uscourts.gov

Law Clerk **Jeffrey "Jeff" Izant** . . . . (718) 613-2490
Began Service: September 2015
Term Expires: September 2016

Law Clerk **Erin Semler** . . . . (718) 613-2490
Began Service: October 2015
Term Expires: October 2016

Judicial Secretary **Chris Corcoran** . . . . (718) 613-2490
E-mail: chris_corcoran@ca2.uscourts.gov

Chambers of Circuit Judge Richard C. Wesley

US Courthouse, 500 Pearl Street, New York, NY 10007
Tel: (585) 243-7910
E-mail: richard_wesley@ca2.uscourts.gov

Richard C. Wesley
Circuit Judge

Date of Birth: 1949
Education: SUNY (Albany) 1971 BA; Cornell 1974 JD
Began Service: 2003
Appointed By: President George W. Bush
Political Affiliation: Republican

Government: Assistant Counsel to Republican Leader, Minority Leader James L. Emery (R-NY), New York State Assembly (1979-1982); Member, One Hundred Thirty Six Assembly District, New York State Assembly (1983-1987)

Judicial: Associate Justice, New York Supreme Court, Seventh Judicial District (1987-1996); Associate Justice, New York Supreme Court, Appellate Division, Fourth Department (1994-1996); Associate Judge, New York Court of Appeals (1997-2003)

Legal Practice: Harris, Beach & Wilcox (1974-1976); Associate then Partner, Streb, Porter, Meyer and Wesley (1976-1986)

Current Memberships: The American Law Institute; Livingston County Bar Association; New York State Bar Association

Staff

Law Clerk **Qais Ghafary** . . . . (585) 243-7910
Began Service: January 2015
Term Expires: January 2016
E-mail: qais_ghafary@ca2.uscourts.gov

Law Clerk **Aidan Grano** . . . . (585) 243-7910
Began Service: August 2015
Term Expires: August 2016
E-mail: aidan_grano@ca2.uscourts.gov

Law Clerk **Lynne Kolodinsky** . . . . (585) 243-7910
Began Service: August 2015
Term Expires: August 2016
E-mail: lynne_kolodinsky@ca2.uscourts.gov

Chambers of Circuit Judge Richard C. Wesley *continued*

Law Clerk **Lauren Moxley** . . . . (585) 243-7910
Began Service: August 2015
Term Expires: August 2016
E-mail: lauren_moxley@ca2.uscourts.gov

Secretary **Suzan J. "Sue" Meyer** . . . . (585) 243-7910
E-mail: sue_meyer@ca2.uscourts.gov

Chambers of Circuit Judge Peter W. Hall

P.O. Box 885, Rutland, VT 05702
Tel: (802) 775-3712 Fax: (802) 773-0962
E-mail: peter_hall@ca2.uscourts.gov

Peter W. Hall
Circuit Judge

Education: North Carolina 1971 BA, 1975 MA; Cornell 1977 JD
Began Service: July 7, 2004
Appointed By: President George W. Bush

Clerkships: Law Clerk, Chambers of District Judge Albert W. Coffrin, United States District Court for the District of Vermont (1977-1978)

Government: Assistant U.S. Attorney, Vermont District, Executive Office for United States Attorneys, United States Department of Justice (1978-1982); First Assistant U.S. Attorney, Vermont District, Executive Office for United States Attorneys, United States Department of Justice (1982-1986); U.S. Attorney, Vermont District, Executive Office for United States Attorneys, United States Department of Justice (2001-2004)

Profession: Private Practice (1986-2001)

Membership: President, Vermont Bar Association (1995-1996)

Staff

Fax: (802) 773-0962

Judicial Assistant **Barbara Whelton** . . . . (802) 775-3712
E-mail: barbara_whelton@ca2.uscourts.gov

Chambers of Circuit Judge Debra Ann Livingston

U.S. Courthouse, 40 Foley Square, New York, NY 10007
Tel: (212) 857-8500
E-mail: debra_livingston@ca2.uscourts.gov

Debra Ann Livingston
Circuit Judge

Date of Birth: 1959
Education: Princeton 1980 BA; Harvard 1984 JD
Began Service: May 17, 2007
Appointed By: President George W. Bush

Academic: Assistant Law Professor, University of Michigan (1992-1994); Associate Professor, Columbia Law School (1994-2000); Law Professor, Columbia University (2000-2007); Vice Dean, Columbia Law School (2005-2006)

Clerkships: Law Clerk, Circuit Judge Joseph Edward Lumbard, United States Court of Appeals for the Second Circuit (1984-1985)

Government: Assistant U.S. Attorney, Office of the United States Attorneys, Southern District of New York, United States Department of Justice (1986-1991); Commissioner, Civilian Complaint Review Board, City of New York, New York (1994-2003)

Legal Practice: Associate, Paul, Weiss, Rifkind, Wharton & Garrison LLP (1985-1986); Associate, Paul, Weiss, Rifkind, Wharton & Garrison LLP (1991-1992)

Nonprofit: Legal Consultant, United Nations High Commissioner for Refugees in Bangkok (1982-1983)

Staff

Law Clerk **Giselle Barcia** . . . . (212) 857-8500
Began Service: September 2015
Term Expires: September 2016
E-mail: thomas_burnett@ca2.uscourts.gov

(continued on next page)

Chambers of Circuit Judge Debra Ann Livingston *continued*

Law Clerk **Richard Cleary** .... (212) 857-8500
Began Service: September 2015
Term Expires: September 2016
E-mail: richard_cleary@ca2.uscourts.gov

Law Clerk **Jodie Liu** .... (212) 857-8500
Began Service: September 2015
Term Expires: September 2016
E-mail: jodie_liu@ca2.uscourts.gov

Law Clerk **Jacob Rosen** .... (212) 857-8500
Began Service: September 2015
Term Expires: September 2016
E-mail: jacob_rosen@ca2.uscourts.gov

Judicial Assistant **Jeanette Santos** .... (212) 857-8500
E-mail: jeanette_santos@ca2.uscourts.gov

Chambers of Circuit Judge Gerard E. Lynch

40 Foley Square, New York, NY 10007
Tel: (212) 857-2320
E-mail: ca02_gelchambers@ca2.uscourts.gov

Gerard E. Lynch
Circuit Judge

Date of Birth: 1951
Education: Columbia 1972 BA, 1975 JD
Began Service: September 21, 2009
Appointed By: President Barack Obama

Clerkships: Law Clerk, Chambers of Senior Judge Wilfred Feinberg, United States Court of Appeals for the Second Circuit (1975-1976); Law Clerk, Chambers of Associate Justice William J. Brennan, Jr., Supreme Court of the United States (1976-1977)

Government: Assistant U.S. Attorney, New York - Southern District, Executive Office for United States Attorneys, United States Department of Justice (1980-1983); Associate Counsel, United States Office of the Independent Counsel (1988-1990); Criminal Division Chief, New York - Southern District, Executive Office for United States Attorneys, United States Department of Justice (1990-1992)

Judicial: District Judge, Chambers of District Judge Gerard E. Lynch, United States District Court for the Southern District of New York (2000-2009)

Legal Practice: Counsel, Howard, Darby & Levin (1992-2000)

Staff

Law Clerk **Jennesa Calvo-Friedman** .... (212) 857-2320
Began Service: September 2015
Term Expires: September 2016
E-mail: jennesa_calvo-friedman@ca2.uscourts.gov

Law Clerk **Remi Jaffre** .... (212) 857-2320
Began Service: September 2015
Term Expires: September 2016
E-mail: remi_jaffre@ca2.uscourts.gov

Law Clerk **Kaitlin Morrison** .... (212) 857-2320
Began Service: August 2015
Term Expires: August 2016
E-mail: kaitlin_morrison@ca2.uscourts.gov

Law Clerk **Anne Silver** .... (212) 857-2320
Began Service: August 2015
Term Expires: August 2016
E-mail: anne_silver@ca2.uscourts.gov

Judicial Assistant **Cheryl Galsini** .... (212) 857-2320
E-mail: cheryl_galsini@ca2.uscourts.gov

Chambers of Circuit Judge Denny Chin

40 Foley Square, New York, NY 10007
Tel: (212) 857-8500
E-mail: denny_chin@ca2.uscourts.gov

Denny Chin
Circuit Judge

Date of Birth: 1954
Education: Princeton 1975 BA; Fordham 1978 JD
Began Service: April 26, 2010
Appointed By: President Barack Obama

Affiliation: Member, The Association of the Bar of the City of New York; Member, Asian American Bar Association of New York; Member, New York County Lawyers' Association

Clerkships: Law Clerk The Honorable Henry F. Werker, United States District Court for the Southern District of New York (1978-1980)

Government: Assistant United States Attorney, Southern District of New York, Civil Division, Office of the United States Attorney, United States Department of Justice (1982-1986)

Judicial: District Judge, Chambers of District Judge Denny Chin, United States District Court for the Southern District of New York (1994-2010)

Legal Practice: Associate, Davis Polk & Wardwell (1980-1982); Partner, Campbell, Patrick & Chin (1986-1990); Counsel and Partner, Vladeck, Waldman, Elias & Engelhard, P.C. (1990-1994)

Current Memberships: Asian American Bar Association of New York; The Association of the Bar of the City of New York; New York County Lawyers' Association

Staff

Law Clerk **Alison Coutifaris** .... (212) 857-8500
Began Service: September 2015
Term Expires: September 2016
E-mail: alison_coutifaris@ca2.uscourts.gov

Law Clerk **Anna Estevao** .... (212) 857-8500
Began Service: September 2015
Term Expires: September 2016
E-mail: anna_estevao@ca2.uscourts.gov

Law Clerk **Dennis Fan** .... (212) 857-8500
Began Service: September 2015
Term Expires: September 2016
E-mail: dennis_fan@ca2.uscourts.gov

Law Clerk **Cristina Rincon** .... (212) 857-8500
Began Service: September 2015
Term Expires: September 2016
E-mail: cristina_rincon@ca2.uscourts.gov

Legal Assistant **Sharon Volckhausen** .... (212) 857-8500
E-mail: sharon_volckhausen@ca2.uscourts.gov

Chambers of Circuit Judge Raymond Joseph Lohier Jr.

40 Foley Square, Room 730, New York, NY 10007
Tel: (212) 857-8500 Fax: (212) 857-8680
E-mail: raymond_lohier@ca2.uscourts.gov

Raymond Joseph Lohier, Jr.
Circuit Judge

Education: Harvard 1988; NYU 1991 JD
Began Service: January 3, 2011
Appointed By: President Barack Obama

Government: Deputy Narcotics Chief, Criminal Division, New York - Southern District, United States Department of Justice; Narcotics Chief, Criminal Division, New York - Southern District, United States Department of Justice; Securities and Commodities Fraud Task Force Deputy Chief, Securities and Commodities Fraud Task Force, New York - Southern District, United States Department of Justice (2007-2009); Chief, Securities and Commodities Fraud Task Force, New York - Southern District, United States Department of Justice (2009-2010)

Chambers of Circuit Judge Raymond Joseph Lohier Jr. *continued*

Staff
Judicial Assistant **Patrice Parris** . . . . (212) 857-8500
E-mail: patrice_parris@ca2.uscourts.gov

Chambers of Circuit Judge Susan Laura Carney

40 Foley Square, New York, NY 10007
Tel: (212) 857-8500 Fax: (212) 857-8710
E-mail: susan_carney@ca2.uscourts.gov

Susan Laura Carney
Circuit Judge

Education: Harvard 1973 AB; Chicago 1975 (Attended); Harvard 1977 JD
Began Service: June 21, 2011
Appointed By: President Barack Obama

Academic: Associate General Counsel, Yale University (1998-2001)

Government: Associate General Counsel, Office of the General Counsel, Peace Corps (1996-1998)

Legal Practice: Of Counsel, Bredhoff & Kaiser PLLC (1994-1996)

Chambers of Circuit Judge Christopher F. Droney

450 Main Street, Hartford, CT 06103
Tel: (860) 240-2635
E-mail: christopher_droney@ca2.uscourts.gov

Christopher F. Droney
Circuit Judge

Date of Birth: 1954
Education: Holy Cross Col 1976 BA; Connecticut 1979 JD
Began Service: March 12, 2012
Appointed By: President Barack Obama
Political Affiliation: Democrat

Government: Member, Town Council, Town of West Hartford, Connecticut (1983-1989); Special Master, United States District Court for the District of Connecticut (1985-1993); U.S. Attorney, Connecticut District, Executive Office for United States Attorneys, United States Department of Justice, William J. Clinton Administration (1993-1997)

Judicial: Connecticut Law Review; District Judge, Chambers of District Judge Christopher F. Droney, United States District Court for the District of Connecticut (1997-2011)

Legal Practice: Associate, Day, Berry & Howard (1979-1981); Associate, Buckley & Santos PC (1981-1984); Associate, Reid & Riege PC (1984-1994); Vice President and Stockholder, Reid & Riege PC (1987-1994)

Current Memberships: Federal Bar Council

Staff
Law Clerk **Jennifer Kwapisz** . . . . (860) 240-2635
Began Service: December 29, 2014
Term Expires: December 31, 2015
E-mail: jennifer_kwapisz@ca2.uscourts.gov
Law Clerk **Emily Damrau** . . . . (860) 240-2635
Began Service: August 17, 2015
Term Expires: August 19, 2016
E-mail: emily_damrau@ca2.uscourts.gov
Law Clerk **William Moccia** . . . . (860) 240-2635
Began Service: January 7, 2015
Term Expires: December 31, 2015
E-mail: william_moccia@ca2.uscourts.gov
Law Clerk **Bonnie Doyle** . . . . (860) 240-2635
Began Service: August 24, 2015
Term Expires: August 26, 2016
E-mail: bonnie_doyle@ca2.uscourts.gov
Education: Yale 2012 JD

Chambers of Senior Judge Robert D. Sack

U.S. Courthouse, 40 Foley Square, New York, NY 10007
Tel: (212) 857-2140 Fax: (212) 857-2149
E-mail: robert_sack@ca2.uscourts.gov

Robert D. Sack
Senior Judge

Date of Birth: 1939
Education: Rochester 1960 BA; Columbia 1963 LLB
Began Service: August 6, 1998
Appointed By: President William J. Clinton

Clerkships: Law Clerk, Judge Arthur S. Lane, United States District Court for the District of New Jersey (1963-1964)

Corporate: Secretary, Ottaway Newspapers, Inc. (1978-1998)

Government: Associate Special Counsel/Senior Associate Special Counsel, Watergate Impeachment Inquiry Staff, Committee on the Judiciary, United States House of Representatives (1974)

Legal Practice: Associate then Partner, Patterson, Belknap, Webb & Tyler (and predecessor firms) (1964-1986); Partner, Gibson, Dunn & Crutcher, LLP (1986-1998)

Current Memberships: American Bar Foundation; American Bar Association; The Association of the Bar of the City of New York

Staff
Law Clerk **Benjamin "Ben" Jackson** . . . . (212) 857-2140
Began Service: September 2015
Term Expires: September 2016
E-mail: benjamin_jackson@ca2.uscourts.gov
Law Clerk **Jessica Ly** . . . . (212) 857-2140
Began Service: September 2015
Term Expires: October 2016
Education: Berkeley Law 2013 JD
Law Clerk **Ned Hirschfeld** . . . . (212) 857-2140
Began Service: October 2015
Term Expires: October 2016
E-mail: ned_hirschfeld@ca2.uscourts.gov
Education: Yale 2013 JD
Judicial Assistant **Ann Pisacano** . . . . (212) 857-2142
E-mail: ann_pisacano@ca2.uscourts.gov
Education: NYU BA

Chambers of Senior Judge Barrington D. Parker

Daniel Patrick Moynihan U.S. Courthouse, 500 Pearl Street, New York, NY 10007
Tel: (212) 857-2211 Fax: (212) 857-2225
E-mail: ca02_bdpchambers@ca2.uscourts.gov

Barrington D. Parker, Jr.
Senior Judge

Date of Birth: 1944
Education: Yale 1965 BA, 1969 LLB
Began Service: October 10, 2001
Appointed By: President George W. Bush

Academic: Instructor, Phillips Exeter Academy (1965-1966)

Clerkships: Law Clerk The Honorable Aubrey E. Robinson, Jr., United States District Court for the District of Columbia (1969-1970)

Judicial: District Judge, United States District Court for the Southern District of New York (1994-2001); Circuit Judge, United States Court of Appeals for the Second Circuit (2001-2009)

Legal Practice: Associate, Sullivan & Cromwell LLP (1970-1977); Partner, Parker, Auspitz, Neesemann & Delehanty, P.C. (1977-1987); Partner, Morrison & Foerster (1987-1994)

(continued on next page)

Chambers of Senior Judge Barrington D. Parker *continued*

Staff

Law Clerk **Joshua Wesneski** .... (212) 857-2211
Began Service: September 2015
Term Expires: September 2016
E-mail: joshua_wesneski@ca2.uscourts.gov

Law Clerk **Laurence Tai** .... (212) 857-2211
Began Service: September 2015
Term Expires: September 2016
E-mail: laurence_tai@ca2.uscourts.gov

Law Clerk **Brandon Trice** .... (212) 857-2211
Began Service: September 2015
Term Expires: September 2016
E-mail: brandon_trice@ca2.uscourts.gov

Judicial Assistant **Yvonne Croft** .... (212) 857-2211
E-mail: yvonne_croft@ca2.uscourts.gov

Chambers of Senior Judge Jon O. Newman

450 Main Street, Hartford, CT 06103
Tel: (212) 857-8500
E-mail: jon_newman@ca2.uscourts.gov

Jon O. Newman

Senior Judge

Date of Birth: 1932
Education: Princeton 1953 AB; Yale 1956 LLB
Began Service: June 25, 1979
Appointed By: President Jimmy Carter
Political Affiliation: Democrat

Clerkships: Law Clerk, Chambers of Circuit Judge George T. Washington, United States Court of Appeals for the District of Columbia Circuit (1956-1957); Senior Law Clerk, Chambers of Chief Justice Earl Warren, Supreme Court of the United States (1957-1958)

Government: Counsel to the Majority, Connecticut General Assembly (1959); Special Counsel, Office of the Governor, State of Connecticut (1960); Executive Assistant, Office of the Secretary, United States Department of Health, Education and Welfare (1961-1962); Administrative Assistant (D-CT), Office of Senator Abraham A. Ribicoff, United States Senate (1963-1964); U.S. Attorney, Connecticut District, Executive Office for United States Attorneys, United States Department of Justice (1964-1969)

Judicial: District Judge, United States District Court for the District of Connecticut (1972-1979)

Legal Practice: Partner, Ritter, Satter & Newman (1958-1960); Private Practice (1969-1971)

Military Service: United States Army Reserve, United States Department of the Army (1954-1962)

Nonprofit: Consultant, Ford Foundation (1969-1970)

Current Memberships: American Bar Foundation; American Bar Association; The American Law Institute; Connecticut Bar Association, Inc.; Hartford County Bar

Staff

Judicial Assistant **Kimberly Gay** .... (860) 240-3260
E-mail: kimberly_gay@ca2.uscourts.gov

Chambers of Senior Judge Ralph K. Winter

U.S. Courthouse, 141 Church Street, New Haven, CT 06510
Tel: (203) 782-3682 Fax: (203) 782-3686
E-mail: ralph_winter@ca2.uscourts.gov

Ralph K. Winter

Senior Judge

Date of Birth: 1935
Education: Yale 1957 BA, 1960 LLB, 1968 MA
Began Service: January 5, 1982
Appointed By: President Ronald Reagan

Academic: Professor of Law, Yale University (1962-1982); Adjunct Professor of Law, University of Chicago (1966)

Clerkships: Law Clerk The Honorable Caleb Wright, United States District Court for the District of Delaware (1960-1961); Law Clerk The Honorable Thurgood Marshall, United States Court of Appeals for the Second Circuit (1961-1962)

Corporate: Senior Fellow, The Brookings Institution (1968-1970)

Judicial: Circuit Judge, Chambers of Circuit Judge Ralph K. Winter, United States Court of Appeals for the Second Circuit (1981-1997); Chief Judge, Chambers of Chief Judge Ralph K. Winter, United States Court of Appeals for the Second Circuit (1997-2000)

Staff

Law Clerk **Nicholas Makarov** .... (203) 782-3682
Began Service: August 2015
Term Expires: August 30, 2016
E-mail: nicholas_makarov@ca2.uscourts.gov

Law Clerk **Adam Sowlati** .... (203) 782-3682
Began Service: June 2015
Term Expires: June 2016
E-mail: adam_sowlati@ca2.uscourts.gov

Judicial Assistant **Maggie Debicella** .... (203) 782-3682
E-mail: maggie_debicella@ca2.uscourts.gov

Judicial Assistant **Gerri Malloy** .... (203) 782-3682
E-mail: gerri_malloy@ca2.uscourts.gov

Chambers of Senior Judge Amalya L. Kearse

Thurgood Marshall U.S. Courthouse, 40 Foley Square,
New York, NY 10007
Tel: (212) 857-2250 Fax: (212) 857-2259
E-mail: ca02_alkchambers@ca2.uscourts.gov

Amalya Lyle Kearse

Senior Judge

Date of Birth: 1937
Education: Wellesley 1959 BA; Michigan 1962 JD
Began Service: June 1979
Appointed By: President Jimmy Carter

Academic: Adjunct Lecturer, New York University (1968-1969)

Judicial: Circuit Judge, Chambers of Circuit Judge Amalya L. Kearse, United States Court of Appeals for the Second Circuit (1979-2002)

Legal Practice: Associate, Hughes Hubbard & Reed LLP (1962-1969); Partner, Hughes Hubbard & Reed LLP (1969-1979)

Current Memberships: American Bar Association; American College of Trial Lawyers; The American Law Institute; The Association of the Bar of the City of New York

Staff

Law Clerk **Brandon Fetzer** .... (212) 857-2250
Began Service: September 2015
Term Expires: September 2016
E-mail: brandon_fetzer@ca2.uscourts.gov

Law Clerk **T. Dietrich Hill** .... (212) 857-2250
Began Service: September 2015
Term Expires: September 2016
E-mail: dietrich_hill@ca2.uscourts.gov

Chambers of Senior Judge Amalya L. Kearse *continued*

Law Clerk **Aisha Rich** .... (212) 857-2250
Began Service: September 2015
Term Expires: September 2016
E-mail: aisha_rich@ca2.uscourts.gov

Judicial Assistant **Saundra Wallace** .... (212) 857-2250
E-mail: saundra_wallace@ca2.uscourts.gov

Chambers of Senior Judge Pierre N. Leval

U.S. Courthouse, 40 Foley Square, Room 1901, New York, NY 10007
Tel: (212) 857-2310 Fax: (212) 857-2319
E-mail: ca02_pnlchambers@ca2.uscourts.gov

Pierre N. Leval
Senior Judge

Date of Birth: 1936
Education: Harvard 1959 AB, 1963 JD
Began Service: 1993
Appointed By: President William J. Clinton

Clerkships: Law Clerk The Honorable Henry J. Friendly, United States Court of Appeals for the Second Circuit (1963-1964)

Government: Assistant United States Attorney, Southern District of New York, United States Department of Justice (1964-1968); Chief Appellate Attorney, State of New York (1967-1968); First Assistant District Attorney, Office of the District Attorney, County of New York, New York (1975-1976); Chief Assistant District Attorney, Office of the District Attorney, County of New York, New York (1976-1977)

Judicial: District Judge, United States District Court for the Southern District of New York (1977-1993)

Legal Practice: Attorney, Cleary Gottlieb Steen & Hamilton LLP (1969-1975)

Military Service: United States Army (1959)

Staff

Law Clerk **Robert "Rob" Cobbs** .... (212) 857-2310
Began Service: 2015
Term Expires: January 2016
E-mail: robert_cobbs@ca2.uscourts.gov

Law Clerk **Charlie Gerstein** .... (212) 857-2310
Began Service: August 18, 2015
Term Expires: August 2016
E-mail: charlie_gerstein@ca2.uscourts.gov
Education: Michigan 2013 JD

Law Clerk **Heather Gregorio** .... (212) 857-2310
Began Service: July 2015
Term Expires: July 2016
E-mail: heather_gregorio@ca2.uscourts.gov

Judicial Assistant **Joanne Falletta** .... (212) 857-2310
E-mail: joanne_falletta@ca2.uscourts.gov

Chambers of Senior Judge John M. Walker, Jr.

U.S. Court of Appeals, 157 Church Street, New Haven, CT 06510
Tel: (203) 773-2181 Fax: (203) 773-2179
E-mail: john_walker@ca2.uscourts.gov

John M. Walker, Jr.
Senior Judge

Date of Birth: 1940
Education: Yale 1962 BA; Michigan 1966 JD
Began Service: 1989
Appointed By: President George H.W. Bush
Political Affiliation: Republican

Government: Assistant U.S. Attorney, New York - Southern District, Executive Office for United States Attorneys, United States Department of Justice (1970-1975); Assistant Secretary, United States Department of the Treasury, Ronald Reagan Administration (1981-1985); Special Counsel, Administrative Conference of the United States (1987-1992)

Chambers of Senior Judge John M. Walker, Jr. *continued*

Judicial: Judge, United States District Court for the Southern District of New York (1985-1989); Circuit Judge, United States Court of Appeals for the Second Circuit (1989-2000); Member, Judicial Conference of the United States

Legal Practice: Associate, Davis Polk & Wardwell (1969-1970); Associate, Carter Ledyard & Milburn LLP (1975-1981)

Military Service: United States Marine Corps (1963-1967)

Current Memberships: American Bar Association; The Association of the Bar of the City of New York; The District of Columbia Bar

Staff

Law Clerk **Ariela Anhalt** .... (203) 773-2181
Began Service: September 2015
Term Expires: September 2016
E-mail: ariela_anhalt@ca2.uscourts.gov

Law Clerk **Benjamin Cavataro** .... (203) 773-2181
Began Service: October 2015
Term Expires: October 2016
E-mail: benjamin_cavataro@ca2.uscourts.gov

Law Clerk **Katherine Mackey** .... (203) 773-2181
Began Service: August 2015
Term Expires: August 2016
E-mail: Katherine_mackey@ca2.uscourts.gov

Judicial Assistant **Aneita H. Delgado** .... (203) 773-2181
E-mail: aneita_delgado@ca2.uscourts.gov

Chambers of Senior Judge Chester J. Straub

40 Foley Square, New York, NY 10007
Tel: (212) 857-8500 Fax: (212) 857-8710
E-mail: chester_straub@ca2.uscourts.gov

Chester J. Straub
Senior Judge

Date of Birth: 1937
Education: St Peter's Col 1958 BA; Virginia 1961 JD
Began Service: June 3, 1998
Appointed By: President William J. Clinton
Political Affiliation: Democrat

Government: Member, New York State Assembly (1967-1972); Member, New York State Senate (1973-1975)

Judicial: Special Master, New York State Supreme Court (1977-1984); Mediator, United States District Court for the Southern District of New York (1993-1998); Neutral Evaluator/Mediator, United States District Court for the Eastern District of New York (1994-1998); Circuit Judge, United States Court of Appeals for the Second Circuit (1998-2008); Senior Judge, Chambers of Senior Judge Chester J. Straub, United States Court of Appeals for the Second Circuit (2008-2009)

Legal Practice: Associate, Willkie Farr & Gallagher (1963-1970); Partner, Willkie Farr & Gallagher (1971-1998)

Current Memberships: American Bar Association; The Association of the Bar of the City of New York; New York State Bar Association

Staff

Law Clerk **Robert Sobelman** .... (212) 857-8500
Began Service: February 2015
Term Expires: February 2016
E-mail: robert_sobelman@ca2.uscourts.gov
Education: Brooklyn Law 2012 JD

Judicial Assistant **Mary Wieczorek** .... (212) 857-8500
E-mail: mary_wieczorek@ca2.uscourts.gov

Chambers of Senior Judge Guido Calabresi

U.S. Courthouse, 157 Church Street, New Haven, CT 06510-2030
Tel: (203) 773-2291 Fax: (203) 773-2401
E-mail: guido_calabresi@ca2.uscourts.gov

Guido Calabresi
Senior Judge

Date of Birth: 1932
Education: Yale 1953 BS; Oxford (UK) 1955 BA, 1959 MA; Yale 1958 LLB
Began Service: September 16, 1994
Appointed By: President William J. Clinton

Academic: Professor, Law School, Yale University (1959-1964); Dean, Law School, Yale University (1985-1994)

Judicial: Circuit Judge, Chambers of Circuit Judge Guido Calabresi, United States Court of Appeals for the Second Circuit (1994-2009)

Current Memberships: American Association of Justice; American Bar Association; The American Law Institute; Association of American Law Schools; Connecticut Bar Association, Inc.; National Association of Women Lawyers; National Bar Association; Society of American Law Teachers

Staff

Law Clerk **Andrew T. Davis** .... (203) 773-2291
Began Service: August 2015
Term Expires: August 2016
E-mail: andrew_davis@ca2.uscourts.gov

Law Clerk **Shayak Sarkar** .... (203) 773-2291
Began Service: August 2015
Term Expires: August 2016
E-mail: shayak_sarkar@ca2.uscourts.gov

Law Clerk **Brooke Willig** .... (203) 773-2291
Began Service: August 2015
Term Expires: August 2016
E-mail: brooke_willig@ca2.uscourts.gov

Judicial Assistant **Marjorie S. Greenblatt** .... (203) 773-2291
E-mail: marjorie_greenblatt@ca2.uscourts.gov

Judicial Assistant **Susan A. Lucibelli** .... (203) 773-2291
E-mail: susan_lucibelli@ca2.uscourts.gov
Education: New Haven 1972 BA

United States Court of Appeals for the Third Circuit

U.S. Courthouse, 601 Market Street, Philadelphia, PA 19106
Tel: (215) 597-0718
Tel: (215) 597-7371 (Electronic Opinions & Dockets Data)
Fax: (215) 597-8656
Internet: www.ca3.uscourts.gov

Number of Judgeships: 14

Number of Vacancies: 2

Supreme Court Justice: Associate Justice Samuel A. Alito Jr.

Areas Covered: Delaware, New Jersey, Pennsylvania and the Virgin Islands

Court Staff

Circuit Executive **Margaret A. Wiegand** .... (215) 597-0718
E-mail: margaret_wiegand@ca3.uscourts.gov

Deputy Circuit Executive **Joel McHugh** .... (215) 597-0718
E-mail: joel_mchugh@ca3.uscourts.gov

Assistant Circuit Executive for Human Resources
Shelly Wulff .... (215) 597-0718

Assistant Circuit Executive for Budget **Lori A. Casner** ... (215) 597-0718
E-mail: lori_casner@ca3.uscourts.gov

Assistant Circuit Executive for Legal Affairs
Jeanne Donnelly .... (215) 597-0718
E-mail: jeanne_donnelly@ca3.uscourts.gov

United States Court of Appeals for the Third Circuit *continued*

Deputy Circuit Executive for Information Technology
P. Mark Soltys .... (215) 597-0718
Education: Goshen 1983 BA; Temple 1992 JD

Clerk of Court **Marcia M. Waldron** .... (215) 597-2995
E-mail: marcia_waldron@ca3.uscourts.gov Fax: (215) 597-6956
Education: Pennsylvania 1973 BA; Villanova 1976 MA; Dickinson Law 1986 JD

Director, Legal Division **Marisa J. G. Watson** .... (267) 299-7902
William J. Green Federal Bldg., 600 Arch St., Philadelphia, PA 19106
E-mail: marisa_watson@ca3.uscourts.gov
Education: Wisconsin 1991 JD

Supervisory Staff Attorney **Elizabeth Cormier** .... (267) 299-7901
William J. Green Federal Bldg., 600 Arch St., Philadelphia, PA 19106
E-mail: elizabeth_cormier@ca3.uscourts.gov
Education: Pennsylvania 1986 JD

Circuit Librarian **Judith F. Ambler** .... (267) 299-4301
E-mail: judith_ambler@ca3.uscourts.gov Fax: (267) 299-5110
Education: Widener 1992 JD

Chief Circuit Mediator **Joseph A. Torregrossa** .... (267) 299-4130
E-mail: joseph_torregrossa@ca3.uscourts.gov

Chambers of Chief Judge Theodore A. McKee

U.S. Courthouse, 601 Market Street, Room 20614, Philadelphia, PA 19106
Tel: (215) 597-9601 Fax: (215) 597-0104
E-mail: chambers_of_judge_theodore_mckee@ca3.uscourts.gov

Theodore A. McKee
Chief Judge

Date of Birth: 1947
Education: SUNY (Cortland) 1969 BA; Syracuse 1975 JD
Began Service: June 20, 1994
Appointed By: President William J. Clinton

Academic: Director, Minority Recruitment and Admissions, State University of New York at Binghamton (1969-1972); Lecturer, Rutgers, The State University of New Jersey (1980-1991)

Government: Assistant U.S. Attorney, Pennsylvania - Eastern District, Executive Office for United States Attorneys, United States Department of Justice (1977-1980); Deputy City Solicitor, Law Department, City of Philadelphia, Pennsylvania (1980-1983); General Counsel, Philadelphia Parking Authority, City of Philadelphia, Pennsylvania (1983)

Judicial: Judge, First Judicial District of Pennsylvania (1984-1994)

Legal Practice: Associate, Wolf, Block, Schorr and Solis-Cohen LLP (1975-1977)

Current Memberships: Barristers' Association of Philadelphia; National Bar Association; Pennsylvania Bar Association; Philadelphia Bar Association

Staff

Law Clerk **Hannah Brennan** .... (215) 597-9601
Began Service: September 2015
Term Expires: September 2016

Law Clerk **Francesca Corbacho** .... (215) 597-9601
Began Service: September 2015
Term Expires: September 2016

Law Clerk **Gerald S. Dickinson** .... (215) 597-9601
Began Service: September 2015
Term Expires: September 2016
E-mail: gerald_dickinson@ca3.uscourts.gov

Law Clerk **Rose Goldberg** .... (215) 597-9601
Began Service: September 2015
Term Expires: September 2016

Career Law Clerk **James Robinson** .... (215) 597-9601
E-mail: james_robinson@ca3.uscourts.gov
Education: Saint Louis U 1974 JD

Secretary **Yvette Childs** .... (215) 597-9601
E-mail: yvette_childs@ca3.uscourts.gov

Judicial Assistant **Anna Hatchett** .... (215) 597-9601
E-mail: anna_hatchett@ca3.uscourts.gov

Chambers of Circuit Judge Thomas L. Ambro

J. Caleb Boggs Federal Courthouse, 844 King Street, Lockbox #32, Wilmington, DE 19801
Tel: (302) 573-6500 Fax: (302) 573-6512
E-mail: judge_thomas_ambro@ca3.uscourts.gov

Thomas L. Ambro
Circuit Judge

Date of Birth: 1949
Education: Georgetown 1971 BA, 1975 JD
Began Service: June 19, 2000
Appointed By: President William J. Clinton

Clerkships: Law Clerk The Honorable Daniel L. Herrmann, Delaware Supreme Court (1975-1976)

Legal Practice: Richards, Layton & Finger, PA (1976-2000)

Current Memberships: Section on Litigation, American Bar Association; American College of Bankruptcy; American College of Commercial Finance Lawyers, Inc

Staff
Law Clerk **Daniel Asher** .... (302) 573-6500
Began Service: August 2015
Term Expires: August 2016
E-mail: daniel_asher@ca3.uscourts.gov
Law Clerk **Matthew Klayman** .... (302) 573-6500
Began Service: August 2015
Term Expires: August 2016
E-mail: matthew_klayman@ca3.uscourts.gov
Law Clerk **Matthew Letten** .... (302) 573-6500
Began Service: August 2015
Term Expires: August 2016
E-mail: matthew_letten@ca3.uscourts.gov
Law Clerk **Rob Silverblatt** .... (302) 573-6500
Began Service: August 2015
Term Expires: August 2016
E-mail: robert_silverblatt@ca3.uscourts.gov
Judicial Assistant **Linda J. Vodovis** .... (302) 573-6500
E-mail: linda_vodovis@ca3.uscourts.gov

Chambers of Circuit Judge Julio M. Fuentes

Martin Luther King, Jr. Federal Building & U.S. Courthouse, 50 Walnut Street, Room 5032, Newark, NJ 07102
Tel: (973) 645-3831 Fax: (973) 645-3681
E-mail: chambers_of_judge_julio_fuentes@ca3.uscourts.gov

Julio M. Fuentes
Circuit Judge

Date of Birth: 1946
Education: Southern Illinois 1971 BA; NYU 1972 MA; SUNY (Buffalo) 1975 JD; Rutgers 1993 MA
Began Service: May 15, 2000
Appointed By: President William J. Clinton

Judicial: Municipal Judge (part time), Newark Municipal Court (1978-1981); Judge, Newark Municipal Court (1981-1987); Judge, New Jersey Superior Court (1987-2000)

Legal Practice: Associate, Miller, Hochman, Meyerson & Schaeffer (1975-1977); Partner, Fuentes, Plant & Velazquez (1977-1981)

Military Service: First Lieutenant, United States Army (1966-1969); United States Army Reserve, United States Department of the Army (1969-1972)

Current Memberships: American Bar Association; Essex County Bar Association; National Hispanic Bar Association; New Jersey Hispanic Bar Association; New Jersey State Bar Association

Staff
Law Clerk **Kari D'Ottavio** .... (973) 645-3831
Began Service: September 2015
Term Expires: August 31, 2016
E-mail: kari_dottavio@ca3.uscourts.gov

Chambers of Circuit Judge Julio M. Fuentes *continued*

Law Clerk **Sean Murray** .... (973) 645-3831
Began Service: September 2015
Term Expires: August 31, 2016
E-mail: sean_murray@ca3.uscourts.gov
Law Clerk **Patrick Reinikainen** .... (973) 645-3831
Began Service: September 2015
Term Expires: August 31, 2016
E-mail: patrick_reinikainen@ca3.uscourts.gov
Law Clerk **Daniel Young** .... (973) 645-3831
Began Service: September 2015
Term Expires: August 31, 2016
E-mail: daniel_young@ca3.uscourts.gov
Judicial Assistant **Suzanne Makwinski** .... (973) 645-3831
E-mail: suzanne_makwinski@ca3.uscourts.gov

Chambers of Circuit Judge D. Brooks Smith

Allegheny Professional Center, 1798 Old Route 220 North, Suite 203, Duncansville, PA 16635
Tel: (814) 693-0570 Fax: (814) 693-0575

D. Brooks Smith
Circuit Judge

Date of Birth: 1951
Education: Franklin & Marshall 1973 BA; Dickinson Law 1976 JD
Began Service: September 23, 2002
Appointed By: President George W. Bush

Government: Assistant District Attorney (part-time), Office of the District Attorney, County of Blair, Pennsylvania (1981-1984); District Attorney (part-time), Commonwealth of Pennsylvania (1983-1984)

Judicial: Judge, Pennsylvania Court of Common Pleas, County of Blair, Pennsylvania (1984-1988); Judge, United States District Court for the Western District of Pennsylvania (1988-2002); Chief Judge, United States District Court for the Western District of Pennsylvania (2001-2002)

Legal Practice: Associate, Jubelirer, Carothers, Krier, Halpern & Smith (1976-1979); Partner, Jubelirer, Carothers, Krier, Halpern & Smith (1980-1984)

Current Memberships: Allegheny County Bar Association; The American Law Institute; Federal Bar Association; Federal Judges Association; Pennsylvania Bar Association

Staff
Career Law Clerk **Dawn Svirsko** .... (814) 693-0570
E-mail: dawn_svirsko@ca3.uscourts.gov
Education: Dickinson Law 1988 JD
Judicial Assistant **Kim Fedesco** .... (814) 693-0570
E-mail: kimberly_fedesco@ca3.uscourts.gov

Chambers of Circuit Judge D. Michael Fisher

U.S. Courthouse, 700 Grant Street, Room 5360, Pittsburgh, PA 15219-1906
Tel: (412) 208-7320 Fax: (412) 208-7327
E-mail: chambers_of_judge_d_michael_fisher@ca3.uscourts.gov

D. Michael Fisher
Circuit Judge

Education: Georgetown 1966 AB, 1969 JD
Began Service: December 11, 2003
Appointed By: President George W. Bush
Political Affiliation: Republican

Staff
Law Clerk **Benjamin Ristau** .... (412) 208-7320
Began Service: September 2015
Term Expires: September 2016
E-mail: benjamin_ristau@ca3.uscourts.gov
Law Clerk **Douglas Baker** .... (412) 208-7320
Began Service: September 2015
Term Expires: September 2016
E-mail: doug_baker@ca3.uscourts.gov

(continued on next page)

Chambers of Circuit Judge D. Michael Fisher *continued*

Law Clerk **Meredith Woods** .... (412) 208-7320
Began Service: September 2015
Term Expires: September 2016
E-mail: meredith_woods@ca3.uscourts.gov

Law Clerk **Elizabeth M. Thomas** .... (412) 208-7320
Began Service: September 2015
Term Expires: September 2016
E-mail: elizabeth_thomas@ca3.uscourts.gov
Education: West Virginia 2013 JD

Judicial Assistant **Kelly LaMantia** .... (412) 208-7320
E-mail: kelly_lamantia@ca3.uscourts.gov

Chambers of Circuit Judge Michael A. Chagares

357 U.S. Post Office and Courthouse, 50 Walnut Street,
Newark, NJ 07102
Tel: (973) 368-6486 Fax: (973) 368-6265
E-mail: chambers_of_judge_michael_chagares@ca3.uscourts.gov

Michael A. Chagares

Circuit Judge

Date of Birth: 1962
Education: Gettysburg 1984 BA; Seton Hall 1987 JD
Began Service: April 24, 2006
Appointed By: President George W. Bush

Academic: Adjunct Professor, School of Law, Seton Hall University (1991-2006)

Clerkships: Law Clerk, Judge Morton I. Greenberg, United States Court of Appeals for the Third Circuit (1988-1990)

Government: Assistant U.S. Attorney, District of New Jersey, U.S. Attorneys Office (1990-2004); Chief, Civil Division, New Jersey District, United States Department of Justice (1999-2004)

Legal Practice: Private Practice (2004-2006)

Staff

Law Clerk **Andrew Macurdy** .... (973) 368-6486
Began Service: September 2015
Term Expires: September 2016
E-mail: andrew_macurdy@ca3.uscourts.gov

Law Clerk **Jonathan Sidhu** .... (973) 368-6486
Began Service: September 2015
Term Expires: September 2016
E-mail: jonathan_sidhu@ca3.uscourts.gov

Law Clerk **Richard Lvedeman** .... (973) 368-6486
Began Service: September 2015
Term Expires: September 2016
E-mail: richard_lvedeman@ca3.uscourts.gov

Law Clerk **Arianna Markel** .... (973) 368-6486
Began Service: September 2015
Term Expires: September 2016
E-mail: arianna_markel@ca3.uscourts.gov
Education: Harvard 2013 JD

Judicial Assistant **Sylvia Lock** .... (973) 368-6486
E-mail: sylvia_lock@ca3.uscourts.gov

Chambers of Circuit Judge Kent A. Jordan

J. Caleb Boggs Federal Building, 844 King Street, Lockbox #10,
Wilmington, DE 19801
Tel: (302) 573-6001
E-mail: chambers_of_judge_kent_jordan@ca3.uscourts.gov

Kent A. Jordan

Circuit Judge

Date of Birth: October 24, 1957
Education: BYU 1981 BA; Georgetown 1984 JD
Began Service: December 2006
Appointed By: President George W. Bush

Academic: Adjunct Professor of Law, School of Law, Widener University (1995-1996); Adjunct Professor of Law, Vanderbilt University (2003-2006); Adjunct Professor, University of Pennsylvania (2005); Adjunct Professor of Law, School of Law, Widener University (2006)

Clerkships: Law Clerk The Honorable James L. Latchum, United States District Court for the District of Delaware (1984-1985)

Corporate: Vice President and General Counsel, Corporation Service Company (1998-2002)

Government: Assistant U.S. Attorney, Delaware District, United States Department of Justice (1987-1992)

Judicial: District Judge, United States District Court District of Delaware (2002-2006)

Legal Practice: Associate, Potter Anderson & Corroon LLP (1985-1987); Associate, Morris, James, Hitchens & Williams LLP (1992-1993); Partner, Morris, James, Hitchens & Williams LLP (1993-1997)

Current Memberships: The American Law Institute

Staff

Secretary **Cheryl Stein** .... (302) 573-6001
E-mail: cheryl_stein@ca3.uscourts.gov

Chambers of Circuit Judge Thomas Michael Hardiman

U.S. Post Office & Courthouse, 700 Grant Street, Suite 2270,
Pittsburgh, PA 15219
Tel: (412) 208-7440 Fax: (412) 208-7447
E-mail: chambers_of_judge_thomas_hardiman@ca3.uscourts.gov

Thomas Michael Hardiman

Circuit Judge

Date of Birth: July 8, 1965
Education: Notre Dame 1987 BA; Georgetown 1990 JD
Began Service: April 2007
Appointed By: President George W. Bush

Legal Practice: Associate, Skadden, Arps, Slate, Meagher & Flom LLP (1989-1992); Associate, Cindrich & Titus (1992-1994); Associate, Titus & McConomy LLP (1994-1996); Partner, Titus & McConomy LLP (1996-1999); Partner, Reed Smith LLP (1999-2003)

Nonprofit: Director, Big Brothers Big Sisters of Greater Pittsburgh, Inc. (1995-2006); President, Big Brothers Big Sisters of Greater Pittsburgh, Inc. (1999-2000); Chair, Board of Excellence Committee, Big Brothers Big Sisters of Greater Pittsburgh, Inc. (2001-2005)

Staff

Law Clerk **Ryan Nelson** .... (412) 208-7440
Began Service: August 2015
Term Expires: August 2016
E-mail: ryan_nelson@ca3.uscourts.gov

Law Clerk **Michael O'Brien** .... (412) 208-7440
Began Service: August 2015
Term Expires: August 2016
E-mail: michael_obrien@ca3.uscourts.gov

Law Clerk **John Robinson** .... (412) 208-7440
Began Service: August 2015
Term Expires: August 2016
E-mail: john_robinson@ca3.uscourts.gov

Chambers of Circuit Judge Thomas Michael Hardiman *continued*

Law Clerk **Anthony "Tony" Sheh** .... (412) 208-7440
Began Service: August 2015
Term Expires: August 2016
E-mail: alexander_kritikos@ca3.uscourts.gov

Judicial Assistant **Melanie Hallums** .... (412) 208-7440
E-mail: melanie_hallums@ca3.uscourts.gov

Chambers of Circuit Judge Joseph A. Greenaway, Jr.

Frank R. Lautenberg U.S. Post Office & Courthouse, Room 411, Newark, NJ 07101-0999
P.O. Box 999, Newark, NJ 07101-0999
Tel: (973) 622-4828 Fax: (973) 622-4806

Joseph A. Greenaway, Jr.
Circuit Judge

Date of Birth: 1957
Education: Columbia 1978 BA; Harvard 1981 JD
Began Service: February 12, 2010
Appointed By: President Barack Obama
Political Affiliation: Democrat

Clerkships: Law Clerk The Honorable Vincent L. Broderick, United States District Court for the Southern District of New York (1982-1983)

Corporate: In-House Counsel, Johnson & Johnson (1990-1996)

Government: Assistant United States Attorney, Criminal Division, United States Attorney's Office, United States Department of Justice, Ronald Reagan Administration (1985-1989); Assistant United States Attorney, Chief Narcotics Division, United States Attorney's Office, United States Department of Justice, George H.W. Bush Administration (1989-1990)

Judicial: District Judge, Chambers of District Judge Joseph A. Greenaway, Jr., United States District Court for the District of New Jersey (1996-2010)

Legal Practice: Associate, Kramer, Levin, Nessen Kamin & Frankel (1981-1982); Associate, Kramer, Levin, Nessen Kamin & Frankel (1983-1985)

Current Memberships: American Bar Association; Columbia College Black Alumni Council; Garden State Bar Association; National Bar Association

Staff

Law Clerk **Caroline Hatton** .... (973) 622-4828
Began Service: September 2015
Term Expires: September 2016
E-mail: caroline_hatton@ca3.uscourts.gov

Law Clerk **Omar Madhany** .... (973) 622-4828
Began Service: September 2015
Term Expires: September 2016
E-mail: omar_madhany@ca3.uscourts.gov

Law Clerk **Pamela Terry** .... (973) 622-4828
Began Service: September 2015
Term Expires: September 2016
E-mail: pamela_terry@ca3.uscourts.gov

Law Clerk **Michele Yankson** .... (973) 622-4828
Began Service: September 2015
Term Expires: September 2016
E-mail: michele_yankson@ca3.uscourts.gov

Permanent Law Clerk **Lynne C. Kosobucki** .... (973) 622-4828
E-mail: lynne_kosobucki@ca3.uscourts.gov
Education: Georgetown 1983 BSChem, 1988 JD

Chambers of Circuit Judge Thomas I. Vanaskie

William J. Nealon Federal Building, 235 North Washington Avenue, Scranton, PA 18501
P.O. Box 913, Scranton, PA 18501
Tel: (570) 207-5720 Fax: (570) 207-5729
E-mail: judge_vanaskie@ca3.uscourts.gov

Thomas I. Vanaskie
Circuit Judge

Date of Birth: 1953
Education: Lycoming 1975 BA; Dickinson Law 1978 JD
Began Service: April 28, 2010
Appointed By: President Barack Obama

Clerkships: Law Clerk The Honorable William J. Nealon, United States District Court for the Middle District of Pennsylvania (1978-1980)

Judicial: Member, Judicial Conference of the United States (2006); District Judge, Chambers of District Judge Thomas I. Vanaskie, United States District Court for the Middle District of Pennsylvania (1994-2010)

Legal Practice: Attorney, Dilworth, Paxson, Kalish & Kauffman (1980-1992); Partner, Elliott, Vanaskie & Riley (1992-1994)

Current Memberships: Federal Bar Association; Lackawanna Bar Association; Pennsylvania Bar Association

Staff

Law Clerk **Amanda Cox** .... (570) 207-5720
Began Service: September 6, 2015
Term Expires: September 2016
E-mail: thomas_burke@ca3.uscourts.gov

Law Clerk **Rebecca Gauthier** .... (570) 207-5720
Began Service: September 6, 2015
Term Expires: September 2016
E-mail: rebecca_gauthier@ca3.uscourts.gov

Law Clerk **Thomas Helbig, Jr.** .... (570) 207-5720
Began Service: September 2015
Term Expires: September 2016
E-mail: thomas_helbig@ca3.uscourts.gov

Law Clerk **Sean Suber** .... (570) 207-5720
Began Service: September 6, 2015
Term Expires: September 2016
E-mail: sean_suber@ca3.uscourts.gov

Case Administrator **Lorna Yzkanin** .... (570) 207-5720
E-mail: lorna_yzkanin@ca3.uscourts.gov

Chambers of Circuit Judge Patty Shwartz

Two Federal Square, Newark, NJ 07102
Tel: (973) 645-6596 Fax: (215) 597-8656
E-mail: chambers_of_judge_patty_shwartz@ca3.uscourts.gov

Patty Shwartz
Circuit Judge

Education: Rutgers 1983 BA; Pennsylvania 1986 JD
Began Service: April 10, 2013
Appointed By: President Barack Obama

Clerkships: Law Clerk The Honorable Harold A. Ackerman, United States District Court for the District of New Jersey (1987-1989)

Government: Assistant U.S. Attorney, District of New Jersey, U.S. Attorney's Office, United States Department of Justice (1989-2003); Deputy Chief, Criminal Division, U.S. Attorney's Office, United States Department of Justice (1995-1999); Chief, Criminal Division, U.S. Attorney's Office, United States Department of Justice (1999-2001); Chief, Criminal Division, U.S. Attorney's Office, United States Department of Justice (2002-2003)

Judicial: Magistrate Judge, Chambers of Magistrate Judge Patty Shwartz, United States District Court for the District of New Jersey (2003-2013)

Current Memberships: The John C. Lifland American Inn of Court, The American Inns of Court; Federal Magistrate Judges Association

(continued on next page)

Chambers of Circuit Judge Patty Shwartz *continued*

Staff

Law Clerk **Halley W. Epstein** .... (973) 645-6596
Term Expires: September 2016
E-mail: halley_epstein@ca3.uscourts.gov
Education: Yale 2014 JD

Law Clerk **Seth Fiur** .... (973) 645-6596
Term Expires: September 2016
E-mail: seth_fiur@ca3.uscourts.gov
Education: Fordham 2013 JD

Law Clerk **Elizabeth Grosso** .... (973) 645-6596
Term Expires: September 2016
E-mail: elizabeth_grosso@ca3.uscourts.gov

Law Clerk **Paul Kleist** .... (973) 645-6596
Term Expires: September 2016
E-mail: paul_kleist@ca3.uscourts.gov

Judicial Assistant **Iris Liriano** .... (973) 645-6596
E-mail: iris_liriano@ca3.uscourts.gov

Chambers of Circuit Judge Cheryl Ann Krause

601 Market Street, Philadelphia, PA 19106
Tel: (267) 232-0202
E-mail: chambers_of_judge_cheryl_ann_krause@ca3.uscourts.gov

Cheryl Ann Krause
Circuit Judge

Education: Pennsylvania 1989 BA; Stanford 1993 JD
Began Service: July 9, 2014
Appointed By: President Barack Obama

Clerkships: Law Clerk, Chambers of Associate Justice Anthony M. Kennedy, Supreme Court of the United States (1994-1995)

Legal Practice: Law Clerk, Heller, Erhman White & McAuliffe (1995-1996); Associate, Davis Polk & Wardwell LLP (1996-1997); Shareholder, Hangley Aronchick Segal Pudlin & Schiller (2003-2006); Partner, Litigation Department, Dechert LLP (2006-2014)

Chambers of Senior Judge Leonard I. Garth

Martin Luther King, Jr. Federal Building & U.S. Courthouse,
50 Walnut Street, Room 5040, Newark, NJ 07102
U.S. Courthouse, 601 Market Street, Room 20613, Philadelphia, PA 19106
Tel: (973) 645-6521 Tel: (215) 597-3925 (Philadelphia Chambers)
Fax: (973) 645-6119 Fax: (215) 597-9157 (Philadelphia Chambers)
E-mail: chambers_of_judge_leonard_garth@ca3.uscourts.gov

Leonard I. Garth
Senior Judge

Date of Birth: 1921
Education: Columbia 1942 BA; Harvard 1952 LLB
Began Service: 1973
Appointed By: President Richard M. Nixon

Academic: Lecturer, Rutgers Law School (1978-1998); Lecturer, School of Law, Seton Hall University (1980-1996)

Government: Board Member, New Jersey Board of Bar Examiners, Supreme Court of New Jersey (1964-1965)

Judicial: District Judge, United States District Court for the District of New Jersey (1970-1973)

Legal Practice: Partner, Cole, Berman & Garth (1952-1970)

Military Service: United States Army (1943-1946)

Nonprofit: President, Harvard Law School Association (1962-1963)

Chambers of Senior Judge Dolores K. Sloviter

U.S. Courthouse, 601 Market Street, Room 18614, Philadelphia, PA 19106
Tel: (215) 597-1588 Fax: (215) 597-2371
E-mail: Chambers_of_Judge_Dolores_Sloviter@ca3.uscourts.gov

Dolores K. Sloviter
Senior Judge

Date of Birth: 1932
Education: Temple 1953 AB; Pennsylvania 1956 LLB
Began Service: 1979
Appointed By: President Jimmy Carter

Current Memberships: American Bar Association; The American Law Institute; Federal Bar Association; Federal Judges Association; National Association of Women Judges; Pennsylvania Women's Forum; Philadelphia Bar Association

Staff

Judicial Assistant **Rosemarie Rao** .... (215) 597-1588
E-mail: rosemarie_rao@ca3.uscourts.gov

Chambers of Senior Judge Walter K. Stapleton

U.S. Courthouse, 844 King Street, Lockbox 33, Wilmington, DE 19801
Tel: (302) 573-6165 Fax: (302) 573-6313
E-mail: chambers_of_judge_walter_stapleton@ca3.uscourts.gov

Walter K. Stapleton
Senior Judge

Date of Birth: 1934
Education: Princeton 1956 AB; Harvard 1959 LLB; Virginia 1984 LLM
Began Service: May 1985
Appointed By: President Ronald Reagan

Government: Deputy Attorney General, United States Department of Justice (1963)

Judicial: Judge, United States District Court for the District of Delaware (1970-1985)

Legal Practice: Associate, Morris, Nichols, Arsht & Tunnell LLP (1959-1965); Partner, Morris, Nichols, Arsht & Tunnell LLP (1965-1970)

Current Memberships: American Bar Association; Delaware State Bar Association

Staff

Judicial Assistant **Fran Wilfong** .... (302) 573-6165
E-mail: fran_wilfong@ca3.uscourts.gov

Chambers of Senior Judge Morton I. Greenberg

U.S. Courthouse, 402 East State Street, Room 219, Trenton, NJ 08608
Tel: (609) 989-0436 Fax: (609) 989-2112
E-mail: chambers_of_judge_morton_greenberg@ca3.uscourts.gov

Morton I. Greenberg
Senior Judge

Date of Birth: March 20, 1933
Education: Pennsylvania 1954 AB; Yale 1957 JD
Began Service: June 18, 1987
Appointed By: President Ronald Reagan

Government: Law Clerk and Deputy Attorney General, Office of the Attorney General, State of New Jersey (1957-1960); County Attorney, County of Mercer, New Jersey (1970-1971); Assistant Attorney General (Civil Litigation), Office of the Attorney General, State of New Jersey (1971-1973); First Assistant County Prosecutor, State of New Jersey (1971)

Judicial: Judge, New Jersey Superior Court, Law Division (1973-1976); Judge, New Jersey Superior Court, Chancery Division (1976-1980); Judge, New Jersey Superior Court, Appellate Division (1980-1987); Circuit Judge, United States Court of Appeals for the Third Circuit (1987-2000)

Current Memberships: New Jersey State Bar Association

Chambers of Senior Judge Morton I. Greenberg *continued*

Staff

Law Clerk **Desiree Grace** . . . . (609) 989-0436
Began Service: September 2015
Term Expires: August 30, 2016
E-mail: zach_shapiro@ca3.uscourts.gov

Law Clerk **Justin Louis Rand** . . . . (609) 989-0436
Began Service: September 2015
Term Expires: August 30, 2016
E-mail: justin_rand@ca3.uscourts.gov

Judicial Assistant **Mary Ann Gartner** . . . . (609) 989-0436

Chambers of Senior Judge Anthony Scirica

U.S. Courthouse, 601 Market Street, Room 22614, Philadelphia, PA 19106
Tel: (215) 597-2399 Fax: (215) 597-7373
E-mail: anthony_scirica@ca3.uscourts.gov

Senior Judge **Anthony J. Scirica**
Began Service: September 11, 1987
E-mail: anthony_scirica@ca3.uscourts.gov
Education: Wesleyan U 1962 BA;
Michigan 1965 JD

Staff

Secretary **LaToya Corprew** . . . . (215) 597-2399
E-mail: latoya_corprew@ca3.uscourts.gov

Chambers of Senior Judge Robert E. Cowen

U.S. Courthouse, 402 East State Street, Room 207,
Trenton, NJ 08608-1507
Tel: (609) 989-2188 Fax: (609) 989-2195
E-mail: chambers_of_judge_robert_cowen@ca3.uscourts.gov

Robert E. Cowen
Senior Judge

Date of Birth: 1930
Education: Drake 1952 BS; Rutgers (Newark) 1958 LLB
Began Service: November 1987
Appointed By: President Ronald Reagan

Affiliation: Lecturer, Institute of Continuing Legal Education

Clerkships: Law Clerk The Honorable Walter Conklin, New Jersey Superior Court (1958-1959)

Government: Assistant Prosecutor, County of Essex, New Jersey (1969-1970); Deputy Attorney General, Organized Crime and Special Prosecutions Section, Criminal Justice Division, United States Department of Justice (1970-1973); Director, Division of Ethics & Professional Services, Administrative Office of the Courts, State of New Jersey (1973-1978)

Judicial: Magistrate Judge, United States District Court for the District of New Jersey (1978-1985); District Judge, United States District Court for the District of New Jersey (1985-1987)

Legal Practice: Associate, Schreiber, Lancaster & Demos (1959-1961); Private Practice (1961-1969)

Military Service: United States Army (1953-1954)

Current Memberships: American Bar Association; Federal Judges Association; National Association of Bat Counsel; New Jersey State Bar Association

Staff

Career Law Clerk **Michael Devlin** . . . . (609) 989-2188
E-mail: michael_devlin@ca3.uscourts.gov
Education: Temple 2000 JD

Judicial Assistant **Deborah A. Jablonski** . . . . (609) 989-2188
E-mail: deborah_jablonski@ca3.uscourts.gov

Chambers of Senior Judge Richard L. Nygaard

17 South Park Row, Suite B - 230, Erie, PA 16501
Tel: (814) 464-9640 Fax: (814) 464-9647
E-mail: chambers_of_judge_richard_nygaard@ca3.uscourts.gov

The Honorable Richard L. Nygaard
Senior Judge

Date of Birth: 1940
Education: USC 1969 BS; Michigan 1971 JD
Began Service: November 1988
Appointed By: President Ronald Reagan

Academic: Senior Lecturer, The Pennsylvania State University (1999-2003)

Government: County Councilman, County of Erie, Pennsylvania (1977-1981)

Judicial: Judge, Pennsylvania Court of Common Pleas, Sixth District (1981-1988)

Legal Practice: Associate, Orton, Nygaard & Dunlavey (1972-1981)

Military Service: United States Naval Reserve (1958-1964)

Current Memberships: Erie County Bar Association (PA); Pennsylvania Bar Association

Staff

Judicial Assistant **Judy Paullet** . . . . (814) 464-9640
E-mail: judy_paullet@ca3.uscourts.gov
Education: Indiana (PA) 1986 BS

Chambers of Senior Judge Jane R. Roth

U. S. Courthouse, 601 Market Street, Room 18316,
Philadelphia, PA 19106
Tel: (215) 597-7803 Fax: (267) 299-5109
E-mail: chambers_of_judge_jane_roth@ca3.uscourts.gov

Jane R. Roth
Senior Judge

Date of Birth: 1935
Education: Smith 1956 BA; Harvard 1965 LLB
Began Service: July 22, 1991
Appointed By: President George H.W. Bush

Government: Administrative Assistant and Clerk, United States Department of State (1956-1962)

Judicial: District Judge, United States District Court for the District of Delaware (1985-1991); Circuit Judge, United States Court of Appeals for the Third Circuit (1991-2006)

Legal Practice: Attorney, Richards, Layton & Finger, P.A. (1965-1985)

Current Memberships: Delaware State Bar Association; Federal Judges Association

Staff

Law Clerk **Lyric Chen** . . . . (215) 597-7803
Began Service: August 17, 2015
Term Expires: August 2016
E-mail: lyric_chen@ca3.uscourts.gov

Law Clerk **Jeffrey Golimowski** . . . . (215) 597-7803
Began Service: August 24, 2015
Term Expires: August 31, 2016
E-mail: jeffrey_golimowski@ca3.uscourts.gov

Law Clerk **Eric Holmes** . . . . (215) 597-7803
Began Service: August 31, 2015
Term Expires: August 31, 2016
E-mail: eric_holmes@ca3.uscourts.gov

Law Clerk **Sarah Magen** . . . . (215) 597-7803
Began Service: August 24, 2015
Term Expires: August 31, 2016
E-mail: sarah_magen@ca3.uscourts.gov

Judicial Assistant **Dana Moore** . . . . (267) 299-4052
E-mail: dana_moore@ca3.uscourts.gov

Chambers of Senior Judge Maryanne Trump Barry

U.S. Post Office & Courthouse, P.O. Box 999, Newark, NJ 07101-0999
Tel: (973) 645-2133 Fax: (973) 645-6628
E-mail: chambers_of_judge_maryanne_trump_barry@ca3.uscourts.gov

Maryanne Trump Barry
Senior Judge

Date of Birth: 1937
Education: Mount Holyoke 1958 BA; Columbia 1961 MA; Hofstra 1974 JD
Began Service: September 13, 1999
Appointed By: President William J. Clinton
Political Affiliation: Republican

Current Memberships: American Bar Foundation; Association of the Federal Bar of New Jersey; New Jersey State Bar Association; New York State Bar Association

Staff
Law Clerk **Ryan Montefusco** .... (973) 645-2133
Began Service: August 2015
Term Expires: August 2016
E-mail: ryan_montefusco@ca3.uscourts.gov
Law Clerk **William Walsh, Jr.** .... (973) 645-2133
Began Service: August 2015
Term Expires: August 2016
E-mail: william_walsh@ca3.uscourts.gov
Career Law Clerk **Katherine Romano** .... (973) 645-2133
Began Service: August 2013
E-mail: katherine_romano@ca3.uscourts.gov
Judicial Secretary **Trinidad Heim** .... (973) 645-2133
Education: U Guam 1976 BA

Chambers of Senior Judge Franklin S. Van Antwerpen

601 Market Street, Philadelphia, PA 19106
Tel: (215) 597-0718

Franklin S. Van Antwerpen
Senior Judge

Date of Birth: 1941
Education: Maine 1964 BS; Temple 1967 JD

Current Memberships: American Bar Association; Federal Bar Association; Federal Judges Association; Northampton County Bar Association; Pennsylvania Bar Association

Chambers of Senior Judge Marjorie O. Rendell

U.S. Courthouse, 601 Market Street, Room 21613,
Philadelphia, PA 19106-1598
Tel: (215) 597-3015 Fax: (215) 580-2393
E-mail: Chambers_of_Judge_Marjorie_Rendell@ca3.uscourts.gov

Marjorie O. Rendell
Senior Judge

Date of Birth: 1947
Education: Pennsylvania 1969 BA; Villanova 1973 JD
Began Service: November 21, 1997
Appointed By: President William J. Clinton

Current Memberships: American Bankruptcy Institute; American College of Bankruptcy; The J. Willard O'Brien Inn of Court, The American Inns of Court; The American Law Institute; Federal Judges Association; National Association of Women Judges

Staff
Law Clerk **Amy Bowles** .... (267) 299-4044
Began Service: September 2015
Term Expires: September 2016
E-mail: amy_bowles@ca3.uscourts.gov

Chambers of Senior Judge Marjorie O. Rendell *continued*

Law Clerk **Patrick Huyett** .... (267) 299-4045
Began Service: August 27, 2015
Term Expires: September 1, 2016
E-mail: daniel_huyett@ca3.uscourts.gov
Law Clerk **Henry Phillips** .... (267) 299-4043
Began Service: September 2015
Term Expires: September 2016
E-mail: henry_phillips@ca3.uscourts.gov
Judicial Assistant **JoAnn Van Heest** .... (215) 597-3015
E-mail: joann_vanheest@ca3.uscourts.gov

United States Court of Appeals for the Fourth Circuit

Lewis F. Powell, Jr. U.S. Courthouse, 1100 East Main Street,
Suite 501, Richmond, VA 23219
Tel: (804) 916-2184
Tel: (804) 771-2028 (Electronic Opinions & Docket Data)
Fax: (804) 916-2188
Internet: www.ca4.uscourts.gov

Number of Judgeships: 15

Supreme Court Justice: Chief Justice John G. Roberts Jr.

Areas Covered: Maryland, North Carolina, South Carolina, Virginia and West Virginia

Court Staff

Circuit Executive **Samuel W. Phillips** .... (804) 916-2184
E-mail: samuel_phillips@ca4.uscourts.gov
Education: William & Mary 1953 BS, 1956 LLB
Deputy Circuit Executive **Thomas Schrinel** .... (804) 916-2184
E-mail: thomas_schrinel@ca4.uscourts.gov
Education: Richmond 1977 BA;
American U 1982 MS
Assistant Circuit Executive **Caron Paniccia** .... (804) 916-2184
E-mail: caron_paniccia@ca4.uscourts.gov
Assistant Circuit Executive for Automation and
Technology **Costa G. Constantino** .... (804) 916-2184
E-mail: costa_constantino@ca4.uscourts.gov
Education: Virginia 1975 BA;
Colorado Tech 1980 BS
Assistant Circuit Executive for Space and Facilities
MajGen Paul W. Brier .... (804) 916-2184
Affiliation: USMCR
E-mail: paul_brier@ca4.uscourts.gov
Education: VMI 1981 BS;
Army War Col 2003 MSS
Circuit Clerk **Patricia S. Connor** .... (804) 916-2706
Education: Georgetown 1975 BA; Virginia 1981 JD Fax: (804) 916-2737
Chief Deputy Clerk **Mark J. Zanchelli** .... (804) 916-2705
E-mail: mark_zanchelli@ca4.uscourts.gov Fax: (804) 916-2759
Education: SUNY (Oswego) 1978 BS;
Tulane 1982 JD
Calendar Clerk **Joseph L. Coleman, Jr.** .... (804) 916-2705
E-mail: joseph_coleman@ca4.uscourts.gov Fax: (804) 916-2759
Counsel to Clerk's Office **Judy Henry** .... (804) 916-2184
E-mail: judy_henry@ca4.uscourts.gov
Chief Circuit Mediator **Thomas F. "Tom" Ball** .... (434) 589-1480
17 Brassie Terrace, Palmyra, VA 22963 Fax: (434) 589-1381
E-mail: tom_ball@ca4.uscourts.gov
Systems Manager **Beth Walton** .... (804) 916-2708
E-mail: beth_walton@ca4.uscourts.gov Fax: (804) 916-2796
Senior Staff Attorney (Acting) **Melissa Wood** .... (804) 916-2900
600 E. Main St., Ste. 2200, Richmond, VA 23219 Fax: (804) 916-2920
E-mail: melissa_wood@ca4.uscourts.gov
Circuit Librarian **Elaine Woodward** .... (804) 916-2319
E-mail: elaine_woodward@ca4.uscourts.gov Fax: (804) 916-2364

Chambers of Chief Judge William B. Traxler, Jr.

300 East Washington Street, Suite 222, Greenville, SC 29601
Tel: (864) 241-2730 Fax: (864) 241-2732
E-mail: wbt@ca4.uscourts.gov

William B. Traxler, Jr.
Chief Judge

Date of Birth: 1948
Education: Davidson 1970 BA; South Carolina 1973 JD
Began Service: October 21, 1998
Appointed By: President William J. Clinton

Government: Chief Deputy Solicitor, Thirteenth Judicial Circuit, State of South Carolina (1975-1981); Solicitor, Thirteenth Judicial Circuit, State of South Carolina (1981-1985)

Judicial: Resident Judge, Thirteenth Judicial Circuit (1985-1992); Judge, United States District Court for the District of South Carolina (1992-1998)

Legal Practice: William Byrd Traxler, Sr. (1973-1974)

Military Service: United States Army Reserve, United States Department of the Army (1970-1978)

Current Memberships: Federal Judges Association; Greenville County Bar Association; South Carolina Bar

Staff

Career Law Clerk **Dodd M. Davis** .... (864) 241-2733
E-mail: dodd_davis@ca4.uscourts.gov
Education: South Carolina 1992 JD
Career Law Clerk **Matthew Fitzer** .... (864) 241-2736
E-mail: matthew_fitzer@ca4.uscourts.gov
Education: South Carolina 1995 JD
Career Law Clerk **Amy C. Hendrix** .... (864) 241-2734
E-mail: amy_hendrix@ca4.uscourts.gov
Education: South Carolina 1989 JD
Career Law Clerk **Thorne B. Loggins** .... (864) 241-2735
E-mail: thorne_loggins@ca4.uscourts.gov
Education: South Carolina 1992 JD
Secretary **Mary Lee Mowry** .... (864) 241-2730
Education: Presbyterian Col BA

Chambers of Circuit Judge J. Harvie Wilkinson III

255 West Main Street, Room 230, Charlottesville, VA 22902
Tel: (434) 296-7063 Fax: (434) 293-6920
E-mail: JHW@ca4.uscourts.gov

J. Harvie Wilkinson III
Circuit Judge

Date of Birth: 1944
Education: Yale 1967 BA; Virginia 1972 JD
Began Service: August 13, 1984
Appointed By: President Ronald Reagan
Political Affiliation: Republican

Academic: Assistant then Associate Professor of Law, University of Virginia (1973-1984)

Clerkships: Law Clerk The Honorable Lewis F. Powell, Supreme Court of the United States (1972-1973)

Corporate: Editor, The Virginian-Pilot (1978-1981)

Government: Deputy Assistant Attorney General, Civil Rights Division, United States Department of Justice (1982-1983)

Judicial: Chief Judge, United States Court of Appeals for the Fourth Circuit

Military Service: United States Army Reserve, United States Department of the Army (1968-1969)

Current Memberships: The American Law Institute; The Virginia Bar Association

Chambers of Circuit Judge J. Harvie Wilkinson III *continued*

Staff

Law Clerk **Matthew Brooker** .... (434) 296-7063
Began Service: June 2015
Term Expires: June 2016
E-mail: matthew_brooker@ca4.uscourts.gov
Law Clerk **Kurt Johnson** .... (434) 296-7063
Began Service: June 2015
Term Expires: June 2016
E-mail: kurt_johnson@ca4.uscourts.gov
Law Clerk **Joseph Schroeder** .... (434) 296-7063
Began Service: June 2015
Term Expires: June 2016
E-mail: joseph_schroeder@ca4.uscourts.gov
Law Clerk **Meng Jia Yang** .... (434) 296-7063
Began Service: June 2015
Term Expires: June 2016
E-mail: mengjia_yang@ca4.uscourts.gov
Judicial Administrative Assistant **Lisa Thacker** .... (434) 296-7063
E-mail: lisa_thacker@ca4.uscourts.gov

Chambers of Circuit Judge Paul V. Niemeyer

U.S. Courthouse, 101 West Lombard Street, Baltimore, MD 21201
Tel: (410) 962-4210 Fax: (410) 962-2277
E-mail: pvn@ca4.uscourts.gov

Paul V. Niemeyer
Circuit Judge

Date of Birth: 1941
Education: Kenyon 1962 AB; Notre Dame 1966 JD
Began Service: 1990
Appointed By: President George H.W. Bush
Political Affiliation: Republican

Academic: Lecturer in Advanced Business Law, Johns Hopkins University (1971-1975)

Judicial: Judge, United States District Court for the District of Maryland (1988-1990)

Legal Practice: Associate, Piper & Marbury LLP (1966-1974); Partner, Piper & Marbury LLP (1974-1988)

Current Memberships: American Bar Foundation; American College of Trial Lawyers; The American Law Institute; Federal Bar Association; Maryland Bar Foundation, Maryland State Bar Association, Inc.; Wednesday Law Club

Staff

Law Clerk **Andrew Lawrence** .... (410) 962-4210
Began Service: August 2015
Term Expires: August 2016
E-mail: andrew_lawrence@ca4.uscourts.gov
Law Clerk **Lide Paterno** .... (410) 962-4210
Began Service: August 2015
Term Expires: August 2016
E-mail: lide_paterno@ca4.uscourts.gov
Secretary **Janice Bures** .... (410) 962-4210
E-mail: janice_bures@ca4.uscourts.gov
Career Law Clerk **Nicole Ellington-Grady** .... (410) 962-4210
Began Service: August 2012

Chambers of Circuit Judge Diana Gribbon Motz

U.S. Courthouse, 101 West Lombard Street, Room 920,
Baltimore, MD 21201
Tel: (410) 962-3606 Fax: (410) 962-2855
E-mail: dgm@ca4.uscourts.gov

Diana Gribbon Motz
Circuit Judge

Date of Birth: 1943
Education: Vassar 1965 BA; Virginia 1968 JD
Began Service: June 1994
Appointed By: President William J. Clinton

Government: Assistant Attorney General, Office of the Attorney General, State of Maryland (1972-1981); Chief of Litigation, Office of the Attorney General, State of Maryland (1981-1986)

Judicial: Associate Judge, Maryland Court of Special Appeals (1991-1994)

Legal Practice: Associate, Piper & Marbury LLP (1968-1971); Partner, Frank, Bernstein, Conaway & Goldman (1986-1991)

Current Memberships: American Bar Foundation; American Bar Association; The Bar Association of Baltimore City; Maryland State Bar Association, Inc.; Maryland Bar Foundation, Maryland State Bar Association, Inc.; Women's Bar Association of Maryland

Staff

Law Clerk **Lindsay Fritchman** .... (410) 962-3606
Began Service: August 2015
Term Expires: August 2016
E-mail: lindsay_fritchman@ca4.uscourts.gov

Law Clerk **Patrick Looby** .... (410) 962-3606
Began Service: August 2015
Term Expires: August 2016
E-mail: patrick_looby@ca4.uscourts.gov

Law Clerk **Stephany Reaves Couper** .... (410) 962-3606
Began Service: August 2015
Term Expires: August 2016
E-mail: stephany_couper@ca4.uscourts.gov

Law Clerk **Kristin Saetveit** .... (410) 962-3606
Began Service: August 2015
Term Expires: August 2016
E-mail: kristin_saetveit@ca4.uscourts.gov

Secretary **Phyllis Hundley** .... (410) 962-3606
E-mail: phyllis_hundley@ca4.uscourts.gov

Chambers of Circuit Judge Robert B. King

Robert C. Byrd U.S. Courthouse, 300 Virginia Street East,
Suite 7602, Charleston, WV 25301
Tel: (304) 347-3533 Fax: (304) 347-3534
E-mail: RBK@ca4.uscourts.gov

Robert B. King
Circuit Judge

Date of Birth: 1940
Education: West Virginia 1961 BA, 1968 JD
Began Service: October 23, 1998
Appointed By: President William J. Clinton

Academic: School Teacher, Rural Greenbrier County (1964-1965); Research Assistant, Center for Appalachian Studies and Development, West Virginia University (1966-1968)

Clerkships: Law Clerk The Honorable John A. Field, Jr., United States District Court for the Southern District of West Virginia (1968-1969)

Government: Assistant United States Attorney, Southern District of West Virginia, United States Attorney's Office, United States Department of Justice, Richard M. Nixon Administration (1970-1974); United States Attorney, Southern District of West Virginia, United States Attorney's Office, United States Department of Justice, Jimmy Carter Administration (1977-1981)

Legal Practice: Associate, Haynes & Ford (1969-1970); Associate then Partner, Spilman, Thomas, Battle & Klostermeyer (1975-1977); Partner, Spilman, Thomas, Battle & Klostermeyer (1981); Partner, King, Allen, Guthrie & McHugh (and predecessor firms) (1981-1998)

Military Service: West Virginia National Guard (1957-1959); United States Air Force (1961-1964)

Current Memberships: American Bar Foundation; American Bar Association; American College of Trial Lawyers; Federal Judges Association; Greenbrier County Bar Association; Kanawha County Bar Association; The West Virginia State Bar

Staff

Law Clerk **Kevin Elliker** .... (304) 347-3537
Began Service: August 2015
Term Expires: August 2016
E-mail: kevin_elliker@ca4.uscourts.gov

Law Clerk **Stephen "Steve" Halpin** .... (304) 347-3537
Began Service: August 2015
Term Expires: August 2016
E-mail: stephen_halpin@ca4.uscourts.gov

Law Clerk **Scott Weingart** .... (304) 347-3537
Began Service: August 2015
Term Expires: August 2016
E-mail: scott_m_weingart@ca4.uscourts.gov

Career Law Clerk **Rochelle Lantz Glover** .... (304) 347-3539
E-mail: rochelle_glover@ca4.uscourts.gov
Education: Wake Forest 1992 BA;
West Virginia 2000 JD

Executive Judicial Assistant **Kim Sassler** .... (304) 347-3535
E-mail: kim_sassler@ca4.uscourts.gov
Education: Marshall 1982 AAS, 1992 AAS

Chambers of Circuit Judge Roger L. Gregory

Lewis F. Powell, Jr. U.S. Courthouse, 1000 East Main Street,
Suite 212, Richmond, VA 23219-3517
Tel: (804) 916-2607 Fax: (804) 916-3055
E-mail: rlg@ca4.uscourts.gov

Roger Lee Gregory
Circuit Judge

Date of Birth: 1953
Education: Virginia State 1975 BA; Michigan 1978 JD
Began Service: January 18, 2001
Appointed By: President William J. Clinton

Academic: Adjunct Professor, Virginia State University (1981-1985)

Legal Practice: Associate, Butzel Long (1978-1980); Associate, Hunton & Williams LLP (1980-1982); Managing Partner, Wilder, Gregory and Associates

Staff

Law Clerk **Rachel Braver** .... (804) 916-2607
Began Service: August 2015
Term Expires: August 2016
E-mail: rachel_braver@ca4.uscourts.gov

Law Clerk **Brandon Hasbrouck** .... (804) 916-2607
Began Service: August 2015
Term Expires: August 2016
E-mail: brandon_hasbrouck@ca4.uscourts.gov

Law Clerk **Trevor Lovell** .... (804) 916-2607
Began Service: August 2015
Term Expires: August 2016
E-mail: trevor_lovell@ca4.uscourts.gov

Chambers of Circuit Judge Roger L. Gregory *continued*

Law Clerk **Katy Robinette** . . . . . (804) 916-2607
Began Service: August 2015
Term Expires: August 2016
E-mail: kathryn_robinette@ca4.uscourts.gov

Judicial Assistant **Thelma Brewer** . . . . . (804) 916-2607
E-mail: thelma_brewer@ca4.uscourts.gov

Chambers of Circuit Judge Dennis W. Shedd

1100 Laurel Street, Columbia, SC 29201-2431
Tel: (803) 732-8250
E-mail: dennis_shedd@ca4.uscourts.gov

Dennis W. Shedd
Circuit Judge

Date of Birth: January 28, 1953
Education: Wofford 1975 BA; South Carolina 1978 JD; Georgetown 1980 LLM
Began Service: December 10, 2002
Appointed By: President George W. Bush

Academic: Adjunct Professor of Law, University of South Carolina (1989-1992)

Government: Administrative Assistant (R-SC), Office of Senator Strom Thurmond, United States Senate (1982-1984); Chief Counsel and Staff Director, Committee on the Judiciary, United States Senate (1985-1986)

Judicial: District Judge, United States District Court for the District of South Carolina (1991-2002)

Legal Practice: Law Clerk, Harry Dent & Associates (1977-1978); Of Counsel, Bethea, Jordan & Griffin, P.A. (1988-1991); Sole Practitioner, Law Offices of Dennis W. Shedd (1989-1991)

Current Memberships: South Carolina Bar

Staff

Law Clerk **John Kammerer** . . . . . (803) 732-8250
E-mail: john_kammerer@ca4.uscourts.gov
Education: George Washington 2003 JD

Law Clerk **Kathleen "Katie" Stoughton** . . . . . (803) 732-8250
Began Service: August 2015
Term Expires: August 2016
E-mail: katie_stoughton@ca4.uscourts.gov

Law Clerk **Kirby Thomas** . . . . . (803) 732-8250
Began Service: August 2015
Term Expires: August 2016
E-mail: kirby_thomas@ca4.uscourts.gov

Career Law Clerk **Tony Emanuel** . . . . . (803) 732-8250
E-mail: tony_emanuel@ca4.uscourts.gov
Education: South Carolina 1984 BS, 1988 JD

Secretary **Kathy Peeples** . . . . . (803) 732-8250
E-mail: kathy_peeples@ca4.uscourts.gov

Chambers of Circuit Judge Allyson K. Duncan

4140 Parklake Avenue, Suite 520, Raleigh, NC 27612
Tel: (919) 782-2554
E-mail: akd@ca4.uscourts.gov

Allyson Kay Duncan
Circuit Judge

Education: Hampton 1972 BA; Duke 1975 JD
Began Service: August 15, 2003
Appointed By: President George W. Bush

Academic: Associate Professor, School of Law, North Carolina Central University (1986-1990)

Clerkships: Law Clerk, Chambers of Associate Justice Julia Cooper Mack, District of Columbia Court of Appeals (1977-1978)

Government: Attorney, United States Equal Employment Opportunity Commission (1978-1986); Commissioner, Utilities Commission, State of North Carolina (1991-1998)

Chambers of Circuit Judge Allyson K. Duncan *continued*

Judicial: Associate Judge, North Carolina Court of Appeals (1990)

Current Memberships: The American Law Institute

Profession: Private Practice (1998-2003)

Staff

Law Clerk **Anna Diakun** . . . . . (919) 782-2554
Began Service: August 2015
Term Expires: August 2016
E-mail: anna_diakun@ca4.uscourts.gov

Law Clerk **Alison Moe** . . . . . (919) 782-2554
Began Service: August 2015
Term Expires: August 2016

Law Clerk **Jack Pararas** . . . . . (919) 782-2554
Began Service: August 2015
Term Expires: August 2016
E-mail: jack_pararas@ca4.uscourts.gov

Law Clerk **Jonathan "Gray" Wilson** . . . . . (919) 782-2554
Began Service: July 2015
Term Expires: July 2016
E-mail: gray_wilson@ca4.uscourts.gov

Judicial Assistant **Pearl Eldridge White** . . . . . (919) 782-2554
E-mail: pearl_white@ca4.uscourts.gov

Chambers of Circuit Judge G. Steven Agee

Lewis F. Powell, Jr. U.S. Courthouse Annex, 1100 East Main Street, Suite 501, Richmond, VA 23219
Tel: (540) 378-5066
E-mail: gsa@ca4.uscourts.gov

G. Steven Agee
Circuit Judge

Date of Birth: 1952
Education: Bridgewater Col 1974 BA; Virginia 1977 JD; NYU 1978 LLM
Began Service: July 2, 2008
Appointed By: President George W. Bush

Government: Member, Virginia House of Delegates (1982-1994); Escheator, 23rd Judicial Circuit, Virginia Circuit Courts (1994-2000); Commissioner, 23rd Judicial Circuit, Virginia Circuit Courts (1996-2000); Member, Virginia Criminal Sentencing Commission, Commonwealth of Virginia (1997-2001)

Judicial: Judge, Court of Appeals of Virginia (2001-2003); Justice, Supreme Court of Virginia (2003-2008)

Legal Practice: Osterhoudt, Ferguson, Natt, Aheron, & Agee, P.C. (1980-2000)

Military Service: United States Army Reserve, JAG Corps (1985-1997)

Current Memberships: The Virginia Bar Association

Staff

Law Clerk **Kyle Dudek** . . . . . (804) 916-2184
Term Expires: August 2016
E-mail: kyle_dudek@ca4.uscourts.gov

Law Clerk **Emma Kozlowski** . . . . . (540) 378-5066
Began Service: August 2015
Term Expires: August 2016
E-mail: emma_kozlowski@ca4.uscourts.gov

Law Clerk **Jake Pugh** . . . . . (804) 916-2184
Began Service: August 2014
Term Expires: August 2016
E-mail: jacob_pugh@ca4.uscourts.gov

Career Law Clerk **Kristina Rutledge** . . . . . (804) 916-2184
E-mail: kristina_rutledge@ca4.uscourts.gov

Judicial Assistant **Deborah L. Estep** . . . . . (804) 916-2184
E-mail: deborah_estep@ca4.uscourts.gov

Chambers of Circuit Judge Barbara Milano Keenan

Lewis F. Powell Jr. U.S. Courthouse, 1100 East Main Street,
Suite 501, Richmond, VA 23219
Tel: (703) 518-8180 Fax: (703) 518-8185
E-mail: bmk@ca4.uscourts.gov

Barbara Milano Keenan
Circuit Judge

Date of Birth: 1950
Education: Cornell 1971 BA; George Washington 1974 JD; Virginia 1992 LLM
Began Service: March 9, 2010
Appointed By: President Barack Obama

Government: Prosecutor, County of Fairfax, Virginia

Judicial: Judge, 19th Judicial District of Virginia - Fairfax County, Virginia District Courts (1980-1982); Judge, Virginia Circuit Courts (1982-1985); Judge, Court of Appeals of Virginia (1985-1991)

Staff

Law Clerk **(Vacant)** . . . . (703) 518-8180
Began Service: 2013
Term Expires: 2015
E-mail: sean_douglass@ca4.uscourts.gov

Law Clerk **Carrie L. Gray** . . . . (703) 518-8180
E-mail: carrie_gray@ca4.uscourts.gov
Education: George Mason 2004 JD

Judicial Assistant **Tiffany Hill** . . . . (703) 518-8180
E-mail: tiffany_hill@ca4.uscourts.gov

Chambers of Circuit Judge James A. Wynn, Jr.

Lewis F. Powell Jr. U.S. Courthouse, 1100 East Main Street,
Suite 501, Richmond, VA 23219
Tel: (804) 916-2700
E-mail: JAW@ca4.uscourts.gov

James Andrew Wynn, Jr.
Circuit Judge

Date of Birth: 1954
Education: North Carolina 1975 BA; Marquette 1979 JD; Virginia 1995 LLM
Began Service: August 10, 2010
Appointed By: President Barack Obama
Political Affiliation: Democrat

Government: Assistant Appellate Defender, State of North Carolina (1983-1984)

Judicial: Judge, North Carolina Court of Appeals (1990-1998); Associate Justice, North Carolina Supreme Court (1998)

Legal Practice: Fitch, Wynn & Associates (1984-1990)

Nonprofit: Director, American Judicature Society

Current Memberships: National Bar Association; Naval Reserve Judge Advocate Association; The North Carolina State Bar; State Bar of Wisconsin

Staff

Career Law Clerk **Sarah L. Buthe** . . . . (804) 916-2700
E-mail: sarah_buthe@ca4.uscourts.gov

Judicial Assistant **Crystal Wright** . . . . (804) 916-2700
E-mail: crystal_wright@ca4.uscourts.gov
Education: East Carolina 1992 BA; Meredith 1997

Chambers of Circuit Judge Albert Diaz

Lewis F. Powell Jr. U.S. Courthouse, 1100 East Main Street,
Suite 501, Richmond, VA 23219
Tel: (704) 333-8025
E-mail: albert_diaz@ca4.uscourts.gov

Albert Diaz
Circuit Judge

Date of Birth: 1960
Education: Wharton 1983 BS; NYU 1988 JD; Boston U 1993 MBA
Began Service: December 22, 2010
Appointed By: President Barack Obama

Judicial: Resident Superior Court Judge, Chambers of Resident Superior Court Judge Albert Diaz (2001-2002); Special Superior Court Judge, North Carolina Business Court (2002-2005); Special Superior Court Judge for Complex Business Cases, Chambers of Judge Albert Diaz, Charlotte Business Court, North Carolina Business Court (2005-2010)

Staff

Law Clerk **Jesse Cuevas** . . . . (704) 333-8025
Began Service: August 2015
Term Expires: August 2016
Education: Northwestern 2015 JD

Law Clerk **Alice Cullina** . . . . (704) 333-8025
Began Service: August 2015
Term Expires: August 2016
E-mail: alice_cullina@ca4.uscourts.gov

Law Clerk **Jordan Rice** . . . . (704) 333-8025
Began Service: August 2015
Term Expires: August 2016
E-mail: jordan_rice@ca4.uscourts.gov
Education: Stanford JD

Law Clerk **Dave Twombly** . . . . (704) 333-8025
Began Service: August 2015
Term Expires: August 2016
E-mail: dave_twombly@ca4.uscourts.gov

Judicial Assistant **Lori Whitcomb** . . . . (704) 333-8025
E-mail: lori_whitcomb@ca4.uscourts.gov

Chambers of Circuit Judge Henry F. Floyd

Lewis F. Powell Jr. U.S. Courthouse, 1100 East Main Street,
Suite 501, Richmond, VA 23219
Tel: (864) 591-5300 Fax: (864) 898-5792
E-mail: henry_floyd@ca4.uscourts.gov

Henry F. Floyd
Circuit Judge

Date of Birth: November 5, 1947
Education: Wofford 1970 BA; South Carolina 1973 JD
Began Service: October 5, 2011
Appointed By: President Barack Obama

Government: Commissioner, Forestry Commission, State of South Carolina (1979-1991)

Judicial: Circuit Judge, Thirteenth Judicial Circuit Court of South Carolina (1992-2003); District Judge, Chambers of District Judge Henry F. Floyd, United States District Court for the District of South Carolina (2003-2011)

Staff

Judicial Assistant **Cindy Chapman** . . . . (864) 591-5300

Chambers of Circuit Judge Stephanie Thacker
300 Virginia Street, Charleston, WV 25301
Tel: (304) 347-3516
E-mail: sdt@ca4.uscourts.gov

Stephanie Dawn Thacker
Circuit Judge

Education: Marshall 1987 BA; West Virginia 1990 JD
Began Service: May 29, 2012
Appointed By: President Barack Obama

Staff
Judicial Assistant **Carolyn Young** .... (304) 347-3516
E-mail: carolyn_young@ca4.uscourts.gov

Chambers of Circuit Judge Pamela A. Harris
1100 East Main Street, Richmond, VA 23219
Tel: (804) 416-2184

Pamela A. Harris
Circuit Judge

Date of Birth: 1962
Education: Yale 1985 BA, 1990 JD
Began Service: July 29, 2014
Appointed By: President Barack Obama

Government: Principal Deputy Assistant Attorney General, Office of Legal Policy, Office of the Deputy Attorney General, United States Department of Justice (2010-2012)

Legal Practice: Associate, Goodwin Procter LLP; Partner, O'Melveny & Myers LLP

Chambers of Senior Judge Clyde H. Hamilton
Bank of America Plaza, 1901 Main Street, Compartment 704, Suite 1250, Columbia, SC 29201
Tel: (803) 765-5461 Fax: (803) 765-5571

Clyde H. Hamilton
Senior Judge

Date of Birth: 1934
Education: Wofford 1956 BS; George Washington 1961 JD
Began Service: July 22, 1991
Appointed By: President George H.W. Bush
Political Affiliation: Republican

Government: Editorial Staff, Cumulative Index of Congressional Commission Hearings (1955-1958); Reference Assistant, United States Senate Library, Office of the Secretary of the Senate (1961-1963)

Judicial: Judge, United States District Court for the District of South Carolina (1982-1991)

Legal Practice: Associate, J. R. Folk, Esquire (1961-1963); Attorney, Butler, Means, Evins & Browne (1963-1982)

Military Service: United States Army (1956-1958); United States Army Reserve, United States Department of the Army (1959-1962)

Current Memberships: South Carolina Bar

Staff
Career Law Clerk **John M. Meyers** .... (803) 765-5461
E-mail: john_meyers@ca4.uscourts.gov
Education: NYU 1990 JD
Career Law Clerk **Robin Reid Tidwell** .... (803) 765-5461
E-mail: robin_tidwell@ca4.uscourts.gov
Education: South Carolina 1994 JD
Secretary **Paula P. Harris** .... (803) 765-5461
E-mail: paula_harris@ca4.uscourts.gov

Chambers of Senior Judge Andre M. Davis
1100 East Main Street, Richmond, VA 23219
Tel: (410) 962-0801
E-mail: AMD@ca4.uscourts.gov

Andre M. Davis
Senior Judge

Date of Birth: 1949
Education: Pennsylvania 1971 BA; Maryland 1978 JD
Began Service: November 12, 2009
Appointed By: President Barack Obama

Current Memberships: American Bar Association; Maryland State Bar Association, Inc.; Monumental City Bar Association; National Judicial College

United States Court of Appeals for the Fifth Circuit
John Minor Wisdom U.S. Court of Appeals Building, 600 Camp Street, Room 100, New Orleans, LA 70130-3425
Tel: (504) 310-7700
Internet: www.ca5.uscourts.gov

Number of Judgeships: 17

Number of Vacancies: 2

Supreme Court Justice: Associate Justice Antonin Scalia

Areas Covered: Louisiana, Mississippi and Texas

Court Staff
Circuit Executive **Paul Benjamin Anderson, Jr.** .... (504) 310-7777
Education: Samford 1970 BA;
Cumberland 1972 JD;
Indust'l Col Armed Forces 1977 MS
Deputy Circuit Executive **Theodore P. Cominos** .... (504) 310-7777
Assistant Circuit Executive for Conferences and Training **Donna B. Dusang** .... (504) 310-7777
E-mail: donna_dusang@ca5.uscourts.gov
Assistant Circuit Executive for Automation
Robert A. Pons .... (504) 310-7796
E-mail: robert_pons@ca5.uscourts.gov
Assistant Circuit Executive for Court Administration
Kyle M. Boudreau .... (504) 310-7777
E-mail: kyle_boudreau@ca5.uscourts.gov
Education: Loyola U (New Orleans) 1983 BS
Assistant Circuit Executive for Space and Facilities
Jesse D. Cannon, Jr. .... (504) 310-7777
E-mail: jesse_cannon@ca5.uscourts.gov
Education: LSU 1972 BArch;
New Orleans 1991 MURP
Circuit Clerk **Lyle Cayce** .... (504) 310-7700
E-mail: lyle_cayce@ca5.uscourts.gov
Deputy Circuit Clerk **Thomas B. Plunkett** .... (504) 310-7656
E-mail: thomas_plunkett@ca5.uscourts.gov
Senior Staff Attorney **Michael E. Schneider** .... (504) 310-8504
Education: West Point 1970 BS;
Marquette 1977 JD; Central Michigan MA;
Indust'l Col Armed Forces MS
Senior Appellate Conference Attorney
Joseph L. S. St. Amant .... (504) 310-7799
Education: Rice 1968 BA;
Santa Barbara Law 1970 MA; Duke 1974 JD
Circuit Librarian **Sue Creech** .... (504) 310-7797
Room 106
E-mail: sue_creech@ca5.uscourts.gov
Head of Library Technical Services **(Vacant)** .... (504) 310-7798

Chambers of Chief Judge Carl E. Stewart

U.S. Courthouse, 300 Fannin Street, Suite 5226, Shreveport, LA 71101
Tel: (318) 676-3765 Fax: (318) 676-3768
E-mail: carl_stewart@ca5.uscourts.gov

Carl Edmund Stewart
Chief Judge

Date of Birth: 1950
Education: Dillard 1971 BA; Loyola U (New Orleans) 1974 JD
Began Service: May 9, 1994
Appointed By: President William J. Clinton
Political Affiliation: Democrat

Current Memberships: American Bar Association; The Harry V. Booth - Judge Henry A. Politz American Inn of Court, The American Inns of Court; Black Lawyers Association of Shreveport-Bossier; Louisiana Conference of Judges of Courts of Appeal; Louisiana State Bar Association; National Bar Association; Shreveport Bar Association

Staff

Law Clerk **Stanley E. Blackmon** .... (318) 676-3765
Began Service: August 2015
Term Expires: August 2016
E-mail: stanley_blackmon@ca5.uscourts.gov

Law Clerk **Nathan G. Harill** .... (318) 676-3765
Began Service: August 2015
Term Expires: August 2016

Law Clerk **Eric D. Lawson** .... (318) 676-3765
Began Service: August 2015
Term Expires: August 2016
E-mail: eric_lawson@ca5.uscourts.gov

Law Clerk **Cadene A. Russell** .... (318) 676-3765
Began Service: August 2015
Term Expires: August 2016
E-mail: cadene_russell@ca5.uscourts.gov

Career Law Clerk **Melissa Allen** .... (318) 676-3765
E-mail: melissa_allen@ca5.uscourts.gov

Judicial Assistant **Marilyn W. Myers** .... (318) 676-3765
E-mail: marilyn_myers@ca5.uscourts.gov
Education: Northwestern State 1983 BS; Grambling State 1997 MS

Chambers of Circuit Judge E. Grady Jolly

501 Court Street, Suite 3850, Jackson, MS 39201
Tel: (601) 608-4745 Fax: (601) 608-4754

E. Grady Jolly
Circuit Judge

Date of Birth: 1937
Education: Mississippi 1959 BA, 1962 LLB
Began Service: August 2, 1982
Appointed By: President Ronald Reagan
Political Affiliation: Republican

Government: Trial Attorney, National Labor Relations Board (1962-1964); Assistant United States Attorney, Northern District of Mississippi, United States Department of Justice (1964-1967); Trial Attorney, Tax Division, United States Department of Justice (1967-1969)

Legal Practice: Partner, Jolly, Miller & Milam (1969-1982)

Staff

Judicial Assistant **Alice O. Gilbert** .... (601) 608-4745
E-mail: alice_gilbert@ca5.uscourts.gov

Chambers of Circuit Judge W. Eugene Davis

800 Lafayette Street, Suite 5100, Lafayette, LA 70501
Tel: (337) 593-5280 Fax: (337) 593-5309

W. Eugene Davis
Circuit Judge

Date of Birth: 1936
Education: Tulane 1960 JD
Began Service: 1983
Appointed By: President Ronald Reagan

Judicial: Judge, United States District Court for the Western District of Louisiana (1976-1983)

Legal Practice: Associate, Phelps, Dunbar, Marks, Claverie & Sims (1960-1964); Associate then Partner, Caffery, Duhe & Davis (1964-1976)

Current Memberships: American Bar Association; Louisiana State Bar Association; Maritime Law Association of the United States

Staff

Law Clerk **Leon Whitten** .... (337) 593-5280
Began Service: September 2015
Term Expires: September 2016
E-mail: leon_whitten@ca5.uscourts.gov

Career Law Clerk **Stuart Welch** .... (337) 593-5290
E-mail: stuart_welch@ca5.uscourts.gov

Judicial Assistant **Linda Henshaw** .... (337) 593-5280
E-mail: linda_henshaw@ca5.uscourts.gov
Education: LSU 1971 BS

Judicial Assistant **Deborah Mahony** .... (337) 593-5280
E-mail: deborah_mahony@ca5.uscourts.gov

Chambers of Circuit Judge Edith Hollan Jones

12505 U.S. Courthouse, 515 Rusk Avenue, Houston, TX 77002
Tel: (713) 250-5484 Fax: (713) 250-5017
E-mail: edith_jones@ca5.uscourts.gov

Edith Hollan Jones
Circuit Judge

Date of Birth: 1949
Education: Cornell 1971 BA; Texas 1974 JD
Began Service: 1985
Appointed By: President Ronald Reagan

Current Memberships: American Bar Association; Fifth Circuit Bar Association; Houston Bar Association; State Bar of Texas

Staff

Judicial Assistant **Pam Wood** .... (713) 250-5485
E-mail: pam_wood@ca5.uscourts.gov

Chambers of Circuit Judge Jerry E. Smith

12621 U.S. Courthouse, 515 Rusk Avenue, Houston, TX 77002-2698
Tel: (713) 250-5101 Fax: (713) 250-5719
E-mail: jerry_smith@ca5.uscourts.gov

Jerry E. Smith
Circuit Judge

Date of Birth: 1946
Education: Yale 1969 BA, 1972 JD
Began Service: January 7, 1988
Appointed By: President Ronald Reagan
Political Affiliation: Republican

Clerkships: Law Clerk The Honorable Halbert O. Woodward, United States District Court for the Northern District of Texas (1972-1973)

Government: Board Member, Harris County Housing Authority, Community and Economic Development Department, County of Harris, Texas (1978-1980); Chairman, Civil Service Commission, City of Houston, Texas (1982-1984); City Attorney, Legal Department, City of Houston, Texas (1984-1988)

Chambers of Circuit Judge Jerry E. Smith *continued*

Legal Practice: Attorney, Fulbright & Jaworski L.L.P. (1973-1984)

Current Memberships: Houston Bar Association; State Bar of Texas

Staff

Law Clerk **Robert "Bob" Belden** .... (713) 250-5101
Began Service: August 24, 2015
Term Expires: August 2016

Law Clerk **Justin Patrick** .... (713) 250-5101
Began Service: August 24, 2015
Term Expires: August 2016
E-mail: justin_patrick@ca5.uscourts.gov

Law Clerk **Jessica Wagner** .... (713) 250-5101
Began Service: August 24, 2015
Term Expires: August 2016
E-mail: jessica_wagner@ca5.uscourts.gov
Education: Virginia JD

Law Clerk **John Wei** .... (713) 250-5101
Began Service: September 5, 2015
Term Expires: August 2016
E-mail: john_wei@ca5.uscourts.gov

Secretary **Penelope "Penny" Stautberg** .... (713) 250-5101
E-mail: penny_stautberg@ca5.uscourts.gov
Education: Trinity U 1971 BA

Chambers of Circuit Judge James L. Dennis

John Minor Wisdom U.S. Court of Appeals Building, 600 Camp Street, Room 219, New Orleans, LA 70130
Tel: (504) 310-8000 Fax: (504) 310-8024
E-mail: james_dennis@ca5.uscourts.gov

James L. Dennis
Circuit Judge

Date of Birth: 1936
Education: Louisiana Tech U 1959 BS; LSU 1962 JD; Virginia 1984 LLM
Began Service: October 2, 1995
Appointed By: President William J. Clinton
Political Affiliation: Democrat

Academic: Visiting Professor, Louisiana State University and Agricultural and Mechanical College; Visiting Professor, Tulane University

Government: State Representative James Dennis (R-LA), Louisiana State House of Representatives (1968-1972)

Judicial: Judge, Louisiana District Court, Fourth Judicial District (1972-1974); Judge, Louisiana Court of Appeal, Second Circuit (1974-1975); Justice, Supreme Court of Louisiana (1975-1995)

Legal Practice: Private Practice (1962-1972)

Military Service: United States Army (1955-1957)

Current Memberships: American Bar Association; Federal Bar Association; Louisiana State Bar Association

Staff

Judicial Assistant **Terri Hooper** .... (504) 310-8000
E-mail: terri_hooper@ca5.uscourts.gov

Chambers of Circuit Judge Edith Brown Clement

John Minor Wisdom U.S. Court of Appeals Building, 600 Camp Street, Room 200, New Orleans, LA 70130
Tel: (504) 310-8068 Fax: (504) 310-8069
E-mail: edith_clement@ca5.uscourts.gov

Edith Brown Clement
Circuit Judge

Date of Birth: 1948
Education: Alabama 1969 BA; Tulane 1972 JD
Began Service: December 27, 2001
Appointed By: President George W. Bush
Political Affiliation: Republican

Clerkships: Law Clerk The Honorable H.W. Christenberry, United States District Court for the Eastern District of Louisiana (1973-1975)

Judicial: District Judge, United States District Court for the Eastern District of Louisiana (1991-2001)

Legal Practice: Jones, Walker, Waechter, Poitevent, Carrere & Denegre (1975-1991)

Current Memberships: The American Inns of Court; The American Law Institute; Federal Bar Association; Louisiana State Bar Association; Maritime Law Association of the United States

Staff

Law Clerk **Christopher Baum** .... (504) 310-8068
Began Service: August 2015
Term Expires: August 2016
E-mail: christopher_baum@ca5.uscourts.gov

Law Clerk **John Guenard** .... (504) 310-8068
Began Service: August 2015
Term Expires: August 2016
E-mail: john_guenard@ca5.uscourts.gov

Law Clerk **Stephanie Maloney** .... (504) 310-8068
Began Service: August 2015
Term Expires: August 2016
E-mail: stephanie_maloney@ca5.uscourts.gov

Law Clerk **McClain Schonekas** .... (504) 310-8068
Began Service: August 2015
Term Expires: August 2016
E-mail: mcclain_schonekas@ca5.uscourts.gov

Secretary **Susan M. Barrios** .... (504) 310-8068
E-mail: susan_barrios@ca5.uscourts.gov

Chambers of Circuit Judge Edward Charles Prado

John Minor Wisdom U.S. Court of Appeals Building, 600 Camp Street, New Orleans, LA 70130-3425
755 East Mulberry Avenue, Room 350, San Antonio, TX 78212
Tel: (504) 310-8311 (New Orleans) Tel: (210) 472-4060 (San Antonio)
E-mail: edward_prado@ca5.uscourts.gov

Edward Charles Prado
Circuit Judge

Date of Birth: 1947
Education: Texas 1969 BA, 1972 JD
Began Service: May 14, 2003
Appointed By: President George W. Bush

Government: Assistant District Attorney, Office of the District Attorney, County of Bexar, Texas (1972-1976); Federal Public Defender, Western District of Texas, State of Texas (1976-1980); United States Attorney, Western District of Texas, United States Department of Justice (1981-1984); District Judge, Chambers of District Judge Edward C. Prado, United States District Court for the Western District of Texas (1984-2003)

Judicial: Judge, Texas District Court, Bexar County (1980)

Military Service: United States Army Reserve, United States Department of the Army (1972-1980)

Current Memberships: American Bar Association; The American Inns of Court; Federal Bar Association; San Antonio Bar Association; San Antonio Bar Foundation; State Bar of Texas

(continued on next page)

Chambers of Circuit Judge Edward Charles Prado *continued*

Staff

Law Clerk **Dustin Brockner** . . . . (210) 472-4060
Term Expires: August 2016
E-mail: dustin_brockner@ca5.uscourts.gov

Law Clerk **Kate Ergenbright** . . . . (210) 472-4060
Term Expires: August 2016
E-mail: kate_ergenbright@ca5.uscourts.gov

Law Clerk **Aaron Markel** . . . . (210) 472-4060
Term Expires: August 2016
E-mail: aaron_markel@ca5.uscourts.gov

Law Clerk **Zain Yoonas** . . . . (210) 472-4060
Term Expires: August 2016
E-mail: zain_yoonas@ca5.uscourts.gov

Judicial Assistant **Mary Beth Byrd** . . . . (210) 472-4060
E-mail: marybeth_byrd@ca5.uscourts.gov

Chambers of Circuit Judge Priscilla R. Owen

Homer Thornberry Judicial Building, 903 San Jacinto Boulevard, Room 434, Austin, TX 78701-2450
Tel: (512) 916-5167
E-mail: priscilla_owen@ca5.uscourts.gov

Priscilla R. Owen
Circuit Judge

Date of Birth: 1954
Education: Baylor 1976 BA, 1977 JD
Began Service: June 3, 2005
Appointed By: President George W. Bush
Political Affiliation: Republican

Judicial: Justice, Supreme Court of Texas (1995-2005)

Legal Practice: Andrews & Kurth L.L.P. (1977-1994)

Current Memberships: American Bar Foundation; American Bar Association; The American Law Institute; Houston Bar Association; Houston Bar Foundation, Houston Bar Association

Staff

Judicial Administrative Assistant **Michele Johnson** . . . . . . (512) 916-5167
E-mail: michele_johnson@ca5.uscourts.gov

Chambers of Circuit Judge Jennifer Walker Elrod

515 Rusk Street, Room 12014, Houston, TX 77002-2600
Tel: (713) 250-7590
E-mail: jennifer_elrod@ca5.uscourts.gov

Jennifer Walker Elrod
Circuit Judge

Education: Baylor 1988 BA; Harvard 1992 JD
Began Service: October 2007
Appointed By: President George W. Bush

Clerkships: Law Clerk, Chambers of District Judge Sim Lake, United States District Court for the Southern District of Texas (1992-1994)

Judicial: 190th District Court Judge, County of Harris, Texas (2002-2007)

Legal Practice: Attorney, Baker Botts L.L.P. (1994-2002)

Staff

Judicial Administrative Assistant **Maria Valdez** . . . . (713) 250-7590
E-mail: maria_valdez@ca5.uscourts.gov

Chambers of Circuit Judge Leslie Southwick

501 East Court Street, Suite 3750, Jackson, MS 39201
Tel: (601) 608-4760
E-mail: leslie_southwick@ca5.uscourts.gov

Leslie H. Southwick
Circuit Judge

Date of Birth: 1950
Education: Rice 1972 BA; Texas 1975 JD
Began Service: October 2007
Appointed By: President George W. Bush

Academic: Adjunct Professor of Law, Mississippi College (1985-1989); Adjunct Professor of Law, Mississippi College (1998-2006)

Clerkships: Law Clerk The Honorable John Onion, Texas Court of Criminal Appeals (1975-1976); Law Clerk, Chambers of Circuit Judge Charles Clark, United States Court of Appeals for the Fifth Circuit (1976-1977)

Government: Deputy Assistant Attorney General, Civil Division, Office of the Associate Attorney General, United States Department of Justice (1989-1993)

Judicial: Judge, Mississippi Court of Appeals (1995-2006)

Legal Practice: Associate then Partner, Brunini, Grantham, Grower & Hewes (1977-1989)

Military Service: United States Army Reserve, United States Department of the Army (1992-1997); Mississippi National Guard, United States Department of the Army (1997-2006)

Current Memberships: The Charles Clark American Inn of Court, The American Inns of Court; The American Law Institute; The Mississippi Bar; The Theodore Roosevelt Association

Staff

Judicial Administrative Assistant **Sharon Berryman** . . . . . (601) 608-4076
E-mail: sharon_berryman@ca5.uscourts.gov

Chambers of Circuit Judge Catharina Haynes

1100 Commerce Street, Room 1452, Dallas, TX 75242
Tel: (214) 753-2750
E-mail: catharina_haynes@ca5.uscourts.gov

Catharina Haynes
Circuit Judge

Education: Florida Tech 1993 BS; Emory 1986 JD
Began Service: April 22, 2008
Appointed By: President George W. Bush

Judicial: District Judge, 191st District Court, Texas District Courts (1999-2006)

Legal Practice: Associate, Thompson & Knight LLP (1986-1988); Associate, Baker Botts L.L.P. (1988-1994); Partner, Baker Botts L.L.P. (1995-1998); Partner, Dallas, TX Office, Baker Botts L.L.P. (2007-2008)

Nonprofit: Volunteer Judge, Legal Aid of NorthWest Texas (2003-2006)

Current Memberships: College of the State Bar of Texas; College of the State Bar of Texas; Insurance Law Section, State Bar of Texas; Professional Ethics Committee, State Bar of Texas

Staff

Law Clerk **Phil Chang** . . . . (214) 753-2750
Began Service: September 2015
Term Expires: September 2016
E-mail: phil_chang@ca5.uscourts.gov

Law Clerk **Megan Coker** . . . . (214) 753-2750
Began Service: September 2014
Term Expires: September 2016
E-mail: megan_coker@ca5.uscourts.gov

Law Clerk **Dina McKenney** . . . . (214) 753-2750
Began Service: September 2015
Term Expires: September 2016
E-mail: dina_mckenney@ca5.uscourts.gov

Chambers of Circuit Judge Catharina Haynes *continued*

Law Clerk **Jessica Underwood** .... (214) 753-2750
Began Service: September 2015
Term Expires: September 2016
E-mail: jessica_underwood@ca5.uscourts.gov

Judicial Assistant **Susan Hudson** .... (214) 753-2750
E-mail: susan_hudson@ca5.uscourts.gov
Education: Southern Methodist 1985 BA, 1985 BS

Chambers of Circuit Judge James E. Graves, Jr.

501 East Court Street, Suite 3550, Jackson, MS 39201
Tel: (601) 608-4775
E-mail: james_graves@ca5.uscourts.gov

James E. Graves, Jr.
Circuit Judge

Education: Millsaps 1975 BA; Syracuse 1980 JD, 1981 MPA
Began Service: February 17, 2011
Appointed By: President Barack Obama

Judicial: Judge, Mississippi 7th Circuit (1991-2001); Justice, Mississippi Supreme Court (2001-2009); Presiding Justice, Chambers of Presiding Justice James E. Graves, Jr., Mississippi Supreme Court (2009-2011)

Staff

Law Clerk **Nick Hart** .... (601) 608-4775
Began Service: August 2015
Term Expires: September 2016
E-mail: nicholas_hart@ca5.uscourts.gov

Law Clerk **J.D. Cooley** .... (601) 608-4775
Began Service: August 2015
Term Expires: September 2016
E-mail: jahviah_cooley@ca5.uscourts.gov

Law Clerk **Sarah Primrose** .... (601) 608-4775
Began Service: August 2015
Term Expires: September 2016
E-mail: sarah_primrose@ca5.uscourts.gov

Judicial Assistant **Jackie Losset** .... (601) 608-4775
E-mail: jackie_losset@ca5.uscourts.gov

Career Law Clerk **Susan Hewitt** .... (601) 608-4775
E-mail: susan_hewitt@ca5.uscourts.gov

Chambers of Circuit Judge Stephen Higginson

600 Camp Street, New Orleans, LA 70130-3425
Tel: (504) 310-8228
E-mail: stephen_higginson@ca5.uscourts.gov

Stephen A. Higginson
Circuit Judge

Education: Harvard 1983 AB; Cambridge (UK) 1984 MPHIL; Yale 1987 JD
Began Service: November 2, 2011
Appointed By: President Barack Obama

Academic: Associate Professor of Law, College of Law, Loyola University New Orleans (2004-2011)

Clerkships: Law Clerk, Chambers of Circuit Judge Patricia M. Wald, United States Court of Appeals for the District of Columbia Circuit (1987-1988); Law Clerk, Chambers of Associate Justice Byron R. White, Supreme Court of the United States (1988-1989)

Government: Appellate Division Chief and Assistant U.S. Attorney, Louisiana - Eastern District, Executive Office for United States Attorneys, United States Department of Justice (1995-2011)

Chambers of Circuit Judge Gregg Jeffrey Costa

515 Rusk Street, Room 4627, Houston, TX 77002-2694
Tel: (713) 250-5030
E-mail: gregg_costa@ca5.uscourts.gov

Gregg Jeffrey Costa
Circuit Judge

Education: Texas JD
Began Service: June 2, 2014
Appointed By: President Barack Obama

Government: Assistant U.S. Attorney, Brownsville (TX) Office, Texas - Southern District, United States Department of Justice; Assistant U.S. Attorney, Criminal Division, Texas - Southern District, United States Department of Justice

Judicial: District Judge, Chambers of District Judge Gregg Jeffrey Costa, United States District Court for the Southern District of Texas (2012-2014)

Chambers of Senior Judge Thomas M. Reavley

515 Rusk Street, Room 11009, Houston, TX 77002-2605
Tel: (713) 250-5185
E-mail: tmr@ca5.uscourts.gov

Thomas M. Reavley
Senior Judge

Date of Birth: 1921
Education: Texas 1942 BA; Harvard 1948 JD; Virginia 1983 LLM
Began Service: 1979
Appointed By: President Jimmy Carter

Academic: Adjunct Professor of Law, Texas (1958-1959); Lecturer on Law, Baylor University (1976); Lecturer on Law, Texas (1978-1979)

Government: Assistant District Attorney, Office of the District Attorney, State of Texas (1948-1949); Secretary of State, State of Texas (1955-1957)

Judicial: Judge, Texas District Court, 167th Judicial District (1964-1968); Justice, Texas Supreme Court (1968-1977)

Legal Practice: Partner, Bell & Reavley (1949-1950); Private Practice (1950-1951); Collins, Garrison, Renfro & Zeleskey (1951-1952); Partner, Fisher & Reavley (1952-1955); Partner, Powell, Rauhut, McGinnis & Reavley (1957-1964); Counsel, Scott & Douglass (1977-1979)

Military Service: United States Navy (1942-1946)

Current Memberships: American Bar Foundation; American Bar Association; The American Law Institute; State Bar of Texas

Staff

Secretary **Terry Reeves** .... (713) 250-5185
E-mail: terry_reeves@ca5.uscourts.gov

Chambers of Senior Judge Patrick E. Higginbotham

903 San Jacinto Boulevard, Room 400, Austin, TX 78701
Tel: (512) 916-5723
E-mail: patrick_higginbotham@ca5.uscourts.gov

Patrick E. Higginbotham
Senior Judge

Date of Birth: 1938
Education: Alabama 1960 BA, 1961 LLB
Began Service: August 3, 1982
Appointed By: President Ronald Reagan

Judicial: Judge, United States District Court for the Northern District of Texas (1976-1982)

Legal Practice: Partner, Coke & Coke (1964-1975)

Military Service: United States Air Force (1961-1964)

(continued on next page)

Chambers of Senior Judge Patrick E. Higginbotham *continued*

Current Memberships: American Bar Foundation; American Bar Association; American Inns of Court Foundation, The American Inns of Court; The American Law Institute; Bench & Bar Legal Honor Society; Dallas Bar Association; Dallas Bar Foundation, Dallas Bar Association; Maritime Law Association of the United States; Southwest Legal Foundation

Staff

Law Clerk **Taylor Steffan** . . . . (512) 916-5723
Began Service: August 2015
Term Expires: August 2016
E-mail: taylor_steffan@ca5.uscourts.gov

Law Clerk **Zachary Arnold** . . . . (512) 916-5723
Began Service: August 2015
Term Expires: August 2016
E-mail: zachary_arnold@ca5.uscourts.gov

Law Clerk **David Friedman** . . . . (512) 916-5723
Began Service: August 2015
Term Expires: August 2016
E-mail: david_friedman@ca5.uscourts.gov
Education: Stanford 2014 JD

Administrative Secretary **Gina Rogers** . . . . (512) 916-5723
E-mail: gina_rogers@ca5.uscourts.gov

Chambers of Senior Judge John Duhé Jr.

600 Camp Street, New Orleans, LA 70130
Tel: (504) 310-7777

John M. Duhé, Jr.
Senior Judge

Date of Birth: 1933
Education: Tulane 1955 BS, 1957 LLB
Began Service: October 17, 1988
Appointed By: President Ronald Reagan
Political Affiliation: Republican

Judicial: Judge, Louisiana District Court, 16th Judicial District (1979-1984); Judge, United States District Court for the Western District of Louisiana (1984-1988)

Legal Practice: Partner, Helm, Simon, Caffrey & Duhé (1957-1978)

Current Memberships: Federal Judges Association; Iberia Parish Bar Association; Louisiana State Bar Association

Chambers of Senior Judge Jacques L. Wiener, Jr.

John Minor Wisdom U.S. Court of Appeals Building, 600 Camp Street, Room 244, New Orleans, LA 70130
Tel: (504) 310-8098 Fax: (504) 310-8099
E-mail: jacques_wiener@ca5.uscourts.gov

Jacques L. Wiener, Jr.
Senior Judge

Date of Birth: 1934
Education: Tulane 1956 BA, 1961 JD
Began Service: May 25, 1990
Appointed By: President George H.W. Bush
Political Affiliation: Republican

Judicial: Circuit Judge, Chambers of Circuit Judge Jacques L. Wiener, Jr., United States Court of Appeals for the Fifth Circuit (1990-2010)

Legal Practice: Partner, Wiener, Weiss & Madison (1961-1990)

Military Service: United States Navy (1956-1958)

Current Memberships: American Bar Foundation; American Bar Association; American College of Trust and Estate Counsel; The American Law Institute; The International Academy of Estate and Trust Law; Louisiana State Bar Association; Louisiana Bar Foundation, Louisiana State Bar Association; Shreveport Bar Association

Chambers of Senior Judge Jacques L. Wiener, Jr. *continued*

Staff

Law Clerk **Andrew Kingsley** . . . . (504) 310-8098
Began Service: August 2015
Term Expires: August 2016
E-mail: andrew_kingsley@ca5.uscourts.gov

Law Clerk **Samuel Perrone** . . . . (504) 310-8098
Began Service: August 2015
Term Expires: August 2016
E-mail: samuel_perrone@ca5.uscourts.gov
Education: Tulane 2014 JD

Judicial Assistant **Velora Spencer** . . . . (504) 310-8098

Judicial Assistant **Carolyn Springman** . . . . (504) 310-8098
E-mail: carolyn_springman@ca5.uscourts.gov

Chambers of Senior Judge Rhesa H. Barksdale

501 East Court Street, Suite 3.800, Jackson, MS 39201
Tel: (601) 608-4730
E-mail: rhesa_barksdale@ca5.uscourts.gov

Rhesa H. Barksdale
Senior Judge

Date of Birth: 1944
Education: West Point 1966 BS; Mississippi 1972 JD
Began Service: May 12, 1990
Appointed By: President George H.W. Bush

Academic: Assistant Professor of Military Science, The University of Akron (1969-1970); Instructor, School of Law, The University of Mississippi (1975-1976); Instructor, School of Law, Mississippi College (1976)

Clerkships: Law Clerk The Honorable Byron R. White, Supreme Court of the United States (1972-1973)

Legal Practice: Attorney, Butler, Snow, O'Mara, Stevens & Cannada, PLLC (1973-1990)

Military Service: United States Army (1966-1970)

Staff

Judicial Assistant **Jonna H. Welch** . . . . (601) 608-4730
E-mail: jonna_welch@ca5.uscourts.gov

Chambers of Senior Judge Fortunato P. Benavides

903 San Jacinto Boulevard, Room 450, Austin, TX 78701
Tel: (512) 916-5796
E-mail: fortunato_benavides@ca5.uscourts.gov

Fortunato P. Benavides
Senior Judge

Date of Birth: 1947
Education: Houston 1968 BBA, 1972 JD
Began Service: 1994
Appointed By: President William J. Clinton
Political Affiliation: Democrat

Current Memberships: American Bar Association; Hidalgo County Bar Association; Hispanic National Bar Association; State Bar of Texas

Staff

Law Clerk **Natasha Breaux** . . . . (512) 916-5796
Began Service: September 1, 2015
Term Expires: August 28, 2016
E-mail: natasha_breaux@ca5.uscourts.gov
Education: Texas A&M 2006 BS; Houston 2013 JD, 2013 MBA

Law Clerk **Michael Foster** . . . . (512) 916-5796
Began Service: September 1, 2015
Term Expires: August 28, 2016
E-mail: michael_foster@ca5.uscourts.gov
Education: Texas 2015 JD

Career Law Clerk **Stephani Stelmach** . . . . (512) 916-5796
E-mail: stephani_stelmach@ca5.uscourts.gov
Education: Kentucky 1990 JD

Chambers of Senior Judge Fortunato P. Benavides *continued*

Secretary **Luz Probus** .... (512) 916-5796
E-mail: luz_probus@ca5.uscourts.gov

Chambers of Senior Judge Carolyn Dineen King

11020 U.S. Courthouse, 515 Rusk Street, Houston, TX 77002-2694
Tel: (713) 250-5750 Fax: (713) 250-5050

Carolyn Dineen King
Senior Judge

Date of Birth: 1938
Education: Smith 1959 AB; Yale 1962 LLB
Began Service: July 13, 1979
Appointed By: President Jimmy Carter
Political Affiliation: Independent

Current Memberships: American Bar Association; The American Law Institute; Federal Bar Association; Houston Bar Association; State Bar of Texas

Staff

Law Clerk **Yuri Fuchs** .... (713) 250-5753
Began Service: August 2015
Term Expires: August 2016
E-mail: yuri_fuchs@ca5.uscourts.gov

Law Clerk **Benjamin J. McMichael** .... (713) 250-5753
Began Service: August 2015
Term Expires: August 2016
E-mail: benjamin_mcmichael@ca5.uscourts.gov

Law Clerk **Steven "Steve" Seybold** .... (713) 250-5753
Began Service: August 2015
Term Expires: August 2016
E-mail: steven_seybold@ca5.uscourts.gov

Secretary **Starla Barker** .... (713) 250-5756
E-mail: starla_barker@ca5.uscourts.gov

United States Court of Appeals for the Sixth Circuit

Potter Stewart U.S. Couthouse, 100 East Fifth Street, Room 540, Cincinnati, OH 45202
Tel: (513) 564-7200
Tel: (513) 564-7000 (Electronic Opinions & Dockets Voice)
Tel: (513) 684-2842 (Electronic Opinions & Docket Data)
Fax: (513) 564-7210
Internet: www.ca6.uscourts.gov

Number of Judgeships: 16

Number of Vacancies: 1

Supreme Court Justice: Associate Justice Elena Kagan

Areas Covered: Kentucky, Michigan, Ohio and Tennessee

Court Staff

Circuit Executive **Clarence G. Maddox** .... (513) 564-7200
E-mail: clarence_maddox@ca6.uscourts.gov

Secretary to the Circuit Executive **Lisa Balli** .... (513) 564-7200
E-mail: lisa_balli@ca6.uscourts.gov Fax: (513) 564-7206

Assistant Circuit Executive - Finance **Larry McManis** .... (513) 564-7218
E-mail: larry_mcmanis@ca6.uscourts.gov

Assistant Circuit Executive - Court Operations **Kimberly De Graaf** .... (513) 564-7215
E-mail: kimberly_degraaf@ca6.uscourts.gov

Assistant Circuit Executive, Automation **Ronald Dowling** .... (513) 564-7235
E-mail: ron_dowling@ca6.uscourts.gov

Assistant Circuit Executive, Space and Facilities **Barbara Wieliczka** .... (513) 564-7211
E-mail: barbara_wieliczka@ca6.uscourts.gov

Administrative Analyst **Allison Bresser** .... (513) 564-7200
E-mail: allison_bresser@ca6.uscourts.gov

United States Court of Appeals for the Sixth Circuit *continued*

Human Resource Specialist **Lorna Parson** .... (513) 564-7205
E-mail: lorna_parson@ca6.uscourts.gov

Financial Specialist **Lelona Walker** .... (513) 564-7200
E-mail: lelona_walker@ca6.uscourts.gov

Technology Division Manager, Applications **Kelly Mocahbee** .... (513) 564-7211
E-mail: kelly_mocahbee@ca6.uscourts.gov

Systems Manager **Mike Nagel** .... (513) 564-7230
Fax: (513) 564-7243

Data Network Administrator **Mike Davison** .... (513) 564-7233
Fax: (513) 564-7243

PC Systems Administrator **Sharon Mahoney** .... (513) 564-7225
E-mail: sharon_mahoney@ca6.uscourts.gov Fax: (513) 564-7243

Clerk of Court **Deborah S. Hunt** .... (513) 564-7000
E-mail: deborah_hunt@ca6.uscourts.gov Fax: (513) 564-7096

Chief Deputy Clerk **Susan Rogers** .... (513) 564-7000
E-mail: susan_rogers@ca6.uscourts.gov Fax: (513) 564-7096

Secretary to the Chief Deputy Clerk **Dixie Aerni** .... (513) 564-7075
E-mail: dixie_aerni@ca6.uscourts.gov Fax: (513) 564-7096

Transcript and En Banc Coordinator **Bev Harris** .... (513) 564-7000
Fax: (513) 564-7096

Operations Manager **Yvonne Henderson** .... (513) 564-7031
E-mail: yvonne_henderson@ca6.uscourts.gov Fax: (513) 564-7097

Administrative Services Manager **Patrick Dinan** .... (513) 564-7000
E-mail: patrick_dinan@ca6.uscourts.gov Fax: (513) 564-7098

Calendar Clerk **Teresa Bertke** .... (513) 564-7000
Fax: (513) 564-7098

Opinions Deputy **Cathryn Lovely** .... (513) 564-7062
E-mail: cathryn_lovely@ca6.uscourts.gov Fax: (513) 564-7098

Financial, Procurement **Carol Field** .... (513) 564-7078
E-mail: carol_field@ca6.uscourts.gov Fax: (513) 564-7096

Senior Staff Attorney **Timothy D. Schroeder** .... (513) 564-7360
Fax: (513) 564-7399

Supervising Staff Attorney **Tom Armine** .... (513) 564-7360
Fax: (513) 564-7399

Supervising Staff Attorney **Janice Platt** .... (513) 564-7361
E-mail: janice_platt@ca6.uscourts.gov Fax: (513) 564-7399

Administrative Manager, Budget Analyst **Micki Conroy** .... (513) 564-7363
E-mail: micki_conroy@ca6.uscourts.gov Fax: (513) 564-7399

Chief Circuit Mediator **Paul B. Calico** .... (513) 564-7330
E-mail: paul_calico@ca6.uscourts.gov Fax: (513) 564-7349
Education: Western Kentucky 1976 BS; Kentucky 1980 JD

Conference Administrator **Theresa Mack** .... (513) 564-7345
Fax: (513) 564-7349

Circuit Librarian **Owen Smith** .... (513) 564-7321
E-mail: owen_smith@ca6.uscourts.gov Fax: (513) 564-7329

Deputy Librarian **Pam Schaffner** .... (513) 564-7300
Fax: (513) 564-7329

Reference Librarian **Barbara Overshiner** .... (513) 564-7303
Fax: (513) 564-7329

Chambers of Chief Judge R. Guy Cole, Jr.

U.S. Courthouse, 85 Marconi Boulevard, Suite 255, Columbus, OH 43215
Tel: (614) 719-3350 Fax: (614) 719-3360
E-mail: ca06-Cole_Chambers@ca6.uscourts.gov

R. Guy Cole, Jr.
Chief Judge

Date of Birth: 1951
Education: Tufts 1972 BA; Yale 1975 JD
Began Service: January 2, 1996
Appointed By: President William J. Clinton

Current Memberships: American Bar Association; Columbus Bar Association; National Bar Association

Staff

Law Clerk **Robert O'Loughlin** .... (614) 719-3350
Term Expires: August 2016
E-mail: robert_o'loughlin@ca6.uscourts.gov

(continued on next page)

Chambers of Chief Judge R. Guy Cole, Jr. *continued*

Law Clerk **Andrew Talai** .... (614) 719-3350
Term Expires: August 2016
E-mail: andrew_talai@ca6.uscourts.gov
Law Clerk **Elizabeth Cary** .... (614) 719-3350
Term Expires: August 2016
E-mail: elizabeth_cary@ca6.uscourts.gov
Administrative Manager **Angela A. Vann** .... (614) 719-3350
E-mail: angela_vann@ca6.uscourts.gov
Judicial Assistant **Diane M. Stash** .... (614) 719-3350
E-mail: diane_stash@ca6.uscourts.gov

Chambers of Circuit Judge Alice M. Batchelder

Potter Stewart U.S. Courthouse, 100 East Fifth Street, Room 532, Cincinnati, OH 45202-3988
Tel: (330) 764-6026 Fax: (330) 725-7760

Alice M. Batchelder
Circuit Judge

Date of Birth: 1944
Education: Ohio Wesleyan 1964 BA; Akron 1971 JD; Virginia 1988 LLM
Began Service: December 1991
Appointed By: President George H.W. Bush

Current Memberships: American Bar Association; Federal Bar Association; Federal Judges Association; Medina County Bar Association

Staff
Career Law Clerk **Christopher Curtin** .... (330) 764-6026
E-mail: christopher_curtin@ca6.uscourts.gov
Education: Akron JD
Administrative Manager **Yvette Gerhard** .... (330) 764-6026
E-mail: yvette_gerhard@ca6.uscourts.gov

Chambers of Circuit Judge Danny J. Boggs

220 U.S. Courthouse, 601 West Broadway, Louisville, KY 40202
Tel: (502) 625-3900 Fax: (502) 625-3929

Danny J. Boggs
Circuit Judge

Date of Birth: 1944
Education: Harvard 1965 AB; Chicago 1968 JD
Began Service: March 27, 1986
Appointed By: President Ronald Reagan
Political Affiliation: Republican

Academic: Bigelow Fellow and Instructor, Law School, University of Chicago (1968-1969)

Government: Deputy Commissioner, Department of Economic Security, Commonwealth of Kentucky (1969-1970); Administrative Assistant, Education and Legal Counsel, Governor Louie B. Nunn (R-KY), Commonwealth of Kentucky (1970-1971); Legislative Counsel to the Minority Leader, Kentucky House of Representatives (1972); Consultant, Office of Economic Opportunity, Commonwealth of Kentucky (1972); Attorney-Adviser, United States Department of Commerce (1973); Assistant to the Solicitor General, Office of the Solicitor General, United States Department of Justice (1973-1975); Assistant to the Chairman, Federal Power Commission (1975-1977); Deputy Counsel, Committee on Energy and Natural Resources, United States Senate (1977-1979); Senior Policy Advisor, Office of Policy Development, Executive Office of the President, Ronald Reagan Administration (1981-1982); Special Assistant to the President & Assistant Director, Energy, Agriculture & Natural Resources, Office of Policy Development, Executive Office of the President, Ronald Reagan Administration (1982-1983); Deputy Secretary, United States Department of Energy (1983-1986)

Current Memberships: American Bar Association; Kentucky Bar Association

Chambers of Circuit Judge Danny J. Boggs *continued*

Staff
Law Clerk **Avi Kupfer** .... (502) 625-3919
Began Service: August 2015
Term Expires: August 2016
E-mail: avi_kupfer@ca6.uscourts.gov
Law Clerk **Cory Liu** .... (502) 625-3919
Began Service: August 2015
Term Expires: August 2016
E-mail: cory_liu@ca6.uscourts.gov
Law Clerk **Karthik Reddy** .... (502) 625-3919
Began Service: August 2015
Term Expires: August 2016
E-mail: karthik_reddy@ca6.uscourts.gov
Administrative Manager **Delores Williamson** .... (502) 625-3900

Chambers of Circuit Judge Karen Nelson Moore

Carl B. Stokes U.S. Courthouse, 801 West Superior Avenue, Cleveland, OH 44113-1831
Tel: (216) 357-7290 Fax: (216) 357-7296
E-mail: ca06-Moore_Chambers@ca6.uscourts.gov

Karen Nelson Moore
Circuit Judge

Education: Harvard 1970 AB, 1973 JD
Began Service: March 29, 1995
Appointed By: President William J. Clinton

Academic: Assistant Professor of Law, Case Western Reserve University (1977-1980); Associate Professor of Law, Case Western Reserve University (1980-1982); Professor of Law, Case Western Reserve University (1982-1995); Visiting Professor of Law, Harvard University (1990-1991); Arthur E. Petersilge Professor of Law, Case Western Reserve University (1994-1995)

Clerkships: Law Clerk The Honorable Malcolm R. Wilkey, United States Court of Appeals for the District of Columbia Circuit (1973-1974); Law Clerk The Honorable Harry A. Blackmun, Supreme Court of the United States (1974-1975)

Legal Practice: Associate, Jones, Day, Reavis & Pogue (1975-1977)

Current Memberships: The American Law Institute

Staff
Law Clerk **Jason Bertoldi** .... (216) 357-7293
Began Service: August 2015
Term Expires: August 21, 2016
E-mail: jason_bertoldi@ca6.uscourts.gov
Law Clerk **Courtney Dixon** .... (216) 357-7293
Began Service: August 2015
Term Expires: August 21, 2016
E-mail: courtney_dixon@ca6.uscourts.gov
Law Clerk **Benjamin "Ben" Hazlewood** .... (216) 357-7293
Began Service: August 2015
Term Expires: August 21, 2016
Law Clerk **Megan Kiernan** .... (216) 357-7293
Began Service: August 2015
Term Expires: August 21, 2016
Administrative Manager **Marilyn T. Burks** .... (216) 357-7290
E-mail: ca06-Moore_Chambers@ca6.uscourts.gov
Education: South Carolina State 1984 BS

Chambers of Circuit Judge Eric Lee Clay

481 Theodore Levin U.S. Courthouse, 231 West Lafayette Boulevard, Detroit, MI 48226
Tel: (313) 234-5260 Fax: (313) 234-5398
E-mail: eric_clay@ca6.uscourts.gov

Eric Lee Clay
Circuit Judge

Date of Birth: 1948
Education: North Carolina 1969 BA; Yale 1972 JD
Began Service: August 15, 1997
Appointed By: President William J. Clinton

Clerkships: Law Clerk The Honorable Damon J. Keith, United States District Court for the District of Michigan (1972-1973)

Government: Hearing Panelist, Attorney Discipline Board, State of Michigan (1985-1997)

Legal Practice: Attorney, Shareholder and Director, Lewis, White & Clay, P.C. (1973-1997)

Current Memberships: American Bar Association; Detroit Bar Association; National Bar Association; Wolverine Bar Association

Staff

Law Clerk **Kevin Cole** .... (313) 234-5288
Began Service: September 2015
Term Expires: September 2016
E-mail: kevin_cole@ca6.uscourts.gov

Law Clerk **Julia Schlozman** .... (313) 234-5262
Began Service: September 2015
Term Expires: September 4, 2016
E-mail: julia_schlozman@ca6.uscourts.gov

Law Clerk **Alisha Johnson** .... (313) 234-5263
Began Service: September 2015
Term Expires: September 4, 2016
E-mail: alisha_johnson@ca6.uscourts.gov

Law Clerk **Nicholas "Nick" Hartmann** .... (313) 234-5263
Began Service: September 2015
Term Expires: September 4, 2016
E-mail: nicholas_hartmann@ca7.uscourts.gov

Administrative Manager **Diane Marion** .... (313) 234-5260
E-mail: diane_marion@ca6.uscourts.gov

Chambers of Circuit Judge Julia Smith Gibbons

970 Federal Building, 167 North Main Street, Memphis, TN 38103
Tel: (901) 495-1265 Fax: (901) 495-1270
E-mail: julia_gibbons@ca6.uscourts.gov

Julia Smith Gibbons
Circuit Judge

Date of Birth: December 23, 1950
Education: Vanderbilt 1972 BA; Virginia 1975 JD
Began Service: August 2, 2002
Appointed By: President George W. Bush

Clerkships: Law Clerk The Honorable William E. Miller, United States Court of Appeals for the Sixth Circuit (1975-1976)

Government: Deputy Counsel and Legal Advisor, Governor Lamar Alexander (R-TN), State of Tennessee (1979-1981)

Judicial: Judge, Tennessee Circuit Court, 15th Judicial Circuit (1981-1983); Judge, Judicial Panel on Multidistrict Litigation; Judge, United States District Court for the Western District of Tennessee (1983-2002); Chief Judge, United States District Court for the Western District of Tennessee (1994-2000)

Legal Practice: Associate, Farris, Hancock, Gilman, Branan & Lanier (1976-1979)

Current Memberships: Association of Women Attorneys; Memphis Bar Association; Tennessee Women's Forum

Chambers of Circuit Judge Julia Smith Gibbons *continued*

Staff

Law Clerk **Emily Kveselis** .... (901) 495-1353
Began Service: September 2, 2015
Term Expires: September 4, 2016
E-mail: emily_kveselis@ca6.uscourts.gov

Law Clerk **Jessica Dragonetti** .... (901) 495-1267
Began Service: August 18, 2015
Term Expires: August 21, 2016
E-mail: jessica_dragonetti@ca6.uscourts.gov

Law Clerk **Brianna Powell** .... (901) 495-1268
Began Service: August 18, 2015
Term Expires: August 21, 2016
E-mail: brianna_powell@ca6.uscourts.gov

Law Clerk **Scott Shelton** .... (901) 495-1344
Began Service: September 2, 2015
Term Expires: September 4, 2016
E-mail: scott_shelton@ca6.uscourts.gov

Administrative Manager **Loretta Carswell** .... (901) 495-1266
E-mail: loretta_carswell@ca6.uscourts.gov

Chambers of Circuit Judge John M. Rogers

Community Trust Bank Building, 100 East Vine Street, Suite 400, Lexington, KY 40507-1442
Tel: (859) 233-2680 Fax: (859) 233-2679
E-mail: john_rogers@ca6.uscourts.gov

John M. Rogers
Circuit Judge

Date of Birth: June 26, 1948
Education: Stanford 1970 BA; Michigan 1974 JD
Began Service: November 2002
Appointed By: President George W. Bush

Academic: Fulbright Professor, Foreign Affairs College Beijing (1987-1988); Fulbright Professor, Zhongshan University (1994-1995); Visiting Professor, School of Law, University of San Diego (1998-1999)

Government: Appellate Staff/Appellate Lawyer, Civil Division, United States Department of Justice (1974-1978); Appellate Staff, Civil Division, United States Department of Justice, Ronald Reagan Administration (1983-1985)

Military Service: Lieutenant Colonel United States Army Reserve, United States Department of the Army

Staff

Administrative Manager **Sandra Hamilton** .... (859) 233-2680
E-mail: sandy_hamilton@ca6.uscourts.gov

Chambers of Circuit Judge Jeffrey S. Sutton

85 Marconi Boulevard, Columbus, OH 43215
Tel: (614) 849-0134
E-mail: jeffrey_sutton@ca6.uscourts.gov

Jeffrey S. Sutton
Circuit Judge

Education: Williams 1983 BA; Ohio State 1990 JD
Began Service: May 5, 2003
Appointed By: President George W. Bush

Government: State Solicitor, State of Ohio (1995-1998)

Legal Practice: Associate, Jones, Day, Reavis & Pogue (1992-1995); Partner, Jones, Day, Reavis & Pogue (1998-2003)

Current Memberships: Columbus Bar Association

Membership: Past Member, Federal Bar Association

Staff

Law Clerk **Peter Bozzo** .... (614) 849-0134
Began Service: September 2015
Term Expires: September 2016

(continued on next page)

Chambers of Circuit Judge Jeffrey S. Sutton *continued*

Law Clerk **Nicole Frazer** .... (614) 849-0134
Began Service: September 2015
Term Expires: September 2016
Law Clerk **James Saywell** .... (614) 849-0134
Began Service: September 2015
Term Expires: September 2016
Law Clerk **Jordan Wish** .... (614) 849-0134
Began Service: September 2015
Term Expires: September 2016
Administrative Manager **June Flynn** .... (614) 849-0134
E-mail: june_flynn@ca6.uscourts.gov

Chambers of Circuit Judge Deborah L. Cook

U.S. Courthouse, Two South Main Street, Suite 433, Akron, OH 44308
Tel: (330) 252-6248
E-mail: deborah_cook@ca6.uscourts.gov

Deborah L. Cook
Circuit Judge

Date of Birth: 1952
Education: Akron 1974 BA, 1978 JD
Began Service: May 7, 2003
Appointed By: President George W. Bush
Political Affiliation: Republican

Judicial: Judge, Ohio Court of Appeals, Ninth District (1991-1994); Justice, Supreme Court of Ohio (1995-2003)

Legal Practice: Partner, Roderick, Myers & Linton (1976-1991)

Current Memberships: Akron Bar Association; Ohio State Bar Association

Staff

Law Clerk **Richard Jolly** .... (330) 252-6248
Began Service: August 2015
Term Expires: August 2016
E-mail: richard_jolly@ca6.uscourts.gov
Law Clerk **Calland Kluchar** .... (330) 252-6248
Began Service: August 2015
Term Expires: August 2016
E-mail: calland_kluchar@ca6.uscourts.gov
Law Clerk **Zachary Miller** .... (330) 252-6248
Began Service: August 2015
Term Expires: August 2016
E-mail: zachary_miller@ca6.uscourts.gov
Law Clerk **Ann Yackshaw** .... (330) 252-6248
Began Service: March 2015
Term Expires: May 2016
E-mail: ann_yackshaw@ca6.uscourts.gov

Chambers of Circuit Judge David W. McKeague

100 East Fifth Street, Cincinnati, OH 45202-3988
Tel: (513) 564-7200

David William McKeague
Circuit Judge

Date of Birth: 1946
Education: Michigan 1968 BBA, 1971 JD
Began Service: July 22, 2005
Appointed By: President George W. Bush

Academic: Adjunct Professor, Michigan State University School of Law (1998)

Judicial: District Judge, United States District Court for the Western District of Michigan (1992-2005)

Legal Practice: Officer and Senior Partner, Foster, Swift, Collins & Smith, P.C. (1971-1992)

Military Service: United States Army Reserve, United States Department of the Army (1969-1975)

Chambers of Circuit Judge David W. McKeague *continued*

Current Memberships: The District of Columbia Bar; Federal Bar Association; The Federalist Society for Law and Public Policy Studies; State Bar of Michigan

Staff

Judicial Assistant **Bonnie Dabb** .... (513) 564-7200
E-mail: bonnie_dabb@ca6.uscourts.gov

Chambers of Circuit Judge Richard Allen Griffin

13919 South West Bayshore Drive, Suite 208, Traverse City, MI 49684
Tel: (231) 929-3190
E-mail: richard_griffin@ca6.uscourts.gov

Richard Allen Griffin
Circuit Judge

Date of Birth: 1952
Education: Western Michigan 1973 BA; Michigan 1977 JD
Began Service: June 26, 2005
Appointed By: President George W. Bush

Clerkships: Law Clerk The Honorable Ross W. Campbell, Michigan Circuit Court, 22nd Judicial Circuit (1975-1977)

Judicial: Judge, Michigan Court of Appeals (1989-2005)

Legal Practice: Associate, Williams, Coulter, Cunningham, Davison & Read (1977-1981); Partner, Coulter, Cunningham, Davison & Read (1981-1985); Partner, Read & Griffin (1985-1988)

Current Memberships: Federal Bar Association; State Bar of Michigan

Staff

Law Clerk **Heather R. Abraham** .... (231) 929-3190
Began Service: August 2014
Term Expires: August 2016
E-mail: heather_abraham@ca6.uscourts.gov
Education: Minnesota 2012 JD
Law Clerk **David Porter** .... (231) 929-3190
Began Service: August 2015
Term Expires: August 2016
E-mail: david_porter@ca6.uscourts.gov
Law Clerk **Lauren Kwapis** .... (231) 929-3190
Began Service: August 2015
Term Expires: August 2016
E-mail: lauren_kwapis@ca6.uscourts.gov
Career Law Clerk **Susan Peterson Rodgers** .... (231) 564-7000
Education: Michigan 1978 JD

Chambers of Circuit Judge Raymond M. Kethledge

Potter Stewart U.S. Courthouse, 100 East Fifth Street, Cincinnati, OH 45202-3988
Tel: (513) 564-7200
E-mail: raymond_kethledge@ca6.uscourts.gov

Raymond Michael Kethledge
Circuit Judge

Education: Michigan 1993 JD
Began Service: July 11, 2008
Appointed By: President George W. Bush

Clerkships: Law Clerk The Honorable Ralph B. Guy, Jr., United States Court of Appeals for the Sixth Circuit; Law Clerk, Justice Anthony M. Kennedy, Supreme Court of the United States

Government: Judiciary Counsel, Office of Senator Spencer Abraham, United States Senate (1995-1997)

Legal Practice: Counsel, Private Pratice; Partner, Litigation Department, Honigman Miller Schwartz and Cohn

Chambers of Circuit Judge Raymond M. Kethledge *continued*

Staff

Judicial Assistant **Marcia Carter** .... (513) 564-7200
E-mail: Marcia_carter@ca6.uscourts.gov

Chambers of Circuit Judge Helene Nita White

Theodore Levin U.S. Courthouse, 231 West Lafayette, Detroit, MI 48226
Tel: (313) 226-0003
E-mail: helene_white@ca6.uscourts.gov

Helene Nita White
Circuit Judge

Date of Birth: 1954
Education: Barnard 1975 AB; Pennsylvania 1978 JD
Began Service: August 12, 2008
Appointed By: President George W. Bush

Clerkships: Law Clerk The Honorable Charles L. Levin, Michigan Supreme Court (1978-1980)

Judicial: Judge, Detroit Court of Common Pleas (1981); Judge, Michigan District Court, 36th Judicial District (1981-1983); Judge, Michigan Circuit Court, Third Judicial Circuit (1983-1992); Judge, Michigan Court of Appeals (1992-2008)

Current Memberships: American Bar Association; Detroit Bar Association; Michigan Judges Association; National Association of Women Judges; Pennsylvania Bar Association; State Bar of Michigan; Women Lawyers Association of Michigan

Staff

Law Clerk **Andrew Elgin** .... (313) 226-0003
Began Service: August 2015
Term Expires: August 2016
E-mail: andrew_elgin@ca6.uscourts.gov

Law Clerk **Daniel Halainen** .... (313) 226-0003
Began Service: August 2015
Term Expires: August 2016
E-mail: daniel_halainen@ca6.uscourts.gov

Law Clerk **Jessica Weiner** .... (313) 226-0003
Began Service: August 2015
Term Expires: August 2016
E-mail: jessica_weiner@ca6.uscourts.gov

Career Law Clerk **Martha Seijas** .... (313) 226-0003
Began Service: 2008
E-mail: martha_seijas@ca6.uscourts.gov
Education: Michigan 1980 BA;
Eastern Michigan 1982 MA;
George Washington 1991 JD

Administrative Manager **Louise Harris** .... (313) 226-0003
E-mail: louise_harris@ca6.uscourts.gov

Chambers of Circuit Judge Jane Branstetter Stranch

701 Broadway, Room 330, Nashville, TN 37203
Tel: (615) 695-4294 Fax: (615) 742-1601
E-mail: jane_stranch@ca6.uscourts.gov

Jane Branstetter Stranch
Circuit Judge

Date of Birth: 1953
Education: Vanderbilt 1975, 1978 JD
Began Service: October 1, 2010
Appointed By: President Barack Obama

Academic: Lecturer, Labor Law, Belmont University

Judicial: Attorney, Branstetter, Stranch & Jennings, PLLC

Nonprofit: Board Chair, Bellevue, YMCA of Middle Tennessee

Current Memberships: American Bar Association; Nashville Bar Association; Nashville Bar Foundation, Nashville Bar Association; Tennessee Bar Association

Chambers of Circuit Judge Jane Branstetter Stranch *continued*

Staff

Law Clerk **Cody McBride** .... (615) 695-4294
Began Service: August 2015
Term Expires: August 2016
E-mail: cody_mcbride@ca6.uscourts.gov

Law Clerk **Laura Heiman** .... (615) 695-4294
Began Service: August 2015
Term Expires: August 2016
E-mail: laura_heiman@ca6.uscourts.gov

Law Clerk **Margaret Artz** .... (615) 695-4294
Began Service: August 2015
Term Expires: August 2016
E-mail: margaret_artz@ca6.uscourts.gov

Career Law Clerk **Jeannine Huber** .... (615) 695-4294
E-mail: jeannine_huber@ca6.uscourts.gov

Administrative Manager **Sara Goodman** .... (615) 695-4294
E-mail: sara_goodman@ca6.uscourts.gov

Chambers of Circuit Judge Bernice B. Donald

Potter Stewart U.S. Courthouse, 100 East Fifth Street, Room 540, Cincinnati, OH 45202
Tel: (513) 564-7200 Fax: (513) 564-7210
E-mail: bernice_donald@ca6.uscourts.gov

Bernice B. Donald
Circuit Judge

Date of Birth: 1951
Education: Memphis State 1974 BA, 1979 JD
Began Service: October 20, 2011
Appointed By: President Barack Obama

Academic: Adjunct Professor (part-time), Shelby State Community College (1980-1984); Adjunct Professor (part-time), University of Memphis School of Law (1985-1988)

Clerkships: District Judge, Chambers of District Judge Bernice B. Donald, United States District Court for the Western District of Tennessee (1996-2011)

Corporate: Clerk and Manager, South Central Bell Telephone Company (1971-1980)

Government: Staff Attorney, Memphis Area Legal Services, Inc. (1980); Assistant Public Defender, Office of the Public Defender, State of Tennessee (1980-1982)

Judicial: Judge, Tennessee General Sessions Criminal Court (1982-1988); Bankruptcy Judge, United States Bankruptcy Court for the Western District of Tennessee (1988-1995)

Legal Practice: Sole Practitioner (1979-1980)

Nonprofit: Secretary, American Bar Association (2008-2011)

Current Memberships: American Bar Foundation; American Association for Justice; American Bar Association; Association of Women Attorneys; International Women's Forum; Memphis Bar Association; National Association of Women Judges; National Bankruptcy Conference; National Bar Association; National Judicial College; Tennessee Bar Association

Chambers of Senior Judge Damon Jerome Keith

240 Theodore Levin U.S. Courthouse, 231 West Lafayette Boulevard, Detroit, MI 48226
Tel: (313) 234-5245 Fax: (313) 234-5382
E-mail: damon_keith@ca6.uscourts.gov

Damon Jerome Keith
Senior Judge

Date of Birth: 1922
Education: West Virginia State Col 1943 BA; Howard U 1949 JD; Wayne State U 1956 LLM
Began Service: October 1977
Appointed By: President Jimmy Carter

Judicial: District Judge, United States District Court for the Eastern District of Michigan (1967-1977)

Legal Practice: Private Practice (1950-1964); Attorney, Office of the Friend of the Court (1951-1955); Senior Partner, Keith, Conyers, Anderson, Brown & Whals (1964-1967)

Military Service: United States Army (1943-1946)

Current Memberships: American Bar Association; Detroit Bar Association; National Bar Association; National Lawyers Guild; State Bar of Michigan

Staff

Law Clerk **Robert Gray** .... (313) 234-5245
Began Service: August 2015
Term Expires: August 2016
E-mail: robert_gray@ca6.uscourts.gov
Law Clerk **Ahmad Huda** .... (313) 234-5245
E-mail: ahmad_huda@ca6.uscourts.gov
Law Clerk **Ammee Smith** .... (313) 234-5245
E-mail: ammee_smith@ca6.uscourts.gov
Administrative Manager **Kimberly Kendrick** .... (313) 234-5245
E-mail: kimberly_kendrick@ca6.uscourts.gov

Chambers of Senior Judge Gilbert S. Merritt

303 Customs House, 701 Broadway, Nashville, TN 37203
Tel: (615) 736-5957

Gilbert S. Merritt
Senior Judge

Date of Birth: 1936
Education: Yale 1957 BA; Vanderbilt 1960 LLB; Harvard 1962 LLM
Began Service: November 18, 1977
Appointed By: President Jimmy Carter
Political Affiliation: Democrat

Academic: Assistant Dean and Instructor, Law School, Vanderbilt University (1960-1961); Part-Time Lecturer, Law School, Vanderbilt University (1962-1969); Associate Professor, Law School, Vanderbilt University (1969-1970)

Government: Associate, Office of the Metropolitan Attorney, City of Nashville, Tennessee (1963-1966); United States Attorney, Middle District of Tennessee, United States Department of Justice (1966-1969); Executive Secretary, Code Commission, State of Tennessee (1977)

Legal Practice: Associate, Boult, Hunt, Cummings & Conners (1962-1963); Partner, Gullett, Steele, Sanford, Robinson & Merritt (1970-1977)

Current Memberships: American Bar Association; Federal Bar Association; Tennessee Bar Association

Staff

Career Law Clerk **Pamela Eddy** .... (615) 736-5957
Education: UMass (Amherst) 1979 BS; Columbus Law 1990 JD
Administrative Manager **Sara Pettit** .... (615) 736-5957

Chambers of Senior Judge Ralph B. Guy, Jr.

200 East Liberty Street, Room 226, Ann Arbor, MI 48104
P.O. Box 7910, Ann Arbor, MI 48107
Tel: (734) 741-2300
E-mail: ralph_guy@ca6.uscourts.gov

Ralph Bright Guy, Jr.
Senior Judge

Date of Birth: 1929
Education: Michigan 1951 AB, 1953 JD
Began Service: October 17, 1985
Appointed By: President Ronald Reagan

Government: Assistant Corporation Counsel, City of Dearborn, Michigan (1955-1958); Corporation Counsel, City of Dearborn, Michigan (1958-1969); Chief Assistant United States Attorney, Eastern District of Michigan, United States Department of Justice (1969-1970); United States Attorney, Eastern District of Michigan, United States Department of Justice (1970-1976)

Judicial: District Judge, United States District Court for the District of Eastern Michigan (1976-1985)

Legal Practice: Partner, Guy & Guy (1954-1955)

Current Memberships: American Bar Association; Cincinnati Bar Association; Dearborn Bar Association; Federal Bar Association; Federal Judges Association; State Bar of Michigan

Staff

Law Clerk (part-time) **Betsy Blake** .... (734) 741-2300
E-mail: betsy_blake@ca6.uscourts.gov
Career Law Clerk **Patricia Kenny** .... (734) 741-2300
E-mail: patricia_kenny@ca6.uscourts.gov
Education: Michigan 1984 BA; Wayne State U 1987 JD
Administrative Manager **Carolyn Shoptaw** .... (734) 741-2300
E-mail: carolyn_shoptaw@ca6.uscourts.gov

Chambers of Senior Judge Alan E. Norris

328 U.S. Courthouse, 85 Marconi Boulevard, Columbus, OH 43215
Tel: (614) 719-3330 Fax: (614) 469-5867
E-mail: alan_norris@ca6.uscourts.gov

Alan E. Norris
Senior Judge

Date of Birth: 1935
Education: Otterbein 1957 BA; NYU 1960 LLB; Virginia 1986 LLM
Began Service: 1986
Appointed By: President Ronald Reagan

Academic: Instructor, Otterbein College (1976-1980)

Clerkships: Law Clerk The Honorable Kingsley A. Taft, Ohio Supreme Court (1960-1961)

Government: City Prosecutor, City of Westerville, Ohio (1962-1966); State Representative (R-OH), Ohio House of Representatives (1967-1980)

Judicial: Judge, Ohio Court of Appeals (1981-1986)

Legal Practice: Attorney, Vorys, Sater, Seymour and Pease LLP (1961-1962); Partner, Metz, Bailey, Norris & Spicer (1965-1980)

Current Memberships: American Bar Association; Columbus Bar Association; Ohio State Bar Association

Staff

Career Law Clerk **James L. Zafris** .... (614) 719-3332
E-mail: jim_zafris@ca6.uscourts.gov
Education: Harvard 1989 JD
Secretary **Terrie Carter** .... (614) 719-3331
E-mail: terrie_carter@ca6.uscourts.gov

Chambers of Senior Judge Richard F. Suhrheinrich

241 Federal Building, 315 West Allegan Street, Lansing, MI 48933
Tel: (517) 377-1513 Fax: (517) 377-1527
E-mail: richard_suhrheinrich@ca6.uscourts.gov

Richard F. Suhrheinrich
Senior Judge

Date of Birth: 1936
Education: Wayne State U 1960 BS; Detroit Law 1963 JD
Began Service: August 1990
Appointed By: President George H.W. Bush

Academic: Associate Professor, Detroit College of Law (1975-1985)

Government: Assistant Prosecutor, County of Macomb, Michigan (1967-1968)

Judicial: District Judge, United States District Court for the Eastern District of Michigan (1984-1990)

Legal Practice: Associate, Moll, Desenberg, Purdy, Glover & Bayer (1963-1967); Partner, Rogensues, Ricard & Suhrheinrich (1967); Associate, Moll, Desenberg, Purdy, Glover & Bayer (1967-1968); Partner, Kitch, Suhnheinrich, Saurbier & Drutchas (1968-1984)

Current Memberships: Ingham County Bar Association; State Bar of Michigan

Staff

Law Clerk **Emily Bodtke** .... (517) 377-1513
Began Service: September 2015
Term Expires: September 2016
E-mail: emily_bodtke@ca6.uscourts.gov

Career Law Clerk **Molly Carrier Hamilton** .... (517) 377-1513
E-mail: molly_hamilton@ca6.uscourts.gov
Education: Michigan 1988 JD

Secretary **Michele Pazur** .... (517) 377-1513
E-mail: michele_pazur@ca6.uscourts.gov

Chambers of Senior Judge Eugene E. Siler, Jr.

310 South Main Street, Suite 333, London, KY 40741
Tel: (606) 877-7930 Fax: (606) 877-7935

Eugene E. Siler, Jr.
Senior Judge

Date of Birth: 1936
Education: Vanderbilt 1958 BA; Virginia 1963 LLB; Georgetown 1964 LLM; Virginia 1995 LLM
Began Service: September 17, 1991
Appointed By: President George H.W. Bush
Political Affiliation: Republican

Government: County Attorney, Office of the County Attorney, County of Whitley, Kentucky (1965-1970); United States Attorney, Eastern District of Kentucky, United States Department of Justice (1970-1975)

Judicial: United States District Judge, United States District Courts for the Eastern and Western Districts of Kentucky (1975-1991)

Legal Practice: Private Practice (1964-1970)

Military Service: United States Navy (1958-1960); United States Naval Reserve (1961-1983)

Current Memberships: The District of Columbia Bar; Federal Bar Association; Federal Judges Association; Kentucky Bar Association; Virginia State Bar

Staff

Administrative Manager **Katherine Smith** .... (606) 877-7930
E-mail: katherine_smith@ca6.uscourts.gov

Chambers of Senior Judge Martha Craig Daughtrey

701 Broadway, Nashville, TN 37203
Tel: (513) 564-7000

Martha Craig Daughtrey
Senior Judge

Date of Birth: 1942
Education: Vanderbilt 1964 BA, 1968 JD
Began Service: November 22, 1993
Appointed By: President William J. Clinton

Academic: Assistant Law Professor, Vanderbilt University (1972-1975)

Government: Assistant United States Attorney, Middle District of Tennessee, United States Department of Justice (1968-1969); Assistant District Attorney, Office of the District Attorney, State of Tennessee (1969-1972)

Judicial: Associate Judge, Tennessee Court of Criminal Appeals (1975-1990); Associate Justice, Tennessee Supreme Court (1990-1993); Circuit Judge, United States Court of Appeals for the Sixth Circuit (1993-2009)

Current Memberships: American Bar Foundation; American Bar Association; The Harry Phillips American Inn of Court, The American Inns of Court; Nashville Bar Association; Napier-Looby Bar Association, Nashville Bar Association; Nashville Bar Foundation, Nashville Bar Association; National Association of Women Judges; Tennessee Bar Association; Tennessee Bar Foundation; Tennessee Judicial Conference

Chambers of Senior Judge Ronald Lee Gilman

1176 Federal Building, 167 North Main Street, Memphis, TN 38103
Tel: (901) 495-1575 Fax: (901) 495-1580
E-mail: ronald_gilman@ca6.uscourts.gov

Ronald Lee Gilman
Senior Judge

Date of Birth: 1942
Education: Harvard 1967 JD
Began Service: November 21, 1997
Appointed By: President William J. Clinton
Political Affiliation: Democrat

Current Memberships: American Bar Foundation; The American Law Institute

Staff

Law Clerk **Conor Craft** .... (901) 495-1575
Began Service: August 2015
Term Expires: August 2016
E-mail: conor_craft@ca6.uscourts.gov

Law Clerk **Peter Fielding** .... (901) 495-1575
Began Service: August 2015
Term Expires: August 2016
E-mail: peter_fielding@ca6.uscourts.gov

Law Clerk **Sheila E. Menz** .... (901) 495-1575
Began Service: August 2015
Term Expires: August 2016
E-mail: sheila_menz@ca6.uscourts.gov

Judicial Assistant **Carol Lutrell** .... (901) 495-1575
E-mail: carol_lutrell@ca6.uscourts.gov

United States Bankruptcy Appellate Panel for the Sixth Circuit

540 Potter Stewart U.S. Courthouse, 100 East Fifth Street, Cincinnati, OH 45202
Tel: (513) 564-7000 Fax: (513) 564-7098

Number of Judgeships: 6

Court Staff

Bankruptcy Appellate Panel Clerk **Deborah S. Hunt** ..... (513) 564-7000
Bankruptcy Appellate Panel Case Manager
Paula Moore ..... (513) 564-7055
E-mail: paula_moore@ca6.uscourts.gov

Chambers of Chief Bankruptcy Judge C. Kathryn Preston

170 North High Street, Columbus, OH 43215
Tel: (614) 469-6638 ext. 5795

C. Kathryn Preston
Chief Bankruptcy Judge

Education: Stetson, JD

Chambers of Bankruptcy Judge Marian F. Harrison

701 Broadway, Room 232, Nashville, TN 37203
Tel: (615) 736-5589

Marian F. Harrison
Bankruptcy Judge

Education: Vanderbilt 1972 BA; Georgia 1975 JD

Current Memberships: American Bar Association; Nashville Bar Association; National Conference of Bankruptcy Judges; Tennessee Bar Association; Tennessee Lawyers' Association for Women

Chambers of Bankruptcy Judge Guy R. Humphrey

120 West Third Street, Dayton, OH 45402
Tel: (937) 225-2863

Guy R. Humphrey
Bankruptcy Judge

Education: Ohio State 1984 JD

Chambers of Bankruptcy Judge Joan A Lloyd

Gene Snyder Federal Courthouse, 601 West Broadway, Louisville, KY 40202
Tel: (502) 627-5525

Joan A. Lloyd
Bankruptcy Judge

Date of Birth: 1961
Education: Kentucky 1982 BA; Brandeis 1985 JD

Current Memberships: American Bankruptcy Institute; The District of Columbia Bar; Kentucky Bar Association; Louisville Bar Association; National Conference of Bankruptcy Judges

Staff

Judicial Assistant **Elaine Fountain** ..... (502) 627-5525
Career Law Clerk **Barbara A. Wetzel** ..... (502) 627-5525
Education: Louisville 1990 JD

Chambers of Bankruptcy Judge Daniel S. Opperman

111 First Street, Bay City, MI 48708
Tel: (989) 894-8850

Daniel S. Opperman
Bankruptcy Judge

Chambers of Bankruptcy Judge Paulette J. Delk

200 Jefferson Avenue, Suite 625, Memphis, TN 38103
Tel: (901) 328-3552

Paulette J. Delk
Bankruptcy Judge

United States Court of Appeals for the Seventh Circuit

U.S. Courthouse, 219 South Dearborn Street, Room 2722, Chicago, IL 60604
Tel: (312) 435-5850
Internet: www.ca7.uscourts.gov

Number of Judgeships: 11

Number of Vacancies: 2

Supreme Court Justice: Associate Justice Elena Kagan

Areas Covered: Illinois, Indiana and Wisconsin

Court Staff

Circuit Executive **Collins T. Fitzpatrick** ..... (312) 435-5803
E-mail: collins_fitzpatrick@ca7.uscourts.gov
Circuit Clerk **Gino J. Agnello** ..... (312) 435-5850
E-mail: gino_agnello@ca7.uscourts.gov Fax: (312) 435-5797
Education: Chicago-Kent JD
Senior Conference Attorney **Joel N. Shapiro** ..... (312) 435-6883
Room 1120
E-mail: joel_shapiro@ca7.uscourts.gov
Settlement Conference Attorney **Jillisa Brittan** ..... (312) 435-6883
E-mail: jillisa_brittan@ca7.uscourts.gov
Education: Latin (Chicago, IL) 1981; Northwestern BA; Columbia 1986 MA; Chicago JD
Settlement Conference Attorney **Rocco J. Spagna** ..... (312) 435-6883
E-mail: rocco_spagna@ca7.uscourts.gov
Counsel to the Circuit Executive **Donald J. Wall** ..... (312) 435-5805
Senior Staff Attorney **Michael Fridkin** ..... (312) 435-5381
E-mail: michael_fridkin@ca7.uscourts.gov
Deputy Senior Staff Attorney **Alan W. Lepp** ..... (312) 435-5880
E-mail: alan_lepp@ca7.uscourts.gov
Deputy Senior Staff Attorney **Philip E. Police** ..... (312) 435-5524
E-mail: philip_police@ca7.uscourts.gov
Supervisory Staff Attorney **Mia Furlong** ..... (312) 435-5779
E-mail: mia_furlong@ca7.uscourts.gov
Supervisory Staff Attorney **Julie Lyons** ..... (312) 435-5663
Systems and Network Manager **(Vacant)** ..... (312) 435-5844
Fax: (312) 408-7886
Financial & Procurement Manager **Edward Stack** ..... (312) 435-5896
E-mail: Ed_Stack@ca7.uscourts.gov Fax: (312) 554-8077
Personnel Specialist **Grace Moriarty** ..... (312) 435-5513
E-mail: Grace_Moriarty@ca7.uscourts.gov Fax: (312) 554-8077
Director of Human Resources **Kathleen O'Malley** ..... (312) 435-5884
E-mail: Kathy_O'Malley@ca7.uscourts.gov Fax: (312) 435-8077
Circuit Librarian **Gretchen Van Dam** ..... (312) 435-5660
Room 1637 Fax: (312) 408-5031
Deputy Circuit Librarian **(Vacant)** ..... (312) 435-5660 ext. 2644
Fax: (312) 408-5031

Chambers of Chief Judge Diane P. Wood

219 South Dearborn Street, Room 2688, Chicago, IL 60604
Tel: (312) 435-5521 Fax: (312) 408-5117
E-mail: dwood@ca7.uscourts.gov

Diane Pamela Wood
Chief Judge

Date of Birth: July 4, 1950
Education: Texas 1971 BA, 1975 JD
Began Service: July 24, 1995
Appointed By: President William J. Clinton
Political Affiliation: Democrat

Current Memberships: American Academy of Arts and Sciences; The American Law Institute; American Society of International Law; The Bar Association of the District of Columbia; Illinois State Bar Association

Staff
Fax: (312) 408-5117
E-mail: chambers_of_judge_d_wood@ca7.uscourts.gov

Law Clerk **Matthew Blumenthal** .... (312) 435-3012
Began Service: August 2015
Term Expires: August 2016
E-mail: matthew_blumenthal@ca7.uscourts.gov
Education: Harvard 2008 AB; Yale 2015 JD

Law Clerk **Rachel Homer** .... (312) 435-3012
Began Service: August 2015
Term Expires: August 2016
E-mail: rachel_homer@ca7.uscourts.gov
Education: Yale 2009 BA; Harvard 2015 JD

Law Clerk **Shira Tevah** .... (312) 435-3012
Began Service: August 2015
Term Expires: August 2016
E-mail: shira_tevah@ca7.uscourts.gov
Education: Chicago 2009 BA;
Berkeley Law 2015 JD

Judicial Assistant **Linda A. Rux** .... (312) 435-5521
E-mail: linda_rux@ca7.uscourts.gov

Chambers of Circuit Judge Richard A. Posner

U.S. Courthouse, 219 South Dearborn Street, Room 2788,
Chicago, IL 60604
Tel: (312) 435-5806 Fax: (312) 435-7545
E-mail: richard_posner@ca7.uscourts.gov

Richard A. Posner
Circuit Judge

Date of Birth: 1939
Education: Yale 1959 AB; Harvard 1962 LLB
Began Service: December 4, 1981
Appointed By: President Ronald Reagan

Academic: Associate Professor of Law, Stanford University (1968); Professor of Law, University of Chicago (1969-1981); Senior Lecturer, University of Chicago (1981)

Clerkships: Law Clerk The Honorable William J. Brennan, Jr., Supreme Court of the United States (1962-1963)

Corporate: President, Lexecon, Inc. (1977-1981)

Government: Legal Assistant to Commissioner, Federal Trade Commission (1963-1965); Attorney, Office of the Solicitor General, United States Department of Justice (1965-1967); General Counsel, President's Task Force on Communications, Executive Office of the President, Lyndon B. Johnson Administration (1967-1968); Research Associate, National Bureau of Economic Research (1971-1981)

Current Memberships: American Economic Association; The American Law Institute

Chambers of Circuit Judge Richard A. Posner *continued*

Staff
Law Clerk **Miriam Hinman** .... (312) 435-5806
Began Service: June 2015
Term Expires: June 2016
E-mail: miriam_hinman@ca7.uscourts.gov

Law Clerk **Matthew Kugler** .... (312) 435-5806
Began Service: July 2015
Term Expires: July 2016
E-mail: matthew_kugler@ca7.uscourts.gov

Law Clerk **Julia Schwartz** .... (312) 435-5806
Began Service: August 2015
Term Expires: August 2016
E-mail: julia_schwartz@ca7.uscourts.gov

Secretary **Patricia Goldrick** .... (312) 435-5806
E-mail: patricia_goldrick@ca7.uscourts.gov

Chambers of Circuit Judge Joel M. Flaum

U.S. Courthouse, 219 South Dearborn Street, Room 2702,
Chicago, IL 60604
Tel: (312) 435-5626 Fax: (312) 435-7539
E-mail: joel_flaum@ca7.uscourts.gov

Joel M. Flaum
Circuit Judge

Date of Birth: 1936
Education: Union Col (NY) 1958 BA; Northwestern 1963 JD, 1964 LLM
Began Service: June 1, 1983
Appointed By: President Ronald Reagan

Academic: Lecturer, Northwestern University School of Law (1967-1969); Lecturer, College of Law, DePaul University (1987-1988); Adjunct Professor, Northwestern University School of Law (1993-2000)

Government: Assistant State's Attorney, Office of the State's Attorney, County of Cook, Illinois (1965-1969); Assistant Attorney General, Office of the Attorney General, State of Illinois (1969-1970); First Assistant Attorney General, Office of the Attorney General, State of Illinois (1970-1972); First Assistant U.S. Attorney, Northern District of Illinois, United States Department of Justice (1972-1975)

Judicial: Judge, United States District Court for the Northern District of Illinois (1975-1983); Chief Judge, United States Court of Appeals for the Seventh Circuit (2000-2006)

Legal Practice: Associate, Schimberg, Greenberger, Kraus & Jacobs (1964-1965)

Military Service: United States Naval Reserve (1981-1992); Lieutenant Commander Judge, Advocate General's Corps

Current Memberships: American Bar Association; The Chicago American Inn of Court, The American Inns of Court; The American Law Institute; The Chicago Bar Association; Chicago Bar Foundation; Federal Bar Association; The Seventh Circuit Bar Association, Federal Bar Association; Illinois State Bar Association; Lawyers Club of Chicago; Naval Justice School Foundation; Naval Reserve Maritime Law Association; Navy-Marine Corps Retired Judges Advocates Association

Staff
Law Clerk **Ashley Cheung**
Began Service: August 2015
Term Expires: August 28, 2016
E-mail: ashley_cheung@ca7.uscourts.gov

Law Clerk **Meryl Holt**
Began Service: August 2015
Term Expires: August 28, 2016
E-mail: meryl_holt@ca7.uscourts.gov

Law Clerk **Jordan Joachim**
Began Service: August 2015
Term Expires: August 28, 2016
E-mail: jordan_joachim@ca7.uscourts.gov

Law Clerk **Dorothy Shapiro**
Began Service: August 2015
Term Expires: August 28, 2016
E-mail: dorothy_shapiro@ca7.uscourts.gov

(continued on next page)

Chambers of Circuit Judge Joel M. Flaum *continued*

Secretary **Sharon E. Anderson** . . . . (312) 435-5626
E-mail: sharon_anderson@ca7.uscourts.gov

Chambers of Circuit Judge Frank H. Easterbrook

219 South Dearborn Street, Room 274, Chicago, IL 60604
Tel: (312) 435-5808
E-mail: frank_easterbrook@ca7.uscourts.gov

Frank H. Easterbrook
Circuit Judge

Date of Birth: 1948
Education: Swarthmore 1970 BA; Chicago 1973 JD
Began Service: 1985
Appointed By: President Ronald Reagan

Staff
Law Clerk **Alan Freedman** . . . . (312) 435-5808
Began Service: August 2015
Term Expires: August 2016
E-mail: alan_freedman@ca7.uscourts.gov
Law Clerk **John Grein** . . . . (312) 435-5808
Began Service: August 2015
Term Expires: August 2016
E-mail: john_grein@ca7.uscourts.gov
Secretary **Kathleen Engel** . . . . (312) 435-5808
E-mail: kathleen_engel@ca7.uscourts.gov

Chambers of Circuit Judge Michael S. Kanne

U.S. Courthouse, 219 South Dearborn Street, Room 2744H,
Chicago, IL 60604
Halleck Federal Building, 4th and Ferry Streets, Lafayette, IN 47902-1340
P.O. Box 1340, Lafayette, IN 47902-1340
Tel: (312) 435-5764 (Illinois Chambers) Tel: (765) 420-6200
Fax: (765) 420-6240 Fax: (312) 435-7540 (Illinois Chambers)
E-mail: michael_kanne@ca7.uscourts.gov

Michael S. Kanne
Circuit Judge

Date of Birth: 1938
Education: Indiana 1962 BS, 1968 JD
Began Service: May 20, 1987
Appointed By: President Ronald Reagan
Political Affiliation: Republican

Academic: Lecturer on Law, St. Joseph's College (1976-1987)

Government: City Attorney, Office of the City Attorney, City of Rensselaer, Indiana (1972)

Judicial: Judge, Indiana Circuit Court, 30th Judicial Circuit (1972-1982); Judge, United States District Court for the Northern District of Indiana (1982-1987)

Legal Practice: Associate, Nesbitt & Fisher (1968-1971); Sole Practitioner (1971-1972)

Military Service: United States Air Force (1962-1965)

Current Memberships: Federal Bar Association; Indiana State Bar Association; Jasper County Bar Association

Staff
Law Clerk **Sarah Hogarth** . . . . (765) 420-6216
Began Service: August 2015
Term Expires: August 2016
E-mail: sarah_hogarth@ca7.uscourts.gov
Law Clerk **Thomas Rybarczyk** . . . . (765) 420-6216
Began Service: August 2015
Term Expires: August 2016
E-mail: thomas_rybarczyk@ca7.uscourts.gov

Chambers of Circuit Judge Michael S. Kanne *continued*

Law Clerk **Andrew Sand** . . . . (765) 420-6216
Began Service: August 2015
Term Expires: August 2016
E-mail: andrew_sand@ca7.uscourts.gov
Judicial Secretary **Neva Kanelos** . . . . (312) 435-5764
E-mail: neva_kanelos@ca7.uscourts.gov
Judicial Secretary **M. Arvilla Mitchell** . . . . (765) 420-6210
Judicial Assistant **Jonna C. Anderson** . . . . (765) 420-6219
E-mail: jonna_anderson@ca7.uscourts.gov Fax: (765) 420-6240

Chambers of Circuit Judge Ilana Diamond Rovner

U.S. Courthouse, 219 South Dearborn Street, Room 2774,
Chicago, IL 60604
Tel: (312) 435-5608 Fax: (312) 408-5011
E-mail: ilana_rovner@ca7.uscourts.gov

Ilana Diamond Rovner
Circuit Judge

Date of Birth: 1938
Education: Bryn Mawr 1960 AB; Chicago-Kent 1966 JD
Began Service: August 17, 1992
Appointed By: President George H.W. Bush

Clerkships: Law Clerk, Chief Judge James B. Parsons, United States District Court for the Northern District of Illinois (1972-1973)

Government: Assistant U.S. Attorney, Northern District of Illinois, Office of the United States Attorney, United States Department of Justice (1973-1977); Deputy Chief, Northern District of Illinois, Public Protection Unit, United States Department of Justice (1975-1976); Chief, Northern District of Illinois, Public Protection Unit, United States Department of Justice (1976-1977); Deputy Governor and Legal Counsel, Office of the Governor, State of Illinois (1977-1984)

Current Memberships: The Chicago Bar Association; Chicago Council of Lawyers; The Decalogue Society of Lawyers; Federal Bar Association; The Seventh Circuit Bar Association, Federal Bar Association; Federal Judges Association; Jewish Judges Association of Illinois; Women's Bar Association of Illinois

Staff
Career Law Clerk **Mary Cameli** . . . . (312) 435-3003
E-mail: mary_cameli@ca7.uscourts.gov
Education: Chicago-Kent 1992 JD
Career Law Clerk **Mariah Christensen** . . . . (312) 846-8726
E-mail: mariah_christensen@ca7.uscourts.gov
Education: Northwestern 2002 JD
Career Law Clerk **Mark Dupont** . . . . (312) 435-3001
E-mail: mark_dupont@ca7.uscourts.gov
Education: Stanford 1986 JD
Career Law Clerk **Peggy Healy** . . . . (312) 435-3002
E-mail: peggy_healy@ca7.uscourts.gov
Education: Loyola U (Chicago) 1989 JD
Career Law Clerk **Lauren Raphael** . . . . (312) 435-5894
E-mail: lauren_raphael@ca7.uscourts.gov
Education: Michigan 1996 JD
Administrative Assistant **Julie Diaz** . . . . (312) 435-5608
E-mail: julie_diaz@ca7.uscourts.gov

Chambers of Circuit Judge Ann Claire Williams

2722 U.S. Courthouse, 219 South Dearborn Street, Room 2602, Chicago, IL 60604
Tel: (312) 435-5532 Fax: (312) 408-5141
E-mail: ann_c_williams@ca7.uscourts.gov

Ann Claire Williams
Circuit Judge

Date of Birth: 1949
Education: Wayne State U 1970 BS; Michigan 1972 MA; Notre Dame 1975 JD
Began Service: November 15, 1999
Appointed By: President William J. Clinton

Clerkships: Law Clerk The Honorable Robert A. Sprecher, United States Court of Appeals for the Seventh Circuit (1975-1976)

Government: Assistant United States Attorney, Northern District of Illinois, United States Department of Justice (1976-1985)

Judicial: District Judge, United States District Court for the Northern District of Illinois (1985-1999)

Nonprofit: Secretary and Board Member and Faculty, National Institute for Trial Advocacy (1979); Equal Justice Works (2001); Secretary, Board of Trustees, The University of Notre Dame; Member, Delta Sigma Theta Sorority, Inc.

Current Memberships: Cook County Bar Association; Federal Bar Association; Federal Judges Association; Illinois Judicial Council; Board of Directors, Just the Beginning Foundation; Women's Bar Association of Illinois

Staff

Law Clerk **Sheerine Alenzadah** .... (312) 435-5532
Began Service: August 2015
Term Expires: August 2016

Law Clerk **Tony Balkissoon** .... (312) 435-5532
Began Service: August 2015
Term Expires: August 2016
E-mail: tony_balkissoon@ca7.uscourts.gov

Law Clerk **Kapri Saunders** .... (312) 435-5532
Began Service: February 2015
Term Expires: January 2016
E-mail: kapri_saunders@ca7.uscourts.gov

Career Law Clerk **Erin McGinley** .... (312) 435-5532
E-mail: erin_mcginley@ca7.uscourts.gov
Education: Loyola U (Chicago) 2003 JD

Judicial Assistant **Debra Perdue-Toney** .... (312) 435-3099
E-mail: debra_perdue@ca7.uscourts.gov

Chambers of Circuit Judge Diane S. Sykes

716 U.S. Courthouse and Federal Building, 517 East Wisconsin Avenue, Milwaukee, WI 53202
Tel: (414) 727-6988 Fax: (414) 727-6991
E-mail: chambers_of_judge_sykes@ca7.uscourts.gov

Diane S. Sykes
Circuit Judge

Date of Birth: 1957
Education: Northwestern 1980 BS; Marquette 1984 JD
Began Service: July 4, 2004
Appointed By: President George W. Bush

Clerkships: Law Clerk The Honorable Terence T. Evans, United States District Court for the Eastern District of Wisconsin (1984-1985)

Corporate: Reporter, Milwaukee Journal (1980-1981)

Judicial: Judge, Milwaukee County Circuit Court Branch (1992-1999); Justice, Wisconsin Supreme Court (1999-2004)

Legal Practice: Attorney, Whyte Hirschboeck Dudek S.C. (1985-1992)

Current Memberships: The American Inns of Court; The American Law Institute; The Seventh Circuit Bar Association, Federal Bar Association; Milwaukee Bar Association; National Association of Women Lawyers; St. Thomas More Legal Society; State Bar of Wisconsin

Chambers of Circuit Judge Diane S. Sykes *continued*

Staff

Law Clerk **Kian Hudson** .... (414) 727-6988
Began Service: August 2015
Term Expires: August 2016
E-mail: kian_hudson@ca7.uscourts.gov

Law Clerk **Kevin LeRoy** .... (414) 727-6988
Began Service: August 2015
Term Expires: August 2016
E-mail: kevin_leroy@ca7.uscourts.gov

Law Clerk **Anne-Louise Mittal** .... (414) 727-6988
Began Service: August 2015
Term Expires: August 2016
E-mail: anne-louise_mittal@ca7.uscourts.gov

Law Clerk **Kelli Mulder** .... (312) 435-5824
Began Service: August 2015
Term Expires: August 2016
E-mail: kelli_mulder@ca7.uscourts.gov

Judicial Assistant **Christine L. Petrie** .... (414) 727-6988

Chambers of Circuit Judge David F. Hamilton

46 East Ohio Street, Indianapolis, IN 46204
Tel: (317) 229-3640
E-mail: david_hamilton@ca7.uscourts.gov

David F. Hamilton
Circuit Judge

Date of Birth: 1957
Education: Haverford 1979 BA; Yale 1983 JD
Began Service: November 2009
Appointed By: President Barack Obama

Clerkships: Law Clerk The Honorable Richard D. Cudahy, United States Court of Appeals for the Seventh Circuit (1983-1984)

Government: Counsel, Governor Evan Bayh (D-IA), State of Indiana (1989-1991); Chairman, State Ethics Commission, State of Indiana (1991-1994)

Legal Practice: Associate, Barnes & Thornburg LLP (1984-1988); Partner, Barnes & Thornburg LLP (1991-1994)

Current Memberships: The Sagamore American Inn of Court, The American Inns of Court

Staff

Law Clerk **Alexander Kasner** .... (317) 229-3640
Began Service: August 2015
Term Expires: August 2016
E-mail: alex_kasner@ca7.uscourts.gov

Law Clerk **Kendra N. Key** .... (317) 229-3640
Began Service: August 2015
Term Expires: August 2016
E-mail: kendra_key@ca7.uscourts.gov
Education: Alabama 2010 AB

Law Clerk **Daniel Leigh** .... (317) 229-3640
Began Service: August 2015
Term Expires: August 2016
E-mail: daniel_leigh@ca7.uscourts.gov

Law Clerk **Monica Mark** .... (317) 229-3640
Began Service: August 2015
Term Expires: August 2016
E-mail: monica_mark@ca7.uscourts.gov

Career Law Clerk **(Vacant)** .... (317) 229-3640

Judicial Assistant **Jennifer J. McGinnis** .... (317) 229-3640
Education: Butler 1982 BA

Chambers of Senior Judge William J. Bauer

U.S. Courthouse, 219 South Dearborn Street, Room 2754, Chicago, IL 60604
Tel: (312) 435-5810 Fax: (312) 435-7548
E-mail: chambers_of_judge_bauer@ca7.uscourts.gov

William J. Bauer
Senior Judge

Date of Birth: 1926
Education: Elmhurst 1949 AB; DePaul 1952 JD
Began Service: 1974
Appointed By: President Gerald Ford
Political Affiliation: Republican

Academic: Instructor, Elmhurst College (1952-1959); Adjunct Professor, DePaul University (1978-1991)

Government: Assistant State's Attorney, Office of the State's Attorney, DuPage County, Illinois (1952-1958); State's Attorney, Office of the State's Attorney, DuPage County, Illinois (1959-1964); United States Attorney, United States Department of Justice (1970-1971)

Judicial: Judge, Illinois Circuit Court, 18th Judicial Circuit (1964-1970); Judge, United States District Court for the Northern District of Illinois (1971-1974)

Legal Practice: Erlenborn & Bauer (1953-1964)

Military Service: United States Army (1945-1947)

Current Memberships: American Bar Association; The Chicago Bar Association; DuPage County Bar Association; Federal Bar Association; Illinois Association of Circuit and Appellate Court Judges; Illinois State Bar Association; Illinois States Attorneys Association; National District Attorneys Association

Staff

Law Clerk **Matthew T. Connelly** .... (312) 435-5810
Began Service: September 2015
Term Expires: September 2016
E-mail: matthew_connelly@ca7.uscourts.gov

Law Clerk **Ben O'Connor** .... (312) 435-5810
Began Service: September 2015
Term Expires: September 2016
E-mail: ben_oconnor@ca7.uscourts.gov

Chambers of Senior Judge Kenneth F. Ripple

208 Robert A. Grant Federal Building, 204 South Main Street, South Bend, IN 46601-2122
Tel: (574) 246-8150 Tel: (312) 435-5510 (Chicago Office)
Fax: (574) 246-8157 Fax: (312) 408-5042 (Chicago Office)
E-mail: chambers_of_judge_ripple@ca7.uscourts.gov

Kenneth F. Ripple
Senior Judge

Date of Birth: 1943
Education: Fordham 1965 AB; Virginia 1968 JD; George Washington 1972 LLM
Began Service: June 10, 1985
Appointed By: President Ronald Reagan

Corporate: Attorney, International Business Machines Corporation (1968)

Government: Legal Officer, Supreme Court of the United States (1972-1973); Legal Assistant, Supreme Court of the United States (1973-1977)

Military Service: Commander, United States Naval Reserve, Judge Advocate General's Corps (1968-1972); Office of the Judge Advocate General, Department of the Navy (1969-1972)

Current Memberships: American Bar Association; The American Law Institute; Federal Bar Association; New York State Bar Association; The Supreme Court Historical Society

Chambers of Senior Judge Kenneth F. Ripple *continued*

Staff

Law Clerk **Andrew Guy** .... (574) 246-8150
Began Service: September 2015
Term Expires: September 2016
E-mail: andrew_guy@ca7.uscourts.gov

Law Clerk **Charles Jones** .... (574) 246-8150
Began Service: September 2015
Term Expires: September 2016
E-mail: charles_johnson@ca7.uscourts.gov

Career Law Clerk **Kari A. Gallagher** .... (574) 246-8150
E-mail: kari_gallagher@ca7.uscourts.gov
Education: Notre Dame 1993 JD

Career Law Clerk **Dory Mitros Durham** .... (574) 246-8150
E-mail: dory_durham@ca7.uscourts.gov

Judicial Assistant **Kim Daniels** .... (574) 246-8150
E-mail: kim_daniels@ca7.uscourts.gov

Chambers of Senior Judge Daniel A. Manion

301 Robert A. Grant Federal Building, 204 South Main Street, South Bend, IN 46601
Tel: (574) 246-8060 Fax: (574) 246-8068
E-mail: daniel_manion@ca7.uscourts.gov

Daniel A. Manion
Senior Judge

Date of Birth: 1942
Education: Notre Dame 1964 AB; Indiana 1973 JD
Began Service: 1986
Appointed By: President Ronald Reagan

Corporate: Manion Forum Trust (1967); Mountain Valley Water Co. (1967-1968); Alexander Hamilton Life Insurance Co. (1968); Director, St. Joseph Bank and Trust Co. (1979-1986)

Government: Director, Industrial Development, Department of Commerce, State of Indiana (1968-1973); Deputy Attorney General, United States Department of Justice (1973-1974); State Senator (R-IA), Indiana State Senate (1978-1982)

Judicial: Circuit Judge, Chambers of Circuit Judge Daniel A. Manion, United States Court of Appeals for the Seventh Circuit (1986-2007)

Legal Practice: Attorney, Doran, Manion, Boynton, Kamm & Esmont (1974-1986)

Military Service: United States Army (1965-1966)

Staff

Law Clerk **Benjamin Bogos** .... (574) 246-8060
Began Service: August 2015
Term Expires: August 2017
E-mail: ben_bogos@ca7.uscourts.gov

Law Clerk **John Tuttle** .... (574) 246-8060
Began Service: August 2014
Term Expires: August 31, 2016
E-mail: john_tuttle@ca7.uscourts.gov

Career Law Clerk **Margot Cleveland** .... (574) 246-8060
E-mail: margot_cleveland@ca7.uscourts.gov
Education: Notre Dame 1992 JD

Judicial Assistant **Catherine A. Bruckbauer** .... (574) 246-8060

Judicial Secretary **Neva Kanelos** .... (312) 435-7536
2640 U.S. Courthouse, 219 S. Dearborn St., Chicago, IL 60604
E-mail: neva_kanelos@ca7.uscourts.gov

United States Court of Appeals for the Eighth Circuit

Thomas F. Eagleton U.S. Courthouse, 111 South Tenth Street, Suite 24.327, St. Louis, MO 63102
Tel: (314) 244-2400 Tel: (314) 244-2479 (Electronic Opinions Data)
Fax: (314) 244-2405
Internet: www.ca8.uscourts.gov

Number of Judgeships: 11

Number of Vacancies: 1

Supreme Court Justice: Associate Justice Samuel A. Alito Jr.

Areas Covered: Arkansas, Iowa, Minnesota, Missouri, Nebraska, North Dakota and South Dakota

Court Staff

Circuit Executive **Millie Adams** .... (314) 244-2600
E-mail: millie_adams@ca8.uscourts.gov Fax: (314) 244-2605
Education: Missouri (St Louis) 1976 BS; Webster 1984 MA

Assistant Circuit Executive, Administrative Services **Michelle Braun** .... (314) 244-2622
E-mail: michelle_braun@ca8.uscourts.gov

Assistant Circuit Executive, Finance **Duane E. Ewell** ..... (314) 244-2620
E-mail: duane_ewell@ca8.uscourts.gov
Education: Missouri BA

Assistant Circuit Executive, Information Services **William Woods** .... (314) 244-2631
E-mail: william_woods@ca8.uscourts.gov
Education: Illinois BA; Southern Illinois MS

Assistant Circuit Executive, Policy **Frenchette Prince** .... (314) 244-2623
E-mail: frechette_prince@ce8.uscourts.gov
Education: Missouri 1982 BS; Saint Louis U 1987 JD

Assistant Circuit Executive, Space and Facilities **Carol Rouw** .... (314) 244-2610
E-mail: carol_rouw@ca8.uscourts.gov

Clerk of Court **Michael E. Gans** .... (314) 244-2400
E-mail: michael_gans@ca8.uscourts.gov
Education: Shimer 1973 BA; Washington U (MO) 1977 JD

Chief Deputy Clerk **Robin Weinberger** .... (314) 244-2434
E-mail: robin_weinberger@ca8.uscourts.gov
Education: Indiana 1977 AB; Washington College of Law 1980 JD

Counsel to the Clerk **Kathryn L. Preston** .... (314) 244-2410

Deputy Clerk-in-Charge **Maureen Watz Gornik** .... (651) 848-1301
500 Federal Courts Building, 316 N. Robert St., St. Paul, MN 55101
E-mail: maureen_gornik@ca8.uscourts.gov
Education: Notre Dame 1983 BA, 1986 JD

Senior Staff Attorney **Kim Patricia Jones** .... (314) 244-2889
Education: Harvard 1980 AB; Michigan 1984 JD Fax: (314) 244-2885

Supervisory Staff Attorney **Beth Dockery** .... (314) 244-2889
E-mail: Beth_Dockery@ca8.uscourts.gov Fax: (314) 244-2885
Education: Saint Louis U 1973 AB, 1977 JD

Supervisory Staff Attorney **Michele Long** .... (314) 244-2889
E-mail: Michele_Long@ca8.uscourts.gov Fax: (314) 244-2885
Education: Eastern Michigan 1978 BA; Saint Louis U 1984 JD

Supervisory Staff Attorney **Julie Tang** .... (314) 244-2889
E-mail: julie_tang@ca8.uscourts.gov Fax: (314) 244-2885

Circuit Librarian **Eric W. Brust** .... (314) 244-2665
U.S. Courthouse, Room 22.300 Fax: (314) 244-2676
E-mail: eric_brust@ca8.uscourts.gov

Chief Settlement Director **John H. Martin** .... (312) 244-2499
Education: Saint Louis U 1965 JD

Chambers of Chief Judge William Jay Riley

Roman L. Hruska Courthouse, 111 South 18th Plaza, Suite 4303, Omaha, NE 68102-1322
Tel: (402) 661-7575 Fax: (402) 661-7574
E-mail: william_riley@ca8.uscourts.gov

William Jay Riley
Chief Judge

Date of Birth: 1947
Education: Nebraska 1969 BA, 1972 JD
Began Service: August 16, 2001
Appointed By: President George W. Bush
Political Affiliation: Republican

Academic: Adjunct Professor, Trial Practice, College of Law, University of Nebraska-Lincoln

Clerkships: Law Clerk The Honorable Donald P. Lay, United States Court of Appeals for the Eighth Circuit (1972-1973)

Legal Practice: Associate, Fitzgerald, Schorr, Barmettler & Brennan, PC, LLO (1973-1979); Partner, Fitzgerald, Schorr, Barmettler & Brennan, PC, LLO (1979-2001)

Current Memberships: American Board of Trial Advocates; American College of Trial Lawyers

Staff

Law Clerk **Katherine Powers** .... (402) 661-7577
Began Service: August 2015
Term Expires: August 2017
E-mail: katherine_powers@ca8.uscourts.gov

Law Clerk **Philip Sancilio** .... (402) 661-7577
Began Service: August 2015
Term Expires: August 2017
E-mail: philip_sancilio@ca8.uscourts.gov

Law Clerk **Alexandria Shasteen** .... (402) 661-7577
Began Service: August 2015
Term Expires: August 2017
E-mail: alexandria_shasteen@ca8.uscourts.gov

Career Law Clerk **Jeffrey Mindrup** .... (402) 661-7579
Began Service: August 16, 2010
E-mail: jeffrey_mindrup@ca8.uscourts.gov

Administrative Assistant **Kristine Schneiss** .... (402) 661-7575
E-mail: kschneiss@ce8.uscourts.gov

Chambers of Circuit Judge James B. Loken

U.S. Courthouse, 300 South Fourth Street, 11W, Minneapolis, MN 55415
Tel: (612) 664-5810 Fax: (612) 664-5817

James B. Loken
Circuit Judge

Date of Birth: 1940
Education: Wisconsin 1962 BS; Harvard 1965 LLB
Began Service: 1991
Appointed By: President George H.W. Bush

Clerkships: Law Clerk The Honorable J. Edward Lumbard, United States Court of Appeals for the Second Circuit (1965-1966); Law Clerk The Honorable Byron R. White, Supreme Court of the United States (1966-1967)

Government: General Counsel, President's Committee on Consumer Interests, Executive Office of the President (1970); Staff Assistant to the President, Executive Office of the President, Richard M. Nixon Administration (1970-1972)

Legal Practice: Associate, Faegre & Benson LLP (1967-1970); Partner, Faegre & Benson LLP (1972-1990)

Current Memberships: Hennepin County Bar Association; Minnesota State Bar Association

Staff

Law Clerk **Rachel Kitze** .... (612) 664-5810
E-mail: rachel_kitze@ca8.uscourts.gov

(continued on next page)

Chambers of Circuit Judge James B. Loken *continued*

Law Clerk **Neil Nandi** .... (612) 664-5810
E-mail: neil_nandi@ca8.uscourts.gov
Law Clerk **William Thomson** .... (612) 664-5810
Judicial Assistant **Tammy Haglin** .... (612) 664-5810
E-mail: tammy_haglin@ca8.uscourts.gov

Chambers of Circuit Judge Roger L. Wollman

315 U.S. Courthouse, 400 South Phillips Avenue,
Sioux Falls, SD 57104-6851
Tel: (605) 330-6680
E-mail: roger_wollman@ca8.uscourts.gov

Roger L. Wollman
Circuit Judge

Date of Birth: 1934
Education: Tabor 1957 BA; South Dakota 1962 JD; Harvard 1964 LLM
Began Service: September 6, 1985
Appointed By: President Ronald Reagan

Clerkships: Law Clerk The Honorable George T. Mickelson, United States District Court for the District of South Dakota (1962-1963)

Judicial: Associate Justice, South Dakota Supreme Court (1971-1985); Member, Judicial Conference of the United States (1999-2002)

Legal Practice: Associate, Law Office of Douglas W. Bantz (1964-1971)

Military Service: United States Army (1957-1959)

Current Memberships: State Bar of South Dakota

Staff

Law Clerk **Garrett F. Mannchen** .... (605) 330-6680
Began Service: August 2015
Term Expires: August 2016
E-mail: garrett_mannchen@ca8.uscourts.gov
Career Law Clerk **Amy N. Softich** .... (605) 848-1375
E-mail: amy_softich@ca8.uscourts.gov
Education: Minnesota 2005 JD
Judicial Assistant **Evelyn M. Carlson** .... (605) 330-6680

Chambers of Circuit Judge Diana E. Murphy

U.S. Courthouse, 300 South Fourth Street, 11E,
Minneapolis, MN 55415-2249
Tel: (612) 664-5820 Fax: (612) 664-5821
E-mail: Judge_Diana_Murphy@ca8.uscourts.gov

Diana E. Murphy
Circuit Judge

Date of Birth: 1934
Education: Minnesota 1954 BA, 1974 JD
Began Service: October 11, 1994
Appointed By: President William J. Clinton

Affiliation: Trustee, Board of Trustees, University of St. Thomas

Judicial: Judge, Hennepin County Municipal Court (1976-1978); Judge, Minnesota District Court, Fourth Judicial District (1978-1980); Judge, United States District Court for the District of Minnesota (1980-1994); Chief Judge, United States District Court for the District of Minnesota (1992-1994); Chair, United States Sentencing Commission (1999-2004)

Legal Practice: Associate, Lindquist & Vennum PLLP (1974-1976)

Current Memberships: American Bar Association; The American Law Institute; Federal Judges Association; Minnesota State Bar Association; Minnesota Women Lawyers; National Association of Women Judges

Staff

Law Clerk **Michael Biehl** .... (612) 664-5820
Began Service: August 2015
Term Expires: August 2016

Chambers of Circuit Judge Diana E. Murphy *continued*

Law Clerk **Sam Eisenberg** .... (612) 664-5820
Began Service: August 2015
Term Expires: August 2016
E-mail: sam_eisenberg@ca8.uscourts.gov
Law Clerk **Jake Vandelist** .... (612) 664-5820
Began Service: August 2015
Term Expires: August 2017
E-mail: jake_vandelist@ca8.uscourts.gov
Law Clerk **Irina Vaynerman** .... (612) 664-5820
Began Service: August 2015
Term Expires: August 2016
E-mail: irina_vaynerman@ca8.uscourts.gov
Judicial Assistant **Marilyn Neitz** .... (612) 664-5827 ext. 5827
E-mail: marilyn_neitz@ca8.uscourts.gov

Chambers of Circuit Judge Lavenski R. Smith

Richard Sheppard Arnold U.S. Courthouse, 600 West Capitol Avenue,
Suite A502, Little Rock, AR 72201
Tel: (501) 324-7310 Fax: (501) 324-7305

Lavenski R. Smith
Circuit Judge

Date of Birth: 1958
Education: Arkansas 1981 BA, 1987 JD
Began Service: July 19, 2002
Appointed By: President George W. Bush

Academic: Assistant Professor, John Brown University (1994-1996)

Government: Regulatory Liaison, Office of the Governor, State of Arkansas (1996-1997); Chairman, Public Service Commission, State of Arkansas (1997-1999)

Judicial: Associate Justice, Arkansas Supreme Court (1999-2000)

Legal Practice: Law Clerk, Hall, Wright & Morris (1985-1987); Staff Attorney, Ozark Legal Services (1987-1991); Sole Proprietor, Smith Law Office (1991-1994)

Staff

Law Clerk **Jonathan Hornok** .... (501) 324-7310
Began Service: September 2015
Term Expires: September 2016
E-mail: jonathan_hornok@ca8.uscourts.gov
Law Clerk **Josh Turner** .... (501) 324-7310
Began Service: September 2015
Term Expires: September 2016
Career Law Clerk **Tiffany Brown** .... (501) 324-7310
Began Service: 2008
E-mail: tiffany_brown@ca8.uscourts.gov
Education: Arkansas (Little Rock) 2002 BA, 2005 JD
Judicial Administrator **Girtrude Simmons** .... (501) 324-7310
E-mail: girtrude_simmons@ca8.uscourts.gov
Judicial Assistant **J. Diann Duty** .... (501) 324-7310
E-mail: diann_duty@ca8.uscourts.gov

Chambers of Circuit Judge Steven M. Colloton

110 East Court Avenue, Suite 461, Des Moines, IA 50309
Tel: (515) 284-6356 Fax: (515) 284-6353

Steven M. Colloton
Circuit Judge

Date of Birth: January 9, 1963
Education: Princeton 1985 BA; Yale 1988 JD
Began Service: September 30, 2003
Appointed By: President George W. Bush

Staff

Law Clerk **Kyle Essley** .... (515) 284-6356
Began Service: September 2015
Term Expires: September 2016
E-mail: kyle_essley@ca8.uscourts.gov

Chambers of Circuit Judge Steven M. Colloton *continued*

Law Clerk **Daniel Khay** . . . . (515) 284-6356
Began Service: September 2015
Term Expires: September 2016
E-mail: daniel_khay@ca8.uscourts.gov

Law Clerk **Mark Kubisch** . . . . (515) 284-6356
Began Service: September 2015
Term Expires: September 2016
E-mail: mark_kubisch@ca8.uscourts.gov

Law Clerk **Abigail Molitor** . . . . (515) 284-6356
Began Service: September 2015
Term Expires: September 2016
E-mail: abigail_molitor@ca8.uscourts.gov

Judicial Assistant **Tammy Courter** . . . . (515) 284-6356
E-mail: tammy_courter@ca8.uscourts.gov

Chambers of Circuit Judge Raymond W. Gruender III

111 South Tenth Street, Suite 23.365, St. Louis, MO 63102-1116
Tel: (314) 244-2820

Raymond W. Gruender III
Circuit Judge

Date of Birth: 1963
Education: Washington U (MO) 1984 BA, 1987 MBA, 1987 JD
Began Service: June 28, 2004
Appointed By: President George W. Bush

Government: U.S. Attorney, Eastern District of Missouri, United States Attorney's Office, United States Department of Justice, George H.W. Bush Administration (1990-1994)

Legal Practice: Associate, Lewis, Rice & Fingersh, L.C. (1987-1990); Partner, Thompson Coburn LLP (1994-2000)

Staff

Judicial Assistant **Nikki Penberthy** . . . . (314) 244-2820
E-mail: nikki_penberthy@ca8.uscourts.gov

Chambers of Circuit Judge Duane Benton

400 East Ninth Street, Suite 1020, Kansas City, MO 64106
Tel: (816) 512-5815 Fax: (816) 512-5829
E-mail: duane_benton@ca8.uscourts.gov

Duane Benton
Circuit Judge

Date of Birth: 1950
Education: Northwestern 1972 BA; Yale 1975 JD; Memphis State 1979 MBA; Virginia 1995 LLM
Began Service: July 8, 2004
Appointed By: President George W. Bush

Academic: Adjunct Professor, Westminster College; Adjunct Professor, School of Law, University of Missouri, Columbia

Government: Administrative Assistant (R-MO, District 8), Office of Representative R. Wendell Bailey, United States House of Representatives (1980-1982); Director, Revenue Department, State of Missouri (1989-1991)

Judicial: Judge, Missouri Supreme Court (1991-2004); Chief Justice, Missouri Supreme Court (1997-1999)

Military Service: United States Navy (1975-1979); Judge Advocate General CAPT, United States Navy Reserve, United States Department of the Navy (1979-2002)

Current Memberships: American Bar Association; American Institute of Certified Public Accountants; The Missouri Bar; Missouri Society of Certified Public Accountants

Staff

Career Law Clerk and Chief of Staff **Elizabeth Healey** . . . (816) 512-5815
E-mail: elizabeth_healey@ca8.uscourts.gov
Education: Missouri BA, 1986 JD

Chambers of Circuit Judge Bobby E. Shepherd

Thomas F. Eagleton U.S. Courthouse, 111 South Tenth Street, St. Louis, MO 63102
Tel: (870) 863-3173

Bobby E. Shepherd
Circuit Judge

Date of Birth: 1951
Education: Ouachita Baptist 1973 BA; Arkansas 1976 JD
Began Service: October 2006
Appointed By: President George W. Bush

Judicial: Circuit-Chancery Judge, Arkansas 13th Judicial District (1991-1993); Magistrate Judge, United States District Court for the Western District of Arkansas (1993-2006)

Legal Practice: Private Practice (1976-1990)

Military Service: United States Army Reserve, United States Department of the Army (1976-1981)

Current Memberships: Arkansas Bar Association; Federal Magistrate Judges Association; Union County Bar Association

Staff

Law Clerk **Britta Stamps** . . . . (870) 863-3173
E-mail: samantha_leflar@ca8.uscourts.gov

Law Clerk **Robin Wright** . . . . (870) 863-3173
E-mail: robin_wright@ca8.uscourts.gov

Law Clerk **Katherine Wutchiett** . . . . (870) 863-3173

Career Law Clerk **Spencer Singleton** . . . . (870) 863-3173
E-mail: spencer_singleton@ca8.uscourts.gov
Education: Arkansas (Little Rock) 2001 JD

Judicial Assistant **Becky Kaldem** . . . . (870) 863-3173
E-mail: becky_kaldem@ca8.uscourts.gov
Education: Arkansas Tech 1976 BA

Chambers of Circuit Judge Jane Kelly

111 Seventh Avenue SE, Box 20, Cedar Rapids, IA 52401
Tel: (319) 423-6110
E-mail: jane_kelly@ca8.uscourts.gov

Jane Kelly
Circuit Judge

Education: Duke 1987 BA; Harvard 1991 JD
Began Service: April 25, 2013
Appointed By: President Barack Obama

Clerkships: Law Clerk, Chambers of Judge David R. Hansen, United States Court of Appeals for the Eighth Circuit

Chambers of Senior Judge Myron H. Bright

340 Quentin N. Burdick U.S. Courthouse, 655 North First Avenue, Fargo, ND 58102-4952
Tel: (701) 297-7260 Fax: (701) 297-7265
E-mail: judge_myron_bright@ca8.uscourts.gov

Myron H. Bright
Senior Judge

Date of Birth: 1919
Education: Minnesota 1941 BSL, 1947 JD
Began Service: 1968
Appointed By: President Lyndon B. Johnson
Political Affiliation: Democrat

Academic: Distinguished Professor of Law, Saint Louis University (1985-1990); Professor Emeritus, School of Law, Saint Louis University (1990-1995)

Legal Practice: Partner, Wattam, Vogel, Vogel, Bright and Peterson (1947-1968)

Military Service: Captain, United States Army Air Corps (1942-1946)

(continued on next page)

Chambers of Senior Judge Myron H. Bright *continued*

Current Memberships: American Bar Association; The Bar Association of Metropolitan St. Louis; Cass County Bar Association; Federal Judges Association; State Bar Association of North Dakota

Staff

Law Clerk **Elise Larson** .... (701) 297-7263
Began Service: February 2015
Term Expires: August 2016
E-mail: elise_larson@ca8.uscourts.gov
Education: Minnesota 2012 JD

Executive Assistant **Lana Schultz** .... (701) 297-7261
E-mail: lana_schultz@ca8.uscourts.gov
Education: Moorhead State 1994 BS

Chambers of Senior Judge Pasco M. Bowman II

10-50 Charles Evans Whittaker U.S. Courthouse, 400 East Ninth Street, Kansas City, MO 64106
Tel: (816) 512-5800 Fax: (816) 512-5814

Pasco M. Bowman II
Senior Judge

Date of Birth: 1933
Education: Bridgewater Col 1955 BA; NYU 1958 JD; Virginia 1986 LLM
Began Service: August 1, 1983
Appointed By: President Ronald Reagan

Academic: Professor of Law, The University of Georgia (1964-1970); Dean and Professor of Law, Wake Forest University (1970-1978); Visiting Professor of Law, University of Virginia (1978-1979); Dean and Professor of Law, University of Missouri-Kansas City (1979-1983)

Judicial: Circuit Judge, United States Court of Appeals for the Eighth Circuit (2003)

Legal Practice: Associate, Cravath, Swaine & Moore LLP (1958-1964)

Military Service: United States Army Reserve, United States Department of the Army (1959-1984)

Current Memberships: The Missouri Bar; New York State Bar Association; State Bar of Georgia

Staff

Career Law Clerk **Linda Dees** .... (816) 512-5800
E-mail: linda_dees@ca8.uscourts.gov
Education: Missouri 1976 BS;
Missouri (Kansas City) 1989 JD

Judicial Assistant **Arla Woerth** .... (816) 512-5800
E-mail: arla_woerth@ca8.uscourts.gov

Chambers of Senior Judge C. Arlen Beam

435 Federal Building, 100 Centennial Mall North, Lincoln, NE 68508
Tel: (402) 437-1600 Fax: (402) 437-1607

C. Arlen Beam
Senior Judge

Date of Birth: 1930
Education: Nebraska 1951 BS, 1965 JD
Began Service: November 9, 1987
Appointed By: President Ronald Reagan
Political Affiliation: Republican

Government: Staff Member, United States House of Representatives (1971-1973)

Judicial: Judge, United States District Court for the District of Nebraska (1982-1987)

Legal Practice: Partner, Chambers, Holland, Dudgeon & Beam (1968-1971); Partner, Knudson, Berkheimer, Beam, Richardson & Endacott (1971-1981)

Military Service: United States Army (1951-1953); United States Army Reserve, United States Department of the Army (1953-1964)

Chambers of Senior Judge C. Arlen Beam *continued*

Current Memberships: Lincoln Bar Association; Nebraska State Bar Association; Omaha Bar Association

Staff

Law Clerk **Nathan Clark** .... (402) 437-1600
Began Service: September 2015
Term Expires: September 2016
E-mail: nathan_clark@ca8.uscourts.gov

Law Clerk **Jacquelyn Swanner** .... (402) 437-1600
Began Service: September 2015
Term Expires: September 2016
E-mail: jacquelyn_swanner@ca8.uscourts.gov

Career Law Clerk **Kris Brenneis** .... (402) 437-1605
Education: Nebraska JD

Career Law Clerk **Amy Vyhlidal** .... (402) 437-1604
E-mail: amy_vyhlidal@ca8.uscourts.gov
Education: Nebraska JD

Administrative Assistant **Gini Russell** .... (402) 437-1600
E-mail: gini_russell@ca8.uscourts.gov

Chambers of Senior Judge Michael J. Melloy

111 Seventh Avenue SE, Box 22, Cedar Rapids, IA 52401-2101
Tel: (319) 423-6080 Fax: (319) 363-6363
E-mail: michael_melloy@ca8.uscourts.gov

Michael J. Melloy
Senior Judge

Date of Birth: 1948
Education: Loras 1970 BA; Iowa 1974 JD
Began Service: February 26, 2002
Appointed By: President George W. Bush

Current Memberships: The Dean Mason Ladd American Inn of Court, The American Inns of Court; Dubuque County Bar Association; Iowa State Bar Association; Linn County Bar Association

Staff

Law Clerk **Roseann Romano** .... (319) 423-6080
Began Service: August 2015
Term Expires: August 2016

Law Clerk **David Waterman** .... (319) 423-6080
Began Service: August 2015
Term Expires: August 2016
E-mail: david_waterman@ca8.uscourts.gov

Career Law Clerk **Douglas Stilwell** .... (319) 363-7580
Education: Iowa 1998 JD

Judicial Assistant **Anita Wolrab** .... (319) 363-7580
E-mail: anita_wolrab@ca8.uscourts.gov

Chambers of Senior Judge Kermit Edward Bye

Quentin N. Burdick U.S. Courthouse, 655 North First Avenue, Chambers 330, Fargo, ND 58102-4952
Tel: (701) 297-7270 Fax: (701) 297-7275
E-mail: kermit_bye@ca8.uscourts.gov

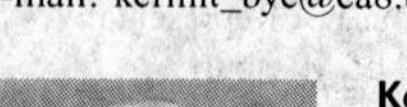

Kermit Edward Bye
Senior Judge

Date of Birth: 1937
Education: North Dakota 1959 BSBA, 1962 JD
Began Service: April 22, 2000
Appointed By: President William J. Clinton
Political Affiliation: Democrat

Current Memberships: American Bar Foundation; American Bar Association; Federal Judges Association; State Bar Association of North Dakota

Chambers of Senior Judge Kermit Edward Bye *continued*

Staff
Law Clerk **Hannah C. Haksgaard** .... (701) 297-7274
Began Service: August 2013
Term Expires: August 2016
E-mail: hannah_haksgaard@ca8.uscourts.gov
Law Clerk **Ross Pearson** .... (701) 297-7273
Began Service: August 2015
Term Expires: August 2016
E-mail: ross_pearson@ca8.uscourts.gov
Law Clerk **Mikala Steenholdt** .... (701) 297-7276
Began Service: August 6, 2015
Term Expires: August 2016
E-mail: mikala_steenholdt@ca8.uscourts.gov
Career Law Clerk **James E. Nicolai** .... (701) 297-7272
E-mail: jim_nicolai@ca8.uscourts.gov
Education: North Dakota 1990 JD
Judicial Assistant **Zue Zan Hanna** .... (701) 297-7270
E-mail: zhanna@ce8.uscourts.gov
Education: North Dakota 1982 BSBA

United States Bankruptcy Appellate Panel for the Eighth Circuit

Thomas F. Eagleton U.S. Courthouse, 111 South Tenth Street, Suite 24.306, St. Louis, MO 63102
Tel: (314) 244-2430 Fax: (314) 244-2780
Internet: www.ca8.uscourts.gov

Number of Judgeships: 6

Court Staff
Bankruptcy Appellate Panel Clerk **Michael E. Gans** ..... (314) 244-2430
E-mail: michael_gans@ca8.uscourts.gov
Bankruptcy Appellate Panel Coordinator
Cindy Harrison .... (314) 244-2430
E-mail: cindy_harrison@ca8.uscourts.gov
Education: Saint Louis U 1981 BSSW

Chambers of Chief Bankruptcy Judge Arthur Federman

6552 Charles Evans Whittaker U.S. Courthouse, 400 East Ninth Street, Kansas City, MO 64106
Tel: (816) 512-1910 Fax: (816) 512-1923
E-mail: arthur.federman@mow.uscourts.gov

Arthur Federman
Chief Bankruptcy Judge

Date of Birth: 1951
Education: Kansas 1973 BA; Missouri (Kansas City) 1976 JD
Began Service: December 18, 1989
Term Expires: December 17, 2017

Staff
Career Law Clerk **Erica Garrett** .... (816) 512-1913
E-mail: erica_garrett@mow.uscourts.gov
Education: Missouri (Kansas City) 1993 JD
Judicial Assistant **Joan D. Brown** .... (816) 512-1911
E-mail: joan_brown@mow.uscourts.gov
Courtroom Deputy **Sharon Stanley** .... (816) 512-1924

Chambers of Bankruptcy Judge Robert J. Kressel

U.S. Courthouse, 300 South Fourth Street, 8 W, Minneapolis, MN 55415
Tel: (612) 664-5250

Robert J. Kressel
Bankruptcy Judge

Date of Birth: 1947
Education: Notre Dame 1969 AB; Harvard 1972 JD
Began Service: 1996

Current Memberships: Federal Bar Association; National Conference of Bankruptcy Judges

Staff
Law Clerk **Natasha Wells** .... (612) 664-5250
Began Service: August 2015
Term Expires: August 2016

Chambers of Bankruptcy Judge Barry S. Schermer

Thomas F. Eagleton U.S. Courthouse, 111 South Tenth Street, St. Louis, MO 63102
Tel: (314) 244-4500 Fax: (314) 244-4535

Barry S. Schermer
Bankruptcy Judge

Date of Birth: 1947
Education: Washington U (MO) 1973 JD
Began Service: 1997
Term Expires: September 10, 2017

Academic: Adjunct Professor, Washington University School of Law

Staff
Law Clerk **Bryan Uelk** .... (314) 244-4531
Education: Washington U (MO) 2014 JD
Career Law Clerk **Emily K. Cohen** .... (314) 244-4532
Education: Washington U (MO) 2000 JD

Chambers of Bankruptcy Judge Thomas L. Saladino

463 Federal Building, 100 Centennial Mall North, Lincoln, NE 68508
Tel: (402) 661-7444

Thomas L. Saladino
Bankruptcy Judge

Began Service: 2009

Staff
Judicial Assistant **Cheryl Belmont** .... (402) 437-1620
Career Law Clerk **Joan Kramer** .... (402) 437-1616
Education: Creighton 1988 BA, 1991 JD

Chambers of Bankruptcy Judge Charles L. Nail Jr.

Federal Building, 225 South Pierre Street, Room 211, Pierre, SD 57501
Tel: (605) 945-4490 Fax: (605) 945-4491

Charles L. Nail, Jr.
Bankruptcy Judge

Education: South Dakota BS; Minnesota 1982 JD

Chambers of Bankruptcy Judge Anita L. Shodeen
U.S. Courthouse Annex, 110 East Court Avenue, Room 300,
Des Moines, IA 50309
Tel: (515) 284-6118
E-mail: anita_shodeen@iasb.uscourts.gov

Anita L. Shodeen
Bankruptcy Judge

Education: Drake JD

United States Court of Appeals for the Ninth Circuit
James R. Browning U.S. Courthouse, 95 Seventh Street,
San Francisco, CA 94103-1526
P.O. Box 193939, San Francisco, CA 94119-3939
Tel: (415) 355-8000 (General Information)
Tel: (415) 355-7830 (Docketing-Civil)
Tel: (415) 355-7840 (Docketing-Criminal)
Tel: (415) 355-7900 (Mediation)
Internet: www.ca9.uscourts.gov

Number of Judgeships: 29

Supreme Court Justice: Associate Justice Anthony M. Kennedy

Areas Covered: Alaska, Arizona, California, Guam, Hawaii, Idaho, Montana, Nevada, Northern Mariana Islands, Oregon and Washington

Court Staff
Circuit and Court of Appeals Executive
Cathy A. Catterson . . . . (415) 355-8800
E-mail: cathy_catterson@ca9.uscourts.gov
Clerk of the Court **Molly C. Dwyer** . . . . (415) 355-8000
E-mail: molly_dwyer@ca9.uscourts.gov
Deputy Circuit Executive **(Vacant)** . . . . (415) 355-8970
Assistant Circuit Executive - Automation **Don Vincent** . . . (415) 355-8990
E-mail: don_vincent@ca9.uscourts.gov
Assistant Circuit Executive - Court Management and Research **Robert Rucker** . . . . (415) 355-8940
E-mail: bob_rucker@ca9.uscourts.gov
Assistant Circuit Executive - Human Resources
Tina Brier . . . . (415) 355-8910
E-mail: tina_brier@ca9.uscourts.gov
Assistant Circuit Executive - Judicial Conference and Education **Renée Lorda** . . . . (415) 355-8920
E-mail: renee_lorda@ca9.uscourts.gov
Assistant Circuit Executive - Legal Affairs
Marcy Mills . . . . (415) 355-8980
E-mail: marcy_mills@ca9.uscourts.gov
Assistant Circuit Executive - Space and Facilities
Clifford Harlan . . . . (415) 355-8954
E-mail: cliff_harlan@ca9.uscourts.gov
Assistant Circuit Executive - Public Information
David Madden . . . . (415) 355-8930
E-mail: david_madden@ca9.uscourts.gov
Procurement Supervisor **Meredith Blain** . . . . (415) 355-8051
E-mail: meredith_blain@ca9.uscourts.gov
Chief Deputy-Legal **Lisa Fitzgerald** . . . . (415) 355-7954
E-mail: lisa_fitzgerald@ca9.uscourts.gov
Chief Deputy-Operations **(Vacant)** . . . . (415) 355-7990
Senior Deputy Clerk **James E. "Jim" Hochstadt** . . . . (415) 355-8297
E-mail: jim_hochstadt@ca9.uscourts.gov
Senior Deputy Clerk, Pasadena **Eve Fisher** . . . . (626) 229-7250
Richard H. Chambers U.S. Court of Appeals Bldg.,
125 S. Grand Ave., Pasadena, CA 91105-1652
P.O. Box 91510, Pasadena, CA 91109-1510
E-mail: eve_fisher@ca9.uscourts.gov
Senior Deputy Clerk, Portland **Robert M. Walch** . . . . (503) 833-5305
Pioneer Courthouse, 700 SW 6th Avenue,
Suite 110, Portland, OR 97204-1434
E-mail: robert_walch@ca9.uscourts.gov
Deputy Clerk, Seattle **Stacy Lee Brebner** . . . . (206) 224-2200
US Court of Appeals, 1010 Fifth Avenue, Fax: (206) 224-2201
Suite 430, Seattle, WA 98104
E-mail: stacy_brebner@ca9.uscourts.gov

United States Court of Appeals for the Ninth Circuit *continued*

Chief Circuit Mediator **Claudia Bernard** . . . . (415) 355-7900
E-mail: claudia_bernard@ca9.uscourts.gov
Circuit Mediator **Roxane Ashe** . . . . (415) 355-7900
E-mail: roxane_ashe@ca9.uscourts.gov
Circuit Mediator **Margaret Corrigan** . . . . (415) 355-7900
E-mail: margaret_corrigan@ca9.uscourts.gov
Circuit Mediator **Lisa Jaye** . . . . (415) 355-7900
E-mail: lisa_evans@ca9.uscourts.gov
Circuit Mediator **Ann Julius** . . . . (415) 355-7900
E-mail: ann_julius@ca9.uscourts.gov
Circuit Mediator **Stephen Liacouras** . . . . (415) 355-7900
E-mail: stephen_liacouras@ca9.uscourts.gov
Circuit Mediator **C. Lewis Ross** . . . . (415) 355-7900
Circuit Mediator **Peter Sherwood** . . . . (415) 355-7900
E-mail: peter_sherwood@ca9.uscourts.gov
Circuit Mediator, Seattle **Chris Goelz** . . . . (206) 224-2320
1010 Fifth Avenue, Suite 730, Seattle, WA 98104
E-mail: chris_goelz@ca9.uscourts.gov
Mediation Administrator **Mary G. Schlepp** . . . . (415) 355-7900
E-mail: mary_schlepp@ca9.uscourts.gov
Mediation Assistant **Lynn Warton** . . . . (206) 224-2320
1010 Fifth Avenue, Suite 730, Seattle, WA 98104
E-mail: lynn_warton@ca9.uscourts.gov
Information Technology Manager **Ryan Means** . . . . (415) 355-7890
E-mail: ryan_means@ca9.uscourts.gov
Personnel Officer **Lisa Lauer** . . . . (415) 355-7868
Secretary **Joan E. Gee** . . . . (415) 355-8962
E-mail: joan_gee@ca9.uscourts.gov
Case Administration Supervisor **Jennifer Flowers** . . . . (415) 355-7830
E-mail: jennifer_flowers@ca9.uscourts.gov
Circuit Librarian **Eric Wade** . . . . (415) 355-8650
Fax: (415) 355-8696
Lead Court Security Officer **Andrew Ballantyne** . . . . (626) 229-7160

Chambers of Chief Judge Sidney R. Thomas
P.O. Box 31478, Billings, MT 59107-1478
Tel: (406) 373-3200 Fax: (406) 373-3250
E-mail: judge_sr_thomas@ca9.uscourts.gov

Sidney R. Thomas
Chief Judge

Date of Birth: 1953
Education: Montana State 1975 BA; Montana 1978 JD
Began Service: March 11, 1996
Appointed By: President William J. Clinton

Current Memberships: American Bar Association; Federal Judges Association; State Bar of Montana; Yellowstone County Bar Association

Staff
Law Clerk **Zachary Abrahamson** . . . . (406) 373-3206
Began Service: August 2015
Term Expires: August 2016
E-mail: zachary_abrahamson@ca9.uscourts.gov
Law Clerk **Caitlinrose Fisher** . . . . (406) 373-3206
Began Service: August 2015
Term Expires: August 2016
E-mail: caitlinrose_fisher@ca9.uscourts.gov
Law Clerk **Raphael Graybill** . . . . (406) 373-3206
Began Service: August 2015
Term Expires: August 2016
E-mail: raphael_graybill@ca9.uscourts.gov
Law Clerk **Catriona Lavery** . . . . (406) 373-3206
Began Service: August 2015
Term Expires: August 2016
E-mail: catriona_lavery@ca9.uscourts.gov
Law Clerk **Alejandra Salinas** . . . . (406) 373-3206
Began Service: August 2015
Term Expires: August 2016
E-mail: alejandra_salinas@ca9.uscourts.gov
Judicial Assistant **Susan Ando** . . . . (406) 373-3200
E-mail: susan_ando@ca9.uscourts.gov

Chambers of Circuit Judge Alex Kozinski

125 South Grand Avenue, Pasadena, CA 91105
Tel: (626) 229-7150 Fax: (626) 229-7444
E-mail: kozinski@usc.edu

Alex Kozinski
Circuit Judge

Date of Birth: 1950
Education: UCLA 1972 AB, 1975 JD
Began Service: November 7, 1985
Appointed By: President Ronald Reagan

Staff

Law Clerk **James Dawson** . . . . . (626) 229-7154
Began Service: May 2015
Term Expires: May 2016
Education: Yale 2014 JD

Law Clerk **Derek Fischer** . . . . . (626) 229-7156
Began Service: June 2015
Term Expires: June 2016
Education: Columbia 2015 JD

Law Clerk **Francisco Morales** . . . . . (626) 229-7153
Began Service: May 2015
Term Expires: May 2016
Education: Pennsylvania 2013 JD

Law Clerk **Anuradha Sivaram** . . . . . (626) 229-7155
Began Service: June 2015
Term Expires: June 2016
Education: Berkeley Law 2014 JD

Secretary **Kathi Davis** . . . . . (626) 229-7151
E-mail: kathi_davis@ca9.uscourts.gov

Administrative Assistant **Donna Salter** . . . . . (626) 229-7150

Chambers of Circuit Judge Harry Pregerson

21800 Oxnard Street, Suite 1140, Woodland Hills, CA 91367-3633
Tel: (818) 710-7791 Fax: (818) 710-7816
E-mail: harry_pregerson@ca9.uscourts.gov

Harry Pregerson
Circuit Judge

Date of Birth: 1923
Education: UCLA 1947 BA; Boalt Hall 1950 LLB
Began Service: 1979
Appointed By: President Jimmy Carter

Judicial: Judge, Los Angeles Municipal Court (1965-1966); Judge, California Superior Court, Los Angeles County (1966-1967); Judge, United States District Court for the Central District of California (1967-1979)

Legal Practice: I. H. Prinzmetal (1951); Private Practice (1951); Morris D. Coppersmith (1952); Clifford Hemmerling (1953); Private Practice (1953); Partner, William M. Costley (1953-1965)

Military Service: United States Navy (1943-1944); United States Marine Corps Reserve (1944-1946)

Current Memberships: American Bar Association; Los Angeles County Bar Association; San Fernando Valley Bar Association; State Bar of California

Staff

Law Clerk **Amanda Carlin** . . . . . (818) 710-7791
Began Service: August 2015
Term Expires: August 2016
E-mail: amanda_carlin@ca9.uscourts.gov

Law Clerk **Jamie Hoffman** . . . . . (818) 710-3627
Term Expires: August 2016
E-mail: jamie_hoffman@ca9.uscourts.gov
Education: UCLA JD

Chambers of Circuit Judge Harry Pregerson *continued*

Law Clerk **Elena Sadowsky** . . . . . (818) 710-3626
Began Service: August 2014
Term Expires: August 2016
E-mail: elena_sadowsky@ca9.uscourts.gov

Law Clerk **Steven Shafer** . . . . . (818) 710-7791
Began Service: August 2015
Term Expires: August 2016
E-mail: steven_shafer@ca9.uscourts.gov

Law Clerk **Lynn Ta** . . . . . (818) 710-7791
Began Service: August 2015
Term Expires: August 2016
E-mail: lynn_ta@ca9.uscourts.gov

Judicial Assistant **Kathy Sistilli** . . . . . (818) 710-7791
E-mail: kathy_sistilli@ca9.uscourts.gov

Chambers of Circuit Judge Stephen Reinhardt

1747 U.S. Courthouse, 312 North Spring Street, Los Angeles, CA 90012
Tel: (213) 894-3639 Fax: (213) 894-0060
E-mail: Judge_Reinhardt@ca9.uscourts.gov

Stephen Reinhardt
Circuit Judge

Date of Birth: 1931
Education: Pomona 1951 BA; Yale 1954 LLB
Began Service: 1980
Appointed By: President Jimmy Carter
Political Affiliation: Democrat

Academic: Adjunct Professor, Loyola Law School, Loyola Marymount University

Clerkships: Law Clerk The Honorable Luther W. Youngdahl, United States District Court for the District of Minnesota (1955-1957)

Government: President, Board of Recreation and Park Commissioners, Department of Recreation and Parks, City of Los Angeles, California (1974-1976); President and Member, Board of Police Commissioners, Police Department, City of Los Angeles, California (1976-1980)

Legal Practice: Associate, O'Melveny & Myers (1957-1959); Partner, Fogel, Julber, Reinhardt, Rothschild & Feldman (1959-1980)

Military Service: United States Air Force (1954-1956)

Current Memberships: American Bar Association; Los Angeles County Bar Association; State Bar of California

Staff

Law Clerk **Edward Fox** . . . . . (213) 894-5218
Began Service: June 2015
Term Expires: June 2016
E-mail: edward_fox@ca9.uscourts.gov

Law Clerk **Andrew Kushner** . . . . . (213) 894-5252
Began Service: June 2015
Term Expires: June 2016
E-mail: andrew_kushner@ca9.uscourts.gov

Law Clerk **Casey Raymond** . . . . . (213) 894-5252
Began Service: August 2015
Term Expires: August 2016
E-mail: casey_raymond@ca9.uscourts.gov

Law Clerk **Jennifer Utrecht** . . . . . (213) 894-5263
Began Service: August 2015
Term Expires: August 2016
E-mail: jennifer_utrecht@ca9.uscourts.gov
Education: Michigan 2014 JD

Judicial Assistant **Aneita Rodriguez** . . . . . (213) 894-3639
E-mail: aneita_rodriguez@ca9.uscourts.gov

Chambers of Circuit Judge Diarmuid F. O'Scannlain

The Pioneer Courthouse, 700 SW 6th Avenue, Suite 313,
Portland, OR 97204-1396
Tel: (503) 833-5380 Fax: (503) 833-5390
E-mail: diarmuid_o'scannlain@ca9.uscourts.gov

Diarmuid F. O'Scannlain
Circuit Judge

Date of Birth: 1937
Education: St John's U (NY) 1957 BA; Harvard 1963 JD; Virginia 1992 LLM; Notre Dame 2002 LLD; Lewis & Clark 2003 LLD
Began Service: September 26, 1986
Appointed By: President Ronald Reagan
Political Affiliation: Republican

Academic: Adjunct Professor, Northwestern School of Law, Lewis & Clark College

Government: Deputy Attorney General, Office of the Attorney General, United States Department of Justice (1969-1971); Commissioner, Public Utility Commission, State of Oregon (1971-1973); Director, Department of Environmental Quality, State of Oregon (1973-1974); Consultant, Ronald Reagan Transition Team (1980-1981); Team Leader, Grace Commission (1982-1983); Chairman, Advisory Panel to the Secretary of Energy, United States Department of Energy (1983-1985)

Legal Practice: Tax Attorney, Tax Department, Standard Oil Company (1963-1965); Davies, Biggs, Strayer, Stoel & Boley (1965-1969); Partner, Keane, Harper, Pearlman & Copeland (1975-1978); Partner, Ragen, Roberts & O'Scannlain (1978-1986)

Military Service: United States Army Reserve, United States Department of the Army (1955-1978)

Current Memberships: American Bar Association; Federal Bar Association; Federal Judges Association; Harvard Law School Association; Multnomah County Bar Association; New York State Bar Association; Oregon State Bar; Ninth Judicial Circuit Historical Society, United States Court of Appeals for the Ninth Circuit; United States District Court of Oregon Historical Society

Staff

Law Clerk **Bill Lane** .... (503) 833-5380
Began Service: September 2015
Term Expires: August 2016
E-mail: bill_lane@ca9.uscourts.gov

Law Clerk **Grant Martinez** .... (503) 833-5380
Began Service: September 2015
Term Expires: August 2016
E-mail: grant_martinez@ca9.uscourts.gov

Law Clerk **Kevin Neylan** .... (503) 833-5380
Began Service: September 2015
Term Expires: August 2016
E-mail: kevin_neylan@ca9.uscourts.gov

Law Clerk **Mark Storslee** .... (503) 833-5380
Began Service: September 2015
Term Expires: August 2016
E-mail: mark_storslee@ca9.uscourts.gov

Judicial Assistant **Brenda J. Hart** .... (503) 833-5380
E-mail: brenda_hart@ca9.uscourts.gov

Career Law Clerk **John Meiser** .... (503) 833-5380
Began Service: June 2015
E-mail: john_meiser@ca9.uscourts.gov

Chambers of Circuit Judge Barry G. Silverman

Sandra Day O'Connor U.S. Courthouse, 401 West Washington Street, SPC 78, Phoenix, AZ 85003
Tel: (602) 322-7330 Fax: (602) 322-7339
E-mail: judge_silverman@ca9.uscourts.gov

Barry G. Silverman
Circuit Judge

Date of Birth: 1951
Education: Arizona State 1973 BA, 1976 JD
Began Service: February 1998
Appointed By: President William J. Clinton

Affiliation: Lecturer in Community Property, BAR/BRI Bar Review

Government: Court Commissioner, Superior Court of Arizona (1979-1984)

Judicial: Judge, Superior Court of Arizona (1984-1995); Magistrate Judge, United States District Court for the District of Arizona (1995-1998)

Current Memberships: American Bar Association; Federal Bar Association; Maricopa County Bar Association; State Bar of Arizona

Staff

Law Clerk **Raejean M. Battin** .... (602) 322-7330
Began Service: September 2015
Term Expires: September 2016
Education: Boston Col 1996 JD

Permanent Law Clerk **Denise K. McKinney** .... (602) 322-7330
E-mail: Denise_McKinney@ca9.uscourts.gov
Education: Arizona State 1989 JD

Secretary **Rebecca Arenas** .... (602) 322-7330
E-mail: rebecca_arenas@ca9.uscourts.gov

Chambers of Circuit Judge Susan P. Graber

Pioneer Courthouse, 700 SW 6th Avenue, Portland, OR 97204
Tel: (503) 833-5360 Fax: (503) 833-5370
E-mail: susan_graber@ca9.uscourts.gov

Susan P. Graber
Circuit Judge

Date of Birth: 1949
Education: Wellesley 1969 BA; Yale 1972 JD
Began Service: April 1, 1998
Appointed By: President William J. Clinton

Government: Assistant Attorney General, Bureau of Revenue, State of Oregon (1972-1974); Arbitrator, Fourth Judicial District, Oregon Circuit Court (1985-1988); Mediator, United States District Court for the District of Oregon (1986-1988)

Judicial: Judge Pro Tem, Multnomah County District Court (1983-1988); Judge, Oregon Court of Appeals (1988-1990); Justice, Oregon Supreme Court (1990-1998)

Current Memberships: American Bar Association; The American Law Institute

Staff

Law Clerk **Jacob Goldberg** .... (503) 833-5360
Began Service: September 2015
Term Expires: September 2016
E-mail: jacob_goldberg@ca9.uscourts.gov

Law Clerk **Franco Muzzio** .... (503) 833-5360
Began Service: September 2015
Term Expires: September 2016
E-mail: franco_muzzio@ca9.uscourts.gov
Education: UCLA 2015 JD

Career Law Clerk **Jamey Harris** .... (503) 833-5360
Began Service: 2007
E-mail: jamey_harris@ca9.uscourts.gov

Secretary **Jane Glenn** .... (503) 833-5360
E-mail: jane_glenn@ca9.uscourts.gov

Secretary **Joan Stevens** .... (503) 833-5360
E-mail: joan_stevens@ca9.uscourts.gov

Chambers of Circuit Judge M. Margaret McKeown

401 West A Street, Suite 2000, San Diego, CA 92101-7908
Tel: (619) 557-5300 Fax: (619) 557-5720
E-mail: judge_mckeown@ca9.uscourts.gov

M. Margaret McKeown
Circuit Judge

Date of Birth: May 11, 1951
Education: Wyoming 1972 BA; Georgetown 1975 JD
Began Service: May 28, 1998
Appointed By: President William J. Clinton

Government: White House Fellow, Executive Office of the President, Jimmy Carter Administration (1980-1981)

Legal Practice: Associate then Partner, Perkins Coie, Washington, DC (1975-1998)

Current Memberships: American Bar Foundation; American Bar Association; American Intellectual Property Law Association; The American Law Institute; King County Bar Association; Washington State Bar Association; Washington Women Lawyers

Staff

Law Clerk **Laura Hill** ....(619) 557-5300
Began Service: August 31, 2015
Term Expires: August 31, 2016
E-mail: laura_hill@ca9.uscourts.gov

Law Clerk **Julia Lisztwan** ....(619) 557-5300
Began Service: August 31, 2015
Term Expires: August 31, 2016
E-mail: julia_lisztwan@ca9.uscourts.gov

Law Clerk **Clare Frances Ryan** ....(619) 557-5300
Began Service: August 31, 2015
Term Expires: August 31, 2016
E-mail: clare_ryan@ca9.uscourts.gov

Law Clerk **Tatiana Sainati** ....(619) 557-5300
Began Service: August 31, 2015
Term Expires: August 31, 2016
E-mail: tatiana_sainati@ca9.uscourts.gov

Law Clerk **Dan Walters** ....(619) 557-5300
Began Service: August 31, 2015
Term Expires: August 31, 2016
E-mail: dan_walter@ca9.uscourts.gov

Judicial Assistant **Wendye Lyn Conn** ....(619) 557-5300
E-mail: wendye_conn@ca9.uscourts.gov

Chambers of Circuit Judge Kim McLane Wardlaw

U.S. Court of Appeals Building, 125 South Grand Avenue,
Suite 500, Pasadena, CA 91105
Tel: (626) 229-7130 Fax: (626) 229-7458
E-mail: judge_wardlaw@ca9.uscourts.gov

Kim McLane Wardlaw
Circuit Judge

Education: UCLA 1976 AB, 1979 JD
Began Service: August 3, 1998
Appointed By: President William J. Clinton

Clerkships: Law Clerk The Honorable William Gray, United States District Court for the Central District of California (1979-1980)

Judicial: Judge, United States District Court for the Central District of California (1996-1998)

Legal Practice: Associate, O'Melveny & Myers (1980-1987); Partner, O'Melveny & Myers (1987-1995)

Staff

Law Clerk **Caitlin Halpern** ....(626) 229-7130
Began Service: September 2015
E-mail: caitlin_halpern@ca9.uscourts.gov
Education: Harvard 2014 JD

Law Clerk **Patrick Hayden** ....(626) 229-7130
Began Service: September 2015
E-mail: patrick_hayden@ca9.uscourts.gov

Chambers of Circuit Judge Kim McLane Wardlaw *continued*

Law Clerk **Leah Judge** ....(626) 229-7130
Began Service: September 2015
E-mail: leah_judge@ca9.uscourts.gov

Law Clerk **Robert Quigley** ....(626) 229-7130
Began Service: September 2015
E-mail: robert_quigley@ca9.uscourts.gov

Judicial Assistant **Sandra Van Over** ....(626) 229-7130
E-mail: sandra_vanover@ca9.uscourts.gov

Chambers of Circuit Judge William A. Fletcher

95 Seventh Street, San Francisco, CA 94103-1526
Tel: (415) 355-8140
E-mail: judge_w_fletcher@ca9.uscourts.gov

William A. Fletcher
Circuit Judge

Date of Birth: 1945
Education: Harvard 1968 AB; Oxford (UK) 1970 BA; Yale 1975 JD
Began Service: January 31, 1999
Appointed By: President William J. Clinton

Academic: Professor, Boalt Hall School of Law, University of California, Berkeley (1977-1998)

Clerkships: Law Clerk The Honorable Stanley A. Weigel, United States District Court for the Northern District of California (1975-1976); Law Clerk The Honorable William J. Brennan, Jr., United States Supreme Court (1976-1977)

Military Service: United States Navy (1970-1972)

Current Memberships: The American Law Institute; State Bar of California

Staff

Judicial Secretary **Uyen Koh** ....(415) 355-8000
E-mail: uyen_koh@ca9.uscourts.gov

Chambers of Circuit Judge Ronald M. Gould

William K. Nakamura Courthouse, 1010 Fifth Avenue, Seattle, WA 98104
Tel: (206) 224-2280
E-mail: ronald_gould@ca9.uscourts.gov

Ronald Murray Gould
Circuit Judge

Date of Birth: 1946
Education: Pennsylvania 1968 BS; Michigan 1973 JD
Began Service: January 3, 2000
Appointed By: President William J. Clinton

Academic: Adjunct Teacher of Dispute Resolution, School of Law, University of Washington (1988-1989)

Clerkships: Law Clerk The Honorable Wade H. McCree, Jr., United States Court of Appeals for the Sixth Circuit (1973-1974); Law Clerk The Honorable Potter Stewart, United States Supreme Court (1974-1975)

Legal Practice: Summer Associate, Arnold & Porter LLP (1972); Associate, Perkins Coie LLP (1975-1980); Partner, Perkins Coie LLP (1981-1999)

Current Memberships: American Bar Association; King County Bar Association; The Supreme Court Historical Society; Ninth Judicial Circuit Historical Society, United States Court of Appeals for the Ninth Circuit; Washington State Bar Association

Staff

Secretary **Kathy Butler** ....(206) 224-2280
E-mail: kathy_butler@ca9.uscourts.gov

Chambers of Circuit Judge Richard A. Paez

Richard H. Chambers U.S. Court of Appeals Building, 125 South Grand Avenue, Pasadena, CA 91105
Tel: (626) 229-7180
E-mail: richard_paez@ca9.uscourts.gov

Richard A. Paez
Circuit Judge

Date of Birth: 1947
Education: BYU 1969 BA; Boalt Hall 1972 JD
Began Service: March 14, 2000
Appointed By: President William J. Clinton
Political Affiliation: Democrat

Judicial: Judge, Los Angeles Municipal Court (1981-1994); Assigned Justice, California Court of Appeal, Second District, Division Seven (1983); Assigned Judge, Los Angeles Superior Court (1993-1994); District Judge, United States District Court for the Central District of California (1994-2000)

Legal Practice: Staff Attorney, California Rural Legal Assistance (1972-1974); Staff Attorney, Western Center on Law and Poverty (1974-1976); Senior Counsel, Legal Aid Foundation of Los Angeles (1976-1978); Acting Executive Director, Director of Litigation, Legal Aid Foundation of Los Angeles (1978-1981)

Current Memberships: California Judges Association; Los Angeles County Bar Association; Mexican American Bar Association of Los Angeles; State Bar of California

Staff

Law Clerk **Rachel Foodman** .... (626) 229-7180
Began Service: September 2015
Term Expires: September 2016
E-mail: rachel_foodman@ca9.uscourts.gov

Law Clerk **Stanley "Stan" Molever** .... (626) 229-7180
Began Service: September 2015
Term Expires: September 2016
E-mail: stan_molever@ca9.uscourts.gov

Law Clerk **Camille Pannu** .... (626) 229-7180
Began Service: September 2015
Term Expires: September 2016
E-mail: camille_pannu@ca9.uscourts.gov

Law Clerk **Devon Porter** .... (626) 229-7180
Began Service: September 2015
Term Expires: September 2016
E-mail: devon_porter@ca9.uscourts.gov

Judicial Assistant **Lydia Martin** .... (626) 229-7180
E-mail: lydia_martin@ca9.uscourts.gov

Chambers of Circuit Judge Marsha S. Berzon

95 Seventh Street, San Francisco, CA 94103-1526
Tel: (415) 355-8160 Fax: (415) 355-8161
E-mail: marsha_berzon@ca9.uscourts.gov

Marsha S. Berzon
Circuit Judge

Date of Birth: 1945
Education: Radcliffe 1966 BA; Boalt Hall 1973 JD
Began Service: March 21, 2000
Appointed By: President William J. Clinton

Academic: Faculty Lecturer, University of California, Berkeley, School of Social Welfare (1992); Practitioner-in-Residence, Cornell Law School (1994); Practitioner-in-Residence, Indiana University Law School (1998); Lecturer, Paul M. Hebert Law Center, Louisiana State University System (2003)

Clerkships: Law Clerk The Honorable James R. Browning, United States Court of Appeals for the Ninth Circuit (1973-1974); Law Clerk The Honorable William J. Brennan, Jr., United States Supreme Court (1974-1975)

Judicial: Of Counsel, Altshuler & Berzon (1978-1990)

Chambers of Circuit Judge Marsha S. Berzon *continued*

Legal Practice: Associate, Woll & Mayer (1975-1977); Partner, Altshuler, Berzon, Nussbaum, Berzon & Rubin (1990-2000)

Current Memberships: American Bar Foundation; The American Law Institute; The District of Columbia Bar; Federal Bar Association; National Association of Women Judges; State Bar of California

Staff

Law Clerk **Daniel Crossen** .... (415) 355-8160
Began Service: June 2015
Term Expires: August 2016
E-mail: daniel_crossen@ca9.uscourts.gov

Law Clerk **Daniel Townsend** .... (415) 355-8160
Began Service: August 2015
Term Expires: August 2016
E-mail: daniel_townsend@ca9.uscourts.gov

Law Clerk **Julie Veroff** .... (415) 355-8160
Began Service: July 15, 2015
Term Expires: July 13, 2016
E-mail: julie_veroff@ca9.uscourts.gov

Law Clerk **Jessica Winter** .... (415) 355-8160
Began Service: August 2015
Term Expires: August 2016
E-mail: jessica_winter@ca9.uscourts.gov

Judicial Assistant **Therese Barquet** .... (415) 355-8160
E-mail: therese_barquet@ca9.uscourts.gov

Chambers of Circuit Judge Richard C. Tallman

William K. Nakamura U.S. Courthouse, 1010 5th Avenue, Room 902, Seattle, WA 98104
Tel: (206) 224-2250 Fax: (206) 224-2251
E-mail: judge_tallman@ca9.uscourts.gov

Richard C. Tallman
Circuit Judge

Date of Birth: 1953
Education: Northwestern 1978 JD
Began Service: May 24, 2000
Appointed By: President William J. Clinton

Clerkships: Law Clerk The Honorable Morell E. Sharp, United States District Court for the Western District of Washington (1978-1979)

Government: Trial Attorney, Criminal Division, United States Department of Justice (1979-1980); Assistant United States Attorney, Western District of Washington, Criminal Division, United States Department of Justice (1980-1983)

Legal Practice: Schweppe, Krug, Tausend & Beezer (1983-1990); Bogle & Gates (1990-1998); Tallman & Severin (1999-2000)

Staff

Law Clerk **Clare Diegel** .... (206) 224-2250
Began Service: September 2015
Term Expires: September 2016
E-mail: clare_diegel@ca9.uscourts.gov

Law Clerk **K.C. Harding** .... (206) 224-2250
Began Service: September 2015
Term Expires: September 2016

Law Clerk **Katherine Kieckhafer** .... (206) 224-2250
Began Service: September 2015
Term Expires: September 2016
E-mail: katherine_kieckhafer@ca9.uscourts.gov

Law Clerk **Amanda McDowell** .... (206) 224-2250
Began Service: September 2015
Term Expires: September 2016
E-mail: amanda_mcdowell@ca9.uscourts.gov

Judicial Assistant **Alice Rosenbach** .... (206) 224-2250
E-mail: alice_rosenbach@ca9.uscourts.gov
Education: U Washington 1976 BS

Chambers of Circuit Judge Johnnie B. Rawlinson

Lloyd D. George U.S. Courthouse, 333 Las Vegas Boulevard South, Room 7072, Las Vegas, NV 89101
Tel: (702) 464-5670 Fax: (702) 464-5671
E-mail: judge_rawlinson@ca9.uscourts.gov

Johnnie B. Rawlinson
Circuit Judge

Date of Birth: 1952
Education: North Carolina A&T 1974 BS; McGeorge 1979 JD
Began Service: July 21, 2000
Appointed By: President William J. Clinton

Government: Deputy District Attorney, County of Clark, Nevada (1980-1989); Chief Deputy District Attorney, County of Clark, Nevada (1989-1995); Assistant District Attorney, County of Clark, Nevada (1995-1998)

Judicial: District Judge, United States District Court for the District of Nevada (1998-2000)

Legal Practice: Staff Attorney, Nevada Legal Services (1980)

Current Memberships: Federal Judges Association; Just the Beginning Foundation; National Bar Association; Southern Nevada Women Attorneys Association; State Bar of California; State Bar of Nevada

Staff

Law Clerk **Elham "Ellie" Roohani** .... (702) 464-5670
Began Service: September 2014
Term Expires: September 2016
E-mail: ellie_roohani@ca9.uscourts.gov

Law Clerk **Salah Hawkins** .... (702) 464-5670
Began Service: September 2015
Term Expires: September 2016
E-mail: salah_hawkins@ca9.uscourts.gov
Education: Berkeley Law 2015 JD

Law Clerk **Scott McAbee** .... (702) 464-5670
Began Service: August 2015
Term Expires: August 2016
E-mail: scott_mcabee@ca9.uscourts.gov
Education: Brooklyn Law 2013 JD

Career Law Clerk **Stan Shoffner** .... (702) 464-5670
E-mail: stan_shoffner@ca9.uscourts.gov
Education: Emory 1991 BA; UNLV 2002 JD; Georgetown 2004 LLM

Judicial Secretary **Leah D'Onofrio** .... (702) 464-5670
E-mail: Leah_D'Onofrio@ca9.uscourts.gov
Education: Valdosta State U 1986 BS

Chambers of Circuit Judge Richard R. Clifton

999 Bishop Street, Suite 2010, Honolulu, HI 96813
Tel: (808) 522-7474 Fax: (808) 522-7477
E-mail: judge_clifton@ca9.uscourts.gov

Richard R. Clifton
Circuit Judge

Date of Birth: November 13, 1950
Education: Princeton 1972 AB; Yale 1975 JD
Began Service: August 5, 2002
Appointed By: President George W. Bush

Academic: Adjunct Professor of Law, University of Hawaii (1979-1981); Adjunct Professor of Law, University of Hawaii (1983-1989)

Clerkships: Law Clerk The Honorable Herbert Y.C. Choy, United States Court of Appeals for the Ninth Circuit (1975-1976)

Legal Practice: Partner, Cades Schutte Fleming & Wright (1977-2002)

Chambers of Circuit Judge Richard R. Clifton *continued*

Staff

Law Clerk **Rachel Dempsey** .... (808) 525-5366
Began Service: September 2015
Term Expires: September 2016
E-mail: rachel_dempsey@ca9.uscourts.gov

Law Clerk **Kaliko'onalani Fernandes** .... (808) 525-5366
Began Service: September 2015
Term Expires: September 2016
E-mail: kaliko_fernandes@ca9.uscourts.gov

Law Clerk **Joshua Korr** .... (808) 525-5366
Began Service: September 2015
Term Expires: September 2016
E-mail: joshua_korr@ca9.uscourts.gov

Law Clerk **Dean Rosenberg** .... (808) 525-5366
Began Service: September 2015
Term Expires: September 2016
E-mail: dean_rosenberg@ca9.uscourts.gov

Judicial Assistant **JoAnn Ota-Young** .... (808) 522-7474
E-mail: joann_ota-young@ca9.uscourts.gov

Chambers of Circuit Judge Jay S. Bybee

Lloyd D. George U.S. Courthouse, 333 Las Vegas Boulevard South, Las Vegas, NV 89101
Tel: (702) 464-5650
E-mail: jay_bybee@ca9.uscourts.gov

Jay S. Bybee
Circuit Judge

Date of Birth: October 27, 1953
Education: BYU 1977 BA; J Reuben Clark Law 1980 JD
Began Service: March 28, 2003
Appointed By: President George W. Bush

Academic: Assistant Professor, Paul M. Hebert Law Center, Louisiana State University System (1991-1994); Associate Professor, Paul M. Hebert Law Center, Louisiana State University System (1994-1998); Professor, Paul M. Hebert Law Center, Louisiana State University System (1998); Professor, University of Nevada, Las Vegas (1999-2000)

Clerkships: Law Clerk, Circuit Judge Donald Russell, United States Court of Appeals for the Fourth Circuit (1980-1981)

Government: U.S. Attorney, Office of Legal Policy, United States Department of Justice (1984-1986); U.S. Attorney, Appellate Staff, Civil Division, United States Department of Justice (1986-1989); Associate Counsel to the President, Executive Office of the President, George H.W. Bush Administration (1989-1991); Assistant Attorney General, Office of Legal Counsel, United States Department of Justice (2001)

Legal Practice: Associate, Sidley Austin LLP (1981-1984)

Chambers of Circuit Judge Consuelo Maria Callahan

501 I Street, Room 12-700, Sacramento, CA 95814
Tel: (916) 930-4160
E-mail: consuelo_callahan@ca9.uscourts.gov

Consuelo Maria Callahan
Circuit Judge

Date of Birth: 1950
Education: Stanford 1972 BA; McGeorge 1975 JD; Virginia 2004 LLM
Began Service: 2003
Appointed By: President George W. Bush
Political Affiliation: Republican

Government: Deputy City Attorney, Office of the Mayor and City Council, City of Stockton, California (1975-1976); Deputy District Attorney, Office of the District Attorney, County of San Joaquin, California (1976-1986)

Judicial: Commissioner, Stockton Municipal Court (1986-1992); Judge, California Superior Court, San Joaquin County (1992-1996); Associate Justice, California Court of Appeal, Third Appellate District (1996-2003)

(continued on next page)

FEDERAL COURTS–UNITED STATES COURTS OF APPEALS

Chambers of Circuit Judge Consuelo Maria Callahan *continued*

Staff

Law Clerk **Jinnifer D. Pitcher** . . . . (916) 930-4167
Began Service: September 2014
Term Expires: October 2016
E-mail: jinnifer_pitcher@ca9.uscourts.gov
Education: U Pacific 2007 JD

Law Clerk **Richard Ramsey** . . . . (916) 930-4167
Began Service: September 2015
Term Expires: October 2016

Law Clerk **Ross W. Tucker** . . . . (916) 930-4167
Began Service: September 2013
Term Expires: October 2016
E-mail: ross_tucker@ca9.uscourts.gov
Education: Chicago 2008 JD

Law Clerk **Tyler Welti** . . . . (916) 930-4167
Began Service: September 2014
Term Expires: October 2016
E-mail: tyler_welti@ca9.uscourts.gov
Education: Virginia 2008 JD

Career Law Clerk **Richard Schickele** . . . . (916) 930-4167
E-mail: richard_schickele@ca9.uscourts.gov

Judicial Assistant **Beverly Hing** . . . . (916) 930-4160
E-mail: beverly_hing@ca9.uscourts.gov

Chambers of Circuit Judge Carlos T. Bea

95 Seventh Street, San Francisco, CA 94103-1526
Tel: (415) 355-8180 Fax: (415) 355-8181
E-mail: judge_bea@ca9.uscourts.gov

Carlos T. Bea
Circuit Judge

Date of Birth: 1934
Education: Stanford 1956 BA, 1958 JD
Began Service: October 2003
Appointed By: President George W. Bush

Judicial: Judge, San Francisco Superior Court (1990-2003)

Chambers of Circuit Judge Milan D. Smith Jr.

222 North Sepulveda Boulevard, Room 2325, El Segundo, CA 90245
Tel: (310) 607-4020 Fax: (310) 607-4039
E-mail: milan_smith@ca9.uscourts.gov

Milan D. Smith, Jr.
Circuit Judge

Education: BYU 1966 BA; Chicago 1969 JD
Began Service: June 2006
Appointed By: President George W. Bush

Government: President, Governing Board of the Los Angeles State Building Authority (1984-1992); Vice Chairman, Fair Employment and Housing Commission

Legal Practice: Associate Attorney, O'Melveny & Myers LLP (1969-1972); Managing Partner, Smith, Crane, Robinson & Parker LLP (1972-2006)

Staff

Law Clerk **Elizabeth Song** . . . . (310) 607-4020
Began Service: August 2015
Term Expires: August 2016
E-mail: elizabeth_song@ca9.uscourts.gov

Law Clerk **Athul Acharya** . . . . (310) 607-4020
Began Service: August 2015
Term Expires: August 2016
E-mail: athul_acharya@ca9.uscourts.gov

Law Clerk **Rebecca Van Tassell** . . . . (310) 607-4020
Began Service: August 2015
Term Expires: August 2016
E-mail: rebecca_vantassell@ca9.uscourts.gov

Law Clerk **Jonathan Rotter** . . . . (310) 607-4020
Began Service: August 2015
Term Expires: August 2016
E-mail: jonathan_rotter@ca9.uscourts.gov

Chambers of Circuit Judge Milan D. Smith Jr. *continued*

Judicial Assistant **Amalia Chevalier** . . . . (310) 607-4020
E-mail: amalia_chevalier@ca9.uscourts.gov

Chambers of Circuit Judge Sandra Segal Ikuta

Richard H. Chambers Court of Appeals Building, 125 South Grand Avenue, Pasadena, CA 91105
Tel: (626) 229-7339 Fax: (626) 229-7446
E-mail: judge_ikuta@ca9.uscourts.gov

Sandra Segal Ikuta
Circuit Judge

Date of Birth: June 1954
Education: UC Berkeley 1976 AB; Columbia 1978 MS; UCLA 1988 JD
Began Service: June 2006
Appointed By: President George W. Bush

Clerkships: Law Clerk, Circuit Judge Alex Kozinski, United States Court of Appeals for the Ninth Circuit (1988-1989); Law Clerk The Honorable Sandra Day O'Connor, Supreme Court of the United States (1989-1990)

Government: Deputy Secretary/General Counsel, Resources Agency, State of California (2004-2006)

Legal Practice: Associate, O'Melveny & Myers LLP (1990-1997); Partner, O'Melveny & Myers (1997-2004); Co-Chair, Environmental Practice Group, O'Melveny & Myers LLP

Chambers of Circuit Judge Norman Randy Smith

801 East Sherman Street, Pocatello, ID 83201
Tel: (208) 478-4140
E-mail: judge_smith@ca9.uscourts.gov

Norman Randy Smith
Circuit Judge

Date of Birth: 1949
Education: BYU 1974 BS; J Reuben Clark Law 1977 JD
Began Service: March 19, 2007
Appointed By: President George W. Bush

Academic: Adjunct Professor, Boise State University (1979-1981)

Corporate: General Counsel, J.R. Simplot Company (1977-1981)

Judicial: District Judge, Idaho Sixth District Court (1995-2004); Administrative Judge, Idaho Sixth District Court (2004-2007)

Legal Practice: Associate, Merrill & Merrill, Chartered (1982-1995); Partner, Merrill & Merrill, Chartered (1984-1995)

Staff

Career Law Clerk **Carole Wesenberg** . . . . (208) 478-4140
E-mail: carole_wesenberg@ca9.uscourts.gov

Judicial Assistant **Patti Richmond** . . . . (208) 478-4140
E-mail: patti_richmond@ca9.uscourts.gov

Chambers of Circuit Judge Mary H. Murguia
401 West Washington Street, Phoenix, AZ 85003
Tel: (602) 322-7580
E-mail: mary_murguia@ca9.uscourts.gov

Mary Helen Murguia
Circuit Judge

Date of Birth: 1960
Education: Kansas 1982 BA, 1982 BS, 1985 JD
Began Service: January 4, 2011
Appointed By: President Barack Obama

Government: Assistant District Attorney, Office of the District Attorney, County of Wyandotte, Kansas (1985-1990); Assistant United States Attorney, District of Arizona, United States Attorney's Office, United States Department of Justice, George H.W. Bush Administration (1990-2000); Director, United States Attorney's Executive Office, United States Department of Justice, William J. Clinton Administration (1999-2000)

Judicial: District Judge, Chambers of District Judge Mary H. Murguia, United States District Court for the District of Arizona (2000-2011)

Staff
Law Clerk **Daniel Arellano** . . . . (602) 322-7580
Began Service: September 2015
Term Expires: September 2016
E-mail: daniel_arellano@ca9.uscourts.gov
Law Clerk **Lauren Capaccio** . . . . (602) 322-7580
Began Service: September 2015
Term Expires: September 2016
E-mail: lauren_capaccio@ca9.uscourts.gov
Law Clerk **Kelsey Helland** . . . . (602) 322-7580
Began Service: September 2015
Term Expires: September 2016
E-mail: kelsey_helland@ca9.uscourts.gov
Law Clerk **Paul Meyer** . . . . (602) 322-7580
Began Service: September 2015
Term Expires: September 2016
E-mail: paul_meyer@ca9.uscourts.gov
Judicial Assistant **Kristen Parris** . . . . (602) 322-7580
E-mail: kristen_parris@ca9.uscourts.gov

Chambers of Circuit Judge Morgan B. Christen
95 Seventh Street, San Francisco, CA 94103-1526
P.O. Box 193939, San Francisco, CA 94119-3939
Tel: (907) 677-6295
E-mail: morgan_christen@ca9.uscourts.gov

Morgan B. Christen
Circuit Judge

Education: U Washington 1983 BA; Golden Gate 1986 JD
Began Service: January 11, 2012
Appointed By: President Barack Obama

Current Memberships: Alaska Bar Association

Staff
Law Clerk **Trevor Lee** . . . . (907) 677-6295
Began Service: August 2015
Term Expires: August 2016
E-mail: trevor_lee@ca9.uscourts.gov
Law Clerk **Anit Jindal** . . . . (907) 677-6295
Began Service: August 2015
Term Expires: August 2016
E-mail: anit_jindal@ca9.uscourts.gov
Law Clerk **Lauren Watts** . . . . (907) 677-6295
Began Service: August 2015
Term Expires: August 2016
E-mail: lauren_watts@ca9.uscourts.gov
Education: U Washington 2014 JD
Law Clerk **Jared Gardner** . . . . (907) 677-6295
Began Service: August 2015
Term Expires: August 2016
E-mail: jared_gardner@ca9.uscourts.gov

Chambers of Circuit Judge Morgan B. Christen *continued*

Judicial Assistant **Sonja Amundsen** . . . . (907) 677-6220
E-mail: sonja_amundsen@ca9.uscourts.gov

Chambers of Circuit Judge Jacqueline H. Nguyen
95 Seventh Street, San Francisco, CA 94103-1526
P.O. Box 193939, San Francisco, CA 94119-3939
Tel: (626) 229-7242
E-mail: jacqueline_nguyen@ca9.uscourts.gov

Jacqueline H. Nguyen
Circuit Judge

Education: Occidental 1987; UCLA 1991 JD
Began Service: 2012
Appointed By: President Barack Obama

Staff
Law Clerk **Connor Williams** . . . . (626) 229-7242
Began Service: August 2015
Term Expires: August 2016
E-mail: connor_williams@ca9.uscourts.gov
Law Clerk **Mary Tharin** . . . . (626) 229-7242
E-mail: mary_tharin@ca9.uscourts.gov
Law Clerk **William Rollins** . . . . (626) 229-7242
Law Clerk **Joel Mallord** . . . . (626) 229-7242
Began Service: September 2015
Term Expires: September 2016
E-mail: joel_mallord@ca9.uscourts.gov
Judicial Assistant **Alicia Mamer** . . . . (626) 229-7248
E-mail: alicia_mamer@ca9.uscourts.gov

Chambers of Circuit Judge Paul J. Watford
95 Seventh Street, San Francisco, CA 94103-1526
P.O. Box 193939, San Francisco, CA 94119-3939
Tel: (626) 229-7300
E-mail: paul_watford@ca9.uscourts.gov

Paul J. Watford
Circuit Judge

Education: UC Berkeley 1989 BA; UCLA 1994 JD
Began Service: June 1, 2012
Appointed By: President Barack Obama

Staff
Judicial Assistant **Marie Baltierra** . . . . (626) 229-7300
E-mail: marie_baltierra@ca9.uscourts.gov

Chambers of Circuit Judge Andrew David Hurwitz
95 Seventh Street, San Francisco, CA 94103-1526
P.O. Box 193939, San Francisco, CA 94119-3939
Tel: (602) 322-7690
E-mail: andrew_hurwitz@ca9.uscourts.gov

Andrew D. Hurwitz
Circuit Judge

Education: Princeton 1968 AB; Yale 1971 JD
Began Service: 2012
Appointed By: President Barack Obama

Staff
Law Clerk **Peter Brody** . . . . (602) 322-7650
Began Service: September 2015
Term Expires: September 2016
E-mail: peter_brody@ca9.uscourts.gov
Law Clerk **Joshua "Josh" Bendor** . . . . (602) 322-7650
Began Service: September 2015
Term Expires: September 2016
E-mail: josh_bendor@ca9.uscourts.gov

(continued on next page)

Chambers of Circuit Judge Andrew David Hurwitz *continued*

Law Clerk **Jillian Hewitt** .... (602) 322-7650
Began Service: September 2015
Term Expires: September 2016
E-mail: jillian_hewitt@ca9.uscourts.gov

Career Law Clerk **Elizabeth Walker** .... (602) 322-7650
Began Service: September 2015
Term Expires: September 2016
E-mail: elizabeth_walker@ca9.uscourts.gov
Education: Stanford 2004 JD

Chambers of Circuit Judge John B. Owens

95 Seventh Street, San Francisco, CA 94103-1526
Tel: (619) 557-6400
E-mail: john_owens@ca9.uscourts.gov

John B. Owens
Circuit Judge

Education: UC Berkeley 1993 BA; Stanford 1996 JD
Began Service: April 25, 2014
Appointed By: President Barack Obama

Chambers of Circuit Judge Michelle T. Friedland

95 Seventh Street, San Francisco, CA 94103-1526
Tel: (415) 355-8000
E-mail: michelle_friedland@ca9.uscourts.gov

Michelle T. Friedland
Circuit Judge

Education: Stanford 1995 BA, 2000 JD
Began Service: 2014
Appointed By: President Barack Obama

Chambers of Senior Judge Alfred T. Goodwin

506 Richard H. Chambers U.S. Court of Appeals Building,
125 South Grand Avenue, Pasadena, CA 91105
P.O. Box 91510, Pasadena, CA 91109-1510
Tel: (626) 229-7100 Fax: (626) 229-7453
E-mail: alfred_goodwin@ca9.uscourts.gov

Alfred T. Goodwin
Senior Judge

Date of Birth: 1923
Education: Oregon 1947 BA, 1951 JD
Began Service: 1972
Appointed By: President Richard M. Nixon

Academic: Adjunct Professor, Oregon (1952-1953)

Judicial: Judge, Oregon Circuit Court, Second Judicial District (1955-1960); Associate Justice, Oregon Supreme Court (1960-1969); Judge, United States District Court for the District of Oregon (1969-1971)

Legal Practice: Attorney, Darling, Vonderheit & Goodwin (1951-1955)

Military Service: United States Army (1942-1946); United States Army Reserve, United States Department of the Army (1946-1969)

Current Memberships: American Bar Foundation; American Bar Association; The American Law Institute; Oregon State Bar

Staff

Law Clerk **Megan Thompson** .... (541) 431-4121
Began Service: August 2014
E-mail: megan_thompson@ca9.uscourts.gov

Law Clerk **(Vacant)** .... (626) 229-7104

Secretary **Karen Navarrete** .... (626) 229-7100
E-mail: Karen_Navarrete@ca9.uscourts.gov

Chambers of Senior Judge J. Clifford Wallace

4192 Edward J. Schwartz U.S. Courthouse & Federal Building,
940 Front Street, San Diego, CA 92101-8918
Tel: (619) 557-6114 Fax: (619) 557-6887
E-mail: Judge_Wallace@ca9.uscourts.gov

J. Clifford Wallace
Senior Judge

Date of Birth: 1928
Education: San Diego State 1952 BA; Boalt Hall 1955 LLB
Began Service: 1972
Appointed By: President Richard M. Nixon

Academic: Visiting Professor, Brigham Young University; Adjunct Professor and Lecturer, University of San Diego; Adjunct Professor and Lecturer, California Western University; Faculty Member, Salzburg Seminar (1985); Faculty Member, Kings College London (1987)

Judicial: Judge, United States District Court for the Southern District of California (1970-1972)

Legal Practice: Associate, Gray, Cary, Ames & Frye (1955-1962); Partner, Gray, Cary, Ames & Frye (1962-1970)

Military Service: United States Navy (1946-1949)

Current Memberships: American Board of Trial Advocates; Federal Bar Association

Staff

Law Clerk **Eric Ashcroft** .... (619) 557-6114
Began Service: August 2015
Term Expires: August 2016
E-mail: eric_ashcroft@ca9.uscourts.gov

Law Clerk **Natalie Holzaepfel** .... (619) 557-6114
Began Service: August 2015
Term Expires: August 2016
E-mail: natalie_holzaepfel@ca9.uscourts.gov

Secretary **Teresa Gonzalez** .... (619) 557-6114
E-mail: teresa_gonzalez@ca9.uscourts.gov

Career Law Clerk **Sarah Wellman** .... (619) 557-6114
E-mail: sarah_wellman@ca9.uscourts.gov

Chambers of Senior Judge Procter Hug, Jr.

708 Bruce Thompson U.S. Courthouse, 400 South Virginia Street,
Reno, NV 89501
Tel: (775) 686-5949 Fax: (775) 686-5958
E-mail: judge_hug@ca9.uscourts.gov

Procter Hug, Jr.
Senior Judge

Date of Birth: 1931
Education: Nevada (Reno) 1953 BS; Stanford 1958 JD
Began Service: September 16, 1977
Appointed By: President Jimmy Carter
Political Affiliation: Democrat

Government: Deputy Attorney General, United States Department of Justice (1972-1976)

Legal Practice: Partner, Springer, McKissick & Hug (1958-1963); Partner, Woodburn, Wedge, Blakey, Folsom & Hug (1963-1977)

Military Service: United States Navy (1953-1955)

Nonprofit: General Counsel, University of Nevada System (1972-1976)

Current Memberships: American Bar Association; The American Law Institute; State Bar of Nevada

Staff

Career Law Clerk **Sandy Roth** .... (775) 686-5949
E-mail: sandy_roth@ca9.uscourts.gov
Education: UCLA 1991 JD

Administrative Assistant **Mary K. Smotony** .... (775) 686-5949
E-mail: Mary_Smotony@ca9.uscourts.gov

Judicial Assistant **Troy Seegmiller** .... (775) 686-5951
E-mail: troy_seegmiller@ca9.uscourts.gov

Chambers of Senior Judge Mary M. Schroeder

Sandra Day O'Connor U.S. Courthouse, 401 West Washington Street, SPC 54, Suite 610, Phoenix, AZ 85003-2156
Tel: (602) 322-7320 Fax: (602) 322-7329
E-mail: judge_schroeder@ca9.uscourts.gov

Mary M. Schroeder
Senior Judge

Date of Birth: 1940
Education: Swarthmore 1962 BA; Chicago 1965 JD
Began Service: October 1979
Appointed By: President Jimmy Carter

Current Memberships: American Bar Association; The American Law Institute; Arizona Women Lawyers Association; The District of Columbia Bar; Federal Bar Association; Illinois State Bar Association; National Association of Women Judges; National Association of Women Lawyers; State Bar of Arizona

Staff

Law Clerk **Sara Hershman** .... (602) 322-7320
Began Service: August 2015
Term Expires: August 2016
E-mail: sara_hershman@ca9.uscourts.gov

Law Clerk **Adriane Peralta** .... (602) 322-7338
Began Service: August 2015
Term Expires: August 2016
E-mail: adriane_peralta@ca9.uscourts.gov
Education: UCLA JD

Administrative Assistant **Tonica R. Firth** .... (602) 322-7322
E-mail: tonica_firth@ca9.uscourts.gov

Judicial Assistant **Stacy Pavese** .... (602) 322-7321
E-mail: stacy_pavese@ca9.uscourts.gov

Chambers of Senior Judge Jerome Farris

1010 Fifth Avenue, Room 1030, Seattle, WA 98104
Tel: (206) 224-2260 Fax: (206) 224-2261
E-mail: jerome_farris@ca9.uscourts.gov

Jerome Farris
Senior Judge

Date of Birth: 1930
Education: Morehouse Col 1951 BS; Atlanta 1955 MSW; U Washington 1958 JD
Began Service: October 16, 1979
Appointed By: President Jimmy Carter

Academic: Faculty, National College State Judiciary, University of Nevada (1973); Lecturer, School of Law, University of Washington (1976); Board of Regents, University of Washington (1985-1997); President, Board of Regents, University of Washington (1990-1991)

Judicial: Judge, Washington Court of Appeals (1969-1979)

Legal Practice: Partner, Farris, Bangs & Horowitz (1965-1969)

Military Service: United States Army (1952-1953)

Current Memberships: American Bar Foundation; Senior Lawyers Division, American Bar Association; King County Bar Association

Staff

Law Clerk **Matthew "Matt" Henry** .... (206) 224-2260
Began Service: September 2015
Term Expires: September 2016

Law Clerk **Francesca Procaccini** .... (206) 224-2260
Began Service: September 2015
Term Expires: September 2016
E-mail: francesca_procaccini@ca9.uscourts.gov

Law Clerk **Andrew Spore** .... (206) 224-2260
Began Service: September 2015
Term Expires: September 2016
E-mail: andrew_spore@ca9.uscourts.gov

Chambers of Senior Judge Jerome Farris *continued*

Secretary (Part-Time) **Laurie Cuaresma** .... (206) 224-2260

Secretary **Kelly Boudreau** .... (206) 224-2260
E-mail: kelly_boudreau@ca9.uscourts.gov

Chambers of Senior Judge Dorothy Wright Nelson

Richard H. Chambers U.S. Court of Appeals Federal Building, 125 South Grand Avenue, Suite 303, Pasadena, CA 91105-1652
P.O. Box 91510, Pasadena, CA 91109-1510
Tel: (626) 229-7400 Fax: (626) 229-7455
E-mail: dorothy_nelson@ca9.uscourts.gov

Dorothy Wright Nelson
Senior Judge

Date of Birth: 1928
Education: UCLA 1950 AB, 1953 JD; USC 1956 LLM
Began Service: 1980
Appointed By: President Jimmy Carter

Academic: Instructor, USC Law School, University of Southern California (1957-1958); Assistant Professor, USC Law School, University of Southern California (1958-1961); Associate Professor, USC Law School, University of Southern California (1961-1967); Professor, USC Law School, University of Southern California (1967); Interim Dean, USC Law School, University of Southern California (1967); Dean, USC Law School, University of Southern California (1968-1980)

Current Memberships: American Bar Foundation; American Bar Association; The American Law Institute; Association of American Law Schools; Beverly Hills Bar Association; Federal Bar Association; International Association of Judges/Union Internationale des Magistrats; International Bar Association; Los Angeles County Bar Association; National Association of Public Administration; State Bar of California; Women Lawyers Association of Los Angeles; World Association of Lawyers

Staff

Law Clerk **Andrew Wiener** .... (626) 229-7400
Began Service: August 2015
Term Expires: August 2016
E-mail: andrew_wiener@ca9.uscourts.gov

Law Clerk **Katherine Lin** .... (626) 229-7405
Began Service: August 2015
Term Expires: August 2016
E-mail: katherine_lin@ca9.uscourts.gov

Career Law Clerk **Mary Beth Lippsmith** .... (626) 229-7407
Began Service: August 2011
E-mail: marybeth_lippsmith@ca9.uscourts.gov
Education: USC 2002 JD

Secretary **Julie Tooley** .... (626) 229-7400
E-mail: julie_tooley@ca9.uscourts.gov

Chambers of Senior Judge William C. Canby, Jr.

Sandra Day O'Connor U.S. Courthouse, 401 West Washington Street, SPC 55, Room 612, Phoenix, AZ 85003-2156
Tel: (602) 322-7300
E-mail: william_canby@ca9.uscourts.gov

William C. Canby, Jr.
Senior Judge

Date of Birth: 1931
Education: Yale 1953 BA; Minnesota 1956 LLB
Began Service: 1980
Appointed By: President Jimmy Carter
Political Affiliation: Democrat

Academic: Assistant to the President, State University of New York at Old Westbury (1967); Professor, Arizona State University (1967-1980); Visiting Fulbright Professor of Law, Makerere University (1970-1971)

Clerkships: Law Clerk The Honorable Charles E. Whittaker, Supreme Court of the United States (1958-1959)

(continued on next page)

Chambers of Senior Judge William C. Canby, Jr. *continued*

Government: Associate Director and Deputy Director, Ethiopia, Peace Corps (1962-1964); Director, Uganda, Peace Corps (1964-1966); Special Assistant (D-MN), Office of Senator Walter F. Mondale, United States Senate (1966)

Legal Practice: Associate, Oppenheimer, Hodgson, Brown, Baer & Wolff (1959-1962)

Military Service: United States Air Force (1956-1958)

Current Memberships: Maricopa County Bar Association; Minnesota State Bar Association; State Bar of Arizona

Staff

Secretary **Sandy Gebbia** .... (602) 322-7300
E-mail: sandy_gebbia@ca9.uscourts.gov

Chambers of Senior Judge John T. Noonan, Jr.

95 Seventh Street, San Francisco, CA 94103-1526
P.O. Box 193939, San Francisco, CA 94119-3939
Tel: (415) 355-8130
E-mail: judge_noonan@ca9.uscourts.gov

John T. Noonan, Jr.
Senior Judge

Date of Birth: 1926
Education: Harvard 1946 AB; Catholic U 1949 MA, 1951 PhD; Harvard 1954 LLB
Began Service: January 16, 1986
Appointed By: President Ronald Reagan

Academic: Assistant Professor, The University of Notre Dame (1961-1963); Professor, The University of Notre Dame (1963-1966); Visiting Professor, Southern Methodist University (1966); Professor and Chairman, University of California, Berkeley (1967-1985); Visiting Professor, Stanford University (1970); Visiting Professor, University of California, Los Angeles (1974); Visiting Professor, Harvard University (1989)

Government: Special Staff, National Security Council (1954-1955); Chairman, Brookline Redevelopment Authority (1958-1962); Advisor, Rockefeller Commission on Population Growth and the American Future (1972); Consultant, National Institutes of Health, United States Department of Health and Human Services (1973); Consultant, National Endowment for the Humanities (1973-1975)

Legal Practice: Herrick & Smith (1955-1960)

Staff

Law Clerk **Mariel Bird** .... (415) 355-8130
Began Service: September 2015
Term Expires: September 2016
E-mail: mariel_bird@ca9.uscourts.gov

Law Clerk **Max Carter-Oberstone** .... (415) 355-8130
Began Service: September 2015
Term Expires: September 2016

Law Clerk **Tamara Crepet** .... (415) 355-8130
Began Service: September 2015
Term Expires: September 2016
E-mail: tamara_crepet@ca9.uscourts.gov

Law Clerk **Jason George** .... (415) 355-8130
Began Service: September 2015
Term Expires: September 2016
E-mail: jason_george@ca9.uscourts.gov
Education: Stanford 2015 JD

Judicial Assistant **Evelyn Lew** .... (415) 355-8130
E-mail: evelyn_lew@ca9.uscourts.gov

Chambers of Senior Judge Edward Leavy

700 Southwest Sixth Avenue, Suite 226, Portland, OR 97204
Tel: (503) 833-5350 Fax: (503) 833-5355
E-mail: judge_leavy@ca9.uscourts.gov

Edward Leavy
Senior Judge

Date of Birth: 1929
Education: Portland 1950 AB; Notre Dame 1953 LLB
Began Service: March 23, 1987
Appointed By: President Ronald Reagan

Judicial: Judge, Lane County District Court (1957-1961); Circuit Judge, Oregon Circuit Court, Second Judicial District (1961-1976); Magistrate Judge, United States District Court for the District of Oregon (1976-1984); Judge, United States District Court for the District of Oregon (1984-1987)

Staff

Career Law Clerk **Kathy Dodds** .... (503) 833-5353
E-mail: kathy_dodds@ca9.uscourts.gov
Education: Vermont 1975 BA; Oregon 1979 JD

Chambers of Senior Judge Stephen S. Trott

U.S. Courthouse, 550 West Fort Street, Room 667, Boise, ID 83724-0040
Tel: (208) 334-1612 Fax: (208) 334-9715
E-mail: judge_trott@ca9.uscourts.gov

Stephen S. Trott
Senior Judge

Date of Birth: 1939
Education: Wesleyan U 1962 BA; Harvard 1965 LLB
Began Service: April 1988
Appointed By: President Ronald Reagan

Government: Deputy District Attorney, County of Los Angeles, California (1966-1981); United States Attorney, Central District of California, United States Department of Justice (1981-1983); Assistant Attorney General, Criminal Division, United States Department of Justice (1983-1986); Associate Attorney General, Office of the Attorney General, United States Department of Justice (1986-1988)

Staff

Law Clerk **Joshua Goyden** .... (208) 334-1612
Began Service: September 2012
Term Expires: September 2016
E-mail: joshua_goyden@ca9.uscourts.gov

Administrative Officer **Toni Smith** .... (208) 334-1612
E-mail: toni_smith@ca9.uscourts.gov

Chambers of Senior Judge Ferdinand Francis Fernandez

602 Richard H. Chambers U.S. Court of Appeals Building,
125 South Grand Avenue, Pasadena, CA 91105
P.O. Box 91510, Pasadena, CA 91109-1510
Tel: (626) 229-7121 Fax: (626) 229-7451
E-mail: ferdinand_fernandez@ca9.uscourts.gov

Ferdinand Francis Fernandez
Senior Judge

Date of Birth: 1937
Education: USC 1958 BS, 1962 JD; Harvard 1963 LLM
Began Service: 1989
Appointed By: President George H.W. Bush

Clerkships: Law Clerk The Honorable William M. Byrne, United States District Court for the Central District of California (1963-1964)

Judicial: Judge, California Superior Court, San Bernardino County (1980-1985); Judge, United States District Court for the Central District of California (1985-1989)

Chambers of Senior Judge Ferdinand Francis Fernandez *continued*

Legal Practice: Attorney, Allard, Shelton & O'Connor (1964-1980)

Current Memberships: American Bar Association; Eastern Bar Association of Los Angeles; Federal Bar Association; Federal Judges Association; Hispanic National Bar Association; Ninth Circuit District Judges Association

Chambers of Senior Judge Andrew J. Kleinfeld

Courthouse Square, 250 Cushman Street, Suite 3 A,
Fairbanks, AK 99701-4665
Tel: (907) 456-0564 Fax: (907) 456-0284
E-mail: judge_kleinfeld@ca9.uscourts.gov

Andrew J. Kleinfeld
Senior Judge

Date of Birth: 1945
Education: Wesleyan U 1966; Harvard 1969 JD
Began Service: September 16, 1991
Appointed By: President George H.W. Bush
Political Affiliation: Republican

Clerkships: Law Clerk The Honorable Jay A. Rabinowitz, Alaska Supreme Court (1969-1971)

Judicial: Magistrate Judge (part-time), United States District Court for the District of Alaska (1971-1974); Judge, United States District Court for the District of Alaska (1986-1991)

Current Memberships: Alaska Bar Association; Tanana Valley Bar Association

Staff

Law Clerk **Ian Brekke** .... (907) 456-0569
Began Service: August 14, 2015
Term Expires: August 14, 2016
E-mail: ian_brekke@ca9.uscourts.gov

Law Clerk **Benjamin Fischer** .... (907) 456-0568
Began Service: August 28, 2015
Term Expires: August 28, 2016
E-mail: benjamin_fischer@ca9.uscourts.gov

Law Clerk **Nathan Kinard** .... (907) 456-0567
Began Service: August 18, 2015
Term Expires: August 18, 2016
E-mail: nathan_kinard@ca9.uscourts.gov

Judicial Assistant **Barbara Frone** .... (907) 456-0565
E-mail: barbara_frone@ca9.uscourts.gov

Secretary **Mary E. Huskey** .... (907) 456-0564
E-mail: mary_huskey@ca9.uscourts.gov

Chambers of Senior Judge Michael Daly Hawkins

Sandra Day O'Connor U.S. Courthouse, 401 West Washington Street,
SPC 47, Suite 510, Phoenix, AZ 85003-2151
Tel: (602) 322-7310 Fax: (602) 322-7319
E-mail: judge_hawkins@ca9.uscourts.gov

Michael Daly Hawkins
Senior Judge

Date of Birth: 1945
Education: Arizona State 1967 BA, 1970 JD; Virginia 1998 LLM
Began Service: 1994
Appointed By: President William J. Clinton

Government: United States Attorney, District of Arizona, United States Department of Justice (1977-1980)

Legal Practice: Daughton Feinstein & Wilson (1973-1976); Hofman Salcito & Stevens (1976-1977); Dushoff & Sacks (1980-1986); Partner, Daughton Hawkins & Bacon (1986-1988); Attorney, Bryan Cave LLP (1988-1992); Partner, Daughton Hawkins Brokelman Guinan & Patterson (1992-1994)

Military Service: Captain, Special Court Military Judge, United States Marine Corps (1970-1973)

Chambers of Senior Judge Michael Daly Hawkins *continued*

Current Memberships: The Horace Rumpole American Inn of Court; Federal Bar Association; Maricopa County Bar Association; National Association of Former United States Attorneys; State Bar of Arizona

Staff

Law Clerk **Neha Gupta** .... (602) 322-7310
Began Service: September 2015
Term Expires: September 2016
E-mail: neha_gupta@ca9.uscourts.gov

Law Clerk **Cynthia Liao** .... (602) 322-7310
Began Service: September 6, 2015
Term Expires: September 2016
E-mail: cynthia_liao@ca9.uscourts.gov

Career Law Clerk **Julia Morse** .... (602) 322-7310
E-mail: julia_morse@ca9.uscourts.gov
Education: Carson-Newman 1991 BA;
Virginia 1995 JD

Judicial Assistant **Laura Ferguson** .... (602) 322-7310
E-mail: laura_ferguson@ca9.uscourts.gov
Education: Arizona State 1983 BS

Chambers of Senior Judge A. Wallace Tashima

406 Richard H. Chambers U.S. Court of Appeals Building,
125 South Grand Avenue, Pasadena, CA 91105
Tel: (626) 229-7373
E-mail: judge_tashima@ca9.uscourts.gov

A. Wallace Tashima
Senior Judge

Date of Birth: 1934
Education: UCLA 1958 AB; Harvard 1961 LLB
Began Service: 1995
Appointed By: President William J. Clinton

Government: Deputy Attorney General, United States Department of Justice (1962-1968)

Judicial: District Judge, United States District Court for the Central District of California (1980-1995)

Legal Practice: Partner, Morrison & Foerster LLP (1977-1980)

Military Service: United States Marine Corps (1953-1955)

Current Memberships: American Bar Association; Los Angeles County Bar Association; State Bar of California

Staff

Law Clerk **Sara McDermott** .... (626) 229-7373
Began Service: September 2015
Term Expires: September 2016
E-mail: sara_mcdermott@ca9.uscourts.gov

Law Clerk **Susan Har** .... (626) 229-7373
Began Service: September 2015
Term Expires: September 2016
E-mail: susan_har@ca9.uscourts.gov

Law Clerk **Nina Kozalenko** .... (626) 229-7373
Began Service: September 2015
Term Expires: September 2016

Secretary **Naomi Rosenblum** .... (626) 229-7373
E-mail: naomi_rosenblum@ca9.uscourts.gov

Chambers of Senior Judge Raymond C. Fisher

Richard H. Chambers U.S. Court of Appeals Building, 125 South Grand Avenue, Suite 400, Pasadena, CA 91105
Tel: (626) 229-7110 Fax: (626) 229-7452
E-mail: raymond_fisher@ca9.uscourts.gov

Raymond C. Fisher
Senior Judge

Date of Birth: 1939
Education: Stanford 1966 LLB
Began Service: October 29, 1999
Appointed By: President William J. Clinton

Staff

Law Clerk **Sean Arenson** .... (626) 229-7110
Began Service: August 2015
Term Expires: August 2016
E-mail: sean_arenson@ca9.uscourts.gov
Education: Yale 2015 JD

Law Clerk **Kellam Conover** .... (626) 229-7110
Began Service: August 2015
Term Expires: August 2016
E-mail: kellam_conover@ca9.uscourts.gov

Law Clerk **Michael Mestitz** .... (626) 229-7110
Began Service: August 2015
Term Expires: August 2016
E-mail: michael_mestitz@ca9.uscourts.gov

Career Law Clerk **Michael Evans** .... (626) 229-7110
E-mail: michael_evans@ca9.uscourts.gov

Secretary **Catherine "Katie" Johnson** .... (626) 229-7110
E-mail: catherine_johnson@ca9.uscourts.gov

United States Bankruptcy Appellate Panel for the Ninth Circuit

U.S. Courthouse, 125 South Grand Avenue, Pasadena, CA 91105
Tel: (626) 229-7225 Fax: (626) 229-7475
Internet: www.ca9.uscourts.gov/bap

Number of Judgeships: 6

Court Staff

Bankruptcy Appellate Panel Clerk **Susan M. Spraul** .... (626) 229-7220
Education: North Carolina 1990 JD Fax: (626) 229-7475

Assistant to the Clerk **Cherri E. Yuen** .... (626) 229-7225
Education: Cal State (Los Angeles) 1987 BS Fax: (626) 229-7475

Deputy Clerk **Vincent J. Barbato** .... (626) 229-7220
E-mail: vincent_barbato@ca9.uscourts.gov

Deputy Clerk **Edwina M. Clay** .... (626) 229-7225
E-mail: edwina_clay@ca9.uscourts.gov

Deputy Clerk **Patricia Ippolito** .... (626) 229-7220

Deputy Clerk **Vicky Jackson-Walker** .... (626) 229-7225
E-mail: vicky_jackson-walker@ca9.uscourts.gov

Staff Attorney **Sarah Stevenson** .... (626) 229-7233
E-mail: sarah_stevenson@ca9.uscourts.gov
Education: Wellesley 1998 BA; USC 2001 JD

Staff Attorney **Mele R. Wood** .... (626) 229-7231
E-mail: mele_wood@ca9.uscourts.gov
Education: Hawaii 1992 BA; UC Davis 1995 JD

Deputy Clerk **Freddie Brown** .... (626) 229-7235
E-mail: freddie_brown@ca9.uscourts.gov

Chambers of Chief Judge of the Bankruptcy Appellate Panel Randall L. Dunn

1001 SW Fifth Avenue, Room 700, Portland, OR 97204
Tel: (503) 326-4175 Fax: (503) 326-5693

Randall L. Dunn
Chief Judge of the Bankruptcy Appellate Panel

Date of Birth: 1950
Education: Northwestern 1972 BA; Stanford 1975 JD
Began Service: 2006

Current Memberships: American Bankruptcy Institute; American Bar Association; National Conference of Bankruptcy Judges; Oregon State Bar; Portland Opera; Washington State Bar Association

Chambers of Bankruptcy Judge Jim D. Pappas

James A. McClure Federal Building, 550 West Fort Street, Boise, ID 83724-0040
Tel: (208) 334-9571 Fax: (208) 334-1334

Jim D. Pappas
Bankruptcy Judge

Date of Birth: 1952
Education: Idaho 1977 JD
Began Service: 2010

Current Memberships: National Conference of Bankruptcy Judges

Staff

Career Law Clerk **Jonathan Derek** .... (208) 334-9136
Education: St Vincent Col 1971 BA; St John's U (NY) 1999 JD, 2009 LLM

Chambers of Bankruptcy Judge Robert J. Faris

1132 Bishop Street, Suite 250L, Honolulu, HI 96813
Tel: (808) 522-8111

Robert J. Faris
Bankruptcy Judge

Education: Reed 1980 BA; Boalt Hall 1983 JD

Chambers of Bankruptcy Judge Meredith A. Jury

3420 12th Street, Riverside, CA 92501
Tel: (951) 774-1043

Meredith A. Jury
Bankruptcy Judge

Date of Birth: 1947
Education: Colorado 1969 BA; Wisconsin 1971 MA, 1972 MS; UCLA 1976 JD
Began Service: 2007

Legal Practice: Associate, Best Best & Krieger LLP (1976-1997)

Current Memberships: Federal Bar Association; Riverside County Bar Association; State Bar of California

Staff

Judicial Assistant **Christine Rhambo** .... (951) 774-1043

Chambers of Bankruptcy Judge Ralph B. Kirscher
400 North Main Street, Room 215, Butte, MT 59701
Tel: (406) 782-3338

Ralph B. Kirscher
Bankruptcy Judge

Date of Birth: 1951
Education: Montana; American U MPA; Montana JD
Began Service: 1999

Academic: Adjunct Lecturer, School of Law, The University of Montana-Missoula (1992-1997)

Current Memberships: National Conference of Bankruptcy Judges; Silver Bow County Bar Association; State Bar of Montana

Chambers of Bankruptcy Judge Laura S. Taylor
325 West F Street, San Diego, CA 92010
Tel: (626) 229-7225

Laura S. Taylor
Bankruptcy Judge

Education: North Carolina 1979 BA; Duke 1983 JD

Chambers of Bankruptcy Judge Frank L. Kurtz
904 West Riverside Avenue Suite 304, Spokane, WA 99201
Tel: (509) 576-6122

Frank L. Kurtz
Bankruptcy Judge

Date of Birth: 1946
Education: Gonzaga 1974 JD

United States Court of Appeals for the Tenth Circuit
Byron White U.S. Courthouse, 1823 Stout Street, Denver, CO 80257
Tel: (303) 844-3157
Tel: (303) 844-5682 (Electronic Opinions and Dockets Data)
Fax: (303) 844-2540
Internet: www.ca10.uscourts.gov

Number of Judgeships: 12

Supreme Court Justice: Associate Justice Sonia Sotomayor

Areas Covered: Colorado, Kansas, New Mexico, Oklahoma, Utah and Wyoming

Court Staff
Circuit Executive **David Tighe** . . . . (303) 844-2067
E-mail: dave_tighe@ca10.uscourts.gov Fax: (303) 335-2838
Education: Penn State 1974 BS; Colorado 1989 JD
Deputy Circuit Executive **Leslee Faathallah** . . . . (303) 335-2067
Fax: (303) 335-2838
Director of Information Services **Mike Kopatich** . . . . (303) 335-3046
E-mail: mike_kopatich@ca10.uscourts.gov Fax: (303) 335-3022
Education: Colorado State 1987 BA
Assistant Circuit Executive for Space and Facilities
Laura Nelson . . . . (303) 335-2067
E-mail: laura_nelson@ca10.uscourts.gov Fax: (303) 335-2838
Clerk of the Court **Elizabeth A. "Betsy" Shumaker** . . . . (303) 844-3157
E-mail: Betsy_Shumaker@ca10.uscourts.gov Fax: (303) 844-2540
Chief Deputy Clerk **Chris Wolpert** . . . . (303) 335-3077
E-mail: chris_wolpert@ca10.uscourts.gov
Chief Staff Counsel **Niki Heller** . . . . (303) 844-5306
E-mail: niki_heller@ca10.uscourts.gov Fax: (303) 844-3733
Education: Wyoming 1984 BS, 1988 JD
Supervising Staff Attorney **Taye Sanford** . . . . (303) 844-5306
E-mail: taye_sanford@ca10.uscourts.gov Fax: (303) 844-3733
Education: Wesleyan U 1980 BA;
William & Mary 1983 JD

United States Court of Appeals for the Tenth Circuit *continued*

Chief Circuit Mediator **David W. Aemmer** . . . . (303) 844-6017
E-mail: david_aemmer@ca10.uscourts.gov Fax: (303) 844-6437
Education: Ohio State 1977 BA; Toledo 1980 JD;
Tufts 1989 MA
Financial and Budget Officer **Jodi Elnicki** . . . . (303) 335-2067
E-mail: jodi_elnicki@ca10.uscourts.gov Fax: (303) 335-2838
Circuit Librarian **Madeline R. Cohen** . . . . (303) 844-3591
1929 Stout Street, 4th Floor, Denver, CO 80294 Fax: (303) 844-5958
E-mail: madeline_cohen@ca10.uscourts.gov
Telecommunications and User Support **(Vacant)** . . . . (303) 335-3044
Fax: (303) 335-3022

Chambers of Chief Judge Timothy M. Tymkovich
1823 Stout Street, Room 102 G, Denver, CO 80257
Tel: (303) 335-3300 Fax: (303) 335-2517
E-mail: timothy_m_tymkovich@ca10.uscourts.gov

Timothy M. Tymkovich
Chief Judge

Date of Birth: November 2, 1956
Education: Colorado Col 1979 BA; Colorado 1982 JD
Began Service: June 19, 2003
Appointed By: President George W. Bush

Current Memberships: American Bar Association; The American Law Institute; Colorado Bar Foundation, Colorado Bar Association; International Society of Barristers

Staff
Secretary **Pearl Donder** . . . . (303) 335-3300
E-mail: pearl_donder@ca10.uscourts.gov

Chambers of Circuit Judge Mary Beck Briscoe
645 Massachusetts, Suite 400, Lawrence, KS 66044
Tel: (785) 843-4067 Fax: (785) 843-4322

Mary Beck Briscoe
Circuit Judge

Date of Birth: 1947
Education: Kansas 1969 BA, 1973 JD; Virginia 1990 LLM
Began Service: May 31, 1995
Appointed By: President William J. Clinton

Staff
Law Clerk **Stephanie Jo Grant** . . . . (785) 843-4067
Began Service: September 2015
Term Expires: August 2016
E-mail: stephanie_grant@ca10.uscourts.gov
Law Clerk **Kevin J. Holt** . . . . (785) 843-4067
Began Service: September 2015
Term Expires: August 2016
E-mail: kevin_holt@ca10.uscourts.gov
Law Clerk **Carrie Phillips** . . . . (785) 843-4067
Began Service: September 2015
Term Expires: August 2016
E-mail: carrie_phillips@ca10.uscourts.gov
Career Law Clerk **Tracy Venters** . . . . (785) 843-4067
E-mail: tracy_venters@ca10.uscourts.gov
Education: Kansas 1988 JD
Secretary **Carol Barnthson** . . . . (785) 843-4067
E-mail: carol_barnthson@ca10.uscourts.gov

Chambers of Circuit Judge Paul J. Kelly, Jr.

120 U.S. Courthouse, South Federal Plaza, Santa Fe, NM 87501
P.O. Box 10113, Santa Fe, NM 87504
Tel: (505) 988-6541 Fax: (505) 988-6545

Paul J. Kelly
Circuit Judge

Date of Birth: 1940
Education: Notre Dame 1963 BBA; Fordham 1967 JD
Began Service: April 14, 1992
Appointed By: President George H.W. Bush
Political Affiliation: Republican

Government: State Representative (R-NM), New Mexico House of Representatives (1977-1981)

Legal Practice: Associate, Hinkle, Bondurant, Cox & Eaton (1967-1971); Partner, Hinkle, Cox, Eaton, Coffield & Hensley (1971-1992)

Current Memberships: The Oliver Seth American Inn of Court, The American Inns of Court; Federal Bar Association; Santa Fe County Bar Association; State Bar of New Mexico

Staff

Law Clerk **Rachel Herd** .... (505) 988-6541
Began Service: August 2015
Term Expires: August 2016
E-mail: rachel_herd@ca10.uscourts.gov
Education: Seattle 2015 JD

Law Clerk **Devon Lash** .... (505) 988-6541
Began Service: August 2015
Term Expires: August 2016
E-mail: devon_lash@ca10.uscourts.gov
Education: Fordham 2015 JD

Law Clerk **Catherine Schmucker** .... (505) 988-6541
Began Service: August 2015
Term Expires: August 2016
E-mail: catherine_schmucker@ca10.uscourts.gov
Education: Texas Tech 2015 JD

Career Law Clerk **Robert Tepper** .... (505) 988-6541
E-mail: robert_tepper@ca10.uscourts.gov
Education: New Mexico 1983 JD

Judicial Assistant **Rita Gallegos** .... (505) 988-6541
E-mail: rita_gallegos@ca10.uscourts.gov

Chambers of Circuit Judge Carlos F. Lucero

Byron White U.S. Courthouse, 1823 Stout Street, Denver, CO 80257
Tel: (303) 844-2200 Fax: (303) 844-2201
E-mail: Carlos_F_Lucero@ca10.uscourts.gov

Carlos F. Lucero
Circuit Judge

Date of Birth: 1940
Education: Adams State 1961 BA; George Washington 1964 JD
Began Service: July 22, 1995
Appointed By: President William J. Clinton
Political Affiliation: Democrat

Clerkships: Law Clerk The Honorable William E. Doyle, United States District Court for the District of Colorado (1964-1965)

Government: Staff Assistant, Subcommittee on Administrative Practice and Procedure, Committee on the Judiciary, United States Senate (1963-1964)

Legal Practice: Associate, Law Office of Jesse E. Pound (1965-1966); Partner, Pound & Lucero (1966-1980); Partner, Lucero, Lester & Sigmond (1980-1995)

Current Memberships: American College of Trial Lawyers; International Academy of Trial Lawyers; International Society of Barristers

Staff

Law Clerk **Sarah Judkins** .... (303) 844-2200
Began Service: August 2015
Term Expires: August 2016
E-mail: sarah_judkins@ca10.uscourts.gov
Education: Colorado 2014 JD

Chambers of Circuit Judge Carlos F. Lucero *continued*

Law Clerk **Michael Lane** .... (303) 844-2200
Began Service: August 2015
Term Expires: August 2016
E-mail: michael_lane@ca10.uscourts.gov

Law Clerk **Mikael Gatsby Miller** .... (303) 844-2200
Began Service: August 2015
Term Expires: August 2016
Education: Columbia 2015 JD

Career Law Clerk **Joshua Glasgow** .... (303) 844-2200
Began Service: 2009
E-mail: joshua_glasgow@ca10.uscourts.gov
Education: Yale 2006 JD

Judicial Assistant **Stephanie Morelee** .... (303) 844-2200
E-mail: stephanie_morelee@ca10.uscourts.gov
Education: Metro State Col Denver 1989 BS

Chambers of Circuit Judge Harris L Hartz

201 Third Street NW, Suite 1870, Albuquerque, NM 87102
Tel: (505) 843-6196 Fax: (505) 843-6202

Harris L Hartz
Circuit Judge

Date of Birth: 1947
Education: Harvard 1967 AB, 1972 JD
Began Service: December 2001
Appointed By: President George W. Bush

Academic: Visiting Assistant Professor, University of Illinois College of Law (1976)

Government: Assistant United States Attorney, District of New Mexico, United States Attorney's Office, United States Department of Justice, Gerald Ford Administration (1972-1975); Counsel and Executive Director, Governor's Commission on Organized Crime Prevention, Office of the Governor, State of New Mexico (1976-1979)

Judicial: Judge, New Mexico Court of Appeals (1988-1999)

Legal Practice: Associate, Poole, Tinnin & Martin, PA (1979-1982); Associate, Miller, Stratvert & Torgerson, P.A. (1982-1983); Shareholder, Miller, Stratvert & Torgerson, P.A. (1983-1988); Special Counsel, Stier, Anderson & Malone (1999-2001)

Current Memberships: American Bar Association; The American Law Institute

Staff

Law Clerk **Jeff Nardinelli** .... (505) 843-6196
Began Service: August 2015
Term Expires: August 2016
E-mail: jeff_nardinelli@ca10.uscourts.gov

Law Clerk **Tom Ryan** .... (505) 843-6196
Began Service: August 2015
Term Expires: August 2016
E-mail: tom_ryan@ca10.uscourts.gov

Law Clerk **Angela Rollins** .... (505) 843-6196
Began Service: August 2015
Term Expires: August 2016
E-mail: angela_rollins@ca10.uscourts.gov

Career Law Clerk **Serge Voronov** .... (505) 843-6196
Began Service: August 2015
E-mail: serge_voronov@ca10.uscourts.gov

Judicial Assistant **Claudette Romero** .... (505) 843-6196
E-mail: claudette_romero@ca10.uscourts.gov
Education: Albuquerque BS

Chambers of Circuit Judge Jerome A. Holmes

215 Dean A. McGee Avenue, Room 315, Oklahoma City, OK 73102
Tel: (405) 609-5480
E-mail: jerome_a_holmes@ca10.uscourts.gov

Jerome A. Holmes
Circuit Judge

Education: Wake Forest 1983 BA; Georgetown 1988 JD; John F Kennedy 2000 MPA
Began Service: August 2006
Appointed By: President George W. Bush

Clerkships: Law Clerk, District Judge Wayne E. Alley, United States District Court for the Western District of Oklahoma (1988-1990); Law Clerk, Chief Judge William J. Holloway, Jr., United States Court of Appeals for the Tenth Circuit (1990-1991)

Government: Assistant U.S. Attorney, Criminal Division, Oklahoma - Western District, United States Department of Justice (1994-2005); Deputy Chief, Criminal Division, Oklahoma - Western District, United States Department of Justice (1996-2004); Anti-Terrorism Coordinator, Office of the Assistant U.S. Attorney, Oklahoma - Western District, United States Department of Justice (2003-2005)

Legal Practice: Chair, Diversity Committee, Crowe & Dunlevy

Current Memberships: Oklahoma Bar Association

Staff
Judicial Assistant **Mary Stricklin** . . . . . . (405) 609-5480
E-mail: mary_stricklin@ca10.uscourts.gov

Chambers of Circuit Judge Neil M. Gorsuch

Byron White U.S. Courthouse, 1823 Stout Street, Denver, CO 80257
Tel: (303) 335-2800

Neil M. Gorsuch
Circuit Judge

Date of Birth: 1967
Education: Columbia 1988 BA; Harvard 1991 JD; Oxford (UK) 2004 DPhil
Began Service: August 2006
Appointed By: President George W. Bush

Clerkships: Law Clerk, Circuit Judge David B. Sentelle, United States Court of Appeals for the District of Columbia Circuit (1991-1992); Law Clerk, Associate Justice Byron R. White, Supreme Court of the United States (1993-1994); Law Clerk, Associate Justice Anthony M. Kennedy, Supreme Court of the United States (1993-1994)

Government: Principal Deputy to the Associate Attorney General, Office of the Associate Attorney General, Office of the Deputy Attorney General, United States Department of Justice (2005-2006); Principal Deputy Associate Attorney General, Office of the Associate Attorney General, Office of the Deputy Attorney General, United States Department of Justice

Legal Practice: Attorney, Private Practice (1995-2005)

Staff
Law Clerk **Alex Harris** . . . . . . (303) 335-2800
Began Service: August 2015
Term Expires: August 2016
E-mail: gerard_cedrone@ca10.uscourts.gov
Education: Harvard 2015 JD
Law Clerk **Stefan Hasselblad** . . . . . . (303) 335-2800
Began Service: August 2015
Term Expires: August 2016
E-mail: stefan_hasselblad@ca10.uscourts.gov
Education: Harvard 2015 JD
Law Clerk **Jordan Moran** . . . . . . (303) 335-2800
Began Service: August 2015
Term Expires: August 2016
E-mail: hamilton_jordan@ca10.uscourts.gov
Education: Harvard 2015 JD

Chambers of Circuit Judge Neil M. Gorsuch *continued*

Law Clerk **Allison Turbiville** . . . . . . (303) 335-2800
Began Service: August 2015
Term Expires: August 2016
E-mail: allison_turbiville@ca10.uscourts.gov
Education: Yale 2015 JD
Judicial Assistant **Holly Cody** . . . . . . (303) 844-3157
E-mail: holly_cody@ca10.uscourts.gov

Chambers of Circuit Judge Scott M. Matheson Jr.

125 South State Street, Suite 5402, Salt Lake City, UT 84138
Tel: (801) 524-5145
E-mail: scott_matheson@ca10.uscourts.gov

Scott M. Matheson, Jr.
Circuit Judge

Date of Birth: July 18, 1953
Education: Stanford 1975 AB; Oxford (UK) MA; Yale 1980 JD
Began Service: January 6, 2011
Appointed By: President Barack Obama
Political Affiliation: Democrat

Academic: Dean, S.J. Quinney College of Law, University of Utah (1998-2006)

Government: Unites States Attorney, District of Utah, United States Attorney's Office, United States Department of Justice (1993-1998); Chairman, Utah Mine Safety Commission, Oil, Gas and Mining Division, State of Utah (2007-2008)

Legal Practice: Associate, Williams & Connolly LLP (1981-1985)

Staff
Law Clerk **Travis Hunt** . . . . . . (801) 524-5145
Began Service: August 2015
Term Expires: August 2016
E-mail: travis_hunt@ca10.uscourts.gov
Law Clerk **Richard "Dick" Baldwin** . . . . . . (801) 524-5145
Term Expires: January 2016
E-mail: dick_baldwin@ca10.uscourts.gov
Law Clerk **Cullen Macbeth** . . . . . . (801) 524-5145
Began Service: August 2015
Term Expires: August 2016
E-mail: cullen_macbeth@ca10.uscourts.gov
Education: Harvard 2014 JD
Law Clerk **Lara Tumeh** . . . . . . (801) 524-5145
Began Service: August 2015
Term Expires: August 2016
E-mail: lara_tumeh@ca10.uscourts.gov
Judicial Assistant **Ana Kahn** . . . . . . (801) 524-5145

Chambers of Circuit Judge Robert E. Bacharach

1823 Stout Street, Denver, CO 80257
Tel: (405) 609-5320

Robert E. Bacharach
Circuit Judge

Date of Birth: 1959
Education: Washington U (MO) 1985 JD
Began Service: March 1, 2013
Appointed By: President Barack Obama

Clerkships: Law Clerk The Honorable William J. Holloway, Jr., United States Court of Appeals for the Tenth Circuit (1985-1987); Magistrate Judge, Chambers of Magistrate Judge Robert E. Bacharach, United States District Court for the Western District of Oklahoma (1999-2013)

Legal Practice: Crowe & Dunlevy (1987-1999)

Staff
Law Clerk **Emilie Blanchard** . . . . . . (405) 609-5320
E-mail: emilie_blanchard@ca10.uscourts.gov
Law Clerk **Sean Delphey** . . . . . . (405) 609-5320
E-mail: sean_delphey@ca10.uscourts.gov

(continued on next page)

Chambers of Circuit Judge Robert E. Bacharach *continued*

Law Clerk **Katherine "Kate" Holey** .... (405) 609-5320
Education: Oklahoma City JD

Law Clerk **Elliott Hood** .... (405) 609-5320
E-mail: elliott_hood@ca10.uscourts.gov

Judicial Assistant **Rosene Coleman** .... (405) 609-5320
E-mail: rosene_coleman@ca10.uscourts.gov

Chambers of Circuit Judge Gregory Alan Phillips

1823 Stout Street, Denver, CO 80257
Tel: (303) 844-3157

Gregory Alan Phillips
Circuit Judge

Education: Wyoming 1983 BS, 1987 JD
Began Service: July 22, 2013
Appointed By: President Barack Obama

Chambers of Circuit Judge Carolyn B. McHugh

125 South State Street, Salt Lake City, UT 84138-1181
Tel: (801) 401-8150
E-mail: carolyn_mchugh@ca10.uscourts.gov

Carolyn B. McHugh
Circuit Judge

Education: Utah 1978 BA, 1982 JD
Began Service: March 17, 2014
Appointed By: President Barack Obama

Judicial: Associate Presiding Judge, Chambers of Associate Presiding Judge Carolyn B. McHugh, Utah Court of Appeals (2005-2012); Presiding Judge, Utah Court of Appeals (2012-2014)

Current Memberships: Utah State Bar

Chambers of Circuit Judge Nancy L. Moritz

1823 Stout Street, Denver, CO 80257
Tel: (303) 844-3157
E-mail: nancy_moritz@ca10.uscourts.gov

Nancy L. Moritz
Circuit Judge

Date of Birth: March 3, 1960
Education: Washburn 1982 BBA, 1985 JD
Began Service: July 29, 2014
Appointed By: President Barack Obama

Clerkships: Justice, Chambers of Justice Nancy Moritz, Kansas Supreme Court (2011-2014)

Government: Research Attorney, Chambers of Justice Harold Herd, Kansas Supreme Court (1985-1987); Assistant U.S. Attorney, Civil Division, Topeka (KS) Office, United States Department of Justice

Judicial: Judge, Chambers of Judge Nancy Caplinger, Kansas Court of Appeals (2004-2011)

Legal Practice: Associate, Spencer Fane Britt & Browne LLP (1989-1995)

Current Memberships: Kansas Bar Association; Topeka Bar Association; Women Attorneys Association of Topeka

Chambers of Senior Judge Monroe G. McKay

6012 Federal Building, 125 South State Street,
Salt Lake City, UT 84138-1181
Tel: (801) 524-5252 Fax: (801) 524-6796

Monroe G. McKay
Senior Judge

Date of Birth: 1928
Education: BYU 1957 BS; Chicago 1960 JD
Began Service: December 1, 1977
Appointed By: President Jimmy Carter

Academic: Professor, Brigham Young University (1974-1977)

Clerkships: Law Clerk The Honorable Jesse A. Udall (1960-1961)

Government: Country Director, Malawi, Africa, Peace Corps (1966-1968)

Legal Practice: Associate, Lewis and Roca LLP (1961-1966); Partner, Lewis and Roca LLP (1968-1974)

Military Service: United States Marine Corps (1946-1948)

Current Memberships: State Bar of Arizona

Staff

Law Clerk **Darren Gardner** .... (801) 524-5252
E-mail: darren_gardner@ca10.uscourts.gov

Law Clerk **Cynthia Ricks** .... (801) 524-5252
Began Service: August 2007
E-mail: cynthia_ricks@ca10.uscourts.gov
Education: Washington U (MO) 2006 JD

Judicial Assistant **Carolyn Dennis** .... (801) 524-5252
E-mail: carolyn_dennis@ca10.uscourts.gov

Chambers of Senior Judge John C. Porfilio

Byron White U.S. Courthouse, 1823 Stout Street, Denver, CO 80257
Tel: (303) 844-3157

John C. Porfilio
Senior Judge

Date of Birth: 1934
Education: Denver 1956 BA, 1959 LLB
Began Service: May 14, 1985
Appointed By: President Ronald Reagan

Government: Assistant Attorney General, Office of the Attorney General, United States Department of Justice (1962-1968); Deputy Attorney General, United States Department of Justice (1968-1972); Attorney General, United States Department of Justice (1972-1974)

Judicial: Bankruptcy Judge, United States Bankruptcy Court for the District of Colorado (1975-1982); District Judge, United States District Court for the District of Colorado (1982-1985)

Legal Practice: Carbone & Walsmith (1959-1962)

Current Memberships: American Bar Association; Colorado Bar Association; Denver Bar Association

Chambers of Senior Judge Stephen H. Anderson

4201 Wallace F. Bennett Federal Building, 125 South State Street,
Salt Lake City, UT 84138-1102
Tel: (801) 524-6950 Fax: (801) 524-5776
E-mail: stephen_h_anderson@ca10.uscourts.gov

Stephen H. Anderson
Senior Judge

Date of Birth: 1932
Education: Utah 1960 LLB
Began Service: November 1985
Appointed By: President Ronald Reagan

Academic: Lecturer, University of Utah; Teacher, South High School

Chambers of Senior Judge Stephen H. Anderson *continued*

Government: Trial Attorney, Tax Division, United States Department of Justice (1960-1964); Grand Jury Special Counsel, Salt Lake County Justice Court (1975)

Legal Practice: Attorney, Ray Quinney & Nebeker P.C. (1964-1985)

Military Service: United States Army (1953-1955)

Staff

Career Law Clerk **Lydia Berggren** .... (801) 524-6950
E-mail: lydia_berggren@ca10.uscourts.gov
Education: Harvard 1977 AB; Oxford (UK) BA; Boalt Hall JD

Judicial Assistant **Nancy D. Hughes** .... (801) 524-6950
E-mail: nancy_hughes@ca10.uscourts.gov

Chambers of Senior Judge Bobby R. Baldock

P.O. Box 2388, Roswell, NM 88202
Tel: (575) 625-2388 Fax: (575) 625-0829

Bobby R. Baldock
Senior Judge

Date of Birth: 1936
Education: Arizona 1960 JD
Began Service: 1985
Appointed By: President Ronald Reagan

Academic: Adjunct Professor, Eastern New Mexico University (1962-1981)

Judicial: District Judge, United States District Court for the District of New Mexico (1983-1985)

Legal Practice: Partner, Sanders, Bruin & Baldock (1960-1983)

Military Service: United States Army Reserve, United States Department of the Army (1960-1969)

Nonprofit: Arbitrator, American Arbitration Association (1972-1974)

Current Memberships: New Mexico Trial Lawyers Association; State Bar of Arizona; State Bar of New Mexico

Staff

Administrative Assistant **Lynda Brown** .... (575) 625-2388
E-mail: lynda_brown@ca10.uscourts.gov

Chambers of Senior Judge Stephanie K. Seymour

4562 U.S. Courthouse, 333 West Fourth Street, Tulsa, OK 74103-3877
Tel: (918) 699-4745

Stephanie K. Seymour
Senior Judge

Date of Birth: 1940
Education: Smith 1962 BA; Harvard 1965 JD
Began Service: November 16, 1979
Appointed By: President Jimmy Carter

Legal Practice: Associate, Goodwin, Procter & Hoar, LLP (1965-1966); Associate, Lupardus, Holliman & Huffman (1966-1967); Associate, Baker and Botts (1968-1969); Associate, Doerner, Stuart, Saunders, Daniel & Anderson LLP (1971-1975); Partner, Doerner, Stuart, Saunders, Daniel & Anderson LLP (1975-1979)

Current Memberships: The Council Oak/Johnson-Sontag American Inn of Court; American Bar Association; Federal Judges Association; National Association of Women Judges; Oklahoma Bar Association; Tulsa County Bar Association

Staff

Law Clerk **Max Hellman** .... (918) 699-4745
Began Service: August 2013
E-mail: max_hellman@ca10.uscourts.gov

Judicial Assistant **Joan Swope** .... (918) 699-4745
E-mail: joan_swope@ca10.uscourts.gov

Chambers of Senior Judge David M. Ebel

Byron White U.S. Courthouse, 1823 Stout Street, Room 109L, Denver, CO 80257
Tel: (303) 844-3800 Fax: (303) 844-4541
E-mail: David_M_Ebel@ca10.uscourts.gov

David Milton Ebel
Senior Judge

Date of Birth: 1940
Education: Northwestern 1962 BA; Michigan 1965 JD
Began Service: July 1988
Appointed By: President Ronald Reagan

Academic: Adjunct Professor, College of Law, University of Denver (1986-1988); Senior Lecturing Fellow, School of Law, Duke University (1992-1994)

Clerkships: Law Clerk The Honorable Byron White, Supreme Court of the United States (1965-1966)

Legal Practice: Attorney, Davis Graham & Stubbs LLP (1966-1988)

Current Memberships: American College of Trial Lawyers

Staff

Law Clerk **Zach Fitzgerald** .... (303) 844-3800
Began Service: August 2015
Term Expires: August 2016
E-mail: zach_fitzgerald@ca10.uscourts.gov

Law Clerk **Corinne Johnson** .... (303) 844-3800
Began Service: August 2015
Term Expires: August 2016
E-mail: corinne_johnson@ca10.uscourts.gov

Career Law Clerk **Joan Buhler** .... (303) 844-3800
E-mail: joan_buhler@ca10.uscourts.gov

Judicial Assistant **Jana Dillingham** .... (303) 844-3800
E-mail: jana_dillingham@ca10.uscourts.gov

Chambers of Senior Judge Michael R. Murphy

5438 Wallace F. Bennett Federal Building, 125 South State Street, Salt Lake City, UT 84138-1181
Tel: (801) 524-5955 Fax: (801) 524-5979
E-mail: Judge_Michael_R_Murphy@ca10.uscourts.gov

Michael R. Murphy
Senior Judge

Date of Birth: 1947
Education: Creighton 1969 BA; Wyoming 1972 JD
Began Service: October 5, 1995
Appointed By: President William J. Clinton

Current Memberships: American Bar Foundation; American Bar Association; The Giles S. Rich American Inn of Court, The American Inns of Court; Utah Bar Association

Staff

Career Law Clerk **Susan G. Lawrence** .... (801) 524-5955
E-mail: susan_lawrence@ca10.uscourts.gov
Education: Syracuse 1988 JD

Career Law Clerk **Del J. Ross** .... (801) 524-5955
E-mail: del_ross@ca10.uscourts.gov
Education: Utah 1993 JD

Chambers of Senior Judge Terrence L. O'Brien
2120 Carey Avenue, Room 2107, Cheyenne, WY 82001
Tel: (307) 433-2400 Fax: (307) 433-2415
E-mail: terrence_l_obrien@ca10.uscourts.gov

Terrence L. O'Brien
Senior Judge

Date of Birth: 1943
Education: Wyoming 1965 BS, 1972 JD
Began Service: April 23, 2002
Appointed By: President George W. Bush

Staff
Career Law Clerk **Nicole Kean** . . . . (307) 433-2400
E-mail: nicole_kean@ca10.uscourts.gov
Education: Washburn JD
Career Law Clerk **(Vacant)** . . . . (307) 433-2400
Administrative Judicial Assistant **(Vacant)** . . . . (307) 433-2400

United States Bankruptcy Appellate Panel for the Tenth Circuit
Byron White U.S. Courthouse, 1823 Stout Street, Denver, CO 80257
Tel: (303) 335-2900 Fax: (303) 335-2999
E-mail: 10th_circuit_bap@ca10.uscourts.gov
Internet: www.bap10.uscourts.gov

Number of Judgeships: 9

Court Staff
Bankruptcy Appellate Panel Clerk **Blaine F. Bates** . . . . (303) 335-2900
Panel Attorney **(Vacant)** . . . . (303) 335-2900
Deputy Clerk/Attorney **(Vacant)** . . . . (303) 335-2900

Chambers of Chief Bankruptcy Judge Janice Miller Karlin
Byron White U.S. Courthouse, 1823 Stout Street, Denver, CO 80257
Tel: (785) 338-5950

Janice Miller Karlin
Chief Bankruptcy Judge

Education: Kansas 1975 BA, 1980 JD
Began Service: June 2008
Term Expires: 2016

Chambers of Bankruptcy Judge William T. Thurman
Byron White U.S. Courthouse, 1823 Stout Street, Denver, CO 80257
Tel: (801) 524-6572

William T. Thurman
Bankruptcy Judge

Date of Birth: 1947
Education: Utah 1971 BA, 1974 JD
Began Service: May 6, 2008
Term Expires: 2016

Current Memberships: American Bankruptcy Institute; National Conference of Bankruptcy Judges

Staff
Career Law Clerk **Julia Attwood** . . . . (801) 524-6572

Chambers of Bankruptcy Judge Tom R. Cornish
209 U.S. Post Office & Courthouse, 111 West Fourth Street, Okmulgee, OK 74447
P.O. Box 1347, Okmulgee, OK 74447
Tel: (918) 549-7205 Fax: (918) 549-7208

Tom R. Cornish
Bankruptcy Judge

Education: Oklahoma State 1966 BS; Oklahoma 1968 JD; Virginia 1982 LLM
Began Service: February 7, 1996
Term Expires: January 19, 2017

Judicial: Judge, Oklahoma Court of Criminal Appeals (1977-1984); Chief Bankruptcy Judge, Chambers of Chief Bankruptcy Judge Tom R. Cornish, United States Bankruptcy Appellate Panel for the Tenth Circuit (1996-2012)

Current Memberships: Oklahoma Bar Association

Staff
Career Law Clerk **Melanie Trump** . . . . (918) 549-7205
Began Service: August 2006
Education: Kansas 1983 JD
Judicial Assistant **Alexia Bible** . . . . (918) 549-7205

Chambers of Bankruptcy Judge Terrence L. Michael
224 South Boulder Avenue, Tulsa, OK 74103-3015
Tel: (918) 699-4065 Fax: (918) 699-4061

Terrence L. Michael
Bankruptcy Judge

Date of Birth: 1958
Education: Doane 1980 BA; USC 1983 JD
Began Service: June 9, 1997

Affiliation: Chief Bankruptcy Judge, Chambers of Chief Bankruptcy Judge Terrence L. Michael, United States Bankruptcy Court for the Northern District of Oklahoma

Judicial: Chief Bankruptcy Judge, United States Bankruptcy Court for the Northern District of Oklahoma (1999-2001)

Legal Practice: Baird, Holm Law Offices (1983-1997)

Current Memberships: National Conference of Bankruptcy Judges

Staff
Career Law Clerk **Janie Phelps** . . . . (918) 699-4062
Education: Lewis & Clark 2004 JD
Courtroom Deputy **Sue Haskins** . . . . (918) 699-4068
Judicial Assistant **Odie Gonzales** . . . . (918) 699-4065

Chambers of Bankruptcy Judge Robert E. Nugent
104 U.S. Courthouse, 401 North Market Street, Wichita, KS 67202
Tel: (316) 315-4150 Fax: (316) 315-4111

Robert E. Nugent
Bankruptcy Judge

Date of Birth: 1955
Education: Kansas 1980 JD
Began Service: 2007
Term Expires: 2017

Affiliation: Chief Bankruptcy Judge, Chambers of Chief Bankruptcy Judge Robert E. Nugent, United States Bankruptcy Court for the District of Kansas

Staff
Career Law Clerk (part-time) **Samantha H. Seang** . . . . . . (316) 315-4150
E-mail: sam_seang@ksb.uscourts.gov
Education: Kansas 1996 JD
Judicial Assistant **Janet Swonger** . . . . (316) 315-4150

Chambers of Bankruptcy Judge Michael E. Romero
1823 Stout Street, Denver, CO 80257
Tel: (720) 904-7413 Fax: (303) 335-2999

Michael E. Romero
Bankruptcy Judge

Date of Birth: June 30, 1955
Education: Denver 1977 BA; Michigan 1980 JD
Began Service: March 30, 2009

Legal Practice: Associate, Holland & Hart LLP (1980-1983); Associate, Issac, Rosenbaum, Woods, Levy and Snow (1983-1987); Shareholder/Director, Pendleton, Friedberg, Wilson & Hennessey, P.C. (1987-2003)

Nonprofit: Director/President, Longmont Theatre Company (1992-1996)

Chambers of Bankruptcy Judge Dale L. Somers
444 South East Quincy Street, Room 225, Topeka, KS 66683
Tel: (785) 338-5960 Fax: (785) 338-5949

Dale L. Somers
Bankruptcy Judge

Began Service: 2011

Chambers of Bankruptcy Judge Robert H. Jacobvitz
1823 Stout Street, Denver, CO 80257
Tel: (505) 348-2545

Robert H. Jacobvitz
Bankruptcy Judge

Began Service: November 8, 2012

Chambers of Bankruptcy Judge Sarah Hall
215 Dean A. McGee Avenue, Oklahoma City, OK 73102
Tel: (405) 609-5660

Sarah A. Hall
Bankruptcy Judge

United States Court of Appeals for the Eleventh Circuit
Elbert P. Tuttle U.S. Court of Appeals Building, 56 NW Forsyth Street, Atlanta, GA 30303
Tel: (404) 335-6100
Internet: www.ca11.uscourts.gov

Number of Judgeships: 12

Number of Vacancies: 1

Supreme Court Justice: Associate Justice Clarence Thomas

Areas Covered: Alabama, Florida and Georgia

Court Staff
Circuit Executive **COL James P. Gerstenlauer** . . . . (404) 335-6535
Affiliation: USA
E-mail: james_gerstenlauer@ca11.uscourts.gov
Education: Penn State BA; Boston U MBA; Kansas JD
Clerk of the Court (Acting) **Amy Nerenberg** . . . . (404) 335-6100
Senior Staff Attorney **Jason Brener** . . . . (404) 335-6411
E-mail: jason_brener@ca11.uscourts.gov
Chief Circuit Mediator (Acting) **Caleb Davies** . . . . (404) 335-6260
E-mail: caleb_davies@ca11.uscourts.gov
Circuit Librarian **Elaine P. Fenton** . . . . (404) 335-6500
E-mail: elaine_fenton@ca11.uscourts.gov
Education: Emory 1970 BA, 1972 MLS

Chambers of Chief Judge Ed Carnes
U.S. Courthouse, One Church Street, Montgomery, AL 36104
Tel: (334) 954-3580

Edward Carnes
Chief Judge

Date of Birth: 1950
Education: Alabama 1972 BS; Harvard 1975 JD
Began Service: October 2, 1992
Appointed By: President George H.W. Bush

Staff
Judicial Administrator **Blanche Baker** . . . . (334) 954-3580
E-mail: blanche_baker@ca11.uscourts.gov

Chambers of Circuit Judge Gerald Bard Tjoflat
56 NW Forsyth Street, Atlanta, GA 30303
Tel: (904) 301-5670 Fax: (904) 301-5680
E-mail: gerald_tjoflat@ca11.uscourts.gov

Gerald Bard Tjoflat
Circuit Judge

Date of Birth: 1929
Education: Duke 1957 LLB
Began Service: November 21, 1975
Appointed By: President Gerald Ford

Judicial: Judge, Florida Circuit Court, Fourth Judicial Circuit (1968-1970); Judge, United States District Court for the Northern District of Florida (1970-1975)

Legal Practice: Associate, Howell & Kirby (1957-1958); Partner, Adams & Tjoflat (1958-1960); Partner, Botts, Mahoney, Whitehead, Ramsaur & Hadlow (1960-1968)

Military Service: United States Army (1953-1955)

Current Memberships: American Bar Association; The American Law Institute; Federal Bar Association; The Florida Bar; Jacksonville Bar Association

Staff
Law Clerk **James Lambert** . . . . (904) 301-6570
Began Service: August 2015
Term Expires: August 2016
E-mail: james_lambert@ca11.uscourts.gov
Law Clerk **Darlena Kern** . . . . (904) 301-6570
Began Service: August 2015
Term Expires: August 2016
E-mail: darlena_kern@ca11.uscourts.gov
Law Clerk **Kyle Druding** . . . . (904) 301-6570
Began Service: August 2015
Term Expires: August 2016
E-mail: kyle_druding@ca11.uscourts.gov
Law Clerk **William Friedman** . . . . (904) 301-6570
Began Service: August 2015
Term Expires: August 2016
E-mail: william_friedman@ca11.uscourts.gov
Law Clerk **William Alex Smith** . . . . (904) 301-6570
Began Service: August 2015
Term Expires: August 2016
Secretary **Barbara A. Lay** . . . . (904) 301-6570
E-mail: barbara_lay@ca11.uscourts.gov

FEDERAL COURTS—UNITED STATES COURTS OF APPEALS

Chambers of Circuit Judge Frank M. Hull

56 Forsyth Street, NW, Atlanta, GA 30303
Tel: (404) 335-6550
E-mail: frank_hull@ca11.uscourts.gov

Frank M. Hull
Circuit Judge

Date of Birth: 1948
Education: Randolph-Macon 1970 BA; Emory 1973 JD
Began Service: October 3, 1997
Appointed By: President William J. Clinton

Clerkships: Law Clerk The Honorable Elbert P. Tuttle, United States Court of Appeals for the Fifth Circuit (1973-1974)

Judicial: Judge, State Court of Fulton County (1984-1990); Judge, Georgia Superior Court, Fulton County, Atlanta Judicial Circuit (1990-1994); Judge, United States District Court for the Northern District of Georgia (1994-1997)

Legal Practice: Attorney, Powell, Goldstein, Frazer & Murphy LLP (1974-1984)

Current Memberships: American Bar Foundation; Federal Bar Association; Order of the Coif; State Bar of Georgia

Staff

Law Clerk **Matthew Friedlander** .... (404) 335-6550
Began Service: August 2015
Term Expires: August 2016
E-mail: matthew_friedlander@ca11.uscourts.gov

Law Clerk **Shanna Reulbach** .... (404) 335-6550
Began Service: August 2015
Term Expires: August 2016
E-mail: shanna_reulbach@ca11.uscourts.gov

Law Clerk **Milton Wilkins** .... (404) 335-6550
Began Service: August 2015
Term Expires: August 2016
E-mail: milton_wilkins@ca11.uscourts.gov

Law Clerk **Jameson Bilsborrow** .... (404) 335-6550
Began Service: August 2015
Term Expires: August 2016
E-mail: jameson_bilsborrow@ca11.uscourts.gov

Career Law Clerk **Laura Story** .... (404) 335-6550
E-mail: laura_story@ca11.uscourts.gov
Education: Florida State 1987 BA;
Georgia State 1995 JD

Judicial Administrator **Darlene Buchanan** .... (404) 335-6550
E-mail: darlene_buchanan@ca11.uscourts.gov

Chambers of Circuit Judge Stanley Marcus

99 NE Fourth Street, Room 1235, Miami, FL 33132
Tel: (305) 536-4841
E-mail: stanley_marcus@ca11.uscourts.gov

Stanley Marcus
Circuit Judge

Date of Birth: 1946
Education: Queens Col (NY) 1967 BA; Harvard 1971 JD
Began Service: November 24, 1997
Appointed By: President William J. Clinton

Government: Associate, United States Department of Justice (1975); Assistant United States Attorney, Eastern District of New York, United States Department of Justice (1975-1978); Deputy Chief, Detroit Office, Organized Crime Strike Force (1978-1979); Deputy-in-Charge, Detroit Office, Organized Crime Strike Force (1980-1982); United States Attorney, Southern District of Florida, United States Department of Justice (1982-1985)

Judicial: District Judge, United States District Court for the Southern District of Florida (1985-1997)

Legal Practice: Botein, Hays, Sklar & Herzberg (1974)

Military Service: United States Army (1968-1974)

Chambers of Circuit Judge Stanley Marcus *continued*

Staff

Judicial Administrator **Lynn White** .... (305) 536-4841
E-mail: lynn_white@ca11.uscourts.gov

Chambers of Circuit Judge Charles R. Wilson

Sam M. Gibbons Courthouse, 801 North Florida Avenue, Suite 16-B, Tampa, FL 33602
Tel: (813) 301-5650 Fax: (813) 301-5659
E-mail: charles_wilson@ca11.uscourts.gov

Charles Reginald Wilson
Circuit Judge

Date of Birth: 1954
Education: Notre Dame 1976 BA, 1979 JD
Began Service: September 30, 1999
Appointed By: President William J. Clinton

Clerkships: Law Clerk Joseph W. Hatchett, United States Court of Appeals for the Fifth Circuit (1980)

Government: United States Attorney, Middle District of Florida, United States Department of Justice (1994-1999)

Judicial: County Judge, Thirteenth Judicial Circuit of Florida (1986-1990); Magistrate Judge, United States District Court for the Middle of the District of Florida (1990-1994)

Legal Practice: Private Practice (1981-1986)

Current Memberships: American Bar Association; The C.H. Ferguson-M.E. White American Inn of Court, The American Inns of Court; The American Law Institute; Federal Bar Association; The Florida Bar

Staff

Judicial Administrator **Beth Banister** .... (813) 301-5650
E-mail: Beth_Banister@ca11.uscourts.gov
Education: Florida State 1980 BS

Chambers of Circuit Judge William H. Pryor Jr.

1729 Fifth Avenue North, Suite 900, Birmingham, AL 35203
Tel: (205) 278-2030 Fax: (205) 278-2025

William Holcombe "Bill" Pryor, Jr.
Circuit Judge

Education: Northeast Louisiana 1984 BA; Tulane 1987 JD
Began Service: February 20, 2004
Appointed By: President George W. Bush

Academic: Adjunct Professor, Cumberland School of Law (1989-1995)

Government: Deputy Attorney General, Office of the Attorney General, State of Alabama (1995-1997); Attorney General, Office of the Attorney General, State of Alabama (1997-2004)

Staff

Staff Attorney **Stephanie Morman** .... (205) 278-2030
E-mail: stephanie_morman@ca11.uscourts.gov

Judicial Administrator **Deanna Stone** .... (205) 278-2030
E-mail: deanna_stone@ca11.uscourts.gov

Chambers of Circuit Judge Beverly Baldwin Martin

56 Forsyth Street, NW, Atlanta, GA 30303
Tel: (404) 335-6630

Beverly Baldwin Martin
Circuit Judge

Date of Birth: 1955
Education: Stetson 1976 BA; Georgia 1981 JD
Began Service: January 28, 2010
Appointed By: President Barack Obama

Government: Assistant Attorney General, Office of the Attorney General, State Law Department (1984-1994); Assistant United States Attorney, Georgia - Middle District, Office of the Attorney General, United States Department of Justice (1994-1997); United States Attorney, Middle District of Georgia (1997-2000)

Judicial: District Judge, Chambers of District Judge Beverly Baldwin Martin, United States District Court for the Northern District of Georgia (2000-2010)

Staff

Law Clerk **Corey Brady** .... (404) 335-6100
Term Expires: September 2016
E-mail: corey_brady@ca11.uscourts.gov

Law Clerk **Jessica Jensen** .... (404) 335-6100
Began Service: September 2015
Term Expires: September 2016
E-mail: jessica_jensen@ca11.uscourts.gov

Law Clerk **Shakeer Rahman** .... (404) 335-6100
Term Expires: September 2016
E-mail: shakeer_rahman@ca11.uscourts.gov
Education: Harvard 2015 JD

Law Clerk **Sarah Beth Solomon** .... (404) 335-6100
Term Expires: September 2016
E-mail: sarah_solomon@ca11.uscourts.gov

Staff Attorney **(Vacant)** .... (404) 335-6100

Chambers of Circuit Judge Adalberto Jordán

56 NW Forsyth Street, Atlanta, GA 30303
Tel: (305) 523-5560
E-mail: adalberto_jordan@ca11.uscourts.gov

Adalberto José Jordán
Circuit Judge

Date of Birth: 1961
Education: Miami 1984 BA, 1987 JD
Began Service: 2012
Appointed By: President Barack Obama

Clerkships: Law Clerk The Honorable Thomas Clark, United States Court of Appeals for the Eleventh Circuit (1987-1988); Law Clerk The Honorable Sandra Day O'Connor, United States Supreme Court (1988-1989)

Government: Assistant United States Attorney, Southern District of Florida, United States Attorney's Office, United States Department of Justice (1994-1996); Deputy Chief of the Appellate Division, Southern District of Florida, United States Attorney's Office, United States Department of Justice (1996-1998); Chief of the Appellate Division, Southern District of Florida, United States Attorney's Office, United States Department of Justice (1998-1999)

Legal Practice: Litigation Associate, Steel Hector & Davis LLP (1989-1993); Partner, Steel Hector & Davis LLP (1994-1994)

Current Memberships: American Bar Association; The Florida Bar

Chambers of Circuit Judge Robin S. Rosenbaum

56 NW Forsyth Street, Atlanta, GA 30303
Tel: (954) 769-5670

Robin S. Rosenbaum
Circuit Judge

Education: Cornell 1988 BA; Miami 1991 JD
Began Service: June 3, 2014
Appointed By: President Barack Obama

Government: Chief, Economic Crimes Section, Executive Office for United States Attorneys, United States Department of Justice (1998-2007)

Judicial: Magistrate Judge, Chambers of Magistrate Judge Robin S. Rosenbaum, United States District Court for the Southern District of Florida (2007-2012); District Judge, Chambers of District Judge Robin S. Rosenbaum, United States District Court for the Southern District of Florida (2012-2014)

Staff

Law Clerk **Carel Ale** .... (954) 769-5670
Term Expires: August 2016
E-mail: carel_ale@ca11.uscourts.gov

Law Clerk **John Langford** .... (954) 769-5670
Term Expires: October 2016
E-mail: john_langford@ca11.uscourts.gov

Law Clerk **Brendon Olson** .... (954) 769-5670
Term Expires: August 2016
E-mail: brendon_olson@ca11.uscourts.gov

Career Law Clerk **Kristie Myers** .... (954) 769-5670
E-mail: kristie_myers@ca11.uscourts.gov

Judicial Assistant **Helen Pantaleo** .... (954) 769-5670
Term Expires: August 2016

Chambers of Circuit Judge Julie E. Carnes

56 NW Forsyth Street, Atlanta, GA 30303
Tel: (404) 335-6100
E-mail: julie_carnes@ca11.uscourts.gov

Julie E. Carnes
Circuit Judge

Date of Birth: 1950
Education: Georgia 1972 AB, 1975 JD
Began Service: July 31, 2014
Appointed By: President Barack Obama

Government: Appellate Chief, Office of the United States Attorney, Northern District of Georgia, United States Department of Justice (1978-1990); Special Counsel, United States Sentencing Commission (1989); Commissioner, United States Sentencing Commission (1990-1996)

Judicial: District Judge, United States District Court for the Northern District of Georgia (1992-2009); Chief Judge, Chambers of Chief Judge Julie E. Carnes, United States District Court for the Northern District of Georgia (2009-2014)

Chambers of Circuit Judge Jill A. Pryor

56 NW Forsyth Street, Atlanta, GA 30303
Tel: (404) 335-6100

Jill A. Pryor
Circuit Judge

Education: William & Mary 1985 BA; Yale 1988 JD
Began Service: October 6, 2014
Appointed By: President Barack Obama

Legal Practice: Associate, Bondurant, Mixson & Elmore, LLP (1989-1997)

Nonprofit: President, Georgia Association for Women Lawyers; Chair, State Bar of Georgia; Member, Lawyers Advisory Committee

Chambers of Senior Judge James C. Hill

US Courthouse, 300 North Hogan Street, Suite 14-400,
Jacksonville, FL 32202-4258
Tel: (904) 301-6630 Fax: (904) 301-6635
E-mail: james_hill@ca11.uscourts.gov

James C. Hill
Senior Judge

Date of Birth: 1924
Education: South Carolina 1948 BS; Emory 1948 JD
Began Service: May 1976
Appointed By: President Gerald Ford
Political Affiliation: Republican

Judicial: Judge, United States District Court for the Northern District of Georgia (1974-1976)

Legal Practice: Attorney, Gambrell, Russell, Killorin & Forbes (1948-1963); Partner, Hurt, Hill & Richardson (1963-1974)

Military Service: United States Army Air Corps (1943-1945)

Current Memberships: American Bar Foundation; American Bar Association; American College of Trial Lawyers; The American Law Institute; Lawyers Club of Atlanta, Inc.; State Bar of Georgia; World Association of Judges

Staff

Career Law Clerk **Sharon Kennedy** .... (904) 301-6630
Education: Florida State 1969 BA, 1971 MS; Florida 1977 PhD, 1982 JD

Career Law Clerk **Barbara P. Lanahan** .... (904) 301-6630
E-mail: barbara_lanahan@ca11.uscourts.gov
Education: Florida 1974 BA, 1977 JD, 1978 LLM

Judicial Administrator **Earleen Shord** .... (904) 301-6630
E-mail: earleen_shord@ca11.uscourts.gov
Education: Columbia 1980 MA

Chambers of Senior Judge Peter T. Fay

Federal Justice Building, 99 NE Fourth Street, Room 1255,
Miami, FL 33132
Tel: (305) 579-4390 Fax: (305) 579-4395

Peter T. Fay
Senior Judge

Date of Birth: 1929
Education: Rollins 1951 BA; Florida 1956 JD
Began Service: 1976
Appointed By: President Gerald Ford

Judicial: Judge, United States District Court for the Southern District of Florida (1970-1976); Judge, Panel for the Appointment of Independent Counsel

Legal Practice: Partner, Nichols, Gaither, Green, Frates & Beckham (1956-1961); Partner, Frates, Fay, Floyd & Pearson (1961-1970)

Military Service: United States Air Force (1951-1953)

Current Memberships: American Bar Association; Dade County Bar Association

Staff

Law Clerk **Monika Woodard** .... (305) 579-4393
Began Service: August 2015
Term Expires: August 2016
E-mail: monika_woodard@ca11.uscourts.gov

Career Law Clerk **Eugenia Gates** .... (305) 579-4394
Began Service: July 2013
E-mail: eugenia_gates@ca11.uscourts.gov
Education: Tulane 1985 JD

Chambers of Senior Judge Phyllis A. Kravitch

56 Forsyth Street, Room 202, Atlanta, GA 30303
Tel: (404) 335-6300 Fax: (404) 335-6308
E-mail: phyllis_kravitch@ca11.uscourts.gov

Phyllis A. Kravitch
Senior Judge

Date of Birth: 1920
Education: Goucher 1941 BA; Pennsylvania 1943 LLB
Began Service: April 10, 1979
Appointed By: President Jimmy Carter

Judicial: Judge, Georgia Superior Court (1977-1979)

Legal Practice: Kravitch & Hendrix (and predecessor firms) (1965-1970)

Current Memberships: American Bar Foundation; American Bar Association; The American Law Institute; Atlanta Bar Association; Eleventh Circuit Historical Society; Federal Judges Association; Lawyers Club of Atlanta, Inc.; Savannah Bar Association; State Bar of Georgia

Staff

Executive Administrator **Bridgett Godwin** .... (404) 335-6300
E-mail: bridgett_godwin@ca11.uscourts.gov

Chambers of Senior Judge R. Lanier Anderson III

475 Mulberry Street, Room 302, Macon, GA 31201
P.O. Box 977, Macon, GA 31202-0977
Tel: (478) 752-8101 Fax: (478) 752-3473

R. Lanier Anderson III
Senior Judge

Date of Birth: 1936
Education: Yale 1958 AB; Harvard 1961 LLB
Began Service: August 1979
Appointed By: President Jimmy Carter

Judicial: Circuit Judge, United States Court of Appeals for the Eleventh Circuit (1979-2009)

Legal Practice: Attorney, Anderson, Walker & Reichert, LLP (1963-1979)

Military Service: United States Army Reserve, United States Department of the Army (1958-1961); United States Army (1961-1963)

Current Memberships: American Bar Association; Macon Bar Association; State Bar of Georgia

Membership: Member, Judicial Conference of the United States (1999-2002)

Staff

Law Clerk **Daniel Cassman** .... (478) 752-8101
Began Service: September 2015
Term Expires: September 2016
E-mail: daniel_cassman@ca11.uscourts.gov

Law Clerk **Jason W. Schnier** .... (478) 752-8101
Began Service: September 2015
Term Expires: September 2016
E-mail: jason_schnier@ca11.uscourts.gov
Education: Columbia 2015 JD

Career Law Clerk **Anne Tunnessen** .... (478) 752-8101
E-mail: anne_tunnessen@ca11.uscourts.gov

Judicial Administrator **Sharon Bowers** .... (478) 752-8101
E-mail: sharon_bowers@ca11.uscourts.gov

Chambers of Senior Judge J. L. Edmondson
56 NW Forsyth Street, Room 416, Atlanta, GA 30303
Tel: (404) 335-6230 Fax: (404) 335-6238

J. L. Edmondson
Senior Judge

Date of Birth: 1947
Education: Emory 1968 BA; Georgia 1971 JD; Virginia 1990 LLM
Began Service: June 9, 1986
Appointed By: President Ronald Reagan

Staff
Career Law Clerk **Sarah Whalin** . . . . (404) 335-6230
Began Service: August 2011
E-mail: sarah_whalin@ca11.uscourts.gov
Secretary **Margie Browning** . . . . (404) 335-6230
E-mail: margie_browning@ca11.uscourts.gov

Chambers of Senior Judge Emmett R. Cox
113 St. Joseph Street, Room 433, Mobile, AL 36602
Tel: (251) 690-2055 Fax: (251) 694-4491
E-mail: emmett_cox@ca11.uscourts.gov

Emmett Ripley Cox
Senior Judge

Date of Birth: 1935
Education: Alabama 1957 AB, 1959 LLB
Began Service: 1988
Appointed By: President Ronald Reagan

Judicial: Judge, United States District Court for the Southern District of Alabama (1981-1988)

Legal Practice: Associate, Mead & Norman (1959-1964); Attorney, Gaillard, Wilkins, Smith & Cox (1964-1970); Partner, Nettles, Cox & Barker (1970-1981)

Military Service: Air National Guard (1958-1964)

Current Memberships: Alabama State Bar; Maritime Law Association of the United States; Mobile Bar Association

Staff
Administrative Assistant **Rhonda Case** . . . . (251) 690-2055
E-mail: rhonda_case@ca11.uscourts.gov

Chambers of Senior Judge Joel Dubina
U.S. Courthouse, One Church Street, Montgomery, AL 36104
Tel: (334) 954-3560 Fax: (334) 954-3579
E-mail: joel_dubina@ca11.uscourts.gov

Joel F. Dubina
Senior Judge

Date of Birth: October 26, 1947
Education: Alabama 1970 BS; Cumberland 1973 JD
Began Service: 1990
Appointed By: President George H.W. Bush

Staff
Law Clerk **Sarah Osbourne** . . . . (334) 954-3560
Began Service: August 2015
Term Expires: September 1, 2016
E-mail: sarah_osbourne@ca11.uscourts.gov
Career Law Clerk **Ruth Williamson** . . . . (334) 954-3560
E-mail: ruth_williamson@ca11.uscourts.gov
Education: Alabama 1989 JD
Judicial Assistant **Debbie Venable** . . . . (334) 954-3560
E-mail: debbie_venable@ca11.uscourts.gov
Secretary **(Vacant)** . . . . (334) 954-3560

Chambers of Senior Judge Susan H. Black
300 North Hogan Street, Suite 14-150, Jacksonville, FL 32202-4258
Tel: (904) 301-5610
E-mail: Susan_Black@ca11.uscourts.gov

Susan Harrell Black
Senior Judge

Date of Birth: 1943
Education: Florida State 1965 BA; Florida 1967 JD; Virginia 1984 LLM
Began Service: August 12, 1992
Appointed By: President George H.W. Bush

Government: Attorney, Corps of Engineers, United States Army (1968-1969); Assistant State Attorney, Office of the State Attorney, State of Florida (1969-1972)

Judicial: Judge, Duval County Court (1973-1975); Judge, Florida Circuit Court (1975-1979); Judge, United States District Court for the Middle District of Florida (1979-1992); Circuit Judge, Chambers of Circuit Judge Susan H. Black, United States Court of Appeals for the Eleventh Circuit (1992-2011)

Current Memberships: American Inns of Court Foundation, The American Inns of Court; The Chester Bedell American Inn of Court, The American Inns of Court; The Florida Bar; Jacksonville Bar Association

Staff
Judicial Administrator **Sandra Madison** . . . . (904) 301-5610

United States Court of Appeals for the District of Columbia Circuit
E. Barrett Prettyman U.S. Courthouse, 333 Constitution Avenue, NW, Washington, DC 20001-2866
Tel: (202) 216-7000 Tel: (202) 216-7300 (Clerk's Office)
Tel: (202) 216-7312 (Calendar) Tel: (202) 216-7280 (Intake)
Tel: (202) 273-0926 (Appellate Case Voice Information)
Tel: (202) 216-7296 (Electronic Opinions Voice) Fax: (202) 273-0988
Internet: www.cadc.uscourts.gov

Number of Judgeships: 11

Supreme Court Justice: Chief Justice John G. Roberts Jr.

Court Staff
Circuit Executive **Elizabeth H. "Betsy" Paret** . . . . (202) 216-7340
E-mail: elizabeth_paret@cadc.uscourts.gov Fax: (202) 273-0331
Education: American U 1987 BA; USC 1994 MPA
Circuit Clerk **Mark J. Langer** . . . . (202) 216-7300
E-mail: mark_langer@cadc.uscourts.gov
Education: Kalamazoo 1979 BA; Duke 1983 JD
Chief Deputy Clerk **Marilyn R. Sargent** . . . . (202) 216-7300
E-mail: marilyn_sargent@cadc.uscourts.gov
Legal Division Director **Martha J. Tomich** . . . . (202) 216-7500
E-mail: martha_tomich@cadc.uscourts.gov Fax: (202) 273-0384
Education: Beaver 1975 BA;
Columbus Law 1978 JD
Chief Circuit Mediator **Amy Wind** . . . . (202) 216-7350
E-mail: amy_wind@cadc.uscourts.gov
Education: Scripps Col BA; Hastings JD
Circuit Librarian **Patricia Michalowskij** . . . . (202) 216-7400
E-mail: patricia_michalowskij@cadc.uscourts.gov Fax: (202) 273-0915

Chambers of Chief Judge Merrick B. Garland

333 Constitution Avenue, NW, Washington, DC 20001-2866
Tel: (202) 216-7460 Tel: (202) 208-2449
E-mail: merrick_garland@cadc.uscourts.gov

Merrick B. Garland
Chief Judge

Date of Birth: 1952
Education: Harvard 1974 AB, 1977 JD
Began Service: April 9, 1997
Appointed By: President William J. Clinton

Staff
Administrative Assistant **Marcia Davidson** . . . . (202) 216-7460
E-mail: marcia_davidson@cadc.uscourts.gov

Chambers of Circuit Judge Karen LeCraft Henderson

E. Barrett Prettyman U.S. Courthouse, 333 Constitution Avenue, NW, Room 3118, Washington, DC 20001
Tel: (202) 216-7370 Fax: (202) 273-0983
E-mail: karen_henderson@cadc.uscourts.gov

Karen LeCraft Henderson
Circuit Judge

Date of Birth: 1944
Education: Duke 1966 BA; North Carolina 1969 JD
Began Service: July 11, 1990
Appointed By: President George H.W. Bush

Government: Assistant Attorney General, Office of the Attorney General, State of South Carolina (1973-1978); Senior Assistant Attorney General and Director, Special Litigation Section, Office of the Attorney General, State of South Carolina (1978-1982); Deputy Attorney General and Director, Criminal Division, Office of the Attorney General, State of South Carolina (1982)

Judicial: Judge, United States District Court for the District of South Carolina (1986-1990)

Legal Practice: Partner, Wright & Henderson (1969-1970); Sinkler, Gibbs & Simons, PA (1983-1986)

Current Memberships: American Bar Association; The Federal American Inn of Court, The American Inns of Court; The American Law Institute; Federal Judges Association; North Carolina Bar Association; South Carolina Bar; The Supreme Court Historical Society

Staff
Law Clerk **Ryan Baasch** . . . . (202) 216-7374
Began Service: August 2015
Term Expires: August 2016
E-mail: ryan_basch@cadc.uscourts.gov
Education: Virginia 2015 JD
Law Clerk **Charles Andrew Davis** . . . . (202) 216-7373
Began Service: September 2015
Term Expires: September 2016
E-mail: charles_davis@cadc.uscourts.gov
Education: George Washington 2013 JD
Law Clerk **John Harris** . . . . (202) 216-7373
Began Service: September 2015
Term Expires: September 2016
E-mail: john_harris@cadc.uscourts.gov
Education: North Carolina JD
Judicial Administrator **Mary Gigliotti** . . . . (202) 216-7376
E-mail: mary_gigliotti@cadc.uscourts.gov

Chambers of Circuit Judge Judith W. Rogers

William B. Bryant Annex, 333 Constitution Avenue, NW, Room 5907, Washington, DC 20001-2866
Tel: (202) 216-7260 Fax: (202) 482-2546
E-mail: judith_rogers@cadc.uscourts.gov

Judith W. Rogers
Circuit Judge

Education: Radcliffe 1961 AB; Harvard 1964 LLB; Virginia 1988 LLM
Began Service: March 21, 1994
Appointed By: President William J. Clinton

Clerkships: Law Clerk, District of Columbia Juvenile Court (1964-1965)

Government: Assistant U.S. Attorney, District of Columbia District, Executive Office for United States Attorneys, United States Department of Justice (1965-1968); Trial Attorney, Criminal Division, United States Department of Justice (1969-1971); General Counsel, Commission on the Organization of the District Government (1971-1972); Legislative Program Coordinator, Office of the Assistant to the Mayor-Commissioner, District of Columbia (1972-1974); Special Assistant, Mayor Walter Washington (D-DC), Office of the Mayor, District of Columbia (1974-1979); Assistant City Administrator, Office of the City Administrator, District of Columbia; Corporation Counsel, District of Columbia (1979-1983)

Judicial: Judge, District of Columbia Court of Appeals (1983-1990); Chief Judge, District of Columbia Court of Appeals (1990-1994)

Nonprofit: Staff Attorney, San Francisco Neighborhood Legal Assistance Foundation (1968-1969)

Current Memberships: American Bar Association; The American Law Institute; The District of Columbia Bar; National Association of Women Judges; National Bar Association

Staff
Secretary **Doreen Greenan** . . . . (202) 216-7260
E-mail: doreen_greenan@cadc.uscourts.gov

Chambers of Circuit Judge David S. Tatel

E. Barrett Prettyman U.S. Courthouse, 333 Constitution Avenue, NW, 5004 William B. Bryant Annex, Washington, DC 20001-2826
Tel: (202) 216-7160 Fax: (202) 208-1922
E-mail: dtatel@cadc.uscourts.gov

David S. Tatel
Circuit Judge

Date of Birth: 1942
Education: Michigan 1963 BA; Chicago 1966 JD
Began Service: October 11, 1994
Appointed By: President William J. Clinton

Academic: Instructor, Michigan (1966-1967); Lecturer, Stanford University (1991-1992)

Corporate: Acting General Counsel, Legal Services Corporation (1975-1976)

Government: Director, Office for Civil Rights, United States Department of Health, Education and Welfare (1977-1979)

Legal Practice: Associate, Sidley & Austin (1967-1969); Associate, Sidley & Austin (1970-1972); Associate, Hogan & Hartson LLP (1974-1977); Partner, Hogan & Hartson LLP (1979-1994)

Nonprofit: Director, Chicago Lawyers Committee for Civil Rights Under Law (1969-1970); Director, National Lawyers' Committee for Civil Rights Under Law (1972-1974)

Current Memberships: National Academy of Education

Staff
Law Clerk **Sylvanus Polky** . . . . (202) 216-7165
Began Service: August 2015
Term Expires: August 2016
E-mail: sylvanus_polky@cadc.uscourts.gov

Chambers of Circuit Judge David S. Tatel *continued*

Law Clerk **Heather Welles** .... (202) 216-7164
Began Service: August 2015
Term Expires: August 2016
E-mail: heather_welles@cadc.uscourts.gov

Law Clerk **Emma Simson** .... (202) 216-7162
Began Service: August 2015
Term Expires: August 2016
E-mail: emma_simson@cadc.uscourts.gov
Education: Yale 2013 JD

Law Clerk **Matthew Rubenstein** .... (202) 216-7163
Began Service: August 2015
Term Expires: August 2016
E-mail: matthew_rubenstein@cadc.uscourts.gov

Reader **Nathan Blevins** .... (202) 216-7166
E-mail: nathan.blevins@cadc.uscourts.gov

Secretary **Jana Frieslander** .... (202) 216-7161
E-mail: jfrieslander@cadc.uscourts.gov

Chambers of Circuit Judge Janice Rogers Brown

333 Constitution Avenue, NW, Washington, DC 20001-2866
Tel: (202) 216-7220
E-mail: janice_brown@cadc.uscourts.gov

Janice Rogers Brown
Circuit Judge

Date of Birth: 1949
Education: Cal State (Sacramento) 1974 BA; UCLA 1977 JD
Began Service: July 1, 2005
Appointed By: President George W. Bush
Political Affiliation: Republican

Academic: Adjunct Professor, McGeorge School of Law

Government: Deputy Legislative Counsel, Legislative Counsel Office, State of California (1977-1979); Deputy Attorney General, State of California (1979-1987); Deputy Secretary, Business, Transportation and Housing Agency, State of California (1987-1990); Legal Affairs Secretary, Governor Pete Wilson (R-CA), Office of the Governor, State of California (1991-1994)

Judicial: Associate Justice, California Court of Appeal, Third District (1994-1996); Associate Justice, California Supreme Court (1996-2005)

Legal Practice: Senior Associate, Nielson, Merksamer, Hodgson, Parinello & Mueller (1990-1991)

Current Memberships: California Judges Association; The Federalist Society for Law and Public Policy Studies

Staff

Law Clerk **Brendan Groves** .... (202) 216-7220
Began Service: September 2015
Term Expires: September 2016
E-mail: brendan_groves@cadc.uscourts.gov

Law Clerk **Bradley "Brad" Masters** .... (202) 216-7220
Began Service: September 2015
Term Expires: September 2016
E-mail: bradley_masters@cadc.uscourts.gov

Law Clerk **Mary K. "Katie" McCarthy** .... (202) 216-7220
Began Service: September 2015
Term Expires: September 2016

Law Clerk **Theodore Wold** .... (202) 216-7220
Began Service: September 2015
Term Expires: September 2016
E-mail: theodore_wold@cadc.uscourts.gov
Education: Notre Dame 2011 JD

Secretary **Audry Owens** .... (202) 216-7220

Chambers of Circuit Judge Thomas B. Griffith

333 Constitution Avenue, NW, Washington, DC 20001-2866
Tel: (202) 216-7170 Fax: (202) 208-0173
E-mail: Thomas_Griffith@cadc.uscourts.gov

Thomas B. Griffith
Circuit Judge

Education: BYU 1978 BA; Virginia 1985 JD
Began Service: June 29, 2005
Appointed By: President George W. Bush

Academic: Assistant to the President and General Counsel, Brigham Young University (2000-2005)

Government: Senate Legal Counsel, United States Senate (1995-1999)

Legal Practice: Attorney, Robinson, Bradshaw & Hinson, P.A. (1985-1989); Partner, Wiley Rein LLP (1989-1995)

Staff

Law Clerk **Cynthia Barmore** .... (202) 216-7176
Began Service: August 2015
Term Expires: August 2016
E-mail: cynthia_barmore@cadc.uscourts.gov
Education: Stanford 2015 JD

Law Clerk **Elizabeth Bewley** .... (202) 216-7175
Began Service: August 2015
Term Expires: August 2016
E-mail: elizabeth_bewley@cadc.uscourts.gov

Law Clerk **Natalie Hausknecht** .... (202) 216-7173
Began Service: August 2015
Term Expires: August 2016
E-mail: natalie_hausknecht@cadc.uscourts.gov

Law Clerk **Ivano Ventresca** .... (202) 216-7174
Began Service: August 2015
Term Expires: August 2016
E-mail: ivano_ventresca@cadc.uscourts.gov

Secretary **Candy Umin** .... (202) 216-7172
E-mail: candace_umin@cadc.uscourts.gov

Chambers of Circuit Judge Brett M. Kavanaugh

E. Barrett Prettyman U.S. Courthouse, 333 Constitution Avenue, NW, Room 3004, Washington, DC 20001
Tel: (202) 216-7180
E-mail: brett_kavanaugh@cadc.uscourts.gov

Brett M. Kavanaugh
Circuit Judge

Education: Yale 1987 BA, 1990 JD
Began Service: May 30, 2006
Appointed By: President George W. Bush

Clerkships: Law Clerk, Senior Judge Walter K. Stapleton, United States Court of Appeals for the Third Circuit (1990-1991); Law Clerk, Circuit Judge Alex Kozinski, United States Court of Appeals for the Ninth Circuit (1991-1992); Law Clerk, Associate Justice Anthony M. Kennedy, Supreme Court of the United States (1993-1994)

Government: Attorney, Office of the Solicitor, United States Department of Justice (1992-1993); Associate Counsel, Office of Independent Counsel (1994-1997); Senior Associate Counsel to the President, Executive Office of the President (2001-2004); Assistant to the President and Staff Secretary, Office of the Staff Secretary, Executive Office of the President, George W. Bush Administration (2004-2006)

Legal Practice: Partner, Kirkland & Ellis LLP (1997-2001)

Current Memberships: The American Law Institute

Staff

Law Clerk **Marguerite Colson** .... (202) 216-7180
Began Service: August 2015
Term Expires: August 2016
E-mail: marguerite_colson@cadc.uscourts.gov

(continued on next page)

Chambers of Circuit Judge Brett M. Kavanaugh *continued*

Law Clerk **Nick Harper** .... (202) 216-7180
Began Service: August 2015
Term Expires: August 2016
E-mail: nick_harper@cadc.uscourts.gov
Education: Chicago 2015 JD

Law Clerk **Julie Karaba** .... (202) 216-7180
Began Service: August 2015
Term Expires: August 2016
E-mail: julie_karaba@cadc.uscourts.gov

Law Clerk **Sean Mirski** .... (202) 216-7180
Began Service: August 2015
Term Expires: August 2016
E-mail: sean_mirski@cadc.uscourts.gov

Chambers of Circuit Judge Srikanth Srinivasan

333 Constitution Avenue, NW, Washington, DC 20001-2866
Tel: (202) 216-7080
E-mail: srikanth_srinivasan@cadc.uscourts.gov

Srikanth "Sri" Srinivasan
Circuit Judge

Education: Stanford 1989 AB, 1995 MBA, 1995 JD
Began Service: June 17, 2013
Appointed By: President Barack Obama

Chambers of Circuit Judge Patricia Ann Millett

E. Barry Prettyman U.S. Courthouse, 333 Constitution Avenue, NW, Washington, DC 20001-2866
Tel: (202) 216-7110
E-mail: patricia_millett@cadc.uscourts.gov

Patricia Ann Millett
Circuit Judge

Education: Illinois 1985 BA; Harvard 1988 JD
Began Service: February 28, 2014
Appointed By: President Barack Obama

Government: Assistant to the Solicitor General, Office of the Solicitor General, United States Department of Justice (1996-2007)

Legal Practice: Partner and Head of Practice Area, Supreme Court & Appellate Practice Group, Akin Gump Strauss Hauer & Feld LLP

Staff

Law Clerk **John Capehart** .... (202) 216-7110
Term Expires: July 2016
E-mail: john_capehart@cadc.uscourts.gov
Education: Oklahoma 2006 BA; Cambridge (UK) 2007 MPhil; Southern Methodist 2010 JD

Law Clerk **Teresa Reed** .... (202) 216-7110
Term Expires: July 2016
E-mail: teresa_reed@cadc.uscourts.gov

Law Clerk **Anne Lee Jang** .... (202) 216-7110
Term Expires: July 2016
E-mail: anne_jang@cadc.uscourts.gov

Law Clerk **Ashwin Phatak** .... (202) 216-7110
Term Expires: July 2016
E-mail: ashwin_phatak@cadc.uscourts.gov
Education: Harvard 2014 JD

Judicial Assistant **Adriana Bowen** .... (202) 216-7110
E-mail: adriana_bowen@cadc.uscourts.gov

Chambers of Circuit Judge Cornelia Pillard

E. Barry Prettyman U.S. Courthouse, 333 Constitution Avenue, NW, Washington, DC 20001-2866
Tel: (202) 216-7120
E-mail: cornelia_pillard@cadc.uscourts.gov

Cornelia T. L. "Nina" Pillard
Circuit Judge

Education: Yale 1983 BA; Harvard 1987 JD
Began Service: December 18, 2013
Appointed By: President Barack Obama

Staff

Law Clerk **Rachel Shalev** .... (202) 216-7120
E-mail: rachel_shalev@cadc.uscourts.gov

Law Clerk **Raymond "Ray" Tolentino** .... (202) 216-7120
E-mail: ray_tolentino@cadc.uscourts.gov

Law Clerk **Gabriel Daly** .... (202) 216-7120
E-mail: gabriel_daly@cadc.uscourts.gov

Law Clerk **Turner H. Smith** .... (202) 216-7120
E-mail: turner_smith@cadc.uscourts.gov

Chambers of Circuit Judge Robert L. Wilkins

E. Barry Prettyman U.S. Courthouse, 333 Constitution Avenue, NW, Washington, DC 20001-2866
Tel: (202) 216-7240
E-mail: rwilkins@cadc.uscourts.gov

Robert Leon Wilkins
Circuit Judge

Education: Rose-Hulman 1986 BS; Harvard 1989 JD
Began Service: January 24, 2014
Appointed By: President Barack Obama

Staff

Courtroom Deputy **(Vacant)** .... (202) 354-3179

Chambers of Senior Judge Douglas H. Ginsburg

E. Barrett Prettyman U.S. Courthouse, 333 Constitution Avenue, NW, Room 5128, Washington, DC 20001
Tel: (202) 216-7190 Fax: (202) 273-0678
E-mail: douglas_ginsburg@cadc.uscourts.gov

Douglas H. Ginsburg
Senior Judge

Date of Birth: 1946
Education: Cornell 1970 BS; Chicago 1973 JD
Began Service: October 14, 1986
Appointed By: President Ronald Reagan

Current Memberships: American Bar Association; American Economic Association; Illinois State Bar Association

Staff

Law Clerk **Amelia Frenkel** .... (202) 216-7190
Began Service: January 2015
Term Expires: January 2016
E-mail: amelia_frenkel@cadc.uscourts.gov
Education: Georgetown 2008 BA; NYU 2014 JD

Law Clerk **Joshua Hazan** .... (202) 216-7190
Began Service: August 2015
Term Expires: August 2016
E-mail: joshua_hazen@cadc.uscourts.gov

Judicial Assistant **Sharon Deare** .... (202) 216-7190
E-mail: sharon_deare@cadc.uscourts.gov

Chambers of Senior Judge David Bryan Sentelle

333 Constitution Avenue, NW, Washington, DC 20001-2866
Tel: (202) 216-7330
E-mail: david_sentelle@cadc.uscourts.gov

David Bryan Sentelle
Senior Judge

Date of Birth: 1943
Education: North Carolina 1965 BA, 1968 JD
Began Service: October 19, 1987
Appointed By: President Ronald Reagan
Political Affiliation: Republican

Current Memberships: The Edward Bennett Williams American Inn of Court, The American Inns of Court

Staff
Law Clerk **Dominique Caamano** .... (202) 216-7334
Began Service: August 2015
Term Expires: August 2016
Law Clerk **Catharine Wright** .... (202) 216-7336
Began Service: August 2015
Term Expires: August 2016
Law Clerk **Chase Zachary** .... (202) 216-7335
Began Service: August 2015
Term Expires: August 2016
Career Law Clerk **George Morris** .... (202) 216-7337
E-mail: george_morris@cadc.uscourts.gov
Secretary **Annette Huskey** .... (202) 216-7333
E-mail: annette_huskey@cadc.uscourts.gov

Chambers of Senior Judge Laurence H. Silberman

E. Barrett Prettyman U.S. Courthouse, 333 Constitution Avenue, NW, Room 3500, Washington, DC 20001-2866
Tel: (202) 216-7353 Fax: (202) 273-0831
E-mail: lsilberman@cadc.uscourts.gov

Laurence H. Silberman
Senior Judge

Date of Birth: 1935
Education: Dartmouth 1957 AB; Harvard 1961 LLB
Began Service: November 1, 1985
Appointed By: President Ronald Reagan

Academic: Adjunct Professor, The Law Center, Georgetown University (1987-1994); Adjunct Professor, School of Law, New York University (1995-1996); Adjunct Professor, Harvard Law School (1998); Adjunct Professor, The Law Center, Georgetown University (1999-2001); Adjunct Professor, The Law Center, Georgetown University (2002-2005)

Corporate: Executive Vice President of Strategic Planning, Legal and Government Affairs, Crocker National Bank (1979-1983)

Government: Attorney, Appellate Court Branch, Office of the General Counsel, National Labor Relations Board (1967-1969); Solicitor, Office of the Solicitor, United States Department of Labor (1969-1970); Under Secretary, United States Department of Labor, Richard M. Nixon Administration (1970-1973); Deputy Attorney General, United States Department of Justice, Gerald Ford Administration (1974-1975); Ambassador, Embassy of the United States, Yugoslavia, United States Department of State, Gerald Ford Administration (1975-1977); President's Special Envoy on ILO Affairs, Executive Office of the President (1976)

Legal Practice: Partner, Moore, Silberman & Schulze (and predecessor firms) (1961-1967); Attorney, Steptoe & Johnson LLP (1973-1974); Attorney, Morrison & Foerster LLP (1978-1979); Attorney, Morrison & Foerster LLP (1983-1985)

Military Service: United States Army Reserve, United States Department of Defense (1957-1958)

Nonprofit: Senior Fellow, American Enterprise Institute for Public Policy Research (1977-1978)

Current Memberships: Hawaii State Bar Association

Chambers of Senior Judge Laurence H. Silberman *continued*

Staff
Law Clerk **Jeffrey "Jeff" Long** .... (202) 216-7353
Began Service: September 2015
Term Expires: September 2016
E-mail: jeffrey_long@cadc.uscourts.gov
Secretary **Lisa Einsel** .... (202) 216-7353
E-mail: lisa_einsel@cadc.uscourts.gov

Chambers of Senior Judge Stephen F. Williams

E. Barrett Prettyman U.S. Courthouse, 333 Constitution Avenue, NW, Room 3700, Washington, DC 20001-2866
Tel: (202) 216-7210 Fax: (202) 273-0976
E-mail: sfwilliams@cadc.uscourts.gov

Stephen F. Williams
Senior Judge

Date of Birth: 1936
Education: Yale 1958 BA; Harvard 1961 JD
Began Service: 1986
Appointed By: President Ronald Reagan
Political Affiliation: Republican

Academic: Professor of Law, The University of Colorado System (1969-1986); Visiting Professor of Law, University of California, Los Angeles (1975-1976); Visiting Professor of Law, University of Chicago (1979-1980); Visiting Professor of Law, Southern Methodist University (1983-1984)

Government: Assistant United States Attorney, United States Department of Justice (1966-1969)

Legal Practice: Attorney, Debevoise, Plimpton, Lyons & Gates (1962-1966)

Military Service: United States Army (1961-1962)

Current Memberships: American Bar Association; The American Law Institute; Energy Bar Association

Staff
Law Clerk **David Hausman** .... (202) 216-7215
Began Service: August 2015
Term Expires: August 2016
E-mail: david_hausman@cadc.uscourts.gov
Law Clerk **Zachary Liscow** .... (202) 216-7213
Began Service: August 2015
Term Expires: August 2016
E-mail: zachary_liscow@cadc.uscourts.gov
Law Clerk **Olga Zverovich** .... (202) 216-7214
Began Service: August 2015
Term Expires: August 2016
E-mail: olga_zverovich@cadc.uscourts.gov
Judicial Administrator **Mary Catherine Matera** .... (202) 216-7210

Chambers of Senior Judge Harry T. Edwards

E. Barrett Prettyman U.S. Courthouse, 333 Constitution Avenue, NW, Room 5500, Washington, DC 20001-2805
Tel: (202) 216-7380 Fax: (202) 273-0119
E-mail: hedwards@cadc.uscourts.gov

Harry T. Edwards
Senior Judge

Date of Birth: 1940
Education: Cornell 1962 BS; Michigan 1965 JD
Began Service: February 20, 1980
Appointed By: President Jimmy Carter
Political Affiliation: Independent

Academic: Professor of Law, Law School, University of Michigan (1970-1975); Visiting Professor of Law, Program for International Legal Cooperation, Free University of Brussels (1974); Visiting Professor of Law, Harvard Law School (1975-1976); Professor of Law, Harvard Law School (1976-1977); Faculty Member, Institute for Educational Management, Harvard University (1976-1982); Professor of Law, Law School, University of Michigan (1977-1980); Lecturer in Law, School of Law, University of Pennsylvania (1981-1982); Lecturer in Law, Harvard Law School (1982-1988); Senior Lecturer in Law, School of Law, Duke University (1983-1989); Lecturer in Law, The Law Center, Georgetown University (1985-1986); Lecturer in Law, Law School, University of Michigan (1988-1989)

Corporate: Member, Editorial and Advisory Board, West Publishing Company (1978-1980)

Government: Public Member, Administrative Conference of the United States (1976-1980); Chairman, Board of Directors, AMTRAK [National Railroad Passenger Corporation] (1978-1980)

Judicial: Neutral Arbitrator (1970-1980); Member, Judicial Conference of the United States (1994-2001)

Legal Practice: Associate, Seyfarth, Shaw, Fairweather & Geraldson (1965-1970); Chairman, Ann Arbor Model Cities Legal Services Center, Inc. (1971-1972)

Current Memberships: American Academy of Arts and Sciences; American Bar Association; The American Law Institute; American Society of International Law; Association of American Law Schools; Federal Judges Association; The Supreme Court Historical Society

Staff
Judicial Assistant **Alva M. Hurd** .... (202) 216-7382
E-mail: alva_hurd@cadc.uscourts.gov

Chambers of Senior Judge A. Raymond Randolph

E. Barrett Prettyman U.S. Courthouse, 333 Constitution Avenue, NW, Room 5010, Washington, DC 20001-2866
Tel: (202) 216-7425 Fax: (202) 273-0004
E-mail: raymond_randolph@cadc.uscourts.gov

A. Raymond Randolph
Senior Judge

Date of Birth: 1943
Education: Drexel 1966 BS; Pennsylvania 1969 JD
Began Service: July 20, 1990
Appointed By: President George H.W. Bush

Academic: Adjunct Professor, The Law Center, Georgetown University (1974-1978)

Clerkships: Law Clerk The Honorable Henry J. Friendly, United States Court of Appeals for the Second Circuit (1969-1970)

Government: Assistant to the Solicitor General, Office of the Solicitor General, United States Department of Justice (1970-1973); Deputy Solicitor General, United States Department of Justice (1975-1977); Special Counsel, Committee on Standards of Official Conduct, United States House of Representatives (1980)

Judicial: Circuit Judge, United States Court of Appeals for the District of Columbia Circuit (1990-2008)

Chambers of Senior Judge A. Raymond Randolph *continued*

Legal Practice: Miller, Cassidy, Larroca & Lewin (1973-1975); Partner, Sharp, Randolph & Janis (1977-1979); Partner, Sharp, Randolph & Green (1979-1983); Partner, Randolph & Fox (1983-1984); Partner, Randolph & Truitt (1984-1987); Pepper, Hamilton & Scheetz (1987-1990)

Current Memberships: The American Law Institute; The Bar Association of the District of Columbia; State Bar of California

Staff
Law Clerk **Samuel Liefer** .... (202) 216-7425
Began Service: August 2015
Term Expires: August 2016
E-mail: samuel_liefer@cadc.uscourts.gov
Law Clerk **Stephen Tensmeyer** .... (202) 216-7425
Began Service: August 2015
Term Expires: August 2016
E-mail: stephen_tensmeyer@cadc.uscourts.gov

United States District Courts

Most federal cases are initially tried and decided in the United States District Courts, the federal courts of general trial jurisdiction. There are 94 courts in the 50 states, the District of Columbia, the Commonwealth of Puerto Rico, and the territories of Guam, the United States Virgin Islands, and the Northern Mariana Islands. Listed in this section for each district court are: U.S. District Court Staff, U.S. District Court judges and staff, U.S. Magistrate judges and staff, U.S. Senior judges and staff, and U.S. Bankruptcy judges and staff. The jurisdiction of the district courts extends to cases involving the U.S. constitution or federal laws, the U.S. government, or controversies between states or between the U.S. and foreign governments. The courts also hear cases involving citizens of different states, or between U. S. citizens and citizens from another country. With the exception of the territorial courts, all district court judges are appointed for life by the President with the advice and consent of the Senate. In each district, the judge who has served on the court the longest and who is under 65 years of age is designated as the chief judge. The chief judge has administrative duties in addition to a caseload. Within each district, the United States Bankruptcy Court hears and decides petitions of individuals and businesses seeking relief from bankruptcy. Bankruptcy judges are appointed by the court of appeals for a term of 14 years. The judges of each district appoint one or more magistrate judges, who discharge many of the ancillary duties of the district judges.

The district-by-district listings include both "active" and "senior" federal judges. Active Judges are listed by date of appointment. Senior judges are listed in the order in which they assumed senior status. Under current rules, an appellate or district court judge with 15 years of active service may "retire on salary" or assume "senior status" at age 65. A sliding scale makes judges with a minimum of 10 years of service eligible at age 70. Federal judges cannot be required to retire or take senior status when they become eligible, because they have life tenure under Article III of the Constitution, which is why they are called "Article III" judges. Those who take senior status continue to hear cases, though at a reduced level.

U.S. Magistrate judges play an important role in the federal litigation process. In civil cases it is not uncommon for magistrate judges to conduct almost all pretrial proceedings, preparing the case for trial before the assigned district judge. There are both full-time and part-time magistrate judge positions, and these positions are assigned to the district courts according to caseload criteria. A full-time magistrate judge serves a term of eight years; a part-time magistrate judge's term is four years.

United States District Court for the Middle District of Alabama

Frank M. Johnson, Jr. Federal Building & U.S. Courthouse,
One Church Street, Suite B - 110, Montgomery, AL 36104
P.O. Box 711, Montgomery, AL 36101
Tel: (334) 954-3600
Internet: www.almd.uscourts.gov

Number of Judgeships: 3

Number of Vacancies: 2

Circuit: Eleventh

Areas Covered: Counties of Autauga, Barbour, Bullock, Butler, Chambers, Chilton, Coffee, Coosa, Covington, Crenshaw, Dale, Elmore, Geneva, Henry, Houston, Lee, Lowndes, Macon, Montgomery, Pike, Randolph, Russell and Tallapoosa

Court Staff

District Clerk **Debra P. "Debbie" Hackett** . . . . (334) 954-3600
E-mail: Debbie_Hackett@almd.uscourts.gov
Chief Deputy Clerk **Trey Granger** . . . . (334) 954-3600
E-mail: trey_granger@almd.uscourts.gov
Education: Birmingham-Southern BA; Alabama JD
Chief Probation Officer **Dwayne Spurlock** . . . . (334) 954-3226
P.O. Box 39, Montgomery, AL 36102

Chambers of Chief Judge W. Keith Watkins

Frank M. Johnson, Jr. Federal Building & U.S. Courthouse,
One Church Street, Room 300-E, Montgomery, AL 36104
Tel: (334) 954-3760

W. Keith Watkins
Chief Judge

Education: Auburn 1973 BS; Alabama 1976 JD
Began Service: January 12, 2006
Appointed By: President George W. Bush

Legal Practice: Partner, Strudwick & Watkins (1976-1978); Partner, Clower & Watkins (1978-1986); Partner, Calhoun, Watkins & Clower (1987-1990); Partner, Calhoun, Faulk, Watkins, Clower & Cox (1990-1994)

Staff
Law Clerk **Patrick Hill** . . . . (334) 954-3766
Began Service: September 2015
Term Expires: September 2017
Career Law Clerk **Laura F. Wright** . . . . (334) 954-3764
Education: Mercer 1994 JD
Court Reporter **Risa Entrekin** . . . . (334) 240-2405
E-mail: risa_entrekin@almd.uscourts.gov
Judicial Assistant **Patricia Newkirk** . . . . (334) 954-3760

Chambers of Senior Judge Truman M. Hobbs

Frank M. Johnson, Jr. Federal Building & U.S. Courthouse,
One Church Street, D-300, Montgomery, AL 36104
Tel: (334) 954-3750 Fax: (334) 954-3615

Truman M. Hobbs
Senior Judge

Date of Birth: 1921
Education: North Carolina 1942 AB; Yale 1948 LLB
Began Service: April 14, 1980
Appointed By: President Jimmy Carter
Political Affiliation: Democrat

Clerkships: Law Clerk The Honorable Hugo Black, Supreme Court of the United States (1948-1949)

Government: Chairman, Unemployment Appeal Board, State of Alabama (1952-1958)

Legal Practice: Partner, Hobbs, Copeland, Franco & Screws (1949-1980)

Military Service: United States Navy (1942-1946)

Current Memberships: Alabama State Bar; American Association of Justice; American Bar Association; American College of Trial Lawyers; International Academy of Trial Lawyers; Montgomery County Bar Association

Staff
Courtroom Deputy **(Vacant)** . . . . (334) 954-3750

Chambers of Senior Judge W. Harold Albritton III

Frank M. Johnson, Jr. Federal Building & U.S. Courthouse,
One Church Street, Montgomery, AL 36104
P.O. Box 629, Montgomery, AL 36101
Tel: (334) 954-3710 Fax: (334) 954-3615

W. Harold Albritton III
Senior Judge

Date of Birth: 1936
Education: Alabama 1959 AB, 1960 LLB
Began Service: May 1991
Appointed By: President George H.W. Bush

Corporate: Director, The Commercial Bank (1983-1985); Director, First Alabama Bank (1985-1991)

(continued on next page)

Chambers of Senior Judge W. Harold Albritton III *continued*

Judicial: Chief Judge, United States District Court for the Middle District of Alabama (1998-2004)

Legal Practice: Partner, Albrittons, Givhan & Clifton (1962-1991)

Military Service: United States Army (1960-1962); United States Army Reserve, United States Department of the Army (1962-1968)

Current Memberships: American Bar Foundation; Alabama Bar Foundation; Alabama State Bar; American College of Trial Lawyers; The Montgomery American Inn of Court, The American Inns of Court; United States District Judges Association

Staff

Career Law Clerk **Lisa Harden** .... (334) 954-3710
E-mail: lisa_harden@almd.uscourts.gov
Education: Rhodes 1993 BA; Alabama 1996 JD

Judicial Assistant **Elna B. Behrman** .... (334) 954-3710
E-mail: elna_behrman@almd.uscourts.gov
Education: Troy State 1998 BA

Chambers of Senior Judge Myron H. Thompson

One Church Street, Montgomery, AL 36104
Tel: (334) 954-3650
E-mail: myron_thompson@almd.uscourts.gov

Myron H. Thompson
Senior Judge

Date of Birth: 1947
Education: Yale 1969 BA, 1972 JD
Began Service: September 29, 1980
Appointed By: President Jimmy Carter

Current Memberships: Alabama Lawyers Association; American Bar Association; National Bar Association

Staff

Law Clerk **Trinity Brown** .... (334) 954-3652
Began Service: August 2015
Term Expires: August 2016
E-mail: trinity_brown@almd.uscourts.gov

Law Clerk **Aaron Littman** .... (334) 954-3654
Term Expires: August 2016
Education: Yale 2014 JD

Law Clerk **William Williams** .... (334) 954-3654
Term Expires: August 2016

Career Law Clerk **Marion Chartoff** .... (334) 954-3651
E-mail: marion_chartoff@almd.uscourts.gov

Chambers of Chief Magistrate Judge Susan Russ Walker

Frank M. Johnson, Jr. Federal Building & U.S. Courthouse,
One Church Street, Suite 501-B, Montgomery, AL 36104
Tel: (334) 954-3670
E-mail: susan_walker@almd.uscourts.gov

Susan Russ Walker
Chief Magistrate Judge

Date of Birth: 1956
Education: Eckerd 1977 BA; Oxford (UK) 1980 MA; Yale 1986 JD
Began Service: April 2008
Term Expires: 2020

Clerkships: Law Clerk The Honorable Frank M. Johnson, Jr. (1985-1986)

Government: Assistant Attorney General, State of Alabama (1987-1989)

Legal Practice: Miller, Hamilton, Snider & Odom, L.L.C. (1989-1996)

Staff

Career Law Clerk **Sandra Gooding Marsh** .... (334) 954-3670
E-mail: sandra_marsh@almd.uscourts.gov
Education: Mississippi Women 1979 BS;
Arizona 1985 JD

Chambers of Chief Magistrate Judge Susan Russ Walker *continued*

Secretary **Sandi Edwards** .... (334) 954-3670
E-mail: sandi_edwards@almd.uscourts.gov

Chambers of Magistrate Judge Wallace Capel, Jr.

Frank M. Johnson, Jr. Federal Building & U.S. Courthouse,
One Church Street, Room 501-A, Montgomery, AL 36104
Tel: (334) 954-3730
E-mail: wallace_capel@almd.uscourts.gov

Wallace Capel, Jr.
Magistrate Judge

Date of Birth: 1955
Education: Utah 1977 BS; Auburn 1979 MPA; Wayne State U 1982 JD
Began Service: December 2006
Term Expires: December 2022

Government: Assistant Attorney General, Office of the Attorney General, Office of the Governor, Virgin Islands of the United States (1992-1995)

Judicial: Magistrate Judge, United States District Court for the Eastern District of Michigan (1999-2007)

Legal Practice: Staff Attorney, Wayne County Neighborhood Services (1984-1985); Deputy Defender, Legal Aid and Defenders Association of Detroit (1985-1991); Wallace Capel Attorney at Law (1991-1992); Deputy Federal Defender, Legal Aid and Defender Association (1995-1999)

Staff

Law Clerk **Kristi White** .... (334) 954-3730
Began Service: 2011
E-mail: kristi_white@almd.uscourts.gov

Career Law Clerk **Robert Illman** .... (334) 954-3730
E-mail: robert_illman@almd.uscourts.gov
Education: Alabama 2003 JD

Courtroom Deputy Clerk **Kelli Fuller** .... (334) 954-3977
E-mail: kelli_fuller@almd.uscourts.gov

Chambers of Magistrate Judge Charles S. Coody

Frank M. Johnson, Jr. Federal Courthouse Annex, One Church Street, Room 401-B, Montgomery, AL 36104
Tel: (334) 954-3700 Fax: (334) 954-3709

Charles S. Coody
Magistrate Judge

Date of Birth: 1946
Education: Spring Hill 1968 BS; Alabama 1975 JD
Began Service: May 1, 1987
Term Expires: December 31, 2016

Clerkships: Law Clerk The Honorable T. Embry, Alabama Supreme Court (1975)

Government: General Counsel, State Board of Education, State of Alabama (1978-1987)

Legal Practice: Associate, Smith, Bowman, Thaggard, Crook & Culpepper (1976-1978)

Military Service: United States Army (1968-1972)

Current Memberships: The Hugh Maddox American Inn of Court; Alabama State Bar

Staff

Career Law Clerk **Corrie Long** .... (334) 954-3700
Began Service: 2000
E-mail: corrie_p_long@almd.uscourts.gov
Education: Georgia 1988 JD

Courtroom Deputy Clerk **Wanda Stinson** .... (334) 954-3971
E-mail: wanda_stinson@almd.uscourts.gov

Chambers of Magistrate Judge Terry F. Moorer
Frank M. Johnson, Jr. Federal Courthouse Annex, One Church Street, A-401, Montgomery, AL 36104
P.O. Box 430, Montgomery, AL 36101
Tel: (334) 954-3740 Fax: (334) 954-3741
E-mail: terry_moorer@almd.uscourts.gov

Terry F. Moorer
Magistrate Judge

Began Service: January 2007

Government: Assistant U.S. Attorney/Organized Crime Drug Enforcement Task Force, Criminal Division, Alabama - Middle District, United States Department of Justice

Military Service: Military Judge Lieutenant Colonel United States Army National Guard

Staff
Law Clerk **Jimmie Birley** .... (334) 954-3740
E-mail: jimmie_birley@almd.uscourts.gov
Career Law Clerk **Cindy Torbert** .... (334) 954-3740
Career Law Clerk **Wynn Dee Allen** .... (334) 954-3740
Courtroom Deputy **Chiquita Baxter** .... (334) 954-3968
E-mail: chiquita_baxter@almd.uscourts.gov

Chambers of Magistrate Judge (recalled) Paul W. Greene
One Church Street, Montgomery, AL 36104
Tel: (334) 954-3960

Paul W. Greene
Magistrate Judge (recalled)

Education: South Alabama 1970 BA; Cumberland 1981 JD

United States Bankruptcy Court for the Middle District of Alabama
One Church Street, Montgomery, AL 36104
Tel: (334) 954-3800 Fax: (334) 954-3819
Tel: (866) 222-8029 (Voice Case Information System VCIS)
Internet: www.almb.uscourts.gov

Number of Judgeships: 2

Court Staff
Clerk of the Court **Juan-Carlos Guerrero** .... (334) 954-3800
E-mail: jc_guerrero@almb.uscourts.gov Fax: (334) 954-3817
Chief Deputy Clerk **Tonya Hagmaier** .... (334) 954-3811
E-mail: tonya_hagmaier@almb.uscourts.gov Fax: (334) 954-3817
Courtroom Deputy **Bill Livingston** .... (334) 954-3845
E-mail: bill_livingston@almb.uscourts.gov Fax: (334) 954-3819
Financial Administrator **Janet Clark** .... (334) 954-3839
E-mail: janet_clark@almb.uscourts.gov Fax: (334) 954-3817
Education: Auburn 1981 BA
Human Resource Manager **Henrietta Foster** .... (334) 954-3850
Education: Auburn (Montgomery) 1993 BS; Troy St (Montgomery) 2004 MS
Electronic Court Recorder Operator **Desma Russell** .... (334) 954-3847
E-mail: desma_hamilton@almb.uscourts.gov
Data Quality Analyst **DeAnna Williams** .... (334) 954-3853
E-mail: deanna_williams@almb.uscourts.gov
Director, Information Technology
John "Scooter" LeMay .... (334) 954-3848
E-mail: scooter_lemay@almb.uscourts.gov
Case Administration Supervisor **Yvonne Pelham** .... (334) 954-3859
Case Administrator **Linda Overton** .... (334) 954-3852
E-mail: linda_overton@almb.uscourts.gov Fax: (334) 954-3819

Chambers of Chief Bankruptcy Judge William R. Sawyer
One Church Street, Montgomery, AL 36102-0035
P.O. Box 35, Montgomery, AL 36102-0035
Tel: (334) 954-3880

William R. Sawyer
Chief Bankruptcy Judge

Date of Birth: 1955
Education: Valparaiso 1982 JD
Began Service: May 24, 1999
Term Expires: May 31, 2028

Staff
Career Law Clerk **Jerrod Maddox** .... (334) 954-3882
Courtroom Deputy **Bill Livingston** .... (334) 354-3846
E-mail: bill_livingston@almb.uscourts.gov
Administrative Assistant **Julie Caro** .... (334) 954-3881

Chambers of Bankruptcy Judge Dwight H. Williams, Jr.
One Church Street, 4th Floor, Montgomery, AL 36104
Tel: (334) 954-3890 Fax: (334) 954-3883
E-mail: DHW@almb.uscourts.gov

Dwight H. Williams, Jr.
Bankruptcy Judge

Date of Birth: 1952
Education: Auburn 1976 BS; Jones Law 1990 JD
Began Service: October 1999
Term Expires: October 2027

Current Memberships: Alabama State Bar; Montgomery County Bar Association

Staff
Law Clerk **Jessica Shavers-Brown** .... (334) 954-3892
Began Service: August 2015
Term Expires: August 2017
Courtroom Deputy **Jacqueline McLain** .... (334) 954-3800
E-mail: jacqueline_mclain@almb.uscourts.gov
Judicial Assistant **LaDonna W. Vinson** .... (334) 954-3891
E-mail: ladonna_vinson@almb.uscourts.gov
Education: Alabama State 1990 BS

United States District Court for the Northern District of Alabama
Hugo L. Black U.S. Courthouse, 1729 Fifth Avenue North, Birmingham, AL 35203-2040
Tel: (205) 278-1700
Internet: www.alnd.uscourts.gov

Number of Judgeships: 8

Number of Vacancies: 2

Circuit: Eleventh

Areas Covered: Counties of Bibb, Blount, Calhoun, Cherokee, Clay, Cleburne, Colbert, Cullman, DeKalb, Etowah, Fayette, Franklin, Greene, Jackson, Jefferson, Lamar, Lauderdale, Lawrence, Limestone, Madison, Marion, Marshall, Morgan, Pickens, Shelby, St. Clair, Sumter, Talladega, Tuscaloosa, Walker and Winston

Court Staff
District Court Clerk **Sharon N. Harris** .... (205) 278-1700
E-mail: sharon_harris@alnd.uscourts.gov
Administrative Assistant **Angela Day** .... (205) 278-1701
Chief Probation Officer **David A. Russell** .... (205) 716-2900

Chambers of Chief Judge Karon O. Bowdre

Hugo L. Black U.S. Courthouse, 1729 Fifth Avenue North,
Birmingham, AL 35203
Tel: (205) 278-1800 Fax: (205) 278-1806
E-mail: karon_bowdre@alnd.uscourts.gov

Karon O. Bowdre
Chief Judge

Date of Birth: 1955
Education: Samford 1977 BA; Cumberland 1981 JD
Began Service: November 8, 2001
Appointed By: President George W. Bush

Staff
Career Law Clerk **Ann Morris Watson** . . . . (205) 278-1800
E-mail: ann_watson@alnd.uscourts.gov
Education: Vanderbilt 1980 BA; Alabama 1983 JD
Staff Attorney **Michelle Wales** . . . . (205) 278-1802
E-mail: michelle_wales@alnd.uscourts.gov

Chambers of District Judge R. David Proctor

1729 Fifth Avenue North, Birmingham, AL 35203-2040
Tel: (205) 278-1980
E-mail: proctor_chambers@alnd.uscourts.gov

R. David Proctor
District Judge

Date of Birth: December 5, 1960
Education: Carson-Newman 1983 BA; Tennessee 1986 JD
Began Service: September 24, 2003
Appointed By: President George W. Bush

Clerkships: Law Clerk H. Emory Widener, Jr., United States Court of Appeals for the Fourth Circuit (1986-1987)

Legal Practice: Sirote & Permutt, P.C. (1987-1993); Proctor, Lehr Middlebrooks Price (1993-2003)

Current Memberships: Alabama State Bar; Birmingham Bar Association

Staff
Career Law Clerk **Laura Taaffe** . . . . (205) 278-1980
E-mail: laura_taaffe@alnd.uscourts.gov
Education: Vanderbilt 2003 JD
Career Law Clerk **Sally Waudby** . . . . (205) 278-1980
E-mail: sally_waudby@alnd.uscourts.gov
Judicial Assistant **Sharon Richards** . . . . (205) 278-1982
E-mail: sharon_richards@alnd.uscourts.gov

Chambers of District Judge L. Scott Coogler

2005 University Boulevard, Room 2300, Tuscaloosa, AL 35401
Tel: (205) 561-1670

L. Scott Coogler
District Judge

Education: Alabama 1981 BA, 1984 JD
Began Service: June 3, 2003
Appointed By: President George W. Bush

Academic: Adjunct Professor, School of Law, University of Alabama - Tuscaloosa (2000-2003)

Clerkships: Law Clerk, Judge Paul Conger, Alabama Sixth Judicial Circuit Court (1984)

Judicial: Judge, Alabama Sixth Judicial Circuit Court (1999-2003)

Staff
Law Clerk **Caroline Cease** . . . . (205) 561-1670
Began Service: August 2015
Term Expires: August 2016
E-mail: caroline_cease@alnd.uscourts.gov

Chambers of District Judge L. Scott Coogler *continued*
Law Clerk **Christopher Driver** . . . . (205) 561-1672
Began Service: August 2015
Term Expires: August 2016
E-mail: christopher_driver@alnd.uscourts.gov
Administrative Law Clerk **Annabel Norton** . . . . (205) 561-1670

Chambers of District Judge Virginia Emerson Hopkins

Hugo L. Black U.S. Courthouse, 1729 Fifth Avenue North,
Suite 619, Birmingham, AL 35203
Tel: (205) 278-1950
E-mail: hopkins_chambers@alnd.uscourts.gov

Virginia Emerson Hopkins
District Judge

Date of Birth: 1952
Education: Alabama 1974 BA; Virginia 1977 JD
Began Service: June 2004
Appointed By: President George W. Bush

Legal Practice: Attorney, Private Practice (1977-2004)

Chambers of District Judge Abdul K. Kallon

1729 Fifth Avenue North, Birmingham, AL 35203-2040
Tel: (205) 278-1850
E-mail: abdul_kallon@alnd.uscourts.gov

Abdul K. Kallon
District Judge

Education: Dartmouth 1990 AB; Pennsylvania 1993 JD
Began Service: February 1, 2010
Appointed By: President Barack Obama

Clerkships: Law Clerk, Chambers of District Judge U. W. Clemon, United States District Court for the Northern District of Alabama (1993-1994)

Corporate: President, Board of Directors, Legal Aid Society of Birmingham

Staff
Law Clerk **Bevan A. Dowd** . . . . (205) 278-1852
Began Service: August 2015
Term Expires: August 2017
E-mail: bevan_dowd@alnd.uscourts.gov
Law Clerk **Michael Crowder** . . . . (205) 278-1852
Began Service: August 2015
Term Expires: August 2017
E-mail: michael_crowder@alnd.uscourts.gov
Career Law Clerk **Sharon Hamilton Broach** . . . . (205) 278-1852

Chambers of District Judge Madeline Hughes Haikala

1729 Fifth Avenue North, Birmingham, AL 35203-2040
Tel: (205) 278-1700
E-mail: madeline_haikala@alnd.uscourts.gov

Madeline H. Haikala
District Judge

Education: Williams 1986 BA; Tulane 1989 JD
Began Service: October 21, 2013
Appointed By: President Barack Obama

Staff
Law Clerk **Kelley Tynes** . . . . (205) 278-1930
Law Clerk **Courtney Williams** . . . . (205) 278-1930

Chambers of Senior Judge James Hughes Hancock

Hugo L. Black U.S. Courthouse, 1729 Fifth Avenue North, Room 681, Birmingham, AL 35203
Tel: (205) 278-1840
E-mail: james_hancock@alnd.uscourts.gov

James Hughes Hancock
Senior Judge

Date of Birth: 1931
Education: Alabama 1953 BS, 1957 LLB
Began Service: 1973
Appointed By: President Richard M. Nixon

Legal Practice: Partner, Balch, Bingham, Baker, Hawthorne, Ward & Williams (1957-1973)

Military Service: United States Army (1953-1955)

Current Memberships: American Bar Association; Birmingham Bar Association

Staff
Career Law Clerk **Shannon Holt** .... (205) 278-1843
E-mail: shannon_holt@alnd.uscourts.gov
Education: Vanderbilt 2002 JD
Career Law Clerk **Laura Taaffe** .... (205) 278-1843
E-mail: laura_taaffe@alnd.uscourts.gov
Judicial Assistant **(Vacant)** .... (205) 278-1840

Chambers of Senior Judge William M. Acker, Jr.

Hugo L. Black U.S. Courthouse, 1729 Fifth Avenue North, Room 481, Birmingham, AL 35203
Tel: (205) 278-1880 Fax: (205) 278-1885
E-mail: William_Acker@alnd.uscourts.gov

William M. Acker, Jr.
Senior Judge

Date of Birth: 1927
Education: Birmingham-Southern 1949 AB; Yale 1952 LLB
Began Service: September 1982
Appointed By: President Ronald Reagan
Political Affiliation: Republican

Legal Practice: Associate, Graham, Bibb, Wingo & Foster (1952-1957); Partner, Smyer, White, Reid & Acker (1957-1972); Partner, Dominick, Fletcher, Yeilding, Acker, Wood & Lloyd (1972-1982)

Military Service: United States Army (1946-1947)

Current Memberships: Alabama State Bar; Birmingham Bar Association

Staff
Law Clerk **Daniel Harris** .... (205) 278-1884
Began Service: August 2014
Term Expires: August 2016
Law Clerk **Noah Oberlander** .... (205) 278-1883
Began Service: August 2014
Term Expires: August 2016
Judicial Assistant **Sharon Rubin** .... (205) 278-1882
E-mail: sharon_rubin@alnd.uscourts.gov Fax: (205) 278-1885

Chambers of Senior Judge C. Lynwood Smith, Jr.

101 Holmes Avenue, Huntsville, AL 35801
Tel: (256) 533-9490

C. Lynwood Smith, Jr.
Senior Judge

Date of Birth: 1943
Education: Alabama 1966 BA; Rutgers 1967 MA; Alabama 1971 JD
Began Service: January 4, 1996
Appointed By: President William J. Clinton
Political Affiliation: Democrat

Chambers of Senior Judge C. Lynwood Smith, Jr. *continued*

Staff
Career Law Clerk **Amy Dalton** .... (256) 551-2513
E-mail: amy_dalton@alnd.uscourts.gov
Courtroom Deputy **Lisa Waters** .... (256) 533-9490
E-mail: lisa_waters@alnd.uscourts.gov

Chambers of Senior Judge Sharon Lovelace Blackburn

Hugo L. Black U.S. Courthouse, 1729 Fifth Avenue North, Room 882, Birmingham, AL 35203
Tel: (205) 278-1810 Fax: (205) 278-1815
E-mail: sharon_blackburn@alnd.uscourts.gov

Sharon Lovelace Blackburn
Senior Judge

Date of Birth: 1950
Education: Alabama 1973 BA; Cumberland 1977 JD
Began Service: July 8, 1991
Appointed By: President George H.W. Bush

Current Memberships: Birmingham Bar Association; Federal Judges Association

Staff
Career Law Clerk **Rebecca Anthony** .... (205) 278-1813
Education: Cumberland 1990 JD
Judicial Assistant/Paralegal **Stephanie Braswell** .... (205) 278-1812
E-mail: stephanie_braswell@alnd.uscourts.gov

Chambers of Chief Magistrate Judge John E. Ott

Hugo L. Black U.S. Courthouse, 1729 Fifth Avenue North, Birmingham, AL 35203-2040
Tel: (205) 278-1920 Fax: (205) 278-1914
E-mail: John_Ott@alnd.uscourts.gov

John E. Ott
Chief Magistrate Judge

Date of Birth: 1955
Education: Cumberland 1981 JD
Began Service: April 6, 1998
Term Expires: April 6, 2022

Current Memberships: The Birmingham American Inn of Court; Alabama State Bar; Birmingham Bar Association; The Florida Bar

Staff
Career Law Clerk **Stephen Becker** .... (205) 278-1920
Began Service: September 2012
E-mail: stephen_becker@alnd.uscourts.gov
Law Clerk **Bill D. Jones** .... (205) 278-1920
Began Service: September 2014
Term Expires: September 2018

Chambers of Magistrate Judge Terry Michael Putnam

Hugo L. Black U.S. Courthouse, 1729 Fifth Avenue North, Room 361, Birmingham, AL 35203
Tel: (205) 278-1900 Fax: (205) 278-1905

Terry Michael Putnam
Magistrate Judge

Date of Birth: 1954
Education: Alabama 1976 BA, 1979 JD
Began Service: February 9, 1987
Term Expires: February 8, 2019

Legal Practice: Associate, Potts & Young (1979-1983); Partner, Potts, Young, Blasingame & Putnam (1983-1987)

Current Memberships: Alabama State Bar; Federal Magistrate Judges Association

(continued on next page)

Chambers of Magistrate Judge Terry Michael Putnam *continued*

Staff

Law Clerk **Pamela M. Arenberg** .... (205) 278-1903
Education: Cumberland 1993 JD
Law Clerk **Amber Parris** .... (205) 278-1902

Chambers of Magistrate Judge John England III

1729 Fifth Avenue North, Birmingham, AL 35203-2040
Tel: (205) 278-1700
E-mail: john_england@alnd.uscourts.gov

John H. England III
Magistrate Judge

Began Service: 2013

Chambers of Magistrate Judge Harwell G. Davis III

101 Holmes Avenue, Huntsville, AL 35801
Tel: (256) 539-7705 Fax: (256) 551-2525
E-mail: harwell_davis@alnd.uscourts.gov

Harwell G. Davis III
Magistrate Judge

Began Service: March 19, 1998
Term Expires: March 18, 2022

Staff

Career Law Clerk **Lesley Gladden** .... (256) 539-7705
E-mail: lesley_gladden@alnd.uscourts.gov
Education: Alabama 1985 JD
Secretary **Shelia Williams** .... (256) 539-7705
E-mail: shelia_williams@alnd.uscourts.gov

Chambers of Magistrate Judge Staci G. Cornelius

1729 Fifth Avenue North, Birmingham, AL 35203-2040
Tel: (205) 278-1930
E-mail: cornelius_chambers@alnd.uscourts.gov

Staci G. Cornelius
Magistrate Judge

Education: Alabama 1989 BA, 1992 JD
Began Service: 2014

United States Bankruptcy Court for the Northern District of Alabama

1800 Fifth Avenue North, Birmingham, AL 35203
Tel: (205) 714-4000 Tel: (877) 466-0795 (Toll Free)
Tel: (205) 254-7337 (Voice Case Information System VCIS)
Fax: (205) 714-3941
Internet: www.alnb.uscourts.gov

Number of Judgeships: 6

Court Staff

Clerk of Court **Scott W. Ford** .... (205) 714-4001
E-mail: scott_ford@alnb.uscourts.gov
Chief Deputy Clerk **Douglas E. Wedge** .... (205) 714-4006
E-mail: douglas_wedge@alnb.uscourts.gov
Education: South Carolina 2001 JD
Division Manager - Anniston **Gerald Wilson** .... (256) 741-1552
U.S. Courthouse, 914 Noble St., Fax: (256) 741-1515
Anniston, AL 36201
E-mail: gerald_wilson@alnb.uscourts.gov
Division Manager - Decatur **Brenda Howell** .... (256) 340-2717
P.O. Box 2775, Decatur, AL 35602 Fax: (256) 584-7964
Division Manager - Tuscaloosa **Lorraine Divers** .... (205) 561-1606
2005 University Boulevard, Room 2300, Fax: (205) 561-1638
Tuscaloosa, AL 35401
E-mail: lorraine_divers@alnb.uscourts.gov

United States Bankruptcy Court for the Northern District of Alabama *continued*

Bankruptcy Administrator **James Thomas Corbett** ..... (205) 714-3828
Education: Alabama 1988 JD Fax: (205) 731-3848
Financial Administrator **Becky Walker Brooks** .... (205) 714-4008
E-mail: becky_brooks@alnb.uscourts.gov
Bankruptcy Attorney **James Thomas Corbett** .... (205) 714-3838
Fax: (205) 731-2096
Automation Manager **Scott Stanley** .... (205) 714-3994
E-mail: scott_stanley@alnb.uscourts.gov
Budget and Human Resources Officer **Barbara Monge** ... (205) 714-4024
E-mail: barbara_monge@alnb.uscourts.gov

Chambers of Chief Bankruptcy Judge James J. Robinson

1129 Noble Street, Room 117, Anniston, AL 36201
Tel: (256) 741-1529 Fax: (256) 741-1515

James J. Robinson
Chief Bankruptcy Judge

Began Service: February 2006

Staff

Law Clerk **Alyssa Ross** .... (256) 741-1500
Began Service: August 2011
Term Expires: August 2016
E-mail: alyssa_ross@alnb.uscourts.gov
Judicial Assistant **Ramona Baker** .... (256) 741-1529

Chambers of Bankruptcy Judge Tamara O. Mitchell

112 Robert S. Vance Federal Building, 1800 Fifth Avenue North, Birmingham, AL 35203
Tel: (205) 714-3850 Fax: (205) 714-3860

Tamara O. Mitchell
Bankruptcy Judge

Education: South Alabama 1974 BS; Whittier 1980 JD
Began Service: January 4, 1992
Term Expires: January 3, 2020

Legal Practice: Sole Practitioner (1981-1983); Partner, Gradsky & Mitchell (1983-1991)

Staff

Law Clerk **Donna McGee** .... (205) 714-3850
Judicial Assistant **Monica Tabb** .... (205) 714-3850
E-mail: monica_tabb@alnb.uscourts.gov

Chambers of Bankruptcy Judge Jennifer H. Henderson

2005 University Boulevard, Tuscaloosa, AL 35401
Tel: (205) 561-1623

Jennifer H. Hudson
Bankruptcy Judge

Staff

Law Clerk **Josh Johnson** .... (205) 561-1623
E-mail: josh_johnson@alnb.uscourts.gov
Courtroom Deputy **Shirley Porter** .... (205) 561-1623
Judicial Assistant **Andrea Smith** .... (205) 561-1623
E-mail: andrea_smith@alnb.uscourts.gov

Chambers of Bankruptcy Judge Clifton R. Jessup Jr.
400 Well Street, NE, Decatur, AL 35601
Tel: (256) 340-2700

Clifton R. Jessup, Jr.
Bankruptcy Judge

Education: Oakwood 1976 BA; Michigan 1978 JD
Began Service: 2015

Staff
Law Clerk **Melissa Brown** .... (256) 340-2700
E-mail: melissa_brown@alnb.uscourts.gov
Courtroom Deputy **MeShae Bogue** .... (256) 340-2700
E-mail: meshae_bogue@alnb.uscourts.gov
Judicial Assistant **Michelle Bracken** .... (256) 340-2700
E-mail: michelle_bracken@alnb.uscourts.gov

Chambers of Bankruptcy Judge Margaret Mahoney
1800 Fifth Avenue North, Birmingham, AL 35203
Tel: (205) 714-3865

Margaret A. Mahoney
Bankruptcy Judge

Date of Birth: 1949
Education: Col St Catherine 1971 BA; Minnesota 1974 JD
Began Service: 2015

United States District Court for the Southern District of Alabama
U.S. Courthouse, 113 St. Joseph Street, Mobile, AL 36602-3621
Tel: (251) 690-2371 Fax: (251) 694-4297
Internet: www.alsd.uscourts.gov

Number of Judgeships: 3

Circuit: Eleventh

Areas Covered: Counties of Baldwin, Choctaw, Clarke, Conecuh, Dallas, Escambia, Hale, Marengo, Mobile, Monroe, Perry, Washington and Wilcox

Court Staff
Clerk **Charles R. "Chuck" Diard, Jr.** .... (251) 690-2371
E-mail: chuck_diard@alsd.uscourts.gov
Chief Deputy Clerk **Jeff L. Reinert** .... (251) 694-4298
E-mail: jeff_reinert@alsd.uscourts.gov
Chief Probation Officer **Jennifer Childress** .... (251) 441-6800
201 St. Michael Street, Second Floor, Mobile, AL 36602 Fax: (251) 441-6810
E-mail: jennifer_childress@alsp.uscourts.gov
United States Probation Office Deputy Chief **Wade Farrish** .... (251) 441-6800
201 St. Michael Street, Second Floor, Mobile, AL 36602 Fax: (251) 441-6810
E-mail: wade_farrish@alsp.uscourts.gov

Chambers of Chief Judge William H. Steele
U.S. Courthouse, 113 St. Joseph Street, Mobile, AL 36602
Tel: (251) 690-3239 Fax: (251) 694-4668
E-mail: william_steele@alsd.uscourts.gov

William H. Steele
Chief Judge

Date of Birth: June 8, 1951
Education: Southern Mississippi 1972 BA; Alabama 1980 JD
Began Service: March 14, 2003
Appointed By: President George W. Bush

Government: Assistant District Attorney, Office of the District Attorney, County of Mobile, Alabama (1981-1985); Assistant U.S. Attorney, Southern District of Alabama, United States Department of Justice (1987-1989)

Chambers of Chief Judge William H. Steele *continued*

Judicial: Judge, Alabama Municipal Court (1989-1990); Magistrate Judge, United States District Court for the Southern District of Alabama (1990-2003)

Legal Practice: Private Practice (1988-1990)

Military Service: Officer, Pilot, Instructor Pilot, United States Marine Corps (1972-1979); Alabama National Guard (1979-1990)

Current Memberships: Alabama State Bar; Federal Association of Magistrate Judges; Mobile Bar Association

Staff
Career Law Clerk **Christopher Ekman** .... (251) 436-5254
E-mail: christopher_ekman@alsd.uscourts.gov
Career Law Clerk **David R. Peeler** .... (251) 690-3280
E-mail: david_peeler@alsd.uscourts.gov
Education: Alabama 1983 JD
Judicial Assistant **Teresa R. Cornell** .... (251) 690-3239
E-mail: teresa_cornell@alsd.uscourts.gov
Judicial Assistant **Karla Roche** .... (251) 690-3239
E-mail: karla_roche@alsd.uscourts.gov

Chambers of District Judge Callie V. S. Granade
U.S. Courthouse, 113 St. Joseph Street, Mobile, AL 36602
Tel: (251) 690-3133 Fax: (251) 694-4451
E-mail: ginny_granade@alsd.uscourts.gov

Callie V. S. "Ginny" Granade
District Judge

Date of Birth: 1950
Education: Hollins Col 1972 BA; Texas 1975 JD
Began Service: February 20, 2002
Appointed By: President George W. Bush

Clerkships: Law Clerk The Honorable John Godbold, United States Court of Appeals for the Fifth Circuit (1975-1976)

Government: Assistant United States Attorney, Southern District of Alabama, Office of the United States Attorney, United States Department of Justice (1977-2002)

Staff
Law Clerk **(Vacant)** .... (251) 690-3133
Law Clerk **Megan Scanlon** .... (251) 690-3133
Career Law Clerk **Lynn Dekle** .... (251) 690-3133
E-mail: lynn_dekle@alsd.uscourts.gov
Education: Florida 1989 BS, 1992 JD

Chambers of District Judge Kristi K. DuBose
U.S. Courthouse, 113 St. Joseph Street, Mobile, AL 36602
Tel: (251) 690-2020 Fax: (251) 690-3065
E-mail: kristi_dubose@alsd.uscourts.gov

Kristi K. DuBose
District Judge

Date of Birth: 1964
Education: Huntingdon 1986 BA; Emory 1989 JD
Began Service: December 28, 2005
Appointed By: President George W. Bush

Clerkships: Law Clerk, District Judge Peter Hill Beer, United States District Court for the Eastern District of Louisiana (1989-1990)

Government: Assistant United States Attorney, Southern District of Alabama, United States Department of Justice (1990-1993); Assistant District Attorney, District Attorney's Office, County of Covington, Alabama (1994); Deputy Attorney General, Office of the Attorney General, State of Alabama (1994-1996); Chief Counsel (R-AL), Office of Senator Jeff Sessions, United States Senate (1997-1999)

(continued on next page)

Chambers of District Judge Kristi K. DuBose *continued*

Staff

Career Law Clerk **Karen H. Carr** .... (251) 690-2020
E-mail: karen_carr@alsd.uscourts.gov

Career Law Clerk **G. Cameron Pfeiffer** .... (251) 690-2020
Education: Vanderbilt 1994 BA;
American U 2000 MA;
Washington College of Law 2000 JD

Chambers of Senior Judge Charles R. Butler, Jr.

U.S. Courthouse, 113 St. Joseph Street, Mobile, AL 36602
Tel: (251) 690-2175 Fax: (251) 694-4218
E-mail: charles_butler@alsd.uscourts.gov

Charles R. Butler, Jr.
Senior Judge

Date of Birth: 1940
Education: Washington and Lee 1962 BA; Alabama 1966 LLB
Began Service: November 1, 1988
Appointed By: President Ronald Reagan

Academic: Adjunct Professor, University of South Alabama (1975-1976)

Government: Assistant Public Defender, State of Alabama (1969-1970); District Attorney, State of Alabama (1971-1975)

Judicial: Chief Judge, United States District Court for the Southern District of Alabama (1995-2003); Member, Judicial Conference of the United States (1999-2002); Member of the Executive Committee, Judicial Conference of the United States (2000-2002)

Legal Practice: Associate, Hamilton, Butler, Riddick & Latour (1966-1969); Partner, Butler & Sullivan (1975-1984); Partner, Hamilton, Butler, Riddick, Tarlton & Latour (1984-1988)

Military Service: United States Army (1962-1964)

Current Memberships: Mobile Bar Association

Staff

Career Law Clerk **Marilyn Fisher** .... (251) 690-2175
E-mail: marilyn_fisher@alsd.uscourts.gov
Education: Alabama 1985 JD

Judicial Administrative Assistant **Ann E. Nielsen** .... (251) 690-2175
E-mail: ann_nielsen@alsd.uscourts.gov

Chambers of Magistrate Judge William E. Cassady

U.S. Courthouse, 113 St. Joseph Street, Room 306, Mobile, AL 36602
Tel: (251) 690-2345 Fax: (251) 694-4198
E-mail: william_cassady@alsd.uscourts.gov

William E. Cassady
Magistrate Judge

Date of Birth: 1950
Education: Jones Law 1977 JD
Began Service: 1985
Term Expires: March 11, 2017

Government: Assistant District Attorney, Fourth Judicial Circuit, State of Alabama (1980-1985)

Legal Practice: Private Practice (1978-1985)

Current Memberships: American Bar Association; The Paul W. Brock American Inn of Court, The American Inns of Court; Mobile Bar Association; Rotary Club of Mobile, Rotary International, Inc.

Staff

Law Clerk **Evan Parrott** .... (251) 690-2345
Began Service: June 2015
Term Expires: July 31, 2017

Career Law Clerk **Laura L. Youngpeter** .... (251) 690-2345
E-mail: laura_youngpeter@alsd.uscourts.gov
Education: Alabama 1987 JD

Chambers of Magistrate Judge Bert W. Milling, Jr.

U.S. Courthouse, 113 St. Joseph Street, Mobile, AL 36602
Tel: (251) 690-3202 Fax: (251) 694-4319
E-mail: bert_milling@alsd.uscourts.gov

Bert W. Milling, Jr.
Magistrate Judge

Date of Birth: 1946
Education: William & Mary 1968 AB; Alabama 1971 JD
Began Service: 1986
Term Expires: November 2018

Government: Special Assistant, Office of the Attorney General, United States Department of Justice (1974-1975); Assistant District Attorney, State of Alabama (1977-1978); Counsel, Subcommittee on Security and Terrorism, Committee on the Judiciary, United States Senate (1981-1983); Assistant U.S. Attorney, Alabama - Southern District, Executive Office for United States Attorneys, United States Department of Justice (1983-1986)

Judicial: Court Referee, Alabama Circuit Court, 13th Judicial Circuit (1978-1981)

Legal Practice: Private Practice (1975-1977)

Military Service: United States Army (1971-1974); Alabama National Guard, United States Department of the Army (1975-1987)

Current Memberships: Christian Legal Society; Federal Magistrate Judges Association; Mobile Bar Association

Staff

Law Clerk **Anna Lundy** .... (251) 690-3202
Began Service: October 2012
Term Expires: October 2016
E-mail: anna_lundy@alsd.uscourts.gov

Career Law Clerk **Michael A. Smith** .... (251) 690-3204
E-mail: michael_smith@alsd.uscourts.gov
Education: Alabama 1987 JD

Chambers of Magistrate Judge Sonja Faye Bivins

113 St. Joseph Street, Mobile, AL 36602
Tel: (251) 694-4545 Fax: (251) 694-4238
E-mail: sonja_bivins@alsd.uscourts.gov

Sonja Faye Bivins
Magistrate Judge

Date of Birth: February 22, 1963
Education: Spring Hill 1985 BS; Alabama 1988 JD
Began Service: February 2, 2004
Term Expires: February 2, 2020

Current Memberships: Alabama State Bar; State Bar of Georgia

Staff

Law Clerk **Chelsey Collins** .... (251) 694-4545
Began Service: October 2015
Term Expires: October 2016

Career Law Clerk **Karen Turner** .... (251) 694-4548
Began Service: 2007
E-mail: karen_turner@alsd.uscourts.gov

Chambers of Magistrate Judge Katherine P. Nelson

113 Saint Joseph Street., Mobile, AL 36602
Tel: (251) 690-3200
E-mail: katherine_nelson@alsd.uscourts.gov

Katherine P. Nelson
Magistrate Judge

Began Service: June 2009

Clerkships: Career Law Clerk, Chambers of District Judge Kristi K. DuBose, United States District Court for the Southern District of Alabama (2009)

Chambers of Magistrate Judge Katherine P. Nelson *continued*

Staff
Law Clerk **Clifford "Cliff" Nelson** .... (251) 690-3038
E-mail: clifford_nelson@alsd.uscourts.gov
Law Clerk **Mark Harris** .... (251) 690-3037
E-mail: mark_harris@alsd.uscourts.gov

United States Bankruptcy Court for the Southern District of Alabama

201 St. Louis Street, Mobile, AL 36602
Tel: (251) 441-5391 Tel: (251) 441-5638 (PACER)
Tel: (251) 441-5637 (Voice Case Information System VCIS)
Internet: www.alsb.uscourts.gov

Number of Judgeships: 2

Court Staff
Clerk of Court **Leonard N. Maldonado** .... (251) 441-5391 ext. 4103
E-mail: leonard_maldonado@alsb.uscourts.gov
Bankruptcy Administrator (Acting) **Mark Zimlich** .... (251) 441-5433
P.O. Box 3083, Mobile, AL 36602

Chambers of Chief Bankruptcy Judge William S. Shulman

201 St. Louis Street, Mobile, AL 36602
Tel: (251) 441-5625 Fax: (251) 441-5399
E-mail: william_shulman@alsb.uscourts.gov

William S. Shulman
Chief Bankruptcy Judge

Date of Birth: 1950
Education: Alabama 1975 JD
Began Service: 1996

Current Memberships: Alabama State Bar; Mobile Bar Association

Staff
Career Law Clerk **Susan Powers** .... (251) 441-5625 ext. 4131
E-mail: susan_powers@alsb.uscourts.gov
Education: Alabama 1990 JD
Judicial Assistant **M. Faith Hoffman** .... (251) 441-5625 ext. 4130
E-mail: faith_hoffman@alsb.uscourts.gov

United States District Court for the District of Alaska

Federal Building & U.S. Courthouse, 222 West Seventh Avenue, #4, Anchorage, AK 99513-7564
Tel: (907) 677-6100 Tel: (866) 243-3814 (Toll Free)
Fax: (907) 677-6180
Internet: www.akd.uscourts.gov

Number of Judgeships: 3

Circuit: Ninth

Court Staff
Clerk of the Court **Marvel Hansbraugh** .... (907) 677-6100
E-mail: marvel_hansbraugh@akd.uscourts.gov Fax: (907) 677-6181
Chief Deputy Clerk **Jan Welch** .... (907) 677-6100
E-mail: jan_welch@akd.uscourts.gov Fax: (907) 677-6181
Deputy Clerk, Fairbanks **Jennifer Meismer-House** ...... (907) 451-5791
101 12th Ave., Rm. 332, Fairbanks, AK 99701 Fax: (907) 456-0439
E-mail: jennifer_house@akd.uscourts.gov
Deputy Clerk, Juneau **April Kleinman** .... (907) 586-7458
P.O. Box 020349, Juneau, AK 99802-0349 Fax: (907) 586-7780
Deputy Clerk, Ketchikan **Heidi Boles** .... (907) 247-7576
648 Mission St., Rm. 507, Ketchikan, AK 99901 Fax: (907) 225-2335
Deputy Clerk, Nome **Tracey Buie** .... (907) 443-5216
P.O. Box 130, Nome, AK 99762 Fax: (907) 443-2192
Chief Probation Officer **Karen Brewer** .... (907) 271-5492
Fax: (907) 271-3060

United States District Court for the District of Alaska *continued*

Librarian **Catherine Davidson** .... (907) 271-5655
Fax: (907) 271-5640

Chambers of Chief Judge Ralph R. Beistline

Federal Building & U.S. Courthouse, 222 West Seventh Avenue, Box 49, Anchorage, AK 99513-7564
Tel: (907) 677-6257 Fax: (907) 677-6264
E-mail: ralph_beistline@akd.uscourts.gov

Ralph R. Beistline
Chief Judge

Date of Birth: 1948
Education: Alaska 1972 BA; U Puget Sound 1974 JD
Began Service: May 19, 2002
Appointed By: President George W. Bush

Clerkships: Law Clerk, Judge The Honorable Taylor, Superior Court of Alaska (1974-1975)

Judicial: Judge, Superior Court of Alaska (1992-2002)

Legal Practice: Associate, Hughes, Thorsness, Gantz, Powell & Brundin, LLC (1975-1978); Partner, Hughes, Thorsness, Gantz, Powell & Brundin, LLC (1979-1992)

Staff
Law Clerk **Dustin Glazier** .... (907) 677-6209
Began Service: August 2014
Term Expires: August 2016
Career Law Clerk **Ruth Tronnes** .... (907) 677-6210
E-mail: ruth_tronnes@akd.uscourts.gov
Secretary **Jan Short** .... (907) 677-6257
E-mail: jan_short@akd.uscourts.gov

Chambers of District Judge Timothy Mark Burgess

Federal Building & U.S. Courthouse, 222 West Seventh Avenue, #4, Anchorage, AK 99513-7564
Tel: (907) 677-6203 Tel: (866) 243-3814 (Toll Free)

Timothy Mark Burgess
District Judge

Date of Birth: 1956
Education: Alaska 1978 BA, 1982 MBA; Northeastern 1987 JD
Began Service: January 2006
Appointed By: President George W. Bush

Government: U.S. Attorney, Alaska District, Executive Office for United States Attorneys, United States Department of Justice (1989-2001); U.S. Attorney, District of Alaska, Executive Office for United States Attorneys, United States Department of Justice (2001-2005)

Legal Practice: Attorney, Private Practice (1987-1989)

Staff
Judicial Assistant **Stephanie Lawley** .... (907) 677-6203
E-mail: stephanie_lawley@akd.uscourts.gov

Chambers of District Judge Sharon L. Gleason

222 West Seventh Avenue, #4, Anchorage, AK 99513-7564
Tel: (907) 677-6253

Sharon L. Gleason
District Judge

Education: Washington U (MO) 1979 BA; UC Davis 1983 JD
Began Service: January 4, 2012
Appointed By: President Barack Obama

Clerkships: Law Clerk, Chambers of Chief Justice Edmond Burke, Alaska Supreme Court (1983-1984)

(continued on next page)

Chambers of District Judge Sharon L. Gleason *continued*

Judicial: Presiding Judge, Chambers of Presiding Judge Sharon L. Gleason, Third Judicial District, Alaska Superior Court (2009-2011)

Legal Practice: Attorney, Reese, Rice and Volland (1984-1995)

Profession: Sole Practitioner (1995-2001)

Staff
Staff Assistant **Anne Masneri** .... (907) 677-6253
E-mail: anne_masneri@akd.uscourts.gov

Chambers of Senior Judge John W. Sedwick

Federal Building & U.S. Courthouse, 222 West Seventh Avenue, #32, Anchorage, AK 99513-7545
Tel: (907) 677-6251
E-mail: john_sedwick@akd.uscourts.gov

John W. Sedwick
Senior Judge

Date of Birth: 1946
Education: Dartmouth 1968 BA; Harvard 1972 JD
Began Service: October 15, 1992
Appointed By: President George H.W. Bush

Government: Director, Natural Resources Division, State of Alaska (1981-1982)

Judicial: Chief Judge, United States District Court for the District of Alaska (2002-2009); District Judge, Chambers of District Judge John W. Sedwick, United States District Court for the District of Alaska (1992-2011)

Legal Practice: Attorney, Burr, Pease & Kurtz (1972-1981); Attorney, Burr, Pease & Kurtz (1983-1992)

Military Service: United States Air National Guard (1969-1971)

Current Memberships: American Bar Association; Anchorage Bar Association, Inc.

Membership: Member, Alaska Bar Association

Staff
Career Law Clerk **Elizabeth Perry** .... (907) 677-6251
Judicial Assistant **Gail Morgan** .... (907) 677-6251
E-mail: gail_morgan@akd.uscourts.gov

Chambers of Senior Judge James K. Singleton, Jr.

Federal Building & U.S. Courthouse, 222 West Seventh Avenue, #41, Anchorage, AK 99513-7524
Tel: (907) 677-6250

James K. Singleton, Jr.
Senior Judge

Date of Birth: 1939
Education: UC Berkeley 1961 AB; Boalt Hall 1964 LLB
Began Service: May 14, 1990
Appointed By: President George H.W. Bush
Political Affiliation: Republican

Judicial: Judge, Alaska Superior Court, Third District (1970-1980); Judge, Alaska Court of Appeals (1980-1990); Judge, United States District Court for the District of Alaska (1990-2004); Chief Judge, United States District Court for the District of Alaska (1995-2002)

Legal Practice: Attorney, DeLaney, Wiles, Moore and Hayes (1963); Attorney, DeLaney, Wiles, Moore and Hayes (1965-1968); Attorney, Roger Cremo Law Office (1968-1970)

Current Memberships: Alaska Bar Association; American Bar Association; Anchorage Bar Association, Inc.; State Bar of California

Staff
Career Law Clerk **Maria-Teresa Davenport** .... (907) 677-6250
Education: American U 2000 BA; Northwestern 2007 JD

Chambers of Senior Judge H. Russel Holland

Federal Building & U.S. Courthouse, 222 West Seventh Avenue, Unit 54, Anchorage, AK 99513-7545
Tel: (907) 677-6252

H. Russel Holland
Senior Judge

Date of Birth: 1936
Education: Michigan 1958 BBA, 1961 LLB
Began Service: 1984
Appointed By: President Ronald Reagan

Clerkships: Law Clerk, Alaska Supreme Court (1961-1963)

Legal Practice: Stevens & Savage (1965-1966); Partner, Stevens, Savage, Holland, Erwin & Edwards (1967-1968); Sole Practitioner, Law Office of H. Russel Holland (1968-1970); Partner, Holland & Thornton (1970-1978); Partner, Holland, Thornton & Trefry; Partner, Holland & Trefry (1978-1984); Trefry & Brecht

Staff
Secretary **Marty Stafford** .... (907) 677-6252
E-mail: marty_stafford@akd.uscourts.gov

Chambers of Chief Magistrate Judge Deborah M. Smith

Federal Building & U.S. Courthouse, 222 West Seventh Avenue, #4, Anchorage, AK 99513-7564
Tel: (907) 677-6256 Tel: (866) 243-3814 (Toll Free)

Deborah M. Smith
Chief Magistrate Judge

Began Service: February 2007
Term Expires: February 2023

Government: First Assistant U.S. Attorney, Alaska District, Executive Office for United States Attorneys, United States Department of Justice; U.S. Attorney, Alaska District, Executive Office for United States Attorneys, United States Department of Justice

Staff
Career Law Clerk **(Vacant)** .... (907) 677-6256
Judicial Assistant **Erikia Harmon** .... (907) 677-6256
E-mail: erikia_harmon@akd.uscourts.gov

Chambers of Magistrate Judge (part-time) Scott A. Oravec

U.S. Federal Building, 101 12th Avenue, Fairbanks, AK 99701
Tel: (907) 451-5795
E-mail: scott_oravec@akd.uscourts.gov

Scott A. Oravec
Magistrate Judge (Part-Time)

Began Service: 2009

Staff
Career Law Clerk **Connie Ledlow** .... (907) 456-0370

Chambers of Magistrate Judge (part-time) Leslie Longenbaugh

U.S. Courthouse, 709 West Ninth Street, Room 979, Juneau, AK 99802
Tel: (907) 321-3402

Leslie Longenbaugh
Magistrate Judge (Part-Time)

Began Service: February 2007
Term Expires: February 2016

Chambers of Magistrate Judge (part-time) Leslie Longenbaugh *continued*

Staff
Secretary **Steve Hildebrand** .... (907) 586-7337

Chambers of Magistrate Judge (part time) Kevin F. McCoy

222 West Seventh Avenue, #4, Anchorage, AK 99513-7564
Tel: (907) 677-6100

Kevin McCoy
Magistrate Judge (Part-Time)

United States Bankruptcy Court for the District of Alaska

605 West Fourth Avenue, Room 138, Anchorage, AK 99501-2296
Tel: (907) 271-2655 Tel: (800) 859-8059 (Toll Free within Alaska)
Tel: (907) 271-2695 (PACER)
Tel: (866) 222-8029 (Voice Case Information System VCIS)
Fax: (907) 271-2645
Internet: www.akb.uscourts.gov

Number of Judgeships: 2

Court Staff
Clerk of the Court **Jan S. Ostrovsky** .... (907) 271-4000
E-mail: jan_ostrovsky@akb.uscourts.gov
Personnel Specialist and Human Resources Administrator **Margaret I. Bondi** .... (907) 271-3923
E-mail: maggie_bondi@akb.uscourts.gov
Deputy-In-Charge, Fairbanks **Maia Bennett** .... (907) 456-0349
101 12th Avenue, Fairbanks, AK 99501-2296
Deputy-In-Charge, Ketchikan **(Vacant)** .... (907) 247-7576
507 Federal Bldg., 648 Mission St., Ketchikan, AK 99501-2296
Financial Deputy **Peggy Gingras** .... (907) 271-2627
E-mail: peggy_gingras@akb.uscourts.gov
Systems Administrator **Leon Cargile** .... (907) 271-2626
E-mail: leon_cargile@akb.uscourts.gov
Generalist, Juneau **April Kleinman** .... (907) 271-2655
709 West Ninth Street, Room 979, Juneau, AK 99802
P.O. Box 020349, Juneau, AK 99802-0349

Chambers of Bankruptcy Judge Gary Allan Spraker

605 West Fourth Avenue, Anchorage, AK 99501-2296
Tel: (907) 271-2667

Gary Allan Spraker
Bankruptcy Judge

Began Service: 2012

Staff
Law Clerk **Amy McFarlane** .... (907) 271-2621
E-mail: amy_mcfarlane@akb.uscourts.gov
Education: Loyola Marymount 1980 JD

Chambers of Bankruptcy Judge (recalled) Herbert A. Ross

605 West 4th Avenue, Room 138, Anchorage, AK 99501-2253
Tel: (907) 271-2630 Fax: (907) 271-2692
E-mail: herb_ross@akb.uscourts.gov

Herbert A. Ross
Bankruptcy Judge (recalled)

Date of Birth: 1935
Education: U San Francisco 1964 LLB
Began Service: 2007
Term Expires: October 8, 2016

Chambers of Bankruptcy Judge (recalled) Herbert A. Ross *continued*

Staff
Deputy Clerk **Cheryl Rapp** .... (907) 271-2630

United States District Court for the District of Arizona

Sandra Day O'Connor U.S. Courthouse, 401 West Washington Street, Room 130, Phoenix, AZ 85003
Tel: (602) 322-7200 Tel: (602) 514-7113 (PACER)
Internet: www.azd.uscourts.gov

Number of Judgeships: 13

Circuit: Ninth

Court Staff
Clerk of the Court and District Court Executive
Brian Karth .... (602) 322-7100
E-mail: brian_karth@azd.uscourts.gov
Chief Deputy Clerk **Debra Lucas** .... (602) 322-7100
E-mail: debra_lucas@azd.uscourts.gov
Chief Deputy Clerk - Tucson **Michael O'Brien** .... (520) 205-4200
E-mail: michael_obrien@azd.uscourts.gov
Chief U.S. Pretrial Services Officer **David L. Martin** ..... (520) 205-4394
E-mail: david_martin@azd.uscourts.gov Fax: (520) 205-4399
Chief U.S. Probation Officer **Mario Moreno** .... (602) 322-7400
O'Connor U.S. Courthouse, Suite 160
E-mail: mario_moreno@azd.uscourts.gov
Librarian **Timothy J. Blake** .... (602) 322-7295
Librarian, Tucson **Deo Maynard** .... (520) 205-4661
Evo A. DeConcini U.S. Courthouse, 405 West Congress Street, Tucson, AZ 85701

Chambers of Chief Judge Raner C. Collins

405 West Congress Street, Suite 5190, Tucson, AZ 85701-5061
Tel: (520) 205-4540
E-mail: Raner_Collins@azd.uscourts.gov

Raner C. Collins
Chief Judge

Date of Birth: 1952
Education: Arkansas Tech 1973 BA; Arizona 1975 JD
Began Service: August 19, 1998
Appointed By: President William J. Clinton
Political Affiliation: Democrat

Current Memberships: Arizona Minority Bar Association; State Bar of Arizona

Staff
Law Clerk **Ana Castillo** .... (520) 205-4540
Began Service: March 2014
Term Expires: March 2016
E-mail: ana_castillo@azd.uscourts.gov
Law Clerk **Tanya Miller** .... (520) 205-4545
Began Service: August 2015
Term Expires: August 2016
E-mail: tanya_miller@azd.uscourts.gov
Court Reporter **Erica Grund** .... (520) 205-4267
E-mail: erica_grund@azd.uscourts.gov
Judicial Secretary **Tara Reid** .... (520) 205-4540
E-mail: Tara_Reid@azd.uscourts.gov
Judicial Secretary **Sandra M. McCullar** .... (520) 205-4541
E-mail: sandra_mccullar@azd.uscourts.gov

Chambers of District Judge Susan R. Bolton

Sandra Day O'Connor U.S. Courthouse, 401 West Washington Street, SPC 50, Suite 522, Phoenix, AZ 85003
Tel: (602) 322-7570 Fax: (602) 322-7579
E-mail: susan_bolton@azd.uscourts.gov

Susan R. Bolton
District Judge

Date of Birth: 1951
Education: Iowa 1973 BA, 1975 JD
Began Service: October 2000
Appointed By: President William J. Clinton
Political Affiliation: Independent

Clerkships: Law Clerk The Honorable Laurance T. Wren, Arizona State Court of Appeals (1975-1977)

Judicial: Judge, Superior Court of Maricopa County, Arizona (1989-2000)

Legal Practice: Associate, Shimmel, Hill, Bishop & Gruender (1977-1982); Partner, Shimmel, Hill, Bishop & Gruender (1982-1989)

Staff

Law Clerk **Sanessa Griffiths** .... (602) 322-7570
Began Service: 2015
Term Expires: October 1, 2016
E-mail: sanessa_griffiths@azd.uscourts.gov

Law Clerk **Courtney Burks** .... (602) 322-7576
Began Service: September 2014
Term Expires: October 1, 2016
E-mail: courtney_burks@azd.uscourts.gov

Court Reporter **Liz Lemke** .... (602) 322-7247

Judicial Assistant **Debbie Norman** .... (602) 322-7570
E-mail: debbie_norman@azd.uscourts.gov

Chambers of District Judge Cindy K. Jorgenson

Evo A. DeConcini U.S. Courthouse, 405 West Congress Street, Suite 5180, Tucson, AZ 85701-5052
Tel: (520) 205-4550 Fax: (520) 205-4559
E-mail: cindy_jorgenson@azd.uscourts.gov

Cindy K. Jorgenson
District Judge

Date of Birth: 1953
Education: Arizona 1974 BS, 1977 JD
Began Service: March 15, 2002
Appointed By: President George W. Bush

Government: Deputy County Attorney, Office of the County Attorney, County of Pima, Arizona (1977-1986); Assistant United States Attorney, District of Arizona, Office of the United States Attorney, United States Department of Justice (1986-1996)

Judicial: Judge, Arizona Superior Court, Pima County (1996-2002)

Staff

Law Clerk **Suzanne King** .... (520) 205-4551
Began Service: 2014
Term Expires: 2016
E-mail: suzanne_king@azd.uscourts.gov

Career Law Clerk **Elizabeth J. Jarecki** .... (520) 205-4552
E-mail: elizabeth_jarecki@azd.uscourts.gov
Education: Arizona 1991 JD

Judicial Assistant **Penny Bradford** .... (520) 205-4550
E-mail: penny_bradford@azd.uscourts.gov

Chambers of District Judge David G. Campbell

401 West Washington Street, Suite 623, Phoenix, AZ 85003
Tel: (602) 322-7645 Fax: (602) 322-7649
E-mail: david_campbell@azd.uscourts.gov

David G. Campbell
District Judge

Education: Utah 1976 BS, 1979 JD
Began Service: July 3, 2003
Appointed By: President George W. Bush

Academic: Adjunct Professor, Arizona State University Law School (1985-1986); Visiting Professor, Brigham Young University (1990)

Clerkships: Law Clerk, Circuit Judge J. Clifford Wallace, United States Court of Appeals for the Ninth Circuit (1979-1980); Law Clerk, Associate Justice William H. Rehnquist, Supreme Court of the United States (1982)

Staff

Law Clerk **Phillip Londen** .... (602) 322-7647
Began Service: August 2015
Term Expires: August 2016
E-mail: phillip_londen@azd.uscourts.gov

Law Clerk **David Baake** .... (602) 322-7647
Began Service: August 2015
Term Expires: August 14, 2016
E-mail: david_baake@azd.uscourts.gov

Court Reporter **Patricia Lyons** .... (602) 322-7257
E-mail: patricia_lyons@azd.uscourts.gov

Judicial Assistant **Nancy Outley** .... (602) 322-7645
E-mail: nancy_outley@azd.uscourts.gov

Chambers of District Judge Neil V. Wake

401 West Washington Street, SPC 52, Suite 524, Phoenix, AZ 85003
Tel: (602) 322-7640
E-mail: neil_wake@azd.uscourts.gov

Neil V. Wake
District Judge

Education: Arizona State 1971 BA; Harvard 1974 JD
Began Service: March 15, 2004
Appointed By: President George W. Bush

Profession: Private Practice (1974-2004)

Staff

Court Reporter **Laurie Adams** .... (602) 322-7256
E-mail: laurie_adams@azd.uscourts.gov

Chambers of District Judge G. Murray Snow

Sandra Day O'Connor U.S. Courthouse, 401 West Washington Street, SPC 80, Suite 622, Phoenix, AZ 85003-2156
Tel: (602) 322-7650

G. Murray Snow
District Judge

Date of Birth: 1959
Education: BYU 1984 BA; J Reuben Clark Law 1987 JD
Began Service: November 7, 2008
Appointed By: President George W. Bush

Academic: Adjunct Professor of Political Sciences, Arizona State University (1992-1999)

Clerkships: Law Clerk, Circuit Judge Stephen H. Anderson, United States Court of Appeals for the Tenth Circuit (1987-1988)

Judicial: Judge, Arizona Court of Appeals, Division One (2002-2008)

Legal Practice: Attorney, Meyer, Hendricks, Victor, Osborn & Maledon (1988-1995); Partner, Osborn Maledon (1995-2002)

Current Memberships: J. Reuben Clark Law Society; State Bar of Arizona

Chambers of District Judge G. Murray Snow *continued*

Staff

Court Reporter **Gary Moll** .... (602) 322-7263
E-mail: gary_moll@azd.uscourts.gov

Chambers of District Judge Jennifer G. Zipps

Evo A. DeConcini U.S. Courthouse, 405 West Congress Street, Suite 5170, Tucson, AZ 85701-5061
Tel: (520) 205-4610

Jennifer C. Guerin Zipps
District Judge

Education: Arizona 1986 BA; Georgetown 1990 JD
Began Service: October 5, 2011
Appointed By: President Barack Obama

Clerkships: Law Clerk, Chambers of Circuit Judge William C. Canby, Jr., United States Court of Appeals for the Ninth Circuit (1990-1991)

Government: Chief, Tucson (AZ) Office, Arizona District, United States Department of Justice (2002); Chief Assistant U.S. Attorney, Tucson (AZ) Office, Arizona District, United States Department of Justice (2002-2005)

Judicial: Magistrate Judge, United States District Court for the District of Arizona (2005-2011)

Legal Practice: Associate, Molloy, Jones & Donahue (1991-1995)

Chambers of District Judge Diane J. Humetewa

401 West Washington Street, Suite 625, Phoenix, AZ 85003
Tel: (602) 322-7600
E-mail: diane_humetewa@azd.uscourts.gov

Diane J. Humetewa
District Judge

Education: Arizona State 1987 BA, 1993 JD
Began Service: May 16, 2014
Appointed By: President Barack Obama

Chambers of District Judge Steven Paul Logan

401 West Washington Street, Suite 521, Phoenix, AZ 85003
Tel: (602) 322-7550
E-mail: steven_logan@azd.uscourts.gov

Steven Paul Logan
District Judge

Education: Louisville 1988 BS; Oklahoma 1992 JD
Began Service: May 16, 2014
Appointed By: President Barack Obama

Government: Assistant U.S. Attorney, Criminal Division, Arizona District, United States Department of Justice; Acting Chief, Criminal Division, Arizona District, United States Department of Justice (2009-2010); Immigration Judge, U.S. Immigration Court - Eloy (AZ) Detention Center, Office of the Chief Immigration Judge, United States Department of Justice (2010-2012)

Judicial: Magistrate Judge, Chambers of Magistrate Judge Steven P. Logan, United States District Court for the District of Arizona (2012-2014)

Chambers of District Judge John Joseph Tuchi

401 West Washington Street, Suite 525, Phoenix, AZ 85003
Tel: (602) 322-7660
E-mail: john_tuchi@azd.uscourts.gov

John Joseph Tuchi
District Judge

Education: West Virginia 1987 BS; Arizona 1989 MS; Arizona State 1994 JD
Began Service: May 16, 2014
Appointed By: President Barack Obama

Government: Chief, Criminal Division, Arizona District, United States Department of Justice (2007-2009); Acting U.S. Attorney, Arizona District, Executive Office for United States Attorneys, United States Department of Justice (2009); Tribal Relations Senior Litigation Counsel, Arizona District, Executive Office for United States Attorneys, United States Department of Justice (2010-2013)

Chambers of District Judge Rosemary Márquez

405 West Congress Street, Suite 5160, Tucson, AZ 85701-5061
Tel: (520) 205-4620
E-mail: rosemary_marquez@azd.uscourts.gov

Rosemary Márquez
District Judge

Education: Arizona 1990 BA, 1993 JD
Began Service: May 19, 2014
Appointed By: President Barack Obama

Government: Public Defender, Legal Defender's Office, County of Pima, Arizona (1994-1996); Assistant Federal Public Defender, United States Court of Appeals for the Ninth Circuit (1996-2000)

Profession: Private Practice (2000-2011)

Chambers of District Judge Douglas L. Rayes

401 West Washington Street, Suite 526., Phoenix, AZ 85003
Tel: (602) 322-7530
E-mail: douglas_rayes@azd.uscourts.gov

Douglas L. Rayes
District Judge

Education: Arizona State 1975 BSE, 1978 JD
Began Service: May 28, 2014
Appointed By: President Barack Obama

Legal Practice: Associate, McGroder, Pearlstein, Pepler & Tryon (1982-1984); Partner, McGroder, Tryon, Heller & Rayes (1986-1989); Partner, Tryon, Heller & Rayes (1989-2000)

Staff

Law Clerk **Kyle LaRose** .... (602) 322-7530
Began Service: June 2014
Term Expires: June 2016
Law Clerk **Kaitlyn M. Quigley** .... (602) 322-7530
Began Service: June 2014
Term Expires: June 2016
Judicial Assistant **Mary Farmer** .... (602) 322-7530

FEDERAL COURTS—UNITED STATES DISTRICT COURTS

Chambers of District Judge James Alan Soto

405 West Congress Street, Suite 6160, Tucson, AZ 85701-5061
Tel: (520) 205-4510
E-mail: james_soto@azd.uscourts.gov

James Alan Soto
District Judge

Began Service: June 9, 2014
Appointed By: President Barack Obama

Judicial: Presiding Judge, Chambers of Presiding Judge James A. Soto, Santa Cruz County Superior Court, Arizona County Courts

Chambers of Senior Judge Stephen M. McNamee

Sandra Day O'Connor U.S. Courthouse, 401 West Washington Street, SPC 60, Suite 625, Phoenix, AZ 85003-2158
Tel: (602) 322-7555 Fax: (602) 322-7509
E-mail: Stephen_McNamee@azd.uscourts.gov

Stephen M. McNamee
Senior Judge

Date of Birth: 1942
Education: Cincinnati 1964 BA; Arizona 1967 MA, 1969 JD
Began Service: June 8, 1990
Appointed By: President George H.W. Bush

Academic: Lecturer, School of Business and Public Administration, The University of Arizona (1975-1979); Assistant Director, Attorney General's Advocacy Institute (1979-1980)

Government: Assistant United States Attorney, District of Arizona, United States Department of Justice (1971-1979); First Assistant United States Attorney, District of Arizona, United States Department of Justice (1980); Chief Assistant United States Attorney, District of Arizona, United States Department of Justice (1981-1985); United States Attorney, District of Arizona, United States Department of Justice (1985-1990)

Judicial: Chief Judge, United State District Court for the District of Arizona (1999-2006)

Current Memberships: Maricopa County Bar Association; State Bar of Arizona

Staff

Law Clerk **Kimball Smith** .... (602) 322-7504
E-mail: kimball_smith@azd.uscourts.gov
Law Clerk **Owen Mcgeehon** .... (602) 322-7501
Began Service: September 2011
E-mail: owen_mcgeehon@azd.uscourts.gov
Judicial Assistant **Linda Petersen** .... (602) 322-7555
E-mail: linda_petersen@azd.uscourts.gov

Chambers of Senior Judge Paul G. Rosenblatt

Sandra Day O'Connor U.S. Courthouse, 401 West Washington Street, SPC 56, Suite 621, Phoenix, AZ 85003-2156
Tel: (602) 322-7510
E-mail: paul_rosenblatt@azd.uscourts.gov

Paul G. Rosenblatt
Senior Judge

Date of Birth: 1928
Education: Arizona 1958 AB, 1963 JD
Began Service: 1984
Appointed By: President Ronald Reagan
Political Affiliation: Republican

Government: Assistant Attorney General, Office of the Attorney General, United States Department of Justice (1963-1966); Administrative Assistant (R-AZ, District 3), Office of Representative Sam Steiger, United States House of Representatives (1967-1972)

Judicial: Presiding Judge, Arizona Superior Court, Yavapai County (1973-1984)

Chambers of Senior Judge Paul G. Rosenblatt *continued*

Legal Practice: Private Practice (1971-1973)

Military Service: United States Army Reserve, United States Department of the Army (1951-1953)

Staff

Career Law Clerk **Richard Corson** .... (602) 322-7510
E-mail: richard_corson@azd.uscourts.gov
Education: Georgetown 1972 BS; Arizona 1976 JD
Judicial Assistant **Tina DeMonaco** .... (602) 322-7510
E-mail: tina_demonaco@azd.uscourts.gov

Chambers of Senior Judge Frank R. Zapata

Evo A. DeConcini U.S. Courthouse, 405 West Congress Street, Suite 5160, Tucson, AZ 85701-5050
Tel: (520) 205-4530 Fax: (520) 205-4539

Frank R. Zapata
Senior Judge

Date of Birth: 1944
Education: Arizona 1966 BA, 1973 JD
Began Service: August 2, 1994
Appointed By: President William J. Clinton

Academic: Tutor, Special Services, Pima Community College District (1970-1973); Assistant Adjunct Professor, College of Law, The University of Arizona (1988-1990)

Government: Teacher, Hayden-Winkelman Unified School District (1967-1969); Teacher, Tucson Unified School District (1969-1970); Assistant Federal Public Defender, District of Arizona, State of Arizona (1974-1984); Chief Assistant Federal Public Defender, United States District Court for the District of Arizona (1984-1994)

Judicial: Magistrate Judge, United States District Court for the District of Arizona (1994-1996)

Legal Practice: Staff Attorney, Southern Arizona Legal Aid, Inc. (1973-1974)

Current Memberships: The Morris K. Udall American Inn of Court, The American Inns of Court; Arizona Minority Bar Association; Tuscon Chapter, Federal Bar Association; National Hispanic Bar Association; Pima County Bar Association; State Bar of Arizona; United States District Judges Association

Staff

Career Law Clerk **Cindy Reyna** .... (520) 205-4530
E-mail: cindy_reyna@azd.uscourts.gov
Education: Arizona 1982 BFA, 1985 MA, 1990 JD
Law Clerk **Amanda Damaianakos** .... (520) 205-4530
E-mail: amanda_damaianakos@azd.uscourts.gov
Court Reporter **Traci Walker** .... (520) 205-4266
Judicial Assistant **Michelle Mejia** .... (520) 205-4530

Chambers of Senior Judge David C. Bury

Evo A. Deconcini U.S. Courthouse, 405 West Congress, Suite 6170, Tucson, AZ 85701-5065
Tel: (520) 205-4560 Fax: (520) 205-4569
E-mail: david_bury@azd.uscourts.gov

David C. Bury
Senior Judge

Date of Birth: 1942
Education: Oklahoma State 1964 BS; Arizona 1967 JD
Began Service: March 29, 2002
Appointed By: President George W. Bush

Staff

Career Law Clerk **Greer Barkley** .... (520) 205-4560
E-mail: greer_barkley@azd.uscourts.gov
Education: Arizona State 1979 BA; Arizona 1992 JD

Chambers of Senior Judge David C. Bury *continued*

Career Law Clerk **Cynthia McMahon Lorge** . . . . (520) 205-4560
E-mail: cynthia_lorge@azd.uscourts.gov
Education: Southern Methodist 1976 BA; McGeorge 1981 JD
Judicial Assistant **Mary Ellen Druckenbrod** . . . . (520) 205-4560
E-mail: mary_ellen_druckenbrod@azd.uscourts.gov

Chambers of Senior Judge Frederick J. Martone

401 West Washington Street, SPC 62, Suite 526, Phoenix, AZ 85003
Tel: (602) 322-7590
E-mail: frederick_martone@azd.uscourts.gov

Frederick J. Martone
Senior Judge

Date of Birth: 1943
Education: Col Holy Cross 1965 BS; Notre Dame 1972 JD; Harvard 1975 LLM
Began Service: January 30, 2002
Appointed By: President George W. Bush

Current Memberships: American Bar Association; Federal Judges Association; State Bar of Arizona

Chambers of Senior Judge James A. Teilborg

Sandra Day O'Connor U.S. Courthouse, 401 West Washington Street, Suite 523, Phoenix, AZ 85003
Tel: (602) 322-7560
E-mail: teilborg_chambers@azd.uscourts.gov

James A. Teilborg
Senior Judge

Date of Birth: 1942
Education: Arizona 1966 JD
Began Service: October 17, 2000
Appointed By: President William J. Clinton
Political Affiliation: Republican

Current Memberships: Colorado Bar Association; Federal Bar Association; Lawyer Pilots Bar Association; Maricopa County Bar Association; State Bar of Arizona

Staff

Career Law Clerk **Elicia Giroux** . . . . (602) 322-7560
E-mail: elicia_giroux@azd.uscourts.gov
Education: UC Santa Barbara 1994 BA; Arizona State 1997 JD
Court Reporter **David C. German** . . . . (602) 322-7251
E-mail: david_german@azd.uscourts.gov

Chambers of Senior Judge Roslyn O. Silver

401 West Washington Street, Suite 624, Phoenix, AZ 85003
Tel: (602) 322-7520
E-mail: Roslyn_Silver@azd.uscourts.gov

Roslyn O. Silver
Senior Judge

Date of Birth: 1946
Education: UC Santa Barbara 1968 BA; Arizona State 1971 JD
Began Service: October 14, 1994
Appointed By: President William J. Clinton
Political Affiliation: Independent

Current Memberships: Arizona Women Lawyers Association; Federal Bar Association; National Association of Women Judges; State Bar of Arizona

Chambers of Senior Judge Roslyn O. Silver *continued*

Staff

Law Clerk **Joel Edman** . . . . (602) 322-7521
Began Service: September 2015
Term Expires: September 2016
E-mail: joel_edman@azd.uscourts.gov
Career Law Clerk **Michael Newman** . . . . (602) 322-7522
E-mail: michael_newman@azd.uscourts.gov
Court Deputy **Teddy Bengtson** . . . . (602) 322-7225
E-mail: teddy_bengtson@azd.uscourts.gov Fax: (602) 322-7529
Court Reporter **Elva Cruz-Lauer** . . . . (602) 322-7245
E-mail: elva_cruz-lauer@azd.uscourts.gov Fax: (602) 322-7509
Judicial Assistant **Kelly Branding** . . . . (602) 322-7520
E-mail: kelly_branding@azd.uscourts.gov

Chambers of Magistrate Judge Bernardo P. Velasco

Evo A. DeConcini U.S. Courthouse, 405 West Congress Street, Suite 5650, Tucson, AZ 85701-5054
Tel: (520) 205-4630 Fax: (520) 205-4639
E-mail: bernardo_velasco@azd.uscourts.gov

Bernardo P. Velasco
Magistrate Judge

Date of Birth: 1949
Education: Arizona 1971 BS, 1974 JD
Began Service: September 29, 2000
Term Expires: September 29, 2016
Political Affiliation: Democrat

Government: Assistant Federal Public Defender, United States District Court for the District of Arizona (1976-1982)

Judicial: Judge, Arizona Superior Court (1985-2000)

Legal Practice: Legal Aid Society (1974-1975); Haralson, Kinerk & Morey (1983-1984)

Military Service: Inactive United States Army Reserve, United States Department of the Army (1971-1979)

Current Memberships: Arizona Judges Association; Arizona Minority Bar Association; National Wild Turkey Federation; Pima County Bar Association; State Bar of Arizona

Staff

Career Law Clerk **Rebecca Huerta** . . . . (520) 205-4631
E-mail: rebecca_huerta@azd.uscourts.gov
Education: Georgetown 1997 JD
Judicial Assistant **Charlotte Molina** . . . . (520) 205-4630
E-mail: charlotte_molina@azd.uscourts.gov

Chambers of Magistrate Judge David K. Duncan

Sandra Day O'Connor U.S. Courthouse, 401 West Washington Street, SPC 14, Suite 325, Phoenix, AZ 85003-2120
Tel: (602) 322-7630 Fax: (602) 322-7639
E-mail: david_duncan@azd.uscourts.gov

David K. Duncan
Magistrate Judge

Date of Birth: 1958
Education: Arizona 1984 BA, 1987 JD
Began Service: June 14, 2001
Term Expires: June 13, 2017

Clerkships: Law Clerk The Honorable William D. Browning, United States District Court for the District of Arizona (1987-1989)

Government: Assistant United States Attorney, United States Department of Justice (1997-2001)

Legal Practice: Associate, Meyer, Hendricks, Victor, Osborn & Maledon; Partner, Osborn Maledon (1995-1997)

Current Memberships: American Bar Association; Arizona Women Lawyers Association; Federal Bar Association; Maricopa County Bar Association

(continued on next page)

Chambers of Magistrate Judge David K. Duncan *continued*

Staff

Career Law Clerk **Sarah Selzer** . . . . (602) 322-7630
E-mail: sarah_selzer@azd.uscourts.gov

Judicial Assistant **Armida Herrera** . . . . (602) 322-7630
E-mail: armida_herrera@azd.uscourts.gov
Education: Arizona State 2003 BS

Chambers of Magistrate Judge Charles R. Pyle

Evo A. DeConcini U.S. Courthouse, 405 West Congress Street, Suite 5660, Tucson, AZ 85701-5055
Tel: (520) 205-4650 Fax: (520) 205-4659
E-mail: charles_pyle@azd.uscourts.gov

Charles R. Pyle
Magistrate Judge

Date of Birth: 1948
Education: Stanford 1970 BA; Arizona 1973 JD
Began Service: June 28, 2002
Term Expires: June 28, 2018
Political Affiliation: Democrat

Government: Assistant, Office of the County Attorney, County of Pima, Arizona (1987-1989); Associate, District of Arizona, Office of the Attorney General, United States Department of Justice (1989-2001)

Legal Practice: Southern Arizona Legal Aid (1977-1987)

Current Memberships: Federal Bar Association; Pima County Bar Association

Staff

Law Clerk **Suzanne McKee** . . . . (520) 205-4651
Began Service: 2009
E-mail: suzanne_mckee@azd.uscourts.gov

Law Clerk **Cassidy L. James** . . . . (520) 205-4650
E-mail: cassidy_james@azd.uscourts.gov

Chambers of Magistrate Judge Jacqueline J. Rateau

Evo A. DeConcini U.S. Courthouse, 405 West Congress Street, Suite 6650, Tucson, AZ 85701-5063
Tel: (520) 205-4232
E-mail: jacqueline_marshall@azd.uscourts.gov

Jacqueline J. Rateau
Magistrate Judge

Date of Birth: 1961
Education: Arizona State 1983 BS; Arizona 1986 JD
Began Service: July 11, 2001
Political Affiliation: Democrat

Clerkships: Law Clerk The Honorable Alfredo C. Marquez, United States District Court for the District of Arizona (1997-2001)

Government: Assistant Public Defender, State of Arizona (1987-1990)

Legal Practice: Law Office of Bertram Polls (1986-1987); Ralls, Fox & Jones, PC (1990-1997)

Current Memberships: Arizona Minority Bar Association; Arizona Women Lawyers Association; Federal Bar Association; State Bar of Arizona

Staff

Career Law Clerk **Gary Kraft** . . . . (520) 205-4232
E-mail: gary_kraft@azd.uscourts.gov
Education: Arizona 1992 BA, 1996 JD

Judicial Assistant **Yvette Gonzalez** . . . . (520) 205-4232
E-mail: yvette_gonzalez@azd.uscourts.gov

Chambers of Magistrate Judge Michelle H. Burns

Sandra Day O'Connor U.S. Courthouse, 401 West Washington Street, SPC 12, Suite 323, Phoenix, AZ 85003-2120
Tel: (602) 322-7610
E-mail: michelle_burns@azd.uscourts.gov

Michelle H. Burns
Magistrate Judge

Education: Michigan 1981 BA; Toledo 1985 JD
Began Service: February 2007
Term Expires: February 2023

Current Memberships: Federal Bar Association

Staff

Courtroom Clerk **Kathy Lara** . . . . (602) 322-7242
E-mail: kathy_lara@azd.uscourts.gov

Chambers of Magistrate Judge D. Thomas Ferraro

404 West Congress Street, Suitee 6660, Tucson, AZ 85701-5065
Tel: (520) 205-4590

D. Thomas Ferraro
Magistrate Judge

Began Service: December 31, 2008

Chambers of Magistrate Judge Bridget S. Bade

401 West Washington Street, Suite 321, Phoenix, AZ 85003
Tel: (602) 322-7680
E-mail: bridget_bade@azd.uscourts.gov

Bridget S. Bade
Magistrate Judge

Education: Arizona State JD
Began Service: September 2012

Staff

Career Law Clerk **Susan Q. Stuart** . . . . (602) 322-7680
E-mail: susan_stuart@azd.uscourts.gov
Education: Washington U (MO) 1994 JD

Judicial Assistant **Ellen Weber** . . . . (602) 322-7680
E-mail: ellen_weber@azd.uscourts.gov

Chambers of Magistrate Judge Leslie A. Bowman

Evo A. DeConcini U.S. Courthouse, 405 West Congress Street, Suite 3170, Tucson, AZ 85701-5061
Tel: (520) 205-4500
E-mail: leslie_bowman@azd.uscourts.gov

Leslie A. Bowman
Magistrate Judge

Staff

Career Law Clerk **Alan Kahn** . . . . (520) 205-4500
E-mail: alan_kahn@azd.uscourts.gov

Judicial Assistant **Carrie Ryan** . . . . (520) 205-4500
E-mail: carrie_ryan@azd.uscourts.gov

Chambers of Magistrate Judge Bruce G. Macdonald

405 West Congress Street, Suite 3180, Tucson, AZ 85701-5061
Tel: (520) 205-4520
E-mail: bruce_macdonald@azd.uscourts.gov

Bruce G. Macdonald
Magistrate Judge

Chambers of Magistrate Judge Bruce G. Macdonald *continued*

Staff
Career Law Clerk **Marcia Delanty** . . . . (520) 205-4520
E-mail: marcia_delanty@azd.uscourts.gov
Judicial Assistant **Karen Straub** . . . . (520) 205-4520
E-mail: karen_straub@azd.uscourts.gov

Chambers of Magistrate Judge Eric J. Markovich
405 West Congress Street, Tucson, AZ 85701-5061
Tel: (520) 205-4600

Eric M. Markovich
Magistrate Judge

Chambers of Magistrate Judge Eileen S. Willett
401 West Washington Street, Suite 321, Phoenix, AZ 85003
Tel: (602) 322-7620

Eileen S. Willett
Magistrate Judge

Began Service: 2014

Chambers of Magistrate Judge John Z. Boyle
401 West Washington Street, Suite 321, Phoenix, AZ 85003
Tel: (602) 322-7670

John Z. Boyle
Magistrate Judge

Began Service: 2014

Chambers of Magistrate Judge Deborah M. Fine
123 North San Francisco Street, Suite 200, Flagstaff, AZ 86001
Tel: (928) 774-2566

Deborah M. Fine
Magistrate Judge

Began Service: 2015

Chambers of Magistrate Judge (part-time) James F. Metcalf
John M. Roll U.S. Courthouse, 98 West 1st Street, Yuma, AZ 85364
Tel: (928) 329-4766
E-mail: james_metcalf@azd.uscourts.gov

James F. Metcalf
Magistrate Judge (Part-Time)

Began Service: June 24, 2009

Chambers of Magistrate Judge (Part-Time) John A. Buttrick
98 West 1st Street, Yuma, AZ 85364
Tel: (928) 329-4766

John A. Buttrick
Magistrate Judge (Part-Time)

United States Bankruptcy Court for the District of Arizona
230 North 1st Avenue, Suite 101, Phoenix, AZ 85003
Tel: (602) 682-4000 (Phoenix)
Tel: (520) 202-7500 (Tucson) Tel: (928) 783-2288 (Yuma)
Tel: (888) 549-5336 (Voice Case Information System VCIS)
Internet: www.azb.uscourts.gov

Number of Judgeships: 8

Court Staff
Clerk of Court **George D. Prentice II** . . . . (602) 682-4024
Chief Deputy **Nancy B. Dickerson** . . . . (602) 682-4030
E-mail: nancy_dickerson@azb.uscourts.gov
Education: Cornell 1977 BS;
Lewis & Clark 1982 JD
Case Administrator **Jennifer Manning** . . . . (928) 783-2288 ext. 245
325 W. 19th St., Ste. D, Yuma, AZ 85364 Fax: (928) 782-9460
Divisional Manager (Tucson) **Dean Axelrod** . . . . (520) 202-7530
38 South Scott Avenue, Tucson, AZ 85707
Administrative Services Manager **Warner Orr** . . . . (602) 682-4120
Human Resources Specialist **Annette Fischer** . . . . (602) 682-4074
Operations Manager **Randy Merrill** . . . . (602) 682-4040
Financial Specialist **Janet Spiker** . . . . (602) 682-4132

Chambers of Chief Bankruptcy Judge Daniel P. Collins
230 North First Avenue, Suite 101, Phoenix, AZ 85003-1706
Tel: (602) 682-4224

Daniel P. Collins
Chief Bankruptcy Judge

Staff
Judicial Assistant **Shirley A. Dunbar** . . . . (602) 682-4224

Chambers of Bankruptcy Judge George B. Nielsen, Jr.
230 North First Avenue, Suite 101, Phoenix, AZ 85003-1706
Tel: (602) 682-4164 Fax: (602) 682-4165
E-mail: george_nielsen@azb.uscourts.gov

George B. Nielsen, Jr.
Bankruptcy Judge

Date of Birth: 1944
Began Service: 1983

Judicial: Chief Bankruptcy Judge, United States Bankruptcy Court for the District of Arizona

Chambers of Bankruptcy Judge Eddward Ballinger Jr.
230 North First Avenue, Suite 101, Phoenix, AZ 85003-1706
Tel: (602) 682-4184

Eddward P. Ballinger, Jr.
Bankruptcy Judge

Staff
Judicial Assistant **Linda Gray** . . . . (602) 682-4184

Chambers of Bankruptcy Judge Brenda Moody Whinery
38 South Scott Avenue, Tucson, AZ 85701
Tel: (602) 682-4268

Brenda Moody Whinery
Bankruptcy Judge

Chambers of Bankruptcy Judge Madeleine C. Wanslee
230 North First Avenue, Phoenix, AZ 85003-1706
Tel: (602) 682-4244

Madeleine C. Wanslee
Bankruptcy Judge

Education: Arizona 1985 BA; Gonzaga 1988 JD
Began Service: 2014

Chambers of Bankruptcy Judge Paul Sala
230 North First Avenue, Phoenix, AZ 85003-1706
Tel: (602) 682-4146

Paul Sala
Bankruptcy Judge

Began Service: 2014

Chambers of Bankruptcy Judge Brenda K. Martin
230 North First Avenue, Phoenix, AZ 85003-1706
Tel: (602) 682-4264

Brenda K. Martin
Bankruptcy Judge

Education: Willamette 1987 BA; Arizona State 1990 JD

Chambers of Bankruptcy Judge Scott H. Gan
38 South Scott Avenue, Tucson, AZ 85701
Tel: (520) 202-7964

Scott H. Gan
Bankruptcy Judge

Chambers of Bankruptcy Judge (recalled) Eileen W. Hollowell
38 South Scott Avenue, Tucson, AZ 85701
Tel: (520) 202-7964

Eileen W. Hollowell
Bankruptcy Judge (recalled)

Date of Birth: 1945
Education: UMass (Amherst) BA; Michigan MSW; Arizona 1981 JD

Current Memberships: American Bar Association; Arizona Women Lawyers Association; National Council of Bankruptcy Judges; Pima County Bar Association; State Bar of Arizona

United States District Court for the Eastern District of Arkansas
U.S. Courthouse, 500 West Capitol Avenue, Room A-149,
Little Rock, AR 72201-3325
Tel: (501) 604-5351 Tel: (501) 604-5300 (General Info)
Tel: (501) 324-6190 (Civil Cases PACER) Fax: (501) 604-5321
Internet: www.are.uscourts.gov

Number of Judgeships: 5

Circuit: Eighth

Areas Covered: Counties of Arkansas, Chicot, Clay, Cleburne, Cleveland, Conway, Craighead, Crittenden, Cross, Dallas, Desha, Drew, Faulkner, Fulton, Grant, Greene, Independence, Izard, Jackson, Jefferson, Lawrence, Lee, Lincoln, Lonoke, Mississippi, Monroe, Perry, Phillips, Poinsett, Pope, Prairie, Pulaski, Randolph, Saline, Sharp, St. Francis, Stone, Van Buren, White, Woodruff and Yell

United States District Court for the Eastern District of Arkansas *continued*

Court Staff
Clerk of Court **James W. McCormack** . . . . (501) 604-5351
600 West Capitol Avenue, Room A149,
Little Rock, AR 72201
E-mail: james_mccormack@ared.uscourts.gov
Chief Deputy **Marcy Davenport** . . . . (501) 604-5129
E-mail: marcy_davenport@ared.uscourts.gov
Chief U.S. Probation Officer
G. Edward "Eddie" Towe . . . . (501) 604-5240
Operations Supervisor **Tammy Downs** . . . . (501) 604-5357
E-mail: tammy_downs@ared.uscourts.gov
Docket Clerk **Megan Frost** . . . . (501) 604-5359
600 West Capitol Avenue,
Little Rock, AR 72201-3325
Financial Administrator **Jason Cauley** . . . . (501) 604-5127
E-mail: jason_cauley@ared.uscourts.gov
Jury Administrator **Shauna Bostic** . . . . (501) 604-5107
Network Administrator **John William French** . . . . (501) 604-5346
E-mail: john_french@ared.uscourts.gov
Senior Systems Administrator **Dale Souza** . . . . (501) 604-5347
Procurement and Property Management Administrator
Steve Elliott . . . . (501) 604-5311
E-mail: steve_elliott@ared.uscourts.gov
Deputy Clerk - Jonesboro **Jake Kornegay** . . . . (870) 972-4610
312 Federal Bldg., 615 S Main St., Room 312, Fax: (870) 972-4612
Jonesboro, AR 72401
E-mail: jake_kornegay@ared.uscourts.gov
Deputy Clerk - Pine Bluff **Brenda Johnson** . . . . (870) 536-1190
100 East 8th Street, Room 3103, Fax: (870) 536-6330
Pine Bluff, AR 71601
Administrative Generalist **Chase Ferguson** . . . . (501) 604-5303
Jury Clerk **(Vacant)** . . . . (501) 604-5319
Administrative Assistant to the Clerk **Cindy Peters** . . . . . (501) 604-5300
E-mail: cindy_peters@ared.uscourts.gov
Criminal Docket Clerk **Katelyn Cameron** . . . . (501) 604-5313
E-mail: katelyn_cameron@ared.uscourts.gov
Criminal Docketing Clerk **Carrie Young** . . . . (501) 604-5310
E-mail: carrie_young@ared.uscourts.gov
Civil Docket Clerk **Laura Bichlmeier** . . . . (501) 604-5364
Jury Clerk **Brandy Dunlap** . . . . (501) 604-5356
Generalist Clerk **Robbie Mixon** . . . . (501) 604-5306
E-mail: robbie_mixon@ared.uscourts.gov
Generalist Clerk **Kyle Smith** . . . . (501) 604-5394
Generalist Clerk **Tenesha Brown** . . . . (501) 604-5355
E-mail: tenesha_jones@ared.uscourts.gov
Generalist Clerk **Michelle Daniel** . . . . (501) 604-5394
Generalist Clerk **Hallie Yates** . . . . (501) 604-5189
E-mail: hallie_yates@ared.uscourts.gov
Generalist Clerk **Kristy Rochelle** . . . . (501) 604-5359
E-mail: kristy_rochelle@ared.uscourts.gov
Intake Clerk **Forrest Dunn** . . . . (501) 604-5341
E-mail: forrest_dunn@ared.uscourts.gov
Intake Clerk **Joyce Pigee** . . . . (501) 604-5353
E-mail: joyce_pigee@ared.uscourts.gov
Financial Specialist **Michelle Toliver** . . . . (501) 604-5304
Courtroom Deputy **Melanie Beard** . . . . (501) 604-5160
Courtroom Deputy **LaShawn Coleman** . . . . (501) 604-5174
E-mail: lashawn_coleman@ared.uscourts.gov
Courtroom Deputy **Suzy Flippen** . . . . (501) 604-5114
E-mail: suzy_flippen@ared.uscourts.gov
Courtroom Deputy **Martha Fugate** . . . . (501) 604-5410
600 West Capitol Avenue,
Little Rock, AR 72201-3325
E-mail: martha_fugate@ared.uscourts.gov
Courtroom Deputy **Kacie Glenn** . . . . (501) 604-5154
E-mail: kacie_glenn@ared.uscourts.gov
Courtroom Deputy **Donna Jackson** . . . . (501) 604-5319
Courtroom Deputy **Lorna Jones** . . . . (501) 604-5184
E-mail: lorna_jones@ared.uscourts.gov
Courtroom Deputy **Cecilia Norwood** . . . . (501) 604-5104
E-mail: cecilia_norwood@ared.uscourts.gov
Courtroom Deputy **Kathy Swanson** . . . . (501) 604-5234
Education: Southern Mississippi BS;
Mississippi State 1993 MPA

United States District Court for the Eastern District of Arkansas *continued*

Courtroom Deputy **Betty Tyree** . . . . (501) 604-5404
E-mail: betty_m_tyree@ared.uscourts.gov
Courtroom Deputy **Tracy Washington** . . . . (501) 604-5420
Courtroom Deputy **Cory Wilkins** . . . . (501) 604-5384
E-mail: cory_wilkins@ared.uscourts.gov
Courtroom Deputy **(Vacant)** . . . . (501) 604-5194
Operations Analyst **Patricia Murray** . . . . (501) 604-5124
E-mail: patricia_murray@ared.uscourts.gov
Education: Arkansas 1983 BS
Operations Analyst **(Vacant)** . . . . (501) 604-5308
Librarian **Crata Castleberry** . . . . (501) 604-5215
Education: USC 1983 MSLS Fax: (501) 324-5217
Assistant Librarian **Stephanie Beavers** . . . . (501) 604-5216
Mail Room Clerk **A. D. Edgerson, Jr.** . . . . (501) 604-5354
Data Quality Analyst **(Vacant)** . . . . (501) 604-5309
Space Manager **(Vacant)** . . . . (501) 960-5311
Systems Manager **Linda Shields** . . . . (501) 604-5343
E-mail: linda_shields@ared.uscourts.gov
Courtroom Technology Coordinator **Jeremy Canitz** . . . . . . (501) 604-5395
E-mail: jeremy_canitz@ared.uscourts.gov
IT Technician II **Cade Bailey** . . . . (501) 604-5345
E-mail: cade_bailey@ared.uscourts.gov
IT Technician II **Micah Hughes** . . . . (501) 604-5340
E-mail: michah_hughes@ared.uscourts.gov
Computer Tech Administrator **James Harrison** . . . . (501) 604-5228
E-mail: james_harrison@ared.uscourts.gov
Generalist Clerk **Mary Zelhof** . . . . (501) 604-5358
E-mail: mary_zelhof@ared.uscourts.gov

Chambers of Chief Judge Brian Stacy Miller

U.S. Courthouse, 600 West Capitol Avenue, Room D258,
Little Rock, AR 72201
Tel: (501) 604-5400
E-mail: bsmchambers@ared.uscourts.gov
E-mail: brian_miller@ared.uscourts.gov

Brian Stacy Miller
Chief Judge

Education: Central Arkansas 1992 BS; Vanderbilt 1995 JD
Began Service: June 27, 2008
Appointed By: President George W. Bush

Current Memberships: American Bar Association; Arkansas Bar Association; National Bar Association; Tennessee Bar Association

Staff
Law Clerk **Brice Kenfack** . . . . (501) 604-5403
E-mail: brice_kenfack@ared.uscourts.gov
Law Clerk **Lauren Eldridge** . . . . (501) 604-5401
E-mail: lauren_eldridge@ared.uscourts.gov
Law Clerk **Steven Williamson** . . . . (501) 604-5402
Began Service: 2013
E-mail: steven_williamson@ared.uscourts.gov
Courtroom Deputy **Betty Tyree** . . . . (501) 604-5404
E-mail: betty_m_tyree@ared.uscourts.gov

Chambers of District Judge Leon Holmes

500 West Capitol Avenue, Room D-469, Little Rock, AR 72201-3325
Tel: (501) 604-5380 Fax: (501) 604-5389
E-mail: jlhchambers@ared.uscourts.gov
E-mail: Leon_Holmes@ared.uscourts.gov

Leon Holmes
District Judge

Education: Arkansas 1973 BA; Northern Illinois 1976 MA; Duke 1979 PhD; Arkansas 1982 JD
Began Service: July 19, 2004
Appointed By: President George W. Bush

Chambers of District Judge Leon Holmes *continued*

Staff
Law Clerk **Michael A. Cantrell** . . . . (501) 604-5385
Law Clerk **Nicole Swisher** . . . . (501) 604-5382
Began Service: 2015
E-mail: nicole_swisher@ared.uscourts.gov
Career Law Clerk **(Vacant)** . . . . (501) 604-5314
Secretary **Lisa Cox** . . . . (501) 604-5383
E-mail: lisa_cox@ared.uscourts.gov
Courtroom Deputy **Cory Wilkins** . . . . (501) 604-5384
E-mail: cory_wilkins@ared.uscourts.gov

Chambers of District Judge Denzil Price Marshall, Jr.

600 West Capitol Avenue, B155, Little Rock, AR 72201
Tel: (501) 604-5410 Fax: (501) 604-5417
E-mail: dpmchambers@ared.uscourts.gov
E-mail: price_marshall@ared.uscourts.gov

Denzil Price Marshall
District Judge

Education: Arkansas State 1985 BA; Harvard 1989 JD
Began Service: May 14, 2010
Appointed By: President Barack Obama

Clerkships: Law Clerk, Chambers of Circuit Judge Richard S. Arnold, United States Court of Appeals for the Eighth Circuit (1989-1991)

Government: Reporter, Committee on Civil Practice, Arkansas Supreme Court (2004)

Judicial: Judge, Chambers of Judge D. P. Marshall, Jr., Arkansas Court of Appeals (2006-2010)

Legal Practice: Attorney, Barrett & Deacon (1991-2006)

Current Memberships: American Bar Association; Arkansas Bar Association

Staff
Law Clerk **Chelsea Cash** . . . . (501) 604-5413
Began Service: 2015
Term Expires: August 2016
E-mail: chelsea_cash@ared.uscourts.gov
Law Clerk **Adam Skarda** . . . . (501) 604-5413
Began Service: 2015
Term Expires: August 2016
E-mail: adam_skarda@ared.uscourts.gov
Law Clerk **Caroline Winningham** . . . . (501) 604-5411
Began Service: 2015
Term Expires: August 2016
E-mail: caroline_winningham@ared.uscourts.gov
Courtroom Deputy **Martha Fugate** . . . . (501) 604-5410
E-mail: martha_fugate@ared.uscourts.gov

Chambers of District Judge Kristine Gerhard Baker

U.S. Courthouse, 500 West Capitol Avenue, Room D444,
Little Rock, AR 72201-3325
Tel: (501) 604-5420 Fax: (501) 604-5321
E-mail: kgbchambers@ared.uscourts.gov

Kristine Gerhard Baker
District Judge

Education: Saint Louis U 1993 BA; Arkansas 1996 JD
Began Service: October 19, 2012
Appointed By: President Barack Obama

Clerkships: Law Clerk, Chambers of District Judge Susan Webber Wright, United States District Court for the Eastern District of Arkansas (1996-1998)

Legal Practice: Attorney, Williams & Anderson PLC (1998-2000); Associate, Quattlebaum, Grooms, Tull & Burrow PLLC (2000-2002)

Staff
Law Clerk **Adam J. Bailey** . . . . (501) 604-5420
Law Clerk **Preston Eldridge** . . . . (501) 604-5420

(continued on next page)

Chambers of District Judge Kristine Gerhard Baker *continued*

Law Clerk **(Vacant)** .... (501) 604-5420
Courtroom Deputy **Tracy Washington** .... (501) 604-5420

Chambers of District Judge James Maxwell Moody Jr.

U.S. Courthouse, 500 West Capitol Avenue, Little Rock, AR 72201-3325
Tel: (501) 604-5157
E-mail: jmmchambers@ared.uscourts.gov

James Maxwell Moody, Jr.
District Judge

Education: Arkansas 1986 BSBA, 1989 JD
Began Service: March 10, 2014
Appointed By: President Barack Obama

Legal Practice: Associate, Wright, Lindsey & Jennings LLP (1989-1994); Partner, Wright, Lindsey & Jennings LLP (1994-2003)

Staff

Law Clerk **Deborah Bliss** .... (501) 604-5150
Law Clerk **Stacy Hatfield** .... (501) 604-5150
Education: Arkansas 1996 JD
Law Clerk **Amy Russell** .... (501) 604-5150
Courtroom Deputy **Kacie Glenn** .... (501) 604-5150

Chambers of Senior Judge Garnett Thomas Eisele

U.S. Courthouse, 500 West Capitol Avenue, Room C 244,
Little Rock, AR 72201
P.O. Box 3684, Little Rock, AR 72203
Tel: (501) 604-5160 Fax: (501) 604-5167

Garnett Thomas Eisele
Senior Judge

Date of Birth: 1923
Education: Washington U (MO) 1947 AB; Harvard 1950 LLB, 1951 LLM
Began Service: August 1970
Appointed By: President Richard M. Nixon

Government: Assistant United States Attorney, Eastern District of Arkansas, United States Department of Justice (1953-1956); Legal Advisor, Governor Winthrop Rockefeller (AR), Office of the Governor, State of Arkansas (1966-1969); Delegate, Seventh Arkansas Constitutional Convention (1969-1970)

Legal Practice: Wootton, Land & Matthews (1951-1952); Owens, McHaney, Lofton & McHaney (1956-1960); Private Practice (1961-1969)

Military Service: United States Army (1943-1946); United States Naval Reserve (1952-1961)

Current Memberships: American Bar Association; The American Law Institute; Arkansas Bar Association; Pulaski County Bar Association; World Association of Judges

Staff

Career Law Clerk **Edie Ervin** .... (501) 604-5160
Education: Hendrix 1988 BA; Arkansas (Little Rock) 1993 JD
Court Reporter **Karen Baker** .... (501) 604-5165
E-mail: karen.baker@ared.uscourts.gov
Courtroom Deputy/Secretary **Cherie Westbrook** .... (501) 604-5160

Chambers of Senior Judge Billy Roy Wilson

600 West Capitol Avenue, Room A403, Little Rock, AR 72201
Tel: (501) 604-5140 Fax: (501) 604-5149
E-mail: william_wilson@ared.uscourts.gov

Billy Roy Wilson
Senior Judge

Date of Birth: 1939
Education: Hendrix 1962 BA; Vanderbilt 1965 JD
Began Service: October 1, 1993
Appointed By: President William J. Clinton

Government: Deputy Prosecuting Attorney, State of Arkansas (1965-1966)

Judicial: District Judge, United States District Court for the Eastern District of Arkansas (1993-2010)

Legal Practice: Autrey & Goodson (1965-1966); Attorney, Wright, Lindsey & Jennings LLP (1969-1972); Partner, Wilson & Hodge (1972-1974); Private Practice (1974-1980); Partner, Wilson & Engstrom (1980-1983); Partner, Wilson, Engstrom & Vowell; Partner, Wilson, Engstrom, Corum & Dudley (1984-1993)

Military Service: United States Navy (1966-1969)

Current Memberships: American Bar Association; American Board of Trial Advocates; American College of Trial Lawyers; Arkansas Bar Association; Arkansas Trial Lawyers Association; International Academy of Trial Lawyers; International Society of Barristers; Miller County Bar Association; Southwest Arkansas Bar Association

Staff

Law Clerk **(Vacant)** .... (501) 604-5142
Law Clerk **Bruce Davis** .... (501) 604-5140
Career Law Clerk **Matt Morgan** .... (501) 604-5141
Courtroom Deputy **Melanie Beard** .... (501) 604-5144
Court Reporter **Christa Jacimore** .... (501) 604-5145
E-mail: christa.jacimore@aredcourtreporters.com
Secretary **J. Kay Holt** .... (501) 604-5140

Chambers of Senior Judge Susan Webber Wright

U.S. Courthouse, 500 West Capitol Avenue, Room 157D,
Little Rock, AR 72201
Tel: (501) 604-5100 Fax: (501) 604-5169

Susan Webber Wright
Senior Judge

Date of Birth: 1948
Education: Randolph-Macon Woman's 1970 BA; Arkansas 1973 MPA, 1975 JD
Began Service: May 11, 1990
Appointed By: President George H.W. Bush

Current Memberships: The American Law Institute; Arkansas Association of Women Lawyers; Arkansas Bar Association; Federal Judges Association; Pulaski County Bar Association; United States Foreign Intelligence Surveillance Court

Staff

Career Law Clerk **Jo-Jo Baldwin** .... (501) 604-5102
Education: Arkansas 1998 JD
Career Law Clerk **Lucille DeGostin** .... (501) 604-5101
Education: Georgetown 1975 JD
Career Law Clerk **Barry Ward** .... (501) 604-5103
Education: Arkansas 1988 JD
Courtroom Deputy **Cecilia Norwood** .... (501) 604-5104
E-mail: cecilia.norwood@ared.uscourts.gov
Court Reporter **Cheryl Kellar** .... (501) 604-5105
E-mail: cbnrealtime@yahoo.com

Chambers of Chief Magistrate Judge J. Thomas Ray
500 West Capitol Avenue, Room D-144, Little Rock, AR 72201-3325
Tel: (501) 604-5230 Fax: (501) 604-5237
E-mail: Thomas_Ray@ared.uscourts.gov

J. Thomas Ray
Chief Magistrate Judge

Date of Birth: 1951
Education: LSU 1973 BS; Tulane 1976 JD
Began Service: June 28, 2000
Term Expires: June 27, 2016

Clerkships: Law Clerk The Honorable G. Thomas Eisele, United States District Court for the Eastern District of Arkansas (1976-1978)

Judicial: Magistrate Judge, Chambers of Magistrate Judge J. Thomas Ray, United States District Court for the Eastern District of Arkansas

Legal Practice: Partner, Shults & Ray, LLP (1978-2000)

Current Memberships: American Bar Association; The Judge William R. Overton American Inn of Court, The American Inns of Court; Arkansas Bar Association; Arkansas Bar Foundation, Arkansas Bar Association; Pulaski County Bar Association

Staff
Career Law Clerk **Suzanne Sims** .... (501) 604-5230
E-mail: suzanne_sims@ared.uscourts.gov
Career Law Clerk **Paul Wood** .... (501) 604-5233
E-mail: paul_wood@ared.uscourts.gov
Education: Arkansas 1993 BA;
Arkansas (Little Rock) 1996 JD
Courtroom Deputy **Kathy Swanson** .... (501) 604-5234

Chambers of Magistrate Judge Beth Deere
500 West Capitol Avenue, Suite C 150, Little Rock, AR 72201-3325
Tel: (501) 604-5110
E-mail: bdchambers@ared.uscourts.gov
E-mail: beth_deere@ared.uscourts.gov

Beth Deere
Magistrate Judge

Education: Arkansas (Little Rock) 1986 JD
Began Service: January 8, 2007
Term Expires: January 8, 2023

Staff
Law Clerk **Josh King** .... (501) 604-5112
E-mail: josh_king@ared.uscourts.gov
Law Clerk **Debra W. Williams** .... (501) 604-5111
E-mail: debra_williams@ared.uscourts.gov
Courtroom Deputy **Suzy Flippen** .... (501) 604-5114
E-mail: suzy_flippen@ared.uscourts.gov

Chambers of Magistrate Judge Joe J. Volpe
500 West Capitol, Room D245, Little Rock, AR 72201
Tel: (501) 604-5190 Fax: (501) 604-5378
E-mail: jjvchambers@ared.uscourts.gov
E-mail: joe_volpe@ared.uscourts.gov

Joe Volpe
Magistrate Judge

Education: West Point 1988 BS; Arkansas (Little Rock) 1995 JD
Began Service: July 30, 2009

Staff
Career Law Clerk **Stacy Williams** .... (501) 604-5191
E-mail: stacy_williams@ared.uscourts.gov
Courtroom Deputy **(Vacant)** .... (501) 604-5194
Secretary **Anita J. Lee** .... (501) 604-5190
E-mail: anita_lee@ared.uscourts.gov

Chambers of Magistrate Judge Jerome T. Kearney
500 West Capitol Avenue, Little Rock, AR 72201-3325
Tel: (501) 604-5170 Fax: (501) 604-5178
E-mail: jtkchambers@ared.uscourts.gov
E-mail: jerome_kearney@ared.uscourts.gov

Jerome T. Kearney
Magistrate Judge

Began Service: April 2010

Staff
Law Clerk **Ryan Loofbourrow** .... (501) 604-5171
E-mail: ryan_loofbourrow@ared.uscourts.gov
Law Clerk **Gwendolyn Rucker** .... (501) 604-5173
Began Service: April 2010
E-mail: gwendolyn_rucker@ared.uscourts.gov
Education: Arkansas (Little Rock) 2001 JD
Courtroom Deputy **LaShawn Coleman** .... (501) 604-5174
E-mail: lashawn_coleman@ared.uscourts.gov

Chambers of Magistrate Judge (recalled) Jerry W. Cavaneau
500 West Capitol, Suite C163, Little Rock, AR 72201-3325
Tel: (501) 604-5200 Fax: (501) 604-5207

Jerry W. Cavaneau
Magistrate Judge (recalled)

Began Service: January 7, 1991

Staff
Courtroom Deputy **Shauna Bostic** .... (501) 604-5204
Secretary **Donna Jackson** .... (501) 604-5200

Chambers of Magistrate Judge Patricia S. Harris
500 West Capitol Avenue, Little Rock, AR 72201-3325
Tel: (501) 604-5180

Patricia Harris
Magistrate Judge

Education: Arkansas (Little Rock) 1986 BA, 1989 JD
Began Service: October 6, 2015
Term Expires: 2023

Staff
Law Clerk **John Courtway** .... (501) 604-5180
Law Clerk **Doug Ward** .... (501) 604-5180

United States Bankruptcy Court for the Eastern District of Arkansas
300 West Second Street, Little Rock, AR 72201
Tel: (501) 918-5500 Tel: (800) 676-6856 (Toll Free PACER)
Tel: (866) 222-8029 (Voice Case Information System McVCIS)
Fax: (501) 918-5520
Internet: www.arb.uscourts.gov

Number of Judgeships: 3

Court Staff
Bankruptcy Clerk **Jean Rolfs** .... (501) 918-5506
E-mail: jean_rolfs@areb.uscourts.gov Fax: (501) 918-5505
Chief Deputy Clerk **Philip R. Principe** .... (501) 918-5509
Education: Georgetown 1994 BSFS; Fax: (501) 918-5505
Columbus Law 1997 JD
Property and Procurement Officer
Charlotte Gomlicker .... (501) 918-5513
E-mail: charlotte_gomlicker@areb.uscourts.gov Fax: (501) 918-5514
Chief Financial Officer **DeeDee Morehead** .... (501) 918-5510
E-mail: deedee_morehead@areb.uscourts.gov Fax: (501) 918-5511
Education: Arkansas (Little Rock) 1987 BA

Chambers of Chief Bankruptcy Judge Richard D. Taylor

300 West Second Street, Little Rock, AR 72201
Tel: (501) 918-5620 Fax: (501) 918-5621
E-mail: rick_taylor@areb.uscourts.gov

Richard D. Taylor
Chief Bankruptcy Judge

Date of Birth: June 23, 1955
Education: Centenary (LA) 1976 BA; Arkansas 1980 JD
Began Service: January 2010
Term Expires: January 2017

Legal Practice: Friday Eldridge & Clark (1980-2002)

Current Memberships: Arkansas Bar Association; Washington County Bar Association

Staff

Staff Attorney **Allison Albritton** .... (501) 918-5620
Began Service: September 2008
E-mail: allison_albritton@areb.uscourts.gov
Education: Arkansas (Little Rock) 2008 JD

Staff Attorney **Linda Bird Green** .... (501) 918-5620
Began Service: August 13, 2012
E-mail: Linda_bird_green@areb.uscourts.gov

Courtroom Deputy **Erika Scales** .... (501) 918-5620
E-mail: erika_scales@areb.uscourts.gov

Chambers of Bankruptcy Judge Ben T. Barry

35 East Mountain Street, Fayetteville, AR 72701
Tel: (479) 582-9801

Ben T. Barry
Bankruptcy Judge

Began Service: April 2007
Term Expires: April 2021

Affiliation: Bankruptcy Judge, Chambers of Bankruptcy Judge Ben T. Barry, United States Bankruptcy Court for the Western District of Arkansas

Staff

Staff Attorney **Erika Stolzer** .... (479) 582-9821
E-mail: erika_stolzer@arwb.uscourts.gov
Education: Arkansas 2007 JD

Staff Attorney **Jim Longino** .... (479) 582-9807
E-mail: jim_longino@arwb.uscourts.gov
Education: Arkansas 1975 BA, 1995 JD

Courtroom Deputy **Marcy Payne** .... (479) 582-9809
E-mail: marcy_payne@arwb.uscourts.gov

Chambers of Bankruptcy Judge Phyllis M. Jones

300 West Second Street, Little Rock, AR 72201
Tel: (501) 918-5640

Phyllis M. Jones
Bankruptcy Judge

Staff

Staff Attorney **Mardi Blissard** .... (501) 918-5643
E-mail: mardi_blissard@areb.uscourts.gov

Staff Attorney **Laura Westbrook** .... (501) 918-5644
E-mail: laura_westbrook@arb.uscourts.gov

Courtroom Deputy **Mary Beth Mansfield** .... (501) 918-5640

United States District Court for the Western District of Arkansas

Isaac C. Parker Federal Building, 30 South Sixth Street, Room 1038, Fort Smith, AR 72901-2437
Tel: (479) 783-6833 Tel: (479) 783-6833 (PACER Registration)
Tel: (479) 783-3538 (PACER) Fax: (479) 783-6308
Internet: www.arwd.uscourts.gov

Number of Judgeships: 3

Circuit: Eighth

Areas Covered: Counties of Ashley, Baxter, Benton, Boone, Bradley, Calhoun, Carroll, Clark, Columbia, Crawford, Franklin, Garland, Hempstead, Hot Spring, Howard, Johnson, Lafayette, Little River, Logan, Madison, Marion, Miller, Montgomery, Nevada, Newton, Ouachita, Pike, Polk, Scott, Searcy, Sebastian, Sevier, Union and Washington

Court Staff

Clerk of Court **Christopher R. Johnson** .... (479) 783-6833
E-mail: chris_johnson@arwd.uscourts.gov
Education: Pittsburg State 1971 BA; Arkansas 1975 MPA

Chief Deputy Clerk **John Stauffer** .... (479) 783-6833
E-mail: john_stauffer@arwd.uscourts.gov
Education: Central Arkansas 1974 BS

Deputy Clerk-in-Charge -El Dorado **Carol Nesbit** .... (870) 862-1202
205 Federal Bldg., 101 S. Jackson Avenue, El Dorado, AR 71730-6133 Fax: (870) 863-4880
E-mail: carol_nesbit@arwd.uscourts.gov

Deputy Clerk-in-Charge - Fayetteville **June Newland** .... (479) 521-6980
510 Federal Bldg., 35 E. Mountain St., Fayetteville, AR 72701-5354 Fax: (479) 575-0774
E-mail: june_newland@arwd.uscourts.gov

Deputy Clerk-in-Charge - Hot Springs **(Vacant)** .... (501) 623-6411
100 Reserve Street, Room 347, Hot Springs, AR 71901-4141 Fax: (501) 623-8606

Deputy Clerk-in-Charge -Texarkana **Marcie Long** .... (870) 773-3381
500 North State Line Avenue, Room 302, Texarkana, AR 71854-5961 Fax: (870) 772-4802
E-mail: marcie_long@arwd.uscourts.gov

Chief Probation Officer **Scott Thibodeaux** .... (479) 783-8050
Room 1064 Fax: (479) 783-5761

Systems Manager **Dale Wellman** .... (479) 582-0905
E-mail: dale_wellman@arwd.uscourts.gov Fax: (479) 575-0774
Education: Rose-Hulman 1980 BS

Financial Administrator **Brenda Smith** .... (479) 783-6833
E-mail: brenda_smith@arwd.uscourts.gov

Procurement Administrator **Tracy Day** .... (479) 783-6833
E-mail: tracy_day@arwd.uscourts.gov Fax: (479) 783-2242

Chambers of Chief Judge Paul K. Holmes III

30 South Sixth Street, Room 317, Fort Smith, AR 72901-2437
Tel: (479) 783-1466 Fax: (479) 709-5421
E-mail: PKHinfo@arwd.uscourts.gov

Paul Kinloch Holmes III
Chief Judge

Education: Westminster (MO) 1973 BA; Arkansas 1978 JD
Began Service: February 14, 2011
Appointed By: President Barack Obama

Government: U.S. Attorney, Arkansas - Western District, Executive Office for United States Attorneys, United States Department of Justice (1993-2001)

Judicial: District Judge, Chambers of District Judge Paul K. Holmes III, United States District Court for the Western District of Arkansas (2011-2012)

Legal Practice: Associate, Warner & Smith (1978-1980); Partner, Warner & Smith (1980-1993); Partner, Warner, Smith & Harris (2001-2009); Of Counsel, Warner, Smith & Harris (2009-2011)

Chambers of Bankruptcy Judge Ben T. Barry
35 East Mountain Street, Fayetteville, AR 72701
Tel: (479) 582-9801 Fax: (479) 582-9824

Ben T. Barry
Bankruptcy Judge

Began Service: April 26, 2007
Term Expires: April 2021

Affiliation: Bankruptcy Judge, Chambers of Bankruptcy Judge Ben T. Barry, United States Bankruptcy Court for the Eastern District of Arkansas

Staff
Senior Staff Attorney **Jim Longino** .... (479) 582-9807
E-mail: jim_longino@arwb.uscourts.gov
Staff Attorney **Erika Stolzer** .... (479) 582-9821
E-mail: erika_stolzer@arwb.uscourts.gov
Courtroom Deputy **Marcy Payne** .... (479) 582-9809
E-mail: marcy_payne@arwb.uscourts.gov
EC RO/Relief Deputy Clerk **Angie Squires-Carter** ...... (479) 582-9810
E-mail: angie_squires@arwb.uscourts.gov

United States District Court for the Central District of California
312 North Spring Street, Los Angeles, CA 90012
Tel: (213) 894-1565 Tel: (213) 894-2215
Tel: (213) 894-3625 (Civil Cases PACER)
Tel: (213) 894-3535 (Intake) Fax: (213) 894-6860
Internet: www.cacd.uscourts.gov

Number of Judgeships: 28

Number of Vacancies: 1

Circuit: Ninth

Areas Covered: Counties of Los Angeles, Orange, Riverside, San Bernardino, San Luis Obispo, Santa Barbara and Ventura

Court Staff
District Court Executive and Clerk of the Court (Acting) **Kiry Gray** .... (213) 894-1565
E-mail: kiry_gray@cacd.uscourts.gov
Chief Deputy, Administration **Kenneth Young** .... (213) 894-1565
Chief Deputy, Case Processing **Carla Ortega** .... (213) 894-1837
Deputy-in-Charge, Eastern Division **Kiry Gray** .... (951) 328-4450
U.S. Courthouse, 3470 Twelfth St., Riverside, CA 92501
E-mail: kiry_gray@cacd.uscourts.gov
Assistant Deputy-in-Charge, Eastern Division **Lisa Adams** .... (951) 328-4450
U.S. Court House, 3470 Twelfth Street, Riverside, CA 92501
E-mail: lisa_adams@cacd.uscourts.gov
Assistant Deputy-in-Charge, Southern Division **Kathy Peterson** .... (714) 338-4760
E-mail: kathy_peterson@cacd.uscourts.gov
Librarian **Jane Kim** .... (213) 894-8901
Fax: (213) 894-8906
Managing Attorney **Jennifer Commings** .... (213) 894-5790
E-mail: jennifer_commings@cacd.uscourts.gov
Executive Assistant **Anna Hernandez-Torres** .... (213) 894-3102
Chief of Pretrial Services Officer **George M. Walker** .... (213) 894-4727
Room 754
Chief Probation Officer **Michelle Carey** .... (213) 894-3600

Chambers of Chief Judge George H. King
Edward R. Roybal Federal Building, 255 East Temple Street, Suite 660, Los Angeles, CA 90012
Tel: (213) 894-5766
E-mail: george_king@cacd.uscourts.gov

George H. King
Chief Judge

Date of Birth: 1951
Education: UCLA 1971 AB; USC 1974 JD
Began Service: July 3, 1995
Appointed By: President William J. Clinton

Staff
Law Clerk **Martin Freeman** .... (213) 894-5766
Term Expires: August 2016
Law Clerk **Kyle M. Grossman** .... (213) 894-5766
Term Expires: August 2016
Court Clerk **Beatrice Herrera** .... (213) 894-6907
E-mail: beatrice_herrera@cacd.uscourts.gov
Secretary **Nadine H. Johnson** .... (213) 894-5766
E-mail: nadine_johnson@cacd.uscourts.gov

Chambers of District Judge Manuel L. Real
U.S. Courthouse, 312 North Spring Street, Los Angeles, CA 90012
Tel: (213) 894-5267
E-mail: manuel_real@cacd.uscourts.gov

Manuel L. Real
District Judge

Date of Birth: 1924
Education: USC 1944 BS; Loyola U (New Orleans) 1951 LLB
Began Service: November 13, 1966
Appointed By: President Lyndon B. Johnson
Political Affiliation: Democrat

Government: Assistant United States Attorney, Southern District of California, United States Department of Justice (1952-1955); United States Attorney, Southern District of California, United States Department of Justice (1964-1966)

Legal Practice: Attorney, Private Practice (1955-1964)

Military Service: United States Navy (1943-1945)

Current Memberships: American Bar Association; Federal Bar Association; Los Angeles County Bar Association; State Bar of California

Staff
Law Clerk **Eric Bell** .... (213) 894-5267
Began Service: September 2014
Term Expires: September 2016
E-mail: eric_bell@cacd.uscourts.gov
Law Clerk **John Korevec** .... (213) 894-5267
Began Service: September 2015
Term Expires: September 2016
Law Clerk **Ali Moghaddas** .... (213) 894-5267
Began Service: September 2015
Term Expires: September 2016
Law Clerk **Shaina Shapiro** .... (213) 894-5267
Began Service: January 2015
Term Expires: January 2016
E-mail: shaina_shapiro@cacd.uscourts.gov
Court Clerk **Christine Chung** .... (213) 894-5696
E-mail: christine_chung@cacd.uscourts.gov
Secretary **Loyette Fisher** .... (213) 894-5267
E-mail: loyette_fisher@cacd.uscourts.gov

Chambers of District Judge Stephen V. Wilson

U.S. Courthouse, 312 North Spring Street, Room 217J,
Los Angeles, CA 90012
Tel: (213) 894-4327
E-mail: stephen_wilson@cacd.uscourts.gov

Stephen V. Wilson
District Judge

Date of Birth: 1941
Education: Lehigh 1963 BA; Brooklyn Law 1967 JD; George Washington 1973 LLM
Began Service: 1985
Appointed By: President Ronald Reagan

Academic: Adjunct Professor of Law, Loyola Law School, Loyola Marymount University (1977-1979); Adjunct Professor of Law, School of Law, University of San Diego (1984)

Government: Trial Attorney, Tax Division, United States Department of Justice (1968-1971); Assistant U.S. Attorney, Central District of California, Executive Office for United States Attorneys, United States Department of Justice (1971-1977); Attorney, Central District of California, Executive Office for United States Attorneys, Fraud and Special Prosecutions Section, United States Department of Justice (1973-1977)

Legal Practice: Partner, Hochman, Salkin & DeRoy (1977-1985)

Current Memberships: American Bar Association; The District of Columbia Bar; Los Angeles County Bar Association; New York State Bar Association; State Bar of California

Staff

Law Clerk **Jesse King** .... (213) 894-4327
Began Service: August 2015
Term Expires: August 2016
Law Clerk **John Pyun** .... (213) 894-4327
Began Service: August 2015
Term Expires: August 2016
Court Clerk **Paul Cruz** .... (213) 894-2881
E-mail: paul_cruz@cacd.uscourts.gov
Secretary **Yvonne Gonzalez** .... (213) 894-4327
E-mail: yvonne_gonzalez@cacd.uscourts.gov

Chambers of District Judge Dean D. Pregerson

U.S. Courthouse, 312 North Spring Street, Los Angeles, CA 90012
Tel: (213) 894-3913 Fax: (213) 894-6848
E-mail: dean_pregerson@cacd.uscourts.gov

Dean D. Pregerson
District Judge

Date of Birth: 1951
Education: UCLA 1972 BA; UC Davis 1976 JD
Began Service: August 1, 1996
Appointed By: President William J. Clinton

Corporate: Vice President and Counsel, The Torrance Company (1985)

Government: Parole Hearing Officer, Department of Corrections and Rehabilitation, State of California (1977); Assistant Public Defender, Guam Public Defender Service Corporation (1978-1980)

Legal Practice: Partner, Pregerson & Pregerson (1978); Sole Practitioner (1980-1981); Partner, Pregerson & McCully (1982); Partner, Pregerson, McCully & Pregerson (1982); Associate, Brian Silver, Attorney at Law (1982); Partner, Harney & Moore (1983-1985); Partner, Berman & Wedner (1986-1988); Sole Practitioner (1988-1989); Partner, Pregerson & Richman (1989-1991); Partner, Pregerson, Richman & Luna (1991-1996)

Staff

Law Clerk **Jonathan Marcus** .... (213) 894-3913
Began Service: September 2010
Term Expires: September 2016
E-mail: jonathan_marcus@cacd.uscourts.gov

Chambers of District Judge Dean D. Pregerson *continued*

Law Clerk **Anne Conley** .... (213) 894-3913
Began Service: September 2015
Term Expires: September 2016
E-mail: anne_conley@cacd.uscourts.gov
Courtroom Deputy Clerk **John Chambers** .... (213) 894-3913
E-mail: john_chambers@cacd.uscourts.gov
Judicial Assistant **Eugenia Paquet** .... (213) 894-3913
E-mail: eugenia_paquet@cacd.uscourts.gov

Chambers of District Judge Fernando M. Olguin

312 North Spring Street, Fifth Floor, Room 22,
Los Angeles, CA 90012-8533
Tel: (213) 894-5105
E-mail: fernando_olguin@cacd.uscourts.gov

Fernando M. Olguin
District Judge

Education: Harvard 1985 BA; Boalt Hall 1989 JD; UC Berkeley 1989 MA
Began Service: 2012
Appointed By: President Barack Obama

Government: Trial Attorney, Civil Rights Division, United States Department of Justice (1991-1994)

Judicial: Magistrate Judge, Chambers of Magistrate Judge Fernando M. Olguin, United States District Court for the Central District of California (2001-2012)

Legal Practice: Partner, Traber, Voorhees & Olguin (1995-2001)

Staff

Career Law Clerk **Sandra Sepulveda** .... (213) 894-0215
E-mail: sandra_sepulveda@cacd.uscourts.gov
Education: Stanford 2002 JD
Deputy Courtroom Clerk **Vanessa Figueroa** .... (213) 894-0215
E-mail: vanessa_figueroa@cacd.uscourts.gov

Chambers of District Judge Christina A. Snyder

U.S. Courthouse, 312 North Spring Street, Courtroom 5,
Los Angeles, CA 90012
Tel: (213) 894-8551
E-mail: christina_snyder@cacd.uscourts.gov

Christina A. Snyder
District Judge

Date of Birth: 1947
Education: Pomona BA; Stanford 1972 JD
Began Service: November 24, 1997
Appointed By: President William J. Clinton

Legal Practice: Partner, Corinblit & Seltzer (1994-1998); Partner, Katten, Muchin, Zavis & Weitzman; Partner, Wyman, Bautzer, Kuchel & Silbert

Staff

Law Clerk **Zachary Dekel** .... (213) 894-8551
Term Expires: August 2016
E-mail: zachary_dekel@cacd.uscourts.gov
Law Clerk **Jonathan N. Soleimani** .... (213) 894-8551
Term Expires: August 2016
E-mail: jonathan_soleimani@cacd.uscourts.gov
Courtroom Deputy Clerk **Catherine Jeang** .... (213) 894-3433
E-mail: catherine_jeang@cacd.uscourts.gov
Education: UCLA 1986 BA
Judicial Secretary **Ravi Ball** .... (213) 894-8551
E-mail: ravi_ball@cacd.uscourts.gov

Chambers of District Judge Margaret M. Morrow

255 East Temple Street, Suite 770, Los Angeles, CA 90012-3332
Tel: (213) 894-2949 Fax: (213) 894-2952
E-mail: margaret_morrow@cacd.uscourts.gov

Margaret M. Morrow
District Judge

Date of Birth: 1950
Education: Bryn Mawr 1971 AB; Harvard 1974 JD
Began Service: March 8, 1998
Appointed By: President William J. Clinton

Legal Practice: Associate, Kadison, Pfaelzer, Woodard, Quinn & Rossi (1974-1979); Partner, Kadison, Pfaelzer, Woodard, Quinn & Rossi (1980-1987); Shareholder, Quinn, Kully and Morrow (1987-1996); Partner, Arnold & Porter (1996-1998)

Staff
Law Clerk **Alexandra "Lexi" Rubow** ....(213) 894-2960
Began Service: August 2015
Term Expires: August 2016
E-mail: alexandra_rubow@cacd.uscourts.gov
Law Clerk **Joshua Rubin** ....(213) 894-2960
Term Expires: August 2016
E-mail: joshua_rubin@cacd.uscourts.gov
Courtroom Deputy Clerk **Anel Huerta** .... (213) 894-7857
E-mail: anel_huerta@cacd.uscourts.gov
Court Reporter **Cindy Nirenberg** ....(213) 663-3494
E-mail: cindy_nirenberg@cacd.uscourts.gov
Judicial Secretary **Celeste Gallegos** .... (213) 894-2949
E-mail: celeste_gallegos@cacd.uscourts.gov

Chambers of District Judge David O. Carter

9-160 Ronald Reagan Federal Building & Courthouse, 411 West Fourth Street, Santa Ana, CA 92701-4516
Tel: (714) 338-4543 Fax: (714) 338-4539
E-mail: david_carter@cacd.uscourts.gov

David O. Carter
District Judge

Date of Birth: 1944
Education: UCLA 1967 BA, 1972 JD
Began Service: October 22, 1998
Appointed By: President William J. Clinton

Government: Assistant District Attorney, County of Orange, California (1972-1981)

Judicial: Judge, Orange County Municipal Court, West (1981-1982); Judge, Orange County Municipal Court, South (1982); Judge, California Superior Court, Orange County (1982-1998)

Military Service: United States Marine Corps (1967-1969)

Current Memberships: The American Law Institute; Orange County Bar Association

Staff
Deputy Court Clerk **Deborah Goltz** .... (714) 338-4543
Judicial Administrative Assistant **Linda Enneman** ....(714) 338-4543
E-mail: linda_enneman@cacd.uscourts.gov

Chambers of District Judge Jesus G. Bernal

3470 Twelfth Street, Riverside, CA 92501
Tel: (951) 328-4410
E-mail: jesus_bernal@cacd.uscourts.gov

Jesus G. Bernal
District Judge

Education: Yale 1986 BA; Stanford 1989 JD
Began Service: January 4, 2013
Appointed By: President Barack Obama

Clerkships: Law Clerk, Chambers of District Judge David V. Kenyon, United States District Court for the Central District of California (1989-1991)

Legal Practice: Litigation Associate, Heller, Ehrman, White & McAuliffe LLP

Staff
Courtroom Deputy **Maynor Galvez** ....(951) 328-2259
E-mail: maynor_galvez@cacd.uscourts.gov
Judicial Assistant **Irma Macias** ....(951) 328-4410
E-mail: irma_macias@cacd.uscourts.gov

Chambers of District Judge Virginia A. Phillips

3470 Twelfth Street, Room 280, Riverside, CA 92501
Tel: (951) 328-4461
E-mail: virginia_phillips@cacd.uscourts.gov

Virginia A. Phillips
District Judge

Date of Birth: 1957
Education: UC Riverside 1979 BA; Boalt Hall 1982 JD
Began Service: December 30, 1999
Appointed By: President William J. Clinton

Academic: Teaching Assistant, University of California, Berkeley (1981)

Government: Court Commissioner, Superior Court of California (1991-1995)

Judicial: Magistrate Judge, United States District Court for the Central District of California (1995-1999)

Legal Practice: Summer Clerk, Best Best & Krieger LLP (1981); Associate, Best Best & Krieger LLP (1982-1988); Partner, Best Best & Krieger LLP (1988-1991)

Current Memberships: California Women Lawyers Bar Association

Staff
Law Clerk **Jason Kim** ....(951) 328-4420
Began Service: August 2015
Term Expires: August 2016
Law Clerk **Omar H. Noureldin** .... (951) 328-4420
Began Service: August 2015
Term Expires: August 2016
E-mail: omar_noureldin@cacd.uscourts.gov
Law Clerk **Shauna Woods** .... (951) 328-4420
Began Service: August 2015
Term Expires: August 2016
E-mail: shauna_woods@cacd.uscourts.gov
Courtroom Deputy Clerk **Marva Dillard** .... (951) 328-4461
E-mail: marva_dillard@cacd.uscourts.gov
Judicial Assistant **Julie Cicero** ....(951) 328-4420
E-mail: julie_cicero@cacd.uscourts.gov

Chambers of District Judge Percy Anderson

U.S. Courthouse, 312 North Spring Street, Los Angeles, CA 90012
Tel: (213) 894-5774 Fax: (213) 894-0125
E-mail: percy_anderson@cacd.uscourts.gov

Percy Anderson
District Judge

Date of Birth: 1948
Education: UCLA 1970 AB, 1975 JD
Began Service: May 1, 2002
Appointed By: President George W. Bush

Academic: Lecturer at Law, School of Law, University of California, Los Angeles (1977-1978)

Government: Assistant United States Attorney, Central District of California, Office of the United States Attorney, United States Department of Justice (1979-1985)

Legal Practice: Directing Attorney, San Fernando Valley Neighborhood Legal Services, Inc. (1975-1978); Consultant, Legal Services Corporation (1978-1979); Partner, Byan Cave, L.L.P. (1985-1996); Partner, Sonnenschein Nath & Rosenthal LLP (1996-2002)

Staff

Courtroom Deputy **Paul Songco** .... (213) 894-1795
E-mail: paul_songco@cacd.uscourts.gov
Court Reporter **Leandra Amber** .... (213) 613-0179
E-mail: leandra_amber@cacd.uscourts.gov

Chambers of District Judge R. Gary Klausner

255 East Temple Street, Los Angeles, CA 90012
Tel: (213) 894-3938 Fax: (213) 894-3923
E-mail: gary_klausner@cacd.uscourts.gov

R. Gary Klausner
District Judge

Date of Birth: August 4, 1941
Education: Notre Dame 1963 BA, 1964 BS; Loyola Marymount 1967 JD
Began Service: December 4, 2002
Appointed By: President George W. Bush

Government: Deputy District Attorney, Office of the District Attorney, County of Los Angeles, California (1969-1974); Court Commissioner, Municipal Court, City of Pasadena, California (1974-1980)

Judicial: Judge, Pasadena Municial Court (1980-1985); Judge, Los Angeles Superior Court (1985-2002)

Military Service: Captain, United States Army (1967-1969)

Staff

Career Law Clerk **Vivian K. Center** .... (213) 894-3938
E-mail: vivian_center@cacd.uscourts.gov
Education: Texas; UCLA 1996 JD
Courtroom Deputy **Sharon L. Williams** .... (213) 894-2649
E-mail: sharon_williams@cacd.uscourts.gov
Secretary **Michelle Clark** .... (213) 620-0431
E-mail: michelle_clark@cacd.uscourts.gov

Chambers of District Judge S. James Otero

U.S. Courthouse, 312 North Spring Street, Suite 244-P, Los Angeles, CA 90012
Tel: (213) 894-4806 Fax: (213) 894-4811
E-mail: sjo_chambers@cacd.uscourts.gov

S. James Otero
District Judge

Date of Birth: December 30, 1951
Education: Cal State (Northridge) 1973 BA; Stanford 1976 JD
Began Service: February 28, 2003
Appointed By: President George W. Bush
Political Affiliation: Republican

Corporate: Vice President and General Counsel, Regional Counsel Southern Pacific Transportation (1987-1988)

Government: Law Clerk/Attorney, Office of the City Attorney, City of Los Angeles, California (1976-1987)

Judicial: Judge, Municipal Court of Los Angeles County, California (1988-1990); Judge, Superior Court of California, County of California (1990-2003)

Staff

Law Clerk **Anuj Nadadur** .... (213) 894-4806
Began Service: August 2015
Term Expires: August 2016
E-mail: anuj_nadadur@cacd.uscourts.gov
Law Clerk **Matthew Samuels** .... (213) 894-4807
Began Service: August 2015
Term Expires: August 2016
E-mail: matthew_samuels@cacd.uscourts.gov
Law Clerk **Amanda Schwartz** .... (213) 894-4808
Began Service: August 2015
Term Expires: August 2016
E-mail: amanda_schwartz@cacd.uscourts.gov

Chambers of District Judge James V. Selna

Ronald Reagan Federal Building & U.S. Courthouse, 411 West Fourth Street, Santa Ana, CA 92701-4516
Tel: (714) 338-2841 Fax: (714) 338-2826
E-mail: james_selna@cacd.uscourts.gov

James V. Selna
District Judge

Date of Birth: February 22, 1945
Education: Stanford 1967 AB, 1970 JD
Began Service: April 30, 2003
Appointed By: President George W. Bush

Judicial: Judge, Superior Court of California, County of Orange (1998-2003)

Legal Practice: Associate, O'Melveny & Myers LLP (1970-1977); Partner, O'Melveny & Myers LLP (1978-1998)

Military Service: Captain United States Army Reserve, United States Department of the Army (1967-1978)

Nonprofit: President, Newport Harbor Art Museum (1994-1996); Vice Chairman, Orange County Art Museum (1996-2000)

Staff

Fax: (714) 338-2826

Law Clerk **Charlie Sarosy** .... (714) 338-2842
Began Service: 2014
E-mail: charlie_sarosy@cacd.uscourts.gov
Law Clerk **Laura Sucheski** .... (714) 338-2843
E-mail: laura_sucheski@cacd.uscourts.gov
Court Clerk **Karla Tunis** .... (714) 338-2848
E-mail: karla_tunis@cacd.uscourts.gov
Court Reporter **Sharon Seffens** .... (714) 543-0870
E-mail: sharon_seffens@cacd.uscourts.gov

Chambers of District Judge James V. Selna *continued*

Judicial Assistant **Jewel Lenn** . . . . (714) 338-2841
E-mail: jewel_lenn@cacd.uscourts.gov

Chambers of District Judge Cormac J. Carney

Ronald Reagan Federal Building and U.S. Courthouse, 411 West 4th Street, Santa Ana, CA 92701-4516
Tel: (714) 338-4720 Fax: (714) 338-4724
E-mail: cormac_carney@cacd.uscourts.gov

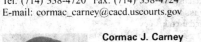

Cormac J. Carney
District Judge

Date of Birth: May 6, 1959
Education: UCLA 1983 BA; Harvard 1987 JD
Began Service: April 30, 2003
Appointed By: President George W. Bush

Judicial: Judge, Superior Court of California, County of Orange (2001-2003)

Legal Practice: Latham & Watkins (1987-1991); Associate/Partner, O'Melveny & Myers LLP (1991-2001)

Staff

Law Clerk **Brian Hardingham** . . . . (714) 338-4720
Began Service: August 24, 2015
Term Expires: August 2016
Law Clerk **Stephen Richards** . . . . (714) 338-4720
Began Service: August 10, 2015
Term Expires: August 2016
Judicial Assistant **Lucy Sicairos** . . . . (714) 338-4720
E-mail: lucia_sicairos@cacd.uscourts.gov

Chambers of District Judge Dale S. Fischer

255 East Temple Street, Los Angeles, CA 90012
Tel: (213) 894-7115 Fax: (213) 894-5676
E-mail: Dale_Fischer@cacd.uscourts.gov

Dale S. Fischer
District Judge

Date of Birth: October 17, 1951
Education: Florida 1977 BA; Harvard 1980 JD
Began Service: November 18, 2003
Appointed By: President George W. Bush

Judicial: Judge, Los Angeles Municipal Court (1997-2000); Judge, California Superior Court (2000-2003)

Legal Practice: Associate, Kindel & Anderson (1980-1986); Partner, Kindel & Anderson (1986-1996); Special Counsel, Heller Ehrman White & McAuliffe LLP (1996-1997)

Current Memberships: Association of Business Trial Lawyers; Federal Judges Association; National Association of Women Judges; Women Lawyers Association of Los Angeles

Staff

Law Clerk **Michelle Roberts** . . . . (213) 894-7115
Began Service: September 2015
Term Expires: August 15, 2016
Career Law Clerk **James P. Fellers** . . . . (213) 894-2609
E-mail: james_fellers@cacd.uscourts.gov
Education: Stanford 2003 JD
Courtroom Deputy **Debra Plato** . . . . (213) 894-0435
E-mail: debra_plato@cacd.uscourts.gov
Court Reporter **Pat Cuneo** . . . . (213) 687-0446
E-mail: pat_cuneo@cacd.uscourts.gov
Judicial Assistant **Tisa Kasik** . . . . (213) 894-7115

Chambers of District Judge Andrew J. Guilford

411 West Fourth Street, Santa Ana, CA 92701-4593
Tel: (714) 338-4757
E-mail: andrew_guilford@cacd.uscourts.gov

Andrew J. Guilford
District Judge

Date of Birth: November 1950
Education: UCLA 1972 AB, 1975 JD
Began Service: June 2006
Appointed By: President George W. Bush

Legal Practice: Associate, Sheppard, Mullin, Richter & Hampton LLP (1975-1983); Partner, Sheppard, Mullin, Richter & Hampton LLP (1983-2006)

Staff

Courtroom Deputy **Lisa Bredahl** . . . . (714) 338-4757
E-mail: lisa_bredahl@cacd.uscourts.gov
Judicial Assistant **Pamela Wiebel** . . . . (714) 338-4757

Chambers of District Judge Philip S. Gutierrez

255 East Temple Street, Room 880, Los Angeles, CA 90012
Tel: (213) 894-8899
E-mail: philip_gutierrez@cacd.uscourts.gov

Philip S. Gutierrez
District Judge

Date of Birth: 1959
Education: Notre Dame 1981 BA; UCLA 1984 JD
Began Service: February 2007
Appointed By: President George W. Bush

Judicial: Judge, Los Angeles County Superior Court (1997-2007)

Legal Practice: Associate, LaFollette, Johnson, DeHaas, Fesler & Ames (1986); Associate, Kern & Wooley (1986-1988); Managing Partner, Cotkin & Collins (1988-1997)

Staff

Courtroom Deputy **Wendy Hernandez** . . . . (213) 894-8899
E-mail: wendy_hernandez@cacd.uscourts.gov
Judicial Assistant **Jovita Grady** . . . . (213) 894-8899
E-mail: jovita_grady@cacd.uscourts.gov

Chambers of District Judge Otis D. Wright, II

U.S. Courthouse, 312 North Spring Street, Los Angeles, CA 90012
Tel: (213) 894-8266
E-mail: otis_wright@cacd.uscourts.gov

Otis D. Wright II
District Judge

Date of Birth: 1944
Education: Cal State (Los Angeles) 1969 BA; Southwestern 1980 JD
Began Service: April 17, 2007
Appointed By: President George W. Bush

Government: Deputy Sheriff, Office of the Sheriff, County of Los Angeles, California (1969-1980); Deputy District Attorney, United States Department of Justice (1980-1983)

Judicial: Judge, Superior Court of California (2005-2007)

Legal Practice: Partner, Wilson, Elser, Moskowitz, Edelman & Dicker LLP (1983-2005)

Military Service: United States Marine Corps, United States Department of Defense (1963-1966); United States Marine Corps Reserve, United States Department of Defense (1966-1969)

Staff

Law Clerk **Kent Shum** . . . . (213) 894-8266
E-mail: kent_shum@cacd.uscourts.gov

(continued on next page)

Chambers of District Judge Otis D. Wright, II *continued*

Law Clerk **(Vacant)** .... (213) 894-8266
Administrative Law Clerk **Haitham Kahwaji** .... (213) 894-0413
Court Reporter **Katie E. Thibodeaux** .... (213) 894-8676
E-mail: katie_thibodeaux@cacd.uscourts.gov
Courtroom Deputy **Sheila English** .... (213) 894-0249
E-mail: sheila_english@cacd.uscourts.gov

Chambers of District Judge George H. Wu

U.S. Courthouse, 312 North Spring Street, Los Angeles, CA 90012
Tel: (213) 894-0191
E-mail: george_wu@cacd.uscourts.gov

George H. Wu
District Judge

Date of Birth: 1950
Education: Pomona 1972 BA; Chicago 1975 JD
Began Service: April 17, 2007
Appointed By: President George W. Bush

Academic: Assistant Professor of Law, University of Tennessee at Knoxville (1979-1982)

Clerkships: Law Clerk, Senior Judge Stanley N. Barnes, United States Court of Appeals for the Ninth Circuit (1976-1977); Law Clerk, Senior Judge Stanley N. Barnes, United States Court of Appeals for the Ninth Circuit (1979)

Government: Assistant United States Attorney, California - Central District, Executive Office for United States Attorneys, United States Department of Justice (1982-1989); Assistant United States Attorney, California - Central District, Executive Office for United States Attorneys, United States Department of Justice (1991-1993)

Judicial: Judge, Los Angeles Municipal Court (1993-1996); Judge, Superior Court of California (1996-2007)

Legal Practice: Associate, Latham & Watkins LLP (1975-1976); Associate, Latham & Watkins LLP (1977-1979); Associate, LeBoeuf, Lamb, Leiby & MacRae (1989-1991)

Staff
Courtroom Deputy **Javier Gonzalez** .... (213) 894-0191
E-mail: javier_gonzalez@cacd.uscourts.gov
Judicial Assistant **Maria Bejarano** .... (213) 894-0191
E-mail: maria_bejarano@cacd.uscourts.gov

Chambers of District Judge Dolly M. Gee

312 North Spring Street, Los Angeles, CA 90012
Tel: (213) 894-5452
E-mail: dolly_gee@cacd.uscourts.gov

Dolly M. Gee
District Judge

Education: UCLA 1981 BA, 1984 JD
Began Service: January 4, 2010
Appointed By: President Barack Obama

Clerkships: Law Clerk, Chambers of District Judge Milton Lewis Schwartz, United States District Court for the Eastern District of California (1984-1986)

Corporate: Regional Coordinator, International Brotherhood of Teamsters (1995-2006)

Government: Member, Federal Service Impasses Panel, United States Federal Labor Relations Authority (1994-1999)

Nonprofit: President, Southern California Chinese Lawyers Association; Trustee, Los Angeles County Bar Association

Current Memberships: Southern California Chinese Lawyers Association

Chambers of District Judge Dolly M. Gee *continued*

Staff
Law Clerk **Sophia Chang** .... (213) 894-8688
E-mail: sophia_chang@cacd.uscourts.gov
Education: Harvard 2002 JD
Law Clerk **(Vacant)** .... (213) 894-8690
Administrative Law Clerk **Karen Uyekawa** .... (213) 894-5452
E-mail: karen_uyekawa@cacd.uscourts.gov
Courtroom Deputy **Valencia Vallery** .... (213) 894-5452
E-mail: valencia_vallery@cacd.uscourts.gov
Court Reporter **Anne Kielwasser** .... (213) 894-2969
E-mail: anne_kielwasser@cacd.uscourts.gov

Chambers of District Judge Josephine Staton Tucker

411 West Fourth Street, Santa Ana, CA 92701-4593
Tel: (714) 338-4738
E-mail: josephine_tucker@cacd.uscourts.gov

Josephine Staton Tucker
District Judge

Education: William Jewell 1983 BA; Harvard 1986 JD
Began Service: August 2, 2010
Appointed By: President Barack Obama

Judicial: Judge, Chambers of Judge Josephine Staton Tucker, County of Orange (2002-2010)

Legal Practice: Attorney, Morrison & Foerster LLP (1987-2002)

Staff
Courtroom Deputy **Ellen Matheson** .... (714) 338-4738
E-mail: ellen_matheson@cacd.uscourts.gov
Judicial Assistant **Terry Guerrero** .... (714) 338-4738
E-mail: terry_guerrero@cacd.uscourts.gov

Chambers of District Judge John A. Kronstadt

312 North Spring Street, Los Angeles, CA 90012
Tel: (213) 894-2156 Fax: (213) 894-6860
E-mail: john_kronstadt@cacd.uscourts.gov

John A. Kronstadt
District Judge

Education: Cornell 1973 BA; Yale 1976 JD
Began Service: April 25, 2011
Appointed By: President Barack Obama

Legal Practice: Partner, Arnold & Porter LLP (1984-1985); Partner, Blanc Williams Johnston & Kronstadt (1985-2000); Partner, Los Angeles, CA Office, Arnold & Porter LLP (2000-2002)

Staff
Courtroom Deputy **Andrea Keifer** .... (213) 894-2156
E-mail: andrea_keifer@cacd.uscourts.gov
Judicial Assistant **(Vacant)** .... (213) 894-2156

Chambers of District Judge Michael Walter Fitzgerald

312 North Spring Street, Los Angeles, CA 90012
Tel: (213) 894-1565 Fax: (213) 894-6860
E-mail: michael_fitzgerald@cacd.uscourts.gov

Michael Walter Fitzgerald
District Judge

Education: Harvard 1981 AB; Boalt Hall 1985 JD
Began Service: 2012
Appointed By: President Barack Obama

Staff
Courtroom Deputy **Rita Sanchez** .... (213) 894-1527
E-mail: rita_sanchez@cacd.uscourts.gov

Chambers of District Judge Michael Walter Fitzgerald *continued*

Court Reporter **Rosalyn Adams** . . . . (213) 626-1056
E-mail: rosalyn_adams@cacd.uscourts.gov

Chambers of District Judge John F. Walter

U.S. Courthouse, 312 North Spring Street, Los Angeles, CA 90012
Tel: (213) 894-5396
E-mail: john_walter@cacd.uscourts.gov

John F. Walter
District Judge

Date of Birth: 1944
Education: Loyola Marymount 1966 BA, 1969 JD
Began Service: May 1, 2002
Appointed By: President George W. Bush

Government: Assistant United States Attorney, Central District of California, Office of the United States Attorney, United States Department of Justice (1970-1972)

Legal Practice: Associate, Kindel & Anderson (1969-1970); Associate, Kindel & Anderson (1972-1976); Partner, Walter, Finestone & Richter (1976-2002)

Staff

Courtroom Deputy Clerk **Shannon Reilly** . . . . (213) 894-5396
E-mail: shannon_reilly@cacd.uscourts.gov
Court Reporter **Victoria Valine** . . . . (213) 894-5396
E-mail: victoria.valine@sbcglobal.net

Chambers of District Judge Beverly Reid O'Connell

312 North Spring Street, Los Angeles, CA 90012-8533
Tel: (213) 894-5283

Beverly Reid O'Connell
District Judge

Education: UCLA 1986 BA; Pepperdine 1990 JD
Began Service: April 30, 2013
Appointed By: President Barack Obama

Government: Assistant U.S. Attorney, California - Central District, Executive Office for United States Attorneys, United States Department of Justice (1995-2005)

Legal Practice: Attorney, Morrison & Foerster LLP (1990-1995)

Staff

Courtroom Deputy **Renee Fisher** . . . . (213) 894-5283
E-mail: renee_fisher@cacd.uscourts.gov

Chambers of District Judge Andre Birotte, Jr.

255 East Temple Street, Los Angeles, CA 90012
Tel: (213) 894-2833
E-mail: ab_chambers@cacd.uscourts.gov

André Birotte, Jr.
District Judge

Education: Tufts 1987; Pepperdine 1991 JD
Began Service: August 3, 2014
Appointed By: President Barack Obama

Staff

Courtroom Deputy **Carla Badirian** . . . . (213) 894-2833

Chambers of Senior Judge Terry J. Hatter, Jr.

U.S. Courthouse, 312 North Spring Street, Los Angeles, CA 90012
Tel: (213) 894-5746 Fax: (213) 894-0029
E-mail: terry_hatter@cacd.uscourts.gov

Terry J. Hatter, Jr.
Senior Judge

Date of Birth: 1933
Education: Wesleyan U 1954 AB; Chicago 1960 JD
Began Service: February 1, 1980
Appointed By: President Jimmy Carter

Academic: Associate Clinical Professor of Law, University of Southern California (1970-1974); Acting Professor of Law, Loyola Marymount University (1973-1976)

Government: Adjudicator, Veterans Administration (1960-1961); Assistant Public Defender, Office of the Public Defender, County of Cook California (1961-1962); Assistant U.S. Attorney, California - Northern District, Executive Office for United States Attorneys, United States Department of Justice (1962-1966); Special Assistant U.S. Attorney, California - Northern District, Executive Office for United States Attorneys, United States Department of Justice (1966); Chief Counsel, San Francisco Neighborhood Legal Assistance Foundation (1966-1967); Regional Legal Services Director, Office of Economic Opportunity, Executive Office of the President (1967-1970); Executive Director, Western Center on Law and Poverty (1970-1973); Executive Assistant/Director of Criminal Justice Planning, Office of the Mayor, City of Los Angeles, California (1974-1975); Special Assistant/Urban Development Director, Office of the Mayor, City of Los Angeles, California (1975-1977)

Judicial: Judge, Superior Court of California (1977-1980)

Legal Practice: Attorney, Harold M. Calhoun Law Office (1961-1962)

Military Service: Special Category Army with the Air Force (SCARWAF), United States Department of Defense (1954-1956)

Current Memberships: Illinois State Bar Association; Los Angeles County Bar Association; National Legal Aid and Defender Association; State Bar of California

Staff

Career Law Clerk **Kenneth Reichman** . . . . (213) 894-0565
E-mail: kenneth_reichman@cacd.uscourts.gov
Education: UCLA 1987 BA; Southwestern 1989 JD
Career Law Clerk **Richard D. Smith** . . . . (213) 894-2088
E-mail: richard_smith@cacd.uscourts.gov
Education: Southwestern 1980 JD
Court Clerk **Yolanda Skipper** . . . . (213) 894-5276
E-mail: yolanda_skipper@cacd.uscourts.gov Fax: (213) 894-6860
Judicial Administrative Secretary **Christine Moiseve** . . . . . (213) 894-5746
E-mail: christine_moiseve@cacd.uscourts.gov

Chambers of Senior Judge Consuelo B. Marshall

U.S. Courthouse, 312 North Spring Street, Los Angeles, CA 90012
Tel: (213) 894-6314 Fax: (213) 894-0045
E-mail: consuelo_marshall@cacd.uscourts.gov

Consuelo B. Marshall
Senior Judge

Date of Birth: 1936
Education: Howard U 1958 BA, 1961 LLB
Began Service: September 30, 1980
Appointed By: President Jimmy Carter

Government: Deputy Attorney, City of Los Angeles, California (1962-1967)

Judicial: Commissioner, California Superior Court, Juvenile Court Division, Los Angeles County (1970-1976); Judge, Los Angeles County Municipal Court, Inglewood Judicial District (1976-1977); Judge, California Superior Court, Los Angeles County (1977-1980)

Legal Practice: Cochran, Atkins & Evans (1968-1970)

(continued on next page)

FEDERAL COURTS–UNITED STATES DISTRICT COURTS

Chambers of Senior Judge Consuelo B. Marshall *continued*

Current Memberships: American Bar Association; Association of Business Trial Lawyers; California Women Lawyers Bar Association; International Association of Women Judges; Los Angeles County Bar Association; State Bar of California

Staff
Law Clerk **Christina Davis** .... (213) 894-8573
E-mail: christina_davis@cacd.uscourts.gov
Law Clerk **Beata Ng** .... (213) 894-8573
Began Service: February 2015
Term Expires: February 2016
E-mail: beata_ng@cacd.uscourts.gov
Court Deputy **Yolanda Skipper** .... (213) 894-5276
E-mail: yolanda_skipper@cacd.uscourts.gov
Office Manager **Amy Emi** .... (213) 894-6314
E-mail: amy_emi@cacd.uscourts.gov

Chambers of Senior Judge William D. Keller

U.S. Courthouse, 312 North Spring Street, Los Angeles, CA 90012
Tel: (213) 894-2659 Fax: (213) 894-1384
E-mail: william_keller@cacd.uscourts.gov

William D. Keller
Senior Judge

Date of Birth: 1934
Education: UC Berkeley 1956 BS; UCLA 1960 LLB
Began Service: 1984
Appointed By: President Ronald Reagan

Academic: Instructor, Trial Advocacy Institute, University of Southern California

Government: Assistant United States Attorney, Southern District of California, United States Department of Justice (1961-1964); United States Attorney, Central District of California, United States Department of Justice (1972-1977)

Legal Practice: Dryden, Harrington, Horgan & Swatz (1964-1972); Partner, Rosenfeld, Meyer & Susman (1977-1978); Partner, Hahn & Cazier (1981-1984)

Staff
Courtroom Deputy **Kelly Davis** .... (213) 894-0539
E-mail: kelly_davis@cacd.uscourts.gov
Judicial Assistant **Linda Kanter** .... (213) 894-5350
E-mail: linda_kanter@cacd.uscourts.gov

Chambers of Senior Judge Ronald S. W. Lew

U.S. Courthouse, 312 North Spring Street, Los Angeles, CA 90012
Tel: (213) 894-3508 Fax: (213) 894-0394
E-mail: ronald_lew@cacd.uscourts.gov

Ronald S. W. Lew
Senior Judge

Date of Birth: 1941
Education: Loyola Marymount 1964 BA; Southwestern Law 1971 JD
Began Service: May 7, 1987
Appointed By: President Ronald Reagan

Government: Deputy City Attorney, City of Los Angeles, California (1972-1974); Commissioner, Fire and Police Pensions, City of Los Angeles, California (1976-1982)

Judicial: Judge, Los Angeles County Municipal Court (1982-1984); Justice Pro Tem, California Court of Appeal, Second Appellate District, Division Seven (1984); Judge, California Superior Court, Los Angeles County (1984-1987); Justice Pro Tem, California Supreme Court (1985)

Legal Practice: Partner, Avans & Lew (1974-1981)

Military Service: United States Army (1967-1969)

Current Memberships: California Asian Judges Association; Southern California Chinese Lawyers Association

Chambers of Senior Judge Ronald S. W. Lew *continued*

Staff
Law Clerk **Jillian Chou** .... (213) 894-3508
Began Service: August 2015
Term Expires: August 2016
E-mail: jillian_chou@cacd.uscourts.gov
Law Clerk **Olivia Hardinge** .... (213) 894-3508
Began Service: August 2015
Term Expires: August 2016
Court Clerk **Joseph Remigio** .... (213) 894-2682
E-mail: joseph_remigio@cacd.uscourts.gov
Secretary **Karen Dansker** .... (213) 894-3508
E-mail: karen_dansker@cacd.uscourts.gov

Chambers of Senior Judge Robert James Timlin

312 North Spring Street, Room 233, Los Angeles, CA 90012
Tel: (213) 894-5275
E-mail: robert_timlin@cacd.uscourts.gov

Robert James Timlin
Senior Judge

Date of Birth: 1932
Education: Georgetown 1954 BA, 1959 JD, 1964 LLM
Began Service: October 18, 1994
Appointed By: President William J. Clinton
Political Affiliation: Democrat

Academic: Instructor, California Southern Law School (1976-1977)

Government: Special Attorney, Criminal Division, United States Department of Justice (1961-1964); Assistant United States Attorney, Central District of California, United States Department of Justice (1964-1966); City Attorney, State of California (1967-1976)

Judicial: Magistrate Judge, United States District Court for the Central District of California (1971-1975); Judge, Western Riverside Municipal Court (1976-1980); Judge, California Superior Court (1980-1990); Associate Justice, Court of Appeal, 4th Appellate District, Division Two (1990-1994)

Legal Practice: Associate, Douglas, Obear & Campbell (1960-1961); Associate, Hennigan, Ryneal & Butterwick (1966-1967); Partner, Shareholder and Officer, Hunt, Palladino & Timlin (1970-1974); Private Practice (1974-1976)

Military Service: United States Army (1955-1957)

Current Memberships: California Judges Association

Staff
Career Law Clerk **Rebecca Schafler** .... (213) 894-5275
E-mail: rebecca_schafler@cacd.uscourts.gov
Education: Williams; Hastings JD
Courtroom Deputy **Patricia Gomez** .... (213) 894-0539
E-mail: patricia_gomez@cacd.uscourts.gov

Chambers of Senior Judge Valerie Baker Fairbank

U.S. Courthouse, 312 North Spring Street, Los Angeles, CA 90012-8533
Tel: (213) 894-0066
E-mail: valerie_fairbank@cacd.uscourts.gov

Valerie Baker Fairbank
Senior Judge

Date of Birth: 1949
Education: UC Santa Barbara 1971 BA, 1972 MA; Boalt Hall 1975 JD
Began Service: February 16, 2007
Appointed By: President George W. Bush

Staff
Courtroom Deputy **Joseph Remigio** .... (213) 894-0066
E-mail: joseph_remigio@cacd.uscourts.gov

Chambers of Chief Magistrate Judge Suzanne H. Segal

U.S. Courthouse, 312 North Spring Street, 3rd Floor, Courtroom 23, Los Angeles, CA 90012
Tel: (213) 894-1420
E-mail: suzanne_segal@cacd.uscourts.gov

Suzanne H. Segal
Chief Magistrate Judge

Education: Claremont McKenna 1982 BA; Cornell 1987 JD
Began Service: July 31, 2002
Term Expires: 2018

Staff
Career Law Clerk **Robert "Bob" Postawko** .... (213) 894-1420
E-mail: bob_postawko@cacd.uscourts.gov
Courtroom Deputy **Marlene Ramirez** .... (213) 894-0958
E-mail: marlene_ramirez@cacd.uscourts.gov

Chambers of Magistrate Judge Charles F. Eick

U.S. Courthouse, 312 North Spring Street, Room 342, Los Angeles, CA 90012
Tel: (213) 894-2964
E-mail: charles_eick@cacd.uscourts.gov

Charles F. Eick
Magistrate Judge

Date of Birth: 1954
Education: Tulane 1975 BA; Texas 1978 JD
Began Service: 1988

Legal Practice: Attorney, Mitchell Silberberg & Knupp LLP (1978-1988)

Staff
Career Law Clerk **Mary E. Miller** .... (213) 894-2964
E-mail: mary_miller@cacd.uscourts.gov
Education: UCLA BA; Harvard 1977 JD
Court Clerk **Stacey Pierson** .... (213) 894-5234
E-mail: stacey_pierson@cacd.uscourts.gov
Secretary **Christine Sato** .... (213) 894-2964
E-mail: christine_sato@cacd.uscourts.gov

Chambers of Magistrate Judge Andrew J. Wistrich

Edward R. Roybal Federal Building, 255 East Temple Street, Los Angeles, CA 90012
Tel: (213) 894-2523
E-mail: andrew_wistrich@cacd.uscourts.gov

Andrew J. Wistrich
Magistrate Judge

Date of Birth: 1951
Education: UC Berkeley 1972 AB, 1973 AB; Chicago 1976 JD
Began Service: March 30, 1994
Term Expires: April 2018
Political Affiliation: Democrat

Clerkships: Law Clerk The Honorable Charles Clark, United States Court of Appeals for the Fifth Circuit (1976-1977)

Legal Practice: Associate, McCutchen Doyle Brown & Enersen (1978-1983); Partner, Brown & Bain, P.A. (1985-1994)

Current Memberships: The American Law Institute

Staff
Career Law Clerk **Jordonna Grace** .... (213) 894-2523
Career Law Clerk **Victoria Shabanian** .... (213) 894-2523
E-mail: victoria_shabanian@cacd.uscourts.gov
Courtroom Deputy **Ysela Benavides** .... (213) 894-6509
E-mail: ysela_benavides@cacd.uscourts.gov
Judicial Assistant **Valencia Munroe** .... (213) 894-2523
E-mail: valencia_munroe@cacd.uscourts.gov

Chambers of Magistrate Judge Robert N. Block

411 West Fourth Street, Santa Ana, CA 92701-4593
Tel: (714) 338-4754
E-mail: robert_block@cacd.uscourts.gov

Robert N. Block
Magistrate Judge

Began Service: 1995

Judicial: Chief Magistrate Judge, United States District Court for the Central District of California (2000-2005)

Staff
Courtroom Deputy **Kerri Hays** .... (714) 338-4754
E-mail: kerri_hays@cacd.uscourts.gov
Judicial Assistant **Jazmin Dorado** .... (714) 338-4754
E-mail: jazmin_dorado@cacd.uscourts.gov

Chambers of Magistrate Judge Carla M. Woehrle

630 Edward R. Roybal Federal Building, 255 East Temple Street, Los Angeles, CA 90012
Tel: (213) 894-4904 Fax: (213) 894-5614
E-mail: carla_woehrle@cacd.uscourts.gov

Carla M. Woehrle
Magistrate Judge

Education: Pomona 1972 BA; Loyola Law 1977 JD
Began Service: June 10, 1996
Term Expires: June 2020

Clerkships: Law Clerk, United States District Court for the Central District of California (1977-1978)

Legal Practice: Partner, Talcott, Lightfoot, Vandevelde, Woehrle & Sadowsky (1978-1996)

Staff
Career Law Clerk **Bruce Hall** .... (213) 894-4904
E-mail: bruce_hall@cacd.uscourts.gov
Education: Hawaii 1974 BA; USC 1995 JD
Career Law Clerk **Carol Klauschie** .... (213) 894-4904
E-mail: carol_klauschie@cacd.uscourts.gov
Pro Se Law Clerk **Emily Dorsett** .... (213) 894-4904
E-mail: emily_dorsett@cacd.uscourts.gov
Courtroom Deputy **Gay Roberson** .... (213) 894-6825
E-mail: gay_roberson@cacd.uscourts.gov

Chambers of Magistrate Judge Arthur Nakazato

Ronald Reagan Federal Building & U.S. Courthouse, 411 West Fourth Street, Santa Ana, CA 92701-4516
Tel: (714) 338-4756 Fax: (714) 338-4719
E-mail: arthur_nakazato@cacd.uscourts.gov

Arthur Nakazato
Magistrate Judge

Date of Birth: 1952
Education: Temple 1978 JD
Began Service: August 13, 1996
Term Expires: August 2028

Legal Practice: Private Practice (1978-1985); Kircher & Nakazato (1985-1996)

Current Memberships: Orange County Chapter, Federal Bar Association

Staff
Courtroom Deputy **Ivette Gomez** .... (714) 338-4756
Career Law Clerk **Eric Shannon** .... (714) 338-4756
Judicial Assistant **Gina Laroff** .... (714) 338-4714
E-mail: gina_laroff@cacd.uscourts.gov

Chambers of Magistrate Judge Patrick J. Walsh

U.S. Courthouse, 312 North Spring Street, Room 323,
Los Angeles, CA 90012
Tel: (213) 894-5722 Fax: (213) 894-5734
E-mail: patrick_walsh@cacd.uscourts.gov

Patrick J. Walsh
Magistrate Judge

Date of Birth: 1959
Education: John Marshall 1985 JD; Rosary 1985 MBA
Began Service: July 18, 2001
Term Expires: July 18, 2017

Clerkships: Law Clerk, United States District Court for the Northern Mariana Islands (1985-1989)

Government: Trial Attorney, United States Department of Justice (1989-1992); Assistant U.S. Attorney, Civil Division, United States Attorney's Office, United States Department of Justice (1992-1996); Assistant U.S. Attorney, Criminal Division, United States Attorney's Office, United States Department of Justice (1996-2001)

Staff
Law Clerk **Luke W. Howitt** .... (213) 894-5722
E-mail: luke_howitt@cacd.uscourts.gov
Education: Leeds (UK) 1992 BA;
UC Berkeley 2002 MPP; Boalt Hall 2003 JD
Career Law Clerk **T. J. Wentz** .... (213) 894-5736
E-mail: theodore_wentz@cacd.uscourts.gov
Education: Northwestern 1991 BA; UCLA 1994 JD
Courtroom Deputy **Celia Anglon-Reed** .... (213) 894-8958
E-mail: celia_anglon-reed@cacd.uscourts.gov

Chambers of Magistrate Judge Paul L. Abrams

U.S. Courthouse, 312 North Spring Street, 9th Floor,
Los Angeles, CA 90012
Tel: (213) 894-7103
E-mail: paul_abrams@cacd.uscourts.gov

Paul L. Abrams
Magistrate Judge

Education: UC Berkeley BA; Boalt Hall JD
Began Service: 2002
Term Expires: January 2018

Staff
Courtroom Deputy Clerk **Christiana Howard** .... (213) 894-7103

Chambers of Magistrate Judge Jacqueline Chooljian

312 North Spring Street, Los Angeles, CA 90012
Tel: (213) 894-2921
E-mail: jacqueline_chooljian@cacd.uscourts.gov

Jacqueline Chooljian
Magistrate Judge

Began Service: January 13, 2006

Government: Assistant U.S. Attorney, Criminal Division, Department of Justice; Chief, Criminal Division, California - Central District, Department of Justice; Assistant U.S. Attorney, Criminal Division, Executive Office for United States Attorneys, United States Department of Justice; Assistant U.S. Attorney, Criminal Division, California - Central District, United States Department of Justice

Staff
Courtroom Deputy **Hana Rashad** .... (213) 894-2921
E-mail: hana_rashad@cacd.uscourts.gov
Judicial Assistant **Cindy Dietze** .... (213) 894-2921

Chambers of Magistrate Judge Frederick F. Mumm

U.S. Courthouse, 312 North Spring Street, Los Angeles, CA 90012-8533
Tel: (213) 894-3046
E-mail: frederick_mumm@cacd.uscourts.gov

Frederick F. Mumm
Magistrate Judge

Began Service: 2006

Legal Practice: Partner, Davis Wright Tremaine LLP

Staff
Courtroom Deputy **James Munoz II** .... (213) 894-3046
E-mail: james_munoz@cacd.uscourts.gov
Judicial Assistant **Diana Hernandez** .... (213) 894-3046
E-mail: diana_hernandez@cacd.uscourts.gov

Chambers of Magistrate Judge Alicia G. Rosenberg

312 North Spring Street, Los Angeles, CA 90012-8533
Tel: (213) 894-5419
E-mail: alicia_rosenberg@cacd.uscourts.gov

Alicia G. Rosenberg
Magistrate Judge

Began Service: March 2007
Term Expires: March 2023

Staff
Courtroom Deputy **Marine Pogosyan** .... (213) 894-5419
E-mail: marine_pogosyan@cacd.uscourts.gov
Judicial Assistant **Angela Santana** .... (213) 894-5419
E-mail: angela_santana@cacd.uscourts.gov

Chambers of Magistrate Judge David T. Bristow

3470 Twelfth Street, Riverside, CA 92501
Tel: (951) 328-4466
E-mail: david_bristow@cacd.uscourts.gov

David T. Bristow
Magistrate Judge

Began Service: October 2009
Term Expires: October 2017

Staff
Courtroom Deputy **Danalyn Castellanos** .... (951) 328-4466
Judicial Assistant **Julie Ruschell** .... (951) 328-4466
E-mail: julie_ruschell@cacd.uscourts.gov

Chambers of Magistrate Judge John E. McDermott

312 North Spring Street, Los Angeles, CA 90012
Tel: (213) 894-0216
E-mail: john_mcdermott@cacd.uscourts.gov

John E. McDermott
Magistrate Judge

Education: Ohio Wesleyan 1968 BA; Harvard 1971 JD
Began Service: July 2009
Term Expires: 2017

Staff
Courtroom Deputy **ShaRon Anthony** .... (213) 894-0216
E-mail: sharon_anthony@cacd.uscourts.gov
Judicial Assistant **Christiane Shertz** .... (213) 894-0216
E-mail: christiane_shertz@cacd.uscourts.gov

Chambers of Magistrate Judge Jay C. Gandhi

312 North Spring Street, Los Angeles, CA 90012-8533
Tel: (714) 338-4776 Fax: (213) 894-6860
E-mail: jay_gandhi@cacd.uscourts.gov

Vijay C. "Jay" Gandhi
Magistrate Judge

Education: UCLA JD
Began Service: April 2010

Staff
Administrative Law Clerk **Melody Chang** . . . . (213) 894-5369
E-mail: melody_chang@cacd.uscourts.gov
Courtroom Deputy **Beatriz Martinez** . . . . (213) 894-5369
E-mail: beatriz_martinez@cacd.uscourts.gov

Chambers of Magistrate Judge Michael R. Wilner

312 North Spring Street, Los Angeles, CA 90012-8533
Tel: (213) 894-5496
E-mail: michael_wilner@cacd.uscourts.gov

Michael R. Wilner
Magistrate Judge

Education: Dartmouth 1988; Pennsylvania 1991 JD
Began Service: April 1, 2011

Staff
Courtroom Deputy **Veronica McKamie** . . . . (213) 894-5496
E-mail: veronica_mckamie@cacd.uscourts.gov
Administrative Law Clerk **Stephanie Delgado** . . . . (213) 894-5496

Chambers of Magistrate Judge Sheri Pym

3470 Twelfth Street, Riverside, CA 92501
Tel: (951) 328-4467
E-mail: sheri_pym@cacd.uscourts.gov

Sheri Pym
Magistrate Judge

Education: Williams 1989 BA; UCLA 1994 JD
Began Service: April 15, 2011

Staff
Administrative Law Clerk **Dorothy R. McLaughlin** . . . . . . (951) 328-4467
Education: Northwestern 2002 JD
Courtroom Deputy **Kimberly Carter** . . . . (951) 328-4467
E-mail: kimberly_carter@cacd.uscourts.gov

Chambers of Magistrate Judge Jean P. Rosenbluth

411 West Fourth Street, Santa Ana, CA 92701-4593
Tel: (213) 894-5369
E-mail: jean_rosenbluth@cacd.uscourts.gov

Jean P. Rosenbluth
Magistrate Judge

Staff
Courtroom Deputy **Joe Roper** . . . . (714) 338-4776
E-mail: joe_roper@cacd.uscourts.gov

Chambers of Magistrate Judge Kenly Kato

3470 Twelfth Street, Riverside, CA 92501
Tel: (951) 328-4463

Kenly Kiya Kato
Magistrate Judge

Education: UCLA 1993 BA; Harvard 1996 JD
Began Service: July 1, 2014

Chambers of Magistrate Judge Louise A. LaMothe

255 East Temple Street, Suite 181-L, Los Angeles, CA 90012
Tel: (213) 894-3787

Louise A. LaMothe
Magistrate Judge

Chambers of Magistrate Judge Douglas F. McCormick

411 West Fourth Street, Santa Ana, CA 92701-4593
Tel: (714) 338-4755
E-mail: DFM_Chambers@cacd.uscourts.gov

Douglas F. McCormick
Magistrate Judge

Chambers of Magistrate Judge Alka Sagar

312 North Spring Street, Los Angeles, CA 90012-8533
Tel: (213) 894-4583

Alka Sagar
Magistrate Judge

Chambers of Magistrate Judge Rozella A. Oliver

312 North Spring Street, Los Angeles, CA 90012
Tel: (213) 894-3922

Rozella A. Oliver
Magistrate Judge

Began Service: 2015

Staff
Courtroom Deputy **Gay Roberson** . . . . (213) 894-3922

Chambers of Magistrate Judge Alexander F. MacKinnon

312 North Spring Street, Los Angeles, CA 90012-8533
Tel: (213) 894-4583
E-mail: afm_chambers@cacd.uscourts.gov

Alexander F. MacKinnon
Magistrate Judge

Began Service: 2015

United States Bankruptcy Court for the Central District of California

Edward R. Roybal Federal Building and Courthouse, 255 East Temple Street, Room 940, Los Angeles, CA 90012
Tel: (213) 894-3118 (Los Angeles General Information)
Tel: (951) 774-1000 (Riverside General Information)
Tel: (714) 338-5300 (Santa Ana General Information)
Tel: (805) 884-4800 (Santa Barbara General Information)
Tel: (818) 587-2900 (San Fernando Valley General Information)
Tel: (213) 894-4111 (Voice Case Information System VCIS)
Tel: (866) 522-6053 (Voice Case Information System VCIS)
Internet: www.cacb.uscourts.gov

Number of Judgeships: 24

Court Staff

Executive Officer/Clerk of Court
Kathleen J. "Kathy" Campbell .... (213) 894-6244
E-mail: kathy_campbell@cacb.uscourts.gov Fax: (213) 894-0225
Chief Deputy [Operations] **Benjamin Varela** .... (213) 894-3257
Fax: (213) 894-0416
Administrative Manager **(Vacant)** .... (213) 894-1296
Fax: (213) 894-8928
Human Resources Manager **(Vacant)** .... (213) 894-3128
Fax: (213) 894-7498
Procurement Manager **Leo Roeder** .... (213) 894-3836
E-mail: leo_roeder@cacb.uscourts.gov Fax: (213) 894-4960
Technology Administration Division Manager
John Kohler .... (213) 894-1296
E-mail: john_kohler@cacb.uscourts.gov
Special Projects Manager **Sandi Brask** .... (213) 894-3127
Fax: (213) 894-5906
Fiscal Supervisor **James Sandino** .... (213) 894-0999
E-mail: james_sandino@cacb.uscourts.gov Fax: (213) 894-1411
Senior Deputy-in-Charge - San Fernando Valley
(Vacant) .... (818) 587-2811
21041 Burbank Blvd., Woodland Hills, CA 91367
Senior Deputy-in-Charge - Santa Barbara **(Vacant)** .... (805) 884-4876
1415 State St., Santa Barbara, CA 93101-2501 Fax: (805) 881-4068
Deputy-in-Charge - Los Angeles **Dennis Tibayan** .... (213) 894-1156
E-mail: dennis_tibayan@cacb.uscourts.gov Fax: (213) 894-4578
Deputy-in-Charge - Riverside **Dennis Tibayan** .... (951) 774-1005
3420 Twelfth St., Riverside, CA 92501-3819 Fax: (951) 276-2908
E-mail: dennis_tibayan@cacb.uscourts.gov
Operations Manager - Santa Ana **Kevin Hernandez** ...... (714) 338-5348
Ronald Reagan Federal Bldg. & U.S. Courthouse, Tel: (213) 894-3732
411 W. Fourth St., Santa Ana, CA 92701-4593 Fax: (714) 338-5393
Facilities Project Coordinator **Leanne O'Brien** .... (213) 894-8263
E-mail: leanne_o'brien@cacb.uscourts.gov Fax: (213) 894-0979
Courtroom Tech Specialist **Jose Fuentes, Jr.** .... (213) 894-8264
E-mail: jose_fuentes@cacb.uscourts.gov Fax: (213) 894-5418

Chambers of Chief Bankruptcy Judge Sheri Bluebond

Edward R. Roybal Federal Building, 255 East Temple Street, Suite 1482, Los Angeles, CA 90012
Tel: (213) 894-8980 Fax: (213) 894-1336
E-mail: sheri_bluebond@cacb.uscourts.gov

Sheri Bluebond
Chief Bankruptcy Judge

Date of Birth: 1961
Education: UCLA 1982 BA, 1985 JD
Began Service: February 1, 2001
Term Expires: January 2027

Current Memberships: American Bankruptcy Institute; American Bar Association; Financial Lawyers Conference of Southern California; Los Angeles Bankruptcy Forum; Los Angeles County Bar Association

Chambers of Chief Bankruptcy Judge Sheri Bluebond *continued*

Staff

Law Clerk **Rina Welles** .... (213) 894-8981
E-mail: rina_welles@cacb.uscourts.gov
Education: USC; Pepperdine 1995 JD
Career Law Clerk **Marie Houle** .... (213) 894-8981
E-mail: marie_houle@cacb.uscourts.gov
Education: San Diego 1992 BA; Oregon 1995 JD
Career Law Clerk **Jennifer Paul Wolfberg** .... (213) 894-8982
E-mail: jennifer_wolfberg@cacb.uscourts.gov
Education: UCLA; Pepperdine 2002 JD
Courtroom Deputy **Wendy Wesley** .... (213) 894-3688
E-mail: wendy_wesley@cacb.uscourts.gov
Courtroom Services Clerk **Sandra Peters** .... (213) 894-1480
E-mail: sandra_peters@cacb.uscourts.gov

Chambers of Bankruptcy Judge Peter H. Carroll

Edward R. Roybal Federal Building, 255 East Temple Street, Room 1468, Los Angeles, CA 90012
Tel: (213) 894-6343 Fax: (213) 894-1312
E-mail: peter_carroll@cacb.uscourts.gov

Peter H. Carroll
Bankruptcy Judge

Education: UC Berkeley 1974 AB; St Mary's U (TX) 1978 JD
Began Service: August 1, 2002
Term Expires: August 2016

Current Memberships: American Bankruptcy Institute; National Conference of Bankruptcy Judges

Staff

Law Clerk **Keith Banner** .... (213) 894-6123
Began Service: 2011
Law Clerk **Richard Solow** .... (213) 894-4185
Began Service: 2012
Term Expires: August 2016
E-mail: richard_solow@cacb.uscourts.gov
Courtroom Deputy **Elaine Garcia** .... (213) 894-0995
E-mail: elaine_garcia@cacb.uscourts.gov
Courtroom Services Clerk **Gabriela Huerta** .... (213) 894-3303
E-mail: gabriela_huerta@cacb.uscourts.gov

Chambers of Bankruptcy Judge Barry Russell

Edward R. Roybal Federal Building, 255 East Temple Street, Suite 1660, Los Angeles, CA 90012
Tel: (213) 894-6091 Fax: (213) 894-2243
E-mail: barry_russell@cacb.uscourts.gov

Barry Russell
Bankruptcy Judge

Date of Birth: 1940
Education: UCLA 1962 BS, 1966 JD
Began Service: September 1974
Term Expires: August 2028

Academic: Faculty member, Federal Judicial Center; Associate Clinical Professor of Psychiatry (Law), University of Southern California

Government: Estate & Gift Tax Examiner, California, United States Department of the Treasury (1966-1967); Deputy Public Defender, Office of the Public Defender, County of Los Angeles, California (1967-1970); Assistant United States Attorney, Central District of California, United States Department of Justice (1970-1974)

Chambers of Bankruptcy Judge Barry Russell *continued*

Judicial: Judge, United States Bankruptcy Appellate Panel of the Ninth Circuit (1988-1999); President, Federal Bar Association (1990-1991); Presiding Judge, United States Bankruptcy Appellate Panel for the Ninth Circuit (1999-2001); Chief Bankruptcy Judge, United States Bankruptcy Court for the Central District of California (2003-2007)

Current Memberships: American Bankruptcy Institute; American College of Bankruptcy; Federal Bar Association; Los Angeles County Bar Association

Staff

Judicial Law Clerk **Sue Doherty** .... (213) 894-6093
E-mail: susan_doherty@cacb.uscourts.gov
Education: Brown U 1974 BA; USC 1984 JD

Courtroom Deputy **Stacey Fortier** .... (213) 894-3687
E-mail: stacey_fortier@cacb.uscourts.gov

Courtroom Services Clerk **Pat Mendoza-Espinoza** ...... (213) 894-7202

Judicial Assistant **Kathryn Kwok** .... (213) 894-6092
E-mail: kathryn_kwok@cacb.uscourts.gov

Chambers of Bankruptcy Judge Robert N. Kwan

Edward R. Roybal Federal Building and Courthouse, 255 East Temple Street, Suite 1682, Los Angeles, CA 90012
Tel: (213) 894-2775 Fax: (213) 894-0787
E-mail: robert_kwan@cacb.uscourts.gov

Robert N. Kwan
Bankruptcy Judge

Education: Yale 1975 BA
Began Service: February 2007
Term Expires: February 2021

Government: Assistant U.S. Attorney, Tax Division, California - Central District, United States Department of Justice

Staff

Law Clerk **Jennifer Spinella** .... (213) 894-2577
E-mail: jennifer_spinella@cacb.uscourts.gov

Career Law Clerk **(Vacant)** .... (213) 894-2578

Courtroom Deputy **Mary Bakchellian** .... (213) 894-3385

Courtroom Services Clerk **Phyllis Jones** .... (213) 894-5860

Chambers of Bankruptcy Judge Robin L. Riblet

1415 State Street, Santa Barbara, CA 93101
Tel: (805) 884-4825 Fax: (805) 963-5973

Robin L. Riblet
Bankruptcy Judge

Date of Birth: 1949
Education: Florida 1971 BA; San Diego 1975 JD; NYU 1979 LLM

Current Memberships: American College of Bankruptcy; California Bankruptcy Forum; Federal Bar Association; Financial Lawyers Conference of Southern California; Los Angeles County Bar Association; Santa Barbara Bar Association

Chambers of Bankruptcy Judge Alan M. Ahart

21041 Burbank Boulevard, Suite 342, Woodland Hills, CA 91367
Tel: (818) 587-2836 Fax: (818) 587-2951
E-mail: alan_ahart@cacb.uscourts.gov

Alan M. Ahart
Bankruptcy Judge

Education: UC Berkeley 1970 AB; SUNY (Albany) 1975 JD; Pennsylvania 1979 LLM
Began Service: April 1988
Term Expires: April 2016

Current Memberships: Federal Bar Association; National Conference of Bankruptcy Judges

Staff

Career Law Clerk **Deborah Chang** .... (818) 587-2837
E-mail: deborah_chang@cacb.uscourts.gov
Education: Loyola Marymount 2003 JD

Courtroom Deputy **Kathleen Ogier** .... (818) 587-2853
E-mail: kathleen_ogier@cacb.uscourts.gov

Courtroom Services Clerk **Nancy Donovan** .... (213) 894-6498

Chambers of Bankruptcy Judge Ernest M. Robles

Edward R. Roybal Federal Building, 255 East Temple Street, Los Angeles, CA 90012
Tel: (213) 894-1522 Fax: (213) 894-1536
E-mail: ernest_robles@cacb.uscourts.gov

Ernest M. Robles
Bankruptcy Judge

Date of Birth: 1956
Education: UC Berkeley 1978 BA; Michigan 1981 JD
Began Service: June 12, 1993
Term Expires: June 11, 2021
Political Affiliation: Republican

Government: Assistant United States Trustee, United States Department of Justice (1988-1993)

Legal Practice: Musick, Peeler & Garrett (1981-1982); Hancock, Rothert & Bunshoft (1982-1987); Kornblum & McBride (1987-1988)

Current Memberships: American Bankruptcy Institute; Los Angeles Bankruptcy Forum; Los Angeles County Bar Association; National Conference of Bankruptcy Judges

Staff

Law Clerk **James Yu** .... (213) 894-0294
Began Service: September 2015
Term Expires: September 2016

Career Law Clerk **Daniel Koontz** .... (213) 894-0295

Courtroom Deputy **Lydia Gonzalez** .... (213) 894-4843
E-mail: lydia_gonzalez@cacb.uscourts.gov

Courtroom Services Clerk **(Vacant)** .... (213) 894-6233

Chambers of Bankruptcy Judge Thomas B. Donovan

Edward R. Roybal Federal Building and Courthouse, 255 East Temple Street, Room 1352, Los Angeles, CA 90012
Tel: (213) 894-3728 Fax: (213) 894-0418
E-mail: thomas_donovan@cacb.uscourts.gov

Thomas B. Donovan
Bankruptcy Judge

Date of Birth: 1935
Education: UC Berkeley 1957 BA; Boalt Hall 1962 JD
Began Service: March 21, 1994
Term Expires: March 20, 2022

Legal Practice: Associate, Covington & Burling LLP (1962-1963); Associate, Dinkelspiel & Dinkelspiel (1964-1969); Partner, Dinkelspiel, Donovan & Reder (1969-1993)

Military Service: United States Army (1957-1959)

Current Memberships: American Bankruptcy Institute; American College of Bankruptcy; California Bankruptcy Forum; Financial Lawyers Conference of Southern California; Los Angeles County Bar Association; National Conference of Bankruptcy Judges

Staff
Law Clerk **(Vacant)** . . . . (213) 894-1577
Career Law Clerk **Candace L. Crociani** . . . . (213) 894-3746
E-mail: candace_crociani@cacb.uscourts.gov
Education: St Olaf 1994 BA; Hamline 2002 JD
Courtroom Deputy **Pat Pennington** . . . . (213) 894-6172
E-mail: pat_pennington@cacb.uscourts.gov
Courtroom Services Clerk **Wanda Toliver** . . . . (213) 894-5011
E-mail: wanda_toliver@cacb.uscourts.gov

Chambers of Bankruptcy Judge Erithe A. Smith

411 West Fourth Street, Suite 5033, Santa Ana, CA 92701
Tel: (714) 338-5440
E-mail: erithe_smith@cacb.uscourts.gov

Erithe A. Smith
Bankruptcy Judge

Date of Birth: 1957
Education: Loyola Marymount 1979 BA; Boalt Hall 1982 JD
Began Service: May 2, 1994
Term Expires: May 1, 2022

Clerkships: Law Clerk The Honorable Marcus M. Kaufman, California Court of Appeals (1982-1983); Law Clerk The Honorable Peter M. Elliott, United States Bankruptcy Court (1983-1985)

Legal Practice: McKittrick, Jackson, DeMarco & Peckenpaugh (1985-1987); Lobel, Winthrop & Broker (1987-1994)

Current Memberships: American Bankruptcy Institute; American Bar Association; National Conference of Bankruptcy Judges; Orange County Bankruptcy Forum

Staff
Law Clerk **Melissa Prochilo** . . . . (714) 338-5443
Law Clerk **Leslie Seibert** . . . . (714) 338-5441
Began Service: 2013
Term Expires: August 2016
Courtroom Deputy **Tina Duarte** . . . . (714) 338-5360
E-mail: tina_duarte@cacb.uscourts.gov
Courtroom Services Clerk **Rick Reid** . . . . (714) 338-5361
E-mail: rick_reid@cacb.uscourts.gov

Chambers of Bankruptcy Judge Meredith A. Jury

3420 12th Street, Room 301, Riverside, CA 92501
Tel: (951) 774-1043
E-mail: meredith_jury@cacb.uscourts.gov

Meredith A. Jury
Bankruptcy Judge

Date of Birth: 1947
Education: Colorado 1969 BA; Wisconsin 1971 MA, 1972 MS; UCLA 1976 JD
Began Service: November 24, 1997

Legal Practice: Associate, Best Best & Krieger LLP (1976-1997)

Current Memberships: Federal Bar Association; Riverside County Bar Association; State Bar of California

Staff
Law Clerk **Annie Hsieh** . . . . (951) 774-1045
Began Service: 2013
Term Expires: 2015
Courtroom Deputy **Janna Tolleson** . . . . (951) 774-1091 ext. 2093
E-mail: janna_tolleson@cacb.uscourts.gov
Court Recorder **Janna Tolleson** . . . . (951) 774-1091
E-mail: janna_tolleson@cacb.uscourts.gov
Judicial Assistant **Christine Rhambo** . . . . (951) 774-1043
E-mail: christine_rhambo@cacb.uscourts.gov

Chambers of Bankruptcy Judge Maureen A. Tighe

21041 Burbank Boulevard, Woodland Hills, CA 91367
Tel: (818) 587-2806
E-mail: maureen_tighe@cacb.uscourts.gov

Maureen A. Tighe
Bankruptcy Judge

Education: Rutgers 1979 BA, 1984 JD
Began Service: November 2003
Term Expires: November 2017

Clerkships: Law Clerk, District Judge Harold Ackerman, United States District Court for the District of New Jersey (1984-1986)

Government: U.S. Trustee, Region 16, Department of Justice; Assistant U.S. Attorney, United States Attorney's Office, United States Department of Justice, Ronald Reagan Administration (1988-1998)

Legal Practice: Sullivan & Cromwell (1986-1988)

Current Memberships: American Bankruptcy Institute; Los Angeles Bankruptcy Forum; Los Angeles County Bar Association

Staff
Law Clerk **Hilda Montes De-Oca** . . . . (818) 587-2806
Began Service: 2011
Education: UCLA 2010 JD
Lead Courtroom Services Deputy **Jewell Williams** . . . . . . (818) 587-2815
E-mail: jewell_williams@cacb.uscourts.gov

Chambers of Bankruptcy Judge Theodor C. Albert
411 West Fourth Street, Suite 5073, Santa Ana, CA 92701-4593
Tel: (714) 338-5430
E-mail: theodor_albert@cacb.uscourts.gov

Theodor C. Albert
Bankruptcy Judge

Education: Stanford 1975 BA; UCLA 1978 JD
Began Service: June 2005
Term Expires: June 2019

Legal Practice: Buchalter, Nemer, Fields & Younger (1983-1995); Co-Founder, Albert, Weiland & Golden (1995)

Current Memberships: Orange County Bankruptcy Forum; Orange County Bar Association; State Bar of California

Staff
Career Law Clerk **Amna Riaz Chaudhary** . . . . (714) 338-5432
E-mail: amna_chaudhary@cacb.uscourts.gov
Education: UCLA, 2002 JD
Lead Courtroom Services Deputy **Elizabeth Steinberg** . . . (714) 338-5383
Judicial Assistant **Cricket Hong** . . . . (714) 338-5431
E-mail: cricket_hong@cacb.uscourts.gov

Chambers of Bankruptcy Judge Richard M. Neiter
Edward R. Roybal Federal Building and Courthouse, 255 East Temple Street, Suite 1652, Los Angeles, CA 90012
Tel: (213) 894-4080 Fax: (213) 894-4198
E-mail: richard_neiter@cacb.uscourts.gov

Richard M. Neiter
Bankruptcy Judge

Education: UCLA 1959 BS; USC 1962 JD
Began Service: February 8, 2006
Term Expires: February 18, 2020

Corporate: Member, Sutman, Treister & Glatt Professional Corporation (1962-2006)

Judicial: Central Mediator of Disputes, United States Bankruptcy Court for the Central District of California (1995-2006)

Current Memberships: Section of Business Law, American Bar Association; Los Angeles County Bar Association; State Bar of California

Staff
Law Clerk **Albert Sheen** . . . . (213) 894-1804
Began Service: 2014
Term Expires: August 2016
Career Law Clerk **Lovee Sarenas** . . . . (213) 894-4082
E-mail: lovee_sarenas@cacb.uscourts.gov
Education: Southwestern 1999 JD
Courtroom Deputy **Phyllis Jones** . . . . (213) 894-5860

Chambers of Bankruptcy Judge Victoria S. Kaufman
San Fernando Valley Courthouse, 21041 Burbank Boulevard, Suite 354, Woodland Hills, CA 91367
Tel: (818) 587-2823

Victoria S. Kaufman
Bankruptcy Judge

Education: Bryn Mawr 1986 AB; Harvard 1989 JD
Began Service: May 2006
Term Expires: May 2020

Clerkships: Law Clerk, Bankruptcy Judge Marilyn Shea-Stonum, United States Bankruptcy Court for the Northern District of Ohio

Legal Practice: Attorney, Private Practice; Of Counsel, Paul, Hastings, Janofsky & Walker LLP

Staff
Law Clerk **Jennifer Leinbach** . . . . (818) 587-2823

Chambers of Bankruptcy Judge Victoria S. Kaufman *continued*

Courtroom Deputy **Patty Garcia** . . . . (818) 587-2850
E-mail: patty_garcia@cacb.uscourts.gov
Court Recorder **Sabine Bever** . . . . (818) 587-2875
E-mail: sabine_bever@cacb.uscourts.gov

Chambers of Bankruptcy Judge Catherine E. Bauer
Ronald Reagan Federal Building and U.S. Courthouse, 411 West Fourth Street, Santa Ana, CA 92701-4593
Tel: (714) 338-5450 Fax: (714) 338-5459
E-mail: catherine_bauer@cacb.uscourts.gov

Catherine E. Bauer
Bankruptcy Judge

Education: UCLA 1982; USC 1985 JD
Began Service: 2010

Government: Assistant U.S. Attorney, Civil Division, California - Central District, United States Department of Justice (2001-2009)

Legal Practice: General Counsel, Bank of America Corporation (1985-2000)

Staff
Law Clerk **Donna Marie Curtis** . . . . (714) 338-5451
E-mail: donna_curtis@cacb.uscourts.gov
Education: Cal State (Northridge); Loyola Law JD
Law Clerk **Isra Shah** . . . . (714) 338-5452
Began Service: 2009
E-mail: isra_shah@cacb.uscourts.gov

Chambers of Bankruptcy Judge Deborah J. Saltzman
3420 -12th Street, Riverside, CA 92501-3819
Tel: (951) 774-1026 Fax: (951) 276-0314
E-mail: deborah_saltzman@cacb.uscourts.gov

Deborah J. Saltzman
Bankruptcy Judge

Education: Amherst 1991 BA; Virginia 1996 JD
Began Service: 2010

Legal Practice: Attorney, O'Melveny & Myers LLP (1996-2000); Attorney, Klee, Tuchin, Bogdanoff & Stern LLP (2000-2001); Attorney, O'Melveny & Myers LLP (2001-2006); Attorney, Hennigan, Bennett & Dorman LLP (2006-2008); Associate, (Downtown) Los Angeles, CA Office, DLA Piper (2008-2010)

Staff
Law Clerk **James Behrens** . . . . (951) 774-1027
Began Service: 2011
E-mail: james_behrens@cacb.uscourts.gov
Law Clerk **Jeffrey Kwong** . . . . (951) 774-1027
Courtroom Deputy **Cynthia Jeanmarie** . . . . (951) 774-1075
E-mail: cynthia_jeanmarie@cacb.uscourts.gov

Chambers of Bankruptcy Judge Vincent P. Zurzolo

Edward R. Roybal Federal Building and Courthouse, 255 East Temple Street, Room 1360, Los Angeles, CA 90012
Tel: (213) 894-3755 Fax: (213) 894-5048
E-mail: vincent_zurzolo@cacb.uscourts.gov

Vincent P. Zurzolo
Bankruptcy Judge

Date of Birth: 1956
Education: UC San Diego 1978 BA; UC Davis 1982 JD
Began Service: April 18, 1988
Term Expires: April 2016

Judicial: Chief Bankruptcy Judge, Chambers of Chief Bankruptcy Judge Vincent P. Zurzolo, United States Bankruptcy Court for the Central District of California (2007-2011)

Legal Practice: Associate, Greenberg Glusker Fields Claman & Machtinger LLP (1982-1988)

Current Memberships: Los Angeles County Bar Association; National Conference of Bankruptcy Judges; State Bar of California

Staff

Career Law Clerk **Jeffrey Randall Cozad** . . . . (213) 894-3721
E-mail: jeffrey_cozad@cacb.uscourts.gov
Education: UCLA; Pepperdine JD
Career Law Clerk **Judy Rose Villa** . . . . (213) 894-3635
E-mail: judy_villa@cacb.uscourts.gov
Education: UCLA; Pepperdine 1999 JD
Courtroom Deputy **Tina Johnson** . . . . (213) 894-5855
E-mail: tina_johnson@cacb.uscourts.gov
Courtroom Services Clerk **(Vacant)** . . . . (213) 894-3150

Chambers of Bankruptcy Judge Sandra R. Klein

Edward R. Roybal Federal Building, 255 East Temple Street, Suite 1582, Los Angeles, CA 90012
Tel: (213) 894-7741 Fax: (213) 894-6407
E-mail: sandra_klein@cacb.uscourts.gov

Sandra R. Klein
Bankruptcy Judge

Education: UMass (Lowell) 1982 BM; Loyola U (Los Angeles) 1992 JD; UCLA 2009 MBA
Began Service: April 22, 2011
Term Expires: April 21, 2025

Clerkships: Law Clerk, Chambers of District Judge Lourdes G. Baird, United States District Court for the Central District of California (1992-1994); Law Clerk, United States Court of Appeals for the Ninth Circuit (1994-1995)

Government: Assistant Director for Criminal Enforcement, Executive Office for United States Trustees, United States Department of Justice (2011-2011)

Legal Practice: Associate, O'Melveny & Myers LLP (1995-1997)

Staff

Law Clerk **Stephanie Rettier** . . . . (213) 894-0992
Began Service: 2011
Education: Pepperdine 2003 JD
Law Clerk **Jared Ahern** . . . . (213) 894-0994
Began Service: 2011
E-mail: jared_ahern@cacb.uscourts.gov
Courtroom Deputy **Thais May** . . . . (213) 894-5856
Began Service: 2011
E-mail: thais_may@cacb.uscourts.gov

Chambers of Bankruptcy Judge Wayne Johnson

3420 -12th Street, Riverside, CA 92501-3819
Tel: (951) 774-1031 Fax: (951) 276-1208
E-mail: wayne_johnson@cacb.uscourts.gov

Wayne Johnson
Bankruptcy Judge

Education: Cornell 1989 BA; Pennsylvania 1992 JD
Began Service: February 28, 2011
Term Expires: February 27, 2025

Clerkships: Law Clerk, Chambers of Bankruptcy Judge David N. Naugle, United States District Court for the Central District of California (1992-1994)

Legal Practice: Attorney, Lewis, D'Amato, Brisbois & Bisgaard (1994-1996); Attorney, Brobeck, Phleger & Harrison LLP (1996-2003); Sole Practitioner, Law Office of Wayne Johnson (2003-2011)

Staff

Law Clerk **Lisa Choi** . . . . (951) 774-1028
Began Service: 2011
Judicial Assistant **Diane Robinson** . . . . (951) 774-1031
Began Service: 2011
E-mail: diane_robinson@cacb.uscourts.gov
Courtroom Deputy **Yvonne Gooch-Carter** . . . . (951) 774-1098
Began Service: 2011

Chambers of Bankruptcy Judge Mark S. Wallace

411 West Fourth Street, Suite 6113, Santa Ana, CA 92701-4593
Tel: (714) 338-5470 Fax: (714) 338-5479
E-mail: mark_wallace@cacb.uscourts.gov

Mark S. Wallace
Bankruptcy Judge

Education: Princeton 1975 BA; Columbia 1977 JD
Began Service: January 20, 2011
Term Expires: January 19, 2025

Clerkships: Law Clerk, Chambers of Senior Judge William B. Enright, United States District Court for the Southern District of California (1977-1979)

Legal Practice: Attorney, Meyer, Hendricks, Victor, Osborn & Maledon (1979-1991); Attorney, Stutman Treister & Glatt (1991-2011)

Nonprofit: Notes and Comments Editor, Columbia Law Review (1977)

Staff

Law Clerk **Erica Lee** . . . . (714) 338-5473
Began Service: 2011
E-mail: erica_lee@cacb.uscourts.gov
Law Clerk **Claudia Lee** . . . . (714) 338-5471
Began Service: 2011
E-mail: claudia_lee@cacb.uscourts.gov
Courtroom Deputy **Nickie Bolte** . . . . (714) 338-5378
Began Service: 2011
E-mail: nickie_bolte@cacb.uscourts.gov

Chambers of Bankruptcy Judge Neil W. Bason

Edward R. Roybal Federal Building, 255 East Temple Street,
Los Angeles, CA 90012
Tel: (213) 894-6098 Fax: (213) 894-4288
E-mail: neil_bason@cacb.uscourts.gov

Neil Bason
Bankruptcy Judge

Education: Johns Hopkins 1984 BA; Boston U 1988 JD
Began Service: October 24, 2011
Term Expires: October 23, 2025

Clerkships: Law Clerk, Chambers of Chief Justice Paul J. Liacos, Massachusetts Supreme Judicial Court (1988-1989); Career Law Clerk, Chambers of Bankruptcy Judge Dennis Montali, United States Bankruptcy Court for the Northern District of California (2000-2008); Career Law Clerk, Chambers of Bankruptcy Judge Dennis Montali, United States Bankruptcy Appellate Panel for the Ninth Circuit (2000-2008)

Legal Practice: Associate, Palmer & Dodge LLP (1989-1992); Attorney, Hovis, Smith, Stewart, Lipscomb & Cross (1992-2000); Special Counsel, Howard Rice Nemerovski Canady Falk & Rabkin (2008-2009); Special Counsel, Duane Morris LLP (2009-2011)

Staff
Law Clerk **David Riley** .... (213) 894-4951
Career Law Clerk **Angella Yates** .... (213) 894-6084
Education: Loyola Law 2006 JD

Chambers of Bankruptcy Judge Julia W. Brand

Edward R. Roybal Federal Building, 255 East Temple Street,
Los Angeles, CA 90012
Tel: (213) 894-6080 Fax: (213) 894-6409

Julia W. Brand
Bankruptcy Judge

Education: UCLA 1981 BA; USC 1985 JD
Began Service: 2011

Legal Practice: Attorney, Bolton Dunn & Moore (1985-1989); Attorney, Gendel, Raskoff, Shapiro & Quittner (1989-1991); Attorney, Katten Muchin Rosenman LLP (1991-2007); Attorney, Liner Grode Stein Yankelevitz Sunshine Regenstreif & Taylor LLP (2007-2009); Attorney, Danning Gill Diamond & Kollitz LLP (2009-2010); Attorney, Brownstein Hyatt Farber Schreck, LLP (2010-2011)

Staff
Law Clerk **Anna Smith** .... (213) 894-3592
Began Service: 2011
E-mail: anna_smith@cacb.uscourts.gov
Law Clerk **Lily Tran** .... (213) 894-1481
Began Service: 2011
Education: Loyola U (Los Angeles) 2009 JD
Courtroom Deputy **Sandra Bryant** .... (213) 894-7341
Began Service: 2011
E-mail: sandra_bryant@cacb.uscourts.gov

Chambers of Bankruptcy Judge Mark D. Houle

3420 -12th Street, Suite 302, Riverside, CA 92501-3819
Tel: (951) 774-1021 Fax: (951) 276-1428
E-mail: mark_houle@cacb.uscourts.gov

Mark D. Houle
Bankruptcy Judge

Began Service: February 17, 2012

Staff
Law Clerk **Jolene Tanner** .... (951) 774-1022
E-mail: jolene_tanner@cacb.uscourts.gov
Law Clerk **Jorge Gaitan** .... (951) 774-1023
E-mail: jorge_gaitan@cacb.uscourts.gov
Courtroom Deputy **Rita Cargill** .... (951) 774-1085

Chambers of Bankruptcy Judge Scott C. Clarkson

411 West Fourth Street, Suite 5C, Santa Ana, CA 92701-4593
Tel: (714) 338-5460 Fax: (714) 338-5469
E-mail: scott_clarkson@cacb.uscourts.gov

Scott C. Clarkson
Bankruptcy Judge

Staff
Law Clerk **Eve Marsella** .... (714) 338-5460
E-mail: eve_marsella@cacb.uscourts.gov
Law Clerk **Christine Fitzgerald** .... (714) 338-5460
E-mail: christine_fitzgerald@cacb.uscourts.gov
Courtroom Deputy **John Craig** .... (951) 774-1097
E-mail: john_craig@cacb.uscourts.gov

Chambers of Bankruptcy Judge Martin R. Barash

21041 Burbank Boulevard, Suite 342, Woodland Hills, CA 91367
Tel: (818) 587-2836

Martin R. Barash
Bankruptcy Judge

Began Service: 2015

Chambers of Bankruptcy Judge (recalled) Geraldine Mund

21041 Burbank Boulevard, Suite 342, Woodland Hills, CA 91367
Tel: (818) 587-2840 Fax: (818) 587-2951
E-mail: geraldine_mund@cacb.uscourts.gov

Geraldine Mund
Bankruptcy Judge (recalled)

Date of Birth: 1943
Education: Brandeis 1965 BA; Smith 1967 MS; Loyola Marymount 1977 JD
Began Service: February 1984

Academic: Assistant Supervisor Physical Activities, University of California System (1967-1971)

Judicial: Chief Bankruptcy Judge, United States Bankruptcy Court for the Central District of California (1997-2002); Bankruptcy Judge, Chambers of Bankruptcy Judge Geraldine Mund, United States Bankruptcy Court for the Central District of California (1984-2011)

Legal Practice: Associate, Frandzel & Share (1977-1982); Partner, Frandzel & Share (1982-1984)

Current Memberships: American Bankruptcy Institute; American Bar Association; Los Angeles County Bar Association; National Conference of Bankruptcy Judges

Staff
Career Law Clerk **Bruce Baron** .... (818) 587-2840
E-mail: bruce_baron@cacb.uscourts.gov
Education: La Verne 1988 JD

United States District Court for the Eastern District of California

Robert T. Matsui United States Courthouse, 501 I Street, Sacramento, CA 95814
Tel: (916) 930-4000 Tel: (916) 498-6567 (PACER)
Tel: (800) 530-7680 (Toll Free Pacer)
Internet: www.caed.uscourts.gov

Number of Judgeships: 6

Number of Vacancies: 1

Circuit: Ninth

Areas Covered: Counties of Alpine, Amador, Butte, Calaveras, Colusa, El Dorado, Fresno, Glenn, Inyo, Kern, Kings, Lassen, Madera, Mariposa, Merced, Modoc, Mono, Nevada, Placer, Plumas, Sacramento, San Joaquin, Shasta, Sierra, Siskiyou, Solano, Stanislaus, Sutter, Tehama, Trinity, Tulare, Tuolumne, Yolo and Yuba

Court Staff

Clerk of the Court **Marianne Matherly** . . . . (916) 930-4000
Room 4-200
E-mail: mmatherly@caed.uscourts.gov
Chief Deputy **Keith Holland** . . . . (559) 499-5600
2500 Tulare Street, Fresno, CA 93721
E-mail: kholland@caed.uscourts.gov
Chief Probation Officer **Richard A. Ertola** . . . . (916) 930-4300
Suite 2-500
Chief of Pretrial Services **Gina Faubion** . . . . (916) 930-4350
Librarian **Jana Maginness** . . . . (916) 930-4155
Fax: (916) 930-4159
Librarian, Fresno **Daniella Lee-Garcia** . . . . (559) 499-5615
2500 Tulare St, Fresno, CA 93721 Fax: (559) 498-7295

Chambers of Chief Judge Morrison C. England, Jr.

Robert T. Matsui United States Courthouse, 501 I Street, Suite 14-230, Sacramento, CA 95814
Tel: (916) 930-4205 Fax: (916) 930-4106
E-mail: mengland@caed.uscourts.gov

Morrison C. England, Jr.
Chief Judge

Date of Birth: December 17, 1954
Education: U Pacific 1977 BA; McGeorge 1983 JD
Began Service: August 2, 2002
Appointed By: President George W. Bush

Staff

Law Clerk **Amanda Alley** . . . . (916) 930-4208
Began Service: September 2013
E-mail: aalley@caed.uscourts.gov
Education: McGeorge 2008 JD
Law Clerk **Eric Olah** . . . . (916) 930-4708
Began Service: March 2015
Term Expires: April 2016
E-mail: eolah@caed.uscourts.gov
Career Law Clerk **Greg Madsen** . . . . (916) 930-4209
E-mail: gmadsen@caed.uscourts.gov
Education: UC Davis 1979 BA; UCLA 1983 JD
Courtroom Deputy **Stephanie Deutsch** . . . . (916) 930-4207
E-mail: sdeutsch@caed.uscourts.gov
Education: UC Davis 2001 BA
Court Reporter **(Vacant)** . . . . (916) 554-7460
Fax: (916) 554-7460
Judicial Assistant **Adele Espana-Purpur** . . . . (916) 930-4205
E-mail: aespana-purpur@caed.uscourts.gov

Chambers of District Judge Lawrence J. O'Neill

Robert E. Coyle U.S. Courthouse, 2500 Tulare Street, Suite 7701, Fresno, CA 93721
Tel: (559) 499-5680 Fax: (559) 499-5959
E-mail: loneill@caed.uscourts.gov

Lawrence J. O'Neill
District Judge

Date of Birth: 1952
Education: UC Berkeley 1973 BA; Golden Gate 1976 MPA; Hastings 1979 JD
Began Service: February 2, 2007
Appointed By: President George W. Bush
Political Affiliation: Republican

Academic: Adjunct Professor, San Joaquin College of Law (1986-1992)

Clerkships: Law Clerk The Honorable Robert F. Kane, California First District Court of Appeal (1978-1979)

Government: Police Officer, County of Alameda, California (1973-1976)

Judicial: Judge, California Superior Court, Fresno (1990-1999); Magistrate Judge, United States District Court for the Eastern District of California (1999-2007)

Legal Practice: Associate, McCormick, Barstow, Sheppard, Wayte & Carruth LLP (1979-1983); Partner, McCormick, Barstow, Sheppard, Wayte & Carruth LLP (1983-1990)

Staff

Career Law Clerk **Lisa B. Coffman** . . . . (559) 499-5683
E-mail: lcoffman@caed.uscourts.gov

Chambers of District Judge John A. Mendez

Robert T. Matsui United States Courthouse, 501 I Street, 14th Floor, Sacramento, CA 95814
Tel: (916) 930-4250 Fax: (916) 930-4106
E-mail: jmendez@caed.uscourts.gov

John A. Mendez
District Judge

Education: Stanford 1977 BA; Harvard 1980 JD
Began Service: 2008; April 17, 2008
Appointed By: President George W. Bush

Government: Assistant U.S. Attorney, California - Northern District, Executive Office for United States Attorneys, United States Department of Justice (1984-1986); Assistant U.S. Attorney, California - Northern District, Executive Office for United States Attorneys, United States Department of Justice (1992-1993)

Judicial: Judge, Superior Court of Sacramento, County of Sacramento, California (2001-2008)

Legal Practice: Associate, Chickering & Gregory (1980-1981); Associate, Orrick, Herrington & Sutcliffe LLP (1981-1984); Partner, Downey Brand LLP (1986-1992); Counsel, Brobeck, Phleger & Harrison LLP (1993-1995); Shareholder, Somach, Simmons & Dunn (1995-2001)

Staff

Law Clerk **Alexander Anzalone** . . . . (916) 930-4250
E-mail: aanzalone@caed.uscourts.gov
Law Clerk **Mia Crager** . . . . (916) 930-4250
Began Service: December 2014
Term Expires: August 2016
E-mail: mcrager@caed.uscourts.gov
Law Clerk **Christian Kurpiewski** . . . . (916) 930-4250
Began Service: September 2013
Term Expires: September 2016
E-mail: ckurpiewski@caed.uscourts.gov
Judicial Assistant **Jane Pratt** . . . . (916) 930-4250
E-mail: jpratt@caed.uscourts.gov Fax: (916) 930-4106

Chambers of District Judge Kimberly J. Mueller

Robert T. Matsui United States Courthouse, 501 I Street,
Sacramento, CA 95814
Tel: (916) 930-4260
E-mail: kmueller@caed.uscourts.gov

Kimberly J. Mueller
District Judge

Education: Pomona 1981 BA; Stanford 1995 JD
Began Service: December 21, 2010
Appointed By: President Barack Obama

Government: Council Member, Office of the Mayor and City Council, City of Sacramento, California (1987-1992)

Judicial: Magistrate Judge, Chambers of Magistrate Judge Kimberly J. Mueller, United States District Court for the Eastern District of California (2003-2010)

Legal Practice: Associate, Orrick, Herrington & Sutcliffe LLP (1994); Associate, Orrick, Herrington & Sutcliffe LLP (1995-2000)

Staff

Law Clerk **Schuyler Brooks** .... (916) 930-4260
Term Expires: September 2016
Law Clerk **Joy Ping** .... (916) 930-4260
Term Expires: September 2016
E-mail: jping@caed.uscourts.gov
Law Clerk **Bryant Pulsipher** .... (916) 930-4260
Term Expires: September 2016
E-mail: bpulsipher@caed.uscourts.gov
Law Clerk **Rukayatu Tijani** .... (916) 930-4260
Term Expires: September 2016
E-mail: rtijani@caed.uscourts.gov
Career Law Clerk **(Vacant)** .... (916) 930-4260
Judicial Assistant **Patti Andrews** .... (916) 930-4260
E-mail: pandrews@caed.uscourts.gov

Chambers of District Judge Troy L. Nunley

Robert T. Matsui United States Courthouse, 501 I Street,
Sacramento, CA 95814
Tel: (916) 930-4163
E-mail: tnunley@caed.uscourts.gov

Troy L. Nunley
District Judge

Education: St Mary's Col (CA) 1986 BA; Hastings 1990 JD
Began Service: 2013
Appointed By: President Barack Obama

Government: District Attorney, Office of the District Attorney, County of Alameda, California (1991-1994); District Attorney, Office of the District Attorney, County of Sacramento, California (1996-1999); Deputy Attorney General, Office of the Attorney General, State of California (1999-2002)

Staff

Judicial Assistant **Deanna Morrison** .... (916) 930-4630
E-mail: dmorrison@caed.uscourts.gov
Courtroom Deputy **Michele Krueger** .... (916) 930-4163
E-mail: mkrueger@caed.uscourts.gov

Chambers of District Judge Dale A. Drozd

501 I Street, Sacramento, CA 95814
Tel: (916) 930-4210
E-mail: dale_drozd@caed.uscourts.gov

Dale A. Drozd
District Judge

Note: On October 6, 2015, the Senate confirmed Dale Drozd to be District Judge on the United States District Court for the Eastern District of California.
Education: San Diego State 1977 BA; UCLA 1980 JD
Began Service: October 2015
Appointed By: President Barack Obama

Staff

Elbow Clerk **Blaze Van Dine** .... (916) 930-4210
E-mail: bvandine@caed.uscourts.gov
Staff Attorney **Ederlina Co** .... (916) 930-4210
E-mail: eco@caed.uscourts.gov
Staff Attorney **(Vacant)** .... (916) 930-4210
Staff Attorney **Diane Uebell** .... (916) 930-4210

Chambers of Senior Judge William B. Shubb

Robert T. Matsui United States Courthouse, 501 I Street,
Sacramento, CA 95814
Tel: (916) 930-4230 Fax: (916) 930-4075
E-mail: wshubb@justice.com

William B. Shubb
Senior Judge

Date of Birth: 1938
Education: UC Berkeley 1960 AB; Boalt Hall 1963 LLB
Began Service: October 29, 1990
Appointed By: President George H.W. Bush

Clerkships: Law Clerk The Honorable Sherrill Halbert (1963-1965)

Government: Assistant United States Attorney, Eastern District of California, United States Department of Justice (1965-1974); United States Attorney, Eastern District of California, United States Department of Justice (1980-1981)

Judicial: Chief Judge, United States District Court for the Eastern District of California

Legal Practice: Attorney, Diepenbrock, Wulff, Plant & Hannegan (1974-1980)

Current Memberships: American Bar Association; American Board of Trial Advocates; The Anthony M. Kennedy American Inn of Court, The American Inns of Court; Federal Bar Association; Sacramento County Bar Assocaition; State Bar of California

Staff

Law Clerk **Zaur D. Gajiev** .... (916) 930-4104
Began Service: September 2015
Term Expires: September 2016
E-mail: zgajiev@caed.uscourts.gov
Law Clerk **Caroline Sesser** .... (916) 930-4104
Began Service: September 2015
Term Expires: September 2016
E-mail: csesser@caed.uscourts.gov
Career Law Clerk **Breann Moebius** .... (916) 930-4236
E-mail: bmoebius@caed.uscourts.gov
Education: McGeorge 2007 JD
Courtroom Deputy **Karen Kirskey-Smith** .... (916) 930-4234

Chambers of Senior Judge Garland E. Burrell, Jr.

Robert T. Matsui United States Courthouse, 501 I Street,
Sacramento, CA 95814
Tel: (916) 930-4115 Fax: (916) 491-3938
E-mail: gburrell@caed.uscourts.gov

Garland E. Burrell, Jr.
Senior Judge

Date of Birth: 1947
Education: Cal State (Sacramento) 1972 BA; Washington U (MO) 1976 MSW; Cal Western 1976 JD
Began Service: March 3, 1992
Appointed By: President George H.W. Bush

Staff
Career Law Clerk **Elizabeth Dankof** .... (916) 930-4115
E-mail: edankof@caed.uscourts.gov
Education: Texas 2002 JD
Court Reporter **(Vacant)** .... (916) 442-8420
Courtroom Deputy **Shani Furstenau** .... (916) 930-4115
E-mail: sfurstenau@caed.uscourts.gov

Chambers of Senior Judge Anthony W. Ishii

Robert E. Coyle U.S. Courthouse, 2500 Tulare Street, Eighth Floor, Suite 1501, Fresno, CA 93721
Tel: (559) 499-5660 Fax: (559) 499-5662
E-mail: aishii@caed.uscourts.gov

Anthony W. Ishii
Senior Judge

Date of Birth: 1946
Education: U Pacific 1970 PharmD; Boalt Hall 1973 JD
Began Service: October 14, 1997
Appointed By: President William J. Clinton

Current Memberships: Asian Pacific Bar Association of Sacramento; Association of Business Trial Lawyers; California Asian Judges Association; Eastern District Historical Society; Federal Judges Association; Fresno County Women Lawyers Association; Ninth Circuit District Judges Association; Ninth Judicial Circuit Historical Society, United States Court of Appeals for the Ninth Circuit

Staff
Career Law Clerk **Richard Corp** .... (559) 499-5663
E-mail: rcorp@caed.uscourts.gov
Education: Santa Clara U BA, 2000 JD
Career Law Clerk **(Vacant)** .... (559) 499-5665
Career Law Clerk **Michael Sowards** .... (559) 499-5666
E-mail: msowards@caed.uscourts.gov
Education: Baylor 2000 JD

Chambers of Magistrate Judge Sandra M. Snyder

Robert E. Coyle U.S. Courthouse, 2500 Tulare Street, Suite 6801,
Fresno, CA 93721
Tel: (559) 499-5690 Fax: (559) 494-3920
E-mail: ssnyder@caed.uscourts.gov

Sandra M. Snyder
Magistrate Judge

Date of Birth: 1946
Education: Golden Gate 1976 JD
Began Service: May 3, 1993
Term Expires: May 2, 2017

Current Memberships: Federal Magistrate Judges Association; Fresno County Women Lawyers Association

Chambers of Magistrate Judge Sandra M. Snyder *continued*

Staff
Career Law Clerk **Cynthia Scharf** .... (559) 499-5690
E-mail: cscharf@caed.uscourts.gov
Courtroom Deputy **Michelle Rooney** .... (559) 499-5690
E-mail: mrooney@caed.uscourts.gov
Court Recorder **Otilia Rosales** .... (559) 499-5928
E-mail: ofigueroa@caed.uscourts.gov
Judicial Assistant **(Vacant)** .... (559) 499-5690

Chambers of Magistrate Judge Gregory G. Hollows

Robert T. Matsui United States Courthouse, 501 I Street,
Sacramento, CA 95814
Tel: (916) 930-4195
E-mail: ghollows@caed.uscourts.gov

Gregory G. Hollows
Magistrate Judge

Date of Birth: 1947
Education: Loyola Marymount 1978 JD
Began Service: March 1990
Term Expires: 2022

Government: Assistant United States Attorney, United States Department of Justice (1982-1988); Assistant United States Attorney, Chief Civil Division, United States Department of Justice (1988-1990)

Legal Practice: Attorney, Gibson, Dunn & Crutcher LLP (1978-1982)

Military Service: United States Marine Corps (1969-1974)

Staff
Career Law Clerk **Julie Vincent** .... (916) 930-4195
E-mail: jvincent@caed.uscourts.gov
Judicial Assistant **Donna Dal Porto** .... (916) 930-4195
E-mail: ddalporto@caed.uscourts.gov

Chambers of Magistrate Judge Dennis L. Beck

Robert E. Coyle U.S. Courthouse, 2500 Tulane Street, Room 6601,
Fresno, CA 93721
Tel: (559) 499-5670
E-mail: dennis_beck@caed.uscourts.gov

Dennis L. Beck
Magistrate Judge

Date of Birth: 1947
Education: William & Mary 1969 BA, 1972 JD
Began Service: March 14, 1990
Term Expires: March 14, 2022

Government: Deputy District Attorney, Fresno County, State of California (1972-1977); Deputy District Attorney, Fresno County, State of California (1978-1983); Assistant District Attorney, Fresno County, State of California (1987-1990)

Judicial: Judge, California Superior Court, Kings County (1983-1985)

Legal Practice: Crossland, Crossland, Caswell & Bell (1977-1978); Thomas, Snell, Jamison, Russel & Asperger (1985-1987)

Staff
Career Law Clerk **Jennifer Larson** .... (559) 499-5670
E-mail: jlarson@caed.uscourts.gov
Education: Boston U 2001 JD

Chambers of Magistrate Judge Gary S. Austin

Robert E. Coyle U.S. Courthouse, 2500 Tulare Street, Sixth Floor, Suite 1501, Fresno, CA 93721
Tel: (559) 499-5962
E-mail: gaustin@caed.uscourts.gov

Gary S. Austin
Magistrate Judge

Education: Cal State (Fresno) 1972 BA; San Joaquin Law 1976 JD
Began Service: October 12, 2007

Clerkships: Law Clerk, Chambers of District Judge M.D. Crocker, United States District Court for the Eastern District of California (1976-1977)

Government: Deputy District Attorney, Office of the District Attorney, County of Fresno, California (1977-1984); Senior Deputy District Attorney and Lead Attorney for the Career Criminal Unit, Office of the District Attorney, County of Fresno, California (1984-1986)

Judicial: Municipal Court Judge, County of Fresno (1986-1988); Superior Court Judge, County of Fresno, Superior Court of California (1988-2007)

Staff
Law Clerk **Samya Burney** .... (559) 499-5962
E-mail: sburney@caed.uscourts.gov
Law Clerk **Claire Carroll** .... (559) 499-5962
E-mail: ccarroll@caed.uscourts.gov
Law Clerk **Tyler Onitsuka** .... (559) 499-5962
Career Law Clerk **Tim Bertalotto** .... (559) 499-5962
E-mail: tbertalotto@caed.uscourts.gov
Education: San Joaquin Law 1995 JD
Courtroom Deputy **Amanda Martinez** .... (559) 499-5962
E-mail: amartinez@caed.uscourts.gov

Chambers of Magistrate Judge Craig M. Kellison

2986 Bechelli Lane, Redding, CA 96002
Tel: (530) 246-5416 Fax: (530) 246-5419
E-mail: ckellison@caed.uscourts.gov

Craig M. Kellison
Magistrate Judge

Date of Birth: 1950
Education: Nevada (Reno) 1972 BS; Gonzaga 1976 JD
Began Service: October 1, 1988
Political Affiliation: Republican

Academic: Instructor in Law, Lassen College (1988-1994)

Clerkships: Law Clerk The Honorable Bruce Thompson, United States District Court for the District of Nevada (1976)

Government: Office of the United States Attorney, District of Nevada, United States Department of Justice (1976-1978)

Current Memberships: Lassen County Bar Association; Oregon State Bar; State Bar of California; State Bar of Nevada; Washoe County Bar Association

Staff
Career Law Clerk **Danika McClelland** .... (530) 246-5040
E-mail: dmcclelland@caed.uscourts.gov
Education: U San Francisco 1999 JD
Career Law Clerk **Erik Stewart** .... (530) 246-5045
E-mail: estewart@caed.uscourts.gov
Courtroom Deputy **Christy L. Pine** .... (530) 246-5417
E-mail: cpine@caed.uscourts.gov

Chambers of Magistrate Judge Edmund F. Brennan

Robert T. Matsui United States Courthouse, 501 I Street, Room 4-200, Sacramento, CA 95814
Tel: (916) 930-4170
E-mail: ebrennan@caed.uscourts.gov

Edmund F. Brennan
Magistrate Judge

Began Service: August 21, 2006
Term Expires: August 21, 2022

Government: Defensive Civil Litigation Chief, Civil Division, California - Eastern District, United States Department of Justice; Civil Chief, Civil Division, California - Eastern District, United States Department of Justice

Staff
Courtroom Deputy **Nic Cannarozzi** .... (916) 930-4172
E-mail: ncannarozzi@caed.uscourts.gov Fax: (916) 491-3931
Judicial Assistant **Tim Hinkle** .... (916) 930-4170
E-mail: tim_hinkle@caed.uscourts.gov

Chambers of Magistrate Judge Jennifer L. Thurston

510 19th Street, Suite 200, Bakersfield, CA 93301
Tel: (661) 326-6620
E-mail: jthurston@caed.uscourts.gov

Jennifer Thurston
Magistrate Judge

Education: Cal State (Bakersfield) 1989 BS; Pacific Coast Law 1997 JD
Began Service: 2009

Staff
Law Clerk **David Saine** .... (661) 326-6620
E-mail: dsaine@caed.uscourts.gov
Law Clerk **Leandra Rayford** .... (661) 326-6620
E-mail: lrayford@caed.uscourts.gov
Courtroom Deputy **Susan Hall** .... (661) 326-6620
E-mail: shall@caed.uscourts.gov

Chambers of Magistrate Judge Kendall J. Newman

501 I Street, 8th Floor, Sacramento, CA 95814
Tel: (916) 930-4187
E-mail: knewman@caed.uscourts.gov

Kendall J. Newman
Magistrate Judge

Education: Cornell 1980 BS; William & Mary 1984 JD
Began Service: 2010

Staff
Courtroom Deputy **Matt Caspar** .... (916) 930-4187
E-mail: mcaspar@caed.uscourts.gov
Court Reporter **Jonathan Anderson** .... (916) 930-4187
E-mail: janderson@caed.uscourts.gov
Judicial Assistant **Robbin Maloney** .... (916) 930-4187
E-mail: rmaloney@caed.uscourts.gov

Chambers of Magistrate Judge Barbara A. McAuliffe

2500 Tulare Street, Fresno, CA 93721
Tel: (559) 499-5788
E-mail: bmcauliffe@caed.uscourts.gov

Barbara A. McAuliffe
Magistrate Judge

Education: LSU 1980 BS; San Diego 1989 JD
Began Service: 2011

(continued on next page)

Chambers of Magistrate Judge Barbara A. McAuliffe *continued*

Staff

Law Clerk **Cathleen Hall** .... (559) 499-5788
E-mail: chall@caed.uscourts.gov
Law Clerk **Marianne Pansa** .... (559) 499-5788
E-mail: mpansa@caed.uscourts.gov
Law Clerk **Sophia Lecky** .... (559) 499-5788
E-mail: slecky@caed.uscourts.gov
Courtroom Deputy **Harriet Herman** .... (559) 499-5788
E-mail: hherman@caed.uscourts.gov

Chambers of Magistrate Judge Carolyn K. Delaney

501 I Street, Sacramento, CA 95814
Tel: (916) 930-4004
E-mail: cdelaney@caed.uscourts.gov

Carolyn K. Delaney
Magistrate Judge

Education: Wesleyan U 1984 BA; Stanford 1988 JD
Began Service: 2011

Staff

Courtroom Deputy **Kyle Owen** .... (916) 930-4004
E-mail: kowen@caed.uscourts.gov
Court Reporter **Jonathan Anderson** .... (916) 930-4072
E-mail: janderson@caed.uscourts.gov
Judicial Assistant **Danielle Eichhorn** .... (916) 930-4004
E-mail: deichhorn@caed.uscourts.gov

Chambers of Magistrate Judge Sheila K. Oberto

2500 Tulare Street, Fresno, CA 93721
Tel: (559) 499-5975
E-mail: soberto@caed.uscourts.gov

Sheila K. Oberto
Magistrate Judge

Education: USC 1977 BS; UCLA 1979 MS; USC 1985 JD
Began Service: 2011

Staff

Law Clerk **Susan Andritch** .... (559) 499-5975
E-mail: sandritch@caed.uscourts.gov
Law Clerk **Natalie Hayen** .... (559) 499-5975
E-mail: nhayen@caed.uscourts.gov
Law Clerk **Deborah Owdom** .... (559) 499-5975
E-mail: dowdom@caed.uscourts.gov
Education: Stanford 1971 BA;
San Joaquin Law 1976 JD
Law Clerk **Kirsten Ronholt** .... (559) 499-5975
E-mail: kronholt@caed.uscourts.gov
Courtroom Deputy **Alice Timken** .... (559) 499-5975
E-mail: atimken@caed.uscourts.gov

Chambers of Magistrate Judge Stanley A. Boone

2500 Tulare Street, Sixth Floor, Fresno, CA 93721
Tel: (559) 499-5672
E-mail: sboone@caed.uscourts.gov

Stanley A. Boone
Magistrate Judge

Education: UC Berkeley 1988 BA; McGeorge 1995 JD

Staff

Law Clerk **Marjorie Webb** .... (559) 499-5672
E-mail: mwebb@caed.uscourts.gov
Law Clerk **Andrew Woo** .... (559) 499-5672
E-mail: awoo@caed.uscourts.gov
Courtroom Deputy **Mamie Hernandez** .... (559) 499-5672
E-mail: mhernandez@caed.uscourts.gov

Chambers of Magistrate Judge Michael J. Seng

P.O. Box 575, Yosemite National Park, CA 95389
Tel: (209) 372-0320 Fax: (209) 372-0324
E-mail: mseng@caed.uscourts.gov

Michael J. Seng
Magistrate Judge

Began Service: May 2010
Term Expires: May 2018

Staff

Law Clerk **Maryam Baqi** .... (209) 372-0321
Law Clerk **Jeremy Clar** .... (559) 499-5659
E-mail: jclar@caed.uscourts.gov
Education: UC Berkeley 1999 BA;
McGeorge 2004 JD
Law Clerk **Monique Drew** .... (559) 499-5978
E-mail: mdrew@caed.uscourts.gov
Career Law Clerk **Cerise Fritsch** .... (559) 499-5674
E-mail: cfritsch@caed.uscourts.gov
Courtroom Deputy Clerk **Laurie Yu** .... (209) 372-0320 ext. 8917
E-mail: lyu@caed.uscourts.gov

Chambers of Magistrate Judge Allison Claire

Robert T. Matsui United States Courthouse, 501 I Street,
Sacramento, CA 95814
Tel: (916) 930-4199
E-mail: aclaire@caed.uscourts.gov

Allison Claire
Magistrate Judge

Education: UC Santa Cruz 1990 BA;
Boalt Hall 1993 JD
Began Service: November 19, 2012

Clerkships: Law Clerk, Chambers of Senior Judge Lawrence K. Karlton, United States District Court for the Eastern District of California (1993-1995)

Government: Federal Public Defender, Office of the Federal Defender for the Eastern District of California, California - Eastern District, Office of the Federal Public Defender (1995-2012)

Staff

Courtroom Deputy **Valerie Callen** .... (916) 930-4199
E-mail: vcallen@caed.uscourts.gov
Court Reporter **Jonathan Anderson** .... (916) 930-4072
E-mail: janderson@caed.uscourts.gov
Judicial Assistant **Donna Dal Porto** .... (916) 930-4120
E-mail: ddalporto@caed.uscourts.gov

United States Bankruptcy Court for the Eastern District of California

Robert T. Matsui United States Courthouse, 501 I Street, Room 3-200,
Sacramento, CA 95814-2322
Tel: (916) 930-4400
Internet: www.caeb.uscourts.gov

Number of Judgeships: 7

Court Staff

Clerk **Wayne Blackwelder** .... (916) 930-4400
E-mail: wayne_blackwelder@caeb.uscourts.gov
Chief Deputy Clerk **Sandy Smith** .... (916) 930-4400
Division Manager - Fresno and Modesto
Robert Herndon .... (559) 499-5800
2500 Tulare Street, Suite 2501, Fresno, CA 93721
E-mail: robert_herndon@caeb.uscourts.gov

United States Bankruptcy Court for the Eastern District of California *continued*

Division Manager - Sacramento **Beverly Collins** .... (916) 930-4400
Operations Coordinator - Fresno **Mary Wellington** ...... (559) 499-5800
2500 Tulare Street, Suite 2501, Fresno, CA 93721
E-mail: mary_wellington@caeb.uscourts.gov
Operations Coordinator - Modesto **Leslie Sousa** .... (209) 521-5160
2500 Tulare Street, Suite 2501, Fresno, CA 93721
Operations Coordinator - Sacramento **Danette Neff** ...... (916) 930-4400
2500 Tulare Street, Suite 2501, Fresno, CA 93721
E-mail: danette_neff@caeb.uscourts.gov
Management Analyst **Diana Holland** .... (916) 930-4400
E-mail: diana_holland@caeb.uscourts.gov
Librarian **Jana Maginness** .... (916) 930-4155
Fax: (916) 930-4159

Chambers of Chief Bankruptcy Judge Christopher M. Klein

Robert T. Matsui United States Courthouse, 501 I Street,
Sacramento, CA 95814
Tel: (916) 930-4510 Fax: (916) 930-4483
E-mail: christopher_klein@caeb.uscourts.gov

Christopher M. Klein
Chief Bankruptcy Judge

Date of Birth: 1946
Education: Brown U 1969 BA, 1969 MA; Chicago 1976 JD, 1976 MBA
Began Service: February 1988
Term Expires: 2016

Government: Trial Attorney, United States Department of Justice, Jimmy Carter Administration (1978-1980)

Judicial: Bankruptcy Judge, United States Bankruptcy Court for the Eastern District of California (1988-2008); Chief Judge of the Bankruptcy Appellate Panel, United States Bankruptcy Appellate Panel for the Ninth Circuit (2007-2008)

Legal Practice: Attorney, Cleary Gottlieb Steen & Hamilton LLP (1980-1983); Deputy General Counsel, National Railroad Passenger Corporation (1983-1987)

Military Service: United States Marine Corps (1969-1978)

Staff
Law Clerk **Joe Boniwell** .... (916) 930-4483
Judicial Assistant **Katherine Nolan** .... (916) 930-4510

Chambers of Bankruptcy Judge Michael S. McManus

U.S. Courthouse, 501 I Street, Room 3-200, Sacramento, CA 95814
Tel: (916) 930-4540 Fax: (916) 930-4552
E-mail: michael_mcmanus@caeb.uscourts.gov

Michael S. McManus
Bankruptcy Judge

Date of Birth: 1953
Education: UC Berkeley 1975 BA; UCLA 1978 JD
Began Service: January 11, 1994
Term Expires: January 10, 2022

Judicial: Chief Bankruptcy Judge, United States Bankruptcy Court for the Eastern District of California

Legal Practice: Associate, Morris & Polich (1978-1979); Partner, Diepenbrock, Wulff, Plant & Hannegan (1979-1994)

Current Memberships: American Bankruptcy Institute; National Conference of Bankruptcy Judges; Sacramento Valley Bankruptcy Forum; State Bar of California

Chambers of Bankruptcy Judge Michael S. McManus *continued*

Staff
Career Law Clerk **Valery P. Loumber** .... (916) 930-4501
E-mail: valery_loumber@caeb.uscourts.gov
Education: McGeorge 2000 JD
Judicial Assistant **Susan C. Cox** .... (916) 930-4537
E-mail: susan_c_cox@caeb.uscourts.gov
Education: Tennessee 1979 BS

Chambers of Bankruptcy Judge W. Richard Lee

Robert E. Coyle U.S. Courthouse, 2500 Tulare Street, Suite 2501,
Fresno, CA 93721
Tel: (559) 499-5870 Fax: (559) 499-5874
E-mail: richard_lee@caeb.uscourts.gov

W. Richard Lee
Bankruptcy Judge

Education: USC BS, MBA; San Joaquin Law JD
Began Service: January 17, 2001
Term Expires: January 16, 2027

Current Memberships: State Bar of California

Staff
Career Law Clerk **Sharlene Roberts-Caudle** .... (559) 499-5870
E-mail: sharlene_roberts-caudle@caeb.uscourts.gov
Judicial Assistant **Virginia Guajardo** .... (559) 499-5870
E-mail: virginia_guajardo@caeb.uscourts.gov

Chambers of Bankruptcy Judge Robert S. Bardwil

Robert T. Matsui United States Courthouse, 501 I Street,
Sacramento, CA 95814
Tel: (916) 930-4400
E-mail: robert_bardwil@caeb.uscourts.gov

Robert S. Bardwil
Bankruptcy Judge

Education: Southwestern Law 1979 JD
Began Service: July 6, 2005
Term Expires: July 2019

Staff
Career Law Clerk **Paula Tanner** .... (916) 930-4400
Courtroom Deputy **Nancy Williams** .... (916) 930-4400
E-mail: nancy_williams@caeb.uscourts.gov
Judicial Assistant **Andrea Lovgren** .... (916) 930-4400
E-mail: andrea_lovgren@caeb.uscourts.gov

Chambers of Bankruptcy Judge Ronald H. Sargis

1200 I Street, Suite 4, Modesto, CA 95354
Tel: (209) 521-5160
E-mail: ronald_sargis@caeb.uscourts.gov

Ronald H. Sargis
Bankruptcy Judge

Began Service: 2010

Staff
Law Clerk **Michael Tomback** .... (209) 521-5160
Courtroom Deputy **Janet Larson** .... (209) 521-5160
E-mail: janet_larson@caeb.uscourts.gov
Judicial Assistant **Dawn Nartker** .... (209) 521-5160
E-mail: dawn_nartker@caeb.uscourts.gov

Chambers of Bankruptcy Judge Fredrick E. Clement

2500 Tulare Street, Fresno, CA 93721
Tel: (559) 499-5860
E-mail: fredrick_clement@caeb.uscourts.gov

Fredrick E. Clement
Bankruptcy Judge

Staff
Career Law Clerk **Joseph Flack** .... (559) 499-5860
Began Service: April 22, 2012
E-mail: joseph_flack@caeb.uscourts.gov
Education: Florida 2011 JD
Judicial Assistant **Kathy Torres** .... (559) 499-5860
E-mail: kathy_torres@caeb.uscourts.gov
Courtroom Deputy - Fresno **Rosalia Estrada** .... (559) 499-5868
Suite 2501

Chambers of Bankruptcy Judge Christopher D. Jaime

501 I Street, Suite 3-200, Sacramento, CA 95814
Tel: (916) 930-4421

Christopher D. Jaime
Bankruptcy Judge

Began Service: January 5, 2015

Staff
Law Clerk **Yolanda Vo** .... (916) 930-4421
Courtroom Deputy **Danielle Mobley** .... (916) 930-4421
Judicial Assistant **Kathy Nolan** .... (916) 930-4421

Chambers of Bankruptcy Judge (recalled) David E. Russell

Robert T. Matsui United States Courthouse, 501 I Street, Suite 3-200, Sacramento, CA 95814
Tel: (916) 930-4502
E-mail: david_russell@caeb.uscourts.gov

David E. Russell
Bankruptcy Judge (recalled)

Date of Birth: 1935
Education: UC Berkeley 1957 BS; Boalt Hall 1960 LLB
Began Service: November 3, 1986

Academic: Lecturer, Cosumnes River College

Legal Practice: Staff Accountant, Lybrand Ross Bros & Montgomery (1960-1963); Robert C. Burnstein (1964-1965); Russell & Humphreys (1965-1966); Partner, Russell, Humphreys & Estabrook (1966-1968); Partner, Russell, Humphreys, Estabrook & Dashiell (1968-1971); Partner, Russell, Jarvis, Estabrook & Dashiell (1971-1986)

Current Memberships: National Conference of Bankruptcy Judges; Sacramento County Bar Assocaition; State Bar of California

Chambers of Bankruptcy Judge (Recalled) Philip H. Brandt

501 I Street, Suite 3-200, Sacramento, CA 95814
Tel: (916) 930-4400

Philip H. Brandt
Bankruptcy Judge (recalled)

Note: Judge Brandt also serves in the United States Bankruptcy Court for the Western District of Washington.
Date of Birth: 1944
Education: Harvard 1966 AB; U Washington 1972 JD

Current Memberships: American Bar Association; King County Bar Association; National Conference of Bankruptcy Judges; Tacoma-Pierce County Bar Association; Washington State Bar Association

Chambers of Bankruptcy Judge (Recalled) Whitney Rimel

2500 Tulare Street, Suite 2501, Fresno, CA 93721
Tel: (559) 499-5800

Whitney Rimel
Bankruptcy Judge (recalled)

Education: Oberlin BA; Chicago MA; UC Davis JD

Current Memberships: American Bankruptcy Institute; Federal Bar Association; National Conference of Bankruptcy Judges

United States District Court for the Northern District of California

Federal Building, 450 Golden Gate Avenue, 16th Floor, San Francisco, CA 94102
P.O. Box 36060, San Francisco, CA 94102
Tel: (415) 522-2000 Tel: (415) 522-2144 (PACER)
Fax: (415) 522-3605
Internet: www.cand.uscourts.gov

Number of Judgeships: 15

Circuit: Ninth

Areas Covered: Counties of Alameda, Contra Costa, Del Norte, Humboldt, Lake, Marin, Mendocino, Monterey, Napa, San Benito, San Francisco, San Mateo, Santa Clara, Santa Cruz and Sonoma

Court Staff

Clerk of Court **Susan Y. Soong** .... (415) 522-2000
E-mail: susan_soong@cand.uscourts.gov
Supervisor, Property and Procurement **Helene McVanner** .... (415) 522-2095
E-mail: helene_mcvanner@cand.uscourts.gov Fax: (415) 522-3605
Financial Administrator **Grace Ligh** .... (415) 522-4621
E-mail: grace_ligh@cand.uscourts.gov Fax: (415) 522-4103
Office Manager - Oakland **Keely Kirkpatrick** .... (510) 637-3530
Ronald V. Dellums Federal Bldg., 1301 Clay St., Ste. 400 South, Oakland, CA 94612 Fax: (510) 637-3545
E-mail: keely_kirkpatrick@cand.uscourts.gov
Office Manager - San Jose **Keely Kirkpatrick** .... (408) 535-5364
U.S. Courthouse, 280 S. First St., Rm. 2112, San Jose, CA 95113 Fax: (408) 535-5360
E-mail: keely_kirkpatrick@cand.uscourts.gov
Capital Habeas Staff Attorney **Veronica Gushin** .... (415) 522-4177
E-mail: veronica_gushin@cand.uscourts.gov
Death Penalty Law Clerk [Oakland] **Julie Bibb Davis** .... (510) 637-3523
Pro Se Law Clerk **Christine Allen** .... (408) 535-5560
E-mail: christine_allen@cand.uscourts.gov
Pro Se Law Clerk **Gina Ramos Campbell** .... (510) 637-3586
1301 Clay St., Oakland, CA 94612
Pro Se Law Clerk **Ronnie Hersler** .... (415) 522-2004
E-mail: ronnie_hersler@cand.uscourts.gov
Education: Boalt Hall 1994 JD
Pro Se Law Clerk **Michael Deibert** .... (415) 522-2080
E-mail: michael_deibert@cand.uscourts.gov

United States District Court for the Northern District of California *continued*

Pro Se Law Clerk **James Eder** .... (415) 522-4758
E-mail: james_eder@cand.uscourts.gov

Pro Se Law Clerk **Luis L. Hernandez** .... (415) 522-2078
E-mail: luis_hernandez@cand.uscourts.gov
Education: Yale 1990 JD

Pro Se Law Clerk **Monica Hunt** .... (415) 522-2094

Pro Se Law Clerk **Emily C. Klein** .... (510) 637-3677

Pro Se Law Clerk **Hannah Lee** .... (408) 535-5444
E-mail: hannah_lee@cand.uscourts.gov

Pro Se Law Clerk **Christine Thornton** .... (415) 522-2024
E-mail: christine_thornton@cand.uscourts.gov

Pro Se Law Clerk **Adam Burns** .... (415) 522-2085
E-mail: adam_burns@cand.uscourts.gov

Chief Probation Officer **Yador Harrell** .... (415) 436-7540
P.O. Box 36057, San Francisco, CA 94102 Fax: (415) 436-7572

Chief Pretrial Services Officer **Roy Saenz** .... (415) 436-7500
P.O. Box 36108, San Francisco, CA 94102

Librarian **Susan Wong Caulder** .... (415) 436-8130
Fax: (415) 436-8134

Librarian, San Jose **Lee Van Duzer** .... (408) 535-5323
280 S. First St., Rm. 5152, San Jose, CA 95113 Fax: (408) 535-5322
Education: New Hampshire 2005 JD;
Arizona 2009 MLIS

Chambers of Chief Judge Phyllis J. Hamilton

Oakland Courthouse, 1301 Clay Street, Room 3, Oakland, CA 94612
Tel: (510) 637-3530
E-mail: phyllis_hamilton@cand.uscourts.gov

Phyllis J. Hamilton
Chief Judge

Education: Stanford 1974 BA; Santa Clara U 1976 JD
Began Service: July 7, 2000
Appointed By: President William J. Clinton

Current Memberships: California Women Lawyers Bar Association; Charles Houston Bar Association; National Association of Women Judges

Staff

Career Law Clerk **Alexandra Petrich** .... (510) 637-3530
E-mail: alexandra_petrich@cand.uscourts.gov
Education: Hastings JD

Career Law Clerk **(Vacant)** .... (510) 637-3530

Courtroom Deputy **Nicole Peric** .... (510) 637-3530
E-mail: nicole_peric@cand.uscourts.gov

Chambers of District Judge Jeremy Fogel

U.S. Courthouse, 280 South First Street, San Jose, CA 95113
Tel: (408) 535-5426 Fax: (408) 535-5163
E-mail: jeremy_fogel@cand.uscourts.gov

Jeremy D. Fogel
District Judge

Date of Birth: 1949
Education: Stanford 1971 BA; Harvard 1974 JD
Began Service: March 31, 1998
Appointed By: President William J. Clinton
Political Affiliation: Democrat

Academic: Lecturer, Human Development, California State University, Hayward (1977-1978)

Judicial: Judge, Municipal Court, Santa Clara County (1981-1986); Judge, County of Santa Clara, Superior Court of California, California (1986-1998)

Chambers of District Judge Jeremy Fogel *continued*

Legal Practice: Member, Smith, Johnson, Fogel & Ramo (1974-1978); Directing Attorney, Mental Health Advocacy Project, Santa Clara County Bar Association Law Foundation, Inc (1978-1981); Executive Director, Santa Clara County Bar Association Law Foundation, Inc (1980-1981)

Current Memberships: California Judges Association; Federal Judges Association; Santa Clara County Bar Association; State Bar of California

Staff

Administrative Law Clerk **Christian Delaney** .... (408) 535-5426
E-mail: christian_delaney@cand.uscourts.gov
Education: Hastings 1992 JD

Courtroom Deputy **Tiffany Salinas-Harwell** .... (408) 535-5166

Chambers of District Judge William Alsup

Federal Building, 450 Golden Gate Avenue, San Francisco, CA 94102
Tel: (415) 522-3684
E-mail: william_alsup@cand.uscourts.gov

William Alsup
District Judge

Date of Birth: 1945
Education: Mississippi State 1967 BS; Harvard 1971 JD;
JFK School Govt 1971 MPP
Began Service: August 17, 1999
Appointed By: President William J. Clinton

Clerkships: Law Clerk The Honorable William O. Douglas, United States Supreme Court (1971-1972)

Government: Assistant Solicitor General, Office of the Solicitor General, United States Department of Justice (1978-1980); Special Counsel, Antitrust Division, United States Department of Justice (1998)

Legal Practice: Attorney, Pyles & Tucker (1972-1973); Associate/Partner, Morrison & Foerster LLP (1973-1978); Partner, Morrison & Foerster LLP (1980-1999)

Current Memberships: American Bar Association; American College of Trial Lawyers; California Supreme Court Historical Society; San Francisco Bar Association; State Bar of California

Staff

Courtroom Deputy **Dawn Toland** .... (415) 522-3684

Chambers of District Judge Jeffrey S. White

450 Golden Gate Avenue, 19th, Courtroom 11, San Francisco, CA 94102
Tel: (510) 637-1820 Fax: (510) 637-1826
E-mail: jeffrey_white@cand.uscourts.gov

Jeffrey S. White
District Judge

Date of Birth: September 2, 1945
Education: Queens Col (NY) 1967 BA; SUNY (Buffalo) 1970 JD
Began Service: January 2, 2003
Appointed By: President George W. Bush

Government: Trial Attorney, Criminal Division, United States Department of Justice, Richard M. Nixon Administration (1970-1971); Assistant U.S. Attorney, Maryland District, United States Department of Justice (1971-1977); Trial Attorney, Criminal Division, Public Integrity Section, United States Department of Justice, Jimmy Carter Administration (1977-1978)

Legal Practice: Associate, Orrick, Herrington & Sutcliffe LLP (1978-1980); Partner, Orrick, Herrington & Sutcliffe LLP (1980-2002)

Current Memberships: American Bar Association; The Bar Association of San Francisco

Staff

Career Law Clerk **Melissa Goldberg** .... (510) 637-1820
E-mail: melissa_goldberg@cand.uscourts.gov

(continued on next page)

Chambers of District Judge Jeffrey S. White *continued*

Career Law Clerk **Margaret "Daisy" Salzman** ....(510) 637-1820
Education: Yale 1992 BA
Administrative Law Clerk **Kristin Ring** ....(510) 637-1820
E-mail: kristin_ring@cand.uscourts.gov
Courtroom Deputy **Jennifer Ottolini** ....(510) 637-1820
E-mail: jennifer_ottolini@cand.uscourts.gov

Chambers of District Judge Richard Seeborg

450 Golden Gate Avenue, San Francisco, CA 94102
Tel: (415) 522-2123
E-mail: richard_seeborg@cand.uscourts.gov

Richard Seeborg
District Judge

Date of Birth: 1956
Education: Yale 1978 BA; Columbia 1981 JD
Began Service: January 4, 2010
Appointed By: President Barack Obama

Clerkships: Law Clerk The Honorable John H. Pratt, United States District Court for the District of Columbia (1981-1982)

Government: Assistant United States Attorney, Northern District of California, United States Attorney's Office, United States Department of Justice, William J. Clinton Administration (1991-1998)

Judicial: Magistrate Judge, Chambers of Magistrate Judge Richard Seeborg, United States District Court for the Northern District of California (2001-2009)

Legal Practice: Associate, Morrison & Foerster LLP; Partner, Morrison & Foerster LLP; Partner, Morrison & Foerster LLP (1998-2000)

Staff
Courtroom Deputy **Corinne Lew** ....(415) 522-2123
E-mail: corinne_lew@cand.uscourts.gov

Chambers of District Judge Lucy H. Koh

280 South First Street, San Jose, CA 95113
Tel: (408) 535-5357 Fax: (508) 535-5360
E-mail: lucy_koh@cand.uscourts.gov

Lucy H. Koh
District Judge

Education: Harvard 1990 BA, 1993 JD
Began Service: June 11, 2010
Appointed By: President Barack Obama

Government: Assistant U.S. Attorney, California - Central District, Executive Office for United States Attorneys, United States Department of Justice (1997-2000)

Judicial: Judge, Chambers of Judge Lucy H. Koh, County of Santa Clara, Superior Court of California (2008-2010)

Membership: Fellow, Committee on the Judiciary (1993-1994)

Profession: Private Practice, Litigation (2000-2008)

Staff
Courtroom Deputy **Martha Parker-Brown** ....(408) 535-5346
E-mail: martha_brown@cand.uscourts.gov

Chambers of District Judge Edward J. Davila

280 South First Street, San Jose, CA 95113
Tel: (408) 535-5356 Fax: (415) 522-3605
E-mail: edward_davila@cand.uscourts.gov

Edward J. Davila
District Judge

Date of Birth: 1952
Education: San Diego State 1976 BA; Hastings 1979 JD
Began Service: March 4, 2011
Appointed By: President Barack Obama

Government: Deputy Public Defender, Office of the Public Defender, County of Santa Clara, California (1981-1988)

Judicial: Judge, Chambers of Judge Edward J. Davila, County of Santa Clara, Superior Court of California (2001-2011)

Legal Practice: Partner, Davila & Polverino, Attorneys at Law (1988-2001)

Staff
Courtroom Deputy **Elizabeth Garcia**..................(408) 535-5356
E-mail: elizabeth_garcia@cand.uscourts.gov

Chambers of District Judge Edward M. Chen

450 Golden Gate Avenue, San Francisco, CA 94102
Tel: (415) 522-2034
E-mail: edward_chen@cand.uscourts.gov

Edward Milton Chen
District Judge

Date of Birth: 1953
Education: UC Berkeley 1975 AB; Boalt Hall 1979 JD
Began Service: May 17, 2011
Appointed By: President Barack Obama

Clerkships: Law Clerk The Honorable James Browning, United States Court of Appeals for the Ninth Circuit (1981-1982)

Judicial: Magistrate Judge, Chambers of Magistrate Judge Edward M. Chen, United States District Court for the Northern District of California (2001-2011)

Legal Practice: Coblentz, Patch, Duffy & Bass (1982-1985); American Civil Liberties Union of Northern California (1985-2001)

Current Memberships: Asian American Bar Association of the Greater Bay Area

Staff
Career Law Clerk **Shao-Bai Wu** ....(415) 522-2034
Education: Stanford 2000 JD
Court Clerk **Betty P. Lee**...........................(415) 522-2034
E-mail: betty_p_lee@cand.uscourts.gov
Secretary **Leni Doyle-Hickman** ....(415) 522-4050
E-mail: leni_doyle-hickman@cand.uscourts.gov
Education: UC Berkeley 1990 BA

Chambers of District Judge Yvonne Gonzalez Rogers

1301 Clay Street, 400 South, Oakland, CA 94612
Tel: (510) 637-3540 Fax: (510) 637-3545
E-mail: ygrcrd@cand.uscourts.gov
E-mail: ygrcrd@cand.uscourts.gov

Yvonne Gonzalez Rogers
District Judge

Education: Princeton 1987; Texas 1991 JD
Began Service: November 21, 2011
Appointed By: President Barack Obama

Staff
Courtroom Deputy **Frances Stone**....................(510) 637-3540
E-mail: frances_stone@cand.uscourts.gov

Chambers of District Judge Jon S. Tigar
Federal Building, 450 Golden Gate Avenue, San Francisco, CA 94102
Tel: (415) 522-2036
E-mail: jon_tigar@cand.uscourts.gov

Jon S. Tigar
District Judge

Education: UC Berkeley 1984 BA; Boalt Hall 1989 JD
Began Service: January 18, 2013
Appointed By: President Barack Obama

Government: Public Defender, Office of the Public Defender, City and County of San Francisco, California (1993-1994)

Judicial: Judge, Chambers of Judge Jon S. Tigar, County of Alameda, Superior Court of California (2002-2012)

Legal Practice: Litigation Associate, Morrison & Foerster LLP (1990-1992); Attorney, Keker & Van Nest LLP (1994-2002)

Staff
Calendar Clerk and Courtroom Deputy **William Noble** . . . (415) 522-2036
E-mail: jstcrd@cand.uscourts.gov
Docketing Clerk **Thelma Nudo** . . . . (415) 522-2067
E-mail: thelma_nudo@cand.uscourts.gov
Docketing Clerk **Ruby Woo** . . . . (415) 522-2076
E-mail: ruby_woo@cand.uscourts.gov
Docketing Clerk **Lori Murray** . . . . (415) 522-2093
E-mail: lori_murray@cand.uscourts.gov
Docketing Clerk **Mark Jenkins** . . . . (415) 522-2067
E-mail: mark_jenkins@cand.uscourts.gov

Chambers of District Judge William H. Orrick
Federal Building, 450 Golden Gate Avenue, San Francisco, CA 94102
Tel: (415) 522-2077
E-mail: william_orrick@cand.uscourts.gov

William Horsley Orrick III
District Judge

Education: Yale 1976 BA; Boston Col 1979 JD
Began Service: August 1, 2013
Appointed By: President Barack Obama

Government: Counselor, Civil Division, United States Department of Justice (2009-2010); Deputy Assistant Attorney General, Office of Immigration Litigation, Civil Division, United States Department of Justice (2010-2013)

Staff
Calendar Clerk and Courtroom Deputy **Jean Davis** . . . . . . (415) 522-2077
E-mail: WHOcrd@cand.uscourts.gov

Chambers of District Judge James Donato
Federal Building, 450 Golden Gate Avenue, San Francisco, CA 94102
Tel: (415) 522-2066
E-mail: james_donato@cand.uscourts.gov

James Donato
District Judge

Education: UC Berkeley 1983 BA; Harvard 1984 MA; Stanford 1988 JD
Began Service: March 21, 2014
Appointed By: President Barack Obama

Staff
Career Law Clerk **Jiyoun Chung** . . . . (415) 522-2066

Chambers of District Judge Beth Labson Freeman
280 South First Street, Fifth Floor, San Jose, CA 95113
Tel: (408) 535-5381
E-mail: beth_freeman@cand.uscourts.gov

Beth Labson Freeman
District Judge

Education: UC Berkeley 1976 AB; Harvard 1979 JD
Began Service: February 28, 2014
Appointed By: President Barack Obama

Judicial: Assistant Presiding Judge, Chambers of Assistant Presiding Judge Beth Labson Freeman, County of San Mateo, Superior Court of California; Presiding Judge, Chambers of Presiding Judge Beth Labson Freeman, County of San Mateo, Superior Court of California

Chambers of District Judge Vince Girdhari Chhabria
Federal Building, 450 Golden Gate Avenue, San Francisco, CA 94102
P.O. Box 36060, San Francisco, CA 94102
Tel: (415) 522-2000
E-mail: vince_chhabria@cand.uscourts.gov

Vince Girdhari Chhabria
District Judge

Education: UC Santa Cruz 1991 BA; Boalt Hall 1998 JD
Began Service: March 7, 2014
Appointed By: President Barack Obama

Clerkships: Law Clerk The Honorable James R. Browning, United States District Court for the Ninth Circuit (1999-2000)

Government: Deputy City Attorney for Government Litigation, Office of the City Attorney, City and County of San Francisco, California (2005-2014)

Legal Practice: Litigation Associate, Covington & Burling LLP (2002-2004)

Staff
Courtroom Deputy **Kristen Melen** . . . . (415) 522-4173

Chambers of District Judge Haywood Stirling Gilliam Jr.
450 Golden Gate Avenue, San Francisco, CA 94102
Tel: (415) 522-2039

Haywood Stirling Gilliam, Jr.
District Judge

Began Service: December 19, 2014
Appointed By: President Barack Obama

Government: Assistant U.S. Attorney, Criminal Division, California - Northern District, United States Department of Justice; Major Frauds Chief, Criminal Division, California - Northern District, United States Department of Justice

Staff
Courtroom Deputy **Nikki Riley** . . . . (415) 522-2039
E-mail: hsgcrd@cand.uscourts.gov

Chambers of Senior Judge Samuel Conti

Federal Building, 450 Golden Gate Avenue, San Francisco, CA 94102
P.O. 36060, San Francisco, CA 94102
Tel: (415) 522-4080 Fax: (415) 522-2153
E-mail: samuel_conti@cand.uscourts.gov

Samuel Conti
Senior Judge

Date of Birth: 1922
Education: Santa Clara U 1945 BS; Stanford 1948 JD
Began Service: 1970
Appointed By: President Richard M. Nixon

Government: Assistant City Attorney, Office of the City Attorney, City of Concord, California (1960-1965); City Attorney, Office of the City Attorney, City of Concord, California (1965-1967)

Judicial: Judge, Superior Court of California (1967-1970)

Legal Practice: Partner, Coll & Conti (1948-1950)

Military Service: United States Army (1942-1944)

Current Memberships: American Bar Association; Contra Costa County Bar Association; State Bar of California

Staff
Law Clerk **Christopher Bower** .... (415) 522-4080
Began Service: May 2015
Term Expires: May 2016
Law Clerk **Aaron Gershbock** .... (415) 522-4080
Began Service: June 2015
Term Expires: June 2016
Judicial Assistant **Letty Whitworth** .... (415) 522-4080
E-mail: letty_whitworth@cand.uscourts.gov

Chambers of Senior Judge Thelton E. Henderson

Federal Building, 450 Golden Gate Avenue, 19th Floor, Courtroom 12, San Francisco, CA 94102
P.O. Box 36060, San Francisco, CA 94102
Tel: (415) 522-2047
E-mail: thelton_henderson@cand.uscourts.gov

Thelton E. Henderson
Senior Judge

Date of Birth: 1933
Education: UC Berkeley 1956 BA; Boalt Hall 1962 JD
Began Service: 1980
Appointed By: President Jimmy Carter

Academic: Assistant Dean, Stanford University (1968-1976); Associate Professor of Law, Golden Gate University (1978-1980)

Government: Attorney, Civil Rights Division, United States Department of Justice (1962-1963); Directing Attorney, Legal Aid Society of San Mateo County (1966-1968)

Legal Practice: Associate, FitzSimmons & Petris (1964-1966); Rosen, Remcho & Henderson (1977-1980)

Military Service: United States Army (1956-1958)

Current Memberships: American Bar Association; The Edward McFetridge American Inn of Court, The American Inns of Court; The American Law Institute; Charles Houston Bar Association; Federal Judges Association; National Bar Association

Staff
Career Law Clerk **Michael Chu** .... (415) 522-2047
E-mail: michael_chu@cand.uscourts.gov
Courtroom Deputy **Tana Ingle** .... (415) 522-2047
E-mail: tana_ingle@cand.uscourts.gov

Chambers of Senior Judge Saundra Brown Armstrong

Ronald V. Dellums Federal Building, 1301 Clay Street, Suite 400 South, Oakland, CA 94612-5212
Tel: (510) 879-3550
E-mail: saundra_armstrong@cand.uscourts.gov

Saundra Brown Armstrong
Senior Judge

Date of Birth: 1947
Education: Cal State (Fresno) 1969 BA; U San Francisco 1977 JD
Began Service: June 21, 1991
Appointed By: President George H.W. Bush
Political Affiliation: Republican

Current Memberships: Alameda County Bar Association; American Bar Association; California Judges Association; Charles Houston Bar Association; Federal Judges Association; National Association of Women Judges; National Bar Association; National Council of Negro Women, Inc.; State Bar of California; Wiley Manuel Bar Association

Staff
Law Clerk **(Vacant)** .... (510) 637-3559
Career Law Clerk **Keith K. Fong** .... (510) 637-3559
Began Service: 2009
E-mail: keith_fong@cand.uscourts.gov
Education: UC Berkeley 1985 BA; UC Davis 1990 JD
Court Reporter **Raynee Mercado** .... (510) 451-7530
E-mail: raynee_mercado@cand.uscourts.gov
Courtroom Deputy **Nikki Riley** .... (510) 637-3542
Judicial Assistant **Lorene DeBose** .... (510) 637-3559
E-mail: lorene_debose@cand.uscourts.gov
Education: UC Berkeley 1970 AB; Hastings 1975 JD

Chambers of Senior Judge Ronald M. Whyte

U.S. Courthouse, 280 South First Street, San Jose, CA 95113
Tel: (408) 535-5331 Fax: (408) 535-5329
E-mail: ronald_whyte@cand.uscourts.gov

Ronald M. Whyte
Senior Judge

Date of Birth: 1942
Education: Wesleyan U 1964 AB; USC 1967 JD
Began Service: February 10, 1992
Appointed By: President George H.W. Bush
Political Affiliation: Republican

Judicial: Judge, California Superior County, Santa Clara County (1989-1992)

Legal Practice: Nichols, Stead, Boileau & Lamb (1967-1968); Attorney, Hoge, Fenton, Jones & Appel, Inc. (1971-1989)

Military Service: United States Naval Reserve (1968-1971)

Current Memberships: American Bar Association; The American Inns of Court; Northern California Chapter, Association of Business Trial Lawyers; California Judges Association; Federal Judges Association; San Francisco Bay Area Intellectual Property Inn of Court; Santa Clara County Bar Association; State Bar of California

Staff
Law Clerk **Roman Swoopes** .... (408) 535-5326
Began Service: August 2015
Term Expires: August 2016
E-mail: roman_swoopes@cand.uscourts.gov
Law Clerk **Frances Cheevers** .... (408) 535-5332
Began Service: October 2015
Term Expires: October 2016
E-mail: frances_cheevers@cand.uscourts.gov
Judicial Assistant **Jacqueline Cruz** .... (408) 535-5331
E-mail: jacqueline_cruz@cand.uscourts.gov

Chambers of Senior Judge Maxine M. Chesney

Federal Building, 450 Golden Gate Avenue, 19th Floor,
San Francisco, CA 94102
P.O. Box 36060, San Francisco, CA 94102-3489
Tel: (415) 522-2041 Fax: (415) 522-2184
E-mail: maxine_chesney@cand.uscourts.gov

Maxine M. Chesney
Senior Judge

Date of Birth: 1942
Education: UC Berkeley 1964 BA; Boalt Hall 1967 JD
Began Service: 1995
Appointed By: President William J. Clinton

Government: Assistant Chief Deputy, Office of the District Attorney, State of California (1976-1979)

Judicial: Judge, San Francisco County Municipal Court (1979-1983); Judge, California Superior Court (1983-1994); District Judge, United States District Court for the Northern District of California (1995-2009)

Current Memberships: Federal Circuit Bar Association; Federal Judges Association; Queens Bench Bar Association; United States Association of Constitutional Law; Ninth Judicial Circuit Historical Society, United States Court of Appeals for the Ninth Circuit

Staff
Courtroom Deputy **Tracy Lucero** .... (415) 522-2041
E-mail: tracy_lucero@cand.uscourts.gov

Chambers of Senior Judge Charles R. Breyer

Federal Building, 450 Golden Gate Avenue, San Francisco, CA 94102
P.O. Box 36060, San Francisco, CA 94102
Tel: (415) 522-2062
E-mail: charles_breyer@cand.uscourts.gov

Charles R. Breyer
Senior Judge

Date of Birth: 1941
Education: Harvard 1963 AB; Boalt Hall 1966 LLB
Began Service: January 1, 1998
Appointed By: President William J. Clinton

Current Memberships: American Bar Association; San Francisco Bar Association

Staff
Law Clerk **(Vacant)** .... (415) 522-3186
Career Law Clerk **Rebecca "Rebe" Glass** .... (415) 522-3187
Education: Harvard BA; Boalt Hall JD
Courtroom Deputy **Barbara Espinosa** .... (415) 522-2062
Judicial Assistant **Judith Stoyko** .... (415) 522-3660
E-mail: judith_stoyko@cand.uscourts.gov

Chambers of Senior Judge Susan Illston

Federal Building, 450 Golden Gate Avenue, 19th Floor,
San Francisco, CA 94102
P.O. Box 36060, San Francisco, CA 94102
Tel: (415) 522-2028 Fax: (415) 522-2184

Susan Yvonne Illston
Senior Judge

Date of Birth: 1948
Education: Duke 1970 BA; Stanford 1973 JD
Began Service: June 2, 1995
Appointed By: President William J. Clinton
Political Affiliation: Democrat

Current Memberships: American Bar Foundation; American Association of Justice; Section on Litigation, American Bar Association; American Board of Trial Advocates; American College of Trial Lawyers; Association of Business Trial Lawyers; Consumer Attorneys of California; International Academy of Trial Lawyers; International Society of Barristers; National Association of Women Judges

Staff
Law Clerk **(Vacant)** .... (415) 522-2028
Began Service: August 2014
Term Expires: August 2015
Career Law Clerk **Alison Aubrejuan** .... (415) 522-2028
E-mail: alison_aubrejuan@cand.uscourts.gov
Education: Stanford 1997 JD
Administrative Law Clerk **Cara Sandberg** .... (415) 522-2028
E-mail: cara_sandberg@cand.uscourts.gov
Education: Brown U 2005 BA; Tufts 2006 MAT; UC Berkeley 2012 JD

Chambers of Senior Judge Claudia A. Wilken

Ronald V. Dellums Federal Building, 1301 Clay Street, 4th Floor, Suite 400 South, Oakland, CA 94612-5212
Tel: (510) 637-3542 Fax: (510) 637-3545
E-mail: claudia_wilken@cand.uscourts.gov

Claudia A. Wilken
Senior Judge

Date of Birth: 1949
Education: Stanford 1971 BA; Boalt Hall 1975 JD
Began Service: December 1993
Appointed By: President William J. Clinton

Staff
Administrative Law Clerk **Elizabeth Eng** .... (510) 637-3542
E-mail: elizabeth_eng@cand.uscourts.gov
Education: Boalt Hall 2005 JD
Courtroom Deputy **Tana Ingle** .... (510) 637-3542
E-mail: tana_ingle@cand.uscourts.gov

Chambers of Chief Magistrate Judge Joseph C. Spero

Federal Building, 450 Golden Gate Avenue, San Francisco, CA 94102
Tel: (415) 522-3691 Fax: (415) 522-3636

Joseph C. Spero
Chief Magistrate Judge

Date of Birth: 1955
Education: Columbia 1981 JD
Began Service: March 13, 1999
Term Expires: March 13, 2023

Staff
Law Clerk **Sam Wheeler** .... (415) 522-3691
Began Service: August 2014
Term Expires: August 2016
E-mail: sam_wheeler@cand.uscourts.gov

(continued on next page)

Chambers of Chief Magistrate Judge Joseph C. Spero *continued*

Career Law Clerk **Melissa Dawson** .... (415) 522-3691
E-mail: melissa_dawson@cand.uscourts.gov
Education: Boalt Hall 1995 JD

Chambers of Magistrate Judge Elizabeth D. Laporte

Federal Building, 450 Golden Gate Avenue, San Francisco, CA 94102
P.O. Box 36060, San Francisco, CA 94102
Tel: (415) 522-3694 Fax: (415) 522-2002

Elizabeth D. Laporte
Magistrate Judge

Date of Birth: 1953
Education: Princeton 1975 BA; Oxford (UK) 1977 MA; Yale 1982 JD
Began Service: April 4, 1998
Term Expires: April 3, 2022

Current Memberships: Board of Governors, Northern California Chapter, Association of Business Trial Lawyers; The Association of Marshall Scholars, Inc.; Litigation Section Executive Committee, The Bar Association of San Francisco; Federal Magistrate Judges Association; State Bar of California

Staff
Administrative Law Clerk
Frederick "Fred" Braunstein .... (415) 522-3694
Career Law Clerk **Sarah Abbott** .... (415) 522-3694
Courtroom Deputy **Stephen H. Ybarra** .... (415) 522-3694

Chambers of Magistrate Judge Maria-Elena James

Federal Building, 450 Golden Gate Avenue, San Francisco, CA 94102
Tel: (415) 522-4698 Fax: (415) 522-4711
E-mail: maria-elena_james@cand.uscourts.gov

Maria-Elena James
Magistrate Judge

Date of Birth: 1953
Education: UC Irvine 1975 BA; U San Francisco 1978 JD
Began Service: October 11, 1994
Term Expires: October 2018

Current Memberships: Charles Houston Bar Association; San Francisco Bar Association

Staff
Law Clerk **Samantha Elboim** .... (415) 522-4698
Term Expires: 2016
E-mail: samantha_elboim@cand.uscourts.gov
Career Law Clerk **Christopher D. Nathan** .... (415) 522-4698
Education: San Francisco State U 1998 BA; Hastings 2001 JD
Courtroom Deputy **Rose Maher** .... (415) 522-4708
E-mail: rose_maher@cand.uscourts.gov

Chambers of Magistrate Judge Howard R. Lloyd

280 South First Street, San Jose, CA 95113
Tel: (408) 535-5411 Fax: (408) 535-5410
E-mail: howard_lloyd@cand.uscourts.gov

Howard R. Lloyd
Magistrate Judge

Date of Birth: October 26, 1941
Education: William & Mary 1963 BA; Michigan 1968 JD
Began Service: June 4, 2002
Term Expires: June 2018

Legal Practice: Litigator and Appellate Specialist, Hoge, Fenton, Jones & Appel, Inc. (1969-1999)

Chambers of Magistrate Judge Howard R. Lloyd *continued*

Staff
Law Clerk **Kevin Potter** .... (408) 535-5411
Began Service: September 2015
Term Expires: September 2016
E-mail: kevin_potter@cand.uscourts.gov
Career Law Clerk **Kristine Ching** .... (408) 535-5411
E-mail: kristine_ching@cand.uscourts.gov
Education: Stanford JD
Courtroom Deputy **Patricia "Patty" Cromwell** .... (408) 535-5365
E-mail: patricia_cromwell@cand.uscourts.gov

Chambers of Magistrate Judge Nandor J. Vadas

3140 Boeing Avenue, Mckinleyville, CA 95519
Tel: (707) 445-3612
E-mail: nandor_vadas@cand.uscourts.gov

Nandor J. Vadas
Magistrate Judge

Education: UC Santa Cruz; Hastings JD
Began Service: June 18, 2004
Term Expires: June 2016

Government: Deputy District Attorney, Office of the District Attorney, City and County of San Francisco, California (1983-1989); Assistant U.S. Attorney, California - Northern District, Executive Office for United States Attorneys, United States Department of Justice (1989-1998); Deputy District Attorney, County of Humboldt, California; Special Assistant U.S. Attorney, California - Northern District, Executive Office for United States Attorneys, United States Department of Justice

Judicial: Magistrate Judge (part-time), United States District Court for the Northern District of California (2004-2009)

Staff
Secretary and Courtroom Deputy **Gloria Knudson** .... (707) 445-3612
E-mail: gloria_knudson@cand.uscourts.gov

Chambers of Magistrate Judge Laurel Beeler

450 Golden Gate Avenue, 15th Floor, San Francisco, CA 94102
Tel: (415) 522-3140
E-mail: laurel_beeler@cand.uscourts.gov

Laurel Beeler
Magistrate Judge

Education: Bowdoin BA; U Washington JD
Began Service: 2009

Government: Deputy Chief, Criminal Division, California - Northern District, Department of Justice; Staff Attorney, United States Court of Appeals for the Ninth Circuit (1989-1990); Civil Appeals Division Chief, United States Court of Appeals for the Ninth Circuit (1990-1992)

Staff
Docket Clerk **Felicia Reloba** .... (415) 522-2063
E-mail: felicia_reloba@cand.uscourts.gov
Courtroom Deputy **Lashanda Scott** .... (415) 522-3140
E-mail: lashanda_scott@cand.uscourts.gov

Chambers of Magistrate Judge Donna M. Ryu
1301 Clay Street, Room 400 South, Oakland, CA 94612
Tel: (510) 637-3639

Donna M. Ryu
Magistrate Judge

Education: Yale BA; Boalt Hall JD
Began Service: 2010

Legal Practice: Attorney, McCutchen, Doyle, Brown and Enersen, LLP; Attorney, Saperstein Seligman Mayeda & Larkin; Co-Founder, Ryu Dickey & Larkin

Nonprofit: Associate Director, Women's Employment Rights Clinic, Golden Gate University; Associate Professor, Golden Gate University; Professor, University of California Hastings College of the Law (2002-2010)

Staff
Docket Clerk (Civil) **Valerie Kyono** . . . . (510) 637-3537
E-mail: valerie_kyono@cand.uscourts.gov
Docket Clerk (Criminal) **Kelly Collins** . . . . (510) 637-3539
E-mail: kelly_collins@cand.uscourts.gov
Calendar Clerk **Ivy Garcia** . . . . (510) 637-3639
E-mail: ivy_garcia@cand.uscourts.gov

Chambers of Magistrate Judge Paul S. Grewal
280 South First Street, San Jose, CA 95113
Tel: (408) 535-5378
E-mail: paul_grewal@cand.uscourts.gov

Paul S. Grewal
Magistrate Judge

Education: MIT 1993 SB; Chicago 1996 JD
Began Service: December 1, 2010

Staff
Courtroom Deputy **Oscar Rivera** . . . . (408) 535-5378
E-mail: oscar_rivera@cand.uscourts.gov

Chambers of Magistrate Judge Jacqueline Scott Corley
450 Golden Gate Avenue, San Francisco, CA 95110
Tel: (415) 522-2015

Jacqueline Scott Corley
Magistrate Judge

Education: UC Berkeley 1988 BA; Harvard 1991 JD
Began Service: 2011

Clerkships: Law Clerk, Chambers of District Judge Robert E. Keeton, United States District Court for the District of Massachusetts (1991-1992); Career Law Clerk, Chambers of District Judge Charles R. Breyer, United States District Court for the Northern District of California (1998-2009)

Legal Practice: Litigation Associate, Goodwin, Procter & Hoar, LLP (1992-1994); Litigation Associate, Coblentz, Cahen, McCabe & Breyer (1994-1997); Partner, Kerr & Wagstaffe LLP (2009-2011)

Staff
Courtroom Deputy **Ada Means** . . . . (415) 522-2015
E-mail: ada_means@cand.uscourts.gov

Chambers of Magistrate Judge Nathanael Cousins
280 South First Street, San Jose, CA 95113
Tel: (415) 522-2039

Nathanael Cousins
Magistrate Judge

Began Service: July 5, 2011

Chambers of Magistrate Judge Nathanael Cousins *continued*

Staff
Courtroom Deputy **Lili Harrell** . . . . (415) 522-2039
E-mail: lili_harrell@cand.uscourts.gov

Chambers of Magistrate Judge Kandis A. Westmore
1301 Clay Street, Oakland, CA 94612-5212
Tel: (510) 637-3525
E-mail: kandis_westmore@cand.uscourts.gov

Kandis A. Westmore
Magistrate Judge

Began Service: February 21, 2012

Staff
Courtroom Deputy **Sue Imbriani** . . . . (510) 637-3525
E-mail: sue_imbriani@cand.uscourts.gov

United States Bankruptcy Court for the Northern District of California
1300 Clay Street, 20th Floor, Oakland, CA 94612
P.O. Box 7341, San Francisco, CA 94120-7341
Tel: (415) 268-2300
Tel: (888) 457-0604 (Voice Case Information System VCIS)
Fax: (415) 268-2303
Internet: pacer.canb.uscourts.gov

Number of Judgeships: 9

Court Staff
Clerk of Court **Edward "Eddy" Emmons** . . . . (415) 268-2300
Chief Deputy **(Vacant)** . . . . (415) 268-2300
Manager, Oakland Division **Tracie Williams** . . . . (510) 879-3600
1300 Clay St., 3rd Fl., Oakland, CA 94612
P.O. Box 2070, Oakland, CA 94604-2070
E-mail: tracie_williams@canb.uscourts.gov
Manager, San Francisco Division **Elizabeth Lucero** . . . . . (415) 268-2300
235 Pine St., 19th Fl., San Francisco, CA 94104
E-mail: elizabeth_lucero@canb.uscourts.gov
Manager, San Jose Division **Roger White** . . . . (408) 535-5118
280 S. First St., Rm. 3035,
San Jose, CA 95113-3099
E-mail: roger_white@canb.uscourts.gov
Manager, Santa Rosa Division **Dennis Bilecki** . . . . (707) 525-8539
99 S."E" St., Santa Rosa, CA 95404
E-mail: dennis_bilecki@canb.uscourts.gov
Administrative Analyst, Web Design, and Content Coordinator **Wendy Kan** . . . . (415) 268-2300
E-mail: wendy_kan@canb.uscourts.gov

Chambers of Chief Bankruptcy Judge Roger L. Efremsky
1300 Clay Street, Suite 300, Oakland, CA 94612
Tel: (510) 879-3540
E-mail: roger_efremsky@canb.uscourts.gov

Roger L. Efremsky
Chief Bankruptcy Judge

Education: Menlo 1978 BS; Santa Clara U 1983 JD
Began Service: August 2006
Term Expires: August 2020

Staff
Career Law Clerk **Jane Fabian** . . . . (510) 879-3540
E-mail: jane_fabian@canb.uscourts.gov
Career Law Clerk **Shannon Mounger-Lum** . . . . (510) 879-3540
E-mail: shannon_mounger-lum@canb.uscourts.gov
Courtroom Deputy **Monica Burley** . . . . (510) 879-3540
E-mail: monica_burley@canb.uscourts.gov

Chambers of Bankruptcy Judge Alan Jaroslovsky

99 South East Street, Santa Rosa, CA 95404
Tel: (707) 547-5900 Fax: (707) 579-0374
E-mail: alan_jaroslovsky@canb.uscourts.gov

Alan Jaroslovsky
Bankruptcy Judge

Date of Birth: 1948
Education: UCLA 1970 BA; Golden Gate 1977 JD
Began Service: January 1, 1987
Term Expires: January 6, 2027

Staff
Law Clerk **Kara Kim** .... (707) 547-5900
Courtroom Deputy **Tara Arruda** .... (707) 547-5920
E-mail: tara_arruda@canb.uscourts.gov
Judicial Administrator **(Vacant)** .... (707) 547-5900

Chambers of Bankruptcy Judge Thomas E. Carlson

235 Pine Street, 19th Floor, San Francisco, CA 94104-7341
P.O. Box 7341, San Francisco, CA 94120-7341
Tel: (415) 268-2360 Fax: (415) 268-2363
E-mail: thomas_carlson@canb.uscourts.gov

Thomas E. Carlson
Bankruptcy Judge

Date of Birth: 1947
Education: Beloit 1969 BA; Harvard 1975 JD; NYU 1985 LLM
Began Service: September 23, 1985
Term Expires: September 22, 2028

Clerkships: Law Clerk The Honorable Thomas Roberts, Rhode Island Supreme Court (1975-1976); Law Clerk The Honorable Donald Wright, California Supreme Court (1976-1977)

Government: Deputy Staff Director, United States Court of Appeals for the Ninth Circuit (1978-1984); Consultant, Committee on the Judiciary, United States House of Representatives (1984)

Legal Practice: Associate, Cooper, White & Cooper LLP (1977-1978)

Current Memberships: National Conference of Bankruptcy Judges

Staff
Law Clerk **(Vacant)** .... (415) 268-2360
Courtroom Deputy **Gordon Hom** .... (415) 268-2362
E-mail: gordon_hom@canb.uscourts.gov
Judicial Assistant **Jane Galvani** .... (415) 268-2367
E-mail: jane_galvani@canb.uscourts.gov

Chambers of Bankruptcy Judge Arthur S. Weissbrodt

U.S. Courthouse, 280 South First Street, Room 3035,
San Jose, CA 95113-3099
Tel: (408) 278-7575
E-mail: arthur_weissbrodt@canb.uscourts.gov

Arthur S. Weissbrodt
Bankruptcy Judge

Education: Penn State 1966 BA; Columbia 1969 JD
Began Service: December 1989
Term Expires: December 2017

Government: Attorney, Bureau of Competition, Federal Trade Commission (1974-1978)

Staff
Career Law Clerk **Audrey Gervasi** .... (408) 278-7575
E-mail: audrey_gervasi@canb.uscourts.gov
Career Law Clerk **Kristi S. Gerrior** .... (408) 278-7575
E-mail: kristi_gerrior@canb.uscourts.gov
Career Law Clerk **Juliana Zolynas** .... (408) 278-7575
E-mail: juliana_zolynas@canb.uscourts.gov

Chambers of Bankruptcy Judge Arthur S. Weissbrodt *continued*

Courtroom Deputy **Brooke Esparza** .... (408) 278-7555

Chambers of Bankruptcy Judge Dennis Montali

235 Pine Street, 22nd Floor, San Francisco, CA 94104
P.O. Box 7341, San Francisco, CA 94120
Tel: (415) 268-2320
E-mail: dennis_montali@canb.uscourts.gov

Dennis Montali
Bankruptcy Judge

Date of Birth: 1940
Education: Notre Dame 1961 AB; Boalt Hall 1968 JD
Began Service: April 23, 1993
Term Expires: April 22, 2028

Legal Practice: Associate then Partner, Rothschild, Phelan, & Montali (1968-1980); Partner, Dinkelspiel, Pelavin, Steefel, and Levitt (1980); Partner, Pillsbury, Madison, & Sutro (1981-1993)

Military Service: United States Naval Reserve

Current Memberships: American Bar Association; American College of Bankruptcy; San Francisco Bar Association

Staff
Career Law Clerk **Peggy E. Brister** .... (415) 268-2320
E-mail: peggy_brister@canb.uscourts.gov
Education: Southern Methodist 1987 JD
Calendar Clerk and Courtroom Deputy **Lorena Parada** ... (415) 268-2323
E-mail: lorena_parada@canb.uscourts.gov
Judicial Assistant **Dorothy A. Timo** .... (415) 268-2320
E-mail: dorothy_timo@canb.uscourts.gov

Chambers of Bankruptcy Judge Charles Daniel Novack

1300 Clay Street, Suite 215, Oakland, CA 94612
Tel: (510) 879-3525
E-mail: charles_novack@canb.uscourts.gov

Charles Daniel Novack
Bankruptcy Judge

Education: Rutgers 1980 BA; Hastings 1983 JD
Began Service: 2010

Academic: Legal Writing and Research Instructor, University of California Hastings College of the Law (1990-1994)

Clerkships: Law Clerk, Chambers of Bankruptcy Judge Randall J. Newsome, United States District Court for the Northern District of California (1991-1993)

Legal Practice: Associate, Kornfield, Nyberg, Bendes & Kuhner, P.C.; Shareholder, Kornfield, Nyberg, Bendes & Kuhner, P.C.

Staff
Law Clerk **David Zubkis** .... (408) 278-7538
E-mail: david_zubkis@canb.uscourts.gov
Education: Brooklyn Law 2008 JD
Judicial Assistant **Dina Kakalia** .... (408) 278-7538
E-mail: dina_kakalia@canb.uscourts.gov
Courtroom Deputy **Ruby Bautista** .... (408) 278-7578

Chambers of Bankruptcy Judge Stephen L. Johnson

280 South First Street, Room 3035, San Jose, CA 95113
Tel: (408) 278-7515
E-mail: stephen_johnson@canb.uscourts.gov

Stephen L. Johnson
Bankruptcy Judge

Education: U San Francisco BS; Hastings JD
Began Service: 2010

Chambers of Bankruptcy Judge Stephen L. Johnson *continued*

Staff

Law Clerk **Laurent Chen** .... (408) 278-7515
E-mail: laurent_chen@canb.uscourts.gov
Education: UC Davis 1997 JD

Judicial Assistant **Anna E. Lee** .... (408) 278-7515

Courtroom Deputy **Tanya Bracegirdle** .... (408) 278-7556
E-mail: tanya_bracegirdle@canb.uscourts.gov

Chambers of Bankruptcy Judge William J. Lafferty

1300 Clay Street, Oakland, CA 94612
Tel: (510) 879-3530 Fax: (415) 268-2303
E-mail: william_lafferty@canb.uscourts.gov

William J. Lafferty
Bankruptcy Judge

Education: UC Berkeley 1978 BA; Hastings 1985 JD
Began Service: April 20, 2011

Clerkships: Law Clerk, Chambers of Bankruptcy Judge Thomas E. Carlson, United States Bankruptcy Court for the Northern District of California (1985-1987)

Legal Practice: Attorney, Howard Rice Nemerovski Canady Falk & Rabkin (1987-2011); Director, Bankruptcy and Reorganization, Howard Rice Nemerovski Canady Falk & Rabkin (1993-2011)

Staff

Law Clerk **Michael Maloney** .... (510) 879-3530
E-mail: michael_maloney@canb.uscourts.gov

Law Clerk **Sam Diamante** .... (510) 879-3530

Courtroom Deputy **Dianna Passadore** .... (510) 879-3530
E-mail: dianna_passadore@canb.uscourts.gov

Chambers of Bankruptcy Judge M. Elaine Hammond

280 South First Street, Room 3035, San Jose, CA 95113
Tel: (408) 278-7538

M. Elaine Hammond
Bankruptcy Judge

Education: Duke BA; North Carolina JD
Began Service: 2012
Term Expires: 2026

Staff

Law Clerk **Steven Nunes** .... (408) 278-7578
Began Service: September 2013
Term Expires: September 2016
E-mail: steven_nunes@canb.uscourts.gov
Education: UCLA 2009 BA;
Washington and Lee 2013 JD

Courtroom Deputy **Millie McGowan** .... (408) 278-7578
E-mail: millie_mcgowan@canb.uscourts.gov

Judicial Assistant **Raenna J. Rorabeck** .... (408) 278-7538
E-mail: raenna_rorabeck@canb.uscourts.gov

Chambers of Bankruptcy Judge Hannah Blumenstiel

235 Pine Street, 19th Floor, San Francisco, CA 94104
Tel: (415) 268-2455
E-mail: hannah_blumenstiel@canb.uscourts.gov

Hannah Blumenstiel
Bankruptcy Judge

Education: Ohio State 1992 BA; Capital U 1997 JD

Staff

Law Clerk **John C. Cannizzaro** .... (415) 268-2455
E-mail: john_cannizzaro@canb.uscourts.gov
Education: Capital U 2009 JD

Chambers of Bankruptcy Judge Hannah Blumenstiel *continued*

Law Clerk **Emily Keller** .... (415) 268-2455
E-mail: emily_keller@canb.uscourts.gov

Courtroom Deputy **Benjamin V. Gapuz** .... (415) 268-2362
E-mail: benjamin_gapuz@canb.uscourts.gov

United States District Court for the Southern District of California

333 West Broadway, Suite 420, San Diego, CA 92101
Tel: (619) 557-5600 Tel: (800) 676-6856 (PACER Information)
Tel: (619) 557-5176 (Juror Information Recording)
Tel: (800) 998-9035 (Toll Free Juror Information) Fax: (619) 702-9900
Internet: www.casd.uscourts.gov

Number of Judgeships: 13

Circuit: Ninth

Areas Covered: Counties of Imperial and San Diego

Court Staff

Clerk of Court (Acting) **John Morrill** .... (619) 557-6348
E-mail: john_morrill@casd.uscourts.gov

Secretary **Lisa Christensen** .... (619) 557-6348
E-mail: lisa_christensen@casd.uscourts.gov

Chief Deputy of Administration **Alan Counts** .... (619) 557-6738
E-mail: alan_counts@casd.uscourts.gov

Chief Deputy of Operations **(Vacant)** .... (619) 557-5083

Financial Supervisor **Mickey Ochoa** .... (619) 557-7347
E-mail: mickey_ochoa@casd.uscourts.gov

Jury Administrator **Irma Fletes** .... (619) 557-3750
E-mail: irma_fletes@casd.uscourts.gov

Human Resources Supervisor **Gary Balog** .... (619) 557-6152
E-mail: gary_balog@casd.uscourts.gov Fax: (619) 702-9911

Facilities/Procurement Supervisor **Richard Virgallito** .... (619) 557-7370
E-mail: richard_virgallito@casd.uscourts.gov

Pro Se Law Clerk - Civil Rights **Karen Beretsky** .... (619) 557-5693
E-mail: karen_beretsky@casd.uscourts.gov

Pro Se Law Clerk - Civil Rights **Susan Ravellette** .... (619) 557-7061
E-mail: susan_ravellette@casd.uscourts.gov

Pro Se Law Clerk - Habeas Corpus
Laura Allan-Dadmun .... (619) 557-3426
E-mail: laura_allan-dadmun@casd.uscourts.gov

Pro Se Law Clerk - Habeas Corpus **Karen Gallagher** .... (619) 446-3721
E-mail: karen_gallagher@casd.uscourts.gov

Pro Se Law Clerk - Habeas Corpus **Will Stansfield** .... (619) 557-5346
E-mail: william_stansfield@casd.uscourts.gov

Pro Se Law Clerk - Habeas Corpus **Monica Sullivan** .... (619) 446-3993
E-mail: monica_sullivan@casd.uscourts.gov
Education: San Diego 2003 JD

Pro Se Law Clerk - Death Penalty [Death Penalty]
Jessica Harry .... (619) 557-6631
E-mail: jessica_harry@casd.uscourts.gov

Manager of Interpreter Services **Rebeca Calderon** .... (619) 557-5205
E-mail: rebeca_calderon@casd.uscourts.gov Fax: (619) 702-9998

Chief Pretrial Services Officer **Lori A. Garofalo** .... (619) 557-7610
101 W. Broadway, Ste. 505, San Diego, CA 92243 Fax: (619) 557-6729

Deputy Chief Pretrial Services Officer **Sean Keohane** .... (619) 557-7206
101 W. Broadway, Ste. 505, San Diego, CA 92243 Fax: (619) 557-6729

Chief Probation Officer **David J. Sultzbaugh** .... (619) 557-6617
101 West Broadway, Suite 700, Fax: (619) 615-6017
San Diego, CA 92101-7991

Deputy Chief Probation Officer **Trisha K. Yamauchi** .... (619) 557-6487
101 West Broadway, Suite 700, Fax: (619) 615-6095
San Diego, CA 92101

Court Librarian **Valerie Railey** .... (619) 557-5066
Fax: (619) 557-5077

Chambers of Chief Judge Barry Ted Moskowitz

333 West Broadway, Suite 1580, San Diego, CA 92101
Tel: (619) 557-5583 Fax: (619) 702-9966

Barry Ted Moskowitz
Chief Judge

Date of Birth: 1950
Education: Rutgers 1972 BA; Rutgers (Newark) 1975 JD
Began Service: January 2, 1996
Appointed By: President William J. Clinton

Staff

Law Clerk **Edwin Howell** .... (619) 557-5583
Began Service: 2015
Term Expires: September 2016
E-mail: edwin_howell@casd.uscourts.gov
Administrative Law Clerk **Jenny Y. Williams** .... (619) 557-5583
E-mail: jenny_williams@casd.uscourts.gov
Courtroom Deputy **Richard "Rick" Messig** .... (619) 557-5492
E-mail: richard_messig@casd.uscourts.gov
Career Law Clerk **Christine Yoon Friedman** .... (619) 557-5583
E-mail: christine_friedman@casd.uscourts.gov
Education: Haverford 1993 BA; Michigan 1996 JD
Judicial Assistant **Veronica Trujillo** .... (619) 557-5583
E-mail: veronica_trujillo@casd.uscourts.gov

Chambers of District Judge Marilyn L. Huff

Edward J. Schwartz United States Courthouse, 940 Front Street, Suite 5135, San Diego, CA 92101-8913
Tel: (619) 557-6016 Fax: (619) 702-9922

Marilyn L. Huff
District Judge

Date of Birth: 1951
Education: Calvin Col 1972 BA; Michigan 1976 JD
Began Service: May 14, 1991
Appointed By: President George H.W. Bush

Judicial: Chief Judge, United States District Court for the Southern District of California (1998-2004); President, American Inns of Court, Lewis M. Welsh Chapter; Chairperson, Judicial Conference Statistics Subcommittee; Member, Judicial Conference Judicial Resources Committee

Legal Practice: Associate, Gray, Cary, Ames & Frye (1976-1983); Partner, Gray, Cary, Ames & Frye (1983-1991)

Current Memberships: American Bar Association; American Board of Trial Advocates; The Louis M. Welsh American Inn of Court, The American Inns of Court; California Women Lawyers Bar Association; Lawyers Club of San Diego; San Diego Bar Foundation; State Bar of California

Staff

Courtroom Deputy **Steven Yaptangco** .... (619) 557-6418
E-mail: steven_yaptangco@casd.uscourts.gov
Court Recorder **Lynnette Lawrence** .... (619) 557-5002
E-mail: lynnette_lawrence@casd.uscourts.gov

Chambers of District Judge Larry Alan Burns

James M. Carter and Judith N. Keep US Courthouse, 333 West Broadway, Suite 1410, San Diego, CA 92101
Tel: (619) 557-5874 Fax: (619) 702-9936

Larry Alan Burns
District Judge

Date of Birth: 1954
Education: Point Loma 1976 BA; San Diego 1979 JD
Began Service: September 29, 2003
Appointed By: President George W. Bush
Political Affiliation: Republican

Academic: Instructor, San Diego State University (1988-1996); Director, Bank of Commerce (1994-1997)

Government: Deputy District Attorney, Office of the District Attorney, County of San Diego, California (1979-1985); Assistant United States Attorney, Southern District of California, United States Attorney's Office, United States Department of Justice, Ronald Reagan Administration (1985-1997)

Judicial: Magistrate Judge, United States District Court for the Southern District of California (1997-2003)

Current Memberships: American Board of Trial Advocates; American College of Trial Lawyers

Staff

Law Clerk **John Burns** .... (619) 557-5874
E-mail: john_burns@casd.uscourts.gov
Career Law Clerk **Mark D. Myers** .... (619) 557-5874
E-mail: mark_d_myers@casd.uscourts.gov
Courtroom Deputy **Tisha Weisbeck** .... (619) 557-6038
E-mail: tisha_weisbeck@casd.uscourts.gov
Court Reporter **Debbie Henson** .... (619) 615-3103
E-mail: debbie_henson@casd.uscourts.gov
Judicial Assistant **Roseanna L. Stovall** .... (619) 557-5874
E-mail: Roseanna_Stovall@casd.uscourts.gov

Chambers of District Judge Dana M. Sabraw

James M. Carter and Judith N. Keep US Courthouse, 333 West Broadway, Suite 1310, San Diego, CA 92101
Tel: (619) 557-6262 Fax: (619) 702-9942
E-mail: dana_sabraw@casd.uscourts.gov

Dana M. Sabraw
District Judge

Date of Birth: July 3, 1958
Education: San Diego State 1980 BA; McGeorge 1985 JD
Began Service: September 29, 2003
Appointed By: President George W. Bush

Legal Practice: Associate, Price Postel & Parma, LLP (1985-1989); Associate, Baker & McKenzie (1989-1992); Partner, Baker & McKenzie (1992-1999)

Staff

Career Law Clerk **Moana McMullan** .... (619) 557-6262
E-mail: moana_mcmullan@casd.uscourts.gov
Career Law Clerk **Marjeta D. Six** .... (619) 557-6262
E-mail: marjeta_six@casd.uscourts.gov
Education: San Diego State 1990 BA; San Diego 1994 JD
Courtroom Deputy **Jamie Klosterman** .... (619) 557-6399
E-mail: jamie_klosterman@casd.uscourts.gov
Court Reporter **Lee Ann Pence** .... (619) 977-7653
E-mail: leeann_pence@casd.uscourts.gov
Secretary **Isabel Smith** .... (619) 557-6262
E-mail: isabel_smith@casd.uscourts.gov

Chambers of District Judge William Q. Hayes
940 Front Street, 4th Floor, Suite 4135, San Diego, CA 92101
Tel: (619) 557-6420

William Q. Hayes
District Judge

Date of Birth: 1956
Education: Syracuse 1979 BS, 1983 JD, 1983 MBA
Began Service: October 8, 2003
Appointed By: President George W. Bush

Government: Assistant U.S. Attorney, Southern District of California, U.S. Attorney's Office, United States Department of Justice (1987-2003); Chief, Criminal Division, U.S. Attorney's Office, United States Department of Justice (1999-2003)

Legal Practice: Associate, Scheid & Horlbeck (1983-1984); Associate, Stone and Associates (1984-1986)

Staff
Administrative Law Clerk **Patricia Wlodarczyk** .... (619) 557-7311
E-mail: patricia_wlodarczyk@casd.uscourts.gov
Courtroom Deputy **Suzie Rogers** .... (619) 557-7360
Court Reporter **Melinda Fetterman** .... (619) 236-0368

Chambers of District Judge John A. Houston
James M. Carter and Judith N. Keep US Courthouse, 333 West Broadway, Suite 1380, San Diego, CA 92101
Tel: (619) 557-5716 Fax: (619) 702-9920
E-mail: john_houston@casd.uscourts.gov

John A. Houston
District Judge

Date of Birth: 1952
Education: Miami 1977 JD
Began Service: October 9, 2003
Appointed By: President George W. Bush

Government: Assistant United States Attorney, Southern District of California, United States Attorney's Office, United States Department of Justice, Ronald Reagan Administration (1981-1998)

Judicial: Magistrate Judge, United States District Court (1998-2003)

Military Service: United States Army (1978-1981)

Staff
Law Clerk **David Middleton** .... (619) 557-5716
Began Service: September 2015
Term Expires: September 2016
E-mail: david_middleton@casd.uscourts.gov
Career Law Clerk **Laura Bostwick** .... (619) 557-5716
E-mail: laura_bostwick@casd.uscourts.gov
Education: Thomas Jefferson 1998 JD
Career Law Clerk **Tara Velez** .... (619) 557-5716
E-mail: tara_velez@casd.uscourts.gov
Education: Cal Western 1996 JD
Courtroom Deputy **Larry McDowell** .... (619) 557-6424
E-mail: larry_mcdowell@casd.uscourts.gov
Court Reporter **Cami Kircher** .... (619) 239-4588

Chambers of District Judge Roger T. Benitez
221 West Broadway, 4th Floor, San Diego, CA 92101-8909
Tel: (619) 446-3589 Fax: (619) 702-9918
E-mail: roger_benitez@casd.uscourts.gov

Roger T. Benitez
District Judge

Began Service: June 2004
Appointed By: President George W. Bush

Judicial: Superior Court Judge, Imperial County (1997-2001); Magistrate Judge, United States District Court for the Southern District of California (2001-2004)

Staff
Law Clerk **Hannah Newkirk** .... (619) 446-3589
Began Service: 2013
Term Expires: 2016
E-mail: hannah_newkirk@casd.uscourts.gov
Administrative Law Clerk **Robert J. Newmeyer** .... (619) 446-3589
E-mail: robert_newmeyer@casd.uscourts.gov
Education: Oral Roberts 1981 ALB;
Regent U 1986 Dr Jur
Courtroom Deputy **Glenn Rivera** .... (619) 557-6422
E-mail: glenn_rivera@casd.uscourts.gov
Court Reporter **Debbie O'Connell** .... (619) 732-1075

Chambers of District Judge Janis L. Sammartino
333 West Broadway, Suite 420, San Diego, CA 92101
Tel: (619) 557-5542

Janis L. Sammartino
District Judge

Education: Occidental 1972 AB; Notre Dame 1975 JD
Began Service: September 21, 2007
Appointed By: President George W. Bush

Clerkships: Deputy City Attorney, Office of the City Attorney, City of San Diego, California (1976-1994)

Judicial: Municipal Court Judge, City of San Diego, California (1994-1995); Superior Court Judge, County of San Diego, California (1995-2008)

Staff
Administrative Law Clerk **Marcia Hartshorne** .... (619) 557-5542
E-mail: marcia_hartshorne@casd.uscourts.gov
Education: Arizona 1990 JD
Courtroom Deputy **Alex Ramos** .... (619) 557-5291
E-mail: alex_ramos@casd.uscourts.gov
Court Reporter **Gayle Wakefield** .... (619) 239-0652
E-mail: gayle_wakefield@casd.uscourts.gov

Chambers of District Judge Michael M. Anello
221 West Broadway, Suite 3130, San Diego, CA 92101-8909
Tel: (619) 557-5960
E-mail: michael_anello@casd.uscourts.gov

Michael M. Anello
District Judge

Education: Bowdoin 1965 BA; Georgetown 1968 JD
Began Service: October 10, 2008
Appointed By: President George W. Bush

Government: Deputy City Attorney, Office of the City Attorney, City of San Diego, California (1972-1973)

Legal Practice: Associate, Todd, Toothacre & Wingert (1973-1974); Partner, Wingert, Grebing, Anello & Brubaker (1974-1998)

Staff
Career Law Clerk **Anne Kammer** .... (619) 557-5960
E-mail: anne_kammer@casd.uscourts.gov

(continued on next page)

Chambers of District Judge Michael M. Anello *continued*

Courtroom Deputy **Patricia Dela Cruz** .... (619) 557-2921
E-mail: patricia_delacruz@casd.uscourts.gov
Court Reporter **Elizabeth Cesena** .... (619) 237-0100
E-mail: elizabeth_cesena@casd.uscourts.gov

Chambers of District Judge Anthony J. Battaglia

221 West Broadway, Courtroom 2A, San Diego, CA 92101-8909
Tel: (619) 557-3446 Fax: (619) 702-9988

Anthony J. Battaglia
District Judge

Date of Birth: 1949
Education: US International U 1971 BA; Cal Western 1974 JD
Began Service: March 10, 2011
Appointed By: President Barack Obama

Judicial: Magistrate Judge, Chambers of Magistrate Judge Anthony J. Battaglia, United States District Court for the Southern District of California (1993-2011)

Legal Practice: Sole Proprietor, Anthony J. Battaglia, A Professional Corporation (1981-1991); Partner, Battaglia, Fitzpatrick & Battaglia (1991-1993)

Current Memberships: American Bar Association; Federal Bar Association; Federal Magistrate Judges Association; San Diego County Bar Association; San Diego County Judges Association

Staff

Law Clerk **Erika Oliver** .... (619) 557-3446
Began Service: September 2015
Term Expires: September 2016
E-mail: erika_oliver@casd.uscourts.gov
Law Clerk **Allexanderia Verdian** .... (619) 557-3446
Began Service: September 2014
Term Expires: September 2016
E-mail: allexanderia_verdian@casd.uscourts.gov
Courtroom Deputy **Yolanda Madueno** .... (619) 557-6423
Secretary **Susan Chilton** .... (619) 557-3446

Chambers of District Judge Cathy Ann Bencivengo

333 West Broadway, Suite 420, San Diego, CA 92101
Tel: (619) 557-5600 Fax: (619) 702-9900

Cathy Ann Bencivengo
District Judge

Education: Rutgers 1980 BA, 1981 MA; Michigan 1988 JD
Began Service: 2012
Appointed By: President Barack Obama

Legal Practice: Litigation Associate, Gray, Cary, Ames & Frye (1988-1996); Partner, DLA Piper (1996-2005)

Staff

Courtroom Deputy **Lori Hernandez** .... (619) 557-6901
E-mail: lori_hernandez@casd.uscourts.gov
Court Reporter **Mauralee Ramirez** .... (619) 994-2526
E-mail: mauralee_ramirez@casd.uscourts.gov

Chambers of District Judge Gonzalo P. Curiel

221 West Broadway, Suite 2190, San Diego, CA 92101
Tel: (619) 557-5600 Fax: (619) 702-9900
E-mail: gonzalo_curiel@casd.uscourts.gov

Gonzalo P. Curiel
District Judge

Education: Indiana 1976 JD, 1979 JD
Began Service: 2012
Appointed By: President Barack Obama

Chambers of District Judge Gonzalo P. Curiel *continued*

Staff

Courtroom Deputy **Lynn Fuchigami** .... (619) 557-5539
E-mail: lynn_fuchigami@casd.uscourts.gov

Chambers of District Judge Cynthia Ann Bashant

221 West Broadway, Suite 4145, San Diego, CA 92101-8900
Tel: (619) 321-0256
E-mail: cynthia_bashant@casd.uscourts.gov

Cynthia Ann Bashant
District Judge

Education: Smith 1982 AB; Hastings 1986 JD
Began Service: May 8, 2014
Appointed By: President Barack Obama

Government: Assistant U.S. Attorney, California - Southern District, Executive Office for United States Attorneys, United States Department of Justice (1989-2000)

Legal Practice: Associate, Macdonald Halsted & Laybourne (1986-1988); Associate, Baker & McKenzie (1988-1989)

Staff

Courtroom Deputy **Stephanie Michele** .... (619) 321-0256
E-mail: stephanie_michele@casd.uscourts.gov

Chambers of Senior Judge William B. Enright

221 West Broadway, Suite 5195, San Diego, CA 92101-8976
Tel: (619) 557-5537 Fax: (619) 702-9934

William B. Enright
Senior Judge

Date of Birth: July 12, 1925
Education: Dartmouth 1947 BA; Loyola Marymount 1950 LLB
Began Service: July 14, 1972
Appointed By: President Richard M. Nixon

Government: Deputy District Attorney, Office of the District Attorney, County of San Diego, California (1951-1954)

Legal Practice: Harelson, Enright, Levitt & Knutson (1954-1972)

Staff

Career Law Clerk **Karen S. Hughes** .... (619) 557-5537
E-mail: karen_hughes@casd.uscourts.gov
Education: UCLA BA; Hastings 1989 JD

Chambers of Senior Judge Jeffrey T. Miller

U.S. Courthouse, 940 Front Street, 5th Floor, Suite 5190, San Diego, CA 92101-8906
Tel: (619) 557-6627 Fax: (619) 702-9986
E-mail: jeffrey_miller@casd.uscourts.gov

Jeffrey T. Miller
Senior Judge

Date of Birth: 1943
Education: UCLA 1964 BA, 1967 JD
Began Service: May 1997
Appointed By: President William J. Clinton

Government: Deputy Attorney General, State of California (1968-1973); Supervising Deputy Attorney General, State of California (1974-1987)

Judicial: Judge, California Superior Court, County of San Diego (1987-1997)

Current Memberships: The American Inns of Court; The Honorable William B. Enright American Inn of Court, The American Inns of Court; California Judges Association; Ninth Circuit District Judges Association; United States Supreme Court Bar

Chambers of Senior Judge Jeffrey T. Miller *continued*

Staff

Law Clerk **Arevik Stepanyan** . . . . (619) 557-6627
Began Service: August 2015
Term Expires: September 2016
E-mail: arevik_stepanyan@casd.uscourts.gov

Career Law Clerk **Randy Rein** . . . . (619) 557-6627
E-mail: randy_rein@casd.uscourts.gov
Education: U Washington 1975 BS;
Seattle 1990 JD; San Diego 1995 LLM

Court Clerk **Gabriela Cazares** . . . . (619) 557-7439
E-mail: gabriela_cazares@casd.uscourts.gov

Court Reporter **(Vacant)** . . . . (619) 238-4538

Judicial Assistant **Kathleen Walford** . . . . (619) 557-6627
E-mail: kathleen_walford@casd.uscourts.gov

Chambers of Senior Judge Thomas J. Whelan

U.S. Courthouse, 940 Front Street, 3rd Floor, Suite 3155,
San Diego, CA 92101
Tel: (619) 557-6625

Thomas J. Whelan
Senior Judge

Date of Birth: 1940
Education: San Diego 1961 BBA, 1965 JD
Began Service: November 5, 1998
Appointed By: President William J. Clinton

Academic: Planner/Estimator, Engineering Department, Convair Division, General Dynamics Corporation (1961-1965); Contracts Administrator, New Product Development, Customer Service Department, Convair Division, General Dynamics Corporation (1965-1969)

Government: Deputy District Attorney, County of San Diego, California (1969-1989)

Judicial: Judge, Superior Court of California, County of San Diego (1990-1997); Presiding Judge, Superior Court of California, County of San Diego (1998); Board of Governors, Association of Business Trial Lawyers (2002-2004)

Current Memberships: The Honorable William B. Enright American Inn of Court, The American Inns of Court; Association of Business Trial Lawyers; California Judges Association; Federal Judges Association

Staff

Law Clerk **Daniel Covarrubias-Klein** . . . . (619) 557-6625
Began Service: October 2014
Term Expires: October 2016

Career Law Clerk **Steven Uribe** . . . . (619) 557-6625
Education: Columbia 1995 JD

Courtroom Deputy **Bernadette Borja** . . . . (619) 557-6417
E-mail: bernadette_borja@casd.uscourts.gov

Court Reporter **(Vacant)** . . . . (619) 702-7508

Judicial Assistant **Rosie Cerda** . . . . (619) 557-6625
E-mail: rosie_cerda@casd.uscourts.gov

Chambers of Senior Judge M. James Lorenz

U.S. Courthouse, 940 Front Street, 5th Floor, Room 5145,
San Diego, CA 92101-8911
Tel: (619) 557-7669 Fax: (619) 702-9944

M. James Lorenz
Senior Judge

Date of Birth: 1935
Education: UC Berkeley 1957 BA;
Cal Western 1965 JD
Began Service: October 5, 1999
Appointed By: President William J. Clinton

Government: Deputy District Attorney, Office of the District Attorney, County of San Diego, California (1966-1978); First Assistant United States Attorney, California - Southern District, Office of the Attorney General, United States Department of Justice (1978-1979); United States Attorney, California - Southern District, Office of the Attorney General, United States Department of Justice (1980-1981)

Legal Practice: Partner, Lorenz Alhadeff Fellmeth Arkin & Multer (1982); Partner, Finley, Kumble, Wagner, Heine, Underberg & Casey (1983-1987); Founding Partner, Lorenz Alhadeff Cannon & Rose, LLP (1988-1999)

Military Service: United States Marine Corps (1957-1960)

Current Memberships: Federal Judges Association; National Association of Former United States Attorneys; Ninth Circuit District Judges Association; San Diego County Bar Association; State Bar of California

Staff

Law Clerk **Benjamin White** . . . . (619) 557-7669
Term Expires: November 2015
E-mail: benjamin_white@casd.uscourts.gov

Career Law Clerk **Rosemary Thomas** . . . . (619) 557-7669
Education: Indiana 1990 JD

Administrative Law Clerk **DaMarr Boyd** . . . . (619) 557-7669
E-mail: damarr_boyd@casd.uscourts.gov

Courtroom Deputy **Stephanie Michele** . . . . (619) 557-6414
E-mail: stephanie_michele@casd.uscourts.gov

Chambers of Presiding Magistrate Judge Nita L. Stormes

U.S. Courthouse, 940 Front Street, 1st Floor, Room 1101,
San Diego, CA 92101-8910
Tel: (619) 557-5391

Nita L. Stormes
Presiding Magistrate Judge

Date of Birth: 1954
Education: Duke 1979 JD
Began Service: January 2000
Term Expires: January 2016

Government: Assistant United States Attorney, Southern District of California, United States Attorney's Office, United States Department of Justice (1983-1999)

Staff

Law Clerk **Mylimh Arnett** . . . . (619) 557-5391

Career Law Clerk **Elizabeth Pietanza** . . . . (619) 557-5391
E-mail: elizabeth_pietanza@casd.uscourts.gov

Courtroom Deputy **George Perrault** . . . . (619) 557-7749
E-mail: george_perrault@casd.uscourts.gov

Career Law Clerk **Christine Semmer** . . . . (619) 557-5391

FEDERAL COURTS—UNITED STATES DISTRICT COURTS

Chambers of Magistrate Judge Ruben B. Brooks

1185 U.S. Courthouse, 940 Front Street, 1st Floor, San Diego, CA 92101
Tel: (619) 557-3404 Fax: (619) 702-9940

Ruben B. Brooks
Magistrate Judge

Education: Yale 1974 JD
Began Service: September 2, 1993
Term Expires: September 1, 2017

Staff
Courtroom Deputy **Vicky Lee** .... (619) 557-7143
E-mail: vicky_lee@casd.uscourts.gov
Secretary **Marcia Garcia** .... (619) 557-3404
E-mail: marcia_garcia@casd.uscourts.gov

Chambers of Magistrate Judge Jan M. Adler

Edward J. Schwartz U.S. Courthouse, 221 West Broadway, Suite 2140, San Diego, CA 92101-8909
Tel: (619) 557-5585 Fax: (619) 702-9939
E-mail: Jan_Adler@casd.uscourts.gov

Jan M. Adler
Magistrate Judge

Date of Birth: May 17, 1953
Education: Cornell 1975 AB; Duke 1978 JD
Began Service: July 8, 2003
Term Expires: July 7, 2018

Academic: Instructor, Maricopa County Bar Association High School Teaching Project (1980-1981); Alumni of San Diego President, School of Law, Duke University (1990-2003)

Legal Practice: Jennings, Strouss & Salmon, P.L.C. (1978-1982); Associate, Milberg Weiss Bershad Hynes & Lerach LLP (1982-1986); Partner, Milberg Weiss Bershad Hynes & Lerach LLP (1987-2003)

Membership: Member, Board of Directors, San Diego Volunteer Lawyer Program (1995-2006)

Staff
Career Law Clerk **Kelly Becker** .... (619) 557-5585
Began Service: 2009
E-mail: kelly_becker@casd.uscourts.gov
Education: Cal Western 1997 JD
Career Law Clerk **Christine Cotner** .... (619) 557-5585
E-mail: Christine_Cotner@casd.uscourts.gov
Education: UC San Diego 1994 BA; San Diego 1999 JD
Courtroom Deputy **Rhea Andrews** .... (619) 557-6412
E-mail: rhea_andrews@casd.uscourts.gov

Chambers of Magistrate Judge Barbara L. Major

333 West Broadway, 11th Floor, Suite 1110, San Diego, CA 92101
Tel: (619) 557-7372
E-mail: barbara_major@casd.uscourts.gov

Barbara L. Major
Magistrate Judge

Education: Stanford BA; UC Berkeley JD
Began Service: January 2004

Government: Major Fraud Deputy Chief, Criminal Division, California - Southern District, Department of Justice

Staff
Courtroom Deputy **Michelle Behning** .... (619) 557-7099
E-mail: michelle_behning@casd.uscourts.gov

Chambers of Magistrate Judge Peter C. Lewis

2003 West Adams Avenue, Suite 220, El Centro, CA 92243
Tel: (760) 339-4248

Peter C. Lewis
Magistrate Judge

Education: Cal Western 1978 JD
Began Service: June 28, 2004
Term Expires: June 28, 2020

Staff
Courtroom Deputy **Erika Flores** .... (760) 339-4248
E-mail: erika_flores@casd.uscourts.gov

Chambers of Magistrate Judge William V. Gallo

221 West Broadway, San Diego, CA 92101-8909
Tel: (619) 557-6384

William V. Gallo
Magistrate Judge

Began Service: October 15, 2009

Staff
Career Law Clerk **Mark Schwartz** .... (619) 557-5600
E-mail: mark_schwartz@casd.uscourts.gov
Education: San Diego 1985 JD
Courtroom Deputy **(Vacant)** .... (619) 557-7141

Chambers of Magistrate Judge Bernard G. Skomal

James M. Carter and Judith N. Keep US Courthouse, 333 West Broadway, Suite 1280, San Diego, CA 92101-8900
Tel: (619) 557-2993

Bernard G. Skomal
Magistrate Judge

Education: Col Holy Cross; Suffolk 1983 JD
Began Service: 2010

Staff
Courtroom Deputy **Trish Lopez** .... (619) 557-7104
E-mail: trish_lopez@casd.uscourts.gov
Career Law Clerk **Alexa Zanolli** .... (619) 557-2993
E-mail: alexa_zanolli@casd.uscourts.gov

Chambers of Magistrate Judge David H. Bartick

U.S. Courthouse, 221 West Broadway, Suite 5140, San Diego, CA 92101-8909
Tel: (619) 557-5383 Fax: (619) 702-9925

David H. Bartick
Magistrate Judge

Began Service: April 2, 2012

Staff
Law Clerk **Matthew Riley** .... (619) 557-5383
E-mail: matthew_riley@casd.uscourts.gov
Career Law Clerk **W. Damarr Boyd** .... (619) 557-5383
Courtroom Deputy **Angela Everill** .... (619) 557-6695
E-mail: angela_everill@casd.uscourts.gov

Chambers of Magistrate Judge Karen S. Crawford
221 West Broadway, 10th Floor, Suite 1010, San Diego, CA 92101-8900
Tel: (619) 446-3964

Karen Shichman Crawford
Magistrate Judge

Education: Boston U 1977 BA; Cal Western 1980 JD

Staff
Courtroom Deputy **Jennifer Rocha** .... (619) 446-3964
E-mail: jennifer_rocha@casd.uscourts.gov

Chambers of Magistrate Judge Mitchell D. Dembin
221 West Broadway, San Diego, CA 92101-8900
Tel: (619) 446-3972

Mitchell D. Dembin
Magistrate Judge

Staff
Courtroom Deputy **Marisa Zvers** .... (619) 446-3972
E-mail: marisa_zvers@casd.uscourts.gov

Chambers of Magistrate Judge Jill L. Burkhardt
221 West Broadway, Suite 5140, San Diego, CA 92101-8900
Tel: (619) 557-6425

Jill L. Burkhardt
Magistrate Judge

Began Service: 2014
Term Expires: 2022

United States Bankruptcy Court for the Southern District of California
Jacob W. Weinberger U.S. Courthouse, 325 West F Street,
San Diego, CA 92101-6991
Tel: (619) 557-5620 Tel: (210) 301-6440 (PACER)
Tel: (800) 676-6856 (Toll Free PACER)
Tel: (866) 222-8029 (Voice Case Information System VCIS)
Fax: (619) 557-5536
Internet: www.casb.uscourts.gov

Number of Judgeships: 4

Court Staff
Bankruptcy Clerk **Barry K. Lander** .... (619) 557-6582
E-mail: barry_lander@casb.uscourts.gov Fax: (619) 557-2646
Education: Cal State (Los Angeles) 1977 BA; USC 1979 MPA
Executive Assistant to the Clerk of Court **Toni Aron** ..... (619) 557-6582
E-mail: toni_aron@casb.uscourts.gov Fax: (619) 557-2646
Chief Deputy Clerk **David M. Grube** .... (619) 557-6428
Education: U Redlands 1984 BA; USC 1986 MS Fax: (619) 557-2646
Executive Assistant to the Chief Deputy Clerk **(Vacant)** .... (619) 557-6428
Fax: (619) 557-2646
Court Reporter **Nancy Wingis** .... (858) 775-0283
P.O. Box 496, Solana Beach, CA 92075
E-mail: nancy.wingis@mindspring.com
Financial Administrator **Russ Reynolds** .... (619) 557-6213
E-mail: russ_reynolds@casb.uscourts.gov Fax: (619) 557-5903
Education: USC 1982 BS
Budget Administrator **Daniel Wiebel** .... (619) 557-5274
E-mail: dan_wiebel@casb.uscourts.gov Fax: (619) 557-5903
Information Systems Manager **Russ Reynolds** .... (619) 557-6213
E-mail: russ_reynolds@casb.uscourts.gov Fax: (619) 557-5903
Human Resources and Training Manager **Kathy Noel** .... (619) 557-5771
E-mail: kathy_noel@casb.uscourts.gov Fax: (619) 557-5536
Public Services Supervisor **Audria Hakow** .... (619) 557-5111
E-mail: audria_hakow@casb.uscourts.gov Fax: (619) 557-5536

Chambers of Chief Bankruptcy Judge Laura S. Taylor
Jacob W. Weinberger U.S. Courthouse, 325 West F Street,
Room 129, San Diego, CA 92101-6991
Tel: (619) 557-6580
E-mail: laura_taylor@casb.uscourts.gov

Laura S. Taylor
Chief Bankruptcy Judge

Education: North Carolina 1979 BA; Duke 1983 JD
Began Service: January 2008
Term Expires: January 2022

Staff
Law Clerk **Linda Fox** .... (619) 557-3455
E-mail: linda_fox@casb.uscourts.gov
Law Clerk **Corina Pandeli** .... (619) 557-2657
Courtroom Deputy **Shawna Dahl** .... (619) 557-6018
E-mail: shawna_dahl@casb.uscourts.gov
Judicial Assistant **Regina Fabre** .... (619) 557-7554
E-mail: regina_fabre@casb.uscourts.gov

Chambers of Bankruptcy Judge Louise DeCarl Adler
Jacob W. Weinberger U.S. Courthouse, 325 West F Street,
San Diego, CA 92101
Tel: (619) 557-5661 Fax: (619) 557-6975
E-mail: louise_adler@casb.uscourts.gov

Louise DeCarl Adler
Bankruptcy Judge

Date of Birth: 1945
Education: Chatham 1966 BA; Loyola U (Chicago) 1970 JD
Began Service: March 5, 1984
Term Expires: January 1, 2029

Government: Standing Trustee in Bankruptcy, United States Bankruptcy Court for the Southern District of California (1974-1979)

Current Memberships: American Bankruptcy Institute; American College of Bankruptcy; INSOL International; National Conference of Bankruptcy Judges; San Diego Bankruptcy Forum; San Diego County Bar Association

Staff
Career Law Clerk **Jeanne Bender** .... (619) 557-5623
E-mail: jeanne_bender@casb.uscourts.gov
Education: Cal Western 1992 JD
Judicial Assistant **Roma London** .... (619) 557-5661
E-mail: roma_london@casb.uscourts.gov
Courtroom Deputy **Karen Fearce** .... (619) 557-6594
E-mail: karen_fearce@casb.uscourts.gov

Chambers of Bankruptcy Judge Margaret M. Mann
325 West F Street, San Diego, CA 92101
Tel: (619) 557-5848 Fax: (619) 557-7026
E-mail: margaret_mann@casb.uscourts.gov

Margaret M. Mann
Bankruptcy Judge

Education: Illinois 1978 BA; USC 1981 JD
Began Service: April 2010

Legal Practice: Firmwide Chair, Hiring Committee, Heller Ehrman LLP; Chair, Restructuring and Insolvency, Heller Ehrman LLP; Shareholder, Heller Ehrman LLP (2003-2008); Partner, Sheppard, Mullin, Richter & Hampton LLP (2008-2010)

Staff
Judicial Assistant **Michele McConnell** .... (619) 557-7560
E-mail: michele_mcconnell@casb.uscourts.gov

(continued on next page)

Chambers of Bankruptcy Judge Margaret M. Mann *continued*

Career Law Clerk **Megan Seliber** .... (619) 557-6692
E-mail: megan_seliber@casb.uscourts.gov
Education: Clemson 2005 BA;
Washington and Lee 2008 JD

Chambers of Bankruptcy Judge Christopher B. Latham

325 West F Street, Room 318, San Diego, CA 92101-6991
Tel: (619) 557-7570

Christopher B. Latham
Bankruptcy Judge

Staff

Law Clerk **Brian Hayag** .... (619) 557-7422
Law Clerk **Daniel Nadal** .... (619) 557-7419
Courtroom Deputy **Jillmarie McGrew** .... (619) 557-6019

United States District Court for the District of Colorado

Alfred A. Arraj U.S. Courthouse, 901 19th Street, Denver, CO 80294
Tel: (303) 844-3433 Tel: (303) 844-3454 (PACER)
Internet: www.cod.uscourts.gov

Number of Judgeships: 7

Circuit: Tenth

Court Staff

Clerk of the Court **Col Jeffrey P. Colwell** .... (303) 844-3433
Affiliation: USMC
Chief Deputy Clerk **Terrance Sheahan** .... (303) 844-3433
Chief Probation Officer **Lavetra S. Castles** .... (303) 844-5424
1929 Stout St., Denver, CO 80294
Chief Deputy Probation Officer **Elizabeth Miller** .... (303) 844-5424
1929 Stout Street, Denver, CO 80294
Director of Information Technology **Diann Duino** .... (303) 335-2322
E-mail: diann_duino@cod.uscourts.gov
Financial Administrator **Thomas O'Malley** .... (303) 335-2244
Fax: (303) 335-2240
Human Resources Administrator **Ronna Duncan** .... (303) 335-2494
1929 Stout Street, Suite C102, Denver, CO 80294 Fax: (303) 335-2495
E-mail: ronna_duncan@cod.uscourts.gov

Chambers of Chief Judge Marcia S. Krieger

Alfred A. Arraj U.S. Courthouse, 901 19th Street, Room A-105,
Denver, CO 80294
Tel: (303) 335-2289
E-mail: marcia_krieger@cod.uscourts.gov

Marcia S. Krieger
Chief Judge

Date of Birth: 1954
Education: Lewis & Clark 1975 BA; Colorado 1979 JD
Began Service: March 1, 2002
Appointed By: President George W. Bush

Staff

Career Law Clerk **Brian J. Bergevin** .... (303) 335-2289
E-mail: brian_bergevin@cod.uscourts.gov
Education: Albany Law 1994 JD
Judicial Assistant **Janine Aguero** .... (303) 844-3433
E-mail: janine_aguero@cod.uscourts.gov

Chambers of District Judge Robert E. Blackburn

Alfred A. Arraj U.S. Courthouse, 901 19th Street, Room A1041,
Denver, CO 80294
Tel: (303) 335-2350

Robert E. Blackburn
District Judge

Date of Birth: 1950
Education: Western State Col 1972 BA; Colorado 1974 JD
Began Service: March 8, 2002
Appointed By: President George W. Bush

Government: Deputy District Attorney (part-time), 16th Judicial District (1980-1986); County Attorney, County of Bent, Colorado (1980-1988)

Judicial: Municipal Judge (1985-1988); Judge, Colorado District Court, Sixteenth Judicial District (1988-2002)

Legal Practice: Law Clerk, Oakley Wade Law Office (1975); Partner, Wade & Blackburn (1975-1980); Private Practice (1980-1988)

Staff

Career Law Clerk **Jeffrey P. Kelson** .... (303) 335-2350
Education: Colorado 1985 JD
Career Law Clerk **Hazel Landwehr Porter** .... (303) 335-2350
E-mail: hazel_porter@cod.uscourts.gov
Education: Duke 1994 JD
Courtroom Deputy **Kathleen Finney** .... (303) 335-2099
E-mail: kathleen_finney@cod.uscourts.gov
Court Reporter **Tracy Weir** .... (303) 335-2358
E-mail: tracy_weir@cod.uscourts.gov
Secretary **Nel Steffens** .... (303) 335-2350
E-mail: nel_steffens@cod.uscourts.gov

Chambers of District Judge Christine M. Arguello

Alfred A. Arraj U.S. Courthouse, 901 19th Street, Room A638,
Denver, CO 80294
Tel: (303) 335-2174 Fax: (303) 335-2317
E-mail: arguello_chambers@cod.uscourts.gov

Christine M. Arguello
District Judge

Date of Birth: 1955
Education: Colorado 1977 BS; Harvard 1980 JD
Began Service: October 21, 2008
Appointed By: President George W. Bush

Academic: Associate Professor, School of Law, University of Kansas (1991-1998); Professor, School of Law, University of Kansas (1998-1999); Managing Senior Associate Counsel, University of Colorado at Boulder (2006-2008)

Government: Deputy Attorney General for States Services, Office of the Attorney General, State of Colorado (1999-2000); Chief Deputy Attorney General, Office of the Attorney General, State of Colorado (2000-2002)

Legal Practice: Shareholder and Managing Partner, Duncan, Green, Brown & Langeness, PC (2003-2004); Partner, Davis Graham & Stubbs LLP (2004-2006)

Current Memberships: Colorado Bar Association; The Florida Bar; Iowa State Bar Association

Chambers of District Judge Philip A. Brimmer
Alfred A. Arraj U.S. Courthouse, 901 19th Street, Room A601, Denver, CO 80294
Tel: (303) 335-2794 Fax: (303) 335-2782
E-mail: brimmer_chambers@cod.uscourts.gov

Philip A. Brimmer
District Judge

Date of Birth: 1959
Education: Harvard 1981 AB; Yale 1985 JD
Began Service: October 14, 2008
Appointed By: President George W. Bush

Clerkships: Law Clerk, Chambers of Senior Judge Zita L. Weinshienk, United States District Court for the District of Colorado (1985-1987)

Government: Deputy District Attorney, Denver District Attorney's Office, Office of the City Council, City and County of Denver, Colorado (1994-2001); Chief Deputy District Attorney, Denver District Attorney's Office, Office of the City Council, City and County of Denver, Colorado (2001); Assistant U.S. Attorney, Criminal Division, Colorado District, United States Department of Justice (2001-2006); Major Crimes Section Chief, Colorado District, Executive Office for United States Attorneys, United States Department of Justice (2006); Special Prosecutions Section Chief/Anti-terrorism Coordinator, Special Prosecutions Division, Colorado District, United States Department of Justice

Legal Practice: Associate, Kirkland & Ellis LLP (1987-1994)

Current Memberships: Colorado Bar Association

Chambers of District Judge William J. Martinez
Alfred A. Arraj United States Courthouse, 901 19th Street, Room A841, Denver, CO 80294
Tel: (303) 335-2805

William J. Martinez
District Judge

Education: Illinois 1977 BA, 1977 BS; Chicago 1980 JD
Began Service: January 10, 2011
Appointed By: President Barack Obama

Government: Regional Attorney, Denver (CO) Field Office, Phoenix (AZ) District Office, United States Equal Employment Opportunity Commission (1992-1996)

Legal Practice: Attorney, Legal Assistance Foundation of Chicago (1980-1987); Associate, Pendleton, Friedberg, Wilson & Hennessey, P.C. (1988-1992)

Current Memberships: Colorado Bar Foundation, Colorado Bar Association; Colorado Hispanic Bar Association

Profession: Sole Practitioner (1997-2001)

Staff
Judicial Assistant **Sharon Kindred** .... (303) 335-2805
E-mail: sharon_kindred@cod.uscourts.gov

Chambers of District Judge R. Brooke Jackson
901 19th Street, Room A738, Denver, CO 80294
Tel: (303) 844-4694

Richard Brooke Jackson
District Judge

Education: Dartmouth 1969 AB; Harvard 1972 JD
Began Service: September 16, 2011
Appointed By: President Barack Obama

Judicial: Chief Judge, Chambers of Chief Judge R. Brooke Jackson, First Judicial District, Colorado District Courts (1998-2011)

Legal Practice: Associate, Holland & Hart LLP (1972-1978); Partner, Holland & Hart LLP (1978-1998)

Chambers of District Judge R. Brooke Jackson *continued*

Staff
Law Clerk **Katherine Hinde** .... (303) 335-2253
E-mail: katherine_hinde@cod.uscourts.gov
Law Clerk **Garen Gervey** .... (303) 335-2253
Education: Colorado 2009 JD
Judicial Assistant **Mary DeRosa** .... (303) 844-3433
E-mail: mary_derosa@cod.uscourts.gov

Chambers of District Judge Raymond P. Moore
901 19th Street, Room A601, Denver, CO 80294
Tel: (303) 335-2784

Raymond P. Moore
District Judge

Education: Yale 1975 BA, 1978 JD
Began Service: April 30, 2013
Appointed By: President Barack Obama

Government: Assistant United States Attorney, Colorado District, Executive Office for United States Attorneys, United States Department of Justice (1982-1986); Federal Public Defender, Colorado and Wyoming Federal Public Defender, Colorado and Wyoming (2004-2013)

Legal Practice: Attorney, Davis Graham & Stubbs LLP (1986-1992); Associate, Davis Graham & Stubbs LLP (1978-1982)

Staff
Judicial Assistant **Deanne Bader** .... (303) 335-2784

Chambers of Senior Judge Richard P. Matsch
Byron White U.S. Courthouse, 1823 Stout Street, Denver, CO 80257
Tel: (303) 844-4627

Richard Paul Matsch
Senior Judge

Date of Birth: 1930
Education: Michigan 1951 AB, 1953 JD
Began Service: 1974
Appointed By: President Richard M. Nixon

Government: Assistant United States Attorney, District of Colorado, United States Department of Justice (1959-1961); Deputy City Attorney, Law Department, City and County of Denver, Colorado (1961-1963)

Judicial: Bankruptcy Judge, United States District Court for the District of Colorado (1965-1974)

Legal Practice: Private Practice (1956-1959); Private Practice (1963-1965)

Military Service: United States Army (1953-1955)

Staff
Secretary **Ginger Wentz** .... (303) 844-4627
E-mail: ginger_wentz@cod.uscourts.gov

Chambers of Senior Judge John Lawrence Kane

Alfred A. Arraj U.S. Courthouse, 901 19th Street, Room A838, Denver, CO 80294-3589
Tel: (303) 844-6118 Fax: (303) 335-2211
E-mail: john_l_kane@cod.uscourts.gov

John Lawrence Kane
Senior Judge

Date of Birth: 1937
Education: Colorado 1958 BA; Denver 1960 JD, 1997 LLD
Began Service: 1977
Appointed By: President Jimmy Carter

Academic: Instructor, Metropolitan State College of Denver (1975); Adjunct Professor, University of Denver (1976); Guest Lecturer, Trinity College Dublin (1989); Distinguished Visiting Professor, University of Denver (1994)

Clerkships: Law Clerk, Colorado District Court, Seventeenth Judicial District

Government: Deputy District Attorney, State of Colorado (1961-1962); Public Defender, Adams County, State of Colorado (1964-1967); Deputy Director, Eastern Region of India, Peace Corps (1967-1969)

Legal Practice: Gaunt, Byrne & Dirrim (1961-1962); Partner, Andrews & Kane (1963-1964); Partner, Holme Roberts & Owen LLP (1970-1977)

Staff
Law Clerk **David Pennington** . . . . (303) 844-6118
Permanent Law Clerk **Karen Robertson** . . . . (303) 844-6118
E-mail: karen_robertson@cod.uscourts.gov
Education: William & Mary 1986 BA; Virginia 1989 JD
Secretary **Deb Wilhelm** . . . . (303) 844-6118

Chambers of Senior Judge Lewis Thornton Babcock

Alfred A. Arraj U.S. Courthouse, 901 19th Street, C450, Denver, CO 80294
Tel: (303) 844-2527

Lewis Thornton Babcock
Senior Judge

Date of Birth: 1943
Education: Denver 1965 BA, 1968 JD; Virginia 1988 LLM; Denver 2004 LLD
Began Service: November 21, 1988
Appointed By: President Ronald Reagan

Government: City Attorney, Office of the City Attorney, City of Las Animas, Colorado (1969-1974); City Attorney, Office of the City Attorney, City of Rocky Ford, Colorado (1970-1976); Assistant District Attorney, 16th Judicial Circuit, State of Colorado (1973-1976); Escrow and Loan Closing Agent, Farmers Home Administration, United States Department of Agriculture (1973-1976)

Judicial: Judge, Colorado District Court, 16th Judicial Circuit (1976-1983); Judge, Colorado Court of Appeals (1983-1988); District Judge, United States District Court for the District of Colorado (1988-2000); Chief Judge, United States District Court for the District of Colorado (2000-2007)

Legal Practice: Mitchell & Babcock (1968-1976); Member of the Board of Directors, Colorado Rural Legal Services Inc. (1974-1976)

Military Service: Colorado National Guard (1968-1974)

Current Memberships: American Bar Association; The James E. Doyle American Inn of Court, The American Inns of Court; Colorado Bar Association; Colorado Bar Foundation, Colorado Bar Association; Denver Bar Association

Staff
Law Clerk **(Vacant)** . . . . (303) 844-2527
Career Law Clerk **Rita Mahoney** . . . . (303) 844-2527
E-mail: rita_mahoney@cod.uscourts.gov
Career Law Clerk **Jennifer Roberts** . . . . (303) 844-2527

Chambers of Senior Judge Lewis Thornton Babcock *continued*

Secretary **Judy Poor** . . . . (303) 844-2527
E-mail: judy_poor@cod.uscourts.gov

Chambers of Senior Judge Wiley Y. Daniel

Alfred A. Arraj U.S. Courthouse, 901 19th Street, Room A1038, Denver, CO 80294
Tel: (303) 335-2170 Fax: (303) 335-2178
E-mail: daniel_chambers@cod.uscourts.gov

Wiley Y. Daniel
Senior Judge

Date of Birth: 1946
Education: Howard U 1968 BA, 1971 JD
Began Service: September 1, 1995
Appointed By: President William J. Clinton

Current Memberships: American Bar Foundation; American Bar Association; The Thompson G. Marsh American Inn of Court, The American Inns of Court; Colorado Bar Association; Colorado Bar Foundation, Colorado Bar Association; Denver Bar Association; National Bar Association; Sam Cary Bar Association

Staff
Law Clerk **Marcus McKinvra** . . . . (303) 335-2170
Began Service: September 2014
Term Expires: October 2016
Career Law Clerk **Chessa Ronning** . . . . (303) 335-2170
E-mail: chessa_ronning@cod.uscourts.gov
Career Law Clerk **Sharon Shahidi** . . . . (303) 335-2170
E-mail: sharon_shahidi@cod.uscourts.gov
Education: Denver 1988 JD
Court Reporter **Tamara Hoffschildt** . . . . (303) 623-3080
E-mail: tamara_hoffschildt@cod.uscourts.gov
Courtroom Deputy **Robb Keech** . . . . (303) 335-2170
E-mail: robb_keech@cod.uscourts.gov

Chambers of Magistrate Judge Michael J. Watanabe

Alfred A. Arraj U.S. Courthouse, 901 19th Street, Suite A532, Denver, CO 80294-3589
Tel: (303) 844-2403 Fax: (303) 335-2199

Michael J. Watanabe
Magistrate Judge

Began Service: February 12, 1999
Term Expires: February 2023

Staff
Career Law Clerk **Alison Andrews** . . . . (303) 844-2403
Education: Pace 1980 BBA; Albany Law 1983 JD
Courtroom Deputy **Ellen Miller** . . . . (303) 335-2101
E-mail: ellen_miller@cod.uscourts.gov
Law Clerk **Joseph Peters** . . . . (303) 844-2403
E-mail: joseph_peters@cod.uscourts.gov

Chambers of Magistrate Judge Craig B. Shaffer
Alfred A. Arraj U.S. Courthouse, 901 19th Street, Room A432, Denver, CO 80294-3589
Tel: (303) 844-2117 Fax: (303) 335-2188
E-mail: shaffer_chambers@cod.uscourts.gov

Craig B. Shaffer
Magistrate Judge

Date of Birth: 1954
Education: Tulane 1979 JD
Began Service: January 18, 2001
Term Expires: January 17, 2017

Government: United States Department of Justice (1983-1991)

Legal Practice: Dufford & Brown, P.C. (1991-1999); Giles, O'Keefe, Vermeire & Gorrel, LLP (2000-2001)

Military Service: United States Navy JAG Corps (1979-1983)

Staff
Career Law Clerk **Charlotte Aycrigg** .... (303) 844-2117
E-mail: shaffer_chambers@cod.uscourts.gov
Education: Colorado 1985 JD
Career Law Clerk **Stephanie Gaddy** .... (303) 844-2117
E-mail: stephanie_gaddy@cod.uscourts.gov
Education: Colorado State 2001 BA; Colorado 2009 JD
Judicial Assistant **Yvonne Moffatt Davis** .... (303) 844-2117
E-mail: shaffer_chambers@cod.uscourts.gov

Chambers of Magistrate Judge Michael E. Hegarty
901 19th Street, Room A542, Denver, CO 80294
Tel: (303) 844-4507

Michael E. Hegarty
Magistrate Judge

Began Service: February 15, 2006

Government: Deputy Chief, Civil Division, Department of Justice; Chief, Civil Division, Colorado District, United States Department of Justice

Chambers of Magistrate Judge Kristen L. Mix
1929 Stout Street, Room C253, Denver, CO 80294
Tel: (303) 335-2770
E-mail: mix_chambers@cod.uscourts.gov

Kristen L. Mix
Magistrate Judge

Began Service: August 2007
Term Expires: August 2023

Staff
Career Law Clerk **Michael West** .... (303) 335-2770
Began Service: August 29, 2011
Career Law Clerk **Elizabeth Young** .... (303) 335-2770
E-mail: elizabeth_young@cod.uscourts.gov

Chambers of Magistrate Judge Kathleen M. Tafoya
1929 Stout Street, Suite C251, Denver, CO 80294
Tel: (303) 335-2780 Fax: (303) 335-2762
E-mail: tafoya_chambers@cod.uscourts.gov

Kathleen M. Tafoya
Magistrate Judge

Began Service: January 2008
Term Expires: 2016

Government: Assistant U.S. Attorney, Criminal Division, United States Attorney's Office, Department of Justice; Senior Litigation Chief and Assistant U.S. Attorney/Organized Crime Drug Enforcement Task Force Assistant U.S. Attorney, Criminal Division, Colorado District, United States Department of Justice; Organized Crime Drug Enforcement Task Force Assistant U.S. Attorney, Criminal Division, Colorado District, United States Department of Justice

Staff
Career Law Clerk **Jamie L. Hodges** .... (303) 335-2780
Began Service: 2008
E-mail: jamie_hodges@cod.uscourts.gov
Education: Denver 2007 JD
Courtroom Deputy **Sabrina Grimm** .... (303) 335-2180
E-mail: sabrina_grimm@cod.uscourts.gov

Chambers of Magistrate Judge Gordon P. Gallagher
Wayne Aspinall Federal Building, 402 Rood Avenue, Grand Junction, CO 81501
P.O. Box 3208, Grand Junction, CO 81501
Tel: (970) 241-8932

Gordon P. Gallagher
Magistrate Judge

Chambers of Magistrate Judge Nina Y. Wang
901 19th Street, Denver, CO 80294
Tel: (303) 335-2600

Nina Y. Wang
Magistrate Judge

Chambers of Magistrate Judge (part-time) David L. West
U.S. Courthouse/Federal Building, 103 Sheppard Drive, Suite 202, Durango, CO 81303
P.O. Box 2906, Durango, CO 81303
Tel: (970) 259-0542

David L. West
Magistrate Judge (Part-Time)

Began Service: 2004

United States Bankruptcy Court for the District of Colorado
U.S. Custom House, 721 19th Street, Denver, CO 80202-2508
Tel: (720) 904-7300
Tel: (303) 844-0267 (Voice Case Information System VCIS)
Internet: www.cob.uscourts.gov

Number of Judgeships: 5

Court Staff
Clerk of Court **Kenneth S. Gardner** .... (720) 904-7300
Education: Western Illinois 1984 BA; Denver 1986 MS

Chambers of Chief Bankruptcy Judge Michael E. Romero
721 19th Street, 5th Floor, Denver, CO 80202-2508
Tel: (720) 904-7413 Fax: (720) 904-7415
E-mail: michael_romero@cob.uscourts.gov

Michael E. Romero
Chief Bankruptcy Judge

Date of Birth: June 30, 1955
Education: Denver 1977 BA; Michigan 1980 JD
Began Service: December 22, 2003
Term Expires: December 2017

Staff
Law Clerk **Matthew Faga** .... (720) 904-7323
Began Service: 2012
Term Expires: August 2016
E-mail: matthew_faga@cob.uscourts.gov
Career Law Clerk **Kelly B. Lambert** .... (720) 904-7417
E-mail: kelly_lambert@cob.uscourts.gov
Education: Colorado Col 1979 BA; Lesley Col 1982 MEd; Boston Col 1985 JD
Judicial Assistant **Deborah L. Beatty** .... (720) 904-7413
E-mail: deborah_beatty@cob.uscourts.gov
Education: Wyoming 1979 BM; Colorado (Denver) 2005 MS

Chambers of Bankruptcy Judge Howard R. Tallman
U.S. Custom House, 721 19th Street, Denver, CO 80202-2508
Tel: (720) 904-7438 Fax: (720) 904-7436
E-mail: howard_tallman@cob.uscourts.gov

Howard R. Tallman
Bankruptcy Judge

Date of Birth: 1950
Education: Denver 1975 JD; Colorado 1984 MBA
Began Service: December 2002
Term Expires: December 2016

Current Memberships: American Bankruptcy Institute; Colorado Bar Association; Faculty of Federal Advocates; National Conference of Bankruptcy Judges

Staff
Law Clerk **K. Lane Cutler** .... (720) 904-7440
Began Service: 2009
E-mail: lane_cutler@cob.uscourts.gov
Law Clerk **Kathryn "Kathy" Plonsky** .... (720) 904-7349
Began Service: 2012
E-mail: kathryn_a_plonsky@cob.uscourts.gov
Career Law Clerk **Thomas N. Lane** .... (720) 904-7439
E-mail: thomas_lane@cob.uscourts.gov
Courtroom Deputy **Margaret Muff** .... (720) 904-7435
E-mail: margaret_muff@cob.uscourts.gov

Chambers of Bankruptcy Judge Sidney B. Brooks
U.S. Custom House, 721 19th Street, Denver, CO 80202-2508
Tel: (720) 904-7338

Sidney B. Brooks
Bankruptcy Judge

Date of Birth: 1945
Education: Denver 1967 BA, 1971 JD
Began Service: 1988
Term Expires: 2016

Current Memberships: American Bankruptcy Institute; Colorado Bar Association; Denver Bar Association; National Conference of Bankruptcy Judges

Chambers of Bankruptcy Judge Sidney B. Brooks *continued*

Staff
Career Law Clerk **Sunika Pawar** .... (720) 904-7339
Courtroom Deputy **Anne Sekera** .... (720) 904-7334
E-mail: anne_sekera@cob.uscourts.gov
Judicial Assistant **Linda Kimes** .... (720) 904-7338
E-mail: linda_kimes@cob.uscourts.gov

Chambers of Bankruptcy Judge Elizabeth E. Brown
U.S. Custom House, 721 19th Street, Denver, CO 80202
Tel: (720) 904-7346
E-mail: elizabeth_brown@cob.uscourts.gov

Elizabeth E. Brown
Bankruptcy Judge

Date of Birth: 1958
Education: Colorado Col 1980 BA; Colorado 1986 JD
Began Service: April 16, 2001
Term Expires: April 15, 2027

Legal Practice: Associate, Davis Graham & Stubbs LLP (1986-1990); Associate, Rothgerber, Appel, Powers & Johnson LLP; Partner, Holme Roberts & Owen LLP (1997-2001)

Current Memberships: American Bankruptcy Institute; Colorado Bar Association; Colorado Bar Foundation, Colorado Bar Association; Denver Bar Association; National Conference of Bankruptcy Judges

Staff
Law Clerk **Bruce Mares** .... (720) 904-7346
Began Service: July 2015
Term Expires: July 2016
Career Law Clerk **Kerstin Cass** .... (720) 904-7361
E-mail: kerstin_cass@cob.uscourts.gov
Courtroom Deputy **Mariah Reynolds** .... (720) 904-7346

Chambers of Bankruptcy Judge Thomas B. McNamara
721 19th Street, Denver, CO 80202-2508
Tel: (720) 904-7310

Thomas B. McNamara
Bankruptcy Judge

Staff
Law Clerk **Kate Swan** .... (720) 904-7312
E-mail: kate_swan@cob.uscourts.gov
Law Clerk **Anne Tunnell** .... (720) 904-7359
E-mail: anne_tunnell@cob.uscourts.gov
Courtroom Deputy **Jaime Escudero** .... (720) 904-7359
E-mail: jaime_escudero@cob.uscourts.gov

United States District Court for the District of Connecticut
U.S. Courthouse, 141 Church Street, New Haven, CT 06510
Tel: (203) 773-2140 Tel: (203) 773-2451 (PACER)
Fax: (203) 773-2334
Internet: www.ctd.uscourts.gov

Number of Judgeships: 8

Circuit: Second

Court Staff
District Clerk **Robin D. Tabora** .... (203) 773-2140
E-mail: robin_tabora@ctd.uscourts.gov
Chief Deputy Clerk **Dinah Milton Kenney** .... (203) 773-2140
Deputy-in-Charge - Bridgeport **Bryan Blough** .... (203) 579-5861
915 Lafayette Blvd., Bridgeport, CT 06604 Fax: (203) 579-5867
E-mail: bryan_blough@ctd.uscourts.gov

United States District Court for the District of Connecticut *continued*

Deputy-in-Charge - Hartford **Melissa Ruocco** .... (860) 240-3200
U.S. Courthouse, 450 Main St., Hartford, CT 06103 Fax: (860) 240-3211
E-mail: melissa_ruocco@ctd.uscourts.gov
Operations Manager - New Haven **Jane Bauer** .... (203) 773-2140
E-mail: jane_bauer@ctd.uscourts.gov Fax: (203) 773-2334
Chief Probation Officer **Edward Scott Chinn** .... (203) 773-2100
Fax: (203) 773-2200
Deputy Chief Probation Officer **C. Warren Maxwell** ..... (203) 773-2100
Human Resources Manager **Andrea Perce** .... (203) 773-5497
E-mail: andrea_perce@ctd.uscourts.gov Fax: (203) 773-2189
Information Systems Manager **Chris Newton** .... (203) 773-2206
Financial/Budget Administrator **Daniel Cohn** .... (203) 773-2140
E-mail: daniel_cohn@ctd.uscourts.gov

Chambers of Chief Judge Janet C. Hall

141 Church Street, New Haven, CT 06510
Tel: (203) 773-2428
E-mail: janet_hall@ctd.uscourts.gov

Janet C. Hall
Chief Judge

Date of Birth: 1948
Education: Mount Holyoke 1970 AB; NYU 1973 JD
Began Service: October 14, 1997
Appointed By: President William J. Clinton

Current Memberships: American Bar Foundation; Connecticut Bar Association, Inc.

Staff

Law Clerk **Virginia McCalmont** .... (203) 773-2058
Began Service: September 2015
Term Expires: September 2016
E-mail: virginia_mccalmont@ctd.uscourts.gov
Law Clerk **Caleb Fountain** .... (203) 773-2058
Began Service: September 2015
Term Expires: September 2016
E-mail: caleb_fountain@ctd.uscourts.gov
Law Clerk **Benjamin Weintraub** .... (203) 773-2059
Began Service: June 2015
Term Expires: June 2016
E-mail: benjamin_weintraub@ctd.uscourts.gov
Court Reporter **Terri Fidanza** .... (203) 910-4567
E-mail: fnza@aol.com
Judicial Assistant **Bernadette Derubeis** .... (203) 773-2427
E-mail: bernadette_derubeis@ctd.uscourts.gov
Courtroom Deputy **Diahann Lewis** .... (203) 773-2421
E-mail: diahann_lewis@ctd.uscourts.gov

Chambers of District Judge Alvin W. Thompson

U.S. Courthouse, 450 Main Street, Suite 240, Hartford, CT 06103
Tel: (860) 240-3224
E-mail: alvin_thompson@ctd.uscourts.gov

Alvin W. Thompson
District Judge

Education: Princeton 1975 BA; Yale 1978 JD
Began Service: October 11, 1994
Appointed By: President William J. Clinton

Staff

Law Clerk **Katherine Calle** .... (860) 240-3224
Began Service: August 2015
Term Expires: August 2016
E-mail: katherine_calle@ctd.uscourts.gov
Law Clerk **Emily Rock** .... (860) 240-3224
Began Service: September 2015
Term Expires: September 2016
E-mail: emily_rock@ctd.uscourts.gov
Courtroom Deputy **Sandy Smith** .... (860) 240-3880
E-mail: sandy_smith@ctd.uscourts.gov

Chambers of District Judge Alvin W. Thompson *continued*

Judicial Assistant **Marion Bock** .... (860) 240-3224
E-mail: marion_bock@ctd.uscourts.gov

Chambers of District Judge Robert N. Chatigny

U.S. Courthouse, 450 Main Street, Hartford, CT 06103-9998
Tel: (860) 240-3659

Robert N. Chatigny
District Judge

Date of Birth: 1951
Education: Brown U 1973 AB; Georgetown 1978 JD
Began Service: 1994
Appointed By: President William J. Clinton

Clerkships: Law Clerk The Honorable Samuel Conti, United States District Court for the Northern District of California (1979-1980); Law Clerk The Honorable Jose A. Cabranes, United States District Court for the District of Connecticut (1980); Law Clerk The Honorable Jon O. Newman, United States Court of Appeals for the Second Circuit (1980-1981)

Government: Member, Prison and Jail Overcrowding Commission, State of Connecticut (1991-1993); Member, Judicial Selection Commission, State of Connecticut (1993)

Legal Practice: Associate, Williams & Connolly (1981-1983); Partner, Chatigny & Palmer (1984-1986); Law Offices of Robert N. Chatigny (1986-1990); Partner, Chatigny & Cowdery (1991-1994)

Current Memberships: American Bar Foundation; The Oliver Ellsworth American Inn of Court, The American Inns of Court; Connecticut Bar Foundation, Connecticut Bar Association, Inc.; Hartford County Bar

Staff

Law Clerk **Ivan Panchenko** .... (860) 240-3659
Began Service: August 2015
Term Expires: August 2016
E-mail: ivan_panchenko@flmd.uscourts.gov
Law Clerk **Jessica Samuels** .... (860) 240-3659
Began Service: August 2015
Term Expires: August 2016
E-mail: jessica_samuels@ctd.uscourts.gov
Courtroom Deputy **Terri Glynn** .... (860) 240-3495
E-mail: terri_glynn@ctd.uscourts.gov
Court Reporter **Darlene Warner** .... (860) 547-0580
Judicial Assistant **Lisa Rickevicius** .... (860) 240-3659
E-mail: lisa_rickevicius@ctd.uscourts.gov

Chambers of District Judge Stefan R. Underhill

915 Lafayette Boulevard, Suite 411, Bridgeport, CT 06604
Tel: (203) 579-5714 Fax: (203) 579-5704
E-mail: stefan_underhill@ctd.uscourts.gov

Stefan R. Underhill
District Judge

Date of Birth: 1956
Education: Virginia 1978 BA; Oxford (UK) 1981 BA; Yale 1984 JD
Began Service: September 1, 1999
Appointed By: President William J. Clinton

Clerkships: Law Clerk The Honorable Jon O. Newman, United States Court of Appeals for the Second Circuit (1984-1985)

Legal Practice: Associate/Partner, Day, Berry & Howard LLP (1985-1999)

Staff

Law Clerk **Michael Landman** .... (203) 579-5714
Began Service: September 2015
Term Expires: September 1, 2017
E-mail: michael_landman@ctd.uscourts.gov
Law Clerk **Robert Pollack** .... (203) 579-5714
Began Service: September 2014
Term Expires: September 2016
E-mail: robert_pollack@ctd.uscourts.gov

(continued on next page)

Chambers of District Judge Stefan R. Underhill *continued*

Law Clerk **Alice Buttrick** . . . . (203) 579-5714
Began Service: September 2015
Term Expires: September 1, 2017
E-mail: alice_buttrick@ctd.uscourts.gov
Courtroom Deputy **Barbara Sbalbi** . . . . (203) 579-5714
E-mail: barbara_sbalbi@ctd.uscourts.gov
Court Reporter **Susan Catucci** . . . . (203) 579-5714
E-mail: susan_catucci@ctd.uscourts.gov

Chambers of District Judge Vanessa Lynne Bryant

450 Main Street, Room 320, Hartford, CT 06103
Tel: (860) 240-3123 Fax: (860) 240-3126
E-mail: vanessa_bryant@ctd.uscourts.gov

Vanessa Lynne Bryant
District Judge

Education: Howard U 1975 BA; Connecticut 1978 JD
Began Service: April 2, 2007
Appointed By: President George W. Bush

Corporate: Counsel, Aetna Life & Casualty (1981-1989); Counsel, Shawmut Bank of Boston, N.A. (1989-1990)

Government: Vice President and General Counsel, Connecticut Housing Finance Authority (1990-1992)

Judicial: Judge, Connecticut Superior Court, Connecticut (1998-2007)

Legal Practice: Associate, Day, Berry & Howard (1978-1981); Partner, Hawkins, Delafield & Wood (1992-1998)

Staff
Law Clerk **Ross Thomas** . . . . (860) 240-3123
Began Service: September 2015
Term Expires: September 2016
E-mail: ross_thomas@ctd.uscourts.gov
Law Clerk **Seth Nadler** . . . . (860) 240-3123
Began Service: September 2014
Term Expires: September 2016
E-mail: seth_nadler@ctd.uscourts.gov
Law Clerk **Neal Schecter** . . . . (860) 240-3123
Began Service: September 2015
Term Expires: September 2017
E-mail: neal_schecter@ctd.uscourts.gov
Courtroom Deputy **Loraine Lalone** . . . . (860) 240-3040
E-mail: loraine_lalone@ctd.uscourts.gov

Chambers of District Judge Michael P. Shea

141 Church Street, New Haven, CT 06510
Tel: (203) 773-2140
E-mail: michael_shea@ctd.uscourts.gov

Michael P. Shea
District Judge

Education: Amherst 1989 BA; Yale 1993 JD
Began Service: December 31, 2012
Appointed By: President Barack Obama

Clerkships: Law Clerk, United States Court of Appeals for the District of Columbia Circuit (1993-1994)

Legal Practice: Associate, Cleary Gottlieb Steen & Hamilton LLP (1994-1998); Associate, Day Pitney LLP (1998-2003)

Staff
Law Clerk **Kathryn Bradley** . . . . (203) 773-2140
E-mail: kathryn_bradley@ctd.uscourts.gov
Law Clerk **Drew Hillier** . . . . (203) 773-2140
E-mail: drew_hillier@ctd.uscourts.gov
Law Clerk **Daniel Osher** . . . . (203) 773-2140
E-mail: daniel_osher@ctd.uscourts.gov
Courtroom Deputy **Devorah Johnson** . . . . (860) 240-3205
E-mail: devorah_johnson@ctd.uscourts.gov

Chambers of District Judge Michael P. Shea *continued*

Court Reporter **Martha Marshall** . . . . (860) 214-7929
E-mail: martha_marshall@ctd.uscourts.gov

Chambers of District Judge Jeffrey Alker Meyer

915 Lafayette Boulevard, Suite 335, Bridgeport, CT 06604
Tel: (203) 579-5554 Tel: (203) 579-5681

Jeffrey Alker Meyer
District Judge

Education: Yale 1985 BA, 1989 JD
Began Service: February 25, 2014
Appointed By: President Barack Obama

Clerkships: Law Clerk, Chambers of Senior Judge James L. Oakes, United States Court of Appeals for the Second Circuit (1989-1990); Law Clerk, Chambers of Associate Justice Harry A. Blackmun, Supreme Court of the United States (1991-1992)

Government: Assistant U.S. Attorney, Connecticut District, United States Department of Justice (1995-2004); Appeals Supervisor, Criminal Division, Connecticut District, United States Department of Justice (2000-2004)

Staff
Law Clerk **Samuel Adriance** . . . . (203) 579-5554
E-mail: samuel_adriance@ctd.uscourts.gov
Law Clerk **Allison Gorsuch** . . . . (203) 579-5554
E-mail: allison_gorsuch@ctd.uscourts.gov
Law Clerk **Amanda Oakes** . . . . (203) 579-5554
E-mail: amanda_oakes@ctd.uscourts.gov
Judicial Assistant **Carolyn Della Pietra** . . . . (203) 579-5554

Chambers of District Judge Victor Allen Bolden

915 Lafayette Boulevard, Suite 335, Bridgeport, CT 06604
Tel: (203) 579-5562 Fax: (203) 579-5844
E-mail: victor_bolden@ctd.uscourts.gov

Victor Allen Bolden
District Judge

Education: Columbia 1986 AB; Harvard 1989 JD
Began Service: January 7, 2015
Appointed By: President Barack Obama
Military: Esq.

Government: Corporation Counsel, Corporation Counsel, Town and City of New Haven, Connecticut (2009-2014)

Staff
Law Clerk **Stewart Dearing** . . . . (203) 579-5562
E-mail: stewart_dearing@ctd.uscourts.gov
Law Clerk **Daniel Shin** . . . . (203) 579-5562
E-mail: daniel_shin@ctd.uscourts.gov
Law Clerk **Eric LaPre** . . . . (203) 579-5562
E-mail: eric_lapre@ctd.uscourts.gov
Courtroom Deputy **Kenneth Ghilardi** . . . . (203) 579-5539
E-mail: kenneth_ghilardi@ctd.uscourts.gov
Court Reporter **Sharon Montini** . . . . (203) 579-5562
E-mail: sharon_montini@ctd.uscourts.gov

Chambers of Senior Judge Alfred Vincent Covello

U.S. Courthouse, 450 Main Street, Hartford, CT 06103-9998
Tel: (860) 240-3218 Fax: (860) 240-2694
E-mail: alfred_covello@ctd.uscourts.gov

Alfred Vincent Covello
Senior Judge

Date of Birth: 1933
Education: Harvard 1954 AB; Connecticut 1960 LLB, 1960 JD
Began Service: September 2, 1992
Appointed By: President George H.W. Bush
Political Affiliation: Republican

Judicial: Justice of the Peace, State of Connecticut (1973-1974); Judge, Connecticut Circuit Court (1974-1975); Judge, Connecticut Court of Common Pleas (1975-1978); Judge, Connecticut Superior Court (1978-1992); Justice, Connecticut Supreme Court (1987-1992); Chief Judge, United States District Court for the District of Connecticut (1998-2003)

Legal Practice: Partner, Bieluch, Barry & Covello (1960-1964); Partner, Gross, Hyde & Williams (1964-1974)

Military Service: United States Army (1955-1959)

Current Memberships: American Bar Foundation; American Bar Association; Connecticut Bar Association, Inc.; Federal Judges Association; Hartford County Bar

Staff

Law Clerk **Sean LaPorta** .... (860) 240-3218
Began Service: September 2015
Term Expires: September 2016
E-mail: sean_laporta@ctd.uscourts.gov
Law Clerk **Sarah Ricciardi** .... (860) 240-3218
Began Service: September 2015
Term Expires: September 2016
E-mail: sarah_ricciardi@ctd.uscourts.gov
Senior Career Law Clerk **Katherine Codeanne** .... (860) 240-3218
E-mail: katherine_codeanne@ctd.uscourts.gov
Judicial Assistant **Renee Alexander** .... (860) 240-3218
E-mail: renee_alexander@ctd.uscourts.gov
Education: Augustana (IL) 1983 BA

Chambers of Senior Judge Warren W. Eginton

915 Lafayette Boulevard, Suite 335, Bridgeport, CT 06604-4765
Tel: (203) 579-5819 Fax: (203) 579-5768
E-mail: warren_eginton@ctd.uscourts.gov

Warren W. Eginton
Senior Judge

Date of Birth: 1924
Education: Princeton 1948 BA; Yale 1951 JD
Began Service: 1979
Appointed By: President Jimmy Carter

Corporate: Editor-in-Chief, Product Liability Law Journal, Butterworth Legal Publishers (1988-1993)

Legal Practice: Associate, Davis Polk & Wardwell (1951-1953); Attorney, Cummings & Lockwood LLC (1954-1979)

Military Service: United States Army (1943-1946); United States Army Reserve, United States Department of the Army (1946-1972)

Current Memberships: American Bar Foundation; American Bar Association; The American Inns of Court; Connecticut Bar Association, Inc.; Connecticut Bar Foundation, Connecticut Bar Association, Inc.; Federal Bar Association; Federal Bar Council; Stamford Regional Bar Association

Staff

Law Clerk **Ivan Ladd-Smith** .... (203) 579-5818
Began Service: 2011
Term Expires: August 2016
Career Law Clerk **Talbot A. Welles** .... (203) 579-5817
E-mail: talbot_welles@ctd.uscourts.gov
Education: Arizona 1997 JD

Chambers of Senior Judge Warren W. Eginton *continued*

Judicial Administrative Assistant **Deborah H. Candee** ... (203) 579-5819
E-mail: deborah_candee@ctd.uscourts.gov

Chambers of Senior Judge Dominic J. Squatrito

U.S. Courthouse, 450 Main Street, Suite 108, Hartford, CT 06103
Tel: (860) 240-3873
E-mail: dominic_squatrito@ctd.uscourts.gov

Dominic J. Squatrito
Senior Judge

Date of Birth: 1939
Education: Wesleyan U 1961 BA; Yale 1965 LLB
Began Service: October 6, 1994
Appointed By: President William J. Clinton

Government: Counsel, Housing Authority, Town of Manchester, Connecticut (1972-1979); Clerk, Legislative Committee on Executive Nominations, State of Connecticut (1974-1978); Assistant Counsel, Committee on the Judiciary, Connecticut State Legislature (1974); Chief Counsel, Connecticut Senate (1976-1980)

Legal Practice: Bayer & Phelon (and successor firms) (1966-1994)

Current Memberships: American Bar Association; Connecticut Bar Association, Inc.; Federal Judges Association; Hartford County Bar; Manchester Bar Association

Staff

Career Law Clerk **Tom Ring** .... (860) 240-3873
E-mail: tom_ring@ctd.uscourts.gov
Courtroom Deputy **Terri Glynn** .... (860) 240-3495
E-mail: terri_glynn@ctd.uscourts.gov
Judicial Assistant **Corinne L. Pike** .... (860) 240-3873
E-mail: corinne_pike@ctd.uscourts.gov

Chambers of Senior Judge Janet Bond Arterton

U.S. Courthouse, 141 Church Street, New Haven, CT 06510
Tel: (203) 773-2456
E-mail: janet_arterton@ctd.uscourts.gov

Janet Bond Arterton
Senior Judge

Date of Birth: 1944
Education: Mount Holyoke 1966 BA; Northeastern 1977 JD
Began Service: May 15, 1995
Appointed By: President William J. Clinton

Current Memberships: American Bar Foundation; Connecticut Bar Association, Inc.; Connecticut Bar Foundation, Connecticut Bar Association, Inc.; Federal Judges Association

Staff

Law Clerk **Jessica Harris** .... (203) 773-2046
Began Service: 2014
Term Expires: August 2016
E-mail: jessica_harris@ctd.uscourts.gov
Law Clerk **Margaux Poueymirou** .... (203) 773-2046
Began Service: August 2015
Term Expires: August 2017
E-mail: margaux_poueymirou@ctd.uscourts.gov
Courtroom Deputy **Betty Torday** .... (203) 773-2046
E-mail: betty_torday@ctd.uscourts.gov
Judicial Assistant **Aimee Magnan-Tooker** .... (203) 773-2456

Chambers of Magistrate Judge Joan G. Margolis

U.S. Courthouse, 141 Church Street, Room 303,
New Haven, CT 06510-2030
Tel: (203) 773-2350 Fax: (203) 773-2304
E-mail: joan_margolis@ctd.uscourts.gov

Joan G. Margolis
Magistrate Judge

Date of Birth: 1953
Education: Connecticut 1978 JD
Began Service: February 4, 1985
Term Expires: February 3, 2017

Clerkships: Law Clerk The Honorable Ellen B. Burns, United States District Court for the District of Connecticut

Legal Practice: Attorney, Wiggin and Dana LLP

Staff

Career Law Clerk **Monica Watson** .... (203) 773-2350
E-mail: monica_watson@ctd.uscourts.gov
Education: Fordham 1998 BS;
George Washington 2002 JD
Judicial Assistant **Rebecca Rodko** .... (203) 773-2350
E-mail: rebecca_rodko@ctd.uscourts.gov

Chambers of Magistrate Judge Donna F. Martinez

450 Main Street, Room 262, Hartford, CT 06103
Tel: (860) 240-3605
E-mail: donna_martinez@ctd.uscourts.gov

Donna F. Martinez
Magistrate Judge

Education: Connecticut 1973 BA, 1975 MSW, 1978 JD
Began Service: February 8, 1994
Term Expires: February 2018

Academic: Instructor, United States Department of Justice Advocacy Institute; Instructor, Law School, Yale University

Government: Assistant Corporation Counsel, Office of the Corporation Counsel, Town and City of Hartford, Connecticut; Assistant U.S. Attorney, Office the the United States Attorney, District of Connecticut, United States Department of Justice (1980-1989); Chief, Organized Crime/Drug Enforcement Task Force, Office the the United States Attorney, District of Connecticut, United States Department of Justice (1989-1994)

Current Memberships: The American Inns of Court; Connecticut Bar Association, Inc.; Federal Magistrate Judges Association

Staff

Law Clerk **Kristen Brierley** .... (860) 240-3605
Began Service: 2015
E-mail: kristen_brierley@ctd.uscourts.gov
Law Clerk **Elizabeth Jones** .... (860) 240-3605
Began Service: 2015
E-mail: elizabeth_jones@ctd.uscourts.gov
Career Law Clerk **Amy Constantine** .... (860) 240-3605
E-mail: amy_constantine@ctd.uscourts.gov
Education: Connecticut 1997 JD
Courtroom Deputy **Robert Wood** .... (860) 240-3210
E-mail: robert_wood@ctd.uscourts.gov

Chambers of Magistrate Judge William I. Garfinkel

915 Lafayette Boulevard, Suite 429, Bridgeport, CT 06604
Tel: (203) 579-5593 Fax: (203) 579-5946
E-mail: william_garfinkel@ctd.uscourts.gov

William I. Garfinkel
Magistrate Judge

Date of Birth: 1956
Education: Yale 1977 BA, 1981 JD
Began Service: November 22, 1996
Term Expires: November 2020

Academic: Visiting Lecturer, Yale College, Yale University (1984-1985); Clinical Instructor, School of Law, University of Bridgeport (1984-1986); Assistant Professor, School of Law, University of Bridgeport (1986-1988); Visiting Lecturer, Yale College (2003)

Clerkships: Law Clerk The Honorable Frederick Lacey, United States District Court for the District of New Jersey (1981-1982)

Government: Assistant District Attorney, City of New York, New York (1982-1983)

Legal Practice: Private Practice (1983-1984); Private Practice (1987-1996)

Current Memberships: Connecticut Bar Foundation, Connecticut Bar Association, Inc.

Staff

Career Law Clerk **Mary Mann Smith** .... (203) 579-5725
Education: Vanderbilt 1976 JD
Court Deputy **Kathi Torres** .... (203) 579-5656
E-mail: kathi_torres@ctd.uscourts.gov
Secretary/Judicial Assistant **Carol Sanders** .... (203) 579-5593
E-mail: carol_sanders@ctd.uscourts.gov

Chambers of Magistrate Judge Sarah A. L. Merriam

141 Church Street, New Haven, CT 06510
Tel: (203) 773-2022 Fax: (203) 773-2631
E-mail: sarah_merriam@ctd.uscourts.gov

Sarah A. L. Merriam
Magistrate Judge

Education: Yale 2000 JD
Began Service: 2015

Staff

Law Clerk **Samantha Katz** .... (203) 773-2022
E-mail: samantha_katz@ctd.uscourts.gov
Career Law Clerk **Alyssa G. Esposito** .... (203) 773-2022
E-mail: alyssa_espisito@ctd.uscourts.gov
Education: Boston Col; Quinnipiac 1993 JD
Courtroom Deputy **Breigh Freberg** .... (203) 773-2414
E-mail: breigh_freberg@ctd.uscourts.gov

United States Bankruptcy Court for the District of Connecticut

U.S. Courthouse, 450 Main Street, Hartford, CT 06103
Tel: (860) 240-3675 Tel: (203) 240-3570 (PACER)
Tel: (203) 240-3345 (Voice Case Information System VCIS)
Tel: (800) 800-5113 (Toll Free Voice Case Information System VCIS)
Fax: (860) 240-3595
Internet: www.ctb.uscourts.gov

Number of Judgeships: 3

Court Staff

Clerk of the Court **Gary M. Gfeller** .... (860) 240-3845
E-mail: gary_gfeller@ctb.uscourts.gov Fax: (860) 240-3680
Chief Deputy **Myrna Atwater** .... (203) 579-5809
U.S. Courthouse, 915 Lafayette Blvd.,
Bridgeport, CT 06604
E-mail: myrna_atwater@ctb.uscourts.gov

United States Bankruptcy Court for the District of Connecticut *continued*

Divisional Manager **Nancy Humlicek** . . . . (860) 221-7757
E-mail: nancy_humlicek@ctb.uscourts.gov
Divisional Manager **Regina Miltenberger** . . . . (203) 773-2752
CT Financial Ctr., 157 Church St.,
New Haven, CT 06510
E-mail: regina_miltenberger@ctb.uscourts.gov
Divisional Manager **Sue Waterbury** . . . . (203) 579-5513
U.S. Courthouse, 915 Lafayette Blvd., Fax: (203) 579-5827
Bridgeport, CT 06604
E-mail: sue_waterbury@ctb.uscourts.gov
Personnel Manager **(Vacant)** . . . . (860) 221-7755
Systems Manager **Dee Allegro** . . . . (860) 221-7753
E-mail: dee_allegro@ctb.uscourts.gov

Chambers of Chief Bankruptcy Judge Julie A. Manning

157 Church Street, New Haven, CT 06510
Tel: (203) 773-2717

Julie A. Manning
Chief Bankruptcy Judge

Chambers of Bankruptcy Judge Alan H. W. Shiff

915 Lafayette Boulevard, Room 104, Bridgeport, CT 06604
Tel: (203) 579-5806 Fax: (203) 579-5515
E-mail: Alan_H_W_Shiff@ctb.uscourts.gov

Alan H. W. Shiff
Bankruptcy Judge

Date of Birth: 1934
Education: Yale 1957 BA; Virginia 1960 LLB
Began Service: 1981
Term Expires: March 19, 2017

Judicial: Chief Judge, U.S Bankruptcy Court for the District of Connecticut (1981-2000)

Legal Practice: Partner, Shiff, Shiff & Schancupp (1960-1981)

Current Memberships: Connecticut Bar Association, Inc.

Staff

Career Law Clerk **Patricia A. Killigrew** . . . . (203) 551-3362
Began Service: 2008
E-mail: pat_killigrew@ctb.uscourts.gov
Education: Vermont Law 1998 JD
Court Reporter **(Vacant)** . . . . (203) 579-5806 ext. 5502
Fax: (203) 579-5827
Judicial Assistant **Rosemary Rizzico** . . . . (203) 551-3361
E-mail: rosemary_rizzico@ctb.uscourts.gov

Chambers of Bankruptcy Judge Ann M. Nevins

450 Main Street, 7th Floor, Hartford, CT 06103
Tel: (860) 240-3176 Fax: (860) 240-3848

Ann M. Nevins
Bankruptcy Judge

Staff

Career Law Clerk **Patricia Adams** . . . . (203) 240-3176
E-mail: patricia_adams@ctb.uscourts.gov
Education: Hunter 1970 BA; Connecticut 1998 JD
Courtroom Deputy **Lisa Durrenberger** . . . . (860) 240-3176
E-mail: lisa_durrenberger@ctb.uscourts.gov

United States District Court for the District of Delaware

J. Caleb Boggs Federal Building, 844 North King Street,
Wilmington, DE 19801
Tel: (302) 573-6170 Tel: (302) 573-6395 (PACER)
Internet: www.ded.uscourts.gov

Number of Judgeships: 4

Circuit: Third

Court Staff

Clerk of the Court **John A. Cerino** . . . . (302) 573-6170
Room 4209
E-mail: john_cerino@ded.uscourts.gov
Chief Deputy Clerk **George Wylesol** . . . . (302) 573-6170
E-mail: george_wylesol@ded.uscourts.gov
Systems Manager **Timothy O'Hora** . . . . (302) 573-6685
E-mail: tim_ohora@ded.uscourts.gov
Intake Supervisor **Bob Cruikshank** . . . . (302) 573-6158
Chief Probation Officer **(Vacant)** . . . . (302) 252-2950
824 Market Street, Unit 39, Wilmington, DE 19801

Chambers of Chief Judge Leonard P. Stark

844 North King Street, Unit 26, Room 6100, Wilmington, DE 19801-3556
Tel: (302) 573-4571
E-mail: judge_leonard_stark@ded.uscourts.gov

Leonard P. Stark
Chief Judge

Education: Delaware 1991; Yale 1996 JD
Began Service: August 16, 2010
Appointed By: President Barack Obama

Staff

Courtroom Deputy **Ron Golden** . . . . (302) 573-4538

Chambers of District Judge Gregory M. Sleet

J. Caleb Boggs Federal Building, 844 North King Street, Lockbox 19, Room 4324, Wilmington, DE 19801
Tel: (302) 573-6470 Fax: (302) 573-6472
E-mail: judge_gregory_sleet@ded.uscourts.gov

Gregory M. Sleet
District Judge

Date of Birth: 1951
Education: Hampton 1973 BA; Rutgers (Camden) 1976 JD
Began Service: September 28, 1998
Appointed By: President William J. Clinton

Staff

Courtroom Deputy **Mark Buckson** . . . . (302) 573-6471
Case Manager **April Walker** . . . . (302) 573-6651
E-mail: april_walker@ded.uscourts.gov
Court Reporter **Kevin Maurer** . . . . (302) 573-6196
E-mail: kevin_maurer@ded.uscourts.gov
Judicial Administrator **Cynthia Tyer-Daly** . . . . (302) 573-6470
E-mail: cynthia_tyerdaly@ded.uscourts.gov

Chambers of District Judge Sue L. Robinson

J. Caleb Boggs Federal Building, 844 North King Street, Unit 31, Room 4124, Wilmington, DE 19801
Tel: (302) 573-6310 Fax: (302) 573-6064

Sue L. Robinson
District Judge

Date of Birth: 1952
Education: Delaware 1974 BA; Pennsylvania 1978 JD
Began Service: 1991
Appointed By: President George H.W. Bush

Government: Assistant United States Attorney, District of Delaware, United States Department of Justice (1983-1988)

Judicial: Magistrate Judge, United States District Court for the District of Delaware (1988-1991); Judge, United States District Court for the District of Delaware (1991-2000); Member, Judicial Conference of the United States (2000-2003); Chief Judge, United States District Court District of Delaware (2000-2007)

Legal Practice: Associate, Potter Anderson & Corroon LLP (1978-1983)

Staff
Law Clerk **Tinna Otero** .... (302) 573-6310
E-mail: tinna_otero@ded.uscourts.gov
Law Clerk **Laura Gordon** .... (302) 573-6310
Courtroom Deputy/Docketing Clerk **Francesca Scarpato** .... (302) 573-6356
E-mail: francesca_scarpato@ded.uscourts.gov
Case Manager **Nicole Nolt** .... (302) 573-6129
Court Reporter **Valerie Gunning** .... (302) 573-6194
E-mail: valerie_gunning@ded.uscourts.gov
Attorney/Office Manager **Maria Alvino** .... (302) 573-6310
E-mail: maria_alvino@ded.uscourts.gov
Education: St Joseph's U 1986 BA; Widener 1989 JD

Chambers of District Judge Richard G. Andrews

844 North King Street, Unit 9, Room 6325, Wilmington, DE 19801
Tel: (302) 573-4581
E-mail: judge_richard_andrews@ded.uscourts.gov

Richard G. Andrews
District Judge

Education: Haverford 1977 BA; Boalt Hall 1987 JD
Began Service: February 13, 2012
Appointed By: President Barack Obama

Clerkships: Law Clerk, Chambers of Circuit Judge Collins J. Seitz, United States Court of Appeals for the Third Circuit (1981-1982)

Government: Assistant U.S. Attorney, Delaware District, Executive Office for United States Attorneys, United States Department of Justice (1983-2006); First Assistant U.S. Attorney, Delaware District, Executive Office for United States Attorneys, United States Department of Justice; Chief, Criminal Division, Delaware District, United States Department of Justice

Staff
Case Manager **Nicole Selmyer** .... (302) 573-6137
Court Reporter **Leonard Dibbs** .... (302) 573-6195
E-mail: leonard_dibbs@ded.uscourts.gov
Courtroom Deputy **Kristin Ringgold** .... (302) 573-4536
E-mail: kristin_ringgold@ded.uscourts.gov

Chambers of Magistrate Judge Mary Pat Thynge

J. Caleb Boggs Federal Building, 844 North King Street, Unit 8, Wilmington, DE 19801
Tel: (302) 573-6173 Fax: (302) 573-6445

Mary Pat Thynge
Magistrate Judge

Date of Birth: 1951
Education: Miami U (OH) 1972 BS; Ohio Northern 1975 JD
Began Service: June 17, 1992
Term Expires: June 2016

Legal Practice: Associate, Biggs & Battaglia (1975-1989); Managing Attorney, White and Williams LLP (1989-1992)

Current Memberships: Delaware State Bar Association; Federal Magistrate Judges Association; National Association of Women Judges

Staff
Career Law Clerk **Robert Anderson** .... (302) 573-4537
Began Service: 2004
E-mail: robert_anderson@ded.uscourts.gov
Education: Alabama 1987 BA; Georgia 1998 BS, 2001 JD
Courtroom Deputy **Keith Kincaid** .... (302) 573-6128
E-mail: keith_kincaid@ded.uscourts.gov
Judicial Assistant **Cathleen A. Kennedy** .... (302) 573-6173
E-mail: cathleen_kennedy@ded.uscourts.gov

Chambers of Magistrate Judge Christopher J. Burke

844 North King Street, Room 6100, Wilmington, DE 19801-3555
Tel: (302) 573-4591
E-mail: judge_christopher_burke@ded.uscourts.gov

Christopher J. Burke
Magistrate Judge

Education: Michigan 2000 JD
Began Service: August 4, 2011

Staff
Courtroom Deputy **Deborah Krett** .... (302) 573-4591
E-mail: deborah_krett@ded.uscourts.gov

Chambers of Magistrate Judge Sherry R. Fallon

844 North King Street, Wilmington, DE 19801
Tel: (302) 573-4551
E-mail: judge_sherry_fallon@ded.uscourts.gov

Sherry R. Fallon
Magistrate Judge

Began Service: April 25, 2012

Staff
Courtroom Deputy **Larisha Hicks** .... (302) 573-4551
E-mail: larisha_hicks@ded.uscourts.gov

United States Bankruptcy Court for the District of Delaware

824 Market Street, Wilmington, DE 19801
Tel: (302) 252-2900 Tel: (800) 676-6856 (Toll Free PACER)
Tel: (302) 252-2560 (Voice Case Information System VCIS)
E-mail: helpdesk@deb.uscourts.gov
Internet: www.deb.uscourts.gov

Number of Judgeships: 6

Court Staff
Clerk of Court **David D. Bird** .... (302) 252-2900
E-mail: david_bird@deb.uscourts.gov

United States Bankruptcy Court for the District of Delaware *continued*

Executive Assistant to Clerk of Court
Marjorie C. Ciunci . . . . (302) 252-2900
E-mail: marjorie_ciunci@deb.uscourts.gov
Chief Deputy Clerk **Stacey Dreschler** . . . . (302) 252-2900
E-mail: stacey_manley@deb.uscourts.gov
Administrative Services Director **Jan Morrill** . . . . (302) 252-2900
E-mail: jan_morrill@deb.uscourts.gov
Facilities and Procurement Specialist **Todd Kirk** . . . . (302) 252-2900
E-mail: todd_kirk@deb.uscourts.gov

Chambers of Chief Bankruptcy Judge Brendan L. Shannon

824 Market Street, 6th Floor, Wilmington, DE 19801
Tel: (302) 252-2915

Brendan L. Shannon
Chief Bankruptcy Judge

Education: Princeton; William & Mary JD
Began Service: 2006

Staff
Courtroom Deputy **Rachel Bello** . . . . (302) 252-2915
E-mail: rachel_bello@deb.uscourts.gov
Judicial Assistant **Jill Walker** . . . . (302) 252-2915
E-mail: jill_walker@deb.uscourts.gov

Chambers of Bankruptcy Judge Kevin Gross

824 Market Street, 6th Floor, Wilmington, DE 19801
Tel: (302) 252-2913

Kevin Gross
Bankruptcy Judge

Began Service: 2006

Staff
Courtroom Deputy **Sherry Scaruzzi** . . . . (302) 252-2913
E-mail: sherry_scaruzzi@deb.uscourts.gov
Judicial Assistant **Laura Haney** . . . . (302) 252-2913
E-mail: laura_strong@deb.uscourts.gov

Chambers of Bankruptcy Judge Kevin J. Carey

824 Market Street, 5th Floor, Wilmington, DE 19801
Tel: (302) 252-2927

Kevin J. Carey
Bankruptcy Judge

Date of Birth: 1954
Education: Penn State 1976 BA; Villanova 1979 JD
Began Service: December 9, 2005
Term Expires: December 2019

Staff
Career Law Clerk **Janet I. Moore** . . . . (302) 252-2927 ext. 4
E-mail: janet_moore@deb.uscourts.gov
Courtroom Deputy **Nancy Hunt** . . . . (302) 252-2927 ext. 3
E-mail: nancy_hunt@deb.uscourts.gov
Judicial Assistant **Donna Jean Grottini** . . . . (302) 252-2927 ext. 2

Chambers of Bankruptcy Judge Mary F. Walrath

824 Market Street, 5th Floor, Wilmington, DE 19801
Tel: (302) 252-2929

Mary F. Walrath
Bankruptcy Judge

Began Service: 1998

Chambers of Bankruptcy Judge Mary F. Walrath *continued*

Staff
Courtroom Deputy **Laurie Capp** . . . . (302) 252-2929
E-mail: laurie_capp@deb.uscourts.gov
Judicial Assistant **Catherine Farrell** . . . . (302) 252-2929
E-mail: catherine_farrell@deb.uscourts.gov

Chambers of Bankruptcy Judge Christopher S. Sontchi

824 Market Street, 5th Floor, Wilmington, DE 19801-4917
Tel: (302) 252-2888

Christopher S. Sontchi
Bankruptcy Judge

Began Service: 2006
Term Expires: February 22, 2020

Staff
Career Law Clerk **Rachel Werkheiser** . . . . (302) 252-2888
Began Service: September 2009
E-mail: rachel_werkheiser@deb.uscourts.gov
Courtroom Deputy **Danielle Gadson** . . . . (302) 252-2888
E-mail: danielle_gadson@deb.uscourts.gov
Judicial Assistant **Cheryl A. Szymanski** . . . . (302) 252-2888

Chambers of Bankruptcy Judge Laurie Selber Silverstein

824 Market Street, 6th Floor, Wilmington, DE 19801
Tel: (302) 252-2925

Laurie Selber Silverstein
Bankruptcy Judge

Education: Delaware 1982 BA; George Washington 1985 JD

Staff
Courtroom Deputy **Lora Johnson** . . . . (302) 252-2925
Judicial Assistant **Cacia Batts** . . . . (302) 252-2925

United States District Court for the Middle District of Florida

U.S. Courthouse & Federal Building, 401 West Central Boulevard, Suite 1200, Orlando, FL 32801
Tel: (407) 835-4200 Tel: (800) 676-6856 (Toll Free PACER)
Fax: (407) 835-4207
Internet: www.flmd.uscourts.gov

Number of Judgeships: 15

Number of Vacancies: 2

Circuit: Eleventh

Areas Covered: Counties of Baker, Bradford, Brevard, Charlotte, Citrus, Clay, Collier, Columbia, DeSoto, Duval, Flagler, Glades, Hamilton, Hardee, Hendry, Hernando, Hillsborough, Lake, Lee, Manatee, Marion, Nassau, Orange, Osceola, Pasco, Pinellas, Polk, Putnam, Sarasota, Seminole, St. Johns, Sumter, Suwannee, Union and Volusia

Court Staff

Clerk of Court **Sheryl L. Loesch** . . . . (407) 835-4222
E-mail: sheryl_loesch@flmd.uscourts.gov Fax: (407) 835-4228
Division Manager, Fort Myers Division
Drew Heathcoat . . . . (239) 461-2002
U.S. Courthouse & Federal Bldg., 2110 First St., Rm. 2-194, Fort Myers, FL 33901 Fax: (239) 461-2034
E-mail: drew_heathcoat@flmd.uscourts.gov
Jacksonville Division Manager **Jim Leanhart** . . . . (904) 549-1313
300 North Hogan Street, 9th Floor, Jacksonville, FL 32202-4242
E-mail: jim_leanhart@flmd.uscourts.gov

(continued on next page)

United States District Court for the Middle District of Florida *continued*

Operations Manager **Shannon Shoulders** . . . . (904) 549-1984
U.S. Courthouse, 300 North Hogan Street, 9th Floor, Jacksonville, FL 32202 Fax: (904) 549-1969
E-mail: shannon_shoulders@flmd.uscourts.gov
Ocala Operations Supervisor **Jim Leanhart** . . . . (352) 369-7402
E-mail: jim_leanhart@flmd.uscourts.gov
Tampa Division Manager **Mark Middlebrook** . . . . (813) 301-5394
E-mail: mark_middlebrook@flmd.uscourts.gov
Division Manager, Orlando Division and Ocala Division **Sara Boswell** . . . . (407) 835-4201
E-mail: sara_boswell@flmd.uscourts.gov Fax: (407) 835-4207
Chief Probation Officer **Joseph Collins** . . . . (813) 301-5600
U.S. Probation Office, 501 E. Polk Street, Room 3955, Tampa, FL 33602-3945 Fax: (813) 301-5569
Chief Pretrial Services Officer **Shelia Arrington Jacoby** . . . . (407) 835-3950
Fairwinds Bank Building, 135 West Central Boulevard, Suite 740, Orlando, FL 32801 Fax: (407) 648-6826
Chief Deputy of Operations **Elizabeth Warren** . . . . (407) 835-4351
E-mail: elizabeth_warren@flmd.uscourts.gov Fax: (407) 835-4228
Chief Deputy of Administration **Johnnie Prophet** . . . . (813) 301-5158
Fax: (813) 301-5390

Chambers of Chief Judge Steven D. Merryday

Sam M. Gibbons U.S. Courthouse, 801 North Florida Avenue, Tampa, FL 33602-3800
Tel: (813) 301-5001
E-mail: steven_merryday@flmd.uscourts.gov

Steven D. Merryday
Chief Judge

Date of Birth: 1950
Education: Florida 1972 BA, 1975 JD
Began Service: March 16, 1992
Appointed By: President George H.W. Bush

Current Memberships: Federal Bar Association; The Florida Bar

Staff
Law Clerk **Chiseul "Kylie" Kim** . . . . (813) 301-5001
Began Service: August 2015
Term Expires: August 2017
Law Clerk **Andrew Peluso** . . . . (813) 301-5001
E-mail: andrew_peluso@flmd.uscourts.gov
Court Reporter **Howard Jones** . . . . (813) 301-5024
E-mail: howard_jones@flmd.uscourts.gov
Courtroom Deputy **Lindsay Meadows** . . . . (813) 301-5006
E-mail: lindsay_meadows@flmd.uscourts.gov
Judicial Assistant **Becky Kline** . . . . (813) 301-5001
E-mail: becky_kline@flmd.uscourts.gov

Chambers of District Judge Elizabeth A. Kovachevich

Sam M. Gibbons U.S. Courthouse, 801 North Florida Avenue, Tampa, FL 33602
Tel: (813) 301-5730
E-mail: elizabeth_kovachevich@flmd.uscourts.gov

Elizabeth A. Kovachevich
District Judge

Date of Birth: 1936
Education: Miami 1958 BBA; Stetson 1961 JD
Began Service: 1982
Appointed By: President Ronald Reagan

Judicial: Secretary, St. Petersburg Bar Association (1969); Member, Board of Regents, Florida (1970-1972); Circuit Judge, Florida Circuit Court, Sixth Judicial Circuit (1973-1982); Judicial Member and Co-Chairman, St. Petersburg Bar Association (1978-1982); Chief Judge, United States District Court for the Middle District of Florida (1996-2002)

Legal Practice: Associate, DiVito & Speer (1961-1962); Private Practice (1962-1973)

Chambers of District Judge Elizabeth A. Kovachevich *continued*

Current Memberships: The Florida Bar

Staff
Law Clerk **Ryan McGee** . . . . (813) 301-5730
E-mail: ryan_mcgee@flmd.uscourts.gov
Career Law Clerk **Julie C. Meisner** . . . . (813) 301-5730
E-mail: julie_meisner@flmd.uscourts.gov
Education: Stetson 1997 JD
Career Law Clerk **Sherrill Newton** . . . . (813) 301-5730
E-mail: sherrill_newton@flmd.uscourts.gov
Education: Florida JD
Staff Attorney **Sheila McNeill** . . . . (813) 301-5700
E-mail: sheila_mcneill@flmd.uscourts.gov
Courtroom Deputy **Cindy Leigh-Martin** . . . . (813) 301-5737
E-mail: cindy_leigh-martin@flmd.uscourts.gov
Court Reporter **Sandra K. Provenzano** . . . . (813) 301-5699
E-mail: sandra_lee@flmd.uscourts.gov

Chambers of District Judge James D. Whittemore

Sam M. Gibbons U.S. Courthouse, 801 North Florida Avenue, Suite 13-B, Tampa, FL 33602
Tel: (813) 301-5880 Fax: (813) 301-5610
E-mail: james_whittemore@flmd.uscourts.gov

James D. Whittemore
District Judge

Education: Florida 1974 BS; Stetson 1977 JD
Began Service: May 27, 2000
Appointed By: President William J. Clinton

Government: Assistant Federal Public Defender, Office of the Federal Public Defender (1978-1981)

Judicial: Circuit Judge, 13th Judicial Circuit Court, County of Hillsborough, Florida (1990-2000)

Legal Practice: Law Clerk and Associate, Bauer, Morlan & Wells, PA (1977); Associate, Whittemore & Seybold, PA (1981-1982); Associate, Whittemore & Campbell, PA (1982-1987); Sole Practitioner (1987-1990)

Staff
Law Clerk **Sarah Anderson** . . . . (813) 301-5880
E-mail: sarah_anderson@flmd.uscourts.gov
Law Clerk **Marena Bard** . . . . (813) 301-5880
E-mail: marena_bard@flmd.uscourts.gov
Law Clerk **Joseph Logan Murphy** . . . . (813) 301-5880
E-mail: joseph_murphy@flmd.uscourts.gov
Court Reporter **Lynann Nicely** . . . . (813) 301-5252
E-mail: lynann_nicely@flmd.uscourts.gov
Courtroom Deputy **Anne Ohle** . . . . (813) 301-5886
E-mail: anne_ohle@flmd.uscourts.gov
Judicial Assistant **Kristin Esposito** . . . . (813) 301-5886
E-mail: kristin_esposito@flmd.uscourts.gov

Chambers of District Judge Timothy J. Corrigan

300 North Hogan Street, Jacksonville, FL 32202-4247
Tel: (904) 549-1300
E-mail: timothy_corrigan@flmd.uscourts.gov

Timothy J. Corrigan
District Judge

Date of Birth: 1956
Education: Notre Dame 1978 BA; Duke 1981 JD
Began Service: September 14, 2002
Appointed By: President George W. Bush

Staff
Law Clerk **Bradley Bulthuis** . . . . (904) 549-1302
E-mail: bradley_bulthuis@flmd.uscourts.gov
Law Clerk **William Guappone** . . . . (904) 549-1311
E-mail: william_guappone@flmd.uscourts.gov

Chambers of District Judge Timothy J. Corrigan *continued*

Career Law Clerk **Susanne R. Weisman** . . . . (904) 549-1304
E-mail: susanne_weisman@flmd.uscourts.gov
Education: Florida Coastal 1999 JD
Court Reporter **Shannon Bishop** . . . . (904) 549-1307
E-mail: shannon_bishop@flmd.uscourts.gov
Courtroom Deputy **Marielena Diaz** . . . . (904) 549-1303
E-mail: marielena_diaz@flmd.uscourts.gov

Chambers of District Judge Virginia M. Hernandez Covington

801 North Florida Avenue, 14th Floor, Tampa, FL 33602-3899
Tel: (813) 301-5340 Fax: (813) 301-5630
E-mail: virginia_covington@flmd.uscourts.gov

Virginia M. Hernandez Covington
District Judge

Date of Birth: 1955
Education: Tampa 1976 BS, 1977 MBA; Georgetown 1980 JD
Began Service: September 10, 2004
Appointed By: President George W. Bush

Government: Trial Attorney, Federal Trade Commission (1980-1981); Assistant State Attorney, County of Hillsborough, Florida (1982-1983); Assistant United States Attorney, Florida - Middle District, Office of the Attorney General, United States Department of Justice (1983-2001)

Judicial: Appellate Judge, Florida District Court of Appeal, Second District (2001-2004)

Staff
Law Clerk **Kendyl Tash** . . . . (813) 301-5344
Began Service: 2014
E-mail: kendyl_tash@flmd.uscourts.gov
Law Clerk **Krista Cammack** . . . . (813) 301-5346
E-mail: krista_cammack@flmd.uscourts.gov
Career Law Clerk **Kelley A. Keller Landkammer** . . . . (813) 301-5347
Education: Stetson 2003 JD
Court Reporter **Scott N. Gamertsfelder** . . . . (813) 301-5898
E-mail: scott_n_gamertsfelder@flmd.uscourts.gov
Courtroom Deputy **Julia Wright** . . . . (813) 301-5348

Chambers of District Judge Marcia Morales Howard

300 North Hogan Street, Jacksonville, FL 32202
Tel: (904) 301-6750 Fax: (904) 301-6757
E-mail: marcia_howard@flmd.uscourts.gov

Marcia Morales Howard
District Judge

Date of Birth: July 16, 1965
Education: Vanderbilt 1987 BS; Florida 1990 JD
Began Service: February 2007
Appointed By: President George W. Bush

Corporate: Counsel, Shawmut Bank of Boston, N.A. (1989-1990)

Judicial: Magistrate Judge, United States District Court for the Middle District of Florida (2003-2007)

Legal Practice: Associate, Commander, Legler, Werber, Dawes, Sadler & Howell (1990-1991); Associate, Foley & Lardner LLP (1991-1994); Partner, Hawkins Delafield & Wood LLP (1992-1998); Associate, McGuireWoods LLP (1994-1998); Partner, McGuireWoods LLP (1998-2003)

Current Memberships: American Bar Association; Federal Bar Association; Federal Magistrate Judges Association; The Florida Bar; Hispanic Bar Association of Northeast Florida; Jacksonville Bar Association

Staff
Law Clerk **Kelly Blair** . . . . (904) 301-6750
E-mail: kelly_blair@flmd.uscourts.gov
Law Clerk **Lauren Blocker** . . . . (904) 301-6750
E-mail: lauren_blocker@flmd.uscourts.gov

Chambers of District Judge Marcia Morales Howard *continued*

Law Clerk **Jane Lester** . . . . (904) 301-6750
E-mail: jane_lester@flmd.uscourts.gov
Education: Florida 1984 JD
Law Clerk **Margaret Peggy Miller** . . . . (904) 301-6750
E-mail: peggy_miller@flmd.uscourts.gov
Courtroom Deputy **Jodi Wiles** . . . . (904) 301-6750
E-mail: jodi_wiles@flmd.uscourts.gov

Chambers of District Judge Mary Stenson Scriven

401 West Central Boulevard, Orlando, FL 32801
Tel: (813) 301-5710 Fax: (407) 835-3849
E-mail: mary_scriven@flmd.uscourts.gov

Mary Stenson Scriven
District Judge

Date of Birth: 1962
Education: Florida State 1987 JD
Began Service: September 30, 2008
Appointed By: President George W. Bush

Current Memberships: George Edgecomb Bar Association; Hillsborough County Bar Association

Staff
Law Clerk **Kayla M. Scarpone** . . . . (407) 835-3841
Term Expires: August 2016
E-mail: kayla_scarpone@flmd.uscourts.gov
Law Clerk **Kenya J. Reddy** . . . . (407) 835-3843
Term Expires: June 2016
E-mail: kenya_reddy@flmd.uscourts.gov
Education: Virginia 2000 JD
Law Clerk **Brian Porter** . . . . (407) 835-3844
Term Expires: August 2016
E-mail: brian_porter@flmd.uscourts.gov
Courtroom Deputy **Anaida Vinza** . . . . (407) 835-4219
E-mail: anaida_vinza@flmd.uscourts.gov

Chambers of District Judge Charlene Edwards Honeywell

401 West Central Boulevard, Orlando, FL 32801
Tel: (407) 835-3840 Fax: (407) 835-3849
E-mail: charlene_honeywell@flmd.uscourts.gov

Charlene Edwards Honeywell
District Judge

Date of Birth: 1957
Education: Howard U 1979; Florida 1981 JD
Began Service: November 2009
Appointed By: President Barack Obama

Government: Public Defender, Office of the Public Defender, County of Leon, Florida (1982-1985); Assistant Public Defender, Office of the Public Defender, County of Hillsborough, Florida (1985-1987); Assistant City Attorney, Office of the City Attorney, City of Tampa, Florida (1987-1994)

Judicial: County Court Judge, Thirteenth Judicial Circuit, Florida Circuit Court (1994)

Legal Practice: Attorney, Hill Ward Henderson (1995-2000)

Current Memberships: American Bar Association; National Bar Association

Staff
Law Clerk **Amanda Clay** . . . . (239) 461-2173
Term Expires: June 30, 2016
E-mail: amanda_clay@flmd.uscourts.gov
Law Clerk **Alexander Hu** . . . . (239) 461-2174
Term Expires: June 30, 2016
E-mail: alexander_hu@flmd.uscourts.gov
Court Reporter **(Vacant)** . . . . (239) 461-2064
Courtroom Deputy **Willye MalVeaux Dent** . . . . (239) 461-2005

(continued on next page)

Chambers of District Judge Charlene Edwards Honeywell *continued*

Judicial Assistant **Bettye G. Samuel** . . . . (239) 461-2170
E-mail: bettye_samuel@flmd.uscourts.gov

Chambers of District Judge Roy B. Dalton, Jr.

401 West Central Boulevard, Orlando, FL 32801
Tel: (407) 835-2590 Fax: (407) 835-2596
E-mail: chambers_flmd_dalton@flmd.uscourts.gov

Roy Bale Dalton, Jr.
District Judge

Date of Birth: 1952
Education: Florida 1974 BA, 1976 JD
Began Service: May 4, 2011
Appointed By: President Barack Obama

Legal Practice: Counsel, Office of Senator Mel R. Martinez, United States Senate (2005)

Current Memberships: American College of Trial Lawyers

Staff

Law Clerk **Lauren Millcarek** . . . . (407) 835-2590
E-mail: lauren_millcarek@flmd.uscourts.gov
Law Clerk **Colleen Conley** . . . . (407) 835-2590
E-mail: colleen_conley@flmd.uscourts.gov
Law Clerk **Ryan T. Hopper** . . . . (407) 835-2590
E-mail: ryan_t_hopper@flmd.uscourts.gov
Court Reporter **Diane Peede** . . . . (407) 835-2590
E-mail: diane_peede@flmd.uscourts.gov
Courtroom Deputy (Acting) **Virginia "Ginny" Flick** . . . . . (407) 835-2590
E-mail: virginia_flick@flmd.uscourts.gov
Education: Penn State 1976 BA; Duquesne 1980 JD

Chambers of District Judge Sheri Polster Chappell

2110 First Street, Fort Myers, FL 33901
Tel: (239) 461-2060 Fax: (239) 461-2139
E-mail: sheri_chappell@flmd.uscourts.gov

Sheri Polster Chappell
District Judge

Date of Birth: May 30, 1962
Education: Wisconsin 1984 BA; Nova Southeastern 1987 JD
Began Service: May 28, 2013
Appointed By: President Barack Obama

Government: Assistant State Attorney, Twentieth Judicial Circuit, Florida Circuit Court (1987-2000)

Judicial: Judge, Lee County Court, Florida (2000-2003); Magistrate Judge, Chambers of Magistrate Judge Sheri Polster Chappell, United States District Court for the Middle District of Florida (2003-2013)

Current Memberships: The Calusa American Inn of Court, The American Inns of Court; Federal Bar Association; Lee County Bar Association

Staff

Law Clerk **Anitra Raiford** . . . . (239) 461-2060
E-mail: anitra_raiford@flmd.uscourts.gov
Education: Florida 2012 JD
Career Law Clerk **Douglas Kemp** . . . . (239) 461-2060
E-mail: douglas_kemp@flmd.uscourts.gov
Education: Baylor BA; Millsaps MA; Stetson 2002 JD
Courtroom Deputy **Leslie Friedmann** . . . . (239) 461-2068
E-mail: leslie_m_friedmann@flmd.uscourts.gov
Court Reporter **Lori Bundy** . . . . (239) 461-2064

Chambers of District Judge Brian J. Davis

401 West Central Boulevard, Orlando, FL 32801
Tel: (904) 301-6625 Fax: (904) 301-6866
E-mail: brian_davis@flmd.uscourts.gov

Brian J. Davis
District Judge

Education: Princeton 1974 BA; Florida 1980 JD
Began Service: December 30, 2013
Appointed By: President Barack Obama

Staff

Career Law Clerk **Michael Gropper** . . . . (904) 301-6625
E-mail: michael_gropper@flmd.uscourts.gov
Career Law Clerk **Michael White** . . . . (904) 301-6625
E-mail: michael_white@flmd.uscourts.gov
Courtroom Deputy **Emily Morin** . . . . (904) 301-6625
E-mail: emily_morin@flmd.uscourts.gov
Judicial Assistant **Agnes Prelow** . . . . (904) 301-6625
E-mail: agnes_prelow@flmd.uscourts.gov

Chambers of District Judge Paul G. Byron

401 West Central Boulevard, Orlando, FL 32801
Tel: (407) 835-4321 Fax: (407) 835-4277
E-mail: chambers_flmd_byron@flmd.uscourts.gov

Paul G. Byron
District Judge

Education: Michigan 1983 AB; LSU Hebert Law 1986 JD
Began Service: June 27, 2014
Appointed By: President Barack Obama

Government: Assistant U.S. Attorney, Florida - Middle District, Executive Office for United States Attorneys, United States Department of Justice (1991-2001); Senior Trial Attorney, International Criminal Tribunal for the Former Yugoslavia (2001-2003)

Legal Practice: Partner, NeJame, Lefay, Barker, Byron, P.A. (2003-2004)

Staff

Law Clerk **Robin Lucas** . . . . (407) 835-4321
E-mail: robin_lucas@flmd.uscourts.gov
Law Clerk **Steven Nauman** . . . . (407) 835-4321
E-mail: steven_nauman@flmd.uscourts.gov
Law Clerk **Melanie Weese-Bennett** . . . . (407) 835-4321
Court Reporter **Koretta Stanford** . . . . (407) 872-1715
E-mail: koretta_stanford@flmd.uscourts.gov
Courtroom Deputy **Nancy Leiter** . . . . (407) 835-4321
E-mail: nancy_leiter@flmd.uscourts.gov

Chambers of District Judge Carlos Eduardo Mendoza

401 West Central Boulevard, Orlando, FL 32801
Tel: (407) 835-4310 Fax: (407) 835-5800
E-mail: carlos_mendoza@flmd.uscourts.gov

Carlos Eduardo Mendoza
District Judge

Education: West Virginia 1993 BA, 1997 JD
Began Service: 2014
Appointed By: President Barack Obama

Government: Assistant State Attorney, Seventh Judicial Circuit, Florida Circuit Courts (2005-2008)

Chambers of Senior Judge Henry Lee Adams, Jr.
U.S. Courthouse, 300 North Hogan Street, Suite 11-200,
Jacksonville, FL 32202-4245
Tel: (904) 549-1930
E-mail: henry_adams@flmd.uscourts.gov

Henry Lee Adams, Jr.
Senior Judge

Date of Birth: 1945
Education: Florida A&M 1966 BS; Howard U 1969 JD
Began Service: December 10, 1993
Appointed By: President William J. Clinton

Government: Assistant Public Defender, Fourth Judicial Circuit, State of Florida (1970-1972)

Judicial: Judge, Florida Circuit Court, Fourth Judicial Circuit (1979-1993)

Legal Practice: Partner, Sheppard, Fletcher, Hand & Adams (1972-1976); Partner, Marshall & Adams (1976-1979)

Current Memberships: D.W. Perkins Bar Association; The Florida Bar; Jacksonville Bar Association; National Bar Association

Staff
Courtroom Deputy **Marsha Grant** .... (904) 549-1902
E-mail: marsha_grant@flmd.uscourts.gov
Judicial Assistant **Mary Oliver** .... (904) 549-1930
E-mail: mary_oliver@flmd.uscourts.gov

Chambers of Senior Judge William J. Castagna
801 North Florida Avenue, Chambers 7A, Tampa, FL 33602-3800
Tel: (813) 301-5935 Fax: (813) 301-5335
E-mail: william_castagna@flmd.uscourts.gov

William J. Castagna
Senior Judge

Date of Birth: June 24, 1924
Education: Florida 1949 LLB
Began Service: July 24, 1979
Appointed By: President Jimmy Carter

Legal Practice: Private Practice (1949-1970); Partner, MacKenzie, Castagna, Bennison & Gardner (1970-1979)

Military Service: United States Air Force (1943-1945)

Staff
Career Law Clerk **Raequel Tomsich** .... (813) 301-5535
E-mail: raequel_tomsich@flmd.uscourts.gov
Education: Eastern Michigan 1991 BS;
Stetson 1994 JD

Chambers of Senior Judge Wm. Terrell Hodges
207 NW Second Street, Ocala, FL 34475-6666
Tel: (352) 690-6907

William Terrell Hodges
Senior Judge

Date of Birth: 1934
Education: Florida 1956 BSBA, 1958 LLB, 1967 JD
Began Service: 1971
Appointed By: President Richard M. Nixon

Academic: Instructor, University of South Florida (1961-1966); Lecturer, Federal Judicial Center (1984)

Legal Practice: Macfarlane, Ferguson, Allison & Kelly (1958-1971)

Current Memberships: The American Inns of Court; The Florida Bar; Hillsborough County Bar Association

Chambers of Senior Judge Wm. Terrell Hodges *continued*

Staff
Career Law Clerk **Leslie Hoffman** .... (352) 690-6907
E-mail: leslie_hoffman@flmd.uscourts.gov
Education: Florida JD
Courtroom Deputy **Mari Jo Taylor** .... (352) 369-4861
E-mail: maurya_mcsheehy@flmd.uscourts.gov
Court Reporter **(Vacant)** .... (352) 342-0414
Secretary **Barbara Wood** .... (352) 690-6907
E-mail: barbara_wood@flmd.uscourts.gov

Chambers of Senior Judge George Kendall Sharp
U.S. Courthouse Annex, 401 West Central Boulevard,
Orlando, FL 32801-0660
Tel: (407) 835-4260 Fax: (407) 835-4267

George Kendall Sharp
Senior Judge

Date of Birth: 1934
Education: Yale 1957 BA; Virginia 1963 JD
Began Service: 1983
Appointed By: President Ronald Reagan

Academic: Faculty, Indian River Community College

Government: Public Defender, 19th Judicial Circuit, State of Florida (1964-1968); Attorney, School Board, County of Indian River, Florida (1968-1978)

Judicial: Judge, Florida Circuit Court, 19th Judicial Circuit (1978-1983)

Legal Practice: Partner, Sharp, Johnston & Brown (1963-1978)

Military Service: United States Naval Reserve (1957-1988)

Staff
Judicial Assistant **Sherri L. Cohen** .... (407) 835-4260
E-mail: sherri_l_cohen@flmd.uscourts.gov

Chambers of Senior Judge Harvey E. Schlesinger
U.S. Courthouse, 300 North Hogan Street, Suite 11-150,
Jacksonville, FL 32202-4246
Tel: (904) 549-1990 Fax: (904) 549-1921
E-mail: harvey_schlesinger@flmd.uscourts.gov

Harvey E. Schlesinger
Senior Judge

Date of Birth: 1940
Education: Citadel 1962 BA; Richmond 1965 JD
Began Service: July 2, 1991
Appointed By: President George H.W. Bush

Academic: Instructor, John Marshall Law School (1967-1968); Adjunct Professor, University of North Florida (1984-1991)

Government: Assistant United States Attorney, Middle District of Florida, United States Department of Justice (1970-1975); District Judge, United States District Court for the Middle District of Florida (1991-2006)

Judicial: Magistrate Judge, United States District Court for the Middle District of Florida (1975-1991)

Legal Practice: Corporate Counsel, SCL Railroad Co. (1968-1970)

Military Service: United States Army (1965-1968)

Current Memberships: American Bar Association; Federal Bar Association; Jacksonville Bar Association; Maritime Law Association of the United States; The Virginia Bar Association

Staff
Law Clerk **Jacquie Thomas** .... (904) 549-1990
Began Service: June 2014
Term Expires: June 2016
E-mail: jacquie_thomas@flmd.uscourts.gov
Administrative/Career Law Clerk **Eric K. Shaddock** ..... (904) 549-1990
E-mail: eric_shaddock@flmd.uscourts.gov
Education: Florida Coastal 1999 JD

(continued on next page)

Chambers of Senior Judge Harvey E. Schlesinger *continued*

Courtroom Deputy **Marsha Grant** .... (904) 549-1982
E-mail: marsha_grant@flmd.uscourts.gov

Chambers of Senior Judge Patricia C. Fawsett

401 West Central Boulevard, Orlando, FL 32801
Tel: (407) 835-4250
E-mail: patricia_fawsett@flmd.uscourts.gov

Patricia C. Fawsett
Senior Judge

Date of Birth: 1943
Education: Florida 1965 BA, 1966 MA, 1973 JD
Began Service: 1986
Appointed By: President Ronald Reagan

Legal Practice: Attorney, Akerman Senterfitt and Edison, P.A. (1973-1986)

Staff
Courtroom Deputy **(Vacant)** .... (407) 835-4218

Chambers of Senior Judge Susan Cawthon Bucklew

Sam M. Gibbons U.S. Courthouse, 801 North Florida Avenue, Suite 1430, Tampa, FL 33602
Tel: (813) 301-5858 Fax: (813) 301-5757
E-mail: susan_bucklew@flmd.uscourts.gov

Susan Cawthon Bucklew
Senior Judge

Date of Birth: 1942
Education: Florida State 1964 BA; South Florida 1968 MA; Stetson 1977 JD
Began Service: December 1993
Appointed By: President William J. Clinton

Current Memberships: American Bar Association; The Herbert G. Goldburg Criminal Law American Inn of Court, The American Inns of Court; The William Glenn Terrell American Inn of Court, The American Inns of Court; Florida Association for Women Lawyers; The Florida Bar; Hillsborough Association for Women Lawyers; Hillsborough County Bar Association

Staff
Law Clerk **Allison Kirkwood** .... (813) 301-5858
Began Service: September 2014
E-mail: allison_kirkwood@flmd.uscourts.gov
Law Clerk **Kathryn Williams** .... (813) 301-5858
E-mail: kathryn_williams@flmd.uscourts.gov
Career Law Clerk **Jennifer M. Deeb** .... (813) 301-5858
E-mail: jennifer_deeb@flmd.uscourts.gov
Education: Florida 1997 BS, 1997 MS, 2000 JD
Courtroom Deputy **Susan Saylor** .... (813) 301-5859
E-mail: susan_saylor@flmd.uscourts.gov

Chambers of Senior Judge Richard Alan Lazzara

Sam M. Gibbons U.S. Courthouse, 801 North Florida Avenue, 15th Floor, Tampa, FL 33602-3800
Tel: (813) 301-5350
E-mail: richard_lazzara@flmd.uscourts.gov

Richard Alan Lazzara
Senior Judge

Date of Birth: 1945
Education: Loyola U (New Orleans) 1967 BA; Florida 1970 JD
Began Service: November 1, 1997
Appointed By: President William J. Clinton

Current Memberships: American Bar Association; The C.H. Ferguson-M.E. White American Inn of Court, The American Inns of Court; Hillsborough County Bar Association; Order Sons of Italy in America

Chambers of Senior Judge Richard Alan Lazzara *continued*

Staff
Career Law Clerk **Douglas M. Bates, Jr.** .... (813) 301-5353
E-mail: douglas_bates@flmd.uscourts.gov
Education: Stetson 1993 JD
Career Law Clerk **Cynthia A. Bedell** .... (813) 301-5352
Education: Stetson 1984 JD
Courtroom Deputy **Susan Saylor** .... (813) 301-5354
E-mail: susan_saylor@flmd.uscourts.gov
Judicial Assistant **Sandra Hartman** .... (813) 301-5351

Chambers of Senior Judge Gregory A. Presnell

401 West Central Boulevard, Suite 5750, Orlando, FL 32801-0575
Tel: (407) 835-4301

Gregory A. Presnell
Senior Judge

Date of Birth: 1942
Education: William & Mary 1964 BA; Florida 1966 JD
Began Service: August 2, 2000
Appointed By: President William J. Clinton

Staff
Law Clerk **Sarah Naseery** .... (407) 835-4309
Began Service: September 1, 2015
Term Expires: August 31, 2016
Career Law Clerk **Eric Dentel** .... (407) 835-4308
Education: Florida 1999 JD
Judicial Assistant **Tomlyn K. Wright** .... (407) 835-4301
E-mail: tomlyn_wright@flmd.uscourts.gov

Chambers of Senior Judge John Antoon II

U.S. Courthouse & Federal Building, 401 West Central Boulevard, Orlando, FL 32801
Tel: (407) 835-4334
E-mail: chambers_flmd_antoon@flmd.uscourts.gov

John Antoon II
Senior Judge

Date of Birth: 1946
Education: Florida Southern 1968 BA; Florida State 1971 JD; Florida Tech 1993 MS; Virginia 2001 LLM
Began Service: June 2, 2000
Appointed By: President William J. Clinton

Staff
Law Clerk **Dustin Mauser-Claassen** .... (407) 835-4334
Began Service: August 2015
Term Expires: August 2016
Administrative Law Clerk **Barbara R. Smith** .... (407) 835-4334
E-mail: barbara_smith@flmd.uscourts.gov

Chambers of Senior Judge John E. Steele

U.S. Courthouse & Federal Building, 2110 First Street, Suite 6-109, Fort Myers, FL 33901
Tel: (239) 461-2140 Fax: (239) 461-2149
E-mail: chambers_flmd_steele@flmd.uscourts.gov

John E. Steele
Senior Judge

Date of Birth: 1949
Education: Detroit 1971 BA, 1973 JD
Began Service: July 28, 2000
Appointed By: President William J. Clinton

Current Memberships: Federal Bar Association; The Florida Bar; State Bar of Michigan

Staff

Law Clerk **Michael A. Watsula** .... (239) 461-2140
Term Expires: January 2016
E-mail: michael_a_watsula@flmd.uscourts.gov

Law Clerk **Alexis Barker** .... (239) 461-2140
Began Service: September 2015
Term Expires: September 2016
E-mail: alexis_barker@flmd.uscourts.gov

Career Law Clerk **Radhika K. Rivera** .... (239) 461-2140
E-mail: radhika_rivera@flmd.uscourts.gov
Education: Florida Coastal 1999 JD

Court Reporter **Jeffrey G. Thomas** .... (239) 461-2033
E-mail: jeffrey_thomas@flmd.uscourts.gov

Courtroom Deputy **Brenda M. Alexander** .... (239) 461-2037
E-mail: brenda_m_alexander@flmd.uscourts.gov

Chambers of Senior Judge James S. Moody, Jr.

Sam M. Gibbons U.S. Courthouse, 801 North Florida Avenue, Suite 17, Tampa, FL 33602
Tel: (813) 301-5680 Fax: (813) 301-5688

James S. Moody, Jr.
Senior Judge

Education: Florida 1969 BS, 1972 JD
Began Service: 2000
Appointed By: President William J. Clinton

Staff

Law Clerk [Even Numbered Cases]
Jennifer Gundlach .... (813) 301-5683
Began Service: 2009
E-mail: jennifer_gundlach@flmd.uscourts.gov

Law Clerk [Odd Numbered Cases] **Randall Leonard** .... (813) 301-5684
Began Service: August 2015
Term Expires: August 2016

Courtroom Deputy **Ariana Romero** .... (813) 301-5697
E-mail: ariana_romero@flmd.uscourts.gov

Judicial Assistant **Leslie Norberg** .... (813) 301-5680
E-mail: leslie_norberg@flmd.uscourts.gov

Chambers of Senior Judge Anne C. Conway

U.S. Courthouse & Federal Building, 401 West Central Boulevard, Suite 6750, Orlando, FL 32801
Tel: (407) 835-4270
E-mail: anne_conway@flmd.uscourts.gov

Anne C. Conway
Senior Judge

Date of Birth: 1950
Education: John Carroll 1972 BA; Florida 1975 JD
Began Service: 1992
Appointed By: President George H.W. Bush

Chambers of Senior Judge Anne C. Conway *continued*

Staff

Law Clerk **Maureen Kelly** .... (407) 835-4270
Began Service: September 2015
E-mail: maureen_kelly@flmd.uscourts.gov

Career Law Clerk **Christine Bilodeau** .... (407) 835-4270
E-mail: christine_bilodeau@flmd.uscourts.gov
Education: Florida JD

Career Law Clerk **Steve Branyon** .... (407) 835-4270
Education: Florida JD

Chambers of Magistrate Judge Thomas G. Wilson

1232 Sam M. Gibbons U.S. Courthouse, 801 North Florida Avenue, Tampa, FL 33602
Tel: (813) 301-5588
E-mail: thomas_wilson@flmd.uscourts.gov

Thomas G. Wilson
Magistrate Judge

Date of Birth: 1939
Education: Michigan State 1961 BA; Duke 1964 LLB
Began Service: April 6, 1979
Term Expires: April 6, 2019

Clerkships: Law Clerk The Honorable Joseph P. Lieb, United Stated District Court for the Middle District of Florida (1964-1966); Law Clerk The Honorable Paul H. Roney, United States Court of Appeals for the Fifth Circuit (1970-1972)

Government: Attorney, United States Court of Appeals for the Fifth Circuit (1965); Attorney, United States District Court for the Middle District of Florida (1965); Assistant United States Attorney, Middle District of Florida, United States Department of Justice (1966-1970); Attorney, Supreme Court of the United States (1968); Senior Attorney, Civil Division, Appellate Section, United States Department of Justice (1972-1979); Attorney, United States Court of Appeals for the Eleventh Circuit (1981)

Legal Practice: Associate, Law Firm of Miller and McKendree (1970)

Current Memberships: The Florida Bar

Staff

Career Law Clerk **Melissa Millican** .... (813) 301-5588
E-mail: melissa_millican@flmd.uscourts.gov
Education: Florida 1976 JD

Courtroom Deputy **Dawn Saucier** .... (813) 301-5588
E-mail: dawn_saucier@flmd.uscourts.gov

Chambers of Magistrate Judge Elizabeth A. Jenkins

Sam M. Gibbons U.S. Courthouse, 801 North Florida Avenue, Tampa, FL 33602
Tel: (813) 301-5774
E-mail: elizabeth_jenkins@flmd.uscourts.gov

Elizabeth A. Jenkins
Magistrate Judge

Date of Birth: 1949
Education: Vanderbilt 1971 BA; Florida 1976 JD
Began Service: 1985
Term Expires: December 9, 2017

Government: Attorney-Advisor, United States Department of Justice (1976-1978); Assistant United States Attorney, Middle District of Florida, United States Department of Justice (1978-1982); Assistant United States Attorney, Southern District of Florida, United States Department of Justice (1982-1985)

Current Memberships: American Bar Association; The William Glenn Terrell American Inn of Court, The American Inns of Court; The District of Columbia Bar; Federal Magistrate Judges Association; The Florida Bar

(continued on next page)

FEDERAL COURTS—UNITED STATES DISTRICT COURTS

Chambers of Magistrate Judge Elizabeth A. Jenkins *continued*

Staff

Law Clerk **Kelly Gay** . . . . (813) 301-5774
E-mail: kelly_gay@flmd.uscourts.gov

Law Clerk **Adam Labonte** . . . . (813) 301-5774
E-mail: adam_labonte@flmd.uscourts.gov

Courtroom Deputy **Cathy Morgan** . . . . (813) 301-5774
E-mail: cathy_morgan@flmd.uscourts.gov

Chambers of Magistrate Judge David A. Baker

401 West Central Boulevard, Suite 6550, Orlando, FL 32801-0655
Tel: (407) 835-4290 Fax: (407) 835-4299
E-mail: david_baker@flmd.uscourts.gov

David A. Baker
Magistrate Judge

Date of Birth: 1951
Education: North Carolina 1973 AB; Virginia 1976 JD
Began Service: December 13, 1991
Term Expires: December 13, 2015

Academic: Adjunct Instructor, University of Central Florida (1993-1995)

Clerkships: Law Clerk The Honorable J. Calvitt Clarke, Jr., United States District Court for the Eastern District of Virginia (1976-1977)

Legal Practice: Attorney, Foley & Lardner LLP (1977-1985); Attorney, Foley & Lardner LLP (1985-1991)

Current Memberships: The Florida Bar; State Bar of Wisconsin

Chambers of Magistrate Judge Thomas B. McCoun III

Sam M. Gibbons U.S. Courthouse, 801 North Florida Avenue, Tampa, FL 33602
Tel: (813) 301-5550 Fax: (813) 301-5560
E-mail: thomas_mccoun@flmd.uscourts.gov

Thomas B. McCoun III
Magistrate Judge

Date of Birth: 1950
Education: Georgia Tech 1973 BS; Stetson 1977 JD
Began Service: February 1, 1994
Term Expires: January 31, 2018

Government: Assistant State Attorney, State of Florida (1977-1980)

Current Memberships: The Florida Bar; Hillsborough County Bar Association; St. Petersburg Bar Association

Staff

Law Clerk **Amanda Lee** . . . . (813) 301-5505

Career Law Clerk **Susan Butler** . . . . (813) 301-5565
E-mail: Susan_L_Butler@flmd.uscourts.gov
Education: Georgia State 1992 BS; Georgia 1998 JD

Judicial Assistant **Sonya Cohn** . . . . (813) 301-5553
E-mail: sonya_cohn@flmd.uscourts.gov

Chambers of Magistrate Judge Mark A. Pizzo

1154 Sam M. Gibbons U.S. Courthouse, 801 North Florida Avenue, Tampa, FL 33602
Tel: (813) 301-5011 Fax: (813) 301-5020
E-mail: mark_pizzo@flmd.uscourts.gov

The Honorable Mark A. Pizzo
Magistrate Judge

Education: Loyola U (New Orleans) 1974 BA, 1977 JD
Began Service: May 22, 1995

Staff

Law Clerk **Sara Whitehead** . . . . (813) 301-5011
E-mail: sara_whitehead@flmd.uscourts.gov

Chambers of Magistrate Judge Mark A. Pizzo *continued*

Career Law Clerk **Dana Kanfer** . . . . (813) 301-5012
E-mail: Dana_Kanfer@flmd.uscourts.gov
Education: Florida 1991 BS; Stetson 1994 JD

Career Law Clerk **Anna Smith** . . . . (813) 301-5012
E-mail: anna_smith@flmd.uscourts.gov
Education: Virginia JD

Courtroom Deputy **James O. Gordon, Jr.** . . . . (813) 301-5895
E-mail: james_gordon@flmd.uscourts.gov

Chambers of Magistrate Judge Karla Rae Spaulding

U.S. Courthouse & Federal Building, 401 West Central Boulevard, Orlando, FL 32801
Tel: (407) 835-4320
E-mail: chambers_flmd_spaulding@flmd.uscourts.gov

Karla Rae Spaulding
Magistrate Judge

Date of Birth: 1954
Education: Western Michigan 1975 BA; Northwestern 1980 JD
Began Service: December 29, 1997
Term Expires: December 28, 2021

Staff

Courtroom Deputy **Edward Jackson** . . . . (407) 835-5809
E-mail: edward_jackson@flmd.uscourts.gov

Chambers of Magistrate Judge Douglas N. Frazier

U.S. Courthouse and Federal Building, 2110 First Street, Room 5-181, Fort Myers, FL 33901
Tel: (239) 461-2120
E-mail: douglas_frazier@flmd.uscourts.gov

Douglas N. Frazier
Magistrate Judge

Date of Birth: 1950
Education: Naval Acad 1972 BS; Mississippi 1979 JD
Began Service: January 8, 2000
Term Expires: January 8, 2016
Military: USAR

Government: Assistant United States Attorney, Eastern District of Louisiana, United States Department of Justice (1984-1987); Assistant United States Attorney, Middle District of Florida, Organized Crime Drug Enforcement Task, United States Department of Justice (1987-1990); Senior Litigation Counsel, United States Executive Attorney's Office, United States Department of Justice (1990-1992); First Assistant United States Attorney, Southern District of Florida, United States Department of Justice (1992); Interim United States Attorney, District of Nevada, United States Department of Justice (1992); Associate Deputy Attorney General, United States Department of Justice (1992-1993); Interim United States Attorney, Middle District of Florida, United States Department of Justice (1992-1993); Senior Litigation Counsel, United States Attorney's Executives Office, United States Department of Justice (1993-1994); Assistant Director for Evaluation and Review, United States Attorney's Executive Office, United States Department of Justice (1994-2000)

Military Service: Artillery Officer, United States Marine Corps (1972-1984)

Staff

Career Law Clerk **Beth R. Heise** . . . . (239) 461-2126
E-mail: beth_heise@flmd.uscourts.gov
Education: Carleton 1982 BA; DePaul 1987 JD

Courtroom Deputy **Bette-Jo Herren** . . . . (239) 461-2007
E-mail: bette-jo_herren@flmd.uscourts.gov

Law Clerk **Corey A. Smith** . . . . (239) 461-2120

Chambers of Magistrate Judge Monte C. Richardson
300 North Hogan Street, Suite 5-411, Jacksonville, FL 32202-4242
Tel: (904) 301-6740
E-mail: monte_richardson@flmd.uscourts.gov

Monte C. Richardson
Magistrate Judge

Date of Birth: July 15, 1961
Education: Valdosta State U BA; American U JD
Began Service: June 2, 2003
Term Expires: 2019

Current Memberships: The Herbert G. Goldburg Criminal Law American Inn of Court, The American Inns of Court; Criminal Law Section, Hillsborough County Bar Association

Staff
Career Law Clerk **Aneta D. Mincheva** . . . . (904) 301-6743
E-mail: aneta_mincheva@flmd.uscourts.gov
Courtroom Deputy **Sharon Spaulding** . . . . (904) 301-6742
E-mail: sharon_spaulding@flmd.uscourts.gov

Chambers of Magistrate Judge James R. Klindt
United States Courthouse, 300 North Hogan Street, Room 5-111, Jacksonville, FL 32202-4242
Tel: (904) 360-1520
E-mail: james_klindt@flmd.uscourts.gov

James R. Klindt
Magistrate Judge

Began Service: October 2007
Term Expires: October 2023

Government: First Assistant U.S. Attorney, Tampa (FL) Office, Executive Office for United States Attorneys, United States Department of Justice; U.S. Attorney, Tampa (FL) Office, Executive Office for United States Attorneys, United States Department of Justice (2007-2008)

Staff
Law Clerk **Erin Heaney** . . . . (904) 360-1520
E-mail: erin_heaney@flmd.uscourts.gov
Law Clerk **Kara Wood** . . . . (904) 360-1520
E-mail: kara_wood@flmd.uscourts.gov
Education: Florida Coastal 2008 JD
Courtroom Deputy **Megan Chaddock** . . . . (904) 360-1520
E-mail: megan_chaddock@flmd.uscourts.gov

Chambers of Magistrate Judge Gregory J. Kelly
U.S. Courthouse & Federal Building, 401 West Central Boulevard, Suite 5550, Orlando, FL 32801-0120
Tel: (407) 835-3855

Gregory J. Kelly
Magistrate Judge

Education: SUNY Col (Buffalo) 1984 BS; Toledo 1988 JD
Began Service: January 2008
Term Expires: January 2016

Legal Practice: Attorney, Akerman Senterfitt

Staff
Career Law Clerk **Patrick Brackins** . . . . (407) 835-3854
Education: St Thomas U 2006 JD
Law Clerk **Matthew Hainen** . . . . (407) 835-3856
E-mail: matthew_hainen@flmd.uscourts.gov
Courtroom Deputy **Kimberly Anderson** . . . . (407) 835-5808
E-mail: kimberly_anderson@flmd.uscourts.gov

Chambers of Magistrate Judge Anthony E. Porcelli
801 North Florida Avenue, Room 1034, Tampa, FL 33602-3899
Tel: (813) 301-5540 Fax: (813) 301-5549
E-mail: anthony_porcelli@flmd.uscourts.gov

Anthony E. Porcelli
Magistrate Judge

Began Service: 2009

Government: Narcotics Assistant U.S. Attorney, Criminal Division, Tampa (FL) Office, United States Department of Justice; General Crimes Assistant U.S. Attorney, Criminal Division, Tampa (FL) Office, United States Department of Justice

Staff
Law Clerk (Even-Numbered Cases) **Diana Evans** . . . .(813) 301-5542
Began Service: 2013
E-mail: diana_evans@flmd.uscourts.gov
Law Clerk (Odd-Numbered Cases)
Jennifer M. Faggion . . . .(813) 301-5541
E-mail: jennifer_faggion@flmd.uscourts.gov
Education: Florida 2003 BS, 2007 MS, 2007 JD
Courtroom Deputy **Lynne Vito** . . . .(813) 301-5547
E-mail: lynne_vito@flmd.uscourts.gov

Chambers of Magistrate Judge Joel B. Toomey
300 North Hogan Street, Jacksonville, FL 32202
Tel: (904) 549-1960 Fax: (904) 549-1967
E-mail: joel_toomey@flmd.uscourts.gov

Joel B. Toomey
Magistrate Judge

Education: Duke 1982 JD
Began Service: July 6, 2010

Staff
Courtroom Deputy **Tracee Perrotti** . . . . (904) 549-1963
E-mail: tracee_perrotti@flmd.uscourts.gov

Chambers of Magistrate Judge Thomas B. Smith
401 West Central Boulevard, Suite337, Orlando, FL 32801
Tel: (407) 835-4305 Fax: (407) 835-4315
E-mail: thomas_smith@flmd.uscourts.gov

Thomas B. Smith
Magistrate Judge

Education: Florida 1977 JD
Began Service: 2011

Legal Practice: Shareholder, Maguire, Voorhis, and Wells, P.A.; Partner, Holland & Knight LLP

Staff
Law Clerk **Kristen Hardy** . . . .(407) 835-4305
Law Clerk **(Vacant)** . . . .(407) 835-4305
E-mail: scott_weingart@flmd.uscourts.gov
Courtroom Deputy **Trish LeGros** . . . . (407) 835-4356

Chambers of Magistrate Judge Philip R. Lammens
207 NW Second Street, Ocala, FL 34475-6666
Tel: (352) 369-4869 Fax: (352) 622-1274
E-mail: philip_lammens@flmd.uscourts.gov

Philip R. Lammens
Magistrate Judge

Staff
Law Clerk **Amanda Reed** . . . . (352) 369-4869
Education: Bowdoin 1998 BA; Florida 2002 JD

(continued on next page)

Chambers of Magistrate Judge Philip R. Lammens *continued*

Law Clerk **Erin Quinn** .... (352) 369-4869
E-mail: erin_quinn@flmd.uscourts.gov
Law Clerk **Jessica W. McCausland** .... (352) 369-4869
Education: Florida 1998 JD
Courtroom Deputy **(Vacant)** .... (352) 369-4869

Chambers of Magistrate Judge Patricia D. Barksdale

300 North Hogan Street, Jacksonville, FL 32202-4242
Tel: (904) 549-1950

Patricia Barksdale
Magistrate Judge

Education: Florida 1996 JD
Began Service: 2013

Staff

Law Clerk **Brian Kelley** .... (904) 549-1950
Law Clerk **Chad Pennington** .... (904) 549-1950
Courtroom Deputy **Angela Loeschen** .... (904) 549-1952

Chambers of Magistrate Judge Carol Mirando

2110 First Street, Fort Myers, FL 33901
Tel: (239) 461-2170

Carol Mirando
Magistrate Judge

Began Service: 2014

Staff

Law Clerk **Ashley Ward-Singleton** .... (239) 461-2170
Law Clerk **Abby Barfelz** .... (239) 461-2170
Courtroom Deputy **Windy Winkel** .... (239) 461-2170

Chambers of Magistrate Judge Julie S. Sneed

801 North Florida Avenue, Tampa, FL 33602-3899
Tel: (813) 301-5260

Julie S. Sneed
Magistrate Judge

Began Service: 2015

United States Bankruptcy Court for the Middle District of Florida

400 West Washington Street, Suite 5100, Orlando, FL 32801
Tel: (407) 237-8000
Tel: (866) 222-8029 (Voice Case Information System VCIS)
Internet: www.flmb.uscourts.gov

Number of Judgeships: 9

Court Staff

Clerk of the Court **LeeAnn Bennett** .... (407) 237-8080
E-mail: leeann_bennett@flmb.uscourts.gov Fax: (407) 237-8079
Chief Deputy **Jason Kadzban** .... (407) 237-8080
Deputy-in-Charge - Jacksonville **Gull Weaver** .... (904) 301-6500
E-mail: gull_weaver@flmb.uscourts.gov Fax: (904) 301-6494
Deputy-in-Charge - Orlando **Kathy J. Deetz** .... (407) 237-8055
E-mail: kathy_deetz@flmb.uscourts.gov Fax: (407) 237-8005
Education: Cal State (Northridge) 1987 BS
Deputy-in-Charge - Tampa **Chuck Kilcoyne** .... (813) 301-5037
Education: South Florida 1974 BA Fax: (813) 301-5112
Financial Manager **Susan Magaditsch** .... (813) 301-5177
E-mail: susan_magaditsch@flmb.uscourts.gov Fax: (813) 301-5054
Human Resources Manager **Celia Rodenmeyer** .... (813) 301-5027
E-mail: Rcelia@flmb.uscourts.gov Fax: (813) 301-5054
Education: Indiana 1978 BS

United States Bankruptcy Court for the Middle District of Florida *continued*

Systems Manager **William Miguenes** .... (813) 301-5105
E-mail: mbill@flmb.uscourts.gov Fax: (813) 301-5054

Chambers of Chief Bankruptcy Judge Karen S. Jennemann

400 West Washington Street, Suite 6100, Orlando, FL 32801
Tel: (407) 237-8110 Fax: (407) 648-6692
E-mail: karen_jennemann@flmb.uscourts.gov

Karen S. Jennemann
Chief Bankruptcy Judge

Education: William & Mary 1983 JD
Began Service: November 1993
Term Expires: 2021

Staff

Law Clerk **Matthew Hale** .... (407) 648-6365 ext. 6523
Began Service: August 2013
Term Expires: August 2016
Judicial Assistant **Kim Osment** .... (407) 237-8111
E-mail: kimosment@flmb.uscourts.gov
Education: Central Florida 1989 BA

Chambers of Bankruptcy Judge Paul M. Glenn

300 North Hogan Street, Suite 4-204, Jacksonville, FL 32202-4242
Tel: (904) 301-6550

Paul M. Glenn
Bankruptcy Judge

Date of Birth: 1945
Education: Florida State 1967 BA; Duke 1970 JD
Began Service: November 24, 1993

Current Memberships: American Bar Association; American College of Bankruptcy; The C.H. Ferguson-M.E. White American Inn of Court, The American Inns of Court; The Florida Bar; National Conference of Bankruptcy Judges; Tampa Bay Bankruptcy Bar Association

Staff

Career Law Clerk **Kristyn Leedekerken** .... (904) 301-6553
E-mail: kristyn_leedekerken@flmb.uscourts.gov
Education: North Florida 1997 BA; Florida 2001 JD
Career Law Clerk **Cindy L. Turner** .... (813) 301-5052
E-mail: cindy_turner@flmb.uscourts.gov
Education: Mercer 1983 JD
Courtroom Administrator **Barry Clark** .... (904) 301-6554
E-mail: barry_clark@flmb.uscourts.gov

Chambers of Bankruptcy Judge Jerry A. Funk

300 North Hogan Street, Suite 4-104, Jacksonville, FL 32202-4254
Tel: (904) 301-6560

Jerry A. Funk
Bankruptcy Judge

Date of Birth: 1945
Education: Cumberland 1970 LLB
Began Service: November 3, 1993
Term Expires: November 3, 2021

Legal Practice: Private Practice (1970-1993)

Military Service: United States Army Reserve, United States Department of the Army (1968-1974)

Current Memberships: American Bar Association; The Florida Bar

Chambers of Bankruptcy Judge Jerry A. Funk *continued*

Staff

Career Law Clerk **Jodie Hollingsworth** . . . . (904) 301-6562
E-mail: jodie_hollingsworth@flmb.uscourts.gov
Education: Florida 1999 JD

Law Clerk **Anna Haugen** . . . . (904) 301-6564
E-mail: anna_haugen@flmb.uscourts.gov

Courtroom Administrator **Ray Readdick** . . . . (904) 301-6566
E-mail: ray_readdick@flmb.uscourts.gov

Chambers of Bankruptcy Judge Michael G. Williamson

Sam M. Gibbons U.S. Courthouse, 801 North Florida Avenue,
Suite 840, Tampa, FL 33602-3899
Tel: (813) 301-5520 Fax: (813) 301-5527
E-mail: mwilliamson@flmb.uscourts.gov

Michael G. Williamson
Bankruptcy Judge

Date of Birth: 1951
Education: Duke 1973 BA; Georgetown 1976 JD
Began Service: March 1, 2000
Term Expires: 2028

Legal Practice: Member and President, McGuire, Voorhis & Wells, P.A.

Current Memberships: The American Law Institute; The Florida Bar

Staff

Career Law Clerk **Edward J. Comey** . . . . (813) 301-5521
Began Service: September 2011

Courtroom Administrator **Marti Malone** . . . . (813) 301-5522
E-mail: mmarti@flmb.uscourts.gov

Judicial Assistant **Mary F. Maddox** . . . . (813) 301-5520
E-mail: marym@flmb.uscourts.gov

Supervisor **Jill Norris** . . . . (813) 301-5032
E-mail: jill_norris@flmb.uscourts.gov

Chambers of Bankruptcy Judge K. Rodney May

801 North Florida Avenue, Tampa, FL 33602-3899
Tel: (813) 301-5200

K. Rodney May
Bankruptcy Judge

Began Service: December 2003
Term Expires: December 2017

Staff

Law Clerk **Heather Reel** . . . . (813) 301-5300

Courtroom Administrator **Kim Murphy** . . . . (813) 301-5118
E-mail: kim_murphy@flmb.uscourts.gov

Supervisor **Tina Mason** . . . . (813) 301-5131
E-mail: tina_mason@flmb.uscourts.gov

Judicial Assistant **Yvonne Shepherd** . . . . (813) 301-5200
E-mail: yvonne_shepherd@flmb.uscourts.gov

Chambers of Bankruptcy Judge Catherine Peek McEwen

Sam M. Gibbons U.S. Courthouse, 801 North Florida Avenue,
Suite 555, Tampa, FL 33602-3899
Tel: (813) 301-5082

Catherine Peek McEwen
Bankruptcy Judge

Began Service: 2005
Term Expires: 2019

Staff

Career Law Clerk **Lisa Scotten** . . . . (813) 301-5088
Began Service: 2009
E-mail: lisa_scotten@flmb.uscourts.gov

Chambers of Bankruptcy Judge Catherine Peek McEwen *continued*

Judicial Assistant **Mary Morrison** . . . . (813) 301-5082
Education: Florida State 1967 BS

Courtroom Administrator **Denise Garcia** . . . . (813) 301-5083
E-mail: denise_garcia@flmb.uscourts.gov

Supervisor **Jill Norris** . . . . (813) 301-5032
E-mail: jill_norris@flmb.uscourts.gov

Chambers of Bankruptcy Judge Caryl E. Delano

Sam M. Gibbons U.S. Courthouse, 801 North Florida Avenue,
Suite 555, Tampa, FL 33602-3899
Tel: (813) 301-5190

Caryl E. Delano
Bankruptcy Judge

Education: South Florida 1976 BA; Indiana 1979 JD
Began Service: 2008
Term Expires: 2022

Staff

Career Law Clerk **Philip Nodhturft III** . . . . (813) 301-5196

Court Administrator **Lisa M. Mills** . . . . (813) 301-5195
E-mail: lisa_mills@flmb.uscourts.gov
Education: Southern Illinois 1993 BS, 2002 JD

Supervisor **Tina Mason** . . . . (813) 301-5137
E-mail: tina_mason@flmb.uscourts.gov

Judicial Assistant **Laura Stevenson** . . . . (813) 301-5190
E-mail: laura_stevenson@flmb.uscourts.gov
Education: Florida 1986 BA

Chambers of Bankruptcy Judge Cynthia Carson Jackson

400 West Washington Street, Suite 5100, Orlando, FL 32801
Tel: (407) 237-8141

Cynthia C. "Cyndi" Jackson
Bankruptcy Judge

Education: Florida State 1981 BS; Florida 1984 JD
Began Service: June 24, 2013

Staff

Judicial Assistant **Gena Whitsett** . . . . (407) 237-8141
E-mail: gena_whitsett@flmb.uscourts.gov

Courtroom Administrator **Lexie Lewis** . . . . (407) 237-8142
E-mail: lexie_lewis@flmb.uscourts.gov

Supervisor **Maggie Moyet** . . . . (407) 237-8010
E-mail: maggie_moyet@flmb.uscourts.gov

Chambers of Bankruptcy Judge (recalled) Arthur B. Briskman

400 West Washington Street, Suite 950, Orlando, FL 32801
Tel: (407) 237-8121

Arthur B. Briskman
Bankruptcy Judge (recalled)

Date of Birth: 1947
Education: Alabama 1969 BA; Cumberland 1972 JD

Current Memberships: Alabama State Bar; American Bankruptcy Institute; Central Florida Bankruptcy Law Association; National Conference of Bankruptcy Judges; Orange County Bar Association, Inc.

Staff

Judicial Assistant **Kim Guerrieri** . . . . (407) 237-8121
E-mail: kim_guerrieri@flmb.uscourts.gov

Courtroom Administrator **Wendy Chatham** . . . . (407) 237-8015
E-mail: wendy_chatham@flmb.uscourts.gov

Supervisor **Maggie Moyet** . . . . (407) 237-8121
E-mail: maggie_moyet@flmb.uscourts.gov

United States District Court for the Northern District of Florida

U.S. Courthouse, 111 North Adams Street, Tallahassee, FL 32301
Tel: (850) 521-3501 Fax: (850) 521-3656
Internet: www.flnd.uscourts.gov

Number of Judgeships: 4

Circuit: Eleventh

Areas Covered: Counties of Alachua, Bay, Calhoun, Dixie, Escambia, Franklin, Gadsden, Gilchrist, Gulf, Holmes, Jackson, Jefferson, Lafayette, Leon, Levy, Liberty, Madison, Okaloosa, Santa Rosa, Taylor, Wakulla, Walton and Washington

Court Staff

Clerk of Court **Jessica J. Lyublanovits** .... (850) 435-8440
E-mail: jessica_lyublanovits@flnd.uscourts.gov
Chief Deputy **(Vacant)** .... (850) 521-3501
Deputy-in-Charge - Gainesville **Blair Patton** .... (352) 380-2400
U.S. Courthouse, 401 SE First Ave., Rm. 243, Gainesville, FL 32601 Fax: (352) 380-2424
E-mail: blair_patton@flnd.uscourts.gov
Deputy-in-Charge - Panama City **Richard Lindenburger** .... (850) 769-4556
30 West Government Street, Panama City, FL 32401 Fax: (850) 769-7528
Deputy-in-Charge - Pensacola **Travis Green** .... (850) 435-8440
U.S. Courthouse, One N. Palafox St., Pensacola, FL 32501 Fax: (850) 433-5972
E-mail: travis_green@flnd.uscourts.gov
Federal Public Defender **Randall Murrell** .... (850) 942-8818
227 N. Bronough St., Suite 4200, Tallahassee, FL 32301 Fax: (850) 942-8809
Director, Information Technology **Stephen Mandel** ...... (850) 470-8186
E-mail: stephen_mandel@flnd.uscourts.gov
Administrative Coordinator **(Vacant)** .... (850) 521-3531
Chief Probation Officer **Mark Cook** .... (850) 521-3551
Suite 100
Financial Administrator **Agatha Carter** .... (850) 521-3521
E-mail: agatha_carter@flnd.uscourts.gov Fax: (850) 521-3692

Chambers of Chief Judge M. Casey Rodgers

One North Palafox Street, Pensacola, FL 32502-5658
Tel: (850) 435-8448 Fax: (850) 437-7897
E-mail: casey_rodgers@flnd.uscourts.gov

M. Casey Rodgers
Chief Judge

Date of Birth: August 13, 1964
Education: West Florida 1989 BA; Cal Western 1991 JD
Began Service: November 24, 2003
Appointed By: President George W. Bush

Staff

Law Clerk **Marc McAllister** .... (850) 435-8448
Career Law Clerk **Annette O. Williams** .... (850) 435-8448
E-mail: annette_williams@flnd.uscourts.gov
Education: Iowa 1989 JD
Court Reporter **Donna Boland** .... (850) 470-8189
E-mail: donna_boland@flnd.uscourts.gov
Judicial Assistant **Kathy Rock** .... (850) 435-8448
E-mail: Kathy_Rock@flnd.uscourts.gov

Chambers of District Judge Robert Lewis Hinkle

U.S. Courthouse, 111 North Adams Street, Tallahassee, FL 32301
Tel: (850) 521-3601 Fax: (850) 521-3610
E-mail: robert_hinkle@flnd.uscourts.gov

Robert Lewis Hinkle
District Judge

Date of Birth: 1951
Education: Florida State 1972 BA; Harvard 1976 JD
Began Service: August 6, 1996
Appointed By: President William J. Clinton

Academic: Adjunct Professor of Law, Trial Practice, College of Law, Florida State University (1981)

Clerkships: Law Clerk The Honorable Irving L. Goldberg, United States Court of Appeals for the Fifth Circuit (1976-1977)

Corporate: Assistant Auditor, Barnett Bank of Tallahassee (1972-1973)

Legal Practice: Associate, Sutherland, Asbill & Brennan (1977-1978); Associate, Thompson, Wadsworth, Messer, Turner & Rhodes (1978-1979); Shareholder, Hinkle & Battaglia, P.A. (1979-1982); Partner, Wadsworth, Davis & Hinkle (1982-1984); Partner, Holland & Knight (1984-1985); Shareholder, Radey Hinkle McArthur Polston & Frehn, P.A. (and predecessor firms) (1985-1996); Chairman of Board of Directors, Radey Hinkle McArthur Polston & Frehn, P.A. (and predecessor firms) (1994-1996)

Current Memberships: The American Inns of Court; The Florida Bar; Jefferson County Bar Association; Tallahassee Bar Association

Staff

Judicial Assistant **Sherrye M. Stephens** .... (850) 521-3601
E-mail: sherrye_stephens@flnd.uscourts.gov

Chambers of District Judge John Richard Smoak, Jr.

30 West Government Street, Panama City, FL 32401
Tel: (850) 785-9761 Fax: (850) 763-6254
E-mail: richard_smoak@flnd.uscourts.gov

John Richard Smoak, Jr.
District Judge

Education: West Point 1965 BS; Florida 1972 JD
Began Service: November 7, 2005
Appointed By: President George W. Bush

Legal Practice: Associate, Isler, Higby, Brown and Smoak (1973-1975); Partner, Isler, Higby, Brown and Smoak (1975-1984); Partner, Sale, Brown and Smoak (1984-1991)

Military Service: U.S. Army (1965-1970)

Staff

Law Clerk **Jonathan Lott** .... (850) 785-9761
Law Clerk **(Vacant)** .... (850) 785-9761

Chambers of District Judge Mark E. Walker

111 North Adams Street, Tallahassee, FL 32301
Tel: (850) 521-3631

Mark E. Walker
District Judge

Education: Florida 1989 BA, 1992 JD
Began Service: December 7, 2012
Appointed By: President Barack Obama

Government: Assistant Public Defender, Second Judicial Circuit (1997-1999)

Judicial: Judge, Chambers of Judge Mark E. Walker, Florida Circuit Courts (2009-2012)

Chambers of District Judge Mark E. Walker *continued*

Staff

Law Clerk **Timothy Moore** . . . . (850) 521-3631
E-mail: timothy_moore@flnd.uscourts.gov
Law Clerk **Tony Bajoczky** . . . . (850) 521-3631
E-mail: tony_bajoczky@flnd.uscourts.gov
Judicial Assistant **Rebecca Jones** . . . . (850) 521-3631

Chambers of Senior Judge William H. Stafford, Jr.

U.S. Courthouse, 111 North Adams Street, Tallahassee, FL 32301-7717
Tel: (850) 521-3611 Fax: (850) 521-3618
E-mail: william_stafford@flnd.uscourts.gov

William H. Stafford, Jr.
Senior Judge

Date of Birth: 1931
Education: Temple 1953 BS, 1956 LLB, 1968 JD
Began Service: May 30, 1975
Appointed By: President Gerald Ford

Academic: Adjunct Instructor, Pensacola Junior College (1964); Instructor, College of Law, Florida State University (1992); Instructor, College of Law, Florida State University (1996-1997); Instructor, College of Law, Florida State University (1999)

Corporate: Claims Representative, State Farm Mutual Automobile Insurance Company (1960)

Government: State Attorney, First Judicial Circuit, State of Florida (1967-1969); United States Attorney, Northern District of Florida, United States Department of Justice (1969-1975)

Legal Practice: Attorney, Robinson & Roark (1961-1964); Private Practice (1964-1969)

Military Service: United States Navy (1956-1960)

Current Memberships: The American Inns of Court; Federal Judges Association; The Florida Bar; Tallahassee Bar Association

Chambers of Senior Judge Maurice M. Paul

U.S. Courthouse, 401 SE First Avenue, Gainesville, FL 32601
Tel: (352) 380-2415 Fax: (352) 380-2435
E-mail: maurice_paul@flnd.uscourts.gov

Maurice M. Paul
Senior Judge

Date of Birth: 1932
Education: Florida 1954 BSBA, 1960 LLB
Began Service: 1982
Appointed By: President Ronald Reagan

Academic: Interim Instructor, College of Law, University of Florida

Judicial: Judge, Florida Circuit Court, Ninth Judicial Circuit (1973-1982)

Legal Practice: Associate, Sanders, McEwan, Mims & MacDonald (1960-1964); Partner, Akerman, Senterfitt, Eidson, Mesmer & Robinson (1965-1966); Partner, Pitts, Eubanks, Ross & Paul (1968-1969)

Military Service: United States Air Force (1954-1957)

Staff

Law Clerk **John Janousek** . . . . (352) 380-2415
Began Service: January 2014
Term Expires: January 2016
E-mail: john_janousek@flnd.uscourts.gov
Career Law Clerk **Michael Dupee** . . . . (352) 380-2415
E-mail: michael_dupee@flnd.uscourts.gov
Education: Florida JD

Chambers of Senior Judge Lacey A. Collier

U.S. Courthouse, One North Palafox Street, Pensacola, FL 32502
Tel: (850) 444-0174 Fax: (850) 444-0177
E-mail: lacey_collier@flnd.uscourts.gov

Lacey A. Collier
Senior Judge

Date of Birth: 1935
Education: Naval Postgrad 1970 BA; West Florida 1972 MA, 1975 BA; Florida State 1977 JD
Began Service: November 20, 1991
Appointed By: President George H.W. Bush

Academic: Adjunct Professor, University of West Florida (1973)

Government: Assistant State Attorney, First Judicial Circuit, State of Florida (1977-1984); Advisor to Grand Juries, First Judicial Circuit, State of Florida (1978-1984)

Judicial: Judge, Florida Circuit Court, First Judicial Circuit (1984-1991)

Military Service: United States Navy (1955-1975)

Current Memberships: The American Inns of Court; Escambia-Santa Rosa Bar Association; The Florida Bar; Okaloosa-Walton Bar Association

Staff

Career Law Clerk **Rick Jank** . . . . (850) 444-0174
E-mail: rick_jank@flnd.uscourts.gov
Education: Stetson 1992 JD
Judicial Assistant **Dene R. Brooke** . . . . (850) 444-0174
E-mail: dene_brooke@flnd.uscourts.gov

Chambers of Senior Judge Roger Vinson

Arnow Federal Building, 100 North Palafox Street,
Pensacola, FL 32502-5658
Tel: (850) 435-8444 Fax: (850) 435-8489
E-mail: roger_vinson@flnd.uscourts.gov

Roger Vinson
Senior Judge

Date of Birth: 1940
Education: Naval Acad 1962 BS; Vanderbilt 1971 JD
Began Service: 1983
Appointed By: President Ronald Reagan

Legal Practice: Attorney, Beggs & Lane (1971-1983)

Military Service: United States Navy (1962-1968)

Staff

Career Law Clerk **Timothy J. Inacio** . . . . (850) 435-8444
E-mail: timothy_inacio@flnd.uscourts.gov
Education: West Florida 1998 BA;
Brooklyn Law 2002 JD
Judicial Assistant **Val Harmon** . . . . (850) 435-8444
E-mail: val_harmon@flnd.uscourts.gov

Chambers of Magistrate Judge Charles A. Stampelos

U.S. Courthouse, 111 North Adams Street, Tallahassee, FL 32301
Tel: (850) 521-3621 Fax: (850) 521-3630
E-mail: charles_stampelos@flnd.uscourts.gov

Charles Stampelos
Magistrate Judge

Began Service: 2012

Staff

Career Law Clerk **Kay Judkins** . . . . (850) 521-3617
E-mail: kay_judkins@flnd.uscourts.gov
Judicial Assistant **Marilyn Holland** . . . . (850) 521-3611
E-mail: marilyn_holland@flnd.uscourts.gov

FEDERAL COURTS—UNITED STATES DISTRICT COURTS

Chambers of Magistrate Judge Elizabeth M. Timothy
One North Palafox Street, Pensacola, FL 32502-5658
Tel: (850) 437-6823 Fax: (850) 437-7760
E-mail: elizabeth_timothy@flnd.uscourts.gov

Elizabeth M. Timothy
Magistrate Judge

Began Service: June 10, 2004

Staff
Judicial Assistant **Teresa Milstead** . . . . (850) 437-6823

Chambers of Magistrate Judge Gary R. Jones
401 SE First Avenue, Suite 383, Gainesville, FL 32601
Tel: (352) 380-2746 Fax: (352) 380-2754
E-mail: gary_r_jones@flnd.uscourts.gov

Gary R. Jones
Magistrate Judge

Date of Birth: 1951
Education: Boston U 1976 BA; Miami 1981 JD; NYU 1983 LLM
Began Service: September 13, 2010
Term Expires: September 12, 2018

Current Memberships: American Bar Association; The D.R. Smith American Inn of Court, The American Inns of Court; Federal Bar Association; Federal Magistrate Judges Association; The Florida Bar

Staff
Law Clerk **Jamie Bowers** . . . . (352) 380-2753
Term Expires: August 2016
E-mail: jamie_bowers@flnd.uscourts.gov
Law Clerk **Erin Sales** . . . . (352) 380-2746
Began Service: August 2, 2015
Term Expires: August 1, 2017
E-mail: erin_sales@flnd.uscourts.gov
Courtroom Deputy **Adelita Tinaya-Miller** . . . . (352) 380-2402
E-mail: adelita_tinaya-miller@flnd.uscourts.gov

Chambers of Magistrate Judge Charles Kahn, Jr
One North Palafox Street, Pensacola, FL 32502
Tel: (850) 470-3090 Fax: (850) 470-8148
E-mail: charles_kahn@flnd.uscourts.gov

Charles J. Kahn, Jr.
Magistrate Judge

Date of Birth: 1951
Education: Vanderbilt 1973 BA; Florida 1977 JD
Began Service: March 4, 2011

Staff
Law Clerk **David Ricci** . . . . (850) 470-3090
E-mail: david_ricci@flnd.uscourts.gov
Law Clerk **Jennifer Wood** . . . . (850) 470-3090
E-mail: jennifer_wood@flnd.uscourts.gov
Education: Gustavus Adolphus 1986 BA; Minnesota 1995 JD
Administrative Law Clerk **Amy Klotz** . . . . (850) 470-3090
E-mail: amy_klotz@flnd.uscourts.gov

Chambers of Magistrate Judge (half-time) Larry A. Bodiford
620 McKenzie Avenue, Panama City, FL 32401
P.O. Box 2528, Panama City, FL 32402
Tel: (850) 763-0723 Fax: (850) 872-8402
E-mail: larry_bodiford@flnd.uscourts.gov

Larry A. Bodiford
Magistrate Judge (part-time)

Date of Birth: 1939
Education: Stetson JD
Began Service: 1985
Term Expires: August 2022

Staff
Judicial Assistant **Susan Mayo** . . . . (850) 763-0723
E-mail: susan_mayo@flnd.uscourts.gov

United States Bankruptcy Court for the Northern District of Florida
110 East Park Avenue, Suite 100, Tallahassee, FL 32301
Tel: (850) 521-5001 (Tallahassee) Tel: (866) 639-4615 (All Divisions)
Tel: (888) 765-1751 (Voice Case Information System VCIS)
Fax: (850) 521-5004
Internet: www.flnb.uscourts.gov

Number of Judgeships: 1

Court Staff
Fax: (850) 521-5004

Clerk of Court **Traci Abrams** . . . . (850) 521-5001
E-mail: traci_abrams@flnb.uscourts.gov
Chief Deputy Clerk **Paul Neely** . . . . (850) 521-5001
E-mail: paul_neely@flnb.uscourts.gov

Chambers of Bankruptcy Judge Karen K. Specie
110 East Park Avenue, Tallahassee, FL 32301
Tel: (850) 521-5031 Fax: (850) 521-5035

Karen K. Specie
Bankruptcy Judge

Began Service: July 25, 2012
Term Expires: July 25, 2026

Staff
Law Clerk **Thomas Powell** . . . . (850) 521-5032
Law Clerk **Michael Niles** . . . . (850) 521-5032
Judicial Assistant **Lisa Murrill** . . . . (850) 521-5031
Courtroom Deputy **Janet Nah** . . . . (850) 521-5009

United States District Court for the Southern District of Florida
U.S. Courthouse, 400 North Miami Avenue, Miami, FL 33128
Tel: (305) 523-5100 Tel: (305) 536-7265 (PACER)
Internet: www.flsd.uscourts.gov

Number of Judgeships: 18

Number of Vacancies: 1

Circuit: Eleventh

Areas Covered: Counties of Broward, Dade, Highlands, Indian River, Martin, Miami-Dade, Monroe, Okeechobee, Palm Beach and St. Lucie

Court Staff
Clerk of Court **Steven M. Larimore** . . . . (305) 523-5001
E-mail: steven_larimore@flsd.uscourts.gov

United States District Court for the Southern District of Florida
continued

Court Administrator **Steven M. Larimore** . . . . (305) 523-5001
E-mail: steven_larimore@flsd.uscourts.gov
Chief Deputy, Administration [Administration]
Kevin Kappes . . . . (305) 523-5010
E-mail: kevin_kappes@flsd.uscourts.gov
Chief Deputy, Operations [Operations]
Debra K. Kempi . . . . (305) 523-5020
E-mail: debra_kempi@flsd.uscourts.gov
Deputy-in-Charge - Fort Pierce **Colette Griffin-Arnold** . . . (772) 467-2300
300 S. Sixth St., Fort Pierce, FL 34950
E-mail: colette_griffin-arnold@flsd.uscourts.gov
Court Reporter Scheduling Coordinator **Jean Vera** . . . . (305) 523-5632
E-mail: jean_vera@flsd.uscourts.gov
Human Resources Manager **Cathyanne Mathis** . . . . (305) 523-5035
E-mail: cathyanne_mathis@flsd.uscourts.gov Tel: (305) 523-5288 (Jobline)
Projects Administration Manager
Pasquale "Pat" Papaianni . . . . (305) 523-5071
E-mail: pasquale_papaianni@flsd.uscourts.gov
Northern Division Operations Manager **John Ditullio** . . . . (561) 803-3400
U.S. Courthouse, 701 Clematis St., Room 402,
West Palm Beach, FL 33401
E-mail: john_ditullio@flsd.uscourts.gov
Computer Operations Manager **Juan C. Vega** . . . .(305) 523-5612
Chief Probation Officer **Reginald D. Michael** . . . .(305) 523-5300
301 North Miami Avenue, Room 315,
Miami, FL 33128
Jury Administrator **Liz Chapas** . . . .(305) 523-5190
E-mail: liz_chapas@flsd.uscourts.gov
Software Services Administrator **Ana Gonzalez-Ruiz** . . . . (305) 523-5605
E-mail: ana_gonzalez-ruiz@flsd.uscourts.gov
CJA & Case Assignment Administrator **Lucy Lara** . . . .(305) 523-5655
E-mail: lucy_lara@flsd.uscourts.gov
Interpreter Supervisor **Irene B. Tomassini** . . . . (305) 523-5620
E-mail: irene_tomassini@flsd.uscourts.gov
Operations Administrator, Appeals, Intake and Docketing **Vanessa Powell-Bacourt** . . . . (305) 523-5299
E-mail: vanessa_powell-bacourt@flsd.uscourts.gov
Records Management Supervisor **Randy Tobie** . . . .(305) 523-5210
E-mail: randy_tobie@flsd.uscourts.gov
Divisional Operations Manager **Michael Beck** . . . . (954) 769-5400
299 East Broward Boulevard,
Fort Lauderdale, FL 33301
E-mail: michael_beck@flsd.uscourts.gov
Executive Services Administrator
Catherine Wade-Babyak . . . . (305) 523-5001

Chambers of Chief Judge K. Michael Moore

Wilkie D. Ferguson Federal Courthouse, 400 North Miami Avenue,
Room 13-1, Miami, FL 33128
Tel: (305) 523-5160 Fax: (305) 523-5169
E-mail: moore@flsd.uscourts.gov

K. Michael Moore
Chief Judge

Date of Birth: 1951
Education: Florida State 1972 BA; Fordham 1976 JD
Began Service: February 10, 1992
Appointed By: President George H.W. Bush
Political Affiliation: Republican

Current Memberships: The Florida Bar

Staff
Law Clerk **Jane Mackenzie Duane** . . . . (305) 523-5160
Began Service: September 2013
Term Expires: November 2015
Education: Fordham 2013 JD
Law Clerk **Michael Glenn** . . . . (305) 523-5160
Courtroom Deputy **Robin Godwin** . . . . (305) 523-5165
E-mail: robin_godwin@flsd.uscourts.gov

Chambers of District Judge William J. Zloch

U.S. Courthouse, 299 East Broward Boulevard, Room 202B,
Fort Lauderdale, FL 33301
Tel: (954) 769-5480 Fax: (954) 769-5429
E-mail: zloch@flsd.uscourts.gov

William J. Zloch
District Judge

Date of Birth: 1944
Education: Notre Dame 1966 BA, 1974 JD
Began Service: November 1985
Appointed By: President Ronald Reagan

Judicial: Chief District Judge, United States District Court for the Southern District of Florida (2000-2007)

Legal Practice: Attorney, Private Practice (1974-1985)

Military Service: United States Navy (1967-1970)

Staff
Law Clerk **David Coulter** . . . .(954) 769-5480
Began Service: 2015
Term Expires: August 30, 2016
E-mail: david_coulter@flsd.uscourts.gov
Law Clerk **Elizabeth Roper** . . . .(954) 769-5480
Began Service: 2012
Term Expires: 2016
Career Law Clerk **Erin Whitcomb** . . . .(954) 769-5480
Began Service: 2009
E-mail: erin_whitcomb@flsd.uscourts.gov
Courtroom Deputy **Barbara L. Coats** . . . . (954) 769-5480
E-mail: barbara_coats@flsd.uscourts.gov
Court Reporter **Tammy Nestor** . . . . (954) 769-5488
E-mail: tammy_nestor@flsd.uscourts.gov

Chambers of District Judge Federico A. Moreno

Wilkie D. Ferguson Courthouse, 400 North Miami Avenue,
Room 13-3, Miami, FL 33128
Tel: (305) 523-5110 Fax: (305) 523-5119
E-mail: moreno@flsd.uscourts.gov

Federico A. Moreno
District Judge

Date of Birth: 1952
Education: Notre Dame 1974 AB; Miami 1978 JD
Began Service: 1990
Appointed By: President George H.W. Bush

Current Memberships: American Judges Association; Federal Bar Association

Staff
Law Clerk **Brendan Ryan** . . . .(305) 523-5110
Law Clerk **Jordi Martinez-Cid** . . . . (305) 523-5110
Began Service: September 2015
Term Expires: September 2016
Career Law Clerk **Mariela Martinez-Cid** . . . . (305) 523-5110
E-mail: mariela_martinez-cid@flsd.uscourts.gov
Education: Yale 2000 JD
Court Reporter **Gilda Pastor-Hernandez** . . . . (305) 523-5118
E-mail: gilda_pastor-hernandez@flsd.uscourts.gov
Courtroom Deputy **Shirley Christie** . . . .(305) 523-5110
E-mail: shirley_christie@flsd.uscourts.gov

Chambers of District Judge Ursula Ungaro

U.S. Courthouse, 301 North Miami Avenue, 11th Floor, Miami, FL 33128
Tel: (305) 523-5550

Ursula Ungaro
District Judge

Date of Birth: 1951
Education: Miami 1973 BA; Florida 1975 JD
Began Service: 1992
Appointed By: President George H.W. Bush

Judicial: Judge, Florida Circuit Court, 11th Judicial Circuit (1987-1992)

Legal Practice: Frates, Floyd, Pearson, Stewart, Richman & Greer (1976-1978); Blackwell, Walker, Gray, Powers, Flick & Hoehl (1978-1980); Finley, Kumble, Heine, Underberg, Manley & Casey (1980-1985); Sparber, Shevin, Shapo & Heilbronner (1985-1987)

Current Memberships: The Spellman-Hoeveler American Inn of Court, The American Inns of Court; Dade County Bar Association; Federal Judges Association; Florida Association for Women Lawyers; The Florida Bar; Florida Conference of Circuit Court Judges

Staff

Law Clerk [Even Numbered Cases] **Brian Shack** .... (305) 523-5550
E-mail: brian_shack@flsd.uscourts.gov
Courtroom Deputy **Kathryn B. Harlan** .... (305) 523-5555
E-mail: kathryn_harlan@flsd.uscourts.gov
Court Reporter **William Romanishin** .... (305) 523-5558

Chambers of District Judge Joan A. Lenard

U.S. Courthouse, 400 North Miami Avenue, Room 12-1,
Miami, FL 33128
Tel: (305) 523-5500 Fax: (305) 523-5509
E-mail: lenard@flsd.uscourts.gov

Joan A. Lenard
District Judge

Date of Birth: 1952
Education: Roger Williams 1973 BA; Antioch Law 1976 JD
Began Service: March 1, 1996
Appointed By: President William J. Clinton

Government: Assistant State Attorney, Consumer Fraud Division, Eleventh Judicial Circuit, State of Florida (1976-1978); Chief, Consumer Fraud Division, Office of the State Attorney, Eleventh Judicial Circuit, State of Florida (1978-1980); Chief, Consumer & Electronic Crime Division, Office of the State Attorney, Eleventh Judicial Circuit, State of Florida (1980-1982)

Judicial: Judge, Dade County Court (1982-1993); Judge (Acting), Florida Circuit Court, 11th Judicial Circuit (1982-1993); Judge, Florida Circuit Court, 11th Judicial District (1993-1995)

Current Memberships: Dade County Bar Association; The District of Columbia Bar; Federal Judges Association; Florida Association for Women Lawyers; The Florida Bar

Staff

Law Clerk **Gregory Ingalsbe** .... (305) 523-5500
Began Service: September 2013
Term Expires: September 2016
E-mail: gregory_ingalsbe@flsd.uscourts.gov
Education: Salmon P Chase 2011 JD
Law Clerk **Trevor Jones** .... (305) 523-5500
Term Expires: July 2016
E-mail: trevor_jones@flsd.uscourts.gov
Courtroom Deputy **Patricia Mitchell** .... (305) 523-5506
E-mail: patricia_mitchell@flsd.uscourts.gov
Court Reporter **Lisa Edwards** .... (305) 523-5499
E-mail: lisa_edwards@flsd.uscourts.gov Fax: (305) 523-5509
Secretary **Diana Pizarro** .... (305) 523-5500
E-mail: diana_pizarro@flsd.uscourts.gov

Chambers of District Judge Donald M. Middlebrooks

U.S. Courthouse, 701 Clematis Street, Room 257,
West Palm Beach, FL 33401
Tel: (561) 514-3720 Fax: (561) 514-3729
E-mail: middlebrooks@flsd.uscourts.gov

Donald M. Middlebrooks
District Judge

Date of Birth: 1946
Education: Florida 1968 BA, 1968 BS, 1972 JD; Virginia 2004 LLM
Began Service: July 28, 1997
Appointed By: President William J. Clinton

Corporate: Managing Partner, Lake Lucy Groves (1994-1997)

Government: Governmental Assistant, Assistant General Counsel and General Counsel, Governor Reubin O'Donovan Askew (D-FL), State of Florida (1974-1977)

Legal Practice: Askerman, Senterfitt & Eidson (1973-1974); Associate, Steel Hector & Davis (1977-1979); Director, Florida Legal Service, Inc. (1977-1979); Equity Partner, Steel, Hector & Davis (1979-1997); President, Florida Legal Services, Inc. (1980-1981); Director, Volunteer Lawyers Resource Center, Inc. (1988-1992); Director, Florida Bar Children's Fund, Inc. (1989-1997)

Military Service: United States Army (1972-1979)

Current Memberships: American Bar Foundation; American Bar Association; Dade County Bar Association; The Florida Bar; Palm Beach County Bar Association

Staff

Career Law Clerk **Kristina Cooper Castillo** .... (561) 514-3720
Began Service: 2014
E-mail: kristina_castillo@flsd.uscourts.gov
Law Clerk **Jarred Klorfein** .... (561) 514-3720
Began Service: 2015
Term Expires: August 2016
E-mail: jarrod_florfein@flsd.uscourts.gov
Law Clerk **Kathryn Clifford** .... (561) 514-3720
E-mail: kathryn_clifford@flsd.uscourts.gov
Courtroom Deputy **Genevieve McGee** .... (561) 514-3725
Court Reporter **Diane Miller** .... (561) 514-3728
E-mail: diane_miller@flsd.uscourts.gov

Chambers of District Judge William P. Dimitrouleas

U.S. Courthouse, 299 East Broward Boulevard, Room 205F,
Fort Lauderdale, FL 33301
Tel: (954) 769-5650 Fax: (954) 769-5656
E-mail: dimitrouleas@flsd.uscourts.gov

William P. Dimitrouleas
District Judge

Date of Birth: 1951
Education: Furman 1973 BA; Florida 1975 JD
Began Service: June 1, 1998
Appointed By: President William J. Clinton

Academic: Adjunct Professor, Trial Advocacy, Shepard Broad Law Center, Nova Southeastern University (1994-1998)

Government: Assistant Public Defender, Seventeenth Judicial Circuit, Office of the Public Defender, State of Florida (1976-1977); Assistant State Attorney, Seventeenth Judicial Circuit, Office of the State Attorney, State of Florida (1977-1989)

Judicial: Judge, Florida Circuit Court, Seventeenth Judicial Circuit (1989-1998)

Current Memberships: American Bar Association; Broward County Bar Association

Staff

Law Clerk **Maria D. Kunz** .... (954) 769-5650
Began Service: September 2010
E-mail: maria_kunz@flsd.uscourts.gov
Education: Stanford 2004 JD

Chambers of District Judge William P. Dimitrouleas *continued*

Law Clerk **(Vacant)** .... (954) 769-5650
Courtroom Deputy **Karen A. Carlton** .... (954) 769-5655
E-mail: karen_carlton@flsd.uscourts.gov
Education: Bryant Col 1985 BS
Court Reporter **Francine Salopek** .... (954) 769-5657
E-mail: francine_salopek@flsd.uscourts.gov
Judicial Secretary **Tammy L. Barlow** .... (954) 769-5650
E-mail: tammy_barlow@flsd.uscourts.gov

Chambers of District Judge Kenneth A. Marra

701 Clematis Street, Room 316, West Palm Beach, FL 33401
Tel: (561) 514-3760
E-mail: marra@flsd.uscourts.gov

Kenneth A. Marra
District Judge

Date of Birth: 1951
Education: SUNY (Stony Brook) 1973 BA; Stetson 1977 JD
Began Service: September 16, 2002
Appointed By: President George W. Bush

Government: Trial Attorney, United States Department of Justice (1977-1980)

Judicial: Circuit Judge, Fifteen Judicial Circuit (1996-2002)

Legal Practice: Associate Attorney, Wender, Murase & White (1980-1983); Associate and Partner, Nason, Gildan, Yeager, Gerson & White, P.A. (1984-1996)

Current Memberships: The Florida Bar

Staff
Law Clerk **Jeremy Kahn** .... (561) 514-3763
Began Service: September 2015
Term Expires: September 2016
Law Clerk **Mindy Levinson** .... (561) 514-3762
E-mail: mindy_levinson@flsd.uscourts.gov
Law Clerk (part-time) **Ann W. Herman** .... (561) 514-3766
E-mail: ann_herman@flsd.uscourts.gov
Judicial Administrator/Law Clerk **H. Lila Hubert** .... (561) 514-3761
E-mail: lila_hubert@flsd.uscourts.gov
Courtroom Deputy **Irene Ferrante Rivera** .... (561) 514-3765
E-mail: irene_rivera@flsd.uscourts.gov
Court Reporter **Stephen Franklin** .... (561) 514-3768
E-mail: stephen_franklin@flsd.uscourts.gov

Chambers of District Judge Jose E. Martinez

400 North Miami Avenue, Room 10-1, Miami, FL 33128-1807
Tel: (305) 523-5590
E-mail: martinez@flsd.uscourts.gov

Jose E. Martinez
District Judge

Date of Birth: 1941
Education: Miami 1962 BBA, 1965 JD
Began Service: September 17, 2002
Appointed By: President George W. Bush

Clerkships: Clerk, Law Offices of Jonathan E. Ammerman (1965)

Government: Legal Officer, United States Department of the Navy, United States Department of Defense (1965-1968); Assistant U.S. Attorney, Florida - Southern District, Executive Office for United States Attorneys, United States Department of Justice (1968-1970); Regional Director, Office for Drug Abuse Law Enforcement, United States Department of Justice (1972-1974)

Legal Practice: Attorney, Helliwell, Melrose & DeWolf (1970-1980); Partner, Leib & Martinez (1980-1982); Partner, English, McCaughan & O'Bryan, PA (1982-1985); Partner, Martinez & Mattox (1985-1989); Attorney, Adorno & Zeder, PA (1989-1991); Partner, Martinez & Gutierrez (1991-2002)

Chambers of District Judge Jose E. Martinez *continued*

Staff
Law Clerk [Even Numbered Cases] **Rania Kajan** .... (305) 523-5592
Began Service: September 2015
Term Expires: September 2017
E-mail: rania_kajan@flsd.uscourts.gov
Career Law Clerk [Odd Numbered Cases]
Terrance Dee .... (305) 523-5593
E-mail: terrance_dee@flsd.uscourts.gov
Courtroom Deputy **Wanda Holston** .... (305) 523-5595
E-mail: wanda_holston@flsd.uscourts.gov
Court Reporter **Dawn Whitmarsh** .... (305) 523-5598
E-mail: dawn_whitmarsh@flsd.uscourts.gov Fax: (305) 523-5599
Judicial Administrator **Diane Quinn** .... (305) 523-5590
E-mail: diane_quinn@flsd.uscourts.gov

Chambers of District Judge Cecilia M. Altonaga

Federal Courthouse Square, 400 North Miami Avenue, Room 12-2, Miami, FL 33128
Tel: (305) 523-5510
E-mail: cecilia_altonaga@flsd.uscourts.gov

Cecilia Maria Altonaga
District Judge

Education: Florida International 1983 BA; Yale 1986 JD
Began Service: May 2003
Appointed By: President George W. Bush

Clerkships: Law Clerk, Chief Judge Edward B. Davis, United States District Court for the Southern District of Florida (1987-1988)

Government: Assistant County Attorney, Office of the County Attorney, County of Miami-Dade, Florida (1988-1996)

Judicial: County Court Judge, Miami-Dade County (1996-1999); Circuit Court Judge, Miami-Dade County, Eleventh Judicial Circuit (1999-2003)

Current Memberships: Cuban American Bar Association; Dade County Bar Association; Florida Association for Women Lawyers; The Florida Bar

Staff
Law Clerk **Jamie Friedland** .... (305) 523-5510
Law Clerk **Leigh Kobrinski** .... (305) 523-5510
E-mail: leigh_kobrinski@flsd.uscourts.gov
Law Clerk **Christopher Wall** .... (305) 523-5510
Court Reporter **Stephanie McCarn** .... (305) 523-5518
E-mail: stephanie_mccarn@flsd.uscourts.gov
Courtroom Deputy **Patricia Snead** .... (305) 523-5515
E-mail: patricia_snead@flsd.uscourts.gov

Chambers of District Judge James I. Cohn

299 East Broward Boulevard, Room 203, Fort Lauderdale, FL 33301
Tel: (954) 769-5490
E-mail: cohn@flsd.uscourts.gov

James I. Cohn
District Judge

Education: Alabama BS; Cumberland JD
Began Service: August 5, 2003
Appointed By: President George W. Bush

Judicial: Circuit Judge, 17th Judicial Circuit (1995-2003)

Legal Practice: Assistant Public Defender, Broward Public Defender's Office (1975); Assistant State Attorney, Broward State Attorney's Office (1975-1978); Attorney, Private Practice (1978-1995)

Current Memberships: Federal Judges Association

(continued on next page)

Chambers of District Judge James I. Cohn *continued*

Staff

Law Clerk [Cases Ending 4, 6, 8] **Kaitlin Sahni** .... (954) 769-5490
Began Service: September 2015
Term Expires: September 2017
E-mail: kaitlin_sahni@flsd.uscourts.gov

Law Clerk [Cases Ending 5, 7, 9] **Derick Vollrath** .... (954) 769-5490
Began Service: August 15, 2014
Term Expires: August 31, 2016
E-mail: derick_vollrath@flsd.uscourts.gov

Career Law Clerk/Administrator [Civil Cases Ending in 0-3] **Shane Raley** .... (954) 769-5492
E-mail: shane_raley@flsd.uscourts.gov

Court Reporter **Pauline Stipes** .... (954) 769-5496
E-mail: pauline_stipes@flsd.uscourts.gov

Courtroom Deputy **Valarie Thompkins** .... (954) 769-5495
E-mail: valarie_thompkins@flsd.uscourts.gov

Chambers of District Judge Marcia G. Cooke

U.S. Courthouse, 301 North Miami Avenue, 6th Floor, Miami, FL 33128
Tel: (305) 523-5150
E-mail: marcia_cooke@flsd.uscourts.gov

Marcia G. Cooke
District Judge

Education: Georgetown 1975 BSFS; Wayne State U 1977 JD
Began Service: May 18, 2004
Appointed By: President George W. Bush

Government: Executive Assistant U.S. Attorney, Southern District of Florida, United States Attorney's Office, United States Department of Justice (1992-1994); Acting Administrative Officer, Southern District of Florida, United States Attorney's Office, United States Department of Justice, William J. Clinton Administration (1996-1997); Chief Inspector General, Executive Office of the Governor, State of Florida (1999-2002); Assistant County Attorney, County of Miami-Dade, Florida (2002)

Judicial: Magistrate Judge, United States District Court for the Eastern District of Michigan (1984-1992)

Legal Practice: Associate, Miro, Miro & Weiner (1983-1984)

Staff

Law Clerk **Anshu Budhrani** .... (305) 523-5150
E-mail: anshu_budhrani@flsd.uscourts.gov

Law Clerk **Lorayne Perez** .... (305) 523-5150
Began Service: January 2015
Term Expires: January 2016
E-mail: lorayne_perez@flsd.uscourts.gov

Courtroom Deputy **Ivan Marchena** .... (305) 523-5155
E-mail: ivan_marchena@flsd.uscourts.gov

Judicial Administrator **Tamara A. "Tammy" McIntyre** ... (305) 523-5150
E-mail: tamara_mcintyre@flsd.uscourts.gov

Chambers of District Judge Kathleen M. Williams

U.S. Courthouse, 400 North Miami Avenue, Miami, FL 33128
Tel: (305) 523-5540
E-mail: kathleen_williams@flsd.uscourts.gov

Kathleen Mary Williams
District Judge

Education: Duke 1978 BA; Miami 1982 JD
Began Service: August 8, 2011
Appointed By: President Barack Obama

Government: Assistant United States Attorney, Florida - Southern District, Executive Office for United States Attorneys, United States Department of Justice (1984-1988); Chief Assistant Federal Public Defender, Southern District of Florida, Office of the Federal Public Defender, Administrative Office of the United States Courts (1990-1995); Federal Public Defender, Southern District of Florida, Office of the Federal Public Defender, Administrative Office of the United States Courts (1995-2011); Acting Federal Public Defender, Middle District of Florida, Office of the Federal Public Defender, Administrative Office of the United States Courts (1999-2000)

Staff

Law Clerk **Christopher Cheek** .... (305) 523-5545
Began Service: 2014
E-mail: christopher_cheek@flsd.uscourts.gov

Law Clerk **Danielle Rosborough** .... (305) 523-5543

Law Clerk **Scott Hiaasen** .... (305) 523-5542
Began Service: 2011
E-mail: scott_hiaasen@flsd.uscourts.gov

Courtroom Deputy **Anita Greer** .... (305) 523-5540

Court Reporter **Patricia Sanders** .... (305) 523-5548
E-mail: patricia_sanders@flsd.uscourts.gov

Chambers of District Judge Robert N. Scola, Jr.

400 North Miami Avenue, Miami, FL 33128
Tel: (305) 523-5140
E-mail: scola@flsd.uscourts.gov

Robert N. Scola, Jr.
District Judge

Date of Birth: 1955
Education: Brown U 1977 BA; Boston Col 1980 JD
Began Service: October 20, 2011
Appointed By: President Barack Obama

Government: Attorney, Office of the State Attorney (11th Judicial Circuit of Florida), County of Miami-Dade, Florida (1980-1986)

Judicial: Judge, Chambers of Judge Robert N. Scola, Eleventh Judicial Circuit, Florida Circuit Courts (1995-2011)

Legal Practice: Partner, Quinon, Strafer & Scola (1992-1993)

Nonprofit: Adjunct Professor, University of Miami (1994-2011); Adjunct Professor, Florida International University (2007-2011)

Staff

Law Clerk **Lindsey Lazopoulos** .... (305) 523-5140
E-mail: lindsey_lazopoulos@flsd.uscourts.gov

Law Clerk **Richard Schevis** .... (305) 523-5140
Began Service: 2011
E-mail: richard_schevis@flsd.uscourts.gov

Law Clerk **Jared Kessler** .... (305) 523-5140
Began Service: 2014
E-mail: jared_kessler@flsd.uscourts.gov

Chambers of District Judge Darrin P. Gayles

400 North Miami Avenue, Room 10-2, Miami, FL 33128
Tel: (305) 523-5170
E-mail: darrin_gayles@flsd.uscourts.gov

Darrin P. Gayles
District Judge

Education: Howard U 1990 BA; George Washington 1993 JD
Began Service: June 19, 2014
Appointed By: President Barack Obama

Government: Assistant State Attorney, Office of the State Attorney (11th Judicial Circuit of Florida), County of Miami-Dade, Florida (1993-1997); Assistant U.S. Attorney, Narcotics Section, Florida - Southern District, United States Department of Justice (1999-2004)

Staff
Law Clerk **Ariel Lett** ....(305) 523-5172
Law Clerk **Heather L. Sarafoglu** ....(305) 523-5173
Education: Indiana 1999 JD

Chambers of District Judge Beth Bloom

299 East Broward Boulevard, Room 207, Fort Lauderdale, FL 33301
Tel: (954) 769-5680
E-mail: Bloom@flsd.uscourts.gov

Beth Bloom
District Judge

Education: Florida 1984 BS; Miami 1988 JD
Began Service: June 25, 2014
Appointed By: President Barack Obama

Judicial: County Judge, Eleventh Judicial Circuit, Florida Circuit Courts (1995-2010)

Legal Practice: Attorney, Floyd Pearson Richman Greer Weil Brumbaugh & Russomanno, P.A (1988-1995)

Staff
Law Clerk **Benjamin Davis** ....(954) 769-5680
Law Clerk **Jarred Reiling** ....(407) 835-4321

Chambers of District Judge Robin L. Rosenberg

101 South U.S. Highway One, Fort Pierce, FL 34950
Tel: (772) 467-2340
E-mail: robin_rosenberg@flsd.uscourts.gov

Robin L. Rosenberg
District Judge

Education: Princeton 1983 BA; Duke 1989 JD, 1989 MA
Began Service: July 24, 2014
Appointed By: President Barack Obama

Corporate: Vice President and General Counsel, Slim Fast Foods (1999-2001)

Government: Assistant City Attorney, Office of the City Attorney, City of West Palm Beach, Florida (1995-1997)

Legal Practice: Partner, Holland & Knight LLP (1997-1999); Partner, Rosenberg & McAuliffe, PL (2001-2006)

Staff
Law Clerk **Benjamin Kennard** ....(772) 467-2340
Judicial Assistant **Saiidia Johnson** ....(772) 467-2343

Chambers of Senior Judge James Lawrence King

James Lawrence King Federal Justice Building, 99 NE Fourth Street, Room 1127, Miami, FL 33132
Tel: (305) 523-5000 Fax: (305) 523-5109
E-mail: king@flsd.uscourts.gov

James Lawrence King
Senior Judge

Date of Birth: 1927
Education: Florida 1949 BS, 1953 LLB
Began Service: October 30, 1970
Appointed By: President Richard M. Nixon
Political Affiliation: Democrat

Judicial: Judge, Florida Circuit Court, 11th Judicial Circuit, Dade County (1964-1970); Associate Justice, Florida Supreme Court; Associate Judge, Florida Court of Appeal, Third District (1966-1967); Temporary Chief Judge for Administration, United States District Court of the Canal Zone (1977-1978); Chief Judge, United States District Court for the Southern District of Florida (1984-1991)

Legal Practice: Sibley & Davis (1955-1964)

Military Service: United States Air Force (1953-1955)

Current Memberships: American Bar Association; Dade County Bar Association; The Florida Bar; Miami Asset Management Company

Staff
Law Clerk **Peter J. Klock II** ....(305) 523-5000
E-mail: peter_klock@flsd.uscourts.gov
Education: Miami 2012 JD
Law Clerk **Robert Dunlap** ....(305) 523-5000
E-mail: robert_dunlap@flsd.uscourts.gov
Courtroom Deputy **Joyce Williams** ....(305) 523-5105
E-mail: joyce_williams@flsd.uscourts.gov
Secretary **Sandra Diaz** ....(305) 523-5000
E-mail: sandra_diaz@flsd.uscourts.gov

Chambers of Senior Judge Jose A. Gonzalez, Jr.

205-D U.S. Courthouse, 299 East Broward Boulevard, Fort Lauderdale, FL 33301
Tel: (954) 769-5560
E-mail: gonzalez@flsd.uscourts.gov

Jose A. Gonzalez, Jr.
Senior Judge

Date of Birth: 1931
Education: Florida 1952 BA, 1957 JD
Began Service: July 28, 1978
Appointed By: President Jimmy Carter
Political Affiliation: Democrat

Corporate: Claim Representative, State Farm Mutual Automobile Insurance Company (1957-1958)

Government: Assistant State Attorney, 15th Judicial Circuit, State of Florida (1961-1964)

Judicial: Judge, Florida Circuit Court, 17th Judicial Circuit (1964-1978)

Legal Practice: Associate, Watson, Hubert & Sousley (1958-1961); Partner, Watson, Hubert & Sousley (1961-1964)

Military Service: Lieutenant, United States Army (1952-1954); Captain United States Army Reserve, United States Department of the Army (1954-1960)

Current Memberships: American Bar Association; Broward County Bar Association; Federal Bar Association; The Florida Bar

Staff
Career Law Clerk **Patricia Burton** ....(954) 769-5563
E-mail: patricia_burton@flsd.uscourts.gov
Secretary **(Vacant)** ....(954) 769-5560

Chambers of Senior Judge Kenneth L. Ryskamp

Paul G. Rogers Federal Building, 701 Clematis Street, Room 416, West Palm Beach, FL 33401
Tel: (561) 803-3420 Fax: (561) 803-3429
E-mail: ryskamp@flsd.uscourts.gov

Kenneth L. Ryskamp
Senior Judge

Date of Birth: 1932
Education: Calvin Col 1955 AB; Miami 1956 JD
Began Service: 1986
Appointed By: President Ronald Reagan

Clerkships: Law Clerk The Honorable Mallory H. Horton, Florida Court of Appeal, Third District (1957-1959)

Legal Practice: Private Practice (1959-1961); Partner, Goodwin, Ryskamp, Welcher & Carrier (1961-1984); Attorney, Squire, Sanders & Dempsey L.L.P. (1984-1986)

Current Memberships: Federal Judges Association; The Florida Bar; State Bar of Michigan

Staff

Law Clerk (Odd-Numbered Cases)
Shannon O'Shea Darsch .... (561) 803-3420
Began Service: 2014
Career Law Clerk (Even-Numbered Cases)
Kari M. Dahlin .... (561) 803-3420
E-mail: kari_dahlin@flsd.uscourts.gov
Education: Minnesota 2001 JD
Courtroom Deputy **Linda Brown** .... (561) 803-3422
Court Reporter **(Vacant)** .... (561) 651-3865

Chambers of Senior Judge Daniel T. K. Hurley

U.S. Courthouse, 701 Clematis Street, Room 352, West Palm Beach, FL 33401-5196
Tel: (561) 803-3450
E-mail: hurley@flsd.uscourts.gov

Daniel T. K. Hurley
Senior Judge

Date of Birth: 1943
Education: St Anselm 1964 AB; George Washington 1968 JD
Began Service: April 1, 1994
Appointed By: President William J. Clinton

Clerkships: Law Clerk The Honorable John Pratt, United States District Court for the District of Columbia; Law Clerk The Honorable Roger Robb, United States Court of Appeals for the District of Columbia Circuit

Government: Assistant County Solicitor, County of Palm Beach, Florida (1970-1973); Executive Assistant State Attorney, 15th Judicial Circuit of Florida, State of Florida (1973-1975)

Judicial: Judge, West Palm Beach County Court (1975-1977); Judge, Florida Circuit Court, 15th Judicial Circuit (1977-1979); Judge, Florida Court of Appeal, Fourth District (1979-1986); Judge, Florida Circuit Court, 15th Judicial Circuit (1986-1994); Chief Judge, Florida Circuit Court, 15th Judicial Circuit (1988-1993)

Current Memberships: American Bar Association; The District of Columbia Bar; The Florida Bar; Palm Beach County Bar Association; State Bar of California

Staff

Law Clerk [Odd Numbered Cases] **(Vacant)** .... (561) 803-3450
Career Law Clerk [Even Numbered Cases]
Theresa A. DiPaola .... (561) 803-3450
E-mail: theresa_dipaola@flsd.uscourts.gov
Education: Boston U 1983 JD
Courtroom Deputy **James Caldwell** .... (561) 803-3452
E-mail: james_caldwell@flsd.uscourts.gov
Court Reporter **(Vacant)** .... (305) 523-5632
Judicial Administrator **Linda Lipps Rosi** .... (561) 803-3450
E-mail: linda_rosi@flsd.uscourts.gov

Chambers of Senior Judge Paul C. Huck

400 North Miami Avenue, Room 13-2, Miami, FL 33128
Tel: (305) 523-5520
E-mail: huck@flsd.uscourts.gov

Paul C. Huck
Senior Judge

Date of Birth: 1940
Education: Florida 1962 BA, 1965 JD
Began Service: August 5, 2000
Appointed By: President William J. Clinton

Staff

Fax: (305) 523-5529

Law Clerk **Erica Perdomo** .... (305) 523-5522
E-mail: erica_perdomo@flsd.uscourts.gov
Law Clerk **Daniel Balmori** .... (305) 523-5524
Began Service: September 2015
Term Expires: September 2016
E-mail: daniel_balmori@flsd.uscourts.gov
Law Clerk **Lauren "Vanessa" Lopez** .... (305) 523-5523
Began Service: September 2015
Term Expires: September 2016
Courtroom Deputy/Judicial Assistant **(Vacant)** .... (305) 523-5525

Chambers of Senior Judge Patricia A. Seitz

U.S. Courthouse, 400 North Miami Avenue, Courtroom 11-4, Miami, FL 33128
Tel: (305) 523-5530
E-mail: seitz@flsd.uscourts.gov

Patricia A. Seitz
Senior Judge

Date of Birth: 1946
Education: Kansas State 1968 BA; Georgetown 1973 JD
Began Service: November 16, 1998
Appointed By: President William J. Clinton

Current Memberships: American Bar Foundation; American Board of Trial Advocates; The District of Columbia Bar; The Florida Bar; International Society of Barristers; International Women's Forum

Staff

Note: For cases ending in 9, the number preceding 9 identifies the responsible clerk.

Law Clerk [Cases Ending 0, 1, 2] **Aatif Iqbal** .... (305) 523-5531
E-mail: aatif_iqbal@flsd.uscourts.gov
Law Clerk [Cases Ending 3, 5, 7] **Yvonne Saadi** .... (305) 523-5533
E-mail: arun_ravindran@flsd.uscourts.gov
Career Law Clerk/Chief of Staff [Cases Ending 4, 6, 8]
Cynthia Bulan .... (305) 523-5532
Began Service: August 18, 2008
E-mail: cynthia_bulan@flsd.uscourts.gov
Courtroom Deputy **Clara Foster** .... (305) 523-5534
E-mail: clara_foster@flsd.uscourts.gov

Chambers of Senior Judge Donald L. Graham

Wilkie D. Ferguson Jr. US Courthouse, 400 North Miami Avenue, Chambers 13-4, Miami, FL 33128
Tel: (305) 523-5130
E-mail: graham@flsd.uscourts.gov

Donald L. Graham
Senior Judge

Date of Birth: 1948
Education: West Virginia State Col 1971 BA; Ohio State 1974 JD
Began Service: October 1991
Appointed By: President George H.W. Bush

Current Memberships: American Association for Justice; American Bar Association; Council of Florida Bar Presidents; Dade County Bar Association; District Judges Association of the Eleventh Circuit; Federal Bar Association; The Florida Bar; National Association of Criminal Defense Lawyers; National Bar Association; Wilkie D. Ferguson, Jr. Bar Association

Staff

Career Law Clerk [Odd Numbered Cases]
Anika Hardmon .... (305) 523-5130
Began Service: November 2009
E-mail: anika_hardmon@flsd.uscourts.gov

Law Clerk [Even Numbered Cases]
John Thornton, Jr. .... (305) 523-5130
Began Service: July 2015
Term Expires: July 12, 2017
E-mail: john_thornton@flsd.uscourts.gov

Courtroom Deputy **Clara Foster** .... (305) 523-5135
E-mail: clara_foster@flsd.uscourts.gov

Judicial Administrator **Gina Wong** .... (305) 523-5130
E-mail: gina_wong@flsd.uscourts.gov
Education: Miami 1982 BBA

Chambers of Chief Magistrate Judge Frank J. Lynch, Jr.

Alto Lee Adams, Sr. United States Courthouse, 101 South U.S. Highway One, 4th Floor, Fort Pierce, FL 34950
Tel: (772) 467-2320
E-mail: frank_lynch@flsd.uscourts.gov

Frank J. Lynch, Jr.
Chief Magistrate Judge

Date of Birth: 1952
Education: Loyola U (New Orleans) 1973 BA, 1976 JD
Began Service: April 1, 1995
Term Expires: 2019

Staff

Career Law Clerk **Ian E. Pate** .... (772) 467-2322
E-mail: ian_pate@flsd.uscourts.gov

Magisterial Support **Colette Griffin-Arnold** .... (772) 467-2308
E-mail: colette_griffin-arnold@flsd.uscourts.gov

Judicial Administrator **Elizabeth Lambertson** .... (772) 467-2320
E-mail: elizabeth_lambertson@flsd.uscourts.gov

Chambers of Magistrate Judge Barry S. Seltzer

299 East Broward Boulevard, Fort Lauderdale, FL 33301
Tel: (954) 769-5450
E-mail: seltzer@flsd.uscourts.gov

Barry S. Seltzer
Magistrate Judge

Date of Birth: 1954
Education: Hamilton 1976 BA; NYU 1980 MBA, 1980 JD, 1984 LLM
Began Service: 2012

Current Memberships: American Bar Association; The Stephen R. Booher American Inn of Court, The American Inns of Court; B'nai Birth Justice Unit; Broward County Bar Association; Federal Bar Association; Federal Magistrate Judges Association; The Florida Bar

Staff

Career Law Clerk **Andrea "Kay" Adams** .... (954) 769-5450
Education: Kentucky JD

Career Law Clerk/Administrator **Channon Coffey** .... (954) 769-5450
E-mail: channon_coffey@flsd.uscourts.gov
Education: Florida 1996 JD

Courtroom Deputy **Aaron Tijerino** .... (954) 769-5450
E-mail: aaron_tijerino@flsd.uscourts.gov

Chambers of Magistrate Judge William C. Turnoff

U.S. Courthouse, 301 North Miami Avenue, 11th Floor, Miami, FL 33128
Tel: (305) 523-5710 Fax: (305) 523-5719
E-mail: turnoff@flsd.uscourts.gov

William C. Turnoff
Magistrate Judge

Date of Birth: 1948
Education: Franklin & Marshall 1970 AB; Cornell 1973 JD
Began Service: 1986

Government: Assistant District Attorney, Commonwealth of Pennsylvania (1973-1980); Assistant United States Attorney, Southern District of Florida, United States Department of Justice (1980-1986)

Staff

Career Law Clerk **Maria Arias-Morgado** .... (305) 523-5710
E-mail: maria_arias-morgado@flsd.uscourts.gov

Career Law Clerk **Lizbeth Michel-Escandell** .... (305) 523-5710
E-mail: lizbeth_michel@flsd.uscourts.gov

Courtroom Deputy **LaKeshia A. Williams** .... (305) 523-5284
E-mail: lakeshia_williams@flsd.uscourts.gov

Chambers of Magistrate Judge Lurana S. Snow

299 East Broward Boulevard, Room 204, Fort Lauderdale, FL 33301
Tel: (954) 769-5460
E-mail: snow@flsd.uscourts.gov

Lurana S. Snow
Magistrate Judge

Date of Birth: 1951
Education: Radcliffe 1972 AB; Harvard 1975 JD; Barry 1998 MA
Began Service: 1986

Academic: Adjunct Faculty, Nova Southeastern University Law School

Clerkships: Law Clerk The Honorable Joe Eaton, United States District Court for the Southern District of Florida (1975-1977)

Government: Assistant Federal Public Defender, State of Florida (1977-1979); Assistant United States Attorney, United States Department of Justice (1980-1986)

Current Memberships: The District of Columbia Bar; The Florida Bar; Massachusetts Bar Association

(continued on next page)

Chambers of Magistrate Judge Lurana S. Snow *continued*

Staff

Career Law Clerk **Naomi Seligman** .... (954) 769-5462
E-mail: naomi_seligman@flsd.uscourts.gov
Courtroom Deputy **Debbie Donovan** .... (954) 769-5407
Secretary **Judy Zanotti** .... (954) 769-5460
E-mail: judy_zanotti@flsd.uscourts.gov

Chambers of Magistrate Judge Andrea M. Simonton

U.S. Courthouse, 301 North Miami Avenue, 8th Floor, Miami, FL 33128
Tel: (305) 523-5930 Fax: (305) 523-5939
E-mail: simonton@flsd.uscourts.gov

Andrea M. Simonton
Magistrate Judge

Date of Birth: 1953
Education: Miami 1978 JD
Began Service: April 1, 1999
Term Expires: March 31, 2023

Staff

Career Law Clerk **Pamela Armour** .... (305) 523-5930
E-mail: pamela_armour@flsd.uscourts.gov
Education: Ohio State 1990 AB; DePaul 1994 JD
Magisterial Support **Alicia Williams** .... (305) 523-5293
E-mail: alicia_williams@flsd.uscourts.gov

Chambers of Magistrate Judge John J. O'Sullivan

301 North Miami Avenue, 5th Floor, Miami, FL 33128
Tel: (305) 523-5920
E-mail: osullivan@flsd.uscourts.gov

John J. O'Sullivan
Magistrate Judge

Date of Birth: 1956
Education: Miami 1985 JD
Began Service: April 1, 1999
Term Expires: March 30, 2023
Military: CPA

Government: Criminal Division Chief, Florida - Southern District, Executive Office for United States Attorneys, United States Department of Justice (1986-1999); Deputy Independent Counsel, United States Office of the Independent Counsel (1995-1996)

Legal Practice: Fowler White et al. (1985-1986)

Current Memberships: The Spellman-Hoeveler American Inn of Court, The American Inns of Court

Staff

Career Law Clerk **Maria Kleppinger** .... (305) 523-5920
E-mail: maria_kleppinger@flsd.uscourts.gov
Career Law Clerk (Part-Time) **Maria McGuinness** ...... (305) 523-5920
E-mail: maria_mcguinness@flsd.uscourts.gov
Career Law Clerk (Part-Time) **Tobi Rousso** .... (305) 523-5920
E-mail: tobi_rousso@flsd.uscourts.gov
Courtroom Deputy **Cherle Griffin** .... (305) 523-5816
E-mail: cherle_griffin@flsd.uscourts.gov

Chambers of Magistrate Judge Patrick A. White

301 North Miami Avenue, 3rd Floor, Miami, FL 33128
Tel: (305) 523-5780
E-mail: white@flsd.uscourts.gov

Patrick A. White
Magistrate Judge

Education: Colgate BA; Howard U JD
Began Service: April 2003

Chambers of Magistrate Judge Patrick A. White *continued*

Staff

Career Law Clerk **Jenny Page** .... (305) 523-5780
E-mail: jenny_page@flsd.uscourts.gov
Education: Miami 2003 BS
Pro Se Writ Clerk **Troy Walker** .... (305) 523-5780
E-mail: troy_walker@flsd.uscourts.gov
Supervising Staff Attorney **(Vacant)** .... (305) 523-5780
Staff Attorney **John Barker** .... (305) 523-5780
E-mail: john_barker@flsd.uscourts.gov
Staff Attorney **Debra Cholodofsky** .... (305) 523-5780
E-mail: debra_cholodofsky@flsd.uscourts.gov
Education: Nova Southeastern 1981 JD
Staff Attorney **(Vacant)** .... (305) 523-5780
Staff Attorney **Erin Kinney McLachlan** .... (305) 523-5780
E-mail: erin_kinney@flsd.uscourts.gov
Staff Attorney **Elena Marlow** .... (305) 523-5780
E-mail: elena_marlow@flsd.uscourts.gov
Education: U Washington 1994 JD
Staff Attorney **Norma B. Nin** .... (305) 523-5780
E-mail: norma_nin@flsd.uscourts.gov
Education: Lewis & Clark 1999 JD
Staff Attorney **Elisabeth Reid** .... (305) 523-5780
E-mail: elisabeth_reid@flsd.uscourts.gov
Courtroom Deputy **Betty Rodriguez** .... (305) 523-5282
E-mail: betty_rodriguez@flsd.uscourts.gov
Secretary **Leonor Rodriguez** .... (305) 523-5780
E-mail: leonor_rodriguez@flsd.uscourts.gov

Chambers of Magistrate Judge James M. Hopkins

701 Clematis Street, Room 331, West Palm Beach, FL 33401
Tel: (561) 514-3710
E-mail: james_hopkins@flsd.uscourts.gov

James M. Hopkins
Magistrate Judge

Began Service: October 2003
Term Expires: 2019

Staff

Law Clerk **Sarah Jeck** .... (561) 514-3710
E-mail: sarah_jeck@flsd.uscourts.gov
Career Law Clerk **Heather D. Kenney** .... (561) 514-3710
E-mail: heather_kenney@flsd.uscourts.gov
Education: Boston U 1998 JD
Courtroom Deputy **Tanya McClendon** .... (561) 803-3483
E-mail: tanya_mcclendon@flsd.uscourts.gov

Chambers of Magistrate Judge Edwin G. Torres

301 North Miami Avenue, Miami, FL 33128
Tel: (305) 523-5750
E-mail: torres@flsd.uscourts.gov

Edwin G. Torres
Magistrate Judge

Began Service: 2003
Term Expires: 2019

Staff

Law Clerk **Andrew Fremming** .... (305) 523-5750
Term Expires: February 2016
E-mail: andrew_fremming@flsd.uscourts.gov
Law Clerk **Alexandra Block** .... (305) 523-5750
Room 234
E-mail: alexandra_block@flsd.uscourts.gov
Education: Yale JD
Courtroom Deputy **Maedon Clark** .... (305) 523-5297
Room 234
E-mail: maedon_clark@flsd.uscourts.gov

Chambers of Magistrate Judge Chris M. McAliley
301 North Miami Avenue, Room 105, Miami, FL 33128
Tel: (305) 523-5890
E-mail: chris_mcaliley@flsd.uscourts.gov

Chris M. McAliley
Magistrate Judge

Education: Tufts 1979 BA; NYU 1983 JD
Began Service: March 25, 2004
Term Expires: March 24, 2020

Staff
Law Clerk **Nicole Sulsky** . . . . (305) 523-5890
E-mail: nicole_sulsky@flsd.uscourts.gov
Career Law Clerk **Rima Mullins** . . . . (305) 523-5890
E-mail: rima_mullins@flsd.uscourts.gov
Education: Florida 1991 JD
Courtroom Deputy **Nancy Flood** . . . . (305) 523-5298
E-mail: nancy_flood@flsd.uscourts.gov

Chambers of Magistrate Judge Jonathan Goodman
400 North Miami Avenue, Miami, FL 33128
Tel: (305) 523-5720 Fax: (305) 536-7265
E-mail: jonathan_goodman@flsd.uscourts.gov

Jonathan Goodman
Magistrate Judge

Began Service: 2010

Staff
Law Clerk **Timothy Rodes** . . . . (305) 523-5720
Term Expires: August 2016
E-mail: timothy_rodes@flsd.uscourts.gov
Law Clerk **Mirels Davila** . . . . (305) 523-5720
Term Expires: August 2017
E-mail: mirels_davila@flsd.uscourts.gov
Magisterial Support **Michael Santorufo** . . . . (305) 523-5720
E-mail: michael_santorufo@flsd.uscourts.gov

Chambers of Magistrate Judge Dave Lee Brannon
701 Clematis Street, West Palm Beach, FL 33401
Tel: (561) 803-3470
E-mail: dave_brannon@flsd.uscourts.gov

Dave Lee Brannon
Magistrate Judge

Began Service: 2012

Staff
Career Law Clerk **Jessica Rodriguez** . . . . (561) 803-3470
E-mail: jessica_rodriguez@flsd.uscourts.gov
Courtroom Deputy **Sandra Acevedo** . . . . (561) 803-3412
E-mail: sandra_acevedo@flsd.uscourts.gov

Chambers of Magistrate Judge Alicia M. Otazo-Reyes
400 North Miami Avenue, Miami, FL 33128
Tel: (305) 523-5740

Alicia Otazo-Reyes
Magistrate Judge

Began Service: 2012

Staff
Law Clerk **Edward Nazarro** . . . . (305) 523-5740
E-mail: edward_nazarro@flsd.uscourts.gov
Law Clerk **Alyssa Hazelwood** . . . . (305) 523-5740
Courtroom Deputy **Stephanie Lee** . . . . (305) 523-5740
E-mail: stephanie_lee@flsd.uscourts.gov

Chambers of Magistrate Judge William Matthewman
701 Clematis Street, West Palm Beach, FL 33401
Tel: (561) 803-3440
E-mail: william_matthewman@flsd.uscourts.gov

William Matthewman
Magistrate Judge

Began Service: 2012

Staff
Law Clerk **Nicole Odrobina** . . . . (561) 803-3440
Law Clerk **London Ott** . . . . (561) 803-3440
E-mail: london_ott@flsd.uscourts.gov
Education: Nova Southeastern 2011 JD

Chambers of Magistrate Judge Barry L. Garber
U.S. Courthouse, 99 NE 4th Street, Room 1061, Miami, FL 33132
Tel: (305) 523-5730
E-mail: garber@flsd.uscourts.gov

Barry L. Garber
Magistrate Judge

Date of Birth: 1930
Education: Emory 1951 AB; Miami 1954 JD
Began Service: September 13, 1991
Political Affiliation: Democrat

Government: Assistant State Attorney, Dade County, State of Florida (1957-1959); Special Counsel, Commerce Committee, Florida Legislature (1968); Grand Jury Special Counsel, Office of the State Attorney (11th Judicial Circuit of Florida), Dade County, Florida (1972)

Legal Practice: Partner, Garber & Chadroff (1959-1972); Sole Practitioner (1972-1974); Partner, Garber & Buoniconti (1974-1984); Partner, Dubbin, Berkman, Garber & Bloom (1986-1991)

Current Memberships: American Bar Association; The American Inns of Court; Federal Bar Association; The Florida Bar

Staff
Career Law Clerk **Kimberly Brown Eve** . . . . (305) 523-5730
E-mail: kimberly_eve@flsd.uscourts.gov

Chambers of Magistrate Judge Patrick M. Hunt
299 East Broward Boulevard, Room 205E, Fort Lauderdale, FL 33301
Tel: (954) 769-5470

Patrick M. Hunt
Magistrate Judge

Began Service: 2014

Staff
Law Clerk **Shari Lefton** . . . . (954) 769-5470
Education: Florida 1990 JD
Law Clerk **Trevor Jones** . . . . (954) 769-5470

Chambers of Magistrate Judge Alicia O. Valle
299 East Broward Boulevard, Fort Lauderdale, FL 33301
Tel: (954) 769-5750

Alicia O. Valle
Magistrate Judge

Began Service: 2014

Staff
Law Clerk **Cary Aronovitz** . . . . (954) 769-5750
Law Clerk **Silvia Duarte** . . . . (954) 769-5750

Chambers of Senior Magistrate Judge (recalled) Peter R. Palermo

James Lawrence King Federal Justice Building, 99 NE 4th Street, Room 1067, Miami, FL 33132
Tel: (305) 523-5760 Fax: (305) 523-5769
E-mail: palermo@flsd.uscourts.gov

Peter R. Palermo
Magistrate Judge (recalled)

Date of Birth: 1918
Education: Penn State 1941 BA; Miami 1950 JD
Began Service: January 1, 1971

Current Memberships: Peter T. Fay American Inn of Court, The American Inns of Court; Dade County Bar Association; Eleventh Circuit Historical Society; Federal Bar Association; Federal Magistrate Judges Association; Florida Association for Women Lawyers; The Florida Bar; Florida Historical Society; The Justinian Society; League of Municipal Judges

United States Bankruptcy Court for the Southern District of Florida

Claude Pepper Federal Building, 51 SW First Avenue, Room 1510, Miami, FL 33130-1669
Tel: (305) 714-1800
Tel: (305) 536-5979 (Voice Case Information System VCIS)
Tel: (305) 536-5696 (Voice Case Information System VCIS)
Tel: (800) 473-0226 (Toll Free Voice Case Information System VCIS)
Tel: (800) 676-6856 (Toll Free PACER Registration)
Fax: (305) 714-1801
Internet: www.flsb.uscourts.gov

Number of Judgeships: 7

Court Staff
Clerk of Court **Joseph "Joe" Falzone** . . . . . (305) 714-1800
Chief Deputy Clerk **Jose A. Rodriguez** . . . . . (305) 714-1894
E-mail: jose_rodriguez@flsb.uscourts.gov
Deputy-in-Charge - Fort Lauderdale **Maggie Ferere** . . . . . (954) 769-5701
310 U.S. Courthouse, 299 E. Broward Blvd., Rm. 112, Fort Lauderdale, FL 33301 Fax: (954) 769-5799
E-mail: chris_lacoursiere@flsb.uscourts.gov
Deputy-in-Charge - West Palm Beach **Cameron Cradic** . . . . . (561) 514-4107
Flagler Waterview Building, 1515 North Flagler Drive, 8th Floor, West Palm Beach, FL 33401 Fax: (561) 514-4139
E-mail: cameron_cradic@flsb.uscourts.gov
Financial Administrator **Juany McKiernan** . . . . . (305) 714-1841
E-mail: juany_mckiernan@flsb.uscourts.gov
Contracting Officer **Denise Eyerman** . . . . . (305) 714-1824
E-mail: denise_eyerman@flsb.uscourts.gov
Human Resources Administrator **Lourdes T. Strong** . . . . . (305) 714-1854
E-mail: lourdes_strong@flsb.uscourts.gov
Information Technology - Applications Manager **Erwin Ruiz** . . . . . (305) 714-1855
E-mail: erwin_ruiz@flsb.uscourts.gov Fax: (305) 714-1806
Information Technology - Networking Manager **Tony Diaz** . . . . . (305) 714-1865
E-mail: tony_diaz@flsb.uscourts.gov
Director of Administrative Services **Jose A. Rodriguez** . . . . . (305) 714-1825
E-mail: jose_rodriguez@flsb.uscourts.gov Fax: (305) 714-1803

Chambers of Chief Bankruptcy Judge Paul G. Hyman, Jr.

1515 North Flagler Drive, 8th Floor, West Palm Beach, FL 33401
Tel: (561) 514-4109 Fax: (561) 514-4139
E-mail: paul_hyman@flsb.uscourts.gov

Paul G. Hyman, Jr.
Chief Bankruptcy Judge

Date of Birth: 1952
Education: Vanderbilt 1974 BA; Miami 1977 JD
Began Service: October 4, 1993
Term Expires: October 3, 2021

Government: Assistant United States Attorney, Southern District of Florida, United States Department of Justice (1979-1981)

Legal Practice: Britton, Cohen, Kaufman & Schantz (1977-1979); Britton, Cohen, Kaufman & Schantz (1981-1983); Attorney, Holme Roberts & Owen LLP (1983-1993)

Staff
Law Clerk **Jordan Wiegele** . . . . . (561) 514-4125
Began Service: 2011
E-mail: jordan_wiegele@flsb.uscourts.gov
Education: Emory 2008 BA; Mercer 2011 JD
Law Clerk **(Vacant)** . . . . . (561) 514-4126
Courtroom Deputy **Vivian Corrales** . . . . . (561) 514-4109
E-mail: vivian_corrales@flsb.uscourts.gov

Chambers of Bankruptcy Judge Robert A. Mark

301 North Miami Avenue, Room 417, Miami, FL 33128
Tel: (305) 714-1760 Fax: (305) 714-1769
E-mail: robert_mark@flsb.uscourts.gov

Robert A. Mark
Bankruptcy Judge

Date of Birth: 1951
Education: Boalt Hall 1978 JD
Began Service: 1990
Term Expires: August 2018

Clerkships: Law Clerk The Honorable Sidney Aronovitz, United States District Court for the Southern District of Florida (1978-1979)

Judicial: Chief Bankruptcy Judge, United States Bankruptcy Court for the Southern District of Florida

Legal Practice: Attorney, Stearns Weaver Miller Weissler Alhadeff & Sitterson, P.A. (1979-1990)

Staff
Law Clerk **Luis Casas** . . . . . (305) 714-1763
E-mail: luis_casas@flsb.uscourts.gov
Courtroom Deputy **Elaine Howlan** . . . . . (305) 714-1766
E-mail: elaine_howlan@flsb.uscourts.gov
Judicial Assistant **Marcy Gatell** . . . . . (305) 714-1762
E-mail: marcy_gatell@flsb.uscourts.gov

Chambers of Bankruptcy Judge A. Jay Cristol

301 North Miami Avenue, Miami, FL 33128
Tel: (305) 714-1770 Fax: (305) 714-1777
E-mail: a_jay_cristol@flsb.uscourts.gov

A. Jay Cristol
Bankruptcy Judge

Date of Birth: 1929
Education: Miami 1958 BA, 1959 JD, 1997 PhD
Began Service: April 1985
Term Expires: April 2027

Government: Special Assistant to the Attorney General for Legislative Session, State of Florida (1959); Special Assistant to the Attorney General for Legislative Session, State of Florida (1961); Special Assistant to the Attorney General for Legislative Session, State of Florida (1963); Special Assistant to the Attorney General for Legislative Session, State of Florida (1965)

Legal Practice: Partner, Cristol, Mishan & Sloto (and predecessor firms) (1959-1985)

Military Service: United States Naval Reserve (1951-1988)

Current Memberships: American Bankruptcy Institute; American Bar Association; American College of Bankruptcy; Dade County Bar Association; The Florida Bar; National Conference of Bankruptcy Judges

Staff
Career Law Clerk **Cheryl A. Kaplan** .... (305) 714-1773
E-mail: Cheryl_Kaplan@flsb.uscourts.gov
Education: Boston U 1984 BA;
John Marshall 1987 JD
Courtroom Deputy **Barbara Cargill** .... (305) 714-1770
E-mail: barbara_cargill@flsb.uscourts.gov
Judicial Assistant **Jennifer Rolph** .... (305) 714-1772
E-mail: Jennifer_Rolph@flsb.uscourts.gov
Education: Florida 1984 BA

Chambers of Bankruptcy Judge Raymond B. Ray

112 U.S. Courthouse, 299 East Broward Boulevard, Room 306,
Fort Lauderdale, FL 33301
Tel: (954) 769-5760 Fax: (954) 769-5769

Raymond B. Ray
Bankruptcy Judge

Date of Birth: 1943
Education: South Florida 1965 BA; Florida 1971 JD
Began Service: November 9, 1993
Term Expires: November 9, 2021

Government: Assistant United States Attorney, Southern District of Florida, United States Department of Justice (1971-1974)

Legal Practice: Raymond B. Ray, P.A.

Military Service: United States Naval Reserve (1961-1985)

Current Memberships: American Bankruptcy Institute; American Bar Association; Broward County Bar Association; Colorado Bar Association; Federal Bar Association; The Florida Bar

Staff
Career Law Clerk **Amanda Finley** .... (954) 769-5762
Began Service: September 2013
E-mail: amanda_finley@flsb.uscourts.gov
Courtroom Deputy **Edy Gomez** .... (954) 769-5765
E-mail: edy_gomez@flsb.uscourts.gov
Judicial Assistant **Betty Robaina** .... (954) 769-5761
E-mail: betty_robaina@flsb.uscourts.gov

Chambers of Bankruptcy Judge Laurel M. Isicoff

300 North Miami Avenue, Room 817, Miami, FL 33128
Tel: (305) 714-1750

Laurel M. Isicoff
Bankruptcy Judge

Education: Miami JD
Began Service: 2006
Term Expires: 2020

Legal Practice: Partner, Kozyak, Tropin & Throckmorton

Staff
Law Clerk **Carly Krupnick** .... (305) 714-1750
Began Service: August 2015
Term Expires: August 2017
E-mail: carly_krupnick@flsb.uscourts.gov
Courtroom Deputy **Noemi Sanabria** .... (305) 714-1877
E-mail: noemi_sanabria@flsb.uscourts.gov
Judicial Assistant **Emily Maza** .... (305) 714-1752
E-mail: emily_maza@flsb.uscourts.gov

Chambers of Bankruptcy Judge John K. Olson

299 East Broward Boulevard, Room 303, Fort Lauderdale, FL 33301
Tel: (954) 769-5772 Fax: (954) 769-5779
E-mail: jko_chambers@flsb.uscourts.gov

John K. Olson
Bankruptcy Judge

Staff
Law Clerk **Aaron Brownell** .... (954) 769-5773
Began Service: September 2014
Term Expires: September 2016
E-mail: aaron_brownell@flsb.uscourts.gov
Courtroom Deputy **Christina Romero** .... (954) 769-5774
E-mail: christina_romero@flsb.uscourts.gov
Judicial Assistant **Joseph Costanzo** .... (954) 769-5772
E-mail: joseph_costanzo@flsb.uscourts.gov

Chambers of Bankruptcy Judge Erik P. Kimball

1515 North Flagler Drive, West Palm Beach, FL 33401
Tel: (561) 514-4140 Fax: (561) 514-4147

Erik B. Kimball
Bankruptcy Judge

Began Service: 2010

Staff
Law Clerk **Michelle Jaffe** .... (561) 514-4140
E-mail: michelle_jaffe@flsb.uscourts.gov
Law Clerk **Tristan Axelrod** .... (561) 514-4140
E-mail: tristan_axelrod@flsb.uscourts.gov
Courtroom Deputy **Cindy Klopp** .... (561) 514-4143
E-mail: cindy_klopp@flsb.uscourts.gov

United States District Court for the Middle District of Georgia

William Augustus Bootle U.S. Courthouse, 475 Mulberry Street, Macon, GA 31201
P.O. Box 128, Macon, GA 31202
Tel: (478) 752-3497 Tel: (478) 752-8170 (PACER)
Fax: (478) 752-3496
Internet: www.gamd.uscourts.gov

Number of Judgeships: 4

Circuit: Eleventh

Areas Covered: Counties of Baker, Baldwin, Ben Hill, Berrien, Bibb, Bleckley, Brooks, Butts, Calhoun, Chattahoochee, Clarke, Clay, Clinch, Colquitt, Cook, Crawford, Crisp, Decatur, Dooly, Dougherty, Early, Echols, Elbert, Franklin, Grady, Greene, Hancock, Harris, Hart, Houston, Irwin, Jasper, Jones, Lamar, Lanier, Lee, Lowndes, Macon, Madison, Marion, Miller, Mitchell, Monroe, Morgan, Muscogee, Oconee, Oglethorpe, Peach, Pulaski, Putnam, Quitman, Randolph, Schley, Seminole, Stewart, Sumter, Talbot, Taylor, Terrell, Thomas, Tift, Turner, Twiggs, Upson, Walton, Washington, Webster, Wilcox, Wilkenson and Worth

Court Staff

Clerk of Court **David Bunt** .... (478) 752-0711
Fax: (478) 752-3450
Chief Deputy Clerk **Tachunta Thomas** .... (478) 752-3497
Case Administrator III - Albany **Wanda Sanders** .... (229) 430-8432
C.B. King U.S. Courthouse, 201 Broad Ave., Albany, GA 31701 Fax: (229) 430-8538
E-mail: wanda_sanders@gamd.uscourts.gov
Case Administrator - Athens **Gail G. Sellers** .... (706) 227-1094
115 E. Hancock Ave., Athens, GA 30601 Fax: (706) 546-2190
P.O. Box 1106, Athens, GA 30603
E-mail: gail_sellers@gamd.uscourts.gov
Case Administrator - Columbus **Tim Frost** .... (706) 649-7816
216 U.S. Courthouse, 120 12th St., Columbus, GA 31901 Fax: (706) 649-7790
P.O. Box 124, Columbus, GA 31902
E-mail: tim_frost@gamd.uscourts.gov
Case Administrator - Valdosta **Sandra DeCesare** .... (229) 242-3616
212 U.S. Courthouse, 401 N. Patterson St., Valdosta, GA 31601 Fax: (229) 244-9547
P.O. Box 68, Valdosta, GA 31601
E-mail: sandra_decesare@gamd.uscourts.gov
Case Administrator - Valdosta **Robin Walsh** .... (229) 242-3616
212 U.S. Courthouse, 401 N. Patterson St., Valdosta, GA 31601 Fax: (229) 244-9547
P.O. Box 68, Valdosta, GA 31601
E-mail: robin_walsh@gamd.uscourts.gov
Chief Probation Officer **Ellen S. Moore** .... (478) 752-8106
431 Walnut St., Macon, GA 31201 Fax: (478) 752-8165
P.O. Box 1736, Macon, GA 31202-1736
Financial Manager **Twranna Hicks** .... (478) 752-0745
E-mail: twranna_hicks@gamd.uscourts.gov
Director of Information Technology **(Vacant)** .... (478) 752-0700
Administrative Analyst **David Lee** .... (478) 752-0709
E-mail: david_lee@gamd.uscourts.gov
Operations Specialist **Debra Boone** .... (478) 752-0725
Jury Administrator **Kellie Sise** .... (478) 752-0708
E-mail: kellie_sise@gamd.uscourts.gov
Personnel Specialist **Daryl Sherwood** .... (478) 752-0710
E-mail: daryl_sherwood@gamd.uscourts.gov

Chambers of Chief Judge Clay D. Land

120 - 12th Street, Columbus, GA 31902-2017
P.O. Box 2017, Columbus, GA 31902-2017
Tel: (706) 649-7812 Fax: (706) 649-7813

Clay D. Land

Chief Judge

Date of Birth: 1960
Education: Georgia 1982 BBA, 1985 JD
Began Service: December 28, 2001
Appointed By: President George W. Bush

Current Memberships: American Bar Association; Columbus Bar Association; State Bar of Georgia

Staff

Career Law Clerk **Caroline G. Castle** .... (706) 649-7812
Courtroom Deputy Clerk/Secretary **Elizabeth Long** .... (706) 649-7812

Chambers of District Judge C. Ashley Royal

William Augustus Bootle U.S. Courthouse, 475 Mulberry Street, Macon, GA 31202
P.O. Box 129, Macon, GA 31202-0129
Tel: (478) 752-3445 Fax: (478) 752-3446
E-mail: ashley_royal@gamd.uscourts.gov

C. Ashley Royal

District Judge

Date of Birth: 1949
Education: Georgia 1971 AB, 1974 JD, 1976 MS
Began Service: December 28, 2001
Appointed By: President George W. Bush

Staff

Law Clerk **Jennifer Findley** .... (478) 752-3445
Began Service: October 2014
Term Expires: October 2016
E-mail: jennifer_findley@gamd.uscourts.gov
Law Clerk **Chelsea Lamb** .... (478) 752-3445
Began Service: August 2015
Term Expires: August 2017
Career Law Clerk **Sally Sanders Hatcher** .... (478) 752-3445
E-mail: sally_hatcher@gamd.uscourts.gov
Education: Col Charleston 1998 BA; Georgia 2001 JD
Scheduling and Courtroom Clerk **Lee Anne Purvis** .... (478) 752-0739
E-mail: leeanne_purvis@gamd.uscourts.gov

Chambers of District Judge Marc T. Treadwell

P.O. Box 65, Macon, GA 31202
Tel: (478) 752-0717
E-mail: marc_treadwell@gamd.uscourts.gov

Marc Thomas Treadwell

District Judge

Education: Valdosta State U 1978 BA; Mercer 1981 JD
Began Service: June 25, 2010
Appointed By: President Barack Obama

Staff

Scheduling/Courtroom Clerk **Teri Hatcher** .... (478) 752-0717
E-mail: teri_hatcher@gamd.uscourts.gov

Chambers of District Judge Leslie Joyce Abrams
201 West Broad Street, Albany, GA 31701
Tel: (229) 431-2510

Leslie J. Abrams
District Judge

Education: Brown U 1997 BA; Yale 2002 JD
Began Service: 2014
Appointed By: President Barack Obama

Staff
Courtroom Deputy **Monica Cooper** .... (229) 431-2510

Chambers of Senior Judge Hugh Lawson
William Augustus Bootle U.S. Courthouse, 475 Mulberry Street, Macon, GA 31202
P.O. Box 838, Macon, GA 31202-0838
Tel: (478) 752-3591 Fax: (478) 752-8164
E-mail: Hugh_Lawson@gamd.uscourts.gov

Hugh Lawson
Senior Judge

Date of Birth: 1941
Education: Emory 1963 BA, 1964 LLB
Began Service: December 29, 1995
Appointed By: President William J. Clinton

Current Memberships: Federal Judges Association

Staff
Law Clerk **Lindsey Stephens** .... (478) 752-3591 ext. 0724
Began Service: July 29, 2015
Term Expires: August 2017
E-mail: lindsey_stephens@gamd.uscourts.gov
Career Law Clerk **Amanda K. Smith** .... (478) 752-3591 ext. 0723
Court Reporter **Sally Gray** .... (478) 752-0804
E-mail: Sally_Gray@gamd.uscourts.gov
Courtroom Clerk/Scheduling **Nora Paul** .... (478) 752-3591 ext. 0725
E-mail: nora_paul@gamd.uscourts.gov

Chambers of Senior Judge W. Louis Sands
201 West Broad Avenue, Albany, GA 31701
Tel: (229) 430-8553 Fax: (229) 430-8559

W. Louis Sands
Senior Judge

Date of Birth: 1949
Education: Mercer 1971 BA, 1974 JD
Began Service: May 1994
Appointed By: President William J. Clinton

Current Memberships: Albany County Bar Association; State Bar of Georgia

Staff
Law Clerk **Mitchell Robinson** .... (229) 430-8553
Began Service: June 2014
Term Expires: June 2016
E-mail: mitchell_robinson@gamd.uscourts.gov
Law Clerk **Caitlin Sandley** .... (229) 430-8553
Began Service: August 2014
Term Expires: August 2016
E-mail: caitlin_sandley@gamd.uscourts.gov
Law Clerk **Tiffany Watkins** .... (229) 430-8553
Began Service: August 2015
Term Expires: August 2017
E-mail: tiffany_watkins@gamd.uscourts.gov

Chambers of Senior Judge W. Louis Sands *continued*

Courtroom Deputy/Scheduling Clerk **Joan King** .... (229) 903-1332
E-mail: joan_king@gamd.uscourts.gov

Chambers of Magistrate Judge Thomas Q. Langstaff
201 West Broad Street, Albany, GA 31701
Tel: (229) 903-1312
E-mail: thomas_langstaff@gamd.uscourts.gov

Thomas Q. Langstaff
Magistrate Judge

Began Service: June 2010

Staff
Career Law Clerk **Alicia S. Brown** .... (229) 430-8577
E-mail: alicia_brown@gamd.uscourts.gov
Education: Emory 1993 JD
Law Clerk **Lisa Fox** .... (229) 430-8577
E-mail: lisa_fox@gamd.uscourts.gov
Courtroom Clerk/Scheduling **Bill Lawrence** .... (229) 903-1316
E-mail: bill_lawrence@gamd.uscourts.gov

Chambers of Magistrate Judge M. Stephen Hyles
P.O. Box 117, Columbus, GA 31902-0117
Tel: (706) 649-7860

M. Stephen Hyles
Magistrate Judge

Began Service: 2010

Staff
Scheduling/Courtroom Clerk **Terrie Smith** .... (706) 649-7860
E-mail: terrie_smith@gamd.uscourts.gov

Chambers of Magistrate Judge Charles H. Weigle
P.O. Box 48, Macon, GA 31202
475 Mulberry Street, Macon, GA 31201
Tel: (478) 752-0730 Fax: (478) 752-8125

Charles H. Weigle
Magistrate Judge

Education: Virginia 1996 JD
Began Service: October 19, 2010
Term Expires: October 19, 2018

Staff
Law Clerk **Luke Caselman** .... (478) 752-0730
Began Service: September 1, 2015
Term Expires: September 1, 2017
E-mail: luke_caselman@gamd.uscourts.gov
Law Clerk **Jake Carroll** .... (478) 752-0730
Began Service: September 1, 2014
Term Expires: September 1, 2016
Career Law Clerk **(Vacant)** .... (478) 752-0730
Scheduling/Courtroom Clerk **Charlene Lunsford** .... (478) 752-0730

United States Bankruptcy Court for the Middle District of Georgia

433 Cherry Street, Macon, GA 31201
P.O. Box 1957, Macon, GA 31202
Tel: (478) 752-3506 Tel: (800) 546-7343 (Toll Free PACER)
Tel: (478) 752-8183 (Voice Case Information System VCIS)
Tel: (800) 211-3015 (Toll Free Voice Case Information System VCIS)
Fax: (478) 752-8157
Internet: www.gamb.uscourts.gov

Number of Judgeships: 3

Court Staff
Bankruptcy Clerk **Kyle George** . . . . (478) 749-6842
Education: Georgia 1986
Chief Deputy **Scott Poupard** . . . . (478) 749-6852
Budget Analyst/Procurement Clerk **Vicki DuBose** . . . . (478) 749-6845
E-mail: vicki_dubose@gamb.uscourts.gov
Financial Administrator **Benita Stripling** . . . . (478) 749-6844
E-mail: Benita_Stripling@gamb.uscourts.gov
Systems Manager **Robley Willis** . . . . (478) 749-6850
E-mail: robley_willis@gamb.uscourts.gov
Administrative Services Specialist **Teresa Waite** . . . . (478) 749-6840
E-mail: teresa_waite@gamb.uscourts.gov

Chambers of Chief Bankruptcy Judge James P. Smith

433 Cherry Street, Macon, GA 31201
Tel: (478) 752-3506 Fax: (478) 752-8157
E-mail: james_smith@gamb.uscourts.gov

James P. Smith
Chief Bankruptcy Judge

Began Service: 2010

Staff
Law Clerk **J. Alvin Brown** . . . . (478) 749-6864
Education: Mercer 1987 JD
Judicial Assistant **Cheryl Spilman** . . . . (478) 749-6861

Chambers of Bankruptcy Judge John T. Laney III

One Arsenal Place, 901 Front Avenue, Room 309, Columbus, GA 31901
P.O. Box 1540, Columbus, GA 31902-1540
Tel: (706) 596-7150 Fax: (706) 649-7871
E-mail: john_laney@gamb.uscourts.gov

John T. Laney III
Bankruptcy Judge

Date of Birth: 1942
Education: Mercer 1964 AB, 1966 JD
Began Service: October 1, 1986
Term Expires: October 1, 2028

Current Memberships: American Bankruptcy Institute; American Bar Association; Columbus Bar Association; Federal Bar Association; National Conference of Bankruptcy Judges; State Bar of Georgia

Staff
Law Clerk **Nicholas Garcia** . . . . (706) 596-7154
Began Service: August 2015
Term Expires: August 2017
E-mail: nicholas_garcia@gamb.uscourts.gov
Secretary **Cathy Dunlap** . . . . (706) 596-7151
E-mail: cathyd_dunlap@gamb.uscourts.gov

Chambers of Bankruptcy Judge Austin E. Carter

433 Cherry Street, Macon, GA 31201
P.O. Box 96, Macon, GA 31202
Tel: (478) 749-6880
E-mail: austin_carter@gamb.uscourts.gov

Austin E. Carter
Bankruptcy Judge

Began Service: May 20, 2014

Staff
Law Clerk **Jacob A. Johnson** . . . . (478) 749-6880
E-mail: jacob_johnson@gamb.uscourts.gov
Courtroom Deputy **Valerie Vaughn** . . . . (478) 749-6885
Judicial Assistant **Shirley Penix** . . . . (478) 749-6881
E-mail: shirley_penix@gamb.uscourts.gov

United States District Court for the Northern District of Georgia

U.S. Courthouse, 75 Spring Street, SW, Room 2211,
Atlanta, GA 30303-3309
Tel: (404) 215-1600
Tel: (404) 215-1655 (Civil and Criminal Case Information)
Tel: (404) 215-1300 (District Executive)
Tel: (404) 215-1635 (Filing and Fee Information)
Tel: (404) 215-1640 (Jury Information)
Internet: www.gand.uscourts.gov

Number of Judgeships: 11

Number of Vacancies: 1

Circuit: Eleventh

Areas Covered: Counties of Banks, Barrow, Bartow, Carroll, Catoosa, Chattooga, Cherokee, Clayton, Cobb, Coweta, Dade, Dawson, DeKalb, Douglas, Fannin, Fayette, Floyd, Forsyth, Fulton, Gilmer, Gordon, Gwinnett, Habersham, Hall, Haralson, Heard, Henry, Jackson, Lumpkin, Meriwether, Murray, Newton, Paulding, Pickens, Pike, Polk, Rabun, Rockdale, Spalding, Stephens, Towns, Troup, Union, Walker, White and Whitfield

Court Staff
District Court Executive and Clerk of Court
James N. Hatten . . . . (404) 215-1610
E-mail: james_hatten@gand.uscourts.gov
Education: Alabama 1976 JD
Resident Deputy-in-Charge - Gainesville **Stacey Kemp** . . . (678) 450-2760
201 Federal Building, 121 Spring Street, SE,
Gainesville, GA 30501-3789
Resident Deputy-in-Charge - Newnan **Robin Harlan** . . . . . (678) 423-3060
18 Greenville Street, Room 352,
Newnan, GA 30263
P.O. Box 939, Newnan, GA 30263
E-mail: robin_harlan@gand.uscourts.gov
Resident Deputy-in-Charge - Rome **Sam Johnston** . . . . . . (706) 378-4060
600 E. First St., Rome, GA 30161
E-mail: sam_johnston@gand.uscourts.gov
Chief Probation Officer **Thomas Bishop** . . . . (404) 215-1950
Russell Federal Building, Suite 900
Human Resources Manager **Linda G. Cooke** . . . . (404) 215-1750
E-mail: linda_cooke@gand.uscourts.gov
Information Systems Manager **Vickie Mullings** . . . . (404) 215-1650
E-mail: vickie_mullings@gand.uscourts.gov
Financial Administrator **Kathy Farmer** . . . . (404) 215-1625
E-mail: kathy_farmer@gand.uscourts.gov
Librarian **Nancy Adams** . . . . (404) 215-1320

Chambers of Chief Judge Thomas W. Thrash, Jr.

U.S. Courthouse, 75 Spring Street, SW, Room 2188,
Atlanta, GA 30303-3309
Tel: (404) 215-1550 Fax: (404) 215-1559
E-mail: Thomas_W_Thrash@gand.uscourts.gov

Thomas W. Thrash, Jr.
Chief Judge

Date of Birth: 1951
Education: Virginia 1973 BA; Harvard 1976 JD
Began Service: August 15, 1997
Appointed By: President William J. Clinton

Current Memberships: Atlanta Bar Association; Cobb County Bar Association; Cobb Justice Foundation; State Bar of Georgia

Staff
Law Clerk **Evelyn French** .... (404) 215-1552
Began Service: August 2015
Term Expires: August 2017
E-mail: evelyn_french@gand.uscourts.gov
Law Clerk **Maggy Randels** .... (404) 215-1510
Began Service: August 2014
Term Expires: August 2016
E-mail: maggy_randels@gand.uscourts.gov
Courtroom Deputy Clerk **Sheila Sewell** .... (404) 215-1555
E-mail: Sheila_Sewell@gand.uscourts.gov
Court Reporter **Susan Baker** .... (404) 215-1558
E-mail: susan_baker@gand.uscourts.gov
Judicial Assistant **Lydia B. Howard** .... (404) 215-1550
E-mail: lydia_howard@gand.uscourts.gov

Chambers of District Judge Harold L. Murphy

600 East First Street, Room 311, Rome, GA 30161
Tel: (706) 378-4080 Fax: (706) 291-3905

Harold L. Murphy
District Judge

Date of Birth: 1927
Education: Georgia 1949 LLB
Began Service: August 9, 1977
Appointed By: President Jimmy Carter

Government: State Representative Harold L. Murphy (GA), Georgia General Assembly (1951-1961); Assistant Solicitor General, Tallapoosa Judicial Circuit, State of Georgia (1956)

Judicial: Superior Court Judge, Georgia Superior Court, Tallapoosa Judicial Circuit (1971-1977)

Legal Practice: Private Practice (1949-1958); Partner, Howe & Murphy (1958-1971)

Military Service: United States Navy (1945-1946)

Current Memberships: American Bar Association; The Joseph Henry Lumpkin American Inn of Court, The American Inns of Court; District Judges Association of the Eleventh Circuit; Federal Judges Association; State Bar of Georgia

Staff
Law Clerk **Brian Abrams** .... (706) 378-4080
Began Service: September 2014
Term Expires: September 1, 2016
E-mail: brian_abrams@gand.uscourts.gov
Career Law Clerk **Mary S. Kirby** .... (706) 378-4080
E-mail: mary_kirby@gand.uscourts.gov
Education: Georgia 1997 JD

Chambers of District Judge Richard W. Story

U.S. Courthouse, 75 Spring Street, SW, Room 2121,
Atlanta, GA 30303-3361
Tel: (404) 215-1350 Fax: (404) 215-1356

Richard W. Story
District Judge

Date of Birth: 1953
Education: LaGrange 1975 BA; Georgia 1978 JD
Began Service: 1998
Appointed By: President William J. Clinton

Academic: Instructor, North Georgia College & State University (1995)

Government: Special Assistant Attorney General, Office of the Attorney General, State of Georgia (1980-1985)

Judicial: Judge, Hall County Juvenile Court (1985-1986); Judge, Georgia Superior Court, Hall County (1986-1998)

Legal Practice: Partner, Kenyon, Hulsey & Oliver (1978-1986)

Current Memberships: Gainsville Northeastern Bar Association

Staff
Law Clerk **Ellen Clarke** .... (404) 215-1660
Began Service: August 2014
Term Expires: August 2016
E-mail: ellen_clarke@gand.uscourts.gov
Law Clerk **Philip Biegler** .... (404) 215-1350
Began Service: August 2015
Term Expires: August 2017
E-mail: philip_biegler@gand.uscourts.gov
Judicial Assistant **Joyce Elliott** .... (404) 215-1350
E-mail: joyce_elliott@gand.uscourts.gov
Education: Georgia 1975 BS

Chambers of District Judge William S. Duffey, Jr.

U.S. Courthouse, 75 Spring Street, SW, Suite 1721,
Atlanta, GA 30303-3309
Tel: (404) 215-1480 Fax: (404) 215-1485
E-mail: william_s_duffey@gand.uscourts.gov

William S. Duffey, Jr.
District Judge

Education: Drake 1973 BA; South Carolina 1977 JD
Began Service: July 1, 2004
Appointed By: President George W. Bush

Government: U.S. Attorney, Georgia - Northern District, United States Attorney's Office, United States Department of Justice, George W. Bush Administration (2001)

Staff
Law Clerk **Omar Jafri** .... (404) 215-1482
Law Clerk **Josh Zugerman** .... (404) 215-1483
Judicial Assistant **Lauren Weaver** .... (404) 215-1480
E-mail: lauren_weaver@gand.uscourts.gov

Chambers of District Judge Timothy C. Batten Sr.

U.S. Courthouse, 75 Spring Street, SW, Room 1756,
Atlanta, GA 30303-3361
Tel: (404) 215-1420
E-mail: timothy_c_batten@gand.uscourts.gov

Timothy C. Batten, Sr.
District Judge

Education: Georgia Tech 1981 BS; Georgia 1984 JD
Began Service: April 2006
Appointed By: President George W. Bush

Legal Practice: Associate, Schreeder, Wheeler & Flint, LLP (1984-1993); Partner, Schreeder, Wheeler & Flint, LLP (1993)

Staff
Law Clerk **(Vacant)** .... (404) 215-1420
Law Clerk **Alice Snedeker** .... (404) 215-1420
E-mail: alice_snedeker@gand.uscourts.gov
Education: Georgia 2010 JD
Courtroom Deputy **Julee G. Smilley** .... (404) 215-1420
E-mail: julee_smilley@gand.uscourts.gov
Education: Westminster (UT) 1991 BS

Chambers of District Judge Steven C. Jones

U.S. Courthouse, 75 Spring Street, SW, Room 1967,
Atlanta, GA 30303-3309
Tel: (404) 215-1228

Steven CarMichael Jones
District Judge

Date of Birth: 1957
Education: Georgia 1978 BBA, 1987 JD
Began Service: March 4, 2011
Appointed By: President Barack Obama

Government: Director, Child Support Recovery Unit, District Attorney, Unified Government of Athens-Clarke County, Georgia (1978-1985); Intern, District Attorney, Unified Government of Athens-Clarke County, Georgia (1986-1987); Assistant District Attorney, District Attorney, Unified Government of Athens-Clarke County, Georgia (1987-1993)

Judicial: Municipal Court Judge, Athens-Clarke County Municipal Court (1993-1995); Judge, Chambers of Judge Steve C. Jones, Georgia (1995-2011)

Staff
Law Clerk **Ashley Barnett Heard** .... (404) 215-1228
E-mail: ashley_heard@gand.uscourts.gov
Law Clerk **Chittam Thakore** .... (404) 215-1228
Law Clerk **Brendan White** .... (404) 215-1228
E-mail: brendan_white@gand.uscourts.gov
Courtroom Deputy Clerk **Pamela Wright** .... (404) 215-1228
E-mail: pamela_wright@gand.uscourts.gov

Chambers of District Judge Amy Totenberg

U.S. Courthouse, 75 Spring Street, SW, Room 2388,
Atlanta, GA 30303-3309
Tel: (404) 215-1438
E-mail: amy_totenberg@gand.uscourts.gov

Amy Mil Totenberg
District Judge

Date of Birth: 1950
Education: Radcliffe 1974 AB; Harvard 1977 JD
Began Service: March 4, 2011
Appointed By: President Barack Obama

Academic: Adjunct Professor, School of Law, Emory University (2004-2007)

Chambers of District Judge Amy Totenberg *continued*

Government: General Counsel, Board of Education, Atlanta Public Schools, City of Atlanta, Georgia (1994-1998); Special Master, United States District Court for the District of Maryland (2000-2011); Court Appointed Mediator, United States District Court for the District of Columbia (2005-2006); Court Monitor, United States District Court for the District of Columbia, United States District Courts (2006-2011)

Legal Practice: Attorney, Law Office of Amy Totenberg (1982-1994); Attorney, Law Office of Amy Totenberg (1998-2011)

Staff
Law Clerk **Noah Grynberg** .... (404) 215-1436
Law Clerk **Michael Baumrind** .... (404) 215-1419
E-mail: michael_baumrind@gand.uscourts.gov
Law Clerk/Judicial Assistant **Holly Cole** .... (404) 215-1404
E-mail: holly_cole@gand.uscourts.gov
Court Reporter **Elise Evans** .... (404) 215-1456
E-mail: elise_evans@gand.uscourts.gov
Courtroom Deputy **Amy McConochie** .... (404) 215-1437
E-mail: amy_mcconochie@gand.uscourts.gov

Chambers of District Judge Leigh Martin May

75 Spring Street, SW, Room 2167, Atlanta, GA 30303-3309
Tel: (404) 215-1510

Leigh Martin May
District Judge

Education: Georgia Tech 1993 BA; Georgia 1998 JD
Began Service: 2014
Appointed By: President Barack Obama

Chambers of District Judge Eleanor Louise Ross

75 Spring Street, SW, Room 1788, Atlanta, GA 30303-3309
Tel: (404) 215-1520

Eleanor Louise Ross
District Judge

Began Service: 2014
Appointed By: President Barack Obama

Chambers of District Judge Mark Howard Cohen

75 Spring Street, SW, Room 1909, Atlanta, GA 30303-3309
Tel: (404) 215-1310

Mark Howard Cohen
District Judge

Education: Emory 1976 BA, 1979 JD
Began Service: 2014
Appointed By: President Barack Obama

Government: Assistant Attorney General, Office of the Attorney General, State of Georgia (1981-1994); Chief State Administrative Law Judge, Office of State Administrative Hearings, State of Georgia (1994-1995); Executive Counsel, Office of Governor Zell Miller, State of Georgia (1995-1998); Executive Secretary, Office of Governor Zell Miller, State of Georgia (1998-1999)

Chambers of Senior Judge Orinda D. Evans

U.S. Courthouse, 75 Spring Street, SW, Room 1988, Atlanta, GA 30303
Tel: (404) 215-1490

Orinda D. Evans
Senior Judge

Date of Birth: 1943
Education: Duke 1965 AB; Emory 1968 JD; Virginia 1998 LLM
Began Service: August 1979
Appointed By: President Jimmy Carter
Political Affiliation: Democrat

Current Memberships: American Bar Association; Atlanta Bar Association; State Bar of Georgia

Staff
Judicial Assistant **Anne Marie Carver** . . . . (404) 215-1490
E-mail: anne_marie_carver@gand.uscourts.gov

Chambers of Senior Judge William C. O'Kelley

U.S. Courthouse, 75 Spring Street, SW, Room 1942,
Atlanta, GA 30303-3309
Tel: (404) 215-1530 Fax: (404) 215-1538

William C. O'Kelley
Senior Judge

Date of Birth: 1930
Education: Emory 1951 AB, 1953 LLB
Began Service: October 23, 1970
Appointed By: President Richard M. Nixon
Political Affiliation: Republican

Affiliation: Senior Judge (R), Chambers of Senior Judge William C. O'Kelley, Alien Terrorist Removal Court

Government: Assistant United States Attorney, Northern District of Georgia, United States Department of Justice (1959-1961); Special Hearing Officer, United States Department of Justice (1962-1968)

Judicial: Judge, United States Foreign Intelligence Surveillance Court (1980-1987)

Legal Practice: Partner, O'Kelley, Hopkins & Van Gerpen (1961-1970); General Counsel, Georgia Republican Party (1968-1970)

Military Service: United States Air Force (1953-1957); United States Air Force Reserve (1957-1966)

Current Memberships: American Bar Association; Atlanta Bar Association; Federal Bar Association; Gainsville Northeastern Bar Association; Lawyers Club of Atlanta, Inc.; Old War Horse Lawyers' Club; State Bar of Georgia

Staff
Law Clerk **Elliott A. Foote** . . . . (404) 215-1533
Began Service: September 3, 2015
Term Expires: August 2017
Career Law Clerk **Seunhee Pike** . . . . (404) 215-1532
E-mail: seunhee_pike@gand.uscourts.gov
Education: Oberlin 1983 BA; Georgia 1988 JD
Secretary **Geri Graham** . . . . (404) 215-1531
E-mail: geri_graham@gand.uscourts.gov

Chambers of Senior Judge Marvin H. Shoob

U.S. Courthouse, 75 Spring Street, SW, Room 1767,
Atlanta, GA 30303-3361
Tel: (404) 215-1470 Fax: (404) 215-1477

Marvin H. Shoob
Senior Judge

Date of Birth: 1923
Education: Georgia 1948 JD
Began Service: 1979
Appointed By: President Jimmy Carter
Political Affiliation: Democrat

Legal Practice: Associate, Andrews & Nall (1948-1949); Partner, Brown & Shoob (1949-1955); Partner, Phillips, Johnson & Shoob (1955-1956); Senior Partner, Shoob, McLain & Merritt (1956-1979)

Military Service: United States Army (1943-1945)

Current Memberships: American Bar Association; The American Law Institute; Atlanta Bar Association; Lawyers Club of Atlanta, Inc.; State Bar of Georgia

Staff
Career Law Clerk **(Vacant)** . . . . (404) 215-1472
Career Law Clerk **Michael Robinson** . . . . (404) 215-1473
E-mail: michael_robinson@gand.uscourts.gov
Education: South Carolina 1974 BA;
Emory 1977 MA; Georgia 1982 JD
Judicial Assistant **Janet Reed** . . . . (404) 215-1471

Chambers of Senior Judge Willis B. Hunt, Jr.

U.S. Courthouse, 75 Spring Street, SW, Room 1756,
Atlanta, GA 30303-3309
Tel: (404) 215-1450 Fax: (404) 215-1455
E-mail: willis_b_hunt@gand.uscourts.gov

Willis B. Hunt, Jr.
Senior Judge

Date of Birth: 1932
Education: Emory 1954 LLB; Virginia 1990 LLM
Began Service: July 1, 1995
Appointed By: President William J. Clinton

Government: Associate, Federal Bureau of Investigation, United States Department of Justice (1957-1959)

Judicial: Judge, Georgia Superior Court, Houston County (1971-1986); Justice, Supreme Court of Georgia (1986-1994); Chief Justice, Supreme Court of Georgia (1994-1995)

Legal Practice: Shoob & McLain (1960-1966); Nunn, Geiger & Hunt (1967-1971)

Military Service: United States Army (1955-1957)

Current Memberships: American Bar Association; The Joseph Henry Lumpkin American Inn of Court, The American Inns of Court; The Lamar American Inn of Court, The American Inns of Court; The American Law Institute; State Bar of Georgia

Staff
Career Law Clerk **Erich Kimbrough** . . . . (404) 215-1450
E-mail: erich_kimbrough@gand.uscourts.gov
Administrative Judicial Assistant/Courtroom Deputy
Clerk **Sue Coalson** . . . . (404) 215-1451
E-mail: sue_coalson@gand.uscourts.gov

Chambers of Senior Judge Clarence Cooper

U.S. Courthouse, 75 Spring Street, SW, Room 1701,
Atlanta, GA 30303-3309
Tel: (404) 215-1390 Fax: (404) 215-1397
E-mail: clarence_cooper@gand.uscourts.gov

Clarence Cooper
Senior Judge

Date of Birth: 1942
Education: Clark Col 1964 BA; Emory 1967 JD; Harvard 1978 MA
Began Service: May 9, 1994
Appointed By: President William J. Clinton

Government: Assistant District Attorney, Office of the District Attorney, State of Georgia (1968-1975)

Judicial: Judge, Atlanta Municipal Court (1975-1980); Judge, Georgia Superior Court, Fulton County (1980-1990); Judge, Georgia Court of Appeals (1990-1993); District Judge, Chambers of District Judge Clarence Cooper, United States District Court for the Northern District of Georgia (1994-2009)

Legal Practice: Atlanta Legal Aid Society (1967-1968)

Military Service: United States Army (1968-1970)

Current Memberships: American Bar Association; Atlanta Bar Association; Federal Bar Association; Gate City Bar Association; Lawyers Club of Atlanta, Inc.; National Bar Association; Old War Horse Lawyers' Club; State Bar of Georgia

Staff
Law Clerk **Jessica Nwokocha** . . . . (404) 215-1390
Began Service: September 2015
Term Expires: September 2017
E-mail: jessica_nwokocha@gand.uscourts.gov
Career Law Clerk **Nicole Lawson Jenkins** . . . . (404) 215-1390
E-mail: nicole_lawson@gand.uscourts.gov
Education: Harvard 2002 JD
Court Reporter **Amanda Lohnaas** . . . . (404) 215-1546
E-mail: amanda_lohnaas@gand.uscourts.gov Fax: (404) 215-1397
Administrative Judicial Assistant **Velma Shanks** . . . . (404) 215-1390
E-mail: velma_shanks@gand.uscourts.gov

Chambers of Senior Judge Charles A. Pannell Jr.

U.S. Courthouse, 75 Spring Street, SW, Atlanta, GA 30303-3309
Tel: (404) 215-1580

Charles A. Pannell, Jr.
Senior Judge

Date of Birth: 1946
Education: Georgia 1967 BA, 1970 JD
Began Service: December 1, 1999
Appointed By: President William J. Clinton
Political Affiliation: Democrat

Current Memberships: State Bar of Georgia

Staff
Law Clerk **Austin King** . . . . (404) 215-1580
Began Service: September 2014
Term Expires: September 2016
E-mail: austin_king@gand.uscourts.gov
Law Clerk **Joseph Saul** . . . . (404) 215-1580
Began Service: September 2015
Term Expires: September 2017
E-mail: joseph_saul@gand.uscourts.gov
Career Law Clerk **Marti Minor** . . . . (404) 215-1580
E-mail: marti_minor@gand.uscourts.gov
Education: North Carolina 1991 BA;
Georgia 1995 JD
Courtroom Deputy **Don Stanhope** . . . . (404) 215-1580
Court Reporter **(Vacant)** . . . . (404) 215-1573

Chambers of Magistrate Judge Janet F. King

U.S. Courthouse, 75 Spring Street, SW, Suite 2007,
Atlanta, GA 30303-3361
Tel: (404) 215-1385 Fax: (404) 215-1387
E-mail: janet_f_king@gand.uscourts.gov

Janet F. King
Magistrate Judge

Date of Birth: 1955
Education: Georgia 1980 JD
Began Service: October 20, 1998
Term Expires: October 20, 2022

Current Memberships: Atlanta Bar Association; Federal Magistrate Judges Association; Lawyers Foundation of Georgia

Staff
Career Law Clerk **Kathleen O. Feldbaum** . . . . (404) 215-1385
E-mail: kathleen_feldbaum@gand.uscourts.gov
Career Law Clerk **Jeffrey W. Redding** . . . . (404) 215-1385
Education: Texas Tech 1998 JD

Chambers of Magistrate Judge Gerrilyn G. Brill

2211 U.S. Courthouse, 75 Spring Street, SW, Atlanta, GA 30303-3361
Tel: (404) 215-1365 Fax: (404) 215-1364
E-mail: gerrilyn_brill@gand.uscourts.gov

Gerrilyn G. Brill
Magistrate Judge

Date of Birth: 1951
Education: Emory 1975 JD
Began Service: January 1995

Current Memberships: Atlanta Bar Association; State Bar of Georgia

Staff
Law Clerk **Evan Weiss** . . . . (404) 215-1365
Began Service: May 2015
Term Expires: May 2016
E-mail: frank_budde@gand.uscourts.gov
Law Clerk **Adam Sparks** . . . . (404) 215-1365
E-mail: adam_sparks@gand.uscourts.gov

Chambers of Magistrate Judge Linda T. Walker

U.S. Courthouse, 75 Spring Street, SW, Room 1856, Atlanta, GA 30303
Tel: (404) 215-1370

Linda T. Walker
Magistrate Judge

Education: Southern U A&M 1983 BS; Atlanta 1987 MS; Georgia 1989 JD
Began Service: January 3, 2000
Term Expires: 2016

Current Memberships: Atlanta Bar Association; Federal Magistrate Judges Association; Georgia Association of Black Women Attorneys; Lawyers Foundation of Georgia

Staff
Career Law Clerk **Kathy Duncan** . . . . (404) 215-1370
Began Service: September 2009
E-mail: kathy_duncan@gand.uscourts.gov
Courtroom Deputy/Judicial Assistant **Sonya Coggins** . . . . (404) 215-1370

Chambers of Magistrate Judge Alan J. Baverman

U.S. Courthouse, 75 Spring Street, SW, Room 1885,
Atlanta, GA 30303-3309
Tel: (404) 215-1395 Fax: (404) 215-1339
E-mail: alan_j_baverman@gand.uscourts.gov

Alan J. Baverman
Magistrate Judge

Date of Birth: 1956
Education: Maryland 1978 BA; Emory 1981 JD
Began Service: February 1, 2001
Term Expires: January 31, 2017

Clerkships: Law Clerk The Honorable Harold L. Murphy, United States District Court for the Northern District of Georgia (1981-1983)

Legal Practice: Kadish & Kadish, P.C. (1983-1986); Chilivis & Grindler (1986-1989); Alan J. Baverman, P.C. (1989-2001)

Current Memberships: American Bar Association; Atlanta Bar Association; Federal Magistrate Judges Association; State Bar of Georgia

Staff
Law Clerk **Stephanie Williams** .... (404) 215-1378
E-mail: stephanie_williams@gand.uscourts.gov
Career Law Clerk **Caroline Placey** .... (404) 215-1344
E-mail: caroline_placey@gand.uscourts.gov
Education: Emory 2007 JD
Deputy Clerk **Lisa Enix** .... (404) 215-1398
E-mail: lisa_enix@gand.uscourts.gov
Education: Georgia State 1991 BA

Chambers of Magistrate Judge Walter E. Johnson

600 East First Street, Room 212, Rome, GA 30161-3187
Tel: (706) 378-4090 Fax: (706) 378-4099

Walter E. Johnson
Magistrate Judge

Education: Georgia 1982 AB, 1985 JD
Began Service: March 18, 2002

Corporate: Principal Counsel for Labor and Employment, Georgia-Pacific Corporation

Legal Practice: Partner, Kilpatrick Stockton LLP

Staff
Law Clerk **(Vacant)** .... (706) 378-4090
Began Service: September 2013
Term Expires: September 2015
E-mail: james_mcgehee@gand.uscourts.gov
Career Law Clerk **Vita Salvemini Rutledge** .... (706) 378-4090
Began Service: August 2008
E-mail: vita_rutledge@gand.uscourts.gov
Education: Georgia 2005 JD
Courtroom Deputy **Kari Butler** .... (706) 378-4090
E-mail: kari_butler@gand.uscourts.gov

Chambers of Magistrate Judge J. Clay Fuller

121 Spring Street, SE, Suite 106, Gainesville, GA 30501
Tel: (678) 450-2790

J. Clay Fuller
Magistrate Judge

Chambers of Magistrate Judge Russell G. Vineyard

U.S. Courthouse, 75 Spring Street, SW, Room 2027, Atlanta, GA 30303
Tel: (404) 215-1375 Fax: (404) 215-1377

Russell G. Vineyard
Magistrate Judge

Began Service: October 23, 2006
Term Expires: October 23, 2022

Government: Deputy Chief, Assistant U.S. Attorney, Public Corruption and Government Fraud Section, Georgia - Northern District, United States Department of Justice

Staff
Law Clerk **Amanda Trull** .... (404) 215-1372
Began Service: September 2015
Term Expires: September 2017
E-mail: amanda_trull@gand.uscourts.gov
Career Law Clerk **Sonya Sheth Nuckolls** .... (404) 215-1375
E-mail: sonya_nuckolls@gand.uscourts.gov
Education: Alabama 2001 JD
Courtroom Deputy **Pat Montgomery** .... (404) 215-1358

Chambers of Magistrate Judge Justin S. Anand

U.S. Courthouse, 75 Spring Street, SW, Room 1909,
Atlanta, GA 30303-3309
Tel: (404) 215-1440

Justin S. Anand
Magistrate Judge

Staff
Career Law Clerk **Cheryl Jenkins** .... (404) 215-1440
E-mail: cheryl_jenkins@gand.uscourts.gov
Education: Duke 1989 AB; Virginia 1993 JD
Career Law Clerk **John Ganz** .... (404) 215-1440
E-mail: john_ganz@gand.uscourts.gov
Secretary **Belqyise Graves** .... (404) 215-1440

Chambers of Magistrate Judge Catherine M. Salinas

75 Spring Street, SW, Suite 1807, Atlanta, GA 30303-3309
Tel: (404) 215-1380

Catherine M. Salinas
Magistrate Judge

Began Service: 2015

United States Bankruptcy Court for the Northern District of Georgia

U.S. Courthouse, 75 Spring Street, SW, Room 1340,
Atlanta, GA 30303-3367
Tel: (404) 215-1000 Tel: (404) 730-3264 (PACER)
Tel: (800) 676-6856 (Toll Free PACER)
Tel: (404) 730-2867 (Voice Case Information System VCIS)
Tel: (404) 730-2866 (Voice Case Information System VCIS)
Fax: (404) 730-2216
Internet: www.ganb.uscourts.gov

Number of Judgeships: 9

Court Staff
Clerk of Court **M. Regina Thomas** .... (404) 215-1000
E-mail: regina_thomas@ganb.uscourts.gov Fax: (404) 215-1223
Chief Deputy Clerk **Charles F. "Fred" Childers** .... (404) 215-1000
E-mail: fred_childers@ganb.uscourts.gov
Chief Deputy Clerk - Information Technology
Michael G. Smith .... (404) 215-1000
E-mail: michael_g_smith@ganb.uscourts.gov Fax: (404) 730-2216
Education: Georgia State BBA
Chief Deputy Clerk - Operations **(Vacant)** .... (404) 215-1000

(continued on next page)

United States Bankruptcy Court for the Northern District of Georgia *continued*

Deputy-in-Charge - Gainesville **Linda Westbrook** . . . . (678) 450-2700
121 Spring Street, South East, Room 120, Gainesville, GA 30501 Fax: (770) 535-2224
E-mail: linda_westbrook@ganb.uscourts.gov
Deputy-in-Charge - Newnan **Donna Collins** . . . . (678) 423-3000
220 Federal Bldg., 18 Greenville St., Newnan, GA 30263 Fax: (770) 251-8538
P.O. Box 2328, Newnan, GA 30264
E-mail: donna_collins@ganb.uscourts.gov
Deputy-in-Charge - Rome **Cherie B. Parris** . . . . (706) 378-4000
600 E. First St., Rome, GA 30161 Fax: (706) 291-5647
E-mail: cherie_parris@ganb.uscourts.gov
Education: Berry 1980 BS, 1984 MBA
Manager of Human Resources **Jason LeFevers** . . . . (404) 215-1143
Manager of Financial Administration **Lynn Saunders** . . . . (404) 215-1132
E-mail: lynn_saunders@ganb.uscourts.gov
Information Technology Manager **John Halloran** . . . . (404) 215-1134

Chambers of Chief Bankruptcy Judge C. Ray Mullins

U.S. Courthouse, 75 Spring Street, SW, Room 1270, Atlanta, GA 30303
Tel: (404) 215-1002 Fax: (404) 215-1117
E-mail: ray_mullins@ganb.uscourts.gov

C. Ray Mullins
Chief Bankruptcy Judge

Date of Birth: 1952
Education: Bowling Green State 1974 BS, 1977 MBA; Toledo 1982 JD
Began Service: February 29, 2000
Term Expires: February 28, 2028

Current Memberships: American Bankruptcy Institute; Commercial Law League of America; National Conference of Bankruptcy Judges; Southeastern Bankruptcy Law Institute

Staff
Career Law Clerk **Alexandra Ragan** . . . . (404) 215-1005
Began Service: August 15, 2011
Courtroom Deputy Clerk **Monique Chapple** . . . . (404) 215-1004
E-mail: monique_chapple@ganb.uscourts.gov
Judicial Assistant **Linnie Patterson** . . . . (404) 215-1002
E-mail: linnie_patterson@ganb.uscourts.gov

Chambers of Bankruptcy Judge W. Homer Drake, Jr.

U.S. Courthouse, 18 Greenville Street, Newnan, GA 30263
P.O. Box 1408, Newnan, GA 30264-1408
Tel: (678) 423-3080 Fax: (678) 423-3099
E-mail: Homer_Drake@ganb.uscourts.gov

Walter Homer Drake, Jr.
Bankruptcy Judge

Date of Birth: 1932
Education: Mercer 1954 AB, 1956 LLB
Began Service: September 1, 1964
Term Expires: February 1, 2016

Academic: Adjunct Professor, School of Law, The University of Georgia (1971-1972); Adjunct Professor, School of Law, Emory University (1973-1975); Walter Homer Drake Professorship of Bankruptcy Law, Mercer University (1996)

Clerkships: Law Clerk The Honorable Lewis R. Morgan, United States District Court for the Northern District of Georgia (1961-1964)

Judicial: President, National Conference of Bankruptcy Judges (1972-1973); Member, Committee on the Administration of the Bankruptcy System, Judicial Conference of the United States (1989-1995); Founder and Advisor, Southeastern Bankruptcy Law Institute

Legal Practice: Partner, Swift, Currie, McGhee & Hiers, LLP (1976-1979)

Military Service: Judge Advocate General, United States Army (1956-1959)

Chambers of Bankruptcy Judge W. Homer Drake, Jr. *continued*

Current Memberships: American College of Bankruptcy; National Conference of Bankruptcy Judges; Southeastern Bankruptcy Law Institute

Staff
Career Law Clerk **Michael Hill** . . . . (678) 423-3084
Secretary **Karen Balkcom** . . . . (678) 423-3080
E-mail: karen_balkcom@ganb.uscourts.gov

Chambers of Bankruptcy Judge Barbara Ellis - Monro

U.S. Courthouse, 75 Spring Street, SW, Room 1431, Atlanta, GA 30303-3309
Tel: (404) 215-1030

Barbara Ellis-Monro
Bankruptcy Judge

Began Service: 2012

Staff
Career Law Clerk **Roberto Bazzani** . . . . (404) 215-1030
Career Law Clerk **Amber Nikell** . . . . (404) 215-1030
Courtroom Deputy **Janette Washington** . . . . (404) 215-1030

Chambers of Bankruptcy Judge Paul W. Bonapfel

U.S. Courthouse, 75 Spring Street, SW, Room 1492, Atlanta, GA 30303
Tel: (404) 215-1018 Fax: (404) 215-1114
E-mail: paul_bonapfel@ganb.uscourts.gov

Paul W. Bonapfel
Bankruptcy Judge

Education: Florida State 1972 BA; Georgia 1975 JD
Began Service: April 10, 2002

Staff
Career Law Clerk **Beth Anne Harrill** . . . . (404) 215-1020
E-mail: beth_harrill@ganb.uscourts.gov
Education: Emory 1995 JD
Courtroom Deputy Clerk **Connie Mason** . . . . (404) 215-1021
Judicial Assistant **Victoria Rodriguez** . . . . (404) 215-1018
E-mail: victoria_rodriguez@ganb.uscourts.gov

Chambers of Bankruptcy Judge Mary Grace Diehl

75 Spring Street, SW, Room 1215, Atlanta, GA 30303
Tel: (404) 215-1202
E-mail: mgdchambers@ganb.uscourts.gov

Mary Grace Diehl
Bankruptcy Judge

Date of Birth: September 3, 1952
Education: Canisius 1974 BA; Harvard 1977 JD
Began Service: February 23, 2004
Term Expires: February 23, 2018

Legal Practice: Practice Group Leader, Bankruptcy, Troutman Sanders LLP

Current Memberships: American Bankruptcy Institute; Atlanta Bar Association; Georgia Association for Women Lawyers; National Conference of Bankruptcy Judges

Staff
Law Clerk **Jamie Stone** . . . . (404) 215-1028
Career Law Clerk **Elizabeth Rose** . . . . (404) 215-1259

Chambers of Bankruptcy Judge Wendy L. Hagenau
75 Spring Street, SW, Atlanta, GA 30303-3309
Tel: (404) 215-1190

Wendy L. Hagenau
Bankruptcy Judge

Began Service: 2010

Chambers of Bankruptcy Judge James R. Sacca
75 Spring Street, SW, Room 1481, Atlanta, GA 30303-3309
Tel: (404) 215-1790
E-mail: jrschambers@ganb.uscourts.gov

James R. Sacca
Bankruptcy Judge

Began Service: October 21, 2010

Staff
Law Clerk **David Fass** .... (404) 215-1792
E-mail: david_fass@ganb.uscourts.gov
Law Clerk **Benjamin Keck** .... (404) 215-1793
E-mail: benjamin_keck@ganb.uscourts.gov
Courtroom Deputy Clerk **Cynthia Eadon** .... (404) 215-1179

Chambers of Bankruptcy Judge Paul M. Baisier
75 Spring Street, SW, Atlanta, GA 30303-3309
Tel: (404) 215-1010

Paul M. Baisier
Bankruptcy Judge

Education: Illinois 1987 BS; Harvard 1990 JD

United States District Court for the Southern District of Georgia
P.O. Box 8286, Savannah, GA 31412
125 Bull Street, Room 306, Savannah, GA 31401
Tel: (912) 650-4020 Tel: (912) 650-4042 (PACER)
Fax: (912) 650-4029
Internet: www.gasd.uscourts.gov

Number of Judgeships: 3

Circuit: Eleventh

Areas Covered: Counties of Appling, Atkinson, Bacon, Brantley, Bryan, Bulloch, Burke, Camden, Candler, Charlton, Chatham, Coffee, Columbia, Dodge, Effingham, Emanuel, Evans, Glascock, Glynn, Jeff Davis, Jefferson, Jenkins, Johnson, Laurens, Liberty, Lincoln, Long, McDuffie, McIntosh, Montgomery, Pierce, Richmond, Screven, Taliaferro, Tattnall, Telfair, Toombs, Treutlen, Ware, Warren, Wayne, Wheeler and Wilkes

Court Staff
Clerk of Court **Scott L. Poff** .... (912) 650-4031
E-mail: scott_poff@gas.uscourts.gov
Education: North Carolina 1987 BA
Chief Deputy Clerk **Robert D. Fritts** .... (912) 650-4020
E-mail: robert_fritts@gas.uscourts.gov Fax: (912) 650-4030
Education: Armstrong 1984 BBA
Resident Deputy-in-Charge - Augusta **Joe Howell** .... (706) 849-4400
Federal Justice Center, 600 James Brown Boulevard, Fax: (706) 849-4401
Augusta, GA 30901
E-mail: joe_howell@gas.uscourts.gov
Resident Deputy-in-Charge - Brunswick **Sherry Taylor** ... (912) 280-1330
Federal Bldg., 801 Gloucester St., Fax: (912) 280-1331
Brunswick, GA 31520
E-mail: sherry_taylor@gas.uscourts.gov
Chief Probation Officer **Richard A. Long** .... (912) 650-4150
P.O. Box 8165, Savannah, GA 31412 Fax: (912) 650-4148
Room 237
E-mail: richard_long@gas.uscourts.gov

United States District Court for the Southern District of Georgia *continued*

Court Reporter **Kelly Dorsey** .... (912) 650-4065
E-mail: cart757@bellsouth.net
Court Reporter **Victoria Root** .... (912) 650-4066

Chambers of Chief Judge Lisa Godbey Wood
801 Gloucester Street, Suite 220, Brunswick, GA 31520
Tel: (912) 262-2600
E-mail: lisa_wood@gas.uscourts.gov

Lisa Godbey Wood
Chief Judge

Date of Birth: 1963
Education: Georgia 1985 BA, 1990 JD
Began Service: February 2007
Appointed By: President George W. Bush

Clerkships: Law Clerk, District Judge Anthony A. Alaimo, United States District Court for the Southern District of Georgia (1990)

Government: U.S. Attorney, Georgia - Southern District, Executive Office for United States Attorneys, United States Department of Justice (2004-2007)

Judicial: Magistrate Judge (part-time), Glynn County Magistrate Court (1998-2000)

Legal Practice: Associate, Gilbert, Harrell, Sumerford & Martin, P.C. (1991-1994); Partner, Gilbert, Harrell, Sumerford & Martin, P.C. (1995-2004)

Staff
Law Clerk **Michelle Dowst** .... (912) 262-2600
Law Clerk **Wes Jackson** .... (912) 262-2600
Judicial Assistant **Kim Mixon** .... (912) 262-2600
E-mail: kim_mixon@gas.uscourts.gov

Chambers of District Judge William T. Moore, Jr.
U.S. Courthouse, 125 Bull Street, Savannah, GA 31401
P.O. Box 10245, Savannah, GA 31412-0445
Tel: (912) 650-4173 Fax: (912) 650-4177

William T. Moore, Jr.
District Judge

Date of Birth: May 7, 1940
Education: Georgia Military 1960 AA; Georgia 1964 JD; Virginia 2001 LLM
Began Service: October 31, 1994
Appointed By: President William J. Clinton
Political Affiliation: Democrat

Government: United States Attorney, Southern District of Georgia, United States Department of Justice (1977-1981); Member, Attorney General's Advisory Committee, Office of the Attorney General, United States Department of Justice (1978-1981)

Judicial: Pro Tem Judge, Recorders Court (1984-1994)

Legal Practice: Pierce, Ranitz and Lee (1964-1965); Richardson, Doremus and Karsman (1965-1968); Partner, Corish, Smith, Remler & Moore (1968-1977); Partner, Sparkman, Harris & Moore (1981-1988); Partner, Oliver Maner & Gray (1988-1994)

Current Memberships: American Board of Criminal Lawyers; Eleventh Circuit District Judges Association; Federal Judges Association; Savannah Bar Association; State Bar of Georgia

(continued on next page)

Chambers of District Judge William T. Moore, Jr. *continued*

Staff

Law Clerk **John P. Harper III** . . . . (912) 650-4181
Began Service: 2008
Term Expires: August 2016
E-mail: john_harper@gas.uscourts.gov
Education: Furman 1998 BA, 1998 BS; South Carolina 2008 JD

Law Clerk **Brian Lake** . . . . (912) 650-4182
E-mail: brian_lake@gas.uscourts.gov

Court Reporter **Victoria Root** . . . . (912) 650-4066
E-mail: victoria_root@gas.uscourts.gov

Judicial Assistant **Becky D. Overstreet** . . . . (912) 650-4173
E-mail: becky_overstreet@gas.uscourts.gov

Chambers of District Judge James Randal Hall

600 James Brown Boulevard, Augusta, GA 30901
Tel: (706) 823-6460

James Randal Hall
District Judge

Education: Augusta 1979 BA; Georgia 1982 JD
Began Service: May 1, 2008
Appointed By: President George W. Bush

Corporate: Vice President and Legal Counsel, Bankers First Corporation (1985-1996)

Legal Practice: Associate, Sanders, Mottola, Haugen & Goodson (1982-1984); Partner, Avrett & Hall, P.C. (1984-1985); Partner, Hall & Millins, P.C. (1996-1999); Partner, Hunter, Maclean, Exley & Dunn, P.C. (1999-2003); Partner, Warlick, Tritt, Stebbins and Hall, LLP (2004-2008)

Staff

Law Clerk **Austin Atkinson** . . . . (706) 823-6460
Began Service: August 31, 2015
Term Expires: September 2017

Law Clerk **Cameron Roberts** . . . . (706) 823-6460
Began Service: August 31, 2015
Term Expires: September 2016

Judicial Assistant **Gail Shafer** . . . . (706) 823-6460
E-mail: gail_shafer@gas.uscourts.gov

Chambers of Senior Judge Dudley H. Bowen, Jr.

Federal Justice Center, 600 James Brown Boulevard, Augusta, GA 30901
P.O. Box 2106, Augusta, GA 30903
Tel: (706) 849-4440
E-mail: dudley_bowen@gas.uscourts.gov

Dudley H. Bowen, Jr.
Senior Judge

Date of Birth: 1941
Education: Georgia 1964 BA, 1965 LLB
Began Service: December 5, 1979
Appointed By: President Jimmy Carter

Current Memberships: American Bar Association; Augusta Bar Association; Federal Judges Association; State Bar of Georgia

Staff

Courtroom Deputy **Jeanne Hyder** . . . . (706) 849-4403
E-mail: jeanne_hyder@gas.uscourts.gov

Chambers of Magistrate Judge George R. "G.R." Smith

U.S. Courthouse, 125 Bull Street, Savannah, GA 31401
P.O. Box 9563, Savannah, GA 31412
Tel: (912) 650-4180 Fax: (912) 650-4184

G. R. Smith
Magistrate Judge

Began Service: 1988
Term Expires: August 2020

Staff

Career Law Clerk **James C. Desmond** . . . . (912) 650-4180
Education: Buffalo 1983 JD

Career Law Clerk **Lennon B. Haas** . . . . (912) 650-4180
E-mail: lennon_b_haas@gas.uscourts.gov

Secretary **Princess P. Mason** . . . . (912) 650-4180
E-mail: princess_mason@gas.uscourts.gov
Education: Bluefield State BS

Chambers of Magistrate Judge James E. Graham

226 U.S. Courthouse, 801 Gloucester Street, Brunswick, GA 31520
P.O. Box 250, Brunswick, GA 31521
Tel: (912) 280-1360 Fax: (912) 280-1361
E-mail: James_Graham@gas.uscourts.gov

James E. Graham
Magistrate Judge

Note: Judge Graham has retired but will remain active until his term in expires in February 2016.
Date of Birth: 1949
Education: Mercer 1977 JD
Began Service: 1987
Term Expires: February 2016

Staff

Career Law Clerk **Erin David Dwyer** . . . . (912) 280-1360
E-mail: Erin_Dwyer@gas.uscourts.gov
Education: Mercer 1998 BA, 2002 JD

Chambers of Magistrate Judge Brian K. Epps

P.O. Box 1130, Augusta, GA 30901
Tel: (706) 849-4404

Brian K. Epps
Magistrate Judge

Staff

Courtroom Deputy **Rebecca Cirillo** . . . . (706) 849-4404

Chambers of Magistrate Judge R. Stan Baker

125 Bull Street, Savannah, GA 31401
Tel: (912) 280-1334

R. Stan Baker
Magistrate Judge

Education: Georgia 2004 JD

United States Bankruptcy Court for the Southern District of Georgia

U.S. Courthouse, 125 Bull Street, Savannah, GA 31401
P.O. Box 8347, Savannah, GA 31412
Tel: (912) 650-4100
Internet: www.gasb.uscourts.gov

Number of Judgeships: 3

Court Staff
Bankruptcy Clerk **Lucinda B. Rauback** . . . . (912) 650-4105
E-mail: lucinda_rauback@gas.uscourts.gov
Chief Deputy Clerk **Douglas Young** . . . . (912) 650-4105
Deputy In Charge - Augusta **Courtney Neidel** . . . . (706) 823-6018
Federal Justice Center, 600 James Brown Boulevard, Augusta, GA 30903
P.O. Box 1487, Augusta, GA 30903
Deputy In Charge - Brunswick **Sharon Rankin** . . . . (912) 280-1376
801 Gloucester Street, Third Floor, Brunswick, GA 31520
Deputy In Charge - Savannah **Cherish Amerson** . . . . (912) 650-4137

Chambers of Chief Bankruptcy Judge Susan D. Barrett

600 James Brown Boulevard, Augusta, GA 30903
P.O. Box 31267, Augusta, GA 30903
Tel: (706) 849-4478

Susan D. Barrett
Chief Bankruptcy Judge

Began Service: March 2006
Term Expires: March 2028

Staff
Judicial Assistant **Janet Payton** . . . . (706) 849-4478
E-mail: janet_payton@gas.uscourts.gov

Chambers of Bankruptcy Judge Edward J. Coleman

125 Bull Street, Savannah, GA 31401
Tel: (912) 650-4100

Edward J. Coleman III
Bankruptcy Judge

Chambers of Bankruptcy Judge Lamar W. Davis, Jr.

U.S. Courthouse, 125 Bull Street, Room 240, Savannah, GA 31401
Tel: (912) 650-4109

Lamar W. Davis, Jr.
Bankruptcy Judge

Date of Birth: 1946
Education: Emory 1968 BA; Georgia 1973 JD
Began Service: 1986
Term Expires: 2016

Current Memberships: Savannah Bar Association

Chambers of Bankruptcy Judge John S. Dalis

801 Gloucester Street, 3rd Floor, Brunswick, GA 31520
Tel: (912) 280-1376

John S. Dalis
Bankruptcy Judge

Date of Birth: 1952
Education: Georgia 1974 AB, 1977 JD

Chambers of Bankruptcy Judge John S. Dalis *continued*

Staff
Administrative Law Clerk **Susan Roberts** . . . . (912) 280-1373
Courtroom Deputy **Leigh Morris** . . . . (912) 280-1343
Court Reporter **April Rowe** . . . . (912) 280-1378

United States District Court for the District of Hawaii

U.S. Courthouse, 300 Ala Moana Boulevard, Honolulu, HI 96850
Tel: (808) 541-1300 Fax: (808) 541-1303
Internet: www.hid.uscourts.gov

Number of Judgeships: 4

Circuit: Ninth

Court Staff

District Clerk **Sue Beitia** . . . . (808) 541-1300
E-mail: sue_beitia@hid.uscourts.gov
Education: Boise State 1985 BA
Chief Probation Officer **Felix Mata** . . . . (808) 541-1283
Room 2-300 Fax: (808) 541-1345
Chief Pretrial Services Officer **Carol M. Miyashiro** . . . . . . (808) 541-3412
Room 7-222 Fax: (808) 541-3507
Education: U Washington 1995 JD
Systems Manager **Erik Grubbs** . . . . (808) 541-1300
E-mail: erik_grubbs@hid.uscourts.gov
Librarian **(Vacant)** . . . . (808) 541-1797

Chambers of Chief Judge Susan Oki Mollway

U.S. Courthouse, 300 Ala Moana Boulevard, Room C409, Honolulu, HI 96850-0409
Tel: (808) 541-1720 Fax: (808) 541-1724
E-mail: susan_mollway@hid.uscourts.gov

Susan Oki Mollway
Chief Judge

Date of Birth: 1950
Education: Hawaii 1971 BA, 1973 MA; Harvard 1981 JD
Began Service: June 23, 1998
Appointed By: President William J. Clinton

Academic: Instructor, English Department, University of Hawaii Manoa (1973-1975); Instructor, Takushoku University (1975-1976); Adjunct Professor, William S. Richardson School of Law, University of Hawaii Manoa (1988-1989)

Corporate: Editor, Charles E. Tuttle Publishing Company (1976-1978)

Government: Arbitrator, Court-Annexed Arbitration Program, State of Hawaii (1989-1996)

Legal Practice: Associate, Cades Schutte Fleming & Wright (1981-1986); Partner, Cades Schutte Fleming & Wright (1986-1998)

Current Memberships: The American Law Institute; Federal Judges Association; Hawaii Justice Foundation; Hawaii State Bar Association; Hawaii Women Lawyers; Hawaii Women's Legal Foundation; National Asian Pacific American Bar Association

Staff
Law Clerk **(Vacant)** . . . . (808) 541-1720
Career Law Clerk **Kenneth C. May** . . . . (808) 541-1720
Education: Hawaii 1995 JD
Courtroom Manager **Toni Fujinaga** . . . . (808) 541-1297
Secretary **Joni Gross** . . . . (808) 541-1720
E-mail: joni_gross@hid.uscourts.gov

Chambers of District Judge J. Michael Seabright

300 Ala Moana Boulevard, Room C-435, Honolulu, HI 96850
Tel: (808) 541-1804 Fax: (808) 541-1851

J. Michael Seabright
District Judge

Education: Tulane 1981 BA; George Washington 1984 JD
Began Service: May 17, 2005
Appointed By: President George W. Bush

Academic: Adjunct Professor, William S. Richardson School of Law, University of Hawaii Manoa (1999-2000)

Government: Assistant U.S. Attorney, District of Columbia, Office of the U.S. Attorney (1987-1990); Assistant U.S. Attorney, District of Hawaii, Office of the U.S. Attorney (1990-2001)

Legal Practice: Associate, Greely, Walker & Kowen (1985-1987); Attorney, Anderson, Kill & Olick (1987)

Current Memberships: Federal Judges Association; Hawaii State Bar Association; Ninth Circuit Judges Association

Staff
Fax: (808) 541-1851

Courtroom Manager **Shelli Mizukami** . . . . (808) 541-3085
E-mail: shelli_mizukami@hid.uscourts.gov
Judicial Assistant **Joedy Hu** . . . . (808) 541-1804
E-mail: joedy_hu@hid.uscourts.gov

Chambers of District Judge Leslie E. Kobayashi

U.S. Courthouse, 300 Ala Moana Boulevard, C-423, Honolulu, HI 96850
Tel: (808) 541-1331 Fax: (808) 541-1386
E-mail: leslie_kobayashi@hid.uscourts.gov

Leslie E. Kobayashi
District Judge

Date of Birth: 1957
Education: Wellesley 1979 BA; Boston Col 1983 JD
Began Service: December 22, 2010
Appointed By: President Barack Obama

Academic: Adjunct Professor, William S. Richardson School of Law, University of Hawaii Manoa (2000-2001)

Judicial: Magistrate Judge, Chambers of Magistrate Judge Leslie E. Kobayashi, United States District Court for the District of Hawaii (1999-2010)

Legal Practice: Associate, Fujiyama, Duffy & Fujiyama (1984-1991); Partner, Fujiyama, Duffy & Fujiyama (1991-1999); Managing Partner, Fujiyama, Duffy & Fujiyama (1995-1999)

Current Memberships: The American Inns of Court; Hawaii State Bar Association; Hawaii Women Lawyers

Staff
Law Clerk **Chesley Burrus** . . . . (808) 541-1391
Began Service: July 2015
Term Expires: July 31, 2016
E-mail: derien_meyer@hid.uscourts.gov
Career Law Clerk **Donna Odani** . . . . (808) 541-1332
E-mail: donna_odani@hid.uscourts.gov
Education: Hawaii 1999 JD
Courtroom Manager **Warren Nakamura** . . . . (808) 541-1894
E-mail: warren_nakamura@hid.uscourts.gov
Secretary **Starr Quon** . . . . (808) 541-1331
E-mail: starr_quon@hid.uscourts.gov

Chambers of District Judge Derrick Kahala Watson

300 Ala Moana Boulevard, Honolulu, HI 96850
Tel: (808) 541-1470

Derrick Kahala Watson
District Judge

Education: Harvard 1988 AB, 1991 JD
Began Service: May 6, 2013
Appointed By: President Barack Obama

Government: Assistant U.S. Attorney, California - Northern District, Executive Office for United States Attorneys, United States Department of Justice (1995-2000); Assistant U.S. Attorney, Hawaii District, Executive Office for United States Attorneys, United States Department of Justice (2007-2009); Chief, Hawaii District, Executive Office for United States Attorneys, United States Department of Justice (2009-2013)

Staff
Courtroom Manager **Tammy Kimura** . . . . (808) 541-3073
E-mail: tammy_kimura@hid.uscourts.gov
Court Reporter **Gloria Bediamol** . . . . (808) 541-2060
E-mail: gloria_bediamol@hid.uscourts.gov

Chambers of Senior Judge Helen Gillmor

U.S. Courthouse, 300 Ala Moana Boulevard, Honolulu, HI 96850
Tel: (808) 541-3502 Fax: (808) 541-3579
E-mail: helen_gillmor@hid.uscourts.gov

Helen Gillmor
Senior Judge

Education: Queens Col (NY) 1965 BA; Boston U 1968 LLB
Began Service: 1994
Appointed By: President William J. Clinton

Clerkships: Law Clerk The Honorable William Richardson, Hawaii State Supreme Court (1972)

Government: Deputy Public Defender, State of Hawaii (1972-1974)

Judicial: Judge Per Diem, Hawaii District Court, Family Court, First Circuit (1977-1983); Judge Per Diem, Hawaii District Court, First Circuit (1983-1985)

Legal Practice: Associate, Ropes & Gray LLP (1968-1969); Attorney, El Paso Real Estate Investment Trust (1969); Law Offices of Alexander Gillmor (1970); Associate, Moore, Torkildson & Schultze (1971-1972); Sole Practitioner (part-time) (1974-1977); Partner, Gillmor & Gillmor (1985-1994)

Staff
Law Clerk **Brett Rowan** . . . . (808) 541-3502
E-mail: brett_rowan@hid.uscourts.gov
Law Clerk **Douglas Yang** . . . . (808) 541-3502
Term Expires: September 2016
E-mail: douglas_yang@hid.uscourts.gov

Chambers of Senior Judge Alan C. Kay

U.S. Courthouse, 300 Ala Moana Boulevard, C-415, Honolulu, HI 96850
Tel: (808) 541-1904 Fax: (808) 541-3517
E-mail: alan_kay@hid.uscourts.gov

Alan C. Kay
Senior Judge

Date of Birth: 1932
Education: Princeton 1957 AB; Boalt Hall 1960 LLB
Began Service: 1987
Appointed By: President Ronald Reagan
Political Affiliation: Republican

Legal Practice: Partner, Case, Kay & Lynch (1960-1986)

Military Service: United States Marine Corps (1953-1955)

Chambers of Senior Judge Alan C. Kay *continued*

Current Memberships: The Aloha American Inn of Court, The American Inns of Court

Staff

Law Clerk **Amalia L. Fenton** .... (808) 541-1904
Began Service: October 1, 2013
Term Expires: January 30, 2016
E-mail: amalia_fenton@hid.uscourts.gov

Law Clerk **Elizabeth Hagerty** .... (808) 541-1904
Began Service: January 2015
Term Expires: January 2016
E-mail: elizabeth_hagerty@hid.uscourts.gov

Courtroom Manager **Leslie Sai** .... (808) 541-3089
E-mail: leslie_sai@hid.uscourts.gov

Secretary **Amy Kiguchi** .... (808) 541-1904
E-mail: amy_kiguchi@hid.uscourts.gov

Chambers of Senior Judge David A. Ezra

655 East Cesar E. Chavez Boulevard, San Antonio, TX 78206-1198
Tel: (210) 472-5870 Fax: (210) 472-5847

David Alan Ezra
Senior Judge

Note: Senior Judge Ezra is sitting by designation in the United States District Court for the Western District of Texas.
Date of Birth: 1947
Education: St Mary's U (TX) 1969 BBA, 1972 JD

Current Memberships: American Arbitration Association; American Bar Association; Federal Judges Association; Hawaii State Bar Association

Chambers of Magistrate Judge Barry M. Kurren

U.S. Courthouse, 300 Ala Moana Boulevard, Honolulu, HI 96850-0229
Tel: (808) 541-1306 Fax: (808) 541-3500
E-mail: Barry_Kurren@hid.uscourts.gov

Barry M. Kurren
Magistrate Judge

Date of Birth: 1951
Education: Hawaii 1973 BA, 1977 JD
Began Service: March 1992
Term Expires: March 2016

Clerkships: Law Clerk The Honorable Martin Pence, United States District Court for the District of Hawaii (1977-1978)

Judicial: Judge, Hawaii First Circuit District Court (1991-1992)

Legal Practice: Attorney, Goodsill Anderson Quinn & Stifel LLP (1978-1980); Burke, Sakai, McPheeters, Bordner & Gilardy (1980-1991)

Current Memberships: American Bar Association; The American Inns of Court; Federal Magistrate Judges Association; Hawaii State Bar Association

Staff

Career Law Clerk **Kanoelani Kane** .... (808) 541-1306
E-mail: kanoelani_kane@hid.uscourts.gov
Education: USC 2000 BS; Hawaii 2006 JD

Courtroom Manager **Bernadette Aurio** .... (808) 541-1306
E-mail: bernadette_aurio@hid.uscourts.gov

Chambers of Magistrate Judge Kevin S. C. Chang

U.S. Courthouse, 300 Ala Moana Boulevard, Honolulu, HI 96850
Tel: (808) 541-1308 Fax: (808) 541-3519
E-mail: Kevin_Chang@hid.uscourts.gov

Kevin S. C. Chang
Magistrate Judge

Date of Birth: 1953
Education: Lewis & Clark 1975 BS, 1978 JD
Began Service: December 2000
Term Expires: December 2016

Clerkships: Law Clerk The Honorable Robert C. Belloni, United States District Court District of Oregon (1978-1980)

Government: Deputy Prosecuting Attorney, City and County of Honolulu, Hawaii (1980-1981)

Judicial: Judge, Hawaii First Circuit Court (1993-2000)

Legal Practice: Watanabe Ing & Kawashima (1981-1993)

Current Memberships: The American Inns of Court; Hawaii State Bar Association

Staff

Career Law Clerk **Aimee Lum** .... (808) 541-1308
E-mail: aimee_lum@hid.uscourts.gov

Courtroom Manager **Shari Afuso** .... (808) 541-3091
E-mail: shari_afuso@hid.uscourts.gov

Secretary **Wilma Ara Kaki** .... (808) 541-1308

Chambers of Magistrate Judge Richard L. Puglisi

300 Ala Moana Boulevard, Honolulu, HI 96850
Tel: (808) 541-1900 Fax: (808) 541-3576

Richard L. Puglisi
Magistrate Judge

Date of Birth: 1953
Education: New Mexico 1975 BA, 1979 JD
Began Service: 2011
Political Affiliation: Republican

Current Memberships: American Bar Association; Hawaii State Bar Association; State Bar of New Mexico

Staff

Courtroom Manager **Mary Feria** .... (808) 541-1900
E-mail: mary_feria@hid.uscourts.gov

United States Bankruptcy Court for the District of Hawaii

1132 Bishop Street, Suite 250L, Honolulu, HI 96813
Tel: (808) 522-8100
Tel: (866) 222-8029 (Voice Case Information System VCIS)
Fax: (808) 522-8120
Internet: www.hib.uscourts.gov

Number of Judgeships: 1

Court Staff

Clerk of Court **Michael B. Dowling** .... (808) 522-8115
E-mail: michael_dowling@hib.uscourts.gov

Chief Deputy **Amy S. Young** .... (808) 522-8100 ext. 119
E-mail: amy_young@hib.uscourts.gov

Chambers of Chief Bankruptcy Judge Robert J. Faris
1132 Bishop Street, Suite 250L, Honolulu, HI 96813
Tel: (808) 522-8111 Fax: (808) 522-8120
E-mail: Robert_Faris@hib.uscourts.gov

Robert J. Faris
Chief Bankruptcy Judge

Education: Reed 1980 BA; Boalt Hall 1983 JD
Began Service: February 14, 2002
Term Expires: February 13, 2016

Legal Practice: Gelber, Gelber, Ingersoll, Klevansky & Faris (1983-2002)

Chambers of Bankruptcy Judge (recalled) Lloyd King
1132 Bishop Street, Suite 250L, Honolulu, HI 96813
Tel: (808) 522-8111

Lloyd King
Bankruptcy Judge (recalled)

Began Service: 2008

United States District Court for the District of Idaho
James A. McClure Federal Building & U.S. Courthouse, 550 West Fort Street, Room 400, Boise, ID 83724
Tel: (208) 334-1361 Tel: (866) 496-1250 (Toll Free)
Fax: (208) 334-9362
Internet: www.id.uscourts.gov

Number of Judgeships: 2

Number of Vacancies: 1

Circuit: Ninth

Court Staff
Clerk of Court **Elizabeth A. "Libby" Smith** .... (208) 334-1361
Chief Deputy Administration **John E. Triplett** .... (208) 334-9205
E-mail: john_triplett@id.uscourts.gov
Chief Deputy Operations **Kirsten Wilkinson** .... (208) 334-9464
Fax: (208) 334-9033
Chief Probation Officer **Jeffrey S. Thomason** .... (208) 334-1630
E-mail: jeffrey_thomason@idp.uscourts.gov Fax: (208) 334-1872
Librarian **Emily Quinn** .... (208) 334-9545
E-mail: emily_quinn@lb9.uscourts.gov Fax: (208) 334-9045
ADR Administrator/Pro Bono Director **Susie Headlee** ... (208) 334-9067
E-mail: susie_boring-headlee@id.uscourts.gov

Chambers of Chief Judge B. Lynn Winmill
James A. McClure Federal Building & U.S. Courthouse, 550 West Fort Street, 6th Floor, Boise, ID 83724
Tel: (208) 334-9145 Fax: (208) 334-9209

B. Lynn Winmill
Chief Judge

Date of Birth: 1952
Education: Idaho State 1974 BA; Harvard 1979 JD
Began Service: August 16, 1995
Appointed By: President William J. Clinton

Academic: Adjunct Professor, Idaho State University (1991-1995)

Judicial: Judge, Idaho District Court, Sixth Judicial District (1987-1995)

Legal Practice: Attorney, Holland & Hart LLP; Burnett & Winmill; Manning, Holmes & Winmill; Trial Lawyer, Hawley Troxell Ennis & Hawley LLP

Current Memberships: Idaho State Bar

Chambers of Chief Judge B. Lynn Winmill *continued*

Staff
Law Clerk **Jackie Hovda** .... (208) 334-9363
Law Clerk **Julie Varin** .... (208) 334-9088
E-mail: julie_varin@id.uscourts.gov
Education: Georgia 2004 JD
Career Law Clerk **David L. Metcalf** .... (208) 334-9025
E-mail: dave_metcalf@id.uscourts.gov
Education: UCLA 1979 JD
Career Law Clerk **Jeff Severson** .... (208) 334-9207
E-mail: jeff_severson@id.uscourts.gov
Courtroom Deputy **Jamie Gearhart** .... (208) 334-9021
E-mail: jamie_gearhart@id.uscourts.gov
Court Reporter **Tammy Hoenleitner** .... (208) 334-1500

Chambers of Chief Magistrate Judge Candy W. Dale
550 West Fort Street, 5th Floor, Boise, ID 83724
Tel: (208) 334-9111 Fax: (208) 334-9215
E-mail: candy_dale@id.uscourts.gov

Candy W. Dale
Chief Magistrate Judge

Began Service: March 30, 2008
Appointed By: President George W. Bush

Staff
Law Clerk **Tara Patterson** .... (208) 334-9206
Term Expires: August 2016
E-mail: tara_patterson@id.uscourts.gov
Career Law Clerk **Kirsten Wallace** .... (208) 334-9111
E-mail: kirsten_wallace@id.uscourts.gov
Education: Cornell 1992 BA;
U San Francisco 1996 JD
Pro Se Staff Attorney **Janis Dotson** .... (208) 334-9111
E-mail: janis_dotson@id.uscourts.gov
Pro Se Law Clerk **Sarah Davis** .... (208) 334-9111
E-mail: brandon_karpen@id.uscourts.gov

Chambers of Magistrate Judge Ronald E. Bush
James A. McClure Federal Building & U.S. Courthouse, 550 West Fort Street, Boise, ID 83724
Tel: (208) 334-9150 Fax: (208) 334-9362
E-mail: ronald_bush@id.uscourts.gov

Ronald E. Bush
Magistrate Judge

Education: Idaho 1979 BA; George Washington 1983 JD
Began Service: September 2008

Staff
Career Law Clerk **Kate Ball** .... (208) 334-9013
E-mail: kate_ball@id.uscourts.gov
Career Law Clerk **Lisa Brownson** .... (208) 334-1376
E-mail: lisa_brownson@id.uscourts.gov
Career Law Clerk **Dan Gordon** .... (208) 334-1881

Chambers of Magistrate Judge Mikel H. Williams
James A. McClure Federal Building & U.S. Courthouse, 550 West Fort Street, Boise, ID 83724-0039
Tel: (208) 334-9330 Fax: (208) 334-9229
E-mail: mikel_williams@id.uscourts.gov

Mikel H. Williams
Magistrate Judge

Date of Birth: 1946
Education: Idaho 1969 LLB
Began Service: 1984

Current Memberships: The American Inns of Court; Idaho State Bar

Chambers of Magistrate Judge Mikel H. Williams *continued*

Staff
Law Clerk **Elaine Lee** . . . . (208) 334-9330
E-mail: elaine_lee@id.uscourts.gov
Career Law Clerk **Claire Dwyer** . . . . (208) 334-1365
E-mail: claire_dwyer@id.uscourts.gov

Chambers of Magistrate Judge Larry M. Boyle
James A. McClure Federal Building & U.S. Courthouse, 550 West Fort Street, Room 518, Boise, ID 83724
Tel: (208) 334-9010 Fax: (208) 334-9215
E-mail: larry_boyle@id.uscourts.gov

Larry M. Boyle
Magistrate Judge

Date of Birth: 1943
Education: BYU 1968 BS; Idaho 1972 JD
Began Service: 1992

Current Memberships: The American Inns of Court

Chambers of Senior Judge Edward J. Lodge
James A. McClure Federal Building & U.S. Courthouse, 550 West Fort Street, Boise, ID 83724
Tel: (208) 334-9270 Fax: (208) 334-9229
E-mail: edward_lodge@id.uscourts.gov

Edward J. Lodge
Senior Judge

Date of Birth: 1933
Education: Col Idaho 1957 BS; Idaho 1961 LLB
Began Service: 1989
Appointed By: President George H.W. Bush

Current Memberships: American Bar Association; The American Inns of Court; Federal District Court Judges Association; Idaho District Judges Association; Idaho State Bar; Idaho Trial Lawyers Association

Staff
Career Law Clerk **Nancy Baskin** . . . . (208) 334-9270
E-mail: nancy_baskin@id.uscourts.gov
Education: Idaho 1983 BS, 1991 JD
Career Law Clerk **Lauri Thompson** . . . . (208) 334-9270
E-mail: lauri_thompson@id.uscourts.gov
Education: Idaho JD
Administrative Assistant **Diane Chamberlain** . . . . (208) 334-9270
E-mail: diane_chamberlain@id.uscourts.gov
Court Reporter **Lisa Erstad Yant** . . . . (208) 334-9721
E-mail: lisa_yant@id.uscourts.gov

United States Bankruptcy Court for the District of Idaho
James A. McClure Federal Building & U.S. Courthouse, 550 West Fort Street, Boise, ID 83724
Tel: (208) 334-1074
Tel: (208) 334-9386 (Voice Case Information System VCIS)
Fax: (208) 334-9362
Internet: www.id.uscourts.gov

Number of Judgeships: 2

Court Staff
Clerk of Court **Elizabeth A. "Libby" Smith** . . . . (208) 334-1361
Fax: (208) 334-9033
Chief Deputy **Kirsten Wilkinson** . . . . (208) 334-9464
Fax: (208) 334-9033

Chambers of Chief Bankruptcy Judge Terry L. Myers
James A. McClure Federal Building & U.S. Courthouse, 550 West Fort Street, Boise, ID 83724
Tel: (208) 334-9341 Fax: (208) 334-1334
E-mail: Terry_Myers@id.uscourts.gov

Terry L. Myers
Chief Bankruptcy Judge

Date of Birth: 1955
Education: Idaho 1980 JD
Began Service: August 1, 1998
Term Expires: July 31, 2026

Clerkships: Law Clerk The Honorable J. McFadden, Idaho Supreme Court (1980-1981); Law Clerk The Honorable M. Young, United States Bankruptcy Court for the District of Idaho (1981-1984)

Legal Practice: Givens, Pursley, LLP (1984-1998)

Current Memberships: American Bankruptcy Institute; National Conference of Bankruptcy Judges

Staff
Law Clerk **Mimi Faller** . . . . (208) 334-9341
Began Service: August 2014
Term Expires: August 2016
E-mail: mimi_faller@id.uscourts.gov
Career Law Clerk **Suzanne J. Hickok** . . . . (208) 334-9341
E-mail: Suzanne_Hickok@id.uscourts.gov
Education: Idaho 2001 JD

Chambers of Bankruptcy Judge Jim D. Pappas
James A. McClure Federal Building & U.S. Courthouse, 550 West Fort Street, Boise, ID 83724
Tel: (208) 334-9571 Fax: (208) 334-1334
E-mail: jim_pappas@id.uscourts.gov

Jim D. Pappas
Bankruptcy Judge

Date of Birth: 1952
Education: Idaho 1977 JD
Began Service: 2010
Term Expires: 2018

Academic: Idaho State (1974)

Judicial: Chief Bankruptcy Judge, United States Bankruptcy Court for the District of Idaho

Legal Practice: Attorney, Service, Gasser & Kerl

Current Memberships: National Conference of Bankruptcy Judges

Staff
Law Clerk **(Vacant)** . . . . (208) 334-9369
Career Law Clerk **Jonathan Derek** . . . . (208) 334-9136
E-mail: jonathan_derek@id.uscourts.gov
Education: St Vincent Col 1971 BA; St John's U (NY) 1999 JD, 2009 LLM
Career Law Clerk (Part-Time) **Carol Keating Mills** . . . . . . (208) 334-9369
E-mail: carol_mills@id.uscourts.gov
Education: Utah 1989 BS, 1992 JD
Judicial Assistant **Debbie Jenson** . . . . (208) 334-9369
E-mail: deborah_jenson@id.uscourts.gov

United States District Court for the Central District of Illinois

U.S. Courthouse, 600 East Monroe Street, Room 151,
Springfield, IL 62701
Tel: (217) 492-4020 Tel: (217) 492-4997 (PACER)
Fax: (217) 492-4028
Internet: www.ilcd.uscourts.gov

Number of Judgeships: 4

Circuit: Seventh

Areas Covered: Counties of Adams, Brown, Bureau, Cass, Champaign, Christian, Coles, De Witt, Douglas, Edgar, Ford, Fulton, Greene, Hancock, Henderson, Henry, Iroquois, Kankakee, Knox, Livingston, Logan, Macon, Macoupin, Marshall, Mason, McDonough, McLean, Menard, Mercer, Montgomery, Morgan, Moultrie, Peoria, Piatt, Pike, Putnam, Rock Island, Sangamon, Schuyler, Scott, Shelby, Stark, Tazewell, Vermilion, Warren and Woodford

Court Staff

Clerk of the Court **Kenneth A. Wells** . . . . (217) 492-4707
E-mail: ken_wells@ilcd.uscourts.gov

Chief Deputy - Springfield **Denise Koester** . . . . (217) 492-4707
E-mail: denise_koester@ilcd.uscourts.gov

Deputy-in-Charge - Peoria **Terry Kelch** . . . . (309) 671-7117
305 Federal Bldg., 100 NE Monroe St.,
Peoria, IL 61602
E-mail: terry_kelch@ilcd.uscourts.gov

Deputy-in-Charge - Rock Island **Kerin Burns** . . . . (309) 793-5778
40 Post Office Bldg., 211 19th St.,
Rock Island, IL 61201
E-mail: kerin_burns@ilcd.uscourts.gov

Deputy-in-Charge - Springfield **Michelle Eddings** . . . . (217) 492-4020
E-mail: michelle_eddings@ilcd.uscourts.gov

Deputy-in-Charge - Urbana **Keri Marsh** . . . . (217) 373-5830
218 U.S. Courthouse, 201 S. Vine St.,
Urbana, IL 61801
E-mail: keri_marsh@ilcd.uscourts.gov

Chief Probation Officer **Douglas Heuermann** . . . . (309) 671-7031

Librarian **(Vacant)** . . . . (217) 492-4191
Fax: (217) 492-4028

Chambers of Chief District Judge James E. Shadid

204 U.S. Courthouse, 100 NE Monroe Street, Peoria, IL 61602
Tel: (309) 671-4227 Fax: (309) 671-4228
E-mail: james_shadid@ilcd.uscourts.gov

James E. Shadid
Chief District Judge

Education: Bradley 1979 BS; John Marshall 1983 JD
Began Service: March 11, 2011
Appointed By: President Barack Obama

Staff

Law Clerk **Sam Perkins** . . . . (309) 671-4227
Term Expires: August 30, 2016
E-mail: sam_perkins@ilcd.uscourts.gov

Career Law Clerk **Kimberly P. Klein** . . . . (309) 671-4227
E-mail: kimberly_klein@ilcd.uscourts.gov
Education: Northwestern 1995 JD

Judicial Assistant **Cathy J. Geier** . . . . (309) 671-4227
E-mail: cathy_geier@ilcd.uscourts.gov

Chambers of District Judge Sue E. Myerscough

U.S. Courthouse, 600 East Monroe Street, Room 319,
Springfield, IL 62701
Tel: (217) 492-4000 Fax: (217) 492-4004

Sue E. Myerscough
District Judge

Date of Birth: 1951
Education: Southern Illinois 1973 BA, 1980 JD
Began Service: March 14, 2011
Appointed By: President Barack Obama
Political Affiliation: Democrat

Judicial: Associate Judge (1987-1990); Circuit Judge (1990-1998); Presiding Judge (1994-1998); Chief Judge (1996-1998); Presiding Justice, Chambers of Presiding Justice Susan E. Myerscough, Illinois Appellate Court, Fourth District (2010-2011)

Current Memberships: American Association of Justice; The Lincoln-Douglas American Inn of Court, The American Inns of Court; Appellate Lawyers Association; Central Illinois Women's Bar Association; Illinois Judges Association; Illinois State Bar Association; Sangamon County Bar Association

Staff

Career Law Clerk **Lara L. Quivey** . . . . (217) 492-4000
E-mail: lara_quivey@ilcd.uscourts.gov
Education: Illinois 1991 BS;
Southern Illinois 1996 JD

Law Clerk **Keith Liguori** . . . . (217) 492-4000
Term Expires: September 28, 2016
E-mail: keith_liguori@ilcd.uscourts.gov

Chambers of District Judge Sara Lynn Darrow

48 U.S. Courthouse, 211 Nineteenth Street, Rock Island, IL 61201
Tel: (309) 793-5779 Fax: (309) 793-5878
E-mail: sara_darrow@ilcd.uscourts.gov

Sara Lynn Darrow
District Judge

Education: Marquette 1992 BA; Saint Louis U 1997 JD
Began Service: August 11, 2011
Appointed By: President Barack Obama

Government: Assistant U.S. Attorney, Rock Island (IL) Office, Illinois - Central District, United States Department of Justice

Staff

Law Clerk **Joseph Platt** . . . . (217) 492-4020
Began Service: August 2015
Term Expires: August 31, 2016
E-mail: joseph_platt@ilcd.uscourts.gov

Law Clerk **Samuel Cross** . . . . (217) 492-4020
E-mail: samuel_cross@ilcd.uscourts.gov

Career Law Clerk **Heather Rouleau** . . . . (217) 492-4020
Began Service: August 15, 2011
E-mail: heather_rouleau@ilcd.uscourts.gov
Education: Northern Illinois 2001 JD

Chambers of District Judge Colin Stirling Bruce

201 South Vine Street, Suite 318, Urbana, IL 61802-3348
Tel: (217) 974-7510

Colin Stirling Bruce
District Judge

Education: Illinois 1986 BA, 1989 JD
Began Service: 2013
Appointed By: President Barack Obama

Staff

Law Clerk **Thomas Kelly** . . . . (217) 974-7510

Chambers of District Judge Colin Stirling Bruce *continued*

Career Law Clerk **Diane R. Klock** .... (217) 974-7510
E-mail: diane_klock@ilcd.uscourts.gov
Education: South Dakota State 1973 BS;
Northern Illinois 1985 JD

Chambers of Senior Judge Joe Billy McDade

122 Federal Building, 100 NE Monroe Street, Peoria, IL 61602
Tel: (309) 671-7821 Fax: (309) 671-7876

Joe Billy McDade
Senior Judge

Date of Birth: 1937
Education: Bradley 1959 BS, 1960 MA; Michigan 1963 JD
Began Service: December 13, 1991
Appointed By: President George H.W. Bush

Academic: Executive Trainee, First Federal Savings & Loan Association (1965)

Government: Staff Attorney, Antitrust Division, United States Department of Justice (1963-1965)

Judicial: Associate Judge, Illinois Circuit Court, 10th Judicial Circuit (1982-1988); Judge, Illinois Circuit Court (1988-1991)

Legal Practice: Executive Director, Greater Peoria Legal Aid Society (1965-1969); Partner, Hafele & McDade (1968-1977); Private Practice (1977-1982)

Current Memberships: Peoria County Bar Association

Staff

Law Clerk **Ben Clark** .... (309) 671-7821
Began Service: September 2014
Term Expires: September 2016
E-mail: ben_clark@ilcd.uscourts.gov

Career Law Clerk **Mohammed Ahmed** .... (309) 671-7821
E-mail: mohammed_ahmed@ilcd.uscourts.gov

Administrative Assistant **Audra Russo** .... (309) 671-7821

Chambers of Senior Judge Michael M. Mihm

Federal Building, 100 NE Monroe Street, Room 112, Peoria, IL 61602
Tel: (309) 671-7113 Fax: (309) 671-7375
E-mail: michael_mihm@ilcd.uscourts.gov

Michael M. Mihm
Senior Judge

Date of Birth: 1943
Education: Loras 1964 BA; Saint Louis U 1967 JD
Began Service: August 22, 1982
Appointed By: President Ronald Reagan

Government: Assistant Prosecuting Attorney, Office of the Prosecuting Attorney, County of St. Louis, Missouri (1967-1968); Assistant State's Attorney, Office of the State's Attorney, County of Peoria, Illinois (1968-1969); Police Legal Advisor and Assistant Corporation Counsel, Legal Department, City of Peoria, Illinois (1969-1972); State's Attorney, Office of the State's Attorney, County of Peoria, Illinois (1972-1980)

Judicial: Chief Judge, US District Court for the Central District of Illinois (1991-1998)

Legal Practice: Attorney, Private Practice (1980-1982)

Staff

Law Clerk **Arsenio Mims** .... (309) 671-7113
Began Service: August 2014
Term Expires: August 2016
E-mail: arsenio_mims@ilcd.uscourts.gov

Career Law Clerk **Shig Yasunaga** .... (309) 671-7113
E-mail: shig_yasunaga@ilcd.uscourts.gov

Court Reporter **Jennifer Johnson** .... (309) 671-7034
E-mail: jennifer_johnson@ilcd.uscourts.gov

Chambers of Senior Judge Michael M. Mihm *continued*

Secretary **Kimberly Ritthaler** .... (309) 671-7113
E-mail: kimberly_ritthaler@ilcd.uscourts.gov

Chambers of Senior Judge Harold Albert Baker

201 South Vine Street, Room 338, Urbana, IL 61802-3348
Tel: (217) 373-5835 Fax: (217) 373-5834
E-mail: harold_baker@ilcd.uscourts.gov

Harold Albert Baker
Senior Judge

Date of Birth: 1929
Education: Illinois 1951 BA, 1956 LLB
Began Service: 1978
Appointed By: President Jimmy Carter
Political Affiliation: Democrat

Academic: Adjunct Instructor, College of Law, University of Illinois (1972-1978)

Government: Senior Counsel, Presidential Commission on the Central Intelligence Agency Activities in the United States, Executive Office of the President, Gerald Ford Administration (1974-1975)

Legal Practice: Hatch & Corazza (1956-1960); Partner, Wheat, Hatch, Corazza & Baker (1960-1978)

Military Service: United States Navy (1951-1953)

Current Memberships: American Bar Association; American College of Trial Lawyers; Champaign County Bar Association; Illinois State Bar Association

Staff

Career Law Clerk **Susan Abrams** .... (217) 373-5835
E-mail: susan_abrams@ilcd.uscourts.gov
Education: Illinois 2001 JD

Court Reporter **(Vacant)** .... (217) 373-5835

Judicial Assistant **Michele Babb** .... (217) 373-5835
E-mail: michele_babb@ilcd.uscourts.gov

Chambers of Senior Judge Richard Mills

U.S. Courthouse, 600 East Monroe Street, Room 117,
Springfield, IL 62701-1659
Tel: (217) 492-4340 Fax: (217) 492-4342
E-mail: Judge_Mills@ilcd.uscourts.gov

Richard Mills
Senior Judge

Date of Birth: 1929
Education: Illinois Col 1951 BA; Mercer 1957 JD; Virginia 1982 LLM
Began Service: August 27, 1985
Appointed By: President Ronald Reagan
Political Affiliation: Republican

Government: State's Attorney, State of Illinois (1960-1964)

Judicial: Judge, Illinois Circuit Court, Eighth Judicial Circuit (1966-1976); Justice, Illinois Appellate Court, Fourth District (1976-1985)

Legal Practice: Mills Law Office (1957-1966)

Military Service: Third Infantry Division, United States Army (1952-1954); COL, United States Army Reserve, United States Department of the Army (1954-1985); Brig. General, Illinois Militia (1986-1990); Major General, Illinois Militia (1990)

Current Memberships: American Bar Foundation; American Bar Association; The American Law Institute; The Chicago Bar Association; The Seventh Circuit Bar Association, Federal Bar Association; Federal Judges Association; Illinois State Bar Association

Staff

Career Law Clerk **James O'Neill** .... (217) 492-4340
E-mail: jamie_o'neill@ilcd.uscourts.gov
Education: Mercer 2000 JD

(continued on next page)

Chambers of Senior Judge Richard Mills *continued*

Judicial Secretary **Carolyn K. Patterson** . . . . (217) 492-4340
E-mail: carolyn_patterson@ilcd.uscourts.gov

Chambers of Magistrate Judge David G. Bernthal

114 U.S. Courthouse, 201 South Vine Street, Urbana, IL 61802
Tel: (217) 373-5839 Fax: (217) 373-5840
E-mail: david_bernthal@ilcd.uscourts.gov

David G. Bernthal
Magistrate Judge

Date of Birth: 1950
Education: Illinois 1972 BA, 1976 JD
Began Service: May 1, 1995
Term Expires: April 30, 2019
Political Affiliation: Republican

Judicial: Associate Judge, Illinois Circuit Court, Fifth Judicial Circuit (1987-1995)

Legal Practice: Private Practice (1976-1986)

Current Memberships: Federal Magistrate Judges Association

Staff

Law Clerk **Marcy Zora** . . . . (217) 373-5839
Began Service: 2015
E-mail: marcy_zora@ilcd.uscourts.gov
Law Clerk **Colleen Ramais** . . . . (217) 373-5839
Began Service: 2013
E-mail: colleen_ramais@ilcd.uscourts.gov
Judicial Assistant **(Vacant)** . . . . (217) 373-5839

Chambers of Magistrate Judge Jonathan E. Hawley

100 NE Monroe Street, Room 211, Peoria, IL 61602
Tel: (309) 671-7140

Jonathan E. Hawley
Magistrate Judge

Chambers of Magistrate Judge Thomas Schanzle-Haskins

600 East Monroe Street, Room 124, Springfield, IL 62701
Tel: (217) 492-4396

Thomas Schanzle-Haskins
Magistrate Judge

Chambers of Magistrate Judge Eric I. Long

201 South Vine Street, Urbana, IL 61802-3348
Tel: (217) 373-5839 Fax: (217) 373-5840

Eric I. Long
Magistrate Judge

Began Service: 2015

United States Bankruptcy Court for the Central District of Illinois

226 U.S. Courthouse, 600 East Monroe Street, Springfield, IL 62701
Tel: (217) 492-4551 Tel: (217) 492-4260 (PACER)
Tel: (217) 492-4550 (Voice Case Information System VCIS)
Tel: (800) 827-9005 (Toll Free Voice Case Information System VCIS)
Fax: (217) 492-4556
Internet: www.ilcb.uscourts.gov

Number of Judgeships: 5

Number of Vacancies: 2

Court Staff

Clerk of Court **Khadijia Thomas** . . . . (217) 492-4551
Education: Missouri 2004 MPPA
Chief Deputy Clerk **Jeffrey Gust** . . . . (217) 492-4551
Deputy-in-Charge - Danville **Deborah Townsley** . . . . (217) 431-4820
130 Federal Bldg., 201 N. Vermilion St.,
Danville, IL 61832
Deputy-in-Charge - Peoria **Kathleen Traenkenschuh** . . . . (309) 671-7035
216 Federal Bldg., 100 NE Monroe,
Peoria, IL 61602
Operations Manager **Gerald Miller** . . . . (217) 492-4551

Chambers of Chief Bankruptcy Judge Mary P. Gorman

600 East Monroe Street, Springfield, IL 62701
Tel: (217) 492-4567

Mary P. Gorman
Chief Bankruptcy Judge

Began Service: 2006

Chambers of Bankruptcy Judge Thomas L. Perkins

216 Federal Building, 100 NE Monore Street, Peoria, IL 61602
Tel: (309) 671-7075
E-mail: thomas_perkins@ilcb.uscourts.gov

Thomas L. Perkins
Bankruptcy Judge

Date of Birth: 1958
Education: Iowa 1980 BBA; Indiana 1984 JD
Began Service: July 2000
Term Expires: July 2028

Current Memberships: American Bankruptcy Institute; Real Estate Section, Illinois State Bar Association

Staff

Career Law Clerk **Cathleen Chambers** . . . . (309) 671-7075
Education: Southern Illinois 1982 JD
Secretary **Lyn J. Vespa** . . . . (309) 671-7075
E-mail: lyn_vespa@ilcb.uscourts.gov

Chambers of Bankruptcy Judge (recalled) William V. Altenberger
216 Federal Building, 100 NE Monroe Street, Peoria, IL 61602
Tel: (309) 671-7290

William V. Altenberger
Bankruptcy Judge (recalled)

Date of Birth: 1935
Education: Illinois 1957 BS, 1963 LLB
Began Service: June 20, 2000

Affiliation: Bankruptcy Judge (visiting), Chambers of Bankruptcy Judge (visiting) William V. Altenberger, United States Bankruptcy Court for the Southern District of Illinois

Legal Practice: Kavanagh, Scully, Sudow, White & Frederick (1964-1985)

Military Service: United States Air Force (1957-1960)

Staff
Career Law Clerk **(Vacant)** . . . . (309) 671-9321

United States District Court for the Northern District of Illinois
Everett McKinley Dirksen U.S. Courthouse, 219 South Dearborn Street, Chicago, IL 60604
Tel: (312) 435-5670 Tel: (312) 408-7777 (PACER)
Fax: (312) 554-8512 Fax: (312) 554-8674
Internet: www.ilnd.uscourts.gov

Number of Judgeships: 22

Circuit: Seventh

Areas Covered: Counties of Boone, Carroll, Cook, DeKalb, DuPage, Grundy, Jo Daviess, Kane, Kendall, La Salle, Lake, Lee, McHenry, Ogle, Stephenson, Whiteside, Will and Winnebago

Court Staff
Clerk **Thomas G. Bruton** . . . . (312) 435-6860
E-mail: thomas_bruton@ilnd.uscourts.gov
Secretary to the Clerk **Annette Panter** . . . . (312) 435-6860
E-mail: Annette_Panter@ilnd.uscourts.gov
Financial Administrator **Donald Sippel** . . . . (312) 435-5503
E-mail: Donald_Sippel@ilnd.uscourts.gov Fax: (312) 554-8549
Docketing Director **Anita Moten-Baugard** . . . . (312) 435-6077
E-mail: anita_baugard@ilnd.uscourts.gov Fax: (312) 554-8675
Administrative Support Manager **Donna M. Carey** . . . . . . (312) 435-5502
E-mail: Donna_Carey@ilnd.uscourts.gov Fax: (312) 554-8549
Court Operations Manager **Anita Moten-Baugard** . . . . (312) 435-5505
E-mail: anita_baugard@ilnd.uscourts.gov Fax: (312) 554-8675
Judicial Support Manager **Ted Newman** . . . . (312) 435-5359
E-mail: Ted_Newman@ilnd.uscourts.gov
Education: Ripon 1974 BA; Chicago 1977 MA
Systems Manager **Mark Tortorici** . . . . (312) 435-5664
E-mail: Mark_Tortorici@ilnd.uscourts.gov Fax: (312) 554-8511
Chief Pretrial Services Officer **Ann Marie Carey** . . . . (312) 435-5793
Fax: (312) 435-5545
Chief Probation Officer **Kristine Phillips** . . . . (312) 435-5700
Fax: (312) 408-7882
Human Resources Officer **Michelle Hennings** . . . . (312) 435-5598
E-mail: michelle_hennings@ilnd.uscourts.gov Fax: (312) 554-8674
Administrative Analyst **(Vacant)** . . . . (312) 435-5358
Jury Administrator **Daniel Fitzsimmons** . . . . (312) 439-2085
E-mail: daniel_fitzsimmons@ilnd.uscourts.gov Fax: (312) 554-8673
Courtroom Services Supervisor **Diane Love** . . . . (312) 435-6877
E-mail: Diane_Love@ilnd.uscourts.gov Fax: (312) 554-8675
Court Reporter Coordinator **Brooke M. Wilson** . . . . (312) 435-5885
E-mail: brooke_wilson@ilnd.uscourts.gov Fax: (312) 554-8675
Official Court Interpreter **Victoria Funes** . . . . (312) 435-7627
E-mail: victoria_funes@ilnd.uscourts.gov

United States District Court for the Northern District of Illinois *continued*

Rockford Deputy in Charge **Jaclyn Pieczkiewicz** . . . . (815) 987-4354
211 S. Court St., Rm. 211, Rockford, IL 61101 Fax: (815) 987-4291
E-mail: jaclyn_pieczkiewicz@ilnd.uscourts.gov

Chambers of Chief Judge Ruben Castillo
Everett McKinley Dirksen U.S. Courthouse, 219 South Dearborn Street, Room 2548, Chicago, IL 60604
Tel: (312) 435-5600 Fax: (312) 554-8528
E-mail: ruben_castillo@ilnd.uscourts.gov

Ruben Castillo
Chief Judge

Date of Birth: 1954
Education: Loyola U (Chicago) 1976 BA; Northwestern 1979 JD
Began Service: May 9, 1994
Appointed By: President William J. Clinton

Staff
Law Clerk **Kathleen Flannery** . . . . (312) 435-3065
Began Service: October 2015
Term Expires: October 2016
E-mail: kathleen_flannery@ilnd.uscourts.gov
Law Clerk **Stephen Shaw** . . . . (312) 435-3058
Began Service: August 2015
Term Expires: August 2016
E-mail: stephen_shaw@ilnd.uscourts.gov
Law Clerk **Wendy Stasell** . . . . (312) 435-3063
Began Service: August 2014
E-mail: wendy_stasell@ilnd.uscourts.gov
Education: Chicago 1997 JD
Minute Clerk **Ruth O'Shea** . . . . (312) 435-5814
E-mail: ruth_o'shea@ilnd.uscourts.gov
Court Reporter **Kathleen Fennell** . . . . (312) 435-5569
E-mail: kathleen_fennell@ilnd.uscourts.gov Fax: (312) 386-1226
Judicial Assistant **Gabriela I. Kennedy** . . . . (312) 435-7595
E-mail: gabriela_kennedy@ilnd.uscourts.gov

Chambers of District Judge Charles Ronald Norgle, Sr.
Everett McKinley Dirksen U.S. Courthouse, 219 South Dearborn Street, Room 2346, Chicago, IL 60604
Tel: (312) 435-5634 Fax: (312) 554-8518
E-mail: charles_norgle@ilnd.uscourts.gov

Charles Ronald Norgle, Sr.
District Judge

Date of Birth: 1937
Education: Northwestern 1964 BBA; John Marshall 1969 JD
Began Service: October 1984
Appointed By: President Ronald Reagan

Academic: Adjunct Faculty, John Marshall Law School; Adjunct Faculty, Northwestern University School of Law

Government: Assistant State's Attorney, Office of the State Attorney, State of Illinois (1969-1971); Deputy Public Defender, State of Illinois (1971-1973)

Judicial: Associate Judge, DuPage County Court (1973-1977); Judge, Illinois Circuit Court (1977-1984)

Military Service: United States Army (1955-1957)

Current Memberships: American Bar Association; DuPage County Bar Association; Federal Bar Association; Illinois State Bar Association

Staff
Law Clerk **William Barnes McAllister** . . . . (312) 435-3093
Began Service: 2011
E-mail: william_mcallister@ilnd.uscourts.gov

(continued on next page)

Chambers of District Judge Charles Ronald Norgle, Sr. *continued*

Law Clerk **Jared Schneider** . . . . (312) 435-3092
E-mail: jared_schneider@ilnd.uscourts.gov
Court Reporter **Maellen Pittman** . . . . (312) 435-5576
E-mail: maellen_pittman@ilnd.uscourts.gov
Courtroom Deputy **Eric Fulbright** . . . . (312) 435-5635
E-mail: eric_fulbright@ilnd.uscourts.gov

Chambers of District Judge James B. Zagel

Everett McKinley Dirksen U.S. Courthouse, 219 South Dearborn Street, Room 2588, Chicago, IL 60604
Tel: (312) 435-5713 Fax: (312) 554-8521
E-mail: james_zagel@ilnd.uscourts.gov

James B. Zagel
District Judge

Date of Birth: 1941
Education: Chicago 1962 BA, 1962 MA; Harvard 1965 JD
Began Service: 1987
Appointed By: President Ronald Reagan

Academic: Lecturer, Northwestern University School of Law

Government: Assistant State's Attorney, Office of the State's Attorney, County of Cook, Illinois (1965-1969); Chief Prosecuting Attorney, Illinois Judicial Inquiry Board, State of Illinois (1973-1975); Chief Assistant Attorney General, Office of the Attorney General, State of Arizona (1975); Executive Director, Law Enforcement Commission, State of Illinois (1977-1979); Director, Department of Revenue, State of Illinois (1979-1980); Director, State Police, State of Illinois (1980-1987)

Current Memberships: American Bar Association; The Chicago Bar Association

Staff

Law Clerk **Sophie Glickstein** . . . . (312) 435-5713
Began Service: September 2015
Term Expires: September 2017
E-mail: sophie_glickstein@ilnd.uscourts.gov
Law Clerk **Peter Mclaughlin** . . . . (312) 435-5713
Began Service: September 2014
Term Expires: October 2016
E-mail: peter_mclaughlin@ilnd.uscourts.gov
Courtroom Deputy **Elisa Perez** . . . . (312) 435-5714
E-mail: elisa_perez@ilnd.uscourts.gov
Court Reporter **Blanca Lara** . . . . (312) 435-5895
E-mail: blanca_lara@ilnd.uscourts.gov
Judicial Assistant **Anne M. Wolf** . . . . (312) 435-5713
E-mail: anne_wolf@ilnd.uscourts.gov

Chambers of District Judge Rebecca R. Pallmeyer

Everett McKinley Dirksen U.S. Courthouse, 219 South Dearborn Street, Room 2146, Chicago, IL 60604-1702
Tel: (312) 435-5636
E-mail: rebecca_pallmeyer@ilnd.uscourts.gov

Rebecca R. Pallmeyer
District Judge

Date of Birth: 1954
Education: Valparaiso 1976 BA; Chicago 1979 JD
Began Service: October 21, 1998
Appointed By: President William J. Clinton

Academic: Adjunct Faculty Member, School of Law, Loyola University Chicago

Clerkships: Law Clerk The Honorable Rosalie E. Wahl, Minnesota Supreme Court (1979-1980)

Chambers of District Judge Rebecca R. Pallmeyer *continued*

Judicial: Administrative Law Judge, Illinois Human Rights Commission (1985-1991); Magistrate Judge, United States District Court for the Northern District of Illinois (1991-1998)

Legal Practice: Associate, Hopkins & Sutter (1980-1985)

Current Memberships: The Chicago Bar Association; Federal Bar Association; National Association of Women Judges; Women's Bar Association of Illinois

Staff

Law Clerk **Andrew Bruns** . . . . (312) 435-5636
E-mail: andrew_bruns@ilnd.uscourts.gov
Law Clerk **Jolie Mclaughlin**
Term Expires: September 2016
E-mail: jolie_mclaughlin@ilnd.uscourts.gov
Law Clerk **Justin Tresnowski** . . . . (312) 435-5636
Term Expires: September 2016
E-mail: justin_tresnowski@ilnd.uscourts.gov
Courtroom Deputy **Ena T. Ventura** . . . . (312) 435-5637
E-mail: ena_ventura@ilnd.uscourts.gov
Court Reporter **Frances Ward** . . . . (312) 435-5561
E-mail: frances_ward@ilnd.uscourts.gov
Judicial Assistant **Susan Kelly Lenburg** . . . . (312) 435-5636
E-mail: susan_lenburg@ilnd.uscourts.gov

Chambers of District Judge Matthew F. Kennelly

Everett McKinley Dirksen U.S. Courthouse, 219 South Dearborn Street, Suite 2188, Chicago, IL 60604
Tel: (312) 435-5618 Fax: (312) 554-8678
E-mail: matthew_kennelly@ilnd.uscourts.gov

Matthew F. Kennelly
District Judge

Date of Birth: 1956
Education: Notre Dame 1978 BA; Harvard 1981 JD
Began Service: June 22, 1999
Appointed By: President William J. Clinton

Clerkships: Law Clerk The Honorable Prentice H. Marshall, United States District Court for the Northern District of Illinois (1982-1984)

Legal Practice: Associate, Hedlund, Hunter & Lynch (1981-1982); Associate, Cotsirilos, Stephenson, Tighe & Streicker, Ltd. (1984-1989); Partner, Cotsirilos, Stephenson, Tighe & Streicker, Ltd. (1989-1999)

Nonprofit: Director, Board of Directors, Lawyers Committee for Better Housing (1984-1999)

Current Memberships: American Bar Association; American College of Trial Lawyers; The Chicago American Inn of Court, The American Inns of Court

Staff

Law Clerk **Matthew Heins** . . . . (312) 435-5618
Began Service: August 2015
Term Expires: August 2016
E-mail: matthew_heins@ilnd.uscourts.gov
Law Clerk **Elizabeth Jordan** . . . . (312) 435-5618
Began Service: October 2015
Term Expires: October 2016
E-mail: elizabeth_jordan@ilnd.uscourts.gov
Court Reporter **Laura M. Brennan** . . . . (312) 427-4393
Courtroom Deputy **Pamela Geringer** . . . . (312) 435-5350
E-mail: pam_geringer@ilnd.uscourts.gov
Judicial Assistant **Denise R. Slappey** . . . . (312) 435-5618
E-mail: denise_slappey@ilnd.uscourts.gov

Chambers of District Judge Ronald A. Guzman

Everett McKinley Dirksen U.S. Courthouse, 219 South Dearborn Street, Room 1278, Chicago, IL 60604
Tel: (312) 435-5363
E-mail: ronald_guzman@ilnd.uscourts.gov

Ronald A. Guzman
District Judge

Date of Birth: 1948
Education: Lehigh 1970 BA; NYU 1973 JD
Began Service: November 16, 1999
Appointed By: President William J. Clinton

Government: Assistant States Attorney, County of Cook, Illinois (1975-1980)

Judicial: U.S. Magistrate, U.S. District Court for the Northern District of Illinois (1990-1999)

Legal Practice: Private Practice (1973-1974); Private Practice (1980-1990)

Nonprofit: Staff Attorney, Association House of Chicago (1980-1984)

Staff

Career Law Clerk **Justin Corbalis** .... (312) 435-5363
E-mail: justin_corbalis@ilnd.uscourts.gov
Career Law Clerk **Page Hartzell** .... (312) 435-5363
E-mail: page_hartzell@ilnd.uscourts.gov
Education: Vanderbilt 1995 JD
Courtroom Deputy **Carole Gainer** .... (312) 435-5364
E-mail: carole_gainer@ilnd.uscourts.gov
Court Reporter **Nancy LaBella** .... (312) 435-6890
E-mail: nancy_labella@ilnd.uscourts.gov
Secretary **Varsha Pandya** .... (312) 435-5363
E-mail: varsha_pandya@ilnd.uscourts.gov

Chambers of District Judge John W. Darrah

Everett McKinley Dirksen U.S. Courthouse, 219 South Dearborn Street, Room 1288, Chicago, IL 60604
Tel: (312) 435-5619

John W. Darrah
District Judge

Education: Loyola U (Chicago) 1965 BS, 1969 JD
Began Service: September 1, 2000
Appointed By: President William J. Clinton

Affiliation: Faculty, National Institute for Trial Advocacy; Adjunct Professor, John Marshall Law School

Government: Public Guardian, County of DuPage, Illinois; Public Administrator, County of DuPage, Illinois; Attorney Advisor, Federal Trade Commission (1969-1971); Deputy Public Defender (part-time), Office of the Public Defender, County of DuPage, Illinois (1971-1973); Assistant State's Attorney, Office of the State's Attorney, State of Illinois (1973-1976)

Judicial: Judge, 18th Judicial Circuit Court of Illinois (1986-2000)

Legal Practice: Partner, Cox, Lyle & Darrah (1971-1973); Partner, Ryan & Darrah (1976-1981); Partner, Ryan, Darrah & Stringini (1981-1984); Sole Practitioner (1984-1986)

Membership: Past President, The DuPage American Inns of Court; Past President, DuPage County Bar Association

Staff

Law Clerk **Michelle Vaughan** .... (312) 435-7554
E-mail: michelle_vaughan@ilnd.uscourts.gov
Law Clerk **Matthew Schmidt** .... (312) 435-7553
Began Service: October 2014
E-mail: matthew_schmidt@ilnd.uscourts.gov
Courtroom Deputy **Melanie Foster** .... (312) 435-5556
E-mail: melanie_foster@ilnd.uscourts.gov
Court Reporter **Mary Hacker** .... (312) 435-5564
E-mail: mary_hacker@ilnd.uscourts.gov
Judicial Assistant **Kathryn Bianchetti** .... (312) 435-5619
E-mail: kathryn_bianchetti@ilnd.uscourts.gov

Chambers of District Judge Amy J. St. Eve

Everett McKinley Dirksen U.S. Courthouse, 219 South Dearborn Street, Room 1260, Chicago, IL 60604
Tel: (312) 435-5686 Fax: (312) 554-8477
E-mail: amy_st_eve@ilnd.uscourts.gov

Amy J. St. Eve
District Judge

Date of Birth: November 20, 1965
Education: Cornell 1987 BA, 1990 JD
Began Service: August 30, 2002
Appointed By: President George W. Bush

Corporate: Senior Counsel, Abbott Laboratories (2001-2002)

Government: Associate Independent Counsel, Whitewater Independent Counsel, City of Little Rock, Arkansas (1994-1996); Assistant United States Attorney, Northern District of Illinois, United States Attorney's Office, United States Department of Justice (1996-2001)

Legal Practice: Associate, Davis Polk & Wardwell (1990-1994)

Staff

Law Clerk **Rachel Schweers** .... (312) 408-5686
Began Service: September 2014
Term Expires: September 2016
E-mail: rachel_schweers@ilnd.uscourts.gov
Law Clerk **Troy Edwards** .... (312) 435-5686
Began Service: September 2015
Term Expires: September 2016
E-mail: troy_edwards@ilnd.uscourts.gov
Career Law Clerk **Suzanne Strater** .... (312) 435-5819
E-mail: suzanne_strater@ilnd.uscourts.gov
Courtroom Deputy **Katie Franc** .... (312) 435-5879
Court Reporter **Joseph Rickoff** .... (312) 435-5562

Chambers of District Judge Samuel Der-Yeghiayan

Everett McKinley Dirksen U.S. Courthouse, 219 South Dearborn Street, Room 1988, Chicago, IL 60604
Tel: (312) 435-5675
E-mail: samuel_der-yeghiayan@ilnd.uscourts.gov

Samuel Der-Yeghiayan
District Judge

Began Service: August 4, 2003
Appointed By: President George W. Bush

Staff

Law Clerk **Christine Dadourian** .... (312) 435-5675
E-mail: christine_dadourian@ilnd.uscourts.gov
Law Clerk **William Dunne** .... (312) 435-5675
E-mail: william_dunne@ilnd.uscourts.gov
Law Clerk **David Rutter** .... (312) 435-5675
Education: John Marshall 2002 JD
Courtroom Deputy **Michael Wing** .... (312) 408-5075
E-mail: michael_wing@ilnd.uscourts.gov
Court Reporter **Laura LaCien** .... (312) 408-5032
E-mail: laura_lacien@ilnd.uscourts.gov

Chambers of District Judge Virginia M. Kendall

Everett McKinley Dirksen U.S. Courthouse, 219 South Dearborn Street, Room 2378, Chicago, IL 60604
Tel: (312) 435-5692
E-mail: virginia_kendall@ilnd.uscourts.gov

Virginia M. Kendall
District Judge

Began Service: December 30, 2005
Appointed By: President George W. Bush

Government: Assistant U.S. Attorney, Illinois - Northern District, Executive Office for United States Attorneys, United States Department of Justice

(continued on next page)

Chambers of District Judge Virginia M. Kendall *continued*

Staff
Law Clerk **Sarah Gallo** .... (312) 435-5692
Began Service: September 2015
Term Expires: September 2016
E-mail: sarah_gallo@ilnd.uscourts.gov
Law Clerk **Sean Hennessy** .... (312) 435-5692
Began Service: 2014
E-mail: sean_hennessy@ilnd.uscourts.gov
Law Clerk **Colette Kopon** .... (312) 435-5692
Began Service: 2015
E-mail: colette_kopon@ilnd.uscourts.gov
Courtroom Deputy **Tresa Abraham** .... (312) 408-5153
E-mail: tresa_abraham@ilnd.uscourts.gov
Education: Loyola U (Chicago) 1985 BA
Court Reporter **Gayle McGuigan** .... (312) 408-5154
E-mail: gayle_mcguigan@ilnd.uscourts.gov

Chambers of District Judge Frederick J. Kapala

327 South Church Street, Room 6300, Rockford, IL 61101
Tel: (815) 987-4357
E-mail: frederick_kapala@ilnd.uscourts.gov

Frederick J. Kapala
District Judge

Date of Birth: 1950
Education: Marquette 1972 BA; Illinois 1976 JD
Began Service: May 10, 2007
Appointed By: President George W. Bush

Government: Assistant State's Attorney, Winnebago County, Illinois (1976-1977); Special Assistant Attorney General, Office of the Attorney General, Consumer Protection Division, State of Illinois (1981-1982)

Judicial: Associate Judge, State of Illinois (1982-1994); Circuit Judge, State of Illinois (1994-2001); Justice, Illinois Appellate Court, Second District (2001-2007)

Legal Practice: Attorney, Pedderson, Menzimer, Conde, Stoner & Killoren (1977-1982)

Military Service: United States Army Reserve, United States Department of Justice (1970-1980)

Staff
Law Clerk **Wendell Alford** .... (815) 987-4357
E-mail: wendell_alford@ilnd.uscourts.gov
Career Law Clerk **Christopher J. Drinkwine** .... (815) 987-4357
E-mail: christopher_drinkwine@ilnd.uscourts.gov
Education: Northern Illinois 1996 JD
Career Law Clerk **Paul Maurer** .... (815) 987-4357
E-mail: paul_maurer@ilnd.uscourts.gov
Education: Illinois 2001 BS, 2004 JD
Courtroom Deputy **Susan Bennehoff** .... (815) 987-4357
E-mail: susan_wessman@ilnd.uscourts.gov
Court Reporter **Mary Lindbloom** .... (815) 987-4486
E-mail: mary_lindbloom@ilnd.uscourts.gov

Chambers of District Judge Robert M. Dow, Jr.

Everett McKinley Dirksen U.S. Courthouse, 219 South Dearborn Street, Room 1919, Chicago, IL 60604
Tel: (312) 435-5668
E-mail: robert_dow@ilnd.uscourts.gov

Robert M. "Bob" Dow, Jr.
District Judge

Date of Birth: 1965
Education: Yale 1987 BA; Oxford (UK) 1990 MPhil; Harvard 1993 JD; Oxford (UK) 1997 DPhil
Began Service: December 5, 2007
Appointed By: President George W. Bush

Academic: Teaching Fellow, Harvard College (1992)

Chambers of District Judge Robert M. Dow, Jr. *continued*

Clerkships: Law Clerk, Circuit Judge Joel M. Flaum, United States Court of Appeals for the Seventh Circuit (1993-1994)

Legal Practice: Associate, Mayer Brown LLP (1995-2001); Partner, Mayer Brown LLP (2002-2007)

Current Memberships: Appellate Lawyers Association of Illinois

Staff
Law Clerk **Andrew Hammond** .... (312) 435-5668
E-mail: andrew_hammond@ilnd.uscourts.gov
Education: Yale 2014 JD
Law Clerk **Nissa Imbrock** .... (312) 435-5670
E-mail: nissa_imbrock@ilnd.uscourts.gov
Education: Harvard 2005 JD
Law Clerk **Stanley Wash** .... (312) 435-5362
Began Service: 2015
E-mail: stanley_wash@ilnd.uscourts.gov
Courtroom Deputy **Carolyn Hoesly** .... (312) 435-5668
E-mail: carolyn_hoesly@ilnd.uscourts.gov
Court Reporter **Kristin Ashenhurst** .... (312) 435-5668
E-mail: kristin_ashenhurst@ilnd.uscourts.gov

Chambers of District Judge Gary Scott Feinerman

Everett McKinley Dirksen U.S. Courthouse, 219 South Dearborn Street, Room 2156, Chicago, IL 60604
Tel: (312) 435-5627 Fax: (312) 554-8512
E-mail: gary_feinerman@ilnd.uscourts.gov

Gary Feinerman
District Judge

Education: Yale 1987 BA; Stanford 1991 JD
Began Service: September 13, 2010
Appointed By: President Barack Obama

Government: Solicitor General, Attorney General's Chicago Office, Office of the Attorney General, State of Illinois (2003-2007)

Legal Practice: Partner, Chicago, IL Office, Sidley Austin LLP (2007-2010)

Staff
Law Clerk **Salvatore Bonaccorso** .... (312) 435-5627
E-mail: salvatore_bonaccorso@ilnd.uscourts.gov
Law Clerk **Jesse Kaplan** .... (312) 435-5627
E-mail: jesse_kaplan@ilnd.uscourts.gov
Law Clerk **James Kylstra** .... (312) 435-5627
E-mail: james_kylstra@ilnd.uscourts.gov
Education: Chicago 2014 JD
Court Reporter **Charles Zandi** .... (312) 435-5627
E-mail: charles_zandi@ilnd.uscourts.gov
Courtroom Deputy **Jackie Deanes** .... (312) 435-5568

Chambers of District Judge Sharon Johnson Coleman

Everett McKinley Dirksen U.S. Courthouse, 219 South Dearborn Street, Room 1460, Chicago, IL 60604
Tel: (312) 435-6885

Sharon Johnson Coleman
District Judge

Education: Northern Illinois 1981 BA; Washington U (MO) 1984 JD
Began Service: September 7, 2010
Appointed By: President Barack Obama

Government: Prosecutor, County of Cook, Illinois; Assistant U.S. Attorney, Indiana - Northern District, United States Department of Justice; Head of Public Interest Bureau, Office of the Attorney General, State of Illinois (1993-1996); Circuit Judge, Illinois Circuit Court

Staff
Law Clerk **Jeannice Appenteng** .... (312) 435-6885
E-mail: jeannice_appenteng@ilnd.uscourts.gov

Chambers of District Judge Sharon Johnson Coleman *continued*

Law Clerk **Meaghan Clayton** . . . . (312) 435-6885
Began Service: 2010
E-mail: meaghan_clayton@ilnd.uscourts.gov
Education: John Marshall 2006 JD
Law Clerk **Roshni Shikari** . . . . (312) 435-6885
E-mail: roshni_shikari@ilnd.uscourts.gov
Court Reporter **Tracey McCullough** . . . . (312) 435-5570
E-mail: tracey_mccullough@ilnd.uscourts.gov
Courtroom Deputy **Robbie Hunt** . . . . (312) 408-5159
E-mail: robbie_hunt@ilnd.uscourts.gov

Chambers of District Judge Edmond E. Chang

Everett McKinley Dirksen U.S. Courthouse, 219 South Dearborn Street, Room 2178, Chicago, IL 60604
Tel: (312) 435-5795 Fax: (312) 554-8059
E-mail: edmond_chang@ilnd.uscourts.gov

Edmond E-Min Chang
District Judge

Education: Michigan 1991 BSE; Northwestern 1994 JD
Began Service: December 20, 2010
Appointed By: President Barack Obama

Clerkships: Law Clerk, Chambers of Circuit Judge James L. Ryan, United States Court of Appeals for the Sixth Circuit; Law Clerk, Chambers of District Judge Marvin E. Aspen, United States District Court for the Northern District of Illinois

Government: Appellate Division Chief, Illinois - Northern District, Executive Office for United States Attorneys, United States Department of Justice

Legal Practice: Associate, Chicago, IL Office, Sidley Austin LLP (1997-1999)

Membership: Assistant U.S. Attorney, Illinois - Northern District, Executive Office for United States Attorneys, United States Department of Justice

Staff
Court Reporter **Krista Burgeson** . . . . (312) 435-5567
E-mail: krista_burgeson@ilnd.uscourts.gov
Courtroom Deputy **Sandra Brooks** . . . . (312) 408-5121
E-mail: sandra_brooks@ilnd.uscourts.gov

Chambers of District Judge John Z. Lee

Everett McKinley Dirksen U.S. Courthouse, 219 South Dearborn Street, Room 1262, Chicago, IL 60604
Tel: (312) 435-5670 Fax: (312) 554-8512
E-mail: john_lee@ilnd.uscourts.gov

John Z. Lee
District Judge

Education: Harvard 1989 BA, 1992 JD
Began Service: 2012
Appointed By: President Barack Obama

Staff
Law Clerk **Julia Rickert** . . . . (312) 435-6899
E-mail: julia_rickert@ilnd.uscourts.gov
Law Clerk **Ignacio Sofo** . . . . (312) 435-6899
E-mail: ignacio_sofo@ilnd.uscourts.gov
Courtroom Deputy **Carmen Enid Acevedo** . . . . (312) 435-6899
E-mail: carmen_acevedo@ilnd.uscourts.gov
Court Reporter **Alexandra Roth** . . . . (312) 408-5038
E-mail: alexandra_roth@ilnd.uscourts.gov

Chambers of District Judge John J. Tharp Jr.

Everett McKinley Dirksen U.S. Courthouse, 219 South Dearborn Street, Room 1478, Chicago, IL 60604
Tel: (312) 435-5861 Fax: (312) 554-8512
E-mail: john_tharp@ilnd.uscourts.gov

John J. "Jay" Tharp, Jr.
District Judge

Education: Duke 1982 BA; Northwestern 1990 JD
Began Service: June 26, 2012
Appointed By: President Barack Obama

Staff
Law Clerk **Katherine Agonis** . . . . (312) 435-5861
E-mail: katherine_agonis@ilnd.uscourts.gov
Law Clerk **Guadalupe Laguna** . . . . (312) 435-5861
E-mail: guadalupe_laguna@ilnd.uscourts.gov
Law Clerk **Sarah Losh** . . . . (312) 435-5861
E-mail: sarah_losh@ilnd.uscourts.gov
Court Reporter **Carolyn Cox** . . . . (312) 435-5639
E-mail: carolyn_cox@ilnd.uscourts.gov
Courtroom Deputy **Alberta Rone** . . . . (312) 435-5861
E-mail: alberta_rone@ilnd.uscourts.gov

Chambers of District Judge Thomas M. Durkin

Everett McKinley Dirksen U.S. Courthouse, 219 South Dearborn Street, Room 1764, Chicago, IL 60604
Tel: (312) 435-5840
E-mail: thomas_durkin@ilnd.uscourts.gov

Thomas M. Durkin
District Judge

Education: Illinois 1975 BS; DePaul 1978 JD
Began Service: January 14, 2013
Appointed By: President Barack Obama

Clerkships: Law Clerk, Chambers of District Judge Stanley J. Roszkowski, United States District Court for the Northern District of Illinois (1978-1980)

Government: Criminal Receiving and Appellate Division Chief, Illinois - Northern District, Executive Office for United States Attorneys, United States Department of Justice; Special Prosecutions Division Chief, Illinois - Northern District, Executive Office for United States Attorneys, United States Department of Justice; First Assistant U.S. Attorney, Illinois - Northern District, Executive Office for United States Attorneys, United States Department of Justice

Legal Practice: Partner, Chicago, IL Office, Mayer Brown LLP

Staff
Law Clerk **Lynn Moffa** . . . . (312) 435-5840
E-mail: lynn_moffa@ilnd.uscourts.gov
Law Clerk **Lauren Schrero** . . . . (312) 435-5840
E-mail: lauren_schrero@ilnd.uscourts.gov
Law Clerk **Peter E. Wilhelm** . . . . (312) 435-5840
E-mail: peter_wilhelm@ilnd.uscourts.gov
Courtroom Deputy **Sandy Newland** . . . . (312) 435-6870
E-mail: sandy_newland@ilnd.uscourts.gov

Chambers of District Judge Sara Lee Ellis

219 South Dearborn Street, Chicago, IL 60604
Tel: (312) 435-5560 Fax: (312) 554-8545
E-mail: sara_ellis@ilnd.uscourts.gov

Sara Lee Ellis
District Judge

Education: Indiana 1991 BA; Loyola U (Chicago) 1994 JD
Began Service: 2013
Appointed By: President Barack Obama

Staff
Law Clerk **Susan Willoughby Anderson** . . . . (312) 435-5560

(continued on next page)

FEDERAL COURTS—UNITED STATES DISTRICT COURTS

Chambers of District Judge Sara Lee Ellis *continued*

Law Clerk **Maria Domanskis** .... (312) 435-5560
E-mail: maria_domanskis@ilnd.uscourts.gov
Education: Michigan 2009 JD
Law Clerk **Ashley Powers** .... (312) 435-5560
E-mail: ashley_powers@ilnd.uscourts.gov
Court Reporter **Patrick Mullen** .... (312) 435-5560
E-mail: patrick_mullen@ilnd.uscourts.gov
Courtroom Deputy **Rhonda Johnson** .... (312) 435-5560
E-mail: rhonda_johnson@ilnd.uscourts.gov

Chambers of District Judge Andrea R. Wood

219 South Dearborn Street, Room 1764, Chicago, IL 60604
Tel: (312) 435-5582
E-mail: andrea_wood@ilnd.uscourts.gov

Andrea Robin Wood
District Judge

Education: Chicago 1995 BA; Yale 1998 JD
Began Service: 2013
Appointed By: President Barack Obama

Staff
Law Clerk **Michael Pomeranz** .... (312) 435-5582
E-mail: michael_pomeranz@ilnd.uscourts.gov
Education: Yale 2014 JD
Law Clerk **Anthony Swanagan** .... (312) 435-5582
E-mail: anthony_swanagan@ilnd.uscourts.gov
Law Clerk **Alyse Wu** .... (312) 435-5582
Courtroom Deputy **Enjoli Fletcher** .... (312) 435-5582
E-mail: enjoli_fletcher@ilnd.uscourts.gov
Court Reporter **Colette Kuemmeth** .... (312) 435-5582
E-mail: colette_kuemmeth@ilnd.uscourts.gov

Chambers of District Judge Manish S. Shah

219 South Dearborn Street, Room 1778, Chicago, IL 60604
Tel: (312) 435-5649 Fax: (312) 554-8524
E-mail: manish_shah@ilnd.uscourts.gov

Manish S. Shah
District Judge

Education: Stanford 1994 BA; Chicago 1998 JD
Began Service: May 1, 2014
Appointed By: President Barack Obama

Government: Deputy Section Chief, Financial Crimes and Special Prosecutions, Illinois - Northern District, Executive Office for United States Attorneys, United States Department of Justice (2008-2011); Appellate Division Chief, Illinois - Northern District, Office of the Director, United States Department of Justice (2011-2012); Assistant U.S. Attorney, Illinois - Northern District, Executive Office for United States Attorneys, United States Department of Justice (2001-2013); Criminal Division Chief, Illinois - Northern District, Executive Office for United States Attorneys, United States Department of Justice (2012-2014)

Staff
Law Clerk **Lauren Abendshien** .... (312) 435-5649
E-mail: lauren_abendshien@ilnd.uscourts.gov
Law Clerk **Andrew H. Erskine** .... (312) 435-5649
E-mail: andrew_erskine@ilnd.uscourts.gov
Education: Illinois 2004 BS, 2004 MS
Law Clerk **Mary McCarthy** .... (312) 435-5649
E-mail: mary_mccarthy@ilnd.uscourts.gov
Courtroom Deputy **Susan McClintic** .... (312) 702-8805
E-mail: susan_mcclintic@ilnd.uscourts.gov
Court Reporter **Colleen Conway** .... (312) 435-5594
E-mail: colleen_conway@ilnd.uscourts.gov

Chambers of District Judge Jorge Luis Alonso

219 South Dearborn Street, Room 1756, Chicago, IL 60604
Tel: (312) 435-6044

Jorge Luis Alonso
District Judge

Education: Miami 1988 BA; George Washington 1991 JD
Began Service: December 19, 2014
Appointed By: President Barack Obama

Government: Assistant Public Defender, Law Office of the Public Defender, County of Cook, Illinois (1991-2003)

Staff
Law Clerk **Jill Dennor** .... (312) 435-6044
E-mail: jill_dennor@ilnd.uscourts.gov
Education: Illinois 1998 JD
Law Clerk **Laure Mullaney** .... (312) 435-6044
E-mail: laure_mullaney@ilnd.uscourts.gov
Education: Michigan 1989 JD
Law Clerk **Michael Conte** .... (312) 435-6044
E-mail: michael_conte@ilnd.uscourts.gov
Courtroom Deputy **Nicole Fratto-Butz** .... (312) 435-6044
Court Reporter **Nancy LaBella** .... (312) 435-6044

Chambers of District Judge John Robert Blakey

219 South Dearborn Street, Room 1046, Chicago, IL 60604
Tel: (312) 435-6058

John Robert Blakey
District Judge

Education: Notre Dame 1988 BA, 1992 JD
Began Service: December 19, 2014
Appointed By: President Barack Obama

Staff
Law Clerk **Frederic Shadley** .... (312) 435-6058
E-mail: frederic_shadley@ilnd.uscourts.gov
Law Clerk **Jackie Dunn** .... (312) 435-6058
E-mail: jackie_dunn@ilnd.uscourts.gov
Law Clerk **Ravi Shankar** .... (312) 435-6058
E-mail: ravi_shankar@ilnd.uscourts.gov
Courtroom Deputy **Gloria Lewis** .... (312) 818-6699
E-mail: gloria_lewis@ilnd.uscourts.gov
Court Reporter **Lisa Breiter** .... (312) 818-6683
E-mail: lisa_breiter@ilnd.uscourts.gov

Chambers of Senior Judge Elaine E. Bucklo

Everett McKinley Dirksen U.S. Courthouse, 219 South Dearborn Street, Room 1446, Chicago, IL 60604
Tel: (312) 435-7611
E-mail: elaine_bucklo@ilnd.uscourts.gov

Elaine E. Bucklo
Senior Judge

Date of Birth: 1944
Education: Saint Louis U 1966 AB; Northwestern 1972 JD
Began Service: October 11, 1994
Appointed By: President William J. Clinton

Academic: Lecturer, Northwestern University (1973); Visiting Professor, School of Law, University of California, Davis (1978-1980)

Clerkships: Law Clerk The Honorable Robert A. Sprecher, United States Court of Appeals for the Seventh Circuit (1972-1973)

Judicial: Magistrate Judge, United States District Court for the Northern District of Illinois (1985-1994)

Legal Practice: Private Practice (1973-1985)

Current Memberships: American Bar Association; Section on Litigation, American Bar Association; Chicago Council of Lawyers; Federal Bar Association

Chambers of Senior Judge Elaine E. Bucklo *continued*

Staff
Courtroom Deputy **Jackie Collier** .... (312) 435-7611
E-mail: jackie_collier@ilnd.uscourts.gov
Court Reporter **Sandra Tennis** .... (312) 435-5563
Judicial Assistant **Rosemarie Gayle** .... (312) 435-7610
E-mail: rosemarie_gayle@ilnd.uscourts.gov

Chambers of Senior Judge Robert W. Gettleman

Everett McKinley Dirksen U.S. Courthouse, 219 South Dearborn Street, Room 1788, Chicago, IL 60604
Tel: (312) 435-5543 Fax: (312) 554-8531
E-mail: robert_gettleman@ilnd.uscourts.gov

Robert W. Gettleman
Senior Judge

Date of Birth: 1943
Education: Boston U 1965 BSBA; Northwestern 1968 JD
Began Service: October 11, 1994
Appointed By: President William J. Clinton
Political Affiliation: Democrat

Clerkships: Law Clerk The Honorable Latham Castle, United States Court of Appeals for the Seventh Circuit (1968-1970)

Judicial: District Judge, United States District Court for the Northern District of Illinois (1994-2009)

Legal Practice: Private Practice (1970-1994)

Current Memberships: American Bar Association; The Chicago Bar Association

Staff
Law Clerk **Shy Jackson** .... (312) 435-3067
E-mail: shy_jackson@ilnd.uscourts.gov
Career Law Clerk **Steven E. Gilman** .... (312) 435-3066
E-mail: steven_gilman@ilnd.uscourts.gov
Education: Chicago-Kent 1982 JD
Courtroom Deputy **George Schwemin** .... (312) 435-5545
E-mail: george_schwemin@ilnd.uscourts.gov
Court Reporter **Nancy Bistany** .... (312) 435-7626
E-mail: nancy_bistany@ilnd.uscourts.gov
Secretary **Mary Gartland** .... (312) 435-5543
E-mail: mary_gartland@ilnd.uscourts.gov

Chambers of Senior Judge Marvin E. Aspen

Everett McKinley Dirksen U.S. Courthouse, 219 South Dearborn Street, Room 2578, Chicago, IL 60604
Tel: (312) 435-5696 Fax: (312) 554-8515
E-mail: marvin_aspen@ilnd.uscourts.gov

Marvin E. Aspen
Senior Judge

Date of Birth: 1934
Education: Loyola U (Chicago) 1956 BS; Northwestern 1958 JD
Began Service: July 24, 1979
Appointed By: President Jimmy Carter

Academic: Adjunct Professor, Northwestern University School of Law (1969-1992)

Government: Law Clerk, United States Department of Justice; Assistant State's Attorney, Office of the State Attorney, State of Illinois (1960-1963); Assistant Corporation Counsel,, Head of Appeals and Review Division, Office of the Corporation Counsel, City of Chicago, Illinois (1963-1971)

Judicial: Judge, Illinois Circuit Court, Cook County Judicial Circuit (1971-1979); Judge, United States District Court for the Northern District of Illinois (1979-1995); Chief Judge, United States District Court for the Northern District of Illinois (1995-2002); Member, Judicial Conference of the United States (2000-2003)

Legal Practice: Private Practice (1959); Private Practice (1971)

Chambers of Senior Judge Marvin E. Aspen *continued*

Military Service: Judge Advocate General Section, United States Army; Illinois National Guard (1959); United States Air Force Reserve (1960-1964)

Current Memberships: American Bar Association; The Chicago Bar Association; Illinois State Bar Association

Staff
Law Clerk **Alexandra Caritis** .... (312) 435-5696
Term Expires: September 2016
E-mail: alexandra_caritis@ilnd.uscourts.gov
Law Clerk **Jessica Fricke** .... (312) 435-5696
E-mail: jessica_fricke@ilnd.uscourts.gov
Career Law Clerk **Beth Cammarata** .... (312) 435-5696
Education: Chicago-Kent 2001 JD
Secretary **Linda Surprenant** .... (312) 435-5696
E-mail: linda_surprenant@ilnd.uscourts.gov

Chambers of Senior Judge Milton I. Shadur

Everett McKinley Dirksen U.S. Courthouse, 219 South Dearborn Street, Room 2388, Chicago, IL 60604
Tel: (312) 435-5766
E-mail: milton_shadur@ilnd.uscourts.gov

Milton I. Shadur
Senior Judge

Date of Birth: 1924
Education: Chicago 1943 BS, 1949 JD
Began Service: June 1980
Appointed By: President Jimmy Carter

Legal Practice: Associate, Goldberg, Devoe & Brussell (1949-1951); Partner, Goldberg, Devoe, Brussell & Shadur (1951-1956); Partner, Goldberg, Devoe, Shadur & Mikva (1956-1961); Partner, Devoe, Shadur, Mikva & Plotkin (1961-1968); Partner, Devoe, Shadur, Plotkin, Krupp & Miller (1969-1973); Partner, Devoe, Shadur, Plotkin & Krupp (1973-1979); Partner, Shadur, Krupp & Miller (1979-1980)

Military Service: United States Naval Reserve (1943-1946)

Staff
Law Clerk **Ross Corbett** .... (312) 435-5766
E-mail: ross_corbett@ilnd.uscourts.gov
Law Clerk **Samuel Levine** .... (312) 435-5766
Law Clerk **Michael Schorsch** .... (312) 435-5766
E-mail: michael_schorsch@ilnd.uscourts.gov
Court Reporter **Rosemary Scarpelli** .... (312) 435-5766
E-mail: rosemary_scarpelli@ilnd.uscourts.gov
Education: Elmhurst 1989 BS
Courtroom Deputy **Carol Wing** .... (312) 435-5766
Judicial Assistant **Mary Ann R. Braasch** .... (312) 435-5766

Chambers of Senior Judge William T. Hart

Everett McKinley Dirksen U.S. Courthouse, 219 South Dearborn Street, Room 2502, Chicago, IL 60604
Tel: (312) 435-5776
E-mail: william_hart@ilnd.uscourts.gov

William T. Hart
Senior Judge

Date of Birth: 1929
Education: Loyola U (Chicago) 1951 JD
Began Service: May 1, 1982
Appointed By: President Ronald Reagan

Government: Assistant United States Attorney, Northern District of Illinois, United States Department of Justice (1954-1956); Special Assistant Attorney General, Illinois, United States Department of Justice (1957-1958); Special Assistant State's Attorney, Illinois, United States Department of Justice (1960)

(continued on next page)

FEDERAL COURTS—UNITED STATES DISTRICT COURTS

Chambers of Senior Judge William T. Hart *continued*

Legal Practice: Associate, DeFrees & Fiske (1956-1959); Attorney, Schiff Hardin & Waite (1959-1982)

Military Service: United States Army (1951-1953)

Current Memberships: American Bar Association; The Chicago Bar Association; The Seventh Circuit Bar Association, Federal Bar Association; Illinois State Bar Association

Staff

Courtroom Deputy **Carol Wing** .... (312) 435-7615
E-mail: carol_wing@ilnd.uscourts.gov
Secretary **Karen Giammarese** .... (312) 435-5776
E-mail: karen_giammarese@ilnd.uscourts.gov

Chambers of Senior Judge Harry D. Leinenweber

Everett McKinley Dirksen U.S. Courthouse, 219 South Dearborn Street, Room 1946, Chicago, IL 60604
Tel: (312) 435-7612 Fax: (312) 554-8522
E-mail: harry_leinenweber@ilnd.uscourts.gov

Harry D. Leinenweber
Senior Judge

Date of Birth: June 3, 1937
Education: Notre Dame 1959 BA; Chicago 1962 JD
Began Service: January 17, 1986
Appointed By: President Ronald Reagan
Political Affiliation: Republican

Government: City Attorney, City of Joliet, Illinois (1963-1967); Special Counsel, Office of the Village Attorney, Village of Park Forest, Illinois (1967-1974); Special Prosecutor, Office of the State's Attorney, County of Will, Illinois (1968-1970); State Representative Harry D. Leinenweber (R-IL), Illinois General Assembly (1973-1983); Special Counsel, Village of Bolingbrook, Illinois (1975-1977); Special Counsel, Will County Forest Preserve (2007)

Judicial: District Judge, United States District Court for the Northern District of Illinois (1986-2002)

Legal Practice: Associate then Partner, Dunn, Stefanich, McGarry & Kennedy (1962-1979); Partner, Dunn, Leinenweber & Dunn (1979-1986)

Current Memberships: Illinois State Bar Association; Illinois Trial Lawyers Association; National Conference of Commissioners on Uniform State Laws; Will County Bar Association

Staff

Law Clerk **Allison Kadrmas** .... (312) 435-7612
Began Service: September 2015
Term Expires: September 2016
E-mail: william_green@ilnd.uscourts.gov
Law Clerk **Elizabeth Winkowski** .... (312) 435-7612
Began Service: January 2015
Term Expires: January 2016
E-mail: elizabeth_winkowski@ilnd.uscourts.gov
Courtroom Deputy **Wanda Parker** .... (312) 435-7613
E-mail: wanda_parker@ilnd.uscourts.gov
Court Reporter **Judith Walsh** .... (312) 435-6047
E-mail: judith_walsh@ilnd.uscourts.gov
Judicial Assistant **Mary Quinlivan** .... (312) 435-7612
E-mail: mary_quinlivan@ilnd.uscourts.gov

Chambers of Senior Judge Charles P. Kocoras

Everett McKinley Dirksen U.S. Courthouse, 219 South Dearborn Street, Room 2560, Chicago, IL 60604
Tel: (312) 435-6872 Fax: (312) 554-8516
E-mail: charles_kocoras@ilnd.uscourts.gov

Charles P. Kocoras
Senior Judge

Date of Birth: 1938
Education: DePaul 1961 BS, 1969 JD
Began Service: November 24, 1980
Appointed By: President Jimmy Carter

Government: Revenue Agent, Internal Revenue Service, United States Department of the Treasury (1962-1969); Assistant United States Attorney, Northern District of Illinois, United States Department of Justice (1971-1977); First Assistant United States Attorney, Northern District of Illinois, United States Department of Justice (1975-1977); Chairman, Commerce Commission, State of Illinois (1977-1979)

Judicial: Chief Judge, United States District Court for the Northern District of Illinois (2002-2006)

Legal Practice: Associate, Bishop & Crawford (1969-1971); Partner, Stone, McGuire, Benjamin & Kocoras (1979-1980)

Military Service: Illinois Army National Guard (1961-1967)

Staff

Fax: (312) 554-8516

Law Clerk **Christina Faklis** .... (312) 435-6872
E-mail: christina_faklis@ilnd.uscourts.gov
Law Clerk **Anne Yonover** .... (312) 435-6872
Began Service: 2015
E-mail: anne_yonover@ilnd.uscourts.gov
Secretary **Jeanette Armstrong** .... (312) 435-6872
E-mail: jeanette_armstrong@ilnd.uscourts.gov

Chambers of Senior Judge Philip G. Reinhard

Stanley J. Roszkowski United States Courthouse, 327 South Church Street, Rockford, IL 61101
Tel: (815) 987-4480 Fax: (815) 987-4291
E-mail: philip_reinhard@ilnd.uscourts.gov

Philip G. Reinhard
Senior Judge

Date of Birth: 1941
Education: Illinois 1962 BA, 1964 JD
Began Service: February 12, 1992
Appointed By: President George H.W. Bush

Current Memberships: Winnebago County Bar Association

Staff

Career Law Clerk **J. Mark Doherty** .... (815) 987-4480
E-mail: mark_doherty@ilnd.uscourts.gov
Education: Sangamon State 1979 BA; Illinois 1982 JD
Career Law Clerk **Max H. DeLeon** .... (815) 987-4480
E-mail: max_deleon@ilnd.uscourts.gov
Court Reporter **Mary Lindbloom** .... (815) 987-4486
E-mail: mary_lindbloom@ilnd.uscourts.gov
Judicial Secretary **Cindy Reed** .... (815) 987-4480
E-mail: cynthia_reed@ilnd.uscourts.gov

Chambers of Senior Judge Joan B. Gottschall

Everett McKinley Dirksen U.S. Courthouse, 219 South Dearborn Street, Suite 2356, Chicago, IL 60604
Tel: (312) 435-5640 Fax: (312) 554-8533
E-mail: joan_gottschall@ilnd.uscourts.gov

Joan B. Gottschall
Senior Judge

Date of Birth: 1947
Education: Smith 1969 BA; Stanford 1973 JD
Began Service: September 3, 1996
Appointed By: President William J. Clinton

Current Memberships: American Bar Association; The Chicago Bar Association

Staff

Law Clerk **Cynthia Cohan** .... (312) 435-3068
Began Service: October 2014
E-mail: cynthia_cohan@ilnd.uscourts.gov
Education: Cornell 1991 JD
Law Clerk **Jimmy Arce** .... (312) 435-3069
Began Service: October 2015
Term Expires: October 2016
Courtroom Deputy **Marlan Cowan** .... (312) 435-5641
E-mail: marlan_cowan@ilnd.uscourts.gov
Judicial Assistant **Nancy Novotny Moravecek** .... (312) 408-7767
E-mail: nancy_moravecek@ilnd.uscourts.gov

Chambers of Senior Judge Joan Humphrey Lefkow

Everett McKinley Dirksen U.S. Courthouse, 219 South Dearborn Street, Room 2286, Chicago, IL 60604-1952
Tel: (312) 435-5832 Fax: (312) 554-8520
E-mail: joan_lefkow@ilnd.uscourts.gov

Joan Humphrey Lefkow
Senior Judge

Date of Birth: 1944
Education: Wheaton (IL) 1965 AB; Northwestern 1971 JD
Began Service: September 1, 2000
Appointed By: President William J. Clinton

Current Memberships: The Chicago Bar Association; Chicago Council of Lawyers; The Seventh Circuit Bar Association, Federal Bar Association; National Association of Women Judges

Staff
Fax: (312) 554-8520

Law Clerk **Abraham Souza** .... (312) 435-5832
Began Service: January 2015
Term Expires: December 31, 2016
E-mail: abraham_souza@ilnd.uscourts.gov
Law Clerk **Daisy Ocampo** .... (312) 435-5832
Began Service: August 17, 2015
Term Expires: September 30, 2016
E-mail: daisy_ocampo@ilnd.uscourts.gov
Court Reporter **Pamela Warren** .... (312) 294-8907
E-mail: pswcsr@aol.com
Judicial Assistant **Krys Juleen** .... (312) 435-5832
E-mail: krys_juleen@ilnd.uscourts.gov

Chambers of Senior Judge George M. Marovich

Everett McKinley Dirksen U.S. Courthouse, 219 South Dearborn Street, Room 1874, Chicago, IL 60604
Tel: (312) 435-5590 Fax: (312) 554-8525
E-mail: george_marovich@ilnd.uscourts.gov

George M. Marovich
Senior Judge

Date of Birth: 1931
Education: Illinois 1952 BS, 1954 JD
Began Service: 1988
Appointed By: President Ronald Reagan

Current Memberships: The Chicago Bar Association; Illinois Judges Association; Illinois Judicial Conference; South Suburban Bar Association

Staff

Career Law Clerk **Angela Mersch** .... (312) 435-3086
E-mail: angela_mersch@ilnd.uscourts.gov
Courtroom Deputy **Carol Wing** .... (312) 435-7615
E-mail: carol_wing@ilnd.uscourts.gov

Chambers of Presiding Magistrate Judge Geraldine Soat Brown

Everett McKinley Dirksen U.S. Courthouse, 219 South Dearborn Street, Suite 1822, Chicago, IL 60604
Tel: (312) 435-5612 Fax: (312) 554-8472

Geraldine Soat Brown
Presiding Magistrate Judge

Date of Birth: 1950
Education: Dayton BA; Chicago 1975 JD
Began Service: June 19, 2000
Term Expires: June 18, 2016

Current Memberships: American Bar Association; The Chicago Bar Association; Chicago Council of Lawyers; Illinois State Bar Association; Women's Bar Association of Illinois

Staff

Law Clerk **Paul Stibbe** .... (312) 435-5612
E-mail: paul_stibbe@ilnd.uscourts.gov
Law Clerk **Sarah Finch** .... (312) 435-5612
E-mail: sarah_finch@ilnd.uscourts.gov
Courtroom Deputy **Eunice Tejeda** .... (312) 435-7552

Chambers of Magistrate Judge Sidney I. Schenkier

Everett McKinley Dirksen U.S. Courthouse, 219 South Dearborn Street, Room 1846, Chicago, IL 60604-1976
Tel: (312) 435-5609 Fax: (312) 554-8677
E-mail: sidney_schenkier@ilnd.uscourts.gov

Sidney I. Schenkier
Magistrate Judge

Date of Birth: 1955
Education: Northwestern 1976 BSJ, 1979 JD
Began Service: October 30, 1998
Term Expires: October 30, 2022

Staff

Law Clerk **Jennifer Cromheecke** .... (312) 435-5609
Term Expires: September 2016
E-mail: jennifer_cromheecke@ilnd.uscourts.gov
Law Clerk **Melanie Berkowitz**
Term Expires: September 2016
Career Law Clerk **Tamar Karsh-Fogel** .... (312) 435-3033
Education: Wisconsin 1996 BS; Chicago 2000 JD

(continued on next page)

Chambers of Magistrate Judge Sidney I. Schenkier *continued*

Courtroom Deputy **Jenny Jauregui** . . . . (312) 435-7573
E-mail: jenny_jauregui@ilnd.uscourts.gov
Judicial Assistant **Patricia Hagenmaier** . . . . (312) 435-5609
E-mail: patricia_hagenmaier@ilnd.uscourts.gov

Chambers of Magistrate Judge Michael T. Mason

Everett McKinley Dirksen U.S. Courthouse, 219 South Dearborn Street, Room 2270, Chicago, IL 60604
Tel: (312) 435-5610

Michael T. Mason
Magistrate Judge

Began Service: September 29, 2001

Staff

Law Clerk **Katie Trzyna** . . . . (312) 435-5610
Law Clerk **Maura O'Meara** . . . . (312) 435-5119
Education: Loyola U (Chicago) 2001 JD
Law Clerk **Janna Shell** . . . . (312) 435-5610
E-mail: janna_shell@ilnd.uscourts.gov
Courtroom Deputy **Rosa Franco** . . . . (312) 435-6051
E-mail: rosa_franco@ilnd.uscourts.gov

Chambers of Magistrate Judge Jeffrey Cole

Everett McKinley Dirksen U.S. Courthouse, 219 South Dearborn Street, Room 1088, Chicago, IL 60604
Tel: (312) 435-5601 Fax: (312) 554-8947
E-mail: jeffrey_cole@ilnd.uscourts.gov

Jeffrey Cole
Magistrate Judge

Date of Birth: September 1942
Began Service: May 6, 2005
Term Expires: May 2021

Current Memberships: American Bar Association; The Seventh Circuit Bar Association, Federal Bar Association

Staff

Career Law Clerk **Jeffrey Pakula** . . . . (312) 582-8775
E-mail: jeffrey_pakula@ilnd.uscourts.gov
Education: Marquette 1983 BA; Chicago-Kent 1986 JD
Courtroom Deputy **Jan Smith** . . . . (312) 408-5178
E-mail: jan_smith@ilnd.uscourts.gov
Judicial Assistant **Mary Ellen Podgorny** . . . . (312) 435-5601
E-mail: maryellen_podgorny@ilnd.uscourts.gov

Chambers of Magistrate Judge Maria G. Valdez

Everett McKinley Dirksen U.S. Courthouse, 219 South Dearborn Street, Room 1058, Chicago, IL 60604-1702
Tel: (312) 435-5690
E-mail: maria_valdez@ilnd.uscourts.gov

Maria G. Valdez
Magistrate Judge

Began Service: 2005

Staff

Law Clerk **Andrew Tonelli** . . . . (312) 435-5690
Began Service: 2015
Term Expires: August 2016
E-mail: andrew_tonelli@ilnd.uscourts.gov
Career Law Clerk **Michelle Mills** . . . . (312) 435-5690
E-mail: michelle_mills@ilnd.uscourts.gov
Education: DePaul 1998 JD
Courtroom Deputy **Lisa Provine** . . . . (312) 408-5135
E-mail: lisa_provine@ilnd.uscourts.gov

Chambers of Magistrate Judge Susan E. Cox

Everett McKinley Dirksen U.S. Courthouse, 219 South Dearborn Street, Chamber 1068, Chicago, IL 60604
Tel: (312) 435-5615 Fax: (312) 554-8514

Susan E. Cox
Magistrate Judge

Began Service: August 27, 2007
Term Expires: August 27, 2023

Staff

Career Law Clerk **Michael La Mare** . . . . (312) 435-5615
Courtroom Deputy **Nakita Perdue** . . . . (312) 435-7558
E-mail: nakita_perdue@ilnd.uscourts.gov
Judicial Assistant **Steven Schell** . . . . (312) 435-5615
E-mail: steven_schell@ilnd.uscourts.gov

Chambers of Magistrate Judge Sheila M. Finnegan

Everett McKinley Dirksen U.S. Courthouse, 219 South Dearborn Street, Room 2206, Chicago, IL 60604
Tel: (312) 435-5657
E-mail: sheila_finnegan@ilnd.uscourts.gov

Sheila M. Finnegan
Magistrate Judge

Education: Georgetown 1982 BA; Chicago 1986 JD
Began Service: 2010
Term Expires: 2018

Staff

Law Clerk **Andrew Gordon** . . . . (312) 408-5157
E-mail: andrew_gordon@ilnd.uscourts.gov
Career Law Clerk **Allison M. Engel** . . . . (312) 408-5056
E-mail: allison_engel@ilnd.uscourts.gov
Education: Northwestern 1993 BA; Washington U (MO) 1996 JD
Courtroom Deputy **Imelda Saccomonto** . . . . (312) 408-5110
E-mail: imelda_saccomonto@ilnd.uscourts.gov

Chambers of Magistrate Judge Young B. Kim

Everett McKinley Dirksen U.S. Courthouse, 219 South Dearborn Street, Room 1000, Chicago, IL 60604
Tel: (312) 408-5168 Fax: (312) 554-8051

Young B. Kim
Magistrate Judge

Education: Loyola U (Chicago) 1991 JD
Began Service: May 7, 2010

Staff

Law Clerk **Angela Bradley "Anna" Debush** . . . . (312) 435-5168
Education: Chicago 2004 JD
Law Clerk **Daniel Kim** . . . . (312) 435-5168
E-mail: daniel_kim@ilnd.uscourts.gov
Law Clerk **Vivian Saptharee** . . . . (312) 435-5168
E-mail: vivian_saptharee@ilnd.uscourts.gov
Courtroom Deputy **Michelle Alston** . . . . (312) 408-5168
Room 1922
E-mail: michelle_alston@ilnd.uscourts.gov

Chambers of Magistrate Judge Jeffrey T. Gilbert
Everett McKinley Dirksen U.S. Courthouse, 219 South Dearborn Street, Room 1366, Chicago, IL 60604
Tel: (312) 435-5672 Fax: (312) 554-8063
E-mail: jeffrey_gilbert@ilnd.uscourts.gov

Jeffrey T. Gilbert
Magistrate Judge

Education: Northwestern 1980 JD
Began Service: May 7, 2010

Staff
Law Clerk **Amanda Catalano** .... (312) 435-5672
E-mail: amanda_catalano@ilnd.uscourts.gov
Law Clerk **Catherine Cook** .... (312) 435-5672
E-mail: catherine_cook@ilnd.uscourts.gov
Courtroom Deputy **Brenda Rinozzi** .... (312) 408-5024
E-mail: brenda_rinozzi@ilnd.uscourts.gov
Judicial Assistant **Pat Hagenmaier** .... (312) 435-5672

Chambers of Magistrate Judge Daniel G. Martin
219 South Dearborn Street, Chicago, IL 60604
Tel: (312) 435-5354 Fax: (312) 554-8071

Magistrate Judge **Daniel G. Martin**

Staff
Law Clerk **John Fischer** .... (312) 435-5354
Law Clerk **Margaret Lipman** .... (312) 435-5354
Education: Northwestern 1993 JD; UCLA 1990 BA
Courtroom Deputy **Lynette M. Santiago** .... (312) 435-5354

Chambers of Magistrate Judge Mary M. Rowland
219 South Dearborn Street, Chicago, IL 60604
Tel: (312) 435-5358

Mary M. Rowland
Magistrate Judge

Staff
Law Clerk **Christopher Campbell** .... (312) 435-5358
Law Clerk **Lina Powell** .... (312) 435-5358
Courtroom Deputy **Maya Burke** .... (312) 435-5358

Chambers of Magistrate Judge Iain D. Johnston
327 South Church Street, Rockford, IL 61101
Tel: (815) 987-4255

Iain D. Johnston
Magistrate Judge

Staff
Law Clerk **Charles Beveridge** .... (815) 987-4255
Education: Illinois (Chicago) 1996 JD
Law Clerk **Jamie Noble** .... (815) 987-4255
E-mail: jamie_noble@ilnd.uscourts.gov

United States Bankruptcy Court for the Northern District of Illinois
Everett McKinley Dirksen U.S. Courthouse, 219 South Dearborn Street, Chicago, IL 60604-1702
U.S. Bankruptcy Court, 327 South Church Street, Rockford, IL 61101
Tel: (800) 676-6856 (PACER)
Tel: (866) 222-8029 (Chicago and Rockford McVCIS)
Tel: (312) 408-5000 (Customer Service)
Internet: www.ilnb.uscourts.gov

Number of Judgeships: 11

Court Staff
Clerk of Court **Jeffrey P. Allsteadt** .... (312) 435-6036
E-mail: jeffrey_allsteadt@ilnb.uscourts.gov
Education: Central Michigan 2000 MSA
Deputy-in-Charge **Ray Matlock** .... (779) 772-8322
327 Church Street, Rockford, IL 61101
E-mail: ray_matlock@ilnb.uscourts.gov
Staff Law Clerk **Susana Heredia** .... (312) 725-1026
E-mail: susana_heredia@ilnb.uscourts.gov
Staff Law Clerk **Igor Shleypak** .... (312) 435-7589
E-mail: igor_shleypak@ilnb.uscourts.gov
Information Technology Manager **Steve Horvath** .... (312) 408-7761
E-mail: steve_horvath@ilnb.uscourts.gov
Operations Manager **Jean Dalicandro** .... (312) 435-5680
E-mail: jean_dalicandro@ilnb.uscourts.gov
Public & Courtroom Service Manager
Adrienne Atkins .... (312) 435-6037
E-mail: adrienne_atkins@ilnb.uscourts.gov
Chief Deputy for Administration **Sharon Zurowski** ...... (312) 435-5711
E-mail: sharon_zurowski@ilnb.uscourts.gov
Fiscal Administrator **Fred Horn** .... (312) 435-5622
Court Reporter **Jackie DeFini** .... (312) 987-9722

Chambers of Chief Bankruptcy Judge Bruce W. Black
Everett McKinley Dirksen U.S. Courthouse, 219 South Dearborn Street, Room 756, Chicago, IL 60604
Tel: (312) 435-6867 Fax: (312) 408-5113
E-mail: bruce_black@ilnb.uscourts.gov

Bruce W. Black
Chief Bankruptcy Judge

Education: Bradley 1966 BA; Illinois 1971 JD
Began Service: August 13, 2001
Term Expires: August 12, 2029

Clerkships: Law Clerk The Honorable Robert D. Morgan, United States District Court for the Central District of Illinois (1971-1972)

Government: Assistant State's Attorney, Office of the State Attorney, State of Illinois (1975-1976); State's Attorney, State of Illinois (1976-1985)

Judicial: Circuit Judge, Tenth Judicial Circuit of Illinois (1985-2001)

Staff
Career Law Clerk **Mary Wilson Barry** .... (312) 435-6867
E-mail: Mary_Barry@ilnb.uscourts.gov
Education: John Marshall 2004 JD
Courtroom Deputy **Shurray Winston** .... (312) 435-6868
E-mail: Shurray_Davis@ilnb.uscourts.gov
Judicial Assistant **Linda Montano** .... (312) 435-6867
Began Service: January 2012
E-mail: linda_montano@ilnb.uscourts.gov

Chambers of Bankruptcy Judge Jack B. Schmetterer

Everett McKinley Dirksen U.S. Courthouse, 219 South Dearborn Street, Room 600, Chicago, IL 60604
Tel: (312) 435-5654
E-mail: jack_schmetterer@ilnb.uscourts.gov

Jack B. Schmetterer
Bankruptcy Judge

Date of Birth: 1931
Education: Yale 1952 BA, 1955 LLB, 1955 JD
Began Service: May 9, 1985

Academic: Instructor, Yale University (1954-1955); Instructor, University Georgia (1957-1958); Visiting Professor, University of Illinois, Chicago Circle Campus (1974-1978)

Government: Assistant U.S. Attorney, Illinois - Northern District, Executive Office for United States Attorneys, United States Department of Justice (1963-1970); Assistant U.S. Attorney, Illinois - Northern District, Executive Office for United States Attorneys, United States Department of Justice (1966-1968); First Assistant U.S. Attorney, Illinois - Northern District, Executive Office for United States Attorneys, United States Department of Justice (1968-1970); First Assistant State's Attorney, Office of the State's Attorney, County of Cook, Illinois (1971-1973); Trustee, Board of Trustees, Village of Northbrook, Illinois (1984-1985)

Legal Practice: Partner, Schmetterer & Schmetterer (1958-1963); Partner, Freeman, Schmetterer, Freeman & Salzman (1970-1971); Partner, Gottlieb & Schwartz (1973-1985)

Military Service: United States Army (1956-1958)

Current Memberships: American Bar Association; The Decalogue Society of Lawyers; Federal Bar Association; The John Howard Association; Board of Directors, Just the Beginning Foundation; Lawyers Club of Chicago

Staff

Law Clerk **Susana Heredia** .... (312) 435-6004
Began Service: August 15, 2015 Fax: (312) 554-8910
Term Expires: August 2016
E-mail: susana_heredia@ilnb.uscourts.gov
Courtroom Deputy **Deborah Smith** .... (312) 435-5655
E-mail: deborah_smith@ilnb.uscourts.gov Fax: (312) 554-8910
Court Reporter **Jacqueline DeFini** .... (312) 987-9722
Judicial Assistant **Dorothy Clay** .... (312) 435-5654
E-mail: dorothy_clay@ilnb.uscourts.gov Fax: (312) 554-8910

Chambers of Bankruptcy Judge Carol A. Doyle

Everett McKinley Dirksen U.S. Courthouse, 219 South Dearborn Street, Room 738, Chicago, IL 60604
Tel: (312) 435-6010
E-mail: carol_doyle@ilnb.uscourts.gov

Carol A. Doyle
Bankruptcy Judge

Education: Iowa 1978 BBA; Loyola U (Chicago) 1982 JD
Began Service: July 26, 1999
Term Expires: July 2027

Staff

Career Law Clerk **Erica Wax** .... (312) 435-6010
Began Service: September 2013
Courtroom Deputy **Tina Devine** .... (312) 435-5676
E-mail: tina_devine@ilnb.uscourts.gov
Judicial Assistant **Peter Castaneda** .... (312) 435-6010

Chambers of Bankruptcy Judge Pamela S. Hollis

Everett McKinley Dirksen U.S. Courthouse, 219 South Dearborn Street, Chambers 648, Chicago, IL 60604
Tel: (312) 435-5534
E-mail: pamela_hollis@ilnb.uscourts.gov

Pamela S. Hollis
Bankruptcy Judge

Date of Birth: June 14, 1954
Education: Illinois 1976 BS; Loyola Marymount 1979 JD
Began Service: January 27, 2003
Term Expires: January 2017

Corporate: Principal, Digital Lawyer Ltd.

Judicial: Member, American Bar Association

Legal Practice: Partner, Hollis and Johnson; Partner, Hinshaw & Culbertson LLP; Law Office of Pamela Hollis

Current Memberships: American Bankruptcy Institute; The Florida Bar; The National Association of Bankruptcy Trustees

Staff

Career Law Clerk **Debbie Silverstein** .... (312) 435-6009
E-mail: debbie_silverstein@ilnb.uscourts.gov
Courtroom Deputy **Steven Beckerman** .... (312) 435-5535
E-mail: steven_beckerman@ilnb.uscourts.gov
Judicial Assistant **Amy Sojka** .... (312) 435-5534
E-mail: amy_sojka@ilnb.uscourts.gov

Chambers of Bankruptcy Judge A. Benjamin Goldgar

Everett McKinley Dirksen U.S. Courthouse, 219 South Dearborn Street, Room 638, Chicago, IL 60604-1702
Tel: (312) 435-5642 Fax: (312) 408-5188
E-mail: ABenjamin_Goldgar@ilnb.uscourts.gov

A. Benjamin Goldgar
Bankruptcy Judge

Date of Birth: January 1957
Education: Brown U 1979 AB; Northwestern 1982 JD
Began Service: February 3, 2003
Term Expires: February 2, 2017

Government: Assistant Attorney General, Civil Appeals Division, Office of the Attorney General, State of Illinois (1995-2003); Supervising Attorney, Civil Appeals Division, Office of the Attorney General, State of Illinois (1997-2003)

Legal Practice: Keck, Mahin & Cate (1982-1995)

Nonprofit: President, Illinois Appellate Lawyers Association (2001-2002)

Current Memberships: American Bankruptcy Institute; American Bar Association; Appellate Lawyers Association; The Chicago Bar Association; The Seventh Circuit Bar Association, Federal Bar Association; Illinois State Bar Association; National Conference of Bankruptcy Judges

Staff

Law Clerk **Kimberly L. Krawczyk** .... (312) 435-6005
Began Service: 2012
E-mail: kim_krawczyk@ilnb.uscourts.gov
Education: Loyola U (Chicago) 1984 BS; John Marshall 1989 JD
Law Clerk **Brendan Gage** .... (312) 435-6005
Began Service: 2013
Courtroom Deputy **Nancy Castellano** .... (312) 435-5531

Chambers of Bankruptcy Judge Jacqueline P. Cox

Everett McKinley Dirksen U.S. Courthouse, 219 South Dearborn Street, Chambers 676, Chicago, IL 60604-1702
Tel: (312) 435-5679
E-mail: Jacqueline_Cox@ilnb.uscourts.gov

Jacqueline P. Cox
Bankruptcy Judge

Education: Cornell 1971 BA; Boston U 1974 JD
Began Service: February 3, 2003
Term Expires: February 2, 2017

Government: Defense Attorney, Office of the Public Defender, County of Mercer, New Jersey (1976-1977); Defense Attorney, Office of the State's Attorney, County of Cook, Illinois (1978-1984); Attorney, Law Department, City of Chicago, Illinois (1984-1988); Attorney, Law Department, Housing Authority, City of Chicago, Illinois (1988)

Judicial: Judge, Circuit Court of Cook County, Illinois (1988-2003); Judge, 1st Municipal District, Circuit Court of Cook County, Illinois

Current Memberships: American Bankruptcy Institute; American Bar Association; Association of Black Women Lawyers of Chicago, Inc.; The Chicago Bar Association; Chicago Council of Lawyers; Cook County Bar Association; Illinois Judges Association; Illinois Judicial Council; Illinois State Bar Association; Board of Directors, Just the Beginning Foundation; Lawyers Club of Chicago; National Bar Association; National Conference of Bankruptcy Judges; Women's Bar Association of Illinois

Staff
Law Clerk **Sandra Carolina** . . . . (312) 435-5643
Began Service: 2015
E-mail: sandra_carolina@ilnb.uscourts.gov
Courtroom Deputy **Josephine Green** . . . . (312) 435-5651
E-mail: josephine_green@ilnb.uscourts.gov
Judicial Assistant **Sylvia Stallworth** . . . . (312) 435-5679
E-mail: sylvia_stallworth@ilnb.uscourts.gov

Chambers of Bankruptcy Judge Donald R. Cassling

Everett McKinley Dirksen U.S. Courthouse, 219 South Dearborn Street, Room 656, Chicago, IL 60604
Tel: (312) 435-6056
E-mail: donald_cassling@ilnb.uscourts.gov

Donald R. Cassling
Bankruptcy Judge

Education: Duke 1973 AB; Chicago 1976 JD
Began Service: 2012

Staff
Law Clerk **Lana Koroleva** . . . . (312) 435-6013
Law Clerk **Susan Pistorius** . . . . (312) 435-7591
Education: DePaul 1987 JD
Courtroom Deputy **Shenitha Burton** . . . . (312) 435-7576

Chambers of Bankruptcy Judge Janet S. Baer

Everett McKinley Dirksen U.S. Courthouse, 219 South Dearborn Street, Room 662, Chicago, IL 60604
Tel: (312) 435-6054

Janet S. Baer
Bankruptcy Judge

Education: Wisconsin 1979 BA; DePaul 1982 JD
Began Service: 2012

Staff
Law Clerk **Christopher Pullman** . . . . (312) 435-6054
E-mail: christopher_pullman@ilnb.uscourts.gov

Chambers of Bankruptcy Judge Janet S. Baer *continued*

Law Clerk **Naomi Kogan Dein** . . . . (312) 435-6054
Courtroom Deputy **Anthony Watson** . . . . (312) 435-5653

Chambers of Bankruptcy Judge Timothy A. Barnes

Everett McKinley Dirksen U.S. Courthouse, 219 South Dearborn Street, Room 668, Chicago, IL 60604
Tel: (312) 435-5646

Timothy A. Barnes
Bankruptcy Judge

Education: Miami U (OH) 1989 BA; Ohio State 1992 MA, 1995 JD
Began Service: 2012

Staff
Law Clerk **Caitlin Cahow** . . . . (312) 435-5646
Law Clerk **Lauren Hargrove** . . . . (312) 435-6006
Courtroom Deputy **Annette McClendon** . . . . (312) 435-5647

Chambers of Bankruptcy Judge Thomas M. Lynch

327 South Church Street, Rockford, IL 61101
Tel: (815) 987-4366

Thomas M. Lynch
Bankruptcy Judge

Staff
Law Clerk **John Hardison** . . . . (815) 987-4366
Education: Chicago 1997 BA; Michigan 2005 JD
Law Clerk **Devvrat Sinha** . . . . (815) 987-4366
Courtroom Deputy **Mimi Kuczynski** . . . . (779) 772-8619

United States District Court for the Southern District of Illinois

Melvin Price Federal Courthouse, 750 Missouri Avenue, East St. Louis, IL 62201
Benton Federal Building and U.S. Courthouse, 301 West Main Street, Benton, IL 62812 (Divisional Office)
Tel: (618) 482-9371 Tel: (618) 439-7760 (Benton)
Tel: (866) 867-3169 (CM/ECF East St. Louis)
Tel: (866) 222-2104 (CM/ECF Benton)
Tel: (800) 676-6856 (PACER) Fax: (618) 482-9383
Internet: www.ilsd.uscourts.gov

Number of Judgeships: 4

Circuit: Seventh

Areas Covered: Counties of Alexander, Bond, Calhoun, Clark, Clay, Clinton, Crawford, Cumberland, Edwards, Effingham, Fayette, Franklin, Gallatin, Hamilton, Hardin, Jackson, Jasper, Jefferson, Jersey, Johnson, Lawrence, Madison, Marion, Massac, Monroe, Perry, Pope, Pulaski, Randolph, Richland, Saline, Saint Clair, Union, Wabash, Washington, Wayne, White and Williamson

Court Staff

Clerk of Court (Acting) **Justine Flanagan** . . . . (618) 482-9172
E-mail: justine_flanagan@ilsd.uscourts.gov Fax: (618) 482-9383
Education: Webster 2004 MBA
Chief Deputy **Justine Flanagan** . . . . (618) 482-9373
E-mail: justine_flanagan@ilsd.uscourts.gov Fax: (618) 482-9383
Director of Information Technology
Thomas Galbraith . . . . (618) 482-9188
E-mail: thomas_galbraith@ilsd.uscourts.gov
Operations Supervisor **Mona Zingrich** . . . . (618) 482-9012
E-mail: mona_zingrich@ilsd.uscourts.gov
Property and Procurement **Anne Hale** . . . . (618) 482-9435
Fax: (618) 482-9450
Jury Administrator **Denise Lameyer** . . . . (618) 482-9160
E-mail: denise_lameyer@ilsd.uscourts.gov

(continued on next page)

FEDERAL COURTS—UNITED STATES DISTRICT COURTS

United States District Court for the Southern District of Illinois *continued*

Financial Specialist **Donna Bauer** . . . . (618) 482-9041
E-mail: donna_bauer@ilsd.uscourts.gov Fax: (618) 482-9499
Financial Specialist **Dawn Lawrence** . . . . (618) 482-9446
E-mail: dawn_lawrence@ilsd.uscourts.gov Fax: (618) 482-9499
Human Resources Manager **JoAnn M. Holdener** . . . . (618) 482-9425
E-mail: joann_holdener@ilsd.uscourts.gov Fax: (618) 482-9383
Librarian **Chris Tighe** . . . . (618) 482-9477
E-mail: chris_tighe@lb7.uscourts.gov Fax: (618) 482-9234
Education: Missouri 1996 MALS
Chief Probation Officer **John M. Koechner** . . . . (618) 439-4828

Chambers of Chief Judge Michael J. Reagan

Melvin Price Federal Courthouse, 750 Missouri Avenue, Room 220, East St. Louis, IL 62201
Tel: (618) 482-9225 Fax: (618) 482-9126

Michael J. Reagan
Chief Judge

Date of Birth: 1954
Education: Bradley 1976 BS; Saint Louis U 1980 JD
Began Service: October 23, 2000
Appointed By: President William J. Clinton

Staff

Law Clerk **Michael Armstrong** . . . . (618) 482-9485
E-mail: michael_armstrong@ilsd.uscourts.gov
Education: Washington U (MO) JD
Law Clerk **John L. Steffan** . . . . (618) 482-9424
E-mail: john_steffan@ilsd.uscourts.gov
Career Law Clerk **Sheila O'Malley Hunsicker** . . . . (618) 482-9229
E-mail: sheila_hunsicker@ilsd.uscourts.gov
Education: Eastern Illinois 1982 BA; Southern Illinois 1987 JD
Court Reporter **Barbara Kniepmann** . . . . (618) 482-9482
Courtroom Deputy **Debbie DeRousse** . . . . (618) 482-9298
E-mail: debbie_derousse@ilsd.uscourts.gov

Chambers of District Judge David R. Herndon

Melvin Price Federal Courthouse, 750 Missouri Avenue, East St. Louis, IL 62201
Tel: (618) 482-9077 Fax: (618) 482-9195
E-mail: judge_herndon@ilsd.uscourts.gov

David R. Herndon
District Judge

Date of Birth: 1953
Education: Southern IL Edwardsville 1974 BA; Southern Illinois 1977 JD
Began Service: November 16, 1998
Appointed By: President William J. Clinton
Political Affiliation: Democrat

Current Memberships: Alton-Wood River Jerseyville Bar Association; American Bar Association; Federal Judges Association; Illinois State Bar Association; Madison County Bar Association; The Missouri Bar

Staff

Law Clerk **Leigh M. Perica** . . . . (618) 482-9484
Began Service: 2014
E-mail: leigh_perica@ilsd.uscourts.gov
Law Clerk **Debra Ward** . . . . (618) 482-9484
Began Service: 2012
E-mail: debra_ward@ilsd.uscourts.gov
Senior Law Clerk **Katherine L. Hoffman** . . . . (618) 482-9192
E-mail: katie_hoffman@ilsd.uscourts.gov
Education: Mississippi 1993 BA; Saint Louis U 1996 JD
Court Reporter **Laura Esposito** . . . . (618) 482-9481
E-mail: laura_esposito@ilsd.uscourts.gov
Courtroom Deputy Clerk **Caitlin Fischer** . . . . (618) 482-9013
E-mail: caitlin_fischer@ilsd.uscourts.gov

Chambers of District Judge Nancy J. Rosenstengel

750 Missouri Avenue, East St. Louis, IL 62201
Tel: (618) 482-9172
E-mail: nancy_rosenstengel@ilsd.uscourts.gov

Nancy J. Rosenstengel
District Judge

Education: Illinois 1990 BA; Southern Illinois 1993 JD
Began Service: May 19, 2014
Appointed By: President Barack Obama

Staff

Law Clerk **Blaire Klehm** . . . . (618) 482-9485
E-mail: blaire_klehm@ilsd.uscourts.gov
Law Clerk **Nicholas Lawson** . . . . (618) 482-9390
E-mail: nicholas_lawson@ilsd.uscourts.gov
Law Clerk **Kristen Henke** . . . . (618) 482-9072
E-mail: kristen_henke@ilsd.uscourts.gov
Courtroom Deputy **Deana Brinkley** . . . . (618) 482-9342
E-mail: deana_brinkley@ilsd.uscourts.gov

Chambers of District Judge Staci Michelle Yandle

750 Missouri Avenue, East St. Louis, IL 62201
Tel: (618) 439-7740 Fax: (618) 438-0217

Staci Michelle Yandle
District Judge

Education: Illinois 1983 BS; Vanderbilt 1987 JD
Began Service: June 19, 2014
Appointed By: President Barack Obama

Staff

Law Clerk **Christine Hummert** . . . . (618) 439-7742
E-mail: christine_hummert@ilsd.uscourts.gov
Law Clerk **(Vacant)** . . . . (618) 439-7742
Law Clerk **Rebecca Warren** . . . . (618) 439-7742
E-mail: rebecca_warren@ilsd.uscourts.gov
Court Reporter **Christine Dohack** . . . . (618) 439-7725
E-mail: christine_dohack@ilsd.uscourts.gov
Courtroom Deputy **Kailyn Kramer** . . . . (618) 439-7744
E-mail: kailyn_kramer@ilsd.uscourts.gov

Chambers of Magistrate Judge Philip M. Frazier

Benton Federal Building and U.S. Courthouse, 301 West Main Street, Benton, IL 62812
Tel: (618) 439-7750 Fax: (618) 439-6325

Philip M. Frazier
Magistrate Judge

Education: Southern Illinois 1980 JD
Began Service: 1987
Term Expires: May 2019

Staff

Career Law Clerk **Karen Stallman** . . . . (618) 439-7752
E-mail: karen_stallman@ilsd.uscourts.gov
Education: Southern Illinois 1982 JD
Courtroom Deputy **Karen R. Metheney** . . . . (618) 439-7754
E-mail: karen_metheney@ilsd.uscourts.gov

Chambers of Magistrate Judge Donald G. Wilkerson
750 Missouri Avenue, East St. Louis, IL 62201
Tel: (618) 482-9380 Fax: (618) 482-9277

Donald G. Wilkerson
Magistrate Judge

Education: Illinois State 1973 BS; Southern Illinois 1978 MSEd; Saint Louis U 1993 JD
Began Service: January 4, 2005
Term Expires: January 3, 2019

Staff
Law Clerk **Natalie Stoltz** . . . . (618) 482-9278
E-mail: natalie_stoltz@ilsd.uscourts.gov
Career Law Clerk **Sona Patel** . . . . (618) 482-9382
E-mail: sona_patel@ilsd.uscourts.gov
Education: Emory 2001 JD
Courtroom Deputy **Jackie Payton** . . . . (618) 482-9376
E-mail: jackie_payton@ilsd.uscourts.gov

Chambers of Magistrate Judge Stephen C. Williams
750 Missouri Avenue, East St. Louis, IL 62201
Tel: (618) 482-9467 Fax: (618) 482-9383

Stephen C. Williams
Magistrate Judge

Began Service: 2011

Staff
Law Clerk **Amber Jeralds** . . . . (618) 482-9469
E-mail: amber_jeralds@ilsd.uscourts.gov
Education: Southern Illinois 2008 JD
Law Clerk **Jennifer Pitzer** . . . . (618) 482-9436
E-mail: jennifer_pitzer@ilsd.uscourts.gov
Courtroom Deputy Clerk **Angela "Angie" Vehlewald** . . . (618) 482-9419
E-mail: angie_vehlewald@ilsd.uscourts.gov

Chambers of Magistrate Judge Clifford J. Proud
Melvin Price Federal Courthouse, 750 Missouri Avenue, East St. Louis, IL 62201
Tel: (618) 482-9006 Fax: (618) 482-9010

Clifford J. Proud
Magistrate Judge

Date of Birth: 1945
Education: Saint Louis U 1972 JD
Began Service: February 28, 1994
Term Expires: February 27, 2018

Government: Assistant United States Attorney, Southern District of Illinois, United States Department of Justice (1976-1983); First Assistant United States Attorney, Southern District of Illinois, United States Department of Justice (1983-1993); United States Attorney, Southern District of Illinois, United States Department of Justice (1993)

Legal Practice: Private Practice (1972-1973); Private Practice (1974-1975)

Military Service: United States Marine Corps Reserve

Current Memberships: Illinois State Bar Association; Madison County Bar Association; The Missouri Bar

Staff
Career Law Clerk **Joan M. Tanner** . . . . (618) 482-9006
E-mail: joan_tanner@ilsd.uscourts.gov
Education: Saint Louis U 1983 JD

Chambers of Senior Judge J. Phil Gilbert
Benton Federal Building and U.S. Courthouse, 301 West Main Street, Benton, IL 62812
Tel: (618) 439-7720 Fax: (618) 435-2775

J. Phil Gilbert
Senior Judge

Date of Birth: 1949
Education: Illinois 1971 BS; Loyola U (Chicago) 1974 JD
Began Service: October 1, 1992
Appointed By: President George H.W. Bush

Current Memberships: Illinois State Bar Association; Jackson County Bar Association

Staff
Law Clerk **Sandra Cook** . . . . (618) 439-7723
Began Service: September 2012
Term Expires: September 2016
E-mail: sandra_cook@ilsd.uscourts.gov
Career Law Clerk **Tracy L. Prosser** . . . . (618) 439-7722
E-mail: tracy_prosser@ilsd.uscourts.gov
Education: Michigan 1995 JD
Court Reporter **Stephanie Rennegarbe** . . . . (618) 439-7725
E-mail: stephanie_rennegarbe@ilsd.uscourts.gov
Courtroom Deputy **K. Jane Reynolds** . . . . (618) 439-7724
Judicial Assistant **Jina Hoyt** . . . . (618) 439-7721
E-mail: jina_hoyt@ilsd.uscourts.gov

United States Bankruptcy Court for the Southern District of Illinois
Melvin Price Federal Courthouse, 750 Missouri Avenue, East St. Louis, IL 62201
Tel: (618) 482-9400 Tel: (618) 482-9114 (PACER)
Tel: (618) 482-9365 (Voice Case Information System VCIS)
Tel: (800) 726-5622 (Toll Free Voice Case Information System VCIS)
Tel: (618) 425-2200 (Benton Divisional Office)
Internet: www.ilsb.uscourts.gov

Number of Judgeships: 1

Court Staff
Bankruptcy Clerk **Donna N. Beyersdorfer** . . . . (618) 482-9427
E-mail: donna_beyersdorfer@ilsb.uscourts.gov
Secretary to the Clerk **(Vacant)** . . . . (618) 482-9423
Chief Deputy Clerk **Kathy McCallister** . . . . (618) 482-9427
E-mail: kathy_mccallister@ilsb.uscourts.gov
Deputy-in-Charge - Benton **Katherine Hutchens** . . . . (618) 439-7607
Federal Courthouse, 301 W. Main St., Benton, IL 62812
E-mail: kathy_hutchens@ilsb.uscourts.gov
Information Systems Manager **Jeremy Korbitt** . . . . (618) 482-9308
E-mail: jeremy_korbitt@ilsb.uscourts.gov

Chambers of Bankruptcy Judge Laura K. Grandy
750 Missouri Avenue, East St. Louis, IL 62201
Tel: (618) 482-9401
E-mail: laura_grandy@ilsb.uscourts.gov

Laura K. Grandy
Bankruptcy Judge

Began Service: 2010

Staff
Career Law Clerk **Rebecca S. Brown** . . . . (618) 482-9401
E-mail: rebecca_brown@ilsb.uscourts.gov
Education: Southern Illinois 1992 JD
Law Clerk **Dan Shesner** . . . . (618) 482-9401

Chambers of Bankruptcy Judge (visiting) William V. Altenberger

216 Federal Building, 100 NE Monroe Street, Peoria, IL 61602
Tel: (309) 671-7290

William V. Altenberger
Bankruptcy Judge (visiting)

Date of Birth: 1935
Education: Illinois 1957 BS, 1963 LLB
Began Service: May 2000

Affiliation: Bankruptcy Judge (recalled), Chambers of Bankruptcy Judge (recalled) William V. Altenberger, United States Bankruptcy Court for the Central District of Illinois

Judicial: Bankruptcy Judge (visiting), United States Bankruptcy Court for the Northern District of Indiana

Legal Practice: Kavanagh, Scully, Sudow, White & Frederick (1964-1985)

Military Service: United States Air Force (1957-1960)

United States District Court for the Northern District of Indiana

Robert A. Grant U.S. Courthouse, 204 South Main Street, Room 102, South Bend, IN 46601-2119
Tel: (574) 246-8000 Tel: (800) 371-8843 (Toll Free PACER)
Fax: (574) 246-8002
Internet: www.innd.uscourts.gov

Number of Judgeships: 5

Circuit: Seventh

Court Staff

Clerk of Court **Robert N. Trgovich** .... (574) 246-8000
E-mail: robert_trgovich@innd.uscourts.gov

Chief Deputy Clerk **Todd Steiner** .... (219) 852-6500
5400 Federal Plaza, Hammond, IN 46320-1840 Fax: (219) 852-6509

Deputy Clerk-in-Charge - Fort Wayne **Linda Walker** ..... (260) 423-3000
1108 East Ross Adair Federal Building. &
U.S. Courthouse, 1300 South Harrison Street,
Fort Wayne, IN 46802-3435
E-mail: linda_walker@innd.uscourts.gov

Deputy Clerk-in-Charge - Hammond **Kurt Koch** .... (219) 852-6500
5400 Federal Plaza, Hammond, IN 46320-1840
E-mail: kurt_koch@innd.uscourts.gov

Deputy Clerk-in-Charge - Lafayette **Kurt Koch** .... (765) 420-6250
P.O. Box 1498, Lafayette, IN 47902 Fax: (765) 420-6273
E-mail: kurt_koch@innd.uscourts.gov

Deputy Clerk-in-Charge - South Bend **Linda Walker** ..... (574) 246-8000
E-mail: linda_walker@innd.uscourts.gov

Chief Probation Officer **Derek Plants** .... (219) 852-3620
5400 Federal Plaza, Hammond, IN 46320-1840
E-mail: derek_plants@innd.uscourts.gov

Librarian **Jon Fox** .... (574) 246-8050

Chambers of Chief Judge Philip P. Simon

5400 Federal Plaza, Suite 4400, Hammond, IN 46320-1840
Tel: (219) 852-6740
E-mail: simon_chambers@innd.uscourts.gov

Philip P. Simon
Chief Judge

Date of Birth: July 7, 1962
Education: Iowa 1984 BA; Indiana 1987 JD
Began Service: March 31, 2003
Appointed By: President George W. Bush

Government: Assistant U.S. Attorney, Indiana Northern District, United States Attorney's Office, United States Department of Justice, George H.W. Bush Administration (1990-1997); Assistant U.S. Attorney, District of Arizona, United States Attorney's Office, United States Department of Justice, William J. Clinton Administration (1997-1999); Assistant U.S. Attorney and Chief, Criminal Division, Northern District of Indiana, United States Attorney's Office, United States Department of Justice, William J. Clinton Administration (1999-2003)

Legal Practice: Associate, Kirkland & Ellis LLP (1987-1990)

Nonprofit: Adjunct Professor of Law, School of Law, Valparaiso University (1996-1997); Adjunct Professor of Law, School of Law, Valparaiso University (1999-2000)

Staff

Law Clerk **Allyson Spacht** .... (219) 852-6740
Began Service: September 2015
Term Expires: September 2016
E-mail: allyson_spacht@innd.uscourts.gov

Law Clerk **Shay-Ann Heiser Singh** .... (219) 852-6740
Began Service: September 2015
Term Expires: September 2017

Law Clerk **Lauren Schwartz** .... (219) 852-6740
Began Service: March 2014
Term Expires: June 2016
E-mail: lauren_schwartz@innd.uscourts.gov

Law Clerk **Denise Woodside** .... (219) 852-6740
E-mail: denise_woodside@innd.uscourts.gov

Case Manager **Noel Collins** .... (219) 852-6724

Court Reporter **Stacy Drohosky** .... (219) 852-6728

Chambers of District Judge Robert L. Miller, Jr.

Robert A. Grant U.S. Courthouse, 204 South Main Street, Room 325, South Bend, IN 46601
Tel: (574) 246-8080
E-mail: robert_miller@innd.uscourts.gov

Robert L. Miller, Jr.
District Judge

Date of Birth: 1950
Education: Northwestern 1972 BA; Indiana 1975 JD
Began Service: January 1986
Appointed By: President Ronald Reagan

Current Memberships: American Bar Association; The American Law Institute; Indiana State Bar Association; Saint Joseph County Bar Association

Staff

Law Clerk **Nick Snavely** .... (574) 246-8080
Began Service: August 2015
Term Expires: August 31, 2016

Career Law Clerk **Sheri Potts** .... (574) 246-8080
E-mail: sheri_potts@innd.uscourts.gov
Education: Purdue BA; Valparaiso 1983 JD

Career Law Clerk **Suzanne "Sue" Shead** .... (574) 246-8080
E-mail: Sue_Shead@innd.uscourts.gov
Education: Ball State BS; Valparaiso 1998 JD

Court Reporter **Debra Bonk** .... (574) 246-8039
E-mail: debra_bonk@innd.uscourts.gov

Chambers of District Judge Theresa L. Springmann
Ross Adair Courthouse, 1300 South Harrison Street,
Fort Wayne, IN 46802
Tel: (260) 423-3050 Fax: (260) 423-3055
E-mail: theresa_springmann@innd.uscourts.gov

Theresa L. Springmann
District Judge

Education: Indiana 1977 BA; Notre Dame 1980 JD
Began Service: June 24, 2003
Appointed By: President George W. Bush

Clerkships: Law Clerk The Honorable James T. Moody, United States District Court for the Northern District of Indiana (1980-1984)

Judicial: Magistrate Judge, United States District Court for the Northern District of Indiana (1995-2003)

Legal Practice: Partner and Member, Spangler, Jennings, Spangler & Dougherty (1984-1995)

Current Memberships: Allen County Bar Association; American Bar Association; The American Inns of Court; Federal Bar Association; Indiana State Bar Association

Staff
Law Clerk **Andrew DeMaio** .... (260) 423-3053
Began Service: August 2015
Term Expires: August 2017
E-mail: andrew_demaio@innd.uscourts.gov
Law Clerk **Matthew Kinsman** .... (260) 423-3058
Career Law Clerk **Maci Doden** .... (260) 423-3052
Began Service: June 12, 2003
E-mail: maci_doden@innd.uscourts.gov
Education: Valparaiso 1998 JD

Chambers of District Judge Joseph S. Van Bokkelen
5400 Federal Plaza, Suite 4200, Hammond, IN 46320-1840
Tel: (219) 852-6720
E-mail: joseph_vanbokkelen@innd.uscourts.gov

Joseph S. Van Bokkelen
District Judge

Date of Birth: 1943
Education: Indiana 1966 BA, 1969 JD
Began Service: July 20, 2007
Appointed By: President George W. Bush

Government: Deputy Attorney General, Office of the Attorney General, State of Indiana (1969-1970); Assistant Attorney General, Office of the Attorney General, State of Indiana (1971-1972); Assistant U.S. Attorney, Indiana - Northern District, United States Department of Justice (1972-1975)

Legal Practice: Partner, Wilson, Donnesberger, Van Bokkelen and Reid (1975-1978); Partner, Goodman, Ball, Van Bokkelen and Leonard (1978-2001)

Current Memberships: American Bar Association; Calumet American Inns of Court; Federal Bar Association; Indiana State Bar Association

Staff
Law Clerk **Brian Potts** .... (219) 852-6720
Began Service: August 2015
Term Expires: August 31, 2016
E-mail: brian_potts@innd.uscourts.gov
Career Law Clerk **Vilius Lapas** .... (219) 852-6720
E-mail: vilius_lapas@innd.uscourts.gov
Career Law Clerk **Gail Oosterhof** .... (219) 852-6720
E-mail: gail_oosterhof@innd.uscourts.gov
Courtroom Deputy **Irma Rivera** .... (219) 852-6744
E-mail: irma_rivera@innd.uscourts.gov

Chambers of District Judge Jon E. DeGuilio
Robert A. Grant U.S. Courthouse, 204 South Main Street,
Room 124, South Bend, IN 46601
Tel: (574) 246-8170 Fax: (574) 246-8002
E-mail: jon_deguilio@innd.uscourts.gov

Jon E. DeGuilio
District Judge

Education: Notre Dame 1977 BA; Valparaiso 1981 JD
Began Service: May 20, 2010
Appointed By: President Barack Obama

Government: Prosecutor, Office of the County Prosecutor, County of Lake, Indiana (1989-1993); U.S. Attorney, Indiana - Northern District, Executive Office for United States Attorneys, United States Department of Justice (1993-1999)

Staff
Law Clerk **Scott Quellhorst** .... (574) 246-8170
Term Expires: September 2016
Law Clerk **Jeff Kienstra** .... (574) 246-8170
Term Expires: September 2016
Career Law Clerk **Chanda J. Berta** .... (574) 246-8170
E-mail: chanda_berta@innd.uscourts.gov
Education: Valparaiso 2005 JD

Chambers of Senior Judge William C. Lee
2100 E. Ross Adair Federal Building & U.S. Courthouse,
1300 South Harrison Street, Fort Wayne, IN 46802
Tel: (260) 423-3030
E-mail: william_lee@innd.uscourts.gov

William C. Lee
Senior Judge

Date of Birth: 1938
Education: Yale 1959 BA; Chicago 1962 JD
Began Service: August 19, 1981
Appointed By: President Ronald Reagan

Government: Deputy Prosecuting Attorney, State of Indiana (1963-1969); Chief Deputy Prosecuting Attorney, State of Indiana (1966-1969); United States Attorney, Northern District of Indiana, United States Department of Justice (1970-1973)

Judicial: Chief Judge, United States District Court for the Northern District of Indiana

Legal Practice: Private Practice (1962-1964); Partner, Parry, Krueckeberg & Lee (1964-1970); Partner, Hunt, Suedhoff, Borror, Eilbacher & Lee (1973-1981)

Current Memberships: Allen County Bar Association; American Bar Association; American College of Trial Lawyers; Federal Bar Association; The Seventh Circuit Bar Association, Federal Bar Association; Indiana State Bar Association

Staff
Career Law Clerk **James "Jim" Berles** .... (260) 423-3030
Education: Texas Southern 1992 JD
Career Law Clerk **Lori Kuchmay** .... (260) 423-3031
E-mail: lori_kuchmay@innd.uscourts.gov
Education: Toledo 1995 BA, 1998 JD
Career Law Clerk **Wanda F. Reed** .... (260) 423-3030
E-mail: wanda_reed@innd.uscourts.gov
Education: Ancilla 1983 BA;
Franklin Col (IN) 1985 BA; Valparaiso 1989 JD

Chambers of Senior Judge James T. Moody

5400 Federal Plaza, Suite 4100, Hammond, IN 46320
Tel: (219) 852-3460 Fax: (219) 852-3461
E-mail: moody_chambers@innd.uscourts.gov

James T. Moody
Senior Judge

Education: Indiana 1960 AB, 1963 LLB
Began Service: February 24, 1982
Appointed By: President Ronald Reagan
Political Affiliation: Republican

Academic: Faculty, Business Law, Indiana University System (1977-1980)

Government: City Attorney, Office of the City Attorney, City of Lake Station, Indiana (1964-1973)

Judicial: Judge, Indiana Superior Court, Lake County (1973-1979); Magistrate Judge, United States District Court for the Northern District of Indiana (1979-1982)

Staff

Law Clerk **Rayna Styles** .... (219) 852-3460
Began Service: September 2010
Term Expires: September 2016
E-mail: rayna_styles@innd.uscourts.gov
Education: Chicago-Kent 2005 JD

Law Clerk **Andrew Pendexter** .... (219) 852-3460
Began Service: September 2011
Term Expires: September 2016
E-mail: andrew_pendexter@innd.uscourts.gov

Career Law Clerk **Greg Opfel** .... (219) 852-3460
E-mail: greg_opfel@innd.uscourts.gov
Education: Notre Dame 1985 JD

Chambers of Senior Judge Rudy Lozano

5400 Federal Plaza, Suite 4300, Hammond, IN 46320
Tel: (219) 852-3600 Fax: (219) 852-3610
E-mail: rudy_lozano@innd.uscourts.gov

Rudy Lozano
Senior Judge

Date of Birth: 1942
Education: Indiana 1963 BS, 1966 LLB
Began Service: March 1988
Appointed By: President Ronald Reagan

Legal Practice: Attorney, Spangler, Jennings, Spangler & Dougherty (1966-1988)

Military Service: United States Army Reserve, United States Department of the Army (1966-1973)

Current Memberships: American Association of Justice; American Bar Association; Federal Bar Association; Federal Judges Association; Hispanic Bar Association of Northwest Indiana; Indiana State Bar Association; National Hispanic Bar Association

Staff

Law Clerk **Elizabeth Moore** .... (219) 852-3600
Began Service: September 2008
E-mail: elizabeth_adamec@innd.uscourts.gov

Career Law Clerk **(Vacant)** .... (219) 852-3600

Career Law Clerk **Jennifer Ortiz** .... (219) 852-3600
E-mail: jennifer_ortiz@innd.uscourts.gov
Education: Valparaiso 2002 JD

Career Law Clerk **Kendra Shearer** .... (219) 852-3600
E-mail: kendra_shearer@innd.uscourts.gov
Education: Trinity U 1995 BA; Illinois 1998 JD

Court Reporter **Angela Phipps** .... (219) 852-6557
E-mail: angela_phipps@innd.uscourts.gov

Courtroom Deputy Clerk **Tiffany Rogers** .... (219) 852-3603
E-mail: tiffany_rogers@innd.uscourts.gov

Chambers of Magistrate Judge Christopher A. Nuechterlein

Robert A. Grant U.S. Courthouse, 204 South Main Street, Room 201, South Bend, IN 46601
Tel: (574) 246-8100 Fax: (574) 246-8106

Christopher A. Nuechterlein
Magistrate Judge

Date of Birth: 1951
Education: Valparaiso 1973 BA, 1976 JD
Began Service: January 10, 2000
Term Expires: January 10, 2016

Clerkships: Law Clerk The Honorable Allen Sharp, United States District Court for the Northern District of Indiana (1976-1978)

Government: Trial Attorney, Land and Natural Resources Division, United States Department of Justice (1983-1985); Trial Attorney, Criminal Division, Fraud Section, United States Department of Justice (1985-1989); Assistant Director, Attorney General's Advocacy Institute, United States Department of Justice (1987-1988); Assistant United States Attorney, Eastern District of California, United States Department of Justice (1989-1998); Assistant Commissioner and Chief Counsel, Health Plan Enforcement Division, California Department of Corporations (1998-2000)

Legal Practice: Yoder, Ainlay, Ulmer and Buckingham (1978-1981)

Current Memberships: The Robert A. Grant American Inn of Court, The American Inns of Court; Federal Magistrate Judges Association; Indiana State Bar Association; St. Joseph County Bar Association

Staff

Law Clerk **Candace C. Kilpinen** .... (574) 246-8101
Began Service: August 2012
Term Expires: August 2016
E-mail: candace_kilpinen@innd.uscourts.gov

Case Manager **Sharon Macon** .... (574) 246-8104

Judicial Assistant **Mary Lou Freitag** .... (574) 246-8100

Chambers of Magistrate Judge Paul R. Cherry

5400 Federal Plaza, Suite 3500, Hammond, IN 46320-1840
Tel: (219) 852-6700 Fax: (219) 852-6713
E-mail: cherry_chambers@innd.uscourts.gov

Paul R. Cherry
Magistrate Judge

Date of Birth: February 24, 1951
Education: Huntington Col 1973 BA; Ohio Northern 1977 JD
Began Service: October 1, 2003

Academic: Adjunct Instructor, Huntington University (1980-2003); Adjunct Professor, School of Law, Valparaiso University (2004-2006)

Government: Deputy Prosecuting Attorney, DeKalb County Prosecutor Office, County of DeKalb, Indiana (1980-1982); Prosecuting Attorney, DeKalb County Prosecutor Office, County of DeKalb, Indiana (1983-1988)

Judicial: Judge, Circuit Court, County of DeKalb, Indiana (1989-2003)

Nonprofit: Member, Board of Trustees, Huntington University (1984-2006); Chairman, Board of Trustees, Huntington University (1998-2004)

Current Memberships: DeKalb Bar Association; The Seventh Circuit Bar Association, Federal Bar Association; Federal Magistrate Judges Association

Staff

Law Clerk **Michael Buschbacher** .... (219) 852-6700

Career Law Clerk **Erin Goffette** .... (219) 852-6700
E-mail: erin_goffette@innd.uscourts.gov
Education: Valparaiso 1997 BA, 2003 JD

Chambers of Magistrate Judge John E. Martin
5400 Federal Plaza, Suite 3700, Hammond, IN 46320-1840
Tel: (219) 852-6610
E-mail: john_martin@innd.uscourts.gov

John E. Martin
Magistrate Judge

Staff
Law Clerk **Cathleen Phillips** .... (219) 852-6610
E-mail: cathleen_phillips@innd.uscourts.gov
Education: Virginia 2010 JD
Law Clerk **Adelaida Hernandez** .... (219) 852-6610
E-mail: adelaida_hernandez@innd.uscourts.gov
Case Manager **Pat Miller** .... (219) 852-6610
E-mail: pat_miller@innd.uscourts.gov

Chambers of Magistrate Judge Susan L. Collins
1300 South Harrison Street, Suite 1130, Fort Wayne, IN 46802
Tel: (260) 423-3042

Susan L. Collins
Magistrate Judge

Staff
Career Law Clerk **Cathy Niemeyer** .... (260) 423-3042
Education: Indiana 1986 BS, 1993 MBA; Indianapolis 1999 JD
Case Manager **Mary Renz** .... (260) 423-3047

Chambers of Magistrate Judge Andrew Rodovich
5400 Federal Plaza, Suite 3400, Hammond, IN 46320-1840
Tel: (219) 852-6600

Andrew P. Rodovich
Magistrate Judge

Date of Birth: 1948
Education: Valparaiso 1970 BA, 1973 JD
Political Affiliation: Republican

Current Memberships: Indiana State Bar Association; Lake County Bar Association (IN)

Staff
Law Clerk **Ryan O'Day** .... (219) 852-6600
Case Manager **Ruth Nagy** .... (219) 852-6600

United States Bankruptcy Court for the Northern District of Indiana
Robert K. Rodibaugh U.S. Courthouse, 401 South Michigan Street, South Bend, IN 46601
Tel: (574) 968-2100
Tel: (574) 968-2275 (Voice Case Information System VCIS)
Tel: (800) 755-8393 (Toll Free Voice Case Information System VCIS)
Fax: (574) 968-2231
Internet: www.innb.uscourts.gov

Number of Judgeships: 3

Court Staff
Clerk of the Court **Christopher M. DeToro** .... (574) 968-2100
E-mail: christopher_detoro@innb.uscourts.gov Fax: (574) 968-2231
Chief Deputy **Guy D. Weeks** .... (574) 968-2270
E-mail: guy_weeks@innb.uscourts.gov Fax: (574) 968-2231
Staff Attorney **(Vacant)** .... (574) 968-2235
Fax: (574) 968-2231
Operations Supervisor - Fort Wayne **Tina Feller** .... (260) 420-5100
1188 E. Ross Adair Federal Building & U.S. Courthouse, 1300 South Harrison Street, Fort Wayne, IN 46802-3435

United States Bankruptcy Court for the Northern District of Indiana *continued*

Operations Supervisor - Hammond **Ethel Weems** .... (219) 852-3480
5400 Federal Plaza, Hammond, IN 46320
E-mail: michael_stewart@innb.uscourts.gov
Operations Supervisor - Lafayette **Irma Osborn** .... (765) 420-6300
Charles Halleck Federal Building, 230 North Fourth Street, Lafayette, IN 47901
E-mail: irma_osborn@innb.uscourts.gov
Division Manager - South Bend **Lesa Piech** .... (574) 968-2100
Finance Manager **Nancy K. Noecker** .... (574) 968-2226
E-mail: nancy_noecker@innb.uscourts.gov Fax: (574) 968-2231
Human Resources Manager **(Vacant)** .... (574) 968-2227
Systems Manager **Jay Hershberger** .... (574) 968-2240
E-mail: jay_hershberger@innb.uscourts.gov Fax: (574) 968-2231
Data Quality Administrator **Lisa Grzeskiewicz** .... (260) 423-3061
E-mail: lisa_grzeskiewicz@innb.uscourts.gov
Court Services Administrator **Susan Ivancsics** .... (574) 968-2100
E-mail: susan_ivancsics@innb.uscourts.gov Fax: (574) 968-2231

Chambers of Chief Bankruptcy Judge Robert E. Grant
1300 South Harrison Street, Fort Wayne, IN 46802
Tel: (260) 426-2455 Fax: (260) 424-3716
E-mail: robert_grant@innb.uscourts.gov

Robert E. Grant
Chief Bankruptcy Judge

Date of Birth: 1954
Education: Wabash Col 1977 BA; Dickinson Law 1980 JD
Began Service: August 17, 1987
Term Expires: August 2029

Legal Practice: Attorney, Baker & Daniels LLP (1980-1987)

Staff
Career Law Clerk **Angela Marshall** .... (260) 426-2455
E-mail: angela_marshall@innb.uscourts.gov
Judicial Assistant **Judi Dove** .... (260) 426-2455
E-mail: judi_dove@innb.uscourts.gov

Chambers of Bankruptcy Judge Harry C. Dees, Jr.
Robert K. Rodibaugh U.S. Courthouse, 401 South Michigan Street, Room 234, South Bend, IN 46601
Tel: (574) 968-2280

Harry C. Dees, Jr.
Bankruptcy Judge

Date of Birth: 1945
Education: DePauw 1967 BA; Indiana 1974 JD
Began Service: October 1, 1986
Term Expires: September 30, 2029

Academic: Assistant Professor, Indiana State University (1983-1985)

Government: Deputy Public Defender, State of Indiana (1976-1978); Deputy Prosecutor, State of Indiana (1983-1984)

Judicial: Judge, Vigo County Juvenile Court (1978-1982)

Legal Practice: Attorney, Hertwig & Decker (1974-1975); Attorney, Tabor & Dees (1978-1986)

Military Service: United States Air Force (1967-1971); Indiana Air National Guard (1976-1992)

Current Memberships: American Bankruptcy Institute; The Seventh Circuit Bar Association, Federal Bar Association; Indiana State Bar Association; National Conference of Bankruptcy Judges; National Guard Association of the United States; St. Joseph County Bar Association; Terre Haute Bar Association

Staff
Career Law Clerk **Larry A. Greer** .... (574) 968-2280
Education: Notre Dame 1974 BA; Detroit Law 1978 JD

(continued on next page)

Chambers of Bankruptcy Judge Harry C. Dees, Jr. *continued*

Judicial Assistant **Janell F. Miller** .... (574) 968-2280

Chambers of Bankruptcy Judge J. Philip Klingeberger

5400 Federal Plaza, Suite 3800, Hammond, IN 46320-1840
Tel: (219) 852-3575 Fax: (219) 852-3577

J. Philip Klingeberger
Bankruptcy Judge

Began Service: June 16, 2003
Term Expires: 2017

Staff

Career Law Clerk **Robert Davidson** .... (219) 852-3575
E-mail: robert_davidson@innb.uscourts.gov
Judicial Assistant **Diane Zack** .... (219) 852-3575

Chambers of Bankruptcy Judge (recalled) Kent Lindquist

5400 Federal Plaza, Suite 3600, Hammond, IN 46320-1859
Tel: (219) 852-3550 Fax: (219) 852-3352
E-mail: kent_lindquist@innb.uscourts.gov

Kent Lindquist
Bankruptcy Judge (recalled)

Date of Birth: 1938
Education: Valparaiso 1963 JD
Began Service: May 1985

Judicial: Chief Bankruptcy Judge, United States Bankruptcy Court for the Northern District of Indiana (1986-2003)

Staff

Judicial Assistant **Mary Oberg** .... (219) 852-3550
E-mail: mary_oberg@innb.uscourts.gov

United States District Court for the Southern District of Indiana

U.S. Courthouse, 46 East Ohio Street, Indianapolis, IN 46204
Tel: (317) 229-3700 Fax: (317) 229-3959
Internet: www.insd.uscourts.gov

Number of Judgeships: 5

Number of Vacancies: 1

Circuit: Seventh

Court Staff

Clerk of Court **Laura A. Briggs** .... (317) 229-3700
E-mail: laura_briggs@insd.uscourts.gov Fax: (317) 229-3704
Chief Deputy Clerk **Greg Barnes** .... (317) 229-3703
E-mail: greg_barnes@insd.uscourts.gov Fax: (317) 229-3717
Deputy Clerk - Evansville **Nicole Neff** .... (812) 434-6410
304 U.S. Courthouse, Evansville, IN 47708 Fax: (812) 434-6418
E-mail: nicole_neff@insd.uscourts.gov
Deputy Clerk - New Albany **Janet Mathews** .... (812) 542-4510
121 W. Spring St., New Albany, IN 47150 Fax: (812) 542-4515
E-mail: janet_mathews@insd.uscourts.gov
Deputy Clerk - Terre Haute **Rebekah Farrington** .... (812) 231-1840
921 Ohio Street, Terre Haute, IN 47807 Fax: (812) 231-1844
E-mail: rebekah_farrington@insd.uscourts.gov
Chief Probation Officer **Dwight T. Wharton** .... (317) 229-3750
Room 101
E-mail: dwight_wharton@insp.uscourts.gov
Librarian **Sonja Simpson** .... (317) 229-3925
E-mail: sonja_simpson@insd.uscourts.gov Fax: (317) 229-3927

United States District Court for the Southern District of Indiana *continued*

Library Technician **Christopher McNeely** .... (317) 229-3925
E-mail: christopher_mcneely@insd.uscourts.gov Fax: (317) 229-3927
Court Personnel Administrator **Gayle-Sue Murphy** ...... (317) 229-3702
E-mail: gayle-sue_murphy@insd.uscourts.gov
Financial Manager **Richard Krall** .... (317) 229-3918
E-mail: richard_krall@insd.uscourts.gov Fax: (317) 229-3740

Chambers of Chief Judge Richard L. Young

U.S. Courthouse, 101 NW Martin Luther King Jr. Boulevard, Room 310, Evansville, IN 47708
Tel: (812) 434-6444 Fax: (812) 434-6445
E-mail: rly@insd.uscourts.gov

Richard L. Young
Chief Judge

Date of Birth: 1953
Education: Drake 1975 BA; George Mason 1980 JD
Began Service: March 25, 1998
Appointed By: President William J. Clinton

Government: County Coordinator, Birch Bayh for President (1975-1976); Legislative Assistant (D-IN, District 8), Office of Representative Philip H. Hayes, United States House of Representatives (1976); Corporation Counsel, City of Evansville, Indiana (1985-1987); Public Defender, Vanderburgh First Judicial Circuit Court, County of Vanderburgh, Indiana (1983-1985)

Judicial: Judge, Vanderburgh First Judicial Circuit Court, County of Vanderburgh, Indiana (1990-1998)

Legal Practice: Partner, Hayes and Young, Attorneys at Law (1980-1990)

Current Memberships: Evansville Bar Association; Federal Judges Association; Indiana State Bar Association; Virginia State Bar

Staff

Law Clerk **Matthew B. Miller** .... (812) 434-6443
E-mail: matthew_miller@insd.uscourts.gov
Law Clerk **Christopher D. Wagner** .... (812) 434-6443
Began Service: August 25, 2014
Term Expires: August 26, 2016
E-mail: christopher_wagner@insd.uscourts.gov
Education: Washington and Lee 2014 JD
Career Law Clerk **Kathryn A. Sullivan** .... (812) 434-6442
Began Service: March 25, 1998
E-mail: kathryn_sullivan@insd.uscourts.gov
Education: St Mary's Col (IN) 1990 BA; Indiana 1995 JD

Chambers of District Judge William T. Lawrence

U.S. Courthouse, 46 East Ohio Street, Room 204, Indianapolis, IN 46204
Tel: (317) 229-3610 Fax: (317) 229-3619
E-mail: william_lawrence@insd.uscourts.gov

William T. Lawrence
District Judge

Date of Birth: 1947
Education: Indiana 1970 BS; IU-Purdue U Indianapolis 1973 JD
Began Service: June 26, 2008
Appointed By: President George W. Bush

Government: Public Defender, Office of the Public Defender, County of Marion, Indiana (1974-1983); Executive Director, Merit Selection Commission on Federal Judicial Appointments (1980-1988); Master Commissioner, Circuit Court, County of Marion, Indiana (1983-1996)

Judicial: Judge, Circuit Court, County of Marion, Indiana (1996-2002); Magistrate Judge, United States District Court for the Southern District of Indiana (2002-2008)

Chambers of District Judge William T. Lawrence *continued*

Legal Practice: Poore, Popcheff, Wurster, Dugan, Sullivan & Burke (1973-1978); Lawrence, Carter, Gresk, Leerkamp & Walsh (1979-1988); Johnson, Smith, Pence, Densborn, Wright & Health (1989-1996)

Current Memberships: American Association for Justice; American Bar Association; The Sagamore American Inn of Court, The American Inns of Court; Federal Magistrate Judges Association; Indiana Judges Association; Indiana State Bar Association; Indiana Bar Foundation, Indiana State Bar Association

Staff

Career Law Clerk **Lisa Hamilton Thielmeyer** .... (317) 229-3610
E-mail: lisa_thielmeyer@insd.uscourts.gov
Education: Indiana 1992 JD

Courtroom Deputy **Jennifer H. Ong** .... (317) 229-3615
E-mail: jennifer_ong@insd.uscourts.gov

Case Administrator **Dena Hernandez** .... (317) 229-3708

Secretary **Elizabeth S. "Libby" Morrow** .... (317) 229-3612
E-mail: elizabeth_morrow@insd.uscourts.gov

Chambers of District Judge Jane Magnus-Stinson

46 East Ohio Street, Room 304, Indianapolis, IN 46204
Tel: (317) 229-3670 Fax: (317) 229-3678

Jane E. Magnus-Stinson
District Judge

Education: Butler 1979; IU-Purdue U Indianapolis 1983 JD
Began Service: June 14, 2010
Appointed By: President Barack Obama

Government: Counsel and Deputy Chief of Staff, Office of the Governor, State of Indiana; County Judge, Marion Superior Court (1995-2007)

Judicial: Magistrate Judge, Chambers of Magistrate Judge Jane E. Magnus-Stinson, United States District Court for the Southern District of Indiana (2007-2010)

Current Memberships: Indianapolis Bar Association; Professionalism Committee, Indianapolis Bar Association

Membership: Vice President, Indianapolis Bar Association (2004); Chair, Pro Bono Standing Committee, Indianapolis Bar Association (2005-2006); Past Board of Directors Member, Indiana Judicial Conference; Past Board of Managers Member, Indiana Judges Association; Past Chair, Criminal Jury Instructions Committee, Indiana Judicial Conference; Past President, Big Sisters of Central Indiana

Staff

Law Clerk **Elena Gobeyn** .... (317) 229-3671
E-mail: elena_gobeyn@insd.uscourts.gov

Law Clerk **Kellie Barr** .... (317) 229-3673
E-mail: kellie_barr@insd.uscourts.gov
Education: Indiana 2006 JD

Law Clerk **Roger Sharpe** .... (317) 229-3698
E-mail: roger_sharpe@insd.uscourts.gov

Courtroom Deputy **Michelle Imel** .... (317) 229-3672
E-mail: michelle_imel@insd.uscourts.gov

Chambers of District Judge Tanya Walton Pratt

46 East Ohio Street, Room 524, Indianapolis, IN 46204
Tel: (317) 229-3984 Fax: (317) 229-3990
E-mail: tanya_pratt@insd.uscourts.gov

Tanya Walton Pratt
District Judge

Education: Spelman 1981 BA; Howard U 1984 JD
Began Service: June 25, 2010
Appointed By: President Barack Obama

Judicial: Judge, Civil Division, Marion County Circuit Court, Indiana Superior Courts (1997-2009); Supervising Judge, Juvenile Detention Center, Marion County Superior Court (2007); Judge, Probate Division, Marion County Superior Court, Indiana Superior Courts (2009-2010)

Chambers of District Judge Tanya Walton Pratt *continued*

Staff

Law Clerk **Cassandra Bentley** .... (317) 229-3983
Began Service: January 2013
Term Expires: January 2016
E-mail: cassandra_bentley@insd.uscourts.gov
Education: Indiana (Indianapolis) 2004 JD

Law Clerk **Jonathan Penn** .... (317) 229-3982
Began Service: October 2014
Term Expires: October 2016
E-mail: jonathan_penn@insd.uscourts.gov
Education: Regent U 2009 JD

Courtroom Deputy **Tanesa Genier** .... (317) 229-3916
E-mail: tanesa_genier@insd.uscourts.gov

Judicial Assistant **Tanya L. "TL" Brown** .... (317) 229-3984
E-mail: tl_brown@insd.uscourts.gov

Chambers of Senior Judge Larry J. McKinney

U.S. Courthouse, 46 East Ohio Street, Room 361, Indianapolis, IN 46204
Tel: (317) 229-3650 Fax: (317) 229-3655
E-mail: larry_mckinney@insd.uscourts.gov

Larry J. McKinney
Senior Judge

Date of Birth: 1944
Education: MacMurray 1966 BA; Indiana 1969 JD
Began Service: 1987
Appointed By: President Ronald Reagan

Government: Deputy Attorney General, Office of the Attorney General, State of Indiana (1970-1971)

Judicial: Circuit Judge, Johnson County Court (1979-1987); Chief Judge, United States District Court for the Southern District of Indiana (2001-2007)

Legal Practice: Partner, Rogers & McKinney (1971-1975); Partner, Sargent & McKinney (1975-1979)

Current Memberships: Johnson County Bar Association

Staff

Law Clerk **Karen Reisinger** .... (317) 229-3650
E-mail: karen_reisinger@insd.uscourts.gov

Chambers of Senior Judge Sarah Evans Barker

U.S. Courthouse, 46 East Ohio Street, Room 210, Indianapolis, IN 46204
Tel: (317) 229-3600

Sarah Evans Barker
Senior Judge

Date of Birth: 1943
Education: Indiana 1965 BS; Washington College of Law 1969 JD
Began Service: March 30, 1984
Appointed By: President Ronald Reagan
Political Affiliation: Republican

Current Memberships: Federal Judges Association; Federal Judges Association; Indiana State Bar Association; Indianapolis Bar Association

Staff

Law Clerk **Monica Brownewell-Smith** .... (317) 229-3600
Began Service: September 2014
Term Expires: September 2016

Law Clerk **Taylor Sample** .... (317) 229-3600
E-mail: taylor_sample@insd.uscourts.gov

Career Law Clerk **Sarah W. Dame** .... (317) 229-3600
E-mail: sarah_dame@insd.uscourts.gov
Education: Indiana 2007 JD

Administrative Law Clerk **Susan Haber** .... (317) 229-3600
E-mail: susan_haber@insd.uscourts.gov

Courtroom Deputy **Kelly Rota-Autry** .... (317) 229-3600
E-mail: kelly_rotaautry@insd.uscourts.gov

Chambers of Magistrate Judge William G. Hussmann, Jr.

101 NW Martin Luther King Boulevard, Room 328, Evansville, IN 47708-1951
Tel: (812) 434-6430 Fax: (812) 434-6434

William G. Hussmann, Jr.
Magistrate Judge

Note: Judge Hussman will retire effective January 31, 2016.
Date of Birth: 1950
Education: Valparaiso 1972 BA, 1975 JD
Began Service: April 4, 1988
Term Expires: April 4, 2020

Academic: Associated Insurance Co. (1986-1988)

Government: Deputy Attorney General, Office of the Attorney General, State of Indiana (1981-1983); Staff Attorney, Disciplinary Committee, Indiana Supreme Court (1983-1986)

Legal Practice: Attorney, Rice, Myles & Hussmann (1976-1981)

Current Memberships: Evansville Bar Association; The Seventh Circuit Bar Association, Federal Bar Association

Staff
Law Clerk **Jeremy Votaw** .... (812) 434-6430
E-mail: jeremy_votaw@insd.uscourts.gov
Court Reporter **Judy Farris Mason** .... (812) 459-9805
E-mail: judy_mason@insd.uscourts.gov Fax: (812) 434-6445
Administrative Assistant **Shelly J. James** .... (812) 434-6430
E-mail: shelly_james@insd.uscourts.gov

Chambers of Magistrate Judge Tim A. Baker

U.S. Courthouse, 46 East Ohio Street, Room 234, Indianapolis, IN 46204
Tel: (317) 229-3660 Fax: (317) 229-3664
E-mail: mjbaker@insd.uscourts.gov

Tim A. Baker
Magistrate Judge

Education: Indiana 1984 BA; Valparaiso 1989 JD
Began Service: October 1, 2001

Affiliation: Chair, Federal Judiciary Committee; Member, Indiana State Bar Association

Clerkships: Law Clerk, Chief Judge The Honorable Larry J. McKinney, United States District Court for the Southern District of Indiana (1989-1991)

Government: Assistant United States Attorney, Indiana - Southern District, Office of the Attorney General, United States Department of Justice (1995-2001)

Judicial: Chair, Labor & Employment Law Section, Indianapolis Bar Association (2000); Distinguished Fellow, Indianapolis Bar Foundation (2002); Co-chair, Student Law Division, Indianapolis Bar Association (2002-2003)

Legal Practice: Associate, Barnes & Thornburg LLP (1991-1995)

Current Memberships: Indianapolis Bar Association

Staff
Law Clerk **Susanne Heckler** .... (317) 229-3660
E-mail: susanne_heckler@insd.uscourts.gov
Courtroom Deputy **Amy Holtz** .... (317) 229-3707
E-mail: amy_holtz@insd.uscourts.gov
Administrative Assistant **Becky Sture** .... (317) 229-3660
E-mail: becky_sture@insd.uscourts.gov

Chambers of Magistrate Judge Debra McVicker Lynch

46 East Ohio Street, Room 277, Indianapolis, IN 46204
Tel: (317) 229-3630 Fax: (317) 229-3637

Debra McVicker Lynch
Magistrate Judge

Education: Miami BA; Indiana JD
Began Service: October 24, 2008
Term Expires: October 24, 2016

Current Memberships: The Indianapolis American Inn of Court, The American Inns of Court; Indiana State Bar Association

Chambers of Magistrate Judge Mark J. Dinsmore

46 East Ohio Street, Room 257, Indianapolis, IN 46204
Tel: (317) 229-3901 Tel: (317) 229-3664
E-mail: mark_dinsmore@insd.uscourts.gov

Mark J. Dinsmore
Magistrate Judge

Education: Wabash Col 1983 AB; Toledo JD
Began Service: December 17, 2010
Term Expires: December 17, 2018

Staff
Courtroom Deputy **Nancy Rassbach** .... (317) 229-3908
E-mail: nancy_rassbach@insd.uscourts.gov

Chambers of Magistrate Judge Denise K. LaRue

46 East Ohio Street, Room 243, Indianapolis, IN 46204
Tel: (317) 229-3930 Fax: (317) 229-3931
E-mail: denise_larue@insd.uscourts.gov

Denise K. LaRue
Magistrate Judge

Education: Indiana 1980 BS; Indiana (Indianapolis) 1989 JD
Began Service: May 24, 2011

Staff
Law Clerk **Perry Secrest** .... (317) 229-3930
E-mail: perry_secrest@insd.uscourts.gov
Education: George Washington 1986 JD
Law Clerk **Jennifer Romanick** .... (317) 229-3930
Courtroom Deputy **Ruth Olive** .... (317) 229-3930
E-mail: ruth_olive@insd.uscourts.gov

Chambers of Magistrate Judge Matthew P. Brookman

101 NW Martin Luther King Boulevard, Evansville, IN 47708-1951
Tel: (317) 229-3700

Matthew P. "Matt" Brookman
Magistrate Judge

Note: Effective February 1, 2016.
Education: DePauw 1990 BA; Washington U (MO) 1993 JD

Chambers of Magistrate Judge (part-time) Craig M. Mckee

207 Federal Building, Terre Haute, IN 47808
Tel: (812) 232-4311

Craig M. McKee
Magistrate Judge (Part-Time)

Began Service: August 23, 2007
Term Expires: August 2023

Affiliation: Attorney, Wilkinson, Goeller, Modesitt, Wilkinson & Drummy, LLP

United States Bankruptcy Court for the Southern District of Indiana

U.S. Courthouse, 46 East Ohio Street, Room 116, Indianapolis, IN 46204
P.O. Box 44978, Indianapolis, IN 46244
Tel: (317) 229-3800
Tel: (317) 229-3888 (Voice Case Information System VCIS)
Fax: (317) 229-3801
Internet: www.insb.uscourts.gov

Number of Judgeships: 4

Court Staff
Clerk of Court **Kevin P. Dempsey** .... (317) 229-3800
Education: Augustana (IL); Illinois JD
Chief Deputy Clerk **Rebecca Vail** .... (317) 229-3800
Executive Assistant to the Clerk **Linda Alspaugh** .... (317) 229-3803
E-mail: linda_alspaugh@insb.uscourts.gov
Systems Manager **Alan Cecil** .... (317) 229-3845
E-mail: Alan_Cecil@insb.uscourts.gov
Case Administration Supervisor **(Vacant)** .... (317) 229-3814
Human Resources Tech **Hope Sallee** .... (317) 229-3812
E-mail: hope_sallee@insb.uscourts.gov

Chambers of Chief Bankruptcy Judge Robyn Lynn Moberly

46 East Ohio Street, Indianapolis, IN 46204
Tel: (317) 229-3880 Fax: (317) 229-3886

Robyn Lynn Moberley
Chief Bankruptcy Judge

Began Service: November 1, 2012

Staff
Law Clerk **Patricia Marshall** .... (317) 229-3880
Education: Valparaiso 1980 BA, 1983 JD
Judicial Assistant **Mary Beth Hall** .... (317) 229-3880

Chambers of Bankruptcy Judge Basil H. Lorch III

127 Federal Building, 121 West Spring Street, New Albany, IN 47150
Tel: (812) 542-4570 Fax: (812) 542-4571
E-mail: basil_lorch@insb.uscourts.gov

Basil H. Lorch III
Bankruptcy Judge

Date of Birth: 1949
Education: Indiana 1971 BA, 1974 JD
Began Service: April 14, 1992
Term Expires: April 13, 2020

Academic: Instructor, School of Law, Indiana University Bloomington

Government: Public Defender, Criminal Court, Floyd County, Indiana

Legal Practice: Managing Partner, Lorch and Naville

Current Memberships: American College of Bankruptcy; Floyd County Bar; National Conference of Bankruptcy Judges

Staff
Career Law Clerk **Kathryn S. Willis** .... (812) 542-4570
Education: Kentucky 1988 JD

Chambers of Bankruptcy Judge James M. Carr

46 East Ohio Street, Indianapolis, IN 46204
Tel: (317) 229-3833

James M. Carr
Magistrate Judge

Education: Indiana 1972 BA, 1975 JD

Chambers of Bankruptcy Judge James M. Carr *continued*

Staff
Courtroom Deputy **Heather Butler** .... (317) 229-3833
E-mail: heather_butler@insb.uscourts.gov

Chambers of Bankruptcy Judge Jeffrey J. Graham

46 East Ohio Street, Indianapolis, IN 46204
Tel: (317) 229-3800

Jeffrey J. Graham
Bankruptcy Judge

Education: Notre Dame BA; Valparaiso JD

United States District Court for the Northern District of Iowa

111 Seventh Avenue SE, Cedar Rapids, IA 52401-2101
Tel: (319) 286-2300 Fax: (319) 286-2301
Internet: www.iand.uscourts.gov

Number of Judgeships: 2

Number of Vacancies: 1

Circuit: Eighth

Areas Covered: Counties of Allamakee, Benton, Black Hawk, Bremer, Buchanan, Buena Vista, Butler, Calhoun, Carroll, Cedar, Cerro Gordo, Cherokee, Chickasaw, Clay, Clayton, Crawford, Delaware, Dickinson, Dubuque, Emmet, Fayette, Floyd, Franklin, Grundy, Hamilton, Hancock, Hardin, Howard, Humboldt, Ida, Iowa, Jackson, Jones, Kossuth, Linn, Lyon, Mitchell, Monona, O'Brien, Osceola, Palo Alto, Plymouth, Pocahontas, Sac, Sioux, Tama, Webster, Winnebago, Winneshiek, Woodbury, Worth and Wright

Court Staff
Clerk of Court **Robert L. Phelps II** .... (319) 286-2300
E-mail: robert_phelps@iand.uscourts.gov
Chief Deputy Clerk **Renea Salter-Solmonson** .... (319) 286-2321
E-mail: renea_solmonson@iand.uscourts.gov
Deputy In Charge - Sioux City **Kim Schwartz** .... (712) 233-3900
301 Federal Bldg., 320 Sixth St.,
Sioux City, IA 51101
E-mail: kim_schwartz@iand.uscourts.gov
Chief Probation Officer **John Zielke** .... (319) 286-2386
Court Reporter **Patrice Murray** .... (319) 286-2324
E-mail: Patrice_Murray@iand.uscourts.gov
Court Reporter **Shelly Semmler** .... (712) 233-3846
E-mail: shelly_semmler@iand.uscourts.gov

Chambers of Chief District Judge Linda R. Reade

111 Seventh Avenue SE, Cedar Rapids, IA 52401
Tel: (319) 286-2330 Fax: (319) 286-2331
E-mail: Linda_Reade@iand.uscourts.gov

Linda R. Reade
Chief District Judge

Date of Birth: February 1, 1948
Education: Drake 1970 BA; Iowa State 1973 MS; Drake 1980 JD
Began Service: November 26, 2002
Appointed By: President George W. Bush

Government: Assistant United States Attorney, Southern District of Iowa, United States Attorney's Executive Office, United States Department of Justice (1986-1993)

Judicial: Judge, Iowa District Court for Polk County (1993-2002)

Legal Practice: Law Clerk, Brown, Winick, Graves, Gross, Baskerville & Schoenebaum, P.L.C. (1980-1980); Associate, Brown, Winick, Graves, Gross, Baskerville & Schoenebaum, P.L.C. (1980-1981); Associate, Rosenberg and Margulies (1981-1984); Partner, Rosenberg, Rosenberg and Reade (1984-1986)

(continued on next page)

Chambers of Chief District Judge Linda R. Reade *continued*

Staff
Law Clerk **Zachary Fairlie** .... (319) 286-2330
E-mail: zachary_fairlie@iand.uscourts.gov
Law Clerk **Noah Goerlitz** .... (319) 286-2330
Law Clerk **Emily Kolbe** .... (319) 286-2330
E-mail: emily_kolbe@iand.uscourts.gov
Pro Se Law Clerk **Paul DeYoung** .... (319) 286-2337
E-mail: Paul_DeYoung@iand.uscourts.gov
Court Reporter **Patrice Murray** .... (319) 286-2324
E-mail: patrice_murray@iand.uscourts.gov
Judicial Assistant **Danielle Cripe** .... (319) 286-2330

Chambers of Senior Judge Mark W. Bennett

313 Federal Building, 320 Sixth Street, Sioux City, IA 51102
P.O. Box 838, Sioux City, IA 51102-0838
Tel: (712) 233-3909 Fax: (712) 233-3913
E-mail: mark_bennett@iand.uscourts.gov

Mark W. Bennett
Senior Judge

Date of Birth: 1950
Education: Gustavus Adolphus 1972 BA; Drake 1975 JD
Began Service: August 26, 1994
Appointed By: President William J. Clinton

Current Memberships: Iowa State Bar Association; Woodbury County Bar Association

Staff
Law Clerk **Robert Johnson** .... (712) 233-3853
Education: Iowa 1987 JD
Law Clerk **Roger Mastalir** .... (712) 233-3854
E-mail: roger_mastalir@iand.uscourts.gov
Education: Iowa 1991 JD, 1992 LLM
Legal Advisor **Will Blackton** .... (712) 233-3855
E-mail: will_blackton@iand.uscourts.gov
Court Reporter **Shelly Semmler** .... (712) 233-3846
E-mail: shelly_semmler@iand.uscourts.gov
Legal Secretary **Jennifer Gill** .... (712) 233-3909
E-mail: jennifer_gill@iand.uscourts.gov
Education: Creighton 1996 JD

Chambers of Senior Judge Edward J. McManus

111 Seventh Avenue SE, Box 8, Cedar Rapids, IA 52401
Tel: (319) 286-2350 Fax: (319) 286-2351
E-mail: edward_mcmanus@iand.uscourts.gov

Edward J. McManus
Senior Judge

Date of Birth: 1920
Education: Iowa 1940 BA, 1942 JD
Began Service: 1962
Appointed By: President John F. Kennedy
Political Affiliation: Democrat

Corporate: President, Coca-Cola Bottling Company United, Inc. (1955-1962); President, 1001 Corporation (1960-1962)

Government: City Attorney, Office of the City Attorney, City of Keokuk, Indiana (1946-1955); State Senator Edward Mcmanus, Iowa State Senate (1955-1959); Lieutenant Governor Edward McManus, State of Iowa (1959-1962)

Legal Practice: Partner, McManus & McManus (1946-1962)

Military Service: United States Naval Reserve (1942-1946)

Current Memberships: American Bar Association

Staff
Career Law Clerk **Richard Lipman** .... (319) 286-2355
E-mail: richard_lipman@iand.uscourts.gov

Chambers of Senior Judge Edward J. McManus *continued*

Judicial Assistant **Deborah J. Frank** .... (319) 286-2354
E-mail: deb_frank@iand.uscourts.gov

Chambers of Chief Magistrate Judge Jon S. Scoles

111 Seventh Avenue SE, Cedar Rapids, IA 52401-2101
Tel: (319) 286-2340
E-mail: jon_scoles@iand.uscourts.gov

Jon S. Scoles
Chief Magistrate Judge

Education: Northern Iowa 1973 BA; Iowa 1979 JD
Began Service: 2012

Staff
Career Law Clerk **Aaron Shileny** .... (319) 286-2340
E-mail: aaron_shileny@iand.uscourts.gov
Judicial Assistant **Karo Stigler** .... (319) 286-2340
E-mail: karo_stigler@iand.uscourts.gov

Chambers of Magistrate Judge Leonard T. Strand

320 Sixth Street, Room 104, Sioux City, IA 51102
Tel: (712) 233-3921 Fax: (712) 233-3918
E-mail: leonard_strand@iand.uscourts.gov

Leonard Terry "Len" Strand
Magistrate Judge

Education: Iowa 1987 BA, 1990 JD
Began Service: 2012

Staff
Law Clerk **Sabrina Danielson** .... (712) 233-3921
E-mail: sabrina_danielson@iand.uscourts.gov
Judicial Assistant **Leslie R. Walker** .... (712) 233-3921
E-mail: leslie_walker@iand.uscourts.gov

United States Bankruptcy Court for the Northern District of Iowa

111 Seventh Avenue SE, Box 15, Cedar Rapids, IA 52401-2101
P.O. Box 74890, Cedar Rapids, IA 52407-4890
Tel: (319) 286-2200 Tel: (800) 676-6856 (Toll Free PACER)
Tel: (866) 222-8029 (Toll Free Voice Case Information System VCIS)
Fax: (319) 286-2280
Internet: www.ianb.uscourts.gov

Number of Judgeships: 2

Court Staff
Bankruptcy Clerk **Jean Hekel** .... (319) 286-2200
E-mail: jean_hekel@ianb.uscourts.gov
Chief Deputy **Sharon Mullin** .... (319) 286-2200
E-mail: sharon_mullin@ianb.uscourts.gov
Case Administrator **Nicole Becker** .... (319) 286-2200
E-mail: nicole_becker@ianb.uscourts.gov
Case Administrator **Som Many Greigg** .... (712) 233-3939
Case Administrator **Theresa Stapelman** .... (712) 233-3939
E-mail: theresa_stapelman@ianb.uscourts.gov
Case Administrator **Stacy Stief** .... (319) 286-2200
Case Administrator **Sherrie Waite** .... (319) 286-2200
Courtroom Deputy **Julie Hubbell** .... (319) 286-2200
E-mail: julie_hubbell@ianb.uscourts.gov
Automation Specialist **(Vacant)** .... (319) 286-2200
CM/ECF Administrator **Karen Hanover** .... (319) 286-2200
Human Resources & Training Specialist
Rebecca Hoefer .... (319) 286-2200
E-mail: rebecca_hoefer@ianb.uscourts.gov
Information Technology Director
Thomas "Tom" Gust .... (319) 286-2200
E-mail: thomas_gust@ianb.uscourts.gov

Chambers of Chief Bankruptcy Judge Thad J. Collins
111 Seventh Avenue SE, Box 23, Cedar Rapids, IA 52401
Tel: (319) 286-2230 Fax: (319) 286-2290
E-mail: thad_collins@ianb.uscourts.gov

Thad J. Collins
Chief Bankruptcy Judge

Began Service: March 29, 2010

Staff
Law Clerk **Jessica Uhlenkamp** . . . . . (319) 286-2230
Judicial Assistant **Gail Jones** . . . . . (319) 286-2230

United States District Court for the Southern District of Iowa
U.S. Courthouse, 123 East Walnut Street, Des Moines, IA 50309
P.O. Box 9344, Des Moines, IA 50306-9344
Tel: (515) 284-6248
Internet: www.iasd.uscourts.gov

Number of Judgeships: 3

Number of Vacancies: 1

Circuit: Eighth

Areas Covered: Counties of Adair, Adams, Appanoose, Audubon, Boone, Cass, Clarke, Clinton, Dallas, Davis, Decatur, Des Moines, Fremont, Greene, Guthrie, Harrison, Henry, Jasper, Jefferson, Johnson, Keokuk, Lee Louisa, Lucas, Madison, Mahaska, Marion, Marshall, Mills, Monroe, Montgomery, Muscatine, Page, Polk, Pottawattamie, Poweshiek, Ringgold, Scott, Shelby, Story, Taylor, Union, Van Buren, Wapello, Warren, Washington and Wayne

Court Staff
Clerk of Court **Marjorie E. Krahn** . . . . . (515) 323-2865
E-mail: Marge_Krahn@iasd.uscourts.gov
Education: Idaho BS; Denver MS
Chief Deputy Clerk **John S. Courter** . . . . . (515) 284-6450
E-mail: john_courter@iasd.uscourts.gov
Deputy Clerk - Council Bluffs **Vickie Rule** . . . . . (712) 328-0283
E-mail: vickie_rule@iasd.uscourts.gov
Deputy In Charge - Davenport **Rita Johnson** . . . . . (563) 884-7607
131 East Fourth Street, Suite 150,
Davenport, IA 52801
E-mail: rita_johnson@iasd.uscourts.gov
Chief Probation Officer **Michael J. Elbert** . . . . . (515) 284-6207
Education: Iowa 1991 BA;
Northern Iowa 1993 MA; Nebraska 2004 PhD
Librarian **Melissa Schutjer** . . . . . (515) 284-6228
110 E. Court Ave., Ste. 358, Fax: (515) 284-6451
Des Moines, IA 50309-2054
Court Reporter **Terri Martin** . . . . . (515) 284-6444
E-mail: terri_martin@iasd.uscourts.gov
Court Reporter **Linda Egbers** . . . . . (563) 884-7737
E-mail: linda_egbers@iasd.uscourts.gov
Court Reporter **Kelli Mulcahy** . . . . . (563) 884-7737
E-mail: kelli_mulcahy@iasd.uscourts.gov

Chambers of Chief Judge John A. Jarvey
123 East Walnut, Des Moines, IA 50309
Tel: (563) 884-7727 Fax: (563) 884-7729
E-mail: john_jarvey@iasd.uscourts.gov

John A. Jarvey
Chief Judge

Date of Birth: 1956
Education: Akron 1978 BS; Drake 1981 JD
Began Service: March 2007
Appointed By: President George W. Bush

Current Memberships: Iowa State Bar Association

Chambers of Chief Judge John A. Jarvey *continued*

Staff
Judicial Assistant **Maura McNally-Cavanagh** . . . . . (563) 884-7727
E-mail: maura_mcnally-cavanagh@iasd.uscourts.gov

Chambers of District Judge Stephanie Marie Rose
123 East Walnut Street, Room 420, Des Moines, IA 50309
Tel: (515) 284-6248
E-mail: stephanie_rose@iasd.uscourts.gov

Stephanie M. Rose
District Judge

Education: Iowa 1994 BA, 1996 JD
Began Service: November 13, 2012
Appointed By: President Barack Obama

Staff
Judicial Assistant **Nancy Ryan** . . . . . (515) 284-6453
E-mail: nancy_ryan@iasd.uscourts.gov

Chambers of Senior Judge Harold D. Vietor
U.S. Courthouse, 123 East Walnut Street, Room 485,
Des Moines, IA 50309
Tel: (515) 284-6237 Fax: (515) 284-6460
E-mail: harold_vietor@iasd.uscourts.gov

Harold D. Vietor
Senior Judge

Date of Birth: 1931
Education: Iowa 1955 BA, 1958 JD
Began Service: 1979
Appointed By: President Jimmy Carter

Clerkships: Law Clerk The Honorable Martin Van Oosterhout, United States Court of Appeals for the Eighth Circuit (1958-1959)

Judicial: Judge, Iowa District Court (1965-1979)

Legal Practice: Attorney, Bleakley Law Offices (1959-1965)

Military Service: United States Navy (1952-1954)

Current Memberships: American Bar Association; Eighth Circuit District Judges Association; Federal Judges Association; Iowa State Bar Association

Chambers of Senior Judge Charles R. Wolle
110 East Court Avenue, Room 403, Des Moines, IA 50309
Tel: (515) 284-6289 Fax: (515) 284-6440
E-mail: charles_wolle@iasd.uscourts.gov

Charles R. Wolle
Senior Judge

Date of Birth: 1935
Education: Harvard 1959 AB; Iowa 1961 JD
Began Service: August 1987
Appointed By: President Ronald Reagan

Judicial: Judge, Iowa District Court (1981-1983); Justice, Iowa Supreme Court (1983-1987)

Legal Practice: Attorney, Shull, Marshall & Marks (1961-1980)

Military Service: United States Army Reserve, United States Department of the Army (1961-1967)

Current Memberships: American Bar Association; American College of Trial Lawyers

Staff
Career Law Clerk **Ann Beneke** . . . . . (515) 284-6289
E-mail: ann_beneke@iasd.uscourts.gov
Education: Iowa JD

Chambers of Senior Judge Ronald E. Longstaff

U.S. Courthouse, 123 East Walnut Street, Room 115,
Des Moines, IA 50309
Tel: (515) 284-6235 Fax: (515) 284-6491
E-mail: ronald_longstaff@iasd.uscourts.gov

Ronald E. Longstaff
Senior Judge

Date of Birth: 1941
Education: Pittsburg State 1962 BA; Iowa 1965 JD
Began Service: November 5, 1991
Appointed By: President George H.W. Bush
Political Affiliation: Republican

Academic: Adjunct Professor, Law School, Drake University (1973-1976)

Clerkships: Law Clerk The Honorable Roy L. Stephenson, United States District Court for the Southern District of Iowa (1965-1967)

Judicial: Clerk of Court and Magistrate Judge (part-time), United States District Court for the Southern District of Iowa (1968-1976); Magistrate Judge, United States District Court for the Southern District of Iowa (1976-1991); District Judge, United States District Court for the Southern District of Iowa (1991-2006); Chief Judge, United States District Court for the Southern District of Iowa (2006)

Legal Practice: Associate, McWilliams, Gross & Kirtley (1967-1968)

Current Memberships: The C. Edwin Moore American Inn of Court, The American Inns of Court; Federal Judges Association; Iowa State Bar Association

Staff

Career Law Clerk **Carla J. Hamborg** .... (515) 284-6458
E-mail: carla_hamborg@iasd.uscourts.gov
Education: Drake 1992 JD
Secretary **(Vacant)** .... (515) 284-6235

Chambers of Senior Judge Robert W. Pratt

U.S. Courthouse, 123 East Walnut Street, Room 221,
Des Moines, IA 50309
Tel: (515) 284-6254 Fax: (515) 323-2907
E-mail: Robert_Pratt@iasd.uscourts.gov

Robert W. "Bob" Pratt
Senior Judge

Date of Birth: 1947
Education: Loras 1969 BA; Creighton 1972 JD
Began Service: July 1, 1997
Appointed By: President William J. Clinton

Current Memberships: American Bar Association; Iowa Academy of Trial Lawyers; Iowa Association of Workers Compensation Attorneys; Iowa State Bar Association; National Organization of Social Security Claimants' Representatives; Polk County Bar Association

Staff

Law Clerk **Carrie Weber** .... (515) 284-6254
Career Law Clerk **Nova Janssen** .... (515) 284-6254
E-mail: nova_janssen@iasd.uscourts.gov
Chamber Administrator **Michael L. Messina** .... (515) 284-6254
E-mail: messinam@aol.com

Chambers of Senior Judge James E. Gritzner

U.S. Courthouse, 123 East Walnut Street, Room 130,
Des Moines, IA 50309
Tel: (515) 284-6291 Fax: (515) 284-6205
E-mail: nancy_harris@iasd.uscourts.gov

James E. Gritzner
Senior Judge

Date of Birth: 1947
Education: Dakota Wesleyan 1969 BA; Northern Iowa 1974 MA; Drake 1979 JD
Began Service: February 19, 2002
Appointed By: President George W. Bush

Staff

Law Clerk **Bart Galvin** .... (515) 284-6291
Began Service: August 2015
Term Expires: August 2016
E-mail: bart_galvin@iasd.uscourts.gov
Career Law Clerk **Cheryl M. Murad** .... (515) 284-6291
E-mail: cheryl_murad@iasd.uscourts.gov
Education: Drake 2001 JD
Judicial Assistant **Nancy Harris** .... (515) 284-6291
E-mail: Nancy_Harris@iasd.uscourts.gov

Chambers of Chief Magistrate Judge Celeste F. Bremer

U.S. Courthouse, 123 East Walnut Street, Suite 435,
Des Moines, IA 50309-2036
Tel: (515) 284-6200 Fax: (515) 284-7392
E-mail: celeste_bremer@iasd.uscourts.gov

Celeste F. Bremer
Chief Magistrate Judge

Date of Birth: 1953
Education: St Ambrose 1974 BA; Iowa 1977 JD; Drake 2002 EdD
Began Service: January 1, 1990
Term Expires: January 1, 2024

Current Memberships: American Bar Association; The C. Edwin Moore American Inn of Court, The American Inns of Court; Federal Magistrate Judges Association; Iowa Organization of Women Attorneys; Iowa State Bar Association; National Association of Women Judges; Polk County Bar Association; Polk County Women Attorneys Association

Staff

Law Clerk **Paul Caligiuri** .... (515) 284-6264
E-mail: paul_caligiuri@iasd.uscourts.gov
Secretary **Melanie Ritchey** .... (515) 284-6200
E-mail: melanie_ritchey@iasd.uscourts.gov

Chambers of Magistrate Judge Helen C. Adams

United States Courthouse, 123 East Walnut, Des Moines, IA 50309
Tel: (515) 284-6217
E-mail: helen_adams@iasd.uscourts.gov

Helen Adams
Magistrate Judge

Staff

Judicial Assistant **Debbie Moses** .... (563) 884-7601
E-mail: debbie_moses@iasd.uscourts.gov

Chambers of Magistrate Judge Ross A. Walters
U.S. Courthouse, 123 East Walnut Street, Suite 440,
Des Moines, IA 50309
Tel: (515) 284-6217 Fax: (515) 284-6442
E-mail: ross_a_walters@iasd.uscourts.gov

Ross A. Walters
Magistrate Judge

Date of Birth: 1949
Education: Penn State 1971 BA; Iowa 1977 JD
Began Service: 1994
Term Expires: November 2018

Clerkships: Law Clerk The Honorable William C. Hanson, United States District Court for the Southern District of Iowa (1977-1979)

Judicial: Judge, Iowa District Court, 5-C Judicial District (1990-1994)

Legal Practice: Associate, Herrick, Langdon & Langdon (1979-1982); Partner, Herrick, Langdon & Langdon (1982-1990)

Military Service: United States Naval Reserve (1971-1974)

Staff
Judicial Assistant **Kathy Nutt** . . . . . (515) 284-6217
E-mail: kathy_nutt@iasd.uscourts.gov

Chambers of Magistrate Judge Stephen B. Jackson Jr.
123 East Walnut Street, Des Moines, IA 50309
Tel: (563) 884-7601

Stephen B. Jackson, Jr.
Magistrate Judge

Began Service: 2015

United States Bankruptcy Court for the Southern District of Iowa
U.S. Courthouse Annex, 110 East Court Avenue, Suite 300,
Des Moines, IA 50309
Tel: (515) 284-6230 Tel: (800) 597-5917 (Toll Free PACER)
Tel: (866) 222-8029 (Toll Free Voice Case Information System VCIS)
Fax: (515) 284-6404
E-mail: bankruptcy_court@iasb.uscourts.gov
Internet: www.iasb.uscourts.gov

Number of Judgeships: 2

Court Staff
Clerk of the Court **Virginia L. Satterstrom** . . . . (515) 284-6230 ext. 2843
E-mail: ginny_satterstrom@iasb.uscourts.gov
Chief Deputy Clerk **Megan Weiss** . . . . . (515) 284-6230 ext. 2843
Systems Manager **Douglas Johnston** . . . . . (515) 284-6230 ext. 2832
E-mail: douglas_johnston@iasb.uscourts.gov
Financial Administrator
William J. Freiburger . . . . . (515) 284-6230 ext. 2844
E-mail: bill_freiburger@iasb.uscourts.gov

Chambers of Chief Bankruptcy Judge Anita L. Shodeen
U.S. Courthouse Annex, 110 East Court Avenue, Room 300,
Des Moines, IA 50309
Tel: (515) 284-6118
E-mail: anita_shodeen@iasb.uscourts.gov

Anita L. Shodeen
Chief Bankruptcy Judge

Education: Drake JD
Began Service: August 26, 2009

Chambers of Chief Bankruptcy Judge Anita L. Shodeen *continued*

Staff
Law Clerk **Laura Carrington** . . . . . (515) 284-6234
Began Service: 2009
E-mail: laura_carrington@iasb.uscourts.gov
Education: Denver 2007 JD
Calendar Clerk **Megan Weiss** . . . . . (515) 284-6118

Chambers of Bankruptcy Judge Lee M. Jackwig
U.S. Courthouse Annex, 110 East Court Avenue, Suite 443,
Des Moines, IA 50309-2050
Tel: (515) 284-6229 Fax: (515) 284-6402
E-mail: lee_jackwig@iasb.uscourts.gov

Lee M. Jackwig
Bankruptcy Judge

Date of Birth: 1950
Education: Loyola U (Chicago) 1972 BA; DePaul 1975 JD
Began Service: November 3, 1986
Term Expires: November 2, 2028

Current Memberships: American Bankruptcy Institute; American Bar Association; Federal Bar Association; Iowa State Bar Association; National Conference of Bankruptcy Judges; Polk County Bar Association; Polk County Women Attorneys Association

Staff
Law Clerk **Andrew "Drew" Clark** . . . . . (515) 284-6231
Term Expires: July 2016
Calendar Clerk **Carol A. White** . . . . . (515) 284-7394
Fax: (515) 284-6404

United States District Court for the District of Kansas
Robert J. Dole U.S. Courthouse, 500 State Avenue,
Kansas City, KS 66101
Tel: (913) 735-2200 Fax: (913) 735-2201
Internet: www.ksd.uscourts.gov

Number of Judgeships: 6

Number of Vacancies: 1

Circuit: Tenth

Court Staff
Clerk of Court **Timothy O'Brien** . . . . . (913) 735-2200
Fax: (913) 735-2221
Administrative Assistant to the Clerk **Carla Brogdon** . . . (913) 735-2200
E-mail: carla_brogdon@ksd.uscourts.gov
Chief Deputy Clerk **Ingrid A. Campbell** . . . . . (913) 735-2200
E-mail: ingrid_campbell@ksd.uscourts.gov
Education: Indiana 1985 BS; Valparaiso 1988 JD
Pro Se Law Clerk **Rachel Lyle** . . . . . (785) 338-5455
U.S. Courthouse, 444 SE Quincy St., Fax: (785) 338-5401
Topeka, KS 66683
E-mail: rachel_lyle@ksd.uscourts.gov
Education: Baker U 1978 BA;
North Carolina 1980 MA; Kansas 1985 JD
Deputy Director of Administrative Services
Skyler O'Hara . . . . . (913) 735-2232
E-mail: skyler_ohara@ksd.uscourts.gov Fax: (913) 735-2231
Education: Kansas 2003 JD
Attorney Registration **Leigh Kinzer** . . . . . (913) 735-2200
E-mail: leigh_kinzer@ksd.uscourts.gov
Administrative Services Manager **Ray Waters** . . . . . (913) 735-2235
E-mail: ray_waters@ksd.uscourts.gov Fax: (913) 735-2249
Education: Naval Acad 1971; Duke 1978
Division Manager - Kansas City **Kim Leininger** . . . . . (913) 735-2200
E-mail: kim_leininger@ksd.uscourts.gov
Education: Emporia State 1989 BS;
Kansas State 1991 MS

(continued on next page)

United States District Court for the District of Kansas *continued*

Division Manager - Topeka **Karen Manza** ....(785) 338-5400
U.S. Courthouse, 444 SE Quincy St., Fax: (785) 338-5401
Topeka, KS 66683
E-mail: karen_manza@ksd.uscourts.gov

Division Manager - Wichita **Jamie Haig** ....(316) 315-4200
U.S. Courthouse, 401 N. Market St., Fax: (316) 315-4201
Wichita, KS 67202
E-mail: jamie_haig@ksd.uscourts.gov

Financial Manager **Jeff Breon** ....(913) 735-2200
E-mail: jeff_breon@ksd.uscourts.gov
Education: Kansas State 1990 BSBA

User Support Manager **Michael Keyes** ....(913) 735-2200

Chief Probation Officer **Ronald G. Schweer** ....(913) 735-2424
E-mail: ronald_schweer@ksd.uscourts.gov

Jury Administrator - Topeka **Mary Beth Hill** ....(785) 338-5412
U.S. Courthouse, 444 SE Quincy St.,
Topeka, KS 66683

Assistant Jury Administrator - Kansas City
Heather Wilkerson ....(913) 735-2200
E-mail: heather_wilkerson@ksd.uscourts.gov

Assistant Jury Administrator - Wichita
Marleen Van Ravenswaay ....(316) 315-4212
U.S. Courthouse, 401 N. Market St.,
Wichita, KS 67202

Procurement Administrator **Carie Shirley** ....(913) 735-2242
E-mail: carie_shirley@ksd.uscourts.gov Fax: (913) 735-2239
Education: William Jewell 1999

Court Operations Supervisor - Wichita
Chasity Schoonover ....(316) 315-4200
U.S. Courthouse, 401 N. Market St.,
Wichita, KS 67202
E-mail: chasity_schoonover@ksd.uscourts.gov

Court Operations Supervisor - Topeka **Debra Waylan** ....(785) 338-5400
U.S. Courthouse, 444 SE Quincy St.,
Topeka, KS 66683
E-mail: debra_waylan@ksd.uscourts.gov

Court Operations Supervisor - Kansas City **Mike Mort** ...(913) 735-2200
E-mail: mike_mort@ksd.uscourts.gov
Education: Arkansas State 1985 BS

Librarian **Meg Martin** ....(913) 735-2495
Fax: (913) 735-2496

Chambers of Chief Judge J. Thomas Marten

U.S. Courthouse, 401 North Market Street, Room 232, Wichita, KS 67202
Tel: (316) 315-4300 Fax: (316) 315-4301
E-mail: judge_marten@ksd.uscourts.gov

J. Thomas "Tom" Marten
Chief Judge

Date of Birth: 1951
Education: Washburn 1973 BA, 1976 JD
Began Service: January 5, 1996
Appointed By: President William J. Clinton

Current Memberships: American Bar Foundation; American Bar Association; Federal Judges Association; Kansas Bar Association; Minnesota State Bar Association; Wichita Bar Association

Staff

Law Clerk **Mike Lahey** ....(316) 315-4308
Began Service: 2015
Term Expires: September 2016
E-mail: michael_lahey@ksd.uscourts.gov

Law Clerk **Misha Jacob-Warren** ....(316) 315-4310
Began Service: 2014
Term Expires: September 2016

Career Law Clerk **Brian P. Wood** ....(316) 315-4307
E-mail: brian_wood@ksd.uscourts.gov
Education: Pittsburg State 1983 BA;
Kansas 1986 JD

Chambers of Chief Judge J. Thomas Marten *continued*

Courtroom Deputy **Joyce Roach** ....(316) 315-4306
E-mail: joyce_roach@ksd.uscourts.gov

Court Reporter **Jana McKinney** ....(316) 315-4314
E-mail: jana_mckinney@ksd.uscourts.gov

Judicial Assistant **Jenine Wright** ....(316) 315-4305
E-mail: jenine_wright@ksd.uscourts.gov
Education: Wichita State 1986 BA

Chambers of District Judge Carlos Murguia

Robert J. Dole U.S. Courthouse, 500 State Avenue, Room 537,
Kansas City, KS 66101
Tel: (913) 735-2340 Fax: (913) 735-2341

Carlos Murguia
District Judge

Date of Birth: 1957
Education: Kansas 1979 BS, 1982 JD
Began Service: September 23, 1999
Appointed By: President William J. Clinton

Judicial: Small Claims Court Judge/Judge Pro Tem (part-time), Wyandotte County District Court (1984-1990); District Court Judge, Wyandotte County District Court

Legal Practice: Attorney, Zeigler Legal Services, Chartered (1982-1985)

Nonprofit: Coordinator of Immigration Amnesty Program, El Centro, Inc. (1985-1990)

Current Memberships: American Bar Association; Hispanic National Bar Association; Kansas Bar Association; Wyandotte County Bar Association

Staff

Law Clerk **Kyle O'Brien** ....(913) 735-2340

Career Law Clerk **Amii Castle** ....(913) 735-2340
E-mail: amii_castle@ksd.uscourts.gov
Education: Kansas 1997 JD

Career Law Clerk **Casey Tourtillott** ....(913) 735-2340
E-mail: casey_tourtillott@ksd.uscourts.gov
Education: William Jewell 1995 BA;
Missouri (Kansas City) 2000 JD

Court Reporter **Nancy Wiss** ....(913) 735-2354
E-mail: nancy_wiss@ksd.uscourts.gov

Courtroom Deputy and Judicial Assistant
Sarah Spegal ....(913) 735-2340
E-mail: sarah_spegal@ksd.uscourts.gov

Chambers of District Judge Julie A. Robinson

500 State Avenue, Suite 511, Topeka, KS 66683-3502
Tel: (913) 735-2360 Fax: (913) 735-2361

Julie A. Robinson
District Judge

Date of Birth: 1957
Education: Kansas 1978 BS, 1981 JD
Began Service: December 14, 2001
Appointed By: President George W. Bush

Academic: Adjunct Faculty Member, School of Law, University of Kansas (1989-1990)

Clerkships: Law Clerk The Honorable Benjamin E. Franklin, United States Bankruptcy Court for the District of Kansas (1981-1983)

Government: Assistant United States Attorney, District of Kansas, United States Attorney's Office, United States Department of Justice, Ronald Reagan Administration (1983-1992); Senior Litigation Counsel, Kansas District, Office of the Attorney General, United States Department of Justice (1992-1994)

Judicial: Bankruptcy Judge, United States Bankruptcy Court for the District of Kansas (1994-2001); Bankruptcy Judge, United States Bankruptcy Appellate Panel for the Tenth Circuit (1996-2001)

Legal Practice: Law Clerk, Schneider, Shamberg & May (1981)

Chambers of District Judge Julie A. Robinson *continued*

Current Memberships: American Bar Foundation; American Bar Association; The American Inns of Court; Kansas Bar Association

Staff
Law Clerk **Meredith Schlacter** .... (913) 735-2360
Law Clerk **Grant Treaster** .... (913) 735-2360
Career Law Clerk **Lauren M. Lowry** .... (913) 735-2360
E-mail: lauren_lowry@ksd.uscourts.gov
Education: Washburn 1985 JD
Career Law Clerk **Amy Miller Seymour** .... (913) 735-2360
Began Service: January 2005
E-mail: amy_seymour@ksd.uscourts.gov
Education: Kansas 2003 JD
Courtroom Deputy **Bonnie Wiest** .... (913) 735-2365
E-mail: bonnie_wiest@ksd.uscourts.gov
Court Reporter **Kelli Stewart** .... (785) 338-5354
E-mail: kelli_stewart@ksd.uscourts.gov

Chambers of District Judge Eric F. Melgren
401 North Market, Suite 414, Wichita, KS 67202
Tel: (316) 315-4320 Fax: (316) 315-4321
E-mail: ksd_melgren_chambers@ksd.uscourts.gov

Eric F. Melgren
District Judge

Education: Wichita State 1979 BA; Washburn 1985 JD
Began Service: October 9, 2008
Appointed By: President George W. Bush

Clerkships: Law Clerk, Judge Frank G. Theis, United States District Court for the District of Kansas

Government: U.S. Attorney, Kansas District, Executive Office for United States Attorneys, United States Department of Justice (2002-2008)

Legal Practice: Attorney, Foulston Siefkin LLP (1987-1992); Partner, Foulston Siefkin LLP (1992-2002)

Staff
Law Clerk **Alicia Bodecker** .... (316) 315-4328
E-mail: alicia_bodecker@ksd.uscourts.gov
Law Clerk **Stephanie Nall** .... (316) 315-4328
E-mail: stephanie_nall@ksd.uscourts.gov
Law Clerk **Jon Simpson** .... (316) 315-4328
E-mail: jon_simpson@ksd.uscourts.gov
Law Clerk **Jeff Kuhlman** .... (316) 315-4328
E-mail: jeff_kuhlman@ksd.uscourts.gov
Court Reporter **Jo Wilkinson** .... (316) 315-4334
E-mail: jo_wilkinson@ksd.uscourts.gov
Courtroom Deputy **Cindy McKee** .... (316) 315-4320
E-mail: cindy_mckee@ksd.uscourts.gov

Chambers of District Judge Daniel D. Crabtree
444 SE Quincy Street, Topeka, KS 66683
Tel: (785) 338-5340 Fax: (785) 338-5341
E-mail: ksd_crabtree_chambers@ksd.uscourts.gov

Daniel D. Crabtree
District Judge

Education: Ottawa U 1978 BA; Kansas 1981 JD
Began Service: May 13, 2014
Appointed By: President Barack Obama

Legal Practice: Partner and Practice Leader, Commercial Litigation, Stinson Morrison Hecker LLP (2010-2011); Managing Partner, Overland Park, KS Office, Stinson Morrison Hecker LLP; Practice Leader, Class Actions - Business Litigation, Stinson Morrison Hecker LLP

Nonprofit: Director, Board of Directors, Greater Kansas City Community Foundation (2013-2014)

Chambers of District Judge Daniel D. Crabtree *continued*

Staff
Law Clerk **Anne Emert** .... (785) 338-5340
Term Expires: July 2016
Law Clerk **Carson Hinderks** .... (785) 338-5340
Law Clerk **Genni K. Hursh** .... (785) 338-5340
Term Expires: July 2016
Court Reporter **Sherry A. Harris** .... (785) 338-5354
Courtroom Deputy **Megan Garrett** .... (785) 338-5345

Chambers of Senior Judge Sam A. Crow
444 SE Quincy Street, Room 430, Topeka, KS 66683
Tel: (785) 338-5360 Fax: (785) 338-5361

Sam A. Crow
Senior Judge

Date of Birth: 1926
Education: Kansas 1949 BA; Washburn 1952 JD
Began Service: December 10, 1981
Appointed By: President Ronald Reagan

Academic: Lecturer, School of Law, Washburn University

Judicial: Magistrate Judge, United States District Court for the District of Kansas (1975-1981)

Legal Practice: Law Clerk, Rooney, Dickinson & Prager (1952-1953); Partner, Rooney, Dickinson, Prager & Crow (1953-1963); Partner, Dickinson, Crow, Skoog & Honeyman (1963-1970); Senior Partner, Crow & Skoog (1971-1975)

Military Service: United States Army; United States Army Reserve, United States Department of the Army (1952-1995)

Current Memberships: American Bar Association; The Sam A. Crow American Inn of Court, The American Inns of Court; Kansas Bar Association; National Association of United States Magistrates; Topeka Bar Association; Topeka Lawyers Club; Wichita Bar Association

Staff
Career Law Clerk **Martin K. Albrecht** .... (785) 338-5360
E-mail: martin_albrecht@ksd.uscourts.gov
Career Law Clerk **(Vacant)** .... (785) 338-5360
Judicial Assistant/Courtroom Deputy **Melinda Barnes** .... (785) 338-5360
E-mail: melinda_barnes@ksd.uscourts.gov

Chambers of Senior Judge John Watson Lungstrum
Robert J. Dole U.S. Courthouse, 500 State Avenue, Suite 517, Kansas City, KS 66101
Tel: (913) 735-2320 Fax: (913) 735-2321
E-mail: ksd_lungstrum_chambers@ksd.uscourts.gov

John Watson Lungstrum
Senior Judge

Date of Birth: 1945
Education: Yale 1967 BA; Kansas 1970 JD
Began Service: 1991
Appointed By: President George H.W. Bush

Current Memberships: American Bar Association; Douglas County Bar Association; Kansas Bar Association; Wyandotte County Bar Association

Staff
Law Clerk **Allen Quinlan** .... (913) 735-2320
Began Service: September 2011
Education: Kansas 1999 JD
Career Law Clerk **Kelly A. Martucci** .... (913) 735-2320
E-mail: kelly_martucci@ksd.uscourts.gov
Education: Kansas 1995 JD
Career Law Clerk **David J. Rempel** .... (913) 735-2320
Began Service: 2007
E-mail: david_rempel@ksd.uscourts.gov
Education: Yale 1990 BA; Kansas 1994 JD
Court Reporter **Kim Greiner** .... (913) 735-2314

(continued on next page)

Chambers of Senior Judge John Watson Lungstrum *continued*

Courtroom Deputy **Sharon Scheurer** . . . . (913) 735-2325
E-mail: sharon_scheurer@ksd.uscourts.gov

Chambers of Senior Judge Kathryn Hoefer Vratil

Robert J. Dole U.S. Courthouse, 500 State Avenue, Suite 529,
Kansas City, KS 66101-2435
Tel: (913) 735-2300 Fax: (913) 735-2301
E-mail: ksd_vratil_chambers@ksd.uscourts.gov

Kathryn Hoefer Vratil
Senior Judge

Date of Birth: 1949
Education: Kansas 1971 BA, 1975 JD
Began Service: October 30, 1992
Appointed By: President George H.W. Bush
Political Affiliation: Republican

Current Memberships: American Bar Foundation; The Earl E. O'Connor American Inn of Court, The American Inns of Court; Association for Women Lawyers of Kansas City; Federal Judges Association; Johnson County Bar Association; Johnson County Bar Foundation, Johnson County Bar Association; Kansas Bar Association; Kansas Bar Foundation, Kansas Bar Association; Kansas City Metropolitan Bar Association; Lawyers Association of Kansas City; National Association of Women Judges; Wyandotte County Bar Association

Staff

Career Law Clerk **Brett Gordon** . . . . (913) 735-2300
E-mail: brett_gordon@ksd.uscourts.gov
Education: Chicago 1990 BA;
Pennsylvania 1994 JD

Career Law Clerk **Angela Gupta** . . . . (913) 735-2300
E-mail: angela_gupta@ksd.uscourts.gov
Education: Kansas 1988 BS; Pennsylvania 1991 JD

Career Law Clerk **Mary Matthews** . . . . (913) 735-2300
E-mail: mary_matthews@ksd.uscourts.gov
Education: Kansas 1978 BS;
Emporia State 1981 MS; Washburn 1991 JD

Career Law Clerk **(Vacant)** . . . . (913) 735-2300

Court Reporter **(Vacant)** . . . . (913) 735-2314

Courtroom Deputy Clerk **Sherry Bernhardt** . . . . (913) 735-2300

Chambers of Chief Magistrate Judge James P. O'Hara

Robert J. Dole U.S. Courthouse, 500 State Avenue, Suite 219,
Kansas City, KS 66101
Tel: (913) 735-2280 Fax: (913) 735-2281
E-mail: ksd_ohara_chambers@ksd.uscourts.gov

James P. O'Hara
Chief Magistrate Judge

Date of Birth: 1955
Education: Nebraska 1977 BA; Creighton 1980 JD
Began Service: April 17, 2000
Term Expires: April 16, 2016

Staff

Law Clerk **Megan Miller** . . . . (913) 735-2288
Term Expires: April 2016
E-mail: megan_miller@ksd.uscourts.gov

Career Law Clerk **Amy M. Henson** . . . . (913) 551-6851
E-mail: amy_henson@ksd.uscourts.gov
Education: Nebraska 1996 BA;
Wake Forest 1999 JD

Judicial Assistant/Courtroom Deputy **Kathy Grant** . . . . (913) 735-2280
E-mail: kathy_grant@ksd.uscourts.gov

Chambers of Magistrate Judge Gerald L. Rushfelt

Robert J. Dole U.S. Courthouse, 500 State Avenue, Suite 628,
Kansas City, KS 66101-2428
Tel: (913) 735-2270 Fax: (913) 735-2261
E-mail: KSD_Rushfelt_chambers@ksd.uscourts.gov

Gerald L. Rushfelt
Magistrate Judge

Date of Birth: 1929
Education: Kansas 1953 BA, 1958 LLB, 1958 JD
Began Service: September 9, 1985
Political Affiliation: Democrat

Academic: Instructor, University of Kansas (1980-1992)

Government: Member, Office of the City Council, City of Roeland Park, Kansas (1964-1969)

Judicial: Judge Pro Tem, Leawood Municipal Court (1978-1985)

Legal Practice: Partner, Sullivant & Smith (1958-1969); Partner, Rushfelt, Mueller, Lamar & Druten (1969-1985)

Military Service: United States Army (1953-1955)

Current Memberships: American Bar Association; American Board of Trial Advocates; American College of Trial Lawyers; The Earl E. O'Connor American Inn of Court, The American Inns of Court; International Society of Barristers; Johnson County Bar Association; Kansas Bar Association

Staff

Career Law Clerk **Gloria Clement** . . . . (913) 735-2267
E-mail: gloria_clements@ksd.uscourts.gov
Education: Kansas 2011 JD

Courtroom Deputy **Yolanda Holman** . . . . (913) 735-2265
E-mail: yolanda_holman@ksd.uscourts.gov

Chambers of Magistrate Judge K. Gary Sebelius

U.S. Courthouse, 444 SE Quincy Street, Suite 475, Topeka, KS 66683
Tel: (785) 338-5480 Fax: (785) 338-5481
E-mail: ksd_sebelius_chambers@ksd.uscourts.gov

K. Gary Sebelius
Magistrate Judge

Date of Birth: November 8, 1949
Education: Kansas State 1971 BA; Georgetown 1974 JD
Began Service: February 21, 2003
Term Expires: February 21, 2019

Current Memberships: Kansas Bar Foundation, Kansas Bar Association

Staff

Career Law Clerk **Brooke Hesler** . . . . (785) 338-5486
Began Service: August 11, 2008
E-mail: brooke_hesler@ksd.uscourts.gov
Education: Washburn 2008 JD

Law Clerk **Katherine Marples** . . . . (785) 338-5487
Began Service: August 2014
Term Expires: August 15, 2016
E-mail: katherine_marples@ksd.uscourts.gov

Courtroom Deputy/Judicial Assistant **Sheryl Gilchrist** . . . . (785) 338-5485
Affiliation: PP; PLS
E-mail: sheryl_gilchrist@ksd.uscourts.gov

Chambers of Magistrate Judge Kenneth G. Gale

United States District Court, 401 North Market Street, Suite 403,
Wichita, KS 67202
Tel: (316) 315-4380 Fax: (316) 315-4381

Kenneth G. Gale
Magistrate Judge

Education: Washburn 1980 JD
Began Service: August 2, 2010
Term Expires: August 1, 2018

Chambers of Magistrate Judge Kenneth G. Gale *continued*

Staff
Career Law Clerk **Dwight Fisher** .... (316) 315-4380
Education: Drake 1992 BA; Kansas 1995 JD
Courtroom Deputy **Angela Whittle** .... (316) 315-4386
E-mail: angela_whittle@ksd.uscourts.gov
Judicial Assistant **Cassie Carter** .... (316) 315-4385
E-mail: cassie_carter@ksd.uscourts.gov

Chambers of Magistrate Judge Teresa J. James

500 State Avenue, Suite 208, Kansas City, KS 66101
Tel: (913) 735-2260 Fax: (913) 735-2261
E-mail: ksd_james_chambers@ksd.uscourts.gov

Teresa J. James
Magistrate Judge

Education: Kansas 1981 BA, 1984 JD

Staff
Career Law Clerk **Therese M. Schuele** .... (913) 735-2260
Education: Georgetown 1987 JD
Career Law Clerk **Brenda Yoakum-Kriz** .... (913) 735-2260
Education: Missouri (Kansas City) 1999 JD
Courtroom Deputy **Carol Kuhl** .... (913) 735-2260
E-mail: carol.kuhl@ksd.uscourts.gov

Chambers of Magistrate Judge Gwynne E. Birzer

401 North Market Street, Suite 322, Wichita, KS 67202
Tel: (316) 315-4360 Fax: (316) 315-4361
E-mail: ksd_birzer_chambers@ksd.uscourts.gov

Gwynne E. Birzer
Magistrate Judge

Education: Washburn 1989 BA, 1992 JD
Began Service: 2015
Term Expires: July 1, 2023

Staff
Career Law Clerk **Angela Coble** .... (316) 315-4360
Courtroom Deputy **Amy Merseal** .... (316) 315-4366
Administrative Assistant **Sharilyn A. Jordan** .... (316) 315-4360
E-mail: sharilyn_jordan@ksd.uscourts.gov

Chambers of Magistrate Judge (recalled) David J. Waxse

Robert J. Dole U.S. Courthouse, 500 State Avenue, Suite 630,
Kansas City, KS 66101-2428
Tel: (913) 735-2290 Fax: (913) 735-2261
E-mail: ksd_waxse_chambers@ksd.uscourts.gov

David J. Waxse
Magistrate Judge

Date of Birth: 1945
Education: Kansas 1967 BA; Columbia 1971 JD
Began Service: October 4, 1999
Term Expires: October 3, 2016
Political Affiliation: Democrat

Academic: Dean of Students, Intermediate School 88, New York City Board of Education (1968-1970); Special Education Teacher, New York City Board of Education (1970-1971); Lecturer, University of Kansas (1981-1982)

Government: City Attorney (part-time) (1972-1979)

Judicial: Municipal Judge (part-time) (1974-1980)

Legal Practice: Attorney, Payne & Jones, Chtd. (1971-1984); Counsel, Shook, Hardy & Bacon L.L.P. (1984-1986); Partner, Shook, Hardy & Bacon L.L.P. (1986-1999)

Chambers of Magistrate Judge (recalled) David J. Waxse *continued*

Current Memberships: American Bar Foundation; American Bar Association; The Earl E. O'Connor American Inn of Court, The American Inns of Court; Federal Magistrate Judges Association; Johnson County Bar Association; Kansas City Metropolitan Bar Association; Midwest Bioethics Center

Staff
Career Law Clerk **(Vacant)** .... (913) 735-2268
Courtroom Deputy **Yolanda Holman** .... (913) 735-2210
E-mail: yolanda_holman@ksd.uscourts.gov

Chambers of Magistrate Judge (recalled) Donald W. Bostwick

U.S. Courthouse, 401 North Market Street, Suite 403, Wichita, KS 67202
Tel: (316) 315-4270 Fax: (316) 315-4271

Donald W. Bostwick
Magistrate Judge (recalled)

Date of Birth: 1943
Education: Kansas 1965 BS, 1968 JD

Current Memberships: American Bar Foundation; American Bar Association; American College of Trial Lawyers; Federal Magistrate Judges Association; Kansas Bar Association; Kansas Bar Foundation, Kansas Bar Association; Wichita Bar Association

United States Bankruptcy Court for the District of Kansas

167 U.S. Courthouse, 401 North Market Street, Wichita, KS 67202
Tel: (316) 315-4110
Tel: (316) 315-4101 (Voice Case Information System VCIS)
Tel: (800) 827-9028 (Toll Free Voice Case Information System VCIS)
Fax: (316) 315-4111
Internet: www.ksb.uscourts.gov

Number of Judgeships: 4

Court Staff
Fax: (316) 315-4111

Clerk of Court **David D. Zimmerman** .... (316) 315-4180
Administrative Assistant **(Vacant)** .... (316) 315-4186

Chambers of Chief Bankruptcy Judge Robert E. Nugent

167 U.S. Courthouse, 401 North Market Street, Wichita, KS 67202
Tel: (316) 315-4150 Fax: (316) 315-4111
E-mail: Judge_Nugent@ksb.uscourts.gov

Robert E. Nugent
Chief Bankruptcy Judge

Date of Birth: 1955
Education: Kansas 1980 JD
Began Service: June 14, 2000
Term Expires: June 13, 2028

Affiliation: Bankruptcy Judge, Chambers of Bankruptcy Judge Robert E. Nugent, United States Bankruptcy Appellate Panel for the Tenth Circuit

Staff
Career Law Clerk **Jana D. Abbott** .... (316) 315-4150
E-mail: Jana_Abbott@ksb.uscourts.gov
Education: Kansas 1981 BSBA; Washburn 1984 JD
Judicial Assistant **Janet Swonger** .... (316) 315-4150
E-mail: janet_swonger@ksb.uscourts.gov

Chambers of Bankruptcy Judge Janice Miller Karlin
U.S. Courthouse, 444 SE Quincy Street, Suite 240, Topeka, KS 66683
Tel: (785) 338-5950 Fax: (785) 338-5949

Janice Miller Karlin
Bankruptcy Judge

Education: Kansas 1975 BA, 1980 JD
Began Service: October 17, 2002
Term Expires: October 16, 2016

Government: Assistant U.S. Attorney, Kansas District, United States Department of Justice (1980-2002)

Staff
Career Law Clerk **(Vacant)** .... (785) 338-5950
Judicial Assistant **Donna Johnson** .... (785) 338-5950

Chambers of Bankruptcy Judge Dale L. Somers
444 SE Quincy Street, Room 225, Topeka, KS 66683
Tel: (785) 338-5960 Fax: (785) 338-5949

Dale L. Somers
Bankruptcy Judge

Began Service: 2010

Staff
Law Clerk **Brian D. Caldwell** .... (785) 338-5963
Education: Kansas 1978 BA; Texas 1985 JD
Law Clerk **Anne Baker** .... (785) 338-5962
Judicial Assistant **Donna Johnson** .... (785) 338-5964

Chambers of Bankruptcy Judge Robert D. Berger
500 State Avenue, Room 161, Kansas City, KS 66101
Tel: (913) 735-2150 Fax: (913) 735-2111

Robert D. Berger
Bankruptcy Judge

Began Service: 2003

United States District Court for the Eastern District of Kentucky
U.S. Courthouse, 101 Barr Street, Lexington, KY 40507
Tel: (859) 233-2503 Tel: (800) 676-6856 (PACER)
Fax: (859) 233-2470
Internet: www.kyed.uscourts.gov

Number of Judgeships: 6

Number of Vacancies: 1

Circuit: Sixth

Areas Covered: Counties of Anderson, Bath, Bell, Boone, Bourbon, Boyd, Boyle, Bracken, Breathitt, Campbell, Carroll, Carter, Clark, Clay, Elliott, Estill, Fayette, Fleming, Floyd, Franklin, Gallatin, Garrard, Grant, Greenup, Harlan, Harrison, Henry, Jackson, Jessamine, Johnson, Kenton, Knott, Knox, Laurel, Lawrence, Lee, Leslie, Letcher, Lewis, Lincoln, Madison, Magoffin, Martin, Mason, McCreary, Menifee, Mercer, Montgomery, Morgan, Nicholas, Owen, Owsley, Pendleton, Perry, Pike, Powell, Pulaski, Robertson, Rockcastle, Rowan, Scott, Shelby, Trimble, Wayne, Whitley, Wolfe and Woodford

Court Staff
Clerk of Court **Robert R. Carr** .... (859) 233-2503
Chief Deputy Clerk **Nathan W. Lee** .... (859) 233-2503

United States District Court for the Eastern District of Kentucky *continued*

Deputy In Charge - Ashland **Christina M. McAlister** .... (606) 329-2465
Federal Bldg., 3rd Fl., 1405 Greenup Ave., Ashland, KY 41101
Deputy In Charge - Covington **Tammy Ziegelmeyer** ..... (859) 392-7925
35 W. Fifth St., Rm. 289, Covington, KY 44102
Deputy In Charge - Frankfort **Ada K. Ratliff** .... (502) 223-5225
313 John C. Watts Federal Bldg., 330 W. Broadway, Frankfort, KY 40601
Deputy In Charge - London **Jacqueline Brock** .... (606) 877-7910
Federal Bldg., 310 S. Main St., Rm. 215, London, KY 40741
Deputy In Charge - Pikeville **Tara Adkins** .... (606) 437-6160
203 Federal Bldg., 110 Main St., Pikeville, KY 41501-1100
Chief Probation Officer **Rozel L. Hollingsworth** .... (859) 233-2646

Chambers of Chief Judge Karen K. Caldwell
101 Barr Street, Lexington, KY 40601
Tel: (859) 233-2828 Fax: (859) 233-2413
E-mail: karen.caldwell@kyed.uscourts.gov

Karen K. Caldwell
Chief Judge

Date of Birth: 1956
Education: Transylvania 1977 BA; Kentucky 1980 JD
Began Service: November 13, 2001
Appointed By: President George W. Bush

Current Memberships: American Bar Association; Kentucky Bar Association

Staff
Law Clerk **Michael E. Hill** .... (859) 233-2828
Began Service: September 2015
Term Expires: September 2016
E-mail: michael_hill@kyed.uscourts.gov
Law Clerk **W. Pearce Nesbitt** .... (859) 233-2828
Began Service: September 2015
Term Expires: September 2016
E-mail: pearce_nesbitt@kyed.uscourts.gov
Career Law Clerk **Candace W. Clay** .... (859) 233-2828
E-mail: candace_clay@kyed.uscourts.gov
Education: Kentucky 1988 BA; George Washington 1996 JD
Court Reporter **Rhonda S. Sansom** .... (859) 619-3624
E-mail: rhonda.sansom@gmail.com
Secretary **Jamie T. Chrisman** .... (859) 233-2828
E-mail: jamie_chrisman@kyed.uscourts.gov
Education: Western Kentucky 1985 AA

Chambers of District Judge Danny C. Reeves
101 Barr Street, Room 136, Lexington, KY 40601
Tel: (859) 233-2453 Fax: (859) 233-2430
E-mail: reeves_chambers@kyed.uscourts.gov

Danny C. Reeves
District Judge

Date of Birth: 1957
Education: Eastern Kentucky 1978 BA; Salmon P Chase 1981 JD
Began Service: December 31, 2001
Appointed By: President George W. Bush

Clerkships: Law Clerk The Honorable Eugene E. Siler, Jr., United States District Court for the Eastern and Western Districts of Kentucky (1981-1983)

Legal Practice: Associate, Greenebaum Doll & McDonald PLLC (1983-1988); Partner, Greenebaum Doll & McDonald PLLC (1988-2001)

Current Memberships: Fayette County Bar Association; Federal Bar Association; Kentucky Bar Association

Chambers of District Judge Danny C. Reeves *continued*

Staff

Career Law Clerk **Anne Cook** . . . . (859) 233-2453
Law Clerk **Elizabeth Davis** . . . . (859) 233-2453
Began Service: September 2014
Term Expires: September 2016
E-mail: elizabeth_barrera@kyed.uscourts.gov
Law Clerk **Alesa Craig** . . . . (859) 233-2453
Began Service: August 29, 2015
Term Expires: August 2016
Judicial Assistant **Lisa K. Moore** . . . . (502) 875-4777
E-mail: lisa_k_moore@kyed.uscourts.gov

Chambers of District Judge David L. Bunning

35 West Fifth Street, Room 410, Covington, KY 41012
P.O. Box 232, Covington, KY 41011
Tel: (859) 392-7907 Fax: (859) 392-7945
E-mail: david_bunning@kyed.uscourts.gov

David L. Bunning
District Judge

Date of Birth: 1966
Education: Kentucky 1988 BA, 1991 JD
Began Service: February 21, 2002
Appointed By: President George W. Bush

Government: Law Clerk, Eastern District of Kentucky, Office of the United States Attorney, United States Department of Justice (1991); Assistant United States Attorney, Eastern District of Kentucky, Office of the United States Attorney, United States Department of Justice (1991-2002)

Current Memberships: Kentucky Bar Association

Staff

Law Clerk **Amanda Theetge** . . . . (859) 392-7907
Began Service: September 2015
Term Expires: September 2016
E-mail: amanda_theetge@kyed.uscourts.gov
Law Clerk **Sarah Townzen** . . . . (859) 392-7907
Began Service: September 2013
Term Expires: September 2016
E-mail: sarah_townzen@kyed.uscourts.gov
Court Reporter **Lisa Wiesman** . . . . (859) 291-4410
E-mail: lisa_wiesman@kyed.uscourts.gov Fax: (859) 392-7945

Chambers of District Judge Gregory Van Tatenhove

330 West Broadway, Frankfort, KY 40601
Tel: (606) 877-7950 Fax: (606) 877-7955

Gregory F. Van Tatenhove
District Judge

Education: Asbury Col 1982; Kentucky JD
Began Service: January 6, 2006
Appointed By: President George W. Bush

Clerkships: Law Clerk, District Judge Eugene E. Siler, Jr., United States District Court for the Western District of Kentucky

Government: Chief of Staff and Legal Counsel (KY, District 2), Office of Representative Ron Lewis, United States House of Representatives; U.S. Attorney, Kentucky - Eastern District, Executive Office for United States Attorneys, United States Department of Justice (2001-2006)

Staff

Law Clerk **Dakotah Burns** . . . . (606) 877-7950
Began Service: September 2015
Term Expires: September 2016
E-mail: dakotah_burns@kyed.uscourts.gov
Law Clerk **Holly Iaccarino** . . . . (606) 877-7950
Education: Columbus Law 2010 JD
Law Clerk **Katharine Smith** . . . . (606) 877-7950
Began Service: September 2015
Courtroom Deputy **Rebecca Chaney** . . . . (606) 877-7950

Chambers of District Judge Amul R. Thapar

35 West Fifth Street, Covington, KY 41011
Tel: (606) 877-7966 Fax: (606) 877-7969

Amul R. Thapar
District Judge

Date of Birth: 1969
Education: Boston Col 1991 BS; Boalt Hall 1994 JD
Began Service: January 4, 2008
Appointed By: President George W. Bush

Academic: Adjunct Professor, College of Law, University of Cincinnati (1996-1997); Trial Advocacy Instructor, The Law Center, Georgetown University (1999-2000); Adjunct Professor, College of Law, University of Cincinnati (2002-2006)

Clerkships: Law Clerk, Chambers of District Judge S. Arthur Spiegel, United States District Court for the Southern District of Ohio (1994-1996); Law Clerk, Chambers of Circuit Judge Nathaniel R. Jones, United States Court of Appeals for the Sixth Circuit (1996-1997)

Corporate: General Counsel, Equalfooting.com (2000-2001)

Government: Assistant U.S. Attorney, District of Columbia District, Executive Office for United States Attorneys, United States Department of Justice (1999-2000); Assistant U.S. Attorney, Ohio - Southern District, Executive Office for United States Attorneys, United States Department of Justice (2002-2003); Assistant U.S. Attorney, Criminal Division, Ohio - Southern District, United States Department of Justice (2006); U.S. Attorney, Kentucky - Eastern District, Executive Office for United States Attorneys, United States Department of Justice (2006-2007)

Legal Practice: Associate, Williams & Connolly LLP (1997-1999); Associate, Cincinnati, OH Office, Squire, Sanders & Dempsey L.L.P. (2001-2002)

Chambers of Senior Judge William O. Bertelsman

U.S. Courthouse, 35 West Fifth Street, Suite 505, Covington, KY 41011
P.O. Box 1012, Covington, KY 41012
Tel: (859) 392-7900

William O. Bertelsman
Senior Judge

Date of Birth: 1936
Education: Xavier (OH) 1958 BA; Cincinnati 1961 JD
Began Service: November 29, 1979
Appointed By: President Jimmy Carter

Academic: Faculty, College of Law, University of Cincinnati (1965-1972); Faculty, Federal Judicial Center (1981-1982)

Government: City Attorney and Prosecutor, Office of the City Prosecutor, City of Covington, Kentucky (1962-1969)

Legal Practice: Partner, Bertelsman & Bertelsman (1962-1979)

Military Service: Ohio and Kentucky National Guard (1958-1963); United States Army (1963-1964)

Nonprofit: Faculty, ALI-ABA, The American Law Institute

Current Memberships: American Bar Association; Judicial Conference of the United States; Kentucky Bar Association; Northern Kentucky Bar Association

Staff

Law Clerk **Paul Hendrickson** . . . . (859) 392-7900
Began Service: September 2015
Term Expires: September 2016
E-mail: paul_hendrickson@kyed.uscourts.gov
Law Clerk **Josh McIntosh** . . . . (859) 392-7900
Began Service: September 2015
Term Expires: September 2016
Career Law Clerk **Dawn L. Rogers** . . . . (859) 392-7900
E-mail: dawn_rogers@kyed.uscourts.gov
Education: George Washington 1995 JD
Court Reporter **Joan Averdick** . . . . (859) 291-9666
E-mail: joan_averdick@kyed.uscourts.gov

(continued on next page)

Chambers of Senior Judge William O. Bertelsman *continued*

Secretary **Elaine Oldiges** .... (859) 392-7900

Chambers of Senior Judge Henry Rupert Wilhoit, Jr.

Federal Building, 110 Main Street, Suite 320, Pikeville, KY 41501
Tel: (606) 329-2592 Fax: (606) 324-5186

Henry Rupert Wilhoit, Jr.
Senior Judge

Date of Birth: 1935
Education: Kentucky 1960 LLB
Began Service: 1981
Appointed By: President Ronald Reagan

Government: City Attorney, Office of the City Attorney, City of Grayson, Kentucky (1962-1966); County Attorney, Office of the County Attorney, County of Carter, Kentucky (1966-1970)

Legal Practice: Partner, Wilhoit & Wilhoit (1960-1981)

Current Memberships: American College of Trial Lawyers; Federal Judges Association; Kentucky Bar Association

Staff
Secretary **Janet Solomon** .... (606) 329-2592
E-mail: janet_solomon@kyed.uscourts.gov

Chambers of Senior Judge Joseph M. Hood

101 Barr Street, Lexington, KY 40588
P.O. Box 2227, Lexington, KY 40588-2227
Tel: (859) 233-2415 Fax: (859) 233-2709

Joseph M. Hood
Senior Judge

Date of Birth: 1942
Education: Kentucky 1965 BS, 1972 JD
Began Service: May 1, 1990
Appointed By: President George H.W. Bush

Academic: Graduate Assistant in Economics, University of Kentucky (1965-1966)

Clerkships: Law Clerk The Honorable David Hermansdorfer, United States District Court for the Eastern District of Kentucky (1972-1976)

Judicial: Magistrate Judge, United States District Court for the Eastern District of Kentucky (1976-1990); Chief Judge, United States District Court for the Eastern District of Kentucky (2005-2007)

Military Service: United States Army (1966-1970)

Current Memberships: Fayette County Bar Association; Federal Judges Association; Kentucky Bar Association; Sixth Circuit District Judges Association

Staff
Law Clerk **Haley Dickerson** .... (859) 233-2415
Began Service: August 2015
Term Expires: August 2016
E-mail: haley_dickerson@kyed.uscourts.gov
Law Clerk **Elizabeth Reynolds** .... (859) 233-2415
E-mail: elizabeth_reynolds@kyed.uscourts.gov
Court Reporter **Ann Banta** .... (502) 545-1090
Career Law Clerk **Mary Ann Miranda** .... (859) 233-2415
Education: Transylvania 1997 BA;
Vanderbilt 2002 JD

Chambers of Magistrate Judge Robert E. Wier

U.S. Courthouse, 101 Barr Street, Room 417, Lexington, KY 40507
Tel: (859) 233-2697 Fax: (859) 233-2773

Robert E. Wier
Magistrate Judge

Began Service: September 2006
Term Expires: August 2022

Staff
Law Clerk **Alicia Harden** .... (606) 877-7940
Education: Southern Methodist 2004 JD

Chambers of Magistrate Judge Edward B. Atkins

110 Main Street, Pikeville, KY 41501
Tel: (606) 877-7956 Fax: (606) 324-9292

Edward B. Atkins
Magistrate Judge

Began Service: August 2006
Term Expires: August 2022

Staff
Law Clerk **Nicholas King** .... (606) 887-7956

Chambers of Magistrate Judge Candace J. Smith

35 West Fifth Street, Suite 375, Covington, KY 41011
P.O. Box 122643, Covington, KY 41011
Tel: (859) 392-7903
E-mail: candace_smith@kyed.uscourts.gov

Candace J. Smith
Magistrate Judge

Education: Mount St Joseph 1986 BS; Salmon P Chase 1992 JD
Began Service: 2010

Clerkships: Career Law Clerk, Chambers of District Judge David L. Bunning, United States District Court for the Eastern District of Kentucky (2002-2010)

Staff
Career Law Clerk **Vicki Christian** .... (859) 392-7903
Education: Salmon P Chase 1991 JD

Chambers of Magistrate Judge Hanly A. Ingram

310 South Main Street, Suite 351, London, KY 40741
Tel: (606) 877-7940 Fax: (606) 877-7945
E-mail: hanly_ingram@kyed.uscourts.gov

Hanly A. Ingram
Magistrate Judge

Began Service: October 1, 2010

Chambers of (recalled) Magistrate Judge J. Gregory Wehrman

35 West Fifth Street, Room 310, Covington, KY 41011
Tel: (859) 392-7909 Fax: (859) 392-7913
E-mail: wehrman_chambers@kyed.uscourts.gov

J. Gregory Wehrman
Magistrate Judge (recalled)

Date of Birth: 1944
Education: Cincinnati 1966 BA; Kentucky 1969 JD
Began Service: January 1992
Term Expires: September 1, 2016
Political Affiliation: Republican

Judicial: Magistrate Judge (part-time), United States District Court for the Eastern District of Kentucky (1975-1992)

Legal Practice: Private Practice (1969-1992)

Current Memberships: Kentucky Bar Association; Northern Kentucky Bar Association

Staff
Career Law Clerk **Larry R. Hornsby** .... (859) 392-7909
Education: Cumberland Col 1992 BS; Kentucky 1995 JD

United States Bankruptcy Court for the Eastern District of Kentucky

Community Trust Bank Building, 100 East Vine Street, Suite 200, Lexington, KY 40507
P.O. Box 1111, Lexington, KY 40588-1111
Tel: (859) 233-2608
Tel: (866) 222-8029 (Voice Case Information System VCIS)
Tel: (800) 998-2650 (Toll Free Voice Case Information System VCIS)
Internet: www.kyeb.uscourts.gov

Number of Judgeships: 3

Number of Vacancies: 1

Court Staff
Clerk of Court **Jerry D. Truitt** .... (859) 233-2608
E-mail: jerry_truitt@kyeb.uscourts.gov
Education: Kentucky 1963 BA, 1971 JD

Chambers of Chief Bankruptcy Judge Tracey N. Wise

Community Trust Bank Building, 100 East Vine Street, Lexington, KY 40507
Tel: (859) 233-2465
E-mail: tracey_wise@kyeb.uscourts.gov

Tracey N. Wise
Chief Bankruptcy Judge

Education: Indiana 1980 BA, 1983 JD
Began Service: 2012

Current Memberships: American College of Bankruptcy

Staff
Law Clerk **Jane Elizabeth Miller** .... (859) 233-2465
E-mail: jane_miller@kyeb.uscourts.gov
Career Law Clerk **Lyndon Risner** .... (859) 233-2465
E-mail: lyndon_risner@kyeb.uscourts.gov
Courtroom Deputy **Sheila Sutphin** .... (859) 233-2465

Chambers of Bankruptcy Judge Gregory Schaaf

100 East Vine Street, Lexington, KY 40507
Tel: (859) 233-2814
E-mail: gregory_schaaf@kyeb.uscourts.gov

Gregory R. "Greg" Schaaf
Bankruptcy Judge

Staff
Law Clerk **Holly Lankster** .... (859) 233-2814
E-mail: holly_lankster@kyeb.uscourts.gov
Law Clerk **Stephen Milner** .... (859) 233-2814
E-mail: stephen_milner@kyeb.uscourts.gov
Courtroom Deputy **Ruth Heil** .... (859) 233-2814

United States District Court for the Western District of Kentucky

Gene Snyder U.S. Courthouse, 601 West Broadway, Room 106, Louisville, KY 40202-2249
Tel: (502) 625-3500 Tel: (800) 676-6856 (PACER)
Fax: (502) 625-3880
Internet: www.kywd.uscourts.gov

Number of Judgeships: 4

Number of Vacancies: 1

Circuit: Sixth

Areas Covered: Counties of Adair, Allen, Ballard, Barren, Breckinridge, Bullitt, Butler, Caldwell, Calloway, Carlisle, Casey, Christian, Clinton, Crittenden, Cumberland, Daviess, Edmonson, Fulton, Graves, Grayson, Green, Hancock, Hardin, Hart, Henderson, Hickman, Hopkins, Jefferson, Larue, Livingston, Logan, Lyon, Marion, Marshall, McCracken, McLean, Meade, Metcalfe, Monroe, Muhlenberg, Nelson, Ohio, Oldham, Russell, Simpson, Spencer, Taylor, Todd, Trigg, Union, Warren, Washington and Webster

Court Staff
Clerk of Court **Vanessa L. Armstrong** .... (502) 625-3522
E-mail: vanessa_armstrong@kywd.uscourts.gov Fax: (502) 625-3882
Chief Deputy Clerk **James Vilt** .... (502) 625-3500
Fax: (502) 625-3882
Deputy Clerk-in-Charge - Bowling Green
Celia D. Russell .... (270) 393-2500
241 E. Main St., Bowling Green, KY 42101-2175 Fax: (270) 393-2519
E-mail: celia_furlong@kywd.uscourts.gov
Deputy Clerk-in-Charge - Owensboro **(Vacant)** .... (270) 689-4400
126 Federal Bldg., 423 Frederica St., Owensboro, KY 42301-3013 Fax: (270) 689-4419
Deputy Clerk-in-Charge - Paducah **Kelly P. Harris** .... (270) 415-6400
127 Federal Bldg., 501 Broadway, Paducah, KY 42001-6801 Fax: (270) 415-6419
Financial Administrator **Jillian Harris** .... (502) 625-3594
E-mail: jillian_harris@kywd.uscourts.gov
Chief Probation Officer **Kathryn B. Jarvis** .... (502) 681-1000
Gene Snyder U.S. Courthouse, 601 W. Broadway, Room 400, Louisville, KY 40202-2277 Fax: (502) 681-1100
Director of IT **Trevor Wallis** .... (502) 625-3570
E-mail: trevor_wallis@kywd.uscourts.gov

Chambers of Chief Judge Joseph H. McKinley, Jr.

206 Federal Building, 423 Frederica Street, Owensboro, KY 42301-3013
Tel: (270) 689-4430 Fax: (270) 689-4445

Joseph H. McKinley, Jr.
Chief Judge

Date of Birth: 1954
Education: Kentucky BS; Louisville JD
Began Service: August 25, 1995
Appointed By: President William J. Clinton

Government: Assistant County Attorney, Office of the County Attorney, Daviess County, Kentucky; Commissioner, Kentucky Oil and Gas Commission, Commonwealth of Kentucky

Judicial: Judge, Kentucky Circuit Court, Daviess County (1992-1995); District Judge, United States District Court for the Western District of Kentucky (1995-2011)

Legal Practice: Partner, Meyer, Hutchinson, McKinley & Haines

Staff
Law Clerk **(Vacant)** . . . . (270) 689-4430
Law Clerk **Brian Epling** . . . . (270) 689-4430
Career Law Clerk **Cheryl Gentry Cooper** . . . . (270) 689-4430
Education: Louisville 1994 JD
Court Reporter **(Vacant)** . . . . (270) 689-4417

Chambers of District Judge David J. Hale

601 West Broadway, Room 202, Louisville, KY 40202-2249
Tel: (502) 625-3640 Fax: (502) 625-3659

David J. Hale
District Judge

Date of Birth: 1967
Education: Vanderbilt 1989 BA; Kentucky 1992 JD
Began Service: December 10, 2014
Appointed By: President Barack Obama

Government: Assistant U.S. Attorney, Kentucky - Western District, Executive Office for United States Attorneys, United States Department of Justice (1995-1999); U.S. Attorney, Kentucky - Western District, Office of the Director, United States Department of Justice (2010-2014)

Legal Practice: Counsel, Reed Weitkamp Schell & Vice, PLLC (1999-2002); Partner, Reed Weitkamp Schell & Vice, PLLC (2002-2010)

Staff
Case Manager **Natalie Thompson** . . . . (502) 625-3640

Chambers of District Judge Greg N. Stivers

241 E. Main St., Room 207, Bowling Green, KY 42101-2175
Tel: (270) 393-2440 Fax: (270) 393-2459

Gregory N. Stivers
District Judge

Education: Eastern Kentucky 1982 BA; Kentucky 1985 JD
Began Service: December 5, 2014
Appointed By: President Barack Obama

Staff
Case Manager **Traci Duff** . . . . (270) 393-2505

Chambers of Senior Judge Charles R. Simpson III

Gene Snyder U.S. Courthouse, 601 West Broadway, Room 247, Louisville, KY 40202
Tel: (502) 625-3600 Fax: (502) 625-3619

Charles R. Simpson III
Senior Judge

Date of Birth: 1945
Education: Louisville 1967 BA, 1970 JD
Began Service: October 15, 1986
Appointed By: President Ronald Reagan

Current Memberships: American Judges Association; Federal Bar Association; Federal Circuit Bar Association; Federal Judges Association; Kentucky Bar Association; Louisville Bar Association

Staff
Law Clerk **Brandon Kenney** . . . . (502) 625-3600
Began Service: September 2015
Term Expires: September 2016
Law Clerk **Sarah Reddick** . . . . (502) 625-3600
Began Service: September 2015
Term Expires: September 2016
Career Law Clerk **Sheri B. Weyhing** . . . . (502) 625-3600
E-mail: sheri_weyhing@kywd.uscourts.gov
Education: Louisville 1986 JD
Case Manager **Renee Koch** . . . . (502) 625-3600

Chambers of Senior Judge Thomas B. Russell

Federal Building, 501 Broadway, 1st Floor, Room 121, Paducah, KY 42001
Tel: (270) 415-6430 Fax: (270) 415-6445

Thomas B. Russell
Senior Judge

Date of Birth: 1945
Education: Western Kentucky 1967 BA; Kentucky 1970 JD
Began Service: October 11, 1994
Appointed By: President William J. Clinton

Judicial: District Judge, United States District Court for the Western District of Kentucky (1994-2008); Chief Judge, United States District Court for the Western District of Kentucky (2008-2011)

Legal Practice: Associate, Waller, Threlkeld & Whitlow (1970-1975); Partner, Whitlow, Roberts, Houston & Russell (1975-1994)

Current Memberships: American College of Trial Lawyers; Kentucky Bar Association; McCracken County Bar Association; United States Foreign Intelligence Surveillance Court

Staff
Law Clerk **Jennifer Pekman** . . . . (270) 415-6439
Began Service: August 2015
Term Expires: August 2016
Law Clerk **Ryan Polczynski** . . . . (270) 415-6437
Began Service: August 2014
Term Expires: August 2016
Law Clerk **James B. Shepard** . . . . (270) 415-6439
Began Service: August 2015
Term Expires: August 2016
Courtroom Deputy/Case Manager **Kelly P. Harris** . . . . (270) 415-6405
E-mail: kelly_p_harris@kywd.uscourts.gov
Court Reporter **Terri Turner** . . . . (270) 415-6417
E-mail: terri_turner@kywd.uscourts.gov

Chambers of Magistrate Judge Lanny King

U.S. Courthouse, 501 Broadway, Room 330, Paducah, KY 42001
Tel: (270) 415-6470 Fax: (270) 415-6480
E-mail: judge_king_chambers@kywd.uscourts.gov

Lanny King
Magistrate Judge

Began Service: November 14, 2011
Term Expires: November 14, 2019

Staff
Career Law Clerk **Chad E. Edwards** .... (270) 415-6470
Education: Kentucky 1993 JD
Case Administrator **Mary Butler** .... (270) 415-6470
Administrative Assistant/Secretary **Matt Smith** .... (270) 415-6470
E-mail: matt_smith@kywd.uscourts.gov

Chambers of Magistrate Judge Dave Whalin

Gene Snyder U.S. Courthouse, 601 West Broadway, Room 200,
Louisville, KY 40202-2249
Tel: (502) 625-3830 Fax: (502) 625-3849
E-mail: dwhalin@kywd.uscourts.gov

Dave Whalin
Magistrate Judge

Date of Birth: December 16, 1948
Education: Louisville 1979 BS, 1985 JD
Began Service: July 26, 2004
Term Expires: July 26, 2020

Staff
Career Law Clerk **Jerome E. Wallace** .... (502) 625-3830
Education: Kentucky 1983 JD
Secretary **Karen Brand** .... (502) 625-3830
E-mail: kbrand@kywd.uscourts.gov

Chambers of Magistrate Judge H. Brent Brennenstuhl

241 E. Main St., Room 207, Bowling Green, KY 42101-2175
Tel: (270) 393-2425 Fax: (270) 393-2519

H. Brent Brennenstuhl
Magistrate Judge

Began Service: 2012

Staff
Law Clerk **Walter A. Connolly III** .... (270) 393-2425
Education: Maine 1982 BA;
Washington and Lee 1990 JD
Law Clerk **Julie Rosing** .... (270) 393-2425

Chambers of Magistrate Judge Colin Lindsay

601 West Broadway, Louisville, KY 40202-2249
Tel: (502) 625-3660 Fax: (502) 625-3679

Colin Lindsay
Magistrate Judge

United States Bankruptcy Court for the Western District of Kentucky

Gene Snyder U.S. Courthouse, 601 West Broadway, Suite 450,
Louisville, KY 40202-2264
Tel: (502) 627-5700 Tel: (502) 627-5800 (Administrative Office)
Fax: (502) 627-5710
Internet: www.kywb.uscourts.gov

Number of Judgeships: 3

Court Staff
Clerk of Court **Diane S. Robl** .... (502) 627-5700
E-mail: diane_robl@kywb.uscourts.gov
Education: Louisville 1987 JD
Human Resource Manager **Jeanne Lucas** .... (502) 627-5800
E-mail: jeanne_lucas@kywb.uscourts.gov

Chambers of Chief Bankruptcy Judge Thomas H. Fulton

Gene Snyder U.S. Courthouse, 601 West Broadway, Suite 528,
Louisville, KY 40202-2264
Tel: (502) 627-5550 Fax: (502) 627-5573

Thomas H. Fulton
Chief Bankruptcy Judge

Date of Birth: December 10, 1946
Education: Mississippi State 1967 BA; Columbia 1974 MA, 1976 MPhil; Tulane 1980 JD
Began Service: December 6, 2002
Term Expires: December 2016

Staff
Staff Attorney **(Vacant)** .... (502) 627-5550
Staff Attorney **James W. Lee** .... (502) 627-5550
E-mail: james_lee@kywb.uscourts.gov
Education: Harvard 1990 JD
Courtroom Deputy **Angela Gudgel** .... (502) 627-5615
E-mail: angela_estrada@kywb.uscourts.gov

Chambers of Bankruptcy Judge Joan A. Lloyd

Gene Snyder U.S. Courthouse, 601 West Broadway, Room 541,
Louisville, KY 40202
Tel: (502) 627-5525 Fax: (502) 627-5569
E-mail: joan_lloyd@kywb.uscourts.gov

Joan A. Lloyd
Bankruptcy Judge

Date of Birth: 1961
Education: Kentucky 1982 BA; Brandeis 1985 JD
Began Service: December 22, 1999
Term Expires: December 22, 2027

Current Memberships: American Bankruptcy Institute; The District of Columbia Bar; Kentucky Bar Association; Louisville Bar Association; National Conference of Bankruptcy Judges

Staff
Career Law Clerk **Barbara A. Wetzel** .... (502) 627-5525
E-mail: barbara_wetzel@kywb.uscourts.gov
Education: Louisville 1990 JD
Courtroom Deputy **Brenda Rupe** .... (502) 627-5617
E-mail: brenda_rupe@kywb.uscourts.gov
Judicial Assistant **Elaine Fountain** .... (502) 627-5525
E-mail: Elaine_Fountain@kywb.uscourts.gov

Chambers of Bankruptcy Judge Alan C. Stout
Gene Snyder U.S. Courthouse, 601 West Broadway, Suite 533,
Louisville, KY 40202-2249
Tel: (502) 627-5575 Fax: (502) 627-5573
E-mail: alan_stout@kywb.uscourts.gov

Alan C. Stout
Bankruptcy Judge

Education: Murray State U 1978 BS; Salmon P Chase 1981 JD
Began Service: October 25, 2011

Staff
Staff Attorney **James R. "Jim" Higdon** . . . . (502) 627-5575
E-mail: jim_higdon@kywb.uscourts.gov
Education: Louisville 1991 BA; Alabama 1994 JD
Courtroom Deputy **Sherry Davis** . . . . (502) 627-5600
E-mail: sherry_davis@kywb.uscourts.gov
Secretary **Karen Lynch** . . . . (502) 627-5575
E-mail: karen_lynch@kywb.uscourts.gov

United States District Court for the Eastern District of Louisiana
U.S. Courthouse, 500 Poydras Street, Room C-151,
New Orleans, LA 70130
Tel: (504) 589-7600 Tel: (504) 589-7650 (Clerk's office)
Tel: (800) 676-6856 (PACER) Fax: (504) 589-7697
Internet: www.laed.uscourts.gov

Number of Judgeships: 12

Number of Vacancies: 1

Circuit: Fifth

Areas Covered: Parishes of Assumption, Jefferson, Lafourche, Orleans, Plaquemines, St. Bernard, St. Charles, St. James, St. John the Baptist, St. Tammany, Tangipahoa, Terrebonne and Washington

Court Staff
Clerk of Court **William W. Blevins** . . . . (504) 589-7650
E-mail: william_blevins@laed.uscourts.gov
Executive Assistant **Dawn Fanning** . . . . (504) 589-7650
E-mail: dawn_fanning@laed.uscourts.gov
Chief Deputy Clerk **Carol L. Michel** . . . . (504) 589-7650
Education: Tulane 1984 JD
Docket Manager **Julie Harrison** . . . . (504) 589-7700
E-mail: julie_harrison@laed.uscourts.gov
Intake Supervisor **Julie Harrison** . . . . (504) 589-7700
E-mail: julie_harrison@laed.uscourts.gov
Systems Manager **Patricia Soule** . . . . (504) 589-7762
E-mail: patricia_soule@laed.uscourts.gov
Financial Administrator **Kim Lange** . . . . (504) 589-7786
E-mail: kim_lange@laed.uscourts.gov
Jury Administrator **Claire Trimble** . . . . (504) 589-7740
E-mail: claire_trimble@laed.uscourts.gov
Naturalization **Kristina Haley** . . . . (504) 589-7714
E-mail: kristina_haley@laed.uscourts.gov
Criminal Magistrate Supervisor **Kimberly County** . . . . (504) 589-7682
E-mail: kimberly_county@laed.uscourts.gov
Pro Se Supervisor **Jay Susslin** . . . . (504) 589-7689
E-mail: jay_susslin@laed.uscourts.gov
Chief Probation Officer **Kito Bess** . . . . (504) 589-3200
Hale Boggs Federal Building, 500 Poydras Street,
Room 505, New Orleans, LA 70130-3321
Chief Pretrial Services Officer **Harold Schlumbrecht** . . . . (504) 589-7900
Room 614

Chambers of Chief District Judge Sarah S. Vance
U.S. Courthouse, 500 Poydras Street, Room C255,
New Orleans, LA 70130
Tel: (504) 589-7595
E-mail: sarah_vance@laed.uscourts.gov

Sarah S. Vance
Chief Judge

Date of Birth: 1950
Education: LSU 1971 BA; Tulane 1978 JD
Began Service: September 29, 1994
Appointed By: President William J. Clinton

Legal Practice: Associate, Stone, Pigman, Walther, Wittmann & Hutchinson L.L.P. (1978-1982); Partner, Stone, Pigman, Walther, Wittmann & Hutchinson L.L.P. (1983-1985); Sarah S. Vance Law Corporation (1986-1994)

Staff
Law Clerk **Chloe Chetta** . . . . (504) 589-7595
Began Service: June 2015
Term Expires: June 2016
E-mail: chloe_chetta@laed.uscourts.gov
Law Clerk **Trevor Templeton** . . . . (504) 589-7595
Began Service: August 2015
Term Expires: August 2016
E-mail: trevor_templeton@laed.uscourts.gov
Docket Clerk **Mary Medders** . . . . (504) 589-7657
E-mail: mary_medders@laed.uscourts.gov
Case Manager **Jay Susslin** . . . . (504) 589-7689
Judicial Assistant **Traci Munster** . . . . (504) 589-7595
E-mail: traci_munster@laed.uscourts.gov

Chambers of District Judge Helen G. Berrigan
U.S. Courthouse, 500 Poydras Street, Room C556,
New Orleans, LA 70130
Tel: (504) 589-7515

Helen Ginger Berrigan
District Judge

Date of Birth: 1948
Education: Wisconsin 1969 BA; American U 1971 MA; LSU 1977 JD
Began Service: March 1994
Appointed By: President William J. Clinton
Political Affiliation: Democrat

Government: Volunteer & Staff Researcher, Office of Senator Harold E. Hughes, United States Senate (1971-1972); Legislative Aide, Office of Senator Joseph R. Biden, Jr., United States Senate (1972-1973); Assistant, Mayor Charles Evers (D-MP), Office of the Mayor, City of Fayette, Mississippi (1973-1974); Staff Attorney, Governor's Pardon, Parole and Rehabilitation Commission, Office of the Governor, State of Louisiana (1977-1978); Member, Louisiana Sentencing Commission, State of Louisiana (1987-1994)

Legal Practice: Member and Partner, Gravel Brady & Berrigan (1978-1984); Of Counsel, Berrigan, Litchfield, Schonekas, Mann & Clement (1984-1994)

Current Memberships: New Orleans Chapter, Federal Bar Association; Louisiana State Bar Association; New Orleans Bar Association

Staff
Law Clerk **Dianne Morgan** . . . . (504) 589-7515
Began Service: September 2015
Term Expires: September 2016
E-mail: dianne_morgan@laed.uscourts.gov
Law Clerk (odd cases) **Nicholas W. Roosevelt** . . . . (504) 589-7515
Began Service: September 2015
Term Expires: September 2016
E-mail: nicholas_roosevelt@laed.uscourts.gov
Career Law Clerk (even cases) **Dianne Morgan** . . . . (504) 589-7515

Chambers of District Judge Helen G. Berrigan *continued*

Courtroom Deputy **Kimberly County** .... (504) 589-7682
E-mail: kimberly_county@laed.uscourts.gov
Docket Clerk **Paula Hebert** .... (504) 589-7711
E-mail: paula_hebert@laed.uscourts.gov
Secretary **Denise Barbarin** .... (504) 589-7515
E-mail: denise_barbarin@laed.uscourts.gov

Chambers of District Judge Martin L. C. Feldman

U.S. Courthouse, 500 Poydras Street, C555, New Orleans, LA 70130
Tel: (504) 589-7550 Fax: (504) 589-4470
E-mail: martin_feldman@laed.uscourts.gov

Martin L. C. Feldman
District Judge

Date of Birth: 1934
Education: Tulane 1955 BA, 1957 JD
Began Service: 1983
Appointed By: President Ronald Reagan
Political Affiliation: Republican

Clerkships: Law Clerk The Honorable John Minor Wisdom, United States Court of Appeals for the Fifth Circuit (1957-1959)

Judicial: Member, Judicial Conference of the United States (2001-2004)

Legal Practice: Bronfin, Heller, Feldman, Steinberg & Berins (1959-1983)

Military Service: United States Army (1957-1963)

Current Memberships: United States Foreign Intelligence Surveillance Court

Staff
Law Clerk **Spencer Sinclair** .... (504) 589-7550
Began Service: September 2015
Term Expires: September 2016
E-mail: spencer_sinclair@laed.uscourts.gov
Career Law Clerk **Andrea "Annie" Miller** .... (504) 589-7550
Education: Tulane 2003 JD
Docket Clerk **Crystal Lee-Mitchell** .... (504) 589-7637
Case Manager **Charles Armond** .... (504) 589-7685
E-mail: charles_armond@laed.uscourts.gov
Court Reporter **Toni Tusa** .... (504) 589-7778
E-mail: toni_tusa@laed.uscourts.gov
Judicial Assistant **Donna Wisecarver** .... (504) 589-7550
E-mail: donna_wisecarver@laed.uscourts.gov

Chambers of District Judge Eldon E. Fallon

U.S. Courthouse, 500 Poydras Street, Room C-456,
New Orleans, LA 70130
Tel: (504) 589-7545 Fax: (504) 589-6966
E-mail: eldon_fallon@laed.uscourts.gov

Eldon E. Fallon
District Judge

Date of Birth: 1939
Education: Tulane 1959 BA, 1962 JD; Yale 1963 LLM
Began Service: June 26, 1995
Appointed By: President William J. Clinton
Political Affiliation: Democrat

Academic: Adjunct Professor, Law School, Tulane University (1975-1995); Adjunct Professor, Law School, Tulane University (2002-2003)

Legal Practice: Associate, Kierr & Gainsburgh (1962-1968); Partner, Gainsburgh, Benjamin, Fallon & David (1968-1995)

Current Memberships: American Bar Association; American Board of Trial Advocates; American College of Trial Lawyers; The American Law Institute; Louisiana State Bar Association; New Orleans Bar Association

Chambers of District Judge Eldon E. Fallon *continued*

Staff
Fax: (504) 589-6966

Law Clerk (even cases) **Duncan T. Fulton** .... (504) 589-7545
E-mail: duncan_fulton@laed.uscourts.gov
Education: Tulane 2012 JD
Law Clerk (odd cases) **Ashley Barriere** .... (504) 589-7545
E-mail: ashley_barriere@laed.uscourts.gov
Docket Clerk **Paula Hebert** .... (504) 589-7659
Courtroom Deputy **Dean Oser** .... (504) 589-7686
E-mail: dean_oser@laed.uscourts.gov
Judicial Assistant **Toni Leard** .... (504) 589-7545
E-mail: toni_leard@laed.uscourts.gov

Chambers of District Judge Carl J. Barbier

U.S. Courthouse, 500 Poydras Street, Room C256,
New Orleans, LA 70130
Tel: (504) 589-7525 Fax: (504) 589-4536
E-mail: Barbier@laed.uscourts.gov

Carl J. Barbier
District Judge

Date of Birth: 1944
Education: Southeastern Louisiana 1966 BA; Loyola U (New Orleans) 1970 JD
Began Service: October 12, 1998
Appointed By: President William J. Clinton

Academic: Teacher, Jefferson Parish (1966)

Clerkships: Law Clerk The Honorable Fred J. Cassibry, United States District Court for the Eastern District of Louisiana (1970-1971); Law Clerk The Honorable William V. Redmann, Louisiana 4th Circuit Court of Appeal

Corporate: Accountant, Shell Oil company (1967-1969)

Legal Practice: Associate, Badeaux and Discon (1971-1973); Partner, Badeaux, Discon, Cumberland and Barbier (1974-1982); Law Offices of Carl J. Barbier (1983-1984); Partner, Barbier and Cumberland (1985-1992); Law Offices of Carl J. Barbier (1992-1993); Owner/Attorney, Barbier Law Firm (1993-1998)

Current Memberships: American Bar Association; Federal Bar Association; Jefferson Bar Association; Louisiana State Bar Association; Louisiana Bar Foundation, Louisiana State Bar Association; New Orleans Bar Association

Staff
Law Clerk (even cases) **Stephanie Giglio** .... (504) 589-7525
Began Service: September 2015
Term Expires: September 2016
E-mail: stephanie_giglio@laed.uscourts.gov
Law Clerk (odd cases) **Jeffrey "Jeff" Gelpi** .... (504) 589-7525
Began Service: June 2015
Term Expires: July 2016
E-mail: jeffrey_gelpi@laed.uscourts.gov
Law Clerk (MDL) **Ben Allums** .... (504) 589-7525
Began Service: 2011
E-mail: ben_allums@laed.uscourts.gov
Case Manager **Stephanie Kall** .... (504) 589-7694
E-mail: stephanie_kall@laed.uscourts.gov
Docket Clerk **Gail Chauvin** .... (504) 589-7704
E-mail: gail_chauvin@laed.uscourts.gov
Judicial Assistant **Hope McDonald** .... (504) 589-7525
E-mail: hope_mcdonald@laed.uscourts.gov

Chambers of District Judge Kurt D. Engelhardt

U.S. Courthouse, 500 Poydras Street, Room C-367,
New Orleans, LA 70130
Tel: (504) 589-7645 Fax: (504) 589-4457
E-mail: kurt_engelhardt@laed.uscourts.gov

Kurt D. Engelhardt
District Judge

Date of Birth: 1960
Education: LSU 1982 BA, 1985 JD
Began Service: December 14, 2001
Appointed By: President George W. Bush

Clerkships: Law Clerk The Honorable Charles Grisbaum, Louisiana Court of Appeals, Fifth Circuit (1985-1987)

Legal Practice: Commercial Litigation Attorney, Little & Metzger (1987-1992); Partner, Hailey, McNamara, Hall, Larmann & Papale, LLP (1992-2001)

Current Memberships: American Bar Association; District Judges Association of the Fifth Circuit; Federal Bar Association; Federal Circuit Bar Association; The Federalist Society for Law and Public Policy Studies; Jefferson Bar Association; Louisiana State Bar Association; New Orleans Bar Association; Phi Alpha Delta Law Fraternity International

Staff

Law Clerk **James Clement** .... (504) 589-7645
Began Service: September 2015
Term Expires: September 2016
E-mail: james_clement@laed.uscourts.gov
Career Law Clerk **Jennifer Rogers** .... (504) 589-7645
E-mail: jennifer_rogers@laed.uscourts.gov
Education: LSU 1994 BA, 1997 JD
Docket Clerk **Mary Medders** .... (504) 589-7710
E-mail: mary_medders@laed.uscourts.gov Fax: (504) 589-3199
Courtroom Deputy **Cherie Stouder** .... (504) 589-7683
Fax: (504) 589-3199
Judicial Secretary **Susan Adams** .... (504) 589-7645
E-mail: susan_adams@laed.uscourts.gov

Chambers of District Judge Jay C. Zainey

U.S. Courthouse, 500 Poydras Street, Room C455,
New Orleans, LA 70130
Tel: (504) 589-7590 Fax: (504) 589-4575
E-mail: jay_zainey@laed.uscourts.gov

Jay C. Zainey
District Judge

Date of Birth: 1951
Education: New Orleans 1972 BS; LSU 1975 JD
Began Service: February 19, 2002
Appointed By: President George W. Bush

Judicial: Judge Ad Hoc, Juvenile Court, Jefferson Parish, Louisiana; Judge Ad Hoc, First Parish Court, Jefferson Parish

Legal Practice: Law Clerk, George & George, Ltd. (1971-1975); Associate and Partner, McPherson, Abadie, Weber & Booth (1976-1986); Sole Practitioner (1986-2002)

Military Service: United States Air Force Reserve (1972-1976)

Nonprofit: President, Jefferson Bar Association (1990-1991); President, Louisiana State Bar Association (1995-1996)

Current Memberships: American Bar Association; The Judge John C. Boutall American Inn of Court, The American Inns of Court; Federal Bar Association; The Federalist Society for Law and Public Policy Studies; Jefferson Bar Association; Louisiana State Bar Association

Chambers of District Judge Jay C. Zainey *continued*

Staff

Law Clerk **Samantha Schott** .... (504) 589-7593
Began Service: September 2015
Term Expires: September 2016
E-mail: john_stanton@laed.uscourts.gov
Career Law Clerk **Pam Starns** .... (504) 589-7592
E-mail: pam_starns@laed.uscourts.gov
Education: Loyola U (New Orleans) 1999 JD
Case Manager **James Crull** .... (504) 589-7688
E-mail: james_crull@laed.uscourts.gov
Education: LSU
Docket Clerk **Brad Newell** .... (504) 589-7714
E-mail: brad_newell@laed.uscourts.gov
Judicial Assistant **Pamela Angelette** .... (504) 589-7591
E-mail: pamela_angelette@laed.uscourts.gov

Chambers of District Judge Lance M. Africk

500 Poydras Street, Room C405, New Orleans, LA 70130
Tel: (504) 589-7605 Fax: (504) 589-7608
E-mail: lance_africk@laed.uscourts.gov

Lance M. Africk
District Judge

Date of Birth: 1951
Education: North Carolina 1973 BA, 1975 JD
Began Service: April 17, 2002
Appointed By: President George W. Bush

Academic: Instructor, University of New Orleans

Clerkships: Law Clerk The Honorable James Gulotta, Louisiana Court of Appeals, Fourth Circuit (1975-1976)

Corporate: Attorney, McDermott, Inc. (1981-1982)

Government: Assistant District Attorney, Career Criminal Bureau, Parish of Orleans, Louisiana (1977-1980); Assistant United States Attorney, Eastern District of Louisiana, Criminal Division, Department of Justice (1982-1990)

Legal Practice: Associate, Normann & Normann (1976-1977); Associate, Kierr, Gainsburgh, Benjamin, Fallon & Lewis (1980-1981)

Current Memberships: Federal Bar Association

Staff

Law Clerk (Even-Numbered Cases)
Joseph H. Escandon .... (504) 589-7605
E-mail: joseph_escandon@laed.uscourts.gov
Education: Tulane 2007 JD
Law Clerk (Odd-Numbered Cases) **Chris Hilton** .... (504) 589-7605
Case Manager **Bridget Gregory** .... (504) 589-7752
E-mail: bridget_gregory@laed.uscourts.gov
Docket Clerk **Laura Guillot** .... (504) 589-7702
Secretary **Gwendolyn "Gwen" Hunter** .... (504) 589-7605

Chambers of District Judge Nannette Jolivette Brown

500 Poydras Street, Room C205, New Orleans, LA 70130
Tel: (504) 589-7505 Fax: (504) 589-7507

Nannette Jolivette-Brown
District Judge

Education: Southwestern Louisiana 1985 BA; Tulane 1988 JD, 1998 LLM
Began Service: October 4, 2011
Appointed By: President Barack Obama

Academic: Clinical Law Professor, Law School, Tulane University (1992-1994); Assistant Law Professor, Southern University Law Center (1998-2000); Clinical Law Professor, College of Law, Loyola University New Orleans (2007-2009)

Government: Director, Sanitation Department, City of New Orleans and Orleans Parish, Louisiana (1994-1996); City Attorney, City Attorney's Office, City of New Orleans and Orleans Parish, Louisiana (2010-2011)

Chambers of District Judge Nannette Jolivette Brown *continued*

Legal Practice: Attorney, Adams and Reese LLP (1988-1992); Attorney, Onebane Law Firm (1996-1998); Attorney, Milling Benson Woodward L.L.P. (2000-2003); Attorney, Chaffe McCall, L.L.P. (2004-2007); Attorney, Chaffe McCall, L.L.P. (2009-2010)

Staff
Law Clerk **Jennifer Papa** . . . . . (504) 589-7505
Case Manager **James Crull** . . . . . (504) 589-7658

Chambers of District Judge Jane Triche Milazzo

500 Poydras Street, Room C206, New Orleans, LA 70130
Tel: (504) 589-7585

Jane Margaret Triche Milazzo
District Judge

Education: Nicholls State 1977 BA; LSU 1992 JD
Began Service: October 12, 2011
Appointed By: President Barack Obama

Judicial: Judge, Judicial District Courts of Louisiana (2008-2011)

Legal Practice: Paralegal, Law Office of Risley C. Triche, LLC (1986-1989); Law Clerk, Law Office of Risley C. Triche, LLC (1989-1992); Associate, Law Office of Risley C. Triche, LLC (1992-1998); Partner, Law Office of Risley C. Triche, LLC (1998-2008)

Staff
Law Clerk **Emmy Gill** . . . . . (504) 589-7585
Began Service: October 2014
Law Clerk **Arthur Kraatz** . . . . . (504) 589-7585
Case Manager **Erin Mouledous** . . . . . (504) 589-7695

Chambers of District Judge Susie Morgan

500 Poydras Street, Room C322, New Orleans, LA 70130
Tel: (504) 589-7535 Fax: (504) 589-7524

Susie Morgan
District Judge

Education: Northeast Louisiana 1974 BA, 1976 MA; LSU 1980 JD
Began Service: June 29, 2012
Appointed By: President Barack Obama

Staff
Law Clerk **Christopher Ulfers** . . . . . (504) 589-7535
Law Clerk **Viviana Aldous** . . . . . (504) 589-7535
Judicial Assistant **Tina Flores** . . . . . (504) 589-7535
Case Manager **Cesyle Nelson** . . . . . (504) 589-7680
Docket Clerk **Brad Newell** . . . . . (504) 589-7714

Chambers of Senior Judge Stanwood R. Duval, Jr.

U.S. Courthouse, 500 Poydras Street, Room C-368,
New Orleans, LA 70130
Tel: (504) 589-7540 Fax: (504) 589-2393
E-mail: stanwood_duval@laed.uscourts.gov

Stanwood R. Duval, Jr.
Senior Judge

Date of Birth: 1942
Education: LSU 1964 BA, 1966 JD
Began Service: October 31, 1994
Appointed By: President William J. Clinton
Political Affiliation: Democrat

Current Memberships: The Tulane Law School American Inn of Court, The American Inns of Court; Federal Bar Association

Chambers of Senior Judge Stanwood R. Duval, Jr. *continued*

Staff
Law Clerk **Meghan E. Carter** . . . . . (504) 589-7540
E-mail: meghan_carter@laed.uscourts.gov
Career Law Clerk **Janet Daley** . . . . . (504) 589-7540
E-mail: janet_daley@laed.uscourts.gov
Education: Georgetown 1984 MS, 1984 JD
Docket Clerk **Mia Young** . . . . . (504) 589-7672
E-mail: mia_young@laed.uscourts.gov
Courtroom Deputy **Dean Oser** . . . . . (504) 589-7687
E-mail: dean_oser@laed.uscourts.gov
Judicial Assistant **Marion Barbir** . . . . . (504) 589-7540
E-mail: marion_barbir@laed.uscourts.gov

Chambers of Senior Judge Mary Ann Vial Lemmon

U.S. Courthouse, 500 Poydras Street, Room C406,
New Orleans, LA 70130
Tel: (504) 589-7565 Fax: (504) 589-2239
E-mail: mary_ann_lemmon@laed.uscourts.gov

Mary Ann Vial Lemmon
Senior Judge

Date of Birth: 1941
Education: Loyola U (New Orleans) 1964 JD
Began Service: July 26, 1996
Appointed By: President William J. Clinton

Current Memberships: American Bar Association; Federal Bar Association; Louisiana District Judges Association; Louisiana State Bar Association; Louisiana Bar Foundation, Louisiana State Bar Association; 29th Judicial District Bar Association

Staff
Career Law Clerk **Megan Dupuy** . . . . . (504) 589-7565
E-mail: megan_dupuy@laed.uscourts.gov
Education: Tulane 2006 JD
Courtroom Deputy **Cesyle Nelson** . . . . . (504) 589-7680
E-mail: cesyle_nelson@laed.uscourts.gov
Secretary **Robin Frieze** . . . . . (504) 589-7565
E-mail: robin_frieze@laed.uscourts.gov

Chambers of Senior Judge Ivan L. R. Lemelle

U.S. Courthouse, 500 Poydras Street, Room C525,
New Orleans, LA 70130
Tel: (504) 589-7555 Fax: (504) 589-7623
E-mail: ivan_lemelle@laed.uscourts.gov

Ivan L.R. Lemelle
Senior Judge

Date of Birth: 1950
Education: Xavier (LA) 1971 BS; Loyola U (New Orleans) 1974 JD
Began Service: April 13, 1998
Appointed By: President William J. Clinton

Current Memberships: The Thomas More - Loyola Law School American Inn of Court, The American Inns of Court; Federal Bar Association; Federal Judges Association; Louis A. Martinet Legal Society; Louisiana State Bar Association; Judicial Council, National Bar Association

Staff
Law Clerk (even cases) **Cornelius J. Murray IV** . . . . . (504) 589-7555
Began Service: September 2015
Term Expires: September 2016
E-mail: cornelius_murray@laed.uscourts.gov
Law Clerk (odd cases) **Kaki J. Johnson** . . . . . (504) 589-7555
Began Service: September 2015
Term Expires: September 2016
E-mail: kaki_johnson@laed.uscourts.gov
Docket Clerk **Laura Guillot** . . . . . (504) 589-7702
E-mail: laura_guillot@laed.uscourts.gov

(continued on next page)

Chambers of Senior Judge Ivan L. R. Lemelle *continued*

Case Manager **Isidore Grisoli** .... (504) 589-7747
E-mail: isidore_grisoli@laed.uscourts.gov
Education: New Orleans 1987 BA

Judicial Assistant **Flay Sambrone-Metoyer** .... (504) 589-7555
E-mail: Flay_Sambrone-Metoyer@laed.uscourts.gov

Chambers of Chief Magistrate Judge Joseph C. Wilkinson, Jr.

U.S. Courthouse, 500 Poydras Street, Room B409,
New Orleans, LA 70130
Tel: (504) 589-7630 Fax: (504) 589-7633

Joseph C. Wilkinson, Jr.
Chief Magistrate Judge

Date of Birth: 1955
Education: LSU 1976 BA; Tulane 1980 JD
Began Service: March 27, 1995
Term Expires: March 2019

Current Memberships: The Thomas More - Loyola Law School American Inn of Court, The American Inns of Court; Federal Bar Association; Louisiana State Bar Association; New Orleans Bar Association

Staff

Career Law Clerk **Kathy Manchester** .... (504) 589-7630
E-mail: kathy_manchester@laed.uscourts.gov
Education: Macalester 1975 BA; Tulane 1989 JD

Case Manager **Tanya Lee** .... (504) 589-7707

Judicial Assistant **Marilyn Mosley** .... (504) 589-7630
E-mail: marilyn_mosley@laed.uscourts.gov

Chambers of Magistrate Judge Sally Shushan

U.S. Courthouse, 500 Poydras Street, Room B-345,
New Orleans, LA 70130
Tel: (504) 589-7620
E-mail: sally_shushan@laed.uscourts.gov

Sally Shushan
Magistrate Judge

Began Service: February 1, 1999
Term Expires: 2023

Staff

Career Law Clerk **Michael O'Keefe** .... (504) 589-7620
Education: Tulane 1971 JD

Case Manager **Gail Chauvin** .... (504) 589-7712

Judicial Assistant **Marie Firmin** .... (504) 589-7620
E-mail: marie_firmin@laed.uscourts.gov

Chambers of Magistrate Judge Karen Wells Roby

U.S. Courthouse, 500 Poydras Street, Room B-437,
New Orleans, LA 70130
Tel: (504) 589-7615 Fax: (504) 589-7618
E-mail: karen_roby@laed.uscourts.gov

Karen Wells Roby
Magistrate Judge

Date of Birth: 1961
Education: Xavier (LA) 1983; Tulane 1987 JD
Began Service: February 1999
Term Expires: February 2023

Clerkships: Law Clerk The Honorable Bernette Johnson, Civil District Court, Orleans Parish Division I

Judicial: Judge Pro Tempore, Civil District Court, Orleans Parish Division I

Legal Practice: Deutsch, Kerrigan (1993-1998); Vial, Hamilton, Koch & Knox (1998-1999)

Chambers of Magistrate Judge Karen Wells Roby *continued*

Current Memberships: Federal Bar Association; Federal Magistrate Judges Association; Louisiana State Bar Association; New Orleans Bar Association

Staff

Law Clerk **Justin A. Jack** .... (504) 589-7615
Began Service: August 2015
Term Expires: August 2016
E-mail: justin_jack@laed.uscourts.gov

Case Manager **Crystal Lee** .... (504) 589-7637
E-mail: crystal_lee@laed.uscourts.gov

Judicial Assistant **Carla Gibson Baker** .... (504) 589-7615
E-mail: carla_baker@laed.uscourts.gov
Education: Xavier (LA) 1977 BS

Chambers of Magistrate Judge Daniel E. Knowles III

U.S. Courthouse, 500 Poydras Street, Room B335,
New Orleans, LA 70130
Tel: (504) 589-7575 Fax: (504) 589-4500
E-mail: daniel_knowles@laed.uscourts.gov

Daniel E. Knowles III
Magistrate Judge

Date of Birth: August 29, 1953
Education: LSU 1975 BA; LSU (Alexandria) 1978 JD
Began Service: January 6, 2003
Term Expires: January 2019

Legal Practice: Partner, Burke & Mayer, PLC (1982-2003)

Staff

Career Law Clerk **Jason Johanson** .... (504) 589-7575
E-mail: jason_johanson@laed.uscourts.gov

Case Manager **Paula Hebert** .... (504) 589-7709
E-mail: paula_hebert@laed.uscourts.gov

Judicial Assistant **Hope Taormina** .... (504) 589-7575
E-mail: hope_taormina@laed.uscourts.gov

Chambers of Magistrate Judge Michael B. North

500 Poydras Street, B419, New Orleans, LA 70130
Tel: (504) 589-7610

Michael B. North
Magistrate Judge

Staff

Law Clerk **Barry L. Yager** .... (504) 589-7610
Education: Tulane 1980 BA; LSU 1984 JD

Case Manager **Laura Guillot** .... (504) 589-7702

Judicial Assistant **Blanca Doll** .... (504) 589-7610

United States Bankruptcy Court for the Eastern District of Louisiana

Hale Boggs Federal Building, 500 Poydras Street, Suite B601,
New Orleans, LA 70130
Tel: (504) 589-7878 Tel: (504) 589-6761 (PACER)
Tel: (504) 589-3951 (Voice Case Information System VCIS)
Tel: (866) 222-8029 (Toll Free Voice Case Information System VCIS)
Internet: www.laeb.uscourts.gov

Number of Judgeships: 2

Court Staff

Clerk of the Court **Sheila Booth** .... (504) 589-7878

Chief Deputy Clerk **Brian Richoux** .... (504) 589-7822
E-mail: brian_richoux@laeb.uscourts.gov

Systems Manager **Frank Radosta** .... (504) 589-7870
E-mail: frank_radosta@laeb.uscourts.gov

United States Bankruptcy Court for the Eastern District of Louisiana *continued*

Fiscal and Human Resources Administrator
Cheryl A. Vogel . . . . . (504) 589-7860
E-mail: cheryl_vogel@laeb.uscourts.gov
Property and Procurement Administrator
Denise Sawyer . . . . . (504) 589-7863
E-mail: denise_sawyer@laeb.uscourts.gov
Case Administration Supervisor **Gaynell Donelon** . . . . . (504) 589-7835

Chambers of Chief Bankruptcy Judge Elizabeth W. Magner

Hale Boggs Federal Building, 500 Poydras Street, Suite B-741B,
New Orleans, LA 70130
Tel: (504) 589-7800
E-mail: elizabeth_magner@laeb.uscourts.gov

Elizabeth W. Magner
Chief Bankruptcy Judge

Began Service: 2012

Staff
Law Clerk **Lauren Havrylkoff** . . . . . (504) 589-7802
E-mail: lauren_havrylkoff@laeb.uscourts.gov
Career Law Clerk **Lauren Tebbe** . . . . . (504) 589-7803
E-mail: lauren_tebbe@laeb.uscourts.gov
Education: LSU 1995 BA, 2002 JD
Courtroom Deputy **Chrystal Brooks-Raymond** . . . . . (504) 589-7805
Calendar Clerk **Evelyn Bates Wegener** . . . . . (504) 589-7844

Chambers of Bankruptcy Judge (recalled) Jerry A. Brown

Hale Boggs Federal Building, 500 Poydras Street, Suite B-741A,
New Orleans, LA 70130-3310
Tel: (504) 589-7810 Fax: (504) 589-7813
E-mail: jerry_brown@laeb.uscourts.gov

Jerry A. Brown
Bankruptcy Judge (recalled)

Date of Birth: 1932
Education: Murray State U 1954 BA; Tulane 1959 LLB
Began Service: August 27, 1992
Political Affiliation: Republican

Current Memberships: American Bar Association; Bar Association of the Fifth Federal Circuit; Kentucky Bar Association; Louisiana State Bar Association; New Orleans Bar Association

Staff
Career Law Clerk **Erin K. Arnold** . . . . . (504) 589-7812
E-mail: erin_arnold@laeb.uscourts.gov
Education: Tulane 2004 JD
Courtroom Deputy Clerk **Lisa Matrana** . . . . . (504) 589-7811
E-mail: Lisa_Matrana@laeb.uscourts.gov

United States District Court for the Middle District of Louisiana

Russell B. Long Federal Building, 777 Florida Street, Suite 139,
Baton Rouge, LA 70801-1712
Tel: (225) 389-3500 Tel: (800) 676-6856 (PACER)
Fax: (225) 389-3501
Internet: www.lamd.uscourts.gov

Number of Judgeships: 3

Circuit: Fifth

Areas Covered: Parishes of Ascension, East Baton Rouge, East Feliciana, Iberville, Livingston, Pointe Coupee, St. Helena, West Baton Rouge and West Feliciana

Court Staff

District Clerk **Michael L. McConnell** . . . . . (225) 389-3500
Chief Deputy Clerk **Donna Gregory** . . . . . (225) 389-3500
E-mail: donna_gregory@lamd.uscourts.gov
Chief Probation Officer **Clarence P. Bambo** . . . . . (225) 389-3600
Room 161 Fax: (225) 389-3601
E-mail: clarence_bambo@lamd.uscourts.gov
Deputy Chief Probation Officer **Agnes Gobert-Harrel** . . . . (225) 389-3600
Fax: (225) 389-3601
Librarian **Maralena R. Murphy** . . . . . (225) 389-2990
Fax: (225) 389-2991

Chambers of Chief District Judge Brian A. Jackson

777 Florida Street, Suite 375, Baton Rouge, LA 70801-1712
Tel: (225) 389-3692

Brian A. Jackson
Chief District Judge

Education: Xavier (LA) 1982 BS; Southern U (New Orleans) 1985 JD; Georgetown 2000 LLM
Began Service: June 18, 2010
Appointed By: President Barack Obama

Government: First Assistant U.S. Attorney, Louisiana - Middle District, Executive Office for United States Attorneys, United States Department of Justice (1994-2002); Interim U.S. Attorney, Louisiana - Middle District, Executive Office for United States Attorneys, United States Department of Justice (2001)

Judicial: District Judge, Chambers of District Judge Brian A. Jackson, United States District Court for the Middle District of Louisiana (2010-2011)

Staff
Law Clerk **Max Africk** . . . . . (225) 389-3692
E-mail: max_africk@lamd.uscourts.gov
Law Clerk **Stesanie Jones** . . . . . (225) 389-3692
E-mail: stesanie_jones@lamd.uscourts.gov
Law Clerk **Connie Song** . . . . . (225) 389-3692
E-mail: connie_song@lamd.uscourts.gov

Chambers of District Judge Shelly Deckert Dick

777 Florida Street, Suite 301, Baton Rouge, LA 70801-1712
Tel: (225) 389-3634
E-mail: shelly_dick@lamd.uscourts.gov

Shelly Deckert Dick
District Judge

Education: Texas 1981 BS; LSU 1988 JD
Began Service: May 15, 2013
Appointed By: President Barack Obama

Staff
Courtroom Deputy **Dana Boneventure** . . . . . (225) 389-3636

(continued on next page)

Chambers of District Judge Shelly Deckert Dick *continued*

Judicial Assistant **Barbara Alcon** .... (225) 389-3634

Chambers of District Judge John W. deGravelles

777 Florida Street, Suite 313, Baton Rouge, LA 70801-1712
Tel: (225) 389-3568 Fax: (225) 389-3569
E-mail: john_degravelles@lamd.uscourts.gov

John W. deGravelles
District Judge

Education: LSU 1971 BA; LSU Hebert Law 1974 JD
Began Service: July 23, 2014
Appointed By: President Barack Obama

Staff
Courtroom Deputy **Kristie Causey** .... (225) 389-3574
Judicial Assistant **Jodi Fryoux** .... (225) 389-3568
Court Reporter **Shannon Thompson** .... (225) 389-3568

Chambers of Senior Judge James J. Brady

Russell B. Long Federal Building, 777 Florida Street, Suite 369,
Baton Rouge, LA 70801
Tel: (225) 389-4030 Fax: (225) 389-4031
E-mail: James_Brady@lamd.uscourts.gov

James J. Brady
Senior Judge

Date of Birth: 1944
Education: Southeastern Louisiana 1966 BA; LSU 1969 JD
Began Service: May 29, 2000
Appointed By: President William J. Clinton

Staff
Law Clerk **Heather Hillaker** .... (225) 389-4030
Began Service: August 2015
Term Expires: August 2016
Law Clerk **A.J. Million** .... (225) 389-4030
Began Service: August 2015
Term Expires: August 2016
Career Law Clerk **Marsha Johnson** .... (225) 389-4030
E-mail: Marsha_Johnson@lamd.uscourts.gov
Education: LSU 1979 JD
Courtroom Deputy **Suzanne Edwards** .... (225) 389-4030
E-mail: Suzie_Edwards@lamd.uscourts.gov
Education: Louisiana Tech U 1985 BS
Court Reporter **Shannon Thompson** .... (225) 389-4030
E-mail: shannon_thompson@lamd.uscourts.gov Fax: (225) 389-4031

Chambers of Magistrate Judge Stephen C. Riedlinger

Russell B. Long Federal Building, 777 Florida Street, Room 260,
Baton Rouge, LA 70801-1764
Tel: (225) 389-3584 Fax: (225) 389-3585

Stephen C. Riedlinger
Magistrate Judge

Note: Judge Riedlinger will retire effective December 31, 2015.
Date of Birth: 1950
Education: LSU 1971 BA, 1977 JD
Began Service: May 29, 1986
Term Expires: May 28, 2018

Clerkships: Law Clerk, United States District Court (1977-1978)

Legal Practice: Private Practice (1978-1986)

Military Service: United States Naval Reserve (1971-1977)

Current Memberships: Louisiana State Bar Association

Chambers of Magistrate Judge Stephen C. Riedlinger *continued*

Staff
Pro Se Law Clerk **(Vacant)** .... (225) 389-3584
Career Law Clerk **Clare Zerangue** .... (225) 389-3584
E-mail: clare_zerangue@lamd.uscourts.gov
Education: LSU 1987 JD
Courtroom Deputy **Bridget Wolfe** .... (225) 389-3584
E-mail: bridget_wolfe@lamd.uscourts.gov
Administrative Legal Assistant **Deelee Szczurek** .... (225) 389-3584
E-mail: deelee_szczurek@lamd.uscourts.gov
Education: Loyola U (New Orleans) 1999 BS; LSU 2003 JD

Chambers of Magistrate Judge Richard L. Bourgeois Jr.

777 Florida Street, Suite 278, Baton Rouge, LA 70801-1712
Tel: (225) 389-3602

Richard L. Bourgeois, Jr.
Magistrate Judge

Began Service: February 21, 2013
Term Expires: 2021

United States Bankruptcy Court for the Middle District of Louisiana

U.S. Courthouse, 707 Florida Street, Room 119, Baton Rouge, LA 70801
Tel: (225) 346-3333
Tel: (225) 382-2175 (Voice Case Information System VCIS)
Fax: (225) 346-3334
Internet: www.lamb.uscourts.gov

Number of Judgeships: 1

Court Staff
Bankruptcy Clerk **Monica Menier** .... (225) 346-3333
E-mail: monica_menier@lamb.uscourts.gov
Education: LSU 2001 BA
Chief Deputy **Elizabeth Hager** .... (225) 346-3333 ext. 3308
E-mail: elizabeth_hager@lamb.uscourts.gov
Financial Administrator **Susan Hardy** .... (225) 346-3333 ext. 3315
E-mail: susan_hardy@lamb.uscourts.gov
Case Administrator/Trainer **Chad Smith** .... (225) 346-3333 ext. 3314
E-mail: chad_smith@lamb.uscourts.gov
Case Administrator **Regina Callihan** .... (225) 346-3333 ext. 3313
Case Administrator **Donna Mascaro**
Case Administrator **Jennifer Poche** .... (225) 346-3333 ext. 3309
Network Administrator **Cory Ewing** .... (225) 346-3333 ext. 3305
E-mail: cory_ewing@lamb.uscourts.gov
Quality Assurance **Debra Dickerson** .... (225) 346-3333 ext. 3307
E-mail: debra_dickerson@lamb.uscourts.gov

Chambers of Bankruptcy Judge Douglas D. Dodd

U.S. Courthouse, 707 Florida Street, Room 236, Baton Rouge, LA 70801
Tel: (225) 346-3335 Fax: (225) 346-3336
E-mail: douglas_dodd@lamb.uscourts.gov

Douglas D. Dodd
Bankruptcy Judge

Education: Tulane 1977 BA; Stanford 1982 JD
Began Service: May 2, 2002

Legal Practice: Attorney, Stone, Pigman, Walther, Wittmann & Hutchinson L.L.P.

Staff
Career Law Clerk **Gretchen Thiberville** .... (225) 346-3335 ext. 3321
E-mail: gretchen_thiberville@lamb.uscourts.gov
Courtroom Deputy **Gina Harrison** .... (225) 346-3335 ext. 3320
E-mail: gina_harrison@lamb.uscourts.gov

Chambers of Bankruptcy Judge Douglas D. Dodd *continued*

Judicial Assistant **Susan Miller** . . . . (225) 346-3335 ext. 3325
E-mail: susan_miller@lamb.uscourts.gov

United States District Court for the Western District of Louisiana

U.S. Courthouse, 300 Fannin Street, Room 1167,
Shreveport, LA 71101-3083
Tel: (318) 676-4273 Tel: (318) 676-3957 (PACER)
Fax: (318) 676-3962
Internet: www.lawd.uscourts.gov

Number of Judgeships: 7

Number of Vacancies: 1

Circuit: Fifth

Areas Covered: Parishes of Acadia, Allen, Avoyelles, Beauregard, Bienville, Bossier, Caddo, Calcasieu, Caldwell, Cameron, Catahoula, Claiborne, Concordia, De Soto, East Carroll, Evangeline, Franklin, Grant, Iberia, Jackson, Jefferson Davis, Lafayette, La Salle, Lincoln, Madison, Morehouse, Natchitoches, Ouachita, Rapides, Red River, Richland, Sabine, St. Landry, St. Martin, St. Mary, Tensas, Union, Vermilion, Vernon, Webster, West Carroll and Winn

Court Staff

Clerk of Court **Tony R. Moore** . . . . (318) 676-4273
Began Service: 2009

Chief Deputy Clerk **Amy Greenwald** . . . . (318) 676-4273
Began Service: 2009
E-mail: amy_greenwald@lawd.uscourts.gov

Deputy Clerk-in-Charge - Alexandria **Greta Roaix** . . . . (318) 473-7417
105 Federal Bldg., 515 Murray St., Alexandria, LA 71301 — Fax: (318) 473-7345
P.O. Box 1269, Alexandria, LA 71309-1269
E-mail: greta_roaix@lawd.uscourts.gov

Deputy Clerk-in-Charge - Lafayette **Cathy Bacon** . . . . (337) 593-5000
U.S. Courthouse, 800 Lafayette St., Lafayette, LA 70501 — Fax: (337) 593-5027
E-mail: cathy_bacon@lawd.uscourts.gov

Deputy Clerk-in-Charge - Lake Charles **Jo Ann Benoit** . . . . (337) 437-7246
188 Edwin F. Hunter Jr. Federal Bldg., 611 Broad St., Lake Charles, LA 70601 — Fax: (337) 437-3873

Deputy Clerk-in-Charge - Monroe **Debbie Dickerson** . . . . (318) 322-6740
205 Jackson St., Rm. 215, Monroe, LA 71201 — Fax: (318) 387-9661
P.O. Drawer 3087, Monroe, LA 71210
E-mail: debbie_dickerson@lawd.uscourts.gov

Chief Probation Officer **Lisa Johnson** . . . . (337) 262-6615
800 Lafayette St., Suite 2400,
Lafayette, LA 70501-6936

Staff Attorney **Pam Mitchell** . . . . (318) 676-4232
E-mail: pam_mitchell@lawd.uscourts.gov

Financial Administrator **Teresa Ferguson** . . . . (318) 676-4227
E-mail: teresa_ferguson@lawd.uscourts.gov

Personnel Administrator **Charlotte Deville** . . . . (337) 593-5000
E-mail: charlotte_deville@lawd.uscourts.gov

Librarian **Marian Drey** . . . . (318) 676-3230
E-mail: 5SatLib-Shreveport@ca5.uscourts.gov — Fax: (318) 676-3231

Librarian, Lafayette **Sheree Harper** . . . . (337) 593-5240
800 Lafayette St., Ste. 5300, Lafayette, LA 70501 — Fax: (337) 593-5242
E-mail: 5SatLib-Lafayette@ca5.uscourts.gov

Chambers of Chief Judge Dee D. Drell

Federal Building, 515 Murray Street, Room 233, Alexandria, LA 71301
P.O. Box 1071, Alexandria, LA 71309
Tel: (318) 473-7420 Fax: (318) 473-7425
E-mail: dee_drell@lawd.uscourts.gov

Dee D. Drell
Chief Judge

Date of Birth: November 4, 1947
Education: Tulane 1968 BA, 1971 JD
Began Service: May 9, 2003
Appointed By: President George W. Bush

Current Memberships: Alexandria Bar Association; American Bar Association; The Crossroads Inn of Court of Alexandria-Pineville, The American Inns of Court; Louisiana State Bar Association

Staff

Law Clerk **Alexander Baynham** . . . . (318) 473-7420
Began Service: August 2015
Term Expires: August 2016
E-mail: alexander_baynham@lawd.uscourts.gov

Permanent Law Clerk **Elizabeth Randall** . . . . (318) 473-7420
Education: Louisiana Tech U 1999; LSU 2002 JD

Judicial Assistant **Una Harrison** . . . . (318) 473-7420
E-mail: una_harrison@lawd.uscourts.gov

Chambers of District Judge Robert G. James

201 Jackson Street, Monroe, LA 71201
P.O. Drawer 3107, Monroe, LA 71210
Tel: (318) 322-6230 Fax: (318) 323-9284
E-mail: robert_james@lawd.uscourts.gov

Robert G. James
District Judge

Date of Birth: 1946
Education: Louisiana Tech U 1968 BA; LSU 1971 JD
Began Service: October 31, 1998
Appointed By: President William J. Clinton
Political Affiliation: Democrat

Current Memberships: American Bar Association; American Judges Association; Louisiana Parish Bar Association; Louisiana State Bar Association; Louisiana Bar Foundation, Louisiana State Bar Association

Staff

Career Law Clerk **Kayla D. May** . . . . (318) 322-6230
E-mail: kayla_may@lawd.uscourts.gov
Education: Louisiana Tech U 1995 MA;
Tennessee 1998 JD

Judicial Assistant **Jennifer Floyd** . . . . (318) 322-6230
E-mail: jennifer_floyd@lawd.uscourts.gov

Chambers of District Judge Rebecca F. Doherty

4900 U.S. Courthouse, 800 Lafayette Street, Lafayette, LA 70501
Tel: (337) 593-5050
E-mail: rebecca_doherty@lawd.uscourts.gov

Rebecca F. Doherty
District Judge

Date of Birth: 1952
Education: Northwestern State 1973 BA, 1975 MA; LSU 1981 JD
Began Service: November 18, 1991
Appointed By: President George H.W. Bush

Legal Practice: Attorney, Onebane, Donohoe, Bernard, Torian, Diaz, McNamara & Abell (1981-1991)

Current Memberships: Acadian Association of Women Attorneys; American Bar Association; Lafayette Parish Bar Association; Louisiana State Bar Association

(continued on next page)

Chambers of District Judge Rebecca F. Doherty *continued*

Staff

Career Law Clerk **Stacey Blanke** .... (337) 593-5050
Began Service: October 2007
E-mail: stacey_blanke@lawd.uscourts.gov
Education: Loyola U (New Orleans) 1996 JD

Career Law Clerk **Heather Edwards** .... (337) 593-5050
E-mail: heather_edwards@lawd.uscourts.gov

Judicial Assistant **Carol Boudreaux** .... (337) 593-5050
E-mail: carol_boudreaux@lawd.uscourts.gov

Chambers of District Judge S. Maurice Hicks Jr.

300 Fannin Street, Suite 5101, Shreveport, LA 71101-3083
Tel: (318) 676-3055 Fax: (318) 676-3059
E-mail: maury_hicks@lawd.uscourts.gov

S. Maurice Hicks, Jr.
District Judge

Date of Birth: December 5, 1952
Education: Texas Christian 1974 BA; LSU 1977 JD
Began Service: June 12, 2003
Appointed By: President George W. Bush
Political Affiliation: Republican

Judicial: Staff Attorney, Louisiana Legislature (1975-1977)

Current Memberships: Louisiana State Bar Association; Shreveport Bar Association

Profession: Private Practice (1977-2003)

Staff

Law Clerk **Margaret Pressly** .... (318) 676-3055
Began Service: 2015

Career Law Clerk **Whitney Howell** .... (318) 676-3055
E-mail: whitney_howell@lawd.uscourts.gov

Judicial Assistant (Part-Time) **Betty Gunter** .... (318) 676-3055
E-mail: Betty_Gunter@lawd.uscourts.gov

Judicial Assistant (Part-Time) **Beth Prest** .... (318) 676-3055
E-mail: beth_prest@lawd.uscourts.gov

Chambers of District Judge Patricia Head Minaldi

611 Broad Street, Suite 328, Lake Charles, LA 70601
Tel: (337) 437-3880 Fax: (337) 437-3969
E-mail: patricia_minaldi@lawd.uscourts.gov

Patricia Head Minaldi
District Judge

Date of Birth: September 12, 1958
Education: Wesleyan U 1980 BA; Tulane 1983 JD
Began Service: June 16, 2003
Appointed By: President George W. Bush
Political Affiliation: Republican

Government: Assistant District Attorney, Orleans Parish, New Orleans (1983-1986); Assistant Attorney General, Calcasieu Parish, Louisiana (1986-1996)

Judicial: Judge, 14th Judicial District of Louisiana (1996-2003)

Current Memberships: Louisiana State Bar Association; Southwest Louisiana Bar Association

Staff

Law Clerk **Kara Larson** .... (337) 487-3880
Began Service: 2014

Career Law Clerk **Nanette Cagney** .... (337) 437-3880
E-mail: nanette_cagney@lawd.uscourts.gov
Education: Tulane 1982 JD

Judicial Assistant **Sherry Crick** .... (337) 487-3880
E-mail: sherry_crick@lawd.uscourts.gov

Chambers of District Judge Elizabeth Erny Foote

300 Fannin Street, Suite 4300, Shreveport, LA 71101-3083
Tel: (318) 934-4780
E-mail: elizabeth_foote@lawd.uscourts.gov

Elizabeth Erny Foote
District Judge

Date of Birth: 1953
Education: LSU (Alexandria) 1974 BA; Duke 1975 MA; LSU Hebert Law 1978 JD
Began Service: September 10, 2010
Appointed By: President Barack Obama

Clerkships: Law Clerk, Chambers of Chief Judge William Culpepper, Louisiana Court of Appeal, Third Circuit (1978-1979)

Legal Practice: Partner, The Smith Foote Law Firm (1979-2010)

Membership: President, Louisiana State Bar Association (2008-2009)

Staff

Law Clerk **Drew Burnham** .... (318) 934-4781
Began Service: 2015
Term Expires: 2016

Law Clerk **Alston Walker** .... (318) 934-4781
Began Service: 2015
Education: Tulane 2009

Career Law Clerk **Robin McCoy** .... (318) 934-4781
E-mail: robin_mccoy@lawd.uscourts.gov
Education: Mississippi 2005 JD

Chambers of Senior Judge Donald E. Walter

U.S. Courthouse, 300 Fannin Street, Suite 4200, Shreveport, LA 71101
Tel: (318) 676-3175 Fax: (318) 676-3179
E-mail: donald_walter@lawd.uscourts.gov

Donald E. Walter
Senior Judge

Date of Birth: 1936
Education: LSU 1961 BA, 1964 JD
Began Service: July 15, 1985
Appointed By: President Ronald Reagan

Academic: Adjunct Professor, Centenary College

Government: U.S. Attorney, Louisiana - Western District, Executive Office for United States Attorneys, United States Department of Justice (1969-1977)

Legal Practice: Attorney, Cavanaugh, Brame, Holt & Woodley (1964-1966); Attorney, Holt & Woodley (1966-1969); Attorney, Hargrove, Guyton, Ramey & Barlow (1978-1985)

Military Service: United States Army (1957-1958)

Staff

Law Clerk **Marshall Perkins** .... (318) 676-3175

Career Law Clerk **Caroline Gardner** .... (318) 676-3175
E-mail: caroline_gardner@lawd.uscourts.gov

Judicial Assistant **Deborah Berry** .... (318) 676-3175
E-mail: deborah_berry@lawd.uscourts.gov

Judicial Assistant **Jill Adcock Kennedy** .... (318) 676-3175
E-mail: jill_kennedy@lawd.uscourts.gov

Chambers of Senior Judge James T. Trimble, Jr.

Edwin F. Hunter Jr. Federal Building, 611 Broad Street, Room 237, Lake Charles, LA 70601
Tel: (337) 437-3884 Fax: (337) 437-3899

James T. Trimble, Jr.
Senior Judge

Date of Birth: 1932
Education: LSU 1955 BA, 1956 JD
Began Service: September 12, 1991
Appointed By: President George H.W. Bush
Political Affiliation: Republican

Judicial: Magistrate Judge, United States District Court for the Western District of Louisiana (1986-1991); District Judge, United States District Court for the Western District of Louisiana (1991-2002)

Legal Practice: Attorney, Gist, Murchison, & Gist (1959-1978); Attorney, Trimble, Percy, Smith, Wilson, Foote, Walker & Honeycutt (1979-1986)

Military Service: United States Air Force (1956-1959)

Current Memberships: Federal Judges Association; Louisiana State Bar Association; Louisiana Bar Foundation, Louisiana State Bar Association; Southwest Louisiana Bar Association

Staff
Career Law Clerk **Toni Petrofes** ....(337) 437-3884
E-mail: toni_petrofes@lawd.uscourts.gov
Education: LSU 1999 JD
Career Law Clerk **Elizabeth Randall** ....(318) 473-7375
E-mail: elizabeth_randall@lawd.uscourts.gov
Judicial Assistant **Janet Redner** ....(318) 473-7375
E-mail: jan_redner@lawd.uscourts.gov

Chambers of Senior Judge Richard T. Haik, Sr.

U.S. Courthouse, 800 Lafayette Street, Suite 4200, Lafayette, LA 70501
Tel: (337) 593-5100 Fax: (337) 593-5110
E-mail: richard_haik@lawd.uscourts.gov

Richard T. Haik, Sr.
Senior Judge

Date of Birth: 1950
Education: Southwestern Louisiana 1971 BS; Loyola U (New Orleans) 1975 JD
Began Service: June 14, 1991
Appointed By: President George H.W. Bush
Political Affiliation: Republican

Current Memberships: American Bar Association; Federal Judges Association; Fifth Circuit District Judges Association; Iberia Parish Bar Association; Louisiana State Bar Association; State Bench Bar Committee, Louisiana State Bar Association

Staff
Law Clerk **J.B. McBride** ....(337) 593-5100
Began Service: September 2012
Term Expires: September 2016
Career Law Clerk **Frances Hays** ....(337) 593-5100
E-mail: frances_hays@lawd.uscourts.gov
Education: LSU 1991 JD
Career Law Clerk **Margaret Giglio** ....(337) 593-5100

Chambers of Magistrate Judge James D. Kirk

Federal Building, 515 Murray Street, Room 331, Alexandria, LA 71301
P.O. Drawer 1072, Alexandria, LA 71309-1072
Tel: (318) 473-7510

James D. Kirk
Magistrate Judge

Date of Birth: 1950
Education: LSU 1972 BS, 1975 JD
Began Service: December 15, 1997
Term Expires: December 2021
Political Affiliation: Republican

Clerkships: Law Clerk The Honorable William A. Culpepper, Louisiana Court of Appeal, Third Circuit (1975-1976)

Government: Assistant District Attorney, Office of the District Attorney, Natchitoches Parish, State of Louisiana (1979-1981)

Legal Practice: Sole Practitioner, James D. Kirk, A Professional Law Corporation (1996-1997)

Current Memberships: The American Inns of Court; Louisiana State Bar Association

Staff
Law Clerk **Camille Jackson** ....(318) 473-7510
E-mail: camille_jackson@lawd.uscourts.gov
Law Clerk **Elizabeth Schaff** ....(318) 473-7510
E-mail: elizabeth_schaff@lawd.uscourts.gov

Chambers of Magistrate Judge C. Michael Hill

U.S. Courthouse, 800 Lafayette Street, Suite 3400, Lafayette, LA 70501
Tel: (337) 593-5160 Fax: (337) 593-5171
E-mail: c_michael_hill@lawd.uscourts.gov

C. Michael Hill
Magistrate Judge

Date of Birth: 1950
Education: LSU 1976 JD
Began Service: July 30, 2001
Term Expires: July 30, 2017
Political Affiliation: Democrat

Academic: Staff, Paul M. Hebert Law Center (1976-1977)

Government: Assistant United States Attorney (1977-1982)

Legal Practice: Private Practice (1982-2001)

Current Memberships: American Bar Association; The John M. Duhe, Jr. American Inn of Court, The American Inns of Court; Lafayette Parish Bar Association; Louisiana State Bar Association

Staff
Career Law Clerk **Lisa D. Hanchey** ....(337) 593-5160 ext. 6
E-mail: lisa_hanchey@lawd.uscourts.gov
Education: LSU 1996 JD
Career Law Clerk **Janet F. Hernandez-Weimer** ... (337) 593-5160 ext. 5
E-mail: janet_weimer@lawd.uscourts.gov
Education: Loyola U (New Orleans) 1993 JD

Chambers of Magistrate Judge Mark L. Hornsby

U.S. Courthouse, 300 Fannin Street, Suite 1148, Shreveport, LA 71101-3087
Tel: (318) 676-3265 Fax: (318) 676-3274
E-mail: mark_hornsby@lawd.uscourts.gov

Mark L. Hornsby
Magistrate Judge

Education: LSU 1985 BS, 1988 JD
Began Service: January 14, 2005

Clerkships: Law Clerk The Honorable Tom Stagg, United States District Court for the Western District of Louisiana (1988-1990)

(continued on next page)

Chambers of Magistrate Judge Mark L. Hornsby *continued*

Legal Practice: Wiener, Weiss & Madison (1990-2005)

Current Memberships: The American Inns of Court; Louisiana State Bar Association; Shreveport Bar Association

Staff
Pro Se Law Clerk **Kimberly Tullis** .... (318) 676-3265
Career Law Clerk **Christopher Slatten** .... (318) 676-3265
Education: LSU 1990 JD
Judicial Assistant **Patti Guin** .... (318) 676-3265
E-mail: patti_guin@lawd.uscourts.gov

Chambers of Magistrate Judge Karen L. Hayes

Federal Building, 201 Jackson Street, Monroe, LA 71201
P.O. Box 3087, Monroe, LA 71210-3087
Tel: (318) 388-6036

Karen L. Hayes
Magistrate Judge

Began Service: June 26, 1997
Term Expires: May 9, 2021

Staff
Career Law Clerk **Bill Barkley** .... (318) 388-6036
Began Service: 2007
E-mail: bill_barkley@lawd.uscourts.gov
Education: LSU 1992 JD

Chambers of Magistrate Judge Kathleen Kay

U.S. Courthouse, 611 Broad Street, Suite 209, Lake Charles, LA 70601
Tel: (337) 437-3874 Fax: (337) 437-8264
E-mail: kathleen_kay@lawd.uscourts.gov

Kathleen Kay
Magistrate Judge

Began Service: December 2007

Staff
Law Clerk **Matthew Lognion** .... (337) 437-3874
Began Service: 2014
Career Law Clerk **Elaine Solari** .... (337) 437-3874
E-mail: elaine_solari@lawd.uscourts.gov

Chambers of Magistrate Judge Patrick J. Hanna

800 Lafayette Street, Suite 3500, Lafayette, LA 70501
Tel: (337) 593-5140
E-mail: patrick_hanna@lawd.uscourts.gov

Patrick J. Hanna
Magistrate Judge

Began Service: December 2009

Staff
Career Law Clerk **Sue Nations** .... (337) 593-5140
E-mail: sue_nations@lawd.uscourts.gov
Law Clerk **Nora Stelly** .... (337) 593-5140
Began Service: 2011
E-mail: nora_stelly@lawd.uscourts.gov

United States Bankruptcy Court for the Western District of Louisiana

U.S. Courthouse, 300 Fannin Street, Suite 2201, Shreveport, LA 71101
Tel: (318) 676-4267 Tel: (318) 676-4235 (PACER)
Tel: (888) 523-1976 (Toll Free PACER)
Tel: (318) 676-4234 (Voice Case Information System VCIS)
Tel: (800) 326-4026 (Toll Free Voice Case Information System VCIS)
Internet: www.lawb.uscourts.gov

Number of Judgeships: 3

Court Staff
Bankruptcy Clerk **Edward A. Takara** .... (318) 676-4267
Chief Deputy Clerk **Edmund Brown** .... (318) 676-4267
Division Deputy - Alexandria **Deedra Rollins** .... (318) 445-1890
300 Jackson Street, Suite 116,
Alexandria, LA 71301
Deputy-in-Charge - Lafayette **Jeanette Tizeno** .... (337) 626-6800
214 Jefferson Street, Suite 100,
Lafayette, LA 70501-7050
E-mail: jeanette_tizeno@lawb.uscourts.gov

Chambers of Chief Bankruptcy Judge Robert R. Summerhays

214 Jefferson Street, Suite 120, Lafayette, LA 70501-7050
Tel: (337) 262-6383
E-mail: robert_summerhays@lawb.uscourts.gov

Robert R. Summerhays
Chief Bankruptcy Judge

Began Service: October 2006
Term Expires: October 2020

Staff
Judicial Assistant **Lynda Dupre** .... (337) 262-6383
E-mail: lynda_dupre@lawb.uscourts.gov

Chambers of Bankruptcy Judge Jeffrey P. Norman

300 Fannin Street, Shreveport, LA 71101-3083
Tel: (318) 676-4269

Jeffrey P. Norman
Bankruptcy Judge

Chambers of Bankruptcy Judge John W. Kolwe

300 Jackson Street, Alexandria, LA 71301-8357
Tel: (318) 443-8083

John W. Kolwe
Bankruptcy Judge

Staff
Career Law Clerk **Jennifer Sues** .... (318) 443-8083
E-mail: Jennifer_Sues@lawb.uscourts.gov
Education: LSU 1998 JD
Court Reporter **Martha Branan** .... (318) 445-1890
E-mail: martha_branan@lawb.uscourts.gov
Judicial Assistant **Karen Hess** .... (318) 445-8083
E-mail: karen_hess@lawb.uscourts.gov

United States District Court for the District of Maine

156 Federal Street, Portland, ME 04101
Tel: (207) 780-3356 Tel: (800) 260-9774 (Toll Free PACER)
Internet: www.med.uscourts.gov

Number of Judgeships: 3

Circuit: First

Court Staff

Clerk of Court **Christa K. Berry** . . . . . . (207) 780-3356
E-mail: christa@med.uscourts.gov
Chief Deputy Clerk **Eric M. Storms** . . . . . . (207) 780-3356
E-mail: eric_storms@med.uscourts.gov
Chief Probation Officer **Karen Lee-Moody** . . . . . . (207) 780-3358
Suite 305
Operations Supervisor **Michelle Thibodeau** . . . . (207) 780-3356 ext. 2209
E-mail: michelle@med.uscourts.gov
Information Technology Director
Preston Sanborn . . . . . . (207) 780-3356 ext. 2203
E-mail: preston_sanborn@med.uscourts.gov
Financial Administrator **Sarah Davis McNamara** . . . . . . (207) 780-3356
E-mail: sarah@med.uscourts.gov
Human Resources Specialist **Diane R. Ford** . . . . (207) 780-3356 ext. 2205
E-mail: diane@med.uscourts.gov
Court Reporter **Lori Dunbar** . . . . . . (207) 749-4072
E-mail: lori_dunbar@med.uscourts.gov
Court Reporter **Julie Edgecomb** . . . . . . (207) 945-5856
E-mail: julie_edgecomb@med.uscourts.gov
Court Reporter **Dennis Ford** . . . . . . (207) 831-8056
E-mail: dennis_ford@med.uscourts.gov

Chambers of Chief Judge Nancy Torresen

156 Federal Street, Portland, ME 04101
Tel: (207) 221-0028
E-mail: nancy_torresen@med.uscourts.gov

Nancy Torresen
Chief Judge

Education: Hope 1981 BA; Michigan 1987 JD
Began Service: May 4, 2012
Appointed By: President Barack Obama

Staff

Judicial Assistant **Renee Bender** . . . . . . (207) 221-0028
E-mail: renee_bender@med.uscourts.gov

Chambers of District Judge John A. Woodcock, Jr.

202 Harlow Street, Bangor, ME 04401
Tel: (207) 945-0549

John Alden Woodcock, Jr.
District Judge

Date of Birth: July 6, 1950
Education: Bowdoin 1972 BA; U London 1973 MA; Maine 1976 JD
Began Service: February 2009
Appointed By: President George W. Bush

Current Memberships: The John Waldo Ballou American Inn of Court, The American Inns of Court

Staff

Law Clerk **Thomas Wakefield** . . . . . . (207) 945-0549
Began Service: August 2015
Term Expires: August 2016
E-mail: thomas_wakefield@med.uscourts.gov
Law Clerk **Patrick Lyons** . . . . . . (207) 945-0549
Began Service: August 2015
Term Expires: August 2016
E-mail: patrick_lyons@med.uscourts.gov

Chambers of District Judge John A. Woodcock, Jr. *continued*

Judicial Assistant **Maureen F. Snow** . . . . . . (207) 945-0549
E-mail: maureen_snow@med.uscourts.gov

Chambers of District Judge Jon David Levy

156 Federal Street, Portland, ME 04101
Tel: (207) 780-3356
E-mail: jon_levy@med.uscourts.gov

Jon David Levy
District Judge

Education: Syracuse 1976 BA; West Virginia 1979 JD
Began Service: May 2, 2014
Appointed By: President Barack Obama

Government: Special Court Monitor, United States District Court for the Southern District of Texas (1981-1982)

Judicial: Judge, Maine District Court (1995-2002); Chief Judge, Maine District Court (2001-2002); Associate Justice, Supreme Judicial Court of Maine (2002-2014)

Staff

Case Managers **Neala Dunfrey** . . . . . . (207) 780-3356 ext. 5109
Judicial Assistant **Christie L. Clifford** . . . . . . (207) 245-3200
E-mail: christie_clifford@med.uscourts.gov

Chambers of Senior Judge D. Brock Hornby

156 Federal Street, Portland, ME 04101
Tel: (207) 780-3280 Fax: (207) 780-3152

D. Brock Hornby
Senior Judge

Date of Birth: 1944
Education: Western Ontario 1965 BA; Harvard 1969 JD
Began Service: 1990
Appointed By: President George H.W. Bush

Current Memberships: American Bar Foundation; American Bar Association; The American Law Institute; Cumberland County Bar Association; Maine State Bar Association; Maine Bar Foundation, Maine State Bar Association

Staff

Law Clerk **Sara A. Murphy** . . . . . . (207) 780-3462
Began Service: September 2015
Term Expires: September 25, 2016
E-mail: sara_murphy@med.uscourts.gov
Career Law Clerk **Jack Dafoe** . . . . . . (207) 780-3462
E-mail: jack_dafoe@med.uscourts.gov
Judicial Assistant **Deann L. Harvie** . . . . . . (207) 780-3280
E-mail: deann_harvie@med.uscourts.gov

Chambers of Senior Judge George Z. Singal

156 Federal Street, Portland, ME 04101
Tel: (207) 780-3119

George Z. Singal
Senior Judge

Date of Birth: 1945
Education: Maine 1967 BA; Harvard 1970 JD
Began Service: July 2000
Appointed By: President William J. Clinton

Staff

Law Clerk **(Vacant)** . . . . . . (207) 780-3119

(continued on next page)

Chambers of Senior Judge George Z. Singal *continued*

Career Law Clerk **Jennifer P. Lyons** . . . . (207) 780-3119
E-mail: jennifer@med.uscourts.gov
Education: NYU 1999 JD

Judicial Assistant **Marsha S. Heath** . . . . (207) 780-3119
Began Service: 2007
E-mail: marsha@med.uscourts.gov

Chambers of Magistrate Judge John C. Nivison

202 Harlow Street, Room 300, Bangor, ME 04401
Tel: (207) 945-0315 Fax: (207) 945-0362
E-mail: jcn@med.uscourts.gov

John C. Nivison
Magistrate Judge

Began Service: January 27, 2014
Term Expires: January 27, 2022

Staff

Professional Staff Attorney **Mary Kellogg** . . . . (207) 945-0315
E-mail: mary_kellogg@med.uscourts.gov

Professional Law Clerk **Marc Veilleux** . . . . (207) 945-0315
E-mail: marc_veilleux@med.uscourts.gov
Education: Maine 1999 JD

Judicial Assistant **Carol Plummer** . . . . (207) 945-0315
E-mail: carol@med.uscourts.gov

Chambers of Magistrate Judge John Rich III

156 Federal Street, Portland, ME 04101
Tel: (207) 780-3360 Fax: (207) 780-3772

John Rich III
Magistrate Judge

Began Service: April 2, 2008

United States Bankruptcy Court for the District of Maine

Edward T. Gignoux Courthouse, 156 Federal Street, Portland, ME 04101
Margaret Chase Smith Federal Building and Courthouse, 202 Harlow Street, Bangor, ME 04401
Tel: (207) 780-3482 Tel: (207) 945-0348 (Bangor Office)
Tel: (207) 780-3755 (Voice Case Information System VCIS)
Tel: (800) 650-7253 (Toll-Free Voice Case Information System VCIS)
Fax: (207) 780-3679 Fax: (207) 945-0304 (Bangor Office)
Internet: www.meb.uscourts.gov

Number of Judgeships: 2

Court Staff

Clerk of the Court **Alec Leddy** . . . . (207) 274-5965
Began Service: November 13, 2006
E-mail: alec_leddy@meb.uscourts.gov
Education: Southern Maine 1992 BA; Maine 1995 JD

Chief Deputy Clerk **David K. Lepauloue** . . . . (207) 274-5964
E-mail: david_lepauloue@meb.uscourts.gov
Education: Northeastern 1989 BS

Courtroom Deputy [Full Calendar] **Lori Stocker** . . . . (207) 922-6408
Federal Bldg., 202 Harlow St., Bangor, ME 04401 Fax: (207) 945-0304

Courtroom Deputy [Full Calendar] **Mary-Ellen Paione** . . . (207) 274-5959
Education: Husson 2003 BA

Systems Manager **Jason Scher** . . . . (207) 274-5955
E-mail: jason_scher@meb.uscourts.gov

ECF Case Administrator **Rachel Parker** . . . . (207) 274-5961

ECF Case Administrator **Amy Rydzewski** . . . . (207) 274-5960

ECF Case Administrator/ Administrative Assistant **Sheila R. Dilios** . . . . (207) 780-3482 ext. 5967
E-mail: sheila_r_dilios@meb.uscourts.gov

ECF Case Administrator - Bangor **Kristen E. Ford** . . . . . . (207) 922-6405
Federal Bldg., 202 Harlow St., Bangor, ME 04401 Fax: (207) 945-0304

United States Bankruptcy Court for the District of Maine *continued*

ECF Case Administrator - Bangor **Mary Withee** . . . . (207) 922-6406
Federal Bldg., 202 Harlow St., Bangor, ME 04401 Fax: (207) 945-0304
Education: Husson 1999 BS

Financial Administrator **Karen White** . . . . (207) 274-5966
Education: Southern Maine 2001 BA

Network Administrator/Programmer **Christopher "Chris" Dodd** . . . . (207) 274-5957
E-mail: christopher_dodd@meb.uscourts.gov

Operations Manager **Philip "Phil" Normand** . . . . (207) 922-6404
Federal Bldg., 202 Harlow St., Bangor, ME 04401 Fax: (207) 945-0304
E-mail: philip_normand@meb.uscourts.gov
Education: Maine BA

User Support Specialist - Bangor **Nancy Carter** . . . . (207) 945-0348 ext. 6403
Federal Bldg., 202 Harlow St., Bangor, ME 04401 Fax: (207) 945-0304
Education: Husson 2003 BS

Information Technology Technician - Bangor **Chris Perkins** . . . . (207) 922-6402
E-mail: chris_perkins@meb.uscourts.gov

User Support Specialist **Kelli Felkel** . . . . (207) 274-5956
E-mail: kelli_felkel@meb.uscourts.gov
Education: Southern Maine 2003 BA

Chambers of Chief Bankruptcy Judge Peter G. Cary

537 Congress Street, Portland, ME 04101
Tel: (207) 780-3482 Fax: (207) 780-3679

Peter G. Cary
Chief Bankruptcy Judge

Education: UMass (Amherst) BA; Boston Col JD

Staff

Law Clerk **Kathryn "Katie" Gibson** . . . . (207) 780-3482

Chambers of Bankruptcy Judge Michael A. Fagone

202 Harlow Street, Bangor, ME 04401
Tel: (207) 945-0550 ext. 6490

Michael A. "Mike" Fagone
Bankruptcy Judge

Education: Amherst 1993 BA; Maine 1997 JD
Began Service: 2015

Staff

Law Clerk **James R. "Jim" Wholly** . . . . (207) 945-0550 ext. 6410
Education: Boston Col 1987 JD

Judicial Assistant **Cheryl Dubois** . . . . (207) 945-0550 ext. 6490

United States District Court for the District of Maryland

U.S. Courthouse, 6500 Cherrywood Lane, Greenbelt, MD 20770
101 West Lombard Street, Baltimore, MD 21201
Tel: (410) 962-2600 (Baltimore)
Tel: (410) 962-1812 (Civil Cases PACER)
Tel: (301) 344-0660 (Greenbelt)
Internet: www.mdd.uscourts.gov

Number of Judgeships: 10

Number of Vacancies: 1

Circuit: Fourth

Court Staff

Clerk of Court **Felicia Cannon** . . . . (410) 962-2600
E-mail: felicia_cannon@mdd.uscourts.gov

Chief Deputy Clerk **Jarrett Perlow** . . . . (301) 344-3223
E-mail: jarrett_perlow@mdd.uscourts.gov

United States District Court for the District of Maryland *continued*

Chief Deputy, Administration & IT
Elizabeth Snowden . . . . (410) 962-4429
E-mail: elizabeth_snowden@mdd.uscourts.gov
Chief U.S. Probation/Pretrial Officer **William F. Henry** . . . (410) 962-4740
250 West Pratt Street, Suite 400,
Baltimore, MD 21201
Financial Administrator **Regan Gwin** . . . . (410) 962-3439
E-mail: regan_gwin@mdd.uscourts.gov
Facilities Manager **Brett Gwin** . . . . (410) 962-3831
E-mail: brett_gwin@mdd.uscourts.gov
Human Resources Administrator **Tina Stavrou** . . . . (410) 962-3552
E-mail: tina_stavrou@mdd.uscourts.gov

Chambers of Chief Judge Catherine C. Blake

U.S. Courthouse, 101 West Lombard Street, Room 7D,
Baltimore, MD 21201
Tel: (410) 962-3220 Fax: (410) 962-6836
E-mail: mdd_ccbchambers@mdd.uscourts.gov

Catherine C. Blake
Chief Judge

Date of Birth: 1950
Education: Radcliffe 1972 AB; Harvard 1975 JD
Began Service: August 1995
Appointed By: President William J. Clinton
Political Affiliation: Democrat

Current Memberships: The Bar Association of Baltimore City; Federal Bar Association; Maryland State Bar Association, Inc.; National Association of Women Judges

Staff
Law Clerk **Kaitlin Konkel** . . . . (410) 962-3220
Began Service: August 2015
Term Expires: August 2016
E-mail: kaitlin_konkel@mdd.uscourts.gov
Law Clerk **Jamie Strawbridge** . . . . (410) 962-3220
Began Service: August 2015
Term Expires: August 2016
E-mail: jamie_strawbridge@mdd.uscourts.gov
Law Clerk **Michelle Willauer** . . . . (410) 962-3220
Began Service: August 2015
Term Expires: August 2016
E-mail: michelle_willauer@mdd.uscourts.gov
Secretary **Barbara L. Childs** . . . . (410) 962-3220
E-mail: barbara_childs@mdd.uscourts.gov

Chambers of District Judge William D. Quarles, Jr.

U.S. Courthouse, 101 West Lombard Street, Room 3A,
Baltimore, MD 21201
Tel: (410) 962-0946

William D. Quarles, Jr.
District Judge

Date of Birth: January 16, 1948
Education: Maryland 1976 BS; Columbus Law 1979 JD
Began Service: March 24, 2003
Appointed By: President George W. Bush

Clerkships: Law Clerk, District Judge Joseph C. Howard, United States District Court for the District of Maryland (1979-1981)

Government: Assistant U.S. Attorney, District of Maryland, United States Attorney's Office, United States Department of Justice (1982-1986)

Judicial: Associate Circuit Judge, Circuit Court, City of Baltimore, Maryland (1996-2003)

Legal Practice: Associate, Finley, Kumble, Wagner, Heine, Underberg & Casey (1981-1982); Associate, Venable, Baetjer and Howard, LLP (1986-1987); Equity Partner, Venable, Baetjer and Howard, LLP (1987-1996)

Chambers of District Judge William D. Quarles, Jr. *continued*

Staff
Law Clerk **Kyle Alexandra** . . . . (410) 962-0946
Term Expires: February 2016
E-mail: kyle_alexandra@mdd.uscourts.gov
Law Clerk **Karri Becker** . . . . (410) 962-0946
Began Service: August 2014
Term Expires: February 2016
E-mail: karri_becker@mdd.uscourts.gov
Secretary **Nora E. Taylor** . . . . (410) 962-0946
E-mail: nora_taylor@mdd.uscourts.gov

Chambers of District Judge Richard D. Bennett

U.S. Courthouse, 101 West Lombard Street, Chambers 5.D,
Baltimore, MD 21201
Tel: (410) 962-3190

Richard D. Bennett
District Judge

Date of Birth: August 12, 1947
Education: Pennsylvania 1969 BA; Maryland 1973 JD
Began Service: April 29, 2003
Appointed By: President George W. Bush
Political Affiliation: Republican

Government: Assistant U.S. Attorney, District of Maryland, United States Department of Justice (1976-1980); U.S. Attorney, District of Maryland, United States Department of Justice (1991-1993)

Legal Practice: Associate, Smith, Somerville & Case, L.L.C. (1973-1976); Partner, Marr and Bennett (1981-1988); Partner, Weaver, Bendos, and Bennett (1989-1991); Partner, Miles & Stockbridge P.C. (1993-2003)

Military Service: Maryland Army National Guard, United States Army Reserve (1969-1975); Maryland Army National Guard, United States Army Reserve (1983-1997)

Current Memberships: American Bar Association; Maryland Chapter, Federal Bar Association; Judicial Conference of the Fourth Circuit; Maryland State Bar Association, Inc.; Maryland Bar Foundation, Maryland State Bar Association, Inc.

Staff
Law Clerk **Emily Hankins** . . . . (410) 962-3190
Began Service: August 2014
Term Expires: August 2016
E-mail: emily_hankins@mdd.uscourts.gov
Law Clerk **William King** . . . . (410) 962-3190
Began Service: August 2015
Term Expires: September 2017
E-mail: william_king@mdd.uscourts.gov

Chambers of District Judge James K. Bredar

101 West Lombard Street, Baltimore, MD 21201
Tel: (410) 962-0950 Fax: (410) 962-0070

James K. Bredar
District Judge

Date of Birth: 1957
Education: Harvard 1979 AB; Georgetown 1982 JD
Began Service: December 22, 2010
Appointed By: President Barack Obama

Clerkships: Law Clerk The Honorable Richard P. Matsch, United States District Court for the District of Colorado

Government: Assistant U.S. Attorney, Colorado District, Executive Office for United States Attorneys, United States Department of Justice, Ronald Reagan Administration (1985-1989); Assistant Federal Public Defender, United States District Court for the District of Colorado (1989-1991)

Nonprofit: Project Director, Vera Institute of Justice (1991-1992)

Current Memberships: Federal Bar Association; Maryland State Bar Association, Inc.

(continued on next page)

Chambers of District Judge James K. Bredar *continued*

Staff

Career Law Clerk **Beverly Peyton Griffith** . . . . (410) 962-0950
E-mail: beverly_griffith@mdd.uscourts.gov
Education: Notre Dame JD

Assistant Secretary **(Vacant)** . . . . (410) 962-0950

Judicial Assistant **Valerie Cusatis** . . . . (410) 962-0950

Chambers of District Judge Ellen L. Hollander

101 West Lombard Street, Baltimore, MD 21201
Tel: (410) 962-0742 Fax: (410) 962-0784

Ellen Lipton Hollander
District Judge

Date of Birth: 1949
Education: Goucher 1971 BA; Georgetown 1974 JD
Began Service: January 4, 2011
Appointed By: President Barack Obama

Government: Assistant Attorney General, Civil Division, Office of the Attorney General, State of Maryland (1979); Assistant United States Attorney, District of Maryland, Office of the United States Attorney, United States Department of Justice (1979-1983)

Judicial: Judge, Circuit Court for Baltimore City (1989-1994); Judge, Chambers of Judge Ellen Lipton Hollander, Court of Special Appeals of Maryland (1994-2011)

Legal Practice: Partner, Frank, Bernstein, Conaway & Goldman (1983-1989)

Current Memberships: American Bar Foundation; American Bar Association; The J. Dudley Digges American Inn of Court, The American Inns of Court; Judicial Administration Committee, The Bar Association of Baltimore City; Maryland Judicial Conference; Maryland State Bar Association, Inc.; Maryland Bar Foundation, Maryland State Bar Association, Inc.; National Association of Women Judges; Women's Bar Association of Maryland; Wranglers Law Club

Staff

Law Clerk **Elsa Andriani** . . . . (410) 962-0742

Law Clerk **Mateya Kelley** . . . . (410) 962-0742
E-mail: mateya_kelley@mdd.uscourts.gov

Judicial Assistant **Karen Warren** . . . . (410) 962-0742
E-mail: karen_warren@mdd.uscourts.gov

Chambers of District Judge George Levi Russell III

101 West Lombard Street, Baltimore, MD 21201
Tel: (410) 962-2600

George L. Russell III
District Judge

Education: Morehouse Col 1988 BA; Maryland 1991 JD
Began Service: May 24, 2012
Appointed By: President Barack Obama

Staff

Law Clerk **Debra Carfora** . . . . (410) 962-4055
E-mail: debra_carfora@mdd.uscourts.gov

Law Clerk **K'Shaani Smith** . . . . (410) 962-4055

Judicial Assistant **Deborah Fales** . . . . (410) 962-4055
E-mail: deborah_fales@mdd.uscourts.gov

Chambers of District Judge Paul William Grimm

101 West Lombard Street, Room 8B, Baltimore, MD 21201
Tel: (301) 344-0670

Paul William Grimm
District Judge

Date of Birth: 1951
Education: UC Davis 1973 BA; New Mexico 1976 JD
Began Service: December 10, 2012
Appointed By: President Barack Obama

Government: Assistant States Attorney, County of Baltimore, Maryland (1980-1981); Assistant Attorney General, State of Maryland (1981-1984)

Judicial: Chief Magistrate Judge, Chambers of Chief Magistrate Judge Paul W. Grimm, United States District Court for the District of Maryland (1997-2012)

Staff

Law Clerk **David Borden** . . . . (301) 344-0670
Began Service: August 2015
Term Expires: August 2016
E-mail: david_borden@mdd.uscourts.gov

Law Clerk **Jordan Cafritz** . . . . (301) 344-0670
Began Service: August 2015
Term Expires: August 2016

Career Law Clerk **Lisa Bergstrom** . . . . (301) 344-0670
Began Service: August 2009
E-mail: lisa_bergstrom@mdd.uscourts.gov

Judicial Assistant **Alicia Travers** . . . . (301) 344-0670

Chambers of District Judge Theodore David Chuang

6500 Cherrywood Lane, Greenbelt, MD 20770
Tel: (301) 344-3982

Theodore David Chuang
District Judge

Education: Harvard 1991 AB, 1994 JD
Began Service: May 2, 2014
Appointed By: President Barack Obama

Corporate: Counsel, Wilmer Cutler Pickering Hale and Dorr LLP (2004-2007)

Government: Assistant U.S. Attorney, Massachusetts District, Executive Office for United States Attorneys, United States Department of Justice (1998-2004); Deputy Chief Investigative Counsel, Committee on Oversight and Government Reform, United States House of Representatives (2007-2009); Chief Oversight Counsel, Committee on Energy and Commerce, United States House of Representatives (2009); Deputy General Counsel, Office of General Counsel, United States Department of Homeland Security (2011-2013)

Staff

Law Clerk **Peter DeMarco** . . . . (301) 344-0053
Began Service: June 2015
Term Expires: June 2016

Law Clerk **Benjamin Takemoto** . . . . (301) 344-0053
Began Service: June 2015
Term Expires: June 2016
E-mail: benjamin_takemoto@mdd.uscourts.gov

Career Law Clerk/Judicial Assistant **Naomi Reed** . . . . (301) 344-0053
E-mail: naomi_reed@mdd.uscourts.gov

Chambers of District Judge George Jarrod Hazel
6500 Cherrywood Lane, Greenbelt, MD 20770
Tel: (301) 344-0637

George Jarrod Hazel
District Judge

Education: Morehouse Col 1996 BA; Georgetown 1999 JD
Began Service: May 2, 2014
Appointed By: President Barack Obama

Government: Assistant U.S. Attorney, Greenbelt (MD) Office, Maryland District, United States Department of Justice (2008-2010); Chief Deputy State's Attorney, Office of the State's Attorney for Baltimore City, City of Baltimore, Maryland

Legal Practice: Attorney, Weil, Gotshal & Manges LLP (1999-2004)

Staff
Law Clerk **Dwight Draughon** .... (301) 344-3628
Began Service: June 2015
Term Expires: August 2016
E-mail: dwight_draughon@mdd.uscourts.gov
Law Clerk **Amanda Krause** .... (301) 344-3628
Began Service: June 2015
Term Expires: August 2016
E-mail: amanda_krause@mdd.uscourts.gov
Judicial Assistant **Ashley Migliore** .... (301) 344-3628
E-mail: ashley_migliore@mdd.uscourts.gov

Chambers of Senior Judge William M. Nickerson
U.S. Courthouse, 101 West Lombard Street, Baltimore, MD 21201
Tel: (410) 962-7810 Fax: (410) 962-2577

William M. Nickerson
Senior Judge

Date of Birth: 1933
Education: Virginia 1955 BA; Maryland 1962 LLB
Began Service: 1990
Appointed By: President George H.W. Bush

Clerkships: Law Clerk The Honorable James K. Cullen, Supreme Bench of Baltimore City (1959-1962)

Corporate: Claims Examiner, United States Fidelity and Guaranty Company (1959)

Judicial: Associate Judge, Circuit Court for Baltimore County (1985-1990)

Legal Practice: Associate, Whiteford, Taylor & Preston L.L.P.

Military Service: United States Coast Guard (1955-1959)

Current Memberships: Christian Legal Society; Maryland State Bar Association, Inc.; Wednesday Law Club

Staff
Law Clerk **Bethany Hennemann** .... (410) 962-7810
Began Service: August 2015
Term Expires: August 2016
E-mail: bethany_hennemann@mdd.uscourts.gov
Career Law Clerk **Richard Ames-Ledbetter** .... (410) 962-7810
E-mail: richard_ames-ledbetter@mdd.uscourts.gov
Education: Maryland 1992 JD
Judicial Assistant **Barbara Fox** .... (410) 962-7810
E-mail: barbara_fox@mdd.uscourts.gov Fax: (410) 962-2577

Chambers of Senior Judge Marvin Joseph Garbis
U.S. Courthouse, 101 West Lombard Street, Room 530, Baltimore, MD 21201-2691
Tel: (410) 962-7700 Fax: (410) 962-0896
E-mail: judge_garbis@mdd.uscourts.gov

Marvin Joseph Garbis
Senior Judge

Date of Birth: 1936
Education: Johns Hopkins 1958 BES; Harvard 1961 JD; Georgetown 1962 LLM
Began Service: 1989
Appointed By: President George H.W. Bush
Political Affiliation: Republican

Government: Attorney, Civil Trial Section, Tax Division, United States Department of Justice (1963-1967)

Legal Practice: Sole Practitioner (1967-1971); Partner, Garbis, Marvel & Junghans; Garbis & Schwait (1971-1986); Member, Melnicove, Kaufman, Weiner, Smouse & Garbis (1986-1988); Member, Johnson & Gibbs (1988-1989)

Current Memberships: American Bar Association; Federal Judges Association

Staff
Law Clerk **Jaan G. Raanik** .... (410) 962-7897
E-mail: jaan_rannik@mdd.uscourts.gov
Education: Maryland 2014 JD
Law Clerk **I. Marie Worden** .... (410) 961-7898
E-mail: marie_worden@mdd.uscourts.gov
Education: Thomas M Cooley 2010 JD
Judicial Assistant **Janice R. Whitmore** .... (410) 962-7894
E-mail: jan_whitmore@mdd.uscourts.gov

Chambers of Senior Judge Peter J. Messitte
6500 Cherrywood Lane, Greenbelt, MD 20770
Tel: (301) 344-0632

Peter J. Messitte
Senior Judge

Date of Birth: July 17, 1941
Education: Amherst 1963 BA; Chicago 1966 JD
Began Service: October 20, 1993
Appointed By: President William J. Clinton
Political Affiliation: Democrat

Current Memberships: American Bar Association; The District of Columbia Bar; Federal Bar Association; Maryland State Bar Association, Inc.; Montgomery County Bar Association

Staff
Law Clerk **Christine Bonomo** .... (301) 344-0632
Began Service: September 2015
Term Expires: September 2016
E-mail: christine_bonomo@mdd.uscourts.gov
Law Clerk **Catherine Cooper** .... (301) 344-0632
Began Service: September 2015
Term Expires: September 2016
Secretary **Robin Shea** .... (301) 344-0632
E-mail: robin_shea@mdd.uscourts.gov

Chambers of Senior Judge J. Frederick Motz

U.S. Courthouse, 101 West Lombard Street, Room 510,
Baltimore, MD 21201
Tel: (410) 962-0782 Fax: (410) 962-2698
E-mail: judge_j_frederick_motz@mdd.uscourts.gov

J. Frederick Motz
Senior Judge

Date of Birth: 1942
Education: Wesleyan U 1964 AB; Virginia 1967 LLB
Began Service: 1985
Appointed By: President Ronald Reagan
Political Affiliation: Republican

Current Memberships: American Bar Foundation; American Bar Association; American College of Trial Lawyers; The American Law Institute; The Bar Association of Baltimore City; Maryland State Bar Association, Inc.

Staff
Law Clerk **Emily Alden** .... (410) 962-0782
Began Service: August 2015
Term Expires: August 2016
E-mail: emily_alden@mdd.uscourts.gov
Law Clerk **Albert Teng** .... (410) 962-0782
Began Service: August 2015
Term Expires: August 2016
E-mail: albert_teng@mdd.uscourts.gov
Secretary **Mary Ellen Claypoole** .... (410) 962-0782

Chambers of Senior Judge Roger W. Titus

6500 Cherrywood Lane, Room 255A, Greenbelt, MD 20770
Tel: (301) 344-0052
E-mail: judge_roger_titus@mdd.uscourts.gov

Roger W. Titus
Senior Judge

Date of Birth: December 16, 1941
Education: Johns Hopkins 1963 BA; Georgetown 1966 JD
Began Service: November 2003
Appointed By: President George W. Bush

Staff
Law Clerk **Liz Rhinehart** .... (301) 344-0055
Began Service: September 2015
Term Expires: September 2016
Law Clerk **Emily Yezerski** .... (301) 344-0056
Began Service: August 29, 2015
Term Expires: August 2016
E-mail: emily_yezerski@mdd.uscourts.gov
Judicial Assistant **Christine Collins** .... (301) 344-0057
E-mail: christine_collins@mdd.uscourts.gov

Chambers of Senior Judge Deborah K. Chasanow

U.S. Courthouse, 6500 Cherry Wood Lane, Greenbelt, MD 20770
Tel: (301) 344-0634

Deborah K. Chasanow
Senior Judge

Date of Birth: 1948
Education: Rutgers 1970 BA; Stanford 1974 JD
Began Service: 1993
Appointed By: President William J. Clinton

Current Memberships: The Marlborough American Inn of Court, The American Inns of Court; Federal Judges Association; Maryland State Bar Association, Inc.; National Association of Women Judges; Prince George's County Bar Association; Women's Bar Association of Maryland

Chambers of Senior Judge Deborah K. Chasanow *continued*

Staff
Law Clerk **Andrew Banks** .... (301) 344-0634
Began Service: August 2015
Term Expires: August 2016
E-mail: andrew_banks@mdd.uscourts.gov
Law Clerk **Dan Grant** .... (301) 344-0634
Began Service: August 2015
Term Expires: August 2016
Career Law Clerk **Bryan Hughes** .... (301) 344-0634
Began Service: August 2009
E-mail: bryan_hughes@mdd.uscourts.gov
Judicial Assistant **Sharon A. Townsend** .... (301) 344-0634
E-mail: sharon_townsend@mdd.uscourts.gov

Chambers of Chief Magistrate Judge William G. Connelly

U.S. Courthouse, 101 West Lombard Street, Room 355A,
Baltimore, MD 21201
Tel: (301) 344-0627 Fax: (301) 344-8434
E-mail: Judge_Connelly@mdd.uscourts.gov

William G. Connelly
Chief Magistrate Judge

Date of Birth: 1952
Education: Maryland 1973 BA, 1976 JD; Georgetown 1979 LLM
Began Service: March 31, 1995
Term Expires: March 30, 2019

Clerkships: Law Clerk, Maryland Circuit Court, Prince George's County (1976-1977)

Legal Practice: Partner, Stern & Connelly (1981-1995)

Military Service: Active, United States Air Force (1977-1981); Reserves, United States Air Force (1981-2005)

Staff
Career Law Clerk **Natonne E. Kemp** .... (301) 344-0627
E-mail: Natonne_Kemp@mdd.uscourts.gov
Education: George Washington 1992 JD

Chambers of Magistrate Judge Jillyn K. Schulze

335A U.S. Courthouse, 6500 Cherywood Lane, Greenbelt, MD 20770
Tel: (301) 344-0630 Fax: (301) 344-0629

Jillyn K. Schulze
Magistrate Judge

Date of Birth: 1951
Education: Maryland 1980 JD
Began Service: October 24, 1994
Term Expires: October 2018

Clerkships: Law Clerk, United States District Court (1980-1981)

Government: Assistant Attorney General, Office of the Attorney General, United States Department of Justice (1981-1982); Counsel, Office of the Governor, State of Maryland (1991-1994)

Judicial: Chief Magistrate Judge, United States District Court for the District of Maryland (2006)

Staff
Law Clerk **Brian Crook** .... (301) 344-3592
E-mail: brian_crook@mdd.uscourts.gov
Secretary **Jo Wright** .... (301) 344-3591
E-mail: jo_wright@mdd.uscourts.gov

Chambers of Magistrate Judge Charles B. Day
U.S. Courthouse, 6500 Cherrywood Lane, 235A, Greenbelt, MD 20770
Tel: (301) 344-0393

Charles Bernard Day
Magistrate Judge

Date of Birth: 1957
Education: Maryland 1978 BA; American U 1980 MS; Maryland Law 1984 JD
Began Service: February 18, 1997
Term Expires: February 2021

Current Memberships: American Bar Association; The District of Columbia Bar; Maryland State Bar Association, Inc.

Staff
Law Clerk **(Vacant)** . . . . (301) 344-0393
Secretary **Barbara Barry** . . . . (301) 344-0393
E-mail: barbara_barry@mdd.uscourts.gov

Chambers of Magistrate Judge Beth P. Gesner
U.S. Courthouse, 101 West Lombard Street, Room 7C, Baltimore, MD 21201
Tel: (410) 962-4288 Fax: (410) 962-3844

Beth P. Gesner
Magistrate Judge

Date of Birth: 1958
Education: Indiana (PA) 1979 BA; Georgetown 1983 JD
Began Service: May 1999

Academic: Adjunct Professor, Columbus School of Law, The Catholic University of America (1990-1999)

Clerkships: Law Clerk, Chambers of District Judge William Benson Bryant, United States District Court for the District of Columbia (1983-1984)

Government: Assistant U.S. Attorney, Criminal and Civil Cases, Maryland District, Executive Office for United States Attorneys, United States Department of Justice (1987-1992); Southern Division Chief, Greenbelt (MD) Office, Executive Office for United States Attorneys, United States Department of Justice (1997-1999)

Legal Practice: Litigation Attorney, Washington, DC Office, Hogan & Hartson LLP (1984-1987)

Staff
Law Clerk **Michael Brown** . . . . (410) 962-4288
Began Service: September 2015
Term Expires: September 2016
Secretary **Donna Cowan** . . . . (410) 962-4288
E-mail: donna_cowan@mdd.uscourts.gov

Chambers of Magistrate Judge Thomas M. DiGirolamo
6500 Cherrywood Lane, Greenbelt, MD 20770
Tel: (301) 344-0080
E-mail: judge_digirolamo@mdd.uscourts.gov

Thomas M. DiGirolamo
Magistrate Judge

Date of Birth: 1956
Education: Dickinson Law 1981 JD
Began Service: June 30, 2004
Term Expires: June 2020
Political Affiliation: Democrat

Clerkships: Law Clerk, Maryland Circuit Court, Washington County (1981-1982)

Government: Assistant State Attorney, Office of the State Attorney, County of Washington, Maryland (1983-1988)

Chambers of Magistrate Judge Thomas M. DiGirolamo *continued*

Current Memberships: Federal Magistrate Judges Association; Maryland State Bar Association, Inc.; Washington County Bar Association

Staff
Career Law Clerk **James Raneses** . . . . (301) 344-0800
E-mail: james_raneses@mdd.uscourts.gov
Education: UC San Diego 1994; Thomas Jefferson Law 2000

Chambers of Magistrate Judge Stephanie A. Gallagher
101 West Lombard Street, Baltimore, MD 21201
Tel: (410) 962-7780

Stephanie A. Gallagher
Magistrate Judge

Education: Georgetown 1994 BA; Harvard 1997 JD
Began Service: April 19, 2011
Term Expires: 2019

Staff
Law Clerk **(Vacant)** . . . . (410) 962-7780
Judicial Assistant **Valerie Litzinger** . . . . (410) 962-7780
E-mail: valerie_litzinger@mdd.uscourts.gov

Chambers of Magistrate Judge J. Mark Coulson
101 West Lombard Street, Baltimore, MD 21201
Tel: (410) 962-2600

J. Mark Coulson
Magistrate Judge

Education: La Salle U 1985 BA; Duke 1991 JD

Chambers of Magistrate Judge Timothy Sullivan
101 West Lombard Street, Baltimore, MD 21201
Tel: (410) 962-4560

Timothy J. Sullivan
Magistrate Judge

Education: Marquette 1984 BA; Georgetown 1987 JD
Began Service: 2012

Chambers of Magistrate Judge (part time) C. Bruce Anderson
129 East Main Street, Salisbury, MD 21803
Tel: (410) 749-7990

C. Bruce Anderson
Magistrate Judge (Part-Time)

Began Service: 2012

United States Bankruptcy Court for the District of Maryland
U.S. Courthouse, 101 West Lombard Street, Room 8305, Baltimore, MD 21201
Tel: (410) 962-2688 Tel: (800) 676-6856 (Toll Free PACER)
Tel: (800) 829-0145 (Toll Free Voice Case Information System VCIS)
Internet: www.mdb.uscourts.gov

Number of Judgeships: 9

Court Staff
Clerk **Mark A. Neal** . . . . (410) 962-2688

(continued on next page)

United States Bankruptcy Court for the District of Maryland *continued*

Chief Deputy Clerk **David Smith** . . . . (410) 962-2688
E-mail: david_smith@mdb.uscourts.gov Fax: (410) 962-2981
Greenbelt Division Manager **Betty Giddings** . . . . (301) 344-8017
300 U.S. Courthouse, 6500 Cherrywood Ln., Greenbelt, MD 20770 Fax: (301) 344-0415
E-mail: betty_giddings@mdb.uscourts.gov
Baltimore Division Manager **Kenneth "Ken" Ridgeway** . . . . (410) 962-2787
E-mail: ken_ridgeway@mdb.uscourts.gov
Administrative Manager **Diane Hydovitz** . . . . (410) 962-3690
E-mail: diane_hydovitz@mdb.uscourts.gov
Manager of Information Systems **Rick Thompson** . . . . (410) 962-4468
E-mail: rick_thompson@mdb.uscourts.gov

Chambers of Chief Bankruptcy Judge Nancy V. Alquist

101 West Lombard Street, 2A, Baltimore, MD 21201
Tel: (410) 962-7479 Tel: (410) 962-7857
E-mail: hearings_nva@mdb.uscourts.gov

Nancy V. Alquist
Chief Bankruptcy Judge

Began Service: 2012

Staff
Career Law Clerk **Kimberly Stoker** . . . . (410) 962-4532
E-mail: kimberly_stoker@mdb.uscourts.gov
Education: Baltimore 1990 JD
Courtroom Deputy **Brenda J. Wolfe** . . . . (410) 962-4439
E-mail: brenda_wolfe@mdb.uscourts.gov
Judicial Assistant **Deborah Constable** . . . . (410) 962-7479
E-mail: deborah_constable@mdb.uscourts.gov

Chambers of Bankruptcy Judge James F. Schneider

U.S. Courthouse, 101 West Lombard Street, Room 9442, Baltimore, MD 21201
Tel: (410) 962-2820 Fax: (410) 962-2883
E-mail: hearings_jfs@mdb.uscourts.gov

James F. Schneider
Bankruptcy Judge

Date of Birth: 1947
Education: Baltimore 1969 BA, 1972 JD
Began Service: February 1, 1982
Term Expires: October 2, 2026

Clerkships: Law Clerk The Honorable Albert L. Sklar, Baltimore City Circuit Court (1972-1973)

Government: Assistant State's Attorney, State of Maryland (1973-1978); General Equity Master, Supreme Bench, City of Baltimore, Maryland (1978-1982)

Legal Practice: Private Practice

Current Memberships: American Bar Association; The Bar Association of Baltimore City; Maryland State Bar Association, Inc.

Staff
Law Clerk **Emily Lamasa** . . . . (410) 962-2997
Began Service: September 2011
Term Expires: September 2016
E-mail: emily_lamasa@mdb.uscourts.gov
Education: Maryland 2011 JD
Courtroom Deputy **Anna Marie Komiserak** . . . . (410) 962-2966
Judicial Assistant **Kim Goodwin** . . . . (410) 962-2820
E-mail: kim_goodwin@mdb.uscourts.gov

Chambers of Bankruptcy Judge Paul Mannes

U.S. Courthouse, 6500 Cherrywood Lane, 385A, Greenbelt, MD 20770
Tel: (301) 344-8040 Fax: (301) 344-0385
E-mail: hearings_pm@mdb.uscourts.gov
E-mail: paul_mannes@mdb.uscourts.gov

Paul Mannes
Bankruptcy Judge

Date of Birth: 1933
Education: Dartmouth 1955 AB; Georgetown 1958 LLB, 1961 LLM
Began Service: December 30, 1981
Term Expires: September 30, 2022

Clerkships: Law Clerk The Honorable A.L. Holtzoff, United States District Court for the District of Columbia (1957-1960)

Government: Assistant Corporate Counsel, District of Columbia (1959-1960)

Legal Practice: Partner, Bernstein, Alper, Klavan & Mannes (1960-1968); Partner, Klavan & Mannes (1968-1975); Partner, Mannes, Meyers, Nadonley, Townsend and O'Brien (1975-1981)

Current Memberships: American Bankruptcy Institute; American College of Bankruptcy; Montgomery County Bar Association; National Conference of Bankruptcy Judges

Staff
Career Law Clerk **Tammie A. Geier** . . . . (301) 344-8018
E-mail: tammie_geier@mdb.uscourts.gov
Courtroom Deputy **Gloria Bellman** . . . . (301) 344-8018
E-mail: gloria_bellman@mdb.uscourts.gov
Judicial Assistant **Mary Lee Zimmerman** . . . . (301) 344-8018

Chambers of Bankruptcy Judge Thomas J. Catliota

6500 Cherrywood Lane, Suite 365A, Greenbelt, MD 20770
Tel: (301) 344-3660 Fax: (301) 344-0383
E-mail: hearings_wil@mdb.uscourts.gov
E-mail: judge_catliota@mdb.uscourts.gov

Thomas J. Catliota
Bankruptcy Judge

Date of Birth: 1953
Education: Marquette 1977 BS; Columbus Law 1983 JD; Georgetown 1985 LLM
Began Service: April 2006

Clerkships: Law Clerk The Honorable L. Bragolis, United States Court of Federal Claims (1983-1984)

Corporate: Credit Analyst, First Bank Milwaukee (1976-1982); Commercial Loan Officer, District of Columbia, First American Bank (1979-1982)

Legal Practice: Partner, Pillsbury Winthrop Shaw Pittman

Staff
Law Clerk **Michael Cain** . . . . (301) 344-3662
Began Service: 2014
Term Expires: September 2016
E-mail: michael_cain@mdb.uscourts.gov
Career Law Clerk **Vivian Diokno** . . . . (301) 344-3662
Began Service: September 2009
E-mail: vivian_diokno@mdb.uscourts.gov
Courtroom Deputy **Rita Hester** . . . . (301) 344-3495
E-mail: rita_hester@mdb.uscourts.gov
Education: Tennessee State 1989 BS

Chambers of Bankruptcy Judge Wendelin I. Lipp
6500 Cherrywood Lane, Room 365, Greenbelt, MD 20770
Tel: (301) 344-3377 Fax: (301) 344-0064
E-mail: hearings_wil@mdb.uscourts.gov

Wendelin I. Lipp
Bankruptcy Judge

Began Service: 2006

Staff
Career Law Clerk **Kerry Hopkins** .... (301) 344-3664
E-mail: kerry_hopkins@mdb.uscourts.gov
Courtroom Deputy **Sophia Ward** .... (301) 344-0585
E-mail: sophia_ward@mdb.uscourts.gov
Judicial Assistant **Glenda Reher** .... (301) 344-3377
E-mail: glenda_reher@mdb.uscourts.gov

Chambers of Bankruptcy Judge Robert A. Gordon
101 West Lombard Street, Baltimore, MD 21201
Tel: (410) 962-4162 Fax: (410) 962-4163
E-mail: hearings_rag@mdb.uscourts.gov

Robert A. Gordon
Bankruptcy Judge

Began Service: June 2006

Staff
Law Clerk **Brandon Iskander** .... (410) 962-7758
Term Expires: September 2016
E-mail: brandon_iskander@mdb.uscourts.gov
Courtroom Deputy **Booker Livingston** .... (410) 962-7848
E-mail: booker_livingston@mdb.uscourts.gov
Judicial Assistant **Lisa Collins** .... (410) 962-4162
E-mail: lisa_chick@mdb.uscourts.gov

Chambers of Bankruptcy Judge David E. Rice
101 West Lombard Street, Baltimore, MD 21201
Tel: (410) 962-4211

David E. Rice
Bankruptcy Judge

Education: Pennsylvania 1973 BA; Baltimore 1980 JD
Began Service: April 1, 2011

Staff
Career Law Clerk **Abby Clifton** .... (410) 962-4211
Education: Washington and Lee 2007 JD
Courtroom Deputy **Cherita "Rita" Martin** .... (410) 962-7769
Judicial Assistant **Anna Maria Pacella-Holt** .... (410) 962-4211

Chambers of Bankruptcy Judge (recalled) E. Stephen Derby
U.S. Courthouse, 101 West Lombard Street, Room 9442,
Baltimore, MD 21201
Tel: (410) 962-7801

E. Stephen Derby
Bankruptcy Judge (recalled)

Date of Birth: 1938
Education: Wesleyan U 1960 AB; Harvard 1965 LLB
Began Service: December 9, 1987

Academic: Adjunct Faculty, University System of Maryland (1987-1999)

Clerkships: Clerk, United States District Court for the District of Maryland and United States Court of Appeals for the Fourth Circuit (1965-1966)

Government: Assistant Attorney General, State of Maryland (1971-1973)

Legal Practice: Associate, Piper & Marbury LLP (1966-1971); Partner, Piper & Marbury LLP (1973-1987)

Chambers of Bankruptcy Judge (recalled) E. Stephen Derby *continued*

Current Memberships: American Bankruptcy Institute; The William Paca - Margaret Brent American Inn of Court, The American Inns of Court; Anne Arundel Bar Association; Bankruptcy Bar Association of the District of Maryland; Maryland State Bar Association, Inc.

Staff
Judicial Assistant **Kim Goodwin** .... (410) 962-2820
E-mail: kim_goodwin@mdb.uscourts.gov

Chambers of Bankruptcy Judge (recalled) Duncan W. Keir
101 West Lombard Street, Chambers 1B, Baltimore, MD 21201
Tel: (410) 962-3555 Fax: (410) 962-7400
E-mail: hearings_dwk@mdb.uscourts.gov

Duncan W. Keir
Bankruptcy Judge (recalled)

Education: Maryland 1975 JD
Began Service: 2012

Current Memberships: American College of Bankruptcy; National Conference of Bankruptcy Judges

United States District Court for the District of Massachusetts
John Joseph Moakley U.S. Courthouse, One Courthouse Way,
Suite 2300, Boston, MA 02210
Tel: (617) 748-9152 Fax: (617) 748-9096
Internet: www.mad.uscourts.gov

Number of Judgeships: 13

Number of Vacancies: 1

Circuit: First

Court Staff
Clerk of Court **Robert M. Farrell** .... (617) 748-9165
Chief Deputy Clerk **Michelle Rynne** .... (617) 748-9152
Administrative Assistant **Tracy McLaughlin** .... (617) 748-9165
E-mail: tracy_mclaughlin@mad.uscourts.gov
Lead Pro Se Staff Attorney **Jeanette McGlamery** .... (617) 748-9559
E-mail: jeanette_mcglamery@mad.uscourts.gov
Pro Se Staff Attorney Coordinator [Civil]
Barbara Morse .... (617) 748-4123
E-mail: barbara_morse@mad.uscourts.gov
Pro Se Staff Attorney **(Vacant)** .... (617) 748-9180
Division Manager - Springfield **Bethaney Healy** .... (413) 785-6803
Federal Bldg. & Courthouse, 300 State Street,
Springfield, MA 01105
E-mail: bethaney_healy@mad.uscourts.gov
Education: Regis Col (MA) 1991 BA
Division Manager - Worcester **Robert C. Alba** .... (508) 929-9907
Donohue Federal Bldg., 595 Main St.,
Worcester, MA 01608
E-mail: robert_alba@mad.uscourts.gov
Chief Probation/Pretrial Officer **Christopher Maloney** .... (617) 748-4200
Pro Se Intake Clerk **(Vacant)** .... (617) 748-9130
Appeals Clerk **(Vacant)** .... (617) 748-9154
Human Resources Director **Susan J. Mohr** .... (617) 748-9127
E-mail: susan_mohr@mad.uscourts.gov
Human Resources Coordinator **Nancy M. Cashman** .... (617) 748-9111
E-mail: nancy_cashman@mad.uscourts.gov
Property & Procurement Manager **(Vacant)** .... (617) 748-9077
Outreach/Training Coordinator **Virginia Hurley** .... (617) 748-9166
E-mail: ginny_hurley@mad.uscourts.gov
Appeals, MBD New CR Cases, Training **Karen Folan** .... (617) 748-4232
Operations Supervisor [Criminal Bonds, Collateral,
New Criminal Cases Backup] **(Vacant)** .... (617) 748-9179
Operations Manager **Craig Nicewicz** .... (617) 748-4012
E-mail: craig_nicewicz@mad.uscourts.gov

(continued on next page)

United States District Court for the District of Massachusetts *continued*

Information Technology Manager **Stuart Barer** . . . . (617) 748-9071
E-mail: stuart_barer@mad.uscourts.gov
Data Quality Analyst **Antonia Alves-Baptista** . . . . (617) 748-4419
E-mail: antonia_alves-baptista@mad.uscourts.gov
Data Quality Analyst/ New Criminal Cases
Theresa Catino . . . . (617) 748-4647
E-mail: theresa_catino@mad.uscourts.gov
Data Quality Analyst/ New Criminal Cases
Dianne Smith . . . . (617) 748-9810
E-mail: dianne_m_smith@mad.uscourts.gov
PC Administrator **David Crepeault** . . . . (617) 748-4403
E-mail: david_crepeault@mad.uscourts.gov
Information and Technology Supervisor
Christopher Gross . . . . (617) 748-9088
E-mail: chris_gross@mad.uscourts.gov
Property & Procurement Administrator/ Interpreter
Douglas Holmes . . . . (617) 748-9079
E-mail: douglas_holmes@mad.uscourts.gov
Customer Services Supervisor/New Criminal Cases
Catherine Gawlik . . . . (617) 748-9124
E-mail: cathy_gawlik@mad.uscourts.gov
Court Reporters Supervisor **Deborah Scalfani** . . . . (617) 748-9167
E-mail: deborah_scalfani@mad.uscourts.gov

Chambers of Chief Judge Patti B. Saris

One Courthouse Way, Suite 8110, Boston, MA 02210
Tel: (617) 748-4141 Fax: (617) 748-4582
E-mail: honorable_patti_saris@mad.uscourts.gov

Patti B. Saris
Chief Judge

Date of Birth: 1951
Education: Radcliffe 1973 BA; Harvard 1976 JD
Began Service: November 24, 1993
Appointed By: President William J. Clinton

Staff

Law Clerk **Emma Freeman** . . . . (617) 748-4141
Began Service: September 2014
Term Expires: December 31, 2015
E-mail: emma_freeman@mad.uscourts.gov
Law Clerk **Michael Gaffney** . . . . (617) 748-4141
Note: Effective January 2016.
Began Service: January 2016
Term Expires: December 31, 2016
Law Clerk **Stephen Hassink** . . . . (617) 748-4141
Began Service: September 2015
Term Expires: September 2016
Law Clerk **Genevieve Parshalle** . . . . (617) 748-4141
Began Service: September 2015
Term Expires: September 2016
E-mail: genevieve_parshalle@mad.uscourts.gov
Courtroom Clerk **Maryellen Molloy** . . . . (617) 748-4870
E-mail: maryellen_molloy@mad.uscourts.gov
Education: Northeastern 1984 BS
Docket Clerk **Clarilde Geraldino-Karasek** . . . . (617) 748-9178
Fax: (617) 748-9096
Court Reporter **Lee Marzilli** . . . . (617) 345-6787
E-mail: lee_marzilli@mad.uscourts.gov
Secretary **Marie C. Losco** . . . . (617) 748-4141
E-mail: marie_losco@mad.uscourts.gov

Chambers of District Judge William G. Young

John Joseph Moakley U.S. Courthouse, One Courthouse Way,
Suite 5710, Boston, MA 02210
Tel: (617) 748-9138 Fax: (617) 748-9142
E-mail: William_Young@mad.uscourts.gov

William G. Young
District Judge

Date of Birth: 1940
Education: Harvard 1962 AB, 1967 LLB
Began Service: 1985
Appointed By: President Ronald Reagan

Academic: Lecturer in Law, Boston College Law School (1968-1995); Lecturer in Law, Harvard Law School (1979-2005); Lecturer in Law, School of Law, Boston University (1979-2005)

Clerkships: Law Clerk The Honorable Raymond S. Wilkins, Massachusetts Supreme Judicial Court (1967-1968)

Government: Special Assistant Attorney General, Commonwealth of Massachusetts (1970-1972); Chief Counsel, Office of the Governor, Commonwealth of Massachusetts (1972-1974)

Judicial: Associate Justice, Massachusetts Superior Court (1978-1985); Chief Judge, United States District Court for the District of Massachusetts

Legal Practice: Bingham, Dana & Gould (1968-1978)

Military Service: United States Army (1962-1964)

Current Memberships: American Bar Association; The American Law Institute; Boston Bar Association; Massachusetts Bar Association

Staff

Law Clerk **Michael Pierce** . . . . (617) 748-9140
E-mail: michael_pierce@mad.uscourts.gov
Law Clerk **Olivia Hoffman** . . . . (617) 748-9141
Began Service: October 1, 2015
Term Expires: October 1, 2016
E-mail: olivia_hoffman@mad.uscourts.gov
Courtroom Clerk **Jennifer Gaudet** . . . . (617) 748-9156
E-mail: jennifer_gaudet@mad.uscourts.gov Fax: (617) 748-9096
Docket Clerk **Matthew Paine** . . . . (617) 748-9157
E-mail: matthew_paine@mad.uscourts.gov Fax: (617) 748-9096
Court Reporter **Richard Romanow** . . . . (617) 748-9138
Fax: (617) 261-7141
Secretary **Elizabeth E. Sonnenberg** . . . . (617) 748-4150
E-mail: elizabeth_sonnenberg@mad.uscourts.gov

Chambers of District Judge Nathaniel M. Gorton

John Joseph Moakley U.S. Courthouse, One Courthouse Way,
Suite 3110, Boston, MA 02210
Tel: (617) 748-9247 Fax: (617) 748-9251
E-mail: honorable_nathaniel_gorton@mad.uscourts.gov

Nathaniel M. Gorton
District Judge

Date of Birth: 1938
Education: Dartmouth 1960 AB; Columbia 1966 LLB
Began Service: October 27, 1992
Appointed By: President George H.W. Bush
Political Affiliation: Republican

Legal Practice: Associate, Nutter McClennen & Fish LLP (1966-1969); Partner, Director and Shareholder, Powers & Hall, PC (1970-1992)

Military Service: LTJG, United States Navy (1960-1962)

Current Memberships: Boston Bar Association

Staff

Law Clerk **Christina Liu** . . . . (617) 748-9249
Began Service: September 2015
Term Expires: September 2016
E-mail: christina_liu@mad.uscourts.gov

Chambers of District Judge Nathaniel M. Gorton *continued*

Law Clerk **Kathryn Schmidt** .... (617) 748-9249
Began Service: August 2015
Term Expires: August 2016
Courtroom Clerk **Christine Patch** .... (617) 748-9158
E-mail: christine_patch@mad.uscourts.gov Fax: (617) 748-9096
Docket Clerk **Christopher Danieli** .... (617) 748-4073
Court Reporter **Debra Lajoie** .... (617) 951-4555
Administrative Assistant **Patricia Verrier** .... (617) 748-9248
E-mail: patricia_verrier@mad.uscourts.gov

Chambers of District Judge Richard G. Stearns

John Joseph Moakley U.S. Courthouse, One Courthouse Way,
Suite 7130, Boston, MA 02210
Tel: (617) 748-9283 Fax: (617) 748-4179
E-mail: honorable_richard_stearns@mad.uscourts.gov

Richard G. Stearns
District Judge

Date of Birth: 1944
Education: Stanford 1968 BA; Oxford (UK) 1971 MA; Harvard 1976 JD
Began Service: January 5, 1994
Appointed By: President William J. Clinton
Political Affiliation: Democrat

Academic: Instructor, Harvard Law School (1984-1987)

Government: Special Assistant (D-SD), Office of Senator George McGovern, United States Senate (1972-1973); Assistant District Attorney, Office of the District Attorney, Commonwealth of Massachusetts (1977-1979); Campaign Advisor, Ted Kennedy for President (1979-1980); Assistant District Attorney, Office of the District Attorney, Commonwealth of Massachusetts (1980-1982); Assistant U.S. Attorney, Massachusetts District, Executive Office for United States Attorneys, United States Department of Justice (1982-1990)

Judicial: Associate Justice, Massachusetts Superior Court (1990-1994)

Nonprofit: Deputy Campaign Manager, George McGovern for President (1970-1972)

Current Memberships: American Bar Association

Staff
Career Law Clerk **Marsha K. Zierk** .... (617) 748-9283
E-mail: marsha_zierk@mad.uscourts.gov
Education: Suffolk 1987 JD
Courtroom Clerk **Terri Seelye** .... (617) 748-9162
E-mail: terri_seelye@mad.uscourts.gov
Docket Clerk **Elaine Flaherty** .... (617) 748-9812
E-mail: elaine_flaherty@mad.uscourts.gov

Chambers of District Judge George A. O'Toole, Jr.

John Joseph Moakley U.S. Courthouse, One Courthouse Way,
Suite 4730, Boston, MA 02210
Tel: (617) 748-9618 Fax: (617) 748-4105
E-mail: george_otoole@mad.uscourts.gov

George A. O'Toole, Jr.
District Judge

Date of Birth: 1947
Education: Boston Col 1969 AB; Harvard 1972 JD
Began Service: July 10, 1995
Appointed By: President William J. Clinton

Judicial: Associate Justice, Boston Municipal Court (1982-1990); Associate Justice, Superior Court of Massachusetts (1990-1995)

Legal Practice: Associate, Hale and Dorr LLP (1972-1977); Junior Partner, Hale and Dorr LLP (1978-1982)

Chambers of District Judge George A. O='Toole, Jr. *continued*

Staff
Law Clerk **Tucker DeVoe** .... (617) 748-4174
Began Service: September 2015
Term Expires: September 2016
E-mail: tucker_devoe@mad.uscourts.gov
Law Clerk **Jane Hill Lovins** .... (617) 748-4174
Began Service: September 2015
Term Expires: September 2016
Education: Boston Col 2009 JD
Courtroom Clerk **Paul Lyness** .... (617) 748-9181
E-mail: paul_lyness@mad.uscourts.gov Fax: (617) 748-9096
Docket Clerk **(Vacant)** .... (617) 748-9182
Fax: (617) 748-9096
Secretary **Dianne G. Croke** .... (617) 748-9618
E-mail: dianne_croke@mad.uscourts.gov

Chambers of District Judge F. Dennis Saylor IV

1 Courthouse Way, Boston, MA 02210
Tel: (617) 748-9212
E-mail: dennis_saylor@mad.uscourts.gov

F. Dennis Saylor IV
District Judge

Date of Birth: July 3, 1955
Education: Northwestern 1977 BSJ; Harvard 1981 JD
Began Service: June 15, 2004
Appointed By: President George W. Bush

Government: Assistant U.S. Attorney, District of Massachusetts, United States Attorney's Office, United States Department of Justice (1987-1990); Special Counsel/Chief of Staff to the Assistant Attorney General, Criminal Division, United States Department of Justice (1990-1993)

Legal Practice: Associate, Goodwin Procter, L.L.P (1981-1987); Partner, Goodwin Procter, L.L.P. (1993-2004)

Current Memberships: American Bar Association; Boston Bar Association; United States Foreign Intelligence Surveillance Court; Worcester County Bar Association

Staff
Law Clerk **Ian Stearns** .... (508) 929-9912
Began Service: September 17, 2015
Term Expires: September 17, 2016
E-mail: ian_stearns@mad.uscourts.gov
Law Clerk **Spencer Cox** .... (508) 929-9913
Began Service: September 10, 2015
Term Expires: September 10, 2016
E-mail: spencer_cox@mad.uscourts.gov
Secretary **Julie Piltzecker** .... (508) 929-9909
E-mail: julie_piltzecker@mad.uscourts.gov

Chambers of District Judge Denise Jefferson Casper

One Courthouse Way, Boston, MA 02210
Tel: (617) 748-4829
E-mail: denise_casper@mad.uscourts.gov

Denise J. Casper
District Judge

Education: Wesleyan U 1990 BA; Harvard 1994 JD
Began Service: January 17, 2011
Appointed By: President Barack Obama

Government: Assistant U.S. Attorney, Organized Crime Drug Enforcement Task Force Unit, Massachusetts District, United States Department of Justice (1999-2005); Deputy Chief, Organized Crime Drug Enforcement Task Force Unit, Massachusetts District, United States Department of Justice (2004-2005); Assistant U.S. Attorney, Organized Crime Drug Enforcement Task Force Unit, Department of Justice

Legal Practice: Civil Litigator, Bingham McCutchen LLP (1995-1998)

(continued on next page)

Chambers of District Judge Denise Jefferson Casper *continued*

Staff

Courtroom Clerk **Lisa Hourihan** . . . . (617) 748-9177
E-mail: lisa_hourihan@mad.uscourts.gov
Docket Clerk **Timothy Maynard** . . . . (617) 748-9041
E-mail: timothy_maynard@mad.uscourts.gov
Court Reporter **Debra Joyce** . . . . (617) 737-4410
E-mail: debra_joyce@mad.uscourts.gov
Judicial Assistant **(Vacant)** . . . . (617) 748-4137

Chambers of District Judge Timothy S. Hillman

595 Main Street, Worcester, MA 01608-2076
Tel: (508) 929-9904 Fax: (617) 748-9096
E-mail: honorable_timothy_hillman@mad.uscourts.gov

Timothy S. Hillman
District Judge

Education: Coe 1970 BA; Suffolk 1973 JD
Began Service: 2012
Appointed By: President Barack Obama

Staff

Judicial Assistant **Mary Stacy** . . . . (508) 929-9904
E-mail: mary_stacy@mad.uscourts.gov
Court Reporter **Marianne Kusa-Ryll** . . . . (508) 929-9904
Courtroom Clerk **Martin Castles** . . . . (508) 929-9904
E-mail: martin_castles@mad.uscourts.gov

Chambers of District Judge Indira Talwani

One Courthouse Way, Boston, MA 02210
Tel: (617) 748-9152
E-mail: indira_talwani@mad.uscourts.gov

Indira Talwani
District Judge

Education: Harvard 1982 BA; Boalt Hall 1988 JD
Began Service: May 12, 2014
Appointed By: President Barack Obama

Staff

Judicial Assistant **Olivia M. Blanchette** . . . . (617) 748-9152
E-mail: olivia_blanchette@mad.uscourts.gov

Chambers of District Judge Mark Mastroianni

One Courthouse Way, Boston, MA 02210
Tel: (617) 785-6804

Mark G. Mastroianni
District Judge

Education: American International 1986 BA; Western New England 1989 JD
Began Service: June 1, 2014
Appointed By: President Barack Obama

Government: District Attorney, Office of the District Attorney, County of Hampden, Massachusetts

Staff

Docket Clerk **Maurice Lindsay** . . . . (617) 785-6805
E-mail: maurice_lindsay@mad.uscourts.gov
Docket Clerk **Mary E. Finn** . . . . (617) 785-6806
Court Reporter **Alice Moran** . . . . (413) 731-0086
Courtroom Clerk **Theresa Pelegano** . . . . (617) 785-6804
E-mail: theresa_pelegano@mad.uscourts.gov

Chambers of District Judge Leo T. Sorokin

One Courthouse Way, Boston, MA 02210
Tel: (617) 748-4231

Leo T. Sorokin
District Judge

Education: Yale 1983 BA; Columbia 1991 JD
Began Service: 2014
Appointed By: President Barack Obama

Staff

Courtroom Deputy **Maria Simeone** . . . . (617) 748-4231
E-mail: maria_simeone@mad.uscourts.gov

Chambers of District Judge Allison Dale Burroughs

One Courthouse Way, Boston, MA 02210
Tel: (617) 748-4232

Allison Dale Burroughs
District Judge

Education: Middlebury BA; Pennsylvania 1988 JD
Began Service: January 7, 2015
Appointed By: President Barack Obama

Staff

Courtroom Deputy **Karen Folan** . . . . (617) 748-4232
Judicial Assistant **Terry Manning** . . . . (617) 748-4232
Court Reporter **Carol Scott** . . . . (617) 748-4232

Chambers of Senior Judge Michael A. Ponsor

300 State Street, Springfield, MA 01105
Tel: (413) 785-6824 Fax: (413) 781-9473
E-mail: michael_ponsor@mad.uscourts.gov

Michael A. Ponsor
Senior Judge

Date of Birth: 1946
Education: Harvard 1969 AB; Oxford (UK) 1971 BA; Yale 1974 JD
Began Service: 1994
Appointed By: President William J. Clinton

Current Memberships: Boston Bar Association; Hampshire County Bar Association; Massachusetts Bar Association

Staff

Career Law Clerk **Jennifer Kaplan** . . . . (413) 785-6826
Began Service: September 6, 2012
E-mail: jennifer_kaplan@mad.uscourts.gov
Education: Western New England JD
Law Clerk **Timothy Cook** . . . . (413) 785-6827
Courtroom Clerk **Bethaney Healy** . . . . (413) 785-6804
E-mail: bethaney_healy@mad.uscourts.gov
Court Reporter **Alice Moran** . . . . (413) 731-0086
E-mail: alice_moran@mad.uscourts.gov
Docket Clerk **Mary E. Finn** . . . . (413) 785-6806
E-mail: mary_finn@mad.uscourts.gov
Docket Clerk **Maurice Lindsay** . . . . (413) 785-6805
E-mail: maurice_lindsay@mad.uscourts.gov
Secretary **Elizabeth Collins** . . . . (413) 785-6824
E-mail: elizabeth_collins@mad.uscourts.gov

Chambers of Senior Judge Mark L. Wolf

John Joseph Moakley U.S. Courthouse, One Courthouse Way,
Boston, MA 02210
Tel: (617) 748-9272 Fax: (617) 748-9096
E-mail: mark_wolf@mad.uscourts.gov

Mark L. Wolf
Senior Judge

Date of Birth: 1946
Education: Yale 1968 BA; Harvard 1971 JD
Began Service: 1985
Appointed By: President Ronald Reagan

Staff
Courtroom Clerk **Daniel "Dan" Hohler** . . . . (617) 748-9159
E-mail: daniel_hohler@mad.uscourts.gov
Docket Clerk **Yvonne Franklin** . . . . (617) 748-9155
E-mail: yvonne_franklin@mad.uscourts.gov
Court Reporter **Kelly Mortellite** . . . . (617) 737-0370
E-mail: kelly_mortellite@mad.uscourts.gov
Judicial Assistant **Margaret Priestly** . . . . (617) 748-9272

Chambers of Senior Judge Joseph L. Tauro

John Joseph Moakley U.S. Courthouse, One Courthouse Way,
Boston, MA 02210
Tel: (617) 748-9288 Fax: (617) 748-4656
E-mail: honorable_joseph_tauro@mad.uscourts.gov

Joseph L. Tauro
Senior Judge

Date of Birth: 1931
Education: Brown U 1953 AB; Cornell 1956 LLB
Began Service: 1972
Appointed By: President Richard M. Nixon

Current Memberships: American Bar Foundation; Boston Bar Association; Cornell Law Association; The District of Columbia Bar; Massachusetts Bar Association

Staff
Law Clerk **(Vacant)** . . . . (617) 748-9288
Law Clerk **(Vacant)** . . . . (617) 748-9288
Courtroom Clerk **Zita Lovett** . . . . (617) 748-9183
E-mail: zita_lovett@mad.uscourts.gov
Judicial Assistant **Yvonne Franklin** . . . . (617) 748-9288
E-mail: yvonne_franklin@mad.uscourts.gov

Chambers of Senior Judge Rya W. Zobel

John Joseph Moakley U.S. Courthouse, One Courthouse Way,
Suite 6110, Boston, MA 02210-3008
Tel: (617) 748-9144 Fax: (617) 748-9146
E-mail: rya_zobel@mad.uscourts.gov

Rya W. Zobel
Senior Judge

Date of Birth: 1931
Education: Radcliffe 1953 AB; Harvard 1956 LLB
Began Service: 1979
Appointed By: President Jimmy Carter

Current Memberships: American Bar Foundation; The American Law Institute; Boston Bar Association; Massachusetts Bar Association; National Association of Women Judges

Staff
Law Clerk **Jennifer C. Brown** . . . . (617) 748-9145
Began Service: October 2015
Term Expires: October 2016
E-mail: jennifer_c_brown@mad.uscourts.gov

Chambers of Senior Judge Rya W. Zobel *continued*

Law Clerk **Alexander Westerfield** . . . . (617) 748-4164
Began Service: September 2015
Term Expires: September 2016
E-mail: alexander_westerfield@mad.uscourts.gov
Courtroom Clerk **Lisa Urso** . . . . (617) 748-9187
E-mail: lisa_urso@mad.uscourts.gov
Docket Clerk **Anamaria Gioia** . . . . (617) 748-9085
E-mail: anamaria_gioia@mad.uscourts.gov
Judicial Assistant **Lily DiBlasi** . . . . (617) 748-9145
E-mail: lily_diblasi@mad.uscourts.gov

Chambers of Senior Judge Douglas P. Woodlock

John Joseph Moakley U.S. Courthouse, One Courthouse Way,
Suite 4110, Boston, MA 02210
Tel: (617) 748-9293 Fax: (617) 748-4593
E-mail: honorable_douglas_woodlock@mad.uscourts.gov

Douglas P. Woodlock
Senior Judge

Date of Birth: 1947
Education: Yale 1969 BA; Georgetown 1975 JD
Began Service: 1986
Appointed By: President Ronald Reagan
Political Affiliation: Republican

Current Memberships: American Bar Foundation; American Bar Association; The American Law Institute; Boston Bar Association; Federal Judges Association; Massachusetts Bar Association

Staff
Courtroom Clerk **Jarrett Lovett** . . . . (617) 748-9170
E-mail: jarrett_lovett@mad.uscourts.gov
Education: Brandeis 1997 BA
Docket Clerk **Anamaria Gioia** . . . . (617) 748-9085
E-mail: anamaria_gioia@mad.uscourts.gov
Court Reporter **Brenda Hancock** . . . . (617) 439-3214
E-mail: brenda_hancock@mad.uscourts.gov
Secretary **Claire Colman** . . . . (617) 748-9293
E-mail: claire_colman@mad.uscourts.gov

Chambers of Chief Magistrate Judge Jennifer C. Boal

John Joseph Moakley U.S. Courthouse, One Courthouse Way,
Boston, MA 02210
Tel: (617) 748-9238
E-mail: jennifer_boal@mad.uscourts.gov

Jennifer C. Boal
Chief Magistrate Judge

Education: Haverford 1985; Cornell 1989
Began Service: 2010

Staff
Law Clerk **(Vacant)** . . . . (617) 748-9236
Law Clerk **Hdeisha Sheldon** . . . . (617) 748-4310
Courtroom/Docket Clerk **Steve York** . . . . (617) 748-9238
E-mail: steve_york@mad.uscourts.gov

Chambers of Magistrate Judge Marianne B. Bowler

John Joseph Moakley U.S. Courthouse, One Courthouse Way,
Suite 8420, Boston, MA 02210
Tel: (617) 748-9219 Fax: (617) 204-5833
E-mail: Honorable_Marianne_Bowler@mad.uscourts.gov

Marianne B. Bowler
Magistrate Judge

Date of Birth: 1947
Education: Regis Col (MA) 1967 AB; Suffolk 1976 JD
Began Service: May 7, 1990
Term Expires: May 2022
Political Affiliation: Democrat

Academic: Assistant Director, Attorney General's Advocacy Institute (1987-1988)

Clerkships: Law Clerk, Massachusetts Superior Court (1976-1977); Deputy Chief Law Clerk, Massachusetts Superior Court (1977-1978)

Government: Assistant District Attorney, Commonwealth of Massachusetts (1978); Assistant United States Attorney, District of Massachusetts, Office of the United States Attorney, United States Department of Justice (1978-1990); Senior Litigation Counsel, United States Department of Justice (1989-1990); Assistant Director, Attorney General's Advocacy Institute, United States Department of Justice

Nonprofit: Director, The Boston Foundation (1995-2005); Overseer, National Constitution Center

Staff
Career Law Clerk **Sara B. Cole** .... (617) 748-9219
E-mail: sara_cole@mad.uscourts.gov
Education: Yale 1978 BA; Connecticut 1984 JD
Courtroom Clerk **Brendan Garvin** .... (617) 748-9222
E-mail: brendan_garvin@mad.uscourts.gov Fax: (617) 748-9096
Judicial Assistant **Susan Costa** .... (617) 748-9219
E-mail: susan_costa@mad.uscourts.gov

Chambers of Magistrate Judge Kenneth P. Neiman

U.S. Courthouse, 300 State Street, Suite 252, Springfield, MA 01105
Tel: (413) 785-6818 Fax: (413) 781-9472

Kenneth P. Neiman
Magistrate Judge

Date of Birth: 1945
Education: Tufts 1967 BA; Harvard 1971 JD
Began Service: January 5, 1995
Term Expires: January 2019

Current Memberships: American Bar Association; The Federal Courts Law Review; Hampshire County Bar Association; Massachusetts Bar Association; Massachusetts Bar Foundation, Massachusetts Bar Association

Staff
Law Clerk **Sara Fawk** .... (413) 785-6819
E-mail: sara_fawki@mad.uscourts.gov
Education: Western New England 2010 JD
Law Clerk **Peter Ferony** .... (413) 785-6819
E-mail: peter_ferony@mad.uscourts.gov
Courtroom Clerk **Melissa Calderon** .... (413) 785-6802
E-mail: melissa_calderon@mad.uscourts.gov

Chambers of Magistrate Judge Judith Gail Dein

John Joseph Moakley U.S. Courthouse, One Courthouse Way,
Room 6420, Boston, MA 02210
Tel: (617) 748-4736 Fax: (617) 748-4585
E-mail: judith_dein@mad.uscourts.gov

Judith Gail Dein
Magistrate Judge

Date of Birth: 1955
Education: Union Col (NY) 1976 BA; Boston Col 1979 JD
Began Service: July 2000
Term Expires: July 2016

Clerkships: Law Clerk, Massachusetts Superior Court (1979-1980); Law Clerk The Honorable Robert Braucher, Massachusetts Supreme Judicial Court (1980-1981)

Judicial: Magistrate Judge, United States District Court for the District of Massachusetts (2000-2009); Chief Magistrate Judge, Chambers of Chief Magistrate Judge Judith Gail Dein, United States District Court for the District of Massachusetts (2009-2012)

Legal Practice: Associate, Hale and Dorr LLP; Junior Partner, Hale and Dorr LLP; Partner, Kirkpatrick & Lockhart LLP (1989-2000)

Current Memberships: Boston Bar Association; Federal Magistrate Judges Association; Massachusetts Association of Women Lawyers; Massachusetts Bar Association; Massachusetts Bar Foundation, Massachusetts Bar Association; Women's Bar Association of Massachusetts

Staff
Career Law Clerk **Amy K. Hollman** .... (617) 748-4171
E-mail: amy_hollman@mad.uscourts.gov
Education: Cornell 1991 JD
Courtroom Clerk **Thomas F. Quinn, Jr.** .... (617) 748-9040
E-mail: thomas_quinn@mad.uscourts.gov
Education: Suffolk 1990 JD
Secretary **Jolyne D'Ambrosio** .... (617) 748-4736
E-mail: jolyne_dambrosio@mad.uscourts.gov

Chambers of Magistrate Judge David H. Hennessey

595 Main Street, Worcester, MA 01608-2076
Tel: (508) 929-9905

David H. Hennessey
Magistrate Judge

Education: SUNY (Albany) 1978 BA; Fordham 1985 JD

Staff
Courtroom Clerk **Lisa Belpedio** .... (508) 929-9905
E-mail: lisa_belpedio@mad.uscourts.gov

Chambers of Magistrate Judge M. Page Kelley

One Courthouse Way, Boston, MA 02210
Tel: (617) 748-9183

M. Page Kelley
Magistrate Judge

Education: Smith 1981 BA; Harvard 1986 JD

Chambers of Magistrate Judge Katherine A. Robertson

One Courthouse Way, Boston, MA 02210
Tel: (413) 785-6802

Katherine A. "Katy" Robertson
Magistrate Judge

Education: Princeton 1975 BA; Western New England 1990 JD

Chambers of Magistrate Judge Katherine A. Robertson *continued*

Staff
Courtroom Deputy **Melissa Calderon** . . . . (413) 785-6802

Chambers of Magistrate Judge Donald L. Cabell
One Courthouse Way, Boston, MA 02210
Tel: (617) 748-9233

Donald L. Cabell
Magistrate Judge

Education: UMass (Amherst) 1986 BA; Northeastern 1991 JD

Chambers of Magistrate Judge (recalled) Jerome J. Niedermeier
John Joseph Moakley U.S. Courthouse, One Courthouse Way, Boston, MA 02210
Tel: (617) 748-9155

Jerome J. Niedermeier
Magistrate Judge (recalled)

Date of Birth: 1943
Education: Boston Col 1967 AB; Georgetown 1972 JD
Began Service: 2010

Current Memberships: Connecticut Bar Association, Inc.; The District of Columbia Bar; Vermont Bar Association

Staff
Judicial Assistant **Yvonne Franklin** . . . . (617) 748-9155
E-mail: yvonne_franklin@mad.uscourts.gov

Chambers of Magistrate Judge (recalled) Robert B. Collings
John Joseph Moakley U.S. Courthouse, One Courthouse Way, Suite 7420, Boston, MA 02210-3008
Tel: (617) 748-9229 Fax: (617) 748-9231

Robert B. Collings
Magistrate Judge (recalled)

Date of Birth: 1942
Education: Hamilton 1964 AB; Harvard 1967 JD
Began Service: 1982

Current Memberships: American Bar Association; Boston Bar Association; Federal Magistrate Judges Association; Massachusetts Bar Association

United States Bankruptcy Court for the District of Massachusetts
John W. McCormack Post Office and Courthouse, 5 Post Office Square, Suite 1150, Boston, MA 02109-3945
Tel: (617) 748-5300 Tel: (617) 748-5350 (PACER)
Tel: (617) 748-5311 (PACER) Tel: (888) 201-3571 (Toll Free PACER)
Tel: (888) 201-3572 (Toll Free Voice Case Information System VCIS)
Tel: (508) 770-8900 (Worcester Divisional Office) Fax: (617) 748-5315
Fax: (508) 793-0189 (Worcester Divisional Office Intake Fax)
Internet: www.mab.uscourts.gov

Number of Judgeships: 5

Court Staff
Bankruptcy Clerk **James M. Lynch** . . . . (617) 748-5300
E-mail: james_lynch@mab.uscourts.gov
Education: Providence 1969 BA; George Mason 1980 JD

United States Bankruptcy Court for the District of Massachusetts *continued*

Chief Deputy Clerk **Judith P. Crossen** . . . . (508) 770-8934
211 Donohue Federal Bldg., 595 Main St., Worcester, MA 01608-2076 Fax: (508) 770-8998
E-mail: judith_crossen@mab.uscourts.gov
Education: New England 1990 JD
Personnel Specialist **Paula Charette** . . . . (617) 748-5300
E-mail: paula_s_charette@mab.uscourts.gov Fax: (617) 748-6622
Director of Information Technology **Edwin Perkins** . . . . . . (617) 748-5300
E-mail: edwin_perkins@mab.uscourts.gov
Case Administration Supervisor **Mary E. Murray** . . . . (617) 748-5350

Chambers of Chief Bankruptcy Judge Melvin S. Hoffman
5 Post Office Square, Boston, MA 02109-3945
Tel: (617) 748-5300

Melvin S. Hoffman
Chief Bankruptcy Judge

Chambers of Bankruptcy Judge Frank J. Bailey
Five Post Office Square, Boston, MA 02109-3945
Tel: (617) 748-5300

Frank J. Bailey
Bankruptcy Judge

Education: Georgetown 1977 BSFS; Suffolk 1980 JD
Began Service: 2010

Staff
Courtroom Deputy **Regina Brooks** . . . . (617) 748-5347
E-mail: regina_brooks@mab.uscourts.gov

Chambers of Bankruptcy Judge Joan N. Feeney
John W. McCormack Post Office and Courthouse, 5 Post Office Square, Suite 1150, Boston, MA 02109-3945
Tel: (617) 748-6631 Fax: (617) 748-6635

Joan N. Feeney
Bankruptcy Judge

Date of Birth: 1953
Education: Connecticut Col 1975 BA; Suffolk 1978 JD
Began Service: 1992
Term Expires: 2020

Clerkships: Law Clerk The Honorable James N. Garbriel, United States Bankruptcy Court (1982-1986)

Government: Chief Bankruptcy Judge, United States Bankruptcy Court for the District of Massachusetts

Legal Practice: Associate, Feeney & Freeley (1979-1982); Associate, Hanify & King, PC (1986-1988); Partner, Hanify & King, PC (1988-1992)

Current Memberships: American Bankruptcy Institute; Boston Bar Association; Massachusetts Bar Association; National Conference of Bankruptcy Judges

Membership: Past Member, American Bankruptcy Institute

Staff
Career Law Clerk **Margaret M. Crouch** . . . . (617) 748-6631
Education: Duquesne 1984 JD
Career Law Clerk **Ann Fox** . . . . (617) 748-6631
Courtroom Deputy **Margaret "Peggy" Defren** . . . . (617) 565-6067
Fax: (617) 565-6651

Chambers of Bankruptcy Judge Henry Jack Boroff
United States Bankruptcy Court, 300 State Street, 2nd Floor,
Springfield, MA 01105
Tel: (413) 785-6860 Fax: (413) 781-9478
E-mail: henry.boroff@mab.uscourts.gov

Henry Jack Boroff
Bankruptcy Judge

Date of Birth: 1951
Education: Boston U 1975 JD
Began Service: 1993
Term Expires: December 10, 2021

Staff
Career Law Clerk **Elizabeth Royalty** . . . . (413) 785-6860
E-mail: elizabeth_royalty@mab.uscourts.gov
Education: Cincinnati 2004 JD
Courtroom Deputy **Stephen Reynolds** . . . . (413) 785-6909
U.S. Courthouse Fax: (413) 785-9477
E-mail: stephen_reynolds@mab.uscourts.gov
Law Clerk **Lauren McNair** . . . . (413) 785-6860
E-mail: lauren_mcnair@mab.uscourts.gov

United States District Court for the Eastern District of Michigan
Theodore Levin U.S. Courthouse, 231 West Lafayette Boulevard,
Detroit, MI 48226
Tel: (313) 234-5005 Tel: (313) 226-7249 (PACER)
Tel: (313) 961-4934 (PACER) Fax: (313) 234-5395
Internet: www.mied.uscourts.gov

Number of Judgeships: 15

Circuit: Sixth

Areas Covered: Counties of Alcona, Alpena, Arenac, Bay, Cheboygan, Clare, Crawford, Genesee, Gladwin, Gratiot, Huron, Iosco, Isabella, Jackson, Lapeer, Lenawee, Livingston, Macomb, Midland, Monroe, Montmorency, Oakland, Ogemaw, Oscoda, Otsego, Presque Isle, Roscommon, Saginaw, Sanilac, Shiawassee, St. Clair, Tuscola, Washtenaw and Wayne

Court Staff
Court Administrator and Clerk of the Court
David J. Weaver . . . . (313) 234-5051
E-mail: david_weaver@mied.uscourts.gov Fax: (313) 234-5399
Deputy Court Administrator **Maureen R. Flavin** . . . . (313) 234-5051
E-mail: maureen_flavin@mied.uscourts.gov
Court Services Manager **Michael Kregear** . . . . (313) 234-5055
E-mail: michael_kregear@mied.uscourts.gov
Human Resources Manager **Robyn Ringl** . . . . (313) 234-5065
Information Technology Manager **Joshua Matta** . . . . (313) 234-5537
E-mail: joshua_matta@mied.uscourts.gov
Chief Probation Officer **Philip Miller** . . . . (313) 234-5400
Fax: (313) 234-5390
Chief Pretrial Services Officer **Alan Murray** . . . . (313) 234-5300
Fax: (313) 234-5385
Community Defender Organization **Miriam Siefer** . . . . (313) 961-4150
Fax: (313) 961-0627
Librarian **Elise Keller** . . . . (313) 234-5255
Fax: (313) 234-5383
Courtroom Deputy Services Supervisor **Kim Grimes** . . . . . (313) 234-5043
E-mail: kim_grimes@mied.uscourts.gov
Jury/Court Recording/ECR Supervisor **John Purdy** . . . . . . (734) 234-5132
Fax: (313) 234-5388

Chambers of Chief Judge Gerald E. Rosen
Theodore Levin U.S. Courthouse, 231 West Lafayette Boulevard,
Room 730, Detroit, MI 48226
Tel: (313) 234-5135 Fax: (313) 234-5360
E-mail: gerald_rosen@mied.uscourts.gov

Gerald E. Rosen
Chief Judge

Date of Birth: 1951
Education: Kalamazoo 1973 BA;
George Washington 1979 JD
Began Service: 1990
Appointed By: President George H.W. Bush

Academic: Adjunct Professor, Law School, Wayne State University (1992-1993); Adjunct Professor, School of Law, University of Detroit Mercy (1994-1998)

Government: Legislative Assistant (R-MI), Office of Senator Robert P. Griffin, United States Senate (1974-1979)

Judicial: Member, United States Judicial Conference Committee on Criminal Law (1995-2001); District Judge, United States District Court for the Eastern District of Michigan (1990-2009)

Legal Practice: Law Clerk, Seyfarth, Shaw, Fairweather & Geraldson (1979); Senior Partner, Miller, Canfield, Paddock and Stone, P.L.C. (1990)

Staff
Career Law Clerk **Linda S. Hylenski** . . . . (313) 234-5138
E-mail: linda_hylenski@mied.uscourts.gov
Education: Detroit Law 1985 JD
Career Law Clerk **James David Lewis** . . . . (313) 234-5191
Education: Michigan 1995 JD
Case Manager **Julie Owens** . . . . (313) 234-5137
Court Reporter **Carol Sapala** . . . . (313) 961-7552
E-mail: carol_sapala@mied.uscourts.gov
Judicial Assistant **Donna D. Vinson** . . . . (313) 234-5135
E-mail: donna_vinson@mied.uscourts.gov

Chambers of District Judge Denise Page Hood
Theodore Levin U.S. Courthouse, 231 West Lafayette Boulevard,
Room 251, Detroit, MI 48226
Tel: (313) 234-5165 Fax: (313) 234-5358

Denise Page Hood
District Judge

Date of Birth: 1952
Education: Yale 1974 BA; Columbia 1977 JD
Began Service: June 11, 1994
Appointed By: President William J. Clinton

Government: Assistant Corporation Counsel, City of Detroit, Michigan (1977-1982)

Judicial: Judge, Michigan District Court, 36th District (1983-1989); Judge, Detroit Recorders Court (1989-1992); Judge, Michigan Circuit Court, Wayne County (1993-1994)

Current Memberships: American Bar Association; Association of Black Judges of Michigan; Detroit Bar Association; State Bar of Michigan

Staff
Law Clerk **Sasha Griffin** . . . . (313) 234-5165
Began Service: August 2015
Term Expires: September 2016
E-mail: sasha_griffin@mied.uscourts.gov
Career Law Clerk **Ann E. Y. Malayang-Daley** . . . . (313) 234-5165
Education: Detroit Law 1989 JD
Case Manager **La Shawn Saulsberry** . . . . (313) 234-5167
Court Reporter **Cheryl Warren Daniel** . . . . (313) 234-5165
E-mail: cheryl_daniel@mied.uscourts.gov
Judicial Secretary **Charlene R. Gill** . . . . (313) 234-5165
E-mail: charlene_gill@mied.uscourts.gov

Chambers of District Judge Victoria A. Roberts

Theodore Levin U.S. Courthouse, 231 West Lafayette Boulevard, Room 123, Detroit, MI 48226
Tel: (313) 234-5230 Fax: (313) 234-5493
E-mail: Victoria_Roberts@mied.uscourts.gov

Victoria A. Roberts
District Judge

Date of Birth: 1951
Education: Michigan 1973 BA; Northeastern 1976 JD
Began Service: August 11, 1998
Appointed By: President William J. Clinton

Academic: Legal Research and Teaching Fellow, Detroit College of Law, Michigan State University (1977-1978)

Government: Research Attorney, Michigan Court of Appeals (1976-1977); Assistant United States Attorney, Eastern District of Michigan, United States Attorney's Office, United States Department of Justice, Ronald Reagan Administration (1985-1988)

Legal Practice: Associate, Lewis, White, Clay & Graves, P.C. (and successor firms) (1977-1980); Shareholder, Lewis, White, Clay & Graves, P.C. (and successor firms) (1980-1983); Senior Litigation Attorney, American Motors Corporation (AMC) (1983-1985); Associate, Goodman, Eden, Millender & Bedrosian (1988-1993); Partner, Goodman, Eden, Millender & Bedrosian (1992-1998); Managing Partner, Goodman, Eden, Millender & Bedrosian (1995-1998)

Current Memberships: American Bar Association; State Bar of Michigan; Wolverine Bar Association; Women Lawyers Association of Michigan

Staff

Law Clerk **Garry Hartlieb** .... (313) 234-5230
Began Service: August 2015
Term Expires: August 2016
E-mail: garry_hartlieb@mied.uscourts.gov
Law Clerk **Rebecca Waisanen** .... (313) 234-5230
Began Service: August 2014
Term Expires: August 2016
Case Manager **Carol A. Pinegar** .... (313) 234-5232
Court Reporter **Janice Coleman** .... (313) 234-5230
E-mail: Janice_Coleman@mied.uscourts.gov
Secretary **Linda Vertriest** .... (313) 234-5230
E-mail: Linda_Vertriest@mied.uscourts.gov

Chambers of District Judge Paul D. Borman

Theodore Levin U.S. Courthouse, 231 West Lafayette Boulevard, Room 740, Detroit, MI 48226
Tel: (313) 234-5120 Fax: (313) 234-5350
E-mail: paul_borman@mied.uscourts.gov

Paul David Borman
District Judge

Date of Birth: 1939
Education: Michigan 1962 JD; Yale 1964 LLM
Began Service: September 2, 1994
Appointed By: President William J. Clinton

Academic: Professor of Law, Wayne State University (1968-1979); Adjunct Instructor, Law School, University of Michigan (1979-1995)

Government: Staff Attorney, United States Commission on Civil Rights (1962-1963); Assistant U.S. Attorney, Michigan - Eastern District, Executive Office for United States Attorneys, United States Department of Justice (1964-1965); Special Counsel, Mayor Jerome P. Cavanagh (MI), Office of the Mayor, City of Detroit, Michigan (1967-1968); Assistant Prosecuting Attorney, Office of the Prosecuting Attorney, County of Wayne, Michigan (1974-1975); Chief Federal Defender, Legal Aid and Defender Association (1979-1994)

Legal Practice: Vice President, House Counsel and Member of the Board, Borman Food Stores, Inc. (1965-1967); Private Practice (1977-1979)

Chambers of District Judge Paul D. Borman *continued*

Staff

Law Clerk **Amanda D'Angelo** .... (313) 234-5120
Began Service: September 2012
Term Expires: August 2016
Career Law Clerk **Marybeth Collon** .... (313) 234-5120
E-mail: marybeth_collon@mied.uscourts.gov
Case Manager **Deborah "Deb" Tofil** .... (313) 234-5120
Secretary **Rebecca McGee** .... (313) 234-5120
E-mail: rebecca_mcgee@mied.uscourts.gov
Court Reporter **Leann Lizza** .... (313) 234-5120
E-mail: leann_lizza@mied.uscourts.gov

Chambers of District Judge David M. Lawson

231 West Lafayette Boulevard, Room 802, Detroit, MI 48226
Tel: (313) 234-2660 Fax: (313) 234-2669
E-mail: David_Lawson@mied.uscourts.gov

David M. Lawson
District Judge

Date of Birth: 1951
Education: Notre Dame 1972 BA; Wayne State U 1976 JD
Began Service: August 4, 2000
Appointed By: President William J. Clinton

Clerkships: Law Clerk The Honorable John N. O'Brien, Oakland County Circuit Court (1973-1975); Law Clerk The Honorable James Ryan, Michigan Supreme Court (1976-1977)

Government: Investment Officer, Office of the Treasurer, County of Oakland, Michigan (1975-1976); Special Assistant Attorney General, County of Oakland, Michigan (1979-1980); Special Prosecuting Attorney, Office of the Prosecuting Attorney, County of Livingston, Michigan (1991-1993)

Legal Practice: Partner, Lawson & Lawson (1977-1985); Partner, Lizza, Mulcahy, Casey & Lawson, PC (1985-1994); Member, Clark Hill PLC (1994-2000)

Current Memberships: American Bar Association; Federal Bar Association; Oakland County Bar Association

Staff

Fax: (313) 234-2669

Law Clerk **Erik Johnson** .... (313) 234-2660
Began Service: August 2015
Term Expires: August 2016
E-mail: erik_johnson@mied.uscourts.gov
Senior Law Clerk **Michael Shaffer** .... (313) 234-2660
E-mail: michael_shaffer@mied.uscourts.gov
Judicial Secretary **Susan Pinkowski** .... (313) 234-2660
E-mail: susan_pinkowski@mied.uscourts.gov

Chambers of District Judge Sean F. Cox

231 West Lafayette Boulevard, Room 257, Detroit, MI 48226
Tel: (313) 234-2650
E-mail: sean_cox@mied.uscourts.gov

Sean F. Cox
District Judge

Education: Michigan 1979 BGS; Detroit 1983 JD
Began Service: June 2006
Appointed By: President George W. Bush

Legal Practice: Associate, Kitch, Saurbier, Drutchas, Wagner & Kenney (1984-1989); Associate, Bloom & Kavanaugh (1989-1990); Partner, Cummings, McClorey, Davis & Acho, P.C. (1990-1996)

Staff

Law Clerk **Zainab Hazimi** .... (313) 234-2650
Began Service: September 2015
Term Expires: September 2017
E-mail: zainab_hazimi@mied.uscourts.gov

(continued on next page)

Chambers of District Judge Sean F. Cox *continued*

Career Law Clerk **Katrina Staub** .... (313) 234-2650
E-mail: katrina_staub@mied.uscourts.gov
Education: Western Michigan 1990 BS; Michigan 1992 MPH; Wayne State U 2000 JD
Court Reporter **Marie Metcalf** .... (313) 962-3832
E-mail: marie_metcalf@mied.uscourts.gov
Case Manager **Jennifer McCoy** .... (313) 234-2653

Chambers of District Judge Thomas L. Ludington

1000 Washington Avenue, Bay City, MI 48708
Tel: (989) 894-8810
E-mail: thomas_ludington@mied.uscourts.gov

Thomas L. Ludington
District Judge

Date of Birth: 1953
Education: Albion 1976 BA; San Diego 1979 JD
Began Service: June 30, 2006
Appointed By: President George W. Bush

Judicial: Circuit Judge, 42nd Circuit Court of Michigan (1994-1999); Chief Judge, 42nd Circuit Court of Michigan (1999-2006)

Legal Practice: Attorney, Private Pratice (1980-1994)

Nonprofit: Trustee, Albion College

Staff

Law Clerk **Michael Whalen** .... (989) 894-8810
Term Expires: August 2016
E-mail: michael_whalen@mied.uscourts.gov
Law Clerk **Mary Erler** .... (989) 894-8810
Term Expires: August 2016
E-mail: mary_erler@mied.uscourts.gov
Case Manager **Tracy Jacobs** .... (989) 894-8810
Court Reporter **Carol Harrison** .... (989) 892-2797
Secretary **Suzanne Gammon** .... (989) 894-8810
E-mail: suzanne_gammon@mied.uscourts.gov

Chambers of District Judge Stephen Joseph Murphy III

Theodore Levin U.S. Courthouse, 231 West Lafayette Boulevard, Room 235, Detroit, MI 48226
Tel: (313) 234-2680

Stephen Joseph Murphy III
District Judge

Education: Saint Louis U 1987 JD
Began Service: July 2, 2008
Appointed By: President George W. Bush

Academic: Adjunct Professor, School of Law, University of Detroit; Adjunct Professor, Ave Maria School of Law

Corporate: Attorney, General Motors Corporation

Government: Trial Attorney, Civil Division, United States Department of Justice; Trial Attorney, Tax Division, United States Department of Justice; Assistant U.S. Attorney, United States Attorneys Office, United States Department of Justice

Staff

Law Clerk **William O'Hara** .... (313) 234-2680
E-mail: william_o'hara@mied.uscourts.gov
Law Clerk **Grant Newman** .... (313) 234-2680
Began Service: September 2015
E-mail: grant_newman@mied.uscourts.gov
Law Clerk **Chris Kopp** .... (313) 234-2680
E-mail: chris_kopp@mied.uscourts.gov
Case Manager **Carol Cohron** .... (313) 234-2680
Court Reporter **Linda Cavanagh** .... (248) 884-0327
E-mail: linda_cavanagh@mied.uscourts.gov

Chambers of District Judge Mark A. Goldsmith

231 West Lafayette Boulevard, Detroit, MI 48226
Tel: (313) 234-5240 Tel: (313) 243-5368
E-mail: mark_goldsmith@mied.uscourts.gov

Mark A. Goldsmith
District Judge

Education: Michigan 1974 BA; Harvard 1977 JD
Began Service: June 21, 2010
Appointed By: President Barack Obama

Academic: Adjunct Instructor, College of Law, Wayne State University

Judicial: Judge, Michigan Circuit Courts (2004-2010)

Legal Practice: Litigator, Paul, Weiss, Rifkind, Wharton & Garrison LLP; Litigation Partner, Oakland County/Bloomfield Hills, MI Office, Honigman Miller Schwartz and Cohn LLP

Staff

Case Manager **Carrie Haddon** .... (810) 341-7066
Court Reporter **David Yarbrough** .... (313) 410-7000
E-mail: david_yarbrough@mied.uscourts.gov

Chambers of District Judge Gershwin A. Drain

Theodore Levin U.S. Courthouse, 231 West Lafayette Boulevard, Room 123, Detroit, MI 48226
Tel: (313) 234-5215 Fax: (313) 234-5219
E-mail: gershwin_drain@mied.uscourts.gov

Gershwin A. Drain
District Judge

Education: Western Michigan 1970 BS; Michigan 1972 JD
Began Service: September 29, 2012
Appointed By: President Barack Obama

Staff

Law Clerk **(Vacant)** .... (810) 341-9760
Career Law Clerk **Kelly Dehn** .... (810) 341-9760
Case Manager **Tanya Bankston** .... (313) 234-5213
Court Reporter **Merilyn Jones** .... (313) 244-0909
E-mail: merilyn_jones@mied.uscourts.gov

Chambers of District Judge Terrence G. Berg

Federal Building and U.S. Courthouse, 600 Church Street, Flint, MI 48502
Tel: (810) 341-9760 Fax: (810) 341-9765
E-mail: terrence_berg@mied.uscourts.gov

Terrence G. Berg
District Judge

Note: On Leave.
Education: Georgetown 1981 BS, 1986 JD
Began Service: December 7, 2012
Appointed By: President Barack Obama

Government: High Tech Crime Unit Chief, Office of the Attorney General, State of Michigan (1999-2003); Interim U.S. Attorney, Michigan - Eastern District, Executive Office for United States Attorneys, United States Department of Justice (2008-2009); Acting First Assistant United States Attorney, Georgia - Middle District, Executive Office for United States Attorneys, United States Department of Justice (2010-2011); Attorney, Professional Misconduct Review Unit, Office of the Attorney General, United States Department of Justice (2011-2012)

Chambers of District Judge Judith Ellen Levy

200 East Liberty Street, Suite 300, Ann Arbor, MI 48104
Tel: (734) 887-4700
E-mail: judith_levy@mied.uscourts.gov

Judith Ellen Levy
District Judge

Education: Michigan 1981 BS, 1996 JD
Began Service: March 14, 2014
Appointed By: President Barack Obama

Staff
Case Manager **Felicia Moses** .... (734) 887-4701

Chambers of District Judge Laurie J. Michelson

Theodore Levin U.S. Courthouse, 231 West Lafayette Boulevard, 640, Detroit, MI 48226
Tel: (313) 234-5095
E-mail: laurie_michelson@mied.uscourts.gov

Laurie J. Michelson
District Judge

Education: Michigan 1989 AB; Northwestern 1992 JD
Began Service: March 14, 2014
Appointed By: President Barack Obama

Clerkships: Law Clerk, Chambers of Circuit Judge Cornelia G. Kennedy, United States Court of Appeals for the Sixth Circuit (1992-1993)

Judicial: Magistrate Judge, Chambers of Magistrate Judge Laurie Michelson, United States District Court for the Eastern District of Michigan (2011-2014)

Legal Practice: Practice Group Manager, IP/Media Practice Group, Butzel Long

Staff
Law Clerk **Eric Lee** .... (313) 234-5096
Began Service: 2011
E-mail: eric_lee@mied.uscourts.gov
Education: Michigan 2009 JD
Career Law Clerk **(Vacant)** .... (313) 234-5097
Case Manager **Jane Johnson** .... (313) 234-5095

Chambers of District Judge Matthew Frederick Leitman

Theodore Levin U.S. Courthouse, 231 West Lafayette Boulevard, Room 1013, Detroit, MI 48226
Tel: (313) 234-5125 Fax: (313) 234-5355
E-mail: matthew_leitman@mied.uscourts.gov

Matthew Frederick Leitman
District Judge

Education: Michigan 1990 BA; Harvard 1993 JD
Began Service: March 14, 2014
Appointed By: President Barack Obama

Staff
Case Manager **Holly Monda** .... (313) 234-5125
Judicial Assistant **Alisha Kaszubski** .... (313) 234-5125
E-mail: alisha_kaszubski@mied.uscourts.gov

Chambers of District Judge Linda Vivienne Parker

Theodore Levin U.S. Courthouse, 231 West Lafayette Boulevard, Room 619, Detroit, MI 48226
Tel: (313) 234-5105 Fax: (313) 234-5357
E-mail: linda_parker@mied.uscourts.gov

Linda Vivienne Parker
District Judge

Education: Michigan 1980 BA; George Washington 1983 JD
Began Service: March 17, 2014
Appointed By: President Barack Obama

Government: Staff Attorney, United States Environmental Protection Agency (1985-1989); Executive Assistant U.S. Attorney, Michigan - Eastern District, Executive Office for United States Attorneys, United States Department of Justice (1994-2000); Director, Department of Civil Rights, State of Michigan (2003-2008)

Legal Practice: Attorney, Dickinson Wright PLLC (1989-1994)

Staff
Case Manager **Richard Loury** .... (313) 234-5104
Judicial Assistant **Tracy Young** .... (313) 234-5108

Chambers of Senior Judge Bernard A. Friedman

Theodore Levin U.S. Courthouse, 231 West Lafayette Boulevard, Room 100, Detroit, MI 48226
Tel: (313) 234-5170 Fax: (313) 234-5356
E-mail: bernard_friedman@mied.uscourts.gov

Bernard A. Friedman
Senior Judge

Date of Birth: 1943
Education: Detroit Law 1968 JD
Began Service: June 1, 1988
Appointed By: President Ronald Reagan

Current Memberships: Oakland County Bar Association; State Bar of Michigan

Staff
Law Clerk **Brittany Mouzourakis** .... (313) 234-5151
E-mail: brittany_mouzourakis@mied.uscourts.gov
Career Law Clerk **Stephen B. Thoburn** .... (313) 234-5173
E-mail: stephen_thoburn@mied.uscourts.gov
Education: Kalamazoo 1981 BA; Michigan 1986 JD
Case Manager **Carol Mullins** .... (313) 234-5172
Official Court Reporter **Joan Morgan** .... (313) 234-4809
E-mail: joan_morgan@mied.uscourts.gov
Education: Detroit 1970 BA
Judicial Secretary **Patricia Foster Hommel** .... (313) 234-5171
E-mail: pat_hommel@mied.uscourts.gov

Chambers of Senior Judge John Corbett O'Meara

200 East Liberty Street, Suite 400, Ann Arbor, MI 48104
Tel: (734) 741-2106 Fax: (734) 741-2073
E-mail: john_corbett_omeara@mied.uscourts.gov

John Corbett O'Meara
Senior Judge

Date of Birth: 1933
Education: Harvard 1962 LLB
Began Service: October 4, 1994
Appointed By: President William J. Clinton

Academic: Adjunct Professor, School of Law, University of Detroit (1965-1970)

(continued on next page)

Chambers of Senior Judge John Corbett O='Meara *continued*

Government: Staff Assistant (D-MI), Office of Senator Philip A. Hart, United States Senate (1959-1961)

Legal Practice: Dickinson Wright (1962-1994)

Military Service: United States Navy (1955-1959); United States Naval Reserve (1959-1970)

Staff

Career Law Clerk **Marie Coombs** .... (734) 741-2106
E-mail: marie_coombs@mied.uscourts.gov
Education: Toledo 1990 JD
Career Law Clerk **Michelle Motowski Lund** .... (734) 741-2106
E-mail: michelle_lund@mied.uscourts.gov
Education: Michigan 1996 JD
Case Manager **William Barkholz** .... (734) 741-2106
Court Reporter **Andrea Wabeke** .... (248) 867-2842
E-mail: andrea_wabeke@mied.uscourts.gov
Executive Assistant **Jane E. Freeman** .... (734) 741-2106
E-mail: jane_freeman@mied.uscourts.gov

Chambers of Senior Judge Avern L. Cohn

Theodore Levin U.S. Courthouse, 231 West Lafayette Boulevard, Room 219, Detroit, MI 48226-2792
Tel: (313) 234-5160 Fax: (313) 234-5351
E-mail: Avern_Cohn@mied.uscourts.gov

Avern Levin Cohn

Senior Judge

Date of Birth: July 23, 1924
Education: Michigan 1942; Tarleton Agricultural Col 1943; Stanford 1944; Loyola U (Chicago) 1946; Michigan 1949 JD
Began Service: October 9, 1979
Appointed By: President Jimmy Carter
Political Affiliation: Democrat

Government: Associate, Social Welfare Commission, State of Michigan; Associate, Civil Rights Commission, State of Michigan (1972-1975); Associate, Detroit Board of Police Commissioners, City of Detroit, Michigan (1975-1979)

Legal Practice: Partner, Irwin I. Cohn (1949-1961); Partner, Honigman Miller Schwartz and Cohn LLP (1961-1979)

Military Service: United States Army (1943-1946)

Current Memberships: American Bar Association; The American Law Institute; Detroit Bar Association; Federal Bar Association; Federal Circuit Bar Association; State Bar of Michigan

Staff

Law Clerk **Brittney Kohn** .... (313) 234-5160
Began Service: August 2015
Term Expires: August 2016
Career Law Clerk **Kimberly G. Altman** .... (313) 234-5160
E-mail: Kimberly_Altman@mied.uscourts.gov
Education: Wayne State U 1995 JD
Case Manager **Sakne Chami** .... (313) 234-5160
Court Reporter **Sheri K. Ward** .... (313) 965-4401
E-mail: sward@fedreporter.com
Secretary **Lori A. Van Hove** .... (313) 234-5160
E-mail: Lori_VanHove@mied.uscourts.gov

Chambers of Senior Judge Arthur J. Tarnow

Theodore Levin U.S. Courthouse, 231 West Lafayette Boulevard, Room 124, Detroit, MI 48226
Tel: (313) 234-5180 Fax: (313) 234-5492
E-mail: arthur_tarnow@mied.uscourts.gov

Arthur J. Tarnow

Senior Judge

Date of Birth: 1942
Education: Wayne State U 1963 BA, 1965 JD
Began Service: May 26, 1998
Appointed By: President William J. Clinton

Current Memberships: Michigan State Bar Foundation

Staff

Law Clerk **Tim Martin** .... (313) 234-5180
Began Service: September 2014
Term Expires: September 2016
E-mail: tim_martin@mied.uscourts.gov
Law Clerk **Breta Olsen** .... (313) 234-5180
Began Service: September 2015
Term Expires: September 2017
E-mail: breta_olsen@mied.uscourts.gov
Case Manager **Michael "Mike" Lang** .... (313) 234-5114
Court Reporter **Lawrence Przybysz** .... (313) 414-4460
E-mail: lawrence_przybysz@mied.uscourts.gov
Secretary **Catherine A. Pickles** .... (313) 234-5180
E-mail: catherine_pickles@mied.uscourts.gov

Chambers of Senior Judge Nancy G. Edmunds

Theodore Levin U.S. Courthouse, 231 West Lafayette Boulevard, Room 851, Detroit, MI 48226
Tel: (313) 234-5155
E-mail: nancy_edmunds@mied.uscourts.gov

Nancy G. Edmunds

Senior Judge

Date of Birth: 1947
Education: Cornell 1969 BA; Chicago 1971 MA; Wayne State U 1976 JD
Began Service: February 10, 1992
Appointed By: President George H.W. Bush

Current Memberships: American Bar Association; Federal Bar Association; Federal Judges Association; State Bar of Michigan

Staff

Law Clerk **Alyssa Cantor** .... (313) 234-5155
Began Service: September 2015
Term Expires: September 2016
E-mail: alyssa_cantor@mied.uscourts.gov
Law Clerk **Ruth Tyszka** .... (313) 234-5155
Began Service: January 2, 2015
Term Expires: August 31, 2016
E-mail: ruth_tyszka@mied.uscourts.gov
Career Law Clerk **Adam M. Wenner** .... (313) 234-5155
E-mail: adam_wenner@mied.uscourts.gov
Education: Michigan 2008 BA; Detroit Mercy 2011 JD
Case Manager **Carol Bethel** .... (313) 234-5157
Official Court Reporter **Suzanne Jacques** .... (313) 234-5155
E-mail: suzanne_jacques@mied.uscourts.gov
Judicial Assistant **Karen M. Hillebrand** .... (313) 234-5155
E-mail: karen_hillebrand@mied.uscourts.gov

Chambers of Senior Judge Marianne O. Battani

Theodore Levin U.S. Courthouse, 231 West Lafayette Boulevard,
Detroit, MI 48226
Tel: (313) 234-2625 Fax: (313) 234-2631
E-mail: marianne_battani@mied.uscourts.gov

Marianne O. Battani
Senior Judge

Date of Birth: 1944
Education: Detroit 1966 BA; Detroit Law 1972 JD
Began Service: June 9, 2000
Appointed By: President William J. Clinton

Staff
Law Clerk **Marguerite Bodem** . . . . (313) 234-2632
Career Law Clerk **Molly Jo Roehrig** . . . . (313) 234-2630
E-mail: molly_roehrig@mied.uscourts.gov
Education: Toledo 1990 JD
Case Manager **KaMyra Doaks** . . . . (313) 234-2627
Court Reporter **Robert L. Smith** . . . . (313) 964-3303
E-mail: rob_smith@mied.uscourts.gov
Judicial Secretary **Colette Motowski** . . . . (313) 234-2626
E-mail: colette_motowski@mied.uscourts.gov
Education: Madonna 1990 BS

Chambers of Senior Judge George Caram Steeh

Theodore Levin U.S. Courthouse, 231 West Lafayette Boulevard,
Room 238, Detroit, MI 48226-2788
Tel: (313) 234-5175 Fax: (313) 234-5364
E-mail: george_caram_steeh@mied.uscourts.gov

George Caram Steeh
Senior Judge

Date of Birth: 1947
Education: Michigan 1969 BA, 1972 JD
Began Service: July 2, 1998
Appointed By: President William J. Clinton

Current Memberships: Arab American Bar Association of Michigan; Macomb County Bar Association; State Bar of Michigan

Staff
Career Law Clerk **(Vacant)** . . . . (313) 234-5175
Career Law Clerk **Rosemary Gardey** . . . . (313) 234-5175
E-mail: rosemary_gardey@mied.uscourts.gov
Career Law Clerk **Jill R. Hart** . . . . (313) 234-5175
E-mail: jill_hart@mied.uscourts.gov
Education: Michigan 1988 BGS;
Ohio State 1992 JD
Court Reporter **Ronald DiBartolomeo** . . . . (313) 962-1234
E-mail: ronald_dibartolomeo@mied.uscourts.gov
Case Manager **Marcia Beauchemin** . . . . (313) 234-5175
Secretary **Barbara M. Radke** . . . . (313) 234-5175
E-mail: barbara_radke@mied.uscourts.gov

Chambers of Senior Judge Robert H. Cleland

Theordore Levin U.S. Courthouse, 231 West Lafayette Boulevard,
Detroit, MI 48226
Tel: (313) 234-5525 Fax: (313) 234-5529
E-mail: robert_cleland@mied.uscourts.gov

Robert Hardy Cleland
Senior Judge

Date of Birth: 1947
Education: Michigan State 1969 BA; North Carolina 1972 JD
Began Service: June 19, 1990
Appointed By: President George H.W. Bush

Current Memberships: Federal Bar Association; Federal Judges Association; Prosecuting Attorneys Association of Michigan; State Bar of Michigan

Chambers of Senior Judge Robert H. Cleland *continued*

Staff
Law Clerk **Sean Quinn** . . . . (313) 234-5525
E-mail: sean_quinn@mied.uscourts.gov
Law Clerk **James Heilpern** . . . . (313) 234-5525
Began Service: August 2015
Term Expires: August 2016
E-mail: james_heilpern@mied.uscourts.gov
Career Law Clerk **Christy H. Dral** . . . . (313) 234-5525
E-mail: christy_dral@mied.uscourts.gov
Education: Tennessee 2001 JD
Court Reporter **Christin Russell** . . . . (248) 420-2720
E-mail: christin_russell@mied.uscourts.gov
Case Manager **Lisa Wagner** . . . . (313) 234-5525

Chambers of Magistrate Judge R. Steven Whalen

Theodore Levin U.S. Courthouse, 231 West Lafayette Boulevard,
Room 673, Detroit, MI 48226
Tel: (313) 234-5115 Fax: (313) 234-5117

R. Steven Whalen
Magistrate Judge

Education: Illinois 1970 BA; Wayne State U 1976 JD
Began Service: September 11, 2002
Term Expires: September 10, 2018

Staff
Career Law Clerk **Amy Humphreys** . . . . (313) 234-5115
E-mail: amy_humphreys@mied.uscourts.gov
Education: Detroit 2004 JD
Case Manager **Carolyn Ciesla** . . . . (313) 234-5114
E-mail: carolyn_ciesla@mied.uscourts.gov
Secretary **Terri Hackman** . . . . (313) 234-5115
E-mail: terri_hackman@mied.uscourts.gov

Chambers of Magistrate Judge Mona K. Majzoub

231 West Lafayette Boulevard, Room 642, Detroit, MI 48226
Tel: (313) 234-5205 Fax: (313) 234-5495
E-mail: mona_majzoub@mied.uscourts.gov

Mona K. Majzoub
Magistrate Judge

Date of Birth: June 19, 1949
Education: Michigan 1970 BA, 1972 MA; Detroit 1976 JD
Began Service: January 6, 2004
Term Expires: January 2020

Staff
Career Law Clerk **Lisa Anderson** . . . . (313) 234-5207
E-mail: lisa_anderson@mied.uscourts.gov
Case Manager **Lisa Bartlett** . . . . (313) 234-5206

Chambers of Magistrate Judge Michael Hluchaniuk

Federal Building and U.S. Courthouse, 600 Church Street,
Room 112, Flint, MI 48502
Tel: (810) 341-7850 Fax: (810) 341-7854
E-mail: michael_hluchaniuk@mied.uscourts.gov

Michael Hluchaniuk
Magistrate Judge

Began Service: January 2008
Term Expires: January 2016

Government: Supervisory Assistant U.S. Attorney, Bay City (MI) Office, Executive Office for United States Attorneys, United States Department of Justice

(continued on next page)

Chambers of Magistrate Judge Michael Hluchaniuk *continued*

Staff

Law Clerk **Karen Benjamin** .... (810) 341-7850
Term Expires: August 2016
Law Clerk **Kimberly Horsley** .... (810) 341-7850
Term Expires: August 2016
Case Manager **Tammy Hallwood** .... (810) 341-7887

Chambers of Magistrate Judge David R. Grand

200 East Liberty Street, Suite 100, Ann Arbor, MI 48104
Tel: (734) 741-2485 Fax: (734) 741-2483
E-mail: david_grand@mied.uscourts.gov

David R. Grand
Magistrate Judge

Education: Indiana BS; Michigan JD
Began Service: November 1, 2011

Staff

Law Clerk **Deb Conry** .... (734) 741-2481
Education: Brown U 1994 BA; Pennsylvania 1994 MA; Roger Williams 2008 JD
Case Manager **Eddrey Butts** .... (734) 741-2484

Chambers of Magistrate Judge Patricia T. Morris

1000 Washington Avenue, Room 323, Bay City, MI 48708
Tel: (989) 894-8820

Patricia T. Morris
Magistrate Judge

Staff

Case Manager **Kristen Krawczyk** .... (989) 894-8821

Chambers of Magistrate Judge Anthony P. Patti

231 West Lafayette Boulevard, Detroit, MI 48226
Tel: (313) 234-5200 Fax: (313) 234-5497

Anthony P. Patti
Magistrate Judge

Chambers of Magistrate Judge Elizabeth A. Stafford

231 West Lafayette Boulevard, Room 619, Detroit, MI 48226
Tel: (313) 234-5105 Fax: (313) 234-5109

Elizabeth Stafford
Magistrate Judge

United States Bankruptcy Court for the Eastern District of Michigan

211 West Fort Street, Detroit, MI 48226
Tel: (313) 234-0068 Tel: (313) 234-0065 (General Info)
Tel: (313) 961-4934 (PACER)
Tel: (313) 961-4940 (Voice Case Information System VCIS)
Internet: www.mieb.uscourts.gov

Number of Judgeships: 5

Court Staff

Bankruptcy Clerk **Katherine B. Gullo** .... (313) 234-0065
E-mail: katherine_gullo@mieb.uscourts.gov
Chief Deputy Clerk **Todd M. Stickle** .... (313) 234-0076
E-mail: todd_stickle@mieb.uscourts.gov
Supervisor - Bay City **Nicole Smith** .... (989) 894-8840
111 First Street, Bay City, MI 48708
P.O. Box 911, Bay City, MI 48707

United States Bankruptcy Court for the Eastern District of Michigan *continued*

Supervisor - Flint **Jennifer Clark** .... (810) 235-4126
226 West Second Street, Flint, MI 48502-1203

Chambers of Chief Bankruptcy Judge Phillip J. Shefferly

211 West Fort Street, Suite 1950, Detroit, MI 48226
Tel: (313) 234-0040 Fax: (313) 226-2933
E-mail: phillip_shefferly@mieb.uscourts.gov

Phillip J. Shefferly
Chief Bankruptcy Judge

Education: Wayne State U JD
Began Service: 2008
Term Expires: 2017

Staff

Career Law Clerk **Barbara A. Bailey** .... (313) 234-0042
E-mail: barbara_bailey@mieb.uscourts.gov
Education: Wayne State U 1988 JD
Courtroom Deputy **Cheryl London** .... (313) 234-0043
E-mail: cheryl_london@mieb.uscourts.gov
Chambers Support Clerk **Kathleen Wiacek** .... (313) 234-0044
E-mail: kathleen_wiacek@mieb.uscourts.gov
Judicial Assistant **Janice "Jan" Zielinski** .... (313) 234-0040

Chambers of Bankruptcy Judge Marci B. McIvor

211 West Fort Street, Suite 1850, Detroit, MI 48226
Tel: (313) 234-0010
E-mail: marci_mcivor@mieb.uscourts.gov

Marci B. McIvor
Bankruptcy Judge

Began Service: 2003
Term Expires: March 14, 2017

Staff

Career Law Clerk **Cindy Person** .... (313) 234-0010
E-mail: cindy_person@mieb.uscourts.gov
Career Law Clerk **Emily Sherman** .... (313) 234-0010
E-mail: emily_sherman@mieb.uscourts.gov
Courtroom Deputy **Patti O'Hara** .... (313) 234-0014
Chambers Support Clerk **Leslie Binion** .... (313) 234-0013
E-mail: leslie_binion@mieb.uscourts.gov
Judicial Assistant **Susan P. Maruszewski** .... (313) 234-0010
E-mail: susan_maruszewski@mieb.uscourts.gov

Chambers of Bankruptcy Judge Thomas J. Tucker

211 West Fort Street, Suite 1900, Detroit, MI 48226
Tel: (313) 234-0030
E-mail: thomas_tucker@mieb.uscourts.gov

Thomas J. Tucker
Bankruptcy Judge

Began Service: March 21, 2003

Staff

Career Law Clerk **Lisa Barnett** .... (313) 234-0032
E-mail: lisa_harris@mieb.uscourts.gov
Courtroom Deputy **Mary Vozniak** .... (313) 234-0033
E-mail: mary_vozniak@mieb.uscourts.gov
Chambers Support Clerk **Jamie Laskaska** .... (313) 234-0038
Judicial Assistant **Sherie Sands** .... (313) 234-0030
E-mail: sherie_sands@mieb.uscourts.gov

Chambers of Bankruptcy Judge Daniel S. Opperman

111 First Street, Bay City, MI 48708
226 West Second Street, Flint, MI 48502-1203
Tel: (989) 894-8850
E-mail: daniel_opperman@mieb.uscourts.gov

Daniel S. Opperman
Bankruptcy Judge

Began Service: July 2006
Term Expires: July 2020

Legal Practice: Attorney, Braun Kendrick Finkbeiner P.L.C.

Staff
Courtroom Deputy **Wendy Erickson** .... (989) 894-8844
E-mail: wendy_erickson@mieb.uscourts.gov
Courtroom Deputy **Jill McFarland** .... (810) 235-2039
Judicial Assistant **Suzanne Hert** .... (989) 894-8850
E-mail: suzanne_hert@mieb.uscourts.gov

Chambers of Bankruptcy Judge (recalled) Walter Shapero

Theodore Levin Courthouse, 231 West Lafayette Boulevard, Room 1029, Detroit, MI 48226
Tel: (313) 234-2640 Fax: (313) 234-2614
E-mail: walter_shapero@mieb.uscourts.gov

Walter Shapero
Bankruptcy Judge (recalled)

Date of Birth: 1930
Education: Michigan 1951 AB; Virginia 1954 LLB
Began Service: July 15, 2002

Clerkships: Law Clerk, Michigan Supreme Court (1954-1956)

Current Memberships: American Bar Association; Detroit Bar Association; National Conference of Bankruptcy Judges; State Bar of Michigan

Staff
Law Clerk **Mark Bassily** .... (313) 234-2642
E-mail: mark_bassily@mieb.uscourts.gov
Judicial Assistant **Marsha Heinonen** .... (313) 234-2640
E-mail: marsha_heinonen@mieb.uscourts.gov

Chambers of Bankruptcy Judge Mark A. Randon

211 West Fort Street, Suite 1820, Detroit, MI 48226
Tel: (313) 234-0026

Bankruptcy Judge **Mark A. Randon**

Staff
Law Clerk **Krystal Player** .... (313) 234-0026
Law Clerk **Iveory Perkins** .... (313) 234-0026
Chambers Support Clerk **Letrice Calloway** .... (313) 234-0026
Courtroom Deputy **Leslie Binion** .... (313) 234-0026

United States District Court for the Western District of Michigan

Federal Building, 110 Michigan Street, NW, Room 399, Grand Rapids, MI 49503
Tel: (616) 456-2381 Tel: (616) 732-2765 (PACER)
Tel: (800) 547-6398 (Toll Free PACER) Fax: (616) 456-2066
Internet: www.miwd.uscourts.gov

Number of Judgeships: 5

Circuit: Sixth

Areas Covered: Counties of Alger, Allegan, Antrim, Baraga, Barry, Benzie, Berrien, Branch, Calhoun, Cass, Charlevoix, Chippewa, Clinton, Delta, Dickinson, Eaton, Emmet, Gogebic, Grand Traverse, Hillsdale, Houghton, Ingham, Ionia, Iron, Kalamazoo, Kalkaska, Kent, Keweenaw, Lake, Leelanau, Luce, Mackinac, Manistee, Marquette, Mason, Mecosta, Menominee, Missaukee, Montcalm, Muskegon, Newaygo, Oceana, Ontonagon, Osceola, Ottawa, Schoolcraft, St. Joseph, Van Buren and Wexford

Court Staff

Clerk of the Court (Acting) **Michelle Benham** .... (616) 456-2381
E-mail: michelle_benham@miwd.uscourts.gov
Chief Deputy Clerk **Michelle Benham** .... (616) 456-2381
E-mail: michelle_benham@miwd.uscourts.gov
Resident Deputy-in-Charge - Kalamazoo **(Vacant)** .... (269) 337-5706
Federal Bldg., 410 W. Michigan Ave., Kalamazoo, MI 49007 Fax: (269) 337-5703
Resident Deputy-in-Charge - Lansing **Jodi Gerona** ...... (517) 377-1559
Federal Bldg., 315 W. Allegan, Lansing, MI 48933 Fax: (517) 377-1576
E-mail: jodi_gerona@miwd.uscourts.gov
Resident Deputy-in-Charge - Marquette **Carole Poggi** .... (906) 226-2021
229 Federal Bldg., 202 W. Washington St., Marquette, MI 49855 Fax: (906) 226-6735
E-mail: carole_poggi@miwd.uscourts.gov
Chief Probation Officer **Rebecca Howell** .... (616) 456-2384
Room 137 Fax: (616) 456-2223

Chambers of Chief Judge Robert James Jonker

Federal Building, 110 Michigan Street, NW, Room 640, Grand Rapids, MI 49503
Tel: (616) 456-2551 Fax: (616) 732-2703
E-mail: robert_jonker@miwd.uscourts.gov

Robert James Jonker
Chief Judge

Date of Birth: 1960
Education: Calvin Col 1982 BA; Michigan 1985 JD
Began Service: July 18, 2007
Appointed By: President George W. Bush

Current Memberships: Federal Bar Association; Grand Rapids Bar Association; State Bar of Michigan

Staff
Law Clerk **Jacob Byl** .... (616) 456-2551
Began Service: September 2015
Term Expires: September 2016
E-mail: jacob_byl@miwd.uscourts.gov
Career Law Clerk **Margaret Khayat Bratt** .... (616) 456-2551
E-mail: margaret_bratt@miwd.uscourts.gov
Case Manager **Melva Ludge** .... (616) 456-2551
Judicial Assistant **Yvonne Carpenter** .... (616) 456-2551
E-mail: yvonne_carpenter@miwd.uscourts.gov

FEDERAL COURTS—UNITED STATES DISTRICT COURTS

Chambers of District Judge Paul Lewis Maloney

137 Federal Building, 410 West Michigan Avenue, Kalamazoo, MI 49007
Tel: (269) 381-4741 Fax: (269) 337-4736
E-mail: paul_maloney@miwd.uscourts.gov

Paul Lewis Maloney
District Judge

Date of Birth: 1949
Education: Lehigh 1972 BA; Detroit 1975 JD
Began Service: July 18, 2007
Appointed By: President George W. Bush

Staff

Law Clerk **Andrew Klopton** .... (269) 381-4741
Began Service: September 2015
Term Expires: September 2017
E-mail: andrew_klopton@miwd.uscourts.gov

Career Law Clerk **Rod Phares** .... (269) 381-4741
E-mail: rod_phares@miwd.uscourts.gov

Judicial Assistant **Christina Cavazos** .... (269) 381-4741
E-mail: christina_cavazos@miwd.uscourts.gov

Chambers of District Judge Robert Holmes Bell

Federal Building, 110 Michigan Street, NW, Room 602,
Grand Rapids, MI 49503
Tel: (616) 456-2021

Robert Holmes Bell
District Judge

Date of Birth: 1944
Education: Wheaton (IL) 1966 BA; Wayne State U 1969 JD
Began Service: August 6, 1987
Appointed By: President Ronald Reagan

Academic: Adjunct Professor, Thomas M. Cooley Law School

Government: Assistant Prosecuting Attorney, State of Michigan (1969-1973)

Judicial: Judge, Michigan District Court, 55th Judicial Court (1973-1979); Judge, Michigan Circuit Court, 30th Judicial Circuit (1979-1987)

Legal Practice: Private Practice (1970-1972)

Current Memberships: Christian Legal Society; District Judges Association of the Sixth Circuit; Western District of Michigan, Federal Bar Association; The Federalist Society for Law and Public Policy Studies; State Bar of Michigan

Staff

Law Clerk **Kyle Asher** .... (616) 456-2021
Began Service: September 2015
Term Expires: September 2016
E-mail: kyle_asher@miwd.uscourts.gov

Career Law Clerk **Todd Broberg** .... (616) 456-2021
Note: Effective December 10, 2015.

Career Law Clerk **Julie VanWyk Clough** .... (616) 456-2021
Note: Until December 10, 2015.
E-mail: julie_clough@miwd.uscourts.gov
Education: Hope 1977 BS; Western New England 1981 JD

Case Manager **Susan Bourque** .... (616) 456-2021
Education: Central Michigan 1981 BS

Court Reporter **Kevin Gaugier** .... (616) 456-6133
E-mail: kevin_gaugier@miwd.uscourts.gov

Judicial Assistant **Kimberly C. Briggs** .... (616) 456-2021
E-mail: Kim@miwd.uscourts.gov

Chambers of District Judge Janet T. Neff

Federal Building, 110 Michigan Street, NW, Room 401,
Grand Rapids, MI 49503
Tel: (616) 456-6774 Fax: (616) 456-6947
E-mail: janet_neff@miwd.uscourts.gov

Janet T. Neff
District Judge

Date of Birth: 1945
Education: Wayne State U 1970 JD
Began Service: August 2007
Appointed By: President George W. Bush

Clerkships: Law Clerk, Michigan Court of Appeals (1970-1971)

Government: Assistant City Attorney, Office of the City Attorney, City of Grand Rapids, Michigan (1971-1973); Commissioner, Michigan Supreme Court (1978-1980); Assistant United States Attorney, Western District of Michigan, United States Department of Justice (1980)

Legal Practice: VanderVeen, Freihofer & Cook (1973-1978); William G. Reamon, PC (1980-1988)

Current Memberships: Grand Rapids Bar Association; State Bar of Michigan

Staff

Career Law Clerk **Rita Buitendorp** .... (616) 456-6774
E-mail: rita_buitendorp@miwd.uscourts.gov
Education: Calvin Col 1993 AB; Valparaiso 1996 JD

Career Law Clerk **Kathleen Geiger** .... (616) 456-6774
E-mail: kathleen_geiger@miwd.uscourts.gov
Education: Thomas M Cooley 1998 JD

Case Manager **Rick Wolters** .... (616) 456-6774

Court Reporter **Kathy Anderson** .... (616) 456-6774
E-mail: kathy_anderson@miwd.uscourts.gov

Judicial Assistant **Christine Bockheim** .... (616) 456-6774
E-mail: chris_bockheim@miwd.uscourts.gov

Chambers of Senior Judge R. Allan Edgar

P.O. Box 698, Marquette, MI 49855
Tel: (906) 226-2084 Fax: (906) 226-6735

R. Allan Edgar
Senior Judge

Date of Birth: 1940
Education: Davidson 1962 BA; Duke 1965 LLB
Began Service: May 16, 1985
Appointed By: President Ronald Reagan

Current Memberships: Chattanooga Bar Association; Federal Bar Association

Staff

Law Clerk **A.J. Peterman** .... (906) 226-2084

Chambers of Senior Judge Gordon J. Quist

110 Michigan Street, NW, Room 482, Grand Rapids, MI 49503
Tel: (616) 456-2253 Fax: (616) 456-2243
E-mail: gordon_j_quist@miwd.uscourts.gov

Gordon J. Quist
Senior Judge

Date of Birth: 1937
Education: Michigan State 1959 BA; George Washington 1962 JD
Began Service: August 28, 1992
Appointed By: President George H.W. Bush

Current Memberships: Michigan State Bar Foundation

Chambers of Senior Judge Gordon J. Quist *continued*

Staff

Law Clerk **Elizabeth "Liz" Geary** . . . . (616) 456-2253
Began Service: September 2013
Term Expires: September 2016
E-mail: elizabeth_geary@miwd.uscourts.gov

Career Law Clerk **Philip G. Henderson** . . . . (616) 456-2253
E-mail: philip_henderson@miwd.uscourts.gov
Education: Toledo 1988 JD

Judicial Assistant **Jane M. Tepper** . . . . (616) 456-2253
E-mail: jane_tepper@miwd.uscourts.gov

Chambers of Magistrate Judge Timothy P. Greeley

330 Federal Building, 202 West Washington Street, Marquette, MI 49855
P.O. Box 698, Marquette, MI 49855
Tel: (906) 226-3854 Fax: (906) 226-6231
E-mail: timothy_greeley@miwd.uscourts.gov

Timothy P. Greeley
Magistrate Judge

Education: Western Michigan 1976 BA; Wayne State U 1980 JD
Began Service: January 11, 1988
Term Expires: December 2021

Staff

Career Law Clerk **Rodney B. Kurzawa** . . . . (906) 226-3854
E-mail: rodney_kurzawa@miwd.uscourts.gov
Education: Wayne State U 1989 JD

Pro Se Law Clerk **Catherine Halverson** . . . . (906) 226-3854
E-mail: catherine_halverson@miwd.uscourts.gov

Judicial Assistant **Pamela Chant** . . . . (906) 226-3854

Chambers of Magistrate Judge Ellen S. Carmody

Federal Building, 110 Michigan Street, NW, Room 664,
Grand Rapids, MI 49503
Tel: (616) 456-2528 Fax: (616) 456-2072
E-mail: ellen_carmody@miwd.uscourts.gov

Ellen S. Carmody
Magistrate Judge

Date of Birth: 1952
Education: Michigan 1983 JD
Began Service: October 11, 2000
Term Expires: October 11, 2016

Academic: Adjunct Professor, Michigan State University College of Law

Clerkships: Law Clerk The Honorable Douglas W. Hillman, United States District Court for the Western District of Michigan (1983-1985)

Legal Practice: Law, Weathers & Richardson (1985-2000)

Current Memberships: Federal Bar Association; Federal Magistrate Judges Association; State Bar of Michigan

Staff

Career Law Clerk **Russell Ambrose** . . . . (616) 456-2528
E-mail: russ_ambrose@miwd.uscourts.gov
Education: Nebraska (Omaha) 1991 BS;
Illinois 1998 JD

Courtroom Deputy **Julie Lenon** . . . . (616) 456-2528
E-mail: julie_lenon@miwd.uscourts.gov

Judicial Assistant **Cynthia Hosner** . . . . (616) 456-2528
E-mail: cynthia_hosner@miwd.uscourts.gov

Chambers of Magistrate Judge Phillip J. Green

110 Michigan Street, NW, Room 712, Grand Rapids, MI 49503
Tel: (616) 456-2309

Phillip J. Green
Magistrate Judge

Education: St Meinrad Col 1982 BA; Saint Louis U 1990 JD

Staff

Law Clerk **Christopher Williams** . . . . (616) 456-2309
Courtroom Deputy **Diane Hand** . . . . (616) 456-2309
Judicial Assistant **Jessica Wright** . . . . (616) 456-2309

Chambers of Magistrate Judge Ray Kent

110 Michigan Street, NW, Grand Rapids, MI 49503
Tel: (616) 456-2381

Ray Kent
Magistrate Judge

United States Bankruptcy Court for the Western District of Michigan

One Division Avenue, North, Room 200, Grand Rapids, MI 49503
Tel: (616) 456-2693 Tel: (800) 676-6856 (Toll Free PACER)
Tel: (866) 222-8029 (Toll Free Voice Case Information System VCIS)
Fax: (616) 456-2919
E-mail: clerk_miwb@miwb.uscourts.gov
Internet: www.miwb.uscourts.gov

Number of Judgeships: 3

Court Staff

Clerk of Court **Daniel M. LaVille** . . . . (616) 456-2693
E-mail: dan_laville@miwb.uscourts.gov
Education: Ohio State 1973 BS;
Notre Dame 1978 JD

Secretary to Clerk **Deborah Morse** . . . . (616) 456-2693
E-mail: debe_morse@miwb.uscourts.gov

Chief Deputy Clerk **Michael Ley** . . . . (616) 456-2540
E-mail: mike_ley@miwb.uscourts.gov
Education: Wisconsin (Stevens Point) 1981 BS;
Denver 1982 MS

Procurement Specialist **Jeff TerAvest** . . . . (616) 456-2582
E-mail: jeff_teravest@miwb.uscourts.gov

Chambers of Chief Bankruptcy Judge Scott W. Dales

One Division Avenue, North, Room 210, Grand Rapids, MI 49503
Tel: (616) 456-2949 Fax: (616) 456-2928
E-mail: scott_dales@miwb.uscourts.gov

Scott W. Dales
Chief Bankruptcy Judge

Began Service: October 5, 2007
Term Expires: 2021

Staff

Career Law Clerk **Jahel Nolan** . . . . (616) 456-2959
Education: Detroit Law 1989 JD

Judicial Assistant **Katrina Shellman** . . . . (616) 456-2949
E-mail: katrina_shellman@miwb.uscourts.gov

United States District Court for the District of Minnesota

U.S. Courthouse, 300 South Fourth Street, Room 202,
Minneapolis, MN 55415
Tel: (612) 664-5000 Tel: (612) 664-5170 (PACER)
Tel: (800) 818-8761 (Toll Free)
Internet: www.mnd.uscourts.gov

Number of Judgeships: 7

Number of Vacancies: 1

Circuit: Eighth

Court Staff

Clerk of Court **Richard D. Sletten** .... (612) 664-5000
Chief Deputy Clerk - Minneapolis **Tricia Pepin** .... (612) 664-5129
E-mail: tricia_pepin@mnd.uscourts.gov Fax: (612) 664-5034
Deputy-in-Charge - Duluth **Michael Vicklund** .... (218) 529-3500
U.S. Courthouse, 515 W. First St.,
Duluth, MN 55802
Facilities Manager **Kristina Thomas** .... (612) 664-5000
E-mail: kristina_thomas@mnd.uscourts.gov
Financial Manager **Katie Uline** .... (612) 664-5016
E-mail: kathryn_uline@mnd.uscourts.gov
Human Resources Manager
Marina Contreras Mentzos .... (612) 664-5000
E-mail: marina_contreras_
mentzos@mnp.uscourts.gov
Information Services Manager **Andy Seldon** .... (612) 664-5000
E-mail: andy_seldon@mnd.uscourts.gov
Operations Manager - Minneapolis **Lou Jean Gleason** ... (612) 664-5009
Fax: (612) 664-5033
Operations Manager - St. Paul **Michael Vicklund** .... (651) 848-1106
E-mail: michael_vicklund@mnd.uscourts.gov Fax: (651) 848-1109
Chief Probation and Pretrial Officer **Kevin Lowry** .... (612) 664-5400
Librarian **Andrea Wambach** .... (651) 848-1320
E-mail: andrea_wambach@ca8.uscourts.gov Fax: (651) 848-1325
Library Technician - Minneapolis and St. Paul
(Vacant) .... (651) 848-1320
Fax: (651) 848-1325
Telecommunications Specialist **Andy Seldon** .... (612) 664-5022

Chambers of Chief Judge John R. Tunheim

U.S. Courthouse, 300 South Fourth Street, Suite 15E,
Minneapolis, MN 55415
Tel: (612) 664-5080 Fax: (612) 664-5087
E-mail: tunheim_chambers@mnd.uscourts.gov

John R. Tunheim
Chief Judge

Date of Birth: 1953
Education: Concordia Col Moorhead MN 1975 BA; Minnesota 1980 JD
Began Service: December 29, 1995
Appointed By: President William J. Clinton

Current Memberships: American Bar Association; The Douglas K. Amdahl American Inn of Court, The American Inns of Court; Federal Bar Association; Federal Judges Association; Judicial Conference of the United States; Minnesota State Bar Association; District 19, Minnesota State Bar Association

Staff

Law Clerk **Matthew Forbes** .... (612) 664-5082
Began Service: August 2015
Term Expires: August 31, 2016
Law Clerk **Adrienne Locke Kaufman** .... (612) 664-5082
Began Service: August 2015
Term Expires: August 31, 2017
E-mail: adrienne_kaufman@mnd.uscourts.gov
Calendar Clerk **Heather Arent-Zachary** .... (612) 664-5083
E-mail: heather_arent-zachary@mnd.uscourts.gov

Chambers of Chief Judge John R. Tunheim *continued*

Court Reporter **Kristine Mousseau** .... (612) 664-5106
E-mail: kristine_mousseau@mnd.uscourts.gov
Judicial Assistant **Debbie Lancette** .... (612) 664-5080
E-mail: Debbie_Lancette@mnd.uscourts.gov

Chambers of District Judge Ann D. Montgomery

U.S. Courthouse, 300 South Fourth Street, Room 13 West,
Minneapolis, MN 55415-1320
Tel: (612) 664-5090 Fax: (612) 664-5097
E-mail: ADMontgomery@mnd.uscourts.gov

Ann D. Montgomery
District Judge

Date of Birth: 1949
Education: Kansas 1971 BS; Minnesota 1974 JD
Began Service: August 6, 1996
Appointed By: President William J. Clinton

Academic: Adjunct Professor, Law School, University of Minnesota (1988-1994)

Clerkships: Law Clerk The Honorable Gerard D. Reilly, District of Columbia Court of Appeals (1974-1976)

Government: Assistant United States Attorney, District of Minnesota, Office of the United States Attorney, United States Department of Justice (1976-1983)

Judicial: Judge, Hennepin County District Court (1983-1985); Judge, Hennepin County District Court (1985-1994); Magistrate Judge, United States District Court for the District of Minnesota (1994-1996)

Current Memberships: Eighth Circuit District Judges Association; Federal Bar Association; Hennepin County Bar Association; Minnesota Judges Association; Minnesota State Bar Association; Minnesota Women Lawyers; National Association of Women Judges

Staff

Law Clerk **Jay Eidsness** .... (612) 664-5091
Began Service: September 2014
Term Expires: September 2016
E-mail: jay_eidsness@mnd.uscourts.gov
Law Clerk **Katie Kimlinger** .... (612) 664-5095
Began Service: February 2009 Tel: (612) 664-5095
E-mail: katie_kimlinger@mnd.uscourts.gov
Education: Saint Martin's U 1987 BA;
Minnesota 1994 JD
Law Clerk **Anna Tobin** .... (612) 664-5092
Began Service: April 2015
Term Expires: September 2016
Calendar Clerk **Jackie Ellingson** .... (612) 664-5093
E-mail: jackie_ellingson@mnd.uscourts.gov
Court Reporter **Timothy Willette** .... (612) 664-5108
E-mail: tim_willette@mnd.uscourts.gov
Chambers Administrator **Tamara Uber** .... (612) 664-5090
E-mail: Tamara_Uber@mnd.uscourts.gov

Chambers of District Judge Donovan W. Frank

Warren E. Burger Federal Building and U.S. Courthouse, 316 North Robert Street, Suite 724, St. Paul, MN 55101
Tel: (651) 848-1290 Fax: (651) 848-1292
E-mail: frank_chambers@mnd.uscourts.gov

Donovan W. Frank
District Judge

Date of Birth: 1951
Education: Luther Col 1973 BA; Hamline 1977 JD
Began Service: November 2, 1998
Appointed By: President William J. Clinton

Government: Assistant County Attorney, County of St. Louis, Minnesota (1977-1985)

Judicial: Judge, Minnesota District Court, Sixth Judicial District (1985-1998); Assistant Chief Judge, Minnesota District Court, Sixth Judicial District (1989-1991); Chief Judge, Minnesota District Court, Sixth Judicial District (1991-1996)

Current Memberships: The Richard T. Oakes American Inn of Court, The American Inns of Court; Board of Directors, Minnesota Chapter, Federal Bar Association; Federal Judges Association; Lawyers Concerned for Lawyers; Minnesota State Bar Association; Range County Bar Association

Staff

Law Clerk **Katherine "Kate" Bruce** .... (651) 848-1293
Began Service: September 2013
Term Expires: September 1, 2016
E-mail: kate_bruce@mnd.uscourts.gov

Law Clerk **Julia Zwak** .... (651) 848-1295
Began Service: August 2015
Term Expires: August 1, 2017
E-mail: julia_zwak@mnd.uscourts.gov

Career Law Clerk **Lisa Converse** .... (651) 848-1294
E-mail: Lisa_Converse@mnd.uscourts.gov
Education: Northwestern 1994 BA; Hastings 1998 JD

Calendar Clerk **Brenda Schaffer** .... (651) 848-1296
E-mail: brenda_schaffer@mnd.uscourts.gov

Court Reporter **Jeanne Anderson** .... (651) 848-1221
E-mail: jeanne_anderson@mnd.uscourts.gov

Judicial Assistant **Rebecca L. Baertsch** .... (651) 848-1290
E-mail: Rebecca_Baertsch@mnd.uscourts.gov

Chambers of District Judge Joan N. Ericksen

300 South Fourth Street, Suite 12 West, Minneapolis, MN 55415
Tel: (612) 664-5890 Fax: (612) 664-5897
E-mail: joanericksen_chambers@mnd.uscourts.gov

Joan N. Ericksen
District Judge

Date of Birth: 1954
Education: St Olaf 1977 BA; Minnesota 1981 JD
Began Service: June 14, 2002
Appointed By: President George W. Bush

Government: Assistant United States Attorney, District of Minnesota, Office of the United States Attorney, United States Department of Justice (1983-1993)

Judicial: Judge, Fourth Judicial District Court, Hennepin County, MN (1995-1998); Associate Justice, Minnesota Supreme Court (1998-2002)

Legal Practice: Associate, Lefevere, Lefler, Kennedy, O'Brien & Drawz (1981-1983); Partner, Leonard, Street and Deinard (1993-1995)

Staff

Law Clerk **Jason Marisam** .... (612) 664-5890
Began Service: August 2014
E-mail: jason_marisam@mnd.uscourts.gov

Law Clerk **Holley C. Horrell** .... (612) 664-5890
Began Service: September 2015
E-mail: holley_horrell@mnd.uscourts.gov

Chambers of District Judge Joan N. Ericksen *continued*

Career Law Clerk **Mark Hamre** .... (612) 664-5890
E-mail: mark_hamre@mnd.uscourts.gov
Education: Middlebury 1995 BA; Minnesota 2001 JD

Court Reporter **Maria Weinbeck** .... (612) 664-5109
E-mail: maria_weinbeck@mnd.uscourts.gov

Judicial Assistant **Catherine Cusack** .... (612) 664-5890
E-mail: cathy_cusack@mnd.uscourts.gov

Chambers of District Judge Patrick Joseph Schiltz

U.S. Courthouse, 300 South Fourth Street, Suite 14 East, Minneapolis, MN 55415
Tel: (612) 664-5480 Fax: (612) 664-5487

Patrick Joseph Schiltz
District Judge

Began Service: September 22, 2006
Appointed By: President George W. Bush

Staff

Law Clerk **Steven Donohue** .... (612) 664-5260
E-mail: steven_donohue@mnd.uscourts.gov

Career Law Clerk **Elizabeth Welter** .... (651) 848-1900
E-mail: elizabeth_welter@mnd.uscourts.gov

Courtroom Deputy **Caryn Glover** .... (651) 848-1900
E-mail: caryn_glover@mnd.uscourts.gov

Court Reporter **Debra Beauvais** .... (651) 848-1900
E-mail: debra_beauvais@mnd.uscourts.gov

Judicial Assistant **Barbara Sauer** .... (651) 848-1900
E-mail: barbara_sauer@mnd.uscourts.gov

Chambers of District Judge Susan Richard Nelson

774 Federal Building, 316 North Robert Street, St. Paul, MN 55106
Tel: (651) 848-1970
E-mail: nelson_chambers@mnd.uscourts.gov

Susan Richard Nelson
District Judge

Education: Oberlin 1971 BA; Pittsburgh 1978 JD
Began Service: December 22, 2010
Appointed By: President Barack Obama

Judicial: Magistrate Judge, Chambers of Magistrate Judge Susan R. Nelson, United States District Court for the District of Minnesota (2000-2010)

Legal Practice: Associate, Tyler Cooper & Alcorn, LLP (1980-1983); Attorney, Robins, Kaplan, Miller & Ciresi L.L.P. (1984-2000); Partner, Robins, Kaplan, Miller & Ciresi L.L.P. (1988-2000)

Staff

Law Clerk **Lindsey Blanchard** .... (651) 848-1970

Law Clerk **Alexander Chiquoine** .... (651) 848-1970

Career Law Clerk **Marilyn Conklin** .... (651) 848-1970
E-mail: marilyn_conklin@mnd.uscourts.gov
Education: Minnesota 1995 JD

Court Reporter **Heather Schuetz** .... (651) 848-1970
E-mail: heather_schuetz@mnd.uscourts.gov

Courtroom Deputy **Susan Del Monte** .... (651) 848-1970

Chambers of Senior Judge Donald D. Alsop

754 Federal Building, 316 North Robert Street, St. Paul, MN 55101
Tel: (651) 848-1170 Fax: (651) 848-1172
E-mail: ddalsop@mnd.uscourts.gov

Donald D. Alsop
Senior Judge

Date of Birth: 1927
Education: Minnesota 1950 BSL, 1952 LLB
Began Service: December 20, 1974
Appointed By: President Richard M. Nixon

Legal Practice: Associate, Felhaber & Larson (1952-1954); Partner, Gislason, Alsop, Dosland & Hunter (1954-1975)

Military Service: United States Army (1945-1946)

Current Memberships: Eighth Circuit District Judges Association; Federal Bar Association

Staff

Judicial Assistant **Lynn Magee** .... (651) 848-1170
E-mail: lynn_magee@mnd.uscourts.gov

Chambers of Senior Judge Paul A. Magnuson

734 Federal Building, 316 North Robert Street, St. Paul, MN 55101
Tel: (651) 848-1150 Fax: (651) 848-1152
E-mail: PAMagnuson@mnd.uscourts.gov

Paul A. Magnuson
Senior Judge

Date of Birth: 1937
Education: Gustavus Adolphus 1959 BA; William Mitchell 1963 JD, 1991 LLD
Began Service: 1981
Appointed By: President Ronald Reagan

Academic: Instructor, William Mitchell College of Law (1984-1992); Jurist in Residence, Hamline University (1985); Jurist in Residence, Augsburg College (1986); Jurist in Residence, Bethel College (1986); Jurist in Residence, Concordia College - St. Paul (1987); Jurist in Residence, University of Minnesota - Morris (1987); Jurist in Residence, St. Johns University (1988); Jurist in Residence, College of St. Benedict (1988)

Legal Practice: Attorney, LeVander, Gillen, Miller & Magnuson

Current Memberships: American Association of Justice; American Bar Association; Dakota County Bar Association; Federal Bar Association; Federal Circuit Bar Association; Federal Judges Association; International Judicial Academy; Minnesota State Bar Association; Tenth Judicial District Bar Association; Washington County Bar Association

Staff

Law Clerk **Marjan Batchelor** .... (651) 848-1150
Began Service: September 2015
Term Expires: August 31, 2016

Career Law Clerk **Anita Terry** .... (651) 848-1150
Began Service: 2007
E-mail: anita_terry@mnd.uscourts.gov
Education: Duke 1995 JD; Colby 1989 BA

Calendar Clerk **Jackie Phipps** .... (651) 848-1156

Judicial Assistant **Lynn Magee** .... (651) 848-1150
E-mail: lynn_magee@mnd.uscourts.gov

Chambers of Senior Judge David S. Doty

U.S. Courthouse, 300 South Fourth Street, Minneapolis, MN 55415
Tel: (612) 664-5060 Fax: (612) 664-5067

David S. Doty
Senior Judge

Date of Birth: 1929
Education: Minnesota 1952 BA, 1961 JD
Began Service: May 1987
Appointed By: President Ronald Reagan

Academic: Instructor, William Mitchell College of Law (1965-1966)

Legal Practice: Associate, Felhaber, Larson, Fenlon & Vogt, P.A. (1961-1962); Partner, Popham, Haik, Schnobrich, Kaufman and Doty Ltd. (1962-1987)

Military Service: United States Marine Corps (1952-1958)

Current Memberships: American Bar Foundation; American Bar Association; The American Law Institute; Federal Bar Association; Hennepin County Bar Association; Minnesota State Bar Association

Staff

Law Clerk **Samuel Bolstad** .... (612) 664-5061
Began Service: August 2015
Term Expires: August 2016
E-mail: sam_bolstad@mnd.uscourts.gov

Law Clerk **Jesseca Cockson** .... (612) 664-5062
Began Service: August 2014
Education: Michigan State 1992 BA; Hamline 1999 JD

Judicial Assistant **Donna O'Kroy** .... (612) 664-5060
E-mail: donna_o'kroy@mnd.uscourts.gov

Court Reporter **Staci Heichert** .... (612) 664-5105
E-mail: staci_heichert@mnd.uscourts.gov

Chambers of Senior Judge Richard H. Kyle

772 Federal Building, 316 North Robert Street, St. Paul, MN 55101
Tel: (651) 848-1160 Fax: (651) 848-1162
E-mail: RHKyle@mnd.uscourts.gov

Richard H. Kyle
Senior Judge

Date of Birth: 1937
Education: Minnesota 1959 BA, 1962 LLB
Began Service: May 15, 1992
Appointed By: President George H.W. Bush

Clerkships: Law Clerk The Honorable Edward J. Devitt (1962-1963)

Government: Solicitor General, State of Minnesota (1968-1970)

Legal Practice: Briggs and Morgan (1963-1968); Briggs and Morgan (1970-1992)

Current Memberships: Minnesota State Bar Association; Ramsey County Bar Association

Staff

Law Clerk **Brittany Resch** .... (651) 848-1160
Began Service: August 2015
Term Expires: August 31, 2016
E-mail: brittany_resch@mnd.uscourts.gov

Career Law Clerk **Marc Betinsky** .... (651) 848-1160
E-mail: marc_betinsky@mnd.uscourts.gov
Education: Cornell 1998 JD

Court Reporter **Carla Bebault** .... (651) 848-1220
E-mail: carla_bebault@mnd.uscourts.gov

Judicial Secretary **Karen Labriola** .... (651) 848-1161
E-mail: karen_labriola@mnd.uscourts.gov

Chambers of Senior Judge Michael J. Davis

U.S. Courthouse, 300 South Fourth Street, Room 15 East, Minneapolis, MN 55415
Tel: (612) 664-5070 Fax: (612) 664-5077
E-mail: MJDavis@mnd.uscourts.gov

Michael J. Davis
Senior Judge

Date of Birth: 1947
Education: Macalester 1969 BA; Minnesota 1972 JD
Began Service: March 30, 1994
Appointed By: President William J. Clinton

Current Memberships: American Bar Association; Federal Bar Association; Federal Judges Association; International Academy of Trial Judges; Minnesota Association of Black Lawyers; Minnesota Lawyers International Human Rights Committee; National Bar Association

Staff
Career Law Clerk **Katie Dunn** ....(612) 664-5071
E-mail: katie_dunn@mnd.uscourts.gov
Career Law Clerk **Clare Priest** ....(612) 664-5074
E-mail: clare_priest@mnd.uscourts.gov
Court Reporter **Lori Simpson** ....(612) 664-5104
E-mail: lori_simpson@mnd.uscourts.gov
Courtroom Deputy **Kristine Wegner** ....(612) 664-5073
E-mail: kristine_wegner@mnd.uscourts.gov
Judicial Assistant **Gerri Rishel** ....(612) 664-5070
E-mail: gerri_rishel@mnd.uscourts.gov

Chambers of Magistrate Judge Franklin L. Noel

U.S. Courthouse, 300 South Fourth Street, Room 9 West, Minneapolis, MN 55415
Tel: (612) 664-5110 Fax: (612) 664-5117

Franklin L. Noel
Magistrate Judge

Date of Birth: 1951
Education: SUNY (Binghamton) 1974 BA; Georgetown 1977 JD
Began Service: November 3, 1989
Term Expires: November 2021
Political Affiliation: Democrat

Government: Assistant District Attorney, Office of the District Attorney, Commonwealth of Pennsylvania (1979-1983); Assistant United States Attorney, District of Minnesota, United States Department of Justice (1983-1989)

Legal Practice: Associate, Arnold & Porter LLP (1977-1979)

Current Memberships: Hennepin County Bar Association; Minnesota State Bar Association

Staff
Law Clerk **Cari Heiklen** ....(612) 664-5112
Term Expires: September 2017
E-mail: cari_heiklen@mnd.uscourts.gov
Law Clerk **Brandon Boese** ....(612) 664-5111
Began Service: September 2014
Term Expires: September 2016
E-mail: brandon_boese@mnd.uscourts.gov
Secretary **Theresa Anderson** ....(612) 664-5110
E-mail: theresa_anderson@mnd.uscourts.gov

Chambers of Magistrate Judge Janie S. Mayeron

632 Federal Building, 316 North Robert Street, St. Paul, MN 55101
Tel: (651) 848-1190 Tel: (651) 848-1192
E-mail: mayeron_chambers@mnd.uscourts.gov

Janie S. Mayeron
Magistrate Judge

Education: Minnesota 1976 JD
Began Service: February 7, 2003

Staff
Law Clerk **Christopher Hanson** ....(651) 848-1190
Law Clerk **Mary Schwind** ....(651) 848-1190
E-mail: mary_schwind@mnd.uscourts.gov
Career Law Clerk **Steven Katras**.....................(651) 848-1190
Judicial Assistant **Katie Haagenson** ....(651) 848-1190
E-mail: katie_haagenson@mnd.uscourts.gov

Chambers of Magistrate Judge Jeffrey J. Keyes

646 Warren E. Burger Federal Courthouse, 316 North Robert Street, Saint Paul, MN 55101
Tel: (651) 848-1180 Fax: (651) 848-1182
E-mail: keyes_chambers@mnd.uscourts.gov

Jeffrey J. Keyes
Magistrate Judge

Education: Notre Dame 1968 BA; Michigan 1972 JD
Began Service: April 28, 2008

Staff
Law Clerk **Brian Pousson** ....(651) 848-1100
Career Law Clerk **Danielle Mair** ....(651) 848-1100
E-mail: danielle_mair@mnd.uscourts.gov
Judicial Assistant **Jackie Phipps** ....(651) 848-1180
E-mail: jackie_phipps@mnd.uscourts.gov

Chambers of Magistrate Judge Leo I. Brisbois

515 West First Street, Room 412, Duluth, MN 55802-1397
Tel: (218) 529-3520

Leo I. Brisbois
Magistrate Judge

Education: Hamline JD
Began Service: 2010

Staff
Law Clerk **Jon C. Kulas** ....(218) 529-3520
Education: Willamette 2009 JD; DePaul 2010 ML
Law Clerk **Emily Tremblay** ....(218) 529-3520
Judicial Assistant **Victoria L. Miller**...................(218) 529-3520

Chambers of Magistrate Judge Steven E. Rau

Warren E. Burger Federal Courthouse, 316 North Robert Street, Room 334, St. Paul, MN 55101
Tel: (651) 848-1620 Tel: (651) 848-1622
E-mail: rau_chambers@mnd.uscourts.gov

Steven E. Rau
Magistrate Judge

Education: Carleton; William Mitchell JD
Began Service: 2011

Staff
Law Clerk **Ellen Ahrens**............................(651) 848-1620
E-mail: ellen_ahrens@mnd.uscourts.gov
Law Clerk **Leah Graff**.............................(651) 848-1620
E-mail: leah_graff@mnd.uscourts.gov
Judicial Assistant **Melissa Erstad** ....(651) 848-1620
E-mail: melissa_erstad@mnd.uscourts.gov

Chambers of Magistrate Judge Tony N. Leung

342 Warren E. Burger Federal Courthouse, 316 North Robert Street, St. Paul, MN 55101
Tel: (651) 848-1870 Fax: (651) 848-1872
E-mail: leung_chambers@mnd.uscourts.gov

Tony N. Leung
Magistrate Judge

Education: Yale 1982 BA; NYU 1985 JD
Began Service: April 29, 2011
Term Expires: April 29, 2019

Staff
Law Clerk **Emily Bucher** .... (651) 848-1870
E-mail: emily_bucher@mnd.uscourts.gov
Education: William Mitchell 2009 JD
Law Clerk **(Vacant)** .... (651) 848-1870
Judicial Assistant **Kathleen Feldman** .... (651) 848-1870

Chambers of Magistrate Judge Hildy Bowbeer

316 North Robert Street, Room 632, St. Paul, MN 55101
Tel: (651) 848-1900 Fax: (651) 848-1907

Hildy Bowbeer
Magistrate Judge

Education: Michigan 1979 JD

Staff
Career Law Clerk **Adrienne Meyers** .... (651) 848-1900
Education: Texas 1994 BA; Stetson 1999 JD
Law Clerk **Andrea Yang** .... (651) 848-1900
Judicial Assistant **Judith Kirby** .... (651) 848-1900

Chambers of Magistrate Judge Becky Thorson

346 Federal Building, 316 North Robert Street, St. Paul, MN 55101
Tel: (651) 848-1210 Fax: (651) 848-1212
E-mail: thorson_chambers@mnd.uscourts.gov

Becky R. Thorson
Magistrate Judge

Education: Hamline BA; William Mitchell JD
Began Service: December 2014

Staff
Law Clerk **Dan Ganin** .... (651) 848-1210
E-mail: dan_ganin@mnd.uscourts.gov
Career Law Clerk **Danielle Mair** .... (651) 848-1210
E-mail: danielle_mair@mnd.uscourts.gov
Judicial Assistant **Melissa Kruger** .... (651) 848-1210
E-mail: melissa_kruger@mnd.uscourts.gov

Chambers of Magistrate Judge (part-time) Jon T. Huseby

519 Anne Street, Bemidji, MN 56601
Tel: (218) 751-0399

Jon T. Huseby
Magistrate Judge (Part-Time)

United States Bankruptcy Court for the District of Minnesota

U.S. Courthouse, 300 South Fourth Street, Room 301, Minneapolis, MN 55415
Tel: (612) 664-5200
Tel: (866) 222-8029 (Toll Free Voice Case Information System)
Fax: (612) 664-5303
Internet: www.mnb.uscourts.gov

Number of Judgeships: 4

Court Staff
Clerk of Court **Lori Vosejpka** .... (612) 664-5200
E-mail: lori_vosejpka@mnb.uscourts.gov
Chief Deputy Clerk **Ming Tan** .... (612) 664-5200
Deputy Clerk-in-Charge - Duluth **Anita Miller** .... (218) 529-3600
416 U.S. Courthouse, 515 W. First St., Duluth, MN 55802 Fax: (218) 529-3606
E-mail: anita_miller@mnb.uscourts.gov
Systems Manager **Ming Tan** .... (612) 664-5270
E-mail: ming_tan@mnb.uscourts.gov
Budget Analyst **Tammy Troje** .... (612) 664-5237
E-mail: tammy_troje@mnb.uscourts.gov

Chambers of Chief Bankruptcy Judge Gregory F. Kishel

Warren E. Burger Federal Building and U.S. Courthouse, 316 North Robert Street, St. Paul, MN 55101-1487
Tel: (651) 848-1060 Fax: (651) 848-1066
E-mail: gregory_kishel@mnb.uscourts.gov

Gregory F. Kishel
Chief Bankruptcy Judge

Date of Birth: 1951
Education: Cornell 1973 BA; Boston Col 1977 JD
Began Service: May 24, 1984
Term Expires: September 30, 2028

Judicial: Bankruptcy Judge, United States Bankruptcy Court for the District of Minnesota (1984-2006); Pro Tem Member, United States Bankruptcy Appellate Panel for the Eighth Circuit (1996-2003); Chief Bankruptcy Judge, Chambers of Chief Bankruptcy Judge Gregory F. Kishel, United States Bankruptcy Court for the District of Minnesota

Legal Practice: Private Practice (1981-1986)

Nonprofit: Attorney, Legal Aid Service of Northeastern Minnesota (1978-1981)

Current Memberships: American Bankruptcy Institute; Minnesota State Bar Association; National Conference of Bankruptcy Judges

Staff
Law Clerk **Ian Rubenstrunk** .... (651) 848-1060
Began Service: August 2012
Term Expires: August 31, 2016
E-mail: ian_rubenstrunk@mnb.uscourts.gov
Court Reporter **Kristin Neff** .... (651) 848-1064
Judicial Assistant **Judy R. Brooks** .... (651) 848-1060
E-mail: judy_brooks@mnb.uscourts.gov
Calendar Clerk **Jamie Smith** .... (651) 848-1061

Chambers of Bankruptcy Judge Robert J. Kressel
U.S. Courthouse, 300 South Fourth Street, Room 8W,
Minneapolis, MN 55415
Tel: (612) 664-5250
E-mail: robert_kressel@mnb.uscourts.gov

Robert J. Kressel
Bankruptcy Judge

Date of Birth: 1947
Education: Notre Dame 1969 AB; Harvard 1972 JD
Began Service: December 6, 1982
Term Expires: December 4, 2015

Academic: Adjunct Professor, Hamline University (1983-1984); Adjunct Professor, William Mitchell College of Law (1986-1994)

Government: Hearing Examiner, Office of Administrative Hearings, State of Minnesota (1978-1980); Referee, Conciliation Court, County of Hennepin, Minnesota (1979); Bankruptcy Analyst, Office of the United States Trustee, United States Department of Justice (1979-1981); Assistant United States Trustee, United States Department of Justice (1981-1982)

Legal Practice: Associate, Kressel, Cecere & Seiler (1972-1976); Partner, Nichols, Kressel & Johnson (1976-1978); Private Practice (1978-1979)

Current Memberships: Federal Bar Association; National Conference of Bankruptcy Judges

Staff
Law Clerk **Abigail McGibbon** . . . . (612) 664-5250
Began Service: 2014
Term Expires: August 2017
Secretary **Lynn M. Hennen** . . . . (612) 664-5250
E-mail: lynn_hennen@mnb.uscourts.gov

Chambers of Bankruptcy Judge Kathleen Sanberg
300 South Fourth Street, Minneapolis, MN 55415
Tel: (612) 664-5280

Kathleen Hvass Sanberg
Bankruptcy Judge

Education: Minnesota 1979 BA, 1982 JD

Chambers of Bankruptcy Judge Katherine A. Constantine
Warren E. Burger Federal Building, 316 North Robert Street,
Room 206, St. Paul, MN 55101
Tel: (651) 848-1050

Katherine A. Constantine
Bankruptcy Judge

Education: Georgetown 1977 BSFS, 1980 JD
Began Service: 2013

Staff
Calendar Clerk **Sandy McMackins** . . . . (651) 848-1050

Chambers of Bankruptcy Judge Michael E. Ridgway
300 South Fourth Street, Minneapolis, MN 55415
Tel: (612) 664-5260

Michael E. Ridgway
Bankruptcy Judge

United States District Court for the Northern District of Mississippi
Federal Building, 911 Jackson Avenue, Room 369, Oxford, MS 38655
Tel: (662) 234-1971 Tel: (662) 236-4706 (PACER)
Fax: (662) 236-5210
Internet: www.msnd.uscourts.gov

Number of Judgeships: 3

Circuit: Fifth

Areas Covered: Counties of Alcorn, Attala, Benton, Bolivar, Calhoun, Carroll, Chickasaw, Choctaw, Clay, Coahoma, DeSoto, Grenada, Humphreys, Itawamba, Lafayette, Lee, Leflore, Lowndes, Marshall, Monroe, Montgomery, Oktibbeha, Panola, Pontotoc, Prentiss, Quitman, Sunflower, Tallahatchie, Tate, Tippah, Tishomingo, Tunica, Union, Washington, Webster, Winston and Yalobusha

Court Staff
Clerk of Court **David Crews** . . . . (662) 234-1971
E-mail: david_crews@msnd.uscourts.gov
Education: Sewanee 1976 BA
Chief Deputy for Administrative Services
Robert Henry III . . . . (662) 234-1971
E-mail: robert_henry@msnd.uscourts.gov
Education: Mississippi 1990 MS
Chief Deputy for Operations **Gina P. Kilgore** . . . . (662) 234-1971
E-mail: gina_kilgore@msnd.uscourts.gov
Education: Mississippi 1981 BA
Deputy Clerk-in-Charge - Aberdeen
Deborah Houston . . . . (662) 369-4952
P.O. Box 704, Aberdeen, MS 39730 Fax: (662) 369-9569
E-mail: deborah_houston@msnd.uscourts.gov
Information Systems Manager **Don Conrad** . . . . (662) 234-1971
E-mail: don_conrad@msnd.uscourts.gov
Chief Probation Officer **Danny Ray McKittrick** . . . . (662) 234-2761
Fax: (662) 236-1458
Financial Administrator **Shawn M. Gardner** . . . . (662) 234-1971
E-mail: shawn_gardner@msnd.uscourts.gov
Librarian **Rose Marie Tominello** . . . . (601) 965-4665
245 E. Capitol St., Rm. 204, Jackson, MS 39201 Fax: (601) 965-4081
E-mail: rosie_tominello@ca5.uscourts.gov
Personnel Specialist **Connie Armstrong** . . . . (662) 234-1971
E-mail: connie_armstrong@msnd.uscourts.gov
Court Reporter **Susan Alford-May** . . . . (662) 801-3366
E-mail: susan_alford@msnd.uscourts.gov
Court Reporter **Phyllis McLarty** . . . . (662) 369-1017
E-mail: phyllis_mclarty@msnd.uscourts.gov
Court Reporter **Rita Young** . . . . (662) 281-3027
E-mail: rita_young@msnd.uscourts.gov

Chambers of Chief Judge Sharion Aycock
301 West Commerce Street, Room 218, Aberdeen, MS 39730
Tel: (662) 369-2628 Fax: (662) 369-8307
E-mail: sharion_aycock@msnd.uscourts.gov

Sharion Aycock
Chief Judge

Date of Birth: 1955
Education: Mississippi State 1977 BA; Mississippi Col 1980 JD
Began Service: October 26, 2007
Appointed By: President George W. Bush

Staff
Law Clerk **Parker Kline** . . . . (662) 369-2628
Began Service: January 2013
E-mail: parker_kline@msnd.uscourts.gov
Law Clerk **Daniel McHugh** . . . . (662) 369-2628
Began Service: August 2015
Term Expires: August 2017
E-mail: daniel_mchugh@msnd.uscourts.gov
Law Clerk **Grafton Bragg** . . . . (662) 369-2628
Began Service: August 2014
Term Expires: August 16, 2016
E-mail: grafton_bragg@msnd.uscourts.gov

(continued on next page)

Chambers of Chief Judge Sharion Aycock *continued*

Courtroom Deputy/Judicial Assistant **Ginger Sisk** .... (662) 369-2628
E-mail: ginger_sisk@msnd.uscourts.gov

Chambers of District Judge Michael P. Mills

Federal Building, 911 Jackson Avenue, Room 335,
Oxford, MS 38655-3622
Tel: (662) 234-1538 Fax: (662) 234-1447
E-mail: judge_mills@msnd.uscourts.gov

Michael P. Mills
District Judge

Date of Birth: 1956
Education: Mississippi 1978 BA, 1980 JD; Virginia 2001 LLM
Began Service: November 1, 2001
Appointed By: President George W. Bush

Staff

Law Clerk **Lucy R. Coolidge** .... (662) 234-1538
Term Expires: August 2016
E-mail: lucy_coolidge@msnd.uscourts.gov
Career Law Clerk **Robert M. Weems** .... (662) 234-1538
E-mail: Robert_Weems@msnd.uscourts.gov
Education: Mississippi 2002 JD
Courtroom Deputy **Sallie Wilkerson** .... (662) 234-1538
E-mail: Sallie_Wilkerson@msnd.uscourts.gov
Court Reporter **Rita Young** .... (662) 234-1538
E-mail: rita_young@msnd.uscourts.gov
Judicial Assistant **Lisa P. Martin** .... (662) 234-1538
E-mail: Lisa_P_Martin@msnd.uscourts.gov

Chambers of District Judge Debra M. Brown

911 Jackson Avenue, Oxford, MS 38655
Tel: (662) 335-4416
E-mail: debra_brown@msnd.uscourts.gov
E-mail: judge_brown@msnd.uscourts.gov

Debra M. Brown
District Judge

Education: Mississippi State 1987 BARC; Mississippi 1997 JD
Began Service: December 19, 2013
Appointed By: President Barack Obama

Legal Practice: Attorney, Phelps Dunbar LLP; Shareholder, Wise Carter Child & Caraway, P.A. (2012-2013)

Staff

Law Clerk **Tyrone Haynes** .... (662) 335-4416
Term Expires: February 2016
E-mail: tyrone_haynes@msnd.uscourts.gov
Law Clerk **Brian Spielman** .... (662) 335-4416
Term Expires: February 2016
E-mail: brian_spielman@msnd.uscourts.gov
Education: Wheaton (IL) 2006 BA; Emory 2009 JD
Law Clerk **Jessica Selecky** .... (662) 335-4416
Term Expires: February 2016
E-mail: jessica_selecky@msnd.uscourts.gov
Courtroom Deputy/Judicial Assistant **Rita Thomas** ...... (662) 335-4416
E-mail: rita_thomas@msnd.uscourts.gov

Chambers of Senior Judge Neal B. Biggers

Federal Building, 911 Jackson Avenue, Suite 388,
Oxford, MS 38655-3622
Tel: (662) 234-3401 Fax: (662) 236-5735
E-mail: neal_biggers@msnd.uscourts.gov

Neal B. Biggers
Senior Judge

Date of Birth: 1935
Education: Millsaps 1956 BA; Mississippi 1963 JD
Began Service: 1984
Appointed By: President Ronald Reagan
Political Affiliation: Democrat

Academic: Assistant Instructor, University of Mississippi (1974)

Government: County Prosecuting Attorney, State of Mississippi (1964); District Attorney, First Judicial District, State of Mississippi (1968-1975)

Judicial: Judge, Mississippi Circuit Court, First Judicial District (1975-1984)

Legal Practice: Private Practice (1963-1968)

Military Service: United States Navy (1956-1960); United States Naval Reserve (1961-1966)

Staff

Law Clerk **Wesley Webb** .... (662) 234-3401
Career Law Clerk **L. Lee Waddle** .... (662) 234-3401
E-mail: Lee_Waddle@msnd.uscourts.gov
Education: Mississippi 1991 BA, 1996 JD
Courtroom Deputy **Karen M. Tidwell** .... (662) 234-3401

Chambers of Senior Judge Glen H. Davidson

U.S. Courthouse, 301 West Commerce Street, Aberdeen, MS 39730
Tel: (662) 369-6486 Fax: (662) 369-8339
E-mail: glen_davidson@msnd.uscourts.gov

Glen H. Davidson
Senior Judge

Date of Birth: 1941
Education: Mississippi 1962 BA, 1965 JD
Began Service: October 29, 1985
Appointed By: President Ronald Reagan

Government: Assistant District Attorney, First Judicial District, Office of the District Attorney, State of Mississippi (1969-1974); District Attorney, First Judicial District, State of Mississippi (1975); United States Attorney, Northern District of Mississippi, United States Department of Justice (1981-1985)

Judicial: Chief Bankruptcy Judge, United States District Court for the Northern District of Mississippi (2000-2007)

Legal Practice: Partner, Riley, Davidson & Weir (1969-1973); Partner, Carnathan & Davidson (1973-1981)

Military Service: United States Air Force (1966-1969)

Current Memberships: American Bar Association; Federal Bar Association; Lee County Bar Association; The Mississippi Bar; The Mississippi Bar Foundation, The Mississippi Bar

Staff

Career Law Clerk **Gina A. Kelley-Smith** .... (662) 369-6486
E-mail: gina_kelley@msnd.uscourts.gov
Secretary **Melba Applewhite** .... (662) 369-6486
E-mail: melba_applewhite@msnd.uscourts.gov

Chambers of Magistrate Judge S. Allan Alexander

Federal Building, 911 Jackson Avenue, Suite 242, Oxford, MS 38655
Tel: (662) 281-3008 Fax: (662) 234-0910
E-mail: judge_alexander@msnd.uscourts.gov

S. Allan Alexander
Magistrate Judge

Date of Birth: 1951
Education: William Woods 1973 BA; Mississippi 1978 JD
Began Service: November 17, 1994

Clerkships: Law Clerk The Honorable William C. Keady, United States District Court for the Northern District of Mississippi

Legal Practice: Holcomb, Dunbar, Connell, Merkel, Tollison & Khayat (1980-1982); Partner, Tollison & Alexander (1982-1992); Partner, Tollison, Austin & Twiford (1992-1994)

Current Memberships: American Bar Association; Federal Bar Association; The Mississippi Bar; The Mississippi Bar Foundation, The Mississippi Bar

Staff
Law Clerk **Liza M. Frugé** . . . . (662) 281-3008
Began Service: August 2012
Term Expires: August 2016
E-mail: liza_fruge@msnd.uscourts.gov
Education: Mississippi 1997 JD
Career Law Clerk **Brooke Driskell** . . . . (662) 281-3007
E-mail: brooke_driskell@msnd.uscourts.gov
Education: Mississippi JD
Courtroom Deputy **Willie Sue Miller** . . . . (662) 281-3009
E-mail: willie_sue_miller@msnd.uscourts.gov
Judicial Assistant **Karen M. Tidwell** . . . . (662) 281-3010
E-mail: karen_tidwell@msnd.uscourts.gov

Chambers of Magistrate Judge David A. Sanders

301 West Commerce Street, Aberdeen, MS 39730
P.O. Box 726, Aberdeen, MS 39730
Tel: (662) 369-2138 Fax: (662) 369-1039
E-mail: judge_sanders@msnd.uscourts.gov

David A. Sanders
Magistrate Judge

Began Service: July 2008

Government: Assistant U.S. Attorney, Criminal Division, Mississippi - Northern District, United States Department of Justice

Staff
Career Law Clerk **D. Elizabeth "Beth" Featherston** . . . . (662) 369-2138
E-mail: beth_featherston@msnd.uscourts.gov
Education: Mississippi State 1977 BA;
Mississippi Col 1980 JD
Law Clerk **Rylee Zalanka** . . . . (662) 369-2138
E-mail: rylee_zalanka@msnd.uscourts.gov
Courtroom Deputy **Jennifer Frantz** . . . . (662) 369-2138
E-mail: jennifer_frantz@msnd.uscourts.gov

Chambers of Magistrate Judge Jane M. Virden

305 Main Street, Room 329, Greenville, MS 38701
Tel: (662) 335-9214 Fax: (662) 332-6881
E-mail: jane_virden@msnd.uscourts.gov

Jane M. Virden
Magistrate Judge

Began Service: 2011

Staff
Law Clerk **Laura Collins** . . . . (662) 335-9214
E-mail: laura_collins@msnd.uscourts.gov
Career Law Clerk **Leneatra "Necee" Brownlee** . . . . (662) 335-9214
E-mail: necee_brownlee@msnd.uscourts.gov
Education: Mississippi 1999 JD

Chambers of Magistrate Judge Jane M. Virden *continued*

Courtroom Deputy **Dean Dacus** . . . . (662) 335-9214
E-mail: dean_dacus@msnd.uscourts.gov

United States Bankruptcy Court for the Northern District of Mississippi

Thad Cochran United States Bankruptcy Courthouse, 703 Highway 145 North, Aberdeen, MS 39730
Tel: (662) 369-2596 Tel: (800) 676-6856 (PACER Subscription)
Tel: (800) 392-8653 (Voice Case Information System)
Internet: www.msnb.uscourts.gov

Number of Judgeships: 2

Court Staff
Clerk of Court **David J. Puddister** . . . . (662) 369-2596
Education: Mississippi State 1978 BA;
Mississippi 1987 JD; Mississippi State 2006 MPPA
Chief Deputy Clerk **Vicki M. Wamble** . . . . (662) 369-2596
E-mail: vicki_wamble@msnb.uscourts.gov
Administrative Secretary/ Human Resources Deputy
Clerk **Nancy R. Patterson** . . . . (662) 369-2596
E-mail: nancy_patterson@msnb.uscourts.gov
Information Systems Manager **Glen A. Jones** . . . . (662) 319-3571
E-mail: glen_jones@msnb.uscourts.gov
Financial Administrator **Edna T. Garth** . . . . (662) 319-3559
E-mail: edna_garth@msnb.uscourts.gov

Chambers of Chief Bankruptcy Judge Jason D. Woodward

703 Highway 145 North, Aberdeen, MS 39730
Tel: (662) 369-2624

Jason D. Woodward
Chief Bankruptcy Judge

Began Service: 2013

Staff
Law Clerk **Jamie F. Wiley** . . . . (662) 369-2624
Law Clerk **(Vacant)** . . . . (662) 369-2624

Chambers of Bankruptcy Judge Neil P. Olack

P.O. Box 2448, Jackson, MS 39225
Tel: (601) 608-4600

Neil P. Olack
Bankruptcy Judge

Education: Lehigh BA; Emory 1981 JD
Began Service: 2006
Term Expires: 2020

United States District Court for the Southern District of Mississippi

316 James O. Eastland U.S. Courthouse, 245 East Capitol Street, Jackson, MS 39201
P.O. Box 23552, Jackson, MS 39225-3552
Tel: (601) 608-4000
Internet: www.mssd.uscourts.gov

Number of Judgeships: 6

Circuit: Fifth

Areas Covered: Counties of Adams, Amite, Claiborne, Clarke, Copiah, Covington, Forrest, Franklin, George, Greene, Hancock, Harrison, Hinds, Holmes, Issaquena, Jackson, Jasper, Jefferson, Jefferson Davis, Jones, Kemper, Lamar, Lauderdale, Lawrence, Leake, Lincoln, Madison, Marion, Neshoba, Newton, Noxubee, Pearl River, Perry, Pike, Rankin, Scott, Sharkey, Simpson, Smith, Stone, Walthall, Warren, Wayne, Wilkinson and Yazoo

Court Staff

Clerk of Court **Arthur Johnston** ....(601) 608-4000
Deputy-in-Charge - Gulfport **Porfiria "Porfi" Stokes** .... (228) 563-1700
2012 15th Street, Suite 403, Gulfport, MS 39501
Deputy-in-Charge - Hattiesburg **Linda Regan** ....(601) 583-2433
701 Main St., Ste. 200, Hattiesburg, MS 39401
Chief Probation Officer **Carolyn Romano** ....(601) 608-4900
2012 15th Street, Suite 1.550, Jackson, MS 39201
Librarian **Rosemarie Tominello** .... (601) 608-4800
2012 15th Street, Jackson, MS 39201
E-mail: 5SatLib-Jackson@ca5.uscourts.gov

Chambers of Chief District Judge Louis Guirola, Jr.

2012 15th Street, Suite 814, Gulfport, MS 39501
Tel: (228) 563-1767

Louis Guirola, Jr.
Chief District Judge

Date of Birth: 1951
Education: William Carey 1973 BA; Mississippi 1979 JD
Began Service: March 22, 2004
Appointed By: President George W. Bush

Government: Assistant District Attorney, 19th Judicial District, District Attorney's Office (1980-1984); Assistant U.S. Attorney, United States Attorney's Office (1990-1993)

Judicial: Magistrate Judge, United States District Court for the Western District of Texas (1993-1996); Magistrate Judge, United States District Court for the Southern District of Mississippi (1996-2003)

Legal Practice: Associate, Boyce, Holleman & Associates, P.A. (1979-1980); Attorney, Guirola & Jackson P.A. (1986-1990)

Staff

Law Clerk **Jennifer Morgan** .... (228) 563-1767
Began Service: September 2014
Term Expires: September 2016
E-mail: jennifer_morgan@mssd.uscourts.gov
Career Law Clerk **Brittany Reid** .... (228) 563-1767
E-mail: brittany_reid@mssd.uscourts.gov
Education: Mississippi 2003 JD
Career Law Clerk **Karla Whitsitt** ....(228) 563-1767
Education: Colorado 1992 JD
Courtroom Deputy **Vicki Kelly** ....(228) 563-1767
E-mail: vicki_kelly@mssd.uscourts.gov

Chambers of District Judge Keith Starrett

701 North Main Street, Suite 228, Hattiesburg, MS 39401
Tel: (601) 583-4422 Fax: (601) 544-7369
E-mail: starrett_chambers@mssd.uscourts.gov
E-mail: keith_starrett@mssd.uscourts.gov

The Honorable Keith Starrett
District Judge

Education: Mississippi State 1972; Mississippi 1974 JD
Began Service: January 1, 2005
Appointed By: President George W. Bush

Current Memberships: The Mississippi Bar

Staff

Law Clerk **Sarah Daley** .... (601) 583-4422
Began Service: August 24, 2015
Term Expires: August 24, 2017
E-mail: sarah_daley@mssd.uscourts.gov
Career Law Clerk **Charles Blanchard** .... (601) 583-4422
Began Service: January 3, 2011
E-mail: charles_blanchard@mssd.uscourts.gov
Courtroom Deputy **Sharon Potin** ....(601) 583-4422
E-mail: sharon_potin@mssd.uscourts.gov
Secretary/Courtroom Deputy **Donna Lampton** ....(601) 583-4422
E-mail: donna_lampton@mssd.uscourts.gov

Chambers of District Judge Daniel Porter Jordan III

2012 15th Street, Suite 5.750, Jackson, MS 39201
Tel: (601) 608-4120

Daniel Porter Jordan III
District Judge

Date of Birth: 1964
Education: Mississippi 1987 BBA; Virginia 1993 JD
Began Service: August 7, 2006
Appointed By: President George W. Bush

Legal Practice: Associate, Butler, Snow, O'Mara, Stevens & Cannada, PLLC (1993-1999); Equity Member, Butler, Snow, O'Mara, Stevens & Cannada, PLLC

Staff

Law Clerk **Ryan Zumwalt** .... (601) 608-4120
Began Service: August 2015
Term Expires: August 2016
E-mail: ryan_zumwalt@mssd.uscourts.gov
Career Law Clerk **Elizabeth Q. Howell** .... (601) 608-4120
E-mail: elizabeth_howell@mssd.uscourts.gov
Education: Virginia 1994 BA; Mississippi Col 2003 JD

Chambers of District Judge Halil Suleyman Ozerden

2012 15th Street, Suite 714, Gulfport, MS 39501
Tel: (228) 679-1070
E-mail: ozerden_chambers@mssd.uscourts.gov

Halil Suleyman Ozerden
District Judge

Date of Birth: 1966
Education: Georgetown 1989 BS; Stanford 1998 JD
Began Service: May 1, 2007
Appointed By: President George W. Bush

Clerkships: Law Clerk, District Judge Eldon E. Fallon, United States District Court for the Eastern District of Louisiana (1998-1999)

Legal Practice: Partner, Dukes, Dukes, Keating & Faneca (1999-2007)

Military Service: LT, United States Navy, United States Department of Defense (1989-1995)

Chambers of District Judge Halil Suleyman Ozerden *continued*

Staff
Law Clerk **Nick Morisani** . . . . (228) 679-1070
E-mail: nick_morisani@mssd.uscourts.gov
Career Law Clerk **Emily Waddell** . . . . (601) 965-4439
E-mail: emily_waddell@mssd.uscourts.gov

Chambers of District Judge Henry T. Wingate

2012 15th Street, Suite 6.750, Jackson, MS 39201
Tel: (601) 608-4100
E-mail: henry_wingate@mssd.uscourts.gov

Henry T. Wingate
District Judge

Date of Birth: 1947
Education: Grinnell 1969 BA; Yale 1972 JD
Began Service: October 1985
Appointed By: President Ronald Reagan

Current Memberships: American Bar Association; Federal Bar Association; Hinds County Bar Association; Magnolia Bar Association; The Mississippi Bar; Judicial Council, National Bar Association

Staff
Law Clerk **Chevon Chatman** . . . . (601) 965-4042
Began Service: December 2014
E-mail: chevon_chatman@mssd.uscourts.gov
Law Clerk **Morgan Miranda** . . . . (601) 965-4042
E-mail: morgan_miranda@mssd.uscourts.gov
Courtroom Deputy Clerk **Twana Summers** . . . . . . (601) 965-4042
E-mail: twana_summers@mssd.uscourts.gov
Education: Belhaven 2002 BABA

Chambers of District Judge Carlton W. Reeves

2012 15th Street, Suite 5.550, Jackson, MS 39201
Tel: (601) 608-4140
E-mail: reeves_chambers@mssd.uscourts.gov

Carlton W. Reeves
District Judge

Education: Jackson State U 1986 BA; Virginia 1989 JD
Began Service: December 30, 2010
Appointed By: President Barack Obama

Government: Assistant U.S. Attorney, Mississippi - Southern District, Executive Office for United States Attorneys, United States Department of Justice (1995-2001); Chief, Civil Division, Mississippi - Southern District, United States Department of Justice

Legal Practice: Associate, Phelps Dunbar LLP (1991-1995); Partner, Pigott Reeves Johnson, P.A. (2001-2010)

Staff
Law Clerk **Elissa Johnson** . . . . (601) 608-4140
Began Service: 2015
Term Expires: August 2016
E-mail: elissa_johnson@mssd.uscourts.gov
Career Law Clerk **Andrew Canter** . . . . (601) 608-4140
E-mail: andrew_canter@mssd.uscourts.gov
Law Clerk **Alicia Netterville** . . . . (601) 608-4140
Began Service: August 2015
Term Expires: August 2016
E-mail: alicia_netterville@mssd.uscourts.gov
Courtroom Deputy **Joyce A. Smith** . . . . (601) 608-4140
E-mail: joyce_smith@mssd.uscourts.gov

Chambers of Senior Judge Walter J. Gex III

2012 15th Street, Suite 572, Gulfport, MS 39501
Tel: (228) 563-1732
E-mail: walter_gex@mssd.uscourts.gov

Walter J. Gex III
Senior Judge

Date of Birth: 1939
Education: Mississippi 1962 BBA, 1963 LLB
Began Service: 1986
Appointed By: President Ronald Reagan

Judicial: Special Master, Mississippi Chancery Court, Hancock County

Legal Practice: Associate, Satterfield, Shell, Williams & Buford; Partner, Gex, Gex & Phillips (1972-1986)

Current Memberships: Federal Bar Association; Fifth Circuit District Judges Association; The Mississippi Bar

Staff
Staff Attorney **Helen Hancock** . . . . (228) 563-1732
E-mail: helen_hancock@mssd.uscourts.gov
Education: Mississippi 1990 JD
Judicial Assistant/Courtroom Deputy Clerk **(Vacant)** . . . . . (228) 563-1732

Chambers of Senior Judge William H. Barbour, Jr.

2012 15th Street, Suite 4.550, Jackson, MS 39201
Tel: (601) 608-4400
E-mail: william_barbour@mssd.uscourts.gov

William H. Barbour, Jr.
Senior Judge

Date of Birth: February 4, 1941
Education: Princeton 1963 BA; Mississippi 1966 JD; NYU 1966
Began Service: April 1983
Appointed By: President Ronald Reagan

Legal Practice: Partner, Henry, Barbour & DeCell (1966-1983)

Current Memberships: American Bar Association; The Charles Clark American Inn of Court, The American Inns of Court

Staff
Career Law Clerk **Sue Collipp** . . . . (601) 608-4400
Secretary/Judicial Assistant **Nijah Lewis** . . . . (601) 608-4400
E-mail: nijah_lewis@mssd.uscourts.gov

Chambers of Senior Judge David C. Bramlette III

P.O. Drawer 928, Natchez, MS 39121
Tel: (601) 442-3006 Tel: (601) 442-9324 (Alternate number)
E-mail: david_bramlette@mssd.uscourts.gov

David C. Bramlette III
Senior Judge

Date of Birth: 1939
Education: Princeton 1962 BA; Mississippi 1965 JD
Began Service: December 1991
Appointed By: President George H.W. Bush

Judicial: Special Circuit Judge, Mississippi District Court, Sixth Judicial District; Judge, Adams County Court

Legal Practice: Associate, Adams, Forman, Truly, Ward & Bramlette

Current Memberships: Adams County Bar Association; American Bar Association; The Mississippi Bar

Staff
Law Clerk **Austin Alexander** . . . . (601) 442-3006
E-mail: austin_alexander@mssd.uscourts.gov
Career Law Clerk **Edwin C. Ward** . . . . (601) 442-3006
E-mail: edwin_ward@mssd.uscourts.gov
Education: Mississippi 1981 JD

(continued on next page)

Chambers of Senior Judge David C. Bramlette III *continued*

Courtroom Deputy **Debra Jackson** .... (601) 442-3006
E-mail: debra_jackson@mssd.uscourts.gov
Secretary **Lorraine Arnold** .... (601) 442-3006
E-mail: lorraine_arnold@mssd.uscourts.gov

Chambers of Senior Judge Tom Stewart Lee

2012 15th Street, Suite 4.756, Jackson, MS 39201
Tel: (601) 608-4420
E-mail: Tom_Lee@mssd.uscourts.gov

Tom Stewart Lee
Senior Judge

Date of Birth: 1941
Education: Mississippi Col 1963 BA; Mississippi 1965 JD
Began Service: June 25, 1984
Appointed By: President Ronald Reagan

Current Memberships: Federal Bar Association; Federal Judges Association; Hinds County Bar Association; The Mississippi Bar; Scott County Bar Association

Staff
Law Clerk (Part-Time) **Dianne Luke** .... (601) 608-4420
E-mail: dianne_luke@mssd.uscourts.gov
Education: Southern Mississippi 1991 BS; Mississippi Col 1996 JD
Career Law Clerk **Caren Peters** .... (601) 608-4420
E-mail: caren_peters@mssd.uscourts.gov
Education: Southern Mississippi 1983 BS; Mississippi 1986 JD
Courtroom Deputy **Lisa Evans** .... (601) 608-4420
E-mail: lisa_evans@mssd.uscourts.gov

Chambers of Magistrate Judge Robert H. Walker

2012 15th Street, Suite 870, Gulfport, MS 39501
Tel: (228) 563-1720
E-mail: robert_walker@mssd.uscourts.gov

Robert H. Walker
Magistrate Judge

Began Service: November 15, 2004

Staff
Career Law Clerk **Scherry Joffe** .... (228) 563-1720
E-mail: scherry_joffe@mssd.uscourts.gov
Career Law Clerk **Stephen King** .... (228) 563-1720
E-mail: stephen_king@mssd.uscourts.gov
Education: William & Mary 1996 JD
Courtroom Deputy **Sandra Ryan** .... (228) 563-1720
E-mail: sandra_ryan@mssd.uscourts.gov

Chambers of Magistrate Judge Michael T. Parker

701 North Main Street, Room 216, Hattiesburg, MS 39401
Tel: (601) 544-9100

Michael T. Parker
Magistrate Judge

Began Service: May 26, 2006

Staff
Law Clerk **(Vacant)** .... (601) 544-9100
Career Law Clerk **Justin Starling** .... (601) 544-9100
E-mail: justin_starling@mssd.uscourts.gov

Chambers of Magistrate Judge Linda R. Anderson

2012 15th Street, Suiet 6.150, Jackson, MS 39201
Tel: (601) 608-4440
E-mail: linda_anderson@mssd.uscourts.gov

Linda R. Anderson
Magistrate Judge

Began Service: July 12, 2006

Government: Assistant District Attorney, District Attorney's Office, County of Hinds, Mississippi; Assistant U.S. Attorney, United States Attorneys Office, United States Department of Justice

Staff
Career Staff Attorney **Cecilia Cameron** .... (601) 608-4440
Began Service: 2007
Education: Loyola U (Chicago) 2000 JD
Career Staff Attorney **Anna Furr** .... (601) 608-4440
E-mail: anna_furr@mssd.uscourts.gov
Education: Mississippi 1980 JD

Chambers of Magistrate Judge F. Keith Ball

2012 15th Street, Suite 5.150, Jackson, MS 39201
Tel: (601) 608-4460
E-mail: ball_chambers@mssd.uscourts.gov
E-mail: keith_ball@mssd.uscourts.gov

F. Keith Ball
Magistrate Judge

Education: Mississippi 1990 JD
Began Service: January 2010

Staff
Law Clerk **Wendy Shelton** .... (601) 608-4460
E-mail: wendy_shelton@mssd.uscourts.gov
Education: Mississippi Col 1990 JD
Career Law Clerk **Yvonne W. Jicka** .... (601) 608-4460
E-mail: yvonne_jicka@mssd.uscourts.gov
Education: Mississippi Col 1988 BS, 1994 JD
Career Law Clerk **Denise Kimble** .... (601) 608-4460
E-mail: denise_kimble@mssd.uscourts.gov
Education: Belhaven 1978 BA; Mississippi Col 1988 JD

Chambers of Magistrate Judge John Gargiulo

245 East Capitol Street, Jackson, MS 39201
Tel: (601) 608-4000

John Gargiulo
Magistrate Judge

Began Service: 2014

United States Bankruptcy Court for the Southern District of Mississippi

2012 15th Street, Jackson, MS 39201
P.O. Box 2448, Jackson, MS 39225-2448
Tel: (601) 608-4600
Tel: (866) 222-8029 (Toll Free Voice Case Information System VCIS)
Internet: www.mssb.uscourts.gov

Number of Judgeships: 3

Court Staff
Bankruptcy Clerk **Danny L. Miller** .... (601) 608-4600
E-mail: danny_miller@mssb.uscourts.gov
Chief Deputy Clerk **Collette Derouen** .... (228) 563-1790

Chambers of Chief Bankruptcy Judge Neil P. Olack
2012 15th Street, Jackson, MS 39201
P.O. Box 2448, Jackson, MS 39225-2448
Tel: (601) 608-4690
E-mail: neil_olack@mssb.uscourts.gov

Neil P. Olack
Chief Bankruptcy Judge

Education: Lehigh BA; Emory 1981 JD
Began Service: May 1, 2006
Term Expires: 2020

Staff
Courtroom Deputy **Beth Harkins** . . . . (601) 608-4690
E-mail: beth_harkins@mssb.uscourts.gov

Chambers of Bankruptcy Judge Edward Ellington
P.O. Box 2448, Jackson, MS 39225
2012 15th Street, Suite 2300, Jackson, MS 39201
Tel: (601) 608-4670
E-mail: edward_ellington@mssb.uscourts.gov

Edward Ellington
Bankruptcy Judge

Date of Birth: 1940
Education: Mississippi State 1962 BS; Mississippi 1967 JD
Began Service: January 15, 1986
Term Expires: January 15, 2019

Staff
Career Law Clerk **Maureen B. "Mimi" Speyerer** . . . . (601) 608-4670
E-mail: mimi_speyerer@mssb.uscourts.gov
Education: Mississippi State 1984 BA; Mississippi 1987 JD
Courtroom Deputy **Rita Greer** . . . . (601) 608-4670
E-mail: rita_greer@mssb.uscourts.gov
Judicial Assistant **Kimber McDowell** . . . . (601) 608-4670
E-mail: kimber_mcdowell@mssb.uscourts.gov

Chambers of Bankruptcy Judge Katharine M. Samson
2012 15th Street, Suite 244, Jackson, MS 39201
Tel: (228) 563-1841
E-mail: katharine_samson@mssb.uscourts.gov

Katharine M. Samson
Bankruptcy Judge

Began Service: 2010

Staff
Career Law Clerk **Carole Evans** . . . . (228) 563-1790
E-mail: carole_evans@mssb.uscourts.gov
Education: Mississippi 1980 BA, 1983 JD
Law Clerk **Ashley Champion** . . . . (228) 563-1790
E-mail: ashley_champion@mssb.uscourts.gov
Courtroom Deputy **Christy Cannette** . . . . (228) 563-1790

United States District Court for the Eastern District of Missouri
Thomas F. Eagleton U.S. Courthouse, 111 South Tenth Street, Room 3.300, St. Louis, MO 63102
Tel: (314) 244-7900 Tel: (314) 244-7775 (PACER)
Fax: (314) 244-7909
Internet: www.moed.uscourts.gov

Number of Judgeships: 9

Circuit: Eighth

Areas Covered: Counties of Adair, Audrain, Bollinger, Butler, Cape Girardeau, Carter, Chariton, Clark, Crawford, Dent, Dunklin, Franklin, Gasconade, Iron, Jefferson, Knox, Lewis, Lincoln, Linn, Macon, Madison, Maries, Marion, Mississippi, Monroe, Montgomery, New Madrid, Pemiscot, Perry, Phelps, Pike, Ralls, Randolph, Reynolds, Ripley, Schuyler, Scotland, Scott, Shannon, Shelby, St. Charles, St. Francois, St. Louis, Ste. Genevieve, Stoddard, Warren, Washington and Wayne

Court Staff
Clerk of Court **Gregory "Greg" Linhares** . . . . (314) 244-7890
E-mail: greg_linhares@moed.uscourts.gov
Chief Probation Officer **Douglas W. Burris** . . . . (314) 244-6700
Education: Saint Louis U 1966 BA; Denver 1970 MSW
Chief Pretrial Services **Mark Reichert** . . . . (314) 244-7000
Chief Deputy Clerk **Lori Miller-Taylor** . . . . (314) 244-7910
Education: Alcorn State BS; Missouri (St Louis) MPP

Chambers of Chief Judge Catherine D. Perry
Thomas F. Eagleton U.S. Courthouse, 111 South Tenth Street, Room 14.182, St. Louis, MO 63102
Tel: (314) 244-7520 Fax: (314) 244-7529
E-mail: catherine_perry@moed.uscourts.gov

Catherine D. Perry
Chief Judge

Date of Birth: 1952
Education: Oklahoma 1977 BA; Washington U (MO) 1980 JD
Began Service: October 21, 1994
Appointed By: President William J. Clinton

Academic: Adjunct Professor, School of Law, Washington University (1981-1984); Adjunct Professor, School of Law, Washington University (1991-1992)

Judicial: Magistrate Judge, United States District Court for the Eastern District of Missouri (1990-1994)

Legal Practice: Armstrong, Teasdale, Shlafly, Davis, and Dicus (1980-1990)

Current Memberships: American Bar Association; The Bar Association of Metropolitan St. Louis; Federal Judges Association; Federal Magistrate Judges Association; The Missouri Bar; National Association of Women Judges; Women Lawyers' Association of Greater St. Louis

Staff
Law Clerk **Mary Michenfelder** . . . . (314) 244-7520
Began Service: August 2015
Term Expires: August 2017
E-mail: mary_michenfelder@moed.uscourts.gov
Law Clerk **Gina Savoie** . . . . (314) 244-7520
Began Service: September 2015
Term Expires: September 2017
Law Clerk **Tessa Schneider** . . . . (314) 244-7520
Began Service: September 2015
Term Expires: September 2017
E-mail: tessa_schneider@moed.uscourts.gov
Career Law Clerk **Jeanette D. Valentine** . . . . (314) 244-7520
E-mail: jeanette_valentine@moed.uscourts.gov
Education: Virginia 1995 JD
Judicial Assistant **Brian Crow** . . . . (314) 244-7520
E-mail: brian_crow@moed.uscourts.gov

Chambers of District Judge Carol E. Jackson

Thomas F. Eagleton U.S. Courthouse, 111 South Tenth Street, Suite 14.148, St. Louis, MO 63102
Tel: (314) 244-7540 Fax: (314) 244-7549
E-mail: carol_jackson@moed.uscourts.gov

Carol E. Jackson
District Judge

Date of Birth: 1952
Education: Wellesley 1973 BA; Michigan 1976 JD
Began Service: October 15, 1992
Appointed By: President George H.W. Bush

Academic: Adjunct Professor, School of Law, Washington University (1989-1992)

Judicial: Magistrate Judge, United States District Court for the Eastern District of Missouri (1986-1992)

Legal Practice: Associate, Thompson & Mitchell (1976-1983); Senior Attorney, Mallinckrodt Inc. (1983-1985)

Current Memberships: The Bar Association of Metropolitan St. Louis; Federal Magistrate Judges Association; The Missouri Bar; Mound City Bar Association; National Association of Women Judges; National Bar Association

Staff

Law Clerk **Lisa Carpenter** .... (314) 244-7540
E-mail: lisa_carpenter@moed.uscourts.gov
Education: Washington U (MO) 2001 JD
Court Reporter **Susan "Sue" Moran** .... (314) 244-7986

Chambers of District Judge Rodney W. Sippel

Thomas F. Eagleton U.S. Courthouse, 111 South Tenth Street, Suite 16.182, St. Louis, MO 61302
Tel: (314) 244-7430 Fax: (314) 244-7439
E-mail: rodney_sippel@moed.uscourts.gov

Rodney W. Sippel
District Judge

Date of Birth: 1956
Education: Tulsa 1978 BS; Washington U (MO) 1981 JD
Began Service: January 27, 1998
Appointed By: President William J. Clinton

Government: Staff Assistant (D-MO), Office of Senator Thomas F. Eagleton, United States Senate (1979-1982); Administrative Assistant (D-MO), Office of Representative Richard A. Gephardt, United States House of Representatives (1993-1995)

Legal Practice: Associate, Husch & Eppenberger, LLC (1982-1988); Partner, Husch & Eppenberger, LLC (1989-1993); Partner, Husch & Eppenberger, LLC (1995-1998)

Staff

Law Clerk **Annie Legomsky** .... (314) 244-7430
E-mail: annie_legomsky@moed.uscourts.gov
Career Law Clerk **Christopher Keefe** .... (314) 244-7430
Education: Saint Louis U 1996 JD
Career Law Clerk **Jeanette D. Valentine** .... (314) 244-7430
E-mail: jeanette_valentine@moed.uscourts.gov
Court Reporter **Shannon White** .... (314) 244-7430
E-mail: shannon_white@moed.uscourts.gov
Judicial Assistant **Brian Crow** .... (314) 244-7430
E-mail: brian_crow@moed.uscourts.gov

Chambers of District Judge Henry Edward Autrey

Thomas F. Eagleton U.S. Courthouse, 111 South Tenth Street, Suite 10.182, St. Louis, MO 63102
Tel: (314) 244-7450 Fax: (314) 244-7459

Henry Edward Autrey
District Judge

Date of Birth: March 18, 1952
Education: Saint Louis U 1974 BS, 1977 JD
Began Service: September 16, 2002
Appointed By: President George W. Bush

Academic: Adjunct Professor, School of Law, Saint Louis University (1991-1997)

Government: Assistant Circuit Attorney, Office of Circuit Attorney, City of St. Louis, Missouri (1977-1984); First Assistant Circuit Attorney, Office of Circuit Attorney, City of St. Louis, Missouri (1984-1986)

Judicial: Associate Circuit Judge, Twenty-second Judicial Circuit Court City of St. Louis (1986-1997); Circuit Judge, Twenty-second Judicial Circuit Court City of St. Louis (1997-2002)

Staff

Law Clerk **Michael R. Dauphin** .... (314) 244-7450
Career Law Clerk **Margaret "Mindy" Finan** .... (314) 244-7450
E-mail: margaret_finan@moed.uscourts.gov
Education: Saint Louis U 1984 JD
Court Reporter **Angela Daley** .... (314) 244-7978
E-mail: angela_daley@moed.uscourts.gov
Judicial Assistant **Heather Krafft** .... (314) 244-7450
E-mail: heather_krafft@moed.uscourts.gov
Court Reporter **Gayle Madden** .... (314) 244-7987
E-mail: gayle_madden@moed.uscourts.gov

Chambers of District Judge Stephen N. Limbaugh, Jr.

555 Independence Street, Suite 4000, Cape Girardeau, MO 63703
Tel: (573) 331-8873

Stephen N. Limbaugh, Jr.
District Judge

Date of Birth: 1952
Education: Southern Methodist 1973 BA, 1976 JD
Began Service: 2008
Appointed By: President George W. Bush

Government: Prosecuting Attorney, Office of the Prosecuting Attorney, County of Cape Girardeau, Missouri (1979-1982)

Judicial: Judge, Missouri Circuit Court, 32nd Judicial Circuit (1987-1992); Judge, Missouri Supreme Court (1992-2008)

Legal Practice: Private Practice (1977-1978); Private Practice (1983-1987)

Current Memberships: American Bar Foundation; American Bar Association; The Missouri Bar; State Bar of Texas

Staff

Career Law Clerk **Amy Trueblood** .... (573) 331-8873
Began Service: August 2010
E-mail: amy_trueblood@moed.uscourts.gov
Education: Harvard 1999; Virginia 2002 JD
Career Law Clerk **Kim Price** .... (573) 331-8873
Court Reporter **Alison Garagnani** .... (573) 331-8832
E-mail: alison_garagnani@moed.uscourts.gov
Judicial Assistant **Sandra Moore** .... (573) 331-8873
E-mail: sandra_moore@moed.uscourts.gov

Chambers of District Judge Audrey Goldstein Fleissig

111 South Tenth Street, Suite 12.182, St. Louis, MO 63102
Tel: (314) 244-7420
E-mail: audrey_fleissig@moed.uscourts.gov

Audrey Goldstein Fleissig
District Judge

Education: Carleton 1976 BA; Washington U (MO) 1980 JD
Began Service: June 11, 2010
Appointed By: President Barack Obama

Current Memberships: National Association of Women Judges

Staff
Law Clerk **Antonia Miceli** . . . . (314) 244-7420
Began Service: 2010
Education: McGeorge 2006 JD
Permanent Law Clerk **Phyllis Shapiro** . . . . (314) 244-7420
E-mail: phyllis_shapiro@moed.uscourts.gov
Judicial Assistant **Sara Armbrecht** . . . . (314) 244-7420
E-mail: sara_armbrecht@moed.uscourts.gov

Chambers of District Judge John A. Ross

Thomas F. Eagleton U.S. Courthouse, 111 South Tenth Street, Room 12.148, St. Louis, MO 63102
Tel: (314) 244-7560 Fax: (314) 244-7909

John A. Ross
District Judge

Education: Emory 1976 BA, 1979 JD
Began Service: November 2, 2011
Appointed By: President Barack Obama

Staff
Case Management Team Leader **Andrea Luisetti** . . . . (314) 244-7933
Case Manager **Lisa Holwitt** . . . . (314) 244-7935
Case Manager **Lisa Wooley** . . . . (314) 244-7936
Case Manager **(Vacant)** . . . . (314) 244-7928
Court Reporter **Lisa Paczkowski** . . . . (314) 244-7983
E-mail: lisa_paczkowski@moed.uscourts.gov
Judicial Assistant **Annette "Dolly" Prock** . . . . . (314) 244-7560
E-mail: annette_prock@moed.uscourts.gov

Chambers of District Judge Brian C. Wimes

Thomas F. Eagleton U.S. Courthouse, 111 South Tenth Street, St. Louis, MO 63102
Tel: (314) 244-7900 Fax: (314) 244-7909

Brian C. Wimes
District Judge

Education: Kansas 1990 BGS; Texas Southern 1994 JD
Began Service: 2012
Appointed By: President Barack Obama

Staff
Judicial Assistant **Denise Halasey** . . . . (314) 244-7900

Chambers of District Judge Ronnie L. White

111 South Tenth Street, Room 17.182, St. Louis, MO 63102
Tel: (314) 244-7580
E-mail: ronnie_white@moed.uscourts.gov

Ronnie L. White
District Judge

Date of Birth: 1953
Education: Saint Louis U 1979 BA; Missouri (Kansas City) 1983 JD
Appointed By: President Barack Obama
Political Affiliation: Democrat

Chambers of District Judge Ronnie L. White *continued*

Staff
Judicial Assistant **Monica Moreland** . . . . (314) 244-7580

Chambers of Senior Judge Edward L. Filippine

Thomas F. Eagleton U.S. Courthouse, 111 South Tenth Street, 10th Floor, St. Louis, MO 63102
Tel: (314) 244-7640 Fax: (314) 244-7909
E-mail: edward_filippine@moed.uscourts.gov

Edward L. Filippine
Senior Judge

Date of Birth: 1930
Education: Saint Louis U 1951 AB, 1957 JD
Began Service: August 1977
Appointed By: President Jimmy Carter

Government: Special Assistant, Office of the Attorney General, State of Missouri (1963-1964); Staff Assistant (D-MO), Office of Senator Thomas F. Eagleton, United States Senate (1969-1974); Campaign Director, Thomas F. Eagleton for United States Senate (1974)

Military Service: United States Air Force (1951-1953)

Current Memberships: American Bar Association; The Bar Association of Metropolitan St. Louis; Lawyers Association of St. Louis; The Missouri Bar

Chambers of Senior Judge E. Richard Webber, Jr.

Thomas F. Eagleton U.S. Courthouse, 111 South Tenth Street, Suite 8 South, St. Louis, MO 63102
Tel: (314) 244-7460 Fax: (314) 244-7469
E-mail: Richard_Webber@moed.uscourts.gov

E. Richard Webber, Jr.
Senior Judge

Date of Birth: 1942
Education: Missouri 1964 BS, 1967 JD
Began Service: December 26, 1995
Appointed By: President William J. Clinton

Government: Prosecuting Attorney, Office of the Prosecuting Attorney, County of Schuyler, Missouri (1967-1975); Prosecuting Attorney, Office of the Prosecuting Attorney, County of Putnam, Missouri; Prosecuting Attorney, Office of the Prosecuting Attorney, County of Scotland, Missouri (1969-1971)

Judicial: Judge, Missouri Circuit Court, First Judicial Circuit (1979-1995)

Legal Practice: E. Richard Webber, Attorney at Law (1967-1971); Webber and Green (1971-1975); E. Richard Webber, Attorney at Law (1975-1979)

Current Memberships: American Bar Association; The Missouri Bar

Staff
Law Clerk **Peter Cosgrove** . . . . (314) 244-7465
Began Service: September 4, 2015
Term Expires: August 29, 2016
E-mail: peter_cosgrove@moed.uscourts.gov
Law Clerk **Melissa Cullman** . . . . (314) 244-7465
Began Service: October 1, 2014
Term Expires: September 30, 2016
E-mail: melissa_cullman@moed.uscourts.gov

Chambers of Senior Judge Jean C. Hamilton

Thomas F. Eagleton U.S. Courthouse, 111 South Tenth Street, Room 16.148, St. Louis, MO 63102
Tel: (314) 244-7600
E-mail: jean_hamilton@moed.uscourts.gov

Jean C. Hamilton
Senior Judge

Date of Birth: 1945
Education: Wellesley 1968 AB; Washington U (MO) 1971 JD; Yale 1982 LLM
Began Service: November 1990
Appointed By: President George H.W. Bush

Current Memberships: American Bar Association; The American Law Institute; The Bar Association of Metropolitan St. Louis; Federal Judges Association; Lawyers Association of St. Louis; The Missouri Bar; National Association of Women Judges; Women Lawyers' Association of Greater St. Louis

Staff
Law Clerk **Jason Schneider** .... (314) 244-7600
Career Law Clerk **Elizabeth Snidman** .... (314) 244-7600
E-mail: elizabeth_snidman@moed.uscourts.gov
Education: Washington U (MO) 1993 JD
Court Reporter **Debbie Kriegshauser** .... (314) 244-7449
Judicial Assistant **Beverly S. Goff** .... (314) 244-7600
E-mail: beverly_goff@moed.uscourts.gov

Chambers of Senior Judge Charles A. Shaw

Thomas F. Eagleton U.S. Courthouse, 111 South Tenth Street, Suite 8.148, St. Louis, MO 63102
Tel: (314) 244-7480 Fax: (314) 244-7489

Charles A. Shaw
Senior Judge

Date of Birth: 1944
Education: Harris-Stowe State 1966 BA; Missouri 1971 MBA; Columbus Law 1974 JD
Began Service: January 3, 1994
Appointed By: President William J. Clinton

Current Memberships: The Bar Association of Metropolitan St. Louis; The District of Columbia Bar; Lawyers Association of St. Louis; The Missouri Bar; Mound City Bar Association

Staff
Career Law Clerk **Susan Heider** .... (314) 244-7480
E-mail: susan_heider@moed.uscourts.gov
Education: Kansas 1984 JD
Career Law Clerk **Maggie B. Peters** .... (314) 244-7480
Began Service: 2007
E-mail: maggie_peters@moed.uscourts.gov
Education: Indiana 1999 JD
Career Law Clerk **Lynn Reid** .... (314) 244-7480
E-mail: lynn_reid@moed.uscourts.gov
Education: Grinnell 1994; Iowa 2000 JD
Court Reporter **Susan "Sue" Moran** .... (314) 244-7983
E-mail: susan_moran@moed.uscourts.gov Fax: (314) 244-7489
Judicial Assistant **Linda Errante Wehner** .... (314) 244-7480
E-mail: linda_errante@moed.uscourts.gov

Chambers of Chief Magistrate Judge Thomas C. Mummert III

Thomas F. Eagleton U.S. Courthouse, 111 South Tenth Street, St. Louis, MO 63102
Tel: (314) 244-7510 Fax: (314) 244-7519
E-mail: thomas_mummert@moed.uscourts.gov

Thomas C. Mummert III
Chief Magistrate Judge

Education: Dayton 1973 BA; St Mary's U (TX) 1976 JD
Began Service: May 15, 1995
Term Expires: 2019

Current Memberships: Legal Advocates for Abused Women

Staff
Career Law Clerk **Anne V. Maloney** .... (314) 244-7510
E-mail: anne_maloney@moed.uscourts.gov
Education: UC Davis 1971 BA; Emory 1972 MLN; Saint Louis U 1978 JD
Law Clerk/Judicial Assistant **Bonnie M. Day** .... (314) 244-7510
E-mail: bonnie_day@moed.uscourts.gov
Education: Smith 1976 BA; Washington U (MO) 1981 JD, 1981 MSW
Judicial Assistant (Part-Time) **Corinne E. Cohen** .... (314) 244-7510
E-mail: corinne_cohen@moed.uscourts.gov

Chambers of Magistrate Judge David D. Noce

Thomas F. Eagleton U.S. Courthouse, 111 South Tenth Street, Suite 17.156, St. Louis, MO 63102
Tel: (314) 244-7630 Fax: (314) 244-7639
E-mail: david_noce@moed.uscourts.gov

David D. Noce
Magistrate Judge

Date of Birth: 1944
Education: Saint Louis U 1966 AB; Missouri 1969 JD
Began Service: October 1, 1976
Term Expires: September 30, 2016

Academic: Adjunct Professor, St. Louis University School of Law; Adjunct Professor, Washington University School of Law

Clerkships: Law Clerk The Honorable H. Kenneth Wangelin, United States District Courts for the Eastern and Western Districts of Missouri (1972-1973); Law Clerk The Honorable John F. Nangle, United States District Court for the Eastern District of Missouri (1973-1975)

Government: Assistant United States Attorney, Eastern District of Missouri, Office of the United States Attorney, United States Department of Justice (1975-1976)

Judicial: Member, Criminal Law Committee, Judicial Conference of the United States (1992-1998)

Military Service: United States Army (1970-1972)

Current Memberships: American Bar Association; The Bar Association of Metropolitan St. Louis; Federal Magistrate Judges Association; The Missouri Bar

Staff
Law Clerk **Rachel Kleinpeter** .... (314) 244-7630
E-mail: rachel_kleinpeter@moed.uscourts.gov
Career Law Clerk **Sheila Brennan** .... (314) 244-7630
E-mail: sheila_brennan@moed.uscourts.gov
Education: Michigan 1984 BA; Cleveland-Marshall 1989 JD

Chambers of Magistrate Judge Nannette A. Baker
Thomas F. Eagleton U.S. Courthouse, 111 South Tenth Street,
Suite 9.152, St. Louis, MO 63102
Tel: (314) 244-7470 Fax: (314) 244-7479
E-mail: nannette_baker@moed.uscourts.gov

Nannette A. Baker
Magistrate Judge

Education: Tennessee BS; Saint Louis U JD
Began Service: February 3, 2011

Staff
Law Clerk **Ebony McCain** . . . . (314) 244-7470
Began Service: 2012
E-mail: ebony_mccain@moed.uscourts.gov
Judicial Assistant **Emily Danker-Feldman** . . . . . . (314) 244-7470
E-mail: emily_danker-feldman@moed.uscourts.gov

Chambers of Magistrate Judge Shirley Padmore Mensah
Thomas F. Eagleton U.S. Courthouse, 111 South Tenth Street,
Suite 14.148, St. Louis, MO 63102
Tel: (314) 244-7490 Fax: (314) 244-7499
E-mail: shirley_mensah@moed.uscourts.gov

Shirley Padmore Mensah
Magistrate Judge

Began Service: 2012
Term Expires: 2020

Staff
Career Law Clerk **Jessica Golby** . . . . (314) 244-7490
E-mail: jessica_golby@moed.uscourts.gov
Judicial Assistant **Sally Keasler** . . . . (314) 244-7490
E-mail: sally_keasler@moed.uscourts.gov

Chambers of Magistrate Judge Noelle Collins
111 South Tenth Street, St. Louis, MO 63102
Tel: (314) 246-7570
E-mail: noelle_collins@moed.uscourts.gov

Noelle C. Collins
Magistrate Judge

Staff
Judicial Assistant **Margaret Guye** . . . . (314) 246-7570
E-mail: margaret_guye@moed.uscourts.gov

Chambers of Magistrate Judge John Bodenhausen
111 South Tenth Street, St. Louis, MO 63102
Tel: (314) 244-7900

John Bodenhausen
Magistrate Judge

Chambers of Magistrate Judge Abbie Crites-Leoni
555 Independence Street, Cape Girardeau, MO 63703
Tel: (573) 331-8870

Abbie Crites-Leoni
Magistrate Judge

Staff
Judicial Assistant **Connie Kenner** . . . . (573) 331-8870

United States Bankruptcy Court for the Eastern District of Missouri
Thomas F. Eagleton U.S. Courthouse, 111 South Tenth Street,
Room 4.380, St. Louis, MO 63102
Tel: (314) 244-4500 Tel: (314) 244-4601 (Clerk's office)
Tel: (800) 676-6856 (PACER)
Tel: (866) 222-8029 ext. 87 (McVIS) Fax: (314) 244-4990
Internet: www.moeb.uscourts.gov

Number of Judgeships: 3

Court Staff
Clerk of Court **Dana C. McWay** . . . . (314) 244-4601
Affiliation: RHIA; FAHIMA
E-mail: dana_mcway@ca8.uscourts.gov
Education: Saint Louis U 1982 BS, 1988 JD
Chief Deputy Clerk **Diana Durkee August** . . . . . . (314) 244-4602
E-mail: diana_durkee@ca8.uscourts.gov
Education: Eastern Illinois 1986 BS;
Webster 1996 MS
Administrative Manager **E.G. Phillips** . . . . (314) 244-4900
E-mail: eg_phillips@moeb.uscourts.gov
Information & Technology Systems Manager
William C. Wolfenbarger . . . . (314) 244-4700
E-mail: bill_wolfenbarger@ca8.uscourts.gov
Education: Tennessee 1977 BS;
Houston Baptist 1986 MS
Operations Manager **Donna E. Bard** . . . . (314) 244-4800
E-mail: donna_bard@ca8.uscourts.gov
Education: National-Louis 1997 MS
Human Resource Manager **Elizabeth Pfister** . . . . . (314) 244-4606
E-mail: beth_pfister@ca8.uscourts.gov
Education: Concordia Col (OR) 2006 BA

Chambers of Chief Bankruptcy Judge Kathy A. Surratt-States
Thomas F. Eagleton U.S. Courthouse, 111 South Tenth Street,
Suite 7 North, St. Louis, MO 63102
Tel: (314) 244-4541 Fax: (314) 244-4545
E-mail: kathy_surratt-states@ca8.uscourts.gov

Kathy A. Surratt-States
Chief Bankruptcy Judge

Date of Birth: January 4, 1967
Education: Oklahoma City 1988 BA; Washington U (MO) 1991 JD
Began Service: March 17, 2003
Term Expires: March 2017

Current Memberships: The Bar Association of Metropolitan St. Louis; The Missouri Bar; Mound City Bar Association

Staff
Law Clerk **Raychelle Tasher** . . . . (314) 244-4543
Began Service: October 2015
Term Expires: October 2017
E-mail: raychelle_tasher@moeb.uscourts.gov
Judicial Assistant **Chicquita Greene** . . . . (314) 244-4541
E-mail: Chicquita_Greene@ca8.uscourts.gov
Education: Saint Louis U 2001 BS;
Fontbonne Col 2003 MM

Chambers of Bankruptcy Judge Barry S. Schermer
Thomas F. Eagleton U.S. Courthouse, 111 South Tenth Street,
St. Louis, MO 63102
Tel: (314) 244-4531 Fax: (314) 244-4535

Barry S. Schermer
Bankruptcy Judge

Date of Birth: 1947
Education: Washington U (MO) 1973 JD
Began Service: 1986
Term Expires: October 14, 2028

(continued on next page)

Chambers of Bankruptcy Judge Barry S. Schermer *continued*

Staff

Career Law Clerk **Emily K. Cohen** .... (314) 244-4532
E-mail: emily_cohen@moeb.uscourts.gov
Education: Washington U (MO) 2000 JD

Judicial Assistant **(Vacant)** .... (314) 244-4531

Chambers of Bankruptcy Judge Charles E. Rendlen, III

Thomas F. Eagleton U.S. Courthouse, 111 South Tenth Street, Suite 7.159, St. Louis, MO 63102
Tel: (314) 244-4511 Fax: (314) 244-4515

Charles E. Rendlen III
Bankruptcy Judge

Education: William Jewell 1972 BS; Missouri 1976 JD
Began Service: May 2006
Term Expires: May 23, 2020

Government: U.S. Trustee, Region 13, Executive Office for United States Trustees, United States Department of Justice (2003-2006)

Legal Practice: Associate, The Rendlen Law Firm, P.C. (1976-1979); Partner, The Rendlen Law Firm, P.C. (1979-1991); Managing Partner, The Rendlen Law Firm, P.C. (1991-2003)

Staff

Career Law Clerk **Abigail B. Willie** .... (314) 244-4512
E-mail: abigail_willie@moeb.uscourts.gov
Education: Southern Methodist 2000 JD

Judicial Assistant **Eva R. Kinzel** .... (314) 244-4511
E-mail: eva_kinzel@moeb.uscourts.gov

United States District Court for the Western District of Missouri

Charles Evans Whittaker U.S. Courthouse, 400 East Ninth Street, Kansas City, MO 64106
Tel: (816) 512-5000 Fax: (816) 512-5078
Internet: www.mow.uscourts.gov
Internet: ecf.mowd.uscourts.gov (Electronic Case Filing)

Number of Judgeships: 6

Circuit: Eighth

Areas Covered: Counties of Andrew, Atchison, Barry, Barton, Bates, Benton, Boone, Buchanan, Caldwell, Callaway, Camden, Carroll, Cass, Cedar, Christian, Clay, Clinton, Cole, Cooper, Dade, Dallas, Daviess, DeKalb Douglas, Gentry, Greene, Grundy, Harrison, Henry, Hickory, Holt, Howard, Howell, Jackson, Jasper, Johnson, Laclede, Lafayette, Lawrence, Livingston, McDonald, Mercer, Miller, Moniteau, Morgan, Newton, Nodaway, Oregon, Osage, Ozark, Pettis, Platte, Polk, Pulaski, Putnam, Ray, Saline, St. Clair, Stone, Sullivan, Taney, Texas, Vernon, Webster, Worth and Wright

Court Staff

Clerk of Court/Court Executive (Acting)
Paige Wymore-Wynn .... (816) 512-5000
Education: Emporia State 1982 BS

Divisional Manager - Jefferson City **Laura Bax** .... (573) 636-4015
U.S. Courthouse, 80 Lafayette Street, Jefferson City, MO 65101 Fax: (573) 636-3456
E-mail: laura_bax@mow.uscourts.gov

Divisional Manager - Springfield **Karyn Williams** .... (417) 865-3869
U.S. Courthouse, 222 N. John Q. Hammons Pkwy., Springfield, MO 65806 Fax: (417) 865-7719
E-mail: karyn_williams@mow.uscourts.gov

Chief Administrative Officer **Paige Wymore-Wynn** ...... (816) 512-5075
E-mail: paige_wymore-wynn@mow.uscourts.gov Fax: (816) 512-5079

Chief Operations Officer **Randall Henderson** .... (816) 512-1851
E-mail: randall_henderson@mow.uscourts.gov Fax: (816) 512-5079

Chief Probation/Pretrial Services Officer **Kevin F. Lyon** ... (816) 512-1300
E-mail: kevin_lyon@mow.uscourts.gov Fax: (816) 512-1313

United States District Court for the Western District of Missouri *continued*

Procurement Officer **Steve Alexopoulos** .... (816) 512-5070
E-mail: steve_alexopoulos@mow.uscourts.gov

Financial Administrator **Laura Schwaller** .... (816) 512-5065
E-mail: laura_schwaller@mow.uscourts.gov Fax: (816) 512-5076

Librarian **Kathryn Winfrey** .... (816) 512-5790
Fax: (816) 512-5799

Human Resource Specialist **Michele Nelson** .... (816) 512-5036
E-mail: michele_nelson@mow.uscourts.gov Fax: (816) 512-5034

Chambers of Chief Judge David Gregory Kays

Charles Evans Whittaker U.S. Courthouse, 400 East Ninth Street, Room 8652, Kansas City, MO 64106
Tel: (816) 512-5600 Fax: (816) 512-5743
E-mail: greg_kays@mow.uscourts.gov

David Gregory Kays
Chief Judge

Education: Southwest Missouri State 1985 BS; Arkansas 1987 JD
Began Service: June 19, 2008
Appointed By: President George W. Bush

Staff

Law Clerk **Steve Platt** .... (816) 512-5603
Began Service: August 2015
Term Expires: August 2016

Law Clerk **Austin Van Tine** .... (816) 512-5603
Began Service: August 2015
Term Expires: August 2016
E-mail: austin_vantine@mow.uscourts.gov

Career Law Clerk **Jonathan H. Lehr** .... (816) 512-5606
E-mail: jonathan_lehr@mow.uscourts.gov
Education: Amherst 1992 BA; Georgetown 2001 JD

Courtroom Deputy **Alexandra Francis** .... (816) 512-5629
E-mail: alexandra_francis@mow.uscourts.gov

Court Reporter **Regina McBride** .... (816) 512-5623
E-mail: regina_mcbride@mow.uscourts.gov

Judicial Assistant **Tracy Strodtman** .... (816) 512-5600
E-mail: tracy_strodtman@mow.uscourts.gov

Chambers of District Judge Gary A. Fenner

Charles Evans Whittaker U.S. Courthouse, 400 East Ninth Street, Room 8452, Kansas City, MO 64106-2607
Tel: (816) 512-5660 Fax: (816) 512-5673
E-mail: gary_fenner@mow.uscourts.gov

Gary A. Fenner
District Judge

Date of Birth: 1947
Education: Kansas 1970 BA; Missouri (Kansas City) 1973 JD
Began Service: July 26, 1996
Appointed By: President William J. Clinton

Academic: Business Law Instructor (part-time), Webster College (1976-1977)

Government: Assistant City Attorney, Office of the City Attorney, City of Saint Joseph, Missouri (1973-1977); Councilman, Office of the City Council, City of Saint Joseph, Missouri (1977-1978)

Judicial: Judge, Missouri Circuit Court, Fifth Judicial Circuit (1979-1988); Judge, Missouri Court of Appeals, Western District (1988-1996)

Legal Practice: Associate of Daniel M. Czamanske, Attorney at Law (1973); Partner, Shoemaker, Summers and Fenner (1977-1978)

Current Memberships: American Bar Association; Clay County Bar Association; Kansas City Metropolitan Bar Association; The Missouri Bar; Platte County Bar Association

Staff

Court Reporter **Kathy Calvert** .... (816) 512-5741
E-mail: kathy_calvert@mow.uscourts.gov

Chambers of District Judge Gary A. Fenner *continued*

Judicial Assistant **Lisa Mitchell** . . . . (816) 512-5660
E-mail: lisa.mitchell@mow.uscourts.gov

Chambers of District Judge Mary Elizabeth Phillips

400 East Ninth Street, Room 7452, Kansas City, MO 64106
Tel: (816) 512-5384 Fax: (816) 512-5388

Mary Elizabeth "Beth" Phillips
District Judge

Education: Chicago 1991 BA, 1992 MA; Missouri 1996 JD
Began Service: March 23, 2012
Appointed By: President Barack Obama

Staff
Law Clerk **Darin Shreves** . . . . (816) 512-5382
E-mail: darin_shreves@mow.uscourts.gov
Education: Missouri 2011 JD
Law Clerk **Jackie Whipple** . . . . (816) 512-5383
Courtroom Deputy **Kelly McIlvain** . . . . (816) 512-5744
E-mail: kelly_mcilvain@mow.uscourts.gov
Judicial Assistant **Annette Cordell** . . . . (816) 512-5384
E-mail: annette_cordell@mow.uscourts.gov

Chambers of District Judge Brian C. Wimes

Charles Evans Whittaker U.S. Courthouse, 400 East Ninth Street, Room 7652, Kansas City, MO 64106
Tel: (816) 512-5391 Fax: (816) 512-5078
E-mail: brian_wimes@mow.uscourts.gov

Brian C. Wimes
District Judge

Education: Kansas 1990 BGS; Texas Southern 1994 JD
Began Service: 2012
Appointed By: President Barack Obama

Staff
Law Clerk **Maggie Boyd** . . . . (816) 512-5392
E-mail: maggie_boyd@mow.uscourts.gov
Law Clerk **Matt Sparks** . . . . (816) 512-5393
E-mail: matt_sparks@mow.uscourts.gov
Judicial Assistant **Claudia Wells** . . . . (816) 512-5391
E-mail: claudia_wells@mow.uscourts.gov
Courtroom Deputy **Joella Baldwin** . . . . (816) 512-5052
E-mail: joella_baldwin@mow.uscourts.gov
Court Reporter **Katie Wirt** . . . . (816) 512-5657
E-mail: katie_wirt@mow.uscourts.gov

Chambers of District Judge M. Douglas Harpool

222 North John Q. Hammons Parkway, Suite 3100, Springfield, MO 65806
Tel: (417) 865-3741

M. Douglas Harpool
District Judge

Education: Missouri State U 1977 BS; Missouri 1990 JD
Began Service: March 28, 2014
Appointed By: President Barack Obama
Political Affiliation: Democrat

Staff
Law Clerk **Kristen Roubal** . . . . (417) 865-3741
E-mail: kristen_roubal@mow.uscourts.gov
Law Clerk **Breanna Hance** . . . . (417) 865-3741
E-mail: breanna_hance@mow.uscourts.gov
Court Reporter **Jeannine Rankin** . . . . (417) 865-3741
E-mail: jeannine_rankin@mow.uscourts.gov
Courtroom Deputy **Linda Howard** . . . . (417) 225-7704
E-mail: linda_howard@mow.uscourts.gov

Chambers of District Judge M. Douglas Harpool *continued*

Judicial Assistant **Patricia View** . . . . (417) 225-7711
E-mail: patricia_view@mow.uscourts.gov

Chambers of District Judge Stephen R. Bough

400 East Ninth Street, Room 7462, Kansas City, MO 64106
Tel: (816) 512-5370

Stephen R. Bough
District Judge

Education: Missouri State U 1993 BS; Missouri (Kansas City) 1997 JD
Began Service: 2014
Appointed By: President Barack Obama

Staff
Law Clerk **Amber Sholes** . . . . (816) 512-5370
Law Clerk **Joselyn Verschelden** . . . . (816) 512-5370
Courtroom Deputy **Tracy Diefenbach** . . . . (816) 512-5055
Judicial Assistant **Gloria Amos** . . . . (816) 512-5372

Chambers of District Judge Roseann A. Ketchmark

400 East Ninth Street, Kansas City, MO 64106
Tel: (816) 512-5000

Roseann A. Ketchmark
District Judge

Note: On September 9, 2015, the Senate confirmed Roseann A. Ketchmark to be District Judge for the United States District Court for the Western District of Missouri.
Education: Oklahoma 1986 BN; Kansas 1990 JD

Chambers of Senior Judge Howard F. Sachs

Charles Evans Whittaker U.S. Courthouse, 400 East Ninth Street, Room 7462, Kansas City, MO 64106
Tel: (816) 512-5715 Fax: (816) 512-5728
E-mail: howard_sachs@mow.uscourts.gov

Howard F. Sachs
Senior Judge

Date of Birth: 1925
Education: Williams 1947 AB; Harvard 1950 JD
Began Service: October 5, 1979
Appointed By: President Jimmy Carter

Clerkships: Law Clerk The Honorable Albert A. Ridge, United States District Court (1950-1951)

Legal Practice: Associate, Phineas Rosenberg (1951-1956); Associate, Spencer Fane Britt & Browne LLP

Military Service: United States Navy (1944-1946)

Current Memberships: American Bar Association; Kansas City Metropolitan Bar Association; Lawyers Association of Kansas City; The Missouri Bar

Staff
Career Law Clerk **Susan Campbell** . . . . (816) 512-5715
E-mail: susan_campbell@mow.uscourts.gov
Chief of Staff **Karen H. Graves** . . . . (816) 512-5715
E-mail: karen_graves@mow.uscourts.gov
Education: St John's U (NY) 1997 JD
Courtroom Deputy **Tina Duer** . . . . (816) 512-5614
E-mail: tina_duer@mow.uscourts.gov
Court Reporter **(Vacant)** . . . . (816) 512-5726
Judicial Assistant **Karen H. Graves** . . . . (816) 512-5715
E-mail: karen_graves@mow.uscourts.gov

Chambers of Senior Judge Dean Whipple

Charles Evans Whittaker U.S. Courthouse, 400 East Ninth Street, Room 8462, Kansas City, MO 64106
Tel: (816) 512-5615 Fax: (816) 512-5628
E-mail: dean_whipple@mow.uscourts.gov

Dean Whipple
Senior Judge

Date of Birth: 1938
Education: Drury Col 1961 BS; Missouri (Kansas City) 1965 JD
Began Service: December 1987
Appointed By: President Ronald Reagan

Government: Prosecuting Attorney, Office of the Prosecuting Attorney, County of Laclede, Missouri (1967-1971)

Judicial: Circuit Judge, Missouri Circuit Court, Division II, 26th Judicial Circuit (1975-1987); Chief Judge, United States District Court for the Western District of Missouri (2000-2007)

Military Service: Missouri National Guard (1956-1961); United States Army Reserve, United States Department of the Army (1961-1966)

Current Memberships: The Kansas City - Ross T. Roberts American Inn of Court; American Bar Association; Kansas City Metropolitan Bar Association; Laclede County Bar Association; The Missouri Bar; Missouri Trial Judges Association

Staff

Law Clerk **Dan Ostaszewski** .... (816) 512-5615
E-mail: dan_ostaszewski@mow.uscourts.gov
Career Law Clerk **Benjamin T. Clark** .... (816) 512-5615
E-mail: ben_clark@mow.uscourts.gov
Education: Iowa 2001 JD
Courtroom Deputy **Terri Moore** .... (816) 512-5674
E-mail: terri_moore@mow.uscourts.gov
Court Reporter **Denna Lamken** .... (816) 512-5622
E-mail: denna_lamken@mow.uscourts.gov
Judicial Assistant **Kathy Sage Willis** .... (816) 512-5621
E-mail: kathy_willis@mow.uscourts.gov

Chambers of Senior Judge Ortrie D. Smith

Charles Evans Whittaker U.S. Courthouse, 400 East Ninth Street, Room 8552, Kansas City, MO 64106
Tel: (816) 512-5645 Fax: (816) 512-5658
E-mail: ortrie_smith@mow.uscourts.gov

Ortrie D. Smith
Senior Judge

Date of Birth: 1946
Education: Missouri BA, JD
Began Service: August 1995
Appointed By: President William J. Clinton

Staff

Law Clerk **Anne Hucker** .... (816) 512-5645
Began Service: September 2014
Term Expires: September 2016
Career Law Clerk **Julia Kitsmiller** .... (816) 512-5645
E-mail: julia_kitsmiller@mow.uscourts.gov
Education: Missouri (Kansas City) 2002 JD
Courtroom Deputy **Renea Matthes** .... (816) 512-5689
E-mail: renea_matthes@mow.uscourts.gov
Court Reporter **Gayle Wambolt** .... (816) 512-5657
E-mail: gayle_wambolt@mow.uscourts.gov
Secretary **Karen A. Hopkins** .... (816) 512-5645
E-mail: karen_hopkins@mow.uscourts.gov

Chambers of Senior Judge Nanette Kay Laughrey

80 Lafayette Street, Room 4112, Jefferson City, MO 65101
Tel: (573) 632-6623 Fax: (573) 636-5108
E-mail: nanette_laughrey@mow.uscourts.gov

Nanette Kay Laughrey
Senior Judge

Date of Birth: 1946
Education: UCLA 1967 BA; Missouri 1975 JD
Began Service: August 26, 1996
Appointed By: President William J. Clinton

Academic: Associate Professor of Law, University of Missouri School of Law (1983-1987); Professor of Law, University of Missouri School of Law (1987-1989); William H. Pittman Professor of Law, University of Missouri School of Law (1989-1996); Visiting Professor of Law, University of Iowa College of Law (1990)

Government: Volunteer, AmeriCorps Volunteers in Service to America, Corporation for National and Community Service (1969-1972); Assistant Attorney General, Office of the Attorney General, State of Missouri (1975-1979); Commissioner, Columbia Arts Commission, City of Columbia, Missouri (1986-1988); Commissioner, Housing Authority, City of Columbia, Missouri (1992-1998); Deputy Attorney General, Office of the Attorney General, State of Missouri (1992-1993)

Judicial: Judge, Municipal Court, City of Columbia, Missouri (1979-1983)

Legal Practice: Staff Attorney (part-time), Craig Van Matre, P.C. (1980-1983)

Nonprofit: Director, Voluntary Action Center (1972)

Current Memberships: American Bar Association; The American Law Institute; Association of Women Lawyers of Greater Kansas City; Kansas City Metropolitan Bar Association; The Missouri Bar

Staff

Law Clerk **Elizabeth Hatting** .... (573) 556-7542
E-mail: elizabeth_hatting@mow.uscourts.gov
Law Clerk **Daniel Rosenbaum** .... (573) 556-7547
Term Expires: August 2016
E-mail: daniel_rosenbaum@mow.uscourts.gov
Courtroom Deputy **Renea Matthes** .... (816) 512-5689
E-mail: renea_matthes@mow.uscourts.gov
Court Reporter **Kathleen Wirt** .... (816) 512-5608
Chief of Staff **Alana M. Barragán-Scott** .... (573) 632-6623
Education: Missouri 1985, 1990 JD

Chambers of Senior Judge Fernando J. Gaitan, Jr.

Charles Evans Whittaker U.S. Courthouse, 400 East Ninth Street, Room 7552, Kansas City, MO 64106
Tel: (816) 512-5630
E-mail: fernando_gaitan@mow.uscourts.gov

Fernando J. Gaitan, Jr.
Senior Judge

Date of Birth: 1948
Education: Pittsburg State 1970 BS; Missouri (Kansas City) 1974 JD
Began Service: 1991
Appointed By: President George H.W. Bush

Current Memberships: American Bar Foundation; Jackson County Bar Association; Kansas City Metropolitan Bar Association; The Missouri Bar

Staff

Court Reporter **Gayle Wambolt** .... (816) 512-5641
E-mail: gayle_wambolt@mow.uscourts.gov
Courtroom Deputy **Rhonda Enss** .... (816) 512-5644
E-mail: rhonda.enss@mow.uscourts.gov
Judicial Assistant **Marylynn Shawver** .... (816) 512-5630
E-mail: marylynn.shawver@mow.uscourts.gov

Chambers of Chief Magistrate Judge Sarah Hays
Charles Evans Whittaker U.S. Courthouse, 400 East Ninth Street,
Kansas City, MO 64106
Tel: (816) 512-5775 Fax: (816) 512-5788
E-mail: sarah_hays@mow.uscourts.gov

Sarah Hays
Chief Magistrate Judge

Education: LSU 1977 JD
Began Service: 1992
Term Expires: February 2016

Staff
Career Law Clerk **Suzanne L. Bliss** .... (816) 512-5777
E-mail: suzanne.bliss@mow.uscourts.gov
Judicial Assistant **Stacy O'Connor** .... (816) 512-5775
E-mail: stacy.oconnor@mow.uscourts.gov

Chambers of Magistrate Judge Robert E. Larsen
Charles Evans Whittaker U.S. Courthouse, 400 East Ninth Street,
Kansas City, MO 64106
Tel: (816) 512-5760 Fax: (816) 512-5773
E-mail: robert_larsen@mow.uscourts.gov

Robert E. Larsen
Magistrate Judge

Date of Birth: 1946
Education: Rockhurst Col 1969 BA; Missouri (Kansas City) 1973 JD
Began Service: May 24, 1991
Term Expires: May 24, 2023

Current Memberships: The Missouri Bar

Staff
Career Law Clerk **Carol Wilson** .... (816) 512-5760
E-mail: carol_wilson@mow.uscourts.gov
Education: Missouri (St Louis) 1988 BS;
Missouri (Kansas City) 1991 JD
Career Law Clerk **Rebecca Suroff** .... (816) 512-5763
E-mail: rebecca_suroff@mow.uscourts.gov
Education: Kansas State 1999 BA;
Missouri (Kansas City) 2004 JD
Courtroom Deputy **Dorothy Myers** .... (816) 512-5774
E-mail: dorothy_myers@mow.uscourts.gov

Chambers of Magistrate Judge John T. Maughmer
Charles Evans Whittaker U.S. Courthouse, 400 East Ninth Street,
Room 7662, Kansas City, MO 64106
Tel: (816) 512-5745 Fax: (816) 512-5758
E-mail: john_maughmer@mow.uscourts.gov

John T. Maughmer
Magistrate Judge

Date of Birth: 1954
Education: Missouri 1977 BS, 1980 JD
Began Service: September 29, 1988
Term Expires: September 30, 2020

Clerkships: Law Clerk The Honorable Elmo B. Hunter, United States District Court for the Western District of Missouri (1980-1982)

Judicial: Chief Magistrate Judge, United States District Court for the Western District of Missouri (1991-2005)

Legal Practice: Lathrop, Koontz & Norquist (1982-1988)

Staff
Career Law Clerk **Pam Alexander** .... (816) 512-5745
E-mail: Pamela.Alexander@mow.uscourts.gov
Education: Missouri (Kansas City) 1988 JD
Courtroom Deputy **Kerry Martinez** .... (816) 512-5759
E-mail: kerry_martinez@mow.uscourts.gov
Education: Baker U 1997 BS

Chambers of Magistrate Judge John T. Maughmer *continued*

Judicial Assistant **Sandy Rollheiser** .... (816) 512-5745
E-mail: Sandy.Rollheiser@mow.uscourts.gov

Chambers of Magistrate Judge Matt J. Whitworth
80 Lafayette Street, Suite 3114, Jefferson City, MO 65101
Tel: (573) 634-3418
E-mail: matt_whitworth@mow.uscourts.gov

Matt J. Whitworth
Magistrate Judge

Date of Birth: 1958
Education: Baker U 1980; Arkansas 1983 JD
Began Service: January 24, 2010

Staff
Career Law Clerk **Heather Richenberger** .... (573) 556-7553
E-mail: heather_richenberger@mow.uscourts.gov
Education: Sam Houston State 1995 BS;
Missouri 2001 JD
Courtroom Deputy **Jackie Price** .... (573) 556-7561
E-mail: jackie_price@mow.uscourts.gov
Judicial Assistant **Kay Bode** .... (573) 556-7551
E-mail: kay_bode@mow.uscourts.gov

Chambers of Magistrate Judge David P. Rush
222 N. John Q. Hammons Parkway, Suite 2000, Springfield, MO 65806
Tel: (417) 865-3761
E-mail: david_rush@mow.uscourts.gov

David P. Rush
Magistrate Judge

Education: Missouri State U 1983 BS; Iowa 1986 JD

Staff
Career Law Clerk **Holly Stone** .... (417) 225-7722
E-mail: holly_stone@mow.uscourts.gov
Education: Washington U (MO) 2001 JD
Judicial Assistant **Karla Berziel** .... (417) 865-3761
E-mail: karla_berziel@mow.uscourts.gov
Courtroom Deputy **Glenda Elayer** .... (417) 225-7723

United States Bankruptcy Court for the Western District of Missouri
Charles Evans Whittaker U.S. Courthouse, 400 East Ninth Street,
Kansas City, MO 64106
Tel: (816) 512-1800
Tel: (816) 512-5110 (Voice Case Information System VCIS)
Tel: (888) 205-2527 (Toll Free Voice Case Information System VCIS)
Fax: (816) 512-1832
Internet: www.mow.uscourts.gov
Internet: ecf.mowb.uscourts.gov (Electronic Case Filing)

Number of Judgeships: 3

Court Staff
Court Executive (Acting) **Paige Wymore-Wynn** .... (816) 512-5000
Chief, Procurement **Steve Alexopoulos** .... (816) 512-5070
E-mail: steve_alexopoulos@mow.uscourts.gov Fax: (816) 512-5079
Financial Administrator **Laura Schwaller** .... (816) 512-5065
E-mail: laura_schwaller@mow.uscourts.gov Fax: (816) 512-5076
Chief Administrative Officer **Paige Wymore-Wynn** ...... (816) 512-5075
E-mail: paige_wymore-wynn@mow.uscourts.gov Fax: (816) 512-5079
Chief Operations Officer **Randall Henderson** .... (816) 512-1851
E-mail: randall_henderson@mow.uscourts.gov Fax: (816) 512-5079

FEDERAL COURTS—UNITED STATES DISTRICT COURTS

Chambers of Chief Bankruptcy Judge Arthur Federman

Charles Evans Whittaker U.S. Courthouse, 400 East Ninth Street, Room 6552, Kansas City, MO 64106
Tel: (816) 512-1910 Fax: (816) 512-1923
E-mail: arthur.federman@mow.uscourts.gov

Arthur Federman
Chief Bankruptcy Judge

Date of Birth: 1951
Education: Kansas 1973 BA; Missouri (Kansas City) 1976 JD
Began Service: December 18, 1989
Term Expires: December 17, 2017

Staff
Career Law Clerk **Erica Garrett** . . . . (816) 512-1910
E-mail: erica_garrett@mow.uscourts.gov
Education: Missouri (Kansas City) 1993 JD
Courtroom Deputy **Sharon Stanley** . . . . (816) 512-1924
E-mail: sharon_stanley@mow.uscourts.gov
Judicial Assistant **Joan D. Brown** . . . . (816) 512-1911
E-mail: joan_brown@mow.uscourts.gov

Chambers of Bankruptcy Judge Dennis R. Dow

400 East Ninth Street, Room 6562, Kansas City, MO 64106
Tel: (816) 512-1880
E-mail: dennis_dow@mow.uscourts.gov

Dennis R. Dow
Bankruptcy Judge

Education: Wyoming 1975 BA; Washburn 1978 JD
Began Service: November 10, 2003

Current Memberships: American Bar Association; Kansas City Metropolitan Bar Association

Staff
Career Law Clerk **Lori Locke** . . . . (816) 512-1886
E-mail: lori_locke@mow.uscourts.gov
Education: Kansas 1999 JD
Career Law Clerk **Sharon Loftspring** . . . . (816) 512-1885
E-mail: sharon_loftspring@mow.uscourts.gov
Courtroom Deputy **Kim Anson** . . . . (816) 512-1894
E-mail: kim_anson@mow.uscourts.gov
Judicial Assistant **Kerry Brown** . . . . (816) 512-1880
E-mail: kerry_brown@mow.uscourts.gov

Chambers of Bankruptcy Judge Cynthia A. Norton

400 East Ninth Street, Kansas City, MO 64106

Cynthia Norton
Bankruptcy Judge

United States District Court for the District of Montana

Missouri River Courthouse, 125 Central Avenue West, Great Falls, MT 59404
Tel: (406) 727-1922 Tel: (406) 452-9581 (Civil Cases PACER)
Tel: (800) 305-5235 (Toll Free Civil Cases PACER) Fax: (406) 727-7648

Number of Judgeships: 3

Circuit: Ninth

Court Staff

Clerk of Court **Tyler Gilman** . . . . (406) 542-7260
E-mail: tyler_gilman@mtd.uscourts.gov
Education: Texas 2003 JD

United States District Court for the District of Montana *continued*

Automation Manager **Cecil Chandler** . . . . (406) 247-4493
E-mail: cecil_chandler@mtd.uscourts.gov Fax: (406) 247-7013
Chief Financial Officer **(Vacant)** . . . . (406) 542-7278
E-mail: lynn_anderson@mtd.uscourts.gov
Chief Probation Officer **Tom Holter** . . . . (406) 542-7105
201 East Broadway, Missoula, MT 59802 Fax: (406) 542-7119
E-mail: tom_holter@mtp.uscourts.gov
Librarian **Lucille Fercho** . . . . (406) 657-5970
E-mail: lucille_fercho@lb9.uscourts.gov Fax: (406) 657-5971

Chambers of Chief Judge Dana L. Christensen

201 East Broadway, Missoula, MT 59802
Tel: (406) 829-7140 Fax: (406) 542-7284

Dana L. Christensen
Chief Judge

Education: Stanford 1973 BA; Montana 1976 JD
Began Service: December 6, 2011
Appointed By: President Barack Obama

Staff
Law Clerk **John Newman** . . . . (406) 829-7140
Term Expires: August 2016
Judicial Assistant **Deborah Etheridge** . . . . (406) 829-7140

Chambers of District Judge Brian Morris

125 Central Avenue West, Great Falls, MT 59404
Tel: (406) 727-7800

Brian Morris
District Judge

Date of Birth: September 1963
Education: Stanford 1986 BA, 1987 MA
Began Service: December 18, 2013
Appointed By: President Barack Obama

Clerkships: Law Clerk William H. Rehnquist, Supreme Court of the United States

Government: Solicitor, Office of the Attorney General, State of Montana (2001)

Judicial: Justice, Montana Supreme Court (2004-2013)

Staff
Judicial Assistant **Sara Luoma** . . . . (406) 727-8877

Chambers of District Judge Susan P. Watters

2601 2nd Avenue North, Room 1200, Billings, MT 59101
Tel: (406) 247-2350

Susan P. Watters
District Judge

Education: Eastern Montana 1980 BA; Montana 1988 JD
Began Service: December 19, 2013
Appointed By: President Barack Obama

Staff
Law Clerk **Colin Gerstner** . . . . (406) 727-2350
Career Law Clerk **Sabrina Manning** . . . . (406) 727-2350
Judicial Assistant **Laura Reyes** . . . . (406) 727-2350

Chambers of Senior Judge Charles C. Lovell

U.S. Courthouse, 901 Front Street, Suite 3100, Helena, MT 59626
Tel: (406) 441-1350 Fax: (406) 441-1352
E-mail: charles_lovell@mtd.uscourts.gov

Charles C. Lovell
Senior Judge

Date of Birth: 1929
Education: Montana 1952 BS, 1959 JD
Began Service: April 1985
Appointed By: President Ronald Reagan

Government: Chief Counsel, Appellate Division, Office of the Attorney General, State of Montana (1969-1972)

Judicial: District Judge, United States District Court for the District of Montana (1985-2000)

Legal Practice: Church, Harris, Johnson & Williams (1959-1985)

Military Service: United States Air Force (1952-1954)

Current Memberships: American Association for Justice; American Bar Association; American College of Mortgage Attorneys; Cascade County Bar Association; Montana Defense Counsel Association; Montana Trial Lawyers Association; State Bar of Montana

Staff

Career Law Clerk **Margaret Bentwood** . . . . (406) 441-1350
E-mail: margaret_bentwood@mtd.uscourts.gov
Education: Montana 1993 JD

Administrative Assistant **Jean Smith** . . . . (406) 441-1350
E-mail: jean_smith@mtd.uscourts.gov
Education: Montana 1983 MBA

Chambers of Senior Judge Donald W. Molloy

Russell Smith Federal Building, 201 East Broadway, Missoula, MT 59802
Tel: (406) 542-7286 Fax: (406) 542-7284
E-mail: donald_molloy@mtd.uscourts.gov

Donald W. Molloy
Senior Judge

Date of Birth: 1946
Education: Montana 1968 BA, 1976 JD
Began Service: August 16, 1996
Appointed By: President William J. Clinton

Current Memberships: Aircraft Owners & Pilots Association; American Association of Justice; American Bar Association; American Board of Trial Advocates; American College of Trial Lawyers; The American Law Institute; The American Legion; Montana Trial Lawyers Association; Pennsylvania Trial Lawyers Association; Roscoe Pound American Trial Lawyers Foundation; State Bar of Montana

Staff

Law Clerk **Stephanie Holstein** . . . . (406) 542-7286
Began Service: September 2, 2014
Term Expires: August 29, 2016
Education: Montana 2013 JD

Law Clerk **Samantha Stephens** . . . . (406) 542-7286
Began Service: August 2013
Term Expires: August 2017
Education: Montana JD

Court Reporter **(Vacant)** . . . . (406) 829-7123
Fax: (406) 542-7284

Judicial Assistant **Deborah Ethridge** . . . . (406) 542-7286
E-mail: deborah_ethridge@mtd.uscourts.gov

Chambers of Senior Judge Sam E. Haddon

Paul G. Hatfield Courthouse, 901 Front Street, Suite 3100A, Helena, MT 59626
Tel: (406) 457-4910

Sam E. Haddon
Senior Judge

Date of Birth: 1937
Education: Rice 1959 BS; Montana 1965 JD
Began Service: July 26, 2001
Appointed By: President George W. Bush

Current Memberships: American Bar Foundation; American Academy of Appellate Lawyers; American Bar Association; American Board of Trial Advocates; American College of Trial Lawyers; The American Law Institute; National Institute of Trial Advocacy; State Bar of Montana

Staff

Law Clerk **Ryan G. Hennen** . . . . (406) 727-8877
Term Expires: September 2016

Law Clerk **Katelyn Hepburn** . . . . (406) 727-8877
Term Expires: September 2016

Court Reporter **(Vacant)** . . . . (406) 454-7805

Judicial Administrative Assistant **Lisa J. Ferkovich** . . . . . . (406) 457-4910
E-mail: lisa_ferkovich@mtd.uscourts.gov

Chambers of Magistrate Judge Carolyn S. Ostby

James F. Battin United States Courthouse, 2601 2nd Avenue North, Billings, MT 59101
Tel: (406) 247-7025 Fax: (406) 247-7027
E-mail: Carolyn_Ostby@mtd.uscourts.gov

Carolyn S. Ostby
Magistrate Judge

Date of Birth: 1951
Education: Macalester 1972 BA; Montana 1977 JD
Began Service: February 2002
Term Expires: February 22, 2018

Clerkships: Law Clerk, Chief Judge The Honorable Russell E. Smith, United District Court for the District of Montana (1977-1979)

Government: Attorney-Advisor, Office of Legal Counsel, United States Department of Justice (1979-1981)

Legal Practice: Partner, Crowley, Haughey, Hanson, Toole & Dietrich, P.L.L.P. (1980-2001)

Current Memberships: American Bar Foundation; American Bar Association; American College of Trial Lawyers; Cascade County Bar Association; State Bar of Montana

Staff

Law Clerk **Pamela Garman** . . . . (406) 247-7025
Began Service: August 2014
Term Expires: August 2016
E-mail: pamela_garman@mtd.uscourts.gov

Career Law Clerk **James Conwell** . . . . (406) 247-7025
Began Service: September 1994
E-mail: James_Conwell@mtd.uscourts.gov
Education: Montana 1986 BA, 1994 JD

Chambers of Magistrate Judge Jeremiah C. Lynch
Russell Smith Federal Building, 201 East Broadway, Missoula, MT 59802
Tel: (406) 542-7280 Fax: (406) 542-7292

Jeremiah C. Lynch
Magistrate Judge

Began Service: June 10, 2006
Term Expires: June 9, 2022

Clerkships: Law Clerk, District Judge Paul G. Hatfield, United States District Court for the District of Montana (1981-1995)

Legal Practice: Attorney, Private Practice (1995-2006)

Staff
Career Law Clerk **Tracey Baldwin** .... (406) 542-7280
E-mail: tracey_baldwin@mtd.uscourts.gov
Education: Montana 1995 JD
Career Law Clerk **Timothy C. Line** .... (406) 542-7280
E-mail: tim_line@mtd.uscourts.gov
Education: Montana JD

Chambers of Magistrate Judge John T. Johnston
125 Central Avenue West, Great Falls, MT 59404
Tel: (406) 727-1922

John T. Johnston
Magistrate Judge

Chambers of Magistrate Judge (recalled) Richard W. Anderson
James F. Battin United States Courthouse, 2601 Second Avenue North, Room 1200, Billings, MT 59101
Tel: (406) 247-7000 Fax: (406) 247-7008
E-mail: richard_anderson@mtd.uscourts.gov

Richard W. Anderson
Magistrate Judge (recalled)

Began Service: January 1, 1991

Chambers of Magistrate Judge (recalled) Robert M. Holter
125 Central Avenue West, Suite 110, Great Falls, MT 59403-2386
Tel: (406) 727-0028 Fax: (406) 727-6309

Robert M. Holter
Magistrate Judge (recalled)

Began Service: January 21, 1988; January 3, 2003

United States Bankruptcy Court for the District of Montana
Federal Building, 400 North Main Street, Butte, MT 59701
Tel: (406) 497-1240
Internet: www.mtb.uscourts.gov

Number of Judgeships: 2

Court Staff
Clerk of Court **Tyler Gilman** .... (406) 497-1243
E-mail: tyler_gilman@mtb.uscourts.gov
Systems Manager **Kou Maou** .... (406) 497-1253
Financial Administrator **Jane Markovich** .... (406) 497-1251
E-mail: Jane_Markovich@mtb.uscourts.gov

Chambers of Bankruptcy Judge Ralph B. Kirscher
400 North Main Street, Room 215, Butte, MT 59701
Tel: (406) 497-1240 Fax: (406) 782-1178
E-mail: ralph_kirscher@mtb.uscourts.gov

Ralph B. Kirscher
Bankruptcy Judge

Date of Birth: 1951
Education: Montana; American U MPA; Montana JD
Began Service: November 18, 1999
Term Expires: May 17, 2028

Academic: Adjunct Lecturer, School of Law, The University of Montana-Missoula (1992-1997)

Current Memberships: National Conference of Bankruptcy Judges; Silver Bow County Bar Association; State Bar of Montana

Staff
BAP Law Clerk **Valerie Grubich** .... (406) 750-2294
Education: Montana 2007 JD
Career Law Clerk **Kelli Harrington** .... (406) 497-1240
Career Law Clerk **Terry Healow** .... (406) 782-1240

United States District Court for the District of Nebraska
Roman L. Hruska U.S. Courthouse, 111 South 18th Plaza, Suite 1152, Omaha, NE 68102-1322
Tel: (402) 661-7350 Tel: (866) 220-4381 (Toll Free)
Fax: (402) 661-7387
Internet: www.ned.uscourts.gov

Number of Judgeships: 3

Number of Vacancies: 1

Circuit: Eighth

Court Staff
Clerk of Court **Denise Lucks** .... (402) 661-7350
E-mail: denise_lucks@ned.uscourts.gov Fax: (402) 661-7386
Education: Nebraska (Omaha) BA, BS, MBA
Chief Deputy Clerk **M. Therese Bollerup** .... (402) 661-7350
E-mail: therese_bollerup@ned.uscourts.gov Fax: (402) 661-7386
Education: Nebraska 1981 JD
Court Services Supervisor **Colleen Beran** .... (402) 437-1900
Federal Bldg., 100 Centennial Mall N., Lincoln, NE 68508 Fax: (402) 437-1911
E-mail: colleen_beran@ned.uscourts.gov
Chief Probation and Pretrial Services Officer
Mary Lee Ranheim .... (402) 661-7555
E-mail: mary_lee_ranheim@nep.uscourts.gov Fax: (402) 661-7550
Librarian **Jeri Kay Hopkins** .... (402) 661-7590
Fax: (402) 661-7591

Chambers of Chief Judge Laurie Smith Camp
Roman L. Hruska U.S. Courthouse, 111 South 18th Plaza, Suite 3210, Omaha, NE 68102-1322
Tel: (402) 661-7323 Fax: (402) 661-7326
E-mail: laurie_smith_camp@ned.uscourts.gov

Laurie Smith Camp
Chief Judge

Date of Birth: 1953
Education: Stanford 1974 BA; Nebraska 1977 JD
Began Service: November 2, 2001
Appointed By: President George W. Bush
Political Affiliation: Republican

Corporate: Associate General Counsel, First National Bank and Trust Company (1977-1978)

Chambers of Chief Judge Laurie Smith Camp *continued*

Government: General Counsel, Department of Correctional Services, State of Nebraska (1980-1991); Chief, Civil Rights Section, Department of Justice, State of Nebraska (1991-1995); Chief Deputy Attorney General for Criminal Matters, Department of Justice, State of Nebraska (1995-2001)

Judicial: District Judge, Chambers of District Judge Laurie Smith Camp, United States District Court for the District of Nebraska (2001-2011)

Legal Practice: Associate, Turner & Boisseau (1978-1979); Solo Practicioner (1980)

Current Memberships: Nebraska Bar Foundation; Nebraska State Bar Association; Omaha Bar Association

Staff

Law Clerk **Brian Fahey** .... (402) 661-7324
Began Service: August 9, 2015
Term Expires: August 13, 2016

Career Law Clerk **Robert A. Stark** .... (402) 661-7325
E-mail: robert_stark@ned.uscourts.gov
Education: Creighton 2009 JD

Court Reporter **Brenda Fauber** .... (402) 661-7322

Judicial Assistant **Janet L. Bartels** .... (402) 661-7323
E-mail: janet_bartels@ned.uscourts.gov

Chambers of District Judge John M. Gerrard

586 Federal Building, 100 Centennial Mall North, Lincoln, NE 68508
Tel: (402) 437-1660 Fax: (402) 437-1665
E-mail: gerrard@ned.uscourts.gov

John M. Gerrard
District Judge

Date of Birth: 1953
Education: Nebraska Wesleyan 1976 BS; Arizona 1977 MPA; McGeorge 1981 JD
Began Service: February 5, 2012
Appointed By: President Barack Obama
Political Affiliation: Democrat

Government: City Attorney, City of Battle Creek, Nebraska (1982-1995)

Judicial: Associate Justice, Chambers of Associate Justice John M. Gerrard, Nebraska Supreme Court (1995-2012)

Legal Practice: Litigation Associate, Jewell, Otte, Gatz, Collins & Domina (1981-1982); Partner, Domina, Gerrard, Copple & Stratton, PC (1982-1990); Senior Partner, Gerrard, Stratton & Ptak, P.C. (1990-1995)

Current Memberships: American Bar Association; American Board of Trial Advocates; National Board of Trial Advocacy

Staff

Law Clerk **Andrew "Andy" Conroy** .... (402) 437-1660
Began Service: February 2012
E-mail: andrew_conroy@ned.uscourts.gov

Career Law Clerk **David Dirgo** .... (402) 437-1660
E-mail: david_dirgo@ned.uscourts.gov
Education: Creighton 1998 JD

Chambers of Senior Judge Lyle E. Strom

Roman L. Hruska U.S. Courthouse, 111 South 18th Plaza, Suite 3190, Omaha, NE 68102-1322
Tel: (402) 661-7320 Fax: (402) 661-7318
E-mail: lyle_strom@ned.uscourts.gov

Lyle E. Strom
Senior Judge

Date of Birth: 1925
Education: Creighton 1950 AB, 1953 JD
Began Service: November 1, 1985
Appointed By: President Ronald Reagan
Political Affiliation: Republican

Academic: Adjunct Professor, School of Law, Creighton University

Legal Practice: Fitzgerald, Brown, Leahy, Strom, Schorr & Barmettler (1953-1985)

Military Service: United States Merchant Marines (1943-1946)

Current Memberships: American Bar Foundation; American College of Trial Lawyers; International Academy of Trial Lawyers; Nebraska State Bar Association; Omaha Bar Association

Staff

Law Clerk **Jordan Hasan** .... (402) 661-7320
Began Service: August 2014
Term Expires: August 2016
E-mail: jordan_carlton@ned.uscourts.gov

Law Clerk **Skyler Pearson** .... (402) 661-7320
Began Service: August 2015
Term Expires: August 2017
E-mail: skyler_pearson@ned.uscourts.gov

Secretary **Jean Roeder** .... (402) 661-7320
E-mail: jean_roeder@ned.uscourts.gov

Chambers of Senior Judge Richard G. Kopf

561A Federal Building, 100 Centennial Mall North, Lincoln, NE 68508
Tel: (402) 437-1640 Fax: (402) 437-1641
E-mail: richard_kopf@ned.uscourts.gov

Richard G. Kopf
Senior Judge

Date of Birth: 1946
Education: Nebraska (Kearney) 1969 BA; Nebraska 1972 JD
Began Service: May 26, 1992
Appointed By: President George H.W. Bush

Current Memberships: American Bar Foundation; American Bar Association; Nebraska Bar Foundation; Nebraska State Bar Association

Staff

Career Law Clerk **James A. Eske** .... (402) 437-1640
E-mail: Jim_Eske@ned.uscourts.gov
Education: Nebraska 1976 JD

Career Law Clerk **Janine E. Rempe** .... (402) 437-1640
E-mail: Jan_Rempe@ned.uscourts.gov
Education: Nebraska 1990 JD

Judicial Assistant **Kris Leininger** .... (402) 437-1640
E-mail: kristin_leininger@ned.uscourts.gov

Chambers of Senior Judge Joseph F. Bataillon

Roman L. Hruska U.S. Courthouse, 111 South 18th Plaza,
Suite 3259, Omaha, NE 68102-1322
Tel: (402) 661-7302 Fax: (402) 661-7306
E-mail: Bataillon@ned.uscourts.gov

Joseph F. "Joe" Bataillon
Senior Judge

Date of Birth: 1949
Education: Creighton 1971 BA, 1974 JD
Began Service: October 1997
Appointed By: President William J. Clinton
Political Affiliation: Democrat

Current Memberships: American Bar Association; Judicial Division, American Bar Association; Federal Bar Association; Nebraska State Bar Association; Omaha Bar Association

Staff
Career Law Clerk **Melinda G. Cummings** . . . . (402) 661-7302
E-mail: melinda_cummings@ned.uscourts.gov
Education: Creighton 1982 JD
Career Law Clerk **Moira White Kennedy** . . . . (402) 661-7302
E-mail: moira_kennedy@ned.uscourts.gov
Education: Creighton 1983 JD
Courtroom Deputy and Judicial Assistant
Tiwauna Lawrence . . . . (402) 661-7384
E-mail: tiwauna_lawrence@ned.uscourts.gov
Court Reporter **Susan DeVetter** . . . . (402) 661-7309
E-mail: sue_devetter@ned.uscourts.gov
Court Reporter **Rogene Schroder** . . . . (402) 661-7383
E-mail: rogene_schroder@ned.uscourts.gov
Courtroom Deputy and Judicial Assistant
Amy Brunswick . . . . (402) 661-7349
E-mail: amy_brunswick@ned.uscourts.gov

Chambers of Magistrate Judge Thomas D. Thalken

Roman L. Hruska U.S. Courthouse, 111 South 18th Plaza,
Suite 2271, Omaha, NE 68102-1322
Tel: (402) 661-7343 Fax: (402) 661-7345
E-mail: thalken@ned.uscourts.gov

Thomas D. Thalken
Magistrate Judge

Date of Birth: 1942
Education: Creighton 1964 BA, 1966 JD
Began Service: January 4, 1993
Term Expires: January 4, 2017

Government: Assistant United States Attorney, District of Nebraska, Office of the United States Attorney, United States Department of Justice (1971-1980); First Assistant United States Attorney, District of Nebraska, Office of the United States Attorney, United States Department of Justice (1981-1993)

Military Service: United States Army (1964-1970)

Current Memberships: Nebraska State Bar Association; Omaha Bar Association

Staff
Career Law Clerk **Tanya R. Langton** . . . . (402) 661-7343
E-mail: tanya_langton@ned.uscourts.gov
Education: Denver 1997 JD
Judicial Assistant **(Vacant)** . . . . (402) 661-7343

Chambers of Magistrate Judge F. A. Gossett, III

111 South 18th Plaza, Suite 2210, Omaha, NE 68102
Tel: (402) 661-7340 Fax: (402) 661-7338

F. A. Gossett III
Magistrate Judge

Education: Midland Col 1967 BA; Creighton 1972 JD
Began Service: May 29, 2003
Term Expires: May 29, 2019

Chambers of Magistrate Judge Cheryl Renae Zwart

566 Federal Building, 100 Centennial Mall North, Lincoln, NE 68508
Tel: (402) 437-1670 Fax: (402) 437-1675

Cheryl Renae Zwart
Magistrate Judge

Education: South Dakota 1980 BA; Nebraska 1988 JD
Began Service: January 15, 2010

Clerkships: Career Law Clerk, Chambers of Magistrate Judge David L. Piester, United States District Court for the District of Nebraska

Legal Practice: Associate, Knudsen Law Firm; Partner, Knudsen Law Firm

Staff
Career Law Clerk **Bren H. Chambers** . . . . (402) 437-1670
Education: Nebraska Wesleyan 1997 BS;
Doane 2001 MA; Nebraska 2005 JD
Judicial Assistant **Deborah Schwab** . . . . (402) 437-1670

United States Bankruptcy Court for the District of Nebraska

Roman L. Hruska U.S. Courthouse, 111 South 18th Plaza,
Suite 1125, Omaha, NE 68102
Tel: (402) 661-7444
Tel: (866) 222-8029 (Toll Free Voice Case Information System)
Fax: (402) 661-7492
Internet: www.neb.uscourts.gov

Number of Judgeships: 2

Court Staff
Clerk **Diane L. Zech** . . . . (402) 661-7444
E-mail: Diane_Zech@neb.uscourts.gov
Chief Deputy **Eva Roeber** . . . . (402) 661-7444
E-mail: eva_roeber@neb.uscourts.gov
Deputy-in-Charge - Lincoln **Lisa Marie Smith** . . . . (402) 437-1625
460 Federal Bldg., 100 Centennial Mall N., Fax: (402) 437-1624
Lincoln, NE 68508
E-mail: lisamarie_smith@neb.uscourts.gov
Director, Information Technology Services **(Vacant)** . . . . . . (402) 661-7444
Budget Analyst **Susanne Bartmess** . . . . (402) 661-7444
E-mail: Susanne_Bartmess@neb.uscourts.gov

Chambers of Chief Bankruptcy Judge Thomas L. Saladino

Roman L. Hruska U.S. Courthouse, 111 South 18th Plaza,
Suite 2144, Omaha, NE 68102-1322
Tel: (402) 661-7482

Thomas L. Saladino
Chief Bankruptcy Judge

Began Service: August 2006
Term Expires: August 2020

Staff
Law Clerk **Joan Kramer** . . . . (402) 661-7484

United States District Court for the District of Nevada

Lloyd D. George U.S. Courthouse, 333 Las Vegas Boulevard South, Las Vegas, NV 89101
Tel: (702) 464-5400 Fax: (702) 464-5457
Internet: www.nvd.uscourts.gov

Number of Judgeships: 7

Circuit: Ninth

Court Staff

Clerk of the Court **Lance S. Wilson** .... (702) 464-5400
E-mail: lance_wilson@nvd.uscourts.gov
Education: Denver 1981 MA

Chief Deputy Clerk - Las Vegas **Cindy Jensen** .... (702) 464-5400
E-mail: cindy_jensen@nvd.uscourts.gov Fax: (702) 464-5424
Education: American U 1982 MA

Chief Deputy Clerk - Reno **Jake Herb** .... (775) 686-5800
400 S. Virginia St., Ste. 301, Reno, NV 89501 Fax: (775) 686-5851
E-mail: jake_herb@nvd.uscourts.gov

Chief U.S. Probation Officer **Chad Boardman** .... (702) 527-7300
300 Las Vegas Boulevard South, Suite 1100, Las Vegas, NV 89101

Chief Pretrial Services Officer **Shiela Adkins** .... (702) 464-5630
Room 1112 Fax: (702) 464-5631

Librarian **Ann Jarrell** .... (702) 464-5693
Fax: (702) 464-5691

Librarian, Reno **Cheryl Kidd** .... (775) 686-5776
Bruce R. Thompson Courthouse & Federal Bldg., 400 S. Virginia St., 10th Fl., Reno, NV 89501 Fax: (775) 686-5779

Chambers of Chief Judge Gloria M. Navarro

333 Las Vegas Boulevard South, Las Vegas, NV 89101
Tel: (702) 464-5490
E-mail: gloria_navarro@nvd.uscourts.gov

Gloria M. Navarro
Chief Judge

Education: UNLV 1989 BA; Arizona State 1992 JD
Began Service: May 25, 2010
Appointed By: President Barack Obama

Staff

Law Clerk **(Vacant)** .... (702) 464-5490
Law Clerk **(Vacant)** .... (702) 464-5490
Judicial Assistant **Pamela Ellison** .... (702) 464-5490
E-mail: pamela_ellison@nvd.uscourts.gov

Chambers of District Judge Robert C. Jones

U.S. Courthouse, 400 South Virginia Street, Suite 805, Reno, NV 89501
Tel: (775) 686-5670

Robert C. Jones
District Judge

Date of Birth: July 21, 1947
Education: BYU 1971 BS; UCLA 1975 JD
Began Service: November 30, 2003
Appointed By: President George W. Bush
Political Affiliation: Republican

Current Memberships: American Bar Association; Clark County Bar Association; State Bar of California; State Bar of Nevada; Washoe County Bar Association

Staff

Law Clerk **Matt Piccolo** .... (775) 686-5670
Began Service: 2015
Term Expires: 2016

Career Law Clerk **Elliot Held** .... (775) 686-5670

Judicial Assistant **Carrie Lipparelli** .... (775) 686-5670
E-mail: carrie_lipparelli@nvd.uscourts.gov

Chambers of District Judge James C. Mahan

Lloyd D. George U.S. Courthouse, 333 Las Vegas Boulevard South, Las Vegas, NV 89101
Tel: (702) 464-5520 Fax: (702) 464-5521
E-mail: James_Mahan@nvd.uscourts.gov

James C. Mahan
District Judge

Date of Birth: 1943
Education: Charleston 1965 BA; Vanderbilt 1973 JD
Began Service: February 1, 2002
Appointed By: President George W. Bush
Political Affiliation: Republican

Judicial: District Judge, Eighth Judicial District Court of Nevada (1999-2002)

Legal Practice: Law Clerk, Lee & Beasey, Ltd.; Attorney, John Peter Lee, Ltd. (1975-1982); Senior Partner, Mahan & Ellis, Chartered (1982-1999)

Military Service: United States Navy (1966-1969)

Staff

Law Clerk **Christine Carletta** .... (702) 464-5520
Began Service: August 11, 2015
Term Expires: August 11, 2016

Law Clerk **Kyle Ewing** .... (702) 464-5520
Began Service: August 11, 2015
Term Expires: August 11, 2016

Court Reporter **Katherine "Kathy" Eismann** .... (702) 431-1919
E-mail: katherine_eismann@nvd.uscourts.gov Fax: (702) 384-4670

Courtroom Administrator **David Oakes** .... (702) 464-5413
E-mail: david_oakes@nvd.uscourts.gov

Judicial Executive Assistant **Susan Briare** .... (702) 464-5520
E-mail: Susan_Briare@nvd.uscourts.gov

Chambers of District Judge Miranda Du

400 South Virginia Street, Reno, NV 89501
Tel: (775) 686-5919 Fax: (702) 464-5457
E-mail: miranda_du@nvd.uscourts.gov

Miranda Du
District Judge

Education: UC Davis 1991 BA; Boalt Hall 1994 JD
Began Service: June 18, 2012
Appointed By: President Barack Obama

Staff

Courtroom Administrator **Peggie Vannozzi** .... (702) 464-5429

Chambers of District Judge Andrew Patrick Gordon

333 Las Vegas Boulevard South, Las Vegas, NV 89101
Tel: (702) 868-4940
E-mail: andrew_gordon@nvd.uscourts.gov

Andrew Patrick Gordon
District Judge

Education: Claremont McKenna 1984 BA; Harvard 1987 JD
Began Service: April 15, 2013
Appointed By: President Barack Obama

Legal Practice: Associate, McDonald Carano Wilson LLP (1994-1997); Partner, McDonald Carano Wilson LLP (1997-2013)

Staff

Courtroom Administrator **Kandy Riscen** .... (702) 464-5432

Chambers of District Judge Jennifer A. Dorsey

333 Las Vegas Boulevard South, Las Vegas, NV 89101
Tel: (702) 868-4960

Jennifer A. Dorsey
District Judge

Education: UNLV 1994 BA; Pepperdine 1997 JD
Began Service: July 9, 2013
Appointed By: President Barack Obama

Legal Practice: Attorney, Kemp, Jones, & Coulthard LLP (1997-2004); Partner, Kemp, Jones, & Coulthard LLP (2004-2013)

Staff
Courtroom Administrator **Donna Sherwood** .... (702) 464-5426

Chambers of District Judge Richard Franklin Boulware II

333 Las Vegas Boulevard South, Las Vegas, NV 89101
Tel: (702) 868-4970
E-mail: richard_boulware@nvd.uscourts.gov

Richard Franklin Boulware II
District Judge

Education: Harvard 1993 AB; Columbia 2002 JD
Began Service: June 10, 2014
Appointed By: President Barack Obama

Clerkships: Law Clerk, Chambers of Senior Judge Denise Cote, United States District Court for the Southern District of New York (2002-2003)

Legal Practice: Trial Attorney, Federal Defenders of New York, Inc. (2003-2007)

Staff
Courtroom Administrator **Blanca Lenzi** .... (702) 868-4970

Chambers of Senior Judge Lloyd D. George

Lloyd D. George U.S. Courthouse, 333 Las Vegas Boulevard South, Room 6073, Las Vegas, NV 89101
Tel: (702) 464-5500 Fax: (702) 464-5501
E-mail: lloyd_george@nvd.uscourts.gov

Lloyd D. George
Senior Judge

Date of Birth: 1930
Education: BYU 1955 BS; Boalt Hall 1961 JD
Began Service: May 1984
Appointed By: President Ronald Reagan

Judicial: Judge, United States Bankruptcy Court for the District of Nevada (1974-1984); Judge, Ninth Circuit Bankruptcy Appellate Panel (1984)

Legal Practice: Albright, George, Johnson & Steffen (1969-1971)

Military Service: United States Air Force (1955-1958)

Current Memberships: American Association for Justice; American Bar Association; Clark County Bar Association; State Bar of Nevada; Washoe County Bar Association

Staff
Career Law Clerk **Troy Healey** .... (702) 464-5500
E-mail: troy_healey@nvd.uscourts.gov
Education: J Reuben Clark Law 1986 JD
Career Law Clerk **Garon Dee Salway** .... (702) 464-5500
E-mail: garon_salway@nvd.uscourts.gov
Education: U Washington 1991 JD
Secretary **Lee Hughes** .... (702) 464-5500
E-mail: lee_hughes@nvd.uscourts.gov

Chambers of Senior Judge Howard D. McKibben

Bruce R. Thompson U.S. Courthouse and Federal Building, 400 South Virginia Street, Room 607, Reno, NV 89501
Tel: (775) 686-5880
E-mail: howard_mckibben@nvd.uscourts.gov

Howard D. McKibben
Senior Judge

Date of Birth: 1940
Education: Bradley 1962 BS; Pittsburgh 1964 MPA; Michigan 1967 JD
Began Service: October 12, 1984
Appointed By: President Ronald Reagan

Academic: Faculty, National Judicial College

Government: Deputy District Attorney, State of Nevada (1969-1971); District Attorney, State of Nevada (1971-1977)

Judicial: Judge, Nevada District Court (1977-1984); Chief Judge, United States District Court for the District of Nevada (1997-2002)

Legal Practice: George W. Abbott Law Office (1967-1971)

Current Memberships: The American Inns of Court; Ninth Circuit District Judges Association

Staff
Law Clerk **Duncan Burke** .... (775) 686-5880
Career Law Clerk **Emily Gust** .... (775) 686-5880
E-mail: emily_gust@nvd.uscourts.gov
Education: Arizona 2006 JD
Courtroom Administrator **Paris Rich** .... (775) 686-5827
E-mail: paris_rich@nvd.uscourts.gov
Judicial Assistant **Candice Rowe** .... (775) 686-5880
E-mail: candice_rowe@nvd.uscourts.gov
Education: Nevada (Reno) 1994 MA

Chambers of Senior Judge Roger L. Hunt

6202 Lloyd D. George U.S. Courthouse, 333 Las Vegas Boulevard South, Las Vegas, NV 89101
Tel: (702) 464-5530 Fax: (702) 464-5531
E-mail: roger_hunt@nvd.uscourts.gov

Roger L. Hunt
Senior Judge

Date of Birth: 1942
Education: BYU 1966 BA; George Washington 1970 JD
Began Service: May 26, 2000
Appointed By: President William J. Clinton

Current Memberships: American Bar Association; Clark County Bar Association

Staff
Law Clerk **Shannon Clarke** .... (702) 464-5530
Term Expires: August 2016
E-mail: shannon_clarke@nvd.uscourts.gov
Courtroom Administrator **Melissa Johansen** .... (702) 464-5415
E-mail: melissa_johansen@nvd.uscourts.gov
Judicial Assistant **Zoretta Smith-Gipson** .... (702) 464-5530
E-mail: zo_gipson@nvd.uscourts.gov

Chambers of Senior Judge Kent J. Dawson

Lloyd D. George U.S. Courthouse, 333 Las Vegas Boulevard South, Suite 4085, Las Vegas, NV 89101
Tel: (702) 464-5560
E-mail: kent_dawson@nvd.uscourts.gov

Kent J. Dawson
Senior Judge

Date of Birth: 1944
Education: Weber State 1969 BS; Utah 1971 JD
Began Service: July 17, 2000
Appointed By: President William J. Clinton

Staff
Law Clerk **(Vacant)** . . . . (702) 464-5565
Career Law Clerk **Bryce Jones** . . . . (702) 464-5564
E-mail: bryce_jones@nvd.uscourts.gov
Education: Houston 1999 JD
Courtroom Administrator **Denise Saavedra** . . . . (702) 464-5429
E-mail: denise_saavedra@nvd.uscourts.gov
Secretary **Donna M. Silva** . . . . (702) 464-5560
E-mail: donna_silva@nvd.uscourts.gov

Chambers of Senior Judge Larry R. Hicks

Bruce R. Thompson U.S. Courthouse, 400 South Virginia Street, Suite 506, Reno, NV 89501
Tel: (775) 686-5700 Fax: (775) 686-5704
E-mail: larry_hicks@nvd.uscourts.gov

Larry R. Hicks
Senior Judge

Date of Birth: 1943
Education: Nevada (Reno) 1965 BS; Colorado 1968 JD
Began Service: November 29, 2001
Appointed By: President George W. Bush

Staff
Judicial Assistant **Elaine Muhlebach** . . . . (775) 686-5700
E-mail: elaine_muhlebach@nvd.uscourts.gov

Chambers of Magistrate Judge Valerie P. Cooke

Bruce R. Thompson U.S. Courthouse and Federal Building, 400 South Virginia Street, Suite 404, Reno, NV 89501
Tel: (775) 686-5855 Fax: (775) 686-5864
E-mail: valerie_cooke@nvd.uscourts.gov

Valerie P. Cooke
Magistrate Judge

Date of Birth: 1953
Education: Nevada (Reno) 1976 BA; Northwestern 1983 JD
Began Service: November 1, 1999
Term Expires: November 1, 2023

Academic: Teacher, Sacred Heart Academy (1976-1979); Teacher, Reno High School (1979-1980)

Clerkships: Law Clerk The Honorable William N. Forman, Second Judicial District Court, Nevada (1983-1984)

Legal Practice: Attorney, Guild & Hagen, Ltd. (1984-1994); Attorney, McDonald Carano Wilson, LLP (1995-1999)

Current Memberships: Federal Magistrate Judges Association; State Bar of Nevada; Washoe County Bar Association

Staff
Law Clerk **Kristen Casey Strong** . . . . (775) 686-5855
Began Service: August 2015
Term Expires: August 2016
Courtroom Administrator **Lisa Mann** . . . . (775) 686-5855
E-mail: lisa_mann@nvd.uscourts.gov

Chambers of Magistrate Judge Valerie P. Cooke *continued*

Secretary **Debra Newman** . . . . (775) 686-5855
E-mail: debra_newman@nvd.uscourts.gov

Chambers of Magistrate Judge Peggy A. Leen

Lloyd D. George U.S. Courthouse, 333 Las Vegas Boulevard South, Las Vegas, NV 89101
Tel: (702) 464-5570 Fax: (702) 464-5571
E-mail: peggy_leen@nvd.uscourts.gov

Peggy A. Leen
Magistrate Judge

Date of Birth: 1954
Education: UNLV 1976 BA; San Diego 1979 JD
Began Service: January 16, 2001
Term Expires: January 16, 2017

Government: Law Clerk and Deputy Public Defender, Office of the Public Defender, County of Clark, Nevada (1976-1981); Clark County District Attorney's Office, Criminal Division, Major Violators Unit (1996-1999); Clark County District Attorney's Office, Civil Division (1999-2000)

Legal Practice: Associate, Thorndal, Backus, Maupin & Armstrong

Current Memberships: American College of Trial Lawyers; International Academy of Trial Lawyers; International Society of Barristers

Staff
Career Law Clerk **Leslie Nino Piro** . . . . (702) 464-5570
Courtroom Administrator **Jeff Miller** . . . . (702) 464-5420
E-mail: jeff_miller@nvd.uscourts.gov

Chambers of Magistrate Judge George W. Foley, Jr.

333 Las Vegas Boulevard South, Suite 3099, Las Vegas, NV 89101
Tel: (702) 464-5575 Fax: (702) 464-5576
E-mail: george_foley@nvd.uscourts.gov

George W. Foley, Jr.
Magistrate Judge

Education: UNLV 1977 BA; McGeorge 1980 JD
Began Service: August 2005

Staff
Law Clerk **Robson Hauser** . . . . (702) 464-5578
Began Service: September 2014
Term Expires: September 2016
E-mail: robson_hauser@nvd.uscourts.gov
Courtroom Administrator **Elvia Garcia** . . . . (702) 464-5513
E-mail: elvia_garcia@nvd.uscourts.gov
Judicial Assistant **Julia Wright** . . . . (702) 464-5575
E-mail: julia_wright@nvd.uscourts.gov

Chambers of Magistrate Judge Carl W. Hoffman

333 Las Vegas Boulevard South, Las Vegas, NV 89101
Tel: (702) 464-5580

Carl W. Hoffman
Magistrate Judge

Began Service: 2011

Staff
Law Clerk **Lindsay Hansen** . . . . (702) 464-5580
Began Service: 2011
E-mail: lindsay_hansen@nvd.uscourts.gov
Courtroom Administrator **Donna Smith** . . . . (702) 464-5418
Began Service: 2011
E-mail: donna_smith@nvd.uscourts.gov

Chambers of Magistrate Judge William G. Cobb

US District Court - Reno, 400 S. Virginia St., Reno, NV 89501
Tel: (775) 686-5858
E-mail: william_cobb@nvd.uscourts.gov

William G. Cobb
Magistrate Judge

Began Service: 2011

Staff

Courtroom Administrator **Katie Ogden** . . . . (775) 686-5758
E-mail: katie_ogden@nvd.uscourts.gov
Judicial Assistant **Susan Davis** . . . . (775) 686-5758
Began Service: 2011
E-mail: susan_davis@nvd.uscourts.gov

Chambers of Magistrate Judge Vincent Ferenbach

Lloyd D. George U.S. Courthouse, 333 Las Vegas Boulevard South, Las Vegas, NV 89101
Tel: (702) 464-5540

Vincent "Cam" Ferenbach
Magistrate Judge

Began Service: October 2011
Term Expires: October 2019

Staff

Judicial Assistant **Mai Tieu** . . . . (702) 464-5540
Began Service: October 2011
E-mail: mai_tieu@nvd.uscourts.gov
Courtroom Administrator **Jerry Ries** . . . . (702) 464-5435
E-mail: jerry_ries@nvd.uscourts.gov

Chambers of Magistrate Judge Nancy Koppe

333 Las Vegas Boulevard South, Las Vegas, NV 89101
Tel: (702) 464-5550
E-mail: nancy_koppe@nvd.uscourts.gov

Nancy Koppe
Magistrate Judge

Staff

Law Clerk **Tim Martin-Vasquez** . . . . (702) 464-5554
E-mail: tim_martin-vazquez@nvd.uscourts.gov
Courtroom Administrator **Ari Caytuero** . . . . (702) 464-5554

Chambers of Magistrate Judge (Recalled) Robert A. McQuaid, Jr.

505 Bruce R. Thomson U.S. Courthouse, 400 South Virginia Street, Reno, NV 89501
Tel: (775) 686-5654 Fax: (775) 686-5963
E-mail: bob_mcquaid@nvd.uscourts.gov

Robert A. McQuaid, Jr.
Magistrate Judge (recalled)

Education: Nevada (Reno) 1968 BA; Willamette 1971 JD
Began Service: April 15, 1996

United States Bankruptcy Court for the District of Nevada

Foley Federal Building, 300 Las Vegas Boulevard South, 4th Floor, Las Vegas, NV 89101
Clifton Young Federal Building, 300 Booth Street, 1st Floor, Reno, NV 89509
Tel: (702) 527-7000 Tel: (775) 326-2100
Tel: (866) 222-8029 (Toll Free Voice Case Information System VCIS)
Internet: www.nvb.uscourts.gov

Number of Judgeships: 4

Court Staff

Clerk of Court **Mary A. Schott** . . . . (702) 527-7000
E-mail: mary_schott@nvb.uscourts.gov
Deputy Clerk-in-Charge **(Vacant)** . . . . (775) 326-2100
Young Federal Bldg., 300 Booth St., Reno, NV 89509
Chief Deputy **Maria Sanders** . . . . (702) 527-7000
Courtroom and Calendar Deputy **Harriette Whitehouse** . . . . (702) 527-7000
E-mail: Harriette_Whitehouse@nvb.uscourts.gov
Courtroom and Calendar Deputy **(Vacant)** . . . . (702) 527-7000
Courtroom and Calendar Deputy - Las Vegas **Benji Rawling** . . . . (702) 527-7000
E-mail: benji_rawling@nvb.uscourts.gov
Electronic Court Recorder **(Vacant)** . . . . (775) 326-2100
Clifton Young Federal Bldg., 300 Booth St., Reno, NV 89509
Electronic Court Recorder/Court Services **Helen Smith** . . . . (702) 527-7000
E-mail: helen_smith@nvb.uscourts.gov
Human Resources Manager **Denise Kirkling-Styles** . . . . . (702) 527-7000
E-mail: Denise_Kirkling-Styles@nvb.uscourts.gov
Operations Manager **Linda Duffy** . . . . (702) 527-7000
Procurement Specialist **Angie Bigas** . . . . (702) 527-7000
E-mail: angie_bigas@nvb.uscourts.gov
Space and Facilities Manager **Robert Wotas** . . . . (702) 527-7000

Chambers of Chief Bankruptcy Judge Mike K. Nakagawa

Foley Federal Building, 300 Las Vegas Boulevard South, 4th Floor, Las Vegas, NV 89101
Tel: (702) 527-7138
E-mail: mike_nakagawa@nvb.uscourts.gov

Mike K. Nakagawa
Chief Bankruptcy Judge

Education: U Pacific 1977 BA; UC Davis 1980 JD
Began Service: 2009

Clerkships: Law Clerk, Chief Judge Philip Wilkins, United States District Court for the Eastern District of California (1980-1984)

Government: Chairperson, Civil Service Commission, County of Sacramento, California

Legal Practice: Principal, Nakagawa and Rico

Current Memberships: Asian Pacific Bar Association of Sacramento; State Bar of California; State Bar of Nevada

Staff

Courtroom Deputy **Benji Rawling** . . . . (702) 527-7000

Chambers of Bankruptcy Judge Gregg W. Zive
300 Booth Street, 5th Floor, Reno, NV 89509
Tel: (775) 326-2100
E-mail: gregg_zive@nvb.uscourts.gov

Gregg W. Zive
Bankruptcy Judge

Date of Birth: 1945
Education: Nevada (Reno) 1967 BA; Notre Dame 1973 JD
Began Service: January 23, 1995
Term Expires: January 22, 2017

Legal Practice: Partner, Hale Lane Peek Dennison and Howard (1976-1990); Partner, Lionel Sawyer & Collins (1990-1992); Partner, Bible, Hoy, Trachok, Wadhams & Zive (1992-1995)

Military Service: United States Army

Current Memberships: American Bankruptcy Institute; American Bar Association; National Conference of Bankruptcy Judges; State Bar of California; State Bar of Nevada; Washoe County Bar Association

Staff
Career Law Clerk **Molly Davenport** .... (775) 326-2100
Courtroom Deputy **Linda Duffy** .... (775) 326-2107
Judicial Assistant **(Vacant)** .... (775) 326-2100

Chambers of Bankruptcy Judge Bruce T. Beesley
Foley Federal Building, 300 Las Vegas Boulevard South, Las Vegas, NV 89101
Tel: (702) 527-7000

Bruce T. Beesley
Bankruptcy Judge

Education: McGeorge 1978 JD

Chambers of Bankruptcy Judge Laurel E. Davis
300 Las Vegas Boulevard South, Las Vegas, NV 89101
Tel: (702) 527-7030

Laurel E. Davis
Bankruptcy Judge

Chambers of Bankruptcy Judge August B. Landis
300 Las Vegas Boulevard South, Las Vegas, NV 89101
Tel: (702) 527-7010

August B. Landis
Bankruptcy Judge

Began Service: November 27, 2013

United States District Court for the District of New Hampshire
Warren B. Rudman U.S. Courthouse, 55 Pleasant Street, Concord, NH 03301
Tel: (603) 225-1423 Tel: (800) 361-7205 (Toll Free PACER)
Internet: www.nhd.uscourts.gov

Number of Judgeships: 3

Circuit: First

Court Staff
Clerk of Court **Daniel Lynch** .... (603) 225-1477
E-mail: daniel_lynch@nhd.uscourts.gov
Chief Deputy **Pamela Phelan** .... (603) 226-7792
E-mail: pamela_phelan@nhd.uscourts.gov

United States District Court for the District of New Hampshire *continued*

Chief U.S. Probation Officer **Jonathan Hurtig** .... (603) 225-1599
Administrative Clerk **Erin Callahan** .... (603) 225-7781
Case Manager **Judy Barrett** .... (603) 225-1587
Case Manager **Kathy DuPont** .... (603) 225-1441
Case Manager **Deb Eastman-Proulx** .... (603) 225-1474
Case Manager **Maryanne Michaelis** .... (603) 225-1478
Case Manager **Vincent Negron** .... (603) 226-7733
Case Manager **Charli Pappas** .... (603) 226-7733
Intake **Janice Boucher** .... (603) 225-1533
E-mail: janice_boucher@nhd.uscourts.gov
Court Reporter **Sandy Bailey** .... (603) 225-1454
E-mail: sandy_bailey@nhd.uscourts.gov
Court Reporter **Susan Bateman** .... (603) 225-1453
E-mail: susan_bateman@nhd.uscourts.gov
Court Reporter **Diane Churas** .... (603) 225-1442
E-mail: diane_churas@nhd.uscourts.gov
Director of Information Technology **Dana Bauer** .... (603) 225-1476
Human Resources Administrator **Thomas Van Beaver** ... (603) 225-1489
E-mail: tom_vanbeaver@nhd.uscourts.gov
Financial Administrator **Dale Trombley** .... (603) 226-7732
E-mail: dale_trombley@nhd.uscourts.gov
Jury Administrator **Cathy Dube** .... (603) 225-7791
E-mail: cathy_dube@nhd.uscourts.gov
Network Administrator **Paul Guest** .... (603) 225-1498
Procurement Administrator **Valerie Allen** .... (603) 225-1472
E-mail: valerie_allen@nhd.uscourts.gov
UNIX Systems Administrator **Eric Swanson** .... (603) 226-7773
Interpreter/Naturalization Liaison **Jennifer Sackos** ...... (603) 225-1475
E-mail: jennifer_sackos@nhd.uscourts.gov
Court Technology Specialist **James Chiavaras** .... (603) 225-1176
E-mail: jim_chiavaras@nhd.uscourts.gov

Chambers of Chief Judge Joseph N. Laplante Jr.
110 Warren B. Rudman U.S. Courthouse, 55 Pleasant Street, Room 401, Concord, NH 03301
Tel: (603) 225-1423
E-mail: joseph_laplante@nhd.uscourts.gov

Joseph N. Laplante, Jr.
Chief Judge

Date of Birth: 1965
Education: Georgetown 1987 AB, 1990 JD
Began Service: December 28, 2007
Appointed By: President George W. Bush

Government: Senior Assistant Attorney General, Office of the Attorney General, State of New Hampshire (1993-1998); Trial Attorney, Criminal Division, United States Department of Justice (1998-1999); Assistant U.S. Attorney, Massachusetts District, United States Department of Justice (2000-2002); First Assistant U.S. Attorney, New Hampshire District, Executive Office for United States Attorneys, United States Department of Justice (2002-2008)

Judicial: District Judge, Chambers of District Judge Joseph N. Laplante Jr., United States District Court for the District of New Hampshire (2007-2012)

Legal Practice: Associate, Wiggin & Nourie, PA (1990-1993)

Nonprofit: Vice Chairman, New Hampshire Charitable Foundation-Nashua Region; Chairman, New Hampshire Charitable Foundation-Nashua Region

Current Memberships: New Hampshire Bar Association

Staff
Career Law Clerk **Eric Kane** .... (603) 225-1423
Began Service: September 2014
E-mail: eric_kane@nhd.uscourts.gov
Law Clerk **Arwyn Carroll** .... (603) 225-1423
E-mail: arwyn_carroll@nhd.uscourts.gov
Judicial Assistant **Jadean Barthelmes** .... (603) 225-1423
E-mail: jadean_barthelmes@nhd.uscourts.gov

Chambers of District Judge Paul James Barbadoro

110 W. B. Rudman Courthouse, 55 Pleasant Street,
Concord, NH 03301-3938
Tel: (603) 226-7303 Fax: (603) 226-7795
E-mail: paul_barbadoro@nhd.uscourts.gov

Paul James Barbadoro
District Judge

Date of Birth: 1955
Education: Gettysburg 1977 BA; Boston Col 1980 JD
Began Service: November 17, 1992
Appointed By: President George H.W. Bush

Academic: Adjunct Professor, Franklin Pierce Law Center (1997-1999)

Government: Assistant Attorney General, State of New Hampshire (1980-1984); Counsel (NH), Office of Senator Warren B. Rudman, United States Senate (1984-1986); Deputy Chief Counsel, Select Committee on Secret Military Assistance to Iran and the Nicaraguan Opposition, United States Senate (1987)

Judicial: Chief Judge, United States District Court for the District of New Hampshire (1997-2004)

Legal Practice: Orr and Reno (1986-1987); Rath, Young, Pignatelli and Oyer (1987-1992)

Current Memberships: First Circuit Court of Appeals Bar Association; Committee on Cooperation With the Courts, New Hampshire Bar Association; New Hampshire Federal District Court Bar Association

Staff

Law Clerk **Andrew J. Haile** .... (603) 226-7303
Began Service: September 2015
Term Expires: August 30, 2016
E-mail: andrew_haile@nhd.uscourts.gov

Law Clerk **Harry D. Hanson** .... (603) 226-7303
Began Service: September 2015
Term Expires: August 30, 2016
E-mail: harry_hanson@nhd.uscourts.gov

Judicial Assistant **Joan N. Ausman** .... (603) 226-7303
E-mail: joan_ausman@nhd.uscourts.gov
Education: Notre Dame 1979 BA

Chambers of District Judge Landya B. McCafferty

55 Pleasant Street, Concord, NH 03301
Tel: (603) 225-1423

Landya Boyer McCafferty
District Judge

Education: Harvard 1984 AB; Northeastern 1991 JM
Began Service: December 21, 2013
Appointed By: President Barack Obama

Staff

Law Clerk **Parker B. Potter, Jr.** .... (603) 225-1423
Education: Franklin Pierce Col 1999 JD

Judicial Assistant **Gail L. Adams** .... (603) 225-1423

Case Manager **(Vacant)** .... (603) 225-1423

Chambers of Senior Judge Joseph A. DiClerico, Jr.

Warren B. Rudman U.S. Courthouse, 55 Pleasant Street, Room 400,
Concord, NH 03301
Tel: (603) 226-7746
E-mail: joseph_diclerico@nhd.uscourts.gov

Joseph A. DiClerico, Jr.
Senior District Judge

Date of Birth: 1941
Education: Williams 1963 BA; Yale 1966 LLB
Began Service: September 11, 1992
Appointed By: President George H.W. Bush

Clerkships: Law Clerk The Honorable Aloysius J. Connor, United States District Court (1966-1967); Law Clerk, New Hampshire Supreme Court (1967-1968)

Government: Assistant Attorney General, State of New Hampshire (1970-1977)

Judicial: Justice, New Hampshire Superior Court (1977-1992); Chief Judge, United States District Court for the District of New Hampshire (1992-1997)

Legal Practice: Cleveland, Waters and Bass (1968-1970)

Current Memberships: American Bar Foundation; American Bar Association; Merrimack County Bar Association; New Hampshire Bar Association; New Hampshire Bar Foundation; New London Bar Association

Staff

Law Clerk **Daniel Fisher** .... (603) 226-7787
Began Service: 2011
E-mail: daniel_fisher@nhd.uscourts.gov

Career Law Clerk **Laura L. Hall** .... (603) 226-7787
E-mail: laura_hall@nhd.uscourts.gov
Education: Franklin Pierce Col 1986 JD

Secretary **Gail L. Adams** .... (603) 226-7746
E-mail: gail_adams@nhd.uscourts.gov

Chambers of Senior Judge Steven James McAuliffe

416 Warren B. Rudman U.S. Courthouse, 55 Pleasant Street,
Concord, NH 03301
Tel: (603) 225-1423 Fax: (603) 230-7604
E-mail: steven_mcauliffe@nhd.uscourts.gov

Steven James McAuliffe
Senior Judge

Date of Birth: 1948
Education: VMI 1970 BA; Georgetown 1973 JD
Began Service: 1992
Appointed By: President George H.W. Bush

Current Memberships: American Association of Justice; American Bar Association; The District of Columbia Bar; Merrimack County Bar Association; National Conference of Bar Presidents; New Hampshire Bar Association; New Hampshire Bar Foundation; New Hampshire Trial Lawyers Association; The Supreme Court Historical Society

Staff

Law Clerk **Emily Feyrer** .... (603) 225-1423

Career Law Clerk **Robert J. Finn** .... (603) 225-1423
Education: Dartmouth 1985 AB;
Vanderbilt 1988 JD

Judicial Assistant **Lorraine A. Temme** .... (603) 225-1423

Chambers of Magistrate Judge Andrea K. Johnstone
55 Pleasant Street, Concord, NH 03301
Tel: (603) 225-1441

Andrea K. Johnstone
Magistrate Judge

Education: Wheaton (IL); Hofstra 1988 JD
Began Service: 2014
Term Expires: 2022

United States Bankruptcy Court for the District of New Hampshire
1000 Elm Street, Suite 1001, Manchester, NH 03101-1708
Tel: (603) 222-2600
Tel: (866) 222-8029 (Voice Case Information System VCIS)
Tel: (800) 676-6856 (PACER Sign up) Fax: (603) 222-2697
Internet: www.nhb.uscourts.gov

Number of Judgeships: 2

Court Staff
Clerk of Court **Bonnie L. McAlary** .... (603) 222-2600
Administrative Manager-Courtroom
Maureen B. Shambo .... (603) 222-2685
E-mail: Maureen_Shambo@nhb.uscourts.gov
Education: Holy Cross Col 1980 BA
Administrative Manager-Operations
Kerri A. Mikolaities .... (603) 222-2618
E-mail: Kerri_Mikolaities@nhb.uscourts.gov
Education: New Hampshire 1980 BA
Career Law Clerk **Jennifer A. Hayes** .... (603) 222-2600
Education: Dartmouth 1992 BA; Boston U 1995 JD

Chambers of Chief Bankruptcy Judge Bruce A. Harwood
1000 Elm Street, Manchester, NH 03101-1708
Tel: (866) 222-8029

Bruce A. Harwood
Chief Bankruptcy Judge

Education: Northwestern 1978 BA; Washington U (MO) 1981 JD

Chambers of Bankruptcy Judge J. Michael Deasy
1000 Elm Street, Suite 1001, Manchester, NH 03101-1708
Tel: (603) 222-2640 Fax: (603) 222-2696

J. Michael Deasy
Bankruptcy Judge

Date of Birth: 1945
Education: Rensselaer Poly 1967 BS; Boston Col 1973 JD
Term Expires: March 11, 2016

Current Memberships: American Bankruptcy Institute; American Bar Association; New Hampshire Bar Association

United States District Court for the District of New Jersey
Martin Luther King, Jr. Federal Building & U.S. Courthouse,
50 Walnut Street, Room 4015, Newark, NJ 07101
P.O. Box 419, Newark, NJ 07101-0419
Tel: (973) 645-3730 Tel: (800) 676-6856 (Toll Free PACER)

Number of Judgeships: 17

Number of Vacancies: 4

Circuit: Third

Court Staff
Clerk of the Court **William T. Walsh** .... (973) 645-3730
Deputy-in-Charge - Camden **Marcy Barratt** .... (856) 757-5059
1050 Mitchell H. Cohen U.S. Courthouse,
One John F. Gerry Plz., Camden, NJ 08102
P.O. Box 2797, Camden, NJ 08101
E-mail: marcy_barratt@njd.uscourts.gov
Deputy-in-Charge - Newark **Andrea Lewis-Walker** ...... (973) 645-4439
E-mail: andrea_walker@njd.uscourts.gov
Deputy-in-Charge - Trenton **Melvin K. Jackson** .... (609) 989-2057
2020 Clarkson S. Fisher Federal Bldg. & U.S.
Courthouse, 402 E. State St., Trenton, NJ 08608
E-mail: melvin_jackson@njd.uscourts.gov
Chief Probation Officer **Wilfredo Torres** .... (973) 645-4747
Room 1005
Director of Court Administration **Alex Minter** .... (609) 989-2314
E-mail: alex_minter@njd.uscourts.gov
Manager of Finance **Denise Howard** .... (609) 989-2314
E-mail: denise_howard@njd.uscourts.gov
Chief Pretrial Services Officer **Christine A. Dozier** ...... (973) 645-2230
Room 1018
Human Resources Manager **Emma Fernandez-Regan** ... (609) 989-2084
E-mail: emma_fernandez-regan@njd.uscourts.gov
Human Resources Specialist **Judith Mancine** .... (609) 989-2084
Human Resources Specialist **Noreen Lyons** .... (609) 989-2084
E-mail: noreen_lyons@njd.uscourts.gov
Human Resources Specialist **Georgeanna VanHise** ...... (609) 989-2084
E-mail: georgeanna_vanhise@njd.uscourts.gov
Librarian **Tom Fasching** .... (609) 989-2345
301 U.S. Courthouse, 402 E. State St., Fax: (609) 989-0485
Trenton, NJ 08608

Chambers of Chief Judge Jerome B. Simandle
6010 Mitchell H. Cohen U.S. Courthouse, One John F. Gerry Plaza, Camden, NJ 08101
P.O. Box 2797, Camden, NJ 08101-0888
Tel: (856) 757-5167 Fax: (856) 757-5459

Jerome B. Simandle
Chief Judge

Date of Birth: 1949
Education: Princeton 1971 BS; U Stockholm (Sweden) 1975; Pennsylvania 1976 JD
Began Service: 1992
Appointed By: President George H.W. Bush

Current Memberships: Camden County Bar Association; Federal Judges Association

Staff
Law Clerk **Hannah Lonky** .... (856) 757-5167
Began Service: September 1, 2015
Term Expires: August 31, 2017
E-mail: hannah_lonky@njd.uscourts.gov
Education: Northwestern 2015 JD
Law Clerk **Logan Pettigrew** .... (856) 757-5167
Began Service: August 2014
Term Expires: August 2016
E-mail: logan_pettigrew@njd.uscourts.gov
Education: Rutgers (Camden) 2013 JD

(continued on next page)

Chambers of Chief Judge Jerome B. Simandle *continued*

Law Clerk **Susan Hu** .... (856) 757-5167
Began Service: September 2014
Term Expires: September 2016
E-mail: susan_hu@njd.uscourts.gov
Courtroom Deputy **Marnie Maccariella** .... (856) 757-5390
E-mail: marnie_maccariella@njd.uscourts.gov
Court Reporter **Lisa Marcus** .... (856) 986-4986
E-mail: lisa_marcus@njd.uscourts.gov
Secretary **Maria Martinez** .... (856) 757-5167
E-mail: maria_martinez@njd.uscourts.gov
Education: Stockton State 1994 BA

Chambers of District Judge Robert B. Kugler

Mitchell H. Cohen U.S. Courthouse, One John F. Gerry Plaza,
Room 6040, Camden, NJ 08101
P.O. Box 889, Camden, NJ 08101-0889
Tel: (856) 757-5019
E-mail: chambers_of_judge_robert_kugler@njd.uscourts.gov

Robert B. Kugler
District Judge

Date of Birth: October 10, 1950
Education: Syracuse 1975 BA; Rutgers (Camden) 1978 JD
Began Service: December 4, 2002
Appointed By: President George W. Bush

Clerkships: Law Clerk The Honorable John F. Gerry, United States District Court for the District of New Jersey (1978-1979)

Government: Assistant Prosecutor, Office of the Prosecutor, County of Camden, New Jersey (1979-1981); Deputy Attorney General, Division of Criminal Justice, Department of Law and Public Safety, State of New Jersey (1981-1982)

Judicial: Magistrate Judge, United States District Court for the District of New Jersey (1992-2002)

Legal Practice: Associate, Partner and Shareholder, Moss, Power & Kugler (1982-1992)

Staff

Law Clerk **Sydney Sgambato** .... (856) 757-5019
Began Service: September 2015
Term Expires: September 2017
E-mail: sydney_sgambato@njd.uscourts.gov
Education: American U 2015 JD
Law Clerk **Stephanie Freudenberg** .... (856) 757-5019
Began Service: September 2015
Term Expires: September 2017
E-mail: stephanie_freudenberg@njd.uscourts.gov
Courtroom Deputy **Barbara Fisher-Arthur** .... (856) 968-4834
Court Reporter **Carl Nami** .... (856) 757-5019
E-mail: carl_nami@njd.uscourts.gov
Secretary **Marcy Golub** .... (856) 757-5019
E-mail: marcy_golub@njd.uscourts.gov

Chambers of District Judge Jose L. Linares

Martin Luther King, Jr. Federal Building and U.S. Courthouse,
50 Walnut Street, Room 5054, Newark, NJ 07101
Tel: (973) 645-6042 Fax: (973) 645-2558
E-mail: Chambers_of_Judge_Jose_Linares@njd.uscourts.gov

Jose L. Linares
District Judge

Date of Birth: November 30, 1953
Education: Jersey City State 1975 BA; Temple 1978 JD
Began Service: December 3, 2002
Appointed By: President George W. Bush

Government: Supervising Attorney, Department of Investigation, City of New York, New York (1978-1980); Judge, Superior Court, County of Essex, New Jersey (2000-2002)

Chambers of District Judge Jose L. Linares *continued*

Legal Practice: Litigation Associate, Horowitz, Bross & Sinins (1980-1982); Partner, Linares & Seradzky, Esqs. (1982-1985); Senior Partner, Linares & Coviello, Esqs. (1985-1999); Senior Partner, Linares, Coviello & Santana, Esqs. (1999-2000)

Nonprofit: President, New Jersey Hispanic Bar Association

Current Memberships: American Bar Foundation; American Association for Justice; Essex County Bar Association; New Jersey Association of Trial Lawyers; New Jersey State Bar Association

Staff

Law Clerk **Gregory Mortenson** .... (973) 645-6042
Began Service: September 2015
Term Expires: September 2016
E-mail: gregory_mortenson@njd.uscourts.gov
Law Clerk **Hope Skibitsky** .... (973) 645-6042
Began Service: September 2015
Term Expires: September 2016
E-mail: hope_skibitsky@njd.uscourts.gov
Career Law Clerk **Stephanie Reger** .... (973) 645-6042
E-mail: stephanie_reger@njd.uscourts.gov
Education: NYU 2008 JD
Courtroom Deputy **Lissette Rodriguez** .... (973) 645-4702
E-mail: lissette_rodriguez@njd.uscourts.gov
Court Reporter **Phyllis Lewis** .... (973) 645-3677
E-mail: phyllis_lewis@njd.uscourts.gov

Chambers of District Judge Freda L. Wolfson

Clarkson S. Fisher Federal Building and U.S. Courthouse,
402 East State Street, Room 5050, Trenton, NJ 08608
Tel: (609) 989-2182 Fax: (609) 989-0496
E-mail: Freda_Wolfson@njd.uscourts.gov

Freda L. Wolfson
District Judge

Date of Birth: May 20, 1954
Education: Rutgers 1976 BA; Rutgers (Newark) 1979 JD
Began Service: December 4, 2002
Appointed By: President George W. Bush
Political Affiliation: Democrat

Judicial: Magistrate Judge, United States District Court for the District of New Jersey (1986-2002)

Legal Practice: Litigation Associate, Lowenstein, Sandler, Kohl, Fisher & Boylan (1979-1981); Litigation Associate, Clapp & Eisenberg (1981-1986)

Current Memberships: American Bar Foundation; New Jersey State Bar Association; Third Circuit Court of Appeals Bar Association

Staff

Law Clerk **Caitlin Jaye** .... (609) 989-2182
Began Service: September 2015
Term Expires: September 2016
E-mail: vinita_andrapalliyal@njd.uscourts.gov
Law Clerk **John Atkin** .... (609) 989-2182
Began Service: September 2015
Term Expires: September 2016
E-mail: john_atkin@njd.uscourts.gov
Career Law Clerk **Wayne Fang** .... (609) 989-2182
Began Service: 2007
E-mail: wayne_fang@njd.uscourts.gov
Education: Rutgers BS; Seton Hall JD
Courtroom Deputy **Jackie Gore** .... (609) 989-2182
E-mail: jackie_gore@njd.uscourts.gov
Court Reporter **Vincent Russoniello** .... (609) 588-9516
E-mail: vincent_russoniello@njd.uscourts.gov

Chambers of District Judge Susan D. Wigenton

Martin Luther King, Jr. Federal Building and U.S. Courthouse,
50 Walnut Street, Room 5060, Newark, NJ 07102
Tel: (973) 645-5903
E-mail: judge_susan_wigenton@njd.uscourts.gov

Susan D. Wigenton
District Judge

Date of Birth: October 12, 1962
Education: Norfolk State BA; William & Mary JD
Began Service: June 2006
Appointed By: President George W. Bush

Clerkships: Law Clerk, Judge Lawrence M. Lawson, Superior Court of New Jersey (1987-1988)

Government: Public Defender, Office of the Public Defender, City of Ashbury Park, New Jersey (1989-1993)

Judicial: Magistrate Judge (part-time), United States District Court for the District of New Jersey (1997-2000); Magistrate Judge (full-time), United States District Court for the District of New Jersey (2000-2006)

Legal Practice: Partner/Shareholder, Giordano, Halleran & Ciesla, P.C.

Staff

Law Clerk **Devon A. Corneal** .... (973) 645-5903
E-mail: devon_corneal@njd.uscourts.gov
Education: Seton Hall 2003 JD

Law Clerk **Eliberty Lopez** .... (973) 645-5903
Began Service: August 2014
Term Expires: August 2016
E-mail: eliberty_lopez@njd.uscourts.gov

Law Clerk **Garen Marshall** .... (973) 645-5903
E-mail: garen_marshall@njd.uscourts.gov

Courtroom Deputy **Carmen D. Soto** .... (973) 645-3095
E-mail: carmen_soto@njd.uscourts.gov

Court Reporter **Carmen Liloia** .... (973) 477-9704
E-mail: carmen_liloia@njd.uscourts.gov

Chambers of District Judge Renée Marie Bumb

Mitchell H. Cohen U.S. Courthouse, One John F. Gerry Plaza,
Camden, NJ 08102-1029
Tel: (856) 757-5020

Renée Marie Bumb
District Judge

Date of Birth: January 25, 1960
Education: Ohio State 1981 BA; Chicago 1983 MA; Rutgers 1987 JD
Began Service: June 2006
Appointed By: President George W. Bush

Clerkships: Law Clerk, Judge Garrett E. Brown, Jr., United States District Court for the District of New Jersey (1987-1988)

Government: Criminal Division Attorney-in-Charge, Camden (NJ) Office, Executive Office for United States Attorneys, United States Department of Justice; Assistant U.S. Attorney-in-Charge, Camden (NJ) Office, Executive Office for United States Attorneys, United States Department of Justice

Legal Practice: Associate, Riker, Danzig, Scherer, Hyland & Perretti (1988-1991)

Staff

Law Clerk **Samuel Harrison** .... (856) 757-5020
Began Service: July 1, 2015
Term Expires: June 30, 2017
E-mail: sam_harrison@njd.uscourts.gov

Law Clerk **Clarissa Lintner** .... (856) 757-5020
Began Service: September 1, 2015
Term Expires: August 31, 2017
E-mail: clarissa_lintner@njd.uscourts.gov

Courtroom Deputy **Art Roney** .... (856) 757-5014

Court Reporter **Ted Formaroli** .... (856) 635-9054
E-mail: ted_formaroli@njd.uscourts.gov

Chambers of District Judge Renée Marie Bumb *continued*

Judicial Assistant **Roberta Costigan** .... (856) 757-5020
E-mail: roberta_costigan@njd.uscourts.gov

Chambers of District Judge Noel Lawrence Hillman

6010 Mitchell H. Cohen U.S. Courthouse, One John F. Gerry Plaza,
Camden, NJ 08101-0887
Tel: (856) 757-5057
E-mail: noel_hillman@njd.uscourts.gov

Noel Lawrence Hillman
District Judge

Date of Birth: 1956
Education: Monmouth U 1981 BA; Seton Hall 1985 JD; NYU 1998 LLM
Began Service: June 2006
Appointed By: President George W. Bush

Clerkships: Law Clerk, District Judge Maryanne Trump Barry, United States District Court for the District of New Jersey (1986-1988)

Government: Assistant U.S. Attorney, Executive Office for United States Attorneys, District of New Jersey, United States Department of Justice (1992-2001); Criminal Division, Deputy Chief, Executive Office for U.S. Attorneys, District of New Jersey, United States Department of Justice (2000-2001); Public Integrity Section Principal Deputy Chief, Criminal Division, Office of the Deputy Attorney General, U.S. Department of Justice (2001-2002); Public Integrity Section Acting Chief, Criminal Division, Office of the Deputy Attorney General, U.S. Department of Justice (2002-2003); Public Integrity Section Chief, Criminal Division, Office of the Deputy Attorney General, United States Department of Justice (2003-2006)

Legal Practice: Attorney, Private Practice (1986); Attorney, Private Pratice (1988-1992)

Staff

Career Law Clerk **Melinda Mueller** .... (856) 757-5057
Began Service: 2009
E-mail: melinda_mueller@njd.uscourts.gov

Courtroom Deputy **Gladys Novoa** .... (856) 968-4982
E-mail: gladys_novoa@njd.uscourts.gov

Chambers of District Judge Peter G. Sheridan

Clarkson S. Fisher Building and United States Courthouse,
402 East State Street, Room 4E, Trenton, NJ 08608
Tel: (609) 989-0508
E-mail: judge_peter_sheridan@njd.uscourts.gov

Peter G. Sheridan
District Judge

Date of Birth: 1950
Education: St Peter's Col 1972 BS; Seton Hall 1977 JD
Began Service: June 2006
Appointed By: President George W. Bush

Clerkships: Law Clerk, Judge James J. Petrella, Superior Court of New Jersey (1977-1978)

Corporate: Vice President and General Counsel, Atlantic City Casino Association (1984-1987)

Government: Attorney, The Port Authority of New York and New Jersey (1978-1981); Executive Director, New Jersey Republican State Committee, Republican National Committee (1993-1994)

Legal Practice: Associate, McCarthy and Schatzman (1981-1984); Of Counsel, Cohen, Shapiro, Polisher, Shiekman & Cohen (1990-1992); Partner, Cullen and Dykman (1994-1995); Shareholder/Director, Graham, Curtin & Sheridan (1995)

(continued on next page)

Chambers of District Judge Peter G. Sheridan *continued*

Staff

Law Clerk **Joshua Katz** .... (609) 989-0508
Began Service: September 2015
Term Expires: September 2016
E-mail: joshua_katz@njd.uscourts.gov

Law Clerk **Lauren Cooper** .... (609) 989-0508
Began Service: September 2015
Term Expires: September 2016
E-mail: lauren_cooper@njd.uscourts.gov

Courtroom Deputy **Dolores Hicks** .... (609) 989-0508
E-mail: dolores_hicks@njd.uscourts.gov

Court Reporter **Frank Gable** .... (856) 889-4761
E-mail: frank_gable@njd.uscourts.gov

Judicial Assistant **Harriet Tyrrell** .... (609) 989-0508
E-mail: harriet_tyrrell@njd.uscourts.gov

Chambers of District Judge Claire C. Cecchi

Martin Luther King Jr. Federal Building & U.S. Courthouse,
50 Walnut Street, Room 4015, Newark, NJ 07101
Tel: (973) 645-6664
E-mail: judge_claire_cecchi@njd.uscourts.gov

Claire C. Cecchi
District Judge

Education: Barnard 1982 BA; Fordham 1989 JD
Began Service: June 14, 2011
Appointed By: President Barack Obama

Staff

Law Clerk **Morgan Davis** .... (973) 645-6664
Began Service: September 2015
Term Expires: September 2016
E-mail: morgan_davis@njd.uscourts.gov

Law Clerk **Alexandra Sadinsky** .... (973) 645-6664
Began Service: September 2015
Term Expires: September 2016
E-mail: alexandra_sadinsky@njd.uscourts.gov

Law Clerk **Adam Stienmetz** .... (973) 645-6664
Began Service: September 2015
Term Expires: September 2016

Career Law Clerk **(Vacant)** .... (973) 645-2578

Courtroom Deputy **Jacqueline Lambiase** .... (973) 645-6664
E-mail: jacqueline_lambiase@njd.uscourts.gov

Court Reporter **Yvonne Davion** .... (908) 229-1221
E-mail: yvonne_davion@njd.uscourts.gov

Chambers of District Judge Esther Salas

Martin Luther King Jr. Federal Building and U.S. Courthouse,
50 Walnut Street, Room 5076, Newark, NJ 07101
Tel: (973) 297-4887
E-mail: judge_esther_salas@njd.uscourts.gov

Esther Salas
District Judge

Education: Rutgers 1991 BA, 1994 JD
Began Service: June 14, 2011
Appointed By: President Barack Obama

Staff

Law Clerk **Simone Silva-Arrindell** .... (973) 297-4887
Began Service: September 2015
Term Expires: September 2016

Law Clerk **Evan Miller** .... (973) 297-4887
Began Service: September 2015
Term Expires: September 2016
E-mail: evan_miller@njd.uscourts.gov

Law Clerk **Amar Mehta** .... (973) 297-4887
Began Service: September 2015
Term Expires: September 2016
E-mail: amar_mehta@njd.uscourts.gov

Court Reporter **Lynne Johnson** .... (609) 896-1836

Chambers of District Judge Esther Salas *continued*

Courtroom Deputy **Philip Selecky** .... (973) 297-4887
E-mail: philip_selecky@njd.uscourts.gov

Chambers of District Judge Kevin McNulty

Martin Luther King, Jr. Federal Building & U.S. Courthouse,
50 Walnut Street, Newark, NJ 07101
Tel: (973) 645-3493

Kevin McNulty
District Judge

Education: Yale 1976 BA; NYU 1983 JD
Began Service: 2012
Appointed By: President Barack Obama

Staff

Law Clerk **Gayle Argon** .... (973) 645-3493
Began Service: August 30, 2015
Term Expires: August 30, 2016
E-mail: gayle_argon@njd.uscourts.gov

Law Clerk **Jonathan Shenker** .... (973) 645-3493
Began Service: August 30, 2015
Term Expires: August 30, 2016
E-mail: jonathan_schenker@njd.uscourts.gov

Law Clerk **Heather Suchorsky** .... (973) 645-3493
Began Service: August 30, 2015
Term Expires: August 30, 2016
E-mail: heather_suchorsky@njd.uscourts.gov

Court Reporter **Mollie Ann Giordano** .... (973) 220-9465
E-mail: mollieann_giordano@njd.uscourts.gov

Courtroom Deputy **Nitza Creegan** .... (973) 645-2578
E-mail: nitza_creegan@njd.uscourts.gov

Chambers of District Judge Michael A. Shipp

Clarkson S. Fisher Building and U.S. Courthouse, 402 East State Street,
Room 7W, Trenton, NJ 08608
Tel: (609) 989-2009

Michael A. Shipp
District Judge

Education: Rutgers 1987 BA; Seton Hall 1994 JD
Began Service: 2012
Appointed By: President Barack Obama

Staff

Law Clerk **Nizritha Ketty** .... (609) 989-2009
Began Service: August 2015
Term Expires: September 2016

Law Clerk **Kimberly Franko** .... (609) 989-2009
Began Service: August 2014
Term Expires: August 2016
E-mail: kimberly_franko@njd.uscourts.gov

Court Reporter **Cathy Ford** .... (609) 367-2777
E-mail: cathy_ford@njd.uscourts.gov

Courtroom Deputy **Nativelis Rodriguez** .... (609) 989-2009
E-mail: nativelis_rodriguez@njd.uscourts.gov

Chambers of District Judge Madeline Cox Arleo

50 Walnut Street, Newark, NJ 07101
Tel: (973) 297-4903
E-mail: madeline_arleo@njd.uscourts.gov

Madeline Cox Arleo
District Judge

Began Service: November 21, 2014
Appointed By: President Barack Obama

Judicial: Magistrate Judge, Chambers of Magistrate Judge Madeline Cox Arleo, United States District Court for the District of New Jersey (2000-2015)

Chambers of District Judge Madeline Cox Arleo *continued*

Staff
Fax: (973) 297-4906

Law Clerk **Amanda Laufer** .... (973) 297-4903
E-mail: amanda_laufer@njd.uscourts.gov
Law Clerk **Alex Silagi** .... (973) 297-4903
Began Service: 2015
Term Expires: August 2016
E-mail: alex_silagi@njd.uscourts.gov
Education: Seton Hall 2014 JD
Courtroom Deputy **Amy Andersonn** .... (973) 297-4903

Chambers of Senior Judge Joseph H. Rodriguez

6060 Mitchell H. Cohen U.S. Courthouse, One John F. Gerry Plaza, Camden, NJ 08102
P.O. Box 886, Camden, NJ 08101
Tel: (856) 757-5002 Fax: (856) 757-5077

Joseph H. Rodriguez
Senior Judge

Date of Birth: 1930
Education: La Salle U 1955 AB; Rutgers (Camden) 1958 LLB, 1968 JD
Began Service: May 23, 1985
Appointed By: President Ronald Reagan

Academic: Chairman, State Board of Higher Education (1971-1973); Instructor, School of Law - Camden, Rutgers, The State University of New Jersey (1972-1982); Lecturer, School of Law, University of Pennsylvania (1989-1992); Instructor, School of Law - Camden, Rutgers, The State University of New Jersey (1993-1994)

Government: Chairman, State Commission of Investigation, State of New Jersey (1974-1979); Public Advocate and Public Defender, State of New Jersey (1982-1985)

Legal Practice: Partner, Brown, Connery, Kulp, Wille, Purnell & Greene (1959-1982)

Military Service: United States Army (1950-1952)

Current Memberships: American Bar Association; American College of Trial Lawyers; International Society of Barristers; New Jersey State Bar Association

Staff
Law Clerk **(Vacant)** .... (856) 757-5002
Career Law Clerk **Maureen Lee Behm** .... (856) 757-5002
E-mail: maureen_behm@njd.uscourts.gov
Education: Rutgers 1996 BS; Rutgers (Camden) 2002 JD
Career Law Clerk **Patricia A. Legge** .... (856) 757-5002
E-mail: Patricia_Legge@njd.uscourts.gov
Education: Rutgers (Camden) 1995 JD
Courtroom Deputy **Dave Bruey** .... (856) 757-5193
E-mail: dave_bruey@njd.uscourts.gov
Court Reporter **(Vacant)** .... (856) 576-7084
Judicial Assistant **Lillian Niedringhaus** .... (856) 757-5002
E-mail: lillian_niedringhaus@njd.uscourts.gov

Chambers of Senior Judge Anne E. Thompson

Clarkson S. Fisher Federal Building & U.S. Courthouse, 402 East State Street, Trenton, NJ 08608
Tel: (609) 989-2123

Anne E. Thompson
Senior Judge

Date of Birth: 1934
Education: Howard U 1955 BA; Temple 1957 MA; Howard U 1964 LLB
Began Service: 1979
Appointed By: President Jimmy Carter
Political Affiliation: Democrat

Government: Staff Attorney, Office of the Solicitor, United States Department of Labor (1964-1965); Assistant Deputy Public Defender, State of New Jersey (1967-1970); Municipal Prosecutor, Office of the Municipal Prosecutor, Township of Lawrence, New Jersey (1970-1972); Prosecutor, Office of the County Prosecutor, County of Mercer, New Jersey (1975-1979)

Judicial: Judge, Trenton Municipal Court (1972-1975); Chief Judge, United States District Court for the District of New Jersey (1994-2001)

Legal Practice: Private Practice (1971-1975)

Current Memberships: American Bar Association; Mercer County Bar Association; New Jersey State Bar Association

Staff
Law Clerk **Rebecca Lipman** .... (609) 989-2123
Began Service: September 2015
Term Expires: September 2016
E-mail: rebecca_lipman@njd.uscourts.gov
Law Clerk **Christina Black** .... (609) 989-2123
Began Service: September 2015
Term Expires: September 2016
E-mail: christina_black@njd.uscourts.gov
Courtroom Deputy **Dana Sledge-Courtney** .... (609) 989-2182
Court Reporter **Jaweia Campbell** .... (609) 588-9516
Secretary **Ann Dello Iacono** .... (609) 989-2123

Chambers of Senior Judge William H. Walls

Martin Luther King, Jr. Federal Building & U.S. Courthouse, 50 Walnut Street, Newark, NJ 07101
Tel: (973) 645-2564
E-mail: chambers_of_judge_william_walls@njd.uscourts.gov

William H. Walls
Senior Judge

Education: Dartmouth 1954 AB; Yale 1957 LLB
Began Service: 1994
Appointed By: President William J. Clinton

Government: Assistant Corporation Counsel, City of Newark, New Jersey (1962-1968); Corporation Counsel, City of Newark, New Jersey (1970-1973); Business Administrator, City of Newark, New Jersey (1974-1977)

Judicial: Judge, Newark Municipal Court (1968-1970); Judge, Essex County Court (1977-1978); Judge, New Jersey Superior Court (1979-1994)

Legal Practice: Law Clerk, Kirkman, Mulligan, Bell & Armstrong (1957-1959); Associate, Herbert Klosk (1959-1962); Sole Practitioner (1968-1970); Partner, Walls, Lester & Smith (1972)

Staff
Law Clerk **Grant Damon** .... (973) 645-2564
Began Service: September 2015
Term Expires: September 2016
E-mail: grant_damon@njd.uscourts.gov
Law Clerk **Alexander Gouzoules** .... (973) 645-2564
Began Service: September 2015
Term Expires: September 2016
E-mail: alexander_gouzoules@njd.uscourts.gov

(continued on next page)

Chambers of Senior Judge William H. Walls *continued*

Courtroom Deputy **Loretta Minott** .... (973) 645-2564
E-mail: loretta_minott@njd.uscourts.gov
Court Reporter **Yvonne Davion** .... (908) 656-1221
E-mail: yvonne_davion@njd.uscourts.gov

Chambers of Senior Judge Mary L. Cooper

Clarkson S. Fisher Federal Building & U.S. Courthouse, 402 East State Street, Room 5000, Trenton, NJ 08608-1507
Tel: (609) 989-2105
E-mail: mary_cooper@njd.uscourts.gov

Mary L. Cooper
Senior Judge

Date of Birth: 1946
Education: Bryn Mawr 1968 AB; Villanova 1972 JD
Began Service: March 1992
Appointed By: President George H.W. Bush
Political Affiliation: Republican

Current Memberships: The John C. Lifland American Inn of Court, The American Inns of Court; Mercer County Bar Association; Princeton Bar Association

Staff

Law Clerk **Katherine S. Linsey** .... (609) 989-2105
Began Service: September 2014
Term Expires: September 2016
E-mail: katherine_linsey@njd.uscourts.gov
Education: Temple 2014 JD
Law Clerk **Megan Lagreca** .... (609) 989-2105
Began Service: September 2015
Term Expires: September 2016
E-mail: megan_lagreca@njd.uscourts.gov
Education: Villanova 2014 JD
Career Law Clerk **Brian Suparnowitz** .... (609) 989-2105
Courtroom Deputy **Elizabeth Heffner** .... (609) 989-2329
E-mail: elizabeth_heffner@njd.uscourts.gov
Court Reporter **Regina Tell** .... (609) 989-2340
E-mail: regina_tell@njd.uscourts.gov

Chambers of Senior Judge Katharine S. Hayden

U.S. Courthouse & Post Office Building, Federal Square, Newark, NJ 07102
Tel: (973) 645-4611

Katharine S. Hayden
Senior Judge

Date of Birth: 1942
Education: Marymount Manhattan 1963 BA; Seton Hall 1971 MA, 1975 JD
Began Service: October 14, 1997
Appointed By: President William J. Clinton

Academic: Adjunct Professor, English Department, Seton Hall University (1967-1972); Adjunct Professor, School of Law, Seton Hall University (2002)

Clerkships: Law Clerk The Honorable Robert L. Clifford, New Jersey Supreme Court (1975-1976)

Corporate: Editorial Assistant, Harper & Row Publishers, Inc. (1964-1965); Assistant Fiction Editor, Good Housekeeping (1965-1967)

Government: Assistant United States Attorney, District of New Jersey, United States Attorney's Office, United States Department of Justice, Gerald Ford Administration (1976-1978)

Judicial: Judge, Superior Court of New Jersey (1991-1997)

Legal Practice: Partner, Sweeney, Bozonelis, Staehle & Woodward, Esqs. (1978-1984); Partner, Boyar, Higgins & Sweeney (1984-1987); Partner, Boyar, Higgins & Hayden (1987-1991)

Chambers of Senior Judge Katharine S. Hayden *continued*

Current Memberships: American Bar Foundation; American Bar Association; New Jersey State Bar Association

Staff

Law Clerk **Katherine St. Romain** .... (973) 645-4611
Began Service: September 2015
Term Expires: September 2016
Law Clerk **Phillip Pavlick** .... (973) 645-4611
Began Service: February 2015
Term Expires: February 2016
E-mail: phillip_pavlick@njd.uscourts.gov
Education: Seton Hall 2013 JD
Courtroom Deputy **RoseMarie Olizieri-Guilloty** .... (973) 645-2487
E-mail: rosemarie_guilloty@njd.uscourts.gov
Court Reporter **Ralph Florio** .... (973) 639-1817
E-mail: ralphflorio@hotmail.com
Secretary **Patricia "Patti" Martirano** .... (973) 645-4611
E-mail: patti_martirano@njd.uscourts.gov

Chambers of Senior Judge William J. Martini

Martin Luther King, Jr. Federal Building and U.S. Courthouse, 50 Walnut Street, Room 4069, Newark, NJ 07101
P.O. Box 419, Newark, NJ 07101-0419
Tel: (973) 645-6340
E-mail: judge_william_martini@njd.uscourts.gov

William J. Martini
Senior Judge

Date of Birth: February 10, 1947
Education: Villanova 1968 BA; Rutgers 1972 JD
Began Service: November 19, 2002
Appointed By: President George W. Bush

Staff

Law Clerk **Ilana Drescher** .... (973) 645-6340
Began Service: August 2015
Term Expires: September 2017
E-mail: ilana_drescher@njd.uscourts.gov
Law Clerk **Rajeev Raghavan** .... (973) 645-6340
Began Service: September 2015
Term Expires: September 2017
E-mail: rajeev_raghavan@njd.uscourts.gov
Law Clerk **Alexander "Alex" Ziccardi** .... (973) 645-6340
Began Service: September 2014
Term Expires: September 2016
Courtroom Clerk **Gail Hansen** .... (973) 645-4562
E-mail: gail_hansen@njd.uscourts.gov
Court Reporter **Walter Perelli** .... (973) 645-2514
E-mail: walter_perelli@njd.uscourts.gov

Chambers of Senior Judge Stanley R. Chesler

Frank R. Lautenberg U.S. Courthouse & Post Office Building, 50 Walnut Street, Newark, NJ 07101
Tel: (973) 645-3136
E-mail: judge_stanley_chesler@njd.uscourts.gov

Stanley R. Chesler
Senior Judge

Date of Birth: June 15, 1947
Education: SUNY (Binghamton) 1968 BA; St John's U (NY) 1974 JD
Began Service: December 4, 2002
Appointed By: President George W. Bush

Current Memberships: American Bar Foundation; The John C. Lifland American Inn of Court, The American Inns of Court; Federal Bar Association

Chambers of Senior Judge Stanley R. Chesler *continued*

Staff

Law Clerk **Allison Schmitt** .... (973) 645-3136
E-mail: allison_schmitt@njd.uscourts.gov

Career Law Clerk **Timothy Bogen** .... (973) 645-3136
E-mail: timothy_bogen@njd.uscourts.gov
Education: Cardozo 2004 JD

Career Law Clerk **Marielena Piriz** .... (973) 645-3136
Began Service: 2007
E-mail: marielena_piriz@njd.uscourts.gov
Education: Georgetown 1997 BS; NYU 2001 JD

Courtroom Deputy **Theresa C. Trivino** .... (973) 645-4705
E-mail: theresa_trivino@njd.uscourts.gov
Education: Seton Hall 1985 BA

Court Reporter **Jackie Kashmer** .... (973) 229-6496
E-mail: jackie_kashmer@njd.uscourts.gov

Chambers of Magistrate Judge Mark Falk

U.S. Post Office and Courthouse, One Federal Square, Room 457,
Newark, NJ 07102-3513
Tel: (973) 645-3110 Fax: (973) 645-3097
E-mail: chambersofmagistratejudgemark_falk@njd.uscourts.gov

Mark Falk
Magistrate Judge

Date of Birth: 1952
Education: Antioch U 1974 BA; New York Law 1977 JD
Began Service: March 1, 2002
Term Expires: February 28, 2018

Clerkships: Law Clerk, Assignment Judge The Honorable John C. Demos, Superior Court of New Jersey (1977-1978)

Legal Practice: Partner, Clapp & Eisenberg (1978-1994); Partner, Barry & McMoran (1994-1998); Partner, Tompkins, McGuire, Wachenfeld & Barry LLP (1998-2002)

Current Memberships: American Bar Association; Essex County Bar Association; Federal Bar Association; New Jersey State Bar Association

Staff

Law Clerk **Gerhard Buehning** .... (973) 645-3110
Began Service: September 2015
Term Expires: September 2016
E-mail: gerhard_buehning@njd.uscourts.gov

Career Law Clerk **Justin Conlon** .... (973) 645-3110
Began Service: September 2009

Deputy Clerk **Lorraine G. McNerney** .... (973) 645-3110
E-mail: lorraine_mcnerney@njd.uscourts.gov

Chambers of Magistrate Judge Ann Marie Donio

One John F. Gerry Plaza, Camden, NJ 08101
Tel: (856) 757-5211

Ann Marie Donio
Magistrate Judge

Date of Birth: June 6, 1960
Began Service: March 24, 2003
Term Expires: March 2019

Staff

Law Clerk **Christine Gaddis** .... (856) 757-5211
Began Service: September 2015
Term Expires: September 2016
E-mail: christine_gaddis@njd.uscourts.gov

Courtroom Deputy **Susan Bush** .... (856) 757-5319
E-mail: susan_bush@njd.uscourts.gov

Secretary **Sharon L. Crescenti** .... (856) 757-5211
E-mail: sharon_crescenti@njd.uscourts.gov

Chambers of Magistrate Judge Tonianne J. Bongiovanni

Clarkson S. Fisher Federal Building, and United States Courthouse,
402 East State Street, Trenton, NJ 08608-1507
Tel: (609) 989-2040
E-mail: tjb_orders@njd.uscourts.gov

Tonianne J. Bongiovanni
Magistrate Judge

Date of Birth: May 3, 1958
Education: New Jersey City U BA; Seton Hall JD
Began Service: April 14, 2003
Term Expires: 2019

Staff
Tel: (609) 989-2040

Law Clerk **Michael Westwood-Booth** .... (609) 989-2040
Began Service: September 2015
Term Expires: September 2016
E-mail: michael_westwoodbooth@njd.uscourts.gov

Career Law Clerk **Sharon Bray** .... (609) 989-2040
Began Service: 2007
E-mail: sharon_bray@njd.uscourts.gov
Education: Harvard 2004 JD

Courtroom Deputy **Mark J. Morelli** .... (609) 989-2133
E-mail: mark_morelli@njd.uscourts.gov

Chambers of Magistrate Judge Joel Schneider

2060 Mitchell H. Cohen US Courthouse, One John F. Gerry Plaza,
Room 3C, Camden, NJ 08101
Tel: (856) 757-5446

Joel Schneider
Magistrate Judge

Began Service: October 2006
Term Expires: 2022

Staff

Law Clerk **John Marshall** .... (856) 757-5446
Began Service: September 2015
Term Expires: September 2016
E-mail: john_marshall@njd.uscourts.gov

Courtroom Deputy **Sarah Eckert** .... (856) 757-5488
E-mail: sarah_eckert@njd.uscourts.gov

Secretary **Jackie Kotarski** .... (856) 757-5446
E-mail: jackie_kotarski@njd.uscourts.gov

Chambers of Magistrate Judge Karen Williams

One John F. Gerry Plaza, Camden, NJ 08102-1029
Tel: (856) 757-6843

Karen Williams
Magistrate Judge

Began Service: May 1, 2009

Staff

Courtroom Deputy **Denise Wolk** .... (856) 757-6844
E-mail: denise_wolk@njd.uscourts.gov

Chambers of Magistrate Judge Douglas E. Arpert

Clarkson S. Fisher U.S. Courthouse, 402 East State Street,
Trenton, NJ 08608
Tel: (609) 989-2144

Douglas E. Arpert
Magistrate Judge

Began Service: April 2009

(continued on next page)

Chambers of Magistrate Judge Douglas E. Arpert *continued*

Staff

Law Clerk **Jessica Biamonte** .... (609) 989-2144
Began Service: September 2015
Term Expires: September 2016
E-mail: jessica_biamonte@njd.uscourts.gov
Courtroom Deputy **Charmaine Ellington** .... (609) 989-2144
E-mail: charmaine_ellington@njd.uscourts.gov
Judicial Assistant **Ruth Hawkins** .... (609) 989-2144
E-mail: ruth_hawkins@njd.uscourts.gov

Chambers of Magistrate Judge Lois H. Goodman

Clarkson S. Fisher Building and U.S. Courthouse, 402 East State Street, Room 7E, Trenton, NJ 08608
Tel: (609) 989-2138

Lois H. Goodman
Magistrate Judge

Education: Rutgers 1977 BA; NYU 1986 JD
Began Service: 2009

Staff

Career Law Clerk **Phillip Gonzalez** .... (609) 989-2138
Began Service: September 2013
E-mail: phillip_gonzalez@njd.uscourts.gov
Law Clerk **Emily Dupraz** .... (609) 989-2138
Began Service: September 2015
Term Expires: September 2016
E-mail: emily_dupraz@njd.uscourts.gov
Courtroom Deputy **Ivannya Jimenez** .... (609) 989-2114
E-mail: ivannya_jimenez@njd.uscourts.gov

Chambers of Magistrate Judge Michael A. Hammer

50 Walnut Street, Newark, NJ 07101
Tel: (973) 776-7858

Michael A. Hammer, Jr.
Magistrate Judge

Began Service: August 12, 2011

Staff

Law Clerk **Tara A. Dunican** .... (973) 776-7858
Began Service: 2015
Term Expires: September 2016
E-mail: tara_dunican@njd.uscourts.gov
Education: Seton Hall 1994 JD
Law Clerk **Carissa Gomez** .... (973) 776-7858
Began Service: 2015
Term Expires: September 2016
Courtroom Deputy **Jacquetta Baker** .... (973) 645-4620
E-mail: jacquetta_baker@njd.uscourts.gov

Chambers of Magistrate Judge Joseph A. Dickson

Martin Luther King, Jr. Federal Building and U.S. Courthouse, 50 Walnut Street, Newark, NJ 07101
Tel: (973) 645-2580

Joseph A. Dickson
Magistrate Judge

Began Service: 2010

Staff

Law Clerk **Timothy Duva** .... (973) 645-2580
Began Service: September 2013
Term Expires: September 2016
E-mail: timothy_duva@njd.uscourts.gov
Law Clerk **Christina Yousef** .... (973) 645-2580
Began Service: September 2014
Term Expires: September 2016
E-mail: christina_yousef@njd.uscourts.gov

Chambers of Magistrate Judge Joseph A. Dickson *continued*

Courtroom Deputy **Nadine Mauro** .... (973) 645-2580
E-mail: nadine_mauro@njd.uscourts.gov

Chambers of Magistrate Judge Cathy L. Waldor

50 Walnut Street, Newark, NJ 07101
Tel: (973) 776-7862 Fax: (973) 776-7865

Cathy L. Waldor
Magistrate Judge

Began Service: September 1, 2011

Staff

Law Clerk **Daniel Beauchemin** .... (973) 776-7862
Began Service: September 2015
Term Expires: September 2016
Law Clerk **Brett Katz** .... (973) 776-7862
Began Service: September 2015
Term Expires: September 2016
E-mail: brett_katz@njd.uscourts.gov
Courtroom Deputy **Timothy Gorman** .... (973) 776-7862
E-mail: timothy_gorman@njd.uscourts.gov

Chambers of Magistrate Judge Steven C. Mannion

50 Walnut Street, Newark, NJ 07101
Tel: (973) 645-3827

Steven C. Mannion
Magistrate Judge

Staff

Law Clerk **Ryan Lamb** .... (973) 645-3827
Term Expires: September 2016
E-mail: ryan_lamb@njd.uscourts.gov
Career Law Clerk **Joyce Chen** .... (973) 645-3827
E-mail: joyce_chen@njd.uscourts.gov
Courtroom Deputy **Murtura Akbari** .... (973) 645-3827

Chambers of Magistrate Judge James B. Clark III

50 Walnut Street, Newark, NJ 07101
Tel: (973) 776-7700 Fax: (973) 645-3020

James B. Clark III
Magistrate Judge

Staff

Law Clerk **Kashif Chand** .... (973) 776-7700
Term Expires: September 2016
E-mail: kashif_chand@njd.uscourts.gov
Law Clerk **Mercedes Jefferis** .... (973) 776-7700
Term Expires: September 2016
E-mail: mercedes_jefferis@njd.uscourts.gov
Courtroom Deputy **Marquis Whitney** .... (973) 776-7700
E-mail: marquis_whitney@njd.uscourts.gov

Chambers of Magistrate Judge Leda Dunn Wettre

50 Walnut Street, Newark, NJ 07101
Tel: (973) 645-3574 Fax: (973) 645-3535
E-mail: leda_wettre@njd.uscourts.gov

Leda Dunn Wettre
Magistrate Judge

Staff

Courtroom Deputy **Kimberly Darling** .... (973) 645-3574
E-mail: kimberly_darling@njd.uscourts.gov

Chambers of Magistrate Judge (part-time) Anthony R. Mautone

500 Prospect Avenue, 2nd Floor, West Orange, NJ 07052-4101
Tel: (973) 325-5900 Fax: (973) 325-2288
E-mail: Judge_Anthony_Mautone@njd.uscourts.gov

Anthony R. Mautone
Magistrate Judge (Part-Time)

Date of Birth: 1943
Education: Villanova 1964 BS; Seton Hall 1967 JD
Began Service: October 12, 2000
Term Expires: October 2016
Political Affiliation: Democrat

Current Memberships: The Seton Hall Alumni American Inn of Court, The American Inns of Court; Essex County Bar Association; Federal Bar Association; New Jersey State Bar Association

Staff
Office Manager **Angela DiAndrea** .... (973) 325-5900
E-mail: angela_diandrea@njd.uscourts.gov
Secretary **Angela DiAndrea** .... (973) 325-5900
E-mail: angela_diandrea@njd.uscourts.gov

United States Bankruptcy Court for the District of New Jersey

Martin Luther King, Jr. Federal Building & U.S. Courthouse, 50 Walnut Street, 3rd Floor, Newark, NJ 07102
P.O. Box 1352, Newark, NJ 17101-1352
Tel: (973) 645-4764 (Phone) Tel: (800) 676-6856 (PACER)
Tel: (866) 222-8029 ext. 88 (Voice Case Information System VCIS)
Internet: www.njb.uscourts.gov

Number of Judgeships: 9

Court Staff
Clerk of Court **James J. Waldron** .... (973) 776-3460
Chief Deputy Clerk **Jeanne Naughton** .... (973) 645-6181
Clarkson S. Fisher Federal Bldg. & U.S. Courthouse, 402 E. State St., Trenton, NJ 08608
E-mail: jeanne_naughton@njb.uscourts.gov
Deputy-in-Charge - Camden **Mary Shashaty** .... (856) 361-2340
P.O. Box 2067, Camden, NJ 08102-2067
E-mail: mary_shashaty@njb.uscourts.gov
Deputy-in-Charge - Newark **Edward Gordon** .... (973) 776-3422
E-mail: edward_gordon@njb.uscourts.gov
Deputy-in-Charge - Trenton **Nancy Figueroa** .... (609) 858-9380
Clarkson S. Fisher Federal Bldg. & U.S. Courthouse, 402 E. State St., Trenton, NJ 08608
E-mail: nancy_figueroa@njb.uscourts.gov

Chambers of Chief Bankruptcy Judge Kathryn C. Ferguson

Clarkson S. Fisher Federal Building, 402 East State Street, Trenton, NJ 08608
Tel: (609) 858-9350 Fax: (609) 989-0555

Kathryn C. Ferguson
Chief Bankruptcy Judge

Date of Birth: 1958
Education: Rutgers 1980 BA; Rutgers (Camden) 1983 JD
Began Service: November 10, 1993
Term Expires: November 10, 2021

Current Memberships: Mercer County Bar Association; National Conference of Bankruptcy Judges; New Jersey State Bar Association

Chambers of Chief Bankruptcy Judge Kathryn C. Ferguson *continued*

Staff
Career Law Clerk **Christy McDonald** .... (609) 858-9354
E-mail: christy_mcdonald@njb.uscourts.gov
Education: Rutgers 1990 BA; Rutgers (Camden) 1993 JD
Court Recorder **Geraldine Holly-Mack** .... (609) 858-9391
Judicial Assistant **Dana Marie Muccie** .... (609) 858-9351
E-mail: dana_muccie@njb.uscourts.gov

Chambers of Bankruptcy Judge Rosemary Gambardella

MLK Federal Building, 50 Walnut Street, Newark, NJ 07101
P.O. Box 1352, Newark, NJ 07101-1352
Tel: (973) 645-2326 Fax: (973) 645-2610
E-mail: chambers_of_rg@njb.uscourts.gov

Rosemary Gambardella
Bankruptcy Judge

Began Service: May 3, 1985
Term Expires: May 3, 2027

Judicial: Chief Bankruptcy Judge, United States Bankruptcy Court for the District of New Jersey (1998-2005)

Staff
Law Clerk **Colleen Maker** .... (973) 645-2326
Began Service: September 2015
Term Expires: September 2016
E-mail: colleen_maker@njb.uscourts.gov
Courtroom Deputy **Sharon Moore** .... (973) 645-4763
E-mail: sharon_moore@njb.uscourts.gov
Court Reporter **Keri Travis** .... (973) 645-4764 ext. 2663
Judicial Assistant **Rosemary Paul** .... (973) 645-2326
E-mail: rosemary_paul@njb.uscourts.gov

Chambers of Bankruptcy Judge Michael B. Kaplan

Clarkson S. Fisher US Courthouse, 402 East State Street, Trenton, NJ 08608
Tel: (609) 989-9397
E-mail: chambers_of_mbk@njb.uscourts.gov

Michael B. Kaplan
Bankruptcy Judge

Education: Georgetown 1984 AB; Fordham 1987 JD
Began Service: October 2006
Term Expires: October 2020

Staff
Law Clerk **(Vacant)** .... (609) 989-2002
Career Law Clerk **Sean Quigley** .... (609) 989-2002
Began Service: September 2011
E-mail: sean_quigley@njb.uscourts.gov
Court Reporter **Kathleen Feeley** .... (609) 989-9386
E-mail: kathleen_feeley@njb.uscourts.gov
Courtroom Deputy **Wendy Romero** .... (609) 989-9397
E-mail: wendy_romero@njb.uscourts.gov

Chambers of Bankruptcy Judge Christine M. Gravelle

402 East State Street, Trenton, NJ 08608
Tel: (609) 858-9370

Christine M. Gravelle
Bankruptcy Judge

Staff
Law Clerk **Michael Tedesco** .... (609) 858-9374
E-mail: michael_tedesco@njb.uscourts.gov
Judicial Assistant **Gina Price** .... (609) 656-2565

FEDERAL COURTS—UNITED STATES DISTRICT COURTS

Chambers of Bankruptcy Judge Andrew B. Altenburg Jr.

401 Market Street, Camden, NJ 08101
Tel: (856) 361-2321

Andrew B. Altenburg, Jr.
Bankruptcy Judge

Staff
Law Clerk **Martha L. Lemmond** .... (856) 361-2321
E-mail: martha_lemmond@njb.uscourts.gov
Law Clerk **Gloria Melunis** .... (856) 361-2321
E-mail: gloria_melunis@njb.uscourts.gov

Chambers of Bankruptcy Judge Vincent Papalia

50 Walnut Street, Newark, NJ 07101
Tel: (973) 368-1244
E-mail: chambers_of_vfp@njb.uscourts.gov

Vincent F. Papalia
Bankruptcy Judge

Education: Pace 1981 BBA; Fordham 1984 JD

Staff
Law Clerk **Margaret S. Hall** .... (973) 368-1244
Education: Rutgers BA, MA; Rutgers (Newark) JD
Judicial Assistant **Margaret Cohen** .... (973) 645-3262
E-mail: margaret_cohen@njb.uscourts.gov
Education: Kean U BA
Courtroom Deputy **Juan Filgueiras** .... (973) 368-1244
Court Reporter **Mariela Primo** .... (973) 776-3457
E-mail: mariela_primo@njb.uscourts.gov

Chambers of Bankruptcy Judge John K. Sherwood

50 Walnut Street, Newark, NJ 07101
Tel: (973) 645-4693
E-mail: chambers_of_jks@njb.uscourts.gov

John K. Sherwood
Bankruptcy Judge

Chambers of Bankruptcy Jerrold N. Poslusny Jr.

50 Walnut Street, Newark, NJ 07101
Tel: (856) 361-2310

Jerrold N. Poslusny, Jr.
Bankruptcy Judge

United States District Court for the District of New Mexico

333 Lomas Boulevard, NW, Albuquerque, NM 87102
Tel: (505) 348-2000 Fax: (505) 348-2028
Internet: www.nmcourt.fed.us/dcdocs

Number of Judgeships: 7

Circuit: Tenth

Court Staff

Clerk of Court **Matthew J. Dykman** .... (505) 348-2000
E-mail: mdykman@nmcourt.fed.us Fax: (505) 348-2028
Chief Deputy Clerk **Mitchell R. Elfers** .... (505) 348-2082
E-mail: melfers@nmcourt.fed.us Fax: (505) 348-2028
Deputy Clerk-in-Charge [Las Cruces] **Lincoln Sorrell** .... (575) 528-1400
U.S. Courthouse, 100 North Church Street, Fax: (575) 528-1425
Las Cruces, NM 88001
Education: New Mexico 1989 BA

United States District Court for the District of New Mexico *continued*

Chief U.S. Probation Officer **Margaret Vigil** .... (505) 348-2600
Case Management Supervision [Santa Fe] **Pat Zold** ...... (505) 988-6481
Administrative Services Manager **(Vacant)** .... (505) 348-2084
Information Technology Manager **Paul O'Brien** .... (505) 348-2104
Fax: (505) 348-2028
Librarian **Gregory Townsend** .... (505) 348-2136
E-mail: gtownsend@nmcourt.fed.us Fax: (505) 348-2795
Education: St Mary's U (TX) 1991 JD

Chambers of Chief District Judge M. Christina Armijo

U.S. Courthouse, 333 Lomas Boulevard, NW, Suite 760,
Albuquerque, NM 87102
Tel: (505) 348-2310 Fax: (505) 348-2315
E-mail: marmijo@nmcourt.fed.us

M. Christina Armijo
Chief District Judge

Date of Birth: 1951
Education: New Mexico 1972 BA, 1975 JD
Began Service: November 15, 2001
Appointed By: President George W. Bush
Political Affiliation: Republican

Current Memberships: The Oliver Seth American Inn of Court; The American Inns of Court; State Bar of New Mexico

Staff
Career Law Clerk **Clark C. Varnell** .... (505) 348-2310
Education: New Mexico 1986 JD
Courtroom Deputy **Carol Bevel** .... (505) 348-2310
E-mail: cbevel@nmcourt.fed.us
Court Reporter **Julie Ghoel** .... (505) 348-2207

Chambers of District Judge Martha Vázquez

Santiago E. Campos U.S. Courthouse, 106 South Federal Place,
Second Floor, Santa Fe, NM 87501
Tel: (505) 988-6330 Fax: (505) 988-6332
E-mail: vazquezchambers@nmcourt.fed.us

Martha A. Vázquez
District Judge

Date of Birth: 1953
Education: Notre Dame 1975 BA, 1979 JD
Began Service: 1993
Appointed By: President William J. Clinton
Political Affiliation: Democrat

Current Memberships: American Bar Association; New Mexico Women's Bar Association; State Bar of New Mexico; The U.S.-Mexico Law Institute

Staff
Law Clerk **Andrew Kincaid** .... (505) 988-6330
Law Clerk **Yvonne Co** .... (505) 988-6330
Career Law Clerk **Jacqueline E. Davis** .... (505) 988-6330
Education: Harvard 1994 JD
Administrative Assistant **Toni Cowden** .... (505) 988-6330

Chambers of District Judge William P. Johnson

U.S. Courthouse, 333 Lomas Boulevard, NW, Suite 640, Albuquerque, NM 87102
Tel: (505) 348-2330 Fax: (505) 348-2335
E-mail: wjohnson@nmcourt.fed.us

William P. Johnson
District Judge

Date of Birth: 1959
Education: VMI 1981 BA; Washington and Lee 1985 JD
Began Service: December 28, 2001
Appointed By: President George W. Bush

Judicial: Judge, New Mexico Fifth Judicial District Court (1995-2001)

Legal Practice: Associate, Bracewell & Patterson, L.L.P. (1985-1986); Associate, Hinkle, Hensley, Shanor & Martin, L.L.P. (1986-1989); Partner, Hinkle, Hensley, Shanor & Martin, L.L.P. (1990-1995)

Military Service: United States Army Reserve, United States Department of the Army (1981-1990)

Staff

Law Clerk **Andrew Squires** .... (505) 348-2330
Began Service: September 2015
Term Expires: September 2016
E-mail: andrew_squires@nmcourt.fed.us

Career Law Clerk **Phyllis Amato** .... (505) 348-2330
E-mail: pamato@nmcourt.fed.us
Education: New Mexico 1994 JD

Courtroom Deputy **Richard Garcia** .... (505) 348-2333
E-mail: rgarcia@nmcourt.fed.us
Education: New Mexico 1995 BA

Administrative Assistant **Martha A. Garcia** .... (505) 348-2330
E-mail: magarcia@nmcourt.fed.us

Chambers of District Judge James O. Browning

333 Lomas Boulevard, Suite 660, Albuquerque, NM 87102
Tel: (505) 348-2280 Fax: (505) 348-2285
E-mail: jbrowning@nmcourt.fed.us

James O. Browning
District Judge

Education: Yale 1978 BA; Virginia 1981 JD
Began Service: August 6, 2003
Appointed By: President George W. Bush

Clerkships: Law Clerk, Circuit Judge Collins J. Seitz, United States Court of Appeals for the Third Circuit (1981-1982); Law Clerk Lewis F. Powell, Jr., Supreme Court of the United States (1982-1983)

Government: Deputy Attorney General, Office of the Attorney General, State of New Mexico (1987-1988)

Legal Practice: Associate, Rodey, Dickason, Sloan, Akin & Robb, P.A. (1983-1987)

Staff

Law Clerk **Alexander Galicki** .... (505) 348-2280
Began Service: September 2015
Term Expires: September 2016
E-mail: agalicki@nmcourt.fed.us

Law Clerk **David Hirsch** .... (505) 348-2280
Began Service: September 2015
Term Expires: September 2016
E-mail: dhirsch@nmcourt.fed.us

Law Clerk **Carolina Stewart** .... (505) 348-2280
Began Service: September 2015
Term Expires: September 2016
E-mail: cstewart@nmcourt.fed.us

Secretary **Mary Garcia** .... (505) 348-2281

Chambers of District Judge Robert C. Brack

100 North Church Street, Suite 590, Las Cruces, NM 88001
Tel: (575) 528-1450 Fax: (575) 528-1455
E-mail: Robert_Brack@nmcourt.fed.us

Robert C. Brack
District Judge

Education: Eastern New Mexico 1975 BA; New Mexico 1978 JD
Began Service: July 28, 2003
Appointed By: President George W. Bush

Judicial: District Judge, Ninth Judicial District, New Mexico (1997-2003)

Profession: Private Practice (1978-1997)

Staff
Fax: (575) 528-1455

Law Clerk **Xochitl Torres-Small** .... (575) 528-1453
Began Service: August 2015
Term Expires: August 2016
E-mail: xochitl_torres-small@nmcourt.fed.us

Career Law Clerk **Anne Morgan Lyman** .... (575) 528-1452
E-mail: anne_lyman@nmcourt.fed.us
Education: New Mexico 1991 JD

Court Deputy **Jessica Chavez** .... (575) 528-1402
E-mail: jessica_chavez@nmcourt.fed.us

Court Reporter **Vanessa Alyce** .... (575) 528-1430
E-mail: vanessa_alyce@nmcourt.fed.us

Judicial Assistant **Annette Ortiz** .... (575) 528-1451
E-mail: annette_ortiz@nmcourt.fed.us

Chambers of District Judge Judith C. Herrera

333 Lomas Boulevard, NW, Suite 710, Albuquerque, NM 87102
Tel: (505) 348-2390 Fax: (505) 348-2395
E-mail: herrerachambers@nmcourt.fed.us

Judith C. Herrera
District Judge

Education: New Mexico 1976 BA; Georgetown 1979 JD
Began Service: June 2004
Appointed By: President George W. Bush

Academic: Regent, Board of Regents, University of New Mexico

Government: Assistant District Attorney, City of Santa Fe, New Mexico (1979-1980); Council Member, Office of the Mayor and City Council, City of Santa Fe, New Mexico (1981-1986)

Chambers of District Judge Kenneth John Gonzales

333 Lomas Boulevard, Albuquerque, NM 87102
Tel: (505) 348-2000

Kenneth John Gonzales
District Judge

Education: New Mexico 1988, 1991 JD
Began Service: October 18, 2013
Appointed By: President Barack Obama

Government: Assistant U.S. Attorney, Criminal Division, New Mexico District, United States Department of Justice (2008-2010); U.S. Attorney, New Mexico District, Executive Office for United States Attorneys, United States Department of Justice, Barack Obama Administration (2010-2013)

Chambers of Senior Judge James A. Parker
421 Gold Avenue, SW, Sixth Floor, Albuquerque, NM 87102
P.O. Box 669, Albuquerque, NM 87103
Tel: (505) 348-2220 Fax: (505) 348-2225
E-mail: jparker@nmcourt.fed.us

James A. Parker
Senior Judge

Date of Birth: 1937
Education: Rice 1959 BA; Texas 1962 LLB
Began Service: November 13, 1987
Appointed By: President Ronald Reagan

Legal Practice: Modrall, Sperling, Roehl, Harris & Sisk, PA (1962-1987)

Current Memberships: Albuquerque Bar Association; American Board of Trial Advocates; Federal Judges Association; State Bar of New Mexico; New Mexico Bar Foundation, State Bar of New Mexico

Staff
Law Clerk **Allison Jaros** .... (505) 348-2222
Began Service: August 2015
Term Expires: August 2016
E-mail: ajaros@nmcourt.fed.us
Career Law Clerk **Mary Woodward** .... (505) 348-2205
E-mail: cbaca@nmcourt.fed.us
Education: Michigan State 1978 BA; Wisconsin 1981 MA; New Mexico 1994 JD
Career Law Clerk (Part-Time) **Ellen C. Snyder** .... (505) 348-2223
E-mail: esnyder@nmcourt.fed.us
Education: Texas 1982 BA, 1989 JD
Administrative Assistant **Debbie MacDonald** .... (505) 348-2220
E-mail: dmacdonald@nmcourt.fed.us

Chambers of Senior Judge C. LeRoy Hansen
421 Gold Avenue, SW, 5th Floor, Albuquerque, NM 87102
P.O. Box 669, Albuquerque, NM 87103
Tel: (505) 348-2240 Fax: (505) 348-2246

C. LeRoy Hansen
Senior Judge

Date of Birth: 1933
Education: Iowa 1956 BS; New Mexico 1961 JD
Began Service: October 1992
Appointed By: President George H.W. Bush
Political Affiliation: Republican

Clerkships: Law Clerk The Honorable Irwin S. Moise, New Mexico Supreme Court (1961-1962)

Legal Practice: Snead & Hansen (1962-1964); Civerolo, Hansen & Wolf, PA (1964-1992)

Current Memberships: Albuquerque Bar Association; American Board of Trial Advocates; American College of Trial Lawyers; State Bar of New Mexico

Staff
Term Law Clerk **Hajra I. Malik** .... (505) 348-2243
Education: New Mexico 2010 JD
Law Clerk **Nancy Ackermann** .... (505) 348-2241
E-mail: nancy_ackermann@nmcourt.fed.us
Education: New Mexico 1989 JD
Career Law Clerk **Mary E. Lebeck** .... (505) 348-2242
E-mail: mary_lebeck@nmcourt.fed.us
Education: New Mexico 1981 JD
Courtroom Deputy [Criminal] **Juan Gonzales** .... (505) 348-2247
E-mail: juan_gonzales@nmcourt.fed.us
Court Reporter **John De La Rosa** .... (505) 348-2249
E-mail: john_delarosa@nmcourt.fed.us

Chambers of Chief Magistrate Judge Karen Ballard Molzen
U.S. Courthouse, 333 Lomas Boulevard, Suite 730, Albuquerque, NM 87102
Tel: (505) 348-2290 Fax: (505) 348-2294
E-mail: kmolzen@nmcourt.fed.us

Karen Ballard Molzen
Chief Magistrate Judge

Education: New Mexico 1985 JD
Began Service: April 26, 1999
Term Expires: April 26, 2023

Current Memberships: Federal Magistrate Judges Association

Staff
Law Clerk **Michael Timm** .... (505) 348-2292
E-mail: michael_timm@nmcourt.fed.us
Career Law Clerk **Anna McDowell** .... (505) 348-2290
E-mail: anna_mcdowell@nmcourt.fed.us
Education: Washburn 2005 JD

Chambers of Magistrate Judge Lourdes A. Martinez
100 North Church Street, Suite 540, Las Cruces, NM 88001
Tel: (575) 528-1650 Fax: (575) 528-1655
E-mail: lmartinez@nmcourt.fed.us

Lourdes A. Martinez
Magistrate Judge

Began Service: April 1, 2011

Chambers of Magistrate Judge William P. Lynch
United States District Court, 100 North Church Street, Suite 550, Las Cruces, NM 88001
Tel: (575) 528-1660 Fax: (575) 528-1665
E-mail: wlynch@nmcourt.fed.us

William P. Lynch
Magistrate Judge

Education: Northern Illinois BA; Illinois JD
Began Service: 2005

Staff
Law Clerk **Rachel Nathanson** .... (505) 528-1660

Chambers of Magistrate Judge Carmen E. Garza
United States District Court, 100 North Church Street, Suite 520, Las Cruces, NM 88001
Tel: (575) 528-1670 Fax: (575) 528-1675
E-mail: garzaschambers@nmcourt.fed.us

Carmen E. Garza
Magistrate Judge

Began Service: August 25, 2006

Staff
Law Clerk **(Vacant)** .... (505) 528-1670

Chambers of Magistrate Judge Gregory B. Wormuth
United States District Court, 100 North Church Street, Suite 530, Las Cruces, NM 88001
Tel: (575) 528-1460 Fax: (575) 528-1465
E-mail: gwormuth@nmcourt.fed.us

Gregory B. Wormuth
Magistrate Judge

Began Service: 2009

Staff
Career Law Clerk **Juliana MacPherson** . . . . (575) 528-1480

Chambers of Magistrate Judge Stephan M. Vidmar
United States District Court, 100 North Church Street, Suite 510, Las Cruces, NM 88001
Tel: (575) 528-1480 Fax: (575) 528-1485
E-mail: vidmarchambers@nmcourts.fed.us
E-mail: svidmar@nmcourt.fed.us

Stephan M. Vidmar
Magistrate Judge

Education: West Point 1974 BS; Michigan 1982 JD
Began Service: December 27, 2011

Staff
Career Law Clerk **Annie Mason** . . . . (575) 528-1480

Chambers of Magistrate Judge Steven C. Yarbrough
333 Lomas Boulevard, Albuquerque, NM 87102
Tel: (505) 348-2270 Fax: (505) 348-2275

Steven C. Yarbrough
Magistrate Judge

Chambers of Magistrate Judge Kirtan Khalsa
333 Lomas Boulevard, Suite 630, Albuquerque, NM 87102
Tel: (505) 348-2340 Fax: (505) 348-2345
E-mail: kirtan_khalsa@nmcourt.fed.us

Kirtan Khalsa
Magistrate Judge

Chambers of Magistrate Judge Laura Fashing
333 Lomas Boulevard, Suite 680, Albuquerque, NM 87102
Tel: (505) 348-2360 Fax: (505) 348-2365

Laura Fashing
Magistrate Judge

Chambers of Magistrate Judge (recalled) Lorenzo F. Garcia
U.S. Courthouse, 333 Lomas Boulevard, NW, Suite 680, Albuquerque, NM 87102
Tel: (505) 348-2320 Fax: (505) 348-2324

Lorenzo F. Garcia
Magistrate Judge (recalled)

Date of Birth: 1947
Education: Col Santa Fe 1969 BA; New Mexico 1973 JD

Chambers of Magistrate Judge (part time) B. Paul Briones
407 North Auburn Avenue, Farmington, NM 87401
Tel: (505) 955-8823 Fax: (505) 955-8824
E-mail: paul_briones@nmcourt.fed.us

B. Paul Briones
Magistrate Judge (Part-Time)

United States Bankruptcy Court for the District of New Mexico
500 Gold Avenue, SW, Albuquerque, NM 87102
P.O. Box 546, Albuquerque, NM 87103-0546
Tel: (505) 348-2500 Tel: (866) 291-6805 (Toll Free)
Tel: (888) 435-7822 (Toll Free Voice Case Information System VCIS)
Tel: (888) 821-8813 (Toll Free PACER) Fax: (505) 348-2473
Internet: www.nmcourt.fed.us

Number of Judgeships: 2

Court Staff
Clerk of the Court **Norman H. Meyer, Jr.** . . . . (505) 348-2450
E-mail: norman_meyer@nmcourt.fed.us Fax: (505) 348-2445
Education: New Mexico 1977 BA; Denver 1979 MS
Chief Deputy Clerk **Lana Merewether** . . . . (505) 348-2490
E-mail: lana_merewether@nmcourt.fed.us Fax: (505) 348-2493
Education: New Mexico State 1992 BS, 1994 MS; New Mexico 2000 MBA
Administrative Manager **Debbie Siner** . . . . (505) 348-2437
E-mail: debra_siner@nmcourt.fed.us Fax: (505) 348-2440
Education: Col Santa Fe 1993 BA
Systems Manager **Lana Merewether** . . . . (505) 348-2490
E-mail: lana_merewether@nmcourt.fed.us Fax: (505) 348-2493
Human Resource Specialist **Maribel Roybal** . . . . (505) 348-2436
E-mail: maribel_roybal@nmcourt.fed.us Fax: (505) 348-2440
Education: Col Santa Fe 1999 MBA

Chambers of Bankruptcy Judge Robert H. Jacobvitz
Dennis Chavez Federal Building, 500 Gold Avenue, SW, 13th Floor, Albuquerque, NM 87102
P.O. Box 546, Albuquerque, NM 87103-0546
Tel: (505) 348-2545
E-mail: robert_jacobvitz@nmcourt.fed.us

Robert H. Jacobvitz
Bankruptcy Judge

Began Service: August 2009
Term Expires: August 2023

Staff
Law Clerk **Jacob Masters** . . . . (505) 348-2545
Career Law Clerk **Patti G. Hennessy** . . . . (505) 348-2545
E-mail: patti_hennessy@nmcourt.fed.us
Education: Notre Dame 1986 BA; New Mexico 1998 JD
Courtroom Deputy **Chris Wilson** . . . . (505) 348-2539

Chambers of Bankruptcy Judge David T. Thuma
Dennis Chavez Federal Building, 500 Gold Avenue, SW, 13th Floor West, Albuquerque, NM 87102
P.O. Box 546, Albuquerque, NM 87103
Tel: (505) 348-2420 Fax: (505) 348-2432
E-mail: thumastaff@nmcourt.fed.us

David T. Thuma
Bankruptcy Judge

Began Service: August 29, 2012

(continued on next page)

Chambers of Bankruptcy Judge David T. Thuma *continued*

Staff

Law Clerk **Nicolas DeRosa** . . . . (505) 348-2420
Term Expires: August 2016
Career Law Clerk **Jaya Rhodes** . . . . (505) 348-2420
Courtroom Deputy **Christa Lucero** . . . . (505) 348-2420

United States District Court for the Eastern District of New York

U.S. Courthouse, 225 Cadman Plaza East, Brooklyn, NY 11201
Tel: (718) 613-2600 Tel: (718) 330-7200 (PACER)
Fax: (718) 613-2333
Internet: www.nyed.uscourts.gov

Number of Judgeships: 15

Number of Vacancies: 2

Circuit: Second

Areas Covered: Counties of Kings, Nassau, Queens, Richmond and Suffolk

Court Staff

District Court Executive **Eugene James Corcoran** . . . . . . (718) 613-2260
E-mail: eugene_corcoran@nyed.uscourts.gov
Education: SUNY (Albany) BA; Marist MPA
Clerk of Court **Douglas C. Palmer** . . . . (718) 613-2270
E-mail: douglas_palmer@nyed.uscourts.gov
Chief Deputy for Information Services **Corey Nguyen** . . . (718) 613-2290
E-mail: corey_nguyen@nyed.uscourts.gov
Chief Deputy for Operations **Brenna Mahoney** . . . . (718) 613-2331
E-mail: brenna_mahoney@nyed.uscourts.gov
Administrative Supervisor **Marc Brown** . . . . (718) 613-2600
E-mail: marc_v_brown@nyed.uscourts.gov
Deputy-in-Charge **Carol McMahon** . . . . (631) 712-6031
E-mail: carol_mcmahon@nyed.uscourts.gov
Chief Court Reporter **Gene Rudolph** . . . . (718) 613-2538
E-mail: gene_rudolph@nyed.uscourts.gov Fax: (718) 613-2661
Chief Pretrial Services Officer **Roberto Cordeiro** . . . . (718) 613-2570
E-mail: roberto_cordeiro@nyept.uscourts.gov
Chief Probation Officer **Eileen Kelly** . . . . (347) 534-3501
E-mail: eileen_kelly@nyep.uscourts.gov Fax: (347) 534-3509
Administrative Specialist/Budget Analyst
August Marziliano . . . . (718) 613-2332
E-mail: august_marziliano@nyed.uscourts.gov
Chief Librarian **Sandra Phillips** . . . . (718) 613-2320
E-mail: sandra_phillips@ca2.uscourts.gov Fax: (718) 613-2395

Chambers of Chief Judge Carol Bagley Amon

U.S. Courthouse, 225 Cadman Plaza East, Brooklyn, NY 11201
Tel: (718) 613-2410 Fax: (718) 613-2416
E-mail: carol_amon@nyed.uscourts.gov

Carol Bagley Amon
Chief District Judge

Date of Birth: 1946
Education: William & Mary 1968 BS; Virginia 1971 JD
Began Service: 1990
Appointed By: President George H.W. Bush

Corporate: Staff Attorney, COMSAT Corporation (1971-1973)

Government: Trial Attorney, United States Department of Justice (1973-1974); Assistant United States Attorney, Eastern District of New York, Office of the United States Attorney, United States Department of Justice (1974-1986)

Judicial: Magistrate Judge, United States District Court for the Eastern District of New York (1986-1990)

Current Memberships: The District of Columbia Bar; Virginia State Bar

Chambers of Chief Judge Carol Bagley Amon *continued*

Staff

Law Clerk **Ryan Chabot** . . . . (718) 613-2410
Began Service: September 2015
Term Expires: September 2016
E-mail: ryan_chabot@nyed.uscourts.gov
Law Clerk **Stephanie Goldfarb** . . . . (718) 613-2410
Began Service: May 2015
Term Expires: May 2016
E-mail: stephanie_goldfarb@nyed.uscourts.gov
Law Clerk **Alex Sinha** . . . . (718) 613-2410
Began Service: August 2015
Term Expires: August 2016
E-mail: alex_sinha@nyed.uscourts.gov
Secretary **Maria Liberatore** . . . . (718) 613-2410
Courtoom Deputy **Vanessa Holley** . . . . (718) 613-2415
E-mail: vanessa_holley@nyed.uscourts.gov

Chambers of District Judge John Gleeson

U.S. Courthouse, 225 Cadman Plaza East, Brooklyn, NY 11201-1818
Tel: (718) 613-2450 Fax: (718) 613-2456
E-mail: john_gleeson@nyed.uscourts.gov

John Gleeson
District Judge

Date of Birth: 1953
Education: Georgetown 1975 BA; Virginia 1980 JD
Began Service: October 24, 1994
Appointed By: President William J. Clinton

Academic: Adjunct Professor of Law, Brooklyn Law School (1990-1997); Visiting Professor of Law, University of Virginia (1994); Adjunct Professor, School of Law, New York University (1995-2006)

Clerkships: Law Clerk The Honorable Boyce F. Martin, United States Court of Appeals for the Sixth Circuit (1980-1981)

Government: Assistant United States Attorney, Eastern District of New York, Office of the United States Attorney, United States Department of Justice (1985-1994)

Legal Practice: Associate, Cravath, Swaine & Moore LLP (1981-1985)

Current Memberships: Federal Bar Council

Profession: Author (1995-2005)

Staff

Law Clerk **Kayla Bensing** . . . . (718) 613-2450
Began Service: October 2015
Term Expires: October 2016
E-mail: kayla_bensing@nyed.uscourts.gov
Law Clerk **Ethan P. Fallon** . . . . (718) 613-2450
Began Service: September 2015
Term Expires: September 2016
E-mail: ethan_fallon@nyed.uscourts.gov
Education: UCLA 2014 JD
Law Clerk **Samia Hossain** . . . . (718) 613-2450
Began Service: August 2015
Term Expires: August 2016
E-mail: samia_hossain@nyed.uscourts.gov

Chambers of District Judge Dora L. Irizarry

225 Cadman Plaza East, Room 928S, Brooklyn, NY 11201
Tel: (718) 613-2150 Fax: (718) 613-2156
E-mail: Dora_L_Irizarry@nyed.uscourts.gov

Dora Lizette Irizarry
District Judge

Date of Birth: January 26, 1955
Education: Yale 1976 BA; Columbia JD
Began Service: August 30, 2004
Appointed By: President George W. Bush

Government: Assistant District Attorney, Bronx County District Attorney, City of New York, New York (1979); Special Assistant District Attorney, Office of the Prosecutor, City of New York, New York (1981-1995); Assistant District Attorney, New York County District Attorney (1987)

Judicial: Judge, New York City Criminal Court, City of New York, New York (1995); Judge, The New York State Court of Claims (1997)

Legal Practice: Hoguet Newman & Regal, L.L.P.

Current Memberships: Federal Bar Council; Hispanic National Bar Association; New York State Bar Association

Staff
Fax: (718) 613-2156

Law Clerk **Richard Fox** . . . . . (718) 613-2150
Term Expires: June 20, 2016
E-mail: richard_fox@nyed.uscourts.gov
Law Clerk **Damani Sims** . . . . . (718) 613-2150
E-mail: damani_sims@nyed.uscourts.gov
Deputy Clerk **Christy Carosella** . . . . . (718) 613-2155
E-mail: christy_carosella@nyed.uscourts.gov

Chambers of District Judge Eric Nicholas Vitaliano

225 Cadman Plaza East, Brooklyn, NY 11201
Tel: (718) 613-2130
E-mail: eric_vitaliano@nyed.uscourts.gov

Eric Nicholas Vitaliano
District Judge

Education: Fordham 1968 BA; NYU 1971 JD
Began Service: December 30, 2005
Appointed By: President George W. Bush

Clerkships: Law Clerk, District Judge Mark A. Costantino, United States District Court for the Eastern District of New York (1971-1972)

Government: Member, New York State Assembly (1983-2002)

Judicial: Judge, New York State Unified Court System (2002-2005)

Staff
Law Clerk **Torie Atkinson** . . . . . (718) 613-2130
Began Service: September 2015
Term Expires: September 2016
E-mail: torie_atkinson@nyed.uscourts.gov
Law Clerk **Samuel Hershey** . . . . . (718) 613-2130
Began Service: September 2015
Term Expires: September 2016
E-mail: samuel_hershey@nyed.uscourts.gov
Law Clerk **Liane Rice** . . . . . (718) 613-2130
Began Service: September 2015
Term Expires: September 2016
E-mail: liane_rice@nyed.uscourts.gov
Education: Columbia 2009 JD

Chambers of District Judge Joseph F. Bianco

100 Federal Plaza, Central Islip, NY 11722
Tel: (631) 712-5670 Fax: (631) 712-5677
E-mail: joseph_bianco@nyed.uscourts.gov

Joseph F. Bianco
District Judge

Education: Georgetown 1988 BA; Columbia 1991 JD
Began Service: January 3, 2006
Appointed By: President George W. Bush

Academic: Professor, Fordham Law School

Clerkships: Law Clerk, District Judge Peter K. Leisure, United States District Court for the Southern District of New York (1992-1993)

Government: Organized Crime and Terrorism Chief, Criminal Division, Department of Justice; Deputy Assistant Attorney General, Criminal Division, United States Department of Justice; Deputy Assistant Attorney General, Criminal Division, Office of the Deputy Attorney General, United States Department of Justice

Legal Practice: Litigation Associate, Simpson Thacher & Bartlett LLP; Counsel (Litigation Section), Debevoise & Plimpton LLP

Staff
Law Clerk **Lauren Dolecki** . . . . . (631) 712-5670
Began Service: October 2015
Term Expires: October 2016
E-mail: lauren_dolecki@nyed.uscourts.gov
Law Clerk **David Mesrobian** . . . . . (631) 712-5670
Began Service: September 2014
Term Expires: November 2015
E-mail: david_mesrobian@nyed.uscourts.gov
Law Clerk **Zoe Shea** . . . . . (631) 712-5670
Began Service: October 2015
Term Expires: October 2016
E-mail: zoe_shea@nyed.uscourts.gov
Deputy Clerk **Michele Savona** . . . . . (631) 712-5670
E-mail: michele_savona@nyed.uscourts.gov

Chambers of District Judge Brian M. Cogan

225 Cadman Plaza East, Brooklyn, NY 11201
Tel: (718) 613-2230 Fax: (718) 613-2236
E-mail: brian_cogan@nyed.uscourts.gov

Brian M. Cogan
District Judge

Education: Illinois 1975 BS; Cornell 1979 JD
Began Service: June 2006
Appointed By: President George W. Bush

Government: Vice Chairman, Appointment of City Marshal's Commission, City of New York, New York; Member, Disciplinary Committee, New York Appellate Division, First Department

Legal Practice: General Counsel, Stroock & Stroock & Lavan LLP

Military Service: Legal Affairs Officer, New York Guard

Staff
Law Clerk **Johanna Hudgens** . . . . . (718) 613-2230
Began Service: August 2015
Term Expires: August 2016
E-mail: johanna_hudgens@nyed.uscourts.gov
Law Clerk **Emily Weissler** . . . . . (718) 613-2230
Began Service: August 2015
Term Expires: August 2016
E-mail: emily_weissler@nyed.uscourts.gov

Chambers of District Judge Roslynn Renee Mauskopf

U.S. Courthouse, 225 Cadman Plaza East, Brooklyn, NY 11201
Tel: (718) 613-2210
E-mail: roslynn_mauskopf@nyed.uscourts.gov

Roslynn Renee Mauskopf
District Judge

Education: Brandeis; Georgetown 1982 JD
Began Service: October 2007
Appointed By: President George W. Bush

Government: Assistant District Attorney, Trial Division, New York County District Attorney; Assistant District Attorney, Investigation Division, New York County District Attorney; Deputy Chief, Special Prosecutions Bureau, New York County District Attorney; Chief, Frauds Bureau, New York County District Attorney; Inspector General, State of New York (1995-2002)

Staff
Law Clerk **Dan Karmel** .... (718) 613-2210
Began Service: January 2015
Term Expires: January 2016
E-mail: dan_karmel@nyed.uscourts.gov
Law Clerk **Laurah Samuels** .... (718) 613-2210
Began Service: 2015
Term Expires: September 2016
E-mail: laurah_samuels@nyed.uscourts.gov
Law Clerk **Annie Turner** .... (718) 613-2210
Began Service: 2015
Term Expires: September 2016
E-mail: annie_turner@nyed.uscourts.gov

Chambers of District Judge Kiyo A. Matsumoto

U.S. Courthouse, 225 Cadman Plaza East, Brooklyn, NY 11201
Tel: (718) 613-2180
E-mail: kiyo_matsumoto@nyed.uscourts.gov

Kiyo A. Matsumoto
District Judge

Education: UC Berkeley; Georgetown JD
Began Service: July 22, 2008
Appointed By: President George W. Bush

Academic: Adjunct Professor, Brooklyn Law School

Government: Civil Division Chief/Professional Responsibility Officer, Civil Division, New York - Eastern District, Department of Justice; Financial Litigation Unit Chief, Civil Division, New York - Eastern District, United States Department of Justice; Civil Health Care Fraud Coordinator, Civil Division, New York - Eastern District, United States Department of Justice; Trial Advocacy and Civil and Financial Litigation Instructor, Office of Legal Education (National Advocacy Center), United States Department of Justice; Senior Trial Counsel, Civil Division, New York - Eastern District, United States Department of Justice

Judicial: Magistrate Judge, United States District Court for the Eastern District of New York (2004-2008)

Legal Practice: Litigation Associate, MacDonald, Hoague and Bayless

Staff
Law Clerk **LiJia Gong** .... (718) 613-2180
Began Service: September 2014
Term Expires: April 2016
E-mail: lijia_gong@nyed.uscourts.gov
Education: Georgetown 2013 JD
Law Clerk **Jonathan Jacobson** .... (718) 613-2180
Began Service: October 2015
Term Expires: October 2016
E-mail: jonathan_jacobson@nyed.uscourts.gov
Law Clerk **John McNulty** .... (718) 613-2180
Began Service: September 2015
Term Expires: September 2016
E-mail: john_mcnulty@nyed.uscourts.gov

Chambers of District Judge William Francis Kuntz II

225 Cadman Plaza East, Brooklyn, NY 11201
Tel: (718) 613-2200 Fax: (718) 613-2333
E-mail: william_kuntz@nyed.uscourts.gov

William F. Kuntz II
District Judge

Education: Harvard 1972 AB, 1974 MA, 1977 JD, 1979 PhD
Began Service: October 4, 2011
Appointed By: President Barack Obama

Legal Practice: Associate, Shearman & Sterling LLP (1978-1986); Partner, Milgrim, Thomajan, Jacobs & Lee (1986-1994); Adjunct Associate Professor of Law, Brooklyn Law School (1987-2003); Partner, Seward & Kissel LLP (1994-2001); Partner, Torys LLP (2001-2004); Counsel, Constantine Cannon LLP (2004-2005); Partner, Baker & Hostetler LLP

Nonprofit: Trustee, Board of Trustees, Practising Law Institute

Chambers of District Judge Margo Kitsy Brodie

225 Cadman Plaza East, Brooklyn, NY 11201
Tel: (718) 613-2140 Fax: (718) 613-2333
E-mail: margo_brodie@nyed.uscourts.gov

Margo Kitsy Brodie
District Judge

Education: St Francis Col (NY) 1988 BA; Pennsylvania 1991 JD
Began Service: January 29, 2012
Appointed By: President Barack Obama

Staff
Law Clerk **Anna Deknatel** .... (718) 613-2600
E-mail: anna_deknatel@nyed.uscourts.gov
Law Clerk **Rafael Reyneri** .... (718) 613-2600
E-mail: rafael_reyneri@nyed.uscourts.gov
Education: Boston Col 2007 BA; NYU 2015 JD
Law Clerk **Drew Rolle** .... (718) 613-2600
E-mail: drew_rolle@nyed.uscourts.gov
Case Manager **Ogoro Francis-McLeish** .... (718) 613-2600
E-mail: ogoro_francis@nyed.uscourts.gov

Chambers of District Judge Pamela Ki Mai Chen

225 Cadman Plaza East, Brooklyn, NY 11201
Tel: (718) 613-2510
E-mail: chen_chambers@nyed.uscourts.gov

Pamela Ki Mai Chen
District Judge

Education: Michigan 1983 BA; Georgetown 1986 JD
Began Service: March 19, 2013
Appointed By: President Barack Obama

Government: Trial Attorney, Special Litigation Section, Civil Rights Division, United States Department of Justice (1991-1998); Deputy Commissioner (Enforcement), Division of Human Rights, State of New York (2008); Civil Rights Litigation Section Chief, Criminal Division, New York - Eastern District, United States Department of Justice (2009-2013)

Legal Practice: Attorney, Arnold & Porter LLP (1986-1989); Attorney, Asbill, Junkin & Myers, Chtd. (1989-1991)

Staff
Law Clerk **Jenny Pelaez** .... (718) 613-2510
Began Service: January 2015
Term Expires: January 2016
E-mail: jenny_pelaez@nyed.uscourts.gov
Education: Pennsylvania 2008 BA; Cardozo 2011 JD
Law Clerk **Neta Levanon** .... (718) 613-2510
Began Service: October 2015
Term Expires: October 2016
E-mail: neta_levanon@nyed.uscourts.gov

Chambers of District Judge Pamela Ki Mai Chen *continued*

Law Clerk **Grace Chan** .... (718) 613-2510
Began Service: October 2015
Term Expires: October 2016
E-mail: grace_chan@nyed.uscourts.gov
Courtroom Deputy **Fida Abdallah** .... (718) 613-2510
E-mail: fida_abdallah@nyed.uscourts.gov

Chambers of District Judge Joan Marie Azrack

225 Cadman Plaza East, Brooklyn, NY 11201
Tel: (718) 613-2530 (Brooklyn) Tel: (631) 712-5600 (Central Islip)
E-mail: joan_azrack@nyed.uscourts.gov

Joan Marie Azrack
District Judge

Date of Birth: 1951
Education: Rutgers 1974 BS; New York Law 1979 JD
Began Service: 2014
Appointed By: President Barack Obama

Government: Attorney, Criminal Division, United States Department of Justice Honors Program (1979-1981); Assistant United States Attorney, Eastern District of New York, Office of the United States Attorney, United States Department of Justice (1981-1990)

Judicial: Magistrate Judge, Chambers of Magistrate Judge Joan M. Azrack, United States District Court for the Eastern District of New York (1990-2014)

Staff
Law Clerk **Jennifer Prevete** .... (718) 613-2530
Began Service: September 2015
Term Expires: September 2016
E-mail: jennifer_prevete@nyed.uscourts.gov
Law Clerk **Harry Jacobs** .... (718) 613-2530
Began Service: September 1, 2015
Term Expires: September 1, 2016
E-mail: harry_jacobs@nyed.uscourts.gov
Law Clerk **Robert Terranova** .... (718) 613-2530
Began Service: September 2011
E-mail: robert_terranova@nyed.uscourts.gov
Education: NYU 2005 JD

Chambers of District Judge Ann M. Donnelly

225 Cadman Plaza East, Brooklyn, NY 11201
Tel: (718) 613-2220 Fax: (718) 613-2226

Ann M. Donnelly
District Judge

Education: Michigan 1981 BA; Ohio State 1984 JD
Began Service: 2015
Appointed By: President Barack Obama

Chambers of Senior Judge Jack B. Weinstein

U.S. Courthouse, 225 Cadman Plaza East, Brooklyn, NY 11201
Tel: (718) 613-2520 Fax: (718) 613-2527
E-mail: jack_weinstein@nyed.uscourts.gov

Jack B. Weinstein
Senior Judge

Date of Birth: 1921
Education: Brooklyn 1943 BA; Columbia 1948 LLB; Embry-Riddle 1987 MS
Began Service: April 15, 1967
Appointed By: President Lyndon B. Johnson

Academic: Professor, Columbia Law School (1956-1967)

Clerkships: Law Clerk The Honorable Stanley H. Fuld, New York Court of Appeals (1949-1950)

Government: County Attorney, County of Nassau, New York (1963-1965)

Chambers of Senior Judge Jack B. Weinstein *continued*

Legal Practice: Partner, Rosenfeld & Weinstein (1950-1952); Private practice (1952-1960)

Military Service: United States Navy (1942-1946); United States Naval Reserve

Current Memberships: American Academy of Arts and Sciences; American Bar Association; The American Law Institute; The Association of the Bar of the City of New York; International Association of Jewish Lawyers and Jurists; Nassau County Bar Association; New York State Bar Association

Staff
Law Clerk **Giulia Previti** .... (718) 613-2524
Began Service: September 30, 2015
Term Expires: September 2016
E-mail: nora_ahmed@nyed.uscourts.gov
Secretary **Jean Capobianco** .... (718) 613-2520
E-mail: jean_capobianco@nyed.uscourts.gov
Case Manager **June Lowe** .... (718) 613-2525

Chambers of Senior Judge Raymond J. Dearie

U.S. Courthouse, 225 Cadman Plaza East, Brooklyn, NY 11201
Tel: (718) 613-2430 Fax: (718) 613-2437
E-mail: raymond_dearie@nyed.uscourts.gov

Raymond J. Dearie
Senior Judge

Date of Birth: 1944
Education: Fairfield 1966 AB; St John's U (NY) 1969 JD
Began Service: March 21, 1986
Appointed By: President Ronald Reagan

Current Memberships: American Bar Association; The Association of the Bar of the City of New York; Federal Bar Council; New York State Bar Association; United States Foreign Intelligence Surveillance Court

Staff
Law Clerk **Jon Bodansky** .... (718) 613-2430
Began Service: October 2015
Term Expires: October 2016
E-mail: jon_bodansky@nyed.uscourts.gov
Law Clerk **Michael Brodlieb** .... (718) 613-2430
E-mail: michael_brodlieb@nyed.uscourts.gov
Career Law Clerk **John R. Quinn** .... (718) 613-2430
E-mail: john_quinn@nyed.uscourts.gov

Chambers of Senior Judge I. Leo Glasser

U.S. Courthouse, 225 Cadman Plaza East, Brooklyn, NY 11201-1818
Tel: (718) 613-2440 Fax: (718) 613-2446
E-mail: leo_glasser@nyed.uscourts.gov

I. Leo Glasser
Senior Judge

Date of Birth: 1924
Education: CCNY 1943 BA; Brooklyn Law 1948 LLB
Began Service: 1982
Appointed By: President Ronald Reagan

Academic: Professor of Law, Brooklyn Law School (1948-1969); Dean, Brooklyn Law School (1977-1981)

Judicial: Judge, New York Family Court (1969-1977)

Military Service: United States Army (1943-1946)

Current Memberships: American Bar Association; The Association of the Bar of the City of New York; The Supreme Court Historical Society

Staff
Law Clerk **Lily Katz** .... (718) 613-2440
Began Service: September 2015
Term Expires: September 2016
E-mail: lily_katz@nyed.uscourts.gov

(continued on next page)

Chambers of Senior Judge I. Leo Glasser *continued*

Law Clerk **Adam Shamah** .... (718) 613-2440
Began Service: September 2015
Term Expires: September 2016
E-mail: adam_shamah@nyed.uscourts.gov
Secretary **Marie J. Chiodo** .... (718) 613-2440
E-mail: marie_chiodo@nyed.uscourts.gov

Chambers of Senior Judge Leonard D. Wexler

Alfonse M. D'Amato Federal Courthouse, 944 Federal Plaza, Central Islip, NY 11722
Tel: (631) 712-5640 Fax: (631) 712-5642
E-mail: leonard_wexler@nyed.uscourts.gov

Leonard D. Wexler
Senior Judge

Date of Birth: 1924
Education: Indiana 1947 BS; NYU 1950 JD
Began Service: 1983
Appointed By: President Ronald Reagan

Legal Practice: Sidney R. Siben Law Office, County of Suffolk, New York (1950-1956); Partner, Meyer & Wexler (1957-1983)

Military Service: United States Army (1943-1945)

Current Memberships: New York State Bar Association; Suffolk County Bar Association

Staff

Law Clerk **Helen M. Sweeney** .... (631) 712-5646
E-mail: helen_sweeney@nyed.uscourts.gov
Career Law Clerk **Peter Ausili** .... (631) 712-5643
E-mail: peter_ausili@nyed.uscourts.gov
Education: St John's U (NY) 1989 JD
Career Law Clerk **Deanna Minerva** .... (631) 712-5644
E-mail: deanna_minerva@nyed.uscourts.gov
Education: Hofstra 2002 JD

Chambers of Senior Judge Sterling Johnson, Jr.

225 Cadman Plaza East, Room 720S, Brooklyn, NY 11201
Tel: (718) 613-2460 Fax: (718) 613-2466
E-mail: sterling_johnson@nyed.uscourts.gov

Sterling Johnson, Jr.
Senior Judge

Date of Birth: 1934
Education: Brooklyn 1963 BA; Brooklyn Law 1966 LLB
Began Service: 1991
Appointed By: President George H.W. Bush

Government: Assistant United States Attorney, Southern District of New York, Office of the United States Attorney, United States Department of Justice (1967-1970); Special Narcotics Prosecutor, United States Department of Justice (1975-1991); Member, United States Sentencing Commission (1999-2002)

Military Service: United States Marine Corps (1952-1955); United States Naval Reserve (1955-1975)

Current Memberships: National Black Prosecutors Association; New York State Bar Association; New York State District Judges Association

Staff

Law Clerk **Ndidi Igboeli** .... (718) 613-2460
Began Service: January 12, 2015
Term Expires: January 12, 2016
E-mail: ndidi_igboeli@nyed.uscourts.gov
Law Clerk **Davina Figeroux** .... (718) 613-2460
Began Service: August 2011
E-mail: davina_figeroux@nyed.uscourts.gov
Education: Pennsylvania 1999 BA; Georgetown 2002 JD

Chambers of Senior Judge Sterling Johnson, Jr. *continued*

Courtroom Deputy **Ana Rodriguez** .... (718) 613-2465
E-mail: ana_rodriguez@nyed.uscourts.gov
Secretary **Sharon Taylor** .... (718) 613-2460
E-mail: sharon_taylor@nyed.uscourts.gov

Chambers of Senior Judge Arthur D. Spatt

100 Federal Plaza, Central Islip, NY 11722-9014
Tel: (631) 712-5620
E-mail: arthur_spatt@nyed.uscourts.gov

Arthur D. Spatt
Senior Judge

Date of Birth: 1925
Education: Ohio State 1947; Brooklyn Law 1949 LLB
Began Service: December 15, 1989
Appointed By: President George H.W. Bush

Judicial: Justice, New York Supreme Court, 10th Judicial Circuit (1978-1982); Administrative Judge, Nassau County (1982-1986); Associate Justice, New York Supreme Court, Second Judicial Department, Appellate Division (1986-1989)

Legal Practice: Associate, Davidson & Davidson; Associate, Lane, Winard, Robinson & Schorr; Associate, Alfred S. Julien (1951-1952); Associate, Florea & Florea; Sole Practitioner (1953-1967); Partner, Spatt & Bauman (1967-1978)

Military Service: United States Navy (1944-1946)

Current Memberships: American Bar Association; Association of Justices of the Supreme Court of the State of New York; Federal Bar Association; Jewish Lawyers Association of Nassau County; Long Beach Lawyers Association; Nassau County Bar Association

Staff

Law Clerk **Anthony Bagnuola** .... (631) 712-5620
Began Service: July 2015
Term Expires: September 2017
E-mail: anthony_bagnuola@nyed.uscourts.gov
Law Clerk **Jonathan Fayer** .... (631) 712-5620
Began Service: October 2014
Term Expires: October 2016
E-mail: jonathan_fayer@nyed.uscourts.gov
Judicial Secretary **Valerie Cohen** .... (631) 712-5620
E-mail: valerie_j_cohen@nyed.uscourts.gov

Chambers of Senior Judge Denis R. Hurley

Alfonse M. D'Amato Federal Courthouse, 100 Federal Plaza, Central Islip, NY 11722-4447
Tel: (631) 712-5650 Fax: (631) 712-5651
E-mail: denis_hurley@nyed.uscourts.gov

Denis R. Hurley
Senior Judge

Date of Birth: 1937
Education: Wharton 1959 BS; Columbia 1962 MBA; Fordham 1966 LLB
Began Service: December 1991
Appointed By: President George H.W. Bush
Political Affiliation: Republican

Academic: Instructor, Long Island University (1971-1973); Instructor, Suffolk County Community College (1984-1990); Adjunct Professor, Touro (1995-1997)

Government: Principal Assistant District Attorney, State of New York (1968-1970); Legislator, County of Suffolk, New York (1978-1979); Senior Assistant County Attorney, County of Suffolk, New York (1980-1981)

Judicial: Judge, New York State Family Court (1983-1987); Acting Justice, New York Supreme Court (1987-1988); Judge, New York State County Court (1988-1991)

Chambers of Senior Judge Denis R. Hurley *continued*

Legal Practice: Associate, Bond, Schoenck & King, LLP (1966-1968); Associate, Pike, Behringer & Hurley

Military Service: New York Army National Guard (1960-1966)

Nonprofit: Member, Little Flower Union Free School Board (1972-1977)

Current Memberships: Suffolk County Bar Association

Staff

Law Clerk **Regina Kaley** .... (631) 712-5650
E-mail: regina_kaley@nyed.uscourts.gov

Career Law Clerk **Michele Gapinski** .... (631) 712-5650
E-mail: michele_gapinski@nyed.uscourts.gov
Education: St John's U (NY) JD

Judicial Assistant **Karen M. Costantini** .... (631) 712-5650
E-mail: karen_costantini@nyed.uscourts.gov

Chambers of Senior Judge Frederic Block

U.S. Courthouse, 225 Cadman Plaza East, Brooklyn, NY 11201
Tel: (718) 613-2420 Fax: (718) 613-2426
E-mail: frederic_block@nyed.uscourts.gov

Frederic Block
Senior Judge

Date of Birth: 1934
Education: Indiana 1956 AB; Cornell 1959 LLB
Began Service: 1994
Appointed By: President William J. Clinton

Academic: Adjunct Professor, Jacob D. Fuchsberg Law Center, Touro College (1992-1994)

Clerkships: Law Clerk, New York Supreme Court, Appellate Division, Third Judicial Department (1959-1961)

Government: Counsel, Education Committee, New York State Constitutional Convention (1967)

Legal Practice: Associate, Dranitzke & Lechtrecker (1961-1962); Sole Practitioner (1962-1963); Partner, Burns & Block (1963-1965); Sole Practitioner (1965-1968); Partner, Baranello, Block & Namm (1968-1974); Sole Practitioner (1974-1979); Partner, Hull, Block & Grundfast (1977-1979); Sole Practitioner (1979-1981); Partner, Block & Costa (1981-1983); Sole Practitioner (1983-1985); Partner, Block & Hamburger (1985-1988); Partner, Block, Amelkin & Hamburger (1988-1994)

Current Memberships: American Bar Association; New York State Bar Association; Suffolk County Bar Association

Staff

Law Clerk **Daniel Horowitz** .... (718) 613-2420
Began Service: August 2015
Term Expires: August 2016
E-mail: daniel_horowitz@nyed.uscourts.gov

Law Clerk **Colleen K. Faherty** .... (718) 613-2420
Began Service: September 2015
Term Expires: September 2016
E-mail: colleen_faherty@nyed.uscourts.gov

Career Law Clerk **Charles Tyler Cone** .... (718) 613-2423
E-mail: charles_cone@nyed.uscourts.gov
Education: Virginia 1998 JD

Courtroom Deputy/Case Manager
Michael "Mike" Innelli .... (718) 613-2425
E-mail: mike_innelli@nyed.uscourts.gov

Chambers of Senior Judge Edward R. Korman

U.S. Courthouse, 225 Cadman Plaza East, Brooklyn, NY 11201
Tel: (718) 613-2470 Fax: (718) 613-2477
E-mail: edward_korman@nyed.uscourts.gov

Edward R. Korman
Senior Judge

Date of Birth: 1942
Education: Brooklyn 1963 BA; Brooklyn Law 1966 LLB; NYU 1971 LLM
Began Service: 1985
Appointed By: President Ronald Reagan

Academic: Professor, Brooklyn Law School (1984)

Clerkships: Law Clerk The Honorable Kenneth B. Keating, New York Court of Appeals (1966-1968)

Government: Assistant United States Attorney, Eastern District of New York, Office of the United States Attorney, United States Department of Justice (1970-1972); Assistant to the Solicitor General of the United States, Office of the Solicitor General, United States Department of Justice (1972-1974); Chief Assistant United States Attorney, Eastern District of New York, United States Department of Justice (1974-1978); United States Attorney, Eastern District of New York, Office of the United States Attorney, United States Department of Justice (1978-1982); Member, Commission of Investigation, State of New York (1983-1985); Chairman, Mayor's Committee on City Marshals, City of New York, New York (1983-1985)

Judicial: Chief Judge, United States District Court for the Eastern District of New York (2000-2007)

Legal Practice: Associate, Paul, Weiss, Rifkind, Wharton & Garrison LLP; Stroock, Stroock & Lavan (1982-1985)

Staff
Fax: (718) 613-2477

Law Clerk **Tristan Ellis** .... (718) 613-2470
Began Service: September 2015
Term Expires: September 2016
E-mail: tristan_ellis@nyed.uscourts.gov

Law Clerk **Christopher Sarma** .... (718) 613-2470
Began Service: September 2015
Term Expires: September 2016
E-mail: christopher_sarma@nyed.uscourts.gov

Law Clerk **Joshua Tannen** .... (718) 613-2470
Began Service: September 2015
Term Expires: September 2016
E-mail: joshua_tannen@nyed.uscourts.gov

Chambers of Senior Judge Nina Gershon

225 Cadman Plaza East, Brooklyn, NY 11201
Tel: (718) 613-2650
E-mail: nina_gershon@nyed.uscourts.gov

Nina Gershon
Senior Judge

Date of Birth: 1940
Education: Cornell 1962 BA; Yale 1965 LLB
Began Service: 1996
Appointed By: President William J. Clinton

Academic: Lecturer in Law and Political Science, University of California, San Diego (1969-1970); Adjunct Professor of Law, Benjamin N. Cardozo School of Law, Yeshiva University (1986-1988)

Government: Staff Attorney, New York Supreme Court, Appellate Division (1966-1968); Assistant Corporation Counsel, Appeals and Opinions Division, State of New York (1968-1969); Chief, Federal Appeals, State of New York (1972-1975); Chief, Consumer Protection Board, State of New York (1975-1976)

Judicial: Magistrate Judge, United States District Court for the Southern District of New York (1976-1996); District Judge, United States District Court for the Eastern District of New York (1996-2008)

(continued on next page)

Chambers of Senior Judge Nina Gershon *continued*

Staff

Law Clerk **Debra Aboodi** . . . . (718) 613-2950
E-mail: debra_aboodi@nyed.uscourts.gov

Law Clerk **Miriam Alinikoff** . . . . (718) 613-2650
E-mail: miriam_alinikoff@nyed.uscourts.gov

Law Clerk **Ben Harrington** . . . . (718) 613-2650
Term Expires: October 2016
E-mail: ben_harrington@nyed.uscourts.gov

Chambers of Senior Judge Allyne R. Ross

U.S. Courthouse, 225 Cadman Plaza East, Room 915 S,
Brooklyn, NY 11201
Tel: (718) 613-2380 Fax: (718) 613-2386
E-mail: allyne_ross@nyed.uscourts.gov

Allyne R. Ross
Senior Judge

Date of Birth: 1946
Education: Wellesley 1967 BA; Harvard 1970 JD
Began Service: 1994
Appointed By: President William J. Clinton

Current Memberships: The Association of the Bar of the City of New York; Federal Bar Council

Staff

Law Clerk **Lauren Hartz** . . . . (718) 613-2380
Began Service: October 2015
Term Expires: October 2016
E-mail: lauren_hartz@nyed.uscourts.gov

Law Clerk **David M. Berman** . . . . (718) 613-2380
Began Service: October 2015
Term Expires: October 2016
E-mail: david_berman@nyed.uscourts.gov
Education: Columbia 2012 JD

Law Clerk **Peter Gil-Montllor** . . . . (718) 613-2380
Began Service: March 2015
Term Expires: March 2016

Chambers of Senior Judge Joanna Seybert

Long Island Federal Courthouse, 100 Federal Plaza, Room 1034,
Central Islip, NY 11722-9014
Tel: (631) 712-5610 Fax: (631) 712-5611
E-mail: joanna_seybert@nyed.uscourts.gov

Joanna Seybert
Senior Judge

Date of Birth: 1946
Education: Cincinnati 1967 BS; St John's U (NY) 1971 JD
Began Service: January 12, 1994
Appointed By: President William J. Clinton

Current Memberships: Federal Judges Association; International Association of Judges/Union Internationale des Magistrats; Suffolk County Bar Association

Staff

Law Clerk **Theodore Hawkins** . . . . (631) 712-5610
Began Service: November 2014
Term Expires: November 21, 2016
E-mail: theodore_hawkins@nyed.uscourts.gov

Law Clerk **Kristin McGrath Seibert** . . . . (631) 712-5610
Began Service: October 2015
Term Expires: October 2016

Deputy Clerk **Charles Baran** . . . . (631) 712-5615
E-mail: charles_baran@nyed.uscourts.gov

Secretary **Bonnie Nohs** . . . . (631) 712-5610
E-mail: bonnie_nohs@nyed.uscourts.gov

Chambers of Senior Judge Nicholas G. Garaufis

U.S. Courthouse, 225 Cadman Plaza East, Brooklyn, NY 11201-1818
Tel: (718) 613-2540 Fax: (718) 613-2546
E-mail: nicholas_garaufis@nyed.uscourts.gov

Nicholas G. Garaufis
Senior Judge

Date of Birth: 1948
Education: Columbia 1969 AB, 1974 JD
Began Service: August 28, 2000
Appointed By: President William J. Clinton

Current Memberships: American Bar Association; The Association of the Bar of the City of New York; Queens County Bar Association

Staff

Law Clerk **Evan Ezray** . . . . (718) 613-2540
Began Service: August 2015
Term Expires: August 2016
E-mail: evan_ezray@nyed.uscourts.gov

Law Clerk **Ryan Goldstein** . . . . (718) 613-2540
Began Service: February 2015
Term Expires: February 2016
E-mail: ryan_goldstein@nyed.uscourts.gov

Law Clerk **Jack Nelson** . . . . (718) 613-2540
Began Service: September 2015
Term Expires: September 2016
E-mail: jack_nelson@nyed.uscourts.gov

Court Deputy **Joseph Reccoppa** . . . . (718) 613-2545
Education: Adelphi 1996 BA

Chambers of Senior Judge Thomas C. Platt, Jr.

P.O. Box 9014, Central Islip, NY 11722-9014
Tel: (631) 712-6031 Fax: (631) 712-5606

Thomas C. Platt, Jr.
Senior Judge

Note: Judge Platt is not currently hearing cases.
Date of Birth: 1925
Education: Yale 1947 BA, 1950 LLB

Chambers of Senior Judge Sandra L. Townes

225 Cadman Plaza East, Room 905S, Brooklyn, NY 11201
Tel: (718) 613-2160 Fax: (718) 613-2166
E-mail: sandra_townes@nyed.uscourts.gov

Sandra L. Townes
Senior Judge

Education: Johnson C Smith 1966 BA; Syracuse 1976 JD
Began Service: September 2004
Appointed By: President George W. Bush

Current Memberships: New York State Bar Association; Onondaga County Bar Association; Women's Bar Association of the State of New York

Staff

Law Clerk **Anjna Kapoor** . . . . (718) 613-2160
Began Service: September 2015
Term Expires: September 2016
E-mail: anjna_kapoor@nyed.uscourts.gov

Law Clerk **Susan Nabet** . . . . (718) 613-2160
Began Service: September 2015
Term Expires: September 2016

Career Law Clerk **Alexander "Alex" Caspari** . . . . (718) 613-2160
E-mail: alexander_caspari@nyed.uscourts.gov

Chambers of Senior Judge Sandra J. Feuerstein

1014 Federal Plaza, Room 1024, Central Islip, NY 11722
Tel: (631) 712-5630 Fax: (631) 712-5636
E-mail: sandra_feuerstein@nyed.uscourts.gov

Sandra J. Feuerstein
Senior Judge

Date of Birth: 1946
Education: Vermont 1966 BA; Hunter MA; Cardozo 1979 JD
Began Service: October 23, 2003
Appointed By: President George W. Bush

Current Memberships: Nassau County Bar Association; Nassau County Women's Bar; Suffolk Women's Bar Association; Women's Bar Association of the State of New York

Staff
Law Clerk **Lisa C. Chan** .... (631) 712-5634
Began Service: September 2015
Term Expires: September 2016
E-mail: lisa_chan@nyed.uscourts.gov
Career Law Clerk **April Adell** .... (631) 712-5633
E-mail: april_adell@nyed.uscourts.gov
Education: Hofstra 1996 JD
Law Clerk and Judicial Assistant **Daniel Belzil** .... (631) 712-5632
E-mail: daniel_belzil@nyed.uscourts.gov

Chambers of Chief Magistrate Judge Steven M. Gold

U.S. Courthouse, 225 Cadman Plaza East, Brooklyn, NY 11201
Tel: (718) 613-2560 Fax: (718) 613-2565
E-mail: steven_gold@nyed.uscourts.gov

Steven M. Gold
Chief Magistrate Judge

Date of Birth: 1955
Education: Wesleyan U 1977 BA; Yale 1980 JD
Began Service: February 23, 1993
Term Expires: 2016

Clerkships: Law Clerk The Honorable Herbert F. Murray, United States District Court for the District of Maryland (1980-1981)

Government: Assistant United States Attorney, Eastern District of New York, Office of the United States Attorney, United States Department of Justice (1985-1989); Assistant United States Attorney and Deputy Chief, Criminal Division, Office of the United States Attorney, United States Department of Justice (1989-1990); General Counsel, Department of Investigation, City of New York, New York (1990-1992)

Legal Practice: Associate, Orans, Elsen & Lupert (1981-1985)

Staff
Law Clerk **Anne J. Collins** .... (718) 613-2560
Began Service: September 2015
Term Expires: September 2016
E-mail: anne_j_collins@nyed.uscourts.gov
Law Clerk **Maxwell Faubion** .... (718) 613-2560
Began Service: September 2015
Term Expires: September 2016
E-mail: maxwell_faubion@nyed.uscourts.gov
Judicial Assistant **Lea D. Vasquez** .... (718) 613-2560
E-mail: lea_vasquez@nyed.uscourts.gov

Chambers of Magistrate Judge Marilyn D. Go

U.S. Courthouse, 225 Cadman Plaza East, Brooklyn, NY 11201
Tel: (718) 613-2550 Fax: (718) 613-2555
E-mail: marilyn_go@nyed.uscourts.gov

Marilyn D. Go
Magistrate Judge

Date of Birth: 1950
Education: Radcliffe 1973 BA; Harvard 1977 JD
Began Service: March 10, 1993
Term Expires: March 9, 2017

Clerkships: Law Clerk The Honorable William M. Marutani, Pennsylvania Court of Common Pleas (1977-1978)

Government: Assistant United States Attorney, Eastern District of New York, Office of the United States Attorney, United States Department of Justice (1978-1982)

Legal Practice: Partner, Baden, Kramer, Huffman, Brodsky & Go, P.C. (1982-1992)

Staff
Law Clerk **Jillian Moo-Young** .... (718) 613-2554
E-mail: jillian_moo-young@nyed.uscourts.gov
Career Law Clerk **Josh Proujansky** .... (718) 613-2553
E-mail: joshua_proujansky@nyed.uscourts.gov
Education: NYU 1999 JD
Courtroom Deputy **Lewis Hugh** .... (718) 613-2550
E-mail: lewis_hugh@nyed.uscourts.gov

Chambers of Magistrate Judge Arlene Rosario Lindsay

Long Island Federal Courthouse, 814 Federal Plaza,
Central Islip, NY 11722
Tel: (631) 712-5730 Fax: (631) 712-5735
E-mail: arlene_lindsay@nyed.uscourts.gov

Arlene Rosario Lindsay
Magistrate Judge

Education: Dayton 1968 BA; NYU 1975 JD
Began Service: 1994
Term Expires: 2018

Academic: Adjunct Professor, Touro Law School

Government: Assistant District Attorney, Office of the District Attorney, County of Bronk, New York (1975-1978); Assistant United States Attorney, Eastern District of New York, Office of the United States Attorney, United States Department of Justice (1978-1983); Deputy County Attorney, Office of the County Attorney, County of Suffolk, New York (1983-1988); Town Attorney, Office of the Town Attorney, Town of Huntington, New York (1988-1990); Chief, Eastern District of New York, Office of the United States Attorney, United States Department of Justice (1990-1994)

Staff
Career Law Clerk **Dina Miller** .... (631) 712-5730
E-mail: dina_miller@nyed.uscourts.gov
Education: Brooklyn Law 2001 JD

Chambers of Magistrate Judge Roanne L. Mann

U.S. Courthouse, 225 Cadman Plaza East, Brooklyn, NY 11201
Tel: (718) 613-2350 Fax: (718) 613-2355
E-mail: roanne_mann@nyed.uscourts.gov

Roanne L. Mann
Magistrate Judge

Date of Birth: 1951
Education: Yale 1972 BA; Stanford 1975 JD
Began Service: March 2, 1994
Term Expires: March 2, 2018

Clerkships: Law Clerk, United States Court of Appeals for the District of Columbia (1976-1977)

Government: Assistant District Attorney, Office of the District Attorney, Borough of Manhattan, New York (1975-1976); Special Assistant to Assistant Attorney General, Civil Division, United States Department of Justice (1977-1978); Chief of Appeals, Southern District of New York and Senior Litigation Counsel, Deputy Chief of Criminal Division, United States Department of Justice (1978-1986)

Legal Practice: Attorney, Stein Zauderer Ellenhorn Frischer & Sharp (1986-1994)

Current Memberships: The Association of the Bar of the City of New York; Federal Bar Council

Staff

Law Clerk **Thomas Dollar** .... (718) 613-2350
Began Service: August 25, 2015
Term Expires: August 2016
E-mail: thomas_dollar@nyed.uscourts.gov

Law Clerk **Jennifer Williams** .... (718) 613-2350
Began Service: August 29, 2011
E-mail: jennifer_williams@nyed.uscourts.gov
Education: Brooklyn Law 2007 JD

Judicial Assistant **Geraldine P. Maynard** .... (718) 613-2350

Chambers of Magistrate Judge Robert M. Levy

U.S. Courthouse, 225 Cadman Plaza East, Brooklyn, NY 11201
Tel: (718) 613-2340 Fax: (718) 613-2345

Robert M. Levy
Magistrate Judge

Education: Harvard 1971; NYU 1975 JD
Began Service: March 20, 1995
Term Expires: March 2019

Academic: Adjunct Professor, Columbia Law School; Adjunct Professor, New York University Law School; Adjunct Professor, Brooklyn Law School

Legal Practice: Senior Staff Attorney, New York Civil Liberties Union (1986-1993); General Counsel, New York Lawyers for the Public Interest (1993-1994)

Current Memberships: The Association of the Bar of the City of New York; Public Service Committee, Federal Bar Council; Second Circuit Courts Committee, Federal Bar Council

Staff

Law Clerk **Hannah Roth** .... (718) 613-2344
Began Service: August 2014
Term Expires: August 2016
E-mail: hannah_roth@nyed.uscourts.gov

Career Law Clerk **Leslie Rubin** .... (718) 613-2343
E-mail: leslie_rubin@nyed.uscourts.gov
Education: NYU 1991 JD

Judicial Assistant **Janine Marino** .... (718) 613-2340
E-mail: janine_marino@nyed.uscourts.gov

Chambers of Magistrate Judge Viktor V. Pohorelsky

U.S. Courthouse, 225 Cadman Plaza East, Room 1207-S, Brooklyn, NY 11201
Tel: (718) 613-2400 Fax: (718) 613-2405
E-mail: viktor_pohorelsky@nyed.uscourts.gov

Viktor V. Pohorelsky
Magistrate Judge

Date of Birth: 1949
Education: Tulane 1971 BA, 1980 JD
Began Service: 1995

Clerkships: Law Clerk The Honorable Earl Veron Summer (1980); Law Clerk The Honorable John Minor Wisdom (1980-1981)

Corporate: Capital National Bank (1971-1972)

Government: Assistant United States Attorney, Southern District of New York, Office of the United States Attorney, United States Department of Justice (1984-1989); Assistant United States Attorney and Deputy Chief, Criminal Division, Southern District of New York, Office of the United States Attorney, United States Department of Justice (1989-1991)

Legal Practice: Associate, Debevoise & Plimpton LLP (1981-1984); Partner, Gold & Wachtel (1991-1994)

Profession: Musician (1972-1975)

Staff

Judicial Assistant **Joan Newton** .... (718) 613-2402
E-mail: joan_newton@nyed.uscourts.gov

Chambers of Magistrate Judge Cheryl L. Pollak

U.S. Courthouse, 225 Cadman Plaza East, Room 1230, Brooklyn, NY 11201
Tel: (718) 613-2360 Fax: (718) 613-2365
E-mail: cheryl_pollak@nyed.uscourts.gov

Cheryl L. Pollak
Magistrate Judge

Date of Birth: 1953
Education: Princeton 1975 AB; Chicago 1978 JD
Began Service: November 1995
Term Expires: November 2019

Clerkships: Law Clerk The Honorable Wm. H. Timbers, United States Court of Appeals for the Second Circuit (1978-1979)

Government: Associate, Eastern District of New York, Office of the United States Attorney, United States Department of Justice (1986-1991); Chief, Eastern District of New York, OCDETF Unit, Office of the United States Attorney, United States Department of Justice (1991-1994); International and National Security Advisor, Eastern District, Office of the United States Attorney, United States Department of Justice (1991-1995); Deputy Chief of Criminal Division, Eastern District of New York, Office of the United States Attorney, United States Department of Justice (1994-1995)

Legal Practice: Associate, Davis Polk & Wardwell (1979-1986)

Current Memberships: American Bar Association; The Association of the Bar of the City of New York; Federal Bar Council

Staff

Law Clerk **Ashok Chandran** .... (718) 613-2360
Began Service: September 2015
Term Expires: September 2016
E-mail: ashok_chandran@nyed.uscourts.gov

Law Clerk **Stefanie Williams** .... (718) 613-2360
Began Service: September 2015
Term Expires: September 2016
E-mail: stefanie_williams@nyed.uscourts.gov

Judicial Assistant **Diana Caggiano** .... (718) 613-2360
E-mail: diana_caggiano@nyed.uscourts.gov

Chambers of Magistrate Judge Lois Bloom

U.S. Courthouse, 225 Cadman Plaza East, Brooklyn, NY 11201
Tel: (718) 613-2170 Fax: (718) 613-2175
E-mail: lois_bloom@nyed.uscourts.gov

Lois Bloom
Magistrate Judge

Education: SUNY (Stony Brook) 1981 BA; SUNY (Buffalo) 1985 JD
Began Service: May 18, 2001

Academic: Instructor, Columbia Law School (1998); Adjunct Professor, New York Law School (1999-2000)

Government: Senior Staff Attorney, United States District Court for the Southern District of New York (1988-2001)

Legal Practice: Staff Attorney, West Side SRO Law Project (1985-1988)

Staff
Law Clerk **Lillian Marquez** .... (718) 613-2170
Began Service: August 2014
Term Expires: August 2016
E-mail: lillian_marquez@nyed.uscourts.gov
Law Clerk **Rebecca Wallach** .... (718) 613-2170
Began Service: January 2015
Term Expires: January 2017
E-mail: rebecca_walsh@nyed.uscourts.gov
Courtroom Deputy/Law Clerk **Rebecca Gannon** .... (718) 613-2170
E-mail: rebecca_gannon@nyed.uscourts.gov

Chambers of Magistrate Judge James Orenstein

225 Cadman Plaza East, Brooklyn, NY 11201
Tel: (718) 613-2110
E-mail: james_orenstein@nyed.uscourts.gov

James Orenstein
Magistrate Judge

Education: Harvard BA; NYU 1986 JD
Began Service: 2004

Staff
Law Clerk **Thomas Howley** .... (718) 613-2110
E-mail: thomas_howley@nyed.uscourts.gov
Law Clerk **Jocelyn Smerd** .... (718) 613-2110
E-mail: jocelyn_smerd@nyed.uscourts.gov

Chambers of Magistrate Judge Ramon E. Reyes, Jr.

225 Cadman Plaza East, Brooklyn, NY 11201
Tel: (718) 613-2120 Fax: (718) 613-2125
E-mail: ramon_reyes@nyed.uscourts.gov

Ramon E. Reyes, Jr.
Magistrate Judge

Education: Cornell 1988 BS; Brooklyn Law 1992 JD; NYU 1993 LLM
Began Service: February 13, 2006

Current Memberships: Association of Judges of Hispanic Heritage; Hispanic National Bar Association; Puerto Rican Bar Association

Staff
Law Clerk **Emmanuel Fashakin, Jr.** .... (718) 613-2120
Began Service: September 2015
Term Expires: September 2016
E-mail: emmanuel_fashakin@nyed.uscourts.gov
Law Clerk **Adrienne Yasunaga** .... (718) 613-2120
Began Service: September 2011
Term Expires: September 2016
E-mail: adrienne_yasunaga@nyed.uscourts.gov

Chambers of Magistrate Judge Gary R. Brown

225 Cadman Plaza East, Brooklyn, NY 11201
Tel: (631) 712-5700
E-mail: gary_brown@nyed.uscourts.gov

Gary R. Brown
Magistrate Judge

Education: Columbia 1985 BA; Yale 1988 JD
Began Service: 2011

Staff
Law Clerk **Kevin Yim** .... (631) 712-5700
Began Service: September 2014
Term Expires: September 2016
E-mail: kevin_yim@nyed.uscourts.gov
Education: Temple 2014 JD
Law Clerk **Linda Johnston** .... (631) 712-5700
E-mail: linda_johnston@nyed.uscourts.gov
Education: St John's U (NY) JD
Judicial Assistant **Karen McMorrow** .... (631) 712-5700
E-mail: karen_mcmorrow@nyed.uscourts.gov

Chambers of Magistrate Judge A. Kathleen Tomlinson

Alfonse M. D'Amato U.S. Courthouse, 100 Federal Plaza, Central Islip, NY 11722-4449
Tel: (631) 712-5760 Fax: (631) 712-5766

A. Kathleen Tomlinson
Magistrate Judge

Education: Rutgers 1972 BA; Long Island 1975 MA; St John's U (NY) 1987 JD
Began Service: February 24, 2006

Staff
Law Clerk **Erin Kandel** .... (631) 712-5760
E-mail: erin_kandel@nyed.uscourts.gov
Career Law Clerk **Katherine Buckel** .... (631) 712-5760
E-mail: katherine_buckel@nyed.uscourts.gov

Chambers of Magistrate Judge Vera M. Scanlon

U.S. Courthouse, 225 Cadman Plaza East, Room 504N, Brooklyn, NY 11201
Tel: (718) 613-2300 Fax: (718) 316-2305
E-mail: scanlon_chambers@nyed.uscourts.gov

Vera M. Scanlon
Magistrate Judge

Began Service: August 14, 2012

Staff
Law Clerk **Corey Calabrese** .... (718) 613-2300
Began Service: September 2015
Term Expires: September 2016
E-mail: corey_calabrese@nyed.uscourts.gov
Education: Fordham 2010 JD
Law Clerk **Richard Weingarten** .... (718) 613-2300
Began Service: September 2015
Term Expires: September 2016
E-mail: richard_weingarten@nyed.uscourts.gov
Courtroom Deputy **Tina Priftakis** .... (718) 613-2300
E-mail: tina_priftakis@nyed.uscourts.gov

Chambers of Magistrate Judge Steven I. Locke

100 Federal Plaza, Central Islip, NY 11722-4447
Tel: (631) 712-5724
E-mail: steven_locke@nyed.uscourts.gov

Steven I. Locke
Magistrate Judge

Began Service: 2014

Chambers of Magistrate Judge Anne Y. Shields

100 Federal Plaza, Central Islip, NY 11722-4447
Tel: (631) 712-5710

Anne Shields
Magistrate Judge

Education: St John's U (NY) 1984 JD

Staff

Law Clerk **Rosalinde Casalini** . . . . (631) 712-5713
E-mail: rosalinde_casalini@nyed.uscourts.gov
Law Clerk **Alison Berson** . . . . (631) 712-5712
E-mail: alison_berson@nyed.uscourts.gov
Courtroom Deputy **Jasmine Torres** . . . . (631) 712-5714

United States Bankruptcy Court for the Eastern District of New York

271 Cadman Plaza East, Suite 1595, Brooklyn, NY 11201
Tel: (347) 394-1700
Tel: (800) 252-2537 (Toll Free Voice Case Information System VCIS)
Internet: www.nyeb.uscourts.gov
Internet: ecf.nyeb.uscourts.gov (PACER)

Number of Judgeships: 6

Court Staff

Clerk of the Court **Robert A. Gavin, Jr.** . . . . (347) 394-1741
E-mail: robert_gavin@nyeb.uscourts.gov Tel: (631) 712-6281 (Central Islip)
Chief Deputy Clerk **Paul Dickson** . . . . (347) 394-1753
E-mail: paul_dickson@nyeb.uscourts.gov
Court Services Generalist- Brooklyn
Gaspare Pellegrino . . . . (347) 394-1727
E-mail: gaspare_pellegrino@nyeb.uscourts.gov
Deputy Clerk in charge - Central Islip **Nancy Profit** . . . . . (631) 712-6204
Long Island Federal Courthouse, 290 Federal Plz., Central Islip, NY 11722-4437
E-mail: nancy_profit@nyeb.uscourts.gov
Operations Manager **Amy Stewart** . . . . (347) 394-1709
E-mail: amy_stewart@nyeb.uscourts.gov Tel: (631) 712-6200 (Brooklyn Office)
Systems Manager **James DiGiacomo** . . . . (347) 394-1755
E-mail: james_digiacomo@nyeb.uscourts.gov
Financial Administrator **Max Bonga** . . . . (631) 712-6269
Long Island Federal Courthouse, 290 Federal Plz., Central Islip, NY 11722-4437
E-mail: max_bonga@nyeb.uscourts.gov
Human Resources Specialist **Shirley Jenkins** . . . . (347) 394-1746
E-mail: shirley_jenkins@nyeb.uscourts.gov
Procurement **James Guzman** . . . . (347) 394-1721
E-mail: james_guzman@nyeb.uscourts.gov

Chambers of Chief Bankruptcy Judge Carla E. Craig

271 Cadman Plaza East, Suite 1595, Brooklyn, NY 11201-1800
Tel: (347) 394-1840
E-mail: carla_craig@nyeb.uscourts.gov

Carla Elizabeth Craig
Chief Bankruptcy Judge

Date of Birth: 1954
Education: Williams 1976 BA; Michigan 1979 JD
Began Service: February 28, 2000
Term Expires: February 28, 2028

Legal Practice: Associate, Milbank, Tweed, Hadley & McCloy LLP (1980-1983); Partner, Hertzog, Calamari & Gleason (1983-1998); Partner, Brown Raysman Millstein Felder & Steiner LLP (1998-2000)

Current Memberships: American Bar Association; The Association of the Bar of the City of New York; Brooklyn Bar Association; National Conference of Bankruptcy Judges

Staff

Law Clerk **Michael Guippone** . . . . (347) 394-1843
E-mail: michael_guippone@nyeb.uscourts.gov
Law Clerk **Phillip Khezri** . . . . (631) 712-5680
E-mail: phillip_khezri@nyeb.uscourts.gov
Career Law Clerk **Sharon L. Weiss** . . . . (347) 394-1843
E-mail: sharon_weiss@nyeb.uscourts.gov
Education: Brooklyn Law 2005 JD
Courtroom Deputy **Tracie M. Leonard** . . . . (347) 394-1844
E-mail: tracie_leonard@nyeb.uscourts.gov

Chambers of Bankruptcy Judge Elizabeth S. Stong

271 Cadman Plaza East, Brooklyn, NY 11201
Tel: (347) 394-1862
E-mail: elizabeth_stong@nyeb.uscourts.gov

Elizabeth S. Stong
Bankruptcy Judge

Education: Harvard 1978 AB, 1982 JD
Began Service: September 2, 2003

Affiliation: Chair, National Conference of Bankruptcy Judges

Clerkships: Law Clerk, United States District Court for the District of Massachusetts (1982-1983)

Legal Practice: Associate, Cravath, Swaine & Moore LLP (1983-1987); Associate, Willkie Farr & Gallagher LLP (1987-1992); Partner, Willkie Farr & Gallagher LLP (1993-2003)

Nonprofit: President, Harvard Law School Association; Vice President, Board of Directors, City Bar Fund, Inc.

Current Memberships: American Bar Foundation; American Bankruptcy Institute; American Bar Association; The American Law Institute; The Association of the Bar of the City of New York; Brooklyn Bar Association; Federal Bar Council; National Conference of Bankruptcy Judges; New York Law Institute; New York State Bar Association

Staff

Law Clerk **Ciara Foster** . . . . (347) 394-1863
Began Service: September 2015
Term Expires: September 2016
E-mail: ciara_foster@nyeb.uscourts.gov
Law Clerk **Caitlin Griffin** . . . . (347) 394-1863
Began Service: September 2015
Term Expires: September 2016
E-mail: caitlin_griffin@nyeb.uscourts.gov
Law Clerk **Adam Lanza** . . . . (347) 394-1862
Began Service: September 2015
Term Expires: September 2016
Career Law Clerk **Joan Gottesman** . . . . (347) 394-1861
E-mail: joan_gottesman@nyeb.uscourts.gov

Chambers of Bankruptcy Judge Elizabeth S. Stong *continued*

Courtroom Deputy **Sheree Jackson** .... (347) 394-1864
E-mail: sheree_jackson@nyeb.uscourts.gov
Electronic Court Reporter **Fanny Randazzo** .... (347) 394-1732
E-mail: fanny_randazzo@nyeb.uscourts.gov

Chambers of Bankruptcy Judge Alan S. Trust

Long Island Federal Court House, 290 Federal Plaza, Room 960, Central Islip, NY 11722
Tel: (631) 712-5680
E-mail: alan_trust@nyeb.uscourts.gov

Alan S. Trust
Bankruptcy Judge

Began Service: April 2, 2008

Staff

Law Clerk **Jason Blanchard** .... (631) 712-5684
Began Service: August 22, 2013
Term Expires: August 2016
E-mail: jason_blanchard@nyeb.uscourts.gov
Law Clerk **Richard Corbi** .... (631) 712-5684
Began Service: August 25, 2014
Term Expires: August 2016
E-mail: richard_corbi@nyeb.uscourts.gov
Courtroom Deputy **Yvette Mills** .... (631) 712-6277

Chambers of Bankruptcy Judge Robert E. Grossman

290 Federal Plaza, Room 860, Central Islip, NY 11722
Tel: (631) 712-5740
E-mail: robert_grossman@nyeb.uscourts.gov

Robert E. Grossman
Bankruptcy Judge

Began Service: 2008

Staff

Law Clerk **Rashida Adams** .... (631) 712-5743
Career Law Clerk **Catherine Cozzette** .... (631) 712-5691
E-mail: catherine_cozzette@nyeb.uscourts.gov
Education: George Washington 1988 JD
Career Law Clerk **(Vacant)** .... (631) 712-5752
Career Law Clerk **Lynn Ryan** .... (631) 712-5683
E-mail: lynn_ryan@nyeb.uscourts.gov
Education: St John's U (NY) 1996 JD
Courtroom Deputy **Madrie Tagle** .... (631) 712-6276
E-mail: madrie_tagle@nyeb.uscourts.gov

Chambers of Bankruptcy Judge Nancy Hershey Lord

271 Cadman Plaza East, Brooklyn, NY 11201
Tel: (347) 394-1850
E-mail: nancy_lord@nyeb.uscourts.gov

Nancy Hershey Lord
Bankruptcy Judge

Began Service: April 1, 2012

Staff

Law Clerk **Allison Arotsky** .... (347) 394-1851
E-mail: allison_arotsky@nyeb.uscourts.gov
Law Clerk **Cassandra Aquart** .... (347) 394-1853
E-mail: cassandra_aquart@nyeb.uscourts.gov
Courtroom Deputy **Angela Howard** .... (347) 394-1854
E-mail: angela_howard@nyeb.uscourts.gov

Chambers of Bankruptcy Judge Louis A. Scarcella

290 Federal Plaza, Central Islip, NY 11722
Tel: (631) 712-6278

Louis A. Scarcella
Bankruptcy Judge

Education: Providence BA; Hofstra JD
Term Expires: May 15, 2028

United States District Court for the Northern District of New York

Federal Building, 100 South Clinton Street, Syracuse, NY 13261
Tel: (315) 234-8500 Tel: (315) 448-0537 (PACER)
Tel: (800) 480-7525 (Toll Free PACER) Fax: (315) 234-8501
Internet: www.nynd.uscourts.gov

Number of Judgeships: 5

Circuit: Second

Areas Covered: Counties of Albany, Broome, Cayuga, Chenango, Clinton, Columbia, Cortland, Delaware, Essex, Franklin, Fulton, Greene, Hamilton, Herkimer, Jefferson, Lewis, Madison, Montgomery, Oneida, Onondaga, Oswego, Otsego, Rensselaer, Saratoga, Schenectady, Schoharie, St. Lawrence, Tioga, Tompkins, Ulster, Warren and Washington

Court Staff

Clerk of Court **Lawrence K. Baerman** .... (315) 234-8516
Albany Division Chief Deputy Clerk
John M. Domurad .... (518) 257-1800
James T. Foley U.S. Courthouse, 445 Broadway, Albany, NY 12207 Fax: (518) 257-1801
E-mail: john_domurad@nynd.uscourts.gov
Deputy of Operations **Daniel McAllister** .... (315) 234-8505
Systems Manager **E. Scott Fuller** .... (315) 234-8524
Utica Division Manager (Acting) **Susan Evans** .... (315) 793-8151
Alexander Pirnie Federal Bldg., 10 Broad St., Utica, NY 13501 Fax: (315) 793-8186
E-mail: susan_evans@nynd.uscourts.gov
Chief Probation Officer **Matthew L. Brown** .... (315) 234-8700
Fax: (315) 234-8701
Financial Administrator **Maria Devins** .... (315) 234-8521
E-mail: maria_devins@nynd.uscourts.gov
Syracuse Division Supervisor **Penny Price** .... (315) 234-8512
E-mail: penny_price@nynd.uscourts.gov
Human Resources and Personnel Specialist
Michelle Louise .... (315) 234-8731

Chambers of Chief Judge Glenn T. Suddaby

Federal Building, 100 South Clinton Street, Syracuse, NY 13261
Tel: (315) 234-8580
E-mail: glenn_suddaby@nynd.uscourts.gov

Glenn T. Suddaby
Chief Judge

Education: SUNY (Plattsburgh) 1980 BA; Syracuse 1985 JD
Began Service: September 5, 2008
Appointed By: President George W. Bush

Staff

Courtroom Clerk **Lori Welch** .... (315) 234-8583
E-mail: lori_welch@nynd.uscourts.gov
Judicial Assistant **Kelly Easton** .... (315) 234-8580
E-mail: kelly_easton@nynd.uscourts.gov

Chambers of District Judge Gary L. Sharpe
James T. Foley Courthouse, 445 Broadway, Albany, NY 12207-2924
Tel: (518) 257-1870 Fax: (518) 257-1871
E-mail: glsharpe@nynd.uscourts.gov

Gary L. Sharpe
District Judge

Date of Birth: 1947
Education: Cornell 1974 JD
Began Service: January 2004
Appointed By: President George W. Bush

Current Memberships: New York State Bar Association

Staff
Law Clerk **Julie Nociolo** .... (518) 257-1870
Began Service: September 2015
Term Expires: September 2016
Career Law Clerk **Benjamin Loefke** .... (518) 257-1870
E-mail: benjamin_loefke@nynd.uscourts.gov
Education: Albany Law 2010 JD
Courtroom Deputy **John Law** .... (518) 257-1870
E-mail: john_law@nynd.uscourts.gov

Chambers of District Judge David N. Hurd
U.S. Courthouse, 10 Broad Street, Room 300, Utica, NY 13501
Tel: (315) 793-9571 Fax: (315) 793-8034
E-mail: david_hurd@nynd.uscourts.gov

David N. Hurd
District Judge

Date of Birth: 1937
Education: Cornell 1959 BS; Syracuse 1963 JD
Began Service: September 24, 1999
Appointed By: President William J. Clinton

Government: Assistant District Attorney, Office of the District Attorney, County of Oneida, New York (1966-1967)

Judicial: Magistrate Judge, United States District Court for the Northern District of New York (1991-1999)

Legal Practice: Associate, Coughlin, Dermody, Ingalls & Guy (1963-1964); Associate, Abelove & Myers (1964-1966); Associate (Part-time), Ferris, Kehoe, Tenney & Murnane (1966-1967); Associate, O'Shea, Griffin, Jones & McLaughlin (1967-1970); Partner, O'Shea, Griffin, McDonald, Hurd & Stevens (1970-1991)

Current Memberships: Albany County Bar Association; American College of Trial Lawyers; Federal Judges Association; New York State Bar Association; Oneida County Bar Association; Rome Bar Association (NY)

Staff
Law Clerk **Steven Huntzinger** .... (315) 793-9571
Began Service: September 3, 2015
Term Expires: September 2, 2016
E-mail: steven_huntzinger@nynd.uscourts.gov
Career Law Clerk **Chelsea L. Scaramuzzino** .... (315) 793-9571
Began Service: September 3, 2013
E-mail: chelsea_selby@nynd.uscourts.gov
Education: SUNY (Buffalo) 2010 JD

Chambers of District Judge Mae A. D'Agostino
445 Broadway, Albany, NY 12207
Tel: (518) 257-1880 Fax: (518) 257-1881
E-mail: mae_dagostino@nynd.uscourts.gov

Mae A. D'Agostino
District Judge

Date of Birth: 1954
Education: Siena Col 1977 BA; Syracuse 1980 JD
Began Service: September 19, 2011
Appointed By: President Barack Obama

Legal Practice: Associate, Maynard, O'Connor & Smith (1981-1985); Partner, Maynard, O'Connor & Smith (1985-1997)

Staff
Law Clerk **Max Lindsey** .... (518) 257-1885
E-mail: max_lindsey@nynd.uscourts.gov
Law Clerk **Brian Onofry** .... (518) 257-1884
Began Service: 2011
E-mail: brian_onofry@nynd.uscourts.gov
Law Clerk **Mia Vanauken** .... (518) 257-1880
E-mail: mia_vanauken@nynd.uscourts.gov
Courtroom Deputy **Britney Norton** .... (518) 257-1883
E-mail: britney_norton@nynd.uscourts.gov

Chambers of District Judge Brenda K. Sannes
100 South Clinton Street, Syracuse, NY 13261
Tel: (315) 234-8500

Brenda K. Sannes
District Judge

Education: Carleton 1980; Wisconsin 1983 JD
Began Service: 2014
Appointed By: President Barack Obama

Chambers of Senior Judge Thomas J. McAvoy
U.S. Courthouse, 15 Henry Street, Room 206, Binghamton, NY 13901
Tel: (607) 773-2892
E-mail: thomas_mcavoy@nynd.uscourts.gov

Thomas J. McAvoy
Senior Judge

Date of Birth: 1938
Education: Villanova 1960 AB; Albany Law 1964 JD
Began Service: 1986
Appointed By: President Ronald Reagan

Government: Legislator, County of Broome, New York (1971-1986); Associate, Broome County Industrial Development Agency, County of Broome, New York (1976-1986)

Legal Practice: Associate, Hinman, Howard & Kattell, LLP (1964-1969); Partner, Kramer, Wales & McAvoy (1969-1984); Partner, McAvoy & Hickey, P.C. (1984-1986)

Current Memberships: American Bar Association; Broome County Bar Association; The Justinian Society

Staff
Career Law Clerk **James Connor** .... (607) 773-2892
Career Law Clerk **Richard S. Lindstrom** .... (607) 773-2892
E-mail: richard_lindstrom@nynd.uscourts.gov
Education: Northwestern 2006 JD
Courtroom Clerk **Colleen Ligas** .... (607) 773-2909
E-mail: colleen_ligas@nynd.uscourts.gov
Secretary/Judicial Assistant **Marlene Price** .... (607) 773-2892
E-mail: marlene_price@nynd.uscourts.gov

Chambers of Senior Judge Frederick J. Scullin, Jr.

Federal Building, 100 South Clinton Street, Syracuse, NY 13261
P.O. Box 7255, Syracuse, NY 13261-7255
Tel: (315) 234-8560 Fax: (315) 234-8561
E-mail: FScullin@nynd.uscourts.gov

Frederick J. Scullin, Jr.
Senior Judge

Date of Birth: 1939
Education: Niagara 1961 BS; Syracuse 1964 LLB
Began Service: March 13, 1992
Appointed By: President George H.W. Bush
Political Affiliation: Republican

Government: Assistant District Attorney, Office of the Attorney General, Onondaga County, State of New York (1969-1970); Special Assistant Attorney General, Organized Crime Task Force, State of New York (1971-1978); United States Attorney, Northern District of New York, United States Department of Justice (1982-1992)

Judicial: District Judge, United States District Court for the Northern District of New York (1992-2000); Chief Judge, United States District Court for the Northern District of New York

Legal Practice: Germain & Germain (1967-1968); Private Practice (1980-1982)

Military Service: United States Army Reserve, United States Department of the Army (1961-1991); United States Army (1964-1966)

Current Memberships: Federal Bar Association; Federal Bar Council; Onondaga County Bar Association

Staff
Law Clerk **Michael Tyszka** .... (315) 234-8560
Began Service: August 2015
Term Expires: August 2016
Career Law Clerk **Debbie Moore** .... (315) 234-8560
E-mail: debbie_moore@nynd.uscourts.gov
Education: Skidmore 1974 BA; Syracuse 1991 JD
Courtroom Deputy **Nicole Eallonardo** .... (315) 234-8560
E-mail: nicole_eallonardo@nynd.uscourts.gov
Judicial Assistant **Rosemary Riley** .... (315) 234-8560
E-mail: rosemary_riley@nynd.uscourts.gov

Chambers of Senior Judge Lawrence E. Kahn

James T. Foley U.S. Courthouse, 445 Broadway, Albany, NY 12207
Tel: (518) 257-1830 Fax: (518) 257-1831
E-mail: lawrence_kahn@nynd.uscourts.gov

Lawrence E. Kahn
Senior Judge

Date of Birth: 1937
Education: Union Col (NY) 1959 AB; Harvard 1962 JD
Began Service: August 1, 1996
Appointed By: President William J. Clinton

Government: Assistant Corporation Counsel, City of Albany, New York (1963-1968)

Judicial: Judge, Albany County Surrogate Court (1974-1979); Justice, New York Supreme Court (1980-1996)

Legal Practice: Partner, Kahn & Kahn, Esqs. (1963-1973)

Military Service: New York State National Guard (1955-1965)

Staff
Law Clerk **Jenna Smith** .... (518) 257-1830
Law Clerk **Matthew Ahn** .... (518) 257-1830
Began Service: September 2015
Term Expires: September 2016
Education: Columbia 1998; Harvard 2002 JD
Law Clerk **Casey Clausen** .... (518) 257-1830
Began Service: January 2015
Term Expires: January 2016
E-mail: casey_clausen@nynd.uscourts.gov

Chambers of Senior Judge Lawrence E. Kahn *continued*

Courtroom Deputy **Scott Snyder** .... (518) 257-1833
E-mail: scott_snyder@nynd.uscourts.gov
Education: SUNY (Albany) 1994

Chambers of Senior Judge Norman A. Mordue

100 South Clinton Street, Syracuse, NY 13261
Tel: (315) 234-8570 Fax: (315) 234-8571
E-mail: norman_mordue@nynd.uscourts.gov

Norman A. Mordue
Senior Judge

Date of Birth: 1942
Education: Syracuse 1966 BA, 1971 JD
Began Service: December 4, 1998
Appointed By: President William J. Clinton

Current Memberships: American Bar Association; Association of Justices of the Supreme Court of the State of New York; New York State Bar Association; Onondaga County Bar Association; Central New York Women's Bar Association, Women's Bar Association of the State of New York

Staff
Law Clerk **Briton Nelson** .... (315) 234-8570
E-mail: briton_nelson@nynd.uscourts.gov
Principal Career Law Clerk **Annelle McCullough** .... (315) 234-8570
E-mail: annelle_mccullough@nynd.uscourts.gov
Education: St Lawrence 1972 BA; Syracuse 1977 JD
Courtroom Clerk **Judi McNicholas** .... (315) 234-8573
E-mail: judi_mcnicholas@nynd.uscourts.gov
Judicial Assistant **Jeanne Linsday** .... (315) 234-8570
E-mail: jeanne_linsday@nynd.uscourts.gov

Chambers of Magistrate Judge David E. Peebles

Federal Building, 100 South Clinton Street, Syracuse, NY 13261
P.O. Box 7345, Syracuse, NY 13261-7345
Tel: (315) 234-8620 Fax: (315) 234-8621
E-mail: dpeebles@nynd.uscourts.gov

David E. Peebles
Magistrate Judge

Date of Birth: 1949
Education: Georgia Tech 1972 BA; Syracuse 1975 JD
Began Service: May 22, 2000
Term Expires: May 22, 2016

Clerkships: Confidential Law Clerk The Honorable Howard G. Munson, United States District Court for the Northern District of New York (1976-1978)

Government: Assistant District Attorney, County of Onondaga, New York (1974-1976)

Legal Practice: Partner, Hancock & Estabrook, LLP (1978-2000)

Current Memberships: Onondaga County Bar Association

Staff
Career Law Clerk **Anne LaFex** .... (315) 234-8624
E-mail: anne_lafex@nynd.uscourts.gov
Courtroom Deputy **Shelly Muller** .... (315) 234-8624
E-mail: shelly_muller@nynd.uscourts.gov
Judicial Assistant **Cindy McNulty** .... (315) 234-8620
E-mail: cmcnulty@nynd.uscourts.gov

Chambers of Magistrate Judge Andrew Baxter
100 South Clinton Street, Syracuse, NY 13261
Tel: (315) 234-8603
E-mail: andrew_baxter@nynd.uscourts.gov

Andrew T. Baxter
Magistrate Judge

Date of Birth: 1956
Education: Princeton 1978 AB; Harvard 1981 JD
Began Service: January 2010

Staff
Law Clerk **(Vacant)** . . . . (315) 234-8600
Career Law Clerk **Gioia A. Gensini** . . . . (315) 234-8600
Began Service: 1987
E-mail: gioia_gensini@nynd.uscourts.gov
Education: Cornell 1978 BS; Syracuse 1982 JD
Courtroom Clerk **Melissa Frisch** . . . . (315) 234-8603
E-mail: melissa_frisch@nynd.uscourts.gov

Chambers of Magistrate Judge Christian F. Hummel
441 James T. Foley U.S. Courthouse, 445 Broadway,
Albany, NY 12207-2924
Tel: (518) 257-1850 Fax: (518) 257-1851
E-mail: christian_hummel@nynd.uscourts.gov

Christian F. Hummel
Magistrate Judge

Staff
Law Clerk **Cynthia Weaver** . . . . (518) 257-1850
E-mail: cynthia_weaver@nynd.uscourts.gov
Career Law Clerk **Adrienne A. Foederer** . . . . (518) 257-1854
E-mail: adrienne_foederer@nynd.uscourts.gov
Education: Albany Law JD
Courtroom Deputy **Cynthia Bury-Mezoff** . . . . (518) 257-1853
Education: SUNY (Albany) 1991 BA

Chambers of Magistrate Judge Therese Wiley Dancks
100 South Clinton Street, Syracuse, NY 13261
Tel: (315) 234-8500
E-mail: therese_dancks@nynd.uscourts.gov

Therese Wiley Dancks
Magistrate Judge

Chambers of Magistrate Judge Gary L. Favro
100 South Clinton Street, Syracuse, NY 13261
Tel: (315) 234-8500
E-mail: gary_favro@nynd.uscourts.gov

Gary Favro
Magistrate Judge

Began Service: 2014

Chambers of Magistrate Judge Daniel J. Stewart
445 Broadway, Albany, NY 12207-2924
Tel: (518) 257-1843

Daniel J. Stewart
Magistrate Judge

Began Service: 2015

Chambers of Magistrate Judge (recalled) William B. Mitchell Carter
100 South Clinton Street, Syracuse, NY 13261
Tel: (315) 234-8500

William B. Mitchell Carter
Magistrate Judge (recalled)

Date of Birth: 1942
Education: North Carolina 1965 BA; Vanderbilt 1968 JD; Tennessee 1972 MBA
Began Service: 2015

United States Bankruptcy Court for the Northern District of New York
James T. Foley Courthouse, 445 Broadway, Suite 330, Albany, NY 12207
Tel: (518) 257-1661 Tel: (518) 431-0175 (PACER)
Tel: (800) 390-8432 (Toll Free PACER)
Tel: (866) 222-8029 (Toll Free Voice Case Information System VCIS)
Fax: (518) 257-1648
Internet: www.nynb.uscourts.gov

Number of Judgeships: 3

Court Staff
Clerk **Kim F. Lefebvre** . . . . (518) 257-1661
E-mail: kim_lefebvre@nynb.uscourts.gov
Chief Deputy Clerk **Diann M. Freeman** . . . . (315) 266-1120
Alexander Pirnie Federal Bldg., 10 Broad St., Utica, NY 13501 Fax: (315) 793-8125
E-mail: diann_freeman@nynb.uscourts.gov
Courtroom Deputy, Full Calendar **Colleen Johnson** . . . . (315) 266-1102
Alexander Pirnie Federal Bldg., 10 Broad St., Utica, NY 13501 Fax: (315) 793-8128
E-mail: colleen_johnson@nynb.uscourts.gov
Courtroom Services Manager **Elizabeth Vadney** . . . . (518) 257-1615
E-mail: elizabeth_vadney@nynb.uscourts.gov Fax: (518) 431-0192
IT Director **Ann Marie Waters** . . . . (518) 257-1635
E-mail: annmarie_waters@nynb.uscourts.gov Fax: (518) 257-1645
Human Resources Specialist **Sean Garrow** . . . . (518) 257-1641
E-mail: sean_garrow@nynb.uscourts.gov
Training Specialist **Dina Ventura** . . . . (315) 266-1109
Alexander Pirnie Federal Bldg., 10 Broad St., Utica, NY 13501 Fax: (315) 793-8128
E-mail: dina_ventura@nynb.uscourts.gov

Chambers of Chief Bankruptcy Judge Margaret Cangilos-Ruiz
100 South Clinton Street, Syracuse, NY 13202
Tel: (315) 295-1682
E-mail: margaret_cangilos-ruiz@nynb.uscourts.gov

Margaret Cangilos-Ruiz
Chief Bankruptcy Judge

Education: Cornell 1974 AB; Albany Law 1979 JD
Began Service: February 2007
Term Expires: February 2021

Staff
Law Clerk **Robert Nussbaum** . . . . (315) 295-1684
Career Law Clerk **Dawn Simmons** . . . . (315) 295-1683
E-mail: dawn_simmons@nynb.uscourts.gov

Chambers of Bankruptcy Judge Robert E. Littlefield, Jr.

James T. Foley U.S. Courthouse, 445 Broadway, Albany, NY 12207
Tel: (518) 257-1668 Fax: (518) 431-0192
E-mail: robert_littlefield@nynb.uscourts.gov

Robert E. Littlefield, Jr.
Bankruptcy Judge

Date of Birth: 1951
Education: Denver 1973 BA; Albany Law 1976 JD
Began Service: 2009

Current Memberships: Albany County Bar Association; New York State Bar Association

Staff
Career Law Clerk **Cynthia A. Platt** .... (518) 257-1620
E-mail: cynthia_platt@nynb.uscourts.gov
Education: Albany Law 1989 JD
Law Clerk **Ryan Hays** .... (518) 257-1605
E-mail: ryan_hays@nynb.uscourts.gov

Chambers of Bankruptcy Judge Diane Davis

220 Alexander Pirnie Federal Building, 10 Broad Street, Utica, NY 13501
Tel: (315) 793-8111 Fax: (315) 793-8792

Diane Davis
Bankruptcy Judge

Education: Albany Law 1991 JD
Began Service: March 6, 2009
Term Expires: March 6, 2023

Academic: Assistant Director of Career Planning, Albany Law School

Clerkships: Law Clerk, Chambers of Magistrate Judge Ralph W. Smith, Jr., United States District Court for the Northern District of New York

Government: Civil Justice Reform Commission, Counsel, United States District Court for the Northern District of New York; Chapter 13 Trustee, Albany (NY) District Office, Executive Office for United States Trustees, United States Department of Justice (1995-2009)

Current Memberships: Albany County Bar Association; Capital Region Bankruptcy Bar Association

Staff
Law Clerk **Jaclyn Weissgerber** .... (315) 266-1122
Career Law Clerk **Jill N. Dalrymple** .... (315) 266-1127
E-mail: jill_n_dalrymple@nynb.uscourts.gov
Education: Albany Law JD

United States District Court for the Southern District of New York

Daniel Patrick Moynihan U.S. Courthouse, 40 Foley Square, New York, NY 10007
Tel: (212) 805-0136 Tel: (212) 791-8050 (PACER)
Internet: www.nysd.uscourts.gov

Number of Judgeships: 28

Number of Vacancies: 1

Circuit: Second

Areas Covered: Counties of Bronx, Dutchess, New York, Orange, Putnam, Rockland, Sullivan and Westchester

Court Staff

Clerk of the Court **Ruby J. Krajick** .... (212) 805-0140
E-mail: ruby_krajick@nysd.uscourts.gov
Education: Wells 1987 BA
District Court Executive **Edward Friedland** .... (212) 805-0500
E-mail: edward_friedland@nysd.uscourts.gov
Secretary to District Court Executive **Eleanor Harrold** ... (914) 805-0500

United States District Court for the Southern District of New York *continued*

Chief Deputy Clerk (Administration) **Richard Wilson** .... (212) 805-0136
E-mail: richard_wilson@nysd.uscourts.gov
Chief Deputy Clerk (Operations) **John Gencarello** ...... (212) 805-0136
E-mail: john_gencarello@nysd.uscourts.gov
Chief Probation Officer **Michael Fitzpatrick** ... (212) 805-0040 ext. 5141
E-mail: michael_fitzpatrick@nysp.uscourts.gov
Chief Pretrial Services Officer **Arthur Penny** .... (212) 805-0015
E-mail: art_penny@nyspt.uscourts.gov
Human Resources Manager **Nazila Peterman-Winfrey** ... (212) 805-0660
Financial Administrator **Diana Gustaferri** .... (212) 805-0610
E-mail: diana_gustaferri@nysd.uscourts.gov

Chambers of Chief Judge Loretta A. Preska

Daniel Patrick Moynihan U.S. Courthouse, 500 Pearl Street, Room 2220, New York, NY 10007
Tel: (212) 805-0240
E-mail: preskanysdchambers@nysd.uscourts.gov

Loretta A. Preska
Chief Judge

Date of Birth: 1949
Education: Col St Rose 1970 BA; Fordham 1973 JD; NYU 1978 LLM
Began Service: August 2, 1992
Appointed By: President George H.W. Bush

Government: Legislative Aide, State Senator John T. Buckley (NY), New York Senate (1968-1970)

Legal Practice: Associate, Cahill Gordon & Reindel LLP (1973-1982); Partner, Hertzog, Calamari & Gleason (1982-1992)

Current Memberships: Federal Bar Council; New York County Lawyers' Association; New York State Bar Association

Staff
Law Clerk **Austin Murnane** .... (212) 805-0240
Began Service: October 2015
Term Expires: October 2016
E-mail: austin_murnane@nysd.uscourts.gov
Law Clerk **Devin Ness** .... (212) 805-0240
E-mail: devin_ness@nysd.uscourts.gov
Law Clerk **Elinor Tarlow** .... (212) 805-0240
Began Service: September 2015
Term Expires: September 2016
E-mail: elinor_tarlow@nysd.uscourts.gov
Courtroom Deputy **Megan Phillips** .... (212) 805-0116
E-mail: megan_phillips@nysd.uscourts.gov
Judicial Assistant **Samantha Gencarello** .... (212) 805-4848
E-mail: samantha_gencarello@nysd.uscourts.gov

Chambers of District Judge John G. Koeltl

1030 Daniel Patrick Moynihan U.S. Courthouse, 500 Pearl Street, Room 1030, New York, NY 10007
Tel: (212) 805-0222 Fax: (212) 805-7912
E-mail: koeltlnysdchambers@nysd.uscourts.gov

John G. Koeltl
District Judge

Date of Birth: 1945
Education: Georgetown 1967 AB; Harvard 1971 JD
Began Service: 1994
Appointed By: President William J. Clinton

Clerkships: Law Clerk The Honorable Edward Weinfield, United States District Court for the Southern District of New York (1971-1972); Law Clerk The Honorable Potter Stewart, Supreme Court of the United States (1972-1973)

Government: Assistant Special Prosecutor, Watergate Special Prosecution Force, United States Department of Justice (1973-1974)

Legal Practice: Debevoise & Plimpton (1975-1994)

(continued on next page)

Chambers of District Judge John G. Koeltl *continued*

Military Service: United States Army Reserve, United States Department of the Army (1968-1974)

Current Memberships: American Bar Foundation; American Bar Association; The American Law Institute; American Society of International Law; The Association of the Bar of the City of New York; Federal Bar Council; Federal Communications Bar Association; Harvard Law School Association of New York; New York County Lawyers' Association; New York State Bar Association; Phi Beta Kappa Society; The Supreme Court Historical Society

Staff

Law Clerk **Gabriela Bersuder** .... (212) 805-0222
Began Service: August 2015
Term Expires: August 2016
E-mail: gabriela_bersuder@nysd.uscourts.gov

Law Clerk **Matthew Ferraro** .... (212) 805-0222
Began Service: August 2015
Term Expires: August 2016
E-mail: matthew_ferraro@nysd.uscourts.gov

Courtroom Deputy **Don Fletcher** .... (212) 805-0107
Education: Syracuse 1990 BA

Judicial Assistant **Kathleen Donald** .... (212) 805-0222

Chambers of District Judge Colleen McMahon

500 Pearl Street, New York, NY 10007
Tel: (212) 805-6325 Fax: (212) 805-6326
E-mail: colleen_mcmahon@nysd.uscourts.gov

Colleen McMahon
District Judge

Date of Birth: 1951
Education: Ohio State 1973 BA; Harvard 1976 JD
Began Service: October 26, 1998
Appointed By: President William J. Clinton

Government: Speechwriter/Special Assistant to U.S. Permanent Representative Donald F. McHenry, United States Permanent Mission to the European Office of the United Nations and Other International Organizations in Geneva, United States Department of State (1979-1980)

Judicial: Judge, New York Court of Claims (1995-1998)

Legal Practice: Associate, Paul Weiss Rifkind Wharton & Garrison (1976-1979); Associate, Paul Weiss Rifkind Wharton & Garrison (1980-1984); Partner, Paul Weiss Rifkind Wharton & Garrison (1984-1995)

Current Memberships: American Judges Association; The American Law Institute; Federal Bar Council

Staff

Law Clerk **Jacob Charles** .... (212) 805-6325
Began Service: September 2015
Term Expires: September 2016
E-mail: jacob_d_charles@nysd.uscourts.gov

Law Clerk **Sarah Evans** .... (212) 805-6325
Began Service: September 2015
Term Expires: September 2016
E-mail: sarah_evans@nysd.uscourts.gov

Career Law Clerk **James O'Neill** .... (212) 805-6325
E-mail: james_oneill@nysd.uscourts.gov
Education: New York Law 1997 JD

Chambers of District Judge William H. Pauley III

U.S. Courthouse, 500 Pearl Street, New York, NY 10007-1581
Tel: (212) 805-6387 Fax: (212) 805-6390
E-mail: William_Pauley@nysd.uscourts.gov

William H. Pauley III
District Judge

Date of Birth: 1952
Education: Duke 1974 BA, 1977 JD
Began Service: October 28, 1998
Appointed By: President William J. Clinton

Government: Deputy County Attorney, Office of the County Attorney, County of Nassau, New York (1978); Assistant Counsel, Assembly Minority Leader, New York State Assembly (1984-1998)

Legal Practice: Associate, Orenstein, Snitow, Sutak & Pollack, P.C. (1978-1983); Member, Orenstein, Snitow & Pauley, P.C. (1983-1985); Partner, Snitow & Pauley (1985-1998)

Current Memberships: The Association of the Bar of the City of New York; Nassau County Bar Association

Staff

Law Clerk **Alison Bonelli** .... (212) 805-6387
Began Service: 2014
E-mail: alison_bonelli@nysd.uscourts.gov
Education: Pennsylvania 2013 JD

Law Clerk **William O'Connell** .... (212) 805-6387
E-mail: william_o'connell@nysd.uscourts.gov

Law Clerk **Dean McGee** .... (212) 805-6387
Began Service: 2015
E-mail: dean_mcgee@nysd.uscourts.gov

Courtroom Deputy/Law Clerk **Kyle O. Wood** .... (212) 805-6387
E-mail: kyle_wood@nysd.uscourts.gov
Education: St John's U (NY) 2001 JD

Chambers of District Judge George B. Daniels

Daniel Patrick Moynihan U.S. Courthouse, 500 Pearl Street, Room 1310, New York, NY 10007
Tel: (212) 805-6735 Fax: (212) 805-6737
E-mail: George_Daniels@nysd.uscourts.gov

George B. Daniels
District Judge

Date of Birth: 1953
Education: Yale 1975 BA; Boalt Hall 1978 JD
Began Service: April 17, 2000
Appointed By: President William J. Clinton

Academic: Adjunct Professor, Brooklyn Law School

Clerkships: Clerk The Honorable Rose E. Bird, California Supreme Court (1980)

Government: Assistant United States Attorney, Eastern District of New York, Office of the United States Attorney, United States Department of Justice (1983-1989); Counsel, Mayor David N. Dinkins (D-NY), City of New York, New York (1990-1993)

Judicial: Judge, Criminal Court (1989-1990); Judge, Criminal Court (1993-1995); Justice, New York Supreme Court (1995-2000)

Legal Practice: Criminal Defense Attorney, Legal Aid Society (1978); Litigation Attorney, Skadden, Arps, Slate, Meagher & Flom LLP (1981-1983)

Nonprofit: Trial Advocacy Instructor, National Institute for Trial Advocacy

Staff

Law Clerk **Russell T. Gorkin** .... (212) 805-6735
Term Expires: September 2016
E-mail: russell_t_gorkin@nysd.uscourts.gov
Education: Duke 2012 JD

Chambers of District Judge George B. Daniels *continued*

Law Clerk **Angela Makabali** .... (212) 805-6735
Term Expires: September 2016
E-mail: angela_makabali@nysd.uscourts.gov
Law Clerk **Nikolai Krylov** .... (212) 805-6735
Term Expires: October 2016
E-mail: nikolai_krylov@nysd.uscourts.gov
Secretary **Elizabeth Vega** .... (212) 805-6735
E-mail: Elizabeth_Vega@nysd.uscourts.gov

Chambers of District Judge Laura Taylor Swain

755 Daniel Patrick Moynihan U.S. Courthouse, 40 Foley Square, New York, NY 10007
Tel: (212) 805-0417 Fax: (212) 805-0426
E-mail: swainnysdchambers@nysd.uscourts.gov

Laura Taylor Swain
District Judge

Date of Birth: 1958
Education: Radcliffe 1979 BA; Harvard 1982 JD
Began Service: August 31, 2000
Appointed By: President William J. Clinton

Clerkships: Law Clerk The Honorable Constance Baker Motley, United States District Court for the Southern District of New York (1982-1983)

Government: Member, State Board of Law Examiners, State of New York (1986-1996)

Judicial: Bankruptcy Judge, United States Bankruptcy Court for the Eastern District of New York (1996-2000)

Legal Practice: Debevoise & Plimpton (1983-1996)

Current Memberships: American Bar Association; The Association of the Bar of the City of New York; Federal Judges Association; Metropolitan Black Bar Association; National Association of Women Judges; National Conference of Bankruptcy Judges; New York State Bar Association

Staff

Law Clerk **Lina Peng** .... (212) 805-0420
Began Service: June 2015
Term Expires: June 2017
E-mail: lina_peng@nysd.uscourts.gov
Law Clerk **Craig Convissar** .... (212) 805-0423
Began Service: August 2014
Term Expires: August 2016
E-mail: craig_convissar@nysd.uscourts.gov
Education: Harvard 2011 JD
Law Clerk **Christopher R. Ford** .... (212) 805-0421
Began Service: August 2015
Term Expires: August 2017
E-mail: chris_ford@nysd.uscourts.gov

Chambers of District Judge P. Kevin Castel

40 Foley Square, New York, NY 10007
Tel: (212) 805-0262 Fax: (212) 805-7949
E-mail: castelnysdchambers@nysd.uscourts.gov

P. Kevin Castel
District Judge

Date of Birth: August 5, 1950
Education: St John's U (NY) 1972 BS, 1975 JD
Began Service: November 4, 2003
Appointed By: President George W. Bush

Clerkships: Law Clerk Kevin Thomas Duffy, United States District Court for the Southern District of New York (1975-1977)

Legal Practice: Associate, Cahill Gordon & Reindel LLP (1977-1983); Partner, Cahill Gordon & Reindel LLP (1983-2003)

Nonprofit: Chair, Commercial and Federal Litigation Section, The New York State Bar Association (1993-1994); President, Federal Bar Council (2000-2002)

Chambers of District Judge P. Kevin Castel *continued*

Current Memberships: American Bar Foundation; New York Bar Foundation, New York State Bar Association

Staff

Law Clerk **Jeffrey Eldridge** .... (212) 805-4644
E-mail: jeff_eldridge@nysd.uscourts.gov
Law Clerk **Matthew King** .... (212) 805-4642
E-mail: matthew_king@nysd.uscourts.gov
Law Clerk **Matthew "Matt" Aglialoro** .... (212) 805-4643
E-mail: matthew_aglialoro@nysd.uscourts.gov
Deputy Clerk **Florence Nacanther** .... (212) 805-0131
E-mail: florence_nacanther@nysd.uscourts.gov

Chambers of District Judge Kenneth M. Karas

300 Quarropas Street, White Plains, NY 10601-4150
Tel: (914) 390-4145
E-mail: karasnysdchambers@nysd.uscourts.gov

Kenneth M. Karas
District Judge

Education: Georgetown 1986 BA; Columbia 1991 JD
Began Service: October 2004
Appointed By: President George W. Bush

Government: Organized Crime and Terrorism Chief, Criminal Division, New York - Southern District, United States Department of Justice (1992-1994)

Staff

Law Clerk **Rebecca Moses** .... (914) 390-4145
Began Service: September 2015
Term Expires: September 2016
E-mail: rebecca_moses@nysd.uscourts.gov
Education: Harvard 2015 JD
Law Clerk **Stephen Secchio** .... (914) 390-4145
Began Service: September 2015
Term Expires: September 2016
E-mail: stephen_secchio@nysd.uscourts.gov
Law Clerk **Christopher Yeager** .... (914) 390-4145
Began Service: September 2015
Term Expires: September 2016
E-mail: christopher_yeager@nysd.uscourts.gov
Courtroom Deputy **Dawn Bordes** .... (914) 390-4145

Chambers of District Judge Richard J. Sullivan

40 Centre Street, New York, NY 10007
Tel: (212) 805-0264
E-mail: richard_sullivan@nysd.uscourts.gov

Richard J. Sullivan
District Judge

Date of Birth: 1964
Education: William & Mary 1986 BA; Yale 1990 JD
Began Service: August 2007
Appointed By: President George W. Bush

Clerkships: Law Clerk, Circuit Judge David M. Ebel, United States Court of Appeals for the Tenth Circuit (1990-1991)

Government: Assistant United States Attorney, Executive Office for United States Attorneys, New York - Southern District, United States Department of Justice (1994-2005)

Legal Practice: Summer Associate, Gibson, Dunn & Crutcher LLP (1990); Summer Associate, McCutchen Doyle Brown & Enersen (1990); Associate, Wachtell, Lipton, Rosen & Katz (1991-1994)

Staff

Law Clerk **Christine Buzzard** .... (212) 805-0264
Began Service: February 31, 2015
Term Expires: February 2016
E-mail: christine_buzzard@nysd.uscourts.gov

(continued on next page)

Chambers of District Judge Richard J. Sullivan *continued*

Law Clerk **Rebecca Dell** . . . . (212) 805-0264
Began Service: August 2015
Term Expires: August 2016
E-mail: rebecca_dell@nysd.uscourts.gov

Law Clerk **David Felton** . . . . (212) 805-0264
Began Service: December 2014
Term Expires: December 2015
E-mail: david_felton@nysd.uscourts.gov

Law Clerk **Claire Guehenno** . . . . (212) 805-0264
Began Service: August 2015
Term Expires: August 2016
E-mail: claire_guehenno@nysd.uscourts.gov
Education: Harvard 2014 JD

Law Clerk **Sarah Kushner** . . . . (212) 805-0264
Began Service: August 2015
Term Expires: August 2016
E-mail: sarah_kushner@nysd.uscourts.gov

Chambers of District Judge Paul G. Gardephe

40 Centre Street, New York, NY 10007
Tel: (212) 805-0224
E-mail: gardephenysdchambers@nysd.uscourts.gov

Paul G. Gardephe
District Judge

Education: Pennsylvania 1979 BA, 1979 MA; Columbia 1982 JD
Began Service: October 3, 2008
Appointed By: President George W. Bush

Clerkships: Law Clerk, United States Court of Appeals for the Sixth Circuit

Corporate: Vice President and Deputy General Counsel, Time Inc.

Government: Federal Prosecutor, New York - Southern District, United States Department of Justice

Legal Practice: Chair, Litigation, Patterson Belknap Webb & Tyler LLP; Co-Chair, Appellate, Patterson Belknap Webb & Tyler LLP; Chair, White Collar Defense and Investigations, Patterson Belknap Webb & Tyler LLP

Staff

Law Clerk **Tara Norris** . . . . (212) 805-0224
Began Service: October 2015
Term Expires: October 2016
E-mail: tara_norris@nysd.uscourts.gov

Law Clerk **Alexandra Messiter** . . . . (212) 805-0224
Began Service: October 2015
Term Expires: October 2016
E-mail: alexandra_messiter@nysd.uscourts.gov

Law Clerk **Rajan Trehan** . . . . (212) 805-0224
Began Service: October 2015
Term Expires: October 2016
E-mail: rajan_trehan@nysd.uscourts.gov

Courtroom Deputy Clerk **Michael P. Ruocco** . . . . (212) 805-0102
E-mail: michael_ruocco@nysd.uscourts.gov

Chambers of District Judge Cathy Seibel

300 Quarropas Street, Room 275, White Plains, NY 10601-4150
Tel: (914) 390-4271
E-mail: cathy_seibel@nysd.uscourts.gov

Cathy Seibel
District Judge

Education: Princeton 1982 AB; Fordham 1985 JD
Began Service: July 30, 2008
Appointed By: President George W. Bush

Clerkships: Law Clerk, Chambers of Senior Judge Joseph M. McLaughlin, United States District Court for the Eastern District of New York (1985-1987)

Chambers of District Judge Cathy Seibel *continued*

Government: Assistant U.S. Attorney, New York - Southern District, Executive Office for United States Attorneys, United States Department of Justice (1987-1991); Special Assistant U.S. Attorney, Washington - Western District, Executive Office for United States Attorneys, United States Department of Justice (1991-1993); Assistant U.S. Attorney, New York - Southern District, Executive Office for United States Attorneys, United States Department of Justice (1993-1997); Assistant U.S. Attorney-in-Charge, New York - Southern District, Executive Office for United States Attorneys, United States Department of Justice (1997-1999); Senior Trial Counsel, New York - Southern District, Executive Office for United States Attorneys, United States Department of Justice (1999-2005); Deputy U.S. Attorney, New York - Southern District, Executive Office for United States Attorneys, United States Department of Justice (2005-2008)

Staff

Law Clerk **Michael Fresco** . . . . (914) 390-4271
E-mail: michael_fresco@nysd.uscourts.gov
Education: Fordham 2013 JD

Law Clerk **Kim Channick** . . . . (914) 390-4271
Began Service: August 2015
Term Expires: August 2016
E-mail: kim_channick@nysd.uscourts.gov

Law Clerk **Alexander Wolf** . . . . (914) 390-4271
Term Expires: January 2016
E-mail: alexander_wolf@nysd.uscourts.gov

Chambers of District Judge Vincent L. Briccetti

300 Quarropas Street, Room 630, White Plains, NY 10601-4150
Tel: (914) 390-4166
E-mail: briccettinysdchambers@nysd.uscourts.gov
Internet: http://www.nysd.uscourts.gov/judge/Briccetti

Vincent L. Briccetti
District Judge

Education: Columbia 1976 BA; Fordham 1980 JD
Began Service: April 21, 2011
Appointed By: President Barack Obama

Government: Assistant U.S. Attorney, New York - Southern District, Office of the Director, United States Department of Justice (1985-1989); Deputy Chief of Appeals, New York - Southern District, Office of the Director, United States Department of Justice

Legal Practice: Associate, Paul, Hastings, Janofsky & Walker LLP (1989-1992); Partner, Briccetti, Calhoun & Lawrence, LLP (1992-2011)

Staff

Law Clerk **Alex Delisi** . . . . (914) 390-4164
Term Expires: October 2016
E-mail: alexander_delisi@nysd.uscourts.gov

Law Clerk **Michael Hardin** . . . . (914) 390-4165
Term Expires: September 2016
E-mail: michael_hardin@nysd.uscourts.gov

Law Clerk **Stephen J. "Steve" Kress** . . . . (914) 390-4163
Term Expires: January 2016
E-mail: stephen_kress@nysd.uscourts.gov
Education: Holy Cross Col 2007; Fordham 2010 JD

Courtroom Deputy **Donna Hilbert** . . . . (914) 390-4167
E-mail: donna_hilbert@nysd.uscourts.gov

Chambers of District Judge J. Paul Oetken

40 Centre Street, New York, NY 10007
Tel: (212) 805-0266
E-mail: oetkennysdchambers@nysd.uscourts.gov

J. Paul Oetken
District Judge

Education: Iowa 1988 BA; Yale 1991 JD
Began Service: July 20, 2011
Appointed By: President Barack Obama

Clerkships: Law Clerk, Chambers of Circuit Judge Richard D. Cudahy, United States Court of Appeals for the Seventh Circuit (1991-1992); Law Clerk, Chambers of District Judge Louis F. Oberdorfer, United States District Court for the District of Columbia (1992-1993); Law Clerk, Chambers of Associate Justice Harry A. Blackmun, Supreme Court of the United States (1993-1994)

Government: Counsel, Debevoise & Plimpton LLP (2003-2004)

Legal Practice: Associate, Debevoise & Plimpton LLP (2001-2003)

Staff

Law Clerk **Emma Kaufman** .... (212) 805-0266
Term Expires: September 2016
E-mail: emma_kaufman@nysd.uscourts.gov

Law Clerk **Alec Schierenbeck** .... (212) 805-0266
Term Expires: September 2016
E-mail: alec_schierenbeck@nysd.uscourts.gov

Law Clerk **Andrew Rohrbach** .... (212) 805-0266
Began Service: September 2015
Term Expires: September 2016
E-mail: andrew_rohrboch@nysd.uscourts.gov

Deputy Clerk **Brandon Skolnik** .... (212) 805-0266
E-mail: brandon_skolnik@nysd.uscourts.gov

Chambers of District Judge Paul A. Engelmayer

40 Centre Street, New York, NY 10007
Tel: (212) 805-0268
E-mail: paul_engelmayer@nysd.uscourts.gov

Paul A. Engelmayer
District Judge

Education: Harvard 1983 BA, 1987 JD
Began Service: July 27, 2011
Appointed By: President Barack Obama

Clerkships: Law Clerk, Chambers of Circuit Judge Patricia M. Wald, United States Court of Appeals for the District of Columbia Circuit (1987-1988); Law Clerk, Chambers of Associate Justice Thurgood Marshall, Supreme Court of the United States (1988-1989)

Government: Assistant U.S. Attorney, New York - Southern District, Office of the Deputy Attorney General, United States Department of Justice (1989-1994); Deputy Chief Appellate Attorney, New York - Southern District, Office of the Deputy Attorney General, United States Department of Justice (1994); Assistant to the Solicitor General, Office of the Solicitor General, Office of the Deputy Attorney General, United States Department of Justice (1994-1996); Major Crimes Chief, Criminal Division, New York - Southern District, United States Department of Justice

Legal Practice: Contact, New York, NY Office, Wilmer Cutler Pickering LLP; Partner, New York, NY Office, Wilmer Cutler Pickering Hale and Dorr LLP; Partner-in-Charge, New York, NY Office, Wilmer Cutler Pickering Hale and Dorr LLP

Staff

Law Clerk **Samuel "Sam" Barr** .... (212) 805-0268
Term Expires: September 2016
E-mail: samuel_j_barr@nysd.uscourts.gov

Law Clerk **Jordana Confino** .... (212) 805-0268
Term Expires: September 2016
E-mail: jordana_confino@nysd.uscourts.gov

Law Clerk **Brett Kalikow** .... (212) 805-0268
Term Expires: September 2016
E-mail: brett_kalikow@nysd.uscourts.gov

Chambers of District Judge Paul A. Engelmayer *continued*

Courtroom Deputy **June Hummel** .... (212) 805-0268
E-mail: june_hummel@nysd.uscourts.gov

Chambers of District Judge Alison J. Nathan

40 Centre Street, New York, NY 10007
Tel: (212) 805-0278
E-mail: alison_nathan@nysd.uscourts.gov

Alison J. Nathan
District Judge

Education: Cornell 1994 AB, 2000 JD
Began Service: October 17, 2011
Appointed By: President Barack Obama

Academic: Visiting Assistant Professor of Law, School of Law, Fordham University (2006-2008); Fritz Alexander Fellow, School of Law, New York University (2008-2009)

Clerkships: Law Clerk, Chambers of Circuit Judge Betty B. Fletcher, United States Court of Appeals for the Ninth Circuit (2000-2001); Law Clerk, Chambers of Associate Justice John Paul Stevens, Supreme Court of the United States (2001-2002)

Government: Special Assistant to the President and Associate Counsel to the President, Office of the White House Counsel, Office of the Chief of Staff, Executive Office of the President, Barack Obama Administration (2009-2010); Special Counsel, Appeals and Opinions Division, Office of the Attorney General, State of New York (2010-2011)

Legal Practice: Associate, Wilmer Cutler Pickering Hale and Dorr LLP (2002-2006)

Chambers of District Judge Katherine B. Forrest

40 Foley Square, New York, NY 10007
Tel: (212) 805-0276
E-mail: katherine_forrest@nysd.uscourts.gov

Katherine B. Forrest
District Judge

Education: Wesleyan U 1986 BA; NYU 1990 JD
Began Service: October 17, 2011
Appointed By: President Barack Obama

Government: Deputy Assistant Attorney General for Criminal Enforcement, Criminal Enforcement, Antitrust Division, United States Department of Justice (2010-2011)

Legal Practice: Partner, Cravath, Swaine & Moore LLP (1998-2010)

Chambers of District Judge Andrew L. Carter Jr.

40 Centre Street, New York, NY 10007
Tel: (212) 805-0280
E-mail: andrew_carter@nysd.uscourts.gov

Andrew L. Carter, Jr.
District Judge

Education: Texas 1991 BA; Harvard 1994 JD
Began Service: December 12, 2011
Appointed By: President Barack Obama

Judicial: Magistrate Judge, Chambers of Magistrate Judge Andrew L. Carter Jr., United States District Court for the Eastern District of New York (2009-2011)

Legal Practice: Program Assistant, Ford Foundation (1994-1996); Attorney, Criminal Defense Division, Legal Aid Society of New York (1996-2000); Attorney, Federal Defender Division, Legal Aid Society of New York (2000-2005)

(continued on next page)

Chambers of District Judge Andrew L. Carter Jr. *continued*

Staff

Law Clerk **Anna Arons** .... (212) 805-0136
E-mail: anna_arons@nysd.uscourts.gov

Law Clerk **Anthony Enriquez** .... (212) 805-0136
Began Service: May 2015
Term Expires: May 2016
E-mail: anthony_enriquez@nysd.uscourts.gov

Law Clerk **Kevin Jason** .... (212) 805-0136
Began Service: October 2015
Term Expires: October 2016
E-mail: kevin_jason@nysd.uscourts.gov

Chambers of District Judge Edgardo Ramos

300 Quarropas Street, White Plains, NY 10601-4150
Tel: (212) 805-0294
E-mail: edgardo_ramos@nysd.uscourts.gov

Edgardo Ramos
District Judge

Education: Yale 1982 BA; Harvard 1987 JD
Began Service: December 6, 2011
Appointed By: President Barack Obama

Government: Assistant U.S. Attorney, New York - Eastern District, Executive Office for United States Attorneys, United States Department of Justice (1992-2002)

Legal Practice: Associate, Simpson Thacher & Bartlett LLP (1987-1992)

Chambers of District Judge Jesse M. Furman

40 Centre Street, New York, NY 10007
Tel: (212) 805-0282
E-mail: jesse_furman@nysd.uscourts.gov

Jesse M. Furman
District Judge

Education: Harvard 1994 BA; Yale 1998 JD
Began Service: 2012
Appointed By: President Barack Obama

Chambers of District Judge Ronnie Abrams

40 Foley Square, New York, NY 10007
Tel: (212) 805-0284
E-mail: ronnie_abrams@nysd.uscourts.gov

Ronnie Abrams
District Judge

Education: Cornell 1990 BA; Yale 1993 JD
Began Service: 2012
Appointed By: President Barack Obama

Staff

Law Clerk **Kyle Wirshba** .... (212) 805-0284
Term Expires: October 2016
E-mail: kyle_wirshba@nysd.uscourts.gov

Law Clerk **Elizabeth Denniston** .... (212) 805-0284
Term Expires: October 2016
E-mail: elizabeth_denniston@nysd.uscourts.gov

Law Clerk **Jacob Tracer** .... (212) 805-0284
Term Expires: September 2016
E-mail: jacob_tracer@nysd.uscourts.gov

Referred Associate **Denise Sohn** .... (212) 805-0284

Courtroom Deputy **Allison Cavale** .... (212) 805-0284
E-mail: allison_cavale@nysd.uscourts.gov

Chambers of District Judge Lorna G. Schofield

40 Centre Street, New York, NY 10007
Tel: (212) 805-0288
E-mail: lorna_schofield@nysd.uscourts.gov

Lorna G. Schofield
District Judge

Education: Indiana 1977 BA; NYU 1981 JD
Began Service: March 28, 2013
Appointed By: President Barack Obama

Legal Practice: Associate, Cleary Gottlieb Steen & Hamilton LLP (1981-1984); Associate, Debevoise & Plimpton LLP (1988-1991); Partner, Debevoise & Plimpton LLP (1991-2011)

Staff

Law Clerk **Christina Liebolt** .... (212) 805-0288
Began Service: September 2015
Term Expires: September 2016
E-mail: christina_lieobolt@nysd.uscourts.gov

Law Clerk **Andrew Villacastin** .... (212) 805-0288
Began Service: September 2015
Term Expires: September 2016
E-mail: andrew_villacastin@nysd.uscourts.gov

Law Clerk **Roman Rodriguez** .... (212) 805-0288
Began Service: September 2015
Term Expires: September 2016
E-mail: roman_rodriguez@nysd.uscourts.gov

Law Clerk **Sok Tea Jiang** .... (212) 805-0288
Began Service: September 2015
Term Expires: September 2016
E-mail: sok_t_jiang@nysd.uscourts.gov

Chambers of District Judge Katherine Polk Failla

40 Foley Square, Room 618, New York, NY 10007
Tel: (212) 805-0290
E-mail: faillanysdchambers@nysd.uscourts.gov

Katherine Polk Failla
District Judge

Education: William & Mary 1990 BA; Harvard 1993 JD
Began Service: 2013
Appointed By: President Barack Obama

Government: Law Clerk, Chambers of Senior Judge Joseph E. Irenas, United States District Court for the District of New Jersey (1993-1994); Deputy Chief Appellate Attorney, Criminal Division, New York - Southern District, United States Department of Justice (2004-2008); Chief Appellate Attorney, Criminal Division, New York - Southern District, United States Department of Justice (2008-2013)

Staff

Law Clerk **Alison Deich** .... (212) 805-0290
Term Expires: September 2016
E-mail: alison_deich@nysd.uscourts.gov

Law Clerk **Katherine Peaslee** .... (212) 805-0290
Began Service: September 2015
Term Expires: September 2016
E-mail: katherine_peaslee@nysd.uscourts.gov

Law Clerk **Jonathan Shaub** .... (212) 805-0290
Began Service: September 2015
Term Expires: September 2016
E-mail: jonathan_shaub@nysd.uscourts.gov

Chambers of District Judge Analisa Torres
40 Foley Square, New York, NY 10007
Tel: (212) 805-0292
E-mail: analisa_torres@nysd.uscourts.gov

Analisa Torres
District Judge

Education: Harvard 1981 AB; Columbia 1984 JD
Began Service: April 23, 2013
Appointed By: President Barack Obama

Government: Commissioner, City Planning Commission, Department of City Planning, City of New York, New York (1993-1995)

Judicial: Judge, Chambers of Judge Analisa Torres, New York City Criminal Court (2000-2002); Judge, Chambers of Judge Analisa Torres, New York City Civil Court (2002-2004)

Staff
Law Clerk **Michael McDonald** . . . . (212) 805-0292
Began Service: September 2015
Term Expires: September 2016
E-mail: michael_mcdonald@nysd.uscourts.gov
Law Clerk **Kevin Hu** . . . . (212) 805-0292
Began Service: September 2015
Term Expires: September 2016
E-mail: kevin_hu@nysd.uscourts.gov
Law Clerk **David Shieh** . . . . (212) 805-0292
Began Service: September 2015
Term Expires: September 2016
E-mail: david_shieh@nysd.uscourts.gov

Chambers of District Judge Nelson Stephen Román
300 Quarropas Street, White Plains, NY 10601-4150
Tel: (914) 390-4177
E-mail: romannysdchambers@nysd.uscourts.gov

Nelson Stephen Román
District Judge

Education: Brooklyn Law 1989 JD; Fordham 1984 BA
Began Service: May 13, 2013
Appointed By: President Barack Obama

Government: Assistant District Attorney, Kings County District Attorney, City of New York, New York (1989-1991); Special Narcotics Assistant District Attorney, Kings County District Attorney, City of New York, New York (1992-1994); Felony Trial Assistant District Attorney, Kings County District Attorney, City of New York, New York (1994-1995)

Judicial: Judge, Bronx County, New York Supreme Court, Civil Term (2001-2002); Associate Justice, Chambers of Associate Justice Nelson Román, New York Supreme Court, Appellate Division, First Department (2009-2013)

Current Memberships: Bronx County Bar Association; Puerto Rican Bar Association

Staff
Law Clerk **Samantha Glazer** . . . . (914) 390-4177
Began Service: August 2015
Term Expires: August 2016
E-mail: samantha_glazer@nysd.uscourts.gov
Law Clerk **Lauren Pignataro** . . . . (914) 390-4177
Began Service: September 2015
Term Expires: September 2016
E-mail: lauren_pignataro@nysd.uscourts.gov
Law Clerk **Alex Weinberg** . . . . (914) 390-4177
Began Service: May 2015
Term Expires: May 2016
E-mail: alex_weinberg@nysd.uscourts.gov

Chambers of District Judge Valerie E. Caproni
40 Foley Square, New York, NY 10007
Tel: (212) 805-6350
E-mail: capronin ysdchambers@nysd.uscourts.gov

Valerie E. Caproni
District Judge

Education: Tulane 1976 BA; Georgia 1979 JD
Began Service: 2013
Appointed By: President Barack Obama

Corporate: Vice President and Deputy General Counsel, Litigation and Investigations, Northrop Grumman Corporation (2011-2013)

Government: General Counsel, Office of the General Counsel, Federal Bureau of Investigation, United States Department of Justice (2003-2011)

Legal Practice: Counsel, Simpson Thacher & Bartlett LLP (2001-2003)

Staff
Law Clerk **Moira Heiges-Goepsert** . . . . (212) 805-6350
Law Clerk **Amanda Hollis** . . . . (212) 805-6350
E-mail: amanda_hollis@nysd.uscourts.gov
Law Clerk **Crystal M. Johnson** . . . . (212) 805-6350
E-mail: crystal_johnson@nysd.uscourts.gov
Education: Georgia 2013 JD
Law Clerk **Nicholas "Nick" Moscow** . . . . (212) 805-6350
E-mail: nicholas_moscow@nysd.uscourts.gov
Education: Columbia 2011 JD
Law Clerk **Cecilia Vogell** . . . . (212) 805-6350

Chambers of District Judge Vernon S. Broderick
40 Foley Square, New York, NY 10007
Tel: (212) 805-6165
E-mail: brodericknysdchambers@nysd.uscourts.gov

Vernon S. Broderick
District Judge

Education: Yale 1985 BA; Harvard 1988 JD
Began Service: 2013
Appointed By: President Barack Obama

Government: Violent Crimes Unit Chief, New York - Southern District, Executive Office for United States Attorneys, United States Department of Justice (1999-2002); Assistant U.S. Attorney, New York - Southern District, Executive Office for United States Attorneys, United States Department of Justice (1994-2002)

Legal Practice: Partner, Securities Litigation Department, Weil, Gotshal & Manges LLP (2005-2013); Counsel, Weil, Gotshal & Manges LLP (2002-2005); Associate, Weil, Gotshal & Manges LLP (1988-1994)

Chambers of District Judge Gregory Howard Woods
40 Foley Square, New York, NY 10007
Tel: (212) 805-0296
E-mail: gregory_woods@nysd.uscourts.gov

Gregory Howard Woods
District Judge

Education: Williams 1991 BA; Yale 1995 JD
Began Service: November 18, 2013
Appointed By: President Barack Obama

Government: Partner, Debevoise & Plimpton LLP (2004-2009); Deputy General Counsel, Office of the General Counsel, Office of the Deputy Secretary, United States Department of Transportation; General Counsel, Office of the General Counsel, United States Department of Energy (2012-2013)

(continued on next page)

Chambers of District Judge Gregory Howard Woods *continued*

Staff

Law Clerk **Nwamaka Ejebe**........................(212) 805-0296
Began Service: January 2015
Term Expires: January 2016
E-mail: nwamaka_ejebe@nysd.uscourts.gov

Law Clerk **Haryle Kaldis**........................(212) 805-0296
Began Service: September 2015
Term Expires: September 2016
E-mail: haryle_kaldis@nysd.uscourts.gov
Education: Columbia 2011 JD

Law Clerk **Sarah Edwards**........................(212) 805-0296
Began Service: September 2015
Term Expires: September 2016
E-mail: sarah_edwards@nysd.uscourts.gov

Chambers of Senior Judge Kimba M. Wood

Daniel Patrick Moynihan U.S. Courthouse, 500 Pearl Street,
New York, NY 10007
Tel: (212) 805-0258 Fax: (212) 805-7900
E-mail: woodnysdchambers@nysd.uscourts.gov

Kimba M. Wood
Senior Judge

Date of Birth: 1944
Education: Connecticut Col 1965 BA; London School Econ (UK) 1966 MSc; Harvard 1969 JD
Began Service: April 20, 1988
Appointed By: President Ronald Reagan

Government: Attorney, Office of Legal Services, Office of Economic Opportunity (1970-1971)

Legal Practice: Attorney, Steptoe & Johnson LLP (1969-1970); Attorney, LeBoeuf, Lamb, Leiby & MacRae (1971-1988)

Current Memberships: American Bar Association; The American Law Institute; The Association of the Bar of the City of New York; Federal Bar Council; New York State Bar Association

Staff

Law Clerk **Leigh Barnwell**........................(212) 805-0258
Began Service: August 2015
Term Expires: August 2016
E-mail: leigh_e_barnwell@nysd.uscourts.gov

Law Clerk **Farbod Faraji**........................(212) 805-0258
Began Service: August 2015
Term Expires: August 2016
E-mail: farbod_faraji@nysd.uscourts.gov

Judicial Assistant **Janice B. Young**........................(212) 805-0258
E-mail: janice_b_young@nysd.uscourts.gov

Chambers of Senior Judge Robert W. Sweet

Daniel Patrick Moynihan U.S. Courthouse, 500 Pearl Street,
Room 1920, New York, NY 10007-1312
Tel: (212) 805-0254 Fax: (212) 805-7925
E-mail: sweetnysdchambers@nysd.uscourts.gov

Robert W. Sweet
Senior Judge

Date of Birth: 1922
Education: Yale 1944 BA, 1948 LLB
Began Service: 1978
Appointed By: President Jimmy Carter
Political Affiliation: Republican

Government: Assistant United States Attorney, Office of the United States Attorney, United States Department of Justice (1953-1955); Deputy Mayor, Mayor John V. Lindsay (NY), City of New York, New York (1966-1969)

Legal Practice: Associate, Simpson Thacher & Bartlett LLP (1948-1953); Partner, Casey, Lane & Mittendorf (1955-1965); Partner, Skadden, Arps, Slate, Meagher & Flom LLP (1970-1977)

Chambers of Senior Judge Robert W. Sweet *continued*

Military Service: United States Naval Reserve (1943-1945)

Current Memberships: American Bar Association; The Association of the Bar of the City of New York; New York County Lawyers' Association; New York Law Institute; New York State Bar Association

Staff

Law Clerk **James Thompson**........................(718) 613-2470
Began Service: April 1, 2015
Term Expires: April 1, 2016
E-mail: james_thompson@nysd.uscourts.gov

Law Clerk **Talia Nissimyan**........................(718) 613-2470
Began Service: September 2015
Term Expires: September 2016
E-mail: talia_nissimyan@nysd.uscourts.gov

Courtroom Deputy **Tsz Chan**........................(212) 805-0124
E-mail: tsz_man_chan@nysd.uscourts.gov

Judicial Assistant **Margaret Acquista**........................(212) 805-0254
E-mail: margaret_acquista@nysd.uscourts.gov

Chambers of Senior Judge John F. Keenan

1930 Daniel Patrick Moynihan U.S. Courthouse, 500 Pearl Street,
New York, NY 10007-1312
Tel: (212) 805-0220 Fax: (212) 805-7911
E-mail: john_f._keenan@nysd.uscourts.gov

John F. Keenan
Senior Judge

Date of Birth: 1929
Education: Manhattan Col 1951 BBA; Fordham 1954 LLB
Began Service: October 21, 1983
Appointed By: President Ronald Reagan

Academic: Lecturer on Criminal Law and Trial Techniques, Northwestern University School of Law (1968-1990); Adjunct Professor, John Jay College of Criminal Justice (1979-1983); Lecturer, Harvard Law School (1979-1983); Lecturer, Harvard Law School (1989); Adjunct Professor, School of Law, Fordham University (1992-1993); Lecturer, Harvard Law School (1994); Lecturer, Harvard Law School (1998)

Government: Assistant District Attorney, Office of the District Attorney, County of New York, New York (1956-1976); Chief Assistant District Attorney, Queens County District Attorney (1973); Administrative Assistant District Attorney, In Charge of Trials, County of New York, New York (1974); Chief Assistant District Attorney, New York County District Attorney (1974-1976); Deputy Attorney General, Special Prosecutor of Corruption in New York City, State of New York (1976-1979); Chairman and President, New York City Off-Track Betting Corporation, City of New York, New York (1979-1982); Criminal Justice Coordinator, City of New York, New York (1982-1983)

Judicial: Senior Judge, Judicial Panel on Multidistrict Litigation (1998-2006)

Legal Practice: Halpin, Keogh & St. John (1956)

Military Service: Army Security Agency, United States Army (1954-1956)

Staff

Law Clerk **George Adams**........................(212) 805-0220
Began Service: August 2014
Term Expires: December 15, 2015
E-mail: george_adams@nysd.uscourts.gov

Law Clerk **Thomas Rosso**........................(212) 805-0220
Began Service: August 2015
Term Expires: October 31, 2016
E-mail: thomas_rosso@nysd.uscourts.gov

Judicial Assistant **Marian A. Quintela**........................(212) 805-0220
E-mail: marian_quintela@nysd.uscourts.gov

Chambers of Senior Judge Miriam Goldman Cedarbaum

Daniel Patrick Moynihan U.S. Courthouse, 500 Pearl Street,
Room 1330, New York, NY 10007-1312
Tel: (212) 805-0198
E-mail: cedarbaumnysdchambers@nysd.uscourts.gov

Miriam Goldman Cedarbaum
Senior Judge

Date of Birth: 1929
Education: Barnard 1950 BA; Columbia 1953 LLB
Began Service: March 27, 1986
Appointed By: President Ronald Reagan
Political Affiliation: Democrat

Clerkships: Law Clerk The Honorable Edward Jordan Dimock, United States District Court for the Southern District of New York (1953-1954)

Government: Assistant U.S. Attorney, New York - Southern District, Executive Office for United States Attorneys, United States Department of Justice (1954-1957); First Assistant Counsel, New York State Moreland Commission on the Alcoholic Beverage Control Law (1963-1964)

Judicial: Acting Village Justice, Scarsdale, New York (1978-1982); Village Justice, Scarsdale, New York (1982-1986)

Legal Practice: Co-Counsel, Scarsdale Open Society Association (1968-1986); Associate and Senior Attorney, Davis Polk & Wardwell (1979-1986)

Nonprofit: Associate Counsel, The Museum of Modern Art (1965-1979)

Current Memberships: American Bar Association; The American Law Institute; The Copyright Society of the U.S.A.; Federal Bar Council

Staff
Law Clerk **(Vacant)** . . . . (212) 805-0198
Courtroom Deputy **Michael Lee** . . . . (212) 805-0198
E-mail: michael_lee@nysd.uscourts.gov
Secretary **Donna Curro** . . . . (212) 805-0198

Chambers of Senior Judge Thomas P. Griesa

Daniel Patrick Moynihan U.S. Courthouse, 500 Pearl Street,
Room 1630, New York, NY 10007
Tel: (212) 805-0210 Fax: (212) 805-7908
E-mail: thomas_griesa@nysd.uscourts.gov

Thomas P. Griesa
Senior Judge

Date of Birth: 1930
Education: Harvard 1952 AB; Stanford 1958 LLB
Began Service: 1972
Appointed By: President Richard M. Nixon

Government: Attorney, United States Department of Justice (1958-1960)

Legal Practice: Symmers, Fish & Warner (1960-1961); Davis Polk & Wardwell (1961-1970); Partner, Davis Polk & Wardwell (1970-1972)

Military Service: United States Coast Guard (1952-1954)

Current Memberships: The Association of the Bar of the City of New York; Washington State Bar Association

Staff
Law Clerk **Jay Cohen** . . . . (212) 805-0210
Began Service: September 2015
Term Expires: September 30, 2016
E-mail: jay_cohen@nysd.uscourts.gov
Law Clerk **Thomas Kadri** . . . . (212) 805-0210
Term Expires: August 24, 2016
E-mail: thomas_kadri@nysd.uscourts.gov
Law Clerk **Sarah Milstein** . . . . (212) 805-0210
Began Service: October 2015
Term Expires: October 2016

Chambers of Senior Judge Kevin Thomas Duffy

500 Pearl Street, Room 2540, New York, NY 10007-1312
Tel: (212) 805-6125 Fax: (212) 805-6131
E-mail: duffynysdchambers@nysd.uscourts.gov

Kevin Thomas Duffy
Senior Judge

Date of Birth: 1933
Education: Fordham 1954 AB, 1958 LLB
Began Service: November 28, 1972
Appointed By: President Richard M. Nixon

Academic: Adjunct Professor, Brooklyn Law School (1975-1980); Adjunct Professor, School of Law, New York University (1983-1984); Adjunct Professor, School of Law, Pace University (1984-1986); Adjunct Professor in Trial Advocacy, Fordham University (1993-1997)

Clerkships: Law Clerk The Honorable J. Edward Lumbard, United States Court of Appeals for the Second Circuit (1955-1958)

Government: Assistant U.S. Attorney, New York - Southern District, Executive Office for United States Attorneys, United States Department of Justice (1958-1959); Assistant Chief, Criminal Division, Office of the Attorney General, United States Department of Justice (1959-1961); Regional Administrator, United States Securities and Exchange Commission (1969-1972)

Legal Practice: Associate, Whitman, Ransom & Coulson (1961-1966); Partner, Gordon & Gordon (1966-1969)

Current Memberships: The American Law Institute; The Association of the Bar of the City of New York; Federal Bar Council; Fordham Law Alumni Association

Staff
Law Clerk **Patrick R. Harrington** . . . . (212) 805-6125
Began Service: July 2015
Term Expires: July 2016
E-mail: patrick_harrington@nysd.uscourts.gov
Education: Michigan 2007 JD
Law Clerk **Francesca Brody** . . . . (212) 805-6129
Began Service: November 2014
Term Expires: December 2015
E-mail: francesca_brody@nysd.uscourts.gov
Secretary **William J. Donald** . . . . (212) 805-6125
E-mail: william_donald@nysd.uscourts.gov

Chambers of Senior Judge Charles Sherman Haight, Jr.

U.S. District Court, 141 Church Street, New Haven, CT 06510
Tel: (203) 773-2052
E-mail: haightnysdchambers@nysd.uscourts.gov

Charles Sherman Haight, Jr.
Senior Judge

Date of Birth: 1930
Education: Yale 1952 BA, 1955 LLB
Began Service: May 3, 1976
Appointed By: President Gerald Ford

Government: Trial Attorney, Civil Division, United States Department of Justice (1955-1957)

Legal Practice: Haight, Gardner, Poor & Havens (1976)

Current Memberships: The Association of the Bar of the City of New York; Federal Bar Council; Maritime Law Association of the United States; New York State Bar Association

Staff
Law Clerk **Yuanheng "Sally" Wang** . . . . (203) 773-2051
E-mail: sally_wang@ctd.uscourts.gov
Law Clerk **(Vacant)** . . . . (203) 773-2051
Career Law Clerk **Lori Dorais** . . . . (203) 773-2052
E-mail: lori_dorais@ctd.uscourts.gov

(continued on next page)

FEDERAL COURTS—UNITED STATES DISTRICT COURTS

Chambers of Senior Judge Charles Sherman Haight, Jr. *continued*

Courtroom Deputy **Kathleen Falcone** . . . . (203) 773-2407
Began Service: 2011
E-mail: kathleen_falcone@nysd.uscourts.gov

Chambers of Senior Judge Louis L. Stanton

Daniel Patrick Moynihan U.S. Courthouse, 500 Pearl Street,
New York, NY 10007
Tel: (212) 805-0252
E-mail: louis_stanton@nysd.uscourts.gov

Louis L. Stanton
Senior Judge

Date of Birth: 1927
Education: Yale 1950 BA; Virginia 1955 LLB, 1955 JD
Began Service: September 1985
Appointed By: President Ronald Reagan

Legal Practice: Associate, Davis Polk & Wardwell (1955-1966); Partner, Carter Ledyard & Milburn LLP (1966-1985)

Military Service: United States Merchant Marines (1945-1947); United States Marine Corps Reserve (1950-1952)

Current Memberships: American College of Trial Lawyers; Federal Bar Council; New York Bar Foundation, New York State Bar Association; The Virginia Bar Association

Staff

Law Clerk **Brandon Chamberlin** . . . . (212) 805-0252
Began Service: September 2014
Term Expires: August 2016
E-mail: brandon_chamberlin@nysd.uscourts.gov
Law Clerk **Steven Shuldman** . . . . (212) 805-0252
Began Service: August 2015
Term Expires: August 2017
E-mail: steve_shuldman@nysd.uscourts.gov
Secretary **Emilie Tropiano** . . . . (212) 805-0252
Courtroom Deputy **Gloria Daley** . . . . (212) 805-0252
E-mail: gloria_daley@nysd.uscourts.gov

Chambers of Senior Judge Sidney H. Stein

Daniel Patrick Moynihan U.S. Courthouse, 500 Pearl Street,
New York, NY 10007-1312
Tel: (212) 805-0192 Fax: (212) 805-7924
E-mail: sidney_h_stein@nysd.uscourts.gov

Sidney H. Stein
Senior Judge

Education: Princeton 1967 AB; Yale 1972 JD
Began Service: May 1, 1995
Appointed By: President William J. Clinton

Current Memberships: American Bar Foundation; American Bar Association; The Association of the Bar of the City of New York; Federal Bar Council; New York State Bar Association; New York Bar Foundation, New York State Bar Association

Staff

Law Clerk **Lee Crain** . . . . (212) 805-0192
Began Service: August 2015
Term Expires: September 2016
E-mail: lee_crain@nysd.uscourts.gov
Education: Michigan 2014 JD
Law Clerk **Ava McAlpin** . . . . (212) 805-0192
Began Service: September 2015
Term Expires: September 2016
E-mail: ava_mcalpin@nysd.uscourts.gov

Chambers of Senior Judge Sidney H. Stein *continued*

Courtroom Deputy **Laura Blakely** . . . . (212) 805-0087
E-mail: laura_blakely@nysd.uscourts.gov

Chambers of Senior Judge Alvin K. Hellerstein

Daniel Patrick Moynihan U.S. Courthouse, 500 Pearl Street,
Room 1050, New York, NY 10007-1312
Tel: (212) 805-0152 Fax: (212) 805-7942
E-mail: alvin_hellerstein@nysd.uscourts.gov

Alvin K. Hellerstein
Senior Judge

Date of Birth: 1933
Education: Columbia 1954 BA, 1956 LLB
Began Service: November 30, 1998
Appointed By: President William J. Clinton
Political Affiliation: Democrat

Current Memberships: American Bar Foundation; The American Association of Jewish Lawyers and Jurists; American Bar Association; The American Law Institute; The Association of the Bar of the City of New York; Federal Bar Council; International Association of Jewish Lawyers and Jurists; New York State Bar Association

Staff

Law Clerk **Sarah Wilensky** . . . . (212) 805-0152
Began Service: September 2015
Term Expires: September 2016
E-mail: sarah_wilensky@nysd.uscourts.gov
Law Clerk **Mollie Bracewell** . . . . (212) 805-0152
Began Service: October 2015
Term Expires: October 2016
E-mail: mollie_bracewell@nysd.uscourts.gov
Courtroom Deputy **Brigitte Jones** . . . . (212) 805-0152
E-mail: brigitte_jones@nysd.uscourts.gov
Education: SUNY (Buffalo) 1990 BS
Judicial Assistant **Nancy Wong** . . . . (212) 805-0152
E-mail: nancy_wong@nysd.uscourts.gov

Chambers of Senior Judge Victor Marrero

Daniel Patrick Moynahan U.S. Courthouse, 40 Foley Square,
Room 660, New York, NY 10007
Tel: (212) 805-6374 Fax: (212) 805-6382
E-mail: Victor_Marrero@nysd.uscourts.gov

Victor Marrero
Senior Judge

Date of Birth: 1941
Education: NYU 1964 BA; Yale 1968 LLB
Began Service: December 1, 1999
Appointed By: President William J. Clinton

Academic: Visiting Lecturer (part-time), Law School, Yale University (1985-1987); Visiting Lecturer (part-time), Columbia Law School (1990-1993)

Corporate: Director, NYNEX Corporation (1987-1993); Trustee, Consolidated Edison Company of New York, Inc. (1989-1993)

Chambers of Senior Judge Victor Marrero *continued*

Government: Intern (D-NY), Office of Senator Robert F. Kennedy, United States Senate (1965); Assistant to the Mayor, Mayor John V. Lindsay (R-NY), City of New York, New York (1968-1970); First Assistant Counsel, Governor Hugh L. Carey (D-NY), State of New York (1975-1976); Chairman, City Planning Commission, City Planning Department, City of New York, New York (1976-1977); Commissioner, Housing and Community Renewal Division, State of New York (1978-1979); Under Secretary, United States Department of Housing and Urban Development, Jimmy Carter Administration (1979-1981); Member, Board of Standards and Appeals, Office of the Mayor, City of New York, New York (1983-1984); Member, New York City Rent Guidelines Board, Office of the Mayor, City of New York, New York (1990-1992); Ambassador, United Nations Economic and Social Council (1993-1997); Ambassador and Permanent Representative, Organization of American States (1998-1999)

Legal Practice: Summer Associate, Cravath, Swaine & Moore LLP (1966-1967); Partner, Tufo & Zuccotti (1982-1985); Partner, Brown and Wood LLP (1986-1993)

Current Memberships: The Association of the Bar of the City of New York

Staff

Law Clerk **Daniella A. Schmidt** .... (212) 805-6374
Began Service: November 9, 2015
Term Expires: November 2016
Education: Michigan 2013 JD

Law Clerk **Margaret Marie Siller** .... (212) 805-6374
Began Service: September 8, 2015
Term Expires: September 2016
E-mail: margaret_siller@nysd.uscourts.gov
Education: Northwestern 2013 JD

Law Clerk **Alyssa Work** .... (212) 805-6374
Began Service: August 31, 2015
Term Expires: August 2016
E-mail: alyssa_work@nysd.uscourts.gov
Education: Swarthmore 2008 JD

Judicial Assistant **Maria C. Ramos** .... (212) 805-6374
E-mail: maria_ramos@nysd.uscourts.gov

Chambers of Senior Judge Jed S. Rakoff

1340 Daniel Patrick Moynihan U.S. Courthouse, 500 Pearl Street, New York, NY 10007
Tel: (212) 805-0401 Fax: (212) 805-7935
E-mail: Jed_S_Rakoff@nysd.uscourts.gov

Jed S. Rakoff
Senior Judge

Date of Birth: 1943
Education: Swarthmore 1964 BA; Oxford (UK) 1966 MPhil; Harvard 1969 JD; Swarthmore 2003 LLD; U St Francis 2005 LLD
Began Service: March 1, 1996
Appointed By: President William J. Clinton

Clerkships: Law Clerk The Honorable Abraham Freedman, United States Court of Appeals for the Third Circuit (1969-1970)

Government: Assistant United States Attorney, Southern District of New York, Office of the United States Attorney, United States Department of Justice (1973-1978); Assistant United States Attorney and Chief, Southern District, Business & Securities Fraud Prosecutions, Office of the United States Attorney, United States Department of Justice (1978-1980)

Legal Practice: Associate, Debevoise, Plimpton, Lyons & Gates (1970-1972); Partner, Mudge, Rose, Guthrie, Alexander & Ferdon (1980-1990); Partner, Fried, Frank, Harris, Shriver & Jacobson LLP (1990-1996)

Current Memberships: American College of Trial Lawyers; The American Law Institute; The Association of the Bar of the City of New York

Chambers of Senior Judge Jed S. Rakoff *continued*

Staff

Law Clerk **Rachel Bayefsky** .... (212) 805-0401
Began Service: August 2015
Term Expires: August 2, 2016
E-mail: rachel_l_bayefsky@nysd.uscourts.gov
Education: Yale 2015 JD

Law Clerk **Adam Goodman** .... (212) 805-0401
Began Service: August 2015
Term Expires: August 2, 2016
E-mail: adam_goodman@nysd.uscourts.gov
Education: Harvard 2013 JD

Law Clerk **Steven Kochevar** .... (212) 805-0401
Began Service: August 2015
Term Expires: August 2, 2016
E-mail: steven_kochevar@nysd.uscourts.gov
Education: Yale 2014 JD

Courtroom Deputy **Linda Kotowski** .... (212) 805-0129
E-mail: linda_kotowski@nysd.uscourts.gov

Chambers of Senior Judge Lewis A. Kaplan

Daniel Patrick Moynihan U.S. Courthouse, 500 Pearl Street, New York, NY 10007
Tel: (212) 805-0216
E-mail: kaplannysdchambers@nysd.uscourts.gov

Lewis A. Kaplan
Senior Judge

Date of Birth: 1944
Education: Rochester 1966 AB; Harvard 1969 JD
Began Service: 1994
Appointed By: President William J. Clinton

Clerkships: Law Clerk The Honorable Edward McEntee, United States Court of Appeals for the First Circuit (1969-1970)

Legal Practice: Paul, Weiss, Rifkind, Wharton & Garrison (1970-1994)

Current Memberships: American Bar Association; American College of Trial Lawyers; The American Law Institute; The Association of the Bar of the City of New York; Federal Bar Council; Federal Judges Association; New York State Bar Association

Staff

Law Clerk **David Kronig** .... (212) 805-0216
Began Service: September 2015
Term Expires: September 2016
E-mail: david_kronig@nysd.uscourts.gov

Law Clerk **Daniel Sinnreich** .... (212) 805-0216
Began Service: September 2015
Term Expires: September 2016
E-mail: daniel_sinnreich@nysd.uscourts.gov

Courtroom Deputy **Andrew Mohan** .... (212) 805-0104
E-mail: andrew_mohan@nysd.uscourts.gov
Education: Iona 1996 MS

Judicial Assistant **Elizabeth Menard** .... (212) 805-0216
E-mail: elizabeth_menard@nysd.uscourts.gov

Chambers of Senior Judge Deborah A. Batts

2510 Daniel Patrick Moynihan U.S. Courthouse, 500 Pearl Street, New York, NY 10007-1312
Tel: (212) 805-0186
E-mail: battsnysdchambers@nysd.uscourts.gov

Deborah A. Batts
Senior Judge

Date of Birth: 1947
Education: Radcliffe 1969 AB; Harvard 1972 JD
Began Service: June 23, 1994
Appointed By: President William J. Clinton

Current Memberships: American Bar Association; The Association of the Bar of the City of New York; Lesbian and Gay Law Association of Greater New York; Metropolitan Black Bar Association

Staff

Law Clerk **Mae Ackerman-Brimberg** . . . . (212) 805-4615
Began Service: September 2014
Term Expires: September 2016
E-mail: mae_brimberg@nysd.uscourts.gov

Law Clerk **Lauren Giudice** . . . . (212) 805-4617
Began Service: August 2014
Term Expires: September 2016
E-mail: lauren_giudice@nysd.uscourts.gov

Law Clerk **David Pollock** . . . . (212) 805-4616
Began Service: September 2014
Term Expires: September 2016
E-mail: david_pollock@nysd.uscourts.gov

Chambers of Senior Judge Shira A. Scheindlin

1620 Daniel Patrick Moynihan U.S. Courthouse, 500 Pearl Street, New York, NY 10007-1312
Tel: (212) 805-0246 Fax: (212) 805-7920
E-mail: Shira_A_Scheindlin@nysd.uscourts.gov

Shira A. Scheindlin
Senior Judge

Date of Birth: 1946
Education: Michigan 1967 BA; Columbia 1969 MA; Cornell 1975 JD
Began Service: November 14, 1994
Appointed By: President William J. Clinton

Current Memberships: The Association of the Bar of the City of New York; Federal Bar Council; Judicial Conference of the United States; New York County Lawyers' Association; New York State Bar Association

Staff

Law Clerk **Peter Dubrowski** . . . . (212) 805-0474
Began Service: October 2015
Term Expires: October 2016
E-mail: peter_dubrowski@nysd.uscourts.gov

Law Clerk **Anuja Thatte** . . . . (212) 805-0475
Began Service: August 2015
Term Expires: August 2016
E-mail: anuja_thatte@nysd.uscourts.gov

Deputy Law Clerk **Clifford D. Bloomfield** . . . . (212) 805-0120
E-mail: clifford_bloomfield@nysd.uscourts.gov

Courtroom Deputy **Angela Del Signore** . . . . (212) 805-0246
E-mail: angela_delsignore@nysd.uscourts.gov

Chambers of Senior Judge Denise Cote

Daniel Patrick Moynihan U.S. Courthouse, 500 Pearl Street, Room 1040, New York, NY 10007
Tel: (212) 805-0202 Fax: (212) 805-7907
E-mail: cotenysdchambers@nysd.uscourts.gov

Denise Cote
Senior Judge

Date of Birth: 1946
Education: St Mary Col 1968; Columbia 1969 MA, 1975 JD
Began Service: August 11, 1994
Appointed By: President William J. Clinton

Staff

Law Clerk **Timothy Gray** . . . . (212) 805-0202
Began Service: January 2015
Term Expires: January 2016
E-mail: timothy_gray@nysd.uscourts.gov
Education: Columbia 2014 JD

Law Clerk **Lise Rahdert** . . . . (212) 805-0202
Began Service: August 2015
Term Expires: August 2016
E-mail: lise_rahdert@nysd.uscourts.gov

Law Clerk **Ravi Ramanathan** . . . . (212) 805-0202
Began Service: August 2015
Term Expires: August 2016
E-mail: ravi_ramanathan@nysd.uscourts.gov

Deputy Clerk **Gloria Rojas** . . . . (212) 805-0097
E-mail: gloria_rojas@nysd.uscourts.gov

Chambers of Senior Judge Richard M. Berman

U.S. Courthouse, 500 Pearl Street, 13th Floor, New York, NY 10007
Tel: (212) 805-6715
E-mail: richard_berman@nysd.uscourts.gov

Richard M. Berman
Senior Judge

Date of Birth: 1943
Education: Cornell 1964 BS; NYU 1967 JD; Fordham 1996 MSW
Began Service: November 23, 1998
Appointed By: President William J. Clinton
Political Affiliation: Republican

Current Memberships: New York State Bar Association

Staff

Law Clerk **Peter Berg** . . . . (212) 805-6715
Began Service: October 2015
Term Expires: October 2016
E-mail: peter_berg@nysd.uscourts.gov

Law Clerk **David Kusnetz** . . . . (212) 805-6715
Began Service: October 2015
Term Expires: October 2016
E-mail: david_kusnetz@nysd.uscourts.gov

Law Clerk **Daniel Passeser** . . . . (212) 805-6715
Term Expires: June 2016
E-mail: daniel_passeser@nysd.uscourts.gov

Law Clerk **Jason Short** . . . . (212) 805-6715
Began Service: October 2015
Term Expires: October 2016
E-mail: jason_short@nysd.uscourts.gov

Career Law Clerk/Courtroom Deputy
Christine Murray . . . . (212) 805-6715
E-mail: christine_murray@nysd.uscourts.gov
Education: St John's U (NY) 1992 JD

Chambers of Senior Judge Naomi Reice Buchwald

2270 Daniel Patrick Moynihan U.S. Courthouse, 500 Pearl Street,
New York, NY 10007-1312
Tel: (212) 805-0194 Fax: (212) 805-7927
E-mail: buchwaldnysdchambers@nysd.uscourts.gov

Naomi Reice Buchwald
Senior Judge

Date of Birth: 1944
Education: Brandeis 1965 BA; Columbia 1968 LLB
Began Service: September 13, 1999
Appointed By: President William J. Clinton

Current Memberships: The Association of the Bar of the City of New York; Federal Bar Council; New York State Bar Association

Staff
Law Clerk **David Friedman** .... (212) 805-0194
Began Service: September 2015
Term Expires: September 2016
Law Clerk **Jeffrey J. Hughes** .... (212) 805-0194
Began Service: August 2015
Term Expires: August 2016
E-mail: jeff_hughes@nysd.uscourts.gov
Law Clerk **David Salant** .... (212) 805-0194
Began Service: September 2015
Term Expires: September 2016
E-mail: david_salant@nysd.uscourts.gov
Secretary **Karen Harris** .... (212) 805-4794
E-mail: karen_harris@nysd.uscourts.gov

Chambers of Senior Judge Paul A. Crotty

500 Pearl Street, Room 1350, New York, NY 10007-1312
Tel: (212) 805-6309 Fax: (212) 805-6304
E-mail: crottynysdchambers@nysd.uscourts.gov

Paul A. Crotty
Senior Judge

Education: Notre Dame 1962 BA; Cornell 1967 JD
Began Service: August 1, 2005
Appointed By: President George W. Bush

Staff
Law Clerk **Michael Schwartz** .... (212) 805-6313
Began Service: September 2015
Term Expires: September 2016
E-mail: michael_schwartz@nysd.uscourts.gov
Law Clerk **Stephen Wirth** .... (212) 805-6314
Began Service: August 2015
Term Expires: August 2016
E-mail: stephen_wirth@nysd.uscourts.gov
Courtroom Deputy **Marlon Ovalles** .... (212) 805-6312
E-mail: marlon_ovalles@nysd.uscourts.gov
Judicial Assistant **Camille A. Pacifico** .... (212) 805-6311
E-mail: camille_pacifico@nysd.uscourts.gov

Chambers of Chief Magistrate Judge Frank Maas

500 Pearl Street, Room 740, New York, NY 10007
Tel: (212) 805-6727 Fax: (212) 805-6724
E-mail: Frank_Maas@nysd.uscourts.gov

Frank Maas
Chief Magistrate Judge

Date of Birth: 1950
Education: SUNY (Binghamton) 1972 BA; NYU 1976 JD
Began Service: June 1999
Term Expires: June 1, 2023

Current Memberships: The Association of the Bar of the City of New York; Federal Bar Council; Federal Magistrate Judges Association; New York State Bar Association

Chambers of Chief Magistrate Judge Frank Maas *continued*

Staff
Law Clerk **Bettina Roberts** .... (212) 805-6727
Began Service: September 2015
Term Expires: September 2016
E-mail: bettina_roberts@nysd.uscourts.gov
Law Clerk **Matthew Simon** .... (212) 805-6727
Began Service: September 2015
Term Expires: September 2016
E-mail: matthew_simon@nysd.uscourts.gov
Courtroom Deputy **Marilyn Ong** .... (212) 805-6734
E-mail: marilyn_ong@nysd.uscourts.gov

Chambers of Magistrate Judge Kevin Nathaniel Fox

U.S. Courthouse, 40 Centre Street, Room 425, New York, NY 10007
Tel: (212) 805-6705 Fax: (212) 805-6712

Kevin Nathaniel Fox
Magistrate Judge

Began Service: October 2, 1997
Term Expires: October 2021

Staff
Law Clerk/Courtroom Deputy **Laura M. Midwood** ...... (212) 805-6710
Education: Rice 1989 MA, 1989 PhD;
Hofstra 2001 JD
Career Law Clerk **Sanja Zgonjanin** .... (212) 805-6708
Began Service: September 3, 2010
E-mail: sanja_zgonjanin@nysd.uscourts.gov
Education: U Sarajevo 1986 BA;
Queens Col (NY) 1999 MLS; Columbia 2000 MA;
CUNY 2006 JD
Secretary **Sabrina Broussard** .... (212) 805-6705

Chambers of Magistrate Judge Henry B. Pitman

Daniel Patrick Moynihan U.S. Courthouse, 500 Pearl Street,
New York, NY 10007
Tel: (212) 805-6105 Fax: (212) 805-6111

Henry B. Pitman
Magistrate Judge

Date of Birth: 1953
Education: Fordham 1975 BA, 1978 JD
Began Service: July 8, 1996
Term Expires: July 8, 2020

Clerkships: Law Clerk The Honorable Lloyd F. McMahon, United States District Court for the Southern District of New York (1978-1979)

Government: Assistant United States Attorney, Southern District of New York, United States Attorney's Office, United States Department of Justice, Ronald Reagan Administration (1985-1990)

Current Memberships: The Association of the Bar of the City of New York

Staff
Law Clerk **Sogol Somekh** .... (212) 805-6105
Began Service: September 2015
Term Expires: September 1, 2016
E-mail: sogol_somekh@nysd.uscourts.gov
Education: Fordham 2007 JD
Law Clerk **Stephen Della Fera** .... (212) 805-6105
Began Service: September 2015
Term Expires: September 1, 2016
E-mail: stephen_dellafera@nysd.uscourts.gov
Courtroom Deputy **Bruce Hampton** .... (212) 805-6112
E-mail: bruce_hampton@nysd.uscourts.gov

Chambers of Magistrate Judge Lisa Margaret Smith

U.S. Courthouse, 300 Quarropas Street, White Plains, NY 10601
Tel: (914) 390-4130

Lisa Margaret Smith
Magistrate Judge

Date of Birth: 1955
Education: Earlham 1977 BA; Duke 1980 JD
Began Service: March 20, 1995
Term Expires: March 19, 2019

Academic: Adjunct Professor, Pace University School of Law (2006)

Government: Assistant District Attorney, Office of the District Attorney, County of Kings, New York (1980-1985); Assistant Attorney General, Department of Law, Office of the Attorney General, State of New York (1985-1986); Assistant District Attorney, Office of the District Attorney, County of Kings, New York (1986-1987); Assistant United States Attorney, Southern District of New York, Office of the United States Attorney, United States Department of Justice (1987-1995)

Judicial: Chief Magistrate Judge, United States District Court for the Southern District of New York (2006-2007)

Current Memberships: Editorial Board of the Federal Bar Council Quarterly, Federal Bar Council; Federal Magistrate Judges Association; Judger and Lawyers' Breast Cancer Alert; National Association of Women Judges; Westchester County Bar Association; Board of Directors, Women's Bar Association of the State of New York

Membership: Past Member of the Board of Directors, Alumni Association, School of Law, Duke University

Staff

Law Clerk **Laura Draper** .... (914) 390-4130
Began Service: September 2014
Term Expires: September 2016
E-mail: laura_draper@nysd.uscourts.gov

Law Clerk **Orrie Levy** .... (914) 390-4130
Began Service: September 2015
Term Expires: September 2017
E-mail: orrie_levy@nysd.uscourts.gov

Career Law Clerk **Karen Jason** .... (914) 390-4130
E-mail: karen_jason@nysd.uscourts.gov
Education: NYU 1993 JD

Chambers of Magistrate Judge Andrew J. Peck

Daniel Patrick Moynihan U.S. Courthouse, 500 Pearl Street, Room 1370, New York, NY 10007-1312
Tel: (212) 805-0036 Fax: (212) 805-7933

Andrew J. Peck
Magistrate Judge

Date of Birth: 1953
Education: Cornell 1974 AB; Duke 1977 JD
Began Service: February 27, 1995
Term Expires: February 26, 2019

Affiliation: Member of the Board of Directors, Berkshire Hills-Emanuel Camps

Clerkships: Law Clerk The Honorable Paul Roney, United States Court of Appeals for the Fifth Circuit (1977-1978)

Legal Practice: Associate, Paul, Weiss, Rifkind, Wharton & Garrison LLP

Nonprofit: Member of the Board of Directors, Mystery Writers of America, Inc. (2002-2004)

Current Memberships: American Bar Association; Federal Magistrate Judges Association

Chambers of Magistrate Judge Andrew J. Peck *continued*

Staff

Law Clerk **Alexander Stone-Tharp** .... (212) 805-0036
Began Service: August 2014
Term Expires: August 2016
E-mail: alexander_stone-tharp@nysd.uscourts.gov
Education: NYU 2011 JD

Law Clerk **Lindsey Keenan** .... (212) 805-0036
Began Service: August 2014
Term Expires: August 2016
E-mail: lindsey_keenan@nysd.uscourts.gov

Secretary **Diane Kelly** .... (212) 805-0036
E-mail: diane_kelly@nysd.uscourts.gov

Chambers of Magistrate Judge Michael H. Dolinger

1670 Daniel Patrick Moynihan U.S. Courthouse, 500 Pearl Street, New York, NY 10007-1312
Tel: (212) 805-0204 Fax: (212) 805-7928

Michael H. Dolinger
Magistrate Judge

Note: Judge Dolinger will retire at the end of his term.
Date of Birth: 1946
Education: Columbia 1968 BA, 1972 JD
Began Service: March 12, 1984
Term Expires: March 11, 2016

Clerkships: Law Clerk The Honorable Wilfred Feinberg, United States Court of Appeals for the Second Circuit (1972-1973)

Government: Assistant United States Attorney, Southern District of New York, Office of the United States Attorney, United States Department of Justice (1976-1984)

Legal Practice: Nickerson, Kramer, Lowenstein, Nessen, Kamin & Soll (1973-1976)

Chambers of Magistrate Judge James Clark Francis IV

1960 Daniel Patrick Moynihan U.S. Courthouse, 500 Pearl Street, New York, NY 10007
Tel: (212) 805-0206 Fax: (212) 805-7930

James Clark Francis IV
Magistrate Judge

Date of Birth: 1952
Education: Yale 1974 BA, 1978 JD; Harvard 1978 MPP
Began Service: October 28, 1985
Term Expires: October 27, 2017
Political Affiliation: Democrat

Academic: Adjunct Professor, School of Law, Fordham University (2003-2006)

Clerkships: Law Clerk The Honorable Robert L. Carter, United States District Court for the Southern District of New York (1978-1979)

Legal Practice: Staff Attorney, Legal Aid Society (1979-1985)

Current Memberships: The Association of the Bar of the City of New York; Federal Bar Council; Federal Magistrate Judges Association; New York State Bar Association

Staff

Law Clerk **Michael Bacchus** .... (212) 805-0206
Began Service: January 2012
E-mail: michael_bacchus@nysd.uscourts.gov
Education: Pennsylvania 2003 JD

Law Clerk **Maria DaSilva** .... (212) 805-0206
Began Service: August 2015
Term Expires: August 2016
E-mail: maria_dasilva@nysd.uscourts.gov

Chambers of Magistrate Judge James Clark Francis IV *continued*

Law Clerk **Colin Stroud** .... (212) 805-0206
Began Service: August 2015
Term Expires: August 2016
E-mail: colin_stroud@nysd.uscourts.gov

Chambers of Magistrate Judge Ronald L. Ellis

Daniel Patrick Moynihan U.S. Courthouse, 500 Pearl Street, Suite 1970, New York, NY 10007
Tel: (212) 805-0242 Fax: (212) 805-7929

Ronald L. Ellis
Magistrate Judge

Date of Birth: 1950
Education: NYU 1975 JD
Began Service: November 16, 1993
Term Expires: November 15, 2017

Academic: Adjunct Professor, School of Law, New York University (1984-1994)

Legal Practice: Attorney, NAACP Legal Defense and Education Fund, Inc. (1976-1993)

Staff

Law Clerk **Janeen Hall** .... (212) 805-0564
Began Service: September 2015
Term Expires: September 2016
E-mail: janeen_hall@nysd.uscourts.gov

Law Clerk **Emily Farrell** .... (212) 805-0562
Began Service: September 2015
Term Expires: September 2016
E-mail: emily_farrell@nysd.uscourts.gov

Courtroom Deputy **Rupa Shah** .... (212) 805-0242
E-mail: rupa_shah@nysd.uscourts.gov

Chambers of Magistrate Judge Debra Freeman

40 Foley Square, Room 1660, New York, NY 10007
Tel: (212) 805-4250 Fax: (212) 805-4258
E-mail: debra_freeman@nysd.uscourts.gov

Debra Freeman
Magistrate Judge

Date of Birth: 1957
Education: Yale 1979 BA; NYU 1986 JD
Began Service: March 2, 2001

Legal Practice: Associate, Parker, Auspitz, Neesemann & Delehanty, P.C. (1986-1987); Associate, Morrison & Foerster LLP (1987-1994); Partner, Morrison & Foerster LLP (1995-2001)

Current Memberships: Federal Bar Council

Staff

Law Clerk **Stephanie Baez** .... (212) 805-4254
Began Service: April 2015
Term Expires: April 2016

Law Clerk **Steven Heller** .... (212) 805-4253
Began Service: September 2015
Term Expires: September 2016
E-mail: steven_heller@nysd.uscourts.gov

Courtroom Deputy **Aisha Bams** .... (212) 805-4250
E-mail: aisha_bams@nysd.uscourts.gov

Chambers of Magistrate Judge Gabriel W. Gorenstein

U.S. Courthouse, 40 Centre Street, Room 431, New York, NY 10007
Tel: (212) 805-4260 Fax: (212) 805-4268

Gabriel William Gorenstein
Magistrate Judge

Date of Birth: 1957
Education: Yale 1979 BA; Columbia 1984 JD
Began Service: March 2, 2001
Term Expires: March 2, 2017

Clerkships: Law Clerk The Honorable Spotswood W. Robinson III, United States Court of Appeals for the District of Columbia Circuit (1984-1985)

Government: Assistant United States Attorney, Southern District of New York, United States Attorney's Office, United States Department of Justice, Ronald Reagan Administration (1987-1994); General Counsel and Deputy Commissioner, Human Resources Administration, City of New York, New York (1994-1998)

Judicial: Judge, Criminal Court of the City of New York (1998-2001)

Staff

Law Clerk **Christopher Coyne** .... (212) 805-4260
Began Service: August 2015
Term Expires: August 2016
E-mail: christopher_coyne@nysd.uscourts.gov

Law Clerk **Mark Goldberg** .... (212) 805-4260
Began Service: September 2015
Term Expires: September 2016
E-mail: mark_goldberg@nysd.uscourts.gov

Courtroom Deputy **Sylvia Gonzalez** .... (212) 805-4260
E-mail: sylvia_gonzalez@nysd.uscourts.gov

Chambers of Magistrate Judge Paul E. Davison

300 Quarropas Street, White Plains, NY 10601-4150
Tel: (914) 390-4250

Paul E. Davison
Magistrate Judge

Began Service: 2009

Staff

Courtroom Deputy **Frank Cangelosi** .... (914) 390-4251
E-mail: frank_cangelosi@nysd.uscourts.gov

Chambers of Magistrate Judge James L. Cott

40 Foley Square, New York, NY 10007
Tel: (212) 805-0250
E-mail: james_cott@nysd.uscourts.gov

James L. Cott
Magistrate Judge

Began Service: 2009

Staff

Courtroom Deputy **David Tam** .... (212) 805-0533
E-mail: david_tam@nysd.uscourts.gov

Chambers of Magistrate Judge Sarah Netburn

40 Foley Square, New York, NY 10007
Tel: (212) 805-0286
E-mail: netburn_NYSDChamber@nysd.uscourts.gov

Sarah Netburn
Magistrate Judge

Staff

Law Clerk **Sarah Heim** .... (212) 805-0286
E-mail: sarah_heim@nysd.uscourts.gov

(continued on next page)

Chambers of Magistrate Judge Sarah Netburn *continued*

Law Clerk **Richard "Rick" Sawyer** . . . . (212) 805-0286
E-mail: richard_sawyer@nysd.uscourts.gov
Courtroom Deputy **Joseph Mendieta** . . . . (212) 805-0286
E-mail: joseph_mendieta@nysd.uscourts.gov

Chambers of Magistrate Judge Judith C. McCarthy

300 Quarropas Street, White Plains, NY 10601-4150
Tel: (914) 390-4124

Judith C. McCarthy
Magistrate Judge

Education: Barnard BA; CUNY 1991 JD
Began Service: January 2014

Staff

Law Clerk **Carly Grant** . . . . (914) 390-4124
Education: Pace 2008 JD
Law Clerk **Rachel K. Clapp** . . . . (914) 390-4124
E-mail: rachel_clapp@nysd.uscourts.gov
Judicial Assistant **Jessica Hummel** . . . . (914) 390-4124
E-mail: mccarthy_nysdchambers@nysd.uscourts.gov

Chambers of Magistrate Judge (part-time) Martin R. Goldberg

225 Dolson Avenue, Middletown, NY 10940
P.O. Box 2083, Middletown, NY 10940
Tel: (845) 343-1130 Fax: (845) 344-5547
E-mail: Martin_R_Goldberg@nysd.uscourts.gov

Martin R. Goldberg
Magistrate Judge (Part-Time)

Date of Birth: 1945
Education: New York Law 1969 JD
Began Service: 1992

Staff

Secretary **Ella Cavaliere** . . . . (845) 343-1130
Courtroom Deputy **Frances J. Fredericks** . . . . (845) 451-6372
Fax: (845) 452-8375

United States Bankruptcy Court for the Southern District of New York

Alexander Hamilton Custom House, One Bowling Green,
New York, NY 10004-1408
Tel: (212) 668-2870 Tel: (212) 668-2896 (PACER)
Tel: (800) 676-6856 (Toll Free PACER)
Tel: (212) 668-2772 (Voice Case Information System VCIS)
Fax: (212) 668-2878
Internet: www.nysb.uscourts.gov

Number of Judgeships: 10

Court Staff

Clerk of Court **Vito Genna** . . . . (212) 668-2870
E-mail: vito_genna@nysb.uscourts.gov
Chief Deputy Clerk **Una O'Boyle** . . . . (212) 668-2870
E-mail: una_o'boyle@nysb.uscourts.gov
Education: New York Law 1991 JD
Divisional Manager - Poughkeepsie
Frances J. Fredericks . . . . (845) 452-4200
355 Main Street, Poughkeepsie, NY 12601
E-mail: frances_fredericks@nysb.uscourts.gov
Divisional Manager - White Plains **Eddie Andino** . . . . (914) 390-4060
300 Quarropas St., White Plains, NY 10601
E-mail: eddie_andino@nysb.uscourts.gov
Court Security Officer **Gerald Durden** . . . . (212) 284-4090

Chambers of Chief Bankruptcy Judge Cecelia G. Morris

355 Main Street, Poughkeepsie, NY 12601-4165
Tel: (845) 452-4200 Fax: (845) 452-8375
E-mail: cecelia_morris@nysb.uscourts.gov

Cecelia G. Morris
Chief Bankruptcy Judge

Date of Birth: 1946
Education: West Texas State BA; John Marshall JD
Began Service: July 1, 2000
Term Expires: June 30, 2028

Staff

Law Clerk **Robert Johnson** . . . . (845) 452-4200 ext. 6373
E-mail: robert_johnson@nysb.uscourts.gov
Law Clerk **Kenneth Williams** . . . . (845) 452-4200 ext. 6373
E-mail: kenneth_williams@nysb.uscourts.gov
Career Law Clerk **Brenda Giuliano** . . . . (845) 452-4200 ext. 6374
E-mail: brenda_giuliano@nysb.uscourts.gov
Management Analyst **Frances J. Fredericks** . . . . (845) 452-4200 ext. 6372
E-mail: frances_fredericks@nysb.uscourts.gov

Chambers of Bankruptcy Judge Robert E. Gerber

Alexander Hamilton Custom House, One Bowling Green,
New York, NY 10004-1408
Tel: (212) 668-5660 Fax: (212) 668-3357
E-mail: judge_gerber@nysb.uscourts.gov

Robert E. Gerber
Bankruptcy Judge

Date of Birth: 1947
Education: Rutgers 1967 BS; Columbia 1970 JD
Began Service: September 5, 2000
Term Expires: September 5, 2028

Legal Practice: Associate, Fried, Frank, Harris, Shriver & Jacobson LLP

Military Service: United States Air Force (1971-1972)

Current Memberships: American Bankruptcy Institute; American Bar Association; American College of Bankruptcy; The Association of the Bar of the City of New York; Federal Bar Council; National Conference of Bankruptcy Judges

Staff

Law Clerk **Kara Neaton** . . . . (212) 668-5660
Began Service: August 2014
Term Expires: August 2016
E-mail: kara_neaton@nysb.uscourts.gov
Law Clerk **Michael Turkel** . . . . (212) 668-5660
E-mail: michael_turkel@nysb.uscourts.gov
Courtroom Deputy **Arlene Plum** . . . . (212) 668-5660

Chambers of Bankruptcy Judge Robert Dale Drain

Alexander Hamilton Custom House, One Bowling Green, Room 632, New York, NY 10004-1408
Tel: (914) 390-4155 Fax: (212) 668-3187
E-mail: RDD.Chambers@nysb.uscourts.gov

Robert Dale Drain
Bankruptcy Judge

Date of Birth: June 1957
Education: Yale 1979 BA; Columbia 1984 JD
Began Service: May 2002
Term Expires: May 2016

Legal Practice: Partner, Paul, Weiss, Rifkind, Wharton & Garrison LLP

Current Memberships: The Association of the Bar of the City of New York

Staff
Law Clerk **(Vacant)** .... (914) 390-4153
Law Clerk **Shlomo Maza** .... (914) 390-4156
Career Law Clerk **Rosemary DiSalvo** .... (914) 390-4157
E-mail: rosemary_disalvo@nysb.uscourts.gov
Education: Iona 1988 BA; Fordham 1992 JD
Courtroom Deputy **Dorothy Li** .... (914) 390-4155
E-mail: dorothy_li@nysb.uscourts.gov
Chapter 13 Specialist **Arturo Tavarez** .... (914) 390-4154
E-mail: arturo_tavarez@nysb.uscourts.gov

Chambers of Bankruptcy Judge Martin Glenn

One Bowling Green, Room 606, New York, NY 10004-1408
Tel: (212) 284-4551 Fax: (212) 668-5614
E-mail: martin_glenn@nysb.uscourts.gov

Martin Glenn
Bankruptcy Judge

Began Service: November 2006
Term Expires: November 2020

Clerkships: Law Clerk, Chief Judge Henry J. Friendly, United States Court of Appeals for the Second Circuit (1971-1972)

Legal Practice: Attorney, O'Melveny & Myers (1972-2006)

Staff
Law Clerk **Mariloly Orozco** .... (718) 613-2470
Began Service: September 2015
Term Expires: September 5, 2016
E-mail: mariloly_orozco@nysb.uscourts.gov
Education: Cornell 2013 JD
Law Clerk **Sean Mitchell** .... (718) 613-2470
Began Service: September 2015
Term Expires: August 27, 2016
E-mail: sean_mitchell@nysb.uscourts.gov
Courtroom Deputy **Deanna Anderson** .... (212) 284-4037
E-mail: deanna_anderson@nysb.uscourts.gov

Chambers of Bankruptcy Judge Sean H. Lane

One Bowling Green, New York, NY 10004-1408
Tel: (212) 668-5637
E-mail: sean_lane@nysb.uscourts.gov

Sean H. Lane
Bankruptcy Judge

Education: NYU 1987 BA, 1991 JD
Began Service: September 7, 2010

Clerkships: Law Clerk, Chambers of District Judge Edmund V. Ludwig, United States District Court for the Eastern District of Pennsylvania (1991-1992); Law Clerk, Chambers of District Judge Charles R. Richey, United States District Court for the District of Columbia (1992-1993)

Chambers of Bankruptcy Judge Sean H. Lane *continued*

Government: Trial Attorney, Civil Division, New York - Southern District, United States Department of Justice (2000-2010); Tax and Bankruptcy Unit Chief, Civil Division, New York - Southern District, United States Department of Justice (2007-2010)

Legal Practice: Attorney, Baker & Hostetler LLP (1993-1997)

Current Memberships: Federal Bar Council

Staff
Law Clerk **Steven Schwartz** .... (212) 284-4048
E-mail: steven_schwartz@nysb.uscourts.gov
Career Law Clerk **Christine Azzaro** .... (212) 284-4047
E-mail: christine_azzaro@nysb.uscourts.gov
Education: St John's U (NY) 2001 JD
Courtroom Deputy **Liza Ebanks** .... (212) 284-4045
E-mail: liza_ebanks@nysb.uscourts.gov

Chambers of Bankruptcy Judge Stuart M. Bernstein

Alexander Hamilton Custom House, One Bowling Green, Room 729, New York, NY 10004
Tel: (212) 668-2304 Fax: (212) 809-9674
E-mail: judge_bernstein@nysb.uscourts.gov

Stuart M. Bernstein
Bankruptcy Judge

Date of Birth: 1950
Education: Fordham 1975 JD
Began Service: November 24, 1993
Term Expires: November 23, 2021

Current Memberships: American Bar Association; The Association of the Bar of the City of New York

Staff
Law Clerk **Michael Byun** .... (212) 284-4027
Began Service: September 2014
Term Expires: September 2016
E-mail: michael_byun@nysb.uscourts.gov
Law Clerk **Jacob Gartman** .... (212) 284-4028
Began Service: September 2015
Term Expires: September 2017
E-mail: jacob_gartman@nysb.uscourts.gov
Law Clerk **Mike Paek** .... (212) 284-4027
Began Service: September 2014
Term Expires: September 2016
E-mail: mike_paek@nysb.uscourts.gov
Courtroom Deputy **Chantel Greene** .... (212) 668-2870 ext. 3723
E-mail: chantel_greene@nysb.uscourts.gov

Chambers of Bankruptcy Judge Shelley C. Chapman

One Bowling Green, New York, NY 10004-1408
Tel: (212) 668-2301

Shelley C. Chapman
Bankruptcy Judge

Education: Cornell 1978 BA; Harvard 1981 JD
Began Service: March 5, 2010

Staff
Law Clerk **Ryan Lifland** .... (212) 284-4027
E-mail: ryan_lifland@nysb.uscourts.gov
Law Clerk **Jamie Eisen** .... (212) 668-2301
E-mail: jamie_eisen@nysb.uscourts.gov
Courtroom Deputy **Greg White** .... (212) 668-2870 ext. 4029
E-mail: greg_white@nysb.uscourts.gov

Chambers of Bankruptcy Judge James L. Garrity Jr.
One Bowling Green, New York, NY 10004-1408
Tel: (212) 668-2870

James L. Garrity, Jr.
Bankruptcy Judge

Education: NYU ML
Began Service: 2015

Chambers of Bankruptcy Judge Michael E. Wiles
One Bowling Green, New York, NY 10004-1408
Tel: (212) 668-5663

Michael E. Wiles
Bankruptcy Judge

Education: Georgetown 1975 AB; Yale 1978 JD

United States District Court for the Western District of New York
Robert H. Jackson U.S. Courthouse, 2 Niagara Square, Buffalo, NY 14202
Kenneth B. Keating Federal Building, 100 State Street,
Rochester, NY 14614 (Rochester Office)
Tel: (716) 551-1700 Fax: (716) 551-4850
Tel: (585) 613-4000 (Rochester Office phone number)
Internet: www.nywd.uscourts.gov

Number of Judgeships: 4

Number of Vacancies: 1

Circuit: Second

Areas Covered: Counties of Allegany, Cattaraugus, Chautauqua, Chemung, Erie, Genesee, Livingston, Monroe, Niagara, Ontario, Orleans, Schuyler, Seneca, Steuben, Wayne, Wyoming and Yates

Court Staff
Clerk of the Court **Michael J. Roemer** .... (716) 332-1700
E-mail: michael_roemer@nywd.uscourts.gov Fax: (716) 551-3288
Education: Cornell 1990 JD
Chief Deputy Clerk **(Vacant)** .... (716) 332-1756
Deputy Clerk-in-Charge **(Vacant)** .... (585) 613-4000
2120 U.S. Courthouse, 100 State St.,
Rochester, NY 14614
Chief U.S. Probation Officer
Anthony M. San Giacomo .... (716) 551-4241
E-mail: anthony_sangiacomo@nywd.uscourts.gov
Information Technology Manager **Patrick J. Healy** .... (716) 332-1770
E-mail: patrick_healy@nywd.uscourts.gov
Financial Operations Supervisor **Lisa G. Ball** .... (716) 332-1731
E-mail: lisa_ball@nywd.uscourts.gov
Personnel Supervisor **Doreen E. Griebel** .... (716) 332-1755
E-mail: doreen_griebel@nywd.uscourts.gov
Librarian **Jay Deveau** .... (716) 551-1561
E-mail: jay_deveau@ca2.uscourts.gov

Chambers of Chief Judge Frank Paul Geraci Jr.
U.S. Courthouse, 100 State Street, Room 4230, Rochester, NY 14614
Tel: (585) 613-4090 Tel: (585) 613-4095
E-mail: frank_geraci@nywd.uscourts.gov

Frank Paul Geraci, Jr.
Chief Judge

Education: Dayton 1973 BA, 1977 JD
Began Service: March 22, 2013
Appointed By: President Barack Obama

Staff
Law Clerk **Connie Walker** .... (585) 613-4090
E-mail: connie_walker@nywd.uscourts.gov

Chambers of Chief Judge Frank Paul Geraci Jr. *continued*
Judicial Assistant **Susan Travis** .... (585) 613-4090
E-mail: susan_travis@nywd.uscourts.gov

Chambers of District Judge Elizabeth A. Wolford
100 State Street, Rochester, NY 14614
Tel: (585) 613-4320 Fax: (585) 613-4325
E-mail: elizabeth_wolford@nywd.uscourts.gov

Elizabeth A. Wolford
District Judge

Education: Colgate 1989 BA; Notre Dame 1992 JD
Began Service: December 17, 2013
Appointed By: President Barack Obama

Legal Practice: Partner, The Wolford Law Firm LLP

Nonprofit: President, Greater Rochester Association for Women Attorneys (2003-2004)

Staff
Law Clerk **Colleen Holland** .... (585) 613-4322
E-mail: colleen_holland@nywd.uscourts.gov
Law Clerk **Caitlin Loughran** .... (585) 613-4322
E-mail: caitlin_loughran@nywd.uscourts.gov
Law Clerk **Kimberly Rowles** .... (585) 613-4322
E-mail: kimberly_rowles@nywd.uscourts.gov
Courtroom Deputy **Lisa M. Duque** .... (585) 613-4320
E-mail: lisa_duque@nywd.uscourts.gov
Court Reporter **Karen Bush** .... (585) 613-4320
E-mail: karen_bush@nywd.uscourts.gov

Chambers of District Judge Lawrence Joseph Vilardo
2 Niagara Square, Buffalo, NY 14202
Tel: (716) 551-1700

Lawrence Joseph Vilardo
District Judge

Note: On October 27, 2015, the Senate confirmed Lawrence Joseph Vilardo to be District Judge for the United States District Court for the Western District of New York.
Education: Canisius 1977 BA; Harvard 1980 JD
Began Service: 2015
Appointed By: President Barack Obama

Chambers of Senior Judge John T. Curtin
Robert H. Jackson U.S. Courthouse, 2 Niagara Square, Room 774, Buffalo, NY 14202
Tel: (716) 551-1830 Fax: (716) 332-7835
E-mail: john_curtin@nywd.uscourts.gov

John T. Curtin
Senior Judge

Date of Birth: 1921
Education: Canisius 1946 BS; SUNY (Buffalo) 1949 LLB
Began Service: December 23, 1967
Appointed By: President Lyndon B. Johnson
Political Affiliation: Democrat

Government: United States Attorney, Western District of New York, United States Department of Justice (1961-1967)

Legal Practice: Sole Practitioner (1949-1961)

Military Service: United States Marine Corps Reserve (1942-1945); United States Marine Corps Reserve (1952-1954)

Current Memberships: American Bar Association; Erie County Bar Association (NY); New York State Bar Association

Chambers of Senior Judge John T. Curtin *continued*

Staff
Career Law Clerk **Karen McMahon** .... (716) 551-1830
E-mail: karen_mcmahon@nywd.uscourts.gov
Education: SUNY (Buffalo) BA, 1986 JD
Career Law Clerk **William C. Schoellkopf** .... (716) 551-1830
E-mail: william_schoellkopf@nywd.uscourts.gov
Education: Siena Col 1972 BA; SUNY (Buffalo) 1987 JD
Judicial Assistant **Janet E. Curry** .... (716) 551-1830
E-mail: janet_curry@nywd.uscourts.gov
Education: SUNY (Buffalo) 1985 BS

Chambers of Senior Judge Michael A. Telesca

272 U.S. Courthouse, 100 State Street, Rochester, NY 14614
Tel: (585) 613-4060 Fax: (585) 613-4065
E-mail: michael_telesca@nywd.uscourts.gov

Michael A. Telesca
Senior Judge

Date of Birth: 1929
Education: Rochester 1952 AB; SUNY (Buffalo) 1955 JD
Began Service: 1982
Appointed By: President Ronald Reagan
Political Affiliation: Republican

Affiliation: Senior Judge (R), Chambers of Senior Judge Michael A. Telesca, Alien Terrorist Removal Court

Judicial: Judge, Surrogate Court, Monroe County (1973-1982)

Legal Practice: Partner, Lamb, Webster, Walz & Telesca (1957-1973)

Military Service: United States Marine Corps (1955-1957)

Current Memberships: American Bar Association; The American Inns of Court; The Justinian Society of Jurists; Monroe County Bar Association (NY); New York State Bar Association

Staff
Law Clerk **Erin Tubbs** .... (585) 613-4067
Term Expires: October 2018
E-mail: erin_tubbs@nywd.uscourts.gov
Career Law Clerk **Andrea Basso** .... (585) 613-4067
E-mail: andrea_basso@nywd.uscourts.gov
Education: Vermont 1996 JD
Court Reporter **(Vacant)** .... (585) 613-4312
Secretary **Joan M. Countryman** .... (585) 613-4060
E-mail: joan_countryman@nywd.uscourts.gov

Chambers of Senior Judge David G. Larimer

250 U.S. Courthouse, 100 State Street, Rochester, NY 14614
Tel: (585) 613-4040 Fax: (585) 613-4045
E-mail: david_larimer@nywd.uscourts.gov

David G. Larimer
Senior Judge

Date of Birth: 1944
Education: St John Fisher 1966 BA; Notre Dame 1969 JD
Began Service: November 6, 1987
Appointed By: President Ronald Reagan
Political Affiliation: Republican

Clerkships: Law Clerk The Honorable Joseph C. McGarraghy (1969-1970)

Government: Assistant United States Attorney, Western District of New York, Office of the United States Attorney, United States Department of Justice (1970-1975); Chief Appellate Law Assistant, Appellate Division, United States Supreme Court (1979-1981); Personal Law Assistant, Appellate Division, United States Supreme Court (1982)

Judicial: Magistrate Judge, United States Court for the Western District of New York (1983-1987); Chief Judge, United States District Court for the Western District of New York

Chambers of Senior Judge David G. Larimer *continued*

Current Memberships: The District of Columbia Bar; Monroe County Bar Association (NY); New York State Bar Association

Staff
Career Law Clerk **David P. Chapus** .... (585) 613-4042
E-mail: david_chapus@nywd.uscourts.gov
Education: Georgetown 1983 BA; Buffalo 1986 JD
Career Law Clerk **Rayne Hammond-Benz** .... (585) 613-4043
Education: Grove City 1998 BA; Buffalo 2001 JD
Courtroom Deputy **Paula Rand** .... (585) 613-4044
E-mail: paula_rand@nywd.uscourts.gov
Secretary **Eileen M. Aleo** .... (585) 613-4041
E-mail: eileen_aleo@nywd.uscourts.gov

Chambers of Senior Judge Charles J. Siragusa

1360 U.S. Courthouse, 100 State Street, Rochester, NY 14614
Tel: (585) 613-4050 Fax: (585) 613-4055
E-mail: charles_siragusa@nywd.uscourts.gov

Charles J. Siragusa
Senior Judge

Date of Birth: 1947
Education: Le Moyne 1969 BA; Albany Law 1976 JD
Began Service: December 15, 1997
Appointed By: President William J. Clinton

Current Memberships: Federal Bar Association; Federal Judges Association; Monroe County Bar Association (NY)

Staff
Career Law Clerk **J. Michael Kehoe** .... (585) 613-4050
E-mail: michael_kehoe@nywd.uscourts.gov
Education: Vermont Law 1993 JD
Career Law Clerk **Mark W. Pedersen** .... (585) 613-4050
E-mail: mark_pedersen@nywd.uscourts.gov
Education: SUNY (Buffalo) 1982 JD
Courtroom Deputy Clerk **Kathy Allen** .... (585) 613-4054
E-mail: kathy_allen@nywd.uscourts.gov
Court Reporter **(Vacant)** .... (585) 613-4312
Judicial Assistant **Kelly A. Pruden** .... (585) 613-4050
E-mail: kelly_pruden@nywd.uscourts.gov
Education: SUNY (Geneseo) 1988 BA

Chambers of Senior Judge William M. Skretny

Robert H. Jackson United States Courthouse, 2 Niagara Square, Buffalo, NY 14202-3350
Tel: (716) 551-1820 Fax: (716) 551-1825
E-mail: william_skretny@nywd.uscourts.gov

William M. Skretny
Senior Judge

Date of Birth: 1945
Education: Canisius 1966 AB; Howard U 1969 JD; Northwestern 1972 LLM
Began Service: October 1, 1990
Appointed By: President George H.W. Bush
Political Affiliation: Republican

Current Memberships: Federal Judges Association

Staff
Law Clerk **Jennifer Phillips** .... (716) 551-1840
E-mail: jennifer_phillips@nywd.uscourts.gov
Career Law Clerk **Andrew W. Moeller** .... (716) 551-1822
E-mail: andrew_moeller@nywd.uscourts.gov
Education: Franklin Pierce Col 1999 JD; SUNY (Buffalo State Col) 1995 BSCrim
Courtroom Deputy **Mary E. Labuzzetta** .... (716) 551-1824
E-mail: mary_labuzzetta@nywd.uscourts.gov

(continued on next page)

Chambers of Senior Judge William M. Skretny *continued*

Court Reporter **Michelle L. McLaughlin** .... (716) 332-3560
E-mail: michelle_mclaughlin@nywd.uscourts.gov
Judicial Assistant **Jennifer Dzielski** .... (716) 551-1821
E-mail: jennifer_dzielski@nywd.uscourts.gov

Chambers of Senior Judge Richard J. Arcara

2 Niagara Square, Buffalo, NY 14202
Tel: (716) 551-1810
E-mail: richard_arcara@nywd.uscourts.gov

Richard J. Arcara
Senior Judge

Date of Birth: 1940
Education: St Bonaventure 1962 BA; Villanova 1965 JD
Began Service: June 1, 1988
Appointed By: President Ronald Reagan
Political Affiliation: Republican

Current Memberships: National Association of Former United States Attorneys

Staff

Law Clerk **Molly Miranda** .... (716) 551-1810
E-mail: molly_miranda@nywd.uscourts.gov
Career Law Clerk **William J. Gillmeister** .... (716) 551-1810
E-mail: william_gillmeister@nywd.uscourts.gov
Education: SUNY (Buffalo) 1984 JD
Courtroom Deputy **Denise J. Daniels** .... (716) 551-1810
E-mail: denise_daniels@nywd.uscourts.gov
Education: Buffalo 1976 BA
Judicial Assistant **Lisa Staff** .... (716) 551-1810

Chambers of Magistrate Judge Jonathan W. Feldman

2330 U.S. Courthouse, 100 State Street, Rochester, NY 14614
Tel: (585) 613-4070 Fax: (585) 613-4075
E-mail: jonathan_feldman@nywd.uscourts.gov

Jonathan W. Feldman
Magistrate Judge

Date of Birth: 1956
Education: Cornell 1978 BA; Syracuse 1981 JD
Began Service: November 1995
Term Expires: November 2019

Clerkships: Law Clerk The Honorable Michael A. Telesca, United States District Court for the Western District of New York

Government: Assistant United States Attorney, Western District of New York, Office of the United States Attorney, United States Department of Justice; Federal Public Defender, Western District of New York, United States Department of Justice

Legal Practice: Associate, Harris, Beach & Wilcox; Geraci & Feldman

Staff

Career Law Clerk **Carey Ann Denefrio** .... (585) 613-4072
E-mail: careyann_denefrio@nywd.uscourts.gov
Education: Boston Col BA; Albany Law JD
Law Clerk **Lisa Schmidt** .... (585) 613-4073
E-mail: lisa_schmidt@nywd.uscourts.gov

Chambers of Magistrate Judge H. Kenneth Schroeder, Jr.

Robert H. Jackson U.S. Courthouse, 2 Niagara Square, Room 593, Buffalo, NY 14202-3498
Tel: (716) 551-1870 Fax: (716) 551-3305

H. Kenneth Schroeder, Jr.
Magistrate Judge

Education: Canisius 1958 BS; SUNY (Buffalo) 1961 JD; Georgetown 1962 LLM
Began Service: June 1, 2000
Term Expires: June 2016

Government: Trial Attorney, United States Department of Justice (1962-1963); Special Assistant United States Attorney, District of Columbia, United States Department of Justice (1963); United States Attorney, Western District of New York, United States Department of Justice (1969-1972)

Legal Practice: Trial Attorney, Hodgson Russ Andrews Woods & Goodyear LLP

Staff

Career Law Clerk **Allison P. Gioia** .... (716) 551-1870
E-mail: allison_gioia@nywd.uscourts.gov
Education: Albany Law 1997 JD
Career Law Clerk **Karen E. Richardson** .... (716) 551-1870
E-mail: karen_richardson@nywd.uscourts.gov
Education: SUNY (Buffalo) 1997 JD
Courtroom Deputy **Llane Guidotti** .... (716) 551-1870
E-mail: llane_guidotti@nywd.uscourts.gov

Chambers of Magistrate Judge Marian W. Payson

2310 U.S. Courthouse, 100 State Street, Rochester, NY 14614
Tel: (585) 613-4080 Fax: (585) 613-4085
E-mail: marian_payson@nywd.uscourts.gov

Marian W. Payson
Magistrate Judge

Date of Birth: 1959
Education: Duke 1981 BA; Northwestern 1984 JD
Began Service: April 14, 2003
Term Expires: April 13, 2019

Government: Assistant U.S. Attorney, Criminal Division, New York - Southern District, United States Department of Justice (1990-1994); Deputy Chief Appellate Attorney, Civil Division, New York - Southern District, United States Department of Justice (1994-1996)

Legal Practice: Litigation Associate, Debevoise & Plimpton LLP (1985-1989)

Current Memberships: American Bar Foundation; American Bar Association; The Association of the Bar of the City of New York; Greater Rochester Association for Women Attorneys; Monroe County Bar Association (NY); New York State Bar Association

Staff

Career Law Clerk **Christin Murphy Cornetta** .... (585) 613-4080
E-mail: christin_cornetta@nywd.uscourts.gov
Courtroom Deputy **Catherine A. Marr** .... (585) 613-4084
Judicial Secretary **Kimberly A. Hardies** .... (585) 613-4080
E-mail: kimberly_hardies@nywd.uscourts.gov

Chambers of Magistrate Judge Jeremiah J. McCarthy
643 Court Street, Buffalo, NY 14202
Tel: (716) 551-1880
E-mail: jeremiah_mccarthy@nywd.uscourts.gov

Jeremiah J. McCarthy
Magistrate Judge

Education: Notre Dame 1974 AB; Cornell 1978 JD
Began Service: April 13, 2007

Staff
Courtroom Deputy **Christine Chiriboya** . . . . (716) 551-1884

Chambers of Magistrate Judge (Recalled) Leslie G. Foschio
Robert H. Jackson United States Courthouse, 2 Niagara Square, Room 724, Buffalo, NY 14202
Tel: (716) 551-1850 Fax: (716) 551-3855
E-mail: leslie_foschio@nywd.uscourts.gov

Leslie G. Foschio
Magistrate Judge (recalled)

Date of Birth: 1940
Education: Buffalo 1962 BA; SUNY (Buffalo) 1965 LLB
Began Service: February 1, 1991
Term Expires: January 31, 2016
Political Affiliation: Democrat

Current Memberships: American Bar Foundation; Bar Association of Erie County; Federal Magistrate Judges Association; New York Bar Foundation, New York State Bar Association

Staff
Career Law Clerk (part-time) **Rebecca McCauley** . . . . (716) 551-1850
E-mail: rebecca_mccauley@nywd.uscourts.gov
Education: Ithaca 1985 SB; Cornell 1999 PMD; SUNY (Buffalo) 2003 Dr Jur
Career Law Clerk (part-time) **Thérèse A. Hopkins** . . . . . . (716) 551-1850
E-mail: therese_hopkins@nywd.uscourts.gov
Education: SUNY (Buffalo) 1994 JD
Secretary **Sandra D. Wilson** . . . . (716) 551-1850
E-mail: sandra_wilson@nywd.uscourts.gov

United States Bankruptcy Court for the Western District of New York
Olympic Towers, 300 Pearl Street, Suite 250, Buffalo, NY 14202-2501
100 State Street, Rochester, NY 14614
Tel: (585) 613-4200 (Rochester) Tel: (716) 362-3200 (Buffalo)
Tel: (716) 362-3201 (Voice Case Information System VCIS)
Tel: (866) 222-8029 (Toll Free Voice Case Information System VCIS)
Internet: www.nywb.uscourts.gov

Number of Judgeships: 3

Court Staff
Clerk of the Court **Lisa Bertino-Beaser** . . . . (716) 362-3200 (Buffalo)
Education: SUNY (Buffalo) 2000 JD Tel: (585) 613-4200 (Rochester)
Chief Deputy Clerk **Michael Powers** . . . . (585) 613-4223

Chambers of Chief Bankruptcy Judge Carl L. Bucki
Olympic Towers, 300 Pearl Street, Suite 350, Buffalo, NY 14202-2510
Tel: (716) 362-3281

Carl L. Bucki
Chief Bankruptcy Judge

Date of Birth: 1953
Education: Cornell 1974 BA, 1976 JD
Began Service: December 30, 1993
Term Expires: December 2021

Clerkships: Law Clerk The Honorable Matthew J. Jasen, New York Court of Appeals

Legal Practice: Associate, Moot & Sprague; Partner, Cohen Swados Wright Hanifin Bradford & Brett, LLP (1990-1993)

Current Memberships: American Bar Association; Erie County Bar Association (NY); New York State Bar Association

Staff
Career Law Clerk **Adolph C. Iannaccone** . . . . (716) 362-3282
E-mail: adolph_iannaccone@nywb.uscourts.gov
Education: Boston Col 1972 AB; Rutgers (Newark) 1975 JD; Jesuit Berkeley 1987 MDiv
Secretary **Marcia A. Bannister** . . . . (716) 362-3281
E-mail: marcia_bannister@nywb.uscourts.gov

Chambers of Bankruptcy Judge Michael J. Kaplan
Olympic Towers, 300 Pearl Street, Suite 350, Buffalo, NY 14202-2501
Tel: (716) 362-3271

Michael J. Kaplan
Bankruptcy Judge

Date of Birth: 1947
Education: Columbia 1968 BA; Boston U 1971 JD
Began Service: October 7, 1991
Term Expires: October 6, 2019

Academic: Adjunct Assistant Professor of Business Law, Monroe Community College (1973-1979); Adjunct Faculty of Business Law, Rochester Institute of Technology (1979-1981)

Corporate: Senior Editor, Lawyers Co-Operative Publishing Company (1981)

Government: Bankruptcy Clerk, United States Bankruptcy Court for the Western District of New York (1981-1988); Clerk of the Court, United States District Courts (1988-1991)

Legal Practice: Private Practice (1974-1981)

Current Memberships: Erie County Bar Association (NY); National Conference of Bankruptcy Judges

Staff
Career Law Clerk **Christopher K. Reed** . . . . (716) 362-3272
E-mail: christopher_k_reed@nywb.uscourts.gov
Education: SUNY (Buffalo) 1982 JD
Secretary **Christine Klimko** . . . . (716) 362-3271
E-mail: christine_klimko@nywb.uscourts.gov

Chambers of Bankruptcy Judge Paul R. Warren
100 State Street, Rochester, NY 14614
Tel: (585) 613-4250

Paul R. Warren
Bankruptcy Judge

Education: St John Fisher 1979 BA; Dayton 1982 JD

Staff
Law Clerk **Melanie Bailey** . . . . (585) 613-4253
Law Clerk **Jane Marie Lewis** . . . . (585) 613-4251
Courtroom Deputy **Tina Folwell** . . . . (585) 613-4214

United States District Court for the Eastern District of North Carolina

Terry Sanford Federal Building, 310 New Bern Avenue,
Raleigh, NC 27601
P.O. Box 25670, Raleigh, NC 27611
Tel: (919) 645-1700 Tel: (919) 856-4768 (Civil Cases PACER)
Fax: (919) 645-1750
Internet: www.nced.uscourts.gov

Number of Judgeships: 4

Number of Vacancies: 1

Circuit: Fourth

Areas Covered: Counties of Beaufort, Bertie, Bladen, Brunswick, Camden, Chowan, Columbus, Craven, Cumberland, Currituck, Dare, Duplin, Edgecombe, Franklin, Gates, Granville, Greene, Halifax, Harnett, Hertford, Hyde, Johnson, Sones, Lenoir, Martin, Nash, New Hanover, Northampton, Onslow, Pamlico, Pasquotank, Pender, Perquimans, Pitt, Robeson, Sampson, Tyrrell, Vance, Wake, Warren, Washington, Wayne and Wilson

Court Staff

Clerk of Court **Julie Richards Johnston** .... (919) 645-1700
E-mail: julie_richards@nced.uscourts.gov
Deputy Clerk - Greenville **Lisa Lee** .... (252) 830-2331
201 S. Evans St., Rm. 209, Greenville, NC 27858-1137 Fax: (252) 830-2790
E-mail: lisa_lee@nced.uscourts.gov
Deputy Clerk - Wilmington **Susan Edwards** .... (910) 815-4663
P.O. Box 338, Wilmington, NC 28402 Fax: (910) 815-4518
E-mail: Susan_Edwards@nced.uscourts.gov
Chief Probation Officer **James Corpening** .... (919) 861-8660
Fax: (919) 861-5555
Deputy Clerk - New Bern **Lenora Fogle** .... (252) 638-8534
E-mail: lenora_fogle@nced.uscourts.gov

Chambers of Chief Judge James C. Dever III

310 New Bern Avenue, Raleigh, NC 27601
P.O. Box 25670, Raleigh, NC 27611
Tel: (919) 645-6570 Fax: (919) 856-4009
E-mail: james_dever@nced.uscourts.gov

James C. Dever III
Chief Judge

Date of Birth: May 25, 1962
Education: Notre Dame 1984 BBA; Duke 1987 JD
Began Service: May 3, 2005
Appointed By: President George W. Bush

Current Memberships: American Bar Association; North Carolina Bar Association

Staff

Law Clerk **Lyndsey Haas** .... (919) 645-6570
Began Service: August 2015
Term Expires: August 2016
Law Clerk **Matthew Patrick O'Sullivan** .... (919) 645-6570
Began Service: October 2015
Term Expires: October 2016
Case Manager - Civil **(Vacant)** .... (919) 645-1728
Case Manager - Criminal **Crystal Jenkins** .... (919) 645-1728
Judicial Assistant **Lyndsay Duté Hayes** .... (919) 645-6570
E-mail: documents_Judge_Dever@nced.uscourts.gov

Chambers of District Judge Terrence W. Boyle

Federal Building, 306 East Main Street, Elizabeth City, NC 27909
Tel: (252) 338-4033 Fax: (252) 338-2471
E-mail: terrence_boyle@nced.uscourts.gov

Terrence W. Boyle
District Judge

Date of Birth: 1945
Education: Brown U 1967 AB; Washington College of Law 1970 JD
Began Service: January 1, 1984
Appointed By: President Ronald Reagan

Government: Staff Assistant, Committee on Banking and Currency, United States House of Representatives (1968-1970); Minority Counsel, Committee on Banking and Currency, United States House of Representatives (1970-1973); Legislative Assistant (D-NC), Office of Senator Jesse Helms, United States Senate (1973-1974)

Legal Practice: LeRoy, Wells, Shaw, Hornthal & Riley (1974-1984)

Staff

Law Clerk **Lucy Partain** .... (252) 338-4033
Began Service: September 2015
Term Expires: September 2016
E-mail: Lucy_partain@nced.uscourts.gov
Career Law Clerk **India White** .... (252) 338-4033
Began Service: September 2011
E-mail: india_white@nced.uscourts.gov
Case Manager - Criminal **Linda Downing** .... (919) 645-1732
Case Manager - Civil **Lindsay Romine** .... (919) 645-1738
Secretary **Gladys S. Brothers** .... (252) 338-4033
E-mail: gladys_brothers@nced.uscourts.gov

Chambers of District Judge Louise W. Flanagan

413 Middle Street, New Bern, NC 28560
Tel: (252) 638-3068 Fax: (252) 637-9143

Louise W. Flanagan
District Judge

Date of Birth: 1962
Education: Wake Forest 1984 BA; Virginia 1988 JD
Began Service: July 21, 2003
Appointed By: President George W. Bush

Staff

Law Clerk **Ian Erickson** .... (252) 638-3068
E-mail: ian_erickson@nced.uscourts.gov
Education: North Carolina 1998 BA, 2001 JD
Law Clerk **Bradley Harder** .... (252) 638-3068
E-mail: bradley_harder@nced.uscourts.gov
Law Clerk **Christopher Edwards** .... (252) 638-3068
E-mail: christopher_edwards@nced.uscourts.gov
Case Manager - Prisoner **Marsha Castania** .... (252) 638-8534
Case Manager - Criminal **Susan Tripp** .... (252) 638-8534
Case Manager - Civil **Christa Baker** .... (252) 638-8534

Chambers of Senior Judge W. Earl Britt

310 New Bern Avenue, Raleigh, NC 27601
P.O. Box 27504, Raleigh, NC 27611
Tel: (919) 645-1745 Fax: (919) 645-1753
E-mail: W_Earl_Britt@nced.uscourts.gov

W. Earl Britt
Senior Judge

Date of Birth: 1932
Education: Campbell 1952 AA; Wake Forest 1956 BS, 1958 LLB
Began Service: 1980
Appointed By: President Jimmy Carter
Political Affiliation: Democrat

Clerkships: Law Clerk The Honorable Emery B. Denny, North Carolina Supreme Court (1958-1959)

Legal Practice: Private Practice (1959-1973); Partner, Page & Britt (1973-1980)

Military Service: United States Army (1953-1955)

Current Memberships: Federal Judges Association; North Carolina Bar Association

Staff
Law Clerk **Amanda Avery** .... (919) 645-1748
E-mail: amanda_avery@nced.uscourts.gov
Career Law Clerk **Amy C. Petty** .... (919) 645-1799
E-mail: amy_petty@nced.uscourts.gov
Education: North Carolina 1988 BS; Campbell 1994 JD
Case Manager - Criminal and Civil **Keah Marsh** .... (919) 645-1700

Chambers of Senior Judge James C. Fox

Alton Lennon Federal Building, Two Princess Street, Wilmington, NC 28401
P.O. Box 2143, Wilmington, NC 28402
Tel: (910) 815-4738 Fax: (910) 815-4628
E-mail: james_fox@nced.uscourts.gov

James C. Fox
Senior Judge

Date of Birth: 1928
Education: North Carolina 1950 BS, 1957 JD
Began Service: September 30, 1982
Appointed By: President Ronald Reagan
Political Affiliation: Republican

Clerkships: Law Clerk The Honorable Don Gilliam, United States District Court of the Eastern District of North Carolina (1957-1958)

Corporate: Vice President and General Manager, Dillard Paper Company (1952-1954)

Government: County Attorney, County of New Hanover, North Carolina (1967-1981)

Legal Practice: Associate, Carter & Murchison (1958-1959); Partner, Murchison, Fox & Newton (1960-1982)

Military Service: United States Army Reserve, United States Department of the Army (1951-1959)

Staff
Law Clerk **Ryan Fairchild** .... (910) 815-4738
Began Service: August 2014
Term Expires: August 2016
E-mail: ryan_fairchild@nced.uscourts.gov
Career Law Clerk **Alyssa Hockaday** .... (910) 815-4738
E-mail: alyssa_hockaday@nced.uscourts.gov
Education: North Carolina 2003 JD
Career Law Clerk **Ashley Maddox** .... (910) 815-4738
E-mail: ashley_maddox@nced.uscourts.gov
Education: Campbell 1998 BA, 2001 JD
Case Manager - Civil **Susan Edwards** .... (252) 830-6009
Case Manager - Criminal **Shelia Foell** .... (252) 830-6009

Chambers of Senior Judge Malcolm J. Howard

U.S. Courthouse, 201 South Evans Street, Greenville, NC 27858-1137
P.O. Box 5006, Greenville, NC 27835
Tel: (252) 830-4990 Fax: (252) 830-0102
E-mail: malcolm_howard@nced.uscourts.gov

Malcolm J. Howard
Senior Judge

Date of Birth: 1939
Education: West Point 1962 BS; Wake Forest 1970 JD
Began Service: March 11, 1988
Appointed By: President Ronald Reagan

Government: Assistant United States Attorney, Eastern District of North Carolina, Office of the United States Attorney, United States Department of Justice (1973-1974); Deputy Special Counsel to the President, Executive Office of the President (1974)

Legal Practice: Partner, Howard, Browning, Sams & Poole (1975-1988)

Military Service: United States Army (1962-1972); United States Army Reserve, United States Department of the Army (1972-1982)

Staff
Law Clerk **Jacob Warner** .... (252) 830-4990
Began Service: November 2014
Term Expires: November 2016
E-mail: jacob_warner@nced.uscourts.gov
Career Law Clerk **Stacey Wiggins** .... (252) 830-4990
Began Service: 2003
E-mail: stacey_wiggins@nced.uscourts.gov
Education: North Carolina 2003 JD
Case Manager - Criminal **Lisa Lee** .... (252) 830-6009
Case Manager - Civil **Donna Rudd** .... (252) 830-6009
Judicial Assistant **Carol Leccesse** .... (252) 830-4990
E-mail: carol_leccesse@nced.uscourts.gov

Chambers of Magistrate Judge James E. Gates

310 New Bern Avenue, Raleigh, NC 27601
Tel: (919) 645-1790 Fax: (919) 645-1751
E-mail: james_gates@nced.uscourts.gov

James E. Gates
Magistrate Judge

Education: Ursinus 1977 BA; Georgetown 1981 JD
Began Service: 2006

Staff
Career Law Clerk **Melynda G. Broomfield** .... (919) 645-1790
E-mail: melynda_broomfield@nced.uscourts.gov
Education: Boston U 1996 JD
Career Law Clerk **Candace Murphy-Farmer** .... (919) 645-1790
Case Manager **Shari Powers** .... (919) 645-1734

Chambers of Magistrate Judge Robert B. Jones, Jr.

Alton Lennon Federal Building, Two Princess Street, Wilmington, NC 28401
Tel: (910) 815-4663
E-mail: robert_jones@nced.uscourts.gov

Robert B. Jones, Jr.
Magistrate Judge

Education: Davidson 1991 BA; Campbell 1997 JD
Began Service: October 12, 2007

Staff
Case Manager **Liz Eggleston** .... (910) 815-4663

Chambers of Magistrate Judge Kimberly A. Swank
201 South Evans Street, Greenville, NC 27858-1137
Tel: (252) 830-6009

Kimberly A. Swank
Magistrate Judge

Education: Campbell 1991 JD

Chambers of Magistrate Judge Robert T. Numbers II
310 New Bern Avenue, Raleigh, NC 27601
Tel: (919) 645-1714

Robert T. Numbers II
Magistrate Judge

Education: Wake Forest 2002 BA; Notre Dame 2005 JD

Staff
Courtroom Deputy **Lauren Herrmann** . . . . . (919) 645-1714

United States Bankruptcy Court for the Eastern District of North Carolina
150 Reade Circle, Greenville, NC 27858
Tel: (919) 856-4752
Tel: (866) 222-8029 (Voice Case Information System VCIS)
Internet: www.nceb.uscourts.gov

Number of Judgeships: 3

Court Staff
Clerk of the Court **Stephanie J. Edmondson** . . . . . (919) 856-4752
E-mail: stephanie_edmondson@nceb.uscourts.gov Fax: (252) 243-4870
Chief Deputy Clerk **Christine A. Castelloe** . . . . . (919) 856-4752
E-mail: christine_castelloe@nceb.uscourts.gov Fax: (252) 243-4870
Case Management/ Administrative Supervisor
Carolyn Baker . . . . . (919) 856-4752
Director, Information Technology **(Vacant)** . . . . . (252) 237-0248
Fax: (252) 243-4870
Financial Specialist **Terry McKeel** . . . . . (919) 237-0248
Fax: (252) 243-4870
Budget Analyst **Heather Nichols** . . . . . (252) 237-0248
E-mail: heather_nichols@nceb.uscourts.gov
Personnel Specialist **Heather Nichols** . . . . . (252) 237-0248
E-mail: heather_nichols@nceb.uscourts.gov Fax: (252) 243-4870
Training Specialist **(Vacant)** . . . . . (252) 237-0248 ext. 124
Fax: (252) 243-4870
Courtroom Deputy Clerk **Anne Moell** . . . . . (919) 856-4752 ext. 101
E-mail: anne_moell@nceb.uscourts.gov
Courtroom Deputy Clerk **Allyson McNeill** . . . . . (919) 856-4752 ext. 126
E-mail: allyson_mcneill@nceb.uscourts.gov
Courtroom Deputy Clerk **Sharon Angel** . . . . . (252) 237-0248 ext. 162
Property/Procurement Administrator
Chris Boswell . . . . . (252) 237-0248 ext. 150
E-mail: chris_boswell@nceb.uscourts.gov

Chambers of Bankruptcy Judge Stephani Humrickhouse
300 Fayetteville Street, Second Floor, Raleigh, NC 27601-1799
Tel: (919) 856-4194

Stephani Humrickhouse
Bankruptcy Judge

Education: Cornell BA; North Carolina JD
Began Service: 2010

Staff
Career Law Clerk **Bess Hilliard** . . . . . (919) 856-4194
Staff Attorney **Tracy Davis** . . . . . (919) 856-4194
E-mail: tracy_davis@nceb.uscourts.gov
Education: North Carolina 1988 BA, 1992 JD

Chambers of Bankruptcy Judge Stephani Humrickhouse *continued*

Judicial Assistant (Acting) **Cathy S. Barnes** . . . . . (919) 856-4194
E-mail: cathy_barnes@nceb.uscourts.gov
Education: Campbell BS

Chambers of Bankruptcy Judge David M. Warren
150 Reade Circle, Greenville, NC 27858
Tel: (919) 856-4033

David M. Warren
Bankruptcy Judge

Staff
Judicial Assistant **Cathy S. Barnes** . . . . . (919) 856-4033
E-mail: cathy_barnes@nceb.uscourts.gov

United States District Court for the Middle District of North Carolina
324 West Market Street, Room 401, Greensboro, NC 27401
P.O. Box 2708, Greensboro, NC 27402
Tel: (336) 332-6000 Tel: (336) 332-6010 (PACER)
Fax: (336) 332-6060
Internet: www.ncmd.uscourts.gov

Number of Judgeships: 4

Circuit: Fourth

Areas Covered: Counties of Alamance, Cabarrus, Caswell, Chatham, Davidson, Davie, Durham, Forsyth, Guilford, Hoke, Lee, Montgomery, Moore, Orange, Person, Randolph, Richmond, Rockingham, Rowan, Scotland, Stanly, Stokes, Surry and Yadkin

Court Staff
Clerk of Court **John Brubaker** . . . . . (336) 332-6000
E-mail: john_brubaker@ncmd.uscourts.gov
Financial Administrator **Sandra "Sandy" Carter** . . . . . (336) 332-6016
E-mail: sandy_carter@ncmd.uscourts.gov Fax: (336) 332-6029
Docket Clerk Supervisor **Lisa Israel** . . . . . (336) 332-6052
E-mail: lisa_israel@ncmd.uscourts.gov
Chief Probation Officer **Melissa Alexander** . . . . . (336) 333-5341
101 South Edgeworth Street, Suite R312,
Greensboro, NC 27402
External Operations Manager **Gloria Powell** . . . . . (336) 332-6035
E-mail: gloria_powell@ncmd.uscourts.gov
Director, Court Information Systems **Grady Franklin** . . . . . (336) 332-6021
E-mail: grady_franklin@ncmd.uscourts.gov
Personnel Specialist, Mediation Coordinator and Secretary to Clerk **Cheryl Gammon** . . . . . (336) 332-6013
E-mail: Cheryl_Gammon@ncmd.uscourts.gov

Chambers of Chief Judge William Lindsay Osteen, Jr.
324 West Market Street, Room 401, Greensboro, NC 27401
Tel: (336) 332-6090

William Lindsay Osteen, Jr.
Chief Judge

Date of Birth: 1960
Education: North Carolina 1983 BS, 1987 JD
Began Service: September 19, 2007
Appointed By: President George W. Bush

Staff
Law Clerk **Christina Phillips** . . . . . (336) 332-6090
Began Service: September 2015
Term Expires: September 2016
E-mail: christina_phillips@ncmd.uscourts.gov
Law Clerk **Zack Dawson** . . . . . (336) 332-6090
Began Service: September 2015
Term Expires: September 2016
E-mail: zack_dawson@ncmd.uscourts.gov

Chambers of Chief Judge William Lindsay Osteen, Jr. *continued*

Judicial Assistant **Frances Cable** .... (336) 332-6090
E-mail: frances_cable@ncmd.uscourts.gov

Chambers of District Judge Thomas D. Schroeder

251 North Main Street, Winston-Salem, NC 27101
Tel: (336) 734-2530

Judge Thomas David Schroeder
District Judge

Date of Birth: 1959
Education: Kansas 1981 BS; Notre Dame 1984 JD
Began Service: January 2008
Appointed By: President George W. Bush

Clerkships: Law Clerk, Chambers of Circuit Judge George E. MacKinnon, United States Court of Appeals for the District of Columbia Circuit (1984-1985)

Legal Practice: Associate, Womble Carlyle Sandridge & Rice, PLLC (1985-1991); Partner, Womble Carlyle Sandridge & Rice, PLLC (1991-2007)

Staff

Law Clerk **Troy Shelton** .... (336) 734-2530
Began Service: 2015
Law Clerk **Nicholas Deuschle** .... (336) 734-2530
Judicial Assistant **Kathy Stevenson** .... (336) 734-2530

Chambers of District Judge Catherine C. Eagles

324 West Market Street, Greensboro, NC 27401
Tel: (336) 332-6070

Catherine C. Eagles
District Judge

Began Service: December 23, 2010
Appointed By: President Barack Obama

Judicial: Senior Resident Superior Court Judge, Chambers of Senior Resident Superior Court Judge Catherine C. Eagles, Judicial District 18, Superior Court of North Carolina

Staff

Law Clerk **Kevin Denny** .... (336) 332-6073
Law Clerk **Nathan Harrill** .... (336) 332-6074
Judicial Assistant **Linda Bostick** .... (336) 332-6070
E-mail: linda_bostick@ncmd.uscourts.gov

Chambers of District Judge Loretta Copeland Biggs

251 North Main Street, Winston-Salem, NC 27101
Tel: (336) 726-2250

Loretta Copeland Biggs
District Judge

Date of Birth: 1954
Education: Spelman 1976 BA; Howard U 1979 JD
Began Service: 2014
Appointed By: President Barack Obama
Political Affiliation: Democrat

Government: Principal Advisor, Executive Office for United States Attorneys, United States Department of Justice (1994-1998); Executive Assistant U.S. Attorney, North Carolina - Middle District, Executive Office for United States Attorneys, United States Department of Justice (1998-2001)

Judicial: District Court Judge, Forsyth County District Court, County of Forsyth, North Carolina (1987-1994); Associate Judge, North Carolina Court of Appeals (2001-2002)

Chambers of District Judge Loretta Copeland Biggs *continued*

Staff

Law Clerk **Malan Cui** .... (336) 726-2250
Law Clerk **Jonathan Peterson** .... (336) 726-2250

Chambers of Senior Judge N. Carlton Tilley, Jr.

324 West Market Street, Greensboro, NC 27401
P.O. Box 3443, Greensboro, NC 27402-3443
Tel: (336) 332-6080 Fax: (336) 332-6085

Norwood Carlton "Woody" Tilley, Jr.
Senior Judge

Date of Birth: 1943
Education: Wake Forest 1966 BS, 1969 JD
Began Service: November 4, 1988
Appointed By: President Ronald Reagan

Current Memberships: American Bar Association; The Greensboro Bar Association, Inc.; North Carolina Academy of Trial Lawyers; The North Carolina State Bar

Staff

Law Clerk **Laura Dildine** .... (336) 332-6083
Began Service: August 2014
E-mail: gregory_knudsen@ncmd.uscourts.gov
Education: Wake Forest 2010 JD
Career Law Clerk **Caroline Carrison** .... (336) 332-6084
E-mail: caroline_carrison@ncmd.uscourts.gov
Court Reporter **Jane Allen-Calhoun** .... (336) 332-6033
Judicial Assistant **Sheila Blumke** .... (336) 332-6082
E-mail: sheila_blumke@ncmd.uscourts.gov

Chambers of Senior Judge James A. Beaty, Jr.

248 Hiram H. Ward Federal Building & U.S. Courthouse, 251 North Main Street, Winston-Salem, NC 27101
Tel: (336) 734-2540 Fax: (336) 631-5004

James A. Beaty, Jr.
Senior Judge

Date of Birth: 1949
Education: Western Carolina 1971 BA; North Carolina 1974 JD
Began Service: November 1, 1994
Appointed By: President William J. Clinton
Political Affiliation: Democrat

Current Memberships: Forsyth County Bar Association; North Carolina Association of Black Lawyers; North Carolina Bar Association; The North Carolina State Bar

Staff

Law Clerk **Ramona McGee** .... (336) 734-2540
Law Clerk **Janie R. Richardson** .... (336) 734-2540
E-mail: amber_melton@ncmd.uscourts.gov
Education: Ohio State 2012 JD
Judicial Assistant **Bonnie Fleming** .... (336) 734-2540
E-mail: bonnie_fleming@ncmd.uscourts.gov

Chambers of Magistrate Judge L. Patrick Auld

P.O. Box 3195, Greensboro, NC 27402
Tel: (336) 332-6120

L. Patrick Auld
Magistrate Judge

Began Service: 2010

Staff

Law Clerk **Jeremy Demmitt** .... (336) 332-6120
Began Service: August 2014
Term Expires: August 2016
E-mail: jeremy_demmitt@ncmd.uscourts.gov

(continued on next page)

Chambers of Magistrate Judge L. Patrick Auld *continued*

Law Clerk **Logan Starr** . . . . . (336) 734-2520
E-mail: logan_starr@ncmd.uscourts.gov

Chambers of Magistrate Judge Joi Peake

251 North Main Street, Winston-Salem, NC 27101
Tel: (336) 734-2520
E-mail: joi_peake@ncmd.uscourts.gov

Joi Peake
Magistrate Judge

Staff

Law Clerk **Gregory O. Spivey** . . . . . (336) 734-2520
Education: Campbell 1983 BS; Wake Forest 1988 JD

Law Clerk **Allison L. Bennett** . . . . . (336) 734-2520
E-mail: allison_bennett@ncmd.uscourts.gov
Education: Davidson 2000 BA; Wake Forest 2006 JD

Judicial Assistant **(Vacant)** . . . . . (336) 734-2520

Chambers of Magistrate Judge Joe L. Webster

333 East Chapel Hill Street, Durham, NC 27702
Tel: (919) 425-8900

Joe L. Webster
Magistrate Judge

Staff

Law Clerk **Pedra D. Lee** . . . . . (919) 425-8900
E-mail: pedra_lee@ncmd.uscourts.gov

Law Clerk **Patricia Jordan** . . . . . (919) 425-8900
E-mail: patti_jordan@ncmd.uscourts.gov

United States Bankruptcy Court for the Middle District of North Carolina

101 South Edgeworth Street, Greensboro, NC 27401
P.O. Box 26100, Greensboro, NC 27402-6100
Tel: (336) 358-4000
Tel: (866) 222-8029 (Voice Case Information System VCIS)
Internet: www.ncmb.uscourts.gov

Number of Judgeships: 3

Court Staff

Clerk of Court **Reid Wilcox** . . . . . (336) 358-4000
Education: North Carolina 1989 BA, 1993 JD

Chief Deputy **Jeanette M. Stark** . . . . . (336) 358-4000
Education: Wake Forest 2003 JD

Director of Automation **Joe Markley** . . . . . (336) 358-4000
Education: North Carolina Wesleyan 1986 BS; North Carolina Greensboro 1996 MBA

Chambers of Chief Bankruptcy Judge Catharine R. Aron

P.O. Box 448, Greensboro, NC 27402
101 South Edgeworth Street, Greensboro, NC 27401
Tel: (336) 358-4150 Fax: (336) 358-4095

Catharine R. Aron
Chief Bankruptcy Judge

Date of Birth: 1954
Education: Wake Forest 1980 JD
Began Service: July 24, 1995
Term Expires: July 24, 2023

Current Memberships: Forsyth County Bar Association; The North Carolina State Bar

Staff

Law Clerk **Julie Grimley** . . . . . (336) 358-4150
Began Service: September 2015
Term Expires: September 2016

Law Clerk **Pat Wallace** . . . . . (336) 358-4150
Began Service: September 2014
Term Expires: September 2016

Chambers of Bankruptcy Judge Benjamin A. Kahn

101 South Edgeworth Street, Greensboro, NC 27401
Tel: (336) 358-4018

Benjamin A. Kahn
Bankruptcy Judge

Staff

Law Clerk **Catherine Clodfelter** . . . . . (336) 358-4092
Law Clerk **(Vacant)** . . . . . (336) 358-4092
Courtroom Deputy **Karen Champagne** . . . . . (336) 358-4018

Chambers of Bankruptcy Judge Lena M. James

101 South Edgeworth Street, Greensboro, NC 27401
Tel: (336) 397-7789

Lena M. James
Bankruptcy Judge

Education: North Carolina 1998 JD

Staff

Law Clerk **Alana Williams** . . . . . (336) 397-7872
Education: Emory 1982 MBA, 1982 JD

Law Clerk **Rebecca Fiss** . . . . . (336) 397-7871
Courtroom Deputy **Janice Leonard** . . . . . (336) 397-7789

United States District Court for the Western District of North Carolina

Charles R. Jonas Federal Building, 401 West Trade Street, Room 212, Charlotte, NC 28202
Tel: (704) 350-7400 Fax: (704) 344-6703
Internet: www.ncwd.uscourts.gov

Number of Judgeships: 5

Circuit: Fourth

Areas Covered: Counties of Alexander, Alleghany, Anson, Ashe, Avery, Buncombe, Burke, Caldwell, Catawba, Cherokee, Clay, Cleveland, Gaston, Graham, Haywood, Henderson, Iredell, Jackson, Lincoln, Macon, Madison, McDowell, Mecklenburg, Mitchell, Polk, Rutherford, Swain, Transylvania, Union, Watauga, Wilkes and Yancey

United States District Court for the Western District of North Carolina
continued

Court Staff

Clerk of Court **Frank G. Johns** .... (704) 350-7413
Education: Denver 1980 JD

Chief Deputy Clerk **Terry Leitner** .... (704) 350-7416
E-mail: terry_leitner@ncwd.uscourts.gov
Education: North Carolina State 1979 BA

Deputy Clerk-in-Charge - Asheville
Tammy Hightower .... (828) 771-7200
309 U.S. Courthouse, 100 Otis St., Fax: (828) 271-4343
Asheville, NC 28801-2611
E-mail: tammy_hightower@ncwd.uscourts.gov

Deputy Clerk-in-Charge - Statesville **Susan Johnson** .... (704) 883-1002
200 W. Broad St., Statesville, NC 28677 Fax: (704) 873-0903
P.O. Box 466, Statesville, NC 28687
Education: Erskine 1975 BA

Chief Information Officer **Kent Creasy** .... (704) 350-7424
E-mail: kent_creasy@ncwd.uscourts.gov

Chief U.S. Probation Officer **Greg Forest** .... (704) 350-7608
200 South College Street, Suite 1650, Fax: (704) 344-6319
Charlotte, NC 28202-2005

Budget Analyst **Brittany Fickling** .... (704) 350-7417
E-mail: brittany_fickling@ncwd.uscourts.gov

Chambers of Chief Judge Frank D. Whitney

401 West Trade Street, Room 195, Charlotte, NC 28202
Tel: (704) 350-7480 Fax: (704) 350-7485
E-mail: frank_whitney@ncwd.uscourts.gov

Frank D. Whitney
Chief Judge

Date of Birth: November 1959
Education: Wake Forest 1982 BA; North Carolina 1987 MBA, 1987 JD
Began Service: July 2006
Appointed By: President George W. Bush

Staff

Law Clerk **(Vacant)** .... (704) 350-7480
Career Law Clerk **Tricia Magee** .... (704) 350-7480
E-mail: tricia_magee@ncwd.uscourts.gov
Judicial Assistant **Ruth Blackmon** .... (704) 350-7480
E-mail: ruth_blackmon@ncwd.uscourts.gov

Chambers of District Judge Robert J. Conrad, Jr.

401 West Trade Street, Room 235, Charlotte, NC 28202
Tel: (704) 350-7460 Fax: (704) 350-7469
E-mail: robert_conrad@ncwd.uscourts.gov

Robert J. Conrad, Jr.
District Judge

Education: Clemson 1980 BA; Virginia 1983 JD
Began Service: June 3, 2005
Appointed By: President George W. Bush

Staff

Career Law Clerk **TJ Haycox** .... (704) 350-7464
E-mail: tj_haycox@ncwd.uscourts.gov
Secretary **Gail Jackson** .... (704) 350-7462
E-mail: gail_jackson@ncwd.uscourts.gov

Chambers of District Judge Richard Lesley Voorhees

250 Charles R. Jonas Federal Building, 401 West Trade Street, Charlotte, NC 28202
Tel: (704) 350-7442 Fax: (704) 350-7447
E-mail: richard_voorhees@ncwd.uscourts.gov

Richard Lesley Voorhees
District Judge

Date of Birth: 1941
Education: Davidson 1963 BA; North Carolina 1968 JD
Began Service: October 28, 1988
Appointed By: President Ronald Reagan
Political Affiliation: Republican

Academic: Instructor (part-time), Gaston College (1980)

Government: Member, Board of Elections, County of Gaston, North Carolina (1970-1972)

Judicial: Chief Judge, United States District Court for the Western District of North Carolina (1991-1998); Chief Judge, United States District Court for the Western District of North Carolina (2006)

Legal Practice: Associate, Garland, Alala, Bradley & Gray; Partner, Garland & Alala (1974-1980); Richard L. Voorhees Law Firm (1980-1988)

Military Service: United States Army (1963-1965); United States Army Reserve, United States Department of the Army (1965-1969)

Current Memberships: Federal Judges Association; North Carolina Bar Association; The North Carolina State Bar

Staff

Law Clerk **Matthew Brandon Howard** .... (704) 350-7440
Began Service: September 2015
Term Expires: August 31, 2016
E-mail: matthew_howard@ncwd.uscourts.gov
Career Law Clerk **Kelly Goodrich** .... (704) 350-7440
E-mail: kelly_goodrich@ncwd.uscourts.gov
Education: Campbell 1999 JD
Court Reporter **Cheryl Nuccio** .... (704) 350-7494
E-mail: cheryl_nuccio@ncwd.uscourts.gov
Judicial Assistant **Terry Gibson** .... (704) 350-7442
E-mail: Terry_Gibson@ncwd.uscourts.gov

Chambers of District Judge Martin Karl Reidinger

U.S. Courthouse Building, 100 Otis Street, Asheville, NC 28801
Tel: (828) 771-7260 Fax: (828) 771-7265
E-mail: martin_reidinger@ncwd.uscourts.gov

Martin Karl Reidinger
District Judge

Date of Birth: 1958
Education: North Carolina 1981 BS, 1984 JD
Began Service: September 17, 2007
Appointed By: President George W. Bush

Legal Practice: Associate, Adams Hendon Carson Crow & Saenger, P.A. (1984-1989); Shareholder, Adams Hendon Carson Crow & Saenger, P.A. (1989-2007)

Staff

Career Law Clerk **Lori Ritter** .... (828) 771-7260
E-mail: lori_ritter@ncwd.uscourts.gov
Education: Tennessee Tech 1994 BS; Tennessee 1999 JD
Administrative Law Clerk **Adam Peoples** .... (828) 771-7260
Courtroom Deputy **Karen Miller** .... (828) 771-7260
E-mail: nancy_day@ncwd.uscourts.gov

Chambers of District Judge Max O. Cogburn, Jr.

100 U.S. Courthouse Building, 100 Otis Street, Asheville, NC 28801
Tel: (828) 771-7250
E-mail: max_cogburn@ncwd.uscourts.gov

Max Oliver Cogburn, Jr.
District Judge

Date of Birth: 1951
Education: North Carolina 1973 AB; Cumberland 1976 JD
Began Service: March 14, 2011
Appointed By: President Barack Obama

Judicial: Magistrate Judge, Chambers of Magistrate Judge Max O. Cogburn, United States District Court for the Western District of North Carolina (1995-2004)

Legal Practice: Partner, Cogburn, Cogburn, Goosmann & Brazil, P.A. (1995); Partner, Cogburn, Goosmann, Brazil & Rose, P.A. (2004-2006); Partner, Cogburn & Brazil, P.A. (2006-2011)

Current Memberships: American Bar Association; North Carolina Bar Association; The North Carolina State Bar

Staff

Career Law Clerk **David K. Davis** .... (828) 771-7250
E-mail: david_davis@ncwd.uscourts.gov
Education: Campbell 1988 JD

Judicial Assistant **Kathy Lancaster** .... (828) 771-7250
E-mail: kathy_lancaster@ncwd.uscourts.gov

Chambers of Senior Judge Graham C. Mullen

Charles R. Jonas Federal Building, 401 West Trade Street, Room 230, Charlotte, NC 28202
Tel: (704) 350-7450 Fax: (704) 350-7456
E-mail: Graham_Mullen@ncwd.uscourts.gov

Graham C. Mullen
Senior Judge

Date of Birth: 1940
Education: Duke 1962 BA, 1969 JD
Began Service: October 25, 1990
Appointed By: President George H.W. Bush
Political Affiliation: Republican

Judicial: Chief Judge, United States District Court for the Western District of North Carolina

Legal Practice: Partner, Mullen, Holland, Cooper, Morrow, Wilder & Sumner (1969-1990)

Military Service: United States Navy (1962-1966)

Current Memberships: Mecklenburg County Bar Association; The North Carolina State Bar

Staff

Law Clerk **Mary Pat Dwyer** .... (704) 350-7454
Began Service: October 2015
Term Expires: August 2016

Career Law Clerk **Debbie Q. Coble** .... (704) 350-7453
E-mail: debbie_coble@ncwd.uscourts.gov
Education: North Carolina Charlotte 1988 BA; North Carolina 1991 JD

Judicial Assistant **Suzanne Barber** .... (704) 350-7450
E-mail: Suzanne_Barber@ncwd.uscourts.gov

Chambers of Magistrate Judge David C. Keesler

Charles R. Jonas Federal Building, 401 West Trade Street, Room 238, Charlotte, NC 28202
Tel: (704) 350-7430 Fax: (704) 350-7435
E-mail: David_Keesler@ncwd.uscourts.gov

David C. Keesler
Magistrate Judge

Date of Birth: July 10, 1962
Education: North Carolina 1984 BA; Virginia 1987 JD
Began Service: May 3, 2004
Term Expires: May 30, 2020

Current Memberships: American Bar Association; Mecklenburg County Bar Association; North Carolina Bar Association

Staff

Career Law Clerk **Andrew D. Taylor III** .... (704) 350-7433
Began Service: January 1, 2010
E-mail: dustin_taylor@ncwd.uscourts.gov
Education: Vermont 2004 JD

Judicial Assistant **Karen A. Burton** .... (704) 350-7432
E-mail: karen_burton@ncwd.uscourts.gov

Chambers of Magistrate Judge David S. Cayer

168 Charles R. Jonas Federal Building, 401 West Trade Street, Charlotte, NC 28202
Tel: (704) 350-7470
E-mail: david_cayer@ncwd.uscourts.gov

David S. Cayer
Magistrate Judge

Began Service: 2009

Staff

Law Clerk **Kristen Arnold** .... (704) 350-7470

Career Law Clerk **David L. Grigg, Jr.** .... (704) 350-7473
E-mail: david_grigg@ncwd.uscourts.gov Fax: (704) 350-7474
Education: North Carolina 1988 BA, 1991 JD

Chambers of Magistrate Judge Dennis Howell

302 U.S. Courthouse, 100 Otis Street, Asheville, NC 28801
Tel: (828) 771-7240 Fax: (828) 771-7244
E-mail: dennis_howell@ncwd.uscourts.gov

Dennis L. Howell
Magistrate Judge

Began Service: October 5, 2004

Staff

Career Law Clerk **Stewart Alford** .... (828) 771-7242
E-mail: stewart_alford@ncwd.uscourts.gov

Secretary **Sharon Hughes** .... (828) 771-7240
E-mail: sharon_hughes@ncwd.uscourts.gov

United States Bankruptcy Court for the Western District of North Carolina

Charles R. Jonas Federal Building, 401 West Trade Street,
Suite 111, Charlotte, NC 28202
Tel: (704) 350-7500 Tel: (704) 344-6121 (PACER)
Tel: (704) 344-6311 (Voice Case Information System VCIS)
Fax: (704) 350-7503
E-mail: clerk@ncbankruptcy.org
Internet: www.ncwb.uscourts.gov

Number of Judgeships: 3

Number of Vacancies: 1

Court Staff

Clerk of Court **COL Steven T. Salata** .... (704) 350-7500
Fax: (704) 350-7504
Chief Deputy Clerk **(Vacant)** .... (704) 350-7500
Fax: (704) 350-7504
Administrative Manager **Christine Winchester** .... (704) 350-7500
E-mail: Chris_Winchester@ncwb.uscourts.gov Fax: (704) 350-7527
Bankruptcy Administrator **Linda W. Simpson** .... (704) 350-7587

Chambers of Chief Bankruptcy Judge Laura Turner Beyer

401 West Trade Street, Charlotte, NC 28202
Tel: (704) 350-7575

Laura Turner Beyer
Chief Bankruptcy Judge

Education: Davidson 1993 BA; North Carolina 1998 JD
Began Service: 2011

Chambers of Bankruptcy Judge J. Craig Whitley

Charles R. Jonas Federal Building, 401 West Trade Street,
Suite 111, Charlotte, NC 28202
P.O. Box 34189, Charlotte, NC 28234-4189
Tel: (704) 350-7575 Fax: (704) 350-7514
E-mail: craig_whitley@ncwb.uscourts.gov

J. Craig Whitley
Bankruptcy Judge

Date of Birth: 1959
Education: Davidson 1981 BA; Wake Forest 1984 JD
Began Service: June 27, 1994
Term Expires: June 26, 2022

Staff
Tel: (704) 350-7575

Law Clerk **Cole Hayes** .... (704) 350-7575
Began Service: September 2014
Term Expires: August 31, 2017
E-mail: cole_hayes@ncwb.uscourts.gov
Judicial Assistant **Ursula Hamilton** .... (704) 350-7575
E-mail: ursula_c_hamilton@ncwb.uscourts.gov

Chambers of Bankruptcy Judge (recalled) George R. Hodges

Charles R. Jonas Federal Building, 401 West Trade Street,
Suite 111, Charlotte, NC 28202
Tel: (704) 350-7575

George R. Hodges
Bankruptcy Judge (recalled)

Began Service: 2011

United States District Court for the District of North Dakota

U.S. Courthouse, 220 East Rosser Avenue, Room 476,
Bismarck, ND 58501
P.O. Box 1193, Bismarck, ND 58502-1193
Tel: (701) 530-2300 Tel: (701) 530-2368 (PACER)
Fax: (701) 530-2312
Internet: www.ndd.uscourts.gov

Number of Judgeships: 2

Circuit: Eighth

Court Staff

Clerk of Court **Robert Ansley** .... (701) 530-2300
E-mail: rob_ansley@ndd.uscourts.gov Fax: (701) 530-2312
Deputy Clerk-in-Charge - Fargo **Todd Dudgeon** .... (701) 297-7000
130 Quentin N. Burdick U.S. Courthouse, Fax: (701) 297-7005
655 First Ave., N., Fargo, ND 58102
E-mail: todd_dudgeon@ndd.uscourts.gov
Chief Probation Officer **Wade Warren** .... (701) 530-2400
220 E. Rosser Avenue, Room 154, Fax: (701) 530-2412
Bismarck, ND 58501
Librarian, Fargo **Suzanne Morrison** .... (701) 297-7280
Quentin N. Burdick U.S. Courthouse, 655 First Ave. Fax: (701) 297-7285
N., Ste. 310, Fargo, ND 58102-4932
E-mail: suzanne_morrison@ca8.uscourts.gov
Court Reporter **Sandie Ehrmantraut** .... (701) 530-2300
E-mail: sandie_ehrmantraut@ndd.uscourts.gov
Court Reporter **Kelly Kroke** .... (701) 297-7000
E-mail: kelly_kroke@ndd.uscourts.gov

Chambers of Chief Judge Ralph R. Erickson

655 First Avenue North, Suite 410, Fargo, ND 58102
Tel: (701) 297-7080 Fax: (701) 297-7085
E-mail: ralph_erickson@ndd.uscourts.gov

Ralph R. Erickson
Chief Judge

Date of Birth: April 28, 1959
Education: Jamestown Col 1980 BA; North Dakota 1984 JD
Began Service: November 1, 2009
Appointed By: President George W. Bush

Judicial: Magistrate Judge, Cass County Court, State of North Dakota (1993-1994); County Judge, Traill, Steele, Nelson and Griggs Counties Court, State of North Dakota (1994); District Judge, East Central Judicial District Court, State of North Dakota (1995-2003)

Legal Practice: Law Clerk, Ohnstad Twichell, P.C. (1984); Associate, Ohnstad Twichell, P.C. (1984-1989); Shareholder, Ohnstad Twichell, P.C. (1989-1991); Sole Proprietor, Erickson Law Office (1992-1994)

Staff

Law Clerk **Doug Nesheim** .... (701) 297-7080
Began Service: August 2015
Term Expires: August 2016
E-mail: doug_nesheim@ndd.uscourts.gov
Career Law Clerk **Susan Hettich** .... (701) 297-7080
E-mail: susan_hettich@ndd.uscourts.gov
Education: North Dakota JD
Career Law Clerk **LaDonne R. Vik** .... (701) 297-7080
E-mail: ladonne_vik@ndd.uscourts.gov
Education: North Dakota 1986 JD

Chambers of District Judge Daniel L. Hovland

220 East Rosser Avenue, Room 411, Bismarck, ND 58501
P.O. Box 670, Bismarck, ND 58502-0670
Tel: (701) 530-2320 Fax: (701) 530-2325
E-mail: ndd_j-hovland@ndd.uscourts.gov

Daniel L. Hovland
District Judge

Date of Birth: November 10, 1954
Education: Concordia Col Moorhead MN 1976 BA; North Dakota 1979 JD
Began Service: November 26, 2002
Appointed By: President George W. Bush

Clerkships: Law Clerk, Chief Justice Ralph J. Erickstad, North Dakota Supreme Court (1979-1980)

Government: Assistant Attorney General, Office of the Attorney General, State of North Dakota (1980-1983); Commissioner, Office of the Commissioner, Parks and Recreation District, City of Bismarck, North Dakota (1992-2006)

Judicial: Administrative Law Judge, Office of Administrative Hearings, State of North Dakota (1994-2002)

Legal Practice: Partner, Fleck, Mather & Strutz (1983-1994); Partner, Smith Bakke Hovland & Oppegard (1994-2002)

Current Memberships: Minnesota State Bar Association; State Bar Association of North Dakota

Staff
Law Clerk **(Vacant)** ....(701) 530-2320
Law Clerk **Rebecca Binstock** ....(701) 530-2320
Law Clerk **(Vacant)** ....(701) 530-2320
Court Reporter **Sandie Ehrmantraut** ....(701) 530-2300
E-mail: sandie_ehrmantraut@ndd.uscourts.gov

Chambers of Magistrate Judge Charles S. Miller, Jr.

220 East Rosser Avenue, Room 426, Bismarck, ND 58501
Tel: (701) 530-2340 Fax: (701) 530-2325

Charles S. Miller, Jr.
Magistrate Judge

Education: North Dakota 1976 JD
Began Service: November 2004

Staff
Judicial Assistant **Brian Gumeringer**..................(701) 530-2342
E-mail: brian_gumeringer@ndd.uscourts.gov
Education: North Dakota 2000 JD

Chambers of Magistrate Judge Alice R. Senechal

Ronald N. Davies U.S. Courthouse and Federal Building, 102 North Fourth Street, Grand Forks, ND 58203
P.O. Box 5576, Grand Forks, ND 58206-5576
Tel: (701) 297-7070 Fax: (701) 775-6274
E-mail: alice_senechal@ndd.uscourts.gov

Alice R. Senechal
Magistrate Judge

Date of Birth: June 25, 1955
Education: North Dakota State 1977 BS; Minnesota 1984 JD
Began Service: November 15, 1990
Term Expires: November 14, 2015

Affiliation: Attorney, Robert Vogel Law Office, P.C.

Current Memberships: American Bar Association; Minnesota State Bar Association; State Bar Association of North Dakota

Chambers of Magistrate Judge Alice R. Senechal *continued*

Staff
Law Clerk **Lindsey Scheel**...........................(701) 775-3117
Career Law Clerk **Amy Strankowski** ....(701) 775-3117
Education: North Dakota 2008 JD

United States Bankruptcy Court for the District of North Dakota

Quentin N. Burdick U.S. Courthouse, 655 First Avenue North, Suite 210, Fargo, ND 58102-4932
Tel: (701) 297-7100 Tel: (800) 676-6856 (PACER)
Tel: (866) 222-8029 (Voice Case Information System VCIS)
Fax: (701) 297-7105
Internet: www.ndb.uscourts.gov

Number of Judgeships: 1

Court Staff
Clerk of Court **Dianne G. Schmitz**..................(701) 297-7100
E-mail: dianne_schmitz@ndb.uscourts.gov
Chief Deputy **Kay Melquist**.........................(701) 297-7100
E-mail: kay_melquist@ndb.uscourts.gov
Education: Minnesota St (Moorhead) BS
Systems Manager **James Snyder**.....................(701) 297-7150
E-mail: jim_snyder@ndb.uscourts.gov
Education: North Dakota State 1983 BS

Chambers of Bankruptcy Judge Shon K. Hastings

350 Quentin N. Burdick U.S. Courthouse, 655 First Avenue North, Fargo, ND 58102-4932
Tel: (701) 297-7140

Shon Kaelberer Hastings
Bankruptcy Judge

Education: North Dakota JD
Began Service: September 13, 2011
Appointed By: President Barack Obama
Term Expires: 2025

Staff
Career Law Clerk **MaryBeth Hegstad** ....(701) 297-7140
Education: North Dakota 2000 JD

United States District Court for the Northern District of Ohio

801 West Superior Avenue, Cleveland, OH 44113-1830
Tel: (216) 357-7000 Fax: (216) 357-7040
Internet: www.ohnd.uscourts.gov

Number of Judgeships: 11

Circuit: Sixth

Areas Covered: Counties of Allen, Ashland, Ashtabula, Auglaize, Carroll, Columbiana, Crawford, Cuyahoga, Defiance, Erie, Fulton, Geauga, Hancock, Hardin, Henry, Holmes, Huron, Lake, Lorain, Lucas, Mahoning, Marion, Medina, Mercer, Ottawa, Paulding, Portage, Putnam, Richland, Sandusky, Seneca, Stark, Summit, Trumbull, Tuscarawas, Van Wert, Wayne, Williams, Wood and Wyandot

Court Staff

Fax: (216) 357-7066

Clerk of Court **Geri M. Smith**........................(216) 357-7068
Deputy-in-Charge - Akron **Stacy Peters**...............(330) 252-6000
568 U.S. Courthouse & Federal Bldg., 25 Main St., Akron, OH 44308
Deputy-in-Charge - Toledo **Debora MacDonell**.........(419) 213-5500
U.S. Courthouse, 1716 Spielbusch Ave., Toledo, OH 43624

United States District Court for the Northern District of Ohio *continued*

Deputy-in-Charge - Youngstown **Linda Rhein** . . . . (330) 884-7400
Thomas D. Lambros Federal Bldg.
& U.S. Courthouse, 125 Market St.,
Youngstown, OH 44503-1787
E-mail: linda_rhein@ohnd.uscourts.gov

Chief Pre-Trial Services Officer and Probation Officer
Burton Maroney . . . . (216) 357-7300

Court Reporting Coordinator **Julie Knabe** . . . . (216) 357-7035
E-mail: julie_knabe@ohnd.uscourts.gov

Chief Court Reporter **Bruce A. Matthews** . . . . (216) 357-7207
Affiliation: RDR; CRR; FAPR
E-mail: bruce_matthews@ohnd.uscourts.gov
Education: Clark State Com Col 1973 AAB

Court Reporter **Sarah E. Nageotte** . . . . (216) 357-7186
Affiliation: RDR; CRR; CBC
E-mail: sarah_nageotte@ohnd.uscourts.gov
Education: Ashtabula Joint Vocational 1996;
Acad Court Reporting and Tech 1997 AAB

Chambers of Chief Judge Solomon Oliver, Jr.

Carl B. Stokes U.S. Court House, 801 West Superior Avenue,
Cleveland, OH 44113-1838
Tel: (216) 357-7171
E-mail: solomon_oliver@ohnd.uscourts.gov

Solomon Oliver, Jr.
Chief Judge

Date of Birth: 1947
Education: Wooster 1969 BA; NYU 1972 JD; Case Western 1974 MA
Began Service: May 9, 1994
Appointed By: President William J. Clinton

Current Memberships: American Bar Association; Cleveland Metropolitan Bar Association; Norman S. Minor Bar Association

Staff
Courtroom Deputy **Maria Dallas** . . . . (216) 357-7173
E-mail: maria_dallas@ohnd.uscourts.gov
Judicial Assistant **Bettye Rhinehart** . . . . (216) 357-7171

Chambers of District Judge Donald C. Nugent

Carl B. Stokes U.S. Courthouse, 801 West Superior Avenue,
Room 15A, Cleveland, OH 44113-1842
Tel: (216) 357-7160 Fax: (216) 357-7165
E-mail: donald_c_nugent@ohnd.uscourts.gov

Donald C. Nugent
District Judge

Date of Birth: 1948
Education: Xavier (OH) 1970 BA; Cleveland-Marshall 1974 JD
Began Service: June 30, 1995
Appointed By: President William J. Clinton
Political Affiliation: Democrat

Academic: Adjunct Professor, Cleveland Marshall College of Law

Government: Assistant Prosecuting Attorney, County of Cuyahoga, Ohio (1975-1985)

Judicial: Judge, Ohio Court of Common Pleas, Cuyahoga County (1985-1993); Judge, Ohio District Court, Eighth District (1993-1995)

Legal Practice: Private Practice (1974-1975); Associate, Laurie, Hull and Ryan (1975-1985)

Military Service: United States Marine Corps (1970-1971)

Current Memberships: Cleveland County Bar Association; Cuyahoga County Bar Association; Ohio State Bar Association

Staff
Career Law Clerk **Betsy A. Breese** . . . . (216) 357-7160
E-mail: BetsyAnn_Breese@ohnd.uscourts.gov
Education: Case Western 1984 JD

Chambers of District Judge Donald C. Nugent *continued*

Career Law Clerk **Amy Carey** . . . . (216) 357-7160
E-mail: amy_carey@ohnd.uscourts.gov
Career Law Clerk **Jennifer Sammon** . . . . (216) 357-7160
Career Law Clerk **Jennifer Stainforth** . . . . (216) 357-7160
E-mail: Jennifer_Stainforth@ohnd.uscourts.gov
Education: Cincinnati 1996 JD
Judicial Assistant/Courtroom Deputy
Jeane M. Wells Ruprecht . . . . (216) 357-7160
E-mail: Jeane_M_Ruprecht@ohnd.uscourts.gov

Chambers of District Judge Patricia A. Gaughan

Carl B. Stokes U.S. Court House, 801 West Superior Avenue,
Cleveland, OH 44113-1835
Tel: (216) 357-7210 Fax: (216) 357-7215

Patricia A. Gaughan
District Judge

Date of Birth: 1953
Education: St Mary's Col (IN) 1975 BA; Notre Dame 1978 JD
Began Service: January 17, 1996
Appointed By: President William J. Clinton

Academic: Adjunct Professor of Law, Cleveland State University (1983-1987)

Government: Assistant Prosecuting Attorney, Criminal Trial Division, County of Cuyahoga, Ohio (1978-1983); Assistant United States Attorney, Economic Crime Division, Northern District of Ohio, United States Attorney's Office, United States Department of Justice, Ronald Reagan Administration (1983-1984)

Judicial: Judge, Ohio Court of Common Pleas, Cuyahoga County (1987-1995)

Legal Practice: Reid, Johnson, Downes, Andrachik and Webster (1984-1987)

Current Memberships: The Sidney Reitman Employment Law American Inn of Court, The American Inns of Court; Cleveland Metropolitan Bar Association; 8th Judicial District Conference; Federal Bar Association; Federal Judges Association; National Conference of Metropolitan Courts

Staff
Law Clerk **Jennifer Cupar** . . . . (216) 357-7214
Began Service: August 2015
Term Expires: August 2016
E-mail: eleanor_hagan@ohnd.uscourts.gov
Career Law Clerk **Joanne D'Emilia** . . . . (216) 357-7214
Education: John Carroll 1985 BA;
Cleveland-Marshall 1989 JD
Career Law Clerk **Sarah E. Nintcheff** . . . . (216) 357-7214
E-mail: sarah_nintcheff@ohnd.uscourts.gov
Education: SUNY (Binghamton) 1995 BS;
Case Western 1998 JD

Chambers of District Judge James S. Gwin

Carl B. Stokes U.S. Courthouse, 801 West Superior Avenue,
Chambers 18A, Cleveland, OH 44113
Tel: (216) 357-7112 Fax: (216) 357-7116
E-mail: james_gwin@ohnd.uscourts.gov

James S. Gwin
District Judge

Date of Birth: 1954
Education: Kenyon 1975 BA; Akron 1979 JD
Began Service: November 10, 1997
Appointed By: President William J. Clinton

Judicial: Judge, Ohio Court of Common Pleas, Stark County (1989-1997)

Legal Practice: Associate, Wise & Gutierrez (1979-1985); Partner, Shareholder, Gutierrez, Mackey & Gwin, L.P.A. (1985-1989)

(continued on next page)

Chambers of District Judge James S. Gwin *continued*

Staff

Courtroom Deputy and Judicial Assistant
Gwen Mackey . . . . (216) 357-7217
U.S. Courthouse, Two South Main Street, Room 403, Akron, OH 44308-1813 Fax: (330) 252-6012
E-mail: gwen_mackey@ohnd.uscourts.gov

Chambers of District Judge Dan A. Polster

Carl B. Stokes U.S. Court House, 801 West Superior Avenue, Room 18B, Cleveland, OH 44113-1837
Tel: (216) 357-7190 Fax: (216) 357-7195
E-mail: Dan_Polster@ohnd.uscourts.gov

Dan A. Polster
District Judge

Date of Birth: 1951
Education: Harvard 1972 AB, 1976 JD
Began Service: August 10, 1998
Appointed By: President William J. Clinton

Academic: Adjunct Professor, Cleveland-Marshall College of Law, Cleveland State University (1980-1981)

Government: Trial Attorney, Antitrust Division, United States Department of Justice, Gerald Ford Administration (1976-1982); Assistant United States Attorney, Economic Crimes Unit, Northern District of Ohio, United States Attorney's Office, United States Department of Justice, Ronald Reagan Administration (1982-1998)

Current Memberships: Criminal Law Committee, Cleveland Metropolitan Bar Association; Federal Bar Association; Jewish Community Federation of Cleveland

Staff

Law Clerk **Brian Choc** . . . . (216) 357-7194
Began Service: 2015
Term Expires: September 10, 2016
E-mail: meheret_kassa@ohnd.uscourts.gov

Career Law Clerk **Mary Jordan Hughes** . . . . (216) 357-7193
E-mail: Mary_Hughes@ohnd.uscourts.gov
Education: Georgetown 1975 BFA; Cleveland-Marshall 1993 JD

Courtroom Deputy Clerk **Robert T. Pitts** . . . . (216) 357-7192
E-mail: Robert_T_Pitts@ohnd.uscourts.gov

Judicial Assistant **Helen Norton** . . . . (216) 357-7190
E-mail: helen_norton@ohnd.uscourts.gov

Chambers of District Judge John R. Adams

510 U.S. Courthouse, Two South Main Street, Akron, OH 44308-1813
Tel: (330) 252-6070 Fax: (330) 252-6077
E-mail: john_adams@ohnd.uscourts.gov

John R. Adams
District Judge

Date of Birth: September 22, 1955
Education: Bowling Green State 1978 BS; Akron 1983 JD
Began Service: February 12, 2003
Appointed By: President George W. Bush

Clerkships: Law Clerk, Judge W. F. Spicer, Summit County Court of Common Pleas, Ohio (1983-1984)

Government: Assistant Prosecutor, Office of the County Prosecutor, County of Summit, Ohio (1986-1989)

Judicial: Judge, Summit County Court of Common Pleas, Ohio (1999-2003)

Legal Practice: Associate, Germano, Rondy, Ciccolini Co., LPA (1984-1989); Partner, Kaufmann & Kaufmann (1989-1999)

Chambers of District Judge John R. Adams *continued*

Staff

Career Law Clerk **Jonathan Little** . . . . (330) 252-6070
Began Service: 2008
E-mail: jonathan_little@ohnd.uscourts.gov
Education: Akron 2004 JD

Law Clerk **Cara Staley** . . . . (330) 252-6070
Began Service: June 2014
Term Expires: June 2018
E-mail: cara_staley@ohnd.uscourts.gov
Education: Akron 2004 JD

Courtroom Deputy **Christin M. Kestner** . . . . (330) 252-6070
E-mail: Christin_Kestner@ohnd.uscourts.gov

Chambers of District Judge Christopher A. Boyko

Carl B. Stokes U.S. Courthouse, 801 West Superior Avenue, Cleveland, OH 44113
Tel: (216) 357-7151
E-mail: christopher_boyko@ohnd.uscourts.gov

Christopher A. Boyko
District Judge

Education: Mount Union 1976 BA; Cleveland-Marshall 1979 JD
Began Service: January 4, 2005
Appointed By: President George W. Bush

Government: Chief Prosecutor, Parma

Judicial: Common Pleas, Cuyahoga County (1996-2004); Parma Municipal Court Judge

Staff

Career Law Clerk **Patricia Rogo** . . . . (216) 357-7151
E-mail: patricia_rogo@ohnd.uscourts.gov

Career Law Clerk **Paul Sikorski** . . . . (216) 357-7151
E-mail: paul_sikorski@ohnd.uscourts.gov

Courtroom Deputy **Chris Huth** . . . . (216) 357-7151

Judicial Assistant **Debra Ress** . . . . (216) 357-7151
E-mail: Debra_Ress@ohnd.uscourts.gov

Chambers of District Judge Jack Zouhary

1716 Spielbusch Avenue, Toledo, OH 43604
Tel: (419) 213-5675 Fax: (419) 213-5680
E-mail: jack_zouhary@ohnd.uscourts.gov

Jack Zouhary
District Judge

Education: Dartmouth 1973 BA; Toledo 1976 JD
Began Service: April 2006
Appointed By: President George W. Bush

Corporate: Senior Vice President/General Counsel, S.E. Johnson Companies, Inc. (2000-2003)

Judicial: Judge, Lucas County Court of Common Pleas (2005-2006)

Legal Practice: Private Practice (1976-1999)

Staff

Judicial Assistant **Nancy Sniegocki** . . . . (419) 213-5675
E-mail: nancy_sniegocki@ohnd.uscourts.gov

Chambers of District Judge Sara Lioi

526 John F. Seiberling Federal Building U.S. Courthouse,
801 West Superior Avenue, Cleveland, OH 44113-1830
Tel: (330) 252-6060
E-mail: sara_lioi@ohnd.uscourts.gov

Sara Lioi
District Judge

Date of Birth: 1960
Education: Bowling Green State 1983 BA; Ohio State 1987 JD
Began Service: March 2007
Appointed By: President George W. Bush

Government: Special Counsel, Stark State College of Technology

Judicial: Judge, Stark County Court of Common Pleas (1997-2007)

Legal Practice: Associate, Day, Ketterer, Raley, Wright & Rybolt, Ltd. (1987-1993); Partner, Day, Ketterer, Raley, Wright & Rybolt, Ltd. (1993-1997)

Staff
Courtroom Deputy **Jackie Porter** .... (330) 252-6060
U.S. Courthouse, Two South Main Street,
Room 526, Akron, OH 44308-1813

Chambers of District Judge Benita Y. Pearson

125 Market Street, Suite 313, Youngstown, OH 44503-1780
Tel: (330) 884-7435 Fax: (330) 884-7450
E-mail: benita_pearson@ohnd.uscourts.gov

Benita Y. Pearson
District Judge

Education: Cleveland-Marshall 1985 BSBA, 1995 JD
Began Service: December 29, 2010
Appointed By: President Barack Obama

Staff
Law Clerk **Keandra Barlow** .... (330) 884-7435
Term Expires: September 2016
E-mail: keandra_barlow@ohnd.uscourts.gov
Law Clerk **Stephen DeGenaro** .... (330) 884-7435
Term Expires: August 2016
E-mail: stephen_degenaro@ohnd.uscourts.gov
Career Law Clerk **Ralph M. Hink** .... (330) 884-7437
E-mail: ralph_m_hink@ohnd.uscourts.gov
Education: John Carroll 1981 BA;
Cleveland-Marshall 1984 JD
Courtroom Deputy **Judy Guyer** .... (330) 884-7433
E-mail: judy_guyer@ohnd.uscourts.gov

Chambers of District Judge Jeffrey J. Helmick

1716 Spielbusch Avenue, Room 210, Toledo, OH 43604
Tel: (419) 213-5690 Fax: (419) 213-5696
E-mail: helmick_chambers@ohnd.uscourts.gov
E-mail: jeffrey_helmick@ohnd.uscourts.gov

Jeffrey J. Helmick
District Judge

Education: Michigan 1983 BA; Ohio State 1988 JD
Began Service: June 19, 2012
Appointed By: President Barack Obama

Staff
Judicial Assistant **Dawn Serna-Gensch** .... (419) 513-5690
Career Law Clerk **Catherine Garcia-Feehan** .... (419) 513-5690
Education: Toledo 1989 JD
Courtroom Deputy **Amy Schroeder** .... (419) 513-5690

Chambers of Senior Judge David A. Katz

307 U.S. Courthouse, 1716 Speilbusch Avenue, Toledo, OH 43604-1363
Tel: (419) 213-5710 Fax: (419) 213-5720
E-mail: david_a_katz@ohnd.uscourts.gov

David A. Katz
Senior Judge

Date of Birth: 1933
Education: Ohio State 1955 BS, 1957 JD
Began Service: October 21, 1994
Appointed By: President William J. Clinton

Legal Practice: Spengler Nathanson (1957-1993)

Current Memberships: American Bar Association; The American Inns of Court; Ohio State Bar Association; Toledo Bar Association

Staff
Law Clerk **Krysten Beech** .... (419) 213-5713
E-mail: krysten_beech@ohnd.uscourts.gov
Secretary **Catherine Goddu** .... (419) 213-5710
E-mail: catherine_c_goddu@ohnd.uscourts.gov
Career Law Clerk **Wayne Kalkwarf**

Chambers of Senior Judge Lesley Wells

328 U.S. Court House, 201 Superior Avenue, Cleveland, OH 44114
Tel: (216) 615-4480 Fax: (216) 615-4371
E-mail: lesley_wells@ohnd.uscourts.gov

Lesley Wells
Senior Judge

Date of Birth: 1937
Education: Chatham 1959 BA; Cleveland-Marshall 1974 JD
Began Service: February 1994
Appointed By: President William J. Clinton

Academic: Adjunct Professor, Cleveland-Marshall College of Law, Cleveland State University (1980-1981)

Judicial: Judge, Ohio Court of Common Pleas, Cuyahoga County (1983-1994)

Legal Practice: Private Practice; Partner, Brooks & Moffet (1975-1979); Schneider, Smeltz, Huston & Ranney (1980-1983)

Current Memberships: American Bar Association; The American Law Institute; Cleveland-Marshall Law Almuni Association; Cleveland Metropolitan Bar Association; Cuyahoga County Bar Association; National Association of Women Judges; Ohio State Bar Association; Ohio Women's Bar Association

Staff
Career Law Clerk **Joshua Miklowski** .... (216) 615-4480
E-mail: joshua_miklowski@ohnd.uscourts.gov
Courtroom Deputy Clerk **Lynn Campbell** .... (216) 615-4479
E-mail: Lynn_S_Campbell@ohnd.uscourts.gov
Judicial Assistant **Kimberly S. Alderton** .... (216) 615-4480
E-mail: Kimberly_S_Alderton@ohnd.uscourts.gov

Chambers of Senior Judge James Gray Carr

U.S. Courthouse, 1716 Spielbusch Avenue, Suite 210, Toledo, OH 43604
Tel: (419) 213-5555 Fax: (419) 213-5563
E-mail: james_g_carr@ohnd.uscourts.gov

James Gray Carr
Senior Judge

Date of Birth: 1940
Education: Kenyon 1962 AB; Harvard 1966 LLB
Began Service: May 12, 1994
Appointed By: President William J. Clinton

Current Memberships: American Bar Association; Toledo Bar Association

Staff

Law Clerk **Evan Creutz** .... (419) 213-5555
Began Service: August 2015
Term Expires: August 2016
E-mail: evan_creutz@ohnd.uscourts.gov
Career Law Clerk **Michael Blankenheim** .... (419) 213-5555
Began Service: August 2013
E-mail: michael_blankenheim@ohnd.uscourts.gov
Education: DePaul JD
Judicial Assistant **Dianne Gowing** .... (419) 213-5555
E-mail: dianne_gowing@ohnd.uscourts.gov

Chambers of Magistrate Judge Nancy A. Vecchiarelli

Carl B. Stokes U.S. Court House, 801 West Superior Avenue, Cleveland, OH 44113
Tel: (216) 357-7130 Fax: (216) 357-7134
E-mail: nancy_vecchiarelli@ohnd.uscourts.gov

Nancy A. Vecchiarelli
Magistrate Judge

Education: Cincinnati 1977 JD
Began Service: April 20, 1998
Term Expires: April 20, 2022

Clerkships: Law Clerk The Honorable Thomas J. Parino, Ohio Court of Appeals, Eighth District (1977-1979)

Government: Assistant United States Attorney, Northern District of Ohio, United States Attorney's Office, United States Department of Justice, Ronald Reagan Administration (1986-1998)

Legal Practice: Associate, Hahn Loeser & Parks LLP (1979-1986)

Current Memberships: The Judge Anthony J. Celebrezze Inn of Court, The American Inns of Court; Federal Bar Association; The Justinian Forum; Ohio Women's Bar Association

Staff

Law Clerk **Monica Frantz** .... (216) 357-7130
Began Service: August 2013
E-mail: monica_giangardella@ohnd.uscourts.gov
Career Law Clerk **Melissa Kelly** .... (216) 357-7130
E-mail: melissa_kelly@ohnd.uscourts.gov
Courtroom Deputy **Wanda F. Golden** .... (216) 357-7130
E-mail: wanda_f_golden@ohnd.uscourts.gov

Chambers of Magistrate Judge George J. Limbert

Thomas D. Lambros Federal Building & U.S. Courthouse, 125 Market Street, Room 229, Youngstown, OH 44503-1780
Tel: (330) 884-7460 Fax: (330) 884-7468
E-mail: George_Limbert@ohnd.uscourts.gov

George J. Limbert
Magistrate Judge

Date of Birth: 1940
Education: Case Western 1965 JD, 1971 LLM
Began Service: November 8, 1999
Term Expires: November 7, 2029
Political Affiliation: Republican

Government: Boardman Township Trustee, County of Mahoning, Ohio (1998-1999)

Judicial: Common Pleas Judge, Mahoning County (1995-1996)

Legal Practice: Private Practice (1965-1995); Private Practice (1997-1999)

Current Memberships: Mahoning County Bar Association; Ohio State Bar Association

Staff

Law Clerk **Halden Schwallie** .... (330) 884-7460
Began Service: May 2015
Term Expires: May 2016
E-mail: halden_schwallie@ohnd.uscourts.gov
Career Law Clerk **Susan A. Burns** .... (330) 884-7460
E-mail: Susan_Burns@ohnd.uscourts.gov
Education: Youngstown State 1992 BS; Akron 1996 JD
Courtroom Deputy **Anita A. Schenker** .... (330) 884-7465
E-mail: Anita_A_Schenker@ohnd.uscourts.gov Fax: (330) 884-7425

Chambers of Magistrate Judge William H. Baughman, Jr.

Carl B. Stokes U.S. Court House, 801 West Superior Avenue, Suite 10-A, Cleveland, OH 44113-1846
Tel: (216) 357-7220
E-mail: william_baughman@ohnd.uscourts.gov

William H. Baughman, Jr.
Magistrate Judge

Date of Birth: 1949
Education: Notre Dame 1974 JD
Began Service: February 15, 2000
Term Expires: February 15, 2016

Academic: Adjunct Faculty, Cleveland-Marshall College of Law, Cleveland State University

Clerkships: Law Clerk The Honorable Roger Kiley, United States Court of Appeals for the Seventh Circuit (1974-1975)

Legal Practice: Partner, Weston Hurd Fallon Paisley & Howley L.L.P. (1985-2000)

Current Memberships: Cleveland Metropolitan Bar Association

Staff

Career Law Clerk **Steven J. Kurdziel** .... (216) 357-7223
E-mail: steven_kurdziel@ohnd.uscourts.gov
Education: Georgetown 1975 BA; Cleveland-Marshall 1980 JD
Courtroom Deputy **Donna Hach** .... (216) 357-7222
E-mail: donna_m_hach@ohnd.uscourts.gov
Judicial Assistant **(Vacant)** .... (216) 357-7220

Chambers of Magistrate Judge Kenneth S. McHargh
Carl B. Stokes United States Courthouse, 801 West Superior Avenue, Cleveland, OH 44113-1849
Tel: (216) 357-7230 Fax: (216) 357-7234
E-mail: kenneth_mchargh@ohnd.uscourts.gov

Kenneth S. McHargh
Magistrate Judge

Education: Wooster 1966 BA; Connecticut 1974 JD
Began Service: March 2004

Government: Deputy Chief, Criminal Division, Northern District of Ohio, United States Department of Justice, Ronald Reagan Administration (1983-2004)

Staff
Law Clerk **Kristen Suber** .... (216) 357-7230
Began Service: 2015
Term Expires: September 2017
E-mail: kristen_suber@ohnd.uscourts.gov
Career Law Clerk **Bob Quartell** .... (216) 357-7230
Courtroom Deputy **Deborah Mattei** .... (216) 357-7230
E-mail: deborah_mattei@ohnd.uscourts.gov

Chambers of Magistrate Judge Gregory A. White
801 West Superior Avenue, Cleveland, OH 44113-1830
Tel: (216) 357-7135 Fax: (216) 357-7139

Gregory A. White
Magistrate Judge

Education: Kent State 1973 BSCrimJ; Cleveland-Marshall 1977 JD
Began Service: March 1, 2008

Staff
Fax: (216) 357-7139

Law Clerk **Ellen A. Siebenschuh** .... (216) 357-7137
E-mail: ellen_siebenschuh@ohnd.uscourts.gov
Education: Grinnell 1992 BA;
Case Western 1995 JD
Career Law Clerk **Zoltan Hargitai** .... (216) 357-7135
E-mail: zoltan_hargitai@ohnd.uscourts.gov
Education: Cleveland-Marshall 2004 JD
Courtroom Deputy **Stacey Swonger** .... (216) 357-7135
E-mail: stacey.swonger@ohnd.uscourts.gov

Chambers of Magistrate Judge James R. Knepp II
James M. Ashley and Thomas W.L. Ashley U.S. Courthouse, 1716 Spielbusch Avenue, Room 318, Toledo, OH 43604-1363
Tel: (419) 213-5570 Fax: (419) 213-5575
E-mail: knepp_chambers@ohnd.uscourts.gov

James R. Knepp II
Magistrate Judge

Education: Mount Union 1986 BA; Bowling Green State 1987 MA; Toledo 1992 JD
Began Service: July 30, 2010

Current Memberships: American Bar Association; Federal Bar Association

Staff
Law Clerk **Sarah Cunningham** .... (419) 213-5570
E-mail: sarah_cunningham@ohnd.uscourts.gov
Law Clerk **Sarah Stephens** .... (419) 213-5570
E-mail: sarah_stephens@ohnd.uscourts.gov
Courtroom Deputy **Pam Armstrong** .... (419) 213-5570

Chambers of Magistrate Judge Kathleen B. Burke
Two South Main Street, Room 480, Akron, OH 44308-1813
Tel: (330) 252-6170 Tel: (330) 252-6175
E-mail: kathleen_burke@ohnd.uscourts.gov

Kathleen Burke
Magistrate Judge

Began Service: August 20, 2011

Government: Executive Director, Lottery Commission, State of Ohio (2009-2011)

Staff
Law Clerk **Susan Waszak** .... (330) 252-6170
E-mail: susan_waszak@ohnd.uscourts.gov
Law Clerk **Pamela "Pam" DeGeeter** .... (330) 252-6170
E-mail: pamela_degeeter@ohnd.uscourts.gov
Courtroom Deputy **Ivonne Davis** .... (330) 252-6170
E-mail: ivonne_davis@ohnd.uscourts.gov

United States Bankruptcy Court for the Northern District of Ohio
Howard M. Metzenbaum U.S. Courthouse, 201 Superior Avenue, Cleveland, OH 44114
Tel: (216) 615-4300 Tel: (800) 579-5735 (Toll Free PACER)
Tel: (866) 222-8029 (Toll Free Voice Case Information System VCIS)
Fax: (216) 615-4364
Internet: www.ohnb.uscourts.gov

Number of Judgeships: 8

Court Staff
Clerk of Court **Kenneth J. Hirz** .... (216) 615-4300
Fax: (216) 615-4364

Chambers of Chief Bankruptcy Judge Patricia E. Morgenstern-Clarren
Howard M. Metzenbaum U.S. Courthouse, 201 Superior Avenue, Cleveland, OH 44114-1235
Tel: (216) 615-4422 Fax: (216) 615-4361
E-mail: pat_morgenstern-clarren@ohnb.uscourts.gov

Patricia E. Morgenstern-Clarren
Chief Bankruptcy Judge

Date of Birth: 1952
Education: Michigan 1974 AB; Case Western 1977 JD; London School Econ (UK) 1979 LLM
Began Service: December 1, 1995
Term Expires: December 1, 2023

Clerkships: Law Clerk The Honorable Jack Grant Day, Court of Appeals of Ohio, Eighth District (1977-1978)

Judicial: Bankruptcy Judge, United States Bankruptcy Appellate Panel for the Sixth Circuit (1999-2002); Bankruptcy Judge, Chambers of Bankruptcy Judge Pat E. Morgenstern-Clarren, United States Bankruptcy Court for the Northern District of Ohio (1995-2012)

Legal Practice: Attorney, Hahn Loeser & Parks LLP (1979-1987); Partner, Hahn Loeser & Parks LLP (1987-1995)

Current Memberships: American Bar Association; The William K. Thomas American Inn of Court, The American Inns of Court; The American Law Institute; Cleveland Metropolitan Bar Association; National Association of Women Judges; National Conference of Bankruptcy Judges; Ohio State Bar Association; Ohio Women's Bar Association

Staff
Career Law Clerk **Mara Doganiero** .... (216) 615-4425
E-mail: mara_doganiero@ohnb.uscourts.gov
Education: Case Western 1980 JD
Courtroom Deputy **Gregory "Greg" Nunn** .... (216) 615-4431
E-mail: gregory_nunn@ohnb.uscourts.gov

(continued on next page)

FEDERAL COURTS—UNITED STATES DISTRICT COURTS

Chambers of Chief Bankruptcy Judge Patricia E. Morgenstern-Clarren
continued

Court Reporter **Erick Jones** . . . . (216) 615-4319
Judicial Assistant **Joyce Gordon** . . . . (216) 615-4422
E-mail: joyce_gordon@ohnb.uscourts.gov

Chambers of Bankruptcy Judge Mary Ann Whipple

U.S. Courthouse, 1716 Spielbusch Avenue, Room 111, Toledo, OH 43604
Tel: (419) 213-5621

Mary Ann Whipple
Bankruptcy Judge

Date of Birth: 1956
Education: Michigan 1977 AB; Stanford 1981 JD
Began Service: May 1, 2001
Term Expires: May 30, 2029

Legal Practice: Attorney, Fuller & Henry Ltd (1981-2001)

Current Memberships: American Bankruptcy Institute; American Bar Association; National Conference of Bankruptcy Judges; Ohio State Bar Association; State Bar of Michigan; Toledo Bar Association

Staff
Career Law Clerk **Karen Declercq** . . . . (419) 213-5621
E-mail: karen_declercq@ohnb.uscourts.gov
Secretary **Andrea Schultz** . . . . (419) 213-5621
E-mail: andrea_schultz@ohnb.uscourts.gov

Chambers of Bankruptcy Judge Russ Kendig

Ralph Regula Federal Building and United States Courthouse, 401 McKinley Ave.,S.W., Canton, OH 44702
Tel: (330) 458-2440 Fax: (330) 458-2445

Russ Kendig
Bankruptcy Judge

Date of Birth: 1957
Education: Northwestern 1980 BS; Ohio State 1984 JD
Began Service: February 28, 2001

Academic: Instructor, Walsh College (1994-1995)

Government: Special Counsel, Office of the Attorney General, State of Ohio (1991-1995)

Legal Practice: Krugliak, Wilkins, Griffiths & Dougherty Co., LPA (1984-1995); Lovells (1995-1996); Ross, Kendig & Arnold, Ltd. (1997-1998); Day Ketterer, Ltd. (1999-2001)

Staff
Law Clerk **Brendan Heil** . . . . (330) 458-2483
Began Service: September 2015
Term Expires: September 2016
E-mail: brendan_heil@ohnb.uscourts.gov
Career Law Clerk **Annette M. Durben** . . . . (330) 458-2441
E-mail: annette_durben@ohnb.uscourts.gov
Education: Wittenberg 1992 BA; Cincinnati 1999 JD

Chambers of Bankruptcy Judge Arthur I. Harris

Howard M. Metzenbaum U.S. Courthouse, 201 Superior Avenue, Cleveland, OH 44114-1235
Tel: (216) 615-4405 Fax: (216) 615-4362
E-mail: arthur_harris@ohnb.uscourts.gov

Arthur Isaac Harris
Bankruptcy Judge

Date of Birth: September 15, 1957
Education: Cornell 1979 AB; Michigan 1982 JD
Began Service: October 7, 2002
Term Expires: October 2016

Clerkships: Law Clerk, District Judge John M. Manos, United States District Court for the Northern District of Ohio (1982-1984)

Government: Assistant U.S. Attorney, Northern Division, Civil Division, United States Attorney's Office, United States Department of Justice, Ronald Reagan Administration (1984-2002)

Staff
Law Clerk **Marta Stewart-Dates** . . . . (216) 615-4404
Began Service: August 2014
Term Expires: August 2016
Law Clerk **Nelson Leese** . . . . (216) 615-4404
Term Expires: August 2016
E-mail: nelson_leese@ohnb.uscourts.gov
Courtroom Deputy **Stephanie Zelman-Thanasiu** . . . . (216) 615-4402
E-mail: stephanie_zelman-thanasiu@ohnb.uscourts.gov

Chambers of Bankruptcy Judge Kay Woods

Nathaniel R. Jones Federal Building & U.S. Courthouse, 10 East Commerce Street, Youngstown, OH 44503
Tel: (330) 742-0900 Fax: (330) 742-0959

Kay Woods
Bankruptcy Judge

Education: Bowling Green State BSEd; Ohio State JD
Began Service: July 7, 2004
Term Expires: July 2018

Legal Practice: Attorney, Jones Day; Attorney, LTV Steel Company, Inc.

Staff
Law Clerk **Audrey Aleskovsky** . . . . (330) 742-0900
Began Service: August 2013
Term Expires: August 2017
E-mail: audrey_aleskovsky@ohnb.uscourts.gov
Career Law Clerk **M. Scott Serfozo** . . . . (330) 742-0900
Began Service: August 2009
E-mail: scott_serfozo@ohnb.uscourts.gov
Education: Ohio 2006 BBA; Cincinnati 2009 JD

Chambers of Bankruptcy Judge Jessica E. Price Smith

201 Superior Avenue, Cleveland, OH 44114-1235
Tel: (216) 615-4451

Jessica E. Price Smith
Bankruptcy Judge

Education: Ohio Northern 1997 JD
Began Service: 2011

Staff
Law Clerk **Donna Parks** . . . . (216) 615-4449
Law Clerk **Ariel Olah** . . . . (216) 615-4448
Courtroom Deputy **Jessica Griffin** . . . . (216) 615-4451

Chambers of Bankruptcy Judge John P. Gustafson
1716 Spielbusch Avenue, Toledo, OH 43604
Tel: (419) 213-5631 Fax: (419) 213-5637

John P. Gustafson
Bankruptcy Judge

Staff
Law Clerk **Adam Motycka** .... (419) 213-5631
Courtroom Deputy **Melinda Hutton** .... (419) 213-5631
Judicial Assistant **Jean McCoy** .... (419) 213-5631

Chambers of Bankruptcy Judge Alan M. Koschik
Two South Main Street, Suite 240, Akron, OH 44308
Tel: (330) 252-6130
E-mail: alan_koschik@ohnb.uscourts.gov

Alan M. Koschik
Bankruptcy Judge

Staff
Law Clerk **Erica Green** .... (330) 252-6130
Judicial Assistant **Renee Bowers** .... (330) 252-6130
Courtroom Deputy **Mary Knotts** .... (330) 252-6134

United States District Court for the Southern District of Ohio
260 Joseph P. Kinneary U.S. Courthouse, 85 Marconi Boulevard,
Columbus, OH 43215
Tel: (614) 719-3000 Tel: (210) 301-6440 (PACER)
Tel: (800) 676-6856 (Toll Free PACER) Fax: (614) 719-3500
Internet: www.ohsd.uscourts.gov

Number of Judgeships: 8

Circuit: Sixth

Areas Covered: Counties of Adams, Athens, Belmont, Brown, Butler, Champaign, Clark, Clermont, Clinton, Coshocton, Darke, Delaware, Fairfield, Fayette, Franklin, Gallia, Greene, Guernsey, Hamilton, Harrison, Highland, Hocking, Jackson, Jefferson, Knox, Lawrence, Licking, Logan, Madison, Meigs, Miami, Monroe, Montgomery, Morgan, Morrow, Muskingum, Noble, Perry, Pickaway, Pike, Preble, Ross, Scioto, Shelby, Union, Vinton, Warren and Washington

Court Staff
Clerk of Court **Richard W. Nagel** .... (614) 719-3000
Fax: (614) 719-3037

Division Manager-Cincinnati **Jeffrey Garey** .... (513) 564-7500
Potter Stewart U.S. Courthouse, 100 E. Fifth St., Cincinnati, OH 45202 Fax: (513) 564-7505
E-mail: jeffrey_garey@ohsd.uscourts.gov
Education: Dayton 1986 BS

Division Manager - Columbus **Scott E. Miller** .... (614) 719-3000
E-mail: chris_williams@ohsd.uscourts.gov Fax: (614) 719-3500

Division Manager-Dayton **Jeffrey Garey** .... (937) 512-1400
Federal Bldg., 200 W. Second St., Dayton, OH 45402 Fax: (937) 512-1660
E-mail: jeffrey_garey@ohsd.uscourts.gov

Chief Pretrial Services Officer **Melanie Furry** .... (614) 719-3080
Potter Stewart U.S. Courthouse, 100 East Fifth Street, Suite 301, Cincinnati, OH 45202-3905 Fax: (614) 469-2484
Joseph P. Kenneary Courthouse, Room 512

Chief Probation Officer **John Dierna** .... (513) 564-7575
Potter Stewart U.S. Courthouse, 100 East Fifth Street, Room 110, Cincinnati, OH 45202-3905 Fax: (513) 564-7587

Chambers of Chief Judge Edmund A. Sargus, Jr.
Joseph P. Kinneary U.S. Courthouse, 85 Marconi Boulevard,
Room 301, Columbus, OH 43215-2823
Tel: (614) 719-3240 Fax: (614) 719-3246
E-mail: sargus_chambers@ohsd.uscourts.gov

Edmund A. Sargus, Jr.
Chief Judge

Date of Birth: 1953
Education: Brown U 1975 AB; Case Western 1978 JD
Began Service: August 23, 1996
Appointed By: President William J. Clinton

Current Memberships: American Bar Association; Belmont County Bar Association; Ohio State Bar Association

Staff
Law Clerk **Jonathan Olivito** .... (614) 719-3240
Began Service: August 2015
Term Expires: September 1, 2016
E-mail: jonathan_olivito@ohsd.uscourts.gov

Career Law Clerk **Penny L. Barrick** .... (614) 719-3240
Began Service: January 1, 2012
E-mail: penny_barrick@ohsd.uscourts.gov
Education: Ohio State 2001 JD

Courtroom Deputy **Andy F. Quisumbing** .... (614) 719-3240
E-mail: andy_quisumbing@ohsd.uscourts.gov
Education: Ohio 1977 MA

Secretary **Debra A. Hepler** .... (614) 719-3240
E-mail: debra_a._hepler@ohsd.uscourts.gov

Chambers of District Judge Susan J. Dlott
227 Potter Stewart U.S. Courthouse, 100 East Fifth Street,
Cincinnati, OH 45202-3927
Tel: (513) 564-7630 Fax: (513) 564-7638
E-mail: susan_dlott@ohsd.uscourts.gov

Susan J. Dlott
District Judge

Date of Birth: 1949
Education: Pennsylvania 1970 BA; Boston U 1973 JD
Began Service: December 29, 1995
Appointed By: President William J. Clinton

Current Memberships: American Bar Association; The Potter Stewart American Inn of Court, The American Inns of Court; Cincinnati Bar Association; Dayton Bar Association; Federal Bar Association; Ohio State Bar Association

Staff
Law Clerk **Jennifer Johnson** .... (513) 564-7630
E-mail: jennifer_johnson@ohsd.uscourts.gov

Career Law Clerk **Peggy Fechtel** .... (513) 564-7630
Education: Ohio State 1997 JD

Law Clerk **Rob Honkonen** .... (513) 564-7630

Court Reporter **Julie A. Wolfer** .... (513) 564-7606
E-mail: julie_wolfer@ohsd.uscourts.gov Fax: (513) 564-7638

Judicial Assistant **Vicki Penley** .... (513) 564-7630
E-mail: vicki_penley@ohsd.uscourts.gov
Education: Cincinnati BS

Chambers of District Judge Algenon L. Marbley

Joseph P. Kinneary U.S. Courthouse, 85 Marconi Boulevard, Room 319, Columbus, OH 43215
Tel: (614) 719-3260 Fax: (614) 719-3264
E-mail: Algenon_Marbley@ohsd.uscourts.gov

Algenon L. Marbley
District Judge

Date of Birth: 1954
Education: North Carolina 1976 BA; Northwestern 1979 JD
Began Service: November 11, 1997
Appointed By: President William J. Clinton

Academic: Adjunct Professor of Criminal Law and Procedure, Northeastern Illinois University (1985-1986); Adjunct Professor of Trial Advocacy, Capital University Law School

Government: Assistant General Counsel, Office of the Regional Attorney, United States Department of Health and Human Services, Region V (1980-1986)

Legal Practice: Associate, James D. Montgomery and Associates (1979-1981); Associate, Vorys, Sater, Seymour and Pease (1986-1991); Partner, Vorys, Sater, Seymour and Pease (1991-1997)

Current Memberships: American Bar Association; Columbus Bar Association; National Bar Association; National Institute of Trial Advocacy; Ohio State Bar Association

Staff

Law Clerk **Emily Brown** .... (614) 719-3260
Began Service: October 2015
Term Expires: October 2016
E-mail: emily_brown@ohsd.uscourts.gov

Law Clerk **Daniel Brown** .... (614) 719-3260
Began Service: November 2015
Term Expires: October 31, 2016

Deputy Clerk **Betty Clark** .... (614) 719-3260
E-mail: Betty_Clark@ohsd.uscourts.gov

Judicial Secretary **Cherida West** .... (614) 719-3260
E-mail: Cherida_West@ohsd.uscourts.gov

Chambers of District Judge Thomas M. Rose

Federal Building, 200 West Second Street, Room 910, Dayton, OH 45402
Tel: (937) 512-1600 Fax: (937) 512-1610
E-mail: rose_chambers@ohsd.uscourts.gov

Thomas M. Rose
District Judge

Date of Birth: 1948
Education: Ohio 1970 BS; Cincinnati 1973 JD
Began Service: June 21, 2002
Appointed By: President George W. Bush

Government: Assistant Prosecutor, Office of the County Prosecutor, County of Greene, Ohio (1973-1975); Chief Juvenile Court Referee, Juvenile Division, Greene County Common Pleas Court (1976-1977); Chief Assistant in Charge, Civil Division, Office of the County Prosecutor, County of Greene, Ohio (1978-1991)

Judicial: Judge, Greene County Common Pleas Court (1991-2002)

Legal Practice: Associate, Nicholas Carrera Law Office (1973-1975); Partner, DeWine & Rose (1975-1976); Partner, DeWine, Schenck & Rose (1978-1991)

Staff

Career Law Clerk **Joseph A. Brossart** .... (937) 512-1600
E-mail: joseph_brossart@ohsd.uscourts.gov
Education: Miami 1987 BA; Notre Dame 1998 JD

Career Law Clerk **Peter T. Snow** .... (937) 512-1600
E-mail: peter_snow@ohsd.uscourts.gov

Courtroom Deputy **Elizabeth Penski** .... (937) 512-1603
E-mail: liz_penski@ohsd.uscourts.gov

Administrative Assistant **Doris J. Evers** .... (937) 512-1600
E-mail: doris_evers@ohsd.uscourts.gov

Chambers of District Judge Gregory L. Frost

Joseph P. Kinneary U.S. Courthouse, 85 Marconi Boulevard, Room 169, Columbus, OH 43215
Tel: (614) 719-3300 Fax: (614) 719-3305
E-mail: greg_frost@ohsd.uscourts.gov

Gregory L. Frost
District Judge

Date of Birth: April 17, 1949
Education: Wittenberg 1971 BA; Ohio Northern 1974 JD
Began Service: March 19, 2003
Appointed By: President George W. Bush
Political Affiliation: Republican

Affiliation: Instructor, Ohio Judicial College; Instructor, Ohio Continuing Legal Education Institute; Instructor, Licking County Peace Officers Training Academy

Government: Assistant County Prosecutor, Office of the Prosecutor, County of Licking, Ohio (1974-1978)

Judicial: Judge, Licking County Municipal Court (1983-1990); Judge, Licking County Commons Pleas Court (1990-2003)

Legal Practice: Partner, Schaller, Frost, Hostetter & Campbell (1978-1983)

Nonprofit: President, Licking County Bar Association (1999)

Staff

Law Clerk **Katherine Ball** .... (614) 719-3302
E-mail: katherine_ball@ohsd.uscourts.gov

Law Clerk **(Vacant)** .... (614) 719-3307

Career Law Clerk **Shawn K. Judge** .... (614) 719-3303
E-mail: Shawn_Judge@ohsd.uscourts.gov
Education: Ohio State 1998 JD

Courtroom Deputy **Kristen Keppler** .... (614) 719-3018
E-mail: kristen_keppler@ohsd.uscourts.gov

Court Reporter **Denise Errett** .... (614) 719-3029
E-mail: denise_errett@ohsd.uscourts.gov

Administrative Assistant **Kristin Sherrard** .... (614) 719-3300
E-mail: kristin_sherrard@ohsd.uscourts.gov

Chambers of District Judge Michael H. Watson

Joseph P. Kinneary Courthouse, 85 Marconi Boulevard, Room 109, Columbus, OH 43215
Potter Stewart U.S. Courthouse, 100 East Fifth Street, Room 815, Cincinnati, OH 45202-3905
Tel: (614) 719-3280 (Columbus) Tel: (513) 564-7692 (Cincinnati)
Fax: (614) 719-3294 (Columbus) Fax: (513) 567-7697 (Cincinnati)
E-mail: watson_chambers@ohsd.uscourts.gov

Michael H. Watson
District Judge

Date of Birth: November 7, 1956
Education: Ohio State BA; Capital U JD
Began Service: October 2004
Appointed By: President George W. Bush

Judicial: Judge, Franklin County Common Pleas Court (1996-2003); Judge, Ohio Court of Appeals, Tenth District (2003-2004)

Current Memberships: Columbus Bar Association; Ohio State Bar Association

Staff

Law Clerk **Caitlin Cline** .... (614) 719-3280
E-mail: caitlin_cline@ohsd.uscourts.gov

Law Clerk **Ranya Elzein** .... (614) 719-3280
E-mail: ranya_elzein@ohsd.uscourts.gov

Career Law Clerk **(Vacant)** .... (614) 719-3280

Chambers of District Judge Michael R. Barrett

Potter Stewart U.S. Courthouse, 100 East Fifth Street, Room 239, Cincinnati, OH 45202
Tel: (513) 564-7660

Michael R. Barrett
District Judge

Date of Birth: January 14, 1951
Education: Cincinnati 1974 BA, 1977 JD
Began Service: May 2006
Appointed By: President George W. Bush

Government: Administrative Hearing Officer, State of Ohio (1977-1978); Assistant Prosecuting Attorney/Chief Assistant, County of Hamilton, Ohio (1978-1984)

Legal Practice: Associate/Partner, Graydon, Head & Richey (1984-1994); Shareholder, Barrett & Weber, LPA (1995-2006)

Staff
Courtroom Deputy **Barbara Crum** .... (513) 564-7666
E-mail: barbara_crum@ohsd.uscourts.gov
Judicial Assistant **Christina Dougherty** .... (513) 564-7660

Chambers of District Judge Timothy S. Black

Potter Stewart U.S. Courthouse, 100 East Fifth Street, Room 815, Cincinnati, OH 45202
Federal Building, 200 West Second Street, Room 902, Dayton, OH 45402
Tel: (513) 564-7640 Tel: (937) 512-1620

Timothy S. Black
District Judge

Date of Birth: 1953
Education: Harvard 1975 AB; Salmon P Chase 1983 JD
Began Service: June 21, 2010
Appointed By: President Barack Obama

Chambers of Senior Judge Herman J. Weber

801 Potter Stewart U.S. Courthouse, 100 East Fifth Street, Cincinnati, OH 45202-3905
Tel: (513) 564-7600 Fax: (513) 564-7601
E-mail: herman_weber@ohsd.uscourts.gov

Herman J. Weber
Senior Judge

Date of Birth: 1927
Education: Otterbein 1949 BA; Ohio State 1951 JD
Began Service: 1985
Appointed By: President Ronald Reagan

Government: Deputy Mayor, City of Fairborn, Ohio (1956-1958)

Judicial: Acting Judge, Fairborn Municipal Court (1958-1961); Judge, Ohio Common Pleas Court, Greene County (1961-1982); Judge, Ohio Court of Appeals, Second District (1982-1985)

Legal Practice: Partner, Weber & Hogue (1952-1961)

Military Service: United States Navy (1945-1946)

Current Memberships: American Bar Association; Federal Bar Association; Federal Judges Association; Greene County Bar Association (OH); Ohio State Bar Association; Ohio State Bar Foundation

Chambers of Senior Judge George C. Smith

Joseph P. Kinneary U.S. Courthouse, 85 Marconi Boulevard, Room 101, Columbus, OH 43215
Tel: (614) 719-3220 Fax: (614) 719-3232

George C. Smith
Senior Judge

Date of Birth: 1935
Education: Ohio State 1957 BA, 1959 JD
Began Service: 1987
Appointed By: President Ronald Reagan
Political Affiliation: Republican

Academic: Judge in Residence, University of Cincinnati College of Law

Government: Clerk, Office of the Attorney General, State of Ohio (1956-1957); Clerk, Governor C. William O'Neill (OH), Office of the Governor, State of Ohio; Assistant City Attorney, Office of the City Attorney, State of Ohio (1959-1962); Executive Assistant, Mayor Ralph S. Locher (D-OH), Office of the Mayor, City of Columbus, Ohio (1962-1964); Assistant Attorney General, Office of the Attorney General, State of Ohio (1964); Chief Counsel, State of Ohio (1965-1970); Prosecuting Attorney, State of Ohio (1971-1980)

Judicial: Judge, Franklin County Municipal Court (1980-1985); Judge, Franklin County Common Pleas Court (1985-1987)

Current Memberships: Columbus Bar Association; Columbus Bar Foundation, Columbus Bar Association; Federal Bar Association

Staff
Law Clerk **Jillian Boone** .... (614) 719-3220
Law Clerk **Bryant Gramlich** .... (614) 719-3220
Career Law Clerk **Stephanie Michelle Rawlings** .... (614) 719-3220
E-mail: stephanie_rawlings@ohsd.uscourts.gov
Education: Denison 1999 AB; Ohio State 2002 Dr Jur
Courtroom Deputy **Lisa Wright** .... (614) 719-3220
E-mail: lisa_wright@ohsd.uscourts.gov
Judicial Secretary **Lisa Wright** .... (614) 719-3220
E-mail: lisa_wright@ohsd.uscourts.gov

Chambers of Senior Judge James L. Graham

349 Joseph P. Kinneary U.S. Courthouse, 85 Marconi Boulevard, Columbus, OH 43215
Tel: (614) 719-3200 Fax: (614) 719-3210

James L. Graham
Senior Judge

Date of Birth: 1939
Education: Ohio State 1962 BA, 1962 JD
Began Service: 1986
Appointed By: President Ronald Reagan

Government: Chairman, Board of Bar Examiners, Supreme Court of Ohio (1969-1974)

Legal Practice: Crabbe, Brown, Jones, Potts & Schmidt (1962-1969); Partner, Graham, Dutro & Nemeth (1969-1986)

Current Memberships: American College of Trial Lawyers; Columbus Bar Association

Staff
Law Clerk **David Boylan** .... (614) 719-3200
Career Law Clerk **Jason Everetts** .... (614) 719-3200
E-mail: jason_everetts@ohsd.uscourts.gov
Education: Ohio State 2000 JD
Career Law Clerk **Karen Martin** .... (614) 719-3200
E-mail: karen_martin@ohsd.uscourts.gov
Education: Ohio State 1975 BA, 1978 JD

Chambers of Senior Judge Walter H. Rice

909 Federal Building, 200 West Second Street, Dayton, OH 45402
Tel: (937) 512-1500 Fax: (937) 512-1522
E-mail: walter_rice@ohsd.uscourts.gov

Walter Herbert Rice
Senior Judge

Date of Birth: 1937
Education: Northwestern 1958 BA; Columbia 1962 JD, 1962 MBA
Began Service: June 4, 1980
Appointed By: President Jimmy Carter

Academic: Adjunct Professor of Business, Wright State University (1975-1976); Adjunct Professor, School of Law, University of Dayton (1976-1996)

Government: Assistant County Prosecutor, Office of the County Prosecutor, County of Montgomery, Ohio (1964-1966); First Assistant County Prosecutor, Office of the County Prosecutor, County of Montgomery, Ohio (1969)

Judicial: Judge, Municipal Court (1970-1971); Judge, Ohio Court of Common Pleas (1971-1980)

Legal Practice: Law Clerk, Third National Bank (1962-1963); Gallon & Miller (1966-1969)

Current Memberships: Dayton Bar Association; Federal Bar Association

Staff
Law Clerk **Zachary Farquhar** . . . . (937) 512-1500
E-mail: zachary_farquhar@ohsd.uscourts.gov
Career Law Clerk **Lisa M. Woodward** . . . . (937) 512-1500
E-mail: lisa_woodward@ohsd.uscourts.gov
Education: Central Michigan 1984 BS; Capital U 1999 JD
Courtroom Deputy **Cindy Fugate** . . . . (937) 512-1501
E-mail: rice_deputy@ohsd.uscourts.gov
Judicial Assistant **Donna Vinolus** . . . . (937) 512-1502
E-mail: donna_vinolus@ohsd.uscourts.gov

Chambers of Senior Judge Sandra S. Beckwith

Potter Stewart U.S. Courthouse, 100 East Fifth Street, Suite 810, Cincinnati, OH 45202
Tel: (513) 564-7610 Fax: (513) 564-7617
E-mail: Sandra_Beckwith@ohsd.uscourts.gov

Sandra S. Beckwith
Senior Judge

Date of Birth: 1943
Education: Cincinnati 1965 BA, 1968 JD
Began Service: February 21, 1992
Appointed By: President George H.W. Bush

Current Memberships: American Judges Association; Federal Bar Association; Federal Circuit Bar Association; Federal Judges Association

Staff
Career Law Clerk **Laurie Jane Nicholson** . . . . (513) 564-7610
E-mail: laurie_nicholson@ohsd.uscourts.gov
Education: Michigan 1979 JD
Career Law Clerk **Patrick F. Smith** . . . . (513) 564-7610
E-mail: Patrick_Smith@ohsd.uscourts.gov
Education: Toledo 1997 JD
Court Reporter **Maryann Ranz** . . . . (513) 564-7626
E-mail: maryann_ranz@ohsd.uscourts.gov Fax: (513) 564-7627
Administrative Assistant **Gail Seibert** . . . . (513) 564-7610
E-mail: gail_seibert@ohsd.uscourts.gov

Chambers of Chief Magistrate Judge Sharon L. Ovington

Federal Building, 200 West Second Street, Room 523, Dayton, OH 45402
Tel: (937) 512-1570
E-mail: sharon_ovington@ohsd.uscourts.gov

Sharon L. Ovington
Chief Magistrate Judge

Date of Birth: October 22, 1956
Education: Cincinnati 1978 BA; Dayton 1981 JD
Began Service: October 28, 2002
Term Expires: October 2018

Staff
Law Clerk **Robert M. Schultz** . . . . (937) 512-1570
E-mail: robert_schultz@ohsd.uscourts.gov
Career Law Clerk **Michael B. McShea** . . . . (937) 512-1570
E-mail: michael_mcshea@ohsd.uscourts.gov
Education: Dayton 1989 JD
Courtroom Deputy **Rose Plummer** . . . . (937) 512-1571
E-mail: rose_plummer@ohsd.uscourts.gov

Chambers of Magistrate Judge Terence P. Kemp

Joseph P. Kinneary U.S. Courthouse, 85 Marconi Boulevard, Room 172, Columbus, OH 43215
Tel: (614) 719-3410 Fax: (614) 719-3420
E-mail: terry_kemp@ohsd.uscourts.gov

Terence P. Kemp
Magistrate Judge

Date of Birth: 1953
Education: Brown U 1974 BA; Virginia 1977 JD
Began Service: September 18, 1987

Current Memberships: Federal Bar Association; Federal Magistrate Judges Association; Ohio State Bar Association

Staff
Law Clerk **Halle Hara** . . . . (614) 719-3410
Began Service: January 2013
E-mail: halle_hara@ohsd.uscourts.gov
Education: Ohio State 1998 JD
Law Clerk **Jill Rogers Spiker** . . . . (614) 719-3410
Education: Columbia 2004 JD
Law Clerk **Joan Veri** . . . . (614) 719-3410
E-mail: joan_veri@ohsd.uscourts.gov
Pro Se Law Clerk **Kimberly Hoffman** . . . . (614) 719-3393
Education: Capital U JD

Chambers of Magistrate Judge Norah McCann King

235 Joseph P. Kinneary U.S. Courthouse, 85 Marconi Boulevard, Columbus, OH 43215-2823
Tel: (614) 719-3390 Fax: (614) 719-3399
E-mail: Norah_McCann_King@ohsd.uscourts.gov

Norah McCann King
Magistrate Judge

Date of Birth: 1949
Education: Dominican U (IL) 1971 BA; Ohio State 1975 JD
Began Service: June 17, 1982
Term Expires: June 2022

Academic: Assistant Professor, Ohio State University (1980-1982)

Clerkships: Law Clerk The Honorable Joseph P. Kinneary, United States District Court for the Southern District of Ohio (1975-1979)

Legal Practice: Counsel, Frost, King, Freytag & Carpenter (1979-1982)

Current Memberships: Columbus Bar Association; Federal Association of Magistrate Judges; Federal Bar Association

Chambers of Magistrate Judge Norah McCann King *continued*

Staff

Law Clerk **Hunter West** .... (614) 719-3390
Began Service: August 2015
Term Expires: August 2017
E-mail: hunter_west@ohsd.uscourts.gov

Career Law Clerk **Sarah Hopp** .... (614) 719-3390
Began Service: September 4, 2007
E-mail: sarah_hopp@ohsd.uscourts.gov
Education: Ohio State 2002 JD

Chambers of Magistrate Judge Michael R. Merz

Federal Building, 200 West Second Street, Room 501, Dayton, OH 45402
Tel: (937) 512-1550 Fax: (937) 512-1650
E-mail: michael_merz@ohsd.uscourts.gov

Michael R. Merz
Magistrate Judge

Date of Birth: 1945
Education: Harvard 1967 AB, 1970 JD
Began Service: November 21, 1984
Term Expires: November 2016
Political Affiliation: Republican

Current Memberships: American Bar Association; Dayton Bar Association; Federal Bar Association; Federal Magistrate Judges Association; Ohio State Bar Association

Staff

E-mail: merz_chambers@ohsd.uscourts.gov

Career Law Clerk **Stephanie L. Winquist** .... (937) 512-1550
E-mail: stephanie_winquist@ohsd.uscourts.gov
Education: Dayton 2002 JD

Death Penalty Law Clerk **Janice R. Konya-Grabill** ...... (937) 512-1550
E-mail: jan_konya@ohsd.uscourts.gov
Education: Dayton 1997 JD

Judicial Assistant and Courtroom Deputy
Kelly A. Kopf .... (937) 512-1551
E-mail: kelly_kopf@ohsd.uscourts.gov

Chambers of Magistrate Judge Elizabeth A. Preston Deavers

Joseph P. Kinneary Courthouse, 85 Marconi Boulevard, Room 208, Columbus, OH 43215
Tel: (614) 719-3460

Elizabeth A. Deavers
Magistrate Judge

Education: Ohio State 1989 BA; Capital U 1994 JD
Began Service: March 15, 2010
Term Expires: March 2018

Staff

Courtroom Deputy **Sherry Nichols** .... (614) 719-3461
E-mail: sherry_nichols@ohsd.uscourts.gov

Chambers of Magistrate Judge Stephanie K. Bowman

Potter Stewart U.S. Courthouse, 100 East Fifth Street, Room 706, Cincinnati, OH 45202
Tel: (513) 564-7680
E-mail: stephanie_bowman@ohsd.uscourts.gov

Stephanie K. Bowman
Magistrate Judge

Education: Illinois 1997 BA; DePaul 2000 JD
Began Service: October 28, 2010

Current Memberships: The Potter Stewart American Inn of Court, The American Inns of Court; Federal Magistrate Judges Association; Ohio Women's Bar Association

Chambers of Magistrate Judge Karen L. Litkovitz

Potter Stewart U.S. Courthouse, 100 East Fifth Street, Room 716, Cincinnati, OH 45202
Tel: (513) 564-7690
E-mail: karen_litkovitz@ohsd.uscourts.gov

Karen Litkovitz
Magistrate Judge

Education: Bowling Green State 1981 BS; Cincinnati 1984 JD
Began Service: October 14, 2010
Term Expires: October 2018

Current Memberships: The Potter Stewart American Inn of Court, The American Inns of Court; Cincinnati Bar Association; Federal Magistrate Judges Association

Chambers of Magistrate Judge Michael J. Newman

Federal Building, 200 West Second Street, Room 505, Dayton, OH 45402
Tel: (937) 512-1640
E-mail: michael_newman@ohsd.uscourts.gov

Michael J. Newman
Magistrate Judge

Education: NYU 1982 BFA; Washington College of Law 1989 JD
Began Service: July 25, 2011

Staff

Law Clerk **Suzanne Firestone** .... (937) 512-1640
Career Law Clerk **Michael Rhinehart** .... (937) 512-1640
Judicial Assistant **Diane Marcus** .... (937) 512-1640
E-mail: diane_marcus@ohsd.uscourts.gov

Chambers of Magistrate Judge (recalled) Mark R. Abel

Joseph P. Kinneary U.S. Courthouse, 85 Marconi Boulevard, Room 208, Columbus, OH 43215-2823
Tel: (614) 719-3370 Fax: (614) 719-3505
E-mail: Mark_Abel@ohsd.uscourts.gov

Mark R. Abel
Magistrate Judge (recalled)

Date of Birth: 1944
Education: Ohio 1966 BA; Ohio State 1969 JD
Began Service: May 1, 1971

Clerkships: Law Clerk The Honorable Joseph Kinneary, United States District Court for the Southern District of Ohio (1969-1971)

Current Memberships: Columbus Bar Association; Federal Bar Association; Ohio State Bar Association

Staff

Career Law Clerk **Rachel Rubey** .... (614) 719-3372
E-mail: Rachel_Rubey@ohsd.uscourts.gov
Education: Ohio State 2003 JD

United States Bankruptcy Court for the Southern District of Ohio

221 East Fourth Street, Cincinnati, OH 45202-4133
170 North High Street, Columbus, OH 43215
120 West Third Street, Dayton, OH 45402
Tel: (614) 469-6638 Tel: (937) 225-7561 (PACER)
Tel: (800) 793-7003 (Toll Free PACER) Tel: (937) 225-2516 (Dayton)
Tel: (866) 222-8029 (Dayton & Cincinnati Toll Free VCIS)
Tel: (513) 684-2572 (Cincinnati)
Internet: www.ohsb.uscourts.gov

Number of Judgeships: 8

Court Staff

Clerk of Court **Kenneth Jordan** . . . . (513) 684-2572 ext. 3201
E-mail: kenneth_jordan@ohsb.uscourts.gov
Chief Deputy **Ronald L. Ammon** . . . . (937) 225-2516 ext. 7269
E-mail: ronald_ammon@ohsb.uscourts.gov
Deputy-in-Charge - Cincinnati
Lynnetta Suggs Rollinson . . . . (513) 684-2572 ext. 2026
Atrium Two, Ste. 800, 221 E. Fourth St., Fax: (513) 684-2138
Cincinnati, OH 45202
E-mail: lynnetta_rollinson@ohsb.uscourts.gov
Deputy-in-Charge - Columbus
Mecca S. Carter . . . . (614) 469-6638 ext. 5442
170 N. High St., Columbus, OH 43215 Fax: (614) 469-2478
E-mail: mecca_carter@ohsb.uscourts.gov
Deputy-in-Charge - Dayton **Tolanda Gilmer** . . . (937) 225-2516 ext. 7683
E-mail: tolanda_gilmer@ohsb.uscourts.gov Fax: (937) 225-7574

Chambers of Chief Bankruptcy Judge Jeffery P. Hopkins

Atrium Two, 221 East Fourth Street, Suite 800, Cincinnati, OH 45202
Tel: (513) 684-2852 Fax: (513) 357-5420
E-mail: jeffery_hopkins@ohsb.uscourts.gov

Jeffery P. Hopkins
Chief Bankruptcy Judge

Date of Birth: 1960
Education: Bowdoin 1982 AB; Ohio State 1985 JD
Began Service: 1996
Term Expires: March 1, 2024

Current Memberships: American Bankruptcy Institute; Cincinnati Bar Association; Federal Bar Association; National Conference of Bankruptcy Judges

Staff

Career Law Clerk **Richard B. Jones** . . . . (513) 684-2635
E-mail: Richard_Jones@ohsb.uscourts.gov
Education: Toledo 1996 JD
Judicial Assistant/Courtroom Deputy **Patricia Francis** . . . . (513) 684-2852
E-mail: Patricia_Francis@ohsb.uscourts.gov

Chambers of Bankruptcy Judge Charles M. Caldwell

170 North High Street, Columbus, OH 43215-2403
Tel: (614) 469-6638 ext. 260 Fax: (614) 469-5506
E-mail: charles_caldwell@ohsb.uscourts.gov

Charles M. Caldwell
Bankruptcy Judge

Date of Birth: 1954
Education: Evansville 1976 BS; Northwestern 1979 JD
Began Service: May 26, 1993
Term Expires: May 25, 2021

Staff

Law Clerk **Christopher Baxter** . . . . (614) 469-6638 ext. 260
E-mail: christopher_baxter@ohsb.uscourts.gov

Chambers of Bankruptcy Judge Charles M. Caldwell *continued*

Law Clerk **Brian J.K. Sisto** . . . . (614) 469-6638 ext. 242
E-mail: brian_sisto@ohsb.uscourts.gov
Courtroom Deputy **Kathleen Tourgeman** . . . . (614) 469-6638 ext. 260

Chambers of Bankruptcy Judge John E. Hoffman, Jr.

170 North High Street, Columbus, OH 43215
Tel: (614) 469-7704 Fax: (614) 469-2218
E-mail: john_hoffman@ohsb.uscourts.gov

John E. Hoffman, Jr.
Bankruptcy Judge

Date of Birth: 1959
Education: Wheeling Jesuit 1980 BA; Ohio State 1983 JD
Began Service: February 25, 2000
Term Expires: February 24, 2028

Staff

Law Clerk **John W. Kennedy** . . . . (614) 469-7706
E-mail: john_kennedy@ohsb.uscourts.gov
Career Law Clerk **Brian Gifford** . . . . (614) 469-7710
E-mail: brian_gifford@ohsb.uscourts.gov
Courtroom Deputy/Judicial Assistant **Kristie Vickers** . . . . . (614) 469-7704
E-mail: kristie_vickers@ohsb.uscourts.gov

Chambers of Bankruptcy Judge Lawrence S. Walter

120 West Third Street, Dayton, OH 45402
Tel: (937) 225-2516 ext. 7684

Lawrence S. Walter
Bankruptcy Judge

Education: Kansas 1972 BA; Michigan 1973 MA; Cincinnati 1986 JD
Began Service: 2003

Current Memberships: National Conference of Bankruptcy Judges

Staff

Career Law Clerk **Jessica Baxley** . . . . (937) 225-2516 ext. 7271
E-mail: jessica_baxley@ohsb.uscourts.gov
Career Law Clerk **Colleen R. Militello** . . . . (937) 225-2516 ext. 2829
E-mail: colleen_militello@ohsb.uscourts.gov
Education: Dayton 1996 JD
Courtroom Deputy **Vickie Hensley** . . . . (937) 225-2516 ext. 7684
E-mail: vickie_hensley@ohsb.uscourts.gov

Chambers of Bankruptcy Judge Beth A. Buchanan

221 East Fourth Street, Atrium Two, Suite 800, Cincinnati, OH 45202
Tel: (513) 684-2572 ext. 6725

Beth A. Buchanan
Bankruptcy Judge

Education: Dayton 1997 JD
Began Service: May 10, 2011

Staff

Law Clerk **Carolyn Buffington** . . . . (513) 684-2785
Education: Miami U (OH) 1978 BA, 1980 MS; Cincinnati 1985 JD
Law Clerk **Anthony Ryan Cunningham** . . . . (513) 684-6725
Courtroom Deputy **Glenn Brown** . . . . (513) 684-2468

Chambers of Bankruptcy Judge C. Kathryn Preston
170 North High Street, Columbus, OH 43215
Tel: (614) 469-6638 ext. 5795

C. Kathryn Preston
Bankruptcy Judge

Education: Stetson, JD
Began Service: 2005

Staff
Law Clerk **Philip Stovall** .... (614) 469-6638 ext. 5797
E-mail: philip_stovall@ohsb.uscourts.gov
Career Law Clerk **Kristin Wehrmann** .... (614) 469-6638 ext. 7784
Began Service: 2011
E-mail: kristin_wehrmann@ohsb.uscourts.gov
Education: Capital U 2000 JD
Courtroom Deputy/Judicial Assistant
Kelly Story .... (614) 469-6638 ext. 5795

Chambers of Bankruptcy Judge Guy R. Humphrey
120 West Third Street, Dayton, OH 45402
Tel: (937) 225-2516
E-mail: guy_humphrey@ohsb.uscourts.gov

Guy R. Humphrey
Bankruptcy Judge

Education: Ohio State 1984 JD
Began Service: October 2007
Term Expires: October 2021

Legal Practice: Attorney, Private Practice

Staff
Career Law Clerk **Neil Berman** .... (937) 225-2516 ext. 336
E-mail: neil_berman@ohsb.uscourts.gov
Education: Miami 1992 BA; Toledo 1995 JD
Career Law Clerk **Tom Kisor** .... (937) 225-2516 ext. 352
Courtroom Deputy **Joni Behnken** .... (937) 225-2516 ext. 338
E-mail: joni_behnken@ohsb.uscourts.gov

Chambers of Bankruptcy Judge (recalled) Burton Perlman
Atrium Two, 221 East Fourth Street, Suite 800, Cincinnati, OH 45202
Tel: (513) 684-2572 ext. 6944 Fax: (513) 684-6008
E-mail: Burton_Perlman@ohsb.uscourts.gov

Burton Perlman
Bankruptcy Judge (recalled)

Date of Birth: 1924
Education: Yale 1944 BE, 1947 ME; Michigan 1952 LLB
Began Service: 1976

Academic: Adjunct Professor, University of Cincinnati College of Law

Judicial: Magistrate Judge, United States District Court (1971-1976)

Legal Practice: Private Practice (1952-1971); Private Practice (1958-1971)

Military Service: United States Army (1944-1946)

Current Memberships: American Bar Association; Cincinnati Bar Association; Federal Bar Association

Staff
Law Clerk **(Vacant)** .... (513) 684-2572 ext. 2861
Courtroom Deputy **Cindy Doyle** .... (513) 684-2572 ext. 2471
E-mail: cindy_doyle@ohsb.uscourts.gov
Judicial Assistant **Monica M. Page** .... (513) 684-2572 ext. 6944
E-mail: monica_m._page@ohsb.uscourts.gov

United States District Court for the Eastern District of Oklahoma
U.S. Courthouse, 101 North Fifth Street, Room 208,
Muskogee, OK 74401
P.O. Box 607, Muskogee, OK 74402
Tel: (918) 684-7920 Fax: (918) 684-7902
Internet: www.oked.uscourts.gov

Number of Judgeships: 2

Circuit: Tenth

Areas Covered: Counties of Adair, Atoka, Bryan, Carter, Cherokee, Choctaw, Coal, Haskell, Hughes, Johnson, Latimer, Le Flore, Love, Marshall, McCurtain, McIntosh, Murray, Muskogee, Okfuskee, Okmulgee, Pittsburg, Pontotoc, Pushmataha, Seminole, Sequoyah and Wagoner

Court Staff
Clerk **Patrick Keaney** .... (918) 684-7920
Began Service: March 2013
E-mail: pat_keaney@oked.uscourts.gov
Education: Tulsa 1985 JD
Chief Deputy Clerk **Tami Collins** .... (918) 684-7920
E-mail: tami_collins@oked.uscourts.gov
Chief Probation and Pretrial Services Officer
William H. Bliss, Jr. .... (918) 687-2366
Room 118 Fax: (918) 687-2369
P.O. Box 1645, Muskogee, OK 74401
Systems Administrator **Susan Schwebke** .... (918) 684-7920
E-mail: susan_schwebke@oked.uscourts.gov
Financial Specialist **Susan Gilmartin** .... (918) 684-7920
E-mail: susan_gilmartin@oked.uscourts.gov
Court Reporter **Karla McWhorter** .... (918) 684-7936
E-mail: karla_mcwhorter@oked.uscourts.gov
Court Reporter **Ken Sidwell** .... (918) 684-7935
E-mail: ken_sidwell@oked.uscourts.gov

Chambers of Chief Judge James Hardy Payne
200 U.S. Courthouse, 101 North Fifth Street, Muskogee, OK 74401
P.O. Box 2459, Muskogee, OK 74402-2549
Tel: (918) 684-7940 Fax: (918) 684-7941
E-mail: james_payne@oked.uscourts.gov

James Hardy Payne
Chief Judge

Date of Birth: 1941
Education: Oklahoma 1963 BS, 1966 JD
Began Service: December 17, 2001
Appointed By: President George W. Bush

Affiliation: District Judge, Chambers of District Judge James Hardy Payne, United States District Court for the Northern District of Oklahoma

Government: Assistant United States Attorney, Eastern District of Oklahoma, Office of the United States Attorney, United States Department of Justice (1970-1973)

Judicial: Magistrate Judge, United States District Court for the Eastern District of Oklahoma (1988-2001)

Legal Practice: Sandlin & Payne (1973-1988)

Military Service: United States Air Force (1966-1970); United States Air Force Reserve (1971-1991)

Current Memberships: American Bar Association; Muskogee County Bar Association; Oklahoma Bar Association

Staff
Law Clerk **Vicky Hildebrand** .... (918) 684-7940
Began Service: June 1, 2015
Term Expires: June 7, 2017
E-mail: vicky_hildebrand@oked.uscourts.gov
Career Law Clerk **Gail Jacobs Seward** .... (918) 684-7940
E-mail: gail_seward@oked.uscourts.gov
Education: Oklahoma 1985 BA, 1989 JD
Secretary **Linda Ambrose** .... (918) 684-7940
E-mail: linda_ambrose@oked.uscourts.gov

Chambers of District Judge Ronald A. White

P.O. Box 1009, Muskogee, OK 74402
Tel: (918) 684-7965 Fax: (918) 684-7966
E-mail: ronald_white@oked.uscourts.gov

Ronald A. White
District Judge

Date of Birth: 1961
Education: Oklahoma 1983 BA, 1986 JD
Began Service: October 6, 2003
Appointed By: President George W. Bush

Legal Practice: Associate Attorney, Hall, Estill, Hardwick, Gable, Golden & Nelson, P.C. (1986-1992); Shareholder, Hall, Estill, Hardwick, Gable, Golden & Nelson, P.C. (1992-2003)

Current Memberships: Oklahoma Bar Association

Staff
Career Law Clerk **Kevin L. Smith** .... (918) 684-7965
Education: Oklahoma City 1984 JD
Secretary **Teresa A. Watson** .... (918) 684-7965
E-mail: teresa_campbell@oked.uscourts.gov
Career Law Clerk **Heather Laffitte** .... (918) 684-7965
E-mail: heather_laffitte@oked.uscourts.gov

Chambers of Senior Judge Frank H. Seay

327 U.S. Courthouse, 101 North Fifth Street, Muskogee, OK 74401
P.O. Box 828, Muskogee, OK 74402
Tel: (918) 684-7950
E-mail: frank_seay@oked.uscourts.gov

Frank H. Seay
Senior Judge

Date of Birth: 1938
Education: Oklahoma 1961 BA, 1963 LLB
Began Service: November 5, 1979
Appointed By: President Jimmy Carter
Political Affiliation: Democrat

Government: Assistant to the District Attorney, Office of the District Attorney, State of Oklahoma (1963-1966); First Assistant District Attorney, Office of the District Attorney, State of Oklahoma (1967-1968)

Judicial: Associate Judge, Oklahoma District Court (1968-1979); Chief Judge, United States District Court for the Eastern District of Oklahoma; Member, Judicial Conference of the United States (2003)

Legal Practice: Private Practice (1963-1966)

Current Memberships: American Bar Association; Muskogee County Bar Association; Oklahoma Bar Association; Seminole County Bar Association

Staff
Career Law Clerk **Denise Graham** .... (918) 684-7946
E-mail: denise_graham@oked.uscourts.gov
Career Law Clerk **Jan Cunningham** .... (918) 684-7946
E-mail: jan_cunningham@oked.uscourts.gov

Chambers of Magistrate Judge Kimberly E. West

101 North Fifth Street, Muskogee, OK 74401
P.O. Box 2999, Muskogee, OK 74402-2999
Tel: (918) 684-7930 Fax: (918) 684-7931
E-mail: kimberly_west@oked.uscourts.gov

Kimberly E. West
Magistrate Judge

Date of Birth: April 22, 1958
Education: Oklahoma 1980 BA; Oklahoma City 1983 JD
Began Service: March 15, 2002
Term Expires: March 2018
Political Affiliation: Democrat

Judicial: Judge, Workers' Compensation Court (1990-1996)

Staff
Career Law Clerk **Kurt Anderson** .... (918) 684-7930
E-mail: kurt_anderson@oked.uscourts.gov
Education: Oklahoma 1987 JD
Personal Secretary **Sally Winkle** .... (918) 684-7930
E-mail: sally_winkle@oked.uscourts.gov

Chambers of Magistrate Judge Steven P. Shreder

101 North Fifth Street, Muskogee, OK 74401
P.O. Box 7002, Muskogee, OK 74402
Tel: (918) 684-7960
E-mail: steven_shreder@oked.uscourts.gov

Steven P. Shreder
Magistrate Judge

Began Service: 2003

Staff
Career Law Clerk **Kara Davis** .... (918) 684-7960
Judicial Assistant **Tracy Beeson** .... (918) 684-7960

United States Bankruptcy Court for the Eastern District of Oklahoma

111 West Fourth Street, Second Floor, Okmulgee, OK 74447
P.O. Box 1347, Okmulgee, OK 74447
Tel: (918) 549-7200
Tel: (877) 377-1221 (Voice Case Information System VCIS)
Fax: (918) 549-7248
Internet: www.okeb.uscourts.gov

Number of Judgeships: 1

Court Staff
Clerk **Therese Buthod** .... (918) 549-7221
E-mail: therese_buthod@okeb.uscourts.gov
Education: Oklahoma 1984 JD
Chief Deputy Clerk **C. Fred Burks** .... (918) 549-7224
E-mail: fred_burks@okeb.uscourts.gov
Education: Oklahoma State 1991 MBA
Systems Manager **Jeff Evans** .... (918) 549-7229
E-mail: jeff_evans@okeb.uscourts.gov
Data Quality Analyst **Wanda J. Been** .... (918) 549-7235
E-mail: wanda_been@okeb.uscourts.gov
Operations Supervisor **Debra L. "Debi" Anderson** ...... (918) 549-7228
E-mail: debi_anderson@okeb.uscourts.gov
Financial Administrator **David Grimmett** .... (918) 549-7222
E-mail: david_grimmett@okeb.uscourts.gov
Education: Northeastern State 1988 BS
Case Administrator **Tina Clark** .... (918) 549-7236
Case Administrator **Cheryl Corley** .... (918) 549-7238
Case Administrator **Denise Morrow** .... (918) 549-7242
Case Administrator **Margaret Prentice** .... (918) 549-7225
System Administrator **Kelly Callicoat** .... (918) 549-7241
E-mail: kelly_callicoat@okeb.uscourts.gov
Education: Langston 1999 BSE

United States Bankruptcy Court for the Eastern District of Oklahoma *continued*

Automation Support Specialist **Cindi Howell** . . . . (918) 549-7240
E-mail: cindi_howell@okeb.uscourts.gov
Judicial Assistant **Alexia Bible** . . . . (918) 549-7226
E-mail: alexia_bible@okeb.uscourts.gov

Chambers of Chief Bankruptcy Judge Tom R. Cornish

206 U.S. Post Office & Courthouse, 111 West Fourth Street,
Okmulgee, OK 74447
P.O. Box 1347, Okmulgee, OK 74447
Tel: (918) 549-7226 Fax: (918) 549-7208

Tom R. Cornish
Chief Bankruptcy Judge

Education: Oklahoma State 1966 BS; Oklahoma 1968 JD; Virginia 1982 LLM
Began Service: February 8, 1994
Term Expires: February 2022

Judicial: Judge, Oklahoma Court of Criminal Appeals (1977-1984)

Current Memberships: Oklahoma Bar Association

Staff
Career Law Clerk **Melanie Trump** . . . . (918) 549-7205
Began Service: August 4, 2003
E-mail: melanie_trump@okeb.uscourts.gov
Education: Kansas 1983 JD
Electronic Court Recorder Operator
Denise Morrow . . . . (918) 758-0126 ext. 242
E-mail: denise_morrow@okeb.uscourts.gov Fax: (918) 756-9248
Judicial Assistant **Alexia Bible** . . . . (918) 549-7226
E-mail: alexia_bible@okeb.uscourts.gov

United States District Court for the Northern District of Oklahoma

U.S. Courthouse, 333 West Fourth Street, Room 411, Tulsa, OK 74103
Tel: (918) 699-4700 Tel: (918) 581-6903 (Civil Cases PACER)
Fax: (918) 699-4756
Internet: www.oknd.uscourts.gov

Number of Judgeships: 4

Circuit: Tenth

Areas Covered: Counties of Craig, Creek, Delaware, Mayes, Nowata, Osage, Ottawa, Pawnee, Rogers, Tulsa and Washington

Court Staff

Clerk of the Court **Phil Lombardi** . . . . (918) 699-4700
E-mail: phil_lombardi@oknd.uscourts.gov
Chief Deputy Clerk **Mark C. McCartt** . . . . (918) 699-4700
E-mail: mark_mccartt@oknd.uscourts.gov
Federal Public Defender **Julie O'Connell** . . . . (918) 581-7656
Systems Technology Division Manager **Melinda Cale** . . . . (918) 699-4732
E-mail: melinda_cale@oknd.uscourts.gov
Chief Probation Officer **Todd Gollihare** . . . . (918) 699-4800
Room 3820
Network Administrator **Vern Hughes** . . . . (918) 699-4733
E-mail: vern_hughes@oknd.uscourts.gov

Chambers of Chief Judge Gregory Kent Frizzell

U.S. Courthouse, 333 West Fourth Street, Tulsa, OK 74103
Tel: (918) 699-4781

Gregory Kent Frizzell
Chief Judge

Began Service: February 2007
Appointed By: President George W. Bush

Chambers of Chief Judge Gregory Kent Frizzell *continued*

Staff
Courtroom Deputy **Howard Overton** . . . . (918) 699-4892
E-mail: howard_overton@oknd.uscourts.gov

Chambers of District Judge Claire V. Eagan

411 U.S. Courthouse, 333 West Fourth Street, Tulsa, OK 74103-3819
Tel: (918) 699-4795 Fax: (918) 699-4787
E-mail: ceagan@oknd.uscourts.gov

Claire V. Eagan
District Judge

Date of Birth: 1950
Education: Trinity Col (DC) 1972 BA; Fordham 1976 JD
Began Service: October 25, 2001
Appointed By: President George W. Bush
Political Affiliation: Republican

Current Memberships: American Bar Foundation; The Council Oak/Johnson-Sontag American Inn of Court, The American Inns of Court; Tulsa Women Lawyers Association; United States Foreign Intelligence Surveillance Court

Staff
Law Clerk **Nicholas Haugen** . . . . (918) 699-4795
Began Service: 2006
E-mail: nicholas_haugen@oknd.uscourts.gov
Education: Tulsa 2005 JD
Law Clerk **Jason L. Callaway** . . . . (918) 699-4795
Began Service: 2014
E-mail: jason_callaway@oknd.uscourts.gov
Courtroom Deputy **Debbie Holland** . . . . (918) 699-4723
E-mail: dholland@oknd.uscourts.gov
Judicial Assistant **Regina Glaze** . . . . (918) 699-4795
E-mail: regina_glaze@oknd.uscourts.gov
Education: Northeastern State 1994 BBA

Chambers of District Judge James Hardy Payne

P.O. Box 2459, Muskogee, OK 74402-2549
333 West Fourth Street, Tulsa, OK 74103
Tel: (918) 699-4790 Fax: (918) 684-7941

James Hardy Payne
District Judge

Date of Birth: 1941
Education: Oklahoma 1963 BS, 1966 JD
Began Service: December 17, 2001
Appointed By: President George W. Bush

Affiliation: Chief Judge, Chambers of Chief Judge James Hardy Payne, United States District Court for the Eastern District of Oklahoma

Government: Assistant United States Attorney, Eastern District of Oklahoma, Office of the United States Attorney, United States Department of Justice (1970-1973)

Judicial: Magistrate Judge, United States District Court for the Eastern District of Oklahoma (1988-2001)

Legal Practice: Sandlin & Payne (1973-1988)

Military Service: United States Air Force (1966-1970); United States Air Force Reserve (1971-1991)

Current Memberships: American Bar Association; Muskogee County Bar Association; Oklahoma Bar Association

Staff
Law Clerk **Vicky Hildebrand** . . . . (918) 684-7940
Began Service: June 1, 2015
Term Expires: June 5, 2017
E-mail: vicky_hildebrand@oked.uscourts.gov
Career Law Clerk **Gail Jacobs Seward** . . . . (918) 684-7940
Secretary **Linda Ambrose** . . . . (918) 684-7940

Chambers of District Judge John E. Dowdell

333 West Fourth Street, Tulsa, OK 74103
Tel: (918) 699-4130

John E. Dowdell
District Judge

Education: Wake Forest 1978 BA; Tulsa 1981 JD
Began Service: December 28, 2012
Appointed By: President Barack Obama

Clerkships: Law Clerk, Chambers of Senior Judge William J. Holloway, Jr., United States Court of Appeals for the Tenth Circuit (1981-1983)

Legal Practice: Partner, Norman Wohlgemuth Chandler & Dowdell, P.C (1983-2012)

Staff
Law Clerk **James M. Blakemore** .... (918) 699-4130
Career Law Clerk **Christine D. Little** .... (918) 699-4130
Courtroom Deputy **Lisa Lyles** .... (918) 699-4130

Chambers of Senior Judge Terence C. Kern

United States District Court, The Federal Building, 224 South Boulder Avenue, Room 241, Tulsa, OK 74103
Tel: (918) 699-4770 Fax: (918) 699-4771

Terence C. "Terry" Kern
Senior Judge

Date of Birth: 1944
Education: Oklahoma State 1966 BS; Oklahoma 1969 JD; Virginia 2004 LLM
Began Service: June 9, 1994
Appointed By: President William J. Clinton
Political Affiliation: Democrat

Government: General Attorney, Federal Trade Commission (1969-1970)

Legal Practice: Partner, Fischl, Culp, McMillin, Kern & Chaffin (1970-1986); President and Shareholder, Kern, Mordy & Sperry, P.C. (1986-1994)

Military Service: Oklahoma Army National Guard (1969-1970); United States Army Reserve, United States Department of the Army (1970-1975)

Current Memberships: American Bar Foundation; American Bar Association; American Board of Trial Advocates; The American Inns of Court; Federal Judges Association; Oklahoma Bar Association; Oklahoma Bar Foundation, Oklahoma Bar Association

Staff
Law Clerk **Ashley Schubert** .... (918) 699-4772
E-mail: ashley_schubert@oknd.uscourts.gov
Career Law Clerk **Jodi F. Jayne** .... (918) 699-4773
E-mail: jodi_jayne@oknd.uscourts.gov
Education: Westminster (MO) 1999 BA; Oklahoma 2002 JD
Judicial Secretary **Vicki Hendryx** .... (918) 699-4770
E-mail: vicki_hendryx@oknd.uscourts.gov

Chambers of Magistrate Judge F. H. McCarthy

U.S. Courthouse, 333 West Fourth Street, Tulsa, OK 74103
Tel: (918) 699-4765

F. H. McCarthy
Magistrate Judge

Date of Birth: 1952
Education: Scranton 1974 BS; Tulsa 1977 JD
Began Service: April 10, 1995
Term Expires: April 9, 2019

Government: Deputy Chief Public Defender, Office of the County Treasurer, County of Tulsa, Oklahoma (1976-1985); Senior Litigation Counsel, United States Department of Justice (1985-1987)

Legal Practice: Barkley, Rodolf & McCarthy (1987-1995)

Chambers of Magistrate Judge F. H. McCarthy *continued*

Current Memberships: Federal Magistrate Judges Association; Oklahoma Bar Association; Tulsa County Bar Association

Staff
Career Law Clerk **Ann Makela Schneider** .... (918) 699-4765
E-mail: ann_schneider@oknd.uscourts.gov
Education: Tulsa 1986 JD
Courtroom Deputy **Tami Calico** .... (918) 699-4765
E-mail: tami_calico@oknd.uscourts.gov
Paralegal **Paige Bruce** .... (918) 699-4765

Chambers of Magistrate Judge Paul J. Cleary

U.S. Courthouse, 333 West Fourth Street, Room 411, Tulsa, OK 74103-3819
Tel: (918) 699-4890 Fax: (918) 699-4794
E-mail: pcleary@oknd.uscourts.gov

Paul J. Cleary
Magistrate Judge

Education: Worcester Polytech 1971 BS; Tulsa 1981 JD
Began Service: July 22, 2002
Term Expires: July 2018

Staff
Career Law Clerk **Rihannon Baker** .... (918) 699-4893
E-mail: rihannon_baker@oknd.uscourts.gov
Career Law Clerk (Part-Time) **Barbara Woltz** .... (918) 699-4890
E-mail: barbara_woltz@oknd.uscourts.gov
Paralegal **Allison Gallant** .... (918) 699-4891
E-mail: allison_gallant@oknd.uscourts.gov
Education: Arizona 1989 BS

Chambers of Magistrate Judge T. Lane Wilson

333 West Fourth, Room 411, Tulsa, OK 74103
Tel: (918) 699-4760

T. Lane Wilson
Judge

Began Service: 2009

Staff
Career Law Clerk **Kimberly Gore** .... (918) 669-4760
Courtroom Deputy **Camie Porpilloz** .... (918) 699-4760

United States Bankruptcy Court for the Northern District of Oklahoma

224 South Boulder Avenue, Room 105, Tulsa, OK 74103
Tel: (918) 699-4000
Tel: (918) 699-4001 (Voice Case Information System VCIS)
Tel: (866) 222-8029 Fax: (918) 699-4045
Internet: www.oknb.uscourts.gov

Number of Judgeships: 2

Court Staff
Clerk of Court **Michael L. Williams** .... (918) 699-4000
E-mail: michael_l_williams@oknb.uscourts.gov
Education: Arizona State 1988 BS; BYU 1990 MPA
Chief Deputy Clerk **Andrea Redmon** .... (918) 699-4000
E-mail: andrea_redmon@oknb.uscourts.gov
Property and Procurement Specialist **(Vacant)** .... (918) 699-4014
Human Resources Administrator **Charlotte Griggs** ...... (918) 699-4841
Fax: (918) 699-4045

Chambers of Chief Bankruptcy Judge Terrence L. Michael

224 South Boulder Avenue, Tulsa, OK 74103-3015
Tel: (918) 699-4065
E-mail: terrence_michael@oknb.uscourts.gov

Terrence L. Michael
Chief Bankruptcy Judge

Date of Birth: 1958
Education: Doane 1980 BA; USC 1983 JD
Began Service: June 9, 1997
Term Expires: June 9, 2025

Affiliation: Bankruptcy Judge, Chambers of Bankruptcy Judge Terrence L. Michael, United States Bankruptcy Appellate Panel for the Tenth Circuit

Judicial: Chief Bankruptcy Judge, United States Bankruptcy Court for the Northern District of Oklahoma (1999-2001); Chief Bankruptcy Judge, United States Bankruptcy Court for the Northern District of Oklahoma (2003-2006)

Legal Practice: Baird, Holm Law Offices (1983-1997)

Current Memberships: National Conference of Bankruptcy Judges

Staff
Career Law Clerk **Janie Phelps** ....(918) 699-4062
E-mail: janie_phelps@oknb.uscourts.gov
Education: Lewis & Clark 2004 JD
Courtroom Deputy **Sue Haskins** .... (918) 699-4068
E-mail: sue_haskins@oknb.uscourts.gov
Judicial Assistant **Odie Gonzales** .... (918) 699-4065
E-mail: odie_gonzales@oknb.uscourts.gov

Chambers of Bankruptcy Judge Dana L. Rasure

224 South Boulder Avenue, Tulsa, OK 74103
Tel: (918) 699-4085 Fax: (918) 699-4090
E-mail: Dana_Rasure@oknb.uscourts.gov

Dana L. Rasure
Bankruptcy Judge

Date of Birth: 1952
Education: Washburn 1973 BA; Michigan 1977 JD
Began Service: 1997
Term Expires: January 2025

Staff
Career Law Clerk **Barbara J. Eden** ....(918) 699-4085
E-mail: Barbara_Eden@oknb.uscourts.gov
Education: Tulsa 1990 JD
Courtroom Deputy **Brenda Nickels** ....(918) 699-4085
E-mail: Brenda_Nickels@oknb.uscourts.gov

United States District Court for the Western District of Oklahoma

U.S. Courthouse, 200 NW Fourth Street, Room 1210,
Oklahoma City, OK 73102
Tel: (405) 609-5000 Fax: (405) 609-5099
Internet: www.okwd.uscourts.gov

Number of Judgeships: 6

Number of Vacancies: 3

Circuit: Tenth

Areas Covered: Counties of Alfalfa, Beaver, Beckham, Blaine, Caddo, Canadian, Cimarron, Cleveland, Comanche, Cotton, Custer, Dewey, Ellis, Garfield, Garvin, Grady, Grant, Greer, Harmon, Harper, Jackson, Jefferson, Kay, Kingfisher, Kiowa, Lincoln, Logan, Major, McClain, Noble, Oklahoma, Payne, Pottawatomie, Roger Mills, Stephens, Texas, Tillman, Washita, Woods and Woodward

United States District Court for the Western District of Oklahoma *continued*

Court Staff

Clerk of Court **Carmelita Reeder Shinn** .... (405) 609-5000
Education: Oregon 1982 JD
Chief Probation Officer **Steve Skinner** .... (405) 609-5800
United States Probation Office, 215 Dean A McGee, Room 201, Oklahoma City, OK 73102 Fax: (405) 609-5859

Chambers of Chief Judge Vicki Miles-LaGrange

U.S. Courthouse, 200 NW Fourth Street, Room 3301,
Oklahoma City, OK 73102
Tel: (405) 609-5400 Fax: (405) 609-5413

Vicki Miles-LaGrange
Chief Judge

Date of Birth: 1953
Education: Vassar 1974 BA; Howard U 1977 JD
Began Service: November 28, 1994
Appointed By: President William J. Clinton
Political Affiliation: Democrat

Current Memberships: American Bar Association; The William J. Holloway, Jr. American Inn of Court, The American Inns of Court; National Bar Association; Oklahoma Association of Black Lawyers; Oklahoma Bar Association

Staff
Law Clerk **Tiece Dempsey** .... (405) 609-5400
Began Service: October 2009
E-mail: tiece_dempsey@okwd.uscourts.gov
Law Clerk **(Vacant)** ....(405) 609-5400
Career Law Clerk **Lori Fagan** ....(405) 609-5400
E-mail: lori_fagan@okwd.uscourts.gov
Education: Oklahoma 1994 BA, 1997 JD
Courtroom Deputy **Kathy Spaulding** .... (405) 609-5402
E-mail: kathy_spaulding@okwd.uscourts.gov
Court Reporter **Lynn Lee** .... (405) 609-5403
E-mail: lynn_lee@okwd.uscourts.gov
Administrative Assistant **Willa Bray** ....(405) 609-5400
E-mail: willa_bray@okwd.uscourts.gov

Chambers of District Judge Joe Heaton

U.S. Courthouse, 200 NW Fourth Street, Room 3108,
Oklahoma City, OK 73102-3092
Tel: (405) 609-5600 Fax: (405) 609-5607

Joe Heaton
District Judge

Date of Birth: 1951
Education: Northwestern Oklahoma St 1973 BA; Oklahoma 1976 JD
Began Service: December 13, 2001
Appointed By: President George W. Bush
Political Affiliation: Republican

Academic: Adjunct Instructor, University of Central Oklahoma (1980-1981); Adjunct Instructor, University of Central Oklahoma (1992-1993)

Government: Legislative Assistant (R-OK), Office of Senator Dewey F. Bartlett, United States Senate (1976-1977); State Representative, Oklahoma House of Representatives (1984-1992); United States Attorney, Western District of Oklahoma, United States Attorney's Office, United States Department of Justice (1992-1993); First Assistant United States Attorney, Western District of Oklahoma, United States Attorney's Office, United States Department of Justice (1996-2001)

Legal Practice: Shareholder, Fuller, Tubb & Pomeroy, PC (1977-1992); Shareholder, Fuller, Tubb & Pomeroy, PC (1993-1996)

(continued on next page)

Chambers of District Judge Joe Heaton *continued*

Current Memberships: American Bar Association; National Association of Former United States Attorneys; Oklahoma Bar Association; Oklahoma County Bar Association

Staff

Law Clerk **Elizabeth Isaacs** .... (405) 609-5600
Began Service: August 2015
Term Expires: August 2016
E-mail: elizabeth_isaacs@okwd.uscourts.gov

Career Law Clerk **Judy J. Thompson** .... (405) 609-5600
E-mail: Judy_J_Thompson@okwd.uscourts.gov
Education: Oklahoma 1982 JD

Courtroom Reporter **Jeanne Ring** .... (405) 609-5603
E-mail: Jeanne_Ring@okwd.uscourts.gov

Judicial Assistant/Courtroom Deputy **Lisa Minter** .... (405) 609-5601
E-mail: Lisa_Minter@okwd.uscourts.gov
Education: Oklahoma 1982 BFA

Chambers of District Judge Timothy D. DeGiusti

U.S. Courthouse, 200 NW Fourth Street, Room 5012,
Oklahoma City, OK 73102
Tel: (405) 609-5120 Fax: (405) 609-5131
E-mail: timothy_degiusti@okwd.uscourts.gov

Timothy D. DeGiusti
District Judge

Date of Birth: 1962
Education: Oklahoma 1985 BA, 1988 JD
Began Service: August 9, 2007
Appointed By: President George W. Bush

Legal Practice: Associate, Andrews Davis Law Firm (1988-1990); Partner, Holladay, Chilton & DeGiusti, PLLC (2000-2007)

Staff

Career Law Clerk **(Vacant)** .... (405) 609-5120

Career Law Clerk **Marcia Rupert** .... (405) 609-5120
E-mail: marcia_rupert@okwd.uscourts.gov
Education: Oklahoma 1987 JD

Courtroom Deputy Clerk **Mike Bailey** .... (405) 609-5122
E-mail: mike_bailey@okwd.uscourts.gov

Court Reporter **Christy Clark** .... (405) 609-5123
E-mail: christina_clark@okwd.uscourts.gov

Judicial Assistant **Sharon A. Henshall** .... (405) 609-5120
E-mail: sharon_henshall@okwd.uscourts.gov

Chambers of Senior Judge Lee R. West

3001 U.S. Courthouse, 200 NW Fourth Street, Oklahoma City, OK 73102
Tel: (405) 609-5140 Fax: (405) 609-5151

Lee R. West
Senior Judge

Date of Birth: 1929
Education: Oklahoma 1952 BA, 1956 JD; Harvard 1963 LLM
Began Service: November 5, 1979
Appointed By: President Jimmy Carter
Political Affiliation: Democrat

Academic: Faculty, University of Oklahoma (1961-1962)

Government: Member, Civil Aeronautics Board (1973-1978)

Judicial: Judge, Oklahoma District Court, 22nd Judicial District (1965-1973); Special Justice, Oklahoma Supreme Court and Court of Criminal Appeals (1973)

Legal Practice: Partner, Busby, Stanfield, Deaton & West (1956-1961); Partner, Deaton, Gassaway & West (1963-1965); Hall, Estill, Hardwick, Gable, Collingsworth & Nelson (1978-1979)

Military Service: United States Marine Corps (1952-1956)

Chambers of Senior Judge Lee R. West *continued*

Current Memberships: Oklahoma Bar Association; Pontotoc County Bar Association

Staff

Career Law Clerk **Cynthia J. Smith** .... (405) 609-5143
Education: Oklahoma City 1981 JD

Career Law Clerk **Jacqueline Stone** .... (405) 609-5144
E-mail: jacqueline_stone@okwd.uscourts.gov
Education: Oklahoma 1990 JD

Secretary **Kadi Burlson** .... (405) 609-5141
E-mail: kadi_burlson@okwd.uscourts.gov

Chambers of Senior Judge Tim Leonard

U.S. Courthouse, 200 NW Fourth Street, Room 4301,
Oklahoma City, OK 73102
Tel: (405) 609-5300 Fax: (405) 609-5313
Internet: http://www.okwd.uscourts.gov/chambers/leonard.htm

Tim Leonard
Senior Judge

Date of Birth: 1940
Education: Oklahoma 1962 BA, 1965 JD
Began Service: August 1992
Appointed By: President George H.W. Bush
Political Affiliation: Republican

Government: Assistant Attorney General, Office of the Attorney General, State of Oklahoma (1969-1971); State Senator (OK), Oklahoma State Senate (1979-1988); United States Attorney, Western District of Oklahoma, United States Department of Justice (1989-1992)

Legal Practice: Partner, Blankenship, Herrold, Russell & Leonard (1971); Partner, Trippet, Leonard & Kee (1971-1988); Of Counsel, Huckaby, Fleming, Frailey, Chaffin & Darrah (1988-1989)

Military Service: United States Navy (1965-1968); United States Naval Reserve (1968-1972)

Current Memberships: American Bar Association; Federal Bar Association; Oklahoma Bar Association; Oklahoma County Bar Association

Staff

Career Law Clerk **Sheila Williams** .... (405) 609-5300
E-mail: sheila_williams@okwd.uscourts.gov
Education: Oklahoma 1989 JD

Courtroom Deputy **Jamie Youngberg** .... (405) 609-5302
E-mail: jamie_youngberg@okwd.uscourts.gov

Chambers of Senior Judge David L. Russell

U.S. Courthouse, 200 NW Fourth Street, Room 3309,
Oklahoma City, OK 73102
Tel: (405) 609-5100 Fax: (405) 609-5113

David L. Russell
Senior Judge

Date of Birth: 1942
Education: Oklahoma Baptist 1963 BS; Oklahoma 1965 JD
Began Service: 1982
Appointed By: President Ronald Reagan
Political Affiliation: Republican

Current Memberships: Federal Bar Association; Oklahoma Bar Association; Oklahoma County Bar Association

Staff

Career Law Clerk **Joan Curran** .... (405) 609-5100
E-mail: joan_curran@okwd.uscourts.gov
Education: William & Mary 1994 JD

Career Law Clerk **Susan Hansen** .... (405) 609-5100
E-mail: susan_hansen@okwd.uscourts.gov
Education: Oklahoma City 1981 JD

Chambers of Senior Judge David L. Russell *continued*

Secretary **Marcia Davis** .... (405) 609-5101
E-mail: marcia_davis@okwd.uscourts.gov

Chambers of Senior Judge Robin J. Cauthron

U.S. Courthouse, 200 NW Fourth Street, Room 4001,
Oklahoma City, OK 73102
Tel: (405) 609-5200 Fax: (405) 609-5213

Robin J. Cauthron
Senior Judge

Date of Birth: 1950
Education: Oklahoma 1970 BA; Central State 1974 MEd; Oklahoma 1977 JD
Began Service: April 5, 1991
Appointed By: President George H.W. Bush

Current Memberships: American Bar Association; National Association of Women Judges; Oklahoma Bar Association; Oklahoma Bar Foundation, Oklahoma Bar Association; Oklahoma County Bar Association; Order of the Coif

Staff
Law Clerk **Nicole Lynn** .... (405) 609-5200
Began Service: August 2015
Term Expires: August 2016
E-mail: nicole_lynn@okwd.uscourts.gov
Career Law Clerk **Jeff E. Lynch** .... (405) 609-5200
Education: Oklahoma City 1996 JD
Court Reporter **Sherri Grubbs** .... (405) 816-5204
E-mail: sherri_grubbs@okwd.uscourts.gov
Administrative Assistant **Lyn Marshala** .... (405) 609-5200
E-mail: lyn_marshala@okwd.uscourts.gov
Courtroom Deputy **Linda Goode** .... (405) 609-5202
E-mail: linda_goode@okwd.uscourts.gov

Chambers of Senior Judge Stephen P. Friot

U.S. Courthouse, 200 NW Fourth Street, Room 3102,
Oklahoma City, OK 73102
Tel: (405) 609-5500 Fax: (405) 609-5513
E-mail: judge_stephen_friot@okwd.uscourts.gov

Stephen P. Friot
Senior Judge

Date of Birth: 1947
Education: Oklahoma 1969 BA, 1972 JD
Began Service: November 19, 2001
Appointed By: President George W. Bush

Staff
Career Law Clerk **Barbara Gilbert** .... (405) 609-5504
Career Law Clerk **Liz Hughes** .... (405) 609-5503
Courtroom Deputy and Case Manager **Lori Gray** .... (405) 609-5502
E-mail: lori_gray@okwd.uscourts.gov
Court Reporter **Tracy Washbourne** .... (405) 609-5505
E-mail: tracy_washbourne@okwd.uscourts.gov
Administrative Assistant **Caral Lock** .... (405) 609-5501
E-mail: caral_lock@okwd.uscourts.gov

Chambers of Magistrate Judge Gary M. Purcell

U.S. Courthouse, 200 NW Fourth Street, Room 2006,
Oklahoma City, OK 73102
Tel: (405) 609-5260 Fax: (405) 609-5267

Gary M. Purcell
Magistrate Judge

Date of Birth: 1950
Education: Oklahoma 1973 BA; Oklahoma City 1975 JD
Began Service: December 28, 1992
Term Expires: December 2016

Clerkships: Law Clerk, United States District Court (1976-1979)

Government: Legal Intern, Oklahoma Court of Criminal Appeals (1975)

Judicial: Special Judge, Oklahoma District Court (1979-1992)

Current Memberships: Cleveland County Bar Association; Federal Bar Association; Oklahoma Bar Association; Oklahoma County Bar Association

Staff
Career Law Clerk **Janice Yeary** .... (405) 609-5260
E-mail: janice_yeary@okwd.uscourts.gov
Education: Oklahoma 1976 BA, 1984 JD
Administrative Assistant **Angie McCombs** .... (405) 609-5260
E-mail: angie_mccombs@okwd.uscourts.gov

Chambers of Magistrate Judge Shon T. Erwin

U.S. Courthouse, 410 SW Fifth Street, Room 102,
Lawton, OK 73501-4628
Tel: (580) 355-6340 Fax: (580) 355-1305

Shon T. Erwin
Magistrate Judge

Date of Birth: 1961
Education: Oral Roberts 1983 BA; Oklahoma 1986 JD
Began Service: June 1, 1995

Affiliation: Partner, Godlove, Mayhall, Dzialo, Dutcher & Erwin, P.C.

Current Memberships: Oklahoma Bar Foundation, Oklahoma Bar Association

Membership: Member, Board of Directors, Young Lawyer's Division, Oklahoma Bar Association (1991-1996); Member, Real Property, Probate and Trust Law Section, Oklahoma Bar Association; Trustee, Oklahoma Bar Foundation, Oklahoma Bar Association (2004)

Staff
Courtroom Deputy **Monja Smith** .... (580) 713-7116
E-mail: monja_smith@okwd.uscourts.gov
Administrative Assistant **Michelle Roudebush** .... (580) 355-6340
E-mail: michelle_roudebush@okwd.uscourts.gov

Chambers of Magistrate Judge Suzanne Mitchell

U.S. Courthouse, 200 Fourth Street NW, First Floor, Room 1301,
Oklahoma City, OK 73102
Tel: (405) 609-5220 Fax: (405) 609-5227

Suzanne Mitchell
Magistrate Judge

Education: Georgetown 1990 BS; George Washington 1996 JD

Staff
Career Law Clerk **Anne Threlkeld** .... (405) 609-5220
Career Law Clerk **Steve Rogers** .... (405) 609-5220
E-mail: steve_rogers@okwd.uscourts.gov
Administrative Assistant **Marsha Thompson** .... (405) 609-5220
E-mail: marsha_thompson@okwd.uscourts.gov

Chambers of Magistrate Judge Charles B. Goodwin

200 NW Fourth Street, First Floor, Room 1305,
Oklahoma City, OK 73102
Tel: (405) 609-5440 Fax: (405) 609-5449
E-mail: charles_goodwin@okwd.uscourts.gov

Charles B. Goodwin
Magistrate Judge

United States Bankruptcy Court for the Western District of Oklahoma

Old Post Office Building, 215 Dean A. McGee Avenue,
Oklahoma City, OK 73102
Tel: (405) 609-5700
Tel: (866) 222-8029 ext. 13 (Voice Case Information System VCIS)

Number of Judgeships: 3

Court Staff
Clerk of the Court **Grant E. Price** .... (405) 609-5700
E-mail: grant_price@okwb.uscourts.gov
Education: Oklahoma 1972 BA;
Oklahoma City 1978 JD
Chief Deputy Court Clerk **Sheila Sewell** .... (405) 609-5767

Chambers of Chief Bankruptcy Judge Sarah A. Hall

215 Dean A. McGee Avenue, 6th Floor, Oklahoma City, OK 73102
Tel: (405) 609-5660 Fax: (405) 609-5671

Sarah A. Hall
Chief Bankruptcy Judge

Began Service: 2012

Staff
Career Law Clerk **Craig Marshall Regens** .... (405) 609-5660
Courtroom Deputy **Denise Calvert** .... (405) 609-5662
Judicial Assistant **Cheryl Shook** .... (405) 609-5660

Chambers of Bankruptcy Judge Janice Loyd

215 Dean A. McGee Avenue, Oklahoma City, OK 73102
Tel: (405) 609-5678

Janice Loyd
Bankruptcy Judge

Staff
Law Clerk **Jim Bellingham** .... (405) 609-5678
Courtroom Deputy **Debbie Rohde** .... (405) 609-5678
Judicial Assistant **Judy Morgan** .... (405) 609-5678

United States District Court for the District of Oregon

Mark O. Hatfield U.S. Courthouse, 1000 SW Third Street,
Portland, OR 97204-2902
Tel: (503) 326-8000 Tel: (503) 326-8904 (PACER)
Fax: (503) 326-8010
Internet: www.ord.uscourts.gov

Number of Judgeships: 6

Circuit: Ninth

Court Staff
Clerk of Court **Mary L. Moran** .... (503) 326-8091
E-mail: mary_moran@ord.uscourts.gov Fax: (503) 326-8080
Chief Deputy Clerk **Susan Kim** .... (503) 326-8090
E-mail: susan_kim@ord.uscourts.gov Fax: (503) 326-8080

Deputy Clerk **(Vacant)** .... (503) 326-8051
Director of Operational Services - Portland (Interim)
Laura M. Brennan .... (503) 326-8163
E-mail: laura_brennan@ord.uscourts.gov Fax: (503) 326-8080
Division Manager - Eugene **Christine Weller** .... (541) 431-4111
405 East Eighth Avenue, Suite 2100, Fax: (541) 431-4109
Eugene, OR 97401
Division Manager - Portland **(Vacant)** .... (503) 326-8092
Budget Director **Adair Fernee** .... (503) 326-8093
E-mail: adair_fernee@ord.uscourts.gov
Director of Information Technology
Stephen J. Sibelman .... (503) 326-8077
E-mail: stephen_sibelman@ord.uscourts.gov Fax: (503) 326-8080
Chief Probation Officer **(Vacant)** .... (503) 326-8601
340 U.S. Courthouse, 1000 SW Third Ave., Fax: (503) 326-8700
Portland, OR 97204
Financial and Budget Administrator
Renee M. Martinez .... (503) 326-8173
E-mail: renee_martinez@ord.uscourts.gov Fax: (503) 326-8080
Court Security Supervisor **Karl Knobbs** .... (503) 326-5007
Personnel Director **Cherie Chapman** .... (503) 326-8192
E-mail: cherie_nelson@ord.uscourts.gov Fax: (503) 326-8080
Personnel Specialist **Megan Morris** .... (503) 326-8169
E-mail: megan_morris@ord.uscourts.gov Fax: (503) 326-8080
Procurement Specialist **Randy Moore** .... (503) 326-8175
Librarian **Julia O. Sathler** .... (503) 326-8140
Fax: (503) 326-8144

Chambers of Chief Judge Ann L. Aiken

Wayne L. Morse U.S. Courthouse, 405 East Eighth Avenue,
Suite 5500, Eugene, OR 97401
Tel: (541) 431-4140 Fax: (541) 431-4149
E-mail: Ann_Aiken@ord.uscourts.gov

Ann L. Aiken
Chief Judge

Date of Birth: 1951
Education: Oregon 1974 BS; Rutgers 1976 MA; Oregon 1979 JD
Began Service: February 4, 1998
Appointed By: President William J. Clinton

Current Memberships: Lane County Bar Association; Lane County Women Lawyers Association; Oregon State Bar; Oregon Women Lawyers

Staff
Staff Attorney **Danette Bloomer** .... (541) 431-4140
E-mail: Danette_Bloomer@ord.uscourts.gov
Education: Oregon 1995 JD
Staff Attorney **Jolie Russo** .... (541) 431-4140
E-mail: Jolie_Russo@ord.uscourts.gov
Education: Lewis & Clark 1988 JD
Courtroom Deputy **Rebecca Henshaw** .... (541) 431-4102
E-mail: rebecca_henshaw@ord.uscourts.gov
Court Reporter **Kristi Anderson** .... (541) 431-4112
E-mail: kristi_anderson@ord.uscourts.gov
Judicial Assistant **Kellie King** .... (541) 431-4141
E-mail: Kellie_King@ord.uscourts.gov
Education: Oregon 1983 BS

Chambers of District Judge Anna J. Brown
Mark O. Hatfield U.S. Courthouse, 1000 SW Third Street,
Room 1407, Portland, OR 97204-2944
Tel: (503) 326-8350
E-mail: anna_brown@ord.uscourts.gov

Anna J. Brown
District Judge

Date of Birth: 1952
Education: Portland State 1975 BS; Lewis & Clark 1980 JD
Began Service: October 27, 1999
Appointed By: President William J. Clinton

Academic: Records Clerk, Dispatcher, Police Community Service Officer, Police Department (1970-1975); Police Emergency Communications Operator (1975-1977)

Clerkships: Judicial Law Clerk The Honorable John C. Beatty, Jr., Multnomah County Circuit Court (1978-1980)

Judicial: District Court Judge, Multnomah County (1992-1994); Circuit Court Judge, Multnomah County (1994-1999)

Legal Practice: Associate, Bullivant, Houser, Bailey, Pendergrass and Hoffman (1980-1986); Partner, Bullivant, Houser, Bailey, Pendergrass and Hoffman (1986-1992)

Current Memberships: American Bar Association; The Gus J. Solomon American Inn of Court, The American Inns of Court; Federal Bar Association; Multnomah County Bar Association; Oregon State Bar; Oregon Women Lawyers; United States District Court of Oregon Historical Society

Staff
Law Clerk **Christopher Riser** .... (503) 326-8352
Term Expires: May 2016
Career Law Clerk **Sandra J. Dixon** .... (503) 326-8351
E-mail: sandra_dixon@ord.uscourts.gov
Education: Oklahoma 1972 MA; Lewis & Clark 1989 JD
Career Law Clerk **Margaret Wells** .... (503) 326-8350
E-mail: margaret_wells@ord.uscourts.gov
Education: Boston Col 1991 BS; Lewis & Clark 1995 JD
Court Reporter **Amanda LeGore** .... (503) 326-8184
E-mail: amanda_legore@ord.uscourts.gov
Courtroom Deputy **Bonnie Boyer** .... (503) 326-8353
E-mail: bonnie_boyer@ord.uscourts.gov

Chambers of District Judge Michael W. Mosman
1000 SW Third Avenue, Room 1615, Portland, OR 97204
Tel: (503) 326-8330
E-mail: michael_mosman@ord.uscourts.gov

Michael W. Mosman
District Judge

Education: Utah State BA; J Reuben Clark Law JD
Began Service: October 3, 2003
Appointed By: President George W. Bush

Government: U.S. Attorney, District of Oregon, United States Attorney's Office, United States Department of Justice (1988)

Current Memberships: United States Foreign Intelligence Surveillance Court

Staff
Courtroom Deputy **Dawn Stephens** .... (503) 326-8024
E-mail: dawn_stephens@ord.uscourts.gov
Judicial Assistant **Mary Jo Peters** .... (503) 326-8331
E-mail: mary_jo_peters@ord.uscourts.gov

Chambers of District Judge Marco A. Hernandez
1427 United States Courthouse, 1000 Southwest Third Avenue,
Portland, OR 97204-2944
Tel: (503) 326-8210
E-mail: marco_hernandez@ord.uscourts.gov

Marco A. Hernandez
District Judge

Education: Western Oregon State 1983 BA; U Washington 1986 JD
Began Service: February 9, 2011
Appointed By: President Barack Obama

Staff
Law Clerk **Robert Doeckel** .... (503) 326-8211
E-mail: robert_doeckel@ord.uscourts.gov
Law Clerk **Maria Witt** .... (503) 326-8210
E-mail: maria_witt@ord.uscourts.gov
Career Law Clerk **Amy Kent** .... (503) 326-8210
E-mail: amy_kent@ord.uscourts.gov
Education: Lewis & Clark 1989 JD
Court Reporter **Nancy Walker** .... (503) 326-8186
E-mail: nancy_walker@ord.uscourts.gov
Courtroom Deputy **Michelle Rawson** .... (503) 326-8051
E-mail: michelle_rawson@ord.uscourts.gov

Chambers of District Judge Michael H. Simon
Mark O. Hatfield U.S. Courthouse, 1000 SW Third Street,
Room 1327, Portland, OR 97204
Tel: (503) 326-8380
E-mail: michael_simon@ord.uscourts.gov

Michael H. Simon
District Judge

Education: UCLA 1978 BA; Harvard 1981 JD
Began Service: June 22, 2011
Appointed By: President Barack Obama

Staff
Law Clerk **(Vacant)** .... (503) 326-8381
Law Clerk **Nicholas Meyers** .... (503) 326-8382
E-mail: nicholas_meyers@ord.uscourts.gov
Law Clerk **Nicholle Winters** .... (503) 326-8383
E-mail: nicholle_winters@ord.uscourts.gov
Courtroom Deputy **Mary Austad** .... (503) 326-8034
E-mail: mary_austad@ord.uscourts.gov

Chambers of District Judge Michael J. McShane
405 East Eighth Avenue, Room 5700, Eugene, OR 97401
Tel: (503) 431-4150
E-mail: michael_mcshane@ord.uscourts.gov

Michael J. McShane
District Judge

Education: Gonzaga 1983 BA; Northwestern 1988 JD
Began Service: June 3, 2013
Appointed By: President Barack Obama

Legal Practice: Public Defender, Metropolitan Public Defender

Staff
Law Clerk **David Svelund** .... (503) 431-4150
E-mail: david_svelund@ord.uscourts.gov
Law Clerk **James Cleavenger** .... (503) 431-4150
E-mail: james_cleavenger@ord.uscourts.gov
Law Clerk **Matthew Berry** .... (503) 431-4150
E-mail: matthew_berry@ord.uscourts.gov
Courtroom Deputy **Charlene Pew** .... (503) 431-4105
E-mail: charlene_pew@ord.uscourts.gov
Court Reporter **Kristi Anderson** .... (503) 431-4150

Chambers of Senior Judge Owen M. Panner

James A. Redden United States Courthouse, 310 West Sixth Street, Medford, OR 97501
Tel: (541) 608-8756
E-mail: owen_panner@ord.uscourts.gov

Owen M. Panner
Senior Judge

Date of Birth: 1924
Education: Oklahoma 1949 LLB
Began Service: February 20, 1980
Appointed By: President Jimmy Carter
Political Affiliation: Republican

Legal Practice: Senior Partner, Panner, Johnson, Marceau, Karnopp, Kennedy & Nash (1950-1980)

Military Service: United States Army (1943-1946)

Current Memberships: American Bar Foundation; American Board of Trial Advocates; American College of Trial Lawyers; Oregon State Bar

Staff

Career Law Clerk **Marc Herzfeld** . . . . (541) 608-8756
E-mail: marc_herzfeld@ord.uscourts.gov
Education: Kansas 1982 BS; Lewis & Clark 1985 JD
Law Clerk **Daniel Philpott** . . . . (541) 608-8756
E-mail: daniel_philpott@ord.uscourts.gov
Judicial Assistant, Medford Office **Wendy Koble** . . . . (541) 608-8756
E-mail: wendy_koble@ord.uscourts.gov

Chambers of Senior Judge James A. Redden, Jr.

Mark O. Hatfield U.S. Courthouse, 1000 SW Third Street, Room 1527, Portland, OR 97204-2902
Tel: (503) 326-8370 Fax: (503) 326-8379
E-mail: james_redden@ord.uscourts.gov

James A. Redden, Jr.
Senior Judge

Date of Birth: 1929
Education: Boston Col 1954 LLB
Began Service: March 24, 1980
Appointed By: President Jimmy Carter
Political Affiliation: Democrat

Government: State Representative (OR), Oregon State House of Representatives (1963-1967); Chairman, Public Employee Relations Board, State of Oregon (1969-1972); Treasurer, State of Oregon (1973-1976); Attorney General, State of Oregon (1977-1980)

Legal Practice: Roberts, Kellington & Branchfield (1956-1957); Partner, Collins, Redden, Ferris & Velure (1957-1973)

Military Service: United States Army (1946-1948)

Current Memberships: American Bar Association; American Board of Trial Advocates; Massachusetts Bar Association; Oregon Association of Defense Counsel; Oregon State Bar

Staff

Career Law Clerk **Michele Friedman** . . . . (503) 326-8370
E-mail: michele_friedman@ord.uscourts.gov
Judicial Assistant/Courtroom Deputy **(Vacant)** . . . . (503) 326-8370

Chambers of Senior Judge Malcolm F. Marsh

Mark O. Hatfield U.S. Courthouse, 1000 SW Third Avenue, Room 1507, Portland, OR 97204-2902
Tel: (503) 326-8360 Fax: (503) 326-8369
E-mail: malcolm_marsh@ord.uscourts.gov

Malcolm F. Marsh
Senior Judge

Date of Birth: 1928
Education: Oregon 1952 BS, 1954 LLB, 1971 JD
Began Service: April 16, 1987
Appointed By: President Ronald Reagan

Legal Practice: Partner, Clark, Marsh, Lindauer & McClinton (1958-1987)

Military Service: United States Army (1946-1947)

Current Memberships: American Bar Association; American College of Trial Lawyers; Oregon State Bar

Staff

Law Clerk **Jackie Holley** . . . . (503) 326-8360
E-mail: jackie_holley@ord.uscourts.gov
Law Clerk **LeAnn Jabs** . . . . (503) 326-8360
Judicial Assistant and Courtroom Deputy **Trish Hunt** . . . . . (503) 326-8360
E-mail: trish_hunt@ord.uscourts.gov

Chambers of Senior Judge Robert E. Jones

Mark O. Hatfield U.S. Courthouse, 1000 SW Third Avenue, Room 1007, Portland, OR 97204-2946
Tel: (503) 326-8340 Fax: (503) 326-8349
E-mail: robert_jones@ord.uscourts.gov

Robert E. Jones
Senior Judge

Date of Birth: 1927
Education: Hawaii 1949 BA; Lewis & Clark 1953 JD
Began Service: May 1990
Appointed By: President George H.W. Bush

Academic: Instructor, College of Law, Willamette University (1988-1990); Adjunct Professor, Lewis & Clark Law School (1964-2006)

Government: State Representative (OK), Oregon House of Representatives (1963)

Judicial: Judge, Oregon Circuit Court, Fourth Judicial District, Multnomah (1963-1983); Justice, Oregon Supreme Court (1983-1990)

Legal Practice: Partner, Windsor, Jones and Briggs (1953-1956); Private Practice (1956-1958); Partner, Anderson, Franklin, Jones, Olsen and Bennett (1959-1963)

Military Service: United States Naval Reserve (1945-1987)

Staff

Career Law Clerk **Nancy Greene** . . . . (503) 326-8343
Career Law Clerk **Daniel Gonzales** . . . . (503) 326-8342
Judicial Assistant and Courtroom Deputy **Becky Peer** . . . . (503) 326-8340

Chambers of Senior Judge Garr M. King

Mark O. Hatfield U.S. Courthouse, 1000 SW Third Street,
Room 907, Portland, OR 97204-2939
Tel: (503) 326-8230 Fax: (503) 326-8239
E-mail: Garr_King@ord.uscourts.gov

Garr M. King
Senior Judge

Date of Birth: 1936
Education: Northwestern 1963 LLB
Began Service: May 1, 1998
Appointed By: President William J. Clinton

Current Memberships: American Bar Foundation; American Bar Association; American College of Trial Lawyers; The Owen M. Panner American Inn of Court, The American Inns of Court; Multnomah County Bar Association; Northwestern Law Alumni Association; Oregon Association of Defense Counsel and Defense Research Institute; Oregon State Bar

Staff
Career Law Clerk **Cindy Canfield** .... (503) 326-8232
E-mail: cindy_canfield@ord.uscourts.gov
Education: Lewis & Clark 1992 JD
Career Law Clerk **Carra L. Sahler** .... (503) 326-8233
E-mail: carra_sahler@ord.uscourts.gov
Courtroom Deputy/Judicial Assistant **Pamela Graham** ... (503) 326-8034
E-mail: pamela_graham@ord.uscourts.gov
Education: Portland 1985 BS

Chambers of Magistrate Judge Thomas M. Coffin

Wayne L. Morse U.S. Courthouse, 405 East Eighth Avenue,
Room 5300, Eugene, OR 97401
Tel: (541) 431-4130 Fax: (541) 431-4139
E-mail: thomas_coffin@ord.uscourts.gov

Thomas M. Coffin
Magistrate Judge

Date of Birth: 1945
Education: St Benedict 1967 BA; Harvard 1970 JD
Began Service: February 5, 1992
Term Expires: 2016
Political Affiliation: Independent

Government: Assistant United States Attorney, Southern District of California, Office of the United States Attorney, United States Department of Justice (1971-1980); Assistant United States Attorney, District of Oregon, Office of the United States Attorney, United States Department of Justice (1980-1992); Supervisory Assistant United States Attorney, District of Oregon, United States Department of Justice (1992)

Staff
Career Law Clerk **David Baker** .... (503) 326-8212
Education: Willamette 1994 JD
Career Law Clerk **Paul Gibson** .... (541) 431-4130
Education: Oregon 1990 JD
Courtroom Deputy **Paul Bruch** .... (541) 431-4111
E-mail: paul_bruch@ord.uscourts.gov

Chambers of Magistrate Judge Janice M. Stewart

1107 Mark O. Hatfield U.S. Courthouse, 1000 SW Third Avenue,
Portland, OR 97204-2902
Tel: (503) 326-8260 Fax: (503) 326-8269
E-mail: janice_stewart@ord.uscourts.gov

Janice M. Stewart
Magistrate Judge

Date of Birth: 1951
Education: Stanford 1972 AB; Chicago 1975 JD
Began Service: October 14, 1993
Term Expires: October 13, 2017

Legal Practice: Associate, Winston & Strawn LLP (1975-1976); Associate, McEwen, Gisvold, Rankin, Carter & Streinz, LLP (1976-1981)

Current Memberships: Federal Bar Association; Multnomah County Bar Association; Oregon State Bar

Staff
Law Clerk **Charlotte Hodde** .... (503) 326-8261
Career Law Clerk **Mary Anne Anderson** .... (503) 326-8263
E-mail: maryanne_anderson@ord.uscourts.gov
Education: Oregon 1990 JD
Courtroom Deputy **Jenny Raun** .... (503) 326-8057
E-mail: jenny_raun@ord.uscourts.gov

Chambers of Magistrate Judge Dennis J. Hubel

1604 Mark O. Hatfield U.S. Courthouse, 1000 SW Third Avenue,
Portland, OR 97204-2902
Tel: (503) 326-8240 Fax: (503) 326-8249
E-mail: dennis_hubel@ord.uscourts.gov

Dennis J. Hubel
Magistrate Judge

Education: Cornell 1969 BS; Lewis & Clark 1976 JD
Began Service: January 1, 1998

Academic: Adjunct Professor, Lewis & Clark Law School (1980-1982)

Judicial: Magistrate Judge (part-time), United States District Court for the District of Oregon (1995-1997)

Legal Practice: Mitchell, Lang & Smith (1976-1987); Karnopp, Petersen, Noteboom, Hubel, Hanson & Arnett (1987-1998)

Military Service: Submarine Officer United States Navy

Current Memberships: Oregon State Bar

Staff
Law Clerk **Tanner Webber** .... (503) 326-8240
E-mail: tanner_webber@ord.uscourts.gov
Education: Oregon 2011 JD
Career Law Clerk **Tomme J. Fent** .... (503) 326-8243
E-mail: tomme_fent@ord.uscourts.gov
Education: Oklahoma 1988 BA, 1990 JD
Courtroom Deputy **Kathleen Bartholomew** .... (503) 326-8060
E-mail: kathleen_bartholomew@ord.uscourts.gov Fax: (503) 326-8010

Chambers of Magistrate Judge Paul J. Papak

1000 SW Third Street, Room 1027, Portland, OR 97204-2902
Tel: (503) 326-8270 Fax: (503) 326-8279
E-mail: paul_papak@ord.uscourts.gov

Paul J. Papak
Magistrate Judge

Education: Princeton 1971 BA; Wisconsin 1975 JD
Began Service: September 19, 2005
Term Expires: 2021

Current Memberships: American Bar Association; Iowa State Bar Association

Staff
Law Clerk **Matthew "Matt" Tripp** .... (503) 326-8271
Began Service: August 2015
Term Expires: September 2016
Career Law Clerk **Steven David Leggett** .... (503) 326-8271
Education: Michigan 1999 JD
Courtroom Deputy **Gary Magnuson** .... (503) 326-8055
E-mail: gary_magnuson@ord.uscourts.gov

Chambers of Magistrate Judge Mark D. Clarke

310 West Sixth Street, Medford, OR 97501
Tel: (541) 608-8750 Fax: (541) 608-8779
E-mail: rebecca_moore@ord.uscourts.gov

Mark D. Clarke
Magistrate Judge

Education: Southern Oregon U 1983 BS; Oregon 1983 JD
Began Service: February 28, 2007
Term Expires: February 28, 2023

Current Memberships: Oregon State Bar

Staff
Law Clerk **Katelyn Mason** .... (541) 608-8750
Began Service: 2012
E-mail: katelyn_mason@ord.uscourts.gov
Law Clerk **Kari Reitan** .... (541) 608-8750
Courtroom Deputy **Rebecca Moore** .... (541) 608-8770
E-mail: rebecca_moore@ord.uscourts.gov

Chambers of Magistrate Judge John V. Acosta

1127 U.S. Courthouse, 1000 SW Third Street, Portland, OR 97204-2902
Tel: (503) 326-8280 Fax: (503) 326-8289
E-mail: john_acosta@ord.uscourts.gov

John V. Acosta
Magistrate Judge

Education: San Diego State 1979 BA; Oregon 1982 JD
Began Service: March 5, 2008

Legal Practice: Associate, Hughes Thorsness Powell Huddleston & Bauman LLC (1982-1986); Partner, Hughes Thorsness Powell Huddleston & Bauman LLC (1987); Associate, Stoel Rives LLP (1987-1993); Partner, Stoel Rives LLP (1994-2002)

Staff
Career Law Clerk **Lynn Barkley** .... (503) 326-8283
E-mail: lynn_barkley@ord.uscourts.gov
Career Law Clerk **Shannon Bronson** .... (503) 326-8282
E-mail: shannon_bronson@ord.uscourts.gov
Education: Willamette 1985 JD
Administrative Law Clerk **Ryan Desjardins** .... (503) 326-8281
E-mail: ryan_desjardins@ord.uscourts.gov
Courtroom Deputy **Paul Gale** .... (503) 326-8056
E-mail: paul_gale@ord.uscourts.gov

Chambers of Magistrate Judge Stacie F. Beckerman

1000 Southwest Third Avenue, Suite 927, Portland, OR 97204-2944
Tel: (503) 326-8240

Stacie Bekcerman
Magistrate Judge

Began Service: 2015

Staff
Courtroom Deputy **Giselle Williams** .... (503) 326-8022

Chambers of Magistrate Judge (part-time) Patricia Sullivan

United States Courthouse, 104 Southwest Dorion, Pendleton, OR 97801-2124
Tel: (503) 326-8028
E-mail: patricia_sullivan@ord.uscourts.gov

Patricia Sullivan
Magistrate Judge (Part-Time)

Date of Birth: July 26, 1946
Education: Loyola U (Chicago) 1973 BS; Georgia 1978 JD
Began Service: September 2005
Term Expires: 2021

Affiliation: Associate, Corey, Byler, Rew, Lorenzen & Hojem LLP

Current Memberships: American Bar Association; Oregon State Bar; Task Force on Professionalism, Oregon State Bar; State Bar of Georgia

Staff
Courtroom Deputy **Jenica Jones** .... (503) 326-8051

Chambers of Magistrate Judge (recalled) John Jelderks

1227 Mark O. Hatfield U.S. Courthouse, 1000 SW Third Avenue, Portland, OR 97204-2902
Tel: (503) 326-8310
E-mail: john_jelderks@ord.uscourts.gov

John Jelderks
Magistrate Judge (recalled)

Date of Birth: 1938
Education: Willamette BA, 1964 JD
Began Service: July 11, 1991

Staff
Courtroom Deputy **Jenica Jones** .... (503) 326-8051
Administrative Law Clerk **Andria Joseph** .... (503) 326-8310
E-mail: andria_joseph@ord.uscourts.gov

United States Bankruptcy Court for the District of Oregon

1001 SW Fifth Avenue, Room 700, Portland, OR 97204
Tel: (503) 326-1500 Tel: (503) 326-5650 (PACER)
Tel: (503) 326-2249 (Voice Case Information System VCIS)
Tel: (866) 222-8029 (Voice Case Information System VCIS)
Tel: (800) 726-2227 (Toll Free Voice Case Information System VCIS)
Internet: www.orb.uscourts.gov

Number of Judgeships: 5

Court Staff
Clerk of the Court **Charlene M. Hiss** .... (503) 326-1500
E-mail: charlene_hiss@orb.uscourts.gov
Education: USC 1996 MPA
Chief Deputy Clerk **Marianne C. Young** .... (503) 326-1500
E-mail: marianne_young@orb.uscourts.gov

United States Bankruptcy Court for the District of Oregon *continued*

Deputy Clerk-in-Charge - Eugene **(Vacant)** . . . . (541) 431-4000
405 East 8th Avenue, Room 2100,
Eugene, OR 97401
Director of Information Technology
Shahin Pourkhesali . . . . (503) 326-1500
Financial Administrator **(Vacant)** . . . . (503) 326-1500

Chambers of Chief Bankruptcy Judge Frank R. Alley III

Wayne L. Morse Federal Courthouse, 405 East Eighth Avenue,
Suite 2600, Eugene, OR 97401
Tel: (541) 431-4055 Fax: (541) 431-4048
E-mail: frank_alley@orb.uscourts.gov

Frank R. Alley III
Chief Bankruptcy Judge

Date of Birth: 1949
Education: Seattle 1976 JD; Wesleyan U 1971 BA
Began Service: January 1995
Term Expires: January 2023

Judicial: Pro Tem, Oregon Circuit Court

Legal Practice: Fowler, Alley & McNair (1977-1995)

Current Memberships: American Bar Association; The Roland K. Rodman American Inn of Court, The American Inns of Court; Oregon State Bar

Staff
Career Law Clerk **Lee Brice** . . . . (541) 431-4057
E-mail: lee_brice@orb.uscourts.gov
Education: Oregon 1992 JD
Judicial Assistant **Barbara Ivey** . . . . (541) 431-4055
E-mail: barb_ivey@orb.uscourts.gov

Chambers of Bankruptcy Judge Randall L. Dunn

1001 SW Fifth Avenue, Room 700, Portland, OR 97204
Tel: (503) 326-1538 Fax: (503) 326-1506
E-mail: randall_dunn@orb.uscourts.gov

Randall L. Dunn
Bankruptcy Judge

Date of Birth: 1950
Education: Northwestern 1972 BA; Stanford 1975 JD
Began Service: February 1, 1998
Term Expires: January 31, 2026

Academic: Second E-Flat Clarinet, Portland Opera

Legal Practice: Associate, Berman & Giauque (1975-1976); Associate then Partner then Managing Partner, Copeland, Landye, Bennett and Wolf, LLP (1977-1997)

Current Memberships: American Bankruptcy Institute; American Bar Association; National Conference of Bankruptcy Judges; Oregon State Bar; Portland Opera; Washington State Bar Association

Staff
Career Law Clerk **Belle S. Na** . . . . (503) 326-1519
Education: UC Davis 2003 JD
Career Law Clerk **JoAnne Sherman** . . . . (503) 326-1533
E-mail: joanne_sherman@orb.uscourts.gov
Education: Texas 1984 BA; Houston 1987 JD
Judicial Assistant **Collin Cole** . . . . (503) 326-1538
E-mail: collin_cole@orb.uscourts.gov

Chambers of Bankruptcy Judge Thomas M. Renn

1001 SW Fifth Avenue, Portland, OR 97204
Tel: (541) 431-5040

Thomas Renn
Bankruptcy Judge

Began Service: 2011

Staff
Career Law Clerk **Howard J. Newman** . . . . (541) 431-4050
Education: Oregon 1984 JD
Judicial Assistant **Virginia Denney** . . . . (541) 431-4050

Chambers of Bankruptcy Judge Trish M. Brown

1001 SW Fifth Avenue, Room 700, Portland, OR 97204-1141
Tel: (503) 326-1592 Fax: (503) 326-4125
E-mail: Trish_Brown@orb.uscourts.gov

Trish M. Brown
Bankruptcy Judge

Date of Birth: 1956
Education: Wharton 1978 BS; Washington and Lee 1981 JD
Began Service: December 3, 1999
Term Expires: December 2, 2027

Clerkships: Law Clerk The Honorable Glen M. Williams, United States District Court for the Western District of Virginia (1981-1982)

Legal Practice: Attorney, Lane Powell Spears Lubersky LLP (1982-1988); Partner, Lane Powell Spears Lubersky LLP (1988-1998); Special Counsel and Shareholder, Farleigh Wada & Witt, PC (1998-1999)

Current Memberships: American Bankruptcy Institute; Oregon State Bar; Virginia State Bar; Washington State Bar Association

Staff
Career Law Clerk **Stephen Raher** . . . . (503) 326-1586
E-mail: stephen_raher@orb.uscourts.gov
Education: Lewis & Clark 2009 JD
Judicial Assistant **Suzanne Marx** . . . . (503) 326-1592
E-mail: Suzanne_Marx@orb.uscourts.gov
Education: Portland State 1978 BA

Chambers of Bankruptcy Judge Peter C. McKittrick

1001 SW Fifth Avenue, Portland, OR 97204
Tel: (503) 326-1536

Peter C. McKittrick
Bankruptcy Judge

United States District Court for the Eastern District of Pennsylvania

U.S. Courthouse, 601 Market Street, Philadelphia, PA 19106-1741
Tel: (215) 597-7704 Fax: (215) 580-2164
Internet: www.paed.uscourts.gov
Internet: pacer.paed.uscourts.gov (PACER)

Number of Judgeships: 22

Number of Vacancies: 1

Circuit: Third

Areas Covered: Counties of Berks, Bucks, Chester, Delaware, Lancaster, Lehigh, Montgomery, Northampton and Philadelphia

(continued on next page)

United States District Court for the Eastern District of Pennsylvania *continued*

Court Staff

Clerk of Court **Michael E. Kunz** .... (215) 597-7704
E-mail: michael_kunz@paed.uscourts.gov
Education: St Joseph's U 1970 BS, 1981 MBA
Chief Deputy **Susan Matlack** .... (267) 299-7051
E-mail: susan_matlack@paed.uscourts.gov
Chief Pretrial Services Officer **Karen D. McKim** .... (267) 299-4400
600 Arch Street, Suite 4408, Fax: (267) 299-5100
Philadelphia, PA 19106
Chief Probation Officer **Ronald DeCastro** .... (215) 597-7950
600 Arch Street, Suite 2400, Fax: (215) 597-8701
Philadelphia, PA 19106
Administrative Services Manager
Michael Sienkiewicz.............................(267) 299-7030

Chambers of Chief Judge Petrese B. Tucker

601 Market Street, Room 9613, Philadelphia, PA 19106-1741
Tel: (267) 299-7610 Fax: (267) 299-5072
E-mail: chambers_of_judge_petrese_b_tucker@paed.uscourts.gov

Petrese B. Tucker
Chief Judge

Date of Birth: 1951
Education: Temple 1973 BA, 1976 JD
Began Service: July 14, 2000
Appointed By: President William J. Clinton
Political Affiliation: Democrat

Current Memberships: American Bar Association; Barristers' Association of Philadelphia; National Bar Association; Pennsylvania Bar Association; Philadelphia Bar Association

Staff

Law Clerk **Katrina Liu** .... (267) 299-7615
Began Service: August 2014
Term Expires: August 2016
E-mail: katrina_liu@paed.uscourts.gov
Law Clerk **Shonterra Jordan** .... (267) 299-7612
Began Service: September 1, 2015
Term Expires: September 1, 2016
E-mail: shonterra_jordan@paed.uscourts.gov
Law Clerk **Bretta Oluyede**..........................(267) 299-7613
Began Service: September 1, 2015
Term Expires: August 1, 2017
E-mail: bretta_oluyede@paed.uscourts.gov
Court Reporter **Lynn McCloskey**.....................(215) 592-4707
E-mail: lynn_mccloskey@paed.uscourts.gov
Secretary **Alisa Ross**..............................(267) 299-7610
E-mail: alisa_ross@paed.uscourts.gov

Chambers of District Judge Legrome D. Davis

6614 U.S. Courthouse, 601 Market Street, Philadelphia, PA 19106
Tel: (267) 299-7650 Fax: (267) 299-5076
E-mail: Chambers_of_judge_legrome_davis@paed.uscourts.gov

Legrome D. Davis
District Judge

Date of Birth: 1952
Education: Princeton 1973 BA; Rutgers 1976 JD
Began Service: May 3, 2002
Appointed By: President George W. Bush

Academic: Attorney, General Counsel's Office, University of Pennsylvania (1987)

Government: Assistant District Attorney, Office of the District Attorney, City of Philadelphia, Pennsylvania (1977-1980); Attorney, Crime Commission, Commonwealth of Pennsylvania (1980-1981); Assistant Deputy District Attorney, Office of the District Attorney, City of Philadelphia, Pennsylvania (1981-1987)

Chambers of District Judge Legrome D. Davis *continued*

Judicial: Judge, Court of Common Pleas, First Judicial District of Pennsylvania (1987-2002)

Staff

Law Clerk **Shreya Fadia**............................(267) 299-7650
Began Service: August 2015
Term Expires: September 2016
E-mail: shreya_fadia@paed.uscourts.gov
Law Clerk **Mario Peia**..............................(267) 299-7650
Began Service: August 2015
Term Expires: September 2016
E-mail: mario_peia@paed.uscourts.gov
Law Clerk **Kali Schellenberg** .... (267) 299-7650
Began Service: September 2015
Term Expires: September 2016
E-mail: kali_schellenberg@paed.uscourts.gov
Civil Deputy/Secretary **Mia Harvey**..................(267) 299-7650
Criminal Court Room Deputy **Donna Croce**............(267) 299-7659

Chambers of District Judge Cynthia M. Rufe

U.S. Courthouse, 601 Market Street, Room 12614,
Philadelphia, PA 19106-1741
Tel: (267) 299-7490 Fax: (267) 299-5077
E-mail: chambers_of_judge_cynthia_m_rufe@paed.uscourts.gov

Cynthia M. Rufe
District Judge

Date of Birth: 1948
Education: Adelphi 1970 BA; SUNY (Buffalo) 1977 JD
Began Service: June 10, 2002
Appointed By: President George W. Bush

Government: Assistant Public Defender, Office of the Public Defender, County of Bucks, Pennsylvania (1977-1982); Deputy Public Defender, Office of the Public Defender, County of Bucks, Pennsylvania (1980-1981); Solicitor, Children & Youth Social Services Agency, County of Bucks, Pennsylvania (1984-1988)

Judicial: Judge, Bucks County Court of Common Pleas (1994-2002)

Staff

Law Clerk **Lauren Hoff-Downing**....................(267) 299-7493
Began Service: September 2015
Term Expires: September 2016
Law Clerk **Nicole L. Herman**........................(267) 299-7493
E-mail: nicole_herman@paed.uscourts.gov
Education: Michigan State 1987 BA;
Pennsylvania 1990 JD
Career Law Clerk **Marybeth Putnick** .... (267) 299-7494
E-mail: marybeth_putnick@paed.uscourts.gov
Courtroom/ Criminal Deputy **Erica Pratt**...............(267) 299-7499
E-mail: erica_pratt@paed.uscourts.gov
Education: St Joseph's U 2003 ABS
Secretary/Civil Deputy **Velma T. White** .... (267) 299-7490
E-mail: velma_white@paed.uscourts.gov

Chambers of District Judge Timothy J. Savage

U.S. Courthouse, 601 Market Street, Room 9614, Philadelphia, PA 19106
Tel: (267) 299-7480
E-mail: chambers_of_judge_timothy_j_savage@paed.uscourts.gov

Timothy J. Savage
District Judge

Date of Birth: 1946
Education: Assumption Col 1968 AB; Temple 1971 JD
Began Service: August 19, 2002
Appointed By: President George W. Bush

Government: Hearing Examiner, Liquor Control Board, Commonwealth of Pennsylvania (1977-2002)

Chambers of District Judge Timothy J. Savage *continued*

Legal Practice: Associate, MacCoy, Evans & Lewis (1971-1974); Partner, Savage and Ciccone (1974-1976); Attorney, Timothy J. Savage, PC (1976-2002)

Staff

Law Clerk **Peggy Greenfeld** .... (267) 299-7480
E-mail: peggy_greenfeld@paed.uscourts.gov
Courtroom Deputy **Harry Grace** .... (267) 299-7489
E-mail: harry_grace@paed.uscourts.gov
Secretary **Roseann Giangiordano** .... (267) 299-7480
E-mail: roseann_giangiordano@paed.uscourts.gov

Chambers of District Judge James Knoll Gardner

Edward N. Cahn U.S. Courthouse and Federal Building, 504 West Hamilton Street, Suite 4701, Allentown, PA 18101
Tel: (610) 434-3457 Fax: (610) 434-3459
E-mail: chambers_of_Judge_James_Knoll_Gardner@paed.uscourts.gov

James Knoll Gardner
District Judge

Date of Birth: September 14, 1940
Education: Yale 1962 BA; Harvard 1965 JD
Began Service: November 27, 2002
Appointed By: President George W. Bush

Government: Solicitor to the County Treasurer, Office of the County Treasurer, County of Lehigh, Pennsylvania (1971-1977); Assistant District Attorney, Office of the District Attorney, County of Lehigh, Pennsylvania (1972-1981); First Assistant District Attorney, Office of the District Attorney, County of Lehigh, Pennsylvania (1977-1981)

Judicial: Judge, Court of Common Pleas of Lehigh County (1981-2002); President Judge, Court of Common Pleas of Lehigh County (1997-2002)

Legal Practice: Associate, Duane, Morris & Heckscher LLP (1965-1966); Associate, Duane, Morris & Heckscher LLP (1969-1970); Partner, Gardner, Gardner & Racines (1970-1981)

Military Service: Judge Advocate General's Corps United States Navy (1966-1969); Judge Advocate General's Corps, United States Naval Reserve (1969-1993)

Staff

Law Clerk **Huaou Yan** .... (610) 434-3457
Began Service: September 26, 2015
Term Expires: September 25, 2017
E-mail: huaou_yan@paed.uscourts.gov
Law Clerk **Laura E. Ploeg** .... (610) 434-3457
Began Service: October 1, 2015
Term Expires: September 30, 2017
E-mail: laura_ploeg@paed.uscourts.gov
Career Law Clerk **Michael S. Daigle** .... (610) 434-3457
E-mail: michael_daigle@paed.uscourts.gov
Education: NYU 1991 BA; Widener 1999 JD
Courtroom Deputy Clerk and Electronic Sound Recorder **Jennifer Fitzko** .... (610) 391-7019
E-mail: jennifer_fitzko@paed.uscourts.gov
Civil Deputy and Secretary **Christine C. Stein** .... (610) 434-3457
E-mail: christine_stein@paed.uscourts.gov

Chambers of District Judge Gene E. K. Pratter

United States Courthouse, 601 Market Street, Room 10613, Philadelphia, PA 19106-1752
Tel: (267) 299-7350 Fax: (267) 299-5070
E-mail: Chambers_of_Judge_Gene_E_K_Pratter@paed.uscourts.gov

Gene E. K. Pratter
District Judge

Date of Birth: February 25, 1949
Education: Stanford 1971 AB; Pennsylvania 1975 JD
Began Service: June 18, 2004
Appointed By: President George W. Bush

Legal Practice: General Counsel, Duane Morris LLP

Staff

Law Clerk **Tyler Dato** .... (267) 299-7350
E-mail: tyler_dato@paed.uscourts.gov
Law Clerk **John Scott** .... (267) 299-7350
Began Service: September 2015
Term Expires: September 2016
E-mail: john_scott@paed.uscourts.gov
Career Law Clerk **Kristina Cole** .... (267) 299-7350
Began Service: 2011
E-mail: kristina_cole@paed.uscourts.gov
Criminal Courtroom Deputy **Michael Coyle** .... (267) 299-7359
E-mail: michael_coyle@paed.uscourts.gov
Secretary/Civil Deputy **Rose A. Barber** .... (267) 299-7352
E-mail: rose_barber@paed.uscourts.gov

Chambers of District Judge Lawrence F. Stengel

601 Market Street, Room 3809, Philadelphia, PA 19106
Tel: (267) 299-7760
E-mail: chambers_of_judge_lawrence_f_stengel@paed.uscourts.gov

Lawrence F. Stengel
District Judge

Education: St Joseph Col 1974 BA; Pittsburgh 1980 JD
Began Service: June 2004
Appointed By: President George W. Bush

Staff

Law Clerk **Jocelyn Hines** .... (267) 299-7760
Began Service: August 31, 2015
Term Expires: August 30, 2016
E-mail: jocelyn_hines@paed.uscourts.gov
Law Clerk **Emilia McKee-Vassallo** .... (267) 299-7760
Began Service: August 2015
Term Expires: August 31, 2017
E-mail: emilia_mckeevassallo@paed.uscourts.gov
Career Law Clerk **Timothy J. Sheehan** .... (267) 299-7760
E-mail: timothy_sheehan@paed.uscourts.gov
Education: St Joseph Col 1977 BS; St Charles Borromeo 1985 MA; Villanova 1992 JD
Criminal Deputy **Laura Buenzle** .... (267) 299-7769
E-mail: laura_buenzle@paed.uscourts.gov
Secretary/Civil Deputy **Patricia A. Cardella** .... (267) 299-7761
E-mail: pat_cardella@paed.uscourts.gov

Chambers of District Judge Paul S. Diamond

601 Market Street, Room 6613, Philadelphia, PA 19106-1741
Tel: (267) 299-7730
E-mail: chambers_of_judge_paul_s_diamond@paed.uscourts.gov

Paul S. Diamond
District Judge

Education: Columbia 1974 BA; Pennsylvania 1977 JD
Began Service: June 22, 2004
Appointed By: President George W. Bush

Academic: Adjunct Professor, James E. Beasley School of Law, Temple University (1990-1992)

(continued on next page)

Chambers of District Judge Paul S. Diamond *continued*

Clerkships: Law Clerk, Chambers of Justice Bruce W. Kauffman, Supreme Court of Pennsylvania (1980)

Government: Assistant District Attorney, Office of the District Attorney, City of Philadelphia, Pennsylvania (1977-1979); Assistant District Attorney, Office of the District Attorney, City of Philadelphia, Pennsylvania (1981-1983)

Profession: Private Practice (1983-2004)

Staff

Law Clerk **Ben Fabens-Lassen** . . . . . (267) 299-7730
Began Service: September 2015
Term Expires: September 2016

Law Clerk **Raphael Janove** . . . . . (267) 299-7730
Began Service: September 2015
Term Expires: September 2016
E-mail: raphael_janove@paed.uscourts.gov
Education: Chicago 2014 JD

Law Clerk **Sara Arrow** . . . . . (267) 299-7730
Began Service: September 2015
Term Expires: September 2016
E-mail: sara_arrow@paed.uscourts.gov
Education: Pennsylvania 2015 JD

Secretary **Carol James** . . . . . (267) 299-7730
E-mail: carol_james@paed.uscourts.gov

Deputy Clerk **Lenora Kashner Wittje** . . . . . (267) 299-7739

Chambers of District Judge Juan R. Sánchez

601 Market Street, Room 11614, Philadelphia, PA 19106-1741
Tel: (267) 299-7780

Juan R. Sánchez
District Judge

Date of Birth: 1955
Education: CUNY 1978 BA; Pennsylvania 1981 JD
Began Service: June 2004
Appointed By: President George W. Bush

Government: Attorney, Office of the Public Defender, County of Chester, Pennsylvania (1983-1997)

Judicial: Judge, Court of Common Pleas, County of Chester, Pennsylvania (1998-2004)

Legal Practice: Attorney, Private Practice (1983-1997)

Nonprofit: Staff Attorney, Legal Aid of Chester County, Pennsylvania (1981-1983)

Staff

Career Law Clerk **Kristen Flynn** . . . . . (267) 299-7780
E-mail: kristen_flynn@paed.uscourts.gov
Education: Amherst 1990 BA; Michigan 1997 JD

Courtroom Deputy **Nancy DeLisle** . . . . . (267) 299-7789
E-mail: nancy_delisle@paed.uscourts.gov
Education: Temple 1992 BA

Deputy Clerk **Stacy Wertz** . . . . . (267) 299-7780
E-mail: stacy_wertz@paed.uscourts.gov

Chambers of District Judge Joel H. Slomsky

601 Market Street, Room 5614, Philadelphia, PA 19106
Tel: (267) 299-7340

Joel H. Slomsky
District Judge

Education: CUNY 1967 BA; NYU 1970 JD
Began Service: October 8, 2008
Appointed By: President George W. Bush

Legal Practice: Attorney, Lipschitz & Danella (1973-1974); Partner, DiGiacomo and Slomsky (1982-1990)

Profession: Private Practice (1974-1982); Private Practice (1990-2008)

Chambers of District Judge Joel H. Slomsky *continued*

Staff

Law Clerk **Jonathan Aronchick** . . . . . (267) 299-7340
Began Service: September 2015
Term Expires: September 2016
E-mail: jonathan_aronchick@paed.uscourts.gov

Law Clerk **Stacy Orvetz** . . . . . (267) 299-7340
Began Service: September 2015
Term Expires: September 2016
E-mail: stacy_orvetz@paed.uscourts.gov

Law Clerk **Terese Schireson** . . . . . (267) 299-7340
Began Service: September 2015
Term Expires: September 2016
E-mail: terese_schireson@paed.uscourts.gov

Courtroom Deputy **Margaret Gallagher** . . . . . (267) 299-7349

Secretary **Kelly Haggerty** . . . . . (267) 299-7340
E-mail: kelly_ann_haggerty@paed.uscourts.gov

Chambers of District Judge C. Darnell Jones II

601 Market Street, Room 5613, Philadelphia, PA 19106
Tel: (267) 299-7750

C. Darnell Jones II
District Judge

Date of Birth: 1949
Education: Southwestern Col (KS) 1972 AB; Washington College of Law 1975 JD
Began Service: October 30, 2008
Appointed By: President George W. Bush

Academic: Curriculum developer/instructor, National Judicial College (1998-2008)

Judicial: Judge, First Judicial District, Pennsylvania Judicial District Courts (1987-2008); President Judge, First Judicial District, Pennsylvania Judicial District Courts (2006-2008)

Legal Practice: Attorney, Defender Association of Philadelphia (1975-1987)

Staff

Law Clerk **Sarah Besnoff** . . . . . (267) 299-7750
E-mail: sarah_besnoff@paed.uscourts.gov

Law Clerk **Jessa DeGroote** . . . . . (267) 299-7750
E-mail: jessa_degroote@paed.uscourts.gov

Career Law Clerk **Candee Cintron** . . . . . (267) 299-7750
E-mail: candee_cintron@paed.uscourts.gov

Courtroom Deputy **A'iShah El-Shabazz** . . . . . (267) 299-7759

Judicial Secretary **Betty J. Harper** . . . . . (267) 299-7750
E-mail: betty_harper@paed.uscourts.gov

Chambers of District Judge Mitchell S. Goldberg

601 Market Street, Room 7614, Philadelphia, PA 19106
Tel: (267) 299-7500

Mitchell S. Goldberg
District Judge

Began Service: November 3, 2008
Appointed By: President George W. Bush

Staff

Law Clerk **Jessica Bocchinfuso** . . . . . (267) 299-7500
Began Service: August 2012
Term Expires: December 2015

Law Clerk **Andrew C. Thomas** . . . . . (267) 299-7500
Began Service: August 2014
Term Expires: August 2016
E-mail: andrew_c_thomas@paed.uscourts.gov

Law Clerk **Hayden Nelson-Major** . . . . . (267) 299-7500
Began Service: October 2014
Term Expires: October 2016

Chambers of District Judge Nitza I. Quiñones Alejandro

601 Market Street, Suite 4000, Philadelphia, PA 19106-1741
Tel: (267) 299-7460

Nitza I. Quiñones Alejandro
District Judge

Education: Puerto Rico 1972 BBA, 1975 JD
Began Service: November 1, 2013
Appointed By: President Barack Obama

Staff
Law Clerk **Christine Beck-Millan** .... (267) 299-7460
E-mail: christine_beck-millan@paed.uscourts.gov
Career Law Clerk **Brian Watson** .... (267) 299-7460
Secretary **Carey Widman** .... (267) 299-7460
Courtroom Deputy **Rosalind Burton-Hoop** .... (267) 299-7467

Chambers of District Judge Luis Felipe Restrepo

U.S. Courthouse, 601 Market Street, Room 8613,
Philadelphia, PA 19106-1741
Tel: (267) 299-7690
E-mail: chambers_of_judge_restrepo@paed.uscourts.gov

Luis Felipe Restrepo
District Judge

Education: Pennsylvania 1981 BA; Tulane 1986 JD
Began Service: 2013
Appointed By: President Barack Obama

Staff
Law Clerk **Nicholas Feltham** .... (267) 299-7690
Began Service: September 2014
Term Expires: September 2016
E-mail: nicholas_s_feltham@paed.uscourts.gov
Law Clerk **Chelsea Steine** .... (267) 299-7690
Began Service: September 2014
Term Expires: September 2016
E-mail: chelsea_c_steine@paed.uscourts.gov
Career Law Clerk **Arnold A. Foley** .... (267) 299-7690
E-mail: arnold_foley@paed.uscourts.gov
Education: Notre Dame 1985 BA;
Dickinson Law 1989 JD
Deputy Clerk/Courtroom Deputy **Nelson Malave** .... (267) 299-7691
E-mail: nelson_malave@paed.uscourts.gov
Secretary/Civil Deputy Clerk **Maryellen Fox** .... (267) 299-7690
E-mail: maryellen_fox@paed.uscourts.gov

Chambers of District Judge Jeffrey L. Schmehl

400 Washington Street, Suite 401, Reading, PA 19601
Tel: (610) 320-5099
E-mail: chambers_of_judge_jeffrey_l_schmehl@paed.uscourts.gov

Jeffrey L. Schmehl
District Judge

Education: Dickinson Col 1977 BA; Toledo 1980 JD
Began Service: September 27, 2013
Appointed By: President Barack Obama

Judicial: President Judge, Chambers of President Judge Jeffrey L. Schmehl, Twenty-Third Judicial District, Pennsylvania Common Pleas Courts (2008-2013)

Legal Practice: Partner, Rhoda, Stoudt & Bradley (1988-1997)

Staff
Law Clerk **Joseph Blowers** .... (610) 320-5099
Began Service: September 2015
Term Expires: September 2016
E-mail: joe_blowers@paed.uscourts.gov
Education: Rutgers (Camden) 2010 JD

Chambers of District Judge Jeffrey L. Schmehl *continued*

Career Law Clerk **Christopher Lyding** .... (610) 320-5099
E-mail: christopher_lyding@paed.uscourts.gov
Education: Ursinus 1982 BA; Rutgers 1985 JD
Career Law Clerk **Jill Radomsky Fisher** .... (610) 320-5099
Education: Penn State 1997 BS;
Dickinson Law 2000 JD
Secretary **Barbara Crossley** .... (610) 320-5099

Chambers of District Judge Gerald Austin McHugh Jr.

601 Market Street, Suite 5918, Philadelphia, PA 19106-1741
Tel: (267) 299-7301
E-mail: chambers_of_judge_gerald_a_mchugh@paed.uscourts.gov

Gerald Austin McHugh, Jr.
District Judge

Education: St Joseph's U 1976 AB; Pennsylvania 1979 JD
Began Service: March 28, 2014
Appointed By: President Barack Obama

Clerkships: Law Clerk, Chambers of Chief Judge Alfred L. Luongo, United States District Court for the Eastern District of Pennsylvania (1979-1981)

Legal Practice: Shareholder, Litvin, Blumberg, Matusow, and Young (1981-2004)

Staff
Law Clerk **Nathan Vogel** .... (267) 299-7301
Began Service: September 2014
Term Expires: September 2016
E-mail: nate_vogel@paed.uscourts.gov
Law Clerk **Katie Rose Beran** .... (267) 299-7301
Began Service: September 2014
Term Expires: September 2016
E-mail: katie_rose_beran@paed.uscourts.gov
Law Clerk **Chelsea Edwards** .... (267) 299-7301
Began Service: September 2015
Term Expires: September 2016
E-mail: chelsea_edwards@paed.uscourts.gov
Secretary **Patricia K. Clark** .... (267) 299-7301
E-mail: patricia_clark@paed.uscourts.gov

Chambers of District Judge Edward G. Smith

101 Larry Holmes Drive, Easton, PA 18042
Tel: (610) 333-1833
E-mail: chambers_of_judge_edward_g_smith@paed.uscourts.gov

Edward G. Smith
District Judge

Education: Franklin & Marshall 1983 BA; Dickinson Law 1986 JD
Began Service: March 31, 2014
Appointed By: President Barack Obama

Legal Practice: Partner, DeRaymond & Smith (1990-2002)

Staff
Law Clerk **Alicia Zito** .... (610) 391-7030
Term Expires: 2016
E-mail: alicia_zito@paed.uscourts.gov
Education: Scranton 1999 BS;
Dickinson Law 2002 JD
Law Clerk **Brett Waldron** .... (610) 391-7030
Term Expires: 2016
E-mail: brett_waldron@paed.uscourts.gov
Career Law Clerk **Steven Holzbaur** .... (610) 391-7030
E-mail: steven_holzbaur@paed.uscourts.gov
Secretary **Shana Restucci** .... (610) 391-7030
E-mail: shana_restucci@paed.uscourts.gov

Chambers of District Judge Wendy Beetlestone

601 Market Street, Room 5918, Philadelphia, PA 19106-1741
Tel: (267) 299-7450

Wendy Beetlestone
District Judge

Education: Liverpool (UK) 1984 BA; Pennsylvania 1993 JD
Began Service: December 21, 2014
Appointed By: President Barack Obama

Government: Member, Higher Education Council, State Board of Education, Commonwealth of Pennsylvania (2011-2014)

Staff
Law Clerk **Katherine Gregory** . . . . (267) 299-7450
Began Service: September 2015
Term Expires: September 2016
E-mail: katherine_gregory@paed.uscourts.gov
Law Clerk **Andrew R. Quirk** . . . . (267) 299-7450
Began Service: September 2015
Term Expires: September 2016
E-mail: andrew_quirk@paed.uscourts.gov
Law Clerk **Shaina Rogozen** . . . . (267) 299-7450
Began Service: February 2015
Term Expires: February 2016
Secretary **Aaris M. Wilson** . . . . (215) 299-7450
Courtroom Deputy **Michael Mani** . . . . (215) 299-7459

Chambers of District Judge Mark A. Kearney

601 Market Street, Room 5118, Philadelphia, PA 19106-1741
Tel: (267) 299-7680

Mark A. Kearney
District Judge

Education: Villanova 1987 JD
Began Service: December 4, 2014
Appointed By: President Barack Obama

Legal Practice: Managing Shareholder, Wilmington, DE Office, Elliott Greenleaf; Shareholder and Co-Chair, Hiring Committee, Elliott Greenleaf

Staff
Secretary **Pamela Hyland** . . . . (215) 299-7680
E-mail: pamela_hyland@paed.uscourts.gov
Courtroom Deputy **Ulie Hevener** . . . . (215) 299-7688

Chambers of District Judge Gerald J. Pappert

601 Market Street, Room 4006, Philadelphia, PA 19106-1741
Tel: (267) 299-7530

Gerald J. "Jerry" Pappert
District Judge

Education: Villanova 1985 BA; Notre Dame 1988 JD
Began Service: 2014
Appointed By: President Barack Obama
Political Affiliation: Republican

Staff
Law Clerk **Andrew Bond** . . . . (267) 299-7530
Began Service: September 2015
Term Expires: September 2016
E-mail: andrew_bond@paed.uscourts.gov
Education: Notre Dame 2015 JD
Law Clerk **Zach Rowen** . . . . (267) 299-7530
Began Service: September 2015
Term Expires: September 2016
E-mail: zach_rowen@paed.uscourts.gov
Education: Virginia 2012 JD
Law Clerk **Peter O'Neill** . . . . (267) 299-7530
Began Service: September 2015
Term Expires: September 2016
E-mail: peter_o'neill@paed.uscourts.gov

Chambers of District Judge Gerald J. Pappert *continued*

Courtroom Deputy **Jeff Lucini** . . . . (215) 299-7537
Secretary **Katie Furphy** . . . . (215) 299-7530
E-mail: katie_furphy@paed.uscourts.gov

Chambers of District Judge Joseph F. Leeson Jr.

504 West Hamilton Street, Suite 3401, Allentown, PA 18101
Tel: (610) 391-7020

Joseph F. Leeson, Jr.
District Judge

Education: DeSales U 1977 BA; Columbus Law 1980 JD
Began Service: December 5, 2014
Appointed By: President Barack Obama

Staff
Law Clerk **Victor Bieger** . . . . (267) 299-7530
Began Service: March 2015
Term Expires: March 2016
E-mail: victor_m_bieger@paed.uscourts.gov
Education: Boston Col 2013 JD
Law Clerk **Charles Skriner** . . . . (267) 299-7530
Began Service: March 2015
Term Expires: March 2016
E-mail: charles_skriner@paed.uscourts.gov
Career Law Clerk **Kelly Jo Sloane** . . . . (267) 299-7530
Began Service: March 2015
Secretary **Diane J. Abeles** . . . . (610) 391-7020

Chambers of Senior Judge J. William Ditter, Jr.

3040 U.S. Courthouse, 601 Market Street, Philadelphia, PA 19106
Tel: (215) 597-9640

J. William Ditter, Jr.
Senior Judge

Date of Birth: 1921
Education: Ursinus 1943 BA; Pennsylvania 1948 LLB
Began Service: December 2, 1970
Appointed By: President Richard M. Nixon
Political Affiliation: Republican

Government: Clerk, Pennsylvania Court of Common Pleas, Fifth Judicial District (1948-1951); Assistant District Attorney, Office of the District Attorney, Commonwealth of Pennsylvania (1951-1955); First Assistant District Attorney, Office of the District Attorney, Commonwealth of Pennsylvania (1956-1960)

Judicial: Judge, Pennsylvania Court of Common Pleas, Montgomery County (1964-1970)

Legal Practice: Partner, Ditter & Jenkins (1941-1963)

Military Service: Captain, United States Naval Reserve (1942-1968)

Staff
Career Law Clerk **Patricia M. Ferlong** . . . . (215) 597-9640
Career Law Clerk **Sherry Hahn** . . . . (215) 597-9640
Began Service: 2010
E-mail: sherry_hahn@paed.uscourts.gov
Career Law Clerk **Heather Tucker** . . . . (215) 597-9640
Began Service: 2010
E-mail: heather_tucker@paed.uscourts.gov
Administrative Secretary **(Vacant)** . . . . (215) 597-9640

Chambers of Senior Judge Norma L. Shapiro

10614 U.S. Courthouse, 601 Market Street, Philadelphia, PA 19106
Tel: (215) 597-9141 Fax: (215) 580-2146

Norma L. Shapiro
Senior Judge

Date of Birth: 1928
Education: Michigan 1948 BA; Pennsylvania 1951 JD
Began Service: September 1978
Appointed By: President Jimmy Carter

Academic: Instructor, School of Law, University of Pennsylvania (1951-1952)

Clerkships: Law Clerk The Honorable Horace Stern, Supreme Court of Pennsylvania (1951-1952)

Legal Practice: Associate Partner, Dechert LLP (1956-1958); Associate Partner, Dechert LLP (1967-1973); Partner, Dechert LLP (1973-1978)

Current Memberships: American Bar Foundation; American Bar Association; The American Law Institute; Federal Bar Association; National Association of Women Judges; National Association of Women Lawyers; Pennsylvania Bar Association; Philadelphia Bar Association; Philadelphia Trial Lawyers Association

Staff
Law Clerk **Benjamin H. Marshal** .... (215) 597-9141
Began Service: September 2015
Term Expires: September 4, 2016
E-mail: benjamin_marshal@paed.uscourts.gov
Law Clerk **Cory Tischbein** .... (215) 597-9141
Began Service: March 2, 2015
Term Expires: September 4, 2016
E-mail: cory_tischbein@paed.uscourts.gov
Deputy Clerk **Danielle Puchon** .... (267) 299-7541
E-mail: danielle_puchon@paed.uscourts.gov

Chambers of Senior Judge Thomas N. O'Neill, Jr.

4007 U.S. Courthouse, 601 Market Street, Philadelphia, PA 19106
Tel: (215) 597-2750 Fax: (215) 580-2137
E-mail: chambers_of_judge_thomas_o'neill@paed.uscourts.gov

Thomas N. O'Neill, Jr.
Senior Judge

Date of Birth: 1928
Education: Catholic U 1950 AB; Pennsylvania 1953 LLB
Began Service: August 30, 1983
Appointed By: President Ronald Reagan

Academic: Instructor in Appellate Advocacy, University of Pennsylvania Law School (1973)

Clerkships: Law Clerk The Honorable Herbert F. Goodrich, United States Court of Appeals for the Third Circuit (1953-1954); Law Clerk The Honorable Harold F. Burton, Supreme Court of the United States (1954-1955)

Legal Practice: Associate, Montgomery, McCracken, Walker & Rhoads, LLP

Military Service: United States Naval Air Reserve (1948-1953)

Current Memberships: American College of Trial Lawyers; The American Law Institute; Pennsylvania Bar Association; Philadelphia Bar Association

Staff
Law Clerk **Dina Kopansky** .... (215) 597-2750
Began Service: September 2015
Term Expires: August 2016
E-mail: dina_kopansky@paed.uscourts.gov
Law Clerk **(Vacant)** .... (215) 597-2750
Career Law Clerk **Meredith Huston** .... (215) 597-2750
Began Service: September 2010
E-mail: meredith_huston@paed.uscourts.gov
Deputy Clerk **Charles Ervin** .... (215) 597-2750
E-mail: charles_ervin@paed.uscourts.gov

Chambers of Senior Judge Thomas N. O='Neill, Jr. *continued*

Secretary **Deborah A. Owens** .... (215) 597-2750
E-mail: deborah_a_owens@paed.uscourts.gov

Chambers of Senior Judge Robert F. Kelly

11613 U.S. Courthouse, 601 Market Street, Philadelphia, PA 19106-1711
Tel: (215) 597-0736 Fax: (215) 580-2143

Robert F. Kelly
Senior Judge

Date of Birth: 1935
Education: Villanova 1957 BS; Temple 1960 LLB
Began Service: 1987
Appointed By: President Ronald Reagan
Political Affiliation: Republican

Academic: Lecturer, Villanova University Law School

Clerkships: Law Clerk The Honorable Francis J. Catania, Pennsylvania Court of Common Pleas (1964-1972)

Government: Prothonotary, County of Delaware, Pennsylvania (1972-1976)

Judicial: Judge, Pennsylvania Court of Common Pleas (1976-1987)

Legal Practice: Private Practice (1961-1962); Private Practice (1962-1964); Private Practice (1964-1976)

Current Memberships: American Bar Association; Delaware County Bar Association; Pennsylvania Bar Association; Pennsylvania Trial Judges Association

Staff
Law Clerk **Kathleen McNabb** .... (267) 299-7312
Began Service: 2010
Term Expires: September 2016
Education: Villanova JD
Career Law Clerk **(Vacant)** .... (267) 299-7316
E-mail: michael_hagan@paed.uscourts.gov
Courtroom Deputy **Mark Rafferty** .... (267) 299-7319
E-mail: mark_rafferty@paed.uscourts.gov
Secretary **Maureen C. Mattern** .... (215) 597-0736

Chambers of Senior Judge Jan E. DuBois

12613 U.S. Courthouse, 601 Market Street, Philadelphia, PA 19106
Tel: (215) 597-5579 Fax: (215) 580-2141
E-mail: chambers_of_judge_jan_e_dubois@paed.uscourts.gov

Jan E. DuBois
Senior Judge

Date of Birth: 1931
Education: Pennsylvania 1952 BS; Yale 1957 LLB
Began Service: 1988
Appointed By: President Ronald Reagan

Academic: Faculty, Academy of Advocacy, Temple University School of Law; Faculty, Pennsylvania Bar Institute; Faculty, American Law Institute

Clerkships: Law Clerk The Honorable Harry E. Kalodner, United States Court of Appeals for the Third Circuit (1957-1958)

Legal Practice: Partner, White and Williams LLP (1958-1988)

Military Service: Captain (retired), United States Army (1952-1954)

Current Memberships: American Bar Association; Pennsylvania Bar Association; Philadelphia Bar Association

Staff
Law Clerk **Daniel Rosenblum** .... (215) 597-5579
Began Service: September 2015
Term Expires: September 2016
E-mail: daniel_rosenblum@paed.uscourts.gov
Law Clerk **Kevin Hoagland-Hanson** .... (215) 597-5579
Began Service: September 2015
Term Expires: September 2016

(continued on next page)

FEDERAL COURTS—UNITED STATES DISTRICT COURTS

Chambers of Senior Judge Jan E. DuBois *continued*

Law Clerk **Amy Nemetz** .... (215) 597-5579
Began Service: September 2015
Term Expires: September 2016
E-mail: amy_nemetz@paed.uscourts.gov
Courtroom Deputy **Milahn Hull** .... (215) 597-5579
E-mail: milahn_hull@paed.uscourts.gov
Secretary **Leesa B. Ciamaichelo** .... (215) 597-5579
E-mail: leesa_ciamaichelo@paed.uscourts.gov

Chambers of Senior Judge Ronald L. Buckwalter

14614 U.S. Courthouse, 601 Market Street, Philadelphia, PA 19106-1755
Tel: (215) 597-3084

Ronald L. Buckwalter
Senior Judge

Date of Birth: 1936
Education: Franklin & Marshall 1958 AB; William & Mary 1962 BCL
Began Service: April 20, 1990
Appointed By: President George H.W. Bush

Clerkships: Law Clerk The Honorable John Bowman (1966-1970)

Government: Assistant District Attorney and District Attorney, Commonwealth of Pennsylvania (1970-1980)

Judicial: Judge, Pennsylvania Court of Common Pleas, Second Judicial Circuit, Lancaster County (1980-1990)

Legal Practice: Sole Practitioner (1963-1971); Attorney, Legal Aid (1964-1966); Partner, Shirk, Reist and Buckwalter (1971-1980)

Military Service: United States Army National Guard (1962-1968)

Current Memberships: Federal Bar Association; Federal Judges Association; Lancaster Bar Association; Pennsylvania Bar Association

Staff

Law Clerk **Kristen Scoville** .... (215) 597-3084
Began Service: September 2014
Term Expires: September 2016
E-mail: kristen_scoville@paed.uscourts.gov
Career Law Clerk **Jennifer Collins Hart** .... (215) 597-3084
Began Service: 2007
E-mail: jennifer_hart@paed.uscourts.gov
Education: Rutgers 1994 BA, 1997 JD
Courtroom Deputy **Matthew J. Higgins** .... (267) 299-7369
Education: Villanova 1981 BA
Judicial Secretary **Sharon Lippi** .... (215) 597-3084
E-mail: sharon_lippi@paed.uscourts.gov

Chambers of Senior Judge Harvey Bartle III

16614 U.S. Courthouse, 601 Market Street, Philadelphia, PA 19106
Tel: (215) 597-2693 Fax: (215) 580-2154

Harvey Bartle III
Senior Judge

Date of Birth: 1941
Education: Princeton 1962 AB; Pennsylvania 1965 LLB
Began Service: September 23, 1991
Appointed By: President George H.W. Bush

Current Memberships: American Bar Association; Philadelphia Bar Association

Staff

Law Clerk **Anna Christiansen** .... (215) 597-2693
Began Service: September 2014 Fax: (215) 580-2154
Term Expires: September 2016
Law Clerk **Jessica Bergin** .... (215) 597-2693
Began Service: September 2015
Term Expires: September 2017
E-mail: jessica_bergin@paed.uscourts.gov
Judicial Secretary **Cheryl Stormes** .... (215) 597-2693
E-mail: cheryl_stormes@paed.uscourts.gov

Chambers of Senior Judge Stewart Dalzell

U.S. Courthouse, 601 Market Street, Room 15613,
Philadelphia, PA 19106-1705
Tel: (215) 597-9773 Fax: (215) 580-2156
E-mail: Chambers_of_Judge_Stewart_Dalzell@paed.uscourts.gov

Stewart Dalzell
Senior Judge

Date of Birth: 1943
Education: Wharton 1965 BS; Pennsylvania 1969 JD
Began Service: October 7, 1991
Appointed By: President George H.W. Bush

Current Memberships: The University of Pennsylvania Law School American Inn of Court, The American Inns of Court; The American Law Institute; Junior Legal Club

Staff

Law Clerk **Harper Seldin** .... (215) 597-9773
Began Service: August 2014
Term Expires: August 2016
Law Clerk **George Donnelly** .... (215) 597-9773
Began Service: April 2015
Term Expires: April 2016
E-mail: george_donnelly@paed.uscourts.gov
Courtroom Deputy **Eileen Adler** .... (267) 299-7399
E-mail: eileen_adler@paed.uscourts.gov
Court Reporter **Kathleen Feldman** .... (215) 627-0184
Secretary **Joanne Tyer** .... (215) 597-9773
E-mail: joanne_tyer@paed.uscourts.gov

Chambers of Senior Judge John R. Padova

U.S. Courthouse, 601 Market Street, Room 17613, Philadelphia, PA 19106
Tel: (215) 597-1178 Fax: (215) 580-2272

John R. Padova
Senior Judge

Date of Birth: 1935
Education: Villanova 1956 AB; Temple 1959 JD
Began Service: March 31, 1992
Appointed By: President George H.W. Bush

Judicial: District Judge, Chambers of District Judge John R. Padova, United States District Court for the Eastern District of Pennsylvania (1992-2008)

Legal Practice: Marcu & Marcu (1960-1961); Partner, Solo, Bergman, Trommer & Padova (1962-1992)

Military Service: United States Army National Guard (1959-1964); United States Army Reserve, United States Department of the Army (1964-1968)

Staff

Career Law Clerk **Debra Nathanson** .... (215) 597-1178
E-mail: debra_nathanson@paed.uscourts.gov
Career Law Clerk **Kaethe Schumacher** .... (215) 597-1178
E-mail: kaethe_schumacher@paed.uscourts.gov
Courtroom Deputy **Patricia Feldman** .... (215) 597-1178
E-mail: patricia_feldman@paed.uscourts.gov
Courtroom Deputy **Michael Beck** .... (267) 299-7409

Chambers of Senior Judge J. Curtis Joyner

U.S. Courthouse, 601 Market Street, Room 17614, Philadelphia, PA 19106
Tel: (215) 597-1537 Fax: (215) 580-2312
E-mail: Chambers_of_Judge_J_Curtis_Joyner@paed.uscourts.gov

J. Curtis Joyner
Senior Judge

Date of Birth: 1948
Education: Central State 1971 BS; Howard U 1974 JD
Began Service: April 13, 1992
Appointed By: President George H.W. Bush
Political Affiliation: Republican

Current Memberships: Chester County Bar Association; Federal Bar Association

Staff
Law Clerk **Elizabeth Grossman** .... (215) 597-1537
Began Service: August 2015
Term Expires: August 2016
E-mail: elizabeth_grossman@paed.uscourts.gov
Career Law Clerk **Sherilyn Frey** .... (215) 597-1537
E-mail: sheri_frey@paed.uscourts.gov
Education: Widener 1984 JD
Courtroom Deputy **Sharon Carter** .... (267) 299-7419
E-mail: sharon_carter@paed.uscourts.gov
Judicial Secretary **Nancy Jussen** .... (215) 597-1537
E-mail: nancy_jussen@paed.uscourts.gov
Education: Delaware 1973 BS

Chambers of Senior Judge Eduardo C. Robreno

U.S. Courthouse, 601 Market Street, Room 15614, Philadelphia, PA 19106
Tel: (215) 597-4073 Fax: (267) 299-5113

Eduardo C. Robreno
Senior Judge

Date of Birth: 1945
Education: Westfield State Col 1967 BA; UMass (Amherst) 1969 MA; Rutgers (Camden) 1978 JD
Began Service: July 27, 1992
Appointed By: President George H.W. Bush

Current Memberships: The American Law Institute

Staff
Law Clerk **Tiffany Engsell** .... (215) 597-4073
Began Service: September 2015
Term Expires: September 2016
E-mail: tiffany_engsell@paed.uscourts.gov
Law Clerk **Karon Fowler** .... (215) 597-4073
Began Service: September 2015
Term Expires: September 2016
E-mail: karon_fowler@paed.uscourts.gov
Law Clerk **Karissa Sauder** .... (215) 597-4073
Began Service: September 2014
Term Expires: September 2016
E-mail: karissa_sauder@paed.uscourts.gov
Courtroom Deputy **Ronald Vance** .... (267) 299-7429
Judicial Secretary **Nicole Spicer** .... (215) 597-4073
E-mail: nicole_spicer@paed.uscourts.gov

Chambers of Senior Judge Anita B. Brody

7613 U.S. Courthouse, 601 Market Street, Philadelphia, PA 19106-1744
Tel: (215) 597-3978 Fax: (215) 580-2356
E-mail: Chambers_of_Judge_Anita_B_Brody@paed.uscourts.gov

Anita B. Brody
Senior Judge

Date of Birth: 1935
Education: Wellesley 1955 BA; Columbia 1958 JD
Began Service: 1992
Appointed By: President George H.W. Bush

Academic: Lecturer, University of Pennsylvania (1979-1980)

Government: Law Apprentice and Deputy Assistant Attorney General, State of New York (1958-1959)

Judicial: Judge, Pennsylvania Court of Common Pleas, 38th Judicial District (1981-1992)

Legal Practice: Duryea, Lazalere & Hepburn (1973-1979); Private Practice (1979-1980); Partner, Brody, Brown & Hepburn (1980-1981)

Nonprofit: Member, Board of Visitors, Columbia Law School, Columbia University (2004-2006)

Current Memberships: The Temple American Inn of Court, The American Inns of Court; The American Law Institute; National Association of Women Judges; Pennsylvania Bar Association

Staff
Law Clerk **Elli Marcus** .... (267) 299-7433
Began Service: August 2015
Term Expires: August 2016
E-mail: elli_marcus@paed.uscourts.gov
Law Clerk **Karun Tilak** .... (267) 299-7433
Began Service: September 2015
Term Expires: September 2016
E-mail: karun_tilak@paed.uscourts.gov
Education: Yale 2014 JD
Permanent Law Clerk **Maya Sosnov** .... (267) 299-7432
Began Service: August 2011
Education: Pennsylvania 2007 JD
Court Reporter and Criminal Deputy Clerk
James F. G. Scheidt .... (267) 299-7439
E-mail: james_scheidt@paed.uscourts.gov Fax: (267) 299-7438
Secretary and Civil Deputy Clerk **Marie O'Donnell** .... (215) 597-3978
E-mail: marie_o'donnell@paed.uscourts.gov

Chambers of Senior Judge Berle M. Schiller

U.S. Courthouse, 601 Market Street, Room 13613, Philadelphia, PA 19106-1797
Tel: (267) 299-7620 Fax: (267) 299-5073

Berle M. Schiller
Senior Judge

Education: Bowdoin 1965 BA; NYU 1968 JD
Began Service: June 6, 2000
Appointed By: President William J. Clinton

Current Memberships: American Bar Association

Staff
Criminal Deputy Clerk **Christopher Campoli** .... (267) 299-7629
E-mail: chris_campoli@paed.uscourts.gov
Civil Deputy Clerk/ Secretary **Jean Pennie** .... (267) 299-7621
E-mail: Jean_Pennie@paed.uscourts.gov

Chambers of Senior Judge Mary A. McLaughlin

13614 U.S. Courthouse, 601 Market Street, Philadelphia, PA 19106
Tel: (267) 299-7600 Fax: (267) 299-5071
E-mail: Chambers_of_Judge_Mary_A_McLaughlin@paed.uscourts.gov

Mary A. McLaughlin
Senior Judge

Date of Birth: 1946
Education: Gwynedd-Mercy 1968 BA; Bryn Mawr 1969 MA; Pennsylvania 1976 JD
Began Service: May 31, 2000
Appointed By: President William J. Clinton

Chambers of Senior Judge R. Barclay Surrick

8614 U.S. Courthouse, 601 Market Street, Philadelphia, PA 19106
Tel: (267) 299-7630 Fax: (267) 299-5074

R. Barclay Surrick
Senior Judge

Education: Dickinson Col 1960 BA; Dickinson Law 1965 JD; Virginia 1982 LLM
Began Service: July 14, 2000
Appointed By: President William J. Clinton

Staff

Law Clerk **Aubrey Chamberlin** .... (267) 299-7634
Began Service: September 10, 2015
Term Expires: September 13, 2016
E-mail: aubrey_chamberlin@paed.uscourts.gov

Law Clerk **Eric Mackie** .... (267) 299-7633
Began Service: August 31, 2015
Term Expires: September 6, 2016
E-mail: eric_mackie@paed.uscourts.gov

Career Law Clerk **Angela Pappas** .... (267) 299-7632
Began Service: September 12, 2011
E-mail: angela_pappas@paed.uscourts.gov

Courtroom Deputy **Christina Franzese** .... (267) 299-7639
E-mail: christina_franzese@paed.uscourts.gov

Civil Deputy/Judicial Assistant
Donna Donohue Marley .... (267) 299-7631
E-mail: donna_marley@paed.uscourts.gov

Chambers of Senior Judge Michael M. Baylson

3810 U.S. Courthouse, 601 Market Street, Philadelphia, PA 19106
Tel: (267) 299-7520 Fax: (267) 299-5078
E-mail: chambers_of_judge_michael_baylson@paed.uscourts.gov

Michael M. Baylson
Senior Judge

Date of Birth: 1939
Education: Pennsylvania 1961 BS, 1964 LLB
Began Service: July 12, 2002
Appointed By: President George W. Bush

Staff

Law Clerk **Selby Brown** .... (267) 299-7520
Began Service: September 2015
Term Expires: September 2016
E-mail: selby_brown@paed.uscourts.gov

Law Clerk **Ilana Cohen** .... (267) 299-7520
Began Service: September 2015
Term Expires: September 2016
E-mail: ilana_cohen@paed.uscourts.gov

Law Clerk **Stephen Henrick** .... (267) 299-7520
Began Service: September 2015
Term Expires: September 2016
E-mail: stephen_henrick@paed.uscourts.gov

Courtroom Deputy [Criminal] **Janice Lutz** .... (267) 299-7571
E-mail: janice_lutz@paed.uscourts.gov

Chambers of Senior Judge Michael M. Baylson *continued*

Secretary and Courtroom Deputy [Civil]
Joanne B. Bryson .... (267) 299-7520
E-mail: joanne_bryson@paed.uscourts.gov

Chambers of Chief Magistrate Judge Carol Sandra Moore Wells

3016 U.S. Courthouse, 601 Market Street, Philadelphia, PA 19106-1725
Tel: (215) 597-7833 Fax: (215) 580-2157
E-mail: chambers_of_magistrate_judge_carol_sandra_moore_wells@paed.uscourts.gov

Carol Sandra Moore Wells
Chief Magistrate Judge

Date of Birth: 1949
Education: Pennsylvania 1985 JD
Began Service: June 3, 1996
Term Expires: June 2020

Current Memberships: The Temple American Inn of Court, The American Inns of Court; Federal Bar Association; Federal Magistrate Judges Association; National Association of Women Judges; National Bar Association; Philadelphia Bar Association

Staff

Career Law Clerk **Camilo Ferrandez** .... (215) 597-7712
E-mail: camilo_ferrandez@paed.uscourts.gov
Education: Pennsylvania 1989 BA, 1989 BS; Temple 1992 JD

Career Law Clerk **Kimberly N. Henderson** .... (215) 597-7713
Education: Virginia BA; Villanova 2004 JD

Deputy/Secretary **Edward Andrews** .... (215) 597-7833
E-mail: edward_andrews@paed.uscourts.gov
Education: Cheyney 1986 BS

Chambers of Magistrate Judge Thomas J. Rueter

U.S. Courthouse, 601 Market Street, Room 3000, Philadelphia, PA 19106
Tel: (215) 597-0048 Fax: (215) 580-2392

Thomas J. Rueter
Magistrate Judge

Date of Birth: 1955
Education: Scranton 1977 BA; Dickinson Law 1980 JD
Began Service: February 22, 1994
Term Expires: February 2018

Current Memberships: The Historical Society of Pennsylvania

Staff

Career Law Clerk **Beth Cannon Bensley** .... (215) 597-0048
E-mail: beth_bensley@paed.uscourts.gov
Education: Villanova 1996 JD

Career Law Clerk **Susan Deasy** .... (215) 597-0048
E-mail: Susan_Deasy@paed.uscourts.gov
Education: Temple 1987 JD

Career Law Clerk **Denise M. Speranza** .... (215) 597-0048
E-mail: Denise_Speranza@paed.uscourts.gov
Education: Temple 1993 JD

Secretary/Deputy Clerk **Lisa Tipping** .... (215) 597-0048

Chambers of Magistrate Judge Linda K. Caracappa

U.S. Courthouse, 601 Market Street, Room 3042, Philadelphia, PA 19106
Tel: (267) 299-7640 Fax: (267) 299-5075

Linda K. Caracappa
Magistrate Judge

Began Service: November 17, 2000

Chambers of Magistrate Judge Linda K. Caracappa *continued*

Staff
Courtroom Deputy Clerk **Ian Broderick** . . . . (267) 299-7640
E-mail: ian_broderick@paed.uscourts.gov

Chambers of Magistrate Judge Timothy R. Rice

U.S. Courthouse, 601 Market Street, Room 3029, Philadelphia, PA 19106
Tel: (267) 299-7660
E-mail: timothy_rice@paed.uscourts.gov

Timothy R. Rice
Magistrate Judge

Began Service: March 2005

Government: Chief, Criminal Division, Pennsylvania - Eastern District, United States Department of Justice

Current Memberships: The American Law Institute

Staff
E-mail: chambers_of_magistrate_judge_timothy_rice@paed.uscourts.gov

Law Clerk **Leslie Kramer** . . . . (267) 299-7660
Began Service: September 12, 2011
Education: Brooklyn Law 2000 JD
Law Clerk **Anna Kessler** . . . . (267) 299-7660
Began Service: September 1, 2015
Term Expires: September 1, 2016
E-mail: anna_kessler@paed.uscourts.gov
Law Clerk (Part-Time) **Nina Russakoff** . . . . (267) 299-7660
Began Service: September 9, 2013
Courtroom Deputy **Chavela M. Settles** . . . . (267) 299-7660
E-mail: chavela_settles@paed.uscourts.gov

Chambers of Magistrate Judge David R. Strawbridge

601 Market Street, Room 3030, Philadelphia, PA 19106
Tel: (267) 299-7790 Fax: (267) 299-5065
E-mail: Chambers_of_Magistrate_Judge_David_Strawbridge@paed.uscourts.gov

David R. Strawbridge
Magistrate Judge

Education: Brown U 1967 BA; Villanova 1971 JD
Began Service: April 26, 2005
Term Expires: April 2021

Staff
Law Clerk **Shannon Zabel** . . . . (267) 299-7790
Began Service: August 2015
Term Expires: August 2016
E-mail: shannon_zabel@paed.uscourts.gov
Career Law Clerk **Maren Reichert** . . . . (267) 299-7790
E-mail: maren_reichert@paed.uscourts.gov
Education: Temple 2000 JD
Secretary/Courtroom Deputy **Lori DiSanti** . . . . (267) 299-7790
E-mail: lori_disanti@paed.uscourts.gov

Chambers of Magistrate Judge Henry S. Perkin

Edward N. Cahn U.S. Courthouse and Federal Building, 504 West Hamilton Street, Suite 4401, Allentown, PA 18101
Tel: (610) 434-3823
E-mail: chambers_of_judge_henry_s_perkin@paed.uscourts.gov

Henry S. Perkin
Magistrate Judge

Date of Birth: December 27, 1947
Education: Duquesne 1969, 1972 JD
Began Service: March 2, 2007
Term Expires: March 2, 2023

Clerkships: Law Clerk, President Judge Alfred T. Williams, Jr., Third Judicial District, Pennsylvania Common Pleas Courts

Government: Assistant Public Defender, County of Lehigh, Pennsylvania (1975-1977); Assistant District Attorney, County of Lehigh, Pennsylvania (1977-1987); Solicitor, County of Lehigh, Pennsylvania (1995-2006); Solicitor, City of Allentown, Pennsylvania (2006-2007)

Staff
Career Law Clerk **Janine Hoffman** . . . . (610) 391-7023
E-mail: janine_hoffman@paed.uscourts.gov
Career Law Clerk **Tricia Tatum** . . . . (610) 391-7024
E-mail: tricia_tatum@paed.uscourts.gov
Deputy Clerk **Helen Nicholas** . . . . (610) 391-7025
E-mail: helen_nicholas@paed.uscourts.gov
Judicial Assistant **Carlene L. Jones** . . . . (610) 434-3823
E-mail: chambers_of_judge_henry_s_perkin@paed.uscourts.gov

Chambers of Magistrate Judge Elizabeth T. Hey

Robert N.C. Nix Federal Building, 900 Market Street, Suite 219, Philadelphia, PA 19107
Tel: (267) 299-7670 Fax: (267) 299-5061
E-mail: chambers_of_magistrate_judge_elizabeth_hey@paed.uscourts.gov

Elizabeth T. Hey
Magistrate Judge

Began Service: April 2007
Term Expires: April 2023

Staff
Career Law Clerk **Anna Marie Plum** . . . . (267) 299-7670
E-mail: anna_marie_plum@paed.uscourts.gov
Education: Temple 1992 JD
Career Law Clerk **Ryan Watts** . . . . (267) 299-7670
E-mail: ryan_watts@paed.uscourts.gov
Secretary **Lara Karlson** . . . . (267) 299-7670
E-mail: lara_karlson@paed.uscourts.gov

Chambers of Magistrate Judge Lynne A. Sitarski

U. S. Courthouse, 601 Market Street, Room 3015, Philadelphia, PA 19106
Tel: (267) 299-7810

Lynne A. Sitarski
Magistrate Judge

Began Service: October 29, 2007

Staff
Law Clerk **Jessica Wirth** . . . . (267) 299-7810
Career Law Clerk **Cory Caswell** . . . . (267) 299-7810
E-mail: cory_caswell@paed.uscourts.gov
Secretary **Regina Zarnowski** . . . . (267) 299-7810
E-mail: regina_zarnowski@paed.uscourts.gov

Chambers of Magistrate Judge Jacob P. Hart
U.S. Courthouse, 601 Market Street, Room 3006, Philadelphia, PA 19106
Tel: (215) 597-2733 Fax: (215) 580-2163
E-mail: Judge_Jacob_Hart@paed.uscourts.gov

Jacob P. Hart
Magistrate Judge

Date of Birth: 1942
Education: Pennsylvania 1963 BA, 1967 JD
Began Service: November 17, 1997
Term Expires: November 2028
Political Affiliation: Democrat

Clerkships: Law Clerk The Honorable Samuel J. Roberts, Pennsylvania Supreme Court (1967-1968)

Government: Director, Enforcement Division, United States Environmental Protection Agency (1972); Director, Appellate Mediation Program, United States Court of Appeals for the Third Circuit (1995-1997)

Legal Practice: Schnader, Harrison, Segal & Lewis (1968-1995)

Staff
Career Law Clerk **Laura Heller** .... (215) 597-2733
E-mail: laura_heller@paed.uscourts.gov
Education: Georgetown 1990 JD
Courtroom Deputy/Secretary **Deborah A. Stevenson** .... (215) 597-2733

Chambers of Magistrate Judge Marilyn Heffley
601 Market Street, Room 4001, Philadelphia, PA 19106-1741
Tel: (267) 299-7420

Marilyn Heffley
Magistrate Judge

Education: Temple 1984 JD

Staff
Courtroom Deputy **Sharon Hall** .... (267) 299-7420
E-mail: sharon_hall@paed.uscourts.gov

Chambers of Magistrate Judge Richard A. Lloret
900 Market Street, Suite 219, Philadelphia, PA 19107-4299
Tel: (267) 299-7410

Richard A. Lloret
Magistrate Judge

Staff
Courtroom Deputy **Sheila McCurry** .... (267) 299-7410
E-mail: sheila_mccurry@paed.uscourts.gov

Chambers of Magistrate Judge (Recalled) M. Faith Angell
Robert N.C. Nix Building, 900 Market Street, Suite 211, Philadelphia, PA 19107
Tel: (215) 597-6079 Fax: (215) 580-2165
E-mail: chambers_of_magistrate_judge_m_faith_angell@paed.uscourts.gov

M. Faith Angell
Magistrate Judge (recalled)

Date of Birth: 1938
Education: Mount Holyoke 1959 AB; Bryn Mawr 1965 MSS; Temple 1971 JD
Began Service: May 14, 1990

Current Memberships: Academy of Certified Social Workers; Federal Magistrate Judges Association; National Association of Women Judges; Philadelphia Bar Association

Staff
Career Law Clerk **Judith J. Kiesel** .... (215) 597-6079
E-mail: judy_kiesel@paed.uscourts.gov
Education: Temple 1990 JD
Career Law Clerk **Leslie F. Stott** .... (215) 597-6079
E-mail: leslie_stott@paed.uscourts.gov
Education: Cleveland-Marshall 1982 JD
Deputy Clerk **Shelli L. MacElderry** .... (215) 597-6079
E-mail: shelli_macelderry@paed.uscourts.gov
Education: Holy Family Col 2002 BA

United States Bankruptcy Court for the Eastern District of Pennsylvania
900 Market Street, Suite 400, Philadelphia, PA 19107-4299
Tel: (215) 408-4411 Tel: (215) 408-2800 (General Information)
Tel: (800) 676-6856 (PACER Registration)
Tel: (888) 584-5853 (VCIS) Fax: (215) 408-2992
Internet: www.paeb.uscourts.gov

Number of Judgeships: 6

Court Staff
Clerk of Court **Timothy B. McGrath** .... (215) 408-4411
E-mail: timothy_mcgrath@paeb.uscourts.gov
Education: Scranton 1984 BS; Temple 1987 JD

Chambers of Chief Bankruptcy Judge Eric L. Frank
900 Market Street, Suite 201, Philadelphia, PA 19107-4299
Tel: (215) 408-2970

Eric L. Frank
Chief Bankruptcy Judge

Education: SUNY (Binghamton) 1973 BA; Pennsylvania 1976 JD
Began Service: February 2006
Term Expires: 2020

Staff
Law Clerk **Karen Muroski** .... (215) 408-2970
E-mail: karen_muroski@paeb.uscourts.gov
Career Law Clerk **Samantha Levy Green** .... (215) 408-2970
E-mail: samantha_levy@paeb.uscourts.gov
Courtroom Deputy **Pamela Blalock** .... (215) 408-2801
E-mail: pamela_blalock@paeb.uscourts.gov
Electronic Court Recorder **Linda LoBosco** .... (215) 408-2849
E-mail: linda_labosco@paeb.uscourts.gov
Judicial Assistant **Laura Frick** .... (215) 408-2970
E-mail: laura_frick@paeb.uscourts.gov

Chambers of Bankruptcy Judge Stephen Raslavich
900 Market Street, Suite 204, Philadelphia, PA 19107
Tel: (215) 408-2982

Stephen Raslavich
Bankruptcy Judge

Date of Birth: 1952
Began Service: 1993
Term Expires: October 2021

Staff
Career Law Clerk **Jeffrey Marchant** . . . . (215) 408-2982
E-mail: jeffrey_marchant@paeb.uscourts.gov
Education: Villanova 1988 JD
Career Law Clerk (Part-Time) **Noreen Walsh** . . . . (215) 408-2982
E-mail: noreen_walsh@paeb.uscourts.gov
Education: Temple 1987 JD
Courtroom Deputy **Nancy Mulvehill** . . . . (215) 408-2820
E-mail: nancy_mulvehill@paeb.uscourts.gov
Electronic Court Recorder **Linda LoBosco** . . . . (215) 408-2849
E-mail: linda_lobosco@paeb.uscourts.gov
Judicial Assistant **Veronica Glanville** . . . . (215) 408-2982
E-mail: veronica_glanville@paeb.uscourts.gov

Chambers of Bankruptcy Judge Richard E. Fehling
Madison Building, 400 Washington Street, Reading, PA 19601
Tel: (610) 208-5040

Richard E. Fehling
Bankruptcy Judge

Education: Yale 1974 BA; Dickinson Law 1979 JD
Began Service: February 2006
Term Expires: 2020

Staff
Career Law Clerk **Pauline Felice Kohler** . . . . (610) 208-5032
E-mail: pauline_kohler@paeb.uscourts.gov
Education: Villanova 1984 JD
Courtroom Deputy **Barbara Spinka** . . . . (610) 208-5035
E-mail: barbara_spinka@paeb.uscourts.gov
Electronic Court Recorder **Sara Roman** . . . . (610) 208-5048
E-mail: sara_roman@paeb.uscourts.gov
Judicial Assistant **Celeste Wilson** . . . . (610) 208-5030

Chambers of Bankruptcy Judge Jean K. FitzSimon
900 Market Street, Room 214, Philadelphia, PA 19107-4299
Tel: (215) 408-2891
E-mail: jean_fitzsimon@paeb.uscourts.gov

Jean K. FitzSimon
Bankruptcy Judge

Began Service: June 2006
Term Expires: 2020

Staff
Career Law Clerk (Part-Time) **Anna R. Marks** . . . . (215) 408-2891
Career Law Clerk (Part-Time) **Noreen Walsh** . . . . (215) 408-2891
E-mail: noreen_walsh@paeb.uscourts.gov
Courtroom Deputy **Joan Ranieri** . . . . (215) 408-2857
Electronic Court Recorder **Tasha Dawsonia** . . . . (215) 408-2846
E-mail: tasha_dawsonia@paeb.uscourts.gov
Judicial Assistant **Michele Boyer** . . . . (215) 408-2891
E-mail: michele_boyer@paeb.uscourts.gov

Chambers of Bankruptcy Judge Magdeline D. Coleman
900 Market Street, Suite 214, Philadelphia, PA 19107-4299
Tel: (215) 408-2978

Magdeline D. Coleman
Bankruptcy Judge

Began Service: 2010

Staff
Law Clerk **DeWitt Brown** . . . . (215) 408-2978
Courtroom Deputy **Eileen Godfrey** . . . . (215) 408-2819
Electronic Court Recorder **Yvette Woods** . . . . (215) 408-2841
Judicial Assistant **Carol Pyle** . . . . (215) 408-2978

Chambers of Bankruptcy Judge Ashely M. Chan
900 Market Street, Suite 214, Philadelphia, PA 19107-4299
Tel: (215) 408-2830

Ashely M. Chan
Bankruptcy Judge

Education: Rutgers (Camden) 1993 BA, 1995 JD

Staff
Law Clerk **Ann Hook** . . . . (215) 408-2830
Courtroom Deputy **Barbara Townsend** . . . . (215) 408-2830
Judicial Assistant **Karen Strupczewski** . . . . (215) 408-2830

United States District Court for the Middle District of Pennsylvania
U.S. Courthouse and Federal Office Building, 240 West Third Street, Suite 218, Williamsport, PA 17701
P.O. Box 1148, Scranton, PA 18501
P.O. Box 983, Harrisburg, PA 17108
Tel: (570) 207-5600 (General Info) Tel: (570) 207-5680 (Clerk's office)
Fax: (570) 207-5689 Tel: (717) 221-3920 (Harrisburg Division)
Fax: (717) 221-3959 (Harrisburg Division)
Tel: (570) 323-6380 (Williamsport Division)
Fax: (570) 323-0636 (Williamsport Division)
E-mail: mdpacourt@pamd.uscourts.gov
Internet: www.pamd.uscourts.gov

Number of Judgeships: 6

Circuit: Third

Areas Covered: Counties of Adams, Bradford, Cameron, Carbon, Centre, Clinton, Columbia, Cumberland, Dauphin, Franklin, Fulton, Huntingdon, Juniata, Lackawanna, Lebanon, Luzerne, Lycoming, Mifflin, Monroe, Montour, Northumberland, Perry, Pike, Potter, Schuylkill, Snyder, Sullivan, Susquehanna, Tioga, Union, Wayne, Wyoming and York

Court Staff
Clerk of Court **Maria Elkins** . . . . (570) 207-5680
E-mail: maria_elkins@pamd.uscourts.gov
Clerk's Sercretary **Roseanne Pucilowski** . . . . (570) 207-5682
E-mail: Roseanne_Pucilowski@pamd.uscourts.gov Fax: (570) 207-5689
Chief Deputy Clerk - Harrisburg **Peter Welsh** . . . . (717) 221-3920
Federal Building and U.S. Courthouse, 228 Walnut Street, Harrisburg, PA 17108 Fax: (717) 221-3959
Chief Deputy Clerk - Scranton **Cathy Dolinish** . . . . (570) 207-5683
E-mail: cathy_dolinish@pamd.uscourts.gov Fax: (570) 207-5689
Deputy-in-Charge - Harrisburg **Pete Welsh** . . . . (717) 221-3920
Federal Building and U.S. Courthouse, 228 Walnut Street, Harrisburg, PA 17108 Fax: (717) 221-3959
E-mail: peter_welsh@pamd.uscourts.gov
Supervisor of Court Services **(Vacant)** . . . . (570) 601-8515
240 West Third Street, Suite 218, Williamsport, PA 17108 Fax: (570) 323-0636
Pro Se Law Clerk **Erin Butler Castanzo** . . . . (570) 207-5642
E-mail: erin_castanzo@pamd.uscourts.gov
Education: Syracuse 1989 JD

(continued on next page)

United States District Court for the Middle District of Pennsylvania *continued*

Pro Se Law Clerk **Sheila M. Flanagan-Sheils** . . . . (570) 207-5647
Pro Se Law Clerk **Alexandra Miller** . . . . (717) 221-3953
100 Chestnut Street, Harrisburg, PA 17101
E-mail: alexandra_a_miller@pamd.uscourts.gov
Education: Dickinson Law 2004 JD
Pro Se Law Clerk **Diana Palevac** . . . . (570) 207-5648
Pro Se Law Clerk **Laurie A. Quinn** . . . . (570) 207-5646
E-mail: laurie_quinn@pamd.uscourts.gov
Pro Se Law Clerk **Pia Taggart** . . . . (570) 207-5641
E-mail: pia_taggart@pamd.uscourts.gov
Pro Se Law Clerk **James P. Van Wie** . . . . (570) 207-5645
E-mail: jim_vanwie@pamd.uscourts.gov
Operations Manager **Kevin T. Calpin** . . . . (570) 207-5600
E-mail: kevin_calpin@pamd.uscourts.gov
Director of Information Technology **Fred Skaluba** . . . . (570) 207-5622
E-mail: fred_skaluba@pamd.uscourts.gov Fax: (570) 207-5650
Chief Probation Officer **Drew Thompson** . . . . (570) 207-5840
P.O. Box 191, Scranton, PA 18501 Fax: (570) 207-5880
235 North Washington Avenue, Room 107,
Scranton, PA 18501-0191
Human Resources Director **Deborah Skopek** . . . . (570) 207-5670
E-mail: Deborah_Skopek@pamd.uscourts.gov Fax: (570) 207-5650
Financial Administrator **Nancy Edmunds** . . . . (570) 207-5665
E-mail: nancy_a_edmunds@pamd.uscourts.gov Fax: (570) 207-5650
Administrative Supervisor/Staff Attorney
Joseph A. Barrett . . . . (570) 207-5622
E-mail: joe_barrett@pamd.uscourts.gov

Chambers of Chief Judge Christopher C. Conner

Federal Building and U.S. Courthouse, 228 Walnut Street,
Room 930, Harrisburg, PA 17101
P.O. Box 847, Harrisburg, PA 17108-0847
Tel: (717) 221-3945 Fax: (717) 221-3949
E-mail: chambers_of_chief_judge_christopher_c_conner@pamd.uscourts.gov

Christopher C. Conner
Chief Judge

Date of Birth: October 25, 1957
Education: Cornell 1979 BA; Dickinson Law 1982 JD
Began Service: August 2, 2002
Appointed By: President George W. Bush

Staff

Law Clerk **Jessica Kyle** . . . . (717) 221-3945
Began Service: August 2015
Term Expires: August 2016
E-mail: jessica_kyle@pamd.uscourts.gov
Law Clerk **Cassandra Roeder** . . . . (717) 221-3945
Term Expires: September 2016
E-mail: cassandra_roeder@pamd.uscourts.gov
Managing Law Clerk **Stefanie Pitcavage** . . . . (717) 221-3945
E-mail: stefanie_pitcavage@pamd.uscourts.gov
Courtroom Deputy **Kimberly McKinney** . . . . (717) 221-3920
E-mail: kimberly_mckinney@pamd.uscourts.gov
Secretary **Gail Sylvia** . . . . (717) 221-3945
E-mail: gail_sylvia@pamd.uscourts.gov

Chambers of District Judge Yvette Kane

U.S. Federal Building and Courthouse, 228 Walnut Street,
8th Floor, Harrisburg, PA 17108
P.O. Box 11817, Harrisburg, PA 17108
Tel: (717) 221-3920 Fax: (717) 221-3959

Yvette Kane
District Judge

Date of Birth: 1953
Education: Nicholls State 1973 BA; Tulane 1976 JD
Began Service: October 27, 1998
Appointed By: President William J. Clinton

Current Memberships: American Bar Association; Dauphin County Bar Association; Federal Bar Association; Federal Judges Association; Pennsylvania Bar Association

Staff

Law Clerk **Miles Babin** . . . . (717) 221-3992
Began Service: August 2014
Term Expires: August 2016
E-mail: miles_c_babin@pamb.uscourts.gov
Law Clerk **Lance Waters** . . . . (717) 221-3991
Began Service: August 2015
Term Expires: August 31, 2016
E-mail: lance_waters@pamd.uscourts.gov
Law Clerk **(Vacant)** . . . . (717) 221-3993
Court Reporter **Lori Shuey** . . . . (717) 215-1270
E-mail: lori_shuey@pamd.uscourts.gov
Judicial Assistant **Dawn McNew** . . . . (717) 221-3920
E-mail: Dawn_McNew@pamd.uscourts.gov

Chambers of District Judge John E. Jones III

P.O. Box 983, Harrisburg, PA 17108
Tel: (717) 221-3986 Fax: (717) 221-3959
E-mail: chambers_of_judge_john_e_jones@pamd.uscourts.gov

John E. Jones III
District Judge

Date of Birth: June 13, 1955
Education: Mercersburg Acad (Mercersburg, PA) 1973; Dickinson Col 1977 BA; Dickinson Law 1980 JD
Began Service: August 2, 2002
Appointed By: President George W. Bush

Clerkships: Law Clerk (part-time) The Honorable Guy A. Bowe, Schuylkill County Court of Common Pleas (1980-1984)

Corporate: Vice President, Secretary, Counsel and Director, Phoenix Contracting Co. (1980-2002); Sole Proprietor, John Jones & Associates, Inc. (1986-2002); Director, Board of Directors, Union Bank & Trust Company (1993-2002)

Government: Assistant Public Defender (part-time), Office of the Public Defender, Commonwealth of Pennsylvania (1984-1995); Chairman, Liquor Control Board, Commonwealth of Pennsylvania (1995-2002)

Legal Practice: Associate, Dolbin, Cori & Jones (1980-1982); Partner, Dolbin, Cori & Jones (1982-1986)

Staff

Law Clerk **Marta Cook** . . . . (717) 221-3986
E-mail: marta_cook@pamd.uscourts.gov
Law Clerk **Juliana van Hoeven** . . . . (717) 221-3986
Began Service: August 2015
Term Expires: August 2017
E-mail: juliana_vanhoeven@pamd.uscourts.gov
Career Law Clerk **Amanda Gaynor** . . . . (717) 221-3986
Education: NYU 2005 JD
Deputy Clerk **Elizabeth A. "Liz" O'Donnell** . . . . (717) 221-3986
E-mail: liz_a._odonnell@pamd.uscourts.gov

Chambers of District Judge Robert David Mariani

235 North Washington Avenue, Scranton, PA 18501
Tel: (570) 207-5750 Fax: (570) 207-5759
E-mail: robert_mariani@pamd.uscourts.gov

Robert David Mariani
District Judge

Education: Villanova 1972 AB; Syracuse 1976 JD
Began Service: October 19, 2011
Appointed By: President Barack Obama

Staff
Courtroom Deputy **Joe Gaughan** .... (570) 207-5750
E-mail: joe_gaughan@pamd.uscourts.gov

Chambers of District Judge Malachy Edward Mannion

235 North Washington Avenue, Scranton, PA 18501
P.O. Box 914, Scranton, PA 18501
Tel: (570) 207-5760 Fax: (570) 207-5769

Malachy Edward Mannion
District Judge

Date of Birth: 1953
Education: Scranton 1976 BS; Pace 1979 JD
Began Service: December 28, 2012
Appointed By: President Barack Obama

Government: Assistant District Attorney, Office of the District Attorney, County of Nassau, New York (1980-1986); Assistant United States Attorney, Middle District of Pennsylvania, United States Department of Justice, Ronald Reagan Administration (1986-1993)

Judicial: Magistrate Judge, Chambers of Magistrate Judge Malachy E. Mannion, United States District Court for the Middle District of Pennsylvania (2001-2012)

Legal Practice: Partner, Hourigan, Kluger, Spohrer & Quinn, P.C. (1993-1997)

Current Memberships: Federal Bar Association; Lackawanna Bar Association; Pennsylvania Bar Association

Staff
Law Clerk **Steven Gavin** .... (570) 207-5760
Law Clerk **John A. Morano** .... (570) 207-5760
E-mail: john_morano@pamd.uscourts.gov
Education: Dickinson Law 1984 JD
Career Law Clerk **Krista Ammenhauser** .... (570) 207-5760
Began Service: 2001
E-mail: krista_ammenhauser@pamd.uscourts.gov
Education: Scranton 1992; Widener 1996 JD
Courtroom Deputy **Barbe Sempa** .... (570) 207-5760
E-mail: barbe_sempa@pamd.uscourts.gov

Chambers of District Judge Matthew N. Brann

U.S. Courthouse and Federal Office Building, 240 West Third Street, Suite 218, Williamsport, PA 17701
Tel: (570) 323-9772
E-mail: matthew_brann@pamd.uscourts.gov

Matthew W. Brann
District Judge

Education: Notre Dame 1987 BA; Dickinson Law 1990 JD
Began Service: February 24, 2013
Appointed By: President Barack Obama

Staff
Law Clerk **Richard Armezzani** .... (570) 323-9772
Term Expires: August 2016
E-mail: richard_armezzani@pamd.uscourts.gov
Law Clerk **Nicholas Caselli** .... (570) 323-9772
Term Expires: August 2016
E-mail: nicholas_caselli@pamd.uscourts.gov

Chambers of District Judge Matthew N. Brann *continued*

Career Law Clerk **Yvonne Campbell** .... (570) 323-9772
E-mail: yvonne_campbell@pamd.uscourts.gov
Education: Pittsburgh 2008 JD
Courtroom Deputy **Kathy A. McLaughlin** .... (570) 323-9772
E-mail: kathy_mclaughlin@pamd.uscourts.gov

Chambers of Senior Judge William J. Nealon, Jr.

William J. Nealon Federal Building & U.S. Courthouse, 235 North Washington Avenue, Scranton, PA 18503
P.O. Box 1146, Scranton, PA 18501-1146
Tel: (570) 207-5700 Fax: (570) 207-5709

William J. Nealon, Jr.
Senior Judge

Date of Birth: 1923
Education: Villanova 1947 BS; Columbus Law 1950 JD
Began Service: December 15, 1962
Appointed By: President John F. Kennedy
Political Affiliation: Democrat

Academic: Lecturer, The University of Scranton (1951-1959)

Government: Hearing Examiner, Liquor Control Board, Commonwealth of Pennsylvania (1955-1959)

Judicial: Judge, Allegheny County Court of Common Pleas (1960-1962)

Legal Practice: Kennedy, O'Brien & O'Brien (1951-1960)

Military Service: United States Marine Corps Reserve (1942-1945)

Current Memberships: Federal Bar Association; Lackawanna Bar Association; Pennsylvania Bar Association

Staff
Career Law Clerk **Kelly Jo Slone** .... (570) 207-5700
Education: Dickinson Law 2001 JD
Career Law Clerk **Paul Keeler** .... (570) 207-5700
E-mail: paul_keeler@pamd.uscourts.gov
Education: Villanova 2003 JD
Courtroom Deputy **(Vacant)** .... (570) 207-5700

Chambers of Senior Judge Richard P. Conaboy

William J. Nealon Federal Building & U.S. Courthouse, 235 North Washington Avenue, Room 405, Scranton, PA 18501
P.O. Box 189, Scranton, PA 18501
Tel: (570) 207-5710 Fax: (570) 207-5719

Richard P. Conaboy
Senior Judge

Date of Birth: 1925
Education: Scranton 1945 BA; Catholic U 1950 LLB
Began Service: 1979
Appointed By: President Jimmy Carter

Government: Deputy Attorney General, State Workmen's Insurance Fund, Commonwealth of Pennsylvania (1953-1959); Hearing Examiner, Liquor Control Board, Commonwealth of Pennsylvania (1959-1962); Chairman, Commission on Sentencing, Commonwealth of Pennsylvania (1979-1981); Chair, United States Sentencing Commission (1994-1998)

Judicial: President Judge, Pennsylvania Court of Common Pleas, Lackawanna County (1962-1979); Chief Judge, United States District Court for the Middle District of Pennsylvania (1989-1992)

Legal Practice: Partner, Powell & Conaboy (1951-1953); Associate, Kennedy, O'Brien & O'Brien (1953-1962)

Military Service: United States Army Air Corps (1945-1947)

Current Memberships: Lackawanna Bar Association; Pennsylvania Conference of State Trial Judges

(continued on next page)

Chambers of Senior Judge Richard P. Conaboy *continued*

Staff
Fax: (570) 207-5719

Law Clerk **Thomas D. Brown** .... (570) 207-5710
Term Expires: January 9, 2016
Career Law Clerk **Joan D. Samuel** .... (570) 207-5710
E-mail: joan_samuel@pamd.uscourts.gov
Education: Widener JD
Courtroom Deputy **Charles T. Cleveland** .... (570) 207-5710
Education: Scranton 1984 BS
Secretary **Kathryn A. Moran** .... (570) 207-5710
E-mail: kathy_moran@pamd.uscourts.gov

Chambers of Senior Judge Sylvia H. Rambo

Federal Building, 228 Walnut Street, Harrisburg, PA 17108
P.O. Box 868, Harrisburg, PA 17108-0868
Tel: (717) 221-3960 Fax: (717) 221-3968
E-mail: chambers_of_judge_sylvia_rambo@pamd.uscourts.gov

Sylvia H. Rambo
Senior Judge

Date of Birth: 1936
Education: Dickinson Law 1958 AB, 1962 JD
Began Service: August 8, 1979
Appointed By: President Jimmy Carter

Academic: Adjunct Professor, The Dickinson School of Law of the Pennsylvania State University (1975-1976)

Government: Chief Public Defender, County of Cumberland, Pennsylvania (1976)

Judicial: Judge, Pennsylvania Court of Common Pleas, Cumberland County (1976-1978)

Legal Practice: Attorney, Trust Department, Bank of Delaware (1962-1963); Private Practice (1963-1976); Private Practice (1978-1979)

Current Memberships: Cumberland County Bar Association; Federal Bar Association; Federal Judges Association; National Association of Women Judges; Pennsylvania Bar Association

Staff
Law Clerk **Tye Bell** .... (717) 221-3960
Began Service: March 2015
Term Expires: August 31, 2017
Law Clerk **Cristin D. Nace** .... (717) 221-3960
Began Service: August 2013
Term Expires: August 31, 2016
E-mail: cristin_nace@pamd.uscourts.gov
Court Reporter **Wendy Yinger** .... (717) 440-1535
E-mail: Wendy_Yinger@pamd.uscourts.gov
Courtroom Deputy Clerk **Mark Armbruster** .... (717) 221-3927
E-mail: mark_armbruster@pamd.uscourts.gov
Administrative Secretary **Kristen Fawcett King** .... (717) 221-3960
E-mail: Kristen_King@pamd.uscourts.gov

Chambers of Senior Judge William W. Caldwell

954 Federal Building, 228 Walnut Street, Harrisburg, PA 17108
P.O. Box 11877, Harrisburg, PA 17108-1877
Tel: (717) 221-3970 Fax: (717) 221-3976

William W. Caldwell
Senior Judge

Date of Birth: 1925
Education: Dickinson Col 1948 AB; Dickinson Law 1951 LLB
Began Service: 1982
Appointed By: President Ronald Reagan

Government: First Assistant District Attorney (part-time), Office of the District Attorney, County of Dauphin, Pennsylvania (1960-1962); Counsel and Chairman, Board of Arbitration of Claims, Commonwealth of Pennsylvania (1963-1970)

Chambers of Senior Judge William W. Caldwell *continued*

Judicial: Judge, Pennsylvania Court of Common Pleas, 12th Judicial District, Dauphin County (1970-1982)

Legal Practice: Partner, Caldwell, Fox & Stoner (1951-1970)

Military Service: United States Army Air Corps (1944-1945)

Current Memberships: Dauphin County Bar Association; Federal Judges Association; Pennsylvania Bar Association

Staff
Law Clerk **Wes Mishoe**
Began Service: September 2015
Term Expires: September 2016
Law Clerk **Langdon Ramsburg** .... (717) 221-3972
Began Service: September 2014
Term Expires: September 2016
E-mail: langdon_ramsburg@pamd.uscourts.gov
Career Law Clerk **Bernard J. Donohue** .... (717) 221-3971
E-mail: bernard_donohue@pamd.uscourts.gov
Courtroom Deputy **Mark Armbruster** .... (717) 221-3929
E-mail: mark_armbruster@pamd.uscourts.gov

Chambers of Senior Judge Edwin M. Kosik

William J. Nealon Federal Building & U.S. Courthouse, 235 North Washington Avenue, Scranton, PA 18501
P.O. Box 856, Scranton, PA 18501-0856
Tel: (570) 207-5730 Fax: (570) 207-5739

Edwin M. Kosik
Senior Judge

Date of Birth: 1925
Education: Wilkes U 1949 BA; Dickinson Law 1951 LLB
Began Service: July 15, 1986
Appointed By: President Ronald Reagan

Government: Assistant United States Attorney, Middle District of Pennsylvania, Office of the United States Attorney, United States Department of Justice (1953-1958); Chairman, Pennsylvania State Workmen's Compensation Board, Commonwealth of Pennsylvania (1964-1969)

Judicial: Judge, Pennsylvania Court of Common Pleas, 45th Judicial District (1969-1979); President Judge, Pennsylvania Court of Common Pleas, 45th Judicial District (1979-1986)

Legal Practice: Needle, Needle & Needle (1958-1969)

Military Service: United States Army (1943-1975)

Current Memberships: Lackawanna Bar Association; Pennsylvania Bar Association

Staff
Law Clerk **Barbara Grimaud** .... (570) 207-5734
Began Service: August 2013
Term Expires: August 16, 2016
E-mail: barbara_grimaud@pamd.uscourts.gov
Career Law Clerk **Carol Kristoff** .... (570) 207-5733
E-mail: carol_kristoff@pamd.uscourts.gov
Education: Dickinson Law 1980 JD
Case Manager **(Vacant)** .... (570) 207-5736
Judicial Assistant **Jennifer Ciccotti** .... (570) 207-5732
E-mail: jennifer_ciccotti@pamd.uscourts.gov

Chambers of Senior Judge A. Richard Caputo

Max Rosenn U.S. Courthouse, 197 South Main Street, Suite 235, Wilkes Barre, PA 18701
Tel: (570) 831-2556 Fax: (570) 829-3948

A. Richard Caputo
Senior Judge

Date of Birth: 1938
Education: Brown U 1960 AB; Pennsylvania 1963 LLB
Began Service: November 12, 1997
Appointed By: President William J. Clinton

Corporate: Secretary and Director, Stegmaier Brewing Company (1973-1992)

Legal Practice: Shea, Shea & Caputo (1968-1997)

Military Service: United States Air Force (1963-1967)

Nonprofit: Director and Secretary/Treasurer, The Luzerne Foundation (1994-1997)

Current Memberships: American Bar Association; Federal Bar Association; Luzerne County Law and Library Association; Pennsylvania Bar Association

Staff

Law Clerk **Chad Sweigart** .... (570) 831-2556
Began Service: 2012
E-mail: chad_sweigart@pamd.uscourts.gov
Education: Dickinson Law 2010 JD

Law Clerk **Sara Chimeme-Weiss** .... (570) 831-2556

Courtroom Deputy/Case Administrator **Judith "Judy" Malave** .... (570) 831-2556
E-mail: judith_malave@pamd.uscourts.gov

Judicial Assistant **Dawn Wychock** .... (570) 831-2556
E-mail: dawn_wychock@pamd.uscourts.gov
Education: King's Col (PA) 1999 AS

Chambers of Senior Judge James M. Munley

P. O. Box 1247, Scranton, PA 18501-1247
Tel: (570) 207-5780 Fax: (570) 207-5789

James M. Munley
Senior Judge

Date of Birth: 1936
Education: Scranton 1958 BS; Temple 1963 LLB
Began Service: October 22, 1998
Appointed By: President William J. Clinton

Current Memberships: Ancient Order of Hibernians in America, Inc.; Knights of Columbus; Lackawanna Bar Association; Pennsylvania Bar Association; The University of Scranton Alumni Association; Veterans of Foreign Wars of the U.S.

Staff

Law Clerk **Sean Camoni** .... (570) 207-5780
Began Service: September 2014
Term Expires: August 2016
E-mail: sean_camoni@pamd.uscourts.gov

Law Clerk **Ted Michel** .... (570) 207-5780
Began Service: October 2012
Term Expires: September 2016

Career Law Clerk **Louis Whitehead** .... (570) 207-5780
E-mail: louis_whitehead@pamd.uscourts.gov
Education: Marywood Col 1993 BA; Dickinson Law 1996 JD

Courtroom Deputy **Sylvia C. Murphy** .... (570) 207-5780
E-mail: sylvia_murphy@pamd.uscourts.gov
Education: Dickinson Col 1982 BA

Chambers of Magistrate Judge Martin C. Carlson

240 West Third Street, Williamsport, PA 17701
Tel: (717) 614-4120
E-mail: martin_carlson@pamd.uscourts.gov

Martin C. Carlson
Magistrate Judge

Education: Penn State 1977 BA; Pennsylvania 1980 JD
Began Service: August 15, 2009

Government: U.S. Attorney, Pennsylvania - Middle District, Executive Office for United States Attorneys, United States Department of Justice (2007-2009); First Assistant U.S. Attorney, Criminal Division, Pennsylvania - Middle District, United States Department of Justice (2002-2007); Chief - Criminal Division, Criminal Division, Pennsylvania - Middle District, United States Department of Justice (1994-2001); Assistant United States Attorney, Pennsylvania - Middle District, United States Department of Justice (1989-1994); Senior Legal Advisor, Criminal Division, District of Columbia District, United States Department of Justice (1988-1989); Trial Attorney, Criminal Division, District of Columbia District, United States Department of Justice (1982-1988)

Current Memberships: Federal Magistrate Judges Association; National Association of Assistant United States Attorneys; National Association of Former United States Attorneys; Pennsylvania Bar Association

Staff

Career Law Clerk **Christian Haugsby** .... (717) 614-4120
E-mail: christian_haugsby@pamd.uscourts.gov
Education: Kenyon 1996 BA; Michigan 2001 JD

Judicial Assistant **Susan Keefer** .... (717) 614-4120

Chambers of Magistrate Judge Susan E. Schwab

228 Walnut Street, Harrisburg, PA 17108
Tel: (717) 221-3980
E-mail: susan_schwab@pamd.uscourts.gov

Susan E. Schwab
Magistrate Judge

Staff

Career Law Clerk **Melissa E. Sayres** .... (717) 221-3980
E-mail: melissa_sayres@pamd.uscourts.gov
Education: Millersville 1989 BA; Dickinson Law 1993 JD

Law Clerk **Sarah McGowan** .... (717) 221-3980
Term Expires: August 2016
E-mail: sarah_mcgowan@pamd.uscourts.gov

Courtroom Deputy **Rashelle Weida** .... (717) 221-3980
E-mail: rashelle_weida@pamd.uscourts.gov

Chambers of Magistrate Judge Karoline Mehalchick

197 South Main Street, Wilkes Barre, PA 18701
Tel: (570) 207-5740 Fax: (570) 821-4009
E-mail: magistrate_judge_mehalchick@pamd.uscourts.gov

Karoline Mehalchick
Magistrate Judge

Education: Penn State; Tulane 2001 JD
Began Service: September 7, 2013

Staff

Law Clerk **Andrew Grow** .... (570) 831-2570
Term Expires: August 2016

Law Clerk **Caitlin Sherrill** .... (570) 831-2570
Term Expires: August 2016
E-mail: caitlin_sherrill@pamd.uscourts.gov

Courtroom Deputy **Corey Wimmer** .... (570) 831-2570
E-mail: corey_wimmer@pamd.uscourts.gov

Chambers of Magistrate Judge Joseph F. Saporito Jr.
197 South Main Street, Wilkes Barre, PA 18701
Tel: (570) 831-2570 Fax: (570) 821-4009
E-mail: magistrate_judge_saporito@pamd.uscourts.gov

Joseph F. Saporito, Jr.
Magistrate Judge

Began Service: April 17, 2015

Chambers of Magistrate Judge (part-time) William I. Arbuckle III
240 West Third Street, Williamsport, PA 17701
Tel: (570) 323-9881
E-mail: william_arbuckle@pamd.uscourts.gov

William I. Arbuckle III
Magistrate Judge

Education: Grove City 1971 BA; Akron 1974 JD
Began Service: July 29, 2008

Current Memberships: Federal Magistrate Judges Association; Pennsylvania Bar Association

United States Bankruptcy Court for the Middle District of Pennsylvania
274 Max Rosenn U.S. Courthouse, 197 South Main Street, Wilkes Barre, PA 18701
Tel: (570) 831-2500 Fax: (570) 829-0249
Internet: www.pamb.uscourts.gov

Number of Judgeships: 3

Court Staff
Clerk of Court **Terrence S. Miller** .... (717) 901-2816
Education: Baltimore 1980 BA; Denver 1986 MS Fax: (717) 901-2848
Chief Deputy Clerk **Seth Eisenberg** .... (570) 831-2500
Information Systems Manager **Chuck Smith** .... (570) 831-2513

Chambers of Chief Bankruptcy Judge Mary D. France
P.O. Box 1263, Harrisburg, PA 17108
Tel: (717) 901-2845 Fax: (717) 901-2844

Mary D. France
Chief Bankruptcy Judge

Began Service: March 3, 2003

Staff
Law Clerk **Vera Kanova** .... (717) 901-2845
Began Service: September 2013
Term Expires: September 2016
E-mail: vera_kanova@pamb.uscourts.gov
Career Law Clerk **John D. Kelly** .... (717) 901-2846
E-mail: john_kelly@pamb.uscourts.gov
Courtroom Deputy **Joan Goodling** .... (717) 901-2818

Chambers of Bankruptcy Judge John J. Thomas
Max Rosenn U.S. Courthouse, 197 South Main Street, Suite 150, Wilkes Barre, PA 18701
Tel: (570) 831-2531 Fax: (570) 829-0164
E-mail: chambers_of_judge_john_thomas@pamb.uscourts.gov

John J. Thomas
Bankruptcy Judge

Date of Birth: 1948
Education: Dickinson Law 1972 JD
Began Service: January 10, 1992
Term Expires: January 10, 2020

Current Memberships: Middle District Bankruptcy Bar Association; National Conference of Bankruptcy Judges; Wilkes-Barre Law and Library Association

Staff
Career Law Clerk **Richard P. Rogers** .... (570) 831-2531
Education: Temple 1983 JD
Judicial Assistant **Catherine M. Sisk** .... (570) 831-2531
E-mail: cathy_sisk@pamb.uscourts.gov

Chambers of Bankruptcy Judge Robert N. Opel
274 Max Rosenn U.S. Courthouse, 197 South Main Street, Suite 144, Wilkes Barre, PA 18701
Tel: (570) 831-2536 Fax: (570) 829-3801

Robert N. Opel
Bankruptcy Judge

Began Service: September 2006
Term Expires: September 2020

Staff
Law Clerk **William Schumacher** .... (570) 831-2536
Began Service: August 1, 2014
Term Expires: August 2016
Courtroom Deputy **Patricia Ratchford** .... (570) 831-2509
Judicial Secretary **Beth Irving** .... (570) 831-2536

United States District Court for the Western District of Pennsylvania
U.S. Post Office & Courthouse, 700 Grant Street, Pittsburgh, PA 15219
Tel: (412) 208-7500 Fax: (412) 208-7530
Internet: www.pawd.uscourts.gov

Number of Judgeships: 10

Number of Vacancies: 3

Circuit: Third

Areas Covered: Counties of Allegheny, Armstrong, Beaver, Bedford, Blair, Butler, Cambria, Clarion, Clearfield, Crawford, Elk, Erie, Fayette, Forest, Greene, Indiana, Jefferson, Lawrence, McKean, Mercer, Somerset, Venango, Warren, Washington and Westmoreland

Court Staff
Clerk of the Court **Robert V. Barth** .... (412) 208-7500
E-mail: robert_barth@pawd.uscourts.gov
Chief Deputy **Colleen Willison** .... (412) 208-7518
E-mail: colleen_willison@pawd.uscourts.gov
Chief U.S. Probation and Pretrial Services Officer
Belinda M. Ashley .... (412) 395-6907
Suite 3330
E-mail: belinda_ashley@pawp.uscourts.gov
Deputy-in-Charge - Erie **Susan Parmeter** .... (814) 464-9600
P.O. Box 1820, Erie, PA 16507 Fax: (814) 464-9607
17 South Park Row, Erie, PA 16501
E-mail: susan_parmeter@pawd.uscourts.gov

United States District Court for the Western District of Pennsylvania *continued*

Deputy-in-Charge - Johnstown **James Graves** .... (814) 533-4504
208 Penn Traffic Bldg., 319 Washington St., Fax: (814) 533-4519
Johnstown, PA 15901
E-mail: james_graves@pawd.uscourts.gov

Chambers of Chief Judge Joy Flowers Conti

5250 U.S. Post Office & Courthouse, 700 Grant Street,
Pittsburgh, PA 15219
Tel: (412) 208-7330 Fax: (412) 208-7337
E-mail: judge_joy_conti@pawd.uscourts.gov

Joy Flowers Conti
Chief Judge

Date of Birth: December 7, 1948
Education: Duquesne 1970 BA, 1973 JD
Began Service: August 30, 2002
Appointed By: President George W. Bush

Current Memberships: American Bar Foundation; Allegheny County Bar Association; American Bankruptcy Institute; American Bar Association; The Pittsburgh American Inn of Court, The American Inns of Court; The American Law Institute; Federal Bar Association; National Association of Women Judges; Pennsylvania Bar Association; Pennsylvania Bar Foundation

Staff

Law Clerk **Benjamin Minegar** .... (412) 208-7330
Began Service: September 2015
Term Expires: September 2016
Career Law Clerk **Katie McGee** .... (412) 208-7330
E-mail: katie_mcgee@pawd.uscourts.gov
Courtroom Deputy **Sharon Conley** .... (412) 208-7330
E-mail: sharon_conley@pawd.uscourts.gov
Judicial Assistant **Carole Leonard** .... (412) 208-7330
E-mail: carole_leonard@pawd.uscourts.gov

Chambers of District Judge David Stewart Cercone

U.S. Courthouse, 700 Grant Street, Room 7270, Pittsburgh, PA 15219
Tel: (412) 208-7363 Fax: (412) 208-7462

David Stewart Cercone
District Judge

Date of Birth: 1952
Education: Westminster (PA) 1974 BA; Duquesne 1977 JD
Began Service: September 12, 2002
Appointed By: President George W. Bush

Academic: Adjunct Faculty, Robert Morris College (1993-1995)

Clerkships: Law Clerk, Judge Paul R. Zavarella, Allegheny County Court of Common Pleas (1978-1979)

Government: Assistant District Attorney, Office of the District Attorney, County of Allegheny, Pennsylvania (1979-1981)

Judicial: District Justice, Commonwealth of Pennsylvania (1982-1985)

Staff

Courtroom Deputy Clerk **Nancy Trapani** .... (412) 208-7363
E-mail: nancy_trapani@pawd.uscourts.gov
Court Reporter **(Vacant)** .... (412) 261-6122
Secretary **Kimberly Kovach** .... (412) 208-7363
E-mail: kimberly_kovach@pawd.uscourts.gov

Chambers of District Judge Arthur J. Schwab

U.S. Courthouse, 700 Grant Street, Suite 7280, Pittsburgh, PA 15219
Tel: (412) 208-7423 Fax: (412) 208-7417

Arthur J. Schwab
District Judge

Date of Birth: December 7, 1946
Education: Grove City 1968 AB; Virginia 1972 JD
Began Service: January 1, 2003
Appointed By: President George W. Bush

Affiliation: Adjunct Professor, Grove City College

Clerkships: Law Clerk, Chief Judge Collins J. Seitz, United States Court of Appeals for the Third Circuit (1972-1973)

Legal Practice: Summer Law Clerk, Jones, Day, Reavis & Pogue (1971); Summer Law Clerk, Reed Smith Shaw & McClay LLP (1972); Deputy Head, Reed Smith Shaw & McClay LLP (1973-1990); Chair of Litigation, Buchanan Ingersoll PC (1990-1999); Chief Counsel-Complex Litigation, Buchanan Ingersoll PC (2000-2002)

Military Service: United States Army National Guard and Army Reserve (1968-1978)

Staff

Law Clerk **Laura C. Bunting** .... (412) 208-7415
Began Service: 2011
E-mail: laura_bunting@pawd.uscourts.gov
Law Clerk **(Vacant)** .... (412) 417-2510
Career Law Clerk **Nicole Moschetta** .... (412) 208-7426
E-mail: nicole_moschetta@pawd.uscourts.gov
Education: Ohio 1996 AB; Pittsburgh 1999 JD
Courtroom Deputy **Linda Krings** .... (412) 208-7425
E-mail: linda_krings@pawd.uscourts.gov
Court Reporter **Virginia Pease** .... (412) 208-7385
Secretary **Melissa Stadelman** .... (412) 208-7423
E-mail: melissa_stadelman@pawd.uscourts.gov

Chambers of District Judge Kim R. Gibson

Penn Traffic Building Courtroom A, 319 Washington Street,
Room 104, Johnstown, PA 15901
Tel: (814) 533-4514

Kim R. Gibson
District Judge

Education: West Point 1970 BS; Dickinson Law 1975 JD
Began Service: 2003
Appointed By: President George W. Bush

Government: Public Defender, Court of Common Pleas, County of Somerset, Pennsylvania (1978-1980); Assistant County Solicitor, Children and Youth Services, County of Somerset, Pennsylvania (1980-1988); Solicitor, County of Somerset, Pennsylvania (1988-1998)

Judicial: Judge, Court of Common Pleas of 16th Judicial District (1998-2003)

Military Service: U.S. Army (1966-1978); Post Judge Advocate, U.S. Army (1975-1978); U.S. Army Reserve (1978-1996)

Staff

Law Clerk **David Brown** .... (814) 533-4514
E-mail: david_brown@pawd.uscourts.gov
Law Clerk **Silvia Costello** .... (814) 533-4514
Courtroom Deputy **Debi Gorgone** .... (814) 533-4514
Began Service: 2003
Judicial Assistant **Kimberly Hochard** .... (814) 533-4514
Began Service: 2003
E-mail: kimberly_hochard@pawd.uscourts.gov

Chambers of District Judge Nora Barry Fischer

U.S. Post Office & Courthouse, 700 Grant Street, Pittsburgh, PA 15219
Tel: (412) 208-7480 Fax: (412) 208-7487

Nora Barry Fischer
District Judge

Date of Birth: 1951
Education: Notre Dame 1976 JD; St Mary's Col (IN) 1973 BA
Began Service: April 2007
Appointed By: President George W. Bush

Academic: National Institute of Trial Advocacy Instructor, School of Law, University of Pittsburgh; National Institute of Trial Advocacy Instructor, School of Law, Duquesne University

Corporate: Editor, Callaghan and Company, Legal Publishers (1976-1977)

Government: Arbitrator, United States District Court for the Western District of Pennsylvania

Judicial: Adjunct Settlement Judge, United States District Court for the Western District of Pennsylvania

Legal Practice: Associate, Meyer, Darragh, Buckler, Bebenek & Eck, PLLC (1977-1980); Junior Partner, Meyer, Darragh, Buckler, Bebenek & Eck, PLLC (1980-1982); Senior Partner, Meyer, Darragh, Buckler, Bebenek & Eck, PLLC (1982-1992); Equity Partner, Pietragallo Bosick & Gordon, LLP (1992-2007)

Staff
Law Clerk **Brian Kravetz** .... (412) 208-7480
E-mail: brian_kravetz@pawd.uscourts.gov
Education: Duquesne 2007 JD
Law Clerk **Alexander Owczarczak** .... (412) 208-7480
E-mail: alexander_owczarczak@pawd.uscourts.gov
Education: New Hampshire 2014 JD
Law Clerk **Nathan Samuel Catanese** .... (412) 208-7480
Began Service: July 2015
Term Expires: July 2016
E-mail: nathan_catanese@pawd.uscourts.gov
Education: Notre Dame 2007 BA
Courtroom Deputy Clerk **John Galovich** .... (412) 208-7480
E-mail: john_galovich@pawd.uscourts.gov
Court Reporter **Sandy Wenger** .... (412) 208-7385

Chambers of District Judge Cathy Bissoon

U.S. Post Office & Courthouse, 700 Grant Street, Pittsburgh, PA 15219
Tel: (412) 208-7460 Fax: (412) 208-7467

Cathy Bissoon
District Judge

Date of Birth: 1968
Education: Alfred 1990 BA; Harvard 1993 JD
Began Service: October 19, 2011
Appointed By: President Barack Obama

Staff
Law Clerk **(Vacant)** .... (412) 208-7460
Career Law Clerk **David C. Donehue** .... (412) 208-7460
E-mail: david_donehue@pawd.uscourts.gov
Education: Pittsburgh 1991 BS, 1996 JD
Courtroom Deputy **James H. Imhof** .... (412) 208-7460
E-mail: Jim_Imhof@pawd.uscourts.gov
Education: Penn State 1985 BA

Chambers of District Judge Mark Raymond Hornak

U.S. Post Office & Courthouse, 700 Grant Street, Pittsburgh, PA 15219
Tel: (412) 208-7433 Fax: (412) 208-7527

Mark R. Hornak
District Judge

Education: Pittsburgh 1978 BS, 1981 JD
Began Service: 2011
Appointed By: President Barack Obama

Current Memberships: American Bar Foundation

Staff
Law Clerk **(Vacant)** .... (412) 208-7433
Law Clerk **Bethany Lipman** .... (412) 208-7433
Courtroom Deputy **Brian Babik** .... (412) 208-7433
E-mail: brian_babik@pawd.uscourts.gov

Chambers of Senior Judge Maurice B. Cohill, Jr.

700 Grant Street, Suite 8170, Pittsburgh, PA 15219
Tel: (814) 464-9620 Fax: (814) 464-9627
E-mail: judge_cohill@pawd.uscourts.gov

Maurice B. Cohill, Jr.
Senior Judge

Date of Birth: 1929
Education: Princeton 1951 AB; Pittsburgh 1956 LLB
Began Service: June 1, 1976
Appointed By: President Gerald Ford
Political Affiliation: Republican

Judicial: Judge, Allegheny Juvenile Court (1965-1969); Judge, Pennsylvania Court of Common Pleas, Allegheny County (1969-1976)

Legal Practice: Kirkpatrick, Pomeroy, Lockhart & Johnson (1957-1965)

Military Service: United States Marine Corps (1951-1953)

Current Memberships: Allegheny County Bar Association; National Council of Juvenile and Family Court Judges

Staff
Law Clerk **Caren A.C. Grau** .... (412) 208-7380
E-mail: caren_grau@pawd.uscourts.gov
Career Law Clerk **Barbara Fisfis Marzina** .... (412) 208-7380
Education: Vassar 1989 BA; Duquesne 1993 JD
Career Law Clerk **Richard T. Williams** .... (412) 208-7380
Education: Pittsburgh 1983 BA, 1992 JD

Chambers of Senior Judge Gustave Diamond

U.S. Post Office & Courthouse, 700 Grant Street, Suite 8270, Pittsburgh, PA 15219
Tel: (412) 208-7390 Fax: (412) 208-7397
E-mail: judge_gustave_diamond@pawd.uscourts.gov

Gustave Diamond
Senior Judge

Date of Birth: 1928
Education: Duke 1951 AB; Duquesne 1956 JD
Began Service: May 2, 1978
Appointed By: President Jimmy Carter

Clerkships: Law Clerk The Honorable Rabe F. Marsh, Jr., United States District Court for the Western District of Pennsylvania (1956-1961)

Government: First Assistant United States Attorney, Western District of Pennsylvania, Office of the United States Attorney, United States Department of Justice (1961-1963); United States Attorney, Western District of Pennsylvania, United States Department of Justice (1963-1969)

Legal Practice: Partner, Cooper, Schwartz, Diamond & Reich (1969-1975); Private Practice (1976-1978)

Military Service: United States Navy (1946-1948)

Chambers of Senior Judge Gustave Diamond *continued*

Current Memberships: Allegheny County Bar Association; American Bar Association; The American Inns of Court; Federal Bar Association; Pennsylvania Bar Association; Washington County Bar Association

Staff
Career Law Clerk **Gary P. Robinson** .... (412) 208-7390
E-mail: gary_robinson@pawd.uscourts.gov
Education: North Carolina 1990 BA; Duquesne 1993 JD
Career Law Clerk **Kristie Woffington** .... (412) 208-7390
E-mail: kristie_woffington@pawd.uscourts.gov
Education: Allegheny 1993 BA; Dickinson Law 1996 JD

Chambers of Senior Judge Alan N. Bloch

U.S. Post Office & Courthouse, 700 Grant Street, Suite 8370, Pittsburgh, PA 15219
Tel: (412) 208-7360 Fax: (412) 208-7367
E-mail: judge_alan_bloch@pawd.uscourts.gov

Alan N. Bloch
Senior Judge

Date of Birth: 1932
Education: Pennsylvania 1953 BS; Pittsburgh 1958 JD
Began Service: November 21, 1979
Appointed By: President Jimmy Carter

Legal Practice: Wirtzman, Sikov & Love (1959-1969); Partner, Flaherty & Bloch (1969-1979)

Military Service: United States Army (1953-1955); Pennsylvania Army National Guard (1955-1959); United States Air Force Reserve (1959-1963)

Current Memberships: Academy of Trial Lawyers of Allegheny County; American Bar Association

Staff
Career Law Clerk **Darren O'Neill** .... (412) 208-7360
Education: Notre Dame 2000 JD
Law Clerk **Lisa Petrick** .... (412) 208-7360
E-mail: lisa_petrick@pawd.uscourts.gov

Chambers of Senior Judge Donetta W. Ambrose

U.S. Post Office & Courthouse, 700 Grant Street, Suite 3280, Pittsburgh, PA 15219-1906
Tel: (412) 208-7350 Fax: (412) 208-7357
E-mail: Judge_Donetta_Ambrose@pawd.uscourts.gov

Donetta W. Ambrose
Senior Judge

Date of Birth: 1945
Education: Duquesne 1967 BA, 1970 JD
Began Service: 1994
Appointed By: President William J. Clinton
Political Affiliation: Democrat

Current Memberships: American Bar Foundation; Allegheny County Bar Association; American Bar Association; The American Inns of Court; National Association of Women Judges; Pennsylvania Bar Association; Commission on Women in the Profession, Pennsylvania Bar Association; Westmoreland Bar Association; Womens Bar Association of Western Pennsylvania

Staff
Law Clerk **Heidi Grogan** .... (412) 208-7353
E-mail: heidi_grogan@pawd.uscourts.gov
Career Law Clerk **Sherry Halfhill** .... (412) 208-7354
E-mail: Sherry_Halfhill@pawd.uscourts.gov
Education: Temple 1993 JD

Chambers of Senior Judge Donetta W. Ambrose *continued*

Career Law Clerk **Anne Salzman Kurzweg** .... (412) 208-7355
Education: Pittsburgh 1998 JD
Career Law Clerk **Susan Schupansky** .... (412) 208-7351
E-mail: susan_schupansky@pawd.uscourts.gov
Education: Pennsylvania 1998 JD

Chambers of Senior Judge Terrence F. McVerry

U.S. Post Office and Courthouse, 700 Grant Street, 6th Floor, Pittsburgh, PA 15219
Tel: (412) 208-7495

Terrence F. McVerry
Senior Judge

Date of Birth: 1943
Education: Duquesne 1962 BA, 1968 JD
Began Service: September 27, 2002
Appointed By: President George W. Bush

Staff
Law Clerk **Matthew Pilsner** .... (412) 208-2485
Began Service: January 2013
Term Expires: September 2016
E-mail: matthew_pilsner@pawd.uscourts.gov
Law Clerk **Ryan Wilk** .... (412) 208-7476
E-mail: ryan_wilk@pawd.uscourts.gov
Education: Penn State 2009 BA; Duquesne 2013 JD
Career Law Clerk **Mark Hall** .... (412) 208-7475
E-mail: mark_hall@pawd.uscourts.gov
Courtroom Deputy Clerk **Keirstin Yost** .... (412) 208-7495
E-mail: keirstin_yost@pawd.uscourts.gov
Court Reporter **Richard Ford** .... (412) 261-6254

Chambers of Magistrate Judge Susan Paradise Baxter

U.S. District Court, 17 South Park Row, Room A280, Erie, PA 16501
Tel: (814) 464-9630 Fax: (814) 464-9637
E-mail: Judge_Susan_Baxter@pawd.uscourts.gov

Susan Paradise Baxter
Magistrate Judge

Date of Birth: 1956
Education: Penn State 1978 BS; Temple 1980 MEd, 1983 JD
Began Service: January 29, 1995
Term Expires: August 27, 2018

Government: Court Solicitor, County of Erie, Pennsylvania (1994)

Legal Practice: Partner, Cole, Raywid & Braverman, LLP (1983-1992)

Staff
Career Law Clerk **Frank C. Fogl III** .... (814) 464-9635
E-mail: frank_fogl@pawd.uscourts.gov
Education: Duquesne 1989 JD
Career Law Clerk **Cynthia Sander** .... (814) 464-9634
E-mail: Cynthia_Sander@pawd.uscourts.gov
Education: Akron 1993 JD
Judicial Assistant/Courtroom Deputy **Leslie R. Wallen** ... (814) 464-9630
E-mail: Leslie_Wallen@pawd.uscourts.gov
Court Reporter **Ron Bench** .... (814) 464-9613
E-mail: ron_bench@pawd.uscourts.gov

FEDERAL COURTS—UNITED STATES DISTRICT COURTS

Chambers of Magistrate Judge Lisa P. Lenihan

U.S. Post Office & Courthouse, 700 Grant Street, Pittsburgh, PA 15219
Tel: (412) 208-7370 Fax: (412) 208-7377
E-mail: judge_lisa_lenihan@pawd.uscourts.gov

The Honorable Lisa Pupo Lenihan
Magistrate Judge

Date of Birth: September 3, 1958
Education: Pittsburgh 1980 BA, 1983 JD
Began Service: April 2, 2004

Legal Practice: Associate, Dickie, McCamey & Chilcote (1983-1986); Managing Partner, Burns, White & Hickton (1997)

Staff
Career Law Clerk **Gina DeMarco** . . . . (412) 208-7370
Career Law Clerk **Jane Rodes** . . . . (412) 208-7370
E-mail: jane_rodes@pawd.uscourts.gov
Courtroom Clerk **Carol Hesz** . . . . (412) 208-7370
E-mail: carol_hesz@pawd.uscourts.gov
Deputy Clerk **Michael Banas** . . . . (412) 208-7370

Chambers of Magistrate Judge Maureen P. Kelly

700 Grant Street, Room 9280, Pittsburgh, PA 15219
Tel: (412) 208-7450 Fax: (412) 208-7457

Maureen P. Kelly
Magistrate Judge

Education: Notre Dame 1983 BA; Duquesne 1987 JD
Began Service: June 13, 2011

Staff
Law Clerk **Ann R. Dickson** . . . . (412) 208-7450
E-mail: ann_dickson@pawd.uscourts.gov
Education: Duquesne 1997 JD
Career Law Clerk **Betsy Brown** . . . . (412) 208-7450
Courtroom Deputy **Elizabeth Abbott** . . . . (412) 208-7450
E-mail: elizabeth_abbott@pawd.uscourts.gov

Chambers of Magistrate Judge Cynthia Reed Eddy

700 Grant Street, Suite 5380, Pittsburgh, PA 15219
Tel: (412) 208-7490 Fax: (412) 208-7583

Cynthia Reed Eddy
Magistrate Judge

Began Service: October 19, 2011

Staff
Career Law Clerk **Brian Pepicelli** . . . . (412) 208-7490
E-mail: brian_pepicelli@pawd.uscourts.gov
Career Law Clerk **Michael J. Lydon** . . . . (412) 208-7490
Education: Duquesne 1977 JD
Courtroom Deputy **Jack Hamilton** . . . . (412) 208-7490
E-mail: jack_hamilton@pawd.uscourts.gov

Chambers of Magistrate Judge (part-time) Keith A. Pesto

Penn Traffic Building, 319 Washington Street, Johnstown, PA 15901
Tel: (814) 536-4342 Fax: (814) 533-4519
E-mail: Judge_Keith_Pesto@pawd.uscourts.gov

Keith A. Pesto
Magistrate Judge (Part-Time)

Date of Birth: September 20, 1960
Education: Johns Hopkins 1980 BA; Pennsylvania 1983 JD
Began Service: March 1994
Term Expires: February 28, 2019
Political Affiliation: Republican

Chambers of Magistrate Judge (part-time) Keith A. Pesto *continued*

Staff
Secretary **Patricia L. Price** . . . . (814) 533-4504
E-mail: Patti_Price@pawd.uscourts.gov

Chambers of Magistrate Judge (recalled) Robert C. Mitchell

U.S. Post Office & Courthouse, 700 Grant Street, Suite 9240, Pittsburgh, PA 15219
Tel: (412) 208-7470 Fax: (412) 208-7477

Robert C. Mitchell
Magistrate Judge (recalled)

Date of Birth: 1940
Education: Dartmouth 1962 AB; Pittsburgh 1964 MBA, 1967 JD
Began Service: February 17, 1972

Current Memberships: Allegheny County Bar Association; American Bar Association; National Council of United States Magistrates

Staff
Law Clerk **Amanda Thomas** . . . . (412) 208-7470
E-mail: amanda_thomas@pawd.uscourts.gov
Career Law Clerk **Sheldon Catz** . . . . (412) 208-7470
E-mail: sheldon_catz@pawd.uscourts.gov
Education: Harvard 1990

United States Bankruptcy Court for the Western District of Pennsylvania

U.S. Steel Tower, 600 Grant Street, Suite 5414, Pittsburgh, PA 15219
Tel: (412) 644-2700 Tel: (800) 676-6856 (PACER)
Tel: (412) 355-3210 (Voice Case Information System VCIS)
Tel: (866) 299-8515 (Voice Case Information System VCIS)
Fax: (412) 644-6812
Internet: www.pawb.uscourts.gov

Number of Judgeships: 6

Number of Vacancies: 2

Court Staff
Clerk of the Court **Michael R. "Mike" Rhodes** . . . . (412) 644-4052
E-mail: michael_rhodes@pawb.uscourts.gov
Executive Assistant to the Clerk **Nicole Shatkoff** . . . . . . (412) 644-4052
E-mail: nicole_shatkoff@pawb.uscourts.gov
Chief Deputy **Joshua Lewis** . . . . (412) 355-3262
E-mail: joshua_lewis@pawb.uscourts.gov

Chambers of Chief Bankruptcy Judge Jeffery A. Deller

U.S. Steel Tower, 600 Grant Street, 54th Floor, Pittsburgh, PA 15219
Tel: (412) 644-4710 Fax: (412) 355-3153

Jeffery A. Deller
Chief Bankruptcy Judge

Education: Pittsburgh BA; Duquesne JD
Began Service: 2005

Staff
Career Law Clerk **Betsy W. Franklin** . . . . (412) 644-4710
E-mail: betsy_franklin@pawb.uscourts.gov
Education: Kenyon 1980 BA; Tulane 1985 JD
Courtroom Deputy **Elsie Martin** . . . . (412) 644-4710
E-mail: elsie_martin@pawb.uscourts.gov
Courtroom Deputy **Mary Schuetz** . . . . (412) 644-4710
E-mail: mary_schuetz@pawb.uscourts.gov
Courtroom Deputy **Jeff Furis** . . . . (412) 355-3685
E-mail: jeff_furis@pawb.uscourts.gov

Chambers of Bankruptcy Judge Thomas P. Agresti
U.S. Courthouse, 17 South Park Row, Room B250, Erie, PA 16501
Tel: (814) 464-9760 Fax: (814) 464-9767

Thomas P. Agresti
Bankruptcy Judge

Began Service: April 2004

Staff
Law Clerk **Margaret Reidy** .... (814) 464-9781
E-mail: margaret_reidy@pawb.uscourts.gov
Career Law Clerk **Ken Wargo** .... (814) 464-9761
E-mail: ken_wargo@pawb.uscourts.gov
Courtroom Deputy **Laurel McWilliams** .... (412) 644-4060 ext. 155
E-mail: laurel_mcwilliams@pawb.uscourts.gov
Courtroom Deputy [for Erie cases] **Vicki Sontheimer**.... (814) 464-9744
Chief Courtroom Deputy **Pamela Jewell** .... (814) 464-9760
E-mail: pamela_jewell@pawb.uscourts.gov
Courtroom Deputy **Julie Markham** .... (814) 464-9748
E-mail: julie_markham@pawb.uscourts.gov

Chambers of Bankruptcy Judge Carlota M. Bohm
5414 U.S. Steel Tower, 600 Grant Street, Pittsburgh, PA 15219
Tel: (412) 644-4328 Fax: (412) 644-4331

Carlota Bohm
Bankruptcy Judge

Education: Pittsburgh 1974 BS; Duquesne 1975 MS, 1979 JD
Began Service: 2011

Staff
Law Clerk **Juliann Haynes-Held**..................... (412) 918-1018
Law Clerk **Kristen Sommers**......................... (412) 644-4330
Courtroom Deputy **Kathy Theis**...................... (412) 644-4328
Judicial Assistant **Donna Sawchak**................... (412) 644-4328
Courtroom Deputy **Diane Rice**....................... (412) 644-6550

Chambers of Bankruptcy Judge Gregory L. Taddonio
5490 U.S. Steel Tower, 600 Grant Street, Pittsburgh, PA 15219
Tel: (412) 644-3541

Gregory L. Taddonio
Bankruptcy Judge

Staff
Law Clerk **Jared Roach** .... (412) 644-4063
Law Clerk **Maribeth Thomas** .... (412) 644-6431
Education: Pittsburgh 2008 JD
Courtroom Deputy **Holly Thurman** .... (412) 644-4064
Courtroom Deputy **Douglas Basinski** .... (412) 644-1661
Courtroom Deputy **Connie Takacs**..................... (412) 644-3541

United States District Court for the District of Rhode Island
Federal Building and U.S. Courthouse, One Exchange Terrace,
Providence, RI 02903-1720
Tel: (401) 752-7200 Tel: (401) 752-7262 (PACER)
Fax: (401) 752-7247
Internet: www.rid.uscourts.gov

Number of Judgeships: 3

Circuit: First

Court Staff
Clerk of Court **David A. DiMarzio** .... (401) 752-7220
E-mail: david_dimarzio@rid.uscourts.gov Fax: (401) 752-7246
Chief Deputy Clerk **Frank Perry** .... (401) 752-7220

United States District Court for the District of Rhode Island *continued*

Systems Manager **John Etchells** .... (401) 752-7220
E-mail: john_etchells@rid.uscourts.gov
ADR Administrator/Mediator-Early Neutral
Berry B. Mitchell .... (401) 752-7229
E-mail: berry_mitchell@rid.uscourts.gov
Financial Administrator **Claire J. Parvin** .... (401) 752-7220
E-mail: claire_parvin@rid.uscourts.gov
Human Resources Specialist **Jill Connolly** .... (401) 752-7220
E-mail: jill_connolly@rid.uscourts.gov
Chief Probation Officer **Barry Weiner** .... (401) 752-7300
Two Exchange Terrace, Third, Providence, RI 02903 Fax: (401) 752-7399
Law Librarian **Stephanie Mutty** .... (401) 752-7240
Administrative Officer **Jennifer Dias**.................. (401) 752-7220
E-mail: jennifer_dias@rid.uscourts.gov Fax: (401) 752-7246

Chambers of Chief Judge William E. Smith
Federal Building and U.S. Courthouse, One Exchange Terrace,
Providence, RI 02903
Tel: (401) 752-7120 Fax: (401) 752-7247

William E. Smith
Chief Judge

Date of Birth: December 31, 1959
Education: Georgetown 1982 BA, 1987 JD
Began Service: December 9, 2002
Appointed By: President George W. Bush

Staff
Court Reporter **Anne Clayton** .... (401) 752-7128
E-mail: anne_clayton@rid.uscourts.gov
Judicial Assistant **Patricia Marseglia**.................. (401) 752-7120
E-mail: Patricia_Marseglia@rid.uscourts.gov

Chambers of District Judge John J. McConnell Jr.
One Exchange Terrace, Providence, RI 02903
Tel: (401) 752-7200 Fax: (401) 752-7247

John J. McConnell, Jr.
District Judge

Education: Brown U 1980 AB; Case Western 1983 JD
Began Service: May 17, 2011
Appointed By: President Barack Obama

Legal Practice: Managing Partner, Providence, RI Office, Motley Rice LLC

Nonprofit: Treasurer, Rhode Island PAC

Staff
Law Clerk **Jenya Parkman** .... (401) 752-7200
Began Service: September 2015
Term Expires: September 2016
Law Clerk **Aileen Sprague** .... (401) 752-7200
Courtroom Reporter **Debra Lajoie** .... (401) 752-7200
Secretary **Kym Monteiro** .... (401) 752-7200

Chambers of Senior Judge Ronald R. Lagueux
225 U.S. District Court, One Exchange Terrace, Providence, RI 02903
Tel: (401) 752-7060 Fax: (401) 752-7068

Ronald R. Lagueux
Senior Judge

Education: Bowdoin 1953 AB; Harvard 1956 LLB
Began Service: September 4, 1986
Appointed By: President Ronald Reagan
Political Affiliation: Republican

Government: Executive Counsel, Governor John H. Chafee (RI), Office of the Governor, State of Rhode Island (1962-1965); Campaign Policy Advisor, John H. Chafee for Governor

(continued on next page)

Chambers of Senior Judge Ronald R. Lagueux *continued*

Judicial: Associate Justice, Rhode Island Superior Court (1968-1986)

Legal Practice: Edwards & Angell (1956-1962)

Current Memberships: Rhode Island Bar Association

Staff

Career Law Clerk **Annie Talbot** . . . . (401) 752-7063
E-mail: annie_talbot@rid.uscourts.gov

Secretary **Janice Cavaco** . . . . (401) 752-7060
E-mail: janice_cavaco@rid.uscourts.gov

Chambers of Senior Judge Mary M. Lisi

Federal Building and U.S. Courthouse, One Exchange Terrace, Providence, RI 02903
Tel: (401) 752-7200 Fax: (401) 752-7247

Mary M. Lisi
Senior Judge

Date of Birth: 1950
Education: Rhode Island 1972 BA; Temple 1977 JD
Began Service: June 13, 1994
Appointed By: President William J. Clinton

Current Memberships: American Bar Association; Rhode Island Bar Association

Staff

Court Reporter **Karen Wischnowsky** . . . . (401) 752-7045

Secretary **Susan Feeley** . . . . (401) 752-7200
E-mail: susan_feeley@rid.uscourts.gov

Chambers of Magistrate Judge Lincoln D. Almond

Two Exchange Terrace, Providence, RI 02903-1720
Tel: (401) 752-7224
E-mail: Mag_Judge_Almond@rid.uscourts.gov

Lincoln D. Almond
Magistrate Judge

Education: Rhode Island 1985 BS; Connecticut 1988 JD
Began Service: September 2004

Clerkships: Law Clerk, Chambers of Senior Judge Peter C. Dorsey, United States District Court for the District of Connecticut (1988-1990)

Legal Practice: Attorney, Edwards and Angell LLP (1990-2004)

Staff

Career Law Clerk **Juliane Realejo** . . . . (401) 752-7160
E-mail: juliane_realejo@rid.uscourts.gov

Executive Assistant **Mara Martinelli** . . . . (401) 752-7160
E-mail: mara_martinelli@rid.uscourts.gov

Chambers of Magistrate Judge Patricia A. Sullivan

One Exchange Terrace, Providence, RI 02903-1720
Tel: (401) 752-7080 Fax: (401) 752-7247

Patricia A. Sullivan
Magistrate Judge

Began Service: October 1, 2012

Staff

Law Clerk **Timothy "Tim" Baldwin** . . . . (401) 752-7080

Career Law Clerk **Carrie E. Mosca** . . . . (401) 752-7080
Education: Suffolk 2004 JD

Courtroom Deputy **Martha Saucier** . . . . (401) 752-7218
Education: Roger Williams 2000 BA

Chambers of Magistrate Judge (recalled) Robert W. Lovegreen

Two Exchange Terrace, Providence, RI 02903-1720
Tel: (401) 752-7110 Fax: (401) 752-7246
E-mail: Mag_Judge_Lovegreen@rid.uscourts.gov

Robert W. Lovegreen
Magistrate Judge (recalled)

Education: Brown U 1960 AB; Virginia 1963 JD
Began Service: March 1993

United States Bankruptcy Court for the District of Rhode Island

The Federal Center, 380 Westminster Street, Providence, RI 02903
Tel: (401) 626-3100
Tel: (866) 222-8029 (Voice Case Information System VCIS)
Fax: (401) 626-3150
Internet: www.rib.uscourts.gov

Number of Judgeships: 1

Court Staff

Fax: (401) 626-3150
E-mail: rib_helpdesk@rib.uscourts.gov

Clerk of the Court **Susan M. Thurston** . . . . (401) 626-3130
E-mail: susan_thurston@rib.uscourts.gov
Education: Suffolk 1987 JD

Chief Deputy Clerk **(Vacant)** . . . . (401) 626-3141

Financial Administrator **April Elderkin** . . . . (401) 626-3142
E-mail: april_elderkin@rib.uscourts.gov

Administrative Specialist **Kristen E. Batty** . . . . (401) 626-3133
E-mail: kristen_batty@rib.uscourts.gov

Systems Manager **Craig Balme** . . . . (401) 626-3140
E-mail: craig_balme@rib.uscourts.gov

Public Information Specialist **Janet Descoteaux** . . . . (401) 626-3111
E-mail: janet_descoteaux@rib.uscourts.gov

Quality Assurance Specialist **Jody Venuti** . . . . (401) 626-3145
E-mail: jody_venuti@rib.uscourts.gov

Automation Support Specialist **Stephen Stricklett** . . . . (401) 626-3126
E-mail: steve_stricklett@rib.uscourts.gov

Courtroom Deputy **Holly D'Agostino** . . . . (401) 626-3135

Case Manager **Jennifer L. Davis** . . . . (401) 626-3110

Case Manager **Dina Fortes** . . . . (401) 626-3122

Case Manager **Christine Lanni** . . . . (401) 626-3112

Case Manager **Pamela Ricciarelli** . . . . (401) 626-3136

Case Manager **Carolyn Sweeney** . . . . (401) 626-3134

Operations Supervisor **Amy Geraghty** . . . . (401) 626-3127
E-mail: amy_geraghty@rib.uscourts.gov

Chambers of Bankruptcy Judge Diane Finkle

The Federal Center, 380 Westminster Street, Room 619, Providence, RI 02903
Tel: (401) 626-3060 Fax: (401) 626-3080

Diane Finkle
Bankruptcy Judge

Staff

Law Clerk **Louisa Gibbs** . . . . (401) 626-3063
Term Expires: August 2016

Career Law Clerk **Jonathan Pincince** . . . . (401) 626-3063
E-mail: jonathan_pincince@rib.uscourts.gov

United States District Court for the District of South Carolina

901 Richland Street, Columbia, SC 29201-2431
Tel: (803) 765-5816 Tel: (803) 765-5871 (PACER)
Fax: (803) 765-5960
Internet: www.scd.uscourts.gov

Number of Judgeships: 10

Number of Vacancies: 2

Circuit: Fourth

Court Staff

Clerk of Court **Robin Blume** . . . . (803) 765-5816
E-mail: robin_blume@scd.uscourts.gov Fax: (803) 765-5960
Deputy Clerk-in-Charge - Charleston
Robbie Shumate . . . . (843) 579-1401
P.O. Box 835, Charleston, SC 29402 Fax: (843) 579-1402
Deputy Clerk-in-Charge - Florence **Susan Roberts** . . . . . . (843) 676-3820
P.O. Box 2317, Florence, SC 29503 Fax: (843) 676-3831
E-mail: susan_roberts@scd.uscourts.gov
Deputy Clerk-in-Charge - Greenville **Kieron Campbell** . . . (864) 241-2700
P.O. Box 10768, Greenville, SC 29603 Fax: (864) 241-2711
E-mail: kieron_campbell@scd.uscourts.gov
Chief Probation and Pretrial Officer **Dickie Brunson** . . . . . (803) 253-3310
1835 Assembly Street, Suite 611, Columbia, SC 29201 Fax: (803) 765-5110
Systems Manager **Judy Matras** . . . . (803) 765-5860
E-mail: judy_matras@scd.uscourts.gov Fax: (803) 765-5108
Financial Administrator **Tyrone Brown** . . . . (803) 253-3473
E-mail: tyrone_brown@scd.uscourts.gov Fax: (803) 765-5283
Personnel Specialist **Sallie Dixon** . . . . (803) 253-3300
E-mail: sallie_dixon@scd.uscourts.gov Fax: (803) 765-5469

Chambers of Chief Judge Terry L. Wooten

901 Richland Street, Columbia, SC 29201-2431
Tel: (803) 253-6420
E-mail: terry_wooten@scd.uscourts.gov

Terry L. Wooten
Chief Judge

Date of Birth: 1954
Education: South Carolina 1976 BA, 1980 JD
Began Service: December 3, 2001
Appointed By: President George W. Bush

Staff

Law Clerk **(Vacant)** . . . . (843) 676-3812
Law Clerk **Mathew Cavender** . . . . (843) 676-3812

Chambers of District Judge David C. Norton

J. Waties Waring Judicial Center, Broad and Meeting Streets, 3rd Floor, Charleston, SC 29401
P.O. Box 835, Charleston, SC 29402
Tel: (843) 579-1450 Fax: (843) 579-1459
E-mail: david_norton@scd.uscourts.gov

David C. Norton
District Judge

Date of Birth: 1946
Education: Sewanee 1968 BA; South Carolina 1975 JD
Began Service: July 13, 1990
Appointed By: President George H.W. Bush

Current Memberships: Federal Judges Association; South Carolina Bar

Chambers of District Judge David C. Norton *continued*

Staff

Law Clerk **Robert "Rob" Wehrman** . . . . (843) 579-1453
Began Service: September 2015
Term Expires: September 2016
E-mail: robert_wehrman@scd.uscourts.gov
Law Clerk **Emily Limehouse** . . . . (843) 579-1454
Began Service: September 2014
Term Expires: September 2016
E-mail: emily_limehouse@scd.uscourts.gov
Secretary **Lisa Richberg** . . . . (843) 579-1452
E-mail: lisa_richberg@scd.uscourts.gov

Chambers of District Judge Robert Bryan Harwell

McMillan Federal Building, 401 West Evans Street, Florence, SC 29501
Tel: (843) 676-3800 Fax: (843) 676-3830
E-mail: harwell_ecf@scd.uscourts.gov
E-mail: harwell_ecf@scd.uscourts.gov

Robert Bryan Harwell
District Judge

Date of Birth: June 4, 1959
Education: Clemson 1980 BA; South Carolina 1982 JD
Began Service: July 13, 2004
Appointed By: President George W. Bush

Academic: Business Law Instructor, Francis Marion University

Clerkships: Law Clerk The Honorable Rodney Peeples, South Carolina Circuit Court (1983); Law Clerk The Honorable Ross Anderson, United States District Court for the District of South Carolina (1983-1984)

Government: Commissioner, Board of Grievances and Discipline (1984-1987); Member, Joint Commission on Alternative Dispute Resolution, State of South Carolina

Legal Practice: Partner, Harwell, Ballenger, Barth & Hoefer (1984-2004)

Military Service: South Carolina Army National Guard, South Carolina Army National Guard (1987-1993)

Current Memberships: American Bar Association; Florence County Bar Association; South Carolina Bar

Staff

Law Clerk **Edmund Neyle** . . . . (843) 676-3800
Began Service: November 2014
Term Expires: November 4, 2015
E-mail: edmund_neyle@scd.uscourts.gov
Law Clerk **Mary Wells** . . . . (843) 676-3802
E-mail: mary_wells@scd.uscourts.gov
Education: South Carolina 1983 JD
Career Law Clerk **J. Thomas McBratney III** . . . . (843) 676-3800
E-mail: thomas_mcbratney@scd.uscourts.gov
Education: Col Charleston 1999 BAM; Cumberland 2004 JD

Chambers of District Judge J. Michelle Childs

901 Richland Street, Columbia, SC 29201
Tel: (803) 253-3850 Fax: (803) 765-5878
E-mail: michelle_childs@scd.uscourts.gov

J. Michelle Childs
District Judge

Date of Birth: 1966
Education: South Florida 1988 BS; South Carolina 1991 MA, 1991 JD
Began Service: August 23, 2010
Appointed By: President Barack Obama

Government: Deputy Director, Department of Labor, Licensing and Regulation (2000-2002); Commissioner, South Carolina Workers' Compensation Commission (2002-2006)

Legal Practice: Lawyer, Nexsen, Pruet, Jacobs and Pollard (1992-2000); Partner, Nexsen, Pruet, Jacobs and Pollard

(continued on next page)

Chambers of District Judge J. Michelle Childs *continued*

Staff

Law Clerk **John Belinga** . . . . (803) 253-3850
Term Expires: September 2016

Law Clerk **Vincent Douglas** . . . . (864) 253-3850
Began Service: August 13, 2013
E-mail: vincent_douglas@scd.uscourts.gov
Education: South Carolina 1999 JD

Law Clerk **Brince Pernell** . . . . (864) 241-2190
Fax: (864) 241-2194

Courtroom Deputy **Jackie Aiken** . . . . (864) 241-2751
E-mail: jackie_aiken@scd.uscourts.gov

Judicial Assistant **Patricia W. Jenkins** . . . . (803) 253-3850
E-mail: patricia_jenkins@scd.uscourts.gov

Chambers of District Judge Richard M. Gergel

P.O. Box 835, Charleston, SC 29402
Tel: (843) 579-2610
E-mail: richard_gergel@scd.uscourts.gov

Richard Mark Gergel
District Judge

Date of Birth: 1954
Education: Duke 1975 BA, 1979 JD
Began Service: August 5, 2010
Appointed By: President Barack Obama

Staff

Law Clerk **Adair Boroughs** . . . . (843) 579-2610
E-mail: adair_boroughs@scd.uscourts.gov

Law Clerk **Sally Newman** . . . . (843) 579-2610
E-mail: sally_newman@scd.uscourts.gov

Case Manager **Sandra Shealy** . . . . (843) 579-1406

Courtroom Deputy **Eunice Ravenel-Bright** . . . . (843) 579-1404
E-mail: eunice_ravenel@scd.uscourts.gov

Judicial Assistant **Lena Tapscott** . . . . (843) 579-2610
E-mail: lena_tapscott@scd.uscourts.gov

Chambers of District Judge Timothy M. Cain

315 South McDuffie Street, First Floor, Anderson, SC 29624
Tel: (864) 261-2030 Fax: (864) 261-2033
E-mail: timothy_cain@scd.uscourts.gov

Timothy M. Cain
District Judge

Education: South Carolina 1983 BS, 1986 JD
Began Service: September 26, 2011
Appointed By: President Barack Obama

Judicial: Judge, Chambers of Judge Timothy M. Cain, Tenth Judicial Circuit, South Carolina Circuit Courts (2000-2011)

Profession: Private Practice (1990-2000)

Staff

Law Clerk **Jeff K. Gurney** . . . . (864) 261-2030
E-mail: jeffery_gurney@scd.uscourts.gov

Judicial Assistant **Jane M. White** . . . . (864) 261-2030
E-mail: jane_white@scd.uscourts.gov

Chambers of District Judge Mary Geiger Lewis

901 Richland Street, Columbia, SC 29201-2431
Tel: (864) 591-5340
E-mail: lewis_ecf@scd.uscourts.gov

Mary Geiger Lewis
District Judge

Date of Birth: December 18, 1958
Education: Clemson 1980 BA; South Carolina 1984 JD
Began Service: 2012
Appointed By: President Barack Obama

Staff

Law Clerk **Allison Ford** . . . . (864) 591-5340
E-mail: allison_ford@scd.uscourts.gov

Career Law Clerk **Jeff St. John** . . . . (864) 591-5340
Education: Harvard 2010 JD

Courtroom Deputy **Mary Floyd** . . . . (864) 591-5340
E-mail: mary_floyd@scd.uscourts.gov

Chambers of District Judge Bruce Howe Hendricks

300 East Washington Street, Greenville, SC 29601
Tel: (864) 239-5710
E-mail: bruce_hendricks@scd.uscourts.gov

Bruce H. Hendricks
District Judge

Date of Birth: October 3, 1957
Education: Col Charleston 1983 BA; South Carolina 1990 JD
Began Service: 2014
Appointed By: President Barack Obama

Clerkships: Magistrate Judge, Chambers of Magistrate Judge Bruce H. Hendricks, United States District Court for the District of South Carolina (2002-2014)

Government: Assistant U.S. Attorney, District of South Carolina, United States Attorney's Office, United States Department of Justice (1991-2002)

Staff

Law Clerk **Chris B. Schoen** . . . . (864) 239-5710
E-mail: chris_schoen@scd.uscourts.gov
Education: Virginia 2010 JD

Career Law Clerk **Joe Brewer** . . . . (864) 239-5710
E-mail: joe_brewer@scd.uscourts.gov
Education: South Carolina JD

Judicial Assistant **Vickie Hearn** . . . . (864) 239-5710
E-mail: vickie_hearn@scd.uscourts.gov

Chambers of Senior Judge Henry M. Herlong, Jr.

300 East Washington Street, Room 324, Greenville, SC 29601
Tel: (864) 241-2720 Fax: (864) 241-2728
E-mail: henry_herlong@scd.uscourts.gov

Henry M. Herlong, Jr.
Senior Judge

Date of Birth: 1944
Education: Clemson 1967 BA; South Carolina 1970 JD
Began Service: May 14, 1991
Appointed By: President George H.W. Bush

Government: Legislative Assistant (R-SC), Office of Senator Strom Thurmond, United States Senate (1970-1972); Assistant United States Attorney, South Carolina District, Executive Office for United States Attorneys, United States Department of Justice (1972-1976); Deputy Civil Division Chief and Assistant U.S. Attorney, South Carolina District, Executive Office for United States Attorneys, United States Department of Justice (1983-1986)

Judicial: Magistrate Judge, United States District Court for the District of South Carolina (1986-1991)

Legal Practice: Partner, Coleman & Herlong (1976-1983)

Chambers of Senior Judge Henry M. Herlong, Jr. *continued*

Military Service: United States Army Reserve, United States Department of the Army (1967-1973)

Current Memberships: American Bar Association; Edgefield County Bar Association; South Carolina Bar

Staff

Law Clerk **Rhett Ricard** . . . . . (864) 241-2720
Began Service: August 2015
Term Expires: August 2016
E-mail: rhett_ricard@scd.uscourts.gov

Career Law Clerk **Christine M. Schanen** . . . . . (864) 241-2720
E-mail: christine_schanen@scd.uscourts.gov
Education: Marquette 2001 JD

Court Reporter **Karen Martin** . . . . . (864) 233-2624

Judicial Assistant **Brenda S. Edwards** . . . . . (864) 241-2720
E-mail: brenda_edwards@scd.uscourts.gov

Chambers of Senior Judge Patrick Michael Duffy

J. Waties Waring Judicial Center, 85 Broad Street, Charleston, SC 29401
P.O. Box 835, Charleston, SC 29402
Tel: (843) 579-1460 Fax: (843) 579-1469

Patrick Michael Duffy
Senior Judge

Date of Birth: 1943
Education: Citadel 1965 BA; South Carolina 1968 JD
Began Service: December 1995
Appointed By: President William J. Clinton

Government: Assistant County Attorney (part-time), County of Charleston, South Carolina (1973-1975)

Legal Practice: Staff Attorney, Neighborhood Legal Assistance Office (1968-1969); Private Practice (1971-1972); Associate then Partner, Hollings and Hawkins (Hawkins and Morris) (1972-1981); Partner, Morris, Duffy and Boone (1981-1987); Shareholder, McNair Law Firm, P.A. (1987-1995)

Military Service: United States Army (1969-1971)

Current Memberships: American Bar Association; Charleston County Bar Association; South Carolina Bar

Staff

Law Clerk **Andrew R. deHoll** . . . . . (843) 579-1463
Began Service: September 4, 2015
Term Expires: September 3, 2016
Education: South Carolina 2010 JD

Law Clerk **Whit McGreevy** . . . . . (843) 579-1464
Began Service: September 6, 2015
Term Expires: September 5, 2017
E-mail: thomas_limehouse@scd.uscourts.gov

Judicial Assistant **Cindi Hubbard** . . . . . (843) 579-1461
E-mail: cindi_hubbard@scd.uscourts.gov
Education: Col Charleston 1994 BA

Chambers of Senior Judge Sol Blatt, Jr.

J. Waties Waring Judicial Center, Broad & Meeting Sts., Charleston, SC 29401
P.O. Box 835, Charleston, SC 29402-0447
Tel: (843) 579-1470 Fax: (843) 579-1479
E-mail: Sol_Blatt@scd.uscourts.gov

Sol Blatt, Jr.
Senior Judge

Date of Birth: 1921
Education: South Carolina 1941 AB, 1946 LLB
Began Service: July 1971
Appointed By: President Richard M. Nixon

Legal Practice: Partner, Blatt & Fales (1946-1971)

Chambers of Senior Judge Sol Blatt, Jr. *continued*

Military Service: United States Navy (1942-1946)

Staff

Career Law Clerk **Nan S. Williams** . . . . . (843) 579-1470
Began Service: 2006
E-mail: nan_williams@scd.uscourts.gov

Judicial Assistant **Janice Pearce** . . . . . (843) 579-1470
E-mail: Janice_Pearce@scd.uscourts.gov
Education: Columbia 1968 BA

Chambers of Senior Judge C. Weston Houck

P.O. Box 150, Charleston, SC 29402
Tel: (843) 579-1480 Fax: (843) 579-1489

C. Weston Houck
Senior Judge

Date of Birth: 1933
Education: South Carolina 1956 LLB
Began Service: 1979
Appointed By: President Jimmy Carter

Government: Member, South Carolina House of Representatives (1963-1966); Chairman, Florence City-County Building Commission, City and County of Florence, South Carolina (1968-1976)

Legal Practice: Partner, Willcox, Hardee, Houck, Palmer & O'Farrell (1956-1970); Partner, Houck, Clarke & Johnson (1971-1979)

Military Service: United States Army (1957-1958)

Current Memberships: American Bar Association; Florence County Bar Association; South Carolina Bar

Staff

Law Clerk **Michelle McMahon** . . . . . (843) 579-1480
Began Service: August 2012
Term Expires: September 1, 2016
E-mail: michelle_mcmahon@scd.uscourts.gov

Career Law Clerk **Patty Quentel** . . . . . (843) 579-1480
E-mail: patty_quentel@scd.uscourts.gov
Education: Wisconsin 1988 JD

Secretary **(Vacant)** . . . . . (843) 579-1480

Chambers of Senior Judge G. Ross Anderson, Jr.

G. Ross Anderson, Jr. Federal Building & U.S. Courthouse, 315 South McDuffie Street, Anderson, SC 29624
P.O. Box 2147, Anderson, SC 29622-2147
Tel: (864) 226-9799 Fax: (864) 226-0112

G. Ross Anderson, Jr.
Senior Judge

Date of Birth: 1929
Education: Southeastern U 1949 BS; South Carolina 1954 LLB
Began Service: May 23, 1980
Appointed By: President Jimmy Carter
Political Affiliation: Democrat

Government: Legislative Secretary, State Senator Olin D. Johnston (SC), South Carolina Senate (1953-1954); State Representative (SC), South Carolina House of Representatives (1955-1956)

Legal Practice: Private Practice (1954-1980); Partner, Anderson & Chapman (1960-1965); Partner, Anderson & Doyle (1962-1965); Partner, Anderson, Epps & Krause (1971-1980)

Military Service: United States Air Force (1951-1952)

Current Memberships: American Association for Justice; American Bar Association; Fourth Circuit Judicial Conference; Georgia Trial Lawyers Association; International Academy of Trial Lawyers; South Carolina Bar; South Carolina Trial Lawyers Association

(continued on next page)

FEDERAL COURTS—UNITED STATES DISTRICT COURTS

Chambers of Senior Judge G. Ross Anderson, Jr. *continued*

Staff

Law Clerk **Emily Hanis** .... (864) 226-9799
Began Service: May 2015
Term Expires: August 2016
E-mail: emily_hanis@scd.uscourts.gov

Law Clerk **Charles Scarminach** .... (864) 226-9799
Began Service: August 2014
E-mail: charles_scarminach@scd.uscourts.gov

Career Law Clerk **Rita Secreast-Doll** .... (864) 226-9799
E-mail: rita_secreast-doll@scd.uscourts.gov
Education: South Carolina 1986 JD

Chambers of Senior Judge Margaret B. Seymour

Matthew J. Perry, Jr. Courthouse, 901 Richland Street,
Columbia, SC 29201
Tel: (803) 765-5590 Tel: (803) 253-3397
E-mail: margaret_seymour@scd.uscourts.gov

Margaret B. Seymour
Senior Judge

Date of Birth: 1947
Education: Howard U 1969 BA; Washington College of Law 1977 JD
Began Service: October 30, 1998
Appointed By: President William J. Clinton

Staff

Law Clerk **Raymond Jackson** .... (803) 765-5590
Began Service: August 29, 2015
Term Expires: August 2016
E-mail: raymond_jackson@scd.uscourts.gov

Law Clerk **Alyssa Richardson** .... (803) 765-5590
Began Service: August 22, 2015
Term Expires: August 2016
E-mail: alyssa_richardson@scd.uscourts.gov

Career Law Clerk **Deborah P. Morgan** .... (803) 765-5590
E-mail: deborah_morgan@scd.uscourts.gov
Education: South Carolina 1974 BA, 1991 JD

Chambers of Senior Judge Cameron McGowan Currie

901 Richland Street, Columbia, SC 29201
Tel: (803) 253-3680 Fax: (803) 253-3683

Cameron McGowan Currie
Senior Judge

Date of Birth: 1948
Education: South Carolina 1970 BA;
George Washington 1975 JD
Began Service: 1994
Appointed By: President William J. Clinton

Current Memberships: The American Inns of Court; Federal Judges Association; South Carolina Bar; South Carolina Women Lawyers Association

Staff

Law Clerk **(Vacant)** .... (803) 253-3680

Career Law Clerk **Emily Deck Harrill** .... (803) 253-3680
E-mail: emily_harrill@scd.uscourts.gov
Education: William & Mary 1988 BA;
South Carolina 2005 JD

Career Law Clerk **Virginia Vroegop** .... (803) 253-3680
E-mail: virginia_vroegop@scd.uscourts.gov
Education: Virginia Tech 1977 BS;
South Carolina 1988 JD

Chambers of Senior Judge Joseph F. Anderson, Jr.

901 Richland Street, Columbia, SC 29201
Tel: (803) 765-5136
E-mail: joe_anderson@scd.uscourts.gov

Joseph F. Anderson, Jr.
Senior Judge

Date of Birth: 1949
Education: Clemson 1972 BA; South Carolina JD
Began Service: 1986
Appointed By: President Ronald Reagan

Current Memberships: American Bar Association; South Carolina Bar; South Carolina Trial Lawyers Association

Staff

Law Clerk **Bettis C. Rainsford, Jr.** .... (803) 765-5136
Began Service: August 2015
Term Expires: August 2016
E-mail: bettis_rainsford@scd.uscourts.gov

Law Clerk **Konstantine Diamaduros** .... (803) 765-5136
Began Service: August 2015
Term Expires: August 2016
E-mail: brittany_mcintosh@scd.uscourts.gov

Paralegal/Judicial Assistant **Gail Hayden** .... (803) 765-5136
E-mail: gail_hayden@scd.uscourts.gov

Chambers of Magistrate Judge Bristow Marchant

P.O. Box 835, Charleston, SC 29402
Tel: (843) 579-2626 Fax: (843) 579-2635
E-mail: bristow_marchant@scd.uscourts.gov

Bristow Marchant
Magistrate Judge

Date of Birth: 1955
Education: Charleston 1977 BA;
South Carolina 1980 JD
Began Service: September 1, 1992
Term Expires: August 31, 2016

Government: Staff Counsel, Committee on the Judiciary, United States Senate (1980-1982); Attorney, Civil Division, Office of Attorney General, State of South Carolina (1982-1983); Assistant Chief Counsel, Department of Highways and Public Transportation, State of South Carolina (1983)

Legal Practice: Partner, Adams, Quackenbush, Herring & Stuart, PA (1983-1992)

Current Memberships: Richland County Bar Association; South Carolina Bar

Staff

Career Law Clerk **Melissa Jones Alexander** .... (843) 579-2626
E-mail: lisa_alexander@scd.uscourts.gov
Education: South Carolina 1982 BA, 1992 JD

Secretary **Elizabeth Lacey** .... (843) 579-2626
E-mail: elizabeth_lacey@scd.uscourts.gov

Chambers of Magistrate Judge Thomas E. Rogers III
401 West Evans Street, Florence, SC 29501
Tel: (843) 676-3805 Fax: (853) 676-3833
E-mail: thomas_rogers@scd.uscourts.gov

Thomas E. Rogers III
Magistrate Judge

Date of Birth: February 8, 1965
Education: Citadel 1987 BS; South Carolina 1992 JD
Began Service: May 8, 2002
Term Expires: May 9, 2018

Clerkships: Law Clerk, Resident Judge John H. Waller, Jr., South Carolina Circuit Court, 12th Judicial District (1992-1993); Law Clerk, District Judge C. Weston Houck, United States District Court for the District of South Carolina (1993-1995)

Legal Practice: Private Practice (1995-2002)

Staff
Career Law Clerk **Susanne K. Hodge** . . . . (843) 676-3805
Began Service: 2006
E-mail: susanne_hodge@scd.uscourts.gov
Career Law Clerk **Lisa A. Lawson** . . . . (843) 676-3807
E-mail: lisa_lawson@scd.uscourts.gov
Education: Francis Marion 1987 BS;
South Carolina 1990 JD

Chambers of Magistrate Judge Paige Jones Gossett
901 Richland Street, Columbia, SC 29201-2431
Tel: (803) 765-5498
E-mail: gossett_ecf@scd.uscourts.gov

Paige Jones Gossett
Magistrate Judge

Began Service: January 30, 2009

Chambers of Magistrate Judge Kevin F. McDonald
300 East Washington Street, Suite 300, Greenville, SC 29601
Tel: (864) 241-2740
E-mail: kevin_mcdonald@scd.uscourts.gov

Kevin F. McDonald
Magistrate Judge

Education: South Carolina 1986, 1990 JD
Began Service: 2010

Chambers of Magistrate Judge Shiva V. Hodges
901 Richland Street, Columbia, SC 29201-2431
Tel: (803) 253-6431
E-mail: hodges_ecf@scd.uscourts.gov

Shiva V. Hodges
Magistrate Judge

Began Service: 2010

Staff
Career Law Clerk **Van Horger** . . . . (803) 253-6431
E-mail: van_horger@scd.uscourts.gov
Law Clerk **Ashley Thompson** . . . . (803) 253-6431
Term Expires: July 2018
E-mail: ashley_thompson@scd.uscourts.gov

Chambers of Magistrate Judge Jacquelyn D. Austin
300 East Washington Street, Greenville, SC 29601
Tel: (864) 241-2700
E-mail: jacquelyn_austin@scd.uscourts.gov

Jacquelyn D. Austin
Magistrate Judge

Began Service: 2012

Staff
Law Clerk **Heath Beard** . . . . (864) 241-2700
E-mail: heath_beard@scd.uscourts.gov
Career Law Clerk **Catie Wilcox** . . . . (864) 241-2700

Chambers of Magistrate Judge Kaymani D. West
401 West Evans Street, Florence, SC 29501
Tel: (843) 292-5630

Kaymani West
Magistrate Judge

Education: South Carolina 2000 JD
Began Service: January 1, 2012

Staff
Law Clerk **Jenny Smith** . . . . (843) 292-5630
Career Law Clerk **Kay Tennyson** . . . . (843) 292-5630
E-mail: kay_tennyson@scd.uscourts.gov

Chambers of Magistrate Judge Mary Gordon Baker
P.O. Box 835, Charleston, SC 29402
Tel: (843) 579-1440

Mary Gordon Baker
Magistrate Judge

Chambers of Magistrate Judge (part-time) Robert L. Buchanan, Jr.
P.O. Box 463, Aiken, SC 29802-0463
Tel: (803) 649-2586 ext. 203 Fax: (803) 649-1392
E-mail: rlbuchananjr@atlanticbbn.net

Robert L. Buchanan, Jr.
Magistrate Judge (Part-Time)

Date of Birth: 1951
Education: Erskine 1973 AB; South Carolina 1976 JD
Began Service: April 1, 1979
Political Affiliation: Independent

Current Memberships: Aiken County Bar Association; American Association for Justice; American Bar Association; South Carolina Bar; South Carolina Trial Lawyers Association

Staff
Paralegal **Pamela Holmes** . . . . (803) 649-2586 ext. 207

United States Bankruptcy Court for the District of South Carolina
J. Bratton Davis U.S. Bankruptcy Courthouse, 1100 Laurel Street, Columbia, SC 29201-2423
Tel: (803) 765-5436 Tel: (866) 222-8029
Internet: http://ecf.scb.uscourts.gov (Electronic Case Files)

Number of Judgeships: 3

Court Staff
Clerk of Court **Laura A. Austin** . . . . (803) 765-5209
E-mail: laura_austin@scb.uscourts.gov

(continued on next page)

United States Bankruptcy Court for the District of South Carolina
continued

Chief Deputy Clerk **Jeff Davis** . . . . . . (803) 765-5005
E-mail: jeff_davis@scb.uscourts.gov
Systems Manager **Mark Tyan** . . . . . . (803) 765-5042

Chambers of Chief Bankruptcy Judge David R. Duncan

1100 Laurel Street, Columbia, SC 29201-2423
Tel: (803) 765-5657 Fax: (803) 253-3996
E-mail: david_duncan@scb.uscourts.gov

David R. Duncan
Chief Bankruptcy Judge

Began Service: May 2006
Term Expires: May 2020

Staff

Law Clerk **Katherine Rea** . . . . . . (803) 765-5657
Term Expires: September 2016
E-mail: katherine_rea@scb.uscourts.gov
Judicial Assistant **Jacqueline Phillips** . . . . . . (803) 765-5657

Chambers of Bankruptcy Judge John E. Waites

J. Bratton Davis U.S. Bankruptcy Courthouse, 1100 Laurel Street, Columbia, SC 29201-2423
Tel: (803) 253-3751 Fax: (803) 253-3464
E-mail: john_waites@scb.uscourts.gov

John E. Waites
Bankruptcy Judge

Began Service: June 1994
Term Expires: June 2022

Staff

Law Clerk **Andrew Powell** . . . . . . (803) 253-3751
Began Service: September 2015
Term Expires: September 2016
Career Law Clerk **Sarah Kistler** . . . . . . (803) 253-3751
E-mail: sarah_kistler@scb.uscourts.gov

Chambers of Bankruptcy Judge Helen Elizabeth Burris

201 Magnolia Street, Spartanburg, SC 29306
Tel: (864) 591-5315 Fax: (864) 591-5317

Helen Elizabeth Burris
Bankruptcy Judge

Began Service: March 2006
Term Expires: March 2020

Staff

Law Clerk **Katherine "Kate" Hendricks** . . . . . . (864) 591-5315
Education: Charleston Law 2013 JD
Career Law Clerk **Lauren T. Maxwell** . . . . . . (864) 591-5315
Education: North Carolina 2010 JD

United States District Court for the District of South Dakota

128 U.S. Courthouse, 400 South Phillips Avenue, Sioux Falls, SD 57104
Tel: (605) 330-6600 Fax: (605) 330-6601
Internet: www.sdd.uscourts.gov

Number of Judgeships: 4

Circuit: Eighth

Court Staff

Clerk of Court **Joseph A. Haas** . . . . . . (605) 330-6606
E-mail: Joe_Haas@sdd.uscourts.gov
Education: U Washington BA, MA; Seattle 1983 JD
Chief Deputy Clerk **Matt Thelen** . . . . . . (605) 330-6600
E-mail: matt_thelen@sdd.uscourts.gov Fax: (605) 399-6601
Deputy Clerk-in-Charge - Pierre **Kathy Hammond** . . . . . . (605) 224-4606
405 Federal Bldg., 225 S. Pierre St., Pierre, SD 57501 Fax: (605) 224-4601
E-mail: kathy_hammond@sdd.uscourts.gov
Deputy Clerk-in-Charge - Rapid City **Tammy Ludeman** . . . . . . (605) 399-6005
P.O. Box 6080, Rapid City, SD 57709-6080
E-mail: tammy_ludeman@sdd.uscourts.gov
Chief Probation and Pretrial Services Officer **John Bentley** . . . . . . (605) 977-8960
314 South Main Avenue, Suite 100, Sioux Falls, SD 57104
Systems Manager **Trae Umstead** . . . . . . (605) 330-6611
E-mail: trae_umstead@sdd.uscourts.gov
Administrative Officer **Kimberly C. Gullickson** . . . . . . (605) 977-8957
Court Reporter **Cheryl Hook** . . . . . . (605) 945-4626
E-mail: cheryl_hook@sdd.uscourts.gov
Court Reporter **Judy Thompson** . . . . . . (605) 348-8610
E-mail: judy_thompson@sdd.uscourts.gov
Court Reporter **Jill Connelly** . . . . . . (605) 330-6669
E-mail: jill_connelly@sdd.uscourts.gov

Chambers of Chief Judge Jeffrey L. Viken

United States Courthouse, 515 Ninth Street, Room 318, Rapid City, SD 57701
Tel: (605) 399-6050 Fax: (605) 330-6051
E-mail: jeffrey_viken@sdd.uscourts.gov

Jeffrey L. Viken
Chief Judge

Education: South Dakota 1974 BA, 1977 JD
Began Service: October 2009
Appointed By: President Barack Obama

Staff

Law Clerk **Alec Bonander** . . . . . . (605) 399-6050
Term Expires: October 2016
E-mail: alec_bonander@sdd.uscourts.gov
Career Law Clerk **Kenneth Dewell** . . . . . . (605) 399-6050
Judicial Assistant **Sheila Belden** . . . . . . (605) 399-6050
E-mail: sheila_belden@sdd.uscourts.gov

Chambers of District Judge Karen E. Schreier

400 South Phillips Avenue, Sioux Falls, SD 57104
Tel: (605) 330-6670
E-mail: karen_schreier@sdd.uscourts.gov

Karen E. Schreier
District Judge

Date of Birth: 1956
Education: Saint Louis U 1978 BA, 1981 JD
Began Service: August 13, 1999
Appointed By: President William J. Clinton
Political Affiliation: Democrat

Current Memberships: American Bar Association; Pennington County Bar Association; State Bar of South Dakota

Staff
Law Clerk **Andrew Fick** .... (605) 330-6670
Began Service: August 2015
Term Expires: August 2017
E-mail: andrew_fick@sdd.uscourts.gov
Law Clerk **James Shanor** .... (605) 330-6670
Began Service: August 2015
Term Expires: August 2016
E-mail: james_shanor@sdd.uscourts.gov
Law Clerk **Mike Snyder** .... (605) 330-6670
Term Expires: August 2016
E-mail: mike_snyder@sdd.uscourts.gov
Court Reporter **Jill Connelly** .... (605) 330-6670
E-mail: jill_connelly@sdd.uscourts.gov

Chambers of District Judge Roberto A. Lange

225 South Pierre Street, Pierre, SD 57501
Tel: (605) 945-4610 Fax: (605) 945-4611
E-mail: roberto_lange@sdd.uscourts.gov

Roberto A. Lange
District Judge

Education: South Dakota 1985 BA; Northwestern 1988 JD
Began Service: November 6, 2009
Appointed By: President Barack Obama

Clerkships: Law Clerk, Chambers of District Judge Donald James Porter, United States District Courts

Legal Practice: Associate, Davenport Evans Hurwitz & Smith LLP (1989-1992)

Staff
Career Law Clerk **Thad Roche** .... (605) 945-4610
Law Clerk **Elizabeth Chrisp** .... (605) 945-4610
Judicial Assistant **Leslie Hicks** .... (605) 945-4610
E-mail: leslie_hicks@sdd.uscourts.gov

Chambers of Senior Judge Charles B. Kornmann

102 Fourth Avenue SE, Suite 408, Aberdeen, SD 57401-4309
Tel: (605) 377-2600 Fax: (605) 377-2601
E-mail: charles_kornmann@sdd.uscourts.gov

Charles B. Kornmann
Senior Judge

Date of Birth: 1937
Education: Col St Thomas 1959; Georgetown 1962 LLB
Began Service: May 1995
Appointed By: President William J. Clinton
Political Affiliation: Democrat

Current Memberships: American Board of Trial Advocates; Brown County Bar Association (SD); State Bar of South Dakota; South Dakota Bar Foundation, State Bar of South Dakota

Staff
Law Clerk **Spencer Werth** .... (605) 377-2600
E-mail: spencer_werth@sdd.uscourts.gov
Career Law Clerk **Susan Margolies** .... (605) 377-2600
E-mail: susan_margolies@sdd.uscourts.gov
Education: Central Col (IA) 1986 BA; Drake 1988 JD
Court Reporter **Cheryl Hook** .... (605) 945-4626
E-mail: cheryl_hook@sdd.uscourts.gov
Judicial Assistant **Barbara J. Paepke** .... (605) 377-2600
E-mail: barb_paepke@sdd.uscourts.gov

Chambers of Senior Judge John B. Jones

400 South Phillips Avenue, Room 202, Sioux Falls, SD 57104-6851
Tel: (605) 330-6640

John B. Jones
Senior Judge

Date of Birth: 1927
Education: South Dakota 1951 BS, 1953 LLB
Began Service: December 5, 1981
Appointed By: President Ronald Reagan

Government: State Representative (R-SD), South Dakota House of Representatives (1956-1960)

Judicial: Judge, Lyman County Court (1953-1956); Judge, South Dakota Circuit Court, 10th Circuit (1967-1974); Judge, South Dakota Circuit Court, Sixth Circuit (1974-1981)

Legal Practice: Private Practice (1953-1962); Partner, Jones & McKeever (1962-1966)

Military Service: United States Naval Reserve (1945-1947)

Current Memberships: Federal Judges Association; State Bar of South Dakota

Chambers of Senior Judge Lawrence L. Piersol

202 U.S. Courthouse, 400 South Phillips Avenue,
Sioux Falls, SD 57104-6851
Tel: (605) 330-6640 Fax: (605) 330-6641

Lawrence L. Piersol
Senior Judge

Date of Birth: 1940
Education: South Dakota 1962 BA, 1965 JD
Began Service: December 11, 1993
Appointed By: President William J. Clinton
Political Affiliation: Democrat

Current Memberships: American Bar Association; Federal Judges Association; State Bar of South Dakota

(continued on next page)

Chambers of Senior Judge Lawrence L. Piersol *continued*

Staff

Law Clerk **Paul Coppock** . . . . (605) 330-6640
E-mail: paul_coppock@sdd.uscourts.gov

Career Law Clerk **Marie Hovland** . . . . (605) 330-6640
E-mail: marie_hovland@sdd.uscourts.gov
Education: Georgetown 1989 JD

Court Reporter **Jill Connelly** . . . . (605) 330-6669
E-mail: jill_connelly@sdd.uscourts.gov

Administrative Assistant **Jackie Hammond** . . . . (605) 330-6640
E-mail: jackie_hammond@sdd.uscourts.gov

Chambers of Magistrate Judge Mark A. Moreno

Federal Building & Courthouse, 225 South Pierre Street, Room 419, Pierre, SD 57501
Tel: (605) 945-4620 Fax: (605) 945-4621
E-mail: Mark_Moreno@sdd.uscourts.gov

Mark A. Moreno
Magistrate Judge

Date of Birth: 1958
Education: Illinois 1980 BA; Creighton 1983 JD
Began Service: February 1, 1993
Term Expires: June 31, 2017
Political Affiliation: Republican

Affiliation: Member, Schmidt, Schroyer, Moreno, Lee & Bachand, P.C.

Current Memberships: Nebraska State Bar Association; State Bar of South Dakota

Staff

Judicial Assistant/Court Reporter
Connie Heckenlaible . . . . (605) 945-4620
E-mail: Connie_Heckenlaible@sdd.uscourts.gov

Chambers of Magistrate Judge Veronica L. Duffy

400 South Phillips Avenue, Sioux Falls, SD 57104
Tel: (605) 330-6655 Fax: (605) 399-6031
E-mail: veronica_duffy@sdd.uscourts.gov

Veronica L. Duffy
Magistrate Judge

Began Service: June 2007
Term Expires: June 2016

Staff

Career Law Clerk **Lori Fossen** . . . . (605) 399-6032
Education: Northern Iowa 1986 BA; Iowa 1992 JD

Judicial Assistant **Christine Gross** . . . . (605) 330-6655

Chambers of Magistrate Judge William D. Gerdes

104 South Lincoln, Room 111, Aberdeen, SD 57401
Tel: (605) 622-2100

William D. Gerdes
Magistrate Judge

Began Service: 2015

United States Bankruptcy Court for the District of South Dakota

104 U.S. Courthouse, 400 South Phillips Avenue, Sioux Falls, SD 57104-6851
P.O. Box 5060, Sioux Falls, SD 57117-5060
Tel: (605) 357-2400
Tel: (800) 768-6218 (Voice Case Information System VCIS)
Fax: (605) 357-2401
Internet: www.sdb.uscourts.gov

Number of Judgeships: 2

Number of Vacancies: 1

Court Staff

Clerk of Court **Rick Entwistle** . . . . (605) 357-2400
Administrative Assistant to the Clerk
Mary Frederickson . . . . (605) 357-2400
E-mail: mary_frederickson@sdb.uscourts.gov

Deputy-in-Charge - Pierre/Sioux Falls **Vicky Reinhard** . . . (605) 945-4460
E-mail: vicky_reinhard@sdb.uscourts.gov Fax: (605) 945-4461

Systems Manager **Harland A. Danielsen** . . . . (605) 357-2400
E-mail: Harland_Danielsen@sdb.uscourts.gov
Education: Augustana (SD) 1987 BS

Chambers of Bankruptcy Judge Charles L. Nail, Jr.

Federal Building, 225 South Pierre Street, Room 211, Pierre, SD 57501
Tel: (605) 945-4490 Fax: (605) 945-4491

Charles L. Nail, Jr.
Bankruptcy Judge

Education: South Dakota BS; Minnesota 1982 JD
Began Service: 2006
Term Expires: 2020

Staff

Career Law Clerk **Kay Cee Hodson** . . . . (605) 945-4490
Education: South Dakota State 1980 BS, 1985 JD

Judicial Assistant **Sally Hanson** . . . . (605) 945-4490
E-mail: sally_hanson@sdb.uscourts.gov

United States District Court for the Eastern District of Tennessee

Howard H. Baker, Jr. U.S. Courthouse, 800 Market Street, Suite 130, Knoxville, TN 37902
Tel: (865) 545-4228 Fax: (865) 545-4247
Internet: www.tned.uscourts.gov

Number of Judgeships: 5

Number of Vacancies: 1

Circuit: Sixth

Areas Covered: Counties of Anderson, Bedford, Bledsoe, Blount, Bradley, Campbell, Carter, Claiborne, Cocke, Coffee, Franklin, Grainger, Greene, Grundy, Hamblen, Hamilton, Hancock, Hawkins, Jefferson, Johnson, Knox, Lincoln, Loudon, Marion, McMinn, Meigs, Monroe, Moore, Morgan, Polk, Rhea, Roane, Scott, Sequatchie, Sevier, Sullivan, Unicoi, Union, Van Buren, Warren and Washington

Court Staff

Clerk of the Court **Debra C. Poplin** . . . . (865) 545-4228
E-mail: debbie_poplin@tned.uscourts.gov Fax: (865) 545-4246
Education: Tennessee 1987 BA; Cincinnati 1990 BA

Chief Deputy Clerk **John Medearis** . . . . (423) 752-5285 ext. 3216
Joel W. Solomon Federal Building & U.S. Courthouse, 900 Georgia Avenue, Suite 309, Chattanooga, TN 37402 Fax: (423) 752-5375
E-mail: john_medearis@tned.uscourts.gov

Chief U.S. Probation Officer **Tony Anderson** . . . . (865) 545-4001
Suite 311 Fax: (865) 545-4003

United States District Court for the Eastern District of Tennessee *continued*

Division Manager - Chattanooga **(Vacant)** ..... (423) 752-5285 ext. 3215
Joel W. Solomon Federal Bldg. & U.S. Courthouse, 900 Georgia Ave., Ste. 309, Chattanooga, TN 37402 Fax: (423) 752-5205

Division Manager - Greeneville **Rick Tipton** ... (423) 639-6235 ext. 1213
James H. Quillen U.S. Courthouse, 220 W. Depot St., Ste. 200, Greeneville, TN 37743 Fax: (423) 639-7134
E-mail: rick_tipton@tned.uscourts.gov

Division Manager- Knoxville **Traci Walker** ..... (865) 545-4234 ext. 2232
Howard H. Baker Jr. U.S. Courthouse
E-mail: traci_walker@tned.uscourts.gov

Circuit Librarian - Chattanooga **(Vacant)** .... (423) 752-5331
Joel W. Solomon Federal Bldg. & U.S. Courthouse, 900 Georgia Ave., Ste. 245, Chattanooga, TN 37402 Fax: (423) 752-5205

Human Resources Specialist
Connie Penland .... (865) 545-4234 ext. 2250
Howard H. Baker Jr. U.S. Courthouse Fax: (865) 545-4246
E-mail: connie_penland@tned.uscourts.gov

Court Reporter **Shannan Andrews** .... (423) 756-5174
P.O. Box 84, Chattanooga, TN 37401
E-mail: shannan_andrews@tned.uscourts.gov

Court Reporter **Karen Bradley** .... (423) 639-3918
220 West Depot Street, Room 402, Greeneville, TN 37743
E-mail: karen_j_bradley@tned.uscourts.gov

Court Reporter **Elizabeth Coffey** .... (423) 267-7333
P.O. Box 1364, Chattanooga, TN 37401
E-mail: elizabeth_coffey@tned.uscourts.gov

Court Reporter [Knoxville] **Donnetta Kocuba** .... (865) 524-4590
Suite 132
E-mail: netta_kocuba@tned.uscourts.gov

Court Reporter [Knoxville] **Jolene Owen** .... (865) 384-6585
Suite 131
E-mail: jolene_owen@tned.uscourts.gov

Chambers of Chief Judge Thomas A. Varlan

800 Market Street, Suite 143, Knoxville, TN 37902
Tel: (865) 545-4762 Fax: (865) 545-4532
E-mail: varlan_chambers@tned.uscourts.gov

Thomas A. Varlan
Chief Judge

Date of Birth: July 8, 1956
Education: Tennessee 1978 BA; Vanderbilt 1981 JD
Began Service: April 5, 2003
Appointed By: President George W. Bush

Current Memberships: The American Inns of Court; The Hamilton Burnett American Inn of Court, The American Inns of Court

Staff

Law Clerk **Batoul Husain** .... (865) 545-4762
Began Service: August 2015
Term Expires: August 2016
E-mail: batoul_husain@tned.uscourts.gov

Law Clerk **Kaitlin Venables** .... (865) 545-4762
Began Service: August 2015
Term Expires: August 2016
E-mail: kaitlin_venables@tned.uscourts.gov

Career Law Clerk **Jill E. McCook** .... (865) 545-4762
Began Service: August 2012
E-mail: jill_mccook@tned.uscourts.gov
Education: Washington and Lee 2007 JD

Judicial Assistant/Paralegal **Lori P. Gibson** .... (865) 545-4762
E-mail: lori_gibson@tned.uscourts.gov

Chambers of District Judge J. Ronnie Greer

220 West Depot Street, Suite 405, Greeneville, TN 37743
Tel: (423) 639-0063 Fax: (423) 638-9069
E-mail: ronnie_greer@tned.uscourts.gov

J. Ronnie Greer
District Judge

Education: East Tennessee State 1974 BS; Tennessee 1980 JD
Began Service: June 25, 2003
Appointed By: President George W. Bush

Government: Special Assistant, Office of the Governor, State of Tennessee (1980-1981); County Attorney, Greene County, Tennessee (1985-1986); State Senator, Tennessee General Assembly (1986-1994)

Profession: Private Practice (1981-2003)

Staff

Career Law Clerk **Carol Sullivan** .... (423) 639-0063
E-mail: carol_sullivan@tned.uscourts.gov
Education: Tennessee Wesleyan 1971 BS; Tennessee 1980 JD

Career Law Clerk **LeAnna R. Wilson** .... (423) 639-0063
E-mail: leanna_wilson@tned.uscourts.gov

Courtroom Deputy **Kathy Hopson** .... (423) 639-6235 ext. 1206
E-mail: kathy_hopson@tned.uscourts.gov

Judicial Assistant **Deborah Daugherty** .... (423) 639-0063
Fax: (423) 638-9069

Chambers of District Judge Harry S. Mattice, Jr.

Joel W. Solomon Federal Building & US Courthouse, 900 Georgia Avenue, Room 104, Chattanooga, TN 37402
Tel: (423) 752-5200 Fax: (423) 386-3596

Harry S. Mattice, Jr.
District Judge

Education: Tennessee 1976 BA, 1981 JD
Began Service: November 18, 2005
Appointed By: President George W. Bush

Government: U.S. Attorney, Tennessee - Eastern District, Executive Office for United States Attorneys, United States Department of Justice

Staff

Law Clerk **Ashley Thompson** .... (423) 752-5200
Began Service: August 2012
Term Expires: August 2016
E-mail: ashley_thompson@tned.uscourts.gov

Law Clerk **Joshua Arocho** .... (423) 752-5200
Began Service: August 19, 2015
Term Expires: August 2017
E-mail: jaclyn_zarack@tned.uscourts.gov

Judicial Assistant **Martha Corts** .... (423) 752-5200
E-mail: martha_corts@tned.uscourts.gov Fax: (423) 386-3596

Chambers of District Judge Pamela L. Reeves

800 Market Street, Suite 145, Knoxville, TN 37902
Tel: (865) 545-4255

Pamela L. Reeves
District Judge

Education: Tennessee 1976 BA, 1979 JD
Began Service: March 5, 2014
Appointed By: President Barack Obama

Staff

Law Clerk **Pat Ferrell** .... (865) 545-4255
E-mail: pat_ferrell@tned.uscourts.gov
Education: Tennessee 1986 BA, 1997 JD

Law Clerk **Sean Solomon** .... (865) 545-4255
E-mail: sean_solomon@tned.uscourts.gov

(continued on next page)

FEDERAL COURTS—UNITED STATES DISTRICT COURTS

Chambers of District Judge Pamela L. Reeves *continued*

Courtroom Deputy **Angela Archer** . . . . (865) 545-4255
E-mail: angela_archer@tned.uscourts.gov
Judicial Assistant **Pam Simpson** . . . . (865) 545-4255
E-mail: pam_simpson@tned.uscourts.gov

Chambers of Senior Judge Robert Leon Jordan

141 Howard H. Baker Jr. U.S. Courthouse, 800 Market Street,
Knoxville, TN 37902-2303
Tel: (865) 545-4224 Fax: (865) 545-4671
E-mail: leon_jordan@tned.uscourts.gov

Robert Leon Jordan
Senior Judge

Date of Birth: 1934
Education: Tennessee 1958 BS, 1960 JD
Began Service: November 15, 1988
Appointed By: President Ronald Reagan
Political Affiliation: Republican

Judicial: Chancellor, Tennessee Chancery Court, First Judicial District (1980-1988)

Legal Practice: Goodpasture, Carpenter, Dale & Woods (1960-1961); Green & Green (1964-1966); Partner, Bryant, Price, Brandt, Jordan & Fox (1971-1980)

Military Service: United States Army (1954-1956)

Current Memberships: The Hamilton Burnett American Inn of Court, The American Inns of Court; Knox County Bar Association; Tennessee Bar Association; Tennessee Bar Foundation

Staff

Career Law Clerk **Brian R. Easley** . . . . (865) 545-4224
E-mail: brian_easley@tned.uscourts.gov
Education: Tennessee 2000 JD
Career Law Clerk **(Vacant)** . . . . (865) 545-4224

Chambers of Senior Judge Curtis L. Collier

900 Georgia Avenue, Room 317, Chattanooga, TN 37402
Tel: (423) 752-5287 Fax: (423) 752-5246
E-mail: curtis_collier@tned.uscourts.gov

Curtis L. Collier
Senior Judge

Date of Birth: 1949
Education: Tennessee State 1971 BS; Duke 1974 JD
Began Service: May 22, 1995
Appointed By: President William J. Clinton

Staff

Law Clerk **Joel Kurtz** . . . . (423) 752-5287
Began Service: September 2015
Term Expires: August 2016
E-mail: joel_kurz@tned.uscourts.gov
Law Clerk **Taylor Crabtree** . . . . (423) 752-5287
Began Service: August 2014
Term Expires: August 2016
Court Reporter **Elizabeth Coffey** . . . . (423) 267-7333
E-mail: elizabeth_coffey@tned.uscourts.gov
Judicial Assistant and Reporter of Decisions
Sheila Hendrix . . . . (423) 752-5287
E-mail: sheila_hendrix@tned.uscourts.gov

Chambers of Senior Judge Thomas W. Phillips

Howard H. Baker, Jr. U.S. Courthouse, 800 Market Street,
Suite 146, Knoxville, TN 37902
Tel: (865) 545-4230

Thomas W. Phillips
Senior Judge

Date of Birth: July 6, 1943
Education: Berea 1965 BA; Vanderbilt 1969 JD;
George Washington 1973 LLM

Current Memberships: American Bar Association; The American Inns of Court; Federal Magistrate Judges Association; Knoxville Bar Association; Scott County Bar Association; Tennessee Bar Association

Chambers of Magistrate Judge Dennis H. Inman

James H. Quillen U.S. Courthouse, 220 West Depot Street,
Greeneville, TN 37743
Tel: (423) 787-7400 Fax: (423) 638-1293
E-mail: dennis_inman@tned.uscourts.gov

Dennis H. Inman
Magistrate Judge

Date of Birth: 1947
Education: Tennessee BS, JD
Began Service: November 14, 1995
Term Expires: November 14, 2019

Judicial: Chancellor, Tennessee Court of Chancery, Third Judicial District (1984-1995)

Staff

Career Law Clerk **John Marshall Smith** . . . . (423) 787-7400
E-mail: john_smith@tned.uscourts.gov
Education: Tennessee 1977 JD
Judicial Assistant **Connie Lamb** . . . .(423) 787-7400
E-mail: connie_lamb@tned.uscourts.gov

Chambers of Magistrate Judge C. Clifford Shirley, Jr.

Howard H. Baker, Jr. U.S. Courthouse, 800 Market Street,
Knoxville, TN 37902
Tel: (865) 545-4260 Fax: (865) 545-4086
E-mail: clifford_shirley@tned.uscourts.gov

C. Clifford Shirley, Jr.
Magistrate Judge

Date of Birth: 1952
Education: David Lipscomb U 1974 BA; Tennessee 1977 JD
Began Service: February 13, 2002
Term Expires: February 2018

Academic: Adjunct Professor, University of Tennessee College of Law

Legal Practice: Partner, Lowe, Shirley & Yeager

Staff

Law Clerk **Danielle Goins** . . . . (865) 545-4260
E-mail: danielle_goins@tned.uscourts.gov
Career Law Clerk **Leah McClanahan** . . . . (865) 545-4260
Began Service: August 4, 2008
E-mail: leah_mcclanahan@tned.uscourts.gov
Education: Tennessee 2008 JD
Career Law Clerk **Michelle Gensheimer** . . . . (865) 545-4260
E-mail: michelle_gensheimer@tned.uscourts.gov
Education: Tennessee (Chattanooga) 1991 BA;
Tennessee 1995 JD
Judicial Assistant **Holly Nease** . . . . (865) 545-4260
E-mail: Holly_Nease@tned.uscourts.gov
Education: Knoxville 2000 AS

Chambers of Magistrate Judge H. Bruce Guyton
800 Market Street, Suite 142, Knoxville, TN 37902
Tel: (865) 545-4260 Fax: (865) 545-4086
E-mail: bruce_guyton@tned.uscourts.gov

H. Bruce Guyton
Magistrate Judge

Education: Rhodes 1978 BA; Virginia 1981 JD
Began Service: June 25, 2003
Term Expires: June 2019

Judicial: President, Hamilton Burnett Chapter of the American Inns of Court; Member, Board of Governors of the KBA

Legal Practice: Baker, Worthington, Crossley, Stansberry & Woolf (1982-1994); Woolf, McClane, Bright, Allen & Carpenter, PLLC (1994-2003)

Staff
Law Clerk **Katherine Blankenship** .... (865) 545-4260
E-mail: katherine_blankenship@tned.uscourts.gov
Career Law Clerk **Michelle Gensheimer** .... (865) 545-4260
E-mail: michelle_gensheimer@tned.uscourts.gov
Career Law Clerk **Leah McClanahan** .... (865) 545-4260
Began Service: August 4, 2008
E-mail: leah_mcclanahan@tned.uscourts.gov
Judicial Assistant **Holly Nease** .... (865) 545-4260
E-mail: holly_nease@tned.uscourts.gov

Chambers of Magistrate Judge Susan K. Lee
900 Georgia Avenue, Room 401, Chattanooga, TN 37402
Tel: (423) 752-5230 Fax: (423) 752-5103
E-mail: susan_k_lee@tned.uscourts.gov

Susan K. Lee
Magistrate Judge

Began Service: April 25, 1988

Staff
Career Law Clerk **Carrie Stefaniak** .... (423) 752-5230
E-mail: carrie_stefaniak@tned.uscourts.gov Fax: (423) 752-5103
Courtroom Deputy **Russell Eslinger** .... (423) 752-5285 ext. 3223
E-mail: russell_eslinger@tned.uscourts.gov
Judicial Assistant **Krista Starnes** .... (423) 752-5230
E-mail: krista_starnes@tned.uscourts.gov Fax: (423) 752-5103

Chambers of Magistrate Judge Christopher H. Steger
900 Georgia Avenue, Chattanooga, TN 37402
Tel: (423) 752-5200

Christopher H. Steger
Magistrate Judge

Education: Baylor 1979 BA, 1983 JD
Began Service: 2015

Chambers of Magistrate Judge Clifton L. Corker
220 West Depot Street, Suite 306, Greeneville, TN 37743
Tel: (423) 787-7400

Clifton L. Corker
Magistrate Judge

Began Service: 2015

United States Bankruptcy Court for the Eastern District of Tennessee
Howard H. Baker, Jr. U.S. Courthouse, 800 Market Street, Suite 330, Knoxville, TN 37902
Tel: (865) 545-4279 Tel: (423) 752-5272 (VCIS)
Tel: (800) 767-1512 (Toll Free Voice Case Information System VCIS)
Fax: (865) 545-4271
Internet: www.tneb.uscourts.gov
Internet: http://pacer.tneb.uscourts.gov (Pacer)

Number of Judgeships: 4

Court Staff
Clerk of the Court **William T. Magill** .... (423) 787-0113
Fax: (423) 787-0714
Deputy-in-Charge **Shelia D. Morgan** .... (865) 545-4279
Fax: (865) 545-4271
Deputy-in-Charge- Chattanooga **Betty G. Shelton** .... (423) 752-5163
Historic U.S. Courthouse, 31 East 11th Street, Chattanooga, TN 37402-2722 Fax: (423) 752-5169
Deputy-in-Charge - Greeneville **(Vacant)** .... (423) 787-0113
U.S. Courthouse, 220 W. Depot St., Greeneville, TN 37743

Chambers of Chief Bankruptcy Judge Marcia Phillips Parsons
James H. Quillen U.S. Courthouse, 220 West Depot Street, Greeneville, TN 37743
Tel: (423) 638-2264 Fax: (423) 639-3598

Marcia Phillips Parsons
Chief Bankruptcy Judge

Date of Birth: 1955
Education: Tennessee 1980 JD
Began Service: November 23, 1993
Term Expires: November 22, 2021

Staff
Law Clerk **(Vacant)** .... (423) 638-2264
Career Law Clerk **Marvin L. Campbell** .... (423) 638-2264
Education: Tennessee 1984 BS, 1987 JD, 1987 MBA
Courtroom Deputy/Chambers Administrator
Merilyn Dunn .... (423) 638-2264

Chambers of Bankruptcy Judge Shelley D. Rucker
31 East 11th Street, Chattanooga, TN 37402-2722
Tel: (423) 752-5104 Fax: (423) 752-5120

Shelley D. Rucker
Bankruptcy Judge

Education: Texas Christian 1979 BA; Georgia 1982 JD
Began Service: 2010

Staff
Law Clerk **Christopher "Chris" Call** .... (423) 752-5104
Term Expires: September 2016
Law Clerk **Ricky Hutchens** .... (423) 752-5104
Courtroom Deputy **Tanya English** .... (423) 752-5104

Chambers of Bankruptcy Judge Suzanne Bauknight
800 Market Street, Suite 330, Knoxville, TN 37902
Tel: (865) 545-4284

Suzanne Bauknight
Bankruptcy Judge

Staff
Law Clerk **Shanna Fuller Veach** .... (865) 545-4284

(continued on next page)

FEDERAL COURTS—UNITED STATES DISTRICT COURTS

Chambers of Bankruptcy Judge Suzanne Bauknight *continued*

Courtroom Deputy **Randi Holden** .... (865) 545-4284
Assistant Courtroom Deputy **Heather Connatser** .... (865) 545-4284
Judicial Assistant **Teresa Wheeler** .... (865) 545-4284

Chambers of Bankruptcy Judge Nicholas W. Whittenburg

800 Market Street, Knoxville, TN 37902
Tel: (865) 545-4279

Nicholas W. "Nick" Whittenburg
Bankruptcy Judge

Education: Vanderbilt 1987 BS; Emory 1990 JD

Staff

Law Clerk **Stephen R. Beckham** .... (865) 545-4279
Education: Ohio State 1981 JD
Law Clerk **Kelly Walsh** .... (865) 545-4279
Courtroom Deputy **Sheri Love** .... (865) 545-4279

United States District Court for the Middle District of Tennessee

U.S. Courthouse, 801 Broadway, Nashville, TN 37203
Tel: (615) 736-5498 Tel: (615) 736-7164 (PACER)
Fax: (615) 736-7488
Internet: www.tnmd.uscourts.gov

Number of Judgeships: 4

Number of Vacancies: 1

Circuit: Sixth

Areas Covered: Counties of Cannon, Cheatham, Clay, Cumberland, Davidson, DeKalb, Dickson, Fentress, Giles, Hickman, Houston, Humphreys, Jackson, Lawrence, Lewis, Macon, Marshall, Maury, Montgomery, Overton, Pickett, Putnam, Robertson, Rutherford, Smith, Stewart, Sumner, Trousdale, Wayne, White, Williamson and Wilson

Court Staff

Clerk of Court **Keith Throckmorton** .... (615) 736-2364 ext. 3225
E-mail: keith_throckmorton@tnmd.uscourts.gov
Chief Deputy Clerk **Vicki Kinkade** .... (615) 736-7551 ext. 3204
E-mail: vicki_kinkade@tnmd.uscourts.gov
Education: Tennessee Tech 1982 BS
Chief U.S. Probation Officer **(Vacant)** .... (615) 736-5771
Director of Information Technology
Mark Blazenyak .... (615) 736-7485 ext. 3214
E-mail: mark_blazenyak@tnmd.uscourts.gov
Operations Manager **Ann Frantz** .... (615) 736-2364 ext. 3201
Financial Administrator **LaRhonda Howard**.... (615) 736-5518 ext. 3216
Jury Administrator **Marcia Knoch** .... (615) 736-5483 ext. 3219
E-mail: marcia_knoch@tnmd.uscourts.gov
Naturalization **Joyce Brooks** .... (615) 736-7445 ext. 3238
Procurement **Tina Webster** .... (615) 736-5498 ext. 3215
E-mail: tina_webster@tnmd.uscourts.gov

Chambers of Chief Judge Kevin H. Sharp

U.S. Courthouse, 801 Broadway, Room A820, Nashville, TN 37203
Tel: (615) 736-2774
E-mail: kevin_sharp@tnmd.uscourts.gov

Kevin Hunter Sharp
Chief Judge

Education: Christian Brothers Col 1990 BS; Vanderbilt 1993 JD
Began Service: May 4, 2011
Appointed By: President Barack Obama

Chambers of Chief Judge Kevin H. Sharp *continued*

Staff

Law Clerk **Christy Chalou** .... (615) 736-2774
E-mail: christy_chalou@tnmd.uscourts.gov
Career Law Clerk **Anthony Genakos** .... (615) 736-2774
E-mail: anthony_genakos@tnmd.uscourts.gov
Education: William & Mary 1978 BA; Valparaiso 1982 JD
Courtroom Deputy **Angela "Angie" Brewer** .... (615) 736-2774
E-mail: angela_brewer@tnmd.uscourts.gov

Chambers of District Judge Todd J. Campbell

U.S. Courthouse, 801 Broadway, Suite A820, Nashville, TN 37203
Tel: (615) 736-5291

Todd J. Campbell
District Judge

Date of Birth: 1956
Education: Vanderbilt 1978 BA; Tennessee 1982 JD
Began Service: 1995
Appointed By: President William J. Clinton

Staff

Career Law Clerk **Charlotte Rappuhn** .... (615) 736-5291
E-mail: charlotte_rappuhn@tnmd.uscourts.gov
Career Law Clerk **Janet Phelps** .... (615) 736-5291
E-mail: janet_phelps@tnmd.uscourts.gov

Chambers of District Judge Aleta Arthur Trauger

U.S. Courthouse, 801 Broadway, Room 825, Nashville, TN 37203
Tel: (615) 736-7143 Fax: (615) 736-7156

Aleta Arthur Trauger
District Judge

Date of Birth: 1945
Education: Cornell Col 1968 BA; Vanderbilt 1972 MAT, 1976 JD
Began Service: December 1, 1998
Appointed By: President William J. Clinton

Academic: Teacher, England and Tennessee (1970-1973); Legal Counsel, College of Charleston (1984-1985); Adjunct Professor, Law School, Vanderbilt University (1986-1988)

Government: Assistant United States Attorney, Middle District of Tennessee and Northern District of Illinois, United States Department of Justice (1977-1982); Chief of Staff, Office of the Metropolitan Mayor, City of Nashville, Tennessee (1991-1992)

Judicial: Bankruptcy Judge, United States Bankruptcy Court for the Middle District of Tennessee (1993-1998)

Legal Practice: Associate, Barrett, Brandt & Barrett P.C. (1976-1977); Associate, Hollins, Wagster & Yarbrough (1983-1984); Counsel & Partner, Wyatt, Tarrant, Combs, Gilbert & Milom (1985-1991)

Current Memberships: American Bar Foundation; American Bar Association; Federal Judges Association; International Women's Forum; Lawyers Association for Women, Marion Griffin Chapter; Nashville Bar Association; Nashville Bar Foundation, Nashville Bar Association; National Association of Women Judges; Tennessee Bar Association; Tennessee Bar Foundation; Tennessee Lawyers' Association for Women

Staff

Law Clerk **Jesse Morris** .... (615) 736-7143
Began Service: August 2015
Term Expires: August 2017
E-mail: jesse_morris@tnmd.uscourts.gov
Law Clerk **Lyndsie Schmalz** .... (615) 736-7143
Began Service: August 2015
Term Expires: August 2016
E-mail: lyndsie_schmalz@tnmd.uscourts.gov

Chambers of District Judge Aleta Arthur Trauger *continued*

Court Reporter **Roxann Harkins** .... (615) 726-4893
E-mail: roxann_harkins@tnmd.uscourts.gov
Secretary **Debbie Sawyer** .... (615) 736-7143
E-mail: becky_cole@tnmd.uscourts.gov

Chambers of Senior Judge John T. Nixon

U.S. Courthouse, 801 Broadway, Room 770, Nashville, TN 37203
Tel: (615) 736-5778 Fax: (615) 736-5324
E-mail: john_nixon@tnmd.uscourts.gov

John T. Nixon
Senior Judge

Date of Birth: 1933
Education: Harvard 1955 AB; Vanderbilt 1960 LLB
Began Service: 1980
Appointed By: President Jimmy Carter
Political Affiliation: Democrat

Government: City Attorney, State of Tennessee (1962-1964); Trial Attorney, Civil Rights Division, United States Department of Justice (1964-1969); Staff Attorney, Office of the Comptroller, State of Tennessee (1971-1976)

Judicial: Judge, Tennessee Circuit Court (1977-1978); Judge, General Sessions Court (1978-1980)

Legal Practice: Private Practice (1960-1962); Private Practice (1969-1971); Private Practice (1976-1977)

Military Service: United States Army (1958)

Current Memberships: American Bar Association; Nashville Bar Association; Tennessee Bar Association

Staff
Law Clerk **Allison Jones** .... (615) 736-5778
Began Service: September 1, 2015
Term Expires: September 1, 2016
E-mail: allison_jones@tnmd.uscourts.gov
Law Clerk **Erin Morgan** .... (615) 736-5778
Began Service: September 1, 2014
Term Expires: September 1, 2016
E-mail: erin_morgan@tnmd.uscourts.gov
Law Clerk **Lilas Taslimi** .... (615) 736-5778
Began Service: September 1, 2014
Term Expires: September 1, 2016
E-mail: lilas_taslimi@tnmd.uscourts.gov
Courtroom Deputy **Mary Conner** .... (615) 736-5778
E-mail: mary_f_conner@tnmd.uscourts.gov

Chambers of Senior Judge William J. Haynes, Jr.

A-845 U.S. Courthouse, 801 Broadway, Nashville, TN 37203
Tel: (615) 736-7217 Fax: (615) 736-5285

William J. Haynes, Jr.
Senior Judge

Date of Birth: 1949
Education: St Thomas Aquinas 1970 BA; Vanderbilt 1973 JD
Began Service: November 1999
Appointed By: President William J. Clinton

Current Memberships: American Bar Foundation; Nashville Bar Foundation, Nashville Bar Association; Tennessee Bar Foundation

Staff
Law Clerk **Jacob Stafford** .... (615) 736-5498 ext. 3152
Began Service: September 2015
Term Expires: September 2016
E-mail: jacob_stafford@tnmd.uscourts.gov
Courtroom Deputy **Megan Gregory** .... (615) 736-5498 ext. 3152
E-mail: megan_gregory@tnmd.uscourts.gov
Career Law Clerk **Kevin Webby** .... (615) 736-5498 ext. 3154
Education: Cumberland 1998 JD

Chambers of Senior Judge William J. Haynes, Jr. *continued*

Judicial Assistant **Megan Gregory** .... (615) 736-7217 ext. 3153
E-mail: megan_gregory@tnmd.uscourts.gov

Chambers of Magistrate Judge E. Clifton Knowles

U.S. Courthouse, 801 Broadway, Suite 649, Nashville, TN 37203-3869
Tel: (615) 736-7344 Fax: (615) 736-7346

E. Clifton Knowles
Magistrate Judge

Date of Birth: 1951
Education: Vanderbilt 1973 BA; Tennessee 1979 JD
Began Service: 2000
Term Expires: 2016

Clerkships: Law Clerk, Chief Judge The Honorable George Edwards, United States Court of Appeal Sixth Circuit (1978-1979)

Legal Practice: Associate and Partner, Bass, Berry & Sims PLC (1979-1999)

Current Memberships: Nashville Bar Association; Nashville Bar Foundation, Nashville Bar Association; Tennessee Bar Association

Staff
Career Law Clerk **Ellie D. Shefi** .... (615) 736-7344
E-mail: ellie_shefi@tnmd.uscourts.gov
Education: Michigan 2002 JD
Courtroom Deputy **Holly Vila** .... (615) 736-7347
E-mail: holly_vila@tnmd.uscourts.gov
Secretary **Barbara Reed** .... (615) 736-7344
E-mail: barbara_reed@tnmd.uscourts.gov

Chambers of Magistrate Judge Barbara D. Holmes

801 Broadway, Nashville, TN 37203
Tel: (615) 736-5164
E-mail: barbara_holmes@tnmd.uscourts.gov

Barbara D. Holmes
Magistrate Judge

Began Service: October 9, 2015

Staff
Law Clerk **William "Will" Woods** .... (615) 736-5164
Began Service: September 2015
Term Expires: September 2016
E-mail: william_woods@tnmd.uscourts.gov
Education: Tennessee 2010 JD
Career Law Clerk **Steve Wilson** .... (615) 736-5164
Education: Notre Dame 1988 BA; Indiana 1991 JD
Courtroom Deputy **Jeanne Cox**
Education: Western Kentucky 1980 BS

Chambers of Magistrate Judge (Recalled) Joe B. Brown

781 U.S. Courthouse, 801 Broadway, Nashville, TN 37203
Tel: (615) 736-2119 Fax: (615) 736-2121
E-mail: joe_b_brown@tnmd.uscourts.gov

Joe B. Brown
Magistrate Judge (recalled)

Date of Birth: 1940
Education: Vanderbilt 1962 BA, 1965 JD
Began Service: August 3, 1998

Current Memberships: Kentucky Bar Association; Nashville Bar Association

(continued on next page)

Chambers of Magistrate Judge (Recalled) Joe B. Brown *continued*

Staff
E-mail: brownchambers@tnmd.uscourts.gov

Law Clerk **Sierra Vierra** . . . . (615) 736-2119
E-mail: sierra_vierra@tnmd.uscourts.gov
Career Law Clerk **Marvin Blair** . . . . (615) 736-2119
E-mail: marvin_blair@tnmd.uscourts.gov
Courtroom Deputy **Robbie Dail** . . . . (615) 736-5097
E-mail: robbie_dail@tnmd.uscourts.gov
Secretary **Joan Hughes** . . . . (615) 736-2119
E-mail: joan_hughes@tnmd.uscourts.gov

Chambers of Magistrate Judge John S. Bryant
U.S. Courthouse, 801 Broadway, Room 797, Nashville, TN 37203
Tel: (615) 736-5878
E-mail: john_bryant@tnmd.uscourts.gov

John S. Bryant
Magistrate Judge

Education: Davidson 1970 BA; Vanderbilt 1973 JD
Began Service: November 1999
Appointed By: President William J. Clinton

Staff
Career Law Clerk **Jason Watson** . . . . (615) 736-5878
Education: Evansville 1995 BA; Tennessee 1998 JD
Courtroom Deputy **Tina McDonald** . . . . (615) 736-5878

United States Bankruptcy Court for the Middle District of Tennessee
Customs House, 701 Broadway, Nashville, TN 37203
Tel: (615) 736-5584 (Clerk's Office)
Tel: (800) 676-6856 (PACER Service)
Tel: (615) 736-5577 (PACER Registration)
Tel: (615) 736-5584 (Voice Case Information Systems)
Fax: (615) 736-2305 (Admin) Fax: (615) 695-4980 (Intake)
E-mail: webmaster@tnmb.uscourts.gov
E-mail: pacer@psc.uscourts.gov
Internet: www.tnmb.uscourts.gov

Number of Judgeships: 3

Court Staff
Clerk of the Court **Matthew T. Loughney** . . . . (615) 736-5590
E-mail: matt_loughney@tnmb.uscourts.gov
Education: West Virginia 2002 JD
Chief Deputy Clerk **Teresa C. Azan** . . . . (615) 736-5590
Began Service: 2009
E-mail: teresa_azan@tnmb.uscourts.gov
Financial Administrator **Alice Dawn Miller** . . . . (615) 736-5590
E-mail: alice_miller@tnmb.uscourts.gov
Procurement and Budget Administrator **Susan Flanary** . . . (615) 736-5590
E-mail: susan_flanary@tnmb.uscourts.gov
Director of Information Technology **Eric J. Fondriest** . . . . (615) 736-5590
E-mail: eric_fondriest@tnmb.uscourts.gov
Human Resources Specialist **Lettie J. Giles** . . . . (615) 736-5590
E-mail: lettie_giles@tnmb.uscourts.gov

Chambers of Chief Bankruptcy Judge Keith M. Lundin
Customs House, 701 Broadway, 2nd Floor, Nashville, TN 37203-3976
Tel: (615) 736-5586 Fax: (615) 736-7705
E-mail: keith_lundin@tnmb.uscourts.gov

Keith M. Lundin
Chief Bankruptcy Judge

Date of Birth: 1951
Education: Brown U 1973 BA; Vanderbilt 1976 JD
Began Service: May 25, 1982
Term Expires: May 24, 2028

Current Memberships: Nashville Bar Association; The National Association of Chapter 13 Trustees; National Conference of Bankruptcy Judges; Tennessee Bar Association

Staff
Career Law Clerk **Sharron B. Lane** . . . . (615) 736-5586
E-mail: sharron_b_lane@tnmb.uscourts.gov
Education: Connecticut 1990 JD
Secretary **Cindy Odle** . . . . (615) 736-5586
E-mail: cindy_odle@tnmb.uscourts.gov

Chambers of Bankruptcy Judge Marian F. Harrison
Customs House, 701 Broadway, Room 232, Nashville, TN 37203
Tel: (615) 736-5589 Fax: (615) 736-7706
E-mail: marian_harrison@tnmb.uscourts.gov

Marian F. Harrison
Bankruptcy Judge

Education: Vanderbilt 1972 BA; Georgia 1975 JD
Began Service: December 21, 1999
Term Expires: 2027

Clerkships: Law Clerk The Honorable Frank Gray, Jr., United States District Court for the Middle District of Tennessee

Legal Practice: Partner, Willis & Knight (1977-1999)

Current Memberships: American Bar Association; Nashville Bar Association; National Conference of Bankruptcy Judges; Tennessee Bar Association; Tennessee Lawyers' Association for Women

Staff
Career Law Clerk **Deborah Lunn** . . . . (615) 736-5589
E-mail: deborah_lunn@tnmb.uscourts.gov
Education: Temple 1989 JD
Secretary/Judicial Assistant **Sharon F. Beers** . . . . (615) 736-5589
E-mail: sharon_beers@tnmb.uscourts.gov

Chambers of Bankruptcy Judge Randal S. Mashburn
701 Broadway, Nashville, TN 37203
Tel: (615) 736-5587

Randal S. Mashburn
Bankruptcy Judge

Education: Tennessee 1976 BS; U Memphis 1982 JD
Began Service: 2011

Staff
Courtroom Deputy **Lolitha Scruggs** . . . . (615) 695-4212
Career Law Clerk **Nancy King** . . . . (615) 736-5587
Education: Rhodes 1990 BA;
Memphis State 1993 JD

United States District Court for the Western District of Tennessee

242 Federal Building, 167 North Main Street, Memphis, TN 38103
Tel: (901) 495-1200 Tel: (901) 495-1259 (PACER)
Tel: (800) 407-4456 (Toll-free) Fax: (901) 495-1250
Internet: www.tnwd.uscourts.gov

Number of Judgeships: 5

Number of Vacancies: 1

Circuit: Sixth

Areas Covered: Counties of Benton, Carroll, Chester, Crockett, Decatur, Dyer, Fayette, Gibson, Hardeman, Hardin, Haywood, Henderson, Henry, Lake, Lauderdale, Madison, McNairy, Obion, Perry, Shelby, Tipton and Weakley

Court Staff

Clerk of Court **Thomas M. Gould** .... (901) 495-1200
Deputy-in-Charge - Eastern Division **Sonya Pettigrew** ... (731) 421-9212
111 S. Highland Ave., Rm. 262, Jackson, TN 38301
E-mail: sonya_pettigrew@tnwd.uscourts.gov
Chief Deputy of Operations **Wendy Oliver** .... (901) 495-1210
E-mail: wendy_oliver@tnwd.uscourts.gov
Chief Probation Officer **Alice Conley** .... (901) 495-1400
Room 234 Fax: (901) 495-1450
E-mail: alice_conley@tnwd.uscourts.gov
Chief Pretrial Services Officer **Carolyn Moore** .... (901) 495-1550
Room 459 Fax: (901) 495-1590
E-mail: carolyn_moore@tnwd.uscourts.gov
Administrative Manager **Tracy Wherry** .... (901) 495-1229
E-mail: tracy_wherry@tnwd.uscourts.gov

Chambers of Chief Judge J. Daniel Breen

111 South Highland Avenue, Room 444, Jackson, TN 38301-6101
Tel: (731) 421-9200 Fax: (731) 421-9255
E-mail: daniel_breen@tnwd.uscourts.gov

J. Daniel Breen
Chief Judge

Date of Birth: July 10, 1950
Education: Spring Hill 1972 BA; Tennessee 1975 JD
Began Service: March 18, 2003
Appointed By: President George W. Bush

Current Memberships: American Bar Foundation; American Bar Association; The Lincoln-Douglas American Inn of Court, The American Inns of Court; Federal Bar Association; Federal Judges Association; Memphis Bar Association; Tennessee Bar Association; Tennessee Bar Foundation

Staff

Law Clerk **Michael Cottone** .... (731) 421-9250
Law Clerk **Matt Waldrop** .... (731) 421-9250
Career Law Clerk **Tina Eubanks McKelvy** .... (731) 421-9250
E-mail: tina_mckelvy@tnwd.uscourts.gov Fax: (731) 421-9255
Education: U Memphis 1991 JD
Secretary **Taffy Elchlepp** .... (731) 421-9250
E-mail: taffy_elchlepp@tnwd.uscourts.gov

Chambers of District Judge Stanley Thomas Anderson

167 North Main Street, Memphis, TN 38103
Tel: (901) 495-1495 Fax: (901) 495-1324

Stanley Thomas Anderson
District Judge

Education: Tennessee 1976 BS
Began Service: May 21, 2008
Appointed By: President George W. Bush

Chambers of District Judge Stanley Thomas Anderson *continued*

Staff

Law Clerk **Kyle Cummins** .... (901) 495-1492
Began Service: 2014
Law Clerk **Shawn McCarver** .... (901) 495-1496
Education: Memphis State 1997 BA, 2001 MA; Mississippi 2006 JD
Case Manager **Terry Haley** .... (901) 495-1276
Judicial Assistant **Betty Guy** .... (901) 495-1495

Chambers of District Judge John Thomas Fowlkes Jr.

951 Federal Building, 167 North Main Street, Memphis, TN 38103
Tel: (901) 495-1326 Fax: (901) 495-1336

John T. Fowlkes, Jr.
District Judge

Education: Valparaiso 1975 BA; Denver 1977 JD
Began Service: August 9, 2012
Appointed By: President Barack Obama

Current Memberships: Judicial Division, American Bar Association; Memphis Area Legal Services, Inc.; Memphis Bar Association; National Bar Association; Tennessee Bar Foundation

Staff

Law Clerk **Cameron Watson** .... (901) 495-1390
Law Clerk **Lorri Fentress** .... (901) 495-1241
Case Manager **Ross Herrin** .... (901) 495-1331
Judicial Assistant **Phyllis Buchanan** .... (901) 495-1326

Chambers of District Judge Sheryl H. Lipman

167 North Main Street, Memphis, TN 38103
Tel: (901) 495-1337
E-mail: ecf_judge_lipman@tnwd.uscourts.gov

Sheryl H. "Sheri" Lipman
District Judge

Education: Michigan 1984 BGS; NYU 1987 JD
Began Service: August 14, 2014
Appointed By: President Barack Obama

Academic: University Counsel, The University of Memphis

Staff

Law Clerk **Samuel Cortina** .... (901) 495-1339
Term Expires: August 2016
Law Clerk **David Goldman** .... (901) 495-1319
Term Expires: August 2016
Judicial Assistant **Cathy Gray** .... (901) 495-1337
Case Manager **Joseph "Joe" Warren** .... (901) 495-1337

Chambers of Magistrate Judge Diane K. Vescovo

341 Federal Building, 167 North Main Street, Memphis, TN 38103
Tel: (901) 495-1307 Fax: (901) 495-1387
E-mail: diane_vescovo@tnwd.uscourts.gov

Diane K. Vescovo
Magistrate Judge

Date of Birth: 1955
Education: Virginia 1977 BA; Memphis State 1980 JD
Began Service: June 15, 1995
Term Expires: June 15, 2019

Clerkships: Law Clerk The Honorable Harry W. Wellford (1980-1981)

Legal Practice: Lloyd C. Kirkland, Jr. (1981-1987); International Paper Company (1987-1992); Wolff Ardis, P.C. (1992-1995)

(continued on next page)

Chambers of Magistrate Judge Diane K. Vescovo *continued*

Current Memberships: Association of Women Attorneys; Federal Magistrate Judges Association; Memphis Bar Association; Tennessee Bar Association

Staff
Law Clerk **Naya Bedini** .... (901) 495-1308
Began Service: August 2014
Term Expires: August 2016
E-mail: naya_bedini@tnwd.uscourts.gov
Secretary **Carol R. Kronquist** .... (901) 495-1307
E-mail: carol_kronqufist@tnwd.uscourts.gov

Chambers of Magistrate Judge Tu M. Pham

Clifford Davis Federal Building, 167 North Main Street, Courtroom 6 Room 338, Memphis, TN 38103-1814
Tel: (901) 495-1351 Fax: (901) 495-1325
E-mail: tu_pham@tnwd.uscourts.gov

Tu M. Pham
Magistrate Judge

Began Service: May 16, 2003

Government: Assistant U.S. Attorney, Northern District of Illinois, United States Attorney's Office, United States Department of Justice, William J. Clinton Administration (1999)

Staff
Law Clerk **Elizabeth Rogers** .... (901) 495-1352
Judicial Assistant **Beverly Gerken** .... (901) 495-1351

Chambers of Magistrate Judge Edward G. Bryant

111 South Highland, Room 345, Jackson, TN 38301
Tel: (731) 421-9200

Edward Glenn "Ed" Bryant
Magistrate Judge

Education: Mississippi 1970 BA, 1972 JD
Began Service: December 15, 2008

Staff
Career Law Clerk **Danielle Hardee** .... (731) 421-9274
E-mail: danielle_hardee@tnwd.uscourts.gov
Case Manager **Emily Strope** .... (731) 421-9206
Judicial Assistant **Andrew Shulman** .... (731) 421-9275
E-mail: andrew_shulman@tnwd.uscourts.gov

Chambers of Magistrate Judge Charmiane G. Claxton

167 North Main Street, Room 357, Memphis, TN 38103
Tel: (901) 495-1326
E-mail: charmiane_claxton@tnwd.uscourts.gov

Charmiane G. Claxton
Magistrate Judge

Education: Spelman; Memphis State JD
Began Service: May 29, 2009

Staff
Career Law Clerk **Sherrill French** .... (901) 495-1313
Began Service: 2009
E-mail: sherrill_french@tnwd.uscourts.gov
Case Manager **Chris Sowell** .... (901) 495-1218
Judicial Assistant **Bernita Henley** .... (901) 495-1312

Chambers of Senior Judge James Dale Todd

U.S. Courthouse, 111 South Highland Avenue, Room 417, Jackson, TN 38301
Tel: (731) 421-9222 Fax: (731) 421-9229
E-mail: james_todd@tnwd.uscourts.gov

James Dale Todd
Senior Judge

Date of Birth: 1943
Education: Lambuth 1965 BS; Mississippi 1968 MCS; Memphis State 1972 JD
Began Service: July 11, 1985
Appointed By: President Ronald Reagan
Political Affiliation: Republican

Academic: Science Teacher and Chairman, Science Department, Lyman High School (1965-1968); Science Teacher and Chairman, Science Department, Memphis University School (1968-1972)

Judicial: Judge, Tennessee Circuit Court, Division II (1983-1985); Chief Judge, Chambers of Chief Judge James D. Todd, United States District Court for the Western District of Tennessee (2001-2007)

Legal Practice: Waldrop, Farmer, Todd & Breen, PA (1972-1983)

Current Memberships: Federal Bar Association; Federal Judges Association; Jackson-Madison County Bar Association

Staff
Career Law Clerk **Rayna Bomar** .... (731) 421-9222
E-mail: rayna_bomar@tnwd.uscourts.gov
Education: Memphis State JD
Career Law Clerk **Lois Cruze** .... (731) 421-9222
E-mail: lois_cruze@tnwd.uscourts.gov
Education: Tennessee JD
Case Manager **Cassandra Ikerd** .... (731) 421-9204
Secretary **Jackie Logue** .... (731) 421-9222
E-mail: jackie_logue@tnwd.uscourts.gov

Chambers of Senior Judge Jon P. McCalla

167 North Main Street, Room 1157, Memphis, TN 38103
Tel: (901) 495-1200 Fax: (901) 495-1295
E-mail: jon_mccalla@tnwd.uscourts.gov

Jon P. McCalla
Senior Judge

Date of Birth: 1947
Education: Tennessee 1969 BS; Vanderbilt 1974 JD
Began Service: 1992
Appointed By: President George H.W. Bush

Current Memberships: American Bar Association; Federal Bar Association; Federal Judges Association; Memphis Bar Association; Tennessee Bar Association

Staff
Law Clerk **Nikki Berkowitz** .... (901) 495-1293
Began Service: August 2015
Term Expires: August 2016
Law Clerk **Anna Han** .... (901) 495-1293
Began Service: August 2015
Term Expires: August 2016
Case Manager **Milton Knox** .... (901) 495-1242
Court Reporter **Brenda Parker** .... (901) 626-8769
E-mail: brenda_parker@tnwd.uscourts.gov
Judicial Secretary **Debbie Baker** .... (901) 495-1291

Chambers of Senior Judge Samuel H. Mays, Jr.
1111 Clifford Davis Federal Building, 167 North Main Street, Memphis, TN 38103
Tel: (901) 495-1283 Fax: (901) 495-1287
E-mail: samuel_mays@tnwd.uscourts.gov

Samuel H. Mays, Jr.
Senior Judge

Date of Birth: 1948
Education: Amherst 1970 BA; Yale 1973 JD
Began Service: June 17, 2002
Appointed By: President George W. Bush

Staff
Law Clerk **Ashley Evans** .... (901) 495-1285
Term Expires: August 2016
Law Clerk **Matthew Sipe** .... (901) 495-1284
Began Service: August 2015
Term Expires: August 2016
Court Reporter **Nicole Warren** .... (901) 572-7252
E-mail: nicole_warren@tnwd.uscourts.gov
Case Manager **Zandra Frazier** .... (901) 495-1277
Judicial Assistant **Jean Lee** .... (901) 495-1283
E-mail: jean_lee@tnwd.uscourts.gov

United States Bankruptcy Court for the Western District of Tennessee
200 Jefferson Avenue, Suite 413, Memphis, TN 38103
Tel: (901) 328-3500 Tel: (800) 406-0190 (Toll Free PACER)
Tel: (901) 328-3617 (PACER)
Tel: (901) 328-3509 (Voice Case Information System VCIS)
Tel: (888) 381-4961 (Toll Free Voice Case Information System VCIS)
Internet: www.tnwb.uscourts.gov

Number of Judgeships: 4

Court Staff
Clerk of Court **Jed G. Weintraub** .... (901) 328-3500
E-mail: jed_weintraub@tnwb.uscourts.gov
Education: Rutgers 1980 BA; USC 1982 MPA, 1982
Chief Deputy Clerk **(Vacant)** .... (901) 328-3500
Deputy-in-Charge - Jackson **Rugena Bivins** .... (731) 421-9300
111 S. Highland Ave., 1st Fl., Jackson, TN 38301
E-mail: rugena_bivins@tnwb.uscourts.gov
Education: Oklahoma 1984 BBA
Systems Manager **Matt Burgess** .... (901) 328-3500
E-mail: matt_burgess@tnwb.uscourts.gov
Director of Human Resources **Lisa Haney** .... (901) 328-3500
E-mail: lisa_haney@tnwb.uscourts.gov
Financial Administrator **Carolyne Avery** .... (901) 328-3500
E-mail: carolyne_avery@tnwb.uscourts.gov
Administrative Secretary **Beth Puckett** .... (901) 328-3557
E-mail: beth_puckett@tnwb.uscourts.gov

Chambers of Chief Bankruptcy Judge David S. Kennedy
200 Jefferson Avenue, Suite 950, Memphis, TN 38103
Tel: (901) 328-3522

David S. Kennedy
Chief Bankruptcy Judge

Date of Birth: 1944
Education: U Memphis 1970 JD
Began Service: November 24, 1980
Term Expires: 2028

Academic: Adjunct Professor, Cecil C. Humphreys School of Law; Faculty, Federal Judicial Center

Clerkships: Law Clerk The Honorable Robert M. McRae, United States District Court (1970-1971)

Chambers of Chief Bankruptcy Judge David S. Kennedy *continued*

Government: Clerk of Court, United States Bankruptcy Court for the Western District of Tennessee (1974-1976); Trustee, United States Bankruptcy Court for the Western District of Tennessee

Legal Practice: Private Practice (1972-1973); Private Practice (1976-1980)

Current Memberships: Memphis Bar Association; National Conference of Bankruptcy Judges; Shelby County Bar Association; Tennessee Bar Association

Staff
Career Law Clerk **Locke Houston** .... (901) 328-3524
Began Service: 2014
Courtroom Deputy **Tonya Lepone** .... (901) 328-3572
Judicial Assistant **Ruth Weymouth** .... (901) 328-3522
E-mail: ruth_weymouth@tnwb.uscourts.gov

Chambers of Bankruptcy Judge Jennie D. Latta
200 Jefferson Avenue, Suite 650, Memphis, TN 38103
Tel: (901) 328-3542 Fax: (901) 328-3545
E-mail: jennie_d_latta@tnwb.uscourts.gov

Jennie D. Latta
Bankruptcy Judge

Date of Birth: January 9, 1961
Education: Memphis State 1981 BA, 1986 JD
Began Service: March 6, 1997
Term Expires: March 2019

Staff
Career Law Clerk **Rhoda Smith** .... (901) 328-3544
E-mail: rhoda_smith@tnwb.uscourts.gov
Education: Memphis State 1984 JD
Courtroom Deputy **Barta Johnson** .... (901) 328-3571
E-mail: barta_johnson@tnwb.uscourts.gov
Judicial Assistant **Sandy Beck** .... (901) 328-3542
E-mail: sandy_beck@tnwb.uscourts.gov

Chambers of Bankruptcy Judge Paulette J. Delk
200 Jefferson Avenue, Suite 413, Memphis, TN 38103
Tel: (901) 328-3534

Paulette J. Delk
Bankruptcy Judge

Began Service: July 2006
Appointed By: President George W. Bush
Term Expires: July 2020

Staff
Law Clerk **Amy Black** .... (901) 328-3544
Career Law Clerk **Donna T. Snow** .... (901) 328-3534
E-mail: donna_snow@tnwb.uscourts.gov
Education: U Memphis 1994 JD
Career Law Clerk **Lisa Whitman** .... (901) 328-3548
E-mail: lisa_whitman@tnwb.uscourts.gov
Education: Notre Dame 2002 JD
Courtroom Deputy **Debra Hayes** .... (901) 328-3570

Chambers of Bankruptcy Judge George W. Emerson, Jr.
200 Jefferson Avenue, Suite 413, Memphis, TN 38103
Tel: (901) 328-3614

George W. Emerson, Jr.
Bankruptcy Judge

Began Service: July 2006
Term Expires: July 2020

Clerkships: Clerk, United States Bankruptcy Court for the Western District of Tennessee (1983-1985)

Legal Practice: Partner, Stevenson and Emerson

Current Memberships: Memphis Bar Association; Tennessee Bar Association

Staff
Career Law Clerk **Rachel H. Wright** .... (901) 328-3615
E-mail: rachel_wright@tnwb.uscourts.gov
Courtroom Deputy **Jenifer Joiner** .... (901) 328-3573
Judicial Assistant **Jennifer McGaugh** .... (901) 328-3614
E-mail: jennifer_mcgaugh@tnwb.uscourts.gov

Chambers of Bankruptcy Judge Jimmy L. Croom
111 South Highland Avenue, Jackson, TN 38301-6101
Tel: (731) 421-9314

Jimmy L. Croom
Bankruptcy Judge

Staff
Courtroom Deputy **Deborah Pulse** .... (731) 421-9314
Law Clerk **Abby Little** .... (731) 421-9372

United States District Court for the Eastern District of Texas
U.S. Courthouse, 211 West Ferguson Street, Room 106, Tyler, TX 75702
Tel: (903) 590-1000 Tel: (903) 531-9210 (PACER)
Fax: (903) 590-1015
Internet: www.txed.uscourts.gov

Number of Judgeships: 8

Number of Vacancies: 2

Circuit: Fifth

Areas Covered: Counties of Anderson, Angelina, Bowie, Camp, Cass, Cherokee, Collin, Cooke, Delta, Denton, Fannin, Franklin, Grayson, Gregg, Hardin, Harrison, Henderson, Hopkins, Houston, Jasper, Jefferson, Lamar, Liberty, Marion, Morris, Nacogdoches, Newton, Orange, Panola, Polk, Rains, Red River, Rusk, Sabine, San Augustine, Shelby, Smith, Titus, Trinity, Tyler, Upshur, Van Zandt and Wood

Court Staff
Clerk of Court **David O'Toole** .... (903) 590-1000
211 W Ferguson Street, Tyler, TX 75702
Chief Deputy **David Provines** .... (903) 590-1000
E-mail: david_provines@txed.uscourts.gov
Education: Texas A&M
Deputy-in-Charge - Lufkin **David Provines** .... (936) 632-2739
104 N. Third St., Lufkin, TX 75902
E-mail: david_provines@txed.uscourts.gov
Deputy-in-Charge - Marshall **Mel Martin** .... (903) 935-2912
P.O. Box 1499, Marshall, TX 75672-1499
E-mail: mel_martin@txed.uscourts.gov
Deputy-in-Charge - Beaumont **Kyla Dean** .... (409) 654-7000
300 Willow Street, Suite 104, Beaumont, TX 77701
E-mail: kyla_dean@txed.uscourts.gov

United States District Court for the Eastern District of Texas *continued*

Deputy-in-Charge - Sherman **Patricia Manning** .... (903) 892-2921
216 Federal Bldg., 101 E. Pecan St.,
Sherman, TX 75090
E-mail: patricia_manning@txed.uscourts.gov
Deputy-in-Charge - Plano **Patricia Manning** .... (214) 872-4800
7940 Preston Road, Plano, TX 75024
E-mail: patricia_manning@txed.uscourts.gov
Deputy-in-Charge - Texarkana **Mel Martin** .... (903) 794-8561
U.S. Courthouse, 500 State Line Ave.,
Texarkana, TX 75501
P.O. Box 2667, Texarkana, TX 75504
E-mail: mel_martin@txed.uscourts.gov
Chief Probation Officer **Shane Ferguson** .... (903) 590-1330
1700 South Southeast Loop 323, Tyler, TX 75701
Librarian **Christina Minter** .... (409) 654-7028
Jack Brooks Federal Bldg. & U.S. Courthouse, Fax: (409) 654-6232
300 Willow St., Rm. 201, Beaumont, TX 77701
Court Interpreter **Melinda Gonzalez-Hibner** .... (214) 872-4856
7940 Preston Road, Plano, TX 75024
E-mail: melinda_gonzalez-hibner@txed.uscourts.gov

Chambers of Chief Judge Ron Clark
P.O. Box 3682, Beaumont, TX 77704
300 Willow Street, Suite 221, Beaumont, TX 77701
Tel: (409) 654-2800 Fax: (409) 654-6280
E-mail: ron_clark@txed.uscourts.gov

Ron Clark
Chief Judge

Date of Birth: January 5, 1953
Education: Connecticut 1973 BA, 1974 MA; Texas 1979 JD
Began Service: November 22, 2002
Appointed By: President George W. Bush

Staff
Law Clerk **Brian Cannon** .... (409) 654-2800
Began Service: January 2015
Term Expires: August 2016
E-mail: brian_cannon@txed.uscourts.gov
Law Clerk **Alex Cockerill** .... (409) 654-2800
Began Service: August 2015
Term Expires: August 31, 2016
Law Clerk **Valerie Lewis** .... (409) 654-2800
Began Service: August 2014
Term Expires: August 2017
E-mail: valerie_lewis@txed.uscourts.gov
Court Reporter **Christina Bickham** .... (409) 654-2800
Courtroom Deputy Clerk **Faith Ann Laurents** .... (409) 654-2800
Judicial Assistant **Brandy O'Quinn** .... (409) 654-2800

Chambers of District Judge Marcia Ann Cain Crone
P.O. Box 1470, Beaumont, TX 77704
300 Willow Street, Suite 239, Beaumont, TX 77701
Tel: (409) 654-2880 Fax: (409) 654-2888
E-mail: Marcia_Crone@txed.uscourts.gov

Marcia Ann Cain Crone
District Judge

Date of Birth: December 12, 1952
Education: Texas 1973 BA; Houston 1978 JD
Began Service: October 3, 2003
Appointed By: President George W. Bush

Current Memberships: Texas Bar Foundation; The American Inns of Court; The District of Columbia Bar; Federal Judges Association; Jefferson County Bar Association; State Bar of Texas

Chambers of District Judge Marcia Ann Cain Crone *continued*

Staff

Law Clerk **Julie Goodrich** .... (409) 654-2880
Began Service: September 2014
Term Expires: September 2016
E-mail: julie_goodrich@txed.uscourts.gov

Law Clerk **Tanner Franklin** .... (409) 654-2880
Began Service: August 2015
E-mail: tanner_franklin@txed.uscourts.gov

Career Law Clerk **Marianne Laine** .... (409) 654-2880
E-mail: marianne_laine@txed.uscourts.gov
Education: South Texas 2008 JD

Courtroom Deputy/Administrator **Patricia Leger** .... (409) 654-2880
E-mail: patricia_leger@txed.uscourts.gov

Court Reporter **Tonya Jackson** .... (409) 654-2880
E-mail: tonya_jackson@txed.uscourts.gov

Chambers of District Judge Michael H. Schneider

211 West Ferguson Street, Room 100, Tyler, TX 75702
Tel: (903) 590-1091 Fax: (903) 590-1095
E-mail: michael_schneider@txed.uscourts.gov

Michael H. Schneider
District Judge

Date of Birth: January 6, 1943
Education: Austin State BS; Houston 1971 JD; Virginia LLM
Began Service: September 2004
Appointed By: President George W. Bush
Political Affiliation: Republican

Corporate: Attorney, Dresser Industries; Vice President and General Counsel, Bawden Drilling, Inc.; General Solicitor, Union Pacific Railroad Company

Government: Assistant District Attorney, Office of the District Attorney, County of Harris, Texas (1971-1975); Municipal Judge (Part-Time), City of West University Place, Texas (1978-1990)

Judicial: Judge, Texas District Court, 157th Judicial District (1991-1996); Chief Justice, Texas Court of Appeals, First District (1996-2002); Justice, Supreme Court of Texas (2002-2004)

Legal Practice: Of Counsel, McFall & Sartwelle

Current Memberships: American Bar Association; Houston Bar Association; Houston Bar Foundation, Houston Bar Association; State Bar of Texas; Texas Law Foundation

Staff

Law Clerk **Melissa Butler** .... (903) 590-1091
Began Service: August 2015
Term Expires: August 31, 2017
E-mail: melissa_butler@txed.uscourts.gov

Law Clerk **John "Roddy" Pace** .... (903) 590-1091
Began Service: August 2015
Term Expires: August 31, 2017

Chief Staff Attorney **Ray Warner** .... (903) 590-1097
E-mail: ray_warner@txed.uscourts.gov

Courtroom Deputy **Rosa Ferguson** .... (903) 590-1091
E-mail: rosa_ferguson@txed.uscourts.gov

Court Reporter **Shea Sloan** .... (903) 590-1171
E-mail: shea_sloan@txed.uscourts.gov

Chambers of District Judge James Rodney Gilstrap

U.S. Courthouse, 100 East Houston, Room 101, Marshall, TX 75670
Tel: (903) 935-3868 Fax: (903) 935-2295

James Rodney Gilstrap
District Judge

Education: Baylor 1978 BA, 1981 JD
Began Service: December 15, 2011
Appointed By: President Barack Obama

Chambers of District Judge James Rodney Gilstrap *continued*

Staff

Law Clerk **Emily Chen** .... (903) 935-3868
Term Expires: September 30, 2016
E-mail: emily_chen@txed.uscourts.gov

Law Clerk **James Wang** .... (903) 935-3868
Began Service: March 9, 2015
Term Expires: March 31, 2016
E-mail: james_wang@txed.uscourts.gov

Law Clerk **Kelsey Jarzombek** .... (903) 935-3868
Term Expires: August 13, 2016
E-mail: kelsey_jarzombek@txed.uscourts.gov

Courtroom Deputy **Jan Lockhart** .... (903) 935-3868
E-mail: jan_lockhart@txed.uscourts.gov

Official Court Reporter **Shelly Holmes** .... (903) 935-3868
E-mail: shelly_holmes@txed.uscourts.gov

Judicial Assistant **Sandre Goldsby** .... (903) 935-3868
E-mail: sandre_goldsby@txed.uscourts.gov

Chambers of District Judge Amos L. Mazzant III

101 East Pecan Street, Sherman, TX 75090
Tel: (903) 893-7008 Fax: (903) 893-9067
E-mail: amos_mazzant@txed.uscourts.gov

Amos L. Mazzant III
District Judge

Education: Pittsburgh 1987 BA; Baylor 1990 JD
Began Service: December 19, 2014
Appointed By: President Barack Obama

Judicial: Justice, Chambers of Justice Amos Mazzant, Texas Court of Appeals, Fifth District (2004-2009); Magistrate Judge, Chambers of Magistrate Judge Amos L. Mazzant, United States District Court for the Eastern District of Texas (2004-2015)

Legal Practice: Of Counsel, Wolfe, Clark, Henderson, Tidwell & McCoy, L.L.P. (2003-2004)

Staff

Law Clerk **Elizabeth Forrest** .... (903) 893-7008
E-mail: elizabeth_forrest@txed.uscourts.gov

Law Clerk **Hayden Lawson** .... (903) 893-7008
E-mail: hayden_lawson@txed.uscourts.gov

Courtroom Deputy **Debbie McCord** .... (903) 893-7008
E-mail: debbie_mccord@txed.uscourts.gov

Judicial Assistant **Terri Scott** .... (903) 893-7008
E-mail: terri_scott@txed.uscourts.gov

Court Reporter **Jan Mason** .... (903) 893-7008
E-mail: jan_mason@txed.uscourts.gov

Chambers of District Judge Robert William Schroeder III

500 North State Line Avenue, Texarkana, TX 75504
Tel: (903) 794-4067

Robert William Schroeder III
District Judge

Education: Arkansas (Little Rock) 1989 BA; Washington College of Law 1994 JD
Began Service: December 19, 2014
Appointed By: President Barack Obama

Staff

Law Clerk **Boone Baxter** .... (903) 794-4067
E-mail: boone_baxter@txed.uscourts.gov

Law Clerk **Elizabeth Chiaviello** .... (903) 794-4067
E-mail: elizabeth_chiaviello@txed.uscourts.gov

Judicial Assistant **Shedera Combs** .... (903) 794-4067
E-mail: shedera_combs@txed.uscourts.gov

Court Reporter **Brenda Butler** .... (903) 794-4067
E-mail: brenda_butler@txed.uscourts.gov

Chambers of Senior Judge Thad Heartfield

212 Jack Brooks Federal Building & U.S. Courthouse, 300 Willow Street, Beaumont, TX 77701
Tel: (409) 654-2860
E-mail: thad_heartfield@txed.uscourts.gov

Thad Heartfield
Senior Judge

Date of Birth: 1940
Education: St Mary's U (TX) 1965 JD
Began Service: May 1, 1995
Appointed By: President William J. Clinton

Government: Assistant District Attorney, Office of the District Attorney, County of Jefferson, Texas (1965-1966); City Attorney, City of Beaumont, Texas (1969-1973)

Legal Practice: Associate, Weller, Wheelus & Green (1966-1969); Partner, O'Brian, Richards & Heartfield (1973-1977); Partner, Crutchfield, DeCordova, Brocato & Heartfield (1977-1981); Private Practice (1981-1995)

Current Memberships: Texas Bar Foundation; Jefferson County Bar Association; State Bar of Texas

Staff
Career Law Clerk **Mary Margaret Groves** .... (409) 654-2860
Court Reporter **(Vacant)** .... (409) 654-2860
Courtroom Deputy **Jill Veazey** .... (409) 654-2860
E-mail: jill_veazey@txed.uscourts.gov
Secretary/Case Manager **Kristi Wernig** .... (409) 654-2860
E-mail: kristi_wernig@txed.uscourts.gov

Chambers of Senior Judge Richard A. Schell

U.S. District Court, 7940 Preston Road, Suite 111, Plano, TX 75024
Tel: (214) 872-4820 Fax: (214) 872-4828
E-mail: richard_schell@txed.uscourts.gov

Richard A. Schell
Senior Judge

Date of Birth: 1950
Education: Southern Methodist 1972 BA, 1975 JD
Began Service: August 15, 1988
Appointed By: President Ronald Reagan

Current Memberships: State Bar of Texas

Staff
Law Clerk **(Vacant)** .... (214) 872-4820
E-mail: amber_reece@txed.uscourts.gov
Career Law Clerk **Aileen Durrett** .... (214) 872-4820
E-mail: aileen_durrett@txed.uscourts.gov
Education: Texas Tech 1993 JD
Court Reporter **(Vacant)** .... (214) 872-4820
Courtroom Deputy **Bonnie Sanford** .... (214) 872-4820
E-mail: bonnie_sanford@txed.uscourts.gov
Judicial Assistant **Lori Stover** .... (214) 872-4820
E-mail: lori_stover@txed.uscourts.gov
Education: Texas (Dallas) BA

Chambers of Magistrate Judge Caroline M. Craven

U.S. Courthouse, 500 State Line Avenue, Room 401, Box 2090, Texarkana, TX 75501
Tel: (903) 792-6424 Fax: (903) 792-0367
E-mail: caroline_craven@txed.uscourts.gov

Caroline M. Craven
Magistrate Judge

Date of Birth: 1964
Education: Arkansas BA, 1990 JD
Began Service: May 26, 1998
Term Expires: May 2022

Clerkships: Law Clerk David Folsom, United States District Court for the Eastern District of Texas (1995-1998)

Legal Practice: Patton, Haltom, Roberts, McWilliams & Greer, LLP (1990-1995)

Staff
Career Law Clerk **Jennifer Orgeron** .... (903) 792-6424
E-mail: jennifer_orgeron@txed.uscourts.gov
Education: Texas 1999 JD
Courtroom Deputy **Lynn Siebel** .... (903) 792-6424
E-mail: lynn_siebel@txed.uscourts.gov
Judicial Assistant **Nicole Peavy** .... (903) 792-6424
E-mail: nicole_peavy@txed.uscourts.gov

Chambers of Magistrate Judge Don D. Bush

U.S. Courthouse, 7940 Preston Road, Plano, TX 75024
Tel: (214) 872-4840 Fax: (214) 872-4846
E-mail: Don_Bush@txed.uscourts.gov

Don D. Bush
Magistrate Judge

Education: Indiana 1968 BA; Southern Methodist 1976 JD, 1986 LLM
Began Service: February 24, 2003
Term Expires: February 24, 2019

Staff
Career Law Clerk **Kirstine Rogers** .... (214) 872-4843
Began Service: 2007
E-mail: kirstine_rogers@txed.uscourts.gov
Courtroom Deputy **Toya McEwen** .... (214) 872-4842
E-mail: toya_mcewen@txed.uscourts.gov
Judicial Assistant **Lori Munoz** .... (214) 872-4841
E-mail: lori_munoz@txed.uscourts.gov

Chambers of Magistrate Judge Keith Giblin

300 Willow Street, Suite 118, Beaumont, TX 77701
Tel: (409) 654-2845
E-mail: keith_giblin@txed.uscourts.gov

Keith F. Giblin
Magistrate Judge

Began Service: October 1, 2004
Term Expires: October 1, 2020

Staff
Career Law Clerk **Alexandra McNicholas** .... (409) 654-2845
E-mail: alexandra_mcnicholas@txed.uscourts.gov
Education: Houston 2002 JD
Courtroom Deputy **Kyla Dean** .... (409) 654-2845
E-mail: kyla_dean@txed.uscourts.gov
Judicial Assistant **Sherre White** .... (409) 654-2845
E-mail: sherre_white@txed.uscourts.gov

Chambers of Magistrate Judge John D. Love

211 West Ferguson Street, Room 210, Tyler, TX 75702
Tel: (903) 590-1164 Fax: (903) 590-1168
E-mail: john_love@txed.uscourts.gov

John D. Love
Magistrate Judge

Began Service: January 2, 2006
Term Expires: January 2, 2022

Staff
Law Clerk **Jenna Gillingham** . . . . . (903) 590-1162
Began Service: August 2015
Term Expires: August 2016
Courtroom Deputy **Mechele Morris** . . . . . (903) 590-1166
E-mail: mechele_morris@txed.uscourts.gov
Judicial Assistant **Sharon Guthrie** . . . . . (903) 590-1164
E-mail: sharon_guthrie@txed.uscourts.gov

Chambers of Magistrate Judge Zachary J. Hawthorn

300 Willow Street, Suite 234, Beaumont, TX 77701
Tel: (409) 654-2815 Fax: (409) 654-6274

Zachary J. Hawthorn
Magistrate Judge

Began Service: August 2, 2011
Term Expires: 2019

Staff
Law Clerk **Russell Welch** . . . . . (409) 654-2815
Began Service: August 2015
E-mail: russell_welch@txed.uscourts.gov
Career Law Clerk **Molly Moore** . . . . . (409) 654-2815
E-mail: molly_moore@txed.uscourts.gov
Courtroom Deputy **Tonya Piper** . . . . . (409) 654-2815
E-mail: tonya_piper@txed.uscourts.gov
Career Law Clerk and Chambers Administrator
Jennifer Fisher . . . . . (409) 654-2815
E-mail: jennifer_fisher@txed.uscourts.gov

Chambers of Magistrate Judge Roy Payne

100 East Houston, Marshall, TX 75670
Tel: (903) 935-2498 Fax: (903) 938-7819
E-mail: roy_payne@txed.uscourts.gov

Roy S. Payne
Magistrate Judge

Date of Birth: 1952
Education: Virginia 1974 BA; LSU 1977 JD; Harvard 1980 LLM
Began Service: December 28, 2011
Term Expires: December 28, 2019
Political Affiliation: Republican

Current Memberships: The Harry V. Booth - Judge Henry A. Politz American Inn of Court, The American Inns of Court; Bar Association of the Fifth Federal Circuit; Louisiana State Bar Association; Shreveport Bar Association

Staff
Law Clerk **Richard Chen** . . . . . (903) 935-2498
E-mail: richard_chen@txed.uscourts.gov
Law Clerk **Alden Harris** . . . . . (903) 935-2498
E-mail: alden_harris@txed.uscourts.gov
Courtroom Deputy **Becky Andrews** . . . . . (903) 935-2498
E-mail: becky_andrews@txed.uscourts.gov

Chambers of Magistrate Judge K. Nicole Mitchell

211 West Ferguson Street, Room 300, Tyler, TX 75702
Tel: (903) 590-1077 Fax: (903) 590-1081
E-mail: nicole_mitchell@txed.uscourts.gov

Nicole Mitchell
Magistrate Judge

Began Service: August 16, 2013
Term Expires: August 16, 2021

Staff
Career Law Clerk **Terri Good** . . . . . (903) 590-1077
E-mail: terri_good@txed.uscourts.gov
Education: LSU 1995 JD
Law Clerk **Timothy Rawson** . . . . . (903) 590-1077
E-mail: tim_rawson@txed.uscourts.gov
Law Clerk **Steven Gray** . . . . . (903) 590-1077
E-mail: stephen_gray@txed.uscourts.gov
Courtroom Deputy **Lisa Hardwick** . . . . . (903) 590-1077
E-mail: lisa_hardwick@txed.uscourts.gov

Chambers of Magistrate Judge Christine A. Nowak

200 North Travis Street, Sherman, TX 75090
Tel: (903) 893-7667 Fax: (903) 892-2415

Christine A. Nowak
Magistrate Judge

Began Service: 2015

Staff
Law Clerk **Melissa Broadway** . . . . . (903) 893-7667
Law Clerk **Emileigh Hubbard** . . . . . (903) 893-7667
Courtroom Deputy **Keary Conrad** . . . . . (903) 893-7667

United States Bankruptcy Court for the Eastern District of Texas

110 North College, 9th Floor, Tyler, TX 75702
Tel: (903) 590-3200
Tel: (903) 590-3251 (Voice Case Information System VCIS)
Fax: (903) 590-3226
Internet: www.txeb.uscourts.gov

Number of Judgeships: 2

Court Staff
Clerk of the Court **Jeanne B. Henderson** . . . . . (903) 590-3200
E-mail: jeanne_henderson@txeb.uscourts.gov
Education: Louisiana Tech U 1972 BA; North Texas 1977 MEd
Deputy-in-charge (Beaumont Office) **Mona Doyle** . . . . . (409) 654-7064
E-mail: mona_doyle@txeb.uscourts.gov
Deputy-in-charge (Plano Office) **Wanda Harpin** . . . . . (972) 509-1244
E-mail: wanda_harpin@txeb.uscourts.gov
Deputy-in-charge (Tyler Office) **Jeanelle Maland** . . . . . (903) 590-3217
E-mail: jeanelle_maland@txeb.uscourts.gov
Finance Administrator **Cheri Bertrand** . . . . . (903) 590-3208
E-mail: cheri_bertrand@txeb.uscourts.gov
Human Resources Specialist **Kim Dixon** . . . . . (903) 590-3212
E-mail: kim_dixon@txeb.uscourts.gov

Chambers of Chief Bankruptcy Judge Brenda T. Rhoades

660 North Central Expressway, Room 300 A, Plano, TX 75074
Tel: (972) 509-1250 Fax: (972) 509-1253
E-mail: brenda_rhoades@txeb.uscourts.gov

Brenda T. Rhoades
Chief Bankruptcy Judge

Began Service: September 1, 2003
Term Expires: August 2017

Staff

Career Law Clerk **Leslie Masterson** .... (972) 509-1252
E-mail: leslie_masterson@txeb.uscourts.gov
Courtroom Deputy Clerk **Shirley Rasco** .... (972) 509-1246
E-mail: shirley_rasco@txeb.uscourts.gov
Courtroom Deputy Clerk **Sheryl Denham** .... (972) 633-4751
E-mail: sheryl_denham@txeb.uscourts.gov
Judicial Assistant **Marianne Denning** .... (972) 509-1250
E-mail: marianne_denning@txeb.uscourts.gov

Chambers of Bankruptcy Judge Bill Parker

110 North College, 9th Floor, Tyler, TX 75702
Tel: (903) 590-3240

Bill Parker
Bankruptcy Judge

Date of Birth: 1955
Education: Austin State 1977 BA; Texas (Permian Basin) 1980 MA; Arkansas 1984 JD
Began Service: October 30, 1998
Term Expires: October 30, 2026

Staff

Law Clerk **Jane Gerber** .... (903) 590-3242
E-mail: jane_gerber@txeb.uscourts.gov
Courtroom Deputy **Mona Doyle** .... (409) 654-7064
Courtroom Deputy **Chasha Traylor** .... (903) 590-3237
Judicial Assistant **Sandy Johnson** .... (903) 590-3240
E-mail: sandy_johnson@txeb.uscourts.gov

United States District Court for the Northern District of Texas

U.S. Courthouse, 1100 Commerce Street, Room 1452, Dallas, TX 75242
Tel: (214) 753-2200 Tel: (800) 676-6856 (Toll Free PACER)
Fax: (214) 753-2266
Internet: www.txnd.uscourts.gov

Number of Judgeships: 12

Number of Vacancies: 2

Circuit: Fifth

Areas Covered: Counties of Archer, Armstrong, Bailey, Baylor, Borden, Briscoe, Brown, Callahan, Carson, Castro, Childress, Clay, Cochran, Coke, Coleman, Collingsworth, Comanche, Concho, Cottle, Crockett, Crosby, Dallam, Dallas, Dawson, Deaf Smith, Dickens, Donley, Eastland, Ellis, Erath, Fisher, Floyd, Foard, Gaines, Garza, Glasscock, Gray, Hale, Hall, Hansford, Hardeman, Hartley, Haskell, Hemphill, Hockley, Hood, Howard, Hunt, Hutchinson, Irion, Jack, Johnson, Jones, Kaufman, Kent, King, Knox, Lamb, Lipscomb, Lubbock, Lynn, Menard, Mills, Mitchell, Montague, Moore, Motley, Navarro, Nolan, Ochiltree, Oldham, Palo Pinto, Parker, Parmer, Potter, Randall, Reagan, Roberts, Rockwall, Runnels, Schleicher, Scurry, Shackelford, Sherman, Stephens, Sterling, Stonewall, Sutton, Swisher, Tarrant, Taylor, Terry, Throckmorton, Tom Green, Wheeler, Wichita, Wilbarger, Wise, Yoakum and Young

Court Staff

Clerk of Court **Karen Mitchell** .... (214) 753-2201
E-mail: karen_mitchell@txnd.uscourts.gov
Education: Abilene Christian 1986 BA; Baylor 1990 JD
Chief Deputy **James Robert "Jim" Barton** .... (214) 753-2201
E-mail: jim_barton@txnd.uscourts.gov
Education: Michigan State 1978 BS; Michigan 1981 JD
Deputy-in-Charge, Abilene Division **Marsha Elliott** ...... (325) 677-6311
341 Pine St., Rm. 2008, Abilene, TX 79601 Fax: (325) 677-6334
P.O. Box 1218, Abilene, TX 79604
E-mail: marsha_elliott@txnd.uscourts.gov
Deputy-in-Charge, Amarillo Division **Danny Aguilera** .... (806) 468-3800
133 Federal Bldg., 205 E. 5th Ave., Amarillo, TX 79101 Fax: (806) 468-3862
E-mail: danny_aguilera@txnd.uscourts.gov
Deputy-in-Charge, Fort Worth Division **Lynn Tedford** .... (817) 850-6601
310 U.S. Courthouse, 501 W. 10th St., Fort Worth, TX 76102-3673 Fax: (817) 850-6633
E-mail: lynn_tedford@txnd.uscourts.gov
Deputy-in-Charge, Lubbock Division **Erik Paltrow** .... (806) 472-1900
C-221 Mahon Federal Bldg., 1205 Texas Ave., Lubbock, TX 79401-4091 Fax: (806) 472-7639
Deputy-in-Charge, San Angelo Division **(Vacant)** .... (325) 655-4506
202 Federal Bldg., 33 E. Twohig St., San Angelo, TX 76903-6451 Fax: (325) 658-6826
Deputy-in-Charge, Wichita Falls Division **Teena Timmons** .... (940) 767-1902
1000 Lamar St., Rm. 203, Wichita Falls, TX 76301 Fax: (940) 767-2526
P.O. Box 1234, Wichita Falls, TX 76307
E-mail: teena_mcneely@txnd.uscourts.gov
Chief U.S. Probation and Pretrial Officer **Mitsi Westendorff** .... (214) 753-2506
Fax: (214) 753-2570
Financial Services Manager **Richard Holt** .... (214) 753-2205
E-mail: richard_holt@txnd.uscourts.gov
Human Resources Manager **Loretta Robinson** .... (214) 753-2242
E-mail: loretta_robinson@txnd.uscourts.gov
Systems Manager **Terry Murphy** .... (214) 753-2223
E-mail: terry_murphy@txnd.uscourts.gov

Chambers of Chief Judge Jorge A. Solis

U.S. Courthouse, 1100 Commerce Street, Room 1654, Dallas, TX 75242
Tel: (214) 753-2342 Fax: (214) 753-2352

Jorge A. Solis
Chief Judge

Date of Birth: 1951
Education: McMurry 1973 BA; Texas 1976 JD
Began Service: 1991
Appointed By: President George H.W. Bush
Political Affiliation: Republican

Staff

Law Clerk **Adam Simon** .... (214) 753-2343
Began Service: August 8, 2015
Term Expires: August 2016
E-mail: adam_simon@txnd.uscourts.gov
Law Clerk **Charles Doraneo** .... (214) 753-2344
Began Service: August 2015
Term Expires: August 2016
E-mail: charles_doraneo@txnd.uscourts.gov
Career Law Clerk **Jennifer Helms** .... (214) 753-2345
E-mail: jennifer_helms@txnd.uscourts.gov
Education: Southern Methodist 1998 JD
Career Law Clerk **Robert Wickham** .... (214) 753-2351
E-mail: robert_wickham@txnd.uscourts.gov
Courtroom Deputy **Kevin K. Frye** .... (214) 753-2346
E-mail: kevin_frye@txnd.uscourts.gov
Court Reporter **Shawn McRoberts** .... (214) 753-2349
E-mail: shawn_mcroberts@txnd.uscourts.gov

Chambers of District Judge Sidney A. Fitzwater

1520 U.S. Courthouse, 1100 Commerce Street, Dallas, TX 75242
Tel: (214) 753-2333
E-mail: judge_fitzwater@txnd.uscourts.gov

Sidney A. Fitzwater
District Judge

Date of Birth: 1953
Education: Baylor 1975 BA, 1976 JD
Began Service: 1986
Appointed By: President Ronald Reagan
Political Affiliation: Republican

Current Memberships: Texas Bar Foundation; The American Law Institute; Dallas Bar Association; State Bar of Texas

Staff
Law Clerk **Allison M. Small** . . . . (214) 753-2333
E-mail: allison_small@txnd.uscourts.gov
Education: Vanderbilt 2006 JD
Court Coordinator **Pat Esquivel** . . . . (214) 753-2336
E-mail: pat_esquivel@txnd.uscourts.gov
Court Reporter **Pam Wilson** . . . . (214) 662-1557
E-mail: pam_wilson@txnd.uscourts.gov
Judicial Secretary **Debra Eubank** . . . . (214) 753-2333

Chambers of District Judge Mary Lou Robinson

205 East 5th Avenue, Room F13248, Amarillo, TX 79101
Tel: (806) 468-3822
E-mail: judge_robinson@txnd.uscourts.gov

Mary Lou Robinson
District Judge

Date of Birth: 1926
Education: Texas 1948 BA, 1950 LLB
Began Service: 1979
Appointed By: President Jimmy Carter

Judicial: Judge, Potter County Court (1955-1959); Judge, Texas District Court, 108th District, Potter County (1960-1973); Justice, Texas Court of Civil Appeals, Seventh Supreme Judicial District (1973-1977); Chief Justice, Texas Court of Civil Appeals, Seventh Supreme Judicial District (1977-1979)

Legal Practice: Partner, Robinson & Robinson (1950-1955)

Current Memberships: Amarillo Bar Association; Federal Judges Association; State Bar of Texas

Staff
Law Clerk **Monica Hart** . . . . (806) 468-3822
Began Service: August 2015
Term Expires: August 2016
E-mail: phil_young@txnd.uscourts.gov
Career Law Clerk **Charles A. Freas** . . . . (806) 468-3822
Education: Texas Tech 1988 JD
Judicial Paralegal **Melba Fenwick** . . . . (806) 468-3822
E-mail: melba_fenwick@txnd.uscourts.gov
Courtroom Deputy **Delynda Smith** . . . . (806) 468-3831
E-mail: delynda_smith@txnd.uscourts.gov
Official Court Reporter **Stacy Mayes Morrison** . . . . (806) 672-6219
E-mail: stacy_morrison@txnd.uscourts.gov

Chambers of District Judge John H. McBryde

401 U.S. Courthouse, 501 West Tenth Street, Fort Worth, TX 76102
Tel: (817) 850-6650 Fax: (817) 850-6660
E-mail: john_mcbryde@txnd.uscourts.gov

John H. McBryde
District Judge

Date of Birth: 1931
Education: Texas Christian 1953 BS; Texas 1956 LLB
Began Service: 1990
Appointed By: President George H.W. Bush

Legal Practice: Associate then Partner, Cantney & Hanger (1956-1969); Partner, McBryde & Bennett (1969-1990)

Current Memberships: American Bar Foundation; Texas Bar Foundation; State Bar of Texas

Staff
Law Clerk **Virginia Burke** . . . . (817) 850-6652
Began Service: August 2015
Term Expires: August 2016
E-mail: virginia_burke@txnd.uscourts.gov
Career Law Clerk **Susanna Johnson** . . . . (817) 850-6653
E-mail: susanna_johnson@txnd.uscourts.gov
Education: Southern Methodist 1985 JD
Secretary **Diane Terry** . . . . (817) 850-6650
E-mail: diane_terry@txnd.uscourts.gov

Chambers of District Judge Sam A. Lindsay

U.S. Courthouse, 1100 Commerce Street, Room 1544,
Dallas, TX 75242-1003
Tel: (214) 753-2365
E-mail: judge_lindsay@txnd.uscourts.gov

Sam A. Lindsay
District Judge

Date of Birth: 1951
Education: St Mary's U (TX) 1974; Texas 1977 JD
Began Service: September 1, 1998
Appointed By: President William J. Clinton

Government: Attorney, City of Dallas, Texas (1979-1998)

Legal Practice: Staff Attorney, Texas Aeronautics Commission (1977-1978)

Current Memberships: The Patrick E. Higginbotham American Inn of Court, The American Inns of Court; Center for American and International Law; Dallas Bar Association; J. L. Turner Legal Association

Staff
Law Clerk [Even Numbered Cases] **Jasmine Tobias** . . . . . (214) 753-2367
Began Service: 2015
Term Expires: August 2016
E-mail: jasmine_tobias@txnd.uscourts.gov
Career Law Clerk [Odd Numbered Cases]
Susan Nassar . . . . (214) 753-2365
E-mail: susan_nassar@txnd.uscourts.gov
Education: Houston 1997 BS, 2000 JD
Courtroom Deputy **Tannica Stewart** . . . . (214) 753-2368
E-mail: tannica_stewart@txnd.uscourts.gov
Court Reporter **Charyse Crawford** . . . . (214) 753-2373
E-mail: charyse_crawford@txnd.uscourts.gov
Judicial Assistant **Michelle L. Goode** . . . . (214) 753-2365
E-mail: michelle_goode@txnd.uscourts.gov

Chambers of District Judge Barbara M. G. Lynn

U.S. Courthouse, 1100 Commerce Street, Room 1572, Dallas, TX 75242
Tel: (214) 753-2420
E-mail: judge_lynn@txnd.uscourts.gov

Barbara M. G. Lynn
District Judge

Date of Birth: 1952
Education: Virginia 1973 BA; Southern Methodist 1976 JD
Began Service: February 14, 2000
Appointed By: President William J. Clinton

Legal Practice: Attorney, Carrington, Coleman, Sloman & Blumenthal, L.L.P. (1976-1999)

Current Memberships: Judicial Division, American Bar Association; Section on Litigation, American Bar Association; American College of Trial Lawyers; The Patrick E. Higginbotham American Inn of Court, The American Inns of Court; Dallas Chapter, International Women's Forum

Staff

Law Clerk **Rebecca Tustin Rutherford** .... (214) 753-2418
Began Service: August 2015
E-mail: brian_young@txnd.uscourts.gov
Education: Southern Methodist 1998 JD

Law Clerk **Jillian Stonecipher** .... (214) 753-2419
Began Service: August 2015
Term Expires: August 2016
E-mail: jillian_stonecipher@txnd.uscourts.gov

Courtroom Deputy **Lori Greco** .... (214) 753-2421
E-mail: lori_greco@txnd.uscourts.gov
Education: Texas (Arlington) 1996 BA

Court Reporter **Keith Johnson** .... (214) 753-2325

Judicial Assistant **Judy Flowers** .... (214) 753-2420
E-mail: judy_flowers@txnd.uscourts.gov

Chambers of District Judge David C. Godbey

U.S. Courthouse, 1100 Commerce Street, 13th Floor, Room 1358, Dallas, TX 75242
Tel: (214) 753-2700 Fax: (214) 753-2707
E-mail: judge_godbey@txnd.uscourts.gov

David C. Godbey
District Judge

Date of Birth: September 17, 1957
Education: Southern Methodist 1978 BSEE; Harvard 1982 JD
Began Service: August 7, 2002
Appointed By: President George W. Bush

Clerkships: Law Clerk The Honorable Irving L. Gorlberg, United States Court of Appeals for the Fifth Circuit (1982-1983)

Judicial: Judge, 160th District Court, State of Texas (1994-2002)

Legal Practice: Associate and Partner, Hughes & Luce, LLP (1983-1994)

Staff

Courtroom Deputy **Carla Moore** .... (214) 753-2706
E-mail: carla_moore@txnd.uscourts.gov
Education: North Texas 1993 BA

Court Reporter **Linda Langford** .... (214) 748-8068
E-mail: linda_langford@txnd.uscourts.gov

Judicial Administrator **Donna Hocker-Beyer** .... (214) 753-2700
E-mail: donna_hocker@txnd.uscourts.gov

Chambers of District Judge Ed Kinkeade

1100 Commerce Street, Room 1625, Dallas, TX 75242-1103
Tel: (214) 753-2720 Fax: (214) 753-2727
E-mail: Judge_Kinkeade@txnd.uscourts.gov

Ed Kinkeade
District Judge

Date of Birth: October 22, 1951
Education: Baylor 1973 BA, 1974 JD; Virginia 1998 LLM
Began Service: November 18, 2002
Appointed By: President George W. Bush
Political Affiliation: Republican

Clerkships: Law Clerk, Brewer & Price Law Firm (1974-1975)

Judicial: Associate Judge, Texas Municipal Court, City of Irving, Texas (1976-1980); Judge, Dallas County Criminal Court No. 10 (1981); Judge, Texas District Court, 194th Judicial District (1981-1988); Justice, Texas Court of Appeals, Fifth District (1988-2002)

Legal Practice: Partner, Power & Kinkeade (1975-1980)

Staff

Courtroom Deputy **Ronnie Jacobson** .... (214) 753-2166
E-mail: ronnie_jacobson@txnd.uscourts.gov

Court Reporter **Todd Anderson** .... (214) 753-2170
E-mail: todd_anderson@txnd.uscourts.gov

Judicial Assistant **Cheri Leatherwood** .... (214) 753-2720
E-mail: Cheri_Leatherwood@txnd.uscourts.gov

Chambers of District Judge Jane J. Boyle

1100 Commerce Street, Room 1520, Dallas, TX 75242
Tel: (214) 753-2740 Fax: (214) 753-2744
E-mail: boyle_clerk@txnd.uscourts.gov

Jane J. Boyle
District Judge

Date of Birth: 1954
Education: Texas 1977 BS; Southern Methodist 1981 JD
Began Service: June 2004
Appointed By: President George W. Bush

Government: Chief Felony Prosecutor, Major Commercial Fraud Unit, Specialized Crime Division, Office of the District Attorney, County of Dallas, Texas (1985-1987); Assistant U.S. Attorney, Criminal Division, Texas - Northern District, Executive Office for United States Attorneys, United States Department of Justice (1987-1989); Assistant U.S. Attorney, Civil Division, Texas - Northern District, Executive Office for United States Attorneys, United States Department of Justice (1989-1990); U.S. Attorney, Texas - Northern District, Executive Office for United States Attorneys, United States Department of Justice, George W. Bush Administration (2002-2004)

Current Memberships: Dallas Bar Association

Staff

Law Clerk **Peter Baumhart** .... (214) 753-2741
Began Service: August 2015
Term Expires: August 2016
E-mail: peter_baumhart@txnd.uscourts.gov

Law Clerk **Samuel Bragg** .... (214) 753-2743
Began Service: September 2015
Term Expires: September 2016
E-mail: samuel_bragg@txnd.uscourts.gov

Law Clerk **Matthew Dolan** .... (214) 753-2742
Began Service: September 2015
Term Expires: September 2016
E-mail: matthew_dolan@txnd.uscourts.gov

Court Reporter **Shawnie Archuleta** .... (214) 753-2747
E-mail: shawnie_archuleta@txnd.uscourts.gov

Courtroom Administrator **Rod Reynolds** .... (214) 753-2740 ext. 0
E-mail: rod_reynolds@txnd.uscourts.gov

Chambers of District Judge Reed Charles O'Connor

501 West Tenth Street, Fort Worth, TX 76102
Tel: (817) 850-6788 Fax: (214) 753-2657
E-mail: judge_o'connor@txnd.uscourts.gov

Reed Charles O'Connor
District Judge

Education: South Texas 1989 JD
Began Service: November 2007
Appointed By: President George W. Bush

Government: Assistant United States Attorney, Executive Office for United States Attorneys, United States Department of Justice; Counsel, Committee on the Judiciary, United States Senate (2003); Counsel, Subcommittee on Immigration, Border Security and Citizenship, Committee on the Judiciary, United States Senate (2005-2006)

Legal Practice: Civil Litigator, Private Practice

Staff
Court Reporter **Denver B. Roden** .... (817) 850-6788
E-mail: denver_roden@txnd.uscourts.gov
Judicial Assistant **Tyler Crowley** .... (817) 850-6788
E-mail: tyler_crowley@txnd.uscourts.gov

Chambers of Senior Judge A. Joe Fish

U.S. Courthouse, 1100 Commerce Street, Room 1528, Dallas, TX 75242
Tel: (214) 753-2310 Fax: (214) 753-2317

A. Joe Fish
Senior Judge

Date of Birth: 1942
Education: Yale 1965 BA, 1968 LLB
Began Service: March 11, 1983
Appointed By: President Ronald Reagan
Political Affiliation: Republican

Current Memberships: American Bar Association; Dallas Bar Association; State Bar of Texas

Staff
Law Clerk **Scott K. Hvidt** .... (214) 753-2310
Began Service: May 2015
Term Expires: May 2016
Career Law Clerk **Cynthia Daley** .... (214) 753-2310
E-mail: cynthia_daley@txnd.uscourts.gov
Education: Southern Methodist 1996 JD
Judicial Assistant [Civil cases only] **Eleanore Piwoni** .... (214) 753-2310
E-mail: eleanore_piwoni@txnd.uscourts.gov

Chambers of Senior Judge Terry Means

U.S. Courthouse, 501 West Tenth Street, Room 502,
Fort Worth, TX 76102
Tel: (817) 850-6670 Fax: (817) 850-6677
E-mail: terry_means@txnd.uscourts.gov

Terry R. Means
Senior Judge

Date of Birth: 1948
Education: Southern Methodist 1971 BA, 1974 JD
Began Service: November 5, 1991
Appointed By: President George H.W. Bush
Political Affiliation: Republican

Current Memberships: American Bar Association; The Eldon B. McMahon American Inn of Court, The American Inns of Court; State Bar of Texas; Tarrant County Bar Association; Waco-McLennan County Bar Association

Chambers of Senior Judge Terry Means *continued*

Staff
Law Clerk **Amber Henderson** .... (817) 850-6670
Began Service: August 2015
Term Expires: August 21, 2016
E-mail: amber_henderson@txnd.uscourts.gov
Career Law Clerk **Cheryl Raper** .... (817) 850-6670
E-mail: cheryl_raper@txnd.uscourts.gov
Education: Southern Methodist 1990 JD
Court Reporter **Ana Warren** .... (817) 850-6681
E-mail: ana_warren@txnd.uscourts.gov
Law Clerk **Michael Foley** .... (817) 850-6670
Began Service: August 2015
Term Expires: August 21, 2018

Chambers of Senior Judge Sam R. Cummings

C-210 Mahon Federal Building, 1205 Texas Avenue, Lubbock, TX 79401
Tel: (806) 472-1922
E-mail: judge_cummings@txnd.uscourts.gov

Sam R. Cummings
Senior Judge

Date of Birth: 1944
Education: Texas Tech 1967 BBA; Baylor 1970 JD
Began Service: December 11, 1987
Appointed By: President Ronald Reagan

Current Memberships: Texas Bar Foundation; State Bar of Texas

Staff
Law Clerk **Andrew Robertson** .... (806) 472-1922
Term Expires: August 11, 2017
E-mail: andrew_robertson@txnd.uscourts.gov
Career Law Clerk **Boyd L. Clark** .... (806) 472-1922
E-mail: boyd_clark@txnd.uscourts.gov
Education: Texas Tech 2003 JD
Courtroom Deputy **Criss Flock** .... (806) 472-1925
E-mail: criss_flock@txnd.uscourts.gov
Judicial Assistant **Delva Hernandez** .... (806) 472-1922
E-mail: delva_hernandez@txnd.uscourts.gov

Chambers of Magistrate Judge Clinton E. Averitte

Federal Building, 205 East Fifth Street, Room 326,
Amarillo, TX 79101-1524
P.O. Box F-13246, Amarillo, TX 79101
Tel: (806) 468-3832

Clinton E. Averitte
Magistrate Judge

Date of Birth: 1948
Education: Texas 1971 BS; Southern Methodist 1974 JD
Began Service: 1987
Term Expires: 2019

Government: Assistant Attorney General, Office of the Attorney General, State of Texas (1974-1977); Assistant District Attorney and Chief, Office of the District Attorney, Business Crimes Division, State of Texas (1979-1980); Assistant United States Attorney, Northern District of Texas, United States Department of Justice (1980-1987)

Legal Practice: Partner, Hiersche, Martens & Averitte (1977-1978)

Current Memberships: Texas Bar Foundation; Amarillo Bar Association; Federal Magistrate Judges Association

Staff
Career Law Clerk **Amanda Mayfield** .... (806) 468-3832
E-mail: amanda_mayfield@txnd.uscourts.gov
Education: Baylor 1989 BA; Texas Tech 1993 JD
Career Law Clerk (part-time) **William Conine** .... (806) 468-3832
Courtroom Deputy **Elodia Brito** .... (806) 468-3816
Judicial Assistant **(Vacant)** .... (806) 468-3832

Chambers of Magistrate Judge Paul Stickney
1549 U.S. Courthouse, 1100 Commerce Street, Dallas, TX 75242
Tel: (214) 753-2409 Fax: (214) 753-2415
E-mail: judge_stickney@txnd.uscourts.gov

Paul Stickney
Magistrate Judge

Date of Birth: 1953
Education: South Dakota 1981 JD
Began Service: 1998
Term Expires: March 2, 2022

Government: First Assistant Federal Public Defender, United States District Court for the Northern District of Texas (1990-1998)

Legal Practice: Breit & Stickney Law Office (1981-1990)

Military Service: United States Air Force (1973-1975)

Current Memberships: Dallas Bar Association; Federal Bar Association; State Bar of Texas

Staff
Law Clerk **Marie Kim** .... (214) 753-2409
E-mail: marie_kim@txnd.uscourts.gov
Career Law Clerk **(Vacant)** .... (214) 753-2412
E-mail: rebecca_rutherford@txnd.uscourts.gov
Courtroom Deputy **Lavenia Price** .... (214) 753-2168
E-mail: lavenia_price@txnd.uscourts.gov

Chambers of Magistrate Judge Nancy M. Koenig
George H. Mahon Federal Building & U.S. Courthouse, 1205 Texas Avenue, Lubbock, TX 79401
Tel: (806) 472-1933 Fax: (806) 472-1963
E-mail: Judge_Koenig@txnd.uscourts.gov

Nancy M. Koenig
Magistrate Judge

Education: Texas 1972 BA, 1975 MA; Texas Tech 1982 JD
Began Service: December 28, 1998
Term Expires: December 28, 2022

Clerkships: Law Clerk The Honorable Halbert O. Woodward, United States District Court for the Northern District of Texas (1982-1984)

Government: Assistant United States Attorney, Northern District of Texas, United States Attorney's Office, United States Department of Justice (1984-1998)

Current Memberships: Texas Bar Foundation; American Bar Association; Lubbock County Bar Association; Lubbock County Women Lawyers Association

Staff
Law Clerk **Lauren McDivitt** .... (806) 472-1934
Began Service: August 2014
Term Expires: August 2016
E-mail: lauren_mcdivitt@txnd.uscourts.gov
Career Law Clerk **Ann Howey** .... (806) 472-1940
E-mail: ann_howey@txnd.uscourts.gov
Education: Texas Tech 2001 JD
Courtroom Deputy **Lana Waits** .... (806) 472-1914
E-mail: lana_waits@txnd.uscourts.gov

Chambers of Magistrate Judge Irma Carrillo Ramirez
U.S. Courthouse, 1100 Commerce Street, Room 1567, Dallas, TX 75242
Tel: (214) 753-2393 Fax: (214) 753-2397

Irma Carrillo Ramirez
Magistrate Judge

Education: West Texas State 1986 BA; Southern Methodist 1991 JD
Began Service: September 9, 2002
Term Expires: September 8, 2018

Government: Assistant U.S. Attorney, Northern District of Texas, United States Department of Justice (1995-2002)

Legal Practice: Associate, Locke Purnell Rain Harrell (1991-1995)

Current Memberships: Dallas Bar Association; Dallas Bar Foundation, Dallas Bar Association; Federal Magistrate Judges Association; State Bar of Texas

Staff
Law Clerk **Deanna Caldwell** .... (214) 753-2396
Began Service: August 2014
Term Expires: August 2016
E-mail: deanna_caldwell@txnd.uscourts.gov
Law Clerk **Cathy Richardson** .... (214) 753-2394
E-mail: cathy_richardson@txnd.uscourts.gov
Courtroom Deputy **Marie Castaneda** .... (214) 753-2167
E-mail: marie_castaneda@txnd.uscourts.gov

Chambers of Magistrate Judge Jeffrey L. Cureton
501 West Tenth Street, Room 520, Fort Worth, TX 76102
Tel: (817) 850-6690
E-mail: judge_cureton@txnd.uscourts.gov

Jeffrey L. Cureton
Magistrate Judge

Education: Baylor 1990 BA, 1993 JD
Began Service: 2010

Staff
Career Law Clerk **Kristi N. Verna** .... (817) 850-6690
E-mail: kristi_verna@txnd.uscourts.gov
Education: Texas A&M 1993 BBA; Washburn 1996 JD
Courtroom Deputy **Julie Harwell** .... (817) 850-6697
E-mail: julie_harwell@txnd.uscourts.gov
Judicial Assistant **Margarita Koye** .... (817) 850-6689
E-mail: margarita_koye@txnd.uscourts.gov

Chambers of Magistrate Judge Renee H. Toliver
1100 Commerce Street, Room 1407, Dallas, TX 75242
Tel: (214) 753-2385

Renee H. Toliver
Magistrate Judge

Staff
Courtroom Deputy **Jane Amerson** .... (214) 753-2169
E-mail: jane_amerson@txnd.uscourts.gov

Chambers of Magistrate Judge E. Scott Frost
341 Pine Street, Room 2313, Abilene, TX 79601
Tel: (325) 677-6311

E. Scott Frost
Magistrate Judge

Chambers of Magistrate Judge David L. Horan
1100 Commerce Street, Room 1549, Dallas, TX 75242
Tel: (214) 753-2400

David L. Horan
Magistrate Judge

Education: Notre Dame 1996 BA; Yale 2000 JD

United States Bankruptcy Court for the Northern District of Texas
1100 Commerce Street, Room 1254, Dallas, TX 75242-1496
Tel: (214) 753-2000 Tel: (800) 676-6856 (Toll Free PACER)
Tel: (866) 222-8029 (Voice Case Information System VCIS)
Fax: (214) 753-2038
Internet: www.txnb.uscourts.gov

Number of Judgeships: 6

Court Staff
Clerk of Court **Tawana C. Marshall** . . . . (214) 753-2000
E-mail: tawana_marshall@txnb.uscourts.gov
Executive Assistant **Pat Blunt** . . . . (214) 753-2000
Chief Deputy Clerk **Robert Colwell** . . . . (214) 753-2000
E-mail: robert_colwell@txnb.uscourts.gov
Education: Texas Christian 1991 BS; Southern Methodist 1994 JD
Court Technology, Facilities and Procurement
Tim Christnagel . . . . (214) 753-2020
E-mail: tim_christnagel@txnb.uscourts.gov
Financial Administrator **Tonya Castillo** . . . . (214) 753-2007
E-mail: mark_burdine@txnb.uscourts.gov
Supervisor - Amarillo **Tina Stevens** . . . . (806) 324-2302
U.S. Courthouse, 306 Federal Building, 1205 Texas Avenue, Lubbock, TX 79401 Fax: (806) 324-2304
E-mail: tina_stevens@txnb.uscourts.gov
Divisional Manager - Dallas **(Vacant)** . . . . (214) 753-2011
1100 Commerce Street, Room 1254, Dallas, TX 75242 Fax: (214) 753-2038
Divisional Manager - Fort Worth **Lisa Holmes** . . . . (817) 333-6000
U.S. Courthouse, 501 W. Tenth St., Fort Worth, TX 76102-3643 Fax: (817) 333-6001
E-mail: lisa_holmes@txnb.uscourts.gov
Divisional Manager - Lubbock **Tina Stevens** . . . . (806) 472-5000
U.S. Courthouse, 306 Federal Building, 1205 Texas Avenue, Lubbock, TX 79401-4002 Fax: (806) 472-5004
E-mail: tina_stevens@txnb.uscourts.gov

Chambers of Chief Bankruptcy Judge Barbara J. Houser
1254 U.S. Courthouse, 1100 Commerce Street, Dallas, TX 75242-1496
Tel: (214) 753-2055

Barbara J. Houser
Chief Bankruptcy Judge

Date of Birth: 1954
Education: Nebraska 1975 BA; Southern Methodist 1978 LLB
Began Service: January 20, 2000
Term Expires: January 20, 2028

Legal Practice: Locke, Purnell, Boren, Laney & Neely (1978-1988); Shareholder, Sheinfeld, Maley & Kay, P.C. (1988-2000)

Current Memberships: American Bar Foundation; Texas Bar Foundation; American Bar Association; American College of Bankruptcy; National Bankruptcy Conference; State Bar of Texas

Staff
Law Clerk **Matthew Brooks** . . . . (214) 753-2056
Began Service: August 2015
Term Expires: August 2016
Career Law Clerk **Michaela Crocker** . . . . (214) 753-2055
E-mail: michaela_crocker@txnb.uscourts.gov

Chambers of Bankruptcy Judge Robert L. Jones
1205 Texas Avenue, Room 312, Lubbock, TX 79401
Tel: (806) 472-5020 Fax: (806) 472-5025

Robert L. Jones
Bankruptcy Judge

Date of Birth: 1955
Education: Texas Tech 1978 BA, 1982 JD
Began Service: April 2000
Term Expires: April 4, 2028

Legal Practice: Jackson, Walker, Winstead, Cantwell & Miller (1982-1985); Crenshaw, Dupree & Milam, LLP (1985-2000)

Staff
Law Clerk **John Eisler** . . . . (806) 472-5021
Began Service: August 2015
Term Expires: August 2016
E-mail: john_eisler@txnb.uscourts.gov
Judicial Assistant **Shelby Wimberley** . . . . (806) 472-5020
E-mail: shelby_wimberley@txnb.uscourts.gov

Chambers of Bankruptcy Judge Harlin D. Hale
1100 Commerce Street, Room 1254, Dallas, TX 75242-1496
Tel: (214) 753-2016 Fax: (214) 753-2036

Harlin DeWayne "Cooter" Hale
Bankruptcy Judge

Date of Birth: March 19, 1957
Education: LSU 1979 BS, 1982 JD
Began Service: November 1, 2002
Term Expires: October 31, 2016

Clerkships: Law Clerk, Associate Justice James L. Dennis, Supreme Court of Louisiana (1982-1983)

Current Memberships: American Bar Association; The Honorable John C. Ford American Inn of Court, The American Inns of Court; Dallas Bankruptcy Bar Association; Dallas Bar Association; Federal Bar Association; Louisiana State Bar Association; National Conference of Bankruptcy Judges; State Bar of Texas

Staff
Law Clerk **Jordan Lewis** . . . . (214) 753-2024
Fax: (214) 753-2036
Career Law Clerk **Stephen Manz** . . . . (214) 753-2017
E-mail: stephen_manz@txnb.uscourts.gov
Courtroom Deputy **Jenni Bergreen** . . . . (214) 753-2060
E-mail: hdh_settings@txnb.uscourts.gov Fax: (214) 753-2072
Electronic Court Recorder Operator
Erica Adams-Williams . . . . (214) 753-2088

Chambers of Bankruptcy Judge Russell F. Nelms
501 West Tenth Street, Fort Worth, TX 76102
Tel: (817) 333-6025 Fax: (817) 333-6029
E-mail: Judge_Russell_Nelms@txnb.uscourts.gov

Russell F. Nelms
Bankruptcy Judge

Education: Texas Tech 1975 BA, 1978 JD
Began Service: November 22, 2004
Term Expires: 2018

Current Memberships: National Conference of Bankruptcy Judges; Tarrant County Bar Association

Staff
Career Law Clerk **Laurie Rea** . . . . (817) 333-6028
E-mail: laurie_rea@txnb.uscourts.gov
Education: Houston 2006 JD
Judicial Assistant **Barbara Groves** . . . . (817) 333-6025
E-mail: barbara_groves@txnb.uscourts.gov

FEDERAL COURTS—UNITED STATES DISTRICT COURTS

Chambers of Bankruptcy Judge Stacey G. C. Jernigan
1100 Commerce Street, Room 1254, Dallas, TX 75242
Tel: (214) 753-2040 Fax: (214) 753-2149
E-mail: sgj_settings@txnb.uscourts.gov

Stacey G. C. Jernigan
Bankruptcy Judge

Education: Southern Methodist 1986 BBA; Texas 1989 JD
Began Service: May 2006
Term Expires: May 2020

Legal Practice: Associate, Haynes and Boone, LLP (1989-1996); Partner, Haynes and Boone, LLP (1997-2006)

Staff
E-mail: sgj_settings@txnb.uscourts.gov

Career Law Clerk **Laura Smith** ....(214) 753-2042
Courtroom Deputy **Traci Davis** ....(214) 753-2046
Judicial Assistant **Anna Saucier** ....(214) 753-2040

Chambers of Bankruptcy Judge Mark X. Mullin
501 West 10th Street, Fort Worth, TX 76102
Tel: (817) 333-6016

Mark X. Mullin
Bankruptcy Judge

Began Service: 2015

United States District Court for the Southern District of Texas
Bob Casey U.S. Courthouse, 515 Rusk Street, Houston, TX 77002
P.O. Box 61010, Houston, TX 77208
Tel: (713) 250-5500 Tel: (800) 676-6856 (Toll Free PACER)
Internet: www.txs.uscourts.gov

Number of Judgeships: 19

Number of Vacancies: 2

Circuit: Fifth

Areas Covered: Counties of Aransas, Austin, Bee, Brazoria, Brazos, Brooks, Calhoun, Cameron, Chambers, Colorado, DeWitt, Duval, Fayette, Fort Bend, Galveston, Goliad, Grimes, Harris, Hidalgo, Jackson, Jim Hogg, Jim Wells, Kenedy, Kleberg, La Salle, Lavaca, Live Oak, Madison, Matagorda, McMullen, Montgomery, Nueces, Refugio, San Jacinto, San Patricio, Starr, Victoria, Walker, Waller, Webb, Wharton, Willacy and Zapata

Court Staff
Clerk of Court **David J. Bradley** ....(713) 250-5500
E-mail: david_bradley@txs.uscourts.gov
Chief Deputy Clerk **Nathan Ochsner** ....(713) 250-5500
E-mail: nathan_ochsner@txs.uscourts.gov
Deputy-in-Charge - Brownsville **Rosalinda D'Venturi** ....(956) 548-2500
600 East Harrison Street, 101,
Brownsville, TX 78520
Deputy-in-Charge - Galveston **Cathy Carnew** ....(409) 766-3530
601 Rosenberg, Room 411, Galveston, TX 77550
Deputy-in-Charge - Laredo **Rosie Rodriguez** ....(956) 723-3542
1300 Victoria Street, Laredo, TX 78040
Deputy-in-Charge - Houston **Darlene Hansen** ....(713) 250-5500
515 Rusk Avenue, Houston, TX 77002
E-mail: darlene_hansen@txs.uscourts.gov
Deputy-in-Charge - McAllen **Velma Barrera** ....(956) 618-7788
601 Rosenberg, Galveston, TX 77550
Deputy-in-Charge - Victoria **Lana Tesch** ....(361) 788-5009
312 South Main, 406, Victoria, TX 77901
Deputy-in-Charge - Corpus Christi **Marianne Serpa** .....(361) 888-3142
1133 North Shoreline Boulevard,
Corpus Christi, TX 78401
E-mail: marianne_serpa@txs.uscourts.gov

United States District Court for the Southern District of Texas *continued*

Chief U.S. Probation Officer **Luis Lopez** ....(713) 250-5266
Suite 2301

Chambers of Chief Judge Ricardo H. Hinojosa
1701 West Business Highway 83, Suite 1100, McAllen, TX 78501
P.O. Box 5007, McAllen, TX 78502-5007
Tel: (956) 618-8100 Fax: (956) 618-8116
E-mail: ricardo_hinojosa@txs.uscourts.gov

Ricardo H. Hinojosa
Chief Judge

Date of Birth: 1950
Education: Texas 1972 BA; Harvard 1975 JD
Began Service: May 5, 1983
Appointed By: President Ronald Reagan

Clerkships: Law Clerk The Honorable Thomas M. Reavley, Texas Supreme Court (1975-1976)

Government: Commissioner, United States Sentencing Commission

Legal Practice: Associate and Partner, Ewers & Toothaker (1976-1983)

Current Memberships: The American Law Institute

Staff
Law Clerk **Jaime Lopez** ....(956) 618-8100
Began Service: 2014
E-mail: jaime_lopez@txs.uscourts.gov
Career Law Clerk **John J. Baker** ....(956) 618-8100
Began Service: 1990
E-mail: john_baker@txs.uscourts.gov
Education: Austin Col 1985 BA;
Notre Dame 1990 JD
Electronic Recorder Operator
Antonio Tijerina ....(956) 618-8065 ext. 8484
E-mail: antonio_tijerina@txs.uscourts.gov
Case Manager **Alex De La Garza** ....(956) 618-8065 ext. 8474
E-mail: alex_dela_garza@txs.uscourts.gov
Judicial Assistant **Hortencia G. Rios** ....(956) 618-8100
E-mail: hortencia_rios@txs.uscourts.gov

Chambers of District Judge Micaela Alvarez
1701 West Business Highway 83, Suite 911, McAllen, TX 78501
Tel: (956) 928-8270
E-mail: micaela_alvarez@txs.uscourts.gov

Micaela Alvarez
District Judge

Education: Texas 1980 BS, 1989 JD
Began Service: December 27, 2004
Appointed By: President George W. Bush

Government: Board Member, Office of Risk Management, State of Texas (1997-2005); Member, Advisory Board, McAllen-Miller International Airport (1998-2003); Chairman, Advisory Board, McAllen-Miller International Airport (2001); Member, Presidential Commission on Educational Excellence for Hispanic Americans, Executive Office of the President, George W. Bush Administration (2002-2003)

Judicial: Presiding Judge, Hidalgo County, Texas, 139th Judicial District Court (1995-1996)

Legal Practice: Litigation Attorney, Atlas & Hall, LLP (1989-1993); Litigation Attorney, Law Offices of Ronald G. Hole (1993-1995); Litigation Attorney, Law Offices of Ronald G. Hole (1997); Litigation Attorney, Hole & Alvarez, LLP (1997-2004)

Nonprofit: Member, Board of Governors, McAllen Medical Center (1998-2001)

Staff
Judicial Assistant **Nereida Perez** ....(956) 618-8492
E-mail: nereida_perez@txs.uscourts.gov

Chambers of District Judge Randy Crane

Bentsen Tower, 1701 West Business Highway 83, Suite 928,
McAllen, TX 78501
Tel: (956) 618-8083 Tel: (956) 928-8273
E-mail: randy_crane@txs.uscourts.gov

Randy Crane
District Judge

Date of Birth: 1965
Education: Texas 1985 BA, 1987 JD
Began Service: March 27, 2002
Appointed By: President George W. Bush

Legal Practice: Associate, Atlas & Hall, LLP

Staff

Law Clerk **Tim Emmons** .... (956) 618-8083
Began Service: September 2014
Career Law Clerk **Samantha Rodriguez** .... (956) 618-8083
Began Service: August 2006
E-mail: samantha_rodriguez@txs.uscourts.gov
Education: Notre Dame 1999 BA;
Texas 2003 Dr Jur
Case Manager **Ludi Cervantes** .... (956) 618-8065
E-mail: ludi_cervantes@txs.uscourts.gov
Deputy-in-Charge **Velma Barrera** .... (956) 618-8065
E-mail: velma_barrera@txs.uscourts.gov
Judicial Assistant **Julie Kittleman** .... (956) 618-8083
E-mail: julie_kittleman@txs.uscourts.gov

Chambers of District Judge Keith Paty Ellison

515 Rusk Street, Room 3716, Houston, TX 77002
Tel: (713) 250-5806 Fax: (713) 250-5503
E-mail: Keith_Ellison@txs.uscourts.gov

Keith Paty Ellison
District Judge

Date of Birth: 1950
Education: Harvard 1972 AB; Oxford (UK) 1974 BA; Yale 1976 JD
Began Service: August 2, 1999
Appointed By: President William J. Clinton

Clerkships: Law Clerk The Honorable J. Skelly Wright, United States Court of Appeals for the District of Columbia (1976-1977); Law Clerk The Honorable Harry A. Blackmun, United States Supreme Court (1977-1978)

Legal Practice: Partner, Conner & Winters, LLP; Partner, Mayor, Day, Caldwell & Keeton, L.L.P. (1985-1986); Partner, Baker and Botts (1986-1994); Of Counsel, Caddell & Conwell (1994-1996); Sole Practitioner, Law Office of Keith P. Ellison (1996-1999)

Current Memberships: American Bankruptcy Institute; The American Law Institute; Association of American Rhodes Scholars; Council on Foreign Relations; Board of Directors, Federal Bar Association; Houston Bar Association; State Bar of Texas

Staff

Case Manager **Stephanie Loewe** .... (713) 250-5181

Chambers of District Judge Vanessa D. Gilmore

Bob Casey U.S. Courthouse, 515 Rusk Avenue, Room 9513,
Houston, TX 77002
Tel: (713) 250-5931 Fax: (713) 250-5477
E-mail: vanessa_gilmore@txs.uscourts.gov

Vanessa D. Gilmore
District Judge

Date of Birth: 1956
Education: Hampton 1977 BS; Houston 1981 JD
Began Service: 1994
Appointed By: President William J. Clinton

Academic: Adjunct Professor of Law, University of Houston

Legal Practice: Associate, Vickery & Kilbride (1981-1985); Associate, Sue Schechter & Associates (1985-1986); Partner, Vickery, Kilbride, Gilmore & Vickery (1986-1994)

Staff

Law Clerk **Jeffrey Miles** .... (713) 250-5933
Began Service: September 2015
Term Expires: September 2017
E-mail: jeffrey_miles@txs.uscourts.gov
Law Clerk **Atticus Lee** .... (713) 250-5934
Began Service: September 2014
Term Expires: September 2016
E-mail: atticus_lee@txs.uscourts.gov
Case Manager **Byron Thomas** .... (713) 250-5512
E-mail: byron_thomas@txs.uscourts.gov
Secretary **Jennifer S. Meeks** .... (713) 250-5931
E-mail: jennifer_meeks@txs.uscourts.gov

Chambers of District Judge Andrew S. Hanen

600 East Harrison Street, Room 301, Brownsville, TX 78520-7114
Tel: (956) 548-2591
E-mail: andrew_hanen@txs.uscourts.gov

Andrew S. Hanen
District Judge

Date of Birth: 1953
Education: Denison 1975 BA; Baylor 1978 JD
Began Service: June 6, 2002
Appointed By: President George W. Bush

Clerkships: Briefing Attorney The Honorable Joe Greenhill, Supreme Court of Texas (1978-1979)

Legal Practice: Associate, Andrews Kurth LLP (1979-1986); Partner, Andrews Kurth LLP (1986-1993); Partner, Hanen, Alexander, Johnson & Spalding, L.L.P. (1993-2002)

Staff

Law Clerk **Francesca M. Genova** .... (956) 548-2591
Began Service: August 2015
Term Expires: August 2016
E-mail: Francesca_genova@txs.uscourts.gov
Law Clerk **Benjamin Lyles** .... (956) 548-2591
Began Service: August 2015
Term Expires: August 2016
E-mail: kathryne_m_gray@txs.uscourts.gov
Case Manager **Cristina Sustaeta** .... (956) 548-2629
Secretary **Adalia Mora** .... (956) 548-2591
E-mail: adalia_mora@txs.uscourts.gov

Chambers of District Judge Melinda Harmon

Bob Casey U.S. Courthouse, 515 Rusk Avenue, Suite 9114,
Houston, TX 77002
Tel: (713) 250-5194
E-mail: melinda_harmon@txs.uscourts.gov

Melinda Harmon
District Judge

Date of Birth: 1946
Education: Radcliffe 1969 AB; Texas 1972 JD
Began Service: 1989
Appointed By: President George H.W. Bush

Clerkships: Law Clerk The Honorable John V. Singleton, Jr., United States District Court for the Southern District of Texas (1973-1975)

Judicial: Judge, Texas District Court, 280th Judicial District, Civil Division (1988-1989)

Legal Practice: Litigation Section, Exxon Company, United States of America (1975-1988)

Current Memberships: Houston Bar Association; State Bar of Texas

Staff

Career Law Clerk **Nancy Benjamin** .... (713) 250-5194
E-mail: nancy_benjamin@txs.uscourts.gov
Education: Smith 1965 BA; NYU 1966 MA;
Houston 1983 PhD, 1987 JD
Judicial Assistant **Rhonda Hawkins** .... (713) 250-5194
E-mail: rhonda_hawkins@txs.uscourts.gov
Case Manager **(Vacant)** .... (713) 250-5518

Chambers of District Judge Lynn Nettleton Hughes

11122 U.S. Courthouse, 515 Rusk Avenue, Houston, TX 77002-2605
Tel: (713) 250-5900 Fax: (713) 250-5650

Lynn Nettleton Hughes
District Judge

Education: Alabama 1963 BA; Texas 1966 JD; Virginia 1992 LLM
Began Service: December 17, 1985
Appointed By: President Ronald Reagan

Academic: Adjunct Professor, South Texas College of Law (1973-2003); Advisor, European Community (1989); Chair, Board of Advisors, Houston Journal of International Law (1989-1999); Adjunct Professor, School of Law, University of Texas at Austin (1990-1991); Advisor, Republic of Moldova's Constitution (1993); Advisor, Romanian privatization (1997); Advisor, George Mason University (1999)

Judicial: Judge, 165th Judicial District of Texas (1979-1980); Judge, 189th Judicial District of Texas (1981-1985)

Legal Practice: Private Practice (1966-1972); Partner, Howard & Hughes (1973-1979)

Current Memberships: The American Law Institute; American Society for Legal History; Council on Foreign Relations; State Bar of Texas

Staff

Law Clerk **Shane O'Neal** .... (713) 250-5900
Began Service: September 2015
Term Expires: September 2016
E-mail: shane_o'neal@txs.uscourts.gov
Law Clerk **Elizabeth Eoff** .... (713) 250-5900
Began Service: September 2014
Term Expires: September 2016
E-mail: elizabeth_eoff@txs.uscourts.gov
Case Manager **Glenda Hassan** .... (713) 250-5516
E-mail: glenda_hassan@txs.uscourts.gov
Secretary **Kathy L. Grant** .... (713) 250-5900
E-mail: kathy_l_grant@txs.uscourts.gov

Chambers of District Judge Sim Lake

Bob Casey U.S. Courthouse, 515 Rusk Street, Room 9535,
Houston, TX 77002-2600
Tel: (713) 250-5177 Fax: (713) 250-5010
E-mail: sim_lake@txs.uscourts.gov

Sim Lake
District Judge

Date of Birth: 1944
Education: Texas A&M 1966 BA; Texas 1969 JD
Began Service: September 2, 1988
Appointed By: President Ronald Reagan

Legal Practice: Associate, Fulbright & Jaworski L.L.P. (1969-1970); Partner, Fulbright & Jaworski L.L.P. (1972-1988)

Military Service: United States Army (1970-1971)

Current Memberships: Texas Bar Foundation; The American Law Institute; Houston Bar Association; Houston Bar Foundation, Houston Bar Association; State Bar of Texas

Staff

Case Manager **Andrew Boyd** .... (713) 250-5514
PO Box 61010, Houston, TX 77208-1010 Fax: (713) 250-5010
Administrative Assistant **Beatrice Adams** .... (713) 250-5177
E-mail: bea_adams@txs.uscourts.gov
Education: East Los Angeles 1965

Chambers of District Judge Gray Hampton Miller

515 Rusk Avenue, Room 9136, Houston, TX 77002
Tel: (713) 250-5377 Fax: (713) 250-5189
E-mail: gray_miller@txs.uscourts.gov

Gray Hampton Miller
District Judge

Education: Houston 1974 BA, 1978 JD
Began Service: May 2006
Appointed By: President George W. Bush

Legal Practice: Associate, Fulbright & Jaworski L.L.P. (1978-1986); Partner, Fulbright & Jaworski L.L.P. (1986-2006)

Current Memberships: Texas Bar Foundation; American Arbitration Association; American Bar Association; Houston Bar Association; Houston Bar Foundation, Houston Bar Association; Maritime Law Association of the United States; State Bar of Texas

Staff

Law Clerk **Clifford Carlson** .... (713) 250-5377
Began Service: 2015
Term Expires: September 2016
E-mail: clifford_carlson@txs.uscourts.gov
Law Clerk **Walter Simon** .... (713) 250-5377
Began Service: September 2015
Term Expires: August 29, 2016
E-mail: walter_simon@txs.uscourts.gov
Career Law Clerk **Anna Archer** .... (713) 250-5379
E-mail: anna_archer@txs.uscourts.gov
Education: Houston BS, 2006 JD
Case Manager **Rhonda Moore-Konieczny** .... (713) 250-5129
Fax: (713) 250-5894

Chambers of District Judge Lee H. Rosenthal

11535 Bob Casey U.S. Courthouse, 515 Rusk Avenue,
Houston, TX 77002
Tel: (713) 250-5980 Fax: (713) 250-5213
E-mail: lee_rosenthal@txs.uscourts.gov

Lee H. Rosenthal
District Judge

Date of Birth: 1952
Education: Chicago 1974 BA, 1977 JD
Began Service: 1992
Appointed By: President George H.W. Bush

Clerkships: Law Clerk The Honorable John R. Brown, United States Court of Appeals for the Fifth Circuit (1977-1978)

Legal Practice: Attorney, Baker Botts L.L.P. (1978-1992)

Current Memberships: Texas Bar Foundation; American Bar Association; The American Inns of Court; The American Law Institute; Houston Bar Association; State Bar of Texas

Staff

Law Clerk **Nicholas "Nick" Brod** .... (713) 250-5980
Began Service: 2015
Term Expires: August 2016
E-mail: nick_brod@txs.uscourts.gov
Law Clerk **Steve Messer** .... (713) 250-5980
Began Service: 2015
Term Expires: August 2016
E-mail: steven_messer@txs.uscourts.gov
Case Manager **Lisa Eddins** .... (713) 250-5517
Secretary **Sheila C. Logullo** .... (713) 250-5980
E-mail: sheila_logullo@txs.uscourts.gov

Chambers of District Judge Diana Saldaña

1300 Victoria Street, Suite 2317, Laredo, TX 78040
Tel: (956) 790-1381 Fax: (956) 794-1027
E-mail: diana_saldana@txs.uscourts.gov

Diana Saldaña
District Judge

Date of Birth: 1971
Education: Texas 1994 BA, 1997 JD
Began Service: February 11, 2011
Appointed By: President Barack Obama

Current Memberships: Federal Magistrate Judges Association; State Bar of Texas; Webb County Bar Association

Staff

Law Clerk **Yamil Farid Yunes** .... (956) 790-1373
E-mail: yamil_yunes@txs.uscourts.gov
Education: Texas 2008 JD
Law Clerk **Kristina Zumita** .... (956) 790-1329
Began Service: August 2015
Term Expires: August 2017
E-mail: kristina_zumita@txs.uscourts.gov
Case Manager **Sara Medellin** .... (956) 790-1356
Judicial Assistant **Irene Sanchez** .... (956) 790-1381
E-mail: irene_sanchez@txs.uscourts.gov

Chambers of District Judge Nelva Gonzales Ramos

1133 North Shoreline Boulevard, Corpus Christi, TX 78401
Tel: (361) 888-3142

Nelva Gonzales Ramos
District Judge

Education: Southwest Texas State 1987 BS; Texas 1991 JD
Began Service: September 27, 2011
Appointed By: President Barack Obama

Judicial: Municipal Court Judge, City of Corpus Christi, Texas (1997-1999); Judge, Chambers of Judge Nelva Gonzales Ramos, Fifth Administrative Judicial Region, Texas District Courts (2000-2011)

Profession: Sole Practitioner (1999)

Chambers of District Judge Marina Garcia Marmolejo

1300 Victoria Street, Laredo, TX 78040
Tel: (713) 250-5500 Tel: (800) 676-6856
E-mail: marina_marmolejo@txs.uscourts.gov

Marina Garcia Marmolejo
District Judge

Education: Incarnate Word Col 1992 BA; St Mary's U (TX) 1996 MA, 1996 JD
Began Service: October 4, 2011
Appointed By: President Barack Obama

Government: Assistant Federal Public Defender, United States District Court for the Western District of Texas (1996-1998); Assistant Federal Public Defender, United States District Court for the Southern District of Texas (1998-1999); Assistant U.S. Attorney, Laredo (TX) Office, Executive Office for United States Attorneys, United States Department of Justice (1999-2007)

Legal Practice: Of Counsel, Thompson & Knight LLP (2007-2009); Partner, Reid Davis LLP (2009-2011)

Current Memberships: State Bar of Texas

Chambers of District Judge Alfred H. Bennett

515 Rusk Street, Houston, TX 77002
Tel: (713) 250-5849

Alfred H. Bennett
District Judge

Education: Houston 1988 BS; Texas 1991 JD
Began Service: April 22, 2015
Appointed By: President Barack Obama

Chambers of District Judge George C. Hanks Jr.

515 Rusk Street, Houston, TX 77002
Tel: (713) 250-5500

George C. Hanks, Jr.
District Judge

Education: LSU 1986 BA; Harvard 1989 JD
Began Service: April 23, 2015
Appointed By: President Barack Obama

Judicial: Judge, 157th State District Court (2001-2002); Magistrate Judge, Chambers of Magistrate Judge George C. Hanks, United States District Court for the Southern District of Texas (2010-2015)

Legal Practice: Attorney, Fulbright & Jaworski L.L.P. (1991-1996)

Current Memberships: American Judges Association; The American Law Institute; Bar Association of the Fifth Federal Circuit; College of the State Bar of Texas; National Bar Association

Staff

Case Manager **Jeanette Gonzalez** .... (713) 250-5757

Chambers of District Judge Jose Rolando Olvera Jr.
515 Rusk Street, Houston, TX 77002
Tel: (956) 548-2595

Jose Rolando Olvera, Jr.
District Judge

Education: Harvard 1985 BS; Texas 1989 JD
Began Service: 2015
Appointed By: President Barack Obama

Government: Commissioner, Lottery Commission, State of Texas

Judicial: Judge, Chambers of Presiding Judge J. Rolando Olvera, Fifth Administrative Judicial Region, Texas District Courts

Staff
Judicial Secretary **Karen Ballard** .... (956) 548-2595

Chambers of Senior Judge George P. Kazen
U.S. Courthouse, 1300 Victoria Street, Laredo, TX 78040
P.O. Box 1060, Laredo, TX 78042
Tel: (956) 726-2237 Fax: (956) 726-2349
E-mail: George_Kazen@txs.uscourts.gov

George P. Kazen
Senior Judge

Date of Birth: 1940
Education: Texas 1960 BBA, 1961 JD
Began Service: May 11, 1979
Appointed By: President Jimmy Carter

Academic: Adjunct Professor, School of Law, St. Mary's University (1990-1999)

Government: Briefing Attorney, Supreme Court of Texas (1961-1962)

Judicial: Chief Judge, United States District Court for the Southern District of Texas (2003)

Legal Practice: Partner, Mann, Freed, Kazen & Hansen (1965-1979)

Military Service: United States Air Force (1962-1965)

Current Memberships: Texas Bar Foundation; Laredo-Webb County Bar Association; State Bar of Texas

Staff
Law Clerk **Juan Roque** .... (956) 726-2237
Law Clerk **Stephen Moulton** .... (956) 726-2237
Secretary **Graciela Sepulveda** .... (956) 726-2237

Chambers of Senior Judge Hayden Head
1133 North Shoreline Boulevard, Room 308, Corpus Christi, TX 78401
Tel: (361) 888-3148 Fax: (361) 888-3179
E-mail: hayden_head@txs.uscourts.gov

Hayden Head
Senior Judge

Date of Birth: 1944
Education: Texas 1967 BA, 1968 LLB
Began Service: October 26, 1981
Appointed By: President Ronald Reagan

Current Memberships: Texas Bar Foundation; Federal Judges Association; Maritime Law Association of the United States; State Bar of Texas

Staff
Law Clerk **Frances Blake** .... (361) 888-3148
Began Service: March 1, 2015
Term Expires: September 1, 2016
Administrative Secretary **(Vacant)** .... (361) 888-3148
Case Manager **Sylvia Syler** .... (361) 888-3669

Chambers of Senior Judge David Hittner
U.S. Courthouse, 515 Rusk Street, Room 8509, Houston, TX 77002
Tel: (713) 250-5711 Fax: (713) 250-5357
E-mail: David_Hittner@txs.uscourts.gov

David Hittner
Senior Judge

Date of Birth: 1939
Education: NYU 1961 BS, 1964 JD
Began Service: June 9, 1986
Appointed By: President Ronald Reagan

Judicial: Judge, Texas District Court, 133rd District (1978-1986)

Legal Practice: Associate, Lynch, Chappell, Allday & Hamilton (1967-1968); Diamond and Totz (1968-1972); Partner, Hittner & Cezeaux (and predecessor firms) (1972-1978)

Military Service: United States Army (1965-1966)

Current Memberships: Texas Bar Foundation; The American Law Institute; Federal Bar Association; Federal Judges Association; Fifth Circuit District Judges Association; Houston Bar Association; Houston Bar Foundation, Houston Bar Association; New York State Bar Association; State Bar of Texas

Staff
Law Clerk **Catherine Eschbach** .... (713) 250-5737
Began Service: August 2015
Term Expires: September 2017
Law Clerk **Jordan Warshauer** .... (713) 250-5738
Began Service: 2014
Term Expires: September 2016
Case Manager **Ellen Alexander** .... (713) 250-5511
Fax: (713) 250-5019
Administrative Judicial Assistant **Karen Harpold** .... (713) 250-5720
E-mail: Karen_Harpold@txs.uscourts.gov Fax: (713) 250-5357

Chambers of Senior Judge Ewing Werlein, Jr.
11521 Bob Casey U.S. Courthouse, 515 Rusk Avenue,
Houston, TX 77002
Tel: (713) 250-5920 Fax: (713) 250-5818
E-mail: ewing_werlein@txs.uscourts.gov

Ewing Werlein, Jr.
Senior Judge

Date of Birth: 1936
Education: Southern Methodist 1958 BA; Texas 1961 LLB
Began Service: May 22, 1992
Appointed By: President George H.W. Bush

Legal Practice: Private Practice (1961); Attorney, Vinson & Elkins L.L.P. (1964-1992)

Military Service: United States Air Force (1961-1964); United States Air Force Reserve (1964-1971)

Current Memberships: American Bar Foundation; Texas Bar Foundation; Federal Bar Association; Houston Bar Association; Houston Bar Foundation, Houston Bar Association; International Society of Barristers; State Bar of Texas

Staff
Case Manager **Marilyn Flores** .... (713) 250-5533
Fax: (713) 250-5550
Secretary **Jill Hawk** .... (713) 250-5920
E-mail: jill_hawk@txs.uscourts.gov

Chambers of Senior Judge Janis Graham Jack

1133 North Shoreline Boulevard, Room 321, Corpus Christi, TX 78401
Tel: (361) 888-3525 Fax: (361) 888-3530
E-mail: janis_jack@txs.uscourts.gov

Janis Graham Jack
Senior Judge

Date of Birth: 1946
Education: Baltimore 1974 BA; South Texas 1981 JD
Began Service: March 14, 1994
Appointed By: President William J. Clinton

Current Memberships: Texas Bar Foundation; American Bar Association; Federal Judges Association; Fifth Circuit District Judges Association; Maritime Law Association of the United States; National Association of Women Judges; Philosophical Society of Texas; State Bar of Texas

Staff
Law Clerk **Ilya Felldsherov** .... (361) 888-3525
Law Clerk **(Vacant)** .... (361) 888-3525
Case Manager **Linda R. Smith** .... (361) 888-3245
Fax: (361) 888-3433
Court Reporter **Arlene Benavidez** .... (361) 693-6596
E-mail: arlene_benavidez@txs.uscourts.gov
Chambers Administrator **Mary Hardin** .... (361) 888-3525
E-mail: mary_hardin@txs.uscourts.gov

Chambers of Senior Judge John D. Rainey

Federal Building, 312 South Main, 4th Floor, Victoria, TX 77901
Tel: (361) 788-5030
E-mail: john_rainey@txs.uscourts.gov

John D. Rainey
Senior Judge

Date of Birth: 1945
Education: Southern Methodist 1967 BBA, 1972 JD
Began Service: May 28, 1990
Appointed By: President George H.W. Bush

Current Memberships: Texas Bar Foundation; State Bar of Texas; Victoria County Bar Association

Staff
Judicial Assistant **Stacie Marthiljohni** .... (361) 788-5034
E-mail: stacie_marthiljohni@txs.uscourts.gov

Chambers of Senior Judge Kenneth M. Hoyt

Bob Casey U.S. Courthouse, 515 Rusk Avenue, Room 11-144, Houston, TX 77002
Tel: (713) 250-5611

Kenneth M. Hoyt
Senior Judge

Date of Birth: 1948
Education: Texas Southern 1969 AB, 1972 JD
Began Service: April 1988
Appointed By: President Ronald Reagan
Political Affiliation: Republican

Current Memberships: National Bar Association; State Bar of Texas

Staff
Law Clerk **Christopher Lopez-Loftis** .... (713) 250-5616
Began Service: September 2014
Term Expires: September 2016
E-mail: chris_lopez@txs.uscourts.gov
Career Law Clerk **Kronsky Sherer** .... (713) 250-5615
Began Service: 2007
E-mail: kronsky_sherer@txs.uscourts.gov
Education: Texas Southern 2001 JD

Chambers of Senior Judge Kenneth M. Hoyt *continued*

Judicial Assistant **Elaine A. Caldwell** .... (713) 250-5613
E-mail: elaine_roberson@txs.uscourts.gov
Education: LeTourneau BM

Chambers of Senior Judge Hilda G. Tagle

Federal Building, 600 East Harrison Street, Room 306, Brownsville, TX 78520
Tel: (956) 548-2510
E-mail: hilda_tagle@txs.uscourts.gov

Hilda G. Tagle
Senior Judge

Date of Birth: 1946
Education: East Texas State BA; North Texas State MLS; Texas JD
Began Service: March 27, 1998
Appointed By: President William J. Clinton

Staff
Career Law Clerk **Eugene Skonicki** .... (956) 548-2510
E-mail: eugene_skonicki@txs.uscourts.gov
Law Clerk **Alia Al-Khatib** .... (956) 548-2510
Began Service: August 2015
Term Expires: August 2016
Case Manager **Estella Cavazos** .... (956) 548-2628
Courtroom Reporter **Heather Hall** .... (956) 548-2510
E-mail: heather_hall@txs.uscourts.gov
Judicial Assistant **Melissa Lothmann** .... (956) 548-2510
E-mail: melissa_lothmann@txs.uscourts.gov

Chambers of Senior Judge Nancy Friedman Atlas

9015 Bob Casey U.S. Courthouse, 515 Rusk Avenue, Suite 9015, Houston, TX 77002-2601
Tel: (713) 250-5990 Fax: (713) 250-5994
E-mail: Nancy_Atlas@txs.uscourts.gov

Nancy Friedman Atlas
Senior Judge

Date of Birth: 1949
Education: Tufts 1971 BS; NYU 1974 JD
Began Service: August 22, 1995
Appointed By: President William J. Clinton

Current Memberships: American Bar Foundation; Texas Bar Foundation; Section on Litigation, American Bar Association; The American Law Institute; The Association of Attorney-Mediators; Federal Bar Association; Houston Bar Association; Houston Bar Foundation, Houston Bar Association; National Association of Women Judges; State Bar of Texas

Staff
Law Clerk **Harold Williford** .... (713) 250-5993
Began Service: September 2015
Term Expires: September 2016
E-mail: harold_w_williford@txs.uscourts.gov
Career Law Clerk **Elizabeth Detweiler** .... (713) 250-5990
Began Service: September 4, 2007
E-mail: elizabeth_detweiler@txs.uscourts.gov
Education: Carleton 1989 AB; Yale 1995 JD
Career Law Clerk **Terri D. Rutt** .... (713) 250-5576
E-mail: Terri_Rutt@txs.uscourts.gov
Education: Cumberland 1983 JD
Case Manager **Shelia Ashabranner** .... (713) 250-5407
Judicial Assistant **Ruth Guerrero** .... (713) 250-5990
E-mail: ruth_guerrero@txs.uscourts.gov

Chambers of Magistrate Judge Frances H. Stacy

Bob Casey U.S. Courthouse, 515 Rusk Avenue, Room 7525,
Houston, TX 77002
Tel: (713) 250-5681 Fax: (713) 250-5188
E-mail: frances_stacy@txs.uscourts.gov

Frances H. Stacy
Magistrate Judge

Date of Birth: 1955
Education: Baylor 1977 BA, 1979 JD
Began Service: February 20, 1990
Term Expires: January 2024

Government: Assistant United States Attorney, Southern District of Texas, Office of the United States Attorney, United States Department of Justice (1980-1990)

Current Memberships: Texas Bar Foundation; Federal Bar Association; Houston Bar Association

Staff
Career Law Clerk **Alice Moore** . . . . . . (713) 250-5681
E-mail: alice_moore@txs.uscourts.gov
Career Law Clerk **Karen M. Schwab** . . . . . . (713) 250-5681
E-mail: karen_schwab@txs.uscourts.gov
Education: Texas (San Antonio) 1989 BA; Houston 1992 JD
Case Manager **Beverly White** . . . . . . (713) 250-5565

Chambers of Magistrate Judge Nancy K. Johnson

7019 Bob Casey U.S. Courthouse, 515 Rusk Avenue, Houston, TX 77002
Tel: (713) 250-5375 Fax: (713) 250-5384

Nancy K. Johnson
Magistrate Judge

Education: Cincinnati 1975 BA, 1978 JD
Began Service: June 12, 1990
Term Expires: June 2022

Government: Assistant Attorney General, Office of the Attorney General, State of Ohio (1978-1980); Assistant Attorney General, Office of the Attorney General, State of Texas (1980-1981); Civil Division, Office of the U.S. Attorney, Southern District of Texas (1982-1986); Tax Prosecution Unit, Office of the U.S. Attorney, Southern District of Texas (1986-1990)

Current Memberships: Federal Bar Association; Houston Bar Association

Staff
Law Clerk **Christopher Dobson** . . . . . . (713) 250-5375
Began Service: August 15, 2014
E-mail: christopher_dobson@txs.uscourts.gov
Career Law Clerk **Linda S. Eckols** . . . . . . (713) 250-5375
E-mail: linda_eckols@txs.uscourts.gov
Education: Texas Tech 1999 JD
Case Manager **Shannon Butler** . . . . . . (713) 250-5703

Chambers of Magistrate Judge John R. Froeschner

601 Rosenberg, Suite 704, Galveston, TX 77550
Tel: (409) 766-3729 Fax: (409) 766-3738
E-mail: john_froeschner@txs.uscourts.gov

John R. Froeschner
Magistrate Judge

Date of Birth: 1950
Education: Elmhurst 1972 BA; Missouri 1976 JD
Began Service: 1991
Term Expires: January 25, 2023

Legal Practice: Private Practice (1976-1991)

Chambers of Magistrate Judge John R. Froeschner *continued*

Current Memberships: Texas Bar Foundation; Board of Directors, Federal Bar Association; Federal Magistrate Judges Association

Staff
Judicial Assistant/Case Manager **Sheila R. Anderson** . . . . (409) 766-3533
E-mail: Sheila_R_Anderson@txs.uscourts.gov
Law Clerk **Jodie Schwab** . . . . . . (409) 766-3740
E-mail: jodie_schwab@txs.uscourts.gov

Chambers of Magistrate Judge Maryrose Milloy

7007 Bob Casey U.S. Courthouse, 515 Rusk Avenue, Houston, TX 77002
Tel: (713) 250-5860 Fax: (713) 250-5348

Maryrose Milloy
Magistrate Judge

Date of Birth: 1952
Education: Texas A&I 1975 BA; Bates 1977
Began Service: October 1992
Term Expires: October 2016

Government: Assistant District Attorney, Office of the District Attorney, State of Texas (1979-1985); Chief, Civil Rights Division, Office of the United States Attorney, United States Department of Justice (1987-1989)

Legal Practice: Practicing Attorney, Leal & Whitworth (1978); Practicing Attorney, Cook, Davids & McFall (1985-1987); Partner, McFall & Sartwelle (1989-1992)

Current Memberships: American Bar Association; Federal Bar Association; State Bar of Texas

Staff
Career Law Clerk **Stephanie Hunter** . . . . . . (713) 250-5860
Began Service: September 2014
E-mail: stephanie_hunter@txs.uscourts.gov
Law Clerk (Part-Time) **Elizabeth Humphrey** . . . . . . (713) 250-5860
Case Manager **Cynthia Jantowski** . . . . . . (713) 250-5158
Secretary **Cynthia Jantowski** . . . . . . (713) 250-5860
E-mail: cynthia_jantowski@txs.uscourts.gov

Chambers of Magistrate Judge Dorina Ramos

1701 West Business Highway 83, Suite 811, McAllen, TX 78501
P.O. Box 4569, McAllen, TX 78502
Tel: (956) 618-8060 Fax: (956) 928-8247
E-mail: dorina_ramos@txs.uscourts.gov

Dorina Ramos
Magistrate Judge

Date of Birth: 1958
Education: Texas 1981 BA; Houston 1985 JD
Began Service: 1996
Term Expires: August 2020

Staff
Career Law Clerk **Laura J. Beaver** . . . . . . (956) 618-8060
E-mail: laura_beaver@txs.uscourts.gov
Administrative Judicial Assistant **Jamie Leyva** . . . . . . (956) 618-8060

Chambers of Magistrate Judge B. Janice Ellington

1133 North Shoreline Boulevard, Room 312, Corpus Christi, TX 78401
Tel: (361) 888-3291 Fax: (361) 888-3269

B. Janice Ellington
Magistrate Judge

Began Service: November 14, 1996
Term Expires: November 2020

Chambers of Magistrate Judge B. Janice Ellington *continued*

Staff
Career Law Clerk **Linda Kring** . . . . (361) 888-3291
E-mail: linda_kring@txs.uscourts.gov
Education: Texas 1990 JD
Case Manager **Dana Terez** . . . . (361) 888-3432
Secretary **Myra Alaniz** . . . . (361) 888-3291
E-mail: myra_alaniz@txs.uscourts.gov

Chambers of Magistrate Judge Peter E. Ormsby
1701 West Business Highway 83, Suite 805, McAllen, TX 78501
Tel: (956) 618-8080
E-mail: peter_ormsby@txs.uscourts.gov

Peter E. Ormsby
Magistrate Judge

Education: J Reuben Clark Law 1984 JD
Began Service: March 1, 2005
Term Expires: March 2021

Staff
Career Law Clerk **Ben K. Miller** . . . . (956) 618-8080
E-mail: ben_miller@txs.uscourts.gov
Education: Houston 2010 JD
Case Manager **Carmel Ramirez** . . . . (956) 618-8080
Judicial Assistant **Nellie A. Davila** . . . . (956) 618-8080
E-mail: nellie_davila@txs.uscourts.gov

Chambers of Magistrate Judge Stephen Wm. Smith
Bob Casey U.S. Courthouse, 515 Rusk Street, Houston, TX 77002
Tel: (713) 250-5100 Fax: (713) 250-5527
E-mail: stephen_smith@txs.uscourts.gov

Stephen Wm. Smith
Magistrate Judge

Date of Birth: 1951
Education: Vanderbilt 1973 BA; Virginia 1977 JD
Began Service: July 22, 2004
Term Expires: July 2020

Clerkships: Law Clerk, United States Court of Federal Claims (1977-1978)

Legal Practice: Attorney, Fulbright & Jaworski L.L.P (1978-2004)

Staff
Courtroom Deputy **Jason Marchand** . . . . (713) 250-5148
E-mail: cm41bt@txs.uscourts.gov

Chambers of Magistrate Judge J. Scott Hacker
United States Courthouse, 1300 Victoria Street, Suite 2276,
Laredo, TX 78040
Tel: (956) 790-1750 Fax: (956) 790-1756

J. Scott Hacker
Magistrate Judge

Began Service: October 17, 2008
Appointed By: President George W. Bush

Chambers of Magistrate Judge Ronald G. Morgan
600 East Harrison Street, Brownsville, TX 78520
Tel: (956) 548-2570

Ronald G. Morgan
Magistrate Judge

Began Service: May 2009

Chambers of Magistrate Judge Ronald G. Morgan *continued*

Staff
Career Law Clerk **Craig Smith** . . . . (956) 548-2570
E-mail: craig_smith@txs.uscourts.gov
Judicial Assistant **Linda Garcia** . . . . (956) 548-2570
E-mail: linda_garcia@txs.uscourts.gov
Case Manager **Bertha Vasquez** . . . . (956) 548-2570

Chambers of Magistrate Judge Guillermo R. Garcia
1300 Victoria Street, Laredo, TX 78040
Tel: (956) 723-3542

Guillermo R. Garcia
Magistrate Judge

Began Service: May 21, 2010
Term Expires: 2018

Chambers of Magistrate Judge Ignacio Torteya III
600 East Harrison Street, Suite 203, Brownsville, TX 78520
Tel: (956) 548-2564
E-mail: ignacio_torteya@txs.uscourts.gov

Ignacio Torteya III
Magistrate Judge

Staff
Case Manager **Sally Garcia** . . . . (956) 548-2564
Career Law Clerk **Jessica Dart** . . . . (956) 982-9660
E-mail: jessica_dart@txs.uscourts.gov
Education: Texas 2000 JD
Secretary **Lydia M. Villarreal** . . . . (956) 548-2564
E-mail: lydia_villarreal@txs.uscourts.gov

Chambers of Magistrate Judge Jason B. Libby
1133 North Shoreline Boulevard, Corpus Christi, TX 78401
Tel: (361) 888-3550

Jason B. Libby
Magistrate Judge

Began Service: 2013

Chambers of Magistrate Judge Diana Song Quiroga
1300 Victoria Street, Suite 2276, Laredo, TX 78040
Tel: (956) 726-2242 Fax: (956) 794-1035

Diana Song Quiroga
Magistrate Judge

Education: UC Berkeley 1998 BA; Harvard 2001 JD

Staff
Law Clerk **Bart Quintans** . . . . (956) 726-2242
Began Service: September 2015
Term Expires: September 2016
E-mail: bart_quintans@txs.uscourts.gov
Case Manager **Cindy Dominguez-DeLeon** . . . . (956) 790-1372
Secretary **Michelle Valdez** . . . . (956) 726-5227
E-mail: michelle_valdez@txs.uscourts.gov

United States Bankruptcy Court for the Southern District of Texas

Bob Casey U.S. Courthouse, 515 Rusk Avenue, Houston, TX 77002
Tel: (713) 250-5500 Tel: (713) 250-5046 (PACER)
Tel: (800) 998-9037 (Toll Free PACER)
Tel: (800) 745-4459 (Toll Free Voice Case Information System VCIS)
Tel: (713) 250-5049 (Voice Case Information System VCIS)
Internet: www.txs.uscourts.gov

Number of Judgeships: 6

Number of Vacancies: 1

Court Staff

Clerk of Court **David J. Bradley** .... (713) 250-5500
E-mail: david_bradley@txs.uscourts.gov
Chief Deputy Clerk **Nathan Ochsner** .... (713) 250-5500
E-mail: nathan_ochsner@txs.uscourts.gov

Chambers of Chief Bankruptcy Judge David R. Jones

515 Rusk Street, Houston, TX 77002
Tel: (713) 250-5713

David R. Jones
Chief Bankruptcy Judge

Staff

Case Manager **Albert Alonzo** .... (713) 250-5467
Courtroom Deputy **Diyana Staples** .... (713) 250-5779
E-mail: diyana_staples@txs.uscourts.gov

Chambers of Bankruptcy Judge Jeffery Bohm

217 Bob Casey U.S. Courthouse, 515 Rusk Street, Houston, TX 77002
Tel: (713) 250-5405

Jeffery Bohm
Bankruptcy Judge

Began Service: 2004

Chambers of Bankruptcy Judge Marvin Isgur

515 Rusk Street, 4th Floor, Room 4636, Courtroom 404,
Houston, TX 77002
Tel: (713) 250-5421

Marvin Isgur
Bankruptcy Judge

Education: Houston BA; Stanford MBA; Houston JD
Began Service: June 1, 2009

Staff

Case Manager **Anita Dolezel** .... (713) 250-5657

Chambers of Bankruptcy Judge Karen Kennedy Brown

4202 Bob Casey U.S. Courthouse, 515 Rusk Avenue, Houston, TX 77002
Tel: (713) 250-5250 Fax: (713) 250-5706

Karen Kennedy Brown
Bankruptcy Judge

Date of Birth: 1947
Education: Pennsylvania 1970 BA; Houston 1973 JD
Began Service: April 2, 1990
Term Expires: April 2018

Clerkships: Law Clerk The Honorable John Brown (1973-1975); Law Clerk The Honorable Woodrow Seals (1975-1976)

Government: Assistant Federal Public Defender, State of Texas (1976-1982)

Chambers of Bankruptcy Judge Karen Kennedy Brown *continued*

Judicial: Magistrate Judge, United States District Court for the Southern District of Texas (1984-1990); Chief Bankruptcy Judge, United States Bankruptcy Court for the Southern District of Texas

Legal Practice: Private Practice (1982-1984)

Current Memberships: American Bar Association; The American Law Institute; Houston Federal Bar Association; National Conference of Bankruptcy Judges; State Bar of Texas

Staff

Career Law Clerk **Kris Thomas** .... (713) 250-5253
Education: Houston 1983 JD
Judicial Assistant **Maureen Bryan** .... (713) 250-5252

Chambers of Bankruptcy Judge Letitia Z. Paul

4019 Bob Casey U.S. Courthouse, 515 Rusk Avenue, Houston, TX 77002
Tel: (713) 250-5410 Fax: (713) 250-5825

Letitia Z. Paul
Bankruptcy Judge

Date of Birth: 1945
Education: Rice 1967 BA; Rutgers 1970 MA; Syracuse 1973 JD
Began Service: 1985
Term Expires: 2027

Government: Attorney, State of Texas (1974-1976); Assistant United States Attorney, Southern District of Texas, Office of the United States Attorney, United States Department of Justice (1982-1985)

Legal Practice: Private Practice (1976-1982)

Staff

Career Law Clerk **Barbara Beck Hibler** .... (713) 250-5410
Education: LSU 1978 JD
Career Law Clerk **Greg Kamen** .... (713) 250-5410
Education: Houston 1991 JD

Chambers of Bankruptcy Judge Eduardo V. Rodriguez

1701 West Business Highway 83, McAllen, TX 78501
Tel: (956) 928-7080

Eduardo Rodriguez
Bankruptcy Judge

United States District Court for the Western District of Texas

John H. Wood, Jr. Federal Courthouse, 655 East Cesar E. Chavez Boulevard, Suite G65, San Antonio, TX 78206-1198
Tel: (210) 472-6550 Tel: (210) 472-5241 (PACER)
Internet: www.txwd.uscourts.gov

Number of Judgeships: 13

Number of Vacancies: 1

Circuit: Fifth

Areas Covered: Counties of Andrews, Atascosa, Bandera, Bastrop, Bell, Bexar, Blanco, Bosque, Brewster, Burleson, Burnet, Caldwell, Comal, Coryell, Crane, Culberson, Dimmit, Ector, Edwards, El Paso, Falls, Freestone, Frio, Gillespie, Gonzales, Guadalupe, Hamilton, Hays, Hill, Hudspeth, Jeff Davis, Karnes, Kendall, Kerr, Kimble, Kinney, Lampasas, Lee, Leon, Limestone, Llano, Loving, Martin, Mason, Maverick, McCulloch, McLennan, Medina, Midland, Milam, Pecos, Presidio, Real, Reeves, Robertson, San Saba, Somervell, Terrell, Travis, Upton, Uvalde, Val Verde, Ward, Washington, Williamson, Wilson, Winkler and Zavalla

Court Staff

Clerk of Court **Jeannette J. Clack** .... (210) 472-4955
Chief Deputy Clerk **Philip Devlin** .... (210) 472-4955

United States District Court for the Western District of Texas *continued*

Chief Pretrial Services Officer **Charles Mason** . . . . (210) 472-4053
727 East Cesar E. Chavez Boulevard, Suite 636, Fax: (210) 472-4052
San Antonio, TX 78205

Chief U.S. Probation Officer **Joe Sanchez** . . . . (210) 472-6590
727 East Cesar E. Chavez Boulevard,
San Antonio, TX 78205
E-mail: joe_sanchez@txwd.uscourts.gov

Divisional Office Manager, Austin **(Vacant)** . . . . (512) 916-5896
U.S. Courthouse, 200 W. Eighth St., Room 130,
Austin, TX 78701

Divisional Office Manager, Del Rio **Rebecca Moore** . . . . (830) 703-2054
L-100 U.S. Courthouse, 111 E. Broadway,
Room L100, Del Rio, TX 78840
E-mail: rebecca_moore@txwd.uscourts.gov

Divisional Office Manager, El Paso **Thomas Hilburger** . . . (915) 534-6725
219 U.S. Courthouse, 511 E. San Antonio St.,
Room 219, El Paso, TX 79901
E-mail: tom_hilburger@txwd.uscourts.gov

Divisional Office Manager, Midland
Laura Fowler-Gonzales . . . . (432) 686-4001
U.S. Courthouse, 200 E. Wall St., Room 107,
Midland, TX 79701
E-mail: laura_gonzales@txwd.uscourts.gov

Divisional Office Manager, Pecos **(Vacant)** . . . . (432) 445-4228
410 S. Cedar St., Pecos, TX 79772

Divisional Office Manager, San Antonio
Michael F. Oakes . . . . (210) 472-6550 ext. 282
655 Cesar Chavez Boulevard, Suite G-65,
San Antonio, TX 78206
E-mail: michael_oakes@txwd.uscourts.gov
Education: West Texas State 1983 BS, 1989 MA

Divisional Office Manager, Waco **Mark G. Borchardt** . . . . (254) 750-1501
U.S. Courthouse, 800 Franklin Avenue, Room 380,
Waco, TX 76701
E-mail: mark_borchardt@txwd.uscourts.gov
Education: Baylor 1987 BBA

Director of Human Resources **Lorre Kukla** . . . . . (210) 249-4034 ext. 505
E-mail: lorre_kukla@txwd.uscourts.gov

Director of Information Technology
James Phillips . . . . (210) 472-4900 ext. 234
E-mail: james_phillips@txwd.uscourts.gov

Financial Manager **Carolyn Mosmeyer** . . . . (210) 472-6550 ext. 249
E-mail: carolyn_mosmeyer@txwd.uscourts.gov

Court Training Administrator **(Vacant)** . . . . (210) 472-4955 ext. 238

Administrative Manager **Phillip Reyes** . . . . (210) 472-4955 ext. 241
E-mail: phillip_reyes@txwd.uscourts.gov

Librarian, Austin **Sue Creech** . . . . (504) 310-7725
Homer Thornberry Judicial Bldg., 903 San Jacinto Fax: (504) 310-7578
Blvd., Rm. 347, Austin, TX 78701
E-mail: sue_creech@txwd.uscourts.gov

Chambers of Chief Judge Fred Biery

John H. Wood, Jr. U.S. Courthouse, 655 Cesar Chavez Boulevard,
San Antonio, TX 78206
Tel: (210) 472-6505 Fax: (210) 472-4246
E-mail: Fred_Biery@txwd.uscourts.gov

Fred Biery
Chief Judge

Date of Birth: 1947
Education: Texas Lutheran 1970 BA; Southern Methodist 1973 JD
Began Service: March 14, 1994
Appointed By: President William J. Clinton
Political Affiliation: Democrat

Judicial: Judge, Bexar County Court at Law (1979-1982); Judge, Texas District Court, 150th District (1983-1988); Justice, Texas Court of Appeals, Fourth District (1989-1994)

Legal Practice: Partner, Biery, Biery, Davis & Myers (1973-1978)

Military Service: United States Army Reserve, United States Department of the Army (1970-1976)

Chambers of Chief Judge Fred Biery *continued*

Current Memberships: Texas Bar Foundation; American Bar Association; The William S. Sessions American Inn of Court, The American Inns of Court; San Antonio Bar Association; San Antonio Bar Foundation; State Bar of Texas

Staff

Judicial Assistant **(Vacant)** . . . . (210) 472-6505

Career Law Clerk **Gloria Christmas** . . . . (210) 472-6505
E-mail: gloria_christmas@txwd.uscourts.gov
Education: St Mary's U (TX) 1990 JD

Career Law Clerk **Joani Sullivan** . . . . (210) 472-6505
E-mail: joani_sullivan@txwd.uscourts.gov
Education: St Mary's U (TX) 1990 JD

Courtroom Deputy **Gloria Vela** . . . . (210) 472-6550 ext. 5022
E-mail: gloria_vela@txwd.uscourts.gov

Court Reporter **Chris Poage** . . . . (210) 472-6550 ext. 5036

Office Manager **Gilbert Rodriguez** . . . . (210) 472-6505
E-mail: gilbert_rodriguez@txwd.uscourts.gov

Chambers of District Judge Walter S. Smith, Jr.

U.S. Courthouse, 800 Franklin Avenue, Suite 301, Waco, TX 76701
Tel: (254) 750-1519 Fax: (254) 750-1516

Walter S. Smith, Jr.
District Judge

Date of Birth: 1940
Education: Baylor 1964 BA, 1966 JD
Began Service: October 6, 1984
Appointed By: President Ronald Reagan

Judicial: Judge, Texas District Court (1980-1983); Magistrate Judge, United States District Court for the Western District of Texas (1983-1984)

Legal Practice: Dunnam & Dunnam (1966-1969); Wallace & Smith (1969-1978); Haley, Fulbright (1978-1980)

Staff

Law Clerk **Erik Jacobson** . . . . (254) 750-1519
Began Service: August 2014
Term Expires: September 2016

Career Law Clerk **Tammy Hooks** . . . . (254) 750-1519
E-mail: Tammy_Hooks@txwd.uscourts.gov
Education: Baylor 1984 JD

Court Reporter **Kristie M. Davis** . . . . (254) 754-7444
E-mail: kristie_davis@txwd.uscourts.gov

Secretary **Sharon M. Schroeder** . . . . (254) 750-1519
E-mail: Sharon_Schroeder@txwd.uscourts.gov

Chambers of District Judge Sam Sparks

501 West Fifth Street, Suite 4120, Austin, TX 78701-3822
Tel: (512) 916-5230

Sam Sparks
District Judge

Date of Birth: 1939
Education: Texas 1961 BA, 1963 LLB
Began Service: December 7, 1991
Appointed By: President George H.W. Bush

Clerkships: Law Clerk, Chambers of District Judge Homer Thornberry, United States District Court for the Western District of Texas (1964-1965)

Government: Aide (D-TX), Office of Representative W. Homer Thornberry, United States House of Representatives (1963-1964)

Legal Practice: Associate Partner, Hardie, Grambling, Sims & Galatzan (1965)

Current Memberships: Texas Bar Foundation; American Board of Trial Advocates; American College of Trial Lawyers; State Bar of Texas

(continued on next page)

Chambers of District Judge Sam Sparks *continued*

Staff

Law Clerk **Kathleen Pritchard** . . . . . (512) 916-5230
Began Service: September 2015
Term Expires: August 28, 2017
E-mail: kathleen_pritchard@txwd.uscourts.gov

Law Clerk **Brittany Artimez** . . . . . (512) 916-5230
Began Service: September 15, 2014
Term Expires: August 29, 2016
E-mail: brittany_artimez@txwd.uscourts.gov

Court Reporter **Lily Reznik** . . . . . (512) 916-5564
E-mail: lily_reznik@txwd.uscourts.gov

Secretary **Linda Mizell** . . . . . (512) 916-5230
E-mail: Linda_D_Mizell@txwd.uscourts.gov

Chambers of District Judge Orlando L. Garcia

John H. Wood, Jr. U.S. Courthouse, 655 Cesar Chavez Blvd,
San Antonio, TX 78206
Tel: (210) 472-6565 Fax: (210) 472-6568

Orlando L. Garcia
District Judge

Date of Birth: 1952
Education: Texas 1975 BA, 1978 JD
Began Service: 1994
Appointed By: President William J. Clinton

Government: Legislative Aide, United States House of Representatives (1974-1983); State Representative Orlando Luis Garcia (R-TX), Texas House of Representatives (1983-1991)

Judicial: Judge, Texas Court of Appeals, Fourth District (1991-1994)

Legal Practice: Associate, Law Office of Matt Garcia (1978-1985); Associate, Heard, Goggan, Blair & Williams (1985-1990)

Current Memberships: Texas Bar Foundation; San Antonio Bar Association; State Bar of Texas

Staff

Law Clerk **Emmanuel Garcia** . . . . . (210) 472-6565
Began Service: 2013
E-mail: emmanuel_garcia@txwd.uscourts.gov

Career Law Clerk **Gail Deml** . . . . . (210) 472-6565
E-mail: gail_deml@txwd.uscourts.gov
Education: Texas (Arlington) 1986 BA;
St Mary's U (TX) 1989 JD

Courtroom Deputy **Jessica Urrutia** . . . . . (210) 472-6550 ext. 296
E-mail: jessica_urrutia@txwd.uscourts.gov

Court Reporter **Leticia Rangel** . . . . . (210) 472-6574
E-mail: leticia_rangel@txwd.uscourts.gov

Judicial Legal Assistant **Christine Anderson Lopez** . . . . . (210) 472-6565
E-mail: christine_anderson_
lopez@txwd.uscourts.gov
Education: Texas (San Antonio) 1994 BA

Chambers of District Judge Philip R. Martinez

U.S. Courthouse, 525 Magoffin Avenue, Suite 661, El Paso, TX 79901
Tel: (915) 534-6736 Fax: (915) 534-6715
E-mail: philip_martinez@txwd.uscourts.gov

Philip R. Martinez
District Judge

Date of Birth: 1957
Education: Texas (El Paso) 1979 BA; Harvard 1982 JD
Began Service: February 15, 2002
Appointed By: President George W. Bush

Judicial: Judge, County Court of Law No. 1 (1991); Judge, 327th Judicial District Court, State of Texas (1991-2002)

Legal Practice: Associate, Kemp, Smith, Duncan & Hammond, P.C.

Chambers of District Judge Philip R. Martinez *continued*

Current Memberships: Texas Bar Foundation; American Bar Association; The American Law Institute; El Paso Bar Association; El Paso Mexican-American Bar Association; Federal Judges Association; National Hispanic Bar Association; Philosophical Society of Texas; State Bar of Texas

Staff

Law Clerk **Christian Orozco** . . . . . (915) 534-6736
Began Service: June 2015
Term Expires: June 2016

Law Clerk **Sara Valenzuela** . . . . . (915) 534-6736
Began Service: August 2015
Term Expires: August 2016
E-mail: sara_valenzuela@txwd.uscourts.gov

Courtroom Deputy **Roberto J. Velez** . . . . . (915) 534-6094 ext. 264

Court Reporter **Laura Stewart** . . . . . (915) 834-0553

Judicial Assistant **Eva A. Gonzalez** . . . . . (915) 534-6736
E-mail: eva_gonzalez@txwd.uscourts.gov

Chambers of District Judge Alia Moses

A-202 U.S. Courthouse, 111 East Broadway, Del Rio, TX 78840-5573
Tel: (830) 703-2038 Fax: (830) 703-2159
E-mail: alia_moses@txwd.uscourts.gov

Alia Moses
District Judge

Date of Birth: January 6, 1962
Education: Texas Woman's 1983 BBA; Texas 1986 JD
Began Service: November 18, 2002
Appointed By: President George W. Bush

Government: Trial Attorney and Chief of Appellate Section, Office of the County Attorney, County of Travis , Texas (1986-1990); Trial Attorney and Chief of Del Rio Division, Western District of Texas, United States Attorney's Office, United States Department of Justice, George H.W. Bush Administration (1990-1997)

Judicial: Magistrate Judge, United States District Court for the Western District of Texas (1997-2002)

Current Memberships: Federal Magistrate Judges Association; Fifth Circuit Bar Association; Hispanic National Bar Association; State Bar of Texas; Val Verde County Bar Association

Staff

Law Clerk **Brandon Bishoff** . . . . . (830) 703-2038
Began Service: September 2015
Term Expires: September 30, 2016
E-mail: brandon_bishoff@txwd.uscourts.gov

Law Clerk **John Adams** . . . . . (830) 703-2038
Began Service: September 2015
Term Expires: September 30, 2016
E-mail: john_adams@txwd.uscourts.gov

Law Clerk **Leslie Turnage** . . . . . (830) 703-2038

Courtroom Deputy Clerk **Debbie Green** . . . . . (830) 703-2038
E-mail: Debbie_Green@txwd.uscourts.gov

Court Reporter **Vickie Garza** . . . . . (830) 703-2054

Chambers of District Judge Xavier Rodriguez

655 East Cesar E. Chavez Boulevard, San Antonio, TX 78206-1198
Tel: (210) 472-6575 Fax: (210) 472-6577
E-mail: xavier_rodriguez@txwd.uscourts.gov

Xavier Rodriguez
District Judge

Date of Birth: September 20, 1961
Education: Harvard 1983 AB; Texas 1987 MPA, 1987 JD
Began Service: August 18, 2003
Appointed By: President George W. Bush

Judicial: Justice, Supreme Court of Texas (2001-2002)

Chambers of District Judge Xavier Rodriguez *continued*

Legal Practice: Partner, Fulbright & Jaworski L.L.P. (1987-2001); Partner, Fulbright & Jaworski L.L.P. (2002-2003)

Military Service: Captain, United States Army Reserve Judge Advocate General Corps

Current Memberships: Texas Bar Foundation; American Bar Association; The American Law Institute; San Antonio Bar Association; San Antonio Bar Foundation; State Bar of Texas

Staff

Law Clerk **Mary Kate Rafetto** . . . . (210) 472-6575
Began Service: August 18, 2015
Term Expires: August 2016

Career Law Clerk **Lauren Laux** . . . . (210) 472-6575
E-mail: lauren_laux@txwd.uscourts.gov
Education: Texas 1996 JD

Court Reporter **Karl Myers** . . . . (210) 244-5037
E-mail: karl_myers@txwd.uscourts.gov

Courtroom Deputy **Becky Greenup** . . . . (210) 472-6550 ext. 5011
E-mail: becky_greenup@txwd.uscourts.gov

Judicial Assistant **Jan Wetzel** . . . . (210) 472-6575
E-mail: jan_wetzel@txwd.uscourts.gov

Chambers of District Judge Lee Yeakel

501 West Fifth Street, Austin, TX 78701
Tel: (512) 916-5756
E-mail: lee_yeakel@txwd.uscourts.gov

Lee Yeakel
District Judge

Date of Birth: 1945
Education: Texas 1966 BA, 1969 JD; Virginia 2001 LLM
Began Service: July 31, 2003
Appointed By: President George W. Bush
Political Affiliation: Republican

Government: Member, National Conference of Commissioners on Uniform State Laws; Member, Licensing and Regulation Commission, State of Texas (1989-1998)

Judicial: Chief Justice, Texas Court of Appeals, Third District (1998); Justice, Texas Court of Appeals, Third District (1998-2003)

Legal Practice: Private Practice (1969-1998)

Military Service: United States Marine Corps (1968-1970)

Current Memberships: American Bar Association; The American Law Institute; State Bar of Texas; Travis County Bar Association

Staff

Law Clerk **Grace Matthews** . . . . (512) 916-5756
Began Service: September 2015
Term Expires: September 2017
E-mail: grace_matthews@txwd.uscourts.gov

Career Law Clerk **Kathryn Baffes** . . . . (512) 916-5756
E-mail: kathryn_baffes@txwd.uscourts.gov
Education: Houston 1982 BS; South Texas 1990 JD

Career Law Clerk **Katie Carmona** . . . . (512) 916-5756
E-mail: katie_carmona@txwd.uscourts.gov
Education: Rice 1990 BA; Texas 1993 JD

Court Reporter **Arlinda Rodriguez** . . . . (512) 916-5143
E-mail: arlinda_rodriguez@txwd.uscourts.gov

Courtroom Deputy **Janie Jones** . . . . (512) 391-8709 ext. 234
E-mail: janie_ney_jones@txwd.uscourts.gov

Chambers of District Judge Frank Montalvo

525 Magoffin Avenue, Courtroom 422, El Paso, TX 79901
Tel: (915) 534-6600 Fax: (915) 534-6604
E-mail: frank_montalvo@txwd.uscourts.gov

Frank Montalvo
District Judge

Education: Puerto Rico 1976 BS; Michigan 1977 MS; Wayne State U 1985 JD
Began Service: August 8, 2003
Appointed By: President George W. Bush

Corporate: Engineer, General Motors Corporation (1983-1988)

Judicial: Judge, 288th Judicial District, Texas District Courts (1995-2003)

Profession: Private Practice (1988-1994)

Staff

Fax: (915) 534-6604

Law Clerk **Rachel Nadas** . . . . (915) 534-6600
Began Service: September 2015
Term Expires: September 5, 2017

Law Clerk **Adam Perkins** . . . . (915) 534-6600
Began Service: September 2014
Term Expires: September 5, 2016
E-mail: adam_perkins@txwd.uscourts.gov

Courtroom Deputy **Adriana Quezada** . . . . (915) 834-0532
E-mail: adriana_quezada@txwd.uscourts.gov Fax: (915) 534-6722

Court Reporter **Nalene Benavides** . . . . (915) 534-6600
E-mail: nalene_benavides@txwd.uscourts.gov

Judicial Assistant **Sandra Flores** . . . . (915) 534-6600
E-mail: sandra_flores@txwd.uscourts.gov

Chambers of District Judge Kathleen Cardone

525 Magoffin Avenue, El Paso, TX 79901
Tel: (915) 534-6740
E-mail: kathleen_cardone@txwd.uscourts.gov

Kathleen Cardone
District Judge

Education: SUNY (Binghamton) 1976 BA; St Mary's U (TX) 1979 JD
Began Service: July 29, 2003
Appointed By: President George W. Bush

Judicial: Judge, Municipal Court, City of El Paso, Texas (1990-1995); Judge, 383th Judicial District, Texas District Courts (1995-1996); Judge, Texas District Courts (1999-2000)

Profession: Private Practice (1980-1990)

Staff

Law Clerk **Sylvia Tsakos** . . . . (915) 534-6740
Began Service: August 2015
Term Expires: August 2016
E-mail: syvlia_tsakos@txwd.uscourts.gov

Law Clerk **Mary Rios** . . . . (915) 534-6740
Began Service: August 2015
Term Expires: August 2016
E-mail: mary_rios@txwd.uscourts.gov

Career Law Clerk **Richard Wallach** . . . . (915) 534-6740
E-mail: richard_wallach@txwd.uscourts.gov

Courtroom Deputy **Javier Martinez** . . . . (915) 534-6725 ext. 229

Chambers of District Judge David C. Guaderrama

525 Magoffin Avenue, El Paso, TX 79901
Tel: (915) 534-6005 Fax: (915) 534-6724
E-mail: david_guaderrama@txwd.uscourts.gov

David Campos Guaderrama
District Judge

Education: New Mexico State 1975 BS; Notre Dame 1979 JD
Began Service: 2012
Appointed By: President Barack Obama

Staff

Law Clerk **Waheed Khan** .... (915) 534-6005
Law Clerk **Cristina Calvar** .... (915) 534-6005
E-mail: cristina_calvar@txwd.uscourts.gov
Education: Col Notre Dame (CA) 2012 JD; Michigan 2009 BA
Courtroom Deputy **Greg Duenas** .... (915) 534-6725 ext. 1509
E-mail: greg_duenas@txwd.uscourts.gov
Education: Texas (El Paso) 1988 BA

Chambers of District Judge Robert Lee Pitman

655 East Cesar E. Chavez Boulevard, San Antonio, TX 78206-1198
Tel: (210) 472-6570 Fax: (210) 472-6572

Robert Lee Pitman
District Judge

Education: Abilene Christian 1985; Texas 1988 JD
Began Service: December 19, 2014
Appointed By: President Barack Obama

Chambers of Senior Judge Harry Lee Hudspeth

903 San Jacinto Boulevard, Suite 440, Austin, TX 78701-2452
Tel: (512) 916-5837 Fax: (512) 916-5831

Harry Lee Hudspeth
Senior Judge

Date of Birth: 1935
Education: Texas 1955 BA, 1958 JD
Began Service: November 1979
Appointed By: President Jimmy Carter
Political Affiliation: Democrat

Government: Trial Attorney, United States Department of Justice (1959-1962); Assistant United States Attorney, Western District of Texas, United States Department of Justice (1962-1969)

Judicial: Magistrate Judge, United States District Court for the Western District of Texas (1977-1979)

Legal Practice: Peticolas, Luscombe & Stephens (1969-1977)

Military Service: United States Marine Corps (1958-1959)

Current Memberships: American Bar Association; Austin Bar Association; El Paso Bar Association; Federal Bar Association; State Bar of Texas

Staff

Law Clerk **Aamir Fiddik** .... (512) 916-5837
Began Service: August 26, 2015
Term Expires: September 2016
Judicial Assistant **Alexis Montgomery** .... (512) 916-5837
E-mail: alexis_montgomery@txwd.uscourts.gov

Chambers of Senior Judge James R. Nowlin

U.S. Courthouse, 501 West Fifth Street, Suite 6400, Austin, TX 78701
Tel: (512) 916-5675 Fax: (512) 916-5680

James Robertson Nowlin
Senior Judge

Date of Birth: 1937
Education: Trinity U 1959 BA, 1962 MA; Texas 1963 JD
Began Service: November 6, 1981
Appointed By: President Ronald Reagan

Academic: Instructor, United States History and Government, San Antonio College (1963)

Government: Associate Legal Counsel, Committee on Labor and Public Welfare, United States Senate (1965-1966); State Representative (R-TX), Texas House of Representatives (1967-1971)

Judicial: Chief Judge, United States District Court for the Western District of Texas

Legal Practice: Associate, Kelso, Locke & King; Associate, Kelso, Locke & Lepick (1963-1975); Law Offices of James R. Nowlin (1975-1981)

Military Service: United States Army (1959-1960); United States Army Reserve, United States Department of the Army (1960-1968)

Current Memberships: American Bar Association; Colorado Bar Association; San Antonio Bar Association; State Bar of Texas; Travis County Bar Association; United States District Judges Association

Staff

Courtroom Deputy **Linda Clevenger** .... (512) 916-5675
E-mail: linda_clevenger@txwd.uscourts.gov

Chambers of Senior Judge David Briones

U.S. Courthouse, 525 Magoffin Avenue, Suite 761, El Paso, TX 79901
Tel: (915) 534-6744 Fax: (915) 534-6881
E-mail: david_briones@txwd.uscourts.gov

David Briones
Senior Judge

Date of Birth: 1943
Education: Texas 1971 JD
Began Service: October 17, 1994
Appointed By: President William J. Clinton

Judicial: Judge, County Court at Law No. 1 (1991-1994)

Legal Practice: Partner, Moreno and Briones, Attorneys at Law (1971-1991)

Military Service: United States Army (1964-1966)

Current Memberships: Texas Bar Foundation; Federal Judges Association; Mexican American Bar Association; State Bar of Texas

Staff

Law Clerk **David Doak** .... (915) 534-6774
Began Service: September 4, 2014
Term Expires: September 2, 2016
E-mail: david_doak@txwd.uscourts.gov
Law Clerk **Stacy Cammarano** .... (915) 534-6774
Began Service: August 26, 2015
Term Expires: September 2, 2017
E-mail: stacy_cammarano@txwd.uscourts.gov
Court Reporter **Maria del Socorro Briggs** .... (915) 534-6744
E-mail: suky_briggs@txwd.uscourts.gov
Secretary **Alice Acosta** .... (915) 534-6744
E-mail: alicia_acosta@txwd.uscourts.gov

Chambers of Senior Judge Robert A. Junell

George H.W. Bush and George W. Bush U.S. Courthouse,
200 West Wall Street, Suite 301, Midland, TX 79701
Tel: (432) 686-4020 Fax: (432) 686-4027
E-mail: rob_junell@txwd.uscourts.gov

Robert A. Junell
Senior Judge

Date of Birth: January 27, 1947
Education: Texas Tech 1969 BS; Arkansas 1974 MS; Texas Tech 1976 JD
Began Service: February 13, 2003
Appointed By: President George W. Bush
Political Affiliation: Democrat

Staff
Law Clerk **Kaitlin Kerr** .... (432) 686-4020
Began Service: August 2015
Term Expires: August 2017
Career Law Clerk **(Vacant)** .... (432) 686-4020
Career Law Clerk **Terri L. Marroquin** .... (432) 686-4020
E-mail: terri_marroquin@txwd.uscourts.gov
Education: Texas 1995 JD
Courtroom Deputy **Monica Serna** .... (432) 685-0349
E-mail: monica_serna@txwd.uscourts.gov
Court Reporter **Ann Record** .... (432) 686-0605
E-mail: ann_record@txwd.uscourts.gov
Judicial Assistant **Debbie S. Baxter** .... (432) 686-4020
E-mail: debbie_baxter@txwd.uscourts.gov

Chambers of Magistrate Judge John W. Primomo

John H. Wood, Jr. U.S. Courthouse, 655 East Cesar E. Chavez Boulevard,
San Antonio, TX 78206-1196
Tel: (210) 472-6357 Fax: (210) 472-6365
E-mail: john_primomo@txwd.uscourts.gov

John W. Primomo
Magistrate Judge

Date of Birth: 1952
Education: St Mary's U (TX) 1976 JD
Began Service: July 18, 1988
Term Expires: July 17, 2020

Clerkships: Law Clerk, United States District Court (1980-1988)

Legal Practice: Private Practice (1977-1980)

Current Memberships: Federal Magistrate Judges Association; San Antonio Bar Association; State Bar of Texas

Staff
Career Law Clerk **Magdalena DeSalme** .... (210) 472-6357
E-mail: magdalena_desalme@txwd.uscourts.gov
Courtroom Deputy **Magda Muzza** .... (210) 472-6550 ext. 5012
E-mail: magda_muzza@txwd.uscourts.gov
Judicial Assistant **Dora M. Samudio** .... (210) 472-6357
E-mail: dora_samudio@txwd.uscourts.gov

Chambers of Magistrate Judge Miguel A. Torres

525 Magoffin Avenue, Room 751, El Paso, TX 79901
Tel: (915) 534-6732 Fax: (915) 534-6714
E-mail: miguel_torres@txwd.uscourts.gov

Miguel A. Torres
Magistrate Judge

Began Service: 2013

Staff
Career Law Clerk **Leslie Wille** .... (915) 534-6732
E-mail: leslie_wille@txwd.uscourts.gov
Education: Texas 1990 JD
Courtroom Deputy **Rita Velez** .... (915) 534-6732

Chambers of Magistrate Judge Miguel A. Torres *continued*

Judicial Assistant **Katherine Hinojos** .... (915) 534-6732
E-mail: katherine_hinojos@txwd.uscourts.gov

Chambers of Magistrate Judge Pamela Ann Mathy

John H. Wood, Jr. U.S. Courthouse, 655 East Cesar Chavez Boulevard,
San Antonio, TX 78206-1198
Tel: (210) 472-6350 Fax: (210) 472-6354
E-mail: pamela_mathy@txwd.uscourts.gov

Pamela Ann Mathy
Magistrate Judge

Date of Birth: 1952
Education: Wisconsin 1978 JD; Georgetown 1982 LLM
Began Service: June 8, 1998
Term Expires: June 8, 2022

Clerkships: Law Clerk and Staff Attorney The Honorable Walter J. Cummings, United States Court of Appeals for the Seventh Circuit (1978-1980)

Government: First Assistant, Western District of Texas, Criminal Division, United States Department of Justice; Senior Staff Attorney, Seventh Circuit, United States Court of Appeals (1981-1983); Assistant United States Attorney, Western District of Texas, United States Attorney's Office, United States Department of Justice, Ronald Reagan Administration (1983-1998)

Current Memberships: American Bar Foundation; Texas Bar Foundation; American Bar Association; The William S. Sessions American Inn of Court, The American Inns of Court; The Bexar County Women's Bar Association; College of the State Bar of Texas; Federal Bar Association; San Antonio Bar Association; San Antonio Bar Foundation; State Bar of Texas; Texas Women Lawyers

Staff
Law Clerk **Robert W. Piatt** .... (210) 472-6350
Began Service: 2014
E-mail: robert_piatt@txwd.uscourts.gov
Law Clerk **Natalee Marion** .... (210) 472-6350
Began Service: 2013
E-mail: natalee_marion@txwd.uscourts.gov
Education: St Mary's U (TX) 2013 JD
Courtroom Deputy **Kathy Hicks** .... (210) 472-6350 ext. 5005

Chambers of Magistrate Judge Andrew W. Austin

U.S. Courthouse, 501 West Fifth Street, Suite 4190, Austin, TX 78701
Tel: (512) 916-5744 Fax: (512) 916-5750

Andrew W. Austin
Magistrate Judge

Date of Birth: 1960
Education: Virginia 1982 BA; Texas 1985 JD; Cambridge (UK) 1990 MPhil
Began Service: November 22, 1999
Term Expires: November 22, 2015

Legal Practice: Briefing Attorney, The Honorable James R. Nowlin, United States District Court for the Western District of Texas (1986-1987); Associate, Vinson & Elkins L.L.P. (1987-1988); Briefing Attorney, The Honorable James R. Nowlin, United States District Court for the Western District of Texas (1988-1989); Associate, Anson, Maloney & Cameron (1990-1992); Partner, Anson, Maloney & Cameron (1993-1994); Shareholder, Sheinfeld, Maley & Kay, P.C. (1994-1999)

Staff
Briefing Attorney **Desiree Durst** .... (512) 916-5744
E-mail: desiree_durst@txwd.uscourts.gov
Education: Texas A&M 1992 BA; Texas 1995 JD

(continued on next page)

Chambers of Magistrate Judge Andrew W. Austin *continued*

Briefing Attorney **Sandy Strubel Wiele** .... (512) 916-5744
E-mail: sandy_strubel@txwd.uscourts.gov
Education: Texas 1993 BA, 1996 JD
Briefing Attorney **Patrick Leahey** .... (512) 916-5744
E-mail: patrick_leahey@txwd.uscourts.gov
Courtroom Deputy **Zing Cheng** .... (512) 916-5896 ext. 244
E-mail: zing_cheng@txwd.uscourts.gov

Chambers of Magistrate Judge Jeffrey C. Manske

U.S. Courthouse, 800 Franklin Avenue, Waco, TX 76701-2499
Tel: (254) 750-1545 Fax: (254) 750-1547
E-mail: jeffrey_manske@txwd.uscourts.gov

Jeffrey C. Manske
Magistrate Judge

Date of Birth: 1961
Education: Baylor 1983; St Mary's U (TX) 1986 JD
Began Service: 2001
Term Expires: 2017

Judicial: Law Clerk, United States District Court for the Western District of Texas (1986-1988)

Staff
Career Law Clerk **John Guinn** .... (254) 750-1545
E-mail: john_guinn@txwd.uscourts.gov
Courtroom Deputy **Lisa Trotter** .... (254) 750-1511
E-mail: lisa_trotter@txwd.uscourts.gov
Law Clerk **Amelia Beck** .... (254) 750-1545

Chambers of Magistrate Judge Victor Roberto García

111 East Broadway, Del Rio, TX 78840
Tel: (830) 703-2170 Fax: (830) 703-2110
E-mail: victor_garcía@txwd.uscourts.gov

Victor Roberto García
Magistrate Judge

Date of Birth: June 7, 1955
Education: Angelo State 1977 BA; Texas Southern 1980 JD
Began Service: May 14, 2003
Term Expires: 2019

Current Memberships: Federal Bar Association; Magistrate Judges Association; State Bar of Texas; Val Verde County Bar Association

Staff
Career Law Clerk **Emily Booth** .... (830) 703-2170
Began Service: August 2009
Judicial Assistant **Sylvia Machado-Aranda** .... (830) 703-2170

Chambers of Magistrate Judge Collis White

111 East Broadway, Del Rio, TX 78840
Tel: (830) 703-2050 Fax: (830) 703-2074
E-mail: collis_white@txwd.uscourts.gov

Collis White
Magistrate Judge

Began Service: 2009

Staff
Courtroom Deputy **Marilyn Burke** .... (830) 703-3753
E-mail: marilyn_burke@txwd.uscourts.gov
Judicial Assistant **Michelle Hester** .... (830) 703-2050

Chambers of Magistrate Judge Norbert Garney

525 Magoffin Avenue, El Paso, TX 79901
Tel: (915) 534-6980
E-mail: norbert_garney@txwd.uscourts.gov

Norbert J. Garney
Magistrate Judge

Began Service: 2000

Staff
Courtroom Deputy **Jode Bejarano** .... (915) 534-6725 ext. 1505
E-mail: jode_bejarano@txwd.uscourts.gov

Chambers of Magistrate Judge Robert F. Castañeda

525 Magoffin Avenue, Suite 651, El Paso, TX 79901
Tel: (915) 534-6028
E-mail: robert_castaneda@txwd.uscourts.gov

Robert F. Castañeda
Magistrate Judge

Began Service: April 1, 2011

Staff
Courtroom Deputy **Veronica Montoya** .... (915) 534-6725 ext. 1520
E-mail: veronica_montoya@txwd.uscourts.gov

Chambers of Magistrate Judge Mark Lane

501 West Fifth Street, Suite 7400, Austin, TX 78701
Tel: (512) 916-5679 Fax: (512) 916-5668

Mark Lane
Magistrate Judge

Education: Texas 1984 BBA; Houston 1987 JD

Chambers of Magistrate Judge Anne T. Berton

525 Magoffin Avenue, El Paso, TX 79901
Tel: (915) 834-0579 Fax: (915) 834-0665

Anne T. Berton
Magistrate Judge

Chambers of Magistrate Judge David Counts

200 East Wall Street, Midland, TX 79701
Tel: (432) 570-4439 Fax: (432) 570-4619

David Counts
Magistrate Judge

Chambers of Magistrate Judge Henry J. Bemporad

655 East Cesar E. Chavez Boulevard, San Antonio, TX 78206-1198
Tel: (210) 472-6363 Fax: (210) 472-6353

Henry J. Bemporad
Magistrate Judge

Staff
Judicial Assistant **Wendy Branham** .... (210) 472-6363
E-mail: wendy_branham@txwd.uscourts.gov
Courtroom Deputy **Kriston Hunt** .... (210) 472-6363
E-mail: kriston_hunt@txwd.uscourts.gov
Law Clerk **Laura Cauley** .... (210) 472-6363
E-mail: laura_cauley@txwd.uscourts.gov

United States Bankruptcy Court for the Western District of Texas
615 East Houston Street, Suite 597, San Antonio, TX 78205
Tel: (210) 472-6720 Tel: (800) 676-6856 (PACER)
Tel: (210) 472-4023 (Voice Case Information System VCIS)
Tel: (888) 436-7477 (Voice Case Information System VCIS)
Fax: (210) 472-5196
Internet: www.txwb.uscourts.gov

Number of Judgeships: 4

Number of Vacancies: 1

Court Staff
Clerk of Court **Yvette M. Taylor** .... (210) 472-6720
E-mail: yvette_taylor@txwb.uscourts.gov Fax: (210) 472-6215
Financial Specialist **Annette Anderson** .... (210) 472-6720 ext. 268
E-mail: annette_anderson@txwb.uscourts.gov
Human Resources Specialist **Patty Nelson** ...... (210) 472-6720 ext. 227
E-mail: patty_nelson@txwb.uscourts.gov
Operations Manager **Maria Dozauer** .... (512) 916-5237 ext. 316
E-mail: maria_dozauer@txwb.uscourts.gov
Information Technology Support Services Manager **Sherry Deering** .... (210) 472-6720 ext. 247
E-mail: sherry_deering@txwb.uscourts.gov

Chambers of Chief Bankruptcy Judge Ronald B. King
615 East Houston Street, San Antonio, TX 78205
P.O. Box 1439, San Antonio, TX 78295-1439
Tel: (210) 472-6609

Ronald B. King
Chief Bankruptcy Judge

Date of Birth: 1953
Education: Southern Methodist 1974 BA; Texas 1977 JD
Began Service: October 1, 1988
Term Expires: September 30, 2016

Legal Practice: Briefing Attorney (1977-1978); Foster, Lewis, Langley, Gardner & Banack, Inc (1978-1988)

Current Memberships: National Conference of Bankruptcy Judges; San Antonio Bankruptcy Bar Association; San Antonio Bar Association

Staff
Law Clerk **Jason Enright** .... (210) 472-6609
Began Service: September 2014
Term Expires: September 2016
E-mail: jason_enright@txwb.uscourts.gov
Courtroom Deputy **Jana Brisiel** .... (210) 472-6720 ext. 235
E-mail: jana_brisiel@txwb.uscourts.gov
Administrative Assistant **Tricia Haass** .... (210) 472-6609
E-mail: tricia_haass@txwb.uscourts.gov

Chambers of Bankruptcy Judge Craig A. Gargotta
Hipolito F. Garcia Federal Building and U.S. Courthouse, 615 East Houston Street, Room 505, San Antonio, TX 78205
Tel: (210) 472-5181

Craig A. Gargotta
Bankruptcy Judge

Began Service: October 2007
Term Expires: October 2021

Government: Deputy Chief, Civil Division, Texas - Western District, United States Department of Justice

Staff
Law Clerk **Amelia Bueche** .... (512) 916-5875
Began Service: September 2015
Term Expires: September 2016
E-mail: amelia_bueche@txwb.uscourts.gov

Chambers of Bankruptcy Judge Craig A. Gargotta *continued*

Law Clerk **Megan Young** .... (512) 916-5875
Began Service: September 2013
Term Expires: September 2016
E-mail: megan_young@txwb.uscourts.gov
Courtroom Deputy **Lisa A. Elizondo** .... (512) 916-5238

Chambers of Bankruptcy Judge H. Christopher Mott
Homer J. Thornberry Federal Judicial Building, 903 San Jacinto Boulevard, Suite 326, Austin, TX 78701
Tel: (512) 916-5800

H. Christopher Mott
Bankruptcy Judge

Began Service: 2010

Staff
Law Clerk **Michael Lutfy** .... (512) 916-5800
Began Service: 2014
E-mail: michael_lutfy@txwb.uscourts.gov
Career Law Clerk **Sarah McHaney** .... (512) 916-5800
E-mail: sarah_mchaney@txwb.uscourts.gov
Education: Texas 1987 JD
Courtroom Deputy **Ronda Farrar** .... (512) 916-5238 ext. 312
E-mail: ronda_farrar@txwb.uscourts.gov

Chambers of Bankruptcy Judge Tony M. Davis
903 San Jacinto Boulevard, Suite 332, Austin, TX 78701
Tel: (512) 916-5875

Tony M. Davis
Bankruptcy Judge

Staff
Law Clerk **Sarah Wood** .... (512) 916-5875
E-mail: sarah_wood@txwb.uscourts.gov
Law Clerk **Marissa Wiesen** .... (512) 916-5875
E-mail: marissa_wiesen@txwb.uscourts.gov
Courtroom Deputy **Jennifer Lopez** .... (512) 916-5875
E-mail: jennifer_lopez@txwb.uscourts.gov

United States District Court for the District of Utah
U.S. Courthouse, 351 South West Temple, Room 1.100, Salt Lake City, UT 84101
Tel: (801) 524-6100 Fax: (801) 526-1175
Internet: www.utd.uscourts.gov

Number of Judgeships: 5

Number of Vacancies: 1

Circuit: Tenth

Court Staff
Clerk of Court **D. Mark Jones** .... (801) 524-6100
E-mail: mark_jones@utd.uscourts.gov
Chief Deputy Clerk **Louise York** .... (801) 524-6100
E-mail: louise_york@utd.uscourts.gov
Computer Systems Manager **Scott Mumford** .... (801) 524-6105
E-mail: scott_mumford@utd.uscourts.gov
UNIX Systems Manager **Robert Janzen** .... (801) 524-6105
E-mail: robert_janzen@utd.uscourts.gov
Human Resources **Tara Curtis** .... (801) 524-6108
E-mail: tara_curtis@utd.uscourts.gov
Appeals Clerk **Jennifer Richards** .... (801) 524-6124
E-mail: jennifer_richards@utd.uscourts.gov
Financial Administrator **Michael Duncan** .... (801) 524-6109
E-mail: michael_duncan@utd.uscourts.gov
Financial Assistant **Trudy Sanderson** .... (801) 524-6110
E-mail: trudy_sanderson@utd.uscourts.gov

(continued on next page)

United States District Court for the District of Utah *continued*

Jury Administrator **Kris Porter** . . . . (801) 524-6285
E-mail: kris_porter@utd.uscourts.gov
Budget Analyst **Gary Serdar** . . . . (801) 524-6107
E-mail: gary_serdar@utd.uscourts.gov
Chief Probation Officer **Dave Christenson** . . . . (801) 524-5176
Circuit Librarian **Pat Hummel** . . . . (801) 524-3505
E-mail: patricia_hummel@utd.uscourts.gov

Chambers of Chief Judge David Nuffer

Frank E. Moss U.S. Courthouse, 351 South West Temple,
Room 10.100, Salt Lake City, UT 84101
Tel: (801) 524-6100 Fax: (801) 526-1175
E-mail: david_nuffer@utd.uscourts.gov

David Nuffer
Chief Judge

Date of Birth: 1952
Education: BYU 1975 BA; J Reuben Clark Law 1978 JD
Began Service: May 28, 2012
Appointed By: President Barack Obama

Current Memberships: Southern Utah Bar Association; State Bar of Arizona

Staff
Court Reporter **Rebecca Janke** . . . . (801) 521-7238
E-mail: rebecca_janke@utd.uscourts.gov
Courtroom Deputy **Anndrea Sullivan-Bowers** . . . . (801) 524-6150

Chambers of District Judge Clark Waddoups

U.S. Courthouse, 351 South West Temple, Room 9.420,
Salt Lake City, UT 84101
Tel: (801) 524-4221
E-mail: clark_waddoups@utd.uscourts.gov

Clark Waddoups
District Judge

Education: BYU; Utah JD
Began Service: October 23, 2008
Appointed By: President George W. Bush

Clerkships: Law Clerk, United States Court of Appeals for the Ninth Circuit

Legal Practice: Partner, Parr Waddoups Brown Gee & Loveless

Staff
Court Reporter **Karen Murakami** . . . . (801) 328-4800
E-mail: karen_murakami@utd.uscourts.gov
Court Reporter **Laura Robinson** . . . . (801) 328-4800
E-mail: laura_robinson@utd.uscourts.gov
Administrative Assistant **S. Adriane Wright** . . . . (801) 524-6600

Chambers of District Judge Robert J. Shelby

Frank E. Moss U.S. Courthouse, 351 South West Temple,
Room 10.220, Salt Lake City, UT 84101
Tel: (801) 524-6100
E-mail: robert_shelby@utd.uscourts.gov

Robert J. Shelby
District Judge

Education: Utah State 1994 BA; Virginia 1998 JD
Began Service: September 25, 2012
Appointed By: President Barack Obama

Staff
Court Reporter **Ray Fenlon** . . . . (801) 809-4634
E-mail: ray_fenlon@utd.uscourts.gov
Courtroom Deputy **Mary Jane McNamee** . . . . (801) 524-6790

Chambers of District Judge Jill N. Parrish

351 South West Temple, Room 9.241, Salt Lake City, UT 84101
Tel: (801) 524-6018

Jill N. Parrish
District Judge

Education: Weber State 1982 BS; Yale 1985 JD
Began Service: 2015
Appointed By: President Barack Obama

Government: Assistant U.S. Attorney, Civil Division, United States Attorney's Office, United States Department of Justice

Judicial: Justice, Utah Supreme Court (2003-2015)

Staff
Courtroom Deputy **Stephanie Schaerrer** . . . . (801) 524-6018
Court Reporter **Patti Walker** . . . . (801) 524-6018

Chambers of Senior Judge Bruce S. Jenkins

351 South West Temple, Salt Lake City, UT 84101
Tel: (801) 524-6507 Fax: (801) 526-1172
E-mail: bruce_jenkins@utd.uscourts.gov
Internet: http://www.utd.uscourts.gov/judges/jenkins.html

Bruce S. Jenkins
Senior Judge

Date of Birth: 1927
Education: Utah 1949 BA, 1952 JD
Began Service: 1978
Appointed By: President Jimmy Carter

Academic: Adjunct Professor, University of Utah (1987-1988); Adjunct Professor, College of Law, University of Utah (1995-1999)

Clerkships: Research Clerk, Supreme Court of Utah

Government: Assistant Attorney General, Office of the Attorney General, State of Utah (1952); Deputy Prosecutor, County of Salt Lake, Utah (1954-1958); State Senator Bruce S. Jenkins (D-UT), Utah State Senate (1959-1965); Vice Chairman, Commission on the Organization of the Executive Branch, State of Utah

Judicial: Bankruptcy Judge, United States Bankruptcy Court for the District of Utah (1965-1978)

Legal Practice: Private Practice (1959-1965)

Military Service: United States Navy (1945-1946)

Current Memberships: American Bar Foundation; American Bar Association; Federal Bar Association; Federal Judges Association; United States Supreme Court Bar; Utah State Bar

Staff
Law Clerk **Ashley Mitchell** . . . . (801) 524-6168
E-mail: ashley_mitchell@utd.uscourts.gov
Court Reporter **(Vacant)** . . . . (801) 328-0837
Courtroom Deputy **Stephanie Schaerrer** . . . . (801) 524-6145
E-mail: stephanie_schaerrer@utd.uscourts.gov
Judicial Assistant **Kathleen Smith** . . . . (801) 524-6507
E-mail: Kathleen_Smith@utd.uscourts.gov

Chambers of Senior Judge Dale A. Kimball

U.S. Courthouse, 351 South West Temple Street,
Salt Lake City, UT 84101
Tel: (801) 524-6610 Fax: (801) 526-1174
E-mail: Dale_Kimball@utd.uscourts.gov

Dale A. Kimball
Senior Judge

Date of Birth: 1939
Education: BYU 1964 BS; Utah 1967 JD
Began Service: November 24, 1997
Appointed By: President William J. Clinton

Academic: Associate Professor, J. Reuben Clark Law School, Brigham Young University (1974-1976); Adjunct Professor, J. Reuben Clark Law School, Brigham Young University (1976-1979); Professor of Law, J. Reuben Clark Law School, Brigham Young University

Judicial: Chairman, Judicial Performance Evaluation Review; Master of the Bench, American Inns of Court; Chairman, Utah State Bar Ethics and Discipline Committee; Chairman, Utah State Bar Committee on the Unauthorized Practice of Law

Legal Practice: Associate then Partner, VanCott, Bagley, Cornwall & McCarthy (1967-1974); Senior Partner, Kimball, Parr, Waddoups, Brown & Gee (1975-1997)

Military Service: Utah Air National Guard (1957-1964)

Nonprofit: Director, Board of Directors, Jordan Education Foundation

Current Memberships: American Bar Foundation; Utah Chapter, Federal Bar Association

Staff
Career Law Clerk **Susie Inskeep Hindley** .... (801) 524-6612
E-mail: susie_hindley@utd.uscourts.gov
Education: Utah 1991 BS, 1995 JD
Career Law Clerk **Anne Morgan** .... (801) 524-6611
E-mail: anne_morgan@utd.uscourts.gov
Education: Stanford 1988 BA; Utah 1993 JD
Case Manager **Kim M. Jones** .... (801) 524-6114
Court Reporter **(Vacant)** .... (801) 521-7238
Court Reporter **(Vacant)** .... (801) 521-7238
Judicial Administrative Assistant **Kim M. Jones** .... (801) 524-6610
E-mail: kim_m_jones@utd.uscourts.gov

Chambers of Senior Judge David Sam

441 Frank E. Moss U.S. Courthouse, 350 South Main Street,
Salt Lake City, UT 84101-2106
Tel: (801) 524-6190 Fax: (801) 526-1156
E-mail: david_sam@utd.uscourts.gov

David Sam
Senior Judge

Date of Birth: 1933
Education: BYU 1957 BS; Utah 1960 JD
Began Service: 1985
Appointed By: President Ronald Reagan
Political Affiliation: Republican

Academic: Institute Director, Church of Jesus Christ of Latter-Day Saints (1964); Institute Director, Church of Jesus Christ of Latter-Day Saints (1969); Part-Time Faculty, Brigham Young University (1977-1985)

Government: County Attorney, Office of the County Attorney, County of Duchesne, Utah (1966-1972); County Commissioner, Office of the County Commissioner, County of Duchesne, Utah (1972-1974)

Judicial: Judge, Utah District Court, Fourth Judicial District (1976-1985)

Legal Practice: Private Practice (1963-1971); Sam & Mangan (1971-1973); Sam, Brown & Park (1973-1976)

Military Service: United States Air Force (1961-1963)

Current Memberships: Federal District Court Judges Association; The Supreme Court Historical Society; Utah State Bar

Chambers of Senior Judge David Sam *continued*

Staff
Career Law Clerk **Mitzi Collins** .... (801) 524-6190
E-mail: mitzi_collins@utd.uscourts.gov
Education: J Reuben Clark Law 1987 JD
Career Law Clerk **David Jones** .... (801) 524-6190
E-mail: david_jones@utd.uscourts.gov
Education: Nebraska 1985 JD
Career Law Clerk **Cindy Lauter** .... (801) 524-6190
Began Service: August 2011
Education: Utah 2011 JD
Career Law Clerk **Shauna Stout** .... (801) 524-6190
E-mail: shauna_stout@utd.uscourts.gov
Education: J Reuben Clark Law 1988 JD
Courtroom Deputy **Kim Forsgren** .... (801) 524-6602

Chambers of Senior Judge Tena Campbell

351 South West Temple, Suite 9.220, Salt Lake City, UT 84101
Tel: (801) 524-6170 Fax: (801) 526-1154
E-mail: Tena_Campbell@utd.uscourts.gov

Tena Campbell
Senior Judge

Date of Birth: 1944
Education: Idaho 1967 BA; Arizona State 1970 MA, 1977 JD
Began Service: July 10, 1995
Appointed By: President William J. Clinton

Staff
Law Clerk **Douglas Crapo** .... (801) 524-6116
Began Service: August 2015
Term Expires: August 2016
Career Law Clerk **Anne E. Rice** .... (801) 524-6172
E-mail: anne_rice@utd.uscourts.gov
Education: Northwestern 1997 JD
Judicial Assistant and Case Manager **Christine F. Ford** ... (801) 524-6170
E-mail: chris_ford@utd.uscourts.gov

Chambers of Senior Judge Dee Benson

Frank E. Moss U.S. Courthouse, 350 South Main Street, Room 253,
Salt Lake City, UT 84101
Tel: (801) 524-6160 Fax: (801) 526-1167
E-mail: dee_benson@utd.uscourts.gov

Dee V. Benson
Senior Judge

Date of Birth: 1948
Education: BYU 1973 BA; J Reuben Clark Law 1976 JD
Began Service: 1991
Appointed By: President George H.W. Bush

Current Memberships: Salt Lake County Bar Association; Utah State Bar

Staff
Law Clerk **Alex Nelson** .... (801) 524-6162
Began Service: October 1, 2015
Term Expires: October 2016
Law Clerk **Tiffany Romney** .... (801) 524-6162
Began Service: October 1, 2014
Term Expires: October 2016
Career Law Clerk **Alison Johnson Adams** .... (801) 524-6162
E-mail: alison_adams@utd.uscourts.gov
Education: Utah 1994 JD
Executive Assistant/Case Manager **Ron Black** .... (801) 524-6160
E-mail: ron_black@utd.uscourts.gov
Education: Utah BA
Court Reporter **Ed Young** .... (801) 328-3202
E-mail: ed_young@utd.uscourts.gov

Chambers of Senior Judge Ted Stewart

Frank E. Moss U.S. Courthouse, 350 South Main Street, Room 148, Salt Lake City, UT 84101
Tel: (801) 524-6617 Fax: (801) 526-1181
E-mail: ted_stewart@utd.uscourts.gov

Ted Stewart
Senior Judge

Date of Birth: 1948
Education: Utah State 1972 BS; Utah 1975 JD
Began Service: December 1999
Appointed By: President William J. Clinton

Current Memberships: Utah Bar Association

Staff
Law Clerk **Margaret Vu** . . . . (801) 524-6516
Began Service: December 2014
Term Expires: December 2016
Law Clerk **Stacie Stewart** . . . . (801) 524-6607
Began Service: September 2015
Term Expires: September 2016
Education: BYU 2014 JD
Law Clerk **(Vacant)** . . . . (801) 524-6609
Career Law Clerk **Thomas Copeland** . . . . (801) 524-6627
E-mail: thomas_copeland@utd.uscourts.gov
Education: Utah 2005 JD
Court Reporter **Patti Walker** . . . . (801) 364-5440
E-mail: patti_walker@utd.uscourts.gov
Courtroom Deputy **Ryan Robertson** . . . . (801) 524-6617
E-mail: ryan_robertson@utd.uscourts.gov

Chambers of Chief Magistrate Judge Brooke C. Wells

350 South Main Street, Room 431, Salt Lake City, UT 84101-2180
Tel: (801) 524-6422 Fax: (801) 526-1173
E-mail: brooke_wells@utd.uscourts.gov

Brooke C. Wells
Chief Magistrate Judge

Education: Utah 1977 JD
Began Service: June 4, 2003
Term Expires: June 2019

Staff
Courtroom Deputy **Lynsie Severnak** . . . . (801) 524-6422
E-mail: lynsie_severnak@utd.uscourts.gov

Chambers of Magistrate Judge Paul M. Warner

351 South West Temple, Room 10.440, Salt Lake City, UT 84101
Tel: (801) 524-6620
E-mail: paul_warner@utd.uscourts.gov

Paul Michael Warner
Magistrate Judge

Date of Birth: June 11, 1949
Education: BYU 1973 BA; J Reuben Clark Law 1976 JD; BYU 1984 MA
Began Service: 2006

Government: Trial Attorney, Office of the Judge Advocate General, United States Department of the Navy, United States Department of Defense; Chief Defense Counsel, San Diego, Office of the Judge Advocate General, United States Department of the Navy, United States Department of Defense; Associate Chief Deputy Attorney General, Office of the Attorney General, State of Utah; First Assistant U.S. Attorney, Utah District, Executive Office for United States Attorneys, United States Department of Justice; U.S. Attorney, Utah District, Executive Office for United States Attorneys, United States Department of Justice, William J. Clinton Administration (1998-2006)

Chambers of Magistrate Judge Paul M. Warner *continued*

Staff
Courtroom Deputy **Kirsten Mumford** . . . . (801) 524-3240
E-mail: kirsten_mumford@utd.uscourts.gov

Chambers of Magistrate Judge Dustin B. Pead

351 South West Temple, Room 9.200, Salt Lake City, UT 84101
Tel: (801) 524-6155
E-mail: utdecf_pead@utd.uscourts.gov

Dustin B. Pead
Magistrate Judge

Began Service: 2012

Staff
Law Clerk **Aimee Nagles** . . . . (801) 524-6155
E-mail: aimee_nagles@utd.uscourts.gov
Law Clerk **(Vacant)** . . . . (801) 524-6155

Chambers of Magistrate Judge Evelyn J. Furse

351 South West Temple, Room 10.200, Salt Lake City, UT 84101
Tel: (801) 524-6180
E-mail: evelyn_furse@utd.uscourts.gov

Evelyn J. Furse
Magistrate Judge

Staff
Law Clerk **(Vacant)** . . . . (801) 524-6180
Courtroom Deputy **Lindsey Pagel** . . . . (801) 524-6180
E-mail: lindsey_pagel@utd.uscourts.gov

Chambers of Magistrate Judge (part-time) Robert T. Braithwaite

206 West Tabernacle, Suite 225, St. George, UT 84770
Tel: (435) 656-7580
E-mail: robert_braithwaite@utd.uscourts.gov

Robert T. Braithwaite
Magistrate Judge (Part-Time)

Education: Utah 1976 JD
Began Service: May 7, 2003
Term Expires: 2016

Staff
Judicial Assistant **Georgia S. Szatlocky** . . . . (435) 656-7580
E-mail: georgia_szatlocky@utd.uscourts.gov

United States Bankruptcy Court for the District of Utah

Frank E. Moss U.S. Courthouse, 350 South Main Street, Room 301, Salt Lake City, UT 84101
Tel: (801) 524-6687 Tel: (800) 676-6856 (Toll Free PACER)
Tel: (866) 222-8029 (Toll Free Voice Case Information System VCIS)
Fax: (801) 524-4409
E-mail: bankruptcy_clerk@utb.uscourts.gov
Internet: www.utb.uscourts.gov

Number of Judgeships: 3

Court Staff
Clerk **David A. Sime** . . . . (801) 524-6565
E-mail: david_sime@utb.uscourts.gov
Chief Deputy Clerk **(Vacant)** . . . . (801) 524-6561
Fax: (801) 526-1197
Systems Manager **Jon Igo** . . . . (801) 524-6550
E-mail: jon_igo@utb.uscourts.gov Fax: (801) 526-1191

United States Bankruptcy Court for the District of Utah *continued*

Human Resources Manager **Jon Willardson** . . . . (801) 524-6593
E-mail: Jon_Willardson@utb.uscourts.gov Fax: (801) 526-1198

Chambers of Chief Bankruptcy Judge R. Kimball Mosier

350 South Main Street, Room 365, Salt Lake City, UT 84101
Tel: (801) 524-6568 Fax: (801) 526-1204

R. Kimball Mosier
Chief Bankruptcy Judge

Education: Utah 1980 JD
Began Service: February 2009

Staff
Career Law Clerk **M. John Straley** . . . . (801) 524-6569
Education: Utah 1974 BA, 1977 MA, 1983 JD
Judicial Assistant **Shannon Robinson** . . . . (801) 524-6568
E-mail: shannon_robinson@utb.uscourts.gov

Chambers of Bankruptcy Judge William T. Thurman

Frank E. Moss U.S. Courthouse, 350 South Main Street, Room 358, Salt Lake City, UT 84101-2195
Tel: (801) 524-6572 Fax: (801) 526-1209
E-mail: william_thurman@utb.uscourts.gov

William T. Thurman
Bankruptcy Judge

Date of Birth: 1947
Education: Utah 1971 BA, 1974 JD
Began Service: September 4, 2001
Term Expires: September 3, 2023

Current Memberships: American Bankruptcy Institute; National Conference of Bankruptcy Judges

Staff
Fax: (801) 526-1209

Law Clerk **Ellen E. Ostrow** . . . . (801) 524-6572
Began Service: August 15, 2013
Term Expires: August 14, 2016
E-mail: ellen_ostrow@utb.uscourts.gov
Judicial Assistant **Thora Searle** . . . . (801) 524-6572
E-mail: thora_searle@utb.uscourts.gov

Chambers of Bankruptcy Judge Joel T. Marker

Frank E. Moss U.S. Courthouse, 350 South Main Street, Salt Lake City, UT 84101
Tel: (801) 524-5749 Fax: (801) 524-4409
E-mail: joel_marker@utb.uscourts.gov

Joel T. Marker
Bankruptcy Judge

Began Service: July 9, 2010
Term Expires: 2024

Staff
Career Law Clerk **Mike Coffman** . . . . (801) 524-5749
Education: Duke 2000 BA; Harvard 2003 JD
Career Law Clerk **Jeffrey Trousdale** . . . . (801) 524-5749
E-mail: jeffrey_trousdale@utb.uscourts.gov
Education: Minnesota 2010 JD

United States District Court for the District of Vermont

U.S. Post Office & Courthouse, 11 Elmwood Avenue, Burlington, VT 05401
P.O. Box 945, Burlington, VT 05402
204 Main Street, Room 201, Brattleboro, VT 05301
P.O. Box 998, Brattleboro, VT 05302-0998
151 West Street, Rutland, VT 05701
P.O. Box 607, Rutland, VT 05702-0607
Tel: (802) 951-6301 Tel: (802) 254-0250 (Brattleboro Office)
Tel: (802) 773-0245 (Rutland Office) Tel: (802) 951-6623 (PACER)
Internet: www.vtd.uscourts.gov

Number of Judgeships: 2

Circuit: Second

Court Staff

Clerk of Court **Jeffrey S. Eaton** . . . . (802) 951-6301
Chief Deputy of Operations **Michael Dunavin** . . . . (802) 951-6301
E-mail: michael_dunavin@vtd.uscourts.gov
Chief Probation Officer **Joseph McNamara** . . . . (802) 652-3000
Director of Technology **Jason Bushey** . . . . (802) 951-6301
E-mail: jason_bushey@vtd.uscourts.gov
Financial Administrator **Julie M. McKenzie** . . . . (802) 951-6301
E-mail: julie_mckenzie@vtd.uscourts.gov
Jury Administrator and Personnel Assistant **Kathleen Carter** . . . . (802) 951-6301
E-mail: kathleen_carter@vtd.uscourts.gov
Operational Supervisor **Lisa A. Wright** . . . . (802) 951-6301
E-mail: lisa_wright@vtd.uscourts.gov

Chambers of Chief Judge Christina Reiss

P.O. Box 446, Burlington, VT 05402-0446
Tel: (802) 951-6622 Fax: (802) 773-0245
E-mail: christina_reiss@vtd.uscourts.gov

Christina Reiss
Chief Judge

Began Service: January 8, 2010
Appointed By: President Barack Obama

Staff
Law Clerk and Judicial Assistant **Elizabeth Hall** . . . . (802) 951-6622
Term Expires: September 2017
Education: Rutgers (Newark) 2003 JD

Chambers of District Judge Geoffrey W. Crawford

11 Elmwood Avenue, Burlington, VT 05401
Tel: (802) 951-6301

Geoffrey W. Crawford
District Judge

Education: Yale 1977 BA; Harvard 1980 JD
Began Service: August 4, 2014
Appointed By: President Barack Obama

Government: Judge, Vermont Superior Court (2002-2013)

Judicial: Associate Justice, Vermont Supreme Court (2013-2014)

Legal Practice: Partner, O'Neill, Crawford & Green (1987-2002)

Chambers of Senior Judge J. Garvan Murtha

204 Main Street, Brattleboro, VT 05301
P.O. Box 760, Brattleboro, VT 05302-0760
Tel: (802) 258-4413 Fax: (802) 254-0267

J. Garvan Murtha
Senior Judge

Date of Birth: 1941
Education: Yale 1963 BA; Connecticut 1968 LLB; Georgetown 1972 LLM
Began Service: May 26, 1995
Appointed By: President William J. Clinton

Government: Deputy County Attorney, Office of the County Attorney, County of Windham, Vermont (1970-1973)

Judicial: District Judge, United States District Court for the District of Vermont

Legal Practice: Associate then Partner, Kristensen, Cummings & Murtha, P.C. (1973-1995)

Current Memberships: American Board of Trial Advocates; Vermont Bar Association; Windham County Bar Association

Staff

Career Law Clerk **Karina J. Martin** .... (802) 258-4413
Began Service: August 11, 2008
E-mail: karina_martin@vtd.uscourts.gov
Education: Elmira 2002 BA; Cornell 2006 JD

Judicial Assistant **Kristine B. Long** .... (802) 258-4413
E-mail: kris_long@vtd.uscourts.gov

Chambers of Senior Judge William K. Sessions III

U.S. Post Office & Courthouse, 11 Elmwood Avenue, Burlington, VT 05401
P.O. Box 928, Burlington, VT 05402
Tel: (802) 951-6350 Fax: (802) 951-6785
E-mail: william_sessions@vtd.uscourts.gov

William K. Sessions III
Senior Judge

Date of Birth: 1947
Education: Middlebury 1969 BA; George Washington 1972 JD
Began Service: August 15, 1995
Appointed By: President William J. Clinton

Staff

Law Clerk **Kendall Hoechft** .... (802) 951-6350

Career Law Clerk **Christopher G. Jernigan** .... (802) 951-6350
E-mail: christopher_jernigan@vtd.uscourts.gov
Education: Boston Col 1994 JD

Judicial Assistant **Elizabeth Evelti** .... (802) 951-6350
E-mail: elizabeth_evelti@vtd.uscourts.gov
Education: Trinity Col (VT) 2000 BA

Chambers of Magistrate Judge John M. Conroy

11 Elmwood Avenue, Burlington, VT 05401
Tel: (802) 951-6308
E-mail: john_conroy@vtd.uscourts.gov

John M. Conroy
Magistrate Judge

Began Service: January 2009

Staff

Law Clerk **Marie Horbar** .... (802) 951-6308
Term Expires: September 2016

Career Law Clerk **Martha Botten** .... (802) 951-6308

United States Bankruptcy Court for the District of Vermont

U.S. Post Office and Courthouse, 151 West Street, Rutland, VT 05701
P.O. Box 6648, Rutland, VT 05702-6648
Tel: (802) 776-2000 Fax: (802) 776-2020
Internet: www.vtb.uscourts.gov

Number of Judgeships: 1

Court Staff
Fax: (802) 776-2020

Clerk of Court **Thomas J. Hart** .... (802) 776-2000

Chief Deputy Clerk **Kathleen A. Ford** .... (802) 776-2000

Finance **Paula S. LaFond** .... (802) 776-2011
E-mail: paula_lafond@vtb.uscourts.gov

Chambers of Bankruptcy Judge Colleen A. Brown

151 West Street, Rutland, VT 05701
P.O. Box 6648, Rutland, VT 05702-6648
Tel: (802) 776-2030 Fax: (802) 776-2028
E-mail: Colleen_Brown@vtb.uscourts.gov

Colleen A. Brown
Bankruptcy Judge

Date of Birth: 1956
Education: Colgate 1979 BA; SUNY (Buffalo) 1983 JD
Began Service: April 10, 2000
Term Expires: April 9, 2022

Clerkships: Law Clerk The Honorable Beryl E. McGuire, United States Bankruptcy Court for the Western District of New York

Government: Assistant U.S. Trustee for the Western District of New York

Legal Practice: Partner, Lawrence, Werner, Kesselring, Swartout & Brown, LLP; In-house Counsel, The Canandaigua National Bank and Trust Company

Current Memberships: American Bar Association; National Conference of Bankruptcy Judges

Staff

Law Clerk **Ha Young Chung** .... (802) 776-2030
Began Service: 2015
Term Expires: September 2016
E-mail: lawclerks@vtb.uscourts.gov

Courtroom Deputy **Terri A. Satterlee** .... (802) 776-2010
E-mail: Terri_Satterlee@vtb.uscourts.gov Fax: (802) 776-2020
Education: Vermont 1980 BA

Judicial Assistant **Maria Dionne** .... (802) 776-2030

United States District Court for the Eastern District of Virginia

Albert V. Bryan Sr. U.S. Courthouse, 401 Courthouse Square, Alexandria, VA 22314-5798
Tel: (703) 299-2100 Tel: (800) 852-5186 (PACER)
Fax: (703) 299-2109
Internet: www.vaed.uscourts.gov

Number of Judgeships: 11

Circuit: Fourth

Areas Covered: Counties of Accomack, Amelia, Arlington, Brunswick, Caroline, Charles City, Chesterfield, Dinwiddie, Essex, Fairfax, Fauquier, Gloucester, Goochland, Greensville, Hanover, Henrico, Isle of Wight, James City, King and Queen, King George, King William, Lancaster, Loudoun, Lunenburg, Mathews, Mecklenburg, Middlesex, New Kent, Northampton, Northumberland, Nottoway, Powhatan, Prince Edward, Prince George, Prince William, Richmond, Southampton, Spotsylvania, Stafford, Surry, Sussex, Westmoreland and York

Court Staff

Clerk of Court **G. Fernando Galindo** . . . . (757) 222-7200
Chief Deputy **Laura Drewa** . . . . (703) 299-2107
E-mail: laura_drewa@vaed.uscourts.gov Fax: (703) 299-2108
Deputy-in-Charge, Newport News Division **Jamie Meyers** . . . . (757) 247-0784
US Courthouse, 2400 West Avenue, Newport News, VA 23607 Fax: (757) 928-0137
E-mail: jamie_meyers@vaed.uscourts.gov
Alexandria Division Manager **Richard Banke** . . . . (703) 299-2179
E-mail: richard_banke@vaed.uscourts.gov
Norfolk Division Manager **Adrian Kellam Glatt** . . . . (757) 222-7200
E-mail: adrian_glatt@vaed.uscourts.gov
Richmond Division Manager **Sharon Cooke** . . . . (804) 916-2200
US Courthouse, 701 East Broad Street, Richmond, VA 23219 Fax: (804) 916-2216
E-mail: sharon_cooke@vaed.uscourts.gov
Chief Probation Officer **Mary Farashahi** . . . . (703) 222-7300

Chambers of Chief Judge Rebecca Beach Smith

358 U.S. Courthouse, 600 Granby Street, Norfolk, VA 23510-2449
Tel: (757) 222-7001
E-mail: rebecca_smith@vaed.uscourts.gov

Rebecca Beach Smith

Chief Judge

Date of Birth: 1949
Education: William & Mary 1971 BA; Virginia 1973 MA; William & Mary 1979 JD
Began Service: 1989
Appointed By: President George H.W. Bush

Current Memberships: American Bar Association; Federal Bar Association; Fourth Circuit Judicial Conference; The Supreme Court Historical Society; Virginia State Bar

Staff

Secretary **Debbie Timlin** . . . . (757) 222-7001
E-mail: debbie_timlin@vaed.uscourts.gov

Chambers of District Judge Leonie M. Brinkema

Albert V. Bryan Sr. U.S. Courthouse, 401 Courthouse Square, Alexandria, VA 22314-5799
Tel: (703) 299-2116 Fax: (703) 299-2238

Leonie M. Brinkema

District Judge

Date of Birth: 1944
Education: Rutgers 1966 BA, 1970 MLS; Cornell 1976 JD
Began Service: October 21, 1993
Appointed By: President William J. Clinton

Government: Assistant United States Attorney, Eastern District of Virginia, Office of the United States Attorney, United States Department of Justice (1977-1983); Trial Attorney, Office of International Affairs, United States Department of Justice (1983-1984)

Judicial: Magistrate Judge, United States District Court for the Eastern District of Virginia (1985-1993)

Legal Practice: Private Practice (1984-1985)

Current Memberships: Alexandria Bar Association; Virginia State Bar; Virginia Women Attorneys Association

Staff

Law Clerk **Kathryn Barber** . . . . (703) 229-2116
Began Service: August 2015
Term Expires: August 2016
E-mail: kathryn_barber@vaed.uscourts.gov
Law Clerk **Michaela Wilkes-Klein** . . . . (703) 229-2116
Began Service: September 2015
Term Expires: September 2016
Court Reporter **Anneliese J. Thomson** . . . . (703) 299-8595
E-mail: anneliese_thomson@vaed.uscourts.gov
Secretary **Beth Richards** . . . . (703) 299-2116
E-mail: beth_richards@vaed.uscourts.gov

Chambers of District Judge Raymond A. Jackson

U.S. Courthouse, 600 Granby Street, Norfolk, VA 23510-2449
Tel: (757) 222-7003 Fax: (757) 222-7023
E-mail: Raymond_Jackson@vaed.uscourts.gov

Raymond A. Jackson

District Judge

Date of Birth: 1949
Education: Norfolk State 1970 BA; Virginia 1973 JD
Began Service: 1993
Appointed By: President William J. Clinton

Academic: Adjunct Faculty, Marshall-Wythe School of Law, The College of William and Mary (1984-1993)

Government: Assistant United States Attorney, Eastern District of Virginia, Office of the United States Attorney, United States Department of Justice (1977-1993)

Legal Practice: Captain, Judge Advocate General's Corp United States Army (1973-1977)

Military Service: United States Army (1973-1977); Colonel United States Army Reserve, United States Department of the Army

Current Memberships: The I'Anson-Hoffman American Inn of Court; Norfolk and Portsmouth Bar Association; Old Dominion Bar Association; South Hampton Roads Bar Association; United States District Judges Association; The Virginia Law Foundation; Virginia State Bar

Staff

Law Clerk **Jazzirelle Sepulveda** . . . . (757) 222-7003
Began Service: August 2015
Term Expires: September 2016
E-mail: jazzirelle_sepulveda@vaed.uscourts.gov
Law Clerk **Brandon Harper** . . . . (757) 222-7003
Began Service: September 2014
Term Expires: September 2016

(continued on next page)

Chambers of District Judge Raymond A. Jackson *continued*

Judicial Administrator and Assistant **Pamela Thorbs** . . . . . (757) 222-7003
E-mail: pamela_thorbs@vaed.uscourts.gov

Chambers of District Judge Gerald Bruce Lee

Albert V. Bryan, Sr. U.S. Courthouse, 401 Courthouse Square, Alexandria, VA 22314-5799
Tel: (703) 299-2117 Fax: (703) 299-3339

Gerald Bruce Lee
District Judge

Date of Birth: 1952
Education: American U 1973 BA; Washington College of Law 1976 JD
Began Service: October 9, 1998
Appointed By: President William J. Clinton

Academic: Adjunct Professorial Lecturer, American University (1974-1978)

Government: Virginia Appointee, Metropolitan Washington Airports Authority (1990-1992)

Judicial: Judge, Virginia Circuit Court, 19th Judicial Circuit (1992-1998)

Legal Practice: Associate, Wiggs & Holland (1976-1977); Attorney/Partner, Wiggs & Lee (1977-1978); Attorney/Partner, Wiggs Lee & McClerklin (1978-1980); Law Offices of Gerald Bruce Lee (1980-1983); Attorney/Partner, Lee & Finch (1983-1985); Law Offices of Gerald Bruce Lee & Associates (1985-1986); Attorney/Principal, Cohen, Dunn & Sinclair, P.C. (1986-1992)

Current Memberships: Alexandria Bar Association; American Bar Association; The George Mason American Inn of Court, The American Inns of Court; Fairfax Bar Association; National Bar Association; Old Dominion Bar Association; Virginia State Bar

Staff

Law Clerk **Miles Galbraith** . . . . (703) 299-2192
Began Service: August 2015
Term Expires: August 2016
Education: UC Santa Barbara 2007 BA

Law Clerk **Katurah Topps** . . . . (703) 299-2192
Began Service: August 2015
Term Expires: August 2016
E-mail: katurah_topps@vaed.uscourts.gov

Court Reporter **Renecia Smith Wilson** . . . . (703) 549-5322
Fax: (703) 549-7334

Judicial Assistant **Avier Gaitan** . . . . (703) 299-2117
E-mail: avier_gaitan@vaed.uscourts.gov

Chambers of District Judge Henry E. Hudson

701 East Broad Street, Suite 6312, Richmond, VA 23219
Tel: (804) 916-2290 Fax: (804) 916-2299
E-mail: henry_hudson@vaed.uscourts.gov

Henry E. Hudson
District Judge

Date of Birth: 1947
Education: American U 1969 BA; Washington College of Law 1974 JD
Began Service: September 3, 2002
Appointed By: President George W. Bush

Government: Assistant Commonwealth Attorney, Office of the Commonwealth Attorney, County of Arlington, Virginia (1974-1979); Assistant U.S. Attorney, Eastern District of Virginia, United States Attorney's Office, United States Department of Justice (1978-1979); Commonwealth Attorney, Office of the Commonwealth Attorney, County of Arlington, Virginia (1980-1986); U.S. Attorney, Eastern District of Virginia, United States Attorney's Office, United States Department of Justice (1986-1991); Director, United States Marshal Service, United States Department of Justice, George H.W. Bush Administration (1992-1993)

Judicial: Judge, Fairfax County Circuit Court (1998-2002)

Chambers of District Judge Henry E. Hudson *continued*

Legal Practice: Counsel, Reed Smith Shaw & McClay LLP (1991-1992); Of Counsel, Mays & Valentine (1993-1995); Of Counsel, Reed Smith Shaw & McClay LLP (1996-1998)

Staff

Law Clerk **Frank Talbott V** . . . . (804) 916-2290
Began Service: August 2015
Term Expires: September 2016
E-mail: frank_talbott@vaed.uscourts.gov
Education: Virginia 2008

Law Clerk **Mark L. Earley, Jr.** . . . . (804) 916-2290
Began Service: August 2015
Term Expires: September 2016
E-mail: kenneth_simon@vaed.uscourts.gov

Judicial Assistant **Robin Belcher** . . . . (804) 916-2290
E-mail: robin_belcher@vaed.uscourts.gov

Chambers of District Judge Liam O'Grady

Albert V. Bryan Sr., U.S. Courthouse, 401 Courthouse Square, Alexandria, VA 22314-5798
Tel: (703) 299-2121

Liam O'Grady
District Judge

Date of Birth: September 24, 1950
Education: Franklin & Marshall 1973 BA; George Mason 1977 JD
Began Service: September 21, 2007
Appointed By: President George W. Bush

Current Memberships: American Bar Association; Arlington County Bar Association; The District of Columbia Bar; Federal Bar Association; The Virginia Bar Association

Staff

Law Clerk **Francesca Fitch** . . . . (703) 299-2121
Began Service: September 2015
Term Expires: September 2016
E-mail: francesca_fitch@vaed.uscourts.gov

Law Clerk **Colleen Smith** . . . . (703) 299-2121
Began Service: September 2015
Term Expires: September 2016

Secretary **Diane Wood** . . . . (703) 299-2121
E-mail: diane_wood@vaed.uscourts.gov

Chambers of District Judge Mark S. Davis

United States Courthouse, 600 Granby Street, Room 132, Norfolk, VA 23510-2449
Tel: (757) 222-7014 Fax: (757) 222-7179

Mark S. Davis
District Judge

Education: Virginia 1984 BA; Washington and Lee 1988 JD
Began Service: June 23, 2008
Appointed By: President George W. Bush

Clerkships: Law Clerk, Chambers of District Judge John A. MacKenzie, United States District Court for the Eastern District of Virginia (1988-1989)

Legal Practice: Associate, McGuireWoods LLP (1989-1996); Partner, McGuireWoods LLP (1996-1998); Partner, Carr & Porter LLC (1998-2003)

Staff

Career Law Clerk **Matthew Carr** . . . . (757) 222-7014
Began Service: August 2011
E-mail: matthew_carr@vaed.uscourts.gov
Education: Wake Forest 2005 JD

Judicial Assistant **Rebecca S. Kois** . . . . (757) 222-7014
E-mail: rebecca_kois@vaed.uscourts.gov

Chambers of District Judge Anthony John Trenga

Albert V. Bryan, Sr. Courthouse, 401 Courthouse Square,
Alexandria, VA 22314-5798
Tel: (703) 299-2113
E-mail: anthony_trenga@vaed.uscourts.gov

Anthony John Trenga
District Judge

Date of Birth: 1949
Education: Princeton 1971 AB; Virginia 1974 JD
Began Service: October 15, 2008
Appointed By: President George W. Bush

Legal Practice: Chair, Litigation/Government Contracts Department, Miller & Chevalier

Staff
Law Clerk **Alejandro Ortega** .... (703) 299-2113
Began Service: August 2015
Term Expires: August 2016
Law Clerk **Robert Farlow** .... (703) 299-2113
Judicial Assistant **Kristina Brown** .... (703) 299-2113

Chambers of District Judge John A. Gibney

701 East Broad Street, Richmond, VA 23219
Tel: (804) 916-2870 Fax: (804) 916-2879
E-mail: john_gibney@vaed.uscourts.gov

John A. Gibney, Jr.
District Judge

Education: William & Mary 1973; Virginia 1976 JD
Began Service: December 27, 2010
Appointed By: President Barack Obama

Clerkships: Law Clerk, Chambers of Justice Harry L. Carrico, Supreme Court of Virginia (1976-1978)

Government: Assistant Attorney General, Office of the Attorney General, Commonwealth of Virginia (1982-1984)

Legal Practice: Shareholder, ThompsonMcMullan, P.C. (2003-2010)

Staff
Law Clerk **Sarah Bennett** .... (804) 916-2872
Term Expires: August 2017
E-mail: sarah_bennett@vaed.uscourts.gov
Law Clerk **Sejal Jhaveri** .... (804) 916-2873
Term Expires: August 2016

Chambers of District Judge Arenda L. Wright Allen

Walter E. Hoffman United States Courthouse, 600 Granby Street,
Norfolk, VA 23510-2449
Tel: (757) 222-7013 Fax: (703) 299-2109

Arenda L. Wright Allen
District Judge

Education: Kutztown 1982 BS; North Carolina Central 1985 JD
Began Service: October 27, 2011
Appointed By: President Barack Obama

Government: Assistant U.S. Attorney, Virginia - Western District, United States Department of Justice (1990-1991); Assistant U.S. Attorney, Criminal Division, Norfolk (VA) Office, United States Department of Justice (1991-2005)

Military Service: United States Navy Reserve, The Judge Advocate General, United States Department of Justice (1992-2005)

Staff
Law Clerk **Megan Bauwens** .... (757) 222-7013
Term Expires: July 2016
E-mail: megan_bauwens@vaed.uscourts.gov
Law Clerk **Peter Rowland** .... (757) 222-7013

Chambers of District Judge Arenda L. Wright Allen *continued*

Career Law Clerk **Michael Reid** .... (757) 222-7013
E-mail: michael_reid@vaed.uscourts.gov
Education: Virginia 1988 JD

Chambers of District Judge M. Hannah Lauck

701 East Broad Street, Richmond, VA 23219
Tel: (804) 916-2890

M. Hannah Lauck
District Judge

Education: Wellesley 1986 BA; Yale 1991 JD
Began Service: June 10, 2014
Appointed By: President Barack Obama

Corporate: Supervising Attorney, Genworth Financial, Inc. (2004-2005)

Government: Assistant U.S. Attorney, Civil Division, Richmond (VA) Office, United States Department of Justice (1994-2004)

Judicial: Magistrate Judge, Chambers of Magistrate Judge M. Hannah Lauck, United States District Court for the Eastern District of Virginia (2005-2014)

Chambers of Senior Judge Claude M. Hilton

Albert V. Bryan Sr. U.S. Courthouse, 401 Courthouse Square,
Alexandria, VA 22314-5799
Tel: (703) 299-2112

Claude M. Hilton
Senior Judge

Date of Birth: 1940
Education: Ohio State 1963 BS; Washington College of Law 1966 JD
Began Service: July 11, 1985
Appointed By: President Ronald Reagan

Government: Deputy Clerk of Courts, Commonwealth of Virginia (1964-1966); Assistant Commonwealth Attorney, Commonwealth of Virginia (1967-1968); Commonwealth Attorney, Commonwealth of Virginia; Member, Planning Commission, County of Arlington, Virginia (1975-1978); Member, Police Trial Board, County of Arlington, Virginia (1980); Chairman, School Board, County of Arlington, Virginia (1984)

Judicial: Commissioner in Chancery, Circuit Court of Arlington County (1976-1985); Chief Judge, United States District Court for the Eastern District of Virginia

Legal Practice: Private Practice (1967-1985)

Current Memberships: American Association for Justice; American Bar Association; Arlington County Bar Association; Virginia State Bar; Virginia Trial Lawyers Association

Staff
Law Clerk **Katherine Davis** .... (703) 299-2112
Began Service: September 2015
Term Expires: September 2016
E-mail: katherine_davis@vaed.uscourts.gov
Law Clerk **Rammy G. Barbari** .... (703) 299-2112
Began Service: August 2015
Term Expires: September 2016
E-mail: rammy_barbari@vaed.uscourts.gov
Judicial Assistant **Jennifer L. Hinkell** .... (703) 299-2112
E-mail: jennifer_hinkell@vaed.uscourts.gov

Chambers of Senior Judge Robert G. Doumar

420 U.S. Courthouse, 600 Granby Street, Norfolk, VA 23510-2449
Tel: (757) 222-7006 Fax: (757) 222-7026
E-mail: robert_doumar@vaed.uscourts.gov

Robert George Doumar
Senior Judge

Date of Birth: 1930
Education: Virginia 1951 BA, 1953 LLB, 1988 LLM
Began Service: 1982
Appointed By: President Ronald Reagan
Political Affiliation: Republican

Legal Practice: Associate, Venable, Parsons, Kyle & Hylton (1955-1958); Senior Partner, Doumar, Pincus, Knight & Harlan (1958-1982)

Military Service: United States Army (1953-1955)

Current Memberships: American Association for Justice; American Bar Association; The American Inns of Court; Defense Research Institute; Federal Bar Association; Federal Judges Association; International Society of Barristers; Maritime Law Association of the United States; The Virginia Bar Association; Virginia State Bar; Virginia Trial Lawyers Association

Staff
Law Clerk **K. Ross Powell** .... (757) 222-7153
Began Service: September 2015
Term Expires: September 2016
Law Clerk **Matthew Skanchy** .... (757) 222-7153
Began Service: September 2015
Term Expires: September 2016
Secretary **Elizabeth Ball** .... (757) 222-7006
E-mail: beth_ball@vaed.uscourts.gov

Chambers of Senior Judge James C. Cacheris

Albert V. Bryan, Sr. U.S. Courthouse, 401 Courthouse Square, Alexandria, VA 22314-5799
Tel: (703) 299-2110 Fax: (703) 299-2249

James C. Cacheris
Senior Judge

Date of Birth: 1933
Education: Pennsylvania 1955 BS; George Washington 1960 JD
Began Service: 1981
Appointed By: President Ronald Reagan

Affiliation: Chief Judge, Chambers of Chief Judge James C. Cacheris, Alien Terrorist Removal Court; Chairman, Intercircuit Assignment Committee

Academic: Lecturer, Law School, The George Washington University (1983-1984)

Government: Assistant Corporation Counsel, Commonwealth of Virginia (1960-1962)

Judicial: Judge, Virginia Circuit Court, 19th Judicial Circuit (1971-1981); Judge, Alien Terrorist Removal Court

Legal Practice: Associate, Miller, Brown & Gildenhorn (1962-1964); Private Practice (1964-1970); Partner, Howard, Stevens, Lynch, Cacheris & Cake (1970-1971)

Military Service: United States Army (1955-1957)

Staff
Law Clerk **Chris White** .... (703) 299-2110
Began Service: August 2015
Term Expires: August 2016
Law Clerk **David Johnson** .... (703) 299-2110
Began Service: August 2015
Term Expires: September 2016
E-mail: david_johnson@vaed.uscourts.gov
Courtroom Deputy **(Vacant)** .... (703) 299-2110
Secretary **Amy Giannetti-Gillespie** .... (703) 299-2110
Began Service: 2007
E-mail: amy_gillespie@vaed.uscourts.gov

Chambers of Senior Judge Henry Coke Morgan, Jr.

307 U.S. Courthouse, 600 Granby Street, Norfolk, VA 23510-2449
Tel: (757) 222-7111 Fax: (757) 222-7022
E-mail: Henry_Morgan@vaed.uscourts.gov

Henry Coke Morgan, Jr.
Senior Judge

Date of Birth: 1935
Education: Washington and Lee 1957 BS, 1960 JD; Virginia 1998 LLM
Began Service: May 1, 1992
Appointed By: President George H.W. Bush

Government: Assistant City Attorney, Office of the City Attorney, Commonwealth of Virginia (1960-1963)

Legal Practice: Partner, Pender & Coward (1963-1992)

Military Service: United States Army Reserve, United States Department of the Army (1958-1959)

Current Memberships: The American Inns of Court; Federal Bar Association; Norfolk and Portsmouth Bar Association; The Virginia Bar Association; Virginia Beach Bar Association; Virginia State Bar

Staff
Law Clerk **Megan Behrman** .... (757) 222-7112
Began Service: August 2015
Term Expires: August 2016
E-mail: megan_behrman@vaed.uscourts.gov
Law Clerk **Nicole Tutrani** .... (757) 222-7113
Term Expires: February 2016
E-mail: nicole_tutrani@vaed.uscourts.gov
Judicial Assistant **Stacie Countess** .... (757) 222-7111
E-mail: stacie_countess@vaed.uscourts.gov

Chambers of Senior Judge T. S. Ellis III

Albert V. Bryan, Sr. U.S. Courthouse, 401 Courthouse Square, Alexandria, VA 22314-5799
Tel: (703) 299-2114

T. S. Ellis III
Senior Judge

Date of Birth: 1940
Education: Princeton 1961 BSE; Harvard 1969 JD
Began Service: 1987
Appointed By: President Ronald Reagan

Academic: Lecturer in Law, The College of William and Mary (1981-1983); Adjunct Professor, Georgetown University (1989-1990); Lecturer, Public Policy Program, The Law Center, Georgetown University (1991-1992)

Legal Practice: Partner, Hunton & Williams LLP (1969-1987)

Military Service: United States Navy (1961-1966)

Staff
Law Clerk **Sarah Buckley** .... (703) 299-2114
Began Service: 2014
E-mail: sarah_buckley@vaed.uscourts.gov
Law Clerk **Archith Ramkumar** .... (703) 299-2114
Career Law Clerk **Erica Petri** .... (703) 299-2114
E-mail: erica_petri@vaed.uscourts.gov

Chambers of Senior Judge Robert E. Payne

701 East Broad Street, Richmond, VA 23219
Tel: (804) 916-2260 Fax: (804) 916-2269
E-mail: robert_payne@vaed.uscourts.gov

Robert E. Payne
Senior Judge

Date of Birth: 1941
Education: Washington and Lee 1963 BA, 1967 LLB
Began Service: May 13, 1992
Appointed By: President George H.W. Bush

Judicial: District Judge, United States District Court for the Eastern District of Virginia (1992-2007)

Legal Practice: Attorney, McGuire, Woods, Battle & Boothe LLP (1971-1992)

Military Service: United States Army (1967-1971)

Current Memberships: American Bar Association; Richmond Bar Association; Virginia Association of Defense Attorneys; The Virginia Bar Association; Virginia State Bar

Staff
Law Clerk **Heidi Siegmund** .... (804) 916-2260
Began Service: August 2015
E-mail: heidi_siegmund@vaed.uscourts.gov
Law Clerk **Emily Rose** .... (804) 916-2260
Began Service: August 2015
Term Expires: August 2016
E-mail: emily_rose@vaed.uscourts.gov
Judicial Assistant **Anna Hooper** .... (804) 916-2260
E-mail: anna_hooper@vaed.uscourts.gov

Chambers of Senior Judge James R. Spencer

U.S. Courthouse, 701 East Broad Street, 7th Floor, Richmond, VA 23219
Tel: (804) 916-2250
E-mail: james_spencer@vaed.uscourts.gov

James R. Spencer
Senior Judge

Date of Birth: 1949
Education: Clark Atlanta 1971 BA; Harvard 1974 JD; Howard U 1985 MDiv
Began Service: 1986
Appointed By: President Ronald Reagan

Current Memberships: American Bar Association; The Bar Association of the District of Columbia; The District of Columbia Bar; Old Dominion Bar Association; Richmond Bar Association; State Bar of Georgia; Virginia State Bar

Staff
Secretary **Teri Scott** .... (804) 916-2250
E-mail: teri_scott@vaed.uscourts.gov

Chambers of Magistrate Judge Theresa Carroll Buchanan

Albert V. Bryan U.S. Courthouse, 401 Courthouse Square, Alexandria, VA 22314
Tel: (703) 299-2120 Fax: (703) 299-2211

Theresa Carroll Buchanan
Magistrate Judge

Date of Birth: 1957
Education: Virginia 1979 BS; William & Mary 1982 JD
Began Service: September 12, 1996
Term Expires: September 2020

Government: Assistant United States Attorney, United States Attorney's Office, United States Department of Justice, George H.W. Bush Administration (1991-1996)

Chambers of Magistrate Judge Theresa Carroll Buchanan *continued*

Legal Practice: Murphy, McGettigan & West, PC (1983-1991)

Current Memberships: Alexandria Bar Association; Northern Virginia Chapter, Federal Bar Association; Virginia State Bar

Staff
Law Clerk **Christian Schreiber** .... (703) 299-2210
Began Service: September 2, 2015
Term Expires: August 27, 2016
E-mail: christian_schreiber@vaed.uscourts.gov
Chambers Administrator **Allison Golden** .... (703) 299-2120
E-mail: allison_golden@vaed.uscourts.gov

Chambers of Magistrate Judge Douglas E. Miller

600 Granby Street, Norfolk, VA 23510-2449
Tel: (757) 222-7012
E-mail: douglas_miller@vaed.uscourts.gov

Douglas E. Miller
Magistrate Judge

Education: William & Mary 1995 JD
Began Service: February 2010

Staff
Judicial Assistant **Deborah Crowder** .... (757) 222-7012
E-mail: deborah_crowder@vaed.uscourts.gov

Chambers of Magistrate Judge John F. Anderson

Albert V. Bryan U.S. Courthouse, 401 Courthouse Square, 5th Floor, Alexandria, VA 22314-5798
Tel: (703) 299-2118 Fax: (703) 299-2215
E-mail: john_anderson@vaed.uscourts.gov

John F. Anderson
Magistrate Judge

Began Service: January 22, 2008

Staff
Law Clerk **Daniel Wallmuth** .... (703) 299-2118
Began Service: August 2015
Term Expires: September 2016
E-mail: daniel_wallmuth@vaed.uscourts.gov
Judicial Assistant **Dilhani Siriwardane** .... (703) 299-2118
E-mail: dilhani_siriwardane@vaed.uscourts.gov

Chambers of Magistrate Judge David J. Novak

701 East Broad Street, 5th Floor, Richmond, VA 23219
Tel: (804) 916-2270 Fax: (804) 916-2279
E-mail: david_novak@vaed.uscourts.gov

David J. Novak
Magistrate Judge

Education: St Vincent's Col 1983 BA; Villanova 1986 JD
Began Service: February 1, 2012
Term Expires: January 31, 2020

Staff
Law Clerk **Alexandra Sur** .... (804) 916-2272
Term Expires: September 2016
E-mail: alexandra_sur@vaed.uscourts.gov
Law Clerk **Patrick Dillard** .... (804) 916-2270
Term Expires: September 2016
E-mail: patrick_dillard@vaed.uscourts.gov

Chambers of Magistrate Judge Ivan D. Davis

Albert V. Bryan U.S. Courthouse, 401 Courthouse Square,
Alexandria, VA 22314
Tel: (703) 299-2119
E-mail: ivan_davis@vaed.uscourts.gov

Ivan D. Davis
Magistrate Judge

Education: Virginia; Howard U JD
Began Service: 2008

Staff
Law Clerk **Nora Fakhri** .... (703) 299-2119
Began Service: September 2015
Term Expires: September 2016
E-mail: nora_fakhri@vaed.uscourts.gov
Judicial Assistant **Gloria Lambert** .... (703) 299-2119
E-mail: gloria_lambert@vaed.uscourts.gov

Chambers of Magistrate Judge Lawrence Leonard

600 Granby Street, Norfolk, VA 23510-2449
Tel: (757) 222-7020
E-mail: lawrence_leonard@vaed.uscourts.gov

Lawrence R. Leonard
Magistrate Judge

Staff
Law Clerk **Leah Stiegler** .... (757) 222-7020
Term Expires: August 2016
Judicial Assistant **Mary Beth Kopso** .... (757) 222-7020

Chambers of Magistrate Judge Roderick C. Young

701 East Broad Street, Richmond, VA 23219
Tel: (804) 916-2240

Roderick C. Young
Magistrate Judge

Began Service: October 29, 2014
Term Expires: October 2022

Staff
Law Clerk **Andrew Tarne** .... (804) 916-2240
Term Expires: October 2016
E-mail: andrew_tarne@vaed.uscourts.gov
Career Law Clerk **Deborah Holloman** .... (804) 916-2240
E-mail: deborah_holloman@vaed.uscourts.gov
Education: Virginia 1986 JD

Chambers of Magistrate Judge Michael S. Nachmanoff

401 Courthouse Square, Alexandria, VA 22314-5798
Tel: (703) 299-3367

Michael S. Nachmanoff
Magistrate Judge

Chambers of Magistrate Judge Thomas Rawles Jones, Jr.

Albert V. Bryan, Sr. U.S. Courthouse, 401 Courthouse Square,
Alexandria, VA 22314-5799
Tel: (703) 299-2122

Thomas Rawles Jones, Jr.
Magistrate Judge

Date of Birth: 1948
Education: Virginia 1973 JD
Began Service: 1994
Term Expires: February 2018

Clerkships: Law Clerk The Honorable Albert V. Bryan, Jr., United States District Court for the Eastern District of Virginia (1973-1974)

Government: Assistant Commonwealth's Attorney, Commonwealth of Virginia (1974-1981)

Legal Practice: Partner, Cohen, Dunn & Sinclair

Chambers of Magistrate Judge Robert J. Krask

600 Granby Street, Norfolk, VA 23510-2449
Tel: (757) 222-7007

Robert "Bob" Krask
Magistrate Judge

Began Service: 2015

Chambers of Magistrate Judge (recalled) William T. Prince

600 Granby Street, Norfolk, VA 23510-1811
Tel: (757) 222-7170 Tel: (757) 222-7008 Fax: (757) 222-7047
E-mail: william_prince@vaed.uscourts.gov

William T. Prince
Magistrate Judge (recalled)

Began Service: March 1, 1990

United States Bankruptcy Court for the Eastern District of Virginia

United States Bankruptcy Court, 701 East Broad Street,
Richmond, VA 23219
Tel: (804) 916-2400 Tel: (800) 676-6856 (Alexandria PACER)
Tel: (800) 676-6856 (Newport News PACER)
Tel: (800) 676-6856 (Richmond PACER)
Tel: (866) 222-8029 (Toll Free Voice Case Information System VCIS)
Fax: (804) 916-2498
Internet: www.vaeb.uscourts.gov

Number of Judgeships: 6

Court Staff
Clerk of Court **William C. Redden** .... (804) 916-2490
E-mail: william_redden@vaeb.uscourts.gov
Chief Deputy Clerk **James V. Ingold** .... (804) 916-2491
E-mail: james_ingold@vaeb.uscourts.gov
Divisional Manager - Alexandria **James W. Reynolds** ... (703) 258-1224
200 South Washington Street, Fax: (703) 258-1206
Alexandria, VA 22314
E-mail: james_reynolds@vaeb.uscourts.gov
Divisional Manager - Norfolk **Stephan C. Kopacki** ...... (757) 222-7570
480 U.S. Courthouse, 600 Granby Street, Fax: (757) 222-7505
Norfolk, VA 23510
E-mail: stephan_kopacki@vaeb.uscourts.gov
Divisional Manager - Richmond **David M. Rabenda** ..... (804) 916-2444
E-mail: david_rabenda@vaeb.uscourts.gov
Lead Court Security Officer **Thomas B. Daniels, Jr.** ..... (804) 916-3020
Fax: (804) 916-3022

Chambers of Chief Bankruptcy Judge Stephen C. St. John
U.S. Courthouse, 600 Granby Street, Norfolk, VA 23510
Tel: (757) 222-7480

Stephen C. St. John
Chief Bankruptcy Judge

Date of Birth: 1952
Education: Virginia 1977 JD
Began Service: 1995
Term Expires: 2023

Staff
Law Clerk **Kathleen Robeson** . . . . (757) 222-7480
Began Service: August 2015
Term Expires: August 2016
E-mail: kathleen_robeson@vaeb.uscourts.gov
Career Law Clerk **Heather Berry** . . . . (757) 222-7480
E-mail: heather_berry@vaeb.uscourts.gov
Education: Richmond 2002 JD

Chambers of Bankruptcy Judge Robert G. Mayer
Martin V.B. Bostetter, Jr. U.S. Courthouse, 200 South Washington Street, Alexandria, VA 22314
Tel: (703) 258-1280 Fax: (703) 258-1291
E-mail: Robert_Mayer@vaeb.uscourts.gov

Robert G. Mayer
Bankruptcy Judge

Date of Birth: 1950
Education: MIT 1972 SB; Virginia 1975 JD
Began Service: October 15, 1999
Term Expires: October 15, 2028

Clerkships: Law Clerk Robert S. Jones, Supreme Court of Virginia (1975-1976); Law Clerk The Honorable Richard H. Poff, Supreme Court of Virginia (1976)

Staff
Law Clerk **David Barnes** . . . . (703) 258-1280
Began Service: August 2015
Term Expires: August 2016
Judicial Assistant **Barbara D. Lewis** . . . . (703) 258-1280

Chambers of Bankruptcy Judge Kevin R. Huennekens
701 East Broad Street, 5th Floor, Richmond, VA 23219
Tel: (804) 916-2455
E-mail: kevin_huennekens@vaeb.uscourts.gov

Kevin R. Huennekens
Bankruptcy Judge

Began Service: September 2006
Term Expires: September 2020

Chambers of Bankruptcy Judge Frank J. Santoro
600 Granby Street, Norfolk, VA 23510-2449
Tel: (757) 222-7471

Frank J. Santoro
Bankruptcy Judge

Began Service: February 21, 2008
Term Expires: February 21, 2022

Staff
Law Clerk **Richard Forzani** . . . . (757) 222-7472
Career Law Clerk **Cynthia Byrne** . . . . (757) 222-7471
Education: Wake Forest 2011 JD

Chambers of Bankruptcy Judge Brian F. Kenney
200 South Washington Street, Alexandria, VA 22314
Tel: (703) 258-1240 Fax: (703) 258-1291

Brian F. Kenney
Bankruptcy Judge

Began Service: September 2011
Term Expires: September 2025

Chambers of Bankruptcy Judge Keith L. Phillips
701 East Broad Street, Richmond, VA 23219
Tel: (804) 916-2461

Keith L. Phillips
Bankruptcy Judge

Began Service: 2013

Staff
Law Clerk **Laurie H. Ross** . . . . (804) 916-2461
Judicial Assistant **Deborah "Deb" Weekley** . . . . (804) 916-2461

United States District Court for the Western District of Virginia
Richard H. Poff Federal Building, 242 Franklin Road, SW, Suite 540, Roanoke, VA 24011
Tel: (540) 857-5100 Fax: (540) 857-5110 Fax: (540) 857-5193
Internet: www.vawd.uscourts.gov

Number of Judgeships: 4

Circuit: Fourth

Areas Covered: Counties of Albemarle, Alleghany, Amherst, Appomattox, Augusta, Bath, Bedford, Bland, Botetourt, Bristol, Buchanan, Buckingham, Buena Vista, Campbell, Carroll, Charlotte, Charlottesville, Clarke, Covington, Craig, Culpeper, Cumberland, Danville, Dickenson, Floyd, Fluvanna, Franklin, Frederick, Galax, Giles, Grayson, Greene, Halifax, Harrisonburg, Henry, Highland, Lee, Lexington, Louisa, Lynchburg, Madison, Martinsville, Montgomery, Nelson, Norton, Orange, Page, Patrick, Pittsylvania, Pulaski, Radford, Rappahannock, Roanoke, Rockbridge, Rockingham, Russell, Salem, Scott, Shenandoah, Staunton, Smyth, Tazewell, Warren, Washington, Waynesboro, Winchester, Wise and Wythe

Court Staff
Clerk of Court **Julia C. Dudley** . . . . (540) 857-5100
E-mail: julie_dudley@vawd.uscourts.gov
Chief Deputy Clerk **Frances McNulty** . . . . (540) 857-5100
E-mail: frances_mcnulty@vawd.uscourts.gov
Supervisory Deputy Clerk **Heather McDonald** . . . . (434) 793-7147
700 Main St., Rm. 202, Danville, VA 24541 Fax: (434) 793-0284
P.O. Box 1400, Danville, VA 24543
E-mail: heather_mcdonald@vawd.uscourts.gov
Supervisory Deputy Clerk - Charlottesville
Joyce Jones . . . . (434) 296-9284
255 W. Main St., Rm. 304, Charlottesville, VA 22902 Fax: (434) 295-8909
E-mail: joyce_jones@vawd.uscourts.gov
Supervisory Deputy Clerk - Harrisonburg **Jody Turner** . . . (540) 434-3181
116 N. Main St., Rm. 314, Harrisonburg, VA 22802 Fax: (540) 434-3319
E-mail: jody_turner@vawd.uscourts.gov
Deputy Clerk **Fay Coleman** . . . . (434) 847-5722
1101 Court Street, Room A66, Lynchburg, VA 24504 Fax: (434) 847-2002
E-mail: fay_coleman@vawd.uscourts.gov
Chief Probation Officer **Philip K. Williams** . . . . (540) 857-5180
P.O. Box 1563, Roanoke, VA 24007
Financial Administrator/Budget Analyst **Jared Martin** . . . . (540) 857-5100
E-mail: jared_martin@vawd.uscourts.gov
Property and Procurement Administrator
Ronda Burton . . . . (540) 857-5100
E-mail: ronda_burton@vawp.uscourts.gov

(continued on next page)

United States District Court for the Western District of Virginia *continued*

Human Resources Administrator **Mary Stovall**..........(540) 857-5100
E-mail: mary_stovall@vawd.uscourts.gov

Property and Procurement Specialist **Ken Harris**.........(540) 857-5100
E-mail: ken_harris@vawd.uscourts.gov

Chambers of Chief District Judge Glen E. Conrad

Richard H. Poff Federal Building, 210 Franklin Road, SW,
Room 206, Roanoke, VA 24011
P.O. Box 2822, Roanoke, VA 24001-2822
Tel: (540) 857-5135 Fax: (540) 857-5125

Glen E. Conrad
Chief Judge

Date of Birth: 1949
Education: William & Mary 1971 AB, 1974 JD
Began Service: October 17, 2003
Appointed By: President George W. Bush

Clerkships: Law Clerk, United States District Court (1975-1976)

Government: United States Probation Office, United States Department of Justice (1975-1976)

Judicial: Magistrate Judge, United States District Court for the Western District of Virginia (1976-2003)

Current Memberships: American Bar Association; The American Inns of Court; The Ted Dalton American Inn of Court, The American Inns of Court; Federal Bar Association; Federal Judges Association; Roanoke Bar Association; The Virginia Bar Association; Virginia Trial Lawyers Association

Staff

Law Clerk **Debbie Wong**..........(540) 857-5135

Career Law Clerk **Jennifer Willis**..........(540) 857-5135
Began Service: 2007
E-mail: jennifer_willis@vawd.uscourts.gov
Education: Wake Forest 2003 JD

Judicial Assistant **Janet Taylor**..........(540) 857-5135
E-mail: janet_taylor@vawd.uscourts.gov

Chambers of District Judge James P. Jones

U.S. Courthouse, 180 West Main Street, Abingdon, VA 24210
Tel: (276) 628-4080 Fax: (276) 628-4597
E-mail: james_jones@vawd.uscourts.gov

James P. Jones
District Judge

Date of Birth: 1940
Education: Duke 1962 AB; Virginia 1965 LLB
Began Service: August 30, 1996
Appointed By: President William J. Clinton

Current Memberships: American Bar Foundation; American Bar Association; American Board of Trial Advocates; American College of Trial Lawyers; City of Bristol Bar Association; United States Foreign Intelligence Surveillance Court; The Virginia Bar Association; Virginia State Bar; Washington County Bar Association

Staff

Law Clerk **Chris Edwards**..........(276) 628-4080
Began Service: September 2015
Term Expires: August 31, 2016

Career Law Clerk **Alexis Tahinci**..........(276) 628-4080
Began Service: September 2015

Court Reporter **Bridget A. Dickert**..........(276) 628-5116 ext. 8119
E-mail: bridgetd@vawd.uscourts.gov Fax: (276) 628-1028

Judicial Assistant **Sharon Callahan**..........(276) 628-4080
E-mail: sharon_callahan@vawd.uscourts.gov
Education: Bristol U 1973 AB

Chambers of District Judge Michael F. Urbanski

210 Franklin Road, SW, Suite 350, Roanoke, VA 24011
Tel: (540) 857-5124 Fax: (540) 857-5129
E-mail: urbanski.ecf@vawd.uscourts.gov

Michael F. Urbanski
District Judge

Date of Birth: November 1, 1956
Education: William & Mary 1978 AB; Virginia 1981 JD
Began Service: May 13, 2011
Appointed By: President Barack Obama

Legal Practice: Associate, Vinson & Elkins (1982-1984); Principal, Woods Rogers PLC (1984-2004)

Current Memberships: American Bar Association; The District of Columbia Bar; Roanoke Bar Association; Virginia State Bar

Staff

Law Clerk **Brett Rector**..........(540) 437-7250
Began Service: August 2015
Term Expires: August 2016

Career Law Clerk **Kristin Johnson**..........(540) 857-5124
E-mail: kristinj@vawd.uscourts.gov
Education: Virginia 2002 BS, 2005 JD

Judicial Assistant **Sue B. DePuy**..........(540) 857-5124
E-mail: sued@vawd.uscourts.gov
Education: Longwood U BS

Chambers of District Judge Elizabeth K. Dillon

242 Franklin Road, SW, Roanoke, VA 24011
Tel: (540) 857-5120

Elizabeth K. Dillon
District Judge

Education: Lenoir-Rhyne 1983 AB; Wake Forest 1986 JD
Began Service: 2014
Appointed By: President Barack Obama

Chambers of Senior Judge Jackson L. Kiser

700 Main Street, Room 202, Danville, VA 24541
P.O. Box 3326, Danville, VA 24543
Tel: (434) 799-8700 Fax: (434) 799-2791
E-mail: jackson_kiser@vawd.uscourts.gov

Jackson L. Kiser
Senior Judge

Date of Birth: 1929
Education: Concord Col 1951 BA; Washington and Lee 1952 LLB
Began Service: January 12, 1982
Appointed By: President Ronald Reagan
Political Affiliation: Republican

Government: Assistant U.S. Attorney, Virginia - Western District, Executive Office for United States Attorneys, United States Department of Justice (1958-1961)

Judicial: U.S. Commissioner, United States District Court for the Western District of Virginia (1956-1958)

Legal Practice: Young, Kiser, Haskins, Mann, Gregory & Young, PC (1961-1982)

Military Service: United States Army (1952-1955); United States Army Reserve, United States Department of the Army (1955-1961)

Current Memberships: American College of Trial Lawyers; Fourth Circuit Judicial Conference; Martinsville-Henry County Bar Association; The Virginia Bar Association; Virginia State Bar; Virginia Trial Lawyers Association

Chambers of Senior Judge Jackson L. Kiser *continued*

Staff

Career Law Clerk **Scott Jones** . . . . (434) 799-8700
Began Service: January 2006
E-mail: scott_jones@vawd.uscourts.gov
Education: Richmond 2009 JD

Judicial Assistant **Denise Hylton** . . . . (434) 799-8700

Chambers of Senior Judge Norman K. Moon

U.S. Courthouse, 1101 Court Street, Lynchburg, VA 24504
P.O. Box 657, Lynchburg, VA 24505
Tel: (434) 845-4891 Fax: (434) 846-4527

Norman K. Moon
Senior Judge

Date of Birth: 1936
Education: Virginia 1959 BA, 1962 BL, 1988 JD
Began Service: November 25, 1997
Appointed By: President William J. Clinton

Judicial: Chief Judge, Court of Appeals of Virginia (1985-1997); District Judge, Chambers of Senior Judge Norman K. Moon, United States District Court for the Western District of Virginia (1997-2010)

Current Memberships: American Bar Association; American Judges Association; National Institute of Trial Advocacy; The Virginia Bar Association; Virginia State Bar

Staff

Law Clerk **Ryan Comer** . . . . (434) 845-4891
Began Service: August 2015
Term Expires: September 2016

Law Clerk **Cagle Juhan** . . . . (434) 845-4891
Began Service: August 2015
Term Expires: September 2016
E-mail: cagle_juhan@vawd.uscourts.gov

Career Law Clerk **James McKinley** . . . . (434) 845-4891
E-mail: james_mckinley@vawd.uscourts.gov
Education: Cal State (Bakersfield) 1998 BA; Hollins Col 1999 MA; Virginia 2001 MPA, 2005 JD

Chambers of Magistrate Judge Pamela Meade Sargent

U.S. Courthouse, 180 West Main Street, Abingdon, VA 24210
P.O. Box 846, Abingdon, VA 24212
Tel: (276) 628-6021 Fax: (276) 628-6072
E-mail: pamela_sargent@vawd.uscourts.gov

Pamela Meade Sargent
Magistrate Judge

Education: Virginia Tech BA; South Carolina JD
Began Service: December 1997
Term Expires: December 2021

Clerkships: Law Clerk The Honorable H. E. Widener, Jr., United States Court of Appeals for the Fourth Circuit (1988-1989)

Legal Practice: Associate, White, Elliott & Bundy (1989-1994); Principal, White Bundy McElroy Hodges & Sargent (1994-1997)

Current Memberships: American Bar Association; The Virginia Bar Association; Virginia State Bar

Staff

Career Law Clerk **Amy Fellhauer** . . . . (276) 628-6021
E-mail: amy_fellhauer@vawd.uscourts.gov
Education: William & Mary 1996 BA; Toledo 2001 JD

Judicial Assistant **Robin Bordwine** . . . . (276) 628-6021
E-mail: robin_bordwine@vawd.uscourts.gov

Chambers of Magistrate Judge Robert S. Ballou

Richard H. Poff Federal Building, 210 Franklin Road, SW, Room 344, Roanoke, VA 24011-2214
Tel: (540) 857-5158 Fax: (540) 857-5159
E-mail: robert_ballou@vawd.uscourts.gov

Robert S. Ballou
Magistrate Judge

Began Service: October 3, 2011
Term Expires: October 3, 2019

Staff

Career Law Clerk **Lindsay Grindo** . . . . (540) 857-5158
E-mail: lindsay_grindo@vawd.uscourts.gov

Law Clerk **Meghan Stubblebine** . . . . (540) 857-5158

Chambers of Magistrate Judge Joel Hoppe

116 North Main Street, Room 314, Harrisonburg, VA 22802
Tel: (540) 434-3181

Joel Hoppe
Magistrate Judge

Education: Richmond 2002 JD
Began Service: 2014

Chambers of Magistrate Judge (part-time) James G. Welsh

116 North Main Street, Harrisonburg, VA 22802
Tel: (540) 434-3181
E-mail: jamesw@vawd.uscourts.gov

James G. Welsh
Magistrate Judge (Part-Time)

Education: Maryland 1964 BA; Virginia 1969 LLB
Began Service: November 16, 2004
Term Expires: November 16, 2016

Staff

Administrative Assistant **Karen Dotson** . . . . (540) 434-3181 ext. 2
E-mail: karen_dotson@vawd.uscourts.gov

United States Bankruptcy Court for the Western District of Virginia

210 Church Avenue, SW, Room 200, Roanoke, VA 24011-0210
Tel: (540) 857-2391 Fax: (540) 857-2873
Internet: www.vawb.uscourts.gov

Number of Judgeships: 3

Court Staff

Clerk of the Court **John W. L. Craig II** . . . . (540) 857-2391
Education: Mercer 1981 JD

Chief Deputy Clerk **A Elizabeth Nichols** . . . . (540) 857-2391 ext. 133

Chambers of Bankruptcy Judge Chief Rebecca B. Connelly

116 North Main Street, Harrisonburg, VA 22802
Tel: (540) 434-6747 Fax: (540) 433-6390

Rebecca B. Connelly
Chief Bankruptcy Judge

Education: Maryland BA; Washington and Lee JD
Began Service: 2012

(continued on next page)

Chambers of Bankruptcy Judge Chief Rebecca B. Connelly *continued*

Staff
Law Clerk **Aaron Williams** .... (540) 434-6747
E-mail: aaron_williams@vawb.uscourts.gov

Chambers of Bankruptcy Judge Paul M. Black
210 Church Avenue, SW, Roanoke, VA 24011-0210
Tel: (540) 857-2394 Fax: (540) 857-2095
E-mail: paul_black@vawb.uscourts.gov

Paul M. Black
Bankruptcy Judge

Education: Washington and Lee 1982 BA; Cambridge (UK) 1983; Richmond 1985 JD

United States District Court for the Eastern District of Washington
Thomas S. Foley U.S. Courthouse, 920 West Riverside Avenue, Room 840, Spokane, WA 99201-1493
P.O. Box 1493, Spokane, WA 99210-1493
Tel: (509) 458-3400 Fax: (509) 458-3420
Internet: www.waed.uscourts.gov

Number of Judgeships: 4

Circuit: Ninth

Areas Covered: Counties of Adams, Asotin, Benton, Chelan, Columbia, Douglas, Ferry, Franklin, Garfield, Grant, Kittitas, Klickitat, Lincoln, Okanogan, Pend Oreille, Spokane, Stevens, Walla Walla, Whitman and Yakima

Court Staff
District Court Executive/Clerk of Court
Sean F. McAvoy .... (509) 458-3400
Chief Probation Officer **Scott M. Morse** .... (509) 742-6300
E-mail: scott_morse@waed.uscourts.gov
Librarian **Julia Seiter** .... (509) 353-3293
Fax: (509) 353-0540

Chambers of Chief Judge Rosanna Malouf Peterson
920 West Riverside Avenue, Spokane, WA 99201-1493
Tel: (509) 458-5260 Fax: (509) 458-3420

Rosanna Malouf Peterson
Chief Judge

Date of Birth: 1951
Education: North Dakota 1977 BA, 1983 MA, 1991 JD
Began Service: January 26, 2010
Appointed By: President Barack Obama

Clerkships: Law Clerk, Chambers of Senior Judge Fred L. Van Sickle, United States District Court for the Eastern District of Washington (1991-1993)

Nonprofit: President, Eastern District of Washington Chapter, Federal Bar Association (2003-2004)

Current Memberships: Eastern District of Washington Chapter, Federal Bar Association

Profession: Attorney (2003-2009)

Staff
Judicial Assistant **Mary Strand** .... (509) 458-5260

Chambers of District Judge Thomas Owen Rice
920 West Riverside Avenue, Spokane, WA 99201-1493
Tel: (509) 458-2470 Fax: (509) 458-3420

Thomas O. Rice
District Judge

Education: Gonzaga 1983 BBA, 1986 JD
Began Service: March 8, 2012
Appointed By: President Barack Obama

Staff
Judicial Administrator **Bridgette Fortenberry** .... (509) 458-2470
Courtroom Deputy **Linda Hanson** .... (509) 458-2470

Chambers of District Judge Stanley Allen Bastian
920 West Riverside Avenue, Spokane, WA 99201-1493
Tel: (414) 397-3372

Stanley Allen Bastian
District Judge

Education: Oregon 1980 BS; U Washington 1983 JD
Began Service: May 1, 2014
Appointed By: President Barack Obama

Government: Assistant City Attorney, Office of the City Attorney/Law Department, City of Seattle, Washington (1985-1988)

Legal Practice: Partner, Jeffers, Danielson, Sonn & Aylward, PS

Chambers of District Judge Salvador Mendoza Jr.
825 Jadwin Avenue, Suite 190, Richland, WA 99352-3586
Tel: (509) 943-8160
E-mail: salvador_mendoza@waed.uscourts.gov

Salvador Mendoza, Jr.
District Judge

Education: U Washington 1994 BA; UCLA 1997 JD
Began Service: June 19, 2014
Appointed By: President Barack Obama

Government: Assistant Attorney General, Office of the Attorney General, State of Washington (1997-1998); Deputy Prosecuting Attorney, Office of the Prosecuting Attorney, County of Franklin, Washington (1998-1999)

Chambers of Senior Judge Robert H. Whaley
Thomas S. Foley U.S. Courthouse, 920 West Riverside Avenue, Spokane, WA 99201
P.O. Box 283, Spokane, WA 99210
Tel: (509) 458-5270 Fax: (509) 458-5271
E-mail: robert_whaley@waed.uscourts.gov

Robert H. Whaley
Senior Judge

Date of Birth: 1943
Education: Princeton 1965 AB; Emory 1968 JD
Began Service: June 30, 1995
Appointed By: President William J. Clinton

Government: Trial Attorney, Land & Natural Resources Division, United States Department of Justice (1969-1971); Assistant United States Attorney, Eastern District of Washington, Office of the United States Attorney, United States Department of Justice (1971-1972)

Judicial: Judge, Washington Superior Court, Spokane County (1992-1995)

Legal Practice: Peek & Whaley (1968-1969); Associate then Partner, Winston & Cashatt (1972-1992)

Military Service: United States Marine Corps (1968)

Chambers of Senior Judge Robert H. Whaley *continued*

Staff
Law Clerk **Kyle Rekofke** .... (509) 458-5270
E-mail: kyle_rekofke@waed.uscourts.gov
Court Reporter **Debra Kinney Clark** .... (509) 458-3433
E-mail: debra_clark@waed.uscourts.gov
Judicial Chambers Administrator **Michelle Fox** .... (509) 458-5270
E-mail: michelle_fox@waed.uscourts.gov

Chambers of Senior Judge Fred L. Van Sickle

Thomas S. Foley U.S. Courthouse, 920 West Riverside Avenue, Spokane, WA 99201
P.O. Box 2209, Spokane, WA 99210
Tel: (509) 458-5250 Fax: (509) 458-5251

Fred L. Van Sickle
Senior Judge

Date of Birth: 1943
Education: Wisconsin 1965 BS; U Washington 1968 JD
Began Service: 1991
Appointed By: President George H.W. Bush

Government: Prosecuting Attorney, Office of the Prosecuting Attorney, County of Douglas, Washington (1971-1975)

Judicial: Judge, Washington Superior Court, Grant and Douglas Counties (1975-1979); Judge, Washington Superior Court, Chelan and Douglas Counties (1979-1991); District Judge, United States District Court for the Eastern District of Washington (1991-2009); Chief Judge, United States District Court for the Eastern District of Washington (2000-2005)

Legal Practice: Clark & Van Sickle (1970-1975)

Military Service: United States Army (1968-1970)

Current Memberships: Superior Court Judges Association (WA); Washington State Bar Association

Staff
Career Law Clerk **Mark Davis** .... (509) 458-5250
Court Reporter **Mark A. Snover** .... (509) 458-3434
E-mail: mark_snover@waed.uscourts.gov
Secretary **(Vacant)** .... (509) 458-5250

Chambers of Senior Judge Justin L. Quackenbush

Thomas S. Foley U.S. Courthouse, 920 West Riverside Avenue, Spokane, WA 99201
P.O. Box 1432, Spokane, WA 99210
Tel: (509) 458-5280 Fax: (509) 458-5281
E-mail: justin_quackenbush@waed.uscourts.gov

Justin L. Quackenbush
Senior Judge

Date of Birth: 1929
Education: Idaho 1951 BA; Gonzaga 1957 LLB
Began Service: 1980
Appointed By: President Jimmy Carter

Academic: Instructor (part-time), School of Law, Gonzaga University (1959-1967)

Government: Deputy Prosecuting Attorney, State of Washington (1957-1959)

Legal Practice: Senior Partner, Quackenbush, Dean, Bailey & Henderson (1959-1980)

Military Service: United States Navy (1951-1954)

Current Memberships: Spokane County Bar; Washington State Bar Association

Staff
Law Clerk **Jake Stillwell** .... (509) 458-5280
E-mail: jake_stillwell@waed.uscourts.gov

Chambers of Senior Judge Justin L. Quackenbush *continued*

Career Law Clerk **Jeremy K. Johnson** .... (509) 458-5280
E-mail: jeremy_johnson@waed.uscourts.gov
Education: Saint Louis U 2002 JD
Career Pro Se Law Clerk **Dennyl McCrorey** .... (509) 458-5280
E-mail: dennyl_mccrorey@waed.uscourts.gov
Education: Gonzaga 1992 JD
Secretary **Lee Ann Mauk** .... (509) 458-5280
E-mail: lee_ann_mauk@waed.uscourts.gov

Chambers of Senior Judge Wm. Fremming Nielsen

Thomas S. Foley U.S. Courthouse, 920 West Riverside Avenue, Suite 904, Spokane, WA 99201
P.O. Box 1493, Spokane, WA 99210-1493
Tel: (509) 458-5290 Fax: (509) 458-5291
E-mail: frem_nielsen@waed.uscourts.gov

Wm. Fremming Nielsen
Senior Judge

Date of Birth: 1934
Education: U Washington 1956 BA, 1962 LLB
Began Service: May 28, 1991
Appointed By: President George H.W. Bush

Academic: Credit Reporter, The Dun & Bradstreet Corporation (1959-1960)

Clerkships: Law Clerk The Honorable Charles L. Powell, United States District Court for the Eastern District of Washington (1963-1964)

Legal Practice: Attorney, Paine, Hamblen, Coffin, Brooke & Miller LLP (1964-1991)

Military Service: United States Air Force (1956-1959); United States Air Force Reserve (1959-1982)

Current Memberships: American College of Trial Lawyers; The American Inns of Court; Eastern District of Washington Chapter, Federal Bar Association; Spokane County Bar; Washington State Bar Association

Staff
Law Clerk **(Vacant)** .... (509) 458-5290
Career Law Clerk **Heather Foe** .... (509) 458-5290
E-mail: heather_foe@waed.uscourts.gov
Education: U Washington 2006 JD
Judicial Assistant **Joanna L. Knutson** .... (509) 458-5290
E-mail: joanna_knutson@waed.uscourts.gov

Chambers of Senior Judge Edward F. Shea

U.S. Courthouse, 825 Jadwin Avenue, Richland, WA 99352-3586
Tel: (509) 943-8190 Fax: (509) 372-3051

Edward F. Shea
Senior Judge

Date of Birth: 1942
Education: Georgetown 1970 JD
Began Service: May 28, 1998
Appointed By: President William J. Clinton

Current Memberships: American Bar Foundation; American Bar Association; Benton-Franklin Bar Association; Federal Bar Association; Washington State Bar Association

Staff
Law Clerk **Casey Bruner** .... (509) 943-8190
Began Service: September 2015
Term Expires: September 2016
E-mail: casey_bruner@waed.uscourts.gov
Career Law Clerk **Erika Hartliep** .... (509) 943-8190
E-mail: erika_hartliep@waed.uscourts.gov
Education: Idaho 2002 JD

(continued on next page)

Chambers of Senior Judge Edward F. Shea *continued*

Deputy Clerk **Cora Vargas** .... (509) 943-8190
E-mail: cora_vargas@waed.uscourts.gov
Judicial Chambers Administrator **Lisa Hernandez** .... (509) 943-8190
E-mail: Lisa_Hernandez@waed.uscourts.gov

Chambers of Senior Judge Lonny R. Suko

William O. Douglas Courthouse, 25 South Third Street,
Yakima, WA 98901
P.O. Box 2706, Yakima, WA 98907
Tel: (509) 573-6650 Fax: (509) 573-6651
E-mail: lonny_suko@waed.uscourts.gov

Lonny R. Suko
Senior Judge

Date of Birth: 1943
Education: Washington State 1965 BA; Idaho 1968 JD
Began Service: August 1, 2003
Appointed By: President George W. Bush

Current Memberships: American Bar Association; Washington State Bar Association

Staff
Career Law Clerk **Fred Karau** .... (509) 573-6653
E-mail: fred_karau@waed.uscourts.gov
Education: Idaho State 1983 BS; Gonzaga 1986 JD
Career Law Clerk **Beth A. Wehrkamp** .... (509) 573-6654
E-mail: beth_wehrkamp@waed.uscourts.gov
Education: Ohio State 1983 BS;
Ohio Northern 1992 JD;
George Washington 1994 LLM
Secretary **Ginger Thompson** .... (509) 573-6650
E-mail: ginger_thompson@waed.uscourts.gov

Chambers of Magistrate Judge James P. Hutton

William O. Douglas Courthouse, 25 South Third Street,
Yakima, WA 98907
P.O. Box 2706, Yakima, WA 98907-2706
Tel: (509) 573-6670 Fax: (509) 573-6671
E-mail: james_hutton@waed.uscourts.gov

James P. Hutton
Magistrate Judge

Education: U Washington 1972 BA; Gonzaga 1976 JD
Began Service: January 2008
Term Expires: January 2016

Judicial: Judge, Yakima County Superior Court, County of Yakima, Washington (1996-2007)

Profession: Attorney, Private Practice (1976-1996)

Staff
Law Clerk **Anna Vowels** .... (509) 573-6670
Education: Idaho 2002 JD
Career Law Clerk **Lauri Boyd**........................(509) 573-6676
E-mail: lauri_boyd@waed.uscourts.gov
Education: Seattle 1986 JD

Chambers of Magistrate Judge John T. Rodgers

P.O. Box 1493, Spokane, WA 99210
Tel: (509) 458-5240

John T. Rodgers
Magistrate Judge

Education: U Washington; Gonzaga 1978 JD

United States Bankruptcy Court for the Eastern District of Washington

U.S. Post Office Building, 904 West Riverside Avenue, Suite 304,
Spokane, WA 99201
P.O. Box 2164, Spokane, WA 99210-2164
402 East Yakima Avenue, Suite 200, Yakima, WA 98901 (Yakima Office)
Tel: (509) 458-5300 (Spokane Office)
Tel: (509) 576-6100 (Yakima Office)
Tel: (800) 519-2549 (Voice Case Information System VCIS)
Fax: (509) 458-2445
Internet: www.waeb.uscourts.gov

Number of Judgeships: 3

Court Staff
Clerk of the Court **Beverly A. Benka** .... (509) 458-5300
Chief Deputy Clerk **Shannon O'Brien** .... (509) 458-5323
Education: Eastern Washington 1978 BA,
1992 MPA

Chambers of Chief Bankruptcy Judge Frederick P. Corbit

904 West Riverside Avenue, Spokane, WA 99201
Tel: (509) 458-5340

Frederick P. Corbit
Chief Bankruptcy Judge

Staff
Law Clerk **Brian Sheehan** .... (509) 458-5340
E-mail: brian_sheehan@waeb.uscourts.gov
Judicial Assistant **Dee Sindlinger** .... (509) 458-5340
E-mail: dee_sidlinger@waeb.uscourts.gov

Chambers of Bankruptcy Judge Frank L. Kurtz

402 East Yakima Avenue, Suite 200, Yakima, WA 98901
Tel: (509) 576-6122
E-mail: frank_kurtz@waeb.uscourts.gov

Frank L. Kurtz
Bankruptcy Judge

Date of Birth: 1946
Education: Gonzaga 1974 JD
Began Service: 2005
Term Expires: 2019

Staff
Career Law Clerk **Tap Menard**.......................(509) 576-6124
Judicial Assistant **Chantelle Sliman** .... (509) 576-6122

Chambers of Bankruptcy Judge (recalled) John A. Rossmeissl

402 East Yakima Avenue, Suite 200, Yakima, WA 98901-5404
Tel: (509) 576-6122

John A. Rossmeissl
Bankruptcy Judge (recalled)

Date of Birth: 1940
Education: Washington State 1962 BA; Chicago 1965 JD
Began Service: 1987

Staff
Judicial Assistant **Chantelle Sliman** .... (509) 576-6122

United States District Court for the Western District of Washington

700 Stewart Street, Suite 2310, Seattle, WA 98101
Tel: (206) 370-8400 Tel: (206) 553-2288 (PACER)
Internet: www.wawd.uscourts.gov

Number of Judgeships: 7

Circuit: Ninth

Areas Covered: Counties of Clallam, Clark, Cowlitz, Grays Harbor, Island, Jefferson, King, Kitsap, Lewis, Mason, Pacific, Pierce, San Juan, Skagit, Skamania, Snohomish, Thurston, Wahkiakum and Whatcom

Court Staff

Clerk of Court **William McCool** . . . . . (206) 370-8400
E-mail: william_mccool@wawd.uscourts.gov
Deputy-in-Charge - Tacoma **Joe Whiteley** . . . . . (253) 882-3808
1717 Pacific Ave., Rm. 3100, Tacoma, WA 98402
E-mail: Joe_Whiteley@wawd.uscourts.gov
Chief Pretrial Services Officer **(Vacant)** . . . . . (206) 370-8950
Chief Probation Officer **Connie Smith** . . . . . (206) 370-8550
Director, Administrative Services **Melissa Muir** . . . . . (206) 370-8488
E-mail: melissa_muir@wawd.uscourts.gov
Librarian **Timothy Sheehy** . . . . . (206) 370-8975
Fax: (206) 553-4385

Chambers of Chief Judge Marsha J. Pechman

U.S. Courthouse, 700 Stewart Street, Room 14229, Seattle, WA 98101
Tel: (206) 370-8820 Fax: (206) 370-8821
E-mail: Marsha_Pechman@wawd.uscourts.gov

Marsha J. Pechman
Chief Judge

Date of Birth: 1951
Education: Cornell 1973 BA; Boston U 1976 JD
Began Service: October 4, 1999
Appointed By: President William J. Clinton

Academic: Instructor and Staff Attorney, School of Law, University of Washington (1979-1981); Adjunct Faculty, School of Law, University of Washington (1983-1987); Visiting Clinical Professor, University of Puget Sound (1986-1987)

Clerkships: Law Clerk/Limited Practice Intern, Greater Boston Legal Services (1975-1976)

Government: Deputy Prosecutor, Office of the Prosecuting Attorney, County of King, Washington (1976-1979)

Judicial: Superior Court Judge, King County Superior Court (1988-1999); District Judge, Chambers of District Judge Marsha J. Pechman, United States District Court for the Western District of Washington (1999-2011)

Legal Practice: Associate, Levinson, Friedman, Vhugen, Duggan, Bland & Horowitz (1981-1986); Partner, Levinson, Friedman, Vhugen, Duggan, Bland & Horowitz (1987-1988)

Current Memberships: Federal Judges Association; King County Bar Association; Washington State Bar Association

Staff

Law Clerk **Puja Mehta** . . . . . (206) 370-8820
Began Service: October 1, 2014
Term Expires: September 30, 2016
E-mail: puja_mehta@wawd.uscourts.gov
Law Clerk **Thomas Rubinsky** . . . . . (206) 370-8820
Began Service: September 2014
Term Expires: September 30, 2016
Law Clerk **Ann "Annie" Wagner** . . . . . (206) 370-8820
Began Service: October 1, 2013
Term Expires: February 29, 2016
E-mail: ann_wagner@wawd.uscourts.gov
Career Law Clerk **Steven Crozier** . . . . . (206) 370-8820
E-mail: Steven_Crozier@wawd.uscourts.gov
Education: UC Davis 1977 JD

Chambers of District Judge Robert S. Lasnik

700 Stewart Street, Suite 15128, Seattle, WA 98101
Tel: (206) 370-8810
E-mail: robert_lasnik@wawd.uscourts.gov

Robert S. Lasnik
District Judge

Date of Birth: 1951
Education: Brandeis 1972 AB; Northwestern 1973 MS, 1974 MA; U Washington 1978 JD
Began Service: December 2, 1998
Appointed By: President William J. Clinton

Academic: Lecturer, School of Law, University of Washington (1980)

Government: Deputy Prosecutor, Office of the Prosecutor, Criminal Division, County of King, Washington (1978-1981); Senior Deputy Prosecutor, Office of the Prosecutor, County of King, Washington (1981-1983); Chief of Staff, Office of the Prosecutor, County of King, Washington (1983-1990)

Judicial: Judge, Washington Superior Court, King County (1990-1998); Chief Judge, Chambers of Chief Judge Robert S. Lasnik, United States District Court for the Western District of Washington (1998-2011)

Current Memberships: Washington State Bar Association

Staff

Law Clerk **Milton Wilkins** . . . . . (206) 370-8810
Began Service: September 2014
Term Expires: September 2016
E-mail: milton_wilkins@wawd.uscourts.gov
Career Law Clerk **LB Kregenow** . . . . . (206) 370-8810
E-mail: lb_kregenow@wawd.uscourts.gov
Education: Dartmouth 1988 BA;
Pennsylvania 1991 JD
Judicial Assistant **Teri DeHaan Roberts** . . . . . (206) 370-8810
E-mail: teri_roberts@wawd.uscourts.gov

Chambers of District Judge Ronald B. Leighton

1717 Pacific Avenue, Tacoma, WA 98402-3241
Tel: (253) 882-3840
E-mail: ronald_leighton@wawd.uscourts.gov

Ronald B. Leighton
District Judge

Date of Birth: May 30, 1951
Education: Whitworth 1973 BA; Hastings 1976 JD
Began Service: November 26, 2002
Appointed By: President George W. Bush

Legal Practice: Partner, Gordon, Thomas, Honeywell, Malanca, Peterson & Daheim L.L.P. (1976-2002)

Staff

Law Clerk **Seamus Molloy** . . . . . (253) 882-3844
E-mail: seamus_molloy@wawd.uscourts.gov
Career Law Clerk **Tiff Seely** . . . . . (253) 882-3843
E-mail: tiff_seely@wawd.uscourts.gov
Education: U Washington 1986 BA;
Colorado 1990 JD
Court Reporter **Julaine Ryen** . . . . . (253) 882-3832
E-mail: julaine_ryen@wawd.uscourts.gov
Judicial Assistant **Debbie Nelson** . . . . . (253) 882-3840
E-mail: debbie_nelson@wawd.uscourts.gov

Chambers of District Judge James L. Robart

700 Stewart Street, Room 14134, Seattle, WA 98101
Tel: (206) 370-8920 Fax: (206) 370-8921
E-mail: james_robart@wawd.uscourts.gov

James L. Robart
District Judge

Date of Birth: September 2, 1947
Education: Whitman 1969 BA; Georgetown 1973 JD
Began Service: June 28, 2004
Appointed By: President George W. Bush

Legal Practice: Partner, Lane Powell Spears Lubersky LLP (1973-1997); Managing Partner, Lane Powell Spears Lubersky LLP (1998-2004)

Staff

Law Clerk **David Martin** .... (206) 370-8920
Term Expires: September 2016
E-mail: david_martin@wawd.uscourts.gov
Law Clerk **Daniel Baris** .... (206) 370-8920
Term Expires: September 2016
E-mail: daniel_baris@wawd.uscourts.gov
Career Law Clerk **Tamara Conrad** .... (206) 370-8920
E-mail: tamara_conrad@wawd.uscourts.gov

Chambers of District Judge Benjamin Hale Settle

1717 Pacific Avenue, Room 3144, Tacoma, WA 98402
Tel: (253) 882-3850
E-mail: benjamin_settle@wawd.uscourts.gov

Benjamin Hale Settle
District Judge

Date of Birth: 1947
Education: Claremont McKenna 1969 BA; Willamette 1972 JD
Began Service: July 9, 2007
Appointed By: President George W. Bush

Legal Practice: Associate, Don Miles Attorneys (1972); Associate, Don Miles Attorneys (1976-1977); Member, Settle & Johnson, P.L.L.C. (1997-2007)

Military Service: CPT, United States Army Reserve, United States Department of Defense (1973-1975)

Staff

Law Clerk **Laura Powell** .... (253) 882-3850
Began Service: September 2014
Term Expires: September 2016
E-mail: laura_powell@wawd.uscourts.gov
Law Clerk **William Burnside** .... (253) 882-3850
Began Service: 2011
Education: Seattle 2004 JD
Courtroom Deputy **Gretchen Craft** .... (253) 882-3825
E-mail: gretchen_craft@wawd.uscourts.gov
Judicial Assistant **Trish Graham** .... (253) 882-3850
E-mail: trish_graham@wawd.uscourts.gov

Chambers of District Judge Ricardo S. Martinez

700 Stewart Street, Suite 13134, Seattle, WA 98101
Tel: (206) 370-8880 Fax: (206) 370-8881
E-mail: ricardo_martinez@wawd.uscourts.gov

Ricardo S. Martinez
District Judge

Date of Birth: June 23, 1951
Education: U Washington 1975 BS, 1980 JD
Began Service: June 2004
Appointed By: President George W. Bush

Judicial: King County Superior Court (1990-1998); Federal Magistrate Judge (1998-2004)

Legal Practice: King County Prosecutor's Office (1980-1990)

Staff

Law Clerk **Sarah Mack** .... (206) 370-8880
Began Service: September 2014
Law Clerk **Stephanie Safdi** .... (206) 370-8880
E-mail: stephanie_safdi@wawd.uscourts.gov
Administrative Assistant **Melody Byrd** .... (206) 370-8880
E-mail: melody_byrd@wawd.uscourts.gov
Administrative Assistant **Carol S. Miller** .... (206) 370-8880
E-mail: carol_miller@wawd.uscourts.gov

Chambers of District Judge Richard A. Jones

700 Stewart Street, Lobby Level, Seattle, WA 98101
Tel: (206) 370-8870

Richard A. Jones
District Judge

Education: Seattle 1972 BPA; U Washington 1975 JD
Began Service: October 29, 2007
Appointed By: President George W. Bush

Government: Community Liaison Officer, Office of the Prosecuting Attorney, County of King, Washington (1975-1977); Deputy Prosecuting Attorney, Office of the Prosecuting Attorney, County of King, Washington (1977-1978); Staff Attorney, Port of Seattle (1978-1983); Assistant United States Attorney, Washington - Western District, Executive Office for United States Attorneys, United States Department of Justice (1988-1994)

Judicial: Judge, King County Superior Court, County of King, Washington (1994-2007)

Legal Practice: Associate, Bogle & Gates (1983-1988)

Chambers of Senior Judge Walter T. McGovern

700 Stewart Street, Suite 13229, Seattle, WA 98101
Tel: (206) 370-8860 Fax: (206) 370-8861
E-mail: walter_mcgovern@wawd.uscourts.gov

Walter T. McGovern
Senior Judge

Date of Birth: May 24, 1922
Education: U Washington 1948 BA, 1950 LLB
Began Service: May 14, 1971
Appointed By: President Richard M. Nixon

Judicial: Judge, Seattle Municipal Court (1959-1965); Judge, Washington Superior Court (1965-1968); Judge, Washington Supreme Court (1968-1971)

Legal Practice: Kerr, McCord, Greenleaf & Moen (1950-1959)

Military Service: United States Naval Reserve (1943-1980)

Current Memberships: King County Bar Association; Washington State Bar Association

Chambers of Senior Judge Walter T. McGovern *continued*

Staff

Judicial Assistant **Dana Scarp** . . . . (206) 370-8862
E-mail: dana_scarp@wawd.uscourts.gov
Education: U Puget Sound 1984 BA

Chambers of Senior Judge Barbara J. Rothstein

700 Stewart Street, Suite 16128, Seattle, WA 98101
Tel: (206) 370-8840 Fax: (206) 370-8841
E-mail: barbara_rothstein@wawd.uscourts.gov

Barbara Jacobs Rothstein
Senior Judge

Note: Judge Rothstein is currently assigned to the District of Columbia District Court as a visiting judge.
Date of Birth: 1939
Education: Cornell 1960 BA; Harvard 1966 LLB
Began Service: February 20, 1980
Appointed By: President Jimmy Carter

Current Memberships: American Bar Foundation; American Association of Justice; American Bar Association; The American Law Institute; King County Bar Association; Massachusetts Bar Association; National Association of Women Judges; Washington State Bar Association

Staff

Law Clerk **Brett D. Weingold** . . . . (206) 370-8844
Began Service: September 5, 2014
Term Expires: September 5, 2016
Education: NYU 2010 JD

Career Law Clerk **Heather Reed** . . . . (206) 370-8847
E-mail: heather_reed@wawd.uscourts.gov
Education: Duke 1998 JD

Secretary **Lois Gamble Duncan** . . . . (206) 370-8842
E-mail: lois_duncan@wawd.uscourts.gov
Education: Missouri 1961 BS

Chambers of Senior Judge Carolyn R. Dimmick

U.S. Courthouse, 700 Stewart Street, Suite 16134, Seattle, WA 98101
Tel: (206) 370-8850 Fax: (206) 370-8851
E-mail: carolyn_dimmick@wawd.uscourts.gov

Carolyn R. Dimmick
Senior Judge

Date of Birth: 1929
Education: U Washington 1951 BA, 1953 JD
Began Service: April 4, 1985
Appointed By: President Ronald Reagan

Government: Assistant Attorney General, Office of the Attorney General, State of Washington (1953-1954); Deputy Prosecuting Attorney, County of King, Washington (1955-1959)

Judicial: Judge, Washington District Court, Northeast District (1965-1975); Judge, Washington Superior Court, King County (1976-1980); Justice, Washington Supreme Court (1981-1985)

Legal Practice: Private Practice (1959-1960)

Current Memberships: American Bar Association; American Judges Association; National Association of Women Judges; Superior Court Judges Association (WA); Washington State Bar Association

Staff

Judicial Assistant **Johanna Moody-Gatlin** . . . . (206) 370-8852
E-mail: johanna_moody@wawd.uscourts.gov

Chambers of Senior Judge Robert J. Bryan

1717 Pacific Avenue, Room 4427, Tacoma, WA 98402
Tel: (253) 882-3870
E-mail: robert_bryan@wawd.uscourts.gov

Robert J. Bryan
Senior Judge

Date of Birth: 1934
Education: U Washington 1956 BA, 1958 JD
Began Service: 1986
Appointed By: President Ronald Reagan

Judicial: Judge, Washington Superior Court (1967-1984)

Legal Practice: Bryan & Bryan (1959-1967); Riddell, Williams, Bullitt & Walkinshaw (1984-1986)

Military Service: United States Army Reserve, United States Department of the Army

Current Memberships: American Bar Association; The Honorable Robert J. Bryan American Inn of Court, The American Inns of Court; Federal Bar Association

Staff

Law Clerk (Part-Time) **Rachel Dolven** . . . . (253) 882-3870
E-mail: rachel_dolven@wawd.uscourts.gov

Law Clerk **Nathan Nanfeld** . . . . (253) 882-3870
E-mail: nathan_nanfeld@wawd.uscourts.gov

Career Law Clerk **Colleen Klein** . . . . (253) 882-3870
E-mail: colleen_klein@wawd.uscourts.gov
Education: Seattle JD

Judicial Assistant **Julie Lemm** . . . . (253) 882-3870
E-mail: julie_lemm@wawd.uscourts.gov
Education: Black Hills State 1989 BS

Chambers of Senior Judge Thomas S. Zilly

700 Stewart Street, Suite 15229, Seattle, WA 98101
Tel: (206) 370-8830 Fax: (206) 370-8831
E-mail: thomas_zilly@wawd.uscourts.gov

Thomas S. Zilly
Senior Judge

Date of Birth: 1935
Education: Michigan 1956 BA; Cornell 1962 JD
Began Service: 1988
Appointed By: President Ronald Reagan

Judicial: Judge Pro Tem, Seattle Municipal Court (1972-1980)

Legal Practice: Lane, Powell, Moss & Miller (1962)

Military Service: United States Naval Reserve (1956-1962)

Current Memberships: American Bar Association; Federal Bar Association; King County Bar Association; Washington State Bar Association

Staff

Law Clerk **Adam Olin** . . . . (206) 370-8830
Began Service: September 30, 2015
Term Expires: September 2016
E-mail: adam_olin@wawd.uscourts.gov

Law Clerk **Kathryn Kim** . . . . (206) 370-8830
Began Service: 2007
E-mail: kathryn_kim@wawd.uscourts.gov
Education: MIT 1986 BS; U Washington 1992 JD

Judicial Assistant **Karen Dews** . . . . (206) 370-8832
E-mail: karen_dews@wawd.uscourts.gov

Chambers of Senior Judge John C. Coughenour
700 Stewart Street, Suite 16229, Seattle, WA 98101
Tel: (206) 370-8800
E-mail: john_coughenour@wawd.uscourts.gov

John C. Coughenour
Senior Judge

Date of Birth: 1941
Education: Kansas State 1963 BS; Iowa 1966 JD
Began Service: 1981
Appointed By: President Ronald Reagan

Academic: Visiting Assistant Professor of Law, University of Washington (1970-1973)

Judicial: District Judge, United States District Court for the Western District of Washington (1981-2006)

Legal Practice: Bogle & Gates (1966-1970); Bogle & Gates (1971-1981)

Current Memberships: American Bar Association; Iowa State Bar Association; Washington State Bar Association

Staff
Law Clerk **Laura Zanzig** .... (206) 370-8804
Began Service: September 2015
Term Expires: September 2017
E-mail: laura_zanzig@wawd.uscourts.gov
Law Clerk **Andrea Woods** .... (206) 370-8800
Began Service: September 2014
Term Expires: September 2016
E-mail: andrea_wood@wawd.uscourts.gov
Law Clerk **Gabriel Ascher** .... (206) 370-8804
Began Service: September 2015
Term Expires: September 2016
E-mail: gabriel_ascher@wawd.uscourts.gov

Chambers of Chief Magistrate Judge James P. Donohue
700 Stewart Street, Seattle, WA 98101
Tel: (206) 370-8940
E-mail: james_donohue@wawd.uscourts.gov

James P. Donohue
Chief Magistrate Judge

Began Service: February 8, 2005

Chambers of Magistrate Judge Mary Alice Theiler
700 Stewart Street, Suite 12141, Seattle, WA 98101
Tel: (206) 370-8890

Mary Alice Theiler
Magistrate Judge

Began Service: April 25, 2003

Chambers of Magistrate Judge Karen L. Strombom
1717 Pacific Avenue, Tacoma, WA 98402
Tel: (253) 882-3890
E-mail: karen_strombom@wawd.uscourts.gov

Karen L. Strombom
Magistrate Judge

Education: Wisconsin (Stevens Point) 1974 BA; Wisconsin 1978 JD
Began Service: 2012

Chambers of Magistrate Judge Brian Tsuchida
700 Stewart Street, Seattle, WA 98101
Tel: (206) 370-8930
E-mail: brian_tsuchida@wawd.uscourts.gov

Brian Tsuchida
Magistrate Judge

Education: Grinnell BA; Oregon JD
Began Service: May 13, 2008

Chambers of Magistrate Judge J. Richard Creatura
Union Station Courthouse, 1717 Pacific Avenue, Room 3100, Tacoma, WA 98402-9800
Tel: (253) 882-3780

J. Richard Creatura
Magistrate Judge

Began Service: March 17, 2009

Staff
Judicial Assistant **Sandy Huntington** .... (253) 882-3780
E-mail: sandy_huntington@wawd.uscourts.gov
Courtroom Deputy **Kelly Miller** .... (253) 882-3780
E-mail: kelly_miller@wawd.uscourts.gov
Career Law Clerk **Victoria E. Stevens** .... (253) 882-3780
E-mail: victoria_stevens@wawd.uscourts.gov
Education: Boalt Hall 2003 JD;
UC Davis 2003 PhD

Chambers of Magistrate Judge David W. Christel
1717 Pacific Avenue, Tacoma, WA 98402
Tel: (360) 993-4990

David W. Christel
Magistrate Judge

Chambers of Magistrate Judge (part-time) Dean Brett
700 Stewart Street, Seattle, WA 98101
Brett & Daugert, PLLC., 119 No. Commercial, Suite 110, Bellingham, WA 98227
Tel: (360) 733-0212
E-mail: dean_brett@wawd.uscourts.gov

Dean Brett
Magistrate Judge (Part-Time)

Education: Whitman 1968 BA; Stanford 1972 JD
Began Service: 2005

Affiliation: Partner, Brett & Coats, PLLC

Current Memberships: American College of Trial Lawyers; Washington State Bar Association

Chambers of Magistrate Judge (recalled) John L. Weinberg

700 Stewart Street, 12th Floor, Seattle, WA 98104
Tel: (206) 370-8910
E-mail: john_weinberg@wawd.uscourts.gov

John L. Weinberg
Magistrate Judge (recalled)

Date of Birth: 1941
Education: Swarthmore 1962 BA; Chicago 1965 JD
Began Service: October 1, 1973

Current Memberships: American Bar Association; Federal Magistrate Judges Association; King County Bar Association; Washington State Bar Association

Chambers of Magistrate Judge (recalled) J. Kelley Arnold

1717 Pacific Avenue, Tacoma, WA 98402-3205
Tel: (253) 882-3800 Fax: (253) 882-3881
E-mail: kelley_arnold@wawd.uscourts.gov

J. Kelley Arnold
Magistrate Judge (recalled)

Date of Birth: 1937
Education: Idaho 1961 JD
Began Service: October 28, 1994
Term Expires: January 2024

Government: Deputy Prosecuting Attorney, County of Pierce, Washington (1963-1964)

Judicial: Judge, Washington Superior Court, Pierce County (1982-1994)

Legal Practice: Partner, McCormick, Hoffman, Rees, Arnold & Faubion (1965-1982)

Military Service: United States Army (1961-1963)

Current Memberships: American Bar Association; The American Inns of Court; Federal Magistrate Judges Association; Tacoma-Pierce County Bar Association; Washington State Bar Association

Staff
Judicial Assistant **Allyson Swan** .... (253) 882-3800

United States Bankruptcy Court for the Western District of Washington

U.S. Courthouse, 700 Stewart Street, Room 6301, Seattle, WA 98101-1271
Tel: (206) 370-5200 Tel: (800) 676-6856 (PACER)
Tel: (888) 409-4662 (Toll free Voice Case Information System VCIS)
Internet: www.wawb.uscourts.gov

Number of Judgeships: 5

Court Staff
Clerk of the Court **Mark L. Hatcher** .... (206) 370-5205
E-mail: mark_hatcher@wawb.uscourts.gov
Chief Deputy **Gina Zadra Walton** .... (206) 370-5200
Operation Manager **(Vacant)** .... (206) 370-5229
Deputy-in-Charge - Tacoma **(Vacant)** .... (253) 882-3900
1717 Pacific Ave., Ste. 2100,
Tacoma, WA 98402-3233
Property and Procurement Administrator **Don Price** ...... (206) 370-5219
E-mail: don_price@wawb.uscourts.gov
Financial Administrator **Brian Futch** .... (206) 370-5221
E-mail: brian_futch@wawb.uscourts.gov
Human Resources Manager **Jim Fenner** .... (206) 370-5214
E-mail: jim_fenner@wawb.uscourts.gov
Courtroom Technology and Services Supervisor
Curtis Udy .... (206) 370-5213
E-mail: curtis_udy@wawb.uscourts.gov
Case Management Supervisor **Suzan Gallup** .... (206) 370-5258

United States Bankruptcy Court for the Western District of Washington *continued*

Training Specialist **Theola Ross** .... (206) 370-5216
E-mail: theola_ross@wawb.uscourts.gov
Administrative Assistant **Susan Shipley** .... (206) 370-5200
E-mail: susan_shipley@wawb.uscourts.gov

Chambers of Chief Bankruptcy Judge Brian D. Lynch

1717 Pacific Avenue, Room 2100, Tacoma, WA 98402
Tel: (253) 882-3900

Brian D. Lynch
Chief Bankruptcy Judge

Began Service: 2011

Staff
Law Clerk **Ben Ellison** .... (253) 882-3900
Law Clerk **Laurie K. Thornton** .... (253) 882-3900
Education: Indiana 1996 BA
Courtroom Deputy **Pattie Adams** .... (253) 882-3952

Chambers of Bankruptcy Judge Paul B. Snyder

1717 Pacific Avenue, Suite 2209, Tacoma, WA 98402-3233
Tel: (253) 882-3950
E-mail: paul_snyder@wawb.uscourts.gov

Paul B. Snyder
Bankruptcy Judge

Date of Birth: 1948
Education: U Washington BA; U Puget Sound 1975 JD; George Washington 1979 LLM
Began Service: November 1, 1996
Term Expires: October 2024

Current Memberships: American Bankruptcy Institute; American Bar Association; National Conference of Bankruptcy Judges

Staff
Career Law Clerk **Dana Manke** .... (253) 882-3953
E-mail: dana_manke@wawb.uscourts.gov
Education: Georgetown JD
Career Law Clerk **Carrie Selby** .... (253) 882-3953
E-mail: carrie_selby@wawb.uscourts.gov
Education: Seattle JD
Career Law Clerk **(Vacant)** .... (253) 882-3959
Courtroom Deputy **Pattie Adams** .... (253) 882-3952
E-mail: pattie_adams@wawb.uscourts.gov
Courtroom Deputy **Shawn Utley** .... (253) 882-3951
E-mail: shawn_utley@wawb.uscourts.gov
Judicial Assistant **Debby Vincent** .... (253) 882-3950
E-mail: debby_vincent@wawb.uscourts.gov

Chambers of Bankruptcy Judge Karen A. Overstreet

700 Stewart Street, Room 7216, Seattle, WA 98101
Tel: (206) 370-5330
E-mail: karen_overstreet@wawb.uscourts.gov

Karen A. Overstreet
Bankruptcy Judge

Date of Birth: 1955
Education: U Washington 1977 BA; Oregon 1982 JD
Began Service: January 3, 1994
Term Expires: January 2022

Current Memberships: American Bar Association; National Conference of Bankruptcy Judges

Staff
Law Clerk **Erin Anderson** .... (206) 370-5330
E-mail: erin_anderson@wawb.uscourts.gov

(continued on next page)

Chambers of Bankruptcy Judge Karen A. Overstreet *continued*

Career Law Clerk **Kerry Holt** . . . . (206) 370-5332
E-mail: kerry_holt@wawb.uscourts.gov
Education: U Washington 1987 JD
Courtroom Deputy **Morgan Brannon** . . . . (206) 370-5331
E-mail: morgan_brannon@wawb.uscourts.gov

Chambers of Bankruptcy Judge Marc Barreca

700 Stewart Street, Room 6301, Seattle, WA 98101
Tel: (206) 370-5310
E-mail: marc_barreca@wawb.uscourts.gov

Marc Barreca
Bankruptcy Judge

Education: U Washington 1983 JD
Began Service: 2010

Staff
Law Clerk **Ramie O'Neill** . . . . (206) 370-5312
Judicial Assistant **Viviane Diaz** . . . . (206) 370-5310
E-mail: viviane_diaz@wawb.uscourts.gov
Courtroom Deputy **Kim Kelley** . . . . (206) 370-5311
E-mail: kim_kelley@wawb.uscourts.gov

Chambers of Bankruptcy Judge Timothy W. Dore

700 Stewart Street, Room 6301, Seattle, WA 98101
Tel: (206) 370-5300

Timothy W. Dore
Bankruptcy Judge

Education: Seattle 1983 BA; U Washington 1987 JD
Began Service: April 4, 2011

Staff
Career Law Clerk **Christopher Dale** . . . . (206) 370-5302
Began Service: April 18, 2011
Courtroom Deputy **Janice Brooks** . . . . (206) 370-5301
E-mail: janice_brooks@wawb.uscourts.gov
Judicial Assistant **Anne K. Hermes** . . . . (206) 370-5300
E-mail: anne_hermes@wawb.uscourts.gov

Chambers of Bankruptcy Judge (recalled) Philip H. Brandt

700 Stewart Street, Suite 8135, Seattle, WA 98101
Tel: (206) 370-5320
E-mail: philip_brandt@wawb.uscourts.gov

Philip H. Brandt
Bankruptcy Judge (recalled)

Date of Birth: 1944
Education: Harvard 1966 AB; U Washington 1972 JD
Began Service: October 11, 1991
Term Expires: October 10, 2019

Government: Attorney, United States Department of Justice (1972); Attorney, Federal Maritime Commission (1972-1973); Deputy Prosecuting Attorney, Office of the Prosecuting Attorney, County of Pierce, Washington (1973-1975); Director, Standards Project, Washington Governor's Committee on Law and Justice (1975-1976)

Judicial: Chief Judge of the Bankruptcy Appellate Panel, United States Bankruptcy Appellate Panel for the Ninth Circuit

Legal Practice: LeCocq, Simonarson et al. (1976-1986); Attorney, Graham & Dunn PC (1986-1991)

Military Service: United States Navy (1966-1969); United States Naval Reserve (1969-1989)

Current Memberships: American Bar Association; King County Bar Association; National Conference of Bankruptcy Judges; Tacoma-Pierce County Bar Association; Washington State Bar Association

United States District Court for the Northern District of West Virginia

U.S. Post Office / U.S. Courthouse, 1125 Chapline Street,
Suite 1000, Wheeling, WV 26301
P.O. Box 471, Wheeling, WV 26003
Tel: (304) 232-0011 Fax: (304) 233-2185 Fax: (304) 636-5746 (Elkins)
Internet: www.wvnd.uscourts.gov

Number of Judgeships: 3

Circuit: Fourth

Areas Covered: Counties of Barbour, Berkeley, Braxton, Brooke, Calhoun, Doddridge, Gilmer, Grant, Hampshire, Hancock, Hardy, Harrison, Jefferson, Lewis, Marion, Marshall, Mineral, Monongalia, Morgan, Ohio, Pendleton, Pleasants, Pocahontas, Preston, Randolph, Ritchie, Taylor, Tucker, Tyler, Upshur, Webster and Wetzel

Court Staff

Clerk of Court **Cheryl Dean Riley** . . . . (304) 232-0011 ext. 228
E-mail: cheryl_riley@wvnd.uscourts.gov Fax: (304) 233-2185
Chief Deputy **Michelle Widmer-Eby** . . . . (304) 623-8513
Deputy Clerk-in-Charge - Clarksburg (Acting)
Michelle Widmer-Eby . . . . (304) 622-8513
Fax: (304) 623-4551
Deputy-in-Charge/HR Specialist **Kelly Fry** . . . . (304) 636-1445
300 Third St., Elkins, WV 26241 Fax: (304) 636-5746
P.O. Box 1518, Elkins, WV 26241
E-mail: kelly_fry@wvnd.uscourts.gov
Chief Probation Officer **Terry Huffman** . . . . (304) 624-5504
320 W. Pike St., Ste. 110, Clarksburg, WV 26302 Fax: (304) 624-7117
Financial Administrator **Evelyn Howell** . . . . (304) 636-1445
P.O. Box 1518, Elkins, WV 26241 Fax: (304) 636-5746
E-mail: evelyn_howell@wvnd.uscourts.gov
Court Reporter **Linda Bachman** . . . . (304) 623-7154
E-mail: linda_bachman@wvnd.uscourts.gov
Court Reporter **Terry C. Hamrick** . . . . (304) 267-5650
E-mail: terry_hamrick@wvnd.uscourts.gov
Court Reporter **Cindy Knecht** . . . . (304) 234-3968
E-mail: cindy_knecht@wvnd.uscourts.gov
Court Reporter **Linda Mullen** . . . . (304) 234-3987

Chambers of Chief Judge Gina Marie Groh

217 West King Street, Martinsburg, WV 25401
Tel: (304) 267-7027 Fax: (304) 267-6965

Gina Marie Groh
Chief Judge

Education: Shepherd U 1986 BS; West Virginia 1989 JD
Began Service: March 20, 2012
Appointed By: President Barack Obama

Chambers of District Judge John Preston Bailey

P.O. Box 551, Wheeling, WV 26003
Tel: (304) 233-1492 Fax: (304) 233-1495

John Preston Bailey
District Judge

Date of Birth: May 2, 1951
Education: Dartmouth 1973 AB; West Virginia 1976 JD
Began Service: March 22, 2007
Appointed By: President George W. Bush

Staff
Law Clerk **Evan Nogay** . . . . (304) 234-3974
Began Service: September 10, 2015
Term Expires: August 2016
Law Clerk **Courtney Hooper** . . . . (304) 234-3975
Began Service: September 2015
Term Expires: September 2016
E-mail: courtney_hooper@wvnd.uscourts.gov

Chambers of District Judge John Preston Bailey *continued*

Career Law Clerk **Jeff Parsons** . . . . (304) 234-3973
Began Service: April 2, 2007
E-mail: jeff_parsons@wvnd.uscourts.gov
Education: West Virginia 2006 JD

Chambers of District Judge Irene M. Keeley

500 West Pike Street, Clarksburg, WV 26301
P.O. Box 2808, Clarksburg, WV 26302-2808
Tel: (304) 624-5850 Fax: (304) 622-1928
E-mail: Judge_Keeley@wvnd.uscourts.gov

Irene M. Keeley
District Judge

Date of Birth: 1944
Education: Col Notre Dame (MD) 1965 BA; West Virginia 1977 MA, 1980 JD
Began Service: 1992
Appointed By: President George H.W. Bush
Political Affiliation: Republican

Academic: Teacher, Prince George's County Maryland Schools (1966-1967); Teacher, Harrison County West Virginia Schools (1968-1975); Adjunct Professor of Law, College of Law, West Virginia University (1990-1991)

Government: Legal Researcher, Civil Rights Division, United States Department of Justice (1965-1965)

Legal Practice: Attorney, Steptoe & Johnson LLP (1980-1992)

Current Memberships: Judicial Division, American Bar Association; Federal Judges Association; Harrison County Bar Association; West Virginia Bar Association; The West Virginia State Bar

Staff

Law Clerk **John Pizzo** . . . . (304) 624-5850
Law Clerk **Shaina Richardson** . . . . (304) 624-5850
Administrative Assistant **Elaine S. Junkins** . . . . . . (304) 624-5850
E-mail: Elaine_Junkins@wvnd.uscourts.gov
Education: Fairmont State Col 1989 BS

Chambers of Senior Judge Frederick P. Stamp, Jr.

U.S. Courthouse, 12th and Chapline Streets, Wheeling, WV 26003
P.O. Box 791, Wheeling, WV 26003
Tel: (304) 233-1120 Fax: (304) 233-0402

Frederick P. Stamp, Jr.
Senior Judge

Date of Birth: 1934
Education: Washington and Lee 1956 BA; Richmond 1959 LLB
Began Service: July 30, 1990
Appointed By: President George H.W. Bush
Political Affiliation: Republican

Government: State Legislator, West Virginia Legislature (1966-1970)

Judicial: District Judge, United States District Court for the Northern District of West Virginia (1990-2006)

Legal Practice: Schrader, Stamp, Byrd, Byrum & Companion (1960-1990)

Military Service: United States Army (1959-1960); United States Army Reserve, United States Department of the Army (1960-1967)

Nonprofit: Trustee, Board of Trustees, University of Richmond

Current Memberships: American Bar Foundation; American Bar Association; American College of Trial Lawyers; National Conference of Commissioners on Uniform State Laws; Ohio County Bar Association; West Virginia Bar Association; The West Virginia State Bar; West Virginia Bar Foundation, Inc., The West Virginia State Bar

Chambers of Senior Judge Frederick P. Stamp, Jr. *continued*

Staff

Law Clerk **Joshua M. Deal** . . . . (304) 233-1120
Began Service: August 2015
Term Expires: August 2017
Law Clerk **Imad S. Matini** . . . . (304) 233-1120
Began Service: August 2014
Term Expires: August 2016
E-mail: imad_matini@wvnd.uscourts.gov
Education: West Virginia 2014 JD
Court Reporter **Cindy Knecht** . . . . (304) 234-3968
Secretary **Marjorie K. Jaworski** . . . . (304) 233-1120

Chambers of Magistrate Judge James E. Seibert

U.S. Courthouse, Wheeling, WV 26003
P.O. Box 471, Wheeling, WV 26003
Tel: (304) 233-1348 Fax: (304) 233-1364

James E. Seibert
Magistrate Judge

Date of Birth: 1944
Education: West Virginia 1969 JD
Began Service: 1985
Term Expires: March 2023

Legal Practice: Seibert & Kasserman, LC (1969-1999)

Staff

Law Clerk **William L. Burner** . . . . (304) 233-1348
Began Service: August 2015
Term Expires: August 2016
E-mail: william_burner@wvnd.uscourts.gov
Pro Se Law Clerk **Mary J. Williams** . . . . (304) 233-1348
E-mail: mary_j_williams@wvnd.uscourts.gov
Secretary **Janet Kalo** . . . . (304) 233-1348
E-mail: Janet_Kalo@wvnd.uscourts.gov

Chambers of Magistrate Judge Robert W. Trumble

217 West King Street, Room 207, Martinsburg, WV 25401
Tel: (304) 267-5611 Fax: (304) 264-2721

Robert W. Trumble
Magistrate Judge

Began Service: June 3, 2014
Term Expires: June 2, 2022

Staff

Career Law Clerk **Deborah Hillyard** . . . . (304) 267-7223 ext. 5611
Education: William & Mary 1992 JD
Law Clerk **Julie Roberts** . . . . (304) 267-7223 ext. 5613

Chambers of Magistrate Judge Michael Aloi

500 West Pike Street, Clarksburg, WV 26301
Tel: (304) 623-7170

Michael J. Aloi
Magistrate Judge

Began Service: October 1, 2015

United States Bankruptcy Court for the Northern District of West Virginia

Federal Building, 12th & Chapline Streets, Wheeling, WV 26003
P.O. Box 70, Wheeling, WV 26003
Tel: (304) 233-1655 Tel: (304) 233-2871 (PACER)
Tel: (304) 233-7318 (Voice Case Information System VCIS)
Fax: (304) 233-0185
Internet: www.wvnb.uscourts.gov

Number of Judgeships: 1

Court Staff

Clerk of the Court **Ryan Johnson** .... (304) 233-1655
E-mail: ryan_johnson@wvnb.uscourts.gov
Education: Loyola U (New Orleans) 2001 JD
Chief Deputy Clerk **Anita Swaton** .... (304) 233-1655
E-mail: Anita_Swaton@wvnb.uscourts.gov
Deputy-in-Charge **Sheree Burlas** .... (304) 623-7866
E-mail: Sheree_Burlas@wvnb.uscourts.gov Fax: (304) 623-9047
Education: West Virginia Wesleyan 1981 BS
Systems Manager **Chris Warsinsky** .... (304) 233-1655
E-mail: chris_warsinsky@industry.net
Education: West Liberty State 1979 BS; Radford 1981 MS
Financial Administrator **Brenda Duvall** .... (304) 233-1655

Chambers of Chief Bankruptcy Judge Patrick M. Flatley

12th & Chapline Streets, Wheeling, WV 26003
Tel: (304) 233-1655

Patrick M. Flatley
Chief Bankruptcy Judge

Began Service: 2006

Staff

Law Clerk **James Voithofer** .... (304) 233-1655
Education: West Virginia 2010 JD
Law Clerk **(Vacant)** .... (304) 233-1655
Courtroom Deputy **Lisa McNeil** .... (304) 233-1655

United States District Court for the Southern District of West Virginia

Robert C. Byrd U.S. Courthouse, 300 Virginia Street East, Suite 7009, Charleston, WV 25301
Tel: (304) 347-3000 Fax: (304) 347-3007
Internet: www.wvsd.uscourts.gov

Number of Judgeships: 5

Circuit: Fourth

Areas Covered: Counties of Boone, Cabell, Clay, Fayette, Greenbrier, Jackson, Kanawha, Lincoln, Logan, Mason, McDowell, Mercer, Mingo, Monroe, Nicholas, Putnam, Raleigh, Roane, Summers, Wayne, Wirt, Wood and Wyoming

Court Staff

Clerk of Court **Teresa L. Deppner** .... (304) 347-3000
Education: Marshall 1988 BA
Chief Deputy Clerk **Krystyna A. Gerencir** .... (304) 347-3086
Fax: (304) 347-3097
Chief Probation Officer **Keith Zutaut** .... (304) 347-3300
E-mail: keith_zutaut@wvsd.uscourts.gov Fax: (304) 347-3301
Deputy Clerk-in-Charge - Beckley
Cassandra D. Staples .... (304) 253-7481
P.O. Drawer 5009, Beckley, WV 25801 Fax: (304) 253-3252
E-mail: cassandra_staples@wvsd.uscourts.gov
Deputy Clerk-in-Charge - Bluefield
Mary Jane Pennington .... (304) 327-9798
P.O. Box 4128, Bluefield, WV 24701 Fax: (304) 327-6668

United States District Court for the Southern District of West Virginia *continued*

Deputy Clerk-in-Charge - Huntington **Marsha Wilson** ... (304) 529-5588
P.O. Box 1570, Huntington, WV 25716 Fax: (304) 529-5131
E-mail: marsha_wilson@wvsd.uscourts.gov
Financial and Budget Administrator **Lisa R. Watts** .... (304) 347-3086
Human Resources Specialist **Korin Parsons** .... (304) 347-3086
E-mail: korin_parsons@wvsd.uscourts.gov
Director of Information Technology **Chad Adkins** .... (304) 347-3005
E-mail: chad_adkins@wvsd.uscourts.gov
Operations Manager **Rowena A. Stiltner** .... (304) 347-3002
E-mail: rowena_stiltner@wvsd.uscourts.gov

Chambers of Chief Judge Robert C. Chambers

Sidney L. Christie Federal Building, 845 Fifth Avenue, 2nd Floor, Huntington, WV 25701
Tel: (304) 528-7583 Fax: (304) 528-7585
E-mail: Judge_Chambers@wvsd.uscourts.gov

Robert C. Chambers
Chief Judge

Date of Birth: 1952
Education: Marshall 1974 AB; West Virginia 1978 JD
Began Service: October 17, 1997
Appointed By: President William J. Clinton

Current Memberships: The West Virginia State Bar

Staff

Law Clerk **Elizabeth Stegeman** .... (304) 528-7583
Began Service: August 2015
Term Expires: August 2016
E-mail: elizabeth_stegeman@wvsd.uscourts.gov
Law Clerk **Jonathan J. Sheffield, Jr.** .... (304) 528-7583
Began Service: September 2015
Term Expires: September 2016
E-mail: jonathan_sheffield@wvsd.uscourts.gov
Career Law Clerk **Sandra Mickle Slack** .... (304) 528-7583
Education: West Virginia 1992 JD
Courtroom Deputy **Terry Justice** .... (304) 528-7583
E-mail: terry_justice@wvsd.uscourts.gov
Court Reporter **Terry Ruffner** .... (304) 528-7583
E-mail: terry_ruffner@wvsd.uscourts.gov

Chambers of District Judge Joseph Robert Goodwin

Robert C. Byrd U.S. Courthouse, 300 Virginia Street East, Suite 5009, Charleston, WV 25301
P.O. Box 2546, Charleston, WV 25329
Tel: (304) 347-3192 Fax: (304) 347-3193
E-mail: joseph_goodwin@wvsd.uscourts.gov

Joseph Robert Goodwin
District Judge

Date of Birth: 1942
Education: West Virginia 1965 BS, 1970 JD
Began Service: May 15, 1995
Appointed By: President William J. Clinton

Staff

Law Clerk **David Bernstein** .... (304) 347-3192
Began Service: November 2015
Term Expires: November 2016
E-mail: david_bernstein@wvsd.uscourts.gov
Law Clerk **Aubrie Kiel** .... (304) 347-3192
Began Service: November 2015
Term Expires: November 2016
E-mail: aubrie_kiel@wvsd.uscourts.gov

Chambers of District Judge Joseph Robert Goodwin *continued*

Law Clerk **Dallas Kratzer** (304) 347-3192
Began Service: August 2015
Term Expires: August 2016
E-mail: skyler_gray@wvsd.uscourts.gov

Law Clerk **Jenna Leary** (304) 347-3192
Began Service: August 2015
Term Expires: August 2016
E-mail: jenna_leary@wvsd.uscourts.gov

Law Clerk **Khushboo Shah** (304) 347-3192
Began Service: November 2015
Term Expires: November 2016
E-mail: khushboo_shah@wvsd.uscourts.gov

Law Clerk **Jonathan Storage** (304) 347-3192
Began Service: August 2015
Term Expires: August 2016
E-mail: jonathan_storage@wvsd.uscourts.gov

Career Law Clerk **Kate Fife** (304) 347-3192
E-mail: kate_fife@wvsd.uscourts.gov
Education: West Virginia 1994 JD

Courtroom Deputy **Robin Clark** (304) 347-3192

Chambers of District Judge John T. Copenhaver, Jr.

6009 Robert C. Byrd U.S. Courthouse, 300 Virginia Street East, Charleston, WV 25301
P.O. Box 2546, Charleston, WV 25329-2546
Tel: (304) 347-3146 Fax: (304) 347-3147

John T. Copenhaver, Jr.
District Judge

Date of Birth: 1925
Education: West Virginia 1947 AB, 1950 LLB
Began Service: September 26, 1976
Appointed By: President Gerald Ford
Political Affiliation: Republican

Academic: Adjunct Professor of Law, College of Law, West Virginia University (1970-1976); Faculty Member, Federal Judicial Center (1970-1976)

Clerkships: Law Clerk The Honorable Ben Moore, United States District Court (1950-1951)

Judicial: Bankruptcy Judge, United States Bankruptcy Court (1958-1976)

Legal Practice: Copenhaver & Copenhaver (1951-1958)

Military Service: United States Army (1944-1946)

Staff

Law Clerk **Edward Dumoulin** (304) 347-3146
Began Service: August 2015
Term Expires: August 2016
E-mail: edward_dumoulin@wvsd.uscourts.gov

Law Clerk **Robert McCaleb** (304) 347-3146
Began Service: August 2015
Term Expires: August 2016
E-mail: robert_mccaleb@wvsd.uscourts.gov

Career Law Clerk **Jonah Fabricant** (304) 347-3146
E-mail: jonah_fabricant@wvsd.uscourts.gov

Courtroom Deputy/Paralegal **Kelley A. Miller** (304) 347-3146
E-mail: Kelley_Miller@wvsd.uscourts.gov

Court Reporter **Catherine Schutte-Stant** (304) 347-3151
Fax: (304) 347-3147

Chambers of District Judge Thomas E. Johnston

300 Virginia Street East, Room 6610, Charleston, WV 25301
Tel: (304) 347-3217 Fax: (304) 347-3218

Thomas E. Johnston
District Judge

Education: West Virginia 1989 BA, 1992 JD
Began Service: April 17, 2006
Appointed By: President George W. Bush

Government: U.S. Attorney, West Virginia - Northern District, Executive Office for United States Attorneys, United States Department of Justice

Staff

Law Clerk **Andrei Popovici** (304) 347-3220
Began Service: December 2014
Term Expires: December 2015
E-mail: andrei_popovici@wvsd.uscourts.gov

Career Law Clerk **Jamie Kastler** (304) 347-3221
E-mail: jamie_kastler@wvsd.uscourts.gov

Courtroom Deputy Clerk **Staci Wilson** (304) 347-3217
E-mail: staci_wilson@wvsd.uscourts.gov

Court Reporter **Ayme Cochran** (304) 347-3217
E-mail: ayme_cochran@wvsd.uscourts.gov

Chambers of District Judge Irene Cornelia Berger

110 North Heber Street, Room 336, Beckley, WV 25801
P.O. Box 5009, Beckley, WV 25801
Tel: (304) 253-2438 Tel: (304) 347-3100 (Charleston Phone Number)
Fax: (304) 347-3007

Irene Cornelia Berger
District Judge

Date of Birth: 1954
Education: West Virginia 1976, 1979 JD
Began Service: December 11, 2009
Appointed By: President Barack Obama

Government: Assistant Prosecuting Attorney, Office of the Prosecuting Attorney, County of Kanawha, West Virginia (1982-1994); Attorney, Virginia - Western District, Executive Office for United States Attorneys, United States Department of Justice (1994)

Judicial: Circuit Judge, Thirteenth Judicial Circuit, West Virginia (1994-2009)

Current Memberships: American Bar Association; West Virginia Bar Association

Staff

Courtroom Deputy **Kierstin K. Tudor** (304) 253-2438
E-mail: kierstin_tudor@wvsd.uscourts.gov
Education: Mountain State 1991 AS; Concord Col 1993 BA

Court Reporter **Lisa A. Cook** (304) 253-2438
E-mail: lisa_cook@wvsd.uscourts.gov

Judicial Assistant **Karen Sword** (304) 253-2438
E-mail: karen_sword@wvsd.uscourts.gov

Chambers of Senior Judge David A. Faber

601 Federal Street, Room 2303, Bluefield, WV 24701
P.O. Box 4278, Bluefield, WV 24701
Tel: (304) 327-8144 (Bluefield Office)
Tel: (304) 347-3170 (Charleston Office) Fax: (304) 325-8344

David A. Faber
Senior Judge

Date of Birth: 1942
Education: West Virginia 1964 BA; Yale 1967 JD; Virginia 1998 LLM
Began Service: December 27, 1991
Appointed By: President George H.W. Bush
Political Affiliation: Republican

Current Memberships: Federal Judges Association; National Association of Former United States Attorneys; West Virginia Bar Association; The West Virginia State Bar

Staff
Law Clerk **Brooke Conkle** .... (304) 327-8144
Began Service: August 2014
Term Expires: August 31, 2016
E-mail: brooke_conkle@wvsd.uscourts.gov
Career Law Clerk **Allison Cox Skinner** .... (304) 327-8144
E-mail: allison_skinner@wvsd.uscourts.gov
Education: William & Mary 1999 JD
Courtroom Deputy **Cindy Lilly** .... (304) 327-8144
E-mail: cindy_lilly@wvsd.uscourts.gov

Chambers of Magistrate Judge R. Clarke VanDervort

1013 Elizabeth Kee Federal Building, 601 Federal Street, Bluefield, WV 24701-3033
110 North Heber Street, Beckley, WV 25801
P.O. Box 5009, Beckley, WV 25801
Tel: (304) 327-0376 Tel: (304) 253-8516 (Beckley Chambers)
Fax: (304) 253-5618 (Beckley Chambers) Fax: (304) 325-7662

R. Clarke VanDervort
Magistrate Judge

Began Service: December 2001
Term Expires: December 19, 2017

Staff
Career Law Clerk **Amy Breeding** .... (304) 327-0376
E-mail: amy_breeding@wvsd.uscourts.gov
Career Law Clerk **Mary Beth Niday** .... (304) 253-8516
E-mail: marybeth_niday@wvsd.uscourts.gov
Education: Virginia Tech 1995 BS; West Virginia 2002 JD
Judicial Assistant **Melissa Keene** .... (304) 327-0376
E-mail: melissa_keene@wvsd.uscourts.gov

Chambers of Magistrate Judge Cheryl A. Eifert

845 Fifth Avenue, Room 109, Huntington, WV 25701
Tel: (304) 529-5709
E-mail: cheryl_eifert@wvsd.uscourts.gov

Cheryl A. Eifert
Magistrate Judge

Education: Miami U (OH) 1980 BA; Ohio State 1983 JD
Began Service: 2010

Staff
Judicial Assistant **Laura Tatman** .... (304) 529-5709
E-mail: laura_tatman@wvsd.uscourts.gov

Chambers of Magistrate Judge Dwane L. Tinsley

Robert C. Byrd U.S. Courthouse, 300 Virginia Street East, Room 5408, Charleston, WV 25301
Tel: (304) 347-3279 Fax: (304) 347-3280
E-mail: dwane_tinsley@wvsd.uscourts.gov

Dwane L. Tinsley
Magistrate Judge

Staff
Judicial Assistant **Karen Stricker** .... (304) 347-3279
E-mail: karen_stricker@wvsd.uscourts.gov
Courtroom Deputy **Tabitha R. Lair** .... (304) 347-3279
E-mail: tabitha_lair@wvsd.uscourts.gov
Education: Charleston 1995 BA
Career Law Clerk **Jennifer L. Stollings-Parr** .... (304) 347-3279

United States Bankruptcy Court for the Southern District of West Virginia

3200 Robert C. Byrd U.S. Courthouse, 300 Virginia Street East, Charleston, WV 25301
Tel: (304) 347-3003
Tel: (866) 222-8029 (Voice Case Information System VCIS)
Fax: (304) 347-3018
Internet: www.wvsb.uscourts.gov

Number of Judgeships: 1

Court Staff
Clerk of the Court **Matthew J. Hayes** .... (304) 347-3003
Chief Deputy Clerk **Rosa C. Maurer** .... (304) 347-3084
E-mail: rosa_maurer@wvsb.uscourts.gov
Financial Manager **Rosa C. Maurer** .... (304) 347-3094
E-mail: rosa_maurer@wvsb.uscourts.gov
Operations/Intake Manager **Leslie J. Gallian** .... (304) 347-3049
E-mail: leslie_gallian@wvsb.uscourts.gov
Deputy-in-charge - Beckley **Cindy McKinney** .... (304) 253-7402
110 North Heber Street, 271, Beckley, WV 25801 Fax: (304) 253-8056
E-mail: cindy_mckinney@wvsb.uscourts.gov
Deputy-in-charge - Huntington (Acting) **Jason Rader** .... (304) 525-0375
845 Fifth Avenue, 336, Huntington, WV 25701 Fax: (304) 525-0243
E-mail: jason_rader@wvsb.uscourts.gov

Chambers of Bankrutpcy Judge Frank Volk

300 Virginia Street East, Charleston, WV 25301
Tel: (304) 347-3003

Frank W. Volk
Bankruptcy Judge

Education: West Virginia 1989 BA, 1992 JD

United States District Court for the Eastern District of Wisconsin

362 U.S. Courthouse, 517 East Wisconsin Avenue, Milwaukee, WI 53202
125 South Jefferson Street, Room 102, Green Bay, WI 54305-2490 (Green Bay Divisional Office)
Tel: (414) 297-3372 Tel: (920) 884-3720 (Green Bay)
Fax: (414) 297-3203 Fax: (920) 884-3724 (Green Bay)
Internet: www.wied.uscourts.gov

Number of Judgeships: 5

Circuit: Seventh

Areas Covered: Counties of Brown, Calumet, Dodge, Door, Florence, Fond du Lac, Forest, Green Lake, Kenosha, Kewaunee, Langlade, Manitowoc, Marinette, Marquette, Menominee, Milwaukee, Oconto, Outagamie, Ozaukee, Racine, Shawano, Sheboygan, Walworth, Washington, Waukesha, Waupaca, Waushara and Winnebago

United States District Court for the Eastern District of Wisconsin
continued

Court Staff

Clerk of Court **Jon W. Sanfilippo** .... (414) 297-3372
E-mail: jon_sanfilippo@wied.uscourts.gov
Chief Probation Officer **Michael Klug** .... (414) 297-1425
Human Resource Manager **Sarah Gunn** .... (414) 297-3130
E-mail: sarah_gunn@wied.uscourts.gov
Librarian **Barbara L. Fritschel** .... (414) 297-1698
Fax: (414) 297-1695

Chambers of Chief Judge William C. Griesbach

Jefferson Court Building, 125 South Jefferson Street, Room 203, Green Bay, WI 54301
P.O. Box 22490, Green Bay, WI 54305-2490
Tel: (920) 884-7775
E-mail: william_griesbach@wied.uscourts.gov

William C. Griesbach
Chief Judge

Date of Birth: 1954
Education: Marquette 1976 BA, 1979 JD
Began Service: May 17, 2002
Appointed By: President George W. Bush

Staff

Law Clerk **Samuel Berg** .... (920) 884-7775
Began Service: April 2015
Term Expires: April 2016
Law Clerk **(Vacant)** .... (920) 884-7775
Career Law Clerk **Steve Dries** .... (920) 884-7775
Judicial Secretary **Mary Fisher** .... (920) 884-7775
E-mail: Mary_Fisher@wied.uscourts.gov

Chambers of District Judge J. P. Stadtmueller

471 U.S. Courthouse, 517 East Wisconsin Avenue, Milwaukee, WI 53202
Tel: (414) 297-1122 Fax: (414) 297-1100

J. P. Stadtmueller
District Judge

Date of Birth: 1942
Education: Marquette 1964 BS, 1967 JD
Began Service: 1987
Appointed By: President Ronald Reagan

Government: Assistant United States Attorney, Eastern District of Wisconsin, United States Department of Justice (1969-1975); Assistant then Deputy United States Attorney, Eastern District of Wisconsin, United States Department of Justice (1977-1981); United States Attorney, Eastern District of Wisconsin, United States Department of Justice (1981-1987)

Judicial: Member, Chambers of Member J.P. Stadtmueller, Judicial Conference of the United States; Chief Judge, United States District Court for the Eastern District of Wisconsin (1995-2002)

Legal Practice: Associate, Kluwin, Dunphy, Hankin & Hayes (1968-1969); Partner, Stepke, Kossow, Trebon & Stadtmueller (1975-1976)

Current Memberships: American Bar Association; The American Law Institute; The Seventh Circuit Bar Association, Federal Bar Association; State Bar of Wisconsin

Staff

Law Clerk **Elleny Christopoulos** .... (414) 297-1122
Began Service: August 2014
Term Expires: August 2016
Law Clerk **Carla Baumel** .... (414) 297-1122
Began Service: August 2015
Term Expires: August 2016
Career Law Clerk **Zachary Willenbrink** .... (414) 297-1122
Began Service: August 2011
Courtroom Deputy/Case Manager **Nancy Monzingo** ..... (414) 297-1122
E-mail: nancy_monzingo@wied.uscourts.gov

Chambers of District Judge Rudolph T. Randa

U.S. Courthouse, 517 East Wisconsin Avenue, Room 310, Milwaukee, WI 53202
Tel: (414) 297-3071 Fax: (414) 297-3089
E-mail: rudolph_randa@wied.uscourts.gov

Rudolph T. Randa
District Judge

Date of Birth: 1940
Education: Wisconsin (Milwaukee) 1963 BS; Wisconsin 1966 JD
Began Service: August 12, 1992
Appointed By: President George H.W. Bush

Government: Office of the City Attorney, City of Milwaukee, Wisconsin (1970-1975)

Judicial: Municipal Judge, City of Milwaukee (1975-1979); Judge, Wisconsin Circuit Court, County of Milwaukee (1979-1992); Judge, Wisconsin Court of Appeals, District One, County of Milwaukee (1981-1984)

Legal Practice: Sole Practitioner (1966-1967)

Military Service: United States Army Reserve, United States Department of the Army (1963-1973); United States Army (1967-1969)

Staff

Career Law Clerk **Troy Martell** .... (414) 297-3071
E-mail: troy_martell@wied.uscourts.gov
Education: Marquette 1998 BA; Illinois 2001 JD
Career Law Clerk **Sandra R. Gegios** .... (414) 297-3071
E-mail: sandra_gegios@wied.uscourts.gov
Education: Wisconsin 1978 BA, 1982 JD
Court Reporter **Heidi J. Trapp** .... (414) 297-3074
E-mail: heidi_trapp@wied.uscourts.gov
Judicial Assistant **Cary Biskupic** .... (414) 297-3071
E-mail: cary_biskupic@wied.uscourts.gov
Courtroom Deputy **Linda Zik** .... (414) 297-3072
E-mail: linda_zik@wied.uscourts.gov

Chambers of District Judge Lynn Adelman

3640U.S. Courthouse, 517 East Wisconsin Avenue, Milwaukee, WI 53202-4583
Tel: (414) 297-1285 Fax: (414) 297-1296
E-mail: lynn_adelman@wied.uscourts.gov

Lynn Adelman
District Judge

Date of Birth: 1939
Education: Princeton 1961 AB; Columbia 1965 LLB
Began Service: December 9, 1997
Appointed By: President William J. Clinton

Government: State Senator (D-WI, 28), Wisconsin State Senate (1977-1997)

Legal Practice: Trial Attorney, Legal Aid Society, Criminal Courts Division (1967-1968); Sole practitioner, Law Office of Lynn Adelman (1968-1972); Associate, Law Office of Coffey, Lerner & Murray (1972-1973); Partner, Law Office of Lerner & Adelman (1973-1978); Sole practitioner, Law Office of Lynn Adelman (1978-1983); Partner, Law Office of Adelman & Adelman (1983-1988); Partner, Law Firm of Adelman, Adelman & Murray, S.C. (1988-1997)

Current Memberships: State Bar of Wisconsin

Staff

Law Clerk **Cary Bloodworth** .... (414) 297-1285
Began Service: September 2014
Term Expires: August 2016
E-mail: cary_bloodworth@wied.uscourts.gov
Career Law Clerk **Michael Ashton** .... (414) 297-1285
E-mail: michael_ashton@wied.uscourts.gov
Education: Wisconsin 2000 BA, 2003 JD

(continued on next page)

Chambers of District Judge Lynn Adelman *continued*

Career Law Clerk **Jonathan I. Deitrich** . . . . (414) 297-1285
E-mail: jon_deitrich@wied.uscourts.gov
Education: Susquehanna 1992 BA; Marquette 1995 JD
Court Reporter **(Vacant)** . . . . (414) 297-3261
Secretary **Dawn Monroe** . . . . (414) 297-1285
E-mail: dawn_monroe@wied.uscourts.gov

Chambers of District Judge Pamela Pepper

517 East Wisconsin Avenue, Milwaukee, WI 53202
Tel: (414) 297-3335 Fax: (414) 297-1596

Pamela Pepper
District Judge

Education: Northwestern 1986 BS; Cornell 1989 JD
Appointed By: President Barack Obama

Chambers of Senior Judge Charles N. Clevert, Jr.

208 U.S. Courthouse, 517 East Wisconsin Avenue, Milwaukee, WI 53202
Tel: (414) 297-1585

Charles N. Clevert, Jr.
Senior Judge

Date of Birth: 1947
Education: Davis & Elkins 1969 BA; Georgetown 1972 JD
Began Service: July 31, 1996
Appointed By: President William J. Clinton

Current Memberships: The Seventh Circuit Bar Association, Federal Bar Association; Federal Judges Association; State Bar of Wisconsin; Wisconsin Association of African-American Lawyers

Staff

Career Law Clerk **Joan Harms** . . . . (414) 297-1585
E-mail: joan_harms@wied.uscourts.gov
Education: Wisconsin 1991 BA, 1994 JD
Career Law Clerk **Margo S. Kirchner** . . . . (414) 297-1585
E-mail: margo_kirchner@wied.uscourts.gov
Education: Notre Dame 1988 BA; Michigan 1991 JD
Courtroom Deputy **Kristine Wilson Brah** . . . . (414) 297-3108
Education: Wisconsin 1984 BS
Judicial Assistant **Catherine Fehrenbach** . . . . (414) 297-1585
E-mail: catherine_fehrenbach@wied.uscourts.gov

Chambers of Magistrate Judge Patricia J. Gorence

264 U.S. Courthouse, 517 East Wisconsin Avenue, Milwaukee, WI 53202
Tel: (414) 297-4165 Fax: (414) 297-3333
E-mail: patricia_gorence@wied.uscourts.gov

Patricia J. Gorence
Magistrate Judge

Education: Marquette 1965 BA; Wisconsin 1968 MA; Marquette 1977 JD
Began Service: April 1, 1994
Term Expires: March 31, 2018

Clerkships: Law Clerk The Honorable Robert W. Warren, United States District Court for the Eastern District of Wisconsin (1977-1979)

Government: Assistant United States Attorney, Eastern District of Wisconsin, United States Department of Justice (1979-1984); First Assistant United States Attorney, Eastern District of Wisconsin, United States Department of Justice (1984-1987); United States Attorney, Eastern District of Wisconsin, United States Department of Justice (1987-1988); Assistant United States Attorney, Eastern District of Wisconsin, United States Department of Justice (1988-1989); First Assistant United States Attorney, Eastern District of Wisconsin, United States Department of Justice (1989-1991); Deputy Attorney General, State of Wisconsin (1991-1993)

Chambers of Magistrate Judge Patricia J. Gorence *continued*

Current Memberships: American Bar Association; The American Law Institute; The Seventh Circuit Bar Association, Federal Bar Association; Federal Magistrate Judges Association; Milwaukee Bar Association; National Association of Women Lawyers; State Bar of Wisconsin

Staff

Career Law Clerk **Kimberly A. Szymborski** . . . . (414) 297-4165
E-mail: kimberly_szymborski@wied.uscourts.gov
Education: Marquette 1997 JD

Chambers of Magistrate Judge William E. Callahan, Jr.

U.S. Courthouse, 517 East Wisconsin Avenue, Room 247, Milwaukee, WI 53202
Tel: (414) 297-1664 Fax: (414) 297-1453
E-mail: William_Callahan@wied.uscourts.gov

William E. Callahan, Jr.
Magistrate Judge

Date of Birth: September 15, 1948
Education: Marquette 1970 BA, 1973 JD
Began Service: August 1, 1995

Government: Eastern District of Wisconsin, Office of the United States Attorney, United States Department of Justice (1975-1984); First Assistant U.S. Attorney, Wisconsin - Eastern District, Executive Office for United States Attorneys, United States Department of Justice (1982-1984)

Legal Practice: Goldberg, Previant & Uelmen (1973-1975); Attorney, Davis & Kuelthau, S.C. (1984-1995)

Current Memberships: The American Inns of Court; Eastern District Bar Association; The Seventh Circuit Bar Association, Federal Bar Association; State Bar of Wisconsin

Staff

Law Clerk **Jeremy Heacox** . . . . (414) 297-1664
Began Service: September 2013
Term Expires: September 2016
Career Law Clerk **Elizabeth Monsils** . . . . (414) 297-1664
Education: Marquette 2009 JD

Chambers of Magistrate Judge Nancy Joseph

U.S. Courthouse, 517 East Wisconsin Avenue, Room 249, Milwaukee, WI 53202
Tel: (414) 297-4167 Fax: (414) 297-3191

Nancy Joseph
Magistrate Judge

Began Service: 2010

Chambers of Magistrate Judge William E. Duffin

517 East Wisconsin Avenue, Room 296, Milwaukee, WI 53202
Tel: (414) 297-3188 Fax: (414) 297-3308

William E. Duffin
Magistrate Judge

Staff

Career Law Clerk **Daryl J. Olszewski** . . . . (414) 297-3188
Education: Marquette 2006 JD

Chambers of Magistrate Judge (part-time) James R. Sickel
125 South Jefferson Street, Suite 101, Green Bay, WI 54301
Tel: (920) 432-7716 Fax: (920) 432-4446

James R. Sickel
Magistrate Judge (Part-Time)

Date of Birth: July 2, 1945
Education: Marquette 1967, 1974 JD
Began Service: December 1991

Current Memberships: The American Trial Lawyers Association; Brown County Bar Association (WI)

Staff
Secretary **Jane Sonetti** ....(920) 432-7716

Chambers of Magistrate Judge (recalled) Aaron E. Goodstein
258 U.S. Courthouse, 517 East Wisconsin Avenue, Milwaukee, WI 53202
Tel: (414) 297-3963 Fax: (414) 297-1199
E-mail: aaron_goodstein@wied.uscourts.gov

Aaron E. Goodstein
Magistrate Judge (recalled)

Date of Birth: 1942
Education: Wisconsin 1964 BA, 1967 JD
Began Service: November 1, 1979
Term Expires: September 30, 2016

Clerkships: Law Clerk The Honorable Myron L. Gordon, United States District Court for the District of Eastern Wisconsin (1967-1968)

Legal Practice: Chernov, Croen and Goodstein (1968-1979)

Current Memberships: American Bar Association; The Seventh Circuit Bar Association, Federal Bar Association; Federal Magistrate Judges Association; Milwaukee Bar Association; State Bar of Wisconsin

Staff
Career Law Clerk **(Vacant)** ....(414) 297-3963
Secretary **(Vacant)** ....(414) 297-3963

United States Bankruptcy Court for the Eastern District of Wisconsin
126 U.S. Courthouse, 517 East Wisconsin Avenue, Milwaukee, WI 53202
Tel: (414) 297-3291
Tel: (866) 222-8029 (Voice Case Information System VCIS)
Tel: (800) 676-6856 (PACER Registration) Fax: (414) 297-4040
Internet: www.wieb.uscourts.gov

Number of Judgeships: 4

Court Staff
Clerk of Court **Janet L. Medlock** ....(414) 297-3291
E-mail: janet_medlock@wieb.uscourts.gov
Chief Deputy Clerk **Sean D. McDermott** ....(414) 297-3291
Fax: (414) 297-4043

Chambers of Chief Bankruptcy Judge Susan V. Kelley
162 U.S. Courthouse, 517 East Wisconsin Avenue, Milwaukee, WI 53202
Tel: (414) 290-2660 Fax: (414) 297-4113
E-mail: susan_v_kelley@wieb.uscourts.gov

Susan V. Kelley
Chief Bankruptcy Judge

Date of Birth: 1954
Education: Marquette 1976 BA; Columbus Law 1979 JD
Began Service: July 1, 2003
Term Expires: June 2017

Current Memberships: American Bankruptcy Institute; American Bar Association; Dane County Bar Association; State Bar of Wisconsin

Staff
Law Clerk **Carrie Theis** ....(414) 290-2663
Term Expires: July 2016
E-mail: carrie_theis@wieb.uscourts.gov
Courtroom Deputy **Jodie A. Primus** ....(414) 290-2662
E-mail: jodie_a_primus@wieb.uscourts.gov
Judicial Assistant **Paula Bartels** ....(414) 290-2661
E-mail: paula_a_bartels@wieb.uscourts.gov

Chambers of Bankruptcy Judge Margaret Dee McGarity
162 U.S. Courthouse, 517 East Wisconsin Avenue,
Milwaukee, WI 53202-4581
Tel: (414) 297-3291 ext. 3203 Fax: (414) 297-4042

Margaret Dee McGarity
Bankruptcy Judge

Date of Birth: 1948
Education: Emory 1969; Wisconsin 1974
Began Service: 1987
Term Expires: February 2016

Current Memberships: American Bankruptcy Institute; American College of Bankruptcy; The American Inns of Court; Milwaukee Bar Association; National Association of Women Lawyers; National Conference of Bankruptcy Judges; State Bar of Wisconsin

Staff
Career Law Clerk **Kristine Trapp** ....(414) 297-3291 ext. 3036
Education: Marquette 1994 JD
Courtroom Deputy **Carolyn Belunas** ....(414) 297-3291 ext. 3034
Judicial Assistant **Stephanie A. Larson** ....(414) 297-3291 ext. 3032

Chambers of Bankruptcy Judge G. Michael Halfenger
517 East Wisconsin Avenue, Room 133, Milwaukee, WI 53202
Tel: (414) 290-2680 Fax: (414) 297-4088

G. Michael "Mike" Halfenger
Bankruptcy Judge

Education: Lawrence U BA; Chicago 1991 JD

Staff
Law Clerk **Shay A. Agsten** ....(414) 290-2680
Law Clerk **Nicholas Chmurski** ....(414) 290-2680

United States District Court for the Western District of Wisconsin

U.S. Courthouse, 120 North Henry Street, Room 320, Madison, WI 53703
Tel: (608) 264-5156 Tel: (608) 264-5914 (PACER)
Fax: (608) 264-5925
Internet: www.wiwd.uscourts.gov

Number of Judgeships: 2

Circuit: Seventh

Areas Covered: Counties of Adams, Ashland, Barron, Bayfield, Buffalo, Burnett, Chippewa, Clark, Columbia, Crawford, Dane, Douglas, Dunn, Eau Claire, Grant, Green, Iowa, Iron, Jackson, Jefferson, Juneau, La Crosse, Lafayette, Lincoln, Marathon, Monroe, Oneida, Pepin, Pierce, Polk, Portage, Price, Richland, Rock, Rusk, Sauk, Sawyer, St. Croix, Taylor, Trempealeau, Vernon, Vilas, Washburn and Wood

Court Staff

Fax: (608) 264-5925

Clerk of Court/Part Time Magistrate **Peter Oppeneer** . . . . (608) 261-5795
E-mail: peter_oppeneer@wiwd.uscourts.gov
Chief Probation Officer **Paul Reed** . . . . (608) 261-5767
E-mail: paul_reed@wiwp.uscourts.gov
Librarian **Marc Weinberger** . . . . (608) 264-5448
E-mail: marc_weinberger@ca7.uscourts.gov Fax: (608) 264-5930

Chambers of Chief Judge William M. Conley

120 North Henry Street, Madison, WI 53703
Tel: (608) 264-5156
E-mail: william_conley@wiwd.uscourts.gov

William M. Conley
Chief Judge

Education: Wisconsin BA, 1984 JD
Began Service: March 30, 2010
Appointed By: President Barack Obama

Chambers of District Judge James D. Peterson

120 North Henry Street, Madison, WI 53703
Tel: (608) 264-5156
E-mail: james_peterson@wiwd.uscourts.gov

James D. Peterson
District Judge

Education: Wisconsin 1979 BS, 1984 MA, 1986 PhD, 1998 JD
Began Service: 2014
Appointed By: President Barack Obama

Chambers of Magistrate Judge Stephen L. Crocker

U.S. Courthouse, 120 North Henry Street, Madison, WI 53703-0591
P.O. Box 591, Madison, WI 53701
Tel: (608) 264-5153
E-mail: stephen_crocker@wiwd.uscourts.gov

Stephen L. Crocker
Magistrate Judge

Date of Birth: 1958
Education: Wesleyan U 1980 BA; Northwestern 1983 JD
Began Service: 1992
Term Expires: January 21, 2016

Clerkships: Judicial Law Clerk The Honorable Barbara Crabb, United States District Court for the Western District of Wisconsin (1983-1984)

Government: Trial Attorney, United States Department of Justice (1984-1986); Assistant United States Attorney, Northern District of Illinois, United States Department of Justice (1986-1990)

Chambers of Magistrate Judge Stephen L. Crocker *continued*

Legal Practice: Associate, Michael, Best & Friedrich (1990-1992)

Staff

Career Law Clerk **Kelly Kinzel O'Driscoll** . . . . (608) 264-5153
E-mail: kelly_odriscoll@wiwd.uscourts.gov
Education: Wisconsin 1992 JD
Career Law Clerk **Lynne Solomon** . . . . (608) 264-5153
Began Service: February 2007
E-mail: lynne_solomon@wiwd.uscourts.gov
Secretary **Connie A. Korth** . . . . (608) 264-5153
E-mail: connie_korth@wiwd.uscourts.gov

Chambers of Senior Judge Barbara B. Crabb

U.S. Courthouse, 120 North Henry Street, Madison, WI 53703-0591
Tel: (608) 264-5447
E-mail: barbara_crabb@wiwd.uscourts.gov

Barbara B. Crabb
Senior Judge

Date of Birth: 1939
Education: Wisconsin 1960 BA, 1962 LLB
Began Service: November 26, 1979
Appointed By: President Jimmy Carter

Academic: Research Assistant, Law School, University of Wisconsin-Madison (1968-1971)

Judicial: Magistrate Judge, United States District Court for the Western District of Wisconsin (1971-1979)

Legal Practice: Associate, Roberts, Boardman, Suhr, Bjork & Curry (1962-1964)

Current Memberships: American Bar Association; The James E. Doyle American Inn of Court, The American Inns of Court; Dane County Bar Association; National Association of Women Judges; State Bar of Wisconsin

Staff

Law Clerk **Samuel Myler** . . . . (608) 264-5447
Began Service: August 2015
Term Expires: August 2016
E-mail: samuel_myler@wiwd.uscourts.gov
Career Law Clerk **Jeffrey Monks** . . . . (608) 264-5447
Began Service: 2007
E-mail: jeff_monks@wiwd.uscourts.gov
Education: Wisconsin 2001 JD
Court Reporter **Cheryl Seeman** . . . . (608) 225-3821
Court Reporter **Lynette Swenson** . . . . (608) 255-3821
E-mail: lynette_swenson@wiwd.uscourts.gov
Secretary **Susan Vogel** . . . . (608) 264-5447
E-mail: susan_vogel@wiwd.uscourts.gov

United States Bankruptcy Court for the Western District of Wisconsin

U.S. Courthouse, 120 North Henry Street, Madison, WI 53703-0548
Tel: (608) 264-5178 Tel: (608) 264-5630 (PACER)
Tel: (800) 373-8708 (Toll Free PACER)
Tel: (608) 264-5035 (Voice Case Information System VCIS)
Tel: (800) 743-8247 (Toll Free Voice Case Information System VCIS)
Fax: (608) 264-5105
Internet: www.wiw.uscourts.gov/bankruptcy

Number of Judgeships: 2

Court Staff

Clerk of Court **MG Marcia M. Anderson** . . . . (608) 264-5178
Affiliation: USAR
Education: Creighton 1979 BA; Rutgers 1984 JD
Chief Deputy Clerk **John Kohler** . . . . (608) 264-5178

United States Bankruptcy Court for the Western District of Wisconsin *continued*

Financial Services Manager **Brenda Welhoefer** . . . . (608) 261-5741
Fax: (608) 264-5030
Human Resources Manager **Kathy Grzybowski** . . . . (608) 264-5178
E-mail: Kathy_Grzybowski@wiwb.uscourts.gov Fax: (608) 264-5090
Systems Manager **Andrew F. Bach** . . . . (608) 264-5178

Chambers of Bankruptcy Judge Robert D. Martin
U.S. Courthouse, 120 North Henry Street, Madison, WI 53703
Tel: (608) 264-5188

Robert D. Martin
Bankruptcy Judge

Date of Birth: 1944
Education: Cornell Col 1966 AB; Chicago 1969 JD
Began Service: 1978

Academic: Lecturer, University of Wisconsin (1981)

Legal Practice: Ross & Stevens (1969-1978)

Current Memberships: American College of Bankruptcy; National Bankruptcy Conference; National Conference of Bankruptcy Judges; State Bar of Wisconsin; Turnaround Management Association, Turnaround Management Association

Staff
Law Clerk **David Ferguson** . . . . (608) 264-5188
Began Service: August 2015
Term Expires: September 2016
Secretary **Penny J. Brellenthin** . . . . (608) 264-5188

Chambers of Bankruptcy Judge Catherine J. Furay
500 South Barstow Street, Eau Claire, WI 54701
Tel: (715) 839-2985

Catherine J. Furay
Bankruptcy Judge

Education: Wisconsin (Eau Claire) 1974 BA; Wisconsin (Stout) 1975 MS; Wisconsin 1980 JD

United States District Court for the District of Wyoming
2120 Capitol Avenue, Room 2131, Cheyenne, WY 82001
Tel: (307) 433-2120 Fax: (307) 433-2152
Internet: www.wyd.uscourts.gov

Number of Judgeships: 3

Circuit: Tenth

Court Staff
Clerk of the Court **Stephan Harris** . . . . (307) 433-2120
E-mail: stephan_harris@wyd.uscourts.gov
Chief Probation Officer **Tambra Loyd** . . . . (307) 433-2300
E-mail: tambra_loyd@wyp.uscourts.gov

Chambers of Chief Judge Nancy D. Freudenthal
2120 Capitol Avenue, Cheyenne, WY 82001
Tel: (307) 433-2190
E-mail: wyojudgendf@wyd.uscourts.gov

Nancy D. Freudenthal
Chief Judge

Education: Wyoming 1976 BA, 1980 JD
Began Service: June 1, 2010
Appointed By: President Barack Obama

Government: Attorney, Office of the Governor, State of Wyoming (1980-1989); Chairman, Wyoming State Board of Equalization

Legal Practice: Associate, Davis & Cannon (1994-1998); Litigation Partner, Davis & Cannon (1998-2010)

Staff
Law Clerk **Ben Rowland** . . . . (307) 433-2190
Began Service: August 2014
Term Expires: August 2016
E-mail: ben_rowland@wyd.uscourts.gov
Career Law Clerk **Brandi Monger** . . . . (307) 433-2190
E-mail: brandi_monger@wyd.uscourts.gov
Judicial Assistant **Kellie Erickson** . . . . (307) 433-2190
E-mail: kellie_erickson@wyd.uscourts.gov

Chambers of District Judge Alan B. Johnson
2120 Capitol Avenue, Room2018, Cheyenne, WY 82001
Tel: (307) 433-2170
E-mail: wyojudgeabj@wyd.uscourts.gov

Alan B. Johnson
District Judge

Date of Birth: 1939
Education: Vanderbilt 1961 BA; Wyoming 1964 JD
Began Service: 1986
Appointed By: President Ronald Reagan

Judicial: Magistrate Judge (part-time), United States District Court for the District of Wyoming (1971-1975); Part-Time Judge, Cheyenne Municipal Court (1972); Judge, Fifth Judicial District, Wyoming (1974-1986)

Legal Practice: Paul B. Godfrey (1968-1971); Hanes, Carmichael, Johnson, Gage & Speight, PC (1971-1974)

Military Service: Judge Advocate, United States Air Force (1964-1967); Col, Wyoming Air National Guard, United States Department of Defense (1973-1992)

Current Memberships: American Bar Association; Laramie County Bar Association; Wyoming Bar Association

Staff
Law Clerk **Sean Larson** . . . . (307) 433-2172
Began Service: September 2015
Term Expires: September 2016
Career Law Clerk **Sherrill Veal** . . . . (307) 433-2173
E-mail: sherrill_veal@wyd.uscourts.gov
Education: Wyoming 1981 BS, 1984 JD

Chambers of District Judge Scott W. Skavdahl
111 South Wolcott, Suite 210, Casper, WY 82601
Tel: (307) 232-2600

Scott W. Skavdahl
District Judge

Education: Wyoming 1989 BS, 1992 JD
Began Service: December 8, 2011
Appointed By: President Barack Obama

(continued on next page)

Chambers of District Judge Scott W. Skavdahl *continued*

Staff

Law Clerk **Kelley Anderson** .... (307) 232-2600
E-mail: kelley_anderson@wyd.uscourts.gov
Education: Wyoming 1993 JD
Law Clerk **William Elliott** .... (307) 232-2600
Judicial Assistant **Kim Blonigen** .... (307) 232-2600
E-mail: kim_blonigen@wyd.uscourts.gov

Chambers of Magistrate Judge Mark L. Carman

1015 Mammoth, Yellowstone National Park, WY 82190
P.O. Box 387, Yellowstone National Park, WY 82190
Tel: (307) 344-2569

Mark L. Carman
Magistrate Judge

Began Service: 2013

Staff

Courtroom Deputy **Karen Angermeier** .... (307) 344-2569

Chambers of Magistrate Judge Kelly H. Rankin

2120 Capitol Avenue, Cheyenne, WY 82001
Tel: (307) 433-2180

Kelly Harrison Rankin
Magistrate Judge

Staff

Career Law Clerk **John Conder** .... (307) 433-2180

Chambers of Magistrate Judge (part-time) Karen Marty

20 East Flaming Gorge Way, Green River, WY 82935
Tel: (307) 875-3235
E-mail: karen_marty@wyd.uscourts.gov

Karen Marty
Magistrate Judge (Part-Time)

Education: Carleton 1978 BA; Washington U (MO) 1981 JD
Began Service: 2003

Current Memberships: American Bar Association; Sweetwater County Bar Association; Wyoming Bar Association

Chambers of Magistrate Judge (part-time) R. Michael Shickich

111 West Second Street, Suite 500, Casper, WY 82601
Tel: (307) 266-5297 Fax: (307) 266-1261

R. Michael Shickich
Magistrate Judge (Part-Time)

Education: Oberlin 1978 BS; Denver 1985 JD
Began Service: January 23, 2004
Term Expires: January 23, 2016

Affiliation: Attorney, Law Office of R. Michael Shickich

Chambers of Magistrate Judge (part-time) Teresa M. Mckee

260 Lincoln Street, Lander, WY 82520
Tel: (307) 332-9406
E-mail: teresa_mckee@wyd.uscourts.gov

Teresa M. McKee
Magistrate Judge (Part-Time)

Began Service: July 2006
Appointed By: President George W. Bush

Affiliation: Attorney, McKee Law Office

Staff

Judicial Assistant **Kathy Shoopman** .... (307) 332-9406
Began Service: 2011

United States Bankruptcy Court for the District of Wyoming

2120 Capitol Avenue, Suite 6004, Cheyenne, WY 82001-3633
Tel: (307) 433-2200
Tel: (307) 433-2238 (Voice Case Information System VCIS)
Tel: (888) 804-5537 (Toll Free Voice Case Information System VCIS)
Internet: www.wyb.uscourts.gov

Number of Judgeships: 1

Court Staff

Clerk of Court **Tim J. Ellis** .... (307) 433-2200

Chambers of Bankruptcy Judge Michael E. Romero

2120 Capitol Avenue, Cheyenne, WY 82001
Tel: (307) 433-2200

Michael E. Romero
Bankruptcy Judge

Note: Judge Romero is currently serving the district of Wyoming on a temporary basis until a permanent replacement has been appointed.
Date of Birth: June 30, 1955
Education: Denver 1977 BA; Michigan 1980 JD

United States District Court for the District of Columbia

E. Barrett Prettyman U.S. Courthouse, 333 Constitution Avenue, NW, Washington, DC 20001-2866
Tel: (202) 354-3000 Tel: (202) 273-0606 (PACER)
Fax: (202) 354-3023
Internet: www.dcd.uscourts.gov

Number of Judgeships: 15

Court Staff

Clerk of Court **Angela D. Caesar** .... (202) 354-3050
E-mail: angela_caesar@dcd.uscourts.gov
Chief Deputy for Administration **Barbara Calhan** .... (202) 354-3010
E-mail: barbara_calhan@dcd.uscourts.gov
Chief Deputy for Operations **Greg Hughes** .... (202) 354-3191
E-mail: greg_hughes@dcd.uscourts.gov
Information Systems Manager **Nick Blend** .... (202) 354-3210
E-mail: nick_blend@dcd.uscourts.gov
Human Resources Director **Sonia Jackson** .... (202) 354-3200
E-mail: sonia_jackson@dcd.uscourts.gov
Chief Probation Officer **Gennine Hagar** .... (202) 565-1302
Fax: (202) 273-0242
Deputy Chief Probation Officer **John A. Hohman** .... (202) 565-1348
E-mail: hohmanj@courts.mi.gov Fax: (202) 273-0193
Deputy Chief Probation Officer **Shari McCoy** .... (202) 565-1348
Fax: (202) 273-0193

United States District Court for the District of Columbia *continued*

Financial Administrator **Tamara Forrest** . . . . (202) 354-3100
E-mail: tamara_forrest@dcd.uscourts.gov

Chambers of Chief Judge Richard W. Roberts

E. Barrett Prettyman U.S. Courthouse, 333 Constitution Avenue, NW, Washington, DC 20001-2866
Tel: (202) 354-3400
E-mail: roberts_chambers@dcd.uscourts.gov

Richard W. Roberts
Chief Judge

Date of Birth: 1953
Education: Vassar 1974 AB; School Intl Training 1978 MIA; Columbia 1978 JD
Began Service: July 31, 1998
Appointed By: President William J. Clinton

Staff

Law Clerk **James Bowden** . . . . (202) 354-3400
Began Service: September 2015
Term Expires: September 2016
E-mail: james_bowden@dcd.uscourts.gov
Law Clerk **Priyanka Gupta** . . . . (202) 354-3400
Began Service: September 2015
Term Expires: September 2016
E-mail: priyanka_gupta@dcd.uscourts.gov
Law Clerk **Jessica Perez** . . . . (202) 354-3400
Began Service: September 2015
Term Expires: September 2016
E-mail: jessica_perez@dcd.uscourts.gov
Career Law Clerk **David Lindquist** . . . . (202) 354-3400
E-mail: david_lindquist@dcd.uscourts.gov
Education: Michigan 2004 JD
Court Reporter **William Zaremba** . . . . (202) 354-3400
E-mail: william_zaremba@dcd.uscourts.gov

Chambers of District Judge Emmet G. Sullivan

E. Barrett Prettyman U.S. Courthouse, 333 Constitution Avenue, NW, Room 4935, Washington, DC 20001-2866
Tel: (202) 354-3260
E-mail: sullivan_chambers@dcd.uscourts.gov

Emmet G. Sullivan
District Judge

Date of Birth: 1947
Education: Howard U 1968 BA, 1971 JD
Began Service: June 15, 1994
Appointed By: President William J. Clinton

Academic: Adjunct Professor, Howard University School of Law

Clerkships: Law Clerk, Judge James A. Washington, Superior Court of the District of Columbia (1972-1973)

Judicial: Associate Judge, Superior Court of the District of Columbia (1984-1992); Associate Judge, District of Columbia Court of Appeals (1992-1994)

Legal Practice: Law Clerk, Neighborhood Legal Services Program (1971-1972); Associate, Houston and Gardner (1973-1974); Partner, Houston and Gardner (1974-1980); Partner, Houston, Sullivan and Gardner (1980-1984)

Current Memberships: American Bar Foundation; American Bar Association; The Bar Association of the District of Columbia; The District of Columbia Bar; National Bar Association

Staff

Law Clerk **Kimberly Stietz** . . . . (202) 354-3260
Began Service: August 2015
Term Expires: August 2016
E-mail: kimberly_stietz@dcd.uscourts.gov

Chambers of District Judge Emmet G. Sullivan *continued*

Law Clerk **Frances Anne Johnson** . . . . (202) 354-3260
Began Service: August 2015
Term Expires: August 2016
E-mail: frances_johnson@dcd.uscourts.gov
Career Law Clerk **Kristy Carroll** . . . . (202) 354-3260
E-mail: kristy_carroll@dcd.uscourts.gov
Courtroom Deputy **Mark Coates** . . . . (202) 354-3152
E-mail: mark_coates@dcd.uscourts.gov
Court Reporter **Scott Wallace** . . . . (202) 354-3187
E-mail: scott_wallace@dcd.uscourts.gov

Chambers of District Judge Colleen Kollar-Kotelly

William Bryant Annex, 333 Constitution Avenue, NW, Room 6939, Washington, DC 20001-2866
Tel: (202) 354-3340
E-mail: colleen_kollar-kotelly@dcd.uscourts.gov

Colleen Kollar-Kotelly
District Judge

Education: Catholic U 1965 BA; Columbus Law 1968 JD
Began Service: May 12, 1997
Appointed By: President William J. Clinton

Clerkships: Law Clerk The Honorable Catherine B. Kelly, District of Columbia Court of Appeals (1968-1969)

Government: Government Attorney, Criminal Division, Appellate Section, United States Department of Justice, Richard M. Nixon Administration (1969-1972); Chief Legal Counsel, Legal Office, Department of Health and Human Services, Saint Elizabeths Hospital (1972-1984)

Judicial: Associate Judge, Superior Court of the District of Columbia (1984-1997)

Current Memberships: The District of Columbia Bar

Staff

Law Clerk **Benjamin Solomon-Schwartz** . . . . (202) 354-3340
Began Service: September 2014
Term Expires: September 2016
Education: Harvard 2013 JD
Law Clerk **Daniel Riegel** . . . . (202) 354-3340
Began Service: October 2015
Term Expires: October 2016
E-mail: daniel_riegel@dcd.uscourts.gov
Courtroom Deputy **Dorothy Jones-Patterson** . . . . (202) 354-3340

Chambers of District Judge Reggie B. Walton

E. Barrett Prettyman U.S. Courthouse, 333 Constitution Avenue, NW, Washington, DC 20001-2866
Tel: (202) 354-3290 Fax: (202) 354-3292
E-mail: reggie_walton@dcd.uscourts.gov

Reggie B. Walton
District Judge

Date of Birth: 1949
Education: West Virginia State Col 1971 BA; Washington College of Law 1974 JD
Began Service: October 29, 2001
Appointed By: President George W. Bush

Government: Executive Assistant U.S. Attorney, District of Columbia District, Executive Office for United States Attorneys, United States Department of Justice (1976-1981); Associate Director, Office of National Drug Control Policy, Executive Office of the President, George H.W. Bush Administration (1989-1991); Senior White House Advisor for Crime, Executive Office of the President, George H.W. Bush Administration (1991)

(continued on next page)

Chambers of District Judge Reggie B. Walton *continued*

Judicial: Associate Judge, Superior Court of the District of Columbia (1981-1989); Associate Judge, Superior Court of the District of Columbia (1991-2001)

Legal Practice: Staff Attorney, Defender Association of Philadelphia (1974-1976)

Staff

Law Clerk **Tabitha Bartholomew** .... (202) 354-3290
Began Service: September 2015
Term Expires: September 2016
E-mail: tabitha_bartholomew@dcd.uscourts.gov

Law Clerk **Hugham Chan** .... (202) 354-3290
Began Service: September 2014
Term Expires: September 2016
E-mail: hugham_chan@dcd.uscourts.gov

Law Clerk **Mark Skerry** .... (202) 354-3290
Term Expires: September 2016
E-mail: mark_skerry@dcd.uscourts.gov
Education: Case Western 2011 JD

Courtroom Deputy Clerk **Mattie Powell-Taylor** .... (202) 354-3184
E-mail: mattie_powell-taylor@dcd.uscourts.gov

Court Reporter **Cathryn Jones** .... (202) 273-0889
E-mail: cathryn_jones@dcd.uscourts.gov

Chambers of District Judge Richard J. Leon

E. Barrett Prettyman U.S. Courthouse, 333 Constitution Avenue, NW, Washington, DC 20001-2866
Tel: (202) 354-3580 Fax: (202) 354-3588
E-mail: richard_leon@dcd.uscourts.gov

Richard J. Leon
District Judge

Date of Birth: 1949
Education: Col Holy Cross 1971 AB; Suffolk 1974 JD; Harvard 1981 LLM
Began Service: March 20, 2002
Appointed By: President George W. Bush

Clerkships: Law Clerk, Massachusetts Superior Court (1974-1975); Law Clerk The Honorable Thomas Kelleher, Rhode Island Supreme Court (1975-1976)

Government: Special Assistant U.S. Attorney, New York - Southern District, Executive Office for United States Attorneys, United States Department of Justice (1977-1978); Deputy Chief Minority Counsel, Iran-Contra Committee, United States House of Representatives (1987-1988); Deputy Assistant Attorney General, Environment and Natural Resources Division, United States Department of Justice (1988-1989); Chief Minority Counsel, Committee on Foreign Affairs, United States House of Representatives (1992-1993); Special Counsel, Whitewater Investigation, Committee on Banking, Finance and Urban Affairs, United States House of Representatives (1994); Special Counsel, Ethics Reform Task Force, United States House of Representatives (1997)

Legal Practice: Partner, Baker & Hostetler LLP (1989-1999); Partner, Vorys, Sater, Seymour and Pease LLP (1999-2002)

Staff

Law Clerk **Sarah Eichenberger** .... (202) 354-3580
E-mail: sarah_eichenberger@dcd.uscourts.gov
Education: Duke 2012 JD

Law Clerk **Kylie Hoover** .... (202) 354-3580
E-mail: kylie_hoover@dcd.uscourts.gov

Law Clerk **Suzanne Salgado** .... (202) 354-3580
Began Service: August 2015
Term Expires: August 2016
E-mail: suzanne_salgado@dcd.uscourts.gov
Education: George Washington 2013 JD

Chambers of District Judge Rosemary M. Collyer

333 Constitution Avenue, NW, Room 2428, Washington, DC 20001
Tel: (202) 354-3560 Fax: (202) 354-3565
E-mail: rosemary_m_collyer@dcd.uscourts.gov

Rosemary M. Collyer
District Judge

Date of Birth: November 19, 1945
Education: Trinity Col (DC) 1968 BA; Denver 1977 JD
Began Service: January 2, 2003
Appointed By: President George W. Bush

Government: Chairman, Federal Mine and Safety Health Review Commission, District of Columbia (1981-1984); General Counsel, National Labor Relations Board, District of Columbia (1984-1989)

Legal Practice: Associate, Sherman & Howard L.L.C. (1977-1981); Partner, Crowell & Moring LLP (1989-2002)

Current Memberships: The Bar Association of the District of Columbia; Colorado Bar Association; United States Foreign Intelligence Surveillance Court

Staff

Law Clerk **Cesar Lopez-Morales** .... (202) 354-3560

Law Clerk **Jason Lynch** .... (202) 354-3560
Began Service: September 2015
Term Expires: September 2016
E-mail: jason_lynch@dcd.uscourts.gov

Career Law Clerk **Kristin Dighe** .... (202) 354-3560
E-mail: kristin_dighe@dcd.uscourts.gov
Education: Michigan 1984 BA; Wayne State U 1987 JD

Courtroom Deputy/Scheduling Clerk
Chashawn White .... (202) 354-3176
E-mail: chashawn_white@dcd.uscourts.gov

Chambers of District Judge Beryl Alaine Howell

333 Constitution Avenue, NW, Room 6600, Washington, DC 20001-2866
Tel: (202) 354-3450
E-mail: howell_chambers@dcd.uscourts.gov

Beryl A. Howell
District Judge

Education: Bryn Mawr 1978 AB; Columbia 1983 JD
Began Service: December 27, 2010
Appointed By: President Barack Obama

Staff

Law Clerk **Perrin Cooke** .... (202) 354-3450
E-mail: perrin_cooke@dcd.uscourts.gov

Law Clerk **Celia Goetzl** .... (202) 354-3450
Term Expires: August 31, 2016
E-mail: celia_goetzl@dcd.uscourts.gov

Law Clerk **Ni Qian** .... (202) 354-3450
Term Expires: August 31, 2016
E-mail: ni_qian@dcd.uscourts.gov
Education: Columbia 2014 JD

Court Reporter **Chantal Geneus** .... (202) 354-3242
E-mail: chantal_geneus@dcd.uscourts.gov

Courtroom Deputy **Teresa Gumiel** .... (202) 354-3124
E-mail: teresa_gumiel@dcd.uscourts.gov

Chambers of District Judge James E. Boasberg
333 Constitution Avenue, NW, Room 6321, Washington, DC 20001-2866
Tel: (202) 354-3300
E-mail: james_boasberg@dcd.uscourts.gov

James Emanuel Boasberg
District Judge

Education: St Albans (Washington, DC) 1981; Yale 1985 BA; Oxford (UK) 1986; Yale 1990 JD
Began Service: April 1, 2011
Appointed By: President Barack Obama

Government: Assistant U.S. Attorney, District of Columbia District, Executive Office for United States Attorneys, United States Department of Justice (1996-2002)

Judicial: Associate Judge, Chambers of Associate Judge James E. Boasberg, Superior Court of the District of Columbia (2002-2011)

Legal Practice: Associate, Keker & Van Nest LLP (1991-1994); Associate, Kellogg, Huber, Hansen, Todd & Evans, P.L.L.C. (1995-1996)

Current Memberships: United States Foreign Intelligence Surveillance Court

Staff
Court Reporter **Lisa Griffith** .... (202) 354-3247
E-mail: lisa_griffith@dcd.uscourts.gov
Courtroom Deputy **Anjanie Desai** .... (202) 354-3066
E-mail: anjanie_desai@dcd.uscourts.gov

Chambers of District Judge Amy Berman Jackson
333 Constitution Avenue, NW, Washington, DC 20001-2866
Tel: (202) 354-3460
E-mail: amy_jackson@dcd.uscourts.gov

Amy Berman Jackson
District Judge

Date of Birth: 1954
Education: Harvard 1976 AB, 1979 JD
Began Service: 2011
Appointed By: President Barack Obama

Clerkships: Law Clerk, Chambers of Circuit Judge Harrison L. Winter, United States Court of Appeals for the Fourth Circuit (1979-1980)

Government: Assistant U.S. Attorney, District of Columbia District, Executive Office for United States Attorneys, United States Department of Justice (1980-1986)

Legal Practice: Partner, Venable, Baetjer and Howard, LLP (1988-1995)

Staff
Career Law Clerk **Dianne Kappler** .... (202) 354-3460
Began Service: 2011
Courtroom Deputy **John Haley** .... (202) 354-3460
E-mail: john_haley@dcd.uscourts.gov

Chambers of District Judge Rudolph Contreras
333 Constitution Avenue, NW, Washington, DC 20001-2866
Tel: (202) 354-3520 Fax: (202) 354-3023
E-mail: rudolph_contreras@dcd.uscourts.gov

Rudolph "Rudy" Contreras
District Judge

Education: Florida State 1984 BS; Pennsylvania 1991 JD
Began Service: June 20, 2012
Appointed By: President Barack Obama

Staff
Courtroom Deputy **Tanya Johnson** .... (202) 354-3141
E-mail: tanya_johnson@dcd.uscourts.gov
Court Reporter **Annette Montalvo** .... (202) 354-3243
E-mail: annette_montalvo@dcd.uscourts.gov

Chambers of District Judge Ketanji Brown Jackson
333 Constitution Avenue, NW, Washington, DC 20001-2866
Tel: (202) 354-3350
E-mail: ketanji_jackson@dcd.uscourts.gov

Ketanji Brown Jackson
District Judge

Education: Harvard 1992 AB, 1996 JD
Began Service: May 10, 2013
Appointed By: President Barack Obama

Clerkships: Law Clerk, Chambers of Associate Justice Stephen G. Breyer, Supreme Court of the United States (1999-2000)

Government: Assistant Special Counsel, United States Sentencing Commission (2003-2005)

Legal Practice: Of Counsel, Washington, DC Office, Morrison & Foerster LLP (2007-2010)

Staff
Law Clerk **Daniel Kanter** .... (202) 354-3350
Term Expires: August 2016
E-mail: daniel_kanter@dcd.uscourts.gov
Law Clerk **Kerrel Murray** .... (202) 354-3350
Term Expires: August 2016
E-mail: kerrel_murray@dcd.uscourts.gov
Career Law Clerk **Jennifer Knight** .... (202) 354-3350
E-mail: jennifer_knight@dcd.uscourts.gov
Courtroom Deputy **Gwen Franklin** .... (202) 354-3350
E-mail: gwen_franklin@dcd.uscourts.gov

Chambers of District Judge Christopher Reid Cooper
333 Constitution Avenue, NW, Washington, DC 20001-2866
Tel: (202) 354-3480
E-mail: christopher_r_cooper@dcd.uscourts.gov

Christopher Reid "Casey" Cooper
District Judge

Education: Yale 1988 BA; Stanford 1993 JD
Began Service: March 28, 2014
Appointed By: President Barack Obama

Government: Team Member, Department of Justice Review Team, President-Elect Obama Transition Team, Executive Office of the President (2008-2009)

Legal Practice: Member, Executive Committee, Baker Botts L.L.P.; Hiring Partner, Washington, DC Office, Baker Botts L.L.P.

Staff
Law Clerk **Ben Moskowitz** .... (202) 354-3480
Began Service: September 2015
Term Expires: September 2016
E-mail: ben_moskowitz@dcd.uscourts.gov
Law Clerk **Daniel Rice** .... (202) 354-3480
Began Service: September 2015
Term Expires: September 2016
E-mail: daniel_rice@dcd.uscourts.gov
Law Clerk **Corinne "Corey" Smith** .... (202) 354-3480
Began Service: September 2015
Term Expires: September 2016
E-mail: corinne_smith@dcd.uscourts.gov
Courtroom Deputy **Terri Robinson** .... (202) 354-3179
E-mail: terri_robinson@dcd.uscourts.gov

Chambers of District Judge Tanya S. Chutkan
333 Constitution Avenue, NW, Washington, DC 20001-2866
Tel: (202) 354-3390

Tanya S. Chutkan
District Judge

Education: George Washington 1983 BA; Pennsylvania 1987 JD
Began Service: June 5, 2014
Appointed By: President Barack Obama

Government: Trial Attorney and Supervisor, Public Defender Service, District of Columbia (1991-2002)

Legal Practice: Attorney, Hogan & Hartson LLP (1987-1990); Attorney, Donovan, Leisure, Rogovin, Huge & Schiller (1990-1991); Recruiting Partner, Washington, DC Office, Boies, Schiller & Flexner LLP (2002-2014)

Staff
Courtroom Deputy **Sarah Moser** .... (202) 354-3032
E-mail: sarah_moser@dcd.uscourts.gov
Career Law Clerk **Delores Simmons** .... (202) 354-3460
E-mail: delores_simmons@dcd.uscourts.gov

Chambers of District Judge Randolph D. Moss
333 Constitution Avenue, NW, Washington, DC 20001-2866
Tel: (202) 354-3000

Randolph D. Moss
District Judge

Education: Hamilton 1983 AB; Yale 1986 JD
Began Service: 2014
Appointed By: President Barack Obama

Chambers of District Judge Amit Priyavadan Mehta
333 Constitution Avenue, NW, Washington, DC 20001-2866
Tel: (202) 354-3000
E-mail: amit_mehta@dcd.uscourts.gov

Amit Priyavadan Mehta
District Judge

Education: Georgetown 1993 BA; Virginia 1997 JD
Began Service: January 22, 2015
Appointed By: President Barack Obama

Government: Staff Attorney, Public Defender Service, District of Columbia (2002-2007)

Legal Practice: Associate, Zuckerman Spaeder LLP (1999-2002); Counsel, Zuckerman Spaeder LLP (2007-2010)

Chambers of Senior Judge Thomas F. Hogan
E. Barrett Prettyman U.S. Courthouse, 333 Constitution Avenue, NW, Room 4012, Washington, DC 20001-2866
Tel: (202) 354-3420 Fax: (202) 354-3422
E-mail: thomas_hogan@dcd.uscourts.gov

Thomas F. Hogan
Senior Judge

Date of Birth: 1938
Education: Georgetown 1960 AB, 1966 JD
Began Service: October 4, 1982
Appointed By: President Ronald Reagan

Academic: Assistant Professor, Potomac School of Law (1977-1979); Adjunct Professor, The Law Center, Georgetown University (1986-1987)

Clerkships: Law Clerk The Honorable William B. Jones, United States District Court for the District of Columbia (1966-1967)

Chambers of Senior Judge Thomas F. Hogan *continued*

Government: Counsel, National Commission on Reform of Federal Criminal Law (1967-1968); Public Member, Board of Examiners for the Foreign Service, United States Department of State

Judicial: Member, Board of Directors, Federal Judicial Center (1996-2000); Chief Judge, United States District Court for the District of Columbia (2001-2008)

Legal Practice: Partner, McCarthy and Wharton (1968-1975); Partner, Kenary, Tietz & Hogan (1975-1981); Partner, Furey, Doolan, Abell & Hogan (1981-1982)

Current Memberships: United States Foreign Intelligence Surveillance Court

Chambers of Senior Judge Gladys Kessler
E. Barrett Prettyman U.S. Courthouse, 333 Constitution Avenue, NW, Washington, DC 20001-2802
Tel: (202) 354-3440 Fax: (202) 354-3442
E-mail: gladys_kessler@dcd.uscourts.gov

Gladys Kessler
Senior Judge

Date of Birth: 1938
Education: Cornell 1959 BA; Harvard 1962 LLB
Began Service: 1994
Appointed By: President William J. Clinton

Government: Staff Attorney, National Labor Relations Board (1962-1964); Legislative Assistant (D-NJ), Office of Senator Harrison A. Williams, United States Senate (1964-1966); Legislative Assistant (D-NY, District 22), Office of Representative Jonathan B. Bingham, United States House of Representatives (1966-1968); Staff Attorney, Office of Labor Relations, New York City Board of Education (1969)

Judicial: Associate Justice, Superior Court of the District of Columbia (1977-1994)

Legal Practice: Partner, Roisman, Kessler & Cashdan (1969-1977)

Current Memberships: American Bar Foundation; Frederick B. Abrahamson Memorial Foundation; American Bar Association; Judicial Administration Division, American Bar Association; The District of Columbia Bar; Einstein Institute for Science, Health and the Courts; National Association of Women Judges; National Center for State Courts

Staff
Law Clerk **Devin Mauney** .... (202) 354-3440
Term Expires: September 2016
E-mail: devin_mauney@dcd.uscourts.gov
Education: Harvard 2013 JD
Law Clerk **Lisa Nowlin** .... (202) 354-3440
Began Service: November 2014
Term Expires: November 2016
E-mail: lisa_nowlin@dcd.uscourts.gov
Education: NYU 2011 JD
Judicial Assistant **Candice Lyons** .... (202) 354-3440
E-mail: candice_lyons@dcd.uscourts.gov

Chambers of Senior Judge Paul L. Friedman

E. Barrett Prettyman U.S. Courthouse, 333 Constitution Avenue, NW, William B. Bryant Annex, Room 6012, Washington, DC 20001-2866
Tel: (202) 354-3490 Fax: (202) 354-3498
E-mail: friedman_chambers@dcd.uscourts.gov

Paul L. Friedman
Senior Judge

Date of Birth: 1944
Education: Cornell 1965 BA; SUNY (Buffalo) 1968 JD
Began Service: August 1, 1994
Appointed By: President William J. Clinton

Academic: Adjunct Professor, Georgetown University (1973-1975); Faculty, National Institute for Trial Advocacy (1984-1988)

Clerkships: Law Clerk The Honorable Aubrey E. Robinson, Jr., United States District Court for the District of Columbia (1968-1969); Law Clerk The Honorable Roger Robb, United States Court of Appeals for the District of Columbia Circuit (1969-1970)

Government: Assistant United States Attorney, District of Columbia, Office of the United States Attorney, United States Department of Justice (1970-1974); Assistant Solicitor General, United States Department of Justice (1974-1976); Associate Independent Counsel, Iran-Contra Investigation (1987-1988)

Legal Practice: Attorney, White & Case LLP (1976-1994)

Current Memberships: American Bar Foundation; American Academy of Appellate Lawyers; American Bar Association; American College of Trial Lawyers; The District of Columbia Bar

Staff

Law Clerk **Geoffrey J. Derrick** . . . . (202) 354-3490
Began Service: September 2015
Term Expires: August 2017
E-mail: geoffrey_derrick@dcd.uscourts.gov

Law Clerk **Nicholas F. Lenning** . . . . (202) 354-3490
Began Service: 2014
Term Expires: August 2016
E-mail: nicholas_lenning@dcd.uscourts.gov
Education: Duke 2011 JD

Judicial Assistant **Marissa V. Ahari** . . . . (202) 354-3490
E-mail: marissa_ahari@dcd.uscourts.gov

Chambers of Senior Judge Barbara J. Rothstein

333 Constitution Avenue, NW, Washington, DC 20001-2866
Tel: (202) 354-3330 Fax: (202) 354-3569
E-mail: barbara_rothstein@dcd.uscourts.gov

Barbara Jacobs Rothstein
Senior Judge

Note: Judge Rothstein is currently assigned to the District of Columbia District Court as a visiting judge.
Date of Birth: 1939
Education: Cornell 1960 BA; Harvard 1966 LLB
Began Service: February 20, 1980
Appointed By: President Jimmy Carter

Current Memberships: American Bar Foundation; American Association of Justice; American Bar Association; The American Law Institute; King County Bar Association; Massachusetts Bar Association; National Association of Women Judges; Washington State Bar Association

Staff

Law Clerk **Graham Cronogue** . . . . (202) 354-3331
Began Service: 2014
Term Expires: September 2016
E-mail: graham_cronogue@dcd.uscourts.gov
Education: Duke 2013 JD

Chambers of Senior Judge Barbara J. Rothstein *continued*

Law Clerk **Brett D. Weingold** . . . . (202) 354-3375
Began Service: 2014
E-mail: brett_weingold@dcd.uscourts.gov

Career Law Clerk **Caroline Danauy** . . . . (202) 354-3375
Began Service: 2011
E-mail: caroline_danauy@dcd.uscourts.gov
Education: Georgetown 2009 JD

Chambers of Senior Judge Royce C. Lamberth

E. Barrett Prettyman U.S. Courthouse, 333 Constitution Avenue, NW, Washington, DC 20001-2866
Tel: (202) 354-3380
E-mail: lamberth_chambers@dcd.uscourts.gov

Royce C. Lamberth
Senior Judge

Date of Birth: 1943
Education: Texas 1965 BA, 1967 LLB
Began Service: November 16, 1987
Appointed By: President Ronald Reagan
Political Affiliation: Republican

Current Memberships: American Bar Association; The District of Columbia Bar; Federal Bar Association; State Bar of Texas

Staff

Law Clerk **Aaron Collins** . . . . (202) 354-3388
Began Service: September 2015
Term Expires: September 2016
E-mail: aaron_collins@dcd.uscourts.gov

Law Clerk **Matthew "Matt" Higgins** . . . . (202) 354-3386
Began Service: September 2015
Term Expires: September 2016

Courtroom Deputy **Harold Smith** . . . . (202) 354-3380
E-mail: harold_smith@dcd.uscourts.gov

Chambers of Senior Judge Ellen Segal Huvelle

E. Barrett Prettyman Courthouse, 333 Constitution Avenue, NW, Washington, DC 20001-2866
Tel: (202) 354-3230 Fax: (202) 354-3232
E-mail: ellen_segal_huvelle@dcd.uscourts.gov

Ellen Segal Huvelle
Senior Judge

Date of Birth: 1948
Education: Wellesley 1970 BA; Yale 1972 MCP; Boston Col 1975 JD
Began Service: January 2000
Appointed By: President William J. Clinton

Current Memberships: American Bar Foundation; American Association for Justice; American Bar Association; The Edward Bennett Williams American Inn of Court, The American Inns of Court; The Bar Association of the District of Columbia; The District of Columbia Bar; Massachusetts Bar Association; National Association of Women Judges; Women's Bar Association of Massachusetts

Staff

Law Clerk **Brian Gilmore** . . . . (202) 354-3230
Began Service: August 2015
Term Expires: September 2016
E-mail: brian_gilmore@dcd.uscourts.gov

Law Clerk **Ben Zweifach** . . . . (202) 354-3230
Began Service: August 2015
Term Expires: September 2016
E-mail: ben_zweifach@dcd.uscourts.gov

Career Law Clerk **Alison E. Grossman** . . . . (202) 354-3230
E-mail: alison_grossman@dcd.uscourts.gov
Education: Virginia 1992 JD

Chambers of Senior Judge John D. Bates

E. Barrett Prettyman U.S. Courthouse, 333 Constitution Avenue NW, Washington, DC 20001-2809
Tel: (202) 354-3430 Fax: (202) 354-3433
E-mail: bates_chambers@dcd.uscourts.gov

John D. Bates
Senior Judge

Date of Birth: 1946
Education: Wesleyan U 1968 BA; Maryland 1976 JD
Began Service: December 20, 2001
Appointed By: President George W. Bush

Current Memberships: The District of Columbia Bar; Maryland State Bar Association, Inc.

Staff

Law Clerk **Graham E. Phillips** .... (202) 354-3430
Term Expires: September 2016
E-mail: graham_phillips@dcd.uscourts.gov
Education: Harvard JD

Law Clerk **Jennifer Bronson** .... (202) 354-3430
Term Expires: September 2016
E-mail: jennifer_bronson@dcd.uscourts.gov
Education: Michigan 2013 JD

Law Clerk **Jeffrey Bengel** .... (202) 354-3430
Term Expires: March 2016
E-mail: jeffrey_bengel@dcd.uscourts.gov

Court Reporter **Bryan A. Wayne** .... (202) 216-0313

Courtroom Deputy **Tim Bradley** .... (202) 354-3430
E-mail: tim_bradley@dcd.uscourts.gov

Chambers of Magistrate Judge Deborah A. Robinson

E. Barrett Prettyman U.S. Courthouse, 333 Constitution Avenue, NW, Courtroom 4, Washington, DC 20001-2866
Tel: (202) 354-3070 Fax: (202) 354-3095

Deborah A. Robinson
Magistrate Judge

Date of Birth: July 12, 1953
Education: Morgan State BA; Emory 1978 JD
Began Service: July 1988
Term Expires: August 18, 2020

Clerkships: Law Clerk The Honorable H. Carl Moultrie, Superior Court of the District of Columbia (1978-1979)

Government: Assistant United States Attorney, District of Columbia, Office of the United States Attorney, United States Department of Justice (1979-1988)

Current Memberships: American Bar Association; The William B. Bryant American Inn of Court, The American Inns of Court; The Bar Association of the District of Columbia; The District of Columbia Bar

Staff

Law Clerk **Brandon R. Wright** .... (202) 354-3077
Began Service: August 2014
Term Expires: January 2016
E-mail: brandon_wright@dcd.uscourts.gov
Education: North Carolina Central 2013 JD

Law Clerk **Chinyere Bun** .... (202) 354-3070
Began Service: March 2015
Term Expires: March 2016
E-mail: chinyere_bun@dcd.uscourts.gov

Chambers of Magistrate Judge Alan Kay

E. Barrett Prettyman U.S. Courthouse, 333 Constitution Avenue NW, Room 2333, Washington, DC 20001-2866
Tel: (202) 354-3030 Fax: (202) 354-3526
E-mail: alan_kay@dcd.uscourts.gov

Alan Kay
Magistrate Judge

Date of Birth: 1934
Education: George Washington 1957 BA, 1959 JD
Began Service: 1991

Clerkships: Law Clerk The Honorable Alexander Holtzoff, United States District Court for the District of Columbia (1960); Law Clerk The Honorable William B. Jones, United States District Court for the District of Columbia (1962-1963)

Government: Public Defender, District of Columbia (1960-1962); Assistant United States Attorney, Office of the United States Attorney, United States Department of Justice (1963-1966); Associate, Office of General Counsel, United States Department of Commerce, Lyndon B. Johnson Administration (1966-1967)

Legal Practice: Bregman, Abell & Kay (1967-1991)

Military Service: District of Columbia National Guard

Current Memberships: The American Inns of Court; The District of Columbia Bar; National Conference of Bar Examiners; The Virginia Bar Association

Staff

Law Clerk **Julia Quinn** .... (202) 354-3030
E-mail: julia_quinn@dcd.uscourts.gov
Education: Texas 2014 JD

Career Law Clerk **Deborah Mulligan** .... (202) 354-3030
E-mail: deborah_mulligan@dcd.uscourts.gov
Education: George Washington 1988 JD

Chambers of Magistrate Judge G. Michael Harvey

333 Constitution Avenue, NW, Washington, DC 20001-2866
Tel: (202) 354-3130

G. Michael Harvey
Magistrate Judge

Education: Duke 1989 BA; Pennsylvania 1993 JD
Began Service: February 12, 2015

United States Bankruptcy Court for the District of Columbia

E. Barrett Prettyman U.S. Courthouse, 333 Constitution Avenue, NW, 1st Floor, Room 1225, Washington, DC 20001-2866
Tel: (202) 354-3280 Tel: (800) 676-6856 (Toll Free PACER)
Tel: (866) 222-8029 (MCVCIS) Fax: (202) 354-3128
Internet: www.dcb.uscourts.gov

Number of Judgeships: 1

Court Staff

Clerk of the Court **Angela D. Caesar** .... (202) 354-3181

Deputy-in-Charge **Michael Wint** .... (202) 354-3188
E-mail: michael_wint@dcb.uscourts.gov

Courtroom Deputy **Aimee Mathewes** .... (202) 354-3178
E-mail: aimee_mathewes@dcb.uscourts.gov

Senior Case Administrator **Renee Jackson** .... (202) 354-3149

Case Manager **Michelle Ryan** .... (202) 354-3024

Case Manager **Vamira Ragland** .... (202) 354-3144

Case Manager **Patti Meador** .... (571) 217-1676

Chambers of Bankruptcy Judge S. Martin Teel, Jr.
E. Barrett Prettyman U.S. Courthouse, 333 Constitution Avenue, NW, Washington, DC 20001-2866
Tel: (202) 354-3530 Fax: (202) 354-3531

S. Martin Teel, Jr.
Bankruptcy Judge

Education: Virginia 1967 BA, 1970 JD
Began Service: February 8, 1988
Term Expires: February 2016

Clerkships: Law Clerk The Honorable Roger Robb, United States Court of Appeals for the District of Columbia Circuit (1970-1971)

Government: Trial Attorney then Assistant Section Chief, Tax Division, United States Department of Justice (1971-1988)

Staff
Law Clerk **Betina Miranda** .... (202) 354-3530
E-mail: betina_miranda@dcb.uscourts.gov
Career Law Clerk **Laura S. Orvald** .... (202) 354-3530
Education: Boston U 2002 JD
Courtroom Deputy **Aimee Mathewes Lee** .... (202) 354-3106
E-mail: aimee_lee@dcb.uscourts.gov

United States District Court for the District of Guam
U.S. Courthouse, 520 West Soledad Avenue, 4th Floor, Hagatna, GU 96910
Tel: (671) 473-9100 Fax: (671) 473-9152
Internet: www.gud.uscourts.gov

Number of Judgeships: 2

Circuit: Ninth

Court Staff
Clerk of Court **Jeanne G. Quinata** .... (671) 473-9100
E-mail: jeanne_quinata@gud.uscourts.gov
Education: Marquette 1996; Wisconsin 1999 JD
Law Clerk **Karen Quitlong** .... (671) 473-9172
E-mail: karen_quitlong@gud.uscourts.gov Fax: (671) 473-9186
Chief Deputy Clerk **Charles B. White** ....(671) 473-9100
E-mail: charles_white@gud.uscourts.gov
Education: Missouri (Rolla) 1987 MS; Washington U (MO) 1983 BS
Courtroom Deputy **Virginia T. Kilgore** .... (671) 473-9100
Intake Clerk **Holly Gumataotao** .... (671) 473-9100
Career Law Clerk/Librarian **Judith P. Hattori** ....(671) 473-9164
E-mail: judith_hattori@gud.uscourts.gov Fax: (671) 473-9118
Education: San Diego State 1991 BS; Hawaii 1997 JD
Case Manager **Francine A. Diaz** .... (671) 473-9100
Case Manager **Carmen B. Santos** ....(671) 473-9100
Case Manager **Walter M. Tenorio** ....(671) 473-9100
Financial Administrator **Shirlene A. Ishizu** ....(671) 473-9100
E-mail: shirlene_ishizu@gud.uscourts.gov
Jury Administrator **Marilyn B. Alcon** .... (671) 473-9100
E-mail: marilyn_alcon@gud.uscourts.gov
Information Systems Manager **Luis Vergel DeVera** ...... (671) 473-9100
E-mail: vergel_devera@gud.uscourts.gov
Information Systems Analyst **(Vacant)** ....(671) 473-9100
Automation Specialist **Rose Mary B. Nanguata** .... (671) 473-9100
Education: U Guam 1998 BA
Procurement/Personnel Specialist **Leilani R. Toves Hernandez** ....(671) 473-9100
E-mail: leilani_hernandez@gud.uscourts.gov
Court Reporter **Veronica Reilly** .... (671) 472-8655
E-mail: veronica_reilly@gud.uscourts.gov

Chambers of Chief Judge Frances Marie Tydingco-Gatewood
520 West Soledad Avenue, Fourth Floor, Hagatna, GU 96910
Tel: (671) 473-9200 Fax: (671) 473-9186

Frances Tydingco-Gatewood
Chief Judge

Began Service: October 2006
Appointed By: President George W. Bush

Clerkships: Law Clerk, Judge Forest W. Hanna, Kansas City Circuit Court (1983-1984)

Government: Assistant Attorney General, Office of the Attorney General, Guam Office, United States Department of Justice (1984-1988); Assistant Prosecuting Attorney, Office of the Prosecuting Attorney, County of Jackson, Missouri (1988-1990); Chief Prosecutor, Office of the Attorney General, Guam Office, United States Department of Justice (1990-1994)

Judicial: Judge, Superior Court of Guam (1994-2001); Associate Justice, Supreme Court of Guam (2001-2006)

Staff
Law Clerk **Jane Lee** .... (671) 473-9200
E-mail: jane_lee@gud.uscourts.gov
Career Law Clerk **Karen Quitlong** .... (671) 473-9200
E-mail: karen_quitlong@gud.uscourts.gov
Judicial Assistant **Cynthia T. Palacios** ....(671) 473-9200
E-mail: cynthia_palacios@gud.uscourts.gov
Pro Se Law Clerk **(Vacant)** ....(671) 473-9200

Chambers of Magistrate Judge Joaquin V. E. Manibusan, Jr.
321 U.S. Courthouse, 520 West Soledad Avenue, 3rd Floor, Hagatna, GU 96910
Tel: (671) 473-9180 Fax: (671) 473-9118

Joaquin V. E. Manibusan, Jr.
Magistrate Judge

Education: UC Berkeley 1971 BA; Boalt Hall 1974 JD
Began Service: February 9, 2004
Term Expires: February 9, 2020

Staff
Career Law Clerk **Judith P. Hattori** ....(671) 473-9164
E-mail: judith_hattori@gud.uscourts.gov
Judicial Assistant **Lolita Toves** ....(671) 473-9180
E-mail: lolita_toves@gud.uscourts.gov
Education: U Guam 1984 BA

United States District Court for the Northern Mariana Islands
Horiguchi Building, Beach Road Garapan, 2nd Floor, Saipan, MP 96950
P.O. Box 500687, Saipan, MP 96950-0687
Tel: (670) 237-1200 Fax: (670) 237-1201
Internet: www.nmid.uscourts.gov

Number of Judgeships: 1

Circuit: Ninth

Areas Covered: Commonwealth of the Northern Marianna Islands.

Court Staff
Clerk of Court **Heather L. Kennedy** ....(670) 237-1210
E-mail: heather_kennedy@nmid.uscourts.gov
Chief Deputy Clerk **William J. Bezzant** ....(670) 237-1211
E-mail: william_bezzant@nmid.uscourts.gov
Education: Cal State (Hayward) 1980 BS
Chambers Administrator **Amanda C. Hayes** ....(670) 236-2900
E-mail: amanda_hayes@nmid.uscourts.gov
Systems Manager **Mario Glenn G. Mendoza** ....(670) 237-1222
E-mail: glenn_mendoza@nmid.uscourts.gov

(continued on next page)

United States District Court for the Northern Mariana Islands *continued*

Financial Administrator **Michelle C. Macaranas** .... (670) 237-1214
E-mail: michelle_macaranas@nmid.uscourts.gov
Courtroom Deputy Clerk **Tina P. Matsunaga** .... (670) 236-2902
E-mail: tina_pangelinan@nmid.uscourts.gov
Jury Administrator/Procurement Specialist
Timothy V. Wesley .... (670) 236-2902
E-mail: timothy_wesley@nmid.uscourts.gov
Court Reporter **Patricia A. Garshak** .... (670) 236-1229
E-mail: patricia_garshak@nmid.uscourts.gov

Chambers of District Judge Ramona Villagomez Manglona

123 Kopa di Oru Street, Saipan, MP 96950
Tel: (670) 237-1230 Fax: (670) 237-1231
E-mail: usdcnmi@nmi.uscourts.gov

Ramona Villagomez Manglona

District Judge

Date of Birth: February 26, 1967
Education: UC Berkeley 1990 BA; New Mexico 1996 JD
Began Service: July 31, 2011
Appointed By: President Barack Obama
Term Expires: 2021

Staff

Law Clerk **Richard C. Miller** .... (670) 237-1235
Began Service: August 22, 2011
Education: Colorado 2005 JD
Law Clerk **Jonathan Wilberscheid** .... (670) 237-1236
Began Service: August 26, 2014

Chambers of Senior Judge Alex R. Munson

P.O. Box 500687, Saipan, MP 96950
Tel: (670) 236-2900 Fax: (670) 236-2911

Alex R. Munson

Senior Judge

Date of Birth: 1941
Education: Cal State (Long Beach) 1964 BA, 1965 MA; USC 1970 EdD; Loyola Marymount 1975 JD
Political Affiliation: Republican

Current Memberships: American Bar Association; State Bar of California

United States District Court for the District of Puerto Rico

Clemente Ruiz-Nazario Courthouse, 150 Carlos Chardon Avenue, San Juan, PR 00918-1767
Tel: (787) 772-3000 Tel: (787) 766-5774 (Civil Cases PACER)
Fax: (787) 766-5693
Internet: www.prd.uscourts.gov

Number of Judgeships: 7

Circuit: First

Court Staff

Fax: (787) 766-5693

Clerk of Court **Frances Ríos De Morán** .... (787) 772-3000
Room 150 Fax: (787) 772-3210
E-mail: Frances_Moran@prd.uscourts.gov
Education: Puerto Rico 1964 JD
Chief Deputy Clerk **(Vacant)** .... (787) 772-3015

United States District Court for the District of Puerto Rico *continued*

Chief of Pre-Trial Services/Chief Probation Officer
Eustaquio Babilonia ... (787) 766-5647 ext. 5240 (Probation Services)
E-mail: eustaquio_babilonia@prp.uscourts.gov Tel: (787) 772-3300
Education: Puerto Rico 1994 MS (Pre-Trial Services)
Fax: (787) 766-5945
Human Resources Manager **Agnes Ferrer-Auffant** .... (787) 772-3006
E-mail: agnes_ferrer@prd.uscourts.gov Fax: (787) 772-3210
Librarian **Ana Milagros Rodríguez** .... (787) 772-3096
E-mail: Ana_Milagros_Rodriguez@prd.uscourts.gov Fax: (787) 766-5747
Education: Puerto Rico 1970 BA, 1976 MLS

Chambers of Chief Judge Aida M. Delgado-Colón

Federico Degetau Federal Building, 150 Carlos Chardon Avenue, Room 111, San Juan, PR 00918
Tel: (787) 772-3195 Fax: (787) 772-3169
E-mail: Aida_Delgado-Colon@prd.uscourts.gov

Aida M. Delgado-Colón

Chief Judge

Education: Puerto Rico 1977 BBA; Columbus Law 1980 JD
Began Service: March 20, 2006
Appointed By: President George W. Bush

Government: Director of Research and Investigations, Labor and Human Resources Department, Commonwealth of Puerto Rico (1981-1982); Assistant Federal Public Defender, United States District Court for the District of Puerto Rico (1982-1988); First Assistant Federal Public Defender, United States District Court for the District of Puerto Rico (1988-1993)

Judicial: Magistrate Judge, United States District Court for the District of Puerto Rico (1993-2006)

Current Memberships: American Bar Association; Association of Magistrate Judges; Federal Bar Association; Puerto Rico Chapter, Federal Bar Association; National Association of Women Judges; National Hispanic Bar Association

Staff

Law Clerk **Edward Sueiro** .... (787) 772-3196
Law Clerk **Adustin Fortouo** .... (787) 772-3196
Began Service: 2015
Term Expires: September 28, 2016
E-mail: adustin_fortouo@prd.uscourts.gov
Career Law Clerk **Eileen Garcia-Wirshing** .... (787) 772-3196
Began Service: October 2008
E-mail: eileen_garcia@prd.uscourts.gov
Education: Puerto Rico 2000 JD
Judicial Secretary **Wanda Marcano** .... (787) 772-3196
E-mail: wanda_marcano@prd.uscourts.gov
Education: Puerto Rico 1979 BSS

Chambers of District Judge José Antonio Fusté

CH-133 Clemente Ruiz-Nazario Courthouse, 150 Carlos Chardon Avenue, San Juan, PR 00918-1758
Tel: (787) 772-3120 Fax: (787) 766-5443

José Antonio Fusté

District Judge

Date of Birth: 1943
Education: Puerto Rico 1965 BBA, 1968 LLB
Began Service: 1985
Appointed By: President Ronald Reagan

Current Memberships: American Association for Justice; American Bar Association; The American Law Institute; Bar Association of Puerto Rico; The Bar Association of the District of Columbia; Federal Bar Association; Maritime Law Association of the United States; Southeastern Admiralty Law Institute

Chambers of District Judge José Antonio Fusté *continued*

Staff
Law Clerk **David Bornstein** .... (787) 772-3120
Began Service: August 2015
Term Expires: August 2016
E-mail: david_bornstein@prd.uscourts.gov
Law Clerk **Caryn Peterson** .... (787) 772-3120
E-mail: caryn_peterson@prd.uscourts.gov
Education: Akron 2011 JD
Judicial Assistant **Mari Rosa Jorge** .... (787) 772-3121
E-mail: mari_rosa_jorge@prd.uscourts.gov
Education: Puerto Rico 1968 BSS

Chambers of District Judge Carmen Consuelo Cerezo

CH-131 Clemente Ruiz-Nazario Courthouse, 150 Carlos Chardon Avenue, San Juan, PR 00918-1764
Tel: (787) 772-3110 Fax: (787) 766-5737
E-mail: carmen_cerezo@prd.uscourts.gov

Carmen Consuelo Cerezo
District Judge

Date of Birth: 1940
Education: Puerto Rico 1963 BA, 1966 LLB
Began Service: 1980
Appointed By: President Jimmy Carter

Clerkships: Law Clerk, United States District Court (1967-1972)

Judicial: Judge, Puerto Rico Superior Court (1972-1976); Judge, Puerto Rico Court of Intermediate Appeals (1976-1980)

Legal Practice: Benny Frankie Cerezo, Esq. (1966-1967)

Current Memberships: Bar Association of Puerto Rico

Staff
Career Law Clerk **Ramon F. Santiago-Velez** .... (787) 772-3116
E-mail: ramon_santiago@prd.uscourts.gov
Education: Puerto Rico 1989 JD
Law Clerk **Mercedes Trigo-Ferraiuoli** .... (787) 772-3114
E-mail: mercedes_trigo@prd.uscourts.gov
Judicial Assistant **Maria Luz Diaz-Santiago** .... (787) 772-3111
E-mail: maria_diaz@prd.uscourts.gov

Chambers of District Judge Jay A. García-Gregory

CH-142 Clemente Ruiz-Nazario Courthouse, 150 Carlos Chardon Avenue, San Juan, PR 00918-0151
Tel: (787) 772-3170 Fax: (787) 772-3209
E-mail: jay_garcia-gregory@prd.uscourts.gov

Jay A. García-Gregory
District Judge

Date of Birth: 1944
Education: Assumption Col 1966 AB; Puerto Rico 1972 LLB
Began Service: August 1, 2000
Appointed By: President William J. Clinton

Academic: Lecturer (part-time), University of Puerto Rico (1975-1976)

Clerkships: Law Clerk The Honorable Hiram R. Cancio, United States District Court for the District of Puerto Rico (1973-1974)

Legal Practice: Associate, Fiddler Gonzalez & Rodriguez, P.S.C.

Military Service: United States Navy Reserve (1962-1964)

Current Memberships: The District of Columbia Bar; Federal Bar Association; Puerto Rico Chapter, Federal Bar Association; Federal Circuit Bar Association; Federal Judges Association; Hispanic National Bar Association

Staff
Law Clerk **Antonio Perez** .... (787) 772-3176
Began Service: September 2015
Term Expires: October 1, 2016
E-mail: antonio_perez@prd.uscourts.gov

Chambers of District Judge Jay A. García-Gregory *continued*

Law Clerk **Maria Alina Castellanos** .... (787) 772-3177
Began Service: September 2014
Term Expires: October 1, 2016
Judicial Assistant **Linda I. Rivera** .... (787) 772-3170

Chambers of District Judge Gustavo A. Gelpi

150 Carlos Chardon Avenue, Suite CH-151, San Juan, PR 00918-0463
Tel: (787) 772-3102
E-mail: gustavo_gelpi@prd.uscourts.gov

Gustavo Antonio Gelpí, Jr.
District Judge

Date of Birth: 1965
Education: Brandeis 1987 BA; Suffolk 1991 JD
Began Service: August 2006
Appointed By: President George W. Bush

Clerkships: Law Clerk The Honorable Juan M. Pérez-Giménez, United States District Court for the District of Puerto Rico (1991-1993)

Government: Assistant Public Federal Defender (1993-1996); Special Counsel, United States Sentencing Commission (1996); Assistant to the Attorney General (1997); Deputy Attorney General (1997-1999); Solicitor General of Puerto Rico (1999-2000)

Judicial: Magistrate Judge, United States District Court for the District of Puerto Rico (2001-2006)

Legal Practice: McConnell Valdés Law Firm (2001)

Current Memberships: Federal Bar Association; Puerto Rico Chapter, Federal Bar Association; Virgin Islands Bar Association

Staff
Law Clerk **Coral Lopez** .... (787) 772-3100
Began Service: October 2015
Term Expires: September 2016
E-mail: coral_lopez@prd.uscourts.gov
Law Clerk **Samantha Drake** .... (787) 772-3104
Began Service: September 2015
Term Expires: September 2016
Law Clerk **Maria E. Torralbas** .... (787) 772-3104
Began Service: September 2014
Term Expires: September 2016

Chambers of District Judge Francisco Augusto Besosa

Clemente Ruiz-Nazario Courthouse, 150 Carlos Chardon Avenue, Room 119, San Juan, PR 00918-1767
Tel: (787) 772-3241 Fax: (787) 772-3249
E-mail: francisco_besosa@prd.uscourts.gov

Francisco Augusto Besosa
District Judge

Date of Birth: 1949
Education: Brown U 1971 AB; Georgetown 1979 JD
Began Service: October 2006
Appointed By: President George W. Bush

Government: Assistant U.S. Attorney, United States Attorneys Office, United States Department of Justice (1983-1986)

Legal Practice: Attorney, Private Practice (1979-1983); Attorney, Private Pratice (1986-2006)

Staff
Fax: (787) 772-3249

Courtroom Deputy **Gladys Romanach** .... (787) 772-3073
E-mail: gladys_romanach@prd.uscourts.gov
Court Reporter **(Vacant)** .... (787) 772-3482
Judicial Assistant **Brunny Rodriguez** .... (787) 772-3241
E-mail: brunny_rodriguez@prd.uscourts.gov

Chambers of District Judge Pedro A. Delgado Hernández

150 Carlos Chardon Avenue, San Juan, PR 00918-0151
Tel: (787) 772-3133

Pedro A. Delgado Hernández
District Judge

Education: Puerto Rico 1979 BS, 1979 JD
Began Service: 2014
Appointed By: President Barack Obama

Staff
Judicial Assistant **Evelyn Baez** . . . . (787) 772-3133

Chambers of Senior Judge Salvador E. Casellas

U.S. Courthouse, 300 Recinto Sur, Suite 342, San Juan, PR 00901
Tel: (787) 977-6060 Fax: (787) 977-6065
E-mail: S._Casellas@prd.uscourts.gov

Salvador E. Casellas
Senior Judge

Date of Birth: 1935
Education: Georgetown 1957 BS; Puerto Rico 1960 LLB; Harvard 1961 LLM
Began Service: November 1, 1994
Appointed By: President William J. Clinton

Government: Secretary of the Treasury, Commonwealth of Puerto Rico (1973-1976); Civilian Aide, Commonwealth of Puerto Rico, Gerald Ford Administration (1985-1989)

Legal Practice: Attorney, Fiddler Gonzalez & Rodriguez, P.S.C. (1962-1972); Attorney, Fiddler Gonzalez & Rodriguez, P.S.C. (1977-1994)

Military Service: United States Army (1961-1962); United States Army Reserve, United States Department of the Army (1963-1967); Civilian Aide to the Secretary of the Army, United States Army (1985-1989)

Current Memberships: American Bar Association; Puerto Rico Chapter, Federal Bar Association; Puerto Rican Academy of Jurisprudence

Staff
Law Clerk **Yasmin Umpierre** . . . . (787) 977-6060
Began Service: September 2010
Term Expires: September 2016
E-mail: yasmin_umpierre@prd.uscourts.gov
Law Clerk **Arturo Bauermeister** . . . . (787) 977-6062

Chambers of Senior Judge Juan M. Pérez-Giménez

Jose V. Toledo Building and U.S. Courthouse, 300 Calle Vel Recinto Sur, Suite 129, San Juan, PR 00901
Tel: (787) 772-3140 Fax: (787) 977-6180

Juan M. Pérez-Giménez
Senior Judge

Date of Birth: 1941
Education: Puerto Rico 1963 BA; George Washington 1965 MBA; Puerto Rico 1968 LLB
Began Service: 1979
Appointed By: President Jimmy Carter

Government: Assistant U.S. Attorney, Puerto Rico District, Executive Office for United States Attorneys, United States Department of Justice (1971-1975)

Judicial: Magistrate Judge, United States District Court for the District of Puerto Rico (1975-1979)

Legal Practice: Associate, Goldman, Antonetti & Davila (1968-1971)

Staff
Law Clerk **Priscila Azevedo** . . . . (787) 772-3140
Began Service: September 2012

Chambers of Senior Judge Juan M. Pérez-Giménez *continued*
Law Clerk **Natalia Del Nido** . . . . (787) 772-3140
Began Service: September 2015
Term Expires: September 2016
Law Clerk **(Vacant)** . . . . (787) 772-3141

Chambers of Senior Judge Daniel R. Domínguez

CH-129 Clemente Ruiz-Nazario Courthouse, 150 Carlos Chardon Avenue, San Juan, PR 00918-1766
Tel: (787) 772-3161 Fax: (787) 766-5408
E-mail: Daniel_Dominguez@prd.uscourts.gov

Daniel R. Domínguez
Senior Judge

Date of Birth: 1945
Education: Boston U 1967 BA; Puerto Rico 1970 LLB
Began Service: November 1, 1994
Appointed By: President William J. Clinton

Current Memberships: American Bar Association; Association of Labor Relations Practitioners; Bar Association of Puerto Rico; Puerto Rico Chapter, Federal Bar Association

Staff
Law Clerk **Manuel Miranda** . . . . (787) 772-3161
Law Clerk **Manuel Franco** . . . . (787) 772-3164
Career Law Clerk **Joan Mulet** . . . . (787) 772-3163
E-mail: joan_mulet@prd.uscourts.gov
Education: Puerto Rico 1971 BA; SUNY (Buffalo) 1976 MA; Inter American 1989 JD; Tulane 1980 LLM
Secretary **(Vacant)** . . . . (787) 772-3161

Chambers of Magistrate Judge Camille L. Velez-Rive

150 Chardon Street, Box 7056, San Juan, PR 00918-1759
Tel: (787) 772-3188 Fax: (787) 772-3179

Camille L. Velez-Rive
Magistrate Judge

Date of Birth: February 5, 1968
Education: Puerto Rico JD
Began Service: March 22, 2004
Term Expires: March 2020

Staff
Career Law Clerk **Ada Sofia Esteves** . . . . (787) 772-3185
E-mail: ada_esteves@prd.uscourts.gov
Judicial Assistant **Laura J. Tossas** . . . . (787) 772-3184
E-mail: laura_tossas@prd.uscourts.gov

Chambers of Magistrate Judge Bruce J. McGiverin

Federico Degetau Federal Building, 150 Carlos Chardon Avenue, Room 483, San Juan, PR 00918-1767
Tel: (787) 772-3341 Fax: (787) 772-3344
E-mail: bruce_mcgiverin@prd.uscourts.gov

Bruce J. McGiverin
Magistrate Judge

Began Service: January 2007
Term Expires: 2023

Staff
Fax: (787) 772-3344

Courtroom Deputy **Melissa Calderon** . . . . (787) 772-3045
Secretary **Jyoti Mehta** . . . . (787) 772-3341
E-mail: jyoti_mehta@prd.uscourts.gov

Chambers of Magistrate Judge Marcos E. Lopez

Federico Degetau Federal Building, 150 Carlos Chardon Avenue, Room 495, San Juan, PR 00918-1767
P.O. Box 7028, San Juan, PR 00918-1767
Tel: (787) 772-3350 Fax: (787) 772-3354
E-mail: marcos_lopez@prd.uscourts.gov

Marcos E. Lopez
Magistrate Judge

Education: Virginia BA; Cornell MBA, JD
Began Service: 2007
Term Expires: 2023

Staff
Tel: (787) 772-3354

Courtroom Deputy **Franchesca Torres** .... (787) 772-3078
E-mail: franchesca_torres@prd.uscourts.gov
Secretary **Janet Hita** .... (787) 772-3351
E-mail: janet_hita@prd.uscourts.gov

Chambers of Magistrate Judge Silvia Carreña-Coll

150 Carlos Chardon Avenue, San Juan, PR 00918-1767
Tel: (787) 772-3190

Silvia Carreño-Coll
Magistrate Judge

Staff
Law Clerk **Nicholas Bacarisse** .... (787) 772-3190
Judicial Assistant **Marirosa Cabrera** .... (787) 772-3190

United States Bankruptcy Court for the District of Puerto Rico

U.S. Post Office and Courthouse Building, 300 Recinto Sur Street, Suite 109, Old San Juan, PR 00901
Tel: (787) 977-6000 Tel: (787) 977-6140 (PACER)
Tel: (800) 676-6856 ext. 225 (Toll Free Pacer) Fax: (787) 977-6008
Internet: www.prb.uscourts.gov

Number of Judgeships: 1

Court Staff
Clerk of the Court **María de los Angeles González** ..... (787) 977-6015
Education: Boston U 1993 LLM;
Pontifical Catholic (Puerto Rico) 1990 JD;
Colgate 1987 BA
Chief Deputy Clerk **Wilma Jaime** .... (787) 977-6125
E-mail: wilma_jaime@prb.uscourts.gov
Administrative Services Coordinator **Mariana Benitez** ... (787) 977-6015
E-mail: mariana_benitez@prb.uscourts.gov
Budget Analyst **Claribel Burgos** .... (787) 977-6106
E-mail: claribel_burgos@prb.uscourts.gov
Property Management **Pablo Vega** .... (787) 977-6108
E-mail: pablo_vega@prb.uscourts.gov
Human Resources Coordinator **Yolanda Benitez** .... (787) 977-6007
E-mail: yolanda_benitez@prb.uscourts.gov
Case Manager **Milagros Irizarry** .... (787) 977-6040
Systems Manager **Félix Martínez** .... (787) 977-6089

Chambers of Chief Bankruptcy Judge Enrique S. Lamoutte

U.S. Post Office and Courthouse Building, 300 Recinto Sur Street, Suite 251, Old San Juan, PR 00901
Tel: (787) 977-6030 Fax: (787) 977-6035
E-mail: Enrique_S._Lamoutte@prb.uscourts.gov

Enrique S. Lamoutte
Chief Bankruptcy Judge

Date of Birth: 1948
Education: Boston Col 1969 BA; Puerto Rico 1976 JD
Began Service: November 1986
Term Expires: November 6, 2028

Affiliation: Bankruptcy Judge, Chambers of Bankruptcy Judge Enrique S. Lamoutte, United States Bankruptcy Appellate Panel for the First Circuit

Clerkships: Law Clerk, United States District Court for the District of Puerto Rico (1977-1979); Law Clerk, United States Bankruptcy Court for the District of Puerto Rico (1979-1983)

Government: Assistant U.S. Attorney, Puerto Rico District, Executive Office for United States Attorneys, United States Department of Justice (1983-1986)

Military Service: Air National Guard (1969)

Current Memberships: American Bar Association; The District of Columbia Bar; Federal Bar Association; Puerto Rico Chapter, Federal Bar Association

Staff
Law Clerk **Gustavo Chico** .... (787) 977-6034
Career Law Clerk **Madeline Mas** .... (787) 977-6033
Began Service: February 2009
E-mail: madeline_mas@prb.uscourts.gov
Education: Puerto Rico JD
Team Coordinator **Darhma Zayas** .... (787) 977-6112
E-mail: darhma_zayas@prb.uscourts.gov

Chambers of Bankruptcy Judge Brian K. Tester

Luis A Ferre US Courthouse & Post Office Building, 93 Atocha Street, 2nd Floor, Ponce, PR 00730
Tel: (787) 977-6040 Fax: (787) 977-6045
E-mail: brian_tester@prb.uscourts.gov

Brian K. Tester
Bankruptcy Judge

Began Service: November 2006
Term Expires: November 2020

Staff
Law Clerk **Gabriel Olivera** .... (787) 977-6040
Began Service: 2012
E-mail: myrna_ruiz@prb.uscourts.gov
Career Law Clerk **Sharon Ramírez** .... (787) 977-6040
E-mail: sharon_ramírez@prb.uscourts.gov

Chambers of Bankruptcy Judge Mildred Caban Flores

Jose V. Toledo Federal Building and U.S. Courthouse, 300 Recinto Sur Street, Courtroom 3, Old San Juan, PR 00901
Tel: (787) 977-6000

Mildred Caban Flores
Bankruptcy Judge

Staff
Career Law Clerk **Sandy Herman** .... (787) 977-6020
Career Law Clerk **Carlos Infante** .... (787) 977-6020

Chambers of Bankruptcy Judge Edward A. Godoy
300 Recinto Sur Street, Old San Juan, PR 00901
Tel: (787) 290-6074

Edward A. Godoy
Bankruptcy Judge

Staff
Career Law Clerk **Javier Vilarino** .... (787) 290-6074
Career Law Clerk **Christopher McParland** .... (787) 290-6074

United States District Court for the District of Virgin Islands
310 U.S. Courthouse, 5500 Veteran's Drive, Charlotte Amalie,
St. Thomas, VI 00802-6424
Tel: (340) 774-0640 Fax: (340) 774-1293
Internet: www.vid.uscourts.gov

Number of Judgeships: 2

Circuit: Third

Court Staff
Clerk of Court **Glenda L. Lake** .... (340) 718-1130
Chief Deputy Clerk, St. Thomas and St. John Division
Joanne U. Barry .... (340) 774-0640
US District Courthouse
E-mail: joanne_barry@vid.uscourts.gov
Financial Clerk **Shervin Clarke** .... (340) 776-0221
E-mail: shervin_clarke@vid.uscourts.gov Fax: (340) 774-1293
Financial Technician **(Vacant)** .... (340) 776-0221 ext. 228
Fax: (340) 777-8614
Management Analyst **Petrani Cornelius** .... (340) 776-0221 ext. 230
E-mail: petrani_cornelius@vid.uscourts.gov Fax: (340) 777-8614
Chief Probation Officer **Larry T. Glenn** .... (340) 718-5515
E-mail: larry_glenn@vid.uscourts.gov Tel: (340) 718-5140 (St. Croix)
Fax: (340) 773-5141 (St. Croix)
Administrative Services Manager **Lorelie Ayala** .... (340) 718-8928
E-mail: lorelie_ayala@vip.uscourts.gov
General Supervisor, St. Croix (Acting) **Marilyn Arroyo** ... (340) 718-1130
Almeric L. Christian Federal Building, 3013 Estate Golden Rock, Lot 13, Christiansted, VI 00820-4355 Fax: (340) 718-1563
General Supervisor, St. Thomas **Cecily Francis** .... (340) 774-0640
Fax: (340) 774-1293
Administrative Services Officer, St. Croix
Marilyn Arroyo .... (340) 718-1130
E-mail: marilyn_arroyo@vid.uscourts.gov Fax: (340) 718-1563
Librarian **Carol Grant** .... (340) 773-2308
Federal Building and U.S. Courthouse, 3013 Estate Golden Rock, Lot 13, St. Croix, VI 00820-4355 Tel: (340) 774-9548 Fax: (340) 774-1293
E-mail: carol_grant@vid.uscourts.gov
Library Technician, St. Croix Division
Coreen Lewis DelSol .... (340) 773-2308
Almeric L. Christian Federal Building, 3013 Estate Golden Rock Lot 13, Christiansted, VI 00820-4355 Fax: (340) 773-1563
E-mail: coreen_lewis@vid.uscourts.gov
Library Technician, St. Thomas Division
Marlene Nesbitt .... (340) 774-9548
Fax: (340) 774-1293
Supervising Court Reporter **Valerie D. Lawrence** .... (340) 773-4979
E-mail: valerie_lawrence@vid.uscourts.gov
Court Reporter **Chandra Kean** .... (340) 774-0640
E-mail: chandra_kean@vid.uscourts.gov

Chambers of Chief Judge Wilma Antoinette Lewis
5500 Veteran's Drive, Charlotte Amalie, St. Thomas, VI 00802-6424
Tel: (340) 774-0640 Fax: (340) 774-1293
E-mail: lewis_chambers@vid.uscourts.gov

Wilma Antoinette Lewis
Chief Judge

Education: Swarthmore 1978 BA; Harvard 1981 JD
Began Service: July 28, 2011
Appointed By: President Barack Obama

Staff
Courtroom Deputy **Margaret Brown** .... (340) 718-1130
Judicial Legal Assistant **Robin Barovick** .... (340) 718-1130
Education: SUNY (Empire State) 1996 BA; SUNY (Buffalo) 2000 JD

Chambers of District Judge Curtis V. Gomez
Ron de Lugo Federal Building & US Courthouse, 5500 Veteran's Drive, St. Thomas, VI 00802-6424
Tel: (340) 774-1800 Fax: (340) 777-8532

Curtis V. Gomez
District Judge

Education: George Washington 1984 BA; Harvard 1989 JD
Began Service: January 3, 2005
Appointed By: President George W. Bush

Current Memberships: Virgin Islands Bar Association

Staff
Law Clerk **Nicholas West** .... (340) 774-2178
Began Service: August 2015
Term Expires: August 2017
E-mail: nicholas_west@vid.uscourts.gov
Law Clerk **Adam Sleeper** .... (340) 774-2178

Chambers of Magistrate Judge George W. Cannon Jr.
3013 Golden Rock, Christiansted, VI 00820-4355
Tel: (340) 718-1601 Fax: (340) 718-7182
E-mail: cannon_chambers@vid.uscourts.gov

George W. Cannon, Jr.
Magistrate Judge

Date of Birth: July 14, 1957
Education: Texas 1977; Antioch Law 1979 JD
Began Service: April 12, 2012
Term Expires: April 12, 2020

Current Memberships: American Bar Association; Federal Bar Association; Virgin Islands Bar Association

Staff
Career Law Clerk **Kimberly D'Eramo** .... (340) 718-1601
E-mail: Kimberly_D'Eramo@vid.uscourts.gov
Education: Notre Dame 1989 JD
Judicial Legal Assistant **Cynthia R. Brown** .... (340) 718-1601
E-mail: cynthia_brown@vid.uscourts.gov
Education: U Virgin Islands 1986

Chambers of Magistrate Judge Ruth Miller
5500 Veteran's Drive, Charlotte Amalie, Suite 345, St. Thomas, VI 00802-6424
Tel: (340) 774-5480 Fax: (340) 777-8119

Ruth Miller
Magistrate Judge

Began Service: June 18, 2010

Chambers of Magistrate Judge Ruth Miller *continued*

Staff

Career Law Clerk **Laura Creasy** .... (340) 774-5480
Courtroom Deputy **Tyrone Hodge** .... (340) 774-5480
Secretary **Amanda Omo-are** .... (340) 774-5480

Chambers of Magistrate Judge (recalled) Geoffrey W. Barnard

5500 Veteran's Drive, Suite 342, St. Thomas, VI 00802-6424
Tel: (340) 774-5480 Fax: (340) 777-8119

Geoffrey W. Barnard
Magistrate Judge (recalled)

Date of Birth: 1945
Began Service: 2010

United States Bankruptcy Court of the Virgin Islands

351 U.S. Courthouse, 5500 Veteran's Drive, St. Thomas, VI 00802-6424
Tel: (340) 774-8310 Fax: (340) 776-5615

Number of Judgeships: 1

Court Staff

Supervisor **Cicely B. Francis** .... (340) 774-8310
E-mail: cicely_francis@vid.uscourts.gov
Deputy Clerk **Kim Bonelli** .... (340) 774-8310
E-mail: kim_bonelli@vid.uscourts.gov
Deputy Clerk **Kimberley Willett** .... (340) 774-8310
E-mail: kimberley_willett@vid.uscourts.gov

Chambers of Bankruptcy Judge Mary Walrath

824 Market Street, Fifth Floor, Wilmington, DE 19801
Tel: (302) 252-2929

Mary F. Walrath
Bankruptcy Judge

Note: Bankruptcy Judge Mary Walrath hears all bankruptcy cases filed in the Virgin Islands in the United States Bankruptcy Court for the District of Delaware.

Judicial Conference of the United States

Thurgood Marshall Federal Judiciary Building, 601 Market Street, Room 7-425 South, Philadelphia, PA 19106-1729
Tel: (202) 502-2400 Fax: (202) 502-1144

The Judicial Conference of the United States is the principal policy making body concerned with the administration of the United States Courts. The specific duties of the Judicial Conference include surveying the conditions of business in the courts of the United States, preparing plans for the assignment of judges to or from courts of appeals or district courts, promoting uniformity of management procedures and the expeditious conduct of court business, the reviewing of circuit council conduct and disability orders, and carrying on a continuous study of the operation and effect of general rules of practice and procedure in use within the federal courts. In addition, the Judicial Conference supervises the Director of the Administrative Office of the United States Courts and operates through a network of committees created to address and advise on a variety of subjects dealing with administration of the courts. The Chief Justice of the United States is the presiding officer of the conference. Membership is comprised of the chief judges of each judicial circuit, the chief judge of the Court of International Trade, and a district judge from each regional judicial circuit. A circuit chief judge's term on the conference is concurrent with his or her term as chief judge of the circuit, seven years or until seventy years of age, whichever comes first. District judge representatives are elected for terms of not less than three nor more than five successive years, as established by majority vote of all circuit and district judges of their circuit. Terms on the conference of elected members are effective and expire on October 1 of any given year. The Director of the Administrative Office of the United States Courts serves as the Judicial Conference Secretary.

Staff

Conference Secretary and Director, Administrative Office of the United States Courts
James C. "Jim" Duff .... (202) 502-3000
Education: Kentucky 1975 BA; Georgetown 1981 JD — Fax: (202) 502-3011

Judicial Conference Secretariat Officer
Katherine H. Simon .... (202) 502-2400
E-mail: katie.simon@ao.uscourts.gov

Attorney Advisor **Helen Bornstein** .... (202) 502-2400
E-mail: helen_bornstein@ao.uscourts.gov

Judicial Conference Secretariat Confidential Assistant
Heidi Marshall-Butler .... (202) 502-2400
E-mail: heidi_marshall-butler@ao.uscourts.gov — Fax: (202) 502-1144

Chambers of Member John G. Roberts, Jr.

U.S. Supreme Court Building, One First Street, NE, Washington, DC 20543
Tel: (202) 479-3000

John G. Roberts, Jr.
Member

Date of Birth: January 27, 1955
Education: Harvard 1976 AB, 1979 JD

Current Memberships: American Academy of Appellate Lawyers; The Edward Coke Appellate American Inn of Court, The American Inns of Court; The American Law Institute

Chambers of Member William Jay Riley

111 South 18th Plaza, Suite 4303, Omaha, NE 68102
Tel: (402) 661-7575 Fax: (402) 661-7574

William Jay Riley
Member

Date of Birth: 1947
Education: Nebraska 1969 BA, 1972 JD
Began Service: April 2, 2010
Term Expires: March 10, 2017
Political Affiliation: Republican

Academic: Adjunct Professor, Trial Practice, College of Law, University of Nebraska-Lincoln

Clerkships: Law Clerk The Honorable Donald P. Lay, United States Court of Appeals for the Eighth Circuit (1972-1973)

Legal Practice: Associate, Fitzgerald, Schorr, Barmettler & Brennan, PC, LLO (1973-1979); Partner, Fitzgerald, Schorr, Barmettler & Brennan, PC, LLO (1979-2001)

Current Memberships: American Board of Trial Advocates; American College of Trial Lawyers

Chambers of Member William B. Traxler, Jr.

300 East Washington Street, Room 222, Greenville, SC 29601
Tel: (864) 241-2730 Fax: (864) 241-2732

William B. Traxler, Jr.
Member

Date of Birth: 1948
Education: Davidson 1970 BA; South Carolina 1973 JD
Began Service: July 9, 2009
Term Expires: July 8, 2016

Government: Chief Deputy Solicitor, Thirteenth Judicial Circuit, State of South Carolina (1975-1981); Solicitor, Thirteenth Judicial Circuit, State of South Carolina (1981-1985)

Judicial: Resident Judge, Thirteenth Judicial Circuit (1985-1992); Judge, United States District Court for the District of South Carolina (1992-1998)

Legal Practice: William Byrd Traxler, Sr. (1973-1974)

Military Service: United States Army Reserve, United States Department of the Army (1970-1978)

Current Memberships: Federal Judges Association; Greenville County Bar Association; South Carolina Bar

Chambers of Member Merrick B. Garland

333 Constitution Avenue, NW, Room 5927, Washington, DC 20001
Tel: (202) 216-7460 Fax: (202) 208-2449

Merrick B. Garland
Member

Date of Birth: 1952
Education: Harvard 1974 AB, 1977 JD
Began Service: February 12, 2013
Term Expires: February 11, 2020

Chambers of Member Carl E. Stewart
300 Fannin Street, Suite 5226, Shreveport, LA 71101
Tel: (318) 676-3765 Fax: (318) 676-3768

Carl Edmund Stewart
Member

Date of Birth: 1950
Education: Dillard 1971 BA; Loyola U (New Orleans) 1974 JD
Began Service: October 1, 2012
Term Expires: September 30, 2019
Political Affiliation: Democrat

Current Memberships: American Bar Association; The Harry V. Booth - Judge Henry A. Politz American Inn of Court, The American Inns of Court; Black Lawyers Association of Shreveport-Bossier; Louisiana Conference of Judges of Courts of Appeal; Louisiana State Bar Association; National Bar Association; Shreveport Bar Association

Chambers of Member Paul J. Barbadoro
55 Pleasant Street, Room 110, Concord, NH 03301-3938
Tel: (603) 226-7303 Fax: (603) 230-7629

Paul James Barbadoro
Member

Date of Birth: 1955
Education: Gettysburg 1977 BA; Boston Col 1980 JD
Began Service: October 1, 2012
Term Expires: October 1, 2016

Current Memberships: First Circuit Court of Appeals Bar Association; Committee on Cooperation With the Courts, New Hampshire Bar Association; New Hampshire Federal District Court Bar Association

Chambers of Member Richard W. Roberts
E. Barrett Prettyman U.S. Courthouse, 333 Constitution Avenue, NW, Room 4535, Washington, DC 20001
Tel: (202) 354-3400 Fax: (202) 354-3256

Richard W. Roberts
Member

Date of Birth: 1953
Education: Vassar 1974 AB; School Intl Training 1978 MIA; Columbia 1978 JD
Began Service: July 6, 2013
Term Expires: July 15, 2018

Chambers of Member Robert A. Katzmann
40 Centre Street, Room 301, New York, NY 10007-1501
Tel: (212) 857-2180 Fax: (212) 857-2189

Robert Allen Katzmann
Member

Date of Birth: 1953
Education: Columbia Col (IL) 1973 AB; Harvard 1977 AM, 1978 PhD; Yale 1980 JD
Began Service: September 1, 2013
Term Expires: August 31, 2020

Chambers of Member William M. Skretny
2 Niagara Square, Room 924, Buffalo, NY 14202-3350
Tel: (716) 551-1820 Fax: (716) 551-1825

William M. Skretny
Member

Date of Birth: 1945
Education: Canisius 1966 AB; Howard U 1969 JD; Northwestern 1972 LLM
Began Service: October 1, 2013
Term Expires: October 1, 2016
Political Affiliation: Republican

Current Memberships: Federal Judges Association

Chambers of Member Theodore A. McKee
601 Market Street, Room 20614, Philadelphia, PA 19106-1729
Tel: (215) 597-9601 Fax: (215) 597-0104

Theodore A. McKee
Member

Date of Birth: 1947
Education: SUNY (Cortland) 1969 BA; Syracuse 1975 JD
Began Service: May 4, 2010
Term Expires: May 3, 2017

Current Memberships: Barristers' Association of Philadelphia; National Bar Association; Pennsylvania Bar Association; Philadelphia Bar Association

Chambers of Member Louis Guirola Jr.
2012 15th Street, Suite 814, Gulfport, MS 39501
Tel: (228) 563-1767 Fax: (228) 563-1768

Louis Guirola, Jr.
Member

Date of Birth: 1951
Education: William Carey 1973 BA; Mississippi 1979 JD
Began Service: October 1, 2013
Term Expires: October 1, 2016

Chambers of Member Paul Lewis Maloney
410 West Michigan Avenue, Room 137, Kalamazoo, MI 49007
Tel: (269) 381-5245 Fax: (269) 337-4736

Paul Lewis Maloney
Member

Date of Birth: 1949
Education: Lehigh 1972 BA; Detroit 1975 JD
Began Service: October 1, 2013
Term Expires: October 1, 2016

Chambers of Member Diane P. Wood
219 South Dearborn Street, Room 2688, Chicago, IL 60604
Tel: (312) 435-5521 Fax: (312) 408-5117

Diane Pamela Wood
Member

Date of Birth: July 4, 1950
Education: Texas 1971 BA, 1975 JD
Began Service: October 1, 2013
Term Expires: July 3, 2020
Political Affiliation: Democrat

Current Memberships: American Academy of Arts and Sciences; The American Law Institute; American Society of International Law; The Bar Association of the District of Columbia; Illinois State Bar Association

Chambers of Member Ed Carnes
One Church Street, Room 403, Montgomery, AL 36104
Tel: (334) 954-3580 Fax: (334) 954-3599

Edward Carnes
Member

Date of Birth: 1950
Education: Alabama 1972 BS; Harvard 1975 JD
Began Service: August 1, 2013
Term Expires: June 2, 2020

Chambers of Member Sharon Prost
717 Madison Place, N.W., Suite 901, Washington, DC 20439
Tel: (202) 275-8700 Fax: (202) 275-9286

Sharon Prost
Member

Date of Birth: 1951
Education: Cornell 1973 BS; George Washington 1975 MBA; Washington College of Law 1979 JD; George Washington 1984 LLM
Began Service: May 31, 2014; May 23, 2021

Chambers of Member Timothy Stanceu
One Federal Plaza, Room 760, New York, NY 10278-0001
Tel: (212) 264-2880 Fax: (212) 264-7568

Timothy C. Stanceu
Member

Date of Birth: July 31, 1951
Education: Colgate 1973 AB; Georgetown 1979 JD
Began Service: July 1, 2014
Term Expires: June 30, 2021
Political Affiliation: Republican

Chambers of Member R. Guy Cole Jr.
85 Marconi Boulevard, Suite 255, Columbus, OH 43215
Tel: (614) 719-3350 Fax: (614) 719-3360

R. Guy Cole, Jr.
Member

Date of Birth: 1951
Education: Tufts 1972 BA; Yale 1975 JD
Began Service: August 15, 2014
Term Expires: May 22, 2021

Current Memberships: American Bar Association; Columbus Bar Association; National Bar Association

Chambers of Member Sidney R. Thomas
P.O. Box 31478, Billings, MT 59107-1478
Tel: (406) 373-3200 Fax: (406) 373-3250

Sidney R. Thomas
Member

Date of Birth: 1953
Education: Montana State 1975 BA; Montana 1978 JD
Began Service: December 1, 2014
Term Expires: November 30, 2021

Current Memberships: American Bar Association; Federal Judges Association; State Bar of Montana; Yellowstone County Bar Association

Chambers of Member Federico A. Moreno
400 North Miami Avenue, Room 13-3, Miami, FL 33128
Tel: (305) 523-5110 Fax: (305) 523-5119

Federico A. Moreno
Member

Date of Birth: 1952
Education: Notre Dame 1974 AB; Miami 1978 JD
Began Service: October 1, 2014
Term Expires: October 1, 2017

Current Memberships: American Judges Association; Federal Bar Association

Chambers of Member Karen E. Schreier
400 South Phillips Avenue, Room 233, Sioux Falls, SD 57104
Tel: (605) 330-6670 Fax: (605) 330-6671

Karen E. Schreier
Member

Date of Birth: 1956
Education: Saint Louis U 1978 BA, 1981 JD
Began Service: October 1, 2014
Term Expires: October 1, 2018
Political Affiliation: Democrat

Current Memberships: American Bar Association; Pennington County Bar Association; State Bar of South Dakota

Chambers of Member Leonard P. Stark
J. Caleb Boggs Federal Building, 844 North King Street, Unit 26, Wilmington, DE 19801-3519
Tel: (302) 573-4571 Fax: (302) 573-6442

Leonard P. Stark
Member

Education: Delaware 1991; Yale 1996 JD
Began Service: October 1, 2014
Term Expires: October 1, 2017

Chambers of Member Jeffrey R. Howard
55 Pleasant Street, Concord, NH 03301-3938
Tel: (603) 225-1525 Fax: (603) 225-1625

Jeffrey R. Howard
Member

Date of Birth: 1955
Education: Plymouth State Col 1978 BA; Georgetown 1981 JD
Began Service: June 16, 2015
Term Expires: June 15, 2022

Chambers of Member Timothy M. Tymkovich
1823 South Street, Suite 102 G, Denver, CO 80257
Tel: (303) 335-3300

Timothy M. Tymkovich
Member

Date of Birth: November 2, 1956
Education: Colorado Col 1979 BA; Colorado 1982 JD
Term Expires: October 2016

Current Memberships: American Bar Association; The American Law Institute; Colorado Bar Foundation, Colorado Bar Association; International Society of Barristers

Chambers of Member Claudia Wilken
1301 Clay Street, 4th Floor, Suite 400, Oakland, CA 94612
Tel: (510) 632-3542

Claudia A. Wilken
Member

Date of Birth: 1949
Education: Stanford 1971 BA; Boalt Hall 1975 JD

Chambers of Member Martha Vazquez
106 South Federal Place, Second Floor, Santa Fe, NM 87501
Tel: (505) 988-6330

Martha A. Vázquez
Member

Date of Birth: 1953
Education: Notre Dame 1975 BA, 1979 JD
Term Expires: October 2016
Political Affiliation: Democrat

Current Memberships: American Bar Association; New Mexico Women's Bar Association; State Bar of New Mexico; The U.S.-Mexico Law Institute

Chambers of Member Michael J. Reagan
750 Missouri Avenue, Room 220, East St. Louis, IL 62201
Tel: (618) 482-9225

Michael J. Reagan
Member

Date of Birth: 1954
Education: Bradley 1976 BS; Saint Louis U 1980 JD

Chambers of Member Robert J. Conrad Jr.
401 West Trade Street, Room 235, Charlotte, NC 28202
Tel: (704) 350-7460

Robert J. Conrad, Jr.
Member

Education: Clemson 1980 BA; Virginia 1983 JD

Administrative Office of the United States Courts

Thurgood Marshall Federal Judiciary Building, One Columbus Circle, NE, Washington, DC 20544
Tel: (202) 502-2600 Tel: (202) 502-3800 (Employee Locator)
Tel: (202) 502-1271 (Job Opportunity Recording)
Tel: (202) 502-3800 (Personnel Office)
Tel: (202) 502-4369 (Post Judgment Interest Rate Recording)
Tel: (202) 502-1441 (Statistical Information)
Tel: (202) 502-2225 (Accounting Operations/Billing Inquiries)
Fax: (202) 502-1155
Internet: www.uscourts.gov

Created by an Act of Congress in 1939, the Administrative Office of the United States Courts provides management and program support and administrative services to the federal courts. It implements the policies of the Judicial Conference of the United States and provides staff support and legal counsel to the Judicial Conference's committees. The services provided by the Administrative Office include program, legal and administrative assistance to Article III, bankruptcy and magistrate judges and court employees. It also handles coordination between and among the judicial branch, the legislative branch, the executive branch and state courts. The Administrative Office is responsible for collecting and reporting judiciary statistics and supports program activity in the areas of court administration, defender services, and probation and pretrial services. Appointment of the Administrative Office Director is made by the Chief Justice of the United States, in consultation with the Judicial Conference of the United States.

Office of the Director

One Columbus Circle, NE, Washington, DC 20544

Director **James C. "Jim" Duff** . . . . (202) 502-3000
Began Service: January 2, 2015
Education: Kentucky 1975 BA; Georgetown 1981 JD

Deputy Director **Jill C. Sayenga** . . . . (202) 502-3015
Thurgood Marshall Federal Judiciary Building, Suite 7100
E-mail: jill_sayenga@ao.uscourts.gov
Education: Fordham 1976 BA; Georgetown 1979 JD

Chief of Staff **Gary A. Bowden** . . . . (202) 502-1300

Long-Range Planning Officer **Brian Lynch** . . . . (202) 502-1300
E-mail: brian_lynch@ao.uscourts.gov

Office of Audit

One Columbus Circle, NE, Washington, DC 20544
Tel: (202) 502-1000

Audit Officer **Veleda Henderson** . . . . (202) 502-1000
E-mail: veleda_henderson@ao.uscourts.gov

General Counsel

One Columbus Circle, NE, Washington, DC 20544
Tel: (202) 502-1100

General Counsel **Sheryl L. Walter** . . . . (202) 502-1100
E-mail: sheryl_walter@ao.uscourts.gov

Deputy General Counsel **(Vacant)** . . . . (202) 502-1100

Judicial Conference Secretariat

One Columbus Circle, NE, Washington, DC 20544
Tel: (202) 502-2400

Judicial Conference Secretariat Officer **Katherine H. Simon** . . . . (202) 502-2400
E-mail: katie.simon@ao.uscourts.gov

Office of Legislative Affairs

One Columbus Circle, NE, Washington, DC 20544
Tel: (202) 502-1700

Legislative Affairs Officer **Cordia A. Strom** . . . . (202) 502-1700
E-mail: cordia_strom@ao.uscourts.gov

Deputy Legislative Affairs Officer **Daniel A. Cunningham** . . . . (202) 502-1700

Office of Public Affairs

One Columbus Circle, NE, Washington, DC 20544
Tel: (202) 502-2600

Public Affairs Officer **David A. Sellers** . . . . (202) 502-2600
E-mail: david_sellers@ao.uscourts.gov
Education: Dickinson Col 1978 BA

Public Information Officer **Karen Redmond** . . . . (202) 502-2600
Education: Syracuse 1976 BA

Department of Administrative Services

One Columbus Circle, NE, Washington, DC 20544
Tel: (202) 502-2000

Associate Director **George H. Schafer** . . . . (202) 502-2000

Chief of Staff **Michael N. Milby** . . . . (202) 502-2000

Office of Administrative Systems

One Columbus Circle, NE, Washington, DC 20544
Tel: (202) 502-2200

Chief **Joseph W. "Joe" Bossi** . . . . (202) 502-2200
E-mail: joe_bossi@ao.uscourts.gov

Office of Budget, Accounting and Procurement

One Columbus Circle, NE, Washington, DC 20544
Tel: (202) 502-2000

Chief Financial Officer **Karin E. O'Leary** . . . . (202) 502-2000
E-mail: karin_oleary@ao.uscourts.gov

Judiciary Budget Officer **James R. Baugher** . . . . (202) 502-2100

Financial Liaison Officer **Edward O'Kane** . . . . (202) 502-2028
E-mail: edward_o'kane@ao.uscourts.gov

Judiciary Procurement Officer **Carey M. Fountain** . . . . (202) 502-1330
E-mail: carey_fountain@ao.uscourts.gov

Office of Facilities and Security

One Columbus Circle, NE, Washington, DC 20544
Tel: (202) 502-1200

Chief **Melanie Gilbert** . . . . (202) 502-1200
E-mail: melanie_gilbert@ao.uscourts.gov

Office of Human Resources

One Columbus Circle, NE, Washington, DC 20544
Tel: (202) 502-3281

Human Resources Officer **Patricia J. Fitzgibbons** . . . . (202) 502-3281
E-mail: patricia_fitzgibbons@ao.uscourts.gov

Department of Program Services

One Columbus Circle, NE, Washington, DC 20544
Tel: (202) 502-3500

Associate Director **Laura C. Minor** .... (202) 502-3500
E-mail: laura_minor@ao.uscourts.gov
Chief of Staff **Michel M. Ishakian** .... (202) 502-3500

Office of Case Management Systems

One Columbus Circle, NE, Washington, DC 20544
Tel: (202) 502-2500

Chief **Andrew Zaso** .... (202) 502-2500

Office of Court Services

One Columbus Circle, NE, Washington, DC 20544
Tel: (202) 502-1500

Chief **Mary Louise Mitterhoff** .... (202) 502-1500
E-mail: mary_louise_mitterhoff@ao.uscourts.gov

Office of Defender Services

One Columbus Circle, NE, Washington, DC 20544
Tel: (202) 502-3030

Chief **Cait T. Clarke** .... (202) 502-3030
E-mail: cait_clarke@ao.uscourts.gov

Office of Judiciary Data and Analysis

One Columbus Circle, NE, Washington, DC 20544
Tel: (202) 502-1440

Chief **Gary Yakimov** .... (202) 502-1440
E-mail: gary_yakimov@ao.uscourts.gov

Office of Judicial Services

One Columbus Circle, NE, Washington, DC 20544
Tel: (202) 502-1800

Chief **Michele E. Reed** .... (202) 502-1800
E-mail: michele_reed@ao.uscourts.gov

Office of Probation and Pretrial Services

One Columbus Circle, NE, Washington, DC 20544
Tel: (202) 502-1600

Chief **Matthew G. Rowland** .... (202) 502-1600
E-mail: matthew_rowland@ao.uscourts.gov
Education: St Francis Col (NY) 1987 BA;
Brooklyn Law 1992 JD

Department of Technology Services

One Columbus Circle, NE, Washington, DC 20544
Tel: (202) 502-2300

Associate Director **Joseph R. Peters, Jr.** .... (202) 502-2300
E-mail: joseph_peters@ao.uscourts.gov
Chief of Staff **Terry A. Cain** .... (202) 502-2300

AO Technology Office

One Columbus Circle, NE, Washington, DC 20544
Tel: (202) 502-2830

Chief **John C. Chang** .... (202) 502-2830
E-mail: john_chang@ao.uscourts.gov

Office of Cloud Technology and Hosting

One Columbus Circle, NE, Washington, DC 20544
Tel: (202) 502-2377

Chief **Robert D. Morse** .... (202) 502-2377
E-mail: robert_morse@ao.uscourts.gov

Office of Infrastructure Management

One Columbus Circle, NE, Washington, DC 20544
Tel: (202) 502-2640

Chief **Timothy "Tim" Hanlon** .... (202) 502-2640
E-mail: tim_hanlon@ao.uscourts.gov

Office of IT Security

One Columbus Circle, NE, Washington, DC 20544
Tel: (202) 502-2350

Chief **Bethany J. De Lude** .... (202) 502-2350
E-mail: bethany_de_lude@ao.uscourts.gov

Office of Systems Deployment and Security

One Columbus Circle, NE, Washington, DC 20544
Tel: (202) 502-2700

Chief **Ronald E. "Ron" Blankenship** .... (202) 502-2700
E-mail: ron_blankenship@ao.uscourts.gov

Office of Technology Solutions

One Columbus Circle, NE, Washington, DC 20544
Tel: (202) 502-2730

Chief Technology Officer **Farhad K. Safaie** .... (202) 502-2730
E-mail: farhad_safaie@ao.uscourts.gov

Federal Judicial Center

Thurgood Marshall Federal Judiciary Building, One Columbus Circle, NE, Washington, DC 20002-8003
Tel: (202) 502-4000 Fax: (202) 502-4099
Internet: www.fjc.gov

The Federal Judicial Center, established by Congress in 1967, is the research and education agency of the federal judicial system. The Center's duties include conducting and promoting orientation and continuing education and training for federal judges, court employees, and others; developing recommendations about the operation and study of the federal courts; and conducting and promoting research on federal judicial procedures, court operations, and history. By statute, the Chief Justice of The Supreme Court of the United States chairs the Center's Board, which also includes the director of the Administrative Office of the United States Courts and seven judges elected by the Judicial Conference of the United States. The Board appoints the Center's director and deputy director and in turn the director appoints the Center's staff.

Staff

Director **Jeremy D. Fogel**............................(202) 502-4160
Education: Stanford 1971 BA; Harvard 1974 JD
Deputy Director **John S. Cooke**......................(202) 502-4060
E-mail: jcooke@fjc.gov
Education: Carleton 1968 BA; USC 1971 JD; Virginia 1977 LLM
Senior Administrative Assistant **Jennifer Krause**........(202) 502-4160
E-mail: jkrause@fjc.gov
Director, Communications Policy and Design Office
Sylvan A. Sobel..................................(202) 502-4250
E-mail: ssobel@fjc.gov Fax: (202) 502-4077
Education: Georgetown 1977 BA; Wisconsin 1983 JD
Director, Education Division **LTG Dana K. Chipman**.....(202) 502-4257
Note: Effective January 2016. Fax: (202) 502-4299
Affiliation: USA (Ret)
Director, Federal Judicial History Office **Clara Altman**... (202) 502-4181
Fax: (202) 502-4077
Director, International Judicial Relations Office
Mira Gur-Arie....................................(202) 502-4191
E-mail: mgurarie@fjc.gov
Education: Cornell 1985 BA; NYU 1988 JD
Director, Research Division **James B. Eaglin**...........(202) 502-4070
E-mail: jeaglin@fjc.gov Fax: (202) 502-4199
Education: Grambling State 1972 BA; SUNY (Buffalo) 1973 MA, 1975 JD
Director, Information and Technology **Esther DeVries**... (202) 502-4195
Fax: (202) 502-4288
Information Services Chief **Matt Sarago**.............. (202) 502-4153
E-mail: msarago@fjc.gov Fax: (202) 502-4077
Financial Management Officer **Norman K. Baker**........(202) 502-4171
E-mail: nbaker@fjc.gov
Education: American U 1975 BA, 1986 MBA
Administrative Services Officer **Michael B. Gross**.......(202) 502-4168
E-mail: mgross@fjc.gov
Education: Bucknell 1973 BA; George Washington 1975 MA, 1981 EdD

United States Sentencing Commission [USSC]

2-500 Thurgood Marshall Federal Judiciary Building, One Columbus Circle, NE, South Lobby, Washington, DC 20002-8002
Tel: (202) 502-4500
Tel: (202) 502-4545 (Guideline Application Assistance Helpline)
Tel: (202) 502-4568 (Public Information and Publications Request Line)
Fax: (202) 502-4699
Internet: www.ussc.gov

The United States Sentencing Commission is a bipartisan, independent agency in the judicial branch of government created by the Sentencing Reform Act provisions of the Comprehensive Crime Control Act of 1984. Its principal purposes are: (1) to establish sentencing policies and practices for the federal courts, including guidelines to be consulted regarding the appropriate form and severity of punishment for offenders convicted of federal crimes; (2) to advise and assist Congress and the executive branch in the development of effective and efficient crime policy; and (3) to collect, analyze, research, and distribute a broad array of information on federal crime and sentencing issues, serving as an information resource for Congress, the executive branch, the courts, criminal justice practitioners, the academic community, and the public.

Staff

Chair **Patti B. Saris** .... (202) 502-4500
Term Expires: October 31, 2015
Education: Radcliffe 1973 BA; Harvard 1976 JD
Vice Chair **Charles R. Breyer** .... (202) 502-4500
Note: On September 10, 2015, President Obama renominated Charles Breyer to be Commissioner for the United States Sentencing Commission.
Education: Harvard 1963 AB; Boalt Hall 1966 LLB
Commissioner **Rachel Elise Barkow** .... (202) 502-4500
Began Service: 2013
Term Expires: October 31, 2017
Education: Northwestern 1993 BA; Harvard 1996 JD
Commissioner-Designate
Richard Franklin Boulware II .... (202) 502-4500
Note: On September 10, 2015, President Obama nominated Richard Franklin Boulware II to be Commissioner for the United States Sentencing Commission.
Term Expires: October 31, 2019
Education: Harvard 1993 AB; Columbia 2002 JD
Commissioner **Dabney L. Friedrich** .... (202) 502-4500
Term Expires: October 31, 2015
Education: Trinity U 1988 BA; Yale 1992 JD
Commissioner **William Holcombe "Bill" Pryor, Jr.** ..... (202) 502-4500
Began Service: 2013
Term Expires: October 31, 2017
Education: Northeast Louisiana 1984 BA; Tulane 1987 JD
Commissioner, ex-officio **Jonathan J. Wroblewski** ..... (202) 502-4500
Commissioner, ex-officio **(Vacant)** .... (202) 502-4500
Staff Director **Kenneth P. Cohen** .... (202) 502-4510
Education: Virginia 1988 BA; Harvard 1993 JD
Administration Director **Susan M. Brazel** .... (202) 502-4610
Legislative and Public Affairs Director
Christine M. Leonard .... (202) 502-4519
Education: Boston Col BA, JD
Training Director and Chief Counsel
Pamela G. Montgomery .... (202) 502-4540
Education: Carleton 1978 BA; Georgia 1981 JD
General Counsel **Kathleen C. Grilli** .... (202) 502-4520
E-mail: kgrilli@ussc.gov
Research and Data Director **Glenn R. Schmitt** .... (202) 502-4530
Education: Indiana State 1983 BS; Notre Dame 1986 JD; Harvard 1994 MPP

State Courts

Alabama

Alabama Administrative Office of Courts

300 Dexter Avenue, Montgomery, AL 36104-3741
Tel: (334) 954-5000 Tel: (866) 954-9411 (Toll free)
Internet: www.alacourt.gov

Staff

Administrative Director of Courts **Rich Hobson** . . . . (334) 954-5080
E-mail: rich.hobson@alacourt.gov
Education: Alabama 1997 PhD

Executive Assistant **Julie Evans** . . . . (334) 954-5014
E-mail: julie.evans@alacourt.gov Fax: (334) 954-3142

Alabama Supreme Court

300 Dexter Avenue, Montgomery, AL 36104-3741
Tel: (334) 229-0700 Fax: (334) 229-0522
Internet: http://judicial.alabama.gov
Internet: http://judicial.alabama.gov/supreme.cfm

Number of Judgeships: 9

The Supreme Court consists of a chief justice and eight associate justices who are elected in statewide partisan elections for six-year terms. Vacancies are filled on an interim basis by the Governor. The Supreme Court has general supervisory authority over all courts in the state and the authority to review any judgment of any other court in the state. The Court has exclusive appellate jurisdiction in actions involving title to or possession of land, in civil cases when the amount exceeds $50,000 and in all appeals involving utility rates approved by the Alabama Public Service Commission. The Court may review decisions of the Alabama Court of Criminal Appeals or the Court of Civil Appeals, as well as all decisions involving capital cases.

The Supreme Court sits in Montgomery and may sit in other locations at the discretion of the Court.

Court Staff

Clerk of the Supreme Court **Julia J. Weller** . . . . (334) 229-0700
Fax: (334) 229-0522

Reporter of Decisions **Bilee K. Cauley** . . . . (334) 229-0649
E-mail: bcauley@appellate.state.al.us

State Law Librarian **Timothy A. Lewis** . . . . (334) 229-0560
E-mail: director@alalinc.net

Supreme Court Marshal **Willie James** . . . . (334) 229-0677
E-mail: willie.james@alacourt.gov

Assistant Clerk **Teresa Allen** . . . . (334) 229-0663
E-mail: tallen@appellate.state.al.us Fax: (334) 229-0522

Chambers of Chief Justice Roy Moore

300 Dexter Avenue, Montgomery, AL 36104-3741
Tel: (334) 229-0700

Roy S. Moore
Chief Justice

Date of Birth: 1947
Education: West Point 1969 BS; Alabama JD
Began Service: January 11, 2013
Political Affiliation: Republican

Chambers of Associate Justice Lyn Stuart

300 Dexter Avenue, Montgomery, AL 36104-3741
Tel: (334) 229-0626 Fax: (334) 229-0537
E-mail: lstuart@appellate.state.al.us

Lyn Stuart
Associate Justice

Date of Birth: 1955
Education: Auburn 1977 BA; Alabama 1980 JD
Began Service: January 15, 2001
Appointed By: Governor Fob James, Jr.
Next Election: November 2018
Term Expires: January 15, 2019
Political Affiliation: Republican

Government: Assistant Attorney General, State of Alabama; Special Assistant Attorney General, Alabama Department of Corrections, State of Alabama; Assistant District Attorney, County of Baldwin, Alabama

Judicial: District Judge (1989-1997); Circuit Judge, 28th Judicial Circuit of Alabama (1997-2001)

Staff

Staff Attorney **Lars Longnecker** . . . . (334) 229-0629
E-mail: llongnecker@appellate.state.al.us
Education: BYU 2000; Chicago 2003 JD

Staff Attorney **Renée Michael** . . . . (334) 229-0628
E-mail: rmichael@appellate.state.al.us
Education: Alabama 1985 BS, 1988 MA, 1996 JD

Chambers of Associate Justice Michael F. Bolin

300 Dexter Avenue, Montgomery, AL 36104-3741
Tel: (334) 229-0620 Fax: (334) 229-0514
E-mail: mbolin@appellate.state.al.us

Michael F. Bolin
Associate Justice

Education: Samford 1970 BS; Cumberland 1973 JD
Began Service: January 18, 2005
Next Election: November 2016
Term Expires: January 2017

Judicial: Probate Judge, Jefferson County (1994-2000)

Staff

Executive Assistant **Zelda Stokes** . . . . (334) 229-0620
E-mail: zstokes@appellate.state.al.us

Chambers of Associate Justice Tom Parker

300 Dexter Avenue, Montgomery, AL 36104-3741
Tel: (334) 229-0648 Fax: (334) 229-0518
E-mail: tparker@appellate.state.al.us

Tom Parker
Associate Justice

Education: Dartmouth BA; Vanderbilt JD
Began Service: January 18, 2005
Next Election: November 2016
Term Expires: January 2017

Government: Deputy Administrative Director of Courts, State of Alabama (2001); General Counsel, Alabama Courts System, State of Alabama (2001); Assistant Attorney General, Office of the Attorney General, State of Alabama

Legal Practice: Partner, Parker & Kotouc, P.C.

Staff

Fax: (334) 229-0518

Senior Staff Attorney **Seth Rhodebeck** . . . . (334) 229-0687
E-mail: srhodebeck@appellate.state.al.us

STATE COURTS – ALABAMA

Chambers of Associate Justice Glenn Murdock

300 Dexter Avenue, Montgomery, AL 36104-3741
Tel: (334) 229-0642
E-mail: gmurdock@appellate.state.al.us

Glenn Murdock
Associate Justice

Date of Birth: 1956
Education: Alabama 1978 BA; Virginia 1981 JD
Began Service: 2007
Next Election: November 2018
Political Affiliation: Republican

Clerkships: Law Clerk The Honorable Clarence W. Allgood, United States District Court for the Northern District of Alabama

Corporate: In-House Counsel, Vulcan Materials Company (1986-1992)

Government: Administrative Law Judge, State of Alabama

Judicial: Judge, Alabama Court of Civil Appeals (2001-2007)

Legal Practice: North, Haskell, Slaughter, Young & Lewis (1982-1986); Wallace, Jordan, Ratliff & Brandt (1992-2001)

Current Memberships: American Bar Association; Birmingham Bar Association

Staff

Staff Attorney **Joey Duke** .... (334) 229-0643
E-mail: jduke@appellate.state.al.us
Staff Attorney **Greg Jones** .... (334) 229-0645
E-mail: gjones@appellate.state.al.us
Staff Attorney **Jim Richey** .... (334) 229-0644
E-mail: jrichey@appellate.state.al.us
Executive Assistant **Ann Owens** .... (334) 229-0642
E-mail: aowens@appellate.state.al.us

Chambers of Associate Justice Greg Shaw

300 Dexter Avenue, Montgomery, AL 36104-3741
Tel: (334) 229-0771 Fax: (334) 229-0525
E-mail: gshaw@appellate.state.al.us

Greg Shaw
Associate Justice

Date of Birth: 1957
Education: Auburn 1979 BS; Cumberland 1982 JD; Virginia 2004 LLM
Began Service: January 2009
Next Election: November 4, 2020
Election Type: General Election
Term Expires: January 2021
Political Affiliation: Republican

Staff

Senior Staff Attorney **Barney A. Butler** .... (334) 229-0773
E-mail: bbutler@appellate.state.al.us
Education: Southern Mississippi 1998 BA; Alabama 2001 JD
Staff Attorney **Jennifer Barber** .... (334) 229-0773
E-mail: jbarber@appellate.state.al.us
Education: Cumberland 2000 JD

STATE COURTS—ALABAMA

Chambers of Associate Justice Alisa Kelli Wise

300 Dexter Avenue, Montgomery, AL 36104-3741
Tel: (334) 229-0777 Fax: (334) 229-0522

Alisa Kelli Wise
Associate Justice

Date of Birth: 1962
Education: Auburn 1985 BS; Jones Law 1994 JD; Auburn 2000 MPA
Began Service: January 17, 2011
Political Affiliation: Republican

Current Memberships: Alabama State Bar; Montgomery County Bar Association

Staff

Staff Attorney **Denice M. Burleson** .... (334) 229-0777
E-mail: dburleson@appellate.state.al.us
Education: Samford 1991 BS; Cumberland 1994 JD
Staff Attorney **Tammy Coughlin** .... (334) 229-0777
E-mail: tcoughlin@appellate.state.al.us
Education: Alabama 1994 BA, 1997 JD
Judicial Assistant **Carolyn Wright** .... (334) 229-0777
E-mail: cwright@appellate.state.al.us

Chambers of Associate Justice James Allen Main

300 Dexter Avenue, Montgomery, AL 36104-3741
Tel: (334) 229-0614 Fax: (334) 229-0522
E-mail: jmain@appellate.state.al.us

James Allen Main
Associate Justice

Education: Auburn BSPh; Alabama JD
Began Service: 2011
Appointed By: Governor Robert R. Riley
Next Election: November 2018

Current Memberships: Alabama State Bar

Staff

Staff Attorney **Chris Howell** .... (334) 229-0765
Staff Attorney **Linda S. Webb** .... (334) 229-0614
E-mail: lwebb@appellate.state.al.us
Education: Northeast Louisiana 1971 BA; Jones Law 1988 JD
Judicial Assistant **Donna Newman** .... (334) 229-0614
E-mail: dnewman@appellate.state.al.us

Chambers of Associate Justice Tommy Bryan

300 Dexter Avenue, Montgomery, AL 36104-3741
Tel: (334) 229-0717

Tommy Elias Bryan
Associate Justice

Date of Birth: May 16, 1956
Education: Troy State BS, MSEd; Jones Law 1983 JD
Began Service: 2013

Current Memberships: Alabama State Bar; Montgomery County Bar Association

Staff

Law Clerk **Jessica Shaver** .... (334) 229-0715
Staff Attorney **Jeremy Veal** .... (334) 229-0714
E-mail: jeremy.veal@alacourt.gov
Education: Alabama JD
Staff Attorney **Megan Rhodebeck** .... (334) 229-0716
Education: Regent U JD
Senior Staff Attorney **Amberly Page** .... (334) 229-0715
E-mail: apage@appellate.state.al.us

Alabama Court of Civil Appeals

300 Dexter Avenue, Montgomery, AL 36104-3741
Tel: (334) 229-0733 Fax: (334) 229-0530
Internet: http://judicial.alabama.gov/civil.cfm

Number of Judgeships: 5

The Court of Civil Appeals, created by the Alabama State Legislature in 1969, consists of a presiding judge and four judges who are elected in statewide partisan elections for six-year terms. The presiding judge is selected based on seniority, and vacancies are filled on an interim basis by the Governor. The Court of Civil Appeals is a court of intermediate appeals in Alabama. The Court has exclusive appellate jurisdiction in all civil cases when the amount in controversy does not exceed $50,000 and also has exclusive appellate jurisdiction in domestic relations cases, workers' compensation cases and all administrative cases (excluding those involving the Alabama Public Service Commission).

The Court of Civil Appeals sits in Montgomery and in other locations at the discretion of the Court.

Court Staff

Clerk of Court **Rebecca C. Oates** .... (334) 229-0733
E-mail: roates@appellate.state.al.us

Chambers of Presiding Judge William C. Thompson

300 Dexter Avenue, Montgomery, AL 36104-3741
Tel: (334) 229-0702 Fax: (334) 229-0536
E-mail: wthompson@appellate.state.al.us

William C. Thompson
Presiding Judge

Date of Birth: 1962
Education: Alabama 1984 BA; Cumberland 1988 JD
Began Service: January 20, 1997
Next Election: November 2020
Election Type: General Election
Term Expires: December 2020
Political Affiliation: Republican

Corporate: Corporate Insurance

Government: Assistant Legal Advisor, Governor Guy Hunt (R-AL), State of Alabama (1992-1993)

Legal Practice: Perry O. Hooper, Sr. & Associates (1993-1994)

Current Memberships: Alabama State Bar; American Bar Association; Montgomery County Bar Association

Staff

Staff Attorney **Morgan Booker** .... (334) 229-0706
Staff Attorney **Shelton Foss** .... (334) 229-0705
E-mail: sfoss@appellate.state.al.us
Senior Staff Attorney **Christine Brannon Nickson** ...... (334) 229-0703
E-mail: cnickson@appellate.state.al.us
Education: Alabama 1991 BS, 1995 JD
Reporter of Decisions **Bilee K. Cauley** .... (334) 229-0649
E-mail: bcauley@appellate.state.al.us
Judicial Assistant **Barbara B. Fischer** .... (334) 229-0702
E-mail: bfischer@appellate.state.al.us
Education: Alabama BA

Chambers of Judge Craig Sorrell Pittman

300 Dexter Avenue, Montgomery, AL 36104-3741
Tel: (334) 229-0709 Fax: (334) 229-0531
E-mail: cpittman@appellate.state.al.us

Craig Sorrell Pittman
Judge

Date of Birth: 1956
Education: Middlebury 1978 BA; Cumberland 1981 JD
Began Service: January 15, 2001
Next Election: November 2018
Term Expires: January 2019
Political Affiliation: Republican

Clerkships: Law Clerk The Honorable T. Virgil Pittman, United States District Court for the Southern District of Alabama (1981-1983)

Government: Deputy Attorney General, State of Alabama; General Counsel, State Docks, Alabama State Port Authority, State of Alabama

Legal Practice: Hamilton, Butler, Riddick, Tarlton and Sullivan (1983-1986); Partner, Pittman, Pittman, Carwie, & Fuquay (1986-2001)

Current Memberships: Alabama State Bar; The Florida Bar; Maritime Law Association of the United States; Mobile Bar Association; Southeastern Admiralty Law Institute

Staff

Staff Attorney **Stuart Wallace** .... (334) 229-0711
E-mail: swallace@appellate.state.al.us
Senior Staff Attorney **Wayne Simms** .... (334) 229-0710
E-mail: WSimms@appellate.state.al.us
Education: Duke 1992 JD
Executive Assistant **Trena Bailey** .... (334) 229-0709
E-mail: tbailey@appellate.state.al.us

Chambers of Judge Terri Willingham Thomas

300 Dexter Avenue, Montgomery, AL 36104-3741
Tel: (334) 229-0719
E-mail: tthomas@appellate.state.al.us

Terri Willingham Thomas
Judge

Education: Cumberland JD; Athens State; Wallace State
Began Service: 2006
Next Election: November 2018

Judicial: District and Juvenile Court Judge, Cullman County, Alabama

Profession: Private Practice

Membership: President, Alabama Juvenile and Family Courts Judges Association (2004-2005)

Staff

Judicial Assistant **(Vacant)** .... (334) 229-0719

Chambers of Judge Terry A. Moore

300 Dexter Avenue, Montgomery, AL 36104-3741
Tel: (334) 229-0724
E-mail: tmoore@appellate.state.al.us

Terry A. Moore
Judge

Education: South Alabama 1990; Alabama 1993 JD
Began Service: 2007
Next Election: November 2018

Legal Practice: Attorney, Adams and Reese LLP (1993-1998); Partner, Vickers, Riis, Murray & Curran, LLC (1998-2004); Co-Founder, Partner, Austill, Lewis, Pipkin & Moore, P.C. (2004-2006)

(continued on next page)

Chambers of Judge Terry A. Moore *continued*

Staff

Staff Attorney **Amanda Cox** .... (334) 229-0725
E-mail: acox@appellate.state.al.us
Staff Attorney **Julia Hatley** .... (334) 229-0726
E-mail: jhatley@appellate.state.al.us
Education: Tulane 2002 AB; Alabama 2005 JD

Chambers of Judge Scott Donaldson

300 Dexter Avenue, Montgomery, AL 36104-3741
Tel: (334) 229-0746

Scott Donaldson
Judge

Education: Alabama 1981 BS; Cumberland 1984 JD
Next Election: November 2020
Term Expires: November 2020

Staff

Staff Attorney **Nathan Wilson** .... (334) 229-0748
Staff Attorney **Michael Higgins** .... (334) 229-0747
E-mail: michael.higgins@alacourt.gov
Staff Attorney **Carl Chang** .... (334) 229-0733
Executive Assistant **(Vacant)** .... (334) 229-0733

Alabama Court of Criminal Appeals

300 Dexter Avenue, Montgomery, AL 36104-3741
Tel: (334) 229-0751 Fax: (334) 229-0521
Internet: http://judicial.alabama.gov/criminal.cfm

Number of Judgeships: 5

The Court of Criminal Appeals is a five-judge court consisting of a presiding judge and four judges who are elected in statewide partisan elections for six-year terms. The presiding judge is elected by peer vote. Vacancies on the Court are temporarily filled by gubernatorial appointment. The Court of Criminal Appeals is a court of intermediate appeals in Alabama. The Court has exclusive appellate jurisdiction over all misdemeanors, including violations of municipal ordinances, all felonies, and all post conviction writs in criminal cases.

The Court sits in Montgomery.

Court Staff

Clerk of Court **D. Scott Mitchell** .... (334) 229-0751
Central Staff Attorney **Carol Surratt** .... (334) 229-0787
E-mail: csurratt@appellate.state.al.us
Education: Alabama JD
Building Manager **Marshal Willie James** .... (334) 229-0677
Fax: (334) 242-4017
Public Information Officer **(Vacant)** .... (334) 954-5147

Chambers of Presiding Judge Mary Windom

300 Dexter Avenue, Montgomery, AL 36104-3741
Tel: (334) 229-0796 Fax: (334) 229-0546
E-mail: mwindom@appellate.state.al.us

Mary Becker Windom
Presiding Judge

Date of Birth: September 7, 1959
Education: Baldwin County High (Bay Minette, Alabama) 1977; South Alabama 1982 BS; Faulkner 1999 JD
Began Service: January 2009
Next Election: November 2020
Election Type: General Election
Term Expires: December 31, 2020

Current Memberships: Mobile Bar Association

Chambers of Presiding Judge Mary Windom *continued*

Staff

Staff Attorney **Mary-Coleman Mayberry Butler** .... (334) 229-0795
E-mail: mbutler@appellate.state.al.us
Education: Auburn 2004 BA; Faulkner 2007 JD
Staff Attorney **Robert Pitman** .... (334) 229-0796
E-mail: rpitman@appellate.state.al.us
Staff Attorney **Courtney Hall** .... (334) 229-0794
Staff Attorney **Jasper Beroujon Roberts, Jr.** .... (334) 229-0793
E-mail: jroberts@appellate.state.al.us
Education: Auburn; Cumberland JD

Chambers of Judge Sam Henry Welch

300 Dexter Avenue, Montgomery, AL 36104-3741
P.O. Box 301555, Montgomery, AL 36130-1555
Tel: (334) 229-0786 Fax: (334) 229-0527
E-mail: swelch@appellate.state.al.us

COL Samuel Henry Welch
Judge

Date of Birth: 1950
Education: Birmingham-Southern 1972 BA; Alabama 1976 JD
Began Service: January 2007
Term Expires: January 2019
Military: USA (Ret)

Current Memberships: The American Legion; The American Legion; First Baptist Church of Monroeville; Omicron Delta Kappa, The National Leadership Honor Society; Veterans of Foreign Wars of the U.S.

Staff

Staff Attorney **Melissa G. Fiore** .... (334) 229-0774
E-mail: mfiore@appellate.state.al.us
Education: Southern Illinois 1979 BA, 1986 JD
Staff Attorney **(Vacant)** .... (334) 229-0769
Senior Staff Attorney **Ethel Ann Holladay** .... (334) 229-0783
E-mail: eholladay@appellate.state.al.us
Education: Sweet Briar 1983 BA; Cumberland 1988 JD
Judicial Assistant **Kelly Kirk** .... (334) 229-0786
E-mail: kkirk@appellate.state.al.us
Education: Alabama 1999 BA, 2002 JD

Chambers of Judge J. Elizabeth Kellum

300 Dexter Avenue, Montgomery, AL 36104-3741
Tel: (334) 229-0770 Fax: (334) 229-0524

J. Elizabeth "Beth" Kellum
Judge

Education: Alabama 1981 BA, 1984 JD
Began Service: January 2009
Next Election: November 2020
Election Type: General Election
Term Expires: December 2020
Political Affiliation: Republican

Current Memberships: The Federalist Society for Law and Public Policy Studies; Landmarks Foundation; Montgomery County Republican Executive Committee

Staff

Staff Attorney **Kasandra Derry** .... (334) 229-0770
Education: Vanderbilt 1994 BA; Florida State 1998 JD
Staff Attorney **Ashley White** .... (334) 229-0770
E-mail: ashley.white@alacourt.gov
Judicial Assistant **Sandy Huovinen** .... (334) 229-0770
Law Clerk **Tommy Gleason** .... (334) 229-0770

Chambers of Judge Liles C. Burke

300 Dexter Avenue, Montgomery, AL 36104-3741
Tel: (334) 229-0762
E-mail: lburke@appellate.state.al.us

Liles C. Burke
Judge

Education: Alabama 1991, 1994 JD
Began Service: 2011
Term Expires: January 2019

Staff

Staff Attorney **Eric Brown** .... (334) 229-0762
E-mail: ebrown@appellate.state.al.us
Staff Attorney **Stephanie Shirley** .... (334) 229-0762
Staff Attorney **Anne McVay Pearson** .... (334) 229-0762
E-mail: apearson@appellate.state.al.us
Education: Vanderbilt 1982 BA; Alabama 1985 JD
Staff Attorney **Beau Womack** .... (334) 229-0762
E-mail: bwomack@appellate.state.al.us
Education: Faulkner 2009 JD

Chambers of Judge J. Michael Joiner

300 Dexter Avenue, Montgomery, AL 36104-3741
Tel: (334) 229-0630

J. Michael Joiner
Judge

Education: Samford 1979 BA; Cumberland 1982 JD
Began Service: 2011
Term Expires: January 2019

Staff

Staff Attorney **Cody Colson** .... (334) 229-0765
Staff Attorney **Stephen Frisby** .... (334) 229-0639
E-mail: sfrisby@appellate.state.al.us
Education: Faulkner 2009 JD
Staff Attorney **Charles Mauney** .... (334) 229-0633
E-mail: cmauney@appellate.state.al.us
Staff Attorney **Aly George** .... (334) 229-0636

Alaska

Office of the Administrative Director of the Alaska Court System

Boney Memorial Courthouse, 303 K Street, Anchorage, AK 99501-2099
Tel: (907) 264-0547 Tel: (907) 264-0585 (Law Library Reference Desk)
Tel: (907) 264-8242 (Personnel Information) Fax: (907) 264-0881

Staff

Administrative Director **Christine E. Johnson** .... (907) 264-0547
E-mail: cjohnson@akcourts.us

Deputy Director **Doug Wooliver** .... (907) 264-8265
820 W. 4th Ave., Anchorage, AK 99501 Tel: (907) 463-4750 (Juneau)
E-mail: dwooliver@akcourts.us Fax: (907) 264-8291

General Counsel **Nancy Meade** .... (907) 264-8264
820 W. 4th Ave, Anchorage, AK 99501 Tel: (907) 463-4736 (Juneau)
E-mail: nmeade@akcourts.us Fax: (907) 264-8291

Human Resource Director **Lee Powelson** .... (907) 264-8248
820 W. 4th Ave., Anchorage, AK 99501 Fax: (907) 264-8262
E-mail: lpowelson@akcourts.us

Facilities Manager **Jack Bailey** .... (907) 264-8282
820 W. 4th Ave., Anchorage, AK 99501 Fax: (907) 264-8291
E-mail: jbailey@akcourts.us

Fiscal Manager **Rhonda McLeod** .... (907) 264-8215
820 W. 4th Ave., Anchorage, AK 99501 Fax: (907) 264-8292
E-mail: rmcleod@akcourts.us

Special Projects Manager **Susan Miller** .... (907) 264-8229
820 W. 4th Ave., Anchorage, AK 99501 Fax: (907) 264-8291
E-mail: smiller@akcourts.us

Technical Operations Manager **Joe Mannion** .... (907) 264-8207
820 W. 4th Ave., Anchorage, AK 99501 Fax: (907) 264-8285
E-mail: jmannion@akcourts.us

Judicial Education Coordinator **Aesha Pallesen** .... (907) 264-0785
820 W. 4th Ave., Anchorage, AK 99501 Fax: (907) 264-8291
E-mail: apallesen@akcourts.us
Education: Michigan 2008 JD

Therapeutic Courts Coordinator **Michelle Bartley** .... (907) 264-8250
820 W. 4th Ave., Anchorage, AK 99501 Fax: (907) 264-8291
E-mail: mbartley@akcourts.us

State Law Librarian **Susan M. Falk** .... (907) 264-0583
E-mail: sfalk@akcourts.us
Education: Boalt Hall JD

Technical Services Librarian **(Vacant)** .... (907) 264-0587
Fax: (907) 264-0733

Administrative Assistant **Lesa Robertson** .... (907) 264-0548
E-mail: lrobertson@akcourts.us

Alaska Supreme Court

Boney Memorial Courthouse, 303 K Street, Anchorage, AK 99501-2084
Tel: (907) 264-0612 Fax: (907) 264-0878
E-mail: supreme_court@appellate.courts.state.ak.us
Internet: http://courts.alaska.gov

Number of Judgeships: 5

The Supreme Court consists of a chief justice and four justices who are appointed by the Governor from nominees of the Alaska Judicial Council and are subject to a retention vote for a ten-year term on a nonpartisan ballot in the first general election held more than three years after the appointment. The chief justice is elected by a peer vote to serve a non-consecutive three-year term. The Supreme Court has final appellate jurisdiction in civil and criminal cases. The Court hears appeals of final judgments entered by the Alaska Superior Court in any civil action. The Court may review decisions of the Alaska Court of Appeals involving criminal cases. The Court has administrative authority over all courts and the practice of law in the state.

The Court sits monthly in Anchorage, periodically in Fairbanks and Juneau, and elsewhere as needed.

Alaska Supreme Court *continued*

Court Staff

Clerk of the Appellate Courts **Marilyn May** .... (907) 264-0608
E-mail: mmay@akcourts.us
Education: Northern Iowa 1975 BA, 1977 MA; Minnesota 1984 JD

Chief Deputy Clerk **Meredith Montgomery** .... (907) 264-0609
E-mail: mmontgomery@akcourts.us

Administrative Assistant **Cheryl Jones** .... (907) 264-0608
E-mail: cajones@akcourts.us

Deputy Clerk **Brandi Alexander** .... (907) 264-0857
E-mail: balexander@akcourts.us

Deputy Clerk **Jolene Hotho** .... (907) 264-0631
E-mail: jhotho@akcourts.us

Deputy Clerk **Mindi Johnson** .... (907) 264-0748
E-mail: mjohnson@akcourts.us

Deputy Clerk **Sara Quinones** .... (907) 264-0612
E-mail: squinones@akcourts.us

Deputy Clerk **Kasey Murphy** .... (907) 264-0611
E-mail: kmurphy@akcourts.us

Deputy Clerk **Beth Pechota** .... (907) 264-0630
E-mail: bpechota@akcourts.us

Chambers of Chief Justice Craig F. Stowers

303 K Street, Anchorage, AK 99501-2099
Tel: (907) 264-0624
E-mail: cstowers@akcourts.us

Craig F. Stowers
Chief Justice

Date of Birth: 1954
Education: Blackburn 1975 BA; UC Davis 1985 JD
Began Service: December 2009
Appointed By: Governor Sean Parnell

Chambers of Justice Dana Fabe

303 K Street, Anchorage, AK 99501-2084
Tel: (907) 264-0622 Fax: (907) 264-0554
E-mail: dfabe@akcourts.us

Dana Fabe
Justice

Note: Justice Fabe will retire effective June 2016.
Date of Birth: 1951
Education: Cornell 1973 BA; Northeastern 1976 JD
Began Service: 1996

Current Memberships: Alaska Bar Association

Staff

Law Clerk **Lauren Bateman** .... (907) 264-0622
Began Service: September 2015
Term Expires: September 1, 2016

Law Clerk **Whitney Leonard** .... (907) 264-0622
Began Service: September 2015
Term Expires: September 1, 2016

Law Clerk **Charmayne Palomba** .... (907) 264-0622
Began Service: September 2015
Term Expires: September 1, 2016

Administrative Assistant **Denise Anthony** .... (907) 264-0622
E-mail: danthony@akcourts.us

Chambers of Justice Daniel E. Winfree

303 K Street, Anchorage, AK 99501-2099
Tel: (907) 452-9301
E-mail: dwinfree@akcourts.us

Daniel E. Winfree
Justice

Education: Oregon 1977 BS; UCLA 1981 MBA, 1981 JD
Began Service: January 2008
Appointed By: Governor Sarah Palin

Academic: Adjunct Faculty Member, Prince William Sound Community College; Adjunct Faculty Member, University of Alaska Tanana Valley Campus

Legal Practice: Attorney, Perkins Coie LLP (1982-1985); Partner, Winfree and Hompesch (1990-1996); Owner, Winfree Law Office

Nonprofit: General Counsel, Greater Fairbanks Community Hospital Foundation, City of Fairbanks, Alaska

Current Memberships: Alaska Academy of Trial Lawyers; Alaska Bar Association; American Bar Association

Profession: Private Practice (1985-1990)

Membership: Member, Greater Fairbanks Chamber of Commerce, City of Fairbanks, Alaska (1987-2006); Member, College of Fellows, University of Alaska Fairbanks (1992-1996); Member, Board of Governors, Alaska Bar Association; Secretary, Board of Governors, Alaska Bar Association; President, Board of Governors, Alaska Bar Association; Member, Western States Bar Conference; President, Western States Bar Conference

Staff
Law Clerk **Yvonne Chi** .... (907) 452-9301
Began Service: September 2015
Term Expires: September 2016
Law Clerk **Sonja Kawasaki** .... (907) 452-9301
Began Service: September 2015
Term Expires: September 2016
E-mail: kparker@akcourts.us
Law Clerk **Julian Marrs** .... (907) 452-9301
Began Service: September 2015
Term Expires: September 2016
Judicial Assistant **Peggy McCoy** .... (907) 452-9301
E-mail: pmccoy@akcourts.us

Chambers of Justice Peter J. Maassen

303 K Street, Anchorage, AK 99501-2084
Tel: (907) 264-0612
E-mail: pmaassen@akcourts.us

Peter J. Maassen
Justice

Education: Hope 1977 BA; Michigan 1980 JD
Began Service: 2012

Staff
Law Clerk **Shane Kanady** .... (907) 264-0618
Law Clerk **Emma Lawton** .... (907) 264-0618
Law Clerk **Joshua Schneider** .... (907) 264-0618
Judicial Assistant **Chris Gilmore** .... (907) 264-0618
E-mail: cgilmore@akcourts.us

Chambers of Justice Joel Bolger

303 K Street, Anchorage, AK 99501-2084
Tel: (907) 264-0612
E-mail: jbolger@akcourts.us

Joel H. Bolger
Justice

Education: Iowa 1976, 1978 JD
Began Service: April 26, 2013
Appointed By: Governor Sean Parnell

Staff
Law Clerk **Marta Darby** .... (907) 264-0751
Term Expires: September 2016
Law Clerk **Shay Elbaum** .... (907) 264-0751
Term Expires: September 1, 2016
Law Clerk **Alexandra Zabierek** .... (907) 264-0751
Term Expires: September 1, 2016

Alaska Court of Appeals

Boney Memorial Courthouse, 303 K Street, Anchorage, AK 99501-2084
Tel: (907) 264-0612 Fax: (907) 264-0878
Internet: http://courts.alaska.gov/appcts.htm

Number of Judgeships: 3

The Court of Appeals, created by the Alaska State Legislature in 1980, consists of a chief judge and two judges. The chief judge serves a consecutive two-year term and is appointed by the chief justice of the Alaska Supreme Court. The judges are appointed by the Governor from nominees submitted by the Alaska Judicial Council and are subject to a retention vote for an eight-year term in the first general election held more than three years after the appointment. The Court of Appeals has appellate jurisdiction in actions and proceedings commenced in the Alaska Superior Court, including appeals from judgments in criminal cases, juvenile delinquency cases, habeas corpus matters and cases involving probation and parole decisions. The Court also has jurisdiction to review sentences imposed by either the Alaska Superior Court or District Court and discretionary review of District Court appeals to the Alaska Superior Court.

The Court sits in Anchorage.

Court Staff
Clerk of the Appellate Courts **Marilyn May** .... (907) 264-0608
E-mail: mmay@akcourts.us
Chief Deputy Clerk **Meredith Montgomery** .... (907) 264-0609
E-mail: badams@akcourts.us
Administrative Assistant **Cheryl Jones** .... (907) 264-0608
E-mail: cjones@akcourts.us
Deputy Clerk **Brandi Alexander** .... (907) 264-0857
E-mail: balexander@akcourts.us
Deputy Clerk **Jolene Hotho** .... (907) 264-0631
E-mail: jhotho@akcourts.us
Deputy Clerk **Mindi Johnson** .... (907) 264-0748
E-mail: mjohnson@akcourts.us
Deputy Clerk **Sara Quinones** .... (907) 264-0612
E-mail: squinones@akcourts.us
Deputy Clerk **Kasey Murphy** .... (907) 264-0611
E-mail: kmurphy@akcourts.us
Deputy Clerk **Beth Pechota** .... (907) 264-0630
E-mail: bpechota@akcourts.us
Central Staff Attorney **Dan Collins** .... (907) 264-0612
E-mail: dcollins@akcourts.us
Central Staff Attorney **Rachel Plumlee** .... (907) 264-0612
E-mail: rplumlee@akcourts.us
Education: Lewis & Clark 2000 JD
Central Staff Attorney **Alyson Pytte** .... (907) 264-0612
E-mail: apytte@akcourts.us

Chambers of Chief Judge David Mannheimer

Boney Memorial Courthouse, 303 K Street, Room 432,
Anchorage, AK 99501-2084
Tel: (907) 264-0754 Fax: (907) 264-0878
E-mail: dmannheimer@appellate.courts.state.ak.us

David Mannheimer
Chief Judge

Date of Birth: 1949
Education: Stanford 1970; Boalt Hall 1974
Began Service: November 29, 1990
Appointed By: Governor Steve Cowper
Next Election: November 2018

Staff

Law Clerk **Kate Bargerhoff** .... (907) 264-0754
Began Service: September 1, 2015
Term Expires: September 2016
E-mail: kbargerhoff@appellate.courts.state.ak.us

Law Clerk **WIlliam Monks** .... (907) 264-0754
Began Service: September 7, 2015
Term Expires: September 2016
E-mail: wmonks@appellate.courts.state.ak.us

Judicial Assistant **Michele Lucas** .... (907) 264-0754

Chambers of Judge Marjorie Allard

303 K Street, Anchorage, AK 99501-2084
Tel: (907) 264-0757
E-mail: mallard@akcourts.us

Marjorie Allard
Judge

Education: Yale, JD

Chambers of Judge Douglas Kossler

303 K Street, Anchorage, AK 99501-2099
Tel: (907) 264-0751
E-mail: dkossler@akcourts.us

Douglas H. Kossler
Judge

Education: William & Mary BBA; Temple JD
Began Service: 2013

Staff

Deputy Clerk **Ryan Montgomery-Sythe** .... (907) 264-0611
E-mail: rjmontgomery@akcourts.us

STATE COURTS – ALASKA

Arizona

Office of the Administrative Director of Arizona Courts

Arizona State Courts Building, 1501 West Washington Street, Phoenix, AZ 85007
Tel: (602) 452-3301 Fax: (602) 452-3484

Staff

Administrative Director **David K. Byers** . . . . (602) 452-3301
E-mail: dbyers@courts.az.gov
Deputy Director **Mike Baumstark** . . . . (602) 452-3301
E-mail: mbaumstark@courts.az.gov
Administrative Services Division Director **Kevin Kluge** . . . (602) 452-3715
Fax: (602) 452-3480
Adult Services Division Director **Kathy Waters** . . . . (602) 452-3461
E-mail: kwaters@courts.az.gov Fax: (602) 452-3673
Certification & Licensing Division Director **Mark Wilson** . . . . (602) 452-3378
E-mail: mwilson@courts.az.gov Fax: (602) 452-3958
Commission on Judicial Conduct Executive Director **George A. Riemer** . . . . (602) 452-3200
E-mail: griemer@courts.az.gov Fax: (602) 452-3201
Court Services Division Director **Marcus Reinkensmeyer** . . . . (602) 452-3358
E-mail: mreinkensmeyer@courts.az.gov Fax: (602) 452-3659
Dependent Children's Services Division Director **Caroline Lautt-Owens** . . . . (602) 452-3408
E-mail: clowens@courts.az.gov Fax: (602) 452-3478
Juvenile Justice Services Division Director **Joe Kelroy** . . . (602) 452-3450
Fax: (602) 452-3879
Information Technology Division Director **Karl Heckart** . . . . (602) 452-3347
E-mail: kheckart@courts.az.gov Fax: (602) 452-3480
CASA Program Manager **(Vacant)** . . . . (602) 452-3683
Financial Services Officer **Melba Davidson** . . . . (602) 452-3714
E-mail: mdavidson@courts.az.gov Fax: (602) 452-3735
Human Resources Officer **Kim Cantoni** . . . . (602) 452-3311
E-mail: kcantoni@courts.az.gov Fax: (602) 452-3652
Legislative Officer **Jerry Landau** . . . . (602) 452-3361
E-mail: jlandau@courts.az.gov
Public Information Officer **Heather Murphy** . . . . (602) 452-3656
Information Technology **Karl Heckart** . . . . (602) 452-3347
E-mail: kheckart@courts.az.gov Fax: (602) 452-3480
Juvenile Automation **Pam Peet** . . . . (602) 452-3646
E-mail: ppeet@courts.az.gov
Appointments & Committees **Blanca Moreno** . . . . (602) 452-3311
Fax: (602) 452-3652
Attorney Admissions **Carole Mitchell** . . . . (602) 452-3378
E-mail: eholliday@courts.az.gov Fax: (602) 452-3958
Budget **Kevin Kluge** . . . . (602) 452-3715
E-mail: kkluge@courts.az.gov
Confidential Intermediary Program & Parent Assistant **(Vacant)** . . . . (602) 452-3378
Fax: (602) 452-3758
Manager of Compliance **Anne Hunter** . . . . (602) 452-3378
Fax: (602) 452-3958
Facilities Management **Dave Summers** . . . . (602) 452-3476
E-mail: dsummers@courts.az.gov Fax: (602) 452-3139
Foster Care Review Board **Caroline Lautt-Owens** . . . . (602) 452-3402
E-mail: clowens@courts.az.gov Fax: (602) 452-3478
Legal Services **David Withey** . . . . (602) 452-3323
E-mail: dwithey@courts.az.gov
Private Fiduciary Program **(Vacant)** . . . . (602) 452-3378
Fax: (602) 452-3958
Program Manager **Julee Bruno** . . . . (602) 452-3060
E-mail: jbruno@courts.az.gov Fax: (602) 452-3004
Research & Statistics **(Vacant)** . . . . (602) 452-3358
Fax: (602) 452-3659

Supreme Court of Arizona

Arizona State Courts Building, 1501 West Washington Street, Phoenix, AZ 85007
Tel: (602) 452-3300
Internet: http://www.azcourts.gov

Number of Judgeships: 5

The Supreme Court of Arizona consists of a chief justice and four justices who are appointed by the Governor for initial two-year terms. Subsequent terms of six years are by retention vote in the first general election after two years. The chief justice is elected by peer vote to a five-year term. Retirement is mandatory at age seventy; however, the chief justice may assign retired justices as needed. The Supreme Court has final appellate jurisdiction over all other courts in the state (except in some actions arising in Justice and Municipal Courts) and exclusive appellate jurisdiction in cases involving the death penalty. The Court has discretionary review of decisions made by the Arizona Court of Appeals, and has exclusive jurisdiction in cases between counties.

The Supreme Court of Arizona sits in Phoenix.

Court Staff

Clerk of the Court **Janet Johnson** . . . . (602) 452-3396
Deputy Clerk - Supervisor **Sarah Jones** . . . . (602) 452-3396
Chief Communications Officer **Heather Murphy** . . . . (602) 452-3656
E-mail: hmurphy@courts.az.gov
Director of Security **Danny Cardova** . . . . (602) 452-3170
Educational Services Division Director **Jeff Schrade** . . . . (602) 452-3060
E-mail: jschrade@courts.az.gov

Chambers of Chief Justice W. Scott Bales

1501 West Washington Street, Phoenix, AZ 85007
Tel: (602) 452-3534

W. Scott Bales
Chief Justice

Education: Michigan State 1978 BA; Harvard 1980 MA, 1983 JD
Began Service: September 16, 2005
Next Election: November 2020
Election Type: Retention Election
Term Expires: December 2020

Current Memberships: The American Law Institute

Chambers of Justice John Pelander

1501 West Washington Street, Phoenix, AZ 85007
Tel: (602) 452-3300

A. John Pelander
Justice

Date of Birth: 1951
Education: Wittenberg 1973 BA; Arizona 1976 JD; Virginia 1998 LLM
Began Service: September 5, 2009
Next Election: 2018
Election Type: Retention Election
Political Affiliation: Republican

Current Memberships: American Bar Association; American Board of Trial Advocates; Pima County Bar Association; State Bar of Arizona

Chambers of Justice Robert Brutinel
1501 West Washington Street, Phoenix, AZ 85007
Tel: (602) 452-3396
E-mail: rbrutinel@courts.az.gov

Robert M. Brutinel
Justice

Education: Arizona State 1979; Arizona 1982 JD
Began Service: January 10, 2011
Appointed By: Governor Jan Brewer
Next Election: November 2020
Term Expires: December 2020

Chambers of Justice Ann Scott Timmer
1501 West Washington Street, Phoenix, AZ 85007
Tel: (602) 452-3300
E-mail: atimmer@courts.az.gov

Ann Scott Timmer
Justice

Date of Birth: 1960
Education: Arizona State 1985 JD
Began Service: 2012
Appointed By: Governor Jan Brewer
Next Election: 2016
Election Type: Retention Election
Political Affiliation: Republican

Current Memberships: The Lorna E. Lockwood American Inn of Court, The American Inns of Court; Arizona Judges Association; Arizona Women Lawyers Association

Staff
Law Clerk **Hannah Russell** . . . . (602) 452-3532
Began Service: August 2015
Term Expires: August 2016
E-mail: hrussell@courts.az.gov
Law Clerk **Maria Hubbard** . . . . (602) 452-3532
Began Service: August 2015
Term Expires: August 2016
E-mail: mhubbard@courts.az.gov
Judicial Assistant **Linda Schneider** . . . . (602) 452-3532
E-mail: lschneider@courts.az.gov

Arizona Court of Appeals
The Arizona Court of Appeals hears and decides cases in three-judge panels. Judges are appointed by the Governor for initial two-year terms and are then subject to retention votes every six years. The chief judge and vice chief judge of each of the two divisions are elected annually by peer vote. Retirement is mandatory at age seventy; however, the Chief Justice of the Arizona Supreme Court may assign retired judges to serve as needed, usually for a period of six months. The Court of Appeals exercises appellate jurisdiction over cases appealed from the Arizona Superior Court, except those cases involving the death penalty, which must be appealed directly to the Arizona Supreme Court. In addition, the Arizona Court of Appeals, Division One has statewide responsibility to review decisions of the Industrial Commission, unemployment compensation appeals from the Arizona Department of Economic Security, and the Arizona Tax Court.

The Court of Appeals sits primarily in Phoenix and Tucson.

Arizona Court of Appeals, Division One
Arizona State Courts Building, 1501 West Washington Street, Phoenix, AZ 85007
Tel: (602) 542-4821 Fax: (602) 542-4833
Internet: www.azcourts.gov

Number of Judgeships: 16

Areas Covered: Counties of Apache, Coconino, La Paz, Maricopa, Mohave, Navajo, Yavapai and Yuma

Court Staff
Clerk of the Court **Ruth A. Willingham** . . . . (602) 542-4821
E-mail: rwillingham@appeals.az.gov
Chief Staff Attorney **Barbara Vidal-Vaught** . . . . (602) 542-4824
Fax: (602) 542-7801
Vice Chief Staff Attorney **Anthony "Tony" Mackey** . . . . . (602) 542-4824
E-mail: tmackey@appeals.az.gov Fax: (602) 542-7801
Staff Attorney **Benjamin Armstrong** . . . . (602) 542-4824
E-mail: barmstrong@appeals.az.gov Fax: (602) 542-7801
Staff Attorney **Erica Bianchi-Jones** . . . . (602) 542-4824
Fax: (602) 542-7801
Staff Attorney **Melina Brill** . . . . (602) 542-4824
E-mail: mbrill@appeals.az.gov Fax: (602) 542-7801
Staff Attorney **Geoffrey Butzine** . . . . (602) 542-4824
E-mail: gbutzine@appeals.az.gov Fax: (602) 542-7801
Staff Attorney **Cynthia Coates** . . . . (602) 542-4824
E-mail: ccoates@appeals.az.gov Fax: (602) 542-7801
Education: Mount Holyoke 1973 BA; Arizona 1992 JD
Staff Attorney **Fred Cole** . . . . (602) 542-4824
E-mail: fcole@appeals.az.gov Fax: (602) 542-7801
Staff Attorney **Bonnie Gordon** . . . . (602) 542-4824
E-mail: bgordon@appeals.az.gov Fax: (602) 542-7801
Staff Attorney **Karen Hines** . . . . (602) 542-4824
E-mail: khines@courts.az.gov Fax: (602) 542-7801
Staff Attorney **Steven T. Lawrence** . . . . (602) 542-4824
E-mail: slawrence@appeals.az.gov Fax: (602) 542-7801
Education: Cal State (Sacramento) 1990 BS; McGeorge 1994 JD; Arizona State 2001 MBA
Staff Attorney **Michelle Miernik** . . . . (602) 542-4824
E-mail: mmiernik@appeals.az.gov Fax: (602) 542-7801
Staff Attorney **Jennifer Prendiville** . . . . (602) 542-4824
E-mail: jprendiville@appeals.az.gov Fax: (602) 542-7801

Chambers of Chief Judge Michael J. Brown
Arizona State Courts Building, 1501 West Washington Street, Room 318, Phoenix, AZ 85007
Tel: (602) 542-1480
E-mail: mbrown@appeals.az.gov

Michael J. Brown
Chief Judge

Began Service: 2012
Next Election: November 2016
Term Expires: December 2016

Chambers of Vice Chief Judge Samuel A. Thumma
1501 West Washington Street, Phoenix, AZ 85007
Tel: (602) 542-3492

Samuel A. Thumma
Vice Chief Judge

Education: Iowa State 1984 BS; Iowa 1988 JD
Began Service: 2012
Next Election: November 2020
Election Type: Retention Election

Staff
Law Clerk **Bryan Martz** . . . . (602) 542-3492
Law Clerk **Molly Schiffer** . . . . (602) 542-3492
Judicial Assistant **Heather Marking** . . . . (602) 542-3492

Chambers of Judge Jon W. Thompson

Arizona State Courts Building, 1501 West Washington Street,
Room 309, Phoenix, AZ 85007
Tel: (602) 542-5304 Fax: (602) 542-7801
E-mail: jthompson@appeals.az.gov

Jon W. Thompson
Judge

Date of Birth: 1954
Education: Colorado 1979 JD
Began Service: April 1995
Appointed By: Governor Fife Symington
Term Expires: December 2016
Political Affiliation: Republican

Academic: Associate Professor of Law, Northern Arizona University (1988-1989)

Government: Deputy County Attorney, County of Yuma, Arizona (1980-1983); Deputy County Attorney, Office of the County Attorney, County of Coconino, Arizona (1983-1988)

Judicial: Judge, Arizona Superior Court, Coconino County (1989-1990)

Legal Practice: Sole practitioner (1979-1980); Partner, Mangum, Wall, Stoops & Warden (1990-1995)

Current Memberships: American Bar Association; The Federalist Society for Law and Public Policy Studies; Arizona Foundation for Legal Services and Education, State Bar of Arizona

Staff

Career Law Clerk **Lisa Cullins** ....(602) 542-5304
Career Law Clerk **Jill Hendrix** ....(602) 542-5304
E-mail: jhendrix@appeals.az.gov
Education: Gonzaga 1996 JD
Career Law Clerk **Kim Miles** ....(602) 542-5304
E-mail: kmiles@appeals.az.gov
Education: Arizona State 1996 JD

Chambers of Judge John C. Gemmill

Arizona State Courts Building, 1501 West Washington Street,
Room 321, Phoenix, AZ 85007
Tel: (602) 542-4828 Fax: (602) 542-7801

John C. Gemmill
Judge

Date of Birth: 1948
Education: Arizona 1971 BS, 1976 JD
Began Service: May 11, 2001
Appointed By: Governor Jane Dee Hull
Next Election: November 2016
Term Expires: January 2017
Political Affiliation: Republican

Staff

Law Clerk **Isaiah Richie** ....(602) 542-4828
Began Service: August 2015
Term Expires: August 2016
Judicial Assistant **Linda Botsko** ....(602) 542-4828

Chambers of Judge Lawrence F. Winthrop

Arizona State Courts Building, 1501 West Washington Street,
Room 322, Phoenix, AZ 85007
Tel: (602) 542-1430 Fax: (602) 542-7801
E-mail: lwinthrop@appeals.az.gov

Lawrence F. Winthrop
Judge

Date of Birth: 1952
Education: Whittier 1974 BA; Cal Western 1977 JD
Began Service: October 15, 2002
Appointed By: Governor Jane Dee Hull
Next Election: November 2016

Current Memberships: American Board of Trial Advocates; Board of Directors, Arizona Foundation for Legal Services & Education; Maricopa County Bar Foundation, Maricopa County Bar Association; State Bar of Arizona; Arizona Foundation for Legal Services and Education, State Bar of Arizona; State Bar of California; Board of Directors, Valley of the Sea School

Staff

Law Clerk **Raoqiong "Rachel" Bennett** ....(602) 542-1430
Began Service: August 2015
Term Expires: August 2016
Career Law Clerk **Mark W. Schultz** ....(602) 542-1430
E-mail: mschultz@appeals.az.gov
Education: Arizona State 1998 JD
Judicial Assistant **Cecilia Samarripas** ....(602) 542-1430
E-mail: csamarripas@appeals.az.gov

Chambers of Judge Maurice Portley

Arizona State Courts Building, 1501 West Washington Street,
Room 308, Phoenix, AZ 85007
Tel: (602) 542-5303
E-mail: mportley@appeals.az.gov

Maurice Portley
Judge

Education: Arizona State 1975 BS; Michigan 1978 JD
Began Service: 2003
Next Election: 2018
Election Type: Retention Election
Term Expires: 2018

Judicial: Maricopa County Superior Court (1991-2003); Presiding Judge, Southeast District (1992-1997); Presiding Judge, Juvenile Court (1998-2001)

Legal Practice: Partner, Jennings, Strouss & Salmon, P.L.C. (1984-2001)

Staff

Law Clerk **Elizabeth Garcia** ....(602) 542-5303
Term Expires: August 15, 2016
Law Clerk **Alejandro Barrientos Borjas** ....(602) 542-5303
Term Expires: August 15, 2016
Judicial Assistant **Kathy Welch** ....(602) 542-5303

Chambers of Judge Donn Kessler

Arizona State Courts Building, 1501 West Washington Street, Room 307, Phoenix, AZ 85007
Tel: (602) 542-4827
E-mail: dkessler@appeals.az.gov

Donn Kessler
Judge

Education: Virginia 1972 BA; Yale 1975 JD
Began Service: 2003
Next Election: November 6, 2018
Election Type: Retention Election
Term Expires: January 21, 2019

Government: Deputy Attorney General, State of Hawaii (1975-1977); Assistant Attorney General, Commonwealth of Virginia (1978-1979)

Legal Practice: Appellate Attorney & Litigator, Christian Barton & Chappell (1979-1982); Appellate Attorney and Litigator, Jennings, Strouss & Salmon, P.L.C. (1982-1990); Appellate Attorney and Litigator, Ulrich, Kessler & Anger, P.C. (1991-2000)

Staff
Law Clerk **Kate Myers** .... (602) 542-4827
Term Expires: August 2016
Judicial Assistant/Law Clerk **Jaleh Najafi** .... (602) 542-4827
Career Law Clerk **Anya Stangl** .... (602) 542-4827

Chambers of Judge Patricia K. Norris

1501 West Washington Street, Suite 327, Phoenix, AZ 85007
Tel: (602) 542-4867
E-mail: pnorris@appeals.az.gov

Patricia K. Norris
Judge

Education: Arizona State 1974 BA, 1977 JD
Began Service: 2003
Next Election: 2018
Term Expires: 2018

Clerkships: Law Clerk Mary M. Schroeder, Arizona Court of Appeals, Division One (1977-1978)

Legal Practice: Attorney, Lewis and Roca LLP (1978-2003)

Current Memberships: American Bar Association; The Lorna E. Lockwood American Inn of Court, The American Inns of Court; Arizona Women Lawyers Association; Maricopa County Bar Association; State Bar of Arizona

Staff
Law Clerk **Susan Russo** .... (602) 542-4867
Began Service: August 2015
Term Expires: August 2016
Law Clerk **Josh Rayes** .... (602) 542-4867
Began Service: 2015
Term Expires: August 2016
Law Clerk **Pamela Witte** .... (602) 542-4867
Fax: (602) 542-7801

Chambers of Judge Patricia A. Orozco

Arizona State Courts Building, 1501 West Washington Street, Room 333, Phoenix, AZ 85007
Tel: (602) 542-3491
E-mail: porozco@appeals.az.gov

Patricia A. Orozco
Judge

Education: Arizona 1977 BA, 1989 JD
Began Service: 2004
Next Election: November 2020
Election Type: Retention Election
Term Expires: December 2020

Staff
Law Clerk **Brandon Arents** .... (602) 542-3491
Term Expires: July 2016

Chambers of Judge Margaret H. Downie

1501 West Washington Street, Phoenix, AZ 85007
Tel: (602) 542-4821
E-mail: mdownie@appeals.az.gov

Margaret H. Downie
Judge

Began Service: 2008
Appointed By: Governor Jan Brewer

Chambers of Judge Peter B. Swann

1501 West Washington Street, Phoenix, AZ 85007
Tel: (602) 542-4821
E-mail: pswann@appeals.az.gov

Peter B. Swann
Judge

Education: UC Berkeley 1987 BA; Maryland Baltimore 1991 JD
Began Service: 2008
Next Election: 2018
Term Expires: 2019

Chambers of Judge Andrew W. Gould

Arizona State Courts Building, 1501 West Washington Street, Phoenix, AZ 85007
Tel: (602) 542-1434 Fax: (602) 542-4833

Andrew W. Gould
Judge

Education: Montana 1986 BA; Northwestern 1990 JD
Began Service: February 17, 2012
Appointed By: Governor Jan Brewer
Next Election: November 2020

Government: Prosecutor, Attorney's Office, County of Yuma, Arizona (1994-1998); Prosecutor, Attorney's Office, County of Maricopa, Arizona (1998-1999); Chief Civil Deputy, Attorney's Office, County of Yuma, Arizona (1999-2001)

Judicial: Presiding Judge, Chambers of Presiding Judge Andrew W. Gould, Yuma County Superior Court, Arizona County Courts (2001-2011)

Legal Practice: Attorney, Snell & Wilmer L.L.P. (1990-1992); Attorney, Gallagher & Kennedy, P.A. (1992-1993)

Staff
Law Clerk **Erica Gadberry** .... (602) 542-1434
Career Law Clerk **Jillian Schultz** .... (602) 542-1434
Judicial Assistant **Donna Lewandowski** .... (602) 542-1434

Chambers of Judge Randall M. Howe
1501 West Washington Street, Phoenix, AZ 85007
Tel: (602) 542-3493 Fax: (602) 542-7801

Randall M. Howe
Judge

Education: Arizona State 1985 BS, 1988 JD
Began Service: 2012
Next Election: November 2020

Staff
Law Clerk **Jennifer Londono** . . . . (602) 542-3493
Law Clerk **Alanna Duong** . . . . (602) 542-3493
E-mail: aduong@appeals.az.gov
Judicial Assistant **Anna Banks** . . . . (602) 542-3493

Chambers of Judge Diane M. Johnsen
Arizona State Courts Building, 1501 West Washington Street, Phoenix, AZ 85007
Tel: (602) 542-1432
E-mail: djohnsen@appeals.az.gov

Diane M. Johnsen
Judge

Education: Arizona 1975 BA; Stanford 1982 JD
Began Service: 2006
Appointed By: Governor Janet Napolitano
Next Election: November 2020
Election Type: Retention Election
Term Expires: December 2020

Current Memberships: American Bar Association

Chambers of Judge Kent E. Cattani
1501 West Washington Street, Phoenix, AZ 85007
Tel: (602) 542-1479 Fax: (602) 542-7801

Kent Cattani
Judge

Chambers of Judge Kenton D. Jones
1501 West Washington Street, Phoenix, AZ 85007
Tel: (602) 542-4826

Kenton D. Jones
Judge

Education: Northern Arizona 1984 BA; Arizona State 1986 JD
Began Service: 2013
Appointed By: Governor Jan Brewer

Arizona Court of Appeals, Division Two
North Building, State Office Complex, 400 West Congress Street, Room 200, Tucson, AZ 85701-1374
Tel: (520) 628-6954 Fax: (520) 628-6959
Internet: www.apltwo.ct.state.az.us

Number of Judgeships: 6

Areas Covered: Counties of Cochise, Gila, Graham, Greenlee, Pima, Pinal and Santa Cruz

Court Staff
Clerk of the Court **Jeffrey P. Handler** . . . . (520) 628-6954
E-mail: handler@appeals2.az.gov
Deputy Clerk Specialist **Maria Campos** . . . . (520) 628-6954
E-mail: mcampos@courts.az.gov
Deputy Clerk **Renee Brooks** . . . . (520) 628-6954

Arizona Court of Appeals, Division Two *continued*

Deputy Clerk **Teresa Hiatt** . . . . (520) 628-6954
Deputy Clerk **Debra Schudel** . . . . (520) 628-6954
Deputy Clerk **(Vacant)** . . . . (520) 628-6954
Deputy Clerk Supervisor (Acting) **Itza French** . . . . (520) 628-6954
E-mail: ifrench@courts.az.gov
Chief Information Officer **Mohyeddin Abdulaziz** . . . . (520) 628-6955
E-mail: abdulaziz@appeals2.az.gov
Information Technology Officer
Nathaniel "Nat" Marler . . . . (520) 628-6954
Finance Officer I **(Vacant)** . . . . (520) 628-6954
Finance Manager **Rachel Garza** . . . . (520) 628-6954
Manager **Itza French** . . . . (520) 628-6954
E-mail: ifrench@courts.az.gov
Chief Staff Attorney **Beth Capin Beckmann** . . . . (520) 628-6955
Staff Attorney **Jennie Boulet** . . . . (520) 628-6955
E-mail: boulet@appeals2.az.gov
Staff Attorney **Geri Mose Mahrt** . . . . (520) 628-6955
E-mail: mahrt@appeals2.az.gov
Staff Attorney **Mac McCallum** . . . . (520) 628-6955
E-mail: mccallum@appeals2.az.gov
Staff Attorney **Lisa Howell** . . . . (520) 628-6955
Education: Arizona 2004 JD
Secretary **Therese Sadorf** . . . . (520) 628-6955
E-mail: sadorf@appeals2.az.gov

Chambers of Chief Judge Peter J. Eckerstrom
State Office Complex, 400 West Congress Street, Tucson, AZ 85701-1374
Tel: (520) 628-6950 Fax: (520) 770-3560 Fax: (520) 628-6959
E-mail: eckerstrom@appeals2.az.gov

Peter J. Eckerstrom
Chief Judge

Date of Birth: October 8, 1960
Education: Yale 1982 BA; Stanford 1986 JD
Began Service: July 3, 2003
Appointed By: Governor Janet Napolitano
Political Affiliation: Democrat

Current Memberships: State Bar of Arizona; State Bar of California

Staff
Law Clerk **David Buechel** . . . . (520) 770-3572
E-mail: buechel@appeals2.az.gov
Education: Arizona 2007 JD
Law Clerk **Jennifer Blum** . . . . (520) 209-4009
E-mail: blum@appeals2.az.gov
Judicial Secretary **Ruth Kea** . . . . (520) 770-3585
E-mail: kea@appeals2.az.gov

Chambers of Vice Chief Judge Garye L. Vasquez
North building, State Office Complex, 400 West Congress Street, Tucson, AZ 85701-1374
Tel: (520) 628-6949 Fax: (520) 628-6959
E-mail: vasquez@appeals2.az.gov

Garye L. Vasquez
Vice Chief Judge

Date of Birth: 1958
Education: Arizona State 1981 BS; Arizona 1984 JD
Began Service: 2005
Appointed By: Governor Janet Napolitano
Next Election: November 2020
Election Type: Retention Election
Term Expires: December 2020

Staff
Secretary **Ruth Kea** . . . . (520) 628-6949
E-mail: kea@appeals2.az.gov

STATE COURTS—ARIZONA

Chambers of Judge Joseph W. Howard
State Office Complex, 400 West Congress Street, Tucson, AZ 85701-1374
Tel: (520) 628-6946 Fax: (520) 628-6959
E-mail: howard@appeals2.az.gov

Joseph W. Howard
Judge

Date of Birth: 1950
Education: Arizona State 1972 BA, 1976 JD
Began Service: April 21, 1997
Appointed By: Governor Fife Symington
Next Election: November 2018
Term Expires: December 31, 2018
Political Affiliation: Republican

Current Memberships: Pima County Bar Association; Pinal County Bar Association; State Bar of Arizona

Staff
Law Clerk **Kaitlin Hollywood** .... (520) 628-6946
Began Service: 2013
Term Expires: June 2017
E-mail: hollywood@appeals2.az.gov
Law Clerk **Alex Winkelman** .... (520) 628-6946
Began Service: 2015
Term Expires: August 2017
Judicial Secretary **Karen Rogers** .... (520) 628-6946
E-mail: rogers@appeals2.az.gov
Education: Arizona 1988 BSBA

Chambers of Judge Philip G. Espinosa
State Office Complex, 400 West Congress Street, Suite 302, Tucson, AZ 85701-1374
Tel: (520) 628-6948 Fax: (520) 628-6959
E-mail: espinosa@appeals2.az.gov

Philip G. Espinosa
Judge

Date of Birth: 1952
Education: Arizona 1978 BA, 1983 JD
Began Service: 1992
Term Expires: 2018

Government: Assistant United States Attorney, District of Arizona, United States Department of Justice (1983-1992); Deputy Chief Assistant United States Attorney, District of Arizona, Criminal Division, United States Department of Justice (1990-1992)

Judicial: Chief Judge, Arizona Court of Appeals, Division Two

Staff
Law Clerk **Carol Lamoureus** .... (520) 209-4008
Law Clerk **Mariette Ambri** .... (520) 770-3580
Secretary **Darcy Meyer** .... (520) 770-3580
E-mail: meyer@appeals2.az.gov

Chambers of Judge Michael Owen Miller
400 West Congress Street, Tucson, AZ 85701-1374
Tel: (520) 628-6954

Michael Owen Miller
Judge

Began Service: 2012
Appointed By: Governor Jan Brewer

Chambers of Judge Christopher Staring
400 West Congress Street, Tucson, AZ 85701-1374
Tel: (520) 628-6954

Christopher Staring
Judge

Began Service: 2015

STATE COURTS—ARIZONA

Arkansas

Arkansas Administrative Office of the Courts

Justice Building, 625 Marshall Street, Suite 1100,
Little Rock, AR 72201-1020
Tel: (501) 682-9400 Fax: (501) 682-9410 Tel: (501) 682-9412 (T.D.D.)
Internet: http://courts.arkansas.gov

Staff

Director **James D. Gingerich** .... (501) 682-9400
Education: Central Arkansas 1977 BA; Arkansas 1980 JD

Deputy Director **John Stewart** .... (501) 682-9400
E-mail: john.stewart@arkansas.gov
Education: Henderson State 1973 BA; Arkansas 1976 MPA

Office Manager **Beth Jacks** .... (501) 682-9400
E-mail: beth.jacks@arkansas.gov

Administrative Secretary **Lillie Kaur** .... (501) 682-9401
E-mail: lillie.kaur@arkansas.gov

Administrative Secretary **Mary Ann Rose** .... (501) 682-9400

Court Services Director **Larry Brady** .... (501) 682-9401
E-mail: larry.brady@arkansas.gov
Education: Arkansas 1977 BA; Washington U (MO) JD

Foreign Language Interpretation **Mara Simmons** .... (501) 682-9400
E-mail: mara.simmons@arkansas.gov

Administrative Assistant **Jessica Bowen** .... (501) 682-9400
E-mail: jessica.bowen@arkansas.gov

Attorney, Circuit Court-Civil and Criminal **Krystal Mann** .... (501) 682-9401
E-mail: krystal.mann@arkansas.gov

Attorney, Circuit Court-Domestic Relations/Probate **Donna Gay** .... (501) 682-9400
E-mail: donna.gay@arkansas.gov
Education: U Memphis 1973 BA; Arkansas (Little Rock) 1981 JD

Attorney, District Courts **Keith Caviness** .... (501) 682-9401
E-mail: keith.caviness@arkansas.gov
Education: Arkansas (Little Rock) 1974 BS, 1977 JD

AD Litem Coordinator **Renia Robinette** .... (501) 682-9400
E-mail: renia.robinette@arkansas.gov

Alternate Dispute Resolution Coordinator **Jennifer Jones Taylor** .... (501) 682-9400
E-mail: Jennifer.Taylor@arkansas.gov
Education: Arkansas 1999 JD

Assistant to Alternate Dispute Resolution Coordinator **James Tapscott** .... (501) 682-9400
E-mail: james.tapscott@arkansas.gov

Judicial Branch Education Director **Marty Sullivan** .... (501) 682-9400
E-mail: marty.sullivan@arkansas.gov

Juvenile Court Coordinator **Connie Hickman-Tanner** .... (501) 682-9400
Education: Hendrix 1986 BA; Arkansas (Little Rock) 1991 JD

Training Coordinator **(Vacant)** .... (501) 682-9400

Website Coordinator **Rhea Clougherty** .... (501) 682-9400
E-mail: rhea.clougherty@arkansas.gov

Research Analyst **Joe Beard** .... (501) 682-9400
E-mail: joe.beard@arkansas.gov

Financial Officer **Joyce French** .... (501) 682-9400
E-mail: joyce.french@arkansas.gov

Financial Officer **(Vacant)** .... (501) 682-9400

Public Education Coordinator **(Vacant)** .... (501) 682-9400
E-mail: corey.gilmore@arkansas.gov

State CASA Coordinator **Mary Beth Luibel** .... (501) 682-9400
E-mail: marybeth.luibel@arkansas.gov

Information Systems Director **Tim Holthoff** .... (501) 682-9400
E-mail: tim.holthoff@arkansas.gov

Judicial Education Specialist **Jasmine Medley** .... (501) 682-9400
E-mail: jasmine.medley@arkansas.gov

Personal Computer Support Specialist **Wade Hankins** .... (501) 682-9400
E-mail: wade.hankins@arkansas.gov

Arkansas Administrative Office of the Courts *continued*

Personal Computer Support Specialist **Jimmy Don Page** .... (501) 682-9400

Arkansas Supreme Court

Justice Building, 625 Marshall Street, First Floor North, Room 130,
Little Rock, AR 72201
Tel: (501) 682-6849 Tel: (501) 682-2147 (Supreme Court Library)
Fax: (501) 682-6877 (Supreme Court Library)
Internet: www.courts.state.ar.us
E-mail: arsclib@arkansas.gov

Number of Judgeships: 7

The Supreme Court consists of a chief justice and six justices who are elected statewide for eight-year terms in partisan elections. Vacancies are filled temporarily by the Governor; however, appointees are not eligible to run for the position in the next general election. Retirement is mandatory at age seventy. The Supreme Court has appellate jurisdiction over cases from the Arkansas Courts involving interpretation of the state constitution; elections; attorney and judicial discipline; a prior decision by the Supreme Court; and criminal cases in which a sentence of life or the death penalty is imposed. The Court may also review decisions from the Arkansas Court of Appeals.

The Arkansas Supreme Court sits in Little Rock.

Court Staff

Clerk of the Court **Stacey Pectol** .... (501) 682-6849
E-mail: stacey.pectol@arkansas.gov
Education: Hendrix 1987 BA; Arkansas (Little Rock) 1990 JD

Chief Deputy Clerk **Sue Clayton** .... (501) 682-6849
E-mail: sue.clayton@arkansas.gov

Deputy Clerk **Rose Allen** .... (501) 682-6849
E-mail: rose.allen@arkansas.gov

Deputy Clerk **Christy Lute** .... (501) 682-6849
E-mail: christy.lute@arkansas.gov

Deputy Clerk **Amanda Hagar** .... (501) 682-6849
E-mail: amanda.hagar@arkansas.gov

Deputy Clerk **Renee Herndon** .... (501) 682-6849
E-mail: renee.herndon@arkansas.gov

Deputy Clerk **Bobby Jackson** .... (501) 682-6849
E-mail: bobby.jackson@arkansas.gov

Deputy Clerk **Rayanne Hinton** .... (501) 682-6849
E-mail: rayanne.hinton@arkansas.gov

Deputy Clerk **Heather Lyvers-Clark** .... (501) 682-6849
E-mail: heather.lyvers@arkansas.gov

Deputy Clerk/Office Manager **Denise Parks** .... (501) 682-6849
E-mail: denise.parks@arkansas.gov

Criminal Justice Coordinator **Sue Newbery** .... (501) 682-6840

Deputy Criminal Coordinator **(Vacant)** .... (501) 682-6878

Secretary to Criminal Justice Coordinator **Michelle Daniel** .... (501) 682-1637
E-mail: michelle.daniel@arkansas.gov

Assistant Criminal Justice Coordinator **Charlotte Aceituno** .... (501) 682-2479

Assistant Criminal Justice Coordinator **Susan Stevens** .... (501) 682-9416
E-mail: susan.stevens@arkansas.gov

Judicial Education Coordinator **Marty Sullivan** .... (501) 682-9400
E-mail: marty.sullivan@arkansas.gov Fax: (501) 682-9410

Appellate Review Attorney **Courtney Umeda** .... (501) 682-6821
Education: Arkansas 2004 BA; Arkansas (Little Rock) 2007 JD

Financial Officer **Melanie Fleming** .... (501) 682-6256
E-mail: melanie.fleming@arkansas.gov

Financial Officer **Rusty Taylor** .... (501) 682-6256

Records Supervisor **Holli North** .... (501) 682-6846
E-mail: holli.north@arkansas.gov

Reporter of Decisions **Susan P. Williams** .... (501) 682-6208
E-mail: susan.williams@arkansas.gov

Assistant Reporter of Decisions **Elizabeth Perry** .... (501) 682-6851
E-mail: elizabeth.perry@arkansas.gov

Appellate Automation Specialist **Brian Lindsey** .... (501) 682-5314
E-mail: brian.lindsey@arkansas.gov

(continued on next page)

Arkansas Supreme Court *continued*

Director of Security **Eddie Davis** .... (501) 682-6068
E-mail: eddie.davis@arkansas.gov Fax: (501) 683-4013
Librarian **Ava Hicks** .... (501) 682-2147
E-mail: ava.hicks@arkansas.gov

Chambers of Chief Justice Howard Brill

625 Marshall Street, Little Rock, AR 72201-1020
Tel: (501) 682-6849

Howard W. Brill
Chief Justice

Chambers of Justice Rhonda Wood

625 Marshall Street, Little Rock, AR 72201-1020
Tel: (501) 682-6838 Fax: (501) 683-4004
E-mail: Rhonda.Wood@arkansas.gov

Rhonda Wood
Justice

Began Service: 2015

Chambers of Justice Paul E. Danielson

Justice Building, 625 Marshall Street, Little Rock, AR 72201
Tel: (501) 682-6861 Fax: (501) 683-4002
E-mail: paul.danielson@arkansas.gov

Paul E. Danielson
Justice

Education: Florida State 1968 BA; Arkansas 1975 JD
Began Service: January 2007
Next Election: November 2016
Election Type: General Election
Term Expires: January 5, 2017

Academic: Law Instructor, University of Arkansas

Clerkships: Law Clerk, Associate Justice Frank Holt, Arkansas Supreme Court

Government: Deputy Prosecuting Attorney, Arkansas 6th Judicial District; Deputy Prosecuting Attorney, 15th Judicial District of Arkansas; City Attorney, City of Booneville, Arkansas

Judicial: Circuit Judge, 15th Judicial District of Arkansas

Legal Practice: Attorney, Private Practice

Current Memberships: Arkansas Bar Association; Arkansas Bar Foundation, Arkansas Bar Association; Arkansas Judicial Council

Staff

Career Law Clerk **Rebecca Miller-Rice** .... (501) 682-6860
E-mail: rebecca.miller-rice@arkansas.gov
Education: Rhodes 1993 BA;
Arkansas (Little Rock) 2000 JD
Career Law Clerk **Tina Bowers Lee** .... (501) 682-6858
E-mail: tina.bowers.lee@arkansas.gov
Education: Arkansas (Little Rock) 1995 BA,
1999 JD
Administrative Assistant **Marilyn Cuffman** .... (501) 682-6861
E-mail: marilyn.cuffman@arkansas.gov

Chambers of Justice Karen R. Baker

625 Marshall Street, Little Rock, AR 72201
Tel: (501) 682-6867 Fax: (501) 683-4005
E-mail: karen.baker@arkansas.gov

Karen R. Baker
Justice

Date of Birth: 1963
Education: Arkansas Tech 1983 BS; Arkansas (Little Rock) 1987 JD
Began Service: January 10, 2011
Political Affiliation: Democrat

Current Memberships: Arkansas Bar Association; Faulkner County Bar Association; Searcy County Bar Association; Van Buren County Bar Association

Staff

Career Law Clerk **Jaletta Smith** .... (501) 682-6867
E-mail: jaletta.smith@arkansas.gov
Education: Arkansas 2010 JD
Career Law Clerk **Allison P. Hatfield** .... (501) 682-6867
E-mail: allison.p.hatfield@arkansas.gov
Administrative Assistant **Katie Webb** .... (501) 682-6867
E-mail: katie.webb@arkansas.gov

Chambers of Justice Courtney Hudson Goodson

625 Marshall Street, Little Rock, AR 72201
Tel: (501) 682-6870 Fax: (501) 683-4000
E-mail: courtney.goodson@arkansas.gov

Courtney Hudson Goodson
Justice

Education: Arkansas 1994 BA, 1998 JD
Began Service: January 10, 2011

Current Memberships: Arkansas Association of Women Lawyers; Arkansas Bar Association; Benton County Bar Association; Pulaski County Bar Association

Staff

Law Clerk **Heather Zachary** .... (501) 682-6870
E-mail: heather.zachary@arkansas.gov
Law Clerk **Melanie Carlson** .... (501) 682-6870
E-mail: melanie.carlson@arkansas.gov
Education: Arkansas (Little Rock) 1987 JD
Administrative Assistant **Michalene Zionce** .... (501) 682-6870
E-mail: michalene.zionce@arkansas.gov

Chambers of Justice Josephine Linker Hart

625 Marshall Street, Little Rock, AR 72201-1020
Tel: (501) 682-6876 Fax: (501) 683-4001
E-mail: jo.hart@arkansas.gov

Josephine Linker Hart
Justice

Education: Arkansas Tech 1965; Arkansas 1971 JD
Began Service: January 2013

Judicial: Judge, Chambers of Judge Josephine Linker Hart, Arkansas Court of Appeals (1999-2012)

Legal Practice: Greg, Hart & Farris (1972-1998)

Current Memberships: American Bar Association; Arkansas Bar Association

Staff

Law Clerk **Timothy D. Sopel** .... (501) 682-6876
E-mail: timothy.sopel@arkansas.gov
Education: Colby 1978 BA;
Arkansas (Little Rock) 1996 JD
Law Clerk **Gil Dudley** .... (501) 682-6876
E-mail: gil.dudley@arkansas.gov

Chambers of Justice Josephine Linker Hart *continued*

Administrative Assistant **Sue Wolfe** . . . . (501) 682-6876
E-mail: sue.wolfe@arkansas.gov

Chambers of Justice Robin Wynne

625 Marshall Street, Little Rock, AR 72201-1020
Tel: (501) 682-6864 Fax: (501) 683-4003
E-mail: robin.wynne@arkansas.gov

Robin F. Wynne
Justice

Staff

Law Clerk **John Webster** . . . . (501) 682-6852
E-mail: john.webster@arkansas.gov
Law Clerk **Courtney Nosari-Wall** . . . . (501) 682-6863
E-mail: courtney.nosari-wall@arkansas.gov
Education: Arkansas 2007 JD
Administrative Assistant **Katy Wilson** . . . . (501) 682-6864
E-mail: katy.wilson@arkansas.gov

Arkansas Court of Appeals

Justice Building, 625 Marshall Street, Little Rock, AR 72201
Tel: (501) 682-7460 Fax: (501) 682-7494
Internet: www.courts.state.ar.us

Number of Judgeships: 12

The Court of Appeals, established in 1978, consists of a chief judge and eleven judges who are elected in partisan elections to eight-year terms from the seven Court of Appeals districts in the state. The chief judge is appointed by the chief justice of the Arkansas Supreme Court for a consecutive four-year term. Retirement is mandatory at age seventy; however, retired judges may serve by assignment of the chief justice. The Court of Appeals has appellate jurisdiction over the Arkansas Circuit and Chancery Courts except in those cases appealed directly to the Arkansas Supreme Court.

The Court of Appeals sits in Little Rock and, at its discretion, may sit in any county seat.

Court Staff

Clerk of the Court **Stacey Pectol** . . . . (501) 682-6845
E-mail: stacey.pectol@arkansas.gov
Chief Deputy Clerk **Linda Ryerson** . . . . (501) 682-6844
E-mail: linda.ryerson@arkansas.gov
Chief Deputy Clerk **Heather Lyver Clark** . . . . (501) 682-6848
Director of Security **Eddie Davis** . . . . (501) 682-6068
E-mail: eddie.davis@arkansas.gov Fax: (501) 682-4013
Librarian **Ava Hicks** . . . . (501) 682-2147
E-mail: ava.hicks@arkansas.gov
Chief Staff Attorney **Rita Cunningham** . . . . (501) 682-7464
E-mail: rita.cunningham@arkansas.gov
Staff Attorney **Anne White** . . . . (501) 682-7465
E-mail: anne.white@arkansas.gov
Staff Attorney **James Bradley** . . . . (501) 682-7466
E-mail: james.bradley@arkansas.gov
Staff Attorney **Valerie Denton** . . . . (501) 682-7463
E-mail: valerie.denton@arkansas.gov

Chambers of Chief Judge Robert J. Gladwin

Justice Building, 625 Marshall Street, Little Rock, AR 72201-1020
Tel: (501) 682-7474 Fax: (501) 682-7494
E-mail: robert.gladwin@arkansas.gov

Robert J. Gladwin
Chief Judge

Education: Arkansas 1978 BA, 1981 JD
Began Service: January 1, 2003
Term Expires: May 2016

Current Memberships: American Judges Association; Arkansas Bar Association; Arkansas Judicial Council; Washington County Bar Association

Staff

Career Law Clerk **Kala Dean** . . . . (501) 682-7476
E-mail: kala.dean@arkansas.gov
Education: Arkansas 1994 JD
Career Law Clerk **Kathleen Pitcock** . . . . (501) 682-7475
E-mail: kathleen.pitcock@arkansas.gov
Education: Arkansas MA, 1993 JD
Administrative Assistant **Teresa Singleton** . . . . (501) 682-7474
E-mail: Teresa.Singleton@arkansas.gov

Chambers of Judge Larry D. Vaught

Justice Building, 625 Marshall Street, Little Rock, AR 72201-2330
Tel: (501) 682-7491 Fax: (501) 682-7494
E-mail: larry.vaught@arkansas.gov

Larry D. Vaught
Judge

Date of Birth: 1947
Education: Washington U (MO) 1969 BA; Arkansas (Little Rock) 1979 JD
Term Expires: May 20, 2022
Political Affiliation: Democrat

Current Memberships: American Bar Association; Arkansas Bar Association; Arkansas Judicial Council; Pulaski County Bar Association

Chambers of Judge David M. Glover

625 Marshall Street, Little Rock, AR 72201
Tel: (501) 682-7977 Fax: (501) 682-7972
E-mail: david.glover@arkansas.gov

David M. "Mac" Glover
Judge

Education: Arkansas 1966 BA, 1969 JD
Began Service: January 3, 2005
Next Election: November 2020
Term Expires: December 31, 2020

Judicial: District Judge, Malvern District Court, Arkansas District Courts (2003-2004)

Profession: Attorney (1971-2004)

Staff

Career Law Clerk **Patti Luppen** . . . . (501) 682-7976
E-mail: patti.luppen@arkansas.gov
Career Law Clerk **Shay Raycher** . . . . (501) 682-7975
E-mail: shay.raycher@arkansas.gov
Education: Hendrix 1991 BA;
Arkansas (Little Rock) 1994 JD
Secretary **Nina White Fitts** . . . . (501) 682-7977
E-mail: nina.fitts@arkansas.gov

STATE COURTS—ARKANSAS

Chambers of Judge Rita Williamson Gruber

Justice Building, 625 Marshall Street, Little Rock, AR 72201
Tel: (501) 682-7478 Fax: (501) 682-7972
E-mail: rita.gruber@arkansas.gov

Rita Williamson Gruber
Judge

Education: Arkansas BA, JD
Began Service: January 7, 2009
Next Election: November 2016
Election Type: General Election
Term Expires: January 2017

Judicial: Circuit Court Judge, County of Pulaski, Arkansas

Staff
Career Law Clerk **Ann Grimes** .... (501) 682-7479
E-mail: ann.grimes@arkansas.gov
Education: Arkansas (Little Rock) 1989 JD
Career Law Clerk **Allison Warner** .... (501) 682-7480
E-mail: allison.warner@arkansas.gov
Education: Colorado Col 1987 BA;
Arkansas (Little Rock) 1991 JD
Administrative Assistant **Mary Ann Furrer** .... (501) 682-7478

Chambers of Judge Waymond M. Brown

625 Marshall Street, Little Rock, AR 72201
Tel: (501) 682-7987
E-mail: waymond.brown@arkansas.gov

Waymond M. Brown
Judge

Began Service: January 7, 2009
Next Election: November 2016
Election Type: General Election
Term Expires: January 2017

Staff
Career Law Clerk **Lakesha Bolden** .... (501) 682-7981
E-mail: lakesha.bolden@arkansas.gov
Education: Talladega 1998 AB; Arkansas 2001 JD;
Jacksonville State 2004 MPPA
Career Law Clerk **Anisha Phillips** .... (501) 682-7985
Began Service: January 2009
E-mail: anisha.phillips@arkansas.gov
Administrative Assistant **Charlie Cunningham** .... (501) 682-7987
E-mail: charlie.cunningham@arkansas.gov

Chambers of Judge Brandon Harrison

625 Marshall Street, Little Rock, AR 72201-1020
Tel: (501) 682-7983
E-mail: brandon.harrison@arkansas.gov

Brandon J. Harrison
Judge

Began Service: 2013

Clerkships: Law Clerk, Chambers of District Judge Denzil Price Marshall, Jr., United States District Court for the Eastern District of Arkansas (2010-2011)

Staff
Career Law Clerk **Beth Cloud** .... (501) 682-7990
E-mail: beth.cloud@arkansas.gov
Career Law Clerk **Martha Ayres** .... (501) 682-7991
E-mail: martha.ayres@arkansas.gov
Administrative Assistant **Joshua Manuel** .... (501) 682-7983
E-mail: joshua.manuel@arkansas.gov

Chambers of Judge Phillip Whiteaker

625 Marshall Street, Little Rock, AR 72201-1020
Tel: (501) 682-7460
E-mail: phillip.whiteaker@arkansas.gov

Phillip Whiteaker
Judge

Began Service: 2013

Staff
Law Clerk **Stephanie Holder** .... (501) 682-7460
E-mail: stephanie.holder@arkansas.gov
Law Clerk **Shannon Padilla** .... (501) 682-7460
E-mail: shannon.padilla@arkansas.gov
Education: Chicago 1992 BA;
Arkansas (Little Rock) 1999 JD
Administrative Assistant **Joan Owens** .... (501) 682-7460
E-mail: joan.owens@arkansas.gov

Chambers of Judge Kenneth Hixson

625 Marshall Street, Little Rock, AR 72201-1020
Tel: (501) 682-7481 Fax: (501) 682-7972
E-mail: kenneth.hixson@arkansas.gov

Kenneth Hixson
Judge

Began Service: 2013

Staff
Law Clerk **Pam Hathaway** .... (501) 682-7484
E-mail: pam.hathaway@arkansas.gov
Education: Arkansas (Little Rock) 1989 BA,
1992 JD
Law Clerk **Bill Scott** .... (501) 682-7483
E-mail: bill.scott@arkansas.gov
Administrative Assistant **Janet R. Armour** .... (501) 682-7481
E-mail: janet.armour@arkansas.gov
Education: Henderson State 1979 BSE

Chambers of Judge Mike Kinard

625 Marshall Street, Little Rock, AR 72201-1020
Tel: (501) 682-7460

M. Michael "Mike" Kinard
Judge

Date of Birth: July 13, 1939
Education: Southern Arkansas U; Arkansas JD

Current Memberships: American Bar Association; Arkansas Bar Association; Arkansas Bar Foundation, Arkansas Bar Association

Chambers of Judge Cliff Hoofman

625 Marshall Street, Little Rock, AR 72201
Tel: (501) 682-7989
E-mail: cliff.hoofman@arkansas.gov

Cliff Hoofman
Judge

Staff
Law Clerk **Shelly D'Atrio** .... (501) 682-6864
Law Clerk **Carrie B. Mensik** .... (501) 682-6864
E-mail: carrie.mensik@arkansas.gov
Education: Arkansas 1996 BA;
Arkansas (Little Rock) 2001 JD
Administrative Assistant **Martha Patton** .... (501) 682-6864
E-mail: martha.patton@arkansas.gov
Education: Arkansas (Little Rock) 1995 MA

Chambers of Judge Bart F. Virden

625 Marshall Street, Little Rock, AR 72201-1020
Tel: (501) 682-7951
E-mail: bart.virden@arkansas.gov

Bart Virden
Judge

Education: Arkansas 1982 BA, 1985 JD
Began Service: 2015

California

California Administrative Office of the Courts

455 Golden Gate Avenue, San Francisco, CA 94102-3688
Tel: (415) 865-4200 Fax: (415) 865-4205
Internet: www.courts.ca.gov

Staff

Administrative Director of the Courts
Martin A. Hoshino . . . . (415) 865-4200
Chief Administrative Officer **Curt Soderlund** . . . . (415) 865-4200
Leadership Services Division **Jody Patel** . . . . (415) 865-4200
E-mail: jody.patel@jud.ca.gov Fax: (415) 865-8795
Chief Counsel **Deborah Brown** . . . . (415) 865-7684
E-mail: deborah.brown@jud.ca.gov
Center for Families, Children and the Courts Director
Diane Nunn . . . . (415) 865-7739
E-mail: diane.nunn@jud.ca.gov Fax: (415) 865-7217
Center for Judiciary Education and Research Director
Diane E. Cowdrey . . . . (415) 865-7745
E-mail: diane.cowdrey@jud.ca.gov Fax: (415) 865-4335
Court Operations Special Services Office Director
Donna Hershkowitz . . . . (415) 865-4250
E-mail: donna.hershkowitz@jud.ca.gov Fax: (415) 865-4588
Governmental Affairs Director **Cory Jasperson** . . . . (916) 323-3121
770 L St., Ste. 700, Sacramento, CA 95814-3393 Fax: (916) 323-4347
E-mail: cory.jasperson@jud.ca.gov
Human Resources Director **(Vacant)** . . . . (415) 865-4260
Fax: (415) 865-4328
Information Technology Director **Mark Dusman** . . . . (415) 865-4949
E-mail: mark.dusman@jud.ca.gov Fax: (415) 865-7496
Capital Program Director **William "Bill" Guerin** . . . . (415) 865-4017
Fax: (415) 865-8885
Chief Financial Officer **Zlatko Theodorovic** . . . . (916) 263-1397
E-mail: zlatko.theodorovic@jud.ca.gov Fax: (415) 865-4325

California Supreme Court

350 McAllister Street, Room 1295, San Francisco, CA 94102
Tel: (415) 865-7000 Tel: (213) 830-7050 (Los Angeles Office)
Tel: (916) 653-0284 (Sacramento Office) Fax: (415) 865-7183
Internet: www.courtinfo.ca.gov

Number of Judgeships: 7

The Supreme Court consists of a chief justice and six associate justices appointed by the Governor and confirmed by the Commission on Judicial Appointments. After confirmation, justices serve until the next gubernatorial election and then run unopposed on a nonpartisan ballot for election to twelve year terms. The Supreme Court has original jurisdiction in mandamus, certiorari, prohibition and habeas corpus proceedings. The Court may review decisions of the California Courts of Appeal, and the Court has final appellate jurisdiction over all cases in which a judgment of death has been pronounced. The Court also reviews the recommendations of the Commission on Judicial Performance and the State Bar of California concerning the removal and suspension of judges and attorneys for misconduct.

The Court sits in San Francisco, Los Angeles and Sacramento, and may hear sessions elsewhere.

Court Staff

Court Executive Officer **Frank McGuire** . . . . . . (415) 865-7000 ext. 57015
Reporter of Decisions **(Vacant)** . . . . (415) 865-7168
Public Information Officer **Peter Allen** . . . . (415) 865-7726

Chambers of Chief Justice Tani G. Cantil-Sakauye

350 McAllister Street, San Francisco, CA 94102
Tel: (415) 865-7000 Tel: (213) 830-7050 Tel: (916) 653-0284
Fax: (415) 865-7183

Tani G. Cantil-Sakauye
Chief Justice

Education: Sacramento 1978 AA; UC Davis 1980 BA, 1984 JD
Began Service: December 3, 2010
Appointed By: Governor Arnold Schwarzenegger

Judicial: Judge, Municipal Court, City of Sacramento, California (1990-1997); Judge, Superior Court of California (1997-2005); Associate Justice, Chambers of Associate Justice Tani Cantil-Sakauye, California Court of Appeal, Third Appellate District (2005-2010)

Chambers of Associate Justice Kathryn Mickle Werdegar

350 McAllister Street, San Francisco, CA 94102-4797
Tel: (415) 865-7032 Fax: (415) 355-5428

Kathryn Mickle Werdegar
Associate Justice

Date of Birth: 1936
Education: UC Berkeley 1957 BA; George Washington 1962 JD; Boalt Hall 1990 JD
Began Service: June 3, 1994
Appointed By: Governor Pete Wilson
Next Election: November 4, 2026
Term Expires: January 5, 2027
Political Affiliation: Republican

Academic: Associate, Center for the Study of Law and Society, University of California, Berkeley (1965-1967); Consultant and Author, California Center for Judicial Education and Research, Berkeley (1968-1971); Associate Professor and Associate Dean, Academic and Student Affairs, School of Law, University of San Francisco (1978-1981); Regents' Lecturer, University of California, Berkeley (2000)

Government: Legal Assistant, Civil Rights Division, United States Department of Justice (1962-1963); Research Attorney and Author, California State Study Commission on Mental Retardation, State of California (1963-1964); Special Consultant, Department of Mental Health, State of California (1967-1968); Senior Staff Attorney, California Court of Appeal, First Appellate District (1981-1985); Senior Staff Attorney, California Supreme Court (1985-1991)

Judicial: Associate Justice, California Court of Appeal, First Appellate District, Division Three (1991-1994)

Legal Practice: Director, Criminal Law Division, Continuing Education of the Bar (1971-1978)

Current Memberships: The American Law Institute; California Judges Association; California/Nevada Women Judges Association; California Supreme Court Historical Society; National Association of Women Judges

Staff

Reporter of Decisions **(Vacant)** . . . . (415) 865-7160
Judicial Assistant **Pauline Stafne** . . . . (415) 865-7032

Chambers of Associate Justice Ming W. Chin
350 McAllister Street, San Francisco, CA 94102-4797
Tel: (415) 865-7050 Fax: (415) 865-7186

Ming W. Chin
Associate Justice

Date of Birth: 1942
Education: U San Francisco 1964 BA, 1967 JD
Began Service: March 1, 1996
Appointed By: Governor Pete Wilson
Next Election: November 2022
Term Expires: January 2023
Political Affiliation: Republican

Academic: Adjunct Professor of Law, University of San Francisco (1989-1993)

Government: Deputy District Attorney, County of Alameda, California (1970-1972)

Judicial: Judge, California Superior Court, Alameda County (1988-1990); Justice, California Court of Appeal, First Appellate District, Division Three (1990-1996)

Legal Practice: Associate, Aiken, Kramer & Cummings (1973-1976); Partner, Aiken, Kramer & Cummings (1976-1988)

Military Service: United States Army (1967-1969); United States Army Reserve, United States Department of the Army (1969-1971)

Current Memberships: Alameda County Bar Association; American Bar Association; Asian American Bar Association of the Greater Bay Area; California Judges Association; The Commonwealth Club of California

Staff
Judicial Assistant **Jonathan Lipsky** .... (415) 865-7052
E-mail: jonathan.lipsky@jud.ca.gov

Chambers of Associate Justice Carol A. Corrigan
350 McAllister Street, San Francisco, CA 94102
Tel: (415) 865-7000
E-mail: carol.corrigan@jud.ca.gov

Carol A. Corrigan
Associate Justice

Date of Birth: 1948
Education: Holy Names 1970 BA; Hastings 1975 JD
Began Service: January 4, 2006
Appointed By: Governor Arnold Schwarzenegger
Next Election: November 6, 2018
Term Expires: January 7, 2019

Academic: University of Puget Sound Law School (1981); Hastings College of Law (1981-1987); Boalt Hall School of Law (1984-1987); University of San Francisco Law School (1988-1990); Hastings College of Law (1989); Boalt Hall School of Law (1989-1994)

Government: Deputy District Attorney, County of Alameda, California (1975-1985); Senior Deputy District Attorney, County of Alameda, California (1985-1987)

Judicial: Judge, Oakland Municipal Court (1987-1991); Judge, California Superior Court, Alameda County (1991-1994); Associate Justice, California Court of Appeal, First Appellate District, Division Three (1994-2006)

Staff
Judicial Assistant **Shelly Mason** .... (415) 865-7074

Chambers of Associate Justice Goodwin Liu
350 McAllister Street, San Francisco, CA 94102
Tel: (415) 865-7000 Fax: (415) 865-7183

Goodwin Liu
Associate Justice

Education: Stanford 1991 BS; Oxford (UK) 1993 MA; Yale 1998 JD
Began Service: September 1, 2011
Appointed By: Governor Jerry Brown
Next Election: November 2026

Chambers of Associate Justice Mariano-Florentino Cuéllar
350 McAllister Street, San Francisco, CA 94102
Tel: (415) 865-7000

Dr. Mariano-Florentino "Tino" Cuéllar
Associate Justice

Education: Harvard 1993 AB; Stanford 1996 MA; Yale 1997 JD; Stanford 2000 PhD
Began Service: January 21, 2015
Appointed By: Governor Jerry Brown

Chambers of Associate Justice Leondra R. Kruger
350 McAllister Street, San Francisco, CA 94102
Tel: (415) 865-7000

Leondra R. Kruger
Associate Justice

Education: Harvard BA; Yale 2001 JD
Began Service: January 21, 2015
Appointed By: Governor Jerry Brown

California Court of Appeal
Internet: www.courts.ca.gov

The California Courts of Appeal are comprised of six districts, three of which are separated into divisions. Each division (or district, if there are no divisions) has a presiding justice. All justices of the Courts of Appeal are initially appointed by the Governor and confirmed by the Commission on Judicial Appointments. After confirmation, justices serve until the next gubernatorial election, at which time they run unopposed on a nonpartisan ballot for election to the remaining portion of the term. A full term is twelve years. The Courts of Appeal have jurisdiction in cases on appeal from the California Superior Courts, except when judgment of death has been pronounced and in other cases as prescribed by statute.

California Court of Appeal, First Appellate District
350 McAllister Street, San Francisco, CA 94102
Tel: (415) 865-7300 Fax: (415) 865-7309
Internet: www.courts.ca.gov/1dca.htm

Number of Judgeships: 20

Areas Covered: Counties of Alameda, Contra Costa, Del Norte, Humboldt, Lake, Marin, Mendocino, Napa, San Francisco, San Mateo, Solano and Sonoma

Court Staff
Fax: (415) 865-7209

Clerk/Administrator **Diana Herbert** .... (415) 865-7264
E-mail: diana.herbert@jud.ca.gov
Assistant Clerk/Administrator **Susan Graham** .... (415) 865-7263

California Court of Appeal, First Appellate District, Division One

350 McAllister Street, San Francisco, CA 94102
Tel: (415) 865-7300 Fax: (415) 865-7309
Internet: www.courts.ca.gov/1dca.htm

Number of Judgeships: 4

Court Staff

Deputy Clerk **Fred Abad** . . . . (415) 865-7290
E-mail: fred.abad@jud.ca.gov
Deputy Clerk **Laura Fredericks** . . . . (415) 865-7291

Chambers of Presiding Justice James M. Humes

350 McAllister Street, San Francisco, CA 94102
Tel: (415) 865-7300

James M. Humes
Presiding Justice

Chambers of Associate Justice Sandra L. Margulies

350 McAllister Street, San Francisco, CA 94102
Tel: (415) 865-7300 Fax: (415) 865-7309

Sandra L. Margulies
Associate Justice

Education: UCLA BA; Southwestern JD
Began Service: January 2002
Appointed By: Governor Gray Davis
Term Expires: January 2019

Staff

Research Attorney **(Vacant)** . . . . (415) 865-7300
Research Attorney **Todd Elliott Thompson** . . . . (415) 865-7300
E-mail: todd.thompson@jud.ca.gov
Education: UC Santa Barbara; Boalt Hall JD
Judicial Assistant **Stella Pereira** . . . . (415) 865-7300

Chambers of Associate Justice Robert L. Dondero

350 McAllister Street, San Francisco, CA 94102
Tel: (415) 865-7300 Tel: (415) 865-7309
E-mail: robert.dondero@jud.ca.gov

Robert L. Dondero
Associate Justice

Date of Birth: 1946
Education: Santa Clara U BA; Boalt Hall JD
Began Service: June 2009
Appointed By: Governor Arnold Schwarzenegger
Next Election: November 2022
Election Type: Retention Election
Political Affiliation: Republican

Government: Deputy District Attorney, Office of the District Attorney, City and County of San Francisco, California (1971-1978); U.S. Attorney, California - Northern District, Executive Office for United States Attorneys, United States Department of Justice (1978-1992)

Judicial: Judge, County of San Francisco, Superior Court of California (1992-2009)

Chambers of Associate Justice Kathleen M. Banke

350 McAllister Street, San Francisco, CA 94102
Tel: (415) 865-7300 Fax: (415) 865-7309
E-mail: kathleen.banke@jud.ca.gov

Kathleen M. Banke
Associate Justice

Date of Birth: 1953
Education: Cal State (Sacramento) 1973 BA; Colorado 1979 JD
Began Service: June 2009
Appointed By: Governor Arnold Schwarzenegger
Next Election: November 2022
Election Type: Retention Election
Political Affiliation: Republican

Judicial: Judge, County of Alameda, Superior Court of California (2006-2009)

Legal Practice: Associate, Crosby, Heafy, Roach & May (1982-1989); Partner, Crosby, Heafy, Roach & May (1989-2003); Partner, Reed Smith LLP (2003-2006)

California Court of Appeal, First Appellate District, Division Two

350 McAllister Street, San Francisco, CA 94102
Tel: (415) 865-7300 Fax: (415) 865-7309
Internet: www.courts.ca.gov/1dca.htm

Number of Judgeships: 4

Court Staff

Deputy Clerk **Imelda Santos** . . . . (415) 865-7293
E-mail: imelda.santos@jud.ca.gov
Deputy Clerk **Stacy Wheeler** . . . . (415) 865-7292

Chambers of Presiding Justice J. Anthony Kline

350 McAllister Street, San Francisco, CA 94102
Tel: (415) 865-7300 Fax: (415) 865-7309
E-mail: anthony.kline@jud.ca.gov

J. Anthony Kline
Presiding Justice

Date of Birth: 1938
Education: Johns Hopkins 1960 BA; Cornell 1962 MPA; Yale 1965 JD
Began Service: December 24, 1982
Appointed By: Governor Edmund G. Brown, Jr.
Term Expires: January 5, 2027
Political Affiliation: Democrat

Clerkships: Law Clerk The Honorable Raymond E. Peters (1965-1966)

Government: Legal Affairs Secretary, Governor Edmund G. Brown, Jr. (CA), State of California (1975-1980)

Judicial: Judge, California Superior Court, San Francisco County (1980-1982)

Legal Practice: Davis Polk & Wardwell (1966-1970); Attorney, Public Advocates, Inc. (1970-1975)

Current Memberships: California Judges Association

Staff

Senior Research Attorney **Winifred A. Berman** . . . . (415) 865-7300
E-mail: winifred.berman@jud.ca.gov
Education: Hampshire 1980 BA; Yale 1985 JD
Senior Research Attorney **Marnie Sayles** . . . . (415) 865-7300
Senior Research Attorney **Maria Kivel** . . . . (415) 865-7300
E-mail: maria.kivel@jud.ca.gov
Education: UC Berkeley 1982 BA; Stanford 1987 JD
Judicial Assistant **Stacy Guerrier** . . . . (415) 865-7372

STATE COURTS—CALIFORNIA

Chambers of Associate Justice James A. Richman

350 McAllister Street, San Francisco, CA 94102
Tel: (415) 865-7232 Fax: (415) 865-7213
E-mail: james.richman@jud.ca.gov

James A. Richman
Associate Justice

Education: U San Francisco 1965 JD
Began Service: March 2006
Appointed By: Governor Arnold Schwarzenegger
Term Expires: January 2019

Academic: Adjunct Professor, School of Law, University of San Francisco (1972-1997)

Clerkships: Law Clerk, Chambers of Associate Justice Raymond L. Sullivan, California Court of Appeal, First Appellate District

Judicial: Superior Court Judge, County of Alameda, California (1996-2006)

Legal Practice: Partner, Cooley Godward LLP (1972-1996)

Staff
Judicial Assistant **Suzanne O'Rourke Scanlon** . . . . (415) 865-7232

Chambers of Associate Justice Therese M. Stewart

350 McAllister Street, San Francisco, CA 94102
Tel: (415) 865-7300

Therese M. Stewart
Associate Justice

Chambers of Associate Justice Marla J. Miller

350 McAllister Street, San Francisco, CA 94102
Tel: (415) 865-7300

Marla J. Miller
Associate Justice

Education: Harvard 1976, 1980 JD
Began Service: November 2014

California Court of Appeal, First Appellate District, Division Three

350 McAllister Street, San Francisco, CA 94102
Tel: (415) 865-7300 Fax: (415) 865-7309
Internet: www.courts.ca.gov/1dca.htm

Number of Judgeships: 4

Court Staff
Deputy Clerk **Mery Chang** . . . . (415) 865-7294
E-mail: mery.chang@jud.ca.gov
Deputy Clerk **Beth Robbins** . . . . (415) 865-7295
E-mail: beth.robbins@jud.ca.gov

Chambers of Administrative Presiding Justice William R. McGuiness

350 McAllister Street, San Francisco, CA 94102
Tel: (415) 865-7300 Fax: (415) 865-7309

William R. McGuiness
Administrative Presiding Justice

Date of Birth: 1946
Education: Santa Clara U 1968 BA; U San Francisco 1972 JD
Began Service: December 21, 1998
Appointed By: Governor Pete Wilson
Next Election: November 2018
Term Expires: January 2019
Political Affiliation: Republican

Government: Deputy District Attorney, Office of the District Attorney, County of Alameda, California (1973-1980); Senior Deputy District Attorney, Office of the District Attorney, County of Alameda, California (1980-1983); Counsel, PresidentsTask Force on Victims of Crime (1982); Associate Deputy Attorney General, United States Attorney General, United States Department of Justice, Ronald Reagan Administration (1985-1986)

Judicial: Judge, Superior Court of California (1986-1997); Associate Justice, California Court of Appeal, First Appellate District, Division Four (1997-1998)

Current Memberships: Alameda County Bar Association; The American Inns of Court; California Judges Association

Staff
Research Attorney **James Lawrence Heideman** . . . . (415) 865-7255
E-mail: james.heideman@jud.ca.gov
Education: Harvard; Stanford JD
Research Attorney **Ai Mori** . . . . (415) 865-7227
E-mail: ai.mori@jud.ca.gov
Executive Judicial Assistant **Kristina Zaldana** . . . . (415) 865-7212

Chambers of Associate Justice Stuart R. Pollak

350 McAllister Street, San Francisco, CA 94102-4712
Tel: (415) 865-7300 Fax: (415) 865-7309

Stuart R. Pollak
Associate Justice

Date of Birth: August 24, 1937
Education: Stanford 1959 AB; Harvard 1962 LLB
Began Service: January 2002
Appointed By: Governor Gray Davis
Term Expires: January 5, 2027
Political Affiliation: Democrat

Clerkships: Law Clerk, Chief Justice Earl Warren, The Supreme Court of the United States (1962-1963); Law Clerk, Justice Harold Burton, The Supreme Court of the United States (1962-1963); Law Clerk, Justice Stanley Forman Reed, The Supreme Court of the United States (1962-1963)

Government: Special Assistant to the Assistant Attorney General, United States Department of Justice (1963-1965)

Judicial: Judge, San Francisco Superior Court (1982-2002)

Legal Practice: Associate and Partner, Howard, Rice, Nemerovski, Canady & Pollak (1965-1982)

Staff
Administrative Specialist **Charles Johnson** . . . . (415) 865-7389

Chambers of Associate Justice Peter Siggins
350 McAllister Street, San Francisco, CA 94102
Tel: (415) 865-7300 Fax: (415) 865-7309
E-mail: first.district@jud.ca.gov

Peter Siggins
Associate Justice

Education: Loyola Marymount BA; Hastings 1975 JD
Began Service: January 9, 2006
Appointed By: Governor Arnold Schwarzenegger
Next Election: November 2022

Government: Legal Affairs Chief Deputy, Attorney General (Justice Department), California; Legal Affairs Secretary, Legal Affairs Office, Office of the Governor, State of California

Staff
Research Attorney **Hannah Rabkin** .... (415) 865-7300
E-mail: hannah.rabkin@jud.ca.gov
Education: Yale 1982 BA; Boalt Hall 1987 JD
Research Attorney **Paul Kenney** .... (415) 865-7300
E-mail: paul.kenney@jud.ca.gov
Education: Harvard 1980 JD
Judicial Assistant **Sheena Green** .... (415) 865-7300

Chambers of Associate Justice Martin J. Jenkins
350 McAllister Street, San Francisco, CA 94102
Tel: (415) 865-7300 Fax: (415) 865-7309
E-mail: martin.jenkins@jud.ca.gov

Martin J. Jenkins
Associate Justice

Date of Birth: 1953
Education: Santa Clara U 1976 BA; U San Francisco 1980 JD
Began Service: April 2008
Next Election: November 2022
Election Type: Retention Election

Corporate: Professional Football Player, Seattle Seahawks (1977)

Government: Deputy District Attorney, Office of the District Attorney, County of Alameda, California (1980-1983); Trial Attorney, Civil Rights Division-Criminal Section, United States Department of Justice, Ronald Reagan Administration (1983-1985)

Judicial: Judge, Oakland-Piedmont-Emeryville Municipal Court (1989-1992); Judge, California Superior Court, Alameda County (1992-1997); District Judge, United States District Court for the Northern District of California (1997-2008)

Legal Practice: General Litigation Department, Legal Department, Pacific Bell Company (1985-1989)

Current Memberships: The American Inns of Court; Charles Houston Bar Association

Staff
Staff Attorney **(Vacant)** .... (415) 865-7319
Staff Attorney **Lee G. Sullivan** .... (415) 865-7253
E-mail: lee.sullivan@jud.ca.gov
Education: North Carolina; Georgetown JD
Secretary **Susan Clancy** .... (415) 865-7379

California Court of Appeal, First Appellate District, Division Four
350 McAllister Street, San Francisco, CA 94102
Tel: (415) 865-7300 Fax: (415) 865-7309
Internet: www.courts.ca.gov/1dca.htm

Number of Judgeships: 4

Court Staff
Deputy Clerk **Ann Reasoner** .... (415) 865-7297
E-mail: ann.reasoner@jud.ca.gov

California Court of Appeal, First Appellate District, Division Four *continued*

Deputy Clerk **Channing Hoo** .... (415) 865-7296
E-mail: channing.hoo@jud.ca.gov

Chambers of Presiding Justice Ignazio J. Ruvolo
350 McAllister Street, San Francisco, CA 94102
Tel: (415) 865-7300 Fax: (415) 865-7213
E-mail: Ignazio.Ruvolo@jud.ca.gov

Ignazio J. Ruvolo
Presiding Justice

Date of Birth: 1947
Education: Rutgers 1969 BA; San Diego 1972 JD; Virginia 2004 LLM
Began Service: January 2006
Appointed By: Governor Arnold Schwarzenegger
Term Expires: January 5, 2027

Government: Trial Attorney, Civil Division, United States Department of Justice, Richard M. Nixon Administration (1972-1977)

Judicial: Judge, California Superior Court, Contra Costa County (1994-1996); Associate Justice, California Court of Appeal, First Appellate District, Division Two (1996-2006)

Legal Practice: Associate, Bronson, Bronson & McKinnon (1977-1983); Partner, Bronson, Bronson & McKinnon (1983-1994)

Current Memberships: California Judges Association

Staff
Judicial Assistant **Lisa Wenter** .... (415) 865-7362
Education: St Mary's Col (CA) 2003 BA

Chambers of Associate Justice Timothy A. Reardon
350 McAllister Street, San Francisco, CA 94102-4712
Tel: (415) 865-7300 Fax: (415) 865-7309
E-mail: first.district@jud.ca.gov

Timothy A. Reardon
Associate Justice

Date of Birth: 1941
Education: Notre Dame 1963 BA; Hastings 1966 JD
Began Service: August 20, 1990
Appointed By: Governor George Deukmejian
Next Election: November 2022
Term Expires: January 4, 2023
Political Affiliation: Democrat

Government: Deputy Attorney General, State of California (1966-1979); Senior Assistant Attorney General, State of California (1979-1983); Deputy District Attorney, County of Alameda, California; Special Assistant United States Attorney, Northern District of California, United States Department of Justice

Judicial: Judge, San Francisco Municipal Court; Judge, California Superior Court, City and County of San Francisco

Current Memberships: Lawyers Club of San Francisco

Chambers of Associate Justice Maria P. Rivera

350 McAllister Street, San Francisco, CA 94102-4712
Tel: (415) 865-7240 Fax: (415) 865-7309

Maria P. Rivera
Associate Justice

Education: Smith BA; U San Francisco JD
Began Service: January 2002
Appointed By: Governor Gray Davis
Next Election: November 2018
Election Type: General Election
Term Expires: January 2019

Government: Deputy District Attorney, Office of the District Attorney, City and County of San Francisco, California (1978-1979); Assistant U.S. Attorney, California - Northern District, Executive Office for United States Attorneys, United States Department of Justice (1979-1981)

Judicial: Judge, Contra Costa County Superior Court, County of Contra Costa, California (1997-2002)

Legal Practice: Associate, Morrison & Foerster LLP (1974-1978); Van Voorhis & Skaggs (1981-1985); McCutchen, Doyle, Brown & Enersen (1985-1996)

Staff

Research Attorney **A. Margaret Bielak** . . . . (415) 865-7300
E-mail: margaret.bielak@jud.ca.gov
Education: U San Francisco; Boalt Hall 1991 JD

Research Attorney **Gloria Maria Gonzalez** . . . . (415) 865-7300
E-mail: gloria.gonzalez@jud.ca.gov
Education: UC Berkeley; Boalt Hall 1981 JD

Judicial Assistant **Melissa Hernandez** . . . . (415) 865-7242

Chambers of Associate Justice Jon B. Streeter

350 McAllister Street, San Francisco, CA 94102
Tel: (415) 865-7300

Jon B. Streeter
Associate Justice

Education: Stanford 1978 AB; Boalt Hall 1981 JD
Began Service: November 2014

California Court of Appeal, First Appellate District, Division Five

350 McAllister Street, San Francisco, CA 94102
Tel: (415) 865-7300 Fax: (415) 865-7309
Internet: www.courts.ca.gov/1dca.htm

Number of Judgeships: 4

Court Staff

Deputy Clerk **Felix Castuera** . . . . (415) 865-7298
E-mail: felix.castuera@jud.ca.gov

Chambers of Presiding Justice Barbara J. R. Jones

350 McAllister Street, San Francisco, CA 94102-3600
Tel: (415) 865-7300 Fax: (415) 865-7309
E-mail: barbara.jones@jud.ca.gov

Barbara J. R. Jones
Presiding Justice

Date of Birth: 1943
Education: Duke 1965 BA; U San Francisco 1974 JD
Began Service: December 6, 1996
Appointed By: Governor Pete Wilson
Next Election: November 7, 2018
Election Type: Retention Election
Term Expires: January 2019
Political Affiliation: Republican

Judicial: Member, Panel of Arbitrators, California Superior Court, City and County of San Francisco (1980-1992); Judge, San Francisco Superior Court (1992); Judge, California Superior Court, City and County of San Francisco (1992-1996); Associate Justice, California Court of Appeal, First Appellate District, Division Five (1996-1998)

Legal Practice: Associate, Hoberg, Finger & Brown (1975); Associate then Partner, Abramson & Bianco (1975-1982); Partner, Bianco, Brandi & Jones (1982-1992)

Staff

Senior Attorney **John Moore** . . . . (415) 865-7300
E-mail: john.moore@jud.ca.gov

Staff Attorney **Adrienne Rogers** . . . . (415) 865-7300
E-mail: adrienne.rogers@jud.ca.gov
Education: Harvard 2000 BA; Hastings 2003 JD

Judicial Assistant **Cathy Gifford** . . . .(415) 865-7300

Chambers of Associate Justice Mark B. Simons

350 McAllister Street, San Francisco, CA 94102
Tel: (415) 865-7300 Fax: (415) 865-7309
E-mail: first.district@jud.ca.gov

Mark B. Simons
Associate Justice

Education: Michigan 1967 BA; Chicago 1970 JD
Began Service: January 29, 2001
Appointed By: Governor Gray Davis

Academic: Dean, Bernard E. Witkin Judicial College; Adjunct Professor, Hastings College of the Law

Government: Deputy Public Defender, County of Contra Costa, California (1980)

Judicial: Judge, Mount Diablo Municipal Court (1980-1995); Judge, Contra Costa County Superior Court (1995-2000); Supervising Judge, Family Law Division, Contra Costa County Superior Court (1996-1997); Presiding Judge, Contra Costa County Superior Court (1999-2000); Justice Pro Tempore, First District Court of Appeal

Legal Practice: Associate, Cooley Godward LLP (1980)

Current Memberships: The Robert G. McGrath American Inn of Court, The American Inns of Court; Board of Governors, Northern California Chapter, Association of Business Trial Lawyers

Staff

Judicial Assistant **Craig Dahlquiest** . . . .(415) 865-7300
E-mail: first.district@jud.ca.gov

Chambers of Associate Justice Henry E. Needham, Jr.
350 McAllister Street, San Francisco, CA 94102
Tel: (415) 865-7300 Fax: (415) 865-7309
E-mail: henry.needham@jud.ca.gov

Henry E. Needham, Jr.
Associate Justice

Education: Fisk 1965 BA; San Francisco Law 1979 JD
Began Service: January 2007
Next Election: November 2022
Election Type: Retention Election

Judicial: Superior Court Judge, County of Alameda, California (1996-2006)

Legal Practice: Attorney, Anderson, Galloway & Lucchese (1988-1996)

Chambers of Associate Justice Terence L. Bruiniers
2424 Ventura Street, Fresno, CA 93721
Tel: (559) 445-5491 Fax: (559) 445-5769
E-mail: terence.bruiniers@jud.ca.gov

Terence L. Bruiniers
Associate Justice

Education: UC Berkeley BA; Boalt Hall 1973 JD
Began Service: June 15, 2009
Appointed By: Governor Arnold Schwarzenegger
Next Election: November 2022

STATE COURTS – CALIFORNIA

California Court of Appeal, Second Appellate District
Ronald Reagan State Building, 300 South Spring Street, Room 2217,
Los Angeles, CA 90013
Tel: (213) 830-7000 Fax: (213) 897-2430
Internet: www.courts.ca.gov/2dca.htm

Number of Judgeships: 32

Number of Vacancies: 6

Areas Covered: Counties of Los Angeles, San Luis Obispo, Santa Barbara and Ventura

Court Staff
Clerk of Court **Joseph A. Lane** . . . . (213) 830-7000
E-mail: joseph.lane@jud.ca.gov

California Court of Appeal, Second Appellate District, Division One
Ronald Reagan State Building, 300 South Spring Street,
Los Angeles, CA 90013
Tel: (213) 830-7000 Fax: (213) 897-7813
Internet: www.courts.ca.gov/2dca.htm

Number of Judgeships: 4

Court Staff
Deputy Clerk **Connie Han** . . . . (213) 830-7120
Deputy Clerk **Shirley Stahl** . . . . (213) 830-7121

Chambers of Presiding Justice Frances Rothschild
300 South Spring Street, Los Angeles, CA 90013
Tel: (213) 830-7530 Fax: (213) 830-7011
E-mail: frances.rothschild@jud.ca.gov

Frances Rothschild
Presiding Justice

Education: UCLA BA
Began Service: April 5, 2005
Appointed By: Governor Arnold Schwarzenegger
Term Expires: 2019

Staff
Career Law Clerk **(Vacant)** . . . . (213) 830-7530
Career Law Clerk **Daniel McCarthy** . . . . (213) 830-7530
Career Law Clerk **Judith Posner** . . . . (213) 830-7530
E-mail: judith.posner@jud.ca.gov
Education: UCLA 1993 JD
Secretary **Tracey Bumgarner** . . . . (213) 830-7530
E-mail: tracey.bumgarner@jud.ca.gov

Chambers of Associate Justice Victoria Gerrard Chaney
300 South Spring Street, Los Angeles, CA 90013
Tel: (213) 830-7500 Fax: (213) 897-7813
E-mail: victoria.chaney@jud.ca.gov

Victoria Gerrard Chaney
Associate Justice

Date of Birth: 1946
Education: Mount St Mary's Sem BA; Loyola Marymount JD
Began Service: June 11, 2009
Appointed By: Governor Arnold Schwarzenegger
Next Election: November 2022
Election Type: Retention Election
Political Affiliation: Republican

Government: Assistant City Attorney, Office of the City Attorney, City of Los Angeles, California (1979-1990)

Judicial: Judge, Los Angeles County Municipal Court (1990-1994); Judge, County of Los Angeles, Superior Court of California (1994-2009)

Legal Practice: Associate, Veatch, Carlson, Grogan and Nelson (1982-1983)

Chambers of Associate Justice Jeffrey W. Johnson
300 South Spring Street, Los Angeles, CA 90013
Tel: (213) 830-7000 Fax: (213) 897-7813
E-mail: jeffrey.johnson@jud.ca.gov

Jeffrey W. Johnson
Associate Justice

Date of Birth: 1960
Education: Duke 1982 BA; Yale 1985 JD
Began Service: June 2009
Appointed By: Governor Arnold Schwarzenegger
Next Election: November 2022
Political Affiliation: Democrat

Government: Assistant U.S. Attorney, California - Central District, Executive Office for United States Attorneys, United States Department of Justice (1989-1999)

Legal Practice: Associate, Manatt, Phelps, Rothenberg & Phillips, LLP (1985-1989)

California Court of Appeal, Second Appellate District, Division Two

Ronald Reagan State Building, 300 South Spring Street,
Los Angeles, CA 90013
Tel: (213) 830-7102 Fax: (213) 897-5811
Internet: www.courts.ca.gov/2dca.htm

Number of Judgeships: 4

Court Staff
Senior Clerk **Orlando Carbone** .... (213) 830-7000
E-mail: orlando.carbone@jud.ca.gov
Senior Deputy Clerk **Joyce Hatter** .... (213) 830-7000
E-mail: joyce.hatter@jud.ca.gov

Chambers of Presiding Justice Roger Wayne Boren

Ronald Reagan State Building, 300 South Spring Street,
Los Angeles, CA 90013
Tel: (213) 830-7300 Fax: (213) 897-9005

Roger Wayne Boren
Presiding Justice

Date of Birth: 1941
Education: UC Berkeley 1966 BA; San José State 1968 MA; UCLA 1973 JD
Began Service: January 12, 1993
Term Expires: December 31, 2018
Political Affiliation: Republican

Government: Deputy, Office of the Attorney General, State of California (1973-1984)

Judicial: Judge, Newhall Municipal Court, Los Angeles County; Judge, California Superior Court, Los Angeles County

Military Service: United States Army (1968-1970); United States Army Reserve, United States Department of the Army (1970-1979)

Current Memberships: California Judges Association; State Bar of California

Staff
Secretary **Loren Cooper** .... (213) 830-7300

Chambers of Associate Justice Judith M. Ashmann-Gerst

Ronald Reagan State Building, 300 South Spring Street,
Los Angeles, CA 90013
Tel: (213) 830-7323 Fax: (213) 897-9005
E-mail: judith.ashmanngerst@jud.ca.gov

Judith M. Ashmann-Gerst
Associate Justice

Date of Birth: 1944
Education: UCLA 1965 BA; Whittier 1972 JD
Began Service: December 7, 2001
Appointed By: Governor Gray Davis
Next Election: November 2022
Term Expires: November 2022
Political Affiliation: Democrat

Government: Deputy Attorney General (1972-1976); Deputy City Attorney (1976-1979); Executive Assistant United States Attorney (1979-1981)

Judicial: Judge, Los Angeles Municipal Court (1981-1986); Judge, Los Angeles Superior Court (1986-2001)

Current Memberships: California Judges Association; California Women Lawyers Bar Association; Los Angeles County Bar Association; National Association of Women Judges

Chambers of Associate Justice Judith M. Ashmann-Gerst *continued*

Staff
Appellate Court Attorney **Melissa Shalit** .... (213) 830-7322
E-mail: melissa.shalit@jud.ca.gov
Education: Brandeis 1991 BA; Cardozo 1994 JD
Appellate Court Attorney **Derek Rogers** .... (213) 830-7321
E-mail: derek.rogers@jud.ca.gov
Education: U Pacific 1989 BA; UC Davis 1992 JD
Appellate Court Attorney **Allison Stuart** .... (213) 830-7311
E-mail: allison.stuart@jud.ca.gov
Education: Loyola U (Los Angeles) JD

Chambers of Associate Justice Victoria M. Chavez

Ronald Reagan State Building, 300 South Spring Street,
Los Angeles, CA 90013
Tel: (213) 830-7000

Victoria M. Chavez
Associate Justice

Education: U San Francisco 1975 BA; Loyola Law 1978 JD
Began Service: December 2005
Appointed By: Governor Arnold Schwarzenegger

Judicial: Municipal Judge, City of Los Angeles, California (1988-1992); Judge, Los Angeles County Superior Court, County of Los Angeles, California (1992-2005)

Legal Practice: Attorney, Pomerantz and Chavez (1979-1988)

Staff
Judicial Assistant **Ann Bird** .... (213) 830-7000
E-mail: ann.bird@jud.ca.gov

Chambers of Associate Justice Brian M. Hoffstadt

300 South Spring Street, Los Angeles, CA 90013
Tel: (213) 830-7102

Brian M. Hoffstadt
Associate Justice

Began Service: 2014
Appointed By: Governor Jerry Brown

California Court of Appeal, Second Appellate District, Division Three

Ronald Reagan State Building, 300 South Spring Street,
Los Angeles, CA 90013
Tel: (213) 830-7000 Fax: (213) 830-7003
Internet: www.courts.ca.gov/2dca.htm

Number of Judgeships: 4

Court Staff
Deputy Clerk **Valorie Gray** .... (213) 830-7000
Deputy Clerk **Zaida Clayton** .... (213) 830-7000
E-mail: zaida.clayton@jud.ca.gov

Chambers of Presiding Justice Lee S. Edmon

300 South Spring Street, Los Angeles, CA 90013
Tel: (213) 830-7000

Lee Smalley Edmon
Presiding Justice

Education: Illinois 1981 JD

Chambers of Associate Justice Patti S. Kitching
Ronald Reagan State Building, 300 South Spring Street, Fourth Floor North, Los Angeles, CA 90013
Tel: (213) 830-7468 Fax: (213) 897-7933

Patti S. Kitching
Associate Justice

Date of Birth: 1941
Education: UCLA 1963 BA; Loyola Marymount 1974 JD
Began Service: January 12, 1993
Appointed By: Governor Pete Wilson
Term Expires: January 7, 2019
Political Affiliation: Republican

Government: Deputy Attorney General, United States Department of Justice (1975-1986)

Judicial: Judge, Los Angeles Municipal Court, Los Angeles Judicial District (1986-1988); Judge, California Superior Court, Los Angeles County (1990-1993)

Legal Practice: Senior Counsel, Bank of America (1986-1988)

Chambers of Associate Justice Richard D. Aldrich
Ronald Reagan State Building, 300 South Spring Street, Los Angeles, CA 90013
Tel: (213) 830-7475 Fax: (213) 830-7003

Richard D. Aldrich
Associate Justice

Date of Birth: 1938
Education: Loyola Marymount 1960 BS; UCLA 1963 LLB
Began Service: August 29, 1994
Appointed By: Governor Pete Wilson
Term Expires: January 7, 2019

Academic: President and General Counsel, Casualty Insurance Corporation of California (1967-1969)

Corporate: General Counsel, Equitable Savings and Loan Association (1970-1971)

Judicial: Judge, Superior Court, County of Ventura, California (1991-1994)

Nonprofit: Chairman Emeritus, Board of Regents, Loyola Marymount University

Current Memberships: American Bar Association; American Board of Trial Advocates; American College of Trial Lawyers; California Judges Association; International Academy of Trial Judges; International Academy of Trial Lawyers; Los Angeles County Bar Association

Staff
Staff Attorney **Janet Dickson** .... (213) 830-7462
E-mail: janet.dickson@jud.ca.gov
Staff Attorney **Janet Tongsuthi** .... (213) 830-7477
E-mail: janet.tongsuthi@jud.ca.gov
Education: UCLA 1992, 1995 JD
Staff Attorney **Sarah Waldstein** .... (213) 830-7476
E-mail: sarah.waldstein@jud.ca.gov
Judicial Assistant **Gina Buhay** .... (213) 830-7475
E-mail: gina.buhay@jud.ca.gov

California Court of Appeal, Second Appellate District, Division Four
Ronald Reagan State Building, 300 South Spring Street, Los Angeles, CA 90013
Tel: (213) 830-7000
Internet: www.courts.ca.gov/2dca.htm

Number of Judgeships: 4

Court Staff
Fax: (213) 897-7933

Deputy Clerk **Vivian Guzman** .... (213) 830-7000
Deputy Clerk **Sandy Veverka** .... (213) 830-7000

Chambers of Presiding Justice Norman L. Epstein
Ronald Reagan State Building, 300 South Spring Street, Los Angeles, CA 90013
Tel: (213) 830-7438 Fax: (213) 830-7020

Norman L. Epstein
Presiding Justice

Date of Birth: 1933
Education: UCLA 1955 BA, 1958 LLB
Began Service: April 1, 1990
Term Expires: 2019

Academic: General Counsel, The California State University System (1962-1975); Visiting Professor, California State (Los Angeles) (1968); Visiting Professor, California State (Northridge) (1973); Vice Chancellor and General Counsel, The California State University System; Associate Dean, California Judicial College (1980-1981); Dean, California Judicial College (1981-1983); Lecturer in Law, University of Southern California (1989-1990); Faculty, California Continuing Judicial Studies Program; Lecturer, National Judicial College

Government: Deputy Attorney General, State of California (1959-1962)

Judicial: Judge, Los Angeles County Municipal Court, Los Angeles Judicial District (1975-1980); Judge, Los Angeles Superior Court (1980); Judge, California Superior Court, Los Angeles County (1980-1990); Associate Justice pro tempore, California Court of Appeal, Second Appellate District, Division Five; Associate Justice pro tempore, California Court of Appeal, Second Appellate District, Division One

Current Memberships: American Bar Foundation; American Bar Association; The American Law Institute; California Judges Association; Lawyers Club of Los Angeles; Los Angeles County Bar Association; National Association of College and University Attorneys

Chambers of Associate Justice Thomas L. Willhite, Jr.
Ronald Reagan State Building, 300 South Spring Street, Los Angeles, CA 90013
Tel: (213) 830-7433 Fax: (213) 897-7933

Thomas L. Willhite, Jr.
Associate Justice

Education: UCLA BA; Loyola Marymount JD
Began Service: April 5, 2005
Appointed By: Governor Arnold Schwarzenegger
Term Expires: January 8, 2019

Government: Deputy Attorney General, Office of the Attorney General, State of California

Judicial: Judge, Los Angeles Municipal Court (1990-1997); Judge, Los Angeles Superior Court (1997-2005); Justice Pro Tempore, California Court of Appeal, Second Appellate District, Division Five (2001)

STATE COURTS – CALIFORNIA

Chambers of Associate Justice Nora Manella

Ronald Reagan State Building, Court of Appeal, 300 South Spring Street, Los Angeles, CA 90013
Tel: (213) 830-7443 Fax: (213) 897-7933

Nora Manella
Associate Justice

Date of Birth: 1951
Education: Wellesley 1972 BA; USC 1975 JD
Began Service: May 2006
Appointed By: Governor Arnold Schwarzenegger
Next Election: 2026
Election Type: Retention Election
Term Expires: January 5, 2027

Clerkships: Law Clerk The Honorable John Minor Wisdom, United States Court of Appeals for the Fifth Circuit (1975-1976)

Government: Legal Counsel, Subcommittee on the Constitution, Committee on the Judiciary, United States Senate (1976-1978); Assistant United States Attorney, Major Crimes Unit, Central District of California, United States Attorney's Office, United States Department of Justice, Ronald Reagan Administration (1982-1986); Assistant United States Attorney, Deputy Chief, Criminal Complaints, Central District of Califonia, United States Attorney's Office, United States Department of Justice, Ronald Reagan Administration (1986-1987); Assistant United States Attorney, Chief, Criminal Appeals, Central District of California, United States Attorney's Office, United States Department of Justice, Ronald Reagan Administration (1988-1990); United States Attorney, Central District of California, United States Attorney's Office, United States Department of Justice, William J. Clinton Administration (1994-1998)

Judicial: Judge, Los Angeles Municipal Court (1990-1992); Judge, California Superior Court, Los Angeles County (1992-1993); District Judge, United States District Court for the Central District of California (1998-2006)

Legal Practice: Associate, O'Melveny & Myers (Washington, DC; Los Angeles, CA) (1978-1982); Associate, O'Melveny & Myers (1979-1982)

Current Memberships: The American Law Institute; Federal Bar Association; National Association of Women Judges

Staff
Career Law Clerk **Meri A. de Kelaita** .... (213) 830-7443
Education: UCLA 1981 JD
Career Law Clerk **Gary Gleb** .... (213) 830-7443
Education: UCLA 1992 JD
Career Law Clerk **Hieu T. Hoang** .... (213) 830-7443
Education: Pennsylvania 2001 JD
Judicial Assistant **Arlene Chavez** .... (213) 830-7443

Chambers of Associate Justice Audrey B. Collins

300 South Spring Street, Los Angeles, CA 90013
Tel: (213) 830-7000

Audrey B. Collins
Associate Justice

Date of Birth: 1945
Education: Howard U 1967 BA; American U 1969 MA; UCLA 1977 JD

Current Memberships: American Bar Association; Black Women Lawyers Association of Los Angeles, Inc.; California Women Lawyers Bar Association; The John M. Langston Bar Association; Los Angeles County Bar Association; National Association of Women Judges; National Bar Association; Women Lawyers Association of Los Angeles

California Court of Appeal, Second Appellate District, Division Five

Ronald Reagan State Building, 300 South Spring Street, North Tower, Los Angeles, CA 90013
Tel: (213) 830-7000
Internet: www.courts.ca.gov/2dca.htm

Number of Judgeships: 4

Court Staff
Senior Deputy Clerk **Joshua Dunn** .... (213) 830-7105
Senior Deputy Clerk **Deborah Lee** .... (213) 830-7105
E-mail: dru.nolan@jud.ca.gov

Chambers of Presiding Justice Paul Turner

Ronald Reagan State Building, 300 South Spring Street, Suite 200, Los Angeles, CA 90013
Tel: (213) 830-7000 Fax: (213) 897-2430

Paul Turner
Presiding Justice

Date of Birth: 1947
Education: Cal State (Long Beach) 1969 BA; UCLA 1972 JD
Began Service: November 2, 1989
Appointed By: Governor George Deukmejian
Next Election: November 2026
Term Expires: January 2027
Political Affiliation: Republican

Judicial: Judge, Los Angeles County Municipal Court, Los Angeles Judicial District (1983-1985); Judge, California Superior Court, Los Angeles County (1985-1989)

Legal Practice: Associate, Richard H. Levin (1973-1975); Associate, Axelrad, Sevilla and Ross (1975-1979); Alan D. Ross Law Corp. (1979-1983)

Military Service: United States Army National Guard (1970-1976)

Current Memberships: California Judges Association

Staff
Research Attorney **Karen T. Grey** .... (213) 830-7000
E-mail: karen.grey@jud.ca.gov
Research Attorney **Hoa Hoang** .... (213) 830-7000
E-mail: hoa.hoang@jud.ca.gov
Research Attorney **Lela J. Huckabee** .... (213) 830-7000
E-mail: lela.huckabee@jud.ca.gov
Judicial Assistant **Eric Sowatsky** .... (213) 830-7000

Chambers of Associate Justice Richard M. Mosk

Ronald Reagan State Building, 300 South Spring Street, Los Angeles, CA 90013
Tel: (213) 830-7000 Fax: (213) 897-2430

Richard M. Mosk
Associate Justice

Date of Birth: 1939
Education: Stanford 1960 AB; Harvard 1963 JD
Began Service: October 2001
Appointed By: Governor Gray Davis
Next Election: November 2026
Term Expires: January 2027
Political Affiliation: Democrat

Academic: Lecturer, University of Southern California Law Center (1978); Chairman and Co-Chairman, Classification and Rating Administration of Motion Picture Association of America (1994-2000)

Clerkships: Law Clerk The Honorable Matthew Tobriner, California Supreme Court (1964-1965)

Government: Staff Member, President's Commission on the Assassination of President Kennedy (1964); Deputy Public Defender (1975-1976)

(continued on next page)

Chambers of Associate Justice Richard M. Mosk *continued*

Judicial: Judge, Iran-United States Claims Tribunal (1981-1984); Judge, Iran-United States Claims Tribunal (1997-2001)

Legal Practice: Associate, Mitchell Silberberg & Knupp LLP; Principal, Sanders, Barnet, Goldman, Simons & Mosk (1987-2001)

Military Service: Air National Guard (1963-1965); United States Naval Reserve (1965-1975)

Current Memberships: American Bar Foundation; American Bar Association; Beverly Hills Bar Association; California Judges Association; College of Commercial Arbitrators; Federal Bar Association; Los Angeles County Bar Association

Staff

Research Attorney **Michael Egan** .... (213) 830-7000
E-mail: michael.egan@jud.ca.gov
Research Attorney **Terrence King** .... (213) 830-7000
E-mail: terrence.king@jud.ca.gov
Research Attorney **Glenn Savard** .... (213) 830-7000
E-mail: glenn.savard@jud.ca.gov
Judicial Assistant **Lori Jankovic** .... (213) 830-7000
Education: SUNY (Binghamton) 1976 BA

Chambers of Associate Justice Sandy R. Kriegler

Ronald Reagan State Building, 300 South Spring Street,
Los Angeles, CA 90013
Tel: (213) 830-7348 Fax: (213) 897-5990

Sandy R. Kriegler
Associate Justice

Education: Cal State (Northridge) BA; Loyola Marymount JD
Began Service: April 5, 2005
Appointed By: Governor Arnold Schwarzenegger

Judicial: Deputy Attorney General, State of California (1975-1985); Judge, Los Angeles Municipal Court (1985-1989); Judge, Los Angeles Superior Court (1989-2005); Supervising Judge, Northwest Judicial District (2002-2004)

Staff

Administrative Office Assistant **Lucia Brambila** .... (213) 830-7390
E-mail: lucia.brambila@jud.ca.gov Fax: (213) 897-5990

California Court of Appeal, Second Appellate District, Division Six

200 East Santa Clara Street, Ventura, CA 93001-2760
Tel: (805) 641-4700 Fax: (805) 643-8344
Internet: www.courts.ca.gov/2dca.htm

Number of Judgeships: 4

Number of Vacancies: 1

Court Staff

Assistant Clerk/Administrator **Paul T. McGill** .... (805) 641-4711
Education: Loyola Marymount 1972 BA, 1978 MBA
Deputy Clerk **Gay Bents** .... (805) 641-4713
E-mail: gay.bents@jud.ca.gov
Deputy Clerk **Victor Salas** .... (805) 641-4718
Deputy Clerk **Patricia Silva** .... (805) 641-4714
E-mail: patricia.silva@jud.ca.gov
Deputy Clerk **Jim Terry** .... (805) 641-4715
E-mail: jim.terry@jud.ca.gov

Chambers of Presiding Justice Arthur Gilbert

200 East Santa Clara Street, Ventura, CA 93001
Tel: (805) 641-4730 Fax: (805) 643-8345
E-mail: justice.arthur.gilbert@jud.ca.gov

Arthur Gilbert
Presiding Justice

Date of Birth: 1937
Education: UCLA 1960 BA; Boalt Hall 1963 LLB
Began Service: December 1982
Term Expires: January 7, 2019

Academic: Teaching and Research Assistant, University of California, Berkeley (1964); Instructor, Los Angeles Valley Community College (1974); Faculty, California Judicial College, University of California, Berkeley

Government: Deputy City Attorney, Criminal Division, City of Los Angeles, California (1964-1965)

Judicial: Judge, Los Angeles Municipal Court, Los Angeles Judicial District (1975-1980); Judge, California Superior Court, Los Angeles County (1980-1982)

Legal Practice: Private Practice (1965-1975)

Staff

Judicial Attorney **Peter Cooney** .... (805) 641-4734
E-mail: peter.cooney@jud.ca.gov
Education: Hastings 1972 JD
Judicial Attorney **Robert Miller** .... (805) 641-4735
E-mail: robert.miller@jud.ca.gov
Education: USC 1972 JD
Judicial Attorney **Lauren Nelson** .... (805) 641-4733
E-mail: lauren.nelson@jud.ca.gov
Education: Loyola Marymount 1974 JD
Judicial Assistant **Bonnie Edwards** .... (805) 641-4745
E-mail: bonnie.edwards@jud.ca.gov
Judicial Attorney **Katy Graham** .... (805) 641-4734
E-mail: katy.graham@jud.ca.gov
Education: Humboldt State 1989 BA; Santa Barbara Law 1994 JD

Chambers of Associate Justice Kenneth Yegan

200 East Santa Clara Street, Ventura, CA 93001
Tel: (805) 641-4740 Fax: (805) 643-8345
E-mail: kenneth.yegan@jud.ca.gov

Kenneth Yegan
Associate Justice

Date of Birth: 1947
Education: UC Santa Barbara 1969 BA; McGeorge 1972 JD
Began Service: December 27, 1990
Next Election: 2026
Term Expires: January 6, 2027
Political Affiliation: Republican

Government: Deputy Public Defender, County of Ventura, California (1972-1975); Senior Attorney, California Court of Appeal, Second Appellate District (1975-1982)

Judicial: Judge, California Municipal Court, Ventura County (1983-1986); Judge, California Superior Court, Ventura County (1986-1990)

Legal Practice: Private Practice (1982-1983)

Current Memberships: California Judges Association

Staff

Attorney **Richard Gerry** .... (805) 641-4782
E-mail: richard.gerry@jud.ca.gov
Education: Harvard 1973 JD

Chambers of Associate Justice Kenneth Yegan *continued*

Attorney **David Harrell** . . . . (805) 641-4743
E-mail: david.harrell@jud.ca.gov
Education: Ventura 1974 JD

Attorney **Julie Huffman** . . . . (805) 641-4759
E-mail: julie.huffman@jud.ca.gov
Education: USC 1987 JD

Chambers of Associate Justice Steven Z. Perren

200 East Santa Clara Street, Ventura, CA 93001
Tel: (805) 641-4770 Fax: (805) 643-8345

Steven Z. Perren
Associate Justice

Date of Birth: 1942
Education: UCLA 1967 JD
Began Service: November 9, 1999
Appointed By: Governor Gray Davis
Next Election: November 2022
Term Expires: January 1, 2023
Political Affiliation: Democrat

Government: Deputy District Attorney, County of Ventura, California (1969-1972)

Judicial: Ventura County Superior Court (1983-1999); President, UCLA Law Alumni Association (2005-2006)

Legal Practice: Benton, Orr, Duval & Buckingham (1972-1976); Ghitterman, Hourigan, Grossman, Finestone & Perren (1976-1983)

Military Service: Lieutenant/Captain, United States Army (1967-1969)

Current Memberships: California Judges Association

Staff
Fax: (805) 643-8345

Attorney **Douglas S. Irwin** . . . . (805) 641-4774
Education: UCLA 1986 BA; Southwestern 1994 JD

Attorney **Susan Krueger** . . . . (805) 641-4780
E-mail: susan.krueger@jud.ca.gov

Attorney **Toby Roberts** . . . . (805) 641-4773
E-mail: toby.roberts@jud.ca.gov

Attorney **Marilyn White-Redmond** . . . . (805) 641-4780
E-mail: marilyn.white-redmond@jud.ca.gov
Education: Cal State (Northridge) 1974 BA; Loyola Law 1978 JD

Librarian **Susan Hill** . . . . (805) 641-4790
E-mail: Susan.Hill@jud.ca.gov

Judicial Assistant **Sally Doyle** . . . . (805) 641-4772
E-mail: sally.doyle@jud.ca.gov

California Court of Appeal, Second Appellate District, Division Seven

Ronald Reagan State Building, 300 South Spring Street, Room 2217, Los Angeles, CA 90013
Tel: (213) 830-7107
Internet: www.courts.ca.gov/2dca.htm

Number of Judgeships: 4

Court Staff

Deputy Clerk **Eva McClintock** . . . . (213) 830-7130
E-mail: eva.mcclintock@jud.ca.gov

Chambers of Presiding Justice Dennis M. Perluss

Ronald Reagan State Building, 300 South Spring Street, Los Angeles, CA 90013
Tel: (213) 830-7418 Fax: (213) 897-2429
E-mail: dennis.perluss@jud.ca.gov

Dennis M. Perluss
Presiding Justice

Date of Birth: 1948
Education: Stanford 1970 BA; Harvard 1973 JD
Began Service: October 2001
Appointed By: Governor Gray Davis
Next Election: November 2026
Term Expires: January 2027
Political Affiliation: Democrat

Academic: Lecturer, University of Southern California (1982); Visiting Professor of Law, University of California, Los Angeles (1994)

Clerkships: Law Clerk The Honorable Shirley Hufstedler, United States Court of Appeals for the Ninth Circuit (1973-1974); Law Clerk The Honorable Potter Stewart, United States Supreme Court (1974-1975)

Judicial: Judge, Los Angeles Superior Court (1999-2001)

Legal Practice: Associate, Beardsley, Hufstedler & Kemble (1975-1977); Partner, Hufstedler & Kaus (1978-1995); Partner, Morrison & Foerster LLP (1995-1999)

Current Memberships: California Judges Association

Staff

Research Attorney **Randee Barak** . . . . (213) 830-7417
E-mail: randee.barak@jud.ca.gov
Education: UCLA 1992 JD

Research Attorney **Mary Newcombe** . . . . (213) 830-7411
E-mail: mary.newcombe@jud.ca.gov

Research Attorney **Deborah Rosenthal** . . . . (213) 830-7416
E-mail: deborah.rosenthal@jud.ca.gov
Education: Loyola U (Chicago) 1997 JD

Judicial Assistant **Veronica Segura** . . . . (213) 830-7415

Chambers of Associate Justice Laurie D. Zelon

300 South Spring Street, Los Angeles, CA 90013
Tel: (213) 830-7107
E-mail: laurie.zelon@jud.ca.gov

Laurie D. Zelon
Associate Justice

Education: Cornell 1974 BA; Harvard 1977 JD
Began Service: 2003
Next Election: November 2022

Affiliation: Member, California Commission on Access to Justice

California Court of Appeal, Second Appellate District, Division Eight

Ronald Reagan State Building, 300 South Spring Street, Los Angeles, CA 90013
Tel: (213) 830-7000 Fax: (213) 897-2430
Internet: www.courts.ca.gov/2dca.htm

Number of Judgeships: 4

Court Staff

Deputy Clerk **Keisha Lewis** . . . . (213) 830-7108
E-mail: keisha.lewis@jud.ca.gov

Deputy Clerk I **Sina Lui** . . . . (213) 830-7108
E-mail: sina.lui@jud.ca.gov

Chambers of Presiding Justice Patricia A. Bigelow
Ronald Reagan State Building, 300 South Spring Street, Los Angeles, CA 90013
Tel: (213) 830-7000

Patricia A. "Tricia" Bigelow
Presiding Justice

Education: Cal State (Fullerton) BA; Pepperdine JD
Began Service: December 30, 2009
Appointed By: Governor Arnold Schwarzenegger
Next Election: November 2022
Political Affiliation: Republican

Government: Deputy Attorney General, Office of the Attorney General, Justice Department, State of California (1986-1995)

Judicial: Municipal Court Judge, City of Los Angeles, California (1995-1998); Judge, Los Angeles County Superior Court, County of Los Angeles, California (1998-2008)

Chambers of Associate Justice Laurence D. Rubin
Ronald Reagan State Building, 300 South Spring Street, Los Angeles, CA 90013
Tel: (213) 830-7365 Fax: (213) 830-7015
E-mail: laurence.rubin@jud.ca.gov

Laurence D. Rubin
Associate Justice

Date of Birth: September 8, 1946
Education: UCLA 1946 BA, 1971 JD
Began Service: October 2001
Appointed By: Governor Gray Davis

Clerkships: Law Clerk, Judge Stanley Mosk, Superior Court of California (1971-1972)

Judicial: Judge, Municipal Court, City of Santa Monica, California (1982-2000); Judge, Los Angeles Superior Court (2000-2001)

Legal Practice: Associate, Kaplan, Livingston, Goodwin, Berkowitz & Selvin (1973-1978); Partner, Kaplan, Livingston, Goodwin, Berkowitz & Selvin (1978-1982); Of Counsel, Mitchell Silberberg & Knupp LLP (1982)

Staff
Attorney **Sharon Perlmutter** .... (213) 830-7365
E-mail: sharon.perlmutter@jud.ca.gov
Education: UC Berkeley 1988 AB; Yale 1991 JD
Attorney **Stacey Mickell** .... (213) 830-7365
E-mail: stacey.mickell@jud.ca.gov
Attorney **Gary Micon** .... (213) 830-7365
E-mail: gary.micon@jud.ca.gov
Judicial Assistant **Patty Garcia** .... (213) 830-7365
E-mail: patty.garcia@jud.ca.gov

Chambers of Associate Justice Madeleine I. Flier
300 South Spring Street, Los Angeles, CA 90013
Tel: (213) 830-7000

Madeleine I. Flier
Associate Justice

Began Service: 2002

Government: Prosecutor, Office of the City Attorney, City of Los Angeles, California; Assistant City Attorney, Office of the City Attorney, City of Los Angeles, California; Chief, Special Prosecution Division, Office of the City Attorney, City of Los Angeles, California; Attorney Advisor, Board of Police Commissioners, City of Los Angeles, California

Judicial: Municipal Court Judge, City of Los Angeles, California (1977-1980)

Chambers of Associate Justice Elizabeth A. Grimes
300 South Spring Street, Los Angeles, CA 90013
Tel: (213) 830-7000 Fax: (213) 897-2430
E-mail: elizabeth.grimes@jud.ca.gov

Elizabeth A. Grimes
Associate Justice

Education: Texas; Stanford 1980 JD
Began Service: 2010
Next Election: November 2022

California Court of Appeal, Third Appellate District
914 Capitol Mall, Fourth Floor, Sacramento, CA 95814
Tel: (916) 654-0209
Internet: www.courts.ca.gov/3dca.htm

Number of Judgeships: 11

Areas Covered: Counties of Alpine, Amador, Butte, Calaveras, Colusa, El Dorado, Glenn, Lassen, Modoc, Mono, Nevada, Placer, Plumas, Sacramento, San Joaquin, Shasta, Sierra, Siskiyou, Sutter, Tehama, Trinity, Yolo and Yuba

Court Staff
Clerk/Administrator **Deena C. Fawcett** .... (916) 654-0209
E-mail: deena.fawcett@jud.ca.gov
Assistant Clerk/Administrator **Colette M. Bruggman** .... (916) 654-0209
E-mail: colette.bruggman@jud.ca.gov
Education: North Dakota 1984 BBA, 1987 JD

Chambers of Administrative Presiding Justice Vance W. Raye
914 Capitol Mall, Fourth Floor, Sacramento, CA 95814
Tel: (916) 654-0209

Vance W. Raye
Administrative Presiding Justice

Date of Birth: 1946
Education: Oklahoma 1967 BA, 1970 JD
Began Service: January 7, 1991
Appointed By: Governor George Deukmejian
Term Expires: January 5, 2027
Political Affiliation: Republican

Government: Deputy Attorney General, State of California (1974-1980); Senior Assistant Attorney General, State of California (1980-1982); Deputy Legislative Secretary, Governor George Deukmejian (R-CA), State of California (1983); Legal Affairs Secretary, Governor George Deukmejian (R-CA), State of California (1983-1989)

Judicial: Judge, California Superior Court, Sacramento County (1989-1991)

Legal Practice: Associate, Bulla and Horning

Military Service: United States Air Force (1970-1974)

Current Memberships: California Association of Black Lawyers; California Judges Association; Wiley Manuel Bar Association

Staff
Judicial Assistant **Kris Harper** .... (916) 654-0209
E-mail: kris.harper@jud.ca.gov

Chambers of Associate Justice Coleman A. Blease

914 Capitol Mall, Fourth Floor, Sacramento, CA 95814
Tel: (916) 654-0209
E-mail: coleman.blease@jud.ca.gov

Coleman A. Blease
Associate Justice

Date of Birth: 1929
Education: UC Berkeley 1952 BA; Boalt Hall 1955 LLB
Began Service: June 15, 1979
Term Expires: January 7, 2019
Political Affiliation: Democrat

Academic: Vice Chairman, California Center for Judicial Education and Research; Instructor, University of California at Berkeley

Legal Practice: Legislative Advocate (1957-1974); Partner, Blease, Vanderlaan & Rothschild (1967-1979)

Staff
Judicial Assistant **Jack Simpson** .... (916) 654-0209
E-mail: jack.simpson@jud.ca.gov

Chambers of Associate Justice George Nicholson

914 Capitol Mall, Fourth Floor, Sacramento, CA 95814
Tel: (916) 654-0209 Fax: (916) 653-0324
E-mail: george.nicholson@jud.ca.gov

George Nicholson
Associate Justice

Date of Birth: 1941
Education: Cal State (Hayward) 1964 BA; Hastings 1967 JD
Began Service: August 23, 1990
Appointed By: Governor George Deukmejian
Next Election: November 2022
Term Expires: January 2, 2023
Political Affiliation: Republican

Academic: Executive Director, California District Attorneys Association (1976-1979); Director and Chief Counsel, National School Safety Center, Pepperdine University (1984-1986); Adjunct Professor, Pepperdine University, Graduate School of Education and Psychology

Government: Deputy District Attorney, County of Alameda, California (1968-1974); Senior Trial Deputy District Attorney, County of Alameda, California (1975-1976); Special Assistant Attorney General, State of California (1979-1980); Senior Assistant Attorney General, State of California (1980-1983); Deputy Director, Special Projects for the Governor, Governor's Office of Planning and Research, State of California (1983-1984)

Judicial: Associate Justice pro tempore, California Supreme Court; Judge, Sacramento Municipal Court (1987-1989); Judge, California Superior Court, Sacramento County (1989-1990)

Legal Practice: Private Practice (1986-1987)

Current Memberships: The Anthony M. Kennedy American Inn of Court, The American Inns of Court; American Judges Association; California Judges Association; The Federalist Society for Law and Public Policy Studies

Staff
Judicial Assistant **Wendy Lebeck** .... (916) 654-0209

Chambers of Associate Justice Harry E. Hull, Jr.

914 Capitol Mall, Fourth Floor, Sacramento, CA 95814
Tel: (916) 654-0209
E-mail: harry.hull@jud.ca.gov

Harry E. Hull, Jr.
Associate Justice

Education: Illinois 1969 BSBA, 1972 JD
Began Service: February 1998
Appointed By: Governor Pete Wilson
Next Election: November 2022
Term Expires: January 2, 2023

Government: Assistant U.S. Attorney, California - Eastern District, Executive Office for United States Attorneys, United States Department of Justice (1976-1979)

Judicial: Judge, Superior Court of Sacramento, County of Sacramento, California (1995-1998)

Legal Practice: Attorney, McDonough, Holland & Allen PC (1979-1995)

Military Service: Capt, United States Air Force, United States Department of the Air Force (1972-1976)

Staff
Judicial Assistant **Rebekah Thornton** .... (916) 654-0209

Chambers of Associate Justice Ronald B. Robie

914 Capitol Mall, Fourth Floor, Sacramento, CA 95814
Tel: (916) 654-0209 Fax: (916) 653-2168

Ronald B. Robie
Associate Justice

Education: UC Berkeley 1958 AB, 1960 MJ; Pacific U 1967 JD
Began Service: January 2002
Appointed By: Governor Gray Davis
Term Expires: January 5, 2027

Government: Vice Chair, Water Resources Control Board, State of California (1969-1975); Director, Water Resources Department, State of California (1975-1983)

Judicial: Judge, Municipal Court, City of Sacramento, California (1983-2002); Judge, Superior Court of Sacramento (1983-2002)

Staff
Judicial Assistant **Malinda Moore** .... (916) 654-0209

Chambers of Associate Justice M. Kathleen Butz

914 Capitol Mall, Fourth Floor, Sacramento, CA 95814
Tel: (916) 654-0209
E-mail: kathleen.butz@jud.ca.gov

M. Kathleen Butz
Associate Justice

Education: UC Davis 1972 BA, 1981 JD
Began Service: October 2003
Appointed By: Governor Gray Davis
Next Election: November 2022
Term Expires: January 2, 2023

Academic: Instructor, California Center for Judicial Education and Research

Judicial: Judge, Superior Court, County of Nevada, California (1996-2003); Presiding Judge, Superior Court, County of Nevada, California (2001-2002)

Profession: Private Practice (1982-1996)

Staff
Judicial Assistant **Sherri Nelson** .... (916) 654-0209

Chambers of Associate Justice Louis R. Mauro

914 Capitol Mall, Fourth Floor, Sacramento, CA 95814
Tel: (916) 654-0209
E-mail: louis.mauro@jud.ca.gov

Louis Mauro
Associate Justice

Education: UC Santa Barbara 1983 BA; UC Davis 1987 JD
Began Service: August 25, 2010
Appointed By: Governor Arnold Schwarzenegger
Term Expires: January 7, 2019

Staff
Judicial Assistant **Rachel Huisman** .... (916) 654-0209
E-mail: rachel.huizman@jud.ca.gov

Chambers of Associate Justice William J. Murray, Jr.

914 Capitol Mall, Fourth Floor, Sacramento, CA 95814
Tel: (916) 654-0209
E-mail: william.murray@jud.ca.gov

William J. Murray, Jr.
Associate Justice

Education: Frostburg State U 1979 BS; George Washington 1982 JD
Began Service: December 10, 2010
Appointed By: Governor Arnold Schwarzenegger

Staff
Judicial Assistant **Teresa Kropp** .... (916) 654-0209

Chambers of Associate Justice Elena J. Duarte

914 Capitol Mall, Fourth Floor, Sacramento, CA 95814
Tel: (916) 654-0209
E-mail: elena.duarte@jud.ca.gov

Elena J. Duarte
Associate Justice

Education: Stanford JD; USC BA
Began Service: December 10, 2010
Appointed By: Governor Arnold Schwarzenegger

Staff
Judicial Assistant **Kathi Rutherdale** .... (916) 654-0209
E-mail: kathy.rutherdale@jud.ca.gov

Chambers of Associate Justice Andrea Hoch

914 Capitol Mall, Fourth Floor, Sacramento, CA 95814
Tel: (916) 654-0209
E-mail: andrea.hoch@jud.ca.gov

Andrea Lynn Hoch
Associate Justice

Education: Stanford AB; McGeorge 1984 JD
Began Service: January 3, 2011
Appointed By: Governor Arnold Schwarzenegger

Staff
Judicial Assistant **Connie Martins** .... (916) 654-0209
E-mail: connie.martins@jud.ca.gov

Chambers of Associate Justice Jonathan Renner

914 Capitol Mall, Sacramento, CA 95814
Tel: (916) 654-0209

Jonathan K. Renner
Associate Justice

Began Service: 2014
Appointed By: Governor Jerry Brown
Term Expires: December 2026

Staff
Judicial Assistant **Nicole Wallen** .... (916) 654-0209
E-mail: nickie.wallen@jud.ca.gov

California Court of Appeal, Fourth Appellate District

750 B Street, Suite 300, San Diego, CA 92101
Tel: (619) 744-0760 Fax: (619) 645-2495
Internet: www.courts.ca.gov/4dca.htm

Number of Judgeships: 25

Areas Covered: Counties of Imperial, Inyo, Orange, Riverside, San Bernardino and San Diego

Court Staff
Clerk of the Court/Administrator **Kevin J. Lane** .... (619) 744-0760
Librarian **Ruth Gervais** .... (619) 744-0786

California Court of Appeal, Fourth Appellate District, Division One

750 B Street, Suite 300, San Diego, CA 92101-8196
Tel: (619) 744-0760 Fax: (619) 645-2495
Internet: www.courts.ca.gov/4dca.htm

Number of Judgeships: 10

Court Staff
Clerk of the Court/Administrator **Kevin J. Lane** .... (619) 744-0760
E-mail: kevin.lane@jud.ca.gov
Managing Attorney **Kimberly A. Stewart** .... (951) 744-0783
E-mail: kimberly.stewart@jud.ca.gov
Education: Ohio State 1986 JD

Chambers of Presiding Justice Judith McConnell

750 B Street, Suite 300, San Diego, CA 92101-8196
Tel: (619) 744-0760
E-mail: judith.mcconnell@jud.ca.gov

Judith McConnell
Presiding Justice

Education: UC Berkeley 1966 BA; Boalt Hall 1969 JD
Began Service: October 3, 2001
Appointed By: Governor Gray Davis
Next Election: November 2022
Term Expires: January 2, 2023

Academic: Adjunct Professor, School of Law, University of San Diego (1973-1976)

Government: Trial Attorney, Department of Transportation, State of California (1969-1976)

Judicial: Judge, San Diego Municipal Court (1978-1980); Judge, San Diego Superior Court (1980-2001)

Legal Practice: Reed, McConnell & Sullivan (1976-1977)

Current Memberships: American Bar Association

Staff
Senior Attorney **Lisa Cooney** .... (619) 744-0604

STATE COURTS—CALIFORNIA

Chambers of Presiding Justice Judith McConnell *continued*

Senior Attorney **Cindie McMahon** . . . . (619) 744-0603
E-mail: cindie.mcmahon@jud.ca.gov
Executive Judicial Assistant **Joyce Matagulay** . . . . (619) 744-0602

Chambers of Associate Justice Patricia D. Benke

750 B Street, Suite 300, San Diego, CA 92101-8196
Tel: (619) 744-0760 Fax: (619) 645-2981

Patricia D. Benke
Associate Justice

Date of Birth: 1949
Education: San Diego State 1971 BA; San Diego 1974 JD
Began Service: June 3, 1987
Appointed By: Governor George Deukmejian
Next Election: November 2018
Term Expires: January 2019
Political Affiliation: Republican

Academic: Writer, Political Analyst, KPBS - Public Television

Government: Deputy Attorney General, Criminal Law Division, State of California (1974-1983)

Judicial: Judge, San Diego County Municipal Court (1983-1985); Judge, California Superior Court, San Diego County (1985-1987)

Current Memberships: California Judges Association; Lawyers Club of San Diego; San Diego County Bar Association; San Diego County Judges Association

Chambers of Associate Justice Richard D. Huffman

750 B Street, Suite 300, San Diego, CA 92101-8196
Tel: (619) 744-0621 Fax: (619) 645-2969

Richard D. Huffman
Associate Justice

Date of Birth: 1939
Education: Cal State (Long Beach) 1961 AB; USC 1965 JD
Began Service: October 13, 1988
Appointed By: Governor George Deukmejian
Term Expires: January 7, 2019
Political Affiliation: Republican

Academic: Director, Center for Criminal Justice Policy and Management, University of San Diego (1979-1985); Instructor, Oxford University (1985); Instructor, Trinity College, Dublin, Ireland (1990); Director, Comparative Law Program, Oxford University (2002)

Government: Deputy Attorney General, State of California (1966-1971); Chief Deputy District Attorney, County of San Diego, California (1971-1981); Assistant District Attorney, Office of the District Attorney, County of San Diego, California (1981-1985)

Judicial: Judge, California Superior Court, San Diego County (1985-1988)

Current Memberships: American Board of Trial Advocates; American College of Trial Lawyers; California Judges Association

Staff

Research Attorney **Valerie Leman** . . . . (619) 744-0624
E-mail: valerie.leman@jud.ca.gov
Education: Stanford 1979 JD
Research Attorney **Chaise R. Bivin** . . . . (619) 744-0623
E-mail: chaise.bivin@jud.ca.gov
Judicial Assistant **Donna J. Pugh** . . . . (619) 744-0622
E-mail: donna.pugh@jud.ca.gov

Chambers of Associate Justice Gilbert Nares

750 B Street, Suite 300, San Diego, CA 92101-8196
Tel: (619) 744-0632 Fax: (619) 645-3009
E-mail: gilbert.nares@jud.ca.gov

Gilbert Nares
Associate Justice

Date of Birth: 1943
Education: San Diego 1964 BA, 1967 JD
Began Service: October 13, 1988
Appointed By: Governor George Deukmejian
Term Expires: January 5, 2027
Political Affiliation: Republican

Judicial: Judge, San Diego County Municipal Court, North County Branch (1976-1978); Judge, California Superior Court, San Diego County (1978-1988)

Legal Practice: Partner, Daubney, Banche, Patterson & Nares (1968-1976)

Staff

Senior Research Attorney **(Vacant)** . . . . (619) 744-0634
Senior Research Attorney **William M. Bothamley** . . . . (619) 744-0633
E-mail: william.bothamley@jud.ca.gov
Education: San Diego 1985 JD
Judicial Assistant **Sandra Feeny** . . . . (619) 744-0632

Chambers of Associate Justice Judith L. Haller

750 B Street, Suite 300, San Diego, CA 92101-8196
Tel: (619) 744-0760 Fax: (619) 645-2818
E-mail: judith.haller@jud.ca.gov

Judith L. Haller
Associate Justice

Date of Birth: 1946
Education: UCLA 1967 BA; San Diego State 1971 MA; Cal Western 1975 JD
Began Service: August 9, 1994
Appointed By: Governor Pete Wilson
Next Election: November 2018
Term Expires: January 2019

Academic: Administrative Staff, San Diego State (1968-1972)

Government: Deputy District Attorney, County of San Diego, California (1976-1979)

Judicial: Judge, California Superior Court, San Diego County (1989-1994)

Legal Practice: Higgs, Fletcher and Mack (1979-1989)

Staff

Staff Attorney **Helene Cauchon** . . . . (619) 744-0760
E-mail: helene.cauchon@jud.ca.gov
Education: UC San Diego 1979 BA; Hastings 1982 JD
Staff Attorney **Melanie Gold** . . . . (619) 744-0760
E-mail: melanie.gold@jud.ca.gov
Education: UC Santa Barbara BA; Santa Clara U 1984 JD
Judicial Assistant **Cathey Byrd** . . . . (619) 744-0760
E-mail: cathey.byrd@jud.ca.gov
Education: San Diego State 1972

Chambers of Associate Justice Alex C. McDonald

750 B Street, Suite 300, San Diego, CA 92101-8196
Tel: (619) 744-0651 Fax: (619) 645-2965
E-mail: alex.mcdonald@jud.ca.gov

Alex C. McDonald
Associate Justice

Date of Birth: 1936
Education: Stanford 1958 BS; Boalt Hall 1961 LLB; Virginia 2001 LLM
Began Service: June 12, 1995
Appointed By: Governor Pete Wilson
Next Election: 2026
Term Expires: 2027

Clerkships: Law Clerk The Honorable Raymond E. Peters, California Supreme Court (1962-1963)

Legal Practice: Private Practice (1963-1995)

Staff

Research Attorney **Stephen Joplin** .... (619) 744-0654
Education: UCLA 1980 JD
Research Attorney **Greg Miller** .... (619) 744-0653
E-mail: greg.miller@jud.ca.gov
Education: Harvard 1981 JD
Judicial Assistant **Joan Mara** .... (619) 744-0652
E-mail: joan.mara@jud.ca.gov

Chambers of Associate Justice James A. McIntyre

750 B Street, Suite 300, San Diego, CA 92101-8196
Tel: (619) 744-0663 Fax: (619) 645-2921
E-mail: james.mcintyre@jud.ca.gov

James A. McIntyre
Associate Justice

Date of Birth: 1938
Education: Brown U 1960 AB; Stanford 1963 JD
Began Service: June 6, 1996
Appointed By: Governor Pete Wilson
Next Election: November 2026
Term Expires: January 5, 2027

Academic: Adjunct Professor of Law, University of San Diego

Judicial: Judge, San Diego County Superior Court (1993-1996)

Legal Practice: McInnis, Fitzgerald, Rees, Sharkey & McIntyre (1963-1993)

Current Memberships: American College of Trial Lawyers; The Honorable William B. Enright American Inn of Court, The American Inns of Court

Staff

Senior Appellate Court Attorney **Marsha Amin** .... (619) 774-0664
E-mail: marsha.amin@jud.ca.gov
Education: San Diego 2005 JD
Senior Appellate Court Attorney **Susan Mittman** .... (619) 774-0663
E-mail: susan.mittman@jud.ca.gov
Education: Suffolk 1992 JD
Judicial Assistant **Lara Joa** .... (619) 744-0662
E-mail: lara.joa@jud.ca.gov

Chambers of Associate Justice Terry B. O'Rourke

750 B Street,, Suite 300, San Diego, CA 92101-8196
Tel: (619) 744-0672
E-mail: justice.o'rourke@jud.ca.gov

Terry B. O'Rourke
Associate Justice

Date of Birth: 1947
Education: Claremont McKenna 1969 BA; Harvard 1972 JD
Began Service: December 7, 1998
Term Expires: January 5, 2027

Judicial: Judge, California Superior Court, Los Angeles County (1984-1987); Judge, California Superior Court, San Diego County (1987-1998)

Legal Practice: Private Practice (1973-1974); Private Practice (1974-1984)

Staff

Senior Attorney **Laura Loberman** .... (619) 744-0672
E-mail: laura.loberman@jud.ca.gov
Senior Attorney **Allen Palacio** .... (619) 744-0672
E-mail: allen.palacio@jud.ca.gov
Judicial Assistant **Maureen Farias** .... (619) 744-0672

Chambers of Associate Justice Cynthia G. Aaron

750 B Street, Suite 300, San Diego, CA 92101-8196
Tel: (619) 744-0681 Fax: (619) 645-2495
E-mail: cynthia.aaron@jud.ca.gov

Cynthia G. Aaron
Associate Justice

Education: Stanford 1979 BA; Harvard 1984 JD
Began Service: January 10, 2003
Term Expires: January 10, 2019

Judicial: Magistrate Judge, United States District Court for the Southern District of California (1994-2003)

Staff

Senior Appellate Court Attorney **Dylan S. Calsyn** .... (619) 744-0684
E-mail: dylan.calsyn@jud.ca.gov
Education: Yale 1999 JD
Senior Appellate Court Attorney **Stacie Somers** .... (619) 744-0683
E-mail: stacie.somers@jud.ca.gov
Education: Harvard 2001 JD
Judicial Assistant **Debbie Lopardo** .... (619) 744-0682
E-mail: debbie.lopardo@jud.ca.gov

Chambers of Associate Justice Joan K. Irion

750 B Street,, San Diego, CA 92101-8196
Tel: (619) 645-2760
E-mail: joan.irion@jud.ca.gov

Joan K. Irion
Associate Justice

Education: UC Davis 1974
Began Service: 2003
Term Expires: January 7, 2019

Judicial: Superior Court Judge, County of San Diego, California

Legal Practice: Shareholder, Heller Ehrman LLP

Profession: Private Practice

Staff

Senior Attorney **Kirk Fritz** .... (619) 744-0773
Senior Attorney **Jill Parry** .... (619) 744-0773

Chambers of Associate Justice Joan K. Irion *continued*

Secretary **Ellen Siemens** . . . . (619) 744-0773
E-mail: ellen.siemens@jud.ca.gov

California Court of Appeal, Fourth Appellate District, Division Two

3389 12th Street, Riverside, CA 92501-3819
Tel: (951) 782-2500
Internet: www.courts.ca.gov/4dca.htm

Number of Judgeships: 7

Court Staff
Assistant Clerk/Administrator **Paula Garcia** . . . . (951) 782-2500

Chambers of Presiding Justice Manuel A. Ramirez

3389 12th Street, Riverside, CA 92501-3819
Tel: (951) 782-2600 Fax: (951) 248-0235

Manuel A. Ramirez
Presiding Justice

Date of Birth: 1948
Education: Whittier 1970 BA; Loyola Marymount 1974 JD
Began Service: December 27, 1990
Appointed By: Governor George Deukmejian
Next Election: November 2022
Term Expires: January 8, 2023
Political Affiliation: Republican

Academic: Instructor, University of California, Irvine (1988-1996)

Government: Deputy District Attorney, County of Orange, California (1976-1983)

Judicial: Judge, Orange County Municipal Court, Central Orange County Judicial District (1983-1986); Judge, California Superior Court, Orange County (1986-1990)

Current Memberships: Orange County Bar Association

Chambers of Associate Justice Thomas E. Hollenhorst

3389 12th Street, Riverside, CA 92501-3819
Tel: (951) 782-2620 Fax: (951) 248-0346

Thomas E. Hollenhorst
Associate Justice

Date of Birth: 1946
Education: San José State 1968 BA; Hastings 1971 JD; Virginia 1995 LLM
Began Service: August 26, 1988
Appointed By: Governor George Deukmejian
Term Expires: January 5, 2027

Government: Deputy District Attorney, County of Riverside, California (1972-1977); Assistant District Attorney, Office of the District Attorney, County of Riverside, California (1977-1981); Acting District Attorney, County of Riverside, California (1981)

Judicial: Judge, Riverside County Municipal Court; Judge, California Superior Court, Riverside County

Current Memberships: American Bar Association; California Judges Association

Staff
Judicial Assistant **Sandra Simmons** . . . . (951) 782-2620

Chambers of Associate Justice Art W. McKinster

3389 12th Street, Riverside, CA 92501-3819
Tel: (951) 782-2500
E-mail: art.mckinster@jud.ca.gov

Art W. McKinster
Associate Justice

Date of Birth: 1946
Education: USC 1968 BS; Hastings 1971 JD
Began Service: December 27, 1990
Appointed By: Governor George Deukmejian
Next Election: November 2022
Term Expires: January 2, 2023

Government: Deputy District Attorney, Office of the District Attorney, County of San Bernardino, California (1972-1977); Supervising Deputy District Attorney, Office of the District Attorney, County of San Bernardino, California (1977-1978); Chief Deputy District Attorney, Office of the District Attorney, County of San Bernardino, California (1978-1984)

Judicial: Judge, San Bernardino County Municipal Court, Central Division; Judge, California Superior Court, San Bernardino County

Military Service: United States Army Reserve, United States Department of the Army (1971-1978)

Current Memberships: California Judges Association

Staff
Senior Research Attorney **Jorge Chica** . . . . (951) 248-0200
E-mail: jorge.chica@jud.ca.gov
Senior Research Attorney **Jill Prentice** . . . . (951) 248-0200
E-mail: jill.prentice@jud.ca.gov
Judicial Secretary **Jana Nocella** . . . . (951) 248-0307
E-mail: jana.nocella@jud.ca.gov

Chambers of Associate Justice Jeffrey King

3389 12th Street, Riverside, CA 92501-3819
Tel: (951) 782-2630
E-mail: jeffrey.king@jud.ca.gov

Jeffrey King
Associate Justice

Date of Birth: 1950
Education: U Redlands 1972 BA; McGeorge 1976 JD
Began Service: January 13, 2003
Appointed By: Governor Gray Davis
Term Expires: January 7, 2019

Judicial: Judge, Superior Court of California (1995-2003)

Profession: Private Practice (1976-1995)

Chambers of Associate Justice Douglas P. Miller

3389 12th Street, Riverside, CA 92501-3819
Tel: (951) 782-2660
E-mail: douglas.miller@jud.ca.gov

Douglas P. Miller
Associate Justice

Education: BYU 1975 BA; Pepperdine 1978 JD
Began Service: June 9, 2006
Term Expires: January 7, 2019

Chambers of Associate Justice Carol D. Codrington
3389 12th Street, Riverside, CA 92501-3819
Tel: (951) 782-2680
E-mail: carol.codrington@jud.ca.gov

Carol D. Codrington
Associate Justice

Date of Birth: 1959
Education: Loyola Marymount 1981 BA; Loyola Law 1984 JD
Began Service: January 3, 2011
Appointed By: Governor Arnold Schwarzenegger

California Court of Appeal, Fourth Appellate District, Division Three
601 West Santa Ana Boulevard, Santa Ana, CA 92701
P.O. Box 22055, Santa Ana, CA 92702
Tel: (714) 571-2600 Fax: (714) 571-2616
Internet: www.courts.ca.gov/4dca.htm

Number of Judgeships: 8

Court Staff
Assistant Clerk/Administrator **Kevin Stinson** . . . . (714) 571-2600
E-mail: kevin.stinson@jud.ca.gov
Supervising Clerk **Robert Abilez** . . . . (714) 571-2600
Senior Deputy Clerk **Tonny Cajigal** . . . . (714) 571-2600
Senior Deputy Clerk **Shahira Naqshbandy** . . . . (714) 571-2600
Deputy Clerk **Bonnie LeSage** . . . . (714) 571-2600
E-mail: bonnie.lesage@jud.ca.gov
Assistant Deputy Clerk III **Denise Massey** . . . . (714) 571-2600
E-mail: denise.massey@jud.ca.gov
Assistant Deputy Clerk III **Alex Reynoso** . . . . (714) 571-2600
E-mail: alex.reynoso@jud.ca.gov
Court Systems Administrator **Rory Aitken** . . . . (714) 571-2600
Court Systems Administrator **Kevin Trainor** . . . . (714) 571-2600
E-mail: kevin.trainor@jud.ca.gov
Librarian **Holly Gale** . . . . (714) 571-2600
Court Services Officer **Mike Clements** . . . . (714) 571-2600
E-mail: mike.clements@jud.ca.gov
Appellate Court Records Assistant **(Vacant)** . . . . (714) 571-2600

Chambers of Presiding Justice Kathleen E. O'Leary
601 West Santa Ana Boulevard, Santa Ana, CA 92701
Tel: (714) 571-2734 Fax: (714) 571-2735
E-mail: kathleen.oleary@jud.ca.gov

Kathleen E. O'Leary
Presiding Justice

Date of Birth: 1951
Education: Marymount Col (CA) 1972 BA; Southwestern 1975 JD
Began Service: January 21, 2000
Appointed By: Governor Gray Davis
Term Expires: January 2019
Political Affiliation: Democrat

Current Memberships: California Judges Association

Staff
Senior Staff Attorney **Sara J. Annis** . . . . (714) 571-2734
E-mail: sara.annis@jud.ca.gov
Education: Whittier 1992 JD
Senior Staff Attorney **Elizabeth Cowles Forbath** . . . . (714) 571-2734
E-mail: betsy.forbath@jud.ca.gov
Education: McGeorge 1985 JD
Senior Staff Attorney **Richard W. Helms** . . . . (714) 571-2734
E-mail: richard.helms@jud.ca.gov
Education: Western St Orange County 2000 JD
Judicial Assistant **Christi Hermosillo** . . . . (714) 571-2734
E-mail: christi.hermosillo@jud.ca.gov

Chambers of Associate Justice William F. Rylaarsdam
601 West Santa Ana Boulevard, Santa Ana, CA 92701
Tel: (714) 571-2714 Fax: (714) 571-2715
E-mail: william.rylaarsdam@jud.ca.gov

William F. Rylaarsdam
Associate Justice

Date of Birth: 1937
Education: Loyola Law 1964 JD; Virginia 1998 LLM
Began Service: April 10, 1995
Appointed By: Governor Pete Wilson
Term Expires: December 31, 2026

Staff
Lead Appellate Court Attorney **William R. Ball** . . . . (714) 571-2714
E-mail: bill.ball@jud.ca.gov
Education: Northern Illinois 1972 BA; Western St Orange County 1979 JD
Senior Appellate Court Attorney **Josephine M. Chow** . . . (714) 571-2714
E-mail: josephine.chow@jud.ca.gov
Education: UC San Diego 1989 BA; Loyola Law 1992 JD
Senior Appellate Court Attorney **Kelly McCourt** . . . . (714) 571-2714
E-mail: kelly.mccourt@jud.ca.gov
Judicial Assistant **Arlette Chavez** . . . . (714) 571-2714
E-mail: arlette.chavez@jud.ca.gov

Chambers of Associate Justice William W. Bedsworth
601 West Santa Ana Boulevard, Santa Ana, CA 92701
Tel: (714) 571-2724 Fax: (714) 571-2725

William W. Bedsworth
Associate Justice

Date of Birth: 1947
Education: Boalt Hall 1971 JD
Began Service: 1997
Appointed By: Governor Pete Wilson
Next Election: November 2022
Term Expires: December 2023
Political Affiliation: Republican

Government: District Attorney, County of Orange, California (1972-1986)

Judicial: Judge, California Superior Court, Orange County (1987-1997)

Staff
Research Attorney **Julie Bisceglia** . . . . (714) 571-2721
E-mail: julie.bisceglia@jud.ca.gov
Research Attorney **Jeffrey "Jeff" Calkins** . . . . (714) 571-2722
E-mail: jeff.calkins@jud.ca.gov
Education: Ambassador Col 1973 BA; Cal State (Los Angeles) 1978 MA; Loyola Marymount 1982 JD
Research Attorney **Todd Vukson** . . . . (714) 571-2723
E-mail: todd.vukson@jud.ca.gov
Education: Minnesota 1985 BS; Cal Western 1988 JD
Judicial Assistant **Kimberly Forsyth** . . . . (714) 571-2724
E-mail: kimberly.forsyth@jud.ca.gov

Chambers of Associate Justice Eileen C. Moore

601 West Santa Ana Boulevard, Santa Ana, CA 92701
Tel: (714) 571-2744 Fax: (714) 571-2745
E-mail: eileen.moore@jud.ca.gov

Eileen C. Moore
Associate Justice

Education: UC Irvine 1975 BA; Pepperdine 1978 JD; Virginia 2004 LLM
Began Service: December 22, 2000
Appointed By: Governor Gray Davis
Next Election: November 2022

Judicial: Orange County Superior Court (1989-2000); Supervising Judge, Civil Law and Motion Department, Orange County Superior Court (1990-1991); Presiding Judge, Appellate Department, Orange County Superior Court (1993-1994)

Military Service: United States Army Nurse Corps

Staff
Lead Attorney **Danie Spence** .... (714) 571-2744
E-mail: danie.spence@jud.ca.gov
Staff Attorney **Lynn Loschin** .... (714) 571-2744
E-mail: lynn.loschin@jud.ca.gov
Staff Attorney **Kevin Phillips** .... (714) 571-2744
E-mail: kevin.phillips@jud.ca.gov

Chambers of Associate Justice Richard M. Aronson

601 West Santa Ana Boulevard, Santa Ana, CA 92701
Tel: (714) 571-2600 Fax: (714) 571-2755

Richard M. Aronson
Associate Justice

Date of Birth: 1950
Education: San Diego 1972 BA, 1975 JD; Virginia 2004 LLM
Began Service: November 2001
Appointed By: Governor Gray Davis
Term Expires: 2027
Political Affiliation: Republican

Clerkships: Senior Judicial Attorney The Honorable Sheila Sonenshine, California Court of Appeal (1988-1989)

Government: Deputy District Attorney, County of San Bernardino, California (1975-1978); Deputy Public Defender, County of Orange, California (1980-1987)

Judicial: Orange County Superior Court Commissioner (1989-1996); Judge, Orange County Superior Court (1996-2001)

Legal Practice: Law Offices of Sylvan Aronson (1979-1986)

Staff
Senior Appellate Court Attorney **Bill Amsbary** .... (714) 571-2751
E-mail: bill.amsbary@jud.ca.gov
Education: UCLA 1985 BA; Hastings 1988 JD
Senior Appellate Court Attorney **David Hesseltine** ...... (714) 571-2753
E-mail: david.hesseltine@jud.ca.gov
Senior Appellate Court Attorney **John Seckinger** .... (714) 571-2752
E-mail: john.seckinger@jud.ca.gov
Education: Notre Dame 1991 BA; Georgetown 1997 JD
Judicial Assistant to the Appellate Court Justice **Rhonda Tharp** .... (714) 571-2754

Chambers of Associate Justice Richard D. Fybel

601 West Santa Boulevard, Santa Ana, CA 92701
Tel: (714) 571-2600 Fax: (714) 571-2765

Richard D. Fybel
Associate Justice

Date of Birth: 1946
Education: UCLA 1968 BA, 1971 JD
Began Service: February 8, 2002
Appointed By: Governor Gray Davis
Next Election: November 2026

Judicial: Judge, Orange County Superior Court (2000-2002)

Legal Practice: Associate, Nossaman, Guthner, Knox & Elliott, LLP; Partner, Morrison & Foerster LLP (1981-2000)

Staff
Senior Appellate Court Attorney **Julianne Bancroft** ..... (714) 571-2600
E-mail: julianne.bancroft@jud.ca.gov
Education: UCLA 1990 JD
Senior Appellate Court Attorney **Matthew Ross** .... (714) 571-2600
E-mail: matthew.ross@jud.ca.gov
Education: Boalt Hall 1985 JD
Senior Appellate Court Attorney **Michele Troyan** .... (714) 571-2600
E-mail: michele.troyan@jud.ca.gov
Education: Loyola Marymount 1996 JD
Judicial Assistant **Nancy O'Connell** .... (714) 571-2600

Chambers of Associate Justice Raymond J. Ikola

601 West Santa Ana Boulevard, Santa Ana, CA 92701
Tel: (714) 571-2774 Fax: (714) 571-2775

Raymond J. Ikola
Associate Justice

Date of Birth: July 24, 1940
Education: Michigan 1962 BSE, 1963 MSE; Poly Inst Brooklyn 1972 PhD; Hastings 1974 JD
Began Service: January 10, 2003
Appointed By: Governor Gray Davis
Term Expires: January 5, 2019
Political Affiliation: Republican

Corporate: Research Engineer, RCA Laboratories

Judicial: Superior Court Judge, County of Orange, California (1995-2002)

Legal Practice: Partner, Wenke, Evans & Ikola (1974-1987); Partner, Hufstedler & Kaus (1987-1990); Partner, Snell & Wilmer L.L.P. (1990-1995)

Current Memberships: Association of Business Trial Lawyers; California Judges Association; Orange County Bar Association

Staff
Senior Appellate Court Attorney **Kathy Nock** .... (714) 571-2774
E-mail: kathy.nock@jud.ca.gov
Education: UCLA 1977 BA; Harvard 1980 JD
Senior Appellate Court Attorney **Jacob T. Risner** .... (714) 571-2772
E-mail: jacob.risner@jud.ca.gov
Education: Michigan 2003 JD
Appellate Court Attorney **Christopher Pinzon** .... (714) 571-2774
E-mail: christopher.pinzon@jud.ca.gov
Judicial Assistant **Olga Rivera** .... (714) 571-2774

Chambers of Associate Justice David A. Thompson

601 West Santa Ana Boulevard, Santa Ana, CA 92701
Tel: (714) 571-2600
E-mail: david.thompson@jud.ca.gov

David A. Thompson
Associate Justice

Education: Georgetown 1980 BA; UCLA 1983 JD

California Court of Appeal, Fifth Appellate District

2424 Ventura Street, Fresno, CA 93721
Tel: (559) 445-5491 Fax: (559) 445-5769
Internet: www.courts.ca.gov/5dca.htm

Number of Judgeships: 10

Number of Vacancies: 1

Areas Covered: Counties of Fresno, Kern, Kings, Madera, Mariposa, Merced, Stanislaus, Tulare and Tuolumne

Court Staff
Court Administrator/Clerk of the Court
Charlene Ynson .... (559) 445-5491
E-mail: charlene.ynson@jud.ca.gov

Chambers of Presiding Justice Brad R. Hill

2424 Ventura Street, Fresno, CA 93721
Tel: (559) 445-5184 Fax: (559) 445-6687
E-mail: brad.hill@jud.ca.gov

Brad R. Hill
Presiding Justice

Education: Cal State (Fresno) 1977 BSBA, 1979 MBA; Hastings 1983 JD
Began Service: August 2010

Staff
Fax: (559) 445-6687

Executive Judicial Assistant **Renee Ivey** .... (559) 445-5184

Chambers of Associate Justice Herbert I. Levy

2424 Ventura Street, Fresno, CA 93721
Tel: (559) 445-5251 Fax: (559) 445-6683
E-mail: herbert.levy@jud.ca.gov

Herbert I. Levy
Associate Justice

Date of Birth: 1952
Education: UC Davis 1974 BA; McGeorge 1977 JD
Began Service: August 5, 1997
Appointed By: Governor Pete Wilson
Next Election: November 2022
Term Expires: January 2, 2023

Judicial: Judge, Municipal Court, Consolidated Fresno Judicial District, Fresno County (1988-1989); Judge, California Superior Court, Fresno County (1989-1997)

Legal Practice: Private Practice (1977-1988)

Current Memberships: California Judges Association

Chambers of Associate Justice Dennis A. Cornell

2424 Ventura Street, Fresno, CA 93721
Tel: (559) 445-5178 Fax: (559) 445-6685
E-mail: Dennis.Cornell@jud.ca.gov

Dennis A. Cornell
Associate Justice

Date of Birth: 1947
Education: Stanford 1969 AB; George Washington 1972 JD
Began Service: December 21, 2000
Appointed By: Governor Gray Davis
Term Expires: January 2027
Political Affiliation: Democrat

Judicial: Magistrate Judge (part-time), United States District Court for the Eastern District of California (1986-1992); Judge, Merced County Superior Court (1992-2000); Judge, Appellate Department, Merced County Superior Court (1992-2000); Judge, Appellate Department, Mariposa County Superior Court (1992-2000); Presiding Judge, Merced County Superior Court (1997-1999)

Staff
Lead Appellate Court Attorney **Carol Diane Mills** .... (559) 445-5619
E-mail: Carol.Mills@jud.ca.gov
Education: UC Riverside 1976 BA; McGeorge 1979 JD
Staff Attorney **Robert Werth** .... (559) 445-5685
E-mail: Robert.Werth@jud.ca.gov
Education: San José State 1980 BS; McGeorge 1989 JD

Chambers of Associate Justice Gene M. Gomes

2424 Ventura Street, Fresno, CA 93721
Tel: (559) 445-6521 Fax: (559) 445-5769
E-mail: gene.gomes@jud.ca.gov

Gene M. Gomes
Associate Justice

Date of Birth: 1946
Education: Cal State (Fresno) 1969 BA; McGeorge 1972 JD
Began Service: May 31, 2002
Appointed By: Governor Gray Davis
Term Expires: January 2027

Academic: Faculty Member, California Judicial College

Judicial: Judge, Fresno County Municipal Court (1980-1982); Trial Judge, Fresno County Superior Court (1982-2002)

Legal Practice: Deputy District Attorney, Office of the District Attorney, Fresno County, California (1972-1975); Chief Trial Deputy District Attorney, Office of the District Attorney, Fresno County, California (1975-1977); Attorney, Gomes, Gomes, Fiske & Berman (1978-1980)

Nonprofit: Co-Founder and President, Fresno County Prosecutors Association

Staff
Judicial Assistant **Sheila Perkins** .... (559) 445-5491

Chambers of Associate Justice Stephen J. Kane

2424 Ventura Street, Fresno, CA 93721
Tel: (559) 445-5185

Stephen J. Kane
Associate Justice

Education: Notre Dame BA; Hastings 1976 JD
Began Service: June 2006
Appointed By: Governor Arnold Schwarzenegger

Judicial: Superior Court Judge, County of Fresno, California (1992-2006)

Chambers of Associate Justice Stephen J. Kane *continued*

Legal Practice: Associate, McCormick, Barstow, Sheppard, Wayte & Carruth LLP (1976-1981); Partner, McCormick, Barstow, Sheppard, Wayte & Carruth LLP (1981-1992)

Staff
Judicial Assistant **Janice Owen** .... (559) 445-5185
E-mail: janice.owen@jud.ca.gov

Chambers of Associate Justice Charles S. Poochigian
2424 Ventura Street, Fresno, CA 93721
Tel: (559) 445-5227
E-mail: charles.poochigian@jud.ca.gov

Charles S. "Chuck" Poochigian
Associate Justice

Education: Cal State (Fresno) 1972 BA; Santa Clara U JD
Began Service: 2009
Next Election: November 2022
Political Affiliation: Republican

Government: Member, California State Assembly, California State Legislature (1994-1998); Vice Chair, Agriculture Committee, Senate Standing Committees, California State Senate; Republican Caucus Chair, California Senate; Chair, Constitutional Amendments Committee, Senate Standing Committees, California State Senate; Senator, State Senator Chuck Poochigian (R-CA, District 14), California State Senate (1998-2006)

Chambers of Associate Justice Jennifer R.S. Detjen
2424 Ventura Street, Fresno, CA 93721
Tel: (559) 445-5663 Fax: (559) 445-5769
E-mail: jennifer.detjen@jud.ca.gov

Jennifer R.S. Detjen
Associate Justice

Began Service: 2010
Appointed By: Governor Arnold Schwarzenegger
Next Election: November 2022

Chambers of Associate Justice Donald R. Franson, Jr.
2424 Ventura Street, Fresno, CA 93721
Tel: (559) 445-5341 Fax: (559) 445-5769
E-mail: donald.franson@jud.ca.gov

Donald R. Franson, Jr.
Associate Justice

Education: UC Berkeley 1974; Hastings 1978 JD
Began Service: December 29, 2010
Appointed By: Governor Arnold Schwarzenegger

Chambers of Associate Justice Rosendo Peña Jr.
2424 Ventura Street, Fresno, CA 93721
Tel: (559) 445-5324

Rosendo Peña, Jr.
Associate Justice

Education: Cal State (Fresno) 1977 BA; UCLA 1980 JD

Clerkships: Lead Attorney, California Court of Appeal, Fifth Appellate District (1994-2002)

Government: Deputy Attorney General, Office of the Attorney General, State of California (1990-1992)

California Court of Appeal, Sixth Appellate District
333 West Santa Clara Street, Suite 1060, San Jose, CA 95113
Tel: (408) 277-1004 Fax: (408) 277-9916
Internet: www.courts.ca.gov/6dca.htm

Number of Judgeships: 7

Areas Covered: Counties of Monterey, San Benito, Santa Clara and Santa Cruz

Court Staff
Clerk of the Court **Dan Potter** .... (408) 277-1004
Law Librarian **Jocelyn Stilwell-Tong** .... (408) 494-2529
Fax: (408) 277-9021

Chambers of Presiding Justice Conrad L. Rushing
333 West Santa Clara Street, Suite 1060, San Jose, CA 95113
Tel: (408) 277-1004 Fax: (408) 277-9916
E-mail: conrad.rushing@jud.ca.gov

Conrad L. Rushing
Presiding Justice

Education: San José State BA; Boalt Hall LLB
Began Service: January 25, 2002
Appointed By: Governor Gray Davis
Next Election: November 2022

Academic: Guest Lecturer, School of Law, Stanford University; Guest Lecturer, Boalt Hall School of Law

Judicial: Judge, Superior Court of Santa Clara County (1978-2002)

Legal Practice: Attorney, Berliner, Cohen, Flaherty & Rushing (1971-1974); Attorney, Rushing, Ames & Norman (1974-1978)

Membership: President, Santa Clara County Bar Association (1974)

Staff
Research Attorney **Lisa Gallo** .... (408) 277-1004
Research Attorney **Marissa Magilligan** .... (408) 277-1004
Research Attorney **Marina Meyere** .... (408) 277-1004
E-mail: marina.meyere@jud.ca.gov
Education: Santa Clara U 2002 JD
Research Attorney **Drew Trott** .... (408) 277-1004
Judicial Assistant **Patricia Martinez** .... (408) 277-1004

Chambers of Associate Justice Eugene M. Premo
333 West Santa Clara Street, Suite 1060, San Jose, CA 95113
Tel: (408) 494-2504 Fax: (408) 277-9916
E-mail: eugene.premo@jud.ca.gov

Eugene M. Premo
Associate Justice

Date of Birth: 1936
Education: Santa Clara U 1957 BS, 1962 JD
Began Service: September 29, 1988
Term Expires: January 6, 2027
Political Affiliation: Republican

Clerkships: Law Clerk The Honorable James Agee, California Court of Appeal, First Appellate District (1962-1963)

Judicial: Judge, California Municipal Court (1969-1974); Judge, California Superior Court (1975-1988)

Legal Practice: Private Practice (1963-1969)

Military Service: United States Army (1957-1959); United States Army Reserve, United States Department of the Army

Staff
Judicial Secretary **Socorro Saboff** .... (408) 494-2506

STATE COURTS—CALIFORNIA

Chambers of Associate Justice Franklin D. Elia

333 West Santa Clara Street, Suite 1060, San Jose, CA 95113
Tel: (408) 494-2507 Fax: (408) 277-9021
E-mail: franklin.elia@jud.ca.gov

Franklin D. Elia
Associate Justice

Date of Birth: 1950
Education: Santa Clara U 1972 BA, 1975 JD
Began Service: October 1988
Appointed By: Governor George Deukmejian
Next Election: November 2026
Term Expires: January 2027
Political Affiliation: Republican

Academic: Visiting Lecturer, School of Law, Santa Clara University (1993-1994); University of San Francisco School of Law (1994); Visiting Lecturer, Santa Clara School of Law (1996)

Government: Deputy Attorney General, State of California (1975-1980); Chief Trial Counsel, The State Bar of California; City Attorney, City of Palo Alto, California (1980-1983)

Judicial: Judge, Santa Clara Municipal Court, Santa Clara Judicial District (1983-1986); Judge, California Superior Court, Santa Clara County (1986-1988)

Current Memberships: California Judges Association; Santa Clara County Bar Association

Staff
Staff Attorney **Madeleine Kaplan** .... (408) 494-2507
E-mail: madeleine.kaplan@jud.ca.gov
Education: UC Santa Barbara 1978 BA; UC Davis 1981 JD
Staff Attorney **Elizabeth Lowenstein** .... (408) 494-2507
Staff Attorney **Christine A. Pack** .... (408) 494-2507
E-mail: christine.pack@jud.ca.gov
Education: Cambridge (UK) 1976 BEd; Santa Clara U 1999 JD
Judicial Assistant **Bella Aquilar** .... (408) 494-2509

Chambers of Associate Justice Patricia Bamattre-Manoukian

333 West Santa Clara Street, Suite 1060, San Jose, CA 95113
Tel: (408) 494-2512 Fax: (408) 277-9021

Patricia Bamattre-Manoukian
Associate Justice

Date of Birth: 1950
Education: UCLA 1972 BA; USC 1974 MPA; Loyola Marymount 1977 JD; USC 1989 PhD
Began Service: October 16, 1989
Appointed By: Governor George Deukmejian
Political Affiliation: Republican

Academic: Instructor, Santa Clara University (1985-1988)

Government: Deputy District Attorney, County of Orange, California (1977-1983)

Judicial: Judge, Orange County Municipal Court, West Orange County Judicial District (1983-1985); Judge, Santa Clara County Municipal Court (1985-1988); Judge, California Superior Court, Santa Clara County (1988-1989)

Current Memberships: California Judges Association; California Women Lawyers Bar Association; National Association of Women Judges; Santa Clara County Bar Association

Staff
Staff Attorney **Syda Cogliati** .... (408) 494-2551
E-mail: syda.kosofsky@jud.ca.gov
Education: UC Santa Cruz 1991 BA; Hastings 1994 JD

Staff Attorney **Mary Wrightson** .... (408) 494-2552
E-mail: mary.wrightson@jud.ca.gov
Staff Attorney **Wendy Ying** .... (408) 494-2550
E-mail: wendy.ying@jud.ca.gov
Judicial Assistant **Marina Flores** .... (408) 494-2512

Chambers of Associate Justice Nathan D. Mihara

333 West Santa Clara Street, Suite 1060, San Jose, CA 95113
Tel: (408) 277-1662 Fax: (408) 277-9021

Nathan D. Mihara
Associate Justice

Date of Birth: 1950
Education: U Washington 1972 BA; Hastings 1975 JD
Began Service: February 4, 1993
Appointed By: Governor Pete Wilson
Next Election: November 2018
Term Expires: January 2019
Political Affiliation: Republican

Government: Deputy Attorney General, State of California (1976-1985)

Judicial: Judge, Santa Clara County Municipal Court (1985-1988); Judge, Santa Clara County Superior Court (1988-1993)

Legal Practice: Private Practice

Current Memberships: Asian-Pacific Bar Association of the Silicon Valley; California Asian Judges Association; California Judges Association

Staff
Judicial Assistant **Karen Bynum** .... (408) 277-1662
E-mail: karen.bynum@jud.ca.gov

Chambers of Associate Judge Miguel Marquez

333 West Santa Clara Street, San Jose, CA 95113
Tel: (408) 277-1004

Miguel A. Márquez
Associate Justice

Education: Stanford BA; Harvard MPP; Boalt Hall 1996 JD
Began Service: 2012

Government: General Counsel, San Francisco Unified School District, City and County of San Francisco, California; County Counsel, Office of the County Counsel, County of Santa Clara, California (2009-2012)

Chambers of Associate Justice Adrienne M. Grover

333 West Santa Clara Street, San Jose, CA 95113
Tel: (415) 865-7000

Adrienne M. Grover
Associate Justice

Education: UC Berkeley BS; Santa Clara U 1990 JD

Government: County Counsel, Office of the County Counsel, County of Monterey, California

Judicial: Presiding Judge, Chambers of Presiding Judge Adrienne M. Grover, County of Monterey, Superior Court of California (2009-2010)

Colorado

Colorado Office of the State Court Administrator

1300 Broadway, Suite 1200, Denver, CO 80203
Tel: (720) 625-5000 Fax: (720) 625-5933
Internet: www.courts.state.co.us

Staff

State Court Administrator
Gerald A. "Jerry" Marroney . . . . (720) 625-5801
E-mail: gerald.marroney@judicial.state.co.us
Education: Southern Colorado 1973 BS; Oklahoma 1976 JD
Administrative Assistant to the State Court Administrator **Sandy Schweitzer** . . . . (720) 625-5804
E-mail: sandy.schweitzer@judicial.state.co.us
Financial Services **David Kribs** . . . . (720) 625-5841
E-mail: david.kribs@judicial.state.co.us
Chief of Staff **Mindy Masias** . . . . (720) 625-5901
E-mail: mindy.masias@judicial.state.co.us
Judicial Educator **Jennifer Mendoza** . . . . (720) 625-5812
E-mail: jennifer.mendoza@judicial.state.co.us Fax: (303) 837-2340
Legal Counsel **Terri Morrison** . . . . (720) 625-5817
E-mail: terri.morrison@judicial.state.co.us
Court Services **Sherry Stwalley** . . . . (720) 625-5941
E-mail: sherry.stwalley@judicial.state.co.us
Public Information Officer **Rob McCallum** . . . . (720) 625-5815
Probation Service Director **Eric Philp** . . . . (720) 625-5751
E-mail: eric.philp@judicial.state.co.us

Colorado Supreme Court

Ralph L. Carr Judicial Center, 2 East Fourteenth Avenue, Denver, CO 80203
Tel: (720) 625-5150 Tel: (720) 625-5100 (Supreme Court Library)
Internet: http://www.courts.state.co.us

Number of Judgeships: 7

The Supreme Court consists of a chief justice and six justices who are appointed by the Governor from a list of candidates submitted by the Supreme Court Nominating Commission. Justices serve initial two-year terms and thereafter stand for retention in general elections for ten-year terms. The chief justice, who is elected by peer vote for a nonspecific term, is the executive head of the judicial system. Retirement is mandatory at age seventy-two; however, retired justices may serve as senior judges by assignment of the state court administrator. The Supreme Court has initial appellate jurisdiction over cases where a statute has been declared unconstitutional by a district court, decisions or actions of the Colorado Public Utilities Commission, habeas corpus, water priorities, and the election code. The Court also has certiorari review over appeals initiated in the Colorado Court of Appeals and District Courts.

The Court sits in Denver.

Court Staff

Clerk of the Court **Christopher T. Ryan** . . . . (303) 837-3790
Began Service: May 23, 2011
E-mail: christopher.ryan@judicial.state.co.us
Clerk, Attorney Registration Office **Elvia Mondragon** . . . . (303) 866-6554
1560 Broadway, Suite 1810, Denver, CO 80202
E-mail: elvia.mondragon@judicial.state.co.us
Librarian **Daniel Cordova** . . . . (303) 837-3521
E-mail: daniel.cordova@judicial.state.co.us Fax: (303) 864-4510
Deputy Librarian **Jenny Moore** . . . . (303) 837-3176
E-mail: jenny.moore@judicial.state.co.us Fax: (303) 864-4510

Chambers of Chief Justice Nancy E. Rice

2 East Fourteenth Avenue, Denver, CO 80203
Tel: (720) 625-5460 Fax: (303) 861-7429
E-mail: nancy.rice@judicial.state.co.us

Nancy E. Rice
Chief Justice

Date of Birth: 1950
Education: Tufts 1972 BA; Utah 1975 JD
Began Service: August 31, 1998
Appointed By: Governor Roy Romer
Next Election: November 2020
Term Expires: January 2021

Current Memberships: Colorado Bar Association; Colorado Women's Bar Association; Denver Bar Association

Staff

Law Clerk **Lenora Plimpton** . . . . (720) 625-5464
Began Service: September 2015
Term Expires: September 2016
Law Clerk **Kathleen Snow** . . . . (720) 625-5463
Began Service: September 2015
Term Expires: September 2016
E-mail: kathleen.snow@judicial.state.co.us
Judicial Assistant **Sonya Stromberg** . . . . (720) 625-5462
E-mail: sonya.stromberg@judicial.state.co.us

Chambers of Justice Nathan B. Coats

2 East Fourteenth Avenue, Denver, CO 80203
Tel: (720) 625-5420 Fax: (303) 864-4536
E-mail: nathan.coats@judicial.state.co.us

Nathan B. Coats
Justice

Education: Colorado 1971 BA, 1977 JD
Began Service: May 25, 2000
Appointed By: Governor Bill Owens
Next Election: November 2022
Term Expires: January 2023

Academic: Adjunct Law Professor, University of Colorado School of Law (1990)

Government: Assistant Colorado Attorney General, Appellate Section, State of Colorado (1978-1983); Deputy Attorney General, Appellate Section, State of Colorado (1983-1986); Chief Appellate Deputy District Attorney, Second Judicial District, State of Denver (1986-2000)

Legal Practice: Associate, Hough, Grant, McCarren and Bernard (1977-1978)

Staff

Law Clerk **Rick Lee** . . . . (720) 625-5420
Began Service: September 2014
Term Expires: September 2016

Chambers of Justice Allison H. Eid

2 East Fourteenth Avenue, Denver, CO 80203
Tel: (720) 625-5430
E-mail: allison.eid@judicial.state.co.us

Allison H. Eid
Justice

Education: Stanford 1987 AB; Chicago 1991 JD
Began Service: February 15, 2006
Appointed By: Governor Bill Owens
Next Election: November 2018
Election Type: Retention Election
Term Expires: 2018

Academic: Associate Professor of Law, School of Law, University of Colorado at Boulder (1998-2005)

Clerkships: Law Clerk, Judge Jerry Smith, United States Court of Appeals for the Fifth Circuit (1991-1992); Law Clerk, Justice Clarence Thomas, The Supreme Court of the United States (1993-1994)

Corporate: Associate, Arnold & Porter LLP (1992-1993); Associate, Arnold & Porter LLP (1994-1998)

Government: Special Assistant and Speechwriter, Office of the Secretary, United States Department of Education (1987-1988); Solicitor General, Office of the Attorney General, State of Colorado (2005-2006)

Chambers of Justice Monica Marie Márquez

2 East Fourteenth Avenue, Denver, CO 80203
Tel: (720) 625-5450
E-mail: monica.márquez@judicial.state.co.us

Monica Marie Márquez
Justice

Education: Stanford 1991 AB; Yale 1997 JD
Began Service: December 10, 2010
Appointed By: Governor Bill Ritter

Staff
Law Clerk **Corey Longhurst** . . . . (303) 837-3771
E-mail: corey.longhurst@judicial.state.co.us

Chambers of Justice Brian Boatright

Colorado Supreme Court, 2 East Fourteenth Avenue, Denver, CO 80203
Tel: (720) 625-5410
E-mail: brian.boatright@judicial.state.co.us

Brian Boatright
Justice

Began Service: 2011
Appointed By: Governor John Hickenlooper

Staff
Law Clerk **(Vacant)** . . . . (720) 625-5410
Law Clerk **Emily Wasserman** . . . . (720) 625-5410
E-mail: emily.wasserman@judicial.state.co.us

Chambers of Justice William Hood III

2 East Fourteenth Avenue, Denver, CO 80203
Tel: (720) 625-5150
E-mail: william.hood@judicial.state.co.us

William W. Hood III
Justice

Education: Syracuse BA; Virginia JD
Began Service: January 13, 2014
Appointed By: Governor John Hickenlooper

Chambers of Justice Richard L. Gabriel

2 East Fourteenth Avenue, Denver, CO 80203
Tel: (720) 625-5150

Richard Lance Gabriel
Justice

Education: Yale 1984; Pennsylvania 1987 JD
Began Service: 2015
Appointed By: Governor John Hickenlooper

Colorado Court of Appeals

Ralph L. Carr Judicial Center, 2 East Fourteenth Avenue, Denver, CO 80203
Tel: (720) 625-5150 Fax: (720) 625-5148
Internet: www.courts.state.co.us/Courts/Court_Of_Appeals/Index.cfm

Number of Judgeships: 22

The Court of Appeals consists of a chief judge and twenty judges who are appointed by the Governor from a list of candidates submitted by the Supreme Court Nominating Commission. The Court sits in divisions of three judges each on a rotating basis as assigned by the chief judge. Judges serve initial two-year terms and then stand for retention of office in general elections for eight-year terms. The chief judge is appointed by the chief justice of the Colorado Supreme Court to serve a non-specified term. Retirement is mandatory at age seventy-two; however, retired judges may serve as senior judges by assignment of the state court administrator. The Court of Appeals has initial appellate jurisdiction over appeals from final judgments of the Colorado District Courts and Denver Probate and Juvenile Courts, except for those matters which come under the direct jurisdiction of the Colorado Supreme Court. The Court also reviews the decisions of twenty six state administrative agencies.

The Court sits in Denver and is authorized to sit in any county seat in Colorado.

Court Staff

Clerk of the Court **Christopher T. Ryan** . . . . (303) 837-3767
E-mail: christopher.ryan@judicial.state.co.us
Facilities Planner **John Gossett** . . . . (303) 837-2332
State Court Administrator's Office, 1301 Pennsylvania Street, Suite 300, Denver, CO 80203 Fax: (303) 837-2340
E-mail: john.gossett@judicial.state.co.us
Reporter of Decisions **Leah Walker** . . . . (720) 625-5000
E-mail: leah.walker@judicial.state.co.us

Chambers of Chief Judge Alan M. Loeb

Colorado State Judicial Building, 2 East Fourteenth Avenue, Room 800, Denver, CO 80203
Tel: (720) 625-5305 Fax: (303) 837-3702
E-mail: alan.loeb@judicial.state.co.us

Alan Michael Loeb
Chief Judge

Date of Birth: December 27, 1946
Education: Stanford 1968 AB; Michigan 1971 JD
Began Service: July 2, 2003
Appointed By: Governor Bill Owens

Staff
Judicial Assistant **Megan Embrey** . . . . (720) 625-5305
E-mail: megan.embrey@judicial.state.co.us

Chambers of Judge Daniel M. Taubman
Colorado State Judicial Building, 101 West Colfax Avenue,
Room 800, Denver, CO 80202-5315
Tel: (303) 837-3719 Fax: (303) 837-3702
E-mail: daniel.taubman@judicial.state.co.us

Daniel M. Taubman
Judge

Date of Birth: 1948
Education: Cornell 1969 BA; Harvard 1974 JD
Began Service: March 1, 1993
Appointed By: Governor Roy Romer
Term Expires: January 1, 2021
Political Affiliation: Democrat

Clerkships: Law Clerk The Honorable Charles E. Stewart, Jr., United States District Court for the Southern District of New York

Government: Volunteer, Peace Corps (1969-1971)

Legal Practice: Staff Attorney, Pikes Peak Legal Services (1975-1977); Managing Attorney, Pikes Peak Legal Services (1978-1980); Staff Attorney, Center on Social Welfare Policy and Law (1980-1982); Staff Attorney, Colorado Coalition of Legal Services Programs (1982-1983); Director, Colorado Coalition of Legal Services Programs (1983-1993)

Current Memberships: Availability of Legal Services Committee, Colorado Bar Association; Colorado Bar Foundation, Colorado Bar Association; Disability Law Committee, Colorado Bar Association; Ethics Committee, Colorado Bar Association; Pro Bono Task Force, Colorado Bar Association

Staff
Law Clerk **Kayleen Glaser** .... (303) 837-3719
Began Service: August 2015
Term Expires: August 2016
Secretary **Pam Goodman** .... (303) 837-3719
E-mail: pam.goodman@judicial.state.co.us
Education: Metro State Col Denver BA

Chambers of Judge John Daniel Dailey
2 East Fourteenth Avenue, Room 800, Denver, CO 80203
Tel: (720) 625-5340 Fax: (303) 864-4534
E-mail: john.dailey@judicial.state.co.us

John Daniel Dailey
Judge

Date of Birth: 1952
Education: Bucknell 1974 BA; Syracuse 1977 JD
Began Service: January 7, 2000
Appointed By: Governor Bill Owens
Next Election: November 2018
Term Expires: January 2019
Political Affiliation: Republican

Academic: Adjunct Professor of Law, University of Denver (1994); Adjunct Professor of Law, University of Colorado at Boulder (1996); Adjunct Professor of Law, University of Colorado at Boulder (1999)

Clerkships: Law Clerk The Honorable David W. Enoch, Colorado Court of Appeals (1977-1978)

Government: Office of the Attorney General, State of Colorado (1978-2000)

Current Memberships: Colorado Bar Association

Staff
Law Clerk **Sarah Andrzejczak** .... (720) 625-5340
Term Expires: August 2016
E-mail: amanda.walck@judicial.state.co.us
Judicial Assistant **Wanda F. Owens** .... (720) 625-5340
E-mail: wanda.owens@judicial.state.co.us

Chambers of Judge John R. Webb
2 East Fourteenth Avenue, Room 800, Denver, CO 80203
Tel: (720) 625-5345 Fax: (303) 864-4534
E-mail: john.webb@judicial.state.co.us

John R. Webb
Judge

Education: North Dakota 1970; Colorado 1973
Began Service: February 1, 2002
Term Expires: December 2020

Clerkships: Law Clerk, Circuit Judge Robert H. McWilliams, United States Court of Appeals for the Tenth Circuit (1973-1974)

Legal Practice: Attorney, Holmes Roberts and Owen, LLP (1974-2000); Attorney, Jacobs Chase Frick Kleinkopf & Kelley LLC (2001)

Staff
Law Clerk **Shawn Neal** .... (303) 837-3731
Career Judicial Law Clerk **Tiffany Mortier** .... (303) 837-3731
E-mail: tiffany.mortier@judicial.state.co.us
Education: Vermont Law 2001 JD

Chambers of Judge Dennis A. Graham
101 West Colfax Avenue, 800, Denver, CO 80203
Tel: (720) 625-5205 Fax: (720) 625-5148
E-mail: dennis.graham@judicial.state.co.us

Dennis A. Graham
Judge

Date of Birth: February 12, 1946
Education: Colorado State 1968; Nebraska 1975 JD
Began Service: September 6, 2002
Term Expires: January 8, 2021

Affiliation: Managing Editor, Nebraska Law Review

Clerkships: Law Clerk, Circuit Judge Robert H. McWilliams, United States Court of Appeals for the Tenth Circuit (1975-1976)

Legal Practice: Partner, Shareholder and Director, Krys Boyle Freedman P.C.

Staff
Law Clerk **Christopher Carry** .... (720) 625-5208
Term Expires: September 2016
Career Law Clerk **Robin Hoogerhyde** .... (720) 625-5207
E-mail: robin.hoogerhyde@judicial.state.co.us
Education: Michigan State 2008 JD

Chambers of Judge Robert D. Hawthorne
2 East Fourteenth Avenue, Room 800, Denver, CO 80203
Tel: (720) 625-5350
E-mail: robert.hawthorne@judicial.state.co.us

Robert D. Hawthorne
Judge

Education: LSU; Missouri JD
Began Service: 2004
Next Election: November 2016
Election Type: Retention Election
Term Expires: 2016

Staff
Senior Appellate Law Clerk **(Vacant)** .... (720) 625-5350

Chambers of Judge Gilbert M. Román

2 East Fourteenth Avenue, Room 800, Denver, CO 80203
Tel: (720) 625-5325 Fax: (303) 837-3702
E-mail: gilbert.roman@judicial.state.co.us

Gilbert M. Román
Judge

Education: Colorado State 1984 BS; Michigan 1987 JD
Began Service: August 1, 2005
Appointed By: Governor Bill Owens
Next Election: November 4, 2016
Election Type: Retention Election
Term Expires: 2016

Academic: Adjunct Professor, Sturm College of Law, University of Denver

Corporate: Associate General Counsel, Kaiser-Hill Company, LLC

Legal Practice: Associate, Sherman & Howard L.L.C.; Partner, Feiger, Collison & Killmer; Partner, Román, Benezra & Culver, LLC; Partner, Rothgerber Johnson & Lyons LLP

Staff
Judicial Assistant/Law Clerk **Krista Schelhaus** .... (720) 625-5325

Chambers of Judge David M. Furman

2 East Fourteenth Avenue, Room 800, Denver, CO 80203
Tel: (720) 625-5310 Fax: (303) 837-3702
E-mail: david.furman@judicial.state.co.us

David M. Furman
Judge

Education: Wheaton (IL) 1982 BA; Denver 1989 JD
Began Service: January 30, 2006
Appointed By: Governor Bill Owens
Next Election: November 2016
Election Type: Retention Election
Term Expires: 2016

Academic: Adjunct Professor, Denver University (1995-2005)

Government: Deputy Public Defender, Office of the State Public Defender, State of Colorado (1990-1994)

Judicial: District Magistrate, Colorado District Court, Second Judicial District (2003-2005)

Profession: Private Practice (1995-2000)

Staff
Senior Appellate Law Clerk **Zachary Cummings** .... (720) 625-5310
E-mail: zachary.cummings@judicial.state.co.us
Education: Regent U 2008 JD

Chambers of Judge Steven L. Bernard

2 East Fourteenth Avenue, Room 800, Denver, CO 80203
Tel: (720) 625-5240
E-mail: steven.bernard@judicial.state.co.us

Steven L. Bernard
Judge

Date of Birth: 1952
Education: Colorado 1975 BA, 1978 JD
Began Service: July 5, 2006
Appointed By: Governor Bill Owens
Next Election: November 2016
Election Type: Retention Election
Term Expires: 2016

Staff
Career Law Clerk **Jenny Carman** .... (720) 625-5240
E-mail: jenny.carman@judicial.state.co.us
Education: Denver 2007 JD

Chambers of Judge Diana L. Terry

Colorado State Judicial Building, 2 East Fourteenth Avenue, Denver, CO 80203
Tel: (720) 625-5320
E-mail: diana.terry@judicial.state.co.us

Diana L. Terry
Judge

Date of Birth: 1956
Education: Rutgers 1979 BA, 1984 JD
Began Service: July 5, 2006
Appointed By: Governor Bill Owens
Next Election: November 2016
Election Type: Retention Election
Term Expires: 2016

Judicial: Law Clerk, Chambers of Presiding Judge Robert Tarleton, New Jersey Superior Court, Chancery Division (1984-1985)

Legal Practice: Attorney, Sherman & Howard L.L.C. (1985-1989); Attorney, Moye, Giles, O'Keefe, Vermeire & Gorrell (1989-1991); Attorney, McElroy, Deutsch, Mulvaney & Carpenter, LLP (1992-1993); Attorney, White & Steele, PC (2001-2006)

Profession: Private Practice (1993-2001)

Staff
Law Clerk **Spencer Allen** .... (303) 837-3736
Began Service: August 2015
Term Expires: August 2017
E-mail: spencer.allen@judicial.state.co.us
Law Clerk **Matthew "Matt" Pierce** .... (303) 837-3736
Began Service: August 2014
Term Expires: August 2016
E-mail: matthew.pierce@judicial.state.co.us

Chambers of Judge Jerry N. Jones

Colorado State Judicial Building, 2 East Fourteenth Avenue, Denver, CO 80203
Tel: (720) 625-5335
E-mail: jerry.jones@judicial.state.co.us

Jerry N. Jones
Judge

Began Service: 2006
Next Election: November 2016
Election Type: Retention Election
Term Expires: 2016

Government: Chief, Appellate Division, Colorado District, United States Department of Justice

Staff
Law Clerk **Annie Lawson** .... (303) 837-3754
Law Clerk **Kelsey Entner** .... (303) 837-3754

Chambers of Judge Nancy Jean Lichtenstein

2 East Fourteenth Avenue, Room 800, Denver, CO 80203
Tel: (720) 625-5220 Fax: (303) 837-3702
E-mail: nancy.lichtenstein@judicial.state.co.us

Nancy Jean Lichtenstein
Judge

Education: Northwestern 1984 BA; Denver 1988 JD
Began Service: May 5, 2008
Next Election: November 2018
Election Type: Retention Election

Chambers of Judge David Jay Richman

2 East Fourteenth Avenue, Room 800, Denver, CO 80203
Tel: (720) 625-5315
E-mail: david.richman@judicial.state.co.us

David Jay Richman
Judge

Education: Michigan 1972; Harvard 1975 JD
Began Service: July 1, 2008
Appointed By: Governor Bill Ritter
Next Election: November 2018

Clerkships: Law Clerk, Chambers of District Judge Phillip S. Figa, United States District Court for the District of Colorado; Career Law Clerk, United States District Court for the District of Colorado (2003-2008)

Chambers of Judge Gale T. Miller

2 East Fourteenth Avenue, Room 800, Denver, CO 80203
Tel: (720) 625-5210
E-mail: gale.miller@judicial.state.co.us

Gale T. Miller
Judge

Education: Augustana (IL) 1968; Michigan 1971 JD
Began Service: 2008
Appointed By: Governor Bill Ritter

Chambers of Judge Laurie A. Booras

2 East Fourteenth Avenue, Room 800, Denver, CO 80203
Tel: (720) 625-5215
E-mail: laurie.booras@judicial.state.co.us

Laurie A. Booras
Judge

Education: Texas 1982 JD
Began Service: August 14, 2008
Appointed By: Governor Bill Ritter

Chambers of Judge Maria Teresa Fox

2 East Fourteenth Avenue, Room 800, Denver, CO 80203
Tel: (720) 625-5245

Maria Teresa "Terry" Fox
Judge

Education: Colorado Mines 1989 BS; South Texas 1993 JD
Began Service: January 11, 2011
Appointed By: Governor Bill Ritter

Current Memberships: Colorado Hispanic Bar Association; Colorado Women's Bar Association

Staff
Law Clerk **Joseph Mark** .... (720) 625-5245
Term Expires: August 2016
E-mail: joseph.mark@judicial.state.co.us

Chambers of Judge Stephanie Dunn

2 East Fourteenth Avenue, Denver, CO 80203
Tel: (720) 625-5235
E-mail: stephanie.dunn@judicial.state.co.us

Stephanie Dunn
Judge

Education: Colorado BS; Denver JD
Began Service: 2012

Chambers of Judge Stephanie Dunn *continued*

Staff
Administrative Law Clerk **Erik Speicher** .... (720) 625-5235
E-mail: erik.speicher@judicial.state.co.us

Chambers of Judge Anthony Navarro

2 East Fourteenth Avenue, Denver, CO 80203
Tel: (720) 625-5250
E-mail: anthony.navarro@judicial.state.co.us

Anthony "Tony" Navarro
Judge

Education: Colorado; Yale JD
Began Service: 2012
Appointed By: Governor John Hickenlooper

Staff
Law Clerk **Stacy Brownhill** .... (720) 625-5250
Law Clerk **Mike Eitner** .... (720) 625-5250

Chambers of Judge Karen Ashby

Two East 14th Avenue, Denver, CO 80203
Tel: (720) 625-5000
E-mail: karen.ashby@judicial.state.co.us

Karen M. Ashby
Judge

Education: Williams; Denver 1983 JD

Government: Attorney, Denver Trial Office, Office of the State Public Defender, State of Colorado (1993-1998)

Judicial: Presiding Judge, Chambers of Presiding Judge Karen M. Ashby, Denver Juvenile Court, Colorado District Courts

Nonprofit: Trustee, Board of Trustees, National Council of Juvenile and Family Court Judges

Profession: Private Practice

Chambers of Judge Michael H. Berger

2 East Fourteenth Avenue, Denver, CO 80203
Tel: (720) 625-5000
E-mail: michael.berger@judicial.state.co.us

Michael H. Berger
Judge

Education: Cornell; Colorado JD
Began Service: 2013
Appointed By: Governor John Hickenlooper

Chambers of Judge Elizabeth Harris

2 East Fourteenth Avenue, Denver, CO 80203
Tel: (720) 625-5150

Elizabeth Harris
Judge

Education: Georgetown 1989 BA; NYU 1996 JD
Began Service: 2015
Appointed By: Governor John Hickenlooper

Connecticut

Connecticut Office of the Chief Court Administrator

Supreme Court Building, 231 Capitol Avenue, Hartford, CT 06106
Tel: (860) 757-2100 Fax: (860) 757-2130
Internet: www.jud.ct.gov

Staff

Chief Court Administrator **Patrick L. Carroll III** . . . . (860) 757-2100
Deputy Chief Court Administrator **Elliot N. Solomon** . . . (860) 757-2100
E-mail: elliot.solomon@jud.ct.gov
Superior Court Operations Executive Director and Executive Secretary **Joseph D. D'Alesio** . . . . (860) 757-2102
E-mail: joseph.dalesio@jud.ct.gov
Education: Fairfield 1971 BA; John Marshall 1975 JD
Executive Director, Administrative Services **Thomas A. Siconolfi** . . . . (860) 757-2106
231 Capitol Avenue, Hartford, CT 06106 Fax: (860) 757-2130
E-mail: thomas.siconolfi@jud.ct.gov
Education: Fairfield 1976 BA; New Haven 1980 MA
Executive Director, Court Support Services **Stephen Grant** . . . . (860) 721-2100
936 Silas Deane Highway, Wethersfield, CT 06109 Fax: (860) 258-8976
E-mail: stephen.grant@jud.ct.gov
Executive Director, External Affairs **Melissa A. Farley** . . . (860) 757-2270
E-mail: melissa.farley@jud.ct.gov Fax: (860) 757-2215
Education: Trinity Col (CT) 1987 BA; Connecticut 1991 JD
Director, Information Technology **Terry Walker** . . . . (860) 282-6590
Two Riverview Square, 99 East River Drive, 7th Floor, East Hartford, CT 06108 Fax: (860) 282-6501
E-mail: terry.walker@jud.ct.gov
Human Resources Director **Elizabeth Graham** . . . . (860) 706-5221
E-mail: elizabeth.graham@jud.ct.gov
Director, Facilities Unit **Joseph P. McMahon** . . . . (860) 706-5269
E-mail: joseph.mcmahon@jud.ct.gov
Education: Central Conn State U 1972 BA; Connecticut 1977 MPA
Budget, Planning and Internal Audit Unit **Joyce Santoro** . . . . (860) 756-7911
E-mail: joyce.santoro@jud.ct.gov

Connecticut Supreme Court

Supreme Court Building, 231 Capitol Avenue, Hartford, CT 06106
Tel: (860) 757-2200 Fax: (860) 757-2217
Internet: www.jud.ct.gov

Number of Judgeships: 7

The Supreme Court consists of a chief justice and six associate justices who are appointed to eight-year terms by the General Assembly upon nomination of the Governor from a list compiled by the Judicial Selection Commission. The chief justice is appointed by the Governor and approved by the General Assembly to serve an eight-year term. Retirement is mandatory at age seventy; however, justices who voluntarily retire early may continue to serve the court as senior justices until they reach age 70. The Supreme Court has exclusive appellate jurisdiction over certain cases from the Connecticut Superior Court. These cases include appeals involving the validity of a state statute or state constitutional provision, conviction for a capital felony and other specified felonies, review of a death sentence, a dispute over an election or primary, reprimand or censure of a probate judge, judicial removal or suspension of a judge and decisions of the Judicial Review Council.

The Connecticut Supreme Court sits in Hartford.

Court Staff

Chief Clerk **Paul S. Hartan** . . . . (860) 757-2200
E-mail: paul.hartan@conn.app.jud.ct.gov
Chief Administrative Officer **Pamela Meotti** . . . . (860) 757-2145
E-mail: pamela.meotti@connapp.jud.ct.gov Fax: (860) 757-2214

Connecticut Supreme Court *continued*

Chief Staff Attorney **John DeMeo** . . . . (860) 757-2240
E-mail: john.demeo@connapp.jud.ct.gov Fax: (860) 757-2212
Reporter of Judicial Decisions **Thomas G. Smith** . . . . (860) 757-2250
E-mail: thomas.smith@connapp.jud.ct.gov Fax: (860) 757-2213
Court Reporter **(Vacant)** . . . . (860) 566-3400
101 Lafayette Street, Hartford, CT 06106 Fax: (860) 566-1638

Chambers of Chief Justice Chase T. Rogers

Supreme Court Building, 231 Capitol Avenue, Hartford, CT 06106
Tel: (860) 757-2200
E-mail: chase.t.rogers@jud.ct.gov

Chase Theodora Rogers
Chief Justice

Date of Birth: 1956
Education: Stanford 1979 BA; Boston U 1983 JD
Began Service: April 25, 2007
Appointed By: Governor M. Jodi Rell
Term Expires: April 2023

Judicial: Judge, Connecticut Superior Court (1998-2006); Judge, Chambers of Judge Chase T. Rogers, Connecticut Appellate Court (2006-2007)

Legal Practice: Partner, Cummings & Lockwood LLC (1991-1998)

Chambers of Associate Justice Richard N. Palmer

Supreme Court Building, 231 Capitol Avenue, Hartford, CT 06106
Tel: (860) 757-2115 Fax: (860) 757-2214
E-mail: richard.palmer@jud.ct.gov

Richard N. Palmer
Associate Justice

Date of Birth: 1950
Education: Trinity Col (CT) 1972 BA; Connecticut 1977 JD
Began Service: March 18, 1993
Appointed By: Governor Lowell P. Weicker, Jr.
Term Expires: March 18, 2017

Clerkships: Law Clerk The Hon. Jon O. Newman, United States District Court for the District of Connecticut (1977-1978)

Government: Assistant United States Attorney, Office of the United States Attorney, United States Department of Justice (1980-1983); Assistant United States Attorney, Office of the United States Attorney, United States Department of Justice (1986-1990); United States Attorney, United States Department of Justice (1991); Chief State's Attorney, State of Connecticut (1991-1993)

Legal Practice: Private Practice (1978-1980); Partner, Chatigny & Palmer (1983-1986)

Staff
Secretary **Elizabeth Hammell** . . . . (860) 757-2184

Chambers of Associate Justice Peter T. Zarella

Supreme Court Building, 231 Capitol Avenue, Hartford, CT 06106
Tel: (860) 757-2119 Fax: (860) 757-2214

Peter T. Zarella
Associate Justice

Education: Northeastern 1972 BS; Suffolk 1975 JD
Began Service: January 3, 2000
Appointed By: Governor John G. Rowland
Political Affiliation: Republican

Government: Commissioner, Metropolitan District Commission

Judicial: Judge, Rockville Superior Court (1996-1999); Judge, Connecticut Appellate Court (2000-2001)

Legal Practice: Partner, Brown, Paindiris & Zarella, LLP

Chambers of Associate Justice Peter T. Zarella *continued*

Staff

Career Law Clerk **Holly Boots** . . . . (860) 757-2119
Secretary **Elizabeth Hammell** . . . . (860) 757-2184
Law Clerk **Evan O'Roark** . . . . (860) 757-2119
E-mail: evan.o'roark@jud.ct.gov

Chambers of Associate Justice Dennis G. Eveleigh

231 Capitol Avenue, Hartford, CT 06106
Tel: (860) 757-2200 Fax: (860) 757-2217
E-mail: dennis.eveleigh@jud.ct.gov

Dennis G. Eveleigh
Associate Justice

Education: Wittenberg 1969; Connecticut 1972 JD
Began Service: June 1, 2010

Chambers of Associate Justice Andrew J. McDonald

State Supreme Court Building, 231 Capitol Avenue, Hartford, CT 06106
Tel: (860) 757-2200

Andrew J. McDonald
Associate Justice

Education: Cornell 1988 AB; Connecticut 1991 JD
Began Service: January 24, 2013
Political Affiliation: Democrat

Government: Senator (D-CT, District 27), Connecticut State Senate (2003-2011); General Counsel, Office of the Governor, State of Connecticut (2011-2013)

Staff

Career Law Clerk **Michele Morris** . . . . (860) 757-2200
Law Clerk **Mara Schulman Ryan** . . . . (860) 757-2200
Secretary **(Vacant)** . . . . (860) 757-2200

Chambers of Associate Justice Carmen E. Espinosa

231 Capitol Avenue, Hartford, CT 06106
Tel: (860) 757-2192
E-mail: carmen.espinosa@connapp.jud.ct.gov

Carmen Elisa Espinosa
Associate Justice

Education: Central Conn State U BS; Brown U MA; George Washington JD
Began Service: February 4, 2013
Appointed By: Governor Dannel Malloy

Government: Special Agent, Federal Bureau of Investigation, United States Department of Justice; Assistant U.S. Attorney, Connecticut District, Executive Office for United States Attorneys, United States Department of Justice

Judicial: Judge, Chambers of Judge Carmen Elisa Espinosa, Connecticut Appellate Court (2011-2013)

Staff

Law Clerk **Benjamin Arrow** . . . . (860) 757-2200
Career Law Clerk **Lisa M. Piquette** . . . . (860) 757-2200
Education: Assumption Col 1985 BA; Boston Col 1992; Cornell 2000 JD
Secretary **Karen Viklinetz** . . . . (860) 757-2200

Chambers of Associate Justice Richard A. Robinson

231 Capitol Avenue, Hartford, CT 06106
Tel: (860) 757-2200

Richard A. Robinson
Associate Justice

Education: Connecticut 1979 BA; West Virginia 1984 JD
Began Service: 2014
Appointed By: Governor Dannel Malloy

Chambers of Senior Justice Christine S. Vertefeuille

Supreme Court Building, 231 Capitol Avenue, Hartford, CT 06106
Tel: (860) 757-2200

Christine S. Vertefeuille
Senior Associate Justice

Date of Birth: 1950
Education: Trinity Col (CT) 1972 BA; Connecticut 1975 JD
Political Affiliation: Democrat

Connecticut Appellate Court

75 Elm Street, Hartford, CT 06106
Tel: (860) 713-2192 Fax: (860) 713-2216
Internet: www.jud.ct.gov

Number of Judgeships: 9

The Appellate Court, established in 1983, consists of a chief judge and nine judges who are appointed to eight-year terms by the Connecticut General Assembly upon nomination of the Governor from a list compiled by the Judicial Selection Commission. A chief judge is appointed by and serves at the pleasure of the chief justice of the Connecticut Supreme Court. Retirement is mandatory at age seventy; however, judges who voluntarily retire before that time may continue to serve the Court as judge trial referees. The Appellate Court has appellate jurisdiction over the Connecticut Superior Court and Probate Court except when the Connecticut Supreme Court has exclusive jurisdiction.

Note: Filings should be addressed to: Connecticut Appellate Court, 231 Capitol Ave, Hartford, CT 06106.

The Connecticut Appellate Court sits in Hartford.

Court Staff

Fax: (860) 757-2217

Chief Clerk **Paul S. Hartan** . . . . (860) 757-2200
231 Capitol Avenue, Hartford, CT 06106
E-mail: paul.hartan@conn.app.jud.ct.gov
Chief Administrative Officer **Pamela Miotti** . . . . (860) 757-2145
231 Capitol Avenue, Hartford, CT 06106 Fax: (860) 757-2214
E-mail: pamela.miotti@jud.ct.gov
Chief Staff Attorney **John DeMeo** . . . . (860) 757-2240
231 Capitol Avenue, Hartford, CT 06106 Fax: (860) 757-2212
E-mail: john.demeo@jud.ct.gov
Executive Director, External Affairs **Melissa A. Farley** . . . (860) 757-2270
Fax: (860) 757-2215
Director of Fiscal Administration **Thomas N. Sitaro** . . . . (860) 722-5821
Education: Hartford 1969 BS, 1976 MPA Fax: (860) 722-1614
Reporter of Judicial Decisions **Thomas Smith** . . . . (860) 757-2250
231 Capitol Avenue, Hartford, CT 06106 Fax: (860) 757-2213
Deputy Director, Law Libraries **Ann H. Doherty** . . . . (860) 706-5145
90 Washington Street, 3rd Floor, Hartford, CT 06106
Executive Assistant to Chief Judge **Jill Begemann** . . . . . . (860) 713-2192
Fax: (860) 713-2216

STATE COURTS – CONNECTICUT

Chambers of Chief Judge Alexandra D. DiPentima

75 Elm Street, Hartford, CT 06106
Tel: (860) 713-2192 Fax: (860) 713-2216

Alexandra D. DiPentima
Chief Judge

Date of Birth: April 18, 1953
Education: Connecticut 1979 JD; Princeton 1975 AB
Began Service: May 14, 2003
Term Expires: May 12, 2019

Judicial: Judge, Connecticut Superior Court (1993-2003)

Legal Practice: Staff Attorney, Connecticut Legal Services, Inc. (1979-1981); Attorney, Moller, Horton & Fineberg, P.C. (1981-1985); Principal, Moller, Horton & Fineberg, P.C. (1985-1993)

Nonprofit: President, Young Lawyers Section, Connecticut Bar Association (1989-1990); Director, Hartford County Bar (1990-1993); Treasurer, Hartford County Bar (1993-1994); President, Connecticut Judges Association (2001-2002)

Current Memberships: American Bar Association; Connecticut Bar Association, Inc.; Connecticut Bar Foundation, Connecticut Bar Association, Inc.; Connecticut Judges Association

Staff
Career Law Clerk **Christopher Heller** .... (860) 713-2192

Chambers of Judge F. Herbert Gruendel

75 Elm Street, Hartford, CT 06106
Tel: (860) 713-2192 Fax: (860) 713-2216
E-mail: f.gruendel@connapp.jud.ct.gov

F. Herbert Gruendel
Judge

Education: Drew 1969 BA; Maryland 1971 MA; Pennsylvania 1974 MA; Rutgers 1976 MA; Connecticut 1984 JD
Began Service: January 2005
Appointed By: Governor M. Jodi Rell

Judicial: Chief Administrative Judge, Family Division, Connecticut Superior Court; Judge, Connecticut Superior Court (1998-2005)

Legal Practice: Attorney, Jacobs, Grudberg, Belt & Dow (1984-1998)

Staff
Career Law Clerk **Christopher Champagne** .... (860) 713-2192
E-mail: christopher.champagne@connapp.jud.ct.gov

Chambers of Judge Douglas S. Lavine

75 Elm Street, Hartford, CT 06106
Tel: (860) 713-2192 Fax: (860) 713-2216
E-mail: douglas.lavine@connapp.jud.ct.gov

Douglas S. Lavine
Judge

Date of Birth: 1950
Education: Colgate 1973 BA; Connecticut 1977 JD
Began Service: 2006

Judicial: Judge, Connecticut Superior Court (1993-2006)

Legal Practice: Association Litigation Department, Shipman & Goodwin (1981-1986); Assistant U.S. Attorney, Office of the United States Attorney (1986-1997)

Staff
Career Law Clerk **Molly LeVan** .... (860) 713-2192
E-mail: molly.levan@connapp.jud.ct.gov

Chambers of Judge Robert E. Beach, Jr

75 Elm Street, Hartford, CT 06106
Tel: (860) 713-2192 Fax: (860) 713-2216
E-mail: robert.beach@connapp.jud.ct.gov

Robert E. Beach, Jr.
Judge

Education: Yale BA; Virginia JD
Began Service: December 2007
Appointed By: Governor M. Jodi Rell

Judicial: Administrative Judge, Hartford Judicial District, Connecticut; Judge, Middlesex Judicial District, Connecticut; Judge, Connecticut Superior Court, Connecticut

Profession: Private Practice

Staff
Career Law Clerk **Christy Ott** .... (860) 713-2192
E-mail: christy.ott@connapp.jud.ct.gov

Chambers of Judge Bethany J. Alvord

75 Elm Street, Hartford, CT 06106
Tel: (860) 713-2192 Fax: (860) 713-2216

Bethany J. Alvord
Judge

Education: Colgate 1979 BA; Connecticut 1982 JD
Began Service: April 2009
Appointed By: Governor M. Jodi Rell

Corporate: Second Vice President and Associate General Counsel, Law Department, Massachusetts Mutual Life Insurance Company (1982-1992); Assistant Vice President and Counsel, Retirement Services Division, Aetna Inc. (1993-1998)

Government: Family Support Magistrate, Family Support Court (1999-2002)

Judicial: Judge, Connecticut Superior Court (2002-2009)

Staff
Career Law Clerk **Mary Driscoll** .... (860) 713-2192
E-mail: mary.driscoll@connapp.jud.ct.gov

Chambers of Judge Michael R. Sheldon

75 Elm Street, Hartford, CT 06106
Tel: (860) 713-2192
E-mail: michael.sheldon@connapp.jud.ct.gov

Michael R. Sheldon
Judge

Education: Princeton 1971 AB; Yale 1974 JD
Began Service: 2012

Chambers of Judge Christine E. Keller

75 Elm Street, Hartford, CT 06106
Tel: (860) 713-2192
E-mail: christine.keller@conapp.jud.ct.gov

Christine E. Keller
Judge

Education: Smith; Connecticut JD
Began Service: 2013
Appointed By: Governor Dannel Malloy
Term Expires: 2021

Chambers of Judge Eliot D. Prescott

75 Elm Street, Hartford, CT 06106
Tel: (860) 713-2192

Eliot D. Prescott
Judge

Began Service: 2014
Appointed By: Governor Dannel Malloy

Chambers of Judge Raheem Mullins

75 Elm Street, Hartford, CT 06106
Tel: (860) 713-2192

Raheem L. Mullins
Judge

Began Service: 2014
Appointed By: Governor Dannel Malloy

Chambers of Judge (Trial Referee) Joseph P. Flynn

75 Elm Street, Hartford, CT 06106
Tel: (860) 713-2192

Joseph P. Flynn
Judge (Trial Referee)

Date of Birth: 1940
Education: Fairfield 1962 BA; Georgetown 1965 JD
Began Service: February 7, 2001
Appointed By: Governor John G. Rowland
Political Affiliation: Democrat

Academic: Adjunct Professor, Fairfield

Government: State Senator Joseph P. Flynn (CT, District 17), Connecticut State Senate (1975-1979); Deputy Chief Court Administrator, Connecticut Superior Court (1999-2001)

Judicial: Judge, Connecticut Superior Court (1985-2001)

Legal Practice: Private Practice (1965-1985)

Military Service: Lance Corporal, United States Marine Corps Reserve; Lieutenant Commander, United States Naval Reserve, Judge Advocate General's Corps

Current Memberships: Connecticut Bar Association, Inc.; Connecticut Judges Association; Lower Naugatuck Valley Bar Association

Chambers of Judge (Trial Referee) Antoinette L. Dupont

75 Elm Street, Hartford, CT 06106
Tel: (860) 713-2192
E-mail: antoinette.dupont@connapp.jud.ct.gov

Antoinette L. Dupont
Judge (Trial Referee)

Date of Birth: 1929
Education: Brown U 1950 BA; Harvard 1954 JD
Began Service: August 15, 1983
Term Expires: March 2016

Government: Special Counsel, City of New London, Connecticut (1960-1961)

Judicial: Judge, Connecticut Court of Common Pleas (1977-1978); Judge, Connecticut Superior Court (1978-1983)

Legal Practice: Private Practice (1956-1977)

Current Memberships: American Bar Foundation; The American Law Institute; Connecticut Bar Association, Inc.

Chambers of Judge (Trial Referee) Francis M. McDonald

75 Elm Street, Hartford, CT 06106
Tel: (860) 713-2192

Francis M. McDonald
Judge (Trial Referee)

Chambers of Judge (Trial Referee) Socrates H. Mihalakos

75 Elm Street, Hartford, CT 06106
Tel: (860) 713-2192
E-mail: socrates.mihalakos@connapp.jud.ct.gov

Socrates H. Mihalakos
Judge (Trial Referee)

Date of Birth: 1933
Education: Brown U 1955 BA; Connecticut 1962 JD
Appointed By: Governor William O'Neill
Political Affiliation: Republican

Judicial: Judge, Connecticut Superior Court (1986-1999); Senior Judge, Connecticut Appellate Court (1999-2004)

Legal Practice: Partner, Hitt, Mihalakos, Sachner and Coleman (1962-1986)

Military Service: United States Air Force (1955-1958)

Chambers of Judge (Trial Referee) Paul M. Foti

75 Elm Street, Hartford, CT 06106
Tel: (860) 713-2192
E-mail: paul.foti@connapp.jud.ct.gov

Paul M. Foti
Judge (Trial Referee)

Date of Birth: 1935
Education: Fordham 1956 BS; Connecticut 1959 JD

Chambers of Judge (Trial Referee) Thomas G. West

75 Elm Street, Hartford, CT 06106
Tel: (860) 713-2192

Thomas G. West
Judge (Trial Referee)

Date of Birth: November 13, 1934
Education: Western Connecticut St 1966 BA; Connecticut 1969 JD
Began Service: November 13, 2004
Political Affiliation: Democrat

Government: Assistant Corporation Counsel, City of Danbury, Connecticut (1979-1984)

Judicial: Judge, Connecticut Superior Court (1984-2002)

Legal Practice: Partner, Ventura, Ventura & West P.C. (1969-1981)

Chambers of Judge (Trial Referee) Joseph H. Pellegrino
95 Washington Street, Hartford, CT 06106
Tel: (860) 548-2822 Tel: (860) 713-2192

Joseph H. Pellegrino
Judge (Trial Referee)

Date of Birth: 1936
Education: Notre Dame 1958 BA; Fairfield 1962 MA; Boston Col 1963 JD
Began Service: March 2000
Appointed By: Governor John G. Rowland

Judicial: Judge, Connecticut Superior Court (1990-1997); Chief Administrative Judge, Civil Division, Connecticut Superior Court (1997-2000)

Legal Practice: Private Practice (1963-1990)

Current Memberships: Connecticut Bar Foundation, Connecticut Bar Association, Inc.

Chambers of Judge (Trial Referee) David M. Borden
75 Elm Street, Hartford, CT 06106
Tel: (860) 713-2192
E-mail: david.borden@connapp.jud.ct.gov

David M. Borden
Judge (Trial Referee)

Date of Birth: 1937
Education: Amherst 1959 BA; Harvard 1962 LLB
Began Service: 2008
Political Affiliation: Democrat

Current Memberships: The American Law Institute; Hartford County Bar

Chambers of Judge (Trial Referee) Stuart Bear
75 Elm Street, Hartford, CT 06106
Tel: (860) 713-2192

Stuart Bear
Judge (Trial Referee)

Education: Harvard, JD
Began Service: April 2010

Staff
Law Clerk **Jessie Opinion** .... (860) 713-2192
Career Law Clerk **Gail Oakley Pratt** .... (860) 713-2192
E-mail: gail.pratt@connapp.jud.ct.gov

Delaware

Delaware Administrative Office of the Courts

1 South Race Street, Georgetown, DE 19947
Tel: (302) 856-5406 Fax: (302) 856-5408
Internet: www.courts.state.de.us

Staff

State Court Administrator **Patricia W. Griffin** . . . . (302) 856-5406
E-mail: patricia.griffin@state.de.us Fax: (302) 856-5408
Operations Policy Coordinator **Sarah S. Lubin** . . . . (302) 255-2474
E-mail: sarah.lubin@state.de.us
Manager of Human Resources **Patricia Dilenno** . . . . (302) 255-0096
E-mail: patricia.diienno@state.de.us
Manager of Pro Se Services **Ashley Tucker** . . . . (302) 255-2475
E-mail: ashley.tucker@state.de.us
Manager of Support Services **Robin Jenkins** . . . . (302) 255-0079
E-mail: robin.jenkins@state.de.us
Deputy State Court Administrator **Amy Quinlan** . . . . (302) 255-0098
E-mail: amy.quinlan@state.de.us Fax: (302) 255-2218
Deputy State Court Administrator **James H. Wright** . . . . . (302) 255-0092
E-mail: james.wright@state.de.us Fax: (302) 255-2218
Deputy State Court Administrator **Dale Matthews** . . . . . . (302) 323-5369
E-mail: dale.matthews@state.de.us Fax: (302) 323-5399
Chief Financial Officer **Everlyn Nestlerode** . . . . (302) 255-0465
E-mail: everlyn.nestlerode@state.de.us
Manager of Judicial Branch Education **(Vacant)** . . . . (302) 255-0093

Delaware Supreme Court

Elbert N. Carvel State Office Building, 820 North French Street, Wilmington, DE 19801
Tel: (302) 577-8425 Fax: (302) 577-3702
Internet: http://courts.delaware.gov/supreme/

Number of Judgeships: 5

The Supreme Court of Delaware consists of a chief justice and four justices who are appointed for twelve-year terms by the Governor with the consent of the Delaware State Senate from a list of candidates provided by the Judicial Nominating Commission. The Supreme Court has final appellate jurisdiction over all civil cases from the Delaware Chancery, Superior and Family Courts and over criminal cases in which the penalty is death, imprisonment over one month, or a fine exceeding $100. The Court also has original jurisdiction over certain extraordinary writs.

The Delaware Supreme Court sits in Dover.

Court Staff

Clerk of the Court **Cathy L. Howard** . . . . (302) 739-4155
E-mail: Cathy.Howard@state.de.us Fax: (302) 739-3751
Chief Staff Attorney **Gayle P. Lafferty** . . . . (302) 577-8794
E-mail: Gayle.Lafferty@state.de.us
Court Administrator **William Montgomery** . . . . (302) 577-8742
E-mail: william.montgomery@state.de.us

Chambers of Chief Justice Leo E. Strine Jr.

405 North King Street, Suite 505, Wilmington, DE 19801
Tel: (302) 651-3902

Leo E. Strine, Jr.
Chief Justice

Education: Delaware BA; Pennsylvania 1988 JD
Began Service: February 28, 2014
Appointed By: Governor Jack Markell

Chambers of Justice Randy J. Holland

P.O. Box 369, Georgetown, DE 19947
Tel: (302) 856-5363 Fax: (302) 856-5365
E-mail: Randy.Holland@state.de.us

Randy J. Holland
Justice

Date of Birth: 1947
Education: Swarthmore 1969 BA; Pennsylvania 1972 JD; Virginia 1998 LLM
Began Service: December 12, 1986
Appointed By: Governor Michael N. Castle
Political Affiliation: Republican

Academic: Adjunct Professor, Widener University (1991); Adjunct Professor, School of Law, University of Pennsylvania (1993-1994); Adjunct Professor, College of Law, The University of Iowa (1997); Adjunct Professor, Vanderbilt University Law School (2000)

Government: City Solicitor, Office of the City Solicitor, City of Milford, Delaware (1974-1981)

Legal Practice: Partner, Dunlap, Holland & Rich (1973-1980); Partner, Morris, Nichols, Arsht & Tunnell LLP (1980-1986)

Current Memberships: American Bar Association; American Inns of Court Foundation, The American Inns of Court; The American Law Institute; Delaware Bar Foundation, Delaware State Bar Association

Staff

Law Clerk **(Vacant)** . . . . (302) 577-8425
E-mail: brittany.giusini@state.de.us
Judicial Secretary **Sharon McKay** . . . . (302) 856-5363
E-mail: sharon.mckay@state.de.us

Chambers of Justice Karen Valihura

820 North French Street, Wilmington, DE 19801
Tel: (302) 577-8425

Karen Valihura
Justice

Began Service: July 25, 2014
Appointed By: Governor Jack Markell

Chambers of Justice James T. Vaughn Jr.

820 North French Street, Wilmington, DE 19801
Tel: (302) 577-8425

James T. Vaughn, Jr.
Justice

Education: Duke 1971 BA; Georgetown 1976 JD
Began Service: October 30, 2014
Appointed By: Governor Jack Markell

Chambers of Justice Collins J. Seitz Jr.

820 North French Street, Wilmington, DE 19801
Tel: (302) 577-8425

Collins J. "C.J." Seitz
Justice

Education: Delaware 1980 BA; Villanova 1983 JD
Began Service: March 19, 2015
Appointed By: Governor Jack Markell

Delaware Court of Chancery

New Castle County Courthouse, 500 North King Street, Suite 1551, Wilmington, DE 19801-3734
Tel: (302) 255-0544 Fax: (302) 255-2213

The Court of Chancery consists of one chancellor and four vice chancellors. The chancellor and vice chancellors are nominated by the Governor and must be confirmed by the Senate for 12-year terms. The Delaware Court of Chancery is a non-jury trial court that serves as Delaware's court of original and exclusive equity jurisdiction, and adjudicates a wide variety of cases involving trusts, real property, guardianships, civil rights, and commercial litigation. The chancellor and vice chancellors must be learned in the law and must be Delaware citizens.

Court Staff

Court Administrator **Karlis P. Johnson** . . . . (302) 255-0544
Operations Manager, Kent County **Lois B. Holland** . . . . . . (302) 736-2242
38 The Green, Dover, DE 19901
E-mail: lois.holland@state.de.us
Operations Manager, Sussex County **Katrina Kruger** . . . . . (302) 856-5775
34 The Circle, Georgetown, DE 19947
E-mail: katrina.kruger@state.de.us
Office Manager, New Castle County
Kenneth J. Lagowski . . . . (302) 255-0544
E-mail: kenneth.lagowski@state.de.us

Chambers of Chancellor Andre G. Bouchard

500 North King Street, Wilmington, DE 19801-3734
Tel: (302) 255-0850

Andre G. Bouchard
Chancellor

Began Service: 2014
Appointed By: Governor Jack Markell
Military: Esq.

Chambers of Vice Chancellor John W. Noble

Kent County Courthouse, 38 The Green, Dover, DE 19901
Tel: (302) 739-4397
E-mail: john.noble@state.de.us

John W. Noble
Vice Chancellor

Education: Bucknell BSChE; Pennsylvania 1975 JD
Began Service: 2000

Chambers of Vice Chancellor J. Travis Laster

New Castle County Courthouse, 500 North King Street, Wilmington, DE 19801
Tel: (302) 255-0510

J. Travis Laster
Vice Chancellor

Education: Princeton AB; Virginia MA, JD
Began Service: October 9, 2009

Current Memberships: American Bar Association; Delaware State Bar Association

Chambers of Vice Chancellor Sam Glasscock III

34 The Circle, Georgetown, DE 19947
Tel: (302) 856-5424 Tel: (302) 856-5748 (Georgetown)
E-mail: sam.glasscock@state.de.us

Sam Glasscock III
Vice Chancellor

Began Service: 2011

Chambers of Master in Chancery Kim E. Ayvazian

34 The Circle, Georgetown, DE 19947
Tel: (302) 856-4670 Tel: (302) 856-5748 (Georgetown)
E-mail: kim.ayvazian@state.de.us

Kim E. Ayvazian
Master in Chancery

Education: Yale 1975 BA; Chicago 1986 JD

Chambers of Master in Chancery Abigail LeGrow

500 North King Street, Wilmington, DE 19801
Tel: (302) 255-0544
E-mail: abigail.legrow@state.de.us

Abigail Legrow
Master in Chancery

Education: Penn State 2004 JD
Began Service: 2012

Florida

Florida Office of the State Courts Administrator

Supreme Court Building, 500 South Duval Street,
Tallahassee, FL 32399-1900
Tel: (850) 922-5081 Fax: (850) 488-0156
E-mail: osca@flcourts.org
Internet: www.flcourts.org

Staff

State Courts Administrator **Patricia "PK" Jameson** ..... (850) 922-5081
E-mail: osca@flcourts.org
Deputy State Courts Administrator **Blan Teagle** .... (850) 410-2504
E-mail: teagleb@flcourts.org Fax: (850) 410-1342
Education: Florida 1985 JD
Deputy State Courts Administrator **Eric Maclure** .... (850) 488-9922
E-mail: macluree@flcourts.org Fax: (850) 488-3744
Director, Community and Intergovernmental Relations
Sarah Naf .... (850) 922-5692
E-mail: nafs@flcourts.org Fax: (850) 488-0156
Director, Information Systems **Alan Neubauer** .... (850) 488-6568
Fax: (850) 410-1521
Director, Public Information **Craig Waters** .... (850) 414-7641
E-mail: watersc@flcourts.org Fax: (850) 488-6130
Education: Florida 1986 JD
Chief, Personnel Services **Beatriz Caballero** .... (850) 487-0778
Fax: (850) 488-3744
Chief of Court Education **Martha Martin** .... (850) 922-5079
E-mail: martinm@flcourts.org Fax: (850) 922-9185
General Counsel **Tad David** .... (850) 922-5109
E-mail: osca@flcourts.org Fax: (850) 410-5301
Finance and Accounting Manager **Jackie Knight** .... (850) 488-3737
E-mail: knightj@flcourts.org Fax: (850) 414-8388
Reporter of Decisions **Paula Sicard** .... (850) 922-9793
E-mail: sicardp@flcourts.org Fax: (850) 488-6130

Florida Supreme Court

Supreme Court Building, 500 South Duval Street,
Tallahassee, FL 32399-1925
Tel: (850) 488-0125
E-mail: supremecourt@flcourts.org
Internet: www.floridasupremecourt.org

Number of Judgeships: 7

The Supreme Court consists of a chief justice and six justices who are appointed for six-year terms. Vacancies are filled by the Governor from a list of names submitted by a judicial nominating commission. Justices must stand for retention on a nonpartisan ballot in the next general election occurring at least one year after appointment. Retention elections are held every six years thereafter. The senior justice who has not previously served is selected as chief justice to serve a two-year term. Retirement is mandatory at age seventy. The Supreme Court has exclusive jurisdiction over criminal appeals involving the death penalty, bond validation and certificates of indebtedness, and shall review actions of statewide agencies related to rates or service of utilities.

The Florida Supreme Court sits in Tallahassee.

Court Staff

Clerk of the Court **John A. Tomasino** .... (850) 488-0125
Administrative Assistant **Vickie Van Lith** .... (850) 488-0125
E-mail: vanlithv@flcourts.org
Chief Deputy Clerk **Mark Clayton** .... (850) 488-0125
E-mail: claytonm@flcourts.org
Case Disposition Clerk **Kathy Belton** .... (850) 488-0463
E-mail: beltonk@flcourts.org
Capital Case Clerk **Tangy Williams** .... (850) 922-5518
E-mail: williamstr@flcourts.org
Case Circulation Clerk **Shannon Hudson** .... (850) 922-5949
E-mail: hudsons@flcourts.org

Florida Supreme Court *continued*

Deputy Clerk II **Terrance Dorsey** .... (850) 922-6036
E-mail: dorseyt@flcourts.org
Court Calendar/Opinions Clerk **Rebecca Morris** .... (850) 922-5466
New Case Set-Up Clerk **Tammy Galey** .... (850) 488-0882
E-mail: galeyt@flcourts.org
Supervisor/Rules Clerk **Victoria Milton** .... (850) 922-5464
Receptionist **Leann Doty** .... (850) 410-0125
E-mail: dotyl@flcourts.org
Opinions/Attorney Clerk **(Vacant)** .... (850) 922-5466
Florida Bar Clerk **Diana Davis** .... (850) 922-6220
E-mail: davisd@flcourts.org
Supervisor **Barbara Harley-Price** .... (850) 414-6886
E-mail: harleyb@flcourts.org
Attorney/ProSe Clerk **Alecia Bryant** .... (850) 922-5467
E-mail: bryanta@flcourts.org
Staff Attorney **Krys Godwin** .... (850) 488-0125
E-mail: godwink@flcourts.org
Marshal **Silvester Dawson** .... (850) 488-8845
E-mail: dawson@flcourts.org
Public Information Director **Craig Waters** .... (850) 414-7641
E-mail: watersc@flcourts.org
Reporter of Decisions **Paula Sicard** .... (850) 922-9793
E-mail: sicardp@flcourts.org
State Courts Administrator **Elisabeth H. Goodner** ...... (850) 922-5081
Education: Florida State 1978 BA
Supreme Court Librarian **Billie J. Blaine** .... (850) 922-5520
E-mail: blaineb@flcourts.org
Chief of Court Education **Martha Martin** .... (850) 922-5079
E-mail: martinm@flcourts.org Fax: (850) 922-9185

Chambers of Chief Justice Jorge Labarga

Supreme Court Building, 500 South Duval Street, Tallahassee, FL 32399
Tel: (850) 413-8371 Fax: (850) 487-4696
E-mail: labargaj@flcourts.org

Jorge Labarga
Chief Justice

Education: Florida 1976, 1979 JD
Began Service: January 2009
Appointed By: Governor Charlie Crist
Next Election: November 2016
Term Expires: January 2017

Staff
Fax: (850) 487-4696

Staff Attorney **Valencia N. Davis** .... (850) 413-8371
E-mail: porcherr@flcourts.org
Education: Nebraska JD
Staff Attorney **Jorge Perez Santiago** .... (850) 413-8371
E-mail: santiagoj@flcourts.org
Career Staff Attorney **Janice G. Scott** .... (850) 413-8371
E-mail: scottj@flcourts.org
Judicial Assistant **B.J. Vickers** .... (850) 413-8371
E-mail: vickersb@flcourts.org

Chambers of Justice Barbara J. Pariente

Supreme Court Building, 500 South Duval Street,
Tallahassee, FL 32399-1925
Tel: (850) 488-8421

Barbara J. Pariente
Justice

Date of Birth: 1948
Education: Boston U 1970 BS; George Washington 1973 JD
Began Service: December 10, 1997
Appointed By: Governor Lawton M. Chiles
Next Election: November 2018
Election Type: Retention Election
Term Expires: 2019

Clerkships: Law Clerk The Honorable Norman Roettger, United States District Court for the Southern District of Florida (1973-1975)

Judicial: Judge, Florida District Court of Appeal, Fourth District (1993-1997); Founding Member/Master, Palm Beach County Chapter, American Inns of Court; Board of Directors, Legal Aid Society; Liaison, Supreme Court Task Force on Treatment-Based Drug Courts (1998); Member, Florida Bar Commission (2000-2002); Chief Justice, Florida Supreme Court (2004-2006)

Legal Practice: Partner, Cone, Wagner, Nugent (1975-1983); Partner, Pariente & Silber, P.A. (1983-1993)

Current Memberships: American Bar Association; Florida Association for Women Lawyers; National Association of Women Judges

Staff

Law Clerk **Erika Follmer** .... (850) 488-8421
Began Service: August 2014
Term Expires: September 2016

Law Clerk **Joseph T. Eagleton** .... (850) 488-8421
Began Service: August 2012
Term Expires: August 2016
E-mail: eagletoj@flcourts.org

Staff Attorney **Lyyli M. Van Whittle** .... (850) 488-8421
Education: Florida 1993 BS; Florida State 1998 JD

Judicial Assistant **Brenda Williams** .... (850) 488-8421
E-mail: williamb@flcourts.org

Chambers of Justice R. Fred Lewis

Supreme Court Building, 500 South Duval Street,
Tallahassee, FL 32399-1925
Tel: (850) 488-0007 Fax: (850) 487-4696

R. Fred Lewis
Justice

Date of Birth: 1947
Education: Florida Southern 1969; Miami 1972 JD
Began Service: December 7, 1998
Appointed By: Governor Lawton M. Chiles
Next Election: November 2018
Election Type: Retention Election

Judicial: Liaison, Florida Board of Bar Examiners; Liaison, Florida Judicial Management Council

Legal Practice: Private Practice (1972-1998)

Military Service: United States Army

Current Memberships: The District of Columbia Bar; The Florida Bar

Staff

Senior Staff Attorney **Antonio Hernandez** .... (850) 410-0877
E-mail: hernandeza@flcourts.org

Career Staff Attorney **Katie Dillados** .... (850) 922-8926
E-mail: dilladosk@flcourts.org

Staff Attorney **Natalie Harrison** .... (850) 414-7645
Began Service: August 2, 2010
E-mail: harrison@flcourts.org

Chambers of Justice R. Fred Lewis *continued*

Judicial Assistant **Gail Posey** .... (850) 488-0007
E-mail: poseyg@flcourts.org

Chambers of Justice Peggy A. Quince

Supreme Court Building, 500 South Duval Street,
Tallahassee, FL 32399-1925
Tel: (850) 922-5624 Fax: (850) 487-2823
E-mail: larryg@flcourts.org

Peggy A. Quince
Justice

Date of Birth: 1948
Education: Howard U 1970 BS; Columbus Law 1975 JD
Began Service: January 5, 1999
Appointed By: Governor Lawton M. Chiles
Next Election: November 2018
Election Type: Retention Election
Term Expires: January 2019

Government: Hearing Officer, Rental Accommodations Office, District of Columbia (1975-1977); Assistant Attorney General, Criminal Division, Office of the Attorney General, State of Florida (1980-1994)

Judicial: Judge, Florida Court of Appeal, Second District (1994-1998); Chief Justice, Chambers of Justice Peggy A. Quince, Florida Supreme Court (2008-2010)

Legal Practice: Private Practice (1977-1978); Private Practice (1978-1980)

Current Memberships: The Florida Bar; National Bar Association; Tallahassee Association of Women Lawyers; Virginia State Bar

Staff

Staff Attorney **Christina A. Jackson** .... (850) 922-5624
E-mail: jacksonc@flcourts.org

Career Staff Attorney **Jeremy Dicker** .... (850) 922-5624
E-mail: dickerj@flcourts.org

Senior Staff Attorney **Tamara St. Hilaire** .... (850) 922-5624
E-mail: sthilait@flcourts.org

Judicial Assistant **Glenda S. Larry** .... (850) 922-5624
E-mail: larryg@flcourts.org

Chambers of Justice Charles T. Canady

Supreme Court Building, 500 South Duval Street,
Tallahassee, FL 32399-1925
Tel: (850) 410-8092
E-mail: canadyc@flcourts.org

Charles T. Canady
Justice

Date of Birth: June 22, 1954
Education: Haverford 1976 BA; Yale 1979 JD
Began Service: September 8, 2008
Appointed By: Governor Charlie Crist
Next Election: November 2016

Staff

Career Staff Attorney **Dalana W. Johnson** .... (850) 410-8092
E-mail: johnsond@flcourts.org
Education: Florida State 1992 JD

Career Staff Attorney **Renee Rancour** .... (850) 410-8092

Staff Attorney **Joshua Pratt** .... (850) 410-8092
E-mail: loguej@flcourts.org

Judicial Assistant **Jessica Miller** .... (850) 410-8092

Chambers of Justice Ricky L. Polston

Supreme Court Building, 500 South Duval Street, Tallahassee, FL 32399
Tel: (850) 488-2361

Ricky L. Polston
Justice

Date of Birth: 1955
Education: Florida State 1977 BS, 1986 JD
Began Service: October 2, 2008
Appointed By: Governor Charlie Crist
Next Election: November 2016
Election Type: Retention Election
Term Expires: January 2017

Current Memberships: American Bar Association; The William H. Stafford American Inn of Court, The American Inns of Court; American Institute of Certified Public Accountants; Florida Institute of CPA's; Tallahassee Bar Association

Staff

Staff Attorney **Vaishali Desai** . . . . . (850) 488-2361
Staff Attorney **Jessica Slatten** . . . . . (850) 488-2361
E-mail: slattenj@flcourts.org
Senior Staff Attorney **Diane Cashin West** . . . . . (850) 488-2361
E-mail: westd@flcourts.org
Judicial Assistant **Tamara L. Adkins** . . . . . (850) 488-2361
E-mail: adkinst@flcourts.org
Education: Florida State 1986 BS

Chambers of Justice James E. C. Perry

500 South Duval Street, Tallahassee, FL 32399-1900
Tel: (850) 921-1096 Fax: (850) 487-2893
E-mail: perryj@flcourts.org

James E. C. Perry
Justice

Education: St Augustine's Col 1966 BA; Columbia 1972 JD
Began Service: March 16, 2009
Appointed By: Governor Charlie Crist
Next Election: November 2016
Election Type: Retention Election
Term Expires: January 2017

Judicial: Judge, Eighteenth Judicial District, Florida Circuit Court (2000-2009)

Current Memberships: The Florida Bar

Profession: Senior Partner

Staff

Fax: (850) 487-2893

Staff Attorney **Ta'Ronce Stowes** . . . . . (850) 921-1096
Career Staff Attorney **Gregory S. "Greg" Redmon** . . . . . (850) 921-1096
E-mail: redmong@flcourts.org
Senior Staff Attorney **Mireille Fall-Fry** . . . . . (850) 921-1096
E-mail: fall-frym@flcourts.org
Judicial Assistant **Dawn Stallworth** . . . . . (850) 921-1096
E-mail: stallwod@flcourts.org

Florida District Courts of Appeal

2000 Drayton Drive, Tallahassee, FL 32399
Tel: (850) 487-1000 Fax: (850) 488-7989
Internet: www.flcourts.org

The judges of the Florida District Courts of Appeal are elected for six-year terms on a non-partisan ballot in general elections held in their respective districts. The Courts sit on panels of three judges each. Vacancies are filled by the governor from a list of names submitted by the Judicial Nominating Commission. New appellate judges stand for retention in the first general election occurring at least one year after appointment. The chief judges are elected by peer vote for two-year terms. Retirement is mandatory at age seventy. The District Courts of Appeal have jurisdiction over civil and criminal appeals, including those taken as a matter of rights from final judgments of trial courts, review of administrative actions not directly appealable to another court or as prescribed by law, and interlocutory orders as provided by Florida Supreme Court rules.

Florida District Court of Appeal, First District

2000 Drayton Drive, Tallahassee, FL 32399
Tel: (850) 487-1000 Fax: (850) 488-7989
Internet: www.1dca.org

Number of Judgeships: 15

Areas Covered: Counties of Alachua, Baker, Bay, Bradford, Calhoun, Clay, Columbia, Dixie, Duval, Escambia, Franklin, Gadsden, Gilchrist, Gulf, Hamilton, Holmes, Jackson, Jefferson, Lafayette, Leon, Levy, Liberty, Madison, Nassau, Okaloosa, Santa Rosa, Suwannee, Taylor, Union, Wakulla, Walton and Washington

Court Staff

Clerk of the Court **Jon S. Wheeler** . . . . . (850) 717-8100
E-mail: wheelerj@1dca.org
Chief Deputy Clerk of the Court **Karen Roberts** . . . . . (850) 717-8101
E-mail: robertsk@1dca.org
Marshal of the Court **J. Daniel McCarthy** . . . . . (850) 717-8130
Deputy Marshal of the Court **Leslie Tharp** . . . . . (850) 717-8131
E-mail: tharpl@1dca.org

Chambers of Chief Judge L. Clayton Roberts

2000 Drayton Drive, Tallahassee, FL 32399
Tel: (850) 487-1000

L. Clayton Roberts
Chief Judge

Date of Birth: April 11, 1965
Education: West Point 1987 BS; Florida State 1991 JD
Began Service: 2007
Appointed By: Governor Charlie Crist
Next Election: November 4, 2020
Election Type: Retention Election
Term Expires: December 2020

Staff

Law Clerk **Laura Ketchum** . . . . . (850) 487-1000
Began Service: November 2012
Career Law Clerk **Sarah Young** . . . . . (850) 487-1000
E-mail: youngs@1dca.org
Judicial Assistant **Suzanne I. Smith** . . . . . (850) 487-1000
E-mail: suzanneismith@comcast.net
Education: Kutztown BSBA; Johns Hopkins MA

STATE COURTS – FLORIDA

Chambers of Appellate Judge Joseph Lewis, Jr.

2000 Drayton Drive, Tallahassee, FL 32399
Tel: (850) 717-8199 Fax: (850) 921-4768
E-mail: lewisj@1dca.org

Joseph Lewis, Jr.
Appellate Judge

Date of Birth: 1953
Education: Montana 1974 BS; Florida State 1977 JD
Began Service: January 2, 2001
Appointed By: Governor Jeb Bush
Next Election: November 4, 2020
Election Type: Retention Election
Term Expires: December 2020

Current Memberships: The Florida Bar; National Bar Association; Tallahassee Bar Association

Staff
Law Clerk **Susan Huber** .... (850) 717-8202
Education: Florida State 2002 JD
Law Clerk **Krisztina Schlessel** .... (850) 717-8201
Began Service: 2013
E-mail: schlesselk@1dca.org
Judicial Assistant **Corla M. Washington** .... (850) 717-8199
E-mail: corlaw@1dca.org

Chambers of Appellate Judge Robert Tyrie Benton II

2000 Drayton Drive, Tallahassee, FL 32399
Tel: (850) 487-1000 ext. 8181 Fax: (850) 488-3136
E-mail: bentonr@1dca.org

Robert Tyrie Benton II
Appellate Judge

Date of Birth: 1946
Education: Johns Hopkins 1967 BA; Florida 1970 JD; Harvard 1971 LLM
Began Service: January 4, 1994
Appointed By: Governor Lawton M. Chiles
Political Affiliation: Democrat

Current Memberships: The Florida Bar; Tallahassee Bar Association

Staff
Law Clerk **Carol Peacock** .... (850) 487-1000
Began Service: 2009
E-mail: peacockc@1dca.org
Education: Florida State 1987 JD
Law Clerk **Marc Hernandez** .... (850) 487-1000
E-mail: hernandezm@1dca.org
Judicial Assistant **Holly J. Higgins** .... (850) 487-1000
E-mail: higginsh@1dca.org

Chambers of Appellate Judge James R. Wolf

2000 Drayton Drive, Tallahassee, FL 32399
Tel: (850) 487-1000 Fax: (850) 921-4768
E-mail: wolfj@1dca.org

James R. Wolf
Appellate Judge

Date of Birth: 1950
Education: Rutgers 1972 AB; Miami 1975 JD; Virginia 2001 LLM
Began Service: June 19, 1990
Appointed By: Governor Bob Martinez
Next Election: November 2016
Term Expires: January 1, 2017

Government: Assistant State Attorney, 15th Judicial Circuit, Office of the State Attorney, State of Florida (1975-1978); Assistant City Attorney, Office of the City Attorney, City of West Palm Beach, Florida (1978-1980)

Chambers of Appellate Judge James R. Wolf *continued*

Legal Practice: Cladwell, Pacetti, Barrow and Salisbury (1980-1983); General Counsel, Florida League of Cities, Inc. (1983-1990)

Staff
Career Law Clerk **Jessica Poarch** .... (850) 487-1000
Education: Abilene Christian 2004 BA; Florida State 2007 JD
Law Clerk **Stephanie Levitt** .... (850) 487-1000
Judicial Assistant **Judy Tehan** .... (850) 487-1000
E-mail: tehanj@1dca.org

Chambers of Appellate Judge Bradford L. Thomas

2000 Drayton Drive, Tallahassee, FL 32399
Tel: (850) 487-1000 Fax: (850) 488-7989
E-mail: thomasb@1dca.org

Bradford L. Thomas
Appellate Judge

Education: Florida State 1977 BA; Florida 1982 JD
Began Service: January 4, 2005
Next Election: November 2018
Election Type: Retention Election
Term Expires: January 2019

Government: Assistant Attorney General, Office of the Attorney General (Legal Affairs Department), State of Florida (1987-1989); Assistant General Counsel, Parole Commission, State of Florida (1989-1991); Staff Director, Criminal Justice, Florida Senate (1996-1997); Public Safety Policy Coordinator, Office of the Governor, State of Florida (1999-2005)

Judicial: Assistant State Attorney, State of Florida (1991-1996); Justice Council Director, Florida House of Representatives (1997-1999)

Legal Practice: Assistant General Counsel, Department of Environmental Protection, State of Florida (1984-1987)

Profession: Private Practice (1984)

Staff
Law Clerk **Jennifer Isherwood** .... (850) 487-1000
Began Service: 2011
E-mail: isherwoodj@1dca.org
Career Attorney **Todd Sanders** .... (850) 487-1000
E-mail: sanderst@1dca.org
Judicial Assistant **Betsy Johansen** .... (850) 487-1000

Chambers of Appellate Judge T. Kent Wetherell

2000 Drayton Drive, Tallahassee, FL 32399
Tel: (850) 487-1000 Fax: (850) 488-7989

T. Kent Wetherell II
Appellate Judge

Date of Birth: 1970
Education: Florida State 1992 BS, 1995 JD
Began Service: October 2009
Next Election: November 2016

Staff
Career Attorney **Dawn Mackland** .... (850) 487-1000
Education: Florida 1993 BS; Florida State 1999 JD
Law Clerk **Amber Stoner** .... (850) 487-1000
E-mail: stonera@1dca.org
Judicial Assistant **(Vacant)** .... (850) 487-1000

Chambers of Appellate Judge Lori S. Rowe
2000 Drayton Drive, Tallahassee, FL 32399
Tel: (850) 487-1000 Fax: (850) 488-7989
E-mail: rowel@1dca.org

Lori Sellers Rowe
Appellate Judge

Date of Birth: 1970
Education: Vanderbilt 1992 BA; Florida State 1997 MBA, 1997 JD
Began Service: September 15, 2009
Appointed By: Governor Charlie Crist
Next Election: November 2016
Election Type: Retention Election

Staff
Law Clerk **Allison Hunter** .... (850) 487-1000
E-mail: huntera@1dca.org
Career Attorney **Joanna Summers** .... (850) 487-1000
Judicial Assistant **Penny Kuhl** .... (850) 487-1000
E-mail: kuhlp@1dca.org

Chambers of Appellate Judge Simone Marstiller
2000 Drayton Drive, Tallahassee, FL 32399
Tel: (850) 487-1000 Fax: (850) 488-7989
E-mail: marstillers@1dca.org

Simone Marstiller
Appellate Judge

Education: Stetson BA, JD
Began Service: 2010
Appointed By: Governor Charlie Crist

Staff
Law Clerk **Wade Holder** .... (850) 487-1000
Law Clerk **Brandi Thompson** .... (850) 487-1000
Judicial Assistant **Betsy Breeden** .... (850) 487-1000
E-mail: breedenb@1dca.org

Chambers of Appellate Judge Ronald V. Swanson
2000 Drayton Drive, Tallahassee, FL 32399
Tel: (850) 487-1000

Ronald V. Swanson
Judge

Date of Birth: April 16, 1948
Education: Florida State 1970 BS; Florida 1973 JD; George Washington 1982 LLM
Began Service: 2011

Staff
Career Attorney **Diane Scott** .... (850) 487-1000
Career Attorney **Gregory Martinson** .... (850) 487-1000
Education: Florida 1988 BA, 1991 JD
Judicial Assistant **Joni White** .... (850) 487-1000

Chambers of Appellate Judge Stephanie Williams Ray
2000 Drayton Drive, Tallahassee, FL 32399
Tel: (850) 487-1000

Stephanie Williams Ray
Judge

Date of Birth: June 6, 1970
Education: Vanderbilt 1992 BA; Florida State 1995 JD
Began Service: 2011

Staff
Career Attorney **Geneva Fountain** .... (850) 487-1000

Chambers of Appellate Judge Stephanie Williams Ray *continued*
Senior Law Clerk **Lindsey Lawton** .... (850) 487-1000
Education: Florida 2007 JD
Judicial Assistant **C. J. Marston** .... (850) 487-1000

Chambers of Appellate Judge Scott Makar
2000 Drayton Drive, Tallahassee, FL 32399
Tel: (850) 487-1000

Scott D. Makar
Appellate Judge

Education: Mercer 1980 BS; Florida 1982 MA, 1982 MBA, 1987 JD, 1993 PhD

Staff
Law Clerk **Renatha Francis** .... (850) 487-1000
Law Clerk **Lauren Woodruff** .... (850) 487-1000
Judicial Assistant **Doris Brickhouse-Hayes** .... (850) 487-1000

Chambers of Appellate Judge Timothy D. Osterhaus
2000 Drayton Drive, Tallahassee, FL 32399
Tel: (850) 487-1000

Timothy D. Osterhaus
Appellate Judge

Began Service: 2013
Appointed By: Governor Rick Scott

Staff
Law Clerk **Natalie Kirk** .... (850) 487-1000
Law Clerk **Madison Kvamme** .... (850) 487-1000

Chambers of Appellate Judge Ross L. Bilbrey
2000 Drayton Drive, Tallahassee, FL 32399
Tel: (850) 487-1000

Ross L. Bilbrey
Appellate Judge

Education: Florida 1990 BA, 1993 JD
Began Service: December 2014
Appointed By: Governor Rick Scott

Chambers of Appellate Judge Susan L. Kelsey
2000 Drayton Drive, Tallahassee, FL 32399
Tel: (850) 487-1000

Susan L. Kelsey
Appellate Judge

Chambers of Appellate Judge Thomas D. Winokur
2000 Drayton Drive, Tallahassee, FL 32399
Tel: (850) 487-1000

Thomas Winokur
Appellate Judge

Began Service: 2015

Florida District Court of Appeal, Second District

1700 North Tampa Street, Tampa, FL 33601
P.O. Box 327, Lakeland, FL 33802-0327
Tel: (863) 499-2290 Fax: (863) 413-2649
E-mail: 2dca@wpgate.courts.state.fl.us

Number of Judgeships: 14

Areas Covered: Counties of Charlotte, Collier, DeSoto, Glades, Hardee, Hendry, Highlands, Hillsborough, Lee, Manatee, Pasco, Pinellas, Polk and Sarasota

Court Staff

Clerk of the Court **Mary Elizabeth Kuenzel** . . . . (863) 499-2290
Education: Florida State 1984 BA; Stetson 1993 JD
Marshal of the Court **Jacinda Haynes** . . . . (863) 499-2290
E-mail: haynesj@flcourts.org
Librarian **Becky Fisher** . . . . (863) 499-2290
E-mail: fisherb@flcourts.org
Senior User Support Analyst **Lori Holmes** . . . . (863) 499-2290
E-mail: holmesl@flcourts.org
Administrative Assistant II **Holly Tidwell** . . . . (863) 499-2290
E-mail: tidwellh@flcourts.org

Chambers of Chief Judge Judge Craig C. Villanti

1700 North Tampa Street, Suite 300, Tampa, FL 33602
Tel: (813) 272-3430

Craig C. Villanti
Chief Judge

Date of Birth: January 21, 1952
Education: NYU 1974 BA; Stetson 1977 JD
Began Service: February 2003
Appointed By: Governor Jeb Bush
Next Election: November 2016

Staff

Staff Attorney **Bradley A. Muhs** . . . . (863) 272-3430
E-mail: whittlen@flcourts.org
Staff Attorney **Tracy E. Leduc** . . . . (863) 272-3430
E-mail: leduct@flcourts.org
Education: William & Mary 1986 BA; Stetson 1997 JD
Judicial Assistant **Edna Stacy** . . . . (863) 272-3430
E-mail: stacye@flcourts.org

Chambers of Appellate Judge Morris Silberman

1700 North Tampa Street, Suite 300, Tampa, FL 33602
Tel: (813) 272-3430 Fax: (813) 229-6534

Morris Silberman
Appellate Judge

Date of Birth: 1957
Education: Tulane 1979; Florida 1982 JD
Began Service: January 2, 2001
Appointed By: Governor Jeb Bush
Next Election: November 4, 2020
Election Type: Retention Election
Term Expires: December 31, 2020

Current Memberships: Clearwater Bar Association; The Florida Bar

Staff

Career Law Clerk **Debbie Tozier** . . . . (813) 272-3430
E-mail: tozierd@flcourts.org
Education: Stetson JD
Career Law Clerk **Joye Bartok Walford** . . . . (813) 272-3430
E-mail: walfordj@flcourts.org
Judicial Assistant **Amye Scholes Robb** . . . . (813) 272-3430
E-mail: robba@flcourts.org

Chambers of Appellate Judge Chris W. Altenbernd

1700 North Tampa Street, Suite 300, Tampa, FL 33602-3547
Tel: (813) 272-3430 Fax: (813) 229-6534

Chris W. Altenbernd
Appellate Judge

Date of Birth: 1949
Education: Missouri 1972 BA; Harvard 1975 JD; Virginia 1998 LLM
Began Service: January 3, 1989
Appointed By: Governor Bob Martinez
Next Election: November 4, 2020
Election Type: Retention Election
Term Expires: December 2020

Judicial: Chief Judge, Florida District Court of Appeal, Second District (2005)

Legal Practice: Attorney, Fowler, White, Gillen, Boggs, Villareal and Banker, P.A. (1975-1989)

Current Memberships: American Bar Association; American Board of Trial Advocates; The William Glenn Terrell American Inn of Court, The American Inns of Court; The Florida Bar; Hillsborough County Bar Association

Staff

Law Clerk **Nancy Noble Burton** . . . . (813) 272-3430
Began Service: 2011
E-mail: burtonn@flcourts.org
Education: Wesleyan Col 1977 BA; Stetson 1984 JD
Law Clerk **Mariko Outman** . . . . (813) 272-3430
Judicial Assistant **Louise B. Norstrom** . . . . (813) 272-3430
E-mail: norstrol@flcourts.org

Chambers of Appellate Judge Stevan T. Northcutt

1700 North Tampa Street, Suite 300, Tampa, FL 33602
Tel: (813) 272-3430 Fax: (813) 229-6534

Stevan T. Northcutt
Appellate Judge

Date of Birth: August 1, 1954
Education: South Florida 1975 BA; Florida State 1978 JD
Began Service: January 1997
Appointed By: Governor Lawton M. Chiles
Next Election: November 2016

Corporate: Journalist, The Tampa Times; Journalist, Tampa Tribune; Journalist, Chicago Tribune

Legal Practice: Associate, Levine, Freedman, Hirsch & Levinson, P.A.; Partner, Levine, Freedman, Hirsch & Levinson, P.A.; Shareholder, Levine, Hirsch, Segall & Northcutt, P.A. (1986-1997)

Current Memberships: Hillsborough County Bar Association

Staff

Career Law Clerk **(Vacant)** . . . . (813) 272-3430
E-mail: kuenzelm@flcourts.org
Career Law Clerk **Frances H. Toomey** . . . . (813) 272-3430
E-mail: toomeyf@flcourts.org
Education: Oklahoma 1972 BA; Florida 1986 JD
Judicial Assistant **Martha Stem** . . . . (813) 272-3430
E-mail: stemm@flcourts.org

Chambers of Appellate Judge Darryl C. Casanueva

1700 North Tampa Street, Suite 300, Tampa, FL 33602
Tel: (813) 272-3430 Fax: (813) 229-6534

Darryl C. Casanueva
Appellate Judge

Date of Birth: 1951
Education: South Florida 1973 BA; Loyola U (New Orleans) 1976 JD; Virginia 2001 LLM
Began Service: February 14, 1998
Appointed By: Governor Lawton M. Chiles
Next Election: November 2018
Term Expires: January 2019

Current Memberships: The Supreme Court Historical Society

Staff
Career Staff Attorney **Bonnie E. Eshleman** .... (813) 272-3430
Education: Stetson 1990 JD
Career Staff Attorney **Stacy Strohauer Son** .... (813) 272-3430
E-mail: sons@flcourts.org
Judicial Assistant **Lynell Nash** .... (813) 272-3430
E-mail: nashl@flcourts.org
Education: Kilgore 1965 AA

Chambers of Appellate Judge Patricia J. Kelly

1700 North Tampa Street, Suite 300, Tampa, FL 33602
Tel: (813) 272-3430 Fax: (813) 229-6534
E-mail: kellyp@flcourts.org

Patricia J. Kelly
Appellate Judge

Date of Birth: 1956
Education: South Florida 1983 BA; Florida 1986 JD
Began Service: December 2001
Appointed By: Governor Jeb Bush
Next Election: November 2016

Clerkships: Law Clerk The Honorable James Lehan, Florida District Court of Appeal, Second District (1989-1993)

Legal Practice: Private Practice (1986-1989); Private Practice (1993-2001)

Current Memberships: The William Glenn Terrell American Inn of Court, The American Inns of Court; Hillsborough County Bar Association

Staff
Staff Attorney **Lorrie Nertney** .... (813) 272-3430
E-mail: nertneyl@flcourts.org Fax: (813) 229-6534
Education: Florida State 1985 JD
Staff Attorney **Donna K. Valenti** .... (813) 272-3430
E-mail: valentid@flcourts.org Fax: (813) 229-6534
Education: South Texas 1982 JD
Judicial Assistant **M. Gail Byrd** .... (813) 272-3430
E-mail: byrdg@flcourts.org Fax: (813) 229-6534

Chambers of Appellate Judge Douglas A. Wallace

1700 North Tampa Street, Suite 300, Tampa, FL 33602
Tel: (813) 272-3430
E-mail: wallaced@flcourts.org

Douglas A. Wallace
Appellate Judge

Education: Princeton 1969 BA; Yale 1972 JD
Began Service: June 2003
Appointed By: Governor Jeb Bush
Next Election: November 2016

Staff
Staff Attorney **Robin Orr** .... (813) 272-3430
E-mail: orrr@flcourts.org

Chambers of Appellate Judge Douglas A. Wallace *continued*

Staff Attorney **Shari D. Johannes** .... (813) 272-3430
E-mail: johannes@flcourts.org
Appellate Assistant **Geraldine Thomas** .... (813) 272-3430
E-mail: thomasg@flcourts.org

Chambers of Appellate Judge Edward C. LaRose

1700 North Tampa Street, Suite 300, Tampa, FL 33602
Tel: (813) 272-3430 Fax: (813) 229-6534
E-mail: larosee@flcourts.org

Edward C. LaRose
Appellate Judge

Date of Birth: January 20, 1955
Education: Boston Col 1977 BA; Cornell 1980 JD
Began Service: February 16, 2005
Appointed By: Governor Jeb Bush

Legal Practice: Attorney, Howrey & Simon; Associate, Trenam, Kemker, Scharf, Barkin, Frye, O'Neill & Mullis (1983-1987); Shareholder, Trenam, Kemker, Scharf, Barkin, Frye, O'Neill & Mullis

Staff
Career Attorney **Carol Castleberry** .... (813) 272-3430
E-mail: castlebc@flcourts.org
Education: Stetson 1996 JD
Career Attorney **Jennifer Fogle** .... (813) 272-3430
E-mail: foglej@flcourts.org
Judicial Assistant **Michelle Doll** .... (813) 272-3430
E-mail: dollm@flcourts.org

Chambers of Appellate Judge Nelly N. Khouzam

1700 North Tampa Street, Suite 300, Tampa, FL 33601
P.O. Box 327, Lakeland, FL 33802-0327
Tel: (813) 272-3430
E-mail: khouzamn@flcourts.org

Nelly N. Khouzam
Appellate Judge

Education: Florida 1979, 1981 JD
Began Service: 2008
Appointed By: Governor Charlie Crist
Next Election: November 2016

Clerkships: Judicial Clerk/Staff Attorney, Florida District Court of Appeal, Second District (1982-1984)

Legal Practice: Attorney, Fowler, White, Gillen, Boggs, Banker & Villareal, P.A. (1984-1990); Attorney, Silberman & Khouzam (1990-1994)

Staff
Staff Attorney **Austin Roe** .... (813) 272-3430
Began Service: 2011
E-mail: brownn@flcourts.org
Staff Attorney **Gretchan A. Myers** .... (863) 499-2290
Began Service: 2008
E-mail: myersg@flcourts.org
Appellate Assistant **Vicki Bouyoukas** .... (863) 499-2290
Began Service: 2008

Chambers of Appellate Judge Marva L. Crenshaw

1700 North Tampa Street, Tampa, FL 33601
Tel: (863) 499-2290 Fax: (863) 413-2649

Marva L. Crenshaw
Appellate Judge

Education: Tuskegee 1973 BS; Florida 1975 JD
Began Service: January 2009
Appointed By: Governor Charlie Crist
Next Election: November 2016

(continued on next page)

Chambers of Appellate Judge Marva L. Crenshaw *continued*

Staff

Staff Attorney **David Brunell** . . . . (863) 499-2290
E-mail: brunelld@flcourts.org
Staff Attorney **Chance Lyman** . . . . (863) 499-2290
Judicial Assistant **Kimberly Vasquez** . . . . (863) 499-2290
E-mail: vasquezk@flcourts.org

Chambers of Appellate Judge Robert J. Morris, Jr.

1700 North Tampa Street, Tampa, FL 33601
Tel: (863) 499-2290
E-mail: morrisr@flcourts.org

Robert J. Morris, Jr.
Appellate Judge

Education: Florida 1975 BS; DePaul 1980 JD
Began Service: August 1, 2009
Appointed By: Governor Charlie Crist
Next Election: November 2016

Staff

Staff Attorney **Dionne Skelton Kohl** . . . . (863) 499-2290
E-mail: skeltond@flcourts.org
Staff Attorney **Jordan Wells** . . . . (863) 499-2290
E-mail: wellsj@flcourts.org
Education: Florida State
Judicial Assistant **Jeraldine Myers** . . . . (863) 499-2290
E-mail: myersj@flcourts.org

Chambers of Appellate Judge Anthony K. Black

1700 North Tampa Street, Tampa, FL 33601
Tel: (863) 499-2290
E-mail: blacka@flcourts.org

Anthony K. Black
Appellate Judge

Education: Arizona State 1978 BA; Illinois 1983 JD
Began Service: April 22, 2010
Appointed By: Governor Charlie Crist

Staff

Staff Attorney **Susan Dowhan** . . . . (863) 499-2290
E-mail: dowhans@flcourts.org
Staff Attorney **Brenda Freeman** . . . . (863) 499-2290
E-mail: freemanb@flcourts.org
Education: Florida 2007 JD
Judicial Assistant **Susan R. Anders** . . . . (863) 499-2290
E-mail: anderss@flcourts.org

Chambers of Appellate Judge Daniel H. Sleet

1700 North Tampa Street, Tampa, FL 33602-3547
Tel: (863) 499-2290
E-mail: sleetd@flcourts.org

Daniel H. Sleet
Appellate Judge

Education: Furman 1984 BA; Cumberland 1987 JD
Began Service: December 21, 2012
Appointed By: Governor Rick Scott

Staff

Staff Attorney **(Vacant)** . . . . (863) 499-2290
Staff Attorney **Laura Triplett** . . . . (863) 499-2290
Judicial Assistant **Judy Menendez** . . . . (863) 499-2290

Chambers of Appellate Judge Matthew C. Lucas

1700 North Tampa Street, Tampa, FL 33601
Tel: (863) 499-2290

Matthew C. "Matt" Lucas
Appellate Judge

Education: Florida State BS; Florida JD
Began Service: 2014

Chambers of Appellate Judge Samuel J. Salario Jr.

1700 North Tampa Street, Tampa, FL 33601
Tel: (863) 499-2290

Samuel J. "Sam" Salario, Jr.
Appellate Judge

Began Service: 2015

Chambers of Appellate Judge John L. Badalamenti

1700 North Tampa Street, Tampa, FL 33601
Tel: (863) 499-2290

John Badalamenti
Appellate Judge

Florida District Court of Appeal, Third District

2001 SW 117th Avenue, Miami, FL 33175-1716
Tel: (305) 229-3200 Fax: (305) 229-3206
E-mail: 3dca@flcourts.org
Internet: www.3dca.flcourts.org

Number of Judgeships: 10

Areas Covered: Counties of Dade and Monroe

Court Staff

Clerk of the Court **Mary Cay Blanks** . . . . (305) 229-3200
E-mail: 3dca@flcourts.org
Education: Florida International 2000 BA
Chief Deputy Clerk **Debbie McCurdy** . . . . (305) 229-3200
E-mail: 3dca@flcourts.org
Marshal **Veronica Antonoff** . . . . (305) 229-3200
E-mail: 3dca@flcourts.org
Deputy Marshal **Frank Valles** . . . . (305) 229-3200

Chambers of Chief Judge Frank A. Shepherd

2001 SW 117th Avenue, Miami, FL 33175-1716
Tel: (305) 229-3200 Fax: (305) 229-3206
E-mail: shepherf@flcourts.org

Frank A. Shepherd
Chief Judge

Date of Birth: December 11, 1946
Education: Florida 1968 BA; UMass (Amherst) 1970 MA; Michigan 1972 JD
Began Service: September 22, 2003
Appointed By: Governor Jeb Bush
Next Election: November 2016
Term Expires: January 1, 2017

Current Memberships: The District of Columbia Bar; The Florida Bar

Staff

Fax: (305) 229-3206

Research Assistant **(Vacant)** . . . . (305) 229-3200 ext. 3231

Chambers of Chief Judge Frank A. Shepherd *continued*

Research Assistant **Sara Garcia Reyes** . . . . (305) 229-3200 ext. 3244
E-mail: reyess@flcourts.org
Education: Florida International 1984 BA; Miami 1988 JD
Judicial Assistant **Marie Mosley** . . . . (305) 229-3200 ext. 3230
E-mail: mosleym@flcourts.org

Chambers of Appellate Judge Linda Ann Wells

2001 SW 117th Avenue, Miami, FL 33175-1716
Tel: (305) 229-3200 Fax: (305) 229-3206
E-mail: wellsla@flcourts.org

Linda Ann Wells
Judge

Date of Birth: April 3, 1947
Education: Florida 1969 BSMT; Florida State 1976 JD
Began Service: 2003
Appointed By: Governor Jeb Bush
Next Election: November 2016

Current Memberships: American Bar Association; Dade County Bar Association

Staff

Career Law Clerk **Gale Bramnick** . . . . (305) 229-3200
E-mail: bramnicg@flcourts.org
Education: Bridgeport 1972 BS; Florida International 1981 MBA; Miami 1988 JD
Career Law Clerk **Kyle Nickel** . . . . (305) 229-3200
E-mail: nickelk@flcourts.org
Education: Florida 1995 BS; Miami 1999 JD
Appellate Judicial Assistant **Tracy Verrire** . . . . (305) 229-3200
E-mail: verriret@flcourts.org

Chambers of Appellate Judge Richard J. Suarez

2001 SW 117th Avenue, Miami, FL 33175-1716
Tel: (305) 229-3200
E-mail: suarezr@flcourts.org

Richard J. Suarez
Appellate Judge

Education: Miami BM, MM, JD
Began Service: 2004
Appointed By: Governor Jeb Bush
Term Expires: January 7, 2019

Judicial: County Court Judge, Eleventh Judicial Circuit

Legal Practice: Shareholder, Corlett, Killian, P.A.; Hardeman & Suarez (1991)

Nonprofit: Board of Directors, The Ronald McDonald House of South Florida (1991-2002); Board of Directors, WLRN Public Television Station (1997-2002); Board of Directors, Florida Humanities Council (1998-2002)

Current Memberships: American Bar Association; Cuban American Bar Association; Dade County Bar Association; The Florida Bar

Chambers of Appellate Judge Leslie B. Rothenberg

2001 SW 117th Avenue, Miami, FL 33175-1716
Tel: (305) 229-3200

Leslie B. Rothenberg
Appellate Judge

Began Service: 2005
Appointed By: Governor Jeb Bush
Term Expires: January 7, 2019

Government: Prosecutor, Miami-Dade State Attorney's Office (1986); Felony Division Chief, Miami-Dade State Attorney's Office

Chambers of Appellate Judge Leslie B. Rothenberg *continued*

Judicial: Circuit Court Bench (1992-2003)

Legal Practice: Partner, Steel, Hector and Davis LLP (2003)

Chambers of Appellate Judge Barbara Lagoa

2001 SW 117th Avenue, Miami, FL 33175-1716
Tel: (305) 229-3200 Fax: (305) 229-3206
E-mail: lagoab@flcourts.org

Barbara Lagoa
Appellate Judge

Education: Columbia 1992 JD
Began Service: July 2006
Appointed By: Governor Jeb Bush
Next Election: November 4, 2020
Election Type: Retention Election
Term Expires: December 31, 2020

Government: Assistant U.S. Attorney, Major Crimes Division, Florida - Southern District, United States Department of Justice; Assistant U.S. Attorney, Appellate Division, Florida - Southern District, United States Department of Justice

Staff

Career Attorney **Whitney Kouvaris** . . . . (305) 229-3200 ext. 3225
E-mail: kouvaris@flcourts.org
Career Attorney **April Veilleux** . . . . (305) 229-3200 ext. 3226
E-mail: veilleua@flcourts.org
Education: Florida 1995 JD
Appellate Judicial Assistant **Susan Faerber** . . . . (305) 229-3200 ext. 3224
E-mail: faerbers@flcourts.org
Education: Nova 1987 JD

Chambers of Appellate Judge Vance E. Salter

2001 SW 117th Avenue, Miami, FL 33175-1716
Tel: (305) 229-3200 Fax: (305) 229-3206
E-mail: salterv@flcourts.org

Vance E. Salter
Appellate Judge

Education: Brown U; Virginia 1976 JD
Began Service: August 1, 2007
Appointed By: Governor Charlie Crist
Next Election: November 4, 2020
Election Type: Retention Election
Term Expires: December 31, 2020

Legal Practice: Associate, Steel Hector & Davis LLP (1976-1981); Partner, Steel Hector & Davis LLP; Partner, Coll, Davidson, Carter, Smith, Salter & Barkett (1987-2000); Attorney, Hunton & Williams LLP (2000-2007)

Staff

Career Attorney **Chelsea Moore** . . . . (305) 229-3200
E-mail: moorec@flcourts.org
Career Attorney **Mercedes Prieto** . . . . (305) 229-3200
Began Service: September 11, 2008
E-mail: prietom@flcourts.org
Education: Miami 1989 JD
Judicial Secretary **Lupe Diaz** . . . . (305) 229-3200 ext. 3218
E-mail: diazl@flcourts.org

Chambers of Appellate Judge Kevin M. Emas
2001 SW 117th Avenue, Miami, FL 33175-1716
Tel: (305) 229-3200 Fax: (305) 229-3206
E-mail: emask@flcourts.org

Kevin M. Emas
Appellate Judge

Education: Florida 1979 BA; Miami 1982 JD
Began Service: February 18, 2011
Appointed By: Governor Charlie Crist

Staff
Law Clerk **Jennifer Herskowitz** .... (305) 229-3200
Law Clerk **Lauren Davis** .... (305) 229-3200
E-mail: davisl@flcourts.org
Judicial Assistant **Delores Ramos** .... (305) 229-3200
E-mail: ramosd@flcourts.org

Chambers of Appellate Judge Ivan F. Fernandez
2001 SW 117th Avenue, Miami, FL 33175-1716
Tel: (305) 229-3200

Ivan F. Fernandez
Appellate Judge

Began Service: September 1, 2011

Chambers of Appellate Judge Thomas Logue
2001 SW 117th Avenue, Miami, FL 33175-1716
Tel: (305) 229-3200
E-mail: loguet@flcourts.org

Thomas "Tom" Logue
Appellate Judge

Education: Dickinson Col 1977 BA; Duke 1982 JD
Began Service: 2012

Chambers of Appellate Judge Edwin A. Scales III
2001 SW 117th Avenue, Miami, FL 33175-1716
Tel: (305) 229-3200
E-mail: scalese@flcourts.org

Edwin Ayres Scales III
Judge

Education: Florida 1988 BA, 1991 JD
Began Service: 2013
Appointed By: Governor Rick Scott

Florida District Court of Appeal, Fourth District
1525 Palm Beach Lakes Boulevard, West Palm Beach, FL 33401
Tel: (561) 242-2000
Internet: www.4DCA.org

Number of Judgeships: 12

Areas Covered: Counties of Broward, Indian River, Martin, Okeechobee, Palm Beach and St. Lucie

Court Staff
Clerk **Lonn Weissblum** .... (561) 242-2000
E-mail: weissbluml@flcourts.org
Education: Florida 2001 JD
Chief Deputy Clerk **Lynn Colletti** .... (561) 242-2000
Senior User Support Analyst **Laura Plaza** .... (561) 242-2000
E-mail: plazal@flcourts.org
Marshal **Daniel DiGiacomo** .... (561) 242-2111
E-mail: digiacomod@flcourts.org Fax: (561) 242-2100

Florida District Court of Appeal, Fourth District *continued*
Deputy Marshal **Doug Pierce** .... (561) 242-2000

Chambers of Chief Judge Cory J. Ciklin
1525 Palm Beach Lakes Boulevard, West Palm Beach, FL 33401
Tel: (561) 242-2000
E-mail: ciklinc@flcourts.org

Cory Ciklin
Chief Judge

Education: Florida State 1978 BS; Samford 1979; Florida State 1981 JD
Began Service: 2008
Appointed By: Governor Charlie Crist
Next Election: November 2016

Chambers of Appellate Judge Dorian K. Damoorgian
1525 Palm Beach Lakes Boulevard, West Palm Beach, FL 33401
Tel: (561) 242-2000
E-mail: damoorgiand@flcourts.org

Dorian K. Damoorgian
Appellate Judge

Education: American U 1977 BA; Cumberland 1980 JD
Began Service: 2008
Next Election: November 2016

Chambers of Appellate Judge Melanie May
1525 Palm Beach Lakes Boulevard, West Palm Beach, FL 33401
Tel: (561) 242-2025 Fax: (561) 242-2096
E-mail: maymg@4dca.org

The Honorable Melanie May
Appellate Judge

Education: Florida Atlantic 1973 BS; Nova 1981 JD
Began Service: January 2, 2002
Appointed By: Governor Jeb Bush
Next Election: November 2016

Staff
Law Clerk **Stratton Smiley** .... (561) 242-2027
Began Service: August 2014
Term Expires: August 2016
Law Clerk **Rachel Lyons** .... (561) 242-2027
Began Service: December 2012
E-mail: lyonsr@flcourts.org
Judicial Assistant **Anna Serrano** .... (561) 242-2028
E-mail: serranoa@flcourts.org

Chambers of Appellate Judge Robert M. Gross
1525 Palm Beach Lakes Boulevard, West Palm Beach, FL 33401
P.O. Box 3315, West Palm Beach, FL 33402-3315
Tel: (561) 242-2068 Fax: (561) 242-2100
E-mail: grossr@flcourts.org

Robert M. Gross
Appellate Judge

Date of Birth: 1951
Education: Williams 1973 BA; Cornell 1976 JD
Began Service: 2009
Appointed By: Governor Lawton M. Chiles
Next Election: November 2016
Term Expires: January 4, 2017

Current Memberships: American Bar Association; Palm Beach County Bar Association

Chambers of Appellate Judge Robert M. Gross *continued*

Staff
Staff Attorney **Kristen Bond** .... (561) 246-2066
E-mail: bondk@flcourts.org
Staff Attorney **Carrie Hay Rosato** .... (561) 242-2067
E-mail: rosatoc@flcourts.org
Judicial Assistant **Denise August** .... (561) 242-2068
E-mail: augustd@flcourts.org

Chambers of Appellate Judge W. Matthew Stevenson

1525 Palm Beach Lakes Boulevard, West Palm Beach, FL 33401
Tel: (561) 242-2058 Fax: (561) 242-2096

W. Matthew Stevenson
Appellate Judge

Date of Birth: 1953
Education: Florida State 1978 JD
Began Service: November 10, 1993
Appointed By: Governor Lawton M. Chiles
Next Election: November 4, 2020
Election Type: Retention Election
Term Expires: December 31, 2020

Judicial: Judge, Florida Circuit Court, 15th Judicial Circuit (1990-1993); Chief Judge, Florida District Court of Appeal, Fourth District

Military Service: United States Navy

Staff
Staff Attorney **Mishannock Arzt** .... (561) 242-2058
E-mail: arztm@flcourts.org
Education: Stetson 1996 JD
Staff Attorney **Kelly Lenahan** .... (561) 242-2058
Began Service: August 1, 2010
E-mail: lenahank@flcourts.org
Judicial Assistant **Jonzell Holmes** .... (561) 242-2058
E-mail: holmesj@flcourts.org
Education: Fort Valley State 1992 BA

Chambers of Appellate Judge Martha C. Warner

1525 Palm Beach Lakes Boulevard, West Palm Beach, FL 33401
Tel: (561) 242-2023 Fax: (561) 242-2016
E-mail: warnerm@flcourts.org

Martha C. Warner
Appellate Judge

Date of Birth: 1950
Education: Colorado Col 1971 BA; Florida 1974 JD; Virginia 1995 LLM
Began Service: January 3, 1989
Appointed By: Governor Bob Martinez
Next Election: November 4, 2020
Election Type: Retention Election
Term Expires: December 31, 2020

Academic: Faculty, Florida College of Advanced Judicial Studies

Judicial: Judge, Florida Circuit Court, 19th Judicial Circuit (1986-1988)

Legal Practice: Private Practice (1974-1985)

Staff
Staff Attorney **Judith Kolich** .... (561) 242-2023
E-mail: kolichj@flcourts.org
Staff Attorney **Christine Gardner** .... (561) 242-2023
E-mail: gardnerc@flcourts.org
Judicial Assistant **Linda Bowsman** .... (561) 242-2023
E-mail: bowsmanl@flcourts.org

Chambers of Appellate Judge Carole Y. Taylor

1525 Palm Beach Lakes Boulevard, West Palm Beach, FL 33401
Tel: (561) 242-2073 Fax: (561) 242-2096
E-mail: taylorc@flcourts.org

Carole Y. Taylor
Appellate Judge

Date of Birth: 1951
Education: North Carolina 1971 BA, 1974 JD
Began Service: April 1, 1998
Appointed By: Governor Lawton M. Chiles

Government: Public Defender, County of Broward, Florida (1979-1982); Assistant United States Attorney, Southern District of Florida, United States Attorney's Office, United States Department of Justice, Ronald Reagan Administration (1982-1983)

Judicial: Judge, Broward County Court (1991-1995); Florida Circuit Court, Broward County (1995-1997)

Legal Practice: Associate University Attorney, University of Florida (1977-1979); Sams, Ward, Et Al (1983-1984); Carole Yvonne Taylor, PA (1984-1991)

Staff
Staff Attorney **Gillian Harris** .... (561) 242-2073
E-mail: harrisg@flcourts.org
Senior Staff Attorney **Jake Williams** .... (561) 242-2073
Began Service: August 2, 2011
E-mail: williamsj@flcourts.org
Education: Florida 2004 JD
Appellate Judicial Assistant **Carol Shaw** .... (561) 242-2073
E-mail: shawc@flcourts.org

Chambers of Appellate Judge Jonathan D. Gerber

1525 Palm Beach Lakes Boulevard, West Palm Beach, FL 33401
Tel: (561) 242-2000
E-mail: gerberj@flcourts.org

Jonathan D. Gerber
Appellate Judge

Began Service: April 2009
Next Election: November 2016

Judicial: County Judge, Criminal Division, Palm Beach County Court, Fifteenth Judicial Circuit (2002-2003); County Judge, Civil Division, Palm Beach County Court, Fifteenth Judicial Circuit (2004); Circuit Judge, Fifteenth Judicial Circuit, Florida Circuit Court (2004-2009)

Legal Practice: Partner, Shutts & Bowen LLP (2001-2002)

Chambers of Appellate Judge Spencer D. Levine

1525 Palm Beach Lakes Boulevard, West Palm Beach, FL 33401
Tel: (561) 242-2000
E-mail: levines@flcourts.org

Spencer D. Levine
Appellate Judge

Began Service: April 2009
Next Election: November 2016

Government: Assistant State Attorney, Office of the State Attorney, County of Palm Beach, Florida (1987-1996); General Counsel, Office of the Sheriff, County of Palm Beach, Florida (1996-2000); Assistant Attorney General, Office of the Attorney General, State of Florida (2002-2003); Attorney, Criminal Justice Standards and Training Commission, Department of Law Enforcement, State of Florida (2003-2004); Medicaid Fraud Control Director, Office of the Attorney General, State of Florida (2003-2006)

Nonprofit: Chief Compliance Officer, Broward Health (2006-2008)

Current Memberships: American Bar Association; The Florida Bar

Chambers of Appellate Judge Burton C. Conner
1525 Palm Beach Lakes Boulevard, West Palm Beach, FL 33401
Tel: (561) 242-2000
E-mail: connerb@flcourts.org

Burton Conner
Appellate Judge

Education: Duke; Florida JD
Began Service: 2011

Chambers of Appellate Judge Alan O. Forst
1525 Palm Beach Lakes Boulevard, West Palm Beach, FL 33401
Tel: (561) 242-2000
E-mail: forsta@flcourts.org

Alan O. Forst
Appellate Judge

Education: Georgetown; Columbus Law JD
Began Service: April 8, 2013
Appointed By: Governor Rick Scott

Staff
Judicial Assistant **Mary Lanier** .... (561) 242-2000
E-mail: lanierm@flcourts.org

Chambers of Appellate Judge Mark W. Klingensmith
1525 Palm Beach Lakes Boulevard, West Palm Beach, FL 33401
Tel: (561) 242-2000
E-mail: klingensmithm@flcourts.org

Mark W. Klingensmith
Appellate Judge

Education: Florida 1982 BA, 1985 JD

Florida District Court of Appeal, Fifth District
300 South Beach Street, Daytona Beach, FL 32114
Tel: (386) 947-1500 Fax: (386) 947-1565
E-mail: 5dca@flcourts.org

Number of Judgeships: 10

Areas Covered: Counties of Brevard, Citrus, Flagler, Hernando, Lake, Marion, Orange, Osceola, Putnam, St. Johns, Seminole, Sumter and Volusia

Court Staff
Clerk of Court **Joanne P. Simmons** .... (386) 255-8600
E-mail: simmonsj@flcourts.org
Education: Stetson BS; Florida 1984 JD
Chief Deputy Clerk **Sheila Stanbro** .... (386) 947-1538
E-mail: stanbros@flcourts.org
Marshal **Charles Crawford** .... (386) 947-1544
E-mail: crawfordc@flcourts.org
Deputy Marshal **Justine Sierzega** .... (386) 947-1546
E-mail: sierzegaj@flcourts.org

Chambers of Chief Judge C. Alan Lawson
300 South Beach Street, Daytona Beach, FL 32114
Tel: (386) 947-1506 Fax: (386) 947-3443

C. Alan Lawson
Chief Judge

Education: Clemson 1983 BS; Florida State 1987 JD
Began Service: January 1, 2006
Appointed By: Governor Jeb Bush
Next Election: November 4, 2020
Election Type: Retention Election
Term Expires: December 31, 2020

Staff
Career Attorney **David M. Barr** .... (386) 947-1506
E-mail: barrd@flcourts.org
Education: Florida 1994 JD
Career Attorney **Tu-Quynh N. Vu** .... (386) 947-1733
E-mail: vuq@flcourts.org
Education: Richmond JD
Judicial Assistant **Deborah Riddell** .... (386) 947-1506
E-mail: riddelld@flcourts.org

Chambers of Appellate Judge Vincent G. Torpy, Jr.
300 South Beach Street, Daytona Beach, FL 32114
Tel: (386) 947-1523 Fax: (386) 947-3443
E-mail: torpyv@flcourts.org

Vincent G. Torpy, Jr.
Appellate Judge

Date of Birth: December 29, 1955
Education: Central Florida 1981 BA; Florida State 1983 JD
Began Service: January 17, 2003
Appointed By: Governor Jeb Bush
Next Election: November 2016
Term Expires: January 2017

Current Memberships: Brevard County Bar Association

Staff
Law Clerk **Melly Hammer** .... (386) 947-1525
E-mail: hammerm@flcourts.org
Career Attorney **Sandra B. Williams** .... (386) 947-1524
Education: Wisconsin 1986 JD
Judicial Assistant **Patricia Girard** .... (386) 947-1523
E-mail: girardp@flcourts.org

Chambers of Appellate Judge Richard B. Orfinger
300 South Beach Street, Daytona Beach, FL 32114
Tel: (386) 947-1510 Fax: (386) 947-1563
E-mail: orfinger@flcourts.org

Richard B. Orfinger
Appellate Judge

Date of Birth: 1952
Education: Tulane 1974 BA; Florida 1976 JD
Began Service: November 21, 2000
Appointed By: Governor Jeb Bush
Next Election: November 4, 2020
Election Type: Retention Election
Term Expires: December 31, 2020

Staff
Law Clerk **Erika Barger** .... (386) 947-1510
E-mail: bargere@flcourts.org
Career Attorney **Tamzen J. Merchant** .... (386) 947-1512
Education: Miami 1998 JD
Judicial Assistant **Sharon Davis** .... (386) 947-1510
E-mail: daviss@flcourts.org
Education: Central Florida 1981 BA

Chambers of Appellate Judge Thomas D. Sawaya

300 South Beach Street, Daytona Beach, FL 32114-5097
Tel: (386) 947-1555 Fax: (386) 947-1562
E-mail: sawayat@flcourts.org

Thomas D. Sawaya
Appellate Judge

Date of Birth: 1952
Education: South Florida 1974 BA; Stetson 1977 JD
Began Service: February 21, 2000
Appointed By: Governor Jeb Bush
Next Election: November 4, 2020
Election Type: Retention Election
Term Expires: December 31, 2020

Government: Assistant State Attorney (1985-1986)

Judicial: Judge, Marion County (1986-1990); Circuit Judge, Fifth Judicial Circuit, Marion County (1990-2000); Chief Judge, Florida District Court of Appeal, Fifth District (2005)

Legal Practice: Private Practice (1978-1986)

Staff
Law Clerk **Emily Sowell** .... (386) 947-1556
E-mail: sowelle@flcourts.org
Career Attorney **(Vacant)** .... (386) 947-1557
Judicial Assistant **Megan Menard** .... (386) 947-1555
E-mail: menardm@flcourts.org

Chambers of Appellate Judge William D. Palmer

300 South Beach Street, Daytona Beach, FL 32114
Tel: (386) 947-1502 Fax: (386) 947-1562
E-mail: palmerw@flcourts.org

William D. Palmer
Appellate Judge

Date of Birth: 1952
Education: Rensselaer Poly 1973; Boston Col 1976 JD
Began Service: October 18, 2000
Appointed By: Governor Jeb Bush
Next Election: November 4, 2020
Election Type: Retention Election
Term Expires: December 31, 2020

Legal Practice: Attorney, Carlton, Fields, Ward, Emmanuel, Smith & Cutler, P.A. (1976-1997); Attorney, Palmer & Palmer, P.A. (1997-2000)

Current Memberships: The Florida Bar

Staff
Career Attorney **Susan Hopkins** .... (386) 947-1504
E-mail: hopkinss@flcourts.org
Education: Villanova 1986 JD
Career Attorney **Brian Giaquinto** .... (386) 947-1503
E-mail: giaquintob@flcourts.org
Judicial Assistant **Cathy Jack** .... (386) 947-1502
E-mail: jackc@flcourts.org

Chambers of Appellate Judge Kerry I. Evander

300 South Beach Street, Daytona Beach, FL 32114
Tel: (386) 947-1518 Fax: (386) 947-1563
E-mail: evanderk@flcourts.org

Kerry I. Evander
Appellate Judge

Education: Florida 1976 BA, 1980 JD
Began Service: July 1, 2006
Appointed By: Governor Jeb Bush
Next Election: November 4, 2020
Election Type: Retention Election
Term Expires: December 31, 2020

Staff
Law Clerk **Lesley Marks** .... (386) 947-1520
E-mail: marksl@flcourts.org
Career Attorney **(Vacant)** .... (386) 947-1519
E-mail: williame@flcourts.org
Judicial Assistant **Linda J. Hiestand** .... (386) 947-1518
Education: Central Florida 1998 BS

Chambers of Appellate Judge Jay P. Cohen

300 South Beach Street, Daytona Beach, FL 32114
Tel: (386) 947-1576
E-mail: cohenj@flcourts.org

Jay P. Cohen
Appellate Judge

Date of Birth: 1952
Education: Florida 1974 BA, 1978 JD
Began Service: February 1, 2008
Appointed By: Governor Charlie Crist
Next Election: November 2016
Term Expires: January 2017

Judicial: Judge, Orange County, Florida (1990-1993); Circuit Court Judge, County of Osceola, Florida; Circuit Court Judge, County of Osceola, Florida

Legal Practice: Attorney, Private Practice (1982-1990)

Staff
Term Law Clerk **Alexandra Costanza** .... (386) 947-1574
E-mail: costanzaa@flcourts.org
Career Law Clerk **Daniel Gaffney** .... (386) 947-1575
Judicial Assistant **Joanie Woodard** .... (386) 947-1576
E-mail: woodardj@flcourts.org

Chambers of Appellate Judge Wendy W. Berger

300 South Beach Street, Daytona Beach, FL 32114
Tel: (386) 947-1514 Fax: (396) 947-1565
E-mail: bergerw@flcourts.org

Wendy W. Berger
Appellate Judge

Began Service: November 9, 2012

Staff
Senior Law Clerk **Erica Tesh White** .... (386) 947-1516
E-mail: teshe@flcourts.org
Career Attorney **Kurt Koehler** .... (386) 947-1515
Career Attorney **(Vacant)** .... (386) 947-1507
E-mail: serras@flcourts.org
Judicial Assistant **Cynthia Vachon** .... (386) 947-1514
E-mail: vachonc@flcourts.org

Chambers of Appellate Judge F. Rand Wallis

300 South Beach Street, Daytona Beach, FL 32114
Tel: (386) 947-1551

F. Rand Wallis
Appellate Judge

Education: Furman 1989 BA; Stetson 1992 JD
Began Service: 2013
Appointed By: Governor Rick Scott

Staff
Law Clerk **Forrest Pittman** .... (386) 947-1545
E-mail: pittmanf@flcourts.org
Law Clerk **Jacob Monk** .... (386) 947-1567
E-mail: monkj@flcourts.org
Judicial Assistant **Marianne Segren** .... (386) 947-1550
E-mail: segrenm@flcourts.org

Chambers of Appellate Judge Brian D. Lambert

300 South Beach Street, Daytona Beach, FL 32114
Tel: (386) 947-1558

Brian D. Lambert
Appellate Judge

Staff
Law Clerk **Tiffany Walters** .... (386) 947-1500
Law Clerk **Adam Hapner** .... (386) 947-1500

Georgia

Administrative Office of the Georgia Courts

244 Washington Street, SW, Suite 300, Atlanta, GA 30334
Tel: (404) 656-5171 Fax: (404) 651-6449

Staff

Director (Acting) **Cynthia Hinrichs Clanton** .... (404) 656-5171
E-mail: cynthia.clanton@georgiacourts.gov Fax: (404) 651-6449
Education: Mercer 1986 JD
Division Director, Financial Administration
Randy Dennis .... (404) 651-7613
E-mail: randy.dennis@georgiacourts.gov
Division Director, Information Technology
Jorge Basto .... (404) 657-9673
E-mail: jorge.basto@georgiacourts.gov

Supreme Court of Georgia

State Judicial Building, 244 Washington Street, SW, Room 572, Atlanta, GA 30334
Tel: (404) 656-3470 Fax: (404) 656-2253
E-mail: scinfo@gasupreme.us
Internet: www.gasupreme.us

Number of Judgeships: 7

The Supreme Court, established by the Georgia State Legislature in 1845, consists of a chief justice, presiding justice, and five justices. The chief justice and presiding justice, who handle administrative matters for the Court, are elected by peer vote to two-year terms. All justices are elected in statewide, nonpartisan elections for six-year terms. Retirement is mandatory at age seventy-five or on the last day of the term during which the justice turns seventy, whichever is later. The Supreme Court has exclusive appellate jurisdiction in all cases involving the United States or Georgia constitutions, the constitutionality of a law or ordinance, and contested elections. The Court has general appellate jurisdiction in areas of land title, equity, divorce and alimony, the validity or construction of wills, capital felonies, extraordinary remedies, or cases referred to it by the Court of Appeals of Georgia or the United States Court of Appeals for the Eleventh Circuit.

The Court sits in Atlanta, but may hold sessions at other locations throughout Georgia.

Court Staff

Clerk of the Court **Therese S. "Tee" Barnes** .... (404) 656-3470
Education: Virginia 1978 BA; Mercer 1981 JD
Chief Deputy Clerk **Tia C. Milton** .... (404) 656-3470
E-mail: miltont@gasupreme.us
Education: Duke 2004 JD
Deputy Clerk **Pamela M. Fishburne** .... (404) 656-3470
Reporter of Decisions **Jean M. Ruskell** .... (404) 656-3460
E-mail: ruskellj@gasupreme.us Fax: (404) 651-7632
Education: Emory 1978 BA; Duke 1981 JD
Executive Director, Institute of Continuing Judicial Education **Richard D. "Rich" Reaves** .... (706) 369-5842
123 Dean Rusk Hall, University of Georgia, Athens, GA 30602 Fax: (706) 369-5840
E-mail: rich@icje.law.uga.edu
Education: Beloit 1969 BA; Tennessee 1976 JD
Director of Technology **Bob McAteer** .... (404) 656-3470
E-mail: mcateerb@gasupreme.us
Fiscal Officer **Regina Jones** .... (404) 656-3470
Public Information Officer **Jane Hansen** .... (404) 651-9385
E-mail: hansenj@gasupreme.us
Docket Clerk and Records Manager **Adrian Woods** .... (404) 656-3470
E-mail: woodsa@gasupreme.us
Docket Clerk **Tori Little** .... (404) 656-3470
E-mail: littlet@gasupreme.us

Chambers of Chief Justice Hugh P. Thompson

State Judicial Center, 244 Washington Street, SW, Room 507, Atlanta, GA 30334
Tel: (404) 656-3472 Fax: (404) 651-8642

Hugh P. Thompson
Chief Justice

Date of Birth: 1943
Education: Emory 1964; Oglethorpe 1965; Mercer 1969 JD
Began Service: March 1, 1994
Appointed By: Governor Zell Miller
Next Election: 2018
Term Expires: December 31, 2018

Current Memberships: American Bar Association; Baldwin County Bar Association; Ocmulgee Judicial Circuit Bar Association; State Bar of Georgia

Staff

Career Law Clerk **Heidi M. Faenza** .... (404) 656-3472
E-mail: faenzah@gasupreme.us
Education: Florida State 1985 BA, 1989 JD
Career Law Clerk **Anne McGlamry** .... (404) 656-3472
E-mail: mcglamra@gasupreme.us
Career Law Clerk **Steve Schaikewitz** .... (404) 656-3472
E-mail: schaikes@gasupreme.us
Education: Virginia 1970 BA; Emory 1973 JD
Administrative Assistant **Liz Tate** .... (404) 656-3472
Career Law Clerk **(Vacant)** .... (404) 656-3472

Chambers of Presiding Justice P. Harris Hines

244 Washington Street, SW, Atlanta, GA 30334
Tel: (404) 656-3473 Fax: (404) 651-8566

P. Harris Hines
Presiding Justice

Date of Birth: 1943
Education: Emory 1965 BA, 1968 JD
Began Service: July 26, 1995
Appointed By: Governor Zell Miller
Next Election: November 2020
Election Type: General Election
Term Expires: December 31, 2020

Staff

Career Law Clerk **Robert S. Anderson** .... (404) 656-3473
Career Law Clerk **Linda Schwartz** .... (404) 656-3473
Administrative Assistant **Anita Harrison** .... (404) 656-3473
E-mail: harrisona@gasupreme.us

Chambers of Justice Carol W. Hunstein

State Judicial Building, 244 Washington Street, SW, Room 533, Atlanta, GA 30334
Tel: (404) 656-3470

Carol W. Hunstein
Justice

Date of Birth: 1944
Education: Florida Atlantic 1972 BS; Stetson 1976 JD
Began Service: November 23, 1992
Appointed By: Governor Zell Miller
Next Election: 2018
Term Expires: December 31, 2018

Current Memberships: The Bleckley American Inn of Court; American Bar Association; National Association of Women Judges; State Bar of Georgia

(continued on next page)

Chambers of Justice Carol W. Hunstein *continued*

Staff

Law Clerk **Kathryn Wetherbee** .... (404) 656-3475
Began Service: 2015
E-mail: wetherbeek@gasupreme.us

Law Clerk **Elizabeth Chandler Stone** .... (404) 656-3475
Began Service: 2007
E-mail: stonee@gasupreme.us
Education: Duke 1993 BA, 1997 JD

Judicial Assistant **Lynnita Terrell** .... (404) 656-3475
E-mail: terrelll@gasupreme.us

Chambers of Justice Robert Benham

State Judicial Building, 244 Washington Street, SW, Room 527, Atlanta, GA 30334
Tel: (404) 656-3476 Fax: (404) 657-4329
E-mail: benhamr@gasupreme.us

Robert Benham
Justice

Date of Birth: 1946
Education: Tuskegee 1967 BS; Georgia 1970 JD; Virginia 1990 LLM
Began Service: December 1, 1989
Appointed By: Governor Joe Frank Harris
Next Election: November 4, 2020
Election Type: General Election
Term Expires: December 31, 2020

Corporate: Member, Advisory Board, First Southern Bank

Government: Trial Attorney, Atlanta Legal Aid Society; Special Assistant Attorney General, State of Georgia

Judicial: Judge, Georgia Court of Appeals (1984-1989); Presiding Justice, Supreme Court of Georgia

Military Service: United States Army Reserve, United States Department of the Army

Current Memberships: The Bleckley American Inn of Court; American Judges Association; Lawyers Club of Atlanta, Inc.

Staff

Law Clerk **Renee Huskey** .... (404) 651-5916

Career Law Clerk **Diana Suber** .... (404) 651-5914
E-mail: suberd@gasupreme.us

Administrative Assistant **Evelyn S. Brundidge** .... (404) 656-3476
Education: Georgia 1975 BBA

Chambers of Justice Harold D. Melton

State Judicial Building, 244 Washington Street, SW, Atlanta, GA 30334
Tel: (404) 656-3477 Fax: (404) 657-4211
E-mail: meltonh@gasupreme.us

Harold D. Melton
Justice

Education: Auburn 1988 BS; Georgia 1991 JD
Began Service: July 1, 2005
Appointed By: Governor Sonny Perdue
Next Election: 2018
Term Expires: December 31, 2018

Government: Executive Counsel, Office of the Governor, State of Georgia

Chambers of Justice David E. Nahmias

244 Washington Street, SW, Atlanta, GA 30334
Tel: (404) 656-3470
E-mail: nahmiasd@gasupreme.us

David E. Nahmias
Justice

Education: Duke 1986 BA; Harvard 1991 JD
Began Service: September 3, 2009
Appointed By: Governor Sonny Perdue
Next Election: November 2016

Government: Assistant U.S. Attorney, Georgia - Northern District, Executive Office for United States Attorneys, United States Department of Justice (1995-2001); Counsel, Criminal Division, Executive Office for United States Attorneys, United States Department of Justice (2001-2003); Deputy Assistant Attorney General, Criminal Division, Office of the Deputy Attorney General, United States Department of Justice (2003-2004); U.S. Attorney, Georgia - Northern District, Executive Office for United States Attorneys, United States Department of Justice, George W. Bush Administration (2004-2009)

Staff

Law Clerk **John Withers** .... (404) 656-3470
Education: Mercer 1981 JD

Law Clerk **Ed Smith** .... (404) 656-3470

Judicial Assistant **Emily Pierce** .... (404) 656-3470

Chambers of Justice Keith Blackwell

244 Washington Street, SW, Atlanta, GA 30334
Tel: (404) 656-3470

Keith R. Blackwell
Justice

Date of Birth: November 13, 1969
Education: Georgia 1996 BA, 1999 JD
Began Service: July 19, 2012
Appointed By: Governor Nathan Deal

Current Memberships: Board of Advisors, The Federalist Society for Law and Public Policy Studies; State Bar of Georgia

Court of Appeals of Georgia

47 Trinity Avenue, SW, Suite 501, Atlanta, GA 30334
Tel: (404) 656-3450

Number of Judgeships: 12

The Court of Appeals, established by a constitutional amendment in 1906, consists of a chief judge, four presiding judges and seven associate judges. The judges elect one of their own members as chief judge for a two-year term. The chief judge assigns judges to four equal divisions and designates presiding judges for one-year terms for each division. Cases are assigned to each judge in each division on an equal basis, via a random assignment wheel for civil, criminal, discretionary applications and interlocutory applications. The Court of Appeals of Georgia is required by the State Constitution to dispose of every case at the term for which it is entered on the Court's docket for hearing or at the next term. All judges are elected in statewide, nonpartisan elections for six-year terms. Vacancies are temporarily filled by the Governor from a list of candidates provided by the Judicial Nominating Commission. Retirement is mandatory at age seventy-five or on the last day of the six-year term during which the judge turns seventy, whichever is later. The Court of Appeals has appellate jurisdiction in all civil and criminal matters where exclusive jurisdiction or general appellate jurisdiction is not reserved to the Supreme Court of Georgia by the Constitution, or conferred on other courts. The Court hears cases involving appeals from torts, contracts, malpractice, workers compensation, juvenile cases and all criminal cases excepting those in which the sentence of death was imposed or could be imposed.

The Court of Appeals of Georgia sits in Atlanta.

Court of Appeals of Georgia *continued*

Court Staff

Clerk and Court Administrator **Stephen E. Castlen** . . . . . (404) 656-3450
Reporter of Decisions **Jean M. Ruskell** . . . . (404) 656-3460
E-mail: ruskellj@gasupreme.us
Fiscal Officer **Jan Kelley** . . . . (404) 656-3462
Education: Texas (Tyler) 1991 BBA Fax: (404) 651-8497
Director of Technical Services **John Ruggeri** . . . . (404) 651-6417
E-mail: ruggerij@gaappeals.us Fax: (404) 651-6418
Education: Auburn BSAE

Chambers of Chief Judge Sara L. Doyle

State Judicial Building, 40 Mitchell Street, Atlanta, GA 30334
Tel: (404) 656-3450
E-mail: doyles@gaappeals.us

Sara L. Doyle
Chief Judge

Education: Florida; Mercer JD
Began Service: January 1, 2009
Next Election: November 4, 2020
Election Type: General Election
Term Expires: December 2020

Current Memberships: American Bar Association; The Bleckley American Inn of Court, The American Inns of Court; Atlanta Bar Association; Gate City Bar Association; Georgia Association for Women Lawyers; Lawyers Club of Atlanta, Inc.; State Bar of Georgia

Chambers of Presiding Judge John J. Ellington

State Judicial Building, 47 Trinity Avenue, Suite 501, Atlanta, GA 30334
Tel: (404) 463-3026 Fax: (404) 463-5590
E-mail: ellingtj@appeals.courts.state.ga.us

John J. Ellington
Presiding Judge

Date of Birth: 1960
Education: Georgia 1982 BBA, 1985 JD
Began Service: July 12, 1999
Appointed By: Governor Roy E. Barnes
Next Election: November 2018
Term Expires: December 31, 2018

Current Memberships: Lawyers Club of Atlanta, Inc.; President's Club at Abraham Baldwin Agricultural College; State Bar of Georgia; Swainsboro Technical College

Staff

Staff Attorney **Jule Felton** . . . . (404) 463-3023
Staff Attorney **Robin M. Hutchinson** . . . . (404) 463-3025
E-mail: hutchinr@mail.doas.state.ga.us
Education: Emory 1985 BA, 1988 JD
Senior Staff Attorney **Mary H. Hines** . . . . (404) 463-3024
E-mail: hinesmh@yahoo.com
Education: Georgia State 1986 BIS, 1989 JD
Administrative Assistant **Laverne Johnson** . . . . (404) 463-3026
E-mail: johnsonl@appeals.courts.state.ga.us
Administrative Assistant **Cindy Harden** . . . . (404) 463-3026
E-mail: hardenc@appeals.courts.state.ga.us

Chambers of Presiding Judge Anne Elizabeth Barnes

47 Trinity Avenue, SW, Atlanta, GA 30334
Tel: (404) 656-3454 Fax: (404) 463-8303
E-mail: judgebarnes@gmail.com

Anne Elizabeth Barnes
Presiding Judge

Date of Birth: 1955
Education: Georgia State 1979 BA; Georgia 1983 JD; Virginia 2004 LLM
Began Service: January 1, 1999
Next Election: November 2016
Term Expires: December 31, 2016

Current Memberships: American Bar Association; The Lamar American Inn of Court, The American Inns of Court; Atlanta Bar Association; DeKalb Bar Association; Gate City Bar Association; Georgia Association for Women Lawyers; Georgia Association of Black Elected Officials; Georgia Association of Black Women Attorneys; Georgia Public Policy Foundation; Lawyers Club of Atlanta, Inc.; Lawyers Foundation of Georgia; National Association of Women Judges; Old War Horse Lawyers' Club; State Bar of Georgia

Staff

Staff Attorney **Christina Cooley Smith** . . . . (404) 656-4212
E-mail: cooleyc@appeals.courts.state.ga.us
Education: Georgia State 1980 BA; Georgia 1983 JD
Staff Attorney **Gordon Hamrick** . . . . (404) 656-2012
E-mail: hamrickg@appeals.courts.state.ga.us
Staff Attorney **Angela Wright-Rheaves** . . . . (404) 657-2190
E-mail: rheavesa@appeals.courts.state.ga.us
Education: Berry 1986; Georgia State 1998

Chambers of Presiding Judge Gary Blaylock Andrews

State Judicial Building, 40 Mitchell Street, Room 424, Atlanta, GA 30334
Tel: (404) 656-3456 Fax: (404) 463-0546
E-mail: andrewsg@gaappeals.us

Gary Blaylock Andrews
Presiding Judge

Date of Birth: 1946
Education: Georgia 1968 BBA, 1971 JD
Began Service: January 1, 1991
Appointed By: Governor Zell Miller
Next Election: November 4, 2020
Election Type: General Election
Term Expires: December 31, 2020

Current Memberships: Atlanta Bar Association; Lawyers Club of Atlanta, Inc.; Lookout Mountain Bar Association; State Bar of Georgia

Staff

Staff Attorney **Joe Chandler** . . . . (404) 656-3364
Education: Mercer 1979 JD
Staff Attorney **John Pilgrim** . . . . (404) 656-6796
E-mail: jpilgrim@gaappeals.us
Staff Attorney **Chad Jacobs** . . . . (404) 656-3429
E-mail: jacobsc@gaappeals.us
Administrative Assistant **Annette Todd** . . . . (404) 656-3456
E-mail: todda@gaappeals.us

Chambers of Presiding Judge Herbert E. Phipps

State Judicial Building, 40 Mitchell Street, Room 340, Atlanta, GA 30334
Tel: (404) 656-3457 Fax: (404) 657-8945

Herbert E. Phipps
Presiding Judge

Date of Birth: 1941
Education: Morehouse Col 1964 BA; Case Western 1971 JD; Virginia 2004 ML
Began Service: July 12, 1999
Appointed By: Governor Roy E. Barnes
Next Election: November 2018
Term Expires: December 31, 2018

Current Memberships: C.B. King Bar Association

Staff
Career Law Clerk **Pamela Kilpatrick** .... (404) 657-2189
Education: Emory 1982 BA, 1986 JD
Career Law Clerk **Stephany Luttrell** .... (404) 651-7638
Career Law Clerk **Valeri McBride** .... (404) 657-8891
Education: Emory 1997 JD
Administrative Assistant **Deborah Zimmerman** .... (404) 656-3457

Chambers of Judge M. Yvette Miller

State Judicial Building, 47 Trinity Avenue, Suite 501, Atlanta, GA 30334
Tel: (404) 463-3032 Fax: (404) 656-4717
E-mail: millery@appeals.courts.state.ga.us

M. Yvette Miller
Judge

Date of Birth: 1955
Education: Mercer 1977 BA, 1980 JD; Emory 1988 LLM; Virginia 2004 LLM
Began Service: July 12, 1999
Appointed By: Governor Roy E. Barnes
Next Election: November 2018
Term Expires: December 31, 2018

Current Memberships: American Bar Association; Atlanta Bar Association; Delta Sigma Theta Sorority, Inc.; Gate City Bar Association; Lawyers Club of Atlanta, Inc.; National Alliance for the Mentally Ill; National Bar Association; State Bar of Georgia

Staff
Staff Attorney **Charlotte Hoel** .... (404) 463-3030
Staff Attorney **Daniel Hernandez** .... (404) 463-3031
Staff Attorney **Ave Mince-Didiera** .... (404) 463-3029
Administrative Assistant **Benita Roberts** .... (404) 463-3032

Chambers of Judge Stephen Louis A. Dillard

47 Trinity Avenue, Atlanta, GA 30334
Tel: (404) 657-9405
E-mail: dillards@gaappeals.us

Stephen Louis A. Dillard
Judge

Education: Samford 1992 BA; Mississippi Col 1996 JD
Began Service: November 2, 2010
Appointed By: Governor Sonny Perdue

Current Memberships: Board of Advisors, The Federalist Society for Law and Public Policy Studies; Speakers Bureau, The Federalist Society for Law and Public Policy Studies; Macon Bar Association

Staff
Staff Attorney **Tiffany D. Gardner** .... (404) 657-9405
E-mail: gardnert@gaappeals.us
Staff Attorney **Mary C. Davis** .... (404) 657-9405

Chambers of Judge Stephen Louis A. Dillard *continued*

Senior Staff Attorney **Robert Elzey** .... (404) 657-9405
E-mail: elzeyr@gaappeals.us
Education: Georgia 1991 BA; Harvard 1995 JD

Chambers of Judge Christopher J. McFadden

47 Trinity Avenue SW, Suitre 501, Atlanta, GA 30334
Tel: (404) 656-3452

Christopher J. "Chris" McFadden
Judge

Began Service: January 6, 2011

Staff
Judicial Assistant **Judy Mayer** .... (404) 656-3452

Chambers of Judge Michael P. Boggs

47 Trinity Avenue, Atlanta, GA 30334
Tel: (404) 656-3453 Fax: (404) 651-8139

Michael P. Boggs
Judge

Education: Georgia Southern 1985 BA; Mercer 1990 JD
Began Service: 2012

Staff
Staff Attorney **Lynn Johnson** .... (404) 656-4707
E-mail: johnsonl@gaappeals.us
Education: Georgia Tech 1994 BTE; Mercer 1998 JD
Staff Attorney **Martha McGhee-Glisson** .... (404) 656-3453
E-mail: rglisson@america.net
Education: Princeton 1977 BA; Emory 1980 JD
Staff Attorney **Julianne Swilley Whisnant** .... (404) 656-3442
Education: Florida 1987 BA; Georgetown 1990 JD
Administrative Assistant **Sabrina Bishop** .... (404) 656-3453
E-mail: bishops@gaappeals.us

Chambers of Judge William M. Ray II

47 Trinity Avenue, Atlanta, GA 30334
Tel: (404) 656-3450

William M. "Billy" Ray II
Judge

Education: Georgia 1985 BB, 1986 MB
Began Service: September 4, 2012
Appointed By: Governor Nathan Deal

Chambers of Judge Elizabeth Branch

47 Trinity Avenue, Atlanta, GA 30334
Tel: (404) 656-3450

Elizabeth L. "Lisa" Branch
Judge

Education: Davidson BA; Emory JD
Began Service: 2012
Next Election: May 2020
Election Type: Retention Election

Staff
Career Law Clerk **Michael Wakefield** .... (404) 656-3450
Education: Sewanee 1981 BA; Duke 1988 JD
Staff Attorney **David Payne** .... (404) 656-3450
Staff Attorney **Ida P. Dorvee** .... (404) 656-3450
Judicial Assistant **Linda King** .... (404) 656-3450

Chambers of Judge Carla McMillian

State Judicial Building, 47 Trinity Avenue, Atlanta, GA 30334
Tel: (404) 656-3455

Carla McMillian
Judge

Education: Duke BA; Georgia JD
Began Service: 2013
Next Election: May 2020

Clerkships: Law Clerk, Chambers of District Judge William O'Kelley, United States District Court for the Northern District of Georgia

Legal Practice: Partner, Sutherland Asbill and Brennan LLP

Staff

Staff Attorney **Ann Kelley** .... (404) 656-3455
Education: Mercer 1979 BA, 1984 JD
Staff Attorney **Laura Robison** .... (404) 656-3455
Education: Georgia 1980 ABJ, 1985 JD
Staff Attorney **Amanda Shelton** .... (404) 656-3455
Judicial Assistant **Crystal James** .... (404) 656-3455

Guam

Guam Supreme Court

Guam Judicial Center, 120 West O'Brien Drive, Suite 300,
Hagatna, GU 96910-5174
Tel: (671) 475-3120
Internet: www.guamsupremecourt.gov

Court Staff

Clerk of Court **Hannah M. Guttierrez-Arroyo** . . . . (671) 475-3162
E-mail: hgutierrezarroyo@guamsupremecourt.com
Assistant Clerk of the Court **Millie B. Duenas** . . . . (671) 475-3162
E-mail: mduenas@guamsupremecourt.com
Staff Attorney **Danielle T. Rosete** . . . . (671) 475-3396
E-mail: drosete@guamsupremecourt.com

Chambers of Chief Justice Robert J. Torres Jr.

120 West O'Brien Drive, Hagatna, GU 96910-5174
Tel: (671) 475-3300

Robert J. Torres, Jr.
Chief Justice

Education: Notre Dame BBA; Harvard JD
Began Service: April 27, 2003
Appointed By: Governor Felix Camacho

Chambers of Associate Justice F. Phillip Carbullido

120 West O'Brien Drive, Hagatna, GU 96910-5174
Tel: (671) 475-3413

F. Phillip Carbullido
Associate Justice

Date of Birth: February 5, 1953
Education: Oregon 1975 BA; UC Davis 1978 JD
Began Service: 2000
Appointed By: Governor Carl T.C. Gutierrez

Chambers of Associate Justice Katherine A. Maraman

120 West O'Brien Drive, Hagatna, GU 96910-5174
Tel: (671) 475-3109
E-mail: kamaraman@guamsupremecourt.com

Katherine A. Maraman
Associate Justice

Began Service: February 21, 2008
Appointed By: Governor Felix Camacho

Hawaii

State of Hawaii Judiciary Office of the Administrative Director

Ali'iolani Hale, 417 South King Street, Room 206A,
Honolulu, HI 96813-2902
Tel: (808) 539-4900 Fax: (808) 539-4855
Internet: www.courts.state.hi.us

Staff

Administrative Director of the Courts
Rodney A. Maile . . . . (808) 539-4900
E-mail: rodney.a.maile@courts.hawaii.gov
Education: Hawaii BA, 1978 JD

Deputy Administrative Director **Iris T. Murayama** . . . . (808) 539-4902
E-mail: iris.t.murayama@courts.hawaii.gov

Private Secretary **Fay Wakida** . . . . (808) 539-4900
E-mail: fay.wakida@courts.hawaii.gov

Administrative Driver's License Revocation Office
Chief Adjudicator **Marie C. Laderta** . . . . . . (808) 973-9500
E-mail: marie.c.laderta@courts.hawaii.gov Fax: (808) 973-9508
Education: Marquette 1978 BA;
John Marshall 1988 JD

Center for Alternative Dispute Resolution Director
(Vacant) . . . . (808) 539-4237
Fax: (808) 539-4416

Children's Justice Center Director
Jasmine Mau-Mukai . . . . (808) 586-0821
E-mail: jasmine.mau-mukai@courts.hawaii.gov Fax: (808) 595-6978

Human Resources Director **Dee L. Wakabayashi** . . . . (808) 539-4948
E-mail: dee.wakabayashi@courts.hawaii.gov Fax: (808) 539-4955

Judiciary History Center Executive Director
Matt Mattice . . . . (808) 539-4999
E-mail: matt.mattice@courts.hawaii.gov Fax: (808) 539-4996

Office on Equality & Access to the Courts Project
Director **Debi Tulang-DeSilva** . . . . (808) 539-4860
E-mail: debi.tulang-desilva@courts.hawaii.gov Fax: (808) 539-4203

Office of the Public Guardian Director
Moira Chin . . . . (808) 548-0006 ext. 14
E-mail: moira.chin@courts.hawaii.gov Fax: (808) 521-0757

Communications and Community Relations Officer
Tammy Mori . . . . (808) 539-4909
E-mail: tammy.mori@courts.hawaii.gov Fax: (808) 539-4801

Director of Intergovernmental and Community
Relations and Chief Staff Attorney **Susan Gochros** . . . . (808) 539-4990
E-mail: susan.gochros@courts.hawaii.gov Fax: (808) 539-4794

Director of Budget and Program Review
Wendell T. Mick . . . . (808) 539-4866
E-mail: tom.mick@courts.hawaii.gov Fax: (808) 539-4745

Director of Information Technology and Systems
Department **Kevin G. Thornton** . . . . (808) 538-5805
E-mail: kevin.g.thornton@courts.hawaii.gov Fax: (808) 538-5802

Equal Employment Opportunity/Disabilities
Accommodations Officer **Beth Tarter** . . . . . . (808) 539-4336
E-mail: beth.tarter@courts.hawaii.gov Fax: (808) 539-4124

Chief Information Officer **David K. Maeshiro** . . . . (808) 538-5301
E-mail: david.k.maeshiro@courts.hawaii.gov Fax: (808) 538-5377

Judicial Education Officer **Dawn Nagatani** . . . . . (808) 539-4344
E-mail: dawn.nagatani@courts.hawaii.gov Fax: (808) 539-4203

Financial Services Director **Janell Kim** . . . . . . (808) 538-5805
E-mail: janell.kim@courts.hawaii.gov Fax: (808) 538-5802

Planning and Program Evaluation Administrator
Christina E. Uebelein . . . . (808) 539-4850
E-mail: christina.e.uebelein@courts.hawaii.gov Fax: (808) 539-4991

Facilities Manager **Wayne S. Taniguchi** . . . . . . (808) 538-5490
E-mail: wayne.s.taniguchi@courts.hawaii.gov Fax: (808) 538-5494

Internal Audit Manager **Peter S. T. Lam** . . . . . . (808) 539-4242
E-mail: peter.s.lam@courts.hawaii.gov Fax: (808) 539-4020

Law Librarian **Jenny Silbiger** . . . . (808) 539-4964
E-mail: jenny.silbiger@courts.hawaii.gov Fax: (808) 539-4974

Hawaii Supreme Court

Ali'iolani Hale, 417 South King Street, Room 103,
Honolulu, HI 96813-2902
Tel: (808) 539-4919 Fax: (808) 539-4928
Internet: www.state.hi.us/jud/

Number of Judgeships: 5

The Supreme Court consists of a chief justice and four associate justices who are appointed for ten-year terms by the Governor with the consent of the Hawaii State Senate from a list compiled by the Judicial Selection Commission. The Supreme Court has appellate jurisdiction over all questions of law or fact brought before it from any other agency or court. The Court has exclusive jurisdiction in the examination, licensing and discipline of attorneys and has superintending control over all inferior courts.

The Hawaii Supreme Court sits in Honolulu.

Court Staff

Chief Clerk of the Court **Rochelle R. Hasuko** . . . . . (808) 539-4919
E-mail: rochelle.hasuko@courts.hawaii.gov

Deputy Court Clerk **Evelyn M. Rimando** . . . . . . (808) 539-4919
E-mail: evelyn.rimando@courts.hawaii.gov

Appellate Court Clerk **Janice Matsumoto** . . . . . . (808) 539-4919
E-mail: janice.matsumoto@courts.hawaii.gov

Court Fiscal Officer **Sandra Y. Miyasato** . . . . . . (808) 539-4916
E-mail: sandra.y.miyasato@courts.state.hi.us Fax: (808) 539-4779

Court Staff Attorney **Elizabeth M. Zack** . . . . . . (808) 539-4747
E-mail: elizabeth.m.zack@courts.state.hi.us Fax: (808) 539-4703

Court Staff Attorney **Matthew P.S. Chapman** . . . . . (808) 539-4747
E-mail: matthew.chapman@courts.hawaii.gov Fax: (808) 539-4703
Education: Stanford 1987 BA; Boalt Hall 2003 JD

Court Staff Attorney **Shellie K. Park-Hoapili** . . . . . (808) 539-4747
E-mail: shellie.k.park-hoapili@courts.state.hi.us Fax: (808) 539-4703
Education: Hawaii 1998 BA, 2002 JD

Bar Examination Technician **Susan E. Nakahara** . . . . (808) 539-4919

Bar Examination Technician **Koreen C. Yogi** . . . . . (808) 539-4919
E-mail: koreen.yogi@courts.hawaii.gov Fax: (808) 539-4978

Personnel Director **Dee L. Wakabayashi** . . . . . . (808) 539-4948
E-mail: dee.l.wakabayashi@courts.state.hi.us Fax: (808) 539-4955

Court Documents Clerk **Kathleen S. Hamakado** . . . . (808) 539-4919
E-mail: kathleen.hamakado@courts.hawaii.gov

Court Documents Clerk **JoAnn Y. Takeuchi** . . . . . (808) 539-4919
E-mail: joann.y.takeuchi@courts.state.hi.us

Court Documents Clerk **Joyce K. Hidani** . . . . . . (808) 539-4919
E-mail: joyce.hidani@courts.hawaii.gov

Judicial Clerk **Jasmin Khammaloun** . . . . (808) 539-4919
E-mail: jasmin.khammaloun@courts.state.hi.us

Secretary **Lescia E. Shaver** . . . . (808) 539-4919
E-mail: lescia.e.shaver@courts.state.hi.us

Secretary **Karen Yoshioka** . . . . (808) 539-4747
E-mail: karen.yoshioka@courts.state.hi.us Fax: (808) 539-4703

Chambers of Chief Justice Mark E. Recktenwald

Ali'iolani Hale, 417 South King Street, Honolulu, HI 96813-2902
Tel: (808) 539-4919 Fax: (808) 539-4928
E-mail: mark.recktenwald@courts.hawaii.gov

Mark E. Recktenwald
Chief Justice

Education: Harvard 1978 BA; Chicago 1986 JD
Began Service: September 14, 2010
Appointed By: Governor Linda Lingle
Term Expires: September 13, 2020

Staff

Judicial Assistant **Grace Ginoza** . . . . (808) 539-4919
E-mail: grace.ginoza@courts.hawaii.gov

Chambers of Associate Justice Paula A. Nakayama
Ali'iolani Hale, 417 South King Street, Honolulu, HI 96813-2914
Tel: (808) 539-4720 Fax: (808) 539-4703
E-mail: paula.a.nakayama@courts.hawaii.gov

Paula A. Nakayama
Associate Justice

Date of Birth: 1953
Education: Hastings JD
Began Service: April 22, 1993
Term Expires: April 21, 2023

Government: Deputy Prosecuting Attorney, City and County of Honolulu, Hawaii (1979-1982)

Judicial: Judge, Hawaii Circuit Court, First Judicial Circuit (1992-1993)

Legal Practice: Partner, Shim, Tam, Kirimitsu, Kitamura & Chang (1982-1992)

Staff
Administrative Assistant **Lois C. Choy** .... (808) 539-4720
E-mail: lois.c.choy@courts.hawaii.gov

Chambers of Associate Justice Sabrina McKenna
417 South King Street, Honolulu, HI 96813-2902
Tel: (808) 539-4735 Fax: (808) 539-4928
E-mail: sabrina.mckenna@courts.state.hi.us

Sabrina McKenna
Associate Justice

Education: Hawaii BA, 1982 JD
Began Service: March 3, 2011

Staff
Law Clerk **Sasha Hamada** .... (808) 539-4919
E-mail: sasha.hamada@courts.hawaii.gov
Law Clerk **Adrienne Iwamoto Suarez** .... (808) 539-4919
E-mail: adrienne.i.suarez@courts.state.hi.us
Education: Columbia 1997 BA, 2001 MA; Hawaii 2005 JD
Judicial Assistant **Nancy Alota** .... (808) 539-4919
E-mail: nancy.alota@courts.state.hi.us

Chambers of Associate Justice Richard W. Pollack
417 South King Street, Honolulu, HI 96813-2902
Tel: (808) 539-4919
E-mail: richard.pollack@courts.hawaii.gov

Richard W. Pollack
Associate Justice

Education: UC Santa Barbara BA; Hastings JD
Began Service: August 6, 2012

Chambers of Associate Justice Michael Wilson
417 South King Street, Honolulu, HI 96813-2902
Tel: (808) 539-4919
E-mail: michael.wilson@courts.hawaii.gov

Michael D. Wilson
Associate Justice

Began Service: April 17, 2014
Appointed By: Governor Neil Abercrombie

Intermediate Court of Appeals of Hawaii
426 Queen Street, Room 201, Honolulu, HI 96813-2914
Tel: (808) 539-4750 Fax: (808) 539-4644

Number of Judgeships: 6

The Intermediate Court of Appeals, established by the Hawaii State Legislature in 1979, consists of a chief judge and five associate judges. The judges are appointed for ten-year terms by the Governor, with the consent of the Hawaii State Senate, from a list compiled by the Judicial Selection Commission. The chief judge is selected through a merit selection plan for a ten-year term. The Intermediate Court of Appeals has concurrent jurisdiction with the Hawaii Supreme Court with the exception of examinations, licensing and discipline of attorneys and questions reserved by a federal appellate court, which fall under the Hawaii Supreme Court's exclusive jurisdiction.

The Intermediate Court of Appeals sits in Honolulu.

Court Staff
Appellate Clerk **Alison M. Hanamoto** .... (808) 539-4611
E-mail: alison.m.hanamoto@courts.state.hi.us
Appellate Clerk **Shirley Toyama** .... (808) 539-4750
E-mail: shirley.toyama@courts.state.hi.us
Supervising Staff Attorney **Randall Pinal** .... (808) 539-4611
E-mail: randall.pinal@courts.state.hi.us
Staff Attorney **Dustin H. Horie** .... (808) 539-4611
E-mail: dustin.h.horie@courts.state.hi.us
Education: San Diego JD
Staff Attorney **Daniel James Kunkel** .... (808) 539-4611
E-mail: daniel.kunkel@courts.hawaii.gov
Education: Wisconsin 1988 BA; San Diego 1993 JD
Staff Attorney **Arleen Watanabe** .... (808) 539-4611
E-mail: arleen.watanabe@courts.hawaii.gov
Staff Attorney **Natalie S. Younoszai** .... (808) 539-4611
E-mail: natalie.s.younoszai@courts.state.hi.us
Judicial Assistant **Nadine Grace** .... (808) 539-4752
E-mail: nadine.grace@courts.state.hi.us
Judicial Assistant **Joelle Hoke** .... (808) 539-4004
E-mail: joelle.hoke@courts.hawaii.gov
Judicial Assistant **Jean Kikumoto** .... (808) 539-4698
E-mail: jean.kikumoto@courts.hawaii.gov
Judicial Assistant **Ginger L. Matayoshi** .... (808) 539-4750
E-mail: ginger.l.matayoshi@courts.state.hi.us
Judicial Assistant **Helen Ota** .... (808) 539-4751
E-mail: helen.ota@courts.hawaii.gov
Judicial Assistant **Tammy Kaina DeCenzo** .... (808) 539-4206
E-mail: tammy.n.kaina@courts.state.hi.us

Chambers of Chief Judge Craig H. Nakamura
426 Queen Street, 2nd Floor, Honolulu, HI 96813-2914
Tel: (808) 539-4750 Fax: (808) 539-4644
E-mail: craig.nakamura@courts.hawaii.gov

Craig H. Nakamura
Chief Judge

Date of Birth: July 19, 1956
Education: Harvard 1981 JD
Began Service: September 16, 2009
Term Expires: September 15, 2019

Government: Assistant U.S. Attorney, Criminal Division, Hawaii District, United States Department of Justice, Ronald Reagan Administration (1986)

Staff
Law Clerk **Bradley Sava** .... (808) 539-4750
Began Service: September 2015
Term Expires: August 31, 2016
E-mail: sara.ayabe@courts.hawaii.gov
Law Clerk **Keone Nakoa** .... (808) 539-4750
Term Expires: August 31, 2016
E-mail: tiffany.dare@courts.hawaii.gov
Education: Harvard 2008 AB

Chambers of Chief Judge Craig H. Nakamura *continued*

Judicial Assistant **Ginger L. Matayoshi** . . . . (808) 539-4750
E-mail: ginger.l.matayoshi@courts.state.hi.us

Chambers of Associate Judge Daniel R. Foley

426 Queen Street, Room 201, Honolulu, HI 96813-2914
Tel: (808) 539-4698 Fax: (808) 539-4644
E-mail: daniel.foley@courts.hawaii.gov

Daniel R. Foley
Associate Judge

Date of Birth: 1947
Education: U San Francisco 1969 BA, 1974 JD
Began Service: October 2, 2000
Appointed By: Governor Benjamin J. Cayetano
Term Expires: October 1, 2020

Academic: Adjunct Professor of Civil Rights, William S. Richardson School of Law, University of Hawaii Manoa (1984-1987)

Government: Counsel to Micronesian Governments, State of Hawaii (1975-1983)

Legal Practice: Partner, Partington & Foley (1989-2000)

Staff
Judicial Assistant **Jean Kikumoto** . . . . (808) 539-4698
E-mail: jean.kikumoto@courts.hawaii.gov

Chambers of Associate Judge Alexa D.M. Fujise

426 Queen Street, Honolulu, HI 96813-2914
Tel: (808) 539-4004
E-mail: alexa.fujise@courts.hawaii.gov

Alexa D.M. Fujise
Associate Judge

Education: Hawaii, JD
Began Service: June 10, 2004
Appointed By: Governor Linda Lingle
Term Expires: June 9, 2024

Clerkships: Law Clerk, Chambers of Associate Justice Herman T.F. Lum, Hawaii Supreme Court (1980-1984)

Government: Appellate Research Branch Chief, Prosecuting Attorney Department, City and County of Honolulu, Hawaii; Deputy Prosecuting Attorney, Prosecuting Attorney Department, City and County of Honolulu, Hawaii; Research and Reference Support Division Director, Prosecuting Attorney Department, City and County of Honolulu, Hawaii; Assistant Disciplinary Counsel for the Office of Disciplinary Counsel, City and County of Honolulu, Hawaii

Chambers of Associate Judge Katherine G. Leonard

426 Queen Street, Room 201, Honolulu, HI 96813-2914
Tel: (808) 539-4751 Fax: (808) 539-4644
E-mail: katherine.g.leonard@courts.hawaii.gov

Katherine G. Leonard
Associate Judge

Education: Wisconsin (Parkside) 1982; Hawaii 1991 JD
Began Service: January 30, 2008
Term Expires: January 29, 2018

Legal Practice: Partner, Carlsmith Ball LLP (1992-2007)

Staff
Judicial Assistant **Helen Ota** . . . . (808) 539-4069
E-mail: helen.ota@courts.hawaii.gov

Chambers of Associate Judge Lawrence M. Reifurth

426 Queen Street, Honolulu, HI 96813-2914
Tel: (808) 539-4206 Fax: (808) 539-4644
E-mail: lawrence.m.reifurth@courts.state.hi.us

Lawrence M. Reifurth
Associate Judge

Education: Marquette 1979 BA; Northwestern 1981 MM, 1983 JD
Began Service: March 11, 2010
Appointed By: Governor Linda Lingle

Chambers of Associate Judge Lisa M. Ginoza

426 Queen Street, Honolulu, HI 96813-2914
Tel: (808) 539-4750 Fax: (808) 539-4644
E-mail: lisa.m.ginoza@courts.state.hi.us

Lisa M. Ginoza
Associate Judge

Education: Oregon State BS; Hawaii JD
Began Service: May 6, 2010

Idaho

Idaho Administrative Director of the Courts

Supreme Court Building, 451 West State Street, Boise, ID 83720
P.O. Box 83720, Boise, ID 83720-0101
Tel: (208) 334-2246 Fax: (208) 334-2146
Tel: (208) 334-2117 (State Law Library) Fax: (208) 334-2467
Internet: www.isc.idaho.gov (Judicial Web Site)
Internet: www.isll.idaho.gov (Library Web Site)

Staff

Administrative Director of the Courts (Interim)
Linda Copple Trout .... (208) 334-2246
Education: Idaho 1973 BA, 1977 JD
Legal Counsel **Michael Henderson** .... (208) 334-2246
E-mail: mhenderson@idcourts.net
Staff Attorney **Cathy Derden** .... (208) 334-2246
E-mail: cderden@idcourts.net
Clerk of Courts **Stephen W. Kenyon** .... (208) 334-2210
E-mail: skenyon@idcourts.net Fax: (208) 334-2616
Chief Information Officer **Kevin Iwersen** .... (208) 334-3868
E-mail: kiwersen@idcourts.net
Director of Court Management **Janica Bisharat** .... (208) 334-2850
Community and Family Justice Services Director
Kerry Hong .... (208) 947-7520
E-mail: khong@idcourts.net
Financial Executive Officer **Roland Gammill** .... (208) 334-2248
E-mail: rgammill@idcourts.net
Human Resources Director **Andrea Patterson** .... (208) 947-7437
E-mail: apatterson@idcourts.net

STATE COURTS—IDAHO

Idaho Supreme Court

Supreme Court Building, 451 West State Street, Boise, ID 83702
P.O. Box 83720, Boise, ID 83720-0101
Tel: (208) 334-2210 Fax: (208) 334-2616
Internet: www.isc.idaho.gov

Number of Judgeships: 5

The Supreme Court consists of a chief justice and four justices, who are elected in statewide, nonpartisan elections for six-year terms. The chief justice is elected by peer vote to a four-year term. Vacancies are filled by the Governor from a list of candidates provided by the Judicial Council or by election. The Supreme Court has appellate jurisdiction over decisions of the Idaho Court of Appeals, interim rulings and final judgments of the Idaho District Courts, decisions of the Public Utilities Commission and the Industrial Commission, and criminal cases imposing sentences of capital punishment. The Court has original jurisdiction to hear claims against the state, to issue writs and to decide disciplinary actions against attorneys. The Court exercises general supervisory and administrative control over the trial courts.

The Court sits in Boise, Coeur d'Alene, Lewiston, Pocatello, Twin Falls and Idaho Falls.

Court Staff

Clerk of Courts **Stephen W. Kenyon** .... (208) 334-2210
E-mail: skenyon@idcourts.net
Chief Deputy Clerk **Karel Lehrman** .... (208) 334-2210
E-mail: klehrman@idcourts.net
Deputy Clerk **Brad Thies** .... (208) 334-2210
E-mail: bthies@idcourts.net
Deputy Clerk **Kimber Grove** .... (208) 334-2210
E-mail: kgrove@idcourts.net
Deputy Clerk **Jane Hosteny** .... (208) 334-2210
E-mail: jhosteny@idcourts.net
Deputy Clerk **(Vacant)** .... (208) 334-2210
Deputy Clerk **Sara Velasquez** .... (208) 334-2210
E-mail: svelasquez@idcourts.net

Chambers of Chief Justice Jim Jones

P.O. Box 83720, Boise, ID 83720-0101
Tel: (208) 334-3186 Fax: (208) 334-4701
E-mail: jjones@idcourts.net

Jim Jones
Chief Justice

Date of Birth: May 13, 1942
Education: Northwestern 1967 JD
Began Service: January 3, 2005
Term Expires: January 1, 2017

Staff

Law Clerk **Kenny Shumard** .... (208) 334-3186
Began Service: August 2015
Term Expires: July 31, 2016
Law Clerk **Shantel Chapple** .... (208) 334-3186
Began Service: July 2015
Term Expires: July 2016
Judicial Assistant **Tresha Griffiths** .... (208) 947-7577
E-mail: tgriffiths@idcourts.net

Chambers of Justice Roger S. Burdick

P.O. Box 83720, Boise, ID 83720-0101
Tel: (208) 334-3464 Fax: (208) 334-4701
E-mail: rburdick@idcourts.net

Roger S. Burdick
Justice

Education: Colorado BS; Idaho 1974 JD
Began Service: August 1, 2003
Appointed By: Governor Dirk Kempthorne
Term Expires: January 1, 2017

Staff

Law Clerk **Laurie O'Neal** .... (208) 334-3464
Began Service: May 2015
Term Expires: August 2017
E-mail: lo'neal@idcourts.net
Law Clerk **Lindy Hornderger** .... (208) 334-3464
Began Service: August 2014
Term Expires: August 2016
E-mail: lhornderger@idcourts.net
Judicial Assistant **Shirley Sanchotena** .... (208) 334-3464
E-mail: ssanchotena@idcourts.net

Chambers of Justice Daniel T. Eismann

Supreme Court Building, 451 West State Street, Boise, ID 83702
P.O. Box 83720, Boise, ID 83720-0101
Tel: (208) 334-2149 Fax: (208) 334-4701
E-mail: deismann@idcourts.net

Daniel T. Eismann
Justice

Date of Birth: 1947
Education: Idaho 1973 BA, 1976 JD
Began Service: January 2, 2001
Term Expires: January 1, 2019

Current Memberships: The American Legion; National Rifle Association; Veterans of Foreign Wars of the U.S.

Staff

Law Clerk **Jason Blakley** .... (208) 334-2149
Began Service: July 31, 2014
Term Expires: July 13, 2016
E-mail: jblakley@idcourts.net
Law Clerk **Jonathan Sater** .... (208) 334-2149
Began Service: July 31, 2015
Term Expires: July 31, 2016

Chambers of Justice Daniel T. Eismann *continued*

Judicial Assistant **Robin Reider** . . . . (208) 334-2149
E-mail: rreider@idcourts.net

Chambers of Justice Warren E. Jones

Supreme Court Building, 451 West State Street, Boise, ID 83702
Tel: (208) 334-3324
E-mail: wjones@idcourts.net

Warren E. Jones
Justice

Education: Albertson; Chicago JD
Began Service: August 2007
Appointed By: Governor C.L. Otter
Next Election: 2020
Election Type: General Election
Term Expires: January 1, 2021

Legal Practice: Attorney, Eberle Berlin, Kading, Turnbow, McKlveen and Jones (1970-2007)

Staff
Law Clerk **Hunter Smith** . . . . (208) 334-3324
Began Service: August 2015
Term Expires: August 2016
E-mail: hsmith@idcourts.net
Law Clerk **Jack Relf** . . . . (208) 334-3324
Judicial Assistant **Karen Carlon** . . . . (208) 334-3324
E-mail: kcarlon@idcourts.net Fax: (208) 334-4701

Chambers of Justice Joel D. Horton

Supreme Court Building, 451 West State Street, Boise, ID 83720
P.O. Box 83720, Boise, ID 83720-0101
Tel: (208) 334-2207
E-mail: jhorton@idcourts.net

Joel D. Horton
Justice

Education: U Washington 1982 BA; Idaho 1985 JD
Began Service: August 24, 2007
Appointed By: Governor C.L. Otter
Next Election: 2020
Election Type: General Election
Term Expires: January 1, 2021

Government: Deputy Prosecuting Attorney, City of Twin Falls, Idaho (1986-1988); Criminal Deputy, Office of the Prosecuting Attorney, County of Ada, Idaho (1988-1991); Deputy Criminal Prosecutor, Office of the Prosecuting Attorney, County of Ada, Idaho (1992-1994); County Magistrate, County of Ada, Idaho

Judicial: Deputy Attorney General, County of Ada, Idaho (1991)

Staff
Law Clerk **Owen Moroney** . . . . (208) 334-2207
Began Service: August 2014
Term Expires: August 2016
Law Clerk **Anna Courtney** . . . . (208) 334-2207
E-mail: acourtney@idcourts.net
Judicial Assistant **Melanie Gagnepain** . . . . (208) 334-2207
E-mail: mgagnepain@idcourts.net

Idaho Court of Appeals

451 West State Street, Boise, ID 83702-0101
P.O. Box 83720, Boise, ID 83720-0101
Tel: (208) 334-5170 Fax: (208) 334-2526
Internet: http://isc.idaho.gov

Number of Judgeships: 4

The Court of Appeals, established in 1981, consists of a chief judge and two judges who are elected to six-year terms in statewide nonpartisan elections. Vacancies are filled temporarily by the Governor from a list of candidates provided by the Judicial Council. Temporary judges are subject to a retention vote in the next general election for a full, six-year term. The chief judge is appointed by the Idaho Supreme Court to serve a two-year term. Retirement is mandatory at age seventy. The Court of Appeals has appellate jurisdiction over cases assigned by the Idaho Supreme Court. The Court may not hear cases involving the original jurisdiction of the Supreme Court, recommendatory orders of the Bar Commission or the Judicial Council, appeals from imposition of capital punishment or appeals from the Industrial Commission or Public Utilities Commission.

The Court sits in Boise and may sit elsewhere as needed.

Court Staff

Clerk of Courts **Stephen W. Kenyon** . . . . (208) 334-5170
E-mail: skenyon@idcourts.net Fax: (208) 334-2616
Chief Deputy **Karel Lehrman** . . . . (208) 334-5170
E-mail: klehrman@idcourts.net
Deputy **Brad Theis** . . . . (208) 334-5170
E-mail: btheis@idcourts.net
Deputy **Sara Velasquez** . . . . (208) 334-5170
E-mail: svelasquez@idcourts.net
Deputy **Kimber Grove** . . . . (208) 334-5170
E-mail: kgrove@idcourts.net
Deputy **Tina Thomas** . . . . (208) 334-5170
E-mail: tthomas@idcourts.net
Deputy **Jane Hosteny** . . . . (208) 334-5170
E-mail: jhosteny@idcourts.net

Chambers of Chief Judge John M. Melanson

451 West State Street, Boise, ID 83720
Tel: (208) 334-5170
E-mail: jmelanson@idcourts.net

John M. Melanson
Chief Judge

Education: Idaho 1978 BBA, 1981 JD
Began Service: October 2009
Appointed By: Governor C.L. Otter

Staff
Law Clerk **Kade Beorchia** . . . . (208) 334-5170
Began Service: 2015
Term Expires: July 31, 2016
E-mail: kbeorchia@idcourts.net
Law Clerk **Chad Moody** . . . . (208) 334-5170
Began Service: July 31, 2015
Term Expires: July 31, 2017
E-mail: cmoody@idcourts.net
Judicial Assistant **Sue Stover** . . . . (208) 334-5170
E-mail: sstover@idcourts.net

Chambers of Judge Sergio A. Gutierrez

451 West State Street, Boise, ID 83720-0101
P.O. Box 83720, Boise, ID 83720-0101
Tel: (208) 334-5166 Fax: (208) 947-7589
E-mail: sgutierrez@idcourts.net

Sergio A. Gutierrez
Judge

Date of Birth: 1954
Education: Boise State 1980 BA; Hastings 1983 JD
Began Service: January 16, 2002
Appointed By: Governor Dirk Kempthorne
Next Election: 2021
Election Type: General Election
Term Expires: January 2022

Staff
Law Clerk **Lisa Carlson** .... (208) 334-5166
Began Service: August 1, 2015
Term Expires: July 31, 2017
Law Clerk **Jessica Harrison** .... (208) 334-5166
Began Service: August 1, 2015
Term Expires: July 31, 2017
E-mail: jharrison@idcourts.net
Judicial Assistant **Anna Goitandia** .... (208) 334-5166
E-mail: rmcfarland@idcourts.net

Chambers of Judge David W. Gratton

451 West State Street, Boise, ID 83702-0101
P.O. Box 83720, Boise, ID 83720-0101
Tel: (208) 334-5167
E-mail: dgratton@idcourts.net

David W. Gratton
Judge

Education: Boise State; Idaho JD
Began Service: January 5, 2009
Next Election: November 2018
Election Type: General Election
Term Expires: January 1, 2019

Staff
Law Clerk **Kelsie Kirkham** .... (208) 334-5167
Began Service: August 1, 2014
Term Expires: August 2016
Law Clerk **Spencer Holm** .... (208) 334-5167
E-mail: sholm@idcourts.net
Judicial Assistant **Julie Hall** .... (208) 334-5167
E-mail: jhall@idcourts.net

Illinois

Administrative Office of the Illinois Courts

222 North LaSalle Street, 13th Floor, Chicago, IL 60601
3101 Old Jacksonville Road, Springfield, IL 62704-6488
Tel: (312) 793-3250 (Chicago Office)
Tel: (217) 558-4490 (Springfield Office)
Fax: (312) 793-1335 (Chicago Office)
Fax: (217) 785-3905 (Springfield Office)
Internet: www.state.il.us/court

Staff

Director **Michael J. Tardy** .... (217) 558-4490
E-mail: mtardy@illinoiscourts.gov
Deputy Director **Marcia Meis** .... (312) 793-7275
E-mail: mmeis@illinoiscourts.gov
Administrative Services Assistant Director
Kathleen L. "Kathy" O'Hara .... (217) 782-7770
E-mail: kohara@court.state.il.us TTY: (217) 524-6428
Fax: (217) 785-9114
Court Services Assistant Director **Todd A. Schroeder** .... (217) 785-2125
Judicial Education Assistant Director **Cyrana Mott** ...... (312) 793-3250
E-mail: cmott@illinoiscourts.gov Fax: (312) 793-5187
Judicial Management Information Services Assistant
Director **Skip Robertson** .... (217) 785-3906
E-mail: srobertson@illinoiscourts.gov Fax: (217) 782-2702
Probation Services Assistant Director
Margaret "Margie" Groot .... (312) 793-4157
E-mail: mgroot@illinoiscourts.gov Fax: (312) 793-5185

Illinois Supreme Court

Supreme Court Building, 200 East Capitol Avenue, Springfield, IL 62701
Tel: (217) 782-2035 TTY: (217) 524-8132
Internet: www.state.il.us/court

Number of Judgeships: 7

The Supreme Court consists of a chief justice and six justices who are initially elected in partisan elections in one of five judicial districts for a ten-year term. After the first election, justices run for retention in nonpartisan elections in their respective judicial districts for ten-year terms. Three justices are elected from the First Judicial District, and one justice each is elected from the Second through Fifth Judicial Districts. The chief justice is elected by peer vote for a three-year term. A judge is automatically retired at the expiration of the term in which the judge attains the age of seventy-five. The Supreme Court has discretionary original jurisdiction in cases relating to revenue, mandamus, prohibition or habeas corpus, and exclusive jurisdiction over matters of redistricting the Illinois General Assembly and the ability of the Governor to hold office. Generally, the Court considers direct appeals from the Illinois Circuit Courts in cases involving capital punishment and where a statute has been held unconstitutional, and discretionary appeals from the Illinois Appellate Court. The Court has general administrative control over all courts in the state.

The Illinois Supreme Court sits in Springfield.

Court Staff

Clerk of Court **Carolyn Taft Grosboll** .... (217) 782-2035
E-mail: cgrosboll@illinoiscourts.gov
Education: Southern Illinois 1984 BS, 1987 JD
Reporter of Decisions **Amy Tomaszewski** .... (309) 827-8513
P.O. Box 3456, Bloomington, IL 61702 Fax: (309) 828-4651
Supreme Court Librarian **Geoffrey P. Pelzek** .... (217) 782-2425
E-mail: gpelzek@illinoiscourts.gov Fax: (217) 557-6940
Press Secretary **(Vacant)** .... (312) 793-2323
222 North LaSalle Street, Chicago, IL 60601 Fax: (312) 793-0871

Chambers of Chief Justice Rita B. Garman

3607 North Vermilion Street, Suite 1, Danville, IL 61832
Tel: (217) 431-8928 Fax: (217) 431-8945
E-mail: rgarman@illinoiscourts.gov

Rita B. Garman
Chief Justice

Date of Birth: 1943
Education: Illinois 1965 BS; Iowa 1968 JD
Began Service: February 5, 2001
Next Election: November 2022
Term Expires: 2022
Political Affiliation: Republican

Current Memberships: Illinois Judges Association; Illinois State Bar Association; Iowa State Bar Association; Vermillion County Bar Association

Chambers of Justice Thomas L. Kilbride

1819 - 4th Avenue, Rock Island, IL 61201
Tel: (309) 794-3608
E-mail: tkilbride@court.state.il.us

Thomas L. Kilbride
Justice

Education: St Mary Col 1978 BA; Antioch Law 1981 JD
Began Service: 2010
Next Election: November 2020
Election Type: Retention Election

Current Memberships: Illinois State Bar Association; Rock Island County Bar Association

Staff

Judicial Secretary **Linda Carlin** .... (309) 794-3608
E-mail: lcarlin@illinoiscourts.gov

Chambers of Justice Charles E. Freeman

160 North LaSalle Street, 20th Floor, Chicago, IL 60601
Tel: (312) 793-5480
E-mail: cfreeman@illinoiscourts.gov

Charles E. Freeman
Justice

Date of Birth: 1933
Education: Virginia Union 1954 BA; John Marshall 1962 JD
Began Service: December 3, 1990
Next Election: November 2020
Term Expires: December 31, 2021
Political Affiliation: Democrat

Government: Attorney, Circuit Court of Cook County (1962-1976); Assistant Attorney General, Office of the Attorney General, State of Illinois (1964); Assistant State's Attorney, Office of the State's Attorney, County of Cook, Illinois (1964); Attorney, Office of the Board of Commissioners, County of Cook, Illinois (1964-1965); Arbitrator, Workers' Compensation Commission, State of Illinois (1965-1973); Commissioner, Commerce Commission, State of Illinois (1973-1976)

Judicial: Judge, Circuit Court of Cook County (1976-1986); Justice, Illinois Appellate Court, First District (1986-1990)

Military Service: United States Army (1956-1958)

Current Memberships: American Judges Association; Cook County Bar Association; DuPage County Bar Association; Illinois Judges Association; Illinois Judicial Council; Illinois State Bar Association

Staff

Senior Law Clerk **James W. Hilliard** .... (312) 793-5480
E-mail: jhilliard@illinoiscourts.gov
Career Law Clerk **James Fisher** .... (312) 793-1340
E-mail: jfisher@illinoiscourts.gov

(continued on next page)

Chambers of Justice Charles E. Freeman *continued*

Career Law Clerk **Nancy B. Jack** .... (312) 793-4540
E-mail: njack@court.state.il.us
Education: John Marshall 1997 JD
Secretary **Lisa Porter** .... (312) 793-5480
E-mail: lporter@court.state.il.us

Chambers of Justice Robert R. Thomas

1776 South Naperville Road, Suite 207A, Wheaton, IL 60187
Tel: (630) 871-0025 Fax: (630) 871-0028
E-mail: rthomas@court.state.il.us

Robert R. Thomas
Justice

Education: Notre Dame 1974 BA; Loyola U (Chicago) 1981 JD
Began Service: December 4, 2000
Next Election: November 2020
Election Type: Retention Election
Term Expires: December 2020

Staff
Secretary **Vickie Kravcar** .... (630) 871-0025

Chambers of Justice Lloyd A. Karmeier

P.O. Box 266, Nashville, IL 62263
Tel: (618) 327-9751
E-mail: lkarmeier@court.state.il.us

Lloyd A. Karmeier
Justice

Date of Birth: January 12, 1940
Education: Illinois 1962 BS, 1964 JD
Began Service: 2004

Clerkships: Justice Byron O. House, Illinois Supreme Court (1964-1968); District Judge James L. Foreman, United States District Court (1972-1973)

Government: State's Attorney, County of Washington, Illinois (1968-1972)

Judicial: Resident Circuit Judge, County of Washington, Illinois (1986-2004)

Legal Practice: Hohlt, House, DeMoss & Johnson (1964-1986)

Current Memberships: East St. Louis Bar Association; Illinois Judges Association; Illinois State Bar Association; St. Clair County Bar Association; Washington County Bar Association

Staff
Career Law Clerk **David Sanders** .... (618) 327-9751
Career Law Clerk **Kim G. Noffke** .... (618) 327-9751
E-mail: knoffke@illinoiscourts.gov
Education: Southern Illinois 1983 JD
Senior Law Clerk **B. Stephen Miller** .... (618) 327-9751
Education: Harvard 1981 JD
Judicial Secretary **Carol Heggemeier** .... (618) 327-9751
E-mail: cheggemeier@illinoiscourts.gov
Administrative Assistant **Mary M. Nalefski** .... (618) 327-9751
E-mail: mnalefski@illinoiscourts.gov
Education: Saint Louis U 1986 JD

Chambers of Justice Anne M. Burke

160 North LaSalle Street, Suite S-2005, Chicago, IL 60601
Tel: (312) 793-5470 Fax: (312) 793-8224
E-mail: aburke@court.state.il.us

Anne M. Burke
Justice

Date of Birth: 1944
Education: DePaul 1976 BA; Chicago-Kent 1983 JD
Began Service: July 2006
Next Election: November 2018
Election Type: Retention Election
Term Expires: December 31, 2018

Clerkships: Law Clerk The Honorable James C. Murray, Cook County Circuit Court

Government: Special Counsel, Governor Jim Edgar (IL), State of Illinois (1994-1995)

Judicial: Judge, Illinois Court of Claims (1987-1994); Justice, Illinois Appellate Court, First District, Division Two (1995-2006)

Legal Practice: Private Practice (1983-1994)

Current Memberships: Illinois Courts Commission; American Association for Justice; American Bar Association; The American Inns of Court; Catholic Lawyers Guild of Chicago; The Chicago Bar Association; Chicago Bar Foundation; The Chicago Network; The Seventh Circuit Bar Association, Federal Bar Association; Illinois Judges Association; Illinois State Bar Association; National Association of Women Judges; Women's Bar Association of Illinois

Staff
Career Law Clerk **Anne Herbert** .... (312) 793-5470
E-mail: aherbert@illinoiscourts.gov
Education: Marshall 1993 JD
Career Law Clerk **Karen L. Jacobs** .... (312) 793-5470
E-mail: kjacobs@illinoiscourts.gov
Education: Detroit 1987 JD
Career Law Clerk **P. Andrew Smith** .... (312) 793-5470
Education: Chicago-Kent 1994 JD
Career Law Clerk **Anne Starr** .... (312) 793-5470
E-mail: astarr@illinoiscourts.gov
Judicial Secretary **Robin Karpinski** .... (312) 793-5470
E-mail: rkarpinski@court.state.il.us

Chambers of Justice Mary Jane Theis

200 East Capitol Avenue, Springfield, IL 62701
Tel: (312) 793-5490

Mary Jane Theis
Justice

Date of Birth: 1949
Education: Loyola U (Chicago) 1971 BA; U San Francisco 1973 JD
Began Service: October 26, 2010
Term Expires: December 3, 2022

Current Memberships: The Chicago Bar Association; Illinois Judges Association; Illinois State Bar Association; Women's Bar Association of Illinois

Staff
Law Clerk **Matthew A. Clarke** .... (217) 782-2035
E-mail: mclarke@illinoiscourts.gov
Education: DePaul 1998 JD
Law Clerk **Linda Godzicki** .... (217) 782-2035
E-mail: lgodzicki@illinoiscourts.gov
Education: DePaul 1989 BS; Chicago-Kent 1993 JD
Law Clerk **Margaret Malsky** .... (217) 782-2035
Career Law Clerk **Jason Freitag** .... (217) 782-2035
E-mail: jfreitag@illinoiscourts.gov
Education: Northwestern 1991 BA;
Valparaiso 1994 JD; Northwestern 1995 LLM

Illinois Appellate Court

The Illinois Appellate Court is comprised of five districts, some of which are subdivided into divisions. The justices of the Appellate Court are initially elected in partisan elections in their respective districts for ten-year terms. Vacancies may be temporarily filled by Illinois Supreme Court appointment. A presiding justice is elected in each division by peer vote to a one-year term. Retirement is mandatory at the age of seventy-five; however, retired justices may be assigned by the Supreme Court to serve on a temporary basis. The Appellate Court hears appeals of decisions of the Illinois Circuit Courts, except those cases heard directly by the Illinois Supreme Court. The Court may exercise any original jurisdiction it finds necessary and reviews administrative actions as provided by law.

Illinois Appellate Court, First District

160 North LaSalle Street, Suite 1400, Chicago, IL 60601
Tel: (312) 793-5415 Fax: (312) 793-4408
Internet: www.state.il.us/court/appellatecourt

Number of Judgeships: 24

Areas Covered: County of Cook

Court Staff
Clerk of the Court **Steven M. Ravid** .... (312) 793-5950
E-mail: sravid@illinoiscourts.gov

Illinois Appellate Court, First District, Division One

160 North LaSalle Street, Suite 1400, Chicago, IL 60601
Tel: (312) 793-5415 Fax: (312) 793-4408
Internet: www.state.il.us/court/appellatecourt

Number of Judgeships: 4

Chambers of Justice Maureen E. Connors

160 North LaSalle Street, Chicago, IL 60601
Tel: (312) 793-5415
E-mail: mconnors@illinoiscourts.gov

Maureen E. Connors
Justice

Education: Loyola U (Chicago) BA; Chicago-Kent 1979 JD
Began Service: 2010
Term Expires: December 3, 2022

Current Memberships: The Chicago Bar Association

Staff
Career Law Clerk **April Connley** .... (312) 793-5415
E-mail: aconnley@illinoiscourts.gov
Career Law Clerk **Gretchen Sperry** .... (312) 793-5415
Career Law Clerk **James Vanzant** .... (312) 793-5415

Chambers of Justice Joy Virginia Cunningham

160 North LaSalle Street, Suite N-1607, Chicago, IL 60601
Tel: (312) 793-5412
E-mail: jcunningham@illinoiscourts.gov

Joy Virginia Cunningham
Justice

Education: CUNY BS; John Marshall 1982 JD
Began Service: December 2006
Next Election: 2016
Term Expires: December 2016

Academic: Associate General Counsel, Loyola University Chicago

Clerkships: Judicial Clerk, Justice Glenn Johnson, Illinois Appellate Court

Corporate: Associate General Counsel, Loyola University Health System

Chambers of Justice Joy Virginia Cunningham *continued*

Government: Assistant Attorney General, State of Illinois

Judicial: Judge, Circuit Court of Cook County

Legal Practice: Litigator, French, Rogers, Kezelis & Kominiarek

Nonprofit: Senior Vice President, General Counsel and Corporate Secretary, Northwestern Memorial HealthCare

Current Memberships: American Bar Association; The Chicago Bar Association; Cook County Bar Association; Illinois State Bar Association; Women's Bar Association of Illinois

Staff
Career Law Clerk **James Buino** .... (312) 793-1098
Career Law Clerk **Flora Fell** .... (312) 793-5435
E-mail: fchan@court.state.il.us
Secretary **Joan Lettiere** .... (312) 793-5412
E-mail: jlettiere@court.state.il.us
Education: Illinois (Chicago) 1984 BS

Chambers of Justice Mathias W. Delort

160 North LaSalle Street, Chicago, IL 60601
Tel: (312) 793-5484
E-mail: mdelort@illinoiscourts.gov

Mathias W. Delort
Justice

Education: DePaul 1981 BS; John Marshall 1985 JD
Term Expires: 2022

Staff
Career Law Clerk **Karl Bade** .... (312) 793-5467
E-mail: kbade@illinoiscourts.gov
Education: DePaul 1990 JD
Career Law Clerk **Maya Hoffman** .... (312) 793-6197
E-mail: mhoffman@illinoiscourts.gov
Education: John Marshall 2000 JD
Courtroom Deputy **Glenn Sroka** .... (312) 793-5424
E-mail: gsroka@illinoiscourts.gov
Education: Loyola U (Chicago) 2006 JD

Chambers of Justice Sheldon A. Harris

160 North LaSalle Street, Chicago, IL 60601
Tel: (312) 793-5415 Fax: (312) 793-4408
E-mail: sharris@illinoiscourts.gov

Sheldon A. Harris
Justice

Education: Arizona 1963 BSBA; John Marshall 1966 JD
Began Service: 2011

Staff
Career Law Clerk **Lisa Ranson** .... (312) 793-5415
E-mail: lranson@illinoiscourts.gov
Career Law Clerk **Benjamin Vaccaro** .... (312) 793-5415
E-mail: bvaccaro@illinoiscourts.gov
Career Law Clerk **Vickie Yussman** .... (312) 793-5415
E-mail: vyussman@illinoiscourts.gov

Illinois Appellate Court, First District, Division Two

160 North LaSalle Street, Suite 1400, Chicago, IL 60601
Tel: (312) 793-5415 Fax: (312) 793-4408
Internet: www.state.il.us/court/appellatecourt

Number of Judgeships: 4

Chambers of Justice P. Scott Neville
160 North LaSalle Street, Suite N-1911, Chicago, IL 60601
Tel: (312) 793-4484

P. Scott Neville
Justice

Began Service: June 2004
Term Expires: 2022

Current Memberships: Cook County Bar Association; Illinois State Bar Association; National Bar Association

Staff
Law Clerk **Carla Sherieves** .... (312) 793-1150
E-mail: csherieves@illinoiscourts.gov
Senior Law Clerk **Michael Edwalds** .... (312) 793-1388
E-mail: medwalds@illinoiscourts.gov
Education: Chicago 1984 JD
Judicial Secretary **Carolyn Jones** .... (312) 793-4484
E-mail: cjones@illinoiscourts.gov

Chambers of Justice Daniel J. Pierce
160 North LaSalle Street, Chicago, IL 60601
Tel: (312) 793-5415
E-mail: dpierce@illinoiscourts.gov

Daniel J. Pierce
Justice

Staff
Career Law Clerk **Gina M. Ficaro** .... (312) 793-1163
E-mail: gficaro@illinoiscourts.gov
Education: DePaul 2002 JD
Career Law Clerk **Elizabeth Al-Dajani** .... (312) 793-1163
E-mail: ealdajani@illinoiscourts.gov
Secretary **Kate Moore** .... (312) 793-5467
E-mail: kmoore@illinoiscourts.gov

Chambers of Justice John B. Simon
160 North LaSalle Street, Chicago, IL 60601
Tel: (312) 793-5415
E-mail: jsimon@illinoiscourts.gov

John B. Simon
Justice

Education: Wisconsin 1964 BS; DePaul 1967 JD
Began Service: November 16, 2012
Term Expires: December 1, 2024

Staff
Law Clerk **Frank Bieszcat** .... (312) 793-5467
Career Law Clerk **Dan Hartweg** .... (312) 793-4486
E-mail: dhartweg@illinoiscourts.gov
Secretary **Julianne Joyce** .... (312) 793-4403
E-mail: jjoyce@illinoiscourts.gov

Chambers of Justice Laura C. Liu
160 North LaSalle Street, Chicago, IL 60601
Tel: (312) 793-5415

Laura C. Liu
Justice

Illinois Appellate Court, First District, Division Three
160 North LaSalle Street, Suite 1400, Chicago, IL 60601
Tel: (312) 793-5415 Fax: (312) 793-4408
Internet: www.state.il.us/court/appellatecourt

Number of Judgeships: 4

Chambers of Justice Michael B. Hyman
160 North LaSalle Street, Chicago, IL 60601
Tel: (312) 793-5431
E-mail: mhyman@illinoiscourts.gov

Michael B. Hyman
Justice

Education: Northwestern 1974 BS, 1977 JD

Judicial: Judge, Circuit Court of Cook County (2006-2012)

Staff
Judicial Law Clerk **Oliver Khan** .... (312) 793-5431
E-mail: okhan@illinoiscourts.gov
Judicial Law Clerk **Kathleen Maher** .... (312) 793-5431
E-mail: kmaher@illinoiscourts.gov
Education: DePaul 2002 JD
Judicial Law Clerk **Emily Vaccaro** .... (312) 793-5431
E-mail: evaccaro@illinoiscourts.gov
Education: Loyola U (Chicago) 2006 JD

Chambers of Justice Terrence J. Lavin
160 North LaSalle Street, Chicago, IL 60601
Tel: (312) 793-5403 Fax: (312) 793-4408
E-mail: tlavin@illinoiscourts.gov

Terrence J. Lavin
Justice

Education: Illinois 1977 BA; Chicago-Kent 1983 JD
Began Service: 2010
Term Expires: 2022

Staff
Judicial Clerk **Erin Clifford** .... (312) 793-5403
E-mail: eclifford@illinoiscourts.gov
Judicial Clerk **Kimberly Guernsy** .... (312) 793-5403
Judicial Clerk **Marya Lucas** .... (312) 793-5403
E-mail: mlucas@illinoiscourts.gov

Chambers of Justice Mary Anne Mason
160 North LaSalle Street, Chicago, IL 60601
Tel: (312) 793-5484
E-mail: mmason@illinoiscourts.gov

Mary Anne Mason
Justice

Chambers of Justice Aurelia Pucinski
160 North LaSalle Street, Chicago, IL 60601
Tel: (312) 793-5415 Fax: (312) 793-4408
E-mail: apucinski@illinoiscourts.gov

Aurelia Pucinski
Justice

Began Service: 2010

Staff
Career Law Clerk **Jelena Beuk** .... (312) 793-5415
E-mail: jbeuk@illinoiscourts.gov

STATE COURTS—ILLINOIS

Chambers of Justice Aurelia Pucinski *continued*

Career Law Clerk **Erin K. Slattery** .... (312) 793-5415
E-mail: eslattery@illinoiscourts.gov
Education: DePaul 2006 JD
Career Law Clerk **Suzi Slavin** .... (312) 793-5415

Illinois Appellate Court, First District, Division Four

160 North LaSalle Street, Suite 1400, Chicago, IL 60601
Tel: (312) 793-5415 Fax: (312) 793-4408
Internet: www.state.il.us/court/appellatecourt

Number of Judgeships: 4

Chambers of Justice Nathaniel R. Howse, Jr.

160 North LaSalle Street, Chicago, IL 60601
Tel: (312) 793-5415
E-mail: nhowse@illinoiscourts.gov

Nathaniel R. Howse, Jr.
Justice

Education: Loyola U (Chicago) AB, 1976 JD
Began Service: 2009
Term Expires: 2022

Judicial: Judge, Circuit Court of Cook County (1998-2009)

Staff
Career Law Clerk **Seija Benitez** .... (312) 793-5415
E-mail: sbenitez@illinoiscourts.gov
Career Law Clerk **Anthony Gordon** .... (312) 793-5415
Career Law Clerk **Darvionne J. Givhan-Edwards** ...... (312) 793-5415
Education: John Marshall 1997 JD

Chambers of Justice James Fitzgerald Smith

160 North LaSalle Street, Suite 1710-S, Chicago, IL 60601
Tel: (312) 793-5404 Fax: (312) 793-2598
E-mail: jsmith@illinoiscourts.gov

James Fitzgerald Smith
Justice

Date of Birth: January 30, 1943
Education: Marquette 1966 BA, 1966 BS; John Marshall 1975 JD
Began Service: December 2, 2002
Term Expires: December 2022

Current Memberships: American Association for Justice; American Bar Association; The Chicago Bar Association; Illinois State Bar Association; Northwest Suburban Bar Association

Staff
Fax: (312) 793-2598

Career Law Clerk **Sonja Dimitrijevic** .... (312) 793-1090
E-mail: sdimitrijevic@illinoiscourts.gov
Education: Illinois 2005 JD
Career Law Clerk **Maria Gonnella** .... (312) 793-5404
E-mail: mgonnella@illinoiscourts.gov
Education: John Marshall 2000 JD
Career Law Clerk **Julia I. Maness** .... (312) 793-5468
E-mail: jmaness@illinoiscourts.gov
Education: Indiana 2005 JD

Chambers of Justice David Ellis

160 North LaSalle Street, Chicago, IL 60601
Tel: (312) 793-5415

David Ellis
Justice

Chambers of Justice Cynthia Cobbs

160 North LaSalle Street, Chicago, IL 60601
Tel: (312) 793-4488 Fax: (312) 793-4408
E-mail: ccobbs@illinoiscourts.gov

Cynthia Y. Cobbs
Justice

Education: Morgan State BA

Illinois Appellate Court, First District, Division Five

160 North LaSalle Street, Suite 1400, Chicago, IL 60601
Tel: (312) 793-5415 Fax: (312) 793-4408
Internet: www.state.il.us/court/appellatecourt

Number of Judgeships: 4

Chambers of Justice Robert E. Gordon

160 North LaSalle Street, Suite N 1611, Chicago, IL 60601
Tel: (312) 793-4841
E-mail: rgordon@court.state.il.us

Robert E. Gordon
Justice

Date of Birth: 1937
Education: DePaul 1962 JD
Began Service: July 2006
Next Election: 2016
Term Expires: 2016

Staff
Career Law Clerk **Ausra Norusis** .... (312) 793-4843
E-mail: anorusis@court.state.il.us
Education: Chicago-Kent 2009 JD
Career Law Clerk **Karen Straus** .... (312) 793-4485
E-mail: kstraus@illinoiscourts.gov
Judicial Secretary **(Vacant)** .... (312) 793-4841

Chambers of Justice Margaret Stanton McBride

160 North LaSalle Street, Suite S-1608, Chicago, IL 60601
Tel: (312) 793-5462 Fax: (312) 793-2611
E-mail: mmcbride@court.state.il.us

Margaret Stanton McBride
Justice

Date of Birth: 1951
Education: DePaul JD
Began Service: December 1998
Next Election: November 4, 2018
Election Type: Retention Election
Term Expires: December 31, 2018

Current Memberships: The Chicago Bar Association; Illinois Judges Association; Northwest Suburban Bar Association

Staff
Career Law Clerk **Laura Kamps** .... (312) 793-5439
E-mail: lkamps@illinoiscourts.gov
Education: Syracuse 2001 JD

(continued on next page)

Chambers of Justice Margaret Stanton McBride *continued*

Career Law Clerk **Rachel Kates** (312) 793-1089
E-mail: rkates@illinoiscourts.gov
Education: Chicago-Kent JD
Administrative Assistant/Career Law Clerk
Melissa White (312) 793-5462
E-mail: mwhite@illinoiscourts.gov

Chambers of Justice Stuart E. Palmer

160 North LaSalle Street, Chicago, IL 60601
Tel: (312) 793-5415
E-mail: spalmer@illinoiscourts.gov

Stuart E. Palmer
Justice

Began Service: 2012

Staff
Judicial Clerk **Mark Haines** (312) 793-5416
E-mail: mhaines@illinoiscourts.gov
Education: Loyola U (Chicago) 2005 JD
Judicial Clerk **Alice L. Withaar** (312) 793-5416
E-mail: awithaar@illinoiscourts.gov
Education: Case Western 1991 JD
Secretary **Martha Dwyer** (312) 793-5416
Education: Barat 1978 BA

Chambers of Justice Jesse Reyes

160 North LaSalle Street, Chicago, IL 60601
Tel: (312) 793-5415
E-mail: jreyes@illinoiscourts.gov

Jesse G. Reyes
Justice

Term Expires: 2022

Staff
Judicial Clerk **Mark Vazquez** (312) 793-5413
E-mail: mvazquez@illinoiscourts.gov
Judicial Clerk **Abigail Sue** (312) 793-5413
E-mail: asue@illinoiscourts.gov
Judicial Clerk **(Vacant)** (312) 793-5413

Illinois Appellate Court, First District, Division Six

160 North LaSalle Street, Suite 1400, Chicago, IL 60601
Tel: (312) 793-5415 Fax: (312) 793-4408
Internet: www.state.il.us/court/appellatecourt

Number of Judgeships: 4

Chambers of Justice Shelvin Louise Hall

160 North LaSalle Street, Chicago, IL 60601
Tel: (312) 793-5438 Fax: (312) 793-2595
E-mail: shall@illinoiscourts.gov

Shelvin Louise Marie Hall
Justice

Date of Birth: 1948
Education: Hampton 1970 BA; Boston U 1974 JD
Began Service: February 2, 1999
Next Election: November 2020
Term Expires: December 3, 2020
Political Affiliation: Democrat

Academic: Adjunct Professor, John Marshall Law School

Chambers of Justice Shelvin Louise Hall *continued*

Government: Legislative Director (D-TX), Office of Representative Mickey Leland, United States House of Representatives (1980-1982); General Counsel, Department of Human Rights, State of Illinois (1982-1991)

Judicial: Judge, Circuit Court of Cook County (1991-1999); Justice, Illinois Appellate Court, First District, Division Four (1999-2000)

Legal Practice: Private practice (1974-1980)

Current Memberships: Black Women Lawyers Association of Greater Chicago, Inc.; The Chicago Bar Association; Cook County Bar Association; Illinois State Bar Association; National Association of Women Judges; Judicial Council, National Bar Association; Women's Bar Association of Illinois

Staff
Career Law Clerk **Clyde C. Dickens** (312) 793-5411
E-mail: cdickens@illinoiscourts.gov
Education: Chicago-Kent 1996 JD
Career Law Clerk **Charmaine Tellefsen Jones** (312) 793-1077
Education: John Marshall 1976 JD
Paralegal/Secretary **Kerensa R. Jackson-Burton** (312) 793-5438
E-mail: kburton@illinoiscourts.gov
Education: Bradley 1996 BS

Chambers of Justice Thomas E. Hoffman

160 North LaSalle Street, Suite N-1610, Chicago, IL 60601
Tel: (312) 793-5432 Fax: (312) 793-2599
E-mail: thoffman@illinoiscourts.gov

Thomas E. Hoffman
Justice

Date of Birth: 1947
Education: John Marshall 1971 JD
Began Service: January 1993
Political Affiliation: Democrat

Staff
Law Clerk **Laura Jennings** (312) 793-4563
E-mail: ljennings@court.state.il.us
Law Clerk **Jordan Yurchich** (312) 793-5469
E-mail: jyurchich@court.state.il.us
Law Clerk and Judicial Secretary **Teresa Campton** (312) 793-5432

Chambers of Justice Bertina E. Lampkin

160 North LaSalle Street, Chicago, IL 60601
Tel: (312) 793-5415
E-mail: blampkin@illinoiscourts.gov

Bertina E. Lampkin
Justice

Began Service: 2009

Staff
Career Law Clerk **Kristin H. Corradini** (312) 793-5415
E-mail: kcorradini@illinoiscourts.gov
Career Law Clerk **Debbie L. Rudsinski** (312) 793-5415
E-mail: drudsinski@illinoiscourts.gov
Career Law Clerk **Noreen Tanzar** (312) 793-5415
E-mail: ntanzar@illinoiscourts.gov
Education: Chicago-Kent 2000 JD

Chambers of Justice Mary K Rochford

160 North LaSalle Street, Chicago, IL 60601
Tel: (312) 793-5484 Tel: (312) 793-4408
E-mail: mrochford@illinoiscourts.gov

Mary Katherine Rochford
Justice

Began Service: 2011

STATE COURTS—ILLINOIS

Chambers of Justice Mary K Rochford *continued*

Staff
Career Law Clerk **Robert Kalnitz** .... (312) 793-5484
E-mail: rkalnitz@illinoiscourts.gov
Education: Chicago-Kent 2003 JD
Career Law Clerk **Beth Anne Lettiere** .... (312) 793-5484
E-mail: blettiere@illinoiscourts.gov
Career Law Clerk **Howard Yussman** .... (312) 793-5484
E-mail: hyussman@illinoiscourts.gov

Illinois Appellate Court, Second District

Appellate Court Building, 55 Symphony Way, Elgin, IL 60120-5558
Tel: (847) 695-3750 Fax: (847) 695-4949
Internet: www.state.il.us/court/appellatecourt

Number of Judgeships: 9

Areas Covered: Counties of Boone, Carroll, DeKalb, DuPage, Jo Daviess, Kane, Kendall, Lake, Lee, McHenry, Ogle, Stephenson and Winnebago

Court Staff
Clerk of Court **Robert J. Mangan** .... (847) 695-3750
Education: John Marshall 1978 JD
Chief Deputy Clerk **Allison Brown** .... (847) 695-3750
E-mail: awilliams@illinoiscourts.gov
Research Director **Jeffrey H. Kaplan** .... (847) 695-3756
E-mail: jkaplan@court.state.il.us Fax: (847) 695-3547
Education: Michigan 1994 BA;
George Washington 1997 JD

Chambers of Presiding Justice Mary Seminara-Schostok

712 Florshein Drive, Suite 10, Libertyville, IL 60048
Tel: (847) 918-8590
E-mail: mschostok@illinoiscourts.gov

Mary Seminara-Schostok
Presiding Justice

Education: Youngstown State 1982; Capital U 1986 JD
Began Service: 2008
Appointed By: Governor Rod R. Blagojevich
Term Expires: December 2020

Staff
Career Law Clerk **Lauren McFarlane** .... (847) 918-8590
E-mail: lmcfarlane@court.state.il.us
Education: Wesleyan U 1983 BA;
Case Western 1991 JD
Career Law Clerk **Constance L. Zanardo** .... (847) 918-8590
E-mail: czanardo@illinoiscourts.gov
Education: Illinois 1991 BS; Chicago-Kent 2001 JD
Senior Career Law Clerk **Shawn A. Wietbrock** .... (847) 918-8590
E-mail: swietbrock@illinoiscourts.gov
Education: DePauw 1993 BA;
Loyola U (Chicago) 1996 JD

Chambers of Justice Michael J. Burke

55 Symphony Way, Elgin, IL 60120
Tel: (847) 695-3750
E-mail: mburke@illinoiscourts.gov

Michael J. Burke
Justice

Began Service: 2008

Staff
Career Law Clerk **Sandra F. Kravitt** .... (847) 695-3750
E-mail: skravitt@illinoiscourts.gov
Education: Drake 1972 BS; John Marshall 1984 JD
Career Law Clerk **Ethan Bogenrief** .... (847) 695-3750
E-mail: ebogenrief@illinoiscourts.gov

Chambers of Justice Michael J. Burke *continued*

Judicial Assistant **Kathleen Roller** .... (847) 695-3750
E-mail: kroller@illinoiscourts.gov

Chambers of Justice Ann B. Jorgensen

100 West Roosevelt Road, Wheaton, IL 60187
Tel: (630) 668-6009
E-mail: ajorgensen@court.state.il.us

Ann B. Jorgensen
Justice

Education: Loyola U (Chicago); DePaul 1980 JD
Began Service: 2008

Current Memberships: DuPage Association of Women Lawyers; DuPage County Bar Association; Illinois Judges Association Foundation; Illinois State Bar Association

Staff
Career Judicial Clerk **Christine S. Kuenster** .... (630) 668-6009
E-mail: ckuenster@court.state.il.us
Education: Illinois 2005 JD
Career Judicial Clerk **Angela K. LaFratta** .... (630) 668-6009
E-mail: alafratta@illinoiscourts.gov
Education: Illinois 2001 JD
Career Judicial Clerk **Niki Werner** .... (630) 668-6009
E-mail: nwerner@illinoiscourts.gov
Education: Chicago 1988 AB;
Chicago-Kent 1999 JD

Chambers of Justice Robert D. McLaren

115 West Wesley, Suite One, Wheaton, IL 60187
Tel: (630) 682-3090 Fax: (630) 682-8186

Robert D. McLaren
Justice

Date of Birth: 1944
Education: Monmouth Col (IL) 1966 BA; Drake 1969 JD
Began Service: December 5, 1988
Next Election: November 4, 2018
Election Type: Retention Election
Term Expires: December 2018

Government: Assistant State's Attorney and Chief, Civil Division, Office of the State's Attorney, Dupage County, Illinois (1970-1977)

Judicial: Judge, Illinois Circuit Court, 18th Judicial Circuit (1981-1988)

Legal Practice: Private Practice (1977-1981)

Current Memberships: DuPage County Bar Association; Illinois Judges Association

Staff
Career Judicial Clerk **Allyson B. Harris** .... (630) 682-3090
E-mail: aharris@illinoiscourts.gov
Education: DePaul 1987 BA; Chicago-Kent 1994 JD
Career Judicial Clerk **Kathleen M. McGinnis** .... (630) 682-3090
E-mail: kmcginnis@illinoiscourts.gov
Career Judicial Clerk **Frank J. Markov, Jr.** .... (630) 682-3090
E-mail: fmarkov@illinoiscourts.gov
Education: Elmhurst 1984 BS;
John Marshall 1989 JD

Chambers of Justice Susan Fayette Hutchinson

55 Symphony Way, Elgin, IL 60120-5558
Tel: (815) 338-5875 Fax: (815) 338-5878
E-mail: shutchinson@illinoiscourts.gov

Susan Fayette Hutchinson
Justice

Date of Birth: April 1, 1950
Education: Quincy U 1971 BA; DePaul 1977 JD
Began Service: December 1994
Term Expires: December 2024
Political Affiliation: Republican

Government: Assistant State's Attorney, Office of the State's Attorney, County of McHenry, Illinois (1977-1981)

Judicial: Judge, Illinois Circuit Court, 19th Judicial Circuit (1981-1994)

Legal Practice: Private Practice (1977-1981)

Current Memberships: American Bar Association; Illinois State Bar Association; McHenry County Bar Association; National Association of Women Judges

Staff

Career Law Clerk **Richard Harris** . . . . . (815) 338-5875
Career Law Clerk **Scott Jacobson** . . . . . (815) 338-5875
E-mail: sjacobson@illinoiscourts.gov
Career Law Clerk **Stacey Mandell** . . . . . (815) 338-5875
E-mail: smandell@illinoiscourts.gov
Education: Northern Illinois 1996 JD

Chambers of Justice Donald C. Hudson

55 Symphony Way, Elgin, IL 60120
Tel: (847) 695-3750 Fax: (847) 695-4949
E-mail: dhudson@illinoiscourts.gov

Donald C. Hudson
Justice

Education: DePaul BA; John Marshall JD
Began Service: January 8, 2009

Staff

Career Law Clerk **Cary Collender** . . . . . (847) 695-3750
E-mail: ccollender@illinoiscourts.gov
Education: Northern Illinois 1994 JD
Career Law Clerk **Jeffrey Murdoch** . . . . . (847) 695-3750
E-mail: jmurdoch@illinoiscourts.gov
Education: Northern Illinois 2000 JD
Secretary **Deborah Ward** . . . . . (847) 695-3750
E-mail: dward@illinoiscourts.gov

Chambers of Justice Joseph E. Birkett

55 Symphony Way, Elgin, IL 60120-5558
Tel: (847) 695-3750 Fax: (847) 695-4949
E-mail: jbirkett@illinoiscourts.gov

Joseph E. "Joe" Birkett
Justice

Education: North Central Col 1977 BA; John Marshall 1981 JD
Began Service: December 13, 2010
Term Expires: 2022
Political Affiliation: Republican

Staff

Judicial Law Clerk **Lynn Harrington** . . . . . (847) 695-3750
E-mail: lharrington@court.state.il.us
Education: Chicago-Kent 1992 JD
Judicial Law Clerk **Michael M. Kessler** . . . . . (847) 695-3750
E-mail: mkessler@court.state.il.us
Education: Wisconsin (Stevens Point) 1994 BA; Minnesota 1998 JD

Chambers of Justice Joseph E. Birkett *continued*

Judicial Law Clerk **Randy Kalberg** . . . . . (847) 695-3750
E-mail: rkalberg@court.state.il.us

Chambers of Justice Kathryn E. Zenoff

6801 Spring Creek Road, Rockford, IL 61114-7420
Tel: (847) 695-3750 Fax: (815) 639-9162
E-mail: kzenoff@illinoiscourts.gov

Kathryn E. Zenoff
Justice

Date of Birth: 1946
Education: Stanford; Columbia JD
Began Service: May 8, 2007

Staff

Judicial Law Clerk **Gregory Grattan** . . . . . (847) 695-3750
E-mail: ggrattan@court.state.il.us
Judicial Law Clerk **Laura Lee** . . . . . (847) 695-3750
E-mail: llee@court.state.il.us
Judicial Law Clerk **Carl Norberg** . . . . . (847) 695-3750
E-mail: cnorberg@court.state.il.us

Chambers of Justice Robert B. Spence

55 Symphony Way, Elgin, IL 60120
Tel: (847) 695-3750
E-mail: rspence@illinoiscourts.gov

Robert B. Spence
Justice

Education: Taylor 1977 BA; John Marshall 1980 JD
Began Service: 2012

Illinois Appellate Court, Third District

1004 Columbus Street, Ottawa, IL 61350
Tel: (815) 434-5050
Internet: www.state.il.us/court/appellatecourt

Number of Judgeships: 7

Areas Covered: Counties of Bureau, Fulton, Grundy, Hancock, Henderson, Henry, Iroquois, Kankakee, Knox, La Salle, Marshall, McDonough, Mercer, Peoria, Putnam, Rock Island, Stark, Tazewell, Warren, Whiteside and Will

Court Staff

Clerk of the Court **Barbara Trumbo** . . . . . (815) 434-5050
E-mail: btrumbo@illinoiscourts.gov
Chief Deputy Clerk **Kim Lukkari** . . . . . (815) 434-5050
Research Director **Matt Butler** . . . . . (815) 434-5050
E-mail: mbutler@illinoiscourts.gov

Chambers of Presiding Justice Mary W. McDade

401 SW Water Street, Suite 409, Peoria, IL 61602
Tel: (309) 671-3003 Fax: (309) 671-3012
E-mail: mcdade82639@yahoo.com

Mary W. McDade
Presiding Justice

Date of Birth: 1939
Education: Michigan 1961 BA; Illinois 1984 JD
Began Service: December 4, 2000
Next Election: November 2020
Election Type: Retention Election
Term Expires: December 2020
Political Affiliation: Democrat

Current Memberships: American Bar Association; The Abraham Lincoln American Inn of Court, The American Inns of Court; Illinois Judges Association; Illinois State Bar Association; Peoria County Bar Association

Staff

Law Clerk **Matthew G. Butler** .... (309) 671-3003
Education: Benedictine U 2001 BA; John Marshall 2004 JD
Law Clerk **Joseph Edward Couture** .... (309) 671-3003
E-mail: jcouture@illinoiscourts.gov
Education: Marquette 2004 JD
Law Clerk **Tracy Robinson** .... (309) 671-3003
E-mail: trobinson@illinoiscourts.gov
Judicial Secretary **Shelly McDuff**.................... (309) 671-3003
E-mail: smcduff@illinoiscourts.gov

Chambers of Justice Tom M. Lytton

1515 Fifth Avenue, Suite 305, Moline, IL 61265
Tel: (309) 757-9458 Fax: (309) 757-9460
E-mail: tlytton@illinoiscourts.gov

Tom M. Lytton
Justice

Date of Birth: 1943
Education: Northwestern 1965 BA, 1968 JD
Began Service: November 1992
Next Election: 2022
Term Expires: November 2022

Current Memberships: American Bar Association; Illinois State Bar Association; Rock Island County Bar Association; State Bar of California

Staff

Career Law Clerk **Julie Angus** .... (309) 757-9458
E-mail: jangus@illinoiscourts.gov
Education: Illinois 1994 BS; Northern Illinois 1997 JD
Career Law Clerk **Heather K. Johnson** .... (309) 757-9458
E-mail: hjohnson@illinoiscourts.gov
Education: Barton 1988 BA; Northern Illinois 2001 JD
Judicial Secretary **Krista M. Klauer**.................. (309) 757-9458
E-mail: kklauer@illinoiscourts.gov

Chambers of Justice Daniel L. Schmidt

1004 Columbus Street, Ottawa, IL 61350
Tel: (309) 671-7659 Fax: (309) 671-7661
E-mail: dschmidt@illinoiscourts.gov

Daniel L. Schmidt
Justice

Date of Birth: January 12, 1951
Education: Illinois 1974 BA; Washington U (MO) 1983 JD
Began Service: 2012
Term Expires: 2022
Political Affiliation: Republican

Current Memberships: The Abraham Lincoln American Inn of Court, The American Inns of Court; Appellate Lawyers Association; Illinois State Bar Association; Peoria County Bar Association

Staff

Law Clerk **Jessica Sarff**.............................. (309) 671-7665
E-mail: jsarff@illinoiscourts.gov
Law Clerk **Ronald Timmons**........................ (309) 671-7664
Term Expires: November 2022
E-mail: rtimmons@illinoiscourts.gov
Secretary **Jeanene Theissen** .... (309) 671-7659
E-mail: jtheissen@illinoiscourts.gov

Chambers of Justice Robert L. Carter

925 LaSalle Street, Peru, IL 61350
Tel: (815) 433-2905 Fax: (815) 433-2950
E-mail: rcarter@illinoiscourts.gov

Robert L. Carter
Justice

Education: Illinois 1974 JD
Began Service: 2012

Current Memberships: Illinois County Bar Association; LaSalle County Bar Association

Staff

Career Law Clerk **Joseph Mikula** .... (815) 433-2905
Began Service: September 2006
E-mail: jmikula@court.state.il.us
Education: Pepperdine 1994 JD
Career Law Clerk **(Vacant)**.......................... (815) 433-2905
Secretary **Carol Murry** .... (815) 433-2905
E-mail: cmurry@court.state.il.us

Chambers of Justice William E. Holdridge

207 Main Street, Suite 600, Peoria, IL 61602-1323
Tel: (815) 434-5050 Fax: (309) 671-3244
E-mail: wholdridge@illinoiscourts.gov

William E. Holdridge
Justice

Date of Birth: March 30, 1948
Education: Illinois State BS; Illinois MS, PhD; Southern Illinois JD
Began Service: 1990
Term Expires: December 2024
Political Affiliation: Republican

Current Memberships: Fulton County Bar Association; Illinois Judges Association; Illinois State Bar Association; The Missouri Bar; Peoria County Bar Association

Staff

Career Law Clerk **David M. House**.................. (309) 671-3190
E-mail: dhouse@illinoiscourts.gov
Education: MacMurray 1978 BS; Chicago-Kent 1988 JD

(continued on next page)

Chambers of Justice William E. Holdridge *continued*

Career Law Clerk **Steven Winger** .... (309) 671-3190
E-mail: swinger@illinoiscourts.gov
Judicial Secretary **(Vacant)** .... (309) 671-3190

Chambers of Justice Mary K. O'Brien

1360 East Division Street, Coal City, IL 60416
Tel: (815) 634-0041 Fax: (815) 634-0296
E-mail: mobrien@illinoiscourts.gov

Mary K. O'Brien
Justice

Date of Birth: June 4, 1965
Began Service: December 2003
Term Expires: December 1, 2024

Government: State Representative, Illinois House of Representatives; Member, Legislative Audit Commission, Illinois General Assembly; Member, Agriculture and Conservation, House Standing Committees, Illinois General Assembly; Chairman, Judiciary II - Criminal Law, House Standing Committees, Illinois General Assembly; Member, Labor, House Standing Committees, Illinois General Assembly; Member, Transportation and Motor Vehicles, House Standing Committees, Illinois General Assembly

Staff
Career Law Clerk **Natalie Hammer** .... (815) 634-0041
E-mail: nhammer@illinoiscourts.gov
Career Law Clerk **Catherine McCabe** .... (815) 634-0041
E-mail: cmccabe@illinoiscourts.gov
Education: Northern Illinois 2001 JD
Judicial Secretary **Deborah Patarozzi** .... (815) 634-0041
E-mail: dpatarozzi@illinoiscourts.gov

Chambers of Justice Vicki R. Wright

1004 Columbus Street, Ottawa, IL 61350
Tel: (815) 434-5050
E-mail: vwright@illinoiscourts.gov

Vicki R. Wright
Justice

Education: Northwestern 1979; Loyola U (Chicago) 1982 JD
Began Service: 2006

Government: Criminal Prosecutor, Office of the State's Attorney, County of Whiteside, Illinois (1984-1991)

Judicial: Associate Circuit Judge, 14th Judicial Circuit, Illinois Circuit Court (1991-2006)

Illinois Appellate Court, Fourth District

Appellate Court Building, 201 West Monroe, Springfield, IL 62794
P.O. Box 19206, Springfield, IL 62794-9206
Tel: (217) 782-2586
Internet: www.state.il.us/court/appellatecourt

Number of Judgeships: 7

Areas Covered: Counties of Adams, Brown, Calhoun, Cass, Champaign, Clark, Coles, Cumberland, DeWitt, Douglas, Edgar, Ford, Greene, Jersey, Livingston, Logan, Macon, Macoupin, Mason, McLean, Menard, Morgan, Moultrie, Piatt, Pike, Sangamon, Schuyler, Scott, Vermilion and Woodford

Court Staff
Clerk of the Court **Carla Bender** .... (217) 782-2586
E-mail: cbender@court.state.il.us
Research Director **Shirley Wilgenbusch** .... (217) 782-3528
E-mail: swilgenbusch@court.state.il.us
Education: Southern Illinois 1982 JD

Chambers of Presiding Justice Thomas R. Appleton

401 East Capitol Avenue, Suite 401, Springfield, IL 62701-1568
Tel: (217) 558-0365 Fax: (217) 558-0371
E-mail: tappleton@illinoiscourts.gov

Thomas R. Appleton
Presiding Justice

Date of Birth: 1949
Education: Augustana (IL) BA; Illinois MA; Chicago-Kent JD
Began Service: December 17, 2001
Political Affiliation: Republican

Current Memberships: Illinois State Bar Association; Sangamon County Bar Association

Staff
Career Law Clerk **Mark Atterberry** .... (217) 558-0368
E-mail: matterberry@illinoiscourts.gov
Education: Wheaton (IL) 1984 BA; Northwestern 1987 MA; Southern Illinois 1995 JD
Career Law Clerk **Michelle Phillips** .... (217) 558-0369
E-mail: mphillips@illinoiscourts.gov
Education: Illinois 1988 BS; Stetson 1996 JD
Administrative Assistant **Debra A. Landgrebe** .... (217) 558-0365
E-mail: dlandgrebe@illinoiscourts.gov

Chambers of Justice James A. Knecht

318 West Washington Street, Bloomington, IL 61701
Tel: (309) 829-3715 Fax: (309) 829-0155
E-mail: jknecht@illinoiscourts.gov

James A. Knecht
Justice

Date of Birth: May 19, 1944
Began Service: December 1, 1986
Next Election: November 2016
Term Expires: December 2016

Staff
Career Law Clerk **Anthony Gough** .... (309) 829-3715
E-mail: agough@illinoiscourts.gov
Career Law Clerk **Lea Parent** .... (309) 829-3715
E-mail: lparent@illinoiscourts.gov
Education: Chicago-Kent JD
Secretary **Cathy Huff** .... (309) 829-3715
E-mail: chuff@illinoiscourts.gov

Chambers of Justice Robert J. Steigmann

100 West Main Street, Urbana, IL 61801
P.O. Box 815, Urbana, IL 61803-0815
Tel: (217) 278-3131 Fax: (217) 278-3135
E-mail: rsteigmann@illinoiscourts.gov

Robert J. Steigmann
Justice

Date of Birth: 1944
Education: Illinois 1965 BS, 1968 JD
Began Service: December 1994
Term Expires: December 2024
Political Affiliation: Republican

Academic: Adjunct Professor of Law, University of Illinois at Urbana-Champaign; Faculty Member, Institute of Judicial Administration, New York University (1997-1999)

Chambers of Justice Robert J. Steigmann *continued*

Government: Associate, Office of the State's Attorney, Sangamon County, Illinois (1969-1971); Associate, Office of the State's Attorney, County of Champaign, Illinois (1971-1976)

Judicial: Judge, Illinois Circuit Court, Sixth Judicial Circuit (1976-1994); Assigned Justice, Illinois Appellate Court, Fourth Judicial District (1989-1994); Presiding Justice, Illinois Appellate Court, Fourth District (2006-2007)

Current Memberships: Champaign County Bar Association; Illinois State Bar Association

Staff

Career Law Clerk **Evan Bruno** . . . . (217) 278-3131
Career Law Clerk **Antonio Martinez** . . . . (217) 278-3131
E-mail: amartinez@illinoiscourts.gov
Education: Illinois 2007 JD
Administrative Assistant **Rebecca "Becky" Gordon** . . . . . (217) 278-3131
E-mail: bgordon@illinoiscourts.gov

Chambers of Justice John W. Turner

319 West Kickapoo Street, Lincoln, IL 62656
Tel: (217) 732-4043 Fax: (217) 732-4123
E-mail: jturner@illinoiscourts.gov

John W. Turner
Justice

Date of Birth: 1956
Education: Illinois 1978 BA; DePaul 1981 JD
Began Service: June 2001
Term Expires: December 2022
Political Affiliation: Republican

Government: Public Defender, Office of the Public Defender, County of Logan, Illinois (1984-1987); State's Attorney, Office of the State Attorney, County of Logan, Illinois (1988-1992); State Representative (R-IL, District 90), Illinois House of Representatives (1994-2001)

Judicial: Presiding Justice, Illinois Appellate Court, Fourth District

Legal Practice: Private Practice (1984-2001)

Current Memberships: Illinois Judges Association; Illinois State Bar Association; Logan County Bar Association

Staff

Career Law Clerk **Stephanie Anders** . . . . (217) 732-4043
E-mail: sanders@illinoiscourts.gov
Education: Illinois 2000 JD
Career Law Clerk **Robert Shumaker** . . . . (217) 732-4043
E-mail: rshumaker@illinoiscourts.gov
Education: Illinois 2000 JD
Secretary **Carla Harnacke** . . . . (217) 732-4043
E-mail: charnacke@illinoiscourts.gov

Chambers of Justice M. Carol Pope

201 West Monroe, Springfield, IL 62794
Tel: (217) 632-7970

M. Carol Pope
Justice

Education: Illinois 1975 BA; DePaul 1979 JD
Began Service: December 2008
Term Expires: 2022

Staff

Law Clerk **John Gabala** . . . . (217) 632-7970
E-mail: jgabala@illinoiscourts.gov
Law Clerk **Justin Ward** . . . . (217) 632-7970
E-mail: jward@illinoiscourts.gov
Judicial Secretary **Diane Paulauskis** . . . . (217) 632-7970

Chambers of Justice Lisa Holder White

201 W. Monroe Street, Springfield, IL 62794-9206
Tel: (217) 782-2586
E-mail: lwhite@illinoiscourts.gov

Lisa Holder White
Justice

Education: Lewis U 1990 BA; Illinois 1993 JD
Began Service: January 14, 2013

Chambers of Justice Thomas M. Harris Jr.

201 W. Monroe Street, Springfield, IL 62794-9206
Tel: (217) 782-2586
E-mail: tharris@illinoiscourts.gov

Thomas M. Harris, Jr.
Justice

Education: Illinois 1985 BA; Colorado 1988 JD
Began Service: 2013

Illinois Appellate Court, Fifth District

P.O. Box 867, Mount Vernon, IL 62864-0018
Tel: (618) 242-3120
Internet: www.state.il.us/court/appellatecourt

Number of Judgeships: 7

Areas Covered: Counties of Alexander, Bond, Christian, Clay, Clinton, Crawford, Edwards, Effingham, Fayette, Franklin, Gallatin, Hamilton, Hardin, Jackson, Jasper, Jefferson, Johnson, Lawrence, Madison, Marion, Massac, Monroe, Montgomery, Perry, Pope, Pulaski, Randolph, Richland, Saline, Shelby, St Clair, Union, Wabash, Washington, Wayne, White and Williamson

Court Staff

Clerk of the Court **John J. Flood** . . . . (618) 242-3120
Chief Deputy Clerk **Linda Kueker** . . . . (618) 242-3120
E-mail: lkueker@court.state.il.us
Research Director **Michael Greathouse** . . . . (618) 242-6414
E-mail: mgreathouse@court.state.il.us
Education: Southern Illinois 1987 JD
Law Librarian **Holly Austin** . . . . (618) 242-6414
E-mail: haustin@court.state.il.us Fax: (618) 242-9133

Chambers of Presiding Justice Thomas M. Welch

14th & Main Streets, Mount Vernon, IL 62864
Two Crestmont, Collinsville, IL 62234
Tel: (618) 344-1299 Fax: (618) 344-9385
E-mail: twelch@court.state.il.us

Thomas M. Welch
Presiding Justice

Date of Birth: 1939
Education: Illinois 1962 BS; Missouri 1965 JD
Began Service: December 1980
Next Election: November 2020
Election Type: Retention Election
Term Expires: December 2021
Political Affiliation: Republican

Current Memberships: Illinois State Bar Association; Madison County Bar Association; Tri-City Bar Association

Staff

Career Law Clerk **Christine Sankoorikal** . . . . (618) 344-1299
E-mail: csankoorikal@illinoiscourts.gov
Career Law Clerk **Lindsey Hallam** . . . . (618) 344-1299
E-mail: lhallam@illinoiscourts.gov

(continued on next page)

Chambers of Presiding Justice Thomas M. Welch *continued*

Law Clerk & Administrator **Joanna Hirsch** .... (618) 344-1299
E-mail: jhirsch@illinoiscourts.gov

Chambers of Justice James Moore

8341 Express Drive, Suite A, Marion, IL 62959
Tel: (618) 993-7013

James Moore
Justice

Chambers of Justice Melissa A. Chapman

2 Ginger Creek Village, Glen Carbon, IL 62034
Tel: (618) 656-0644 Fax: (618) 656-8591
E-mail: mchapman@illinoiscourts.gov

Melissa A. Chapman
Justice

Date of Birth: 1951
Education: Southern IL Edwardsville 1974 BA, 1975 MA; Saint Louis U 1983 JD
Began Service: September 1, 2001
Next Election: November 2022
Term Expires: December 2, 2022
Political Affiliation: Democrat

Current Memberships: Illinois Judges Association; Madison County Bar Association

Staff
Career Law Clerk **Jennifer I. Hanan** .... (618) 656-0644
E-mail: jhanan@illinoiscourts.gov
Education: Emerson 1990 BS; Golden Gate 1998 JD
Career Law Clerk **Carma L. Smith** .... (618) 656-0644
E-mail: csmith@illinoiscourts.gov
Education: Eastern Illinois 1984 BS; Thomas M Cooley 1988 JD
Judicial Secretary **Machele M. Knobeloch** .... (618) 656-0644
E-mail: mknobeloch@illinoiscourts.gov

Chambers of Justice Bruce D. Stewart

600 Clearwave Building, 2 North Vine Street, Harrisburg, IL 62946
Tel: (618) 294-8481
E-mail: bstewart@court.state.il.us

Bruce D. Stewart
Justice

Date of Birth: August 30, 1952
Education: Southern Illinois 1973, 1976 JD
Began Service: November 2006
Term Expires: 2016

Chambers of Justice Richard P. Goldenhersh

56 South 65th Street, Suite 6, Belleville, IL 62223
Tel: (618) 397-9733 Fax: (618) 397-6280
E-mail: rgoldenhersh@court.state.il.us

Richard P. Goldenhersh
Justice

Date of Birth: 1944
Education: Washington U (MO) 1969
Began Service: December 1988
Next Election: November 4, 2018
Election Type: Retention Election
Term Expires: December 31, 2018

Judicial: Judge, Illinois Circuit Court, 20th Judicial Circuit (1975-1988)

Current Memberships: Illinois Judges Association; Illinois State Bar Association; St. Clair County Bar Association

Staff
Career Law Clerk **Andrew Hoerner** .... (618) 397-9733
Career Law Clerk **Joan Keltner** .... (618) 397-9733
E-mail: jkeltner@court.state.il.us
Education: Southern Illinois 1987 JD
Secretary **Linda Schmulbach** .... (618) 397-9733
E-mail: lschmulbach@illinoiscourts.gov

Chambers of Justice Judy Cates

P.O. Box 867, Mount Vernon, IL 62864-0018
Tel: (618) 257-7575
E-mail: jcates@illinoiscourts.gov

Judy Cates
Justice

Began Service: December 2012
Term Expires: December 2022

Staff
Law Clerk **Diane M. Hurwitz** .... (618) 257-7575
E-mail: dhurwitz@illinoiscourts.gov
Education: Washington U (MO) 1983 JD
Law Clerk **Rosemary McGuire** .... (618) 257-7575
E-mail: rmcguire@illinoiscourts.gov

STATE COURTS—ILLINOIS

Indiana

Indiana Division of State Court Administration

30 South Meridian Street, Suite 500, Indianapolis, IN 46204-3568
Tel: (317) 232-2542 Tel: (317) 232-4706 (Judicial Qualifications)
Tel: (800) 542-0813 (GAL-CASA Toll Free)
Tel: (800) 452-9963 (CLEO Toll Free) Fax: (317) 233-6586
Internet: http://www.courts.in.gov

Staff

Executive Director **Lilia G. Judson** .... (317) 232-2542
E-mail: lilia.judson@courts.in.gov
Education: Indiana; Indianapolis 1975 JD

Chief Deputy Executive Director **David Remondini** ..... (317) 232-2542
E-mail: dave.remondini@courts.in.gov
Education: Ripon 1980 BA; Indiana 1997 JD

Director/Counsel, Trial Court Technology
Mary L. DePrez .... (317) 234-2604
E-mail: mdeprez@jtac.in.gov
Education: Indiana 1974 BA, 1979 JD

Director, Appellate Court Technology **Robert Rath** ...... (317) 234-6529
E-mail: robert.rath@courts.in.gov

Director, Appellate IT Operations **Rusty L. Lowe** .... (317) 233-0225
E-mail: rus.lowe@courts.in.gov

Deputy Director, Appellate IT Operations **Mark Roth** .... (317) 233-3710
E-mail: mark.roth@courts.in.gov

Director/Office and Employment Law Services
Brenda Rodeheffer .... (317) 234-3936
E-mail: brenda.rodeheffer@courts.in.gov

Director, State Office of GAL/CASA (Guardian Ad Litem/Court Appointed Special Advocates)
Leslie S. Dunn .... (317) 233-0224
E-mail: leslie.dunn@courts.in.gov
Education: Indiana 1987 BA;
South Carolina 1990 JD

Director, Trial Court Management **Jeff Wiese** .... (317) 234-5562

Director, Trial Court Services **Thomas Carusillo** .... (317) 233-2779
E-mail: tom.carusillo@courts.in.gov
Education: Notre Dame 1976 BA;
Indianapolis 1979 JD

Program Coordinator, State Office of GAL/CASA (Guardian Ad Litem/Court Appointed Special Advocates) **Teresa E. Lyles** .... (800) 542-0813
E-mail: teresa.lyles@courts.in.gov
Education: Indiana 1997 BS

Family Court Manager **Michael Commons** .... (317) 234-1376
E-mail: michael.commons@courts.in.gov

Counsel, Judicial Qualifications Commission
Adrienne Meiring .... (317) 232-4706
E-mail: adrienne.meiring@courts.in.gov
Education: Ohio State 1990 BA, 1993 JD

Staff Attorney **Elizabeth Daulton** .... (317) 234-7155
E-mail: elizabeth.daulton@courts.in.gov
Education: Cardozo 2009 JD

Staff Attorney **James Maguire** .... (317) 233-3018
E-mail: james.maguire@courts.in.gov
Education: Purdue 1969 BS;
IU-Purdue U Indianapolis 1972 JD

Staff Attorney **(Vacant)** .... (317) 234-3935
Staff Attorney **(Vacant)** .... (317) 234-2905
Staff Attorney **(Vacant)** .... (317) 233-3017
Staff Attorney **(Vacant)** .... (317) 234-3180
Staff Attorney **(Vacant)** .... (317) 234-5398
Staff Attorney **(Vacant)** .... (317) 234-1873

MIS Director/CMS Project Manager, Trial Court Technology **Andy Cain** .... (317) 234-3716
E-mail: acain@jtac.in.gov
Education: Purdue 1989 BS

Office/Fiscal Manager, Trial Court Technology
Anthony Warfield .... (317) 234-2712
E-mail: awarfield@jtac.in.gov
Education: Wabash Col 1983 BA;
Indianapolis 1991 MBA; Savannah Art 1998 MFA

Indiana Division of State Court Administration *continued*

Records Manager **Thomas Q. Jones** .... (317) 233-3695
E-mail: tom.jones@courts.in.gov
Education: Hamline 1971 BA;
North Dakota 1977 MA;
Wisconsin (Eau Claire) 1983 MA;
Indiana 1987 MLS

Public Information Officer **Kathryn Dolan** .... (317) 234-4722
E-mail: kathryn.dolan@courts.in.gov

Court Analyst **James Diller** .... (317) 233-2312
E-mail: jim.diller@courts.in.gov

Court Analyst **Angela James** .... (317) 232-1871
E-mail: angela.james@courts.in.gov

Staff Attorney/CLEO Program Coordinator
Jasmine Parson .... (317) 234-1376
E-mail: jasmine.parson@courts.in.gov

Indiana Supreme Court

200 West Washington Street, Indianapolis, IN 46204-2732
Tel: (317) 232-2540 Fax: (317) 232-8372
Internet: www.in.gov/judiciary/supreme

Number of Judgeships: 5

The Supreme Court consists of a chief justice and four associate justices who are appointed for initial two-year terms by the Governor from a list supplied by the Judicial Nominating Commission. Justices are then subject to a retention vote in the next statewide general election for a ten-year term. The chief justice is selected by the Judicial Nominating Commission to serve a consecutive five-year term. The Supreme Court has original exclusive jurisdiction over cases involving admission to the practice of law; discipline and disbarment of those admitted to the practice of law; unauthorized practice of law; discipline, removal, or retirement of judges; exercise of jurisdiction by other courts; appeals from judgments imposing a sentence of death or life imprisonment; appeals from the denial of post-conviction relief in which the sentence was death; and appealable cases where a state or federal statute has been declared unconstitutional.

The Supreme Court sits in Indianapolis.

Court Staff

Supreme Court Administrator **Kevin S. Smith** .... (317) 232-2540
E-mail: kevin.smith@courts.in.gov
Education: Indiana 1996 JD

Deputy Administrator **Greta M. Scodro** .... (317) 232-2540
E-mail: greta.scodro@courts.state.in.us

Staff Attorney **Harriet Harmon** .... (317) 232-2540
E-mail: harriet.harmon@courts.in.gov

Staff Attorney **Geoff Davis** .... (317) 232-2540
E-mail: geoff.davis@courts.state.in.us

Staff Attorney **Brian Eisenman** .... (317) 232-2540
E-mail: brian.eisenman@courts.state.in.us

Staff Attorney **Lynn Pelley** .... (317) 232-2540
E-mail: lynn.pelley@courts.state.in.us

Clerk of the Supreme and Appellate Courts
Kevin S. Smith .... (317) 232-2540
E-mail: kevin.smith@courts.in.gov Fax: (317) 232-8365

Executive Director [Continuing Legal Education]
Julia Orzeske .... (317) 232-1945
30 South Meridian, Suite 950, Fax: (317) 233-1442
Indianapolis, IN 46204
E-mail: julia.orzeske@courts.in.gov

Supreme Court Law Librarian **Terri Ross** .... (317) 232-2557
E-mail: terri.ross@courts.in.gov

Reference Librarian **Kim L. Schwant** .... (317) 232-2557
E-mail: kim.schwant@courts.in.gov

STATE COURTS – INDIANA

Chambers of Chief Justice Loretta Rush

200 West Washington Street, Indianapolis, IN 46204-3466
Tel: (317) 232-2548
E-mail: loretta.rush@courts.in.gov

Loretta Hogan Rush
Chief Justice

Education: Purdue 1976 BA; Indiana 1983 JD
Began Service: December 28, 2012
Appointed By: Governor Mitch Daniels
Next Election: November 2024
Election Type: Retention Election

Staff
Law Clerk **Jason Bennett** .... (317) 232-2548
E-mail: jason.bennett@courts.in.gov
Law Clerk **Dylan Pittman** .... (317) 232-2548
Law Clerk **Amanda Terrell** .... (317) 232-2548
Judicial Assistant **Amber Holland** .... (317) 232-2548
E-mail: amber.holland@courts.in.gov

Chambers of Associate Justice Brent E. Dickson

306 State House, 200 West Washington Street,
Indianapolis, IN 46204-3466
Tel: (317) 232-2549 Fax: (317) 233-8706
E-mail: brent.dickson@courts.in.gov

Brent E. Dickson
Associate Justice

Note: Justice Dickson will retire effective Spring 2016.
Date of Birth: 1941
Education: Purdue 1964 BA; Indianapolis 1968 JD
Began Service: August 8, 2012
Appointed By: Governor Robert D. Orr
Term Expires: December 31, 2016

Current Memberships: American Bar Association; The American Law Institute; The Seventh Circuit Bar Association, Federal Bar Association; Indiana Judges Association; Indiana State Bar Association; Indianapolis Bar Association

Staff
Law Clerk **Jeffrey Dunn** .... (317) 232-2549
Began Service: 2015
Term Expires: September 2017
E-mail: jeffrey.dunn@courts.in.gov
Law Clerk **Christine File** .... (317) 232-2549
Began Service: 2015
Term Expires: August 2017
E-mail: christine.file@courts.in.gov

Chambers of Associate Justice Robert D. Rucker

312 State House, 200 West Washington Street,
Indianapolis, IN 46204-2732
Tel: (317) 233-3664 Fax: (317) 233-8677
E-mail: robert.rucker@courts.in.gov

Robert D. Rucker
Associate Justice

Education: Indiana Northwest 1974 AB; Valparaiso 1976 JD; Virginia LLM
Began Service: November 1999
Appointed By: Governor Frank O'Bannon
Term Expires: December 2022

Government: Deputy Prosecuting Attorney, County of Lake, Indiana; City Attorney, City of Gary, Indiana

Judicial: Judge, Indiana Court of Appeals, Fifth District (1991-1999)

Chambers of Associate Justice Robert D. Rucker *continued*

Current Memberships: Commission for Continuing Legal Education, Indiana Supreme Court; American Bar Association; Indiana Judges Association; Indiana State Bar Association; Indiana Trial Lawyers Association; Lake County Bar Association (IN); Marion County Bar Association (IN); National Bar Association; Thurgood Marshall and James C. Kimbrough Bar Association

Staff
Law Clerk **Traci Cosby** .... (317) 233-3664
Began Service: August 2012
Term Expires: August 2016
E-mail: traci.cosby@courts.in.gov
Law Clerk **Jenna Shives** .... (317) 233-3664
Began Service: August 16, 2010
Term Expires: August 2016
E-mail: hattie.harman@courts.in.gov
Secretary **Pamela Cody** .... (317) 233-3664
E-mail: pam.cody@courts.in.gov

Chambers of Associate Justice Steven H. David

200 West Washington Street, Indianapolis, IN 46204-3466
Tel: (317) 232-2547 Fax: (317) 232-8711
E-mail: steven.david@courts.state.in.us

Steven H. David
Associate Justice

Education: Murray State U 1979 BS; Indiana 1982 JD
Began Service: October 18, 2010
Appointed By: Governor Mitch Daniels

Current Memberships: Boone County Bar Association; Indiana State Bar Association

Staff
Law Clerk **Michelle Langdon** .... (317) 232-2547
Term Expires: August 2016
Law Clerk **Alyssa Taylor** .... (317) 232-2547
Term Expires: August 2016
E-mail: alyssa.taylor@courts.state.in.us

Chambers of Associate Justice Mark S. Massa

200 West Washington Street, Indianapolis, IN 46204-3466
Tel: (317) 232-2550
E-mail: mark.massa@courts.in.gov

Mark S. Massa
Associate Justice

Education: Indiana 1983, 1989 JD
Began Service: 2012
Next Election: November 2024
Election Type: Retention Election

Staff
Law Clerk **Leah Seigel** .... (317) 232-2550
E-mail: andrew.norris@courts.in.gov
Law Clerk **Alex Preller** .... (317) 232-2550
E-mail: alex.preller@courts.in.gov
Judicial Assistant **Jessica Strange** .... (317) 232-2550

STATE COURTS—INDIANA

Indiana Court of Appeals

200 West Washington Street, Indianapolis, IN 46204
Tel: (317) 232-6906 Fax: (317) 233-4627
Internet: www.in.gov/judiciary/appeals

Number of Judgeships: 15

Each District of the Court of Appeals in Indiana consists of a presiding judge and two judges, who are appointed for initial two-year terms by the Governor from a list supplied by the Judicial Nominating Commission. Following the initial two-year term, judges face a retention vote in their districts for a ten-year term. The Court of Appeals has appellate jurisdiction over all cases except for those where the Indiana Supreme Court has exclusive jurisdiction. The Court also reviews final decisions of administrative agencies. The First, Second and Third Districts of the Court of Appeals hear appeals from specific geographic areas. The Court of Appeals for the Fourth District hears every fourth case from the First, Second and Third Districts, while the Court of Appeals for the Fifth District hears every fifth case.

Court Staff

Administrator for the Court of Appeals
Larry L. Morris .... (317) 232-6906
E-mail: larry.morris@courts.in.gov
Education: Lincoln Christian 1979 BA; Illinois (Springfield) 1983 MA; Indiana 1991 JD

Clerk of the Supreme and Appellate Courts
Kevin S. Smith .... (317) 232-1930
State House, 200 W. Washington St., Indianapolis, IN 46204 Fax: (317) 232-8365
E-mail: kevin.smith@courts.in.gov

Indiana Court of Appeals, First District

State House, 200 West Washington Street, Indianapolis, IN 46204
Tel: (317) 232-6906 Fax: (317) 233-4627

Number of Judgeships: 3

Areas Covered: Counties of Bartholomew, Boone, Brown, Clark, Clay, Crawford, Daviess, Dearborn, Decatur, Dubois, Fayette, Floyd, Fountain, Franklin, Gibson, Greene, Hancock, Harrison, Hendricks, Henry, Jackson, Jefferson, Jennings, Johnson, Knox, Lawrence, Martin, Monroe, Montgomery, Morgan, Ohio, Orange, Owen, Parke, Perry, Pike, Posey, Putnam, Randolph, Ripley, Rush, Scott, Shelby, Spencer, Sullivan, Switzerland, Union, Vanderburgh, Vermillion, Vigo, Warrick, Washington and Wayne

Chambers of Presiding Judge Edward W. Najam, Jr.

423 State House, 200 West Washington Street, Indianapolis, IN 46204-2784
Tel: (317) 232-6884 Fax: (317) 233-6001
E-mail: edward.najam@courts.in.gov

Edward W. Najam, Jr.
Presiding Judge

Date of Birth: 1947
Education: Indiana 1969 BA; Harvard 1972 JD
Began Service: December 30, 1992
Appointed By: Governor Evan Bayh
Next Election: 2016
Election Type: Retention Election
Term Expires: 2016

Government: Assistant to the Mayor, Office of the Mayor, County of Monroe, Indiana (1972-1974)

Judicial: Chair, Appellate Practice Section, Indiana State Bar Association (1997-1998); Member, Supreme Court Committe on Rules of Practice and Procedure; Presiding Judge, Indiana Court of Appeals, First District

Legal Practice: Private Practice (1974-1992)

Chambers of Presiding Judge Edward W. Najam, Jr. *continued*

Staff

Law Clerk **Jonathan B. Warner** .... (317) 232-6884
Began Service: August 2008
E-mail: jonathan.warner@courts.in.gov

Career Law Clerk **Angela J. Hauck** .... (317) 232-6884
E-mail: angela.hauck@courts.in.gov
Education: Indiana 1991 BA; IU-Purdue U Indianapolis 1995 JD

Career Law Clerk **(Vacant)** .... (317) 232-6884

Office Administrator **Kristie A. Utter** .... (317) 232-6884
E-mail: kristie.utter@courts.in.gov

Chambers of Judge John G. Baker

419 State House, 200 West Washington Street, Indianapolis, IN 46204
Tel: (317) 232-6895 Fax: (317) 233-3093
E-mail: john.baker@courts.in.gov

John G. Baker
Judge

Date of Birth: 1946
Education: Indiana 1968 AB, 1971 JD; Virginia 1995 LLM
Began Service: June 2, 1989
Appointed By: Governor Evan Bayh
Term Expires: October 4, 2021
Political Affiliation: Democrat

Current Memberships: American Bar Association; Indiana Judges Association; Indiana State Bar Association; Indianapolis Bar Association

Staff

Law Clerk **Brittany L. West** .... (317) 232-6895
E-mail: brittany.west@courts.in.gov

Secretary **Nancy Collins** .... (317) 232-6895
E-mail: nancy.collins@courts.in.gov

Chambers of Judge L. Mark Bailey

State House, 200 West Washington Street, Indianapolis, IN 46204
Tel: (317) 232-6906 Fax: (317) 233-4627
E-mail: mark.bailey@courts.in.gov

L. Mark Bailey
Judge

Education: Indianapolis 1978 BA, 1982 JD
Began Service: January 30, 1998
Next Election: November 2020

Judicial: Decatur County Court (1991-1992); Decatur Superior Court (1992-1998)

Current Memberships: American Bar Association; Indiana Judges Association; Indiana State Bar Association

Indiana Court of Appeals, Second District

State House, 200 West Washington Street, Indianapolis, IN 46204
Tel: (317) 232-6906 Fax: (317) 233-4627

Number of Judgeships: 3

Areas Covered: Counties of Adams, Blackford, Carroll, Cass, Clinton, Delaware, Grant, Hamilton, Howard, Huntington, Jay, Madison, Marion, Miami, Tippecanoe, Tipton, Wabash, Wells and White

Chambers of Presiding Judge James S. Kirsch

415 State House, 200 West Washington Street, Indianapolis, IN 46204
Tel: (317) 232-6909 Fax: (317) 233-3385
E-mail: james.kirsch@courts.in.gov

James S. Kirsch
Presiding Judge

Date of Birth: 1946
Education: Butler 1968 BA; Indiana 1974 JD
Began Service: March 4, 1994
Appointed By: Governor Evan Bayh
Next Election: November 2016
Election Type: Retention Election
Term Expires: December 31, 2016

Current Memberships: American Bar Association; Indiana Judges Association; Indiana State Bar Association; Indianapolis Bar Association; Indianapolis Bar Foundation, Indianapolis Bar Association

Staff
Career Law Clerk **Melissa Clark** .... (317) 233-0365
E-mail: melissa.clark@courts.in.gov
Education: Kansas 1987 BS; Arizona 1992 JD
Career Law Clerk **Catherine Little** .... (317) 232-0364
E-mail: catherine.little@courts.in.gov
Education: Kenyon 1979 BA;
Case Western 1988 JD
Career Law Clerk **Angela M. Yoon** .... (317) 233-9281
E-mail: angela.yoon@courts.in.gov
Education: Indiana 1998 BS, 2002 JD
Office Administrator **Sue Barnett** .... (317) 232-6909
E-mail: sue.barnett@courts.in.gov
Education: Indianapolis 1968 BA

Chambers of Judge Cale J. Bradford

200 West Washington Street, Indianapolis, IN 46204-3466
Tel: (317) 232-6906 Fax: (317) 233-4627
E-mail: cale.bradford@courts.state.in.us

Cale J. Bradford
Judge

Education: Indiana 1982 BS, 1986 JD
Began Service: August 1, 2007
Appointed By: Governor Mitch Daniels
Next Election: November 2020

Chambers of Judge Robert Altice

200 West Washington Street, Indianapolis, IN 46204-3466
Tel: (317) 232-6906

Robert Altice
Judge

Indiana Court of Appeals, Third District

200 West Washington Street, Indianapolis, IN 46204
Tel: (317) 232-6906 Fax: (317) 233-4627

Number of Judgeships: 3

Areas Covered: Counties of Allen, Benton, DeKalb, Elkhart, Fulton, Jasper, Kosciusko, LaGrange, Lake, LaPorte, Marshall, Newton, Noble, Porter, Pulaski, St. Joseph, Starke, Steuben, Warren and Whitley

Chambers of Presiding Judge Terry A. Crone

200 West Washington Street, Room 420, Indianapolis, IN 46204
Tel: (317) 232-6882 Fax: (317) 233-0392
E-mail: terrie.crone@courts.in.gov

Terry A. Crone
Presiding Judge

Date of Birth: September 28, 1951
Education: DePauw 1974 BA; Notre Dame 1977 JD
Began Service: March 8, 2004
Appointed By: Governor Joseph E. Kernan
Term Expires: November 2016

Current Memberships: Indiana Judges Association; Indiana State Bar Association; St. Joseph County Bar Association

Staff
Career Law Clerk **Cynthia S. Egloff** .... (317) 233-0367
E-mail: cynthia.egloff@courts.in.gov
Education: Indiana 1984 BA, 1994 JD
Career Law Clerk **Allison Gallo** .... (317) 233-0367
E-mail: allison.gallo@courts.in.gov
Education: Indiana JD
Career Law Clerk **Kerry Popowikz** .... (317) 233-0367
E-mail: kerry.popowikz@courts.in.gov
Education: DePaul 1990 JD
Career Senior Law Clerk **Scott B. Brauneller** .... (317) 233-0369
E-mail: scott.brauneller@courts.in.gov
Education: Harvard 1990 AB;
IU-Purdue U Indianapolis 1992 JD
Administrative Assistant **Wendy Hendricks** .... (317) 232-6882
E-mail: wendy.hendricks@courts.in.gov

Chambers of Judge Paul D. Mathias

421 State House, 200 West Washington Street, Indianapolis, IN 46204
Tel: (317) 232-6880 Fax: (317) 233-3100
E-mail: pmathias@courts.state.in.us

Paul D. Mathias
Judge

Date of Birth: 1953
Education: Harvard 1976 AB; Indiana 1979 JD
Began Service: March 2000
Appointed By: Governor Frank O'Bannon
Next Election: November 2022
Term Expires: December 31, 2022

Current Memberships: Allen County Bar Association; American Bar Association; Indiana State Bar Association

Staff
Law Clerk **Ann Lowe** .... (317) 233-0370
Deputy Senior Law Clerk **Jonathan Ballard** .... (317) 233-0371
E-mail: jballard@courts.state.in.us
Education: Indiana 2000 JD
Career Law Clerk **Erin Heuer Lantzer** .... (317) 233-1492
E-mail: elantzer@courts.state.in.us
Education: Indiana 2000 JD
Administrative Assistant **Kristine Weddell** .... (317) 232-6880
E-mail: kweddell@courts.state.in.us

Chambers of Judge Michael P. Barnes
1080 South, PNC Center, 115 West Washington Street, Suite 1080, Indianapolis, IN 46204-3419
Tel: (317) 232-6887 Fax: (317) 234-2985
E-mail: michael.barnes@courts.in.gov

Michael P. Barnes
Judge

Date of Birth: 1947
Education: St Ambrose 1970 BA; Notre Dame 1973 JD
Began Service: May 2000
Appointed By: Governor Frank O'Bannon
Next Election: November 2022

Current Memberships: American Bar Association; Indiana Judges Association; Indiana State Bar Association

Staff
Career Law Clerk **Christina D. Arvin** . . . . (317) 232-6887
E-mail: chris.arvin@courts.in.gov
Education: Purdue 1993 BS; Indiana 1997 JD
Career Law Clerk **Ann C. Coriden** . . . . (317) 232-6887
E-mail: ann.coriden@courts.in.gov
Education: Ohio 1998 BA; Toledo 2001 JD
Career Law Clerk **Glenn R. Johnson** . . . . (317) 232-6887
E-mail: glenn.johnson@courts.in.gov
Education: Butler 1993 BS; Indiana 1999 JD
Secretary **Lynn R. Aldridge** . . . . (317) 232-6887
E-mail: lynn.aldridge@courts.in.gov

Indiana Court of Appeals, Fourth District
200 West Washington Street, Indianapolis, IN 46204
Tel: (317) 232-6906 Fax: (317) 233-4627

Number of Judgeships: 3

The Court of Appeals, Fourth District hears every fourth case from the Courts of Appeals for the First, Second and Third Districts.

Chambers of Presiding Judge Rudolph Pyle III
200 West Washington Street, Indianapolis, IN 46204-3466
Tel: (317) 232-6906 Fax: (317) 233-4627
E-mail: rudolph.pyle@courts.in.gov

Rudolph Pyle III
Presiding Judge

Education: Anderson U 1992 BA; William & Mary 1994 MPP; Indiana 2000 JD
Began Service: August 27, 2012

Staff
Law Clerk **Eileen Euzen** . . . . (317) 232-6900
E-mail: eileen.euzen@courts.in.gov
Education: Indiana 1997 JD
Law Clerk **Russell Hughes** . . . . (317) 232-6900
Law Clerk **Terrance Tharpe** . . . . (317) 232-6900
E-mail: terrance.tharpe@courts.in.gov

Chambers of Judge Patricia A. Riley
411 State House, 200 West Washington Street, Indianapolis, IN 46204
Tel: (317) 232-6902 Fax: (317) 233-3092
E-mail: priley@courts.state.in.us

Patricia A. Riley
Judge

Date of Birth: 1949
Education: Indiana 1971 BA, 1974 JD
Began Service: January 1, 1994
Appointed By: Governor Evan Bayh
Next Election: November 2016
Election Type: Retention Election
Term Expires: December 31, 2016
Political Affiliation: Democrat

Staff
Law Clerk **Katherine Haire** . . . . (317) 233-0380
Law Clerk **Katherine Karanja** . . . . (317) 233-0380
Career Law Clerk **Inge Porter** . . . . (317) 233-3660
Began Service: September 2003
E-mail: iporter@courts.state.in.us
Education: Indiana 2003 JD
Office Administrator **Shari Carr** . . . . (317) 232-6902
E-mail: scarr@courts.state.in.us

Chambers of Judge Melissa May
200 West Washington Street, Indianapolis, IN 46204-3419
Tel: (317) 232-6907 Fax: (317) 233-3084
E-mail: mmay@courts.state.in.us

Melissa May
Judge

Date of Birth: 1957
Education: Indiana (South Bend) 1980 BS; Indiana 1984 JD
Began Service: April 9, 1998
Appointed By: Governor Frank O'Bannon
Next Election: November 2020
Election Type: Retention Election
Term Expires: December 2020

Current Memberships: American Bar Foundation; Commission for Continuing Legal Education, Indiana Supreme Court; American Bar Association; The American Inns of Court; Evansville Bar Association; Indiana Judges Association; Indiana State Bar Association; Indiana Bar Foundation, Indiana State Bar Association; Indianapolis Bar Association; National Association of Women Judges

Staff
Law Clerk **Jessica Ballard-Barnett** . . . . (317) 233-0377
Term Expires: August 2016
E-mail: jessica.ballard@courts.in.gov
Education: Indiana (Indianapolis) 2010 JD
Career Law Clerk **Jennifer D. Warriner** . . . . (317) 233-3659
E-mail: jennifer.warriner@courts.in.gov
Education: Indiana 2000 JD
Senior Law Clerk **Tom Newby** . . . . (317) 233-0378
E-mail: tnewby@courts.state.in.us
Education: Indiana 1987 JD
Administrative Assistant **Kari Byrd** . . . . (317) 232-6907
E-mail: kari.byrd@courts.in.gov

Indiana Court of Appeals, Fifth District
200 West Washington Street, Indianapolis, IN 46204
Tel: (317) 232-6906 Fax: (317) 233-4627

Number of Judgeships: 3

The Court of Appeals, Fifth District hears every fifth case from the Courts of Appeals for the First, Second and Third Districts.

Chambers of Chief Judge Nancy H. Vaidik
200 West Washington Street, Indianapolis, IN 46204-4784
Tel: (317) 234-0883 Fax: (317) 233-4627
E-mail: nancy.vaidik@courts.in.gov

Nancy H. Vaidik
Chief Judge

Date of Birth: 1955
Education: Valparaiso 1980 JD
Began Service: February 7, 2000
Appointed By: Governor Frank O'Bannon
Next Election: November 2022
Term Expires: January 2019

Staff
Law Clerk **Lauren Barth** .... (317) 234-0885
Began Service: 2011
E-mail: lauren.barth@courts.in.gov
Education: Hofstra 2011 JD
Law Clerk **Kristy Murphy** .... (317) 234-0884
Education: Indiana JD
Career Law Clerk **Amanda Bunton** .... (317) 234-0883
E-mail: amanda.bunton@courts.in.gov
Education: Indiana 2000
Administrative Assistant **Amy Holton** .... (317) 234-0883

Chambers of Judge Margret G. Robb
115 West Washington Street, Suite 1270 South Tower,
Indianapolis, IN 46204
Tel: (317) 233-3668
E-mail: margret.robb@courts.state.in.us

Margret G. Robb
Judge

Date of Birth: 1948
Education: Purdue 1970 BS, 1972 MS; Indiana 1978 JD
Began Service: January 1, 2011

Current Memberships: American Bar Foundation; American Bar Association; The American Law Institute; Indiana State Bar Association; Indiana Bar Foundation, Indiana State Bar Association; Indianapolis Bar Association; National Association of Women Judges; Tippecanoe County Bar Association

Staff
Law Clerk **Jonathon Snider** .... (317) 233-3668
Began Service: August 2013
Term Expires: August 2016
E-mail: jonathon.snider@courts.in.gov
Law Clerk **Jennifer Van Dame** .... (317) 233-3668
Began Service: March 2015
Term Expires: August 2016
Senior Law Clerk **Tina Cooper** .... (317) 233-3668
E-mail: tcooper@courts.in.gov
Education: Indiana 1995 JD
Administrative Assistant **Yana Dess** .... (317) 233-3668
E-mail: ydess@courts.in.gov

Chambers of Judge Elaine B. Brown
200 West Washington Street, Indianapolis, IN 46204-3466
Tel: (317) 232-6906 Fax: (317) 233-4627
E-mail: ebrown@courts.state.in.us

Elaine B. Brown
Judge

Education: Indiana 1976, 1982 JD
Began Service: May 5, 2008
Appointed By: Governor Mitch Daniels
Next Election: November 2020

Government: Founder, Dubois County Drug Court, Dubois Superior Court (2005); Chair, Dubois County Substance Abuse Council (2006-2007); Board Member, Dubois County Community Corrections Advisory Board; Founder, Dubois Superior Court Alcohol and Drug Program, Dubois Superior Court (2007)

Judicial: Judge, Dubois Superior Court (1987-1998); Judge, Dubois Superior Court (2005-2008); Special Judge, Indiana Supreme Court (2007)

Legal Practice: Attorney, Fine & Hatfield (1999-2002)

Profession: Attorney, Private Practice (2002-2004)

Indiana Tax Court
115 West Washington Street, 960 South, Indianapolis, IN 46204-2241
Tel: (317) 232-4694 Fax: (317) 232-0644
Internet: www.courts.in.gov/tax

Number of Judgeships: 1

Areas Covered: Counties of Allen, Jefferson, Lake, Marion, St. Joseph, Vigo and Vanderburgh

Established effective July 1, 1986, the Indiana Tax Court has exclusive jurisdiction over any case that arises under the Indiana tax laws. The Court also has exclusive jurisdiction over cases that are initial appeals of final determinations made by the Indiana Department of State Revenue or the Indiana Board of Tax Review. In addition, the Court has jurisdiction over certain appeals from the Department of Local Government Finance. The Court also hears appeals of inheritance tax determinations from the courts of probate jurisdiction. Decisions of the Tax Court may be appealed directly to the Indiana Supreme Court.

Court Staff
Court Administrator **Karyn D. Graves** .... (317) 232-4694
E-mail: karyn.graves@courts.in.gov
Education: Indiana 1988 BS
Clerk of the Supreme and Appellate Courts
Kevin S. Smith .... (317) 232-1930
E-mail: kevin.smith@courts.in.gov Fax: (317) 232-8365

Chambers of Presiding Judge Martha Blood Wentworth
115 West Washington Street, Room 960 South,
Indianapolis, IN 46204-2241
Tel: (317) 232-4694 Fax: (317) 232-0644
E-mail: martha.wentworth@courts.in.gov

Martha Blood Wentworth
Presiding Judge

Education: Bennett; Indiana, JD
Began Service: January 17, 2011
Appointed By: Governor Mitch Daniels
Next Election: November 4, 2020
Term Expires: November 4, 2020

Staff
Law Clerk **Brandee A. Chanin** .... (317) 232-4694
E-mail: brandee.chanin@courts.in.gov
Education: Indiana 2006 JD
Law Clerk **Robert Drew** .... (317) 232-4694
Education: Indiana 1986 JD

Chambers of Presiding Judge Martha Blood Wentworth *continued*

Law Clerk **John Christopher Frankel** . . . . (317) 232-4694
Staff Attorney **Erica E. Aker** . . . . (317) 232-4694
E-mail: erica.aker@courts.in.gov
Education: Valparaiso 1993 JD

Iowa

Iowa Office of State Court Administration

Iowa Judicial Building, 1111 East Court Avenue, Des Moines, IA 50319
Tel: (515) 281-5241 Fax: (515) 242-0014
Internet: www.iowacourts.gov

Staff

State Court Administrator **David K. Boyd** .... (515) 281-5241
E-mail: david.boyd@iowacourts.gov Fax: (515) 242-0014
Education: Arizona MA

Deputy State Court Administrator **John A. Goerdt** ...... (515) 242-0193
E-mail: john.goerdt@iowacourts.gov Fax: (515) 242-0014
Education: Syracuse JD

Clerk of the Courts **Donna Humphal** .... (515) 281-5911
Fax: (515) 242-6164

Deputy Clerk of the Supreme Court
Christine A. Mayberry .... (515) 281-5911
E-mail: christine.mayberry@iowacourts.gov Fax: (515) 242-6164
Education: Iowa JD

Director, Finance and Personnel **Peggy J. Sullivan** ...... (515) 242-0171
E-mail: peggy.sullivan@iowacourts.gov Fax: (515) 242-0197
Education: Central Missouri State BS

Director, Human Resources **(Vacant)** .... (515) 242-0175
Fax: (515) 242-0197

Director, Information Systems and Technology
Ken Bosier .... (515) 281-9765
E-mail: ken.bosier@iowacourts.gov Fax: (515) 281-9764

Director, Judicial Branch Education **Jennifer Juhler** ..... (515) 242-0190
E-mail: jennifer.juhler@iowacourts.gov Fax: (515) 281-9605

Iowa Supreme Court

Iowa Judicial Building, 1111 East Court Avenue, Des Moines, IA 50319
Tel: (515) 281-5174 Fax: (515) 281-3043
Internet: www.iowacourts.gov

Number of Judgeships: 7

The Supreme Court consists of a chief justice and six associate justices who are appointed by the Governor from a list of nominees selected by a judicial nominating commission. Justices face a retention vote for an eight-year term in the first general election following at least one year of service. The chief justice is elected by peer vote for an eight-year term. Retirement is mandatory at age seventy-two; however, retired justices may serve as senior judges with temporary assignments until age seventy-eight. The Supreme Court has general appellate jurisdiction in civil and criminal cases including questions concerning the constitutionality of a legislative or executive act. The Court hears or transfers to the Iowa Court of Appeals all cases appealed from the Iowa District Court, except those concerning real estate interests when the amount involves less than $5000 (or small claims actions when the amount in controversy is $5000 or less) unless the trial judges certifies that the cause is one in which appeals should be allowed. The Court has original jurisdiction in such cases as reapportionment, bar discipline, and the issuance of temporary injunctions. The Court also exercises administrative control and supervisory control over the trial courts.

The Iowa Supreme Court sits in Des Moines.

Court Staff

Clerk of the Supreme Court **Donna Humphal** .... (515) 281-5911
Fax: (515) 242-6164

Deputy Clerk of the Supreme Court
Christine A. Mayberry .... (515) 281-5911
E-mail: Christine.Mayberry@iowacourts.gov Fax: (515) 242-6164

Counsel to the Chief Justice **Molly Kottmeyer**.......... (515) 281-8205
E-mail: molly.kottmeyer@iowacourts.gov Fax: (515) 281-3043
Education: Marquette 1993 BA; Missouri 2004 JD

Director, Facilities **Jim Evans** .... (515) 281-6903
E-mail: jim.evans@iowacourts.gov

Director, Finance and Personnel **Peggy J. Sullivan** ...... (515) 242-0171
E-mail: Peggy.Sullivan@iowacourts.gov Fax: (515) 242-0197

Iowa Supreme Court *continued*

Director, Human Resources **(Vacant)** .... (515) 242-0175
Fax: (515) 242-0197

Director, ICIS **Ken Bosier** .... (515) 281-9765
E-mail: ken.bosier@iowacourts.gov Fax: (515) 281-9764

Director, Judicial Branch Education **Jennifer Juhler** ..... (515) 242-0190
E-mail: jennifer.juhler@iowacourts.gov Fax: (515) 281-9605

Chambers of Chief Justice Mark Cady

Iowa Judicial Building, 1111 East Court Avenue, Des Moines, IA 50319
P.O. Box 507, Fort Dodge, IA 50501
Tel: (515) 281-5911
E-mail: mark.cady@iowacourts.gov

Mark S. Cady
Chief Justice

Date of Birth: 1953
Education: Drake 1975 BS, 1978 JD
Began Service: 1988
Appointed By: Governor Terry E. Branstad
Next Election: December 31, 2016
Election Type: Retention Election
Term Expires: December 31, 2016

Current Memberships: Iowa State Bar Association

Staff

Law Clerk **Lauren Van Waardhuizen** .... (515) 281-3952
Began Service: September 2014
Term Expires: September 2016

Administrative Assistant **Tamara J. Barrett** .... (515) 281-3952
E-mail: tamara.barrett@iowacourts.gov

Chambers of Associate Justice David S. Wiggins

1111 East Court Avenue, Des Moines, IA 50319
Tel: (515) 281-5175
E-mail: david.wiggins@iowacourts.gov

David S. Wiggins
Associate Justice

Date of Birth: October 19, 1951
Education: Illinois (Chicago) 1973 BA; Drake 1976 JD
Began Service: October 7, 2003
Appointed By: Governor Thomas J. Vilsack
Term Expires: December 31, 2020

Legal Practice: Associate, Williams, Hart, Lavorato & Kirtley; Partner, Williams, Hart, Lavorato & Kirtley (1979)

Current Memberships: The C. Edwin Moore American Inn of Court, The American Inns of Court; Iowa State Bar Association

Staff

Law Clerk **Kristy Rogers** .... (515) 281-5175
Began Service: August 2015
Term Expires: August 2016
E-mail: kristy.rogers@iowacourts.gov

Legal Assistant **Julie Cosner** .... (515) 281-5175
E-mail: julie.cosner@iowacourts.gov

Chambers of Associate Justice Daryl L. Hecht
Iowa Judicial Building, 1111 East Court Avenue, Des Moines, IA 50319
Tel: (712) 233-8980 Fax: (712) 233-8981
E-mail: daryl.hecht@iowacourts.gov

Daryl L. Hecht
Associate Justice

Date of Birth: 1952
Education: South Dakota 1977 JD; Virginia 2004 LLM
Began Service: September 2006
Appointed By: Governor Thomas J. Vilsack
Next Election: November 4, 2016
Election Type: Retention Election
Term Expires: December 31, 2016

Judicial: Judge, Iowa Court of Appeals (1999-2006)

Legal Practice: Crary, Huff, Inkster, Hecht & Sheehan, PC (1977-1999)

Current Memberships: Iowa State Bar Association

Staff
Law Clerk **David Ransch** .... (515) 281-5175
Began Service: April 2015
E-mail: david.ransch@iowacourts.gov

Chambers of Associate Justice Brent R. Appel
Iowa Judicial Branch Building, 1111 East Court Avenue, Des Moines, IA 50319
Tel: (515) 281-5911
E-mail: brent.appel@iowacourts.gov

Brent R. Appel
Associate Justice

Education: Stanford 1973; Boalt Hall 1977 JD
Began Service: 2006
Next Election: November 4, 2016
Election Type: Retention Election
Term Expires: December 31, 2016

Government: First Assistant and Deputy Attorney General, State of Iowa

Legal Practice: Attorney, Private Practice

Staff
Law Clerk **Rebecca Barloon** .... (515) 281-5175
Began Service: September 2014
Term Expires: September 2016
E-mail: daniel.zagoren@iowacourts.gov
Judicial Assistant **Julie Cosner** .... (515) 281-5175
E-mail: julie.cosner@iowacourts.gov

Chambers of Associate Justice Thomas Waterman
1111 East Court Avenue, Des Moines, IA 50319
Tel: (515) 281-3952
E-mail: thomas.waterman@iowacourts.gov

Thomas D. Waterman
Associate Justice

Education: Dartmouth 1981 BA; Iowa 1984 JD
Began Service: March 7, 2011
Appointed By: Governor Terry E. Branstad
Term Expires: December 31, 2020

Current Memberships: The American Law Institute

Staff
Law Clerk **Stephanie Koltookian** .... (515) 281-3952
Term Expires: September 2016
E-mail: stephanie.koltookian@iowacourts.gov
Executive Assistant **Tamara J. Barrett** .... (515) 281-3952
E-mail: tamara.barrett@iowacourts.gov

Chambers of Associate Justice Edward M. Mansfield
1111 East Court Avenue, Des Moines, IA 50319
Tel: (515) 281-5174 Fax: (515) 281-3043
E-mail: edward.mansfield@iowacourts.gov

Edward M. Mansfield
Associate Justice

Education: Harvard 1978 AB; Yale 1982 JD
Began Service: March 8, 2011
Appointed By: Governor Terry E. Branstad
Term Expires: December 31, 2020

Staff
Law Clerk **Kyndra Lunquist** .... (515) 281-3952
E-mail: kyndra.lunquist@iowacourts.gov
Secretary **Kathy Higginbotham** .... (515) 281-3952
E-mail: kathy.higginbotham@iowacourts.gov

Chambers of Associate Justice Bruce Zager
1111 East Court Avenue, Des Moines, IA 50319
Tel: (515) 281-5174 Fax: (515) 281-3043
E-mail: bruce.zager@iowacourts.gov

Bruce Zager
Associate Justice

Education: Iowa 1975 BBA; Loyola U (Chicago) 1977 MSIR; Drake 1980 JD
Began Service: March 9, 2011
Appointed By: Governor Terry E. Branstad
Term Expires: December 31, 2020

Staff
Law Clerk **Meredith Lamberti** .... (515) 281-5174
E-mail: meredith_lamberti@iowacourts.gov
Secretary **Kathy Higginbotham** .... (515) 281-5174
E-mail: kathy.higginbotham@iowacourts.gov

Iowa Court of Appeals
Iowa Judicial Building, 1111 East Court Avenue, Des Moines, IA 50319
Tel: (515) 281-5221 Fax: (515) 281-8371
Internet: www.iowacourts.gov

Number of Judgeships: 9

The Court of Appeals consists of a chief judge and eight judges who are appointed by the Governor from a list of nominees selected by a judicial nomination commission. Judges face a retention vote for a six-year term in the first general election after at least one year of service. The chief judge is elected by peer vote for a two-year term. Retirement is mandatory at age seventy-two; however, retired judges may serve as senior judges with temporary assignments until age eighty. The Court of Appeals has appellate jurisdiction over all civil and criminal actions, post-conviction remedy proceedings, small claims actions, writs, orders and other proceedings. The Court hears only those cases which are transferred to it by the Iowa Supreme Court.

The Iowa Court of Appeals sits in Des Moines.

Court Staff
Clerk of the Courts **Donna Humpal** .... (515) 281-5911
E-mail: donna.humpal@iowacourts.gov
Staff Attorney **Kimberly Cook** .... (515) 725-8077
E-mail: kimberly.cook@iowacourts.gov
Education: Iowa 1984 JD
Staff Attorney **Lara Geer Farley** .... (515) 242-6105
E-mail: lara.farley@iowacourts.gov
Staff Attorney **Jennifer James** .... (515) 281-6452
E-mail: jennifer.james@iowacourts.gov
Staff Attorney **Sandee Lyons** .... (515) 725-8052
E-mail: sandee.lyons@iowacourts.gov

(continued on next page)

STATE COURTS—IOWA

Iowa Court of Appeals *continued*

Staff Attorney **Daniel R. Marvin** . . . . (515) 281-8052
E-mail: Daniel.Marvin@iowacourts.gov
Education: Iowa State 1972 BS; Western Sem 1977 MDiv, 1979 ThM; Iowa 1993 JD

Staff Attorney **Ann Meyer** . . . . (515) 281-6451
E-mail: ann.meyer@iowacourts.gov
Education: Drake 1999 JD

Staff Attorney **Carla Scholten** . . . . (515) 281-7287
E-mail: carla_scholten@iowacourts.gov

Secretary **Barbara Harris** . . . . (515) 281-8277

Secretary **Molly Rawls** . . . . (515) 281-5221
E-mail: molly.rawls@iowacourts.gov

Secretary **Anne Reser** . . . . (515) 281-5223
E-mail: anne.reser@iowacourts.gov

Chambers of Chief Judge David Danilson

1111 East Court Avenue, Des Moines, IA 50319
Tel: (515) 281-5221 Fax: (515) 281-8371
E-mail: david.danilson@iowacourts.gov

David Danilson
Chief Judge

Education: Iowa State 1976 BA; Creighton 1979 JD
Began Service: December 2009
Next Election: November 2016
Election Type: Retention Election

Current Memberships: Iowa Judges Association; Iowa State Bar Association

Staff
Law Clerk **Cassie Bonefas** . . . . (515) 281-8053
E-mail: cassie.bonefas@iowacourts.gov

Chambers of Judge Gayle Nelson Vogel

Iowa Judicial Building, 1111 East Court Avenue, Des Moines, IA 50319
Tel: (515) 281-5221 Fax: (515) 281-8371
E-mail: gayle.vogel@iowacourts.gov

Gayle Nelson Vogel
Judge

Date of Birth: 1949
Education: Rockford 1971 BA; Drake 1983 JD
Began Service: May 23, 1996
Appointed By: Governor Terry E. Branstad
Next Election: November 2016
Election Type: Retention Election

Legal Practice: Johnson, Lane & Vogel (1983-1996)

Current Memberships: The C. Edwin Moore American Inn of Court, The American Inns of Court; Iowa Judges Association; Iowa State Bar Association

Staff
Law Clerk **Jennifer Lisankis** . . . . (515) 281-7710
E-mail: jennifer.lisankis@iowacourts.gov

Chambers of Judge Anuradha Vaitheswaran

Iowa Judicial Building, 1111 East Court Avenue, Des Moines, IA 50319
Tel: (515) 281-5221 Fax: (515) 281-8371
E-mail: anuradha.vaitheswaran@iowacourts.gov

Anuradha Vaitheswaran
Judge

Date of Birth: 1959
Education: Grinnell 1980 BA; Iowa 1984 JD
Began Service: September 17, 1999
Appointed By: Governor Thomas J. Vilsack
Next Election: November 2018
Election Type: Retention Election
Term Expires: December 2018

Clerkships: Law Clerk The Honorable Charles R. Wolle, Iowa Supreme Court

Legal Practice: Attorney, Legal Services Corporation

Current Memberships: The C. Edwin Moore American Inn of Court, The American Inns of Court; Iowa State Bar Association; Polk County Bar Association; Polk County Women's Association

Staff
Law Clerk **Timothy Hau** . . . . (515) 281-7218
E-mail: timothy.hau@iowacourts.gov

Chambers of Judge Amanda Potterfield

Iowa Judicial Building, 1111 East Court Avenue, Des Moines, IA 50319
Tel: (515) 281-5221 Fax: (515) 281-8371
E-mail: amanda.potterfield@iowacourts.gov

Amanda Potterfield
Judge

Education: Hollins Col 1969; George Washington 1974 JD
Began Service: 2008
Appointed By: Governor Chester J. Culver
Next Election: November 2016
Election Type: Retention Election

Government: Attorney, Georgia Criminal Justice Council; Attorney, Office of the County Attorney, County of Linn, Iowa

Nonprofit: Attorney, Prisoners' Legal Services of New York

Profession: Private Practice (1989-2001)

Staff
Law Clerk **David Yoshimura** . . . . (515) 281-8980
Began Service: June 2014
E-mail: david.yoshimura@iowacourts.gov

Chambers of Judge Richard H. Doyle

Iowa Judicial Building, 1111 East Court Avenue, Des Moines, IA 50319
Tel: (515) 281-5221
E-mail: richard.doyle@iowacourts.gov

Richard H. Doyle
Judge

Education: Drake 1971 BA, 1976 JD
Began Service: 2008
Appointed By: Governor Thomas J. Vilsack
Next Election: November 2016
Election Type: Retention Election
Term Expires: December 2016

Government: Assistant Attorney General, Criminal Appeals Division, Office of the Attorney General, State of Iowa (1976-1977)

Legal Practice: Attorney, Lawyer & Jackson (1977-1979); Attorney, Verne Lawyer & Associates (1979-1993); Attorney, Reavely, Shinkle, Bauer, Scism, Reavely & Doyle (1993-1994)

Chambers of Judge Richard H. Doyle *continued*

Current Memberships: American Bar Association; Iowa Academy of Trial Lawyers; Iowa State Bar Association; Iowa Trial Lawyers Association; Polk County Bar Association

Staff
Law Clerk **Kerry Carskadon** . . . . (515) 242-6880
Began Service: 2008
E-mail: kerry.carskadon@iowacourts.gov

Chambers of Judge Mary E. Tabor
1111 East Court Avenue, Des Moines, IA 50319
Tel: (515) 281-5221
E-mail: mary.tabor@iowacourts.gov

Mary E. Tabor
Judge

Education: Iowa 1985 BA, 1991 JD
Began Service: June 9, 2010
Next Election: November 2018
Election Type: Retention Election

Current Memberships: The Blackstone American Inn of Court, The American Inns of Court; Iowa State Bar Association

Staff
Law Clerk **Aaron Lindebak** . . . . (515) 281-7189
E-mail: aaron.lindebak@iowacourts.gov

Chambers of Judge Michael R. Mullins
1111 East Court Avenue, Des Moines, IA 50319
Tel: (515) 281-5221 Fax: (515) 281-8371
E-mail: michael.mullins@iowacourts.gov

Michael R. Mullins
Judge

Education: Southwest Baptist 1974; Iowa 1976 MSW; Drake 1982 JD
Began Service: June 2011
Appointed By: Governor Terry E. Branstad
Next Election: November 2018
Election Type: Retention Election

Staff
Law Clerk **Kelcy Whitaker** . . . . (515) 281-6227
E-mail: kelcy.whitaker@iowacourts.gov

Chambers of Judge Thomas N. Bower
Iowa Judicial Building, 1111 East Court Avenue, Des Moines, IA 50319
Tel: (515) 281-5221 Fax: (581) 281-8371
E-mail: thomas.bower@iowacourts.gov

Thomas N. Bower
Judge

Education: Illinois State 1984 BA; Drake 1987 JD
Began Service: January 18, 2012
Appointed By: Governor Terry E. Branstad
Next Election: November 2020
Election Type: Retention Election

Current Memberships: Black Hawk County Bar Association

Staff
Law Clerk **Jeffrey Cook** . . . . (515) 281-6227
E-mail: jeffrey.cook@iowacourts.gov

Chambers of Judge Christopher McDonald
1111 East Court Avenue, Des Moines, IA 50319
Tel: (515) 281-5221
E-mail: christopher.mcdonald@iowacourts.gov

Christopher McDonald
Judge

Education: Grand View 1997 BA; Iowa 2001 JD
Began Service: October 2013
Appointed By: Governor Terry E. Branstad
Next Election: November 2020
Election Type: Retention Election

Staff
Law Clerk **Melissa Knight** . . . . (515) 725-8038
E-mail: melissa.knight@iowacourts.gov

Kansas

Office of the Judicial Administration of Kansas

Kansas Judicial Center, 301 SW Tenth Avenue, Topeka, KS 66612
Tel: (785) 296-2256 Fax: (785) 296-7076
Internet: www.kscourts.org

Staff

Judicial Administrator **Nancy Maydew Dixon** .... (785) 296-4873
E-mail: dixonn@kscourts.org
Education: Kansas 1979 JD
Disciplinary Administrator **Stanton A. Hazlett** .... (785) 296-2486
E-mail: shazlett@kscourts.org Fax: (785) 296-6049
Reporter of Decisions/Court Reporter **Richard D. Ross** ... (785) 296-3214
E-mail: rossr@kscourts.org Fax: (785) 368-6573
Education: Washburn 1974 JD
Assistant Librarian **Claire King** .... (785) 296-3257
E-mail: kingc@kscourts.org Fax: (785) 296-1863
Director of Judicial Education **Denise Kilwein** .... (785) 296-4894
E-mail: kilweind@kscourts.org
Director, Personnel **Patricia Henshall** .... (785) 296-2877
E-mail: henshallp@kscourts.org Fax: (785) 368-6573
Budget and Fiscal Officer **Stephanie Bunten** .... (785) 296-4897
E-mail: buntens@kscourts.org
Education-Information Officer **Lisa Taylor** .... (785) 296-4872
Law Librarian **(Vacant)** .... (785) 296-3257
Fax: (785) 296-1863

Kansas Supreme Court

374 Kansas Judicial Center, 301 SW Tenth Avenue,
Topeka, KS 66612-1507
Tel: (785) 296-3229 Fax: (785) 296-7076
Internet: www.kscourts.org
Internet: http://www.kscourts.org/kansas-courts/supreme-court/justice-bios/default.asp

Number of Judgeships: 7

The Supreme Court consists of a chief justice and six justices who are appointed by the Governor from nominations submitted by a Supreme Court nominating commission. Newly-appointed justices serve initial one-year terms and then face a retention vote for a six-year term in the next general election. The justice with the most seniority serves as chief justice. Retirement is mandatory at age seventy or at the end of the current term; however, retired justices may be appointed by the Supreme Court to serve temporary assignments. The Supreme Court has original jurisdiction in proceedings in quo warranto, mandamus, and habeas corpus. Cases involving the death penalty and off-grid are appealed directly to the Supreme Court. The Court may also review decisions of the Kansas Court of Appeals.

The Kansas Supreme Court sits in Topeka.

Court Staff

Clerk of the Appellate Courts **Heather L. Smith** .... (785) 296-3229
Chief Deputy Clerk **Jason P. Oldham** .... (785) 296-3229
E-mail: oldhamj@kscourts.org
Education: Washburn 1993 JD
Law Librarian **(Vacant)** .... (785) 296-3257
Fax: (785) 296-1863
Director of Judicial Education **Denise Kilwein** .... (785) 296-4894
E-mail: kilweind@kscourts.org Fax: (785) 296-7076
Reporter of Decisions **Richard D. Ross** .... (785) 296-2602
E-mail: rossr@kscourts.org

Chambers of Chief Justice Lawton R. Nuss

389 Kansas Judicial Center, 301 SW Tenth Avenue,
Topeka, KS 66612-1507
Tel: (785) 296-4898 Fax: (785) 296-0534
E-mail: nussl@kscourts.org

Lawton R. Nuss
Chief Justice

Education: Kansas 1975 BA; Naval Acad 1977 BS; Kansas 1982 JD
Began Service: October 17, 2002
Appointed By: Governor Bill Graves
Next Election: November 2016
Term Expires: January 2017

Government: Federal Court Mediator (part-time) (1992-2002); Special Prosecutor, City of Salina, Kansas (1994-1996)

Legal Practice: Shareholder and Vice President, Clark, Mize & Linville, Chartered

Military Service: Second Lieutenant, U.S. Marine Corps

Staff

Law Clerk **Jennifer Marie Cocking** .... (785) 296-4898
Began Service: August 2013
Term Expires: August 2016
E-mail: cockingj@kscourts.org
Education: Washburn JD
Legal Secretary **Sue Macafee** .... (785) 296-4898

Chambers of Justice Marla J. Luckert

Kansas Judicial Center, 301 SW Tenth Avenue, Room 315,
Topeka, KS 66612-1507
Tel: (785) 296-4900 Fax: (785) 291-3274
E-mail: luckertm@kscourts.org

Marla J. Luckert
Justice

Date of Birth: July 20, 1955
Education: Washburn 1977 BA, 1980 JD
Began Service: January 13, 2003
Appointed By: Governor Bill Graves
Next Election: November 2016
Term Expires: January 2017

Academic: Adjunct Professor, Washburn University of Topeka

Judicial: Judge, Kansas District Court, Third Judicial District Court (1992-2003)

Legal Practice: Goodell, Stratton, Edmonds, and Palmer

Current Memberships: American Bar Association; American Judges Association; Kansas Bar Association; National Association of Women Judges; National Center for State Courts

Staff

Law Clerk **Joshua Marrone** .... (785) 296-4900
Career Law Clerk **Stacy Edwards** .... (785) 296-4900
Secretary **Sally Brown** .... (785) 296-4900

Chambers of Justice Carol A. Beier

301 SW Tenth Avenue, Topeka, KS 66612-1507
Tel: (785) 296-5412 Fax: (785) 291-3274
E-mail: beierc@kscourts.org

Carol A. Beier
Justice

Date of Birth: September 27, 1958
Education: Kansas 1981 BS, 1985 JD; Virginia 2004 LLM
Began Service: 2003
Appointed By: Governor Kathleen Sebelius
Next Election: November 2016
Term Expires: January 2016

Current Memberships: American Bar Association; The Bar Association of the District of Columbia; The District of Columbia Bar; Kansas Bar Association; Kansas Women Attorneys Association; National Association of Women Judges; Topeka Bar Association; Wichita Bar Association; Wichita Women Attorneys Association; Women Attorneys Association of Topeka

Staff
Law Clerk **Robert Fitzgerald** . . . . (785) 296-5412
Began Service: August 2012
Term Expires: August 2016
E-mail: fitzgeraldr@kscourts.org
Law Clerk **Betsey Lasister** . . . . (785) 296-5412
Began Service: September 2015
Term Expires: September 2017
Judicial Executive Assistant **Julie A. Meyer** . . . . . . (785) 296-5412
E-mail: meyerj@kscourts.org

Chambers of Justice Eric S. Rosen

301 SW Tenth Avenue, Room 314, Topeka, KS 66612
Tel: (785) 296-6290
E-mail: rosene@kscourts.org

Eric S. Rosen
Justice

Date of Birth: May 25, 1953
Education: Washburn 1984 JD; Kansas BS, MS
Began Service: November 2005
Appointed By: Governor Kathleen Sebelius
Next Election: November 4, 2020
Election Type: Retention Election
Term Expires: December 31, 2020

Academic: Adjunct Professor, School of Law, Washburn University

Government: Assistant Public Defender, County of Shawnee, Kansas; Assistant District Attorney, County of Shawnee, Kansas; Associate General Counsel, Office of the Securities Commissioner, State of Kansas

Judicial: Judge, Thirteenth Judicial District, Kansas District Courts (1993-2005)

Legal Practice: Partner, Hein, Ebert and Rosen

Staff
Law Clerk **Matthew Vogelsberg** . . . . (785) 296-6290
E-mail: vogelsbergm@kscourts.org
Research Attorney/Career Law Clerk
Jonathan Paretsky . . . . (785) 296-6290
E-mail: paretskyj@kscourts.org
Education: Kansas 2002 JD
Judicial Assistant **Cheryl Karns** . . . . (785) 296-6290
E-mail: karnsc@kscourts.org

Chambers of Justice Lee Alan Johnson

301 SW Tenth Avenue, Room 388, Topeka, KS 66612
Tel: (785) 296-5407 Fax: (785) 291-3274
E-mail: johnsonl@kscourts.org

Lee Alan Johnson
Justice

Date of Birth: 1947
Education: Kansas 1969 BA; Washburn 1980 JD
Began Service: January 2007
Appointed By: Governor Kathleen Sebelius
Next Election: November 2020
Election Type: Retention Election
Term Expires: January 2021

Corporate: Insurance Agent (1972-1977)

Judicial: Judge, Kansas Court of Appeals

Legal Practice: Private Practice (1980-2001)

Current Memberships: Kansas Bar Association

Staff
Research Attorney **Ashley Jarmer** . . . . (785) 296-5407
Began Service: 2012
E-mail: jarmera@kscourts.org
Research Attorney **Penny Moylan** . . . . (785) 296-5407
Began Service: 2012 Fax: (785) 291-3274
E-mail: moylanp@kscourts.org
Reporter of Decisions **Richard D. Ross** . . . . (785) 296-2602
E-mail: rossr@kscourts.org
Judicial Executive Assistant **Brenda Smith** . . . . (785) 296-5407
E-mail: smithb@kscourts.org Fax: (785) 291-3274

Chambers of Justice William Daniel Biles

301 SW Tenth Avenue, Topeka, KS 66612
Tel: (785) 368-6212

William Daniel Biles
Justice

Date of Birth: August 12, 1952
Education: Kansas State 1974 BJ; Washburn 1978 JD
Began Service: March 6, 2009
Appointed By: Governor Kathleen Sebelius
Next Election: November 2016
Term Expires: January 2017

Current Memberships: Johnson County Bar Association; Kansas Association for Justice; Kansas Bar Association

Chambers of Justice Caleb Stegall

301 SW Tenth Avenue, Topeka, KS 66612
Tel: (785) 296-3229

Caleb Stegall
Justice

Education: Geneva; Kansas 2000 JD
Began Service: 2014
Appointed By: Sam Brownback

Kansas Court of Appeals

Kansas Judicial Center, 301 SW Tenth Avenue, Topeka, KS 66612-1502
Tel: (785) 296-3229 Fax: (785) 296-7079
Internet: www.kscourts.org

Number of Judgeships: 13

The Court of Appeals consists of a chief judge and eleven judges who are appointed by the Governor from nominations submitted by a Supreme Court nominating commission. Judges serve four-year terms and then stand for retention in the next general election. The chief judge is selected by the Kansas Supreme Court. Judges may not stand for retention after age seventy-five; however, retired judges may serve by assignment of the Kansas Supreme Court. The Court of Appeals has statewide jurisdiction over appeals in civil and criminal matters arising in the Kansas District Court, except where the Kansas Supreme Court has exclusive jurisdiction.

The Court of Appeals sits in panels of three at various sites throughout Kansas.

Court Staff

Clerk of the Appellate Courts **Heather L. Smith** . . . . (785) 296-3229
Fax: (785) 296-1028
Director of Judicial Education **Denise Kilwein** . . . . (785) 296-4894
E-mail: kilweind@kscourts.org Fax: (785) 296-7076
Law Librarian **(Vacant)** . . . . (785) 296-3257

STATE COURTS—KANSAS

Chambers of Chief Judge Thomas E. Malone

301 SW Tenth Avenue, Topeka, KS 66612
Tel: (785) 296-5364
E-mail: malonet@kscourts.org

Thomas E. Malone
Chief Judge

Date of Birth: December 29, 1953
Education: Kansas Newman 1976 BA; Washburn 1979 JD
Began Service: 2003
Next Election: November 2020
Election Type: Retention Election

Current Memberships: American Bar Association; Kansas Bar Association; Kansas Trial Lawyers Association; Wichita Bar Association

Staff
Research Attorney **Cali Selig** . . . . (785) 296-5364
Judicial Executive Assistant **Vicki Streit** . . . . (785) 296-5364
E-mail: streitv@kscourts.org

Chambers of Judge G. Joseph Pierron, Jr.

Kansas Judicial Center, 301 SW Tenth Avenue, Topeka, KS 66612
Tel: (785) 296-5408 Fax: (785) 296-7079
E-mail: pierronj@kscourts.org

G. Joseph Pierron, Jr.
Judge

Date of Birth: 1947
Education: Rockhurst Col 1968 AB; Kansas 1971 JD
Began Service: December 11, 1990
Appointed By: Governor Mike Hayden
Next Election: November 4, 2018
Election Type: Retention Election
Term Expires: 2018
Political Affiliation: Republican

Government: Assistant District Attorney, Office of the District Attorney, State of Kansas (1971-1982)

Judicial: Judge, Spring Hill Municipal Court (1972); Judge, Kansas District Court, 10th Judicial District (1982-1990)

Legal Practice: Private Practice (1971-1973)

Current Memberships: American Bar Association; Kansas Bar Association

Chambers of Judge G. Joseph Pierron, Jr. *continued*

Staff
Research Attorney **Douglas Shima** . . . . (785) 296-5408
Education: Washburn 1994 JD
Judicial Executive Assistant **Rebecca "Becky" Nioce** . . . . (785) 296-5408
E-mail: nioceb@kscourts.org

Chambers of Judge Henry W. Green, Jr.

Kansas Judicial Center, 301 SW Tenth Avenue, Topeka, KS 66612-1507
Tel: (785) 296-5409 Fax: (785) 296-7079
E-mail: greenh@kscourts.org

Henry W. Green, Jr.
Judge

Date of Birth: 1949
Education: Kansas State 1972 BA; Kansas 1975 JD
Began Service: June 1993
Appointed By: Governor Joan Finney
Term Expires: 2020

Academic: Instructor of Business Law (part-time), National College of Business, Shawnee Mission (1975-1977)

Government: Trustee, United States Panel of Bankruptcy Trustees for the District of Kansas (1979-1993)

Legal Practice: Private Practice (1975-1993)

Current Memberships: American Association for Justice; American Bar Association; Kansas Bar Association; Leavenworth County Bar Association

Staff
Research Attorney **(Vacant)** . . . . (785) 296-5409
Research Attorney **Holly Turk** . . . . (785) 296-5409
E-mail: turkh@kscourts.org
Judicial Executive Assistant
Guadalupe "Lupe" Martinez . . . . (785) 296-5409
E-mail: martinezl@kscourts.org

Chambers of Judge Stephen D. Hill

301 SW Tenth Avenue, Topeka, KS 66612
Tel: (785) 296-5410 Fax: (785) 296-7079
E-mail: hills@kscourts.org

Stephen D. Hill
Judge

Date of Birth: December 18, 1950
Education: Kansas 1972 BA; Washburn 1975 JD
Began Service: December 5, 2003
Appointed By: Governor Kathleen Sebelius
Next Election: November 2020
Election Type: Retention Election
Term Expires: 2020

Government: County Attorney, County of Linn, Kansas (1976-1981)

Judicial: Associate District Judge, Sixth Judicial District, Kansas District Courts (1981-1982); District Judge, Sixth Judicial District, Kansas District Courts; Administrative Judge, Sixth Judicial District, Kansas District Courts; Chief Judge, Sixth Judicial District, Kansas District Courts

Legal Practice: Attorney, Hill & Wisler (1975-1976)

Membership: Member, Kansas Judicial Initiative (1998); Member, Executive Committee, Kansas District Judges Association

Staff
Research Attorney **(Vacant)** . . . . (785) 296-5410
Research Attorney **Kevin Grant** . . . . (785) 296-5410
E-mail: grantk@kscourts.org
Judicial Executive Assistant **Lacey Phillips** . . . . (785) 296-5410
E-mail: phillipsl@kscourts.org

Chambers of Judge Patrick D. McAnany
301 SW Tenth Avenue, Topeka, KS 66612-1507
Tel: (785) 296-0571
E-mail: mcananyp@kscourts.org

Patrick D. McAnany
Judge

Date of Birth: November 18, 1943
Education: Rockhurst Col 1965 BA; Missouri (Kansas City) 1968 JD, 1971 LLM
Began Service: 2004
Appointed By: Governor Kathleen Sebelius
Next Election: November 2020

Academic: Business Law Professor, Rockhurst University

Corporate: Assistant Division Attorney, Office of the General Counsel, Mobil Oil Company

Judicial: Judge, Johnson County District Court (1995)

Legal Practice: Miller & O'Laughlin; McAnany, Van Cleave & Phillips

Staff
Research Attorney **Charisse M. Powell** .... (785) 296-0571
E-mail: powellc@kscourts.org
Education: Kansas State 1996 BA; Washburn 1998 JD
Judicial Executive Assistant **Karla Keys** .... (785) 296-0571
E-mail: keysk@kscourts.org

Chambers of Judge Michael B. Buser
301 SW Tenth Avenue, Room 278, Topeka, KS 66612
Tel: (785) 296-8183
E-mail: buserm@kscourts.org

Michael B. Buser
Judge

Education: Georgetown 1974 BA; Kansas 1977 JD
Began Service: January 2005
Appointed By: Governor Kathleen Sebelius
Next Election: November 2020
Election Type: Retention Election

Corporate: General Counsel, Union Pacific Railroad Company (1988-1991)

Government: Assistant District Attorney, County of Johnson, Kansas (1977-1988)

Legal Practice: Attorney, Shook, Hardy & Bacon L.L.P. (1991-2005)

Staff
Research Attorney **John Andra** .... (785) 296-8183
E-mail: andraj@kscourts.org
Education: Kansas 1998 JD
Judicial Executive Assistant **Ann Myers** .... (785) 296-8183
E-mail: myersa@kscourts.org

Chambers of Judge Steve Leben
301 SW Tenth Avenue, Room 278, Topeka, KS 66612
Tel: (785) 296-3807 Fax: (785) 296-7079
E-mail: lebens@kscourts.org

Steve Leben
Judge

Date of Birth: June 23, 1956
Education: Kansas 1978 BS, 1982 JD
Began Service: June 15, 2007
Appointed By: Governor Kathleen Sebelius
Next Election: November 4, 2018
Election Type: Retention Election
Term Expires: 2018

Judicial: District Judge, Tenth Judicial District (1993-2007)

Chambers of Judge Steve Leben *continued*

Legal Practice: Attorney, Stinson Morrison Hecker LLP (1982-1988); Attorney, Private Practice (1988-1993)

Membership: President, American Judges Association (2006-2007)

Staff
Research Attorney **Laura Rossi** .... (785) 296-3807
Judicial Executive Assistant **Justine Greve** .... (785) 296-3807

Chambers of Judge Melissa Taylor Standridge
Kansas Judicial Center, 301 SW Tenth Avenue, Room 277, Topeka, KS 66612
Tel: (785) 296-3025
E-mail: standridgem@kscourts.org

Melissa Taylor Standridge
Judge

Date of Birth: July 12, 1962
Education: Kansas 1984 BS; Missouri (Kansas City) 1993 JD
Began Service: February 29, 2008
Appointed By: Governor Kathleen Sebelius
Next Election: November 2020
Election Type: Retention Election

Clerkships: Law Clerk, Chambers of Magistrate Judge David J. Waxse, United States District Court for the District of Kansas

Current Memberships: Kansas Bar Association

Staff
Research Assistant **Kyle Malone** .... (785) 296-3025
Judicial Executive Assistant **Trish Heim** .... (785) 296-3025
E-mail: heimt@kscourts.org

Chambers of Judge G. Gordon Atcheson
301 SW Tenth Avenue, Topeka, KS 66612-1502
Tel: (785) 296-3229 Fax: (785) 296-7079
E-mail: atchesong@kscourts.org

G. Gordon Atcheson
Judge

Education: Michigan 1976 BA; Kansas 1981 JD
Began Service: September 10, 2010
Appointed By: Governor Mark Parkinson
Next Election: 2018

Staff
Staff Attorney **Whitney Novak** .... (785) 296-3229
Staff Attorney **James M. Gannon** .... (785) 296-3229
Education: Washburn JD
Judicial Assistant **Sandy Reigle** .... (785) 296-3229

Chambers of Judge Karen Arnold-Burger
301 SW Tenth Avenue, Topeka, KS 66612-1502
Tel: (785) 296-6184 Fax: (785) 296-7079
E-mail: arnold-burgerk@kscourts.org

Karen Arnold-Burger
Judge

Education: Kansas 1979, 1981 JD
Began Service: March 4, 2011
Next Election: 2018

Staff
Staff Attorney **Barbara Dye** .... (785) 296-6184
E-mail: dyeb@kscourts.org

Chambers of Judge David E. Bruns

301 SW Tenth Avenue, Topeka, KS 66612-1502
Tel: (785) 296-3229
E-mail: brunsd@kscourts.org

David E. Bruns
Judge

Education: Kansas 1981 BASecEd; Washburn 1984 JD
Began Service: June 3, 2011
Next Election: 2018

Chambers of Judge Anthony Powell

301 SW Tenth Avenue, Topeka, KS 66612
Tel: (785) 296-3229

Anthony Powell
Judge

Education: George Washington BA; Washburn JD
Began Service: 2013

Government: Intern (R-KS), Office of Senator Robert J. Dole, United States Senate; Legislative Director (R-MI, District 18), Office of Representative William S. Broomfield, United States House of Representatives; State Representative, Kansas House of Representatives

Chambers of Judge Kim R. Schroeder

301 SW Tenth Avenue, Topeka, KS 66612
Tel: (785) 296-3229

Kim R. Schroeder
Judge

Education: Washburn 1979 BA, 1982 JD
Began Service: February 15, 2013
Next Election: November 2020
Election Type: Retention Election

Chambers of Judge Kathryn Gardner

301 SW Tenth Avenue, Topeka, KS 66612
Tel: (785) 296-3229

Kathryn Gardner
Judge

Began Service: May 8, 2015
Appointed By: Sam Brownback

Kentucky

Kentucky Administrative Office of the Courts

1001 Vandalay Drive, Frankfort, KY 40601
Tel: (502) 573-2350 Fax: (502) 695-1759

Staff

Director **Laurie K. Dudgeon** . . . . . (502) 573-2350
E-mail: lauriedudgeon@kycourts.net Fax: (502) 782-8707
Education: Kentucky 1994 JD

Deputy Director **Lisa Broaddus** . . . . . (502) 573-2350
E-mail: lisabroaddus@kycourts.net

Administrative Services and Operations General Manager **Leslie Brown** . . . . . (502) 573-2350
E-mail: lesliebrown@kycourts.net

Executive Officer, Department of Statewide Services **Connie Payne** . . . . . (502) 573-2350
E-mail: conniepayne@kycourts.net

Executive Officer, Department of Administrative Services **Scott Brown** . . . . . (502) 573-2350
E-mail: scottbrown@kycourts.net Fax: (502) 573-0357

Human Resources Executive Officer **Jason McGinnis** . . . . (502) 573-2350
E-mail: jasonmcginnis@kycourts.net Fax: (502) 573-1633

Budget Director for the Office of Budget and Policy **Carol Henderson** . . . . . (502) 573-2350
E-mail: carolhenderson@kycourts.net

Executive Officer, Department of Family and Juvenile Services **Rachel Bingham** . . . . . (502) 573-2350
E-mail: rachelb@kycourts.net Fax: (502) 573-1448

General Counsel for the Department of Legal Services **Marc Theriault** . . . . . (502) 573-2350
E-mail: marctheriault@kycourts.net Fax: (502) 573-0343

Chief Operating Officer for the Division of Pretrial Services **Tara Klute** . . . . . (502) 573-2350
E-mail: taraklute@kycourts.net Fax: (502) 573-1669

Public Information Officer **Leigh Anne Hiatt** . . . . . (502) 573-2350
E-mail: lhiatt@kycourts.net

Technology Services Executive Officer **Charles Byers** . . . . (502) 573-2350
E-mail: charlesbyers@kycourts.net Fax: (502) 573-1589

Manager of the Division of Drug Court **Connie Neal** . . . . (502) 573-2350
E-mail: connieneal@kycourts.net

State Law Librarian **Jennifer Frazier** . . . . . (502) 564-4848
State Capitol, 700 Capitol Avenue, Suite 200, Frankfort, KY 40601-3489 Fax: (502) 564-5041
E-mail: jenniferfrazier@kycourts.net

Kentucky Supreme Court

State Capitol Building, 700 Capital Avenue, Room 235,
Frankfort, KY 40601
Tel: (502) 564-5444 Fax: (502) 564-2665
Internet: www.kycourts.net

Number of Judgeships: 7

The Supreme Court consists of seven justices who are elected in nonpartisan elections in separate districts throughout the state for eight-year terms. Temporary appointments may be made by the Governor to fill vacancies. The chief justice is elected by peer vote for a four-year term and serves as the administrative head of the state's court system. The Supreme Court exercises appellate jurisdiction over civil and criminal matters, with direct review over sentences of death, life imprisonment, or imprisonment of more than twenty years.

The Kentucky Supreme Court sits in Frankfort.

Court Staff

Court Administrator, General Counsel and Clerk of the Supreme Court **Susan Stokley Clary** . . . . . (502) 564-4176
E-mail: susanclary@kycourts.net
Education: Kentucky 1978 BA, 1981 JD

Chambers of Chief Justice John D. Minton, Jr.

231 State Capitol, 700 Capital Avenue, Frankfort, KY 40601
Tel: (502) 564-4162 Fax: (502) 564-1933
E-mail: johnminton@kycourts.net

John D. Minton, Jr.
Chief Justice

Date of Birth: March 19, 1952
Education: Western Kentucky 1974 BA; Kentucky 1977 JD
Began Service: July 25, 2006
Appointed By: Governor Ernie Fletcher
Term Expires: December 2022

Judicial: Judge, Division 2, Warren Circuit Court (1992-2003); Chief Administrative Judge, Green River Region of Judicial Circuits (1997-2003); Judge, Kentucky Court of Appeals (2003-2006)

Legal Practice: Cole, Harned & Broderick (1977-1988); Partner, Cole, Broderick, Minton, Moore & Thornton (1988-1991); Partner, Cole, Minton & Moore (1991-1992)

Staff

Fax: (270) 746-7870

Career Law Clerk **Joseph A. Wright** . . . . . (270) 746-7867
E-mail: joeywright@kycourts.net

Career Law Clerk **Ian A. Loos** . . . . . (270) 746-7867
E-mail: ianloos@kycourts.net

Chief of Staff and Counsel to Chief Justice **Katie Shepherd** . . . . . (502) 564-4162
E-mail: katieshepherd@kycourts.net

Executive Assistant to the Chief Justice **Susan E. Railey** . . . . . (270) 746-7867
E-mail: susanrailey@kycourts.net

Administrative Assistant to the Chief of Staff **Kathy R. Stevens** . . . . . (502) 564-4162
E-mail: kathystevens@kycourts.net

Chambers of Deputy Chief Justice Mary C. Noble

300 West Vine Street, Suite 2201, Lexington, KY 40507
Tel: (859) 246-2220 Fax: (859) 246-2705
E-mail: maryn@kycourts.net

Mary C. Noble
Deputy Chief Justice

Date of Birth: 1949
Education: Austin Peay State 1971 BS, 1975 MA; Kentucky 1981 JD
Began Service: November 2006
Next Election: November 2016
Election Type: General Election
Term Expires: 2016

Judicial: Circuit Judge, Fayette County Circuit Court (1991-2005); Chief Regional Circuit Judge, Fayette County Circuit Court (1998-2002)

Legal Practice: Attorney, Private Practice (1981-1991)

Staff

Law Clerk **Shawn Chapman** . . . . . (859) 246-2220
E-mail: shawnchapman@kycourts.net
Education: Kentucky 2002 JD

Law Clerk **Joseph Mankovich** . . . . . (859) 246-2220
Began Service: 2014

Administrative Secretary **Darlene Maybrier** . . . . . (859) 246-2220
E-mail: darlenem@kycourts.net

Chambers of Justice Bill Cunningham
103 West Court Street, Princeton, KY 42445
Tel: (270) 365-3533 Fax: (270) 365-3505
E-mail: billcunningham@kycourts.net

Bill Cunningham
Justice

Education: Murray State U 1962; Kentucky 1969 JD
Began Service: 2007
Term Expires: January 2023

Government: Public Defender, Kentucky State Penitentiary (1974-1976); City Attorney, City of Eddyville, Kentucky (1974-1991); Trial Commissioner, Lyon County District Court (1989-1992)

Judicial: Circuit Judge, 56th Judicial Circuit Court of Kentucky (1991-2007)

Staff
Career Law Clerk **Jennifer Emerson** . . . . (502) 595-3199

Chambers of Justice Lisabeth Hughes Abramson
700 West Jefferson Street, Louisville, KY 40202-4737
Tel: (502) 595-3199
E-mail: lisabethabramson@kycourts.net

Lisabeth Hughes Abramson
Justice

Education: Louisville 1977, 1980 JD
Began Service: September 2007
Appointed By: Governor Ernie Fletcher
Next Election: November 4, 2022
Election Type: General Election
Term Expires: 2023

Judicial: Judge, Kentucky Court of Appeals (1997-1998); Circuit Judge, 30th Judicial Circuit Court of Kentucky (1999-2006); Judge, Kentucky Court of Appeals (2006-2007)

Legal Practice: Attorney, Private Practice

Staff
Career Law Clerk **William L. Bronson** . . . . (502) 595-3199
Education: Louisville 1991 JD

Chambers of Justice Daniel J. Venters
401 South Main Street, Suite 1, Somerset, KY 42501
Tel: (606) 677-4248
E-mail: danielventers@kycourts.net

Daniel J. Venters
Justice

Education: Ohio State 1972; Kentucky 1975 JD
Began Service: August 11, 2008
Appointed By: Governor Steven L. Beshear
Next Election: November 2018
Election Type: General Election
Term Expires: 2019

Government: Assistant Commonwealth's Attorney, Office of the Commonwealth's Attorney, County of Pulaski, Kentucky (1975-1979); District Judge, 28th Judicial District, Kentucky District Courts (1979-1984)

Judicial: Circuit Judge, 28th Judicial Circuit, Kentucky Circuit Courts (1984-2003)

Current Memberships: Kentucky Bar Association; United States Supreme Court Bar

Profession: Private Practice

Membership: Member, Kentucky Board of Bar Examiners

Chambers of Justice Daniel J. Venters *continued*

Staff
Career Law Clerk **Stephen Gilley** . . . . (502) 564-4192
E-mail: stephengilley@kycourts.net

Chambers of Justice Michelle M. Keller
Kenton County Justice Center, Covington, KY 41011
Tel: (859) 291-9966
E-mail: michellekeller@kycourts.net

Michelle M. Keller
Justice

Date of Birth: 1959
Education: Northern Kentucky 1985 BS; Salmon P Chase 1990 JD
Began Service: 2013
Appointed By: Governor Steven L. Beshear
Next Election: November 2022
Military: RN

Government: Hearing Officer, Kentucky Personnel Board

Judicial: Judge, Chambers of Judge Michelle M. Keller, Kentucky Court of Appeals (2007-2013)

Current Memberships: National Association of Administrative Law Judges; Advisory Council, Northern Kentucky Children's Advocacy Center

Staff
Career Law Clerk **Kevin King** . . . . (859) 291-9966
E-mail: kevinking@kycourts.net

Chambers of Justice David A. Barber
700 West Main Street, Morehead, KY 40351
Tel: (606) 780-8384

David A. Barber
Justice

Date of Birth: 1953
Education: Transylvania 1977 BA; Louisville 1980 JD
Began Service: March 24, 2015
Appointed By: Governor Steven L. Beshear
Political Affiliation: Democrat

Current Memberships: Kentucky Academy of Trial Attorneys; Kentucky Bar Association

Chambers of Justice (Elect) Samuel T. Wright III
700 Capital Avenue, Frankfort, KY 40601
Tel: (502) 564-5444

Samuel T. Wright III
Justice-Elect

Note: On November 3, 2015, Samuel T. Wright III was elected Justice in the Kentucky general election. Wright will be sworn in effective January 4, 2016.

STATE COURTS—KENTUCKY

Kentucky Court of Appeals

360 Democratic Drive, Frankfort, KY 40601
Tel: (502) 573-7920 Fax: (502) 573-6795
Internet: www.aoc.state.ky.us

Number of Judgeships: 14

The Court of Appeals consists of fourteen judges who are divided into panels of three to review and decide cases. Two judges are elected in nonpartisan elections in each of the seven Supreme Court districts for eight-year terms. The chief judge is elected by peer vote for a four-year term. Temporary appointments may be made by the Governor to fill vacancies. The Court of Appeals has appellate jurisdiction over final and interlocutory judgments, convictions, orders or decrees of the Kentucky Circuit Court unless such actions involve a judgment dissolving marriage or were rendered in an appeal from the Kentucky District Court. The Court also reviews decisions of administrative agencies.

The Court does not sit in one location, but travels throughout the state to hear cases.

Court Staff

Clerk of the Court **Samuel Givens, Jr.** . . . . (502) 573-7920
E-mail: samg@kycourts.net
Education: Centre 1984 BA;
Salmon P Chase 1987 JD

Chambers of Chief Judge Glenn E. Acree

125 Lisle Industrial Avenue, Lexington, KY 40511-2062
Tel: (859) 246-2734 Fax: (859) 246-2737
E-mail: glennacree@kycourts.net

Glenn E. Acree
Chief Judge

Education: Kentucky; Maryland; Kentucky JD
Began Service: August 16, 2006
Term Expires: December 2022

Staff
Career Law Clerk **Betsy Catron** . . . . (859) 246-2734
Career Law Clerk **Katie Morgan** . . . . (859) 246-2734
E-mail: katiemorgan@kycourts.net
Secretary **Rachael Mayolo** . . . . (859) 246-2734
E-mail: rachaelmayolo@kycourts.net

Chambers of Judge Jeff S. Taylor

Corporate Center, 401 Frederica Street, Owensboro, KY 42301
Tel: (270) 687-7116 Fax: (270) 687-7118
E-mail: judgejstaylor@hotmail.com

Jeff S. Taylor
Judge

Date of Birth: September 28, 1953
Education: Murray State U BS; Memphis State MPA; Louisville JD
Began Service: December 17, 2003
Term Expires: December 31, 2022

Current Memberships: Davies County Bar Association; Greater Owensboro Chamber of Commerce; Kentucky Bar Association; Kentucky Bar Foundation

Staff
Senior Staff Attorney **Christina R. West** . . . . (270) 687-7116
Education: Louisville 1992 JD
Staff Attorney **Angela Fallin-Ward** . . . . (270) 687-7116
E-mail: angelafallin-ward@kycourts.net
Education: Kentucky JD
Judicial Secretary **Theresa Kasinger** . . . . (270) 687-7116
E-mail: theresakasinger@kycourts.net

Chambers of Judge Sara Walter Combs

323 East College Avenue, Stanton, KY 40380
P.O. Box 709, Stanton, KY 40380-0709
Tel: (606) 663-0651 Fax: (606) 663-0726
E-mail: saracombs@kycourts.net

Sara Walter Combs
Judge

Date of Birth: 1948
Education: Louisville 1970 BA, 1971 MA, 1979 JD
Began Service: January 27, 1994
Next Election: November 2022
Term Expires: December 31, 2022

Academic: Teacher, Henryville High School (1971-1980); Professor of Law, University of Louisville (1987-1989)

Corporate: Vice President, Corporate Development and General Counsel, Naegele Outdoor Advertising (1982-1989)

Judicial: Associate Justice, Kentucky Supreme Court (1993)

Legal Practice: Associate, Wyatt, Tarrant & Combs, LLP (1979-1982); Private Practice (1989-1991); Sole Practitioner (1991-1992); Mapother & Mapother (1992-1993)

Current Memberships: Kentucky Bar Association; Louisville Bar Association

Staff
Career Staff Attorney **Mimi White** . . . . (606) 663-0651
E-mail: mimijones@kycourts.net
Education: Louisville 1988 BA;
Wake Forest 1992 JD
Career Staff Attorney **Emily Lucas** . . . . (606) 663-0651
E-mail: emilylucas@kycourts.net
Education: Freed-Hardeman 2000 BA;
Kentucky 2008 JD
Secretary **Vera Patterson** . . . . (606) 663-0651
E-mail: verapatterson@kycourts.net

Chambers of Judge Janet L. Stumbo

311 North Arnold Avenue, Suite 502, Prestonsburg, KY 41653
Tel: (606) 889-1710 Fax: (606) 889-1709
E-mail: janetstumbo@kycourts.net

Janet L. Stumbo
Judge

Date of Birth: 1954
Education: Morehead State 1976 BA; Kentucky 1980 JD
Began Service: January 2007
Term Expires: December 2022

Current Memberships: Floyd County Bar; Kentucky Bar Association; National Association of Women Judges

Staff
Staff Attorney **Joshua Michael Castle** . . . . (606) 889-1710
E-mail: joshuacastle@kycourts.net
Education: Ohio Northern 2006 JD;
Centre 2003 BA
Staff Attorney **Todd Henderson** . . . . (606) 889-1710
E-mail: toddhenderson@kycourts.net
Judicial Secretary **(Vacant)** . . . . (606) 889-1710

Chambers of Judge James H. Lambert Sr.

Rockcastle County Judicial Center, 205 East Main Street, Suite 101, Mt. Vernon, KY 40456
Box 7, Mt. Vernon, KY 40456
Tel: (606) 256-0472 Fax: (606) 256-0182
E-mail: jameslambert@kycourts.net

James H. Lambert, Sr.
Judge

Education: Eastern Kentucky; Salmon P Chase JD
Began Service: January 2007
Term Expires: December 2022

Government: County Attorney, County of Rockcastle, Kentucky (1981-1994); Trial Commissioner, County of Rockcastle, Kentucky (2002-2005)

Judicial: Administrative Law Judge, Corrections Department, Commonwealth of Kentucky

Legal Practice: Attorney, Lambert & Lambert

Staff

Staff Attorney **Sarah Hays** .... (606) 256-0472
E-mail: sarahhays@kycourts.net
Staff Attorney **Lisa Hubbard** .... (606) 256-0472
E-mail: lisahubbard@kycourts.net
Education: Miami 1991 BA; Kentucky 1994 JD
Secretary **Sandy Slusher** .... (606) 256-0472
E-mail: sandyslusher@kycourts.net

Chambers of Judge Christopher Shea Nickell

3235 Olivet Church Road, Suite F, Paducah, KY 42001
Tel: (270) 575-7030 Fax: (270) 575-7032
E-mail: sheanickell@kycourts.net

Christopher Shea Nickell
Judge

Education: DePauw 1981 BA; Kentucky 1984 JD
Began Service: January 2007
Term Expires: December 31, 2022

Academic: Instructor, The University of North Carolina at Chapel Hill; Instructor, Murray State University

Government: Assistant Commonwealth Attorney, 21st Judicial District of Kentucky (1985-1986); Assistant Public Advocate, County of Graves, Kentucky (1999-2000); Assistant County Attorney, County of McCracken, Kentucky (2002-2006)

Legal Practice: Founder and Attorney, Nickell Law Firm; Attorney, Law Office of Truman L. Dehner; Attorney, Boehl Stopher & Graves LLP; Attorney, Saladino Law Firm

Current Memberships: McCracken County Bar Association

Staff

Staff Attorney **Chad A. Kerley** .... (270) 575-7178
E-mail: chadkerley@kycourts.net
Staff Attorney **Carol Ullerich** .... (270) 575-7031
E-mail: carolullerich@kycourts.net
Judicial Secretary **Debbie Staples** .... (270) 575-7177
E-mail: debbiestaples@kycourts.net

Chambers of Judge Joy A. Kramer

Boone County Judicial Center, 6025 Rogers Lane, Suite 238, Burlington, KY 41005
Tel: (859) 334-4870 Fax: (859) 334-4877
E-mail: joymoore@kycourts.net

Joy A. Kramer
Judge

Education: Morehead State; Salmon P Chase 1996 JD
Began Service: January 2007
Next Election: November 2022
Election Type: Retention Election

Clerkships: Law Clerk, Chambers of Senior Judge William O. Bertelsman, United States District Court for the Eastern District of Kentucky

Government: Staff Attorney, Chambers of Judge Daniel Guidugli, Kentucky Court of Appeals; Staff Attorney, Chambers of Judge Robert W. Dyche III, Kentucky Court of Appeals; Member, Personnel Board, State of Kentucky

Legal Practice: Attorney, Hoffman, Hoffman & Grubbs; Attorney, Adams, Stepner, Woltermann & Dusing, PLLC

Current Memberships: Kentucky Bar Association; Northern Kentucky Bar Association; Salmon P. Chase Inn of Court

Staff

Staff Attorney **Chris Harwood** .... (859) 334-4870
Staff Attorney **Tracy A. Richardson** .... (859) 334-4870
E-mail: tracyarichardson@kycourts.net
Judicial Assistant **Betsy Catron** .... (859) 334-4870
E-mail: betsycatron@kycourts.net

Chambers of Judge Kelly Thompson

Warren County Justice Center, 1001 Center Street, Suite 204, Bowling Green, KY 42101
Tel: (270) 746-7219 Fax: (270) 746-7222
E-mail: kellythompson@kycourts.net

Kelly Thompson
Judge

Education: Western Kentucky 1968 BA; Kentucky 1972 JD
Began Service: January 2007
Next Election: November 2022
Term Expires: December 31, 2022

Clerkships: Law Clerk, Kentucky Court of Appeals (1973-1974)

Government: Chief Trial Counsel, Highways Department, Commonwealth of Kentucky (1972-1973)

Legal Practice: Attorney, Private Practice (1974-2006)

Staff

Staff Attorney **Leslie Berry** .... (270) 746-7219
E-mail: leslieberry@kycourts.net
Staff Attorney **Ralaina Hunley** .... (270) 746-7219
E-mail: ralainahunley@kycourts.net
Secretary **Cindy Downey** .... (270) 746-7219
E-mail: cindydowney@kycourts.net

Chambers of Judge Donna L. Dixon
423 South 28th Street, Suite B, Paducah, KY 42003
Tel: (270) 575-7171 Fax: (270) 575-7172
E-mail: donnadixon@kycourts.net

Donna L. Dixon
Judge

Education: Murray State U; Southern Illinois JD
Began Service: July 2006
Term Expires: December 2022

Government: Staff Attorney, Chief Judge J. William Howerton, Kentucky Court of Appeals; Assistant Commonwealth's Attorney, County of McCracken, Kentucky

Judicial: District Judge, County of McCracken, Kentucky

Legal Practice: Attorney, Private Practice

Membership: Past President, United Way of Paducah-McCracken County; Past President, McCracken County Young Lawyers Association

Staff
Staff Attorney **Jill Atkins** .... (270) 889-6537
E-mail: jillatkins@kycourts.net
Staff Attorney **Heather Denton** .... (270) 575-7171
E-mail: heatherdenton@kycourts.net
Education: Salmon P Chase 1995 JD
Secretary **Cathy Stamper** .... (270) 575-7171
E-mail: cathystamper@kycourts.net

Chambers of Judge Denise G. Clayton
Jefferson County Judicial Center, 700 West Jefferson Street, 10th Floor, Suite 1020, Louisville, KY 40202-4737
Tel: (502) 595-3440 Fax: (502) 595-3442

Denise G. Clayton
Judge

Education: Defiance; Louisville JD
Began Service: November 2007
Appointed By: Governor Ernie Fletcher
Next Election: November 4, 2022
Election Type: General Election
Term Expires: 2022

Judicial: Chief Circuit Judge, Circuit Court, County of Jefferson, Kentucky

Staff
Staff Attorney **Ruth Coleman** .... (502) 595-3433
E-mail: ruthcoleman@kycourts.net
Staff Attorney **Mary Jo Gleason** .... (502) 595-3435
E-mail: maryjogleason@kycourts.net
Secretary **Danae Bransford** .... (502) 595-3440
E-mail: danaebransford@kycourts.net

Chambers of Judge Laurance Browning VanMeter
1999 Richmond Road, Suite 2B, Lexington, KY 40502
Tel: (859) 246-2053 Fax: (859) 246-2055
E-mail: lbv@kycourts.net

Laurance Browning VanMeter
Judge

Date of Birth: August 29, 1958
Education: Vanderbilt 1980 BS; Kentucky 1983 JD
Began Service: December 1, 2003
Next Election: November 2022
Term Expires: December 31, 2022

Judicial: Fayette District Court, 22nd Judicial District, 1st Division (1994-1999); Fayette Circuit Court, 22nd Judicial Circuit, 1st Division (1999-2003)

Legal Practice: Stoll, Keenon & Park (1983-1994)

Chambers of Judge Laurance Browning VanMeter *continued*

Staff
Staff Attorney **Ellen Black** .... (859) 246-2053
E-mail: ellenblack@kycourts.net
Staff Attorney **Megan Kleinline** .... (859) 246-2053
E-mail: megankleinline@kycourts.net
Secretary **Kim Lawson** .... (859) 246-2053
E-mail: kiml@kycourts.net

Chambers of Judge Irvin Maze
700 West Jefferson Street, Suite 1010, Louisville, KY 40202-4737
Tel: (502) 595-3430

Irvin "Irv" Maze
Judge

Began Service: 2012
Next Election: 2022
Political Affiliation: Democrat

Staff
Staff Attorney **Timothy M. Buckley** .... (502) 595-3430
E-mail: timothybuckley@kycourts.net
Education: Louisville 1990 JD
Staff Attorney **Thomas Patteson** .... (502) 595-3430
Secretary **Rachel Brawner** .... (502) 595-3430
E-mail: rachelbrawner@kycourts.net

Chambers of Judge Allison Jones
330 York Street, Newport, KY 41071
Tel: (859) 669-1212 Fax: (859) 669-1213
E-mail: allisonjones@kycourts.net

Allison Jones
Judge

Began Service: July 12, 2013
Appointed By: Governor Steven L. Beshear
Next Election: November 2022
Election Type: Retention Election

Staff
Staff Attorney **Brittany Staverman** .... (859) 669-1212
E-mail: brittanystaverman@kycourts.net
Staff Attorney **Meghan Thompson** .... (859) 669-1212
E-mail: meghanthompson@kycourts.net
Secretary **Kathy Burggraf** .... (859) 669-1212
E-mail: kathyburggraf@kycourts.net

Chambers of Judge Debra Hembree Lambert
360 Democratic Drive, Frankfort, KY 40601
Tel: (502) 573-7920

Debra Hembree Lambert
Judge

Louisiana

Office of the Judicial Administrator of Louisiana

400 Royal Street, Suite 1190, New Orleans, LA 70130
Tel: (504) 310-2550 Fax: (504) 310-2587
Internet: www.lasc.org

Staff

Judicial Administrator **Sandra Vujnovich** . . . . (504) 310-2550
Education: LSU 1986 JD
Deputy Judicial Administrator, Accounting Services
Terence Sims . . . . (504) 310-2583
E-mail: tsims@lasc.org Fax: (504) 310-2580
Deputy Judicial Administrator, Community Relations
Valerie S. Willard . . . . (504) 310-2590
E-mail: vsw@lasc.org Fax: (504) 310-2589
Deputy Judicial Administrator, Human Resources
Veronica Cheneau . . . . (504) 310-2550
Fax: (225) 310-3186
Law Librarian **Georgia Chadwick** . . . . (504) 310-2402
E-mail: gchadwick@lasc.org
Education: Denver 1978 MSLS

Supreme Court of Louisiana

400 Royal Street, Suite 4200, New Orleans, LA 70130-2104
Tel: (504) 310-2300
Internet: www.lasc.org

Number of Judgeships: 7

The Supreme Court consists of a chief justice and six justices who are elected on a nonpartisan basis from seven districts throughout the state for ten-year terms. The most senior justice is selected as chief justice and serves until retirement, which is mandatory at age seventy (seventy-five if elected under an earlier constitution). Vacancies are filled within one year by a special election called by the Governor. The Supreme Court has appellate jurisdiction over cases in which an ordinance or law has been declared unconstitutional or the death penalty has been imposed. The Court has exclusive original jurisdiction over disbarment proceedings and petitions for discipline of judges. The Court has discretionary review over decisions of the Louisiana Courts of Appeal and trial courts.

The Supreme Court sits in New Orleans.

Court Staff

Clerk of the Court **John Tarlton Olivier** . . . . (504) 310-2300
E-mail: jolivier@lasc.org
Education: Loyola U (New Orleans) 1976 BBA, 1979 JD
Director of Security **Thomas Anderson** . . . . (504) 310-2456
E-mail: tanderson@lasc.org
Executive Director **Cheney C. Joseph, Jr.** . . . . (225) 578-8825
Lousiana Judicial College, Louisiana State University Law Center, Room W-126, Baton Rouge, LA 70803 Fax: (225) 578-8762
Education: Princeton 1964 AB; LSU 1969 JD

Chambers of Chief Justice Bernette Joshua Johnson

400 Royal Street, New Orleans, LA 70130
Tel: (504) 310-2350 Fax: (504) 310-2359
E-mail: bjohnson@lasc.org

Bernette Joshua Johnson
Chief Justice

Date of Birth: 1943
Education: Spelman 1964 BA; LSU 1969 JD
Began Service: October 31, 1994
Term Expires: 2020
Political Affiliation: Democrat

Current Memberships: American Bar Association; American Judges Association; Louis A. Martinet Legal Society; Louisiana State Bar Association; National Association of Women Judges; National Bar Association

Staff

Research Attorney **Kelly Barbier** . . . . (504) 310-2354
E-mail: kbarbier@lasc.org
Education: LSU 1989 BS; Loyola U (New Orleans) 1992 JD
Research Attorney **Veronica A. Collins** . . . . (504) 310-2352
E-mail: vcollins@lasc.org
Executive Counsel **Angela White-Bazile** . . . . (504) 310-2353
E-mail: abazile@lasc.org
Education: Southwestern Louisiana 1993 BS; Southern U (New Orleans) 1996 JD
Administrative Assistant **Laverne M. Tropez** . . . . (504) 310-2350
E-mail: ltropez@lasc.org
Education: Southern U (New Orleans) 2003 BS

Chambers of Associate Justice Greg G. Guidry

Supreme Court Building, 400 Royal Street, New Orleans, LA 70130
Tel: (504) 310-2330
E-mail: gguidry@lasc.org

Greg Gerard Guidry
Associate Justice

Education: LSU 1985 JD
Began Service: January 2009
Next Election: November 2018
Election Type: General Election
Term Expires: 2018

Government: Assistant U.S. Attorney, Louisiana - Eastern District, United States Department of Justice; Grand Jury Coordinator, Louisiana - Eastern District, United States Department of Justice

Judicial: Judge, 24th Judicial District Court of Louisiana; Judge, Louisiana Court of Appeal, Fifth Circuit

Legal Practice: Attorney, Liskow & Lewis

Current Memberships: Louisiana Bar Foundation, Louisiana State Bar Association

Staff

Career Law Clerk **Jeffery Gregorie** . . . . (504) 310-2334
Career Law Clerk **Leslie M. Langhetee** . . . . (504) 310-2333
E-mail: llanghetee@lasc.org
Education: LSU 1979 JD
Career Law Clerk **Veronica Koclanes** . . . . (504) 310-2336
E-mail: vkoclanes@lasc.org
Judicial Assistant **Wendy McCrossen** . . . . (504) 310-2330
E-mail: wmccrossen@lasc.org

Chambers of Associate Justice Jeannette Theriot Knoll
400 Royal Street, New Orleans, LA 70130
P.O. Box 505, Marksville, LA 71351
Tel: (318) 253-4586 (Marksville Chambers)
Tel: (504) 310-2380 Fax: (504) 310-2389
E-mail: jknoll@lasc.org

Jeannette Theriot Knoll
Associate Justice

Date of Birth: 1944
Education: Loyola U (New Orleans) 1966 BA, 1969 JD; Virginia 1996 LLM
Began Service: January 1, 1997
Term Expires: January 2016
Political Affiliation: Democrat

Government: First Assistant District Attorney, Twelfth Judicial District Court, Office of the District Attorney, Avoyelles Parish, Louisiana (1972-1982)

Judicial: Judge, Louisiana Court of Appeal, Third Circuit (1983-1996)

Current Memberships: American Bar Association; Avoyelles Parish Bar Association; Louisiana State Bar Association; National Association of Women Judges

Staff
Career Law Clerk **Julie Hebert Danos** .... (504) 310-2380
E-mail: jhebert@lasc.org
Education: Loyola U (New Orleans) 2000 BA, 2003 JD
Law Clerk **Mary Watson** .... (504) 310-2380
Began Service: August 2013
Term Expires: August 2016
E-mail: mwatson@lasc.org
Law Clerk **Jessica Orgeron** .... (504) 310-2380
Began Service: August 2013
Term Expires: December 2016

Chambers of Associate Justice John L. Weimer
400 Royal Street, New Orleans, LA 70130
P.O. Box 391, Thibodaux, LA 70302
Tel: (985) 493-8833 Fax: (985) 449-5106
E-mail: jweimer@lasc.org

John L. Weimer
Associate Justice

Date of Birth: October 2, 1954
Education: Nicholls State 1976 BS; LSU 1980 JD
Began Service: January 1, 2002
Next Election: 2022
Political Affiliation: Democrat

Academic: Law Professor, Nicholls State University (1983-1998)

Judicial: Judge Pro Tempore, Louisiana District Court (1993); Judge, Louisiana District Court (1995-1998); Judge, Louisiana First Circuit Court of Appeal (1998-2001)

Legal Practice: Private Practice (1980-1995)

Staff
Career Law Clerk **Raul Efquivel** .... (985) 493-8833
Career Law Clerk **Gaynel Guillot** .... (985) 493-8833
E-mail: gguillot@lasc.org
Education: LSU 1989 JD
Career Law Clerk **Gail N. Wise** .... (985) 493-8833
E-mail: gwise@lasc.org
Education: LSU 1982 JD
Secretary **Stephanie Garrison** .... (985) 493-8833
E-mail: sgarrison@lasc.org
Education: Nicholls State 1989 AS

Chambers of Associate Justice Marcus Clark
400 Royal Street, New Orleans, LA 70130-2199
Tel: (504) 310-2370
E-mail: mclark@lasc.org

Marcus R. Clark
Associate Justice

Date of Birth: 1956
Education: Northeast Louisiana 1978; LSU Hebert Law 1985 JD
Began Service: November 20, 2009

Current Memberships: Louisiana District Judges Association; Louisiana State Bar Association

Staff
Staff Attorney **Julie Eldridge** .... (504) 310-2370
E-mail: jeldridge@lasc.org
Staff Attorney **Rebecca Mighton** .... (504) 310-2370
E-mail: rmighton@lasc.org
Staff Attorney **Patrick Parham** .... (504) 310-2370
E-mail: pparham@lasc.org
Education: Baylor 1996 JD
Administrative Secretary **Karen McCarty** .... (504) 310-2370
E-mail: kmccarty@lasc.org

Chambers of Associate Justice Jefferson D. Hughes
400 Royal Street, New Orleans, LA 70130-2199
Tel: (504) 310-2300

Jefferson D. Hughes III
Associate Justice

Education: LSU, JD

Judicial: Judge, Chambers of Judge Jefferson D. Hughes, III, Louisiana Court of Appeal, First Circuit (2005-2013)

Staff
Research Attorney **Timberly Enete** .... (225) 665-8939
Research Attorney **Hope Normand** .... (225) 665-8939
Judicial Secretary **Simone Macdonald** .... (225) 665-8939

Louisiana Courts of Appeal
Internet: www.lasc.org

The Courts of Appeal are courts of intermediate appellate jurisdiction over all civil cases. The courts also have jurisdiction over all criminal cases triable by a jury, except for those in which the death penalty has been imposed. The jurisdiction of the courts is limited to matters of law in criminal cases and questions of fact and law in civil cases. The courts hear appeals from the Louisiana Family, District and Juvenile Courts; they also may issue writs when necessary. There are five judicial circuits in Louisiana, with a court of appeal in each circuit. These circuits, in turn, are divided into at least three districts. The judges are elected in nonpartisan elections in their respective districts and serve for ten years. The chief judge of each court is the most senior member of its court and may serve in this capacity as long as he serves on the court. Retirement is mandatory at the age of seventy; however, retired judges may serve by assignment of the Supreme Court. A judge who reaches the mandatory age while in office, may complete the term. Each court sits in panels of three judges, but may sit in larger panels when necessary.

Louisiana Court of Appeal, First Circuit

1600 North Third Street, Baton Rouge, LA 70802
P.O. Box 4408, Baton Rouge, LA 70821-4408
Tel: (225) 382-3000 Fax: (225) 382-3010
E-mail: webmaster@la-fcca.org
Internet: www.la-fcca.org

Number of Judgeships: 12

Areas Covered: Parishes of Ascension, Assumption, East Baton Rouge, East Feliciana, Iberville, Lafourche, Livingston, Pointe Coupee, St. Helena, St. Mary, St. Tammany, Tangipahoa, Terrebonne, Washington, West Baton Rouge and West Feliciana

Court Staff

Clerk of Court **Christine L. Crow** .... (225) 382-3000
E-mail: ccrow@la-fcca.org
Education: LSU 1978 BS, 1981 JD, 2000 MPA
Chief Deputy Clerk **Rodd Naquin** .... (225) 382-3000
E-mail: rnaquin@la-fcca.org
Education: LSU 1993 BS, 1997 JD
Business Services Manager **Tammy Meunier** .... (225) 382-3000
E-mail: tmeunier@la-fcca.org Fax: (225) 382-3026
Information Technology Consultant **Bert Lousteau** ...... (225) 382-3000
E-mail: blousteau@la-fcca.org
Chief of Security **Mike Lanier** .... (225) 382-3000
E-mail: mlanier@la-fcca.org

Chambers of Chief Judge Vanessa Guidry-Whipple

1600 North Third Street, Baton Rouge, LA 70802
Tel: (985) 876-4034 Fax: (985) 857-3759

Vanessa Guidry-Whipple
Chief Judge

Began Service: November 1990
Next Election: 2022

Staff

Career Law Clerk **Dana Butler** .... (985) 876-4034
Education: LSU 1988 BS;
Loyola U (New Orleans) 1991 JD
Career Law Clerk **Julie S. Domangue** .... (985) 876-4034
Education: Southeastern Louisiana 1990 BA;
Mississippi Col 1993 JD
Secretary **Judy Ellender** .... (985) 876-4034

Chambers of Judge John Michael Guidry

1600 North Third Street, Baton Rouge, LA 70802
P.O. Box 4408, Baton Rouge, LA 70821-4408
Tel: (225) 382-3080 Fax: (225) 382-3033
E-mail: jguidry@la-fcca.org

John Michael Guidry
Judge

Date of Birth: 1962
Education: LSU 1983; Southern U A&M 1987 JD
Began Service: November 19, 1997
Next Election: November 2020
Term Expires: December 31, 2021
Political Affiliation: Democrat

Government: State Representative (D-LA), Louisiana House of Representatives (1991-1992); State Senator (D-LA), Louisiana State Senate (1993-1997)

Current Memberships: Baton Rouge Bar Association; Louis A. Martinet Legal Society; Louisiana State Bar Association; National Bar Association

Staff

Career Law Clerk **Kacy Renea Collins** .... (225) 382-3080
E-mail: kcollins@la-fcca.org
Education: LSU 1993 BA;
Southern U A&M 1999 JD

Chambers of Judge John Michael Guidry *continued*

Career Law Clerk **Jill Nasello Graves** .... (225) 382-3080
E-mail: jnasello@la-fcca.org
Education: LSU 1997 BA; New England 2001 JD
Secretary **Courtney Harris** .... (225) 382-3080
E-mail: charris@la-fcca.org

Chambers of Judge John T. Pettigrew

7837 Main Street, Houma, LA 70360
P.O. Box 7035, Houma, LA 70361
Tel: (985) 872-3522 Fax: (985) 876-8826
E-mail: jpettigrew@la-fcca.org

John T. Pettigrew
Judge

Date of Birth: 1947
Education: LSU 1972 JD
Began Service: January 1, 1999
Next Election: October 2018
Election Type: General Election
Term Expires: December 31, 2018
Political Affiliation: Democrat

Academic: Adjunct Professor, Nicholls State University

Government: Special Assistant District Attorney, 32nd Judicial District Court of Louisiana (1985-1990)

Judicial: Judge, 32nd Judicial District Court of Louisiana (1991-1998)

Legal Practice: Associate, Ashby W. Pettigrew, Jr. (1973-1974); Private Practice (1974-1975); Waitz, Weigand & Downer (1975-1976); Bosworth & Samanie (1976-1977); Partner, Meyers & Pettigrew (1977-1980); Private Practice (1980-1990)

Military Service: United States Army (1972-1979)

Current Memberships: American Association of Justice; American Bar Association; Louisiana District Judges Association; Louisiana State Bar Association; National Council of Juvenile and Family Court Judges; Terrebonne Parish Bar Association; Terrebonne Parish Chamber of Commerce

Staff

Career Law Clerk **Kristi Maiorana** .... (985) 872-3522
E-mail: kmaiorana@la-fcca.org
Education: Nicholls State 1989 BS;
Loyola U (New Orleans) 1992 JD
Career Law Clerk **Marité Cruz Zietz** .... (225) 382-3162
E-mail: mzietz@la-fcca.org
Education: LSU Hebert Law 1990 JD
Secretary **Sherrill Rodrigue** .... (985) 872-3522
E-mail: srodrigue@la-fcca.org

Chambers of Judge J. Michael McDonald

1600 North Third Street, 3rd Floor, Baton Rouge, LA 70802
P.O. Box 4408, Baton Rouge, LA 70821
Tel: (225) 382-3050 Fax: (225) 382-3142

J. Michael McDonald
Judge

Date of Birth: March 11, 1946
Education: LSU 1968 BA, 1976 JD
Began Service: January 1, 2003
Next Election: 2022
Election Type: General Election
Term Expires: December 31, 2022
Political Affiliation: Republican

Judicial: Judge, 19th Judicial District Court (1986-2002)

Staff

Career Law Clerk **Madalyn Moore** .... (225) 382-3050
E-mail: mmoore@la-fcca.org

STATE COURTS—LOUISIANA

Chambers of Judge J. Michael McDonald *continued*

Career Law Clerk **Connie Young** .... (225) 382-3050
E-mail: cyoung@la-fcca.org
Judicial Assistant **Ellen Blackledge** .... (225) 382-3050
E-mail: eblackledge@la-fcca.org

Chambers of Judge Page McClendon

2140 Eighth Street, Suite A, Mandeville, LA 70471
Tel: (985) 845-2221 Fax: (985) 624-4627
E-mail: pmcclendon@la-fcca.org

Page McClendon
Judge

Education: Sophie Newcomb 1978 BA; Tulane 1981 JD
Began Service: January 1, 2003
Next Election: November 2022
Election Type: General Election
Term Expires: December 31, 2022

Government: Assistant District Attorney, 21st Judicial District, City of Mandeville, Louisiana

Staff
Career Law Clerk **Steven Slayton** .... (225) 382-3121
E-mail: sslayton@la-fcca.org
Career Law Clerk **Kim Kammler** .... (985) 624-3310
E-mail: kkammler@la-fcca.org
Education: LSU 1977 BA, 1981 JD
Secretary **Debi Vicknair** .... (985) 845-2221
E-mail: dvicknair@la-fcca.org

Chambers of Judge Jewel E. Welch

1600 North Third Street, Baton Rouge, LA 70802
P.O. Box 4408, Baton Rouge, LA 70821-4408
Tel: (225) 382-3060 Fax: (225) 382-3143

Jewel E. "Duke" Welch
Judge

Began Service: January 1, 2005
Term Expires: December 31, 2024

Staff
Research Attorney **Charlotte Andrews** .... (225) 382-3060
Research Attorney **Hilary Leblanc** .... (225) 382-3060
Judicial Secretary **Geraldine Simon** .... (225) 382-3061
E-mail: gsimon@la-fcca.org

Chambers of Judge Toni M. Higginbotham

1600 North Third Street, Baton Rouge, LA 70802
Tel: (225) 382-3041
E-mail: thigginbotham@la-fcca.org

Toni M. Higginbotham
Judge

Education: LSU; Southern U (New Orleans)
Began Service: January 5, 2011

Current Memberships: American Judges Association; American Judges Foundation; Baton Rouge Bar Association

Staff
Law Clerk **Ginny Krigler** .... (225) 382-3041
Law Clerk **Theresa Sandifer** .... (225) 382-3041
E-mail: tsandifer@la-fcca.org
Secretary **Stacie Minor** .... (225) 382-3041
E-mail: sminor@la-fcca.org

Chambers of Judge Mitchell R. Theriot

4198 Highway I, Raceland, LA 70394
Tel: (985) 537-2285 Fax: (985) 537-2289

Mitchell R. "Mitch" Theriot
Judge

Education: Nicholls State 1985 BS; Loyola U (New Orleans) 1988 JD
Began Service: 2013

Chambers of Judge William J. Crain

1600 North Third Street, Baton Rouge, LA 70802
Tel: (225) 382-3000

William J. "Will" Crain
Judge

Began Service: 2012

Chambers of Judge Ernest Drake

1600 North Third Street, Baton Rouge, LA 70802
Tel: (225) 382-3156

Ernest G. "Ernie" Drake
Judge

Education: Southeastern Louisiana BS; Tulane 1974 JD

Chambers of Judge Guy Holdridge

1600 North Third Street, Baton Rouge, LA 70802
Tel: (225) 382-3000

Guy Holdridge
Judge

Began Service: 2015

Chambers of Judge Wayne Ray Chutz

1600 North Third Street, Baton Rouge, LA 70802
Tel: (225) 382-3000

Wayne Ray Chutz
Judge

Began Service: 2015

Louisiana Court of Appeal, Second Circuit

Pike Hall, Jr. Courthouse, 430 Fannin Street, Shreveport, LA 71101-5537
Tel: (318) 227-3700 Fax: (318) 227-3735
Internet: www.lacoa2.org

Number of Judgeships: 9

Areas Covered: Parishes of Bienville, Bossier, Caddo, Caldwell, Claiborne, DeSoto, East Carroll, Franklin, Jackson, Lincoln, Madison, Morehouse, Ouachita, Red River, Richland, Tensas, Union, Webster, West Carroll and Winn

Court Staff
Clerk of the Court and Court Administrator
Lillian Evans Richie .... (318) 227-3702
E-mail: lrichie@la2nd.org Fax: (318) 227-3735
Education: LSU Hebert Law 1981 JD
Chief Deputy Clerk **Debbie R. Ware** .... (318) 227-3700
First Deputy Clerk **Karen Greer McGee** .... (318) 227-3700
E-mail: kmcgee@la2nd.org
File Clerk to the Clerk **Pharoah Marable** .... (318) 227-3734
E-mail: pmarable@la2nd.org
Deputy Clerk **(Vacant)** .... (318) 227-3700

(continued on next page)

STATE COURTS—LOUISIANA

Louisiana Court of Appeal, Second Circuit *continued*

Deputy Clerk **Brian Walls** ....(318) 227-3700
E-mail: bwalls@la2nd.org

Chambers of Chief Judge Henry N. Brown, Jr.

Pike Hall, Jr. Courthouse, 430 Fannin Street, Shreveport, LA 71101
P.O. Box 1528, Shreveport, LA 71165-1528
Tel: (318) 227-3766 Fax: (318) 227-3001
E-mail: hnbrown@la2nd.org

Henry N. Brown, Jr.
Chief Judge

Date of Birth: December 30, 1941
Education: LSU 1962, 1966 JD
Began Service: January 1, 1991
Next Election: October 2020
Term Expires: December 31, 2020

Staff

Law Clerk **(Vacant)** ....(318) 227-3739
Career Law Clerk **Jennifer Brown** ....(318) 227-3767
E-mail: jbrown@la2nd.org
Education: LSU 1992 JD
Career Law Clerk **Luke Hutchison** ....(318) 227-3768
Education: Pepperdine 2006 JD
Secretary **Rebecca J. Flippo** ....(318) 227-3766
E-mail: bflippo@la2nd.org

Chambers of Judge Felicia Toney Williams

Pike Hall, Jr. Courthouse, 430 Fannin Street, Shreveport, LA 71101
403 North Cedar Street, Tallulah, LA 71284
P.O. Box 111, Tallulah, LA 71284-0111
Tel: (318) 227-3744 Tel: (318) 574-9500 (Tallulah Chambers)
Fax: (318) 227-3003 Fax: (318) 574-9502 (Tallulah Chambers)
E-mail: fwilliams@la2nd.org

Felicia Toney Williams
Judge

Date of Birth: 1956
Education: Southern U A&M 1977, 1980 JD
Began Service: December 1992
Next Election: 2022

Clerkships: Law Clerk, Louisiana Supreme Court (1981-1982)

Government: Assistant District Attorney, Office of the District Attorney, Madison Parish, Louisiana (1982-1990)

Judicial: Judge, Louisiana District Court, Sixth District (1991-1992)

Legal Practice: Private Practice (1982-1990)

Current Memberships: American Bar Association; Louisiana State Bar Association; National Association of Women Judges; National Association of Women Lawyers

Staff

Career Law Clerk **Victor Killory** ....(318) 227-3747
E-mail: vkillory@la2nd.org Fax: (318) 227-3003
Education: Loyola U (New Orleans) 1987 JD;
Tulane 1995 LLM
Career Law Clerk **Cynthia J. Strickland** ....(318) 227-3746
E-mail: cstrickland@la2nd.org Fax: (318) 227-3003
Education: Grambling State 1989 BS; LSU 1998 JD
Judicial Assistant **Jacqueline "Jackie" Johnson** ....(318) 227-3745
E-mail: jjohnson@la2nd.org Fax: (318) 227-3003

Chambers of Judge James E. Stewart, Sr.

Pike Hall, Jr. Courthouse, 430 Fannin Street, Shreveport, LA 71101
P.O. Box 1528, Shreveport, LA 71165-1528
Tel: (318) 227-3740 Fax: (318) 227-3002
E-mail: jstewart@la2nd.org

James E. Stewart, Sr.
Judge

Date of Birth: August 11, 1955
Education: New Orleans 1977 BA;
Loyola U (New Orleans) 1980 JD
Began Service: September 1, 1994
Term Expires: December 2024
Political Affiliation: Democrat

Government: Legal Assistant, Office of the City Attorney, City of Shreveport, Louisiana (1980); Assistant City Attorney, Office of the City Attorney, City of Shreveport, Louisiana (1980-1982); Assistant District Attorney, Office of the District Attorney, Caddo Parish, Louisiana (1982-1983); Misdemeanor Assistant, Office of the District Attorney, Caddo Parish, Louisiana (1983-1984); Felony Assistant, Office of the District Attorney, Caddo Parish, Louisiana (1984-1985); Section Chief, Office of the District Attorney, Caddo Parish, Louisiana (1985-1987); Division Chief, Office of the District Attorney, Caddo Parish, Louisiana (1987-1989); First Assistant, Office of the District Attorney, Caddo Parish, Louisiana (1989-1990)

Judicial: Judge, Louisiana District Court, First Judicial District (1991-1993)

Current Memberships: American Bar Association; Louisiana Court of Appeals Judges Association; Louisiana State Bar Association; Judicial Council, National Bar Association; Shreveport Bar Association

Staff

Career Law Clerk **Rebecca Armand Edwards** ....(318) 227-3742
E-mail: redwards@la2nd.org
Education: Louisiana (Lafayette) 1992 BA;
LSU 1995 JD
Career Law Clerk **Erica Nicole Jefferson** ....(318) 227-3743
E-mail: ejefferson@la2nd.org
Education: Louisiana (Monroe) 2004 BA;
Southern U (New Orleans) 2007 JD
Judicial Secretary **Roxanne Williams Linnear** ....(318) 227-3741

Chambers of Judge J. Jay Caraway

Pike Hall, Jr. Courthouse, 430 Fannin Street, Shreveport, LA 71101
P.O. Box 1528, Shreveport, LA 71165-1528
Tel: (318) 227-3725 Fax: (318) 227-3008
E-mail: jcaraway@la2nd.org

J. Jay Caraway
Judge

Date of Birth: 1953
Education: Louisiana Tech U 1972 BS, 1975 MBA; LSU 1980 JD
Began Service: March 25, 1996
Next Election: November 2016
Term Expires: December 31, 2016
Political Affiliation: Democrat

Legal Practice: Blanchard, Walker, O'Quin & Roberts (1980-1996)

Staff

Law Clerk **Noah B. Baker** ....(318) 227-3727
E-mail: nbaker@la2nd.org
Career Law Clerk **Jennifer L. Segner** ....(318) 227-3726
Education: Nicholls State 1982 BA; LSU 1986 JD;
Centenary (LA) 1990 MBA
Judicial Assistant **Debi Brewer** ....(318) 227-3725
E-mail: dbrewer@la2nd.org

Chambers of Judge Harmon Drew, Jr.
Pike Hall, Jr. Courthouse, 430 Fannin Street, Shreveport, LA 71101-3132
Tel: (318) 227-3720 Fax: (318) 227-3007

Harmon Drew, Jr.
Judge

Date of Birth: November 11, 1946
Education: LSU 1968 BA, 1971 JD
Began Service: January 1, 1999
Next Election: 2018
Election Type: General Election
Term Expires: December 31, 2018
Political Affiliation: Democrat

Government: Special Assistant (D-LA), Office of Senator J. Bennett Johnston, United States Senate (1973); Assistant District Attorney, State of Louisiana (1974-1984)

Judicial: Judge, Minden City Court (1984-1988); Judge, Louisiana District Court, 26th Judicial District (1988-1998)

Military Service: United States Army (1972)

Current Memberships: American Bar Association; Louisiana Appellate Judges Association; Louisiana State Bar Association; Second Circuit Court of Appels Judges Association

Staff
Career Law Clerk **Jean Talley Drew** .... (318) 227-3723
E-mail: jtdrew@la2nd.org
Education: Hollins Col 1967 BA; LSU 1971 JD
Career Law Clerk **David P. Tullis** .... (318) 227-3722
E-mail: dtullis@la2nd.org
Education: LSU 1992 BA, 1995 JD
Secretary **Brenda C. Baker** .... (318) 227-3721
E-mail: bbaker@la2nd.org

Chambers of Judge D. Milton Moore III
130 DeSiard Street, Suite 608, Monroe, LA 71201-7363
Tel: (318) 325-6244 Fax: (318) 325-6473
E-mail: mmoore@la2nd.org

D. Milton Moore III
Judge

Education: LSU 1973 BA, 1976 JD
Began Service: January 1, 2003
Term Expires: December 31, 2022

Government: Member, Office of the City Council, City of Monroe, Louisiana (1980-1988); Chairman, Office of the City Council, City of Monroe, Louisiana (1984-1986)

Judicial: Chief Judge, Ouachita and Morehouse Parish, Fourth Judicial District Court (1997-1998)

Current Memberships: American Bar Association; American Judges Association; Louisiana State Bar Association

Staff
Career Law Clerk **Hal Odom** .... (318) 227-3762
E-mail: rhodom@la2nd.org
Education: LSU 1980 BA, 1983 JD
Career Law Clerk **Gary F. Strickland** .... (318) 227-3763
E-mail: gstrickland@la2nd.org
Education: LSU 1976 BA, 1990 JD;
Louisiana Tech U 2001 MA
Judicial Assistant **Vicki Rigdon** .... (318) 325-6244
E-mail: vrigdon@la2nd.org

Chambers of Judge John Larry Lolley
PO Box 1528, Shreveport, LA 71165
Tel: (318) 323-7911 Fax: (318) 361-0833

John Larry Lolley
Judge

Date of Birth: October 30, 1945
Education: Northeast Louisiana BA; Loyola U (New Orleans) JD
Began Service: October 31, 2003
Term Expires: December 2018

Government: Assistant City Attorney, City of Monroe, Louisiana (1973-1978)

Judicial: Judge, Monroe City Court (1979-1996); Judge, Fourth Judicial District Court (1997-2003)

Military Service: COL, United States Army (1995)

Staff
Career Law Clerk **Robin Jones** .... (318) 323-7911
E-mail: rjones@la2nd.org
Education: Tulane 1989 BS;
Loyola U (New Orleans) 1995 JD
Career Law Clerk **(Vacant)** .... (318) 323-7911
Judicial Assistant **Teresa Smith** .... (318) 323-7911
E-mail: tsmith@la2nd.org

Chambers of Judge Frances Pitman
430 Fannin Street, Shreveport, LA 71101-5537
Tel: (318) 227-3700

Frances J. Pitman
Judge

Began Service: 2013

Staff
Law Clerk **Margaret McDonald** .... (318) 227-3700
Secretary **Susan Reeves** .... (318) 227-3700

Chambers of Judge Jeanette Garrett
Pike Hall Jr. Courthouse, 430 Fannin Street, Shreveport, LA 71101
Tel: (318) 227-3700

Jeanette Garrett
Judge

Staff
Career Law Clerk **Susan Jiles Lindanger** .... (318) 227-3700
Education: LSU 1983 JD
Career Law Clerk **Ellen E. Davis** .... (318) 227-3700
Education: LSU 1984 JD

Louisiana Court of Appeal, Third Circuit
1000 Main Street, Lake Charles, LA 70615
P.O. Box 16577, Lake Charles, LA 70616
Tel: (337) 433-9403 Fax: (337) 491-2590
Internet: www.la3circuit.org

Number of Judgeships: 12

Areas Covered: Parishes of Acadia, Allen, Avoyelles, Beauregard, Calcasieu, Cameron, Catahoula, Concordia, Evageline, Grant, Iberia, Jefferson Davis, Lafayette, La Salle, Natchitoches, Rapides, Sabine, St. Landry, St. Martin, Vermilion and Vernon

Court Staff
Clerk of the Court **Charles Kelly McNeely** .... (337) 493-3012
Deputy Chief Clerk **Roberta D. Burnett** .... (337) 433-9403
E-mail: rburnett@la3circuit.org

Chambers of Chief Judge Ulysses Gene Thibodeaux

1000 Main Street, Lake Charles, LA 70615
P.O. Box 16577, Lake Charles, LA 70616
Tel: (337) 433-9403 Fax: (337) 491-2830
E-mail: jthibode@la3circuit.org

Ulysses Gene Thibodeaux
Chief Judge

Date of Birth: 1949
Education: Dartmouth 1971 BA; Tulane 1975 JD
Began Service: October 1, 1992
Next Election: October 2020
Term Expires: December 31, 2020
Political Affiliation: Democrat

Government: Assistant District Attorney, Office of the District Attorney, Calcasieu Parish, Louisiana (1976-1979)

Judicial: City Judge Ad Hoc, Lake Charles City Court (1984)

Legal Practice: Private Practice (1975-1976); Private Practice (1979-1992)

Current Memberships: American Judges Association; National Bar Association

Staff
Career Law Clerk **(Vacant)** .... (337) 433-9403 ext. 3072
Career Law Clerk **(Vacant)** .... (337) 433-9403 ext. 3043
Judicial Secretary **Jackie Frank** .... (337) 433-9403 ext. 3041
E-mail: jfrank@la3circuit.org
Education: McNeese State 1980 BS
Administrative General Counsel
Dianne Tynes .... (337) 433-9403 ext. 3043
E-mail: dtynes@la3circuit.org
Education: Southeastern Louisiana 1988 BA; Loyola U (New Orleans) 1995 JD

Chambers of Judge Sylvia R. Cooks

1000 Main Street, Lake Charles, LA 70601
P.O. Box 3841, Lafayette, LA 70502
Tel: (337) 235-2196 Fax: (337) 235-0026

Sylvia R. Cooks
Judge

Date of Birth: 1951
Education: LSU 1973 BA, 1976 JD; Virginia 1998 LLM
Began Service: October 9, 1992
Next Election: October 2022
Term Expires: December 31, 2022
Political Affiliation: Democrat

Clerkships: Law Clerk, Louisiana Supreme Court

Government: Assistant District Attorney, Office of the District Attorney, State of Louisiana

Legal Practice: Private Practice

Current Memberships: American Bar Association; National Bar Association

Staff
Career Law Clerk **Ted Luquette** .... (337) 235-2196
Career Law Clerk **Donald Williams** .... (337) 235-2196
Education: LSU 1988 BA, 1991 JD
Secretary **Evelyn Broussard** .... (337) 235-2196
E-mail: ebroussa@la3circuit.org
Education: Louisiana (Lafayette) 2004 BS

Chambers of Judge John D. Saunders

211 South Coreil Street, Ville Platte, LA 70586-4437
P.O. Box 566, Ville Platte, LA 70586-0566
Tel: (337) 363-5629 Fax: (337) 363-5186
E-mail: jsaunder@la3circuit.org

John D. Saunders
Judge

Date of Birth: June 4, 1943
Education: LSU 1965 BA, 1968 JD
Began Service: October 12, 1992
Term Expires: December 31, 2022
Political Affiliation: Democrat

Government: State Senator John D. Saunders (D-LA, District 26), Louisiana State Senate (1975-1992)

Legal Practice: Attorney, Saunders and Vidrine (1984-1990)

Staff
Law Clerk **Sarah Stephens** .... (337) 363-5629
Career Law Clerk **David LaHaye** .... (337) 363-5629
E-mail: dlahaye@la3circuit.org
Secretary **Carla Dupuis** .... (337) 363-5629
E-mail: cdupuis@la3circuit.org

Chambers of Judge Jimmie C. Peters

709 Versailles Boulevard, Alexandria, LA 71315
P.O. Box 1380, Jena, LA 71342
Tel: (318) 992-6125 Fax: (318) 992-6147
E-mail: jpeters@la3circuit.org

Jimmie C. Peters
Judge

Date of Birth: 1943
Education: LSU 1968 BS, 1970 JD
Began Service: May 4, 1994
Term Expires: December 31, 2016
Political Affiliation: Democrat

Government: City Attorney, Louisiana (1974-1984); Assistant District Attorney, 28th Judicial District, Office of the District Attorney, State of Louisiana (1985-1988)

Judicial: Judge, Louisiana District Court, 28th Judicial District, La Salle Parish (1985-1994)

Legal Practice: Associate, Long, Sleeth and Hughes (1970-1971); Junior Partner, Long, Hughes, Ryland and Peters (1971-1972); Partner, Long and Peters (1972-1978); Senior Partner, Peters, Hennigan and Walters (1981-1984)

Military Service: United States Army Reserve, United States Department of the Army (1968-1974)

Current Memberships: American Bar Association; The Crossroads Inn of Court of Alexandria-Pineville, The American Inns of Court; Louisiana State Bar Association

Staff
Career Law Clerk **Darla Vincent** .... (318) 992-6125
E-mail: dvincent@la3circuit.org
Education: LSU 1991 JD
Research Attorney **Courtney Ray** .... (318) 992-6125
Secretary **Carol Peavy** .... (318) 992-6125
E-mail: cpeavy@la3circuit.org

Chambers of Judge Marc T. Amy

122 North State Street, Abbeville, LA 70510
Tel: (337) 898-1222

Marc T. Amy
Judge

Education: Virginia 2001 LLM
Began Service: 1994
Next Election: 2018
Election Type: General Election
Term Expires: December 31, 2018

Staff
Career Law Clerk **Elizabeth Morehead** .... (337) 898-1222
Secretary **Stephanie Toups** .... (337) 898-1222

Chambers of Judge Elizabeth A. Pickett

657 Main Street, Many, LA 71449
P.O. Box 70, Many, LA 71449
Tel: (318) 256-4180 Fax: (318) 256-4173

Elizabeth A. Pickett
Judge

Date of Birth: 1959
Education: Tulane 1981 BA, 1984 JD
Began Service: April 1997
Next Election: 2022
Election Type: General Election
Term Expires: December 31, 2022
Political Affiliation: Democrat

Government: Assistant District Attorney, Eleventh Judicial District, State of Louisiana (1985-1990)

Judicial: Judge, Louisiana District Court, 11th Judicial District (1990-1997)

Legal Practice: Private Practice (1984-1990)

Staff
Career Law Clerk **Matthew Couvillion** .... (318) 256-4180
E-mail: mcouvili@la3circuit.org
Education: DePaul 1997 BS; LSU 2000 JD
Career Law Clerk **Janet C. Landry** .... (318) 256-4180
E-mail: jlandry@la3circuit.org
Education: McNeese State 1979 BA; LSU 1983 JD
Secretary **Patricia E. Cook** .... (318) 256-4180
E-mail: pcook@la3circuit.org
Education: Northwestern State

Chambers of Judge Billy H. Ezell

P.O. Box 16577, Lake Charles, LA 70616
Tel: (337) 433-9403 Fax: (337) 491-2468
E-mail: jezell@la3circuit.org

Billy H. Ezell
Judge

Date of Birth: July 24, 1943
Education: LSU 1970 JD
Began Service: 2003
Next Election: 2022
Term Expires: December 31, 2022
Political Affiliation: Republican

Clerkships: Law Clerk, Louisiana Court of Appeal, First Circuit

Judicial: Ad Hoc Judge, Ward 3; Judge, Family and Judicial Court, 14th Judicial District Court (1985-2002)

Military Service: Captain, United States Army

Current Memberships: American Bar Association; Judges Association of the Third Circuit Court of Appeal; Judicial Budgetary Control Board, State of Louisiana; Louisiana State Bar Association

Chambers of Judge Billy H. Ezell *continued*

Staff
Career Law Clerk **Priscilla P. Gayle** .... (337) 433-9403
Education: LSU 1991 JD
Career Law Clerk **Joseph B. Kelty** .... (337) 433-9403
Education: LSU 2001 JD
Secretary **Courtney Myers** .... (337) 433-9403

Chambers of Judge James T. Genovese

131 South Court Street, Opelousas, LA 70570
Tel: (337) 942-4240 Fax: (337) 942-2191
E-mail: jgenovese@la3circuit.org

James T. Genovese
Judge

Date of Birth: August 24, 1949
Education: Northwestern State 1971 BS; Loyola U (New Orleans) 1974 JD
Began Service: December 9, 2004
Term Expires: December 31, 2024

Corporate: Attorney, Southland Federal Savings Bank

Judicial: Judge Ad Hoc, Opelousas City Court (1975-1989); Judge, 27th Judicial District Court (1995-2004)

Legal Practice: Trial Attorney

Current Memberships: Colorado Bar Association; Louisiana State Bar Association

Staff
Research Attorney **Joana O. LaBruyere** .... (337) 942-4240
E-mail: jlabruye@la3circuit.org
Education: Southwestern Louisiana 1991 BS; LSU 1994 JD
Research Attorney **Alyce C. Richard** .... (337) 942-4240
E-mail: arichard@la3circuit.org
Education: Southwestern Louisiana 1996 BA; Southern U A&M 2000 JD

Chambers of Judge Shannon J. Gremillion

709 Versailles Boulevard, Alexandria, LA 71315
Tel: (318) 757-4640

Shannon J. Gremillion
Judge

Education: Louisiana (Monroe) 1991 BA; LSU 1995 JD
Began Service: January 19, 2009
Term Expires: December 31, 2016

Legal Practice: Partner and Director, Bolen, Parker, Brenner, Lee & Gremillion, Ltd. (1996-2009)

Current Memberships: Louisiana State Bar Association

Chambers of Judge Phyllis M. Keaty

P.O. Box 2548, Lafayette, LA 70502
Tel: (337) 269-9686

Phyllis M. Keaty
Judge

Began Service: 2010

Staff
Career Law Clerk **Sheryl L. Hoerner** .... (337) 269-9686
Career Law Clerk **Jennifer J. Coussan** .... (337) 269-9686
Judicial Secretary **Janell Broussard** .... (337) 269-9686
Education: Southwestern Louisiana 1980

Chambers of Judge John Conery
709 Versailles Boulevard, Alexandria, LA 71315
Tel: (337) 369-3540

John Conery
Judge

Began Service: 2013
Political Affiliation: Republican

Staff
Career Law Clerk **Sylvia S. Lowe** .... (337) 369-3540
Education: LSU 1989 JD
Law Clerk **Rebecca Autin** .... (337) 369-3540
Began Service: 2013
Term Expires: August 2016
Judicial Assistant **Sally Landry** .... (337) 369-3540

Chambers of Judge D. Kent Savoie
1000 Main Street, Lake Charles, LA 70601
Tel: (337) 433-9403

D. Kent Savoie
Judge

Began Service: 2015

Louisiana Court of Appeal, Fourth Circuit
400 Royal Street, New Orleans, LA 70130-2199
Tel: (504) 412-6001
Internet: www.la4th.org

Number of Judgeships: 12

Areas Covered: Parishes of Orleans, Plaquemines and St. Bernard

Court Staff
Clerk of Court **Danielle A. Schott** .... (504) 412-6001
E-mail: das@la4th.org
Education: Loyola U (New Orleans) 1978 BA
Chief Deputy Clerk **Susan B. Hammer** .... (504) 412-6001

Chambers of Chief Judge James F. McKay III
410 Royal Street, New Orleans, LA 70130-2199
Tel: (504) 412-6050 Fax: (504) 412-6053
E-mail: jfm@la4th.org

James F. McKay III
Chief Judge

Date of Birth: 1947
Education: Loyola U (New Orleans) 1974 JD
Began Service: April 7, 1998
Next Election: November 2022
Term Expires: December 31, 2022
Political Affiliation: Democrat

Current Memberships: American Bar Association; American Judges Association; Ancient Order of Hibernians in America, Inc.; Firemen's Charitable and Benevolent Association; Louisiana State Bar Association

Staff
Career Law Clerk **Nicholas S. Bouzon** .... (504) 412-6052
E-mail: nsb@la4th.org
Education: Tulane 1991 BA;
Loyola U (New Orleans) 1996 JD
Career Law Clerk **Inez M. Bucaro** .... (504) 412-6051
E-mail: imb@la4th.org
Education: Sophie Newcomb 1974 BA;
New Orleans 1993 MA;
Loyola U (New Orleans) 1993 JD
Career Law Clerk **Dawn H. DiRosa** .... (504) 412-6033

Chambers of Chief Judge James F. McKay III *continued*

Executive Assistant **Teri M. Carson** .... (504) 412-6050
E-mail: tmc@la4th.org

Chambers of Judge Dennis R. Bagneris, Sr.
400 Royal Street, New Orleans, LA 70130-2199
Tel: (504) 412-6056
E-mail: drb@la4th.org

Dennis R. Bagneris, Sr.
Judge

Date of Birth: 1948
Education: Xavier (LA) 1970 BA, 1977 MA; Tulane 1981 JD
Began Service: January 1, 1999
Next Election: October 2018
Election Type: General Election
Term Expires: December 31, 2018

Academic: Pre-Med Recruiter, Xavier University of Louisiana (1974-1976); Freshman Counselor, Xavier University of Louisiana (1976-1978)

Corporate: Pfizer Pharmaceuticals, Inc. (1970)

Government: Case Worker, Department of Public Welfare, State of Louisiana (1970-1972); Probation Officer, Alcohol Safety Action Project, City of New Orleans and Orleans Parish, Louisiana (1972-1974); Public Defender, Indigent Defender Program, City of New Orleans and Orleans Parish, Louisiana (1980-1982); State Senator (D-LA), Louisiana State Senate (1983-1998); President, Louisiana Legislative Black Caucus (1989-1990); President Pro Tempore, Louisiana Senate (1992-1999)

Staff
Law Clerk **Elise De La Houssaye** .... (504) 412-6056
Law Clerk **Iris Tate** .... (504) 412-6056
Administrative Assistant **Mary Phaline Williams** .... (504) 412-6056

Chambers of Judge Terri F. Love
410 Royal Street, New Orleans, LA 70130
Tel: (504) 412-6068 Fax: (504) 412-6071
E-mail: tfl@la4th.org

Terri F. Love
Judge

Date of Birth: 1961
Education: Jackson State U 1983 BS; Tulane 1986 JD; Virginia 2004 LLM
Began Service: 2000
Term Expires: December 2024
Political Affiliation: Democrat

Government: Chief Deputy City Attorney (1994-1995)

Judicial: Judge, Civil District Court, Orleans Parish (1995)

Legal Practice: Jefferson, Bryan & Gray; Law Offices of Terri Love

Current Memberships: Louisiana State Bar Association

Staff
Research Attorney **Lisa R. Eidson** .... (504) 412-6069
E-mail: lre@la4th.org
Education: Southern Mississippi 2002 BS;
Loyola U (New Orleans) 2005 JD
Career Law Clerk **Kathryn Autry** .... (504) 412-6070
E-mail: kma@la4th.org
Secretary **Norma K. Lombard** .... (504) 412-6068
E-mail: nkl@la4th.org

Chambers of Judge Max N. Tobias, Jr.

410 Royal Street, New Orleans, LA 70130-2199
Tel: (504) 412-6074 Fax: (504) 412-6077
E-mail: mnt@la4th.org

Max N. Tobias, Jr.
Judge

Date of Birth: 1947
Education: Tulane BA, 1971 JD
Began Service: 2000
Next Election: September 2016
Term Expires: December 31, 2016
Political Affiliation: Democrat

Clerkships: Law Clerk, Supreme Court of Louisiana (1971-1972)

Government: Louisiana Constitutional Convention (1973-1974)

Judicial: Judge, Civil District Court, Orleans Parish, Louisiana (1986-2000)

Legal Practice: Private Practice (1975-1984); Tobias, LeBlanc, Thompson & Waldrup (1984-1986)

Current Memberships: American Bar Association; Association of Women Attorneys; Louisiana State Bar Association; New Orleans Bar Association

Staff
Career Law Clerk **Paige Freeman Rosato** .... (504) 412-6076
E-mail: pfr@la4th.org
Education: Loyola U (New Orleans) 1987 JD
Career Law Clerk **Susan Tart** .... (504) 412-6075
E-mail: st@la4th.org
Education: Loyola U (New Orleans) 1985 JD
Judicial Secretary **Cynthia Kelly Massicot** .... (504) 412-6074
E-mail: ckm@la4th.org

Chambers of Judge Edwin A. Lombard

400 Royal Street, New Orleans, LA 70130-2199
Tel: (504) 412-6086
E-mail: eal@la4th.org

Edwin A. Lombard
Judge

Began Service: January 1, 2003
Term Expires: December 31, 2022

Academic: Adjunct Professor of Political Science and Government, Southern University of New Orleans

Clerkships: Clerk, City of New Orleans and Orleans Parish, Louisiana

Government: Assistant City Attorney, Law Department, City of New Orleans and Orleans Parish, Louisiana

Chambers of Judge Roland L. Belsome

410 Royal Street, New Orleans, LA 70130
Tel: (504) 412-6001
E-mail: rlb@la4th.org

Roland L. Belsome
Judge

Education: New Orleans; Tulane JD
Began Service: 2004

Academic: Adjunct Professor, Tulane University

Judicial: Judge, Civil District Court, City of New Orleans and Orleans Parish, Louisiana

Chambers of Judge Paul A. Bonin

400 Royal Street, New Orleans, LA 70130
Tel: (504) 412-6001
E-mail: pab@la4th.org

Paul A. Bonin
Judge

Began Service: 2009
Next Election: 2018
Term Expires: 2019

Chambers of Judge Daniel L. Dysart

400 Royal Street, New Orleans, LA 70130-2199
Tel: (504) 412-6001
E-mail: dld@la4th.org

Daniel L. Dysart
Judge

Began Service: December 29, 2010

Staff
Law Clerk **Maria Rabieh** .... (504) 412-6001
Law Clerk **Patrice D. Cusimano** .... (504) 412-6001
Education: Loyola U (New Orleans) 1994 JD
Judicial Assistant **Barbara Guerra** .... (504) 412-6001

Chambers of Judge Madeleine M. Landrieu

400 Royal Street, New Orleans, LA 70130-2199
Tel: (504) 412-6001

Madeleine M. Landrieu
Judge

Began Service: January 1, 2012

Staff
Career Law Clerk **Anne M. Otts** .... (504) 412-6001
Education: LSU 1977 BA; Tulane 1981 JD
Career Law Clerk **Julie L. Sirera** .... (504) 412-6001
Education: Mississippi 1980 BBA; Tulane 1983 JD
Judicial Assistant **Sheneta Johnson** .... (504) 412-6001

Chambers of Judge Joyce C. Lobrano

400 Royal Street, New Orleans, LA 70130-2199
Tel: (504) 412-6001

Joy Cossich Lobrano
Judge

Education: Tulane 1983 BA; Loyola U (New Orleans) 1988 JD; NYU 1993 ML
Began Service: January 1, 2012

Chambers of Judge Rosemary Ledet

400 Royal Street, New Orleans, LA 70130-2199
Tel: (504) 412-6001

Rosemary Ledet
Judge

Began Service: January 1, 2012

Chambers of Judge Sandra Cabrina Jenkins
400 Royal Street, New Orleans, LA 70130-2199
Tel: (504) 412-6038

Sandra Cabrina Jenkins
Judge

Education: LSU 1984 BA; Southern U Law 1984 JD; Southern U A&M 1987 MPA
Began Service: 2013

Staff
Career Law Clerk **Barbara Siefken** .... (504) 412-6040
Law Clerk **Emma Kingsdorf** .... (504) 412-6039
Judicial Assistant **Elizabeth Springs** .... (504) 412-6038

Louisiana Court of Appeal, Fifth Circuit
101 Derbigny Street, Gretna, LA 70053
P.O. Box 489, Gretna, LA 70054
Tel: (504) 376-1400 Fax: (504) 376-1498
Internet: www.fifthcircuit.org

Number of Judgeships: 8

Areas Covered: Parishes of Jefferson, St. Charles, St. James and St. John the Baptist

Court Staff
Clerk of the Court **Cheryl Q. Landrieu** .... (504) 376-1400
E-mail: clandrieu@fifthcircuit.org Fax: (504) 376-1498
Education: Loyola U (New Orleans) 1985 JD
Chief Deputy Clerk **Mary E. Legnon** .... (504) 376-1400
E-mail: mlegnon@fifthcircuit.org
First Deputy Clerk **Susan Buchholz** .... (504) 376-1400
E-mail: sbuchholz@fifthcircuit.org
Deputy Clerk **Nancy Vega** .... (504) 376-1400
E-mail: nvega@fifthcircuit.org
Deputy Clerk **Donna Holmes** .... (504) 376-1400
E-mail: dholmes@fifthcircuit.org
Business Services Manager **Maryanne Price** .... (504) 376-1400
IT Director **Bryan Herbert** .... (504) 376-1400
E-mail: bherbert@fifthcircuit.org
Director of Central Staff **Melissa Ledet** .... (504) 376-1494
E-mail: mledet@fifthcircuit.org
Assistant Director of Central Staff **Andrea Courtade** .... (504) 376-1455
E-mail: acourtade@fifthcircuit.org
Security Director **Charles Knopp** .... (504) 376-1481
E-mail: cknopp@fifthcircuit.org

Chambers of Chief Judge Susan M. Chehardy
101 Derbigny Street, Gretna, LA 70053
Tel: (504) 376-1445 Fax: (504) 376-1498
E-mail: schehardy@fifthcircuit.org

Susan M. Chehardy
Chief Judge

Date of Birth: 1957
Education: Loyola U (New Orleans) 1985 JD
Began Service: October 7, 1998
Term Expires: December 31, 2022
Political Affiliation: Republican

Current Memberships: American Bar Association; Jefferson Bar Association; Louisiana State Bar Association; National Association of Women Judges; New Orleans Bar Association

Staff
Career Law Clerk **Candace Chauvin** .... (504) 376-1445
E-mail: cchauvin@fifthcircuit.org
Career Law Clerk **Curtis Pursell** .... (504) 376-1445
E-mail: cpursell@fifthcircuit.org
Secretary **Eddean Jackson** .... (504) 376-1445
E-mail: ejackson@fifthcircuit.org

Chambers of Chief Judge Susan M. Chehardy *continued*
Judicial Secretary II **Lisa Tague** .... (504) 376-1445
E-mail: ltague@fifthcircuit.org

Chambers of Judge Fredericka Homberg Wicker
101 Derbigny Street, Gretna, LA 70053
P.O. Box 489, Gretna, LA 70054
Tel: (504) 376-1420
E-mail: rwicker@fifthcircuit.org

Fredericka Homberg Wicker
Judge

Education: Tulane 1977 JD
Began Service: February 2006
Next Election: November 2020
Term Expires: December 31, 2020

Government: Assistant District Attorney, Orleans Parish, New Orleans; Chief of Narcotics, Office of the Attorney General, United States Department of Justice; District Attorney, Jefferson Parish, Louisiana (1993-1996)

Judicial: Judge, 24th Judicial District Court of Louisiana, Louisiana

Legal Practice: Partner, Kierr, Gainsburgh, Benjamin, Fallon & Lewis

Current Memberships: Louisiana District Judges Association

Chambers of Judge Jude G. Gravois
101 Derbigny Street, Gretna, LA 70053
489, Gretna, LA 70054
Tel: (504) 376-1425
E-mail: jgravois@fifthcircuit.org

Jude G. Gravois
Judge

Began Service: May 1, 2009
Next Election: November 2020
Term Expires: December 31, 2020

Chambers of Judge Marc E. Johnson
101 Derbigny Street, Gretna, LA 70053
489, Gretna, LA 70054
Tel: (504) 376-1440
E-mail: mjohnson@fifthcircuit.org

Marc E. Johnson
Judge

Began Service: May 7, 2009
Term Expires: December 31, 2024
Political Affiliation: Democrat

Chambers of Judge Robert A. Chaisson
101 Derbigny Street, Gretna, LA 70053
P.O. Box 489, Gretna, LA 70054
Tel: (504) 376-1414 Fax: (504) 376-1406

Robert A. Chaisson
Judge

Began Service: 2011
Term Expires: December 31, 2022

Chambers of Judge Stephen J. Windhorst

101 Derbigny Street, Gretna, LA 70053
Tel: (504) 376-1415

Stephen J. "Steve" Windhorst
Judge

Education: Tulane BA, JD
Began Service: 2013

Government: State Representative (R-LA, District 86), Louisiana House of Representatives (1992-2000)

Staff
Law Clerk **Deborah G. Durette** (504) 376-1415
Education: Tulane 1984 JD
Law Clerk **Sheila Hymel** (504) 376-1415
Judicial Assistant **Janelle V. Cranmer** (504) 376-1415

Chambers of Judge Robert M. Murphy

101 Derbigny Street, Gretna, LA 70053
Tel: (504) 376-1430

Robert M. Murphy
Judge

Began Service: 2013

Staff
Career Law Clerk **Troy Broussard** (504) 376-1430
Education: Loyola U (New Orleans) 1997 JD
Career Law Clerk **Stephanie Walsh** (504) 376-1430
Secretary **Judy Kreppein** (504) 376-1430

Chambers of Judge Hans J. Liljeberg

101 Derbigny Street, Gretna, LA 70053
Tel: (504) 376-1410

Hans J. Liljeberg
Judge

Began Service: 2013

Staff
Law Clerk **Jennifer Gleeson** (504) 376-1410
Education: LSU 1997 JD
Law Clerk **Lauren Garvey** (504) 376-1410
Staff Secretary **Deborah Farmer** (504) 376-1410

STATE COURTS—LOUISIANA

Maine

Maine Administrative Office of the Courts

P.O. Box 4820, Portland, ME 04112-4820
Tel: (207) 822-0792 Fax: (207) 822-0781
Internet: www.courts.state.me.us

Staff

State Court Administrator **James T. Glessner** .... (207) 822-0710
E-mail: james.t.glessner@courts.maine.gov
Education: West Chester 1981 MS
Director of Budget and Accounting **Ellen M. Hjelm** ..... (207) 822-0714
E-mail: ellen.hjelm@courts.maine.gov
Chief of Finance and Administration **Dennis Corliss** ..... (207) 822-0709
E-mail: dennis.corliss@courts.maine.gov
Director of Human Resources **Kelly John** .... (207) 822-0757
E-mail: kelly.john@courts.maine.gov
Director of the Office of Information Technology
David Packard .... (207) 287-4645
E-mail: david.packard@courts.maine.gov Fax: (207) 287-4641
Government and Media Counsel **Mary Ann Lynch** ...... (207) 592-5940
State Court Library Supervisor **(Vacant)** .... (207) 822-0718
Fax: (207) 822-0781

Supreme Judicial Court of Maine

Maine Supreme Judicial Court, 205 Newbury Street, Room 139,
Portland, ME 04101-4125
Tel: (207) 822-4146
Internet: www.courts.state.me.us

Number of Judgeships: 7

The Supreme Judicial Court, established in 1820, consists of a chief justice and six associate justices who are appointed by the Governor with consent of the Maine State Legislature for seven-year terms. Three justices are appointed by the chief justice to serve as the Sentence Review Panel for the review of criminal sentences of one year or more. The Supreme Judicial Court hears appeals of civil and criminal cases from the Maine Superior Court, appeals from final judgments, orders and decrees of the Maine Probate Court, appeals of decisions of the Maine Public Utilities Commission and the Workers' Compensation Board, interlocutory criminal appeals and appeals of decisions from a single justice of the Court. The Court makes decisions regarding legislative apportionment and renders advisory opinions concerning important questions of law when requested by the Governor or State Legislature.

The Supreme Judicial Court sits in Portland.

Court Staff

Clerk **Matthew E. Pollack** .... (207) 822-4146
E-mail: matthew.pollack@courts.maine.gov
Associate Clerk **Kim Jaques** .... (207) 822-4146
E-mail: kim.jaques@courts.maine.gov
Director of Judicial Marshals **Michael A. Coty** .... (207) 557-4088
171 State House Station, Augusta, ME 04430
P.O. Box 328, Portland, ME 04112-0328
E-mail: michael_coty@maine.gov

Chambers of Chief Justice Leigh I. Saufley

Main Supreme Judicial Court, 205 Newbury Street, Room 139,
Portland, ME 04101
Tel: (207) 822-4286 Fax: (207) 822-4202
E-mail: chiefjustice@courts.maine.gov

Leigh I. Saufley
Chief Justice

Date of Birth: 1954
Education: Maine 1976, 1980 JD
Began Service: December 6, 2001
Appointed By: Governor Angus S. King, Jr.
Term Expires: February 26, 2016

Judicial: Judge, Maine District Court (1990-1993); Justice, Maine Superior Court (1993-1997); Associate Justice, Supreme Judicial Court of Maine (1997-2001)

Staff

Law Clerk **Laura Shaw** .... (207) 822-3251
Began Service: August 2015
Term Expires: August 2016
Lead Law Clerk to the Chief Justice **Rose M. Everitt** .... (207) 822-3250
E-mail: rose.everitt@courts.maine.gov
Education: Wesleyan U 1995 BA; Maine 1998 JD
Executive Judicial Assistant **Amanda J. Martin** .... (207) 822-4286
E-mail: amanda.j.martin@courts.maine.gov

Chambers of Associate Justice Donald G. Alexander

Main Supreme Judicial Court, 205 Newbury Street, Room 139,
Portland, ME 04101-4125
Tel: (207) 822-4175

Donald G. Alexander
Associate Justice

Education: Bowdoin 1964 AB; Chicago 1967 JD
Began Service: September 2, 1998
Appointed By: Governor Angus S. King, Jr.

Government: Assistant Counsel, Committee on Environment and Public Works, United States Senate (1972-1973); Deputy and Assistant Attorney General, Office of the Attorney General, State of Maine (1974-1978)

Judicial: Judge, United States District Court for the District of Maine (1978-1980); Justice, Maine Superior Court (1980-1998)

Legal Practice: Private Practice (1971)

Nonprofit: Legislative Counsel, National League of Cities (1967-1969)

Current Memberships: Maine State Bar Association

Staff

Law Clerk **Samuel Baldwin** .... (207) 822-4175
Term Expires: August 2016
E-mail: samuel.baldwin@courts.maine.gov
Law Clerk **Caitlin Ross** .... (207) 822-4175
Secretary **Lauri Cincotta** .... (207) 822-4175
E-mail: lauri.cincotta@courts.maine.gov

Chambers of Associate Justice Andrew M. Mead

Penobscot Judicial Center, 78 Exchange Street, Bangor, ME 04401-4913
Tel: (207) 561-2310

Andrew M. Mead
Associate Justice

Education: Maine; NYU JD
Began Service: April 2, 2007
Term Expires: December 2021

Judicial: Chief Judge, Maine Superior Court (1999-2001); Judge, Maine Superior Court (1992-2007)

Chambers of Associate Justice Andrew M. Mead *continued*

Legal Practice: Attorney, Paine, Lynch & Weatherbee; Attorney, Mitchell & Stearns

Nonprofit: President, Maine State Bar Association

Staff
Law Clerk **Steven DiCairano** . . . . (207) 561-2310
Began Service: August 2015
Term Expires: August 2016
E-mail: steven.dicairano@courts.maine.gov
Career Law Clerk **C. Daniel Wood** . . . . (207) 561-2310
Judicial Assistant **Cindy Brochu** . . . . (207) 561-2310
E-mail: cindy.brochu@courts.maine.gov

Chambers of Associate Justice Ellen A. Gorman
Maine Supreme Judicial Court, 205 Newbury Street, Room 139, Portland, ME 04101-4125
Tel: (207) 822-4135

Ellen A. Gorman
Associate Justice

Education: Trinity Col (DC) 1977; Cornell 1982 JD
Began Service: October 1, 2007
Appointed By: Governor John Baldacci
Term Expires: December 2021

Judicial: Judge, Maine Superior Court (2000-2007)

Legal Practice: Associate, Richardson, Tyler and Troubh (1982-1986)

Staff
Fax: (207) 822-4252

Law Clerk **Matthew Gerety** . . . . (207) 822-4239
Began Service: August 2015
Term Expires: August 2016
E-mail: matthew.gerety@courts.maine.gov
Career Law Clerk **Crystal L. Bulges** . . . . (207) 822-4179
E-mail: crystal.bulges@courts.maine.gov
Education: Maine 2000 JD
Judicial Secretary **Lauri Cincotta** . . . . (207) 822-4135
E-mail: lauri.cincotta@courts.maine.gov

Chambers of Associate Justice Joseph M. Jabar
65 Stone Street, Augusta, ME 04330-5222
Tel: (207) 287-6950

Joseph M. Jabar
Associate Justice

Education: Colby; Maine Law 1971 JD
Began Service: 2009

Staff
Secretary **Toni Day** . . . . (207) 287-6950
E-mail: toni.day@courts.maine.gov

Chambers of Associate Justice Jeffrey L. Hjelm
205 Newbury Street, Portland, ME 04101
Tel: (207) 822-4146

Jeffrey L. Hjelm
Associate Justice

Chambers of Associate Justice Thomas E. Humphrey
205 Newbury Street, Portland, ME 04101
Tel: (207) 822-3232

Thomas E. Humphrey
Associate Judge

Began Service: 2015
Appointed By: Governor Paul LePage

Chambers of Associate Justice (Active-Retired) Robert W. Clifford
Two Turner Street, Auburn, ME 04212
Tel: (207) 330-7515

Robert W. Clifford
Justice (Active-Retired)

Date of Birth: 1937
Education: Bowdoin 1959 AB; Boston Col 1962 JD; Virginia 1998 LLM
Began Service: 2009

Current Memberships: Androscoggin County Bar Association; Maine State Bar Association

Maryland

Maryland Administrative Office of the Courts

Maryland Judicial Center, 580 Taylor Avenue, Annapolis, MD 21401
Tel: (410) 260-1400
Tel: (800) 735-2258 (Maryland Relay Service - Voice/TTY)
Fax: (410) 974-2169
E-mail: webmaster@courts.state.md.us
Internet: www.mdcourts.gov

Staff

State Court Administrator **Pamela Q. Harris** .... (410) 260-1295
E-mail: pamela.harris@mdcourts.gov Fax: (410) 974-2066
Deputy State Court Administrator **Faye Matthews** ...... (410) 260-1257
E-mail: faye.matthews@mdcourts.gov
Executive Director - Budget and Finance
Allen C. Clark III .... (410) 260-1579
E-mail: allen.clark@courts.state.md.us Fax: (410) 974-2169
Human Resources Executive Director (Acting)
Faye Matthews .... (410) 260-1280
E-mail: faye.matthews@courts.state.md.us Fax: (410) 974-2849
Judicial Information Systems Executive Director
Mark Bittner .... (410) 260-1001
E-mail: mark.bittner@mdcourts.gov Fax: (410) 974-7170
Judicial Institute Executive Director **Claire Smearman** ... (410) 946-4905
E-mail: claire.smearman@courts.state.md.us Fax: (410) 841-9850
Maryland Mediation and Conflict Resolution Office
Executive Director **Rachel Wohl** .... (410) 260-3540
E-mail: rachel.wohl@courts.state.md.us Fax: (410) 841-2261
Education: Antioch U 1974 BA; Ohio 1976 MA; Maryland 1988 JD
Government Relations Director **Kelley E. O'Connor** ..... (410) 260-1560
E-mail: kelley.o'connor@courts.state.md.us Fax: (410) 974-5291
Internal Audit Director **Ssali Luwemba** .... (410) 260-3673
E-mail: ssali.luwemba@mdcourts.gov
Legal Affairs Director **David R. Durfee, Jr.** .... (410) 260-1405
E-mail: david.durfee@courts.state.md.us Fax: (410) 974-2066
Education: Cornell 1980 BS; Maryland 1984 JD
Procurement Director **Gisela Blades** .... (410) 260-1410
E-mail: gisela.blades@mdcourts.gov Fax: (410) 974-5577
Administrative Services Manager
Roxanne P. McKagan .... (410) 260-1407
E-mail: roxanne.mckagan@mdcourts.gov Fax: (410) 974-2066
Communications and Public Affairs Officer
Angelita Plemmer .... (410) 260-1564
E-mail: angelita.plemmer@mdcourts.gov Fax: (410) 260-1488
Secretary to the Board of Law Examiners
Steven W. Boggs .... (410) 260-3644
E-mail: sble@courts.state.md.us Fax: (410) 260-1944
Reporter to the Standing Committee on Rules of Practice and Procedure **Sandra F. Haines** .... (410) 260-3630
E-mail: sandra.haines@courts.state.md.us Fax: (410) 514-7240
Education: Bucknell 1973 BA; Johns Hopkins 1978 MS; Maryland 1980 JD
Commission on Judicial Disabilities Executive Secretary **Gary J. Kolb** .... (410) 514-7044
E-mail: gary.kolb@mdcourts.gov Fax: (410) 514-7098

STATE COURTS—MARYLAND

Court of Appeals of Maryland

Robert C. Murphy Courts of Appeal Building, 401 Bosley Avenue, Towson, MD 21204
Tel: (410) 260-1500 Tel: (800) 926-2583 (Toll Free)
Internet: www.mdcourts.gov

Number of Judgeships: 7

The Court of Appeals, created by the Maryland Constitution in 1776, is divided into seven appellate judicial circuits and consists of a chief judge and six judges; one elected in each appellate circuit. Judges are initially appointed by the Governor and confirmed by the Maryland State Senate. Appointed judges face a retention vote after one year in a general election for a ten-year term. The chief judge is designated by the Governor as the constitutional administrative head of the Maryland court system and serves until the end of his term. Retirement is mandatory at age seventy; however, retired judges may be recalled for temporary assignment. The Court of Appeals has exclusive appellate jurisdiction in criminal cases when judgment of death has been pronounced or when a question certified under the Uninformed Certified Questions of Law Act is involved. The Court exercises discretionary review of cases pending in or decided by the Court of Special Appeals of Maryland. The Court has rule-making and supervisory control over the lower courts and regulates admission to the bar and the conduct of its members and members of the bench.

The Court of Appeals sits in Annapolis.

Court Staff

Clerk of Court **Bessie M. Decker** .... (410) 260-1500
E-mail: bessie.decker@mdcourts.gov
Chief Deputy Clerk **Terry L. Ruffatto** .... (410) 260-1529
E-mail: terry.ruffatto@mdcourts.gov
Senior Deputy Clerk **Melissa "Missy" Higdon** .... (410) 260-1503
E-mail: missy.higdon@mdcourts.gov
Deputy Clerk **Carol A. Greenstein** .... (410) 260-1504
E-mail: carol.greenstein@mdcourts.gov
Deputy Clerk **Doneice A. Burnette** .... (410) 260-1504
E-mail: doneice.burnette@mdcourts.gov
Deputy Clerk **Kisha Taylor-Wallace** .... (410) 260-1506
E-mail: kisha.wallace@mdcourts.gov
Assistant to State Reporter **Sara Rabe** .... (410) 260-1501
E-mail: sara.rabe@mdcourts.gov
Senior Recorder **Leslie G. Cockrell** .... (410) 260-1509
E-mail: les.cockrell@mdcourts.gov
Recorder **Sandy Belt** .... (410) 260-1539
E-mail: sandy.belt@mdcourts.gov
Administrative Support **Rachael Spicknall** .... (410) 260-1505
E-mail: rachael.spicknall@mdcourts.gov

Chambers of Chief Judge Mary Ellen Barbera

Judicial Center, 50 Maryland Avenue, Rockville, MD 20850
Tel: (240) 777-9320 Fax: (240) 777-9327
E-mail: mary.ellen.barbera@mdcourts.gov

Mary Ellen Barbera
Chief Judge

Date of Birth: 1951
Education: Towson State U 1975 BS; Maryland 1984 JD
Began Service: January 15, 2009
Appointed By: Governor Martin OMalley
Next Election: November 2020

Current Memberships: Citizens Law-Related Education Program; Committee on Criminal Law and Procedure, Maryland Judicial Conference; Maryland State Bar Association, Inc.; Appellate Litigation Committee, Maryland State Bar Association, Inc.; Pattern Jury Instruction Committee, Maryland State Bar Association, Inc.; National Association of Women Judges; Women's Bar Association of Maryland

Staff

Law Clerk **Kaitlin Motley** .... (240) 777-9320
Began Service: August 2015
Term Expires: August 2016
E-mail: kaitlin.motley@mdcourts.gov

Chambers of Chief Judge Mary Ellen Barbera *continued*

Law Clerk **Rebecca Wolf** .... (240) 777-9320
Began Service: August 2015
Term Expires: August 2016
E-mail: rebecca.wolf@mdcourts.gov

Judicial Assistant **Joan Canterbury** .... (240) 777-9320
E-mail: joan.canterbury@mdcourts.gov

Chief of Staff **Suzanne Schneider** .... (240) 777-9320

Chambers of Judge (recalled) Glenn T. Harrell, Jr.

150-B Courthouse Bourne Wing, Upper Marlboro, MD 20772-3004
P.O. Box 209, Upper Marlboro, MD 20773-0209
Tel: (301) 298-4062 Fax: (301) 574-5282
E-mail: glenn.harrell@courts.state.md.us

Glenn T. Harrell, Jr.
Judge (recalled)

Date of Birth: 1945
Education: Maryland 1967 BA, 1970 JD
Began Service: September 10, 1999
Appointed By: Governor Parris N. Glendening
Term Expires: June 27, 2016

Government: Associate County Attorney, Office of the County Attorney, Prince George's County, Maryland (1971-1973)

Judicial: Judge, Court of Special Appeals of Maryland (1991-1999)

Legal Practice: Private Practice (1973-1976); Private Practice (1977-1991)

Current Memberships: J. Franklyn Bourne Bar Association; Maryland State Bar Association, Inc.; Prince George's County Bar Association

Staff

Law Clerk **Virginia Callahan** .... (301) 298-4062
Began Service: August 2015
Term Expires: August 2016

Chambers of Judge Lynne A. Battaglia

Robert C. Murphy Courts of Appeal Building, 361 Rowe Boulevard, Annapolis, MD 21401
Tel: (410) 260-1565 Fax: (410) 260-1543
E-mail: lynne.battaglia@courts.state.md.us

Lynne A. Battaglia
Judge

Date of Birth: 1946
Education: American U 1967 BA, 1968 MA; Maryland 1974 JD
Began Service: January 26, 2001
Appointed By: Governor Parris N. Glendening
Next Election: November 2022
Term Expires: November 2022

Academic: Visiting Professor, School of Law, University of Maryland, Baltimore (1983-1984)

Government: Assistant United States Attorney, District of Maryland, United States Attorney's Office (1978-1982); Senior Trial Attorney, Office of Special Litigation, United States Department of Justice, Ronald Reagan Administration (1984-1988); Chief of Criminal Investigations Division, Office of the Attorney General, State of Maryland (1988-1991); Chief of Staff (D-MD), Office of Senator Barbara A. Mikulski, United States Senate (1991-1993); United States Attorney, District of Maryland, United States Attorney's Office, United States Department of Justice, William J. Clinton Administration (1993-2001)

Legal Practice: Associate, Semmes, Bowen & Semmes (1974-1978)

Current Memberships: The American Law Institute; The Bar Association of Baltimore City; Maryland State Bar Association, Inc.

Staff

Administrative Aide **John Baber** .... (410) 260-1565

Chambers of Judge Clayton Greene, Jr.

Robert C. Murphy Courts of Appeal Building, 361 Rowe Boulevard, Annapolis, MD 21401
Tel: (410) 260-1520 Fax: (410) 260-1545
E-mail: clayton.greene@courts.state.md.us

Clayton Greene, Jr.
Judge

Date of Birth: 1951
Education: Maryland 1973 BA, 1976 JD
Began Service: January 22, 2004
Appointed By: Governor Robert L. Ehrlich, Jr.
Political Affiliation: Democrat

Government: Solicitor, County of Anne Arundel, Maryland (1977-1978); Public Defender, County of Anne Arundel, Maryland (1978-1988); Deputy Public Defender, County of Anne Arundel, Maryland (1985-1988)

Judicial: Judge, District Court of Maryland (1988-1995); Circuit Judge, Anne Arundel County Circuit Court (1995-2002); Judge, Court of Special Appeals of Maryland (2002-2003)

Current Memberships: Anne Arundel Bar Association; The District of Columbia Bar; Maryland State Bar Association, Inc.; National Bar Association

Staff

Executive Assistant and Paralegal **Jean Bowling** .... (410) 260-1537
E-mail: jean.bowling@courts.state.md.us
Education: Maryland 1976 BS

Chambers of Judge Sally D. Adkins

P.O. Box 1029, Salisbury, MD 21803-1029
Tel: (410) 713-3440 Fax: (410) 334-3449
E-mail: sally.adkins@courts.state.md.us

Sally D. Adkins
Judge

Date of Birth: 1950
Education: Lawrence U 1972 BA; Maryland 1975 JD
Began Service: June 25, 2008
Appointed By: Governor Martin OMalley
Next Election: November 4, 2018
Election Type: Retention Election
Term Expires: 2018
Political Affiliation: Republican

Clerkships: Law Clerk The Honorable Marvin H. Smith, Maryland Court of Appeals (1975-1976)

Government: Chair, Maryland Commission on Judicial Disabilities (1999-2006)

Judicial: Associate Judge, Wicomico County Circuit Court (1996-1998); Judge, Court of Special Appeals of Maryland (1998-2008)

Legal Practice: Associate then Partner, Adkins, Potts and Smethurst (1976-1995); Partner, Adkins and Allen (1995-1996)

Nonprofit: Director and Secretary, O.U.R. Community, Inc. (1995-2005)

Current Memberships: American Bar Association; Maryland Bar Foundation, Maryland State Bar Association, Inc.

Membership: Director, Legal Aid Bureau Inc.; Director, Coastal Hospice, Inc.

Staff

Law Clerk **Jason Kornmehl** .... (410) 260-1496
Began Service: August 2015
Term Expires: August 2016
E-mail: jason.kornmehl@courts.state.md.us

Law Clerk **Christopher Chaulk** .... (410) 260-1495
Began Service: August 2015
Term Expires: August 2016
E-mail: christopher.chaulk@courts.state.md.us

(continued on next page)

Chambers of Judge Sally D. Adkins *continued*

Administrative Assistant **Kristin Seal** . . . . (410) 713-3440
E-mail: kristin.seal@courts.state.md.us

Chambers of Judge Robert N. McDonald

401 Bosley Avenue, Towson, MD 21204
Tel: (410) 887-3206
E-mail: robert.mcdonald@mdcourts.gov

Robert N. McDonald
Judge

Education: Harvard 1972 BA, 1977 JD
Began Service: January 24, 2012

Chambers of Judge Shirley M. Watts

626B Courthouse East, 111 North Calvert Street, Baltimore, MD 21202
Tel: (410) 260-1500
E-mail: shirley.watts@mdcourts.gov

Shirley M. Watts
Judge

Education: Rutgers 1983 JD; Howard Col 1980 BA
Appointed By: Governor Martin OMalley

Court of Special Appeals of Maryland

Robert C. Murphy Courts of Appeal Building, 361 Rowe Boulevard, 2nd Floor, Annapolis, MD 21401
Tel: (410) 260-1450
Tel: (888) 200-7444 (Direct line from Washington, DC (Toll-free))
Internet: www.mdcourts.gov

Number of Judgeships: 13

The Court of Special Appeals, established in 1966, is divided into the same seven appellate judicial circuits as the Court of Appeals of Maryland and consists of a chief judge and twelve judges. One judge is appointed from each circuit. The remaining six judges are appointed at large. Judges are initially appointed by the Governor and confirmed by the Maryland State Senate, and they run for retention for ten-year terms at the next general election occurring at least one year after the appointment. The chief judge is appointed by the Governor and serves until the end of his or her term. Retirement is mandatory at age seventy; however, retired judges may be recalled for temporary assignments. The Court of Special Appeals has exclusive initial appellate jurisdiction over any reviewable judgment, decree, order or other action of the Maryland Circuit Court or Orphans' Court except as provided by law.

The Court of Special Appeals sits in Annapolis.

Court Staff

Clerk of the Court **Gregory Hilton** . . . . (410) 260-1459
E-mail: greg.hilton@mdcourts.gov
Chief Deputy **Rachel Dombrowski** . . . . (410) 260-1456
E-mail: rachel.dombrowski@mdcourts.gov
Chief Staff Attorney **Kathryn May** . . . . (410) 260-1472
E-mail: kathryn.may@mdcourts.gov
Staff Attorney **Nancy S. Hoffman** . . . . (410) 887-3115
E-mail: nancy.hoffman@mdcourts.gov
Assistant Staff Attorney **Alyssa Bedell** . . . . (410) 260-1519
Assistant Staff Attorney **Steve Holcomb** . . . . (410) 260-3713
Assistant Staff Attorney **Jessica A. Gray** . . . . (410) 260-1480
E-mail: jessica.gray@courts.state.md.us
Education: Maryland 2004 JD
Assistant Staff Attorney **Ellen Draper** . . . . (410) 887-3113
E-mail: ellen.draper@courts.state.md.us
Assistant Staff Attorney **Caryn A. Jackson** . . . . (410) 260-1475
E-mail: caryn.jackson@courts.state.md.us
Assistant Staff Attorney **John Jeffrey Ross** . . . . (410) 260-1478
Assistant Staff Attorney **(Vacant)** . . . . (410) 260-1450

Court of Special Appeals of Maryland *continued*

Assistant Staff Attorney **Elizabeth Rubin** . . . . (410) 260-1450
Assistant Staff Attorney **Garrick Greenblatt** . . . . (410) 260-1450
E-mail: garrick.greenblatt@mdcourts.gov

Chambers of Chief Judge Peter B. Krauser

Robert C. Murphy Courts of Appeal Building, 361 Rowe Boulevard, Annapolis, MD 21401
Tel: (410) 260-1469 Fax: (410) 268-3102
E-mail: peter.krauser@mdcourts.gov

Peter B. Krauser
Chief Judge

Date of Birth: 1947
Education: Pennsylvania 1972 JD
Began Service: January 31, 2000
Appointed By: Governor Parris N. Glendening
Next Election: November 2020
Term Expires: December 31, 2021
Political Affiliation: Democrat

Clerkships: Law Clerk The Honorable John P. Fullam, United States District Court for the Eastern District of Pennsylvania

Government: Appellate Attorney, Criminal Division, United States Department of Justice; Trial and Appellate Attorney, Defender Association of Philadelphia

Legal Practice: Partner, Margolius, Davis, Finkelstein & Rider; General Counsel, Prince George Center, Inc.; Partner, Pohoryles & Greenstein, PC; Partner, Thompson Hine & Flory LLP; President, Krauser & Taub, PC

Staff

Law Clerk **Cynthia Polasko** . . . . (410) 260-1469
Began Service: August 2013
Term Expires: August 2016
E-mail: cynthia.polasko@mdcourts.gov
Education: Dickinson Col 2006 BA; Maryland 2013 JD
Senior Law Clerk **Peter Goldsmith** . . . . (410) 260-1469
Administrative Aide **Peg Redd** . . . . (410) 260-1469
E-mail: peggy.redd@mdcourts.gov
Education: Col Notre Dame (MD) 2002 BA, 2004 MA

Chambers of Judge Deborah Sweet Eyler

Robert C. Murphy Courts of Appeal Building, 361 Rowe Boulevard, Annapolis, MD 21401
Tel: (410) 260-1485 Fax: (410) 260-1546
E-mail: deborah.eyler@mdcourts.gov

Deborah Sweet Eyler
Judge

Date of Birth: August 11, 1952
Education: Maryland 1981 JD
Began Service: June 17, 1997
Appointed By: Governor Parris N. Glendening
Next Election: November 4, 2018
Election Type: Retention Election
Term Expires: 2018
Political Affiliation: Democrat

Government: Service Member, Peace Corps (1973-1974); Chair, Trial Courts Nominating Commission, County of Baltimore, Maryland (1995-1997)

Legal Practice: Associate, Whiteford, Taylor & Preston (1981-1990); Partner, Whiteford, Taylor & Preston (1990-1997)

Current Memberships: Baltimore County Bar Association; Maryland State Bar Association, Inc.; Maryland Bar Foundation, Maryland State Bar Association, Inc.

Chambers of Judge Deborah Sweet Eyler *continued*

Membership: Board Member, Board of Governors, Maryland State Bar Association, Inc. (1995-1997)

Staff

Law Clerk **Anthony J. May** .... (410) 260-1485
Began Service: August 2015
Term Expires: August 2016
Career Law Clerk **Kathryn Vaeth** .... (410) 260-1485
Education: Vassar 2000 BA; Maryland 2006 JD
Administrative Specialist **Ann Kaiser** .... (410) 260-1485
E-mail: ann.kaiser@mdcourts.gov

Chambers of Judge Timothy E. Meredith

Robert C. Murphy Courts of Appeal Building, 361 Rowe Boulevard, 3rd Floor, Annapolis, MD 21401
Tel: (410) 260-1718
E-mail: timothy.meredith@mdcourts.gov

Timothy E. Meredith
Judge

Date of Birth: May 11, 1952
Education: Western Maryland 1974 BA; Duke 1977 JD
Began Service: August 2, 2004

Affiliation: Member, Woods Memorial Presbyterian Church

Clerkships: Law Clerk, Chambers of Judge Marvin H. Smith, Court of Appeals of Maryland (1977-1978)

Corporate: Co-Host, Lawline Cable TV Show (1995-2000)

Legal Practice: Associate, Corbin, Heller & Warfield (1978-1984); Partner, Corbin, Heller & Warfield (1984); Partner, Corbin, Warfield, Schaffer & Meredith (1984-1995); Partner, Warfield, Meredith & Darrah, P.C. (1995-2004)

Nonprofit: President, Anne Arundel County Bar Association (1993-1994); President, Anne Arundel Bar Foundation (1994-1995)

Current Memberships: American Bar Association; Maryland State Bar Association, Inc.; Maryland Bar Foundation, Maryland State Bar Association, Inc.

Membership: Elder, Woods Memorial Presbyterian Church (1983-1986); Board Member, Board of Governors, Maryland State Bar Association, Inc. (1994-1996); Council Member, Baltimore Area Council, Boy Scouts of America; Clerk of Session, Woods Memorial Presbyterian Church (2001-2005); Board Member, Board of Governors, Maryland State Bar Association, Inc. (2002-2004)

Staff

Law Clerk **Kathryn Bartz** .... (410) 260-1718
E-mail: kathryn.bartz@mdcourts.gov
Senior Law Clerk **Kathryn Buettner** .... (410) 260-1717
Began Service: August 2010
E-mail: kathryn.buettner@mdcourts.gov
Education: Baltimore 2001 JD

Chambers of Judge Patrick L. Woodward

Montgomery County Judicial Center, 50 Maryland Avenue, Rockville, MD 20850
Tel: (240) 777-9351
E-mail: patrick.woodward@mdcourts.gov

Patrick L. Woodward
Judge

Date of Birth: 1948
Education: Princeton 1970 AB; Vanderbilt 1973 JD
Began Service: 2005

Clerkships: Law Clerk, Chambers of Chief Judge Edward S. Northrop, United States District Court for the District of Maryland (1973-1974)

Chambers of Judge Patrick L. Woodward *continued*

Legal Practice: Associate, Law Offices of Rourke J. Sheehan (1974-1978); Partner, Sheehan & Woodward (1978-1980); Partner, Jackson, Campbell & Parkinson; Director, Jackson & Campbell, P.C. (1980-1987); Attorney, Private Practice (1987-1991)

Military Service: CPT, United States Army Reserve, United States Department of Defense (1974-1975)

Current Memberships: Maryland State Bar Association, Inc.

Staff

Administrative Assistant **Levora Cherry** .... (240) 777-9351
E-mail: levora.cherry@mdcourts.gov

Chambers of Judge Robert A. Zarnoch

Robert C. Murphy Courts of Appeals Building, 361 Rowe Boulevard, Annapolis, MD 21401
Tel: (410) 260-1450
E-mail: robert.zarnoch@mdcourts.gov

Robert A. Zarnoch
Judge

Began Service: March 7, 2008
Appointed By: Governor Martin OMalley
Next Election: November 4, 2018
Election Type: Retention Election
Term Expires: 2018

Government: General Assembly Counsel, Office of the Attorney General, State of Maryland

Staff

Law Clerk **Michael "Mike" Sherling** .... (410) 260-3701
Began Service: August 2015
Term Expires: August 31, 2016
E-mail: michael.sherling@mdcourts.gov
Judicial Assistant **(Vacant)** .... (410) 260-3701
E-mail: alexia.smith@mdcourts.gov

Chambers of Judge Alexander Wright, Jr.

County Courts Building, 401 Bosley Avenue, Towson, MD 21204
Tel: (410) 887-3286
E-mail: alexander.wright@mdcourts.gov

Alexander Wright, Jr.
Judge

Education: Morgan State 1971 BA; Maryland 1974 JD
Began Service: February 28, 2008
Appointed By: Governor Martin OMalley
Next Election: November 2020

Staff

Law Clerk **Xheni Llaguri** .... (410) 887-3286
Began Service: August 2015
Term Expires: August 19, 2016
E-mail: xheni.llaguri@mdcourts.gov
Career Law Clerk **Roxanne Smalkin** .... (410) 887-3286
Began Service: February 2008
E-mail: roxanne.reyes@mdcourts.gov
Education: Baltimore 2003 JD

Chambers of Judge Kathryn Grill Graeff
Robert C. Murphy Courts of Appeal Building, 361 Rowe Boulevard, Annapolis, MD 21401
Tel: (410) 260-1466 Fax: (410) 260-1714
E-mail: kathryn.graeff@mdcourts.gov

Kathryn Grill Graeff
Judge

Began Service: September 2008
Appointed By: Governor Martin OMalley
Next Election: November 2020

Staff
Law Clerk **Andrew DiMiceli** . . . . (410) 260-1466
Began Service: August 2015
Term Expires: August 2016
Senior Law Clerk **Suzanne Johnson** . . . . (410) 260-1466
E-mail: suzanne.johnson@mdcourts.gov
Judicial Assistant **Claudia R. Thomas** . . . . (410) 260-1466
E-mail: claudia.thomas@mdcourts.gov
Education: Liberty 1994

Chambers of Judge Christopher B. Kehoe
11 South Washington Street, Suite F, Easton, MD 21601
Tel: (410) 822-3935
E-mail: christopher.kehoe@mdcourts.gov

Christopher B. Kehoe
Judge

Education: Tufts 1975 BA; Duke 1978 JD
Began Service: January 21, 2009
Appointed By: Governor Martin OMalley
Next Election: November 2020
Election Type: Retention Election
Term Expires: 2019

Staff
Law Clerk **Peter Hershey** . . . . (410) 822-3935
Began Service: 2010
E-mail: peter.hershey@mdcourts.gov
Law Clerk **Meredith Schreibseder** . . . . (410) 822-3935
Began Service: 2010

Chambers of Judge Michele D. Hotten
P.O. Box 209, Upper Marlboro, MD 20773-0209
Tel: (301) 298-4075
E-mail: michele.hotten@mdcourts.gov

Michele D. Hotten
Judge

Date of Birth: April 20, 1954
Education: New Col South Florida 1975 BA; Howard U 1979 JD
Began Service: August 17, 2010
Appointed By: Governor Martin OMalley

Staff
Law Clerk **Jeffrey Johnson** . . . . (301) 298-4075
Began Service: August 2015
Term Expires: August 2017
Law Clerk **Alicia Philip** . . . . (301) 298-4075
Began Service: August 2015
Term Expires: August 2017
E-mail: alicia.philip@mdcourts.gov
Administrative Aide **Shelley Lester** . . . . (301) 298-4075
E-mail: shelley.lester@mdcourts.gov

Chambers of Judge Stuart R. Berger
Courthouse East, 111 North Calvert Street, Room 626, Baltimore, MD 21202
Tel: (410) 333-6241

Stuart R. Berger
Judge

Began Service: 2011
Next Election: 2022

Staff
Law Clerk **Bryant Green** . . . . (410) 333-6241
Term Expires: August 2016
Career Law Clerk **Elizabeth Pittman** . . . . (410) 333-6241
Administrative Assistant **Kathy Boone** . . . . (410) 333-6241

Chambers of Judge Douglas R.M. Nazarian
401 Bosley Avenue, Towson, MD 21204
Tel: (410) 260-1450
E-mail: douglas.nazarian@courts.state.md.us

Douglas R.M. Nazarian
Judge

Date of Birth: October 30, 1966
Education: Yale 1988 BA; Duke 1991 JD
Began Service: 2013
Appointed By: Governor Martin OMalley

Chambers of Judge Kevin F. Arthur
111 North Calvert Street, Baltimore, MD 21202
Tel: (410) 260-1450
E-mail: kevin.arthur@mdcourts.gov

Kevin F. Arthur
Judge

Began Service: 2014
Appointed By: Governor Martin OMalley

Chambers of Judge Andrea M. Leahy
361 Rowe Boulevard, Annapolis, MD 21401
Tel: (410) 260-1515
E-mail: andrea.leahy@mdcourts.gov

Andrea M. Leahy
Judge

Began Service: 2014
Appointed By: Governor Martin OMalley

Staff
Law Clerk **Darci Smith** . . . . (410) 260-1515
Term Expires: August 2016
Law Clerk **Anthony Kikendall** . . . . (410) 260-1515
Term Expires: August 2016
Career Law Clerk **Kevin Harp** . . . . (410) 260-1515

Chambers of Judge Michael W. Reed
620 Mitchell Courthouse, 100 North Calvert Street, Baltimore, MD 21202
Tel: (410) 209-6340
E-mail: michael.reed@mdcourts.gov

Michael W. Reed
Judge

Staff
Law Clerk **Timothy Dygert** . . . . (410) 260-1450
Term Expires: August 2016

Chambers of Judge Michael W. Reed *continued*

Law Clerk **Joey Cravath** . . . . (410) 260-1450
Term Expires: August 2016
Judicial Assistant **Artist Arthur** . . . . (410) 260-1450

Chambers of Judge Daniel A. Friedman

401 Bosley Avenue, Suite 342, Towson, MD 21204
Tel: (410) 887-2647

Daniel A. Friedman
Judge

Began Service: 2014

Massachusetts

Massachusetts Supreme Judicial Court

John Adams Courthouse, One Pemberton Square, Suite 2500,
Boston, MA 02108-1750
Tel: (617) 557-1000 Fax: (617) 723-3577
Internet: www.mass.gov/courts/sjc

Number of Judgeships: 7

The Supreme Judicial Court consists of a chief justice and six associate justices who are appointed by the Governor with the consent of the Massachusetts Executive Council to serve until age seventy. The Supreme Judicial Court has concurrent appellate jurisdiction with the Massachusetts Appeals Court over civil and criminal matters in all lower courts. The Court has original appellate jurisdiction in cases of first degree murder and in cases that the Supreme Judicial Court or the Appeals Court certifies for direct review or one that has broad public concern. The Court may render advisory opinions to the State Legislature, the Governor, and the Executive Council.

The Supreme Judicial Court sits in Boston.

Court Staff

Clerk for the Commonwealth **Francis V. Kenneally** . . . . . . (617) 557-1020
E-mail: francis.kenneally@sjc.state.ma.us Fax: (617) 557-1145
Education: Columbus Law 1989 JD
Assistant Clerk **Maura Looney** . . . . (617) 557-1020
E-mail: maura.looney@sjc.state.ma.us Fax: (617) 557-1145
Assistant Clerk Pro Tem **(Vacant)** . . . . (617) 557-1020
Fax: (617) 557-1145
Executive Director **(Vacant)** . . . . (617) 557-1194
Fax: (617) 557-1052
Clerk of the Supreme Judicial Court, Suffolk County
Maura Sweeney Doyle . . . . (617) 557-1180
John Adams Courthouse, One Pemberton Square, First Floor, Suite 1300, Boston, MA 02108 Fax: (617) 523-1540
E-mail: maura.doyle@sjc.state.ma.us
First Assistant Clerk, Boston **Eric Wetzel** . . . . (617) 557-1165
E-mail: eric.wetzel@sjc.state.ma.us Fax: (617) 523-1540
Second Assistant Clerk, Milton **George E. Slyva** . . . . (617) 557-1185
E-mail: george.slyva@sjc.state.ma.us Fax: (617) 523-1540
Third Assistant Clerk, Suffolk **Amy C. Stewart** . . . . (617) 557-1186
E-mail: amy.stewart@sjc.state.ma.us Fax: (617) 523-1540
Chief Staff Counsel **Neal B. Quenzer** . . . . (617) 557-1122
E-mail: neal.quenzer@sjc.state.ma.us Fax: (617) 557-1053
Coordinator of Policy and Development **Carol Lev** . . . . (617) 557-1074
E-mail: carol.lev@sjc.state.ma.us Fax: (617) 557-1052
Reporter of Decisions **Brian H. Redmond** . . . . (617) 557-1196
E-mail: brian.redmond@sjc.state.ma.us Fax: (617) 557-1105
Chief Information Officer **David Lucal** . . . . (617) 557-1119
E-mail: david.lucal@sjc.state.ma.us Fax: (617) 557-1053
Public Information Officer **Jennifer Donahue** . . . . (617) 557-1114
E-mail: jennifer.donahue@sjc.state.ma.us Fax: (617) 742-1807
Business Manager **Robert Burns** . . . . (617) 557-1070
E-mail: robert.burns@sjc.state.ma.us Fax: (617) 723-3577

Chambers of Chief Justice Ralph D. Gants

John Adams Courthouse, One Pemberton Square, Boston, MA 02108
Tel: (617) 557-1020
E-mail: ralph.gants@sjc.state.ma.us

Ralph D. Gants
Chief Justice

Education: Harvard, JD
Began Service: January 29, 2009
Appointed By: Governor Deval L. Patrick

Staff
Executive Assistant **Catherine C. MacInnes** . . . . (617) 557-1020
E-mail: catherine.macinnes@sjc.state.ma.us

Chambers of Associate Justice Francis X. Spina

John Adams Courthouse, One Pemberton Square, Boston, MA 02108
Tel: (617) 557-1000 Fax: (617) 557-1054
E-mail: francis.spina@sjc.state.ma.us

Francis X. Spina
Associate Justice

Date of Birth: 1946
Education: Amherst 1968 BA; Boston Col 1971 JD
Began Service: October 14, 1999
Appointed By: Governor Argeo Paul Cellucci

Government: Assistant City Solicitor, Department of Law, City of Pittsfield, Massachusetts (1975-1977); Special Assistant District Attorney, Office of the District Attorney, County of Berkshire, Massachusetts (1979-1983)

Judicial: Judge, Massachusetts Superior Court (1993-1997); Judge, Massachusetts Appeals Court (1997-1999)

Legal Practice: Katz, LaPointe & Spina

Current Memberships: Berkshire County Bar Association; Hampden County Bar Association; Massachusetts Bar Association

Staff
Law Clerk **Maggi Farrell** . . . . (617) 557-1000
Began Service: September 1, 2012
Term Expires: August 30, 2016
E-mail: maggi.farrell@sjc.state.ma.us
Executive Assistant **Joyce Hurley** . . . . (617) 557-1150
E-mail: joyce.hurley@sjc.state.ma.us

Chambers of Associate Justice Robert J. Cordy

John Adams Courthouse, One Pemberton Square, Suite 2200,
Boston, MA 02108-1735
Tel: (617) 557-1136 Fax: (617) 557-1041
E-mail: robert.cordy@sjc.state.ma.us

Robert J. Cordy
Associate Justice

Date of Birth: 1949
Education: Dartmouth 1971 AB; Harvard 1974 JD
Began Service: February 2001
Appointed By: Governor Argeo Paul Cellucci

Academic: Lecturer, Harvard Law School (1987-1996)

Government: Special Assistant Attorney General, Revenue Department, Administration and Finance Executive Office, Commonwealth of Massachusetts (1978-1979); Associate General Counsel, State Ethics Commission, Commonwealth of Massachusetts (1979-1982); Federal Prosecutor, United States Attorney's Office, Commonwealth of Massachusetts (1982-1987); Chief Legal Counsel, Governor William F. Weld (R-MA), Commonwealth of Massachusetts (1991-1993)

Legal Practice: Defense Attorney, Committee for Public Counsel Services (1974-1978); Partner, Burns & Levinson LLP (1987-1991); Managing Partner, McDermott Will & Emery LLP (1993-2001)

Staff
Law Clerk **Kenneth Kaufman** . . . . (617) 557-1136
Began Service: 2015
Term Expires: August 31, 2016
Law Clerk **Janine Pare** . . . . (617) 557-1136
Began Service: 2015
Term Expires: August 31, 2016
E-mail: janine.pare@sjc.state.ma.us
Executive Assistant **Catherine C. MacInnes** . . . . (617) 557-1136
E-mail: catherine.macinnes@sjc.state.ma.us

Chambers of Associate Justice Margot Botsford
John Adams Courthouse, One Pemberton Square, Suite 2200,
Boston, MA 02108-1735
Tel: (617) 557-1150
E-mail: margot.botsford@sjc.state.ma.us

Margot Botsford
Associate Justice

Date of Birth: 1947
Education: Barnard 1969 BA; Northeastern 1973 JD
Began Service: September 4, 2007
Appointed By: Governor Deval L. Patrick

Clerkships: Law Clerk, Associate Justice Francis J. Quirico, Massachusetts Supreme Judicial Court (1973-1974)

Government: Assistant Attorney General, Commonwealth of Massachusetts (1975-1979); Assistant District Attorney, Office of the District Attorney, Chief Appeals Bureau, County of Middlesex, Massachusetts (1983-1989)

Legal Practice: Associate, Hill & Barlow (1974-1975); Partner, Rosenfeld, Botsford & Krokidas (1979-1983)

Current Memberships: Boston Bar Association; Massachusetts Bar Association; National Association of Women Judges

Staff
Law Clerk **(Vacant)** .... (617) 557-1150
Law Clerk **Elizabeth McEvoy** .... (617) 557-1150
Executive Assistant **Joyce Hurley** .... (617) 557-1150
E-mail: joyce.hurley@sjc.state.ma.us

Chambers of Associate Justice Fernande R.V. Duffly
John Adams Courthouse, One Pemberton Square, Boston, MA 02108
Tel: (617) 557-1000 Fax: (617) 723-3577
E-mail: fernande.duffly@sjc.state.ma.us

Fernande R. V. "Nan" Duffly
Associate Justice

Date of Birth: 1949
Education: Connecticut 1973 BA; Harvard 1978 JD
Began Service: January 25, 2011
Appointed By: Governor Deval L. Patrick

Current Memberships: Massachusetts Chapter, American Academy of Matrimonial Lawyers; Asian American Lawyers Association of Massachusetts; Boston Bar Association; Massachusetts Bar Association; National Association of Women Judges; Women's Bar Association of Massachusetts

Chambers of Associate Justice Barbara A. Lenk
One Pemberton Square, Boston, MA 02108
Tel: (617) 557-1000 Fax: (617) 723-3577
E-mail: barbara.lenk@sjc.state.ma.us

Barbara A. Lenk
Associate Justice

Date of Birth: 1950
Education: Fordham 1972 BA; Yale 1973 MA, 1974 MPhil, 1978 PhD; Harvard 1979 JD
Began Service: June 8, 2011
Appointed By: Governor Deval L. Patrick

Current Memberships: The Boston American Inn of Court, The American Inns of Court; Board of Trustees, Western New England College

Chambers of Associate Justice Geraldine S. Hines
One Pemberton Square, Boston, MA 02108
Tel: (617) 557-1000

Geraldine S. Hines
Associate Justice

Education: Tougaloo 1968 BA; Wisconsin 1971 JD
Began Service: July 31, 2014
Appointed By: Governor Deval L. Patrick

Massachusetts Appeals Court
John Adams Courthouse, One Pemberton Square, Suite 3500,
Boston, MA 02108-1705
Tel: (617) 725-8106
Internet: www.mass.gov/courts/appealscourt

Number of Judgeships: 25

The Appeals Court consists of a chief justice and 24 associate justices who are appointed by the Governor with the consent of the Massachusetts Governor's Council to serve until age seventy. The justices sit in panels of three or more as determined by the chief justice of the Appeals Court. The Appeals Court has concurrent appellate jurisdiction with the Supreme Judicial Court in civil and equity matters, administrative determinations and proceedings related to extraordinary writs, and in criminal matters except appeals from first degree murder convictions. The Court has appellate jurisdiction over final decisions of the Massachusetts Employee Relations Board, the Appellate Tax Board and the Department of Industrial Accidents.

The Massachusetts Appeals Court sits regularly in Boston and periodically in other specially designated locations.

Court Staff
Clerk of the Appeals Court **Joseph F. Stanton** .... (617) 725-8106
E-mail: joseph.stanton@appct.state.ma.us
Education: New England 1994 JD
Court Administrator **Gilbert P. Lima, Jr.** .... (617) 725-8098
Began Service: July 16, 2010 Fax: (617) 523-2845
E-mail: gilbert.lima@appct.state.ma.us
Education: Western New England 1983 JD
First Assistant Clerk **Lena M. Wong** .... (617) 725-8106
E-mail: lena.wong@appct.state.ma.us
Education: Boston Col 1983 JD
Assistant Clerk **Julie Goldman** .... (617) 725-8106
E-mail: julie.goldman@appct.state.ma.us
Assistant Clerk **Ann Thomas** .... (617) 725-8106
E-mail: ann.thomas@appct.state.ma.us
Special Assistant Clerk **Joseph F. Launie** .... (617) 725-8106
E-mail: joseph.launie@appct.state.ma.us
Chief Court Officer **Dana Smith** .... (617) 725-8087
E-mail: dana.smith@appct.state.ma.us Fax: (617) 523-2845
Special Projects Manager **Daniel W. Thurler** .... (617) 725-8096
Managing Staff Attorney **Frank C. Mockler** .... (617) 626-7982
E-mail: frank.mockler@appct.state.ma.us
Fiscal Officer **Karen Zysk** .... (617) 994-4154
E-mail: karen.zysk@appct.state.ma.us
Reporter of Decisions **Brian H. Redmond** .... (617) 557-1075

Chambers of Chief Justice Scott L. Kafker
John Adams Courthouse, One Pemberton Square, Boston, MA 02108
Tel: (617) 725-8085 Fax: (617) 723-1593
E-mail: scott.kafker@appct.state.ma.us

Scott L. Kafker
Chief Justice

Date of Birth: 1959
Education: Amherst 1981 BA; Chicago 1985 JD
Began Service: 2001
Appointed By: Governor Argeo Paul Cellucci

(continued on next page)

Chambers of Chief Justice Scott L. Kafker *continued*

Staff

Law Clerk **Brittany Williams** . . . . (617) 725-8085
Began Service: September 2013
E-mail: alex.brazier@appct.state.ma.us
Judicial Secretary **Gina Demetrio** . . . . (617) 626-7915
E-mail: gina.demetrio@appct.state.ma.us

Chambers of Associate Justice Elspeth B. Cypher

One Pemberton Square, Boston, MA 02108
Tel: (617) 723-1506 Fax: (617) 723-1593
E-mail: Elspeth.Cypher@appct.state.ma.us

Elspeth B. Cypher
Associate Justice

Date of Birth: 1959
Education: Emerson 1980; Suffolk 1986 JD
Began Service: December 27, 2000
Appointed By: Governor Argeo Paul Cellucci

Academic: Adjunct Professor, Southern New England School of Law

Government: Assistant District Attorney, Office of the District Attorney, County of Bristol, Massachusetts (1988-1993); Chief, Appellate Division, Office of the District Attorney, County of Bristol, Massachusetts (1993-2000)

Legal Practice: Associate, Grayer, Brown & Dilday (1986-1988)

Current Memberships: Massachusetts Bar Association

Staff

Career Law Clerk **Richard A. Pline** . . . . (617) 723-1506
E-mail: richard.pline@appct.state.ma.us
Education: Suffolk 1989 JD
Judicial Secretary **Gina Demetrio** . . . . (617) 626-7915
E-mail: gina.demetrio@appct.state.ma.us

Chambers of Associate Justice Marc Kantrowitz

Adams Courthouse, Pemberton Square, Boston, MA 02108
Tel: (617) 626-7915 Fax: (617) 723-1593

Marc Kantrowitz
Associate Justice

Began Service: May 2001
Appointed By: Governor Argeo Paul Cellucci

Government: Assistant District Attorney, Commonwealth of Massachusetts

Legal Practice: Attorney, Private Practice

Staff

Law Clerk **Amal Bama** . . . . (617) 626-7986
E-mail: amal.bala@appct.state.ma.us
Secretary **Gina Demetrio** . . . . (617) 626-7915
E-mail: gina.demetrio@appct.state.ma.us

Chambers of Associate Justice Janis M. Berry

John Adams Courthouse, One Pemberton Square, Suite 3500, Boston, MA 02108
Tel: (617) 626-7922 Fax: (617) 367-7119
E-mail: janis.berry@appct.state.ma.us

Janis M. Berry
Associate Justice

Date of Birth: 1949
Education: Boston U 1971 BA, 1974 JD
Began Service: 2001
Appointed By: Governor Argeo Paul Cellucci

Academic: Instructor, Harvard Law School, Harvard University (1983-1986)

Chambers of Associate Justice Janis M. Berry *continued*

Government: Assistant U.S. Attorney, United States Department of Justice, Ronald Reagan Administration (1980-1986)

Legal Practice: Associate, Bingham, Dana & Gould, LLP (1975-1980); Partner, Ropes & Gray LLP (1986-1994); Partner, Roche, Carens & DeGiacomo, P.C. (1996-1997); Partner, Rubin and Rudman LLP (1997-2001)

Current Memberships: The American Law Institute; Boston Bar Association; Massachusetts Bar Association

Staff

Law Clerk **Matthew Wahrer** . . . . (617) 626-7922
Began Service: September 2014
Term Expires: August 2015
E-mail: matthew_wahrer@app.state.ma.us
Secretary **Jeanie O'Connor** . . . . (617) 626-7908

Chambers of Associate Justice Cynthia J. Cohen

John Adams Courthouse, One Pemberton Square, Suite 3500, Boston, MA 02108
Tel: (617) 626-7900 Fax: (617) 725-8797
E-mail: cynthia.cohen@appct.state.ma.us

Cynthia J. Cohen
Associate Justice

Education: Brown U AB; Chicago MAT; Harvard JD
Began Service: 2001
Appointed By: Governor Argeo Paul Cellucci

Legal Practice: Partner, Meehan, Boyle & Cohen, PC

Staff

Law Clerk **Jodi Guinn** . . . . (617) 994-4117
E-mail: jodi.guinn@appct.state.ma.us
Judicial Secretary **Beverly McDonald** . . . . (617) 723-1509
E-mail: beverly.mcdonald@appct.state.ma.us

Chambers of Associate Justice Mark V. Green

John Adams Courthouse, One Pemberton Square, Suite 3500, Boston, MA 02108
Tel: (617) 725-8673 Fax: (617) 723-1592
E-mail: mark.green@appct.state.ma.us

Mark V. Green
Associate Justice

Date of Birth: 1956
Education: Cornell 1978 AB; Harvard 1982 JD
Began Service: 2001
Appointed By: Governor Jane M. Swift

Judicial: Associate Justice, Massachusetts Land Court (1997-2001)

Legal Practice: Herrick & Smith (1982-1985); Goulston & Storrs, PC (1985-1990); Shawmut Bank, N.A. (1990-1994); TMAC (1994-1995); Bay Bank Boston, N.A. (1995-1996); Bank Boston, N.A. (1996-1997)

Staff

Judicial Assistant **Katherine Boczkowski** . . . . (617) 725-8673

Chambers of Associate Justice Joseph A. Trainor

John Adams Courthouse, One Pemberton Square, Suite 3500, Boston, MA 02108
Tel: (617) 725-8085 Fax: (617) 725-8026
E-mail: joseph.trainor@appct.state.ma.us

Joseph A. Trainor
Associate Justice

Date of Birth: 1948
Education: St Anselm BA; Suffolk JD
Began Service: December 6, 2001

Judicial: First Justice, Middlesex County Juvenile Court, Massachusetts (1996-2001)

Staff
Law Clerk **Nicholas Hasenfus** . . . . (617) 994-4128
Began Service: 2015
Term Expires: August 2017
E-mail: nicholas.hasenfus@appct.state.ma.us
Judicial Secretary **Jennifer L. Martin** . . . . (617) 626-7919
E-mail: jennifer.martin@appct.state.ma.us

Chambers of Associate Justice Gary S. Katzmann

One Pemberton Square, Boston, MA 02108
Tel: (617) 725-8085
E-mail: gary.katzmann@appct.state.ma.us

Gary S. Katzmann
Associate Justice

Education: Yale 1979 MPPM, 1979 JD
Began Service: 2004

Chambers of Associate Justice Ariane D. Vuono

One Pemberton Square, Boston, MA 02108
Tel: (617) 725-8085
E-mail: ariane.vuono@appct.state.ma.us

Ariane D. Vuono
Associate Justice

Began Service: 2006

Government: Criminal Division Assistant U.S. Attorney, Springfield (MA) Office, Executive Office for United States Attorneys, United States Department of Justice (1995-2006)

Chambers of Associate Justice Andrew R. Grainger

One Pemberton Square, Boston, MA 02108
Tel: (617) 626-7920 Fax: (617) 523-2845

Andrew R. Grainger
Associate Justice

Education: Harvard 1969 BA; Michigan 1976 JD
Began Service: May 4, 2006

Academic: Adjunct Professor, Boston University

Government: Assistant Attorney General, Office of the Attorney General, State of New Hampshire

Legal Practice: Partner, Peabody & Brown; General Counsel, Recall Management Corporation

Nonprofit: President, New England Legal Foundation; Chair, Arts Boston; Director, Arts Boston

Staff
Law Clerk **(Vacant)** . . . . (617) 626-7920
Judicial Secretary **Kelli Polizzotti** . . . . (617) 626-7920
E-mail: kelli.polizzotti@appct.state.ma.us

Chambers of Associate Justice William J. Meade

John Adams Courthouse, One Pemberton Square, Boston, MA 02108
Tel: (617) 725-8085
E-mail: william.meade@appct.state.ma.us

William J. Meade
Associate Justice

Education: UMass (Amherst) 1986 BA; Western New England 1989 JD
Began Service: 2006

Chambers of Associate Justice Peter J. Rubin

John Adams Courthouse, One Pemberton Square, Suite 3500, Boston, MA 02108
Tel: (617) 725-8085
E-mail: peter.rubin@appct.state.ma.us

Peter J. Rubin
Associate Justice

Education: Yale BA; Harvard JD
Began Service: 2008

Clerkships: Law Clerk, Chambers of Circuit Judge Collins J. Seitz, United States Court of Appeals for the Third Circuit; Law Clerk, Chambers of Associate Justice David H. Souter, Supreme Court of the United States

Judicial: Professor of Law, Georgetown University

Nonprofit: Founder, American Constitution Society

Chambers of Associate Justice Francis R. Fecteau

John Adams Courthouse, One Pemberton Square, Suite 3500, Boston, MA 02108
Tel: (617) 725-8085
E-mail: francis.fecteau@appct.state.ma.us

Francis R. Fecteau
Associate Justice

Education: Holy Cross Col 1969; Boston Col 1972 JD
Began Service: 2008

Government: Assistant District Attorney, Worcester County District Attorney's Office (1974-1979); Attorney, Healy & Rocheleau (1982-1996)

Chambers of Associate Justice Gabrielle R. Wolohojian

John Adams Courthouse, One Pemberton Square, Suite 3500, Boston, MA 02108
Tel: (617) 725-8085
E-mail: gabrielle.wolohojian@appct.state.ma.us

Gabrielle R. Wolohojian
Associate Justice

Education: Rutgers 1982 BA; Oxford (UK) 1987 PhD; Columbia 1989 JD
Began Service: 2008

Chambers of Associate Justice James R. Milkey
One Pemberton Square, Boston, MA 02108
Tel: (617) 725-8085
E-mail: james.milkey@appct.state.ma.us

James R. Milkey
Associate Justice

Date of Birth: December 17, 1956
Education: Harvard 1978 AB, 1983 JD; MIT 1983 MA
Began Service: April 9, 2009
Appointed By: Governor Deval L. Patrick

Academic: Visiting Associate Professor, School of Law, Pace University (1994-1995)

Government: Environmental Protection Division Deputy Chief, Public Protection and Advocacy Bureau, Office of the Attorney General, Commonwealth of Massachusetts (1990-1996); Environmental Protection Division Chief, Public Protection and Advocacy Bureau, Office of the Attorney General, Commonwealth of Massachusetts (1996-2009)

Nonprofit: Co-Chair, Environmental Law Section, Boston Bar Association (2003-2005)

Chambers of Associate Justice Sydney Hanlon
One Pemberton Square, Boston, MA 02108
Tel: (617) 725-8085
E-mail: sydney.hanlon@appct.state.ma.us

Sydney Hanlon
Associate Justice

Education: Brown U 1972; Harvard 1975 JD
Began Service: April 29, 2009
Appointed By: Governor Deval L. Patrick

Government: Assistant U.S. Attorney, Organized Crime Drug Enforcement Task Force Unit, Massachusetts District, United States Department of Justice (1982-1987); Assistant Attorney General, Office of the Attorney General, Commonwealth of Massachusetts (1987-1990)

Judicial: Associate Justice - Dorchester District Court, Boston Municipal Court Department (1990-1994); First Justice - Dorchester Division, Boston Municipal Court Department (1994-2009)

Chambers of Associate Justice Judd J. Carhart
One Pemberton Square, Boston, MA 02108-1705
Tel: (617) 725-8106
E-mail: judd.carhart@appct.state.ma.us

Judd J. Carhart
Associate Justice

Education: UMass (Amherst) 1971; Suffolk 1974 JD
Began Service: January 7, 2011

Chambers of Associate Justice Peter W. Agnes, Jr.
One Pemberton Square, Boston, MA 02108
Tel: (617) 725-8106

Peter W. Agnes, Jr.
Associate Justice

Date of Birth: April 12, 1950
Education: Boston U 1972 AB; Suffolk 1975 JD
Began Service: 2011

Chambers of Associate Justice Mary T. Sullivan
John Adams Courthouse, One Pemberton Square, Boston, MA 02108
Tel: (617) 626-7919

Mary T. Sullivan
Associate Justice

Education: UMass (Amherst) 1975 BA; Northeastern 1981 JD
Began Service: February 16, 2012
Appointed By: Governor Deval L. Patrick

Staff
Law Clerk **Laura Graham** .... (617) 626-7919
Secretary **Jennifer L. Martin** .... (617) 626-7919

Chambers of Associate Justice Diana L. Maldonado
John Adams Courthouse, One Pemberton Square, Boston, MA 02108
Tel: (617) 725-8106

Diana L. Maldonado
Associate Justice

Education: SUNY (Stony Brook) 1980 BA; Northeastern 1985 JD
Began Service: 2013
Appointed By: Governor Deval L. Patrick

Chambers of Associate Justice Amy Lyn Blake
One Pemberton Square, Boston, MA 02108
Tel: (617) 725-8106

Amy Lyn Blake
Associate Justice

Education: Rochester 1987 BA; New England 1992 JD
Began Service: 2014

Chambers of Associate Justice Gregory I. Massing
One Pemberton Square, Boston, MA 02108
Tel: (617) 725-8106

Gregory I. "Greg" Massing
Associate Justice

Began Service: 2014

Chambers of Recalled Justice Frederick Brown
One Pemberton Square, Boston, MA 02108
Tel: (617) 725-8085
E-mail: frederick.brown@appct.state.ma.us

Frederick Brown
Recalled Justice

Began Service: 2003

Michigan

Michigan State Court Administrative Office

Hall of Justice, 925 West Ottawa Street, Lansing, MI 48913
P.O. Box 30048, Lansing, MI 48909
Tel: (517) 373-0130 Fax: (517) 373-7517

Staff

Trial Court Services Director **Jennifer Warner** . . . .(517) 373-4835
E-mail: warnerj@courts.mi.gov Fax: (517) 373-0974
State Court Administrator **Milton L. Mack, Jr.** . . . .(517) 373-0128
E-mail: msc-info@courts.mi.gov Fax: (517) 373-9831
Chief Operating Officer **Dawn A. Monk** . . . .(517) 373-0128
E-mail: monkd@courts.mi.gov Fax: (517) 373-9831
Child Welfare Services Director **Kelly Wagner** . . . .(517) 373-8036
E-mail: howardk@courts.mi.gov Fax: (517) 373-8922
Judicial Information Systems Director **Marcus Dobek** . . . .(517) 373-8777
E-mail: dobekm@courts.mi.gov Fax: (517) 373-7451
Michigan Judicial Institute Director **Dawn F. McCarty** . . . (517) 373-7171
E-mail: mccartyd@courts.mi.gov Fax: (517) 373-7615
Office of Dispute Resolution Director
Douglas A. Van Epps . . . .(517) 373-4839
E-mail: vaneppsd@courts.mi.gov Fax: (517) 373-5748
Security and Emergency Management Director
John Ort . . . .(517) 373-4427
E-mail: ortj@courts.mi.gov Fax: (517) 373-9831
Region I Administrator **Deborah Green** . . . .(313) 972-3300
P.O. Box 02984, Detroit, MI 48202 Fax: (313) 972-3309
E-mail: greend@courts.mi.gov
Region II Administrator **James P. Hughes** . . . .(517) 373-9353
E-mail: hughesj@courts.mi.gov Fax: (517) 373-8760
Region III Administrator **J. Bruce Kilmer** . . . .(989) 772-5934
P.O. Box 750, Mt. Pleasant, MI 48804-0750 Fax: (989) 773-0457
E-mail: kilmerb@courts.mi.gov
Region IV Administrator **Jerome M. P. Kole** . . . . (989) 732-3311
P.O. Box 100, Gaylord, MI 49734-0100 Fax: (989) 732-4237
E-mail: kolej@courts.mi.gov
Region V Administrator **Jill Booth** . . . .(517) 373-8679
E-mail: boothj@courts.mi.gov Fax: (517) 373-5235

Michigan Supreme Court

Hall of Justice, 925 West Ottawa, Lansing, MI 48909
P.O. Box 30052, Lansing, MI 48909
Tel: (517) 373-0120
Internet: http://courts.michigan.gov/courts/michigansupremecourt/pages

Number of Judgeships: 7

The Supreme Court consists of seven justices who are nominated by political parties and elected in nonpartisan elections for eight-year terms. The chief justice is elected by peer vote for a consecutive two-year term. The Supreme Court has discretionary review of cases from the Michigan Court of Appeals and other state courts. Cases are appealed to the Supreme Court by filing an application for leave to appeal with the Court which has the authority to grant or deny any application. In addition to its judicial duties, the Court is responsible for the general administrative supervision of all courts in the state. The Court also establishes rules for practice and procedure in all courts.

The Michigan Supreme Court sits in Lansing.

Court Staff

Clerk of Court **Larry Royster** . . . .(517) 373-0120
E-mail: roysterl@courts.mi.gov
Education: Michigan State BA;
Thomas M Cooley JD
Deputy Clerk **Inger Z. Meyer** . . . .(517) 373-0120
E-mail: meyeri@courts.mi.gov
Legal Counsel **Joseph J. Baumann** . . . . (517) 373-0128
E-mail: baumannj@courts.mi.gov
Education: Michigan State 2000 BA;
Thomas M Cooley 2006 JD

Michigan Supreme Court *continued*

Finance and Budget Director **Karen Ellis** . . . .(517) 373-5544
E-mail: ellisk@courts.mi.gov
Human Resources Director **Edward Zobeck** . . . .(517) 373-7481
E-mail: zobecke@courts.mi.gov
Judicial Information Systems Director **Marcus Dobek** . . . .(248) 352-8990
E-mail: dobekm@courts.mi.gov
Public Information Officer **John Nevin** . . . .(517) 373-9345
E-mail: nevinj@courts.mi.gov
Reporter of Decisions **Corbin R. Davis** . . . .(517) 373-0120
E-mail: davisc@courts.mi.gov
Court Security and Emergency Management **John Ort** . . . (517) 373-0954
E-mail: ortj@courts.mi.gov

Chambers of Chief Justice Robert P. Young, Jr.

Cadillac Place, 3034 West Grand Boulevard, Suite 8-500,
Detroit, MI 48202-6034
Tel: (313) 972-3250 Fax: (313) 875-9329
E-mail: youngr@courts.mi.gov

Robert P. Young, Jr.
Chief Justice

Date of Birth: 1951
Education: Harvard 1977 JD
Began Service: January 3, 1999
Appointed By: Governor John Engler
Next Election: November 2018
Term Expires: January 2019

Judicial: Judge, Michigan Court of Appeals (1995-1998)

Legal Practice: Partner, Dickinson, Wright, Moon, Van Dusen & Freeman (1978-1992); General Counsel, AAA Michigan (1992-1995)

Staff

Law Clerk **Matthew Muma** . . . .(313) 972-3253
Began Service: August 2015
Term Expires: August 2017
E-mail: mumam@courts.mi.gov
Senior Law Clerk **Tamara York** . . . . (313) 972-3251
E-mail: yorkt@courts.mi.gov
Education: Michigan State 1989 BS;
Detroit Law 1997 JD
Judicial Secretary **Carolyn Adkins** . . . .(313) 972-3250
E-mail: adkinsc@courts.mi.gov

Chambers of Justice Stephen J. Markman

Hall of Justice, 925 West Ottawa Street, Lansing, MI 48913
P.O. Box 30052, Lansing, MI 48909
Tel: (517) 373-9449 Fax: (517) 373-8163
E-mail: markmans@courts.mi.gov

Stephen J. Markman
Justice

Date of Birth: 1949
Education: Duke 1971 BA; Cincinnati 1974 JD
Began Service: 1999
Appointed By: Governor John Engler
Next Election: 2021
Election Type: General Election
Term Expires: January 1, 2021

Government: Legislative Assistant, United States House of Representatives (1975-1978); Chief Counsel, Subcommittee on the Constitution, Committee on the Judiciary, United States Senate (1978-1985); Deputy Chief Counsel, Committee on the Judiciary, United States Senate (1984); Assistant United States Attorney General, Office of Legal Policy, United States Department of Justice, Ronald Reagan Administration (1985-1989); United States Attorney, Department of Justice, State of Michigan (1989-1993)

Judicial: Judge, Michigan Court of Appeals (1996-1998)

(continued on next page)

Chambers of Justice Stephen J. Markman *continued*

Legal Practice: Miller, Canfield, Paddock & Stone (1993-1994)

Current Memberships: The American Inns of Court; The Federalist Society for Law and Public Policy Studies; Michigan State Bar Foundation; The One Hundred Club

Staff
Law Clerk **Alexander "Alex" Gallucci** .... (517) 373-9449
E-mail: galluccia@courts.mi.gov
Education: Notre Dame 2012 JD
Law Clerk **Jesse J. Kirchner** .... (517) 373-9449
E-mail: kirchnerj@courts.mi.gov
Law Clerk **Jonathon M. Regal** .... (517) 373-9449
E-mail: regalj@courts.mi.gov
Education: Thomas M Cooley 2011 JD
Career Law Clerk **Cheryl Nowak** .... (517) 373-9449
E-mail: nowakc@courts.mi.gov
Education: Grand Valley State 1998 BS; Michigan State 2001 JD
Judicial Secretary **Keri Perkins** .... (517) 373-9449
E-mail: perkinsk@courts.mi.gov

Chambers of Justice Brian Zahra
925 West Ottawa, Lansing, MI 48915-1741
Tel: (517) 373-4926
E-mail: zahrab@courts.mi.gov

Brian K. Zahra
Justice

Date of Birth: 1960
Education: Wayne State U 1984 BGS; Detroit 1987 JD
Began Service: January 14, 2011
Term Expires: January 1, 2023

Staff
Law Clerk **Samantha Lynn Cook** .... (517) 373-0120
E-mail: cooks@courts.mi.gov
Law Clerk **Shara Youles** .... (517) 373-0120
E-mail: youless@courts.mi.gov
Law Clerk **Justin Zatkoss** .... (517) 373-0120
Career Law Clerk **Brian Balow** .... (517) 373-0120
E-mail: balowb@courts.mi.gov
Education: Wayne State U 1999 BA; Detroit Mercy 2006 JD

Chambers of Justice Bridget McCormack
925 West Ottawa, Lansing, MI 48909
Tel: (517) 373-0128 Fax: (517) 373-9831
E-mail: mccormackb@courts.mi.gov

Bridget McCormack
Justice

Education: NYU JD
Began Service: January 23, 2013

Chambers of Justice David Viviano
925 West Ottawa, Lansing, MI 48915
Tel: (517) 373-2604
E-mail: vivianod@courts.mi.gov

David Viviano
Justice

Education: Hillsdale; Michigan JD
Began Service: 2013
Appointed By: Governor Rick Snyder
Next Election: 2016

Judicial: Chief Judge, Chambers of Chief Judge David Viviano, Michigan Circuit Courts (2012-2013)

Chambers of Justice David Viviano *continued*

Legal Practice: Attorney, Jenner & Block LLP; Attorney, Dickinson Wright PLLC

Staff
Law Clerk **Adam Dutkiewicz** .... (517) 373-2604
E-mail: dutkiewicza@courts.mi.gov
Law Clerk **Kathryn Loncarich** .... (517) 373-2604
E-mail: loncarichk@courts.mi.gov
Law Clerk **(Vacant)** .... (517) 373-2604
Senior Law Clerk **Lauri Hrydiuszko** .... (517) 373-2604

Chambers of Justice Richard Bernstein
925 West Ottawa, Lansing, MI 48909
Tel: (517) 373-0120
E-mail: bernsteinr@courts.mi.gov

Richard H. Bernstein
Justice

Education: Michigan BGS; Northwestern JD
Began Service: January 1, 2015
Political Affiliation: Democrat

Chambers of Justice Joan Larsen
925 West Ottawa, Lansing, MI 48909
Tel: (517) 373-0120

Joan Larsen
Justice

Began Service: 2015
Appointed By: Governor Rick Snyder

Michigan Court of Appeals
925 West Ottawa, Lansing, MI 48915
P.O. Box 30022, Lansing, MI 48909-7522
Tel: (517) 373-0786 Tel: (313) 972-5678 (Detroit Office)
Tel: (616) 456-1167 (Grand Rapids Office)
Tel: (248) 524-8700 (Troy Office)

Number of Judgeships: 27

The Court of Appeals, established in 1963, is comprised of four districts from which twenty-seven judges are elected in nonpartisan elections for six-year terms. The Chief Judge is designated by the Michigan Supreme Court. Chief Judge Pro Tem is selected by the Chief Judge. The Court sits in panels of three judges each. The Court of Appeals has appellate jurisdiction in both civil and criminal cases from Michigan Circuit Courts.

The Court of Appeals sits in Detroit, Grand Rapids, Lansing and Marquette.

Court Staff
Chief Clerk of Court **Jerome "Jerry" Zimmer** .... (517) 373-2252
E-mail: jzimmer@courts.mi.gov
Secretary to the Chief Clerk **Mary Lu Hickner** .... (517) 373-2252
E-mail: mhickner@courts.mi.gov
District Clerk, First District **John P. Lowe** .... (313) 972-5678
Cadillac Place, 3020 West Grand Boulevard, Suite 14-300, Detroit, MI 48202-6020
Assistant District Clerk, First District **Clare Cylkowski** ... (313) 972-5678
3020 W. Grand Blvd., Ste. 14-300, Detroit, MI 48202
District Clerk, Second District **Angela DiSessa** .... (248) 524-8700
201 West Big Beaver Road, Suite 800, Troy, MI 48084
District Clerk, Third District **Lori Zarzecki** .... (616) 456-1167
State of Michigan Office Bldg., 350 Ottawa, NW, Grand Rapids, MI 49503-2349
E-mail: lzarzecki@courts.mi.gov

STATE COURTS—MICHIGAN

Michigan Court of Appeals *continued*

District Clerk, Fourth District **Kimberly S. Hauser** . . . . . . (517) 373-0786
P.O. Box 30022, Lansing, MI 48909
925 West Ottawa Street, Lansing, MI 48913
E-mail: khauser@courts.mi.gov
Finance Director **Russell Rudd** . . . . (517) 373-5979
E-mail: rrudd@courts.mi.gov
Human Resources Director **Peggy Ruiz-Helmic** . . . . (517) 373-7347
Information Systems Director **Denise Devine** . . . . (517) 373-9820
E-mail: ddevine@courts.mi.gov
Reporter of Decisions **Corbin R. Davis** . . . . (517) 373-5678
E-mail: davisc@courts.mi.gov

Chambers of Chief Judge Michael J. Talbot

Cadillac Place, 3020 West Grand Boulevard, Suite 14-300,
Detroit, MI 48202-6020
Tel: (313) 972-5736
E-mail: mtalbot@courts.mi.gov

Michael J. Talbot
Chief Judge

Date of Birth: 1945
Education: Georgetown 1967 BS; Detroit 1971 JD
Began Service: April 1998
Appointed By: Governor John Engler
Next Election: November 4, 2022
Election Type: General Election
Term Expires: December 2022

Current Memberships: Advisory Board for Catholic Education, Archdiocese of Detroit; Catholic Lawyers Society; Michigan Judicial Tenure Commission

Staff
Law Clerk **John Hiemstra** . . . . (313) 972-5736
Judicial Assistant **Janice Christophel** . . . . (313) 972-5736

Chambers of Chief Judge Pro Tem Christopher M. Murray

Cadillac Place, 3020 West Grand Boulevard, Suite 14-300,
Detroit, MI 48202-6020
Tel: (313) 972-5720 Fax: (313) 972-5715
E-mail: cmurray@courts.mi.gov

Christopher M. Murray
Chief Judge Pro Tem

Date of Birth: 1964
Education: Hillsdale 1985 BA; Detroit 1990 JD
Began Service: January 16, 2002
Appointed By: Governor John Engler
Next Election: November 4, 2022
Election Type: General Election
Term Expires: December 2022

Current Memberships: State Bar of Michigan

Staff
Judicial Assistant **Vicky Patricca** . . . . (313) 972-5720
E-mail: vpatricca@courts.mi.gov

Chambers of Judge David H. Sawyer

State of Michigan Office Building, 350 Ottawa Avenue, NW,
Grand Rapids, MI 49503
Tel: (616) 456-1811 Fax: (616) 456-1321
E-mail: dsawyer@courts.mi.gov

David H. Sawyer
Judge

Date of Birth: 1947
Education: Arizona 1970 BS; Valparaiso 1973 JD
Began Service: January 1, 1987
Next Election: November 2016
Election Type: General Election
Term Expires: January 1, 2017
Political Affiliation: Republican

Current Memberships: The Federalist Society for Law and Public Policy Studies; Grand Rapids Rotary Club; Kent County Justice Center Task Force; Michigan State Bar Foundation; State Bar of Michigan

Staff
Career Law Clerk **Martin J. Hillard** . . . . (616) 456-1811
E-mail: mhillard@courts.mi.gov
Education: Wayne State U 1983 JD
Judicial Assistant **Sandra Justian** . . . . (616) 456-1811
E-mail: sjustian@courts.mi.gov

Chambers of Judge William B. Murphy

State of Michigan Office Building, 350 Ottawa Avenue, NW,
Grand Rapids, MI 49503
Tel: (616) 456-7553 Fax: (616) 456-1105

William B. Murphy
Judge

Date of Birth: 1945
Education: Michigan State 1967 BA; Wayne State U 1970 JD

Current Memberships: American Bar Association; Grand Rapids Bar Association; Michigan State Bar Foundation; State Bar of Michigan

Chambers of Judge Mark J. Cavanagh

201 West Big Beaver Road, Suite 800, Troy, MI 48084
Tel: (248) 524-8730
E-mail: mcavanagh@courts.mi.gov

Mark J. Cavanagh
Judge

Date of Birth: 1953
Education: Michigan BA; Detroit 1982 JD
Began Service: January 1989
Next Election: November 4, 2022
Election Type: General Election
Term Expires: 2023
Political Affiliation: Democrat

Government: Assistant County Prosecutor, Office of the County Prosecutor, County of Wayne, Michigan (1980-1985); Special Assistant Attorney General, State of Michigan (1986-1988)

Legal Practice: Private Practice (1985-1988)

Nonprofit: Domestic Relations Investigator, Wayne County Friend of the Court

Current Memberships: Irish-American Lawyers Association; Michigan Judges Association; Recorder's Court Bar Association; State Bar of Michigan

Staff
Career Law Clerk **Kimberly Harbus** . . . . (248) 524-8730
E-mail: kharbus@courts.mi.gov
Education: Detroit Mercy 1998 JD

(continued on next page)

Chambers of Judge Mark J. Cavanagh *continued*

Judicial Assistant **Anna Campbell** . . . . (248) 524-8730
Education: Wayne State U 1985 BA

Chambers of Judge Kathleen Jansen

Cadillac Place, 3020 West Grand Boulevard, Suite 14-300,
Detroit, MI 48202-6020
Tel: (313) 972-5726 Fax: (313) 972-5716
E-mail: kjansen@courts.mi.gov

Kathleen Jansen
Judge

Date of Birth: 1948
Education: Michigan State 1971 BS; Detroit 1977 JD
Began Service: January 1990
Appointed By: Governor James J. Blanchard
Next Election: November 2018
Term Expires: January 1, 2019

Government: Member, Planning Commission, State of Michigan (1980-1984)

Judicial: Judge, Macomb County Probate Court (1983-1984); Judge, Michigan Circuit Court, 16th Judicial Circuit, Macomb County (1985-1989)

Legal Practice: Attorney, Mancini & Blumenthal, P.C. (1977-1982)

Current Memberships: Macomb County Bar Association; Macomb County Bar Foundation, Macomb County Bar Association; Michigan Judges Association; National Association of Women Judges; State Bar of Michigan; Women Lawyers Association of Michigan

Staff

Career Law Clerk **Nicholas C. "Nick" Krieger** . . . . (313) 972-5726
Education: Michigan State BS;
Wayne State U 2004 JD
Judicial Assistant **Lyn Scharret** . . . . (313) 972-5726
E-mail: lscharrett@courts.mi.gov

Chambers of Judge Henry William Saad

201 West Big Beaver Road, Suite 800, Troy, MI 48084
Tel: (248) 524-8770
E-mail: hsaad@courts.mi.gov

Henry William Saad
Judge

Education: Wayne State U 1971 BA, 1974 JD
Began Service: 1994
Next Election: November 4, 2022
Election Type: General Election
Term Expires: January 1, 2023

Academic: Adjunct Professor, School of Law, University of Detroit Mercy; Adjunct Professor, Law School, Wayne State University

Government: Arbitrator, Bureau of Employment Relations, State of Michigan; Hearing Referee, Department of Civil Rights, State of Michigan

Legal Practice: Attorney, Dickinson, Wright, Moon, Van Dusen & Freeman (1974-1994)

Chambers of Judge Joel P. Hoekstra

The Law Building, 330 Ionia Avenue, NW, Room 201,
Grand Rapids, MI 49503
Tel: (616) 458-3396 Fax: (616) 458-3892
E-mail: jhoekstra@courts.mi.gov

Joel P. Hoekstra
Judge

Date of Birth: 1947
Education: Calvin Col 1970 AB; Valparaiso 1973 JD
Began Service: January 1, 1995
Next Election: November 2016
Election Type: General Election
Term Expires: January 1, 2017

Academic: Adjunct Professor, Calvin College

Government: Assistant Prosecuting Attorney, Office of the Prosecuting Attorney, County of Kent, Michigan (1973-1984)

Judicial: Judge, Michigan District Court, 61st District (1985-1995)

Current Memberships: American Bar Association; Grand Rapids Bar Association; State Bar of Michigan

Staff

Judicial Secretary **Annette Bailey** . . . . (616) 458-3396
E-mail: abailey@courts.mi.gov

Chambers of Judge Jane E. Markey

201 The Law Building, 330 Ionia Avenue, NW, Grand Rapids, MI 49503
Tel: (616) 458-3476 Fax: (616) 458-3892
E-mail: jmarkey@courts.mi.gov

Jane E. Markey
Judge

Date of Birth: 1951
Education: Michigan State 1973 BA; Thomas M Cooley 1981 JD
Began Service: January 1, 1995
Next Election: November 4, 2022
Election Type: General Election
Term Expires: January 1, 2023

Academic: Lansing Community College (1980-1981)

Clerkships: Judicial Law Clerk and Prehearing Attorney, Michigan Court of Appeals (1981-1982)

Judicial: Judge, Michigan District Court, 61st District (1991-1994)

Legal Practice: Baxter & Hammond (1982-1984); Dykema, Gossett (1984-1991)

Current Memberships: American Judges Association; State Bar of Michigan; Women Lawyers Association of Michigan

Staff

Career Law Clerk **Dale Crowley** . . . . (616) 458-3476
E-mail: dcrowley@courts.mi.gov
Education: Wayne State U JD
Judicial Assistant **Donna Fischer** . . . . (616) 458-3476
E-mail: dfischer@courts.mi.gov

Chambers of Judge Peter D. O'Connell

Hall of Justice, 925 West Ottawa Street, Lansing, MI 48913
P.O. Box 30022, Lansing, MI 48909-7522
Tel: (517) 373-9847 Fax: (517) 373-9870
E-mail: POConnell@courts.mi.gov

Peter D. O'Connell
Judge

Date of Birth: 1948
Education: Western Michigan 1971 BBA; Detroit Law 1975 JD; Nevada (Reno) 1987
Began Service: January 1, 1995
Next Election: November 2018
Term Expires: January 1, 2019

Academic: Adjunct Professor of Law, Thomas M. Cooley Law School

Corporate: Lawyers Title Insurance Company (1972-1974)

Government: Chief Assistant Prosecutor, Office of the County Prosecutor, County of Isabella, Michigan (1976-1979)

Judicial: Judge, Michigan District Court, 76th District (1979-1994)

Legal Practice: Mitchell & Leon (1974-1976)

Current Memberships: American Bar Association; Isabella County Bar Association; Michigan District Court Judges Association; State Bar of Michigan

Staff

Law Clerk **Tricia L. B. Warren** .... (517) 373-9847
Began Service: December 2014
E-mail: twarren@courts.mi.gov

Judicial Assistant **Claudette Bexell Frame** .... (517) 373-9847
E-mail: cframe@courts.mi.gov

Chambers of Judge Kurtis T. Wilder

Cadillac Place, 3020 West Grand Boulevard, Suite 14-300, Detroit, MI 48202
Tel: (313) 972-5755 Fax: (313) 972-5718
E-mail: kwilder@courts.mi.gov

Kurtis T. Wilder
Judge

Date of Birth: 1959
Education: Michigan AB, 1984 JD
Began Service: January 1, 1999
Appointed By: Governor John Engler
Term Expires: January 1, 2017

Judicial: Chief Judge, Washtenaw Circuit Court

Current Memberships: Michigan Judges Association

Staff

Law Clerk **Shara Youles** .... (313) 972-5755
E-mail: syoules@courts.mi.gov

Judicial Assistant **Connie Fuller** .... (313) 972-5755
E-mail: cfuller@courts.mi.gov

Chambers of Judge Patrick M. Meter

Hall of Justice, 925 West Ottawa Street, Lansing, MI 48915
P.O. Box 30185, Lansing, MI 48909-7522
Tel: (517) 373-6787 Fax: (517) 373-6897
E-mail: pmeter@courts.mi.gov

Patrick Murphy Meter
Judge

Date of Birth: 1948
Education: Notre Dame BA, JD
Began Service: September 1, 1999
Appointed By: Governor John Engler
Next Election: November 4, 2022
Election Type: General Election
Term Expires: December 31, 2022

Government: Chief Assistant Prosecuting Attorney, Office of the Prosecuting Attorney, County of Saginaw, Michigan

Judicial: Judge, Michigan Tenth Judicial Circuit Court

Legal Practice: Associate, Braun, Kendrick, Finkbeiner, Schafer and Murphy

Current Memberships: Michigan Judges Association; Saginaw County Bar Association

Staff

Career Law Clerk **Lois A. Kline** .... (517) 373-6821
E-mail: lkline@courts.mi.gov
Education: Amherst 1992 BA; Michigan 1997 JD

Judicial Assistant **Heather Childs** .... (517) 373-6787
E-mail: hchilds@courts.mi.gov

Chambers of Judge Donald S. Owens

Hall of Justice, 925 West Ottawa Street, Lansing, MI 48915
P.O. Box 30022, Lansing, MI 48909-7522
Tel: (517) 373-9854 Fax: (517) 373-9817
E-mail: dowens@courts.mi.gov

Donald S. Owens
Judge

Date of Birth: 1943
Education: Michigan 1966 BA, 1967 MBA, 1969 JD
Began Service: December 1999
Appointed By: Governor John Engler
Next Election: November 2016
Election Type: General Election
Term Expires: January 1, 2017

Judicial: Judge, Ingham County Probate Court (1974-1999)

Legal Practice: Associate Attorney, MacLean, Seaman, Laing & Guilford (1969-1974)

Staff

Career Law Clerk **Katie Barron** .... (517) 373-9854
Began Service: 2013

Judicial Secretary **Cheryl Pazur** .... (517) 373-9854
E-mail: cpazur@courts.mi.gov

Chambers of Judge Kirsten Frank Kelly

Cadillac Place, 3020 West Grand Boulevard, Suite 14-300,
Detroit, MI 48202
Tel: (313) 972-5733 Fax: (313) 972-5717
E-mail: kkelly@courts.mi.gov

Kirsten Frank Kelly
Judge

Date of Birth: 1956
Education: Michigan State 1978 BA; Detroit 1981 JD
Began Service: January 1, 2001
Next Election: November 2018
Term Expires: January 1, 2019

Judicial: Judge, Wayne Circuit Court; Presiding Judge, Family Division, Wayne Circuit Court; Judge, Grosse Pointe Park Municipal Court

Staff
Career Law Clerk **Rebecca Dubuque** . . . . (313) 972-5733
E-mail: rdubuque@courts.mi.gov
Education: Detroit Law 1998 JD
Secretary **Colleen Lees** . . . . (313) 972-5733
E-mail: clees@courts.mi.gov

Chambers of Judge Karen Fort Hood

Cadillac Place, 3020 West Grand Boulevard, Suite 14-300,
Detroit, MI 48202-6020
Tel: (313) 972-5723 Fax: (313) 972-5716
E-mail: khood@courts.mi.gov

Karen Fort Hood
Judge

Education: Detroit Law 1989 JD
Began Service: January 2003
Next Election: November 4, 2022
Election Type: General Election
Term Expires: December 2022

Government: Prosecutor, County of Wayne, Michigan

Judicial: Judge, Wayne County Circuit Court; Presiding Judge, Criminal Division, Wayne County Circuit Court (1999-2002)

Staff
Career Law Clerk **Coryelle Christie** . . . . (313) 972-5723
E-mail: cchristie@courts.mi.gov
Judicial Assistant **Renita L. Wilks** . . . . (313) 972-5723

Chambers of Judge Stephen L. Borrello

P.O. Box 30022, Lansing, MI 48909
Tel: (517) 373-1055 Fax: (517) 373-1050
E-mail: sborrello@courts.mi.gov

Stephen L. Borrello
Judge

Date of Birth: June 1959
Education: Albion BA; Detroit Law JD
Began Service: June 9, 2003
Term Expires: 2019

Government: Assistant Prosecuting Attorney, County of Saginaw, Michigan (1988-1990)

Legal Practice: Partner, Gilbert, Smith & Borrello, PC

Staff
Fax: (517) 373-1050

Career Law Clerk **Toby Koenig** . . . . (517) 373-1055
Education: Wayne State U JD
Judicial Assistant **Stefanie Stockwell** . . . . (517) 373-1055
E-mail: sstockwell@courts.mi.gov

Chambers of Judge Deborah A. Servitto

201 West Big Beaver Road, Suite 800, Troy, MI 48084
Tel: (248) 524-8760
E-mail: dservitto@courts.mi.gov

Deborah A. Servitto
Judge

Date of Birth: February 17, 1956
Education: Oakland U 1978 BA; Detroit Law 1982 JD
Began Service: March 2006
Term Expires: January 1, 2019

Government: Assistant City Attorney, Office of the City Attorney, City of Warren, Michigan (1982-1986)

Judicial: Circuit Judge, Macomb County Circuit Court, County of Macomb, Michigan (1990-2006)

Staff
Assistant **Annie Madigan** . . . . (248) 524-8760
E-mail: amadigan@courts.mi.gov

Chambers of Judge Jane M. Beckering

The Law Building, 330 Ionia Avenue, NW, Suite 201,
Grand Rapids, MI 49503-3114
Tel: (616) 456-0244
E-mail: jbeckering@courts.mi.gov

Jane M. Beckering
Judge

Education: Michigan; Wisconsin JD
Began Service: September 2007
Appointed By: Governor Jennifer Granholm
Next Election: November 4, 2018
Election Type: General Election
Term Expires: January 1, 2019

Legal Practice: Attorney, McDermott Will & Emery LLP; Founding Partner, Buchanan & Beckering, PLC

Staff
Law Clerk **Nick Paulucci** . . . . (616) 456-0244
Judicial Assistant **Cheryl Zorin** . . . . (616) 456-0244

Chambers of Judge Elizabeth L. Gleicher

Cadillac Place, 3020 West Grand Boulevard, Suite 14-300,
Detroit, MI 48202-6020
Tel: (313) 972-5646 Fax: (313) 972-5715
E-mail: egleicher@courts.mi.gov

Elizabeth L. Gleicher
Judge

Education: Carleton; Wayne State U JD
Began Service: September 2007
Appointed By: Governor Jennifer Granholm
Next Election: November 4, 2018
Election Type: General Election
Term Expires: January 1, 2019

Government: Adjunct Professor, Law School, Wayne State University

Legal Practice: Attorney, Goodman, Eden, Millender & Bedrosian

Profession: Private Practice

Staff
Career Law Clerk **Amber O. Tykoski** . . . . (313) 972-5617
E-mail: atykoski@courts.mi.gov
Education: Wayne State U 2003 JD
Judicial Assistant **Jennifer Boardman** . . . . (313) 972-5646
E-mail: jboardman@courts.mi.gov

Chambers of Judge Cynthia Diane Stephens

925 West Ottawa, Lansing, MI 48915
Tel: (517) 373-0786
E-mail: cstephens@courts.mi.gov

Cynthia Diane Stephens
Judge

Began Service: 2008
Term Expires: January 1, 2017

Chambers of Judge Michael J. Kelly

Hall of Justice, 925 West Ottawa Street, Lansing, MI 48909-7522
Tel: (517) 373-0599 Fax: (517) 373-4272

Michael J. Kelly
Judge

Date of Birth: April 3, 1962
Education: Michigan (Flint) 1984; Detroit 1988 JD
Began Service: January 2009
Next Election: November 2022
Election Type: General Election
Term Expires: January 1, 2023

Staff
Law Clerk **Stephan M. Fellows** .... (517) 373-0599
Began Service: 2009
E-mail: sfellows@courts.mi.gov
Education: Michigan State 2004 JD
Judicial Assistant **Tracie Dantzler** .... (517) 373-0599
E-mail: tdantzler@courts.mi.gov

Chambers of Judge Douglas B. Shapiro

925 West Ottawa, Lansing, MI 48915
Tel: (517) 373-0899
E-mail: dshapiro@courts.mi.gov

Douglas B. Shapiro
Judge

Began Service: February 2, 2009
Term Expires: January 1, 2019

Staff
Career Law Clerk **James Leiby** .... (517) 373-0899
Judicial Assistant **Deborah Allen** .... (517) 373-0899

Chambers of Judge Amy Ronayne Krause

925 West Ottawa Street, Lansing, MI 48915
P.O. Box 30022, Lansing, MI 48909-7522
Tel: (517) 373-0683
E-mail: akrause@courts.mi.gov

Amy Ronayne Krause
Judge

Education: Michigan BA; Notre Dame JD
Began Service: February 24, 2011
Term Expires: January 1, 2019

Chambers of Judge Michael Riordan

3020 West Grand Boulevard, Detroit, MI 48202-6020
Tel: (313) 972-5678

Michael J. "Mike" Riordan
Judge

Education: Michigan State BA; Detroit Mercy JD
Began Service: 2012
Term Expires: January 1, 2019

Chambers of Judge Mark T. Boonstra

State Office Building, 350 Ottawa Avenue, NW, Grand Rapids, MI 49503
Tel: (517) 373-0875

Mark T. Boonstra
Judge

Education: Michigan State 1975 BA; Michigan 1983 MA, 1983 JD
Began Service: 2012
Term Expires: January 1, 2021

Staff
Law Clerk **Jason Murdey** .... (517) 373-0875
Judicial Assistant **Yvette Brabant** .... (517) 373-0875

Chambers of Judge Michael F. Gadola

925 West Ottawa, Lansing, MI 48909
Tel: (517) 373-0786

Michael F. Gadola
Judge

Began Service: January 5, 2015

Minnesota

Minnesota Office of the State Court Administrator

135 Minnesota Judicial Center, 25 Rev. Dr. Martin Luther King, Jr. Boulevard, St. Paul, MN 55155
Tel: (651) 296-2474 Fax: (651) 297-5636
Internet: www.mncourts.gov

Staff

State Court Administrator **Jeffrey "Jeff" Shorba** .... (651) 296-2474
E-mail: jeff.shorba@courts.state.mn.us Fax: (651) 297-5636
Deputy State Court Administrator **Dawn Torgerson** ..... (651) 297-7801
E-mail: dawn.torgerson@courts.state.mn.us Fax: (651) 297-5636
Director, Court Information Office **Beau Berentson** ..... (651) 296-6043
Fax: (651) 297-5636
Director, Court Services Division **Kay Pedretti** .... (651) 297-7587
E-mail: kay.pedretti@courts.state.mn.us Fax: (651) 296-6609
Director, Finance Division **Dan Ostdiek** .... (651) 215-0044
E-mail: dan.ostdiek@courts.state.mn.us Fax: (651) 205-4441
Director, Human Resources Division
Nancy Dietl-Griffin .... (651) 282-2067
Fax: (651) 284-4341
Director, Information Technology Division (Acting)
Dean Buker .... (651) 297-7636
E-mail: dean.buker@courts.state.mn.us Fax: (651) 297-7595
Law Librarian **Liz Reppe** .... (651) 297-7800
E-mail: liz.reppe@courts.state.mn.us

Minnesota Supreme Court

Minnesota Judicial Center, 25 Rev. Dr. Martin Luther King, Jr. Boulevard, St. Paul, MN 55155
Tel: (651) 297-7650 Tel: (651) 296-2254 (Attorney Registrations)
Fax: (651) 297-5636
Internet: www.mncourts.gov

Number of Judgeships: 7

The Supreme Court consists of a chief justice and six associate justices who are elected in statewide, nonpartisan elections for six-year terms. Vacancies are filled by the Governor. Newly appointed justices serve until the next general election occurring at least one year after appointment, at which time they may run for the position. Retirement is mandatory at age seventy; however, retired justices may be temporarily assigned to serve in any state court. The Supreme Court has original appellate jurisdiction over first degree murder convictions, legislative contest appeals, and appeals from the Minnesota Tax Court and Workers' Compensation Court of Appeals. The Court has discretionary review of decisions of the Minnesota Court of Appeals. The Court also has supervisory control over the lower courts and authority to regulate admission to the bar and review grievance complaints against attorneys.

The Supreme Court sits in St. Paul.

Court Staff

Clerk of the Appellate Courts and Supreme Court Administrator **AnnMarie S. O'Neill** .... (651) 297-5529
Fax: (651) 297-4149
Supreme Court Commissioner **Rita Coyle DeMeules** .... (651) 296-6125
E-mail: rita.demeules@courts.state.mn.us Fax: (651) 282-5115

Chambers of Chief Justice Lorie Skjerven Gildea

25 Rev. Dr. Martin Luther King, Jr. Boulevard, St. Paul, MN 55155
Tel: (651) 297-7650
E-mail: lorie.gildea@courts.state.mn.us

Lorie Skjerven Gildea
Chief Justice

Education: Minnesota (Morris) 1983 BA; Georgetown 1986 JD
Began Service: July 12, 2010
Appointed By: Governor Tim Pawlenty

Academic: Associate General Counsel, University of Minnesota (1993-2004)

Government: Prosecutor, Office of the County Attorney, County of Hennepin, Minnesota (2004-2005)

Legal Practice: Attorney, Arent Fox LLP (1986-1993)

Membership: Director, The YWCA of Minneapolis (2000-2003)

Staff
Judicial Administrative Assistant
Virginia "Ginger" Meyer .... (651) 296-3380
E-mail: ginger.meyer@courts.state.mn.us

Chambers of Associate Justice G. Barry Anderson

25 Rev. Dr. Martin Luther King, Jr. Boulevard, Suite 425, St. Paul, MN 55155
Tel: (651) 297-1007 Fax: (651) 282-5115

G. Barry Anderson
Associate Justice

Date of Birth: 1954
Education: Gustavus Adolphus 1976 BA; Minnesota 1979 JD
Began Service: October 13, 2004
Appointed By: Governor Tim Pawlenty
Term Expires: December 31, 2018

Judicial: Judge, Minnesota Court of Appeals (1998-2004)

Legal Practice: Partner, Arnold, Anderson & Dove PLLP (1983-1998)

Staff
Fax: (651) 282-5115

Judicial Assistant **Jo Ann Gillis** .... (651) 297-1007
E-mail: joann.gillis@courts.state.mn.us

Chambers of Associate Justice Christopher J. Dietzen

Minnesota Judicial Center, 25 Rev. Dr. Martin Luther King, Jr. Boulevard, St. Paul, MN 55155
Tel: (651) 297-7676
E-mail: christopher.dietzen@courts.state.mn.us

Christopher J. Dietzen
Associate Justice

Date of Birth: March 8, 1947
Education: Gonzaga 1973 BA, 1977 JD
Began Service: February 19, 2008
Appointed By: Governor Tim Pawlenty
Next Election: November 2016
Term Expires: January 2017

Judicial: Judge, Chambers of Judge Christopher Dietzen, Minnesota Court of Appeals (2004-2008)

Legal Practice: Attorney and Partner, Richter, Wimberley & Ericson (1973-1978); Senior Litigator, Larkin Hoffman Daly & Lindgren Ltd. (1978-2004)

Current Memberships: American Bar Association; Hennepin County Bar Association; Minnesota State Bar Association

Chambers of Associate Justice Christopher J. Dietzen *continued*

Membership: Member, Board of Directors, Larkin Hoffman Daly & Lindgren Ltd. (1995-2002)

Staff
Law Clerk **James Sadkovich** .... (651) 297-7677
Began Service: August 2015
Term Expires: August 1, 2016
Judicial Administrative Assistant **Mary Lou Kruger** ...... (651) 297-7676
E-mail: marylou.kruger@courts.state.mn.us

Chambers of Associate Justice David R. Stras
25 Rev. Dr. Martin Luther King, Jr. Boulevard, St. Paul, MN 55155
Tel: (651) 297-7650
E-mail: david.stras@courts.state.mn.us

David R. Stras
Associate Justice

Education: Kansas BA, MBA, 1999 JD
Began Service: July 12, 2010
Appointed By: Governor Tim Pawlenty
Term Expires: 2018

Clerkships: Law Clerk, Chambers of Senior Judge Melvin T. Brunetti, United States Court of Appeals for the Ninth Circuit (1999-2000); Law Clerk, Chambers of Circuit Judge J. Michael Luttig, United States Court of Appeals for the Fourth Circuit (2000-2001); Law Clerk, Chambers of Associate Justice Clarence Thomas, Supreme Court of the United States (2002-2003)

Legal Practice: Associate, Sidley Austin LLP (2001-2002)

Chambers of Associate Justice Wilhelmina M. Wright
25 Rev. Dr. Martin Luther King, Jr. Boulevard, St. Paul, MN 55155
Tel: (651) 297-7650
E-mail: wilhelmina.wright@courts.state.mn.us

Wilhelmina M. Wright
Associate Justice

Education: Yale 1986 BA; Harvard 1989 JD
Began Service: October 16, 2012
Appointed By: Governor Mark Dayton
Next Election: November 2022

Staff
Law Clerk **Rachel Bandli** .... (651) 297-7650
Judicial Assistant **Mary Lou Kruger** .... (651) 297-7650
E-mail: marylou.kruger@courts.state.mn.us

Chambers of Associate Justice David Lillehaug
25 Rev. Dr. Martin Luther King, Jr. Boulevard, St. Paul, MN 55155
Tel: (651) 297-7650
E-mail: david.lillehaug@courts.state.mn.us

David Lillehaug
Associate Justice

Education: Augustana (IL) 1976 BA; Harvard 1979 JD
Began Service: June 3, 2013
Appointed By: Governor Mark Dayton
Next Election: November 2022

Government: U.S. Attorney, Minnesota District, Executive Office for United States Attorneys, United States Department of Justice, William J. Clinton Administration (1994-1998)

Legal Practice: Attorney, Fredrikson & Byron, P.A. (2002-2013)

Chambers of Associate Justice Natalie E. Hudson
25 Rev. Dr. Martin Luther King, Jr. Boulevard, St. Paul, MN 55155
Tel: (651) 297-7650

Natalie E. Hudson
Associate Justice

Education: Arizona State; Minnesota

Current Memberships: Minnesota Association of Black Lawyers; Minnesota State Bar Association; Minnesota Women Lawyers; Ramsey County Bar Association

Minnesota Court of Appeals
Minnesota Judicial Center, 25 Rev. Dr. Martin Luther King, Jr. Boulevard, St. Paul, MN 55155
Tel: (651) 297-1000 Fax: (651) 297-8779
Internet: www.mncourts.gov

Number of Judgeships: 19

The Court of Appeals, established by a constitutional amendment which went into effect in 1983, consists of nineteen judges who are elected in statewide, nonpartisan elections to six-year terms. The Court sits in three-judge panels with rotating memberships. Vacancies are filled by the Governor. The chief judge is appointed by the Governor to serve a three-year term. Retirement is mandatory at age seventy; however, retired judges may be assigned to serve in any court except the Minnesota Supreme Court. The Court of Appeals has appellate jurisdiction over final decisions of the trial courts except decisions of conciliation courts and first degree murder convictions, appeals from administrative agency decisions, and appeals from the Minnesota Commissioner of Economic Security.

The Court sits in St. Paul; however, it may sit in any of the state's ten judicial districts.

Court Staff
Clerk of the Appellate Courts and Supreme Court Administrator **AnnMarie S. O'Neill** .... (651) 297-5529
Fax: (651) 297-4149
Chief Attorney **Cynthia L. Lehr** .... (651) 297-1025
E-mail: cindy.lehr@courts.state.mn.us

Chambers of Chief Judge Edward J. Cleary
Minnesota Judicial Center, 25 Rev. Dr. Martin Luther King, Jr. Boulevard, St. Paul, MN 55155
Tel: (651) 297-1000 Fax: (651) 297-8779
E-mail: edward.cleary@courts.state.mn.us

Edward J. Cleary
Chief Judge

Education: Minnesota 1974 BA, 1977 JD
Began Service: November 22, 2011
Next Election: November 2020

Chambers of Judge Matthew E. Johnson
Minnesota Judicial Center, 25 Rev. Dr. Martin Luther King, Jr. Boulevard, St. Paul, MN 55155
Tel: (651) 297-1616
E-mail: matthew.johnson@courts.state.mn.us

Matthew E. Johnson
Judge

Education: St Olaf 1985 BA; William Mitchell 1992 JD
Began Service: January 1, 2008
Appointed By: Governor Tim Pawlenty
Next Election: November 2016
Term Expires: January 3, 2017

(continued on next page)

STATE COURTS—MINNESOTA

Chambers of Judge Matthew E. Johnson *continued*

Staff

Law Clerk **Michael Ervin** .... (651) 296-6165
Began Service: August 2015
Term Expires: August 2016

Law Clerk **Allison Whalen** .... (651) 296-6165
Began Service: August 2015
Term Expires: August 2016
E-mail: allison.whalen@courts.state.mn.us

Judicial Assistant **Helen Alexander** .... (651) 297-1616
E-mail: helen.alexander@courts.state.mn.us

Chambers of Judge Randolph W. Peterson

316 Minnesota Judicial Center, 25 Rev. Dr. Martin Luther King, Jr. Boulevard, St. Paul, MN 55155-6102
Tel: (651) 297-7807 Fax: (651) 297-8779
E-mail: randolph.peterson@courts.state.mn.us

Randolph W. Peterson
Judge

Date of Birth: 1953
Education: Minnesota 1976 BA, 1979 JD
Began Service: December 4, 1990
Appointed By: Governor Rudy Perpich
Next Election: November 2016

Government: State Senator Randolph W. Peterson (R-MN), Minnesota State Senate (1981-1990)

Staff

Secretary **Sandy Wendt** .... (651) 297-7807
E-mail: sandy.wendt@courts.state.mn.us

Chambers of Judge Jill Flaskamp Halbrooks

Minnesota Judicial Center, 25 Rev. Dr. Martin Luther King, Jr. Boulevard, St. Paul, MN 55155-6102
Tel: (651) 297-1002 Fax: (651) 297-8779
E-mail: jill.halbrooks@courts.state.mn.us

Jill Flaskamp Halbrooks
Judge

Date of Birth: 1949
Education: Colorado 1971 BA, 1976 MA; William Mitchell 1985 JD
Began Service: November 2, 1998
Appointed By: Governor Arne H. Carlson
Next Election: November 2018
Term Expires: January 2019

Academic: Department of Housing, University of Colorado (1973-1982)

Legal Practice: Rider, Bennett, Egan & Arundel (1985-1998)

Current Memberships: American Bar Association; American Board of Trial Advocates; International Society of Barristers; Minnesota State Bar Association; Minnesota Women Lawyers; National Association of Women Judges

Staff

Judicial Administrative Assistant II **Jeanine Chagnon** ... (651) 297-1002
E-mail: jeanine.chagnon@courts.state.mn.us

Chambers of Judge Renee Worke

Minnesota Judicial Center 312, 25 Rev. Dr. Martin Luther King, Jr. Boulevard, St. Paul, MN 55155
Tel: (651) 297-1011
E-mail: renee.worke@courts.state.mn.us

Renee Worke
Judge

Education: Minnesota 1980 BS; William Mitchell 1983 JD
Began Service: 2005
Term Expires: 2018

Current Memberships: Minnesota District Judges Association; Minnesota State Bar Association; Minnesota Women Lawyers

Staff

Judicial Administrative Assistant
Brenda Montgomery .... (651) 297-1011
E-mail: brenda.montgomery@courts.state.mn.us

Chambers of Judge Kevin G. Ross

25 Rev. Dr. Martin Luther King, Jr. Boulevard, St. Paul, MN 55155
Tel: (651) 297-1009
E-mail: kevin.ross@courts.state.mn.us

Kevin G. Ross
Judge

Education: Iowa BA, JD
Began Service: February 23, 2006
Appointed By: Governor Tim Pawlenty
Next Election: November 4, 2020
Election Type: General Election
Term Expires: December 31, 2020

Clerkships: Law Clerk, Chambers of Senior Judge Paul A. Magnuson, United States District Court for the District of Minnesota; Law Clerk, Chambers of Senior Judge Donald P. Lay, United States Court of Appeals for the Eighth Circuit

Government: Police Officer, Iowa City, Iowa

Legal Practice: Attorney, Greene Espel

Staff

Judicial Administrative Assistant **Earnestine Milton** ..... (651) 297-1009
E-mail: earnestine.milton@courts.state.mn.us

Chambers of Judge Heidi S. Schellhas

Minnesota Judicial Center, 25 Rev. Dr. Martin Luther King, Jr. Boulevard, St. Paul, MN 55155
Tel: (651) 297-5499
E-mail: heidi.schellhas@courts.state.mn.us

Heidi S. Schellhas
Judge

Education: Minnesota 1975 BA; William Mitchell 1980 JD
Began Service: January 1, 2008
Appointed By: Governor Tim Pawlenty
Term Expires: January 3, 2017

Corporate: Title Examiner, Guaranty Title, Inc. (1977-1978)

Judicial: Judge, Fourth Judicial District, Minnesota District Courts (1996-2007)

Legal Practice: Legal Assistant, Dorsey & Whitney LLP (1978-1979); Partner, Carlsen, Greiner & Law (1979-1988); Sole Proprietor, Heidi S. Schellhas Law Offices (1988-1989); Founding Partner, Rode, Lucas & Schellhas, PLLP (1989-1996)

Current Memberships: Hennepin County Bar Association; Minnesota State Bar Association; Minnesota Women Lawyers

Membership: Member, Minnesota District Judges Association

Chambers of Judge Heidi S. Schellhas *continued*

Staff
Law Clerk **Jeffrey Markowitz** . . . . (651) 297-7831
Law Clerk **Amy McGowan** . . . . (651) 297-7831
Began Service: August 2014
Term Expires: August 2016
Judicial Administrative Assistant **Linda Leegard** . . . . (651) 297-5499
E-mail: linda.leegard@courts.state.mn.us

Chambers of Judge Francis J. Connolly

MInnesota Judicial Center, 25 Rev. Dr. Martin Luther King, Jr. Boulevard, St. Paul, MN 55155
Tel: (651) 297-8769
E-mail: francis.connolly@courts.state.mn.us

Francis J. Connolly
Judge

Education: Columbia 1980 BA; Georgetown 1984 MSFS, 1984 JD
Began Service: January 1, 2008
Appointed By: Governor Tim Pawlenty
Next Election: November 2016
Term Expires: January 3, 2017

Academic: Adjunct Representation Professor, William Mitchell College of Law (2003-2007)

Corporate: Associate General Counsel, Kraus-Anderson Companies, Inc. (1994-1998)

Government: Honors Program Attorney, United States Department of Justice (1984-1986)

Judicial: Assistant Presiding Judge, Fourth Judicial District, Minnesota District Courts (2004-2006); Presiding Judge, Civil Division, Fourth Judicial District, Minnesota District Courts (2006-2007)

Legal Practice: Attorney, Popham, Haik, Schnobrich & Kaufman, Ltd. (1986-1987); Attorney, Dorsey & Whitney LLP (1987-1992); Attorney, Rossini, Nelson & Rossini (1992-1994)

Current Memberships: The Douglas K. Amdahl American Inn of Court, The American Inns of Court; Hennepin County Bar Association; Minnesota State Bar Association

Membership: Member, Minnesota District Judges Association

Staff
Law Clerk **(Vacant)** . . . . (651) 297-8769
Career Law Clerk **Helen Mary Hughesdon** . . . . (651) 297-8769
Education: Col St Catherine 1968 BA; William Mitchell 1989 JD
Judicial Administrative Assistant **Sheri McGruder** . . . . (651) 297-8769

Chambers of Judge Michelle Ann Larkin

25 Rev. Dr. Martin Luther King Jr. Boulevard, St. Paul, MN 55155
Tel: (651) 297-1004
E-mail: michelle.larkin@courts.state.mn.us

Michelle Ann Larkin
Judge

Education: Minnesota 1988 BA; William Mitchell 1992 JD
Began Service: June 24, 2008
Appointed By: Governor Tim Pawlenty
Next Election: November 2016
Term Expires: January 3, 2017

Current Memberships: Minnesota State Bar Association

Staff
Law Clerk **Grant Goerke** . . . . (651) 297-1004
Began Service: September 2014
E-mail: grant.goerke@courts.state.mn.us
Law Clerk **Randall Shimpach** . . . . (651) 297-1004
Began Service: 2011
E-mail: randall.shimpach@courts.state.mn.us

Chambers of Judge Michelle Ann Larkin *continued*

Judicial Assistant **Sheri McGruder** . . . . (651) 297-1004

Chambers of Judge Lawrence B. Stauber Jr.

Minnesota Judicial Center, 25 Rev. Dr. Martin Luther King, Jr. Boulevard, St. Paul, MN 55155-6102
Tel: (651) 297-7650

Lawrence "Larry" Stauber, Jr.
Judge

Education: Minnesota (Duluth) 1970 BA, 1970 BS; Chicago-Kent 1977 JD
Began Service: October 17, 2008
Appointed By: Governor Tim Pawlenty
Next Election: November 2016
Term Expires: January 2017

Chambers of Judge Louise Dovre Bjorkman

25 Rev. Dr. Martin Luther King, Jr. Boulevard, St. Paul, MN 55155
Tel: (651) 297-7650
E-mail: louise.bjorkman@courts.state.mn.us

Louise Dovre Bjorkman
Judge

Education: Luther Col 1982 BA; Minnesota 1985 JD
Began Service: June 2008
Appointed By: Governor Tim Pawlenty
Next Election: November 2016
Term Expires: January 3, 2017

Current Memberships: Minnesota State Bar Association; Minnesota Women Lawyers

Chambers of Judge Carol A. Hooten

25 Rev. Dr. Martin Luther King, Jr. Boulevard, St. Paul, MN 55155
Tel: (651) 297-7650
E-mail: carol.hooten@courts.state.mn.us

Carol A. Hooten
Judge

Education: Minnesota 1973 BA; William Mitchell 1978 JD
Began Service: 2012
Next Election: November 2020

Staff
Law Clerk **Nick Jannakos** . . . . (651) 297-7650
Law Clerk **Nathan Shepherd** . . . . (651) 297-7650
Judicial Assistant **Maggie Hawkins** . . . . (651) 297-7650
E-mail: maggie.hawkins@courts.state.mn.us

Chambers of Judge Margaret H. Chutich

25 Rev. Dr. Martin Luther King, Jr. Boulevard, St. Paul, MN 55155
Tel: (651) 297-7650
E-mail: margaret.chutich@courts.state.mn.us

Margaret H. Chutich
Judge

Education: Minnesota 1980 BA; Michigan 1984 JD
Began Service: December 27, 2011
Term Expires: January 2021

Chambers of Judge John R. Rodenberg

25 Rev. Dr. Martin Luther King, Jr. Boulevard, St. Paul, MN 55155-6102
Tel: (651) 297-7650
E-mail: john.rodenberg@courts.state.mn.us

John R. Rodenberg
Judge

Education: St Olaf 1978 BA; Hamline 1981 JD
Began Service: December 27, 2011
Term Expires: January 2021

Chambers of Judge Michael L. Kirk

25 Rev. Dr. Martin Luther King, Jr. Boulevard, St. Paul, MN 55155
Tel: (651) 297-7650
E-mail: michael.kirk@courts.state.mn.us

Michael L. Kirk
Judge

Began Service: June 27, 2012
Appointed By: Governor Mark Dayton
Next Election: November 2020
Term Expires: January 2021

Staff
Judicial Assistant **Laurie Lahn** .... (651) 297-7650

Chambers of Judge John P. Smith

25 Rev. Dr. Martin Luther King, Jr. Boulevard, St. Paul, MN 55155
Tel: (651) 297-1000
E-mail: john.smith@courts.state.mn.us

John P. Smith
Judge

Note: Judge Smith will retire effective February 2, 2016.
Education: Concordia Col Moorhead MN 1971 BA; William Mitchell 1975 JD; Emory 1987 LLM
Began Service: January 7, 2013
Appointed By: Governor Mark Dayton
Next Election: November 2020

Chambers of Judge Denise D. Reilly

25 Rev. Dr. Martin Luther King, Jr. Boulevard, St. Paul, MN 55155
Tel: (651) 297-1000
E-mail: denise.reilly@courts.state.mn.us

Denise D. Reilly
Judge

Education: Wooster BA; William Mitchell JD

Chambers of Judge Peter M. Reyes

25 Rev. Dr. Martin Luther King, Jr. Boulevard, St. Paul, MN 55155
Tel: (651) 297-1000

Peter M. Reyes, Jr.
Judge

Education: U St Thomas (MN) BA; William Mitchell JD

Mississippi

Mississippi Administrative Office of Courts

450 High Street, Jackson, MS 39201
P.O. Box 117, Jackson, MS 39205
Tel: (601) 576-4630 Fax: (601) 576-4639

Staff

Supreme Court Administrator
Hubbard T. "Hubby" Saunders IV . . . . . (601) 359-2182
E-mail: hsaunders@courts.ms.gov Fax: (601) 359-2443
Education: Mississippi JD
Administrative Office of Courts Director **Kevin Lackey** . . . (601) 576-4636
E-mail: lackeyjk@courts.ms.gov
Education: Vanderbilt 1986 BS; Tulane 1989 JD
Finance Director **Carol Allgood** . . . . . (601) 359-3731
E-mail: callgood@courts.ms.gov Fax: (601) 359-3203
Information Systems Director **Daryl Wingo** . . . . . (601) 359-3709
E-mail: dwingo@courts.ms.gov Fax: (601) 359-3203

Mississippi Supreme Court

Carroll Gartin Justice Building, 450 High Street, Jackson, MS 39201
P.O. Box 117, Jackson, MS 39205
Tel: (601) 359-3697 Fax: (601) 359-2443
E-mail: sctclerk@mssc.state.ms.us
Internet: www.mssc.state.ms.us

Number of Judgeships: 9

The Supreme Court consists of nine justices who are elected in one of three districts for eight-year terms and sit in divisions of three justices each. The Governor appoints temporary justices to fill vacancies, and these appointees serve until the first general election occurring more than nine months after the initial appointment. The longest serving justice is selected as chief justice, and the next two senior justices are selected as presiding justices. The Supreme Court exercises appellate jurisdiction over the lower state courts. The Court also exercises jurisdiction over all matters relating to the state bar.

The Supreme Court sits in Jackson.

Court Staff

Clerk of the Court **Muriel Ellis** . . . . . (601) 359-2175
E-mail: sctclerk@mssc.state.ms.us Fax: (601) 359-2407
Chief Deputy Clerk **Rusty Holmes** . . . . . (601) 359-3694
Fax: (601) 359-2407
Deputy Clerk **Debra Knapp** . . . . . (601) 359-3694
E-mail: dknapp@mssc.state.ms.us Fax: (601) 359-2407
Marshal **Stephen E. Markert** . . . . . (601) 359-2368
E-mail: smarkert@mssc.state.ms.us
Director, Information Technology **Daryl Wingo** . . . . . (601) 359-3709
E-mail: dwingo@mssc.state.ms.us Fax: (601) 359-1981
State Law Librarian **Clara Watson Joorfetz** . . . . . (601) 359-3672
E-mail: cjoorfetz@mssc.state.ms.us Fax: (601) 359-2912
Education: Mississippi BA, MLS

Chambers of Chief Justice William L. Waller, Jr.

Carrol Gartin Justice Building, 450 High Street, Jackson, MS 39201
P.O. Box 117, Jackson, MS 39205-0117
Tel: (601) 359-2139 Fax: (601) 359-2443
E-mail: cjwaller@courts.ms.gov

William L. Waller, Jr.
Chief Justice

Date of Birth: 1952
Education: Mississippi State 1974; Mississippi 1977 JD
Began Service: January 5, 1998
Term Expires: January 2018

Current Memberships: American Bar Association; The American Legion; Christian Legal Society; Hinds County Bar Association; The Mississippi Bar

Staff

Law Clerk **Tyler Ellis** . . . . . (601) 359-5026
Began Service: August 2015
Term Expires: July 31, 2016
Law Clerk **Chad Byrd** . . . . . (601) 359-2204
Began Service: February 2013
Term Expires: July 31, 2016
E-mail: cbyrd@courts.ms.gov
Education: Mississippi JD
Judicial Assistant **Susan Ingram** . . . . . (601) 359-2139
E-mail: singram@courts.ms.gov
Education: Mississippi 1978 BS

Chambers of Presiding Justice Jess Dickinson

450 High Street, Jackson, MS 39201
Tel: (601) 359-2184
E-mail: jdickinson@mssc.state.ms.us

Jess H. Dickinson
Presiding Justice

Date of Birth: 1947
Education: Mississippi State 1978 BS; Mississippi 1982 JD
Began Service: January 2004
Term Expires: January 2020

Current Memberships: The Mississippi Bar

Staff

Judicial Assistant **Cindy Ward** . . . . . (601) 359-2184
E-mail: cward@mssc.state.ms.us

Chambers of Presiding Justice Michael K. Randolph

P.O. Box 117, Jackson, MS 39205
Tel: (601) 359-2100 Fax: (601) 359-2443
E-mail: jrandolph@mssc.state.ms.us

Michael K. Randolph
Presiding Justice

Date of Birth: December 4, 1946
Education: Rollins 1972 BS; Mississippi 1974 JD
Began Service: April 23, 2004
Term Expires: January 2019

Current Memberships: American Bar Association; The Mississippi Bar

Staff

Judicial Assistant **Angela Cossar** . . . . . (601) 359-2100
E-mail: acossar@mssc.state.ms.us

Chambers of Associate Justice Ann Hannaford Lamar

Carroll Gartin Justice Building, 450 High Street, Jackson, MS 39201
P.O. Box 117, Jackson, MS 39205-0117
Tel: (601) 359-2099 Fax: (601) 359-1272
E-mail: alamar@mssc.state.ms.us

Ann Hannaford Lamar
Associate Justice

Education: Delta State 1974 BS; Mississippi 1982 JD
Began Service: May 2007
Appointed By: Governor Haley Barbour
Next Election: November 2016
Election Type: General Election
Term Expires: January 2017

Government: Assistant District Attorney, State of Mississippi (1987-1993); Assistant District Attorney, State of Mississippi (1996-1999); District Attorney, State of Mississippi (2001-2007)

Judicial: Circuit Judge, 17th Judicial District of Mississippi (2001-2006)

Staff
Judicial Assistant **Mary L. Ewing** .... (601) 359-2099
E-mail: mewing@mssc.state.ms.us

Chambers of Associate Justice James W. Kitchens

Carroll Gartin Justice Building, 450 High Street, Jackson, MS 39201
Tel: (601) 359-2180
E-mail: jkitchens@courts.ms.gov

James W. "Jim" Kitchens
Associate Justice

Education: Southern Mississippi 1964; Mississippi 1967 JD
Began Service: January 2009
Next Election: November 2016
Election Type: General Election
Term Expires: January 2017

Current Memberships: Mississippi Prosecutors Association; National District Attorneys Association

Staff
Judicial Assistant **Cindy Henderson** .... (601) 359-2180
E-mail: chenderson@mssc.state.ms.us

Chambers of Associate Justice David Chandler

Carroll Gartin Justice Building, 450 High Street, Jackson, MS 39201
Tel: (601) 359-2107

David A. Chandler
Associate Justice

Date of Birth: 1946
Education: Mississippi State BA, MA, PhD; Mississippi JD; Virginia LLM
Began Service: January 2009
Next Election: November 2016
Election Type: General Election
Term Expires: January 2017

Current Memberships: American Bar Association; The Mississippi Bar; Tupelo Bar Association

Staff
Judicial Assistant **Vera Johnson** .... (601) 359-2107
E-mail: vjohnson@mssc.state.ms.us

Chambers of Associate Justice Randy Pierce

Carroll Gartin Justice Building, 450 High Street, Jackson, MS 39201
Tel: (601) 359-2093
E-mail: rpierce@courts.ms.gov

Randy G. "Bubba" Pierce
Associate Justice

Education: Southern Mississippi 1987 BS, MBA; Mississippi JD
Began Service: January 2009
Next Election: November 2016
Election Type: General Election
Term Expires: January 2017

Current Memberships: The Mississippi Bar; Mississippi Society of Certified Public Accountants

Staff
Judicial Assistant **Julia B. Soutullo** .... (601) 359-2093
E-mail: jsoutullo@mssc.state.ms.us

Chambers of Associate Justice Leslie D. King

450 High Street, Jackson, MS 39201
Tel: (601) 359-2096

Leslie D. King
Associate Justice

Date of Birth: 1949
Education: Mississippi 1970 BA; Texas Southern 1973 JD
Began Service: March 1, 2011
Appointed By: Governor Haley Barbour

Current Memberships: American Association for Justice; American Bar Association; Magnolia Bar Association; Magnolia Bar Foundation, Magnolia Bar Association; The Mississippi Bar; Mississippi Trial Lawyers Association

Staff
Law Clerk **Shalon Love-Wansley** .... (601) 359-2096
E-mail: slove@mssc.state.ms.us
Education: Spelman 2004 BA; Mississippi 2007 JD
Law Clerk **Elise Stewart** .... (601) 359-2096
E-mail: sraffin@mssc.state.ms.us
Judicial Assistant **Mabel Davenport** .... (601) 359-2096
E-mail: mdavenport@mssc.state.ms.us

Chambers of Associate Justice Josiah Coleman

450 High Street, Jackson, MS 39201
Tel: (601) 359-3697
E-mail: jcoleman@courts.ms.gov

Josiah D. Coleman
Associate Justice

Education: Mississippi BA, JD
Began Service: January 7, 2013

Staff
Law Clerk **Warren Stafford** .... (601) 359-3697
Law Clerk **Lindsey Simmons** .... (601) 359-3697
E-mail: lsimmons@courts.ms.gov
Judicial Assistant **Shinyera Johnson** .... (601) 359-3697
E-mail: sjohnson@courts.ms.gov

Court of Appeals of the State of Mississippi

450 High Street, Jackson, MS 39201
Tel: (601) 576-4665 Fax: (601) 576-4708
Internet: www.courts.ms.gov

Number of Judgeships: 10

The judges of the Mississippi Court of Appeals are elected for eight-year terms on a nonpartisan ballot; each court of appeals district elects two judges to serve on the court. The chief judge is appointed by the Chief Justice of the Mississippi Supreme Court. The chief judge, in turn, appoints the two presiding judges of the Court of Appeals. Established by statute in 1995, the Mississippi Court of Appeals hears cases deflected from the Supreme Court. However, the Supreme Court retains cases involving the death penalty, utility rates, bar matters, annexations, bond issues, election contests, and statutes that have been ruled unconstitutional by a lower court. Decisions by the Court of Appeals are final, except for those accepted by a writ of certiorari to the Supreme Court.

The Court of Appeals sits in Jackson.

Court Staff

Clerk of the Court **Muriel Ellis** . . . . (601) 359-2175
Fax: (601) 359-2407
Assistant Court Administrator **Kathryn Cassady** . . . . (601) 576-4725
E-mail: kcassady@courts.ms.gov
Senior Staff Attorney **(Vacant)** . . . . (601) 576-4723
Staff Attorney **Jack Bach** . . . . (601) 576-4655
E-mail: jbach@courts.ms.gov
Education: Wyoming 1988 JD
Staff Attorney **Christen Kazery-Hobbs** . . . . (601) 576-4722
Editor of Opinions **John Grant** . . . . (601) 576-4726
E-mail: jgrant@courts.ms.gov

Chambers of Chief Judge L. Joseph Lee

450 High Street, Jackson, MS 39201
P.O. Box 22847, Jackson, MS 39225-2847
Tel: (601) 576-4645 Fax: (601) 576-4708
E-mail: jlee@courts.ms.gov

L. Joseph Lee
Chief Judge

Date of Birth: 1945
Education: William Carey 1969 BS; Mississippi Col 1973 JD
Began Service: January 1999
Next Election: November 2018
Term Expires: December 2018

Current Memberships: American Bar Association; The Mississippi Bar; State Bar of Texas

Staff

Law Clerk **Christina Sequeira** . . . . (601) 576-4692
Began Service: July 2014
Term Expires: July 2016
Law Clerk **Ashley L. Sulser** . . . . (601) 576-4691
Began Service: August 2002
Education: Millsaps 1999 BA; Mississippi 2002 JD
Judicial Assistant **Peggy Brown** . . . . (601) 576-4645
E-mail: pbrown@courts.ms.gov

Chambers of Presiding Judge Tyree Irving

450 High Street, Jackson, MS 39201
P.O. Box 22847, Jackson, MS 39225-2847
Tel: (601) 576-4644 Fax: (601) 576-4708
E-mail: jirving@courts.ms.gov

Tyree Irving
Presiding Judge

Date of Birth: 1946
Education: Jackson State U 1968 BA; Mississippi 1974 JD
Began Service: January 1, 1999
Next Election: November 2018
Term Expires: December 31, 2018

Academic: English Teacher, Greenville and Leflore County School Districts (1968-1972)

Clerkships: Law Clerk, Mississippi Supreme Court (1975-1976)

Government: Assistant United States Attorney, Northern District of Mississippi, United States Department of Justice (1978)

Legal Practice: Private Practice (1977); Walls, Buck & Irving (1979-1988); Walls & Irving; Solo Practitioner (1989-1998)

Current Memberships: American Bar Association; Leflore County Bar Association; Magnolia Bar Association; The Mississippi Bar

Staff

Law Clerk **Mabel Kimbrough** . . . . (601) 576-4644
Began Service: June 2, 2015
Term Expires: July 31, 2016
Law Clerk **Dorissa Smith** . . . . (601) 576-4644
E-mail: dsmith@mssc.state.ms.us
Judicial Assistant **Wanda H. Zambrano** . . . . (601) 576-4644
E-mail: wzambrano@courts.ms.gov
Education: Florida State 1981 BS

Chambers of Presiding Judge T. Kenneth Griffis, Jr.

450 High Street, Jackson, MS 39201
Tel: (601) 576-4673 Fax: (601) 576-4708
E-mail: jgriffis@courts.ms.gov

T. Kenneth Griffis, Jr.
Presiding Judge

Date of Birth: 1961
Education: Mississippi 1983, 1987 JD
Began Service: January 6, 2003
Next Election: November 2022
Term Expires: January 1, 2023

Legal Practice: Private Practice

Nonprofit: Attorney, Blue Cross and Blue Shield of Mississippi

Current Memberships: Hinds County Bar Association; The Mississippi Bar

Staff

Law Clerk **Emily Lindsay** . . . . (601) 576-4693
Law Clerk **(Vacant)** . . . . (601) 576-4694
Judicial Assistant **Mary Holden Dooley** . . . . (601) 576-4673
E-mail: mdooley@courts.ms.gov

Chambers of Judge Donna M. Barnes

450 High Street, Jackson, MS 39201
P.O. Box 22847, Jackson, MS 39225-2847
Tel: (601) 576-4671 Fax: (601) 576-4708
E-mail: jbarnes@courts.ms.gov

Donna M. Barnes
Judge

Date of Birth: October 30, 1960
Education: Mississippi 1982 BA, 1985 JD; Cambridge (UK) 1997 LLM
Began Service: August 16, 2004
Next Election: November 2018
Term Expires: December 2018

Current Memberships: American Bar Association; Fifth Circuit Bar Association; Lee County Bar Association; The Missouri Bar

Staff
Law Clerk **Kathy Russell** . . . . (601) 576-4688
E-mail: krussell@courts.ms.gov
Education: Mississippi Col 2006 JD
Career Law Clerk **Ann M. Heidke** . . . . (601) 576-4687
Education: Millsaps 1989 BA;
Mississippi Col 1995 MA; Mississippi 2005 JD
Judicial Assistant **Mary Nell Jeffreys** . . . . (601) 576-4671
E-mail: mjeffreys@courts.ms.gov

Chambers of Judge David Ishee

P.O. Box 22847, Jackson, MS 39225-2847
Tel: (601) 576-4714 Fax: (601) 576-4708

David M. Ishee
Judge

Date of Birth: 1963
Education: Southern Mississippi BS; Mississippi JD
Began Service: September 27, 2004
Next Election: November 4, 2016
Election Type: General Election
Term Expires: December 31, 2016

Judicial: Municipal Court Judge, City of Pascagoula, Mississippi

Legal Practice: Attorney, Elmo Lang; Attorney, Lang & Ishee

Current Memberships: The Mississippi Bar

Staff
Career Law Clerk **Rebekah B. Gregory** . . . . (601) 576-4710
Began Service: August 2010
E-mail: rblakeslee@mssc.state.ms.us
Education: Mississippi 2009 JD
Law Clerk **Katherine Alexander** . . . . (601) 576-4710
Began Service: August 2014
Term Expires: August 2016
E-mail: kalexander@mssc.state.ms.us
Judicial Assistant **Debra Dodd** . . . . (601) 576-4714
E-mail: ddodd@courts.ms.gov
Education: Belhaven 2008 BSM

Chambers of Judge Virginia C. Carlton

450 High Street, Jackson, MS 39201
Tel: (601) 576-4678 Fax: (601) 576-4708
E-mail: vcarlton@courts.ms.gov

Virginia C. Carlton
Judge

Education: Mississippi 1986 BBA, 1989 JD
Began Service: January 2007
Next Election: November 2022
Term Expires: 2023
Political Affiliation: Republican

Chambers of Judge Virginia C. Carlton *continued*

Staff
Law Clerk **Avery Shannon** . . . . (601) 576-4704
Began Service: August 2009
E-mail: acarlisle@mssc.state.ms.us
Law Clerk **Lindsey Watkins** . . . . (601) 576-4703
Began Service: November 2010
E-mail: kmcleod@mssc.state.ms.us
Education: Mississippi JD
Judicial Assistant **Kathleen Johnson** . . . . (601) 576-4678
E-mail: kjohnson@courts.ms.gov

Chambers of Judge James D. Maxwell II

450 High Street, Jackson, MS 39201
Tel: (601) 576-4643 Fax: (601) 576-4708
E-mail: jmaxwell@courts.ms.gov

James D. Maxwell II
Judge

Began Service: March 2009
Next Election: November 2022
Term Expires: 2022

Staff
Law Clerk **Elizabeth F. Archer** . . . . (601) 576-4702
Began Service: August 2010
Term Expires: August 2016
E-mail: earcher@mssc.state.ms.us
Education: Virginia 2002 BA; Mississippi 2008 JD
Law Clerk **Jamie Ballard** . . . . (601) 576-4702
Began Service: July 2013
E-mail: jballard@mssc.state.ms.us
Judicial Assistant **Katherine Frye** . . . . (601) 576-4665
Began Service: 2009
E-mail: kfrye@courts.ms.gov

Chambers of Judge Eugene L. Fair, Jr.

450 High Street, Jackson, MS 39201
Tel: (601) 576-4681 Tel: (601) 576-4708
E-mail: efair@courts.ms.gov

Eugene L. "Gene" Fair, Jr.
Judge

Education: Mississippi 1966 BA, 1968 JD
Began Service: January 1, 2012
Appointed By: Governor Haley Barbour

Staff
Law Clerk **Robert L. Bouis III** . . . . (601) 576-4706
E-mail: rbouis@courts.ms.gov
Law Clerk **Sue Ann Bernard** . . . . (601) 576-4705
E-mail: sbernard@courts.ms.gov
Judicial Assistant **Bea Ratcliffe** . . . . (601) 576-4654
E-mail: bratcliffe@courts.ms.gov

Chambers of Judge Ceola James

450 High Street, Jackson, MS 39201
Tel: (601) 576-4665

Ceola James
Judge

Education: Mississippi Col JD
Began Service: January 7, 2013

Staff
Law Clerk **Joseph Hemleben** . . . . (601) 576-4680
Law Clerk **Kathryn McDonald** . . . . (601) 576-4680
E-mail: kmcdonald@courts.ms.gov
Judicial Assistant **Kimberly Davis** . . . . (601) 576-4680
E-mail: kdavis@courts.ms.gov

Chambers of Judge Jack Wilson
450 High Street, Jackson, MS 39201
Tel: (601) 576-4665

Jack Wilson
Judge

Education: U Memphis; Mississippi; Harvard JD
Began Service: 2015

Missouri

Office of the State Courts Administrator of Missouri

2112 Industrial Boulevard, Jefferson City, MO 65109
P.O. Box 104480, Jefferson City, MO 65110
Tel: (573) 751-4377 Fax: (573) 522-6152
Internet: www.courts.mo.gov

Staff

State Courts Administrator **Kathy S. Lloyd** .... (573) 526-8803
Fax: (573) 522-6152
Deputy State Courts Administrator **Earl Kraus** .... (573) 522-1284
E-mail: earl.kraus@courts.mo.gov
Division of Administration Director **Earl Kraus** .... (573) 522-1284
Fax: (573) 522-6152
Court Business Services Director **Sherri Paschal** .... (573) 522-8237
E-mail: sherri.paschal@courts.mo.gov Fax: (573) 522-5961
Human Resources Manager **Paul Buckley** .... (573) 526-8807
E-mail: paul.buckley@courts.mo.gov Fax: (573) 526-8260
Information Technology Services Director **Pat Brooks** .... (573) 522-8222
E-mail: pat.brooks@courts.mo.gov Fax: (573) 526-5430

Missouri Supreme Court

Supreme Court Building, 207 West High Street, Jefferson City, MO 65101
P.O. Box 150, Jefferson City, MO 65102
Tel: (573) 751-4144 Fax: (573) 751-7514
Internet: www.courts.mo.gov

Number of Judgeships: 7

The Supreme Court consists of a chief justice and six judges who are appointed by the Governor from a list of candidates submitted by a nonpartisan Appellate Judicial Commission. Appointed judges face a retention vote in the next general election occurring after one year in office for a twelve-year term. The chief justice is elected by peer vote for a two-year term. Retirement is mandatory at age seventy; however, retired judges may be assigned to serve in state courts. The Supreme Court has exclusive appellate jurisdiction in all cases involving federal or Missouri constitutional law, federal treaties or statutes, Missouri revenue laws, and in any case involving the death penalty or life imprisonment. The Court exercises appellate jurisdiction over cases transferred from the Missouri Court of Appeals. The Court has rule-making authority over the lower courts and regulates admission to the state bar.

The Supreme Court sits in Jefferson City.

Court Staff

Fax: (573) 751-7514

Clerk of Court **Bill L. Thompson** .... (573) 751-4144
E-mail: bill.thompson@courts.mo.gov
Chief Deputy Clerk **Don Dickey** .... (573) 751-7311
E-mail: don.dickey@courts.mo.gov
Deputy Clerk for the Court en Banc **Cynthia L. Turley** ... (573) 751-7313
E-mail: cynthia.turley@courts.mo.gov Fax: (573) 751-2809
Commission Counsel **Betsy AuBuchon** .... (573) 751-0178
Communications Counsel **Beth S. Riggert** .... (573) 751-3676
E-mail: beth.riggert@courts.mo.gov
Assistant to the Clerk and Counsel **Terri Milinkov** .... (573) 751-4144
Fax: (573) 751-7514
Supreme Court Librarian (Acting) **Gail Miller** .... (573) 751-2636
Fax: (573) 751-2573
Assistant Librarian **Gail Miller** .... (573) 751-2636
Fax: (573) 751-2573
Systems Administrator **Tom Fishback** .... (573) 751-4144
E-mail: tom.fishback@courts.mo.gov
Marshal **Robert Stiefferman** .... (573) 751-2117
Judicial Education Director (Acting) **Sherri Paschal** ..... (573) 526-8839
Fax: (573) 522-5013

Chambers of Chief Justice Patricia Breckenridge

Supreme Court Building, 207 West High Street, Jefferson City, MO 65101
P.O. Box 150, Jefferson City, MO 65102
Tel: (573) 751-9652 Fax: (573) 751-7359
E-mail: patricia.breckenridge@courts.mo.gov

Patricia Breckenridge
Chief Justice

Date of Birth: 1953
Education: Arkansas BS; Missouri 1977 JD
Began Service: September 2007
Appointed By: Governor Matt Blunt
Next Election: November 4, 2020
Election Type: Retention Election
Term Expires: December 31, 2020

Current Memberships: American Bar Foundation; American Bar Association; Association for Women Lawyers of Kansas City; The Missouri Bar; National Association of Women Judges

Staff

Law Clerk **Elizabeth Lucas** .... (573) 751-6848
E-mail: elizabeth.lucas@courts.mo.gov
Law Clerk **Carol Jansen** .... (573) 526-9771
Began Service: 2011
E-mail: carol.jansen@courts.mo.gov
Judicial Executive Assistant **Cindy Ruether** .... (573) 751-9652
E-mail: cindy.ruether@courts.mo.gov

Chambers of Judge Mary Rhodes Russell

Supreme Court Building, 207 West High Street, Jefferson City, MO 65101
Tel: (573) 751-6880 Fax: (573) 751-7361
E-mail: mary.russell@courts.mo.gov

Mary Rhodes Russell
Judge

Date of Birth: 1958
Education: Truman State 1980 BA, 1980 BS; Missouri 1983 JD
Began Service: October 8, 2004
Appointed By: Governor Bob Holden
Term Expires: December 31, 2018

Current Memberships: The Bar Association of Metropolitan St. Louis; Cole County Bar Association; Illinois State Bar Association; Kansas City Metropolitan Bar Association; Mid-Missouri Women Lawyers Association; The Missouri Bar; National Association of Women Judges; Springfield Metropolitan Bar Association; Tenth Judicial Circuit Bar Association; Women Lawyers' Association of Greater St. Louis

Staff

Law Clerk **Peter Bay** .... (573) 751-6880
Began Service: August 2014
Term Expires: August 2016
E-mail: peter.bay@courts.mo.gov
Law Clerk **Kristen Johnson** .... (573) 751-6880
Term Expires: August 2016
E-mail: kristen.johnson@courts.mo.gov
Judicial Executive Assistant **Rebecca Fredrick** .... (573) 751-6880

Chambers of Judge Richard B. Teitelman

Supreme Court Building, 207 West High Street, Jefferson City, MO 65101
P.O. Box 150, Jefferson City, MO 65102
Tel: (573) 751-1004 Tel: (573) 751-7161
E-mail: rteitelm@courts.mo.gov

Richard B. Teitelman
Judge

Date of Birth: 1947
Education: Pennsylvania 1969 BA; Washington U (MO) 1973 JD
Began Service: March 1, 2002
Appointed By: Governor Bob Holden
Term Expires: December 31, 2016

Current Memberships: The American Association of Jewish Lawyers and Jurists; Association of Jewish Judges; St. Louis Bar Foundation, The Bar Association of Metropolitan St. Louis; The Missouri Bar

Staff
Career Law Clerk **Eric Peterson** . . . . (573) 751-1004
E-mail: eric.peterson@courts.mo.gov
Education: Washington U (MO) 1999 JD

Chambers of Judge Laura Denvir Stith

Supreme Court Building, 207 West High Street, Jefferson City, MO 65101
P.O. Box 150, Jefferson City, MO 65102
Tel: (573) 751-3570 Fax: (573) 751-7355
E-mail: laura.stith@courts.mo.gov

Laura Denvir Stith
Judge

Date of Birth: 1953
Education: Tufts 1975 BA; Georgetown 1978 JD
Began Service: March 7, 2001
Appointed By: Governor Bob Holden
Next Election: November 2026
Term Expires: December 31, 2026

Clerkships: Law Clerk The Honorable Robert E. Seiler, Missouri Supreme Court (1978-1979)

Judicial: Judge, Missouri Court of Appeals, Western District (1994-2001)

Legal Practice: Associate, Shook, Hardy & Bacon L.L.P.

Current Memberships: American Bar Foundation; American Bar Association; Association of Women Lawyers of Greater Kansas City; Kansas City Metropolitan Bar Association; The Missouri Bar

Staff
Law Clerk **Paul Brusati** . . . . (573) 751-3570
Law Clerk **Kirsten Dunham** . . . . (573) 751-3570
Judicial Executive Assistant **Falena Vittetoe-Moore** . . . . . (573) 751-3570
E-mail: falena.moore@courts.mo.gov

Chambers of Judge Zel Fischer

Supreme Court Building, 207 West High Street, Jefferson City, MO 65101
Tel: (573) 751-4375 Fax: (573) 751-7362
E-mail: zel.fischer@courts.mo.gov

Zel Martin Fischer
Judge

Education: William Jewell 1985 BA; Missouri 1988 JD
Began Service: December 12, 2008
Appointed By: Governor Matt Blunt
Next Election: November 2022
Election Type: Retention Election

Clerkships: Law Clerk, Witt, Boggs, Shaw and VanAmburg; Law Clerk, Law Office of James D. Boggs; Law Clerk, Missouri Supreme Court

Chambers of Judge Zel Fischer *continued*

Judicial: Atchison County Associate Circuit Judge, 4th Judicial Circuit Court, Missouri Judicial Circuit Courts (2006-2008)

Legal Practice: Attorney, Law Office of James D. Boggs (1989-1992); Attorney, Law Offices of Zel M. Fischer (1992-2006)

Current Memberships: American Bar Association; Missouri Association of Trial Attorneys; The Missouri Bar; 4th Circuit Judicial Bar Association, Missouri Judicial Circuit Courts

Staff
Law Clerk **Jacob Lewis** . . . . (573) 751-4375
Law Clerk **Caleb Phillips** . . . . (573) 751-4375
Judicial Executive Assistant **Melanie Barlow** . . . . (573) 751-4375
E-mail: melanie.barlow@courts.mo.gov

Chambers of Judge George W. Draper III

Supreme Court Building, 207 West High Street, Jefferson City, MO 65101
Tel: (573) 751-6644

George W. Draper III
Judge

Date of Birth: 1953
Education: Morehouse Col 1977 BA; Howard U 1981 JD
Began Service: October 20, 2011
Appointed By: Governor Jay Nixon

Staff
Law Clerk **Kelly Dunsford** . . . . (573) 751-6644
E-mail: kelly.dunsford@courts.mo.gov
Education: Missouri 1999 JD
Law Clerk **Misty A. Ramirez** . . . . (573) 751-6644
E-mail: misty.ramirez@courts.mo.gov
Education: Saint Louis U 2000 JD
Judicial Assistant **Kristin Bennett** . . . . (573) 751-6644
E-mail: kristin.bennett@courts.mo.gov

Chambers of Judge Paul Wilson

207 West High Street, Jefferson City, MO 65101
Tel: (573) 751-4144

Paul Wilson
Judge

Education: Drury U BA; Missouri JD
Began Service: 2012
Appointed By: Governor Jay Nixon
Next Election: November 2026
Election Type: Retention Election

Government: Senior Counsel for Budget and Finance, Office of the Governor, State of Missouri

Staff
Law Clerk **Jordon Baehr** . . . . (573) 751-4144
Judicial Executive Assistant **Jeanne Richardson** . . . . (573) 751-4144

Missouri Court of Appeals

Tel: (417) 895-6811 Fax: (417) 895-6817

The judges of the Court of Appeals are initially appointed by the Governor from a list of candidates submitted by a nonpartisan Appellate Judicial Commission. They must then stand for retention in the next general election occurring at least one year after their appointment. Retention elections are held every twelve years. The chief judges are elected by peer vote in each district for a term determined by the district. The method of selection varies with each district, as does the length of term. Retirement is at age seventy, but retired judges may serve as senior judges in any Missouri court, as assigned by the Supreme Court. The Court of Appeals has appellate jurisdiction over civil and criminal cases, except those within the exclusive jurisdiction of the Missouri Supreme Court.

Missouri Court of Appeals, Eastern District

One Post Office Square, 815 Olive Street, St. Louis, MO 63101
Tel: (314) 539-4300 Fax: (314) 539-4324
Internet: www.courts.mo.gov

Number of Judgeships: 14

Areas Covered: Counties of Audrain, Cape Girardeau, Clark, Franklin, Gasconade, Jefferson, Knox, Lewis, Lincoln, Madison, Marion, Monroe, Montgomery, Osage, Perry, Pike, Ralls, St. Charles, St. Francois, St. Genevieve, St. Louis, St. Louis City, Scotland, Shelby, Warren and Washington

Court Staff

Clerk of Court **Laura Thielmeier Roy** .... (314) 539-4300
E-mail: laura.roy@courts.mo.gov
Education: Missouri BJ, JD
Chief Deputy Clerk **Debbie Skinner-Neuhaus** .... (314) 539-4300
E-mail: debbie.skinner-neuhaus@courts.mo.gov
Court Administrator **Douglas Bader** .... (314) 539-4300
E-mail: doug.bader@courts.mo.gov
Education: Kansas BA; Illinois JD
Marshal **Alvin Chamberlain** .... (314) 539-4300
E-mail: alvin.chamberlain@courts.mo.gov

Chambers of Chief Judge Lisa Van Amburg

815 Olive Street, St. Louis, MO 63101
Tel: (314) 539-4300

Lisa Van Amburg
Chief Judge

Education: Washington U (MO) BA; Saint Louis U JD
Began Service: 2012
Appointed By: Governor Jay Nixon
Next Election: November 2026

Chambers of Judge Angela T. Quigless

815 Olive Street, St. Louis, MO 63101
Tel: (314) 539-4300

Angela T. Quigless
Judge

Education: Missouri 1981 BA; Saint Louis U 1984 JD
Began Service: 2012
Next Election: November 2026

Chambers of Judge Robert M. Clayton III

One Post Office Square, 815 Olive Street, St. Louis, MO 63101
Tel: (314) 539-4300 Fax: (314) 539-4324

Robert M. Clayton III
Judge

Education: Southern Methodist 1991 BA; Missouri (Kansas City) 1994 JD
Began Service: 2012

Chambers of Judge Gary M. Gaertner Jr.

815 Olive Street, St. Louis, MO 63101
Tel: (314) 539-4376

Gary M. Gaertner, Jr.
Judge

Education: Saint Louis U 1987 BA, 1990 JD
Began Service: October 2009
Appointed By: Governor Jay Nixon

Staff

Law Clerk **Jessica Eswine** .... (314) 539-4376
Began Service: June 2014
Law Clerk **Alice Wortman** .... (314) 539-4376
E-mail: alice.wortman@courts.mo.gov

Chambers of Judge Kurt S. Odenwald

One Post Office Square, 815 Olive Street, St. Louis, MO 63101
Tel: (314) 539-4340
E-mail: kurt.odenwald@courts.mo.gov

Kurt S. Odenwald
Judge

Education: Missouri (St Louis) 1976 BA; Saint Louis U 1979 JD
Began Service: October 30, 2007
Appointed By: Governor Matt Blunt
Next Election: November 4, 2020
Election Type: Retention Election
Term Expires: December 31, 2020
Political Affiliation: Republican

Staff

Law Clerk **Matthew Hoffman** .... (314) 539-4340
E-mail: adam.johnson@courts.mo.gov
Law Clerk **Zachary Merkle** .... (314) 539-4340
E-mail: zachary.merkle@courts.mo.gov
Administrative Assistant **Karen VanDorn** .... (314) 539-4340
E-mail: karen.vandorn@courts.mo.gov

Chambers of Judge Robert G. Dowd, Jr.

One Post Office Square, 815 Olive Street, St. Louis, MO 63101
Tel: (314) 539-4350 Fax: (314) 539-4339

Robert G. Dowd, Jr.
Judge

Date of Birth: 1951
Education: Quincy Col 1973 BA; St Mary's U (TX) 1977 JD
Began Service: August 18, 1994
Next Election: November 2020
Election Type: Retention Election
Term Expires: December 31, 2020

Judicial: Magistrate Judge, Missouri Circuit Court (1978-1982); Judge, Missouri Circuit Court (1982-1994)

Legal Practice: Private Practice (1978-1979)

Current Memberships: American Bar Association; The Bar Association of Metropolitan St. Louis; The Missouri Bar

Chambers of Judge Robert G. Dowd, Jr. *continued*

Staff
Career Law Clerk **Shannon Williams** . . . . . (314) 539-4352
E-mail: shannon.williams@courts.mo.gov
Career Law Clerk **Jason Sengheiser** . . . . . (314) 539-4352
E-mail: jason.sengheiser@courts.mo.gov
Education: Saint Louis U 2003 JD
Judicial Administrative Assistant **Susan Neal** . . . . . (314) 539-4351
E-mail: sue.neal@courts.mo.gov

Chambers of Judge Mary K. Hoff

815 Olive Street, St. Louis, MO 63101
Tel: (314) 539-4355 Fax: (314) 539-4339
E-mail: mary.hoff@courts.mo.gov

Mary K. Hoff
Judge

Date of Birth: 1953
Education: Missouri BS; Saint Louis U 1978 JD
Began Service: 1996
Appointed By: Governor Mel Carnahan
Next Election: November 2022
Term Expires: December 2022

Academic: High School Teacher (1974-1975)

Government: Assistant Public Defender, Office of the Public Defender, State of Missouri (1978-1982)

Judicial: Judge, Missouri Circuit Court, St. Louis Circuit (1989-1996)

Legal Practice: Leonard Buckley & Associates (1982-1986); Schuchat, Cook & Werner (1986-1989)

Current Memberships: American Bar Association; The Bar Association of Metropolitan St. Louis; The Missouri Bar; National Association of Women Judges; Women Lawyers' Association of Greater St. Louis

Staff
Career Law Clerk **Catherine Lappas** . . . . . (314) 539-4357
Began Service: 2007
E-mail: catherine_lappas@courts.mo.gov
Education: Wellesley 1987 BA;
Saint Louis U 2002 JD
Career Law Clerk **Amy S. Westermann** . . . . . (314) 539-4357
E-mail: amy.westermann@courts.mo.gov
Education: Maryville U 1999 BA;
Saint Louis U 2003 JD
Judicial Administrative Assistant **Karen Taylor** . . . . . (314) 539-4356
E-mail: karen.taylor@courts.mo.gov

Chambers of Judge Lawrence E. Mooney

One Post Office Square, 815 Olive Street, St. Louis, MO 63101
Tel: (314) 539-4360 Fax: (314) 539-4339
E-mail: lawrence.mooney@courts.mo.gov

Lawrence E. Mooney
Judge

Date of Birth: 1949
Education: Saint Louis U 1971 AB, 1974 JD
Began Service: August 14, 1998
Appointed By: Governor Mel Carnahan
Next Election: November 2024
Term Expires: December 31, 2024

Government: Assistant Prosecuting Attorney, County of St. Louis, Missouri (1975-1977); First Assistant Prosecuting Attorney, County of St. Louis, Missouri (1979-1990); Executive Assistant to the County Executive, County of St. Louis, Missouri (1991-1998)

Legal Practice: Private Practice (1974-1975); Private Practice (1977-1978)

Chambers of Judge Lawrence E. Mooney *continued*

Current Memberships: American Bar Association; The Bar Association of Metropolitan St. Louis; International Association of Lesbian and Gay Judges; The Missouri Bar; Women Lawyers' Association of Greater St. Louis

Staff
Career Law Clerk **Lisa Anderson** . . . . . (314) 539-4362
E-mail: landerson@courts.mo.gov
Education: Missouri (Kansas City) 1994 BA;
Saint Louis U 2005 JD
Career Law Clerk **Julie A. Stevens** . . . . . (314) 539-4362
E-mail: julie.stevens@courts.mo.gov
Education: Baylor 1984 BSN;
Saint Louis U 2000 JD
Judicial Administrative Assistant **Cynthia A. Borisch** . . . . (314) 539-4361
E-mail: cynthia.borisch@courts.mo.gov

Chambers of Judge Patricia L. Cohen

815 Olive Street, St. Louis, MO 63101
Tel: (314) 539-4331 Fax: (314) 539-4339
E-mail: patricia.cohen@courts.mo.gov

Patricia L. Cohen
Judge

Education: Michigan BA; Cornell 1982 JD
Began Service: October 2003

Clerkships: Law Clerk, Chambers of District Judge Jean C. Hamilton, Missouri Court of Appeals, Eastern District

Judicial: Judge, 22nd Judicial Circuit, Missouri Judicial Circuit Courts (1997-2003)

Current Memberships: The Bar Association of Metropolitan St. Louis; National Association of Women Judges; Women Lawyers' Association of Greater St. Louis

Profession: Private Practice (1982-1997)

Staff
Research Attorney **Courtney Stirrat** . . . . . (314) 539-4332
E-mail: courtney.stirrat@courts.mo.gov
Judicial Administrative Assistant **Roxane Ellis** . . . . . (314) 539-4331
E-mail: roxane.ellis@courts.mo.gov
Law Clerk **Laura Taylor** . . . . . (314) 539-4331

Chambers of Judge Sherri B. Sullivan

815 Olive Street, St. Louis, MO 63101
Tel: (314) 539-4381 Fax: (314) 539-4339
E-mail: sherri.sullivan@courts.mo.gov

Sherri B. Sullivan
Judge

Education: Missouri (St Louis) BS; Saint Louis U JD
Began Service: August 1999
Appointed By: Governor Mel Carnahan
Next Election: November 2024
Term Expires: December 2024

Judicial: Associate Circuit Judge, State of Missouri; Circuit Judge, State of Missouri

Current Memberships: Metropolitan St. Louis Bar Association; National Association of Women Judges; Women Lawyers' Association of Greater St. Louis

Staff
Career Law Clerk **Lea Mackowiak** . . . . . (314) 539-4382
E-mail: lea.mackowiak@courts.mo.gov
Education: Missouri 2004 JD
Career Law Clerk **Emily M. Tucker** . . . . . (314) 539-4382
E-mail: emily.tucker@courts.mo.gov
Education: Columbus Law 1995 JD

(continued on next page)

Chambers of Judge Sherri B. Sullivan *continued*

Judicial Administrative Assistant **Judith Gonzalez** . . . . . . (314) 539-4381
E-mail: judith.gonzalez@courts.mo.gov

Chambers of Judge Roy L. Richter

One Post Office Square, 815 Olive Street, St. Louis, MO 63101
Tel: (314) 539-4336
E-mail: roy.richter@courts.mo.gov

Roy L. Richter
Judge

Education: Drury Col; Missouri JD
Began Service: 2006
Next Election: November 4, 2020
Election Type: Retention Election
Term Expires: December 31, 2020

Staff

Law Clerk **Paul "Trey" Conklin III** . . . . (314) 539-4336
Began Service: August 2014
Term Expires: July 2016
Law Clerk **Karen Schneider** . . . . (314) 539-4336
Began Service: August 2011
E-mail: karen.schneider@courts.mo.gov
Education: Tulane 1989 JD
Administrative Assistant **Brenda K. Endres** . . . . (314) 539-4300
E-mail: brenda.endres@courts.mo.gov

Chambers of Judge Philip M. Hess

815 Olive Street, St. Louis, MO 63101
Tel: (314) 539-4300

Philip M. Hess
Judge

Education: Rockhurst U; Missouri JD
Began Service: 2013
Appointed By: Governor Jay Nixon
Term Expires: December 31, 2016

Chambers of Judge James M. Dowd

815 Olive Street, St. Louis, MO 63101
Tel: (314) 539-4300

James M. Dowd
Judge

Began Service: October 16, 2015

Missouri Court of Appeals, Southern District

John Q. Hammons Building, 300 Hammons Parkway,
Springfield, MO 65806
Tel: (417) 895-6811 Fax: (417) 895-6817
Internet: www.courts.mo.gov

Number of Judgeships: 7

Areas Covered: Counties of Barry, Barton, Bollinger, Butler, Camden, Carter, Cedar, Christian, Crawford, Dade, Dallas, Dent, Douglas, Dunklin, Greene, Hickory, Howell, Iron, Jasper, Laclede, Lawrence, McDonald, Maries, Mississippi, New Madrid, Newton, Oregon, Ozark, Pemiscot, Phelps, Polk, Pulaski, Reynolds, Ripley, Scott, Shannon, Saint Clair, Stoddard, Stone, Taney, Texas, Wayne, Webster and Wright

Court Staff

Clerk of Court **Sandra L. Skinner** . . . . (417) 895-6811
E-mail: sandra.skinner@courts.mo.gov
Education: Missouri 1976 JD

Missouri Court of Appeals, Southern District *continued*

Chief Deputy Clerk **Connie Platter** . . . . (417) 895-6811
E-mail: connie.platter@courts.mo.gov
Staff Counsel **Craig A. Street** . . . . (417) 895-6811
E-mail: craig.street@courts.mo.gov
Education: Missouri 1998 JD
Marshal **Mike Woods** . . . . (417) 895-6811
Librarian **Amy L. Bailey** . . . . (417) 895-6813
E-mail: amy.bailey@courts.mo.gov
Fiscal Officer **Susan Newton** . . . . (417) 895-6812
E-mail: susan.newton@courts.mo.gov
Computer Information Specialist **Joel Sanders** . . . . (417) 895-5979
E-mail: joel.sanders@courts.mo.gov

Chambers of Chief Judge Mary W. Sheffield

300 Hammons Parkway, Springfield, MO 65806
Tel: (417) 895-6818

Mary W. Sheffield
Chief Judge

Next Election: November 2026

Chambers of Judge William W. Francis Jr.

300 Hammons Parkway, Springfield, MO 65806
Tel: (417) 895-6820

William W. Francis, Jr.
Judge

Education: Southwest Missouri State 1974 BS; Missouri 1977 JD
Began Service: April 2010
Appointed By: Governor Jay Nixon

Current Memberships: The Missouri Bar; Springfield Metropolitan Bar Association

Chambers of Judge Don E. Burrell Jr.

John Q. Hammons Building, 300 Hammons Parkway,
Springfield, MO 65806
Tel: (417) 895-6826 Fax: (417) 895-6599
E-mail: don.burrell@courts.mo.gov

Don E. Burrell, Jr.
Judge

Date of Birth: December 4, 1960
Education: Southwest Missouri State 1983 BS;
Missouri (Kansas City) 1991 JD
Began Service: January 2008
Next Election: November 2022
Election Type: Retention Election

Staff

Law Clerk **Rose Barber** . . . . (417) 895-5885
Began Service: July 2010
E-mail: rose.barber@courts.mo.gov
Education: Southwest Missouri State 1986 BS;
Oklahoma City 1989 JD
Judicial Assistant **Kerry D. Wilson** . . . . (417) 895-6826
E-mail: kerry.wilson@courts.mo.gov

STATE COURTS – MISSOURI

Chambers of Judge Daniel E. Scott
John Q. Hammons Building, 300 Hammons Parkway,
Springfield, MO 65806
Tel: (417) 895-6822

Daniel E. Scott
Judge

Date of Birth: September 29, 1955
Education: Central Missouri State 1977 BS; Missouri 1980 JD
Began Service: September 2006
Appointed By: Governor Matt Blunt
Next Election: November 2020
Election Type: Retention Election
Term Expires: December 31, 2020

Current Memberships: Big Brothers Big Sisters of America; Jasper County Bar Association; The Missouri Bar; Special Committee on Professionalism and Ethics, The Missouri Bar; Ronald McDonald House of the Four States

Chambers of Judge Gary W. Lynch
300 Hammons Parkway, Springfield, MO 65806
Tel: (417) 895-6825
E-mail: gary.lynch@courts.mo.gov

Gary W. Lynch
Judge

Date of Birth: June 19, 1952
Education: Southwest Baptist 1974 BA; Missouri 1976 JD
Began Service: February 1, 2006
Next Election: November 2020
Election Type: Retention Election
Term Expires: December 31, 2020

Judicial: Associate Circuit Judge, 30th Judicial Circuit Court (2003-2006)

Legal Practice: Attorney, Private Practice (1977-2002)

Nonprofit: President, 30th Judicial Circuit Bar Association

Current Memberships: First Baptist Church of Bolivar; The Missouri Bar; Complaint Resolution Program Committee, The Missouri Bar; Lawyer to Lawyer Dispute Resolution Committee, The Missouri Bar; Polk County Bar Association; Springfield Metropolitan Bar Association; 30th Judicial Circuit Bar Association

Chambers of Judge Jeffrey W. Bates
300 Hammons Parkway, Springfield, MO 65806
Tel: (417) 895-6824
E-mail: jeffrey.bates@courts.mo.gov

Jeffrey W. Bates
Judge

Date of Birth: September 28, 1958
Education: Southwest Missouri State 1979 BS; Missouri 1984 JD
Began Service: December 1, 2003
Term Expires: December 2018

Judicial: Chief Judge, Missouri Court of Appeals, Southern District (2005-2007)

Legal Practice: Attorney, Private Practice (1984-2003)

Current Memberships: Campbell United Methodist Church; The Missouri Bar; The International Legal Fraternity of Phi Delta Phi; Springfield Metropolitan Bar Association

Membership: Member, Child Advocacy Council (1990-1992)

Staff
Career Law Clerk **Mary Browne** . . . . (417) 895-6824
E-mail: mary.browne@courts.mo.gov
Judicial Administrative Assistant **Lindy Mense** . . . . (417) 895-6824
E-mail: lindy.mense@courts.mo.gov

Chambers of Judge Nancy Steffen Rahmeyer
John Q. Hammons Building, 300 Hammons Parkway,
Springfield, MO 65806-2546
Tel: (417) 895-6823

Nancy Steffen Rahmeyer
Judge

Date of Birth: 1951
Education: Iowa State 1973 BS; Southwest Missouri State 1981 MEd; Arkansas 1987 JD
Began Service: March 2, 2001
Appointed By: Governor Bob Holden
Next Election: November 2026
Term Expires: December 31, 2026

Clerkships: Law Clerk The Honorable Russell Clark, United States District Court for the Western District of Missouri (1987-1989)

Judicial: Provisional Judge, Municipal Division, Greene County Circuit Court (1993-2000)

Legal Practice: Private Practice (1989-2001)

Current Memberships: The Missouri Bar; Springfield Metropolitan Bar Association

Staff
Law Clerk **Douglas "Doug" Bunch** . . . . (417) 895-6823
Judicial Administrative Assistant **Jayme Travis** . . . . (417) 895-6823
Education: Drury Col 1999 BA

Missouri Court of Appeals, Western District
1300 Oak Street, Kansas City, MO 64106-2970
Tel: (816) 889-3600 Fax: (816) 889-3668

Number of Judgeships: 11

Areas Covered: Counties of Adair, Andrew, Atchison, Bates, Benton, Boone, Buchanan, Caldwell, Callaway, Cass, Chariton, Clay, Clinton, Carroll, Cole, Cooper, Daviess, DeKalb, Gentry, Grundy, Henry, Holt, Howard, Harrison, Jackson, Johnson, Lafayette, Linn, Livingston, Macon, Mercer, Miller, Moniteau, Morgan, Nodaway, Platte, Putnam, Pettis, Randolph, Ray, Saline, Schuyler, Sullivan, Vernon and Worth

Court Staff
Clerk of Court **Terence G. Lord** . . . . (816) 889-3600
E-mail: tlord@courts.mo.gov
Education: Missouri 1977 JD
Staff Counsel **Susan C. Sonnenberg** . . . . (816) 889-3600
Education: Missouri (Kansas City) 1997 JD
Marshal **Brenda Hasty** . . . . (816) 889-3656
E-mail: bhasty@courts.mo.gov
Librarian **Janine Estrada-Lopez** . . . . (816) 889-3600
E-mail: janine_estrada-lopez@courts.mo.gov

Chambers of Chief Judge Alok Ahuja
1300 Oak Street, Kansas City, MO 64106-2970
Tel: (816) 889-3601 Fax: (816) 889-3599
E-mail: alok.ahuja@courts.mo.gov

Alok Ahuja
Chief Judge

Began Service: January 21, 2008
Next Election: November 2022
Election Type: Retention Election
Term Expires: November 2022

Staff
Law Clerk **Jacob Adair** . . . . (816) 889-3601
Began Service: August 2015
Term Expires: August 2017
E-mail: jacob.adair@courts.mo.gov

(continued on next page)

STATE COURTS—MISSOURI

Chambers of Chief Judge Alok Ahuja *continued*

Law Clerk **Heath Hooper** .... (816) 889-3602
Began Service: August 2014
Term Expires: August 2016
Judicial Assistant **Monja Calvert** .... (816) 889-3610
E-mail: monja.calvert@courts.mo.gov
Education: Missouri (Kansas City) 1992 BA
Career: Judicial Administrative Assistant, Chambers of Judge Harold L. Lowenstein, Missouri Court of Appeals, Western District

Chambers of Judge James E. Welsh

1300 Oak Street, Kansas City, MO 64106-2970
Tel: (816) 889-3632
E-mail: james.welsh@courts.mo.gov

James E. Welsh
Judge

Education: Saint Louis U 1969 BS, 1975 JD
Began Service: November 2007
Appointed By: Governor Matt Blunt
Next Election: November 2022
Election Type: Retention Election

Staff
Law Clerk **Marita Griffin** .... (816) 889-3649
Began Service: August 2013
Term Expires: August 2016
E-mail: marita_griffin@courts.mo.gov
Education: Missouri (Kansas City) 1999 JD
Senior Law Clerk **Kimberly Boeding** .... (816) 889-3633
Began Service: November 2007
E-mail: kimberly.boeding@courts.mo.gov
Education: Missouri (Kansas City) 1986 BA, 1988 JD
Judicial Administrative Assistant
Charlotte V. Washington .... (816) 889-3632
E-mail: charlotte.washington@courts.mo.gov
Education: MidAmerica Nazarene; Kansas

Chambers of Judge Lisa White Hardwick

1300 Oak Street, Kansas City, MO 64106
Tel: (816) 889-3611 Fax: (816) 889-3599

Lisa White Hardwick
Judge

Date of Birth: 1960
Education: Missouri 1982 BA; Harvard 1985 JD
Began Service: May 3, 2001
Appointed By: Governor Bob Holden
Next Election: November 2026
Term Expires: December 31, 2026

Current Memberships: Jackson County Bar Association; Kansas City Metropolitan Bar Association; The Missouri Bar; National Association of Women Lawyers; National Bar Association

Staff
Law Clerk **Nick Daugherty** .... (816) 889-3612
E-mail: nick.daugherty@courts.mo.gov
Career Law Clerk **Carol Sevier** .... (816) 889-3646
E-mail: carol.sevier@courts.mo.gov
Judicial Administrative Assistant **Monja Calvert** .... (816) 889-3610
E-mail: monja.calvert@courts.mo.gov

Chambers of Judge Thomas H. Newton

1300 Oak Street, Kansas City, MO 64106-2970
Tel: (816) 889-3629 Fax: (816) 889-3599
E-mail: thomas.newton@courts.mo.gov

Thomas H. Newton
Judge

Date of Birth: 1952
Education: Howard U BA, JD
Began Service: November 1999
Next Election: 2024
Term Expires: 2024

Staff
Law Clerk **Alexandra Alpough** .... (816) 889-3628
Began Service: September 16, 2015
Term Expires: September 16, 2017
E-mail: alexandra.alpough@courts.mo.gov
Career Law Clerk **Katherine Ray** .... (816) 889-3630
E-mail: katherine.ray@courts.mo.gov
Education: Missouri (Kansas City) 2005 JD
Judicial Administrative Assistant
Charlotte V. Washington .... (816) 889-3631
E-mail: Charlotte.Washington@courts.mo.gov

Chambers of Judge Joseph M. Ellis

1300 Oak Street, Kansas City, MO 64106-2970
Tel: (816) 889-3622 Fax: (816) 889-3589
E-mail: joseph.m.ellis@courts.mo.gov

Joseph M. Ellis
Judge

Date of Birth: 1946
Education: Washington U (MO) 1971 JD
Began Service: August 1993
Appointed By: Governor Mel Carnahan
Next Election: November 2018
Election Type: Retention Election
Term Expires: December 31, 2018

Judicial: Judge, Macon Municipal Court

Legal Practice: Private Practice (1972-1993)

Military Service: United States Air Force, Judge Advocate General's Corps (1972)

Current Memberships: American Bar Association; 41st Judicial Circuit Bar Association; Kansas City Metropolitan Bar Association; The Missouri Bar

Staff
Career Law Clerk **David Kennedy** .... (816) 889-3624
E-mail: david.kennedy@courts.mo.gov
Education: Kansas BA; Notre Dame JD
Law Clerk **(Vacant)** .... (816) 889-3623
Judicial Administrative Assistant **Paula Heenan** .... (816) 889-3622
E-mail: paula.heenan@courts.mo.gov

Chambers of Judge Victor C. Howard
1300 Oak Street, Kansas City, MO 64106-2970
Tel: (816) 889-3626
E-mail: victor.howard@courts.mo.gov

Victor C. Howard
Judge

Date of Birth: 1952
Education: Central Missouri State 1973 BS; Missouri (Kansas City) JD
Began Service: November 1996
Appointed By: Governor Mel Carnahan
Next Election: November 2022
Term Expires: December 2022

Clerkships: Law Clerk The Honorable William Marsh, Jackson County Circuit Court (1977)

Government: Deputy County Counsel, Office of the County Counselor, County of Clay, Missouri (1977-1991)

Judicial: Judge, Missouri Circuit Court, Clay County (1993-1996)

Legal Practice: Withers Brant & Howard (1977-1993)

Staff
Law Clerk **Sara Skelton** . . . . (816) 889-3627
Began Service: August 2008
E-mail: sara.skelton@courts.mo.gov
Career Law Clerk **Susan King** . . . . (816) 889-3626
E-mail: susan.king@courts.mo.gov
Education: Missouri (Kansas City) 1994 JD
Judicial Administrative Assistant **Paula Heenan** . . . . (816) 889-3625
E-mail: paula.heenan@courts.mo.gov

Chambers of Judge Mark D. Pfeiffer
1300 Oak Street, Kansas City, MO 64106-2970
Tel: (816) 889-3614 Fax: (816) 889-3599
E-mail: mark.pfeiffer@courts.mo.gov

Mark D. Pfeiffer
Judge

Education: Westminster (MO) 1989 BA; Missouri 1991 JD
Began Service: June 1, 2009
Next Election: November 2022

Current Memberships: The Missouri Bar

Staff
Career Law Clerk **Katherine Werzer** . . . . (816) 889-3614
Career Law Clerk **Donna Stanford** . . . . (816) 889-3614
Judicial Assistant **Tammy Beckert** . . . . (816) 889-3614

Chambers of Judge Karen King Mitchell
1300 Oak Street, Kansas City, MO 64106-2970
Tel: (816) 889-3600
E-mail: karen.mitchell@courts.mo.gov

Karen King Mitchell
Judge

Education: Missouri 1981 BA; Missouri (Kansas City) 1984 JD
Began Service: July 2009
Next Election: November 2022

Government: Chief Deputy Attorney General, Office of Attorney General Jay Nixon, State of Missouri; State Solicitor and Chief Counsel, Governmental Affairs Division, Office of the Attorney General, State of Missouri; Director, Revenue Department, State of Missouri (2009); Director, Revenue Department, State of Missouri

Chambers of Judge Cynthia L. Martin
1300 Oak Street, Kansas City, MO 64106-2970
Tel: (816) 889-3600 Fax: (816) 889-3668

Cynthia L. Martin
Judge

Education: William Jewell 1981; Missouri (Kansas City) 1984 JD
Began Service: October 13, 2009
Appointed By: Governor Jay Nixon

Staff
Law Clerk **Kelsey Whitt** . . . . (816) 889-3600
Began Service: August 2011
Term Expires: August 2016
E-mail: kelsey.whitt@courts.mo.gov
Education: Missouri 2009 JD
Career Law Clerk **Nick Draper** . . . . (816) 889-3600
E-mail: bridget.mcmanus@courts.mo.gov
Judicial Assistant **Jo Carpenter** . . . . (816) 889-3600
E-mail: jo.carpenter@courts.mo.gov

Chambers of Judge Gary D. Witt
1300 Oak Street, Kansas City, MO 64106-2970
Tel: (816) 889-3600
E-mail: gary.witt@courts.mo.gov

Gary D. Witt
Judge

Education: William Jewell 1987 BA; Missouri 1990 JD
Began Service: 2010
Appointed By: Governor Jay Nixon

Government: Associate Circuit Judge, 6th Judicial Circuit Court, Missouri Circuit Courts (1998-2010); State Representative (MO, District 29), Missouri House of Representatives (1991-1997)

Legal Practice: Attorney, Witt, Hicklin and Witt, P.C. (1990-1998)

Chambers of Judge Rex Gabbert
1300 Oak Street, Kansas City, MO 64106-2970
Tel: (816) 889-3600

Rex Gabbert
Judge

Education: Missouri (Kansas City); Mississippi Col JD
Began Service: 2013
Appointed By: Governor Jay Nixon
Next Election: November 2026

Montana

Montana Court Administration

315 Justice Building, 215 North Sanders, Helena, MT 59620-3002
P.O. Box 203002, Helena, MT 59620-3002
Tel: (406) 444-2621 Tel: (406) 442-7660 (Board of Bar Examiners)
Fax: (406) 444-0834
Internet: www.montanacourts.org

Staff

State Court Administrator **Beth McLaughlin** . . . . (406) 841-2966
E-mail: bmclaughlin@mt.gov Fax: (406) 841-2955
Court Services Director **(Vacant)** . . . . (406) 841-2957
Fax: (406) 841-2955
Financial Services Director **Becky Buska** . . . . (406) 444-2698
E-mail: bbuska@mt.gov
Information Technology Director **Lisa Mader** . . . . (406) 841-2956
E-mail: lmader@mt.gov
District and Youth Court Services Bureau Chief
Bob Peake . . . . (406) 841-2961
E-mail: rpeake@mt.gov
Administrative Secretary, Commission on Practice and Judicial Standards **Shelly Nash** . . . . (406) 841-2976
E-mail: snash@mt.gov
Administrative Secretary, Sentence Review Division
Georgia Lovelady . . . . (406) 841-2977
Court Services Coordinator **Shauna Ryan** . . . . (406) 841-2967
E-mail: shryan@mt.gov
Accounting and Fiscal Policy Analyst **(Vacant)** . . . . (406) 444-2672
Accounting and Fiscal Policy Analyst **Cathy Pennie** . . . . . (406) 444-1810
E-mail: cpennie@mt.gov
Application Services Supervisor **Tyler Arnold** . . . . (406) 841-2960
E-mail: tarnold@mt.gov
Education: South Carolina 2008 JD
Reference Librarian **Susan Lupton** . . . . (406) 444-3636
E-mail: slupton@mt.gov
State Law Librarian **Lisa Jackson** . . . . (406) 444-1979
Fax: (406) 444-3603
Technical Services Librarian **Laura Tretter** . . . . (406) 444-1984
E-mail: ltretter@mt.gov Fax: (406) 444-3603
Human Resources Specialist **Shelly Grandy** . . . . (406) 841-2965
Systems Support **Tammy Peterson** . . . . (406) 841-2959
E-mail: tammyp@mt.gov
End User Training and Support **Gregory Warhank** . . . . . . (406) 841-2913
E-mail: gwarhank@mt.gov
Administrative Assistant **Judith Rogers** . . . . (406) 444-3660
E-mail: jurogers@mt.gov Fax: (406) 444-3603
Administrative Assistant **Brandon Ricks** . . . . (406) 841-2950

Montana Supreme Court

323 Justice Building, 215 North Sanders, Helena, MT 59620
P.O. Box 203003, Helena, MT 59620-3001
Tel: (406) 444-3858 Fax: (406) 444-5705

Number of Judgeships: 7

The Supreme Court consists of a chief justice and six justices who are elected in statewide, nonpartisan elections for eight-year terms. Vacancies are filled by appointment by the Governor from a list of nominees submitted by the Judicial Nominations Commission and confirmed by the Montana State Senate. The chief justice is elected to the position by the electorate in a statewide general election. The Supreme Court has appellate jurisdiction over cases from the Montana District Court, has supervisory control over all state courts, and has authority to regulate admission to the state bar and the conduct of its members.

The Supreme Court sits in Helena.

Court Staff

Clerk of Court **Ed Smith** . . . . (406) 444-3858
Education: Montana 1976 BA

Montana Supreme Court *continued*

Deputy Clerk **Rex Renk** . . . . (406) 444-3858
E-mail: rrenk@mt.gov
Education: Carroll Col (MT) 1988 BA; Washington State 1990 MA
Appellate Case Manager **Diane Anderson** . . . . (406) 444-3858
E-mail: danderson@mt.gov
Appellate Case Manager **Darlene Gallagher** . . . . (406) 444-3858
E-mail: dgallagher@mt.gov
Appellate Case Manager **Katrina Martin** . . . . (406) 444-3858
Appellate Case Manager **JoAnne Sherwood** . . . . (406) 444-3858
E-mail: jsherwood@mt.gov
Appellate Case Manager **(Vacant)** . . . . (406) 444-3858
Court Administrator **Beth McLaughlin** . . . . (406) 841-2966
301 South Park Street, Suite 328, Helena, MT 59620 Fax: (406) 841-2955
P.O. Box 203005, Helena, MT 59620-3005
E-mail: bmclaughlin@mt.gov

Chambers of Chief Justice Mike McGrath

Justice Building, 215 North Sanders, Helena, MT 59620
Tel: (406) 444-5490
E-mail: mmcgrath@mt.gov

Mike McGrath
Chief Justice

Education: Montana 1970 BA; Gonzaga 1975 JD
Began Service: January 5, 2009
Next Election: November 2016
Election Type: General Election
Term Expires: January 2017
Political Affiliation: Democrat

Current Memberships: Montana Legal Services Association

Staff

Law Clerk **Samir Aarab** . . . . (406) 444-5490
Began Service: August 31, 2015
Term Expires: September 2016
E-mail: saarab@mt.gov
Career Law Clerk **Allen Chronister** . . . . (406) 444-5490
E-mail: achronister@mt.gov
Education: North Carolina 1969 BA; George Washington 1972 JD
Judicial Assistant **Lorrie Cole** . . . . (406) 444-5490
E-mail: lcole@mt.gov

Chambers of Justice Patricia Cotter

Justice Building, 215 North Sanders, Helena, MT 59620
P.O. Box 203003, Helena, MT 59620-3001
Tel: (406) 444-5570 Fax: (406) 444-3274
E-mail: pcotter@mt.gov

Patricia Cotter
Justice

Date of Birth: 1950
Education: Western Michigan 1972 BS; Notre Dame 1977 JD
Began Service: January 2, 2001
Next Election: November 4, 2016
Election Type: General Election
Term Expires: December 31, 2016

Legal Practice: Private Practice (1977-2000)

Staff

Law Clerk **Caitlin Aarab** . . . . (406) 444-5570
Began Service: August 2015
Term Expires: August 2016
E-mail: caarab@mt.gov
Career Law Clerk **Teresa B. Bass** . . . . (406) 444-5570
E-mail: tbass@mt.gov
Education: Tennessee 1990 JD

Chambers of Justice Patricia Cotter *continued*

Judicial Assistant **Angela Rutherford** . . . . (406) 444-5570
E-mail: astagg2@mt.gov

Chambers of Justice Jim Rice

Justice Building, 215 North Sanders, Helena, MT 59620
P.O. Box 203001, Helena, MT 59620-3001
Tel: (406) 444-5573 Fax: (406) 444-3274
E-mail: jrice@mt.gov

Jim Rice
Justice

Date of Birth: 1957
Education: Montana State 1975 BA; Montana 1982 JD
Began Service: March 15, 2001
Appointed By: Governor Judy Martz
Next Election: November 2026
Term Expires: December 31, 2026

Government: Member, Montana House of Representatives (1988-1994); Chairman, Board of Personnel Appeals, State of Montana (1996-2000)

Legal Practice: Partner, Jackson & Rice (1982-2001)

Staff
Law Clerk **Anna Maria Kecskes** . . . . (406) 444-5597
Began Service: August 2015
Term Expires: August 2016
E-mail: akecske@mt.gov
Law Clerk **John Wolff** . . . . (406) 444-5597
Began Service: August 2015
Term Expires: August 2016
E-mail: mdolphay@mt.gov
Judicial Assistant **Gwyn Gregor** . . . . (406) 444-5573
E-mail: ggregor2@mt.gov

Chambers of Justice Michael E. Wheat

215 North Sanders, Helena, MT 59620-3002
Tel: (406) 444-5494
E-mail: mwheat@mt.gov

Michael E. Wheat
Justice

Education: Montana 1975 BA, 1978 JD
Began Service: January 2010
Next Election: November 2026

Staff
Law Clerk **Andrea Collins** . . . . (406) 444-5498
Term Expires: August 2016
Law Clerk **Dave Bell** . . . . (406) 444-5498
Term Expires: August 2016
Judicial Assistant **Alta Solan** . . . . (406) 444-5494
E-mail: asolan@mt.gov

Chambers of Justice Beth Baker

215 North Sanders, Helena, MT 59620
P.O. Box 203001, Helena, MT 59620-3001
Tel: (406) 444-5573 Fax: (406) 444-3274
E-mail: bbaker@mt.gov

Beth Baker
Justice

Education: U Washington 1982 BA; Montana 1985 JD
Began Service: January 3, 2011

Current Memberships: State Bar of Montana

Chambers of Justice Beth Baker *continued*

Staff
Law Clerk **Leah Tracy** . . . . (406) 444-5599
Began Service: August 2015
Term Expires: August 2016
E-mail: ltracy@mt.gov
Law Clerk **Colin Phelps** . . . . (406) 444-5599
Began Service: August 2015
Term Expires: August 2016
E-mail: cphelps@mt.gov
Judicial Assistant **Gwyn Gregor** . . . . (406) 444-5573
E-mail: ggregor2@mt.gov

Chambers of Justice Laurie McKinnon

215 North Sanders, Helena, MT 59620-3002
Tel: (406) 444-3858
E-mail: lmckinnon@mt.gov

Laurie McKinnon
Justice

Began Service: 2013

Staff
Career Law Clerk **Matthew Dolphay** . . . . (406) 444-3858
E-mail: mdolphay@mt.gov
Career Law Clerk **Jessica Walker-Kelleher** . . . . (406) 444-3858
Judicial Assistant **Angela Ruthersford** . . . . (406) 444-3858
E-mail: aruthersford@mt.gov

Chambers of Justice James Shea

215 North Sanders, Helena, MT 59620-3002
Tel: (406) 444-3858
E-mail: jshea@mt.gov

James Jeremiah "Jim" Shea
Justice

Began Service: 2014

Nebraska

Nebraska Office of the State Court Administrator

1220 State Capitol Building, 1445 K Street, Lincoln, NE 68509
P.O. Box 98910, Lincoln, NE 68509
Tel: (402) 471-3730 Fax: (402) 471-2197
Internet: www.supremecourt.ne.gov/9/administrative-office-courts

Staff

Fax: (402) 471-2197

State Court Administrator **Corey R. Steel** .... (402) 471-3730
E-mail: corey.steel@nebraska.gov
Deputy State Court Administrator **Judy Beutler** .... (402) 471-2921
E-mail: judy.beutler@nebraska.gov
Public Information Officer **Janet Bancroft** .... (402) 471-3205
E-mail: janet.bancroft@nebraska.gov
State Law Librarian **Marie Wiechman** .... (402) 471-3189
E-mail: marie.wiechman@nebraska.gov
Financial Officer **Eric Asboe** .... (402) 471-4138
E-mail: eric.asboe@nebraska.gov
Network Administrator **Shawn Done** .... (402) 471-9042
E-mail: shawn.done@nebraska.gov
Administrative Assistant **Marcie Luhman** .... (402) 471-2249
E-mail: marcie.luhman@nebraska.gov
Administrative Assistant **Eileen Janssen** .... (402) 471-4427
E-mail: eileen.janssen@nebraska.gov

Nebraska Supreme Court

2413 State Capitol Building, 1445 K Street, Lincoln, NE 68509
Tel: (402) 471-3731 Fax: (402) 471-3480
Internet: http://supremecourt.ne.gov

Number of Judgeships: 7

The Supreme Court consists of a chief justice and six associate justices who are appointed by the Governor from a list submitted by a judicial nominating commission. Justices run for retention in the next general election occurring more than three years after the appointment for a six-year term. The chief justice is elected on a statewide ballot, while the six associate justices are elected in six separate judicial districts throughout the state. The judicial districts are approximately equal in population and are redistricted by the State Legislature after every census. The Supreme Court has discretionary review of cases from the Nebraska Court of Appeals and hears cases regarding constitutional issues. The Court also has jurisdiction over all appeals dealing with the death penalty and the sentence of life imprisonment. Appeals are brought to the Court from the Nebraska District Courts, Juvenile Courts, Workers' Compensation Court, and administrative agencies. The Court is responsible for the regulation of the practice of law in the state and oversees the admission of attorneys to the state bar.

The Nebraska Supreme Court sits in Lincoln.

Court Staff

Clerk of Supreme Court and Court of Appeals
Teresa A. "Terri" Brown .... (402) 471-3731
Education: Nebraska 1984 BA, 1987 JD
Staff Attorney **Teresa A. "Terri" Brown** .... (402) 471-2650
E-mail: terri.a.brown@nebraska.gov
Staff Attorney **Erika Schafer** .... (402) 471-6046
E-mail: erika.schafer@nebraska.gov
Law Librarian **Marie Weichman** .... (402) 471-3189
E-mail: marie.weichman@nebraska.gov Fax: (402) 471-1011
Reporter of Decisions **Peggy Polacek** .... (402) 471-3739
E-mail: peggy.polacek@nebraska.gov

Chambers of Chief Justice Michael G. Heavican

2214 State Capitol Building, 1445 K Street, Lincoln, NE 68509
P.O. Box 98910, Lincoln, NE 68509
Tel: (402) 471-3738 Fax: (402) 471-0297
E-mail: mike.heavican@nebraska.gov

Michael G. Heavican
Chief Justice

Date of Birth: 1947
Education: Nebraska 1969 BA, 1974 JD
Began Service: October 2, 2006
Appointed By: Governor David Heineman
Next Election: November 2016
Election Type: Retention Election
Political Affiliation: Republican

Government: Deputy County Attorney, Office of the County Attorney, County of Lancaster, Nebraska (1975-1980); Chief Deputy County Attorney, Office of the County Attorney, County of Lancaster, Nebraska (1981); County Attorney, Office of the County Attorney, County of Lancaster, Nebraska (1981-1990); Assistant U.S. Attorney, Executive Office for United States Attorneys, United States Department of Justice (1991-2001); U.S. Attorney, Executive Office for United States Attorneys, United States Department of Justice (2001-2006)

Staff

Career Law Clerk **(Vacant)** .... (402) 471-4164
Career Law Clerk **Jessica Sidders** .... (402) 471-6219
E-mail: jessica.sidders@nebraska.gov
Education: Nebraska 2002 JD
Administrative Assistant **Jackie M. Hladik** .... (402) 471-3738
E-mail: jackie.hladik@nebraska.gov
Education: Col St Mary 1995 BA

Chambers of Associate Justice John F. Wright

2207 State Capitol Building, 1445 K Street, Lincoln, NE 68509
P.O. Box 98910, Lincoln, NE 68509
Tel: (402) 471-3735 Fax: (402) 471-3480
E-mail: john.wright@nebraska.gov

John F. Wright
Associate Justice

Date of Birth: 1945
Education: Nebraska 1967 BS, 1970 JD
Began Service: February 25, 1994
Appointed By: Governor E. Benjamin Nelson
Political Affiliation: Democrat

Judicial: Judge, Nebraska Court of Appeals (1992-1994)

Legal Practice: Partner, Wright & Simmons (1970-1984); Partner, Wright, Sorensen & Brower (1984-1991)

Military Service: United States Army (1970); Nebraska National Guard (1970-1976)

Staff

Law Clerk **Rachel Hollingsead** .... (402) 471-3735
E-mail: rachel.hollingsead@nebraska.gov
Law Clerk **Greg Ramirez** .... (402) 471-3735
Administrative Assistant **Sandi Peters** .... (402) 471-3735
E-mail: sandi.peters@nebraska.gov

Chambers of Associate Justice William M. Connolly
State Capitol Building, 1445 K Street, Room 2210, Lincoln, NE 68509
P.O. Box 98910, Lincoln, NE 68509-8910
Tel: (402) 471-3733 Fax: (402) 471-2197
E-mail: wconnolly@nsc.state.ne.us

William M. Connolly
Associate Justice

Date of Birth: 1938
Education: Creighton 1963 LLB
Began Service: December 15, 1994
Term Expires: December 2016

Government: Deputy County Attorney, County of Adams, Nebraska (1964-1966); County Attorney, County of Adams, Nebraska (1967-1972)

Judicial: Judge, Nebraska Court of Appeals (1992-1994)

Legal Practice: Partner, Conway, Connolly & Pauley, PC (1972-1991)

Current Memberships: American College of Trial Lawyers

Chambers of Associate Justice Michael McCormack
2218 State Capitol Building, 1445 K Street, Lincoln, NE 68509
P.O. Box 98910, Lincoln, NE 68509
Tel: (402) 471-4345 Fax: (402) 471-3482
E-mail: mike.mccormack@nebraska.gov

Michael McCormack
Associate Justice

Date of Birth: 1939
Education: Creighton 1963 JD
Began Service: March 19, 1997
Appointed By: Governor E. Benjamin Nelson
Next Election: November 2018
Election Type: Retention Election
Term Expires: 2018
Political Affiliation: Democrat

Government: Deputy Public Defender, Douglas County (1963-1966)

Legal Practice: Private Practice (1963-1997)

Staff
Law Clerk **Natalie Sindelar** .... (402) 471-6217
E-mail: natalie.sindelar@nebraska.gov
Career Law Clerk **Brenda Luers** .... (402) 471-4527
E-mail: brenda.luers@nebraska.gov
Administrative Assistant **Tracie McArdle** .... (402) 471-4345
E-mail: tracie.mcardle@nebraska.gov

Chambers of Associate Justice Lindsey Miller-Lerman
2222 State Capitol Building, 1445 K Street, Lincoln, NE 68508
Tel: (402) 471-3734 Fax: (402) 435-7872
E-mail: lindsey.miller-lerman@nebraska.gov

Lindsey Miller-Lerman
Associate Justice

Date of Birth: 1947
Education: Wellesley 1968 BA; Columbia 1973 JD
Began Service: September 23, 1998
Appointed By: Governor E. Benjamin Nelson
Next Election: November 4, 2020
Election Type: Retention Election
Term Expires: December 2020

Clerkships: Law Clerk The Honorable Constance Baker Motley, United States District Court for the Southern District of New York (1973-1975)

Judicial: Judge, Nebraska Court of Appeals (1992-1998)

Legal Practice: Private Practice (1976-1992)

Chambers of Associate Justice Lindsey Miller-Lerman *continued*

Current Memberships: American Bar Association; The Association of the Bar of the City of New York; National Association of Women Judges; Nebraska State Bar Association; Omaha Bar Association

Staff
Law Clerk **Shelly Montgomery** .... (402) 471-3734
Began Service: August 2011
E-mail: shelly.montgomery@nebraska.gov
Career Law Clerk **Michael Watchorn** .... (402) 471-3734
E-mail: mike.watchorn@nebraska.gov
Administrative Assistant **Kara Nielsen** .... (402) 471-3734
E-mail: kara.nielsen@nebraska.gov

Chambers of Associate Justice William B. Cassel
2413 State Capitol Building, 1445 K Street, Room 2219, Lincoln, NE 68509
Tel: (402) 471-3736 Fax: (402) 471-3480
E-mail: william.cassel@nebraska.gov

William B. Cassel
Associate Justice

Date of Birth: September 20, 1955
Education: Nebraska 1979 JD, 1977 BS
Began Service: 2012

Current Memberships: American Bar Association; National Association of Radio and Television Engineers; Nebraska State Bar Association

Staff
Law Clerk **Tyler Spahn** .... (402) 471-3736
E-mail: tyler.spahn@nebraska.gov
Career Law Clerk **Lori Helgoth** .... (402) 471-3736
E-mail: lori.helgoth@nebraska.gov
Administrative Assistant **Sandi Peters** .... (402) 471-3736
E-mail: sandi.peters@nebraska.gov

Chambers of Associate Justice Stephanie Stacy
1445 K Street, Lincoln, NE 68509
Tel: (402) 471-3731

Stephanie Stacy
Associate Justice

Nebraska Court of Appeals

State Capitol Building, 1445 K Street, Lincoln, NE 68508
P.O. Box 98910, Lincoln, NE 68509
Tel: (402) 471-3731 Fax: (402) 471-2197
Internet: court.nol.org/judges/appealsjudges.htm

Number of Judgeships: 6

The Court of Appeals, established in September 1991 as a result of a constitutional amendment, consists of a chief judge and five judges who are appointed by the Governor from a list submitted by judicial nominating commissions. Judges run for retention in the next general election occurring more than three years after appointment for a six-year term. The chief judge is selected by the Nebraska Supreme Court to serve a one-year renewable term. The districts from which the Court's judges are appointed are the same as those used for the six Supreme Court associate judges. The Court is divided into two panels consisting of three judges each. The Court of Appeals hears all appeals from lower courts, except cases involving the death penalty and life imprisonment and cases involving the constitutionality of a statute. In cases appealed to the Court, a petition to bypass may be filled with the Nebraska Supreme Court. If the Supreme Court deems it necessary, the petition will be granted and the case will be moved to the Supreme Court docket without first being heard by the Court of Appeals. A petition for further review may also be filed. This petition is filed after a case has been decided by the Court of Appeals and one of the parties involved is not satisfied with the ruling. The Supreme Court may also grant or deny this petition.

The Court has its primary office in Lincoln and sits in various locations throughout the state.

Court Staff

Clerk of Supreme Court and Court of Appeals
Teresa A. "Terri" Brown .... (402) 471-3731
Fax: (402) 471-3480
Staff Attorney **M. J. Walsh** .... (402) 471-0045
E-mail: mwalsh@nsc.state.ne.us
Education: Creighton JD
Law Librarian **Marie Weichman** .... (402) 471-3189
E-mail: mweichman@nsc.state.ne.us
Public Information Officer **Janet Bancroft** .... (402) 471-3205
The Executive Building, 521 South 14th Street, Suite 200, Lincoln, NE 68509
E-mail: jbancroft@nsc.state.ne.us
Reporter of Decisions **Peggy Polacek** .... (402) 471-3739
E-mail: ppolacek@nsc.state.ne.us Fax: (402) 471-1310
Director of Judicial Education
Carole McMahon-Boies .... (402) 471-3072

Chambers of Chief Judge Frankie Moore

300 East 3rd Street, Suite 254, North Platte, NE 69101
P.O. Box 907, North Platte, NE 69103
State Capitol Building, 1445 K Street, Lincoln, NE 68508
P.O. Box 98910, Lincoln, NE 68509
Tel: (308) 535-8342 Tel: (402) 471-3732 (Lincoln Chambers)
Fax: (308) 535-8344
E-mail: frankie.moore@nebraska.gov

Frankie Moore
Chief Judge

Date of Birth: 1958
Education: Nebraska Wesleyan 1980 BA; Nebraska 1983 JD
Began Service: January 8, 2000

Current Memberships: Nebraska State Bar Association

Staff
Law Clerk **Shannon McCoy** .... (308) 535-8343
Career Law Clerk **Rachel Smith** .... (402) 471-0046
E-mail: rachel.smith@nebraska.gov

Chambers of Judge Everett O. Inbody

112 East Seventh Street, Wahoo, NE 68066
Tel: (402) 443-5180 Fax: (402) 443-5285
E-mail: everett.inbody@nebraska.gov

Everett O. Inbody
Judge

Date of Birth: 1945
Education: Nebraska 1967 BS, 1970 JD
Began Service: April 20, 1995
Appointed By: Governor E. Benjamin Nelson
Term Expires: 2016
Political Affiliation: Democrat

Staff
Law Clerk **Linsey Moran Bryant** .... (402) 443-5180
Began Service: March 2008
E-mail: linsey.bryant@nebraska.gov
Career Law Clerk **Kirs Otoupal Wertz** .... (402) 443-5180
E-mail: kirs.wertz@nebraska.gov
Education: Creighton BSBA; Nebraska JD

Chambers of Judge John F. Irwin

Sarpy County Courthouse, 1210 Golden Gate Drive, Papillion, NE 68046
10709 Poppleton Avenue, Omaha, NE 68124
Tel: (402) 593-4491 Fax: (402) 593-4493
E-mail: jirwin@sarpy.com

John F. Irwin
Judge

Date of Birth: 1952
Education: Nebraska (Omaha) 1974 BA; Creighton 1977 JD
Began Service: February 1992
Appointed By: Governor E. Benjamin Nelson
Next Election: November 4, 2022
Election Type: Retention Election
Term Expires: December 2022
Political Affiliation: Democrat

Government: Chief Deputy County Attorney, County of Sarpy, Nebraska (1981-1992)

Judicial: Chief Judge, Nebraska Court of Appeals (1998-2004)

Legal Practice: Private Practice (1977-1981)

Current Memberships: Appellate Division, American Bar Association

Staff
Law Clerk **Alison Breuning** .... (402) 593-4475
E-mail: abreuning@sarpy.com
Career Law Clerk **Daniel Real** .... (402) 593-4492
E-mail: dreal@sarpy.com
Education: Creighton 1995 JD
Administrative Assistant **Maradelle Hammerstrom** .... (402) 593-4491
E-mail: mhammerstrom@nsc.state.ne.us

Chambers of Judge Michael W. Pirtle

1819 Farnam Street, Omaha, NE 68183
Tel: (402) 595-1112 Fax: (402) 595-1016
E-mail: michael.pirtle@nebraska.gov

Michael W. Pirtle
Judge

Education: Midland Lutheran 1975 BA; Nebraska 1978 JD
Began Service: 2011
Appointed By: Governor David Heineman
Next Election: November 2020
Election Type: Retention Election

Corporate: Senior Staff Attorney, American Family Insurance Group (2000-2006)

Legal Practice: Law Clerk, Pierson, Ackerman, Fitchett & Akin (1976-1978); Associate, Noren & Burns (1978-1979); Director, Gross & Welch P.C., L.L.O (2006-2011)

Chambers of Judge Francie C. Riedmann

1445 K Street, Lincoln, NE 68509
Tel: (402) 332-0781

Francie C. Riedmann
Judge

Education: Kearney State 1985 BS; Creighton 1993 JD

Legal Practice: Associate, Blackwell Sanders LLP (1996-1999); Attorney, Gross & Welch P.C., L.L.O (1999-2008)

Chambers of Judge Riko E. Bishop

P.O. Box 98910, Lincoln, NE 68509
Tel: (402) 471-3732 Fax: (402) 471-4148

Riko E. Bishop
Judge

Education: Kearney State 1977 BA; Nebraska 1992 JD
Began Service: 2013
Appointed By: Governor David Heineman

Nevada

Administrative Office of the Courts of Nevada

Supreme Court Building, 201 South Carson Street, Suite 250,
Carson City, NV 89701-4702
Tel: (775) 684-1700 Fax: (775) 684-1723

Staff

State Court Administrator **Robin Sweet** . . . . (775) 684-1717
E-mail: rsweet@nvcourts.nv.gov
Education: Nevada (Reno); UNLV MPA
Manager of Budget and Accounting **Deanna Bjork** . . . . . . (775) 684-1708
E-mail: dbjork@nvcourts.nv.gov
Human Resources and Payroll Manager **Debra Norvell** . . . (775) 684-1711
E-mail: dnorvell@nvcourts.nv.gov

Nevada Supreme Court

Supreme Court Building, 201 South Carson Street, Suite 201,
Carson City, NV 89701-4702
Tel: (775) 684-1600
Internet: www.nevadajudiciary.us

Number of Judgeships: 7

The Supreme Court consists of a chief justice and six justices who run in nonpartisan elections for six-year terms. Appointees, who serve until the next general election, are selected by the Governor from nominees of the Commission on Judicial Selection to fill temporary vacancies. The chief justice is selected on the basis of seniority and serves a two-year term. The Supreme Court has appellate jurisdiction in all civil cases arising in district courts, and on questions of law alone in all criminal cases of the district courts. The court has power to issue writs of mandamus, certiorari, prohibition, quo warranto, and habeas corpus and all writs necessary or proper to the complete exercise of its appellate jurisdiction. The court also exercises administrative control over the lower courts and adopts rules governing the legal profession in the state.

The Nevada Supreme Court sits in Carson City and Las Vegas.

Court Staff

Clerk of the Court **Tracie Lindeman** . . . . (775) 684-1600
Chief Deputy Clerk **Amanda Ingersoll** . . . . (775) 684-1600
Chief Assistant Clerk **Harriet Cummings** . . . . (775) 684-1600
Law Librarian **Christine Timko** . . . . (775) 684-1671
Assistant Librarian **Paula Doty** . . . . (775) 684-1672
E-mail: pdoty@nvcourts.nv.gov
Catalog Librarian **(Vacant)** . . . . (775) 684-1675
Fax: (775) 684-1662
Library Assistant **Amanda Krause** . . . . (775) 684-1674

Chambers of Chief Justice James Hardesty

Supreme Court Building, 201 South Carson Street,
Carson City, NV 89701-4702
Tel: (775) 684-1590
E-mail: jhardesty@nvcourts.nv.gov

James W. Hardesty
Chief Justice

Education: Nevada (Reno) BA; McGeorge JD
Began Service: January 3, 2005
Next Election: November 2016
Term Expires: January 2017

Staff

Law Clerk **Samantha Peisser** . . . . (775) 684-1590
Began Service: August 2015
Term Expires: August 2016
E-mail: aarger@nvcourts.nv.gov

Chambers of Chief Justice James Hardesty *continued*

Law Clerk **Will Wagner** . . . . (775) 684-1590
Began Service: August 2015
Term Expires: August 2016
Administrator **Michele Shull** . . . . (775) 684-1590
E-mail: mshull@nvcourts.nv.gov

Chambers of Justice Mark Gibbons

Supreme Court Building, 201 South Carson Street,
Carson City, NV 89701-4702
Tel: (775) 684-1500
E-mail: mgibbons@nvcourts.nv.gov

Mark Gibbons
Justice

Date of Birth: 1950
Education: UC Irvine 1972 BA; Loyola Marymount 1975 JD
Began Service: January 6, 2003
Next Election: November 2020
Election Type: General Election
Term Expires: December 2020

Staff

Law Clerk **Erica Nannini** . . . . (775) 684-1502
Began Service: September 2015
Term Expires: September 2016
E-mail: enannini@nvcourts.nv.gov
Law Clerk **Casey Stiteler** . . . . (775) 684-1502
Began Service: August 2015
Term Expires: August 2016
E-mail: cstiteler@nvcourts.nv.gov
Chambers Administrator **Gerri Biegler** . . . . (775) 684-1500
E-mail: gbiegler@nvcourts.nv.gov

Chambers of Justice Kristina Pickering

Regional Justice Center, 200 Lewis Avenue, 17th Floor,
Carson City, NV 89101
Tel: (702) 486-9370 (Las Vegas Office)
Tel: (775) 684-1754 (Carson City Office)

Kristina "Kris" Pickering
Justice

Education: Yale 1974 BA; UC Davis 1977 JD
Began Service: January 2009
Next Election: November 2020
Election Type: General Election
Term Expires: 2021

Current Memberships: The America Law Institute; American Bar Association; Washoe County Bar Association

Staff

Law Clerk **Naveen Dixit** . . . . (702) 486-9370
Began Service: August 2015
Term Expires: August 2016
Law Clerk **Erica Smit** . . . . (702) 486-9370
Began Service: August 2015
Term Expires: August 2016
Judicial Court Administrator **Anita Alexander** . . . . (702) 486-9370

Chambers of Justice Michael A. Cherry

Supreme Court Building, 201 South Carson Street,
Carson City, NV 89701-4702
Tel: (775) 684-1540 Fax: (775) 684-1543

Michael A. Cherry
Justice

Education: Missouri 1966; Washington U (MO) 1969 JD
Began Service: 2012

Chambers of Justice Michael A. Cherry *continued*

Staff

Law Clerk **Gerri Hardcastle** . . . . (775) 684-1541
Began Service: August 2014
Term Expires: August 4, 2016
E-mail: ghardcastle@nvcourts.nv.gov

Law Clerk **Lee Gorlin** . . . . (775) 684-1542
Began Service: August 2015
Term Expires: August 4, 2017
E-mail: lgorlin@nvcourts.nv.gov

Judicial Chambers Assistant **Janice Luevano** . . . . (775) 684-1540
E-mail: jluevano@nvcourts.nv.gov

Chambers of Justice Nancy M. Saitta

Supreme Court Building, 201 South Carson Street,
Carson City, NV 89701-4702
Tel: (775) 684-1530
E-mail: nsaitta@nvcourts.nv.gov

Nancy M. Saitta
Justice

Date of Birth: April 29, 1951
Education: Wayne State U 1983 BS, 1986 JD
Began Service: 2006

Current Memberships: Executive Committee, Clark County Bar Association; Clark County Public Education Foundation

Staff

Law Clerk **Daniel Alejandre** . . . . (775) 684-1530
Began Service: August 2015
Term Expires: August 2016

Law Clerk **Carl Segerblom** . . . . (775) 684-1530
Term Expires: August 2016

Administrator **Vickie Roberts** . . . . (775) 684-1530

Chambers of Justice Michael L. Douglas

Regional Justice Center, 200 Lewis Avenue, 17th Floor,
Las Vegas, NV 89101
Tel: (702) 486-3225 (Las Vegas Office)
Tel: (775) 684-1755 (Carson City Office)
E-mail: mdouglas@nvcourts.nv.gov

Michael L. Douglas
Justice

Education: Cal State (Long Beach) 1971 BA; Hastings 1974 JD
Began Service: April 19, 2004
Appointed By: Governor Kenny Guinn
Term Expires: December 2018

Current Memberships: American Bar Association; American Judges Association; National District Attorneys Association; Nevada District Court Judges Association; Nevada Gaming Attorneys; Pennsylvania Bar Association; Philadelphia Bar Association

Staff

Judicial Court Administrator **Jill Hiatt** . . . . (702) 486-3225

Chambers of Justice Ronald Parraguirre

Supreme Court Building, 201 South Carson Street,
Carson City, NV 89701-4702
Tel: (775) 684-1510

Ronald Parraguirre
Justice

Education: San Diego 1985 JD
Began Service: January 3, 2010
Next Election: November 2016
Term Expires: January 2017

Government: Counsel, Subcommittee on Criminal Law, Committee on the Judiciary, United States Senate

Judicial: Las Vegas Municipal Court (1991-1999); Eighth Judicial District Court (1999)

Staff

Law Clerk **Adam Tully** . . . . (775) 684-1510
Began Service: September 4, 2014
Term Expires: September 2016
E-mail: atully@nvcourts.nv.gov

Law Clerk **Sean Daly** . . . . (775) 684-1510
Began Service: August 2015
Term Expires: August 2017
E-mail: sdaly@nvcourts.nv.gov

Administrator **Roxanne Doyle** . . . . (775) 684-1510
E-mail: rdoyle@nvcourts.nv.gov

Nevada Court of Appeals

200 Lewis Avenue, 17th Floor, Las Vegas, NV 89101
201 South Carson Street, Suite 250, Carson City, NV 89701-4702
Tel: (702) 486-9300

On November 4, 2014, Nevada voters approved an amendment to Article 6 of the Nevada Constitution in order to create an intermediate appellate court also known as the Nevada Court of Appeals. As a result of the approval, all appeals will still be filed with the Nevada Supreme Court, which will then assign cases to the three-judge Court of Appeals. This court will hear roughly one-third of all cases submitted to the Nevada Supreme Court.

Court Staff

Assistant Clerk, Court of Appeals
Thomas "Tom" Harris . . . . (702) 486-9300

Chambers of Chief Judge Michael P. Gibbons

201 South Carson Street, Suite 300, Carson City, NV 89701-4702
Tel: (775) 684-1520

Michael P. Gibbons
Chief Judge

Education: UCLA BA; Idaho JD
Began Service: January 5, 2015
Appointed By: Governor Brian Sandoval

Chambers of Judge Jerome T. Tao

200 Lewis Avenue, Las Vegas, NV 89101
Tel: (702) 486-9360

Jerome T. Tao
Judge

Education: Cornell 1989 BS; George Washington 1992 JD
Began Service: January 5, 2015
Appointed By: Governor Brian Sandoval

Chambers of Judge Abbi Silver

200 Lewis Avenue, Las Vegas, NV 89101
Tel: (702) 486-9340

Abbi Silver
Judge

Education: UNLV 1986 BA; Southwestern 1989 JD
Began Service: January 5, 2015
Appointed By: Governor Brian Sandoval

STATE COURTS – NEVADA

New Hampshire

Administrative Office of the Courts of New Hampshire

Two Charles Doe Drive, Concord, NH 03301-6179
Tel: (603) 271-2521 Fax: (603) 513-5454
E-mail: AOC@courts.state.nh.us
Internet: www.courts.state.nh.us

Staff

Director **Donald D. Goodnow** .... (603) 271-2521
Affiliation: Esq.
E-mail: AOC@courts.state.nh.us
Education: Franklin & Marshall 1972 AB; Suffolk 1977 JD

New Hampshire Supreme Court

Supreme Court Building, One Charles Doe Drive,
Concord, NH 03301-6160
Tel: (603) 271-2646 Tel: (603) 271-3777 (Law Library)
Fax: (603) 513-5475 Fax: (603) 271-2168 (Law Library)
Internet: www.courts.state.nh.us/supreme/index.htm

Number of Judgeships: 5

The Supreme Court consists of a chief justice and four associate justices who are appointed by the Governor and Executive Council to serve until age seventy when retirement is mandatory. The Supreme Court has final appellate jurisdiction over all questions of law and over decisions or appeals of all trial courts and several administrative agencies. The Court exercises administrative control over all lower courts in the state.

The New Hampshire Supreme Court sits in Concord.

Court Staff

Clerk of Court **Eileen Fox** .... (603) 271-2646
E-mail: efox@courts.state.nh.us
Deputy Clerk, Administrative **Allison Cook** .... (603) 271-2646
E-mail: acook@courts.state.nh.us
Deputy Clerk, Legal **Timothy Gudas** .... (603) 271-2646
E-mail: tgudas@courts.state.nh.us
General Counsel **Howard J. Zibel** .... (603) 271-2646
E-mail: hzibel@courts.state.nh.us
Reporter of Decisions **Lorrie Platt** .... (603) 271-2646
E-mail: lplatt@courts.state.nh.us
Communications Director **Carole Alfano** .... (603) 271-2646
E-mail: calfano@courts.state.nh.us
Law Librarian **Mary S. Searles** .... (603) 271-3777
E-mail: msearles@courts.state.nh.us Fax: (603) 513-5450

Chambers of Chief Justice Linda S. Dalianis

One Charles Doe Drive, Concord, NH 03301
Tel: (603) 271-2646 Fax: (603) 513-5475
E-mail: ldalianis@courts.state.nh.us

Linda S. Dalianis
Chief Justice

Education: Northeastern 1970 BA; Suffolk 1974 JD
Began Service: December 15, 2010
Appointed By: Governor John H. Lynch

Staff

Law Clerk **Lynn Huggins** .... (603) 271-2646
E-mail: lhuggins@courts.state.nh.us
Senior Law Clerk **Anne Zinkin** .... (603) 271-2646
E-mail: azinkin@courts.state.nh.us
Education: Trinity Col (CT) 1983 BA; NYU 1988 JD
Executive Assistant **Irene Dalbec** .... (603) 271-2646
E-mail: idalbec@courts.state.nh.us

Chambers of Senior Associate Justice Gary E. Hicks

One Charles Doe Drive, Concord, NH 03301-6160
Tel: (603) 271-2646
E-mail: ghicks@courts.state.nh.us

Gary E. Hicks
Senior Associate Justice

Education: Bucknell 1975 BA; Boston U 1978 JD
Began Service: January 30, 2006
Appointed By: Governor John H. Lynch
Term Expires: November 30, 2023

Judicial: Associate Justice, New Hampshire Superior Court (2001-2005)

Legal Practice: Wiggin & Nourie (1978-2001)

Staff

Career Law Clerk **Mary Beth Kula** .... (603) 271-2646
E-mail: mkula@courts.state.nh.us
Secretary **Irene Dalbec** .... (603) 271-2646 ext. 2360
E-mail: idalbec@courts.state.nh.us

Chambers of Associate Justice Carol Ann Conboy

One Charles Doe Drive, Concord, NH 03301
Tel: (603) 271-2646
E-mail: cconboy@courts.state.nh.us

Carol Ann Conboy
Associate Justice

Education: Connecticut 1969; Pierce Law 1978 JD
Began Service: June 17, 2009

Clerkships: Law Clerk, Chambers of District Judge Shane Devine, United States District Court for the District of New Hampshire (1978-1979)

Legal Practice: Partner, Concord, NH Office, McLane, Graf, Raulerson & Middleton (1979-1992)

Military Service: Lieutenant 1st Lt, United States Air Force, United States Department of the Air Force, United States Department of Defense

Staff

Law Clerk **Emily Lawrence** .... (603) 271-2646
Began Service: August 2013
Term Expires: September 2016
E-mail: elawrence@courts.state.nh.us
Education: New England 2003 JD
Law Clerk **Erin Fitzgerald** .... (603) 271-2646
Began Service: August 2015
Term Expires: September 2016
E-mail: efitzgerald@courts.state.nh.us

Chambers of Associate Justice Robert J. Lynn

One Charles Doe Drive, Concord, NH 03301-6160
Tel: (603) 271-2646 Fax: (603) 513-5475
E-mail: rlynn@courts.state.nh.us

Robert J. Lynn
Associate Justice

Education: New Haven 1971; Connecticut 1975 JD
Began Service: December 17, 2010
Appointed By: Governor John H. Lynch

Staff

Law Clerk **(Vacant)** .... (603) 271-2646
Law Clerk **Michael Varley** .... (603) 271-2646
Judicial Assistant **Irene Dalbec** .... (603) 271-2646
E-mail: idalbec@courts.state.nh.us

Chambers of Associate Justice James P. Bassett
One Charles Doe Drive, Concord, NH 03301-6160
Tel: (603) 271-2646
E-mail: jbassett@courts.state.nh.us

James P. "Jim" Bassett
Associate Justice

Education: Dartmouth AB; Virginia JD
Began Service: July 19, 2012
Appointed By: Governor John H. Lynch

New Jersey

Administrative Office of the Courts of New Jersey

Richard J. Hughes Justice Complex, 25 Market Street,
Trenton, NJ 08625-0037
P.O. Box 037, Trenton, NJ 08625-0037
Tel: (609) 984-0275 Tel: (609) 292-9580 (Public Information)
Fax: (609) 984-6968
Internet: www.njcourts.com

Staff

Administrative Director (Acting) [Judge of the Appellate Division] **Glenn A. Grant** . . . . (609) 984-0275
E-mail: glenn.grant@judiciary.state.nj.us Fax: (609) 984-6968
Director, Communications **Winifred Comfort** . . . . (609) 292-9580
E-mail: winnie.comfort@judiciary.state.nj.us
Director, Information Technology **John P. McCarthy III** . . . (609) 292-8343
E-mail: john.mccarthy@judiciary.state.nj.us Fax: (609) 633-8114
Director, Management and Administrative Services **Shelley Webster** . . . . (609) 292-2166
E-mail: shelley.webster@judiciary.state.nj.us
Director, Professional and Governmental Services **Deirdre Naughton** . . . . (609) 292-8553
E-mail: deirdre.naughton@judiciary.state.nj.us
Chief of Staff **Steven D. Bonville** . . . . (609) 984-5523
E-mail: steven.bonville@judiciary.state.nj.us
Trial Court Services Director **Jennifer M. Perez** . . . . (609) 292-4637
Education: St Joseph's U BA; Rutgers (Camden) JD

Supreme Court of New Jersey

25 West Market Street, Trenton, NJ 08625
P.O. Box 970, Trenton, NJ 08625-0970
Tel: (609) 984-7791 Fax: (609) 396-9056
Internet: www.judiciary.state.nj.us

Number of Vacancies: 1

Number of Judgeships: 7

The Supreme Court consists of a chief justice and six associate justices who are initially appointed by the Governor with consent of the New Jersey State Senate for seven-year terms with tenure granted upon reappointment. Retirement is mandatory at age seventy; however, retired justices may be recalled by the Court. The Supreme Court has final appellate jurisdiction on all constitutional questions, cases of dissent from the Appellate Division of the New Jersey Superior Court, and petitions for certification. The Court also has rule-making authority and regulates admission and discipline of attorneys and judges.

The Supreme Court of New Jersey sits in Trenton.

Court Staff

Clerk of the Court **Mark Neary** . . . . (609) 292-4837
E-mail: mark.neary@judiciary.state.nj.us

Chambers of Chief Justice Stuart Rabner

Richard J. Hughes Justice Complex, 25 Market Street, Trenton, NJ 08625
P.O. Box 023, Trenton, NJ 08625-0023
Tel: (609) 292-2448 Fax: (609) 984-6988
E-mail: stuart.rabner@judiciary.state.nj.us

Stuart Rabner
Chief Justice

Date of Birth: June 30, 1960
Education: Princeton 1982; Harvard 1985 JD
Began Service: June 29, 2007
Appointed By: Governor Jon S. Corzine

Government: Lead Attorney, Organized Crime Drug Enforcement Task Force, New Jersey District, United States Department of Justice; Deputy Chief, Special Prosecutions Division, New Jersey District, United States Department of Justice; Executive Assistant United States Attorney, New Jersey District, United States Department of Justice; First Assistant United States Attorney, New Jersey District, United States Department of Justice; Terrorism Unit Chief, Criminal Division, New Jersey District, United States Department of Justice; Chief, Criminal Division, New Jersey District, United States Department of Justice; Chief Counsel, Governor Jon S. Corzine (D-NJ), State of New Jersey (2006); Attorney General/Homeland Security Head, State of New Jersey (2006-2007); Commission Member, Motor Vehicle Commission, State of New Jersey (2006-2007)

Staff

Law Clerk **Parimal Garg** . . . . (609) 292-2448
Began Service: September 2015
Term Expires: August 22, 2016
E-mail: parimal.garg@judiciary.state.nj.us
Law Clerk **Aaron Webman** . . . . (609) 292-2448
Began Service: September 2015
Term Expires: August 22, 2016
Law Clerk **McKenzie Wilson** . . . . (609) 292-2448
Began Service: September 2015
Term Expires: September 31, 2016
Judicial Assistant **Donna B. Anepete** . . . . (609) 292-2448
E-mail: donna.anepete@judiciary.state.nj.us

Chambers of Associate Justice Jaynee LaVecchia

158 Headquarters Plaza, North Tower, Suite 1101, Morristown, NJ 07960
Tel: (973) 631-6379 Fax: (973) 631-6591
E-mail: jaynee.lavecchia@judiciary.state.nj.us

Jaynee LaVecchia
Associate Justice

Date of Birth: 1954
Education: Douglass 1976 BA; Rutgers 1979 JD
Began Service: February 1, 2000
Appointed By: Governor Christine Todd Whitman

Government: Law Assistant then Deputy Attorney General Division of Land, Department of Law and Public Safety, State of New Jersey (1979-1984); Assistant Counsel, Governor Thomas H. Kean (R-NJ), State of New Jersey (1986-1988); Deputy Chief Counsel, Governor Thomas H. Kean (R-NJ), State of New Jersey (1988-1989); Director, Division of Law, Department of Law and Public Safety, State of New Jersey (1994-1998); Commissioner, Department of Banking and Insurance, State of New Jersey (1998-2000)

Judicial: Director and Chief Administrative Law Judge, Office of Administrative Law (1989-1994)

Legal Practice: Associate, Brach, Eichler, Rosenberg, Silver, Bernstein, Hammer and Gladstone (1984-1986)

Current Memberships: American Bar Association

(continued on next page)

Chambers of Associate Justice Jaynee LaVecchia *continued*

Staff

Judicial Secretary **Linda Gruchacz** .... (973) 631-6379
Began Service: 2008
E-mail: linda.gruchacz@judiciary.state.nj.us
Education: South Carolina BA

Chambers of Associate Justice Barry T. Albin

Post Office Plaza, 50 Division Street, Suite 201, Somerville, NJ 08876
Tel: (908) 704-8109 Fax: (908) 704-8113
E-mail: barry.albin@judiciary.state.nj.us

Barry T. Albin
Associate Justice

Date of Birth: July 7, 1952
Education: Cornell 1976 JD
Began Service: October 3, 2002
Appointed By: Governor James E. McGreevey

Government: Deputy Attorney General, Appellate Section, Criminal Justice Division, State of New Jersey; Assistant Prosecutor, Office of the County Prosecutor, Office of the Board of Chosen Freeholders, County of Middlesex, New Jersey

Legal Practice: Partner, Wilentz Goldman & Spitzer P.A. (1982-2002)

Staff

Law Clerk **Brett Ruber** .... (908) 704-8112
Began Service: September 2015
Term Expires: September 2016
Law Clerk **Alex Kramer** .... (908) 704-8112
Began Service: September 2015
Term Expires: September 2016
Law Clerk **Allison Hollows** .... (908) 704-8112
Began Service: September 2015
Term Expires: September 2016
E-mail: allison.hollows@judiciary.state.nj.us
Secretary **Sara Cronin** .... (908) 704-8109
E-mail: sara.cronin@judiciary.state.nj.us

Chambers of Associate Justice Anne M. Patterson

25 Market Street, Trenton, NJ 08625-0037
Tel: (609) 292-4837 Fax: (609) 396-9056

Anne M. Patterson
Associate Justice

Education: Dartmouth 1980 AB; Cornell 1983 JD
Began Service: September 1, 2011
Appointed By: Governor Chris Christie

Chambers of Associate Justice Mary Catherine Cuff

25 West Market Street, Trenton, NJ 08625
Tel: (732) 229-3702

Mary Catherine Cuff
Associate Justice (Acting)

Date of Birth: 1947
Education: Rosemont 1969 BA; Rutgers (Newark) 1973 JD
Began Service: 2012

Current Memberships: American Bar Association; Monmouth County Bar Association; New Jersey State Bar Association

Staff

Law Clerk **Joanna Laine** .... (732) 229-3702
Began Service: September 2015
Term Expires: September 2016
E-mail: joanna.laine@judiciary.state.nj.us

Chambers of Associate Justice Mary Catherine Cuff *continued*

Law Clerk **Cody Mason** .... (732) 229-3702
Began Service: September 2015
Term Expires: August 31, 2016
E-mail: cody.mason@judiciary.state.nj.us
Law Clerk **Cymetra Williams** .... (732) 229-3702
Began Service: September 2015
Term Expires: August 31, 2016
E-mail: cymetra.williams@judiciary.state.nj.us
Secretary **Marie E. Schenck** .... (732) 229-3702
E-mail: marie.schenck@judiciary.state.nj.us

Chambers of Associate Justice Faustino J. Fernandez-Vina

25 Market Street, Trenton, NJ 08625-0037
Tel: (609) 984-7791

Faustino J. "F.J." Fernandez-Vina
Associate Justice

Began Service: November 19, 2013
Appointed By: Governor Chris Christie

Chambers of Associate Justice Lee Solomon

25 West Market Street, Trenton, NJ 08625
Tel: (609) 984-7791

Lee A. Solomon
Associate Justice

Began Service: October 8, 2014
Appointed By: Governor Chris Christie

New Jersey Superior Court, Appellate Division

Richard J. Hughes Justice Complex, 25 West Market Street, Trenton, NJ 08625
P.O. Box 006, Trenton, NJ 08625-0006
Tel: (609) 292-4822 Fax: (609) 292-9806
Internet: www.judiciary.state.nj.us/appdiv/index.htm

Number of Judgeships: 33

The Appellate Division of the Superior Court consists of thirty-three judges who are assigned to parts of four or five judges. Appellate Division judges, including the presiding judge for administration and the presiding judge for each part, are selected from the Superior Court and assigned to the Division by the Supreme Court chief justice. All Superior Court judges are initially appointed by the Governor with consent of the New Jersey State Senate for seven-year terms with tenure granted upon reappointment. Retirement is mandatory at age seventy; however, retired judges may be recalled by the New Jersey Supreme Court. The Appellate Division of the Superior Court is the intermediate appellate court and hears appeals from the Law and Chancery Divisions of the Superior Court, Tax Court and state administrative agencies.

The Appellate Division of the Superior Court sits in Morristown, Newark, and Trenton, as well as other locations from time to time.

Court Staff

Clerk, Appellate Division **Joseph H. Orlando** .... (609) 292-6995
E-mail: joe.orlando@judiciary.state.nj.us Fax: (609) 292-9806
Deputy Clerk, Appellate Division Administrative Services **Leigh Eastty** .... (609) 292-2644
Fax: (609) 989-7764
Deputy Clerk, Appellate Division Case Processing **John K. Grant** .... (609) 777-4529
E-mail: john.grant@judiciary.state.nj.us
Education: Col New Jersey BS
Chief Counsel **Jack G. Trubenbach** .... (609) 633-3637
Education: Rutgers BA; Brooklyn Law JD

New Jersey Superior Court, Appellate Division *continued*

Director, Central Appellate Research **Ellen T. Wry** . . . . (609) 292-4982
E-mail: ellen.wry@judiciary.state.nj.us
Executive Librarian **Katheryn Spalding** . . . . (609) 292-7231
E-mail: katheryn.spalding@judiciary.state.nj.us Fax: (609) 989-7764

New Jersey Superior Court, Appellate Division, Part A

Chambers of Presiding Judge Jack M. Sabatino
Richard J. Hughes Justice Complex, 25 Market Street,
Trenton, NJ 08625-0977
P.O. Box 977, Trenton, NJ 08625-0977
Tel: (609) 777-0200
E-mail: jack.sabatino@judiciary.state.nj.us

Jack Michael Sabatino
Presiding Judge

Education: Yale 1979 BA; Harvard JD
Began Service: March 1, 2006

Chambers of Judge Marie P. Simonelli
LeRoy F. Smith, Jr. Public Safety Complex, 60 Nelson Place,
8th Floor, Newark, NJ 07102-1501
Tel: (973) 792-5844
E-mail: marie.simonelli@judiciary.state.nj.us

Marie P. Simonelli
Judge

Began Service: 2010

Staff
Law Clerk **Liana Abreu** . . . . (973) 792-5844
Began Service: September 2015
Term Expires: September 2016
Law Clerk **Michael Bachmann** . . . . (973) 792-5844
Began Service: September 2015
Term Expires: September 2016
Legal Secretary **Elizabeth Wilson** . . . . (973) 792-5844
E-mail: elizabeth.wilson@judiciary.state.nj.us

Chambers of Judge Michael A. Guadagno
185 State Route 36, West Long Branch, NJ 07764-1304
Tel: (732) 229-3729

Michael A. Guadagno
Judge

Staff
Secretary **Kimberly Rudolph** . . . . (732) 229-3729
E-mail: kimberly.rudolph@judiciary.state.nj.us

Chambers of Judge George S. Leone
216 Haddon Avenue, Westmont, NJ 08108-2815
Tel: (856) 854-8590

George S. Leone
Judge

New Jersey Superior Court, Appellate Division, Part B

Chambers of Presiding Judge Marie E. Lihotz
216 Haddon Avenue, Westmont, NJ 08108-2815
Tel: (856) 854-8764 Fax: (856) 858-9243
E-mail: marie.lihotz@judiciary.state.nj.us

Marie E. Lihotz
Judge

Began Service: 2006

Staff
Law Clerk **John Weiss, Jr.** . . . . (856) 854-8764
Began Service: September 2015
Term Expires: August 31, 2016
E-mail: john.weiss@judiciary.state.nj.us
Law Clerk **Charles Vaccaro** . . . . (856) 854-8764
Began Service: August 2015
Term Expires: August 31, 2016
Secretary **JoAnn Ruhland** . . . . (856) 854-8764

Chambers of Judge Marianne Espinosa
158 Headquarters Plaza, Suite 1101, Morristown, NJ 07960-3965
Tel: (973) 631-6527

Marianne Espinosa
Judge

Education: NYU; Rutgers JD
Began Service: August 1, 2009

Chambers of Judge Jerome M. St. John
60 Nelson Place, Newark, NJ 07102-1501
Tel: (973) 792-5868

Jerome M. St. John
Judge

Education: Villanova 1971 AB; Seton Hall 1975 JD
Began Service: August 1, 2011

Chambers of Judge Garry S. Rothstadt
158 Headquarters Plaza, Suite 1101, Morristown, NJ 07960-3965
Tel: (973) 631-6365

Garry S. Rothstadt
Judge

New Jersey Superior Court, Appellate Division, Part C

Chambers of Presiding Judge Susan L. Reisner
Middlesex County Courthouse, 56 Paterson Street, The Tower,
4th Floor, New Brunswick, NJ 08903
P.O. Box 112, New Brunswick, NJ 08903-2698
Tel: (732) 591-3875 Fax: (732) 519-3883
E-mail: susan.reisner@judiciary.state.nj.us

Susan L. Reisner
Presiding Judge

Began Service: March 1, 2004

Chambers of Judge Ellen L. Koblitz
Jst. W.J. Brennan Courthouse, 583 Newark Avenue,
Jersey City, NJ 07306-2395
Tel: (201) 963-3230

Ellen L. Koblitz
Judge

Began Service: 2010

Staff
Law Clerk **Janine Stanizz** .... (201) 963-3230
Secretary **Susanne Rodriguez** .... (201) 963-3230

Chambers of Judge Michael J. Haas
216 Haddon Avenue, Westmont, NJ 08108-2815
Tel: (856) 854-8826

Michael Haas
Judge

Staff
Secretary **Sue Kelly** .... (856) 854-8826
E-mail: sue.kelly@judiciary.state.nj.us

New Jersey Superior Court, Appellate Division, Part D

Chambers of Presiding Judge Carmen H. Alvarez
P.O. Box 280, Cape May Court House, NJ 08210
Tel: (609) 465-1566 Fax: (609) 465-3166

Carmen H. Alvarez
Presiding Judge

Education: Bryn Mawr BA; Columbus Law JD
Began Service: August 1, 2007

Staff
Law Clerk **Alicia VanSciver** .... (609) 465-1566
Began Service: August 2014
E-mail: alicia.vansciver@judiciary.state.nj.us
Law Clerk **Daniel Thornton** .... (609) 465-1566
Began Service: August 2014
Legal Secretary **Karen Rafine** .... (609) 465-1566
E-mail: karen.rafine@judiciary.state.nj.us

Chambers of Judge Alexander P. Waugh Jr.
158 Headquarters Plaza, North Tower, Suite 1101,
Morristown, NJ 07960-3965
Tel: (973) 631-6455

Alexander P. Waugh, Jr.
Judge

Education: Columbia; Rutgers (Newark) JD
Began Service: August 1, 2007

Staff
Law Clerk **(Vacant)** .... (973) 631-6455
Law Clerk **(Vacant)** .... (973) 631-6455
Secretary **Jacqueline Berringer** .... (973) 631-6455
E-mail: jacqueline.berringer@judiciary.state.nj.us

Chambers of Judge Susan F. Maven
1201 Bacharach Boulevard, Atlantic City, NJ 08401-4510
Tel: (609) 348-0424
E-mail: susan.maven@judiciary.state.nj.us

Susan F. Maven
Judge

Staff
Secretary **Charlotte Stapleton** .... (609) 348-0424
E-mail: charlotte.stapleton@judiciary.state.nj.us

Chambers of Judge Harry G. Carroll
583 Newark Avenue, Jersey City, NJ 07306-2395
Tel: (201) 659-8710

Harry G. Carroll
Judge

New Jersey Superior Court, Appellate Division, Part E

Chambers of Presiding Judge Carmen Messano
Justice W. J. Brennan Courthouse, 583 Newark Avenue,
Jersey City, NJ 07306-2395
Tel: (201) 659-6869
E-mail: carmen.messano@judiciary.state.nj.us

Carmen Messano
Presiding Judge

Date of Birth: May 23, 1953
Education: Lafayette 1974 BA; Boston Col 1977 JD
Began Service: November 20, 2006
Appointed By: Governor Jon S. Corzine
Term Expires: 2023

Chambers of Judge Mitchel Ostrer
25 Market Street, Trenton, NJ 08625-0037
Tel: (609) 984-2446

Mitchel E. Ostrer
Judge

Began Service: August 1, 2011

Chambers of Judge Margaret M. Hayden
60 Nelson Place, Newark, NJ 07102-1501
Tel: (973) 792-5875

Margaret M. Hayden
Judge

Began Service: August 1, 2011

New Jersey Superior Court, Appellate Division, Part F

Chambers of Presiding Judge Clarkson S. Fisher
185 State Route 36, Suite 1, West Long Branch, NJ 07764-1304
Tel: (732) 229-3710

Clarkson S. Fisher, Jr.
Presiding Judge

Began Service: 2003

Chambers of Judge Allison E. Accurso
56 Paterson Street, New Brunswick, NJ 08903
Tel: (732) 519-3871

Allison E. Accurso
Judge

Staff
Secretary **Linda Comerford** . . . . (732) 519-3871
E-mail: linda.comerford@judiciary.state.nj.us

Chambers of Judge William E. Nugent
Atlantic County Civil Courthouse, 1201 Bacharach Boulevard, Atlantic City, NJ 08401-4510
Tel: (609) 441-3482

William E. Nugent
Judge

Began Service: March 1, 2010

New Jersey Superior Court, Appellate Division, Part G

Chambers of Presiding Judge Joseph L. Yannotti
LeRoy F. Smith, Jr. Public Safety Complex, 60 Nelson Place, 8th Floor, Newark, NJ 07102-1501
Tel: (973) 792-5856
E-mail: joseph.yannotti@judiciary.state.nj.us

Joseph L. Yannotti
Presiding Judge

Education: Syracuse BA, JD
Began Service: August 1, 2004

Chambers of Judge Richard S. Hoffman
216 Haddon Avenue, Westmont, NJ 08108-2815
Tel: (856) 854-8581

Richard S. Hoffman
Judge

Staff
Secretary **Linda Pallies** . . . . (856) 854-8581
E-mail: linda.pallies@judiciary.state.nj.us

Chambers of Judge Douglas M. Fasciale
LeRoy F. Smith, Jr. Public Safety Building, 60 Nelson Place, Newark, NJ 07102-1501
Tel: (973) 792-5847

Douglas M. Fasciale
Judge

Education: Seton Hall, JD

New Jersey Superior Court, Appellate Division, Part H

Chambers of Presiding Judge Jose L. Fuentes
North Tower, 158 Headquarters Plaza, Suite 1101, Morristown, NJ 07960-3965
Tel: (973) 631-6370
E-mail: jose.fuentes@judiciary.state.nj.us

Jose L. Fuentes
Judge

Education: Montclair State Col 1978; Rutgers 1982 JD
Began Service: August 1, 2002

Staff
Law Clerk **Thomas B. Jones** . . . . (973) 631-6370
Began Service: September 2015
Term Expires: September 2016
Law Clerk **Clifford Dawkins** . . . . (973) 631-6370
Began Service: September 2015
Term Expires: September 2016

Chambers of Judge John C. Kennedy
60 Nelson Place, Newark, NJ 07102-1501
Tel: (973) 792-5850

John C. Kennedy
Judge

Began Service: 2011

Chambers of Judge Victor Ashrafi
158 Headquarters Plaza, North Tower, Suite 1101, Morristown, NJ 07960-3965
Tel: (973) 631-6360

Victor Ashrafi
Judge

Education: Amherst; Stanford; Cornell JD
Began Service: 2009

Chambers of Judge Amy O'Connor
158 Headquarters Plaza, Suite 1101, Morristown, NJ 07960-3965
Tel: (973) 631-6362

Amy O'Connor
Judge

New Mexico

Administrative Office of the Courts of New Mexico

Supreme Court Building, 237 Don Gaspar Avenue, Room 25,
Santa Fe, NM 87501
Tel: (505) 827-4800 Fax: (505) 827-4824
Internet: www.nmcourts.com

Staff

Administrative Office of the Courts Director
Arthur W. Pepin . . . . (505) 827-4800
Deputy Director **(Vacant)** . . . . (505) 827-4800
Executive Assistant to the Director **Patricia Wolff** . . . . (505) 827-4800
Court Services Division Director **Louise Baca-Sena** . . . . . (505) 827-4960
Fiscal Services Director **Oscar J. Arevalo** . . . . (505) 827-4832
E-mail: aocoja@nmcourts.gov Fax: (505) 827-8091
Education: Col Santa Fe 1993 BA
Human Resources Director
Lynette Paulman-Rodriguez . . . . (505) 827-4937
Chief Information Officer **Greg Saunders** . . . . (505) 476-6900
Magistrate Court Division Director
Rosemary McCourt . . . . (505) 827-4831
General Counsel (Acting) **Celina Jones** . . . . (505) 827-4800
E-mail: aoccaj@nmcourts.net

New Mexico Supreme Court

Supreme Court Building, 237 Don Gaspar Avenue, Santa Fe, NM 87501
P.O. Box 848, Santa Fe, NM 87504-0848
Tel: (505) 827-4860 Tel: (505) 827-4850 (Library Information)
Fax: (505) 827-4837
Internet: http://nmsupremecourt.nmcourts.gov

Number of Judgeships: 5

The Supreme Court consists of a chief justice and four associate justices who are elected in general elections to eight-year terms. Vacancies are filled by the Governor from a list submitted by the constitutionally created Judicial Selection Commission. Appointees serve until the next general election. The chief justice is elected by peer vote to a two-year term each January of odd-numbered years. The Supreme Court has appellate jurisdiction over all New Mexico District Court decisions in criminal cases imposing a death penalty or life imprisonment and in appeals from the Public Regulation Commission. All other cases are appealed to the New Mexico Court of Appeals. The Court has supervisory and administrative control over all lower courts and exercises disciplinary control over judges and attorneys in the state.

The New Mexico Supreme Court sits in Santa Fe.

Court Staff

Chief Clerk of the Court **Joey Moya** . . . . (505) 827-4860
Education: New Mexico 1988 JD
Administrative Assistant to Chief Clerk
Kathy Bartlett . . . . (505) 827-4860
Chief Disciplinary Counsel **William Slease** . . . . (505) 827-4860
Education: New Mexico 1991 JD
Chief Deputy Clerk **Madeline Garcia** . . . . (505) 827-4860
Deputy Clerk **Amy Mayer** . . . . (505) 827-4860
Deputy Clerk **Debbie A. Romero** . . . . (505) 827-4860
Deputy Clerk **(Vacant)** . . . . (505) 827-4860
Financial Specialist **Eric Catanach** . . . . (505) 827-4860
Court Financial Manager **Wanda M. Gonzales** . . . . (505) 827-4860
Human Resources Administrator **Agnes Wozniak** . . . . (505) 827-4201
State Law Librarian **Lynne Rhys** . . . . (505) 827-4850
P.O. Drawer L, Santa Fe, NM 87504 Fax: (505) 827-4852
Director of Judicial Education Center **John Newell** . . . . . . (505) 277-5006
1117 Stanford Dr., NE, Fax: (505) 277-7064
Albuquerque, NM 87131-0001

Chambers of Chief Justice Barbara Vigil

237 Don Gaspar Avenue, Santa Fe, NM 87501
Tel: (505) 827-4860

Barbara J. Vigil
Chief Justice

Education: New Mexico JD; New Mexico State JD
Began Service: December 7, 2012

Chambers of Justice Petra Jimenez Maes

Supreme Court Building, 237 Don Gaspar Avenue, Santa Fe, NM 87501
P.O. Box 2268, Santa Fe, NM 87504-0848
Tel: (505) 827-4883 Fax: (505) 827-4837
E-mail: suppjm@nmcourts.gov

Petra Jimenez Maes
Justice

Date of Birth: 1947
Education: New Mexico BA, 1973 JD
Began Service: April 4, 2012
Term Expires: December 31, 2018
Political Affiliation: Democrat

Staff

Law Clerk **Nicole Beder** . . . . (505) 827-4819
Began Service: 2015
Term Expires: 2016
Law Clerk **Mark Cox** . . . . (505) 827-4885
Began Service: 2014
Term Expires: 2016
Paralegal **Carolyn Wright** . . . . (505) 827-4883

Chambers of Justice Charles W. Daniels

Supreme Court Building, 237 Don Gaspar Avenue, Santa Fe, NM 87501
P.O. Box 848, Santa Fe, NM 87504-0848
Tel: (505) 827-4889 Fax: (505) 827-4837

Charles W. Daniels
Justice

Education: Arizona; New Mexico JD; Georgetown LLM
Began Service: November 2007
Appointed By: Governor Bill Richardson
Next Election: November 2018
Election Type: Retention Election
Term Expires: 2018

Staff

Law Clerk **Rachel Giron** . . . . (505) 827-4889
Began Service: August 2014
Term Expires: August 2015
Law Clerk **Justin Muehlmeyer** . . . . (505) 827-4889
Began Service: August 2013
Term Expires: August 2015
Paralegal **Phyllis Russo** . . . . (505) 827-4889

Chambers of Justice Edward L. Chavez

P.O. Box 848, Santa Fe, NM 87504-0848
Tel: (505) 827-4880 Fax: (505) 827-4837

Edward L. Chavez
Justice

Education: Eastern New Mexico 1978 BBA; New Mexico 1981 JD
Began Service: March 7, 2003
Next Election: November 2022
Election Type: Retention Election
Term Expires: December 31, 2022

Profession: Attorney, Private Practice

New Mexico Court of Appeals

Supreme Court Building, 237 Don Gaspar Avenue, Santa Fe, NM 87501
P.O. Box 2008, Santa Fe, NM 87504-2008
Tel: (505) 827-4925 Fax: (505) 827-4946
Internet: http://coa.nmcourts.com/

Number of Judgeships: 10

The Court of Appeals consists of ten judges who are elected in general elections for eight-year terms. Vacancies are filled by the Governor and appointees serve until December 31 following the next general election or for the remainder of the unexpired term, whichever is longer. The chief judge is elected by peer vote to serve a two-year term. The Court of Appeals has appellate jurisdiction over most civil cases, all actions under the Workers' Compensation Act, the Occupational Disease Disablement Law, the Health Care Provider Act, the Subsequent Injury Act and the Federal Employers' Liability Act. The Court also has appellate jurisdiction over criminal cases and post-conviction remedy proceedings (except where a sentence of death or life imprisonment has been imposed), decisions of administrative agencies as provided by law, municipal or county ordinance violations involving a fine or imprisonment and tort actions.

The Court of Appeals sits in Santa Fe, but may sit elsewhere in the state as necessary.

Court Staff

Chief Clerk of the Court **Mark Reynolds** .... (505) 827-4925
Chief Staff Attorney **Paul G. Fyfe** .... (505) 827-4875
E-mail: coapgf@nmcourts.com
Education: Harvard 1981 JD
Financial Administrator **Ken Wells** .... (505) 827-4807
Appellate Mediator **Robert Rambo** .... (505) 827-3694
Education: Puget Sound Col 1993 JD

Chambers of Chief Judge Roderick T. Kennedy

2211 Tucker NE, Albuquerque, NM 87131
P.O. Box 25306, Albuquerque, NM 87125-0306
Tel: (505) 841-4611 Fax: (505) 841-4614

Roderick T. Kennedy
Chief Judge

Date of Birth: 1955
Education: Wooster 1977 BA; Toledo 1980 JD
Began Service: January 2002
Appointed By: Governor Gary E. Johnson
Term Expires: December 31, 2020

Current Memberships: American Academy of Forensic Sciences; Colorado Bar Association; International Council on Alcohol, Drugs & Traffic Safety; State Bar of New Mexico

Staff
Law Clerk **Natalie Arvizu** .... (505) 841-4606
Began Service: September 2014
Term Expires: September 2016
Paralegal **Diane C. Chavez** .... (505) 841-4611

Chambers of Judge Cynthia A. Fry

2211 Tucker NE, Albuquerque, NM 87106
P.O. Box 25306, Albuquerque, NM 87125-5306
Tel: (505) 841-4626 Fax: (505) 767-6137
E-mail: coacaf@nmcourts.gov

Cynthia A. Fry
Judge

Date of Birth: 1953
Education: Colorado Col 1975 BA; New Mexico 1981 JD
Began Service: December 2000
Next Election: November 2022
Election Type: Retention Election
Term Expires: December 31, 2022
Political Affiliation: Democrat

Current Memberships: New Mexico Women's Bar Association; State Bar of New Mexico

Staff
Law Clerk **Christopher S. McNair** .... (505) 841-4667
Began Service: September 2012
Term Expires: December 2015
E-mail: coacsm@nmcourts.gov
Paralegal **Sylvia P. Wilson** .... (505) 841-4626
E-mail: coaspw@nmcourts.gov

Chambers of Judge Michael D. Bustamante

P.O. Box 488, Albuquerque, NM 87103-0488
Tel: (505) 841-4650 Fax: (505) 841-4614

Michael D. Bustamante
Judge

Date of Birth: 1949
Education: New Mexico 1971 BA, 1974 JD
Began Service: December 27, 1994
Appointed By: Governor Bruce King
Next Election: November 2018
Term Expires: December 31, 2018
Political Affiliation: Democrat

Judicial: Chief Judge, New Mexico Court of Appeals (2005-2006)

Legal Practice: Partner, Ortega & Snead, PA (1974-1990); Private Practice (1990-1994)

Staff
Law Clerk **Nicole Banks** .... (505) 841-4633
Began Service: May 2012
Term Expires: September 2016
Legal Assistant **Kathleen Ciarlotta** .... (505) 841-4650

Chambers of Judge James J. Wechsler

Supreme Court Building, 237 Don Gaspar Avenue, Santa Fe, NM 87503
P.O. Box 2008, Santa Fe, NM 87504-2008
Tel: (505) 827-4908 Fax: (505) 827-4946
E-mail: coajjw@nmcourts.com

James J. Wechsler
Judge

Date of Birth: 1944
Education: NYU 1969 JD
Began Service: December 23, 1994
Appointed By: Governor Bruce King
Next Election: November 2022
Election Type: Retention Election
Term Expires: December 31, 2022

Government: Assistant Attorney General, Office of the Attorney General, State of New Mexico (1976-1983)

(continued on next page)

Chambers of Judge James J. Wechsler *continued*

Judicial: Chief Judge, New Mexico Court of Appeals

Legal Practice: Hinkle, Cox, Eaton, Coffield & Hensley (1983-1994)

Current Memberships: First Judicial District Bar Association; State Bar of New Mexico

Staff
Law Clerk **Nick Henes** . . . . (505) 827-4908
Began Service: August 2015
Term Expires: July 31, 2016
Law Clerk **Matthew Zidovsky** . . . . (505) 827-4908
Began Service: September 2015
Term Expires: August 31, 2016
Legal Assistant **Amy Meilander** . . . . (505) 827-4908

Chambers of Judge Michael Edward Vigil

P.O. Box 25306, Albuquerque, NM 87125
Tel: (505) 767-6126 Fax: (505) 841-4614

Michael Edward Vigil
Judge

Date of Birth: May 23, 1951
Education: Col Santa Fe; Georgetown 1976 JD
Began Service: March 10, 2003
Appointed By: Governor Bill Richardson
Term Expires: December 2020

Government: Staff Attorney, New Mexico Court of Appeals (1976-1979)

Profession: Private Practice

Membership: Member, National Association of Criminal Defense Lawyers; Member, The American Inns of Court

Staff
Law Clerk **Victor Sanchez** . . . . (505) 767-6129
Began Service: September 2015
Term Expires: September 2016
Legal Assistant **Diane C. Chavez** . . . . (505) 767-6126

Chambers of Judge Linda M. Vanzi

237 Don Gaspar Avenue, Santa Fe, NM 87501
Tel: (505) 767-6134

Linda M. Vanzi
Judge

Education: Marymount Col (CA); New Mexico 1995 JD
Began Service: December 2008
Appointed By: Governor Bill Richardson
Next Election: November 2022
Election Type: Retention Election
Term Expires: December 31, 2022

Current Memberships: Albuquerque Bar Association; New Mexico Bar Association; New Mexico Women's Bar Association

Staff
Judicial Assistant **Brandy R. Alazemi** . . . . (505) 767-6134

Chambers of Judge Jonathan Sutin

2211 Tucker NE, Albuquerque, NM 87106
P.O. Box 25306, Albuquerque, NM 87125-5306
Tel: (505) 841-4609 Fax: (505) 841-4614
E-mail: coajbs@nmcourts.gov

Jonathan Sutin
Judge

Date of Birth: 1938
Education: Colorado 1960 BA; New Mexico 1963 JD
Began Service: March 1999
Appointed By: Governor Gary E. Johnson
Next Election: November 4, 2016
Election Type: General Election
Term Expires: December 31, 2016
Political Affiliation: Republican

Government: Trial Attorney, Civil Rights Division, United States Department of Justice

Legal Practice: Attorney, Sutin Thayer & Browne (1965-1999)

Military Service: United States Marine Corps Reserve

Staff
Law Clerk **Tara Lor** . . . . (505) 841-4607
Began Service: 2010
Term Expires: August 2016
Paralegal **Anna M. Box** . . . . (505) 841-4609
Began Service: March 1999
E-mail: coaamb@nmcourts.gov
Education: Eastern New Mexico 1987 BBA

Chambers of Judge Timothy L. Garcia

P.O. Box 2008, Santa Fe, NM 87504-2008
Tel: (505) 827-4911

Timothy L. Garcia
Judge

Education: New Mexico 1979 BBA, 1984 JD
Began Service: November 12, 2008
Appointed By: Governor Bill Richardson

Staff
Judicial Assistant **Angelique Herrera** . . . . (505) 827-4925

Chambers of Judge M. Monica Zamora

237 Don Gaspar Avenue, Santa Fe, NM 87501
Tel: (505) 767-6125

M. Monica Zamora
Judge

Began Service: 2013

Staff
Judicial Assistant **Nancy Sandstrom** . . . . (505) 767-6125

Chambers of Judge J. Miles Hanisee

237 Don Gaspar Avenue, Santa Fe, NM 87501
Tel: (505) 827-4925

J. Miles Hanisee
Judge

Education: LSU 1990 BA; Pepperdine 1993 JD
Began Service: 2012
Next Election: November 2022

Staff
Judicial Assistant **Christy Lujan-Vigil** . . . . (505) 827-4925

New York

New York Office of Court Administration [OCA]

25 Beaver Street, New York, NY 10004
Tel: (212) 428-2100 Fax: (212) 428-2188
Internet: www.nycourts.gov

Staff

Chief Administrative Judge of the Courts **Lawrence K. Marks** . . . . . (212) 428-2120
Education: SUNY (Albany) 1979 BA; Cornell 1982 JD

Chief of Operations of the Office of Court Administration **Eugene Myers** . . . . . (212) 428-2126
Fax: (212) 428-2190

Deputy Chief Administrative Judge [Courts Outside New York City] **Michael V. Coccoma** . . . . . (518) 474-3828
Agency Building- 4, Empire State Plaza, Albany, NY 12223
E-mail: michael.coccoma@nycourts.gov

Deputy Chief Administrative Judge [Courts in New York City] **Fern A. Fisher** . . . . . (646) 386-3170
E-mail: ffisher@courts.state.ny.us

Administrative Director of the Office of Court Administration **Ronald Younkins** . . . . . (212) 428-2884
E-mail: lawrence.marks@nycourts.gov Fax: (212) 428-2188
Education: Nyack 1970 BA; Rutgers (Camden) 1979 JD

Chief of Staff to the Deputy Chief Administrative Judge [Courts in New York City] **Maria Logus** . . . . . (646) 386-4201
E-mail: mlogus@courts.state.ny.us
Education: NYU 1977 BA; Brooklyn Law 1980 JD

Chief Counsel **John McConnell** . . . . . (212) 428-2160
E-mail: jmcconnell@courts.state.ny.us Fax: (212) 428-2155

Chief Records Officer **Geoffrey A. "Geof" Huth** . . . . . (212) 428-2100

Communications Director **David Bookstaver** . . . . . (212) 428-2500
E-mail: dbooksta@courts.state.ny.us Fax: (212) 428-2507
Education: NYU 1982 BA

Public Affairs Director **Gregory L. Murray** . . . . . (212) 428-2116
E-mail: gmurray@courts.state.ny.us Fax: (212) 428-2117
Education: John Jay Col 1984 BA, 1990 MPA

Librarian **James M. Lee** . . . . . (212) 428-2174
E-mail: jlee@courts.state.ny.us Fax: (212) 428-2155
Education: John Jay Col 1984 BA; New York Law 1989 JD

New York Court of Appeals

Court of Appeals Hall, 20 Eagle Street, Albany, NY 12207-1095
Tel: (518) 455-7700
Internet: www.courts.state.ny.us/ctapps

Number of Judgeships: 6

The Court of Appeals, which is New York's court of last resort, consists of a chief judge and six associate judges who are appointed to fourteen-year terms. Judges are appointed by the Governor with the advice and consent of the New York State Senate from a list of candidates provided by the Commission on Judicial Nominations. The Court of Appeals hears both civil and criminal appeals. The jurisdiction of the Court is limited by Section 3 of Article VI of the New York Constitution to the review of questions of law, except in a criminal case in which the judgment includes a penalty of death or a case in which the Appellate Division of the Supreme Court, in reversing or modifying a final or interlocutory judgment or order, finds new facts and a final judgment or order is entered pursuant to that finding. An appeal may be taken directly from the court of original jurisdiction to the Court of Appeals from a final judgment or order in a civil action or proceeding in which the only question is the constitutionality of a state or federal statute. The Court also reviews determinations of the New York State Commission on Judicial Conduct.

The New York Court of Appeals sits in Albany.

New York Court of Appeals *continued*

Court Staff

Clerk of the Court **John P. Asiello** . . . . . (518) 455-7700
E-mail: coa@courts.state.ny.us

Deputy Clerk **(Vacant)** . . . . . (518) 455-7700

Public Information Officer **Gary Spencer** . . . . . (518) 455-7711
E-mail: gspencer@courts.state.ny.us

Chambers of Chief Judge Jonathan Lippman

780 Third Avenue, New York, NY 10017
Tel: (212) 661-6787
E-mail: jlippman@courts.state.ny.us

Jonathan Lippman
Chief Judge

Note: Judge Lippman will retire effective December 2015.
Education: NYU 1965 BA, 1968 JD
Began Service: February 25, 2009
Term Expires: 2023

Chambers of Associate Judge Eugene F. Pigott, Jr.

Court of Appeals Hall, 20 Eagle Street, Albany, NY 12207
Tel: (518) 455-7700

Eugene F. Pigott, Jr.
Associate Judge

Date of Birth: 1946
Education: LeMoyne-Owen 1968 BA; SUNY (Buffalo) 1973 JD
Began Service: 2006
Political Affiliation: Republican

Current Memberships: American Bar Association; Erie County Bar Association (NY); New York State Bar Association

Chambers of Associate Judge Jenny Rivera

20 Eagle Street, Albany, NY 12207
Tel: (212) 661-2144

Jenny Rivera
Associate Judge

Education: Princeton; NYU JD; Columbia 1993 LLM
Began Service: March 18, 2013
Appointed By: Governor Andrew Cuomo

Clerkships: Law Clerk, Chambers of District Judge Sonia Sotomayor, United States District Court for the Southern District of New York

Government: Member, Commission on Human Rights, City of New York, New York; Special Deputy Attorney General for Civil Rights, Office of Attorney General Andrew Cuomo, State of New York

Nonprofit: Staff Attorney, Legal Aid Society of New York

Staff

Law Clerk **Noel Mendez** . . . . . (212) 661-2144
E-mail: nmendez@courts.state.ny.us

Administrative Assistant **Azahar LaPorte** . . . . . (212) 661-2144
E-mail: alaporte@courts.state.ny.us

Chambers of Associate Justice Sheila Abdus-Salaam

20 Eagle Street, Albany, NY 12207
Tel: (518) 455-7700

Sheila Abdus-Salaam
Associate Justice

Education: Barnard 1974 BA; Columbia 1977 JD
Began Service: June 20, 2013
Appointed By: Governor Andrew Cuomo

STATE COURTS—NEW YORK

Chambers of Associate Justice Leslie E. Stein
20 Eagle Street, Albany, NY 12207
Tel: (518) 455-7700

Leslie E. Stein
Associate Justice

Education: Macalester 1978; Albany Law 1981 JD
Began Service: February 9, 2015
Appointed By: Governor Andrew Cuomo

Current Memberships: American Academy of Matrimonial Lawyers; New York State Judicial Institute on Professionalism in the Law

Chambers of Associate Justice Eugene Fahey
20 Eagle Street, Albany, NY 12207
Tel: (518) 455-7736

Eugene M. Fahey
Associate Justice

Education: SUNY (Buffalo) 1974 BA, 1984 JD, 1998 MA
Began Service: February 9, 2015
Appointed By: Governor Andrew Cuomo

Current Memberships: New York State Bar Association

Staff
Career Law Clerk **Michael Pastrick** .... (518) 455-7736
E-mail: mpastric@nycourts.gov
Education: Buffalo 2004 JD
Career Law Clerk **Gordon Lyon** .... (518) 455-7736
Career Law Clerk **Laura Groschadl** .... (518) 455-7736
Confidential Secretary **Mary K. Welch** .... (518) 455-7736
E-mail: mwelch@nycourts.gov

STATE COURTS—NEW YORK

New York Supreme Court, Appellate Division
Tel: (585) 530-3100 Fax: (585) 530-3247

The four Supreme Court Appellate Divisions located in Albany, Brooklyn, Manhattan and Rochester are courts of intermediate appellate jurisdiction hearing appeals from judgment and intermediate orders as well as certain original proceedings arising from the Supreme and County Courts, the Court of Claims, Surrogate's Court and Family Court. Additionally, the Appellate Divisions have original jurisdiction over applications to practice law and attorney disciplinary matters. Each Supreme Court Appellate Division consists of a Presiding Justice and Associate Justices appointed from the ranks of elected Supreme Court Justices by the Governor. The Appellate Divisions sit in panels of four to five justices to hear and determine those proceedings.

New York Supreme Court, Appellate Division, First Department
27 Madison Avenue, New York, NY 10010
Tel: (212) 340-0400 Fax: (212) 952-6580

Number of Judgeships: 20

Areas Covered: Counties of Bronx and New York

Court Staff
Clerk of the Court **Susanna Rojas** .... (212) 340-0400
E-mail: srojas@nycourts.gov
Deputy Clerk **Eric B. Schumacher** .... (212) 340-0400
E-mail: eric.schumacher@nycourts.gov
Education: Cardozo 1984 JD
Deputy Clerk **Margaret Sowah** .... (212) 340-0400
E-mail: msowah@nycourts.gov
Chief Law Assistant **Matthew V. Grieco** .... (212) 340-0400
E-mail: mgrieco@nycourts.gov
Education: Brown U 1991 BA; Columbia 1994 JD

New York Supreme Court, Appellate Division, First Department *continued*

Deputy Chief Law Assistant **Laura LoCurto** .... (212) 340-0400
E-mail: llocurto@nycourts.gov
Principal Law Librarian **Eugene Preudhomme** .... (212) 340-0400
E-mail: epreudho@nycourts.gov
Education: SUNY (Albany) 1987 MLS; Rutgers (Newark) 1993 JD
Chief of Security **Anthony Cavallo** .... (212) 340-0400
E-mail: acavallo@nycourts.gov

Chambers of Presiding Justice Luis A. Gonzalez
27 Madison Avenue, New York, NY 10010
Tel: (212) 340-0422

Luis A. Gonzalez
Presiding Justice

Education: Columbia 1975 JD
Began Service: March 25, 2009
Appointed By: Governor George E. Pataki
Term Expires: March 2016

Government: Investigator, Department of Investigation, City of New York, New York (1975-1976); General Counsel, Commonwealth of Puerto Rico (1978-1980); Hearing Officer, Housing and Community Renewal Division, State of New York (1981-1985)

Judicial: Housing Court Judge, Civil Court (1985-1986); Judge, Civil Court (1987-1992); Acting Justice, New York Supreme Court, Appellate Division (1992); Justice, New York Supreme Court, 12th Judicial District (1993-2002)

Legal Practice: Private Practice (1976-1978)

Nonprofit: General Counsel, South Bronx Community Housing Corporation (1980-1981)

Staff
Career Law Clerk **Linda M. Byrne** .... (212) 340-0576
E-mail: lbyrne@courts.state.ny.us
Education: Yale 1989 BA; Georgetown 1993 JD

Chambers of Associate Justice Peter Tom
27 Madison Avenue, New York, NY 10010
Tel: (212) 340-0400
E-mail: ptom@nycourts.gov

Peter Tom
Associate Justice

Date of Birth: 1947
Education: CCNY BA; Brooklyn Law 1975 JD
Began Service: January 1994

Current Memberships: Asian American Bar Association of the Greater Bay Area

Chambers of Associate Justice Angela M. Mazzarelli
27 Madison Avenue, New York, NY 10010
Tel: (212) 340-0459 Fax: (212) 340-0578

Angela M. Mazzarelli
Associate Justice

Education: Brandeis 1968 BA; Columbia 1971 JD
Began Service: December 1994

Government: Staff Attorney, Bronx Legal Services (1971-1973); Special Assistant, Housing and Development Administration, City of New York, New York (1973); Law Assistant, New York Supreme Court, Civil Term (1973-1977); Principal Law Assistant The Honorable William P. McCooe, New York Supreme Court, Criminal Term (1978-1980)

Judicial: Justice, New York Supreme Court, Criminal Term (1988-1992)

Chambers of Associate Justice Angela M. Mazzarelli *continued*

Legal Practice: Partner, Wresien & Mazzarelli (1980-1985)

Staff

Career Law Clerk **Robert J. Patchen** .... (212) 340-0459
E-mail: rpatchen@courts.state.ny.us
Secretary **Arlene M. Ursini** .... (212) 340-0459
E-mail: aursini@courts.state.ny.us

Chambers of Associate Justice Richard T. Andrias

27 Madison Avenue, New York, NY 10010
Tel: (212) 340-0436 Fax: (212) 340-0579
E-mail: randrias@nycourts.gov

Richard T. Andrias
Associate Justice

Date of Birth: 1943
Education: Columbia 1970 JD
Began Service: June 1996
Appointed By: Governor George E. Pataki
Term Expires: December 31, 2015
Political Affiliation: Democrat

Academic: Adjunct Professor, School of Law, Pace University

Judicial: Judge, New York City Criminal Court (1983-1986); Justice, New York State Supreme Court (1987-1996)

Legal Practice: Gilbert, Segall & Young (1970-1971); Criminal Division, Legal Aid (1971-1975); Davis & Davis (1975-1981); Gordon & Shechtman (1981-1983)

Military Service: United States Army (1965-1967)

Current Memberships: American Bar Association; The Association of the Bar of the City of New York

Staff

Career Law Clerk **Neil Friedkin** .... (212) 340-0436
E-mail: neil.friedkin@nycourts.gov
Education: New York Law 1980 JD
Secretary **Irene Tossone** .... (212) 340-0436
E-mail: itossone@courts.state.ny.us

Chambers of Associate Justice David B. Saxe

27 Madison Avenue, New York, NY 10010
Tel: (212) 340-0401 Fax: (212) 295-4956

David B. Saxe
Associate Justice

Education: Columbia 1963 BA; Case Western 1966 JD; NYU 1972 LLM
Began Service: 1998

Clerkships: Law Clerk The Honorable Shanley N. Egeth

Government: Consumer Advocate, City of New York, New York; Director of Law Enforcement, Department of Consumer Affairs, City of New York, New York; Special Assistant Corporation Counsel, City of New York, New York (1974-1978)

Judicial: Judge, Civil Court for the City of New York (1982-1985); Acting Justice, New York Supreme Court (1986-1990)

Legal Practice: Krakower & Weissman; Salon, Marrow & Dyckma; Brett, Apfelberg & Epstein; Brett, Apfelberg, Epstein & Saxe

Staff

Career Law Clerk **Lauren Foodim** .... (212) 340-0401
E-mail: lfoodim@courts.state.ny.us
Education: SUNY (Buffalo) 1977 BA; Hastings 1985 JD
Administrative Assistant **Leslie Guevara** .... (212) 340-0401
E-mail: lguevara@courts.state.ny.us
Education: Marymount Col (NY) 1982 BS

Chambers of Associate Justice David Friedman

27 Madison Avenue, New York, NY 10010
Tel: (212) 340-0400
E-mail: dfriedman@nycourts.gov

David Friedman
Associate Justice

Date of Birth: 1950
Education: New York Law 1975 JD
Began Service: 1999
Appointed By: Governor George E. Pataki

Government: Law Assistant, New York Supreme Court, Appellate Division, Second Department (1976-1980); Law Secretary, New York Supreme Court (1981-1989)

Judicial: Civil Court (1990-1993); Acting Justice, Supreme Court (1994-1997); Supreme Court Justice (1998-1999)

Staff

Career Law Clerk **Daniel J. Fish** .... (212) 340-0400
E-mail: dfish@courts.state.ny.us
Education: Columbia 1988 JD
Secretary **David Morgenstern** .... (212) 340-0400
E-mail: david.morgenstern@nycourts.gov

Chambers of Associate Justice John W. Sweeny Jr.

27 Madison Avenue, New York, NY 10010
Tel: (212) 340-0450
E-mail: jsweeny@nycourts.gov

John W. Sweeny, Jr.
Associate Justice

Date of Birth: May 29, 1949
Education: Notre Dame 1971 AB; Fordham 1974 JD
Began Service: May 14, 2004
Appointed By: Governor George E. Pataki
Term Expires: December 31, 2027

Government: Administrative Assistant District Attorney, Office of the District Attorney, County of Putnam, New York (1976-1977)

Legal Practice: Associate, McCann, Ahern and Sommers (1974-1976); Confidential Law Secretary, John P. Donohoe J.S.C. (1976); Confidential Law Secretary, Fred A. Dickinson J.S.C. (1977-1986)

Current Memberships: American Association for Justice; New York State Bar Association; New York State Trial Lawyers Association

Staff

Principal Law Clerk **Joseph D. Cerreto** .... (212) 340-0450
E-mail: jcerreto@courts.state.ny.us
Education: Pace 1971 BA; Hofstra 1974 JD; Fordham 1993 MA
Secretary **Christine O'Donnell** .... (212) 340-0450
E-mail: codonnell@courts.state.ny.us

Chambers of Associate Justice Karla Moskowitz
27 Madison Avenue, New York, NY 10010
Tel: (212) 340-0515

Karla Moskowitz
Associate Justice

Education: Alfred 1963 BA; Columbia 1966 JD
Began Service: January 2, 2008
Political Affiliation: Democrat

Government: Assistant to the First Assistant Attorney General, Office of the Attorney General (Law Department), State of New York (1966-1970); Associate Counsel, Human Resources Administration/Department of Social Services, City of New York, New York (1970-1974); Assistant Counsel, Health and Hospitals Corporation, City of New York, New York (1974-1975); Hearing Officer, Department of Education, City of New York, New York (1976-1980)

Judicial: Administrative Law Judge, Health Department, State of New York (1978-1981)

Legal Practice: Counsel, Moskowitz and Moll (1975-1980)

Staff
Career Law Clerk **Laura Hogan** .... (212) 340-0515
Secretary **Kimberly Nickerson** .... (212) 340-0515
E-mail: knickerson@nycourts.gov

Chambers of Associate Justice Rolando T. Acosta
27 Madison Avenue, New York, NY 10010
Tel: (212) 340-0564
E-mail: racosta@nycourts.gov

Rolando T. Acosta
Associate Justice

Education: Columbia 1979 BA, 1982 JD
Began Service: January 7, 2008
Term Expires: 2016

Government: Attorney-in-Charge, Legal Aid Society of New York (1994-1995); Director of Government and Community Relations, Legal Aid Society of New York; Human Rights Commission Deputy Commissioner for Law Enforcement, City of New York, New York; Commissioner of Human Rights, City of New York, New York

Judicial: Judge, New York County; Acting Justice, New York Supreme Court

Staff
Staff Attorney **Adam Horowitz** .... (212) 340-0564
E-mail: ahorowitz@nycourts.gov
Staff Attorney **Rosali Vazquez** .... (212) 340-0564
E-mail: rvazquez@nycourts.gov

Chambers of Associate Justice Dianne Renwick
27 Madison Avenue, New York, NY 10010
Tel: (212) 340-0400
E-mail: drenwick@nycourts.gov

Dianne T. Renwick
Associate Justice

Education: Cornell 1982 BS; Cardozo 1987 JD
Began Service: 2008

Chambers of Associate Justice Rosalyn H. Richter
27 Madison Avenue, New York, NY 10010
Tel: (212) 340-0400
E-mail: rrichter@nycourts.gov

Rosalyn H. Richter
Associate Justice

Education: Barnard 1976 BA; Brooklyn Law 1979 JD
Began Service: March 19, 2009
Appointed By: Governor David A. Paterson

Government: Supervising Assistant District Attorney, Kings County District Attorney, City of New York, New York (1983-1987)

Judicial: Administrative Law Judge, Office of Administrative Trials and Hearings (1987-1990); Judge, New York City Criminal Court (1990-2003); Associate Justice, Civil Court, New York County Court, New York Supreme Court, Appellate Division, First Department (2003-2009)

Staff
Law Secretary **Thomas Hickey** .... (212) 340-0400
Began Service: March 19, 2009
E-mail: thickey@nycourts.gov
Law Secretary **Shannon Henderson** .... (212) 340-0400
Began Service: October 25, 2012
E-mail: shenderson@nycourts.gov

Chambers of Associate Justice Sallie Manzanet-Daniels
27 Madison Avenue, New York, NY 10010
Tel: (212) 340-0400

Sallie Manzanet-Daniels
Associate Justice

Education: Marymount Col (NY) 1985; Hofstra 1988 JD
Began Service: September 25, 2009
Appointed By: Governor David A. Paterson

Chambers of Associate Justice Paul G. Feinman
27 Madison Avenue, New York, NY 10010
Tel: (212) 340-0400
E-mail: pfeinman@nycourts.gov

Paul G. Feinman
Associate Justice

Education: Columbia 1981 BA; Minnesota 1985 JD
Began Service: October 9, 2012

Staff
Principal Law Clerk **Julia P. Herd** .... (212) 340-0400
E-mail: jherd@nycourts.gov

Chambers of Associate Justice Judith J. Gische
27 Madison Avenue, New York, NY 10010
Tel: (212) 340-0400
E-mail: jgische@nycourts.gov

Judith J. Gische
Associate Justice

Education: SUNY Col (Buffalo) 1977 BA, 1980 JD
Began Service: 2012

Chambers of Associate Justice Darcel D. Clark
27 Madison Avenue, New York, NY 10010
Tel: (212) 340-0400
E-mail: ddclark@nycourts.gov

Darcel D. Clark
Associate Justice

Education: Boston Col 1983 BA; Howard U 1986 JD
Began Service: October 1, 2012

Chambers of Associate Justice Barbara R. Kapnick
27 Madison Avenue, New York, NY 10010
Tel: (212) 340-0400
E-mail: bkapnick@nycourts.gov

Barbara Kapnick
Associate Justice

New York Supreme Court, Appellate Division, Second Department
45 Monroe Place, Brooklyn, NY 11201
Tel: (718) 875-1300 Fax: (718) 858-2446

Number of Judgeships: 19

Areas Covered: Counties of Dutchess, Kings, Nassau, Orange, Putnam, Queens, Richmond, Rockland, Suffolk and Westchester

Court Staff
Clerk of the Court **Aprilanne Agostino** . . . . (718) 722-6307
E-mail: aagostino@courts.state.ny.us
Education: Fordham 1984 JD
Deputy Clerk **Mel E. Harris** . . . . (718) 722-6308
E-mail: mharris@courts.state.ny.us
Education: Brooklyn Law 1969 JD
Deputy Clerk **Karen Hochberg Tommer** . . . . (718) 722-6308
E-mail: ktommer@courts.state.ny.us
Deputy Clerk **Kenneth Band** . . . . (718) 722-6308
E-mail: kband@courts.state.ny.us
Associate Deputy Clerk **Maria Fasulo** . . . . (718) 722-6308
E-mail: mfasulo@courts.state.ny.us
Associate Deputy Clerk **Darrell Joseph** . . . . (718) 722-6308
E-mail: djoseph@courts.state.ny.us
Education: MIT 1983 SB; Pace 1986 JD
Principal Law Librarian **Bruce Bosso** . . . . (718) 722-6356
E-mail: bbosso@nysad2d.org Fax: (718) 722-6302
Education: Pratt Inst 1993 MLS

Chambers of Presiding Justice Randall T. Eng
45 Monroe Place, Brooklyn, NY 11201
Tel: (718) 298-1555 Fax: (718) 520-3557
E-mail: reng@courts.state.ny.us

Randall T. Eng
Presiding Justice

Education: SUNY (Buffalo) 1969 BA; St John's U (NY) 1972 JD
Began Service: 2012

Staff
Career Law Clerk **Wendy Cohen** . . . . (718) 298-1555
E-mail: wcohen@courts.state.ny.us
Education: SUNY (Buffalo) 1984 JD
Secretary **Iris Guzman** . . . . (718) 298-1555
E-mail: iguzman@courts.state.ny.us

Chambers of Associate Justice Justice William F. Mastro
60 Bay Street, Staten Island, NY 10301
Tel: (718) 675-8680 Fax: (718) 816-4587
E-mail: wmastro@courts.state.ny.us

William F. Mastro
Associate Justice

Education: Villanova 1972; New York Law 1977 JD
Began Service: June 7, 2002
Appointed By: Governor George E. Pataki

Staff
Career Law Clerk **Terence Henchey** . . . . (718) 675-8680
E-mail: thenchey@courts.state.ny.us
Secretary **Phyllis Brownfield** . . . . (718) 675-8680

Chambers of Associate Justice Reinaldo E. Rivera
45 Monroe Place, Brooklyn, NY 11201
Tel: (718) 722-6486 Fax: (646) 963-6449
E-mail: rrivera@courts.state.ny.us

Reinaldo E. Rivera
Associate Justice

Education: St Peter's Col 1973; St John's U (NY) 1976 JD; Columbia 1977 LLM
Began Service: June 11, 2002
Appointed By: Governor George E. Pataki
Term Expires: December 31, 2019

Academic: Adjunct Professor, St. John's University School of Law

Judicial: Justice, New York Supreme Court, Second Judicial District (1992-2002)

Military Service: Lieutenant Colonel, New York Guard

Staff
Career Law Clerk **Maria E. Martí** . . . . (718) 722-6486
E-mail: mmarti@courts.state.ny.us
Education: St John's U (NY) 1993 JD
Secretary **Danielle Boyce** . . . . (718) 722-6486

Chambers of Associate Justice Mark C. Dillon
45 Monroe Place, Brooklyn, NY 11201
Tel: (718) 875-1300
E-mail: mdillon@courts.state.ny.us

Mark C. Dillon
Associate Justice

Education: Colgate 1981 BA; Fordham 1984 JD; NYU 1990 MA
Began Service: August 25, 2005
Appointed By: Governor George E. Pataki
Term Expires: December 30, 2027

Government: Assistant District Attorney, Office of the District Attorney, County of Westchester, New York (1985-1987)

Judicial: County Court Judge, County of Westchester, New York (1997); Justice, New York Supreme Court, Appellate Term, Second Judicial Department, 9th & 10th Judicial Districts (1999-2005)

Legal Practice: Attorney, Cerussi & Spring (1988-1997); Partner, Dillon & Sarcone, LLP (1998-1999)

Chambers of Associate Justice Ruth C. Balkin

Nassau County Supreme Courthouse, 100 Supreme Court Drive, Mineola, NY 11501
Tel: (516) 403-2473
E-mail: rbalkin@nycourts.gov

Ruth C. Balkin
Associate Justice

Education: Adelphi 1973 BA; St John's U (NY) 1976 JD
Began Service: January 2007
Term Expires: 2018

Judicial: Judge, Nassau County Family Court, County of Nassau, New York (1995-2004); Presiding Judge, Nassau County Family Court, County of Nassau, New York (2002-2004); Supervising Judge, Nassau County Family Court, County of Nassau, New York (2003-2004)

Legal Practice: Partner, Sutter, Balkin, Marten & Regan (1984-1986); Associate, Meyer, Suozzi, English, and Klein, PC (1986-1987)

Staff

Law Secretary **Jay L. Weiner** . . . . . (718) 722-6406
E-mail: jweiner@nycourts.gov
Education: Dartmouth 1981 AB; Fordham 1984 JD

Secretary **Lisa Carlisi** . . . . . (516) 403-2473
E-mail: lcarlisi@nycourts.gov

Chambers of Associate Justice Thomas A. Dickerson

111 Dr. Martin Luther King Jr. Blvd., White Plains, NY 10601
Tel: (718) 875-1300

Thomas A. Dickerson
Associate Justice

Education: Colgate 1969 BA; Cornell 1973 JD, 1973 MBA
Began Service: January 2007

Government: Councilman, Office of the City Council, City of Yonkers, New York (1989-1993)

Judicial: City Court Judge, City of Yonkers, New York (1994-1999); County Court Judge, County of Westchester, New York (2000-2002)

Legal Practice: Associate, Kaye Scholer LLP (1974-1975); Associate, Shea & Gould (1975-1977)

Profession: Private Practice (1977-1993)

Staff

Principal Law Secretary **Jonathan Glenn** . . . . . (718) 722-6423
E-mail: jglenn@courts.state.ny.us

Secretary **Laura Puja** . . . . . (914) 824-5405
E-mail: lpuja@courts.state.ny.us

Chambers of Associate Justice John M. Leventhal

45 Monroe Place, Brooklyn, NY 11201
Tel: (718) 722-6350

John M. Leventhal
Associate Justice

Education: Case Western BA; Hunter MS; Brooklyn Law JD
Began Service: 2008

Judicial: Associate Justice, New York Supreme Court, Appellate Term, Second Judicial Department, 2nd & 11th Judicial Districts

Legal Practice: Attorney, Private Practice (1982-1994)

Staff

Career Law Clerk **Ben Darvil** . . . . . (718) 722-6350
E-mail: bdarvil@courts.state.ny.us

Chambers of Associate Justice Cheryl E. Chambers

45 Monroe Place, Brooklyn, NY 11201
Tel: (718) 722-6310
E-mail: cchambers@courts.state.ny.us

Cheryl E. Chambers
Associate Justice

Education: Brooklyn 1973 BA; Boston U 1976 JD; Rutgers 1984 MBA
Began Service: February 2008

Government: Domestic Violence Bureau Chief, Kings County District Attorney; Criminal Court and Trial Bureaus Deputy Chief, Kings County District Attorney

Judicial: Judge, Civil Court of the City of New York (1995-1998); Judge, Criminal Court of the City of New York (1995-1998)

Staff

Principal Law Clerk **Michael Carinci** . . . . . (347) 296-1041
E-mail: mcarinci@courts.state.ny.us

Secretary **Audrey Ervin** . . . . . (347) 296-1040
E-mail: aervin@courts.state.ny.us

Chambers of Associate Justice Leonard B. Austin

45 Monroe Place, Brooklyn, NY 11201
Tel: (718) 875-1300
E-mail: laustin@courts.state.ny.us

Leonard B. Austin
Associate Justice

Education: Georgetown 1974 BE; Hofstra 1977 JD
Began Service: March 19, 2009
Term Expires: December 31, 2024

Judicial: Judge, Tenth Judicial District, New York Supreme Court Judicial Districts, New York (1998-1999); Judge, Dedicated Matrimonial Part, Suffolk County Court, New York (1999-2000); Judge, Dedicated Commercial Part, Nassau County Court, New York (2000-2009)

Current Memberships: The Florida Bar; New York State Bar Association

Chambers of Associate Justice L. Priscilla Hall

45 Monroe Place, Brooklyn, NY 11201
Tel: (718) 875-1300
E-mail: lhall@courts.state.ny.us

L. Priscilla Hall
Associate Justice

Education: Howard U 1968 JD; Columbia 1969, 1973 JD
Began Service: March 19, 2009

Government: Assistant District Attorney, New York County District Attorney, City of New York, New York (1974-1979); Inspector General, Human Resources Administration/Department of Social Services (1979-1982); Assistant Attorney General, Labor Department, State of New York (1982)

Judicial: Judge, New York City Criminal Court (1986-1990); Judge, New York State Court of Claims (1990-1994)

Chambers of Associate Justice Sheri S. Roman
45 Monroe Place, Brooklyn, NY 11201
Tel: (718) 875-1300 Fax: (718) 858-2446
E-mail: sroman@courts.state.ny.us

Sheri S. Roman
Associate Justice

Education: Buffalo 1969 BA; Georgetown 1972 JD; NYU 1976 LLM
Began Service: July 2009

Government: Bureau Chief of the Supreme Court, Bronx County District Attorney, City of New York, New York

Judicial: Judge, Criminal Court of the City of New York, Criminal Court of the City of New York, City of New York, New York (1985-1994); Justice, Queens County, New York Supreme Court, Criminal Term; Justice, Queens County, New York Supreme Court, Civil Term; Acting Justice, Queens County, New York Supreme Court, Criminal Term (1992-1995)

Current Memberships: Queens County Bar Association; Women's Bar Association of the State of New York

Chambers of Associate Justice Sandra L. Sgroi
400 Carleton Avenue, Central Islip, NY 11722
Tel: (631) 583-5138
E-mail: ssgroi@courts.state.ny.us

Sandra L. Sgroi
Associate Justice

Education: SUNY (Buffalo State Col) 1974 BA; Hofstra 1978 JD
Began Service: October 15, 2009
Appointed By: Governor David A. Paterson

Chambers of Associate Justice Jeffrey A. Cohen
45 Monroe Place, Brooklyn, NY 11201
Tel: (718) 875-1300
E-mail: jcohen@courts.state.ny.us

Jeffrey A. Cohen
Associate Justice

Education: NYU 1971 BA; Rutgers 1975 JD
Began Service: 2010

Chambers of Associate Justice Robert J. Miller
45 Monroe Place, Brooklyn, NY 11201
Tel: (718) 875-1300
E-mail: rmiller@courts.state.ny.us

Robert J. Miller
Associate Justice

Education: Brooklyn 1971 BA; Georgetown 1974 JD
Began Service: 2010

Chambers of Associate Justice Sylvia O. Hinds-Radix
45 Monroe Place, Brooklyn, NY 11201
Tel: (718) 875-1300
E-mail: sylvia.hindsradix@nycourts.gov

Sylvia O. Hinds-Radix
Associate Justice

Education: Howard U

Current Memberships: National Association of Women Judges; New York State Association of Supreme Court Justices

Chambers of Associate Justice Colleen Duffy
45 Monroe Place, Brooklyn, NY 11201
Tel: (718) 875-1300
E-mail: cduffy@courts.state.ny.us

Colleen Duffy
Associate Justice

Began Service: 2014
Appointed By: Governor Andrew Cuomo

Chambers of Associate Justice Hector D. LaSalle
45 Monroe Place, Brooklyn, NY 11201
Tel: (718) 875-1300
E-mail: hlasalle@courts.state.ny.us

Hector D. LaSalle
Associate Justice

Began Service: 2014
Appointed By: Governor Andrew Cuomo

Chambers of Associate Justice Joseph J. Maltese
45 Monroe Place, Brooklyn, NY 11201
Tel: (718) 875-1300
E-mail: jmaltese@courts.state.ny.us

Joseph J. Maltese
Associate Justice

Began Service: 2014
Appointed By: Governor Andrew Cuomo

Chambers of Associate Justice Betsy Barros
45 Monroe Place, Brooklyn, NY 11201
Tel: (718) 875-1300

Betsy Barros
Associate Justice

Education: Cornell 1979 BA; NYU 1982 JD
Began Service: 2014
Appointed By: Governor Andrew Cuomo

New York Supreme Court, Appellate Division, Third Department
P.O. Box 7288, Capitol Station, Albany, NY 12224-0288
Tel: (518) 471-4777 Fax: (518) 471-4750

Number of Judgeships: 10

Areas Covered: Counties of Albany, Broome, Chemung, Chenango, Clinton, Columbia, Cortland, Delaware, Essex, Franklin, Fulton, Greene, Hamilton, Madison, Montgomery, Otsego, Rensselaer, St. Lawrence, Saratoga, Schenectady, Schoharie, Schuyler, Sullivan, Tioga, Tompkins, Ulster, Warren and Washington

Court Staff
Clerk of the Court **Robert D. Mayberger** . . . . (518) 471-4777
E-mail: rmayberg@courts.state.ny.us
Education: Albany Law 1978 JD
Deputy Clerk **Sean M. Morton** . . . . (518) 471-4777
Education: UMass (Boston) 1991 BS; Albany Law 2001 JD
Chief Appellate Court Attorney **Beth Lifshin** . . . . (518) 471-4777
E-mail: blifshin@courts.state.ny.us

STATE COURTS—NEW YORK

Chambers of Presiding Justice Karen K. Peters

281 Wall Street, Kingston, NY 12401-3817
Tel: (845) 481-9333
E-mail: kpeters@courts.state.ny.us

Karen K. Peters
Presiding Justice

Date of Birth: 1947
Education: George Washington 1969 BA; NYU 1972 JD
Began Service: 2012
Political Affiliation: Democrat

Current Memberships: Association of Justices of the Supreme Court of the State of New York; National Association for the Advancement of Colored People; New York State Bar Association; Ulster County Bar Association; Women's Bar Association of the State of New York

Staff
Career Law Clerk **Anthony Beccari** .... (845) 481-9333
Confidential Secretary **Laura J. Cepeda** .... (845) 481-9333
E-mail: lcepeda@courts.state.ny.us
Special Projects Counsel **(Vacant)** .... (845) 481-9333

Chambers of Associate Justice Robert S. Rose

Broome County Courthouse, Binghamton, NY 13902-1766
Tel: (607) 240-5906 Fax: (607) 240-5939
E-mail: rrose@nycourts.gov

Robert S. Rose
Associate Justice

Date of Birth: 1943
Education: St Lawrence 1965 BA; Albany Law 1968 JD
Began Service: March 2000
Appointed By: Governor George E. Pataki
Term Expires: December 31, 2015
Political Affiliation: Republican

Clerkships: Confidential Law Clerk The Honorable Justice Robert E. Fischer (1974-1976)

Government: Assistant District Attorney, Office of the District Attorney, County of Broome, New York (1976-1978); Commissioner, Elections Board, County of Broome, New York (1985-1987)

Judicial: Justice, New York Supreme Court (1988-2000); Administrative Judge, 6th Judicial District (1999-2000)

Legal Practice: Partner, Twining, Nemia, Hill & Steflik

Military Service: United States Army (1969-1972)

Current Memberships: Association of Justices of the Supreme Court of the State of New York; Broome County Bar Association; New York State Bar Association

Staff
Fax: (607) 240-5939

Career Law Clerk **Michael T. Snyder** .... (607) 240-5906
E-mail: mtsnyder@nycourts.gov

Chambers of Associate Justice John A. Lahtinen

36 Oak Street, Plattsburgh, NY 12901
P.O. Box 38, Plattsburgh, NY 12901
Tel: (518) 562-1446 Fax: (518) 562-1792
E-mail: jlahtine@nycourts.gov

John A. Lahtinen
Associate Justice

Education: Colgate 1967 BA; Albany Law 1970 JD
Began Service: March 6, 2000

Government: Law Secretary, Justice Norman L. Harvey, New York Supreme Court (1970-1975); Town Attorney, Office of the Town Attorney, Town of Schuyler Falls, New York (1971-1973); (Acting) Special District Attorney, Office of the District Attorney, County of Clinton, New York (1972); Legal Advisor, Selective Service System (1974-1976); Attorney, Board of Education, Peru Central School District

Judicial: Special Acting Judge, Plattsburgh City Court, 4th Judicial District (1979)

Staff
Law Clerk **Dana Peck** .... (518) 562-1446
E-mail: dpeck@nycourts.gov
Secretary **Julie Timmons** .... (518) 562-1446
E-mail: jtimmons@nycourts.gov

Chambers of Associate Justice William E. McCarthy

16 Eagle Street, Albany, NY 12207
Tel: (518) 285-8986

William E. McCarthy
Associate Justice

Education: SUNY (Potsdam) 1985 BA; Albany Law 1988 JD
Began Service: January 30, 2009

Current Memberships: Albany County Bar Association; Connecticut Bar Association, Inc.; New York State Bar Association

Staff
Career Law Clerk **Matthew Side** .... (518) 285-8986
E-mail: mside@courts.state.ny.us
Secretary **Laura Warner** .... (518) 285-8986
E-mail: lwarner@courts.state.ny.us

Chambers of Associate Justice Elizabeth A. Garry

6 East Main Street, Suite 201, Norwich, NY 13815
Tel: (607) 337-1724 Fax: (607) 337-1722
E-mail: egarry@courts.state.ny.us

Elizabeth A. Garry
Associate Justice

Education: Alfred 1984; Albany Law 1990 JD
Began Service: March 19, 2009

Staff
Principal Law Clerk **Catherine F. Murphy** .... (607) 337-1724
E-mail: cmurphy@courts.state.ny.us

Chambers of Associate Justice John C. Egan

16 Eagle Street, Albany, NY 12207
Tel: (518) 471-4777
E-mail: jegan@courts.state.ny.us

John C. Egan, Jr.
Associate Justice

Education: Bryant Col 1976 BS; Albany Law 1980 JD
Began Service: January 2010
Appointed By: Governor David A. Paterson

Chambers of Associate Justice Michael C. Lynch
P.O. Box 7344, Albany, NY 12224
Tel: (518) 471-4777

Michael C. Lynch
Justice

Began Service: 2014
Appointed By: Governor Andrew Cuomo

Staff
Law Clerk **Amy Joyce** .... (518) 471-4777

Chambers of Associate Justice Eugene P. Devine
P.O. Box 7344, Albany, NY 12224
Tel: (518) 471-4777

Eugene P. Devine
Justice

Began Service: 2014
Appointed By: Governor Andrew Cuomo

Staff
Law Clerk **Rebecca Chancy** .... (518) 471-4777

Chambers of Associate Justice Christine M. Clark
P.O. Box 7344, Albany, NY 12224
Tel: (518) 471-4777

Christine M. Clark
Justice

Began Service: 2014
Appointed By: Governor Andrew Cuomo

Staff
Law Clerk **Erica Putnam** .... (518) 471-4777

New York Supreme Court, Appellate Division, Fourth Department
50 East Avenue, Suite 200, Rochester, NY 14604
Tel: (585) 530-3100 Fax: (585) 530-3247
Internet: http://www.nycourts.gov/courts/ad4/

Number of Judgeships: 11

Areas Covered: Counties of Allegany, Cattaraugus, Cayuga, Chautauqua, Erie, Genesee, Herkimer, Jefferson, Lewis, Livingston, Monroe, Niagara, Oneida, Onondaga, Ontario, Orleans, Oswego, Seneca, Steuben, Wayne, Wyoming and Yates

Court Staff
Clerk of the Court **Frances Cafarell** .... (585) 530-3101
E-mail: fcafarell@courts.state.ny.us Fax: (585) 530-3246
Deputy Clerk **Alan L. Ross** .... (585) 530-3102
E-mail: aross@courts.state.ny.us
Consultation Clerk **(Vacant)** .... (585) 530-3163
Fax: (585) 530-3248
Librarian **Betsy Vipperman** .... (585) 530-3250
Fax: (585) 530-3270
Management Analyst **Mark Lee** .... (585) 530-3100
Fax: (585) 530-3015
Sergeant **Anthony Ognifffenti** .... (585) 530-3290

Chambers of Presiding Justice Henry J. Scudder
19 East Pulteney Square, Bath, NY 14810
50 East Avenue, Suite 200, Rochester, NY 14604
Tel: (607) 622-8250 Tel: (585) 530-3200 (Rochester Chambers)
Fax: (607) 776-7168
E-mail: hscudder@nycourts.gov

Henry J. Scudder
Presiding Justice

Date of Birth: 1945
Education: Tennessee 1969 JD
Began Service: 1999
Appointed By: Governor George E. Pataki
Term Expires: December 31, 2024
Political Affiliation: Republican

Government: Assistant District Attorney, County of Steuben, New York (1972-1977); First Assistant District Attorney, County of Steuben, New York (1977-1979); County Surrogate (1982-1986)

Legal Practice: Scudder, McCarthy and Plaskov, PC

Military Service: United States Army Reserve, United States Department of the Army

Staff
Career Law Clerk **Mary Hope Benedict** .... (607) 622-8253
E-mail: mhbenedi@nycourts.gov
Education: Le Moyne 1982 BS; SUNY (Buffalo) 1986 JD
Career Law Clerk **Jennifer Powers Iacobucci** .... (585) 530-3215
E-mail: jiacobuc@nycourts.gov
Education: SUNY (Binghamton) 1992 BS; Syracuse 1995 JD
Executive Assistant **James Mulley** .... (585) 530-3165
E-mail: jmulley@nycourts.gov Fax: (585) 530-3245
Secretary **Katherine Hoffman** .... (607) 622-8252
E-mail: kahoffma@nycourts.gov

Chambers of Associate Justice Nancy E. Smith
50 East Avenue, Rochester, NY 14604-2214
Tel: (585) 530-3280 Fax: (585) 530-3193
E-mail: nesmith@courts.state.ny.us

Nancy E. Smith
Associate Justice

Date of Birth: 1954
Education: Allegheny 1976 BA; Vermont 1980 JD
Began Service: March 4, 1999
Appointed By: Governor George E. Pataki
Next Election: November 2025
Term Expires: December 31, 2025

Academic: Instructor, Criminal Justice Training Center (1986-1992)

Government: Assistant District Attorney, County of Monroe, New York (1982-1988); Special District Attorney, County of Monroe, New York (1988-1992); Instructor, Prosecutor's Course, Criminal Justice Services Division, State of New York (1989-1992)

Judicial: Judge, Monroe County (1993-1997); Acting County Court Judge, Sullivan County (1993); Acting Family Court Judge, Livingston County (1993-1995); Acting County Court Judge, Livingston County (1993-1997); Acting County Court Judge, Yates County (1994); Acting County Court Judge, Saratoga County (1995); Acting County Court Judge, Rensselaer County (1996); Acting County Court Judge, Ontario County (1996); Acting Family Court Judge, Monroe County (1996-1998); Supreme Court Justice, New York State Seventh Judicial District (1997-1999); Acting Supreme Court Justice, New York State Fifth Judicial District (1997); Acting Supreme Court Justice, New York State Ninth Judicial District (1998)

Legal Practice: Associate, Greisberger, Zicari, McConville, Cooman, Morin & Welch, P.C. (1984-1985)

Nonprofit: Instructor, The New York State Bar Association (1994-1996)

(continued on next page)

STATE COURTS—NEW YORK

Chambers of Associate Justice Nancy E. Smith *continued*

Current Memberships: Monroe County Bar Association (NY); National Association of Women Judges; New York State Bar Association; Women's Bar Association of the State of New York

Staff

Career Law Clerk **James Stevenson** . . . . (585) 530-3280
E-mail: jdsteven@courts.state.ny.us
Education: SUNY (Albany) 1978 BA; San Diego 1982 JD

Secretary **Lori Quayle** . . . . (585) 530-3280
E-mail: lquayle@courts.state.ny.us

Chambers of Associate Justice John V. Centra

Onondaga County Courthouse, 401 Montgomery Street, Room 401, Syracuse, NY 13202-2127
Tel: (315) 671-1105
E-mail: jcentra@courts.state.ny.us

John V. Centra
Associate Justice

Education: SUNY (Buffalo); Ohio Northern JD
Began Service: October 2006
Appointed By: Governor George E. Pataki

Government: Assistant District Attorney, County of Onondaga, New York; Town Justice, Town of DeWitt, New York (1988-1998)

Legal Practice: Attorney, Carni, Centra & Rose (1989-1991); Attorney, Primo, Primo & Centra (1992-1997); Attorney, Primo, Primo, Centra & Kirwan, LLP (1998-1999)

Current Memberships: New York State Bar Association; New York State Magistrates Association; New York State Trial Lawyers Association

Membership: Past Delegate, New York State Supreme Court Justices Association; Past President, New York State Magistrates Association

Staff

Law Clerk **Colleen Farrell** . . . . (315) 671-1105
E-mail: cfarrell@courts.state.ny.us
Education: SUNY (Buffalo) 1997 JD

Chambers of Associate Justice Erin M. Perradotto

50 East Avenue, Rochester, NY 14604
Tel: (716) 845-9360

Erin M. Peradotto
Associate Justice

Education: SUNY (Buffalo) 1981 BA, 1984 JD
Began Service: December 2006
Appointed By: Governor George E. Pataki

Government: Assistant Attorney General, Office of the Attorney General (Law Department), State of New York (1997-1998)

Legal Practice: Attorney, Private Practice

Current Memberships: New York State Supreme Court Justices Association

Membership: President, Erie County Bar Association (NY) (1997-1998); Past Delegate, House of Delegates, The New York State Bar Association; Past Director, Women Lawyers of Western New York; Member, Attorney Grievance Committee for the 8th Judicial District, State of New York (2001-2003)

Staff

Law Clerk **Elizabeth Fox-Solomon** . . . . (716) 845-9360
Education: SUNY (Buffalo) 2006 JD

Chambers of Associate Justice Edward D. Carni

Onondaga County Supreme Courthouse, 401 Montgomery Street, Room 409, Syracuse, NY 13202-2127
Tel: (315) 671-1117
E-mail: ecarni@courts.state.ny.us

Edward D. Carni
Associate Justice

Education: SUNY (Cortland) 1982 BA; Whittier 1985 JD
Began Service: December 2006
Term Expires: December 31, 2015

Profession: Private Practice (1986-2001)

Staff

Confidential Principal Law Clerk **John Short** . . . . (315) 671-1108
E-mail: jshort@courts.state.ny.us

Secretary **Erika Gallucci** . . . . (315) 671-1108

Chambers of Associate Justice Stephen K. Lindley

50 East Avenue, Rochester, NY 14604
Tel: (585) 530-3227
E-mail: slindley@courts.state.ny.us

Stephen K. Lindley
Associate Justice

Education: Emory 1986 BS; Buffalo 1989 JD
Began Service: 2010
Appointed By: Governor David A. Paterson

Staff

Career Law Clerk **William Clauss** . . . . (585) 530-3227
E-mail: wclauss@courts.state.ny.us

Chambers of Associate Justice Rose H. Sconiers

50 East Avenue, Rochester, NY 14604
Tel: (585) 530-3100

Rose H. Sconiers
Associate Justice

Education: Long Island 1960 BA; SUNY (Buffalo) 1973 JD
Began Service: January 2010

Staff

Law Clerk **John Ziegler** . . . . (716) 845-9495
E-mail: jziegler@courts.state.ny.us

Chambers of Associate Justice Joseph D. Valentino

50 East Avenue, Rochester, NY 14604
Tel: (585) 530-3100
E-mail: jvalentino@courts.state.ny.us

Joseph D. Valentino
Justice

Education: Niagara; St John's U (NY) JD
Began Service: 2012
Appointed By: Governor Andrew Cuomo

Chambers of Associate Justice Gerald J. Whalen

50 East Avenue, Rochester, NY 14604
Tel: (585) 530-3100
E-mail: gwhalen@courts.state.ny.us

Gerald J. Whalen
Associate Justice

Appointed By: Governor Andrew Cuomo

Chambers of Associate Justice Brian F. DeJoseph
50 East Avenue, Rochester, NY 14604
Tel: (585) 530-3100

Brian F. DeJoseph
Associate Justice

Education: Syracuse 1972 BA, 1975 JD
Began Service: 2014
Appointed By: Governor Andrew Cuomo

New York Supreme Court, Appellate Term

The Appellate Term of Supreme Court, which was established by the New York Supreme Court Appellate Division, exercises jurisdiction over civil and criminal appeals from various local courts and certain criminal appeals from County Courts in the Second Judicial Department. Appeals from the Appellate Term are to the Supreme Court Appellate Division in civil matters and to the New York Court of Appeals in criminal matters.

New York Supreme Court, Appellate Term, First Judicial Department, 1st and 12th Judicial Districts
60 Centre Street, New York, NY 10007
Tel: (646) 386-3040

Number of Judgeships: 5

Number of Vacancies: 1

Areas Covered: Counties of Bronx and New York

Court Staff
Clerk of the Court **Frank Polizano** . . . . (646) 386-5955
Chief Court Attorney **(Vacant)** . . . . (646) 386-5955

Chambers of Presiding Justice Richard B. Lowe III
100 Centre Street, Room 1735, New York, NY 10007
Tel: (646) 646-3259
E-mail: rlowe@courts.state.ny.us

Richard B. Lowe III
Presiding Justice

Began Service: 2011

Chambers of Associate Justice Martin Schoenfeld
60 Centre Street, Room 609, New York, NY 10007
Tel: (646) 386-3232 Fax: (212) 374-5622
E-mail: mschoenf@courts.state.ny.us

Martin Schoenfeld
Associate Justice

Date of Birth: 1947
Education: Brooklyn 1968; Syracuse 1971 JD
Began Service: March 2002

Academic: Brooklyn Law School Trial Advocy Program

Clerkships: Principal Law Clerk The Honorable Jerome W. Marks (1979-1984)

Government: Court Attorney, New York Supreme Court

Legal Practice: Attorney, Rogers, Kaufman & Shenkman, P.C. (1972-1978)

Current Memberships: The Association of the Bar of the City of New York; New York State Bar Association

Chambers of Associate Justice Martin Schoenfeld *continued*

Staff
Assistant Law Clerk **William Shepard** . . . . (646) 386-3232
Began Service: January 2012
E-mail: wshepard@courts.state.ny.us
Education: Lehigh 2007 BA; New York Law 2011 JD
Principal Law Clerk **Laura Diamond** . . . . (646) 386-3232
Principal Law Clerk **Monica Selter** . . . . (646) 386-3232
E-mail: mselter@courts.state.ny.us

Chambers of Associate Justice Alexander W. Hunter, Jr.
60 Centre Street, New York, NY 10007
Tel: (646) 386-3040
E-mail: ahunter@courts.state.ny.us

Alexander W. Hunter, Jr.
Associate Judge

Education: Temple 1971 BA; SUNY (Buffalo State Col) 1974 JD
Began Service: August 2009

Clerkships: First Principal Law Clerk, First Judical District, New York Supreme Court Judicial Districts (1978-1986)

Judicial: Judge, New York City Criminal Court (1986-1993); Acting Justice of Supreme Court, Bronx County, New York Supreme Court, Criminal Term (1993-1994); Justice, Bronx County, New York Supreme Court, Criminal Term (1995-2009)

Chambers of Associate Justice Martin Shulman
111 Centre Street, New York, NY 10013
Tel: (646) 386-5687
E-mail: mshulman@courts.state.ny.us

Martin Shulman
Associate Justice

Education: Yeshiva 1978 BA; Cardozo 1981 JD
Began Service: 2009

Staff
Law Secretary **Joanne Balecha** . . . . (646) 386-5687
E-mail: jbalecha@courts.state.ny.us
Law Secretary **Melinda P. Lisanti** . . . . (646) 386-5688
E-mail: mlisanti@courts.state.ny.us

New York Supreme Court, Appellate Term, Second Judicial Department
141 Livingston Street, 15th Floor, Brooklyn, NY 11201
Tel: (347) 401-9580

Number of Judgeships: 10

Areas Covered: Counties of Dutchess, Kings, Nassau, Orange, Putnam, Queens, Richmond, Rockland, Suffolk and Westchester

Court Staff
Chief Clerk of Court **Paul Kenny** . . . . (347) 401-9580
E-mail: pkenny@courts.state.ny.us
Education: CUNY 1986 JD
Deputy Chief Clerk **Jennifer Chan** . . . . (347) 401-9580
E-mail: jennifer.chan@nycourts.gov

STATE COURTS—NEW YORK

New York Supreme Court, Appellate Term, Second Judicial Department, 2nd, 11th and 13th Judicial Districts

141 Livingston Street, 15th Floor, Brooklyn, NY 11201
Tel: (347) 401-9580

Number of Judgeships: 5

Areas Covered: Counties of Kings, Queens and Richmond

Court Staff
Chief Clerk of Court **Paul Kenny** . . . . (347) 401-9580
E-mail: pkenny@courts.state.ny.us
Chief Deputy Clerk **Jennifer Chan** . . . . (347) 401-9580
E-mail: jennifer.chan@nycourts.gov

Chambers of Presiding Justice Michael L. Pesce

Civic Center, 360 Adams Street, Room 1173, Brooklyn, NY 11201
Tel: (347) 296-1007 Fax: (718) 643-8753
E-mail: mpesce@nycourts.gov

Michael L. Pesce
Presiding Justice

Education: Detroit Law 1969 JD
Began Service: February 11, 2002

Government: Legal Aid Society, Civil Division (1969-1972); Member, New York State Assembly (1973-1980)

Judicial: Judge, New York City Civil Court (1981-1983); Acting Supreme Court Justice, New York Supreme Court (1984-1989); Administrative Judge, New York Supreme Court, Second Judicial District (1996-2002)

Legal Practice: Private Practice (1976-1980)

Staff
Career Law Clerk **Margherita Racanelli** . . . . (347) 296-1008
E-mail: mracanel@nycourts.gov
Education: Seton Hall 2007 JD
Confidential Secretary **Celina Collado** . . . . (347) 296-1007
E-mail: ccollado@nycourts.gov

Chambers of Associate Justice Michelle Weston

Civic Center, 360 Adams Street, Brooklyn, NY 11201
Tel: (347) 296-1480
E-mail: mweston@nycourts.gov

Michelle Weston
Associate Justice

Education: St John's U (NY) 1973; Rutgers 1976 JD
Began Service: 1991
Next Election: 2018
Term Expires: 2018

Academic: Adjunct Faculty, New York City Technical College; Adjunct Professor, College of New Rochelle

Government: Trial Attorney, Criminal Defense Division, Legal Aid Society (1976); Administrative Law Judge, Office of Children and Family Services, State of New York

Judicial: Judge, Brooklyn Criminal Court (1989-1990)

Current Memberships: Association of Justices of the Supreme Court of the State of New York; Brooklyn Bar Association; Kings County Judges' Association; Metropolitan Black Bar Association; New York State Bar Association

Staff
Career Law Clerk **Cristina Baiata Martinez** . . . . (347) 296-1480
Education: Brooklyn Law 1995 JD
Career Law Clerk **Iris Cross** . . . . (347) 296-1480
E-mail: icross@nycourts.gov
Education: Pennsylvania 1989 JD

Chambers of Associate Justice Michelle Weston *continued*
Secretary **Marie Nyman** . . . . (347) 296-1480
E-mail: mnyman@nycourts.gov

Chambers of Associate Justice Thomas P. Aliotta

18 Richmond Terrace, Staten Island, NY 10301
Tel: (718) 675-8620
E-mail: taliotta@courts.state.ny.us

Thomas P. Aliotta
Associate Justice

Education: SUNY Col (Buffalo) 1975 BA; Brooklyn Law 1978 JD
Began Service: 2011

Chambers of Associate Justice David Elliott

141 Livingston Street, Brooklyn, NY 11201-5078
Tel: (347) 401-9580

David Elliott
Associate Justice

Began Service: 2014
Appointed By: Governor Andrew Cuomo

Chambers of Associate Justice Martin M. Solomon

360 Adams Street, Brooklyn, NY 11201
Tel: (347) 296-1495

Martin M. Solomon
Associate Justice

Began Service: 2015

New York Supreme Court, Appellate Term, Second Judicial Department, 9th and 10th Judicial Districts

141 Livingston Street, 15th Floor, Brooklyn, NY 11201
Tel: (347) 401-9580

Number of Judgeships: 5

Areas Covered: Counties of Dutchess, Nassau, Orange, Putnam, Rockland, Suffolk and Westchester

Court Staff
Chief Clerk of the Court **Paul Kenny** . . . . (347) 401-9580
E-mail: pkenny@courts.state.ny.us
Deputy Chief Clerk **Jennifer Chan** . . . . (347) 401-9580
E-mail: jennifer.chan@nycourts.gov

Chambers of Associate Justice Bruce E. Tolbert

111 Dr. Martin Luther King Jr. Boulevard, White Plains, NY 10601
Tel: (914) 824-5435

Bruce E. Tolbert
Associate Justice

Chambers of Associate Justice Anthony Marano

100 Supreme Court Drive, Mineola, NY 11501
Tel: (516) 493-3020

Anthony F. Marano
Associate Justice

Education: St John's U (NY) 1966 BA, 1969 JD

STATE COURTS—NEW YORK

Chambers of Associate Justice Angela G. Iannacci

100 Supreme Court Drive, Mineola, NY 11501
Tel: (516) 571-2484

Angela G. Iannacci
Associate Justice

Education: George Washington 1983 BA; Pace 1986 JD
Began Service: 2009

Chambers of Associate Justice Jerry Garguilo

141 Livingston Street, Brooklyn, NY 11201-5078
Tel: (347) 401-9580
E-mail: jerry.garguilo@nycourts.gov

Jerry Garguilo
Associate Justice

Began Service: 2014
Appointed By: Governor Andrew Cuomo

North Carolina

Administrative Office of the Courts of North Carolina

North Carolina Judicial Center, 901 Corporate Center Drive, Raleigh, NC 27607
P.O. Box 2448, Raleigh, NC 27602
Tel: (919) 890-1000 Fax: (919) 890-1915
Internet: www.nccourts.org

Staff

Director **Marion Warren** (919) 890-1391
Deputy Director **Lorrie L. Dollar** (919) 890-1000
Assistant Director **David F. Hoke** (919) 831-5971
E-mail: david.f.hoke@nccourts.org
Education: Davidson 1980 BA; Wake Forest 1983 JD
Senior Deputy Director **Jonathan Williams** (919) 890-1392
Chief Information Officer **Jeffrey Marecic** (919) 890-1330
E-mail: jeffrey.m.marecic@nccourts.org
Deputy Director of Program Services **McKinley Wooten, Jr.** (919) 890-1221
Education: Morehouse Col 1988 BA; Vanderbilt 1991 JD
Financial Services Officer **Bud P. Jennings** (919) 890-1022
E-mail: bud.p.jennings@nccourts.org
Human Resources Officer **Margaret B. Wiggins** (919) 890-1125
Legal Counsel **Pamela W. Best** (919) 890-1304
Judicial Purchasing Officer **Brenda G. Allen** (919) 890-1526
E-mail: brenda.g.allen@nccourts.org
Communications Director **Sharon Gladwell** (919) 890-1394
E-mail: sharon.gladwell@nccourts.org
Guardian ad Litem Administrator **Cindy Bizzell** (919) 890-1221
Human Resources Manager **Michael Smith** (919) 890-1395
Judicial Services Coordinator **Tracie M. Hembrick** (919) 831-5973
North Carolina Justice Building, Two East Morgan Street, Raleigh, NC 27601
E-mail: tracie.m.hembrick@nccourts.org
Court Reporting Manager **David E. Jester** (919) 831-5974
E-mail: david.e.jester@nccourts.org
Interpreting Services Manager **Brooke A. Bogue** (919) 890-1213
E-mail: brooke.a.bogue@nccourts.org

North Carolina Innocence Inquiry Commission

P.O. Box 2448, Raleigh, NC 27602
Tel: (919) 890-1580 Fax: (919) 890-1937
E-mail: nciic@nccourts.org
Internet: www.innocencecommission-nc.gov

Chair **Arnold O. Jones II** (919) 890-1580
Commissioner **Aurelia Sands Belle** (919) 890-1580
Commissioner **Luther Johnson Britt III** (919) 890-1580
Commissioner **Michael A. Grace** (919) 890-1580
Commissioner **Isaac Heard** (919) 890-1580
Commissioner **Susan Johnson** (919) 890-1580
Commissioner **Barbara Pickens** (919) 890-1580
Commissioner **T. Diane Surgeon** (919) 890-1580

Commission Staff

Executive Director **Kendra Montgomery-Blinn** (919) 890-1580
Paralegal **Aschante Pretty** (919) 890-1580
Case Coordinator **(Vacant)** (919) 890-1580
Associate Director **Sharon Stellato** (919) 890-1580
Staff Attorney **(Vacant)** (919) 890-1580
Grant Staff Attorney **Catharine Matoian** (919) 890-1580
Grant Investigator **(Vacant)** (919) 890-1580
Grant Investigator **Sarah Riney** (919) 890-1580
Associate Counsel **Lindsey Smith** (919) 890-1580

North Carolina Supreme Court

100 Justice Building, Two East Morgan Street, Raleigh, NC 27601
P.O. Box 2170, Raleigh, NC 27602
Tel: (919) 831-5700 Fax: (919) 831-5720
Internet: www.nccourts.org

Number of Judgeships: 7

The Supreme Court consists of a chief justice and six associate justices who are elected in statewide elections for eight-year terms. Vacancies may be filled by the Governor. Retirement is mandatory at age seventy-two; however, retired justices may be recalled to serve as needed. The Supreme Court exercises exclusive appellate jurisdiction over first degree murder cases in which the defendant is sentenced to death and over final orders by the North Carolina Utilities Commission for general rate cases. The Court also has appellate jurisdiction over cases involving substantial constitutional issues, cases of dissent in the North Carolina Court of Appeals, and cases which have been granted a review at the Court's discretion. The Court exercises original jurisdiction over the censure and removal of judges and has supervisory control and rule-making authority over the lower courts.

The North Carolina Supreme Court sits in Raleigh.

Court Staff

Clerk of the Court **Christie Speir Cameron Roeder** (919) 831-5700
Education: North Carolina 1979 JD
Assistant Clerk **M.C. Hackney** (919) 831-5700
Librarian **Thomas P. Davis** (919) 831-5709
Education: North Carolina 1978 BA; Syracuse 1988 MLS; Duke 1992 JD
Reporter **H. James Hutcheson** (919) 831-5710

Chambers of Chief Justice Mark D. Martin

Justice Building, Two East Morgan Street, Raleigh, NC 27601
P.O. Box 1841, Raleigh, NC 27602-1841
Tel: (919) 831-5712 Fax: (919) 831-5730
E-mail: mmartin@sc.nccourts.org

Mark D. Martin
Chief Justice

Date of Birth: 1963
Education: Western Carolina 1985 BSBA; North Carolina 1988 JD; Virginia 1998 LLM
Began Service: January 4, 1999
Next Election: November 2022
Term Expires: December 31, 2022
Political Affiliation: Republican

Current Memberships: American Bar Association; The American Law Institute; North Carolina Bar Association; The North Carolina State Bar

Staff

Law Clerk **Daniel Benson** (919) 831-5712
Began Service: August 2015
Term Expires: August 2017
Law Clerk **Alan Rosinus** (919) 831-5712
Began Service: September 7, 2015
Term Expires: September 2016
Executive Assistant **Terry Murray** (919) 831-5712
E-mail: tmurray@sc.thecourts.org

STATE COURTS—NORTH CAROLINA

Chambers of Associate Justice Robert H. Edmunds, Jr.

P.O. Box 1841, Raleigh, NC 27602
Tel: (919) 831-5713 Fax: (919) 831-5720

Robert H. Edmunds, Jr.
Associate Justice

Date of Birth: 1949
Education: North Carolina 1975 JD; Virginia 2004 LLM
Began Service: January 1, 2001
Next Election: November 2016
Election Type: General Election
Term Expires: December 31, 2016
Political Affiliation: Republican

Government: Assistant District Attorney, Guilford County, Eighteenth Prosecutorical District (1978-1982); Assistant U.S. Attorney, North Carolina - Middle District, Office of the Attorney General, United States Department of Justice (1982-1986); United States Attorney, Middle District of North Carolina, United States Department of Justice (1986-1993)

Judicial: Judge, North Carolina Court of Appeals (1999-2000)

Legal Practice: Stern & Klepfer, LLP (1993-1998)

Military Service: United States Navy (1975-1977)

Current Memberships: American Bar Association; North Carolina Bar Association; The North Carolina State Bar; Virginia State Bar

Staff
Law Clerk/Research Assistant **Lauren P. Suber** . . . . (919) 831-5713
Began Service: August 2015
Term Expires: August 2017
Law Clerk/Research Assistant **Debolina Das** . . . . (919) 831-5713
Began Service: August 2014
Term Expires: August 2016
Executive Assistant **Valerie Tart** . . . . (919) 831-5713

Chambers of Associate Justice Paul Newby

Two East Morgan Street, Raleigh, NC 27601
Tel: (919) 831-5715 Fax: (919) 831-5720
E-mail: pnewby@sc.state.nc.us

Paul M. Newby
Associate Justice

Date of Birth: May 5, 1955
Education: Duke BA; North Carolina JD
Began Service: 2004
Next Election: November 2020
Term Expires: 2020

Corporate: Vice President/General Counsel, Cannon Mills Realty and Development Corporation

Government: Assistant U.S. Attorney, North Carolina - Eastern District, U.S. Attorney's Office, United States Department of Justice (1985)

Judicial: Judicial Intern, United States Supreme Court

Legal Practice: Van Winkle, Buck, Wall, Starnes and Davis

Staff
Law Clerk **Alexandra "Alex" Hirsch** . . . . (919) 831-5715
Began Service: 2014
Term Expires: September 2016
E-mail: ahirsch@sc.state.nc.us
Law Clerk **Elizabeth Henderson** . . . . (919) 831-5715
Term Expires: September 2015
Law Clerk **Will Robinson** . . . . (919) 831-5715
Term Expires: August 2015

Chambers of Associate Justice Robin E. Hudson

Justice Building, Two East Morgan Street, Raleigh, NC 27601
Tel: (919) 831-5717 Fax: (919) 831-5720
E-mail: rhudson@sc..state.nc.us

Robin E. Hudson
Associate Justice

Date of Birth: 1952
Education: Yale 1973 BA; North Carolina 1976 JD
Began Service: January 2007
Next Election: November 2022
Election Type: General Election
Term Expires: December 31, 2022
Political Affiliation: Democrat

Government: Assistant Appellate Defender (1984-1987); Chair, Occupational Safety and Health Review Commission, Occupational Safety and Health, State of North Carolina (1994-2000)

Legal Practice: Private Practice (1977-1984); Private Practice (1987-2000)

Current Memberships: American Bar Association; National Association of Women Judges; North Carolina Association of Black Lawyers; North Carolina Bar Association; Wake County Bar Association

Staff
Career Law Clerk **Meghan Martie** . . . . (919) 831-5717
E-mail: mmartie@sc.state.nc.us
Career Law Clerk **Aaron Johnson** . . . . (919) 831-5717
E-mail: ajohnson@sc.state.nc.us
Executive Assistant **Gaynelle P. Little** . . . . (919) 831-5717
E-mail: glittle@sc.state.nc.us

Chambers of Associate Justice Barbara Jackson

Two East Morgan Street, Raleigh, NC 27601
Tel: (919) 831-5714

Barbara Jackson
Associate Justice

Date of Birth: December 25, 1961
Education: North Carolina 1984 BA, 1990 JD
Began Service: January 7, 2011

Current Memberships: North Carolina Association of Women Attorneys; North Carolina Bar Association; Board of Directors, Wake County Bar Association

Staff
Research Assistant **Jordan Sly** . . . . (919) 831-5714
Research Assistant **Brittany Birch** . . . . (919) 831-5714
Judicial Assistant **Lynette Dean Johnson** . . . . (919) 831-5714

Chambers of Associate Justice Cheri Beasley

Two East Morgan Street, Raleigh, NC 27601
Tel: (919) 831-5700

Cheri Beasley
Associate Justice

Education: Rutgers 1988 BA; Tennessee 1991 JD
Began Service: 2012

Current Memberships: American Bar Association; Cumberland County Bar Association; National Bar Association; North Carolina Association of Black Lawyers; North Carolina Association of District Court Judges; North Carolina Association of Women Attorneys

Chambers of Associate Justice Sam Ervin
Two East Morgan Street, Raleigh, NC 27601
Tel: (919) 831-5700

Sam J. "Jimmy" Ervin IV
Associate Justice

Education: Davidson 1978 AB; Harvard 1981 JD
Began Service: 2015
Political Affiliation: Democrat

North Carolina Court of Appeals
One West Morgan Street, Raleigh, NC 27601
P.O. Box 2779, Raleigh, NC 27602-2779
Tel: (919) 831-3600
Tel: (919) 831-5708 (Electronic Access Registration)
Fax: (919) 831-3615
Internet: www.nccourts.org/courts/appellate/appeal

Number of Judgeships: 15

The Court of Appeals, established in 1967, consists of a chief judge and fourteen judges who are elected in statewide elections for eight-year terms. The chief judge is selected by the North Carolina Supreme Court chief justice. Judges sit in panels of three judges each. Retirement is mandatory at age seventy-two, but retired judges may be recalled to serve as needed. The Court of Appeals has appellate jurisdiction over cases appealed from the trial courts except those cases heard directly by the Supreme Court. The Court also hears appeals from the North Carolina Industrial Commission, Commissioner of Insurance, State Board of Contract Appeals, State Bar, Property Tax Commission, Department of Human Resources, Commissioner of Banks, Administrator of Savings and Loans, Governor's Waste Management Board and Utilities Commission in cases other than those concerning general rates.

The Court of Appeals sits in Raleigh.

Court Staff
Clerk of the Court **John H. Connell** .... (919) 831-3600
E-mail: jhc@coa.state.nc.us
Education: North Carolina 1981 AB, 1985 JD
Administrative Counsel **Daniel M. Horne, Jr.** .... (919) 831-3640
E-mail: fed@coa.state.nc.us
Director, Information Services **Marcos De Souza** .... (919) 831-5708
E-mail: mdesouza@coa.state.nc.us

Chambers of Chief Judge Linda M. McGee
P.O. Box 888, Raleigh, NC 27602
Tel: (919) 831-3720 Fax: (919) 831-3615
E-mail: lmcgee@coa.nccourts.org

Linda M. McGee
Chief Judge

Date of Birth: 1949
Education: North Carolina 1971 BA, 1973 JD
Began Service: February 3, 1995
Appointed By: Governor James B. Hunt, Jr.
Term Expires: December 31, 2020
Political Affiliation: Democrat

Current Memberships: American Bar Association; National Association of Women Judges; North Carolina Association of Women Attorneys; North Carolina Bar Association

Staff
Research Assistant **Bryan Anderson** .... (919) 831-3723
E-mail: mga@coa.nccourts.org
Education: North Carolina 2002 JD
Research Assistant **Tracy Nayer** .... (919) 831-3724
E-mail: tnayer@coa.nccourts.org
Education: North Carolina 2007 JD

Chambers of Chief Judge Linda M. McGee *continued*
Research Assistant **Matthew Herr** .... (919) 831-3724
E-mail: mherr@coa.nccourts.org
Executive Assistant **Peggy Seifert** .... (919) 831-3720
E-mail: pseifert@coa.nccourts.org

Chambers of Judge Wanda G. Bryant
One West Morgan Street, Raleigh, NC 27601
P.O. Box 888, Raleigh, NC 27602
Tel: (919) 831-3760 Fax: (919) 831-3615
E-mail: wbryant@coa.state.nc.us

Wanda G. Bryant
Judge

Date of Birth: 1956
Education: Duke 1977; North Carolina Central 1982 JD
Began Service: March 1, 2001
Term Expires: December 31, 2020
Political Affiliation: Democrat

Government: Assistant District Attorney, Thirteenth Prosecutorial District of North Carolina (1983-1987); Assistant United States Attorney, United States Department of Justice (1989-1993); Senior Deputy Attorney General, Office of the Attorney General, Citizens Rights Division, North Carolina Department of Justice (1993-2001)

Legal Practice: Associate Attorney, Walton Fairley & Jess (1982)

Nonprofit: Staff Attorney, Police Executive Research Forum (1987-1989)

Current Memberships: The District of Columbia Bar; North Carolina Association of Black Lawyers; North Carolina Association of Women Attorneys; North Carolina Bar Association; The North Carolina State Bar; Wake County Bar Association

Staff
Research Assistant **Jonathan Eric James** .... (919) 831-3760
E-mail: ejames@coa.state.nc.us
Research Assistant **Caroline Massagee** .... (919) 831-3760
E-mail: jblazich@coa.state.nc.us
Executive Assistant **Mary A. Knight** .... (919) 831-3760
E-mail: mknight@coa.state.nc.us
Education: Campbell BS

Chambers of Judge Ann Marie Calabria
One West Morgan Street, Raleigh, NC 27602
P.O. Box 888, Raleigh, NC 27602
Tel: (919) 831-3770
E-mail: acalabria@coa.state.nc.us

Ann Marie Calabria
Judge

Date of Birth: October 31, 1947
Education: Fairleigh Dickinson 1977 BA; Campbell 1983 JD
Began Service: January 1, 2003
Next Election: November 2018
Term Expires: 2018

Academic: Teacher and Paralegal, Overseas Division, University of Maryland University College (1986-1987)

Government: Contract Specialist, United States Department of Housing and Urban Development (1989-1990)

Judicial: District Court Judge, Wake County District Court, 10th Judicial District (1996-2002)

Legal Practice: Private Practice (1988-1989); Associate, Hutchens & Waple (1990-1991); Private Practice (1991-1996)

Nonprofit: Vice President, North Carolina Bar Association (2000-2001)

Current Memberships: North Carolina Bar Association; Wake County Bar Association

Chambers of Judge Ann Marie Calabria *continued*

Staff

Law Clerk **Bethany Hukill** . . . . (919) 831-3770
Began Service: 2011

Law Clerk **Michael Rogers** . . . . (919) 831-3770
Began Service: August 2009

Executive Assistant **Paula Broome** . . . . (919) 831-3770
E-mail: pbroome@coa.state.nc.us

Chambers of Judge Richard A. Elmore

One West Morgan Street, Raleigh, NC 27601
P.O. Box 888, Raleigh, NC 27602
Tel: (919) 831-3780
E-mail: relmore@coa.state.nc.us

Richard A. "Rick" Elmore
Judge

Education: Guilford Col 1974; North Carolina Central 1982 JD
Began Service: January 1, 2003
Next Election: November 2018
Term Expires: January 1, 2019
Political Affiliation: Republican

Government: Board Member, Planning Board, County of Guilford, North Carolina; Elections Official, Elections Office, County of Guilford, North Carolina

Legal Practice: Attorney, Private Practice

Nonprofit: Volunteer Legal Counsel, Greensboro AAU Basketball

Current Memberships: The Greensboro Bar Association, Inc.; North Carolina Academy of Trial Lawyers; North Carolina Bar Association; The North Carolina State Bar

Staff

Law Clerk **Joanna Dick** . . . . (919) 831-3780

Law Clerk **Dylan Castellino** . . . . (919) 831-3780

Secretary **Julie LaVelle** . . . . (919) 831-3780
E-mail: jlavelle@coa.state.nc.us

Chambers of Judge Robert N. Hunter, Jr.

P.O. Box 888, Raleigh, NC 27602
Tel: (919) 831-3740

Robert Neal "Bob" Hunter, Jr.
Judge

Education: North Carolina 1969 BA, 1973 JD

Current Memberships: The Greensboro Bar Association, Inc.; North Carolina Academy of Trial Lawyers; North Carolina Bar Association

Chambers of Judge Martha A. Geer

P.O. Box 888, Raleigh, NC 27602
Tel: (919) 831-3650 Fax: (919) 831-3615
E-mail: mgeer@coa.state.nc.us

Martha A. Geer
Judge

Education: Bryn Mawr 1980 AB; North Carolina 1983 JD
Began Service: January 2, 2003
Next Election: November 2018
Term Expires: December 31, 2018

Legal Practice: Associate, Paul, Weiss, Rifkind, Wharton & Garrison LLP (1983-1986); Founding Partner, Patterson, Harkavy & Lawrence, L.L.P. (1991-2002)

Current Memberships: American Bar Association; North Carolina Association of Women Attorneys; North Carolina Bar Association

Membership: Past Board Member, Board of Governors, North Carolina Academy of Trial Lawyers

Chambers of Judge Martha A. Geer *continued*

Staff

Executive Assistant **Pam Casper** . . . . (919) 831-3650

Chambers of Judge Linda Stephens

P.O. Box 888, Raleigh, NC 27602
Tel: (919) 831-3670
E-mail: lstephens@coa.state.nc.us

Linda Stephens
Judge

Date of Birth: November 13, 1950
Education: South Carolina 1973 BA; North Carolina 1979 JD
Began Service: 2006
Appointed By: Governor Michael F. Easley
Next Election: November 2016
Election Type: General Election
Term Expires: 2016

Clerkships: Law Clerk, North Carolina Court of Appeals (1979-1980)

Government: Deputy Commissioner, North Carolina Industrial Commission (1980-1984)

Legal Practice: Associate, Teague Campbell Dennis & Gorham, LLP (1984-1988); Partner, Teague Campbell Dennis & Gorham, LLP (1989-2006)

Current Memberships: North Carolina Association of Women Attorneys; North Carolina Bar Association; Wake County Bar Association

Membership: Board Member, Board of Directors, Society for the Prevention of Cruelty to Animals-Wake County

Chambers of Judge Donna S. Stroud

P.O. Box 888, Raleigh, NC 27602
Tel: (919) 831-3680
E-mail: dstroud@coa.state.nc.us

Donna S. Stroud
Judge

Date of Birth: June 28, 1964
Education: Campbell 1985 BA, 1988 JD
Began Service: January 2007
Next Election: November 2022
Election Type: General Election
Term Expires: January 2023

Affiliation: Member, Zebulon Baptist Church

Judicial: Judge, Wake County District Court (2004-2006)

Legal Practice: Attorney, Kirk, Gay, Kirk, Gwynn & Howell (1988-1995); Attorney, Private Practice (1988-2004); Attorney, Gay, Stroud & Jackson, L.L.P. (1995-2004)

Current Memberships: North Carolina Association of Women Attorneys; North Carolina Bar Association; Wake County Bar Association

Membership: Member, North Carolina Academy of Trial Lawyers; Member, Bench-Bar Liaison Committee, Wake County Bar Association

Staff

Law Clerk **David Unwin** . . . . (919) 831-3680
E-mail: dunwin@coa.state.nc.us

Law Clerk **Danyelle Edwards** . . . . (919) 831-3680
Education: Campbell JD

Executive Assistant **Kathy Taylor** . . . . (919) 831-3680
E-mail: ktaylor@coa.state.nc.us

Chambers of Judge J. Douglas McCullough
One West Morgan Street, Raleigh, NC 27601
Tel: (919) 831-3660

J. Douglas McCullough
Judge

Date of Birth: 1945
Education: North Carolina 1967 AB; South Carolina 1970 JD
Began Service: 2011
Political Affiliation: Republican

Current Memberships: North Carolina Bar Association; The North Carolina State Bar; Tenth Judicial District Bar Association; Wake County Bar Association

Staff
Law Clerk **Ross Wilfley** .... (919) 831-3660
Began Service: 2012
Executive Assistant **Betsy Sullivan** .... (919) 831-3662
E-mail: mhs@coa.nccourts.org

Chambers of Judge Chris Dillon
One West Morgan Street, Raleigh, NC 27601
Tel: (919) 831-3600

Chris Dillon
Judge

Began Service: 2013

Chambers of Judge Mark Davis
One West Morgan Street, Raleigh, NC 27601
Tel: (919) 831-3600

Mark Davis
Judge

Next Election: November 2022

Chambers of Judge Richard Dietz
One West Morgan Street, Raleigh, NC 27601
Tel: (919) 831-3600

Richard Dietz
Judge

Education: Wake Forest 2002 JD

Chambers of Judge John Tyson
One West Morgan Street, Raleigh, NC 27601
Tel: (919) 831-3600

John Marsh Tyson
Judge

Date of Birth: July 14, 1953
Education: North Carolina Wilmington 1974 BA; Campbell 1979 JD; Fuqua 1988 MBA; Virginia 2004 LLM
Political Affiliation: Republican

Current Memberships: American Arbitration Association; North Carolina Bar Association; The North Carolina State Bar; United States Supreme Court Bar; Virginia State Bar

Chambers of Judge Lucy Inman
One West Morgan Street, Raleigh, NC 27601
Tel: (919) 831-3600

Lucy Inman
Judge

STATE COURTS—NORTH CAROLINA

North Dakota

North Dakota Office of the State Court Administrator

State Capitol, Judicial Wing, 600 East Boulevard Avenue, Bismarck, ND 58505-0530
Tel: (701) 328-4216 Fax: (701) 328-2092
Internet: www.ndcourts.gov

Staff

State Court Administrator **Sally A. Holewa** .... (701) 328-4216
E-mail: sholewa@ndcourts.gov
Education: North Dakota 2005 MPA
Director, Finance **Donald J. Wolf** .... (701) 328-4216
E-mail: djwolf@ndcourts.gov
Director, Human Resources **Amy Klein** .... (701) 328-4216
E-mail: aklein@ndcourts.gov
Director, Technology **Larry Zubke** .... (701) 328-4218
E-mail: lzubke@ndcourts.gov
Joint Procedure Committee **Michael Hagburg** .... (701) 328-4216
E-mail: mhagburg@ndcourts.gov
Education: Minnesota 1985 BA; North Dakota 1995 JD
Judicial Conduct Commission and Disciplinary Board of the Supreme Court Staff Counsel **Brent Edison** ..... (701) 328-3925
P.O. Box 2297, Bismarck, ND 58502-2297 Fax: (701) 328-3964
E-mail: bedison@nd.gov
Supreme Court Law Librarian **Ted Smith** .... (701) 328-4594
E-mail: tsmith@ndcourts.gov Fax: (701) 328-3609
Education: North Dakota 1986 JD

North Dakota Supreme Court

State Capitol, Judicial Wing, 600 East Boulevard Avenue, 1st Floor, Bismarck, ND 58505-0530
Tel: (701) 328-2221 Fax: (701) 328-4480
E-mail: supclerkofcourt@ndcourts.gov
Internet: www.ndcourts.gov Tel: (800) 366-6888 (TTY)

Number of Judgeships: 5

The Supreme Court consists of a chief justice and four justices who are elected in nonpartisan elections for ten-year terms. Vacancies are filled by the Governor from a list provided by the Judicial Nomination Commission or by special election called by the Governor. Appointees serve at least two years and until the next general election thereafter. The subsequent term for that judgeship may be reduced to allow for the minimum two-year term and for the staggering of judicial elections. The chief justice is selected by justices of the Supreme Court and judges of the District Court for a five-year term or until the end of the elected term. The Supreme Court has final appellate jurisdiction over cases from the North Dakota District Courts. The Court has original jurisdiction with authority to issue, hear and determine such original and remedial writs as maybe necessary to properly exercise its jurisdiction. The Court is responsible for the discipline, admissions and licensing of attorneys and administration of the court system.

The Supreme Court sits in Bismarck.

Court Staff

Clerk of Courts **Penny Miller** .... (701) 328-2221
E-mail: pmiller@ndcourts.gov
Education: North Dakota 1985 JD
Chief Deputy Clerk of Court **Petra Mandigo Hulm** ..... (701) 328-2221
Education: Creighton 2003 JD
Deputy Clerk **Terra Cota** .... (701) 328-4270
E-mail: tcota@ndcourts.gov
Deputy Clerk **Sherrie Johnston** .... (701) 328-2221
Deputy Clerk **Sarah Erck** .... (701) 328-2221
E-mail: serck@ndcourts.gov
Deputy Clerk **Heather Keller** .... (701) 328-4202
E-mail: hkeller@ndcourts.gov
Deputy Clerk **Sheree Locken** .... (701) 328-4440
E-mail: slocken@ndcourts.gov

North Dakota Supreme Court *continued*

Deputy Clerk **Helen Harrison** .... (701) 328-2225
E-mail: hharris@ndcourts.gov

Chambers of Chief Justice Gerald W. VandeWalle

State Capitol, Judicial Wing, Department 180, 600 East Boulevard Avenue, Bismarck, ND 58505-0530
Tel: (701) 328-2221 Fax: (701) 328-4480
E-mail: gvandewalle@ndcourts.gov

Gerald W. VandeWalle
Chief Justice

Date of Birth: 1933
Education: North Dakota 1955 BS, 1958 JD
Began Service: August 15, 1978
Appointed By: Governor Arthur A. Link
Next Election: 2024
Term Expires: December 31, 2024

Government: Special Assistant Attorney General, Office of the Attorney General, State of North Dakota (1958-1974); First Assistant Attorney General, Office of the Attorney General, State of North Dakota (1975-1978)

Current Memberships: American Bar Association

Staff

Law Clerk **Zachary Eiken** .... (701) 328-4493
Began Service: August 2015
Term Expires: August 2016
Judicial Secretary **Cathy Arneson** .... (701) 328-4211
E-mail: carneson@ndcourts.gov

Chambers of Justice Dale V. Sandstrom

State Capitol, Judicial Wing, 600 East Boulevard Avenue, Bismarck, ND 58505-0530
Tel: (701) 328-4212 Fax: (701) 328-4480
E-mail: dsandstrom@ndcourts.gov

Dale V. Sandstrom
Justice

Date of Birth: 1950
Education: North Dakota 1975 JD
Began Service: December 31, 1992
Next Election: November 2016
Term Expires: December 31, 2016

Government: Staff, United States Senate; Staff, Criminal Justice Commission, State of North Dakota; Assistant Attorney General, Office of the Attorney General, State of North Dakota; Securities Commissioner, State of North Dakota; Public Service Commissioner, State of North Dakota

Staff

Fax: (701) 328-4480

Law Clerk **(Vacant)** .... (701) 328-4491
Law Clerk **Krista Thompson** .... (701) 328-4491
Began Service: August 1, 2015
Term Expires: July 31, 2016
Judicial Secretary **Kathryn Williams** .... (701) 328-4212
E-mail: kwilliams@ndcourts.gov

Chambers of Justice Carol Ronning Kapsner

State Capitol, Judicial Wing, Department 180, 600 East Boulevard Avenue, Bismarck, ND 58505-0530
Tel: (701) 328-4494 Fax: (701) 328-4480
E-mail: ckapsner@ndcourts.gov

Carol Ronning Kapsner
Justice

Date of Birth: November 25, 1947
Education: St Catharine Col BA; Indiana MA; Colorado 1977 JD
Began Service: October 30, 1998
Appointed By: Governor Edward T. Schafer
Next Election: November 2020
Term Expires: December 31, 2020

Legal Practice: Attorney, Kapsner and Kapsner (1977-1998)

Membership: Past President, Burleigh County Bar Association

Staff

Law Clerk **Nick Henes** .... (701) 328-2463
Began Service: August 1, 2015
Term Expires: July 31, 2016
E-mail: nhenes@ndcourts.gov
Judicial Secretary **Peggy Ganyo** .... (701) 328-4494
E-mail: pganyo@ndcourts.gov
Education: North Dakota 1975 BS, 1976 MS

Chambers of Justice Daniel J. Crothers

State Capitol, Judicial Wing,, 600 East Boulevard Avenue, 1st Floor, Bismarck, ND 58505-0530
Tel: (701) 328-4205 Fax: (701) 328-4480
E-mail: dcrothers@ndcourts.gov

Daniel J. Crothers
Justice

Date of Birth: January 3, 1957
Education: North Dakota 1979 BA, 1982 JD
Began Service: July 15, 2005
Appointed By: Governor John Hoeven
Term Expires: 2022

Clerkships: Law Clerk, Chambers of Judge Ramon Lopez, New Mexico Court of Appeals (1982-1983)

Government: Assistant State's Attorney, Office of the State's Attorney, County of Walsh, North Dakota (1983-1984)

Profession: Private Practice (1985-2005)

Membership: President, State Bar Association of North Dakota (2001-2002)

Staff

Secretary **Sue Hartley** .... (701) 328-4205
E-mail: shartley@ndcourts.gov

Chambers of Justice Lisa Fair McEvers

600 East Boulevard Avenue, Bismarck, ND 58505-0530
Tel: (701) 328-2221

Lisa K. Fair McEvers
Justice

Education: North Dakota 1997 JD, 1993 BBA
Began Service: 2014

Staff

Law Clerk **Meagan Essen** .... (701) 328-4207
Judicial Assistant **Jeanne L. Walstad** .... (701) 328-2221
Education: Maryland AA

Northern Mariana Islands

Northern Mariana Islands Supreme Court

P.O. Box 502165, Saipan, MP 96950-0307
Tel: (670) 236-9800 Fax: (670) 236-9702
Internet: www.justice.gov.mp/supreme_court.aspx

Number of Judgeships: 3

Court Staff

Clerk of the Courts **Deanna M. Manglona** . . . . (670) 236-9715
Director of Courts **(Vacant)** . . . . (670) 236-9715
Court Administrator and Public Information Officer
Jim Stowell . . . . (670) 236-9715

Chambers of Chief Justice Alexandro C. Castro

P.O. Box 502165, Saipan, MP 96950-0307
Tel: (670) 236-9709

Alexandro C. Castro
Chief Justice

Education: U Papua New Guinea 1979 LLB
Began Service: October 11, 2012

Chambers of Associate Justice John A. Manglona

P.O. Box 502165, Saipan, MP 96950-0307
Tel: (670) 236-9710

John A. Manglona
Associate Justice

Date of Birth: June 12, 1959
Education: UC Berkeley 1981 BA; Creighton 1984 JD
Began Service: May 2000

Chambers of Associate Justice Perry B. Inos

P.O. Box 502165, Saipan, MP 96950-0307
Tel: (670) 236-9708

Perry B. Inos
Associate Justice

Education: U Guam 1987 BBA; New Mexico 1994 JD
Began Service: 2013

Ohio

Supreme Court of Ohio Office of the Administrative Director

65 South Front Street, Columbus, OH 43215-3431
Tel: (614) 387-9500
Tel: (614) 387-9600 (Office of Information Technology)
Fax: (614) 387-9509
E-mail: constituent@sconet.state.oh.us
Internet: www.supremecourtofohio.gov

Staff

Administrative Director **Michael L. Buenger** . . . . (614) 387-9500
Fax: (614) 387-9509

Clerk of Court **Sandra Grosko** . . . . (614) 387-9530
Fax: (614) 387-9539

Deputy Administrative Director **Mindi L. Wells** . . . . (614) 387-9500

Reporter of Decisions **Jason Macke** . . . . (614) 387-9580
Fax: (614) 387-9589

Director, Attorney Services Division
Susan B. Christoff . . . . (614) 387-9327
E-mail: susan.christoff@sc.ohio.gov Fax: (614) 387-9529

Director, Facilities Management Division
W. Craig Morrow . . . . (614) 387-9480
Fax: (614) 387-9489

Director, Judicial Services **W. Milt Nuzum III** . . . . (614) 387-9445
E-mail: nuzumw@sconet.state.oh.us Fax: (614) 387-9449
Education: Indiana JD

Director, Office of Court Security **James Cappelli** . . . . . . (614) 387-9000
E-mail: cappellij@sconet.state.oh.us

Director, Office of Public Information **Bret Crow** . . . . (614) 387-9250
Fax: (614) 387-9259

Information Technology Division Director
Robert D. Stuart . . . . (614) 387-9619
E-mail: stuartr@sconet.state.oh.us Fax: (614) 387-9606

Director, Court Services **Stephanie E. Hess** . . . . (614) 387-9410
Fax: (614) 387-9419

Policy and Research Counsel **Alicia Wolf** . . . . (614) 387-9425
E-mail: wolfa@sconet.state.oh.us Fax: (614) 387-9409

Supreme Court of Ohio

65 South Front Street, Columbus, OH 43215-3431
Tel: (614) 387-9000 Fax: (614) 387-9539
E-mail: constituent@sconet.state.oh.us
Internet: www.supremecourtofohio.gov

Number of Judgeships: 7

The Supreme Court consists of a chief justice and six justices who are nominated in partisan primaries but run on nonpartisan ballots in general elections for six-year terms. The Governor may appoint justices to temporarily fill vacancies which occur between general elections. Retirement is mandatory at the end of the term during which the justice turns seventy; however, retired justices may be recalled for assignment by the chief justice. The Supreme Court has appellate jurisdiction over cases which originate in the Ohio Courts of Appeals, involve the death penalty, involve state or federal constitutional law and cases which are significant or of public interest from any lower court. The Court has exclusive appellate jurisdiction over appeals from the Ohio Public Utilities Commission and concurrent appellate jurisdiction with the Ohio Courts of Appeals over appeals from the Ohio Board of Tax Appeals. The Court has original jurisdiction over matters related to the practice of law and admission to the bar in Ohio.

The Supreme Court sits in Columbus.

Court Staff

Clerk of Court **Sandra Grosko** . . . . (614) 387-9530
Fax: (614) 387-9539

Children, Families and Court Programs Manager
Stephanie Nelson . . . . (614) 387-9385
Fax: (614) 387-9419

Chambers of Chief Justice Maureen O'Connor

65 South Front Street, Columbus, OH 43215-3431
Tel: (614) 387-9060

Maureen O'Connor
Chief Justice

Date of Birth: August 7, 1951
Education: Seton Hill Col 1973 BA; Cleveland-Marshall 1980 JD
Began Service: 2011
Next Election: November 2016

Government: Prosecuting Attorney, Office of the Prosecutor, County of Summit, Ohio (1995-1999); Lieutenant Governor (R), State of Ohio (1999-2003); Director, Department of Public Safety, State of Ohio (1999-2003)

Judicial: Magistrate, Probate Court Summit County, Maryland (1985-1993); Judge, Court of Common Pleas Summit County, Maryland (1993-1995)

Legal Practice: Private Practice (1981-1993)

Staff

Law Clerk **Theresa Dean** . . . . (614) 387-9060
Law Clerk **Sarah R. Stafford** . . . . (614) 387-9060
Career Law Clerk **Amy Ervin** . . . . (614) 387-9060
Education: Capital U 1996 JD
Career Law Clerk **Pierce Reed** . . . . (614) 387-9060
Education: Northeastern 1995 JD
Executive Assistant **Jill Winn** . . . . (614) 387-9060

Chambers of Justice Paul E. Pfeifer

65 South Front Street, Columbus, OH 43215-3431
Tel: (614) 387-9020 Fax: (614) 387-9029
Internet: www.supremecourt.ohio.gov

Paul E. Pfeifer
Justice

Date of Birth: 1942
Education: Ohio State 1966 JD
Began Service: January 2, 1993
Term Expires: January 1, 2017
Political Affiliation: Republican

Government: Assistant Attorney General, Office of the Attorney General, State of Ohio (1967-1970); State Representative Paul Pfeifer (OH), Ohio House of Representatives (1971-1972); Assistant Prosecuting Attorney, Office of the Prosecuting Attorney, Crawford County, Ohio (1973-1976); State Senator Paul E. Pfeifer (OH), Ohio State Senate (1977-1992)

Legal Practice: Partner, Cory, Brown & Pfeifer (1972-1992)

Current Memberships: Ohio State Bar Association

Staff

Career Law Clerk **Robert L. Burpee** . . . . (614) 387-9024
E-mail: bob.burpee@sc.ohio.gov
Education: Suffolk 1995 JD
Career Law Clerk **James W. Sheridan** . . . . (614) 387-9023
E-mail: jim.sheridan@sc.ohio.gov
Education: Ohio State 1989 JD
Administrative Clerk **Kevin L. Diehl** . . . . (614) 387-9022
E-mail: kevin.diehl@sc.ohio.gov
Education: Ohio State 1982 BS; Tufts 1990 MA
Executive Assistant **Sandra Wearly-Messer** . . . . (614) 387-9021
E-mail: sandy.messer@sc.ohio.gov
Education: Bowling Green State 1975 AA

Chambers of Justice Terrence O'Donnell
65 South Front Street, Columbus, OH 43215-3431
Tel: (614) 387-9030 Fax: (614) 387-9039

Terrence O'Donnell
Justice

Date of Birth: February 11, 1946
Education: Kent State 1968 BA; Cleveland-Marshall 1971 JD
Began Service: May 19, 2003
Appointed By: Governor Bob Taft II
Term Expires: December 31, 2018

Academic: Instructor (part-time), Cleveland State University (1974); Instructor (part-time), Dyke College (1974)

Clerkships: Law Clerk, Ohio Supreme Court (1971-1972); Law Clerk, Ohio Court of Appeals, Eighth District (1972-1974)

Judicial: Judge, Ohio Court of Common Pleas, Cuyahoga County (1980-1994); Judge, Ohio Court of Appeals, Eighth District (1994-2003)

Legal Practice: Associate, Marshman, Snyder and Corrigan

Current Memberships: Cleveland Metropolitan Bar Association; Cuyahoga County Bar Association; Ohio Appellate Judges Association; Ohio State Bar Association

Staff
Law Clerk **Tiffany Rinsky** . . . . (614) 387-9030
E-mail: tiffany.rinsky@sc.ohio.gov
Law Clerk **Francis L. Barnes III** . . . . (614) 387-9030
Began Service: August 2008
E-mail: francis.barnes@sc.ohio.gov
Education: Georgia 2006 JD
Law Clerk **Jeffry Hartel** . . . . (614) 387-9030
Began Service: April 2012
E-mail: jeffry.hartel@sc.ohio.gov
Education: Capital U 2000 JD
Judicial Assistant **Ann Schlatter** . . . . (614) 387-9030
E-mail: ann.schlatter@sc.ohio.gov

Chambers of Justice Judith Ann Lanzinger
65 South Front Street, Columbus, OH 43215-3431
Tel: (614) 387-9090

Judith Ann Lanzinger
Justice

Education: Toledo BEd, JD
Began Service: January 1, 2005
Next Election: November 2016
Term Expires: December 31, 2016

Academic: Adjunct Professor, University of Toledo

Judicial: Judge, Toledo Municipal Court (1985-1989); Judge, Lucas County Common Pleas (1989-2003); Judge, Ohio Court of Appeals, Sixth District (2003-2004)

Staff
Career Law Clerk **Kristin Mutchler** . . . . (614) 387-9090
Education: Ohio State 2009 JD
Career Law Clerk **Lora Peters** . . . . (614) 387-9090
Education: Cincinnati 1997 JD
Career Law Clerk **Ron Wadlinger III** . . . . (614) 387-9090
Education: Ohio State 2007 JD
Judicial Assistant **Sandy Ringer** . . . . (614) 387-9090

Chambers of Justice Sharon L. Kennedy
65 South Front Street, Columbus, OH 43215-3431
Tel: (614) 387-9000

Sharon L. Kennedy
Justice

Began Service: December 7, 2012
Term Expires: December 2020

Staff
Law Clerk **David Bartleson** . . . . (614) 387-9000
Education: Otterbein BA; Capital U 1992 JD
Law Clerk **Betsy Clarke** . . . . (614) 387-9000
Law Clerk **Dorci Gass-Lower** . . . . (614) 387-9000
Judicial Assistant **Christy Robe** . . . . (614) 387-9000

Chambers of Justice Judith L. French
65 South Front Street, Columbus, OH 43215-3431
Tel: (614) 387-9000

Judith L. French
Justice

Education: Ohio State 1984 BA, 1988 MA, 1988 JD
Began Service: January 23, 2013
Next Election: November 2022

Staff
Law Clerk **John Schelb** . . . . (614) 387-9000
Judicial Assistant **Kelly A. Peters** . . . . (614) 387-9000

Chambers of Justice William O'Neill
65 South Front Street, Columbus, OH 43215-3431
Tel: (614) 387-9000

William O'Neill
Justice

Began Service: December 27, 2012

Staff
Law Clerk **Michael O'Day** . . . . (614) 387-9000
Law Clerk **Lewis Grube** . . . . (614) 387-9000
Law Clerk **Christina Madriguera** . . . . (614) 387-9000
Executive Assistant **Lisa Sharron** . . . . (614) 387-9000

Ohio Court of Appeals

Ohio Court of Appeals serves as the intermediate appellate court for the state. The Court of Appeals exercises two types of jurisdiction: appellate jurisdiction and original jurisdiction. The twelve districts of the Court of Appeals hear from cases arising in the Courts of Common Pleas, County District Courts, and Municipal Courts within their respective districts. The court has concurrent jurisdiction with the Ohio Supreme Court to hear appeals from a County Board of Tax Appeals. Decisions of the Court of Appeals may be reviewed by the Ohio Supreme Court. The appellate court also has limited original jurisdiction in quo warranto, mandamus, habeas corpus, prohibition and procedendo, and any cause on review as may be necessary to complete its determination. Judgments are subject to review by the Ohio Supreme Court. Each appellate district has a minimum of three judges. These judges are nominated in partisan primaries but run on nonpartisan ballots in general elections for six-year terms. The governor may appoint judges to temporarily fill vacancies that occur between general elections. Retirement is mandatory at the age of seventy; however, retired judges may be recalled for assignment by the Chief Justice of the Ohio Supreme Court. The clerks of court are independently elected officials.

Ohio Court of Appeals, First District

William H. Taft Law Center, 230 East Ninth Street, 12th Floor, Cincinnati, OH 45202-2138
Tel: (513) 946-3500 Fax: (513) 946-3411
Internet: www.hamilton-co.org/appealscourt

Number of Judgeships: 6

Areas Covered: County of Hamilton

Note: The Clerks of the Courts of Ohio are elected officials.

Court Staff
Administrator **Margaret M. "Molly" Leonard** .... (513) 946-3488
E-mail: mleonard@cms.hamilton-co.org
Education: Cincinnati 1988 JD
Assistant Administrator/Conference Attorney
Keith Sauter .... (513) 946-3489
E-mail: ksauter@cms.hamilton-co.org
Education: Cincinnati 1991 JD
Senior Staff Attorney **Kathleen Keeney** .... (513) 946-3432
Fax: (513) 946-3411

Chambers of Presiding Judge Judge Sylvia Sieve Hendon

230 East Ninth Street, 12th Floor, Cincinnati, OH 45202-2138
Tel: (513) 946-3421 Fax: (513) 946-3411
E-mail: shendon@cms.hamilton-co.org

Sylvia Sieve Hendon
Judge

Education: Salmon P Chase 1975 JD
Began Service: February 9, 2005

Staff
Career Law Clerk **Bethany Meyer** .... (513) 946-3431
Career Law Clerk **Kate Murray** .... (513) 946-3427
E-mail: kmurray@cms.hamilton-co.org
Education: Cincinnati 1993 JD
Judicial Assistant **Kathleen Osterday Menchhofer** .... (513) 946-3421
E-mail: kosterda@cms.hamilton-co.org

Chambers of Judge Penelope R. Cunningham

William H. Taft Law Center, 230 East Ninth Street, 12th Floor, Cincinnati, OH 45202-2138
Tel: (513) 946-3424 Fax: (513) 946-3411
E-mail: pcunningham@cms.hamilton-co.org

Penelope R. Cunningham
Judge

Education: Cincinnati 1984 BA, 1987 JD
Began Service: January 1, 2007
Term Expires: February 12, 2019

Staff
Staff Attorney **Thomas W. Langlois** .... (513) 946-3415
Began Service: 2007
E-mail: tlangloi@cms.hamilton-co.org
Education: Cincinnati 1991 JD
Staff Attorney **Mary Minnillo** .... (513) 946-3417
Began Service: 2007
E-mail: mminnillo@cms.hamilton-co.org
Education: Cincinnati 1995 JD
Judicial Administrative Assistant **Marion Hochbein** .... (513) 946-3421
E-mail: mhocbein@cms.hamilton-co.org
Judicial Administrative Assistant **Karen Lumpkins** .... (513) 946-3421
E-mail: klumpkins@cms.hamilton-co.org

Chambers of Judge Patrick F. Fischer

230 East Ninth Street, Cincinnati, OH 45202-2138
Tel: (513) 946-3500 Fax: (513) 946-3411

Patrick F. Fischer
Judge

Education: Harvard 1980 AB, 1983 JD
Began Service: December 24, 2010

Staff
Career Law Clerk **Ashley Coffaro** .... (513) 946-3418
E-mail: acoffaro@cms.hamilton-co.org
Career Law Clerk **Susan Schaen** .... (513) 946-3419
E-mail: sschaen@cms.hamilton-co.org
Education: Cincinnati 1999 JD
Judicial Assistant **Karen Lumpkins** .... (513) 946-3424
E-mail: klumpkins@cms.hamilton-co.org

Chambers of Judge R. Patrick DeWine

230 East Ninth Street, Cincinnati, OH 45202-2138
Tel: (513) 946-3500

R. Patrick DeWine
Judge

Education: Miami U (OH) 1990 BA; Michigan 1994 JD

Staff
Career Law Clerk **Melissa Schuett** .... (513) 946-3416
Career Law Clerk **Mary Stier** .... (513) 946-3425
E-mail: mstier@cms.hamilton-co.org
Education: Miami 1991 BA; Cincinnati 1994 JD
Judicial Assistant **Karen Lumpkins** .... (513) 946-3506

Chambers of Judge Russell Mock

230 East Ninth Street, Cincinnati, OH 45202-2138
Tel: (513) 946-3500

Russell Mock
Judge

Began Service: 2015

Ohio Court of Appeals, Second District

41 North Perry Street, Dayton, OH 45422-2170
Tel: (937) 225-4464 Tel: (800) 608-4652 (Toll-free in Ohio)
Fax: (937) 496-7724
Internet: www.mcohio.org/SecondDistrictAppeals

Number of Judgeships: 5

Areas Covered: Counties of Champaign, Clark, Darke, Greene, Miami and Montgomery

Note: The Clerks of the Courts of Ohio are elected officials.

Court Staff
Court Administrator **Erin Scanlon** .... (937) 225-4464
Deputy Court Administrator **Jim Nealon** .... (937) 225-4464
Assignment Commissioner **Lisa Paul** .... (937) 225-4464
Administrative Coordinator **Angela L. House** .... (937) 225-4464
Docket Clerk **Jessica Mcvey** .... (937) 225-4464

Chambers of Presiding and Administrative Judge Jeffrey E. Froelich
41 North Perry Street, Dayton, OH 45422
Tel: (937) 225-4464

Jeffrey Earl Froelich
Presiding and Administrative Judge

Education: Miami U (OH) BA; Michigan 1972 JD
Began Service: February 9, 2009
Next Election: November 2020
Political Affiliation: Democrat

Current Memberships: American Bar Association; Dayton Bar Association; Ohio Common Pleas Judges Association; Ohio Community Corrections Organization; Ohio State Bar Association

Staff
Staff Attorney **Valerie Finn-Deluca** .... (937) 225-4464
Education: Detroit 1989 BA; Cincinnati 1994 JD
Staff Attorney **Karen Lindsay** .... (937) 225-4464
Education: Johns Hopkins 1993 BA; Dayton 1998 JD
Secretary **Patty Edmondson** .... (937) 225-4464

Chambers of Judge Mike Fain
41 North Perry Street, Dayton, OH 45422-2170
Tel: (937) 225-4464 Tel: (800) 608-4652 (Toll-Free in Ohio)
Fax: (937) 496-7724
E-mail: fainm@mcohio.org

Mike Fain
Judge

Date of Birth: 1946
Education: Yale 1968 BA; Pennsylvania 1972 JD
Began Service: February 11, 1987
Term Expires: February 10, 2017
Political Affiliation: Democrat

Academic: Adjunct Professor, School of Law, University of Dayton (1988-1991)

Government: Counsel, Board of Inquiry, State of Ohio (1978-1979)

Legal Practice: Private Practice (1973-1987)

Military Service: United States Naval Reserve (1969-1975)

Nonprofit: General Counsel, Montgomery County, Ohio Democrat Party (1982-1986)

Current Memberships: American Bar Association; Dayton Bar Association; Ohio Court of Appeals Judges Association; Ohio State Bar Association

Staff
Career Staff Attorney **Pamela Kimberley Allen** .... (937) 496-7440
E-mail: allenkim@mcohio.org
Education: Transylvania 1987 BA; Kentucky 1990 JD
Career Staff Attorney **Nadine Ballard** .... (937) 496-3357
Judicial Secretary **Donna M. Friedman** .... (937) 225-4464
E-mail: friedmand@mcohio.org

Chambers of Judge Mary E. Donovan
41 North Perry Street, Room 515, Dayton, OH 45422-2170
Tel: (937) 225-4464 Fax: (937) 496-7724

Mary E. Donovan
Judge

Education: Cincinnati 1973 BA; Dayton 1977 JD
Began Service: February 9, 2005
Term Expires: February 8, 2017

Government: Public Defender's Office, County of Lake, Ohio (1978-1979); Public Defender's Office, County of Montgomery, Ohio (1979-1988); Prosecutor's Office, City of Cincinnati, Ohio (1989-1990); Public Defender's Office, County of Montgomery, Ohio (1990-1993)

Judicial: Acting Judge, Dayton Municipal Court (1993-1995); General Division, Montgomery County Common Pleas Court (1995-2004); Editorial Staff, Ohio Judicial Conference

Legal Practice: Allbery, Cross, Fogarty and Tuss (1993-1995)

Current Memberships: Dayton Bar Association; Ohio State Bar Association

Staff
Staff Attorney **Mary Berg** .... (937) 225-4464
Education: Sewanee 1984 BA; Dayton 2002 JD
Staff Attorney **Jacob Worsham** .... (937) 225-4464
Education: South Alabama 2000 BS; Dayton 2003 JD
Judicial Secretary **Patty Edmondson** .... (937) 225-4464

Chambers of Judge Michael T. Hall
41 North Perry Street, Dayton, OH 45422-2170
Tel: (937) 225-4464 Fax: (937) 496-7724

Michael T. Hall
Judge

Education: Dayton 1975 BS, 1979 JD
Began Service: February 10, 2011
Term Expires: 2017

Staff
Staff Attorney **Christopher Timmermans** .... (937) 225-4464
Staff Attorney **Douglas Waymire** .... (937) 225-4464
Education: Dayton 1990 BA; Toledo 1995 JD
Judicial Secretary **Donna M. Friedman** .... (937) 225-4464

Chambers of Judge Jeffrey M. Welbaum
41 North Perry Street, Dayton, OH 45422-2170
Tel: (937) 225-4464

Jeffrey M. Welbaum
Judge

Education: Defiance 1974 BS; Ohio Northern 1977 JD

Staff
Staff Attorney **Erin Gay** .... (937) 225-4464
Staff Attorney **Shauna McSherry** .... (937) 225-4464
Education: Bowling Green State 1972 BS; Dayton 1979 JD
Judicial Assistant **Ann Francis** .... (937) 225-4464

STATE COURTS—OHIO

Ohio Court of Appeals, Third District

204 North Main Street, Lima, OH 45801
Tel: (419) 223-1861 Fax: (419) 224-3828
Internet: http://www.third.courts.state.oh.us/

Number of Judgeships: 4

Areas Covered: Counties of Allen, Auglaize, Crawford, Defiance, Hancock, Hardin, Henry, Logan, Marion, Mercer, Paulding, Putnam, Seneca, Shelby, Union, Van Wert and Wyandot

Note: The Clerks of the Courts of Ohio are elected officials.

Court Staff
Court Administrator **Gregory B. Miller** .... (419) 223-1861
E-mail: gmiller@third.courts.state.oh.us
Education: Capital U 1991 JD

Chambers of Presiding Judge Richard M. Rogers

204 North Main Street, Lima, OH 45801
Tel: (419) 223-1861 Fax: (419) 224-3828

Richard M. Rogers
Presiding Judge

Education: Ohio Northern 1966 BA, 1972 JD
Began Service: May 3, 2004
Term Expires: February 8, 2017

Current Memberships: Marion County Bar Association (OH); Ohio Judicial Conference; Ohio State Bar Association; Ohio State Bar Foundation

Staff
Law Clerk **Erin Kelly** .... (419) 223-1861
Began Service: June 2013
Law Clerk **Michael A. Walton** .... (419) 223-1861

Chambers of Administrative Judge Stephen R. Shaw

204 North Main Street, Lima, OH 45801
Tel: (419) 223-1861 Fax: (419) 224-3828

Stephen R. Shaw
Administrative Judge

Date of Birth: 1949
Education: Earlham 1971 BA; Ohio Northern 1975 JD; Virginia 1995 LLM
Began Service: February 11, 1987
Term Expires: February 10, 2017
Political Affiliation: Republican

Current Memberships: Allen County Bar Association; American Bar Association; Ohio Court of Appeals Judges Association; Ohio Judicial Conference; Ohio State Bar Association

Staff
Law Clerk **Ryan Nuss** .... (419) 223-1861
Began Service: January 2011
Education: Ohio Northern 2011 JD
Law Clerk **M. Charlotte Flower** .... (419) 223-1861
Began Service: August 2009
Education: Boston U BA; Ohio Northern JD

Chambers of Judge Vernon L. Preston

204 North Main Street, Lima, OH 45801
Tel: (419) 223-1861 Fax: (419) 224-3828

Vernon L. Preston
Judge

Date of Birth: 1950
Education: Findlay 1972 BS; Toledo 1980 JD
Began Service: January 2, 2007
Next Election: November 4, 2020
Election Type: General Election
Term Expires: February 8, 2021

Current Memberships: Allen County Bar Association; American Bar Association; Hancock County Bar Association; Ohio Judicial Conference

Staff
Law Clerk **Jenelia A. Sarver** .... (419) 223-1861
Law Clerk **Michael A. Wehrkamp** .... (419) 223-1861
Began Service: April 2013

Chambers of Judge John R. Willamowski

204 North Main Street, Lima, OH 45801
Tel: (419) 223-1861 Fax: (419) 224-3828

John R. Willamowski
Judge

Education: Notre Dame BA; Ohio Northern JD
Began Service: February 2007
Term Expires: February 8, 2019
Political Affiliation: Republican

Staff
Law Clerk **Lidia Ebersole** .... (419) 223-1861
Began Service: August 2013
Career Law Clerk **Tamara Bell** .... (419) 223-1861
E-mail: tbell@third.courts.state.oh.us
Education: Hanover 1992 BA; Toledo 1996 JD

Ohio Court of Appeals, Fourth District

Pickaway County Court House, 207 South Court Street, Circleville, OH 43113
Tel: (740) 474-5233 Fax: (740) 477-3976
Internet: www.4thdistrictappeals.com

Number of Judgeships: 4

Areas Covered: Counties of Adams, Athens, Gallia, Highland, Hocking, Jackson, Lawrence, Meigs, Pickaway, Pike, Ross, Scioto, Vinton and Washington

Note: The Clerks of the Courts of Ohio are elected officials.

Court Staff
Court Administrator **Sharon Maerten-Moore** .... (740) 779-6662

Chambers of Judge William H. Harsha

14 South Paint Street, Suite 38, Chillicothe, OH 45601
Tel: (740) 779-6662 Fax: (740) 779-6665

William H. Harsha
Judge

Date of Birth: 1948
Education: Miami U (OH) 1971 BA, 1976 MS; Thomas M Cooley 1981 JD
Began Service: February 10, 1989
Next Election: November 2018
Term Expires: February 9, 2019
Political Affiliation: Republican

Government: Prosecuting Attorney, County of Pickaway, Ohio (1985-1988)

Chambers of Judge William H. Harsha *continued*

Legal Practice: Partner, Bowers and Harsha (1982-1985)

Current Memberships: American Bar Association; American Judges Association; Ohio Association for Justice; Ohio Judicial Conference; Ohio State Bar Association; Pickaway County Bar Association

Staff

Law Clerk **Chris Pon** . . . . (740) 779-6662
Began Service: 2014
Law Clerk **(Vacant)** . . . . (740) 779-6662
Began Service: 2011
Court Administrator **Sharon Maerten-Moore** . . . . (740) 779-6662
Education: Washington College of Law 1998 JD
Administrative Counsel **Lisa Nooris** . . . . (740) 779-6662
Administrative Assistant **Michelle M. Ervin** . . . . (740) 779-6662
Education: Shawnee State 2004 AA; Ohio 2007 BA
Secretary **Heather Smith** . . . . (740) 779-6662

Chambers of Judge Peter B. Abele

Athens County Courthouse, 2nd Floor, Athens, OH 45701
Tel: (740) 592-3247 Fax: (740) 594-3303

Peter B. Abele
Judge

Date of Birth: 1957
Education: Bowling Green State 1979 BS; Capital U 1982 JD
Began Service: 1991
Next Election: November 4, 2020
Election Type: General Election
Term Expires: February 8, 2021

Government: Assistant County Prosecutor, County of Vinton, Ohio (1982-1985); Prosecutor, County of Athens, Ohio (1985-1988)

Staff

Career Law Clerk **Gary Garrison** . . . . (740) 592-3247
Career Law Clerk **Susan Malloy** . . . . (740) 592-3247
Secretary **Teresa Yates** . . . . (740) 592-3247

Chambers of Judge Matthew W. McFarland

Scioto County Court House, 602 Seventh Street, 3rd Floor, Portsmouth, OH 45662
Tel: (740) 891-4762 Fax: (740) 355-3934

Matthew W. McFarland
Judge

Education: Capital U, JD
Began Service: 2004

Staff

Law Clerk **Nikki Smith-Kemper** . . . . (740) 891-4762
Law Clerk **Anna Davis** . . . . (740) 891-4762
Bailiff **Dean Novinger** . . . . (740) 891-4762
Secretary **Kellie Fields** . . . . (740) 891-4762

Chambers of Judge Marie C. Moraleja Hoover

602 Seventh Street, Portsmouth, OH 45662
Tel: (740) 474-5233

Marie C. Moraleja Hoover
Judge

Ohio Court of Appeals, Fifth District

110 Central Plaza South, Suite 320, Canton, OH 44702-1411
Tel: (330) 451-7765 Tel: (800) 369-4528
Tel: (800) 750-0750 (TTY) Fax: (330) 451-7249
Internet: www.fifthdist.org

Number of Judgeships: 6

Areas Covered: Counties of Ashland, Coshocton, Delaware, Fairfield, Guernsey, Holmes, Knox, Licking, Morgan, Morrow, Muskingum, Perry, Richland, Stark and Tuscarawas

Note: The Clerks of the Courts of Ohio are elected officials.

Court Staff

Court Administrator **Melinda S. Cooper** . . . . (330) 451-7765
E-mail: mscooper@co.stark.oh.us
Education: Hiram; Denver 1993 JD
Docket Manager **Lynne M. Frieg** . . . . (330) 451-7912
Administrative Staff Attorney **Angela D. Stone** . . . . (330) 451-7240
E-mail: adstone@co.stark.oh.us
Deputy Court Administrator **Polly Mallett** . . . . (330) 451-7437
E-mail: pemallet@co.stark.oh.us
Education: Akron
Administrative Assistant **Angela R. Miller** . . . . (330) 451-7765
E-mail: armiller@stark.oh.us

Chambers of Presiding Judge W. Scott Gwin

110 Central Plaza South, Suite 320, Canton, OH 44702-1411
Tel: (330) 451-7750 Fax: (330) 451-7249

W. Scott Gwin
Presiding Judge

Date of Birth: November 26, 1951
Education: John Carroll 1973 BA; Akron 1976 JD
Began Service: February 1, 1989
Next Election: November 2018
Term Expires: 2019
Political Affiliation: Democrat

Staff

Career Law Clerk **Carol Andrews** . . . . (330) 451-7911
Education: Baldwin-Wallace 2000 BA; Akron 2004 JD
Career Law Clerk **James S. Manello** . . . . (330) 451-7244
Education: Ohio Northern JD
Judicial Assistant **Cheryl L. Wood** . . . . (330) 451-7750

Chambers of Administrative Judge Sheila G. Farmer

110 Central Plaza South, Suite 320, Canton, OH 44702-1411
Tel: (330) 451-7447 Fax: (330) 451-7249

Sheila G. Farmer
Administrative Judge

Date of Birth: 1945
Education: Marymount Col (NY) 1967 BA; Case Western 1970 JD
Began Service: February 9, 1993
Term Expires: February 8, 2017
Political Affiliation: Republican

Current Memberships: Ohio Judicial College; Ohio State Bar Association; Stark County Bar Association

Staff

Staff Attorney **Diane Burton** . . . . (330) 451-7770
Education: Kent State 1985 BA; Akron 1990 JD
Judicial Administrative Assistant **Sandra Gammill** . . . . . . (330) 451-7447
E-mail: stgammill@co.stark.oh.us

STATE COURTS—OHIO

Chambers of Judge William B. Hoffman
320 Citizens Building, 110 Central Plaza South, Canton, OH 44702-1411
Tel: (330) 451-7909 Fax: (330) 451-7249

William B. Hoffman
Judge

Date of Birth: 1951
Education: Wooster 1973 BA; Akron 1976 JD
Began Service: February 1, 1991
Next Election: November 4, 2020
Election Type: General Election
Term Expires: December 2020
Political Affiliation: Democrat

Current Memberships: Ohio Court of Appeals Judges Association; Ohio State Bar Association; Stark County Bar Association

Staff
Staff Attorney **Jacqueline Marks Dossi** . . . . (330) 451-7242
Education: Grove City 1995 BA; Akron 1998 JD
Staff Attorney **Suzanne Longbrake** . . . . (330) 451-7767
Education: Case Western 1995 JD
Judicial Administrative Assistant **Angela Giavasis** . . . . (330) 451-7448

Chambers of Judge John W. Wise
110 Central Plaza South, Suite 320, Canton, OH 44702-1411
Tel: (330) 451-7701 Fax: (330) 451-7249

John W. Wise
Judge

Date of Birth: December 24, 1951
Education: Bowling Green State BS; Ohio Northern 1979 JD
Began Service: February 9, 1995
Next Election: 2018
Term Expires: February 8, 2019
Political Affiliation: Republican

Current Memberships: Ohio Court of Appeals Judges Association; Ohio State Bar Association; Stark County Bar Association

Staff
Staff Attorney **F. William Dahler** . . . . (330) 451-7241
Education: Akron JD
Staff Attorney **Kristine Scott Witner** . . . . (330) 451-7900
Education: Akron 1989 BA, 1993 JD
Judicial Administrative Assistant **Diane M. Giua** . . . . (330) 451-7701

Chambers of Judge Patricia A. Delaney
20 West Central Avenue, Delaware, OH 43015 (Satellite Office)
Tel: (740) 833-2520 Fax: (740) 833-2519

Patricia A. Delaney
Judge

Education: Toledo, JD
Began Service: February 11, 2007
Next Election: November 2018
Term Expires: February 10, 2019

Current Memberships: Ohio Women's Bar Association

Staff
Staff Attorney **Shaunna Lincoln Dobbs** . . . . (330) 451-7918
Education: Miami U (OH) 1995; Akron 2001 JD
Staff Attorney **Amy Andrews Sabino** . . . . (330) 451-7918
Judicial Administrative Assistant
Katherine Giacomelli-Butcher . . . . (740) 833-2520
E-mail: kgbutcher@co.stark.oh.us

Chambers of Judge Craig R. Baldwin
110 Central Plaza South, Canton, OH 44702-1411
Tel: (740) 670-5477 Fax: (740) 670-5467

Craig R. Baldwin
Judge

Education: Capital U JD; Ohio BA
Began Service: March 2013
Appointed By: Governor John Kasich
Term Expires: February 9, 2017

Staff
Staff Attorney **Deborah Roland** . . . . (330) 451-7765
Education: Washington U (MO) 1984 BA; Chicago 1985 MA; Ohio State 1989 JD
Staff Attorney **Ruthanne Dingwell** . . . . (330) 451-7765
Education: Malone Col 1987 BA; Akron 1990 JD
Administrative Assistant **Christy Sayatovich** . . . . (740) 670-5477
E-mail: cssayatovich@co.stark.oh.us

Ohio Court of Appeals, Sixth District
One Constitution Avenue, Toledo, OH 43604-1681
Tel: (419) 213-4755 Fax: (419) 213-4844
E-mail: 6thca@co.lucas.oh.us
Internet: http://www.co.lucas.oh.us/Appeals/

Number of Judgeships: 5

Areas Covered: Counties of Erie, Fulton, Huron, Lucas, Ottawa, Sandusky, Williams and Wood

Note: The Clerks of the Courts of Ohio are elected officials.

Court Staff
Court Administrator **Jason A. Hill** . . . . (419) 213-4755

Chambers of Judge Mark L. Pietrykowski
One Constitution Avenue, Toledo, OH 43604-2104
Tel: (419) 213-4755 Fax: (419) 213-4844

Mark L. Pietrykowski
Judge

Education: Notre Dame 1976 BA; Ohio Northern 1979 JD
Began Service: February 10, 1999
Next Election: November 2016
Term Expires: February 9, 2017

Government: Council Member, Office of the City Council, City of Toledo, Ohio (1985-1992); Vice Mayor, City of Toledo, Ohio (1987-1989); Commissioner, Office of the Board of Commissioners, County of Lucas, Ohio (1992-1999)

Judicial: Presiding Judge, Ohio Court of Appeals (2008-2009)

Legal Practice: Civil Litigator, Manahan, Pietrykowski, Bamman, and Delaney

Staff
Staff Attorney **Stephen Ahern** . . . . (419) 213-4755
Staff Attorney **Julie Bohmer** . . . . (419) 213-4755
Staff Attorney **Karen Helmick** . . . . (419) 213-4755

Chambers of Judge Arlene Singer
One Constitution Avenue, Toledo, OH 43604-1681
Tel: (419) 213-4755 Fax: (419) 213-4844

Arlene Singer
Judge

Education: Toledo 1972 BA, 1976 JD
Began Service: February 9, 2003
Next Election: November 4, 2020
Election Type: General Election
Term Expires: February 8, 2021

Government: State Representative (D-OH, District 36), Ohio House of Representatives (1987-1988); Assistant Prosecutor, County of Lucas, Ohio (1989-1990)

Judicial: Judge, Municipal Court for Toledo, Ohio; Presiding Judge, Ohio Court of Appeals, Sixth District

Staff
Staff Attorney **Barbara Dudda-Sworden** .... (419) 213-4755
Staff Attorney **Joann K. Miller** .... (419) 213-4755
Education: Toledo 1984 BS, 1988 JD
Staff Attorney **Mary Anne Sullivan** .... (419) 213-4755
Education: Capital U 1986 BA; Toledo 1989 JD

Chambers of Judge Thomas J. Osowik
One Constitution Avenue, Toledo, OH 43604-1681
Tel: (419) 213-4755

Thomas J. Osowik
Judge

Education: Toledo 1977 BA, 1981 JD
Began Service: December 2006
Next Election: November 4, 2020
Election Type: General Election
Term Expires: December 2020

Government: Assistant Attorney General, Office of the Attorney General, State of Ohio

Judicial: Municipal Judge, City of Toledo, Ohio (1991-2004); Judge, Court of Common Pleas, County of Lucas, Ohio (2004-2006)

Profession: Private Practice

Staff
Staff Attorney **Lois Bowlus** .... (419) 213-4755
Staff Attorney **JoAnne Kirby** .... (419) 213-4755
Education: Toledo JD
Staff Attorney **David Lemon** .... (419) 213-4755

Chambers of Judge Stephen A. Yarbrough
One Constitution Avenue, Toledo, OH 43604-1681
Tel: (419) 213-4755

Stephen A. Yarbrough
Judge

Education: Toledo BBA, MBA, JD
Began Service: February 9, 2011
Term Expires: February 8, 2017

Staff
Staff Attorney **Ronald Kreager** .... (419) 213-4755
Staff Attorney **Jeff Rausch** .... (419) 213-4755
Staff Attorney **Lauren Colby** .... (419) 213-4755

Chambers of Judge James Jensen
One Constitution Avenue, Toledo, OH 43604-1681
Tel: (419) 213-4755

James D. Jensen
Judge

Staff
Staff Attorney **Shelly Musshel-Kennedy** .... (419) 213-4755
Staff Attorney **Meredith L. Mercurio** .... (419) 213-4755
Staff Attorney **Katie Thomas Talbott** .... (419) 213-4755

Ohio Court of Appeals, Seventh District
131 West Federal Street, Youngstown, OH 44503-1710
Tel: (330) 740-2180 Fax: (330) 740-2182
Internet: http://www.seventh.courts.state.oh.us/

Number of Judgeships: 4

Areas Covered: Counties of Belmont, Carroll, Columbiana, Harrison, Jefferson, Mahoning, Monroe and Noble

Note: The Clerks of the Courts of Ohio are elected officials.

Court Staff
Court Administrator **Robert Budinsky** .... (330) 740-2180
E-mail: seventhdistricto@aol.com

Chambers of Presiding Judge Gene Donofrio
131 West Federal Street, Youngstown, OH 44503-1710
Tel: (330) 740-2180 Fax: (330) 740-2182

Gene Donofrio
Presiding Judge

Date of Birth: 1953
Education: Youngstown State 1975 BA; Akron 1978 JD
Began Service: February 9, 1993
Term Expires: February 8, 2017
Political Affiliation: Democrat

Current Memberships: American Bar Association; The Florida Bar; Mahoning County Bar Association; Ohio State Bar Association

Staff
Career Law Clerk **Aaron Hively** .... (330) 740-2180
Education: Youngstown State 1993 BS; Akron 1999 JD
Career Law Clerk **Melanie Czopur-Gaffney** .... (330) 740-2180
Education: Youngstown State 1998 BSAS; Akron 2001 JD
Judicial Secretary **Rebecca Hively** .... (330) 740-2180
E-mail: rhively@mahoningcountyoh.gov

Chambers of Judge Mary DeGenaro

131 West Federal Street, Youngstown, OH 44503-1710
Tel: (330) 740-2180 Fax: (330) 740-2182
E-mail: mdegenaro@aol.com

Mary DeGenaro
Judge

Date of Birth: 1961
Education: Youngstown State 1983 BA; Cleveland-Marshall 1986 JD
Began Service: February 9, 2001
Next Election: November 2018
Term Expires: February 8, 2019
Political Affiliation: Republican

Current Memberships: American Bar Association; Columbiana County Bar Association; Jefferson County Bar Association; Board of Trustees, County of Mahoning, Ohio; Board of Trustees, County of Mahoning, Ohio; Ohio Court of Appeals Judges Association; Ohio Judicial Conference; Ohio State Bar Association

Staff
Career Law Clerk **Emily Anglewicz** .... (330) 740-2180
Education: Bryn Mawr 2001 BA; Case Western 2007 JD
Career Law Clerk **Kyde Kelly** .... (330) 740-2180
Secretary **Michelle Bistarkey** .... (330) 740-2180

Chambers of Judge Cheryl L. Waite

131 West Federal Street, Youngstown, OH 44503-1710
Tel: (330) 740-2180 Fax: (330) 740-2182

Cheryl L. Waite
Judge

Date of Birth: 1959
Education: Youngstown State 1982; Cleveland-Marshall 1985 JD
Began Service: February 10, 1997
Next Election: November 4, 2020
Election Type: General Election
Term Expires: February 9, 2021
Political Affiliation: Democrat

Current Memberships: American Bar Association; American Judges Association; Mahoning County Bar Association; Ohio Court of Appeals Judges Association; Ohio State Bar Association

Staff
Senior Law Clerk **Jeffrey E. Hendrickson** .... (330) 740-2180
Education: Wooster 1982 BA; Pittsburgh Sem 1987 MDiv; Akron 2000 JD
Attorney **Laura Canale** .... (330) 740-2180
Secretary **Teresa Y. Barron-Lloyd** .... (330) 740-2180
E-mail: TBarron@MahoningCounty.org

Chambers of Judge Carol Ann Robb

131 West Federal Street, Youngstown, OH 44503-1710
Tel: (330) 740-2180

Carol Ann Robb
Judge

Ohio Court of Appeals, Eighth District

Cuyahoga County Courthouse, One Lakeside Avenue, Cleveland, OH 44113
Tel: (216) 443-6350 Fax: (216) 443-2044
Internet: http://appeals.cuyahogacounty.us

Number of Judgeships: 12

Areas Covered: County of Cuyahoga

Note: The Clerks of the Courts of Ohio are elected officials.

Court Staff
Court Administrator **Ute Lindenmaier Vilfroy** .... (216) 443-6396
E-mail: ulv@8thappeals.com
Education: Cleveland State BA; Cleveland-Marshall JD
Deputy Administrator **Terri Berish** .... (216) 443-6386
Deputy Administrator/Bailiff **Jason Warren Diehl** .... (216) 443-6334
Deputy Administrator/Bailiff **Lillian Elmore** .... (216) 443-6351
Assignment Commissioner **Damon E. Wright** .... (216) 443-6391
Staff Attorney **Erin O'Toole** .... (216) 443-6398
E-mail: emo@8thappeals.com
Education: Cleveland-Marshall
Staff Attorney **David F. Parchem** .... (216) 443-6397
E-mail: dfp@8thappeals.com
Education: Notre Dame 1980 JD
Staff Attorney **Andrew N. Rodak** .... (216) 443-6372
E-mail: anr@8thappeals.com
Education: Cleveland-Marshall 1979 JD
En Banc Attorney **Tina Wallace** .... (216) 443-6321
Conference Attorney **David A. Shively** .... (216) 348-4835
Education: Dayton 1990 JD
Senior Conference/Motions Attorney **Ellen L. Ashwill** .... (216) 443-6331
E-mail: ela@8thappeals.com
Education: Cleveland-Marshall 1985 JD
Conference Secretary **Carolyn Malanij** .... (216) 348-4809
Administrative Assistant **Jeanne Gallagher** .... (216) 443-6382
Information Systems Manager **Stan Zakelj** .... (216) 443-6374

Chambers of Administrative Judge Frank D. Celebrezze, Jr.

Cuyahoga County Courthouse, One Lakeside Avenue, Cleveland, OH 44113
Tel: (216) 443-6352 Fax: (216) 443-2044
E-mail: fdc@8thappeals.com

Frank D. Celebrezze, Jr.
Administrative Judge

Date of Birth: 1952
Education: Cleveland State 1980 BA; Cleveland-Marshall 1983 JD
Began Service: January 1, 2001
Term Expires: December 31, 2018
Political Affiliation: Democrat

Current Memberships: Ohio Common Pleas Judges Association; Ohio Court of Appeals Judges Association; Ohio State Bar Association

Staff
Judicial Attorney **Jacob R. Dicus** .... (216) 443-6389
Began Service: 2009
E-mail: jrd@8thappeals.com
Judicial Attorney **Justin D. Care** .... (216) 443-6385
E-mail: jdc@8thappeals.com
Judicial Secretary **Sharon Keating** .... (216) 443-6352
E-mail: sak@8thappeals.com Fax: (216) 443-2044

Chambers of Judge Mary J. Boyle
Cuyahoga County Courthouse, One Lakeside Avenue,
Cleveland, OH 44113
Tel: (216) 443-6354 Fax: (216) 443-2044

Mary J. Boyle
Judge

Education: Ithaca; Cleveland-Marshall
Began Service: February 2007

Current Memberships: Alternate Dispute Resolution Committee, Ohio Judicial College

Staff
Fax: (216) 443-1755

Judicial Attorney **Michelle L. Krocker** .... (216) 443-6384
Education: Akron 2002 JD
Judicial Attorney **Bridget O'Brien** .... (216) 443-6393
Education: Cleveland-Marshall 2001 JD
Judicial Secretary **Susan C. Needham** .... (216) 443-6354

Chambers of Judge Melody J. Stewart
Cuyahoga County Courthouse, One Lakeside Avenue, Room 202,
Cleveland, OH 44113
Tel: (216) 443-6360 Fax: (216) 443-2044

Melody J. Stewart
Judge

Education: Cincinnati BMus; Cleveland-Marshall JD
Began Service: December 7, 2006
Term Expires: January 1, 2017

Staff
Judicial Attorney **Caitlin Hill** .... (216) 443-6360
Judicial Attorney **Timothy P. Riordan** .... (216) 443-6360
Began Service: December 11, 2006
Education: Cleveland State 1982 BA;
Cleveland-Marshall 1987 JD
Secretary **Joy Iannicca** .... (216) 443-6360

Chambers of Judge Patricia Ann Blackmon
Cuyahoga County Courthouse, One Lakeside Avenue, Room 202,
Cleveland, OH 44113
Tel: (216) 443-6358 Fax: (216) 443-2044

Patricia Ann Blackmon
Judge

Date of Birth: 1950
Education: Cleveland-Marshall 1975 JD
Began Service: February 11, 1991
Next Election: November 4, 2020
Election Type: General Election
Term Expires: December 2020
Political Affiliation: Democrat

Current Memberships: American Bar Association; Cleveland Metropolitan Bar Association; Cuyahoga County Bar Association; National Association of Women Judges; Norman S. Minor Bar Association; Ohio State Bar Association

Staff
Judicial Attorney **Newton S. Cargill** .... (216) 443-6358
E-mail: nsc@8thappeals.com
Education: Howard U 1983 BA;
Cleveland-Marshall 2000 JD
Judicial Attorney **Mary Pat Horwitz** .... (216) 443-6358
E-mail: mph@8thappeals.com
Education: Hiram 1996 BA; Case Western 1992 JD
Judicial Secretary **Marilyn R. Reaves** .... (216) 443-6358
E-mail: mrr@8thappeals.com

Chambers of Judge Mary Eileen Kilbane
One Lakeside Avenue, Cleveland, OH 44113
Tel: (216) 443-6355 Fax: (216) 443-2044
E-mail: mek@8thappeals.com

Mary Eileen Kilbane
Judge

Education: John Carroll 1983 BA; Cleveland-Marshall 1987 JD
Began Service: January 1, 2005

Current Memberships: Cleveland Metropolitan Bar Association; Cuyahoga County Bar Association; Ohio State Bar Association

Staff
Judicial Attorney **Romie Christensen** .... (216) 443-6355
Education: Ursuline Col 1999 BA;
Cleveland-Marshall 2002 JD
Judicial Attorney **Rochelle Dobeck** .... (216) 443-6355
Secretary **Kathleen Jacobs** .... (216) 443-6355

Chambers of Judge Larry A. Jones Sr.
Cuyahoga County Courthouse, One Lakeside Avenue,
Cleveland, OH 44113
Tel: (216) 348-4837

Larry A. Jones
Judge

Education: Wooster BA; Case Western JD
Began Service: February 10, 2009
Political Affiliation: Democrat

Current Memberships: American Judges Association; Association of Municipal/County Judges of Ohio; Cleveland Metropolitan Bar Association; Cuyahoga County Bar Association; National Association of Drug Court Professionals; National Bar Association; Norman S. Minor Bar Association

Staff
Judicial Attorney **Amy Cheatham Tye** .... (216) 348-4837
Judicial Attorney **Anna B. Ferguson** .... (216) 348-4837
Education: Ohio 1996 BA;
Cleveland-Marshall 2001 JD
Judicial Secretary **Stephanie D. Douglas** .... (216) 348-4837
Education: Ohio 1980 BBA;
Baldwin-Wallace 1997 MBA; Tiffin 2005 MA

Chambers of Judge Sean C. Gallagher
Cuyahoga County Courthouse Building, One Lakeside Avenue,
Cleveland, OH 44113
Tel: (216) 348-4838 Fax: (216) 443-2044

Sean C. Gallagher
Judge

Education: Ohio 1978 BA; Cleveland-Marshall 1989 JD
Began Service: February 9, 2003
Next Election: November 4, 2020
Election Type: General Election
Term Expires: February 8, 2021
Political Affiliation: Democrat

Current Memberships: Cuyahoga County Bar Association; Ohio State Bar Association; State Bar of Arizona

Staff
Judicial Attorney **Amy Trejbal Lennon** .... (216) 348-4838
Began Service: February 10, 2003
Education: South Florida BA;
Cleveland-Marshall JD
Judicial Attorney **David Winkelhake** .... (216) 348-4838
Began Service: February 28, 2011
E-mail: dcw@8thappeals.com
Education: New England 2007 JD

(continued on next page)

Chambers of Judge Sean C. Gallagher *continued*

Secretary **Jo Ann Kramer** .... (216) 348-4838

Chambers of Judge Kathleen Ann Keough

One Lakeside Avenue, Cleveland, OH 44113
Tel: (216) 443-6359 Fax: (216) 443-2044

Kathleen Ann Keough
Judge

Began Service: 2011

Staff

Judicial Attorney **Christina Gary** .... (216) 443-6359
Education: Ohio 1998 BA; Capital U 2001 JD
Judicial Attorney **Wendy Asma Ling** .... (216) 443-6359
Education: Michigan 1991 JD
Secretary **Mary Jo O'Toole** .... (216) 443-6359
E-mail: mjo@8thappeals.com

Chambers of Judge Eileen A. Gallagher

One Lakeside Avenue, Cleveland, OH 44113
Tel: (216) 443-6356

Eileen A. Gallagher
Judge

Education: Ohio Dominican Col 1977 BA; Cleveland-Marshall 1987 JD
Began Service: February 9, 2011

Staff

Judicial Attorney **James McGlone** .... (216) 443-6350
Judicial Attorney **Toni G. Farkas** .... (216) 443-6350
Secretary **Lisa M. Handley** .... (216) 443-6356

Chambers of Judge Eileen T. Gallagher

One Lakeside Avenue, Cleveland, OH 44113
Tel: (216) 443-6357

Eileen T. Gallagher
Judge

Staff

Judicial Attorney **Sonia Roche** .... (216) 443-6357
Education: Earlham 1995 BA;
Case Western 1998 JD
Judicial Attorney **Brandon M. French** .... (216) 443-6357
Judicial Secretary **Teddi Brhel** .... (216) 443-6357
E-mail: tab@8thappeals.com

Chambers of Judge Tim McCormack

One Lakeside Avenue, Cleveland, OH 44113
Tel: (216) 348-4807

Tim McCormack
Judge

Education: Miami BA; Cleveland State JD
Political Affiliation: Democrat

Staff

Judicial Attorney **Angela T. Sullivan** .... (216) 348-4807
Education: Cleveland-Marshall 1994 JD
Judicial Attorney **Janice Schwartz** .... (216) 348-4807
Education: National Taiwan U 1981 BA;
Ohio State 1990 PhD; Cleveland-Marshall 2000 JD
Judicial Secretary **Liz Maloney** .... (216) 348-4807

Chambers of Judge Anita Laster Mays

One Lakeside Avenue, Cleveland, OH 44113
Tel: (216) 443-6350

Anita Laster Mays
Judge

Ohio Court of Appeals, Ninth District

161 South High Street, Suite 504, Akron, OH 44308-1671
Tel: (330) 643-2250 Fax: (330) 643-2091
Internet: http://www.ninth.courts.state.oh.us/

Number of Judgeships: 5

Areas Covered: Counties of Lorain, Medina, Summit and Wayne

Note: The Clerks of the Courts of Ohio are elected officials.

Court Staff

Magistrate/Court Administrator **C. Michael Walsh** .... (330) 643-2250
E-mail: cmwalsh@ninth.courts.state.oh.us

Chambers of Administrative Judge Jennifer L. Hensal

161 South High Street, Akron, OH 44308-1671
Tel: (330) 643-2250
E-mail: hensal@ninth.courts.state.oh.us

Jennifer L. Hensal
Administrative Judge

Education: Akron 1989 BA; Toledo 1993 JD
Began Service: February 2013
Term Expires: February 2019

Staff

Career Law Clerk **Joseph Ursic** .... (330) 643-2250
Education: Case Western 2003 JD
Career Law Clerk **Alicia Hathcock** .... (330) 643-2250

Chambers of Judge Carla Moore

161 South High Street, Suite 504, Akron, OH 44308
Tel: (330) 643-2259 Fax: (330) 643-2091
E-mail: moore@ninth.courts.state.oh.us

Carla Moore
Judge

Education: Akron 1974 BA; Ohio State 1977 JD
Began Service: February 9, 2005
Term Expires: February 8, 2017

Current Memberships: Akron County Bar Association; American Bar Association; Lorain County Bar Association; Medina County Bar Association; Ohio State Bar Association; Wayne County Bar Association

Chambers of Judge Beth Whitmore

161 South High Street, Suite 504, Akron, OH 44308-1677
Tel: (330) 643-2259 Fax: (330) 643-2091
E-mail: whitmore@ninth.courts.state.oh.us

Beth Whitmore
Judge

Date of Birth: 1945
Education: Grinnell 1967 BA; Akron 1982 JD
Began Service: February 11, 1999
Term Expires: February 10, 2017
Political Affiliation: Republican

Current Memberships: Akron Bar Association; Ohio State Bar Association

Chambers of Judge Beth Whitmore *continued*

Staff
Career Law Clerk **(Vacant)** .... (330) 643-2250
Career Law Clerk **(Vacant)** .... (330) 643-2250

Chambers of Judge Donna J. Carr
161 South High Street, Suite 504, Akron, OH 44308-1671
Tel: (330) 643-2259 Fax: (330) 643-2091
E-mail: carr@ninth.courts.state.oh.us

Donna J. Carr
Judge

Education: Kent State BA; Akron JD
Began Service: July 1, 1998
Appointed By: Governor George V. Voinovich
Term Expires: February 9, 2017

Staff
Law Clerk **Joann Leong** .... (330) 643-2259

Chambers of Judge Julie A. Schafer
161 South High Street, Akron, OH 44308-1671
Tel: (330) 643-2250

Julie A. Schafer
Judge

Began Service: 2015

Ohio Court of Appeals, Tenth District
373 South High Street, 24th Floor, Columbus, OH 43215-6313
Tel: (614) 525-3580 Fax: (614) 525-7249
Internet: www.franklincountyohio.gov/appeals

Number of Judgeships: 8

Areas Covered: County of Franklin

Note: The Clerks of the Courts of Ohio are elected officials.

Court Staff
Court Administrator **Douglas W. Eaton** .... (614) 525-3580
E-mail: dweaton@franklincountyohio.gov
Education: Ohio State 1988 BA; Capital U 1992 JD
Deputy Court Administrator **Cynthia J. Sgalla** .... (614) 525-3973
E-mail: cjsgalla@franklincountyohio.gov
Education: Ohio State 1996 BS; Capital U 2000 JD

Chambers of Administrative Judge Julia L. Dorrian
373 South High Street, Columbus, OH 43215-6313
Tel: (614) 525-7241

Julia L. Dorrian
Administrative Judge

Education: Notre Dame 1987 BA; Ohio State 1996 JD, 1997 MA
Began Service: 2011

Staff
Staff Attorney **Joseph Wenger** .... (614) 525-7241
Staff Attorney **Joshua A. Kimsey** .... (614) 525-7241
Judicial Secretary **Jan Hutcheson** .... (614) 525-7241

Chambers of Judge Lisa L. Sadler
373 South High Street, 24th Floor, Columbus, OH 43215-6313
Tel: (614) 525-4054 Fax: (614) 525-7249
E-mail: llsadler@co.franklin.oh.us

Lisa L. Sadler
Judge

Date of Birth: December 15, 1957
Education: Ohio State 1980 BSSW; Capital U 1984 JD
Began Service: July 1, 2003
Next Election: November 4, 2020
Election Type: General Election
Term Expires: December 2020
Political Affiliation: Republican

Current Memberships: Columbus Bar Association; The Florida Bar; Ohio State Bar Association

Staff
Career Law Clerk **Erin Porta** .... (614) 525-7250
Career Law Clerk **Luke Pettigrew** .... (614) 525-7242
Judicial Secretary **Susan Shewalter** .... (614) 525-4054

Chambers of Judge William A. Klatt
373 South High Street, 24th Floor, Columbus, OH 43215-6313
Tel: (614) 525-3610 Fax: (614) 525-7249
E-mail: waklatt@co.franklin.oh.us

William A. Klatt
Judge

Date of Birth: 1956
Education: Miami U (OH); Notre Dame 1981 JD
Began Service: March 2002
Appointed By: Governor Bob Taft

Current Memberships: Columbus Bar Association; Board of Governors, Columbus Bar Association; Board of Trustees, Ohio Legal Assistance Foundation; Ohio State Bar Association

Staff
Career Law Clerk **Thea Allendorf** .... (614) 525-3580
E-mail: tlallend@co.franklin.oh.us
Education: Ohio State BA; Northwestern JD
Career Law Clerk **Brett Lieberman** .... (614) 525-3580
E-mail: bhlieber@co.franklin.oh.us
Education: John Carroll BA; Ohio State JD
Judicial Assistant **Katy Ruffner** .... (614) 525-3610
E-mail: katyruffner@franklincountyohio.gov

Chambers of Judge G. Gary Tyack
373 South High Street, 24th Floor, Columbus, OH 43215-6313
Tel: (614) 525-3613 Fax: (614) 525-7249
E-mail: ggtyack@co.franklin.oh.us

G. Gary Tyack
Judge

Date of Birth: July 23, 1946
Education: Wooster 1968 BA; Ohio State 1974 JD; Methodist Theol Ohio 2000 MTheol
Began Service: February 9, 2007
Next Election: November 2018
Term Expires: February 18, 2019
Political Affiliation: Democrat

Current Memberships: American Bar Association; Columbus Bar Association; Ohio Judicial Conference; Ohio State Bar Association

Staff
Staff Attorney **Jonathan S. Tewart** .... (614) 525-3580 ext. 7237
E-mail: jstewart@co.franklin.oh.us

(continued on next page)

STATE COURTS—OHIO

Chambers of Judge G. Gary Tyack *continued*

Career Law Clerk **Marianne Neal** .... (614) 525-3613
E-mail: mxneal@co.franklin.oh.us
Education: Ohio State 1988 JD
Judicial Secretary **Lori Harrison** .... (614) 525-3613

Chambers of Presiding Judge Susan Brown

373 South High Street, 24th Floor, Columbus, OH 43215-6313
Tel: (614) 525-4022 Fax: (614) 525-7249

Susan D. Brown
Presiding Judge

Education: Kent State BS; Ohio State MA; Capital U JD
Began Service: January 3, 1999
Term Expires: January 2, 2017

Current Memberships: Columbus Bar Association; Ohio Court of Appeals Judges Association; Ohio State Bar Association

Staff
Law Clerk **Brad R. Byers** .... (614) 525-3997
Began Service: 2011
Education: Ohio Northern 1989 JD
Law Clerk **Thomas W. Scholl III** .... (614) 525-3979
Education: Capital U 1996 JD
Secretary **Nancy A. Finn** .... (614) 525-4022

Chambers of Judge Betsy Luper Schuster

373 South High Street, Columbus, OH 43215-6313
Tel: (614) 525-3580

Betsy Luper Schuster
Judge

Education: Ohio State 1997 JD
Began Service: 2014
Appointed By: Governor John Kasich

Chambers of Judge Jennifer L. Brunner

373 South High Street, Columbus, OH 43215-6313
Tel: (614) 525-3580

Jennifer Lee Brunner
Judge

Date of Birth: February 5, 1957
Education: Miami U (OH) 1978 BA; Capital U 1982 JD
Began Service: 2015
Political Affiliation: Democrat

Chambers of Judge Timothy S. Horton

373 South High Street, Columbus, OH 43215-6313
Tel: (614) 525-3580

Timothy S. Horton
Judge

Began Service: 2015

Staff
Staff Attorney **Katharine Donnellan** .... (614) 525-3580
Staff Attorney **Mark Wilson** .... (614) 525-3580
Judicial Secretary **(Vacant)**

Ohio Court of Appeals, Eleventh District

111 High Street, NE, Warren, OH 44481
Tel: (330) 675-2650 Fax: (330) 675-2655
Internet: www.11thcourt.co.trumbull.oh.us

Number of Judgeships: 5

Areas Covered: Counties of Ashtabula, Geauga, Lake, Portage and Trumbull

Note: The Clerks of the Courts of Ohio are elected officials.

Court Staff
Court Administrator **Shibani Sheth-Massacci** .... (330) 675-2650
Deputy Administrator **Keitsa Miles** .... (330) 675-2650
Case Coordinator **Sheryl Russell** .... (330) 675-2650
Administrative Assistant **Tanisha Silvers** .... (330) 675-2650

Chambers of Presiding/Administrative Judge Timothy P. Cannon

111 High Street, NE, Warren, OH 44481
Tel: (330) 675-6670 Fax: (330) 675-7786

Timothy P. Cannon
Presiding/Administrative Judge

Education: John Carroll 1977 BA; Cleveland-Marshall 1980 JD
Began Service: August 15, 2007
Next Election: November 4, 2020
Election Type: General Election
Term Expires: February 8, 2021
Political Affiliation: Democrat

Government: Assistant Law Director, Prosecutor, City of Painesville, Illinois (1989-1992); Legal Advisor, Painesville Township Trustees, City of Painesville, Illinois (1997-2007); Legal Advisor, Laketran Regional Transit Authority, County of Lake, Illinois (2003-2007)

Legal Practice: Attorney, Cannon, Stern, and Aveni (1980-2006)

Current Memberships: Lake County Bar Association (IL)

Staff
Judicial Attorney **(Vacant)** .... (330) 675-6670
Judicial Attorney **Tara T. Keating** .... (330) 675-6670
Education: Youngstown State 2002 BA; Akron 2006 JD
Law Clerk **Deanna L. Tuttle** .... (330) 675-6670
Secretary **Sarah Meadors** .... (330) 675-6670

Chambers of Judge Diane V. Grendell

111 High Street, NE, Warren, OH 44481
Tel: (330) 675-6673 Fax: (330) 675-2671

Diane V. Grendell
Judge

Date of Birth: 1945
Education: Baldwin-Wallace 1980 BA; Cleveland-Marshall 1984 JD
Began Service: February 10, 2001
Next Election: November 2018
Term Expires: February 10, 2019
Political Affiliation: Republican

Clerkships: Intern/Clerk The Honorable George White, Federal District Court

Government: Ohio State Representative Diane V. Grendell (R-OH, District 68), Ohio State Senate

Legal Practice: Attorney, Squire, Sanders & Dempsey L.L.P.; Attorney, Grendell & Marrer; Attorney, Jones, Day, Reavis & Pogue; Attorney, Barrett, Sexton & Federman

STATE COURTS—OHIO

Chambers of Judge Diane V. Grendell *continued*

Staff
Law Clerk **Julie Beadle** . . . . . (330) 675-6695
Began Service: August 2010
Term Expires: August 2016
Education: Akron 2010 JD
Career Law Clerk **William R. Knox** . . . . . (330) 675-6694
Education: Cleveland-Marshall 2001 JD
Secretary **Stacie A. Whitney** . . . . . (330) 675-6673

Chambers of Judge Cynthia Westcott Rice

111 High Street, NE, Warren, OH 44481
Tel: (330) 675-2650 Fax: (330) 675-7786

Cynthia Westcott Rice
Judge

Began Service: February 2003
Next Election: November 4, 2020
Election Type: General Election
Term Expires: February 9, 2021
Political Affiliation: Democrat

Judicial: Presiding Judge, Chambers of Judge Presiding Cynthia W. Rice, Ohio Court of Appeals, Eleventh District

Staff
Judicial Attorney **Dax W.A. Kerr** . . . . . (330) 675-2650
Judicial Attorney **John Tremsyn** . . . . . (330) 675-2650
Secretary **Sharon Vigorito** . . . . . (330) 675-2650

Chambers of Judge Thomas R. Wright

111 High Street, NE, Warren, OH 44481
Tel: (330) 675-2650 Fax: (330) 675-2655

Thomas R. Wright
Judge

Began Service: 2011

Staff
Judicial Attorney **Harry T. Raphtis** . . . . . (330) 675-2650
Education: Cleveland-Marshall 2000 JD; John Carroll 1996 BA
Magistrate/Judicial Attorney **Matthew O. Lamb** . . . . . (330) 675-2650
Secretary **Judy Rader** . . . . . (330) 675-2650

Chambers of Judge Colleen O'Toole

111 High Street, NE, Warren, OH 44481
Tel: (330) 675-2650

Colleen M. O'Toole
Judge

Education: John Carroll 1983 BA; Cleveland-Marshall 1990 JD
Began Service: February 9, 2013

Ohio Court of Appeals, Twelfth District

1001 Reinartz Boulevard, Middletown, OH 45042
Tel: (513) 425-6609 Tel: (800) 824-1883 (Toll-Free Ohio)
Fax: (513) 425-8751
Internet: www.twelfth.courts.state.oh.us

Number of Judgeships: 5

Areas Covered: Counties of Brown, Butler, Clermont, Clinton, Fayette, Madison, Preble and Warren

Note: The Clerks of the Courts of Ohio are elected officials.

Court Staff
Court Administrator **Bennett A. Manning** . . . . . (513) 425-6609

Ohio Court of Appeals, Twelfth District *continued*

Assistant Administrator **Scot M. Ritter** . . . . . (513) 425-6609
Assignment Commissioner **Judith F. Eckert** . . . . . (513) 425-6609
Conference Attorney **Sasha A.M. Blaine** . . . . . (513) 425-6609
E-mail: greg.clark@twelfth.courts.state.oh.us Fax: (513) 425-8772
Fiscal Officer **Jennifer LoBuono** . . . . . (513) 425-6609
Judicial Staff Secretary **Barbara Black** . . . . . (513) 425-6609
Administrative Secretary **Nicole Rutherford** . . . . . (513) 425-6609
Judicial Staff Secretary **Leann Gilbert** . . . . . (513) 425-6609

Chambers of Presiding Judge Robin N. Piper

1001 Reinartz Boulevard, Middletown, OH 45042
Tel: (513) 425-6609 Fax: (513) 425-8751

Robin N. Piper
Presiding Judge

Education: Miami U (OH) 1978 BA; Dayton 1981 JD
Began Service: 2011

Chambers of Judge Robert P. Ringland

1001 Reinartz Boulevard, Middletown, OH 45042
Tel: (513) 425-6609

Robert P. Ringland
Judge

Date of Birth: October 6, 1945
Education: Ohio State 1967 BA; Cincinnati 1970 JD
Began Service: January 2009
Political Affiliation: Republican

Current Memberships: American Bar Association; The Potter Stewart American Inn of Court, The American Inns of Court; American Judges Association; Cincinnati Bar Association; Ohio State Bar Association

Chambers of Judge Robert A. Hendrickson

1001 Reinartz Boulevard, Middletown, OH 45042
Tel: (513) 425-6609

Robert A. Hendrickson
Judge

Education: Cincinnati 1981; Capital U 1984 JD
Began Service: February 9, 2009
Next Election: November 2020
Term Expires: February 8, 2021
Political Affiliation: Republican

Staff
Staff Attorney **Renee Karnes** . . . . . (513) 425-6609
Secretary **Barbara Black** . . . . . (513) 425-6609

Chambers of Judge Stephen W. Powell

1001 Reinartz Boulevard, Middletown, OH 45042
Tel: (513) 425-6609 Fax: (513) 425-8751
E-mail: powellsw@twelfth.courts.state.oh.us

Stephen W. Powell
Judge

Date of Birth: 1955
Education: Heidelberg 1977 BA; Dayton 1981 JD
Began Service: February 1, 1995
Next Election: November 2018
Term Expires: February 8, 2019
Political Affiliation: Republican

Current Memberships: American Bar Association; American Judges Association; Butler County Bar Association; Ohio Court of Appeals Judges Association; Ohio State Bar Association

Staff

Staff Attorney **Dave Warren** .... (513) 425-6609
Secretary **Leann Gilbert** .... (513) 425-6609

Chambers of Judge Michael E. Powell

1001 Reinartz Boulevard, Middletown, OH 45042
Tel: (513) 425-6609

Michael E. "Mike" Powell
Judge

Began Service: 2013

Oklahoma

Administrative Office of the Courts of Oklahoma

2100 North Lincoln Boulevard, Suite 3, Oklahoma City, OK 73105
Tel: (405) 556-9300
E-mail: webmaster@oscn.net
Internet: www.oscn.net

Staff

Administrative Director **Jari P. Askins** .... (405) 556-9818
Education: Oklahoma 1975 BJ, 1980 JD
Deputy Director **(Vacant)** .... (405) 522-7880
Asset Management Director **Michael Smith** .... (405) 556-9867
E-mail: michael.smith@oscn.net
Chief Finance Officer, Human Resources Director
April Story .... (405) 556-9699
Legal Information & Law Libraries Director
Debra Charles .... (405) 556-9810
Fax: (405) 521-9688
Management Information Systems Director
Michael Kiss .... (405) 556-9877
E-mail: michael.kiss@oscn.net Fax: (405) 521-9688
Education: West Virginia 1976 BA

Supreme Court of Oklahoma

2100 North Lincoln Boulevard, Suite 1, Oklahoma City, OK 73105
Tel: (405) 556-9300 Fax: (405) 528-1607

Number of Judgeships: 9

The Supreme Court consists of a chief justice, vice chief justice, and seven justices, one from each of the nine Supreme Court judicial districts, serving six-year terms. At the general election preceding the expiration of a term of office, a justice who wants to remain in office must file a candidacy to succeed himself. If a majority of those voters casting ballots in a nonpartisan election vote in favor of retention, the justice will serve another term. A vacancy occurring on the court during a term of office is filled by gubernatorial appointment. The Judicial Nominating Commission provides the Governor with a list of nominees which have been selected by the Commission from applicants living in the appropriate Supreme Court judicial district. The chief justice and vice chief justice are elected by peer vote to two-year terms. The Supreme Court has appellate jurisdiction over all civil cases at law and in equity. The Court has superintending control over all lower courts, agencies, commissions and boards created by law as well as administrative authority over all courts in the state, except the Court on the Judiciary and a Senate Court of Impeachment. The Court has exclusive jurisdiction over admission to the bar and the conduct of its members.

The Supreme Court sits in Oklahoma City.

Court Staff

Clerk of the Court **Michael S. Richie** .... (405) 556-9400
E-mail: michael.richie@oscn.net
Education: Tulane 1975 JD
Administrative Director **Jari P. Askins** .... (405) 556-9818
Marshall of Court **Barbara Swimley** .... (405) 556-9344
E-mail: barbara.swimley@oscn.net

Chambers of Chief Justice John F. Reif

Oklahoma Judicial Center, 2100 North Lincoln Boulevard, Suite 1, Oklahoma City, OK 73105
Tel: (405) 556-9360
E-mail: john.reif@oscn.net

John F. Reif
Chief Justice

Date of Birth: 1951
Education: Tulsa 1973 BS, 1977 JD
Began Service: October 2007
Appointed By: Governor C. Brad Henry
Next Election: November 4, 2020
Election Type: Retention Election
Term Expires: December 2020

Current Memberships: Oklahoma Bar Association

Staff

Judicial Law Clerk **Hilda Harlton** .... (405) 556-9323
E-mail: hilda.harlton@oscn.net
Education: Tulsa 1979 BSBA, 1982 JD
Judicial Law Clerk **Sharon Schooley** .... (405) 556-9341
E-mail: sharon.schooley@oscn.net
Administrative Assistant **Jean R. Mullican** .... (405) 556-9360
E-mail: jean.mullican@oscn.net

Chambers of Vice Chief Justice Douglas L. Combs

2300 North Lincoln Boulevard, Oklahoma City, OK 73105
Tel: (405) 556-9361 Fax: (405) 556-9120
E-mail: douglas.combs@oscn.net

Douglas L. Combs
Vice Chief Justice

Education: St Gregory's; Oklahoma; Oklahoma City 1976 JD
Began Service: January 7, 2011
Appointed By: Governor C. Brad Henry

Staff

Staff Attorney **Selden Jones** .... (405) 556-9361
E-mail: selden.jones@oscn.net
Education: Oklahoma 1991 JD
Staff Attorney **John David Holden** .... (405) 556-9361
E-mail: john.holden@oscn.net
Administrative Assistant **(Vacant)** .... (405) 556-9361

Chambers of Justice Tom Colbert

State Capitol, 2300 North Lincoln Boulevard, Room 204, Oklahoma City, OK 73105
Tel: (405) 521-3843
E-mail: tom.colbert@oscn.net

Tom Colbert
Justice

Education: Kentucky State 1973 BS; Eastern Kentucky 1976 MA; Oklahoma 1982 JD
Began Service: January 3, 2011
Appointed By: Governor C. Brad Henry
Next Election: November 4, 2020
Election Type: Retention Election
Term Expires: December 31, 2020

Current Memberships: American Bar Association; National Bar Association; Tulsa County Bar Association

Chambers of Justice Steven W. Taylor

2100 North Lincoln Boulevard, Room 200, Oklahoma City, OK 73105
Tel: (405) 556-9368
E-mail: steven.taylor@oscn.net

Steven W. Taylor
Justice

Education: Oklahoma State 1971 BA; Oklahoma 1974 JD
Began Service: January 3, 2011
Appointed By: Governor C. Brad Henry

Staff
Judicial Assistant **Kyle P. Rogers** .... (405) 556-9318
E-mail: donna.embry@oscn.net
Judicial Assistant **Barbara Kinney** .... (405) 556-9332
E-mail: barbara.kinney@oscn.net
Education: Oklahoma City 1988 JD

Chambers of Justice Joseph M. Watt

244 State Capitol Building, 2300 North Lincoln Boulevard, Oklahoma City, OK 73105-4801
Tel: (405) 556-9359 Fax: (405) 521-6982
E-mail: joseph.watt@oscn.net

Joseph M. Watt
Justice

Date of Birth: 1947
Education: Texas Tech 1969 BA; Texas 1972 JD
Began Service: May 18, 1992
Appointed By: Governor David Walters
Next Election: November 4, 2020
Election Type: Retention Election
Term Expires: December 31, 2020

Government: City Prosecutor, City of Altus, Oklahoma (1980-1985); General Counsel, Office of the Governor, State of Oklahoma (1991-1992)

Judicial: Special Judge, Oklahoma District Court; Associate Judge, Oklahoma District Court

Legal Practice: Private Practice (1973-1985)

Current Memberships: Oklahoma Judicial Conference

Staff
Staff Attorney **Vicki Angus** .... (405) 556-9359
E-mail: vicki.angus@oscn.net
Education: Oklahoma 1970 BA; Oklahoma City 1982 JD
Staff Attorney **Marissa Lane** .... (405) 556-9359
E-mail: marissa.lane@oscn.net
Administrative Assistant/Legal Assistant **Nancy McVay** .... (405) 556-9359
E-mail: nancy.mcvay@oscn.net
Education: Central Oklahoma 1983 BA

Chambers of Justice Yvonne Kauger

State Capitol Building, 2300 North Lincoln Boulevard, Room 208, Oklahoma City, OK 73105
Tel: (405) 556-9364 Fax: (405) 528-1607
E-mail: yvonne.kauger@oscn.net

Yvonne Kauger
Justice

Date of Birth: 1937
Education: Southwestern Oklahoma St 1958 BS; Oklahoma City 1969 JD
Began Service: 1984
Appointed By: Governor George Nigh
Term Expires: 2018

Clerkships: Staff Attorney The Honorable Ralph B. Hodges, Oklahoma Supreme Court (1972-1984)

Chambers of Justice Yvonne Kauger *continued*

Corporate: Medical Technologist, Medical Arts Laboratory (1959-1968)

Legal Practice: Associate, Rogers, Travis & Jordan (1970-1972)

Current Memberships: Oklahoma Bar Association; Washita County Bar Association

Staff
Staff Attorney **Kyle Shifflett** .... (405) 556-9364
E-mail: Kyle.Shifflett@oscn.net
Education: Oklahoma 1994 JD
Executive Assistant **Vanessa Traylor** .... (405) 556-9364
E-mail: vanessa.traylor@oscn.net

Chambers of Justice James Winchester

Oklahoma Judicial Center, 2100 North Lincoln Boulevard, Room E 205, Oklahoma City, OK 73105-4907
Tel: (405) 556-9367 Fax: (405) 528-1607
E-mail: james.winchester@oscn.net

James Winchester
Justice

Date of Birth: 1952
Education: Oklahoma City 1977 JD
Began Service: February 2, 2000
Appointed By: Governor Frank Keating
Term Expires: December 2016

Judicial: District Judge, County Court (1985-1997); United States Administrative Law Judge (1997-2000); Vice Chief Justice, Supreme Court of Oklahoma (2005-2007)

Current Memberships: Oklahoma Bar Association

Staff
Staff Lawyer **Jill van Egmond** .... (405) 556-9367
E-mail: jill.vanegmond@oscn.net
Education: Oklahoma 1996 JD, 1993 BA
Staff Lawyer **Paul White** .... (405) 556-9367
E-mail: paul.white@oscn.net
Education: Oklahoma Christian 1973 BA; Oklahoma 1982 JD
Judicial Assistant **Gayleen Rabbakukk** .... (405) 556-9367
E-mail: gayleen.rabakukk@oscn.net

Chambers of Justice James E. Edmondson

2100 North Lincoln Boulevard, Room 202, Oklahoma City, OK 73105
Tel: (405) 556-9366 Fax: (405) 528-1607
E-mail: james.edmondson@oscn.net

James E. Edmondson
Justice

Date of Birth: March 7, 1945
Education: Northeastern State 1967 BA; Georgetown 1973 JD
Began Service: January 14, 2004
Next Election: November 2018
Term Expires: December 2018

Current Memberships: Muskogee County Bar Association; Oklahoma Bar Association

Staff
Judicial Assistant **(Vacant)** .... (405) 521-3838
Judicial Assistant **Michael Elliott** .... (405) 556-9317
E-mail: michael.elliott@oscn.net

Chambers of Justice Noma Gurich
2300 North Lincoln Boulevard, Oklahoma City, OK 73105
Tel: (405) 556-9362 Fax: (405) 528-1607
E-mail: noma.gurich@oscn.net

Noma Gurich
Justice

Began Service: February 15, 2011
Appointed By: Governor C. Brad Henry

Staff
Career Law Clerk **Jana Knott** . . . . (405) 556-9362
E-mail: jana.knott@oscn.net
Career Law Clerk **John Turner** . . . . (405) 556-9362
E-mail: john.turner@oscn.net
Administrative Assistant **Katie Craig** . . . . (405) 556-9362
E-mail: katie.craig@oscn.net

Oklahoma Court of Civil Appeals
1915 North Stiles Avenue, Suite 357, Oklahoma City, OK 73105
601 State Office Building, 440 South Houston Avenue, Tulsa, OK 74127
Tel: (405) 521-3751 Tel: (918) 581-2711 (Tulsa Office)
Internet: www.oscn.net

Number of Judgeships: 12

The Court of Civil Appeals consists of a chief judge and eleven judges who are elected from the six judicial districts in nonpartisan retention elections for six-year terms. Two judges are elected from each district. Vacancies are filled by the Governor from a list submitted by the Judicial Nominating Commission. The chief judge is elected by peer vote to a one-year term. The Court sits in four divisions consisting of three judge panels. Divisions one and three sit in Oklahoma City and divisions two and four sit in Tulsa. The Court of Civil Appeals has jurisdiction over all civil cases as assigned to it by the Oklahoma Supreme Court.

The Court of Civil Appeals sits in Oklahoma City and Tulsa.

Court Staff
Clerk of the Court **Michael S. Richie** . . . . (405) 556-9400
E-mail: michael.richie@oscn.net

Chambers of Chief Judge William C. Hetherington
2100 North Lincoln Boulevard, Oklahoma City, OK 73105
Tel: (405) 521-3751
E-mail: william.hetherington@oscn.net

William C. Hetherington, Jr.
Chief Judge

Education: Oklahoma 1970; Oklahoma City 1979 JD
Began Service: October 2009
Appointed By: Governor C. Brad Henry

Staff
Staff Attorney **Beth M. Alonso** . . . . (405) 521-3751
E-mail: beth.alonso@oscn.net
Education: New England 1981 JD
Staff Attorney **M. Elaine Howard** . . . . (405) 521-3751
Education: Oklahoma 1988 JD

Chambers of Vice Chief Judge Jane P. Wiseman
440 South Houston Avenue, Suite 601, Tulsa, OK 74127
Tel: (918) 581-2711
E-mail: jane.wiseman@oscn.net

Jane P. Wiseman
Vice Chief Judge

Education: Cornell 1969 BA; North Carolina 1971 MA; Tulsa 1973 JD
Began Service: April 8, 2005
Appointed By: Governor C. Brad Henry
Next Election: November 4, 2020
Election Type: Retention Election
Term Expires: December 31, 2020

Staff
Judicial Assistant **Tammie Goodell** . . . . (918) 581-2711
E-mail: tammie.goodell@oscn.net
Education: Tulsa 1990 BA, 1995 JD
Judicial Assistant **(Vacant)** . . . . (918) 581-2711
Administrative Assistant **Heather Forsyth** . . . . (918) 581-2711

Chambers of Judge Deborah Barnes
440 South Houston Avenue, Suite 601, Tulsa, OK 74127-8912
Tel: (918) 581-2711
E-mail: deborah.barnes@oscn.net

Deborah Browers Barnes
Judge

Education: Oklahoma BA; Oklahoma City 1983 JD
Began Service: 2008
Appointed By: Governor C. Brad Henry

Staff
Career Law Clerk **Catherine Cullem** . . . . (918) 581-2711
E-mail: catherine.cullem@oscn.net
Education: Tulsa 1980 JD
Career Law Clerk **Michael Klenda** . . . . (918) 581-2711
E-mail: michael.klenda@oscn.net

Chambers of Judge Larry E. Joplin
1915 North Stiles Avenue, Suite 357, Oklahoma City, OK 73105
Tel: (405) 521-3751 Fax: (405) 522-6287
E-mail: larry.joplin@oscn.net

Larry E. Joplin
Judge

Date of Birth: 1946
Education: Oklahoma 1968 BA, 1971 JD
Began Service: November 28, 1994
Appointed By: Governor David Walters
Term Expires: December 31, 2016

Staff
Judicial Clerk **Jennifer Davis Lee** . . . . (405) 521-3751
Began Service: 2008
E-mail: jennifer.lee@oscn.net
Education: Vanderbilt 1990 BA; Oklahoma City 1993 JD
Judicial Counsel **Christopher M. Ruggiers** . . . . (405) 521-3751
Began Service: 1987
E-mail: chris.ruggiers@oscn.net
Education: Oklahoma 1979 BA, 1983 JD

Chambers of Judge John F. Fischer

440 South Houston Avenue, Suite 601, Tulsa, OK 74127-8912
Tel: (918) 581-2711
E-mail: john.fischer@oscn.net

John F. Fischer
Judge

Began Service: January 25, 2007
Appointed By: Governor C. Brad Henry
Next Election: November 4, 2016
Election Type: Retention Election
Term Expires: 2016

Staff
Judicial Assistant **Amanda Janssen** . . . . (918) 581-2711
Judicial Assistant **Christina Romero** . . . . (918) 581-2711
Administrative Assistant **Ashley Smith** . . . . (918) 581-2711
E-mail: ashley.smith@oscn.net

Chambers of Judge Robert Dick Bell

2100 North Lincoln Boulevard, Suite 357, Oklahoma City, OK 73105
Tel: (405) 521-3751
E-mail: robert.bell@oscn.net

Robert Dick Bell
Judge

Education: Oklahoma 1989 BA; Tulsa 1992 JD
Began Service: 2006

Staff
Staff Attorney **Amanda Nixon** . . . . (405) 521-3751
E-mail: amanda.nixon@oscn.net
Staff Attorney **Donald B. Lynn** . . . . (405) 521-3751
E-mail: donald.lynn@oscn.net
Education: Oklahoma 1989 JD

Chambers of Judge E. Bay Mitchell, III

1915 North Stiles Avenue, Suite 357, Oklahoma City, OK 73105
Tel: (405) 521-3751 Fax: (405) 522-6287
E-mail: Bay.Mitchell@oscn.net

E. Bay Mitchell III
Judge

Date of Birth: 1953
Education: Oklahoma 1976 BS, 1979 JD
Began Service: March 2002
Appointed By: Governor Frank Keating
Term Expires: December 31, 2018

Current Memberships: Oklahoma Bar Association; Oklahoma County Bar Association

Staff
Career Law Clerk **Kristin C. McAdams** . . . . (405) 521-3751
E-mail: kristin.mcadams@oscn.net
Education: Baylor 1990 BA, 1991 MA; Oklahoma City 1995 JD
Career Law Clerk **Kimberly Carlson** . . . . (405) 521-3751

Chambers of Judge Kenneth L. Buettner

1915 North Stiles Avenue, Suite 357, Oklahoma City, OK 73105-4914
Tel: (405) 521-3751 Fax: (405) 522-6287
E-mail: kenneth.buettner@oscn.net

Kenneth L. Buettner
Judge

Date of Birth: 1950
Education: Texas Christian 1972 BA; Southern Methodist 1975 JD
Began Service: February 1996
Appointed By: Governor Frank Keating
Next Election: November 2018
Term Expires: January 2019

Academic: Adjunct Professor, Oklahoma City University School of Law (1992-1996)

Judicial: Chief Judge, Oklahoma Court of Civil Appeals

Legal Practice: Associate then Partner, McAfee & Taft (1980-1996)

Military Service: United States Air Force (1976-1980)

Current Memberships: The American Inns of Court; Colorado Bar Association; Oklahoma Bar Association; Oklahoma Bar Foundation, Oklahoma Bar Association; Oklahoma County Bar Association; State Bar of Texas

Staff
Staff Attorney **Susan R. Beaty** . . . . (405) 521-3751
E-mail: susan.beaty@oscn.net
Education: Oklahoma 1991 BA, 1994 JD
Staff Attorney **Bevan Graybill** . . . . (405) 521-3751
E-mail: bevan.graybill@oscn.net

Chambers of Judge Keith Rapp

601 State Office Building, 440 South Houston Avenue, Tulsa, OK 74127-8912
Tel: (918) 581-2711 Fax: (918) 581-2403
E-mail: Rapp@oscn.net

Keith Rapp
Judge

Date of Birth: May 2, 1934
Education: Southwest Missouri State 1958 BS; Tulsa 1968 JD; Virginia 1990 ML
Began Service: December 11, 1984
Appointed By: Governor George Nigh
Next Election: November 2020
Election Type: Retention Election
Term Expires: December 31, 2020

Current Memberships: Oklahoma Bar Association; Tailhook Association

Staff
Career Law Clerk **A. T. Dalton** . . . . (918) 581-2711
E-mail: dalton@oscn.net
Education: Princeton 1959 BS; Oklahoma 1962 JD
Career Law Clerk **Sandra Jarvis** . . . . (918) 581-2711
E-mail: Jarvis@oscn.net
Education: Oklahoma 1981 BBA; Tulsa 1988 JD
Secretary **Judy Parks** . . . . (918) 581-2711
E-mail: judy.parks@oscn.net

Chambers of Judge Jerry L. Goodman

601 State Office Building, 440 South Houston Avenue,
Tulsa, OK 74127-8943
Tel: (918) 581-2711 Fax: (918) 581-2403
E-mail: jerry.goodman@oscn.net

Jerry L. Goodman
Judge

Education: Georgetown 1964 JD
Began Service: July 26, 1994
Appointed By: Governor David Walters
Next Election: November 4, 2020
Election Type: Retention Election
Term Expires: January 13, 2021

Academic: Adjunct Professor, University of Tulsa (1965-1966)

Corporate: Vice President and General Counsel, OTASCO, Inc. (1970-1983); Chairman, President and Chief Executive Officer, OTASCO, Inc. (1983-1989)

Government: Law Clerk, Antitrust Division, Office of the Associate Attorney General, United States Department of Justice; Assistant City Attorney, Office of the City Attorney, City of Tulsa, Oklahoma; Cabinet Secretary of Policy and Management, Office of the Governor, State of Oklahoma; Chief Operating Officer, Office of the Governor, State of Oklahoma; Labor Arbitrator, National Mediation Board

Judicial: Judge, Temporary Emergency Court of Appeals; Chief Judge, Oklahoma Court of Civil Appeals (2000)

Legal Practice: Private Practice (1964-1970); Private Practice (1989-1992)

Military Service: United States Naval Reserve

Current Memberships: Oklahoma Bar Association; Tulsa County Bar Association

Staff

Career Law Clerk **Robert M. Cunningham** .... (918) 581-2711
E-mail: robert.cunningham@oscn.net Fax: (918) 581-2438
Education: Tulsa 1985 JD

Career Law Clerk **Lora Montross** .... (918) 581-2711
E-mail: lora.montross@oscn.net
Education: Tulsa 1995 BSBA; Oklahoma City 1999 JD

Chambers of Judge Brian Goree

1915 North Stiles Avenue, Oklahoma City, OK 73105
Tel: (405) 521-3751
E-mail: brian.goree@oscn.net

Brian Goree
Judge

Education: Oklahoma BS; Tulsa JD
Began Service: 2012

Staff

Staff Attorney **Lu Willis** .... (405) 521-3751
E-mail: lu.willis@oscn.net
Education: Oklahoma 1985 JD

Staff Attorney **Debbie Clark** .... (405) 521-3751
E-mail: debbie.clark@oscn.net
Education: Oklahoma City 1983 JD

Chambers of Judge P. Thomas Thornbrugh

1915 North Stiles Avenue, Oklahoma City, OK 73105
Tel: (405) 521-3751

P. Thomas Thornbrugh
Judge

Began Service: 2011

Oklahoma Court of Criminal Appeals

Oklahoma Judicial Center, 2100 North Lincoln Boulevard,
Suite 2, Oklahoma City, OK 73105-4907
Tel: (405) 556-9600 Fax: (405) 556-9130
Internet: www.okcca.net

Number of Judgeships: 5

The Court of Criminal Appeals is composed of five electoral districts represented by five judges who are initially appointed by the Governor from a list submitted by the Judicial Nominating Commission and thereafter, retained in statewide, nonpartisan elections for six-year terms. The positions of presiding judge and vice presiding judge rotate among the judges every two years. The Court of Criminal Appeals has exclusive appellate jurisdiction in criminal cases appealed from the Oklahoma District Courts and Municipal Criminal Courts of Record.

The Court of Criminal Appeals sits in Oklahoma City.

Court Staff

Fax: (405) 556-9130

Clerk of the Court **Michael S. Richie** .... (405) 556-9400
E-mail: michael.richie@oscn.net

Court Marshal **Kim Donaldson** .... (405) 556-9606
E-mail: kdonaldson@okcca.net

Communications Administrator **Donna Way** .... (405) 556-9627
E-mail: dway@okcca.net

Chambers of Presiding Judge Clancy Smith

2100 North Lincoln Boulevard, Suite 2, Oklahoma City, OK 73105-4907
Tel: (405) 556-9643
E-mail: csmith@okcca.net

Clancy Smith
Presiding Judge

Education: Oklahoma State 1964 BA; Tulsa 1980 JD
Began Service: September 1, 2010
Term Expires: December 31, 2016

Current Memberships: Oklahoma Bar Association; Tulsa County Bar Association

Staff

Career Law Clerk **Lou Ann Kohlman** .... (405) 556-9616
E-mail: lkohlman@okcca.net
Education: Rice 1983 BA; Harvard 1986 JD

Career Law Clerk **Allen Smith** .... (405) 556-9617
E-mail: asmith@oscn.net
Education: Tulsa 1988 JD

Administrative Assistant **Elizabeth Bridgers** .... (405) 556-9629
E-mail: ebridgers@oscn.net

Chambers of Vice Presiding Judge Gary L. Lumpkin

2100 North Lincoln Boulevard, Oklahoma City, OK 73105-4907
Tel: (405) 556-9642
E-mail: glumpkin@okcca.net

Gary L. Lumpkin
Vice Presiding Judge

Date of Birth: July 2, 1946
Education: Southwestern Oklahoma St 1968 BS; Oklahoma 1974 JD
Began Service: January 9, 1989
Appointed By: Governor Henry Bellmon
Next Election: November 4, 2020
Election Type: Retention Election
Term Expires: January 10, 2021

Current Memberships: The William J. Holloway, Jr. American Inn of Court, The American Inns of Court; Marine Corps Reserve Association; Marshall County Bar Association; Oklahoma Bar Association; Oklahoma County Bar Association; Oklahoma Judicial Conference

Staff
Judicial Assistant **Brant M. Elmore** .... (405) 556-9608
E-mail: belmore@okcca.net
Judicial Assistant **Caroline Emerson-Mitchell** .... (405) 556-9621
E-mail: cmitchell@okcca.net
Education: Oklahoma 1985 JD
Administrative Assistant **Carla Odom** .... (405) 556-9603
E-mail: codom@okcca.net

Chambers of Judge David B. Lewis

2100 North Lincoln Boulevard, Oklahoma City, OK 73105-4907
Tel: (405) 556-9611
E-mail: dlewis@okcca.net

David B. Lewis
Judge

Education: Oklahoma 1980 BBA, 1983 JD
Began Service: August 18, 2005
Appointed By: Governor C. Brad Henry
Next Election: November 2018
Election Type: General Election
Term Expires: 2019

Staff
Career Law Clerk **Lendell S. Blosser** .... (405) 556-9602
E-mail: lblosser@okcca.net
Education: Oklahoma 1991 JD
Career Law Clerk **Bryan Dupler** .... (405) 556-9607
E-mail: bdupler@okcca.net
Education: Oklahoma 1991 JD
Administrative Assistant **Cheryl Harris** .... (405) 556-9611
E-mail: charris@okcca.net

Chambers of Judge Arlene Johnson

2100 North Lincoln Boulevard, Suite 2, Oklahoma City, OK 73105-4905
Tel: (405) 556-9640 Fax: (405) 556-9130
E-mail: ajohnson@okcca.net

Arlene Johnson
Judge

Education: Oklahoma BA, JD
Began Service: March 21, 2005
Appointed By: Governor C. Brad Henry
Term Expires: January 2019

Current Memberships: American Bar Association; Oklahoma Bar Association

Chambers of Judge Arlene Johnson *continued*

Staff
Career Law Clerk **Patty Grotta** .... (405) 556-9622
E-mail: pgrotta@okcca.net
Education: Oklahoma 1986 BA; Tulane 1989 JD
Career Law Clerk **Melanie Stucky** .... (405) 556-9626
E-mail: mstucky@okcca.net
Education: Oklahoma City 1989 JD
Administrative Assistant **Patty Frakes** .... (405) 556-9609
E-mail: pfrakes@okcca.net
Education: Rose State 1989 AAS; Oklahoma 2005 BLS

Chambers of Judge Robert Hudson

2100 North Lincoln Boulevard, Oklahoma City, OK 73105
Tel: (405) 556-9600

Robert Hudson
Judge

Education: Oklahoma State; Oklahoma JD
Began Service: 2015

Oregon

Oregon Office of the State Court Administrator

Supreme Court Building, 1163 State Street, Salem, OR 97301-2563
Tel: (503) 986-5500 Fax: (503) 986-5503
Internet: http://courts.oregon.gov/ojd

Staff

Fax: (503) 986-5503
E-mail: ojd.info@ojd.state.or.us

State Court Administrator **Kingsley W. Click** . . . . (503) 986-5500
E-mail: kingsley.w.click@ojd.state.or.us
Education: Kansas 1977 JD

Director, Business and Fiscal Services Division
David T. Moon . . . . (503) 986-5150
E-mail: david.t.moon@ojd.state.or.us Fax: (503) 986-5856

Director, Human Resource Services Division
Terri J. Chandler . . . . (503) 986-5926
Fax: (503) 986-5871

Director, Information Technology Division
Bryant Baehr . . . . (503) 986-4515
E-mail: bryant.baehr@ojd.state.or.us Fax: (503) 986-5616

Director, Education, Training and Outreach
Mollie A. Croisan . . . . (503) 986-5924
E-mail: mollie.a.croisan@ojd.state.or.us

Director, Legal Counsel Division **Karen L. Hightower** . . . (503) 986-5500
E-mail: karen.l.hightower@ojd.state.or.us

Oregon Supreme Court

Supreme Court Building, 1163 State Street, Salem, OR 97301-2563
Tel: (503) 986-5555 Fax: (503) 986-5560
Internet: courts.oregon.gov/supreme

Number of Judgeships: 7

The Supreme Court consists of a chief justice and six justices who are elected in statewide nonpartisan elections for six-year terms. The Governor may appoint a justice to temporarily fill a vacancy until the next general election. The Chief Justice is elected by peer vote for a six-year term. The Supreme Court may review any decision of the Oregon Court of Appeals and hears all appeals from the Oregon Tax Court. The court has general administrative and supervisory authority over the courts of the state and admission to the state bar.

The Supreme Court sits in Salem and occasionally will sit in other parts of the state.

Court Staff

Appellate Courts Records Administrator
Rebecca J. "Becky" Osborne . . . . (503) 986-5589
E-mail: rebecca.j.osborne@ojd.state.or.us

Appellate Legal Counsel [Records Section]
Lisa Norris-Lampe . . . . (503) 986-7023
E-mail: lisa.j.norris-lampe@ojd.state.or.us
Education: Willamette

Director, Internal Auditing **Darrin D. Hotrum** . . . . (503) 986-5531
E-mail: darrin.d.hotrum@ojd.state.or.us

Law Librarian **Cathryn E. Bowie** . . . . (503) 986-5644
E-mail: cathryn.e.bowie@ojd.state.or.us Fax: (503) 986-5623

Judicial Publications Services Specialist
Mary C. Younker . . . . (503) 986-5567

Chambers of Chief Justice Thomas A. Balmer

State Supreme Court Building, 1163 State Street, Salem, OR 97301-2563
Tel: (503) 986-5717

Thomas A. "Tom" Balmer
Chief Justice

Date of Birth: 1952
Education: Oberlin 1974 BA; Chicago 1977 JD
Began Service: 2012

Staff

Law Clerk **Alletta Brenner** . . . . (503) 986-5717
Began Service: August 2015
Term Expires: August 2016

Chambers of Justice Rives Kistler

1163 State Street, Salem, OR 97301-2563
Tel: (503) 986-5713
E-mail: rives.kistler@ojd.state.or.us

Rives Kistler
Justice

Date of Birth: 1949
Education: Williams 1971 BA; Georgetown 1981 JD
Began Service: August 15, 2003
Appointed By: Governor Ted Kulongoski
Term Expires: January 1, 2017

Academic: Adjunct Professor, Lewis & Clark Law School (1997); Adjunct Professor, Lewis & Clark Law School (1999)

Clerkships: Law Clerk The Honorable Charles Clark, United States Court of Appeals for the Fifth Circuit (1981-1982); Law Clerk The Honorable Lewis F. Powell, Jr., Supreme Court of the United States (1982-1983)

Government: Assistant Attorney General, State of Oregon (1987-1999)

Judicial: Judge, Oregon Court of Appeals (1999-2003)

Legal Practice: Stoel, Rives, Boley, Jones & Grey (1983-1987)

Staff

Law Clerk **Philip Thoennes** . . . . (503) 986-5734
Term Expires: August 2016

Judicial Assistant **Julie Reynolds** . . . . (503) 986-5713
Education: Pacific Northwest 1998 BA

Chambers of Justice Martha L. Walters

Supreme Court Building, 1163 State Street, Salem, OR 97301-2563
Tel: (503) 986-5668 Fax: (503) 986-5730

Martha L. Walters
Justice

Began Service: October 2006
Appointed By: Governor Ted Kulongoski
Next Election: November 4, 2020
Election Type: General Election
Term Expires: January 5, 2021

Government: Commissioner, Law Commission, Legislative Commissions, Oregon Legislative Assembly

Staff

Law Clerk **Zara Lukens** . . . . (503) 986-5668
Began Service: August 2015
Term Expires: August 2017

Judicial Assistant **Mechele Surgeon** . . . . (503) 986-5668

Chambers of Justice Virginia L. Linder
Supreme Court Building, 1163 State Street, Salem, OR 97301-2563
Tel: (503) 986-5701 Fax: (503) 986-5730
E-mail: virginia.l.linder@ojd.state.or.us

Virginia L. Linder
Justice

Note: Justice Linder will retire effective December 31, 2015.
Date of Birth: 1953
Education: Willamette 1980 JD
Began Service: January 2007

Judicial: Judge, Oregon Court of Appeals (1997-2006)

Chambers of Justice Jack Landau
1163 State Street, Salem, OR 97301-2563
Tel: (503) 986-5674 Fax: (503) 986-5730
E-mail: jack.l.landau@ojd.state.or.us

Jack L. Landau
Justice

Date of Birth: 1953
Education: Lewis & Clark 1975 BA, 1980 JD
Began Service: January 3, 2011

Staff
Law Clerk **Lauren Eldridge** . . . . . (503) 986-5674
Judicial Assistant **Linda Kinney** . . . . . (503) 986-5674

Chambers of Justice David V. Brewer
1163 State Street, Salem, OR 97301-2563
Tel: (503) 986-5709
E-mail: david.v.brewer@ojd.state.or.us

David V. Brewer
Justice

Date of Birth: 1951
Education: Sonoma State 1974 BA; Oregon 1977 JD
Began Service: January 9, 2013

Current Memberships: Lane County Bar Association; Oregon State Bar

Staff
Law Clerk **Rob Whitsley** . . . . . (503) 986-5709
Law Clerk **(Vacant)** . . . . . (503) 986-5709

Chambers of Justice Richard Baldwin
1163 State Street, Salem, OR 97301-2563
Tel: (503) 986-5555

Richard C. Baldwin
Justice

Began Service: 2013

Staff
Law Clerk **Rachel Marx** . . . . . (503) 986-5707

Oregon Court of Appeals
Supreme Court Building, 1163 State Street, Salem, OR 97301-2563
Tel: (503) 986-5555 Fax: (503) 986-5560
Internet: www.ojd.state.or.us

Number of Judgeships: 13

The Court of Appeals consists of a chief judge and nine judges who are elected in statewide, nonpartisan elections for six-year terms. Vacancies are filled by the Governor until a successor can be elected at the next general election. The Chief Judge is appointed by the Supreme Court Chief Justice for a two-year term. Cases are heard by panels of three judges. The Oregon Court of Appeals has appellate jurisdiction over all matters from the state's circuit courts, and review of most state administrative agency actions.

The Court sits in Salem, and occasionally will sit in other parts of the state.

Court Staff
Appellate Courts Records Administrator
Rebecca J. "Becky" Osborne . . . . . (503) 986-5550
E-mail: rebecca.j.osborne@ojd.state.or.us
Appellate Commissioner [Records Section] **Jim Nass** . . . . (503) 986-5566
Education: Willamette 1971 JD
Staff Attorney **Colm Moore** . . . . . (503) 986-5872
E-mail: colm.moore@ojd.state.or.us Fax: (503) 986-5865
Staff Attorney **Lora Keenan** . . . . . (503) 986-5660
Education: St John's Col (NM) 1985 BA; Lewis & Clark 1995 JD Fax: (503) 986-5865
Staff Attorney **Jean Ann Quinn** . . . . . (503) 986-0281
Education: USC 1989 JD Fax: (503) 986-5865
Staff Attorney **Francine S. Shetterly** . . . . . (503) 986-5682
E-mail: francine.s.shetterly@ojd.state.or.us Fax: (503) 986-5865
Education: Lewis & Clark 1981 JD
Staff Attorney **Julie E. Smith** . . . . . (503) 986-5634
E-mail: julie.e.smith@ojd.state.or.us Fax: (503) 986-5865
Education: Eastern Oregon State 1990 BA; Oregon 1998 JD
Staff Attorney **Theresa Kidd** . . . . . (503) 986-5576
E-mail: theresa.kidd@ojd.state.or.us
Education: Ohio Northern 2002 JD
Staff Attorney **Jeff Schick** . . . . . (503) 986-5679
E-mail: jeffrey.j.schick@ojd.state.or.us Fax: (503) 986-5865

Chambers of Chief Judge Rick Haselton
1163 State Street, Salem, OR 97301-2563
Tel: (503) 986-5678 Fax: (503) 986-5865

Rick Haselton
Chief Judge

Note: Chief Judge Haselton will retire effective December 31, 2015.
Date of Birth: 1953
Education: Stanford 1976 BA; Yale 1979 JD
Began Service: 2012

Staff
Law Clerk **Sadie Forzley** . . . . . (503) 986-5678
Began Service: August 2014
Term Expires: August 15, 2016
Judicial Assistant **Jill D. Howell** . . . . . (503) 986-5678
E-mail: jill.d.howell@ojd.state.or.us

STATE COURTS—OREGON

Chambers of Judge Rex Armstrong

Court of Appeals, Justice Building, 1163 State Street, Salem, OR 97301
Tel: (503) 986-5664 Fax: (503) 986-5865
E-mail: rex.armstrong@ojd.state.or.us

Rex Armstrong
Judge

Date of Birth: 1950
Education: Pennsylvania 1974 BA; Oregon 1977 JD
Began Service: January 3, 1995
Next Election: November 2018
Term Expires: January 2019

Academic: Adjunct Professor of Law, Willamette University (1978); Adjunct Professor of Law, Northwestern School of Law (1987)

Clerkships: Law Clerk The Honorable Hans Linde, Oregon Supreme Court (1977-1978)

Legal Practice: Lindsay, Hart (1978-1981); Kell, Alterman (1982-1985); Bogle & Gates (1986-1994)

Staff
Law Clerk I **Christopher Page** .... (503) 986-5664
Education: Oregon 2010 JD
Law Clerk II **Adam Adkin** .... (503) 986-5664
Judicial Assistant **Melinda Hammelman** .... (503) 986-5664

Chambers of Judge Darleen Ortega

1163 State Street, Salem, OR 97301-2563
Tel: (503) 986-5721 Fax: (503) 986-5865
E-mail: darleen.ortega@ojd.state.or.us

Darleen Rene Ortega
Judge

Date of Birth: July 7, 1962
Education: George Fox Col 1984 BA; Michigan 1989 JD
Began Service: October 13, 2003
Appointed By: Governor Ted Kulongoski
Term Expires: December 31, 2016

Current Memberships: Oregon State Bar; Oregon Women Lawyers

Profession: Private Practice (1989-1992); Private Practice (1992-2003)

Staff
Career Law Clerk **Erin Everett** .... (503) 986-5721
Judicial Assistant **Christina M. Esquivel** .... (503) 986-5721
E-mail: christina.m.esquivel@ojd.state.or.us

Chambers of Judge Timothy J. Sercombe

Judicial Building, 1163 State Street, Salem, OR 97301-2563
Tel: (503) 986-5659 Fax: (503) 986-5865
E-mail: timothy.j.sercombe@ojd.state.or.us

Timothy J. Sercombe
Judge

Education: Northwestern 1971 BA; Oregon 1976 JD
Began Service: March 2007
Appointed By: Governor Ted Kulongoski
Next Election: November 2020
Election Type: General Election
Term Expires: January 5, 2021

Legal Practice: Managing Partner, Portland, OR Office, Preston Gates & Ellis LLP

Staff
Law Clerk **(Vacant)** .... (503) 986-5659
Law Clerk **Jonathan Schlidt** .... (503) 986-5659
Judicial Assistant **Jill D. Howell** .... (503) 986-5659
E-mail: jill.d.howell@ojd.state.or.us

Chambers of Judge Rebecca Duncan

1163 State Street, Salem, OR 97301-2563
Tel: (503) 986-5670 Fax: (503) 986-5865
E-mail: rebecca.a.duncan@ojd.state.or.us

Rebecca A. Duncan
Judge

Began Service: February 4, 2010
Appointed By: Governor Ted Kulongoski
Next Election: November 2016
Election Type: General Election
Term Expires: January 5, 2017

Chambers of Judge Lynn R. Nakamoto

1163 State Street, Salem, OR 97301-2563
Tel: (503) 986-5705 Fax: (503) 986-5865
E-mail: lynn.r.nakamoto@ojd.state.or.us

Lynn R. Nakamoto
Judge

Education: Wellesley 1982 AB; NYU 1985 JD
Began Service: February 3, 2011
Appointed By: Governor Ted Kulongoski

Chambers of Judge Erika L. Hadlock

1163 State Street, Salem, OR 97301-2563
Tel: (503) 986-5666 Fax: (503) 986-5560

Erika L. Hadlock
Judge

Education: Reed BA; Cornell 1991 JD
Began Service: 2011
Appointed By: Governor John A. Kitzhaber

Chambers of Judge James C. Egan

1163 State Street, Salem, OR 97301-2563
Tel: (503) 986-5662

James Egan
Judge

Began Service: 2013

Chambers of Judge Douglas L. Tookey

1163 State Street, Salem, OR 97301-2563
Tel: (503) 986-5423

Douglas L. "Doug" Tookey
Judge

Education: Chicago BA; Cornell JD; National U Singapore LLM
Appointed By: Governor John A. Kitzhaber

Chambers of Judge Erin Lageson

1163 State Street, Salem, OR 97301-2563
Tel: (503) 986-5430

Erin C. Lagesen
Judge

Education: Williams BA; Oregon MS; Harvard MEd; Willamette JD
Appointed By: Governor John A. Kitzhaber

Chambers of Judge Joel DeVore

1163 State Street, Salem, OR 97301-2563
Tel: (503) 986-5431

Joel S. DeVore
Judge

Education: Antioch Col BA; Oregon JD
Appointed By: Governor John A. Kitzhaber

Chambers of Judge Chris Garrett

1163 State Street, Salem, OR 97301-2563
1162 Court Street, NE, Fourth Floor, Salem, OR 97301
Tel: (503) 986-5672 Fax: (503) 986-5865
E-mail: chris.garrett@ojd.state.or.us

Chris Garrett
Judge

Education: Chicago 2000 JD
Began Service: February 3, 2014
Appointed By: Governor John A. Kitzhaber

Staff
Law Clerk **Eamon McCleery** . . . . (503) 986-5672
Judicial Assistant **Julie Boock** . . . . (503) 986-5672

Chambers of Judge Meagan A. Flynn

1163 State Street, Salem, OR 97301-2563
Tel: (503) 986-5555

Meagan A. Flynn
Judge

Education: Gonzaga JD

Pennsylvania

Administrative Office of Pennsylvania Courts

1515 Market Street, Suite 1414, Philadelphia, PA 19102
Tel: (215) 560-6300 Fax: (215) 560-6315
Internet: www.pacourts.us

Staff

Court Administrator **Thomas B. Darr** . . . . (215) 560-6300
E-mail: thomas.darr@pacourts.us
Administrative Assistant **Ellen L. Conaway** . . . . . . (215) 560-6300
E-mail: ellen.conaway@pacourts.us
Assistant Court Administrator **Andrea B. Tuominen** . . . . . (215) 560-6300
E-mail: andrea.tuominen@pacourts.us
Deputy Court Administrator **(Vacant)** . . . . (717) 231-3326
601 Commonwealth Avenue, Suite 1500, Harrisburg, PA 17106 Fax: (717) 231-3327
61260, Harrisburg, PA 17106
Director of Finance **Michael Felice** . . . . . . (717) 231-3300 ext. 4063
E-mail: michael.felice@pacourts.us Fax: (717) 231-3298
Director, Human Resources **David W. Kutz** . . . . . . (717) 231-3309
E-mail: david.kutz@pacourts.us Fax: (717) 231-3310
Director, Judicial Automation **Amy Ceraso** . . . . . . (412) 565-3013
One Oxford Centre, Suite 3135, Pittsburgh, PA 15219 Fax: (412) 565-3025
E-mail: amy.ceraso@pacourts.us
Director, Judicial Programs **Joseph Mittleman** . . . . . (215) 560-6300
E-mail: joseph.mittleman@pacourts.us Fax: (215) 560-5492
Director, Policy Research and Statistics **Kim Nieves** . . . . . (215) 560-6300
E-mail: kim.nieves@pacourts.us Fax: (215) 560-5487
Chief Counsel **Joseph Cosgrove** . . . . (717) 231-3300
E-mail: joseph.cosgrove@pacourts.us Fax: (717) 231-9581

Supreme Court of Pennsylvania

1515 Market Street, Suite 1414, Philadelphia, PA 19102
Tel: (215) 560-6300

Number of Judgeships: 7

Number of Vacancies: 2

The Supreme Court consists of a chief justice and six justices who are initially elected in statewide, partisan elections for ten-year terms, and who then run for retention for additional ten-year terms. The Governor may, with the consent of the State Senate, appoint a justice to temporarily fill a vacancy until the next general election. The senior justice on the Court is designated as chief justice. Retirement is mandatory at age seventy; however, retired judges may be recalled for temporary assignment by the chief justice. The Supreme Court has exclusive appellate jurisdiction over appeals involving the Pennsylvania Court of Common Pleas in cases involving the imposition of capital punishment, right to public office, supersession of a district attorney, suspension or disbarment, public indebtedness and the constitutionality of any law. The Court has exclusive jurisdiction over all appeals of cases originating in the Commonwealth Court of Pennsylvania and over appeals from orders of the Commonwealth Court in cases originating in the Pennsylvania Board of Finance and Revenue. The Court may review decisions of the Pennsylvania Superior Court and Commonwealth Court. The Court exercises general supervisory control and rule-making authority over the court system.

The Supreme Court sits at Harrisburg, Philadelphia and Pittsburgh.

Court Staff

Prothonotary **Irene Bizzoso** . . . . (717) 787-6181
Areas Covered: The Supreme Court Prothonotary is responsible for all court districts.
Pennsylvania Judicial Center, 601 Commonwealth Avenue, Suite 4500, Harrisburg, PA 17106
P.O. Box 62575, Harrisburg, PA 17106
E-mail: irene.bizzoso@pacourts.us
Education: Widener 1992 JD

Supreme Court of Pennsylvania *continued*

Deputy Prothonotary, Harrisburg Office
Amy Dreibelbis . . . . (717) 787-6181
Areas Covered: Middle District - Adams, Bradford, Berks, Bucks, Carbon, Centre, Chester, Clinton, Columbia, Cumberland, Dauphin, Delaware, Franklin, Fulton, Huntingdon, Juniata, Lancaster, Lebanon, Lehigh, Luzerne, Lycoming, Mifflin, Montgomery, Montour, Northampton, Northumberland, Perry, Pike, Shuykill, Snyder, Sullivan, Susquehanna, Tioga, Union, Wayne, Wyoming, and York Counties.
601 Commonwealth Avenue, Harrisburg, PA 17106
P.O. Box 62575, Harrisburg, PA 17106
Deputy Prothonotary, Philadelphia District Office
John W. Person, Jr. . . . . (215) 560-6370
Areas Covered: Eastern District – Pennsylvania County
468 City Hall, Philadelphia, PA 19107
E-mail: john.person@pacourts.us
Education: Rutgers (Camden) 1986 JD
Deputy Prothonotary, Pittsburgh District Office
John Vaskov . . . . (412) 565-2816
Areas Covered: Western District – Allegheny, Armstrong, Beaver, Bedford, Blair, Butler, Cambria, Cameron, Clarion, Clearfield, Crawford, Elk, Erie, Fayette, Forest, Greene, Indiana, Jefferson, Lawrence, McKean, Mercer, Potter, Somerset, Venango, Warren, Washington, and Westmoreland counties
801 City-County Bldg., Pittsburgh, PA 15219
E-mail: john.vaskov@pacourts.us
Education: Pittsburgh 1986 JD

Chambers of Chief Justice Thomas G. Saylor

Fulton Building, 200 North Third Street, 16th Floor, Harrisburg, PA 17101
Tel: (717) 772-1599 Fax: (717) 772-1605

Thomas G. Saylor
Chief Justice

Date of Birth: 1946
Education: Virginia 1969 BA; Columbia 1972 JD; Virginia 2004 LLM
Began Service: January 5, 1998
Next Election: November 2017
Election Type: Retention Election
Term Expires: January 2018
Political Affiliation: Republican

Current Memberships: American Bar Association; The American Law Institute; Pennsylvania Bar Association

Staff

Chief Law Clerk **John A. Witherow, Jr.** . . . . (717) 772-1599
E-mail: john.witherow@pacourts.us
Education: George Washington 1988 JD
Chief Judicial Assistant **Diane L. Frazier** . . . . (717) 772-1599
E-mail: diane.frazier@pacourts.us

Chambers of Justice J. Michael Eakin

4720 Old Gettysburg Road, Suite 405, Mechanicsburg, PA 17055
Tel: (717) 731-0461 Fax: (717) 731-0465

J. Michael Eakin
Justice

Date of Birth: November 18, 1948
Education: Franklin & Marshall 1970 BA; Dickinson Law 1975 JD
Began Service: January 2002
Next Election: 2016
Election Type: Retention Election
Term Expires: January 2017

Government: Assistant District Attorney, Office of the District Attorney, County of Cumberland, Pennsylvania (1975-1983); District Attorney, Office of the District Attorney, County of Cumberland, Pennsylvania (1984-1995)

Judicial: Judge, Superior Court of Pennsylvania (1996-2002)

Legal Practice: Private Practice (1980-1989)

Current Memberships: Cumberland County Bar Association; Pennsylvania Bar Association

Staff

Judicial Clerk **William C. Vohs** .... (717) 731-0461
Education: Temple 1989 BA; Dickinson Law 1992 JD
Deputy Judicial Clerk **Catherine L. Shelly** .... (717) 731-0461
E-mail: catherine.shelly@pacourts.us
Education: Duquesne 1987 BA, 1991 JD
Administrative Secretary **Lynn Zembower** .... (717) 731-0461
E-mail: lynn.zembower@pacourts.us

Chambers of Justice Max Baer

2525 One Oxford Centre, Pittsburgh, PA 15219
Tel: (412) 467-2220 Fax: (412) 467-2221
E-mail: max.baer@pacourts.us

Max Baer
Justice

Date of Birth: December 24, 1947
Education: Pittsburgh 1971 BA; Duquesne 1975 JD
Began Service: January 5, 2004
Term Expires: December 2024

Academic: Lecturer, History Department, Carnegie Mellon University

Corporate: Director, Budd Baer, Inc.

Government: Deputy Attorney General, Pennsylvania Department of Justice, Commonwealth of Pennsylvania (1975-1979)

Judicial: Judge, Court of Common Pleas of Allegheny County, Pennsylvania (1990-2003)

Legal Practice: Partner, Campbell, Sherrard & Burke (1981-1989)

Staff

Law Clerk **Corrin Johnson** .... (412) 467-2220
E-mail: corrin.johnson@pacourts.us
Law Clerk **Anna Venturini** .... (412) 467-2220
Began Service: August 2009
E-mail: anna.venturini@pacourts.us
Law Clerk **Melanie Seigel** .... (412) 467-2220
Law Clerk **Lucinda Pepples** .... (412) 467-2220
E-mail: lucinda.pepples@pacourts.us
Law Clerk **Lisa Sasinoski** .... (412) 467-2220
E-mail: lisa.sasinoski@pacourts.us
Education: Notre Dame 1979 BBA; Pittsburgh 1982 JD
Law Clerk **Erin Wick** .... (412) 467-2220
E-mail: erin.wick@pacourts.us
Chief Clerk **Betsy Ceraso** .... (412) 467-2220
E-mail: betsy.ceraso@pacourts.us

Chambers of Justice Max Baer *continued*

Judicial Secretary **Linda Williams** .... (412) 467-2220
E-mail: linda.williams@pacourts.us
Judicial Secretary **Kristi Matolyak** .... (412) 467-2224
Chief Judicial Administrative Assistant
Michele Makray .... (412) 467-2223
E-mail: michele.makray@pacourts.us

Chambers of Justice Debra Todd

One Oxford Centre, Suite 3130, Pittsburgh, PA 15219
Tel: (412) 565-2680 Fax: (412) 565-2690
E-mail: debra.todd@pacourts.us

Debra Todd
Justice

Date of Birth: 1957
Education: Pittsburgh 1982 JD; Virginia 2004 LLM
Began Service: January 2008
Next Election: November 2017
Term Expires: January 2018
Political Affiliation: Democrat

Judicial: Judge, Superior Court of Pennsylvania (2000-2008)

Staff

Career Law Clerk **Daniel DeLisio** .... (412) 565-3423
E-mail: daniel.delisio@pacourts.us
Education: Duquesne 1992 JD
Career Law Clerk **(Vacant)** .... (412) 565-5295
Career Law Clerk **Lynn Snyderman** .... (412) 565-3422
E-mail: lynn.irwin@pacourts.us
Education: Washington College of Law 1985 JD
Chief Law Clerk **Sean M. Winters** .... (412) 565-3415
E-mail: sean.winters@pacourts.us
Education: Pittsburgh 1996 JD
Deputy Chief Law Clerk **Jeffrey Bauman** .... (412) 565-5034
E-mail: jeff.bauman@pacourts.us
Deputy Chief Law Clerk **Kimberly A. Collins** .... (412) 565-3421
E-mail: kimberly.collins@pacourts.us
Education: Duquesne 1995 JD

Chambers of Justice Correale F. Stevens

1515 Market Street, Philadelphia, PA 19102
Tel: (215) 560-6300
E-mail: correale.stevens@pacourts.us

Correale F. Stevens
Justice

Date of Birth: 1946
Education: Penn State 1964 AB; Dickinson Law 1972 JD
Began Service: July 30, 2013

Chambers of Justice (Elect) David Wecht

1515 Market Street, Philadelphia, PA 19102
Tel: (215) 560-6300

David N. Wecht
Justice-Elect

Note: On November 3, 2015, Judge David Wecht was elected Justice in the Pennsylvania general election. Wecht will be sworn in effective January 4, 2016.

Education: Yale 1984 BA, 1987 JD

Chambers of Justice (Elect) Kevin M. Dougherty
1515 Market Street, Philadelphia, PA 19102
Tel: (215) 560-6300

Kevin Dougherty
Justice-Elect

Note: On November 3, 2015, Kevin Dougherty was elected Justice in the Pennsylvania general election. Dougherty will be sworn in effective January 4, 2016.

Chambers of Justice (Elect) Christine Donohue
1515 Market Street, Philadelphia, PA 19102
Tel: (215) 560-6300

Christine L. Donohue
Justice-Elect

Note: On November 3, 2015, Judge Christine Donohue was elected Justice in the Pennsylvnia general election. Donohue will be sworn in effective January 4, 2016.
Date of Birth: 1952
Education: East Stroudsburg 1974 BA; Duquesne 1980 JD

Current Memberships: Allegheny County Bar Association; American Bar Association; Pennsylvania Bar Association

Superior Court of Pennsylvania
530 Walnut Street, Suite 315, Philadelphia, PA 19106
Tel: (215) 560-5800 Fax: (215) 560-6279

Number of Judgeships: 15

The Superior Court is comprised of three judicial districts and consists of a president judge and fourteen judges who are initially elected in statewide, partisan elections for ten-year terms and who then run for retention for additional ten-year terms. The Governor may, with the consent of the State Senate, appoint a justice to temporarily fill a vacancy until the next general election. The president judge is elected by the Court's commissioned (non-senior) judges for a five year term. Retirement is mandatory at age seventy; however, retired judges may be recalled for temporary assignments by the Supreme Court president judge. The Superior Court has exclusive jurisdiction over all cases at law and equity from Pennsylvania Courts of Common Pleas, except those cases which are under the exclusive jurisdiction of the Pennsylvania Supreme Court or Commonwealth Court. The Court hears appeals involving matters of contract, tort, domestic relations, nongovernment equity except for eminent domain and nonprofit corporation matters and most criminal cases.

The Superior Court sits at Harrisburg, Philadelphia and Pittsburgh.

Court Staff
Prothonotary **Joseph Seletyn** .... (215) 560-5800
Areas Covered: The Superior Court Prothonotary is responsible for all court districts
E-mail: joseph.seletyn@pacourts.us
Deputy Prothonotary, Philadelphia Office
Michael DiPasquale .... (215) 560-5800
Areas Covered: Eastern District – Pennsylvania County
Deputy Prothonotary, Harrisburg Office
Jennifer Traxler .... (717) 772-1294
Fax: (717) 772-1297
Areas Covered: Middle District – Adams, Bradford, Berks, Bucks, Carbon, Centre, Chester, Clinton, Columbia, Cumberland, Dauphin, Delaware, Franklin, Fulton, Huntingdon, Juniata, Lancaster, Lebanon, Lehigh, Luzerne, Lycoming, Mifflin, Montgomery, Montour, Northampton, Northumberland, Perry, Pike, Shuykill, Snyder, Sullivan, Susquehanna, Tioga, Union, Wayne, Wyoming, and York Counties.
100 Pine Street, Suite 400, Harrisburg, PA 17101
E-mail: jennifer.traxler@pacourts.us

Deputy Prothonotary, Pittsburgh Office
Nicholas V. Corsetti .... (412) 565-7592
Fax: (412) 565-7711
Areas Covered: Western District – Allegheny, Armstrong, Beaver, Bedford, Blair, Butler, Cambria, Cameron, Clarion, Clearfield, Crawford, Elk, Erie, Fayette, Forest, Greene, Indiana, Jefferson, Lawrence, McKean, Mercer, Potter, Somerset, Venango, Warren, Washington, and Westmoreland counties
Affiliation: Esq.
310 Grant Street, Suite 600, Pittsburgh, PA 15219
E-mail: nicholas.corsetti@pacourts.us

Chambers of President Judge Susan Peikes Gantman
200 Four Falls Corporate Center, Suite 302,
West Conshohocken, PA 19428
Tel: (610) 832-1651
E-mail: susan.gantman@pacourts.us

Susan Peikes Gantman
President Judge

Date of Birth: August 8, 1952
Education: Pennsylvania 1974 BA, 1974 MA; Villanova 1977 JD
Began Service: January 2004
Term Expires: 2023

Staff
Career Law Clerk **Nicole DeSouza** .... (610) 832-1651
E-mail: nicole.desouza@pacourts.us
Career Law Clerk **Michael Di Pasquale** .... (610) 832-1651
Career Law Clerk **Melissa Scacchitti** .... (610) 832-1651
E-mail: melissa.scacchitti@pacourts.us
Chief Clerk **Evelyn W. Reichman** .... (610) 832-1651
E-mail: evelyn.reichman@pacourts.us
Education: Holy Family Col 1970 BA; West Chester 1985 MA; Temple 1992 JD
Secretary **Eileen Corr** .... (610) 832-1651
E-mail: eileen.corr@pacourts.us
Secretary **Lisa Lombardi** .... (610) 832-1651
E-mail: lisa.lombardi@pacourts.us

Chambers of President Judge Emeritus John T. Bender
105 Freeport Road, Pittsburgh, PA 15215
Tel: (412) 784-7101 Fax: (412) 784-7106
E-mail: Judge.Bender@pacourts.us

John T. Bender
President Judge Emeritus

Date of Birth: 1948
Education: Penn State 1970 BA; Duquesne 1976 JD
Began Service: January 7, 2002
Next Election: November 2016
Term Expires: January 2017
Political Affiliation: Republican

Current Memberships: Allegheny County Bar Association; American Bar Association; Pennsylvania Bar Association

Staff
Career Law Clerk **Sheri Geis** .... (412) 784-7101
Career Law Clerk **Paul Matuch** .... (412) 784-7101
E-mail: paul.matuch@pacourts.us
Career Law Clerk **Jeffrey Murray** .... (412) 784-7101
E-mail: jeffrey.murray@pacourts.us
Judicial Clerk III **Emily J. Yuhaniak** .... (412) 784-7101
Education: Pittsburgh 2005 BA, 2009 JD
Administrative Law Clerk **Gail N. Sanger** .... (412) 784-7101
Education: Boston U 1965 BS, 1968 MEd; Dickinson Law 1988 JD

(continued on next page)

STATE COURTS – PENNSYLVANIA

Chambers of President Judge Emeritus John T. Bender *continued*

Judicial Secretary I **Mary Pat "Mimi" Shento** . . . . (412) 784-7101
E-mail: Mimi.Shento@pacourts.us
Judicial Secretary II **Diane M. Cutrara** . . . . (412) 784-7101
E-mail: Diane.Cutrara@pacourts.us

Chambers of President Judge Emeritus Kate Ford Elliott

Two Chatham Center, Suite 1660, Pittsburgh, PA 15219
Tel: (412) 565-7670 Fax: (412) 565-5613

Kate Ford Elliott
President Judge Emeritus

Date of Birth: 1949
Education: Pittsburgh 1971 BA; Duquesne 1973 MS, 1978 JD
Began Service: January 1990
Next Election: November 2019
Term Expires: January 2020
Political Affiliation: Democrat

Current Memberships: American Bar Foundation; Allegheny County Bar Association; American Bar Association; National Association of Women Judges; Pennsylvania Bar Association; Womens Bar Association of Western Pennsylvania

Staff

Career Law Clerk **Cynthia A. Barowich** . . . . (412) 565-7670
E-mail: cynthia.barowich@pacourts.us
Education: Duquesne 1992 JD
Career Law Clerk **Damon S. Chilcote** . . . . (412) 565-7670
E-mail: damon.chilcote@pacourts.us
Education: Pittsburgh 1998 JD
Career Law Clerk **Stephne Bernacki** . . . . (412) 565-7670
E-mail: stephne.bernacki@pacourts.us
Career Law Clerk **Heather J. Rusert** . . . . (412) 565-7670
E-mail: heather.rusert@pacourts.us

Chambers of Judge Mary Jane Bowes

The Grant Building, 310 Grant Street, Suite 2600, Pittsburgh, PA 15219
Tel: (412) 565-2342 Fax: (412) 565-2317
E-mail: JudgeBowes@pacourts.us

Mary Jane Bowes
Judge

Date of Birth: 1954
Education: Georgetown 1976 BA; Pittsburgh 1979 JD
Began Service: January 7, 2002
Next Election: November 2022
Term Expires: January 1, 2022
Political Affiliation: Republican

Clerkships: Judicial Law Clerk The Honorable Harry Montgomery, Superior Court of Pennsylvania (1980-1981); Judicial Law Clerk, Chief Justice The Honorable Henry X. O'Brien, Supreme Court of Pennsylvania (1981-1982); Judicial Law Clerk The Honorable John P. Hester, Superior Court of Pennsylvania (1982-1986)

Legal Practice: Private Practice (1986-1998); Owner, Bowes & Associates (1994)

Current Memberships: Allegheny County Bar Association; National Association of Women Judges; Appellate Advocacy Committee, Pennsylvania Bar Association; Womens Bar Association of Western Pennsylvania

Staff

Career Law Clerk **Maureen Dunn Harvey** . . . . (412) 565-2342
E-mail: maureen.harvey@pacourts.us
Education: Pittsburgh 1978 JD

Chambers of Judge Mary Jane Bowes *continued*

Career Law Clerk **Michael Payne** . . . . (412) 565-2342
E-mail: michael.payne@pacourts.us
Education: Duquesne 2000 JD
Career Law Clerk **Andrew Salemme** . . . . (412) 565-2342
E-mail: andrew.salemme@pacourts.us
Education: Duquesne 2008 JD
Career Law Clerk **Wendy Taylor** . . . . (412) 565-2342
E-mail: wendy.taylor@pacourts.us
Education: Pittsburgh 1981 JD
Secretary **Lavonne Daw** . . . . (412) 565-2342
E-mail: lavonne.daw@pacourts.us

Chambers of Judge Jack A. Panella

One East Broad Street, Suite 410, Bethlehem, PA 18018
Tel: (610) 694-1121 Fax: (610) 694-1122
E-mail: jack.panella@pacourts.us

Jack A. Panella
Judge

Date of Birth: May 4, 1955
Education: St John's U (NY) 1977 BS; Columbus Law 1980 JD
Began Service: January 4, 2004
Term Expires: December 31, 2023

Clerkships: Law Clerk Michael V. Franciosa, Court of Common Pleas, Northampton County, Third Judicial District (1980-1982)

Government: Assistant County Solicitor, Office of the Solicitor, County of Northampton, Pennsylvania (1982-1987); Solicitor, Office of the Solicitor, County of Northampton, Pennsylvania (1987-1991)

Judicial: Trial Judge, Northampton County Court of Common Pleas (1991-1994)

Legal Practice: Sole Practitioner, Jack A. Panella, Esq. (1982-1991)

Current Memberships: American Bar Association; American Judges Association; The Justinian Society; Pennsylvania Bar Association

Staff

Law Clerk **William Clements** . . . . (610) 694-1121
Education: New Hampshire 1993 BS; Temple 2001 JD
Deputy Career Clerk **Benjamin D. Kohler** . . . . (610) 694-1121
Education: Temple 2002 BA, 2005 JD
Deputy Career Clerk **(Vacant)** . . . . (610) 694-1121
Chief Career Law Clerk **Christopher Nace** . . . . (610) 694-1121
E-mail: christopher.nace@pacourts.us
Education: Moravian 1998 BA; New York Law 2001 JD
Judicial Secretary I **(Vacant)** . . . . (610) 694-1121
Judicial Secretary II **Doreen T. Lipare** . . . . (610) 694-1121
E-mail: doreen.lipare@pacourts.us

Chambers of Judge Christine L. Donohue

One Oxford Centre, Suite 4225, Pittsburgh, PA 15219
Tel: (412) 565-2750
E-mail: christine.donohue@pacourts.us

Christine L. Donohue
Judge

Date of Birth: 1952
Education: East Stroudsburg 1974 BA; Duquesne 1980 JD
Began Service: January 2008

Current Memberships: Allegheny County Bar Association; American Bar Association; Pennsylvania Bar Association

STATE COURTS—PENNSYLVANIA

Chambers of Judge Jacqueline O. Shogan
300 Oxford Drive, Monroeville, PA 15146
Tel: (412) 565-3604

Jacqueline O. Shogan
Judge

Date of Birth: 1953
Education: Temple 1975 BS; Virginia MS; Duke 1990 JD
Began Service: 2007
Next Election: 2016

Government: Attorney, Chambers of District Judge Maurice B. Cohill Jr., United States District Court for the Western District of Pennsylvania

Legal Practice: Attorney, Thorp Reed & Armstrong, LLP (2001-2007)

Current Memberships: American Bar Association; Federal Bar Association; National Association of Women Judges; Pennsylvania Bar Association

Chambers of Judge Cheryl Lynn Allen
301 Grant Street, Suite 810, Pittsburgh, PA 15219
Tel: (412) 565-5230 Fax: (412) 565-7711
E-mail: cheryl.allen@pacourts.us

Cheryl Lynn Allen
Judge

Education: Penn State; Pittsburgh JD
Began Service: 2007
Next Election: 2016
Political Affiliation: Republican

Affiliation: Trustee, Board of Trustees, Waynesburg University

Academic: Associate Professor, Point Park University (2001-2006)

Judicial: Criminal Division Judge, Fifth Judicial District, Pennsylvania Judicial District Courts; Juvenile Section Judge, Fifth Judicial District, Pennsylvania Judicial Districts (1991-2004); Criminal Division Judge, Fifth Judicial District, Pennsylvania Judicial District Courts (2004-2007)

Current Memberships: Pennsylvania Bar Association

Chambers of Judge Anne E. Lazarus
1700 Market Street, Suite 1440, Philadelphia, PA 19103
Tel: (215) 560-6301
E-mail: anne.lazarus@pacourts.us

Anne E. Lazarus
Judge

Began Service: January 2010
Term Expires: December 2019

Staff
Law Clerk **Jonah Eaton** .... (215) 560-6301
Law Clerk **Robert Katz** .... (215) 560-6301
E-mail: robert.katz@pacourts.us
Judicial Clerk **Rayleen Romeo** .... (215) 560-6301
E-mail: rayleen.romeo@pacourts.us
Education: Western New England 1995 JD
Judicial Clerk III **Lisa Quasti** .... (215) 560-6301
E-mail: lisa.quasti@pacourts.us
Education: Widener 1986 JD
Deputy Judicial Clerk **Caroline Lindberg** .... (215) 560-6301
E-mail: caroline.lindberg@pacourts.us

Chambers of Judge Sallie Updyke Mundy
37 Pearl Street, Wellsboro, PA 16901
Tel: (570) 724-0171 Fax: (570) 724-0179
E-mail: sallie.mundy@pacourts.us

Sallie Updyke Mundy
Judge

Began Service: January 2010
Term Expires: December 2019

Chambers of Judge Judith Ference Olson
The Grant Building, 310 Grant Street, Suite 2420, Pittsburgh, PA 15219
Tel: (412) 565-2264
E-mail: judith.olson@pacourts.us

The Honorable Judith Ference "Judy" Olson
Judge

Date of Birth: 1957
Education: St Francis Col (PA) 1979 BA; Duquesne 1982 JD
Began Service: January 2010
Term Expires: December 2019

Current Memberships: Allegheny County Bar Association; Allegheny County Bar Foundation, Allegheny County Bar Association; Federal Bar Association; Pennsylvania Bar Association

Staff
Law Clerk **Ned Spells** .... (412) 565-2264
E-mail: ned.spells@pacourts.us

Chambers of Judge Paula Francisco Ott
15 West Gay Street, Third Floor, West Chester, PA 19380
Tel: (610) 344-2193
E-mail: paula.ott@pacourts.us

Paula Francisco Ott
Judge

Date of Birth: 1950
Education: Delaware 1972 BA, 1975 JD; Temple 1981 LLM
Began Service: January 2010
Term Expires: December 2019

Current Memberships: Chester County Bar Association; National Association of Women Judges; Pennsylvania Bar Association

Chambers of Judge David N. Wecht
One Oxford Centre, Suite 1010, Pittsburgh, PA 15219
Tel: (412) 565-7511
E-mail: david.wecht@pacourts.us

David N. Wecht
Judge

Education: Yale 1984 BA, 1987 JD
Began Service: 2012

Chambers of Senior Judge John L. Musmanno
One Oxford Center, 301 Grant Street, Room 4250, Pittsburgh, PA 15219
Tel: (412) 880-5800 Fax: (412) 880-5806
E-mail: john.musmanno@pacourts.us

John L. Musmanno
Senior Judge

Date of Birth: 1942
Education: Washington & Jefferson 1963 BA; Vanderbilt 1966 JD
Began Service: January 1998
Next Election: November 2017
Election Type: Retention Election
Term Expires: January 2018

Current Memberships: Allegheny County Bar Association; American Bar Association; Pennsylvania Bar Association

Staff
Judicial Assistant **Marybeth Palko** . . . . (412) 880-5800
E-mail: marybeth.palko@pacourts.us

Chambers of Senior Judge James J. Fitzgerald III
530 Walnut Street, Suite 1776, Philadelphia, PA 19106
Tel: (215) 560-6081 Fax: (215) 560-3083
E-mail: james.fitzgerald@pacourts.us

James J. Fitzgerald III
Senior Judge

Education: Pennsylvania 1962 BA; Villanova JD
Began Service: January 7, 2008

Chambers of Senior Judge William H. Platt
640 Hamilton Street, Allentown, PA 18101
Tel: (610) 432-2131
E-mail: william.platt@pacourts.us

William H. Platt
Senior Judge

Date of Birth: 1940
Education: Dickinson Col 1961 BA; Pennsylvania 1964 JD
Began Service: 2011

Current Memberships: American Judges Association

Chambers of Senior Judge Eugene B. Strassburger
City-County Building, 414 Grant Street, Pittsburgh, PA 15219
Tel: (412) 394-6913
E-mail: gene.strassburger@pacourts.us

Eugene B. "Gene" Strassburger
Senior Judge

Date of Birth: 1943
Education: Yale 1964 BA; Harvard 1967 JD
Began Service: 2011

Current Memberships: Allegheny County Bar Association; The American Law Institute

Commonwealth Court of Pennsylvania
Pennsylvania Judicial Center, 601 Commonwealth Avenue,
Suite 2100, Harrisburg, PA 17120
P.O. Box 69185, Harrisburg, PA 17106
Tel: (717) 255-1600

Number of Judgeships: 9

The Commonwealth Court consists of nine judges who are elected for ten-year terms in partisan elections and who may be retained for additional ten-year terms in retention elections. Vacancies are filled by the Governor with the consent of the State Senate. Those appointed to vacant positions serve until the next general election. The president judge of the court is elected by members of the court and serves a five year, non-renewable term. Elected judges must retire at the age of seventy. Senior judges, appointed by the Supreme Court, serve in various capacities. The Commonwealth Court is primarily an intermediate appellate court. It hears appeals from orders of the courts of common pleas, usually involving government-related parties and issues, and petitions for review from orders of state agencies. The court also has limited jurisdiction to hear some civil actions by and against the Commonwealth government and its officers. Significant exceptions to the grant of original jurisdiction place most actions against the Commonwealth in the court of common pleas or an administrative tribunal. The court also has original jurisdiction to hear election matters involving statewide offices.

The Court hears arguments in Harrisburg, Philadelphia and Pittsburgh. Its administrative and filing offices are in Harrisburg.

Court Staff
Executive Administrator **Gary L. Hollinger** . . . . (717) 255-1611
E-mail: gary.hollinger@pacourts.us
Education: Penn State MPA
Prothonotary **Kristen W. Brown** . . . . (717) 255-1600
E-mail: kristen.brown@pacourts.us
Education: Dickinson Law 1975 BA, 1978 JD
Chief Clerk **Michael F. Krimmel** . . . . (717) 255-1661
E-mail: michael.krimmel@pacourts.us
Education: American U 1986 BA; Widener 1995 JD
Deputy Prothonotary **John R. Moyer** . . . . (717) 255-1600
E-mail: john.moyer@pacourts.us
Education: Bloomsburg 1980 BS;
Penn State 1981 MSEd; North Carolina 1990 JD

Chambers of President Judge Dan Pellegrini
609 Frick Building, 437 Grant Street, Pittsburgh, PA 15219-6002
Tel: (412) 565-7919 Fax: (412) 565-5285

Dan Pellegrini
President Judge

Date of Birth: 1945
Education: Duquesne 1967 BA, 1970 JD
Began Service: January 1990
Next Election: November 2018
Term Expires: December 31, 2019

Current Memberships: Allegheny County Bar Association; American Bar Association; Pennsylvania Bar Association

Staff
Career Law Clerk **James Stock** . . . . (412) 565-7919
Secretary **Barbara Craig** . . . . (412) 565-7919
E-mail: barbara.craig@pacourts.us

Chambers of Judge Bernard L. McGinley

5840 Ellsworth Avenue, Suite 104, Pittsburgh, PA 15232-1779
Tel: (412) 665-5503 Fax: (412) 665-5540

Bernard L. McGinley
Judge

Date of Birth: January 7, 1946
Education: John Carroll 1967 BS; Pittsburgh 1970 JD
Began Service: January 1988
Next Election: November 2017
Election Type: General Election
Term Expires: January 2018

Academic: Professor, Allegheny County Community College (1974-1975)

Clerkships: Law Clerk The Honorable Robert A. Doyle, Pennsylvania Court of Common Pleas, Fifth Judicial District (1974-1977)

Government: Assistant District Attorney, County of Allegheny, Pennsylvania (1971-1974); Chairman, Board of Viewers, Court of Common Pleas, Fifth Judicial District, Commonwealth of Pennsylvania (1976-1980)

Judicial: Judge, Pennsylvania Court of Common Pleas, Fifth Judicial District (1982-1987)

Military Service: United States Army Reserve, United States Department of the Army (1970-1977)

Current Memberships: Allegheny County Bar Association; American Bar Association; Pennsylvania Bar Association

Staff

Career Law Clerk **Corinne McGinley-Smith** .... (412) 665-5503
Career Law Clerk **Charles P. Perrone** .... (412) 665-5511
E-mail: charles.perrone@pacourts.us
Education: John Marshall 1979 JD
Career Law Clerk **James Roberts** .... (412) 665-5538
E-mail: james.roberts@pacourts.us
Education: Pittsburgh 1992 JD
Career Law Clerk **Martin Toth** .... (412) 665-5539
Judicial Secretary **(Vacant)** .... (412) 665-5503
Judicial Secretary **Paula Hornberger** .... (412) 665-5503
E-mail: paula.hornberger@pacourts.us

Chambers of Judge Bonnie Brigance Leadbetter

610 Sentry Park East, Suite 210, Blue Bell, PA 19422
Tel: (610) 832-1715 Fax: (610) 832-1719

Bonnie Brigance Leadbetter
Judge

Date of Birth: 1947
Education: Rice 1968 BA; Pittsburgh 1971 JD
Began Service: May 1996
Appointed By: Governor Thomas J. Ridge
Term Expires: January 2018
Political Affiliation: Republican

Staff

Career Law Clerk **Seung Jai Lee** .... (610) 832-1715
E-mail: seung.lee@pacourts.us
Education: Temple 1984 JD
Career Law Clerk **Ellen McCann** .... (610) 832-1715
E-mail: ellen.mccann@pacourts.us
Career Law Clerk **Amy Suhr** .... (610) 832-1715
E-mail: amy.suhr@pacourts.us
Career Law Clerk **Heather Tomb** .... (610) 832-1715
E-mail: heather.tomb@pacourts.us
Education: Penn State 1987 BS; Duquesne 1992 JD
Career Law Clerk **(Vacant)** .... (610) 832-1715
Judicial Secretary **Judy Ferree** .... (610) 832-1715
E-mail: judy.ferree@pacourts.us
Administrative Judicial Secretary **Maureen McNiff** ...... (610) 832-1715
E-mail: maureen.mcniff@pacourts.us

Chambers of Judge Renée Cohn Jubelirer

Pennsylvania Judicial Center, 601 Commonwealth Avenue,
Harrisburg, PA 17106-9185
P.O. Box 69185, Harrisburg, PA 17106-9185
450 Windmere Drive, Suite 250, State College, PA 16801
Tel: (717) 255-1793 Tel: (814) 235-4800 (State College phone contact)
Fax: (814) 235-4804 (State College fax contact) Fax: (717) 787-0796
E-mail: jody.gardner@pacourts.us

Renée Cohn Jubelirer
Judge

Date of Birth: 1957
Education: Penn State 1978 BA; Northwestern 1983 JD
Began Service: January 7, 2002
Next Election: November 2021
Term Expires: December 31, 2021

Academic: Teaching Fellow, School of Law, Stanford University (1983-1984); Assistant Professor, College of Law, DePaul University (1985-1987)

Corporate: Corporate Counsel, ATX Telecommunications (1997-2001)

Government: Assistant County Solicitor, Office of the County Solicitor, County of Lehigh, Pennsylvania (1996-1999); Commissioner, Board of Commissioners, Township of South Whitehall, Pennsylvania (2000-2001)

Legal Practice: Associate, Sidley Austin LLP (1984-1985); Vice President and Shareholder, Frank, Frank, Penn & Bergstein (1988-1996)

Current Memberships: American Bar Association; Lehigh County Bar Association; National Association of Women Judges; Pennsylvania Bar Association

Staff

Law Clerk **Nicholas Krakoff** .... (814) 235-4800
E-mail: nicholas.krakoff@pacourts.us
Judicial Clerk III **Leah Davis** .... (814) 235-4800
E-mail: leah.davis@pacourts.us
Law Clerk **Scott Stedjan** .... (717) 255-1793
E-mail: scott.stedjan@pacourts.us
Deputy Judicial Clerk III **Brenda L. Carver** .... (814) 235-4800
E-mail: brenda.carver@pacourts.us
Education: Duquesne 2005 JD

Chambers of Judge Robert E. Simpson, Jr.

Justice Building, 115 South Broad Street, Nazareth, PA 17101
Tel: (717) 255-1688

Robert E. Simpson, Jr.
Judge

Education: Dickinson Col 1973 BA; Dickinson Law 1976 JD
Began Service: January 7, 2001
Next Election: November 2016

Staff

Secretary **Tracy Wagner** .... (717) 255-1688
E-mail: tracy.wagner@pacourts.us

Chambers of Judge Mary Hannah Leavitt

601 Commonwealth Avenue, Suite 4300, Harrisburg, PA 17120
Tel: (717) 255-1796 Fax: (717) 783-6715
E-mail: judge.leavitt@pacourts.us

Mary Hannah Leavitt
Judge

Date of Birth: 1947
Education: Connecticut Col 1969 BA; Pennsylvania 1972 MA; Dickinson Law 1978 JD
Began Service: January 7, 2002
Next Election: November 2021
Term Expires: January 2022

Academic: Adjunct Professor, The Pennsylvania State University (1996-1998)

Government: Assistant Attorney General, Office of the Attorney General, Commonwealth of Pennsylvania (1978-1981); Chief of Litigation and Chief Counsel, Insurance Department, Commonwealth of Pennsylvania (1981-1987)

Legal Practice: Shareholder, Buchanan Ingersoll PC (1991-2001)

Current Memberships: American Bar Association; Dauphin County Bar Association; Pennsylvania Bar Association

Staff

Law Clerk **Sherry Bainbridge** . . . . (717) 255-1788
Began Service: 2010
E-mail: sherry.bainbridge@pacourts.us
Education: Wilkes U 1992 BA; Dickinson Law 1995 JD

Law Clerk **Joshua Veith** . . . . (717) 255-1798
Began Service: 2014
E-mail: joshua.veith@pacourts.us

Law Clerk **Geoffrey Weyl** . . . . (717) 255-1790
Began Service: 2013

Career Law Clerk **Jennifer Bacon** . . . . (717) 255-1791
Began Service: 2006
E-mail: jennifer.bacon@pacourts.us
Education: Dickinson Col 1994 BA; Dickinson Law 1998 JD

Administrative Law Clerk **Vance A. Fink, Jr.** . . . . (717) 255-1799
Began Service: 2003
E-mail: vance.fink@pacourts.us
Education: Franklin & Marshall 1992 BA; Dickinson Law 1995 JD

Judicial Secretary **Cindy Landis** . . . . (717) 255-1796
E-mail: cynthia.landis@pacourts.us

Judicial Secretary **Donette McPoyle** . . . . (717) 255-1797
E-mail: donette.mcpoyle@pacourts.us

Chambers of Judge P. Kevin Brobson

601 Commonwealth Avenue, Harrisburg, PA 17120
Tel: (717) 255-1600
E-mail: judge.brobson@pacourts.us

P. Kevin Brobson
Judge

Date of Birth: 1970
Education: Lycoming 1992 BA; Widener 1995 JD
Began Service: January 2010
Term Expires: December 2019

Current Memberships: Dauphin County Bar Association; Pennsylvania Bar Association

Chambers of Judge Patricia A. McCullough

Grant Building, 310 Grant Street, Pittsburgh, PA 15219
Tel: (412) 565-5348
E-mail: judge.mccullough@pacourts.us

Patricia A. McCullough
Judge

Date of Birth: 1956
Education: Pittsburg State 1978 BA; Pittsburgh 1981 JD
Began Service: 2010
Term Expires: December 2019

Chambers of Judge Anne E. Covey

400 South River Road, New Hope, PA 18938
Tel: (215) 862-6571
E-mail: judge.covey@pacourts.us

Anne E. Covey
Judge

Education: Delaware 1981 BA; Widener 1984 JD
Began Service: 2011
Term Expires: 2021

Chambers of Senior Judge James Gardner Colins

Widener Building, One South Penn Square, Philadelphia, PA 19107
Tel: (215) 496-4960 Fax: (215) 560-5624
E-mail: judge.colins@pacourts.us

James Gardner Colins
Senior Judge

Date of Birth: 1946
Education: Pennsylvania 1968 BA; Villanova 1971 JD
Began Service: 2012

Current Memberships: Pennsylvania Bar Association; Philadelphia Bar Association

Chambers of Senior Judge Rochelle S. Friedman

313 Hyde Park, Doylestown, PA 18902
Tel: (215) 489-3853

Rochelle S. Friedman
Senior Judge

Date of Birth: 1938
Education: Pittsburgh 1959 BA, 1972 JD
Began Service: January 1992
Political Affiliation: Democrat

Current Memberships: American Bar Association; The Temple American Inn of Court, The American Inns of Court; American Judges Association; Bucks County Bar Association; National Association of Women Judges; Pennsylvania Bar Association

Staff

Career Law Clerk **Matthew McKeon** . . . . (215) 489-3853
E-mail: matthew.mckeon@pacourts.us

Administrative Law Clerk **Diane L. Davis** . . . . (412) 565-5449
601 Commonwealth Avenue, Harrisburg, PA 17120 Fax: (717) 705-5725
E-mail: diane.davis@pacourts.us
Education: Kent State 1986 BA; Pittsburgh 1989 JD

Deputy Law Clerk **Lisa N. Pettit** . . . . (215) 489-3853
E-mail: lisa.pettit@pacourts.us Fax: (215) 489-3857
Education: Villanova 1998 JD

Judicial Secretary **Barbara Hevner** . . . . (215) 489-3853
E-mail: barbara.hevner@pacourts.us

Judicial Secretary **Theresa Rickert** . . . . (717) 255-1648
601 Commonwealth Avenue, Harrisburg, PA 17120
E-mail: theresa.rickert@pacourts.us

Chambers of Senior Judge Rochelle S. Friedman *continued*

Judicial Law Clerk **Rachel M. Stoltenberg** . . . . (412) 565-7787
Frick Building, 437 Grant Street, Suite 601,
Pittsburgh, PA 15219
E-mail: rachel.stoltenberg@pacourts.us
Education: Penn State 1990 BS;
Dickinson Law 1993 JD

Puerto Rico

Supreme Court of Puerto Rico

Ponce de Leon Avenue, Stop #8, San Juan, PR 00902
P.O. Box 9022392, San Juan, PR 00902-2392
Tel: (787) 723-6033 Fax: (787) 723-9199
Internet: www.ramajudicial.pr

Number of Judgeships: 9

Court Staff

Administrative Director of the Courts
Sonia Colon Velez Ivette .... (787) 641-6600
Clerk of the Supreme Court
Aida Ileana Oquendo .... (787) 641-6600 ext. 2072
Chief Information Officer **Felix Bajandas** .... (787) 723-6033

Chambers of Chief Justice Liana Fiol Matta Hon

P.O. Box 9022392, San Juan, PR 00902-2392
Tel: (787) 721-6625

Liana Fiol Matta Hon
Chief Justice

Education: Puerto Rico JD; Columbia LLM
Began Service: February 2004
Term Expires: 2016

Chambers of Associate Justice Anabelle Rodriguez Rodriguez

P.O. Box 9022392, San Juan, PR 00902-2392
Tel: (787) 723-0648

Anabelle Rodriguez Rodriguez
Associate Justice

Education: Puerto Rico 1985 BA, JD
Began Service: August 18, 2004
Term Expires: 2023

Chambers of Associate Justice Rafael L. Martinez Torres

P.O. Box 9022392, San Juan, PR 00902-2392
Tel: (787) 723-0343

Rafael L. Martinez Torres
Associate Justice

Education: Puerto Rico BA, JD
Began Service: March 10, 2009

Chambers of Associate Justice Mildred G. Pabon Charneco

P.O. Box 9022392, San Juan, PR 00902-2392
Tel: (787) 723-0294

Mildred G. Pabon Charneco
Associate Justice

Began Service: February 24, 2009

Chambers of Associate Justice Eric V. Kolthoff Caraballo

P.O. Box 9022392, San Juan, PR 00902-2392
Tel: (787) 723-0856

Eric V. Kolthoff Caraballo
Associate Justice

Began Service: February 4, 2009

Chambers of Associate Justice Edgardo Rivera Garcia

P.O. Box 9022392, San Juan, PR 00902-2392
Tel: (787) 723-0752

Edgardo Rivera Garcia
Associate Justice

Began Service: 2010

Chambers of Associate Justice Robert Cintron Feliberti

P.O. Box 9022392, San Juan, PR 00902-2392
Tel: (787) 724-4547

Robert Cintron Feliberti
Associate Justice

Began Service: 2010

Chambers of Associate Justice Luis Estrella Martinez

P.O. Box 9022392, San Juan, PR 00902-2392
Tel: (787) 725-6474

Luis Estrella Martinez
Associate Justice

Began Service: May 5, 2011

Chambers of Associate Justice Maite Oronoz Rodriguez

Ponce de Leon Avenue, San Juan, PR 00902
Tel: (787) 723-6033

Maite Oronoz Rodriguez
Associate Justice

Began Service: July 17, 2014

Rhode Island

Rhode Island Office of the State Court Administrator

Frank Licht Judicial Complex, 250 Benefit Street, Providence, RI 02903
Tel: (401) 222-3266 TTY: (401) 222-3269 Fax: (401) 222-4224
Internet: www.courts.ri.gov

Staff

State Court Administrator **J. Joseph Baxter, Jr.** .... (401) 222-3266
E-mail: jbaxter@courts.ri.gov
Education: Penn State 1983 BA;
Rhode Island 1993 MPA
Deputy State Court Administrator **Gail M. Valuk** .... (401) 222-3266
E-mail: gvaluk@courts.ri.gov
Education: Connecticut 1986 BS;
Detroit Law 1994 JD
Assistant State Court Administrator, Facilities and
Operations **Stephen Kerr** .... (401) 222-4999
E-mail: skerr@courts.ri.gov
Assistant State Court Administrator, Finance
Darlene Leyden Walsh .... (401) 222-8723
E-mail: dwalsh@courts.ri.gov
Assistant State Court Administrator, Employee
Relations **Marisa White** .... (401) 222-8665
E-mail: mwhite@courts.ri.gov
Assistant State Court Administrator, Judicial
Technology **Peter Panciocco** .... (401) 222-3000
E-mail: ppanciocco@courts.ri.gov
Assistant State Court Administrator, Community
Outreach and Public Relations **Craig Berke** .... (401) 222-8631
E-mail: cberke@courts.ri.gov Fax: (401) 222-8632
Education: Rhode Island 1977 BA
Assistant Director, Policy & Programs Office
Jennifer Olivelli .... (401) 222-8666
E-mail: jolivelli@courts.ri.gov
Education: Rhode Island Col 1993 BA;
Northeastern 1994 MS
Executive Director, MCLE Commission
Holly Hitchcock .... (401) 222-4942
E-mail: hhitchcock@courts.ri.gov
Education: Rhode Island 1976 BS;
Florida Atlantic 1977 MEd
Chief Staff Attorney **Martha Newcomb** .... (401) 222-8671
E-mail: mnewcomb@courts.ri.gov
Education: Smith 1976 AB; Northeastern 1984 JD
Staff Attorney II **Carol Bourcier-Fargnoli** .... (401) 222-6536
E-mail: cfargnoli@courts.ri.gov
Education: Regis Col (MA) 1974 BA;
Rhode Island Col 1980 MAT; Suffolk 1989 JD
General Counsel **Erika Kruse-Weller** .... (401) 222-3266
E-mail: ekruse@courts.ri.gov
Education: Wheaton (IL) 1993 BA;
Suffolk 1996 JD
Chief Disciplinary Counsel **David Curtin** .... (401) 222-3270
E-mail: dcurtin@courts.ri.gov
Education: Rhode Island 1979 BA; Suffolk 1984 JD

Rhode Island Supreme Court

Frank Licht Judicial Complex, 250 Benefit Street, Providence, RI 02903
Tel: (401) 222-3272 TTY: (401) 222-3269 Fax: (401) 222-3599
Internet: www.courts.state.ri.us

Number of Judgeships: 5

The justices of the Supreme Court are appointed to life terms by the Governor and confirmed by the state legislature. All appointments are first nominated by the Judicial Review Committee. The Supreme Court exercises final appellate jurisdiction over all courts, determines the constitutionality of legislation and issue writs necessary to the exercise of proper jurisdiction. The Court has general supervision over all lower court and regulates admission to the bar and discipline of its members.

The Supreme Court sits in Providence.

Rhode Island Supreme Court *continued*

Court Staff

Clerk of Court **Debra Saunders** .... (401) 222-3272
Court Administrator **J. Joseph Baxter, Jr.** .... (401) 222-3263
E-mail: jbaxter@courts.ri.gov
Deputy State Court Administrator **Gail M. Valuk** .... (401) 222-3266
E-mail: gvaluk@courts.ri.gov Fax: (401) 222-2625
Director, Consumer Protection/Education Programs
Holly Hitchcock .... (401) 222-4942
E-mail: hhitchcock@courts.state.ri.us Fax: (401) 222-3599

Chambers of Chief Justice Paul A. Suttell

Frank Licht Judicial Complex, 250 Benefit Street, Providence, RI 02903
Tel: (401) 222-3943 Fax: (401) 222-1059
E-mail: psuttell@courts.ri.gov

Paul A. Suttell
Chief Justice

Date of Birth: January 10, 1949
Education: Northwestern 1971 BA; Suffolk 1976 JD
Began Service: July 16, 2009
Appointed By: Governor Don Carcieri

Judicial: Associate Justice, Family Court (1990-2003)

Current Memberships: American Academy of Adoption Attorney; American Bar Association; National Council of Juvenile and Family Court Judges; Rhode Island Bar Association

Staff

Administrative Assistant **Ronald Tutalo** .... (401) 222-3073
E-mail: rtutalo@courts.ri.gov
Education: Providence 1967 BA; Suffolk 1970 JD

Chambers of Justice Maureen McKenna Goldberg

250 Benefit Street, Providence, RI 02903
Tel: (401) 222-3280

Maureen McKenna Goldberg
Justice

Date of Birth: 1951
Education: Providence 1973 AB; Suffolk 1978 JD
Began Service: February 24, 2001
Appointed By: Governor Lincoln Almond

Current Memberships: American Bar Association; National Association of Women Judges; Pawtucket Bar Association; Rhode Island Bar Association; Rhode Island Trial Judges Association

Staff

Law Clerk **Nicole Verdi** .... (401) 222-3280
Began Service: September 2014
Term Expires: August 31, 2015
Law Clerk **Patrick McBurney** .... (401) 222-3280
Began Service: September 2014
Term Expires: August 31, 2015
Associate Executive Assistant **Celine Goodson** .... (401) 222-3280
E-mail: cgoodson@courts.state.ri.us

Chambers of Justice Francis X. Flaherty
250 Benefit Street, Providence, RI 02903
Tel: (401) 222-3285 Fax: (401) 222-3659
E-mail: fflaherty@courts.ri.gov

Francis X. Flaherty
Justice

Date of Birth: January 8, 1947
Education: Providence 1968 AB; Suffolk 1975 JD
Began Service: May 2, 2003
Appointed By: Governor Don Carcieri

Academic: Governor, University of Rhode Island

Staff
Law Clerk **Chloe Davis** .... (401) 222-3285
Began Service: September 2, 2015
Term Expires: September 4, 2016
Law Clerk **John Scannell, Jr.** .... (401) 222-3285
Began Service: September 2, 2015
Term Expires: September 4, 2016

Chambers of Justice William P. Robinson, III
250 Benefit Street, Providence, RI 02903-2719
Tel: (401) 222-3775
E-mail: wrobinson@courts.ri.gov

William P. Robinson III
Justice

Began Service: September 2004

Academic: Governor, University of Rhode Island

Staff
Law Clerk **Erin Paquette** .... (401) 222-3775
Began Service: September 2013
Term Expires: August 2015
Law Clerk **Paige Schroeder** .... (401) 222-3775
Began Service: August 2013
Term Expires: August 2015
Secretary **Linda F. Tancrell** .... (401) 222-3775

Chambers of Justice Gilbert V. Indeglia
250 Benefit Street, Providence, RI 02903
Tel: (401) 222-3272

Gilbert V. Indeglia
Justice

Began Service: April 28, 2010
Appointed By: Governor Don Carcieri

South Carolina

South Carolina Court Administration

John C. Calhoun Building, 1015 Sumter Street, Suite 200,
Columbia, SC 29201
Tel: (803) 734-1800 Fax: (803) 734-1821
Internet: www.judicial.state.sc.us

Staff

Director **Rosalyn Woodson Frierson** . . . . (803) 734-1800
E-mail: rfrierson@sccourts.org Fax: (803) 734-1355
Education: South Carolina 1979 BA, 1992 JD

Finance and Personnel Director **Carolyn Taylor** . . . . . . (803) 734-1970
E-mail: ctaylor@sccourts.org Fax: (803) 734-1963

Information Technology Director **Joan Assey** . . . . . . (803) 734-0523
E-mail: jassey@sccourts.org Fax: (803) 734-0273
Education: South Carolina 1966 BA, 1976 MEd, 1988 EdD

South Carolina Supreme Court

1231 Gervais Street, Columbia, SC 29201
P.O. Box 11330, Columbia, SC 29211
Tel: (803) 734-1080 Fax: (803) 734-1499
Internet: www.sccourts.org

Number of Judgeships: 5

The Supreme Court consists of a chief justice and four associate justices who are elected by the South Carolina General Assembly for ten-year terms. The Governor may fill vacancies for unexpired terms not exceeding one year. The Supreme Court has appellate jurisdiction over cases involving the death penalty, public utility rates, significant constitutional issues, public bond issues and the elections laws. The Court may review decisions of the South Carolina Court of Appeals and has administrative control over all lower courts in the state. The Court also regulates the admission to the state bar and the practice of law in the state.

The Supreme Court sits in Columbia.

Court Staff

Clerk **Daniel E. Shearouse** . . . . (803) 734-1080
E-mail: dshearouse@sccourts.org
Education: Clemson 1976 BS; South Carolina 1979 JD

Deputy Clerk **Brenda F. Shealy** . . . . (803) 734-1080
E-mail: bshealy@sccourts.org
Education: Midlands Tech 1971 AB

Chief Staff Attorney **Betsy Goodale** . . . . (803) 734-1160
E-mail: bgoodale@sccourts.org Fax: (803) 734-1789

Law Librarian **Janet F. Meyer** . . . . (803) 734-1140
E-mail: jmeyer@sccourts.org Fax: (803) 734-0519
Education: Carson-Newman 1977 BA; South Carolina 1986 MLS

Chambers of Chief Justice Jean Hoefer Toal

Supreme Court Building, 1231 Gervais Street, Columbia, SC 29211
P.O. Box 12456, Columbia, SC 29201
Tel: (803) 734-1584 Fax: (803) 734-1167
E-mail: jtoal@sccourts.org

Jean Hoefer Toal
Chief Justice

Date of Birth: August 11, 1943
Education: Agnes Scott 1965 BA; South Carolina 1968 JD
Began Service: March 17, 1988
Term Expires: December 2024

Government: South Carolina Human Affairs Commission (1972-1974); Member, South Carolina House of Representatives (1975-1988); Chair, House Rules Committee, South Carolina House of Representatives (1980-1988)

Legal Practice: Haynsworth, Perry, Bryant, Marion & Johnstone (1968-1970); Partner, Belser, Baker, Barwick, Ravenel, Toal & Bender (1970-1988)

Current Memberships: American Bar Association; The John Belton O'Neall American Inn of Court, The American Inns of Court; South Carolina Bar; South Carolina Women Lawyers Association

Staff

Law Clerk **Katherine Heminger** . . . . (803) 734-1586
Began Service: August 2013
Term Expires: December 2015
E-mail: kheminger@sccourts.org

Law Clerk **Ashley Robertson** . . . . (803) 734-1088
Term Expires: December 2015
E-mail: arobertson@sccourts.org

Law Clerk **Amelia Waring Walker** . . . . (803) 734-1587
Began Service: May 2012
Term Expires: December 2015
E-mail: awaring@sccourts.org

Counsel to the Chief Justice **Stephanie A. Nye** . . . . . . (803) 734-2898
E-mail: snye@sccourts.org
Education: Duke 1996 BA; South Carolina 1999 JD

Chambers of Justice Costa M. Pleicones

1231 Gervais Street, Columbia, SC 29201
P.O. Box 11330, Columbia, SC 29211
Tel: (803) 734-1438 Fax: (803) 734-0427
E-mail: cpleicones@sccourts.org

Costa M. Pleicones
Justice

Date of Birth: 1944
Education: Wofford 1965; South Carolina 1968 JD
Began Service: 2000
Next Election: February 2016
Term Expires: July 31, 2016

Government: Public Defender, Office of the Public Defender, County of Richland, South Carolina (1973-1977); County Attorney, Office of the County Attorney, County of Richland, South Carolina (1977-1981)

Judicial: Municipal Judge (part-time), City of Columbia (1982-1988); Circuit Judge, South Carolina Circuit Court (1991-2000)

Legal Practice: Private Practice (1975-1991)

Military Service: United States Army (1968-1973)

Current Memberships: Richland County Bar Association; South Carolina Bar

Staff

Law Clerk **(Vacant)** . . . . (803) 734-1438

(continued on next page)

Chambers of Justice Costa M. Pleicones *continued*

Career Law Clerk **Susan Widener** .... (803) 734-1438
E-mail: swidener@sccourts.org
Education: Hollins Col 1978 BA;
South Carolina 1983 JD

Chambers of Justice Donald W. Beatty

P.O. Box 3543, Spartanburg, SC 29304-3543
Tel: (864) 596-3450

Donald W. Beatty
Justice

Education: South Carolina State 1974 BA; South Carolina 1979 JD
Began Service: May 2007

Affiliation: Member, Mount Moriah Baptist Church; Trustee, Board of Trustees, Mount Moriah Baptist Church

Government: Council Member, City Council, City of Spartanburg, South Carolina (1988-1990); South Carolina House of Representatives (1991-1995)

Judicial: Circuit Court Judge, Seventh Judicial Circuit (1995); Associate Judge, Chambers of Associate Judge Donald W. Beatty, South Carolina Court of Appeals (2003-2007)

Legal Practice: Attorney, Private Practice

Military Service: United States Army, United States Department of Defense

Staff

Career Law Clerk **Dawn A. Przirembel** .... (864) 596-3450
E-mail: dprzirembel@sccourts.org
Education: Washington and Lee 1993 JD
Career Law Clerk **Katherine Myers** .... (864) 596-3450
E-mail: kmyers@sccourts.org
Executive Assistant **Majorie Jones** .... (864) 596-3450
E-mail: mjones@sccourts.org

Chambers of Justice John W. Kittredge

305 East North Street, Suite 216, Greenville, SC 29601
P.O. Box 11330, Columbia, SC 29211
Tel: (864) 734-1579
E-mail: jkittredge@sccourts.org

John W. Kittredge
Justice

Date of Birth: September 28, 1956
Education: South Carolina 1979 BA, 1982 JD
Began Service: June 18, 2008
Appointed By: Governor Mark Sanford
Term Expires: 2018

Staff

Law Clerk **Blaire Camp** .... (803) 734-1578
Began Service: August 2011
E-mail: bcamp@sccourts.org
Law Clerk **John Warren** .... (803) 734-1579

Chambers of Justice Kaye G. Hearn

1231 Gervais Street, Columbia, SC 29201
Tel: (803) 734-1080 Fax: (803) 734-1499
E-mail: khearn@sccourts.org

Kaye G. Hearn
Justice

Date of Birth: 1950
Education: Bethany (WV) 1972 BA; South Carolina 1977 JD; Virginia 1998 LLM
Began Service: 2009

South Carolina Court of Appeals

1015 Sumter Street, Columbia, SC 29201
P.O. Box 11629, Columbia, SC 29211
Tel: (803) 734-1890 Fax: (803) 734-1839
Internet: www.sccourts.org

Number of Judgeships: 9

The Court of Appeals, which was established in 1983, consists of a chief judge and eight associate judges elected by the South Carolina General Assembly for six-year terms. The Governor may fill vacancies for unexpired terms not exceeding one year. The Court of Appeals exercises appellate jurisdiction over cases from the South Carolina Circuit Court and Family Court, except cases over which the Supreme Court has exclusive jurisdiction.

The Court of Appeals may sit in any county as needed.

Court Staff

Clerk **Jenny Abbott Kitchings** .... (803) 734-1890
E-mail: jkitchings@sccourts.org Fax: (803) 734-1839
Deputy Clerk **V. Claire Allen** .... (803) 734-1890
E-mail: callen@sccourts.org

Chambers of Chief Judge John C. Few

1015 Sumter Street, Columbia, SC 29201
Tel: (803) 734-1890 Fax: (803) 734-1839
E-mail: jfew@sccourts.org

John C. Few
Chief Judge

Date of Birth: April 9, 1963
Education: Duke 1985 BA; South Carolina 1988 JD
Began Service: February 3, 2010

Staff

Law Clerk **Nick Charles** .... (803) 734-1890
Began Service: 2015
E-mail: ncharles@sccourts.org
Law Clerk **(Vacant)** .... (803) 734-1890
Administrative Assistant/Law Clerk **Kallyn K. Falvo** ..... (803) 734-1890

Chambers of Associate Judge Thomas E. Huff

P.O. Box 11629, Columbia, SC 29211
Tel: (803) 734-1890 (Columbia Chambers)
Fax: (803) 734-1596 (Columbia Chambers)
E-mail: thuffj@sccourts.org

Thomas E. Huff
Associate Judge

Date of Birth: 1949
Education: Augusta 1971 BA; South Carolina 1975 JD
Began Service: March 29, 1996
Next Election: February 2018
Term Expires: June 30, 2018

Corporate: Corporate Counsel, Aiken Electric Cooperative, Inc. (1991-1996)

Government: Member, South Carolina House of Representatives (1979-1996)

Legal Practice: Private Practice (1977-1996)

Current Memberships: Aiken County Bar Association; South Carolina Bar

Staff

Career Law Clerk **Lucia Hoefer Leaman** .... (803) 734-1890
E-mail: lleaman@sccourts.org
Education: Clemson 1983 BS;
South Carolina 1986 JD
Career Law Clerk **Jennifer Bush Madsen** .... (803) 734-1931
E-mail: jmadsen@sccourts.org
Education: Furman 1992 BA;
South Carolina 1996 JD

Chambers of Associate Judge Thomas E. Huff *continued*

Career Law Clerk/Administrative Assistant
Aline Ferguson . . . . (803) 734-1541
E-mail: aferguson@sccourts.org
Education: Converse 1976 BA;
South Carolina 1980 JD

Chambers of Associate Judge Paul E. Short, Jr.

1015 Sumter Street, Columbia, SC 29201
Tel: (803) 734-1890
E-mail: pshort@sccourts.org

Paul E. Short, Jr.
Associate Judge

Education: Citadel 1968 BA; South Carolina 1971 JD
Began Service: May 2004
Term Expires: June 2017

Government: Representative, District 43, South Carolina House of Representatives (1983-1991)

Judicial: Circuit Court Judge, At Large Seat # 8 (1991-1999); Resident Judge, Sixth Judicial Circuit (1999-2004)

Staff
Career Law Clerk **Jeanette F. Barber** . . . . (803) 734-1890
E-mail: jbarber@scourts.org
Education: New Hampshire 1982 BS;
New Hampshire Col 1987 MBA;
South Carolina 1994 JD
Career Law Clerk **Alyssa Stigamier** . . . . (803) 734-2711
E-mail: astigamier@scourts.org
Administrative Assistant **Hethie Burgess** . . . . (803) 581-5011
E-mail: pshortsc@sccourts.org

Chambers of Associate Judge H. Bruce Williams

P.O. Box 11629, Columbia, SC 29211
Tel: (803) 734-1890 Fax: (803) 734-1829
E-mail: hwilliams@sccourts.org

H. Bruce Williams
Associate Judge

Date of Birth: March 13, 1956
Education: Wofford 1978 BA; South Carolina 1982 JD
Began Service: May 25, 2004
Term Expires: June 2017

Profession: Private Practice (1982-1995)

Staff
Law Clerk **Carlisle "Lisle" Traywick** . . . . (803) 734-1575
Began Service: September 2014
Term Expires: September 2017
E-mail: vttraywick@sccourts.org
Law Clerk **Benjamin "Ben" Dudek** . . . . (803) 734-1575
Began Service: September 2015
Term Expires: September 2016
E-mail: bdudek@sccourts.org
Career Law Clerk **Rebecca Goings** . . . . (803) 734-1594
Began Service: August 2011
E-mail: rgoings@sccourts.org

Chambers of Associate Judge Paula H. Thomas

1015 Sumter Street, Columbia, SC 29201
Tel: (803) 734-1890

Paula H. Thomas
Associate Judge

Education: South Carolina 1979 BIS, 1981 MEd, 1986 JD
Began Service: February 7, 2007
Term Expires: June 30, 2017

Government: State Representative, South Carolina House of Representatives (1993-1996)

Judicial: Judge, 15th Judicial Circuit, South Carolina Circuit Court (1998-2007)

Staff
Law Clerk **Mary Au** . . . . (803) 734-1901
E-mail: mau@sccourts.org
Law Clerk **Andrew Joiner** . . . . (803) 734-1919
E-mail: ajoiner@sccourts.org
Administrative Assistant **Elaine Langston** . . . . (843) 545-3551
E-mail: elangston@sccourts.org

Chambers of Associate Judge Aphrodite K. Konduros

1015 Sumter Street, Columbia, SC 29201
Tel: (803) 734-1890 Tel: (864) 467-8496 (Greenville Office)
E-mail: akonduros@sccourts.org

Aphrodite K. Konduros
Associate Judge

Date of Birth: January 30, 1959
Education: South Carolina BA, JD
Began Service: February 6, 2008
Term Expires: June 30, 2021

Affiliation: Judge, South Carolina Family Court

Clerkships: Law Clerk, Third Judicial Circuit, South Carolina

Government: Deputy General Counsel, Disabilities and Special Needs Department, State of South Carolina; County Attorney, Social Services Department, State of South Carolina; Assistant General Counsel, Social Services Department, State of South Carolina; County Director, Social Services Department, City of Greenville, South Carolina

Staff
Career Law Clerk **Jennifer Camp** . . . . (803) 734-1929
E-mail: jcamp@sccourts.org
Career Law Clerk **Meghan "Meg" Newman** . . . . (864) 467-8614
E-mail: mnewman@sccourts.org
Law Clerk/Administrative Assistant **Michael Martinez** . . . (864) 467-8575
E-mail: mmartinez@sccourts.org

Chambers of Associate Judge John D. Geathers

1015 Sumter Street, Columbia, SC 29201
Tel: (803) 734-1890
E-mail: jgeathers@sccourts.org

John D. Geathers
Associate Justice

Education: South Carolina 1983 BA, 1986 JD
Began Service: May 21, 2008
Appointed By: Governor Mark Sanford
Term Expires: June 30, 2017

Government: Senior Staff Counsel, Office of Senate Research, State of South Carolina (1987-1995); Judge, Administrative Law Court, State of South Carolina (1994-2008)

Current Memberships: North Carolina Bar Association; South Carolina Bar

(continued on next page)

STATE COURTS—SOUTH CAROLINA

Chambers of Associate Judge John D. Geathers *continued*

Staff

Law Clerk **Mary Elam** .... (803) 734-1890
E-mail: melam@sccourts.org

Law Clerk **John "Max" Gravlee** ....(803) 734-1890
E-mail: jmgravlee@sccourts.org

Administrative Assistant **Stefanie Anderson** .... (803) 734-1890
E-mail: sjanderson@sccourts.org

Chambers of Associate Judge James E. Lockemy

1015 Sumter Street, Columbia, SC 29201
Tel: (803) 734-1890
E-mail: jlockemy@sccourts.org
E-mail: jlockemy@sccourts.org

James E. Lockemy
Associate Justice

Began Service: May 21, 2008
Term Expires: June 30, 2016

Staff

Law Clerk **William Childers** .... (803) 734-2293

Law Clerk **Catherine Harrison** .... (803) 734-2293
E-mail: charrison@sccourts.org

Administrative Assistant **Patricia Bohachic** .... (843) 774-4166
E-mail: pbohachic@sccourts.org

Chambers of Associate Judge Stephanie P. McDonald

1015 Sumter Street, Columbia, SC 29201
Tel: (803) 734-1890

Stephanie P. McDonald
Associate Judge

Staff

Law Clerk **Sarah Thornton** .... (843) 958-5101
E-mail: sthornton@sccourts.org

Law Clerk **Margaret Strom** .... (843) 598-5102
E-mail: mstrom@sccourts.org

Administrative Assistant **Elyse Clark** .... (843) 958-5102
E-mail: ecclark@sccourts.org

South Dakota

South Dakota Office of the State Court Administrator

State Capitol Building, 500 East Capitol Avenue, Pierre, SD 57501-5070
Tel: (605) 773-3474 Fax: (605) 773-8437
Internet: www.sdjudicial.com

Staff

State Court Administrator **Greg Sattizahn** . . . . (605) 773-3474
Began Service: 2013
E-mail: greg.sattizahn@ujs.state.sd.us
Human Resources Manager **Beth Urban** . . . . (605) 773-3474
E-mail: beth.urban@ujs.state.sd.us Fax: (605) 773-8437
Budget and Finance Director **Janet Borchard** . . . . (605) 773-4872
E-mail: janet.borchard@ujs.state.sd.us
Information Technology Director **Kent Grode** . . . . (605) 773-4876
E-mail: kent.grode@ujs.state.sd.us Fax: (605) 773-8369
Trial Court Services Director **Nancy Allard** . . . . (605) 773-4873
E-mail: nancy.allard@ujs.state.sd.us
Law Librarian **Sheridan Cash Anderson** . . . . (605) 773-4898
E-mail: Sheridan.Anderson@ujs.state.sd.us Fax: (605) 773-8479
Assistant Librarian **Susan "Sue" Zilverberg** . . . . (605) 773-4898
E-mail: susan.zilverberg@ujs.state.sd.us Fax: (605) 773-8479
Court Information and Publications **Jill Gusso** . . . . (605) 773-3474
E-mail: Jill.Gusso@ujs.state.sd.us
Policy and Legal Services Director **Suzanne Kappes** . . . . (605) 773-3474
E-mail: suzanne.kappes@ujs.state.sd.us

South Dakota Supreme Court

State Capitol Building, 500 East Capitol Avenue, Pierre, SD 57501
Tel: (605) 773-3511 Fax: (605) 773-6128
Internet: www.sdjudicial.com

Number of Judgeships: 5

The Supreme Court consists of a chief justice and four justices who are appointed by the Governor from one of five electoral districts throughout the state for initial three-year terms and then run for retention in statewide general elections for eight-year terms. The chief justice is elected by peer vote for a four-year term. Retirement is mandatory at age seventy; however, retired justices may be recalled for temporary assignment. The Supreme Court has original jurisdiction in cases involving interests of the state and exclusive appellate jurisdiction over the South Dakota Circuit Court. The Court may render advisory opinions to the Governor involving the exercise of his or her executive powers. The Court has authority to supervise admission to the state bar and the conduct of its members and the Court has general administrative and rule-making authority over the lower courts.

The Supreme Court sits in Pierre and may sit elsewhere in the state as necessary.

Court Staff

Clerk of the Court **Shirley A. Jameson-Fergel** . . . . (605) 773-3511
E-mail: shirley.jameson-fergel@ujs.state.sd.us
Chief Deputy **Laura J. Graves** . . . . (605) 773-3511
E-mail: laura.graves@ujs.state.sd.us
Deputy Clerk **Sarah L Gallagher** . . . . (605) 773-3511
E-mail: sarah.gallagher@ujs.state.sd.us
Deputy Clerk **Amy Hudson** . . . . (605) 773-3511
E-mail: amy.hudson@ujs.state.sd.us

Chambers of Chief Justice David Gilbertson

State Capitol Building, 500 East Capitol Avenue, Pierre, SD 57501
Tel: (605) 773-4881
E-mail: david.gilbertson@ujs.state.sd.us

David Gilbertson
Chief Justice

Date of Birth: 1949
Education: South Dakota State 1972 BS; South Dakota 1975 JD
Began Service: April 17, 1995
Appointed By: Governor William Janklow
Next Election: November 2018
Election Type: Retention Election
Term Expires: December 2018

Government: Deputy State's Attorney, Office of the State's Attorney, County of Roberts, South Dakota (1975-1986); City Attorney, Office of the City Attorney, City of Sisseton, South Dakota (1975-1986)

Judicial: Judge, South Dakota Circuit Court, Fifth Judicial Circuit (1986-1995)

Legal Practice: Private Practice (1975-1986)

Current Memberships: State Bar of South Dakota

Staff

Judicial Assistant **Kristina Mechaley** . . . . (605) 773-4881
E-mail: kristina.mechaley@ujs.state.sd.us

Chambers of Justice Steven L. Zinter

State Capitol Building, 500 East Capitol Avenue, Pierre, SD 57501-5070
Tel: (605) 773-3511 Fax: (605) 773-6128
E-mail: steven.zinter@ujs.state.sd.us

Steven L. Zinter
Justice

Date of Birth: 1950
Education: South Dakota 1972 BS, 1975 JD
Began Service: April 2, 2002
Appointed By: Governor William Janklow
Next Election: November 2018
Election Type: Retention Election
Term Expires: December 2018

Government: Assistant Attorney General, District of South Dakota, Office of the Attorney General, United States Department of Justice; State Attorney, County of Hughes, South Dakota (1980-1987)

Judicial: Circuit Judge, Sixth Judicial Circuit, South Dakota (1987-1997); Presiding Judge, Sixth Judicial Circuit, South Dakota (1997-2002)

Current Memberships: American Bar Association; South Dakota Judges Association; State Bar of South Dakota

Chambers of Justice Glen A. Severson

500 East Capitol Avenue, Pierre, SD 57501-5070
Tel: (605) 773-4883
E-mail: glen.severson@ujs.state.sd.us

Glen A. Severson
Justice

Education: South Dakota 1972, 1975 JD
Began Service: April 3, 2009
Appointed By: Governor Mike Rounds

Government: Deputy State's Attorney, Office of the State's Attorney, County of Beadle, South Dakota (1975-1976)

Judicial: Presiding Judge, Second Judicial Circuit, South Dakota Circuit Courts (2002-2009)

Current Memberships: American Bar Association

Profession: Attorney (1976-1993)

(continued on next page)

Chambers of Justice Glen A. Severson *continued*

Staff

Law Clerk **Eric Cleveringa** .... (605) 773-4883
Began Service: August 2012
E-mail: eric.cleveringa@ujs.state.sd.us

Chambers of Justice Lori Wilbur

500 East Capitol Avenue, Pierre, SD 57501
Tel: (605) 773-3511 Fax: (605) 773-6128
E-mail: lori.wilbur@ujs.state.sd.us

Lori S. Wilbur
Justice

Education: South Dakota 1974, 1977 JD
Began Service: 2011
Next Election: November 2018

Chambers of Justice Janine Kern

500 East Capitol Avenue, Pierre, SD 57501-5070
Tel: (605) 773-3511

Janine Kern
Justice

Education: Arizona State 1982 BA; Minnesota 1985 JD
Began Service: 2015
Appointed By: Governor Dennis Daugaard

Tennessee

Administrative Office of the Courts of Tennessee

600 Nashville City Center, 511 Union Street, Suite 600, Nashville, TN 37219
Tel: (615) 741-2687 Tel: (800) 448-7970 Fax: (615) 741-6285
E-mail: ib27la3@smtpaoc.tsc.state.tn.us
Internet: www.tsc.state.tn.us

Staff

Administrative Director **Deborah Taylor Tate** . . . . (615) 741-2687
Education: Tennessee 1977 BA, 1980 JD
Assistant Director, Fiscal Services **Pam Hancock** . . . . (615) 741-2687
E-mail: pam.hancock@tscmail.state.tn.us
Assistant Director, Legal/Public Information **(Vacant)** . . . . (615) 741-2687
Assistant Director, Technology Services
Ann Lynn Walker . . . . (615) 741-2687
Human Resources Manager **Cindy Saladin** . . . . (615) 741-2687
E-mail: cindy.saladin@tscmail.state.tn.us
Public Information Officer **Michele Wojciechowski** . . . . . (615) 741-2687
E-mail: michele.wojciechowski@tscmail.state.tn.us

Tennessee Supreme Court

Supreme Court Building, 401 Seventh Avenue North, Nashville, TN 37219-1407 (Middle Division)
Supreme Court Building, 505 Main Street, Suite 200, Knoxville, TN 37902 (Eastern Division)
Six Highway 45 By-Pass, Jackson, TN 38301 (Western Division)
Tel: (615) 741-2681 (Middle Division)
Tel: (865) 594-6700 (Eastern Division)
Tel: (731) 423-5840 (Western Division)
Fax: (615) 532-8757 (Middle Division)
Fax: (865) 594-6497 (Eastern Division)
Fax: (731) 423-6453 (Western Division)
Internet: www.tncourts.gov

Number of Judgeships: 5

The Supreme Court is comprised of three judicial divisions and consists of a chief justice and four justices who are elected in statewide, partisan elections for eight-year terms. The chief justice is elected by peer vote to a four-year term. Retirement is usually at age seventy; however, retired justices may be recalled by the Supreme Court chief justice to serve temporary assignments. The Supreme Court hears direct appeals from the state's trial courts in cases involving a question of the constitutionality of a state law or municipal ordinance, the right to hold public office and other public law issues, workers' compensation, state revenue and death penalty convictions. The Court may review decisions of the state's two intermediate appellate courts by writ of certiorari. The Court exercises rule-making and supervisory control over the lower courts and disciplinary authority over members of the state bar.

The Supreme Court sits in Knoxville, Nashville and Jackson.

Court Staff

Clerk of the Court **James M. Hivner** . . . . (615) 253-1470
E-mail: james.hivner@tncourts.gov
Education: Tennessee 1988 BS; Alabama 1993 JD, 1993 LLM
Chief Deputy Clerk, Eastern Grand Division
Joanne Newsome . . . . (865) 594-6700
Fax: (865) 594-6497
P.O. Box 444, Knoxville, TN 37901-0444
E-mail: joanne.newsome@tncourts.gov
Chief Deputy Clerk, Middle Grand Division
Lisa Marsh . . . . (615) 741-2682 ext. 1104
E-mail: lisa.marsh@tncourts.gov Fax: (615) 532-8757
Chief Deputy Clerk, Western Grand Division
Nancy Acred . . . . (731) 423-5840
Supreme Court Bldg., 6 Highway 45 By-Pass, Jackson, TN 38301 Fax: (731) 423-6453
P.O. Box 909, Jackson, TN 38302-0909
E-mail: nancy.acred@tncourts.gov

Chambers of Chief Justice Sharon Gail Lee

505 Main Street, Suite 200, Knoxville, TN 37902
Tel: (865) 594-5289

Sharon Gail Lee
Chief Justice

Date of Birth: December 8, 1953
Education: Tennessee 1975 BBA, 1978 JD
Began Service: October 2, 2008
Appointed By: Governor Phil Bredesen
Term Expires: October 2022

Staff

Administrative Assistant **Shelly Ward** . . . . (865) 594-5289

Chambers of Justice Cornelia A. Clark

401 Seventh Avenue North, Suite 318, Nashville, TN 37219
Tel: (615) 741-2114 Fax: (615) 741-5809
E-mail: cclark@tncourts.gov

Cornelia A. Clark
Justice

Education: Vanderbilt BA; Harvard MA; Vanderbilt JD
Began Service: September 19, 2005
Appointed By: Governor Phil Bredesen
Term Expires: September 1, 2022

Staff

Law Clerk **Chris Rowe** . . . . (615) 741-2114
Career Law Clerk **Lisa A. Rippy** . . . . (615) 741-2114
Began Service: 2011
E-mail: lisa.rippy@tncourts.gov
Education: Tennessee 1992 JD
Executive Administrative Assistant
Lisa Hazlett-Wallace . . . . (615) 741-2114
E-mail: lisa.hazlett-wallace@tncourts.gov

Chambers of Justice Holly M. Kirby

401 Seventh Avenue North, Nashville, TN 37219-1407
Tel: (615) 741-2681

Holly M. Kirby
Justice

Date of Birth: July 9, 1957
Education: U Memphis 1982 JD
Political Affiliation: Republican

Chambers of Justice Jeffrey Bivins

401 Seventh Avenue North, Nashville, TN 37219-1407
Tel: (615) 741-2681

Jeffrey S. Bivins
Justice

Education: East Tennessee State 1982 BA; Vanderbilt 1986 JD

Tennessee Court of Appeals

Internet: www.tsc.state.tn.us

The three divisions of the Court of Appeals each consists of a presiding judge and three judges who are elected in nonpartisan elections for eight-year terms. Vacancies are filled by the Governor from a list of candidates provided by the Appellate Court Nominating Commission; newly-appointed judges stand for retention in the first August biennial election occurring more than thirty days after their appointment. The presiding judges are elected by peer vote to a one-year term. Retirement is at age seventy. However, retired judges may be recalled by the Tennessee Supreme Court Chief Justice to serve temporary assignments. The Court of Appeals has direct appellate jurisdiction over all civil cases, except when the Supreme Court has exclusive jurisdiction or as provided by law.

Tennessee Court of Appeals, Eastern Grand Division

505 Main Street, Suite 200, Knoxville, TN 37902
P.O. Box 444, Knoxville, TN 37901-0444
Tel: (865) 594-6700 Fax: (865) 594-6497

Number of Judgeships: 4

Areas Covered: Counties of Anderson, Bledsoe, Blount, Bradley, Campbell, Carter, Claiborne, Cocke, Cumberland, Grainger, Greene, Hamblen, Hamilton, Hancock, Hawkins, Jefferson, Johnson, Knox, Loudon, McMinn, Meigs, Monroe, Morgan, Polk, Rhea, Roane, Scott, Sevier, Sullivan, Unicoi, Union and Washington

Court Staff
Chief Deputy Clerk **Joanne Newsome** . . . . (865) 594-6700
E-mail: joanne.newsome@tncourts.gov

Chambers of Presiding Judge Charles D. Susano, Jr.

U.S. Post Office Building, 505 Main Street, Suite 200, Knoxville, TN 37902
P.O. Box 444, Knoxville, TN 37901-0444
Tel: (865) 594-5246 Fax: (865) 594-2825
E-mail: Judge.Charles.D.Susano.Jr@tncourts.gov

Charles D. Susano, Jr.
Presiding Judge

Date of Birth: 1936
Education: Notre Dame 1958; Tennessee 1963 JD
Began Service: March 18, 1994
Appointed By: Governor Ned Ray McWherter
Next Election: August 2022
Term Expires: September 1, 2022
Political Affiliation: Democrat

Current Memberships: American Bar Foundation; American Bar Association; Knoxville Bar Association; Tennessee Bar Association; Tennessee Bar Foundation; Tennessee Judicial Conference

Staff
Career Law Clerk **(Vacant)** . . . . (865) 594-5733
Career Law Clerk **Matthew "Matt" Gerdeman** . . . . (865) 594-5733
E-mail: matt.gerdeman@tncourts.gov
Education: Tennessee 1995 JD
Administrative Assistant **Ryan Mirian** . . . . (865) 594-5246

Chambers of Judge D. Michael Swiney

505 Main Street, Suite 200, Knoxville, TN 37902
P.O. Box 444, Knoxville, TN 37901-0444
Tel: (865) 594-6116

D. Michael Swiney
Judge

Date of Birth: May 25, 1949
Education: Tennessee 1971 BS, 1974 MS, 1978 JD
Began Service: July 1999
Term Expires: December 2022

Academic: Adjunct Law Professor, University of Tennessee at Knoxville (1997-2006)

Legal Practice: Attorney, Private Practice (1979-1999)

Current Memberships: The Hamilton Burnett American Inn of Court, The American Inns of Court; Knoxville Bar Association

Staff
Career Law Clerk **Robin McMillian** . . . . (865) 594-6116
Began Service: October 1, 2007
Education: Tennessee JD
Career Law Clerk **Andrew "Andy" Whaley** . . . .(865) 594-6116
Executive Judicial Assistant **Tammy Capps** . . . . (865) 594-6116
E-mail: tammy.capps@tncourts.gov

Chambers of Judge John Westley McClarty

633 Chestnut Street, Suite 1560, Chattanooga, TN 37450
P.O. Box 11481, Chattanooga, TN 37450
Tel: (423) 634-0590 Fax: (423) 634-0596

John McClarty
Judge

Education: Austin Peay State 1971 BS; Southern U (New Orleans) 1976 JD
Began Service: January 2009

Profession: Attorney

Chambers of Judge Thomas R. Frierson, II

505 Main Street, Knoxville, TN 37902
Tel: (865) 594-6700

Thomas R. "Skip" Frierson
Judge

Education: Tennessee 1980, 1983 JD
Began Service: February 14, 2013
Appointed By: Governor Bill Haslam

Tennessee Court of Appeals, Middle Grand Division

Supreme Court Building, 401 Seventh Avenue North, Nashville, TN 37219-1407
Tel: (615) 741-2681 Fax: (615) 532-8757

Number of Judgeships: 4

Areas Covered: Counties of Bedford, Cannon, Cheatham, Clay, Coffee, Davidson, DeKalb, Dickson, Fentress, Franklin, Giles, Grundy, Hickman, Houston, Humphreys, Jackson, Lawrence, Lewis, Lincoln, Macon, Marion, Marshall, Maury, Montgomery, Moore, Overton, Perry, Pickett, Putnam, Robertson, Rutherford, Sequatchie, Smith, Summer, Stewart, Trousdale, Van Buren, Warren, Wayne, White, Williamson and Wilson

Court Staff
Chief Deputy Clerk **Lisa Marsh** . . . . (615) 741-2681
E-mail: lisa_marsh@tncourts.gov

Chambers of Presiding Judge W. Neal McBrayer
401 Seventh Avenue North, Nashville, TN 37219-1407
Tel: (615) 741-2681

W. Neal McBrayer
Presiding Judge

Education: Maryville Col 1986 BA; William & Mary 1989 JD

Chambers of Judge Frank G. Clement, Jr.
401 Seventh Avenue North, Suite 215, Nashville, TN 37219-1407
Tel: (615) 741-2206 Fax: (615) 741-9880
E-mail: judge.frank.clement@tncourts.gov

Frank G. Clement, Jr.
Judge

Date of Birth: August 1, 1949
Education: Tennessee (Memphis) 1972 BSE; Nashville 1979 JD
Began Service: October 2003
Appointed By: Governor Phil Bredesen
Term Expires: December 2022

Judicial: Circuit and Probate Court Judge, 20th Judicial District, Tennessee Judicial District Courts (1995); Judge, Division VII of Circuit Probate Court, 20th Judicial District, Tennessee Judicial District Courts (1996-2003)

Current Memberships: Board of Trustees, Nashville School of Law; Tennessee Bar Association; Tennessee Bar Foundation

Membership: President, Nashville Kiwanis Club (1987-1988)

Profession: Private Practice (1979-1995)

Membership: Member, The Harry Phillips American Inn of Court (1990-2001); President, Nashville Bar Association (1995); Member, Tennessee Trial Judges Association (1997-2002); Convention Chair, Tennessee Judicial Conference (1998)

Staff
Law Clerk **Nate Lykins** .... (615) 741-2206
Began Service: February 2015
Term Expires: September 2017
E-mail: nate.lykins@tncourts.gov
Law Clerk **Chandler Farmer** .... (615) 741-2206
Began Service: September 2015
Term Expires: September 2017
E-mail: chandler.farmer@tncourts.gov
Judicial Assistant and Law Clerk **Kimberly Faye** .... (615) 741-2206
E-mail: kimberly.faye@tncourts.gov

Chambers of Judge Andy D. Bennett
Supreme Court Building, 401 Seventh Avenue North, Nashville, TN 37219-1407
Tel: (615) 741-6750

Andy D. Bennett
Judge

Began Service: October 5, 2007
Appointed By: Governor Phil Bredesen
Next Election: August 2022
Election Type: Retention Election

Government: Chief Deputy Attorney General, Office of the Attorney General, State of Tennessee

Staff
Career Law Clerk **Diane Nisbet** .... (615) 741-6750
Began Service: 2009
E-mail: diane.nisbet@tncourts.gov

Chambers of Judge Richard H. Dinkins
Supreme Court Building, 401 Seventh Avenue North, Nashville, TN 37219-1407
Tel: (615) 741-6491 Fax: (615) 741-9880

Richard H. Dinkins
Judge

Education: Vanderbilt 1977 JD
Began Service: January 2008
Next Election: August 2022
Election Type: Retention Election

Staff
Law Clerk **Erin Shackelford** .... (615) 741-6491
Term Expires: July 31, 2016
Law Clerk **Emily Patten** .... (615) 741-6491
Administrative Assistant **Martha Tria** .... (615) 741-6491
E-mail: martha.tria@tncourts.gov

Tennessee Court of Appeals, Western Grand Division
Supreme Court Building, Six Highway 45 Bypass, Jackson, TN 38301
P.O. Box 909, Jackson, TN 38302-0909
Tel: (731) 423-5840 Fax: (731) 423-6453

Number of Judgeships: 4

Areas Covered: Counties of Benton, Carroll, Chester, Crockett, Decatur, Dyer, Fayette, Gibson, Hardeman, Hardin, Haywood, Henderson, Henry, Lake, Lauderdale, McNairy, Madison, Obion, Shelby, Tipton and Weakley

Court Staff
Chief Deputy Clerk **Nancy Acred** .... (731) 423-5840
E-mail: nancy.acred@tncourts.gov

Chambers of Judge J. Steven Stafford
100 Main Avenue North, Suite 4, Dyersburg, TN 38025
P.O. Box 1103, Dyersburg, TN 38025
Tel: (731) 286-8387

J. Steven Stafford
Judge

Education: Tennessee; Cumberland JD
Began Service: July 2008
Appointed By: Governor Phil Bredesen
Next Election: August 2022
Election Type: Retention Election

Judicial: Chancellor, 29th Judicial District, Tennessee (1993-2008); Presiding Judge, Tennessee Court of the Judiciary

Current Memberships: Tennessee Bar Association; Tennessee Bar Foundation

Staff
Career Law Clerk **Sarah Day** .... (731) 286-8387
Career Law Clerk **Jennillyn Gibson** .... (731) 286-8387
Judicial Assistant **Pattye Mallard** .... (731) 286-8387
E-mail: pattye.mallard@tncourts.gov

Chambers of Judge Arnold B. Goldin
Six Highway 45 Bypass, Jackson, TN 38301
Tel: (731) 423-5840

Arnold B. Goldin
Judge

Chambers of Judge Kenny W. Armstrong
Six Highway 45 Bypass, Jackson, TN 38301
Tel: (731) 423-5840
E-mail: kenny.armstrong@tncourts.gov

Kenny Armstrong
Judge

Chambers of Judge Brandon O. Gibson
P.O. Box 909, Jackson, TN 38302-0909
Tel: (731) 423-5836

Brandon O. Gibson
Judge

Began Service: October 13, 2014
Appointed By: Governor Bill Haslam

Tennessee Court of Criminal Appeals
Internet: tscaoc.tsc.state.tn.us/

The three divisions of the Court of Criminal Appeals each consist of four judges who are elected in nonpartisan elections for eight-year terms. Vacancies are filled by the Governor from a list of candidates provided by the Appellate Court Nominating Commission; newly-appointed judges stand for retention in the first August biennial election occurring more than thirty days after their appointment. The presiding judge is elected by peer vote to a one-year term. Retirement is at age seventy; however, retired judges may be recalled by the Tennessee Supreme Court Chief Justice to serve temporary assignments. The Court of Criminal Appeals has appellate jurisdiction over felony and misdemeanor criminal cases, habeas corpus and post-conviction proceedings, criminal contempt proceedings and extradition cases.

Tennessee Court of Criminal Appeals, Eastern Grand Division
505 Main Street, Suite 200, Knoxville, TN 37902
P.O. Box 444, Knoxville, TN 37901-0444
Tel: (865) 594-6700 Fax: (865) 594-6497

Number of Judgeships: 4

Areas Covered: Counties of Anderson, Bledsoe, Blount, Bradley, Campbell, Carter. Claiborne, Cocke, Cumberland, Grainger, Greene, Hamblen, Hamilton, Hancock, Hawkins, Jefferson, Johnson, Knox, Loudon, McMinn, Meigs, Monroe, Morgan, Polk, Rhea, Roane, Scott, Sevier, Sullivan, Unicoi, Union and Washington

Court Staff
Chief Deputy Clerk **Joanne Newsome** .... (865) 594-6700
E-mail: joanne.newsome@tncourts.gov

Chambers of Judge James Curwood Witt, Jr.
505 Main Street, Suite 356, Knoxville, TN 37902
Tel: (865) 594-5187 Fax: (865) 594-5235

James Curwood Witt, Jr.
Judge

Date of Birth: 1948
Education: Tennessee 1973 JD
Began Service: January 1997
Appointed By: Governor Don Sundquist
Next Election: August 2022
Election Type: Retention Election
Term Expires: September 1, 2022
Political Affiliation: Republican

Judicial: Judge, Monroe County Juvenile Court (1979-1982)

Chambers of Judge James Curwood Witt, Jr. *continued*

Legal Practice: Private Practice (1973-1997)

Current Memberships: Tennessee Bar Foundation; Tennessee Judicial Conference

Staff
Senior Law Clerk **Renee Hammond** .... (865) 594-2421
E-mail: renee.hammond@tncourts.gov
Education: Tennessee 2001 JD
Junior Law Clerk **Carol Anne Long** .... (865) 594-5279
Education: Tennessee 2000 JD
Secretary **Melissa "Missy" McConkey** .... (865) 594-5187
E-mail: missy.mcconkey@tncourts.gov

Chambers of Judge Norma McGee Ogle
505 Main Street, Suite 350, Knoxville, TN 37902
P.O. Box 444, Knoxville, TN 37901-0444
Tel: (865) 594-6089

Norma McGee Ogle
Judge

Date of Birth: 1952
Education: Tennessee JD
Began Service: November 1998
Appointed By: Governor Don Sundquist

Legal Practice: Ogle, Wynn and Rader

Staff
Law Clerk **Paula L. Calhoun** .... (865) 594-6089
Began Service: 2010
E-mail: paula.calhoun@tncourts.gov
Education: Tennessee 2001 JD
Career Law Clerk **Amy Paul** .... (865) 594-6089
E-mail: amy.paul@tncourts.gov
Education: Mid Tennessee State 1996 BS; Tennessee 2000 JD
Executive Administrative Assistant **Andrea Wingate** ..... (865) 594-6089
E-mail: andrea.wingate@tncourts.gov

Chambers of Judge D. Kelly Thomas, Jr.
505 Main Street, Knoxville, TN 37902
Tel: (865) 594-6400 Fax: (865) 594-5349

D. Kelly Thomas, Jr.
Judge

Education: Tennessee 1974 BA, 1977 JD
Began Service: 2006
Next Election: August 2022
Election Type: Retention Election

Staff
Law Clerk **Elizabeth Hatcher** .... (865) 594-6400
Term Expires: August 2016
Law Clerk **Jason Smith** .... (865) 594-6400
Term Expires: August 2016
E-mail: jason.smith@tncourts.gov
Career Law Clerk **Danielle Greer** .... (865) 594-6400
E-mail: danielle.greer@tncourts.gov

Chambers of Judge Robert H. Montgomery Jr.
400 Clinchfield Street, Suite 210, Kingsport, TN 37660
Tel: (423) 392-4851

Robert H. Montgomery, Jr.
Judge

Began Service: 2014

Tennessee Court of Criminal Appeals, Middle Grand Division

Supreme Court Building, 401 Seventh Avenue North,
Nashville, TN 37219-1407
Tel: (615) 741-2681 Tel: (615) 532-8757

Number of Judgeships: 4

Areas Covered: Counties of Bedford, Cannon, Cheatham, Clay, Coffee, Davidson, DeKalb, Dickson, Fentress, Franklin, Giles, Grundy, Hickman, Houston, Humphreys, Jackson, Lawrence, Lewis, Lincoln, Macon, Marion, Marshall, Maury, Montgomery, Moore, Overton, Perry, Pickett, Putnam, Robertson, Rutherford, Sequatchie, Smith, Sumner, Stewart, Trousdale, Van Buren, Warren, Wayne, White, Williamson and Wilson

Court Staff
Chief Deputy Clerk **Lisa Marsh** . . . . (615) 741-2681
Deputy Clerk **(Vacant)** . . . . (615) 741-2681
Deputy Clerk **Stephanie Wilson** . . . . (615) 741-2681
E-mail: stephanie.wilson@tncourts.gov
Deputy Clerk **Vickie Smith** . . . . (615) 741-2681
E-mail: vickie.smith@tncourts.gov

Chambers of Judge Thomas T. Woodall

103 Sylvis Street, Dickson, TN 37055
P.O. Box 1075, Dickson, TN 37056-1075
Tel: (615) 446-1661

Thomas T. Woodall
Judge

Education: Tennessee Tech BS; U Memphis 1981 JD
Began Service: December 4, 1996
Appointed By: Governor Don Sundquist
Next Election: 2022
Term Expires: September 1, 2022

Government: District Attorney General, State of Tennessee (1984-1990)

Legal Practice: Attorney, Private Practice (1990-1996)

Current Memberships: Dickson County Bar Association; Tennessee Bar Association

Membership: Attorney, Private Practice (1982-1984); Arbitrator, American Arbitration Association (1985-1999)

Staff
Career Law Clerk **Jennifer Bledsoe** . . . . (615) 446-1661
Began Service: July 2008
Career Law Clerk **Lindsay Barrett** . . . . (615) 446-1661
E-mail: lindsay.barrett@tscmail.state.tn.us
Secretary **Kim Hayes** . . . . (615) 446-1661
E-mail: kim.hayes@tscmail.state.tn.us

Chambers of Judge Robert W. Wedemeyer

Supreme Court Building, 401 Seventh Avenue North, Suite 220,
Nashville, TN 37219-1407
Tel: (615) 532-7967 Fax: (615) 741-9880
E-mail: Judge.Robert.Wedemeyer@tscmail.state.tn.us

Robert W. Wedemeyer
Judge

Date of Birth: 1951
Education: Vanderbilt 1973 BA; Memphis State 1976 JD
Began Service: April 14, 2000
Appointed By: Governor Don Sundquist
Next Election: 2022
Term Expires: September 2022

Judicial: Circuit Court Judge (1990-2000)

Legal Practice: Private Law Practice (1977-1990)

Current Memberships: Montgomery County Bar Association; Robertson County Bar Association; Tennessee Judicial Conference

Chambers of Judge Robert W. Wedemeyer *continued*

Staff
Law Clerk **Katherine Merrill** . . . . (615) 532-7967
Law Clerk **Amber Gallina** . . . . (615) 532-9275
Began Service: August 2009
E-mail: amber.gallina@tscmail.state.tn.us
Education: U Memphis 2004 JD
Career Law Clerk **Christy Graves** . . . . (615) 532-7966
E-mail: christy.graves@tscmail.state.tn.us
Education: Tennessee 2001 JD

Tennessee Court of Criminal Appeals, Western Grand Division

Supreme Court Building, Six Highway 45 Bypass, Jackson, TN 38301
P.O. Box 909, Jackson, TN 38302-0909
Tel: (731) 423-5840 Fax: (731) 423-6453

Number of Judgeships: 4

Areas Covered: Counties of Benton, Carroll, Chester, Crockett, Decatur, Dyer, Fayette, Gibson, Hardeman, Hardin, Haywood, Henderson, Henry, Lake, Lauderdale, Madison, McNairy, Obion, Shelby, Tipton and Weakley

Court Staff
Chief Deputy Clerk **Susan Turner** . . . . (731) 423-5840
E-mail: susan.turner@tscmail.state.tn.us
Education: Union U 1977 BA

Chambers of Judge John Everett Williams

115 Court Square, Huntingdon, TN 38344
P.O. Box 88, Huntingdon, TN 38344
Tel: (731) 986-2225 Fax: (731) 986-2226
E-mail: judge.john.e.williams@tncourts.gov

John Everett Williams
Judge

Date of Birth: 1953
Education: Tennessee (Martin) 1977 BS; Cumberland 1981 JD
Began Service: November 12, 1998
Appointed By: Governor Don Sundquist
Political Affiliation: Republican

Legal Practice: Williams & Williams (1981-1998)

Current Memberships: Carroll County Bar Association; Tennessee Bar Association; Tennessee Trial Lawyers Association

Staff
Law Clerk **Davey Douglas** . . . . (731) 986-2225
E-mail: davey.douglas@tncourts.gov
Law Clerk **Emoke K. Pulay** . . . . (731) 986-2225
E-mail: emoke.pulay@tncourts.gov
Career Law Clerk **Jennifer Chick** . . . . (731) 986-2225
Began Service: 1999
E-mail: jennifer.chick@tncourts.gov
Education: U Memphis 2002 JD

Chambers of Judge Alan E. Glenn

5050 Poplar Avenue, Suite 1414, Memphis, TN 38157-1414
Tel: (901) 537-2980 Fax: (901) 537-2998
E-mail: judge.alan.glenn@tncourts.gov

Alan E. Glenn
Judge

Date of Birth: October 3, 1942
Education: Vanderbilt 1965 BA, 1968 JD
Began Service: 1999
Appointed By: Governor Don Sundquist

(continued on next page)

STATE COURTS—TENNESSEE

Chambers of Judge Alan E. Glenn *continued*

Staff

Career Law Clerk **Zora Liggett** . . . . (901) 685-3955
E-mail: zora.liggett@tncourts.gov
Education: U Memphis 1999 JD

Career Law Clerk **Marsha Ishman Phillips** . . . . (901) 685-3954
E-mail: marsha.phillips@tncourts.gov
Education: U Memphis 2005 JD

Executive Administrative Assistant **Judy Ringold** . . . . (901) 537-2980
E-mail: judy.ringold@tncourts.gov

Chambers of Judge Camille R. McMullen

5050 Poplar Avenue, Suite 1416, Memphis, TN 38157
Tel: (901) 537-2983

Camille R. McMullen
Judge

Education: Austin Peay State 1993 BS; Tennessee 1996 JD
Began Service: September 3, 2008
Appointed By: Governor Phil Bredesen
Next Election: August 2022
Election Type: Retention Election

Government: Assistant District Attorney, County of Shelby, Iowa (1998-2001); Assistant U.S. Attorney, Criminal Division, Tennessee - Western District, United States Department of Justice (2001-2008)

Chambers of Judge Roger A. Page

P.O. Box 909, Jackson, TN 38301
Tel: (731) 426-0861

Roger A. Page
Judge

Education: Tennessee 1978 BS; U Memphis 1984 JD
Began Service: 2011

Texas

Office of Court Administration of the Texas Judicial System

600 Tom C. Clark Building, 205 West 14th Street, Austin, TX 78701
P.O. Box 12066, Austin, TX 78711-2066
Tel: (512) 463-1625 Tel: (512) 463-1625 (Texas Judicial Council)
Fax: (512) 463-1648
Internet: www.txcourts.gov/oca

Staff

Administrative Director **David Slayton** .... (512) 463-1625
E-mail: david.slayton@txcourts.gov
Director of Research and Court Services **Scott Griffith** ... (512) 463-1629
E-mail: scott.griffith@txcourts.gov Fax: (512) 463-1648
Chief Financial Officer **(Vacant)** .... (512) 463-1625
Director, Information Services **Casey Kennedy** .... (512) 463-1603
E-mail: casey.kennedy@txcourts.gov Fax: (512) 475-3450
General Counsel **Maria Elena Ramon** .... (512) 463-4829
E-mail: mena.ramon@txcourts.gov
Human Resources Officer **Nancy Simmons** .... (512) 936-1611

Supreme Court of Texas

Supreme Court Building, 201 West 14th Street, Room 104, Austin, TX 78701
P.O. Box 12248, Austin, TX 78711-2248
Tel: (512) 463-1312 Fax: (512) 463-1365
Internet: www.supreme.courts.state.tx.us

Number of Judgeships: 9

The Supreme Court consists of a chief justice and eight justices who are elected in statewide, partisan elections for six-year terms. Vacancies between elections are filled by the Governor with the advice and consent of the State Senate, and newly appointed justices serve until the next general election. The Supreme Court has final appellate jurisdiction over all civil and juvenile cases and authority to determine certain legal matters when no other court has jurisdiction. The Court has the authority to conduct proceedings for the involuntarily retirement or removal of judges and to make rules for the administration of justice, including rules of civil practice and procedure.

The Supreme Court sits in Austin.

Court Staff

Clerk of the Court **Blake A. Hawthorne** .... (512) 463-1312
E-mail: blake.hawthorne@txcourts.gov
Chief Deputy Clerk **Claudia Jenks** .... (512) 463-1312
E-mail: claudia.jenks@txcourts.gov
General Counsel **Nina Hess Suh** .... (512) 475-0938
Staff Attorney for Public Information **Osler McCarthy** ... (512) 463-1441
E-mail: osler.mccarthy@txcourts.gov
Rules Attorney **Marisa Secco** .... (512) 463-1353
Education: Texas 2007 JD
Administrative Assistant to the Court
Nadine Schneider .... (512) 463-1317
E-mail: nadine.schneider@txcourts.gov

Chambers of Chief Justice Nathan L. Hecht

Supreme Court Building, 201 West 14th Street, Austin, TX 78701
P.O. Box 12248, Austin, TX 78711
Tel: (512) 463-1348 Fax: (512) 463-1365
E-mail: nathan.hecht@txcourts.gov

Nathan L. Hecht
Chief Justice

Date of Birth: 1949
Education: Yale 1971 BA; Southern Methodist 1974 JD
Began Service: January 1, 1989
Next Election: November 2018
Term Expires: December 31, 2018
Political Affiliation: Republican

Current Memberships: American Bar Foundation; Texas Bar Foundation; The American Law Institute; The District of Columbia Bar; Philosophical Society of Texas; State Bar of Texas

Staff

Staff Attorney **Sylvia Herrera** .... (512) 463-1348
E-mail: sylvia.herrera@txcourts.gov
Executive Assistant **Kathy Miller** .... (512) 463-1348
E-mail: kathy.miller@txcourts.gov
Education: Baylor 1977 BM, 1979 MM

Chambers of Justice Paul W. Green

201 West 14th Street, Austin, TX 78701
Tel: (512) 463-1312
E-mail: paul.green@txcourts.gov

Paul W. Green
Justice

Date of Birth: 1952
Education: Texas 1974 BBA; St Mary's U (TX) 1977 JD
Began Service: 2004
Next Election: November 2016
Term Expires: December 31, 2016
Political Affiliation: Republican

Judicial: Justice, Texas Court of Appeals, Fourth District (1995-2004)

Legal Practice: Partner, Green, McReynolds & Green (1977-1994)

Current Memberships: Texas Bar Foundation; The American Law Institute; Austin Bar Association; Austin Bar Foundation, Austin Bar Association; San Antonio Bar Association; San Antonio Bar Foundation

Membership: Past President, San Antonio Bar Association; Past Director, State Bar of Texas; Past Member, House of Delegates, American Bar Association; Founding Member, The William S. Sessions American Inn of Court

Staff

Law Clerk **Brittany Greger** .... (512) 463-1312
Began Service: August 2015
Term Expires: August 2016
Law Clerk **Jaclyn Joseph** .... (512) 463-1312
Began Service: August 2015
Term Expires: August 2016
Staff Attorney **Jenny Hodgkins** .... (512) 463-1312
Executive Secretary **Linda Smith** .... (512) 463-1312

Chambers of Justice Phil Johnson

201 West 14th Street, Austin, TX 78701
P.O. Box 12248, Austin, TX 78711-2248
Tel: (512) 463-1336 Fax: (512) 936-2308
E-mail: phil.johnson@txcourts.gov

Phil Johnson
Justice

Date of Birth: October 1944
Education: Texas Tech 1965 BA, 1975 JD
Began Service: April 2005
Next Election: November 4, 2020
Election Type: General Election
Term Expires: December 31, 2020
Political Affiliation: Republican

Judicial: Justice, Texas Court of Appeals, Seventh District (1999-2002); Chief Justice, Texas Court of Appeals, Seventh District (2003-2005)

Legal Practice: Crenshaw, Dupree & Milam, LLP (1975-1998)

Military Service: United States Air Force (1965-1972)

Current Memberships: American Bar Association; The American Law Institute; State Bar of Texas

Staff

Law Clerk **Michael Duncan** .... (512) 463-1336
Began Service: August 2015
Term Expires: August 2016
Law Clerk **Nicole Sears** .... (512) 463-1336
Began Service: August 2015
Term Expires: August 2016
Staff Attorney **Heather Holmes** .... (512) 463-1336
E-mail: heather.holmes@txcourts.gov
Education: Sam Houston State 1997 JD; Texas 2003 JD
Executive Assistant **Georgie Gonzales** .... (512) 463-1336
E-mail: georgie.gonzales@txcourts.gov

Chambers of Justice Don R. Willett

P.O. Box 12248, Austin, TX 78711-2248
Tel: (512) 463-1344 Fax: (512) 463-1365
E-mail: don.willett@courts.state.tx.us

Don R. Willett
Justice

Education: Baylor 1988 BBA; Duke 1992 MA, 1992 JD
Began Service: August 24, 2005
Appointed By: Governor Rick Perry
Next Election: 2018
Term Expires: December 31, 2018

Government: Deputy Attorney General for Legal Counsel, Office of the Attorney General, State of Texas; Deputy Assistant Attorney General for Legal Policy, United States Department of Justice; Special Assistant to the President, Executive Office of the President

Staff

Law Clerk **Ben Aguinaga** .... (512) 463-1344
Law Clerk **Abhishek Banerjee-Shukla** .... (512) 463-1344
E-mail: abhishek.banerjee-shukla@texascourts.gov
Staff Attorney **Robert Brailas** .... (512) 463-1344
Executive Assistant **Ryan Vassar** .... (512) 463-1344
E-mail: ryan.vassar@courts.state.tx.us

Chambers of Justice Eva M. Guzman

201 West 14th Street, Austin, TX 78701
Tel: (512) 463-1340
E-mail: eva.guzman@txcourts.gov

Eva M. Guzman
Justice

Education: Houston BBA; South Texas 1989 JD
Began Service: January 11, 2010
Appointed By: Governor Rick Perry
Political Affiliation: Republican

Judicial: Judge, 309th State District Court; Justice, Chambers of Justice Eva M. Guzman, Texas Court of Appeals, Fourteenth District (2001-2009)

Current Memberships: Texas Bar Foundation; The American Law Institute

Staff

Staff Attorney **Bradley Starr** .... (512) 463-1340
Executive Assistant **Amelia Alvarado** .... (512) 462-1340

Chambers of Justice Debra Lehrmann

201 West 14th Street, Austin, TX 78701
Tel: (512) 463-1320

Debra H. Lehrmann
Justice

Education: Texas 1979, 1982 JD
Began Service: June 21, 2010
Appointed By: Governor Rick Perry
Term Expires: December 31, 2016

Current Memberships: Texas Bar Foundation; The Eldon B. McMahon American Inn of Court, The American Inns of Court; National Conference of Commissioners on Uniform State Laws; Tarrant County Bar Foundation, Tarrant County Bar Association

Staff

Staff Attorney **Ginger Rodd** .... (512) 463-1320
Executive Assistant **Lisa Cabello** .... (512) 463-1320
E-mail: lisa.cabello@courts.state.tx.us

Chambers of Justice Jeffrey Boyd

201 West 14th Street, Austin, TX 78701
Tel: (512) 463-1312

Jeffrey S. "Jeff" Boyd
Justice

Education: Abilene Christian 1983 BA; Pepperdine 1991 JD
Began Service: 2012
Appointed By: Governor Rick Perry
Term Expires: December 2020

Chambers of Justice John Devine

201 West 14th Street, Austin, TX 78701
Tel: (512) 463-1312

John Devine
Justice

Began Service: 2013

Staff

Law Clerk **Joe Greenhill** .... (512) 463-1312
Law Clerk **Jason Muriby** .... (512) 463-1312
Executive Assistant **Suzanne Sweetland** .... (512) 463-1312

Chambers of Justice Jeff Brown
201 West 14th Street, Austin, TX 78701
Tel: (512) 463-1312

Jeffrey V. "Jeff" Brown
Justice

Education: Texas BA; Houston JD
Began Service: 2013
Appointed By: Governor Rick Perry
Next Election: November 2020

Texas Court of Criminal Appeals
Supreme Court Building, 201 West 14th Street, Room 106, Austin, TX 78701
P.O. Box 12308, Capitol Station, Austin, TX 78711
Tel: (512) 463-1551 Fax: (512) 463-7061
Internet: www.cca.courts.state.tx.us

Number of Judgeships: 9

The Court of Criminal Appeals consists of a presiding judge and eight judges who are elected in statewide, partisan elections for six-year terms. Vacancies between elections are filled by the Governor with the advice and consent of the State Senate, and newly-appointed judges serve until the next general election. The Court of Criminal Appeals has final appellate jurisdiction over all criminal cases except as provided by law and exclusive jurisdiction over automatic appeals in death penalty cases.

The Court of Criminal Appeals sits in Austin.

Court Staff
Clerk of the Court **Abel Acosta** .... (512) 936-1620
E-mail: abel.acosta@cca.courts.state.tx.us
Chief Deputy Clerk **John Brown** .... (512) 936-1618
E-mail: john.brown@cca.courts.state.tx.us
Chief Deputy Clerk **Kelley Reyes** .... (512) 936-1641
General Counsel **Sian R. Schilhab** .... (512) 463-1597
E-mail: sian.schilhab@cca.courts.state.tx.us Fax: (512) 936-2436
Attorney **Michael Stauffacher** .... (512) 463-1600
Attorney **Kathy Schneider** .... (512) 463-1600
Judicial Grant Section Auditor **William Hill** .... (512) 475-2312
E-mail: Bill.Hill@cca.courts.state.tx.us Fax: (512) 475-2592

Chambers of Presiding Judge Sharon Keller
Supreme Court Building, 201 West 14th Street, Austin, TX 78711
P.O. Box 12308, Capitol Station, Austin, TX 78711
Tel: (512) 463-1590

Sharon Keller
Presiding Judge

Date of Birth: 1953
Education: Rice 1975 BA; Southern Methodist 1978 JD
Began Service: January 1, 1995
Next Election: November 2018
Term Expires: December 31, 2018
Political Affiliation: Republican

Government: Assistant District Attorney, County of Dallas, Texas (1987-1994)

Legal Practice: Private Practice (1978-1981)

Staff
Attorney **Donald Cimics** .... (512) 463-1590
E-mail: donald.cimics@cca.courts.state.tx.us
Education: Baylor JD
Administrative Assistant **Jeanne Salyer** .... (512) 463-1590
E-mail: jeanne.salyer@cca.courts.state.tx.us

Chambers of Judge Lawrence E. Meyers
Supreme Court Building, 201 West 14th Street, Austin, TX 78701
P.O. Box 12308, Capitol Station, Austin, TX 78711
Tel: (512) 463-1580

Lawrence E. Meyers
Judge

Date of Birth: 1947
Education: Southern Methodist 1970 BA; Kansas 1973 JD
Began Service: January 1, 1993
Next Election: November 2016
Term Expires: December 31, 2016
Political Affiliation: Republican

Academic: Instructor, Texas Christian University

Government: Assistant District Attorney, County of Montgomery, Kansas (1973-1975)

Judicial: Substitute Municipal Judge; Associate Justice, Texas Court of Appeals, Second District (1988-1992)

Legal Practice: Private Practice (1975-1988)

Current Memberships: Kansas Bar Association; State Bar of Texas; Tarrant County Bar Association

Staff
Law Clerk **Kimberly "Kim" Donoghue** .... (512) 463-1580
Began Service: August 2013
Term Expires: August 2016
Research Assistant **Anna Kathryn Price** .... (512) 463-1580
Secretary **Nicole Reedy** .... (512) 463-1580

STATE COURTS—TEXAS

Chambers of Judge Cheryl Johnson
Supreme Court Building, 201 West 14th Street, Austin, TX 78701
P.O. Box 12308, Capitol Station, Austin, TX 78711
Tel: (512) 463-1560 Fax: (512) 463-7061
E-mail: cheryl.johnson@txcourts.gov

Cheryl Johnson
Judge

Date of Birth: 1946
Education: Ohio State 1968 BS; Illinois 1970 MS; John Marshall 1983 JD
Began Service: January 1, 1999
Next Election: November 2016
Term Expires: December 31, 2016
Political Affiliation: Republican

Clerkships: Law Clerk The Honorable Sam Johnson, U.S. Court of Appeals for the Fifth Circuit (1983-1984)

Legal Practice: Private Practice (1984-1998)

Current Memberships: Texas Bar Foundation; College of the State Bar of Texas; State Bar of Texas

Staff
Law Clerk **Clayton Suitt** .... (512) 463-1560
Began Service: September 1, 2015
Term Expires: December 31, 2016
Staff Attorney **Morris Greggs** .... (512) 463-1560
E-mail: morris.greggs@txcourts.gov
Education: Baylor 1984 BS, 1988 JD
Executive Assistant **Barbara McNichol** .... (512) 463-1560
E-mail: barbara.mcnichol@txcourts.gov

Chambers of Judge Michael Keasler

Supreme Court Building, 201 West 14th Street, Austin, TX 78701
P.O. Box 12308, Capitol Station, Austin, TX 78711
Tel: (512) 463-1555 Fax: (512) 463-7061
E-mail: michael.keasler@cca.courts.state.tx.us

Michael Keasler
Judge

Date of Birth: 1942
Education: Texas 1964 BA, 1967 LLB
Began Service: January 4, 1999
Next Election: November 2016
Term Expires: December 31, 2016
Political Affiliation: Republican

Academic: Faculty, Texas College for New Judges (1985-1998)

Government: Senior Felony Chief Prosecutor, Office of the District Attorney, County of Dallas, Texas (1969-1981)

Current Memberships: American Bar Association; National Conference of Metropolitan Courts; State Bar of Texas

Profession: Attorney (1967-1969)

Staff
Staff Attorney **Brian Chandler** .... (512) 463-1555
E-mail: brian.chandler@cca.courts.state.tx.us
Legal Secretary **Laura E. Moorman** .... (512) 463-1555
E-mail: laura.moorman@cca.courts.state.tx.us
Education: Southwest Texas State 1997 BS

Chambers of Judge Barbara P. Hervey

Supreme Court Building, 201 West 14th Street, Austin, TX 78701
P.O. Box 12308, Capitol Station, Austin, TX 78711
Tel: (512) 463-1575 Fax: (512) 463-7061
E-mail: barbara.hervey@cca.courts.state.tx.us

Barbara P. Hervey
Judge

Date of Birth: 1953
Education: North Carolina Greensboro 1975 BA; St Mary's U (TX) 1979 JD
Began Service: January 1, 2001
Next Election: November 2018
Term Expires: December 31, 2018
Political Affiliation: Republican

Government: Assistant Criminal District Attorney, County of Bexar, Texas (1984-2000)

Legal Practice: Private Practice (1979-1984)

Current Memberships: The Bexar County Women's Bar Association; State Bar of Texas

Staff
Law Clerk **Elizabeth Smith** .... (512) 463-1575
Began Service: September 2014
Term Expires: August 31, 2016
Attorney **Carson Guy** .... (512) 463-1575
E-mail: carson.guy@txcourts.gov
Executive Assistant **Deborah Atkinson** .... (512) 463-1575
E-mail: deborah.atkinson@txcourts.gov

Chambers of Judge Elsa Alcala

201 West 14th Street, Austin, TX 78701
Tel: (512) 463-1551 Fax: (512) 463-7061

Elsa Alcala
Judge

Date of Birth: 1964
Education: Texas A&M 1986 BA; Texas 1989 JD
Began Service: 2011
Appointed By: Governor Rick Perry

Current Memberships: Association of Women Attorneys; Houston Bar Association; Mexican American Bar Association; National Association of Women Judges; State Bar of Texas

Staff
Briefing Attorney **Ingrid Grobey** .... (512) 463-1551
Law Clerk **Andrew Fletcher** .... (512) 463-1551
Judicial Assistant **Genoveva Mendoza** .... (512) 463-1551

Chambers of Judge David Newell

201 West 14th Street, Austin, TX 78701
Tel: (512) 463-1551

David Newell
Judge

Began Service: 2015

Chambers of Judge Bert Richardson

201 West 14th Street, Austin, TX 78701
Tel: (512) 463-1551

Bert Richardson
Judge

Began Service: 2015

Chambers of Judge Kevin Patrick Yeary

201 West 14th Street, Austin, TX 78701
Tel: (512) 463-1551

Kevin Yeary
Judge

Texas Court of Appeals

Internet: www.courts.state.tx.us/appcourt.asp

The Court of Appeals is comprised of fourteen judicial districts with between three and thirteen justices each. Each district has a chief justice who is elected to a six-year term by the voters of the district. Justices are also elected from the fourteen districts in partisan elections for six-year terms. Vacancies between elections are filled by the Governor with the advice and consent of the State Senate. The districts of the Court of Appeals have appellate jurisdiction within their respective districts over civil and criminal cases decided in the Texas District or County Courts.

Texas Court of Appeals, First District

301 Fannin Street, Houston, TX 77002
Tel: (713) 274-2700 Fax: (713) 755-9060
E-mail: 1stcoa@courts.state.tx.us
Internet: www.1stcoa.courts.state.tx.us

Number of Judgeships: 9

Areas Covered: Counties of Austin, Brazoria, Chambers, Colorado, Fort Bend, Galveston, Grimes, Harris, Waller and Washington

Texas Court of Appeals, First District *continued*

Court Staff

Clerk of the Court **Christopher A. Prine** . . . . (713) 274-2700
E-mail: christopher.prine@txcourts.gov

Chief Staff Attorney **Janet McVea Williams** . . . . (713) 274-2700
E-mail: janet.williams@txcourts.gov
Education: Millsaps 1986 BA; LSU 1990 JD

Central Staff Attorney **Robert Tobor** . . . . (713) 274-2700
Education: Texas 1997 BA; South Texas 2000 JD

Chambers of Chief Justice Sherry Radack

301 Fannin Street, Houston, TX 77002
Tel: (713) 274-2700 Fax: (713) 755-9060
E-mail: sherry.radack@txcourts.gov

Sherry Radack
Chief Justice

Date of Birth: 1951
Education: Rice BA; Houston JD
Began Service: November 2001
Appointed By: Governor Rick Perry
Political Affiliation: Republican

Judicial: Judge, 55th Judicial District (1999-2002); Judge, Texas Court of Appeals, First District (2002)

Legal Practice: Attorney, Bracewell & Patterson, L.L.P.

Current Memberships: Texas Bar Foundation; The American Inns of Court; American Judges Association; Council of Chief Judges of the State of Texas; Houston Bar Association; State Bar of Texas

Staff

Chief Staff Attorney **Janet McVea Williams** . . . . (713) 274-2700
E-mail: janet.williams@txcourts.gov

Chambers Attorney **Karlene Poll** . . . . (713) 274-2700
E-mail: karlene.poll@txcourts.gov

Chambers of Justice Terry Jennings

301 Fannin Street, Houston, TX 77002
Tel: (713) 274-2700 Fax: (713) 755-9060
E-mail: terry.jennings@txcourts.gov

Terry Jennings
Justice

Date of Birth: 1960
Education: Texas BA; Houston JD
Began Service: January 1, 2001
Next Election: November 2018
Term Expires: December 31, 2018
Political Affiliation: Republican

Government: Trial Bureau, Office of the District Attorney, County of Harris, Texas (1990-1994); Special Crimes Bureau, Office of the District Attorney, County of Harris, Texas (1994-2000)

Legal Practice: Attorney, Young & Hampton; Attorney, Alexander & McEvily

Current Memberships: Houston Bar Association; State Bar of Texas

Chambers of Justice Evelyn Keyes

301 Fannin Street, Houston, TX 77002
Tel: (713) 274-2700 Fax: (713) 755-9060

Evelyn Keyes
Justice

Date of Birth: 1943
Education: Tulane 1965 BA; Texas 1967 MA, 1972 PhD; Rice 1984 MA, 1985 PhD; Houston 1987 JD
Began Service: May 10, 2002
Appointed By: Governor Rick Perry
Political Affiliation: Republican

Clerkships: Intern The Honorable Carolyn R. King, Fifth Circuit Court of Appeals (1987)

Government: Special Assistant Attorney General, Office of the Attorney General, State of Texas (2000-2001)

Legal Practice: Associate, Porter & Clements (1988-1993); Associate, Clements, O'Neill, Pierce & Nickens, L.L.P. (1993-1996); Partner, Clements, O'Neill, Pierce & Nickens, L.L.P. (1996-2000); Of Counsel, Clements, O'Neill, Pierce, Wilson & Fulkerson, L.L.P. (2001-2002)

Current Memberships: Texas Bar Foundation; American Bar Association; College of the State Bar of Texas; Houston Bar Association; Houston Bar Foundation, Houston Bar Association; State Bar of Texas; United States Supreme Court Bar

Staff

Chambers Attorney **Alicia Flarity** . . . . (713) 274-2700
E-mail: alicia.flarity@txcourts.gov

Chambers Attorney **Angela Spoede** . . . . (713) 274-2700
E-mail: angela.spoede@txcourts.gov

Chambers of Justice Laura Carter Higley

301 Fannin Street, Houston, TX 77002
Tel: (713) 274-2700

Laura Carter Higley
Justice

Date of Birth: November 27, 1946
Education: Vanderbilt 1969 BA; Texas 1971 MA; Houston 1989 JD
Began Service: January 1, 2003
Next Election: November 4, 2020
Election Type: General Election
Term Expires: December 31, 2020

Legal Practice: Attorney, Baker Botts L.L.P. (1990-2002)

Nonprofit: Trustee, Houston Museum of Natural Science

Staff

Chambers Attorney **Derek D. Bauman** . . . . (713) 274-2700
E-mail: derek.bauman@txcourts.gov

Chambers Attorney **Lisa Phelps** . . . . (713) 274-2700
E-mail: lisa.phelps@txcourts.gov

Chambers of Justice Jane Bland

301 Fannin Street, Houston, TX 77002
Tel: (713) 274-2700

Jane Bland
Justice

Education: Texas BA, JD
Began Service: December 2003
Appointed By: Governor Rick Perry

Clerkships: Law Clerk Thomas Gibbs gee, United States Court of Appeals for the Fifth Circuit

Judicial: Judge, 281st State District Court (1997-2003)

Legal Practice: Attorney, Baker and Botts

(continued on next page)

STATE COURTS – TEXAS

Chambers of Justice Jane Bland *continued*

Current Memberships: The American Law Institute

Staff
Chambers Attorney **Anne Pike** . . . . (713) 274-2700

Chambers of Justice Russell Lloyd
301 Fannin Street, Houston, TX 77002
Tel: (713) 274-2700

Russell Lloyd
Justice

Chambers of Justice Michael C. Massengale
301 Fannin Street, Houston, TX 77002
Tel: (713) 274-2700

Michael C. Massengale
Justice

Education: Dartmouth; Texas JD
Began Service: August 2009
Appointed By: Governor Rick Perry

Staff
Chambers Attorney **Margot Stander** . . . . (713) 274-2700
Began Service: August 2009
E-mail: margot.stander@txcourts.gov
Education: Alabama 1992 BS; Baylor 2002 JD

Chambers of Justice Harvey Brown
301 Fannin Street, Houston, TX 77002
Tel: (713) 274-2700 Fax: (713) 755-9060

Harvey G. Brown
Justice

Education: Texas 1978 BA, 1981 JD
Began Service: November 2010
Appointed By: Governor Rick Perry

Current Memberships: Texas Bar Foundation; American Bar Association; Houston Bar Association; Houston Bar Foundation, Houston Bar Association; State Bar of Texas

Staff
Chambers Attorney **Jenifer Points** . . . . (713) 274-2700
E-mail: jenifer.points@txcourts.gov

Chambers of Justice Rebeca Huddle
301 Fannin Street, Houston, TX 77002
Tel: (713) 274-2700 Fax: (713) 755-9060

Rebeca Huddle
Justice

Education: Stanford 1995 BA; Texas 1999 JD
Began Service: 2011
Appointed By: Governor Rick Perry

Staff
Chambers Attorney **Sarah Cottrell** . . . . (713) 274-2700
E-mail: sarah.cottrell@txcourts.gov Fax: (713) 755-9060

Texas Court of Appeals, Second District
Tim Curry Criminal Justice Center, 401 West Belknap, Suite 9000, Fort Worth, TX 76196
Tel: (817) 884-1900 Fax: (817) 884-1932
Internet: www.2ndcoa.courts.state.tx.us

Number of Judgeships: 7

Areas Covered: Counties of Archer, Clay, Cooke, Denton, Hood, Jack, Montague, Parker, Tarrant, Wichita, Wise and Young

Court Staff
Clerk of the Court **Debra Spisak** . . . . (817) 884-1900 ext. 226
E-mail: debra.spisak@txcourts.gov
Chief Staff Attorney **Lisa M. West** . . . . (817) 884-1900
E-mail: lisa.west@txcourts.gov
Network Specialist **Carol Baker** . . . . (817) 884-1900
E-mail: carol.baker@txcourts.gov
Education: Baylor 1981 JD

Chambers of Chief Justice Terrie Livingston
Tim Curry Criminal Justice Center, 401 West Belknap, Fort Worth, TX 76196
Tel: (817) 884-1900 Fax: (817) 884-1932
E-mail: terrie.livingston@txcourts.gov

Terrie Livingston
Chief Justice

Date of Birth: 1955
Education: Texas Tech 1977 BA; Texas 1980 JD
Began Service: April 19, 2010
Next Election: November 2018
Election Type: General Election
Term Expires: December 31, 2018
Political Affiliation: Republican

Government: Law Clerk, Special Prosecutor's Division, Office of the Attorney General, State of Texas; Law Clerk, Appellate Division, Office of the District Attorney, County of Tarrant, Texas

Legal Practice: Associate and Partner, Watson, Ice & McGee (1980-1985); Shareholder, Livingston & Todd-Bruse, PC (1985-1988); Partner, Gandy, Michener, Swindle & Whittaker, LLP (1988-1992); Sole Practitioner (1992-1994)

Current Memberships: Texas Bar Foundation; American Bar Association; Judicial Division, American Bar Association; College of the State Bar of Texas; Fort Worth Professional Women's Organization; Parker County Bar Association; State Bar of Texas; Tarrant County Appellate Bar Association; Tarrant County Bar Association; Tarrant County Bar Foundation, Tarrant County Bar Association; Tarrant County Probate Bar Association; Tarrant County Womens Bar Association

Staff
Staff Attorney **Bryce Perry** . . . . (817) 884-1900
Staff Attorney **Lisa M. West** . . . . (817) 884-1900
Secretary **Olivia Hibscher** . . . . (817) 884-1900

Chambers of Justice Lee Ann Dauphinot

Tim Curry Criminal Justice Center, 401 West Belknap, Suite 9000, Fort Worth, TX 76196
Tel: (817) 884-1900 Fax: (817) 884-1932

Lee Ann Dauphinot
Justice

Date of Birth: 1940
Education: Texas Christian 1961 BA; Stanford 1963 MA; Southern Methodist 1978 JD
Began Service: January 1, 1995
Next Election: November 2018
Term Expires: December 31, 2018
Political Affiliation: Republican

Judicial: Judge, Tarrant County Criminal District Court 2 (1989-1995)

Legal Practice: Private Practice (1978-1988)

Current Memberships: American Bar Association; National Association of Women Judges; State Bar of Texas; Tarrant County Bar Association

Staff
Staff Attorney **Lauren Chadwick** .... (817) 884-1900
Education: Southern Methodist 1996 JD
Staff Attorney **Jennifer Roberts** .... (817) 884-1900
Education: Utah 1998 BS, 2002 JD
Secretary **Krystal Spruill** .... (817) 884-1900

Chambers of Justice Anne Gardner

Tim Curry Justice Center, 401 West Belknap, Fort Worth, TX 76196
Tel: (817) 884-1900 Fax: (817) 884-1932
E-mail: anne.gardner@txcourts.gov

Anne Gardner
Justice

Date of Birth: 1942
Education: Texas 1964 BA, 1966 JD
Began Service: January 1, 2000
Appointed By: Governor George W. Bush
Term Expires: December 31, 2016
Political Affiliation: Republican

Clerkships: Law Clerk The Honorable Leo Brewster (1967-1971)

Legal Practice: Partner, Simon, Peebles, Haskell, Gardner & Betty (1971-1985); Partner, McLean & Sanders (1985-1988); Partner, Shannon, Gracey, Ratliff & Miller, L.L.P. (1988-1999)

Current Memberships: American Bar Association; State Bar of Texas; Tarrant County Bar Association

Staff
Staff Attorney **Rebecca Heinemann** .... (817) 884-1900
Education: Texas 2004
Staff Attorney **Dean Swanda** .... (817) 884-1900
Secretary **Cassie Allen** .... (817) 884-1900

Chambers of Justice Sue Walker

Tim Curry Criminal Justice Center, 401 West Belknap, Suite 9000, Fort Worth, TX 76196
Tel: (817) 884-1900 Fax: (817) 884-1932

Sue Walker
Justice

Date of Birth: 1961
Education: Texas 1982 BS; Texas Tech 1986 JD
Began Service: January 1, 2001
Next Election: November 2018
Term Expires: December 31, 2018
Political Affiliation: Republican

Academic: Adjunct Professor, School of Law, Texas Wesleyan University

Chambers of Justice Sue Walker *continued*

Government: Briefing Attorney, Texas Court of Appeals, Fifth District (1986); Staff Attorney, Texas Court of Appeals, Fifth District (1990-1994)

Legal Practice: Private Practice (1994-2000)

Current Memberships: The Eldon B. McMahon American Inn of Court, The American Inns of Court; American Judges Association; College of the State Bar of Texas; State Bar of Texas; Tarrant County Bar Foundation, Tarrant County Bar Association

Staff
Staff Attorney **Alyssa Jurek** .... (817) 884-1900
Staff Attorney **Logan Simmons** .... (817) 884-1900
Secretary **Prentiss Edmondson** .... (817) 884-1900

Chambers of Justice Bill Meier

Tim Curry Justice Center, 401 West Belknap, Suite 9000, Fort Worth, TX 76196
Tel: (817) 884-1900 Fax: (817) 884-1932

William C. "Bill" Meier
Justice

Education: Texas 1964 BS, 1966 JD
Began Service: January 1, 2009
Next Election: November 2020
Term Expires: December 31, 2020

Government: State Senator (TX), Texas State Senate (1973-1983)

Legal Practice: Public Defender, Dallas Legal Services

Staff
Staff Attorney **Cameron Davis** .... (817) 884-1900
Staff Attorney **Johannes Walker** .... (817) 884-1900
Education: Texas Wesleyan U 2007 JD
Secretary **Jeanne Cloward** .... (817) 884-1900

Chambers of Justice Lee Gabriel

401 West Belknap, Suite 9000, Fort Worth, TX 76196
Tel: (817) 884-1900

Lee Gabriel
Justice

Education: Texas Tech BA, JD
Began Service: August 1, 2010
Appointed By: Governor Rick Perry
Next Election: November 2020
Term Expires: December 31, 2020

Current Memberships: Judicial Section, State Bar of Texas

Staff
Staff Attorney **Amy Hennessee** .... (817) 884-1900
Staff Attorney **Kelly Canavan** .... (817) 884-1900
Secretary **Patty Adkinson** .... (817) 884-1900

Chambers of Justice Bonnie Sudderth

401 West Belknap, Fort Worth, TX 76196
Tel: (817) 884-1900

Bonnie Sudderth
Justice

Began Service: 2015

Texas Court of Appeals, Third District

101 Price Daniel, Sr. Building, 209 West 14th Street, Austin, TX 78701
P.O. Box 12547, Austin, TX 78711
Tel: (512) 463-1733 Fax: (512) 463-1685
Internet: www.3rdcoa.courts.state.tx.us

Number of Judgeships: 6

Areas Covered: Counties of Bastrop, Bell, Blanco, Burnet, Caldwell, Coke, Comal, Concho, Fayette, Hays, Irion, Lampasas, Lee, Llano, McCulloch, Milam, Mills, Runnels, San Saba, Schleicher, Sterling, Tom Green, Travis and Williamson

Court Staff
Clerk of the Court **Jeffrey D. Kyle** .... (512) 463-1709
E-mail: jeff.kyle@3rdcoa.courts.state.tx.us

Chambers of Chief Justice Jeff L. Rose

201 West 14th Street, Austin, TX 78701
Tel: (512) 463-1733

Jeff L. Rose
Chief Justice

Education: Baylor BA; Vanderbilt JD
Began Service: December 6, 2010
Next Election: November 2020
Term Expires: December 31, 2020

Chambers of Justice David Puryear

Price Daniel, Sr. Building, 209 West 14th Street, Austin, TX 78701
P.O. Box 12547, Austin, TX 78711
Tel: (512) 463-1689 Fax: (512) 463-1685
E-mail: david.puryear@3rdcoa.courts.state.tx.us

David Puryear
Justice

Date of Birth: 1955
Education: Southwestern 1978 BS; Texas Tech 1983 JD
Began Service: January 1, 2001
Next Election: November 2018
Term Expires: December 31, 2018
Political Affiliation: Republican

Government: Assistant County Attorney, County of Travis, Texas (1983-1990); Assistant Attorney General, State of Texas (1999-2000)

Judicial: Judge, County Court at Law #6, County of Travis, Texas (1991-1998)

Staff
Staff Attorney **Alessandra Beavers** .... (512) 936-6956
E-mail: alessandra_beavers@courts.state.tx.us
Staff Attorney **Ryan Rollans** .... (512) 936-6941
E-mail: ryan.rollans@courts.state.tx.us
Education: Texas 2004 JD

Chambers of Justice Bob Pemberton

P.O. Box 12547, Austin, TX 78711
Tel: (512) 463-1733
E-mail: bob.pemberton@courts.state.tx.us

Bob Pemberton
Justice

Date of Birth: October 30, 1966
Education: Baylor 1989 BBA; Harvard 1992 JD
Began Service: December 15, 2003
Appointed By: Governor Rick Perry
Next Election: November 2018
Term Expires: December 31, 2018

Clerkships: Briefing Attorney, Texas Supreme Court (1992-1993)

Government: Deputy General Counsel, Office of the Governor, State of Texas (2000-2002)

Judicial: Rules Attorney, Texas Supreme Court (1998-2000)

Legal Practice: Associate, Baker and Botts (1993-1998); Senior Counsel, Akin Gump Strauss Hauer & Feld LLP (2003)

Current Memberships: The American Inns of Court; The Robert W. Calvert American Inn of Court, The American Inns of Court; State Bar of Texas; Travis County Bar Association

Chambers of Justice Melissa Goodwin

209 West 14th Street, Austin, TX 78701
Tel: (512) 463-1733 Fax: (512) 463-1685

Melissa Goodwin
Justice

Education: Texas BA; St Mary's U (TX) JD
Began Service: January 1, 2011
Next Election: December 2016
Term Expires: December 31, 2016

Chambers of Justice Scott Field

209 West 14th Street, Austin, TX 78701
Tel: (512) 463-1733

Scott Field
Justice

Began Service: 2013
Term Expires: December 31, 2018

Staff
Staff Attorney **Alice Ortiz** .... (512) 463-1733
Staff Attorney **Alan Hersh** .... (512) 463-1733
Legal Assistant **Elizabeth Bruton** .... (512) 463-1733

Chambers of Justice Cindy Olson Bourland

201 West 14th Street, Austin, TX 78701
Tel: (512) 463-1733

Cindy Olson Bourland
Justice

Began Service: 2015
Appointed By: Governor Rick Perry

Texas Court of Appeals, Fourth District

Cadena-Reeves Justice Center, 300 Dolorosa, Room 3200,
San Antonio, TX 78205-3037
Tel: (210) 335-2635 Fax: (210) 335-2762
Internet: www.4thcoa.courts.state.tx.us

Number of Judgeships: 7

Areas Covered: Counties of Atascosa, Bandera, Bexar, Brooks, Dimmit, Duval, Edwards, Frio, Gillespie, Guadalupe, Jim Hogg, Jim Wells, Karnes, Kendall, Kerr, Kimble, Kinney, LaSalle, Mason, Maverick, McMullen, Medina, Menard, Real, Starr, Sutton, Uvalde, Val Verde, Webb, Wilson, Zapata and Zavala

Court Staff

Clerk of Court **Keith E. Hottle** .... (210) 335-2510
E-mail: keith.hottle@txcourts.gov
Chief Staff Attorney **Wendy Martinez** .... (210) 335-3977
Education: Texas 1986 BBA;
St Mary's U (TX) 1989 JD
Chief Deputy Clerk **Belinda T. Burkhart** .... (210) 335-3979
E-mail: belinda.burkhart@txcourts.gov
Education: Incarnate Word Col 1978 BA

Chambers of Chief Justice Sandee Bryan Marion

Cadena-Reeves Justice Center, 300 Dolorosa, Suite 3200,
San Antonio, TX 78205-3037
Tel: (210) 335-2629
E-mail: sandee.marion@courts.state.tx.us

Sandee Bryan Marion
Chief Justice

Date of Birth: 1956
Education: Texas BA; St Mary's U (TX) 1980 JD
Began Service: January 2002
Appointed By: Governor Rick Perry
Next Election: November 2020
Political Affiliation: Republican

Current Memberships: College of the State Bar of Texas; San Antonio Bar Association

Staff

Law Clerk **(Vacant)** .... (210) 335-3967
Staff Attorney **Pamela Jewell** .... (210) 335-3984
E-mail: pamela.jewell@courts.state.tx.us
Education: Houston 1977 BA, 1991 JD

Chambers of Justice Karen Angelini

300 Dolorosa, San Antonio, TX 78205-3037
Tel: (210) 335-2635 Fax: (210) 335-2762
E-mail: karen.angelini@courts.state.tx.us

Karen Angelini
Justice

Date of Birth: 1951
Education: Texas 1972 BA; St Mary's U (TX) 1979 JD
Began Service: January 2, 1997
Appointed By: Governor George W. Bush
Next Election: November 2018
Term Expires: 2018
Political Affiliation: Republican

Clerkships: Law Clerk, Texas Court of Appeals, Fourth Circuit (1980-1981); Law Clerk, United States District Court (1992-1996)

Legal Practice: Brock & Fuller (1981-1991)

Current Memberships: Texas Bar Foundation; San Antonio Bar Association; San Antonio Bar Foundation; San Antonio Women's Bar Association; State Bar of Texas

Chambers of Justice Karen Angelini *continued*

Staff

Staff Attorney **Valerie Najera** .... (210) 335-2635
E-mail: valerie.najera@courts.state.tx.us
Education: St Mary's U (TX) 1998 JD
Staff Attorney **Diane Palmiotti** .... (210) 335-2635

Chambers of Justice Marialyn Barnard

Cadena-Reeves Justice Center, 300 Dolorosa, San Antonio, TX 78205
Tel: (210) 335-2658

Marialyn Price Barnard
Justice

Education: Texas A&M (Commerce) 1983 BS; St Mary's U (TX) 1992 JD
Began Service: January 1, 2009
Term Expires: December 31, 2018

Staff

Law Clerk **Jobe Jackson** .... (210) 335-3968
Staff Attorney **Andrea Morris** .... (210) 335-2658

Chambers of Justice Rebeca Martinez

300 Dolorosa, San Antonio, TX 78205-3037
Tel: (210) 335-2635

Rebeca Martinez
Justice

Began Service: 2013

Chambers of Justice Patricia Alvarez

300 Dolorosa, San Antonio, TX 78205-3037
Tel: (210) 335-2635

Patricia O'Connell Alvarez
Justice

Education: Texas 1987 JD; Texas (San Antonio) 1982 BBA

Staff

Law Clerk **Matthew Compton** .... (210) 335-2635
Law Clerk **Jennifer Rosenblatt** .... (210) 335-2635

Chambers of Justice Luz Elena Chapa

300 Dolorosa, San Antonio, TX 78205-3037
Tel: (210) 335-2635

Luz Elena Chapa
Justice

Staff

Staff Attorney **Elizabeth A. "Beth" Crabb** .... (210) 335-3975
Education: Texas 1981 BA, 1981 BBA, 1984 JD
Staff Attorney **Michael Ritter** .... (210) 335-2633

Chambers of Justice Jason Pulliam

300 Dolorosa, San Antonio, TX 78205-3037
Tel: (210) 335-2635

Jason Pulliam
Justice

Texas Court of Appeals, Fifth District

George L. Allen, Sr. Courts Building, 600 Commerce Street,
Suite 200, Dallas, TX 75202-4653
Tel: (214) 712-3400 Fax: (214) 745-1083
E-mail: clerk@5th.txcourts.gov
Internet: www.5thcoa.courts.state.tx.us

Number of Judgeships: 13

Areas Covered: Counties of Collin, Dallas, Grayson, Hunt, Kaufman, and Rockwall

Court Staff

Clerk of the Court **Lisa Matz** . . . . (214) 712-0199
E-mail: lisa.matz@5th.txcourts.gov
Chief Staff Attorney **Cliffie Wesson** . . . . (214) 712-3400
E-mail: cliffie.wesson@5th.txcourts.gov
Education: Texas Wesleyan U JD
Business Administrator **Gayle Humpa** . . . . (214) 712-3434
E-mail: gayle.humpa@5th.txcourts.gov
Education: Texas Wesleyan U 1994 JD
Accountant **Susan Fox** . . . . (214) 712-3444
E-mail: susan.fox@5th.txcourts.gov
Education: Texas A&M 1999 BS

Chambers of Chief Justice Carolyn Wright

George L. Allen, Sr. Courts Building, 600 Commerce Street,
Suite 200, Dallas, TX 75202
Tel: (214) 712-3410 Fax: (214) 745-1083

Carolyn Wright
Chief Justice

Education: Strayer Col 1966 AA; DC Teachers Col 1974 BS; Howard U 1978 JD
Began Service: March 1995
Appointed By: Governor George W. Bush
Term Expires: December 31, 2018
Political Affiliation: Republican

Government: Equal Employment Opportunity Commission (1967-1968); Mayor's Office of Youth Advocacy, District of Columbia (1968-1978)

Judicial: Associate Judge (1983-1986); Judge, Texas District Court (1986-1995); Chair, Texas Bar Foundation; Faculty, National Judicial College, Reno, Nevada; Faculty, Texas College for New Judges

Legal Practice: Legal Intern, Lawyer's Committee for Civil Rights, South Africa Project (1978); Private Practice (1978-1983)

Current Memberships: Texas Bar Foundation; American Bar Association; College of the State Bar of Texas; Dallas Association of Young Lawyers; Dallas Bar Association; Dallas Bar Foundation, Dallas Bar Association; Dallas Women Lawyers Association; J. L. Turner Legal Association; National Bar Association; State Bar of Texas

Staff

Career Staff Attorney **Cliffie Wesson** . . . . (214) 712-3410
Career Staff Attorney **Marilyn Houghtalin** . . . . (214) 712-3410
Secretary **Tashonda Carey-Jones** . . . . (214) 712-3417

Chambers of Justice David L. Bridges

George L. Allen, Sr. Courts Building, 600 Commerce Street,
Suite 200, Dallas, TX 75202-4653
Tel: (214) 712-3412 Fax: (214) 745-1083

David L. Bridges
Justice

Date of Birth: 1955
Education: Texas Tech 1984 JD
Began Service: January 1, 1997
Next Election: November 4, 2020
Election Type: General Election
Term Expires: December 31, 2020

Government: Chief Felony Prosecutor, Office of the District Attorney, County of Smith, Texas (1984-1987); First Assistant General Counsel, State Bar of Texas; First Assistant Attorney, Office of the District Attorney, County of Upshur, Texas (1987-1988)

Military Service: United States Army (1973-1974)

Current Memberships: Dallas Bar Association; Rockwall Bar Association

Staff

Staff Attorney **John Dumford** . . . . (214) 712-3400
E-mail: john.dumford@5thcoa.courts.state.tx.us
Secretary **Tashonda Carey-Jones** . . . . (214) 712-3417
E-mail: tashonda.carey-jones@5thcoa.courts.state.tx.us

Chambers of Justice Molly Francis

George L. Allen, Sr. Courts Building, 600 Commerce Street,
Suite 200, Dallas, TX 75202
Tel: (214) 712-3400 Fax: (214) 745-1083

Molly Francis
Justice

Date of Birth: 1956
Education: Baylor 1978 BS, 1981 JD
Began Service: September 12, 2001
Appointed By: Governor Rick Perry
Political Affiliation: Republican

Government: Briefing Attorney, Texas Court of Appeals, First District (1981-1982); Dallas County District Attorney's Office (1982-1983)

Judicial: Judge, County Criminal Court No. 9 (1991-1996); Judge, 283rd District Criminal Court (1996-2001)

Current Memberships: Dallas Bar Association; State Bar of Texas

Chambers of Justice Douglas S. Lang

George L. Allen, Sr. Courts Building, 600 Commerce Street,
2nd Floor, Dallas, TX 75202
Tel: (214) 712-3402 Fax: (214) 745-1083

Douglas S. Lang
Justice

Education: Drake BBA; Missouri JD
Began Service: October 24, 2002
Appointed By: Governor Rick Perry
Next Election: 2018
Term Expires: December 31, 2018

Government: Briefing Attorney, Supreme Court, State of Missouri

Legal Practice: Partner, Gardere Wynne Sewell LLP

Nonprofit: President, Dallas Bar Association; Chair, Texas Center for Legal Ethics and Professionalism; President, National Conference of Bar Presidents

Chambers of Justice Douglas S. Lang *continued*

Current Memberships: American Bar Foundation; Texas Bar Foundation; American Bar Association; The American Law Institute; Dallas Bar Association; Dallas Bar Foundation, Dallas Bar Association; State Bar of Texas

Staff
Briefing Attorney **Haleigh Jones** .... (214) 712-3402

Chambers of Justice Elizabeth Lang-Miers
600 Commerce Street, Suite 200, Dallas, TX 75202-4653
Tel: (214) 712-3403 Fax: (214) 745-1083

Elizabeth Lang-Miers
Justice

Date of Birth: November 26, 1950
Education: Missouri 1972 BA, 1975 JD
Began Service: October 13, 2003
Next Election: 2018
Term Expires: December 31, 2018

Legal Practice: Partner, Locke Liddell & Sapp LLP (1976-2003)

Current Memberships: American Bar Foundation; Texas Bar Foundation; American Bar Association; The American Law Institute; Dallas Bar Foundation, Dallas Bar Association; Dallas Bar Foundation, Dallas Bar Association; State Bar of Texas; Board of Trustees, State Bar of Texas

Staff
Staff Attorney **Judy White** .... (214) 712-3426
Secretary **Cindy Thornton** .... (214) 712-3419

Chambers of Justice Robert M. Fillmore
600 Commerce Street, Dallas, TX 75202-4653
Tel: (214) 712-3409 Fax: (214) 745-1083

Robert M. Fillmore
Justice

Education: Kansas 1975 BS, 1977 JD
Began Service: June 2009
Appointed By: Governor Rick Perry
Next Election: November 2018
Term Expires: December 31, 2018

Staff
Staff Attorney **Ardita Vick** .... (214) 712-3400
Staff Attorney **Sudie Thompson** .... (214) 712-3400
Judicial Assistant **Cindy Thornton** .... (214) 712-3400

Chambers of Justice Lana Myers
600 Commerce Street, Dallas, TX 75202-4653
Tel: (214) 712-3401 Fax: (214) 745-1083

Lana Myers
Justice

Education: Baylor BA, JD
Began Service: December 2009
Appointed By: Governor Rick Perry
Next Election: November 2016
Term Expires: December 31, 2016

Current Memberships: Dallas Bar Association; State Bar of Texas

Staff
Staff Attorney **Douglas Frobese** .... (214) 712-3424
Education: Southwestern 1987 BA; South Texas 1990 JD
Staff Attorney **Richard A. Gonzales** .... (214) 712-3424
Education: St Mary's U (TX) 1992 JD

Chambers of Justice Lana Myers *continued*

Secretary **Captoria Shelby** .... (214) 712-3418

Chambers of Justice David Evans
600 Commerce Street, Dallas, TX 75202-4653
Tel: (214) 712-3400

David Evans
Justice

Began Service: 2013

Chambers of Justice David Lewis
600 Commerce Street, Dallas, TX 75202-4653
Tel: (214) 712-3400

David Lewis
Justice

Began Service: 2013

Chambers of Justice Ada Brown
600 Commerce Street, Dallas, TX 75202-4653
Tel: (214) 712-3450

Ada Brown
Justice

Education: Spelman 1996 BA; Emory 1999 JD

Chambers of Justice Craig Stoddart
600 Commerce Street, Dallas, TX 75202-4653
Tel: (214) 712-3450

Craig Stoddart
Justice

Education: North Texas; Texas Tech JD
Appointed By: Governor Rick Perry

Chambers of Justice Bill White Hill
600 Commerce Street, Dallas, TX 75202-4653
Tel: (214) 712-3400

Bill White Hill
Justice

Chambers of Justice David Schenck
600 Commerce Street, Dallas, TX 75202-4653
Tel: (214) 712-3400

David J. Schenck
Justice

Date of Birth: September 6, 1967
Education: SUNY (Albany) 1989 BA; Baylor 1992 JD
Began Service: 2015
Appointed By: Governor Rick Perry
Political Affiliation: Republican

Texas Court of Appeals, Sixth District

Bi-State Justice Building, 100 North State Line Avenue,
Texarkana, TX 75501
Tel: (903) 798-3046 Fax: (903) 798-3034
Internet: www.6thcoa.courts.state.tx.us

Number of Judgeships: 3

Areas Covered: Counties of Bowie, Camp, Cass, Delta, Fannin, Franklin, Gregg, Harrison, Hopkins, Hunt, Lamar, Marion, Morris, Panola, Red River, Rusk, Titus, Upshur and Wood

Court Staff

Clerk of the Court **Debbie Autrey** .... (903) 798-3046
E-mail: debbie.autrey@txcourts.gov
Education: Texas A&M 2004 MBA
Chief Staff Attorney **Kristi McCasland** .... (903) 798-3046
E-mail: kristi.mccasland@txcourts.gov
Deputy Clerk for Criminal Cases **Molly Pate** .... (903) 798-3047
Deputy Clerk for Civil Cases **Kim Robinson** .... (903) 798-3046
Staff Attorney **Leisa Pearlman** .... (903) 798-3046
E-mail: leisa.pearlman@txcourts.gov
Staff Attorney **James Smith** .... (903) 798-3046
E-mail: james.smith@txcourts.gov
Staff Attorney **Shivali Sharma** .... (903) 798-3046
E-mail: shivali.sharma@txcourts.gov
Staff Attorney **Randall Goodwin** .... (903) 798-3046
E-mail: randy.goodwin@txcourts.gov
Staff Attorney **Michael Skotnik** .... (903) 798-3046
E-mail: michael.skotnik@txcourts.gov
Education: Baylor 1997 JD

Chambers of Chief Justice Josh R. Morriss III

Bi-State Justice Building, 100 North State Line Avenue, Box 20,
Texarkana, TX 75501
Tel: (903) 798-3046 Fax: (903) 798-3034
E-mail: josh.morriss@txcourts.gov

Josh R. Morriss III
Chief Justice

Date of Birth: 1950
Education: Southern Methodist 1972 BBA, 1973 MBA; Texas 1975 JD
Began Service: June 7, 2002
Appointed By: Governor Rick Perry
Term Expires: December 31, 2016
Political Affiliation: Republican

Academic: President, Texas Association of Bank Counsel

Legal Practice: Attorney and Partner, Atchley, Russell, Waldrop & Hlavinka, L.L.P. (1976-2002)

Current Memberships: Texas Bar Foundation; Northeast Texas Bar Association; Texarkana Bar Association; Texas Association of Bank Counsel

Staff

Legal Assistant **Shera Morgan** .... (903) 798-3028
E-mail: shera.morgan@courts.state.tx.us

Chambers of Justice Bailey C. Moseley

Bi-State Justice Building, 100 North State Line Avenue, Room 20,
Texarkana, TX 75501
Tel: (903) 798-3046 Fax: (903) 798-3034
E-mail: bailey.moseley@txcourts.gov

Bailey C. Moseley
Justice

Education: Texas BBA; Houston JD
Began Service: January 1, 2007

Legal Practice: Partner, Moseley and Davis, Associates (1986-1992)

Profession: Private Practice (1992-2007)

Membership: President, Harrison County Bar Association

Chambers of Justice Bailey C. Moseley *continued*

Staff

Legal Assistant **Carol Pope** .... (903) 798-3025
E-mail: carol.pope@txcourts.gov

Chambers of Justice Ralph K. Burgess

100 North State Line Avenue, Texarkana, TX 75501
Tel: (903) 798-3046

Ralph K. Burgess
Justice

Texas Court of Appeals, Seventh District

2-A Potter County Courts Building, 501 South Fillmore Street,
Amarillo, TX 79101-2449
P.O. Box 9540, Amarillo, TX 79105-9540
Tel: (806) 342-2650 Fax: (806) 342-2675
Internet: www.7thcoa.courts.state.tx.us

Number of Judgeships: 4

Areas Covered: Counties of Armstrong, Bailey, Briscoe, Carson, Castro, Childress, Cochran, Collingsworth, Cottle, Crosby, Dallam, Deaf Smith, Dickens, Donley, Floyd, Foard, Garza, Gray, Hale, Hall, Hansford, Hardeman, Hartley, Hemphill, Hockley, Hutchinson, Kent, King, Lamb, Lipscomb, Lubbock, Lynn, Moore, Motley, Ochiltree, Oldham, Parmer, Potter, Randall, Roberts, Sherman, Swisher, Terry, Wheeler, Wilbarger and Yoakum

Court Staff

Clerk of the Court **Vivian Long** .... (806) 342-2652
Chief Deputy Clerk **Rhonda Silverman** .... (806) 342-2650
Deputy Clerk **Donna Artis** .... (806) 342-2650
Deputy Clerk **Donalee Gibson** .... (806) 342-2650

Chambers of Chief Justice Brian Quinn

2-A Potter County Courts Building, 501 South Fillmore Street,
Amarillo, TX 79101-2449
P.O. Box 9540, Amarillo, TX 79105-9540
Tel: (806) 342-2668 Fax: (806) 342-2675
E-mail: brian.quinn@courts.state.tx.us

Brian Quinn
Chief Justice

Date of Birth: 1956
Education: Texas (El Paso) 1978 BA; Texas Tech 1981 JD
Began Service: January 4, 1995
Term Expires: 2016
Political Affiliation: Republican

Academic: Adjunct Professor, Texas Tech School of Law

Clerkships: Law Clerk The Honorable George P. Kazen, United States District Court for the Southern District of Texas (1981-1983)

Legal Practice: McWhorter, Cobb & Johnson, LLP (1983-1994)

Current Memberships: Texas Bar Foundation; Amarillo Bar Association; Lubbock County Bar Association; Panhandle Family Law Association; State Bar of Texas

Staff

Research Attorney **Thomas McMillian** .... (806) 342-2665
E-mail: susan.heady@courts.state.tx.us
Research Attorney II **Elyse D. Blount** .... (806) 342-2676
E-mail: elyse.blount@courts.state.tx.us
Education: Texas Tech 1991 JD
Legal Assistant **Donalee Gibson** .... (806) 342-2668
E-mail: donalee.gibson@courts.state.tx.us

Chambers of Justice James T. Campbell

2-A Potter County Court Building, 501 South Fillmore Street, Amarillo, TX 79101-2449
P.O. Box 9540, Amarillo, TX 79105-9540
Tel: (806) 342-2664 Fax: (806) 342-2675
E-mail: james.campbell@txcourts.gov

James T. Campbell
Justice

Education: Texas Tech 1971 BA; Vanderbilt 1974 JD
Began Service: February 24, 2003
Next Election: November 2016
Term Expires: December 31, 2016
Political Affiliation: Republican

Legal Practice: Attorney, Pioneer Corporation (1978-1986); Attorney, Peterson Farris Doores & Jones P. C. (1986-2003)

Military Service: United States Navy (1974-1977)

Current Memberships: Texas Bar Foundation; Amarillo Bar Association; Lubbock County Bar Association

Staff
Staff Attorney **Tom McIlhany** .... (806) 342-2646
Began Service: 2007
E-mail: tom.mcilhany@txcourts.gov
Education: Texas Tech 1988 JD; McMurry 1980
Staff Attorney **Alison Sanders** .... (806) 342-2661
E-mail: alison.sanders@txcourts.gov
Education: New Mexico 2003 JD
Legal Assistant **Nancy Klein** .... (806) 342-2664
E-mail: nancy.klein@txcourts.gov

Chambers of Justice Mackey K. Hancock

501 South Fillmore Street, Amarillo, TX 79101-2449
Tel: (806) 342-2650
E-mail: mackey.hancock@courts.state.tx.us

Mackey K. Hancock
Justice

Education: Texas Tech 1971 BS, 1974 JD
Began Service: 2005
Term Expires: 2018

Staff
Staff Attorney **Carrie Simpson** .... (806) 342-2650
Education: Texas Tech 2002 JD
Staff Attorney **Stephen Palmer** .... (806) 342-2650
Education: Houston BS; Texas Tech JD
Legal Assistant **Nancy Klein** .... (806) 342-2650

Chambers of Justice Patrick A. Pirtle

2-A Potter County Courts Building, 501 South Fillmore Street, Amarillo, TX 79101-2449
Tel: (806) 342-2650 Fax: (806) 342-2675

Patrick A. Pirtle
Justice

Education: Texas Tech 1974 BA, 1977 JD
Began Service: 2006
Appointed By: Governor Rick Perry
Term Expires: December 31, 2018

Judicial: Justice, Texas Court of Appeals, Seventh District (1988); District Judge, 251st Judicial District, State of Texas (1989-2006)

Legal Practice: Attorney, Sell & Griffin (1977-1981); Attorney, Sell, Griffin & Pirtle (1981-1985), Attorney, Nickum & Pirtle (1985-1987); Attorney, Whittenburg, Whittenburg & Schachter (1988)

Current Memberships: American Bar Association; State Bar of Texas

Chambers of Justice Patrick A. Pirtle *continued*

Staff
Staff Attorney **Minerva McLaughlin** .... (806) 342-2650
E-mail: minerva.mclaughlin@txcourts.gov
Education: Texas 1984 JD
Staff Attorney **Jon Stewart** .... (806) 342-2650
E-mail: jon.stewart@txcourts.gov
Legal Assistant **Rhonda Silverman** .... (806) 342-2654
E-mail: rhonda.silverman@txcourts.gov

Texas Court of Appeals, Eighth District

1203 County Courthouse, 500 East San Antonio Avenue, El Paso, TX 79901
Tel: (915) 546-2240 Fax: (915) 546-2252
E-mail: clerk@8thcoa.courts.state.tx.us
Internet: www.8thcoa.courts.state.tx.us

Number of Judgeships: 3

Areas Covered: Counties of Andrews, Brewster, Crane, Crockett, Culberson, El Paso, Hudspeth, Jeff Davis, Loving, Pecos, Presidio, Reagan, Reeves, Terrell, Upton, Ward and Winkler

Court Staff
Clerk of Court **Denise Pacheco** .... (915) 546-2240
E-mail: clerk@8thcoa.courts.state.tx.us
Chief Staff Attorney **Kay Waters** .... (915) 546-2240 ext. 3506
Education: Corpus Christi State 1980 BBA; Texas Tech 1986 JD, 1986 MBA

Chambers of Chief Justice Ann Crawford McClure

1203 County Courthouse, 500 East San Antonio Avenue, El Paso, TX 79901
Tel: (915) 546-2240 Fax: (915) 546-2252
E-mail: amcclure@8thcoa.courts.state.tx.us

Ann Crawford McClure
Chief Justice

Date of Birth: September 5, 1953
Education: Texas Christian 1974 BFA; Houston 1979 JD
Began Service: October 12, 2011
Appointed By: Governor Rick Perry
Political Affiliation: Democrat

Current Memberships: El Paso Bar Association; State Bar of Texas; Texas Civil Appellate Law Advisory Commission

Staff
Law Clerk **Ali Walker** .... (915) 546-2240
E-mail: awalker@8thcoa.courts.state.tx.us
Chief Staff Attorney **Kay Waters** .... (915) 546-2240
E-mail: kwaters@8thcoa.courts.state.tx.us
Legal Assistant **Yolanda "Yoly" Fisher** .... (915) 546-2240
E-mail: yfisher@8thcoa.courts.state.tx.us

Chambers of Justice Yvonne Rodriguez

500 East San Antonio Avenue, El Paso, TX 79901
Tel: (915) 546-2240

Yvonne Rodriguez
Justice

Began Service: 2013

Staff
Staff Attorney **Aries Solis** .... (915) 546-2240
Education: Texas 1988 JD
Staff Attorney **Kirk Cooper** .... (915) 546-2240
Legal Assistant **Gloria Gravalos** .... (915) 546-2240

Chambers of Justice Steve Hughes
500 East San Antonio Avenue, El Paso, TX 79901
Tel: (916) 546-2240

Steve Hughes
Justice

Education: Texas Tech BA, MA; Texas JD
Began Service: 2014
Appointed By: Governor Rick Perry
Term Expires: November 2016

Texas Court of Appeals, Ninth District
Jefferson County Courthouse, 1001 Pearl Street, Suite 330,
Beaumont, TX 77701-3352
Tel: (409) 835-8402 Fax: (409) 835-8497
Internet: www.9thcoa.courts.state.tx.us

Number of Judgeships: 4

Areas Covered: Counties of Hardin, Jasper, Jefferson, Liberty, Montgomery, Newton, Orange, Polk, San Jacinto and Tyler

Court Staff
Clerk of the Court **Carol Anne Harley** . . . . (409) 835-8402
E-mail: charley@courts.state.tx.us
Education: Texas A&M 1982 BS
Chief Staff Attorney **Leslie A. Saia** . . . . (409) 835-8402
E-mail: leslie.saia@courts.state.tx.us
Education: Texas 1979 BA, 1982 JD

Chambers of Chief Justice Steve McKeithen
330 Jefferson County Courthouse, 1001 Pearl Street,
Beaumont, TX 77701
Tel: (409) 835-8405 Fax: (409) 835-8497
E-mail: steve.mckeithen@courts.state.tx.us

Steve McKeithen
Chief Justice

Education: Houston 1976 BA; South Texas 1984 JD
Began Service: January 1, 2003
Next Election: November 4, 2020
Election Type: General Election
Term Expires: December 31, 2020
Political Affiliation: Republican

Government: Prosecutor, Office of the County Attorney, County of Montgomery, Texas (1989-1992); Chief Justice, Office of the County Attorney, Civil Division, County of Montgomery, Texas (1992-2002)

Staff
Legal Assistant **Becky Jones** . . . . (409) 835-8405
E-mail: becky.jones@courts.state.tx.us

Chambers of Justice Charles Kreger
1001 Pearl Street, Beaumont, TX 77701-3352
Tel: (409) 835-8402
E-mail: charles.kreger@courts.state.tx.us

Charles Kreger
Justice

Date of Birth: June 27, 1959
Education: Houston 1982 BA; South Texas JD
Began Service: 2004

Membership: Director, Montgomery County Bar Association

Chambers of Justice Hollis Horton
1001 Pearl Street, Beaumont, TX 77701-3352
Tel: (409) 835-8402
E-mail: hollis.horton@courts.state.tx.us

Hollis Horton
Justice

Education: Duke 1978 BA; Texas 1980 JD
Began Service: 2004
Appointed By: Governor Rick Perry
Term Expires: 2018

Legal Practice: Attorney, Orgain Bell & Tucker, LLP

Chambers of Justice Leanne Johnson
1001 Pearl Street, Beaumont, TX 77701-3352
Tel: (409) 835-8402

Leanne Johnson
Justice

Education: Southern Arkansas U 1983 BS; Arkansas 1986 JD

Texas Court of Appeals, Tenth District
McLennan County Courthouse, 501 Washington Avenue, Room 415,
Waco, TX 76701-1373
Tel: (254) 757-5200 Fax: (254) 757-2822
Internet: www.10thcoa.courts.state.tx.us

Number of Judgeships: 3

Number of Vacancies: 0

Areas Covered: Counties of Bosque, Brazos, Burleson, Coryell, Ellis, Falls, Freestone, Hamilton, Hill, Johnson, Leon, Limestone, McLennan, Madison, Navarro, Robertson, Somervell and Walker

Court Staff
Clerk of the Court **Sharri Roessler** . . . . (254) 757-5200
E-mail: sharri.roessler@txcourts.gov

Chambers of Chief Justice Tom Gray
415 McLennan County Courthouse, 501 Washington Avenue,
Waco, TX 76701-1327
Tel: (254) 757-5205 Fax: (254) 757-2822
E-mail: tom.gray@txcourts.gov

Tom Gray
Chief Justice

Date of Birth: 1956
Education: Sam Houston State 1978 BBA; Texas A&M 1979 MBA; Baylor 1985 JD
Began Service: January 1999
Next Election: November 2018
Term Expires: December 31, 2018
Political Affiliation: Republican

Academic: Sam Houston State (1979); Navarro College (1986)

Corporate: CPA, Deloitte, Haskins & Sells (1980-1983)

Judicial: Judge, Rice Municipal Court (1998); Justice, Texas Court of Appeals, Tenth District (1999-2003)

Legal Practice: Dawson, Dawson, Sodd, Davis, Moe & Bizzell (1985-1988); Fulbright & Jaworski, LLP (1988-1998)

Staff
Staff Attorney **Jill A. Durbin** . . . . (254) 757-5200
E-mail: jill.durbin@txcourts.gov
Education: Texas Tech 1986 BA; Houston 1989 JD

Chambers of Chief Justice Tom Gray *continued*

Staff Attorney **Pauline Stevens** . . . . (254) 757-5200
E-mail: pauline.stevens@txcourts.gov
Education: Baylor 1993 JD

Chambers of Justice Rex D. Davis

McLennan County Courthouse, 501 Washington Avenue, Room 415, Waco, TX 76701-1373
Tel: (254) 757-5200

Rex D. Davis
Justice

Date of Birth: August 23, 1950
Education: Texas; Baylor 1974 JD
Began Service: January 2009
Next Election: November 2020
Election Type: General Election
Term Expires: December 31, 2020
Political Affiliation: Republican

Current Memberships: Texas Bar Foundation; College of the State Bar of Texas; State Bar of Texas; Waco-McLennan County Bar Association

Staff
Staff Attorney **Casey Kent** . . . . (254) 757-5200
Education: Texas Wesleyan U 2005 JD
Staff Attorney **Stephen W Kotara** . . . . (254) 757-5200
Education: Texas Tech 1987 JD

Chambers of Justice Al Scoggins

McClennan County Courthouse, 501 Washington Avenue, Room 415, Waco, TX 76701-1373
Tel: (254) 757-5200 Fax: (254) 757-2822

Al Scoggins
Justice

Date of Birth: 1955
Education: Baylor 1977 BBA, 1979 JD
Began Service: January 2011
Next Election: November 2016
Election Type: General Election
Term Expires: December 31, 2016

Staff
Staff Attorney **Rick Bradley** . . . . (254) 757-5200
Staff Attorney **Rachelle Gee** . . . . (254) 757-5200

Texas Court of Appeals, Eleventh District

Eastland County Courthouse, 100 West Main Street, 3rd Floor, Eastland, TX 76448
P.O. Box 271, Eastland, TX 76448
Tel: (254) 629-2638 Fax: (254) 629-2191
Internet: www.11thcoa.courts.state.tx.us

Number of Judgeships: 3

Areas Covered: Counties of Baylor, Borden, Brown, Callahan, Coleman, Comanche, Dawson, Eastland, Ector, Erath, Fisher, Gaines, Glasscock, Haskell, Howard, Jones, Knox, Martin, Midland, Mitchell, Nolan, Palo Pinto, Scurry, Shackelford, Stephens, Stonewall, Taylor and Throckmorton

Court Staff
Clerk of the Court **Sherry Williamson** . . . . (254) 629-2638
E-mail: sherry.williamson@txcourts.gov
Chief Staff Attorney **Jill Barrier Stephens** . . . . (254) 629-2638
E-mail: jill.stephens@txcourts.gov

Chambers of Chief Justice Jim R. Wright

Eastland County Courthouse, 100 West Main, Eastland, TX 76448
P.O. Box 271, Eastland, TX 76448
Tel: (254) 629-2638 Fax: (254) 629-2191
E-mail: jim.wright@txcourts.gov

Jim R. Wright
Chief Justice

Date of Birth: 1946
Education: Texas Tech 1971 JD
Began Service: April 14, 1995
Next Election: November 2018
Term Expires: December 31, 2018

Judicial: Judge, Texas District Court, 91st District Court, Eastland County (1979-1995)

Legal Practice: Wagonseller & Cobb (1971-1972); Sole practitioner (1972-1979)

Current Memberships: State Bar of Texas

Chambers of Justice Mike Willson

100 West Main Street, Eastland, TX 76448
Tel: (254) 629-2638

Mike Willson
Justice

Chambers of Justice John Bailey

100 West Main Street, Eastland, TX 76448
Tel: (254) 629-2638

John Bailey
Justice

Texas Court of Appeals, Twelfth District

1517 West Front Street, Suite 354, Tyler, TX 75702
Tel: (903) 593-8471 Fax: (903) 593-2193
Internet: www.12thcoa.courts.state.tx.us

Number of Judgeships: 3

Areas Covered: Counties of Anderson, Angelina, Cherokee, Gregg, Henderson, Houston, Nacogdoches, Rains, Rusk, Sabine, Smith, San Augustine, Shelby, Trinity, Upshur, Van Zandt and Wood

The Court sits in Tyler, Smith County.

Court Staff
Clerk of the Court **Pam Estes** . . . . (903) 593-8471
E-mail: pam.estes@txcourts.gov
Chief Staff Attorney **Margaret L. Hussey** . . . . (903) 593-8471
Education: Austin State 1972 MBA; Baylor 1980 JD

STATE COURTS—TEXAS

Chambers of Chief Justice James T. Worthen

1517 West Front Street, Suite 354, Tyler, TX 75702
Tel: (903) 593-8471 Fax: (903) 593-2193
E-mail: james.worthen@txcourts.gov

James T. Worthen
Chief Justice

Date of Birth: 1954
Education: Texas (Tyler) 1978 BS; South Texas 1980 JD; Virginia 2004 LLM
Began Service: January 1, 1999
Next Election: November 2020
Term Expires: December 31, 2020
Political Affiliation: Republican

Government: City Attorney, Office of the City Attorney, City of Big Sandy, Texas (1981-1985)

Legal Practice: Sammons & Parker (1981-1986); Bain, Files, Worthen & Jarrett (1987-1998)

Current Memberships: American Bar Association; Fifth Circuit Bar Association; Gregg County Bar Association; Smith County Bar Association; State Bar of Texas

Staff

Chief Staff Attorney **Margaret L. Hussey** .... (903) 593-8471
Legal Assistant **Bethena Atwood** .... (903) 593-8471
E-mail: bethena.atwood@txcourts.gov
Education: Southwest Texas State 1982 BA

Chambers of Justice Brian Hoyle

1517 West Front Street, Suite 354, Tyler, TX 75702
Tel: (903) 593-8471 Fax: (903) 593-2193

Brian Hoyle
Justice

Education: Texas 1991 BA; Baylor 1994 JD
Began Service: August 28, 2006
Appointed By: Governor Rick Perry
Term Expires: December 31, 2016

Clerkships: Law Clerk, Texas Farm Bureau Federation; Law Clerk, United States District Court for the Eastern District of Texas (1994-1996)

Legal Practice: Attorney, Merriman, Patterson & Allison (1996-2000); Attorney, Brown McCarroll, L.L.P. (2000-2001); Partner, Brown McCarroll, L.L.P. (2001-2006)

Current Memberships: Gregg County Bar Association; Smith County Bar Association; State Bar of Texas

Chambers of Justice Greg Neeley

1517 West Front Street, Tyler, TX 75702
Tel: (903) 593-8471

Greg Neeley
Justice

Texas Court of Appeals, Thirteenth District

Nueces County Courthouse, 901 Leopard Street, 10th Floor, Corpus Christi, TX 78401
Hidalgo County Administration Building, 100 East Cano Street, 5th Floor, Edinburg, TX 78539
Tel: (361) 888-0416 Tel: (956) 318-2405 (Edinburg Office)
Fax: (361) 888-0794 Fax: (956) 318-2403 (Edinburg Office)
Internet: www.txcourts.gov/13thcoa

Number of Judgeships: 6

Areas Covered: Counties of Aransas, Bee, Calhoun, Cameron, De Witt, Goliad, Gonzales, Hidalgo, Jackson, Kenedy, Kleberg, Lavaca, Live Oak, Matagorda, Nueces, Refugio, San Patricio, Victoria, Wharton and Willacy

Court Staff

Clerk of the Court **Dorian Ramirez** .... (361) 888-0697
E-mail: dorian.ramirez@txcourts.gov
Chief Staff Attorney **Cecile Foy Gsanger** .... (361) 888-0416
E-mail: cecile.gsanger@txcourts.gov
Education: Texas 1986 BA, 1990 JD

Chambers of Chief Justice Rogelio Valdez

100 East Cano Street, 5th Floor, Edinburg, TX 78539
Tel: (956) 318-2405 Fax: (956) 318-2403
E-mail: roy.valdez@courts.state.tx.us

Rogelio Valdez
Chief Justice

Date of Birth: 1951
Education: Texas A&I 1976 BA; Texas Southern 1979 JD
Began Service: January 1, 2001
Next Election: November 2018
Term Expires: December 31, 2018
Political Affiliation: Democrat

Government: Assistant District Attorney, Office of the District Attorney, County of Cameron, Texas

Judicial: Judge, County Court at Law (1983-1986); Judge, 357th District Court (1987-2000)

Legal Practice: Private Practice (1979-1980)

Current Memberships: American Bar Association; Cameron County Bar Association; Mexican American Bar Association; State Bar of Texas; Texas Judges Association

Staff

Chief Staff Attorney **Cecile Foy Gsanger** .... (956) 318-2405
E-mail: cecile.gsanger@courts.state.tx.us
Senior Attorney **Erica Ramos** .... (956) 318-2405
E-mail: erica.ramos@courts.state.tx.us
Briefing Attorney **Christopher G. Gonzalez** .... (956) 318-2405
Legal Assistant **Celinda Coronado** .... (956) 318-2410 ext. 236
Began Service: 2008
E-mail: celinda.coronado@courts.state.tx.us

Chambers of Justice Nelda V. Rodriguez

Nueces County Courthouse, 901 Leopard Street, 10th Floor, Corpus Christi, TX 78401
Tel: (361) 888-0685 Fax: (361) 888-0794
E-mail: nelda.rodriguez@courts.state.tx.us

Nelda V. Rodriguez
Justice

Date of Birth: 1954
Education: Texas Southern 1981 JD
Began Service: 1995
Next Election: November 2018
Term Expires: December 31, 2018
Political Affiliation: Democrat

Judicial: Judge, Municipal Court (1990-1991); Title IV-D Court Master (1991-1993)

Legal Practice: Rodriguez & Associates (1981-1990)

Staff
Legal Assistant **Diana Tello** .... (361) 888-0685
E-mail: diana.tello@courts.state.tx.us

Chambers of Justice Dori Contreras Garza

Hidalgo County Administration Building, 100 East Cano Street, 5th Floor, Edinburg, TX 78539
Tel: (956) 318-2405 Fax: (956) 318-2403

Dori Contreras Garza
Justice

Education: Texas 1980 BABA; Houston 1990 JD
Began Service: January 1, 2003
Next Election: November 4, 2020
Election Type: General Election
Term Expires: December 31, 2020

Legal Practice: Private Practice (1997-2002); Associate, Thurlow & Associates, P.C. (1990-1991); Attorney, Law Offices of Frank Herrera (1991-1997)

Current Memberships: National Association of Women Judges; State Bar of Texas

Staff
Junior Staff Attorney **Cindy Polinard** .... (956) 318-2405
E-mail: cindy.polinard@courts.state.tx.us
Education: Texas Pan American 1979 BA; Texas 1994 JD
Senior Staff Attorney **Andrew G. Monaco** .... (956) 318-2405
E-mail: andrew.monaco@courts.state.tx.us
Legal Assistant **Delia Rodriguez** .... (956) 318-2879
E-mail: delia.rodriguez@courts.state.tx.us

Chambers of Justice Gina M. Benavides

100 East Cano Street, 5th Floor, Edinburg, TX 78539
Tel: (956) 318-2405 Fax: (956) 318-2403
E-mail: gina.benavides@courts.state.tx.us

Gina M. Benavides
Justice

Education: Texas BS; Houston JD
Began Service: January 2007

Legal Practice: Attorney, Adams & Graham; Attorney, Jim Gonzalez & Associates

Membership: President, Cameron County Bar Association; President, Mexican American Bar Association of Texas

Staff
Senior Staff Attorney **Kristalee Guerra** .... (956) 318-2405
E-mail: kristalee.guerra@courts.state.tx.us

Chambers of Justice Gina M. Benavides *continued*

Briefing Attorney **Joshua Caldwell** .... (956) 318-2405
Legal Assistant **Marina Quilantan** .... (956) 318-2405
E-mail: marina.quilantan@courts.state.tx.us

Chambers of Justice Gregory T. Perkes

Tel: (361) 888-0608 Fax: (361) 888-0794
E-mail: greg.perkes@txcourts.gov

Gregory T. Perkes
Justice

Began Service: January 1, 2011

Staff
Briefing Attorney **Joel de la Garza** .... (361) 888-0608
Senior Attorney **Andrew Thompson** .... (361) 888-0608

Chambers of Justice Nora Longoria

100 East Cano Street, Edinburg, TX 78539
Tel: (361) 888-0416

Nora Longoria
Justice

Began Service: January 1, 2013
Term Expires: December 31, 2018

Staff
Staff Attorney **Austin Miller** .... (956) 318-2405
Senior Attorney **Nate Beal** .... (956) 318-2405
Legal Assistant **Joe Paredes** .... (915) 318-2405

Texas Court of Appeals, Fourteenth District

301 Fannin Street, Suite 245, Houston, TX 77002
Tel: (713) 274-2800 Fax: (713) 650-8550
Internet: www.14thcoa.courts.state.tx.us

Number of Judgeships: 9

Areas Covered: Counties of Austin, Brazoria, Chambers, Colorado, Fort Bend, Galveston, Grimes, Harris, Waller and Washington

Court Staff
Clerk of the Court **Christopher A. Prine** .... (713) 274-2800
Chief Staff Attorney **Nina Reilly Indelicato** .... (713) 274-2800
Education: South Texas 1992 JD

Chambers of Chief Justice Kem Thompson Frost

301 Fannin Street, Suite 245, Houston, TX 77002
Tel: (713) 274-2800 Fax: (713) 650-8550

Kem Thompson Frost
Chief Justice

Date of Birth: 1958
Education: Texas 1980 BBA; Texas Tech 1983 JD
Began Service: March 11, 1999
Appointed By: Governor George W. Bush
Next Election: November 4, 2020
Election Type: General Election
Term Expires: December 31, 2020
Political Affiliation: Republican

Current Memberships: American Bar Association; The American Inns of Court; Houston Bar Association; State Bar of Texas

Staff
Junior Staff Attorney **Kara Gansmann** .... (713) 274-2800

(continued on next page)

STATE COURTS—TEXAS

Chambers of Chief Justice Kem Thompson Frost *continued*

Chambers Attorney **Ray Blackwood** . . . . (713) 274-2800
E-mail: ray.blackwood@courts.state.tx.us
Education: Duke 1993 JD

Chambers of Justice William J. Boyce

301 Fannin Street, 11th Floor, Houston, TX 77002
Tel: (713) 274-2800 Fax: (713) 650-8550

William J. Boyce
Justice

Education: Northwestern 1985 BSJ, 1988 JD
Began Service: January 2008
Appointed By: Governor Rick Perry
Next Election: November 4, 2018
Election Type: General Election
Term Expires: 2018

Clerkships: Law Clerk, Chambers of Circuit Judge W. Eugene Davis, United States Court of Appeals for the Fifth Circuit (1988-1989)

Legal Practice: Associate, Fulbright & Jaworski L.L.P. (1989-2006); Partner, Fulbright & Jaworski L.L.P. (1997-2007)

Current Memberships: The American Law Institute

Staff
Junior Staff Attorney **Nick Pavlov** . . . . (713) 274-2800
Chambers Attorney **Belinda Tiosavljevic** . . . . (713) 274-2800

Chambers of Justice Tracy Christopher

301 Fannin Street, Houston, TX 77002
Tel: (713) 274-2800 Fax: (713) 650-8550
E-mail: tracy.christopher@courts.state.tx.us

Tracy Christopher
Justice

Education: Notre Dame 1978 BA; Texas 1981 JD
Began Service: December 2009
Appointed By: Governor Rick Perry

Staff
Briefing Attorney **Dov Rosen** . . . . (713) 274-2800
E-mail: dov.rosen@courts.state.tx.us
Chambers Attorney **Madison Finch** . . . . (713) 274-2800
E-mail: madison.finch@courts.state.tx.us

Chambers of Justice Martha Hill Jamison

301 Fannin Street, Houston, TX 77002
Tel: (713) 274-2800 Fax: (713) 650-8550

Martha Hill Jamison
Justice

Education: Texas 1973 BA, 1977 JD
Began Service: November 29, 2010
Term Expires: 2018

Staff
Junior Staff Attorney **Jennifer Kingaard** . . . . (713) 274-2800
E-mail: jennifer.kingaard@courts.state.tx.us
Chambers Attorney **Steve Carter** . . . . (713) 274-2800
E-mail: steve.carter@courts.state.tx.us

Chambers of Justice John Donovan

301 Fannin Street, Houston, TX 77002
Tel: (713) 274-2800

John Donovan
Justice

Began Service: 2013
Term Expires: December 31, 2018

Chambers of Justice Sharon McCally

301 Fannin Street, Houston, TX 77002
Tel: (713) 274-2800 Fax: (713) 650-8550

Sharon McCally
Justice

Education: Southern Methodist 1981 BA; South Texas 1990 JD

Staff
Staff Attorney **Anna L. Etheridge** . . . . (713) 274-2800
Education: South Texas 1994 JD
Staff Attorney **(Vacant)** . . . . (713) 274-2800

Chambers of Justice Brett Busby

301 Fannin Street, Houston, TX 77002
Tel: (713) 274-2800

Brett Busby
Justice

Education: Duke; Columbia JD
Began Service: 2013

Clerkships: Law Clerk, Supreme Court of the United States; Law Clerk, Chambers of Circuit Judge Gerald Bard Tjoflat, United States Court of Appeals for the Eleventh Circuit

Legal Practice: Partner, Bracewell & Giuliani LLP

Staff
Staff Attorney **Keith Middleton** . . . . (713) 274-2800
Law Clerk **John MacVayne** . . . . (713) 274-2800

Chambers of Justice Marc W. Brown

301 Fannin Street, Houston, TX 77002
Tel: (713) 274-2800

Marc W. Brown
Justice

Appointed By: Governor Rick Perry

Chambers of Justice Ken Wise

301 Fannin Street, Houston, TX 77002
Tel: (713) 274-2800

Ken Wise
Justice

Education: Texas A&M; Houston JD
Began Service: October 2013
Appointed By: Governor Rick Perry

Utah

Administrative Office of the Courts of Utah

Scott M. Matheson Courthouse, 450 South State Street,
Salt Lake City, UT 84111
P.O. Box 140241, Salt Lake City, UT 84114-0241
Tel: (801) 578-3800 Fax: (801) 578-3843

Staff

State Court Administrator **Daniel J. "Dan" Becker** . . . . . . (801) 578-3806
E-mail: danb@utcourts.gov Fax: (801) 578-3843
Education: Florida Atlantic BA, 1977 MPA
Executive Assistant **Jody Gonzales** . . . . (801) 578-3806
E-mail: jodyg@utcourts.gov
District Court Administrator **Debra Moore** . . . . (801) 578-3971
E-mail: debram@utcourts.gov
Deputy Court Administrator **Raymond "Ray" Wahl** . . . . . (801) 578-3805
E-mail: rayw@utcourts.gov
Assistant Court Administrator
Richard "Rick" Schwermer . . . . (801) 578-3816
E-mail: ricks@utcourts.gov
Juvenile Court Administrator **Dawn-Marie Rubio** . . . . (801) 578-3812
E-mail: dawnr@utcourts.gov
Assistant Juvenile Court Administrator **Krista Airam** . . . . . (801) 578-3800
Assistant Juvenile Court Administrator **Katie Gregory** . . . (801) 578-3811
E-mail: katieg@utcourts.gov
General Legal Counsel **Brent Johnson** . . . . (801) 578-3817
E-mail: brentj@utcourts.gov
Senior Staff Attorney **Alison Adams-Perlac** . . . . (801) 578-3808
E-mail: tims@utcourts.gov
ADR Director **Nini Rich** . . . . (801) 578-3982
E-mail: ninir@utcourts.gov
Court Services Director **Kim Allard** . . . . (801) 578-3988
E-mail: kima@utcourts.gov
Guardian Ad Lit Director **Elizabeth Knight** . . . . (801) 578-3848
E-mail: elizabethk@utcourts.gov
Human Resources Director **Rob Parkes** . . . . (801) 578-3802
E-mail: robap@utcourts.gov
Information Technology Director **Ron Bowmaster** . . . . . . (801) 578-3872
E-mail: ronb@utcourts.gov
Associate Physical Resources Coordinator
Alyn Lunceford . . . . (801) 578-3881
E-mail: alynl@utcourts.gov
Audit Manager **Heather MacKenzie-Campbell** . . . . (801) 578-3889
E-mail: heatherm@utcourts.gov
Budget/Accounting Manager **Derek Byrne** . . . . (801) 578-3887
E-mail: derekb@utcourts.gov
Finance Manager **Brian Ross** . . . . (801) 578-3862
E-mail: brianr@utcourts.gov
Communications Director **Nancy Volmer** . . . . (801) 578-3994
E-mail: nancyv@utcourts.gov
Education Director **Tom Langhorne** . . . . (801) 578-3837
E-mail: tomnl@utcourts.gov

Utah Supreme Court

Scott M. Matheson Courthouse, 450 South State Street, 5th Floor,
Salt Lake City, UT 84114
P.O. Box 140210, Salt Lake City, UT 84114-0210
Tel: (801) 238-7967 Tel: (801) 238-7990 (Supreme Court Law Library)
E-mail: supremecourt@utcourts.gov
Internet: courtlink.utcourts.gov

Number of Judgeships: 5

The Supreme Court consists of a chief justice, an associate chief justice and three justices who are initially appointed by the Governor upon recommendation of a Judicial Nominating Commission and then run unopposed for retention for a ten-year term in the first general election occurring not more than three years after appointment. The chief justice is elected by peer vote to a four-year term and the associate chief justice is elected by peer vote to a two-year term. The Supreme Court has exclusive appellate jurisdiction over first degree and capital felony convictions from the Utah District Court and civil judgments other than domestic relations. The Court also has exclusive appellate jurisdiction over cases where the Utah Court of Appeals does not have jurisdiction and over some administrative agencies. The Court exercises constitutional rule-making authority over procedure and evidence and regulates admission to the state bar and the conduct of its members.

The Supreme Court sits in Salt Lake City.

Court Staff

Clerk of the Court **Andrea Martinez** . . . . (801) 238-7974
E-mail: andrearm@utcourts.gov
Judicial Assistant III **Merilyn Hammond** . . . . (801) 578-3904
E-mail: merilynh@utcourts.gov
Judicial Assistant III **Kimberly Shafer** . . . . (801) 238-7977
Judicial Services Manager **Susan Willis** . . . . (801) 238-7976
E-mail: suew@utcourts.gov
Senior Appellate Assistant **Joan Keller** . . . . (801) 238-7935
E-mail: joank@utcourts.gov
Senior Appellate Assistant **Elise Walker Jones** . . . . (801) 238-7950
Appellate Judicial Assistant **Dolores Celio** . . . . (801) 238-7945
E-mail: doloresc@utcourts.gov
Appellate Judicial Assistant **Diane Groesbeck** . . . . (801) 238-7958
E-mail: dianexg@utcourts.gov
Appellate Judicial Assistant **Samantha Hunn** . . . . (801) 238-7937
E-mail: samanthah@utcourts.gov

Chambers of Chief Justice Matthew B. Durrant

Scott M. Matheson Courthouse, 450 South State Street, 5th Floor,
Salt Lake City, UT 84111
P.O. Box 140210, Salt Lake City, UT 84114-0210
Tel: (801) 238-7937 Fax: (801) 738-7980

Matthew B. Durrant
Chief Justice

Date of Birth: 1957
Education: Harvard 1984 JD
Began Service: April 1, 2012

Staff

Law Clerk **Ryan Merriman** . . . . (801) 238-7940
E-mail: thomasg@utcourts.gov
Law Clerk **Erin St. John** . . . . (801) 238-7941
Judicial Secretary **Samantha Hunn** . . . . (801) 238-7937
E-mail: samanthah@utcourts.gov

STATE COURTS—UTAH

Chambers of Justice Christine M. Durham

Scott M. Matheson Courthouse, 450 South State Street,
Salt Lake City, UT 84111
P.O. Box 140210, Salt Lake City, UT 84114-0210
Tel: (801) 238-7945 Fax: (801) 238-7980

Christine M. Durham
Justice

Date of Birth: 1945
Education: Wellesley 1967 AB; Duke 1971 JD
Began Service: April 1, 2012

Current Memberships: American Bar Foundation

Staff
Law Clerk **Larissa Lee** .... (801) 238-7946
Began Service: September 2015
Term Expires: August 31, 2016
E-mail: leel@utcourts.gov
Law Clerk **Kris Bahr** .... (801) 238-7947
Began Service: January 23, 2013
Term Expires: January 30, 2016
E-mail: krisb@utcourts.gov
Administrative Assistant **Dolores Celio** .... (801) 238-7945
E-mail: doloresc@email.utcourts.gov

Chambers of Justice Thomas R. Lee

450 South State Street, Salt Lake City, UT 84111
Tel: (801) 238-7950 Fax: (801) 238-7980

Thomas Rex "Tom" Lee
Justice

Education: BYU 1988 BA; Chicago 1991 JD
Began Service: 2010
Appointed By: Gary R. Herbert

Staff
Law Clerk **Daniel Ortner** .... (801) 238-7954
Term Expires: August 2016
E-mail: danielo@utcourts.gov
Law Clerk **James Phillips** .... (801) 238-7953
Term Expires: August 2016
Judicial Secretary **Elise Jones** .... (801) 238-7950

Chambers of Justice Constandinos Himonas

450 South State Street, Salt Lake City, UT 84111
Tel: (801) 238-7967

Constandinos "Deno" Himonas
Justice

Education: Utah 1986 BA; Chicago 1989 JD
Began Service: March 16, 2015

Utah Court of Appeals

Scott M. Matheson Courthouse, 450 South State Street, 5th Floor,
Salt Lake City, UT 84111
P.O. Box 140230, Salt Lake City, UT 84114-0230
Tel: (801) 578-3900
Tel: (801) 578-3923 (Electronic Bulletin Board Data)
Fax: (801) 578-3999
Internet: courtlink.utcourts.gov/

Number of Judgeships: 7

Number of Vacancies: 1

The Court of Appeals, established in 1987, consists of a presiding judge and six judges who are initially appointed by the Governor upon recommendation of a Judicial Nominating Commission and then run unopposed for retention for six-year terms at the first general election occurring not more than three years after appointment. The presiding judge is elected by peer vote to a two-year term. The Court sits in rotating panels of three judges each. The Court of Appeals exercises appellate jurisdiction over cases from the Utah Juvenile Courts, domestic relations cases, criminal cases (except those appealed directly to the Supreme Court) and cases from administrative agencies which are not appealed directly to the Supreme Court.

The Court of Appeals sits in Salt Lake City.

Court Staff

Clerk of the Court **Lisa A. Collins** .... (801) 578-3907
E-mail: lisaac@email.utcourts.gov
Judicial Assistant **Breeanna Degarmo** .... (801) 578-3948
E-mail: crystalc@utcourts.gov
Judicial Assistant **Ashley Dovidauskas** .... (801) 578-3905
E-mail: celiau@utcourts.gov
Judicial Assistant **Nicole Gray** .... (801) 578-7975
E-mail: nicoleg@utcourts.gov
Judicial Assistant **Kim Shafer** .... (801) 238-7978
E-mail: kimberlyxs@utcourts.gov
Transcripts Coordinator **Crystal Cragun** .... (801) 578-3947
Chief Appellate Mediator **Michele Mattsson** .... (801) 238-7806
E-mail: michelem@utcourts.gov Fax: (801) 238-7014
Education: Utah 1988 JD
Central Staff Attorney **Robert Harrow** .... (801) 578-3950
E-mail: roberth@utcourts.gov Fax: (801) 238-7981
Central Staff Attorney **Bret Hayman** .... (801) 578-3950
E-mail: breth@utcourts.gov Fax: (801) 238-7981
Education: Utah JD
Central Staff Attorney **Karen S. Thompson** .... (801) 578-3950
E-mail: karent@utcourts.gov Fax: (801) 238-7981
Education: Utah 1982 JD
Central Staff Attorney **Mary E. Westby** .... (801) 578-3950
E-mail: maryw@utcourts.gov Fax: (801) 238-7981
Education: Utah 1998 JD
Judicial Secretary **Celia Urcino** .... (801) 578-3950
Fax: (801) 238-7981
Mediation Administrative Assistant **Shauna Hawley** .... (801) 578-7805
E-mail: shaunah@utcourts.gov Tel: (801) 238-7014

Chambers of Presiding Judge J. Frederic Voros Jr.

Scott M. Matheson Courthouse, 450 South State Street,
Salt Lake City, UT 84111
P.O. Box 140230, Salt Lake City, UT 84114-0230
Tel: (801) 578-3950 Fax: (801) 238-7981

J. Frederic "Fred" Voros, Jr.
Presiding Judge

Education: BYU 1975 BA; J Reuben Clark Law 1978 JD
Began Service: October 2009
Appointed By: Gary R. Herbert

Staff
Law Clerk **Sarah Carlquist** .... (801) 578-3950
Began Service: August 2015
Term Expires: August 31, 2016
E-mail: sarahc@utcourts.gov

Chambers of Presiding Judge J. Frederic Voros Jr. *continued*

Law Clerk **Sarah Jenkins** .... (801) 578-3950
Began Service: August 2015
Term Expires: August 2016

Chambers of Associate Presiding Judge Gregory K. Orme

Scott M. Matheson Courthouse, 450 South State Street,
Salt Lake City, UT 84111
P.O. Box 140230, Salt Lake City, UT 84114-0230
Tel: (801) 578-3950 Fax: (801) 238-7981

Gregory K. Orme
Associate Presiding Judge

Date of Birth: 1953
Education: Utah 1975 BA; George Washington 1978 JD
Began Service: February 2, 1987
Appointed By: Governor Norman H. Bangerter
Next Election: November 4, 2020
Election Type: Retention Election
Term Expires: December 2020

Current Memberships: Utah State Bar

Staff
Law Clerk **Wendy Brown** .... (801) 578-3950
Law Clerk **Stephanie Chipley** .... (801) 578-3950

Chambers of Judge Stephen L. Roth

Scott M. Matheson Courthouse, 450 South State Street,
Salt Lake City, UT 84111
P.O. Box 140230, Salt Lake City, UT 84114-0230
Tel: (801) 578-3950 Fax: (801) 238-7981

Stephen L. Roth
Judge

Education: J Reuben Clark Law JD
Began Service: 2010
Appointed By: Gary R. Herbert

Staff
Law Clerk **Gregory Gunn** .... (801) 578-3950
Began Service: March 2010
E-mail: gregg@utcourts.gov
Law Clerk **Elise Carter** .... (801) 578-3950

Chambers of Judge Michele Christiansen

Scott M. Matheson Courthouse, 450 South State Street,
Salt Lake City, UT 84111
P.O. Box 140230, Salt Lake City, UT 84114-0230
Tel: (801) 578-3950 Fax: (801) 238-7981

Michele M. Christiansen
Judge

Education: Lawrence U; Utah 1995 JD
Began Service: July 2010
Appointed By: Gary R. Herbert

Staff
Law Clerk **Adam Bondy** .... (801) 578-3950
Law Clerk **Brooke Wansgaard** .... (801) 578-3950

Chambers of Judge James Z. Davis

Scott M. Matheson Courthouse, 450 South State Street, 5th Floor,
Salt Lake City, UT 84111
P.O. Box 140230, Salt Lake City, UT 84114-0230
Tel: (801) 578-3950 Fax: (801) 238-7981
E-mail: jzdavis@email.utcourts.gov

James Z. Davis
Judge

Education: Utah 1968
Began Service: January 5, 2010
Appointed By: Governor Michael O. Leavitt
Next Election: November 4, 2020
Election Type: Retention Election
Term Expires: December 2020

Current Memberships: American Association for Justice; American Bar Association; Utah State Bar

Staff
Law Clerk **Adrienne Bossi** .... (801) 578-3950
E-mail: adrienneb@utcourts.gov
Education: Boston U 2010 JD
Law Clerk **Jessame Petersen** .... (801) 578-3950
E-mail: jessamep@utcourts.gov
Education: J Reuben Clark Law 2009 JD

Chambers of Judge John A. Pearce

450 South State Street, Salt Lake City, UT 84111
Tel: (801) 578-3900

John A. Pearce
Judge

Education: Utah 1992 BS; Boalt Hall 1996 JD
Began Service: 2013
Appointed By: Gary R. Herbert

Chambers of Judge Kate A. Toomey

450 South State Street, Salt Lake City, UT 84111
Tel: (801) 578-3900

Kate A. Toomey
Judge

Began Service: September 2014
Appointed By: Gary R. Herbert

Vermont

Vermont Office of the Court Administrator

111 State Street, Montpelier, VT 05609-0701
109 State Street, Montpelier, VT 05609-0701
Tel: (802) 828-3278 Fax: (802) 828-3457
Internet: www.vermontjudiciary.org

Staff

Court Administrator and Clerk of Court **Patricia Gabel** . . . (802) 828-3278
E-mail: patricia.gabel@state.vt.us
Education: Albany Law 1975 JD
Chief of Trial Court Operations **Theresa "Tari" Scott** . . . (802) 828-3278
E-mail: theresa.scott@state.vt.us
Planning and Court Services Director **Linda Richard** . . . . . (802) 828-3278
E-mail: linda.richard@state.vt.us
Education: Trinity Col (VT) 2000 MS
Finance and Administration Chief **Matt Riven** . . . . (802) 828-3278
Fax: (802) 828-0414
Chief Information Officer **Jeffery Loewer** . . . . (802) 828-3278
E-mail: jeffery.loewer@state.vt.us Fax: (802) 828-0414
Deputy Director, Research and Information Services
Sean Thomson . . . . (802) 828-3278
E-mail: sean.thomson@state.vt.us Fax: (802) 828-0414
Treatment Court Coordinator **Karen Gennette** . . . . (802) 828-4913
E-mail: karen.gennette@state.vt.us Fax: (802) 828-3457
Education: Vermont 1980 BA
Human Resources Manager **John McGlynn** . . . . (802) 828-3278
E-mail: john.mcglynn@state.vt.us
Deputy Director of Planning and Court Services
Laura Dolgin . . . . (802) 828-3278
E-mail: laura.dolgin@state.vt.us Fax: (802) 828-3457
Programs Manager, Juvenile Justice Systems
Shari Young . . . . (802) 828-5625
E-mail: shari.young@state.vt.us
Education: Vermont Law 1987 JD
Programs Manager, Trial Court Operations
David Kennedy . . . . (802) 828-3278
Security and Safety Program Manager
William F. Gerke, Jr. . . . . (802) 828-3278
E-mail: william.gerke@state.vt.us

Vermont Supreme Court

111 State Street, Montpelier, VT 05609-0701
109 State Street, Montpelier, VT 05609-0801
Tel: (802) 828-3278 Tel: (802) 828-3234 (TTD)
Tel: (802) 828-2729 (Electronic Bulletin Board Data)
Fax: (802) 828-3457
Internet: www.vermontjudiciary.org

Number of Judgeships: 5

The Supreme Court consists of a chief justice and four associate justices who are initially appointed for six-year terms by the Governor with the advice and consent of the State Senate from a list of nominees submitted by the Judicial Nominating Board. Thereafter, the newly-appointed justices are subject to retention votes by the Vermont General Assembly for six-year terms. The chief justice is appointed by the Governor. Retirement is mandatory at age ninety; however, retired justices may be recalled by the chief justice to serve temporary assignments. The Supreme Court has appellate jurisdiction over the Vermont Superior Court, District Court, Family Court, Environmental Court and Judicial Bureau, as well as over the Vermont Probate Court when a question of law is involved. The Court also has appellate jurisdiction over certain administrative agency proceedings. The Court has administrative control over all courts, admittance to the state bar, and the regulation of the practice of law and disciplinary control over judges and attorneys.

The Supreme Court sits in Montpelier.

Vermont Supreme Court *continued*

Court Staff

Court Administrator and Clerk of the Court
Patricia Gabel . . . . (802) 828-3278
E-mail: patricia.gabel@state.vt.us
Deputy Clerk **Ed McSweeney** . . . . (802) 828-3278
E-mail: ed.mcsweeney@state.vt.us
Reporter of Decisions **Larry A. Abbott** . . . . (802) 828-3278
E-mail: larry.abbott@state.vt.us Fax: (802) 828-4750
Education: Chicago 1973 JD
Librarian **(Vacant)** . . . . (802) 828-3268
E-mail: paul.donovan@state.vt.us Fax: (802) 828-2199

Chambers of Chief Justice Paul L. Reiber

109 State Street, Montpelier, VT 05609-0801
Tel: (802) 828-4784 Fax: (802) 828-0536
E-mail: paul.reiber@state.vt.us

Paul L. Reiber
Chief Justice

Education: Hampden-Sydney 1970 BA; Suffolk 1974 JD
Began Service: 2004
Appointed By: Governor Jim Douglas
Term Expires: March 31, 2017

Legal Practice: Partner, Kenlan, Schweibert & Facey (1986-2003)

Staff

Law Clerk **Christian Chorba** . . . . (802) 828-4748
Began Service: August 13, 2015
Term Expires: August 9, 2016
E-mail: zachary.chen@state.vt.us

Chambers of Associate Justice John A. Dooley

109 State Street, Montpelier, VT 05609-0801
Tel: (802) 828-4784 Fax: (802) 828-0536
E-mail: john.dooley@state.vt.us

John A. Dooley
Associate Justice

Date of Birth: 1944
Education: Union Col (NY) 1965 BSEE; Boston Col 1968 LLB
Began Service: June 12, 1987
Appointed By: Governor Madeleine M. Kunin
Term Expires: March 31, 2017

Clerkships: Law Clerk The Honorable Bernard J. Leddy, United States District Court for the District of Vermont (1968-1969)

Government: Consultant, Legal Services Corporation (1978-1981); Legal Counsel, Governor Madeleine M. Kunin (D-VT), State of Vermont (1984-1985); Secretary of Administration, State of Vermont (1985-1987)

Judicial: Magistrate Judge, United States District Court for the District of Vermont (1971-1975)

Legal Practice: Private Practice (1981-1984)

Nonprofit: Deputy Director, Vermont Legal Aid (1969-1972); Director, Vermont Legal Aid (1972-1978)

Current Memberships: Vermont Bar Association

Staff

Law Clerk **Lauren Sampson** . . . . (802) 828-4753
Began Service: August 13, 2015
Term Expires: August 9, 2016
Administrative Assistant **Monica Bombard** . . . . (802) 828-4784
E-mail: monica.bombard@state.vt.us

Chambers of Associate Justice Marilyn S. Skoglund

109 State Street, Montpelier, VT 05609-0801
Tel: (802) 828-4784 Fax: (802) 828-0536
E-mail: marilyn.skoglund@state.vt.us

Marilyn S. Skoglund
Associate Justice

Date of Birth: 1946
Education: Southern Illinois 1971 BA
Began Service: August 27, 1997
Appointed By: Governor Howard Dean
Term Expires: March 31, 2017

Government: Special Assistant Attorney General, Office of the Attorney General, State of Vermont (1978-1981); Assistant Attorney General, State of Vermont (1981-1989); Chief, Law Division, Office of the Attorney General, State of Vermont (1989-1993); Chief, Public Protection Division, Office of the Attorney General, State of Vermont (1993-1994)

Judicial: Judge, Vermont District Court (1994-1997)

Staff

Law Clerk **Devin McKnight** .... (802) 828-4784
Began Service: August 13, 2015
Term Expires: August 9, 2016
E-mail: devin.mcknight@state.vt.us

Administrative Assistant **Monica Bombard** .... (802) 828-4784
E-mail: monica.bombard@state.vt.us

Chambers of Associate Justice Beth Robinson

111 State Street, Montpelier, VT 05609-0701
Tel: (802) 828-3278
E-mail: beth.robinson@state.vt.us

Beth Robinson
Associate Justice

Education: Dartmouth 1986 BA; Chicago 1989 JD
Began Service: November 28, 2011
Term Expires: March 31, 2017

Chambers of Associate Justice Harold Eaton Jr.

111 State Street, Montpelier, VT 05609-0701
Tel: (802) 828-3278

Harold E. Eaton, Jr.
Associate Justice

U.S. Virgin Islands

Supreme Court of the United States Virgin Islands

161B Crown Bay, St. Thomas, VI 00802 (St. Thomas)
P.O. Box 590, St. Thomas, VI 00804 (St. Thomas)
18 Strand Street, Frederiksted, VI 00841 (St. Croix)
P.O. Box 336, Frederiksted, VI 00841 (St. Croix)
Tel: (340) 774-2237 (St. Thomas) Tel: (340) 778-0641 (St. Croix)
Fax: (340) 774-2258 (St. Thomas) Fax: (340) 772-0004 (St. Croix)
Internet: www.visupremecourt.org

Number of Judgeships: 3

Court Staff

Clerk of the Court **Veronica J. Handy** . . . . (340) 774-2237
Affiliation: Esq.
E-mail: veronica.handy@visupremecourt.org
Administrative Director **(Vacant)** . . . . (340) 774-2237

Chambers of Chief Justice Rhys S. Hodge

161B Crown Bay, St. Thomas, VI 00802
Tel: (340) 774-2237

Rhys S. Hodge
Chief Justice

Education: Kansas State 1971 BS; Rutgers (Camden) 1977 JD
Began Service: October 27, 2006
Appointed By: Governor Charles W. Turnbull
Term Expires: October 27, 2016

Chambers of Justice Maria M. Cabret

161B Crown Bay, St. Thomas, VI 00802
Tel: (340) 774-2237

Maria M. Cabret
Justice

Education: Marymount Manhattan 1971 BA; Howard U 1978 JD
Began Service: October 27, 2006
Appointed By: Governor Charles W. Turnbull
Term Expires: October 27, 2016

Chambers of Justice Ive Arlington Swan

161B Crown Bay, St. Thomas, VI 00802
Tel: (340) 774-2237

Ive Arlington Swan
Justice

Education: Morgan State 1967 BA; Howard U 1970 JD
Began Service: October 27, 2006
Appointed By: Governor Charles W. Turnbull
Term Expires: October 27, 2016

Virginia

State Court Administrator's Office of Virginia

Supreme Court Building, 100 North Ninth Street, 3rd Floor,
Richmond, VA 23219
Tel: (804) 786-6455 Fax: (804) 786-4542
Internet: www.courts.state.va.us

Staff

Executive Secretary **Karl R. Hade** .... (804) 786-6455
E-mail: khade@courts.state.va.us
Education: Richmond 1979 BS, 1988 MBA

Assistant Executive Secretary and Legal Counsel
Edward M. Macon .... (804) 786-6455
E-mail: emacon@courts.state.va.us
Education: Virginia 1980 BA; Richmond 1986 JD

Court Improvement Program Director **Lelia B. Hopper** ... (804) 786-6455
E-mail: lhopper@courts.state.va.us
Education: Marshall JD

Educational Services Director **Caroline E. Kirkpatrick** ... (804) 786-6455
E-mail: ckirkpatrick@courts.state.va.us
Education: Virginia 1992 BA;
Virginia Commonwealth 1995 MS, 2001 PhD

Fiscal Services Director **John B. Rickman** .... (804) 786-6455
E-mail: jrickman@courts.state.va.us
Education: William & Mary 1976 BA;
Virginia Commonwealth 1982 MBA

Human Resources Director **Renee Fleming-Mills** .... (804) 786-6455

Judicial Information Technology Director
Robert Smith .... (804) 786-6455
E-mail: bsmith@courts.state.va.us
Education: U Phoenix 2006 BS

Judicial Planning Director **Cyril W. Miller, Jr.** .... (804) 786-6455
E-mail: cmiller@courts.state.va.us
Education: Virginia Commonwealth PhD

Judicial Services Director **Paul DeLosh** .... (804) 786-6455
E-mail: pdelosh@courts.state.va.us
Education: Virginia Commonwealth 1985 BS

Legal Research Director **Steven L. DalleMura** .... (804) 786-6455
E-mail: sdallemura@courts.state.va.us
Education: Virginia 1988 JD

Legislative and Public Relations Director **Kristi Wright** ... (804) 786-6455

Supreme Court of Virginia

100 North Ninth Street, Richmond, VA 23219
Tel: (804) 786-2251
Tel: (804) 371-8611 (Electronic Bulletin Board Data)
Fax: (804) 786-6249
Internet: www.courts.state.va.us/scv

Number of Judgeships: 7

Number of Vacancies: 1

The Supreme Court consists of a chief justice and six justices who are elected by majority vote of the Virginia General Assembly for twelve-year terms. Vacancies on the Court occurring between sessions of the General Assembly may be filled by the Governor for a term expiring thirty days after the commencement of the next session of the General Assembly. The chief justice is elected by the Court for a four-year term. The Supreme Court has appellate jurisdiction over decisions of the lower courts. The Court exercises review over cases involving the death penalty, the disbarment of an attorney, or the State Corporation Commission. The Court has original jurisdiction in matters filed by the Judicial Inquiry and Review Commission relating to judicial censure, retirement and removal of judges. The Court exercises administrative control over the lower courts.

The Supreme Court sits in Richmond.

Court Staff

Clerk of Court **Patricia L. Harrington** .... (804) 786-2251
E-mail: scvclerk@courts.state.va.us Fax: (804) 786-6249
Education: Duke 1979 BA; Richmond 1983 JD

Supreme Court of Virginia *continued*

Chief Deputy Clerk **Doug Robelen** .... (804) 786-2251
E-mail: drobelen@courts.state.va.us

Deputy Clerk **Ebby Edwards** .... (804) 786-2251
E-mail: eedwards@courts.state.va.us

Deputy Clerk **Sirena Kestner** .... (804) 786-2251
E-mail: skestner@courts.state.va.us

Deputy Clerk **Lesley Smith** .... (804) 786-2251
E-mail: lesmith@courts.state.va.us

Chief Staff Attorney **K. Lorraine "Lori" Lord** .... (804) 786-2259
Education: Washington and Lee BA, JD Fax: (804) 371-8530

Reporter of Decisions **Kent Sinclair** .... (434) 924-4663
E-mail: ksinclair@courts.state.va.us Fax: (434) 293-7564
Education: UC Santa Barbara 1968 AB;
Boalt Hall 1971 JD

State Law Librarian **Gail Warren** .... (804) 786-2075
E-mail: gwarren@courts.state.va.us Fax: (804) 786-4542
Education: James Madison 1978 BA;
Richmond 1981 JD; Catholic U 1987 MSLS

Chief of Capitol Police **Anthony S. Pike** .... (804) 786-2567

Chambers of Chief Justice Donald W. Lemons

Supreme Court Building, 100 North Ninth Street, Richmond, VA 23219
Tel: (804) 225-2183 Fax: (804) 371-8530
E-mail: dlemons@courts.state.va.us

Donald W. Lemons
Chief Justice

Education: Virginia 1970 BA, 1976 JD
Began Service: March 2000
Term Expires: March 16, 2024

Staff

Law Clerk **Joanne Rome** .... (804) 225-2188
Began Service: August 2012
E-mail: jrome@courts.state.va.us

Law Clerk **Paul Wiley** .... (804) 225-2184
Began Service: August 2015
Term Expires: August 2017

Law Clerk **Danny Yates** .... (804) 225-2184
Began Service: August 2015
Term Expires: August 2017
E-mail: dyates@courts.state.va.us

Judicial Assistant **Judy L. Gyorko** .... (804) 225-2183
E-mail: jgyorko@courts.state.va.us

Chambers of Justice S. Bernard Goodwyn

Supreme Court Building, 100 North Ninth Street, Richmond, VA 23219
Tel: (757) 382-3075

S. Bernard Goodwyn
Justice

Education: Harvard BS; Virginia 1986 JD
Began Service: October 10, 2007
Appointed By: Governor Timothy M. Kaine
Term Expires: February 8, 2020

Academic: Research Associate Professor of Law, University of Virginia (1994-1995)

Judicial: Judge, General District Court, City of Chesapeake, Virginia; Circuit Judge, Circuit Court, City of Chesapeake, Virginia

Legal Practice: Attorney, Willcox & Savage, P.C.

Chambers of Justice William C. Mims

100 North Ninth Street, Richmond, VA 23219
P.O. Box 1315, Richmond, VA 23218
Tel: (804) 786-2251
E-mail: wmims@courts.state.va.us

William C. "Bill" Mims
Justice

Education: William & Mary 1979 AB; George Washington 1984 JD; Georgetown 1986 LLM
Began Service: April 9, 2010
Term Expires: March 31, 2022
Political Affiliation: Republican

Chambers of Justice Cleo E. Powell

100 North Ninth Street, Richmond, VA 23219
Tel: (804) 786-2251 Fax: (804) 786-6249
E-mail: cpowell@courts.state.va.us

Cleo Elaine Powell
Justice

Education: Virginia, 1982 JD
Began Service: October 21, 2011

Chambers of Justice Elizabeth A. McClanahan

100 North Ninth Street, Richmond, VA 23219
Tel: (704) 786-2251 Fax: (704) 786-6249
E-mail: emcclanahan@courts.state.va.us

Elizabeth A. McClanahan
Justice

Education: William & Mary BS; Dayton JD
Began Service: August 1, 2011

Chambers of Justice D. Arthur Kelsey

100 North Ninth Street, Richmond, VA 23219
Tel: (804) 786-2251

D. Arthur Kelsey
Justice

Education: William & Mary 1985 JD
Began Service: 2015

Chambers of Justice Jane Marum Roush

100 North Ninth Street, Richmond, VA 23219

Jane Marum Roush
Justice

Chambers of Senior Justice Charles S. Russell

100 North Ninth Street, Richmond, VA 23219
Tel: (804) 786-2251
E-mail: crussell@courts.state.va.us

Charles S. Russell
Senior Justice

Began Service: 1991

Chambers of Senior Justice Elizabeth B. Lacy

Supreme Court Building, 100 North Ninth Street, Richmond, VA 23219
P.O. Box 1315, Richmond, VA 23219
Tel: (804) 786-9980 Fax: (804) 371-8530
E-mail: elacy@courts.state.va.us

Elizabeth B. Lacy
Senior Justice

Date of Birth: 1945
Education: St Mary's Col (IN) 1966 BA; Texas 1969 JD; Virginia 1992 LLM
Began Service: 2007

Government: Staff Attorney, Legislative Agencies, Texas Legislature (1969-1972); Special Assistant and Deputy Attorney General, Office of the Attorney General, State of Texas (1973-1976); Legislative Aide to Delegate Carrington Williams, Virginia General Assembly (1976-1977); Deputy Attorney General, Commonwealth of Virginia (1982-1985); Commissioner, State Corporation Commission, Commonwealth of Virginia (1985-1989)

Legal Practice: Justice, Supreme Court of Virginia (1989-2007)

Nonprofit: Executive Committee Member, American Judicature Society; Director, American Judicature Society

Current Memberships: American Bar Foundation; American Bar Association; National Association of Women Judges; State Bar of Texas; The Virginia Bar Association; Virginia State Bar; Virginia Women Attorneys Association

Staff

Judicial Assistant **Judy C. Nunnally** .... (804) 786-9980
E-mail: jnunnally@courts.state.va.us

Chambers of Senior Justice Lawrence L. Koontz, Jr.

305 East Main Street, 2nd Floor, Salem, VA 24153
P.O. Box 687, Salem, VA 24153-0687
Tel: (540) 387-6082 Fax: (540) 387-6151
E-mail: lkoontz@courts.state.va.us

Lawrence L. Koontz, Jr.
Senior Justice

Date of Birth: 1940
Education: Virginia Tech 1962 BS; Richmond 1965 LLB
Began Service: August 16, 1995
Term Expires: August 15, 2019

Current Memberships: American Bar Association; Roanoke Bar Association; Virginia State Bar

Staff

Career Law Clerk **John Koehler** .... (540) 387-6082
E-mail: jkoehler@courts.state.va.us
Education: Catholic U 1983 BA; William & Mary 1993 JD

Secretary **Sharon Board** .... (540) 387-6082
E-mail: sboard@courts.state.va.us

Court of Appeals of Virginia

109 North Eighth Street, Richmond, VA 23219-2321
Tel: (804) 371-8428
Internet: www.courts.state.va.us/coa/coa.htm

Number of Judgeships: 11

The Court of Appeals, established in 1985, consists of a chief judge and ten judges who are elected by majority vote of the Virginia General Assembly for eight-year terms. If a vacancy occurs while the General Assembly is not in session, the Governor may appoint a successor to serve until thirty days after the commencement of the next session of the General Assembly. The chief judge is elected by a majority vote of the judges of the Court to serve a term of four years. The Court of Appeals has authority to hear appeals as a matter of right from: (a) any final judgment, order, or decree of a circuit court involving affirmance or annulment of a marriage, divorce, custody, spousal or child support, or control or disposition of a child, as well as other domestic relations cases; (b) any final decision of the Workers' Compensation Commission; (c) any final decision of a circuit court on appeal from a decision of an administrative agency; and (d) any interlocutory order granting, dissolving, or denying an injunction or adjudicating the principles of a cause in any cases listed above. The Court also has authority to consider petitions for appeal from final orders of conviction in criminal and traffic matters except where a death penalty is imposed, final decisions of a circuit court on an application for a concealed weapons permit, and certain preliminary rulings in felony cases when requested by the Commonwealth.

The Court of Appeals usually sits in Alexandria, Chesapeake, Richmond and Salem.

Court Staff

Clerk of Court **Cynthia L. McCoy** .... (804) 371-8428
E-mail: cmccoy@courts.state.va.us
Education: Messiah 1979 BA

Chief Staff Attorney **John T. Tucker III** .... (804) 786-6739
E-mail: jtucker@courts.state.va.us
Education: Richmond 1985 JD

Court Reporter **Ronald J. "Ron" Bacigal** .... (804) 371-8428
TC Williams School, University of Richmond, Richmond, VA 23173
E-mail: rbacigal@courts.state.va.us
Education: Concord Col BS; Washington and Lee 1967 LLB

Court Reporter **Peter N. Swisher** .... (804) 371-8428
E-mail: pswisher@courts.state.va.us
Education: Amherst 1966 BA; Stanford 1967 MA; Hastings 1973 JD

Chambers of Chief Judge Glen Huff

109 North Eighth Street, Richmond, VA 23219-2321
Tel: (804) 371-8428
E-mail: ghuff@courts.state.va.us

Glen Huff
Chief Judge

Education: Maine 1973 BA; Pierce Law 1976 JD
Began Service: August 1, 2011

Chambers of Judge Robert J. Humphreys

477 Viking Drive, Suite 300, Virginia Beach, VA 23452
Tel: (757) 431-3468 Fax: (757) 431-3467
E-mail: RHumphreys@courts.state.va.us

Robert J. Humphreys
Judge

Date of Birth: 1950
Education: Washington and Lee 1972 BA; Widener 1976 JD
Began Service: April 2000
Term Expires: April 2016

Government: Assistant Attorney General, Department of Justice, State of Delaware (1976-1978); Assistant Commonwealth's Attorney (1979-1982); Chief Deputy Commonwealth's Attorney (1982-1987); Commonwealth Attorney (1990-2000)

Legal Practice: McCardell and Inman, P.C. (1988-1989)

Current Memberships: The Virginia Bar Association

Staff

Law Clerk **Tara Berger** .... (757) 431-3468
Term Expires: September 2016

Law Clerk **Laura Cahill** .... (757) 431-3468
Began Service: August 2014
Term Expires: August 2016
E-mail: lcahill@courts.state.va.us

Paralegal **Paula Drew** .... (757) 431-3468
E-mail: pdrew@courts.state.va.us

Chambers of Judge William G. Petty

109 North Eighth Street, Richmond, VA 23219-2321
Tel: (804) 371-8428
E-mail: wpetty@courts.state.va.us

William G. Petty
Judge

Began Service: 2006

Chambers of Judge Randolph A. Beales

109 North Eighth Street, Richmond, VA 23219-2321
Tel: (804) 371-8428
E-mail: rbeales@courts.state.va.us

Randolph A. Beales
Judge

Education: William & Mary 1982 BA; Virginia 1986 JD
Began Service: 2006

Legal Practice: Chair, Client Development Committee, Christian & Barton, LLP; Chairman, Legislative Affairs Department, Christian & Barton, LLP

Chambers of Judge Rossie D. Alston, Jr.

109 North Eighth Street, Richmond, VA 23219
Tel: (804) 371-8428
E-mail: ralston@courts.state.va.us

Rossie D. Alston, Jr.
Judge

Education: Averett U 1979 BA; North Carolina Central 1982 JD
Began Service: 2009
Term Expires: 2017

Staff

Career Law Clerk **Jacob Shorter** .... (804) 371-8428
E-mail: jshorter@courts.state.va.us

Career Law Clerk **Caitlin Vogus** .... (804) 371-8428
E-mail: cvogus@courts.state.va.us

(continued on next page)

STATE COURTS—VIRGINIA

Chambers of Judge Rossie D. Alston, Jr. *continued*

Secretary **Meggie Holson** .... (804) 371-8428
E-mail: mholson@courts.state.va.us

Chambers of Judge Stephen R. McCullough

109 North Eighth Street, Richmond, VA 23219-2321
Tel: (804) 371-8428
E-mail: smccullough@courts.state.va.us

Stephen R. McCullough
Judge

Began Service: August 1, 2011

Chambers of Judge Teresa M. Chafin

109 North Eighth Street, Richmond, VA 23219-2321
Tel: (804) 371-8428
E-mail: tchafin@courts.state.va.us

Teresa M. Chafin
Judge

Began Service: May 2012

Staff

Law Clerk **Sarah E. Lohman** .... (804) 371-8428
E-mail: slohman@courts.state.va.us
Law Clerk **Erica Parish** .... (804) 371-8428
E-mail: eparish@courts.state.va.us
Education: Appalachian Law 2007 JD
Law Clerk **D. Nathaniel Castle II** .... (804) 371-8428

Chambers of Judge Marla Graff Decker

109 North Eighth Street, Richmond, VA 23219-2321
Tel: (804) 371-8428
E-mail: mdecker@courts.state.va.us

Marla Graff Decker
Judge

Chambers of Judge Richard Y. AtLee Jr.

109 North Eighth Street, Richmond, VA 23219-2321
Tel: (804) 371-8428

Richard Y. Atlee, Jr.
Judge

Chambers of Judge Mary Grace O'Brien

109 North Eighth Street, Richmond, VA 23219-2321
Tel: (804) 371-8428

Mary Grace O'Brien
Judge

Chambers of Judge Wesley G. Russell Jr.

109 North Eighth Street, Richmond, VA 23219-2321
Tel: (804) 371-8428

Wesley G. Russell, Jr.
Judge

Chambers of Senior Judge Rosemarie Annunziata

109 North 8th Street, Richmond, VA 23219
Tel: (804) 371-8428
E-mail: rannunziata@courts.state.va.us

Rosemarie Annunziata
Senior Judge

Date of Birth: 1940
Education: Elmira 1962 BA; Yale 1967 MA; Washington College of Law 1978 JD
Began Service: June 1, 1995

Academic: Teacher (1962-1963); Teacher (1964-1965); Adjunct Professor of Law, George Mason University (1988-1990)

Corporate: Reporter, Alabama Advertiser-Journal (1965-1967)

Government: Hearing Officer, State of Virginia (1979-1986); Hearing Officer, Fairfax County Civil Service Commission, County of Fairfax, Virginia (1986-1989)

Judicial: Judge, Virginia Circuit Court, 19th Judicial Circuit, Fairfax County (1989-1995)

Legal Practice: Sole Practitioner (1978-1981); Associate, Hall, Surovell, Jackson & Colten, P.C. (1981-1984); Partner, Cremins, Snead & Annunziata (1984-1986); Of Counsel, Dickstein, Shapiro & Morin (1986-1989)

Current Memberships: American Bar Association; International Association of Women Judges; National Association of Women Judges; The Virginia Bar Association; Virginia Trial Lawyers Association

Chambers of Senior Judge Rudolph Bumgardner III

109 North Eighth Street, 3rd Floor, Richmond, VA 23219-2321
Tel: (804) 371-8428
E-mail: rbumgardner@courts.state.va.us

Rudolph Bumgardner III
Senior Judge

Date of Birth: 1941
Education: Davidson 1963 AB; Washington and Lee 1966 JD
Began Service: 2005

Judicial: Judge, Court of Appeals of Virginia (1997-2005)

Chambers of Senior Judge Jean Harrison Clements

109 North Eighth Street, Richmond, VA 23219
Tel: (703) 737-7114 Fax: (703) 737-7116
E-mail: jclements@courts.state.va.us

Jean Harrison Clements
Senior Judge

Date of Birth: 1938
Began Service: 2009

Current Memberships: Arlington County Bar Association; Loudon County Bar Association; Virginia State Bar; Virginia Trial Lawyers Association

Chambers of Senior Judge James W. Haley Jr.

109 North Eighth Street, Richmond, VA 23219-2321
Tel: (804) 371-8428
E-mail: jhaley@courts.state.va.us

James W. Haley, Jr.
Senior Judge

STATE COURTS—VIRGINIA

Washington

Washington State Administrative Office of the Courts

1112 Quince Street, SE, Olympia, WA 98501
P.O. Box 41170, Olympia, WA 98504-1170
Tel: (360) 753-3365 Fax: (360) 586-8869
Internet: www.courts.wa.gov

Staff

Administrator **Callie T. Dietz** . . . . (360) 357-2121
E-mail: callie.dietz@courts.wa.gov Fax: (360) 357-2127
Associate Director, Human Resources **Jane Van Camp** . . . (360) 705-5289
E-mail: jane.vancamp@courts.wa.gov
Director, Judicial Services **Dirk A. Marler** . . . . (360) 705-5211
E-mail: dirk.marler@courts.wa.gov Fax: (360) 586-8869
Director, Management Services **Ramsey Radwan** . . . . (360) 357-2406
E-mail: ramsey.radwan@courts.wa.gov Fax: (360) 586-8869
Chief Information Officer **Veronica "Vonnie" Diseth** . . . . (360) 705-5236
E-mail: vonnie.diseth@courts.wa.gov
Public Information Officer **Wendy Ferrell** . . . . (360) 705-5331
E-mail: wendy.ferrell@courts.wa.gov Fax: (360) 586-8869
Executive Assistant **Beth Flynn** . . . . (360) 357-2121
E-mail: beth.flynn@courts.wa.gov Fax: (360) 357-2127
Manager, Legal Services **Shannon Hinchclisse** . . . . (360) 357-2124
Business Manager **Pam Kelly** . . . . (360) 705-5318

Washington Supreme Court

415 12th Avenue SW, Olympia, WA 98501-2314
P.O. Box 40929, Olympia, WA 98504-0929
Tel: (360) 357-2077
E-mail: supreme@courts.wa.gov
Internet: www.courts.wa.gov/court/supreme

Number of Judgeships: 9

The Supreme Court consists of a chief justice and eight justices who are elected in statewide nonpartisan elections to six-year terms. Vacancies are filled by the Governor and newly-appointed justices run for election on nonpartisan ballots in the next general election to complete the unexpired term. The position of chief justice is selected from the Court's own membership to serve a four-year term. Retirement is mandatory at age seventy-five; however, retired judges may be recalled to serve temporary assignments. The Supreme Court has original jurisdiction over petitions against state officers and can review decisions of lower courts if the money or value of property involved exceeds $200. (The $200 limitation is not in effect if the case involves a question of the legality of a tax, duty, assessment, toll, or municipal fine, or the validity of a statute.) Direct review by the Court of a trial court decision is permitted if the action involves a state officer, a trial court rules a statute or ordinance unconstitutional, conflicting statutes or rules of law are involved, or the issue is of broad public interest and requires prompt and ultimate determination. All cases in which the death penalty has been imposed are reviewed directly to the Court. The Court has discretionary review of decisions of the Washington Court of Appeals.

The Supreme Court sits in Olympia.

Court Staff

Clerk **Ronald R. Carpenter** . . . . (360) 357-2077
E-mail: ronald.carpenter@courts.wa.gov
Education: Idaho 1970 JD
Deputy Clerk **Susan L. Carlson** . . . . (360) 357-2077
E-mail: susan.carlson@courts.wa.gov
Commissioner **Narda Pierce** . . . . (360) 357-2058
E-mail: narda.pierce@courts.wa.gov
Deputy Commissioner **Walter M. Burton** . . . . (360) 357-2064
E-mail: walter.burton@courts.wa.gov
Education: UC Davis 1982 JD
Senior Staff Attorney **Michael E. Johnston** . . . . (360) 357-2062
E-mail: michael.johnston@courts.wa.gov
Education: Gonzaga 1998 JD

Washington Supreme Court *continued*

Reporter of Decisions **Rick Neidhart** . . . . (360) 357-2087
Bailiff **Tim Schiewe** . . . . (360) 357-2074
E-mail: tim.schiewe@courts.wa.gov

Chambers of Chief Justice Barbara A. Madsen

415 12th Avenue SW, Olympia, WA 98501-2314
P.O. Box 40929, Olympia, WA 98504-0929
Tel: (360) 357-2037 Fax: (360) 357-2085
E-mail: J_B.Madsen@courts.wa.gov

Barbara A. Madsen
Chief Justice

Date of Birth: 1952
Education: U Washington 1974 BA; Gonzaga 1977 JD
Began Service: January 11, 1993
Term Expires: December 31, 2016

Government: Criminal Defense Attorney, Office of the Public Defender, County of King, Washington; Staff Attorney, Office of the City Attorney/Law Department, City of Seattle, Washington (1982-1984); Special Prosecutor, Office of the City Attorney/Law Department, City of Seattle, Washington (1984); Court Commissioner, Municipal Court of Seattle, City of Seattle, Washington (1985-1988)

Judicial: Judge, Municipal Court of Seattle, City of Seattle, Washington (1988-1993)

Current Memberships: American Judges Association; National Association of Women Judges

Staff

Law Clerk **Randy Perry** . . . . (360) 357-2039
Began Service: August 2014
Term Expires: August 2016
E-mail: randy.perry@courts.wa.gov
Law Clerk **Nicholas "Nick" Carlson** . . . . (360) 357-2040
E-mail: nick.carlson@courts.wa.gov

Chambers of Associate Chief Justice Charles W. Johnson

415 12th Avenue SW, Olympia, WA 98501-2314
P.O. Box 40929, Olympia, WA 98504-0929
Tel: (360) 357-2020 Fax: (360) 357-2103
E-mail: J_C.Johnson@courts.wa.gov

Charles W. Johnson
Associate Chief Justice

Date of Birth: 1951
Education: U Washington 1974 BA; U Puget Sound 1976 JD
Began Service: January 14, 1991
Next Election: November 4, 2020
Election Type: General Election
Term Expires: January 2021

Judicial: Judge Pro Tem, Pierce County District Court (1990); Judge Pro Tem, Mason County District Court; Judge Pro Tem, Washington Court of Appeals, Division II

Legal Practice: Attorney, Private Practice (1977-1990)

Current Memberships: American Bar Association; Tacoma-Pierce County Bar Association; Washington State Bar Association

Staff

Law Clerk **Robert Wilke** . . . . (360) 357-2023
Began Service: August 2015
Term Expires: August 2016
E-mail: robert_wilke@courts.wa.gov
Law Clerk **Tyler Farmer** . . . . (360) 357-2023
Began Service: August 2015
Term Expires: August 2016
E-mail: tyler.farmer@courts.wa.gov

(continued on next page)

STATE COURTS – WASHINGTON

Chambers of Associate Chief Justice Charles W. Johnson *continued*

Administrative Assistant **Cynthia S. Jennings** .... (360) 357-2021
E-mail: cindy.jennings@courts.wa.gov
Education: St Martin's Col 1999 BA

Chambers of Justice Susan Owens

415 12th Avenue SW, Olympia, WA 98501-2314
P.O. Box 40929, Olympia, WA 98504-0929
Tel: (360) 357-2041 Fax: (360) 357-2104
E-mail: J_S.Owens@courts.wa.gov

Susan Owens
Justice

Date of Birth: 1949
Education: Duke 1971 BA; North Carolina 1975 JD
Began Service: January 8, 2001
Next Election: November 2018
Term Expires: December 31, 2018

Judicial: District Court Judge, Clallam County, Washington (1981-2000); Chief Judge, Quileute Tribe (1987-1992); Chief Judge, Lower Elwha S'Klallam Tribe (1994-2001)

Legal Practice: Olympic Legal Services (1976-1978); Private Practice (1978-2000)

Current Memberships: Oregon State Bar; Washington State Bar Association

Staff
Law Clerk **Erin M. Burris** .... (360) 357-2043
Began Service: September 2015
Term Expires: August 2016
E-mail: erin.burris@courts.wa.gov
Law Clerk **Erin L. Lennon** .... (360) 357-2043
E-mail: erin.lennon@courts.wa.gov
Education; U Washington 2002 BA, 2008 JD
Administrative Assistant **Brenda J. Moore** .... (360) 357-2042
E-mail: brenda.moore@courts.wa.gov

Chambers of Justice Mary E. Fairhurst

415 12th Avenue SW, Olympia, WA 98501-2314
P.O. Box 40929, Olympia, WA 98504-0929
Tel: (360) 357-2053 Fax: (360) 357-2103
E-mail: J_M.Fairhurst@courts.wa.gov

Mary E. Fairhurst
Justice

Education: Gonzaga 1979 BA, 1984 JD
Began Service: December 2002
Next Election: November 4, 2020
Election Type: General Election
Term Expires: December 31, 2020

Clerkships: Law Clerk, Chief Justice The Honorable William H. Williams, Washington Supreme Court; Law Clerk, Justice The Honorable William C. Goodloe, Washington Supreme Court

Government: Division Chief, Revenue, Bankruptcy and Collections Division, Office of the Attorney General, State of Washington

Current Memberships: National Association of Women Judges; Washington State Bar Association; Washington Women Lawyers

Staff
Law Clerk **Jessica Erickson** .... (360) 357-2056
Began Service: August 2015
Term Expires: August 2016
Law Clerk **Keaton Hille** .... (360) 357-2055
Began Service: August 2015
Term Expires: August 2016
Reporter of Decisions **Rick Neidhardt** .... (360) 357-2090
E-mail: rick.neidhardt@courts.wa.gov

Chambers of Justice Mary E. Fairhurst *continued*

Administrative Assistant **Cynthia Phillips** .... (360) 357-2054
E-mail: cindy.phillips@courts.wa.gov

Chambers of Justice Debra Stephens

415 12th Avenue SW, Olympia, WA 98501-2314
Tel: (360) 357-2050
E-mail: debra.stephens@courts.wa.gov

Debra L. Stephens
Justice

Began Service: December 31, 2007
Appointed By: Governor Christine O. Gregoire
Next Election: November 4, 2020
Election Type: General Election
Term Expires: December 2020

Judicial: Judge, Washington Court of Appeals, Division III (2007)

Staff
Career Law Clerk **(Vacant)** .... (360) 357-2051
Administrative Assistant **Judy Vandervort** .... (360) 357-2050
E-mail: judy.vandervort@courts.wa.gov

Chambers of Justice Charles K. Wiggins

415 12th Avenue SW, Olympia, WA 98501-2314
Tel: (360) 357-2025

Charles K. Wiggins
Justice

Education: Princeton 1969 BA; Hawaii 1972 MBA; Duke 1976 JD
Began Service: January 7, 2011

Staff
Law Clerk **Jeremy Ciarabellini** .... (360) 357-2025
Began Service: August 2015
Term Expires: September 2016
Law Clerk **Lance Pelletier** .... (360) 357-2025
Began Service: August 2014
Term Expires: September 2016

Chambers of Justice Steven González

415 12th Avenue SW, Olympia, WA 98501-2314
Tel: (360) 357-2030

Steven C. González
Justice

Education: Pitzer BA; Boalt Hall 1991 JD
Began Service: January 9, 2012

Chambers of Justice Sheryl McCloud

415 12th Avenue SW, Olympia, WA 98501-2314
Tel: (360) 357-2045

Sheryl Gordon McCloud
Justice

Began Service: 2013

Chambers of Justice Mary Yu
415 12th Avenue SW, Olympia, WA 98501-2314
Tel: (360) 357-2077

Mary Yu
Justice

Began Service: May 20, 2014
Appointed By: Governor Jay Inslee

Washington Court of Appeals
Tel: (206) 753-3365 (Electronic Access Registration)
Internet: www.courts.wa.gov

Each Court of Appeals has a chief judge, and acting chief judge and two to seven judges who are elected on a nonpartisan ballot by the voters in their division for six-year terms. Vacancies are filled by the Governor, and newly-appointed judges run on the ballot in the next general election to complete the unexpired term. The judges in each division elect a chief judge and an acting chief judge for two-year terms. Retirement is mandatory at age seventy-five; however, retired judges may be recalled to serve temporary assignments. The Court of Appeals has exclusive appellate jurisdiction, except in those cases which are appealed directly to the Washington Supreme Court, and those over which the Supreme Court has asserted jurisdiction.

Washington Court of Appeals, Division I
One Union Square, 600 University Street, Seattle, WA 98101-4170
Tel: (206) 464-7750 Fax: (206) 389-2613

Number of Judgeships: 10

Areas Covered: Counties of Island, King, San Juan, Skagit, Snohomish and Whatcom

Court Staff
Court Administrator/Clerk of Court
Richard D. Johnson .... (206) 464-5871
E-mail: richard.johnson@courts.wa.gov
Education: U Washington 1985 BA;
USC 1987 MPA, 1987
Commissioner **Mary S. Neel** .... (206) 464-7649
E-mail: mary.neel@courts.wa.gov
Education: Lewis & Clark 1972 BA;
U Washington 1973 MEd; U Puget Sound 1982 JD
Commissioner **Masako Kanazawa** .... (206) 464-7649
Staff Attorney **Jennifer Koh** .... (206) 464-7649
Staff Attorney **Loren Rayment** .... (206) 464-7649
Senior Staff Attorney **Frank Lehman** .... (206) 464-7649
E-mail: frank.lehman@courts.wa.gov
Education: Yale 1972 BA, 1973 MA, 1976 MPhil;
U Puget Sound 1985 JD
Senior Staff Attorney **Mark Swanson** .... (206) 464-7749
E-mail: mark.swanson@courts.wa.gov
Education: Colgate 1980 BA;
U Puget Sound 1984 JD

Chambers of Chief Judge Michael S. Spearman
600 University Street, Seattle, WA 98101-4170
Tel: (206) 464-6047

Michael S. Spearman
Chief Judge

Education: Brown U BA; NYU JD
Began Service: 2010
Appointed By: Governor Christine O. Gregoire
Next Election: November 2016

Chambers of Acting Chief Judge James Verellen
600 University Street, Seattle, WA 98101-4170
Tel: (206) 464-7750

James Verellen
Chief Judge (Acting)

Education: Washington State 1973 BA; Willamette 1976 JD
Began Service: October 2012
Appointed By: Governor Christine O. Gregoire

Chambers of Judge J. Robert Leach
600 University Street, One Union Square, Seattle, WA 98101-1176
Tel: (206) 464-7423 Fax: (206) 389-2460

J. Robert Leach
Judge

Education: U Washington 1976 JD
Began Service: March 2008
Appointed By: Governor Christine O. Gregoire
Next Election: November 4, 2020
Election Type: General Election
Term Expires: December 2020

Staff
Law Clerk **Courtney Skiles** .... (206) 464-7423
Began Service: August 2014
Term Expires: August 2016
Law Clerk **Louis Russell** .... (206) 464-7423
Began Service: August 2015
Term Expires: August 2017

Chambers of Judge Stephen Dwyer
One Union Square, 600 University Street, Seattle, WA 98101-4170
Tel: (206) 464-7658 Fax: (206) 389-2460
E-mail: stephen.dwyer@courts.wa.gov

Stephen J. Dwyer
Judge

Education: U Puget Sound 1979; U Washington 1982 JD
Began Service: 2005
Next Election: November 2016

Current Memberships: Washington Bar Association

Staff
Judicial Assistant **Maria T. Porteous** .... (206) 464-7658

Chambers of Judge Ann Schindler
One Union Square, 600 University Street, Seattle, WA 98101-4170
Tel: (206) 464-7659
E-mail: j_a.schindler@courts.wa.gov

Ann Schindler
Judge

Education: U San Francisco 1969 BA; U Washington 1977 JD
Began Service: January 1, 2002
Appointed By: Governor Gary Locke
Next Election: November 4, 2020
Election Type: General Election
Term Expires: December 31, 2020

Government: Attorney, Office of the County Prosecutor, County of King, Washington (1982-1986); Lead Attorney, Land Use and Environmental Law Area, Office of the County Executive, County of King, Washington (1986-1991)

Judicial: Trial Judge, King County Superior Court (1991-2001); Assistant Presiding Judge, King County Superior Court (2000-2001)

(continued on next page)

STATE COURTS – WASHINGTON

Chambers of Judge Ann Schindler *continued*

Legal Practice: Attorney, Culp, Dwyer, Guterson and Grader (1978-1982)

Staff
Law Clerk **Caroline Cress** .... (206) 464-7659
E-mail: caroline.cress@courts.wa.gov
Law Clerk **Kathleen Kline** .... (206) 464-7659
E-mail: kathleen.kline@courts.wa.gov
Secretary **Erin Sanders** .... (206) 464-7659
E-mail: erin.sanders@courts.wa.gov

Chambers of Judge Marlin J. Appelwick
One Union Square, 600 University Street, Seattle, WA 98101-4170
Tel: (206) 389-3926 Fax: (206) 389-2460
E-mail: j_m.appelwick@courts.wa.gov

Marlin J. Appelwick
Judge

Education: Mankato State 1976 BA, 1976 BS; U Washington 1979 JD
Began Service: July 1, 1998
Appointed By: Governor Gary Locke
Next Election: November 2018
Term Expires: January 2019

Staff
Law Clerk **Niki Morrison** .... (206) 389-3926
Began Service: August 2014
Term Expires: August 2016
E-mail: niki.morrison@courts.wa.gov
Law Clerk **Kelsey Martin** .... (206) 389-3926
Began Service: August 16, 2015
Term Expires: August 15, 2017
E-mail: kelsey.martin@courts.wa.gov
Judicial Administrative Assistant **Wendy Davis** .... (206) 389-3926
E-mail: wendy.davis@courts.wa.gov

STATE COURTS—WASHINGTON

Chambers of Judge Mary Kay Becker
One Union Square, 600 University Street, Seattle, WA 98101-4170
Tel: (206) 464-7656 Fax: (206) 389-2460
E-mail: mary.becker@courts.wa.gov

Mary Kay Becker
Judge

Education: Stanford 1966 AB; U Washington 1982 JD
Began Service: January 18, 1994
Next Election: November 2018
Term Expires: January 2019

Government: Member, Washington House of Representatives (1975-1983)

Legal Practice: Paralegal, Northwest Washington Legal Services

Staff
Judicial Assistant **Elaine Asaidali** .... (206) 464-7656
E-mail: elaine.asaidali@courts.wa.gov

Chambers of Judge Linda Lau
One Union Square, 600 University Street, Seattle, WA 98101-4170
Tel: (206) 464-7657

Linda Lau
Judge

Began Service: 2007
Next Election: November 4, 2020
Election Type: General Election
Term Expires: December 2020

Staff
Law Clerk **Jacob Dishion** .... (206) 464-7657

Chambers of Judge Linda Lau *continued*
Law Clerk **Jonathan Collins** .... (206) 464-7657
Began Service: August 2014
Term Expires: August 2016
Judicial Assistant **Saney Nguyen** .... (206) 464-7657

Chambers of Judge Ronald E. Cox
One Union Square, 600 University Street, Seattle, WA 98101-4170
Tel: (206) 464-7654 Fax: (206) 389-2613

Ronald E. Cox
Judge

Date of Birth: 1945
Education: West Point 1966 BS; U Washington 1973 JD
Began Service: 1995
Next Election: November 2018
Term Expires: January 5, 2019

Judicial: Presiding Chief Judge, Washington Court of Appeals, Division I (2007-2008)

Legal Practice: Preston, Gates & Ellis (1973-1994)

Military Service: United States Army (1966-1970)

Current Memberships: American College of Real Estate Lawyers; King County Bar Foundation, King County Bar Association; The Washington State Minority and Justice Commission

Staff
Law Clerk **Pedro Celis** .... (206) 464-7654
Began Service: August 2014
Term Expires: August 2016
E-mail: pedro.celis@courts.wa.gov
Law Clerk **Christal Harrison** .... (206) 464-7654
Began Service: August 2015
Term Expires: August 2017
E-mail: christal.harrison@courts.wa.gov
Judicial Assistant **Denise Stefansson** .... (206) 464-7654
E-mail: denise.stefansson@courts.wa.gov
Education: Hawaii 1982 BA

Chambers of Judge Michael J. Trickey
600 University Street, Seattle, WA 98101-4170
Tel: (206) 464-7655

Michael J. Trickey
Judge

Washington Court of Appeals, Division II
950 Broadway, Suite 300, Tacoma, WA 98402
Tel: (253) 593-2970 Fax: (253) 593-2806
E-mail: coa2filing@courts.wa.gov

Number of Judgeships: 7

Areas Covered: Counties of Clallam, Clark, Cowlitz, Grays Harbor, Jefferson, Kitsap, Lewis, Mason, Pacific, Pierce, Skamania, Thurston and Wahkiakum

Court Staff
Clerk of the Court **David Ponzoha** .... (253) 593-2970
E-mail: dave.ponzoha@courts.wa.gov
Education: Washington State MBA
Commissioner **Eric Schmidt** .... (253) 593-2970
E-mail: eric.schmidt@courts.wa.gov
Education: U Puget Sound 1985 JD
Commissioner **Aurora Bearse** .... (253) 593-2970
E-mail: aurora.bearse@courts.wa.gov
Senior Staff Attorney **Carole Breitenbach** .... (253) 573-2970
E-mail: carole.breitenbach@courts.wa.gov
Education: U Puget Sound 1985 JD

Washington Court of Appeals, Division II *continued*

Senior Staff Attorney **Clair J. Bruggeman** . . . . (253) 573-2970
E-mail: clair.bruggeman@courts.wa.gov
Education: U Puget Sound 1990 JD
Staff Attorney **Michelle E. Chase** . . . . (253) 573-2970
E-mail: michelle.chase@courts.wa.gov
Education: Seattle 1999 JD
Staff Attorney **Peregrin Sorter** . . . . (253) 573-2970
E-mail: peregrin.sorter@courts.wa.gov

Chambers of Chief Judge Jill M. Johanson

950 Broadway, Tacoma, WA 98402
Tel: (253) 593-2204

Jill M. Johanson
Chief Judge

Education: Washington State 1981 BA; Willamette 1985 JD
Began Service: 2011
Next Election: November 2016

Chambers of Acting Chief Judge Thomas Bjorgen

950 Broadway, Tacoma, WA 98402
Tel: (253) 593-2970

Thomas Bjorgen
Chief Judge (Acting)

Began Service: 2014

Chambers of Judge Lisa Worswick

950 Broadway, Suite 300, Tacoma, WA 98402
Tel: (253) 593-2817

Lisa Worswick
Judge

Education: U Washington JD
Began Service: May 3, 2010
Next Election: November 2016

Staff
Law Clerk **(Vacant)** . . . . (253) 593-2970
Judicial Administrative Assistant **Shirley Wilson** . . . . (253) 593-2970
E-mail: shirley.wilson@courts.wa.gov

Chambers of Judge Bradley A. Maxa

950 Broadway, Tacoma, WA 98402
Tel: (253) 593-2975

Bradley A. Maxa
Judge

Began Service: 2013

Staff
Law Clerk **Kristina Southwell** . . . . (253) 593-2975
Term Expires: August 2016
Law Clerk **Kendra Lotstein** . . . . (253) 593-2975
Term Expires: August 2016
Judicial Assistant **Chandra Zimmerman** . . . . (253) 593-2975

Chambers of Judge Linda Lee

950 Broadway, Tacoma, WA 98402
Tel: (253) 593-2970

Linda Lee
Judge

Began Service: 2014

Chambers of Judge Rich Melnick

950 Broadway, Tacoma, WA 98402
Tel: (253) 593-2974

Rich Melnick
Judge

Education: Lewis & Clark JD
Began Service: March 26, 2014
Appointed By: Governor Jay Inslee

Staff
Judicial Assistant **Sonya Porter** . . . . (253) 593-2974

Chambers of Judge Lisa L. Sutton

950 Broadway, Tacoma, WA 98402
Tel: (253) 593-2976

Lisa L. Sutton
Judge

Washington Court of Appeals, Division III

500 North Cedar Street, Spokane, WA 99201-1905
Tel: (509) 456-3082 Fax: (509) 456-4288

Number of Judgeships: 5

Areas Covered: Counties of Adams, Asotin, Benton, Chelan, Columbia, Douglas, Ferry, Franklin, Garfield, Grant, Kittitas, Klickitat, Lincoln, Okanogan, Pend Oreille, Spokane, Stevens, Walla Walla, Whitman and Yakima

Court Staff
Fax: (509) 456-4288

Clerk/Administrator **Renee S. Townsley** . . . . (509) 456-3082
E-mail: renee.townsley@courts.wa.gov
Commissioner **Monica Wasson** . . . . (509) 456-3095
E-mail: monica.wasson@courts.wa.gov Fax: (509) 625-5544
Commissioner **(Vacant)** . . . . (509) 456-3095
Fax: (509) 625-5544

Chambers of Chief Judge Laurel H. Siddoway

500 North Cedar Street, Spokane, WA 99201-1905
Tel: (509) 456-3944

Laurel H. Siddoway
Chief Judge

Education: Utah 1975, 1979 JD
Began Service: May 10, 2010
Next Election: August 2018

Staff
Administrative Assistant **Jo Anne Bergh** . . . . (509) 456-4033

Chambers of Acting Chief Judge George Fearing
500 North Cedar Street, Spokane, WA 99201-1905
Tel: (509) 456-3082

George Barr Fearing
Chief Judge (Acting)

Began Service: July 1, 2013
Appointed By: Governor Jay Inslee
Term Expires: December 2016
Political Affiliation: Republican

Chambers of Judge Kevin M. Korsmo
500 North Cedar Street, Spokane, WA 99210
Tel: (509) 456-4034 Fax: (509) 456-4288

Kevin M. Korsmo
Judge

Education: North Dakota State 1979 BS; U Washington 1982 JD
Began Service: February 13, 2008
Appointed By: Governor Christine O. Gregoire
Next Election: November 4, 2020
Election Type: General Election
Term Expires: December 2020

Staff
Judicial Administrative Assistant **Kathleen Owens** . . . . . . (509) 456-4034

Chambers of Judge Stephen M. Brown
500 North Cedar Street, Spokane, WA 99201
Tel: (509) 456-4028 Fax: (509) 456-4288
E-mail: stephen.brown@courts.wa.gov

Stephen M. Brown
Judge

Date of Birth: 1943
Education: Stetson 1973 JD
Began Service: January 13, 1997
Appointed By: Governor Gary Locke
Next Election: November 4, 2020
Election Type: General Election
Term Expires: December 2020

Government: Commissioner, Washington Supreme Court (1983-1988)

Judicial: Judge, Selah Municipal Court (1982-1983); Judge, Washington Superior Court, Yakima County (1988-1997)

Legal Practice: Velikanje, Moore & Shore (1975-1978); Sole Practice (1979-1983)

Military Service: Colonel, Infantry, United States Army (1965-1970)

Current Memberships: Washington State Bar Association; Yakima County Bar Association

Staff
Law Clerk **Hayley Dean** . . . . (509) 456-4028
Career Law Clerk **Carolyn Zorich** . . . . (509) 456-4028
E-mail: carolyn.zorich@courts.wa.gov
Education: Gonzaga 1997 JD
Judicial Assistant **Michelle Karademos** . . . . (509) 456-4028
E-mail: michelle.karademos@courts.wa.gov

Chambers of Judge Robert Lawrence-Berrey Jr.
500 North Cedar Street, Spokane, WA 99201
Tel: (509) 625-5159

Robert Lawrence-Berrey
Judge

Education: Whitman; Willamette JD
Began Service: 2014
Appointed By: Governor Jay Inslee

West Virginia

West Virginia Office of the Administrative Director of the Courts

Capitol Complex, 1900 Kanawha Boulevard East, Building 1,
Room E-100, Charleston, WV 25305
Tel: (304) 558-0145 Fax: (304) 558-1212
Internet: www.state.wv.us/wvsca

Staff

Administrative Director **Steven D. Canterbury** . . . . (304) 558-0145
E-mail: steve.canterbury@courtswv.gov
Executive Administrative Assistant **Mary Greene** . . . . . . (304) 558-0145
E-mail: mary.greene@courtswv.gov
Executive Administrative Assistant **Joan Mullins** . . . . (304) 558-0145
E-mail: joan.mullins@courtswv.gov
Deputy Director of Administration
Jennifer D. Singletary . . . . (304) 558-0145
E-mail: jennifer.singletary@courtswv.gov
Education: West Virginia State Col 1994 BA;
Marshall 2001 MA; Cincinnati 2001 JD
General Administrative Counsel **Kirk Brandfass** . . . . (304) 558-0145
Special Projects Director **Sarah Johnson** . . . . (304) 558-0145
E-mail: sarah.johnson@courtswv.gov
Court Services Division Director **Angela D. Saunders** . . . (304) 558-0145
E-mail: angelasaunders@courtswv.org
Director, Division of Childrens Services **Nikki Tennis** . . . . (304) 558-0145
E-mail: nikki.tennis@courtswv.gov
Family Services Director **Lisa Tackett** . . . . (304) 558-0145
E-mail: lisatackett@courtswv.org
Financial Management Director **Sue Troy** . . . . (304) 558-0145
E-mail: sue.troy@courtswv.gov
Human Resources Director **Christine Workman** . . . . (304) 558-0145
Judicial Education Director **Sara Thompson** . . . . (304) 558-0145
E-mail: sarathompson@courtswv.org
Probation Services Director **Michael "Mike" Lacy** . . . . . . (304) 558-0145
Administrative Services Director **P. Fletcher Adkins** . . . . . (304) 558-0145
Technology Director **Scott Harvey** . . . . (304) 558-0145
E-mail: scottharvey@courtswv.org
Network Operations Manager **Mark Smith** . . . . (304) 558-0145
E-mail: mark.smith@courtswv.gov
Invoice Auditor **Daniel Hager** . . . . (304) 558-0145
Invoice Auditor **Nikki Preece** . . . . (304) 558-0145
E-mail: nikkipreece@courtswv.org
Public Information Officer **Jennifer Bundy** . . . . (304) 558-0145
E-mail: jenniferbundy@courtswv.org
Public Information Specialist **April Harless** . . . . (304) 558-0145
E-mail: april.harless@courtswv.gov
PEIA Administrator **Linda Foster** . . . . (304) 558-0145
E-mail: lindafoster@courtswv.org
Legislative Analyst **Tina Payne** . . . . (304) 558-0145
E-mail: tina.payne@courtswv.gov
Administrative Assistant for General Counsel
Debra "Debbie" Henley . . . . (304) 558-0145
Director of Magistrate Services **Janie L. Moore** . . . . (304) 558-0145
E-mail: janie.moore@courtswv.gov

West Virginia Supreme Court of Appeals

Capitol Complex, 1900 Kanawha Boulevard East, Room E-317,
Charleston, WV 25305
Tel: (304) 558-2601 Tel: (304) 340-2324 (Supreme Court Library)
Fax: (304) 558-3815
Internet: www.courtswv.gov

Number of Judgeships: 5

The Supreme Court of Appeals consists of a chief justice and four justices who are elected in statewide, partisan elections for twelve-year terms. Vacancies are filled by the Gubernatorial appointment until the next general election. The position of chief justice alternates annually based on seniority among the justices. The Supreme Court of Appeals has appellate jurisdiction in all civil and criminal cases ruled upon by West Virginia's circuit courts. The Supreme Court has original jurisdiction in extraordinary writs (i.e. prohibition, mandamus, certiorari and habeas corpus) and in answering questions posited by federal courts. The Court has administrative authority over the circuit and magistrate courts.

The Supreme Court sits in Charleston.

Court Staff

Clerk **Rory L. Perry II** . . . . (304) 558-2601
E-mail: rory.perry@courtswv.gov
Education: Marshall 1989 BA;
West Virginia 1994 JD
Chief Counsel **Bruce A. Kayuha** . . . . (304) 558-6206
E-mail: bruce.kayuha@courtswv.gov Fax: (304) 558-6045
Education: West Virginia 1972 BA, 1973 MPA;
Washington and Lee 1978 JD
Public Information Officer **Jennifer Bundy** . . . . (304) 340-2305
E-mail: jennifer.bundy@courtswv.gov Fax: (304) 558-1212
Court Marshal **Arthur G. Angus** . . . . (304) 558-1911
E-mail: arthur.angus@courtswv.gov Fax: (304) 558-4308
Deputy Director of Administration
Jennifer D. Singletary . . . . (304) 558-0145
E-mail: jennifer_singletary@courtswv.gov

Chambers of Chief Justice Margaret L. Workman

Capitol Complex, Building 1, 1900 Kanawha Boulevard East,
Room E-306, Charleston, WV 25305
Tel: (304) 558-2606
E-mail: margaret.workman@courtswv.gov

Margaret L. Workman
Chief Justice

Education: West Virginia 1969, 1974 JD
Began Service: January 1, 2009
Next Election: November 2020
Election Type: General Election
Term Expires: December 31, 2020

Staff

Administrative Assistant **Jeanne Stevenson** . . . . (304) 558-2606
E-mail: jeanne.stevenson@courtswv.gov

STATE COURTS—WEST VIRGINIA

Chambers of Justice Robin Jean Davis

Capitol Complex, Building 1, 1900 Kanawha Boulevard East,
Room E-301, Charleston, WV 25305
Tel: (304) 558-4811 Fax: (304) 558-4308
E-mail: robin.davis@courtswv.gov

Robin Jean Davis
Justice

Date of Birth: April 6, 1956
Education: West Virginia Wesleyan 1978 BSA; West Virginia 1982 MA, 1982 JD
Began Service: December 16, 1996
Next Election: 2024
Term Expires: 2024
Political Affiliation: Democrat

Staff

Career Law Clerk **Cynthia Bowman** .... (304) 558-0389
E-mail: cynthiabowman@courtswv.org
Education: West Virginia 1994 JD
Career Law Clerk **Toni Harvey Takarsh** .... (304) 558-0520
E-mail: tonitakarsh@courtswv.org
Education: West Virginia 1995 JD
Per Curiam Law Clerk **(Vacant)** .... (304) 558-4811
Per Curiam Law Clerk **Louis J. Palmer** .... (304) 558-0374
E-mail: louispalmer@courtswv.org
Education: West Virginia 1992 JD
Administrative Assistant **Jennifer Stover** .... (304) 558-4811
E-mail: jenniferstover@courtswv.org

Chambers of Justice Brent D. Benjamin

State Capitol Complex, Room E-302, Charleston, WV 25302
Tel: (304) 558-2602 Fax: (304) 558-5491
E-mail: brent.benjamin@courtswv.gov

Brent D. Benjamin
Justice

Education: Ohio State BA, 1984 JD
Began Service: January 2005
Term Expires: December 31, 2016

Staff

Career Law Clerk **Shannon Akers** .... (304) 558-2602
E-mail: shannon.akers@courtswv.gov
Career Law Clerk **Bobby F. Lipscomb** .... (304) 558-2602
E-mail: bobby.lipscomb@courtswv.gov
Education: West Virginia 1996 JD
Career Law Clerk **Jane Charnock Smallridge** .... (304) 558-2602
Administrative Assistant **Steven Cohen** .... (304) 558-2602
E-mail: steven.cohen@courtswv.gov

Chambers of Justice Menis E. Ketchum

1900 Kanawha Boulevard East, Room E-307, Charleston, WV 25305
Tel: (304) 558-2604
E-mail: menis.ketchum@courtswv.gov

Menis E. Ketchum II
Justice

Date of Birth: 1943
Education: Ohio 1964; West Virginia 1967 JD
Began Service: December 18, 2008
Next Election: November 2020
Election Type: General Election
Term Expires: 2020
Political Affiliation: Democrat

Staff

Career Law Clerk **Peter Chambers** .... (304) 558-2604
E-mail: peter.chambers@courtswv.gov
Education: West Virginia 1993 JD

Chambers of Justice Menis E. Ketchum *continued*

Career Law Clerk **Mark Farrell** .... (304) 558-2604
E-mail: mark.farrell@courtswv.gov
Career Law Clerk **Tom McQuian** .... (304) 558-2604
Career Law Clerk **Robert Pruett** .... (304) 558-2604
E-mail: robert.pruett@courtswv.gov
Judicial Assistant **Ruth Melvine** .... (304) 558-2604

Chambers of Justice Allen Loughry

1900 Kanawha Boulevard East, Building 1, Charleston, WV 25305
Tel: (304) 558-2605
E-mail: allen.loughry@courtswv.gov

Allen H. Loughry II
Justice

Education: West Virginia BS; Capital U JD; U London LLM; American U (London) SJD, LLM
Term Expires: December 31, 2024

Government: Senior Assistant Attorney General, Office of the Attorney General, State of West Virginia (1997-2003)

Staff

Law Clerk **Trina Leone** .... (304) 558-2605
E-mail: trina.leone@courtswv.gov
Law Clerk **Cynthia Nelson** .... (304) 558-2605
E-mail: cynthia.nelson@courtswv.gov
Education: Washington and Lee 1984 JD
Administrative Assistant **Vici Shafer** .... (304) 558-4282
E-mail: vici.shafer@courtswv.gov

Wisconsin

Wisconsin Director of State Courts Office

16 East State Capitol, Madison, WI 53702
P.O. Box 1688, Madison, WI 53701-1688
Tel: (608) 266-6828 Fax: (608) 267-0980
Internet: www.wicourts.gov

Staff

Director of State Courts (Interim) **J. Denis Moran** ...... (608) 266-6828
Education: Temple 1975 JD
Deputy Director, Court Operations
Sara Ward Cassady .... (608) 266-6984
E-mail: sara.ward-cassady@wicourts.gov
Director, Judicial Education **Karla Baumgartner** .... (608) 266-7807
110 East Main Street, Suite 200, Fax: (608) 261-6650
Madison, WI 53703-3328
E-mail: karla.baumgartner@wicourts.gov
Deputy Director, Management Services
Pamela J. "Pam" Radloff .... (608) 266-8914
E-mail: pam.radloff@wicourts.gov
Education: Wisconsin (Whitewater) MPA
Legislative Liaison **Nancy Mary Rottier** .... (608) 267-9733
E-mail: nancy.rottier@wicourts.gov
Personnel Manager **Margaret Brady** .... (608) 267-1940
E-mail: margaret.brady@wicourts.gov Fax: (608) 261-8293
Education: Wisconsin (Stevens Point) BS
Chief Information Officer **Jean Bousquet** .... (608) 267-0678
E-mail: jean.bousquet@wicourts.gov Fax: (608) 261-6655
Court Information Officer
Thomas J. "Tom" Sheehan .... (608) 261-6640
E-mail: tom.sheehan@wicourts.gov Fax: (608) 261-8299
Court Information Officer **(Vacant)** .... (608) 264-6256
Fax: (608) 261-8299
Fiscal Officer **Brian Lamprech** .... (608) 266-6865
E-mail: brian.lamprech@wicourts.gov Fax: (608) 261-8293
Education: Wisconsin (La Crosse) BS
Purchasing and Facility Officer **Dave Korenic** .... (608) 267-7997
E-mail: dave.korenic@wicourts.gov Fax: (608) 261-8293
State Law Librarian **Julie Tessmer** .... (608) 261-2340
120 Martin Luther King,, Madison, WI 53707-7881 Fax: (608) 267-2319
P.O.Box 7881, Madison, WI 53707-7881
E-mail: julie.tessmer@wicourts.gov

Wisconsin Supreme Court

P.O. Box 1688, Madison, WI 53701-1688
16 East State Capitol, Madison, WI 53702
Tel: (608) 266-1880 Fax: (608) 267-0640
Internet: www.wicourts.gov

Number of Judgeships: 7

The Supreme Court consists of a chief justice and six justices who are elected at-large in nonpartisan elections for ten-year terms. Vacancies occurring between terms are filled by the Governor. The justice with the most seniority serves as chief justice. The Supreme Court exercises appellate jurisdiction over all courts and may hear original actions and proceedings. The Court may review judgments of, may remove cases from, and may accept certification by the Wisconsin Court of Appeals. The Court has general superintending control over all lower courts and may hear, determine and issue any writ relevant to its jurisdiction.

The Supreme Court sits in Madison.

Court Staff

Clerk of Supreme Court **Diane Fremgen** .... (608) 266-1880
110 E. Main St., Ste. 215, Fax: (608) 267-0640
Madison, WI 53703-3328
E-mail: diane.fremgen@wicourts.gov
Marshal **Tina Nodolf** .... (608) 266-0231
E-mail: tina.nodolf@wicourts.gov

Wisconsin Supreme Court *continued*

Director, Judicial Education **Karla Baumgartner** .... (608) 266-7807
110 East Main Street, Suite 200, Fax: (608) 261-6650
Madison, WI 53703-3328

Chambers of Chief Justice Patience Drake Roggensack

16 East State Capitol, Madison, WI 53702
Tel: (608) 266-1888 Fax: (608) 261-8275
E-mail: patience.roggensack@wicourts.gov

Patience Drake Roggensack
Chief Justice

Date of Birth: July 1940
Education: Wisconsin 1980 JD
Began Service: August 2003
Term Expires: July 31, 2023

Current Memberships: American Bar Foundation; American Bar Association; Dane County Bar Association; Wisconsin Chapter, International Women's Forum; National Association of Women Judges; State Bar of Wisconsin; Western District of Wisconsin Bar Association

Staff

Law Clerk **Cody Brookhouser** .... (608) 266-1888
Began Service: August 1, 2015
Term Expires: July 31, 2016
E-mail: cody.brookhouser@wicourts.gov
Judicial Assistant **Patti Gotrik** .... (608) 266-1888
E-mail: patti.gotrik@wicourts.gov

Chambers of Justice Shirley S. Abrahamson

16 E. State Capitol, Madison, WI 53702
P.O. Box 1688, Madison, WI 53701-1688
Tel: (608) 266-1885 Fax: (608) 267-0596

Shirley S. Abrahamson
Justice

Date of Birth: 1933
Education: NYU 1953 AB; Indiana 1956 JD; Wisconsin 1962 SJD
Began Service: September 6, 1976
Appointed By: Governor Patrick J. Lucey
Next Election: April 2019
Term Expires: July 31, 2019

Current Memberships: American Bar Foundation; American Philosophical Society; American Bar Association; The American Law Institute; Conference of Chief Justices; Dane County Bar Association; The Seventh Circuit Bar Association, Federal Bar Association; Indiana State Bar Association; National Association of Women Judges; State Bar of Wisconsin

Staff

Law Clerk **Matthew Woleske** .... (608) 266-1885
Began Service: August 1, 2015
Term Expires: August 1, 2016
E-mail: matthew.woleske@wicourts.gov
Judicial Assistant **Ingrid Anna Nelson** .... (608) 266-1885
E-mail: ingrid.nelson@wicourts.gov
Education: Wisconsin 1995 JD

Chambers of Justice Ann Walsh Bradley
16 East State Capitol, Madison, WI 53702
P.O. Box 1688, Madison, WI 53701-1688
Tel: (608) 266-1886 Fax: (608) 261-8273
E-mail: ann.bradley@wicourts.gov

Ann Walsh Bradley
Justice

Date of Birth: 1950
Education: Wisconsin 1976 JD
Began Service: August 1, 1995
Term Expires: July 31, 2025

Judicial: Judge, Wisconsin Circuit Court (1985-1995)

Legal Practice: Private Practice (1976-1985)

Staff
Law Clerk **Katherine Polich** .... (608) 266-1886
Began Service: August 2015
Term Expires: July 31, 2016
E-mail: jen.clark@wicourts.gov
Administrative Assistant **Laura Graham** .... (608) 266-1886
E-mail: laura.graham@wicourts.gov Fax: (608) 261-8273

Chambers of Justice David T. Prosser
16 East State Capitol, Madison, WI 53702
P.O. Box 1688, Madison, WI 53701-1688
Tel: (608) 266-1882 Fax: (608) 261-8299
E-mail: david.prosser@wicourts.gov

David T. Prosser
Justice

Date of Birth: 1942
Education: DePauw 1965 BA; Wisconsin 1968 JD
Began Service: September 9, 1998
Appointed By: Governor Tommy G. Thompson
Term Expires: July 31, 2021

Government: Attorney/Advisor, Office of Criminal Justice, United States Attorney's Office, United States Department of Justice; Administrative Assistant (R-WI), Office of Representative Harold V. Froehlich, United States House of Representatives; District Attorney, County of Outagamie, Wisconsin; Representative, Wisconsin State Assembly (1979-1996); Member, Tax Appeals Commission, State of Wisconsin (1996-1998)

Current Memberships: Dane County Bar Association; Outagamie County Bar Association; State Bar of Wisconsin

Staff
Law Clerk **Joel M. Graczyk** .... (608) 266-1882
Judicial Assistant **Denise L. Croake** .... (608) 266-1882
E-mail: denise.croake@wicourts.gov

Chambers of Justice Annette Kingsland Ziegler
16 East State Capitol, Madison, WI 53701
P.O. Box 1688, Madison, WI 53701-1688
Tel: (608) 266-1881 Fax: (608) 267-6828
E-mail: annette.ziegler@wicourts.gov

Annette Kingsland Ziegler
Justice

Education: Hope 1986 BS; Marquette 1989 JD
Began Service: August 1, 2007
Term Expires: July 31, 2017

Government: Pro Bono Special Assistant District Attorney, County of Milwaukee, Wisconsin (1992-1996); United States Attorney for the Eastern District of Wisconsin, Executive Office for United States Attorneys, United States Department of Justice

Legal Practice: Attorney, Private Practice

Chambers of Justice Annette Kingsland Ziegler *continued*

Current Memberships: The American Law Institute

Staff
Law Clerk **Anthony Lococo** .... (608) 266-1881
Term Expires: July 31, 2016
Judicial Assistant **Susan Gray** .... (608) 266-1881
E-mail: susan.gray@wicourts.gov

Chambers of Justice Michael J. Gableman
16 East State Capitol, Madison, WI 53701
Tel: (608) 266-1884

Michael J. Gableman
Justice

Education: Ripon 1988; Hamline 1993 JD
Began Service: 2008
Appointed By: Governor Jim Doyle
Term Expires: July 31, 2018

Government: Assistant Corporation Counsel, Forest County, Wisconsin; Assistant District Attorney, County of Marathon, Wisconsin; Assistant District Attorney, County of Langlade, Wisconsin; District Attorney, County of Ashland, Wisconsin

Judicial: Administrative Law Judge, Department of Workforce Development, State of Wisconsin; Circuit Court Judge, Burnett County Circuit Court, County of Burnett, Wisconsin (2002-2008)

Staff
Law Clerk **Lisa Fishering** .... (608) 266-1884
Began Service: August 2015
Term Expires: July 31, 2016
Law Clerk **Jennifer McNamee** .... (608) 266-1884
Began Service: August 2015
Term Expires: July 31, 2016

Chambers of Justice Rebecca Bradley
16 East State Capitol, Madison, WI 53701

Rebecca Bradley
Justice

Note: On October 9, 2015, Governor Scott Walker appointed Rebecca Bradley to the Nebraska Supreme Court.

Wisconsin Court of Appeals
Ten East Doty Street, Suite 700, Madison, WI 53703
P.O. Box 1688, Madison, WI 53701-1688
Tel: (608) 266-1880 Fax: (608) 267-0640
Internet: www.wicourts.gov

Number of Judgeships: 16

The Court of Appeal is comprised of four districts and consists of a chief judge and fifteen judges who are elected for six-year terms. The Chief Judge is appointed by the Wisconsin Supreme Court to serve as the administrative head of the court for a three-year term. Presiding judges are appointed in each district by the Chief Judge to serve a two-year term. The Governor may appoint judges to the Court to temporarily fill vacancies that occur before a term has expired. The Court of Appeal has appellate jurisdiction over all final judgments and orders from Wisconsin circuit courts and has original jurisdiction to issue prerogative writs. The Court's decisions may be reviewed by the Wisconsin Supreme Court at its discretion, but there is no automatic appeal process. The Court exercises supervisory control over the lower courts.

The Court of Appeals primarily sits in Madison, Milwaukee, Waukesha and Wausau.

Wisconsin Court of Appeals *continued*

Court Staff

Clerk of Court of Appeals **Diane Fremgen** . . . . (608) 266-1880
110 E. Main St., Ste. 215, Madison, WI 53703-3328 Fax: (608) 267-0640
E-mail: diane.fremgen@wicourts.gov

Chief Staff Attorney **Jennifer Dean Andrews** . . . . (608) 266-9323
E-mail: jennifer.andrews@wicourts.gov Fax: (608) 267-0432

Director, Judicial Education **(Vacant)** . . . . (608) 266-7807
110 East Main Street, Suite 200, Madison, WI 53703-3328 Fax: (608) 261-6650

Wisconsin Court of Appeals, District I

330 East Kilbourn Avenue, Suite 1020, Milwaukee, WI 53202-3161
Tel: (414) 227-4680 Fax: (414) 227-4051
Internet: www.wicourts.gov/appeals

Number of Judgeships: 4

Areas Covered: County of Milwaukee

Court Staff

Staff Attorney **Hillary M. Cothroll** . . . . (414) 227-4971
E-mail: hillary.cothroll@wicourts.gov Fax: (414) 227-4051
Education: Marquette JD

Staff Attorney **Julie Derwinski** . . . . (608) 267-9347
Ten E. Doty St., Ste. 700, Madison, WI 53703-3397 Fax: (608) 261-6644
E-mail: julie.derwinski@wicourts.gov

Staff Attorney **Christina Plum** . . . . (414) 227-4971
E-mail: christina.plum@wicourts.gov Fax: (414) 227-4051
Education: Marquette 1992 BA; Wisconsin 1995 JD

Staff Attorney **Mia Sefarbi** . . . . (608) 261-2343
Ten E. Doty St., Ste. 700, Madison, WI 53703-3397 Fax: (608) 261-6644
E-mail: mia.sefarbi@wicourts.gov

Staff Attorney **Emily Waranka** . . . . (608) 267-9347
Ten E. Doty St., Ste. 700, Madison, WI 53703-3397 Fax: (608) 261-6644
E-mail: emily.waranka@wicourts.gov
Education: Wisconsin 2002 JD

Secretary **Barbara Schlak** . . . . (608) 266-9320
E-mail: barbara.schlak@wicourts.gov Fax: (608) 261-8298

Chambers of Presiding Judge Patricia S. Curley

330 East Kilbourn Avenue, Suite 1020, Milwaukee, WI 53202-3161
Tel: (414) 227-4682 Fax: (414) 227-4051
E-mail: patricia.curley@wicourts.gov

Patricia S. Curley
Presiding Judge

Date of Birth: 1946
Education: Marquette 1973 JD
Began Service: August 1, 1996
Term Expires: July 31, 2020

Government: Assistant District Attorney, Office of the District Attorney, Office of the Board of Supervisors, County of Milwaukee, Wisconsin (1973-1978)

Judicial: Judge, Wisconsin Circuit Court, Milwaukee County

Staff

Career Law Clerk **Jennifer Marsch** . . . . (414) 227-4680
E-mail: jennifer.marsch@wicourts.gov
Education: Wisconsin 2008 JD

Judicial Assistant **Diana L. Mantz** . . . . (414) 227-4680
E-mail: diana.mantz@wicourts.gov

Chambers of Judge Joan F. Kessler

330 East Kilbourn Avenue, Suite 1020, Milwaukee, WI 53202-3161
Tel: (414) 227-4684 Fax: (414) 227-4051
E-mail: joan.kessler@wicourts.gov

Joan F. Kessler
Judge

Education: Kansas 1966 BA; Marquette 1968 JD
Began Service: August 2, 2004
Term Expires: July 31, 2016

Clerkships: Law Clerk John W. Reynolds, United States District Court for the Eastern District of Wisconsin (1968-1969)

Government: U.S. Attorney for the Eastern District of Wisconsin, United States Department of Justice (1978-1981)

Legal Practice: Associate, Warshafsky, Rotler & Tarnoff; Associate, Cook & Franke; Associate then Partner, Foley & Lardner, LLP (1981-2004)

Current Memberships: American Academy of Matrimonial Lawyers; American Bar Association; The American Law Institute; Association for Women Lawyers (WI); Milwaukee Bar Association; State Bar of Wisconsin

Staff

Law Clerk **Soniya Yunus** . . . . (414) 227-4680
E-mail: soniya.yunus@wicourts.gov

Judicial Assistant **Madree K. Williams** . . . . (414) 227-4680
E-mail: madree.williams@wicourts.gov

Chambers of Judge Kitty K. Brennan

330 East Kilbourn Avenue, Milwaukee, WI 53202
Tel: (414) 227-5160
E-mail: kitty.brennan@wicourts.gov

Kitty Brennan
Judge

Education: Wisconsin JD
Began Service: September 8, 2008
Appointed By: Governor Jim Doyle

Government: Assistant District Attorney, Office of the District Attorney, County of Milwaukee, Wisconsin

Judicial: Judge, Milwaukee County Circuit Courts, County of Milwaukee, Wisconsin (1994-2008)

Profession: Private Practice

Staff

Career Law Clerk **Malinda J. Kyle-Eskra** . . . . (414) 227-4680
E-mail: malinda.kyle.eskra@wicourts.gov

Judicial Assistant **Rossetta Hall** . . . . (414) 227-4680
E-mail: rossetta.hall@wicourts.gov

Chambers of Judge William W. Brash III

330 East Kilbourn Avenue, Milwaukee, WI 53202-3161
Tel: (414) 227-4680

William W. Brash III
Judge

Wisconsin Court of Appeals, District II

2727 North Grandview Boulevard, Suite 300, Waukesha, WI 53188-1672
Tel: (262) 521-5230 Fax: (262) 521-5419
Internet: www.wicourts.gov/appeals

Number of Judgeships: 4

Areas Covered: Counties of Calumet, Fond du Lac, Green Lake, Kenosha, Manitowoc, Ozaukee, Racine, Sheboygan, Walworth, Washington, Waukesha and Winnebago

(continued on next page)

Wisconsin Court of Appeals, District II *continued*

Court Staff

Chief Staff Attorney **Jennifer Dean Andrews** .... (608) 261-8266
Ten E. Doty St., Ste. 700, Madison, WI 53703-3397 Fax: (608) 261-6644
E-mail: jennifer.andrews@wicourts.gov

Staff Attorney **Lora B. Cerone** .... (608) 266-9324
Ten E. Doty St., Ste. 700, Madison, WI 53703-3397 Fax: (608) 261-6644
E-mail: lora.cerone@wicourts.gov

Staff Attorney **Erik Kinnunen** .... (608) 266-9323
Ten E. Doty St., Ste. 700, Madison, WI 53703-3397 Fax: (608) 261-6644
E-mail: erik.kinnunen@wicourts.gov
Education: Wisconsin 2003 JD

Staff Attorney **Julie A. Plotkin** .... (608) 266-9321
Ten E. Doty St., Ste. 700, Madison, WI 53703-3397 Fax: (608) 621-6644
E-mail: julie.plotkin@wicourts.gov

Staff Attorney **Clare T. Ryan** .... (262) 521-5117
Fax: (262) 521-5419
E-mail: clare.ryan@wicourts.gov
Education: Wisconsin 1986 BA, 1989 JD

Chambers of Chief Judge Lisa S. Neubauer

2727 North Grandview Boulevard, Suite 300, Waukesha, WI 53188-1672
Tel: (262) 521-5234 Fax: (262) 521-5419
E-mail: lisa.neubauer@wicourts.gov

Lisa S. Neubauer
Chief Judge

Education: Wisconsin 1979 BA; Chicago 1987 JD
Began Service: April 1, 2008
Appointed By: Governor Jim Doyle
Next Election: 2020
Election Type: General Election
Term Expires: July 31, 2020

Staff

Career Law Clerk **Patricia Sommer** .... (262) 521-5230
E-mail: patricia.sommer@wicourts.gov

Legal Secretary **Corrinne Hedtcke** .... (262) 521-5230
E-mail: corrinne.hedtcke@wicourts.gov

STATE COURTS–WISCONSIN

Chambers of Presiding Judge Paul F. Reilly

2727 North Grandview Boulevard, Suite 300, Waukesha, WI 53188-1672
Tel: (262) 521-5230
E-mail: paul.reilly@wicourts.gov

Paul F. Reilly
Presiding Judge

Education: Wisconsin 1984, 1987 JD
Began Service: 2010
Term Expires: July 31, 2016

Staff

Law Clerk **Amy Hetzner** .... (262) 521-5233
E-mail: amy.hetzner@wicourts.gov

Judicial Assistant **Linda Dejewski** .... (262) 521-5233
E-mail: linda.dejewski@wicourts.gov

Chambers of Judge Mark D. Gundrum

2727 North Grandview Boulevard, Suite 300, Waukesha, WI 53188-1672
Tel: (262) 521-5230
E-mail: mark.gundrum@wicourts.gov

Mark Gundrum
Judge

Education: Wisconsin 1992 BA, 1994 JD
Began Service: 2011
Term Expires: July 31, 2019
Political Affiliation: Republican

Chambers of Judge Mark D. Gundrum *continued*

Staff

Law Clerk **Carol Ann Chapman** .... (262) 521-5372
E-mail: carol.chapman@wicourts.gov
Education: Marquette 2011 JD

Judicial Assistant **Deborah Watkins** .... (262) 521-5372
E-mail: deborah.watkins@wicourts.gov

Chambers of Judge Brian K. Hagedorn

2727 North Grandview Boulevard, Waukesha, WI 53188-1672
Tel: (262) 521-5230

Brian K. Hagedorn
Judge

Education: Trinity International 2000 BA; Northwestern 2006 JD
Began Service: 2015
Term Expires: July 31, 2017

Wisconsin Court of Appeals, District III

2100 Stewart Avenue, Suite 310, Wausau, WI 54401-1700
Tel: (715) 848-1421 Fax: (715) 845-4523
Internet: www.wicourts.gov/appeals

Number of Judgeships: 3

Areas Covered: Counties of Ashland, Barron, Bayfield, Brown, Buffalo, Burnett, Chippewa, Door, Douglas, Dunn, Eau Claire, Florence, Forest, Iron, Kewaunee, Langlade, Lincoln, Marathon, Marinette, Menominee, Oconto, Oneida, Outagamie, Pepin, Pierce, Polk, Price, Rusk, Sawyer, Shawano, St. Croix, Taylor, Trempealeau, Vilas and Washburn

Court Staff

Staff Attorney **Fran Garvida** .... (608) 267-9348
Ten E. Doty St., Ste. 700, Madison, WI 53703-3397 Fax: (608) 261-6644
E-mail: fran.garvida@wicourts.gov

Staff Attorney **Donald L. Romundson** .... (715) 842-1501
Fax: (715) 845-4523
E-mail: donald.romundson@wicourts.gov

Staff Attorney **Glen Tritz** .... (608) 267-9349
Ten E. Doty St., Ste. 700, Madison, WI 53703-3397
E-mail: glen.tritz@wicourts.gov

Secretary **Diane Frauchiger** .... (608) 266-1276
Ten E. Doty St., Ste. 700, Madison, WI 53703-3397
E-mail: diane.frauchiger@wicourts.gov

Chambers of Deputy Chief and Presiding Judge Lisa K. Stark

2100 Stewart Avenue, Wausau, WI 54401-1700
Tel: (715) 848-1421
E-mail: lisa.stark@wicourts.gov

Lisa Kay Stark
Deputy Chief and Presiding Judge

Education: Wisconsin (Eau Claire) 1979 BA; Wisconsin 1982 JD
Began Service: 2013
Term Expires: July 31, 2019

Chambers of Judge Thomas M. Hruz

2100 Stewart Avenue, Suite 310, Wausau, WI 54401-1700
Tel: (715) 848-1421

Thomas M. Hruz
Judge

Education: Marquette 2002 JD
Began Service: 2014
Term Expires: July 31, 2016

Chambers of Judge Mark Seidl
2100 Stewart Avenue, Suite 310, Wausau, WI 54401-1700

Mark A. Seidl
Judge

Term Expires: July 31, 2021

Wisconsin Court of Appeals, District IV
Ten East Doty Street, Suite 700, Madison, WI 53703-3397
Tel: (608) 266-9250 Fax: (608) 267-0432
Internet: www.wicourts.gov/appeals

Number of Judgeships: 5

Areas Covered: Counties of Adams, Clark, Columbia, Crawford, Dane, Dodge, Grant, Green, Iowa, Jackson, Jefferson, Juneau, LaCrosse, Lafayette, Marquette, Monroe, Portage, Richland, Rock, Sauk, Vernon, Waupaca, Waushara and Wood

Court Staff
Staff Attorney **Kenneth Fall** .... (608) 267-9423
Fax: (608) 261-6644
Staff Attorney **Elizabeth J. Lawson** .... (608) 266-9322
E-mail: elizabeth.lawson@wicourts.gov Fax: (608) 261-6644
Education: Cal Western 2006 JD
Staff Attorney **Susan Parsons** .... (608) 267-3359
Fax: (608) 261-6644
Staff Attorney **Elizabeth Yockey** .... (608) 261-8288
Fax: (608) 261-6644
Secretary **Sarah Motiff** .... (608) 261-2342
E-mail: sarah.motiff@wicourts.gov Fax: (608) 261-6644

Chambers of Presiding Judge JoAnne F. Kloppenburg
Ten East Doty Street, Madison, WI 53703
Tel: (608) 267-3100 Fax: (608) 267-0432
E-mail: joanne.kloppenburg@wicourts.gov

JoAnne F. Kloppenburg
Presiding Judge

Education: Yale 1974 BA; Princeton 1976 MA; Wisconsin 1988 JD
Began Service: August 1, 2012
Term Expires: July 31, 2018

Staff
Law Clerk **Tram Huynh** .... (608) 266-9250
E-mail: tram_huynh@wicourts.gov
Judicial Assistant **Debe Martin** .... (608) 266-9250
E-mail: debe.martin@wicourts.gov

Chambers of Judge Brian W. Blanchard
Ten East Doty Street, Madison, WI 53703
Tel: (608) 266-9362 Fax: (608) 267-0432
E-mail: brian.blanchard@wicourts.gov

Brian W. Blanchard
Judge

Began Service: August 2010
Term Expires: July 31, 2016
Political Affiliation: Democrat

Staff
Law Clerk **Vanessa Wishart** .... (608) 266-9362
Began Service: 2013
E-mail: vanessa.wishart@wicourts.gov
Judicial Assistant **Rose Marie Vine** .... (608) 266-9362
E-mail: rose.vine@wicourts.gov

Chambers of Judge Paul Lundsten
Ten East Doty Street, Suite 700, Madison, WI 53703-3397
Tel: (608) 266-9361 Fax: (608) 267-0432
E-mail: paul.lundsten@wicourts.gov

Paul Lundsten
Judge

Date of Birth: August 11, 1955
Education: Wisconsin 1980 BA, 1983 JD
Began Service: November 6, 2000
Appointed By: Governor Tommy G. Thompson
Next Election: April 2019
Term Expires: July 31, 2019

Current Memberships: Dane County Bar Association

Staff
Law Clerk **Anthony J. Lucchesi** .... (608) 266-9361
Began Service: September 2013
E-mail: anthony.lucchesi@wicourts.gov
Education: Wisconsin 2000 JD
Legal Secretary **Judy Waddell** .... (608) 266-9361
E-mail: judy.waddell@wicourts.gov

Chambers of Judge Paul B. Higginbotham
Ten East Doty Street, 7th Floor, Madison, WI 53703
Tel: (608) 266-9360 Fax: (608) 267-0432
E-mail: paul.higginbotham@wicourts.gov

Paul B. Higginbotham
Judge

Date of Birth: October 14, 1954
Education: Wisconsin 1981 BA, 1985 JD
Began Service: 2003
Term Expires: July 30, 2017

Academic: Adjunct Professor, Law School, University of Wisconsin-Madison (1995); Adjunct Professor, Law School, University of Wisconsin-Madison (1999)

Judicial: Municipal Judge, City of Madison, Wisconsin (1992-1993); Circuit Court Judge, Dane County (1994-2003)

Legal Practice: Staff Attorney, Legal Aid Society of Milwaukee, Inc. (1985-1986); Attorney, Reynolds, Gruber, Herrick, Flesch & Kasdorf

Current Memberships: Dane County Bar Association; State Bar of Wisconsin

Staff
Law Clerk **Julia Norsetter** .... (608) 266-9360
Judicial Assistant **Vickie L. McNeal** .... (608) 266-9360
E-mail: vickie.mcneal@wicourts.gov

Chambers of Judge Gary E. Sherman
Ten East Doty Street, Madison, WI 53703
Tel: (608) 266-9338 Fax: (608) 267-0432
E-mail: gary.sherman@wicourts.gov

Gary E. Sherman
Judge

Date of Birth: May 5, 1949
Education: Wisconsin 1970 BA, 1973 JD
Began Service: May 2010
Appointed By: Governor Jim Doyle
Term Expires: July 31, 2020
Political Affiliation: Democrat

Staff
Law Clerk **Stephanie Zulkoski** .... (608) 266-9338
Began Service: May 2010
E-mail: stephanie.zulkoski@wicourts.gov

(continued on next page)

Chambers of Judge Gary E. Sherman *continued*

Judicial Assistant **Jane Dixon** . . . . (608) 266-9338
E-mail: jane.dixon@wicourts.gov

Wyoming

Wyoming Supreme Court

Supreme Court Building, 2301 Capitol Avenue, Cheyenne, WY 82002
Tel: (307) 777-7316 Fax: (307) 777-6129
Internet: www.courts.state.wy.us

Number of Judgeships: 5

The Supreme Court consists of a chief justice and four justices initially appointed by the Governor from a list of three nominees submitted by the Judicial Nominating Commission and subject to a retention vote one year after appointment. If retained, a justice serves for the remainder of the eight-year term and subsequent eight-year terms are by a nonpartisan retention vote. The chief justice is elected to serve a four-year term by peer vote. Retirement is mandatory at age seventy; however, retired justices may be recalled by the chief justice to serve temporary assignments. The Supreme Court has final appellate jurisdiction over all cases from the Wyoming District Courts and original jurisdiction to issue extradition writs. The Court exercises superintending control over inferior courts, regulates admission to the state bar and the practice of law, and may issue writs necessary to the exercise of proper jurisdiction.

The Supreme Court sits in Cheyenne.

Court Staff

Clerk of the Court **Carol Thompson** .... (307) 777-7316
E-mail: cthompson@courts.state.wy.us
Education: Wyoming 1991 BS

Chief Deputy Clerk **Laura Mickey** .... (307) 777-5117
E-mail: lmickey@courts.state.wy.us

Court Administrator **Lily Sharpe** .... (307) 777-7581
Fax: (307) 777-7240

Deputy Court Administrator **Ronda Munger** .... (307) 777-7581
E-mail: rmunger@courts.state.wy.us Fax: (307) 777-3447
Education: Wyoming 1988 BA, 2003 MPA

Librarian **Eugenia Charles-Newton** .... (307) 777-7187
Fax: (307) 777-7240

Chambers of Chief Justice E. James Burke

2301 Capitol Avenue, Cheyenne, WY 82002
Tel: (307) 777-7557

E. James Burke
Chief Justice

Education: St Joseph Col 1971 BS; Wyoming 1977 JD
Began Service: January 3, 2005
Appointed By: Governor David D. Freudenthal
Next Election: November 2022
Election Type: Retention Election
Term Expires: December 31, 2022

Staff

Career Staff Attorney **Aaron Blum** .... (307) 777-7680
E-mail: ablum@courts.state.wy.us

Career Staff Attorney **Edward W. Harris** .... (307) 777-5989
Began Service: May 7, 2007
E-mail: eharris@courts.state.wy.us
Education: Harvard 1979 AB; Wyoming 1984 JD

Chambers of Justice William U. Hill

Supreme Court Building, 2301 Capitol Avenue, Cheyenne, WY 82002
Tel: (307) 777-7571 Fax: (307) 777-8668

William U. Hill
Justice

Date of Birth: 1948
Education: Wyoming 1970 BA, 1974 JD
Began Service: November 3, 1998
Appointed By: Governor Jim Geringer
Next Election: November 4, 2016
Election Type: Retention Election
Term Expires: 2016

Government: Chief of Staff/Counsel (R-WY), Office of Senator Malcolm Wallop, United States Senate; Attorney General, State of Wyoming (1995-1998)

Judicial: Chief Justice, Wyoming Supreme Court

Legal Practice: Private Practice; Private Practice

Staff

Career Law Clerk **Lindsay Hoyt** .... (307) 777-5260

Career Law Clerk **Jennifer Golden** .... (307) 777-7582
Education: Wyoming 1992 JD

Judicial Assistant **Ruby Gregorio** .... (307) 777-7571
E-mail: rgregorio@courts.state.wy.us

Chambers of Justice Michael K. Davis

Supreme Court Building, 2301 Capitol Avenue, Cheyenne, WY 82002
Tel: (307) 777-7421

Michael K. Davis
Justice

Education: Wyoming JD
Began Service: 2012
Appointed By: Governor Matt Mead

Chambers of Justice Catherine M. Fox

2301 Capitol Avenue, Cheyenne, WY 82002
Tel: (307) 777-7573 Fax: (307) 777-7503

Catherine M. "Kate" Fox
Justice

Education: Wyoming JD
Began Service: January 7, 2014
Appointed By: Governor Matt Mead
Term Expires: January 2017

Staff

Law Clerk **Elisa M. Butler** .... (307) 777-7573

Law Clerk **(Vacant)** .... (307) 777-7573

Chambers of Justice Keith Kautz

2301 Capitol Avenue, Cheyenne, WY 82002
Tel: (307) 777-7316
E-mail: kgk@courts.state.wy.us

Keith G. Kautz
Justice

Education: Wyoming 1975 BA, 1978 JD
Began Service: September 2, 2015
Appointed By: Governor Matt Mead

District of Columbia

District of Columbia Court of Appeals

430 E Street NW, Washington, DC 20001
Tel: (202) 879-2700 Fax: (202) 626-8840
Internet: www.dcappeals.gov

Number of Judgeships: 9

The Court of Appeals consists of a chief judge and eight associate judges who are appointed for fifteen-year terms by the President of the United States with approval of the United States Senate from a list compiled by the District of Columbia Judicial Nomination Commission. The chief judge is designated by the Judicial Nomination Commission from among the active judges for a four-year term. The Court sits in three-judge panels rotating within three divisions unless a hearing or rehearing before the full Court is ordered. Retirement is mandatory at age seventy-four; however, senior judges may serve by assignment. The Court of Appeals has jurisdiction over appeals from the Superior Court of the District of Columbia and, to the extent provided by law, jurisdiction to review orders and decisions of administrative agencies of the district. The Court's decisions are final regarding nonstatutory common law; however, all decisions concerning statutes of the United States relevant to District of Columbia and the U.S. Constitution may be appealed to the United States Supreme Court.

Court Staff

Clerk of Court **Julio A. Castillo** . . . . (202) 879-2725
E-mail: jcastillo@dcappeals.gov
Chief Deputy Clerk **Tracy B. Nutall** . . . . (202) 879-2722
E-mail: tnutall@dcca.state.dc.us
Education: Howard U 1995 JD
Administration Director **Reginald Turner** . . . . (202) 879-2738
Office on Admissions and the Unauthorized Practice of Law Director **Derek Mitchell** . . . . (202) 879-2710
Public Office Operations Director **Terry Lambert** . . . . (202) 879-2702
E-mail: tlambert@dcappeals.gov
Staff Counsel **Rosanna M. Mason** . . . . (202) 879-2718
E-mail: rmason@dcappeals.gov
Law Librarian **Letty Limbach** . . . . (202) 879-2767
E-mail: llimbach@dcappeals.gov
Special Assistant to Clerk **Ernest M. Brooks** . . . . (202) 879-2723
E-mail: ebrooks@dcappeals.gov

Chambers of Chief Judge Eric T. Washington

Historic Courthouse, 430 E Street NW, Room 319, Washington, DC 20001
Tel: (202) 879-2771 Fax: (202) 824-8580
E-mail: ewashington@dcappeals.gov

Eric T. Washington
Chief Judge

Date of Birth: 1953
Education: Tufts 1976; Columbia 1979 JD
Began Service: July 1, 1999
Appointed By: President William J. Clinton

Government: Legislative Director and Counsel (D-TX), Office of Representative Michael A. Andrews, United States House of Representatives (1983-1985); Special Counsel to the Corporation Counsel, District of Columbia (1987); Principal Deputy Corporation Counsel, District of Columbia (1987-1989)

Judicial: Associate Judge, Superior Court of the District of Columbia (1995-1999)

Legal Practice: Associate Attorney, Fulbright & Jaworski L.L.P. (1979-1982); Participating Associate Attorney, Fulbright & Jaworski L.L.P. (1985-1987); Partner, Hogan & Hartson LLP (1990-1995)

Current Memberships: American Bar Association; Conference of Chief Justices; The District of Columbia Bar; National Bar Association

Chambers of Chief Judge Eric T. Washington *continued*

Staff

Law Clerk **Brandi Howard** . . . . (202) 879-2775
Began Service: August 2015
Term Expires: September 2016
Law Clerk **Mara Jumper** . . . . (202) 879-2775
Began Service: August 2015
Term Expires: September 2016
Judicial Administrative Assistant **Sandra Strawder** . . . . . . (202) 879-2771
E-mail: sstrawder@dcappeals.gov
Education: Alabama 1982 BA
Executive Assistant **Cherylen Walker-Turner** . . . . (202) 879-2773
E-mail: cwalkerturner@dcappeals.gov

Chambers of Associate Judge Stephen H. Glickman

Historic Court House, 430 E Street N.W., Suite 220, Washington, DC 20001
Tel: (202) 879-2740 Fax: (202) 879-9908
E-mail: sglickman@dcappeals.gov

Stephen H. Glickman
Associate Judge

Date of Birth: 1948
Education: Cornell 1969 AB; Yale 1973 JD
Began Service: July 1999
Appointed By: President William J. Clinton

Academic: Instructor, Yale University (1974)

Clerkships: Law Clerk The Honorable Joseph Bogdanski, Connecticut Supreme Court

Government: Staff Attorney, Federal Trade Commission (1974-1976); Public Defender Service (1976-1980)

Legal Practice: Zuckerman, Spaeder, Goldstein, Taylor & Kolker (1980-1999)

Chambers of Associate Judge John R. Fisher

430 E Street NW, Suite 201, Washington, DC 20001
Tel: (202) 879-2751
E-mail: jfisher@dcappeals.gov

John R. Fisher
Associate Judge

Began Service: October 2005
Appointed By: President George W. Bush
Term Expires: 2020

Government: Chief, District of Columbia Court of Appeals, Executive Office for United States Attorneys, United States Department of Justice

Chambers of Associate Judge Anna Blackburne-Rigsby

430 E Street NW, Suite 430, Washington, DC 20001
Tel: (202) 879-2731

Anna Blackburne-Rigsby
Associate Judge

Education: Duke BA; Howard U 1987 JD
Began Service: August 2006
Appointed By: President George W. Bush
Term Expires: 2021

Government: Special Counsel to the Corporation Council, Office of Corporation Counsel, Washington, D.C.; Deputy Corporation Counsel, Office of Corporation Counsel, Family Services Division, Washington, D.C.

Judicial: Hearing Commissioner, Superior Court of the District of Columbia (1996-2000); Associate Judge, Superior Court of the District of Columbia (2000-2006)

Chambers of Associate Judge Anna Blackburne-Rigsby *continued*

Legal Practice: Associate Attorney, Hogan and Hartson (1987-1992)

Chambers of Associate Judge Phyllis D. Thompson

430 E Street NW, Suite 301, Washington, DC 20001
Tel: (202) 879-2781
E-mail: pthompson@dcappeals.gov

Phyllis D. Thompson
Associate Judge

Education: George Washington 1974 BA; Princeton 1976 MA; George Washington 1981 JD
Began Service: September 2006
Term Expires: 2021

Academic: Instructor and Lecturer, Department of Theology, Georgetown University (1977-1981)

Legal Practice: Contact Partner, Federal Benefits Programs Practice Group, Covington & Burling LLP

Chambers of Associate Judge Corinne Ann Beckwith

430 E Street NW, Washington, DC 20001
Tel: (202) 879-2728

Corinne Ann Beckwith
Associate Judge

Education: Kalamazoo BA; Illinois BS; Michigan JD
Began Service: February 6, 2012
Appointed By: President Barack Obama

Chambers of Associate Judge Catharine Friend Easterly

430 E Street NW, Suite 218, Washington, DC 20001
Tel: (202) 879-2786 Tel: (202) 626-8840

Catharine Friend "Kate" Easterly
Associate Judge

Education: Yale BA; Virginia JD
Began Service: February 10, 2012
Appointed By: President Barack Obama

Government: Attorney, Special Litigation Division, Public Defender Service, District of Columbia (2011-2012)

Staff

Law Clerk **Gabe Newland** .... (202) 879-2786
Term Expires: September 2016
Law Clerk **Purba Mukerjee** .... (202) 879-2786
Term Expires: September 2016
Education: UC Berkeley 2015 JD
Law Clerk **Hannah Swanson** .... (202) 879-2786
Term Expires: June 2016

Chambers of Associate Judge Roy Wallace McLeese III

430 E Street NW, Suite 308, Washington, DC 20001
Tel: (202) 879-2762

Roy W. McLeese III
Associate Judge

Education: Harvard BA; NYU 1985 JD
Began Service: September 28, 2012
Appointed By: President Barack Obama

Clerkships: Law Clerk, Chambers of Associate Justice Antonin Scalia, Supreme Court of the United States (1986-1987)

Chambers of Associate Judge Roy Wallace McLeese III *continued*

Government: Deputy Chief, Appellate Division, District of Columbia District, United States Department of Justice (1990-2005); Assistant to the Solicitor General, Office of the Solicitor General (1997-1999); Chief, Appellate Division, District of Columbia District, United States Department of Justice

Chambers of Senior Judge Theodore R. Newman, Jr.

430 E Street NW, Suite 341, Washington, DC 20001
Tel: (202) 879-2757 Fax: (202) 626-8876
E-mail: tnewman@dcappeals.gov

Theodore R. Newman, Jr.
Senior Judge

Date of Birth: 1934
Education: Brown U 1955 AB; Harvard 1958 JD
Began Service: 1976
Appointed By: President Gerald Ford
Political Affiliation: Democrat

Academic: Trustee, Board of Trustees, Brown University; Visiting Lecturer, Harvard Law School; Adjunct Professor, School of Law, Howard University; Adjunct Professor, The Law Center, Georgetown University

Government: Attorney, Civil Rights Division, United States Department of Justice (1961-1962)

Judicial: Associate Judge, Superior Court of the District of Columbia (1970-1976); Chief Judge, District of Columbia Court of Appeals (1976-1984)

Legal Practice: Associate, Houston, Bryant & Gardner; Partner, Pratt, Bowers & Newman (1968-1970)

Military Service: Judge Advocate United States Air Force, United States Department of Defense

Current Memberships: American Bar Foundation

Chambers of Senior Judge William C. Pryor

430 E Street NW, Washington, DC 20001
Tel: (202) 879-2757 Fax: (202) 626-8840
E-mail: wpryor@dcappeals.gov

William C. Pryor
Senior Judge

Education: Dartmouth 1954; Georgetown 1959 JD
Began Service: 1979

Academic: Distinguished Professor of Law, University of the District of Columbia

Government: Associate, Office of the United States Attorney, United States Department of Justice

Judicial: Judge, District of Columbia Superior Court

Current Memberships: American Bar Association

Chambers of Senior Judge Warren R. King

430 E Street NW, 3rd Floor, Washington, DC 20001
Tel: (202) 626-8871 Fax: (202) 626-8869
E-mail: wking@dcappeals.gov

Warren R. King
Senior Judge

Date of Birth: May 9, 1937
Education: Rensselaer Poly 1960 BAE; Washington College of Law 1967 JD; Yale 1969 LLM
Began Service: 1991
Appointed By: President George H.W. Bush

Judicial: Associate Judge, Superior Court of the District of Columbia (1981-1991)

(continued on next page)

Chambers of Senior Judge Warren R. King *continued*

Staff

Judicial Administrative Assistant **Leta F. Walters** . . . . (202) 879-2756
E-mail: lwalters@dcca.state.dc.us

Chambers of Senior Judge John M. Ferren

430 E Street NW, Washington, DC 20001
Tel: (202) 879-2772 Fax: (202) 626-8876
E-mail: jferren@dcappeals.gov

John M. Ferren
Senior Judge

Date of Birth: 1937
Education: Harvard 1959 AB, 1962 LLB
Began Service: 1977
Appointed By: President Jimmy Carter
Political Affiliation: Democrat

Academic: Adjunct Lecturer, University of Iowa College (2006)

Government: Corporation Counsel, District of Columbia (1997-1999)

Legal Practice: Kirkland, Ellis, Hodson, Chaffetz & Masters (1962-1966); Hogan & Hartson (1970-1977)

Nonprofit: Lecturer, Harvard Law School (1966-1970); Fellow, Woodrow Wilson International Center for Scholars (2000-2001)

Staff

Administrative Assistant **Nélida L. Price** . . . . (202) 879-2757
E-mail: mmoore@dcappeals.gov

Chambers of Senior Judge Frank Q. Nebeker

430 E Street NW, 3rd Floor, Washington, DC 20001
Tel: (202) 879-2778 Fax: (202) 626-8869
E-mail: fnebeker@dcappeals.gov

Frank Q. Nebeker
Senior Judge

Date of Birth: April 23, 1930
Education: Utah 1953 BS; Washington College of Law 1956 JD
Began Service: 1969
Appointed By: President Richard M. Nixon

Academic: Instructor, American University (1965-1985)

Government: Correspondence Secretary, The White House Office, Executive Office of the President (1953-1956); Trial Attorney, Internal Security Division, United States Department of Justice (1956-1958); Assistant U.S. Attorney, District of Columbia District, Executive Office for United States Attorneys, United States Department of Justice (1958-1969); Director, United States Office of Government Ethics (1987-1989)

Judicial: Associate Judge, District of Columbia Court of Appeals (1969-1987); Chief Judge, United States Court of Appeals for Veterans Claims (1989-2000)

Military Service: United States National Guard Artillery (1948-1956)

Current Memberships: The American Law Institute; The District of Columbia Bar

Staff

Judicial Administrative Assistant **Leta F. Walters** . . . . (202) 879-2756
E-mail: lwalters@dcca.state.dc.us

Chambers of Senior Judge John M. Steadman

430 E Street NW, 3rd Floor, Washington, DC 20001
Tel: (202) 879-2765 Fax: (202) 626-8869
E-mail: jsteadman@dcappeals.gov

John M. Steadman
Senior Judge

Date of Birth: August 8, 1930
Education: Yale 1952 BA; Harvard 1955 LLB
Began Service: 1985
Appointed By: President Ronald Reagan

Academic: Visiting Professor, School of Law, University of Pennsylvania (1970-1972); Professor, The Law Center, Georgetown University (1972-1985); Associate Dean, The Law Center, Georgetown University (1979-1984)

Government: Attorney, United States Department of Justice (1963-1964); Deputy Undersecretary for International Affairs, United States Department of the Army, United States Department of Defense (1964-1965); Special Assistant, Office of the Secretary of the Army, United States Department of Defense (1965-1968); General Counsel, United States Department of the Air Force, United States Department of Defense (1968-1970)

Judicial: Associate Judge, District of Columbia Court of Appeals (1985-2004)

Legal Practice: Private Practice (1956-1963); Private Practice (Of Counsel) (1979-1985)

Current Memberships: American Bar Association; The American Law Institute

Staff

Judicial Administrative Assistant **Leta F. Walters** . . . . (202) 879-2756
E-mail: lwalters@dcca.state.dc.us

Chambers of Senior Judge Vanessa Ruiz

430 E Street NW, Washington, DC 20001
Tel: (202) 879-2757 Fax: (202) 626-8868
E-mail: vruiz@dcappeals.gov

Vanessa Ruiz
Senior Judge

Date of Birth: 1950
Education: Wellesley 1972 BA; Georgetown 1975 JD
Began Service: November 28, 1994
Appointed By: President William J. Clinton

Current Memberships: American Bar Foundation; The American Law Institute; The District of Columbia Bar; Hispanic National Bar Association; National Association of Women Judges; Women's Bar Association of the District of Columbia

Chambers of Senior Judge John A. Terry
430 E Street NW, Washington, DC 20001
Tel: (202) 879-2768 Fax: (202) 626-8840
E-mail: jterry@dcca.state.dc.us

John A. Terry
Senior Judge

Date of Birth: 1933
Education: Yale 1954 BA; Georgetown 1960 JD
Began Service: September 1, 1982
Appointed By: President Ronald Reagan

Government: Assistant U.S. Attorney, District of Columbia District, Executive Office for United States Attorneys, United States Department of Justice (1962-1967); Attorney, National Commission on Reform of Federal Criminal Law (1967-1968); Appellate Division Chief, Executive Office for United States Attorneys, United States Department of Justice (1969-1982)

Legal Practice: Private Practice (1968-1969)

Current Memberships: American Bar Association; The District of Columbia Bar

Staff
Secretary **Kathy Jackson** .... (202) 879-2795
E-mail: kjackson@dcappeals.gov

Chambers of Senior Judge Michael W. Farrell
430 E Street NW, Washington, DC 20001
Tel: (202) 879-2757
E-mail: mfarrell@dcappeals.gov

Michael W. Farrell
Senior Judge

Date of Birth: 1938
Education: Notre Dame 1960 BA; Columbia 1966 MA; Washington College of Law 1973 JD
Began Service: 1989

Chambers of Senior Judge (retired) Inez Smith Reid
430 E Street NW, Washington, DC 20001
Tel: (202) 879-2726
E-mail: ireid@dcappeals.gov

Inez Smith Reid
Senior Judge (retired)

Date of Birth: 1937
Education: Tufts 1959 BA; Yale 1962 LLB; UCLA MA; Columbia PhD
Began Service: June 23, 1995

Current Memberships: The Association of the Bar of the City of New York; The District of Columbia Bar; State Bar of California

Staff
Judicial Administrative Assistant **Leta F. Walters** .... (202) 879-2756
E-mail: lwalters@dcappeals.gov

Chambers of Senior Judge James A. Belson
430 E Street NW, Washington, DC 20001
Tel: (202) 879-2757
E-mail: jbelson@dcappeals.gov

James A. Belson
Senior Judge

Date of Birth: 1931
Education: Georgetown 1956 JD, 1962 LLM

Current Memberships: The District of Columbia Bar

District of Columbia Judicial Nomination Commission
515 Fifth Street, NW, Suite 235, Washington, DC 20001
Tel: (202) 879-0478 Fax: (202) 737-9126
E-mail: dc.jnc@dc.gov

The District of Columbia Judicial Nomination Commission screens, selects, and recommends candidates for nomination to judicial positions in the District of Columbia. The Commission must present a list of three names to the President of the United States within sixty days of a vacancy on the court. The President then must nominate at least one person from the list for Senate confirmation within sixty days of its receipt. If the President fails to meet the time restriction, the Commission will nominate a candidate to the Senate for confirmation. There are seven members of the Commission. There are two appointed by the Mayor of the District of Columbia, two by the Board of Governors of the District of Columbia Bar, one by the Council of the District of Columbia, one by the Chief Judge of the United States District Court for the District of Columbia, and one by the President of the United States. The members of the Commission serve six-year terms, with the exception of the member appointed by the President, who serves a five-year term.

Commission
Chairperson **Emmet G. Sullivan** .... (202) 354-3260
Education: Howard U 1968 BA, 1971 JD
Member **Ronald S. Flagg** .... (202) 344-4000
Education: Chicago 1975 AB; Harvard 1978 JD
Member **William Lucy** .... (301) 520-0576
E-mail: williamlucy1@comcast.net
Education: UC Berkeley
Member **Natalie O. Ludaway** .... (202) 434-9103
E-mail: noludaway@leftwichlaw.com Fax: (202) 783-3420
Education: Hunter BA, MA; George Washington 1986 JD
Member **Woody N. Peterson** .... (202) 420-2212
E-mail: wpetersonjnc@dicksteinshapiro.com
Education: Harvard 1970 AB, 1976 JD
Member **Rev. Morris L. Shearin, Sr.** .... (202) 269-0288
E-mail: revshearin_jnc@yahoo.com
Member **Grace E. Speights** .... (202) 739-5189
E-mail: gspeights@morganlewis.com

Staff
Executive Director **Katherine L. Garrett** .... (202) 879-0478
Began Service: January 19, 2010 Fax: (202) 737-9126
E-mail: katherine.garrett@dc.gov
Executive Assistant **Irvie Ozier** .... (202) 879-0477
E-mail: irvie.ozier@dc.gov

STATE COURTS—DISTRICT OF COLUMBIA

United States Department of Justice

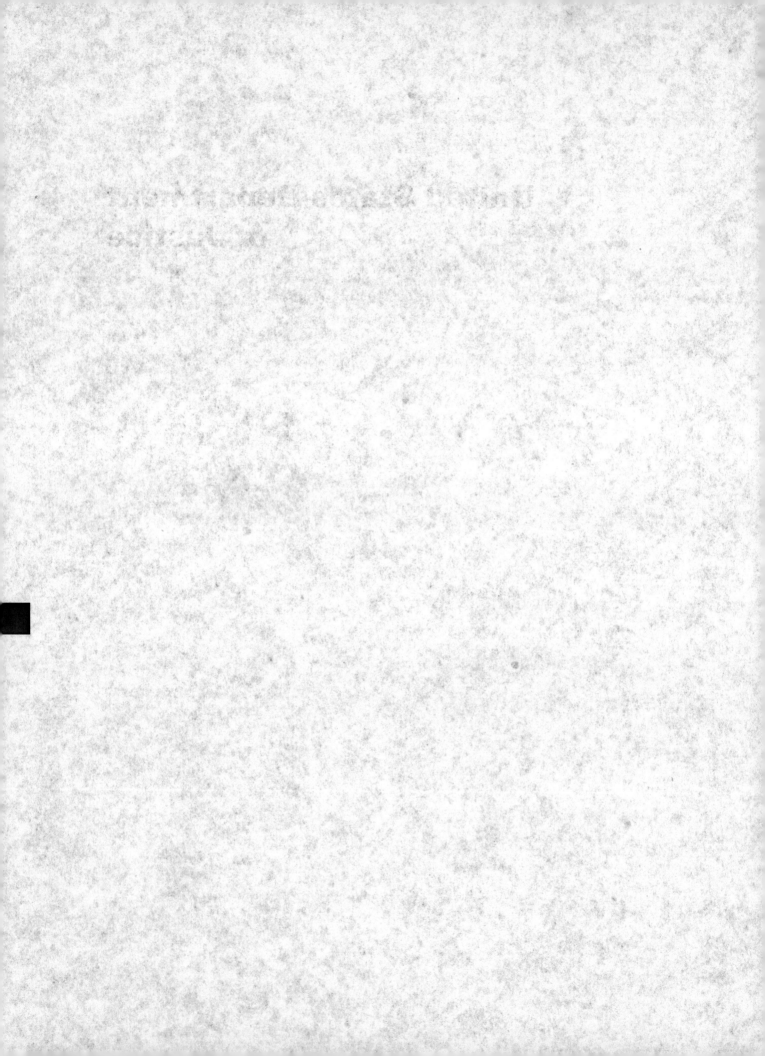

United States Department of Justice [DOJ]

Robert F. Kennedy Building, 950 Pennsylvania Avenue, NW,
Washington, DC 20530-2001
Tel: (202) 514-2000 (Personnel Locator)
Tel: (202) 307-2000 (Procurement Information)
Tel: (202) 514-2007 (Public Information)
Tel: (202) 514-3642 (Freedom of Information/Privacy Act)
Tel: (202) 514-2001 (Office of the Attorney General)
Tel: (800) 869-4499 (Inspector General's Hot Line)
Tel: (202) 514-4330 (Immigration General Information)
Tel: (800) 514-0301 (Americans with Disabilities Act Information)
Tel: (800) 777-7700 (Amnesty Program/Legalization General Information)
Fax: (202) 514-4371
Internet: www.justice.gov
Internet: www.justice.gov/open (Open Government Directive)
Internet: www.usa.gov (Official US Government Website)

The Department of Justice serves as counsel to the U.S. Government, enforces the law, protects the public from criminals and subversion, ensures healthy business competition, and safeguards consumers. In its capacity as counsel, the department manages all cases involving the United States Federal Government.

Office of the Attorney General

Robert F. Kennedy Building, 950 Pennsylvania Avenue, NW,
Washington, DC 20530-2001
Tel: (202) 514-2001 Fax: (202) 307-6777
Internet: www.usdoj.gov/ag

The mission of the Office of the Attorney General is to supervise and direct the administration and operation of the Department of Justice, including the Federal Bureau of Investigation, Drug Enforcement Administration, Bureau of Alcohol, Tobacco, Firearms and Explosives, Bureau of Prisons, Office of Justice Programs, and the U.S. Attorneys and U.S. Marshals Service.

Loretta E. Lynch
Attorney General

Date of Birth: May 21, 1959
Education: Harvard 1981 AB, 1984 JD
Began Service: April 27, 2015

★ Attorney General **Loretta E. Lynch** Room 5111 .... (202) 514-2000
Began Service: April 27, 2015 Fax: (202) 307-6777
E-mail: loretta.lynch@usdoj.gov
E-mail: askdoj@usdoj.gov
Education: Harvard 1981 AB, 1984 JD

□ Confidential Assistant **Bessie L. Meadows** .... (202) 514-2001
E-mail: bessie.l.meadows@usdoj.gov

□ Special Assistant **Sabrina Curtis** .... (202) 514-2291
950 Pennsylvania Avenue, NW, Room 5751, Washington, DC 20530
E-mail: sabrina.curtis@usdoj.gov

○ Chief of Staff and Counselor **Sharon Werner** .... (202) 514-3892
Robert F. Kennedy Building, 950 Pennsylvania Avenue, NW, Room 5115, Washington, DC 20530-2000
E-mail: sharon.werner@usdoj.gov
Education: Penn State 1999 BA; Stanford 2003 JD

○ Deputy Chief of Staff and Counselor **Carolyn Pokorny**
Room 5112 .... (202) 514-9797
E-mail: carolyn.pokorny@usdoj.gov

Office of the Attorney General *continued*

○ Counselor to the Attorney General **Denise Cheung**
Room 5116 .... (202) 305-9798
E-mail: denise.cheung2@usdoj.gov

Counselor to the Attorney General **Eric J. Feigin** .... (202) 514-9798
E-mail: eric.feigin2@usdoj.gov

Counselor to the Attorney General **Paige L. Herwig** ..... (202) 616-2372
950 Pennsylvania Avenue, NW, Room 5214, Washington, DC 20530
E-mail: paige.herwig@usdoj.gov

○ Counselor to the Attorney General **(Vacant)** .... (202) 514-4969
950 Pennsylvania Avenue, NW, Room 5224, Washington, DC 20530

○ Counselor to the Attorney General **(Vacant)** .... (202) 514-9798
950 Pennsylvania Avenue, NW, Room 5119, Washington, DC 20530-2000

□ Director of Advance and Scheduling **Alan Bray**
Room 5133 .... (202) 514-6333
E-mail: alan.bray@usdoj.gov

□ Special Assistant and Scheduler **Christina Sivret**
Room 5129 .... (202) 514-7281
E-mail: christina.sivret@usdoj.gov

□ White House Liaison and Counsel to the Attorney General **Shirlethia V. Franklin** Room 5110 .... (202) 616-2372
E-mail: shirlethia.franklin@usdoj.gov
Education: Howard U 2007 JD

Office for Access to Justice [ATJ]

950 Pennsylvania Avenue, NW, Room 3340, Washington, DC 20530
Tel: (202) 514-5312 Fax: (202) 514-5326
Internet: http://www.justice.gov/atj/index.html

The Access to Justice Initiative was established in March 2010 to address the access-to-justice crisis in the Federal and State justice systems. The mission of this office is to help the justice system efficiently deliver fair and accessible legal services to all, regardless of wealth or status.

Director **Lisa Foster** .... (202) 514-5312
E-mail: lisa.foster2@usdoj.gov
Education: Stanford BA; Harvard JD

Deputy Director **Maha Jweied** .... (202) 514-5312
E-mail: maha.jweied@usdoj.gov

Deputy Director **Karen Ann Lash** .... (202) 514-5312
E-mail: karen.lash@usdoj.gov
Education: UCLA 1983 BA; USC 1987 JD

Senior Counsel **Robert "Bob" Bullock** .... (202) 514-5312
E-mail: bob.bullock@usdoj.gov

Senior Counsel **Andrew Stanner** .... (202) 514-5312
E-mail: andrew.stanner@usdoj.gov

Special Counsel **Anne Traum** .... (202) 514-5312
E-mail: anne.traum@usdoj.gov

Counsel **Helam Gebremariam** .... (202) 514-5312
E-mail: helam.gebremariam@usdoj.gov
Education: NYU 2010 JD

Counsel **Allie Yang-Green** .... (202) 514-5312
E-mail: allie.c.yang-green@usdoj.gov.

Office Manager **Stephan P. Matthews** .... (202) 514-5312
E-mail: stephan.p.matthews@usdoj.gov

Office of Legal Counsel [OLC]

Robert F. Kennedy Building, 950 Pennsylvania Avenue, NW,
Washington, DC 20530
Tel: (202) 514-2051 Fax: (202) 514-0539
Internet: www.usdoj.gov/olc

The mission of the Office of Legal Counsel is to assist the Attorney General in carrying out his or her statutory responsibility of furnishing legal advice to the President and the heads of the executive and military departments, and to provide legal advice and assistance to other components of the Department of Justice upon request.

★ Assistant Attorney General **(Vacant)** Room 5216......... (202) 514-2051

Executive Officer **Valerie H. Yancey** Room 5142 .... (202) 514-3957
E-mail: valerie.yancey@usdoj.gov

Confidential Assistant **Dyone Mitchell** Room 5218 ..... (202) 514-2633
E-mail: dyone.mitchell@usdoj.gov

(continued on next page)

★ Presidential Appointment Requiring Senate Confirmation
☆ Presidential Appointment
□ Schedule C Appointment
◇ Career Senior Foreign Service Appointment
● Career Senior Executive Service (SES) Appointment
○ Non-Career Senior Executive Service (SES) Appointment

Office of Legal Counsel [OLC] *continued*

○ Principal Deputy Assistant Attorney General
Karl Remon Thompson Room 5222 .... (202) 514-2051
Education: Harvard 1991 BA; Cambridge (UK) 1992 MPhil, 1998 PhD; Chicago 2000 JD

○ Deputy Assistant Attorney General **John Bies**
Room 5231 .... (202) 305-8521
E-mail: john.bies@usdoj.gov
Education: Pomona BA; Minnesota MA; Chicago JD

○ Deputy Assistant Attorney General **Brian Boynton**
Room 5235 .... (202) 514-9700
E-mail: brian.boynton@usdoj.gov
Education: Stanford 2000 JD

• Deputy Assistant Attorney General **Daniel L. Koffsky**
Room 5238 .... (202) 514-2030
E-mail: daniel.l.koffsky@usdoj.gov
Education: Harvard 1975 BA; Yale 1978 JD

○ Deputy Assistant Attorney General **Troy A. McKenzie**
Room 5229 .... (202) 514-4038
E-mail: troy.mckenzie@usdoj.gov
Education: Princeton 1997 BSE; NYU 2000 JD

□ Senior Counsel **Matthew Roberts** Room 5235 .... (202) 514-2051
E-mail: matthew.roberts@usdoj.gov
Education: Harvard 1989 JD

• Senior Counsel **Jeffrey P. Singdahlsen** Room 5262 ...... (202) 514-4174
E-mail: jeffrey.singdahlsen@usdoj.gov
Education: Dartmouth AB; Virginia JD

• Special Counsel **Paul P. Colborn** Room 5240 .... (202) 514-2048
E-mail: paul.p.colborn@usdoj.gov
Education: Princeton 1971 BA; Georgetown 1974 JD

• Special Counsel **Rosemary A. Hart** Room 5242 .... (202) 514-2027
E-mail: rosemary.hart@usdoj.gov
Education: UC Santa Cruz 1976 BA; Hastings 1979 JD

Attorney Advisor **Andrew Tutt** .... (202) 514-2051
E-mail: andrew.tutt@usdoj.gov
Education: Yale 2013 JD

Office of the Deputy Attorney General [ODAG]

Robert F. Kennedy Building, 950 Pennsylvania Avenue, NW, Washington, DC 20530
Tel: (202) 514-2101 Fax: (202) 514-0467
Internet: www.justice.gov/dag

The mission of the Deputy Attorney General is to advise and assist the Attorney General in formulating and implementing Department policies and programs and in providing overall supervision and direction to all organizational units of the Department.

★ Deputy Attorney General **Sally Quillian Yates** .... (202) 514-2101
Began Service: May 14, 2015
E-mail: sally.yates@usdoj.gov
Education: Georgia 1982, 1986 JD

Senior Counsel to the Deputy Attorney General
Amin Aminfar .... (202) 305-0071
E-mail: amin.aminfar@usdoj.gov

Senior Counsel to the Deputy Attorney General
Andrew J. Bruck Room 4224 .... (202) 305-0180
E-mail: andrew.bruck@usdoj.gov

Senior Counsel to the Deputy Attorney General
R. Scott Ferber .... (202) 514-3853
E-mail: scott.ferber@usdoj.gov

Senior Counsel to the Deputy Attorney General
G. Scott Hulsey .... (202) 353-3030
E-mail: g.scott.hulsey@usdoj.gov

□ Senior Counsel to the Deputy Attorney General
Brette Steele .... (202) 514-2101
E-mail: brette.steele@usdoj.gov

□ Associate Deputy Attorney General **Armando Bonilla**
Room 4313 .... (202) 616-1621
E-mail: armando.bonilla@usdoj.gov
Education: West Virginia 1989 BA; Seton Hall 1992 JD

Associate Deputy Attorney General
Danielle Y. Conley .... (202) 514-6753
E-mail: danielle.conley@usdoj.gov
Education: Tulane 2000 BA; Howard U 2003 JD

Office of the Deputy Attorney General [ODAG] *continued*

□ Associate Deputy Attorney General **Tashina Gauhar**
Room 4222 .... (202) 353-3030
E-mail: tashina.gauhar@usdoj.gov

Associate Deputy Attorney General **Samir Jain** .... (202) 514-7473
E-mail: samir.jain@usdoj.gov

Associate Deputy Attorney General **Iris Lan**
Room 4311 .... (202) 514-6907
E-mail: iris.lan@usdoj.gov

• Associate Deputy Attorney General **David Margolis**
Room 4113 .... (202) 514-4945
E-mail: david.margolis@usdoj.gov
Education: Brown U 1961; Harvard 1964 JD

Associate Deputy Attorney General
Raphael A. Prober .... (202) 307-1045
E-mail: raphael.prober@usdoj.gov
Education: Georgetown 2000 BS, 2003 JD

□ Associate Deputy Attorney General **Miriam Vogel**
Room 4135 .... (202) 307-2090
E-mail: miriam.vogel@usdoj.gov
Education: Georgetown 2000 JD

□ Confidential Assistant to the Deputy Attorney General **Joshua Mogil** Room 4111 .... (202) 514-1904
E-mail: joshua.mogil@usdoj.gov

• Principal Associate Deputy Attorney General
Matthew S. Axelrod Room 4208 .... (202) 514-2105
E-mail: matthew.axelrod@usdoj.gov
Education: Amherst 1992 BA; Yale 1997 JD

Chief of Staff **Heather G. Childs** Room 4210 .... (202) 514-3712

Senior Counsel for Rule of Law in Afghanistan
Brian Tomney Room 4413 .... (202) 353-8657
E-mail: brian.tomney2@usdoj.gov

Emergency Preparedness and Response Coordinator
Mark E. Michalic Room 4112 .... (202) 514-0438
E-mail: mark.michalic@usdoj.gov

National Coordinator for Child Exploitation Prevention and Interdiction **Jill E. Steinberg** Room 4317 .... (202) 514-9340
E-mail: jill.steinberg@usdoj.gov

• National Criminal Discovery Coordinator
Andrew D. Goldsmith .... (202) 252-1438
E-mail: andrew.goldsmith@usdoj.gov
Education: Cornell; Albany Law JD

White House Fellow **(Vacant)** Room 4116 .... (202) 305-3481

Office of Legal Policy [OLP]

Robert F. Kennedy Building, 950 Pennsylvania Avenue, NW, Washington, DC 20530
Tel: (202) 514-4601 Fax: (202) 514-2424
Internet: www.justice.gov/olp

The mission of the Office of Legal Policy is to develop and implement the Departments significant policy initiatives, handle special projects that implicate the interests of multiple Department components, coordinate with other interested Department components and other Executive Branch agencies, and serve as the primary policy advisor to the Attorney General and the Deputy Attorney General; it also reviews and coordinates all regulations promulgated by the Department and all of its components, assists the Attorney General with responsibilities in recommending candidates for federal judgeships, and coordinates the judicial nomination and confirmation process.

★ Assistant Attorney General **(Vacant)** Room 4238 .... (202) 514-4601
Special Assistant **(Vacant)** Room 4234 .... (202) 514-4601

○ Principal Deputy Assistant Attorney General
Elana J. Tyrangiel Room 4238 .... (202) 514-4601
E-mail: elana.tyrangiel2@usdoj.gov
Education: Brown U 1993 AB; Michigan 1998 JD

• Deputy Assistant Attorney General **Kevin R. Jones**
Room 4248 .... (202) 514-4604
E-mail: kevin.r.jones@usdoj.gov
Education: William & Mary 1975 BA; Virginia 1978 JD

○ Deputy Assistant Attorney General
Alexander G. "Alex" Krulic .... (202) 305-4870
E-mail: alexander.krulic@usdoj.gov

★ Presidential Appointment Requiring Senate Confirmation
☆ Presidential Appointment
□ Schedule C Appointment
◇ Career Senior Foreign Service Appointment
• Career Senior Executive Service (SES) Appointment
○ Non-Career Senior Executive Service (SES) Appointment

Office of Legal Policy *continued*

Deputy Assistant Attorney General
Laurence E. "Larry" Rothenberg Room 3116 . . . . (202) 514-8356
E-mail: laurence.rothenberg@usdoj.gov
● Deputy Assistant Attorney General
Robyn L. Thiemann Room 4237 . . . . (202) 514-8356
E-mail: robyn.thiemann2@usdoj.gov
○ Deputy Assistant Attorney General
Michael Zubrensky Room 4229 . . . . (202) 514-4606
E-mail: michael.zubrensky@usdoj.gov
Chief of Staff **Hannah Fried** . . . . (202) 353-3069
E-mail: hannah.fried@usdoj.gov
Senior Counsel **Eric T. Gormsen** Room 4258 . . . . (202) 514-4087
E-mail: eric.t.gormsen@usdoj.gov
Senior Counsel **Robert Hinchman** Room 4252 . . . . (202) 514-8059
E-mail: robert.hinchman@usdoj.gov
Senior Counsel **David J. Karp** Room 4509 . . . . (202) 514-3273
E-mail: david.j.karp@usdoj.gov
□ Counsel **Sean Douglass** . . . . (202) 514-4601
E-mail: sean.douglass@usdoj.gov
□ Researcher **Tara Ohitman** . . . . (202) 514-4601
E-mail: tara.ohitman@usdoj.gov

Office of Dispute Resolution [ODR]

Tel: (202) 616-9471 Fax: (202) 616-9570
Internet: http://www.justice.gov/olp/alternative-dispute-resolution

The mission of the Office of Dispute Resolution is to develop policy and to promote the effective use of alternative dispute resolution (ADR) processes. The office is responsible for monitoring and evaluating the use of ADR throughout the Department; representing the Department leadership with foreign governments as well as the private sector in ADR matters; and facilitating the effective use of ADR in litigation and agency administrative disputes. The office also represents the Attorney General in leadership of federal ADR through the Interagency ADR Working Group, an organization which was created by the President and convened by the Attorney General to promote the use of ADR throughout the federal government.

● Director and Senior Counsel for Alternative Dispute Resolution **Joanna Martinson Jacobs** Room 4529 . . . . . (202) 616-9471
E-mail: joanna.jacobs@usdoj.gov
Education: New Mexico; Columbus Law 1978 JD
Deputy Director **(Vacant)** Room 4529 . . . . (202) 305-4439

Office of Legislative Affairs [OLA]

Robert F. Kennedy Building, 950 Pennsylvania Avenue, NW, Washington, DC 20530
Tel: (202) 514-2141 Fax: (202) 305-2643
Internet: www.justice.gov/ola

The mission of the Office of Legislative Affairs is to advise appropriate components of the Department on the development of the Departments official policies through legislation initiated by the Department, by other parts of the executive branch, or by Members of Congress, and to explain and advocate the Departments policies to the Congress. The Office also serves as the Attorney Generals focal point for dealing with Department nominees, congressional oversight, congressional correspondence, and congressional requests for documents and access to Department employees.

★ Assistant Attorney General **Peter J. Kadzik** . . . . (202) 514-2141
E-mail: peter.j.kadzik@usdoj.gov
Education: SUNY (Buffalo) 1974 BA; Georgetown 1977 JD
□ Congressional Assistant **Tashi Chogyal** . . . . (202) 514-2141
E-mail: tashi.chogyal@usdoj.gov
□ Legislative Assistant **Maida Johnson** . . . . (202) 514-2141
E-mail: maida.p.johnson@usdoj.gov
○ Principal Deputy Assistant Attorney General
Eric Losick Room 1145 . . . . (202) 514-2141
E-mail: eric.p.losick@usdoj.gov
○ Deputy Assistant Attorney General **Elliot C. Williams**
Room 1143 . . . . (202) 514-2141
E-mail: elliot.williams@usdoj.gov

Office of Legislative Affairs *continued*

□ Attorney Advisor/Chief Of Staff
Daniel L. "Dan" Goldberg . . . . (202) 514-2141
E-mail: daniel.l.goldberg@usdoj.gov
Education: Wisconsin 1998 BA; Harvard 2003 JD
● Special Counsel **M. Faith Burton** . . . . (202) 514-2141
E-mail: faith.burton@usdoj.gov
Office Manager **Saundra M. Callier** Room 1612 . . . . (202) 616-9864
E-mail: saundra.m.callier@usdoj.gov

Office of Privacy and Civil Liberties

National Place Building, 1331 Pennsylvania Avenue, NW, Suite 1000, Washington, DC 20530
Tel: (202) 514-0208 Fax: (202) 307-0693
E-mail: privacy@usdoj.gov
Internet: www.justice.gov/opcl

The Office of Privacy and Civil Liberties (OPCL) supports the duties and responsibilities of the Departments Chief Privacy and Civil Liberties Officer (CPCLO). The principle mission of OPCL is to protect the privacy and civil liberties of the American people by reviewing and overseeing the Departments privacy operations and ensuring its privacy compliance, including compliance with the Privacy Act of 1974 and the E-Government Act of 2002; assisting the CPCLO in developing Departmental privacy policy and refining Department policies relating to the protection of civil liberties of individuals.

○ Chief Privacy and Civil Liberties Officer
Erika Brown-Lee . . . . (202) 307-0697
950 Pennsylvania Avenue, NW, Room 4216, Washington, DC 20530
E-mail: erika.brown.lee@usdoj.gov
Director (Acting) **Kristi Lane Scott** . . . . (202) 514-0208

Office of Public Affairs [OPA]

Robert F. Kennedy Building, 950 Pennsylvania Avenue, NW, Room 1220, Washington, DC 20530
Tel: (202) 514-2007 Fax: (202) 514-5331
Internet: www.justice.gov/opa

The Office of Public Affairs coordinates the relations of the Department of Justice with the news media and serves as the center for information about all organizational units of the Department.

○ Director **Melanie Newman** . . . . (202) 616-2777
E-mail: melanie.newman@usdoj.gov
Education: Florida A&M 2001 BA; American U MA
Deputy Director **Wyn Hornbuckle** . . . . (202) 616-2777
□ Deputy Director **Emily Pierce** . . . . (202) 616-2777
E-mail: emily.pierce@usdoj.gov
□ Press Secretary **Kevin S. Lewis** . . . . (202) 514-2007
E-mail: kevin.s.lewis@usdoj.gov
Public Affairs Specialist **Mark Abueg** . . . . (202) 514-2007
Public Affairs Specialist **Peter Carr** . . . . (202) 514-2007
Public Affairs Specialist **Dena Iverson** . . . . (202) 514-2007
E-mail: dena.w.iverson@usdoj.gov
Education: Oberlin BA
Public Affairs Specialist **Nicole Navas** . . . . (202) 514-2007
Public Affairs Specialist **Marc Raimondi** . . . . (202) 514-2007
Education: UMass (Amherst) BA
Public Affairs Specialist **Patrick Rodenbush** . . . . (202) 514-2007
E-mail: patrick.rodenbush@usdoj.gov
Press Assistant **George Hornedo** . . . . (202) 514-2007
Press Assistant **David Jacobs** . . . . (202) 514-2007
Press Assistant **Kelli James** . . . . (202) 514-2007
Press Assistant **Anthony Juarez** . . . . (202) 514-2007
Press Assistant **Erica Lacy** . . . . (202) 514-2007
Press Assistant **Rebecca Stewart** . . . . (202) 514-2007
□ Chief Speechwriter **Jake Maccoby** . . . . (202) 514-2007
Deputy Speechwriter **Jim Santel** . . . . (202) 514-2007
□ Speechwriter **Sarah Chang** . . . . (202) 514-2007
E-mail: sarah.chang@usdoj.gov
Office Manager **Kelly Creighton** . . . . (202) 514-2007
E-mail: kelly.m.creighton@usdoj.gov
Staff Assistant **Tamara Loper** . . . . (202) 514-2007

US DEPARTMENT OF JUSTICE

★ Presidential Appointment Requiring Senate Confirmation
☆ Presidential Appointment
□ Schedule C Appointment
◇ Career Senior Foreign Service Appointment
● Career Senior Executive Service (SES) Appointment
○ Non-Career Senior Executive Service (SES) Appointment

Office of Tribal Justice [OTJ]

Robert F. Kennedy Building, 950 Pennsylvania Avenue, NW, Room 2200, Washington, DC 20530
Tel: (202) 514-8812 Fax: (202) 514-9078
Internet: www.justice.gov/otj
Internet: www.tribaljusticeandsafety.gov

The Office of Tribal Justice is the primary point of contact for the Department of Justice with federally recognized Native American tribes, and advises the Department on legal and policy matters pertaining to Native Americans.

● Director **Tracy Toulou** .... (202) 514-8812
E-mail: tracy.toulou2@usdoj.gov
Education: New Mexico
Counsel to the Director **Marcia Hurd** .... (202) 514-8812
E-mail: marcia.hurd@usdoj.gov
Executive Assistant **(Vacant)** .... (202) 514-8812
Deputy Director **(Vacant)** .... (202) 514-8812
Policy and Management Analyst **Jeanne Jacobs** .... (202) 514-8812
E-mail: jeanne.jacobs@usdoj.gov

Office of the Associate Attorney General [OASG]

Robert F. Kennedy Building, 950 Pennsylvania Avenue, NW, Room 5706, Washington, DC 20530
Tel: (202) 514-9500 Fax: (202) 514-0238
Internet: www.justice.gov/asg

The Office of the Associate Attorney General advises and assists the Attorney General and the Deputy Attorney General in formulating and implementing Departmental policies and programs pertaining to a broad range of civil justice, federal and local law enforcement, and public safety matters.

★ Associate Attorney General (Acting) [Chief FOIA Officer] **Stuart F. Delery** .... (202) 514-9500
Note: On January 27, 2015 President Obama nominated Stuart Delery to be Associate Attorney General. Mr. Delery is currently acting in this position.
E-mail: stuart.f.delery@usdoj.gov
Education: Virginia 1990 BA; Yale 1993 JD
□ Chief of Staff **James C. Cox** .... (202) 514-9500
E-mail: james.c.cox@usdoj.gov
□ Deputy Chief of Staff and Counsel **Rita Christine Aguilar** .... (202) 514-9500
E-mail: rita.aguilar@usdoj.gov
□ Counsel to the Associate Attorney General **(Vacant)** .... (202) 514-9500
□ Senior Counselor for Access to Justice **Lisa Foster** .... (202) 514-5312
E-mail: lisa.foster2@usdoj.gov
Education: Stanford BA; Harvard JD
Confidential Assistant **Currie Gunn** .... (202) 514-9500
E-mail: currie.gunn@usdoj.gov
○ Principal Deputy Associate Attorney General **Molly Moran** .... (202) 514-9500
E-mail: molly.moran@usdoj.gov
○ Deputy Associate Attorney General **Christopher H. "Chris" Casey** .... (202) 514-9500
E-mail: christopher.casey@usdoj.gov
Education: Col Holy Cross 1983 BA; George Washington 1987 JD
○ Deputy Associate Attorney General **Julie McEvoy** .... (202) 514-9500
E-mail: julie.mcevoy@usdoj.gov
○ Deputy Associate Attorney General **Philippa Scarlett** .... (202) 514-9500
E-mail: philippa.scarlett@usdoj.gov
Deputy Associate Attorney General **Carlos F. Uriarte** .... (202) 514-9500
E-mail: carlos.uriarte@usdoj.gov
Education: Washington U (MO) 2002 BA; Pennsylvania 2005 JD
○ Deputy Associate Attorney General **(Vacant)** .... (202) 514-9500
Staff Assistant **(Vacant)** .... (202) 514-9500

Antitrust Division [ATR]

950 Pennsylvania Avenue, NW, Room 3109, Washington, DC 20530
Tel: (202) 514-2401 Fax: (202) 616-2645
E-mail: antitrust@usdoj.gov
Internet: www.justice.gov/atr

The mission of the Antitrust Division is to promote competition in the U.S. economy through enforcement of, improvements to, and education about antitrust laws and principles.

★ Assistant Attorney General **William Joseph "Bill" Baer** .... (202) 514-2401
Began Service: January 3, 2013
E-mail: bill.baer@usdoj.gov
Education: Lawrence U 1972 BA; Stanford 1975 JD
□ Chief of Staff and Counsel **Juan A. Arteaga** Room 3114 .... (202) 307-2408
E-mail: juan.arteaga@usdoj.gov
Education: Boston Col 1999 BA; Columbia 2002 JD
○ Chief Counsel for Competition Policy and Intergovernmental Relations **Caroline Holland** .... (202) 353-9208
E-mail: caroline.holland@usdoj.gov Fax: (202) 616-2645
Counsel for Legislative and Intergovernmental Affairs **Adrienne M. Hahn** Room 3123 .... (202) 532-4761
E-mail: adrienne.hahn@usdoj.gov Fax: (202) 514-0306
Education: Boston Col JD
Counsel **Ryan J. Danks** Room 3217 .... (202) 514-0128
E-mail: ryan.danks@usdoj.gov
Education: DePauw 1999 BA; Michigan 2002 JD
□ Counsel **Anant Raut** Room 3118 .... (202) 532-6766
E-mail: anant.raut@usdoj.gov Fax: (202) 514-0306
Counsel **(Vacant)** .... (202) 307-1281
Special Counsel for State Relations and Agriculture **Mark B. Tobey** .... (202) 532-4763
450 Fifth Street, NW, Room 11038, Washington, DC 20530 Fax: (202) 514-9082
E-mail: mark.tobey@usdoj.gov
Counsel **(Vacant)** .... (202) 305-8376
● Appellate Section Chief **Kristen C. Limarzi** Room 3222 .... (202) 514-2413
E-mail: kristen.limarzi@usdoj.gov
Education: Georgetown 2002 JD
● Legal Policy Section Chief **Robert A. Potter** .... (202) 514-2512
Liberty Square Building, 450 5th Street, N.W., Room 11700, Washington, DC 20530 Fax: (202) 514-9082
● Legal Policy Section Assistant Chief **Frances E. Marshall, Jr.** .... (202) 307-2130
E-mail: frances.marshall@usdoj.gov
Education: St Joseph's U 1973 BS; Widener 1978 JD
● Legal Policy Section Assistant Chief **Ann M. O'Brien** .... (202) 514-6213
E-mail: ann.obrien@usdoj.gov
□ Confidential Assistant **(Vacant)** .... (202) 514-2401

Executive Office

● Executive Officer (Acting) **Scott J. Cohen** .... (202) 514-7305
Liberty Square Building, 450 Fifth Street, NW, Room 3026, Washington, DC 20530
E-mail: scott.cohen2@usdoj.gov
Deputy Executive Officer **Scott J. Cohen** .... (202) 514-7305
450 Fifth Street, NW, Washington, DC 20530
E-mail: scott.cohen2@usdoj.gov
Deputy Executive Officer **Mark R. Gavin** .... (202) 514-0799
450 Fifth Street, NW, Washington, DC 20530
E-mail: mark.gavin@usdoj.gov
Chief Information Officer **Linda T. Carter** .... (202) 307-3546
E-mail: linda.carter@usdoj.gov
Public Affairs Officer [Chief FOIA Officer] **Sue Ann Slates** .... (202) 514-2692
Fax: (202) 616-4529
Librarian **Bridget Gilhool** .... (202) 514-5870
E-mail: bridget.gilhool@usdoj.gov Fax: (202) 514-9099

Civil Enforcement

○ Deputy Assistant Attorney General for Civil and Criminal Operations **Renata B. Hesse** .... (202) 353-1535
E-mail: renata.hesse@usdoj.gov Fax: (202) 514-6543
Education: Wellesley 1986 BA; Boalt Hall 1990 JD

★ Presidential Appointment Requiring Senate Confirmation
☆ Presidential Appointment
□ Schedule C Appointment
◇ Career Senior Foreign Service Appointment
● Career Senior Executive Service (SES) Appointment
○ Non-Career Senior Executive Service (SES) Appointment

Civil Enforcement *continued*

○ Deputy Assistant Attorney General for Enforcement
Sonia Kuester Pfaffenroth . . . . (202) 307-1342
E-mail: sonia.pfaffenroth@usdoj.gov Fax: (202) 616-2645
Education: Stanford 2002 JD

○ Deputy Assistant Attorney General for Litigation
David I. Gelfand Room 3210 . . . . (202) 514-0731
E-mail: david.gelfand@usdoj.gov Fax: (202) 514-6543
Education: Pennsylvania 1981 BS; Georgetown 1987 JD

Director of Civil Enforcement **Patricia A. Brink** . . . . (202) 514-2562
Counsel to the Director **Anne McFadden** Room 3334 . . . (202) 514-8671
E-mail: anne.mcfadden@usdoj.gov Fax: (202) 353-8435

● Director of Litigation **Eric Mahr** . . . . (202) 532-4753
Liberty Square Building, 450 Fifth Street, NW, Washington, DC 20530
E-mail: eric.mahr@usdoj.gov
Education: Bucknell 1987 BA; Pittsburgh 1990 JD

Litigation I Section
Fax: (202) 307-5802

● Chief **Peter J. Mucchetti** . . . . (202) 307-0001
Liberty Square Building, 450 Fifth Street, NW, Room 4700, Washington, DC 20530 Fax: (202) 514-5802
E-mail: peter.j.mucchetti@usdoj.gov

Litigation II Section
Fax: (202) 514-9033

● Chief **Maribeth Petrizzi** . . . . (202) 307-0924
Liberty Square Building, 450 Fifth Street, NW, Room 8700, Washington, DC 20530
E-mail: maribeth.petrizzi@usdoj.gov

Litigation III Section
Fax: (202) 514-7308

● Chief **David C. Kully** . . . . (202) 307-0468
Liberty Square Building, 450 Fifth Street, NW, Room 4000, Washington, DC 20530
E-mail: david.kully@usdoj.gov

Criminal Enforcement
Fax: (202) 307-9978

● Deputy Assistant Attorney General for Criminal Enforcement **Brent C. Snyder** Room 3216 . . . . . . (202) 514-3543
E-mail: brent.snyder@usdoj.gov
Education: Texas 1992 JD

● Director of Criminal Enforcement **Marvin N. Price, Jr.** . . . (202) 307-0719
E-mail: marvin.price@usdoj.gov
Counsel **Matthew W. Lunder** . . . . (202) 514-6373
E-mail: matthew.lunder@usdoj.gov
Education: Montana 2006 JD

Washington Criminal Section I
Fax: (202) 598-2428

● Chief **Lisa M. Phelan** . . . . (202) 307-6694
Liberty Square Building, 450 Fifth Street, NW, Room 11400, Washington, DC 20530
E-mail: lisa.phelan@usdoj.gov
Education: American U 1983 BA; Washington College of Law 1986 JD
Assistant Chief **Mark Grundvig** . . . . (202) 305-1878
E-mail: mark.grundvig@usdoj.gov
Assistant Chief **Craig Y. Lee** . . . . (202) 307-1044
E-mail: craig.lee@usdoj.gov
Education: Northwestern 1997 BA, 2002 JD

Washington Criminal Section II
Fax: (202) 598-2428

● Chief **Mary N. Strimel** . . . . (202) 616-5949
450 Fifth Street, NW, Washington, DC 20530
E-mail: mary.strimel@usdoj.gov
Assistant Chief **Eric M. Meiring** . . . . (202) 598-2322
450 Fifth Street, NW, Washington, DC 20530
E-mail: eric.meiring@usdoj.gov

General Counsel

● General Counsel to the Assistant Attorney General
J. Robert Kramer II Room 3220 . . . . (202) 514-3543
E-mail: robert.kramer@usdoj.gov
Deputy General Counsel - Criminal
Belinda A. Barnett Room 3311 . . . . (202) 514-3543
E-mail: belinda.barnett@usdoj.gov
Deputy General Counsel - Civil **(Vacant)** Room 3309 . . . . (202) 305-1210
Ethics Officer **Anne Purcell White** . . . . (202) 514-4773
Fax: (202) 307-9978

Economic Analysis
Fax: (202) 514-6543

Deputy Assistant Attorney General for Economic Analysis **Dr. Nancy Lin Rose** . . . . (202) 353-0163
E-mail: nancy.rose@usdoj.gov Fax: (202) 514-0306
Education: Harvard 1980 AB; MIT 1985 PhD

● Economic Director of Enforcement **W. Robert Majure**
Room 3209 . . . . (202) 514-6994
E-mail: robert.majure@usdoj.gov

Competition Policy Section
Fax: (202) 514-8862

Chief **Ronald Drennan** . . . . (202) 307-6603
450 Fifth Street, NW, Room 9400, Washington, DC 20530

Economic Litigation Section
Fax: (202) 307-3372

● Chief **Norman Familant** . . . . (202) 307-6323
450 Fifth Street, NW, Room 9912, Washington, DC 20530
E-mail: norman.familant@usdoj.gov

Economic Regulatory Section
Fax: (202) 514-5847

Chief **Elizabeth Armington** . . . . (202) 307-6332
450 Fifth Street, NW, Room 3700, Washington, DC 20530

Foreign Commerce
Fax: (202) 514-6543

● Section Chief **Edward T. Hand** . . . . (202) 514-2464
Liberty Square Building, 450 5th Street, N.W., Room 11000, Washington, DC 20530 Fax: (202) 514-4508
E-mail: edward.hand@usdoj.gov
Assistant Section Chief **Lynda K. Marshall** . . . . . . (202) 598-2264
450 5th Street, N.W., Washington, DC 20530 Fax: (202) 514-4508
E-mail: lynda.marshall@usdoj.gov

Regulatory Matters
Tel: (202) 514-3543 Fax: (202) 616-7320

● Networks and Technology Section Chief
James J. Tierney . . . . (202) 307-6640
Liberty Square Building, 450 Fifth Street, NW, Room 7700, Washington, DC 20530 Fax: (202) 616-8544
E-mail: james.tierney@usdoj.gov

● Telecommunications and Media Enforcement Section Chief **Scott A. Scheele** . . . . (202) 616-5924
Liberty Square Building, 450 Fifth Street, NW, Room 7000, Washington, DC 20530 Fax: (202) 514-6381
E-mail: scott.scheele@usdoj.gov

● Transportation, Energy and Agriculture Section Chief
Kathleen O'Neill . . . . (202) 307-9323
Liberty Square Building, 450 Fifth Street, NW, Room 8000, Washington, DC 20530 Fax: (202) 307-2784
E-mail: kathleen.oneill@usdoj.gov
Education: NYU 2006 JD

US DEPARTMENT OF JUSTICE

★ Presidential Appointment Requiring Senate Confirmation ☆ Presidential Appointment ☐ Schedule C Appointment ◇ Career Senior Foreign Service Appointment ● Career Senior Executive Service (SES) Appointment ○ Non-Career Senior Executive Service (SES) Appointment

Civil Division [CIV]

Robert F. Kennedy Building, 950 Pennsylvania Avenue, NW,
Washington, DC 20530
Tel: (202) 514-3301 Fax: (202) 514-8071
Internet: www.justice.gov/civil

The Civil Division represents the United States in any civil or criminal matter within its scope of responsibility – protecting the United States Treasury, ensuring that the federal government speaks with one voice in its view of the law, preserving the intent of Congress, and advancing the credibility of the government before the courts.

★ Assistant Attorney General (Acting)
Benjamin C. "Ben" Mizer . . . . (202) 514-3301
E-mail: benjamin.mizer@usdoj.gov
Education: Wooster 1999 JD

☐ Chief of Staff **Nitin Shah** . . . . (202) 514-2793
E-mail: nitin.shah@usdoj.gov
Education: Virginia 2009 JD

☐ Senior Counsel **Natalia Sorgente** . . . . (202) 307-5906
E-mail: natalia.sorgente@usdoj.gov
Education: Harvard 1992; NYU 1996 JD

○ Counselor to the Assistant Attorney General **(Vacant)** . . . . (202) 514-4826

● Principal Deputy Assistant Attorney General
Benjamin C. "Ben" Mizer . . . . (202) 514-3301
E-mail: benjamin.mizer@usdoj.gov
Education: Wooster 1999 JD

☐ Counsel **(Vacant)** . . . . (202) 514-0115
☐ Counsel **(Vacant)** . . . . (202) 616-9928
☐ Counsel **(Vacant)** . . . . (202) 305-0588
Special Counselor **(Vacant)** . . . . (202) 353-5906
Attorney Advisor **(Vacant)** . . . . (202) 514-5739
Director of E-Discovery, FOIA, and Records
Allison Stanton . . . . (202) 514-3301
E-mail: allison.stanton@usdoj.gov
Education: Cornell 1998 BS; Washington College of Law 2001 JD

Appellate Staff

Robert F. Kennedy Building, 950 Pennsylvania Avenue, NW,
Washington, DC 20530
Tel: (202) 514-9367 Fax: (202) 514-8151

The Appellate Staff represents the United States, its agencies, and officers in civil cases in the federal courts of appeals. Established in 1953, the Appellate Staff handles appeals involving all of the subject-matter areas litigated by the Civil Division, including appeals arising out of civil cases handled by the United States Attorneys nationwide. Appellate Staff attorneys practice in all thirteen of the federal courts of appeals, as well as in the United States Supreme Court. The Appellate Staff's portfolio includes many of the most difficult and controversial cases in which the Federal Government is involved.

○ Deputy Assistant Attorney General
Beth S. Brinkmann Room 3133 . . . . (202) 514-9367
E-mail: beth.brinkmann@usdoj.gov Fax: (202) 514-8071
Education: UC Berkeley 1980 AB; Yale 1985 JD

● Appellate Staff Director **Douglas N. Letter** Room 7519 . . . (202) 514-3602
E-mail: douglas.letter@usdoj.gov

● Appellate Litigation Counsel **Michael Raab** . . . . (202) 514-4053
E-mail: michael.raab@usdoj.gov

● Appellate Litigation Counsel **Mark Stern** Room 7531 . . . (202) 514-5089
E-mail: mark.stern@usdoj.gov

Commercial Litigation Branch

1100 L Street, NW, Washington, DC 20530
Fax: (202) 514-7968

The Commercial Litigation Branch both brings claims on behalf of the United States and defends claims brought against the United States. The claims can involve billions of dollars in money damages. The Branchs work falls into six major practice areas, each of which is overseen by a Section: the Corporate and Financial Litigation Section, the Office of Foreign Litigation, the Fraud Section; the Intellectual Property Section, and the National Courts Section.

Commercial Litigation Branch *continued*

● Deputy Assistant Attorney General **Joyce R. Branda** . . . . (202) 514-3306
Robert F. Kennedy Building, Fax: (202) 514-8071
950 Pennsylvania Avenue, NW, Room 3607,
Washington, DC 20530
E-mail: joyce.branda@usdoj.gov

● Fraud Section Director **Michael Granston** . . . . (202) 305-0632
Patrick Henry Building, 601 D Street, NW, Fax: (202) 514-7361
Room 9002, Washington, DC 20530
E-mail: michael.granston@usdoj.gov

● Intellectual Property Section Director **John J. Fargo**
Room 11116 . . . . (202) 514-7223
E-mail: john.fargo@usdoj.gov
Education: SUNY (Buffalo) 1972 BSIE, 1976 JD

● National Courts Section Director **Robert Kirschman**
Room 12124 . . . . (202) 616-0328
E-mail: robert.kirschman@usdoj.gov

● Office of Foreign Litigation Director
Jeanne E. Davidson . . . . (202) 616-8277
E-mail: jeanne.davidson@usdoj.gov
Education: UC Berkeley 1976 AB; NYU 1980 JD

● Special Litigation Counsel **John Stemplewicz**
Room 10136 . . . . (202) 307-1104
E-mail: john.stemplewicz@usdoj.gov

Consumer Protection Branch

National Place Building, 1331 Pennsylvania Avenue, NW,
Washington, DC 20530
Fax: (202) 616-5200

The Consumer Protection Branch (CPB) was established in 1971 in response to considerable Legislative and Executive Branch interest in consumer protection. CPB enforces and defends the consumer protection programs of four client agencies: the Food and Drug Administration (FDA), the Federal Trade Commission (FTC), the Consumer Product Safety Commission, and the Department of Transportation's National Highway Traffic Safety Administration. By regulation, CPB is responsible for litigation under the principal Federal consumer protection laws these agencies enforce.

○ Deputy Assistant Attorney General
Jonathan F. "Jon" Olin . . . . (202) 616-4171
Robert F. Kennedy Building, Fax: (202) 514-8071
950 Pennsylvania Avenue, NW, Room 3611,
Washington, DC 20530
E-mail: jonathan.f.olin@usdoj.gov
Education: Brown U 1999 BA

● Director **Michael S. Blume** . . . . (202) 307-0066
450 Fifth Street, NW, Room 6254, Washington, DC 20530
E-mail: michael.s.blume@usdoj.gov

Deputy Director **Jill Furman** . . . . (202) 307-0090
450 Fifth Street, NW, Room 6000, Washington, DC 20530
E-mail: jill.furman@usdoj.gov

Federal Programs Branch

145 First Street, NE, Washington, DC 20002
Fax: (202) 616-8470

Federal Programs Branch attorneys litigate on behalf of approximately 100 federal agencies, the President, Cabinet officers, and other government officials. They defend against constitutional challenges to federal statutes, suits to overturn government policies and programs, and attacks on the legality of government decisions. The Federal Programs Branch also initiates litigation to enforce regulatory statutes and to remedy statutory and regulatory violations.

○ Deputy Assistant Attorney General
Kathleen R. Hartnett . . . . (202) 514-2331
Robert F. Kennedy Building, Fax: (202) 514-8071
950 Pennsylvania Avenue, NW, Room 3137,
Washington, DC 20530
E-mail: kathleen.r.hartnett@usdoj.gov

● Federal Programs Director **John Griffiths** . . . . (202) 514-4652
20 Massachusetts Avenue, NW, Room 7100, Washington, DC 20530
E-mail: john.griffiths@usdoj.gov

★ Presidential Appointment Requiring Senate Confirmation
☆ Presidential Appointment
☐ Schedule C Appointment
◇ Career Senior Foreign Service Appointment
● Career Senior Executive Service (SES) Appointment
○ Non-Career Senior Executive Service (SES) Appointment

Federal Programs Branch *continued*

- Federal Programs Director **Joseph H. Hunt** . . . . (202) 514-1259
  20 Massachusetts Avenue, NW, Room 7348, Washington, DC 20530
- Federal Programs Director **Jennifer Ricketts** . . . . (202) 514-3671
  20 Massachusetts Avenue, NW, Room 6100, Washington, DC 20530
  E-mail: jennifer.rivera@usdoj.gov
- Special Litigation Counsel **James Gilligan** . . . . (202) 514-3358
  20 Massachusetts Avenue, NW, Room 6102, Washington, DC 20530
  E-mail: james.gilligan@usdoj.gov

Torts Branch
Fax: (202) 616-5200

The Torts Branch represents the United States, including its officers and agents, in suits for monetary damages alleging negligent or wrongful acts and under statutory compensation programs. In addition, Torts Branch attorneys handle claims related to injury and damage to Government property. Four sections handle the Torts Branchs major practice areas: the Aviation and Admiralty Section; the Environmental Tort Litigation Section; the Federal Tort Claims Act Litigation Section; and the Constitutional and Specialized Torts Litigation Section.

○ Deputy Assistant Attorney General **Kali Nneka Bracey** . . . (202) 353-9328
  Robert F. Kennedy Building,
  Tenth Street and Constitution Avenue, NW, Room 3131,
  Washington, DC 20530
  E-mail: kali.n.bracey@usdoj.gov
  Deputy Director **Vincent Matanoski** . . . . (202) 616-4134
  1425 New York Avenue, NW, Room 3114, Fax: (202) 616-4002
  Washington, DC 20005
  E-mail: vincent.matanoski@usdoj.gov
- Aviation and Admiralty Section Director **Peter Frost** . . . . . (202) 616-4000
  1425 New York Avenue, NW, Room 10122, Fax: (202) 616-4002
  Washington, DC 20005
  E-mail: peter.frost@usdoj.gov
  Education: USC 1976 AB; Hastings 1983 JD
- Constitutional and Specialized Tort Litigation Section
  Director **Rupa Bhattacharyya** . . . . (202) 616-0008
  1425 New York Avenue, NW, Room 8122, Washington, DC 20005
  E-mail: rupa.bhattacharyya@usdoj.gov
- Environmental Tort Litigation Section Director
  J. Patrick Glynn . . . . (202) 616-4200
  National Place Building, 1331 Pennsylvania Avenue, NW,
  Room 8028S, Washington, DC 20530
  E-mail: j.patrick.glynn@usdoj.gov
  Education: Saint Louis U 1967 BA; Indiana 1970 JD
- Federal Tort Claims Act Litigation Section Director
  James Touhey, Jr. . . . . (202) 616-4292
  National Place Building, 1331 Pennsylvania Avenue, NW,
  Room 8064N, Washington, DC 20530
  E-mail: james.touhey@usdoj.gov
- Special Litigation Counsel **Barbara B. O'Malley** . . . . (202) 616-4081
  1425 New York Avenue, NW, Room 8026, Fax: (202) 616-4002
  Washington, DC 20005
  E-mail: barbara.o'malley@usdoj.gov

Office of Immigration Litigation
450 Fifth Street, NW, Room 7426, Washington, DC 20530
Tel: (202) 616-4900 (Appellate) Tel: (202) 598-2964 (DCS)
Fax: (202) 616-5200

The Office of Immigration Litigation oversees all civil immigration litigation, both affirmative and defensive, and it is responsible for coordinating national immigration matters before the federal district courts and circuit courts of appeals. It provides support and counsel to all federal agencies involved in alien admission, regulation, and removal under U.S. immigration and nationality statutes. Office of Immigration Litigation attorneys work closely with United States Attorneys' Offices on immigration cases. The Office of Immigration Litigation is divided into two functional sections, an Appellate Section and a District Court Section.

○ Deputy Assistant Attorney General **Leon Fresco** . . . . (202) 307-6482
  Robert F. Kennedy Building, 950 Pennsylvania Avenue, NW,
  Room 3129, Washington, DC 20530
  E-mail: leon.fresco@usdoj.gov
  Education: Yale 2003 JD

Office of Immigration Litigation *continued*

Deputy Director **Donald E. Keener** . . . . (202) 616-4878
  E-mail: donald.keener@usdoj.gov
Deputy Director **Michelle Latour** . . . . (202) 616-4881
  E-mail: michelle.latour@usdoj.gov
- Office of Immigration/District Court Director
  William Peachey Room 2200 . . . . (202) 307-0871
  E-mail: william.peachey@usdoj.gov
- Immigration Litigation Director (Acting) **Colin Kisor** . . . . (202) 532-4331
  E-mail: colin.kisor@usdoj.gov
- Immigration Litigation Director **David McConnell** . . . . . . (202) 616-4852
  E-mail: david.mcconnell@usdoj.gov

Office of Management Programs
1100 L Street, NW, Washington, DC 20530
Fax: (202) 514-7968

- Director **Kenneth L. Zwick** . . . . (202) 514-4552
  Robert F. Kennedy Building, Fax: (202) 514-8071
  Tenth Street and Constitution Avenue, NW,
  Room 3140, Washington, DC 20530
  E-mail: ken.zwick@usdoj.gov
  Education: MIT 1969 BS; Temple 1976 JD
  Human Resources Chief **Donna Cornett** Room 9008 . . . . . (202) 616-7914
  E-mail: donna.cornett@usdoj.gov
  Budget and Planning Office Head (Acting)
  Frankie Free Room 9042 . . . . (202) 307-0842
  E-mail: frankie.free@usdoj.gov
  Litigation Support Office Head **Joshua Wood**
  Room 9126 . . . . (202) 616-5014
  E-mail: joshua.wood@usdoj.gov
  Management Information Office Head
  Parmod Monga Room 8044 . . . . (202) 514-8030
  E-mail: parmod.monga@usdoj.gov
  Management Operations Office Head
  Douglas McManus Room 8128 . . . . (202) 616-8073
  E-mail: doug.mcmanus@usdoj.gov

Civil Rights Division [CRD]
Robert F. Kennedy Building, 950 Pennsylvania Avenue, NW,
Washington, DC 20530
Tel: (202) 514-2151 Fax: (202) 514-0293
Fax: (202) 307-2572 Fax: (202) 307-2839
Internet: www.justice.gov/crt

The Civil Rights Division enforces the Civil Rights Acts; the Voting Rights Act; the Equal Credit Opportunity Act; the Americans with Disabilities Act; the National Voter Registration Act; the Uniformed and Overseas Citizens Absentee Voting Act; the Voting Accessibility for the Elderly and Handicapped Act; and additional civil rights provisions contained in other laws and regulations. These laws prohibit discrimination in education, employment, credit, housing, public accommodations and facilities, voting, and certain federally funded and conducted programs.

★ Assistant Attorney General (Acting) **Vanita Gupta** . . . . . . (202) 514-2151
  E-mail: vanita.gupta@usdoj.gov
  Education: Yale BA; NYU JD
  □ Special Assistant **Makeba Rutahindurwa**
  Room 5642 . . . . (202) 353-3426
  E-mail: makeba.rutahindurwa@usdoj.gov
  Staff Assistant **(Vacant)** Room 5643 . . . . (202) 514-2151
○ Principal Deputy Assistant Attorney General
  Vanita Gupta . . . . (202) 307-6639
  E-mail: vanita.gupta@usdoj.gov
  Education: Yale BA; NYU JD
- Deputy Assistant Attorney General **Gregory B. Friel**
  Room 5744 . . . . (202) 307-0063
  E-mail: gregory.b.friel@usdoj.gov
○ Deputy Assistant Attorney General **Eve L. Hill**
  Room 5637 . . . . (202) 514-9390
  E-mail: eve.hill@usdoj.gov
  Education: Sweet Briar BA; Cornell JD
○ Deputy Assistant Attorney General **Robert Moossy**
  Room 5531 . . . . (202) 514-3845
  E-mail: robert.moossy@usdoj.gov
  Education: Houston 1994 JD

(continued on next page)

★ Presidential Appointment Requiring Senate Confirmation ☆ Presidential Appointment □ Schedule C Appointment ◇ Career Senior Foreign Service Appointment ● Career Senior Executive Service (SES) Appointment ○ Non-Career Senior Executive Service (SES) Appointment

Civil Rights Division *continued*

○ Deputy Assistant Attorney General for Voting Rights
Justin Levitt .... (202) 514-2151
E-mail: justin.levitt@usdoj.gov
Education: Harvard 2002 JD

□ Chief of Staff (Acting) **Kathy Toomey** Room 5746 .... (202) 307-2502
E-mail: kathleen.toomey@usdoj.gov

□ Senior Counsel to the Assistant Attorney General
Chiraag Bains Room 5742A .... (202) 305-1876
E-mail: chiraag.bains@usdoj.gov
Education: Yale 2003 BA; Harvard 2008 JD

□ Senior Counselor to the Assistant Attorney General
James Cadogan Room 5535 .... (202) 305-0864
E-mail: james.cadogan@usdoj.gov

Special Counsel for Fair Lending **(Vacant)** Room 5529 ... (202) 307-3033

FOIA and Public Affairs Branch Chief
Nelson Hermilla Room 3234 .... (202) 514-4209

Office of Special Counsel for Immigration-Related Unfair Employment Practices
1425 New York Avenue, NW, Washington, DC 20005
Tel: (202) 616-5594 Fax: (202) 616-5509
Internet: www.justice.gov/crt/osc

★ Special Counsel **(Vacant)** Room 9032.................. (202) 616-5528

● Deputy Special Counsel **Alberto J. Ruisánchez**
Room 9030 .... (202) 305-1291
E-mail: alberto.ruisanchez@usdoj.gov
Education: Georgetown 1996 BA; Harvard 2001 JD

Special Policy Counsel **Jennifer Sultan** Room 9022...... (202) 305-4154
E-mail: jennifer.sultan@usdoj.gov

Special Litigation Counsel **Sebastian Aloot**
Room 9048 .... (202) 305-9349
E-mail: sebastian.aloot@usdoj.gov

Special Litigation Counsel **(Vacant)**.................. (202) 616-5594

Office of Complaint Adjudication
Robert F. Kennedy Building, 950 Pennsylvania Avenue, NW, Washington, DC 20530
Tel: (202) 514-0545 Fax: (202) 514-0655

Complaint Adjudication Officer **Mark L. Gross**
Room 3712 .... (202) 514-2172
E-mail: mark.l.gross@usdoj.gov
Education: Rutgers (Newark) 1970 BS; Georgetown 1973 JD

Administrative Management Section
600 E Street NW, Washington, DC 20004
Tel: (202) 514-4224

● Executive Officer (Acting) **Gary Wong** Room 3222 ...... (202) 514-4224
E-mail: gary.wong@usdoj.gov

● Deputy Executive Officer **Gary Wong** Room 3218 .... (202) 514-4224
E-mail: gary.wong@usdoj.gov

Appellate Section
Tel: (202) 514-2195
Internet: www.justice.gov/crt/app

● Chief **Diana K. Flynn** .... (202) 514-2195
Robert F. Kennedy Building,
Tenth Street and Constitution Avenue, NW, Room 3704,
Washington, DC 20530
E-mail: diana.k.flynn@usdoj.gov
Education: Rochester 1976 BA; Yale 1979 JD

Criminal Section
Tel: (202) 514-3204

● Chief **Robert Moossy** .... (202) 305-2445
Patrick Henry Building, 601 D Street, NW, Room 5102,
Washington, DC 20530
E-mail: robert.moossy@usdoj.gov
Education: Houston 1994 JD

Disability Rights Section
Tel: (202) 307-0663

● Chief **Rebecca B. Bond** .... (202) 307-2584
1425 New York Avenue, NW, Room 4014, Washington, DC 20005
E-mail: rebecca.bond@usdoj.gov
Education: Yale 1993 BA; Harvard 1997 JD

Educational Opportunities Section
Tel: (202) 514-4092

● Chief **Anurima Bhargava** .... (202) 514-8399
Patrick Henry Building, 601 D Street, NW, Room 4002,
Washington, DC 20530
E-mail: anurima.bhargava@usdoj.gov
Education: Columbia 2000 JD

Employment Litigation Section
Tel: (202) 514-3831 Fax: (202) 514-1005

● Chief **Delora L. Kennebrew** .... (202) 514-3831
Patrick Henry Building, 601 D Street, NW, Room 4040,
Washington, DC 20530
E-mail: delora.kennebrew@usdoj.gov
Education: Vanderbilt 1980 BS; Mercer 1984 JD

Federal Coordination and Compliance Section
Tel: (202) 307-2222 Fax: (202) 307-0595
Internet: www.justice.gov/crt/cor

● Chief **Deeana Laurie Jang** .... (202) 307-2222
1800 G. Street NW, Room 824, Washington, DC 20005
E-mail: deeana.jang@usdoj.gov
Education: Oberlin 1979 BA; UC Davis 1983 JD

Housing and Civil Enforcement Section
Tel: (202) 514-4713

● Chief **Steven H. Rosenbaum** .... (202) 514-4713
1800 G Street, NW, Room 7036, Washington, DC 20530
E-mail: steven.rosenbaum@usdoj.gov
Education: SUNY (Binghamton) 1974 BA; Michigan 1978 JD

Policy and Strategy Section
Tel: (202) 305-4151

Chief **Aaron Schuham** .... (202) 305-4151
Patrick Henry Building, 601 D Street, NW, Room 5006,
Washington, DC 20530
E-mail: aaron.schuham@usdoj.gov

Special Litigation Section
Tel: (202) 514-6255

● Chief (Acting) **Judith "Judy" Preston** .... (202) 514-5393
601 D Street, NW, Room 5034, Washington, DC 20530
E-mail: judy.preston@usdoj.gov

Voting Section
Tel: (202) 307-2767 Fax: (202) 307-3961 (Litigation)
Fax: (202) 307-2569 (Section 5)

● Chief **Christian "Chris" Herren** .... (202) 514-1416
1800 G Street, NW, Room 7254, Washington, DC 20530
E-mail: chris.herren@usdoj.gov

Environment and Natural Resources Division [ENRD]

Robert F. Kennedy Building, 950 Pennsylvania Avenue, NW, Washington, DC 20530
Tel: (202) 514-2701 Fax: (202) 514-0557
E-mail: webcontentmgr.enrd@usdoj.gov
Internet: www.justice.gov/enrd

The mission of the Environment and Natural Resources Division is, through litigation in the federal and state courts, to safeguard and enhance the American environment; acquire and manage public lands and natural resources; and protect and manage Indian rights and property.

★ Presidential Appointment Requiring Senate Confirmation □ Schedule C Appointment ● Career Senior Executive Service (SES) Appointment
☆ Presidential Appointment ◇ Career Senior Foreign Service Appointment ○ Non-Career Senior Executive Service (SES) Appointment

Environment and Natural Resources Division *continued*

★ Assistant Attorney General **John Charles Cruden** . . . . (202) 514-2701
Began Service: January 2015
E-mail: john.cruden@usdoj.gov
Education: West Point 1968 BS; Santa Clara U 1974 JD; Virginia 1975 MA

□ Chief of Staff **Varu Chilakamarri** . . . . (202) 514-0943
Education: Ohio State 2001 BA; Georgetown 2004 JD

General Counsel and Attorney Educational Coordinatior **Patricia McKenna** . . . . (202) 514-4760
E-mail: patricia.mckenna@usdoj.gov
Education: Siena Col BA; William & Mary 1995 JD

Counselor to the Assistant Attorney General for State and Local Matters **Andrea L. Berlowe** . . . . (202) 514-2701
E-mail: andrea.berlowe@usdoj.gov
Education: Vermont BS; Vermont Law MEL, JD

□ Special Assistant **Paulo Palugod** Room 2127 . . . . (202) 616-3088
E-mail: paulo.palugod@usdoj.gov
Education: Bucknell BA; Washington College of Law 2010 JD

Office of the Principal Deputy Assistant Attorney General

○ Principal Deputy Assistant Attorney General **Samuel Hirsch** Room 2603 . . . . (202) 514-3370
E-mail: sam.hirsch@usdoj.gov
Education: Rice BA; Harvard JD

Executive Office

● Executive Officer **Andrew Collier** . . . . (202) 616-3147
Patrick Henry Building, 601 D Street, NW, Room 2038, Washington, DC 20004
E-mail: andrew.collier@usdoj.gov

● Deputy Executive Officer **(Vacant)** . . . . (202) 616-3147
601 D Street, NW, Washington, DC 20004

Natural Resources Section

● Chief **Lisa L. Russell** . . . . (202) 305-0438
Patrick Henry Building, 601 D Street, NW, Room 3102, Washington, DC 20004
E-mail: lisa.russell@usdoj.gov

Office of the Deputy Assistant Attorney General

○ Deputy Assistant Attorney General **Lisa E. Jones** Room 2607 . . . . (202) 514-0624
E-mail: lisa.e.jones@usdoj.gov
Education: Vanderbilt BS; Virginia JD

Appellate Section

● Chief **James C. "Jim" Kilbourne** Room 2339 . . . . (202) 305-0438
E-mail: jim.kilbourne@usdoj.gov
Education: Montana 1974 BA, 1977 JD

Indian Resources Section

● Chief **S. Craig Alexander** . . . . (202) 514-9080
Patrick Henry Building, 601 D Street, NW, Room 3106, Washington, DC 20004
E-mail: craig.alexander@usdoj.gov
Education: Wisconsin 1987 BS; Duke 1991 JD

Office of the Deputy Assistant Attorney General

● Deputy Assistant Attorney General **Bruce Gelber** Room 2611 . . . . (202) 514-2718
E-mail: bruce.gelber@usdoj.gov
Education: Cornell 1972 BA; Harvard 1975 JD

Environmental Enforcement Section

● Chief **W. Benjamin Fisherow** . . . . (202) 514-4624
601 D Street, NW, Room 6002, Washington, DC 20004
E-mail: benjamin.fisherow@usdoj.gov

Land Acquisition Section

● Chief **Andrew Goldfrank** . . . . (202) 305-0314
Patrick Henry Building, 601 D Street, NW, Room 3638, Washington, DC 20004
E-mail: andrew.goldfrank@usdoj.gov

Office of the Deputy Assistant Attorney General

○ Deputy Assistant Attorney General **Jean Williams** Room 2137 . . . . (202) 514-0943
E-mail: jean.williams@usdoj.gov
Education: Goucher 1975 BA; Tulane 1979 JD

Environmental Defense Section

● Chief **Letitia J. Grishaw** . . . . (202) 514-2219
Patrick Henry Building, 601 D Street, NW, Room 8002, Washington, DC 20004
E-mail: letitia.grishaw@usdoj.gov
Education: Michigan 1976 BA; Wisconsin 1980 JD

Law and Policy Section

● Chief **Karen Wardzinski** Room 2613 . . . . (202) 514-2586
E-mail: karen.wardzinski@usdoj.gov

Office of the Deputy Assistant Attorney General

○ Deputy Assistant Attorney General **(Vacant)** . . . . (202) 305-0438

Environmental Crimes Section

● Chief **Deborah L. Harris** . . . . (202) 305-0337
Patrick Henry Building, 601 D Street, NW, Room 2102, Washington, DC 20004
E-mail: deborah.harris@usdoj.gov

Wildlife and Marine Resources Section

● Chief **Seth M. Barsky** . . . . (202) 305-0210
Patrick Henry Building, 601 D Street, NW, Room 3902, Washington, DC 20004
E-mail: seth.barsky@usdoj.gov

Tax Division [TAX]

Robert F. Kennedy Building, 950 Pennsylvania Avenue, NW, Washington, DC 20530
Tel: (202) 514-2901 Fax: (202) 514-5479
Internet: www.justice.gov/tax

The Tax Division's mission is to enforce the nation's tax laws fully, fairly, and consistently, through both criminal and civil litigation, in order to promote voluntary compliance with the tax laws, maintain public confidence in the integrity of the tax system, and promote the sound development of the law.

★ Assistant Attorney General (Acting) **Caroline D. Ciraolo** . . . . (202) 514-2901
E-mail: caroline.d.ciraolo@usdoj.gov Fax: (202) 514-9500

★ Assistant Attorney General-Designate **Cono R. Namorato** . . . . (202) 514-2901
E-mail: crn@capdale.com Fax: (202) 514-9500

□ Confidential Assistant **(Vacant)** . . . . (202) 514-4401

Counsel to the Assistant Attorney General **Norah E. Bringer** Room 4142 . . . . (202) 307-6224
E-mail: norah.e.bringer@usdoj.gov
Education: Harvard 2008 JD

Principal Deputy Assistant Attorney General **Caroline D. Ciraolo** Room 4137 . . . . (202) 514-2901
E-mail: caroline.d.ciraolo@usdoj.gov

□ Special Counsel **(Vacant)** Room 4616 . . . . (202) 353-8900

● Executive Officer **Robert L. Bruffy** . . . . (202) 616-0010
Patrick Henry Building, 601 D Street, NW, Room 10002, Washington, DC 20530
E-mail: robert.bruffy@usdoj.gov
Education: Maryland 1979 BA

Legislative Reference Specialist **(Vacant)** . . . . (202) 307-0957

Office of the Deputy Assistant Attorney General for Appellate and Review

○ Deputy Assistant Attorney General for Appellate and Review **Diana L. Erbsen** Room 4326 . . . . (202) 514-2901
E-mail: diana.l.erbsen@usdoj.gov

★ Presidential Appointment Requiring Senate Confirmation
☆ Presidential Appointment
□ Schedule C Appointment
◇ Career Senior Foreign Service Appointment
● Career Senior Executive Service (SES) Appointment
○ Non-Career Senior Executive Service (SES) Appointment

Civil Appellate Section

• Chief **Gilbert S. Rothenberg** . . . . (202) 514-3361
Robert F. Kennedy Building,
Tenth Street and Constitution Avenue, NW, Room 4326,
Washington, DC 20530
E-mail: gilbert.s.rothenberg@usdoj.gov

Deputy Chief **Thomas J. Clark** Room 4322 . . . . . . (202) 514-9084
E-mail: thomas.j.clark@usdoj.gov

Assistant Chief **Bridget Maria Rowan** Room 4330 . . . . (202) 514-1840
E-mail: bridget.m.rowan@usdoj.gov

Office of Review

• Chief **Ann Carroll Reid** . . . . (202) 514-6636
Judiciary Center Building, 555 Fourth Street, NW, Room 6846,
Washington, DC 20001
E-mail: ann.carroll.reid@usdoj.gov

Office of the Deputy Assistant Attorney General for Civil Trial Matters

• Deputy Assistant Attorney General for Civil Trial Matters **David A. Hubbert** . . . . (202) 514-2901
Robert F. Kennedy Building,
Tenth Street and Constitution Avenue, NW, Room 4603,
Washington, DC 20530
E-mail: david.a.hubbert@usdoj.gov

Civil Trial Sections

• Civil Trial Section Chief (Central Region) **Scott Clark** . . . (202) 307-6647
Judiciary Center Building, 555 Fourth Street, NW, Room 8921B,
Washington, DC 20001

• Civil Trial Section Chief (Eastern Region)
Deborah S. Meland . . . . (202) 307-6567
Judiciary Center Building, 555 Fourth Street, NW, Room 6126,
Washington, DC 20001
E-mail: deborah.s.meland@usdoj.gov
Education: SUNY (Stony Brook) 1980 AB;
Washington College of Law 1983 JD

• Civil Trial Section Chief (Northern Region)
D. Patrick Mullarkey . . . . (202) 307-6533
Judiciary Center Building, 555 Fourth Street, NW, Room 7804B,
Washington, DC 20001
E-mail: d.patrick.mullarkey@usdoj.gov

• Civil Trial Section Chief (Southern Region)
Michael J. Kearns . . . . (202) 514-5905
Judiciary Center Building, 555 Fourth Street, NW, Room 6243A,
Washington, DC 20001
E-mail: michael.j.kearns@usdoj.gov

• Civil Trial Section Chief (Southwestern Region)
Grover Hartt III . . . . (214) 880-9725
Maxus Energy Tower, 717 North Harwood, Room 4100,
Dallas, TX 75201
E-mail: grover.hartt@usdoj.gov

• Civil Trial Section Chief (Western Region) (Acting)
Richard R. "Rick" Ward . . . . (202) 307-6413
Judiciary Center Building, 555 Fourth Street, NW, Room 7917,
Washington, DC 20001
E-mail: richard.r.ward@usdoj.gov

Court of Federal Claims Section Chief **David I. Pincus** . . . (202) 307-6440
Judiciary Center Building, 555 Fourth Street, NW, Room 8804A,
Washington, DC 20001
E-mail: david.i.pincus@usdoj.gov

Litigation Counsels

Chief Senior Litigation Counsel **Dennis M. Donohue** . . . . (202) 307-6492
Judiciary Center Building, 555 Fourth Street, NW, Room 7104,
Washington, DC 20001
E-mail: dennis.donohue@usdoj.gov

Senior Litigation Counsel **Joseph A. Sergi** . . . . . . (202) 305-0868
Judiciary Center Building, 555 Fourth Street, NW, Room 7207,
Washington, DC 20530
E-mail: joseph.a.sergi@usdoj.gov
Education: Pace 1992 BBA; NYU 1999 LLM

Litigation Counsel **Mark F. Daly** . . . . (202) 616-2245
Patrick Henry Building, 601 D Street, NW, Room 6546,
Washington, DC 20530
E-mail: mark.f.daly@usdoj.gov

Litigation Counsel **Judith A. Hagley** Room 4320 . . . . (202) 514-8126

Litigation Counsels *continued*

Litigation Counsel **John A. Lindquist III** . . . . . . (202) 307-6561
Judiciary Center Building, 555 Fourth Street, NW, Room 7203,
Washington, DC 20530
E-mail: john.a.lindquist@usdoj.gov

Office of the Deputy Assistant Attorney General for Criminal Matters

Deputy Assistant Attorney General for Criminal Matters **Caroline D. Ciraolo** Room 4603 . . . . . . (202) 514-2915
E-mail: caroline.d.ciraolo@usdoj.gov

Criminal Appeals and Tax Enforcement Policy Section

• Chief **Frank P. Cihlar** . . . . (202) 514-2839
Patrick Henry Building, 601 D Street, NW, Room 7002,
Washington, DC 20530
E-mail: frank.p.cihlar@usdoj.gov

Assistant Chief **Samuel R. "Bob" Lyons** . . . . . . (202) 514-6512
Patrick Henry Building, 601 D Street, NW, Room 7104,
Washington, DC 20530
E-mail: samuel.r.lyons@usdoj.gov

Criminal Enforcement Sections

• Northern Region Section Chief **Rosemary E. Paguni** . . . . (202) 305-3676
Patrick Henry Building, 601 D Street, NW, Room 7548,
Washington, DC 20530
E-mail: rosemary.e.paguni@usdoj.gov

Northern Region Assistant Chief **Jorge Almonte** . . . . . . (202) 514-8030
Patrick Henry Building, 601 D Street, NW, Room 7140,
Washington, DC 20530
E-mail: jorge.almonte@usdoj.gov
Education: Tulane 2001 JD

Northern Region Assistant Chief **Karen E. Kelly** . . . . . . (202) 616-3864
Patrick Henry Building, 601 D Street, NW, Room 7130,
Washington, DC 20530
E-mail: karen.e.kelly@usdoj.gov

Southern Region Section Chief **Bruce M. Salad** . . . . . . (202) 514-4334
601 D Street, NW, Washington, DC 20530
E-mail: bruce.m.salad@usdoj.gov

Southern Region Assistant Chief **Todd A. Ellinwood** . . . (202) 616-9330
Patrick Henry Building, 601 D Street, NW, Room 7636,
Washington, DC 20530
E-mail: todd.a.ellinwood@usdoj.gov

Southern Region Assistant Chief **Gregory E. Tortella** . . . (202) 616-3866
Patrick Henry Building, 601 D Street, NW, Room 7928,
Washington, DC 20530
E-mail: gregory.e.tortella@usdoj.gov

• Western Region Section Chief **Larry J. Wszalek** . . . . (202) 514-3866
Patrick Henry Building, 601 D Street, NW, Room 7034,
Washington, DC 20530
E-mail: larry.j.wszalek@usdoj.gov

Western Region Assistant Chief **Tino M. Lisella** . . . . (202) 514-5085
Patrick Henry Building, 601 D Street, NW, Room 7030,
Washington, DC 20530
E-mail: tino.m.lisella@usdoj.gov

Office of the Deputy Assistant Attorney General for Policy and Planning

• Deputy Assistant Attorney General for Policy and Planning **(Vacant)** . . . . (202) 514-5109

Office of Legislation, Policy and Management

• Senior Legislative Counsel **Eileen M. Shatz** . . . . . . (202) 307-6419
Robert F. Kennedy Building,
Tenth Street and Constitution Avenue, NW, Room 4134,
Washington, DC 20530
E-mail: eileen.m.shatz@usdoj.gov

Office of Management and Administration

• Executive Officer **Robert L. Bruffy** . . . . (202) 616-0010
Patrick Henry Building, 601 D Street, NW, Room 10002,
Washington, DC 20530
E-mail: robert.bruffy@usdoj.gov
Education: Maryland 1979 BA

US DEPARTMENT OF JUSTICE

★ Presidential Appointment Requiring Senate Confirmation
☆ Presidential Appointment
□ Schedule C Appointment
◇ Career Senior Foreign Service Appointment
● Career Senior Executive Service (SES) Appointment
○ Non-Career Senior Executive Service (SES) Appointment

Office of Training and Career Development
Director **Rachel D. Cramer** . . . . (202) 514-6540
Judiciary Center Building, 555 Fourth Street, NW, Room 6102, Washington, DC 20001
E-mail: rachel.d.cramer@usdoj.gov

Community Oriented Policing Services Office [COPS]

145 N Street, NE, Washington, DC 20530
Tel: (202) 616-2888
Tel: (800) 421-6770 (Department of Justice Response Center)
Internet: www.cops.usdoj.gov

The Community Oriented Policing Services Office was created as a result of the Violent Crime Control and Law Enforcement Act of 1994. As a component of the Justice Department, the mission of the Community Oriented Policing Services Office is to advance community policing in jurisdictions of all sizes across the country. Community policing represents a shift from more traditional law enforcement in that it focuses on prevention of crime and the fear of crime on a local basis. Community policing puts law enforcement professionals on the streets and assigns them a beat, so they can build mutually beneficial relationships with the people they serve. By earning the trust of the members of their communities and making those individuals stakeholders in their own safety, community policing makes law enforcement safer and more efficient, and makes America safer.

○ Director **Ronald L. "Ron" Davis** . . . . (202) 616-2888
E-mail: ronald.davis@usdoj.gov
Chief of Staff **Melanca D. Clark** . . . . (202) 616-9961
Education: Harvard 2002 JD
Facilities Manager **Laurel Matthews** . . . . (202) 616-2888
● Principal Deputy Director (Acting) **Sandra Webb** . . . . (202) 616-2888
E-mail: sandra.webb@usdoj.gov
Deputy Director for Community Policing Advancement
Robert Chapman . . . . (202) 616-3256
E-mail: robert.chapman@usdoj.gov
Deputy Director for Management **Wayne Henry** . . . . (202) 616-9416
E-mail: wayne.henry@usdoj.gov
Deputy Director for Operations (Acting) **Andrew Dorr** . . . (202) 616-2888
E-mail: andrew.dorr@usdoj.gov

Administrative Division
Assistant Director **(Vacant)** . . . . (202) 305-3893

Audit Division
Assistant Director **(Vacant)** . . . . (202) 616-3645

Communications Division
Assistant Director **(Vacant)** . . . . (202) 616-1728

External Affairs Division
Assistant Director **Shannon Long** . . . . (202) 353-9961
E-mail: shannon.long@usdoj.gov
Education: Western Carolina BS, MPA

Finance Division
Finance Officer **Kim Page** . . . . (202) 514-8074
E-mail: kim.page@usdoj.gov

General Counsel
General Counsel **Charlotte C. Grzebien** . . . . (202) 514-3750
E-mail: charlotte.grzebien@usdoj.gov

Grants Administration Division
Assistant Director (Acting) **John Oliphant** . . . . (202) 616-3031

Grants Monitoring Division
Assistant Director **Marcia Samuels** . . . . (202) 514-8507

Program/Policy Support and Evaluation Division
Assistant Director **Matthew Scheider** . . . . (202) 514-2301

Community Relations Service [CRS]

Bicentennial Building, 600 E Street, NW, Suite 6000, Washington, DC 20530
Tel: (202) 305-2935 Fax: (202) 305-3003
Internet: www.justice.gov/crs

The mission of Community Relations Service is to provide violence prevention and conflict resolution services for community conflicts and tensions arising from differences of race, color, or national origin. CRS is the only federal service mandated to help state and local government agencies, public and private organizations, and community groups resolve and prevent community racial conflicts through the use of mediation, conciliation, and other conflict resolution approaches.

★ Director **Grande H. Lum** . . . . (202) 305-2935
Began Service: August 2012
E-mail: grande.lum@usdoj.gov
Education: UC Berkeley 1986 BA; Harvard 1991 JD
Administrative Officer **(Vacant)** . . . . (202) 305-2935
Deputy Director **Gilbert L. Moore** . . . . (202) 305-2950
E-mail: gilbert.moore@usdoj.gov
Associate Director **O. Ben Lieu** . . . . (202) 514-1328
E-mail: ben.lieu@usdoj.gov
□ Chief of Staff and Senior Counsel **Marlene Sallo** . . . . (202) 305-3411
E-mail: marlene.sallo@usdoj.gov
Education: Manhattanville BA; Florida State JD
Legal Counsel **Antoinette Barksdale** . . . . (202) 305-2964
E-mail: antoinette.barksdale2@usdoj.gov
Media Affairs Officer **(Vacant)** . . . . (202) 305-2935
Information Technology Manager **Janet Peterkin** . . . . (202) 514-2388
E-mail: janet.peterkin@usdoj.gov

Executive Office for United States Trustees [EOUST]

441 G Street, NW, Suite 6150, Washington, DC 20530
Tel: (202) 307-1391 Fax: (202) 307-0672
Internet: www.justice.gov/ust

The United States Trustee Program is a component of the Department of Justice that seeks to promote the efficiency and protect the integrity of the Federal bankruptcy system. To further the public interest in the just, speedy and economical resolution of cases filed under the Bankruptcy Code, the Program monitors the conduct of bankruptcy parties and private estate trustees, oversees related administrative functions, and acts to ensure compliance with applicable laws and procedures. It also identifies and helps investigate bankruptcy fraud and abuse in coordination with United States Attorneys, the Federal Bureau of Investigation, and other law enforcement agencies.

● Director **Clifford J. White III** . . . . (202) 307-1391
E-mail: clifford.j.white@usdoj.gov
Education: George Washington 1983 JD
● Deputy Director and General Counsel
Ramona D. Elliott . . . . (202) 353-1399
E-mail: ramona.d.elliott@usdoj.gov
Deputy General Counsel and Senior Counsel
Lisa A. Tracy . . . . (202) 307-1399
E-mail: lisa.tracy@usdoj.gov
Education: Washington College of Law 2001 JD
● Deputy Director for Field Operations (Acting)
William T. Neary . . . . (202) 307-1391
E-mail: william.neary@usdoj.gov
Education: Vanderbilt 1979; Southern Methodist 1982 JD
● Deputy Director for Management **Diedre L. Windsor** . . . . (202) 307-1391
E-mail: diedre.l.windsor@usdoj.gov
Assistant Director for Administration
Monique K. Bourque . . . . (202) 353-3548
E-mail: monique.bourque@usdoj.gov Fax: (202) 307-3960
Assistant Director for Criminal Enforcement
Sandra T. Rasnak . . . . (312) 886-3323
219 South Dearborn Street, Room 873, Chicago, IL 60604 Fax: (312) 886-5794
E-mail: sandra.rasnak@usdoj.gov
Assistant Director for Oversight **Doreen B. Solomon** . . . . (202) 305-0222
Fax: (202) 616-4576

(continued on next page)

US DEPARTMENT OF JUSTICE

★ Presidential Appointment Requiring Senate Confirmation
☆ Presidential Appointment
□ Schedule C Appointment
◇ Career Senior Foreign Service Appointment
● Career Senior Executive Service (SES) Appointment
○ Non-Career Senior Executive Service (SES) Appointment

Executive Office for United States Trustees *continued*

Assistant Director for Planning and Evaluation
Thomas C. Kearns .... (202) 305-7827
E-mail: thomas.c.kearns@usdoj.gov Fax: (202) 616-4576
Chief Information Officer **Barbara A. Brown** .... (202) 353-8754
E-mail: barbara.a.brown@usdoj.gov Fax: (202) 616-1174

Foreign Claims Settlement Commission of the U.S. [FCSC]

Bicentennial Building, 600 E Street, NW, Room 6002, Washington, DC 20579
Tel: (202) 616-6975 Fax: (202) 616-6993
Internet: www.justice.gov/fcsc

The Foreign Claims Settlement Commission of the United States (FCSC) is a quasi-judicial, independent agency within the Department of Justice which adjudicates claims of U.S. nationals against foreign governments, under specific jurisdiction conferred by Congress, pursuant to international claims settlement agreements, or at the request of the Secretary of State. Funds for payment of the Commission's awards are derived from congressional appropriations, international claims settlements, or liquidation of foreign assets in the United States by the Departments of Justice and the Treasury.

Note: Members may continue to serve until reappointed or replaced.

★ Chairman **(Vacant)** .... (202) 616-6975
□ Assistant to the Chairman **(Vacant)** .... (202) 616-6983

Commissioners
Tel: (202) 616-6975 Fax: (202) 616-6993

★ Commissioner **Sylvia M. Becker** .... (202) 616-6975
Began Service: 2013
Term Expires: September 30, 2016
Education: Georgetown BSFS, MSFS, JD
★ Commissioner **Anuj Chang Desai** .... (202) 616-6975
Began Service: April 6, 2012
Term Expires: September 30, 2014
Education: Harvard 1988 AB; Columbia 1990 MA; Boalt Hall 1994 JD
★ Commissioner **(Vacant)** .... (202) 616-6975

Officials and Staff
Chief Counsel **Brian M. Simkin** .... (202) 616-6975
E-mail: brian.simkin@usdoj.gov
Executive Officer **Judith H. Lock** .... (202) 616-6986
E-mail: judith.h.lock@usdoj.gov
Administrative Assistant/Records Management
(Vacant) .... (202) 616-6988

Office of Information Policy [OIP]

1425 New York Avenue, NW, Suite 11050, Washington, DC 20530
Tel: (202) 514-3642 Fax: (202) 514-1009
Internet: www.justice.gov/oip
Internet: www.foia.gov

The Office of Information Policy (OIP) is responsible for encouraging agency compliance with the Freedom of Information Act (FOIA) and for ensuring that the Presidents FOIA Memorandum and the Attorney General's FOIA Guidelines are fully implemented across the government. OIP develops and issues policy guidance to all agencies on proper implementation of the FOIA.

● Director **Melanie Ann Pustay** .... (202) 514-3642
E-mail: melanie.a.pustay@usdoj.gov
Education: George Mason 1979 BA; Washington College of Law 1982 JD
Chief of Staff **Carmen L. Mallon** .... (202) 514-3642

Office of Justice Programs [OJP]

810 Seventh Street, NW, Washington, DC 20531
Tel: (202) 307-5933
Tel: (202) 307-1480 (DOJ Response Center - DC Metropolitan Area)
Tel: (800) 421-6770 (DOJ Response Center - Outside DC Area)
Tel: (800) 458-0786 (Customer Service Center) Fax: (202) 514-7805
Internet: www.ojp.usdoj.gov

The Office of Justice Programs (OJP) provides innovative leadership to federal, state, local, and tribal justice systems, by disseminating state-of-the art knowledge and practices across America, and providing grants for the implementation of crime fighting strategies. Because most of the responsibility for crime control and prevention falls to law enforcement officers in states, cities, and neighborhoods, the federal government can be effective in these areas only to the extent that it can enter into partnerships with these officers. Therefore, OJP does not directly carry out law enforcement and justice activities. Instead, OJP works in partnership with the justice community to identify the most pressing crime-related challenges confronting the justice system and to provide information, training, coordination, and innovative strategies and approaches for addressing these challenges.

★ Assistant Attorney General **Karol Virginia Mason**
Room 6400 .... (202) 307-5933
Began Service: June 3, 2013
E-mail: karol.v.mason@usdoj.gov
Education: North Carolina 1979 AB; Michigan 1982 JD
□ Senior Advisor **Amy L. Solomon** .... (202) 307-5933
E-mail: amy.solomon@usdoj.gov
○ Principal Deputy Assistant Attorney General
Beth McGarry Room 6400 .... (202) 307-5933
E-mail: beth.mcgarry@usdoj.gov
Education: Delaware BN; Hastings JD
● Deputy Assistant Attorney General for Operations and Management **Maureen A. Henneberg** Room 6400 ..... (202) 307-5933
E-mail: maureen.henneberg@usdoj.gov
Education: SUNY (Geneseo) 1988 BA; American U 1990 MPA
Senior Advisor for Tribal Affairs
Eugenia Tyner-Dawson .... (202) 307-5933
E-mail: eugenia.tyner-dawson@usdoj.gov
□ Chief of Staff **Theron Phillip Pride, Jr.** .... (202) 514-1369
E-mail: theron.pride@usdoj.gov
Administrative Officer **Raymond Brian Ridge**
Room 6400 .... (202) 514-0956
E-mail: raymond.b.ridge@usdoj.gov

Office of Administration
Tel: (202) 307-0087 Fax: (202) 307-1020

● Director **Phillip K. Merkle** Room 3424 .... (202) 307-2534
E-mail: phillip.merkle@usdoj.gov
Supervisory Management Analyst **Elizabeth Quinn**
Room 3425 .... (202) 305-2921
E-mail: elizabeth.quinn@usdoj.gov
Administrative Officer **Erica C. Brooks** .... (202) 307-0087
E-mail: erica.brooks@usdoj.gov

Office of the Chief Financial Officer [OCFO]
Tel: (202) 307-0623 Tel: (800) 458-0786 (Customer Service Center)
Internet: www.ojp.usdoj.gov/about/offices/ocfo.htm

● Chief Financial Officer **Leigh Benda** Room 3345 TW .... (202) 353-8153
E-mail: leigh.benda@usdoj.gov
● Deputy Chief Financial Officer **Marilynn Atsatt**
Room 3347 TW .... (202) 305-1802
Associate Chief Financial Officer
Christal McNeil-Wright Room 3319TW .... (202) 307-8122
E-mail: christal.mcneil-wright@usdoj.gov
Associate Chief Financial Officer, Budget Execution Division **Quinntella J. Wilson** Room 3353 TW .... (202) 307-5980
E-mail: quinntella.wilson@usdoj.gov
Associate Chief Financial Officer, Budget Formulation, Liaison, Planning and Performance Division
Gretchen Stiers Room 3349 TW .... (202) 305-1802
E-mail: gretchen.stiers@usdoj.gov
Education: DePauw 1984 BA; UMass (Amherst) MA, PhD

★ Presidential Appointment Requiring Senate Confirmation
☆ Presidential Appointment
□ Schedule C Appointment
◇ Career Senior Foreign Service Appointment
● Career Senior Executive Service (SES) Appointment
○ Non-Career Senior Executive Service (SES) Appointment

Office of the Chief Financial Officer *continued*

Associate Chief Financial Officer, Finance, Accounting and Analysis Division **Joanne Suttington** Room 3315 TW . . . . (202) 305-2122
E-mail: joanne.suttington@usdoj.gov
Assistant Chief Financial Officer, Grants Financial Management Division **Jerry "Angel" Conty** Room 3133 TW . . . . (202) 514-7934
E-mail: jerry.conty@usdoj.gov
Administrative Officer **Linda Jacobs** Room 3344 TW . . . . (202) 307-0625
E-mail: linda.jacobs@usdoj.gov Fax: (202) 514-9028
Manager, MAT **Lisa Palechek** Room 3329 TW . . . . (202) 514-8541
E-mail: lisa.palechek@usdoj.gov

Office of Chief Information Officer [OCIO]
Tel: (202) 305-9071 Fax: (202) 307-2019

• Chief Information Officer **Brian E. McGrath** . . . . (202) 305-9071
Deputy Chief Information Officer **Angel Santa** Room 8425 . . . . (202) 305-9071
E-mail: angel.santa@usdoj.gov
Administrative Officer **Lori Fender** Room 8410 . . . . (202) 307-3984
E-mail: lori.fender@usdoj.gov

Office for Civil Rights [OCR]
Tel: (202) 307-0690
Internet: www.ojp.usdoj.gov/ocr

Director **Michael Alston** Tech World, Room 3411 . . . . (202) 307-0692
E-mail: michael.alston@usdoj.gov
Administrative Officer **Debra J. Saunders** Tech World, Room 3426 . . . . (202) 307-0690
E-mail: debra.saunders@usdoj.gov

Office of Communications [OCOM]
Tel: (202) 307-0703 Fax: (202) 514-5958
Internet: www.ojp.usdoj.gov/ocom

Director (Acting) **Silas Darden** Room 6338 . . . . (202) 307-0703
E-mail: silas.darden@usdoj.gov
Deputy Director **Adam T. Spector** Room 6328 . . . . (202) 307-0703
E-mail: adam.t.spector@usdoj.gov
Deputy Director **Chuck Wagner** . . . . (202) 307-0703
E-mail: chuck.wagner@usdoj.gov
Congressional Affairs Specialist **Sabrina Scott** . . . . (202) 307-8561
Congressional Affairs Specialist **(Vacant)** . . . . (202) 307-0703
Public Affairs Specialist **Sheila Jerusalem** . . . . (202) 307-0703
Public Affairs Specialist **Kara McCarthy** . . . . (202) 307-0703
Public Affairs Specialist **Starr Melissa Stepp** . . . . (202) 514-9870
Administrative Officer **Cynthia A. Ellis-Evans** Room 6327 . . . . (202) 514-1966
E-mail: cynthia.ellis-evans@usdoj.gov

Office of General Counsel [OGC]
Fax: (202) 307-1419
Internet: www.ojp.usdoj.gov/ogc

• General Counsel **Rafael A. Madan** Room 5418 . . . . (202) 307-6235
E-mail: rafael.a.madan@usdoj.gov
Principal Deputy General Counsel **John L. Pensinger** Room 5328 . . . . (202) 616-3254
E-mail: john.pensinger@usdoj.gov
Deputy General Counsel **Rosemary C. Carradini** Room 5417 . . . . (202) 616-3257
E-mail: rosemary.carradini@usdoj.gov
Deputy General Counsel **Carolyn Kennedy** Room 5420 . . . (202) 616-2370
Deputy General Counsel **Charles T. Moses III** Room 5322 . . . . (202) 305-2536
E-mail: charles.moses@usdoj.gov
Deputy General Counsel **Matthew T. Scodellaro** . . . . (202) 305-8219
E-mail: matthew.scodellaro@usdoj.gov
Administrative Officer **Rosa M. Washington** Room 5412 . . . . (202) 616-3269
E-mail: rosa.m.washington@usdoj.gov

Bureau of Justice Assistance [BJA]
810 Seventh Street, NW, Washington, DC 20531
Tel: (202) 616-6500 Fax: (202) 353-0585
Internet: www.ojp.usdoj.gov/bja

The Bureau of Justice Assistance (BJA) supports law enforcement, courts, corrections, treatment, victim services, technology, and prevention initiatives that strengthen the nations criminal justice system. BJA provides leadership, services, and funding to Americas communities by emphasizing local control, building relationships in the field, providing training and technical assistance in support of efforts to prevent crime, drug abuse, and violence at the national, state, and local levels, developing collaborations and partnerships, promoting capacity building through planning, streamlining the administration of grants, and other initiatives.

★ Director **Denise Ellen O'Donnell** Room 4427 . . . . (202) 616-3613
E-mail: denise.odonnell@usdoj.gov
Education: Canisius BS; SUNY (Buffalo) MSW, 1982 JD
☐ Counsel to the Director **(Vacant)** Room 4429 . . . . (202) 307-2858
☐ Senior Advisor **(Vacant)** . . . . (202) 514-5411
☐ Special Assistant **(Vacant)** . . . . (202) 616-6500
Senior Policy Advisor **David P. Lewis** . . . . (202) 616-7829
E-mail: david.p.lewis@usdoj.gov
• Deputy Director for Planning **Eileen M. Garry** Room 4422 . . . . (202) 307-6226
E-mail: eileen.garry@usdoj.gov
• Deputy Director for Policy **Kristen Mahoney** Room 4228 . . . . (202) 616-5140
E-mail: kristen.mahoney@ojp.usdoj.gov
• Deputy Director for Programs **Tracey Trautman** Room 4345 . . . . (202) 805-1491
E-mail: tracey.trautman@usdoj.gov
Education: North Dakota State 1989 BA; George Mason MPA
Administrative Officer **Felicia Evans** Room 4413 . . . . (202) 514-2307
E-mail: felicia.evans@usdoj.gov

Bureau of Justice Statistics [BJS]
810 Seventh Street, NW, Room 2413, Washington, DC 20531
Tel: (202) 307-0765 Tel: (800) 851-3420 (Clearinghouse Hotline)
Fax: (202) 307-5846
Internet: www.bjs.gov

The Bureau of Justice Statistics collects, analyzes, and publishes statistical information on crime, criminal offenders, victims of crime, and the operations of the justice system. The program provides data needed by researchers and policymakers to understand and influence the workings of the criminal justice system.

☆ Director **William J. Sabol** . . . . (202) 514-1062
E-mail: william.sabol@usdoj.gov
Education: Pittsburgh BA, PhD
• Deputy Director **Gerard F. Ramker** . . . . (202) 616-3282
E-mail: gerard.ramker@usdoj.gov
Education: St Joseph's Col (IN) BA; Indiana State MA; Sam Houston State PhD
Statistical Collection and Analysis, Victimization, Corrections, Recidivism, and Special Projects Deputy Director **(Vacant)** Room 2409 . . . . (202) 514-1062
Statistical Planning, Policy, and Operations Deputy Director **Gerard F. Ramker** Room 2402 . . . . (202) 616-3282
E-mail: gerard.ramker@usdoj.gov
Education: St Joseph's Col (IN) BA; Indiana State MA; Sam Houston State PhD
Corrections Statistics Chief **(Vacant)** Room 2239 . . . . (202) 514-1062
Law Enforcement, Adjudication, and Federal Statistics Chief **Howard N. Snyder** Room 2323 . . . . (202) 307-0765
Prosecution and Adjudication Statistics Chief **Howard N. Snyder** Room 2338 . . . . (202) 307-0765
Publications and Dissemination Chief **Doris J. James** Room 2250 . . . . (202) 616-3625
Victimization Statistics Chief **Michael Planty** Room 2215 . . . . (202) 616-3494
Senior Statistical Advisor **Allen J. Beck** Room 2414 . . . . (202) 616-3277
E-mail: allen.beck@usdoj.gov
Education: Michigan PhD

(continued on next page)

★ Presidential Appointment Requiring Senate Confirmation ☐ Schedule C Appointment • Career Senior Executive Service (SES) Appointment
☆ Presidential Appointment ◇ Career Senior Foreign Service Appointment ○ Non-Career Senior Executive Service (SES) Appointment

Bureau of Justice Statistics *continued*

Administrative Officer **Lisa Huff-Gallaway** Room 2406 . . . (202) 616-3497
E-mail: lisa.huff-gallaway@usdoj.gov
Criminal Justice Data Improvement Program Manager
Devon Adams Room 2327 . . . (202) 514-9157

National Institute of Justice [NIJ]

810 Seventh Street, NW, Washington, DC 20531
Tel: (202) 307-2942 Fax: (202) 307-6394
Internet: www.nij.gov

The National Institute of Justice (NIJ) is the research, development, and evaluation agency of the U.S. Department of Justice and is dedicated to researching crime control and justice issues. NIJ provides objective, independent, evidence-based knowledge and tools to meet the challenges of crime and justice, particularly at the State and local levels. The National Institute of Justice's principal authorities are derived from the Omnibus Crime Control and Safe Streets Act of 1968, as amended (see 42 USC § 3721-3723) and Title II of the Homeland Security Act of 2002. The Director is appointed by the President and confirmed by the Senate. The Institute actively solicits the views of criminal justice and other professionals and researchers to inform its search for the knowledge and tools to guide policy and practice.

☆ Director **Nancy Rodriguez** Room 7422 . . . (202) 353-2942
Began Service: February 9, 2015
E-mail: nancy.rodriguez@usdoj.gov
Education: Sam Houston State BA; Washington State 1998 PhD

● Deputy Director [Chief of Staff]
Howard R. Spivak MD Room 7422 . . . (202) 307-2942
E-mail: howard.spivak@usdoj.gov
Education: Rochester MD

● Senior Social Scientist **(Vacant)** . . . (202) 307-2949
Senior Policy Advisor **Nancy Merritt** . . . (202) 307-8748
E-mail: nancy.merritt@usdoj.gov
Policy Advisor **Maureen McGough** . . . (202) 305-4539
E-mail: maureen.mcgough@usdoj.gov

Office of Communications

Director **Jolene Hernon** Room 7118 . . . (202) 307-1464
E-mail: jolene.hernon@usdoj.gov

Office of Investigative and Forensic Sciences

Fax: (202) 307-9907

Director (Acting) **Gerald Laporte** Room 7123 . . . (202) 305-1106
E-mail: gerald.laporte@usdoj.gov

Office of Operations

Director **Portia Graham** . . . (202) 307-2964
E-mail: portia.graham@usdoj.gov
Associate Director **Barry A. Bratburd** . . . (202) 616-5314

Office of Research and Evaluation

Fax: (202) 305-8626

● Director **Seri Irazola** Room 7330 . . . (202) 305-2457
E-mail: seri.irazola@usdoj.gov
Associate Director **(Vacant)** Room 7355 . . . (202) 307-7256
Social Science Analyst **(Vacant)** . . . (202) 353-9254
Research Associate **(Vacant)** . . . (202) 514-7748
Secretary **(Vacant)** . . . (202) 514-8036

Crime, Violence and Victimization Research Division

Fax: (202) 305-8626

Director **John Picarelli** Room 7440 . . . (202) 307-3213
E-mail: john.picarelli@usdoj.gov

Justice Systems Research Division

Fax: (202) 305-8626

Director **Angela Moore Parmley** Room 7344 . . . (202) 307-0145
E-mail: angela.mooreparmley@usdoj.gov
Senior Social Science Analyst **Katharine Browning** . . . (202) 616-4786
E-mail: katharine.browning@usdoj.gov

Justice Systems Research Division *continued*

Senior Social Science Analyst **Linda Truitt** . . . (202) 353-9081
E-mail: linda.truitt@usdoj.gov
Senior Social Science Analyst **(Vacant)** . . . (202) 616-3624

Office of Science and Technology

Fax: (202) 307-9907

● Director **Chris Tillery** Room 7424 . . . (202) 305-9829

Research Division

Fax: (202) 307-9907

Director **William "Bill" Ford** . . . (202) 353-9768
E-mail: william.ford@usdoj.gov

Policy, Standards and Grants Management Division

Fax: (202) 307-9907

Director **Mark Greene** Room 7224 . . . (202) 307-3384
E-mail: mark.greene@ojp.usdoj.gov

Office of Juvenile Justice and Delinquency Prevention [OJJDP]

810 Seventh Street, NW, Washington, DC 20531
Tel: (202) 307-5911 Fax: (202) 353-9093 (Missing Children)
Internet: www.ojjdp.gov/

The Office of Juvenile Justice and Delinquency Prevention (OJJDP) provides national leadership, coordination, and resources to prevent and respond to juvenile delinquency and victimization. OJJDP supports states and communities in their efforts to develop and implement effective and coordinated prevention and intervention programs and to improve the juvenile justice system so that it protects public safety, holds offenders accountable, and provides treatment and rehabilitative services tailored to the needs of juveniles and their families.

☆ Administrator **Robert L. Listenbee, Jr.** . . . (202) 616-3646
E-mail: robert.l.listenbee@usdoj.gov Fax: (202) 307-2093
Education: Harvard BA; UC Berkeley JD
Senior Advisor to the Administrator
Catherine L. Pierce . . . (202) 307-6785
E-mail: catherine.pierce@usdoj.gov
Senior Advisor to the Administrator
Gregory Thompson . . . (202) 616-3663
E-mail: gregory.thompson3@usdoj.gov
Chief of Staff **Shanetta Brown Cutlar** . . . (202) 307-0195
Education: Cal State (Los Angeles) 1988 BS; UCLA 1993 JD
Executive Assistant **Simone Luke** . . . (202) 616-1742
E-mail: simone.luke@usdoj.gov
Executive Assistant **Elizabeth Scott** . . . (202) 305-2448
E-mail: elizabeth.scott@usdoj.gov
Special Assistant **Ellen Williams** . . . (202) 514-5411
E-mail: ellen.williams@usdoj.gov

○ Principal Deputy Administrator **(Vacant)** . . . (202) 353-7105
Deputy Administrator for Operations **(Vacant)** . . . (202) 353-9055
● Deputy Administrator for Policy **(Vacant)** . . . (202) 353-9427
● Deputy Administrator for Programs **Chyrl Jones**
Room 5222 . . . (202) 616-0798
E-mail: chyrl.jones@usdoj.gov

Budget and Administration Division

Associate Administrator **Janet Chiancone** Room 5136 . . . (202) 353-9258
E-mail: janet.chiancone@usdoj.gov
Deputy Associate Administrator **Willie Bronson** . . . (202) 305-2427
E-mail: willie.bronson@usdoj.gov

Innovation and Research Division

Associate Administrator **Catherine M. Doyle** . . . (202) 616-9208
E-mail: catherine.doyle@usdoj.gov
Deputy Associate Administrator **Brecht Donoghue** . . . (202) 616-1270
E-mail: brent.donoghue@usdoj.gov

Juvenile Justice System Improvement Division

Associate Administrator **Kellie Dressler Blue**
Room 5155 . . . (202) 514-4817
E-mail: kellie.dressler@usdoj.gov Fax: (202) 307-2093

US DEPARTMENT OF JUSTICE

★ Presidential Appointment Requiring Senate Confirmation ☐ Schedule C Appointment ● Career Senior Executive Service (SES) Appointment
☆ Presidential Appointment ◇ Career Senior Foreign Service Appointment ○ Non-Career Senior Executive Service (SES) Appointment

Juvenile Justice System Improvement Division *continued*

Deputy Associate Administrator **Nicole Dennis** .... (202) 532-0169
E-mail: nicole.dennis@usdoj.gov

State and Community Development Division

Associate Administrator **Robin Delany-Shabazz**
Room 5306 .... (202) 616-9963
E-mail: robin.delany-shabazz@usdoj.gov Fax: (202) 616-2819
Education: Maryland 1995 MAA

Deputy Associate Administrator **Jennifer Yeh**
Room 5306 .... (202) 616-9135
E-mail: jennifer.yeh2@usdoj.gov

Youth Development, Prevention and Safety Division

Associate Administrator (Acting) **James "Jim" Antal**
Room 5136 .... (202) 514-1289
E-mail: james.antal@usdoj.gov Fax: (202) 514-6382

Deputy Associate Administrator **James "Jim" Antal** ... (202) 514-1289
E-mail: james.antal@usdoj.gov

Deputy Associate Administrator **Jeffrey Gersh** .... (202) 514-5535
E-mail: jeffrey.gersh@usdoj.gov

Office of Sex Offender Sentencing, Monitoring, Apprehending, Registering, and Tracking [SMART]

810 Seventh Street, NW, Room 6108, Washington, DC 20531
Tel: (202) 514-4689 Fax: (202) 354-4200
E-mail: getsmart@usdoj.gov
Internet: www.ojp.usdoj.gov/smart

The Office of Sex Offender Sentencing, Monitoring, Apprehending, Registering, and Tracking was authorized by the Adam Walsh Child Protection and Safety Act of 2006. It performs several crucial missions, including administering the standards for the Sex Offender Registration and Notification Program set forth in Title 1 of the Adam Walsh Act; administering grant programs relating to sex offender registration and notification; and cooperating with and providing technical assistance to states, the District of Columbia, principle U.S. territories, units of local government, tribal governments, and other public and private entities involved in activities related to sex offender registration or notification.

○ Director **Luis E. CdeBaca** .... (202) 353-3040
Education: Iowa State 1990 BA; Michigan 1993 JD

Deputy Director **Dawn Doran** .... (202) 353-3040
E-mail: dawn.doran@usdoj.gov
Education: Tennessee (Martin) BS; Tennessee JD

Office for Victims of Crime [OVC]

810 Seventh Street, NW, Room 8332, Washington, DC 20531
Tel: (202) 307-5983 Fax: (202) 514-6383
Fax: (202) 305-2440 (Alternate)
Internet: www.ojp.usdoj.gov/ovc
Internet: ovc.ncjrs.org/askovc (Ask OVC)

The Office for Victims of Crime provides federal funds to support victim compensation and assistance programs across the Nation. The Office for Victims of Crime also provides training for diverse professionals who work with victims, develops and disseminates publications, supports projects to enhance victims' rights and services, and educates the public about victim issues. Funding for the Office for Victims of Crime programs comes from the Crime Victims Fund.

☆ Director **Joye E. Frost** Room 8331 .... (202) 307-5983
Began Service: June 14, 2013
E-mail: joye.frost@usdoj.gov
Education: Texas 1972 BA; Mary Hardin-Baylor 1997 MHS

● Deputy Director **(Vacant)** Room 8328 .... (202) 353-0420

□ Chief of Staff **(Vacant)** Room 8327 .... (202) 305-2172

Administrative Officer **Lynnell Clark** Room 8340 .... (202) 616-3701
E-mail: lynnell.clarke@usdoj.gov

Office on Violence Against Women [OVW]

145 N Street, NE, Suite 10W.100, Washington, DC 20530
Tel: (202) 307-6026 TTY: (202) 307-2277 Fax: (202) 305-2589
E-mail: ovw.info@usdoj.gov
Internet: www.ovw.usdoj.gov

The mission of the Office on Violence Against Women (OVW) is to provide federal leadership to reduce violence against women, and to administer justice for and strengthen services to all victims of domestic violence, dating violence, sexual assault, and stalking. This is accomplished by developing and supporting the capacity of state, local, tribal, and non-profit entities involved in responding to violence against women.

★ Director **(Vacant)** .... (202) 307-6026

□ Confidential Assistant **Carla Bernal** .... (202) 616-3255
E-mail: carla.bernal@usdoj.gov

□ Special Assistant **Brenda Auterman** .... (202) 532-4482
E-mail: brenda.auterman@usdoj.gov

○ Principal Deputy Director **Beatrice "Bea" Hanson** ...... (202) 307-6026
E-mail: bea.hanson@usdoj.gov
Education: Michigan BA; Hunter MA

Deputy Director, Grant Development and Management
Nadine Neufville .... (202) 305-2590
E-mail: nadine.neufville@usdoj.gov

Deputy Director, Legal Counsel **Jennifer Kaplan** .... (202) 514-0052
E-mail: jennifer.kaplan@usdoj.gov

□ Deputy Director, Policy, Communication and Evaluation Division **Rosie Hidalgo** .... (202) 514-0391
Note: On detail to the Office of the Vice President.
E-mail: rosie.hidalgo@usdoj.gov

Deputy Director, Tribal Affairs **Lorraine Edmo** .... (202) 514-8804
E-mail: lorraine.edmo@usdoj.gov

Associate Director, Grant Development and Management Division **Krista Blakeney-Mitchell** .... (202) 305-2651
E-mail: krista.blakeney-mitchell@usdoj.gov

Associate Director, Grant Development and Management Division **Michelle Brickley** .... (202) 514-3590
E-mail: michelle.brickley@usdoj.gov

Associate Director, Grant Development and Management Division **Darlene Johnson** .... (202) 307-6795
E-mail: darlene.johnson@usdoj.gov

Associate Director, Grant Development and Management Division **Amy Loder** .... (202) 305-2971
E-mail: amy.loder@usdoj.gov

Associate Director, Grant Development and Management Division **Lauren Nassikas** .... (202) 305-1792
E-mail: lauren.nassikas@usdoj.gov

Associate Director, Grants Financial Management Section **Donna Simmons** .... (202) 514-1015
E-mail: donna.simmons@usdoj.gov

Chief of Staff **Allison Randall** .... (202) 532-4548

Executive Officer **Sybil Barksdale** .... (202) 353-7378
E-mail: sybil.barksdale@usdoj.gov

Chief Financial Officer **Angela Wood** .... (202) 353-3982
E-mail: angela.wood@usdoj.gov

Domestic Violence Homicide Prevention Demonstration Initiative [DVHP Initiative]

Tel: (202) 307-6026 Fax: (202) 305-2589

The Domestic Violence Homicide Prevention Demonstration Initiative (DVHP) serves to implement domestic violence homicide reduction and prevention models and to evaluate how well they work in different communities. It also aims for the successful adaptation of key components. The DVHP will help build the capacity of state, local and tribal jurisdictions to improve identification of and services for high-risk victims, along with better monitoring of high-risk offenders to reduce domestic violence related homicide. It also hopes to identify barriers to providing quality assistance and advocacy, as well as documenting and disseminating solutions for replication.

Program Specialist **Anne Hamilton** .... (202) 353-2794

US DEPARTMENT OF JUSTICE

★ Presidential Appointment Requiring Senate Confirmation
☆ Presidential Appointment
□ Schedule C Appointment
◇ Career Senior Foreign Service Appointment
● Career Senior Executive Service (SES) Appointment
○ Non-Career Senior Executive Service (SES) Appointment

Office of the Solicitor General [OSG]

Robert F. Kennedy Building, 950 Pennsylvania Avenue, NW, Washington, DC 20530
Tel: (202) 514-2203 Fax: (202) 514-3648
Internet: www.justice.gov/osg

The task of the Office of the Solicitor General is to supervise and conduct government litigation in the United States Supreme Court. Virtually all such litigation is channeled through the Office of the Solicitor General and is actively conducted by the Office. The United States is involved in approximately two-thirds of all the cases the U.S. Supreme Court decides on the merits each year. Another responsibility of the Office is to review all cases decided adversely to the government in the lower courts to determine whether they should be appealed and, if so, what position should be taken. Moreover, the Solicitor General determines whether the government will participate as an amicus curiae, or intervene, in cases in any appellate court.

★ Solicitor General **Donald B. "Don" Verrilli, Jr.**
Room 5143 ....(202) 514-2201
Began Service: June 9, 2011
Education: Yale 1979 BA; Columbia 1983 JD

□ Confidential Assistant (Acting) **Rebecca Rios**
Room 5143 ....(202) 514-2201

Executive Officer **Valerie H. Yancey** Room 5142 ....(202) 514-3957
E-mail: valerie.hall@usdoj.gov

Supervisory Case Management Specialist
Charlene W. Goodwin Room 5608 ....(202) 514-2218
E-mail: charlene.w.goodwin@usdoj.gov

○ Principal Deputy Solicitor General
Ian Heath Gershengorn ....(202) 514-2206
E-mail: ian.gershengorn@usdoj.gov
Education: Harvard 1988 AB, 1993 JD

● Deputy Solicitor General **Michael R. Dreeben**
Room 5623 ....(202) 514-2255
E-mail: michael.r.dreeben@usdoj.gov
Education: Wisconsin 1976 BA; Chicago 1978 MA; Duke 1981 JD

● Deputy Solicitor General **Edwin S. Kneedler**
Room 5137 ....(202) 514-3261
E-mail: edwin.s.kneedler@usdoj.gov
Education: Lehigh 1967 BS; Virginia 1974 JD

● Deputy Solicitor General **Malcolm L. Stewart**
Room 5137 ....(202) 514-2211
E-mail: malcolm.l.stewart@usdoj.gov

Research and Publications Sections Director
(Vacant) Room 6636 ....(202) 514-4459
Fax: (202) 307-4614

Office of the Inspector General [OIG]

950 Pennsylvania Avenue, NW, Suite 4706, Washington, DC 20530
Tel: (202) 514-3435 Fax: (202) 514-4001
Internet: www.justice.gov/oig

The Office of the Inspector General (OIG) in the U.S. Department of Justice (DOJ) is a statutorily created independent entity whose mission is to detect and deter waste, fraud, abuse, and misconduct in DOJ programs and personnel, and to promote economy and efficiency in those programs. The Inspector General, who is appointed by the President subject to Senate confirmation, reports to the Attorney General and Congress. The OIG investigates alleged violations of criminal and civil laws by DOJ employees and also audits and inspects DOJ programs.

★ Inspector General **Michael E. Horowitz** ....(202) 514-3435
Began Service: 2012
E-mail: michael.e.horowitz@usdoj.gov
Education: Brandeis 1984 BA; Harvard 1987 JD

Senior Counsel to the Inspector General
Jay N. Lerner ....(202) 514-3435
E-mail: jay.lerner@usdoj.gov
Education: Illinois BS; Pennsylvania JD

Counsel to the Inspector General [Media Relations]
John S. Lavinsky ....(202) 514-3435
E-mail: john.s.lavinsky@usdoj.gov

Office of the Inspector General [OIG] *continued*

Counsel to the Inspector General
James A. Mitzelfeld ....(202) 514-3435
E-mail: james.a.mitzelfeld@usdoj.gov
Education: Michigan State 1984 BA; Michigan 1996 JD

● Deputy Inspector General **Robert P. Storch** ....(202) 514-3435
E-mail: robert.p.storch@usdoj.gov
Education: Harvard 1982; Columbia 1985 JD

● General Counsel **William M. Blier** Suite 4726 ....(202) 616-0646
E-mail: william.blier@usdoj.gov Fax: (202) 616-9152

Whistleblower Ombudsperson **Robert P. Storch** ....(202) 514-3435
E-mail: robert.p.storch@usdoj.gov
Education: Harvard 1982; Columbia 1985 JD

Audit Division

1425 New York Avenue, NW, Suite 5000, Washington, DC 20530

● Assistant Inspector General **Jason R. Malmstrom** ......(202) 616-4633
E-mail: jason.r.malmstrom@usdoj.gov Fax: (202) 616-1697

● Deputy Assistant Inspector General (Acting)
Mark L. Hayes ....(202) 616-4633
E-mail: mark.l.hayes@usdoj.gov

Evaluation and Inspections Division

1425 New York Avenue, NW, Suite 6100, Washington, DC 20530

● Assistant Inspector General **Nina S. Pelletier** ....(202) 616-4620
E-mail: nina.pelletier@usdoj.gov Fax: (202) 616-4584

Deputy Assistant Inspector General **Erin A. Lane** ....(202) 616-4620

Deputy Assistant Inspector General **James A. Tyrell** .....(202) 616-4620

Investigations Division

1425 New York Avenue, NW, Suite 7100, Washington, DC 20530

● Assistant Inspector General (Acting) **Eric A. Johnson** ....(202) 616-4760
E-mail: eric.a.johnson@usdoj.gov Fax: (202) 616-9881

● Deputy Assistant Inspector General **Eric A. Johnson** .....(202) 616-4760
E-mail: eric.a.johnson@usdoj.gov

Management and Planning Division

1425 New York Avenue, NW, Room 7000, Washington, DC 20530

● Assistant Inspector General **Gregory T. Peters** ....(202) 616-4550
E-mail: greg.t.peters@usdoj.gov Fax: (202) 616-4532

Deputy Assistant Inspector General **Cynthia A. Lowell** ...(202) 616-4550

Oversight and Review Division

1425 New York Avenue, NW, Room 13100, Washington, DC 20530

● Assistant Inspector General (Acting)
Daniel C. Beckhard ....(202) 616-0645
E-mail: dan.c.beckhard@usdoj.gov Fax: (202) 616-0271

Deputy Assistant Inspector General
Daniel C. Beckhard ....(202) 616-0645

Associate Deputy Assistant Inspector General
Brandy Hamilton ....(202) 616-0645

Associate Deputy Assistant Inspector General
M. Sean O'Neill ....(202) 616-0645

Office of Professional Responsibility [OPR]

950 Pennsylvania Avenue, NW, Room 3525, Washington, DC 20530
Tel: (202) 514-3365 Fax: (202) 514-9508
Internet: www.justice.gov/opr

The Office of Professional Responsibility (OPR) has jurisdiction to investigate allegations of misconduct by Department of Justice attorneys that relate to the exercise of their authority to investigate, litigate, or provide legal advice; and to investigate allegations of misconduct by law enforcement personnel when they are related to allegations of misconduct by attorneys within the jurisdiction of OPR.

● Counsel **Robin C. Ashton** ....(202) 514-3365
E-mail: robin.ashton@usdoj.gov

● Deputy Counsel **G. Bradley Weinsheimer** ....(202) 514-4860
E-mail: bradley.weinsheimer@usdoj.gov

Executive Officer **Jennifer LaPoint** ....(202) 514-8334
E-mail: jennifer.lapoint@usdoj.gov

★ Presidential Appointment Requiring Senate Confirmation
☆ Presidential Appointment
□ Schedule C Appointment
◇ Career Senior Foreign Service Appointment
● Career Senior Executive Service (SES) Appointment
○ Non-Career Senior Executive Service (SES) Appointment

Professional Responsibility Advisory Office [PRAO]

1425 New York Avenue, NW, Suite 12000, Washington, DC 20530
Tel: (202) 514-0458 Fax: (202) 353-7483
Internet: www.justice.gov/prao

The mission of the Professional Responsibility Advisory Office (PRAO) is to provide prompt, consistent advice to Department attorneys and Assistant United States Attorneys with respect to professional responsibility and choice-of-law issues.

• Director (Acting) **Stacy M. Ludwig** .... (202) 514-0458
Deputy Director (Acting) **Matthew Ferguson** .... (202) 514-0458
E-mail: matthew.ferguson@usdoj.gov

Criminal Division [CD]

Robert F. Kennedy Building, 950 Pennsylvania Avenue, NW, Washington, DC 20530
Tel: (202) 514-2601 Fax: (202) 514-9412
Internet: www.justice.gov/criminal

The mission of the Criminal Division is to serve the public interest through the enforcement of criminal statutes in a vigorous, fair, and effective manner; and to exercise general supervision over the enforcement of all federal criminal laws, with the exception of those statutes specifically assigned to the Antitrust, Civil Rights, Environment and Natural Resources, or Tax Divisions.

★ Assistant Attorney General **Leslie Ragon Caldwell**
Room 2107 .... (202) 514-7200
Began Service: June 2, 2014
E-mail: leslie.r.caldwell@usdoj.gov
Education: Penn State 1979 BA; George Washington 1982 JD
Supervisory Administrative Specialist
Michelle Stallings Room 2215 .... (202) 305-4491
E-mail: michelle.stallings@usdoj.gov Fax: (202) 514-0409
• Senior Counsel to the Assistant Attorney General
Nancy Sumption .... (202) 514-2601
E-mail: nancy.sumption@usdoj.gov
• Senior Counsel to the Assistant Attorney General
(Vacant) .... (202) 514-2601
• Counsel to the Assistant Attorney General
Deborah Zerwitz .... (202) 307-3552
E-mail: deborah.zerwitz@usdoj.gov
○ Principal Deputy Assistant Attorney General and Chief of Staff **David Bitkower** Room 2206 .... (202) 307-1154
E-mail: david.bitkower@usdoj.gov
Education: Yale 1997 BA
○ Deputy Chief of Staff and Counselor to the Assistant Attorney General (Acting) **James Craig Mann**
Room 2208 .... (202) 514-2601
E-mail: james.mann@usdoj.gov
○ Executive Officer for the Office of Administration
Tracy Melton .... (202) 514-2811
Bond Building, 1400 New York Avenue, NW, 5th Floor, Washington, DC 20005
E-mail: tracy.melton@usdoj.gov
• Policy and Legislation Office Director
Jonathan J. Wroblewski Room 2218 .... (202) 514-3062
E-mail: jonathan.wroblewski@usdoj.gov
IT Program Director **Donovan Guthrie** .... (202) 616-2183
Bond Building, 1400 New York Avenue, NW, Room 7100, Washington, DC 20005 Fax: (202) 514-1578
E-mail: donovan.guthrie@usdoj.gov

Office of the Deputy Assistant Attorney General

• Deputy Assistant Attorney General **Paul M. O'Brien**
Room 2115 .... (202) 514-0169
E-mail: paul.obrien@usdoj.gov
Education: Texas A&M BA; U Memphis JD

Office of Enforcement Operations

1301 New York Avenue, NW, Room 1209, Washington, DC 20005
Tel: (202) 514-6809

• Director **Monique Perez Roth** .... (202) 514-8178
E-mail: monique.roth@usdoj.gov

Office of Enforcement Operations *continued*

• Deputy Director **Janet Webb** .... (202) 514-8178
E-mail: janet.webb@usdoj.gov

Public Integrity Section

Tel: (202) 514-1412

• Chief **Raymond N. Hulser** .... (202) 514-1412
Bond Building, 1400 New York Avenue, NW, Room 12100, Washington, DC 20005
E-mail: raymond.hulser@usdoj.gov
• Principal Deputy Chief **(Vacant)** .... (202) 514-1412

Office of the Deputy Assistant Attorney General

• Deputy Assistant Attorney General
Kenneth Anthony Blanco Room 2113 .... (202) 616-3027

Asset Forfeiture and Money Laundering Section

• Chief **Kendall Day** .... (202) 514-1263
Bond Building, 1400 New York Avenue, NW, Room 10100, Washington, DC 20005

Child Exploitation and Obscenity Section

• Chief (Acting) **Damon A. King** .... (202) 514-5780
Bond Building, 1400 New York Avenue, NW, 6th Floor, Washington, DC 20005
E-mail: damon.king@usdoj.gov

Narcotic and Dangerous Drug Section

• Chief **Arthur Wyatt** .... (202) 307-2382
Bond Building, 1400 New York Avenue, NW, Room 111000, Washington, DC 20005
E-mail: arthur.wyatt@usdoj.gov

Office of the Deputy Assistant Attorney General

• Deputy Assistant Attorney General and Counselor for International Affairs **Bruce C. Swartz** Room 2119 ...... (202) 514-2333
E-mail: bruce.swartz@usdoj.gov

International Criminal Investigative Training Assistance Program [ICITAP]

• Director **Robert Carr Trevillian IV** .... (202) 305-4243
1331 F Street, NW, Room 540, Washington, DC 20004

Office of International Affairs

• Director (Acting) **Mary D. Rodriguez** .... (202) 514-0000
1301 New York Avenue, NW, Room 900, Washington, DC 20005
E-mail: mary.rodriguez2@usdoj.gov

Office of Overseas Prosecutorial Development, Assistance and Training

Tel: (202) 514-1323

• Director (Acting) **Faye S. Ehrenstamm** .... (202) 616-8388
1331 F Street, NW, Suite 400, Washington, DC 20004
E-mail: faye.s.ehrenstamm@usdoj.gov

Office of the Deputy Assistant Attorney General

Deputy Assistant Attorney General **Sung-Hee Suh** ...... (202) 514-2601
E-mail: sung-hee.suh@usdoj.gov
Education: Radcliffe 1986 AB; Harvard 1986 AM, 1990 JD

Appellate Section

• Chief **Patty M. Stemler** Room 1521 .... (202) 514-2611
E-mail: patty.stemler@usdoj.gov

Capital Case Unit

• Chief **Kevin Carwile** .... (202) 353-7172
1331 F Street NW, Room 337, Washington, DC 20530
E-mail: kevin.carwile@usdoj.gov

Fraud Section

• Chief **Andrew Weissmann** .... (202) 514-7023
1400 New York Avenue, NW, Washington, DC 20005
E-mail: andrew.weissmann@usdoj.gov
Education: Princeton 1980 BA; Columbia 1984 JD

US DEPARTMENT OF JUSTICE

★ Presidential Appointment Requiring Senate Confirmation
☆ Presidential Appointment
□ Schedule C Appointment
◇ Career Senior Foreign Service Appointment
● Career Senior Executive Service (SES) Appointment
○ Non-Career Senior Executive Service (SES) Appointment

Office of the Deputy Assistant Attorney General

○ Deputy Assistant Attorney General (Acting)
David Bitkower Room 2121 .... (202) 616-2601
E-mail: david.bitkower@usdoj.gov
Education: Yale 1997 BA

Computer Crime and Intellectual Property Section [CCIPS]

10th and Constitution Avenue, NW, Suite 600,
Washington, DC 20530-0001
Tel: (202) 514-1026 Fax: (202) 514-6113
Internet: http://www.justice.gov/criminal-ccips

• Chief **John Lynch** .... (202) 514-1026
1301 New York Avenue, NW, Room 609, Washington, DC 20005
E-mail: john.lynch@usdoj.gov

Principal Deputy Chief **Richard Downing** .... (202) 514-1026
Washington, DC 20005
E-mail: richard.downing@usdoj.gov

Principal Deputy Chief for Litigation **James Silver** ...... (202) 514-1026
Washington, DC 20005
E-mail: james.silver@usdoj.gov

Deputy Chief for Intellectual Property
Christopher S. Merriam .... (202) 514-1026
Washington, DC 20005
E-mail: christopher.s.merriam@usdoj.gov

Cybercrime Lab Director **Ovie Carroll** .... (202) 514-1026
Washington, DC 20005
E-mail: ovie.carroll@usdoj.gov

Human Rights and Special Prosecutions Section

Tel: (202) 616-2492
Internet: http://www.justice.gov/criminal/hrsp/

Chief **Teresa L. McHenry** Room 7748 .... (202) 616-2492
E-mail: teresa.mchenry@usdoj.gov
Education: Rice; Harvard JD

• Director of Human Rights Enforcement Strategy and
Policy **Eli M. Rosenbaum** .... (202) 616-2492
1301 New York Avenue, NW, Room 206, Washington, DC 20005
E-mail: eli.rosenbaum@usdoj.gov
Education: Wharton 1976, 1977 MBA; Harvard 1980 JD

Organized Crime and Gang Section

• Chief **James M. Trusty** .... (202) 307-0207
1301 New York Avenue, NW, Room 700, Washington, DC 20005
E-mail: james.trusty@usdoj.gov

Criminal Enterprises [CE]

Robert F. Kennedy Building, 950 Pennsylvania Avenue, NW, Room 2107,
Washington, DC 20530

The purpose of the Criminal Enterprises program is to identify and investigate the local, regional, national, and transnational criminal enterprises that pose the greatest threat to the economic and national security of the United States, with the intent to disrupt and dismantle these organizations.

Program Manager **Bruce G. Ohr** .... (202) 514-2601

National Procurement Fraud Task Force

Bond Building, 4111, 10th and Constitution Avenue, NW,
Washington, DC 20530-0001
Tel: (202) 514-2000
E-mail: npftf@usdoj.gov

Director **William Simmonson** .... (202) 514-2000

Justice Management Division [JMD]

Robert F. Kennedy Building, 950 Pennsylvania Avenue, NW, Room 1111,
Washington, DC 20530
Tel: (202) 514-3101 Fax: (202) 616-6695
Internet: www.justice.gov/jmd

The mission of the Justice Management Division is to provide advice to senior management officials relating to basic Department policy for budget and financial management, personnel management and training, procurement, equal employment opportunity, information processing, telecommunications, security, and all matters pertaining to organization, management, and administration. The Assistant Attorney General for Administration leads the Division serves as the Department's Chief Financial Officer, and his four deputies serve as the Department's Controller, Chief Human Capital Officer, Chief Information Officer, and Senior Procurement Executive.

• Assistant Attorney General for Administration [Senior
Sustainability Officer] **Leon J. "Lee" Lofthus** .... (202) 514-3101
E-mail: lee.j.lofthus@usdoj.gov
Education: American U 1982 MBA

Controller

• Deputy Assistant Attorney General and Controller
[Performance Improvement Officer] **Jolene Lauria**
Room 1117 .... (202) 514-1843
E-mail: jolene.lauria-sullens@usdoj.gov
Education: Maryland Baltimore County 1987 BSc

• Asset Forfeiture Management Staff Director **(Vacant)** .... (202) 616-8000
145 First Street, NE, Suite 5W-725, Fax: (202) 616-8100
Washington, DC 20002

• Budget Staff Director **Robin Funston** Room 7605 .... (202) 514-4082
E-mail: robin.funston@usdoj.gov Fax: (202) 514-0406

• Debt Collection Management Director **(Vacant)** .... (202) 514-5343
145 First Street, NE, Suite 5E-103, Fax: (202) 514-1965
Washington, DC 20002

• Finance Staff Director **Melinda B. Morgan** .... (202) 616-5809
145 First Street NE, Suite 7E-202, Fax: (202) 616-6414
Washington, DC 20002
E-mail: melinda.b.morgan@usdoj.gov

Senior Appropriation Liaison Officer **Daniel Lucas**
Room 1116 .... (202) 514-2147
E-mail: daniel.lucas@usdoj.gov

Human Resources and Administration

• Deputy Assistant Attorney General and Human
Resources Director **Mari Barr Santangelo**
Room 1110 .... (202) 514-5501
E-mail: mari.santangelo@usdoj.gov Fax: (202) 305-4746
Education: Wisconsin BS, MS

• Attorney Recruitment and Management Office Director
Jamila Frone .... (202) 514-8900
Liberty Square, 450 5th Street, N.W., Room 10112, Fax: (202) 514-0713
Washington, DC 20530
E-mail: jamila.frone@usdoj.gov

Consolidated Executive Office Director
Cyntoria E. Carter Room 7113 .... (202) 514-5537
E-mail: cyntoria.carter@usdoj.gov Fax: (202) 514-2028

• Human Resources Staff Director **Terence L. Cook** .... (202) 514-4350
145 First Street NE, Suite 9W-102, Washington, DC 20002

• Security and Emergency Planning Staff Director
James L. Dunlap Room 6217 .... (202) 514-2094
E-mail: james.l.dunlap@usdoj.gov Fax: (202) 307-2069

Office of the Executive Secretariat [OES]

Robert F. Kennedy Building, 950 Pennsylvania Avenue, NW,
Washington, DC 20530
Tel: (202) 514-2063 Fax: (202) 514-4507

Director **Dana E. Paige** Room 4414 .... (202) 616-2374
E-mail: dana.e.paige@usdoj.gov

Special Assistant **(Vacant)** Room 4400 .... (202) 514-2063

Controlled Correspondence Assistant Director
Kimberly G. Tolson Room 4412 .... (202) 514-2063
E-mail: kimberly.g.tolson@usdoj.gov

★ Presidential Appointment Requiring Senate Confirmation ☐ Schedule C Appointment ● Career Senior Executive Service (SES) Appointment
☆ Presidential Appointment ◇ Career Senior Foreign Service Appointment ○ Non-Career Senior Executive Service (SES) Appointment

Office of the Executive Secretariat *continued*

Technical Services Assistant Director **Dorothy Ward**
Room 4414 .... (202) 514-2063
E-mail: dorothy.ward@usdoj.gov

Records Requests/Inquiries **Marcia L. Hines**
Room 4416 .... (202) 514-2063
E-mail: marcia.l.hines@usdoj.gov

Equal Employment Opportunity Staff

Tel: (202) 616-4800 Fax: (202) 616-4823

• Director **Richard Toscano** .... (202) 616-4800
145 First Street NE, Suite 1W-102, Washington, DC 20002
E-mail: richard.toscano@usdoj.gov

Information Resources Management [OCIO]

950 Pennsylvania Avenue, NW, Washington, DC 20530
Tel: (202) 514-0507 Fax: (202) 514-1225

• Deputy Assistant Attorney General and Chief Information Officer **Joseph F. "Joe" Klimavicz**
Room 1310 .... (202) 514-0507
E-mail: joseph.klimavicz@usdoj.gov
Education: Virginia Tech 1983 BS, 1988 ME

• Deputy Chief Information Officer **Kevin Deeley** .... (202) 514-0507
E-mail: kevin.deeley@usdoj.gov

• System Engineering Staff Director and Deputy Chief Information Officer **Eric R. Olson** .... (202) 353-2355
145 N Street, NE, Suite 3W-701, Washington, DC 20530
E-mail: eric.olson@usdoj.gov

Chief Technology Officer **(Vacant)** .... (202) 514-0507
145 N Street, NE, Washington, DC 20530

Enterprise Solutions Staff Director **John Murray** .... (202) 532-5845
145 N Street, NE, Suite 3E.701, Washington, DC 20530
E-mail: john.murray@usdoj.gov

Operation Services Staff Director **(Vacant)** .... (202) 514-0778
145 N Street, NE, Suite 4E-202, Washington, DC 20530

• Information Technology Security Staff Director [Chief Information Security Officer] **Melinda Rogers** .... (202) 305-7017
145 N Street, NE, Suite 4E-206, Washington, DC 20530 Fax: (202) 514-1534
E-mail: melinda.rogers@usdoj.gov

Information Technology Security Staff Deputy Director **Kevin Cox** .... (202) 305-0507
145 N Street, NE, Washington, DC 20530 Fax: (202) 514-1534
E-mail: kevin.cox@usdoj.gov

Policy and Planning Staff Director **Richard "Rick" Chandler** .... (202) 353-2421
145 N Street, NE, Suite 3E.206, Washington, DC 20530
E-mail: richard.chandler@usdoj.gov

Chief Enterprise Architect **(Vacant)** .... (202) 616-1167
145 N Street, NE, Suite 300.122, Washington, DC 20530

Policy, Management and Planning

Tel: (202) 514-3101

• Deputy Assistant Attorney General for Policy, Management and Planning [Open Government Directive Official, Senior Agency Official for Records Management] **Michael H. "Mike" Allen** Room 1113 .... (202) 514-3101
E-mail: michael.allen3@usdoj.gov

• Facilities and Administrative Services Staff Director **Scott Snell** .... (202) 616-2995
145 First Street NE, Suite 9E-206, Washington, DC 20002 Fax: (202) 307-1915
E-mail: scott.snell@usdoj.gov

• General Counsel Office Director **Arthur E. "Art" Gary** ... (202) 514-3452
145 First Street, NE, Suite 8E-528, Washington, DC 20002 Fax: (202) 514-4317
E-mail: arthur.gary@usdoj.gov
Education: Virginia 1980 BA; William & Mary 1983 JD

Internal Review and Evaluation Office Director **Neil Ryder** .... (202) 616-5499
145 First Street, NE, Suite 8W-1419, Washington, DC 20002
E-mail: neil.ryder@usdoj.gov

Policy, Management and Planning *continued*

• Procurement Services Staff Director **Mark Selweski** ..... (202) 307-2000
145 First Street NE, Suite 8E-202, Washington, DC 20002 Fax: (202) 307-1933
E-mail: mselweski@usdoj.gov

Office of Records Management Policy Director **Jeanette Plante** .... (202) 514-3528
145 First Street, NE, Suite 8W-1401, Washington, DC 20002
E-mail: jeanette.plante@usdoj.gov

Departmental Ethics Office

Tel: (202) 514-8196

• Director **Janice Rodgers** .... (202) 514-8196
145 First Street, NE, Suite 8E-310, Washington, DC 20002 Fax: (202) 514-3117
E-mail: janice.rodgers@usdoj.gov

Deputy Director **Cynthia Shaw** .... (202) 514-8196

National Security Division [NSD]

Robert F. Kennedy Building, 950 Pennsylvania Avenue, NW, Room 7339, Washington, DC 20530
Tel: (202) 514-1057
Internet: www.justice.gov/nsd

The National Security Division (NSD) was created in March 2006 by the USA PATRIOT Reauthorization and Improvement Act. The mission of the National Security Division is to carry out the Departments highest priority: to combat terrorism and other threats to national security. The NSDs organizational structure is designed to ensure greater coordination and unity of purpose between prosecutors and law enforcement agencies, on the one hand, and intelligence attorneys and the Intelligence Community, on the other, thus strengthening the effectiveness of the federal governments national security efforts.

★ Assistant Attorney General **John P. Carlin** .... (202) 514-1057
Began Service: April 2, 2014
E-mail: john.carlin@usdoj.gov
Education: Williams 1995 BA; Harvard 1999 JD

• Principal Deputy Assistant Attorney General **Mary B. McCord** .... (202) 514-1057
E-mail: mary.mccord@usdoj.gov

• Chief of Staff and Counselor **Anita Singh** .... (202) 514-1057
E-mail: anita.singh@usdoj.gov
Education: Southern Methodist 2001 BA, 2001 BS; Pennsylvania MA, JD

Deputy Chief of Staff **(Vacant)** .... (202) 514-1057

Senior Litigation Counsel for Cyber Investigations **Timothy Howard** .... (202) 514-1057
E-mail: timothy.howard@usdoj.gov
Education: Georgetown 2000 BS; Harvard 2004 JD

Special Assistant to the Assistant Attorney General **Stephanie Ore-Brooks** .... (202) 514-1057
E-mail: stephanie.ore-brooks@usdoj.gov

Special Assistant to the Assistant Attorney General **Brianna Carbonneau** .... (202) 514-1057
E-mail: brianna.carbonneau@usdoj.gov

• FOIA and Declassification Program Director **Mark A. Bradley** .... (202) 514-1057
E-mail: mark.a.bradley@usdoj.gov

Domestic Terrorism Counsel **(Vacant)** .... (202) 514-1057
Note: On October 14, 2015 Assistant Attorney General John P. Carlin announced the appointment of a new Domestic Terrorism Counsel to serve as the main point of contact for U.S. Attorneys working on domestic terrorism matters.

Executive Office

Executive Officer **Mark A. Jenkins** .... (202) 363-9787
E-mail: mark.a.jenkins@usdoj.gov

Office of Justice for Victims of Overseas Terrorism

• Deputy Assistant Attorney General **Luke Dembosky** ..... (202) 514-1057
E-mail: luke.dembosky@usdoj.gov
Education: Pittsburgh JD

(continued on next page)

★ Presidential Appointment Requiring Senate Confirmation
☆ Presidential Appointment
☐ Schedule C Appointment
◇ Career Senior Foreign Service Appointment
● Career Senior Executive Service (SES) Appointment
○ Non-Career Senior Executive Service (SES) Appointment

Office of Justice for Victims of Overseas Terrorism *continued*

Director **Heather Cartwright** .... (202) 233-0701
600 E Street, NW, Washington, DC 20530
E-mail: heather.cartwright@usdoj.gov
Education: Illinois, JD

Office of Counterterrorism and Counterespionage

● Deputy Assistant Attorney General **George C. Tocas** .... (202) 514-1057
E-mail: gtocas@jmd.usdoj.gov

Counterespionage Section

600 E Street, NW, Washington, DC 20530

● Chief **David H. Laufman** .... (202) 514-1057
E-mail: david.laufman@usdoj.gov
Education: Pennsylvania 1980 BA; Georgetown JD
● Deputy Chief **(Vacant)** .... (202) 233-0980

Counterterrorism Section

950 Pennsylvania Avenue, NW, Room 2649, Washington, DC 20530

● Chief **Michael J. Mullaney** .... (202) 514-0849
E-mail: michael.mullaney@usdoj.gov
Education: Southern Illinois BS; Miami 1988 JD
Principal Deputy Chief (Acting) **Jennifer Smith** .... (202) 514-0849
E-mail: jennifer.smith3@usdoj.gov
Program Support Deputy Chief **(Vacant)** .... (202) 514-0849
International Terrorism Unit I Deputy Chief **(Vacant)** .... (202) 514-0849
International Terrorism Unit II Deputy Chief (Acting)
Stephen Ponticiello .... (202) 514-0849
E-mail: stephen.ponticiello@usdoj.gov
International Terrorism Unit III Deputy Chief
Michael Taxay .... (202) 514-0849
E-mail: michael.taxay@usdoj.gov

Office of Intelligence

● Deputy Assistant Attorney General **Tashina Gauhar** ..... (202) 514-1057
E-mail: tashina.gauhar@usdoj.gov

Office of Law and Policy

○ Deputy Assistant Attorney General **Brad Wiegmann** ..... (202) 514-1057
E-mail: brad.wiegmann@usdoj.gov
Chief **(Vacant)** .... (202) 514-1057
Counsel **Jennifer C. Daskal** .... (202) 514-1057
E-mail: jennifer.daskal@usdoj.gov
Education: Brown U 1994 BA; Cambridge (UK) 1996 BA, 1996 MA; Harvard 2001 JD
Senior Component Official for Privacy **Jocelyn Aqua** .... (202) 514-1057
E-mail: jocelyn.aqua@usdoj.gov
Education: Penn State 1990 BA; George Washington 1994 MA, 1995 JD

Executive Office for Immigration Review [EOIR]

Skyline Towers, 5107 Leesburg Pike, Falls Church, VA 22041
Tel: (703) 305-0289 Fax: (703) 605-0365
E-mail: pao.eoir@usdoj.gov
Internet: www.justice.gov/eoir

The primary mission of the Executive Office for Immigration Review (EOIR) is to adjudicate immigration cases by fairly, expeditiously, and uniformly interpreting and administering the Nation's immigration laws. Under delegated authority from the Attorney General, EOIR conducts immigration court proceedings, appellate reviews, and administrative hearings.

● Director **Juan P. Osuna** Room 2600 .... (703) 305-0289
E-mail: juan.p.osuna@usdoj.gov
Education: George Washington 1985 BA; Washington College of Law 1988 JD; American U 1989 MA
● Deputy Director **Ana Kocur** Room 2600 .... (703) 305-0289
E-mail: ana.kocur@usdoj.gov
Program Director, Office of Legal Access Programs
Steven Lang Room 2600 .... (703) 305-0169
E-mail: steven.lang@usdoj.gov

Executive Office for Immigration Review [EOIR] *continued*

Equal Employment Opportunity and Diversity
Program Manager **(Vacant)** Room 1905 .... (703) 305-0289
Executive Secretariat **Rhonda Caldwell** Room 2600 .... (703) 305-0169
E-mail: rhonda.caldwell@usdoj.gov
Chief Information Officer **Terryne F Murphy**
Room 2300 .... (703) 305-6933
E-mail: terryne.murphy@usdoj.gov
Chief Technology Officer **Ajay Budhraja** .... (703) 305-0289
● General Counsel (Acting) **Jean King** Room 2600 .... (703) 305-0470
E-mail: jean.king@usdoj.gov
Deputy General Counsel **Jean King** Room 2600 .... (703) 305-0470
E-mail: jean.king@usdoj.gov
Administration Assistant Director (Acting)
Edward F. Kelly Room 2300 .... (703) 605-1346
Education: Notre Dame 1982 AB, 1987 JD
● Principal Deputy Director for Administration
(Vacant) Suite 2300 .... (703) 305-0418
Controller Deputy Assistant Director
(Vacant) Room 2200 .... (703) 305-1634
Management Programs Assistant Director (Acting)
James Paul McDaniel Room 2653 .... (703) 305-0289
E-mail: james.p.mcdaniel@usdoj.gov
Management Programs Deputy Assistant Director
(Vacant) Room 2653 .... (703) 305-0289
Counsel for Legislative and Public Affairs
Lauren Alder Reid Room 1902 .... (703) 305-0289
E-mail: lauren.alder.reid@usdoj.gov
E-mail: pao.eoir@usdoj.gov
Security Programs Manager **James Paul McDaniel**
Room 1901 .... (703) 605-1141
E-mail: james.p.mcdaniel@usdoj.gov
Space Management Officer **Mary Jane Graul**
Room 2300 .... (703) 305-1178
E-mail: mary.jane.graul@usdoj.gov
Planning, Analysis and Technology Assistant Director
(Vacant) Room 2600 .... (703) 605-0445

Board of Immigration Appeals [BIA]

5107 Leesburg Pike, Suite 2400, Falls Church, VA 20530
Tel: (703) 605-1007 (General Information)
Internet: www.usdoj.gov/eoir/biainfo.htm

The Board of Immigration Appeals (BIA) is the highest administrative body for interpreting and applying immigration laws. It is authorized up to 15 Board Members, including the Chairman and Vice Chairman who share responsibility for BIA management. The BIA has been given nationwide jurisdiction to hear appeals from certain decisions rendered by immigration judges and by district directors of the Department of Homeland Security (DHS) in a wide variety of proceedings in which the Government of the United States is one party and the other party is an alien, a citizen, or a business firm. In addition, the BIA is responsible for the recognition of organizations and accreditation of representatives requesting permission to practice before DHS, the immigration courts, and the BIA.

● Chairman **David L. Neal** .... (703) 305-1194
Education: Wabash Col 1981 BA; Harvard 1984 MDiv; Columbia 1989 JD
● Vice Chairman **Charles Adkins-Blanch** .... (703) 305-1194
Education: Grinnell BA; George Washington 1990 JM
Chief Clerk of the Board **Donna Carr** .... (703) 605-1007
5107 Leesburg Pike, Suite 2000, Falls Church, VA 22041
P.O. Box 8530, Falls Church, VA 22041
E-mail: donna.carr@usdoj.gov
Director of Operations **Jake Walker** .... (703) 305-1194
E-mail: jake.walker@usdoj.gov
Executive Officer **Michael Porter** .... (703) 305-1194
E-mail: michael.porter@usdoj.gov
Head Librarian **Karen Drumond** .... (703) 605-1102
5201 Leesburg Pike, Falls Church, VA 22041
E-mail: karen.drumond@usdoj.gov

Office of the Chief Administrative Hearing Officer [OCAHO]

Skyline Towers, 5107 Leesburg Pike, Suite 2519, Falls Church, VA 20530
Fax: (703) 305-1515
Internet: www.usdoj.gov/eoir/ocahoinfo.htm

The Office of the Chief Administrative Hearing Officer is responsible for the general supervision and management of Administrative Law Judges who preside at hearings which are mandated by provisions of law enacted in the Immigration Reform and Control Act of 1986 (IRCA) and the Immigration Act of 1990. These acts, among others, amended the Immigration and Nationality Act of 1952 (INA).

● Chief Administrative Hearing Officer
Robin M. Stutman .... (703) 305-0864
Skyline Towers, 5107 Leesburg Pike, Room 2519,
Falls Church, VA 22041
E-mail: robin.m.stutman@usdoj.gov
Education: SUNY (Stony Brook) 1978 BA; UCLA 1982 JD

Administrative Law Judge **Stacy Stiffel Paddack** .... (703) 305-0289
5107 Leesburg Pike, Falls Church, VA 22041
E-mail: stacy.paddack@usdoj.gov
Education: Texas 1989 BA; American U 1994 MA;
Washington College of Law 1997 JD

Administrative Law Judge **Ellen K. Thomas** .... (703) 305-1742
Skyline Towers, 5107 Leesburg Pike, Room 2500,
Falls Church, VA 22041
E-mail: ellen.thomas@usdoj.gov

Office of the Chief Immigration Judge [OCIJ]

Skyline Towers, 5107 Leesburg Pike, Room 2500,
Falls Church, VA 20530
Tel: (703) 305-1247
Internet: www.usdoj.gov/eoir/ocijinfo.htm

The Office of the Chief Immigration Judge (OCIJ) provides overall program direction, articulates policies and procedures, and establishes priorities for over 260 immigration judges in 59 immigration courts throughout the Nation. The Chief Immigration Judge carries out these responsibilities with Deputy and Assistant Chief Immigration Judges, a Chief Clerks Office, a Language Services Unit, and other functions that coordinate management and operation of the immigration courts.

● Chief Immigration Judge (Interim)
Robert P. "Print" Maggard .... (703) 305-1247
5107 Leesburg Pike, Falls Church, VA 22041
E-mail: print.maggard@usdoj.gov
Education: Western Kentucky 1982 BA; Golden Gate 1987 MPA;
McGeorge 1990 JD; George Washington 1999 LLM

Counsel to the Chief Immigration Judge **(Vacant)** ...... (703) 305-1247

Deputy Chief Immigration Judge **Edward F. Kelly** .... (703) 305-1247
Skyline Towers, 5107 Leesburg Pike, Room 2500,
Falls Church, VA 22041
E-mail: ed.kelly@usdoj.gov
Education: Notre Dame 1982 AB, 1987 JD

Deputy Chief Immigration Judge (Acting)
Christopher A. Santoro .... (703) 305-1247
Skyline Towers, 5107 Leesburg Pike, Room 2500,
Falls Church, VA 22041
E-mail: christopher.santoro@usdoj.gov
Education: Tufts 1991 BA; Boston U 1994 JD

Assistant Chief Immigration Judge
Richard J. Bartolomei, Jr. .... (619) 557-6052
401 West A Street, Suite 800, San Diego, CA 92101
Education: Notre Dame 1983 BA; Georgetown 1986 JD

Assistant Chief Immigration Judge **John W. Davis** ...... (303) 844-5815
621 17th Street, Room 300, Denver, CO 80293
E-mail: john.davis@usdoj.gov
Education: Nebraska (Omaha) 1981 BA; Creighton 1987 JD;
Judge Advocate Gen 1997 LLM

Assistant Chief Immigration Judge **Jill H. Dufresne** ..... (703) 305-1247
Skyline Towers, 5107 Leesburg Pike, Room 2500,
Falls Church, VA 22041
E-mail: jill.dufresne@usdoj.gov

Office of the Chief Immigration Judge *continued*

Assistant Chief Immigration Judge
Thomas Y. K. Fong .... (213) 894-2811
Los Angeles Immigration Court, 606 South Olive Street, Suite 1500,
Los Angeles, CA 90014
E-mail: thomas.fong@usdoj.gov
Education: BYU 1972 BS; J Reuben Clark Law 1977 JD

Assistant Chief Immigration Judge (Acting)
Stephen S. Griswold .... (703) 305-1247
Skyline Towers, 5107 Leesburg Pike, Room 2500,
Falls Church, VA 22041
E-mail: stephen.griswold@usdoj.gov
Education: Wesleyan U 1978 BA; George Washington 1985 JD

Assistant Chief Immigration Judge **Mary Beth Keller** .... (703) 305-1247
Skyline Towers, 5107 Leesburg Pike, Room 2500,
Falls Church, VA 22041
Education: Catholic U 1984 BA; Virginia 1987 JD

Assistant Chief Immigration Judge
Robert P. "Print" Maggard .... (415) 705-4415
120 Montgomery Street, Suite 800, San Francisco, CA 94104
E-mail: print.maggard@usdoj.gov
Education: Western Kentucky 1982 BA; Golden Gate 1987 MPA;
McGeorge 1990 JD; George Washington 1999 LLM

Assistant Chief Immigration Judge **Deepali Nadkarni** .... (703) 305-1247
Skyline Towers, 5107 Leesburg Pike, Room 2500,
Falls Church, VA 22041
E-mail: deepali.nadkarni@usdoj.gov

Assistant Chief Immigration Judge **Elisa M. Sukkar** ..... (305) 789-4221
One Riverview Square, 333 South Miami Avenue, Suite 700,
Miami, FL 33133
E-mail: elisa.sukkar@usdoj.gov

Assistant Chief Immigration Judge **Jack H. Weil** .... (210) 472-6637
Note: On detail to the Director's Office.
800 Dolorosa Street, Suite 300, San Antonio, TX 78207
E-mail: jack.weil@usdoj.gov

Assistant Chief Immigration Judge **Robert D. Weisel** .... (917) 454-1040
New York Immigration Court, 26 Federal Plaza, 12th Floor,
Room 1237, New York, NY 10278-0004
E-mail: robert.weisel@usdoj.gov
Education: SUNY (New Paltz) 1973 BA; Hamline 1976 JD

Assistant Chief Immigration Judge **(Vacant)** .... (703) 305-1247
5107 Leesburg Pike, Falls Church, VA 22041

Executive Office for United States Attorneys [EOUSA]

Robert F. Kennedy Building, 950 Pennsylvania Avenue, NW,
Washington, DC 20530
Tel: (202) 252-1000 Fax: (202) 252-1001
Internet: www.justice.gov/usao/eousa

The United States Attorneys serve as the nation's principal litigators under the direction of the Attorney General. One United States Attorney is assigned to each of the judicial districts, with the exception of Guam and the Northern Mariana Islands where a single United States Attorney serves in both districts. Each United States Attorney is the chief federal law enforcement officer of the United States within his or her particular jurisdiction.

The mission of the Executive Office for U.S. Attorneys is to provide general executive assistance to the 94 Offices of the United States Attorneys and to coordinate the relationship between the United States Attorneys and the organizational components of the Department of Justice and other federal agencies.

Office of the Director

Tel: (202) 252-1000 Fax: (202) 252-1001

● Director **Monty Wilkinson** Room 2242 .... (202) 252-1000
E-mail: monty.wilkinson@usdoj.gov
Education: Dartmouth 1983 AB; Georgetown Col 1988 JD

Attorney Advisor **(Vacant)** .... (202) 252-1000

● Principal Deputy Director and Chief of Staff **(Vacant)** .... (202) 252-1000

(continued on next page)

★ Presidential Appointment Requiring Senate Confirmation
☆ Presidential Appointment
☐ Schedule C Appointment
◇ Career Senior Foreign Service Appointment
● Career Senior Executive Service (SES) Appointment
○ Non-Career Senior Executive Service (SES) Appointment

Office of the Director *continued*

Attorney Generals Advisory Committee Liaison, Executive Assistant and Editor, US Attorneys Manual
Karen Winzenburg Room 2262 .... (202) 252-1374
E-mail: karen.winzenburg@usdoj.gov Fax: (202) 252-1373

Data Analysis Staff Assistant Director
Michelle Slusher .... (202) 252-5570
Bicentennial Building, 600 E Street, NW, Room 2000, Washington, DC 20530 Fax: (202) 252-5580
E-mail: michelle.slusher@usdoj.gov

Employee Assistance Program Administrator
Ed Neunlist .... (888) 271-0381
Bicentennial Building, 600 E Street, NW, Room 6800, Washington, DC 20530 Fax: (202) 252-5454
E-mail: ed.neunlist@usdoj.gov

Administrative Officer (Acting) **Joy Smith** .... (202) 252-5553
E-mail: joy.smith@usdoj.gov Fax: (202) 252-5543

Victims' Rights Ombudsman **Marie O'Rourke** .... (202) 252-1317
E-mail: marie.o'rourke@usdoj.gov Fax: (202) 252-1011

• Chief of Planning, Evaluation and Performance
(Vacant) .... (202) 252-1000

National Project Safe Neighborhood Coordinator
Seth Meinero .... (202) 252-5847
E-mail: seth.meinero@usdoj.gov Fax: (202) 252-5861

Office of the Deputy Director for Administration and Management

• Deputy Director for Administration and Management
(Vacant) Room 2242 .... (202) 252-5553

Associate Director **(Vacant)** .... (202) 252-1000

Chief Human Resources Officer **Shawn Flinn** .... (202) 252-5300
Bicentennial Building, 600 E Street, NW, Room 8017, Washington, DC 20530 Fax: (202) 252-5301
E-mail: shawn.flinn@usdoj.gov
Education: Vermont Law 2001 JD

Acquisitions Staff Assistant Director
Stephanie M. Girard .... (202) 252-5400
Bicentennial Building, 600 E Street, NW, Room 8300, Washington, DC 20579 Fax: (202) 252-5401
E-mail: stephanie.girard@usdoj.gov

Facilities and Support Staff Services Assistant Director
Ana Indovina .... (202) 252-5964
Bicentennial Building, 600 E Street, NW, Room 8300, Washington, DC 20530 Fax: (202) 252-5969
E-mail: ana.indovina@usdoj.gov

Security and Emergency Management Staff Assistant Director **Timothy "Tim" George** .... (202) 252-5694
Bicentennial Building, 600 E Street, NW, Room 2600, Washington, DC 20579 Fax: (202) 252-5737
E-mail: timothy.george@usdoj.gov

Resource Management and Planning Staff

Bicentennial Building, 600 E Street, NW, Washington, DC 20530
Tel: (202) 252-5600 Fax: (202) 252-5601

Chief Financial Officer **Paul Suddes** Room 8000 .... (202) 252-5600
E-mail: paul.suddes@usdoj.gov

Assistant Director for Audits **Louisa McCarter-Dadzie** ... (202) 252-5600
E-mail: louisa.mccarter-dadzie@usdoj.gov

Assistant Director for Execution **Tracy Hall** Room 8503 ... (202) 252-5600

Assistant Director for Financial Systems
Jonathan Pelletier .... (202) 252-5600
E-mail: jonathan.pelletier@usdoj.gov

Assistant Director for Formulation **(Vacant)** Room 2200 ... (202) 252-5600

Office of Information Technology [CIO]

Bicentennial Building, 600 E Street, NW, Washington, DC 20530

Chief Information Officer **Mark Fleshman** Room 2300 ... (202) 252-6246
E-mail: mark.fleshman@usdoj.gov Fax: (202) 252-6100

Case Management Staff Assistant Director
Siobhan Sperin Room 7500 .... (202) 252-6234
E-mail: siobhan.sperin@usdoj.gov Fax: (202) 252-6201

Enterprise Voiceover IP Assistant Director
Joe Pfeifer Room 9100 .... (202) 272-4462
E-mail: joe.pfeifer@usdoj.gov Fax: (202) 272-4441

Office of Information Technology *continued*

Office Automation Staff Assistant Director
Glenn Shrieves Room 9100 .... (202) 252-6270
E-mail: glenn.shrieves@usdoj.gov Fax: (202) 252-6100

Records and Information Management Assistant Director **Bonnie Curtin** Room 9100 .... (202) 252-6488
E-mail: bonnie.curtin@usdoj.gov Fax: (202) 252-6481

Telecommunication and Technology Development Assistant Director **Denny Ko** Room 6012 .... (202) 252-6430
E-mail: denny.ko@usdoj.gov Fax: (202) 252-6455

Office of the Deputy Director and Counsel

• Deputy Director and Counsel to the Director
Norman Y. Wong Room 2242 .... (202) 252-1000
E-mail: norman.wong@usdoj.gov

Evaluation and Review Staff Assistant Director
Dayle Elieson .... (202) 252-5900
Bicentennial Building, 600 E Street, NW, Room 8500, Washington, DC 20530 Fax: (202) 252-5902
E-mail: dayle.elieson@usdoj.gov

FOIA and Privacy Unit Assistant Director
Susan Gerson .... (202) 252-1000
Bicentennial Building, 600 E Street, NW, Room 7300, Washington, DC 20530 Fax: (202) 252-6047
E-mail: susan.gerson@usdoj.gov

LECC/Victim Witness Staff Assistant Director
Kristina M. Neal .... (202) 252-5858
Bicentennial Building, 600 E Street, NW, Room 2500, Washington, DC 20530 Fax: (202) 252-5861
E-mail: kristina.neal@usdoj.gov

Office of Legal and Victim Programs

Bicentennial Building, 600 E Street, NW, Washington, DC 20530

Counsel for Legal and Victim Programs
Daniel Villegas Room 7600 .... (202) 252-5858
E-mail: dan.villegas@usdoj.gov Fax: (202) 252-5861

Office of the Deputy Director for Legal Management

Deputy Director for Legal Management
Suzanne L. Bell Room 2242 .... (202) 252-1000
E-mail: suzanne.l.bell@usdoj.gov

Equal Employment Opportunity Staff Assistant Director **Jason M. Osborne** .... (202) 252-1000
National Place Building, 1331 Pennsylvania Avenue, NW, Room 524, Washington, DC 20530 Fax: (202) 252-1011
E-mail: jason.osborne@usdoj.gov

Office of General Counsel

501 3rd Street, NW, Room 5500, Washington, DC 20530
Tel: (202) 252-1649 Fax: (202) 514-1104

General Counsel **Jay Macklin** .... (202) 252-1550
E-mail: jay.macklin@usdoj.gov

Deputy General Counsel **Thomas Anderson** .... (202) 252-1552
E-mail: thomas.anderson@usdoj.gov

Deputy General Counsel **Carol A. Shea** .... (202) 252-1551
E-mail: carol.shea@usdoj.gov

Office of Legal Education (National Advocacy Center)

1620 Pendelton Street, Columbia, SC 29201
Tel: (803) 705-5100 Fax: (803) 705-5110
Internet: www.justice.gov/usao/eousa/ole

• Associate Director **Cammy Chandler** .... (803) 705-5102
E-mail: cammy.chandler@usdoj.gov

Deputy Director **Col Calvin L. Lewis USAF** .... (803) 705-5102
E-mail: calvin.lewis@usdoj.gov

US DEPARTMENT OF JUSTICE

★ Presidential Appointment Requiring Senate Confirmation
☆ Presidential Appointment
☐ Schedule C Appointment
◇ Career Senior Foreign Service Appointment
● Career Senior Executive Service (SES) Appointment
○ Non-Career Senior Executive Service (SES) Appointment

INTERPOL Washington [USNCB]

U.S. Department of Justice, Washington, DC 20530
Tel: (202) 616-9000 Fax: (202) 616-8400
Internet: www.justice.gov/interpol-washington

INTERPOL Washington, the United States National Central Bureau, serves as the designated representative to the International Criminal Police Organization (INTERPOL) on behalf of the Attorney General. INTERPOL Washington is the official U.S. point of contact in INTERPOL's worldwide, police-to-police communications and criminal intelligence network. A component of the U.S. Department of Justice (DOJ), INTERPOL Washington is co-managed by the U.S. Department of Homeland Security (DHS) pursuant to a Memorandum of Understanding that ensures a continuing commitment to the guidance and oversight of the organization and reinforces its role in effectively sharing and exchanging international criminal investigative and humanitarian assistance information.

Office of the Director

Tel: (202) 616-9700 Fax: (202) 616-1048

Director **(Vacant)** .... (202) 616-9700
Executive Assistant **Kelly Jones-Brown** .... (202) 532-4239
E-mail: kelly.jones-brown@usdoj.gov
Deputy Director **Geoffrey S. "Geoff" Shank** .... (202) 616-9700

Office of General Counsel

Tel: (202) 616-9700 Fax: (202) 616-8400

General Counsel **Kevin R. Smith** .... (202) 616-4103
E-mail: kevin.r.smith@usdoj.gov
Supervisory Legal Analyst **Kathleen O'Connell** .... (202) 307-0856
E-mail: kathleen.oconnell@usdoj.gov

Office of the Chief Information Officer

Chief Information Officer **Wayne Towson** .... (202) 616-3855
E-mail: wayne.towson@usdoj.gov
Information Systems Security Officer
Nathree "Nate" Turner .... (202) 305-8764
E-mail: nate.turner@usdoj.gov

Office of the Executive Officer

Tel: (202) 616-9000 Fax: (202) 616-9541

Executive Officer **(Vacant)** .... (202) 616-8810
Administrative Officer **Deborah C. Allen** .... (202) 305-7847
E-mail: deborah.c.allen@usdoj.gov
Compliance Officer **Robin Palmer** .... (202) 616-3587
E-mail: robin.palmer@usdoj.gov
Public and Congressional Affairs Officer
LaTonya N. Turner .... (202) 616-8006

Alien and Fugitive Division

Tel: (202) 616-9000 Fax: (202) 616-3894

Assistant Director **Darrell H. White** .... (202) 616-0310
E-mail: darrell.h.white@usdoj.gov
Supervisor **Crystal Holland** .... (202) 616-3503

Counterterrorism Division

Tel: (202) 616-9000 Fax: (202) 616-7233

Assistant Director **Robert W. Meadows** .... (202) 616-9000
E-mail: robert.w.meadows@usdoj.gov
Supervisor/Program Manager **Wendy Standel** .... (202) 353-0811
E-mail: wendy.standel@usdoj.gov

Drug Division

Tel: (202) 616-9000 Fax: (202) 616-8333

Assistant Director **Richard J. Joyce** .... (202) 616-3379
E-mail: richard.j.joyce@usdoj.gov
Supervisor **Donna Holland-Egerson** .... (202) 616-8259
E-mail: donna.egerson@usdoj.gov

Economic Crimes Division

Tel: (202) 616-9000 Fax: (202) 616-8314

Assistant Director **Gerard Doret** .... (202) 616-5466
E-mail: gerard.doret@usdoj.gov
Supervisor **David Whitmire** .... (202) 353-8171
E-mail: david.whitmire@usdoj.gov

Human Trafficking Division

Tel: (202) 616-9000 Fax: (202) 616-7233

Assistant Director **Paul Layman** .... (202) 616-9000
E-mail: paul.layman@usdoj.gov
Supervisor **Michelle Ford-Stepney** .... (202) 616-1073
E-mail: michelle.ford-stepney@usdoj.gov

INTERPOL Operations and Command Center

Fax: (202) 616-9400 Fax: (202) 616-7999 Fax: (202) 616-8400

Assistant Director **Royce G. Walters** .... (202) 616-3459
E-mail: royce.g.walters@usdoj.gov
Deputy Assistant Director **Mary Ann Brewster** .... (202) 616-8269
E-mail: maryann.brewster@usdoj.gov
Deputy Assistant Director **Edwin Quall** .... (202) 616-7589
E-mail: edwin.quall@usdoj.gov
Supervisor **David M. "Dave" Bonanno** .... (202) 616-8320
E-mail: david.m.bonanno@usdoj.gov
Supervisor **Neville C. Campbell-Adams** .... (202) 305-9264
E-mail: neville.c.campbell-adams@usdoj.gov
Night Supervisor **Marc M. Nakahara** .... (202) 616-7152
E-mail: marc.m.nakahara@usdoj.gov

State and Local Liaison Division

Tel: (202) 616-9000 Fax: (202) 616-1087

Assistant Director **(Vacant)** .... (202) 616-8272

Violent Crime Division [VCD]

Assistant Director **Joseph Trigg** .... (202) 532-4457
E-mail: joseph.trigg@usdoj.gov
Supervisor **Edward A. McCaw** .... (202) 353-0303
E-mail: edward.a.mccaw@usdoj.gov

Office of the Pardon Attorney [OPA]

145 N Street, NE, Room 5E.508, Washington, DC 20530
Tel: (202) 616-6070 Fax: (202) 616-6069
Internet: www.justice.gov/pardon

The Office of the Pardon Attorney, in consultation with the Attorney General or his designee, assists the President in the exercise of executive clemency as authorized under Article II, Section 2, of the Constitution. Under the Constitution, the President's clemency power extends only to federal criminal offenses. All requests for executive clemency for federal offenses are directed to the Pardon Attorney for investigation and review. The Pardon Attorney prepares the Department's recommendation to the President for final disposition of each application.

● Pardon Attorney **Deborah Leff** .... (202) 616-6070
1425 New York Avenue, NW, Suite 11000, Washington, DC 20530
E-mail: deborah.leff@usdoj.gov
Education: Princeton 1973 AB; Chicago 1977 JD
Deputy Pardon Attorney **Lawrence B. Kupers** .... (202) 616-6070
1425 New York Avenue, NW, Suite 11000, Washington, DC 20530
E-mail: lawrence.b.kupers@usdoj.gov
Executive Officer **William Taylor** .... (202) 616-6070
Staff Attorney **Tammy Allison** .... (202) 616-6070
1425 New York Avenue, NW, Suite 11000, Washington, DC 20530
E-mail: tammy.allison2@usdoj.gov
Staff Attorney **Kathleen G. Hatton** .... (202) 616-6070
1425 New York Avenue, NW, Suite 11000, Washington, DC 20530
E-mail: kathleen.hatton@usdoj.gov
Staff Attorney **Kira Horstmeyer** .... (202) 616-6070
1425 New York Avenue, NW, Washington, DC 20530
E-mail: kira.horstmeyer@usdoj.gov
Staff Attorney **Eric M. Opanga** .... (202) 616-6070
1425 New York Avenue, NW, Suite 11000, Washington, DC 20530
E-mail: eric.opanga2@usdoj.gov

(continued on next page)

★ Presidential Appointment Requiring Senate Confirmation ☆ Presidential Appointment ☐ Schedule C Appointment ◇ Career Senior Foreign Service Appointment ● Career Senior Executive Service (SES) Appointment ○ Non-Career Senior Executive Service (SES) Appointment

Office of the Pardon Attorney [OPA] *continued*

Staff Attorney **Rosalind A. Sargent-Burns** .... (202) 616-6070
1425 New York Avenue, NW, Suite 11000, Washington, DC 20530
E-mail: rosalind.sargent-burns@usdoj.gov
Program Specialist **Monique Alexander** .... (202) 514-1669
1425 New York Avenue, NW, Suite 11000, Washington, DC 20530
E-mail: monique.alexander@usdoj.gov

United States Parole Commission [USPC]

90 K. Street NE, Washington, DC 20530
Tel: (202) 346-7000
Internet: www.usdoj.gov/uspc

The United States Parole Commission makes parole release decisions for eligible Federal and District of Columbia (D.C.) prisoners, determines the conditions of parole or supervised release, issues warrants for arrest, and revokes parole and supervised release for violation of the conditions of release. Those individuals under the USPC jurisdiction include Federal Offenders, D.C. Code Offenders, Uniform Code of Military Justice Offenders, State Probationers and Parolees in Federal Witness Protection Program, and U.S. citizens who are serving prison terms imposed by foreign countries and who, pursuant to treaty, have elected to be transferred to the United States for service of that sentence.

Note: Members may continue to serve until reappointed or replaced.

Office of the Chairman

★ Chairman **J. Patricia Wilson Smoot** .... (202) 346-7000
Began Service: May 29, 2015
E-mail: patricia.w.smoot@usdoj.gov
Education: Bucknell 1985 BA; Columbus Law 1988 JD
★ Vice Chairman **Patricia K. Cushwa** .... (202) 346-7000
Began Service: 2004
E-mail: patricia.cushwa@usdoj.gov
Education: Hood BA, MA

Commissioners

★ Commissioner **Charles Thomas Massarone** .... (202) 346-7000
Began Service: 2012
Term Expires: August 16, 2018
E-mail: charles.massarone@usdoj.gov
★ Commissioner **(Vacant)** .... (202) 346-7000

Officials and Staff

General Counsel **Helen Krapels** .... (202) 346-7000
E-mail: helen.krapels@usdoj.gov
Chief Information Officer **Jonathan H. Pinkerton** .... (202) 346-7000
E-mail: jonathan.h.pinkerton@usdoj.gov
Executive Officer **Zelia Carter** .... (202) 346-7000
E-mail: zelia.carter@usdoj.gov
Case Operations Administrator
Stephen J. "Steve" Husk .... (202) 346-7000
E-mail: steve.husk@usdoj.gov
Case Services Administrator **Deirdre McDaniel** .... (202) 346-7000
E-mail: deirdre.mcdaniel@usdoj.gov

Bureau of Alcohol, Tobacco, Firearms and Explosives [ATF]

99 New York Avenue, NE, Washington, DC 20226
Tel: (202) 648-7777 (General Information)
Tel: (888) 283-3473 (Arson Hotline)
Tel: (888) 283-2662 (Bomb Hotline)
Tel: (888) 283-4867 (Report Illegal Firearms Activity)
Tel: (888) 930-9275 (Firearms Theft Hotline)
Tel: (800) 788-7133 (Firearms Tracing Center)
Tel: (800) 578-7223 (Law Enforcement Use)
Tel: (800) 659-6242 (Report Stolen, Hijacked or Seized Cigarettes)
Tel: (800) 283-8477 (Other Criminal Activity)
Internet: www.atf.gov

The Bureau of Alcohol, Tobacco, Firearms and Explosives is a principal law enforcement agency dedicated to preventing terrorism, reducing violent crime, and protecting our Nation. Its responsibilities include the investigation and prevention of federal offenses involving the unlawful use, manufacture, and possession of firearms and explosives, acts of arson and bombings, and illegal trafficking of alcohol and tobacco products. The ATF also regulates via licensing the sale, possession, and transportation of firearms, ammunition, and explosives in interstate commerce.

Office of the Director

99 New York Avenue, NE, Suite 5S.100, Washington, DC 20226
Tel: (202) 648-8700 Fax: (202) 648-9622

★ Director (Acting) **Thomas E. Brandon** .... (202) 648-8700
E-mail: thomas.brandon@atf.gov
● Deputy Director (Acting)
BrigGen Ronald B. Turk ANG .... (202) 648-8710
E-mail: ronald.turk@atf.gov
Education: Sam Houston State BS; Louisville MS
Bureau Deciding Official **Eugenio A. Marquez** .... (256) 261-7538
E-mail: eugenio.marquez@atf.gov
Ombudsman **Grace Reisling** Suite 3E.490 .... (202) 648-8750
Office of Strategic Management Chief
Christopher Pellettiere Suite 5E.417 .... (202) 648-7425
Staff Assistant **Michelle Back** .... (202) 648-8700
E-mail: michelle.back@atf.gov
Staff Assistant **Betty Coleman** .... (202) 648-8700
E-mail: betty.coleman@atf.gov

Office of the Chief of Staff

Tel: (202) 648-7285 Fax: (202) 648-9622

Chief of Staff (Acting) **Robyn L. Thiemann** .... (202) 648-7285
Deputy Chief of Staff **Cherie Knoblock** .... (202) 648-9211

Office of Chief Counsel [OCC]

99 New York Avenue, NE, Washington, DC 20226
Fax: (202) 648-9600

● Chief Counsel **Charles R. Gross** .... (202) 648-7000
E-mail: charles.gross@atf.gov
Education: Wisconsin 1975 BS, 1978 JD
● Deputy Chief Counsel **Joel J. Roessner** .... (202) 648-7000
E-mail: joel.roessner@atf.gov
Chief of Staff **April V. Harris** .... (202) 648-7996
Administrative Officer **Margaret B. Ailstock** .... (202) 648-7000
E-mail: margaret.ailstock@atf.gov
Associate Chief Counsel for Firearms and Explosives
Eric M. Epstein .... (202) 648-7051
E-mail: eric.epstein@atf.gov Fax: (202) 648-9620
○ Associate Chief Counsel for Law Policy
Barry S. Orlow .... (202) 648-7043
E-mail: barry.orlow@atf.gov Fax: (202) 648-9620
Associate Chief Counsel for Litigation
Melissa Anderson .... (202) 648-7056
E-mail: melissa.anderson@atf.gov Fax: (202) 648-9610
○ Associate Chief Counsel for Management **Tara Scaro** .... (202) 648-7023
E-mail: tara.scaro@atf.gov Fax: (202) 648-9610

★ Presidential Appointment Requiring Senate Confirmation
☆ Presidential Appointment
☐ Schedule C Appointment
◇ Career Senior Foreign Service Appointment
● Career Senior Executive Service (SES) Appointment
○ Non-Career Senior Executive Service (SES) Appointment

Office of Equal Opportunity Employment
Tel: (202) 648-8760 Fax: (202) 648-9618

Chief (Acting) **Patricia R. Cangemi** .... (202) 648-8760
E-mail: patricia.cangemi@atf.gov

Office of Enforcement Programs and Services [OEPS]
99 New York Avenue, NE, Washington, DC 20226
Fax: (202) 648-9757

• Assistant Director **Marvin G. Richardson** .... (202) 648-7080
• Deputy Assistant Director **Curtis W. Gilbert** .... (202) 648-7080
Chief of Staff **Sonya Dyer** .... (202) 648-7080
Staff Assistant **Gloria Makel** .... (202) 648-7080

Firearms and Ammunition Technology Division
Division Chief **Earl Griffith** .... (202) 648-7090
Firearms Technology and Industry Services Branch Chief **(Vacant)** .... (304) 648-3414
244 Needy Road, Martinsburg, WV 25401
Firearms Technology Criminal Branch Chief **Max Kingery** .... (304) 648-3414
244 Needy Road, Martinsburg, WV 25401

Firearms and Explosives Industry Division
99 New York Avenue, NE, Washington, DC 20226
Internet: www.atf.gov/firearms

The Firearms program enforces Federal firearms laws and regulations. The strategy prioritizes reducing gun crimes committed by the most violent criminals and curbing illegal transactions of firearms.

Chief (Acting) **Gary Taylor** .... (202) 648-7090
Deputy Chief **(Vacant)** .... (202) 648-7090
Explosives Industry Programs Branch Chief **William E. Frye, Jr.** .... (202) 648-7090
E-mail: william.frye@atf.gov
Firearms Industry Programs Branch Chief **Edward C. Courtney** .... (202) 648-7090

Firearms and Explosives Services Division
244 Needy Road, Martinsburg, WV 25401
Tel: (304) 616-4590 Fax: (304) 616-4591

Chief **Alphonso Hughes** .... (304) 616-4590
E-mail: alphonso.hughes@atf.gov
Deputy Chief **Gary Taylor** .... (304) 616-4590
Firearms and Explosives Import Branch Chief **William Majors** .... (304) 616-4590
National Firearms Act Branch Chief **William J. Boyle III** .... (304) 616-4590
E-mail: william.boyle@atf.gov
Federal Explosives Licensing Center Chief **Christopher Reeves** .... (304) 616-4590
Federal Firearms Licensing Center Chief **Tracey Robertson** .... (304) 616-4608

National Tracing Center Division
244 Needy Road, Martinsburg, WV 25401
Tel: (800) 788-7133 Fax: (304) 260-5342

Division Chief **Charles J. Houser** .... (304) 260-1500
E-mail: charles.houser@atf.gov
Education: Grand Valley State BS; US Army Command
Deputy Chief **Tyson Arnold** .... (304) 260-1500
Firearms Tracing Branch Chief **David A. Scott** .... (304) 260-1500
Industry Records Branch Chief **Brenda Bennett** .... (304) 260-5351
E-mail: brenda.bennett@atf.gov
Law Enforcement Support Branch Chief **(Vacant)** .... (304) 260-1500
Division Operations Officer **(Vacant)** .... (304) 260-1500

Office of Field Operations [OFO]
99 New York Avenue, NE, Washington, DC 20226
Tel: (202) 648-8410 Fax: (202) 648-9608

• Assistant Director **Michael P. "Mike" Gleysteen** .... (202) 648-8410
E-mail: mike.p.gleysteen@atf.gov
• Field Operations Deputy Assistant Director (Programs) **Jeffrey L. Fulton** .... (202) 648-8410
E-mail: jeffrey.fulton@atf.gov
Field Operations Deputy Assistant Director (North - Industry Operations) **(Vacant)** .... (614) 288-7513
• Field Operations Deputy Assistant Director (Central) **Marino F. Vidoli** .... (202) 648-8410
• Field Operations Deputy Assistant Director (East) (Acting) **Essam E. Rabadi** .... (202) 648-8410
Education: Manhattan Col BS
Field Operations Deputy Assistant Director (South) **Andrew R. "Andy" Graham** .... (202) 648-8410
E-mail: andy.graham@atf.gov
• Field Operations Deputy Assistant Director (West) **(Vacant)** .... (202) 648-8410
Field Management Staff Chief **Megan A. Bennett** .... (202) 648-8344
E-mail: megan.bennett@atf.gov

Advanced Firearms and Operations Training Division
99 New York Avenue, NE, Washington, DC 20226
Tel: (202) 648-8440

Deputy Chief **Thomas "Tom" Murray** .... (202) 648-8440
E-mail: thomas.murray@atf.gov
Advanced Investigations Training Branch Chief **(Vacant)** .... (202) 648-8431
Industry Operations Training Branch Chief **(Vacant)** ..... (202) 648-8408

Alcohol and Tobacco Diversion Division [ATDD]
99 New York Avenue, NE, Mailstop 7S-233, Washington, DC 20226
Internet: www.atf.gov/content/alcohol-and-tobacco

Chief **Joseph Fox** .... (202) 648-7117

Arson and Explosives Programs Division
99 New York Avenue, NE, Washington, DC 20226
Tel: (202) 648-7100 Fax: (202) 648-9660

The Arson and Explosives Program combats violent crime and prevents terrorism by regulating the possession and use of explosives. The Arson and Explosives Program also provides training to state, local and other Federal authorities.

Chief **Billy M. Magalassi** .... (256) 261-7606
E-mail: billy.magalassi@atf.gov
Deputy Chief **(Vacant)** .... (202) 648-7100
Arson and Explosives Enforcement Branch Chief **(Vacant)** .... (202) 648-7100
Explosives Industry Programs Branch Chief **(Vacant)** .... (202) 648-7100
Explosives Technology Branch Chief **(Vacant)** .... (202) 648-7100

Arson, Explosives and International Training Division
99 New York Avenue, NE, Washington, DC 20226
Fax: (202) 648-9717

Chief **(Vacant)** .... (202) 648-8470
Deputy Chief **(Vacant)** .... (202) 648-8470
Arson Training Branch Chief **Bradley S. Earman** .... (256) 261-7603
E-mail: bradley.s.earman@atf.gov
Canine Advanced Training and Operations Support Branch Chief **Deborah Dassler** .... (540) 622-6580
E-mail: deborah.dassler@atf.gov
Explosives Training Branch Chief **(Vacant)** .... (804) 633-1555
International Training Branch Chief **Alfredo Phoenix** .... (202) 648-8470
E-mail: alfredo.phoenix@atf.gov

Special Operations Division
99 New York Avenue, NE, Suite 7S-140, Washington, DC 20226
Tel: (202) 648-8620 Fax: (202) 648-9616

• Chief **John Cooper** .... (202) 648-8620
Deputy Chief **Donald Brougher** .... (202) 648-8620

(continued on next page)

★ Presidential Appointment Requiring Senate Confirmation
☆ Presidential Appointment
☐ Schedule C Appointment
◇ Career Senior Foreign Service Appointment
● Career Senior Executive Service (SES) Appointment
○ Non-Career Senior Executive Service (SES) Appointment

US DEPARTMENT OF JUSTICE

Special Operations Division *continued*

Special Agent-in-Charge for Critical Incident Management Branch **(Vacant)** .... (202) 648-8620
Special Agent-in-Charge for Digital Investigations Branch **A. Michelle Collier** .... (202) 648-8620
Special Agent-in-Charge for Emergency Support Function #13 Branch **(Vacant)** .... (202) 648-8620
Special Agent-in-Charge for Enforcement Support Branch **Robert Tolbert** .... (202) 648-8620
Special Agent-in-Charge for Polygraph Branch **Eduardo Fernandez** .... (202) 648-8620
Special Agent-in-Charge for Technical Operations **John Spencer** .... (202) 648-8620
Special Agent-in-Charge for Undercover Branch **Kim Balog** .... (202) 648-8620

Office of Human Resources and Professional Development

99 New York Avenue, NE, Washington, DC 20226
Tel: (202) 648-8416 Fax: (202) 648-9732

● Assistant Director **David L. McCain** .... (202) 648-8416
E-mail: david.mccain@atf.gov
● Deputy Assistant Director **(Vacant)** .... (202) 648-8416
Chief of Staff **Paul A. Leathem** .... (202) 648-8382

Human Resources Operations Division

99 New York Avenue, NE, Washington, DC 20226
Tel: (202) 648-7489

Chief **Lisa Boykin** .... (202) 648-7489
E-mail: lisa.boykin@atf.gov
Deputy Chief **Ralph Bittelairi** .... (202) 648-9100
E-mail: ralph.bittelairi@atf.gov
Classification and Performance Management Branch Chief **Kathryn Greene** .... (202) 648-9079
E-mail: kathryn.greene@atf.gov
Employee and Workforce Benefits Branch Chief (Acting) **Erica Sterling** .... (202) 648-7466
Human Resources Support Staff Branch Chief **Elsa Newland** .... (202) 648-8801
Payroll Processing and Operations Branch Chief **Christopher Kopeck** .... (202) 648-7520
E-mail: christopher.kopeck@atf.gov
Executive and Supervisory Staffing Center Chief **Robin D. McBeth** .... (202) 648-8361
E-mail: robin.mcbeth@atf.gov
Recruitment, Hiring and Staffing Center Chief **(Vacant)** .... (202) 648-9100

Leadership and Professional Development Division

99 New York Avenue, NE, Washington, DC 20226
Tel: (202) 648-8420 Fax: (202) 648-9717

Chief **Rayfield Roundtree** .... (202) 648-8391
E-mail: rayfield.roundtree@atf.gov
Advanced Training Branch Chief **Ann Marie Leinemann** .... (202) 648-9326
E-mail: ann.leinemann@atf.gov
Professional/Technical Training and Development Branch Chief **Elizabeth O'Brien** .... (202) 648-8398
E-mail: elizabeth.o'brien@atf.gov

Center for Talent Solutions

99 New York Avenue, NE, Washington, DC 20226
Tel: (202) 628-8397 Fax: (202) 648-9720

Chief (Acting) **James E. Scott** .... (202) 648-8397
E-mail: james.e.scott@atf.gov
Chief, Talent Analytics **James E. Scott** .... (202) 648-8385
E-mail: james.e.scott@atf.gov

ATF National Academy

Federal Law Enforcement Training Center, 1131 Chapel Crossing Road, Building 681, Glynco, GA 31524
Fax: (912) 267-2901

Chief **Daniel L. Board, Jr.** .... (912) 267-2251
E-mail: daniel.board@atf.gov
Deputy Chief **Tracy L. Hite** .... (912) 267-2828
E-mail: tracy.hite@atf.gov
Logistics and Operations Branch Chief **Delmaria Cole-Bigelow** .... (912) 267-2261
E-mail: delmaria.cole-bigelow@atf.gov
Basic Training Program Branch Chief **Todd Jones** .... (912) 554-4788
E-mail: todd.jones@atf.gov

Office of Management/Chief Financial Officer

99 New York Avenue, NE, Washington, DC 20226
Tel: (202) 648-7800 Fax: (202) 648-9666

● Assistant Director **Christopher C. Schaefer** .... (202) 648-7800
E-mail: christopher.schaefer@atf.gov
● Deputy Assistant Director/Chief Financial Officer **Vivian Michalic** .... (202) 648-7800
E-mail: vivian.michalic@atf.gov
Chief of Staff **Stephen Wills** .... (202) 648-7800
E-mail: stephen.wills@atf.gov

Asset Forfeiture and Seized Property Division

Tel: (202) 648-7890 Fax: (202) 648-9647

Chief **Wanda Bossa** .... (202) 648-7890
E-mail: wanda.bossa@atf.gov
Deputy Chief **Gilbert Salinas** .... (202) 648-7890
E-mail: gilbert.salinas@atf.gov
Asset Management Branch Chief **Kathleen McQueen** .... (202) 648-7890
E-mail: kathleen.mcqueen@atf.gov
Budgetary Operations Branch Chief **George Craig Sabo** .... (202) 648-7890
E-mail: george.sabo@atf.gov
Education and Training Branch Chief **Richard Checo** .... (202) 648-7890
E-mail: richard.checo@atf.gov
Field Assistance Branch Chief **Sonja A. Everitt** .... (202) 648-7890
E-mail: sonja.everitt@atf.gov
Management Support Branch Chief **Sandrica Sams** .... (202) 648-7890
E-mail: sandrica.sams@atf.gov

Financial Management Division

Tel: (202) 648-7830 Fax: (202) 648-9656

Chief and Deputy Chief Financial Officer **Melissa McCoy** .... (202) 648-7830
E-mail: melissa.mccoy@atf.gov
Accounting Branch Chief **Steve Kolcio** .... (202) 648-7830
E-mail: ihor.kolcio@atf.gov
Budget Branch Chief **Elisa Krobot** .... (202) 648-7830
E-mail: elisa.krobot@atf.gov
Financial Systems Branch Chief **Paul Joseph** .... (202) 648-7830
E-mail: paul.joseph@atf.gov
Resources Management Branch Chief **(Vacant)** .... (202) 648-7830

Logistics and Acquisitions Division

99 New York Avenue, NE, Washington, DC 20226
Tel: (202) 648-7410 Fax: (202) 648-9661

Chief **Demetress Smith** .... (202) 648-7410
E-mail: demetress.smith@atf.gov
Acquisitions Branch Chief **Craig Drew** .... (202) 648-7410
E-mail: craig.drew@atf.gov
Material Management Branch Chief **Stacey Washington** .... (202) 648-7410
E-mail: stacey.washington@atf.gov
Policy and Safety Branch Chief **Kenneth Houser** .... (202) 648-7410
E-mail: kenneth.houser@atf.gov
Realty and Building Operations Branch Chief **Brad Dessler** .... (202) 648-7410
E-mail: brad.dessler@atf.gov

★ Presidential Appointment Requiring Senate Confirmation
☆ Presidential Appointment
□ Schedule C Appointment
◇ Career Senior Foreign Service Appointment
● Career Senior Executive Service (SES) Appointment
○ Non-Career Senior Executive Service (SES) Appointment

Office of Professional Responsibility and Security Operations [OPRS]
99 New York Avenue, NE, Washington, DC 20226
Tel: (202) 648-7500 Fax: (202) 648-9663

- • Assistant Director **Melvin D. King** .... (202) 648-7500
  E-mail: melvin.king@atf.gov
- • Deputy Assistant Director **Daryl McCrary** .... (202) 648-7500
  Chief of Staff **Janis Knight** .... (202) 648-7500
  Oversight and Review Division Chief **Kelly Lago** .... (202) 648-9200
  E-mail: kelly.lago@atf.gov
  Security and Emergency Program Division Chief
  Scott Bakka .... (202) 648-7510
  E-mail: scott.bakka@atf.gov
  Special Agent-in-Charge for Internal Affairs Division
  Thomas "Tom" Murray .... (202) 648-5940
  E-mail: thomas.murray@atf.gov

Office of Public and Governmental Affairs [OPGA]
99 New York Avenue, NE, Washington, DC 20226
Tel: (202) 648-8500 Fax: (202) 648-9750

- • Assistant Director **Christopher C. Shaefer** .... (202) 648-8500
- • Deputy Assistant Director **Frederick J. Milanowski** ..... (202) 648-8500
  Chief of Staff **Thomas Klein** .... (202) 648-8500
  Digital Media Division Chief **Brian Nickey** .... (202) 648-8500
  Intergovernmental Affairs Division Chief **Ross Arends** ... (202) 648-8500
  Legislative Affairs Division Chief **Dean M. Kueter, Jr.** ... (202) 648-8510
  Education: Boston Col 1992 BA
  Public Affairs Division Chief **Ginger Colbrun** .... (202) 648-8500
  Public Affairs Division Deputy Chief **Corey Ray** .... (202) 648-8500

Office of Science and Technology [OST]
99 New York Avenue, NE, Washington, DC 20226
Tel: (202) 648-8390

- • Assistant Director and Chief Information Officer
  (Acting) **Roger Beasley** .... (202) 648-8390
  Deputy Assistant Director (Acting) **Francis Frande** ...... (202) 648-8390
  650 Massachusetts Avenue, NW, Room 8150, Washington, DC 20226
  Chief of Staff **Thomas "Tom" Hill** .... (202) 648-8380
  Executive Assistant **(Vacant)** .... (202) 648-8390
  Chief Technology Officer **(Vacant)** .... (202) 648-8390

Financial Investigative Services Division
Chief **Francis Frande** .... (202) 648-8360

Information Technology Services Management Division
Fax: (202) 648-9562

Chief **Walter Bigelow** .... (202) 648-9374
E-mail: walter.bigelow@atf.gov
Information Technology Service Delivery Branch Chief
Dwayne Spriggs .... (202) 648-9306

Laboratory Services Division
National Laboratory Research Center, 6000 Ammendale Road, Ammendale, MD 20705-1250

- • Deputy Assistant Director for Forensic Services
  Gregory P. "Greg" Czarnopys .... (240) 264-3700
  E-mail: greg.czarnopys@atf.gov Fax: (240) 264-1495

Office of Strategic Intelligence and Information [OSII]
99 New York Avenue, NE, Washington, DC 20226
Tel: (202) 648-7600

- • Assistant Director **James E. McDermond** .... (202) 648-7600
  E-mail: james.mcdermond@atf.gov
- • Deputy Assistant Director **Scott Sweetow** .... (202) 648-7600
  Education: Punahou (Honolulu, HI) 1976; Arizona 1988 BA; Norwich 1989; JFK School Govt 2008
  Chief of Staff **Ernest Hickson** .... (202) 648-7600

Office of Strategic Intelligence and Information [OSII] *continued*

- • Deputy Director, TEDAC **Michael B. Boxler** .... (703) 632-8410
  2501 Investigation Parkway, Quantico, VA 22135 Fax: (703) 632-8417
  E-mail: michael.boxler@atf.gov
  International Affairs Branch Chief **(Vacant)** .... (202) 648-7235

Field Intelligence Division
99 New York Avenue, NE, Washington, DC 20226

Chief **Shawn Arthur** .... (202) 648-7600
Deputy Chief **(Vacant)** .... (202) 648-7600
Strategic Projects Branch Chief **Edward Kropke** .... (202) 648-7600
Joint Support and Operations Center Chief
Brian Washington .... (202) 648-7600

Intelligence and Information Systems Division
99 New York Avenue, NE, Washington, DC 20226

Chief **Marion Burrows** .... (202) 648-7600
E-mail: marion.burrows@atf.gov
Intelligence Systems Support Branch Chief
Adolphus Peoples .... (202) 648-7600
NFOCIS Branch Chief **Kenneth Kwak** .... (202) 648-7600

Violent Crimes Intelligence Division
99 New York Avenue, NE, Washington, DC 20226

Chief **Kevin O'Keefe** .... (202) 648-7600
US Bomb Data Chief **Brandt A. Schenken** .... (202) 648-7600

Drug Enforcement Administration [DEA]
Lincoln Place-West, 700 Army Navy Drive, Arlington, VA 22202
Tel: (202) 307-4228
Tel: (800) 882-9539 (Narcotics License Registration Section)
Internet: www.dea.gov

The mission of the Drug Enforcement Administration (DEA) is to enforce the controlled substances laws and regulations of the United States and bring to the criminal and civil justice system of the United States, or any other competent jurisdiction, those organizations and principal members of organizations, involved in the growing, manufacture, or distribution of controlled substances appearing in or destined for illicit traffic in the United States; and to recommend and support non-enforcement programs aimed at reducing the availability of illicit controlled substances on the domestic and international markets.

Office of the Administrator
Lincoln Place-West, 700 Army Navy Drive, Arlington, VA 22202
Fax: (202) 307-4540

- ★ Administrator (Acting)
  Charles P. "Chuck" Rosenberg Room 12060 .... (202) 307-8000
  E-mail: chuck.rosenberg@usdoj.gov
  Education: Tufts 1982 BA; Harvard 1985 MPP; Virginia 1990 JD
  Executive Assistant **(Vacant)** Room 12060 .... (202) 307-6208
- ★ Deputy Administrator (Acting) **John J. "Jack" Riley**
  Room 12058 .... (202) 307-7345
  E-mail: john.j.riley@usdoj.gov
  Executive Assistant **Robert W. Patterson**
  Room 12058 .... (202) 307-6141
  E-mail: robert.w.patterson@usdoj.gov
  Equal Employment Officer **Oliver C. Allen** .... (202) 307-8888
  Lincoln Place-East, 600 Army Navy Drive, Room E11275, Arlington, VA 22202
  E-mail: oliver.c.allen2@usdoj.gov

Office of the Administrative Law Judges [LJ]
1550 Crystal Drive, 9th Floor, Arlington, VA 22202
Tel: (202) 307-8188 Fax: (202) 307-8198

Chief Administrative Law Judge **John J. Mulrooney** .... (202) 307-8686
E-mail: john.j.mulrooney@usdoj.gov

(continued on next page)

Office of the Administrative Law Judges *continued*

Law Clerk **Katherine E. Legel** .... (202) 307-4228
E-mail: katherine.e.legel@usdoj.gov
Law Clerk **Adrienne M. Shergill** .... (202) 307-4228
E-mail: adrienne.m.shergill@usdoj.gov
Secretary **Ikea C. Lewis** .... (202) 307-4228
E-mail: ikea.c.lewis@usdoj.gov
Administrative Law Judge
Col Charles W. Dorman USMC .... (202) 307-8188
E-mail: charles.w.dorman@usdoj.gov
Law Clerk **Jessica M. Krentz** .... (202) 307-4228
E-mail: jessica.m.krentz@usdoj.gov
Secretary **Chakia C. Lyles** .... (202) 307-8188
E-mail: chakia.c.lyles@usdoj.gov
Secretary **Carlene R. Thomas** .... (202) 307-4228
E-mail: carlene.r.thomas@usdoj.gov
Administrative Law Judge **(Vacant)** .... (202) 307-8199
Law Clerk **(Vacant)** .... (202) 307-4228
Administrative Law Judge **(Vacant)** .... (202) 307-8188
Hearing Office Director **Roxann E. Eline** .... (202) 307-4228
E-mail: roxann.e.eline@usdoj.gov
Hearing Clerk **Helen D. Walker** .... (202) 307-4228
E-mail: helen.d.walker@usdoj.gov
Secretary **Debra Rosario** .... (202) 307-8188

Office of Chief Counsel [CC]
Tel: (202) 307-7322

Chief Counsel **Wendy H. Goggin** Room W-12142-C ..... (202) 307-7322
E-mail: wendy.h.goggin@usdoj.gov
Education: Tennessee, 1976 JD
Deputy Chief Counsel for International and Intelligence
Law **Maura F. Quinn** .... (202) 307-4665
Lincoln Place-East, 600 Army Navy Drive, Room E-12149, Arlington, VA 22202
E-mail: maura.f.quinn@usdoj.gov
Deputy Chief Counsel for Litigation and Policy
Bettie E. Goldman .... (202) 307-8049
Lincoln Place-East, 600 Army Navy Drive, Room E-12001, Arlington, VA 22202
E-mail: bettie.e.goldman@usdoj.gov
Deputy Chief Counsel for Operational Law
Robert C. Gleason .... (202) 307-8083
Lincoln Place-East, 600 Army Navy Drive, Room E-12375, Arlington, VA 22202
E-mail: robert.gleason2@usdoj.gov

Office of Congressional and Public Affairs [CP]
Tel: (202) 307-7363

• Chief (Acting) **Gary R. Owen** Room W-12228 .... (202) 307-6747
E-mail: gary.r.owen@usdoj.gov
• Congressional Affairs Section Chief (Acting)
Matthew J. Strait Room W-12104 .... (202) 353-7895
E-mail: matthew.j.strait@usdoj.gov
Demand Reduction Section Chief (Acting)
Deborah S. Augustine .... (202) 307-4777
Lincoln Place-East, 600 Army Navy Drive, Room E-9049, Arlington, VA 22202
E-mail: deborah.s.augustine@usdoj.gov
Public Affairs Section Chief (Acting)
Joseph H. Moses Room W-12200 .... (202) 307-4454

Financial Management Division [FC]

Lincoln Place-West, 700 Army Navy Drive, Room 12138, Arlington, VA 22202

• Chief Financial Officer (Acting) **Christina K. Sisk** .... (202) 307-7330

Office of Acquisition Management [FA]
600 Army Navy Drive, Arlington, VA 22202

Deputy Assistant Administrator **Christina K. Sisk**
Room 8379 .... (202) 307-7777
E-mail: christinia.sisk@usdoj.gov
Special Assistant **Victor N. Painter** Room 8373 .... (202) 307-7822
E-mail: victor.n.painter@usdoj.gov

Office of Acquisition Management *continued*

Acquisition Management Section Chief
Nancy Costello Room 8281 .... (202) 307-7831
Policy and Transportation Section Chief
Carol Burger Room 8165 .... (202) 307-7808
E-mail: carol.burger@usdoj.gov

Office of Finance [FN]
Lincoln Place-East, 600 Army Navy Drive, Arlington, VA 22202

• Deputy Assistant Administrator **Daniel C. Gillette**
Room 7397 .... (202) 307-7002
E-mail: daniel.gillette@usdoj.gov
Financial Operations Section Chief **Daanish Ahmed**
Room 7165 .... (202) 307-9933
Accounts Payable Unit Chief **(Vacant)** Room E-7701 .... (202) 307-7024
Financial Review and Training Unit Chief
Bridgette K. Downs-Tucker Room 7101 .... (202) 307-5580
Reconciliation Unit Chief **Annette R. Ford**
Room 7059 .... (202) 307-7105
E-mail: annette.r.ford@usdoj.gov
Financial Reports Section Chief **Sherri Woodle**
Room E-7297 .... (202) 307-7040
E-mail: sherri.woodle@usdoj.gov
Financial Systems Section Chief **(Vacant)**
Room E-850F .... (202) 307-7043

Office of Resource Management [FR]
Lincoln Place-East, 600 Army Navy Drive, Arlington, VA 22202
Tel: (202) 307-4800 Fax: (202) 307-7849

• Deputy Assistant Administrator **Brian G. Horn**
Room 5156 .... (202) 307-4800
E-mail: brian.g.horn@usdoj.gov
Special Assistant **Bill Connelly** Room 5156 .... (202) 307-4800
Control and Coordination Section Chief
Bryan L. Parks Room 5384 .... (202) 307-5276
Technical Analysis Unit Chief **Peter E. Tavernini**
Room 5360 .... (202) 307-7053
E-mail: peter.e.tavernini@usdoj.gov
Organization and Staffing Management Section Chief
Susan Mosser Room 5284 .... (202) 307-7077
Program Liaison and Analysis Section Chief
(Vacant) Room 5104 .... (202) 353-9545
Statistical Services Section Chief **Gamaliel S. Rose**
Room 5332 .... (202) 307-7088

Human Resources Division [HR]

Lincoln Place-West, 700 Army Navy Drive, Arlington, VA 22202

• Assistant Administrator **Diane E. Filler** Room 12020 ..... (202) 307-4177
E-mail: diane.e.filler@usdoj.gov
Deputy Assistant Administrator **(Vacant)** Room 3166 ..... (202) 307-4000
Career Board Executive Secretary
Michael Rothermund Room 2270 .... (202) 353-1165
Classifications and Program Support Branch Chief
Jill Colburn Room 3126-2 .... (202) 307-4027
E-mail: jill.colburn@usdoj.gov
Compensation and Benefits Chief **Ruth Johnston** .... (202) 307-2461
E-mail: ruth.johnston@usdoj.gov
Employee Relations and Health Chief
Walter C. Morrison .... (202) 307-4015
E-mail: walter.c.morrison@usdoj.gov
Recruitment and Placement Section Chief
Joyce G. Thomas Room 3262 .... (202) 307-4097
E-mail: joyce.g.thomas@usdoj.gov
Suitability Section Chief **Patricia A. Murphy** .... (202) 307-4058
E-mail: patricia.a.murphy@usdoj.gov

Board of Professional Conduct [HRB]
Chairman **Christopher S. Quaglino** Room 9333 .... (202) 307-7382
E-mail: christopher.s.quaglino@usdoj.gov

Office of Training [TR]
P.O. Box 1475, DEA Training Academy, Quantico, VA 22134-1475

Special Agent-in-Charge **James R. "Jay" Gregorius** .... (703) 632-5010

Office of Training *continued*

Assistant Special Agent-in-Charge/Domestic Training Section Chief **Michael Blackwood** .... (703) 632-5310
Leadership Development Unit Chief (Acting) **Craig Williams** .... (703) 632-5027
International Training Section Chief **(Vacant)** .... (703) 632-5330

Inspection Division [IG]

Lincoln Place-West, 700 Army Navy Drive, Arlington, VA 22202

Chief Inspector (Acting) **Jon Ciarletta** Room 12042 ...... (202) 358-1032
Executive Assistant **Bruce McColley** Room 12042B ..... (202) 307-2466

Administrative and Financial Management Unit

Administrative Officer **Brenda D. Poole** .... (202) 307-7685
Lincoln Place-East, 600 Army Navy Drive, Room 4034, Arlington, VA 22202 Fax: (202) 353-9525
E-mail: brenda.d.hodges@usdoj.gov

Office of Inspections [IN]

• Deputy Chief Inspector (Acting) **Michael A. Dixon** Room 4250 .... (202) 307-8200
E-mail: michael.a.dixon@usdoj.gov
Associate Deputy Chief Inspector (Acting) **Gerald E. Kaphing** Room 4250 .... (202) 307-4569

Office of Professional Responsibility [OPR]

Deputy Chief Inspector **(Vacant)** Room 4176 .... (202) 307-8235
Associate Deputy Chief Inspector **Joe "Jesse" Garcia** Room 4036 .... (202) 307-4852

Office of Security Programs [IS]

Tel: (202) 307-4400

Deputy Chief Inspector **(Vacant)** Room 2340-4 .... (202) 307-3465

Intelligence Division [NC]

Lincoln Place-West, 700 Army Navy Drive, Arlington, VA 22202
Tel: (202) 307-3607

• Assistant Administrator and Chief of Intelligence **Douglas W. Poole** Room 12036A .... (202) 307-3607
E-mail: douglas.w.poole@usdoj.gov
Executive Assistant (Acting) **Cheryl E. Hooper** Room 12036 B .... (202) 307-3607
E-mail: cheryl.e.hooper@usdoj.gov
Deputy Assistant Administrator for Intelligence **(Vacant)** Room 12036C .... (202) 307-3607
Warnings, Plans and Programs Section Chief **Lourdes P. Border** Room 8072 .... (202) 307-9284
E-mail: lourdes.p.border@usdoj.gov
Management and Production Support Section Chief **James A. Curtin** Room 7124 .... (202) 307-7534
E-mail: james.curtin@usdoj.gov
Policy and Strategic Planning Section Chief **Patrick J. Lowry** Room W7030 .... (202) 307-8544
E-mail: patrick.j.lowry@usdoj.gov
Executive Assistant **(Vacant)** Room 12036D .... (202) 307-3607

Office of Investigative Intelligence [NI]

Investigative Intelligence Section Chief **Lourdes P. Border** Room 10270 .... (202) 307-9284
E-mail: lourdes.p.border@usdoj.gov

Office of National Security Intelligence [NN]

Deputy Chief of Intelligence **Willard Bond Wells, Jr.** Room 8072 .... (202) 307-7923
E-mail: w.b.wells.jr@usdoj.gov
Requirements and Collection Chief **(Vacant)** Room 8066 .... (202) 307-7923

Office of Special Intelligence [NS]

Fusion Center, 2675 Prosperity Avenue, Fairfax, VA 22031-4906

Deputy Assistant Administrator **Willard Bond Wells, Jr.** .... (703) 561-7100
Data Management Section Chief **Cheryl E. Hooper** ...... (703) 561-7465
E-mail: cheryl.e.hooper@usdoj.gov

Office of Special Intelligence *continued*

Investigative Support Section Chief (Acting) **Scott Springer** .... (703) 488-4246
14560 Avion Parkway, Chantilly, VA 20151
Operational Support Section Chief **Timothy Hutchinson** .... (703) 561-7437
Technical Support Section Chief **Gisele M. Gatjanis** ..... (703) 561-7107
E-mail: gisele.m.gatjanis@usdoj.gov

Office of Strategic Intelligence [NT]

Strategic Intelligence Section Chief (Acting) **Kevin J. O'Brien** Room W8258 .... (202) 353-9581
E-mail: kevin.j.o'brien@usdoj.gov

Operational Support Division [SC]

Lincoln Place-West, 700 Army Navy Drive, Arlington, VA 22202

Assistant Administrator **Preston L. Grubbs** Room 12142 .... (202) 307-4730
E-mail: preston.l.grubbs@usdoj.gov

Office of Administration [SA]

• Deputy Assistant Administrator **Renaldo R. Prillman** Room 9088 .... (202) 307-7708
E-mail: renaldo.r.prillman@usdoj.gov
Administrative Operations Section Chief **Janet M. Gates** Room 5104 .... (202) 307-5240
Facilities Operations Section Chief **Michael A. Barbour** Room 5244 .... (202) 307-7792
E-mail: michael.barbour@usdoj.gov
Freedom of Information and Records Management Section Chief **Stacey K. Strayer** Room 9174 .... (202) 307-7711
E-mail: stacey.strayer@usdoj.gov
Head Librarian **Rosemary M. "Rose" Russo** Lincoln Place- West, Room 7216 .... (202) 307-8932
E-mail: rose.m.russo@usdoj.gov Fax: (202) 307-8939
Investigative Records Unit Chief **Vernon Corbitt** .... (202) 353-7928
Records Management Unit Chief **Janet Gardner** Lincoln Place- West, Room 6188 .... (202) 307-7928

Office of Forensic Sciences [SF]

• Deputy Assistant Administrator **Nelson A. Santos** Room 7342 .... (202) 307-8885
E-mail: nelson.a.santos@usdoj.gov
Forensic Sciences Environmental Section Chief **Ronald A. Leadore** .... (202) 353-9501
Hazardous Waste Disposal Section Chief **Stephen E. Wasem** Room 7308 .... (202) 307-7206
Laboratory Operations Section Chief **(Vacant)** Room 7310 .... (202) 307-8880
Laboratory Support Section Chief **Lance D. Kvetko** Room 7248 .... (202) 307-4028
Quality Assurance Manager **Richard P. Meyers** .... (202) 307-8873
E-mail: richard.p.meyers@usdoj.gov

Office of Information Systems [SI]

600 Army Navy Drive, Arlington, VA 22202
Tel: (202) 307-7454

• Deputy Assistant Administrator **Dennis R. McCrary** Lincoln Place-East, Room 3105 .... (202) 307-3653
E-mail: dennis.r.mccrary@usdoj.gov Fax: (202) 307-4684
Associate Deputy Assistant Administrator **(Vacant)** Lincoln Place-East, Room E-3005 .... (202) 307-9896
Special Assistant **(Vacant)** Lincoln Place-East, Room E-3101 .... (202) 307-8673
Chief Technology Officer **Mark Shafernich** .... (703) 285-7301
Sterling Park Technology Center, 22400 Shaw Road, Sterling, VA 20166
E-mail: mark.shafernich@usdoj.gov
Business Process Management Section Chief **Mildred Tyler** Lincoln Place-East, Room E-3225 .... (202) 307-9895
E-mail: mildred.tyler2@usdoj.gov
Finance and Administration Chief **Maria Hughes** Lincoln Place-East, Room E-3163 .... (202) 307-9885

(continued on next page)

★ Presidential Appointment Requiring Senate Confirmation ☐ Schedule C Appointment ● Career Senior Executive Service (SES) Appointment
☆ Presidential Appointment ◇ Career Senior Foreign Service Appointment ○ Non-Career Senior Executive Service (SES) Appointment

Office of Information Systems *continued*

IT Field Services Section Chief **Venita Phillips**
Lincoln Place-East, Room E-4005 .... (202) 307-9892
E-mail: venita.phillips@usdoj.gov Fax: (202) 353-1055
IT Operations Section Chief **Ruth Torres** .... (703) 307-9883
Sterling Park Technology Center, 22400 Shaw Road, Sterling, VA 20166
E-mail: ruth.torres@usdoj.gov
Software Operations Section Chief **Carl D. Conner**
Lincoln Place-East, Room 3285 .... (202) 307-4684
E-mail: carl.d.conner@usdoj.gov

Office of Investigative Technology [ST]
10555 Furnace Road, Lorton, VA 22079

Deputy Assistant Administrator **Gary Tennant** .... (703) 495-6500

Operations Division [OC]
Lincoln Place-West, 700 Army Navy Drive, Suite 12050, Arlington, VA 22202
Tel: (202) 307-7340

• Chief of Operations **James Soiles** .... (202) 307-7340
E-mail: james.soiles@usdoj.gov
Executive Assistant **Jon C. Delena** .... (202) 307-4907
E-mail: jon.c.delena@usdoj.gov
Executive Assistant **Robert W. Patterson** .... (202) 307-6141
E-mail: robert.w.patterson@usdoj.gov

Aviation Division [OA]
2300 Horizon Drive, Fort Worth, TX 76177-5300
Tel: (817) 837-2000

Special Agent In Charge **Jeffrey B. Stamm** .... (817) 837-2004
E-mail: jeffrey.b.stamm@usdoj.gov

Office of Diversion Control [OD]
Lincoln Place-East, 600 Army Navy Drive, Arlington, VA 22202
Tel: (202) 307-7165

Deputy Assistant Administrator and Deputy Chief of Operations for Diversion Control
Louis Milione Room 6295 .... (202) 307-7165
Deputy Director **(Vacant)** Room 6293-3 .... (202) 307-7163

Office of Financial Operations
Tel: (202) 307-4536

Chief **Anthony C. Marotta** .... (202) 307-4536
E-mail: anthony.c.marotta@usdoj.gov

Office of Global Enforcement [OE]
Deputy Chief of Operations **James Soiles**
Room 11072 .... (202) 307-7927
E-mail: james.soiles@usdoj.gov

Enforcement and Administrative Support Branch [OG]
Assistant Chief of Operations **(Vacant)** .... (202) 307-7927

Special Projects Branch [OT]
Lincoln Place-West, 700 Army Navy Drive, Room 11166, Arlington, VA 22202
Tel: (202) 307-4233

Deputy Chief of Operations **(Vacant)** .... (202) 307-4233

Office of Operations Management [OM]
Tel: (202) 307-4200

Deputy Chief **Michael Dellacorte** Room 11148 .... (202) 307-6080

Office of Special Operations [OS]
Tel: (703) 488-4200

Special Agent-in-Charge (Acting)
Christopher T. Tersigni .... (703) 488-4356
14560 Avion Parkway, Chantilly, VA 20151
E-mail: christopher.t.tersigni@usdoj.gov

Federal Bureau of Investigation [FBI]
J. Edgar Hoover Building, 935 Pennsylvania Avenue, NW, Washington, DC 20535-0001
Tel: (202) 324-3000 (Public Information)
Internet: www.fbi.gov
Internet: www.fbi.gov/espanol/fbi-en-espanol (FBI in Spanish)

The Federal Bureau of Investigation is the primary investigative arm of the United States Department of Justice serving as both a federal criminal investigative body and a domestic intelligence agency. At present, the FBI has investigative jurisdiction over violations of more than 200 categories of federal crimes. The Bureau works to protect and defend the United States against terrorist and foreign intelligence threats, to uphold and enforce the criminal laws of the United States, and to provide leadership and criminal justice services to federal, state, municipal, and international agencies and partners.

Office of the Director [DO]
J. Edgar Hoover Building, 935 Pennsylvania Avenue, NW, Washington, DC 20535-0001

★ Director **James B. "Jim" Comey, Jr.** Room 7176 .... (202) 324-3444
Began Service: September 4, 2013
Term Expires: September 4, 2023
E-mail: james.comey@ic.fbi.gov
Education: William & Mary 1982 BA; Chicago 1985 JD
Chief of Staff and Senior Counsel to the Director
James Rybicki .... (202) 324-3444
Deputy Chief of Staff **Dawn W. Burton** .... (202) 324-5212
E-mail: dawn.burton@ic.fbi.gov
Special Advisor to the Director **Joseph F. Hannigan**
Room 7163 .... (202) 324-4209
Education: Mount St Mary's U 1978; Delaware 1990
Deputy Director **Mark F. Giuliano** .... (202) 324-7045
Education: Wooster BSE
Chief of Staff to the Deputy Director
Joanna P. Baltes .... (202) 324-3000
Education: Arizona 1995 BA; UC San Diego 1999 JD; San Diego 1999 MLL

Office of Congressional Affairs [OCA]
J. Edgar Hoover Building, 935 Pennsylvania Avenue, NW, Room 7240, Washington, DC 20535-0001

Assistant Director **Stephen Dedalus Kelly** .... (202) 324-5051
Education: Vermont 1985; Boston Col 1989 JD

Office of Equal Employment Opportunity Affairs [OEEOA]
J. Edgar Hoover Building, 935 Pennsylvania Avenue, NW, Room 7901, Washington, DC 20535-0001

Equal Employment Opportunity Officer
Kevin M. Walker .... (202) 324-4128
Education: Purdue 1985; Albany Law 1992 JD; Judge Advocate Gen 2000 MLaw

Office of the General Counsel [OGC]
J. Edgar Hoover Building, 935 Pennsylvania Avenue, NW, Washington, DC 20535-0001

General Counsel **James A. Baker** Room 7427 .... (202) 324-6829
E-mail: james.baker@ic.fbi.gov
Education: Notre Dame BA; Michigan MA, JD
Deputy General Counsel **Brian Binney** .... (202) 324-0328
E-mail: brian.binney@ic.fbi.gov
Deputy General Counsel **Tom Bondy** .... (202) 220-9320
Deputy General Counsel **Jason Herring** .... (202) 324-8067
E-mail: jason.herring@ic.fbi.gov
Deputy General Counsel **Elaine M. Lammert** .... (202) 324-1533

US DEPARTMENT OF JUSTICE

★ Presidential Appointment Requiring Senate Confirmation ☐ Schedule C Appointment ● Career Senior Executive Service (SES) Appointment
☆ Presidential Appointment ◇ Career Senior Foreign Service Appointment ○ Non-Career Senior Executive Service (SES) Appointment

Office of Integrity and Compliance [OIC]

• Assistant Director **Patrick W. Kelley** . . . . (202) 324-7330
Education: Michigan State BS; Pennsylvania 1984 LLM; George Washington 1988 MBA; Duke JD

Office of the Ombudsman [OO]

J. Edgar Hoover Building, 935 Pennsylvania Avenue, NW, Room 6065, Washington, DC 20535-0001

Ombudsman **Monique A. Bookstein** . . . . (202) 324-2156

Office of Professional Responsibility [OPR]

J. Edgar Hoover Building, 935 Pennsylvania Avenue, NW, Room PA-444, Washington, DC 20535-0001

Assistant Director **Candice M. Will** . . . . (202) 220-7800
E-mail: candice.will@ic.fbi.gov
Education: New Mexico 1979 BA; Saint Louis U 1982 JD

Office of Public Affairs [OPA]

J. Edgar Hoover Building, 935 Pennsylvania Avenue, NW, Room 7230, Washington, DC 20535-0001
Tel: (202) 324-3691 (National Press Office)

Assistant Director **Michael Kortan** Room 7222 . . . . (202) 324-5352

Criminal, Cyber, Response, and Services Branch [CCRSB]

J. Edgar Hoover Building, 935 Pennsylvania Avenue, NW, Room 7110, Washington, DC 20535-0001

Executive Assistant Director **Robert Anderson, Jr.** . . . . . . (202) 324-0308
E-mail: robert.anderson@ic.fbi.gov
Associate Executive Assistant Director **Joseph M. Demarest, Jr.** . . . . (202) 324-0308
E-mail: joseph.demarest@ic.fbi.gov

Critical Incident Response Group

Assistant Director **Gregory D. Cox** . . . . (703) 632-4100
F.B.I. Academy, Quantico, VA 22135
Education: Wittenberg BA
Deputy Assistant Director **Kimberly K. Mertz** . . . . (703) 632-4100
F.B.I. Academy, Quantico, VA 22135

National Center for the Analysis of Violent Crime

Administrator (Acting) **Kim Tilton** . . . . (703) 632-4100

Intelligence Branch

Executive Assistant Director **Eric Velez-Villar** . . . . (202) 324-3000
E-mail: eric.velez-villar@ic.fbi.gov
Education: Inter American BA

Criminal Investigative Division

J. Edgar Hoover Building, 935 Pennsylvania Avenue, NW, Washington, DC 20535-0001

Assistant Director **Joseph S. Campbell** Room 3012 . . . . . (202) 324-4260
E-mail: joseph.campbell@ic.fbi.gov
Education: Kansas BA; Washburn JD
Deputy Assistant Director **Jayne L. Challman** . . . . (202) 324-5807
E-mail: jayne.challman@ic.fbi.gov
Deputy Assistant Director **J. Chris Warrener** . . . . (202) 324-5740
E-mail: j.warrener@ic.fbi.gov
Education: Oklahoma City 1981 BS; Oklahoma 1986 JD
Deputy Assistant Director **(Vacant)** . . . . (202) 324-4260
Violent Crimes Against Children Section Chief **Calvin A. Shivers** . . . . (202) 324-4260
E-mail: calvin.shivers@ic.fbi.gov

Cyber Division

J. Edgar Hoover Building, 935 Pennsylvania Avenue, NW, Washington, DC 20535-0001

The FBI's cyber mission is four-fold: first and foremost, to stop those behind the most serious computer intrusions and the spread of malicious code; second, to identify and thwart online sexual predators who use the Internet to meet and exploit children and to produce, share, or possess child pornography; third, to counteract operations that target U.S. intellectual property, endangering our national security and competitiveness; and fourth, to dismantle national and transnational organized criminal enterprises engaging in Internet fraud.

Assistant Director **James C. Trainor, Jr.** Room 5835 . . . . . (202) 324-7770
E-mail: james.trainor@ic.fbi.gov
Education: Assumption Col 1987 BA; Connecticut 1994 MPA
Deputy Assistant Director **(Vacant)** . . . . (202) 651-3003
Deputy Assistant Director **(Vacant)** . . . . (202) 651-3080
Unit Chief, Cyber Initiative and Resource Fusion **Eric Strom** . . . . (412) 802-8000 ext. 241

Directorate of Intelligence

J. Edgar Hoover Building, 935 Pennsylvania Avenue, NW, Washington, DC 20535-0001

The purpose of the Federal Bureau of Investigation (FBI) intelligence program is to identify and analyze current and emerging national security and criminal threats to the United States. The program's analysis is used to inform decision-making by both the FBI and other intelligence and law enforcement organizations.

Assistant Director **Rafael J. "Jorge" Garcia, Jr.** Room 7125 . . . . (202) 324-7605
Education: West Point 1982 BS; Military Intelligence Col MS; U Phoenix MCoun
Deputy Assistant Director **Tracey A. North** . . . . (202) 324-4837
E-mail: tracey.north@ic.fbi.gov
Deputy Assistant Director **Amy L. Pepper** . . . . (202) 324-1446
E-mail: amy.pepper@ic.fbi.gov
Deputy Assistant Director **(Vacant)** . . . . (202) 324-0997
Deputy Assistant Director **(Vacant)** . . . . (202) 324-7663

International Operations Division [IOD]

J. Edgar Hoover Building, 935 Pennsylvania Avenue, NW, Room 7443, Washington, DC 20535-0001

Assistant Director **Carlos Cases** . . . . (202) 324-5904
Note: Effective early January 2016.
E-mail: carlos.cases@ic.fbi.gov

National Security Branch [NSB]

J. Edgar Hoover Building, 935 Pennsylvania Avenue, NW, Room 7116, Washington, DC 20535-0001

• Executive Assistant Director **John Giacalone** . . . . (202) 324-7045
E-mail: john.giacalone@ic.fbi.gov
Education: Adelphi BBA; Naval War 2007 MNSSS
Associate Executive Assistant Director **Hal V. Lackey III** . . . . (202) 324-7705

Counterintelligence Division

J. Edgar Hoover Building, 935 Pennsylvania Avenue, NW, Washington, DC 20535-0001

The Federal Bureau of Investigation (FBI) Counterintelligence program protects the U.S. against foreign intelligence operations and espionage. Program activities are carried out by special agents, analysts, and other staff in FBI field offices who integrate intelligence and law enforcement efforts to investigate violations of espionage statutes.

Assistant Director **Randall C. Coleman** Room 4012 . . . . . . (202) 324-4614
E-mail: randall.coleman@ic.fbi.gov
Education: East Central U BA
Deputy Assistant Director **Dina M. Corsi** . . . . (202) 324-8912
Deputy Assistant Director **(Vacant)** . . . . (202) 324-4883

US DEPARTMENT OF JUSTICE

★ Presidential Appointment Requiring Senate Confirmation
☆ Presidential Appointment
☐ Schedule C Appointment
◇ Career Senior Foreign Service Appointment
● Career Senior Executive Service (SES) Appointment
○ Non-Career Senior Executive Service (SES) Appointment

Counterterrorism Division
J. Edgar Hoover Building, 935 Pennsylvania Avenue, NW, Washington, DC 20535-0001
Internet: www.fbi.gov/about-us/investigate/terrorism

The Federal Bureau of Investigation (FBI) Counterterrorism program is designed to protect the United States from terrorist attacks. FBI agents, analysts, and other staff investigate threats to prevent attacks from occurring, pursue sanctions against terrorists, and respond to terror attacks against Americans.

• Assistant Director **Michael B. Steinbach** Room 5012 .... (202) 324-2770
E-mail: michael.steinbach@ic.fbi.gov
Education: Naval Acad 1988 BAE

Deputy Assistant Director, Operational Support Branch
C. Bryan Paarmann .... (571) 280-5281
E-mail: bryan.paarmann@ic.fbi.gov

Deputy Assistant Director, Operations Branch I
J. S. Tabb, Jr. .... (571) 280-5526
1500 Farm Credit Drive, McLean, VA 22102

Deputy Assistant Director, Operations Branch II
Gary Douglas Perdue .... (571) 280-5526
LX-1, 1500 Farm Credit Drive, Room 3W-421, McLean, VA 22102
E-mail: gary.perdue@ic.fbi.gov
Education: Maryland 1988 BS; National Defense U 2008 MS

Deputy Assistant Director, Operations Branch III
(Vacant) .... (703) 553-7990

Terrorist Financing Operations Section Chief
Jane Rhodes-Wolfe .... (202) 324-5082

Weapons of Mass Destruction Directorate
J. Edgar Hoover Building, 935 Pennsylvania Avenue, NW, Room 5829, Washington, DC 20535-0001

Assistant Director **John G. Perren** .... (202) 324-4965
Education: American U BS; Indiana (PA) MS

Deputy Assistant Director **(Vacant)** .... (202) 324-4985

Science and Technology Branch [STB]
Executive Assistant Director **Amy S. Hess** .... (703) 985-6100
E-mail: amy.hess@ic.fbi.gov
Education: Purdue BS

Associate Executive Assistant Director **(Vacant)** .... (703) 985-6100

Criminal Justice Information Services Division [CJIS]
1000 Custer Hollow Road, Clarksburg, WV 26306
Internet: www.fbi.gov/hq/cjisd/cjis.htm

The Criminal Justice Information Services program supports federal, state, and local law enforcement efforts. It conducts fingerprint, DNA, and handgun background checks, and publishes national crime statistics. Some services are the only ones of their type in the country.

Assistant Director **Stephen L. Morris** .... (304) 625-2000
E-mail: stephen.morris@ic.fbi.gov
Education: Hawaii Pacific 1990

Deputy Assistant Director **Randall C. Thysse CPA** ...... (304) 625-2900
Education: U St Thomas (MN) BA; Drake MBA

Deputy Assistant Director **Jeremy Wiltz** .... (304) 625-4400

Laboratory Division
J. Edgar Hoover Building, 935 Pennsylvania Avenue, NW, Washington, DC 20535-0001
Internet: www.fbi.gov/hq/lab/labhome.htm

Assistant Director **Christopher Todd Doss** .... (703) 632-7001
E-mail: todd.doss@ic.fbi.gov

Deputy Assistant Director **(Vacant)** .... (703) 632-7100

Librarian **(Vacant)** .... (202) 324-4384

Operational Technology Division [OTD]
F.B.I. Academy, Quantico, VA 22135

Assistant Director **Stephen E. Richardson** .... (202) 324-0805
E-mail: stephen.richardson@ic.fbi.gov
Education: East Tennessee State BSBA; Duke MABA

Operational Technology Division *continued*

Deputy Assistant Director **James C. Burrell** .... (703) 985-6100
E-mail: james.burrell@ic.fbi.gov

Office of the Associate Deputy Director [OADD]
J. Edgar Hoover Building, 935 Pennsylvania Avenue, NW, 7142, Washington, DC 20535-0001

Associate Deputy Director **Andrew G. McCabe** .... (202) 324-4180
E-mail: andrew.mccabe@ic.fbi.gov
Education: Duke 1990 BA; Washington U (MO) 1993 JD

Office of Law Enforcement Coordination
J. Edgar Hoover Building, 935 Pennsylvania Avenue, NW, Room 7110, Washington, DC 20535-0001
Tel: (202) 324-7126 Fax: (202) 234-0920
E-mail: olec@leo.gov

Assistant Director **Ronald C. Ruecker** .... (202) 324-7126

Facilities and Logistics Services Division
J. Edgar Hoover Building, 935 Pennsylvania Avenue, NW, Room 1B875, Washington, DC 20535-0001

Assistant Director **Patrick G. Findlay** .... (202) 324-2875
E-mail: patrick.findlay@ic.fbi.gov
Education: West Point 1975; American U MPA; Georgia Tech MCE, MME; Missouri MEM

Deputy Assistant Director (Acting) **Teresa L. Carlson** .... (202) 324-2875
Education: Michigan State

Field Operations Support Section Chief
Paul F. Jarvis PE, PMP .... (202) 436-8002
E-mail: paul.jarvis@ic.fbi.gov
Education: VMI 1986 BS; Georgia Tech 1995 MS

Finance Division
J. Edgar Hoover Building, 935 Pennsylvania Avenue, NW, Washington, DC 20535-0001
Tel: (202) 324-4104

Chief Financial Officer and Assistant Director
Richard Lee Haley II Room 6012 .... (202) 324-4104
E-mail: richard.haley@ic.fbi.gov

Deputy Assistant Director **Janice J. Lambert**
Room 6012 .... (202) 324-4104
Education: USC BS; George Washington MPA

Inspection Division
J. Edgar Hoover Building, 935 Pennsylvania Avenue, NW, Washington, DC 20535-0001

Assistant Director **Nancy McNamara** Room 7825 .... (202) 324-2901

Deputy Assistant Director **Mark Alan Morgan** .... (202) 324-2901
Note: On detail.
Education: Central Missouri State BS; Missouri (Kansas City) JD

Records Management Division
J. Edgar Hoover Building, 935 Pennsylvania Avenue, NW, Washington, DC 20535-0001

Assistant Director **Michelle Ann Jupina** .... (540) 868-4400
Education: Virginia Tech; Penn State

Executive Secretariat- Unit Chief **Linda Trigeiro-Pabst** ... (202) 324-2828

FOIA Officer **David M. Hardy** .... (202) 324-5520
E-mail: david.hardy@ic.fbi.gov

Resource Planning Office [RPO]
Assistant Director **David Schlendorf** .... (202) 324-2211
Education: Duke; Harvard 1973 MBA

Human Resources Branch [HRB]
J. Edgar Hoover Building, 935 Pennsylvania Avenue, NW, Room 10903, Washington, DC 20535-0001

Executive Assistant Director **(Vacant)** .... (202) 324-3514

★ Presidential Appointment Requiring Senate Confirmation ☐ Schedule C Appointment ● Career Senior Executive Service (SES) Appointment
☆ Presidential Appointment ◇ Career Senior Foreign Service Appointment ○ Non-Career Senior Executive Service (SES) Appointment

Human Resources Branch [HRB] *continued*

Associate Executive Assistant Director **Timothy Groh** . . . . (202) 324-3514
E-mail: timothy.groh@ic.fbi.gov

Human Resources Division

• Assistant Director **James L. Turgal, Jr.** . . . . (202) 324-3514
Education: Northern Arizona BSB; Thomas M Cooley JD; Georgetown 1993 MLL
Deputy Assistant Director **(Vacant)** . . . . (202) 324-3592

Security Division

J. Edgar Hoover Building, 935 Pennsylvania Avenue, NW, Washington, DC 20535-0001

Assistant Director **Clifford C. Holly** Room 7128 . . . . (202) 324-7112
E-mail: clifford.holly@ic.fbi.gov
Deputy Assistant Director **Brigette Flynn-Class** . . . . (202) 324-2122
Chief Information Security Officer **Arlette Hart** . . . . (202) 324-5706
E-mail: arlette.hart@ic.fbi.gov

Training Division

F.B.I. Academy, Quantico, VA 22135

• Assistant Director **Owen D. Harris** . . . . (703) 632-1100
Education: Indiana (PA) 1986 BA
Deputy Assistant Director **(Vacant)** . . . . (703) 632-1100
New Agents Training Chief **(Vacant)** . . . . (703) 632-1000

Information and Technology Branch

J. Edgar Hoover Building, 935 Pennsylvania Avenue, NW, Room 7125, Washington, DC 20535-0001
Tel: (202) 324-6165

Executive Assistant Director and Chief Information Officer (Acting) **Brian Truchon** . . . . (202) 324-6165
E-mail: brian.truchon@ic.fbi.gov
Education: Arizona State 1984 BS
Associate Executive Assistant Director and Deputy Chief Information Officer **Dean E. Hall** Room 9396 . . . . (202) 324-6080
E-mail: dean.hall@ic.fbi.gov
Education: George Washington BSEE

Information Technology Application and Data Division

J. Edgar Hoover Building, 935 Pennsylvania Avenue, NW, Washington, DC 20535-0001

Assistant Director (Acting) **Jon K. Reid** Room 9396 . . . . . . (703) 872-5056
E-mail: jon.reid@ic.fbi.gov

Information Technology Customer Relationship and Management Division

J. Edgar Hoover Building, 935 Pennsylvania Avenue, NW, Room 9998, Washington, DC 20535-0001

Assistant Director and Chief Technology Officer **Jennifer R. Sanchez** . . . . (703) 324-4507
E-mail: jennifer.sanchez@ic.fbi.gov
Education: George Mason BS, MS

Information Technology Infrastructure Division

J. Edgar Hoover Building, 935 Pennsylvania Avenue, NW, Washington, DC 20535-0001

Assistant Director (Acting) **William Searcy** Room 9939 . . . . (202) 324-4840
E-mail: william.searcy@ic.fbi.gov
Deputy Assistant Director **William Searcy** . . . . (202) 324-4840
E-mail: william.searcy@ic.fbi.gov

Federal Bureau of Prisons [BOP]

Home Owners Loan Corporation Building, 320 First Street, NW, Washington, DC 20534
Tel: (202) 305-2500 (Nationwide Recruiting Information)
Tel: (800) 347-7744 Tel: (202) 307-3198
Internet: www.bop.gov

The Bureau of Prisons (BOP) protects society by confining federal inmates in prisons and other facilities that are safe, humane, cost-efficient and appropriately secure and by providing work and other self-improvement opportunities to assist offenders in becoming law-abiding citizens. The BOP incarcerates offenders in 122 prisons nationwide and houses more than 206,000 inmates in federal prisons, secure privately managed facilities, secure facilities operated by state and local governments, contract halfway houses or under home confinement.

Office of the Director

Home Owners Loan Corporation Building, 320 First Street, NW, Suite 654, Washington, DC 20534
Fax: (202) 514-6878

• Director **Charles E. Samuels, Jr.** . . . . (202) 307-3250
Education: Alabama Birmingham BS
• Deputy Director **Chris L.C. "Ike" Eichenlaub** . . . . (202) 307-3250
E-mail: bop-dir/deputydirector@bop.gov
Chief of Staff **Carla Wilson** . . . . (202) 307-3250
E-mail: bop-dir/chiefofstaff@bop.gov
Executive Secretary **Marla Clayton** . . . . (202) 307-3250
E-mail: m1clayton@bop.gov

Grand Prairie Office Complex

U.S. Armed Forces Reserve Complex, 346 Marine Forces Drive, Grand Prairie, TX 75051

Designation and Sentence Computation Center [DSCC]
Tel: (972) 362-4400 Fax: (972) 352-4395
E-mail: gra-dsc/policycorrespondence@bop.gov

Chief **Jose Santana** . . . . (972) 362-4400

Field Acquisition Office [FAO]
Tel: (972) 352-4200 Fax: (972) 352-4545
E-mail: gra/fieldacquisitionoffice@bop.gov

Chief **Jill Ryan** . . . . (972) 352-4200

Human Resource Services Center [HRSC]
Tel: (972) 352-4200 Fax: (972) 352-4220
E-mail: gra-hrm/chief-cesc@bop.gov

Chief **J. D. Robinson** . . . . (972) 730-8682

Office of General Counsel

Fax: (202) 307-2995

• Assistant Director/General Counsel **Kathleen M. Kenney** Room 958 . . . . (202) 307-3062
E-mail: bop-ogc/assistantdirector@bop.gov
Education: Catholic U 1988 BA; Notre Dame 1992 JD

Program Review Division

Fax: (202) 616-2100

• Assistant Director **Sara M. Revell** Room 1054 . . . . (202) 307-1076
E-mail: bop-prd/assistantdirector@bop.gov

Federal Prison Industries [UNICOR]

400 First Street, NW, Washington, DC 20534
Tel: (202) 305-3500 Fax: (202) 305-7340
Internet: www.unicor.gov

• Chief Executive Officer **Charles E. Samuels, Jr.** . . . . (202) 307-3250
320 First Street, NW, Suite 654, Washington, DC 20534 Fax: (202) 514-6878
Education: Alabama Birmingham BS

(continued on next page)

US DEPARTMENT OF JUSTICE

★ Presidential Appointment Requiring Senate Confirmation ☐ Schedule C Appointment ● Career Senior Executive Service (SES) Appointment
☆ Presidential Appointment ◇ Career Senior Foreign Service Appointment ○ Non-Career Senior Executive Service (SES) Appointment

Federal Prison Industries *continued*

- Chief Operating Officer **Mary Mitchell** 8th Floor . . . . (202) 305-3500

National Institute of Corrections [NIC]

320 First Street, NW, Washington, DC 20534
Tel: (800) 995-6423 Fax: (202) 307-3361
Internet: www.nicic.gov

○ Director **James L. "Jim" Cosby** . . . . (800) 995-6423 ext. 34213
500 First Street, NW, 7th Floor, Washington, DC 20530
E-mail: jcosby@bop.gov
E-mail: bop-nic/assistantdirector@bop.gov

Deputy Director **Robert M. Brown, Jr.** . . . . . . (800) 995-6423 ext. 44254
500 First Street, NW, 7th Floor, Washington, DC 20530
Education: USC MPA

Administration Division

- Assistant Director/Chief Financial Officer
William F. Dalius, Jr. . . . . (202) 307-3230
500 First Street, NW, 9th Floor, Washington, DC 20530 Fax: (202) 514-9481
E-mail: bop-adm/assistantdirector@bop.gov
Education: Bloomsburg 1980 BSBA

Correctional Programs Division

Fax: (202) 307-0509

- Assistant Director **Angela P. Dunbar** Room 554 . . . . (202) 307-3226
E-mail: bop-dpd/assistantdirector@bop.gov

Health Services Division

Fax: (202) 307-0826

Assistant Director/Medical Director
RADM Newton E. Kendig USPHS Room 454 . . . . (202) 307-3055
Education: Jefferson Col 1984 MD

Human Resource Management Division

Fax: (202) 353-4954

- Assistant Director **Daniel Joslin** Room 754 . . . . (202) 307-3082
E-mail: bop-hrm/assistantdirector@bop.gov
Education: Eastern Kentucky 1985 BS, 1987 MS

Industries, Education and Vocational Training Division

Fax: (202) 305-7340

- Assistant Director **Mary Mitchell** . . . . (202) 305-3501
400 First Street, NW, 8th Floor, Washington, DC 20534
E-mail: bop-fpi/assistantdirector@bop.gov

Information, Policy and Public Affairs Division

Fax: (202) 616-2093

- Assistant Director **Judi Simon Garrett** Suite 670 . . . . (202) 514-6537
E-mail: bop-ipp/assistantdirector@bop.gov

Reentry Services Division

400 First Street, NW, Second Floor, Washington, DC 20534
Fax: (202) 307-0215

- Assistant Director **Linda T. McGrew** . . . . (202) 514-8585
E-mail: bop-rsd/assistantdirector@bop.gov

United States Marshals Service [USMS]

United States Marshals Headquarters, 2604 Jefferson Davis Highway, Alexandria, VA 22301
Tel: (202) 307-9100 (Communications Center)
Tel: (202) 336-0162 (Public Affairs After hours)
E-mail: us.marshals@usdoj.gov
Internet: www.usmarshals.gov

The United States Marshals Service is the oldest federal law enforcement agency, and is the enforcement arm of the federal courts, protecting federal courts and ensuring the effective operation of the judicial system. It also operates the Witness Security Program, transports federal prisoners and seizes property acquired by criminals through illegal activity. The Service includes 94 Presidentially appointed U.S. Marshals, each representing a federal judicial district.

Office of the Director

United States Marshals Headquarters, 2604 Jefferson Davis Highway, Alexandria, VA 22301
Fax: (703) 603-7021

★ Director (Acting) **David L. Harlow** . . . . (202) 307-9001
Chief of Staff **Sophia Edwards** . . . . (202) 307-9072

Office of Equal Employment Opportunity

Fax: (703) 603-7005

Equal Employment Opportunity Officer
Marcus Williams . . . . (202) 307-9048

Office of the Deputy Director

- Deputy Director **(Vacant)** . . . . (202) 307-9005

Office of District Affairs Chief (Acting)
James Cunfer . . . . (202) 305-9547
E-mail: james.cunfer@usdoj.gov

Office of General Counsel [GC]

Fax: (703) 603-7022

- General Counsel **Gerald M. Auerbach** . . . . (202) 307-9054
E-mail: gerald.auerbach@usdoj.gov

Office of Professional Responsibility

- Assistant Director **Carl Caulk** . . . . (202) 307-9155
E-mail: carl.caulk@usdoj.gov

Directorate of Administration

- Associate Director for Administration
David F. "Dave" Musel . . . . (202) 307-9319
E-mail: david.musel@usdoj.gov
Education: Creighton BA, 1993 JD

Office of Congressional and Public Affairs

Fax: (703) 603-2819

Chief **William Delaney** . . . . (202) 307-9220
E-mail: william.delaney@usdoj.gov

Office of Congressional Affairs

Deputy Chief **Christie Dawson** . . . . (202) 307-9220
E-mail: christie.dawson@usdoj.gov

Office of Public Affairs

Public Affairs Chief **Drew J. Wade** . . . . (202) 307-9065
Public Affairs Deputy Chief **Donna Sellers** . . . . (202) 307-9065

Asset Forfeiture Division

Tel: (888) 878-3256 Fax: (703) 308-0374

- Assistant Director (Acting) **Timothy Virtue** . . . . (202) 307-9221
E-mail: tim.virtue@usdoj.gov

Deputy Assistant Director **Timothy Virtue** . . . . (202) 353-8345
E-mail: tim.virtue@usdoj.gov

Financial Services Division [FSD]
Fax: (703) 603-2033

• Chief Financial Officer **Holley B. O'Brien** . . . . (202) 307-9037
E-mail: holley.o'brien@usdoj.gov
Deputy Assistant General for Acquisitions and Procurement **Carole O'Brien** . . . . (202) 307-9625

Human Resources Division
Tel: (202) 307-9625 Fax: (703) 603-7023

• Assistant Director **Katherine Mohan** . . . . (202) 307-9871
E-mail: katherine.mohan@usdoj.gov
Deputy Assistant Director **Beth Brown-Ghee** . . . . (202) 307-9625
E-mail: beth.brown-ghee@usdoj.gov

Information Technology Division
Fax: (703) 603-7003

• Assistant Director **Karl Mathias** . . . . (703) 604-2054
E-mail: karl.mathias@usdoj.gov
Deputy Assistant Director **Jarrod Bruner** . . . . (703) 604-2054
E-mail: jarrod.bruner@usdoj.gov

Management Services Division
Fax: (703) 603-2032

• Assistant Director **Thomas "Tom" Sgroi** . . . . (202) 307-9011
E-mail: thomas.sgroi@usdoj.gov
Deputy Assistant Director **Michael Clay** . . . . (202) 307-9011
E-mail: michael.clay@usdoj.gov

Training Division
Fax: (912) 267-2882

• Assistant Director **William T. Fallon** . . . . (912) 267-2505
Federal Law Enforcement Training Center, Building 20, Glynco, GA 31524
E-mail: william.fallon@usdoj.gov
Deputy Assistant Director **David Anderson** . . . . (912) 267-2505

Directorate of Operations
• Associate Director for Operations **William D. Snelson** . . . (202) 307-9001
E-mail: william.snelson@usdoj.gov

Investigative Operations Division
United States Marshals Headquarters, 2604 Jefferson Davis Highway, Alexandria, VA 22301
Internet: www.usmarshals.gov/investigations

In fiscal year 2008, the U.S. Marshals arrested more than 36,600 federal fugitive felons, clearing 39,700 federal felony warrants–more than all other law enforcement agencies combined. Working with authorities at the federal, state, and local levels, U.S. Marshals-led fugitive task forces arrested more than 73,000 state and local fugitives, clearing 90,600 state and local felony warrants.

• Assistant Director **Derrick Driscoll** . . . . (202) 307-9110
E-mail: derrick.driscoll@usdoj.gov Fax: (703) 603-7006
Deputy Assistant Director **Donald P. O'Hearn** . . . . (202) 307-9195
E-mail: donald.o'hearn@usdoj.gov Fax: (703) 603-2024

Judicial Security Division [JSD]
United States Marshals Headquarters, 2604 Jefferson Davis Highway, Alexandria, VA 22301
Internet: www.usmarshals.gov/judicial

The Judicial Security Division is committed to the protection of the judicial process by ensuring the safe and secure conduct of judicial proceedings and protecting federal judges, jurors and other members of the federal judiciary. This mission is accomplished by anticipating and deterring threats to the judiciary, and the continuous development and employment of innovative protective techniques.

• Assistant Director **Noelle Douglas** . . . . (202) 307-9500
E-mail: noelle.douglas@usdoj.gov
Deputy Assistant Director **Thomas Wight** . . . . (202) 307-5213
E-mail: thomas.wight@usdoj.gov

Judicial Security Division *continued*

Deputy Assistant Director, Judicial Services (Acting) **Gary Insley** . . . . (202) 307-9500
E-mail: gary.insley2@usdoj.gov

Justice Prisoner and Alien Transportation System [JPATS]
1251 Northwest Briar Cliff Parkway, Suite 300, Kansas City, MO 64116
Tel: (816) 467-1900 Tel: (405) 680-3400 (Prisoner Transportation)
Fax: (816) 467-1980
Internet: www.usdoj.gov/marshals/jpats

The Justice Prisoner and Alien Transportation System (JPATS) transports sentenced prisoners who are in the custody of the Federal Bureau of Prisons as well as Immigration and Customs Enforcement criminal/administrative aliens to hearings, court appearances and detention facilities. The Justice Prisoner and Alien Transportation System also provides regular international flights for the removal of deportable aliens. Military and civilian law enforcement agencies use the Justice Prisoner and Alien Transportation System to shuttle their prisoners between different jurisdictions at a fraction of what commercial sources would charge.

• Assistant Director **Shannon Brown** . . . . (816) 467-1900
Deputy Assistant Director **Scott Flood** . . . . (816) 467-1900
E-mail: scott.flood@usdoj.gov
Chief of Operations **Nelson Hackmaster** . . . . (816) 467-1900

Prisoner Operations Division
Fax: (703) 603-7008

• Assistant Director **Eben Morales** . . . . (202) 307-5100
E-mail: eben.morales@usdoj.gov
Deputy Assistant Director, Prisoner Operations **Bruce E. Vargo** . . . . (202) 307-5100
Budget, Finance and Forecasting Division Chief **Jim Murphy** . . . . (202) 307-5100
Detention Standards and Compliance Division Chief (Acting) **Theo Anderson** . . . . (202) 307-5100
Information Technology Division Chief **(Vacant)** . . . . (202) 307-5100
Procurement Division Chief **Scott P. Stermer** . . . . (202) 307-5100
E-mail: scott.stermer2@usdoj.gov

Tactical Operations Division
• Assistant Director **Neil DeSousa** . . . . (202) 307-3437
E-mail: neil.desousa@usdoj.gov
Education: John Jay Col
Deputy Assistant Director (Acting) **Marti Stanley** . . . . (800) 336-0102
E-mail: marti.stanley@usdoj.gov
Special Operations Tactical Center Commander **Eric Kessel** . . . . (318) 640-4560
E-mail: eric.kessel@usdoj.gov

Witness Security Division
United States Marshals Headquarters, 2604 Jefferson Davis Highway, Alexandria, VA 22301

• Assistant Director **Michael "Mike" Prout** . . . . (202) 307-9150
E-mail: mike.prout@usdoj.gov
Deputy Assistant Director **Marcus Walker** . . . . (202) 307-9150

★ Presidential Appointment Requiring Senate Confirmation ☐ Schedule C Appointment ● Career Senior Executive Service (SES) Appointment
☆ Presidential Appointment ◇ Career Senior Foreign Service Appointment ○ Non-Career Senior Executive Service (SES) Appointment

Regional Offices - US Attorneys and US Marshals Service

United States Department of Justice [DOJ]

Robert F. Kennedy Building, 950 Pennsylvania Avenue, NW, Washington, DC 20530-2001
Tel: (202) 514-2000 (Personnel Locator)
Tel: (202) 307-2000 (Procurement Information)
Tel: (202) 514-2007 (Public Information)
Tel: (202) 514-3642 (Freedom of Information/Privacy Act)
Tel: (202) 514-2001 (Office of the Attorney General)
Tel: (800) 869-4499 (Inspector General's Hot Line)
Tel: (202) 514-4330 (Immigration General Information)
Tel: (800) 514-0301 (Americans with Disabilities Act Information)
Tel: (800) 777-7700 (Amnesty Program/Legalization General Information)
Fax: (202) 514-4371
Internet: www.justice.gov
Internet: www.justice.gov/open (Open Government Directive)
Internet: www.usa.gov (Official US Government Website)

The Department of Justice serves as counsel to the U.S. Government, enforces the law, protects the public from criminals and subversion, ensures healthy business competition, and safeguards consumers. In its capacity as counsel, the department manages all cases involving the United States Federal Government.

OFFICE OF THE ATTORNEY GENERAL

Robert F. Kennedy Building, 950 Pennsylvania Avenue, NW, Washington, DC 20530-2001
Tel: (202) 514-2001 Fax: (202) 307-6777
Internet: www.usdoj.gov/ag

The mission of the Office of the Attorney General is to supervise and direct the administration and operation of the Department of Justice, including the Federal Bureau of Investigation, Drug Enforcement Administration, Bureau of Alcohol, Tobacco, Firearms and Explosives, Bureau of Prisons, Office of Justice Programs, and the U.S. Attorneys and U.S. Marshals Service.

Office of the Deputy Attorney General [ODAG]

Robert F. Kennedy Building, 950 Pennsylvania Avenue, NW, Washington, DC 20530
Tel: (202) 514-2101 Fax: (202) 514-0467
Internet: www.justice.gov/dag

The mission of the Deputy Attorney General is to advise and assist the Attorney General in formulating and implementing Department policies and programs and in providing overall supervision and direction to all organizational units of the Department.

Executive Office for United States Attorneys [EOUSA]

Robert F. Kennedy Building, 950 Pennsylvania Avenue, NW, Washington, DC 20530
Tel: (202) 252-1000 Fax: (202) 252-1001
Internet: www.justice.gov/usao/eousa

The United States Attorneys serve as the nation's principal litigators under the direction of the Attorney General. One United States Attorney is assigned to each of the judicial districts, with the exception of Guam and the Northern Mariana Islands where a single United States Attorney serves in both districts. Each United States Attorney is the chief federal law enforcement officer of the United States within his or her particular jurisdiction.

The mission of the Executive Office for U.S. Attorneys is to provide general executive assistance to the 94 Offices of the United States Attorneys and to coordinate the relationship between the United States Attorneys and the organizational components of the Department of Justice and other federal agencies.

Office of the Director

Tel: (202) 252-1000 Fax: (202) 252-1001

Office of the Deputy Director for Legal Management

Office of Legal Education (National Advocacy Center)

1620 Pendelton Street, Columbia, SC 29201
Tel: (803) 705-5100 Fax: (803) 705-5110
Internet: www.justice.gov/usao/eousa/ole

• Associate Director **Cammy Chandler** .... (803) 705-5102
E-mail: cammy.chandler@usdoj.gov

Deputy Director **Col Calvin L. Lewis** .... (803) 705-5102
E-mail: calvin.lewis@usdoj.gov
Affiliation: USAF

District Offices

Alabama - Middle District

131 Clayton Street, Montgomery, AL 36104
P.O. Box 197, Montgomery, AL 36101-0197
Tel: (334) 223-7280 Fax: (334) 223-7560
Internet: www.usdoj.gov/usao/alm/index.html

★ U.S. Attorney **George Lamar Beck, Jr.** .... (334) 223-7280
E-mail: george.beck@usdoj.gov
Education: Auburn 1963; Alabama 1966 JD
Secretary to the U.S. Attorney **Brittney Boshell** .... (334) 223-7280
E-mail: brittney.boshell@usdoj.gov

First Assistant U.S. Attorney **A. Clark Morris** .... (334) 223-7280
E-mail: clark.morris@usdoj.gov

Senior Litigation Counsel and Assistant U.S. Attorney **Jerusha T. Adams** .... (334) 223-7280
E-mail: jerusha.adams@usdoj.gov

Executive Coordinator **(Vacant)** .... (334) 223-7280

Asset Forfeiture Assistant U.S. Attorney **Kevin Davidson** .... (334) 223-7280
E-mail: kevin.davidson@usdoj.gov

Drug Task Force Lead Assistant U.S. Attorney **Verne H. Speirs** .... (334) 223-7280
E-mail: verne.speirs@usdoj.gov

Law Enforcement Coordination Manager **Douglas Howard** .... (334) 223-7280
E-mail: douglas.howard@usdoj.gov

Victim/Witness Coordinator **Jacqueline Vickers** .... (334) 223-7280
E-mail: jackie.vickers@usdoj.gov

Administrative Officer **Retta C. Goss** .... (334) 223-7280
E-mail: retta.goss@usdoj.gov

Budget Officer **Sherri Hamilton** .... (334) 223-7280

Information Technology Specialist **Jordan Oakley** .... (334) 223-7280
E-mail: jordan.oakley@usdoj.gov

(continued on next page)

★ Presidential Appointment Requiring Senate Confirmation ☆ Presidential Appointment □ Schedule C Appointment ◇ Career Senior Foreign Service Appointment
● Career Senior Executive Service (SES) Appointment ○ Non-Career Senior Executive Service (SES) Appointment ■ Postal Career Executive Service

Alabama - Middle District *continued*

Information Technology Systems Manager
Randy Durden . . . . (334) 223-7280
E-mail: randy.durden@usdoj.gov
Public Affairs Officer **A. Clark Morris** . . . . (334) 223-7280

Civil Division
Tel: (334) 223-7280 Fax: (334) 223-7560

Chief **Stephen M. Doyle** . . . . (334) 223-7280
E-mail: stephen.doyle@usdoj.gov
Assistant U.S. Attorney **Bob Anderson** . . . . (334) 223-7280
E-mail: bob.anderson@usdoj.gov
Assistant U.S. Attorney **James "Jim" DuBois** . . . . (334) 223-7280
E-mail: james.dubois2@usdoj.gov
Assistant U.S. Attorney **Randolph R. Neeley** . . . . (334) 223-7280
E-mail: rand.neeley@usdoj.gov

Criminal Division
Tel: (334) 223-7280 Fax: (334) 223-7135

Chief **Louis V. Franklin, Sr.** . . . . (334) 223-7280
E-mail: louis.franklin@usdoj.gov
Deputy Chief **Verne H. Speirs** . . . . (334) 223-7280
E-mail: verne.speirs@usdoj.gov
Assistant U.S. Attorney **Gray M. Borden** . . . . (334) 223-7280
E-mail: gray.m.borden@usdoj.gov
Assistant U.S. Attorney **Todd Brown** . . . . (334) 223-7280
E-mail: todd.brown@usdoj.gov
Assistant U.S. Attorney **Kevin Davidson** . . . . (334) 223-7280
E-mail: kevin.davidson@usdoj.gov
Assistant U.S. Attorney **Susan Redmond** . . . . (334) 223-7280
E-mail: susan.redmond@usdoj.gov
Assistant U.S. Attorney **Christopher A. Snyder** . . . . (334) 223-7280
E-mail: christopher.a.snyder@usdoj.gov
Education: Ohio 1996 BA; Ohio State 2000 JD
Assistant U.S. Attorney **(Vacant)** . . . . (334) 223-7280
Assistant U.S. Attorney **(Vacant)** . . . . (334) 223-7280
Assistant U.S. Attorney/Health Care Fraud Coordinator
Denise Simpson . . . . (334) 223-7280
E-mail: denise.simpson@usdoj.gov

Financial Litigation Unit
Tel: (334) 223-7280 Fax: (334) 223-7418

Lead Attorney **Randolph R. Neeley** . . . . (334) 223-7280
E-mail: rand.neeley@usdoj.gov

Alabama - Northern District

1801 Fourth Avenue North, Birmingham, AL 35203-2101
Tel: (205) 244-2001 Fax: (205) 244-2183
Internet: www.usdoj.gov/usao/aln/

★ U.S. Attorney **Joyce White Vance** . . . . (205) 244-2001
E-mail: joyce.vance@usdoj.gov
Education: Bates 1982; Virginia 1985 JD
Executive Assistant to the U.S. Attorney
Stacy M. Crane . . . . (205) 244-2015
E-mail: stacy.crane@usdoj.gov
First Assistant U.S. Attorney **Robert O. Posey** . . . . (205) 244-2216
E-mail: robert.posey@usdoj.gov
Crisis Management Coordinator **Henry B. Cornelius** . . . . (205) 244-2213
Law Enforcement Coordinator Manager
Lyndon J. Laster . . . . (205) 244-2092
E-mail: lyndon.laster@usdoj.gov
Victim-Witness Coordinator
Tonja Benninger Holtkamp . . . . (205) 244-2093
E-mail: tonja.benninger@usdoj.gov
Administrative Officer **China M. Davidson** . . . . (205) 244-2030
E-mail: china.davidson@usdoj.gov
Deputy Administrative Officer **(Vacant)** . . . . (205) 244-2001
Administrative Services Specialist
Christopher J. Givens . . . . (205) 244-2050
E-mail: christopher.givens@usdoj.gov

Alabama - Northern District *continued*

Human Resources Officer **Donzella L. Walton** . . . . (205) 244-2070
E-mail: donzella.walton@usdoj.gov
Human Resources Specialist **Jane M. McGuire** . . . . (205) 244-2071
E-mail: jane.mcguire@usdoj.gov
Intelligence Specialist **Tammy R. Davis** . . . . (205) 244-2188
Litigation Support Specialist **Kayla D. Trudeau** . . . . (205) 244-2087
E-mail: kayla.trudeau@usdoj.gov
Systems Manager **P. Tracy Stewart** . . . . (205) 244-2080
E-mail: tracy.stewart@usdoj.gov

Appellate Division
Chief **Michael B. Billingsley** . . . . (205) 244-2157
E-mail: michael.billingsley@usdoj.gov
Assistant U.S. Attorney **Ramona C. Albin** . . . . (205) 244-2234
E-mail: ramona.albin@usdoj.gov
Assistant U.S. Attorney **Praveen S. Krishna** . . . . (205) 244-2168
E-mail: praveen.krishna@usdoj.gov
Assistant U.S. Attorney **Jenny L. Smith** . . . . (205) 244-2105
E-mail: jenny.smith@usdoj.gov

Civil Division
Chief **Lane H. Woodke** . . . . (205) 244-2107
E-mail: lane.woodke@usdoj.gov
Deputy Chief **(Vacant)** . . . . (205) 244-2121
Assistant U.S. Attorney **Thomas E. Borton IV** . . . . (205) 244-2131
E-mail: thomas.borton@usdoj.gov
Education: Alabama 2001 JD
Assistant U.S. Attorney **Jason R. Cheek** . . . . (205) 244-2104
E-mail: jason.r.cheek@usdoj.gov
Assistant U.S. Attorney **Erin M. Everitt** . . . . (205) 244-2119
E-mail: erin.everitt@usdoj.gov
Assistant U.S. Attorney **Jack B. Hood** . . . . (205) 244-2103
E-mail: jack.hood@usdoj.gov
Assistant U.S. Attorney **Don B. Long** . . . . (205) 244-2106
E-mail: don.long2@usdoj.gov
Education: Texas 2008 JD
Assistant U.S. Attorney **Richard E. O'Neal** . . . . (205) 244-2120
E-mail: richard.o'neal@usdoj.gov
Assistant U.S. Attorney **Edward Q. Ragland** . . . . (205) 244-2109
E-mail: ed.ragland@usdoj.gov
Assistant U.S. Attorney **(Vacant)** . . . . (205) 244-2217

Civil Rights Unit
Tel: (205) 244-2001

Chief **Tamarra Matthews-Johnson** . . . . (205) 244-2001
E-mail: tamarra.matthews-johnson@usdoj.gov

Criminal Division
Chief **(Vacant)** . . . . (205) 244-2241
Deputy Chief (Drugs, Guns, Violent Crimes)
William G. Simpson . . . . (205) 244-2207
E-mail: bill.simpson@usdoj.gov
Deputy Chief (Public Corruption, Fraud, Civil Rights, Environmental) **George A. Martin** . . . . (205) 244-2254
E-mail: george.martin@usdoj.gov
Deputy Chief (Terrorism, Cybercrime, Child Exploitation, Asset Forfeiture) **Daniel J. Fortune** . . . . (205) 244-2156
E-mail: daniel.fortune@usdoj.gov
Asset Forfeiture Unit Assistant U.S. Attorney
Jennifer S. Murnahan . . . . (205) 244-2135
E-mail: jennifer.murnahan@usdoj.gov
Assistant U.S. Attorney **Melissa K. Atwood** . . . . (205) 244-2159
E-mail: melissa.atwood@usdoj.gov
Assistant U.S. Attorney **Erica W Barnes** . . . . (205) 244-2228
E-mail: erica.barnes@usdoj.gov
Assistant U.S. Attorney **Henry B. Cornelius** . . . . (205) 244-2213
E-mail: henry.cornelius@usdoj.gov
Assistant U.S. Attorney **Chinelo Dike-Minor** . . . . (205) 244-2139
E-mail: chinelo.dike-minor@usdoj.gov
Assistant U.S. Attorney **John B. "Brad" Felton** . . . . (205) 244-2256
E-mail: brad.felton@usdoj.gov

★ Presidential Appointment Requiring Senate Confirmation ☆ Presidential Appointment ☐ Schedule C Appointment ◇ Career Senior Foreign Service Appointment
● Career Senior Executive Service (SES) Appointment ○ Non-Career Senior Executive Service (SES) Appointment ■ Postal Career Executive Service

Criminal Division *continued*

Assistant U.S. Attorney **Elizabeth A. Holt** . . . . (205) 244-2022
E-mail: elizabeth.holt@usdoj.gov
Assistant U.S. Attorney **Jacquelyn M. Hutzell** . . . . (205) 244-2158
E-mail: jacquelyn.hutzell@usdoj.gov
Assistant U.S. Attorney **Robin B. Mark** . . . . (205) 244-2154
E-mail: robin.mark@usdoj.gov
Assistant U.S. Attorney **Tamarra Matthews-Johnson** . . . (205) 244-2203
E-mail: tamarra.matthews-johnson@usdoj.gov
Assistant U.S. Attorney **John P. "Pat" Meadows** . . . . (205) 244-2214
E-mail: pat.meadows@usdoj.gov
Assistant U.S. Attorney **Joseph P. Montminy** . . . . (205) 244-2185
E-mail: joe.montminy@usdoj.gov
Assistant U.S. Attorney **Frank M. Salter** . . . . (205) 244-2208
E-mail: frank.salter@usdoj.gov
Assistant U.S. Attorney **Austin D. Shutt** . . . . (205) 244-2001
E-mail: austin.shutt@usdoj.gov
Assistant U.S. Attorney **(Vacant)** . . . . (205) 244-2138

Drug Task Force

Lead Assistant U.S. Attorney **Gregory R. Dimler** . . . . (205) 244-2223
E-mail: greg.dimler@usdoj.gov
Assistant U.S. Attorney **Daniel M. Murdock** . . . . (205) 244-2224
E-mail: daniel.murdock@usdoj.gov
Assistant U.S. Attorney **L. James "Jim" Weil, Jr.** . . . . (205) 244-2242
E-mail: jim.weil@usdoj.gov
Assistant U.S. Attorney **Hunter Wilson** . . . . (205) 244-2242

Huntsville (AL) Office

400 Meridian Street, Suite 304, Huntsville, AL 35801
Tel: (256) 534-8285 Fax: (256) 539-3270

Branch Chief and Assistant U.S. Attorney
Laura D. Hodge . . . . (256) 534-8285
E-mail: laura.hodge@usdoj.gov
Assistant U.S. Attorney **Davis A. Barlow** . . . . (256) 534-8285
E-mail: davis.barlow@usdoj.gov
Assistant U.S. Attorney **Mary Stuart Burrell** . . . . (256) 534-8285
E-mail: mary.stuart.burrell@usdoj.gov
Assistant U.S. Attorney **David H. Estes** . . . . (256) 534-8285
E-mail: david.estes@usdoj.gov
Assistant U.S. Attorney **Russell E. Penfield** . . . . (256) 534-8285
E-mail: russell.penfield@usdoj.gov

Alabama - Southern District

Renaissance Riverview Plaza Office Building, 63 South Royal Street, Suite 600, Mobile, AL 36602
Tel: (251) 441-5845 Fax: (251) 441-5277
Internet: www.justice.gov/usao/als

★ U.S. Attorney **Kenyen Ray Brown** . . . . (251) 441-5845
E-mail: kenyen.brown@usdoj.gov
Education: Alabama 1991 BA; Tennessee 1995 JD
□ Secretary to the U.S. Attorney **Gloria Patton** . . . . (251) 441-5845
E-mail: gloria.patton@usdoj.gov
First Assistant U.S. Attorney **Steven E. Butler** . . . . (251) 441-5845
E-mail: steven.butler@usdoj.gov
Appellate Chief **Adam W. Overstreet** . . . . (251) 411-5845
E-mail: adam.overstreet@usdoj.gov
Law Enforcement Coordination Specialist
Thomas Loftis . . . . (251) 441-5845
E-mail: thomas.loftis@usdoj.gov
Intelligence Specialist **Roy H. Sawyer** . . . . (251) 441-5845
Crisis Management Coordinator **(Vacant)** . . . . (251) 441-5845
Technology Specialist **Joshua Smith** . . . . (251) 415-7108
E-mail: joshua.smith@usdoj.gov Fax: (251) 441-6526
Victim-Witness Specialist **Eric T. Day** . . . . (251) 441-5845
E-mail: eric.day@usdoj.gov
Administrative Officer **James A. "Jim" Tharp, Jr.** . . . . . . (251) 441-5845
E-mail: jim.tharp@usdoj.gov

Civil Division

Chief **Steven E. Butler** . . . . (251) 441-5845
E-mail: steven.butler@usdoj.gov
Assistant U.S. Attorney **Daryl Atchison** . . . . (251) 441-5845
E-mail: daryl.atchison@usdoj.gov
Assistant U.S. Attorney **Charles Baer** . . . . (251) 441-5845
E-mail: charles.baer@usdoj.gov
Assistant U.S. Attorney **Patricia Beyer** . . . . (251) 441-5845
E-mail: patricia.beyer@usdoj.gov
Assistant U.S. Attorney **Deidre Colson** . . . . (251) 441-5845
E-mail: deidre.colson@usdoj.gov
Assistant U.S. Attorney **Erica Hilliard** . . . . (251) 441-5845
E-mail: erica.hilliard@usdoj.gov
Assistant U.S. Attorney **Alex F. Lankford IV** . . . . (251) 441-5845
E-mail: alex.lankford@usdoj.gov
Assistant U.S. Attorney **Suntrease Williams-Maynard** . . . (251) 441-5845
E-mail: suntrease.williams-maynard@usdoj.gov
Assistant U.S. Attorney **Holly Wiseman** . . . . (251) 441-5845
E-mail: holly.wiseman@usdoj.gov

Criminal Division

Chief **Vicki Davis** . . . . (251) 441-5845
E-mail: vicki.davis@usdoj.gov
Deputy Criminal Chief **Sean Costello** . . . . (251) 441-5845
E-mail: sean.costello@usdoj.gov
Assistant U.S. Attorney **Michael D. "Mike" Anderson** . . . (251) 441-5845
E-mail: michael.d.anderson@usdoj.gov
Assistant U.S. Attorney **Lawrence Ballard** . . . . (251) 441-5845
E-mail: lawrence.ballard@usdoj.gov
Assistant U.S. Attorney **Gloria A. Bedwell** . . . . (251) 441-5845
E-mail: gloria.bedwell@usdoj.gov
Assistant U.S. Attorney **Christopher Bodnar** . . . . (251) 441-5845
E-mail: christopher.bodnar@usdoj.gov
Education: Texas 2008 JD
Assistant U.S. Attorney **Greg A. Bordenkircher** . . . . (251) 441-5845
E-mail: greg.bordenkircher@usdoj.gov
Assistant U.S. Attorney **Deborah A. Griffin** . . . . (251) 441-5845
E-mail: deborah.griffin@usdoj.gov
Assistant U.S. Attorney **Sinan Kalayoglu** . . . . (251) 441-5845
E-mail: sinan.kalayoglu@usdoj.gov
Assistant U.S. Attorney **George F. May** . . . . (251) 441-5845
E-mail: george.may@usdoj.gov
Assistant U.S. Attorney **Maria E. Murphy** . . . . (251) 441-5845
E-mail: maria.murphy@usdoj.gov
Assistant U.S. Attorney **Michele O'Brien** . . . . (251) 441-5845
E-mail: michele.obrien@usdoj.gov
Assistant U.S. Attorney **Gina Vann** . . . . (251) 441-5845
E-mail: gina.vann@usdoj.gov
Assistant U.S. Attorney **(Vacant)** . . . . (251) 441-5845
Assistant U.S. Attorney **(Vacant)** . . . . (251) 441-5845
Assistant U.S. Attorney **(Vacant)** . . . . (251) 441-5845

Alaska District

Federal Building and U.S. Courthouse, 222 West Seventh Avenue, #9, Room 253, Anchorage, AK 99513-7567
Tel: (907) 271-5071 Fax: (907) 271-3224
Internet: www.justice.gov/usao/ak

★ U.S. Attorney **Karen Louise Loeffler** . . . . (907) 271-5071
E-mail: karen.loeffler@usdoj.gov
Education: Dartmouth 1979 AB; Harvard 1983 JD
Secretary to the U.S. Attorney **Eileen Frost** . . . . (907) 271-5071
E-mail: eileen.frost@usdoj.gov
First Assistant U.S. Attorney **Kevin Feldis** . . . . (907) 271-5071
E-mail: kevin.feldis@usdoj.gov
Criminal Division Chief and Assistant U.S. Attorney
Kevin Feldis . . . . (907) 271-5071
E-mail: kevin.feldis@usdoj.gov
Deputy Criminal Division Chief and Assistant U.S. Attorney **Frank V. Russo** . . . . (907) 271-5071
E-mail: frank.russo@usdoj.gov

(continued on next page)

★ Presidential Appointment Requiring Senate Confirmation ☆ Presidential Appointment □ Schedule C Appointment ◇ Career Senior Foreign Service Appointment
● Career Senior Executive Service (SES) Appointment ○ Non-Career Senior Executive Service (SES) Appointment ■ Postal Career Executive Service

Alaska District *continued*

Civil Division Chief and Assistant U.S. Attorney
Richard Pomeroy . . . . (907) 271-5071
E-mail: richard.pomeroy@usdoj.gov
Asset Forfeiture Unit Assistant U.S. Attorney
James N. "Jim" Barkeley . . . . (907) 271-5071
E-mail: jim.barkeley@usdoj.gov
Drug Task Force Assistant U.S. Attorney
Stephan Collins . . . . (907) 271-5071
E-mail: stephan.collins@usdoj.gov
Assistant U.S. Attorney **Joseph W. "Joe" Bottini** . . . . . . (907) 271-5071
E-mail: joe.bottini@usdoj.gov
Assistant U.S. Attorney **Thomas "Tom" Bradley** . . . . (907) 271-5071
E-mail: thomas.bradley@usdoj.gov
Assistant U.S. Attorney **Kelly Cavanaugh** . . . . (907) 271-5071
E-mail: kelly.cavanaugh@usdoj.gov
Assistant U.S. Attorney **Stephanie Courter** . . . . (907) 271-5071
E-mail: scourter@usa.doj.gov
Assistant U.S. Attorney **Timothy Edmonds** . . . . (907) 271-2174
E-mail: timothy.edmonds@usdoj.gov
Assistant U.S. Attorney **Jo Ann Farrington** . . . . (907) 271-5071
E-mail: jo.ann.farrington2@usdoj.gov
Assistant U.S. Attorney **Gary Guarino** . . . . (907) 271-5071
E-mail: gary.guarino@usdoj.gov
Education: UC Davis 1981 JD
Assistant U.S. Attorney **Yvonne Lamoureux** . . . . (907) 271-5071
E-mail: yvonne.lamoureux@usdoj.gov
Education: Virginia 2003 JD
Assistant U.S. Attorney **Susan Lindquist** . . . . (907) 271-5071
E-mail: susan.lindquist@usdoj.gov
Assistant U.S. Attorney **Retta-Rae Randall** . . . . (907) 271-5071
E-mail: rettarae.randall@usdoj.gov
Assistant U.S. Attorney **Audrey Renschen** . . . . (907) 271-5071
E-mail: audrey.renschen@usdoj.gov
Assistant U.S. Attorney **Kimberly "Kim" Sayers-Fay** . . . . (907) 271-5071
E-mail: kim.sayers-fay@usdoj.gov
Assistant U.S. Attorney **Bryan Schroder** . . . . (907) 271-5071
E-mail: bryan.schroder@usdoj.gov
Assistant U.S. Attorney **Steven E. "Steve" Skrocki** . . . . . (907) 271-5071
E-mail: steven.skrocki@usdoj.gov
Assistant U.S. Attorney **Andrea "Aunnie" Steward** . . . . . (907) 271-5071
E-mail: aunnie.steward@usdoj.gov
Assistant U.S. Attorney **Bryan Wilson** . . . . (907) 271-5071
E-mail: bryan.wilson@usdoj.gov
Administrative Officer **Brenda Spicer** . . . . (907) 271-5071
E-mail: brenda.spicer@usdoj.gov
Administrative Support Specialist **Lisa Brune** . . . . (907) 271-5071
E-mail: lisa.brune@usdoj.gov
Automated Litigation Support Specialist
Jodi Bradison . . . . (907) 271-5071
E-mail: jodi.bradison@usdoj.gov
Budget Officer **Traci D. Ross** . . . . (907) 271-5071
E-mail: traci.ross@usdoj.gov
Intelligence Officer **(Vacant)** . . . . (907) 271-5071
Law Enforcement Committee Coordinator **(Vacant)** . . . . . . (907) 271-5071
Office Automation Assistant, Administrative Division
(Vacant) . . . . (907) 271-3977
Office Automation Assistant, Criminal Division
Lashelli "Sha" Martin . . . . (907) 271-5071
E-mail: lashelli.martin@usdoj.gov
Legal Assistant - Administration
Ashley Nighswander . . . . (907) 271-5071
Legal Assistant Civil Division **(Vacant)** . . . . (907) 271-5071
Legal Assistant Criminal Division **Chloe Martin** . . . . (907) 271-4244
E-mail: chloe.martin@usdoj.gov
Legal Assistant Criminal Division
Mac Callie Petursson . . . . (907) 271-4802
Legal Assistant Criminal Division **(Vacant)** . . . . (907) 271-3296
Supervisory Paralegal Specialist, Criminal Division
Sean Robinson . . . . (907) 271-5071
E-mail: sean.robinson@usdoj.gov

Alaska District *continued*

Paralegal Specialist, Criminal Division
Monica Johnson . . . . (907) 271-5071
E-mail: monica.johnson2@usdoj.gov
Paralegal Specialist, Criminal Division **Jamie Keen** . . . . . . (907) 271-4262
E-mail: jamie.keen@usdoj.gov
Paralegal Specialist, Criminal Division **Jennifer Lotz** . . . . (907) 271-5071
E-mail: jennifer.lotz@usdoj.gov
Legal Assistant Financial Litigation Unit **(Vacant)** . . . . (907) 271-5071
Paralegal Finance Litigation Unit **David Urrea** . . . . (907) 271-5071
E-mail: david.urrea@usdoj.gov
Paralegal Financial Litigation Unit **Kathey Virgin** . . . . (907) 271-5071
E-mail: kathey.virgin@usdoj.gov
Paralegal Specialist Civil Division
Christine "Christy" Dollerhide . . . . (907) 271-5071
E-mail: christine.dollerhide@usdoj.gov
Paralegal Specialist Civil Division
Deborah "Debbie" Simpson . . . . (907) 271-5071
E-mail: deborah.simpson@usdoj.gov
Systems Manager **Renee Robinson** . . . . (907) 271-5071
E-mail: renee.robinson@usdoj.gov
Victim/Witness Specialist **(Vacant)** . . . . (907) 271-5071
Assistant Information Technology Specialist **(Vacant)** . . . . (907) 271-4054

Fairbanks (AK) Office

Federal Building and U.S. Courthouse, 101 12th Avenue,
Room 310, Box 2, Fairbanks, AK 99701
Tel: (907) 456-0245 Fax: (907) 456-0309

Assistant U.S. Attorney **Stephen "Steve" Cooper** . . . . . . (907) 456-0245
E-mail: stephen.cooper@usdoj.gov
Paralegal Specialist **Sandra Rodriguez** . . . . (907) 456-0245

Juneau (AK) Office

Federal Building & U.S. Courthouse, 709 West Ninth Street,
Room 937, P.O. Box 21627, Juneau, AK 99802
Tel: (907) 796-0400 Fax: (907) 796-0409

Assistant U.S. Attorney **Jack S. Schmidt** . . . . (907) 796-0400
E-mail: jack.schmidt@usdoj.gov
Paralegal **Ryhana Akhund** . . . . (907) 796-0400
E-mail: ryhana.akhund@usdoj.gov

Arizona District

Two Renaissance Square, 40 North Central Avenue,
Suite 1200, Phoenix, AZ 85004-4408
Tel: (602) 514-7500 Fax: (602) 514-7693
Internet: www.usdoj.gov/usao/az

★ U.S. Attorney **John S. Leonardo** . . . . (602) 514-7518
E-mail: john.leonardo@usdoj.gov
Education: Notre Dame 1969; George Washington 1972 JD
Secretary to the U.S. Attorney **Victoria Vasquez** . . . . . . (520) 620-7348
E-mail: victoria.vasquez@usdoj.gov
First Assistant U.S. Attorney
Elizabeth A. "Betsy" Strange . . . . (602) 514-7518
E-mail: elizabeth.strange@usdoj.gov
Executive Assistant U.S. Attorney **Dominic Lanza** . . . . (602) 514-7699
E-mail: dominic.lanza@usdoj.gov
Education: Harvard 2002 JD
Chief Assistant U.S. Attorney **(Vacant)** . . . . (602) 514-7500
Deputy Administrative Officer **Brandon Brokaw** . . . . (602) 514-7600
E-mail: brandon.brokaw@usdoj.gov
Community Outreach Director **Cosme Lopez** . . . . (602) 514-7456
E-mail: cosme.lopez@usdoj.gov
Law Enforcement Coordinator **(Vacant)** . . . . (602) 514-7573
Public Affairs Officer **Cosme Lopez** . . . . (602) 514-7500
E-mail: cosme.lopez@usdoj.gov
Systems Manager **James "Jim" Walsh** . . . . (602) 514-7642
E-mail: james.walsh@usdoj.gov
Victim Witness Coordinator **(Vacant)** . . . . (602) 514-7595

★ Presidential Appointment Requiring Senate Confirmation ☆ Presidential Appointment ☐ Schedule C Appointment ◇ Career Senior Foreign Service Appointment
● Career Senior Executive Service (SES) Appointment ○ Non-Career Senior Executive Service (SES) Appointment ■ Postal Career Executive Service

Appellate Division
Chief **Robert L. Miskell** .... (602) 514-7500
E-mail: robert.miskell@usdoj.gov
Deputy Chief **Krissa M. Lanham** .... (602) 514-7689
E-mail: krissa.lanham@usdoj.gov
Education: Yale JD
Assistant U.S. Attorney **Joan G. Ruffennach** .... (602) 514-7505
E-mail: joan.ruffennach@usdoj.gov

Civil Division
Chief **Diana Varela** .... (602) 514-7743
E-mail: diana.varela@usdoj.gov
Deputy Chief **Peter M. Lantka** .... (602) 514-7739
E-mail: peter.lantka@usdoj.gov
Education: Illinois 1999 BA; Valparaiso 2002 JD
Assistant U.S. Attorney **Paul A. Bullis** .... (602) 514-7659
E-mail: paul.bullis@usdoj.gov
Education: Arizona 1979 BA; Georgetown 1982 JD
Assistant U.S. Attorney **Ann E. Harwood** .... (602) 514-7740
E-mail: ann.harwood@usdoj.gov
Assistant U.S. Attorney **Emory T. Hurley** .... (602) 514-7749
E-mail: emory.hurley@usdoj.gov
Assistant U.S. Attorney **Michael A. "Mike" Johns** ...... (602) 514-7566
E-mail: michael.a.johns@usdoj.gov
Assistant U.S. Attorney **Peter Kozinets** .... (602) 514-7525
E-mail: peter.kozinets@usdoj.gov
Assistant U.S. Attorney **Lon Leavitt** .... (602) 514-7500
E-mail: lon.r.leavitt@usdoj.gov
Assistant U.S. Attorney **Todd F. Lang** .... (602) 514-7500
E-mail: todd.lang@usdoj.gov
Education: Cornell 1993 JD
Assistant U.S. Attorney **Anne E. Nelson** .... (602) 514-7500
E-mail: anne.nelson@usdoj.gov
Education: Arizona 2005 BA; James Rogers Law 2010 JD

Criminal Division
Chief **Gary Restaino** .... (602) 514-7520
E-mail: gary.restaino@usdoj.gov
Deputy Chief **Glenn McCormick** .... (602) 514-7669
E-mail: glenn.mccormick@usdoj.gov
Deputy Chief **Sharon K. Sexton** .... (602) 514-7584
E-mail: sharon.sexton@usdoj.gov
Deputy Chief **Keith Vercauteren** .... (602) 514-7621
E-mail: keith.vercauteren@usdoj.gov
Deputy Chief **(Vacant)** .... (602) 514-7517
Assistant U.S. Attorney **Alison Bachus** .... (602) 514-7599
E-mail: alison.bachus@usdoj.gov
Assistant U.S. Attorney **Kristen Brook** .... (602) 514-7503
Assistant U.S. Attorney **Roger W. Dokken** .... (602) 514-7523
E-mail: roger.dokken@usdoj.gov
Assistant U.S. Attorney **Frank Galati** .... (602) 514-7582
E-mail: frank.galati@usdoj.gov
Assistant U.S. Attorney **Jennifer Green** .... (602) 514-7641
E-mail: jennifer.green@usdoj.gov
Assistant U.S. Attorney **Dyanne Greer** .... (602) 514-7592
E-mail: dyanne.greer@usdoj.gov
Assistant U.S. Attorney **Maria Gutierrez** .... (602) 514-7520
E-mail: maria.gutierrez@usdoj.gov
Assistant U.S. Attorney **Charles F. "Chuck" Hyder** ...... (602) 514-7565
E-mail: chuck.hyder@usdoj.gov
Assistant U.S. Attorney **Melissa Karlen** .... (602) 514-7688
E-mail: melissa.karlen@usdoj.gov
Assistant U.S. Attorney **Christine D. Keller** .... (602) 514-7500
E-mail: christine.keller@usdoj.gov
Assistant U.S. Attorney **James "Jim" Knapp** .... (602) 514-7675
E-mail: james.knapp3@usdoj.gov
Education: Arizona State BA, JD
Assistant U.S. Attorney **Brian G. Larson** .... (602) 514-7532
E-mail: brian.larson@usdoj.gov
Assistant U.S. Attorney **Kathy Lemke** .... (602) 514-7544
E-mail: kathy.lemke@usdoj.gov
Assistant U.S. Attorney **Jennifer Levinson** .... (602) 514-7501
E-mail: jennifer.levinson@usdoj.gov

Criminal Division *continued*
Assistant U.S. Attorney **Jonell L. Lucca** .... (602) 514-7591
Education: Notre Dame 2001 JD
Assistant U.S. Attorney **Karen S. McDonald** .... (602) 514-7558
E-mail: karen.mcdonald@usdoj.gov
Assistant U.S. Attorney **Jane McLaughlin** .... (602) 514-7534
E-mail: jane.mclaughlin@usdoj.gov
Assistant U.S. Attorney **James "Jim" Morse, Jr.** .... (602) 514-7619
E-mail: james.morse@usdoj.gov
Assistant U.S. Attorney **Walter Perkel** .... (602) 514-7572
E-mail: walter.perkel@usdoj.gov
Assistant U.S. Attorney **Reid C. Pixler** .... (602) 514-7630
E-mail: reid.pixler@usdoj.gov
Assistant U.S. Attorney **Kevin Rapp** .... (602) 514-7609
E-mail: kevin.rapp@usdoj.gov
Assistant U.S. Attorney **Theresa Rassas** .... (602) 514-7541
E-mail: theresa.rassas@usdoj.gov
Assistant U.S. Attorney **Dimitra Sampson** .... (602) 514-7567
E-mail: dimitra.sampson@usdoj.gov
Assistant U.S. Attorney **Peter S. Sexton** .... (602) 514-7508
E-mail: peter.sexton@usdoj.gov
Assistant U.S. Attorney **Thomas C. Simon** .... (602) 514-7610
E-mail: thomas.simon@usdoj.gov
Assistant U.S. Attorney **Howard Sukenic** .... (602) 514-7522
E-mail: howard.sukenic@usdoj.gov
Assistant U.S. Attorney **Mark J. Wenker** .... (602) 514-7748
E-mail: mark.wenker@usdoj.gov
Assistant U.S. Attorney **Cassie Woo** .... (602) 514-7691
E-mail: cassie.woo@usdoj.gov
Assistant U.S. Attorney **Raymond Woo** .... (602) 514-7736
E-mail: raymond.woo@usdoj.gov

National Security Section
Chief **David Pimsner** .... (602) 514-7512
E-mail: david.pimsner@usdoj.gov
Legal Assistant **Charles "Chuck" Bailey** .... (602) 514-7577
E-mail: charles.bailey@usdoj.gov

Flagstaff (AZ) Office
123 North San Francisco Street, Suite 410, Flagstaff, AZ 86001
Tel: (928) 556-0833 Fax: (928) 556-0759

Supervisory Assistant U.S. Attorney
Patrick J. Schneider .... (928) 556-0833
E-mail: patrick.schneider@usdoj.gov
Assistant U.S. Attorney **Camille Bibles** .... (928) 556-0833
E-mail: camille.bibles@usdoj.gov
Assistant U.S. Attorney **Paul Stearns** .... (928) 556-0833
E-mail: paul.stearns@usdoj.gov
Assistant U.S. Attorney **Adam Zickerman** .... (928) 556-0833
E-mail: adam.zickerman@usdoj.gov

Tucson (AZ) Office
405 West Congress Street, Suite 4800, Tucson, AZ 85701-5040
Tel: (520) 620-7300 Fax: (520) 620-7320

Chief Assistant U.S. Attorney (Acting)
Elizabeth A. "Betsy" Strange .... (520) 620-7300
E-mail: elizabeth.strange@usdoj.gov

Civil Division
Chief **Janet K. Martin** .... (520) 620-7493
E-mail: janet.martin@usdoj.gov
Assistant U.S. Attorney **Charles A. Davis** .... (520) 620-7408
E-mail: charles.davis@usdoj.gov
Assistant U.S. Attorney **Denise Faulk** .... (520) 620-7442
E-mail: denise.faulk@usdoj.gov
Assistant U.S. Attorney **Jane Westby** .... (520) 620-7333
E-mail: jane.westby@usdoj.gov
Assistant U.S. Attorney **Angela W. Woolridge** .... (520) 620-7339
E-mail: angela.woolridge@usdoj.gov

★ Presidential Appointment Requiring Senate Confirmation ☆ Presidential Appointment □ Schedule C Appointment ◇ Career Senior Foreign Service Appointment
● Career Senior Executive Service (SES) Appointment ○ Non-Career Senior Executive Service (SES) Appointment ■ Postal Career Executive Service

Appellate Division

Chief **Robert L. Miskell** . . . . . (520) 620-7300
E-mail: robert.miskell@usdoj.gov
Assistant U.S. Attorney **Christina M. Cabanillas** . . . . . (520) 620-7377
E-mail: christina.cabanillas@usdoj.gov
Assistant U.S. Attorney **Bruce Michael Ferg** . . . . . (520) 620-7313
E-mail: bruce.ferg@usdoj.gov
Assistant U.S. Attorney **Erica A. McCallum** . . . . . (520) 620-7371

Criminal Division

Chief **Nicole P. Savel** . . . . . (520) 620-7391
E-mail: nicole.savel@usdoj.gov
Deputy Chief **David P. Flannigan** . . . . . (520) 620-7364
E-mail: david.flannigan@usdoj.gov
Deputy Chief **Liza M. Granoff** . . . . . (520) 620-7474
E-mail: liza.granoff@usdoj.gov
Deputy Chief **Craig Russell** . . . . . (520) 620-7351
E-mail: craig.russell2@usdoj.gov
Senior Litigation Counsel, Asset Forfeiture **Reese V. Bostwick** . . . . . (520) 620-7383
E-mail: reese.bostwick@usdoj.gov
Senior Litigation Counsel, OCDETF **Robert Fellrath** . . . . . (520) 620-7473
E-mail: robert.fellrath@usdoj.gov
Assistant U.S. Attorney **Joshua Ackerman** . . . . . (520) 620-7355
E-mail: josh.ackerman@usdoj.gov
Assistant U.S. Attorney **Beverly K. Anderson** . . . . . (520) 620-7330
E-mail: bev.anderson@usdoj.gov
Assistant U.S. Attorney **Raquel N. Arellano** . . . . . (520) 620-7382
Assistant U.S. Attorney **Patrick T. Barry** . . . . . (520) 620-7352
Assistant U.S. Attorney **Christopher Brown** . . . . . (520) 620-7380
E-mail: christopher.brown@usdoj.gov
Assistant U.S. Attorney **Monte C. Clausen** . . . . . (520) 620-7412
E-mail: monte.clausen@usdoj.gov
Assistant U.S. Attorney **Carmen F. Corbin** . . . . . (520) 620-7263
E-mail: carmen.corbin@usdoj.gov
Assistant U.S. Attorney **Ann Demarais** . . . . . (520) 620-7159
E-mail: ann.demarais@usdoj.gov
Assistant U.S. Attorney **Carin C. Duryee** . . . . . (520) 620-7427
E-mail: carin.duryee@usdoj.gov
Assistant U.S. Attorney **Jesse J. Figueroa** . . . . . (520) 620-7372
E-mail: jesse.figueroa@usdoj.gov
Assistant U.S. Attorney **Wallace H. "Wally" Kleindienst** . . . . . (520) 620-7578
Assistant U.S. Attorney **Lawrence Lee** . . . . . (520) 620-7308
Assistant U.S. Attorney **Anthony E. Maingot** . . . . . (520) 620-7472
Assistant U.S. Attorney **Cory M. Picton** . . . . . (520) 620-7426
Assistant U.S. Attorney **Karen E. Rolley** . . . . . (520) 620-7357
Assistant U.S. Attorney **Heather Scachrist** . . . . . (520) 620-7370
E-mail: heather.scachrist@usdoj.gov
Assistant U.S. Attorney **Serra M. Tsethlikai** . . . . . (520) 620-7358
Assistant U.S. Attorney **Rui Wang** . . . . . (520) 620-7422
Assistant U.S. Attorney **Jane Westby** . . . . . (520) 620-7333
E-mail: jane.westby@usdoj.gov
Assistant U.S. Attorney **David R. Zipps** . . . . . (520) 620-7471
Assistant U.S. Attorney **(Vacant)** . . . . . (520) 620-7437
Assistant U.S. Attorney **(Vacant)** . . . . . (520) 620-7355
Victim Witness Specialist **Mary-Anne Estrada** . . . . . (520) 620-7431
E-mail: mary-anne.estrada@usdoj.gov
Victim Witness Specialist **Jovana Uzarraga** . . . . . (520) 620-7367
E-mail: jovava.uzarraga@usdoj.gov

Yuma (AZ) Office

4035 South Avenue A, Yuma, AZ 85365
Tel: (928) 314-6410 Tel: (928) 314-6411

Supervisory Assistant U.S. Attorney **Fred Cocio** . . . . . (928) 314-6410
E-mail: fred.cocio@usdoj.gov
Assistant U.S. Attorney **John Ballos** . . . . . (928) 314-6402
E-mail: john.ballos@usdoj.gov
Assistant U.S. Attorney **Louis Uhl** . . . . . (928) 314-6410
E-mail: louis.uhl@usdoj.gov

Arkansas - Eastern District

Metropolitan National Bank Building, 425 West Capitol Avenue, Suite 500, Little Rock, AR 72201
P.O. Box 1229, Little Rock, AR 72203-1229
Tel: (501) 340-2600 Fax: (501) 340-2728
Internet: www.justice.gov/usao/are

★ U.S. Attorney **Christopher R. "Chris" Thyer** . . . . . (501) 340-2600
E-mail: chris.thyer@usdoj.gov
Education: Arkansas State 1991 BA; Arkansas 1995 JD
Secretary to the U.S. Attorney **Cindy Treazqs** . . . . . (501) 340-2600
Fax: (501) 340-2727
First Assistant U.S. Attorney **Patrick C. Harris** . . . . . (501) 340-2600
E-mail: patrick.harris@usdoj.gov
Intelligence Research Specialist **Scott Hendriks** . . . . . (501) 340-2673
E-mail: scott.hendriks@usdoj.gov
Law Enforcement Committee Coordinator **Paulette Chappelle** . . . . . (501) 340-2648
Systems Manager **Andrew Oyemola** . . . . . (501) 340-2644
E-mail: andrew.oyemola@usdoj.gov
Victim-Witness Coordinator **Amanda Warford** . . . . . (501) 340-2647
E-mail: amanda.warford@usdoj.gov

Civil Division

Tel: (501) 340-2600 Fax: (501) 340-2730

Chief **Richard M. Pence** . . . . . (501) 340-2600
E-mail: richard.pence@usdoj.gov
Assistant U.S. Attorney **Jamie Dempsey** . . . . . (501) 340-2600
E-mail: jamie.dempsey@usdoj.gov
Assistant U.S. Attorney **Lindsey Lorence** . . . . . (501) 340-2600
E-mail: lindsey.lorence@usdoj.gov
Assistant U.S. Attorney **Stacey McCord** . . . . . (501) 340-2600
E-mail: stacey.mccord@usdoj.gov
Assistant U.S. Attorney **Shannon Smith** . . . . . (501) 340-2600
E-mail: shannon.smith@usdoj.gov

Criminal Division

Fax: (501) 340-2725

Chief **John Ray White** . . . . . (501) 340-2600
E-mail: john.white@usdoj.gov
Deputy Chief **Anne Gardner** . . . . . (501) 340-2600
E-mail: anne.gardner2@usdoj.gov
Chief, Organized Crime **Anne Gardner** . . . . . (501) 340-2600
E-mail: anne.gardner2@usdoj.gov
Assistant U.S. Attorney **Ali Ahmad** . . . . . (501) 340-2600
E-mail: ali.ahmad@usdoj.gov
Education: Michigan 2004 JD
Assistant U.S. Attorney **Allison Bragg** . . . . . (501) 340-2600
E-mail: allison.bragg@usdoj.gov
Assistant U.S. Attorney **Hunter Bridges** . . . . . (501) 340-2600
E-mail: hunter.bridges@usdoj.gov
Assistant U.S. Attorney **Kristin Bryant** . . . . . (501) 340-2600
E-mail: kristin.bryant@usdoj.gov
Assistant U.S. Attorney **Chris Givens** . . . . . (501) 340-2600
E-mail: chris.givens@usdoj.gov
Assistant U.S. Attorney **Michael Gordon** . . . . . (501) 340-2600
E-mail: michael.gordon@usdoj.gov
Assistant U.S. Attorney **Jana Harris** . . . . . (501) 340-2600
E-mail: jana.harris@usdoj.gov
Assistant U.S. Attorney **Angela Jegley** . . . . . (501) 340-2600
E-mail: angela.jegley@usdoj.gov
Assistant U.S. Attorney **Linda Lipe** . . . . . (501) 340-2600
E-mail: linda.lipe@usdoj.gov
Assistant U.S. Attorney **Stephanie Mazzanti** . . . . . (501) 340-2600
E-mail: stephanie.mazzanti@usdoj.gov
Education: Arkansas 2006 JD
Assistant U.S. Attorney **Cameron McCree** . . . . . (501) 340-2600
E-mail: cameron.mccree@usdoj.gov
Education: Arkansas JD
Assistant U.S. Attorney **Benecia Moore** . . . . . (501) 340-2600
E-mail: benecia.moore@usdoj.gov

Criminal Division *continued*

Assistant U.S. Attorney **Alex Morgan** . . . . (501) 340-2600
E-mail: alex.morgan@usdoj.gov
Assistant U.S. Attorney **Erin O'Leary-Chalk** . . . . (501) 340-2600
E-mail: erin.o'leary@usdoj.gov
Assistant U.S. Attorney **Julie Peters** . . . . (501) 340-2600
E-mail: julie.peters@usdoj.gov
Assistant U.S. Attorney **Edward O. Walker** . . . . (501) 340-2600
E-mail: edward.o.walker@usdoj.gov
Assistant U.S. Attorney **(Vacant)** . . . . (501) 340-2600

Arkansas - Western District

414 Parker Street, Fort Smith, AR 72901
Tel: (479) 783-5125 Fax: (479) 783-0578 Fax: (479) 785-2442

★ U.S. Attorney (Acting) **Kenneth P. "Kenny" Elser** . . . . . . (479) 783-5125
Secretary to the U.S. Attorney **Joyce Snow** . . . . (479) 783-5125
First Assistant U.S. Attorney
Kenneth P. "Kenny" Elser . . . . (479) 783-5125
E-mail: kenny.elser@usdoj.gov
Administrative Officer **Cathe Bowman** . . . . (479) 783-5125
E-mail: cathe.bowman@usdoj.gov
Intelligence Specialist **Daren Fowler** . . . . (479) 783-5125
E-mail: daren.fowler@usdoj.gov
LECC Coordinator **(Vacant)** . . . . (479) 783-5125
Systems Manager **Justin Trice** . . . . (479) 783-5125
E-mail: justin.trice@usdoj.gov
Victim-Witness Coordinator **Laura Johnson** . . . . (479) 783-5125
E-mail: laura.johnson@usdoj.gov

Civil Division

Chief **Deborah J. "Debbie" Groom** . . . . (479) 783-5125
E-mail: debbie.groom@usdoj.gov

Criminal Division

Chief **Kenneth P. "Kenny" Elser** . . . . (479) 783-5125
E-mail: kenny.elser@usdoj.gov
Deputy Chief **Clay Fowlkes** . . . . (479) 783-5125
E-mail: clay.fowlkes@usdoj.gov
Asset Forfeiture Chief **Aaron Jennen** . . . . (479) 783-5125
E-mail: aaron.jennen@usdoj.gov
Organized Crime Drug Enforcement Task Force Chief
Clay Fowlkes . . . . (479) 783-5125
E-mail: clay.fowlkes@usdoj.gov

California - Central District

312 North Spring Street, Suite 1200, Los Angeles, CA 90012
Tel: (213) 894-2400 (Main Line)
Tel: (213) 894-2434 Fax: (213) 894-0141
Internet: www.justice.gov/usao/cac

★ U.S. Attorney **Eileen M. Decker** . . . . (213) 894-2434
E-mail: eileen.decker@usdoj.gov
Secretary to the U.S. Attorney **Melena Malunao** . . . . . . (213) 894-2434
E-mail: melena.malunao@usdoj.gov
First Assistant U.S. Attorney **Patrick Fitzgerald** . . . . (213) 894-2434
U.S. Courthouse, 312 North Spring Street, Los Angeles, CA 90012
E-mail: patrick.fitzgerald@usdoj.gov
Executive Assistant U.S. Attorney **Wesley L. Hsu** . . . . (213) 894-2434
E-mail: wesley.hsu@usdoj.gov
Education: Yale 1993 BA, 1996 JD
Counsel to the United States Attorney
Bruce K. Riordan . . . . (213) 894-2434
E-mail: bruce.riordan@usdoj.gov
Chief Assistant for Trials, Integrity, and
Professionalism **Robert E. Dugdale** . . . . (213) 894-2400
E-mail: robert.dugdale@usdoj.gov
Director of Administration **Kenneth A. "Ken" Martin** . . . (213) 894-8792
E-mail: ken.martin@usdoj.gov
Assistant Director, Litigation Support
Richard Bernales . . . . (213) 894-2434
E-mail: richard.bernales@usdoj.gov

California - Central District *continued*

Administrative Services Chief **John Frazier** . . . . (213) 894-0608
E-mail: john.frazier@usdoj.gov
Criminal Dockets Chief **Leodegardio Martinez** . . . . (213) 894-2434
Financial Services Chief **Nathan Nguyen** . . . . (213) 894-2434
Human Resources Chief **Ann Quinn** . . . . (213) 894-2434
E-mail: ann.quinn@usdoj.gov
Information Technology Chief **Martin Jones** . . . . (213) 894-2434
Crisis Management Coordinator **(Vacant)** . . . . (213) 894-2434
Law Enforcement Committee Coordinator
Ted Marquez . . . . (213) 894-2434
Librarian **Cornell H. Winston** . . . . (213) 894-2419
U.S. Courthouse, 312 North Spring Street,
Room 1214, Los Angeles, CA 90012
E-mail: cornell.h.winston@usdoj.gov
Public Information Officer **Thom Mrozek** . . . . (213) 894-6947
E-mail: thom.mrozek@usdoj.gov
Intelligence Specialist **Andrea Caston** . . . . (213) 894-2434
E-mail: andrea.caston@usdoj.gov
Victim-Witness Coordinator **Jeff Alabaso** . . . . (213) 894-7627
U.S. Courthouse, 312 North Spring Street,
Room 1311, Los Angeles, CA 90012
E-mail: jeff.alabaso@usdoj.gov

Civil Division

Federal Building, 300 North Los Angeles Street,
Suite 7516, Los Angeles, CA 90012
Tel: (213) 894-2404

Chief **Leon Warren Weidman** . . . . (213) 894-2404
E-mail: lee.weidman@usdoj.gov
Civil Appeals Section Chief **Dorothy A. Schouten** . . . . . . (213) 894-2404
E-mail: dorothy.schouten@usdoj.gov
Civil Fraud Section Chief **David K. Barrett** . . . . (213) 894-0522
E-mail: david.barrett@usdoj.gov
Financial Litigation Section Chief **Zoran J. Segina** . . . . . . (213) 894-2404
E-mail: zoran.segina@usdoj.gov

Criminal Division

312 North Spring Street, Los Angeles, CA 90012
Fax: (213) 894-0141

Chief **Lawrence S. Middleton** . . . . (213) 894-4685
E-mail: lawrence.middleton@usdoj.gov
Deputy Chief **Scott Matthew Garringer** . . . . (213) 894-6772
E-mail: scott.garringer@usdoj.gov
Education: Iowa; UCLA JD
Appeals Section Chief **Jean-Claude Andre** . . . . (213) 894-3391
E-mail: jean-claude.andre@usdoj.gov
Education: Virginia JD
Asset Forfeiture Section Chief **Steven R. Welk** . . . . (213) 894-6166
E-mail: steven.welk@usdoj.gov
Cyber and Intellectual Property Crime Section Chief
(Vacant) . . . . (213) 894-3045
Environmental Crimes Section Chief **Joseph O. Johns** . . . (213) 894-4536
E-mail: joseph.johns@usdoj.gov
General Crimes Chief **Ruth C. Pinkel** . . . . (213) 894-3424
E-mail: ruth.pinkel@usdoj.gov
Major Frauds Section Chief **George S. Cardona** . . . . (213) 894-3868
E-mail: george.s.cardona@usdoj.gov
National Security Section Chief **Patricia A. Donahue** . . . . (213) 894-0721
E-mail: patricia.donahue@usdoj.gov
Organized Crime and Drug Enforcement Task Force
Section Chief **Kevin M. Lally** . . . . (213) 894-2170
E-mail: kevin.lally@usdoj.gov
Public Corruption and Civil Rights Chief
Brandon D. Fox . . . . (213) 894-2434
E-mail: brandon.fox@usdoj.gov
Violent and Organized Crime Section Chief
Elizabeth R. Yang Room 1547 . . . . (213) 894-1785
E-mail: elizabeth.yang@usdoj.gov

(continued on next page)

★ Presidential Appointment Requiring Senate Confirmation ☆ Presidential Appointment ☐ Schedule C Appointment ◇ Career Senior Foreign Service Appointment
● Career Senior Executive Service (SES) Appointment ○ Non-Career Senior Executive Service (SES) Appointment ■ Postal Career Executive Service

Criminal Division *continued*

Assistant U.S. Attorney **Joshua Klein** . . . . (213) 894-3899
E-mail: joshua.klein@usdoj.gov
Education: Stanford 2002 JD

Tax Division
Federal Building, 300 North Los Angeles Street,
Suite 7211, Los Angeles, CA 90012

Chief **Sandra R. Brown** . . . . (213) 894-5810
E-mail: sandra.brown@usdoj.gov

Riverside (CA) Office
3880 Lemon Street, Suite 210, Riverside, CA 92501
Tel: (951) 276-6210 Fax: (951) 276-6202

Chief **Joseph Widman** . . . . (951) 276-6945
E-mail: joseph.widman@usdoj.gov

Santa Ana (CA) Office
411 West Fourth Street, Suite 8000, Santa Ana, CA 92701-4599
Tel: (714) 338-3540 Fax: (714) 338-3708

Assistant U.S. Attorney-in-Charge **Dennise D. Willett** . . . . (714) 338-3500
E-mail: dennise.willett@usdoj.gov

California - Eastern District
501 I Street, Suite 10-100, Sacramento, CA 95814
Tel: (916) 554-2700 TTY: (916) 554-2124 Fax: (916) 554-2900
Internet: www.usdoj.gov/usao/cae

★ U.S. Attorney
Benjamin Alden Belknap "Ben" Wagner . . . . (916) 554-2730
E-mail: ben.wagner@usdoj.gov
Education: Dartmouth 1982 AB; NYU 1986 JD
Secretary to the U.S. Attorney **Mary E. Wenger** . . . . . . (916) 554-2730
E-mail: mary.wenger@usdoj.gov
Senior Counsel to the U.S. Attorney **Duce Rice** . . . . (559) 497-4000
E-mail: duce.rice@usdoj.gov
First Assistant U.S. Attorney **Phillip Talbert** . . . . (916) 554-2798
E-mail: phillip.talbert@usdoj.gov
Press Officer **Lauren Horwood** . . . . (916) 554-2706
Executive Assistant U.S. Attorney **Philip A. Ferrari** . . . . . . (916) 554-2740
E-mail: philip.ferrari@usdoj.gov
Administrative Officer **Jacquelyn C. "Jackie" Strong** . . . (916) 554-2714
E-mail: jackie.strong@usdoj.gov
Anti-Terrorism Advisory Council Coordinator
Jean Hobler . . . . (916) 554-2700
E-mail: jean.hobler@usdoj.gov
District Office Security Manager **James Ham** . . . . (916) 554-2700
E-mail: james.ham@usdoj.gov
Information Technology Specialist **Tammy Metz** . . . . (916) 554-2742
E-mail: tammy.metz@usdoj.gov
Information Technology Specialist **Sharon Sumrak** . . . . . . (916) 554-2753
E-mail: sharon.sumrak@usdoj.gov
Law Enforcement Committee Coordinator **(Vacant)** . . . . . . (916) 554-2712
Records Coordinator **Tracy Remitz** . . . . (916) 554-2700
E-mail: tracy.remitz@usdoj.gov
Supervisor, Computer Technology **Gina Alires** . . . . (916) 554-2746
E-mail: gina.alires@usdoj.gov
Victim-Witness Coordinator **Helene J. Tenette** . . . . (916) 554-2776
E-mail: helene.tenette@usdoj.gov
Special Prosecutions Unit Chief **Matthew D. Segal** . . . . . (916) 554-2700
E-mail: matthew.segal@usdoj.gov
Education: Yale 2002 JD

Civil Division
Civil Chief **David T. Shelledy** . . . . (916) 554-2700
E-mail: david.shelledy@usdoj.gov
Education: Yale 1990 LLM
Affirmative Civil Litigation Chief **Kelli L. Taylor** . . . . (916) 554-2700
E-mail: kelli.l.taylor@usdoj.gov

Civil Division *continued*

Civil Defense Chief **J. Earlene Gordon** . . . . (916) 554-2700
E-mail: earlene.gordon@usdoj.gov
Assistant U.S. Attorney **Edward Baker** . . . . (916) 554-2700
E-mail: ed.baker@usdoj.gov
Assistant U.S. Attorney **Anderson Berry** . . . . (916) 554-2700
E-mail: anderson.berry@usdoj.gov
Assistant U.S. Attorney **Victoria L. Boesch** . . . . (916) 554-2700
E-mail: victoria.boesch@usdoj.gov
Assistant U.S. Attorney **Gregory Broderick** . . . . (916) 554-2700
E-mail: gregory.broderick@usdoj.gov
Assistant U.S. Attorney **Kurt Didier** . . . . (916) 554-2700
E-mail: kurt.didier@usdoj.gov
Assistant U.S. Attorney **Lynn Trinka Ernce** . . . . (916) 554-2700
Assistant U.S. Attorney **Audrey B. Hemesath** . . . . (916) 554-2700
E-mail: audrey.hemesath@usdoj.gov
Assistant U.S. Attorney **Colleen M. Kennedy** . . . . (916) 554-2700
E-mail: colleen.m.kennedy@usdoj.gov
Education: Duke AB; Yale JD
Assistant U.S. Attorney **Kevin Khasigian** . . . . (916) 554-2700
E-mail: kevin.khasigian@usdoj.gov
Education: McGeorge 2007 JD
Assistant U.S. Attorney **Chi Soo Kim** . . . . (916) 554-2700
E-mail: chi.soo.kim@usdoj.gov
Education: Vanderbilt 2004 JD
Assistant U.S. Attorney **Marilee Miller** . . . . (916) 554-2700
E-mail: marilee.miller@usdoj.gov
Education: Northwestern 2001 BS, 2002 MS; Utah 2006 JD
Assistant U.S. Attorney **Bobbie J. Montoya** . . . . (916) 554-2700
E-mail: bobbie.montoya@usdoj.gov
Assistant U.S. Attorney **Edward Olsen** . . . . (916) 554-2700
E-mail: edward.olsen@usdoj.gov
Assistant U.S. Attorney **Catherine J. Swann** . . . . (916) 554-2700
E-mail: catherine.swann@usdoj.gov

Criminal Division
Chief - Criminal Division **John K. Vincent** . . . . (916) 554-2795
E-mail: john.vincent@usdoj.gov
Education: Notre Dame BA, JD
Appeals and Training Chief **Camil A. Skipper** . . . . (916) 554-2700
E-mail: camil.skipper@usdoj.gov
Crisis Management Coordinator **Michael Beckwith** . . . . . . (916) 554-2700
E-mail: michael.beckwith@usdoj.gov
Computer Crimes Chief **(Vacant)** . . . . (916) 554-2700
Narcotics and Violent Crimes Chief
Richard J. Bender . . . . (916) 554-2700
E-mail: richard.bender@usdoj.gov
Special Prosecutions Unit Chief **Matthew D. Segal** . . . . . (916) 554-2700
E-mail: matthew.segal@usdoj.gov
Education: Yale 2002 JD
White Collar Crime Chief **Michael Anderson** . . . . (916) 554-2700
E-mail: michael.anderson@usdoj.gov
Assistant U.S. Attorney **Amanda Beck** . . . . (916) 554-2700
E-mail: amanda.beck@usdoj.gov
Assistant U.S. Attorney **Michele Beckwith** . . . . (916) 554-2700
E-mail: michelel.beckwith@usdoj.gov
Assistant U.S. Attorney **Lee Bickley** . . . . (916) 554-2700
E-mail: lee.bickley@usdoj.gov
Assistant U.S. Attorney **Russell Carlberg** . . . . (916) 554-2700
Assistant U.S. Attorney **Heiko P. Coppola** . . . . (916) 554-2700
E-mail: heiko.coppola@usdoj.gov
Assistant U.S. Attorney **Nirav K. Desai** . . . . (916) 554-2700
E-mail: nirav.desai@usdoj.gov
Assistant U.S. Attorney **Jared Dolan** . . . . (916) 554-2700
E-mail: jared.dolan@usdoj.gov
Education: Stetson 2007 JD
Assistant U.S. Attorney **Andre Espinosa** . . . . (916) 554-2700
E-mail: andre.espinosa@usdoj.gov
Assistant U.S. Attorney **Brian Fogerty** . . . . (916) 554-2700
E-mail: brian.fogerty@usdoj.gov
Assistant U.S. Attorney **Mary L. Grad** . . . . (916) 554-2700
E-mail: mary.grad@usdoj.gov

Criminal Division *continued*

Assistant U.S. Attorney **Christopher Hales** . . . . (916) 554-2700
E-mail: christopher.hales@usdoj.gov
Assistant U.S. Attorney **Sherry Hartel Haus** . . . . (916) 554-2706
E-mail: sherry.haus@usdoj.gov
Assistant U.S. Attorney **Paul Hemesath** . . . . (916) 554-2700
E-mail: paul.hemesath@usdoj.gov
Assistant U.S. Attorney **Christiaan H. Highsmith** . . . . . . (916) 554-2706
E-mail: christiaan.highsmith@usdoj.gov
Assistant U.S. Attorney **Jason Hitt** . . . . (916) 554-2700
E-mail: jason.hitt@usdoj.gov
Assistant U.S. Attorney **Jean Hobler** . . . . (916) 554-2700
E-mail: jean.hobler@usdoj.gov
Assistant U.S. Attorney **Justin Lee** . . . . (916) 554-2700
E-mail: justin.lee@usdoj.gov
Assistant U.S. Attorney **Katherine Lydon** . . . . (916) 554-2700
E-mail: katherine.lydon@usdoj.gov
Assistant U.S. Attorney **Matthew T. Morris** . . . . (916) 554-2700
E-mail: matthew.morris@usdoj.gov
Assistant U.S. Attorney **Todd A. Pickles** . . . . (916) 554-2700
E-mail: todd.pickles@usdoj.gov
Education: Georgetown 1997 BA; San Francisco Law 2001 JD
Assistant U.S. Attorney **Michelle Rodriguez** . . . . (916) 554-2700
E-mail: michelle.rodriguez@usdoj.gov
Assistant U.S. Attorney **Rosanne Rust** . . . . (916) 554-2700
E-mail: rosanne.rust@usdoj.gov
Assistant U.S. Attorney **Matthew D. Segal** . . . . (916) 554-2700
E-mail: matthew.segal@usdoj.gov
Education: Yale 2002 JD
Assistant U.S. Attorney **Robin R. Taylor** . . . . (916) 554-2700
E-mail: robin.taylor@usdoj.gov
Assistant U.S. Attorney **Jill Thomas** . . . . (916) 554-2700
E-mail: jill.thomas@usdoj.gov
Assistant U.S. Attorney **Shelley Weger** . . . . (916) 554-2700
E-mail: shelley.weger@usdoj.gov
Assistant U.S. Attorney **Samuel Wong** . . . . (916) 554-2700
E-mail: samuel.wong@usdoj.gov
Assistant U.S. Attorney **William S. Wong** . . . . (916) 554-2700
E-mail: william.wong@usdoj.gov
Assistant U.S. Attorney **Roger Yang** . . . . (916) 554-2706
E-mail: roger.yang@usdoj.gov
Assistant U.S. Attorney **Matthew Yelovich** . . . . (916) 554-2706
E-mail: matthew.yelovich@usdoj.gov
Special Assistant U.S. Attorney **Josh F. Sigal** . . . . (916) 554-2700
E-mail: josh.sigal@usdoj.gov

Fresno (CA) Office

2500 Tulare Street, Suite 4401, Fresno, CA 93721
Tel: (559) 497-4000 TTY: (559) 498-7499 Fax: (559) 497-4099

Chief **Mark E. Cullers** . . . . (559) 497-4000
E-mail: mark.cullers@usdoj.gov
Chief, Narcotics and Violent Crimes **Kevin P. Rooney** . . . . (559) 497-4000
Chief, White Collar Crime Section **Kirk E. Sherriff** . . . . . . (559) 497-4000
E-mail: kirk.e.sherriff@usdoj.gov
Information Technology Specialist **Donna Dotson** . . . . (559) 497-4000
E-mail: donna.dotson@usdoj.gov

Civil Division

Assistant U.S. Attorney **Alyson Berg** . . . . (559) 497-4000
E-mail: alyson.berg@usdoj.gov
Assistant U.S. Attorney **Benjamin Hall** . . . . (559) 497-4000
E-mail: benjamin.hall@usdoj.gov
Assistant U.S. Attorney **Jeffrey L. Lodge** . . . . (559) 497-4000
E-mail: jeffrey.lodge@usdoj.gov
Assistant U.S. Attorney **Jeffery A. Spivak** . . . . (559) 497-4000
E-mail: jeffrey.spivak@usdoj.gov
Assistant U.S. Attorney **Patrick Suter** . . . . (559) 497-4000
E-mail: patrick.suter@usdoj.gov
Assistant U.S. Attorney **Vincent Tennerelli** . . . . (559) 497-4000
E-mail: vincent.tennerelli@usdoj.gov
Assistant U.S. Attorney **(Vacant)** . . . . (559) 497-4000

Criminal Division

Assistant U.S. Attorney **Melanie Alsworth** . . . . (559) 497-4000
E-mail: melanie.alsworth@usdoj.gov
Assistant U.S. Attorney **Christopher D. Baker** . . . . (559) 497-4000
E-mail: christopher.baker@usdoj.gov
Assistant U.S. Attorney **Henry Carbajal** . . . . (559) 497-4000
E-mail: henry.carbajal@usdoj.gov
Assistant U.S. Attorney **Brian K. Delaney** . . . . (661) 852-2470
E-mail: brian.delaney@usdoj.gov
Education: Illinois (Chicago) BSCrimJ; DePaul JD
Assistant U.S. Attorney **Patrick Delahunty** . . . . (559) 497-4000
E-mail: patrick.delahunty@usdoj.gov
Assistant U.S. Attorney **Brian W. Enos** . . . . (559) 497-4000
E-mail: brian.enos@usdoj.gov
Assistant U.S. Attorney **Karen A. Escobar** . . . . (559) 497-4000
E-mail: karen.escobar@usdoj.gov
Assistant U.S. Attorney **Michael S. Frye** . . . . (559) 497-4000
E-mail: michael.frye@usdoj.gov
Assistant U.S. Attorney **David L. Gappa** . . . . (559) 497-4000
E-mail: david.gappa@usdoj.gov
Assistant U.S. Attorney **Mia Giacomazzi** . . . . (559) 497-4000
E-mail: mia.giacomazzi@usdoj.gov
Education: San Diego 1998 BA; Santa Clara U 2005 JD
Assistant U.S. Attorney **Daniel Griffin** . . . . (559) 497-4000
E-mail: daniel.griffin@usdoj.gov
Assistant U.S. Attorney **Mark J. McKeon** . . . . (559) 497-4000
E-mail: mark.mckeon@usdoj.gov
Assistant U.S. Attorney **Laurel J. Montoya** . . . . (559) 497-4000
E-mail: laurel.j.montoya@usdoj.gov
Assistant U.S. Attorney **Grant B. Rabenn** . . . . (559) 497-4000
E-mail: grant.rabenn@usdoj.gov
Assistant U.S. Attorney **Vincenza Rabenn** . . . . (559) 497-4000
E-mail: vincenza.rabenn@usdoj.gov
Assistant U.S. Attorney **Dawrence W. Rice** . . . . (559) 497-4000
Assistant U.S. Attorney **Megan A.S. Richards** . . . . (559) 497-4000
E-mail: megan.richards@usdoj.gov
Assistant U.S. Attorney **Kimberly Sanchez** . . . . (559) 497-4000
E-mail: kimberly.sanchez@usdoj.gov
Assistant U.S. Attorney **Angela Scott** . . . . (559) 497-4000
E-mail: angela.scott3@usdoj.gov
Assistant U.S. Attorney **Kathleen A. Servatius** . . . . (559) 497-4000
E-mail: kathleen.servatius@usdoj.gov
Assistant U.S. Attorney **Michael G. Tierney** . . . . (559) 497-4000
E-mail: michael.tierney@usdoj.gov

California - Northern District

U.S. Courthouse, 450 Golden Gate Avenue,
11th Floor, San Francisco, CA 94102
Tel: (415) 436-7200 TTY: (415) 436-7221 Fax: (415) 436-7234
Internet: www.usdoj.gov/usao/can

★ U.S. Attorney (Acting) **Brian Stretch** . . . . (415) 436-6938
E-mail: brian.stretch@usdoj.gov
Secretary to the U.S. Attorney **Orisme Carminati** . . . . . . (415) 436-7143
E-mail: orisme.carminati@usdoj.gov
First Assistant U.S. Attorney **Brian Stretch** . . . . (415) 436-6783
E-mail: brian.stretch@usdoj.gov
Executive Assistant U.S. Attorney **Joshua Eaton** . . . . (415) 436-6958
Counsel to the U.S. Attorney **J. Douglas Wilson** . . . . (415) 436-7200
E-mail: douglas.wilson@usdoj.gov
Administrative Officer **Mary Cooper** . . . . (415) 436-6992
E-mail: mary.cooper@usdoj.gov
Administrative Services Supervisor **Peggy Hurdle** . . . . (415) 436-7252
E-mail: peggy.hurdle@usdoj.gov
Administrative Service Specialist **Natalya Labauve** . . . . . . (510) 637-3721
E-mail: natalya.labauve@usdoj.gov
Budget Officer **Denise Zvanovec** . . . . (415) 436-7313
Fax: (415) 436-7333
Information Technology Manager **Brian Wickett** . . . . (415) 436-7183
E-mail: brian.wickett@usdoj.gov
Public Affairs Officer **Abraham Simmons** . . . . (415) 436-6599
Law Enforcement Coordinator **Annemarie Conroy** . . . . . . (415) 436-7067
E-mail: annemarie.conroy@usdoj.gov

(continued on next page)

★ Presidential Appointment Requiring Senate Confirmation ☆ Presidential Appointment □ Schedule C Appointment ◇ Career Senior Foreign Service Appointment
● Career Senior Executive Service (SES) Appointment ○ Non-Career Senior Executive Service (SES) Appointment ■ Postal Career Executive Service

California - Northern District *continued*

Victim-Witness Program Manager **Maureen French** ..... (415) 436-6993
E-mail: maureen.french@usdoj.gov
Intelligence Research Specialist **Michael Gylock** .... (415) 436-7200
E-mail: michael.gylock@usdoj.gov
Librarian **Janice Litten** .... (415) 436-7037
E-mail: janice.litten@usdoj.gov

Civil Division
Tel: (415) 436-7137 Fax: (415) 436-6748

Chief **Alex Tse** .... (415) 436-6855
E-mail: alex.tse@usdoj.gov
Deputy Chief **Jonathan "John" Lee** .... (415) 436-7137
E-mail: jonathan.lee@usdoj.gov
Deputy Chief **Sara Winslow** .... (415) 436-6925
E-mail: sara.winslow@usdoj.gov
Deputy Chief of Financial Litigation Unit
Steven Saltiel .... (415) 436-6996
E-mail: steven.saltiel@usdoj.gov
Assistant U.S. Attorney **Mark Conrad** .... (415) 436-7025
E-mail: mark.conrad@usdoj.gov
Assistant U.S. Attorney **Jerome Mayer-Cantu** .... (415) 436-6962
E-mail: jerome.mayer-cantu@usdoj.gov
Education: Stanford 2010 JD
Assistant U.S. Attorney **Abraham Simmons** .... (415) 436-7264
E-mail: abraham.simmons@usdoj.gov
Environment and Natural Resources Unit Chief
(Vacant) .... (415) 436-7180
Tax Division Chief **Thomas G. Moore** .... (415) 436-7137
E-mail: thomas.moore@usdoj.gov

Criminal Division
Tel: (415) 436-7200 Fax: (415) 436-7009

Chief **David Callaway** .... (415) 436-7200
E-mail: david.callaway@usdoj.gov
Appellate Chief **Barbara J. Valliere** .... (415) 436-7039
E-mail: barbara.valliere@usdoj.gov
Anti-Terrorism Task Force Coordinator **Candace Kelly** ... (415) 436-7200
E-mail: candace.kelly@usdoj.gov
Asset Forfeiture Unit Assistant U.S. Attorney
Stephanie Hinds .... (415) 436-6816
E-mail: stephanie.hinds@usdoj.gov
Asset Forfeiture Unit Assistant U.S. Attorney
Patricia Kenney .... (415) 436-6857
E-mail: patricia.kenney@usdoj.gov
Cybercrimes Chief **Matthew Parrella** .... (415) 436-7200
E-mail: matthew.parrella@usdoj.gov
Economic Crimes and Security Fraud Chief **(Vacant)** ..... (415) 436-7200
Assistant U.S. Attorney **Kirstin Ault** .... (415) 436-6940
E-mail: kirstin.ault@usdoj.gov
Assistant U.S. Attorney **Peter Axelrod** .... (415) 436-6774
E-mail: peter.axelrod@usdoj.gov
Assistant U.S. Attorney **Kathryn R. Haun** .... (415) 436-7200
E-mail: kathryn.haun@usdoj.gov
Education: Boston U BA; Stanford JD
Assistant U.S. Attorney **Wilson Leung** .... (415) 436-6758
E-mail: wilson.leung@usdoj.gov
Assistant U.S. Attorney **Kyle Waldinger** .... (415) 436-6830
E-mail: kyle.waldinger@usdoj.gov
Assistant U.S. Attorney **Hartley West** .... (415) 436-6747
E-mail: hartley.west@usdoj.gov
Assistant U.S. Attorney **Gregg Lowder** .... (415) 436-7044
E-mail: gregg.lowder@usdoj.gov
Narcotics Section Chief **Andrew "Andy" Scoble** .... (415) 436-7249
E-mail: andrew.scoble@usdoj.gov
Assistant U.S. Attorney **Robin Harris** .... (415) 436-7016
Assistant U.S. Attorney **Barbara Silano** .... (415) 436-7223
E-mail: barbara.silano@usdoj.gov
National Security Section Chief **Elise Becker** .... (415) 436-6878
E-mail: elise.becker@usdoj.gov

Criminal Division *continued*

National Security Section Deputy Chief **Jeff Nedrow** ... (408) 535-5061
150 Almaden Blvd., Suite 900, San Jose, CA 95113
E-mail: jeff.nedrow@usdoj.gov
Organized Crime Strike Force Chief **William Frentzen** ... (415) 436-6959
E-mail: william.frentzen@usdoj.gov Fax: (415) 436-6401
Assistant U.S. Attorney **Robert Rees** .... (415) 436-7210
E-mail: robert.rees@usdoj.gov
Education: NYU 2003 JD
Assistant U.S. Attorney **Denise Barton** .... (510) 637-3709
E-mail: denise.barton@usdoj.gov
Assistant U.S. Attorney **Chinhayi Cadet** .... (415) 436-7073
E-mail: chinhayi.cadet@usdoj.gov
Assistant U.S. Attorney **(Vacant)** .... (415) 436-6833

Oakland (CA) Office

1301 Clay Street, Suite 340S, Oakland, CA 94612
Tel: (510) 637-3680 TTY: (510) 637-3678 Fax: (510) 637-3724

Chief **Keslie Stewart** .... (510) 637-3680
E-mail: keslie.stewart@usdoj.gov
Supervisory Legal Assistant
Kathleen "Katie" Turner .... (510) 637-3680
E-mail: kathleen.turner@usdoj.gov

Criminal Division
Chief **(Vacant)** .... (510) 637-3680
Deputy Chief **(Vacant)** .... (510) 637-3680
Assistant U.S. Attorney **Maureen Bessette** .... (510) 637-3771
E-mail: maureen.bessette@usdoj.gov
Assistant U.S. Attorney **Andrew Huang** .... (510) 637-3703
E-mail: andrew.huang@usdoj.gov

Drug Task Force
Assistant U.S. Attorney **Aaron Wegner** .... (510) 637-3709
E-mail: aaron.wegner@usdoj.gov
Education: Harding 1998 BA; Oregon 2003 JD

San Jose (CA) Office

150 Almaden Boulevard, Suite 900, San Jose, CA 95113
Tel: (408) 535-5061 TTY: (408) 535-3960 Fax: (408) 535-5066
Fax: (408) 535-5081

Chief **Jeff Nedrow** .... (408) 535-5061
E-mail: jeff.nedrow@usdoj.gov

Civil Division
Fax: (408) 535-5081

Assistant U.S. Attorney **Claire Cormier** .... (408) 535-5082
E-mail: claire.cormier@usdoj.gov

Criminal Division
Fax: (408) 535-5066

Assistant U.S. Attorney **Gary Fry** .... (408) 535-5051
E-mail: gary.fry@usdoj.gov
Assistant U.S. Attorney **Tim Lucy** .... (408) 535-5054
Assistant U.S. Attorney **Stephen James Meyer** .... (408) 535-5061
E-mail: stephen.meyer@usdoj.gov
Education: Brooklyn Law 2002 JD
Assistant U.S. Attorney **Amber Rosen** .... (408) 535-5046
E-mail: amber.rosen@usdoj.gov
Assistant U.S. Attorney **(Vacant)** .... (408) 535-5061

Computer Hacking and Intellectual Property
Assistant U.S. Attorney **Matthew Parrella** .... (408) 535-5596
E-mail: matthew.parrella@usdoj.gov

Drug Task Force
Assistant U.S. Attorney **John Glang** .... (408) 535-5084
E-mail: john.glang@usdoj.gov

★ Presidential Appointment Requiring Senate Confirmation ☆ Presidential Appointment □ Schedule C Appointment ◇ Career Senior Foreign Service Appointment
● Career Senior Executive Service (SES) Appointment ○ Non-Career Senior Executive Service (SES) Appointment ■ Postal Career Executive Service

Strike Force
Assistant U.S. Attorney **Tim Lucy** .... (408) 535-5054

California - Southern District
Federal Office Building, 880 Front Street,
Room 6293, San Diego, CA 92101-8893
Tel: (619) 557-5610 Fax: (619) 546-0620
Internet: www.usdoj.gov/usao/cas

★ U.S. Attorney **Laura E. Duffy** .... (619) 546-5690
E-mail: laura.duffy@usdoj.gov
Education: Iowa State 1988; Creighton 1993 JD
First Assistant U.S. Attorney **Cindy M. Cipriani** .... (619) 546-9608
E-mail: cindy.cipriani@usdoj.gov
Executive Assistant U.S. Attorney **Blair C. Perez** .... (619) 546-7963
E-mail: blair.perez@usdoj.gov
Administrative Assistant to the First Assistant and Executive Assistant U.S. Attorneys
Hortencia Barajas .... (619) 546-8639
E-mail: hortencia.barajas@usdoj.gov
Administrative Officer **Mary Tracy** .... (619) 546-9966
E-mail: mary.tracy@usdoj.gov
Human Resources Officer **Sylvia Rojas** .... (619) 546-8973
E-mail: sylvia.rojas@usdoj.gov
Law Enforcement Committee Coordinator **(Vacant)** ...... (619) 546-8817
Victim-Witness Coordinator **Polly M. Montano** .... (619) 546-8921
E-mail: polly.montano@usdoj.gov

Civil Division
Assistant U.S. Attorney, Chief **Thomas C. Stahl** .... (619) 546-7767
E-mail: thomas.stahl@usdoj.gov
Education: San Diego State BA; San Diego JD
Assistant U.S. Attorney, Deputy Chief
Katherine L. Parker .... (619) 546-7634
E-mail: katherine.parker@usdoj.gov
Assistant U.S. Attorney, Deputy Chief
Joseph P. Price, Jr. .... (619) 546-7642
E-mail: joseph.price@usdoj.gov
Special Assistant U.S. Attorney **Samuel W. Bettwy** ..... (619) 546-7125
Assistant U.S. Attorney **Dylan Aste** .... (619) 546-7621
E-mail: dylan.aste@usdoj.gov
Assistant U.S. Attorney **Daniel E. Butcher** .... (619) 546-7696
Assistant U.S. Attorney **Steve B. Chu** .... (619) 546-7167
E-mail: steve.chu@usdoj.gov
Assistant U.S. Attorney **Rebecca Church** .... (619) 546-7721
E-mail: rebecca.church@usdoj.gov
Assistant U.S. Attorney **Caroline Clark** .... (619) 546-7183
E-mail: caroline.clark@usdoj.gov
Assistant U.S. Attorney **Beth Clukey** .... (619) 546-7344
E-mail: beth.clukey@usdoj.gov
Assistant U.S. Attorney **Ernesto Cordero, Jr.** .... (619) 546-7478
E-mail: ernesto.cordero@usdoj.gov
Assistant U.S. Attorney **Glen F. Dorgan** .... (619) 546-7665
E-mail: glen.dorgan@usdoj.gov
Assistant U.S. Attorney **Michael Garabed** .... (619) 546-7703
E-mail: michael.garabed@usdoj.gov
Assistant U.S. Attorney **Leslie Gardner** .... (619) 546-7603
E-mail: lgardner@usa.doj.gov
Assistant U.S. Attorney **Kyle W. Hoffman** .... (619) 546-6987
E-mail: kyle.hoffman@usdoj.gov
Assistant U.S. Attorney **Douglas Keehn** .... (619) 546-7573
E-mail: douglas.keehn@usdoj.gov
Assistant U.S. Attorney **George V. Manahan** .... (619) 546-7607
E-mail: george.manahan@usdoj.gov
Education: Harvard
Assistant U.S. Attorney **Brett Norris** .... (619) 546-7620
E-mail: brett.norris@usdoj.gov
Assistant U.S. Attorney **Steven J. Poliakoff** .... (619) 546-7058
E-mail: steve.poliakoff@usdoj.gov
Assistant U.S. Attorney **Joseph J. Purcell** .... (619) 546-7643
E-mail: joseph.purcell@usdoj.gov

Civil Division *continued*
Assistant U.S. Attorney **Dianne M. Schweiner** .... (619) 546-7654
E-mail: dianne.schweiner@usdoj.gov
Assistant U.S. Attorney **Paul L. Starita** .... (619) 546-8402
E-mail: paul.starita@usdoj.gov
Assistant U.S. Attorney **Valerie Torres** .... (619) 546-7644
E-mail: valerie.torres@usdoj.gov
Assistant U.S. Attorney **David B. Wallace** .... (619) 546-7669
E-mail: dave.wallace@usdoj.gov

Criminal Division
Chief **William P. Cole** .... (619) 546-6762
E-mail: william.p.cole@usdoj.gov
Deputy Chief **Timothy D. Coughlin** .... (619) 546-6768
E-mail: timothy.coughlin@usdoj.gov
Education: Whittier JD
Criminal Division Senior Litigation Counsel
Todd W. Robinson .... (619) 546-7699
E-mail: todd.robinson@usdoj.gov
Criminal Division Senior Litigation Counsel
Michael G. Wheat .... (619) 546-8437
E-mail: michael.wheat@usdoj.gov
Foreign Affairs Coordinator **Robert Ciaffa** .... (619) 546-6752
E-mail: robert.ciaffa@usdoj.gov

Appellate Section
Assistant U.S. Attorney, Chief **Peter G. Ko** .... (619) 546-7359
E-mail: peter.ko2@usdoj.gov
Assistant U.S. Attorney **D. Benjamin Holley** .... (619) 546-7952
E-mail: bholley@usa.doj.gov
Assistant U.S. Attorney **Helen Hong** .... (619) 546-6990
E-mail: helen.hong@usdoj.gov
Assistant U.S. Attorney **Colin McDonald** .... (619) 546-9144
E-mail: colin.mcdonald@usdoj.gov
Assistant U.S. Attorney **Mark R. Rehe** .... (619) 546-7986
E-mail: mark.rehe@usdoj.gov
Assistant U.S. Attorney **Daniel E. Zipp** .... (619) 546-8463
E-mail: daniel.zipp@usdoj.gov

Criminal Enterprises Section
Assistant U.S. Attorney, Chief **Linda A. Frakes** .... (619) 546-6793
E-mail: linda.frakes@usdoj.gov
Assistant U.S. Attorney, Deputy Chief
Adam L. Braverman .... (619) 546-6717
E-mail: adam.braverman@usdoj.gov
Education: George Washington 2000 JD
Assistant U.S. Attorney, Deputy Chief
Joseph S. Green .... (619) 546-6955
E-mail: joseph.green@usdoj.gov
Assistant U.S. Attorney, Deputy Chief **David Leshner** .... (619) 546-7921
E-mail: david.leshner@usdoj.gov
Assistant U.S. Attorney, Deputy Chief
Timothy F. Salel .... (619) 546-8055
E-mail: timothy.salel@usdoj.gov
Assistant U.S. Attorney **Patrick Bumatay** .... (619) 546-8450
E-mail: pbumatay@usa.doj.gov
Assistant U.S. Attorney **Luella M. Caldito** .... (619) 546-6732
E-mail: luella.caldito@usdoj.gov
Assistant U.S. Attorney **Jose Castillo** .... (619) 564-6745
E-mail: jose.castillo3@usdoj.gov
Assistant U.S. Attorney **David P. Finn** .... (619) 546-1342
E-mail: david.finn@usdoj.gov
Assistant U.S. Attorney **Orlando B. Gutierrez** .... (619) 546-6758
E-mail: orlando.gutierrez@usdoj.gov
Assistant U.S. Attorney **Sherri Walker Hobson** .... (619) 546-6986
E-mail: sherri.hobson@usdoj.gov
Assistant U.S. Attorney **Joshua Jones** .... (619) 546-9744
E-mail: joshua.jones@usdoj.gov
Assistant U.S. Attorney **Josh Mellor** .... (619) 546-9733
E-mail: jmellor@usa.doj.gov
Assistant U.S. Attorney **Cynthia L. "Cindy" Millsaps** ... (619) 546-7940
E-mail: cynthia.millsaps@usdoj.gov
Education: Wake Forest BA; North Carolina JD

(continued on next page)

★ Presidential Appointment Requiring Senate Confirmation ☆ Presidential Appointment ☐ Schedule C Appointment ◇ Career Senior Foreign Service Appointment
● Career Senior Executive Service (SES) Appointment ○ Non-Career Senior Executive Service (SES) Appointment ■ Postal Career Executive Service

Criminal Enterprises Section *continued*

Assistant U.S. Attorney **Jaime D. Parks** . . . . (619) 546-7955
E-mail: jaime.parks@usdoj.gov
Assistant U.S. Attorney **Jonathan I. Shapiro** . . . . (619) 546-8225
E-mail: jonathan.shapiro@usdoj.gov
Assistant U.S. Attorney **Victor P. White** . . . . (619) 546-8439
E-mail: victor.white2@usdoj.gov
Assistant U.S. Attorney **Lara W. Worm** . . . . (619) 546-9697
E-mail: lara.worm@usdoj.gov
Assistant U.S. Attorney **(Vacant)** . . . . (619) 546-6758
Assistant U.S. Attorney **(Vacant)** . . . . (619) 546-6717

Fast-Track Sentencing Unit

Assistant U.S. Attorney, Deputy Chief
Marietta I. Geckos . . . . (619) 546-6952
E-mail: marietta.geckos@usdoj.gov
Assistant U.S. Attorney **Charlotte E. Kaiser** . . . . (619) 546-7282
E-mail: charlotte.kaiser@usdoj.gov
Education: Chicago 1995 BA; Northwestern 2001 JD
Assistant U.S. Attorney **Susan Park** . . . . (619) 546-6760
E-mail: spark2@usa.doj.gov
Assistant U.S. Attorney **Ryan Sausedo** . . . . (619) 546-9689
E-mail: ryan.sausedo@usdoj.gov

Financial Litigation Unit

Assistant U.S. Attorney, FLU Coordinator
Leah R. Bussell . . . . (619) 546-6727
E-mail: leah.bussell@usdoj.gov
Assistant U.S. Attorney **Carol M. Lee** . . . . (619) 546-7584
E-mail: carol.lee@usdoj.gov
Assistant U.S. Attorney **Daniel C. Silva** . . . . (619) 546-9713
E-mail: daniel.c.silva@usdoj.gov
Assistant U.S. Attorney **Bruce Smith** . . . . (619) 546-8266
E-mail: bruce.smith@usdoj.gov
Assistant U.S. Attorney **Thomas Watkinson III** . . . . (619) 546-8861
E-mail: thomas.watkinson@usdoj.gov

Grand Jury Section

Assistant U.S. Attorney **Janaki S. Ghandi** . . . . (619) 546-8817
E-mail: janaki.ghandi@usdoj.gov
Assistant U.S. Attorney **Connie Wu** . . . . (619) 546-8592
E-mail: connie.wu@usdoj.gov

Intake Unit

Assistant U.S. Attorney, Intake Unit Deputy Chief
Arnold Dale Blankenship . . . . (619) 546-6705
E-mail: dale.blankenship@usdoj.gov
Assistant U.S. Attorney, Intake Unit Deputy Chief
Caroline Han . . . . (619) 546-6968
E-mail: caroline.han@usdoj.gov
Assistant U.S. Attorney **Adriana Ahumada** . . . . (619) 546-8971
E-mail: adriana.ahumada@usdoj.gov
Assistant U.S. Attorney **Francis DiGiacco** . . . . (619) 546-6771
E-mail: francis.digiacco@usdoj.gov
Assistant U.S. Attorney **Kevin Mokhtari** . . . . (619) 546-8402
E-mail: kevin.mokhtari@usdoj.gov

General Crimes Section

Assistant U.S. Attorney, Chief **Seth Askins** . . . . (619) 546-6692
E-mail: seth.askins@usdoj.gov
Assistant U.S. Attorney, Deputy Chief
Joseph M. Orabona . . . . (619) 546-7951
E-mail: joseph.orabona@usdoj.gov
Assistant U.S. Attorney, Deputy Chief **Fred Sheppard** . . . (619) 546-8237
E-mail: fred.sheppard@usdoj.gov
Senior Assistant U.S. Attorney **Michael E. Lasater** . . . . . . (619) 546-7462
E-mail: michael.lasater@usdoj.gov
Education: San Diego JD
Assistant U.S. Attorney **Christopher M. Alexander** . . . . . (619) 546-6665
E-mail: christopher.m.alexander@usdoj.gov
Assistant U.S. Attorney **Lawrence A. Casper** . . . . (619) 546-6734
E-mail: lawrence.casper@usdoj.gov

General Crimes Section *continued*

Assistant U.S. Attorney **Andre M. Espinosa** . . . . (619) 546-9744
E-mail: aespinosa2@usa.doj.gov
Education: Kansas 1997 BA; Rutgers 2002 MPA; Rutgers (Camden) 2003 JD
Assistant U.S. Attorney **Alexandra Foster** . . . . (619) 546-6735
E-mail: afoster@usa.doj.gov
Assistant U.S. Attorney **Andrew R. Haden** . . . . (619) 546-6961
E-mail: andrew.haden@usdoj.gov
Assistant U.S. Attorney **Michael J. Heyman** . . . . (619) 546-9615
E-mail: mheyman@usa.doj.gov
Assistant U.S. Attorney **Scott T. Jones** . . . . (619) 546-8248
E-mail: sjones11@usa.doj.gov
Education: UC Santa Cruz 1980 BA; Columbia 1987 MBA, 1987 JD
Assistant U.S. Attorney **Brian Kasprzyk** . . . . (619) 546-9732
E-mail: bkasprzyk@usa.doj.gov
Assistant U.S. Attorney **Stephen F. Miller** . . . . (619) 546-7938
E-mail: steve.miller2@usdoj.gov
Assistant U.S. Attorney **Alana W. Robinson** . . . . (619) 546-7990
E-mail: alana.robinson@usdoj.gov
Assistant U.S. Attorney **Alessandra P. Serano** . . . . (619) 546-8014
E-mail: alessandra.p.serano@usdoj.gov
Assistant U.S. Attorney **Lara A. Stingley** . . . . (619) 546-8403
E-mail: lara.stingley@usdoj.gov
Assistant U.S. Attorney **Stacey H. Sullivan** . . . . (619) 546-8412
E-mail: stacey.sullivan@usdoj.gov
Assistant U.S. Attorney **Stephen Wong** . . . . (619) 546-9464
E-mail: swong4@usa.doj.gov
Assistant U.S. Attorney **(Vacant)** . . . . (619) 546-9613

Major Frauds

Assistant U.S. Attorney, Chief **Phillip L. B. Halpern** . . . . . (619) 546-6964
E-mail: phillip.halpern@usdoj.gov
Assistant U.S. Attorney, Principal Deputy Chief
Eric J. Beste . . . . (619) 546-6695
E-mail: eric.beste@usdoj.gov
Education: Oxford (UK) 1990 URGD; Pennsylvania 1991 AB; Northwestern 1994 JD
Assistant U.S. Attorney, Deputy Chief
Andrew G. Schopler . . . . (619) 546-8068
E-mail: andrew.schopler@usdoj.gov
Assistant U.S. Attorney **Emily Allen** . . . . (619) 546-9738
E-mail: emily.allen@usdoj.gov
Education: Harvard 2004 JD
Assistant U.S. Attorney **Valerie H. Chu** . . . . (619) 546-6750
E-mail: valerie.chu@usdoj.gov
Assistant U.S. Attorney **Andrew Galvin** . . . . (619) 546-9721
E-mail: agalvin@usa.doj.gov
Assistant U.S. Attorney **Rebecca Kanter** . . . . (619) 546-7304
E-mail: rebecca.kanter@usdoj.gov
Education: UC Irvine BA; UCLA 2003 JD
Assistant U.S. Attorney **Emily J. Keifer** . . . . (619) 546-7319
E-mail: emily.keifer@usdoj.gov
Assistant U.S. Attorney **Joseph M. Orabona** . . . . (619) 546-7951
E-mail: joseph.orabona@usdoj.gov
Assistant U.S. Attorney **Melanie K. Pierson** . . . . (619) 546-7976
E-mail: melanie.pierson@usdoj.gov
Assistant U.S. Attorney **Nicholas W. Pilchak** . . . . (619) 546-9709
E-mail: npilchak@usa.doj.gov
Assistant U.S. Attorney **Mark W. Pletcher** . . . . (619) 546-9714
E-mail: mpletcher1@usa.doj.gov
Assistant U.S. Attorney **Christopher P. Tenorio** . . . . (619) 546-8413
E-mail: christopher.tenorio@usdoj.gov
Assistant U.S. Attorney **Michelle L. Wasserman** . . . . (619) 546-8431
E-mail: michelle.wasserman@usdoj.gov
Education: Harvard 2007 JD
Assistant U.S. Attorney **(Vacant)** . . . . (619) 546-7053
Assistant U.S. Attorney **(Vacant)** . . . . (619) 546-7928
International Coordinator **Mark W. Conover** . . . . (619) 546-6763
E-mail: mark.conover@usdoj.gov

National Security and Cybercrimes Section

Chief of National Security and Cybercrimes
John N. Parmley . . . . (619) 546-7957
E-mail: john.parmley@usdoj.gov
Assistant U.S. Attorney **Sabrina L. Fève** . . . . (619) 546-6786
E-mail: sabrina.feve@usdoj.gov
Education: Williams 1997 BA; Harvard 2002 JD
Assistant U.S. Attorney **Shane P. Harrigan** . . . . (619) 546-6981
E-mail: shane.harrigan@usdoj.gov
Assistant U.S. Attorney **Michael J. Kaplan** . . . . (619) 546-7927
E-mail: mkaplan@usa.doj.gov
Assistant U.S. Attorney **Steven A. Peak** . . . . (619) 546-7958
E-mail: steve.peak@usdoj.gov
Assistant U.S. Attorney **Michelle Pettit** . . . . (619) 546-7972
E-mail: michelle.pettit@usdoj.gov
Assistant U.S. Attorney **(Vacant)** . . . . (619) 546-7957

Reactive Crimes Section

Assistant U.S. Attorney, Principal Deputy Chief
Paul S. Cook . . . . (619) 546-6764
E-mail: paul.cook@usdoj.gov
Assistant U.S. Attorney, Deputy Chief **Tara McGrath** . . . . (619) 546-7930
E-mail: tara.mcgrath@usdoj.gov
Senior Assistant U.S. Attorney **Anne K. Perry** . . . . (619) 546-7964
Senior Assistant U.S. Attorney **Faith A. Devine** . . . . (619) 546-6784
E-mail: faith.devine@usdoj.gov
Diversion Coordinator **Carla J. Bressler** . . . . (619) 564-6720
Assistant U.S. Attorney **Carlos Arguello** . . . . (619) 546-6684
E-mail: carlos.arguello2@usdoj.gov
Assistant U.S. Attorney **Matthew Brehm** . . . . (760) 370-3028
E-mail: mbrehm@usa.doj.gov
Assistant U.S. Attorney **Janet Cabral** . . . . (619) 546-8715
E-mail: jcabral@usa.doj.gov
Education: Notre Dame 1993 JD
Assistant U.S. Attorney **Coretta Catlin** . . . . (619) 546-7937
E-mail: coretta.catlin@usdoj.gov
Assistant U.S. Attorney **Arash Fuladian** . . . . (619) 546-9734
E-mail: arash.fuladian@usdoj.gov
Assistant U.S. Attorney **Jennifer L. Gmitro** . . . . (619) 546-9692
E-mail: jennifer.gmitro@usdoj.gov
Assistant U.S. Attorney **Laura Grimes** . . . . (619) 546-7748
E-mail: lgrimes@usa.doj.gov
Assistant U.S. Attorney **Jarad Hodes** . . . . (619) 546-7432
E-mail: jarad.hodes@usdoj.gov
Assistant U.S. Attorney **Benjamin Katz** . . . . (619) 546-8971
E-mail: benjamin.katz@usdoj.gov
Assistant U.S. Attorney **Brandon Kimura** . . . . (619) 546-9614
E-mail: bkimura@usa.doj.gov
Education: Hawaii 2010 JD
Assistant U.S. Attorney **Joseph S. Smith, Jr.** . . . . (619) 546-8299
E-mail: joseph.smith@usdoj.gov
Assistant U.S. Attorney **Lawrence E. Spong** . . . . (619) 546-8401
E-mail: larry.spong@usdoj.gov
Assistant U.S. Attorney **(Vacant)** . . . . (619) 546-7235

Imperial County Office - El Centro

516 Industry Way, #C, Imperial, CA 92251
Tel: (760) 370-0893 Fax: (760) 335-3975

Assistant U.S. Attorney **Karla Davis** . . . . (760) 370-3037
E-mail: karla.davis@usdoj.gov
Assistant U.S. Attorney **Kyle B. Martin** . . . . (619) 546-8384
E-mail: kyle.martin@usdoj.gov
Assistant U.S. Attorney **Christine M. Ro** . . . . (760) 355-2230
E-mail: christine.ro@usdoj.gov

Colorado District

1225 - 17th Street, Suite 700, Denver, CO 80202
Tel: (303) 454-0100 Fax: (303) 454-0400
Internet: www.usdoj.gov/usao/co

★ U.S. Attorney **John F. Walsh** . . . . (303) 454-0100
E-mail: john.walsh@usdoj.gov
Education: Williams 1983 BA; Stanford 1986 JD
Executive United States Attorney
David M. Gaouette . . . . (303) 454-0100
E-mail: david.gaouette@usdoj.gov
Education: Florida State 1976; Denver 1982 JD
First Assistant U.S. Attorney **Robert C. "Bob" Troyer** . . . . (303) 454-0100
E-mail: robert.troyer@usdoj.gov
Education: Pomona 1984 BA; Boston Col 1990 JD
Project Safe Neighborhood Assistant U.S. Attorney
Kurt Bohn . . . . (303) 454-0100
E-mail: kurt.bohn@usdoj.gov
Law Enforcement Coordinator **David M. Gaouette** . . . . (303) 454-0100
E-mail: david.gaouette@usdoj.gov
Education: Florida State 1976; Denver 1982 JD
Victim-Witness Specialist **Donna Summers** . . . . (303) 454-0100
E-mail: donna.summers@usdoj.gov
Information Technology Specialist and Litigation
Support **Daniel Keener** . . . . (303) 454-0100
E-mail: daniel.keener@usdoj.gov
Intelligence Research Specialist **(Vacant)** . . . . (303) 454-0100
Legal Administration Specialist/FOIA **Charisha Cruz** . . . . (303) 454-0100
E-mail: charisha.cruz@usdoj.gov
Public Affairs Specialist **Jeffrey Dorschner** . . . . (303) 454-0100
E-mail: jeffrey.dorschner@usdoj.gov
Regional Security Specialist **(Vacant)** . . . . (303) 454-0100
Executive Assistant/Office Manager **Cathy Olguin** . . . . (303) 454-0100
E-mail: cathy.olguin@usdoj.gov

Administrative Division

Fax: (303) 454-0405

Chief **Marilyn Ferguson** . . . . (303) 454-0100
E-mail: marilyn.ferguson@usdoj.gov
Human Resources Specialist **Gloria Engle** . . . . (303) 454-0100
E-mail: gloria.engle@usdoj.gov
Human Resources Assistant **Alexandria Suazo** . . . . (303) 454-0100
E-mail: alexandria.suazo@usdoj.gov
Human Resources Assistant **(Vacant)** . . . . (303) 454-0100
Supervisor Administrative Services Specialist
Bonnie Vigil . . . . (303) 454-0100
E-mail: bonnie.vigil@usdoj.gov
Administrative Services Specialist **Jeffrey Hernandez** . . . . (303) 454-0100
E-mail: jeffrey.hernandez@usdoj.gov
Administrative Specialist **Victoria "Tori" Soltis** . . . . (303) 454-0100
E-mail: victoria.soltis@usdoj.gov
Administrative Assistant and Receptionist
Nicholas Smith . . . . (303) 454-0100
E-mail: nicholas.smith@usdoj.gov
Budget Officer **Mary Nevares** . . . . (303) 454-0100
E-mail: mary.nevares@usdoj.gov
Budget Analyst **Joanne Gienger** . . . . (303) 454-0100
E-mail: joanne.gienger@usdoj.gov
Financial Technician **Alexandra Ornelas** . . . . (303) 454-0100
E-mail: alexandra.ornelas@usdoj.gov
Information Technology Director **Mark Pittington** . . . . (303) 454-0100
E-mail: mark.pittington@usdoj.gov
Information Technology Director **(Vacant)** . . . . (303) 454-0100
Information Technology Specialist and Litigation
Support **Ed Medina** . . . . (303) 454-0100
Information Technology Specialist and Litigation
Support **(Vacant)** . . . . (303) 454-0100

Appellate Division

Tel: (303) 454-0461

Appellate Chief **Robert Russel** . . . . (303) 454-0100
E-mail: robert.russel@usdoj.gov

(continued on next page)

★ Presidential Appointment Requiring Senate Confirmation ☆ Presidential Appointment ☐ Schedule C Appointment ◇ Career Senior Foreign Service Appointment
● Career Senior Executive Service (SES) Appointment ○ Non-Career Senior Executive Service (SES) Appointment ■ Postal Career Executive Service

Appellate Division *continued*

Assistant U.S. Attorney **Paul Farley** .... (303) 454-0100
E-mail: paul.farley@usdoj.gov
Education: Colorado BA; Denver JD
Assistant U.S. Attorney **Bishop Grewell** .... (303) 454-0100
E-mail: bishop.grewell@usdoj.gov
Assistant U.S. Attorney **Michael C. Johnson** .... (303) 454-0100
Assistant U.S. Attorney **James C. Murphy** .... (303) 454-0100
E-mail: james.murphy@usdoj.gov
Assistant U.S. Attorney **(Vacant)** .... (303) 454-0100
Library Manager **(Vacant)** .... (303) 454-0100
Paralegal **Ma-Linda LaFollette** .... (303) 454-0100
Paralegal **Carmen Gibson** .... (303) 454-0248
E-mail: carmen.gibson@usdoj.gov Fax: (303) 454-0403

Asset Recovery Division
Fax: (303) 454-0402

Chief **Tonya Andrews** .... (303) 454-0100
E-mail: tonya.andrews@usdoj.gov
Assistant U.S. Attorney **(Vacant)** .... (303) 454-0100
Assistant U.S. Attorney **H. Wayne Campbell** .... (303) 454-0100
E-mail: wayne.campbell@usdoj.gov
Paralegal **Pam Jebens** .... (303) 454-0100
E-mail: pam.jebens@usdoj.gov Fax: (303) 454-0402

Civil Division
Fax: (303) 454-0404

Chief **Kevin Traskos** .... (303) 454-0100
E-mail: kevin.traskos@usdoj.gov
Deputy Chief **Amy Padden** .... (303) 454-0100
E-mail: amy.padden@usdoj.gov
Education: William & Mary 1988 BS; Georgetown 1994 JD
Paralegal **Pauline Moncayo** .... (303) 454-0100
E-mail: pauline.moncayo@usdoj.gov Fax: (303) 454-0402
Paralegal **(Vacant)** .... (303) 454-0100
Fax: (303) 454-0402
Paralegal **(Vacant)** .... (303) 454-0100
Fax: (303) 454-0402
Affirmative Civil Enforcement Assistant U.S. Attorney/Senior Litigation Chief **Amanda Rocque** ..... (303) 454-0100
E-mail: amanda.rocque@usdoj.gov
Affirmative Civil Enforcement Assistant U.S. Attorney **Edwin Winstead** .... (303) 454-0100
E-mail: edwin.winstead@usdoj.gov
Affirmative Civil Enforcement, Mortgage Fraud Assistant U.S. Attorney **Jamie Mendelson** .... (303) 454-0100
E-mail: jamie.mendelson@usdoj.gov
Affirmative Civil Enforcement Auditor **(Vacant)** .... (303) 454-0100
Financial Fraud Assistant U.S. Attorney **J. Chris Larson** .... (303) 454-0100
E-mail: j.chris.larson@usdoj.gov
Financial Analyst, Affirmative Civil Enforcement **(Vacant)** .... (303) 454-0100
Defensive Litigation Assistant U.S. Attorney **Lila Batemen** .... (303) 454-0100
E-mail: lila.bateman@usdoj.gov
Defensive Litigation Assistant U.S. Attorney **J. B. Garcia** .... (303) 454-0100
E-mail: j.b.garcia@usdoj.gov
Defensive Litigation Assistant U.S. Attorney **Timothy Jafek** .... (303) 454-0100
E-mail: timothy.jafek@usdoj.gov
Defensive Litigation Assistant U.S. Attorney **Mark S. Pestal** .... (303) 454-0100
E-mail: mark.pestal@usdoj.gov
Defensive Litigation Assistant U.S. Attorney **Susan Prose** .... (303) 454-0100
E-mail: susan.prose@usdoj.gov
Defensive Litigation Assistant U.S. Attorney **Katherine Ross** .... (303) 454-0100
E-mail: katherine.ross@usdoj.gov

Civil Division *continued*

Defensive Litigation Assistant U.S. Attorney **Juan G. Villaseñor** .... (303) 454-0100
E-mail: juan.villasenor@usdoj.gov
Financial Litigation Unit Supervisor **Patricia McGee-Wake** .... (303) 454-0100
E-mail: patricia.mcgee-wake@usdoj.gov
Financial Litigation Unit Paralegal **Carolyn Dean** .... (303) 454-0100
E-mail: carolyn.dean@usdoj.gov Fax: (303) 454-0407
Affirmative Civil Enforcement, Health Care Fraud Assistant U.S. Attorney **Marcy Cook** .... (303) 454-0100
E-mail: marcy.cook@usdoj.gov
Defensive Litigation, Health Care Fraud Assistant U.S. Attorney **Mark S. Pestal** .... (303) 454-0100
E-mail: mark.pestal@usdoj.gov
Health Care Fraud Paralegal **Lisa Lara** .... (303) 454-0100
E-mail: lisa.lara@usdoj.gov

Criminal Division
Fax: (303) 454-0402

Chief **Matthew Kirsch** .... (303) 454-0100
E-mail: matthew.kirsch@usdoj.gov
Economic Crimes Chief **Suneeta Hazra** .... (303) 454-0100
Economic Crimes Assistant U.S. Attorney **Patricia Davies** .... (303) 454-0100
Economic Crimes Assistant U.S. Attorney **John Haried** .... (303) 454-0100
Economic Crimes Assistant U.S. Attorney **Kenneth Harmon** .... (303) 454-0100
Economic Crimes Assistant U.S. Attorney **Linda S. Kaufman** .... (303) 454-0100
Economic Crimes Assistant U.S. Attorney **Tim Neff** .... (303) 454-0100
Economic Crimes Assistant U.S. Attorney **Thomas M. O'Rourke** .... (303) 454-0100
Economic Crimes Assistant U.S. Attorney **Martha A. Paluch** .... (303) 454-0100
E-mail: martha.paluch@usdoj.gov
Economic Crimes Assistant U.S. Attorney **Pegeen D. Rhyne** .... (303) 454-0100
Auditor of Economic Crimes **Richard "Rich" Zoeter** ... (303) 454-0100
E-mail: richard.zoeter@usdoj.gov
Auditor **Dana Chamberlin** .... (303) 454-0100
E-mail: dana.chamberlin@usdoj.gov
Health Care Fraud Assistant U.S. Attorney/ Senior Litigation Chief **Jaime Peña** .... (303) 454-0100
Major Crimes Section Chief **Bradley W. "Brad" Giles** ... (303) 454-0100
Major Crimes Assistant U.S. Attorney **Mark Barrett** .... (303) 454-0100
E-mail: mark.barrett@usdoj.gov
Major Crimes Assistant U.S. Attorney **Kurt Bohn** ...... (303) 454-0100
Major Crimes Assistant U.S. Attorney **Robert M. Brown** .... (303) 454-0100
Major Crimes Assistant U.S. Attorney **Dave Conner** .... (303) 454-0100
E-mail: dave.conner@justice.usdoj.gov
Major Crimes Assistant U.S. Attorney **Jeremy Sibert** .... (303) 454-0100
E-mail: jeremy.sibert@usdoj.gov
Drug Enforcement Task Force Section Co-Chief **Susan "Zeke" Knox** .... (303) 454-0100
Fax: (303) 454-0401
Drug Enforcement Task Force Section Co-Chief **Zachary "Zak" Phillips** .... (303) 454-0100
Chief Counsel, Special Projects **Stephanie Podolak** .... (303) 454-0100
E-mail: stephanie.podolak@usdoj.gov
Organized Crime Drug Enforcement Task Force Assistant U.S. Attorney **James Boma** .... (303) 454-0100
E-mail: james.boma@usdoj.gov
Organized Crime Drug Enforcement Task Force Assistant U.S. Attorney **Kasandra Carleton** .... (303) 454-0100
Organized Crime Drug Enforcement Task Force Assistant U.S. Attorney **Zeke Knox** .... (303) 454-0100
E-mail: zeke.knox@justice.usdoj.gov Fax: (303) 454-0401

★ Presidential Appointment Requiring Senate Confirmation ☆ Presidential Appointment ☐ Schedule C Appointment ◇ Career Senior Foreign Service Appointment
● Career Senior Executive Service (SES) Appointment ○ Non-Career Senior Executive Service (SES) Appointment ■ Postal Career Executive Service

Criminal Division *continued*

Organized Crime Drug Enforcement Task Force Assistant U.S. Attorney **Michelle Korver** . . . . (303) 454-0100

Organized Crime Drug Enforcement Task Force Assistant U.S. Attorney **Barbara Skalla** . . . . (303) 454-0100
E-mail: barbara.skalla@usdoj.gov

Organized Crime Drug Enforcement Task Force Assistant U.S. Attorney **Guy Till** . . . . (303) 454-0100
E-mail: guy.till@usdoj.gov

Organized Crime Drug Enforcement Task Force Assistant U.S. Attorney **(Vacant)** . . . . (303) 454-0100

Organized Crime Drug Enforcement Task Force Special Assistant U.S. Attorney **(Vacant)** . . . . (303) 454-0100

Organized Crime Drug Enforcement Task Force Auditor **Scott Gammel** . . . . (303) 454-0100
E-mail: scott.gammel@usdoj.gov

Organized Crime Drug Enforcement Task Force Paralegal **Charlotte Musser** . . . . (303) 454-0100
E-mail: charlotte.musser@usdoj.gov

Special Prosecutions Division

Special Prosecutions Section Chief/CHIP **Judith Smith** . . . . (303) 454-0100
Note: CHIP stands for Computer Hacking and Intellectual Property Fax: (303) 454-0403

Special Prosecutions Assistant U.S. Attorney **Colleen Covell** . . . . (303) 454-0100

Special Prosecutions Assistant U.S. Attorney **Gregory Holloway** . . . . (303) 454-0100
E-mail: gregory.holloway@usdoj.gov

Special Prosecutions Assistant U.S. Attorney **Linda A. McMahan** . . . . (303) 454-0100
Note: On detail.

Special Prosecutions Assistant U.S. Attorney **Alecia Riewerts Wolak** . . . . (303) 454-0100

Special Prosecutions Assistant U.S. Attorney **Valeria Spencer** . . . . (303) 454-0100

Special Prosecutions Assistant U.S. Attorney **David Tonini** . . . . (303) 454-0100
E-mail: david.tonini@usdoj.gov

Durango Office

103 Sheppard Drive, Suite 215, Durango, CO 81303
Tel: (970) 247-1514 Fax: (970) 247-8619

Branch Chief and Senior Litigation Chief (Acting) **James Candelaria** . . . . (970) 247-3101
E-mail: james.candelaria@justice.usdoj.gov

Assistant U.S. Attorney **James Candelaria** . . . . (970) 247-3101
E-mail: james.candelaria@justice.usdoj.gov

Assistant U.S. Attorney **Todd Norvell** . . . . (970) 247-3102

Assistant U.S. Attorney **Dondi Osborne** . . . . (970) 247-3103
E-mail: dondi.osborne@usdoj.gov

Paralegal **Melodee Horton** . . . . (970) 247-3104
E-mail: melodee.horton@justice.usdoj.gov

Grand Junction Office

205 North Fourth Street, Suite 400, Grand Junction, CO 81501
Tel: (970) 257-7113 Fax: (970) 248-3630

Assistant U.S. Attorney **Michele M. Heldmyer** . . . . (970) 257-1580
E-mail: michele.heldmyer@justice.usdoj.gov

Assistant U.S. Attorney **(Vacant)** . . . . (970) 257-7113

Legal Assistant **Cosandra Foster** . . . . (970) 241-3843
E-mail: cosandra.foster@usdoj.gov

Connecticut District

Connecticut Financial Center, 157 Church Street, 23rd Floor, New Haven, CT 06510
Tel: (203) 821-3700 Fax: (203) 773-5376
Internet: www.usdoj.gov/usao/ct

★ U.S. Attorney **Deirdre M. Daly** . . . . (203) 821-3700
E-mail: deirdre.daly@usdoj.gov
Education: Dartmouth 1981 BA; Georgetown 1984 JD

Secretary to the U.S. Attorney **Judith "Judi" Dauria** . . . (203) 821-3700
E-mail: judi.dauria@usdoj.gov

First Assistant U.S. Attorney **(Vacant)** . . . . (203) 821-3700

Counsel to the U.S. Attorney **John H. Durham** . . . . (203) 821-3700
E-mail: john.durham@usdoj.gov
Education: Colgate 1972; Connecticut 1975 JD

Executive Assistant U.S. Attorney **Peter S. Jongbloed** . . . (203) 821-3700
E-mail: peter.jongbloed@usdoj.gov

Administrative Officer **Michele Genden** . . . . (203) 821-3700
E-mail: michele.genden@usdoj.gov

Budget Officer **Ruth Matthews** . . . . (203) 821-3700
E-mail: ruth.matthews@usdoj.gov

Human Resources Officer **(Vacant)** . . . . (203) 821-3700

Senior Litigation Counsel **Richard J. Schechter** . . . . (203) 696-3000
E-mail: richard.schechter@usdoj.gov

Systems Manager and Coordinator **(Vacant)** . . . . (203) 821-3700

Law Enforcement Coordination Specialist **Lorelei Vernali** . . . . (860) 947-1101
E-mail: loreliei.vernali@justice.usdoj.gov

Public Affairs Specialist **Thomas Carson** . . . . (203) 821-3722

Victim-Witness Specialist **Linda Corraro** . . . . (203) 821-3700
E-mail: linda.corraro@justice.usdoj.gov

Civil Division

Chief **John B. Hughes** . . . . (203) 821-3700
E-mail: john.hughes@usdoj.gov

Affirmative Civil Enforcement Unit Chief **Richard M. Molot** . . . . (203) 821-3700
E-mail: richard.molot2@usdoj.gov

Defensive Unit Chief **Michelle L. McConaghy** . . . . (203) 821-3700
E-mail: michelle.mcconaghy@usdoj.gov
Education: Roger Williams 2005 JD

Financial Litigation Unit Supervisor **Christine Sciarrino** . . . . (203) 821-3700
E-mail: christine.sciarrino@usdoj.gov

Assistant U.S. Attorney **Douglas Morabito** . . . . (203) 821-3700
E-mail: douglas.morabito@usdoj.gov

Assistant U.S. Attorney **Lauren M. Nash** . . . . (203) 821-3700
E-mail: lauren.nash@usdoj.gov

Assistant U.S. Attorney **Alan M. Soloway** . . . . (203) 821-3700
E-mail: alan.soloway@usdoj.gov

Assistant U.S. Attorney **David X. Sullivan** . . . . (203) 821-3700
E-mail: david.sullivan@usdoj.gov

Assistant U.S. Attorney **Anne F. Thidemann** . . . . (203) 821-3700
E-mail: anne.thidemann@usdoj.gov
Education: Ohio JD

Assistant U.S. Attorney **Julie G. Turbert** . . . . (203) 821-3700
E-mail: julie.turbert@usdoj.gov

Criminal Division

Chief **William J. Nardini** . . . . (203) 821-3700
E-mail: william.nardini@usdoj.gov

Financial Fraud and Public Corruption Unit Chief **Christopher M. Mattei** . . . . (203) 821-3700
E-mail: christopher.mattei@usdoj.gov
Education: Connecticut 2005 JD

Financial Fraud and Public Corruption Unit Deputy Chief **David E. Novick** . . . . (203) 821-3700
E-mail: david.novick@usdoj.gov

Financial Fraud and Public Corruption Unit Deputy Chief **Michael S. McGarry** . . . . (203) 821-3700
E-mail: michael.mcgarry@usdoj.gov

(continued on next page)

★ Presidential Appointment Requiring Senate Confirmation ☆ Presidential Appointment ☐ Schedule C Appointment ◇ Career Senior Foreign Service Appointment
● Career Senior Executive Service (SES) Appointment ○ Non-Career Senior Executive Service (SES) Appointment ■ Postal Career Executive Service

Criminal Division *continued*

National Security and Major Crimes Unit Chief
Raymond F. Miller . . . . (203) 821-3700
E-mail: ray.miller2@usdoj.gov
National Security and Major Crimes Unit Deputy Chief **Jacabed Rodriguez-Coss** . . . . (203) 821-3700
E-mail: jacabed.rodriguez-coss@usdoj.gov
National Security and Major Crimes Unit Deputy Chief **Stephen B. Reynolds** . . . . (203) 821-3700
E-mail: stephen.reynolds@usdoj.gov
Education: Hamilton 1993 BA; Cornell 1997 JD
Anti-Terrorism Advisory Council Coordinator
Stephen B. Reynolds . . . . (203) 821-3700
Education: Hamilton 1993 BA; Cornell 1997 JD
Strike Force Unit Chief **Raymond F. Miller** . . . . (203) 821-3700
E-mail: ray.miller2@usdoj.gov
Violent Crimes and Narcotics Unit Chief **S. Dave Vatti** . . . (203) 821-3700
E-mail: dave.vatti@usdoj.gov
Violent Crimes and Narcotics Unit Deputy Chief
Brian P. Leaming . . . . (203) 821-3700
E-mail: brian.leaming@usdoj.gov
Violent Crimes and Narcotics Unit Deputy Chief
Robert M. Spector . . . . (203) 821-3700
E-mail: robert.spector@usdoj.gov
Drug Enforcement Task Force Chief **Peter D. Markle** . . . (203) 821-3700
E-mail: peter.markle@usdoj.gov
Drug Enforcement Task Force Deputy Chief
H. Gordon Hall . . . . (203) 821-3700
E-mail: gordon.hall@usdoj.gov
Project Safe Neighborhoods Coordinator
S. Dave Vatti . . . . (203) 821-3700
Appellate Unit Chief **Sandra S. Glover** . . . . (203) 821-3700
E-mail: sandra.glover@usdoj.gov
Appellate Unit Deputy Chief **Marc Harris Silverman** . . . (203) 821-3700
E-mail: marc.silverman@usdoj.gov
Education: Yale 2003 BA, 2006 JD
Senior Litigation Counsel **Anthony E. Kaplan** . . . . (203) 821-3700
E-mail: anthony.kaplan@usdoj.gov
Assistant U.S. Attorney **William Brown** . . . . (203) 821-3700
E-mail: william.brown@justice.usdoj.gov
Assistant U.S. Attorney **Patrick F. Caruso** . . . . (203) 821-3700
E-mail: patrick.caruso@usdoj.gov
Assistant U.S. Attorney **Edward Chang** . . . . (203) 821-3700
E-mail: edward.chang@usdoj.gov
Assistant U.S. Attorney **Felice Duffy** . . . . (203) 821-3700
E-mail: felice.duffy@usdoj.gov
Education: Connecticut 1982 BS, 1985 MA, 1991 PhD; Quinnipiac 1999 JD
Assistant U.S. Attorney **David T. Huang** . . . . (203) 821-3700
E-mail: david.huang@usdoj.gov
Assistant U.S. Attorney **Sarah P. Karwan** . . . . (203) 821-3700
E-mail: sarah.p.karwan@usdoj.gov
Education: Connecticut JD
Assistant U.S. Attorney **Anastasia M. King** . . . . (203) 821-3700
E-mail: anastasia.king@usdoj.gov
Assistant U.S. Attorney **Henry K. Kopel** . . . . (203) 821-3700
E-mail: henry.kopel@usdoj.gov
Assistant U.S. Attorney **Michael E. Runowicz** . . . . (203) 821-3700
E-mail: mike.runowicz@usdoj.gov
Assistant U.S. Attorney **Christopher W. Schmeisser** . . . . (203) 821-3700
E-mail: christopher.schmeisser@usdoj.gov
Assistant U.S. Attorney **David J. Sheldon** . . . . (203) 821-3700
E-mail: david.sheldon@usdoj.gov
Assistant U.S. Attorney **Susan Wines** . . . . (203) 821-3700
E-mail: susan.wines@usdoj.gov
Assistant U.S. Attorney **(Vacant)** . . . . (203) 821-3700

Bridgeport (CT) Office

RBS Financial Center, 1000 Lafayette Boulevard, 10th Floor, Bridgeport, CT 06604
Tel: (203) 696-3000 Fax: (203) 579-5550

Supervisory Assistant U.S. Attorney **Tracy L. Dayton** . . . . (203) 696-3000
E-mail: tracy.dayton@usdoj.gov
Civil Division Assistant U.S. Attorney
Brenda Moss Green . . . . (203) 696-3000
E-mail: brenda.green@usdoj.gov
Civil Division Assistant U.S. Attorney **(Vacant)** . . . . (203) 696-3000
Criminal Division Assistant U.S. Attorney
Harold H. Chen . . . . (203) 696-3000
E-mail: harold.chen@usdoj.gov
Education: Yale 1991 BA; Duke 1996 JD
Criminal Division Assistant U.S. Attorney **(Vacant)** . . . . (203) 696-3000
Criminal Division Assistant U.S. Attorney **(Vacant)** . . . . (203) 696-3000
Drug Enforcement Task Force Assistant U.S. Attorney
Alina P. Reynolds . . . . (203) 696-3000
E-mail: alina.reynolds@usdoj.gov

Hartford (CT) Office

Federal Building and U.S. Court House, 450 Main Street, Room 328, Hartford, CT 06103
Tel: (860) 947-1101

Supervisory Assistant U.S. Attorney **Brian P. Leaming** . . . (860) 947-1101
E-mail: brian.leming@usdoj.gov
Intelligence Research Specialist **(Vacant)** . . . . (860) 947-1101
Senior Litigation Counsel **(Vacant)** . . . . (860) 941-1101

Civil Division

Assistant U.S. Attorney **William A. Collier** . . . . (860) 941-1101
E-mail: william.collier@usdoj.gov
Assistant U.S. Attorney **Carolyn Ikari** . . . . (860) 947-1101
E-mail: carolyn.ikari@usdoj.gov
Assistant U.S. Attorney **Gabriel J. Vidoni** . . . . (860) 947-1101
E-mail: gabriel.vidoni@usdoj.gov

Criminal Division

Assistant U.S. Attorney **Sarala Nagala** . . . . (860) 947-1101
E-mail: sarala.nagala@usdoj.gov
Assistant U.S. Attorney **Deborah R. Slater** . . . . (860) 947-1101
E-mail: deborah.slater@usdoj.gov
Assistant U.S. Attorney **Geoffrey M. Stone** . . . . (860) 947-1101
E-mail: geoffrey.stone@usdoj.gov
Assistant U.S. Attorney **S. Dave Vatti** . . . . (860) 947-1101
E-mail: dave.vatti@usdoj.gov

Delaware District

1007 Orange Street, Suite 700, Wilmington, DE 19801
P.O. Box 2046, Wilmington, DE 19899-2046
Tel: (302) 573-6277 Fax: (302) 573-6220
Internet: www.usdoj.gov/usao/de

★ U.S. Attorney **Charles M. Oberly III** . . . . (302) 573-6277
E-mail: charles.oberly@usdoj.gov
Education: Wesley Col (DE) 1966 AA; Penn State 1968 BA; Virginia 1971 JD
Secretary to the U.S. Attorney **Marie Steel** . . . . (302) 573-6277
E-mail: marie.steel@usdoj.gov
First Assistant U.S. Attorney **David C. Weiss** . . . . (302) 573-6277
E-mail: david.weiss@usdoj.gov
Administrative Officer (Acting) **Paulette V. Cryer** . . . . (302) 573-6277
E-mail: paulette.cryer@usdoj.gov
Deputy Administrative Officer **Paulette V. Cryer** . . . . (302) 573-6277
E-mail: paulette.cryer@usdoj.gov
Law Enforcement Coordinator/Press Officer
Kimberlynn Reeves . . . . (302) 573-6277
E-mail: kimberlynn.reeves@usdoj.gov
Victim-Witness Coordinator **Susan Alfree** . . . . (302) 573-6277
E-mail: susan.alfree@usdoj.gov

Delaware District *continued*

Systems Manager **David Flint** . . . . (302) 573-6277
E-mail: david.flint@usdoj.gov

Civil Division

Chief **Jennifer L. Hall** . . . . (302) 573-6277
E-mail: jennifer.hall@usdoj.gov
Assistant U.S. Attorney **Patricia C. Hannigan** . . . . (302) 573-6277
E-mail: patricia.hannigan@usdoj.gov
Assistant U.S. Attorney **Lauren Paxton** . . . . (302) 573-6277
E-mail: lauren.mcevoy@usdoj.gov
Assistant U.S. Attorney **Ellen W. Slights** . . . . (302) 573-6277
E-mail: ellen.slights@usdoj.gov
Assistant U.S. Attorney **Jennifer Welsh** . . . . (302) 573-6277
E-mail: jennifer.welsh@usdoj.gov
Assistant U.S. Attorney **Lesley Wolf** . . . . (302) 573-6277
E-mail: lesley.wolf@usdoj.gov
Assistant U.S. Attorney **(Vacant)** . . . . (302) 573-6277

Criminal Division

Chief **Shannon T. Hanson** . . . . (302) 573-6277
E-mail: shannon.hanson@usdoj.gov
Assistant U.S. Attorney **Ilana Eisenstein** . . . . (302) 573-6277
E-mail: ilana.eisenstein@usdoj.gov
Assistant U.S. Attorney **Edmond Falgowski** . . . . (302) 573-6277
E-mail: edmond.falgowski@usdoj.gov
Assistant U.S. Attorney **David Hall** . . . . (302) 573-6277
E-mail: david.hall@usdoj.gov
Assistant U.S. Attorney **Robert Kravetz** . . . . (302) 573-6277
E-mail: robert.kravetz@usdoj.gov
Assistant U.S. Attorney **Mark Lee** . . . . (302) 573-6277
E-mail: mark.lee@usdoj.gov
Education: North Carolina 1996 BA; Temple 2004 JD
Assistant U.S. Attorney **Edward McAndrew** . . . . (302) 573-6277
E-mail: ed.mcandrew@usdoj.gov
Assistant U.S. Attorney **Jamie McCall** . . . . (302) 573-6277
E-mail: jamie.mccall@usdoj.gov
Assistant U.S. Attorney **Robert J. Prettyman** . . . . (302) 573-6277
E-mail: robert.prettyman@usdoj.gov
Assistant U.S. Attorney **Shawn Weede** . . . . (302) 573-6277
E-mail: shawn.weede@usdoj.gov
Education: Pennsylvania 2002 JD

District of Columbia District

555 Fourth Street, NW, Washington, DC 20530
Tel: (202) 252-7566 Fax: (202) 305-0266
Internet: www.usdoj.gov/usao/dc

★ U.S. Attorney (Acting) **Channing D. Phillips** . . . . (202) 252-6600
Note: On October 16, 2015 President Obama nominated Channing Phillips to be U.S. Attorney. Mr. Phillips is currently acting in the position.
E-mail: channing.d.phillips@usdoj.gov
Education: Virginia 1980; Howard U 1986 JD
Executive Assistant **(Vacant)** . . . . (202) 252-1816
Principal Assistant U.S. Attorney **(Vacant)** . . . . (202) 252-6602
Executive Assistant **(Vacant)** . . . . (202) 252-6615
Executive Assistant U.S. Attorney for External Affairs
Wendy Pohlhaus . . . . (202) 252-6612
E-mail: wendy.pohlhaus@usdoj.gov
Education: Miami 1990 JD
Supervisory Community Outreach Specialist
Brenda J. Horner . . . . (202) 698-0825
E-mail: brenda.j.horner@usdoj.gov
Executive Assistant U.S. Attorney for Management
Denise Simmonds . . . . (202) 252-6621
E-mail: denise.simmonds@usdoj.gov
Executive Assistant U.S. Attorney for Operations
(Vacant) . . . . (202) 252-6603
Administrative Officer **(Vacant)** . . . . (202) 252-7627

District of Columbia District *continued*

Victim/Witness Assistance Unit Chief
Jelahn Stewart . . . . (202) 252-7187
E-mail: jelahn.stewart2@usdoj.gov
Special Counsel to the U.S. Attorney **Renata Cooper** . . . . (202) 252-6606
E-mail: renata.cooper@usdoj.gov
Affiliation: Esq.
Special Counsel to the U.S. Attorney **(Vacant)** . . . . (202) 252-6606
Chief Information Officer **Michael Vasquez** . . . . (202) 252-0882
E-mail: michael.vasquez3@usdoj.gov
Budget Officer **Jonathan Ellsworth** Room 5207 . . . . (202) 252-1723
E-mail: jonathan.ellsworth@usdoj.gov
Librarian **Lisa Kosow** Room 8222-A . . . . (202) 252-6659
E-mail: lisa.kosow2@usdoj.gov
Office Services Manager **Lee Pensmith** . . . . (202) 252-7634
E-mail: lee.pensmith@usdoj.gov
Human Resources Officer
Leslie Haynes Room 5300 I . . . . (202) 252-7629
E-mail: leslie.haynes@usdoj.gov
Intelligence Specialist **John Marsh** . . . . (202) 252-6862
E-mail: john.marsh@usdoj.gov
Systems Manager **Karen T. Kress** . . . . (202) 252-0822
E-mail: karen.kress@usdoj.gov
Special Counsel for Professional Development
Denise Simmonds . . . . (301) 492-5513
E-mail: denise.simmonds@usdoj.gov
Antiterrorism Officer/LECC Manager
Christopher Brophy . . . . (202) 252-6857
E-mail: christopher.brophy@usdoj.gov

Appellate Division

Fax: (202) 514-8779

Chief **Elizabeth Trosman** . . . . (202) 252-6784
E-mail: elizabeth.trosman@usdoj.gov
Deputy Chief **Elizabeth Danello** . . . . (202) 252-6768
E-mail: elizabeth.danello@usdoj.gov
Deputy Chief **Chrisellen R. Kolb** . . . . (202) 252-6833
E-mail: chrisellen.r.kolb@usdoj.gov
Deputy Chief **John Mannarino** . . . . (202) 514-7118
E-mail: john.mannarino@usdoj.gov
Deputy Chief **(Vacant)** . . . . (202) 252-6784
Supervisory Paralegal Specialist **Brandon Tracz** . . . . (202) 514-7694
E-mail: brandon.tracz@usdoj.gov

Civil Division

Tel: (202) 252-2563 Fax: (202) 514-8781 Fax: (202) 514-8780

Chief **Daniel Van Horn** . . . . (202) 514-7151
E-mail: daniel.vanhorn@usdoj.gov
Assistant to the Chief **Cynthia Parker** . . . . (202) 514-7166
E-mail: cindy.parker@usdoj.gov
Deputy Chief **Doris D. Coles-Huff** . . . . (202) 514-7170
E-mail: doris.coles@usdoj.gov
Deputy Chief **Robin Meriweather** . . . . (202) 514-7135
E-mail: robin.meriweather@usdoj.gov
Deputy Chief **Keith V. Morgan** . . . . (202) 514-7228
E-mail: keith.morgan@usdoj.gov
Deputy Chief **(Vacant)** . . . . (202) 514-7168
Appellate Counsel **R. Craig Lawrence** . . . . (202) 278-3307
E-mail: craig.lawrence@usdoj.gov
Support Staff Manager **Pamela Lawson** . . . . (202) 514-6200
E-mail: pamela.lawson@usdoj.gov

Criminal Division

Tel: (202) 252-6766 Fax: (202) 514-8782

Chief **Jonathan M. Malis** . . . . (202) 252-6782
E-mail: jonathan.m.malis@usdoj.gov
Deputy Chief **(Vacant)** . . . . (202) 252-7842
Asset Forfeiture Unit Chief **(Vacant)** . . . . (202) 252-6766
Federal Major Crimes Section Chief **(Vacant)** . . . . (202) 252-7900

(continued on next page)

★ Presidential Appointment Requiring Senate Confirmation ☆ Presidential Appointment □ Schedule C Appointment ◇ Career Senior Foreign Service Appointment
● Career Senior Executive Service (SES) Appointment ○ Non-Career Senior Executive Service (SES) Appointment ■ Postal Career Executive Service

Criminal Division *continued*

Fraud and Public Corruption Section Chief
Deborah L. Connor . . . . (202) 252-7862
E-mail: deborah.connor@usdoj.gov
Education: Miami U (OH) BA; Georgetown JD

National Security Section Chief
Gregg Maisel Room 11-453 . . . . (202) 252-7812
E-mail: gregg.maisel@usdoj.gov
Special Counsel for National Security **(Vacant)** . . . . (202) 353-8831

Organized Crime and Narcotics Trafficking Section Chief **(Vacant)** Room 4804 . . . . (202) 252-7683

Assistant U.S. Attorney **Michael C. DiLorenzo** . . . . (202) 252-6766

Assistant U.S. Attorney **Scott L. Sroka** . . . . (202) 252-6766

Special Proceedings Division

Chief **Leslie Ann Gerardo** Room 10-836 . . . . (202) 252-7578
E-mail: leslie.gerardo@usdoj.gov

Superior Court Division

Tel: (202) 514-7379 Fax: (202) 307-3221

Chief **Richard S. Tischner** Room 3205 . . . . (202) 252-7274
E-mail: richard.s.tischner@usdoj.gov

Deputy Chief **Michelle Jackson** . . . . (202) 252-7275
E-mail: michelle.jackson@usdoj.gov

Homicide Section Chief **Jeffrey R. Ragsdale** . . . . (202) 252-7268

Felony Major Crimes Section Chief
Jeffrey R. Ragsdale . . . . (202) 252-7268

General Crimes Section Chief
Lisa Baskerville-Greene . . . . (202) 252-7279

Sex Offense and Domestic Violence Section Chief
Kelly Higashi . . . . (202) 252-7282
Sex Offense and Domestic Violence Prosecutor
Allison Leotta . . . . (202) 252-7277
Education: Michigan State; Harvard JD

Florida - Middle District

Park Tower, 400 North Tampa Street, Suite 3200, Tampa, FL 33602
Tel: (813) 274-6000 Fax: (813) 274-6358
Internet: www.usdoj.gov/usao/flm/

★ U.S. Attorney **Arthur Lee Bentley** . . . . (813) 274-6000
E-mail: lee.bentley@usdoj.gov
Education: Georgia 1980 BA; Virginia 1983 JD

First Assistant U.S. Attorney **W. Stephen Muldrow** . . . . (813) 274-6467
E-mail: w.stephen.muldrow@usdoj.gov

Executive Assistant U.S. Attorney **Todd Grandy** . . . . (813) 274-6343
E-mail: todd.grandy@usdoj.gov

Public Affairs Specialist **William Daniels** . . . . (813) 274-6388

Law Enforcement Coordination Specialist
Eric Johnson . . . . (813) 274-6092

Administration Division

Fax: (813) 274-6358

Director **Jeffrey Hahn** . . . . (813) 274-6302
E-mail: jeffrey.hahn@usdoj.gov Fax: (813) 274-6074

Budget Officer **Evelyn Restaino** . . . . (813) 274-6007
E-mail: evelyn.restaino@usdoj.gov

Human Resources Officer **Dawn McCourt** . . . . (813) 274-6006
E-mail: dawn.mccourt@usdoj.gov

Litigation Support Manager **Marcia Martaus** . . . . (813) 274-6000
E-mail: marcia.martaus@justice.usdoj.gov

Support Services Manager **Tracy Ray** . . . . (813) 274-6013
E-mail: tracy.ray@usdoj.gov

Systems Manager **Anne Fishkin** . . . . (813) 274-6010
E-mail: anne.fishkin@justice.usdoj.gov

Appellate Division

Fax: (813) 274-6102

Chief **David P. Rhodes** . . . . (813) 274-6305
E-mail: david.rhodes@usdoj.gov

Appellate Division *continued*

Deputy Chief, Appellate Division **Linda McNamara** . . . . (813) 274-6306
E-mail: linda.mcnamara@usdoj.gov

Assistant U.S. Attorney **Todd Grandy** . . . . (813) 274-6307
E-mail: todd.grandy@usdoj.gov

Assistant U.S. Attorney **Yvette Rhodes** . . . . (813) 274-6330
E-mail: yvette.rhodes@usdoj.gov

Assistant U.S. Attorney **Susan Rothstein-Youakim** . . . . (813) 274-6329
E-mail: susan.youakim@usdoj.gov

Assistant U.S. Attorney **Peter J. Sholl** . . . . (813) 274-6327
E-mail: peter.sholl@usdoj.gov

Civil Division

Fax: (813) 274-6198

Chief **Randy Harwell, Jr.** . . . . (813) 274-6332
E-mail: randy.harwell@usdoj.gov

Deputy Chief **Sean J. Flynn** . . . . (813) 274-6333
E-mail: sean.flynn2@usdoj.gov
Education: Colorado 1996 BA; Notre Dame 2002 JD

Assistant U.S. Attorney **Jennifer Corinis** . . . . (813) 274-6310
E-mail: jennifer.corinis@usdoj.gov

Assistant U.S. Attorney **Charles Harden** . . . . (813) 274-6316
E-mail: charles.harden@usdoj.gov

Assistant U.S. Attorney **John Rudy** . . . . (813) 274-6319
E-mail: john.rudy@usdoj.gov

Assistant U.S. Attorney **Kenneth Stegeby** . . . . (813) 274-6303
E-mail: kenneth.stegeby@usdoj.gov

Assistant U.S. Attorney **Patricia Willing** . . . . (813) 274-6321
E-mail: patricia.willing@justice.usdoj.gov

Assistant U.S. Attorney/ACE Coordinator **(Vacant)** . . . . (813) 274-6335

Assistant U.S. Attorney/Social Security **(Vacant)** . . . . (813) 274-6334

Criminal Division

Fax: (813) 274-6108

Chief (North) **Roger B. Handberg** . . . . (813) 274-6000
E-mail: roger.handberg@usdoj.gov

Chief (South) **Rachelle DesVaux Bedke** . . . . (813) 274-6000
E-mail: rachelle.bedke@usdoj.gov

Asset Forfeiture Chief **Anita M. Cream** . . . . (813) 274-6301
E-mail: anita.cream@usdoj.gov Fax: (813) 274-6220
Asset Forfeiture Assistant U.S. Attorney
Josephine "Josie" Thomas . . . . (813) 274-6086
E-mail: josie.thomas@usdoj.gov

Economic Crimes Section Deputy Chief **(Vacant)** . . . . (813) 274-6317
Fax: (813) 274-6103
Economic Crimes Assistant U.S. Attorney **(Vacant)** . . . . (813) 274-6354
Economic Crimes Assistant U.S. Attorney
Cherie Krigsman . . . . (813) 274-6344
E-mail: cherie.krigsman@usdoj.gov
Economic Crimes Assistant U.S. Attorney
David G. Lazarus . . . . (813) 274-6323
Economic Crimes Assistant U.S. Attorney
Thomas Palermo . . . . (813) 274-6355
E-mail: thomas.palermo@usdoj.gov
Education: Florida State 2001 JD; U London 2002 LLM
Economic Crimes Assistant U.S. Attorney
Jay Trezevant . . . . (813) 274-6312
E-mail: jay.trezevant@usdoj.gov
Economic Crimes Assistant U.S. Attorney
Christopher P. Tuite . . . . (813) 274-6339
E-mail: christopher.tuite@usdoj.gov
Economic Crimes Assistant U.S. Attorney
Terry A. Zitek . . . . (813) 274-6336
E-mail: terry.zitek@justice.usdoj.gov

Narcotics Section Senior Deputy Chief **Joseph Ruddy** . . . . (813) 274-6338
E-mail: joseph.ruddy@usdoj.gov Fax: (813) 274-6125
Narcotics Section Deputy Chief
James Conway "Jim" Preston . . . . (813) 274-6326
E-mail: james.preston@usdoj.gov

★ Presidential Appointment Requiring Senate Confirmation ☆ Presidential Appointment ☐ Schedule C Appointment ◇ Career Senior Foreign Service Appointment
● Career Senior Executive Service (SES) Appointment ○ Non-Career Senior Executive Service (SES) Appointment ■ Postal Career Executive Service

Criminal Division *continued*

Narcotics Assistant U.S. Attorney
Maria Chapa Lopez . . . . (813) 274-6353
E-mail: maria.chapa@usdoj.gov

Narcotics Assistant U.S. Attorney
Kelley Howard-Allen . . . . (813) 274-6313
E-mail: kelley.howard@usdoj.gov

Narcotics Assistant U.S. Attorney **Jeffrey Miller** . . . . (813) 274-6348
E-mail: jeffrey.miller2@usdoj.gov

Narcotics Assistant U.S. Attorney **James Muench** . . . . . (813) 274-6345
E-mail: james.muench2@usdoj.gov

Narcotics Assistant U.S. Attorney
Christopher Murray . . . . (813) 274-6356
E-mail: christopher.murray@usdoj.gov

Narcotics Assistant U.S. Attorney **Kathy Peluso** . . . . (813) 274-6341
E-mail: kathy.peluso@usdoj.gov

Narcotics Assistant U.S. Attorney **Matthew H. Perry** . . . (813) 274-6466
E-mail: matthew.perry@usdoj.gov

Narcotics Assistant U.S. Attorney **(Vacant)** . . . . (813) 301-3003

Organized Crime Section Deputy Chief **Walter E. Furr** . . . (813) 274-6324
E-mail: walter.furr@usdoj.gov

Organized Crime Section Assistant U.S. Attorney
Jeffrey Downing . . . . (813) 274-6309
E-mail: jeff.downing@usdoj.gov

Organized Crime Special Assistant U.S. Attorney
Shauna Hale . . . . (813) 274-6347
E-mail: shauna.hale@usdoj.gov

General Crimes Section

Deputy Chief **Simon Gaugush** . . . . (813) 274-6318
E-mail: simon.gaugush@usdoj.gov Fax: (813) 274-6178

Assistant U.S. Attorney **Don Hansen** . . . . (813) 274-6351
E-mail: don.hansen@usdoj.gov

Assistant U.S. Attorney **Stacie Harris** . . . . (813) 274-6346
E-mail: stacie.harris@usdoj.gov

Assistant U.S. Attorney **Amanda Kaiser** . . . . (813) 274-6315
E-mail: amanda.kaiser@usdoj.gov

Assistant U.S. Attorney **Colleen Murphy-Davis** . . . . (813) 274-6331
E-mail: colleen.murphy@usdoj.gov

Assistant U.S. Attorney **Amanda Riedel** . . . . (813) 274-6340
E-mail: amanda.riedel@usdoj.gov

Fort Myers (FL) Office

2110 First Street, Suite 3-137, Fort Myers, FL 33901
Tel: (239) 461-2200 Fax: (239) 461-2219

Chief **Jesus M. Casas** . . . . (239) 461-2200
E-mail: jesus.m.casas@usdoj.gov

Civil Division

Assistant U.S. Attorney **Kyle Cohen** . . . . (239) 461-2245
E-mail: kyle.cohen@usdoj.gov

Criminal Division

Assistant U.S. Attorney **Robert "Bob" Barclift** . . . . (239) 461-2200
E-mail: robert.barclift@usdoj.gov

Assistant U.S. Attorney **David G. Lazarus** . . . . (239) 461-2200
E-mail: david.lazarus@justice.usdoj.gov

Assistant U.S. Attorney **Jeffrey Michelland** . . . . (239) 461-2200
E-mail: jeffrey.michelland@usdoj.gov

Assistant U.S. Attorney **(Vacant)** . . . . (239) 461-2200

Asset Forfeiture

Assistant U.S. Attorney **Michael Bagge-Hernandez** . . . . . (239) 461-2200

Jacksonville (FL) Office

300 North Hogan Street, Suite 700, Jacksonville, FL 32202
Tel: (904) 301-6300 Fax: (904) 301-6310

Chief **Julie Hackenberry** . . . . (904) 301-6300
E-mail: julie.savell@usdoj.gov

Office Manager **Michael J. Brown** . . . . (904) 301-6300
E-mail: michael.j.brown@usdoj.gov

Civil Division

Assistant U.S. Attorney **Ronnie Carter** . . . . (904) 301-6300
E-mail: ronnie.carter@usdoj.gov

Assistant U.S. Attorney **Collette Cunningham** . . . . (904) 301-6300
E-mail: collette.cunningham@usdoj.gov

Assistant U.S. Attorney **Laura Lothman** . . . . (904) 301-6300
E-mail: laura.lothman@usdoj.gov

Assistant U.S. Attorney **Jason Mehta** . . . . (904) 301-6300
E-mail: jason.mehta@usdoj.gov

Criminal Division

Deputy Chief **Mac Heavener** . . . . (904) 301-6300
E-mail: mac.heavener@usdoj.gov

Special Assistant U.S. Attorney **(Vacant)** . . . . (904) 301-6300

Assistant U.S. Attorney **D. Rodney Brown** . . . . (904) 301-6300
E-mail: rodney.brown@usdoj.gov

Assistant U.S. Attorney **Dale Campion** . . . . (904) 301-6300
E-mail: dale.campion@usdoj.gov

Assistant U.S. Attorney
Arnold Bernard "Chip" Corsmeier . . . . (904) 301-6300
E-mail: chip.corsmeier@usdoj.gov

Assistant U.S. Attorney **Mark Devereaux** . . . . (904) 301-6300
E-mail: mark.devereaux@usdoj.gov

Assistant U.S. Attorney **A. Tysen Duva** . . . . (904) 301-6300
E-mail: tysen.duva@usdoj.gov
Education: Florida 2002 JD

Assistant U.S. Attorney **Kevin Frein** . . . . (904) 301-6300
E-mail: kevin.frein@usdoj.gov

Assistant U.S. Attorney **Bonnie Glober** . . . . (904) 301-6300
E-mail: bonnie.glober@usdoj.gov

Assistant U.S. Attorney **Kelly Karase** . . . . (904) 301-6300
E-mail: kelly.karase@usdoj.gov

Assistant U.S. Attorney **Diidri Robinson** . . . . (904) 301-6300
E-mail: diidri.robinson@usdoj.gov

Assistant U.S. Attorney **Jay Taylor** . . . . (904) 301-6300
E-mail: jay.taylor@usdoj.gov

Assistant U.S. Attorney **(Vacant)** . . . . (904) 301-6300

Assistant U.S. Attorney **(Vacant)** . . . . (904) 301-6300

Senior Litigation Counsel **(Vacant)** . . . . (904) 301-6300

Asset Forfeiture

Assistant U.S. Attorney **Bonnie Glober** . . . . (904) 301-6300
E-mail: bonnie.glober@usdoj.gov

Ocala (FL) Office

35 SE First Avenue, Suite 300, Ocala, FL 34471
Tel: (352) 547-3600 Fax: (352) 547-3623

Chief **Carlos A. Perez** . . . . (352) 547-3600
E-mail: carlos.a.perez@usdoj.gov

Assistant U.S. Attorney **Bryon Aven** . . . . (352) 547-3600
E-mail: bryon.aven@usdoj.gov

Assistant U.S. Attorney **Robert E. Bodnar, Jr.** . . . . (352) 547-3605
E-mail: robert.bodnar@usdoj.gov

Officer Manager **Elaine Williams** . . . . (352) 547-3600

Orlando (FL) Office

501 West Church Street, Suite 300, Orlando, FL 32805
Tel: (407) 648-7500 Fax: (407) 648-7643

Chief **Katherine Ho** . . . . (407) 648-7500
E-mail: katherine.ho@usdoj.gov

Deputy Chief **Daniel Irick** . . . . (407) 648-7500
E-mail: daniel.irick@usdoj.gov

Officer Manager **Joey Chigro** . . . . (407) 648-7500
E-mail: joey.chigro@usdoj.gov

Appellate Division

Assistant U.S. Attorney **Roberta Bodnar** . . . . (407) 648-7500
E-mail: roberta.bodnar@usdoj.gov

Assistant U.S. Attorney **Peggy Morris Ronca** . . . . (407) 648-7501
E-mail: peggy.ronca@usdoj.gov

★ Presidential Appointment Requiring Senate Confirmation ☆ Presidential Appointment ☐ Schedule C Appointment ◇ Career Senior Foreign Service Appointment
● Career Senior Executive Service (SES) Appointment ○ Non-Career Senior Executive Service (SES) Appointment ■ Postal Career Executive Service

Civil Division
Assistant U.S. Attorney **Bradley M. Bole** .... (407) 648-7514
E-mail: bradley.bole@usdoj.gov
Assistant U.S. Attorney **Ralph E. Hopkins** .... (407) 648-7500
E-mail: ralph.hopkins@usdoj.gov
Assistant U.S. Attorney **Scott H. Park** .... (407) 648-7500
E-mail: scott.park@usdoj.gov
Assistant U.S. Attorney **Julie Posteraro** .... (407) 648-7500
E-mail: julie.posteraro@usdoj.gov
Assistant U.S. Attorney **(Vacant)** .... (407) 648-7500

Criminal Division
Assistant U.S. Attorney **Bruce S. Ambrose** .... (407) 648-7500
E-mail: bruce.ambrose@usdoj.gov
Assistant U.S. Attorney **Vincent Chiu** .... (407) 648-7500
E-mail: vincent.chiu@usdoj.gov
Assistant U.S. Attorney **Karen L. Gable** .... (407) 648-7500
E-mail: karen.gable@usdoj.gov
Assistant U.S. Attorney **David Haas** .... (407) 648-7537
E-mail: david.haas@usdoj.gov
Assistant U.S. Attorney **Shawn Napier** .... (407) 648-7500
E-mail: shawn.napier@usdoj.gov
Education: Capital U 2001 JD
Assistant U.S. Attorney **J. Bishop Ravenel** .... (407) 648-7500
E-mail: bishop.ravenel@usdoj.gov
Assistant U.S. Attorney **Joseph Schuster** .... (407) 648-7500
E-mail: joseph.schuster@usdoj.gov
Assistant U.S. Attorney **(Vacant)** .... (407) 648-7500
Assistant U.S. Attorney **(Vacant)** .... (407) 540-3606
Assistant U.S. Attorney **(Vacant)** .... (407) 648-7500
Assistant U.S. Attorney **(Vacant)** .... (407) 648-7500
Assistant U.S. Attorney **(Vacant)** .... (407) 648-7500
Assistant U.S. Attorney **(Vacant)** .... (407) 648-7500

Asset Forfeiture
Assistant U.S. Attorney **Nicole Andrejko** .... (407) 648-7500
E-mail: nicole.andrejko@usdoj.gov

Florida - Northern District
111 North Adams Street, 4th Floor, Tallahassee, FL 32301
Tel: (850) 942-8430 Fax: (850) 942-8429
Internet: www.justice.gov/usao/fln

★ U.S. Attorney (Acting) **Christopher Canova** .... (850) 942-8430
E-mail: christopher.canova@usdoj.gov
Secretary to the U.S. Attorney **(Vacant)** .... (850) 942-8430
Counsel to the U.S. Attorney **Stephen M. Kunz** .... (850) 942-8430
E-mail: stephen.kunz@justice.usdoj.gov
First Assistant U.S. Attorney **(Vacant)** .... (850) 942-8430
Law Enforcement Coordination Director
Kenneth S. "Ken" Tucker .... (850) 942-8430
E-mail: kenneth.tucker@usdoj.gov
Education: Central Florida 1983 BA
OCDETF Chief Assistant U.S. Attorney
Eric K. Mountin .... (850) 942-8430
E-mail: eric.mountin@usdoj.gov
Senior Litigation Counsel **(Vacant)** .... (850) 785-3495
Systems Manager **Joshua Watson** .... (850) 942-8530
E-mail: joshua.watson@usdoj.gov

Appellate Division
Chief Assistant U.S. Attorney **Nancy J. Hess** .... (850) 942-8430
E-mail: nancy.hess@usdoj.gov

Civil Division
Chief **Peter G. Fisher** .... (850) 942-8430
E-mail: peter.fisher@usdoj.gov
Chief Assistant U.S. Attorney **(Vacant)** .... (850) 942-8430
Assistant U.S. Attorney **Jonathan D. Letzring** .... (850) 942-8430
E-mail: jonathan.letzring@usdoj.gov
Assistant U.S. Attorney **(Vacant)** .... (850) 942-8430

Criminal Division
Chief **Karen E. Rhew-Miller** .... (850) 942-8430
Supervisory Assistant U.S. Attorney **(Vacant)** .... (850) 942-8430
Assistant U.S. Attorney **Jason Coody** .... (850) 942-8430
Assistant U.S. Attorney **Michael J. Harwin** .... (850) 942-8430
E-mail: michael.harwin@usdoj.gov
Education: Emory 2001 JD
Assistant U.S. Attorney **Herbert Lindsey** .... (850) 942-8430
Assistant U.S. Attorney **Winifred L.A. Nesmith** .... (850) 942-8430
E-mail: winifred.nesmith@usdoj.gov
Assistant U.S. Attorney **Michael T. Simpson** .... (850) 942-8430
Assistant U.S. Attorney **Corey J. Smith** .... (850) 942-8430
Assistant U.S. Attorney **James Ustynoski** .... (850) 942-8430
Assistant U.S. Attorney **(Vacant)** .... (850) 942-8430

Gainesville (FL) Office
300 East University Avenue, Suite 310, Gainesville, FL 32601
Tel: (352) 378-0996 Fax: (352) 338-7981

Chief Assistant U.S. Attorney **(Vacant)** .... (352) 378-0996
Assistant U.S. Attorney **Gregory McMahon** .... (352) 378-0996
E-mail: gregory.mcmahon@usdoj.gov
Assistant U.S. Attorney **Frank T. Williams** .... (352) 378-0996
E-mail: frank.williams@usdoj.gov

Pensacola (FL) Office
21 East Garden Street, Suite 300, Pensacola, FL 32502
Tel: (850) 444-4000

Supervisory Assistant U.S. Attorney **Nancy J. Hess** ..... (850) 444-4000
Administrative Officer **Floyd Boyer** .... (850) 942-8430
E-mail: floyd.boyer@usdoj.gov

Civil/Appellate Division
Appellate Chief **Robert G. Davies** .... (850) 444-4000
Civil Chief **(Vacant)** .... (850) 444-4000
Assistant U.S. Attorney **Leah A. Butler** .... (850) 444-4000
E-mail: leah.butler@usdoj.gov
Assistant U.S. Attorney **Erica A. Hixon** .... (850) 444-4000
E-mail: erica.hixon@usdoj.gov
Assistant U.S. Attorney **Len Register** .... (850) 444-4000
E-mail: len.register@usdoj.gov
Assistant U.S. Attorney **(Vacant)** .... (850) 444-4000

Criminal Division
Assistant U.S. Attorney **Tiffany H. Eggers** .... (850) 444-4000
E-mail: tiffany.eggers@usdoj.gov
Assistant U.S. Attorney **David L. Goldberg** .... (850) 444-4000
E-mail: david.goldberg@usdoj.gov
Assistant U.S. Attorney **Alicia H. Kim** .... (850) 444-4000
E-mail: alicia.kim@usdoj.gov
Assistant U.S. Attorney **Edwin F. Knight** .... (850) 444-4000
E-mail: edwin.knight@usdoj.gov
Assistant U.S. Attorney **J. Ryan Love** .... (850) 444-4000
E-mail: ryan.love@usdoj.gov
Assistant U.S. Attorney **Jeffrey M. Tharp** .... (850) 444-4000
E-mail: jeffrey.tharp@usdoj.gov
Assistant U.S. Attorney **(Vacant)** .... (850) 444-4000

Florida - Southern District
99 NE Fourth Street, Suite 800, Miami, FL 33132
Tel: (305) 961-9001 Fax: (305) 530-7679
Internet: www.justice.gov/usao/fls

★ U.S. Attorney **Wifredo A. "Willy" Ferrer** .... (305) 961-9001
E-mail: wifredo.ferrer@usdoj.gov
Education: Miami 1987; Pennsylvania 1990 JD
Executive Assistant U.S. Attorney **(Vacant)** .... (305) 961-9289
Special Counsel for Public Affairs **(Vacant)** .... (305) 961-9174
Senior Litigation Counsel **Thomas J. Mulvihill** .... (305) 961-9424
E-mail: thomas.mulvihill@usdoj.gov

★ Presidential Appointment Requiring Senate Confirmation ☆ Presidential Appointment ☐ Schedule C Appointment ◇ Career Senior Foreign Service Appointment
● Career Senior Executive Service (SES) Appointment ○ Non-Career Senior Executive Service (SES) Appointment ■ Postal Career Executive Service

Administration Division
Fax: (305) 530-7679

Administrative Officer **Helen Grill** .... (305) 961-9259
E-mail: helen.grill@usdoj.gov
Deputy Administrative Officer **(Vacant)** .... (305) 961-9113
Administrative Services Manager **Sandra Ortiz** .... (305) 961-9250
E-mail: sandra.ortiz@usdoj.gov
Human Resources Officer **Cynthia Hampton** .... (305) 961-9241
E-mail: cynthia.hampton@usdoj.gov
District Security Manager **Juan C. Fernandez** .... (305) 961-9037
E-mail: juan.c.fernandez@usdoj.gov
IT Manager **Jacqueline "Jacquie" Varela-Grajurdo** .... (305) 961-9218
E-mail: jacquie.varela@usdoj.gov

Appellate Division
Tel: (305) 961-9005 Fax: (305) 530-7214

Chief **Anne R. Schultz** .... (305) 961-9117
E-mail: anne.schultz@usdoj.gov
Deputy Chief **Kathleen M. Salyer** .... (305) 961-9130
E-mail: kathleen.salyer@usdoj.gov
Supervisory Assistant U.S. Attorney **(Vacant)** .... (305) 961-9325
Assistant U.S. Attorney **Jonathan Colan** .... (305) 961-9383
E-mail: jonathan.colan@usdoj.gov
Assistant U.S. Attorney **Harriett Galvin** .... (305) 961-9120
E-mail: harriett.galvin@usdoj.gov
Education: Yale 1981 LLM
Assistant U.S. Attorney **Carol Herman** .... (305) 961-9115
E-mail: carol.herman@usdoj.gov
Assistant U.S. Attorney **Lisa Hirsch** .... (305) 961-9214
E-mail: lisa.hirsch@usdoj.gov
Assistant U.S. Attorney **Jeanne Mullenhoff** .... (305) 961-9019
E-mail: jeanne.mullenhoff@usdoj.gov
Assistant U.S. Attorney **Lisette Reid** .... (305) 961-9129
E-mail: lisette.reid@usdoj.gov
Assistant U.S. Attorney **Sally M. Richardson** .... (305) 961-9336
E-mail: sally.richardson@usdoj.gov
Assistant U.S. Attorney **Laura Rivero** .... (305) 961-9433
E-mail: laura.rivero@usdoj.gov
Assistant U.S. Attorney **Lisa Rubio** .... (305) 961-9114
E-mail: lisa.rubio@usdoj.gov
Assistant U.S. Attorney **Stephen Schlessinger** .... (305) 961-9199
E-mail: stephen.schlessinger@usdoj.gov
Education: Yale 1970 BA
Assistant U.S. Attorney **Madeleine R. Shirley** .... (305) 961-9127
E-mail: madeleine.shirley@usdoj.gov
Assistant U.S. Attorney **Emily Smachetti** .... (305) 961-9295
E-mail: emily.smachetti@usdoj.gov
Assistant U.S. Attorney **(Vacant)** .... (305) 961-9123

Asset Forfeiture Division
Tel: (305) 961-9007 Fax: (305) 536-7599

Chief **Gerardo Simms** .... (305) 961-9035
E-mail: gerardo.simms@usdoj.gov
Deputy Chief **Michelle Alvarez** .... (305) 961-9088
E-mail: michelle.alvarez@usdoj.gov
Assistant U.S. Attorney **Alison Lehr** .... (305) 961-9176
E-mail: alison.lehr@usdoj.gov
Assistant U.S. Attorney **Karen E. Moore** .... (305) 961-9030
E-mail: karen.moore@usdoj.gov
Assistant U.S. Attorney **Arimentha Walkins** .... (305) 961-9091
E-mail: arimentha.walkins@usdoj.gov

Civil Division
Tel: (305) 961-9003 Fax: (305) 530-7139

Chief **Wendy Jacobus** .... (305) 961-9301
E-mail: wendy.jacobus@usdoj.gov
Deputy Chief **Maureen Donlan** .... (305) 961-9334
E-mail: maureen.donlan@usdoj.gov

Civil Division *continued*

Deputy Chief **Veronica Harrell-James** .... (305) 961-9327
E-mail: veronica.harrell-james@usdoj.gov
Senior Litigation Counsel **Dexter Lee** .... (305) 961-9320
E-mail: dexter.lee@usdoj.gov
Supervisory Assistant U.S. Attorney **(Vacant)** .... (305) 961-9335
Assistant U.S. Attorney **Jeffrey Dickstein** .... (305) 961-9453
E-mail: jeffrey.dickstein@usdoj.gov
Assistant U.S. Attorney **Stephanie Fidler** .... (305) 961-9073
E-mail: stephanie.fidler@usdoj.gov
Assistant U.S. Attorney **Mark A. Lavine** .... (305) 961-9303
E-mail: mark.lavine@usdoj.gov
Assistant U.S. Attorney **Larry Rosen** .... (305) 961-9321
E-mail: larry.rosen@usdoj.gov
Assistant U.S. Attorney **Susan Torres** .... (305) 961-9331
E-mail: susan.torres@usdoj.gov
Assistant U.S. Attorney **Karin Wherry** .... (305) 961-9016
E-mail: karin.wherry@usdoj.gov
Assistant U.S. Attorney **Charles White** .... (305) 961-9286
E-mail: charles.white@usdoj.gov
Assistant U.S. Attorney **(Vacant)** .... (305) 961-9003
Assistant U.S. Attorney **(Vacant)** .... (305) 961-9333

Financial Litigation Unit
Assistant U.S. Attorney **(Vacant)** .... (305) 961-9310
Assistant U.S. Attorney **(Vacant)** .... (305) 961-9204

Criminal Division
Fax: (305) 530-7950

Chief **Edward N. Stamm** .... (305) 961-9164
E-mail: edward.stamm@usdoj.gov
Deputy Chief **Kenneth Noto** .... (305) 961-9416
E-mail: kenneth.noto@usdoj.gov

Economic and Environmental Crimes Section
Tel: (305) 961-9004 Fax: (305) 530-6168

Chief (Acting) **Joan Silverstein** .... (305) 961-9121
E-mail: joan.silverstein@usdoj.gov
Deputy Chief **Luis Perez** .... (305) 961-9428
E-mail: luis.perez@usdoj.gov
Deputy Chief **Thomas Watts-Fitzgerald** .... (305) 961-9413
E-mail: thomas.watts-fitzgerald@usdoj.gov
Deputy Chief **(Vacant)** .... (305) 961-9322
Senior Litigation Counsel **Caroline Heck Miller** .... (305) 961-9432
E-mail: caroline.miller@usdoj.gov
Assistant U.S. Attorney **Jose Bonau** .... (305) 961-9426
E-mail: jose.bonau@usdoj.gov
Assistant U.S. Attorney **Christopher Clark** .... (305) 961-9167
E-mail: christopher.clark@usdoj.gov
Assistant U.S. Attorney **Michael Davis** .... (305) 961-9027
E-mail: michael.davis2@usdoj.gov
Assistant U.S. Attorney **Wilfredo Fernandez** .... (305) 961-9184
E-mail: wilfredo.fernandez@usdoj.gov
Assistant U.S. Attorney **Lois Foster-Steers** .... (305) 961-9203
E-mail: lois.foster-steers@usdoj.gov
Assistant U.S. Attorney **Randy Katz** .... (954) 356-7255 ext. 3620
E-mail: randy.katz@usdoj.gov
Education: Duke 2001 JD
Assistant U.S. Attorney **Ana Maria Martinez** .... (305) 961-9431
E-mail: ana.maria.martinez@usdoj.gov
Assistant U.S. Attorney **Marc Osborne** .... (305) 961-9198
E-mail: marc.osborne@usdoj.gov
Assistant U.S. Attorney **Peter Outerbridge** .... (305) 961-9326
E-mail: peter.outerbridge@usdoj.gov
Assistant U.S. Attorney **Karen Rochlin** .... (305) 961-9234
E-mail: karen.rochlin@usdoj.gov
Assistant U.S. Attorney **Kimberly A. Selmore** .... (305) 961-9189
E-mail: kim.selmore@usdoj.gov
Assistant U.S. Attorney **Alicia Shick** .... (305) 961-9317
E-mail: alicia.shick@usdoj.gov
Assistant U.S. Attorney **(Vacant)** .... (305) 961-9277

Major Crimes Section
Tel: (305) 961-9006 Fax: (305) 530-7976

Chief **Randy Hummel** .... (305) 961-9043
E-mail: randy.hummel@usdoj.gov
Deputy Chief **Peter R. Forand** .... (305) 961-9060
E-mail: peter.forand@usdoj.gov
Deputy Chief **Rosa Rodriguez-Mera** .... (954) 356-7255
E-mail: rosa.rodriguez-mera@usdoj.gov
Deputy Chief **Alejandro Soto** .... (305) 961-9034
E-mail: alejandro.soto@usdoj.gov
Deputy Chief **(Vacant)** .... (305) 961-9033
Assistant U.S. Attorney **Diane Patrick** .... (305) 961-9414
E-mail: diane.patrick@usdoj.gov
Assistant U.S. Attorney **(Vacant)** .... (305) 961-9023

Narcotics Section
Tel: (305) 961-9007 Fax: (305) 536-7213

Chief **Lynn Kirkpatrick** .... (305) 961-9289
E-mail: lynn.kirkpatrick@usdoj.gov
Deputy Chief **Richard Getchell** .... (305) 961-9281
E-mail: richard.getchell@usdoj.gov
Deputy Chief **Robin W. Waugh** .... (305) 961-9239
E-mail: robin.waugh@usdoj.gov
Deputy Chief **(Vacant)** .... (305) 961-9009
Senior Litigation Counsel **Richard "Dick" Gregorie** ..... (305) 961-9148
E-mail: dick.gregorie@usdoj.gov
OCDETF Coordinator **Mary Virginia King** .... (305) 961-9418
E-mail: mary.v.king@usdoj.gov
Assistant U.S. Attorney **Yvonne Rodriguez-Schack** ..... (305) 961-9014
E-mail: yvonne.rodriguez-schack@usdoj.gov
Assistant U.S. Attorney **Frank Tamen** .... (305) 961-9022
E-mail: frank.tamen@usdoj.gov
Assistant U.S. Attorney **(Vacant)** .... (305) 961-9029
Assistant U.S. Attorney **(Vacant)** .... (305) 715-7646
Assistant U.S. Attorney **(Vacant)** .... (305) 961-9012

High Intensity Drug Trafficking Areas [HIDTA]
Fax: (305) 715-7639

Assistant U.S. Attorney
William Leonard "Lenny" Athas .... (305) 715-7643
E-mail: william.athas@usdoj.gov
Assistant U.S. Attorney
Juan Antonio "Tony" Gonzalez .... (305) 597-1973
E-mail: juan.antonio.gonzalez@usdoj.gov

Organized Crime Section
Assistant U.S. Attorney **Robert Lehner** .... (305) 961-9020
E-mail: robert.lehner@usdoj.gov
Education: Columbia 1961 Dr Jur

Public Integrity and National Security Section
Tel: (305) 961-9001 Fax: (305) 536-4675

Chief **Robert Senior** .... (305) 961-9291
E-mail: robert.senior@usdoj.gov
Deputy Chief **(Vacant)** .... (305) 961-9292
Senior Litigation Counsel **(Vacant)** .... (305) 961-9274
Assistant U.S. Attorney **Eloisa D. Fernandez** .... (305) 961-9025
E-mail: eloisa.d.fernandez@usdoj.gov
Assistant U.S. Attorney **Allyson Fritz** .... (305) 961-9287
E-mail: allyson.fritz@usdoj.gov
Assistant U.S. Attorney **Susan Osborne** .... (305) 961-9104
E-mail: susan.osborne@usdoj.gov

Special Prosecutions Section
Chief **Barbara Martinez** .... (305) 961-9146
E-mail: barbara.martinez@usdoj.gov
Deputy Chief **Anthony Lacosta** .... (305) 961-9280
E-mail: anthony.lacosta@usdoj.gov
Deputy Chief **(Vacant)** .... (305) 961-9013

Special Prosecutions Section *continued*
Assistant U.S. Attorney **Gera R. Peoples** .... (305) 961-9314
E-mail: gera.peoples@usdoj.gov
Assistant U.S. Attorney **Marlene Rodriguez** .... (305) 961-9206
E-mail: marlene.rodriguez@usdoj.gov

Fort Lauderdale Office
500 East Broward Boulevard, 7th Floor, Fort Lauderdale, FL 33394
Tel: (954) 356-7255 Fax: (954) 356-7336

Administrative Officer **Susan "Sue" Fernandez** .... (954) 660-5926
E-mail: sue.fernandez@usdoj.gov

Appellate Division
Assistant U.S. Attorney **Robert B. Cornell** .... (954) 660-5697
E-mail: robert.b.cornell@usdoj.gov
Assistant U.S. Attorney **Phillip DiRosa** .... (954) 660-5959
E-mail: phillip.dirosa@usdoj.gov

Asset Forfeiture Unit
Fax: (954) 356-7336

Assistant U.S. Attorney
William H. Beckerleg .... (954) 660-5774 ext. 3614
E-mail: william.h.beckerleg@usdoj.gov

Civil Unit
Fax: (954) 356-7180

Deputy Chief **Marilynn K. Lindsey** .... (954) 356-7255 ext. 3610
E-mail: marilynn.lindsey@usdoj.gov
Assistant U.S. Attorney **David Mellinger** ...... (954) 356-7255 ext. 3612
E-mail: david.mellinger@usdoj.gov
Assistant U.S. Attorney **(Vacant)** .... (954) 356-7255 ext. 3599

Criminal Division
Deputy Chief and Assistant U.S.
Attorney-in-Charge **(Vacant)** .... (954) 356-7255 ext. 3558

Economic Crimes Section
Fax: (954) 356-7336

Chief (Acting) **Neil Karadbil** .... (954) 356-7255
E-mail: neil.karadbil@usdoj.gov
Senior Litigation Counsel **Neil Karadbil** .... (954) 356-7255
E-mail: neil.karadbil@usdoj.gov
Assistant U.S. Attorney
Laurence M. "Larry" Bardfeld .... (954) 356-7255 ext. 3611
E-mail: laurence.bardfeld@usdoj.gov
Assistant U.S. Attorney **Jennifer Keen** .... (954) 356-7255 ext. 3596
E-mail: jennifer.keene@usdoj.gov
Assistant U.S. Attorney **Bertha Mitrani** .... (954) 356-7255 ext. 3511
E-mail: bertha.mitrani@usdoj.gov
Assistant U.S. Attorney **(Vacant)** .... (954) 356-7255 ext. 3613
Assistant U.S. Attorney **(Vacant)** .... (954) 356-7255 ext. 3593
Special Assistant U.S. Attorney **Marc Anton** ... (954) 356-7255 ext. 3608
E-mail: marc.anton@usdoj.gov

Narcotics and Violent Crimes Section
Fax: (954) 356-7228

Chief **Bruce Brown** .... (954) 356-7255 ext. 3514
E-mail: bruce.brown2@usdoj.gov
Assistant U.S. Attorney **Scott Behnke** .... (954) 660-5698
E-mail: scott.behnke@usdoj.gov
Assistant U.S. Attorney **Donald Chase** .... (954) 660-5693
E-mail: donald.chase@usdoj.gov
Assistant U.S. Attorney **Terry Lindsey** .... (954) 660-5957
E-mail: terry.lindsey@usdoj.gov
Assistant U.S. Attorney **Paul Schwartz** .... (954) 356-7255 ext. 3577
E-mail: paul.schwartz@usdoj.gov
Assistant U.S. Attorney **Julia Vaglienti** .... (954) 356-7255 ext. 3509
E-mail: julia.vaglienti@usdoj.gov

Narcotics and Violent Crimes Section *continued*

Assistant U.S. Attorney **Michael Walleisa** ..... (954) 356-7255 ext. 3548
E-mail: michael.walleisa@usdoj.gov
Assistant U.S. Attorney **(Vacant)** .... (954) 356-7255 ext. 3512

Organized Crime Section
Tel: (954) 356-7392 Fax: (954) 356-7230

Chief **Jeffrey Kaplan** .... (954) 356-7255 ext. 3515
E-mail: jeffrey.kaplan@usdoj.gov
Assistant U.S. Attorney
Lawrence Lavecchio .... (954) 356-7255 ext. 3588
E-mail: lawrence.lavecchio@usdoj.gov
Assistant U.S. Attorney **(Vacant)** .... (954) 356-7255 ext. 3515
Assistant U.S. Attorney **(Vacant)** .... (954) 356-7255 ext. 3587

Fort Pierce Office

1111 SE Federal Highway, Suite 314, Stuart, FL 34994
Tel: (772) 466-0899

Assistant U.S. Attorney **Diana Acosta** .... (772) 466-0899
E-mail: diana.acosta@usdoj.gov
Assistant U.S. Attorney
LTC Theodore M. Cooperstein .... (772) 466-0899
E-mail: theodore.cooperstein2@usdoj.gov
Affiliation: USAR
Education: Dartmouth 1984 AB; Stanford 1987 JD; Georgetown 1999 LLM; Army War Col 2008 MSS

West Palm Beach Office

500 South Australian Avenue, Suite 400, West Palm Beach, FL 33401
Tel: (561) 820-8711

Deputy Chief **Rolando Garcia** .... (561) 820-8711 ext. 3010
E-mail: rolando.garcia@usdoj.gov
Assistant U.S. Attorney **Robert H. Waters, Jr.** .... (561) 209-1036
E-mail: robert.waters@usdoj.gov

Asset Forfeiture Unit
Fax: (561) 655-9785

Assistant U.S. Attorney **Antonia Barnes** .... (561) 209-1035
E-mail: antonia.barnes@usdoj.gov
Assistant U.S. Attorney **Mark Lester** .... (561) 820-8711 ext. 3056
E-mail: mark.lester@usdoj.gov

Criminal I
Fax: (561) 659-4526

Chief **Rolando Garcia** .... (561) 820-8711 ext. 3010
E-mail: rolando.garcia@usdoj.gov
Assistant U.S. Attorney **Stephen Carlton** ...... (561) 820-8711 ext. 3053
E-mail: stephen.carlton@usdoj.gov
Assistant U.S. Attorney **John McMillan** .... (561) 820-8711 ext. 3008
E-mail: john.mcmillan@usdoj.gov
Assistant U.S. Attorney
Alan Lothrop Morris .... (561) 820-8711 ext. 3013
E-mail: lothrop.morris@usdoj.gov
Assistant U.S. Attorney
Ann Marie C. Villafana .... (561) 820-8711 ext. 3047
E-mail: ann.marie.c.villafana@usdoj.gov
Assistant U.S. Attorney **William Zloch** .... (561) 820-8711 ext. 3022
E-mail: william.zloch@usdoj.gov
Assistant U.S. Attorney **Roger Harris Stefin** ... (561) 820-8711 ext. 3034
E-mail: roger.stefin@usdoj.gov

Criminal II
Fax: (561) 820-8777

Chief **Adrienne Rabinowitz** .... (561) 209-1039
E-mail: adrienne.rabinowitz@usdoj.gov
Assistant U.S. Attorney **Kerry S. Baron** .... (561) 209-1043
E-mail: kerry.baron@justice.usdoj.gov

Criminal II *continued*

Assistant U.S. Attorney **Carolyn Bell** .... (561) 209-1042
E-mail: carolyn.bell@usdoj.gov
Assistant U.S. Attorney **Ellen Cohen** .... (561) 209-1046
E-mail: ellen.cohen@usdoj.gov
Assistant U.S. Attorney **Lauren Jorgensen** .... (561) 209-1027
E-mail: lauren.jorgensen@usdoj.gov
Assistant U.S. Attorney **(Vacant)** .... (561) 209-1011

Georgia - Middle District

300 Mulberry Street, Suite 400, Macon, GA 31201
P.O. Box 1702, Macon, GA 31202-1702
Tel: (478) 752-3511 Fax: (478) 621-2655
Fax: (478) 621-2667 (Administration)
Fax: (478) 621-2679 (Personnel)
E-mail: mdga@hom.net
Internet: www.usdoj.gov/usao/gam

★ U.S. Attorney **Michael J. Moore** .... (478) 621-2600
E-mail: michael.j.moore@usdoj.gov Fax: (478) 621-2604
Education: Mercer 1989 BA, 1993 JD
Secretary to the U.S. Attorney **Karen F. Moore** .... (478) 621-2606
E-mail: karen.f.moore@usdoj.gov Fax: (478) 621-2604
First Assistant U.S. Attorney
G. F. "Pete" Peterman III .... (478) 621-2601
E-mail: pete.peterman@usdoj.gov
Chief Administrative Officer **Dale Vaughn** .... (478) 621-2612
E-mail: dale.vaughn@usdoj.gov
Press Information Officer **Pamela "Pam" Lightsey** ...... (478) 621-2602
Information Technology Specialist **Joey Hitchock** .... (478) 621-2734
E-mail: joey.hitchcock@usdoj.gov
Information Technology Specialist **Keli Maire** .... (478) 621-2609
E-mail: keli.maire@usdoj.gov
Law Enforcement Coordinator
Pamela "Pam" Lightsey .... (478) 621-2603
E-mail: pam.lightsey@usdoj.gov
Victim-Witness Coordinator **Cathy Barnes** .... (478) 621-2634
E-mail: cathy.barnes@usdoj.gov

Civil Division
Tel: (478) 752-3511 Fax: (478) 621-2737

Chief **Bernard Snell** .... (478) 621-2732
E-mail: bernard.snell@usdoj.gov
Assistant U.S. Attorney - Senior Litigation Counsel
(Vacant) .... (478) 621-2729
Assistant U.S. Attorney **Stewart Brown** .... (478) 621-2690
E-mail: stewart.brown@usdoj.gov
Assistant U.S. Attorney **Aimee Hall** .... (478) 621-2663
E-mail: aimee.hall@usdoj.gov
Assistant U.S. Attorney **Barbara Parker** .... (478) 621-2733
E-mail: barbara.parker@usdoj.gov
Assistant U.S. Attorney **Todd Swanson** .... (478) 621-2728
E-mail: todd.swanson@usdoj.gov
Assistant U.S. Attorney **(Vacant)** .... (478) 621-2729

Criminal Division
Tel: (478) 752-3511 Fax: (478) 621-2655

Chief **Michael T. "Mike" Solis** .... (478) 621-2640
E-mail: mike.solis@usdoj.gov
Deputy Criminal Division Chief and Assistant U.S. Attorney **Tamara Jarrett** .... (478) 621-2638
E-mail: tamara.jarrett@usdoj.gov
Assistant U.S. Attorney **Danial A. Bennett** .... (478) 621-2731
E-mail: danial.bennett@usdoj.gov
Assistant U.S. Attorney **Julia Bowen** .... (478) 752-3511
E-mail: julia.bowen@justice.usdoj.gov
Assistant U.S. Attorney **Charles Calhoun** .... (478) 621-2649
E-mail: charles.calhoun@usdoj.gov
Assistant U.S. Attorney **Kimberly Easterling** .... (478) 621-2627
E-mail: kimberly.easterling@usdoj.gov

(continued on next page)

REGIONAL OFFICES — US ATTORNEYS AND US MARSHALS SERVICE

★ Presidential Appointment Requiring Senate Confirmation ☆ Presidential Appointment □ Schedule C Appointment ◇ Career Senior Foreign Service Appointment
● Career Senior Executive Service (SES) Appointment ○ Non-Career Senior Executive Service (SES) Appointment ■ Postal Career Executive Service

Criminal Division *continued*

Assistant U.S. Attorney **Lindsay Feinberg** . . . . (478) 621-2685
E-mail: lindsay.feinberg@usdoj.gov
Assistant U.S. Attorney **Elizabeth S. Howard** . . . . (478) 621-2645
E-mail: elizabeth.s.howard@usdoj.gov
Assistant U.S. Attorney **Peter Leary** . . . . (478) 621-2642
E-mail: peter.leary@usdoj.gov
Assistant U.S. Attorney **Paul McCommon** . . . . (478) 621-2632
E-mail: paul.mccommon@usdoj.gov
Assistant U.S. Attorney **Robert McCullers** . . . . (478) 621-2730
E-mail: robert.mccullers@usdoj.gov
Assistant U.S. Attorney **Sonja B. Profit** . . . . (478) 621-2648
E-mail: sonja.b.profit@usdoj.gov
Assistant U.S. Attorney **Michelle L. "Mikki" Schieber** . . . (478) 621-2623
E-mail: mikki.schieber@usdoj.gov
Education: Illinois State 1985 BS; Mercer 1992 JD
Assistant U.S. Attorney **Graham Thorpe** . . . . (478) 621-2637
E-mail: graham.thorpe@justice.usdoj.gov
Community Relations Specialist
Pamela "Pam" Lightsey . . . . (478) 621-2603
E-mail: pam.lightsey@usdoj.gov Fax: (478) 621-2605
Intelligence Research Specialist **Gregory D. Armes** . . . . . . (478) 621-2643
E-mail: gregory.d.armes@usdoj.gov Fax: (478) 621-2682
Victim-Witness Specialist **Cathy Barnes** . . . . (478) 621-2634
E-mail: cathy.barnes@usdoj.gov
Law Enforcement Committee Coordinator
Pamela "Pam" Lightsey . . . . (478) 621-2603
E-mail: pam.lightsey@usdoj.gov

Albany (GA) Branch Office

C.B. King U.S. Courthouse, 201 West Broad Avenue,
2nd Floor, Albany, GA 31701
P.O. Box 366, Albany, GA 31702-9917
Tel: (229) 430-7754 Fax: (229) 430-7766

Assistant U.S. Attorney **Alan Dasher** . . . . (229) 430-7718
E-mail: alan.dasher@usdoj.gov
Criminal Division Assistant U.S. Attorney **Jim Crane** . . . . (229) 430-7756
E-mail: jim.crane@usdoj.gov
Criminal Division Assistant U.S. Attorney **(Vacant)** . . . . . . (229) 430-7758
Assistant U.S. Attorney **Leah E. McEwen** . . . . (229) 430-7757
E-mail: leah.e.mcewen@usdoj.gov

Columbus (GA) Branch Office

Sun Trust Building, 1246 First Avenue,
3rd Floor, Columbus, GA 31901
P.O. Box 2568, Columbus, GA 31902-2568
Tel: (706) 649-7700 Fax: (706) 649-7667

Assistant U.S. Attorney **Chuck Byrd** . . . . (706) 649-7734
E-mail: chuck.byrd@justice.usdoj.gov
Assistant U.S. Attorney **Melvin E. Hyde** . . . . (706) 649-7728
E-mail: melvin.e.hyde@usdoj.gov
Assistant U.S. Attorney **Crawford L. Seals** . . . . (706) 649-7733
E-mail: crawford.l.seals@usdoj.gov
Assistant U.S. Attorney **Sheetul S. Wall** . . . . (706) 649-7731
E-mail: sheetul.s.wall@usdoj.gov

Georgia - Northern District

Richard B. Russell Federal Building, 75 Spring Street, NW,
Suite 600, Atlanta, GA 30303-3309
Tel: (404) 581-6000 Fax: (404) 581-6181
Internet: www.usdoj.gov/usao/gan

★ U.S. Attorney (Acting) **John A. Horn** . . . . (404) 581-6000
E-mail: john.horn@usdoj.gov
First Assistant U.S. Attorney **John A. Horn** . . . . (404) 581-6000
E-mail: john.horn@usdoj.gov
Executive Assistant U.S. Attorney
Charysse L. Alexander . . . . (404) 581-6000
E-mail: charysse.alexander@usdoj.gov

Georgia - Northern District *continued*

Administrative Officer **Gregory R. Marshall** . . . . (404) 581-6000
E-mail: greg.marshall@usdoj.gov
Public Affairs Officer **Robert Page** . . . . (404) 581-6000
E-mail: robert.page@usdoj.gov
Information Technology (Systems) Manager
David W. Houston . . . . (404) 581-6000
E-mail: david.houston@usdoj.gov
Law Enforcement Coordination Manager and
Community Programs **Diane "Didi" Nelson** . . . . (404) 581-6000
E-mail: diane.nelson@justice.usdoj.gov
Intelligence Research Specialist **Eric De La Barre** . . . . (404) 581-6000
E-mail: eric.delabarre@usdoj.gov
Victim/Witness Specialist **Christie Smith Jones** . . . . (404) 581-6000
E-mail: christie.jones@usdoj.gov

Civil Division

Chief, Assistant U.S. Attorney **Amy L. Berne** . . . . (404) 581-6000
E-mail: amy.berne@usdoj.gov
Deputy Chief, Assistant U.S. Attorney
Lori M. Beranek . . . . (404) 581-6000
E-mail: lori.beranek@usdoj.gov

Affirmative Litigation and Civil Defensive Section

Assistant U.S. Attorney **Vania Allen** . . . . (404) 581-6000
E-mail: vania.allen@usdoj.gov
Assistant U.S. Attorney **Lena M. Amanti** . . . . (404) 581-6000
E-mail: lena.amanti@usdoj.gov
Education: Pomona 1998 BA; Pennsylvania 2003 JD
Assistant U.S. Attorney **Neeli Ben-David** . . . . (404) 581-6000
E-mail: neeli.ben-david@usdoj.gov
Assistant U.S. Attorney **Lisa D. Cooper** . . . . (404) 581-6000
E-mail: lisa.cooper@usdoj.gov
Assistant U.S. Attorney **Darcy F. Coty** . . . . (404) 581-6000
E-mail: darcy.coty@usdoj.gov
Assistant U.S. Attorney **Aileen M. Bell Hughes** . . . . (404) 581-6000
E-mail: aileen.bell.hughes@usdoj.gov
Assistant U.S. Attorney **Gabriel Mendel** . . . . (404) 581-6000
E-mail: gabriel.mendel@usdoj.gov
Assistant U.S. Attorney **David O'Neal** . . . . (404) 581-6000
E-mail: david.oneal@usdoj.gov
Assistant U.S. Attorney **R. David Powell** . . . . (404) 581-6000
E-mail: r.david.powell@usdoj.gov
Assistant U.S. Attorney **Emily Shingler** . . . . (404) 581-6000
E-mail: emily.shingler@usdoj.gov
Assistant U.S. Attorney **Melaine A. Williams** . . . . (404) 581-6000
E-mail: melaine.williams@usdoj.gov
Assistant U.S. Attorney **Paris Wynn** . . . . (404) 581-6000
E-mail: paris.wynn@usdoj.gov
Special Assistant U.S. Attorney **Ellen Persons** . . . . (404) 581-6000
E-mail: ellen.persons@usdoj.gov

Financial Litigation Unit

Chief, Assistant U.S. Attorney **Lori M. Beranek** . . . . (404) 581-6000
E-mail: lori.beranek@usdoj.gov
Assistant U.S. Attorney **James Cash** . . . . (404) 581-6000
E-mail: james.cash@usdoj.gov
Assistant U.S. Attorney **Cynthia B. Smith** . . . . (404) 581-6000
E-mail: cynthia.smith@usdoj.gov

Criminal Division

Chief, Assistant U.S. Attorney **F. Gentry Shelnutt, Jr.** . . . (404) 581-6000
E-mail: gentry.shelnutt@justice.usdoj.gov
Senior Litigation Counsel **William L. McKinnon** . . . . (404) 581-6000
E-mail: william.mckinnon@usdoj.gov
Senior Litigation Counsel **William R. Toliver** . . . . (404) 581-6000
E-mail: william.toliver@usdoj.gov
Senior Litigation Counsel **(Vacant)** . . . . (404) 581-6000
Senior Trial Counsel **Thomas A. Devlin, Jr.** . . . . (404) 581-6000
E-mail: thomas.devlin@usdoj.gov

★ Presidential Appointment Requiring Senate Confirmation ☆ Presidential Appointment □ Schedule C Appointment ◇ Career Senior Foreign Service Appointment
● Career Senior Executive Service (SES) Appointment ○ Non-Career Senior Executive Service (SES) Appointment ■ Postal Career Executive Service

Criminal Division *continued*

Outreach Coordinator, Assistant U.S. Attorney
Loranzo M. Fleming . . . . (404) 581-6000
E-mail: loranzo.fleming@usdoj.gov
Public Corruption Chief **Kurt R. Erskine** . . . . (404) 581-6000
E-mail: kurt.erskine@usdoj.gov
Public Corruption Deputy Chief **Jeffrey W. Davis** . . . . (404) 581-6000
E-mail: jeffrey.davis@usdoj.gov

Appellate and Legal Advice Section
Chief, Assistant U.S. Attorney
Lawrence S. Sommerfeld . . . . (404) 581-6000
E-mail: lawrence.sommerfeld@usdoj.gov
Assistant U.S. Attorney **J. Elizabeth McBath** . . . . (404) 581-6000
E-mail: elizabeth.mcbath@usdoj.gov
Special Assistant U.S. Attorney **Erin Sanders** . . . . (404) 581-6000
E-mail: erin.sanders@usdoj.gov

Asset Forfeiture Section
Chief **Dahil D. Goss** . . . . (404) 581-6000
E-mail: dahil.goss@usdoj.gov
Assistant U.S. Attorney **Michael John Brown** . . . . (404) 581-6000
E-mail: michael.brown@usdoj.gov
Assistant U.S. Attorney **Thomas Krepp** . . . . (404) 581-6000
E-mail: thomas.krepp@usdoj.gov
Assistant U.S. Attorney **Jenny R. Turner** . . . . (404) 581-6000
E-mail: jenny.turner@usdoj.gov
Assistant U.S. Attorney **George Jeffrey Viscomi** . . . . (404) 581-6000
E-mail: jeffrey.viscomi@usdoj.gov

Economic Crime Section
Chief, Assistant U.S. Attorney **Randy Chartash** . . . . (404) 581-6000
E-mail: randy.chartash@usdoj.gov
Deputy Chief, Assistant U.S. Attorney **Glenn D. Baker** . . . (404) 581-6000
E-mail: glenn.baker@usdoj.gov
Deputy Chief, Assistant U.S. Attorney
Steven D. Grimberg . . . . (404) 581-6000
E-mail: steven.grimberg@usdoj.gov
Deputy Chief, Assistant U.S. Attorney
Stephen H. McClain . . . . (404) 581-6000
E-mail: stephen.mcclain@usdoj.gov
Deputy Chief, Assistant U.S. Attorney **(Vacant)** . . . . (404) 581-6000
Assistant U.S. Attorney **Lynsey Barron** . . . . (404) 581-6000
E-mail: lynsey.barron@usdoj.gov
Assistant U.S. Attorney **Alana R. Black** . . . . (404) 581-6000
E-mail: alana.black@usdoj.gov
Assistant U.S. Attorney **Christopher C. Bly** . . . . (404) 581-6000
E-mail: chris.bly@usdoj.gov
Education: Emory 2002 JD
Assistant U.S. Attorney **Jeffery A. Brown** . . . . (404) 581-6000
E-mail: jeff.a.brown@usdoj.gov
Assistant U.S. Attorney **David M. Chaiken** . . . . (404) 581-6000
E-mail: david.chaiken@usdoj.gov
Assistant U.S. Attorney **Shanya J. Dingle** . . . . (404) 581-6000
E-mail: shanya.dingle@usdoj.gov
Assistant U.S. Attorney **Kamal Ghali** . . . . (404) 581-6000
E-mail: kamal.ghali@usdoj.gov
Education: Michigan 2006 JD
Assistant U.S. Attorney **Douglas W. Gilfillan** . . . . (404) 581-6000
E-mail: doug.gilfillan@usdoj.gov
Assistant U.S. Attorney **Nekia Shantel Hackworth** . . . . (404) 581-6000
E-mail: nekia.hackworth@usdoj.gov
Education: Harvard 2004 MBA, 2004 JD
Assistant U.S. Attorney **Teresa D. Hoyt** . . . . (404) 581-6000
E-mail: teresa.hoyt@usdoj.gov
Assistant U.S. Attorney **Christopher J. Huber** . . . . (404) 581-6000
E-mail: chris.huber@usdoj.gov
Assistant U.S. Attorney **Samir Kaushal** . . . . (404) 581-6000
E-mail: samir.kaushal@usdoj.gov
Assistant U.S. Attorney **Nathan Kitchens** . . . . (404) 581-6000
E-mail: nathan.kitchens@usdoj.gov
Education: Princeton 2002 AB; Harvard 2006 JD

Economic Crime Section *continued*

Assistant U.S. Attorney **Bernita B. Malloy** . . . . (404) 581-6000
E-mail: bernita.malloy@usdoj.gov
Assistant U.S. Attorney **Jamie L. Mickelson** . . . . (404) 581-6000
E-mail: jamie.l.mickelson@usdoj.gov
Assistant U.S. Attorney **Sally B. Molloy** . . . . (404) 581-6000
E-mail: sally.molloy@usdoj.gov
Assistant U.S. Attorney **John Russell Phillips** . . . . (404) 581-6000
E-mail: russell.phillips@usdoj.gov
Assistant U.S. Attorney **(Vacant)** . . . . (404) 581-6000
Special Assistant U.S. Attorney **Diane Schulman** . . . . (404) 581-6000
E-mail: diane.schulman@usdoj.gov

Intake Section
Chief, Assistant U.S. Attorney **Mary Jane Stewart** . . . . (404) 581-6000
E-mail: mary.jane.stewart@usdoj.gov
Assistant U.S. Attorney **Mary C. Roemer** . . . . (404) 581-6000
E-mail: mary.roemer@usdoj.gov
Assistant U.S. Attorney **Trevor Wilmot** . . . . (404) 581-6000
E-mail: trevor.wilmot@usdoj.gov

Narcotics and Organized Crime Drug Enforcement Task Force (OCDETF) Section
Chief, Assistant U.S. Attorney
Elizabeth M. Hathaway . . . . (404) 581-6000
E-mail: elizabeth.hathaway@usdoj.gov
Deputy Chief, Assistant U.S. Attorney
Michael V. Herskowitz . . . . (404) 581-6000
E-mail: michael.herskowitz@usdoj.gov
Deputy Chief, Assistant U.S. Attorney **Lisa W. Tarvin** . . . . (404) 581-6000
E-mail: lisa.tarvin@usdoj.gov
Deputy Chief, Assistant U.S. Attorney **(Vacant)** . . . . (404) 581-6000
Assistant U.S. Attorney **Laurel R. Boatright** . . . . (404) 581-6000
E-mail: laurel.boatright@usdoj.gov
Assistant U.S. Attorney **Garrett Bradford** . . . . (404) 581-6000
E-mail: garrett.bradford@usdoj.gov
Assistant U.S. Attorney **Brock Brockington** . . . . (404) 581-6000
Assistant U.S. Attorney **Ryan Christian** . . . . (404) 581-6000
Assistant U.S. Attorney **Dashene Cooper** . . . . (404) 581-6000
Assistant U.S. Attorney **Nicholas Hartigan** . . . . (404) 581-6000
E-mail: nicholas.hartigan@usdoj.gov
Assistant U.S. Attorney **Tasheika Hinson** . . . . (404) 581-6000
Assistant U.S. Attorney **Vivek Kothari** . . . . (404) 581-6000
E-mail: vivek.kothari@usdoj.gov
Assistant U.S. Attorney **Cassandra J. Schansman** . . . . (404) 581-6000
E-mail: cassandra.schansman@usdoj.gov
Assistant U.S. Attorney **Sandra E. Strippoli** . . . . (404) 581-6000
E-mail: sand.strippoli@usdoj.gov
Assistant U.S. Attorney **Bret R. Williams** . . . . (404) 581-6000
E-mail: bret.williams@usdoj.gov
Assistant U.S. Attorney **(Vacant)** . . . . (404) 581-6000
OCDETF Coordinator/ Assistant U.S. Attorney
Michael F. Smith . . . . (404) 581-6000
E-mail: michael.f.smith@usdoj.gov
Special Assistant U.S. Attorney **DeLana Jones** . . . . (404) 581-6000
E-mail: delana.jones@usdoj.gov
Special Assistant U.S. Attorney **Katie Terry** . . . . (404) 581-6000
E-mail: katie.terry@usdoj.gov
Special Assistant U.S. Attorney **Jennifer Whitfield** . . . . (404) 581-6000
E-mail: jennifer.whitfield2@usdoj.gov

Major Crime Section
Chief, Assistant U.S. Attorney **Yonette M. Buchanan** . . . . (404) 581-6000
E-mail: yonette.buchanan@usdoj.gov
Deputy Chief, Assistant U.S. Attorney
Kim S. Dammers . . . . (404) 581-6000
E-mail: kim.dammers@usdoj.gov
Deputy Chief, Assistant U.S. Attorney
Katherine M. Hoffer . . . . (404) 581-6000
E-mail: katherine.hoffer@usdoj.gov

(continued on next page)

★ Presidential Appointment Requiring Senate Confirmation ☆ Presidential Appointment ☐ Schedule C Appointment ◇ Career Senior Foreign Service Appointment
● Career Senior Executive Service (SES) Appointment ○ Non-Career Senior Executive Service (SES) Appointment ■ Postal Career Executive Service

Major Crime Section *continued*

Deputy Chief, Assistant U.S. Attorney **Richard S. Moultrie, Jr.** .... (404) 581-6000
E-mail: richard.moultrie@usdoj.gov

Assistant U.S. Attorney **Ryan K. Buchanan** .... (404) 581-6000
E-mail: ryan.buchanan@usdoj.gov
Education: Samford 2001 BS; Vanderbilt 2005 JD

Assistant U.S. Attorney **Matthew Carrico** .... (404) 581-6000
E-mail: matthew.carrico@usdoj.gov

Assistant U.S. Attorney **Phyllis Clerk** .... (404) 581-6000
E-mail: phyllis.clerk@usdoj.gov

Assistant U.S. Attorney **L. Skye Davis** .... (404) 581-6000
E-mail: skye.davis@usdoj.gov

Assistant U.S. Attorney **Stephanie Gabay-Smith** .... (404) 581-6000
E-mail: stephanie.smith@usdoj.gov

Assistant U.S. Attorney **John Ghose** .... (404) 581-6000
E-mail: john.ghose@usdoj.gov

Assistant U.S. Attorney **Brent A. Gray** .... (404) 581-6000
E-mail: brent.gray@usdoj.gov

Assistant U.S. Attorney **Paul R. Jones** .... (404) 581-6000
E-mail: paul.jones@usdoj.gov

Assistant U.S. Attorney **Jennifer Keen** .... (404) 581-6000
E-mail: jennifer.keen@usdoj.gov

Assistant U.S. Attorney **Tricia M. King** .... (404) 581-6000
E-mail: tricia.king@usdoj.gov

Assistant U.S. Attorney **Jessica Morris** .... (404) 581-6000
E-mail: jessica.morris3@usdoj.gov
Education: Dartmouth 2001 BA; Georgia 2007 JD

Assistant U.S. Attorney **Angela M. Munson** .... (404) 581-6000
E-mail: angela.garland@usdoj.gov

Assistant U.S. Attorney **Joseph A. Plummer** .... (404) 581-6000
E-mail: joe.plummer@usdoj.gov

Assistant U.S. Attorney **Jolee Porter** .... (404) 581-6000
E-mail: jolee.porter@usdoj.gov

Assistant U.S. Attorney **Suzette A. Smikle** .... (404) 581-6000
E-mail: suzette.smikle@usdoj.gov

Assistant U.S. Attorney **William G. Traynor** .... (404) 581-6000
E-mail: will.traynor@usdoj.gov

Assistant U.S. Attorney **Mary Webb** .... (404) 581-6000
E-mail: mary.webb@usdoj.gov

Assistant U.S. Attorney **(Vacant)** .... (404) 581-6000

Georgia - Southern District

22 Barnard Street, Suite 300, Savannah, GA 31401
P.O. Box 8970, Savannah, GA 31412
Tel: (912) 652-4422 Fax: (912) 652-4388
Internet: www.usdoj.gov/usao/gas

★ U.S. Attorney **Edward J. Tarver** .... (912) 652-4422
E-mail: edward.tarver@usdoj.gov
Education: Augusta State 1981 BA; Georgia 1991 JD
Secretary to the U.S. Attorney **Katherine "Katie" Guardino** .... (912) 652-4422
E-mail: katherine.guardino@usdoj.gov

First Assistant U.S. Attorney **James Denton Durham** ... (912) 652-4422
E-mail: james.durham@usdoj.gov

Administrative Officer **Marian M. Nelson** .... (912) 652-4422
E-mail: marian.nelson@usdoj.gov

Victim-Witness Specialist **Iverna Campbell** .... (912) 652-4422
E-mail: iverna.campbell@usdoj.gov

Victim-Witness Specialist **Debra Jones** .... (912) 652-4422
E-mail: debra.jones@usdoj.gov

Law Enforcement Committee Coordinator **Dan Drake** .... (912) 652-4422
E-mail: dan.drake@justice.usdoj.gov

Supervisory Computer Specialist **Sherrie N. Page** .... (912) 652-4422
E-mail: sherri.page@usdoj.gov

Appellate Division

Chief **R. Brian Tanner** .... (912) 652-4422
E-mail: brian.tanner@justice.usdoj.gov
Education: Georgia Tech 1998 BS; Emory 2001 JD

Appellate Division *continued*

Assistant U.S. Attorney **James C. Stuchell** .... (912) 652-4422
E-mail: james.stuchell@justice.usdoj.gov

Civil Division

Chief **Edgar D. Bueno** .... (706) 826-4522
E-mail: edgar.bueno@usdoj.gov

Deputy Chief **Shannon Statkus** .... (912) 652-4520
E-mail: shannon.statkus@usdoj.gov

Assistant U.S. Attorney **Kindra Baer** .... (912) 652-4422
E-mail: kindra.baer@usdoj.gov

Assistant U.S. Attorney **Thomas "Tommy" Clarkson** .... (912) 652-4422
E-mail: thomas.clarkson@usdoj.gov

Assistant U.S. Attorney **Sanjay S. Karnik** .... (912) 652-4422
E-mail: sanjay.karnik@usdoj.gov

Assistant U.S. Attorney **Charles Mulaney** .... (912) 652-4422
E-mail: charles.mulaney@usdoj.gov

Assistant U.S. Attorney **Melissa S. Mundell** .... (912) 652-4422
E-mail: melissa.mundell@usdoj.gov

Criminal Division

Chief **Brian T. Rafferty** .... (912) 652-4422
E-mail: brian.rafferty@usdoj.gov

Deputy Chief **Karl I. Knoche** .... (912) 652-4422
E-mail: karl.knoche@usdoj.gov

Counter Terrorism Assistant U.S. Attorney **Charlie Bourne** .... (912) 201-2526
E-mail: charlie.bourne@justice.usdoj.gov

Assistant U.S. Attorney **Jeffrey J. Buerstatte** .... (912) 652-4422
E-mail: jeffrey.buerstatte@justice.usdoj.gov

Assistant U.S. Attorney **Greg Gilluly** .... (912) 652-4422
E-mail: greg.gilluly@usdoj.gov

Assistant U.S. Attorney **Tania Groover** .... (912) 653-4422
E-mail: tania.groover@usdoj.gov

Assistant U.S. Attorney **T. Shane Mayes** .... (912) 652-4422
E-mail: shane.mayes@justice.usdoj.gov
Education: Georgia Southern 1999 BBA; Wake Forest 2002 JD

Assistant U.S. Attorney **Scarlett Nokes** .... (912) 652-4422
E-mail: scarlett.nokes@usdoj.gov

Senior Litigation Counsel **Frederick W. Kramer III** ...... (912) 652-4422
E-mail: frederick.kramer@justice.usdoj.gov

Senior Litigation Counsel **Joseph D. Newman** .... (912) 652-4422
E-mail: joseph.newman@usdoj.gov

Augusta (GA) Office

600 James Brown Boulevard, Suite 200, Augusta, GA 30901
Tel: (706) 724-0517 Fax: (706) 724-7728

Branch Chief **Shannon Statkus** .... (706) 826-4520
E-mail: shannon.statkus@usdoj.gov

Criminal Division Deputy Chief and Assistant U.S. Attorney **Nancy C. Greenwood** .... (706) 724-0517
E-mail: nancy.greenwood@usdoj.gov

Civil Division Assistant U.S. Attorney **Daniel Crumby** ... (706) 826-4520
E-mail: daniel.crumby@usdoj.gov

Civil Division Assistant U.S. Attorney **Shannon Statkus** .... (706) 724-0517
E-mail: shannon.statkus@usdoj.gov

Criminal Division Assistant U.S. Attorney **Lamont A. Belk** .... (706) 724-0517
E-mail: lamont.belk@usdoj.gov

Criminal Division Assistant U.S. Attorney **Troy Clark** .... (706) 724-0517
E-mail: troy.clark@justice.usdoj.gov

Criminal Division Assistant U.S. Attorney **Patricia Green Rhodes** .... (706) 724-0517
E-mail: patricia.rhodes@usdoj.gov

Criminal Division Assistant U.S. Attorney **David Mitchell Stewart** .... (706) 724-0517
E-mail: david.stewart@justice.usdoj.gov

★ Presidential Appointment Requiring Senate Confirmation ☆ Presidential Appointment ☐ Schedule C Appointment ◇ Career Senior Foreign Service Appointment
● Career Senior Executive Service (SES) Appointment ○ Non-Career Senior Executive Service (SES) Appointment ■ Postal Career Executive Service

Guam District - Northern Marianas District
108 Hernan Cortez, Suite 500, Agana, GU 96910
Tel: (671) 472-7332 Fax: (671) 472-7334

★ U.S. Attorney **Alicia Garrido Limtiaco** . . . . (671) 472-7332
E-mail: alicia.limtiaco@usdoj.gov
Education: USC 1985 BBA; UCLA 1990 JD
Secretary **Carmelleta San Nicolas** . . . . (671) 472-7332 ext. 142
E-mail: carmelleta.sannicolas@usdoj.gov
Law Enforcement Committee/Victim-Witness Coordinator **Salome Blas** . . . . (671) 472-7332 ext. 144
E-mail: salome.blas@usdoj.gov
Administrative Officer **Ed Talato** . . . . (671) 472-7332 ext. 106
E-mail: ed.talato@usdoj.gov

Civil Division
Tel: (671) 472-7332 ext. 121 Fax: (671) 472-7215

Chief **Mikel Schwab** . . . . (671) 472-7332 ext. 107
E-mail: mikel.schwab@usdoj.gov
Assistant U.S. Attorney **Jessica F. Cruz** . . . . (671) 472-7332 ext. 139
E-mail: jessica.f.cruz@usdoj.gov

Criminal Division
Fax: (671) 472-7334 Fax: (671) 472-7229

First Assistant U.S. Attorney **(Vacant)** . . . . (671) 472-7332 ext. 116
Assistant U.S. Attorney **Belinda C. Alcantara** . . . (671) 472-7332 ext. 143
E-mail: belinda.alcantara@usdoj.gov
Assistant U.S. Attorney **Frederick A. Black** . . . . . (671) 472-7332 ext. 141
E-mail: frederick.black@usdoj.gov
Assistant U.S. Attorney **Marivic P. David** . . . . (671) 472-7332 ext. 120
E-mail: marivic.david@usdoj.gov
Assistant U.S. Attorney **Rosetta San Nicolas** . . . (671) 472-7332 ext. 115
E-mail: rosetta.sannicolas@usdoj.gov
Asset Forfeiture Unit Assistant U.S. Attorney **(Vacant)** . . . . (671) 472-7332 ext. 146

Commonwealth of the Northern Mariana Islands Office
Horiguchi Building, 3rd Floor, Saipan, MP 96950
P.O. Box 500377, Saipan, MP 96950-0377
Tel: (670) 236-2980 Fax: (670) 236-2945

Assistant U.S. Attorney **Rami Badawy** . . . . (670) 236-2986
E-mail: rami.badawy@usdoj.gov
Assistant U.S. Attorney **Ross Naughton** . . . . (670) 236-2987
E-mail: ross.naughton@usdoj.gov
Education: UCLA 2007 JD
Assistant U.S. Attorney **(Vacant)** . . . . (670) 236-2986
Legal Assistant **Marylynn Yamada-Sablan** . . . . (670) 236-2978
E-mail: marylynn.yamada-sablan@usdoj.gov

Hawaii District
300 Ala Moana Boulevard, Room 6-100, Honolulu, HI 96850
Tel: (808) 541-2850 Fax: (808) 541-2958
Internet: www.usdoj.gov/usao/hi

★ U.S. Attorney **Florence T. Nakakuni** . . . . (808) 541-2850
E-mail: florence.nakakuni@usdoj.gov
Education: Hawaii 1975 BA, 1975 BEd, 1978 JD
Secretary to the U.S. Attorney **Cheri Abing** . . . . (808) 541-2850
E-mail: cheri.abing@justice.usdoj.gov
First Assistant U.S. Attorney **Elliot Enoki** . . . . (808) 541-2850
E-mail: elliot.enoki@usdoj.gov
Administrative Officer **Lian Abernathy** . . . . (808) 541-2850
E-mail: lian.abernathy@usdoj.gov
Law Enforcement Coordinator **Wesley J. Wong** . . . . (808) 541-2850
E-mail: wesley.wong@usdoj.gov
Education: UC Berkeley BA; UC Davis JD; NYU LLM
Systems Manager **Randal Wong** . . . . (808) 541-2850
E-mail: randal.wong@usdoj.gov

Civil Division
Chief **Tom Helper** . . . . (808) 541-2850
E-mail: tom.helper@usdoj.gov
Assistant U.S. Attorney **Michael Albanese** . . . . (808) 541-2850
E-mail: michael.albanese@usdoj.gov
Assistant U.S. Attorney **Edric Ching** . . . . (808) 541-2850
E-mail: edric.ching@usdoj.gov
Assistant U.S. Attorney **Rachel Moriyama** . . . . (808) 541-2850
E-mail: rachel.moriyama@usdoj.gov
Assistant U.S. Attorney **Harry Yee** . . . . (808) 541-2850
E-mail: harry.yee@usdoj.gov

Criminal Division
Chief **Thomas J. "Tom" Brady** . . . . (808) 541-2850
E-mail: tom.brady@usdoj.gov
Assistant U.S. Attorney **Larry Butrick** . . . . (808) 541-2850
E-mail: larry.butrick@usdoj.gov
Assistant U.S. Attorney **Darren Ching** . . . . (808) 541-2850
E-mail: darren.ching@usdoj.gov
Assistant U.S. Attorney **Tracy Hino** . . . . (808) 541-2850
E-mail: tracy.hino@usdoj.gov
Assistant U.S. Attorney **Mark A. Inciong** . . . . (808) 541-2850
E-mail: mark.inciong@usdoj.gov
Assistant U.S. Attorney **Ronald G. Johnson** . . . . (808) 541-2850
E-mail: ron.johnson@usdoj.gov
Assistant U.S. Attorney **Cynthia Lie** . . . . (808) 541-2850
E-mail: clie@usa.doj.gov
Assistant U.S. Attorney **Jonathan Loo** . . . . (808) 541-2850
E-mail: jonathan.loo@usdoj.gov
Assistant U.S. Attorney **Tom Muehleck** . . . . (808) 541-2850
E-mail: tom.muehleck@usdoj.gov
Assistant U.S. Attorney **Jill Otake** . . . . (808) 541-2850
E-mail: jill.otake2@usdoj.gov
Assistant U.S. Attorney **Tony R. Roberts** . . . . (808) 541-2850
E-mail: troberts@usa.doj.gov
Assistant U.S. Attorney **Marshall Silverberg** . . . . (808) 541-2850
E-mail: marshall.silverberg@usdoj.gov
Assistant U.S. Attorney **Ken Sorenson** . . . . (808) 541-2850
E-mail: ken.sorenson@usdoj.gov
Assistant U.S. Attorney **Chris Thomas** . . . . (808) 541-2850
E-mail: chris.thomas@usdoj.gov
Assistant U.S. Attorney **Larry Tong** . . . . (808) 541-2850
E-mail: larry.tong@usdoj.gov
Assistant U.S. Attorney **Marc Wallenstein** . . . . (808) 541-2850
E-mail: marc.wallenstein@usdoj.gov
Education: Harvard 2002 AB; Yale 2006 JD
Assistant U.S. Attorney **(Vacant)** . . . . (808) 541-2850
Drug and Organized Crime Section Chief **Beverly Sameshima** . . . . (808) 541-2850
E-mail: beverly.sameshima@usdoj.gov
Fraud and Financial Crime Section Chief **(Vacant)** . . . . (808) 541-2850
Special Crime Section Chief **Thomas J. "Tom" Brady** . . . (808) 541-2850
E-mail: tom.brady@usdoj.gov

Idaho District
Washington Group Plaza IV, 800 E. Park Boulevard, Suite 600, Boise, ID 83712-7788
Tel: (208) 334-1211 Fax: (208) 334-9375
Internet: www.usdoj.gov/usao/id

★ U.S. Attorney **Wendy J. Olson** . . . . (208) 334-1211 (Boise)
E-mail: wendy.olson@usdoj.gov
Education: Drake 1986; Stanford 1990 JD
First Assistant U.S. Attorney **Rafael M. Gonzalez, Jr.** . . . . (208) 334-1211
E-mail: rafael.gonzalez@usdoj.gov Fax: (208) 334-1038
Secretary to the U.S. Attorney **Becky Early** . . . . (208) 334-1211
E-mail: becky.early@usdoj.gov
Administrative Officer **Lynn M. Clifford** . . . . (208) 334-1211
E-mail: lynn.clifford@justice.usdoj.gov Fax: (208) 334-9375
Law Enforcement Committee Coordinator **Tim Hawkins** . . . . (208) 334-1211
E-mail: tim.hawkins@usdoj.gov Fax: (208) 334-1413

(continued on next page)

REGIONAL OFFICES — US ATTORNEYS AND US MARSHALS SERVICE

★ Presidential Appointment Requiring Senate Confirmation ☆ Presidential Appointment □ Schedule C Appointment ◇ Career Senior Foreign Service Appointment
● Career Senior Executive Service (SES) Appointment ○ Non-Career Senior Executive Service (SES) Appointment ■ Postal Career Executive Service

Idaho District *continued*

Victim-Witness Coordinator **Kristi Johnson** .... (208) 334-1211
E-mail: kristi.johnson@usdoj.gov Fax: (208) 334-1038
Asset Forfeiture Unit Assistant U.S. Attorney
Anthony G. Hall .... (208) 334-1211
E-mail: anthony.hall@usdoj.gov
ALS/Assistant Systems Manager
Pamela J. "Pam" Rocca .... (208) 334-1211
E-mail: pam.rocca2@usdoj.gov
Public Information Officer **Becky Early** .... (208) 334-1211
Systems Manager **Laurie Porter** .... (208) 334-1211
E-mail: laurie.porter@usdoj.gov
IT Specialist **Joel Hawker** .... (208) 334-1211
E-mail: joel.hawker@usdoj.gov Fax: (208) 334-9375

Civil Division
Fax: (208) 334-1414

Chief **Syrena Case Hargrove** .... (208) 334-1211
E-mail: syrena.hargrove@usdoj.gov
Education: Harvard 1997 JD
Senior Litigation Counsel
Nicholas J. "Nick" Woychick .... (208) 334-1211
E-mail: nick.woychick@usdoj.gov
Assistant U.S. Attorney **Christine England** .... (208) 334-1211
E-mail: christine.england@usdoj.gov
Assistant U.S. Attorney **Jessica Gunder** .... (208) 334-1211
E-mail: jessica.gunder@usdoj.gov
Education: Missouri 2007 JD
Assistant U.S. Attorney **William Humphries** .... (208) 334-1211
Assistant U.S. Attorney **Joanne P. Rodriguez** .... (208) 334-1211
E-mail: joanne.rodriguez@usdoj.gov

Criminal Division
Fax: (208) 334-1413

Chief **Aaron N. Lucoff** .... (208) 334-1211
E-mail: aaron.lucoff@usdoj.gov
Assistant U.S. Attorney **Anthony G. Hall** .... (208) 334-1211
E-mail: anthony.hall@usdoj.gov
Assistant U.S. Attorney **D. Marc Haws** .... (208) 334-1211
E-mail: marc.haws@usdoj.gov
Assistant U.S. Attorney **Joshua D. Hurwit** .... (208) 334-1211
E-mail: joshua.hurwit@usdoj.gov
Education: Stanford 2002 BA; Harvard 2006 JD
Assistant U.S. Attorney **Kevin T. Maloney** .... (208) 334-1211
E-mail: kevin.maloney@usdoj.gov
Assistant U.S. Attorney **Christian S. Nafzger** .... (208) 334-1211
E-mail: christian.nafzger@usdoj.gov
Assistant U.S. Attorney **Heather S. Patricco** .... (208) 334-1211
E-mail: heather.patricco@usdoj.gov
Assistant U.S. Attorney **Raymond E. Patricco, Jr.** .... (208) 334-1211
E-mail: raymond.patricco@usdoj.gov
Assistant U.S. Attorney **Justin D. Whatcott** .... (208) 334-1211
E-mail: justin.whatcott@usdoj.gov
Assistant U.S. Attorney **(Vacant)** .... (208) 334-1211
Assistant U.S. Attorney **(Vacant)** .... (208) 334-1211

Coeur d'Alene (ID) Office
6450 North Mineral Drive, Suite 210, Coeur d'Alene, ID 83815
Tel: (208) 667-6568 Fax: (208) 667-0814

Branch Manager **Traci J. Whelan** .... (208) 667-6568
E-mail: traci.whelan@usdoj.gov
Assistant U.S. Attorney **Nancy D. Cook** .... (208) 667-6568
E-mail: nancy.cook@usdoj.gov
Assistant U.S. Attorney **Peggy Johnson** .... (208) 667-6568
E-mail: peggy.johnson@usdoj.gov
Assistant U.S. Attorney **Michael W. "Mike" Mitchell** .... (208) 667-6568
E-mail: mike.mitchell@usdoj.gov

Pocatello (ID) Office
801 East Sherman, Room 192, Pocatello, ID 83201
Tel: (208) 478-4166 Fax: (208) 478-4175

Branch Manager **Jack B. Haycock** .... (208) 478-4166
E-mail: jack.haycock@usdoj.gov
Assistant U.S. Attorney **Ann T. Wick** .... (208) 478-4166
E-mail: ann.wick@usdoj.gov
Assistant U.S. Attorney **Michael J. Fica** .... (208) 478-4166
E-mail: michael.fica@usdoj.gov

Illinois - Northern District
Dirksen Federal Building, 219 South Dearborn Street,
5th Floor, Chicago, IL 60604
Tel: (312) 353-5300 Fax: (312) 353-2067
Internet: www.usdoj.gov/usao/iln

★ U.S. Attorney **Zachary Thomas Fardon** .... (312) 353-5300
E-mail: zachary.fardon@usdoj.gov
Education: Vanderbilt 1988 BA, 1992 JD
Counsel to the U.S. Attorney **Morris O. Pasqual** .... (312) 886-7637
E-mail: morris.pasqual@usdoj.gov
Secretary to the U.S. Attorney **Karen Wheeler-Lee** .... (312) 886-1321
E-mail: karen.wheeler-lee@usdoj.gov
Public Affairs Specialist **(Vacant)** .... (312) 353-5318
First Assistant U.S. Attorney **Joel R. Levin** .... (312) 353-1980
E-mail: joel.levin@usdoj.gov
Senior Litigation Counsel **Daniel W. Gillogly** .... (312) 886-1328
E-mail: dan.gillogly@usdoj.gov
Litigation Counsel **Diane MacArthur** .... (312) 353-5352
E-mail: diane.macarthur@usdoj.gov
Litigation Counsel **April M. Perry** .... (312) 886-5966
E-mail: april.perry@usdoj.gov
Education: Northwestern 2003 JD
Executive Assistant U.S. Attorney **Margaret A. Hickey** .... (312) 886-7633
E-mail: margaret.hickey@usdoj.gov
Executive Assistant U.S. Attorney **(Vacant)** .... (312) 353-1983
Appellate Division Chief **Debra R. Bonamici** .... (312) 353-3741
E-mail: debra.bonamici@usdoj.gov
Civil Division Chief **Thomas P. Walsh** .... (312) 353-5312
E-mail: thomas.walsh2@usdoj.gov
Criminal Division Chief **Julie B. Porter** .... (312) 886-1317
E-mail: julie.porter@usdoj.gov
Criminal Division Associate Chief **(Vacant)** .... (312) 353-1980
Financial Litigation Section Chief **(Vacant)** .... (312) 353-1980
General Crimes Section Chief **Brian Hayes** .... (312) 353-4307
E-mail: brian.hayes@usdoj.gov
Financial Crimes Section Chief **Rick Young** .... (312) 886-7660
E-mail: rick.young@usdoj.gov
National Security and Cybercrimes Section Chief
Christopher K. Veatch .... (312) 886-3389
E-mail: christopher.veatch@usdoj.gov
Narcotics Section Chief **Christopher P. Hotaling** .... (312) 353-5324
E-mail: christopher.hotaling@usdoj.gov
Education: Duke BA; Virginia 2000 JD
Organized Crime Section Chief **Marsha A. McClellan** .... (312) 353-2814
E-mail: marsha.mcclellan@usdoj.gov
Securities and Commodities Fraud Section Chief
Jason Yonan .... (312) 353-0708
E-mail: jason.yonan@usdoj.gov
Education: Illinois State 1997 BS; Illinois 2002 JD
Public Corruption Section Chief **Laurie J. Barsella** .... (312) 353-5300
E-mail: laurie.barsella@usdoj.gov
Violent Crimes Section Chief **Ronald L. DeWald, Jr.** .... (312) 886-4187
E-mail: ronald.dewald@usdoj.gov
Special Assistant U.S. Attorney **Jonathan Baum** .... (312) 353-5349
E-mail: jonathan.baum@usdoj.gov
Special Assistant U.S. Attorney **Catherine Dick** .... (312) 886-3482
E-mail: catherine.dick@usdoj.gov
Education: Harvard 2005 JD
Special Assistant U.S. Attorney **Brooke Harper** .... (312) 697-4087
E-mail: brooke.harper@usdoj.gov

★ Presidential Appointment Requiring Senate Confirmation ☆ Presidential Appointment ☐ Schedule C Appointment ◇ Career Senior Foreign Service Appointment
● Career Senior Executive Service (SES) Appointment ○ Non-Career Senior Executive Service (SES) Appointment ■ Postal Career Executive Service

Illinois - Northern District *continued*

Special Assistant U.S. Attorney **Jared Jodrey** .... (312) 353-5358
E-mail: jared.jodrey@usdoj.gov
Special Assistant U.S. Attorney **Heidi Manschreck** ...... (312) 469-6052
E-mail: heidi.manschreck@usdoj.gov
Special Assistant U.S. Attorney **William P. Novak** .... (312) 697-4073
E-mail: william.novak@usdoj.gov
Special Assistant U.S. Attorney **(Vacant)** .... (312) 353-5361
Assistant U.S. Attorney **Georgia Alexakis** .... (312) 353-8897
E-mail: georgia.alexakis@usdoj.gov
Education: Harvard 2000 AB; Northwestern 2006 JD
Assistant U.S. Attorney **Carol A. Bell** .... (312) 353-8898
E-mail: carol.bell@usdoj.gov
Assistant U.S. Attorney **Yasmin N. Best** .... (312) 469-6024
E-mail: yasmin.best@usdoj.gov
Assistant U.S. Attorney **Amarjeet Bhachu** .... (312) 469-6212
E-mail: amarjeet.bhachu@usdoj.gov
Assistant U.S. Attorney **Bethany K. Biesenthal** .... (312) 886-7629
E-mail: bethany.biesenthal@usdoj.gov
Assistant U.S. Attorney **David E. Bindi** .... (312) 886-7643
E-mail: david.bindi@usdoj.gov
Assistant U.S. Attorney **Steven A. Block** .... (312) 886-7647
E-mail: steven.block@usdoj.gov
Assistant U.S. Attorney **Debra R. Bonamici** .... (312) 353-3741
E-mail: debra.bonamici@usdoj.gov
Assistant U.S. Attorney **Gina E. Brock** .... (312) 353-7919
E-mail: gina.brock@usdoj.gov
Assistant U.S. Attorney **Rachel M. Cannon** .... (312) 353-5357
E-mail: rachel.cannon@justice.usdoj.gov
Assistant U.S. Attorney **Harpreet Chahal** .... (312) 353-1996
E-mail: harpreet.chahal@usdoj.gov
Assistant U.S. Attorney **Timothy J. Chapman** .... (312) 353-1925
E-mail: timothy.chapman@usdoj.gov
Assistant U.S. Attorney **Megan Cuniff Church** .... (312) 886-1173
E-mail: megan.church@usdoj.gov
Education: Georgetown 1999 BA; Northwestern 2003 JD
Assistant U.S. Attorney **Samuel B. Cole** .... (312) 353-4258
E-mail: samuel.cole@usdoj.gov
Assistant U.S. Attorney **John D. Cooke** .... (312) 353-8788
E-mail: john.cooke@usdoj.gov
Assistant U.S. Attorney **Erika L. Csicsila** .... (312) 353-5370
E-mail: erika.csicsila@usdoj.gov
Assistant U.S. Attorney **Yusef Dale** .... (312) 886-7645
E-mail: yusef.dale@usdoj.gov
Assistant U.S. Attorney **Jeremy Daniel** .... (312) 469-6314
E-mail: jeremy.daniel@usdoj.gov
Assistant U.S. Attorney **Steven Dollear** .... (312) 353-5359
E-mail: steven.dollear@usdoj.gov
Education: Loyola U (Chicago) 2002 JD
Assistant U.S. Attorney **Sean Driscoll** .... (312) 469-6151
E-mail: sean.driscoll@usdoj.gov
Assistant U.S. Attorney **Matthew S. Ebert** .... (312) 353-5354
E-mail: matthew.ebert@usdoj.gov
Assistant U.S. Attorney **Scott M. Edenfield** .... (312) 353-5277
E-mail: scott.edenfield@usdoj.gov
Assistant U.S. Attorney **Ryan Fayhee** .... (312) 353-1998
E-mail: ryan.fayhee@usdoj.gov
Assistant U.S. Attorney **Maribel Fernandez** .... (312) 353-4129
E-mail: maribel.fernandez-harvath@usdoj.gov
Assistant U.S. Attorney **Michael Ferrara** .... (312) 886-7649
E-mail: michael.ferrara@usdoj.gov
Education: Boston Col 1998 BA; Stanford 2003 JD
Assistant U.S. Attorney **Peter M. Flanagan** .... (312) 469-6235
E-mail: peter.flanagan@usdoj.gov
Assistant U.S. Attorney **Philip Fluhr, Jr.** .... (312) 697-4050
E-mail: philip.fluhr@usdoj.gov
Assistant U.S. Attorney **Sean J.B. Franzblau** .... (312) 371-4171
E-mail: sean.franzblau@usdoj.gov
Assistant U.S. Attorney **Naana A. Frimpong** .... (312) 353-3540
E-mail: naana.frimpong@usdoj.gov
Assistant U.S. Attorney **Stuart D. Fullerton** .... (312) 353-5266
E-mail: stuart.fullerton@usdoj.gov

Illinois - Northern District *continued*

Assistant U.S. Attorney **Matthew M. Getter** .... (312) 886-7651
E-mail: matthew.getter@usdoj.gov
Assistant U.S. Attorney **Kelly M. Greening** .... (312) 371-3191
E-mail: kelly.greening@usdoj.gov
Assistant U.S. Attorney **Helene B. Greenwald** .... (312) 469-6296
E-mail: helene.greenwald@usdoj.gov
Assistant U.S. Attorney **Kelly Guzman** .... (815) 353-1598
E-mail: kelly.guzman@usdoj.gov
Assistant U.S. Attorney **Jonathan C. Haile** .... (312) 886-2055
E-mail: jonathan.haile@usdoj.gov
Assistant U.S. Attorney **Joel M. Hammerman** .... (312) 353-8881
E-mail: joel.hammerman@usdoj.gov
Assistant U.S. Attorney **Jeffrey M. Hansen** .... (312) 886-1325
E-mail: jeffrey.hansen@usdoj.gov
Assistant U.S. Attorney **Sunil R. Harjani** .... (312) 353-9353
E-mail: sunil.harjani@usdoj.gov
Education: Northwestern 2000 JD
Assistant U.S. Attorney **Brian R. Havey** .... (312) 353-1857
E-mail: brian.havey@usdoj.gov
Assistant U.S. Attorney **Bolling Haxall** .... (312) 353-8728
E-mail: bolling.haxall@usdoj.gov
Assistant U.S. Attorney **Ryan S. Hedges** .... (312) 353-5340
E-mail: ryan.hedges@usdoj.gov
Assistant U.S. Attorney **Stephen L. Heinze** .... (312) 886-1265
E-mail: stephen.heinze@usdoj.gov
Assistant U.S. Attorney **Matthew Hernandez** .... (312) 353-4317
E-mail: matthew.hernandez@usdoj.gov
Assistant U.S. Attorney **Matthew Hiller** .... (312) 697-4088
E-mail: matthew.hiller@justice.usdoj.gov
Assistant U.S. Attorney **William R. Hogan, Jr.** .... (312) 886-4185
E-mail: william.hogan@usdoj.gov
Assistant U.S. Attorney **Erik A. Hogstrom** .... (312) 353-8709
E-mail: erik.hogstrom@usdoj.gov
Education: Michigan 2004 JD
Assistant U.S. Attorney **Christopher P. Hotaling** .... (312) 353-5324
E-mail: christopher.hotaling@usdoj.gov
Education: Duke BA; Virginia 2000 JD
Assistant U.S. Attorney **Nathalina A. Hudson** .... (312) 353-1123
E-mail: nathalina.hudson@usdoj.gov
Education: Duke 2001 JD
Assistant U.S. Attorney **Lindsay Jenkins** .... (312) 353-0962
E-mail: lindsay.jenkins@usdoj.gov
Assistant U.S. Attorney **Lela D. Johnson** .... (312) 353-4320
E-mail: lela.johnson@usdoj.gov
Assistant U.S. Attorney **Patrick W. Johnson** .... (312) 353-5327
E-mail: patrick.johnson@usdoj.gov
Assistant U.S. Attorney **Barry Jonas** .... (312) 886-8027
E-mail: barry.jonas@usdoj.gov
Assistant U.S. Attorney **Andrianna D. Kastanek** .... (312) 886-0974
E-mail: andrianna.kastanek@usdoj.gov
Assistant U.S. Attorney **Erin Kelly** .... (312) 886-9083
E-mail: erin.kelly@usdoj.gov
Assistant U.S. Attorney **Kathryn A. Kelly** .... (312) 353-1936
E-mail: kathryn.kelly@usdoj.gov
Assistant U.S. Attorney **Michael Kelly** .... (312) 353-4220
E-mail: michael.kelly@usdoj.gov
Education: Illinois 2003 BSEE; Chicago 2006 JD
Assistant U.S. Attorney **Nicole Kim** .... (312) 886-7635
E-mail: nicole.kim@usdoj.gov
Education: Wesleyan U 1996 BA; U Washington 2000 JD
Assistant U.S. Attorney **Patrick J. King** .... (312) 353-5341
E-mail: patrick.king@usdoj.gov
Assistant U.S. Attorney **John F. Kness** .... (312) 469-6042
E-mail: john.kness@usdoj.gov
Assistant U.S. Attorney **Edward G. Kohler** .... (312) 353-4086
E-mail: edward.kohler@usdoj.gov
Assistant U.S. Attorney **Prashant Kolluri** .... (312) 886-9085
E-mail: prashant.kolluri@usdoj.gov
Assistant U.S. Attorney **Angel Krull** .... (312) 886-2954
E-mail: angel.krull@usdoj.gov

(continued on next page)

★ Presidential Appointment Requiring Senate Confirmation ☆ Presidential Appointment ☐ Schedule C Appointment ◇ Career Senior Foreign Service Appointment
● Career Senior Executive Service (SES) Appointment ○ Non-Career Senior Executive Service (SES) Appointment ■ Postal Career Executive Service

Illinois - Northern District *continued*

Assistant U.S. Attorney **James M. Kuhn** .... (312) 353-1877
E-mail: james.kuhn@usdoj.gov

Assistant U.S. Attorney **Raj P. Laud** .... (312) 469-6306
E-mail: raj.laud@justice.usdoj.gov
Education: Yale 2008 JD

Assistant U.S. Attorney **Stephen C. Lee** .... (312) 353-4127
E-mail: stephen.lee@usdoj.gov

Assistant U.S. Attorney **Jennie H. Levin** .... (312) 353-5372
E-mail: jennie.levin@usdoj.gov

Assistant U.S. Attorney **David R. Lidow** .... (312) 886-1390
E-mail: david.lidow@usdoj.gov
Education: Chicago 2003 JD

Assistant U.S. Attorney **Kurt N. Lindland** .... (312) 353-4163
E-mail: kurt.lindland@usdoj.gov

Assistant U.S. Attorney **Ernest Y. Ling** .... (312) 353-5870
E-mail: ernest.ling@usdoj.gov

Assistant U.S. Attorney **Donald Lorenzen** .... (312) 353-5330
E-mail: donald.lorenzen@usdoj.gov

Assistant U.S. Attorney **Matthew F. Madden** .... (312) 886-2050
E-mail: matthew.madden@usdoj.gov
Education: Illinois 2002 JD

Assistant U.S. Attorney **Kathryn Malizia** .... (312) 353-5319
E-mail: kathryn.malizia@usdoj.gov

Assistant U.S. Attorney **Renato Mariotti** .... (312) 886-7855
E-mail: renato.mariotti@usdoj.gov

Assistant U.S. Attorney **Daniel E. May** .... (312) 353-8694
E-mail: daniel.may@usdoj.gov

Assistant U.S. Attorney **Christopher McFadden** .... (312) 353-1931
E-mail: christopher.mcfadden@usdoj.gov

Assistant U.S. Attorney **Heather K. McShain** .... (312) 353-1414
E-mail: heather.mcshain@usdoj.gov
Education: Notre Dame 1999 JD

Assistant U.S. Attorney **Sheri H. Mecklenburg** .... (312) 469-6030
E-mail: sheri.mecklenburg@usdoj.gov

Assistant U.S. Attorney **Maureen E. Merin** .... (312) 353-1457
E-mail: maureen.merin@usdoj.gov
Education: Chicago 2004 JD

Assistant U.S. Attorney **John D. Mitchell** .... (312) 353-5159
E-mail: john.mitchell@usdoj.gov
Education: Loyola U (Chicago) 2004 JD

Assistant U.S. Attorney **Madeleine S. Murphy** .... (312) 886-2070
E-mail: madeleine.murphy@usdoj.gov

Assistant U.S. Attorney **Michelle Nasser** .... (312) 469-6201
E-mail: michelle.nasser@usdoj.gov

Assistant U.S. Attorney **Brian P. Netols** .... (312) 353-4128
E-mail: brian.netols@usdoj.gov

Assistant U.S. Attorney **Sarah North** .... (312) 353-1413
E-mail: sarah.north@usdoj.gov

Assistant U.S. Attorney **Craig A. Oswald** .... (312) 886-9080
E-mail: craig.oswald@usdoj.gov

Assistant U.S. Attorney **Patrick M. Otlewski** .... (312) 469-6045
E-mail: patrick.otlewski@usdoj.gov

Assistant U.S. Attorney **Derek R. Owens** .... (312) 697-4071
E-mail: derek.owens@usdoj.gov

Assistant U.S. Attorney **Jordan M. Palmore** .... (312) 697-4090
E-mail: jordan.palmore@usdoj.gov
Education: Pennsylvania 2009 JD

Assistant U.S. Attorney **Christopher V. Parente** .... (312) 353-2447
E-mail: christopher.parente@usa.doj.gov

Assistant U.S. Attorney **Abigail Peluso** .... (312) 353-5342
E-mail: abigail.peluso@usdoj.gov

Assistant U.S. Attorney **Michelle M. Petersen** .... (312) 886-7655
E-mail: michelle.petersen@usdoj.gov

Assistant U.S. Attorney **Shoba Pillay** .... (312) 886-7631
E-mail: shoba.pillay@usdoj.gov

Assistant U.S. Attorney **Andrew K. Polovin** .... (312) 353-5351
E-mail: andrew.polovin@usdoj.gov
Education: Colgate 1995 BA; Northwestern 2001 JD

Assistant U.S. Attorney **Elizabeth Pozolo** .... (312) 469-6131
E-mail: elizabeth.pozolo@usdoj.gov
Education: DePaul 2008 JD

Illinois - Northern District *continued*

Assistant U.S. Attorney **Eric S. Pruitt** .... (312) 353-5496
E-mail: eric.pruitt@usdoj.gov
Education: John Marshall 2001 JD

Assistant U.S. Attorney **Kartik Raman** .... (312) 469-6026
E-mail: kartik.raman@justice.usdoj.gov

Assistant U.S. Attorney **Allison Ray** .... (312) 353-6117
E-mail: allison.ray@usdoj.gov
Education: Harvard AB, 2012 JD

Assistant U.S. Attorney **Tobara Richardson** .... (312) 469-6305
E-mail: tobara.richardson@usdoj.gov

Assistant U.S. Attorney **William Ridgway** .... (312) 469-6233
E-mail: william.ridgway@usdoj.gov
Education: Stanford 2006 JD

Assistant U.S. Attorney **Renai S. Rodney** .... (312) 353-4064
E-mail: renai.rodney@usdoj.gov

Assistant U.S. Attorney **Jessica Romero** .... (312) 353-4137
E-mail: jessica.romero@justice.usdoj.gov

Assistant U.S. Attorney **Peter S. Salib** .... (312) 697-4092
E-mail: peter.salib@usdoj.gov

Assistant U.S. Attorney **Kaarina Salovaara** .... (312) 353-8880
E-mail: kaarina.salovaara@usdoj.gov

Assistant U.S. Attorney **Katherine A. Sawyer** .... (312) 697-4089
E-mail: katherine.sawyer@usdoj.gov
Education: Washington College of Law 2004 JD

Assistant U.S. Attorney **Margaret Schneider** .... (312) 353-1875
E-mail: margaret.schneider@usdoj.gov

Assistant U.S. Attorney **Matthew M. Schneider** .... (312) 886-0973
E-mail: matthew.schneider@usdoj.gov

Assistant U.S. Attorney **Douglas Snodgrass** .... (312) 886-2065
E-mail: douglas.snodgrass@usdoj.gov

Assistant U.S. Attorney **Ankur Srivastava** .... (312) 353-3148
E-mail: ankur.srivastava@usdoj.gov

Assistant U.S. Attorney **Meghan C. Stack** .... (312) 353-4045
E-mail: meghan.stack@usdoj.gov

Assistant U.S. Attorney **Jacqueline O. Stern** .... (312) 353-5329
E-mail: jacqueline.stern@usdoj.gov

Assistant U.S. Attorney **Christopher Stetler** .... (312) 353-7602
E-mail: christopher.stetler@usdoj.gov

Assistant U.S. Attorney **Joseph A. Stewart** .... (312) 469-6008
E-mail: joseph.stewart@usdoj.gov

Assistant U.S. Attorney **Timothy J. "Tim" Storino** ..... (312) 353-5347
E-mail: tim.storino@usdoj.gov
Education: Notre Dame 2002 BA, 2005 JD

Assistant U.S. Attorney **Sarah E. Streicker** .... (312) 353-1415
E-mail: sarah.streicker@usdoj.gov

Assistant U.S. Attorney **Carrie E. Sussman** .... (312) 353-4558
E-mail: carrie.hamilton@usdoj.gov

Assistant U.S. Attorney **Kruti Trivedi** .... (312) 353-5323
E-mail: kruti.trivedi@usdoj.gov

Assistant U.S. Attorney **Paul H. Tzur** .... (312) 697-4032
E-mail: paul.tzur@usdoj.gov

Assistant U.S. Attorney **Brian S. Wallach** .... (312) 886-7625
E-mail: brian.wallach@usdoj.gov
Education: Yale 2003 BA; Georgetown 2007 JD

Assistant U.S. Attorney **Linda A. Wawzenski** .... (312) 353-1994
E-mail: linda.wawzenski@usdoj.gov

Assistant U.S. Attorney **Katherine Welsh** .... (312) 469-6309
E-mail: katherine.welsh@usdoj.gov

Assistant U.S. Attorney **Elizabeth A. Wilson** .... (312) 353-5331
E-mail: elizabeth.wilson@usdoj.gov

Assistant U.S. Attorney **Kenneth E. Yeadon** .... (312) 353-5326
E-mail: kenneth.yeadon@usdoj.gov

Assistant U.S. Attorney **Rick Young** .... (312) 886-7660
E-mail: rick.young@usdoj.gov

Assistant U.S. Attorney **Kate Zell** .... (312) 353-4305
E-mail: kate.zell@usdoj.gov
Education: Taylor 1999 BS; Michigan 2007 JD

Assistant U.S. Attorney **(Vacant)** .... (312) 353-5310

Assistant U.S. Attorney **(Vacant)** .... (312) 353-7223

Assistant U.S. Attorney **(Vacant)** .... (312) 886-7641

Assistant U.S. Attorney **(Vacant)** .... (312) 886-2035

★ Presidential Appointment Requiring Senate Confirmation ☆ Presidential Appointment □ Schedule C Appointment ◇ Career Senior Foreign Service Appointment
● Career Senior Executive Service (SES) Appointment ○ Non-Career Senior Executive Service (SES) Appointment ■ Postal Career Executive Service

Administration

Administrative Officer **Paul J. Borowitz** . . . . (312) 353-5302
E-mail: paul.borowitz@usdoj.gov
Information Technology Officer **Clark Krystopher** . . . . (312) 353-8282
E-mail: clark.krystopher@usdoj.gov
Human Resources Officer **Vicky Gehrt** . . . . (312) 353-8405
E-mail: vicky.gehrt@usdoj.gov
Budget Officer **Amanda Cross** . . . . (312) 353-1124
E-mail: amanda.cross@usdoj.gov
Law Enforcement Committee Coordinator
Kim Nerheim . . . . (312) 353-5489
E-mail: kimberly.nerheim@usdoj.gov
Systems Manager **Denise M. Pec** . . . . (312) 886-7658
E-mail: denise.pec@usdoj.gov

Rockford (IL) Office

327 South Church Street, Rockford, IL 61101
Tel: (815) 987-4444 Fax: (815) 987-4236

Assistant U.S. Attorney-in-Charge **John G. McKenzie** . . . (815) 987-4444
E-mail: john.mckenzie@usdoj.gov
Assistant U.S. Attorney **Talia Bucci** . . . . (815) 987-4451
E-mail: talia.bucci@usdoj.gov
Assistant U.S. Attorney **Michael D. Love** . . . . (815) 987-4444
E-mail: michael.love@usdoj.gov
Assistant U.S. Attorney **Monica V. Mallory** . . . . (815) 987-4444
E-mail: monica.mallory@usdoj.gov
Assistant U.S. Attorney **Scott R. Paccagnini** . . . . (815) 987-4456
E-mail: scott.paccagnini@justice.usdoj.gov
Education: Chicago-Kent JD
Assistant U.S. Attorney **Joseph Pedersen** . . . . (815) 987-4453
E-mail: joseph.pedersen@usdoj.gov
Assistant U.S. Attorney **(Vacant)** . . . . (815) 987-4444

Illinois - Central District

318 South Sixth Street, Springfield, IL 62701-1806
Tel: (217) 492-4450 Fax: (217) 492-4512
Internet: www.usdoj.gov/usao/ilc

★ U.S. Attorney **James A. "Jim" Lewis** . . . . (217) 492-4450
E-mail: jim.lewis2@usdoj.gov
Education: Yale 1962; Chicago 1962 JD; Duke 1975
Secretary to U.S. Attorney **Charlotte McCormick** . . . . . . (217) 492-4469
E-mail: charlotte.mccormick@usdoj.gov
First Assistant U.S. Attorney **Patrick D. Hansen** . . . . (217) 492-4450
E-mail: patrick.hansen@usdoj.gov
Administrative Officer **Jack E. Pascoe** . . . . (217) 492-4450
E-mail: jack.pascoe@usdoj.gov
Appellate Chief **Greggory Walters** . . . . (217) 492-4450
E-mail: greggory.walters@usdoj.gov
Immigration Coordinator **(Vacant)** . . . . (217) 492-4450
Law Enforcement Coordinator **(Vacant)** . . . . (217) 492-4450
Victim-Witness Coordinator **Sharon J. Paul** . . . . (217) 492-4450
E-mail: sharon.paul@usdoj.gov
Librarian **Carol M. Swiney** . . . . (217) 492-4450
E-mail: carol.swiney@usdoj.gov
Systems Manager **Michael Morgan** . . . . (217) 492-4450
E-mail: michael.morgan@usdoj.gov
IT Specialist **James M. "Jimmy" Henton** . . . . (217) 492-4450
E-mail: jimmy.henton@usdoj.gov

Civil Division

Chief **Gregory M. Gilmore** . . . . (217) 492-4450
E-mail: greg.gilmore@usdoj.gov
Assistant U.S. Attorney **Hilary W. Frooman** . . . . (217) 492-4450
E-mail: hilary.frooman@usdoj.gov
Assistant U.S. Attorney **Gail L. Noll** . . . . (217) 492-4450
E-mail: gail.noll@usdoj.gov
Education: Illinois Col 1994 BA; Illinois 1997 JD

Criminal Division

Chief **(Vacant)** . . . . (217) 492-4450

Criminal Division *continued*

Supervisor **John E. Childress** . . . . (217) 492-4450
E-mail: john.childress@usdoj.gov
Education: Indiana; Duke
Asset Forfeiture Unit Chief **Gregory M. Gilmore** . . . . (217) 492-4450
E-mail: greg.gilmore@usdoj.gov
Senior Litigation Counsel **Patrick D. Hansen** . . . . (217) 492-4450
E-mail: patrick.hansen@usdoj.gov
Assistant U.S. Attorney **Timothy A. Bass** . . . . (217) 492-4450
E-mail: tim.bass@usdoj.gov
Assistant U.S. Attorney **Bryan D. Freres** . . . . (217) 492-4450
E-mail: bryan.freres@usdoj.gov
Assistant U.S. Attorney **Gregory K. Harris** . . . . (217) 492-4450
E-mail: gregory.harris@usdoj.gov
Assistant U.S. Attorney **Victory Yanz** . . . . (217) 492-4450

Peoria (IL) Office

One Technology Plaza, 211 Fulton Street,
Suite 400, Peoria, IL 61602-1348
Tel: (309) 671-7050 Fax: (309) 671-7259

Branch Chief **Darilynn J. Knauss** . . . . (309) 671-7050
E-mail: darilynn.knauss@usdoj.gov
Assistant U.S. Attorney **Ronald Hanna** . . . . (309) 671-7050
E-mail: ronald.hanna@usdoj.gov
Assistant U.S. Attorney **Greggory Walters** . . . . (309) 671-7050
E-mail: greggory.walters@usdoj.gov
Civil Division Assistant U.S. Attorney
Gerard A. Brost . . . . (309) 671-7050
E-mail: gerard.brost@usdoj.gov
Criminal Division Assistant U.S. Attorney
John H. Campbell . . . . (309) 671-7050
E-mail: john.campbell@usdoj.gov
Criminal Division Assistant U.S. Attorney
Bradley W. Murphy . . . . (309) 671-7050
E-mail: bradley.murphy@justice.usdoj.gov
Drug Task Force Lead Assistant U.S. Attorney
K. Tate Chambers . . . . (309) 671-7050
E-mail: tate.chambers@usdoj.gov

Rock Island (IL) Office

211 North 19th Street, 2nd Floor, Rock Island, IL 61201
Tel: (309) 793-7760 Fax: (309) 793-5663

Branch Chief **John Mehochko** . . . . (309) 793-7760
E-mail: john.mehochko@usdoj.gov
Assistant U.S. Attorney **Donald B. Allegro** . . . . (309) 671-7760
E-mail: don.allegro@usdoj.gov
Assistant U.S. Attorney **Meredith DeCarlo** . . . . (309) 793-7760
E-mail: meredith.decarlo@usdoj.gov
Assistant U.S. Attorney **Micah Reyner** . . . . (309) 793-7760
E-mail: micah.reyner@usdoj.gov
Assistant U.S. Attorney **(Vacant)** . . . . (309) 793-7760

Urbana (IL) Office

201 South Vine Street, Suite 226, Urbana, IL 61801
Tel: (217) 373-5875 Fax: (217) 373-5891

Branch Supervisor **Ronda Coleman** . . . . (217) 373-5875
E-mail: ronda.coleman@usdoj.gov
Assistant U.S. Attorney **Katherine Boyle** . . . . (217) 373-5875
E-mail: katherine.boyle@usdoj.gov
Assistant U.S. Attorney **Elham Peirson** . . . . (217) 373-5875
E-mail: elly.peirson@usdoj.gov
Civil Division Assistant U.S. Attorney **David H. Hoff** . . . . (217) 373-5875
E-mail: david.hoff@usdoj.gov
Criminal Division Assistant U.S. Attorney
Eugene L. Miller . . . . (217) 373-5875
E-mail: eugene.miller@usdoj.gov
Anti-Terrorism Advisory Council Coordinator
Jason M. Bohm . . . . (217) 373-5875
E-mail: jason.bohm@usdoj.gov
Education: Illinois 2003 JD

★ Presidential Appointment Requiring Senate Confirmation ☆ Presidential Appointment ☐ Schedule C Appointment ◇ Career Senior Foreign Service Appointment
● Career Senior Executive Service (SES) Appointment ○ Non-Career Senior Executive Service (SES) Appointment ■ Postal Career Executive Service

Illinois - Southern District

Nine Executive Drive, Fairview Heights, IL 62208
Tel: (618) 628-3700 Fax: (618) 628-3730
Internet: www.usdoj.gov/usao/ils

★ U.S. Attorney **Stephen R. Wigginton** . . . . . (618) 628-3700
E-mail: stephen.wigginton@usdoj.gov
Education: Southern IL Edwardsville 1985 BS; Saint Louis U 1988 JD
Secretary to U.S. Attorney **Karen Harriman** . . . . . (618) 628-3700
E-mail: karen.harriman@usdoj.gov
First Assistant U.S. Attorney **James L. Porter** . . . . . (618) 628-3700
E-mail: james.porter@usdoj.gov
Administrative Officer **Lindsey Lester-Brutscher** . . . . . (618) 628-3700
E-mail: lindsay.lester-brutscher@justice.usdoj.gov
Law Enforcement Committee Coordinator **Greg Cueto** . . . (618) 628-3700
Victim-Witness Coordinator **Julie Swanston** . . . . . (618) 628-3700
E-mail: julie.swanston@usdoj.gov
Intelligence Specialist **Mario Jimenez** . . . . . (618) 628-3700
E-mail: mario.jimenez@usdoj.gov
IT Specialist **Michael McAfee** . . . . . (618) 628-3700
E-mail: michael.mcafee@usdoj.gov
IT Specialist **Joyce Voss** . . . . . (618) 628-3700
E-mail: joyce.voss@usdoj.gov

Civil Division

Chief **Gerald M. Burke** . . . . . (618) 628-3700
E-mail: gerald.burke@usdoj.gov
Assistant U.S. Attorney **Nicholas Biersbach** . . . . . (618) 628-3770
E-mail: nicholas.biersbach@usdoj.gov
Assistant U.S. Attorney **Adam Hanna** . . . . . (618) 628-3700
E-mail: adam.hanna@usdoj.gov
Assistant U.S. Attorney **Jennifer Hudson** . . . . . (618) 628-3700
E-mail: jennifer.hudson@usdoj.gov
Assistant U.S. Attorney **Laura J. Jones** . . . . . (618) 628-3700
E-mail: laura.jones@usdoj.gov
Assistant U.S. Attorney **David J. Pfeffer** . . . . . (618) 628-3700
E-mail: david.j.pfeffer@usdoj.gov
Assistant U.S. Attorney **Nathan Stump** . . . . . (618) 628-3700
E-mail: nathan.stump@usdoj.gov
Assistant U.S. Attorney **Nathan E. Wyatt** . . . . . (618) 628-3700
E-mail: nathan.wyatt@usdoj.gov
Education: Illinois 2001 JD

Criminal Division

Chief **Suzanne M. Garrison** . . . . . (618) 628-3700
E-mail: suzanne.garrison@usdoj.gov
Organized Crime Drug Enforcement Task Force
Division Chief **Donald S. Boyce** . . . . . (618) 628-3700
E-mail: donald.boyce@justice.usdoj.gov
Fraud and Corruption Chief **Bruce E. Reppert** . . . . . (618) 628-3700
E-mail: bruce.reppert@usdoj.gov
Special Assistant U.S. Attorney **Jonathan Drucker** . . . . . (618) 628-3700
E-mail: jonathan.drucker@usdoj.gov
Special Assistant U.S. Attorney **Michael Hallock** . . . . . (618) 628-3700
E-mail: michael.hallock@usdoj.gov
Education: Arizona 2005 BA; Chicago-Kent 2008 JD
Special Assistant U.S. Attorney **(Vacant)** . . . . . (618) 628-3700
Assistant U.S. Attorney **Stephen B. Clark** . . . . . (618) 628-3700
E-mail: stephen.clark@usdoj.gov
Assistant U.S. Attorney **William E. Coonan** . . . . . (618) 628-3700
E-mail: william.coonan@justice.usdoj.gov
Assistant U.S. Attorney **Deirdre A. Durborow** . . . . . (618) 628-3700
E-mail: deirdre.durborow@usdoj.gov
Assistant U.S. Attorney **Robert L. Garrison** . . . . . (618) 628-3700
E-mail: robert.garrison@justice.usdoj.gov
Assistant U.S. Attorney **Daniel T. Kapsak** . . . . . (618) 628-3828
E-mail: dan.kapsak@usdoj.gov
Assistant U.S. Attorney **Ranley R. Killian** . . . . . (618) 628-3700
E-mail: ranley.killian@usdoj.gov
Assistant U.S. Attorney **Kit R. Morrissey** . . . . . (618) 628-3700
E-mail: kit.morrissey@usdoj.gov
Assistant U.S. Attorney **Michael J. Quinley** . . . . . (618) 628-3700

Criminal Division *continued*

Assistant U.S. Attorney **Laura Reppert** . . . . . (618) 628-3700
E-mail: laura.reppert@usdoj.gov
Assistant U.S. Attorney **Angela Scott** . . . . . (618) 628-3700
E-mail: angela.scott@usdoj.gov
Education: Southern Illinois 1997 BS, 2000 JD
Assistant U.S. Attorney **Norman R. Smith** . . . . . (618) 628-3700
E-mail: norman.smith@usdoj.gov
Assistant U.S. Attorney **Monica A. Stump** . . . . . (618) 628-3700
E-mail: monica.stump@usdoj.gov
Assistant U.S. Attorney **Ali Summers** . . . . . (618) 628-3700
E-mail: ali.summers@usdoj.gov
Assistant U.S. Attorney **Scott A. Verseman** . . . . . (618) 628-3700
E-mail: scott.verseman@usdoj.gov
Assistant U.S. Attorney **Steven Weinhoeft** . . . . . (618) 628-3700
E-mail: steven.weinhoeft@usdoj.gov

Benton (IL) Office

402 West Main Street, Benton, IL 62812
Tel: (618) 439-3808 Fax: (618) 439-2401

Branch Manager **George A. Norwood** . . . . . (618) 439-3808
E-mail: george.norwood@usdoj.gov
Criminal Division Assistant U.S. Attorney
James M. Cutchin . . . . . (618) 439-3808
Criminal Division Assistant U.S. Attorney
Thomas E. Leggans . . . . . (618) 439-3808
E-mail: thomas.leggans@usdoj.gov
Criminal Division Assistant U.S. Attorney
Amanda A. Robertson . . . . . (618) 439-3808
E-mail: amanda.robertson@usdoj.gov

Indiana - Northern District

5400 Federal Plaza, Suite 1500, Hammond, IN 46320
Tel: (219) 937-5500 Fax: (219) 852-2770
Internet: www.usdoj.gov/usao/inn

★ U.S. Attorney **David A. Capp** . . . . . (219) 937-5500 ext. 15601
E-mail: david.capp@usdoj.gov
Education: Wisconsin 1972 BA; Valparaiso 1977 JD
Secretary to the U.S. Attorney
Sandra Clanin . . . . . (219) 937-5500 ext. 15682
E-mail: sandra.clanin@usdoj.gov
First Assistant U.S. Attorney **Clifford D. Johnson** . . . . . (574) 236-8287
E-mail: clifford.johnson@usdoj.gov
Public Affairs Specialist/Information Officer
Ryan Holmes . . . . . (219) 937-5500 ext. 15666
E-mail: ryan.holmes@usdoj.gov
Senior Litigation Counsel **Robin Morlock** . . . . . (219) 937-5500 ext. 5611
E-mail: robin.morlock@usdoj.gov
Victim-Witness Specialist **Sally Haviar** . . . . . (219) 937-5500 ext. 15665
E-mail: sally.haviar@usdoj.gov
Administrative Officer **Kenneth Potchen** . . . . . (219) 937-5500 ext. 15613
E-mail: kenneth.potchen@usdoj.gov
Budget Officer **Jun Zhang** . . . . . (219) 937-5500 ext. 15622
E-mail: jun.zhang3@usdoj.gov
Systems Manager **Chad Hunter** . . . . . (219) 937-5500 ext. 15620
E-mail: chad.hunter@usdoj.gov
Webmaster **Chad Hunter** . . . . . (219) 937-5500 ext. 15620
E-mail: chad.hunter@usdoj.gov

Civil Division

Chief **Orest Szewciw** . . . . . (219) 937-5500 ext. 5612
E-mail: orest.szewciw@usdoj.gov
Assistant U.S. Attorney **Wayne Ault** . . . . . (219) 937-5500 ext. 5650
E-mail: wayne.ault@usdoj.gov
Assistant U.S. Attorney **Sharon Jefferson** . . . . . (219) 937-5500 ext. 5681
E-mail: sharon.johnson@usdoj.gov
Assistant U.S. Attorney **Robin Morlock** . . . . . (219) 937-5500 ext. 5611
E-mail: robin.morlock@usdoj.gov
Assistant U.S. Attorney **Abizer Zanzi** . . . . . (219) 937-5500 ext. 5651
E-mail: abizer.zanzi@usdoj.gov
Education: Pennsylvania 2000 BA; Duke 2005 JD

REGIONAL OFFICES — US ATTORNEYS AND US MARSHALS SERVICE

★ Presidential Appointment Requiring Senate Confirmation ☆ Presidential Appointment □ Schedule C Appointment ◇ Career Senior Foreign Service Appointment
● Career Senior Executive Service (SES) Appointment ○ Non-Career Senior Executive Service (SES) Appointment ■ Postal Career Executive Service

Criminal Division

Chief **Daniel L. Bella** .... (219) 937-5500 ext. 15609
E-mail: daniel.bella@usdoj.gov

Supervisory Assistant U.S. Attorney
Gary Bell .... (219) 937-5500 ext. 15656
E-mail: gary.bell@usdoj.gov

Supervisory Assistant U.S. Attorney
Jacqueline L. Jacobs .... (219) 937-5500 ext. 15634

Assistant U.S. Attorney **Philip Benson** .... (219) 937-5500 ext. 15608
E-mail: philip.benson@usdoj.gov

Assistant U.S. Attorney
Diane L. Berkowitz .... (219) 937-5500 ext. 15657
E-mail: diane.berkowitz@usdoj.gov

Assistant U.S. Attorney
Jennifer S. Chang-Adiga .... (219) 937-5500 ext. 5658
E-mail: jennifer.chang@usdoj.gov
Education: Stanford 2003 JD

Assistant U.S. Attorney **Toi D. Houston** ...... (219) 937-5500 ext. 15653
E-mail: toi.houston@usdoj.gov

Assistant U.S. Attorney **Joshua Kolar** .... (219) 937-5500 ext. 15659
E-mail: joshua.kolar@usdoj.gov

Assistant U.S. Attorney **Jill Koster** .... (219) 937-5500
E-mail: jill.koster@usdoj.gov

Assistant U.S. Attorney **Dean Lanter** .... (219) 937-5500 ext. 15677
E-mail: dean.lanter@usdoj.gov

Assistant U.S. Attorney **David Nozick** .... (219) 937-5500 ext. 15655
E-mail: david.nozick@usdoj.gov

Assistant U.S. Attorney **Nicholas J. Padilla** ... (219) 937-5500 ext. 15652

Assistant U.S. Attorney
Thomas S. Ratcliffe .... (219) 937-5500 ext. 15654
Education: Vanderbilt 1993 BA; Northwestern 1997 JD

Assistant U.S. Attorney
Randall M. Stewart .... (219) 937-5500 ext. 15610
E-mail: randall.stewart@usdoj.gov

Assistant U.S. Attorney **(Vacant)** .... (219) 937-5500 ext. 15678

Fort Wayne (IN) Office

1300 South Harrison Street, Room 3128, Fort Wayne, IN 46802
Tel: (260) 422-2595 Fax: (260) 426-1616

Supervisory Assistant U.S. Attorney **Tina L. Nommay** ... (260) 422-2595
E-mail: tina.nommay@usdoj.gov

Civil Division Assistant U.S. Attorney
Deborah Leonard .... (260) 422-2595
E-mail: deborah.leonard@usdoj.gov

Criminal Division Assistant U.S. Attorney
Anthony Geller .... (260) 422-2595
E-mail: anthony.geller@usdoj.gov

Criminal Division Assistant U.S. Attorney
Nathaniel Henson .... (260) 422-2595
E-mail: nathaniel.henson@usdoj.gov
Education: Valparaiso 2004 JD

Criminal Division Assistant U.S. Attorney
Lovita Morris King .... (260) 422-2595
E-mail: lovita.morris.king@usdoj.gov

Criminal Division Assistant U.S. Attorney
Lesley Miller Lowery .... (260) 422-2595
E-mail: lesley.millerlowery@usdoj.gov

South Bend (IN) Office

204 South Main Street, Room MO-1, South Bend, IN 46601
Tel: (574) 236-8287 Fax: (574) 236-8155

First Assistant U.S. Attorney **Clifford D. Johnson** .... (574) 236-8287
E-mail: clifford.johnson@usdoj.gov

Supervisory Assistant U.S. Attorney **Kenneth Hays** ...... (574) 236-8287
E-mail: kenneth.hays@usdoj.gov

Criminal Division Assistant U.S. Attorney
Jesse Barrett .... (574) 236-8287
E-mail: jesse.barrett@usdoj.gov

Criminal Division Assistant U.S. Attorney
William T. Grimmer .... (574) 236-8287
E-mail: william.grimmer@usdoj.gov

South Bend (IN) Office *continued*

Criminal Division Assistant U.S. Attorney
John Maciejczyk .... (574) 236-8287
E-mail: john.maciejczyk@usdoj.gov

Criminal Division Assistant U.S. Attorney
Frank Schaffer .... (574) 236-8286
E-mail: frank.schaffer@usdoj.gov

Criminal Division Assistant U.S. Attorney
Donald Schmid .... (574) 236-8287
E-mail: donald.schmid@usdoj.gov

Criminal Division Assistant U.S. Attorney **(Vacant)** ...... (574) 236-8287

Senior Litigation Counsel **(Vacant)** .... (574) 236-8287

Indiana - Southern District

10 West Market Street, Suite 2100, Indianapolis, IN 46204
Tel: (317) 226-6333 Fax: (317) 226-6125 (Criminal)
Fax: (317) 226-5027 (Civil)
Internet: www.usdoj.gov/usao/ins

★ U.S. Attorney (Acting) **Joshua J. Minkler** .... (317) 226-6333

Staff Assistant to the U.S. Attorney **Mary Bippus** ...... (317) 226-6333
E-mail: mary.bippus@usdoj.gov

First Assistant U.S. Attorney (Acting) **Joe H. Vaughn** .... (317) 226-6333
E-mail: joe.vaughn@usdoj.gov

Senior Litigation Counsel **Bradley L. Blackington** .... (317) 226-6333
E-mail: bradley.blackington@usdoj.gov

Senior Litigation Counsel **Steven D. DeBrota** .... (317) 226-6333
E-mail: steve.debrota@usdoj.gov

Administrative Officer **Judith Dillard** .... (317) 226-6333
E-mail: judith.dillard@usdoj.gov Fax: (317) 226-5176

Appellate Division

Chief **Bob Wood** .... (317) 226-6333
E-mail: bob.wood@usdoj.gov

Civil Division

Fax: (317) 226-5027

Chief **Jill E. Julian** .... (317) 226-6333

Assistant U.S. Attorney **Jonathan Bont** .... (317) 226-6333
E-mail: jonathan.bont@usdoj.gov

Assistant U.S. Attorney **Gerald A. Coraz** .... (317) 226-6333
E-mail: gerald.coraz@usdoj.gov

Assistant U.S. Attorney **Jeffrey L. Hunter** .... (317) 226-6333

Assistant U.S. Attorney **Thomas E. Kieper** .... (317) 226-6333

Assistant U.S. Attorney **Debra Richards** .... (317) 226-6333
E-mail: debra.richards@usdoj.gov

Assistant U.S. Attorney **Shelese Woods** .... (317) 226-6333
E-mail: shelese.woods@usdoj.gov

Assistant U.S. Attorney **(Vacant)** .... (317) 226-6333

Criminal Division

Fax: (317) 226-6125

Chief (Acting) **Winfield D. Ong** .... (317) 226-6333
E-mail: winfield.ong@usdoj.gov

Assistant U.S. Attorney **Steven D. DeBrota** .... (317) 226-6333
E-mail: steve.debrota@usdoj.gov

Assistant U.S. Attorney **Charnette D. Garner** .... (317) 226-6333
E-mail: charnette.garner@usdoj.gov

Assistant U.S. Attorney **Matthew Lasher** .... (317) 226-6333
E-mail: matthew.lasher@usdoj.gov
Education: Indiana JD

Assistant U.S. Attorney **Nicholas Linder** .... (317) 226-6333
E-mail: nicholas.linder@usdoj.gov

Assistant U.S. Attorney **Jeffrey D. Preston** .... (317) 226-6333
E-mail: jeffrey.preston@usdoj.gov

Assistant U.S. Attorney **Cynthia Ridgeway** .... (317) 226-6333
E-mail: cynthia.ridgeway@usdoj.gov

Assistant U.S. Attorney **Matthew Rinka** .... (317) 226-6333
E-mail: matthew.rinka@usdoj.gov

Assistant U.S. Attorney **Brad Shepard** .... (317) 226-6333
E-mail: brad.shepard@usdoj.gov

(continued on next page)

★ Presidential Appointment Requiring Senate Confirmation ☆ Presidential Appointment □ Schedule C Appointment ◇ Career Senior Foreign Service Appointment
● Career Senior Executive Service (SES) Appointment ○ Non-Career Senior Executive Service (SES) Appointment ■ Postal Career Executive Service

Criminal Division *continued*

Assistant U.S. Attorney **James M. Warden** .... (317) 226-6333
Assistant U.S. Attorney **James R. Wood** .... (317) 226-6333
Asset Forfeiture Assistant U.S. Attorney
Winfield D. Ong .... (317) 226-6333
E-mail: winfield.ong@usdoj.gov

Drug Unit
Fax: (317) 226-5953

Chief **Matthew P. "Matt" Brookman** .... (317) 226-6333
Note: On September 15, 2015 Matthew Brookman was selected to be a magistrate judge for the Southern District of Indiana.
Education: DePauw 1990 BA; Washington U (MO) 1993 JD
Assistant U.S. Attorney **Bradley L. Blackington** .... (317) 226-6333
E-mail: bradley.blackington@usdoj.gov
Assistant U.S. Attorney **Michelle P. Brady** .... (317) 226-6333
E-mail: michelle.brady@usdoj.gov
Assistant U.S. Attorney **Barry D. Glickman** .... (317) 226-6333
E-mail: barry.glickman@usdoj.gov
Assistant U.S. Attorney **William L. McKoscky** .... (317) 226-6333
E-mail: william.mckoscky@usdoj.gov
Education: Indiana 2002 JD
Assistant U.S. Attorney **MaryAnn Mindrum** .... (317) 226-6333
E-mail: maryann.mindrum@usdoj.gov

National Terrorism Unit
Chief **Doris Pryor** .... (317) 226-6333
E-mail: doris.pryor@usdoj.gov

Evansville (IN) Office
101 NW Martin Luther King, Jr. Boulevard,
Suite 250, Evansville, IN 47708
Fax: (812) 465-6444

Assistant U.S. Attorney **Kyle M. Sawa** .... (812) 465-6475
E-mail: kyle.sawa@usdoj.gov
Education: Indiana 2005 BA; George Washington 2009 JD
Assistant U.S. Attorney **Todd Shellenberger** .... (812) 465-6475
Assistant U.S. Attorney **Lauren Wheatley** .... (812) 465-6475
E-mail: lauren.wheatley@usdoj.gov

Iowa - Northern District
111 7th Avenue SE, Box 1, Cedar Rapids, IA 52401
Tel: (319) 363-6333 TTY: (319) 286-9258 Fax: (319) 363-1990
Internet: www.usdoj.gov/usao/ian

★ U.S. Attorney **Kevin W. Techau** .... (319) 363-6333
E-mail: kevin.techau@usdoj.gov
Affiliation: USAF (Ret); ANG (Ret)
Education: Iowa 1981 BBA, 1984 JD
Special Counsel **Richard L. Murphy** .... (319) 363-6333
First Assistant U.S. Attorney **Sean R. Berry** .... (319) 363-6333
E-mail: sean.berry@usdoj.gov
Education: Notre Dame 1982 BBA; Northwestern 1987 JD
Administrative Officer **Misti Kloubec** .... (319) 363-6333
E-mail: misti.kloubec@usdoj.gov
Law Enforcement Committee Coordinator
Steven Young .... (319) 363-6333
Victim-Witness Coordinator **Shari Konarske** .... (319) 363-6333
E-mail: shari.konarske@usdoj.gov
Civil Division Chief **Matthew J. Cole** .... (319) 363-6333
E-mail: matthew.cole@usdoj.gov
Criminal Division Chief **Peter E. Deegan, Jr.** .... (319) 363-6333
E-mail: peter.deegan@usdoj.gov
Senior Litigation Counsel **C. J. Williams** .... (319) 363-6333
Appellate Chief **Mark Tremmel** .... (319) 363-6333
E-mail: mark.tremmel@usdoj.gov
Assistant U.S. Attorney **Dan Chatham** .... (319) 363-6333
E-mail: dan.chatham@usdoj.gov
Education: Iowa 2007 JD
Assistant U.S. Attorney **Justin Lightfoot** .... (319) 363-6333
E-mail: justin.lightfoot@usdoj.gov

Iowa - Northern District *continued*

Assistant U.S. Attorney **Martin J. McLaughlin** .... (319) 363-6333
Assistant U.S. Attorney **Tony Morfit** .... (319) 363-6333
Assistant U.S. Attorney **Ravi Narayan** .... (319) 363-6333
E-mail: ravi.narayan@usdoj.gov
Assistant U.S. Attorney **BG Patrick J. Reinert** .... (319) 363-6333
E-mail: pat.reinert@usdoj.gov
Affiliation: USAR
Education: Iowa State 1983 BA; Central U Iowa 1986 JD; Army War Col 2005 MS
Assistant U.S. Attorney **Jacob A. Schunk** .... (319) 363-6333
Education: Concordia U (WI) 2001 BA; St Thomas U 2004 JD
Assistant U.S. Attorney **Daniel C. Tvedt** .... (319) 363-6333
E-mail: daniel.tvedt@usdoj.gov
Assistant U.S. Attorney **Timothy L. Vavricek** .... (319) 363-6333
E-mail: tim.vavricek@usdoj.gov
Education: Iowa 2000 JD
Assistant U.S. Attorney **Lisa C. Williams** .... (319) 363-6333
E-mail: lisa.williams@usdoj.gov
Assistant U.S. Attorney **Stephanie J. Wright** .... (319) 363-6333
E-mail: stephanie.wright@usdoj.gov
Special Assistant U.S. Attorney **Erin Eldridge** .... (319) 363-6333
E-mail: erin.eldridge@usdoj.gov
Intelligence Specialist **Todd A. Voter** .... (319) 363-6333
Systems Manager **Ashlee Plotz** .... (319) 363-6333
E-mail: ashlee.plotz@usdoj.gov

Sioux City (IA) Office
600 Fourth Street, Suite 670, Sioux City, IA 51101
Tel: (712) 255-6011 TTY: (712) 258-4761 Fax: (712) 252-2034

Branch Chief **Timothy Duax** .... (712) 255-6011
Assistant U.S. Attorney **James D. Bowers, Jr.** .... (712) 255-6011
Assistant U.S. Attorney **Forde Owens Fairchild** .... (712) 255-6011
E-mail: forde.fairchild@usdoj.gov
Assistant U.S. Attorney **Kevin Fletcher** .... (712) 255-6011
E-mail: kevin.fletcher@usdoj.gov
Assistant U.S. Attorney **Jack H. Lammers** .... (712) 255-6011
E-mail: jack.lammers@usdoj.gov
Assistant U.S. Attorney **Shawn S. Wehde** .... (712) 255-6011
E-mail: shawn.wehde@usdoj.gov
Special Assistant U.S. Attorney **Nathan W. Nelson** ..... (712) 255-6011
E-mail: nathan.nelson@usdoj.gov
Education: St John's U (MN) 2002 BA; Minnesota 2005 JD

Iowa - Southern District
U.S. Courthouse Annex, 110 East Court Avenue,
Suite 286, Des Moines, IA 50309-2053
Tel: (515) 473-9300 Fax: (515) 473-9298
Internet: www.usdoj.gov/usao/ias

★ U.S. Attorney **Nicholas A. Klinefeldt** .... (515) 473-9300
Education: Iowa 1995 BA, 2000 JD
Secretary to the U.S. Attorney **Valerie Quast** .... (515) 473-9347
First Assistant U.S. Attorney **Kevin E. VanderSchel** ..... (515) 473-9300
E-mail: kevin.vanderschel@usdoj.gov
Administrative Officer **Deb Harvey** .... (515) 473-9333
E-mail: deb.harvey@usdoj.gov
Law Enforcement Coordinator **(Vacant)** .... (515) 473-9341
Victim-Witness Program Manager **Jennifer Boeding** ..... (515) 473-9341
E-mail: jennifer.boeding@usdoj.gov
Systems Manager **Fred Hanna** .... (515) 473-9331
E-mail: fred.hanna@usdoj.gov

Civil Division
Fax: (515) 284-6492 Fax: (515) 473-9282

Chief **William C. Purdy** .... (515) 473-9315
Assistant U.S. Attorney **Mary C. Luxa** .... (515) 473-9303
E-mail: mary.luxa@usdoj.gov
Assistant U.S. Attorney **Richard L. Richards** .... (515) 473-9357
E-mail: richard.richards@usdoj.gov

★ Presidential Appointment Requiring Senate Confirmation ☆ Presidential Appointment □ Schedule C Appointment ◇ Career Senior Foreign Service Appointment
● Career Senior Executive Service (SES) Appointment ○ Non-Career Senior Executive Service (SES) Appointment ■ Postal Career Executive Service

Criminal Division
Fax: (515) 284-6281

Chief **Andrew H. Kahl** .... (515) 473-9311
E-mail: andrew.kahl@usdoj.gov
Deputy Chief **Debra L. Scorpiniti** .... (515) 473-9316
E-mail: debra.scorpiniti@usdoj.gov
Special Assistant U.S. Attorney **(Vacant)** .... (515) 473-9325
Special Assistant U.S. Attorney **Marc L. Krickbaum** ..... (515) 473-9305
E-mail: marc.krickbaum@usdoj.gov
Special Assistant U.S. Attorney **Mikaela Shotwell** ...... (515) 473-9284
E-mail: mikaela.shotwell@usdoj.gov
Assistant U.S. Attorney **John E. Beamer** .... (515) 473-9304
E-mail: john.beamer@usdoj.gov
Assistant U.S. Attorney **Virginia Bruner** .... (515) 473-9324
E-mail: virginia.bruner@usdoj.gov
Assistant U.S. Attorney **Craig Gaumer** .... (515) 473-9317
Assistant U.S. Attorney **Jason Griess** .... (515) 473-9302
E-mail: jason.griess2@usdoj.gov
Assistant U.S. Attorney **Kelly Mahoney** .... (515) 473-9312
E-mail: kelly.mahoney@usdoj.gov
Assistant U.S. Attorney **Maureen McGuire** .... (515) 473-9354
E-mail: maureen.mcguire@usdoj.gov
Assistant U.S. Attorney **Bradley Price** .... (515) 473-9256
E-mail: bradley.price@usdoj.gov
Assistant U.S. Attorney **Rachel Scherle** .... (515) 473-9329
E-mail: rachel.scherle@usdoj.gov Fax: (515) 473-9292
Assistant U.S. Attorney **Clifford D. Wendel** .... (515) 473-9320

Council Bluffs Branch Office
8 South Sixth Street, Room 348, Council Bluffs, IA 51501
Tel: (712) 328-1612 Fax: (712) 328-4048

Assistant U.S. Attorney **Katherine McNamara** .... (712) 256-5104
E-mail: katherine.mcnamara@usdoj.gov
Assistant U.S. Attorney **Richard Rothrock** .... (712) 328-1612
E-mail: richard.rothrock@usdoj.gov

Quad-Cities Branch Office
131 East Fourth Street, Davenport, IA 52801
Tel: (563) 449-5432 Fax: (563) 449-5433

Assistant U.S. Attorney **Clifford R. Cronk III** .... (563) 449-5415
Assistant U.S. Attorney **Adam Kerndt** .... (563) 449-5422
E-mail: adam.kerndt@usdoj.gov
Assistant U.S. Attorney **Richard Westphal** .... (563) 449-5421
Assistant U.S. Attorney **Melissa Zachringer** .... (563) 449-5426
Special Assistant U.S. Attorney **Ashley Corkery** .... (563) 449-5405
E-mail: ashley.corkery@usdoj.gov

Kansas District
1200 Epic Center, 301 North Main Street, Wichita, KS 67202
Tel: (316) 269-6481 Fax: (316) 269-6484
Internet: www.usdoj.gov/usao/ks

★ U.S. Attorney **Barry R. Grissom** .... (913) 551-6730
E-mail: barry.grissom@usdoj.gov
Education: Kansas 1977 BS; Oklahoma City 1981 JD
Secretary to the U.S. Attorney **Linda Smith** .... (913) 551-6730
E-mail: linda.smith2@usdoj.gov
First Assistant U.S. Attorney **Tom Beall** .... (785) 295-2850
Education: Washburn 2000 JD; Kansas State 1992 MPA; Baker U 1990 BA
Administrative Officer **Randy Miller** .... (316) 269-6481
E-mail: randy.miller@usdoj.gov
Law Enforcement Coordinator **Steve Nevil** .... (316) 269-6481
Victim-Witness Coordinator **Kim Reese** .... (316) 269-6481
E-mail: kim.reese@usdoj.gov
Victim-Witness Coordinator **Vivian Van Vleet** .... (316) 269-6481
E-mail: vivian.vanvleet@usdoj.gov
Budget Officer **Frank Prevost** .... (316) 269-6481
E-mail: frank.prevost@usdoj.gov

Kansas District *continued*

Personnel Officer **Amy Ayala** .... (316) 269-6481
E-mail: amy.ayala@usdoj.gov
Librarian **Phyllis A. Creed** .... (316) 269-6481
E-mail: phyllis.creed@usdoj.gov
Systems Manager **David Steeby** .... (316) 269-6481
E-mail: david.steeby@usdoj.gov

Civil Division
Chief **Emily B. Metzger** .... (316) 269-6481
E-mail: emily.metzger@usdoj.gov
Special Assistant U.S. Attorney **Robin Sommer** .... (316) 269-6481
Assistant U.S. Attorney **Jason Oller** .... (316) 269-6481
E-mail: jason.oller@usdoj.gov
Assistant U.S. Attorney **Brian Sheern** .... (316) 269-6481
E-mail: brian.sheern@usdoj.gov

Criminal Division
Chief **Jared Maag** .... (785) 295-2850
Special Assistant U.S. Attorney **(Vacant)** .... (316) 269-6481
Criminal Division Coordinator/ Assistant U.S. Attorney
Debra L. Barnett .... (316) 269-6481
E-mail: debra.barnett@usdoj.gov
Assistant U.S. Attorney **Brent I. Anderson** .... (316) 269-6481
E-mail: brent.anderson@usdoj.gov
Assistant U.S. Attorney **Mona L. Furst** .... (316) 269-6481
E-mail: mona.furst@usdoj.gov
Assistant U.S. Attorney **Annette B. Gurney** .... (316) 269-6481
E-mail: annette.gurney@usdoj.gov
Assistant U.S. Attorney **Jason Hart** .... (316) 269-6481
Assistant U.S. Attorney **David M. Lind** .... (316) 269-6481
E-mail: david.lind@usdoj.gov
Assistant U.S. Attorney **Alan G. Metzger** .... (316) 269-6481
E-mail: alan.metzger@usdoj.gov
Assistant U.S. Attorney **Aaron Smith** .... (316) 269-6481
Assistant U.S. Attorney **Matt Treaster** .... (316) 269-6481
E-mail: matt.treaster@usdoj.gov

Kansas City (KS) Office
Federal Building, 500 State Avenue, Suite 360, Kansas City, KS 66101
Tel: (913) 551-6730 Fax: (913) 551-6541

Assistant U.S. Attorney/Branch Manager
Christopher Allman .... (913) 551-6730

Civil Division
Assistant U.S. Attorney/Branch Manager
Christopher Allman .... (913) 551-6730
E-mail: chris.allman@usdoj.gov
Assistant U.S. Attorney **Robin Anderson** .... (913) 551-6730
Assistant U.S. Attorney **Jon Fleenor** .... (913) 551-6730
E-mail: jon.fleenor@usdoj.gov
Assistant U.S. Attorney **Leon J. Patton** .... (913) 551-6730
E-mail: leon.patton@usdoj.gov
Assistant U.S. Attorney **Andrea Taylor** .... (913) 551-6730
E-mail: andrea.taylor@usdoj.gov
Assistant U.S. Attorney **(Vacant)** .... (913) 551-6730

Criminal Division
Criminal Division Coordinator **Kim M. Martin** .... (913) 551-6730
E-mail: kim.martin@usdoj.gov
Special Assistant U.S. Attorney **Trent Krug** .... (913) 551-6730
E-mail: trent.krug@usdoj.gov
Assistant U.S. Attorney **Tris Hunt** .... (913) 551-6730
E-mail: tris.hunt@usdoj.gov
Assistant U.S. Attorney **Scott Rask** .... (913) 551-6730
E-mail: scott.rask@usdoj.gov
Assistant U.S. Attorney **Sheri McCracken** .... (913) 551-6730
E-mail: sheri.mccracken@usdoj.gov
Assistant U.S. Attorney **Terra Morehead** .... (913) 551-6730
E-mail: terra.morehead@usdoj.gov
Assistant U.S. Attorney **Christopher "Chris" Oakley** .... (913) 551-6730

(continued on next page)

★ Presidential Appointment Requiring Senate Confirmation ☆ Presidential Appointment □ Schedule C Appointment ◇ Career Senior Foreign Service Appointment
● Career Senior Executive Service (SES) Appointment ○ Non-Career Senior Executive Service (SES) Appointment ■ Postal Career Executive Service

Criminal Division *continued*

Assistant U.S. Attorney **Kurt Shernuk** . . . . (913) 551-6730
E-mail: kurt.shernuk@usdoj.gov
Assistant U.S. Attorney **David Smith** . . . . (913) 551-6730
E-mail: david.smith@usdoj.gov
Assistant U.S. Attorney **Jabari Wamble** . . . . (913) 551-6730
Assistant U.S. Attorney **David Zabel** . . . . (913) 551-6730
E-mail: david.zabel@usdoj.gov

Topeka (KS) Office

Federal Building, 444 SE Quincy Street,
Suite 290, Topeka, KS 66683
Tel: (785) 295-2850 Fax: (785) 295-2853

Assistant U.S. Attorney/Branch Manager
Jackie A. Rapstine . . . . (785) 295-2850
E-mail: jackie.rapstine@usdoj.gov

Civil Division

Assistant U.S. Attorney **D. Brad Bailey** . . . . (785) 295-2850
E-mail: brad.bailey@usdoj.gov
Assistant U.S. Attorney **Thomas G. "Tom" Luedke** . . . . . (785) 295-2850
E-mail: tom.luedke@usdoj.gov
Assistant U.S. Attorney **Tanya S. Wilson** . . . . (785) 295-2850
E-mail: tanya.wilson@usdoj.gov
Assistant U.S. Attorney **(Vacant)** . . . . (785) 295-2850

Criminal Division

Criminal Division Coordinator **Jared Maag** . . . . (785) 295-2850
E-mail: jared.maag@usdoj.gov
Appellate Chief **James Brown** . . . . (785) 295-2850
E-mail: james.brown@usdoj.gov
Senior Litigation Counsel **Tanya J. Treadway** . . . . (785) 295-2850
E-mail: tanya.treadway@usdoj.gov
Assistant U.S. Attorney **Richard L. Hathaway** . . . . (785) 295-2850
E-mail: rich.hathaway@usdoj.gov
Assistant U.S. Attorney **Gregory A. Hough** . . . . (785) 295-2850
E-mail: greg.hough@usdoj.gov
Assistant U.S. Attorney **Christine Kenney** . . . . (785) 295-2850
E-mail: christine.kenney@usdoj.gov
Assistant U.S. Attorney **Anthony W. Mattivi** . . . . (785) 295-2850
E-mail: anthony.mattivi@usdoj.gov
Assistant U.S. Attorney **(Vacant)** . . . . (785) 295-2850
Assistant U.S. Attorney **(Vacant)** . . . . (785) 295-2850

Kentucky - Eastern District

260 West Vine Street, Suite 300, Lexington, KY 40507
Tel: (859) 233-2661 Fax: (859) 233-2666

★ U.S. Attorney **Kerry B. Harvey** . . . . (859) 233-2661
E-mail: kerry.harvey@usdoj.gov
Education: Murray State U 1978 BA; Kentucky 1982 JD
Secretary to the U.S. Attorney **Melanie LeTourneau** . . . (859) 685-4802
E-mail: melanie.letourneau@usdoj.gov
First Assistant U.S. Attorney **Carlton S. Shier IV** . . . . . . (859) 233-2661
E-mail: carlton.shier@usdoj.gov
Managing Assistant U.S. Attorney **Jason Parman** . . . . . . (606) 864-5523
E-mail: jason.parman@usdoj.gov
Administrative Officer **Rhonda Trent** . . . . (859) 685-4804
E-mail: rhonda.trent@usdoj.gov
Law Enforcement Committee Coordinator **Allen Love** . . . . (859) 233-2661
Victim-Witness Coordinator **Jenny Parker** . . . . (859) 685-4899
E-mail: jenny.parker@usdoj.gov
Personnel Officer **Louanne Davis** . . . . (859) 685-4928
E-mail: louanne.davis@usdoj.gov
Systems Manager **Traci Davis-Smith** . . . . (859) 685-4917
E-mail: traci.davis-smith@usdoj.gov
Systems Manager **Robin Gosper** . . . . (859) 685-4918
E-mail: robin.gosper@usdoj.gov

Civil Division

Fax: (859) 233-2533

Chief **Robin Gwinn** . . . . (859) 233-2661
Asset Forfeiture Unit Assistant U.S. Attorney
David Y. Olinger, Jr. . . . . (859) 233-2661
E-mail: david.olinger@usdoj.gov
Assistant U.S. Attorney **Robin Gwenn** . . . . (859) 233-2661
Assistant U.S. Attorney **Cheryl Morgan** . . . . (859) 233-2661
E-mail: cheryl.morgan@usdoj.gov
Assistant U.S. Attorney **Wade Napier** . . . . (859) 233-2661
E-mail: wade.napier@usdoj.gov
Assistant U.S. Attorney **John S. Osborn III** . . . . (859) 233-2661
E-mail: john.osborn@usdoj.gov
Assistant U.S. Attorney **Andrew Sparks** . . . . (859) 233-2661
E-mail: andrew.sparks@usdoj.gov
Assistant U.S. Attorney **(Vacant)** . . . . (859) 233-2661
Assistant U.S. Attorney **(Vacant)** . . . . (859) 233-2661
Assistant U.S. Attorney **(Vacant)** . . . . (859) 233-2661

Criminal Division

Fax: (859) 233-2747

Chief **Kevin C. Dicken** . . . . (859) 233-2661
E-mail: kevin.dicken@usdoj.gov
Senior Litigation Counsel **Hydee Hawkins** . . . . (859) 233-2661
E-mail: hydee.hawkins@usdoj.gov
Assistant U.S. Attorney **James E. "Jim" Arehart** . . . . (859) 233-2661
Assistant U.S. Attorney **Rob Duncan** . . . . (859) 233-2661
E-mail: rob.duncan@usdoj.gov
Assistant U.S. Attorney **John Grant** . . . . (859) 233-2661
Assistant U.S. Attorney **Hydee Hawkins** . . . . (859) 233-2661
E-mail: hydee.hawkins@usdoj.gov
Assistant U.S. Attorney **Erin May-Roth** . . . . (859) 233-2661
Education: Kentucky 2004 JD
Assistant U.S. Attorney **Kenneth R. Taylor** . . . . (859) 233-2661
E-mail: ken.taylor@usdoj.gov
Assistant U.S. Attorney **Ronald L. Walker** . . . . (859) 233-2661
E-mail: ronald.walker@usdoj.gov
Assistant U.S. Attorney **Charles Wisdom** . . . . (859) 233-2661
E-mail: charles.wisdom@usdoj.gov
Assistant U.S. Attorney **(Vacant)** . . . . (859) 233-2661
Assistant U.S. Attorney **(Vacant)** . . . . (859) 233-2661
Assistant U.S. Attorney **(Vacant)** . . . . (859) 233-2661
Assistant U.S. Attorney **(Vacant)** . . . . (859) 233-2661

Fort Mitchell (KY) Office

207 Grandview Drive, Suite 400, Fort Mitchell, KY 41017
Tel: (859) 655-3200 Fax: (859) 655-3211

Managing Assistant U.S. Attorney **Robert McBride** . . . . . (859) 655-3200
E-mail: robert.mcbride@usdoj.gov
Education: Dayton 1992 JD
Assistant U.S. Attorney **Tony Bracke** . . . . (859) 655-3200
E-mail: tony.bracke@usdoj.gov
Assistant U.S. Attorney **Jason Denney** . . . . (859) 655-3200
E-mail: jason.denney@usdoj.gov
Assistant U.S. Attorney **Elaine M. Leonhard** . . . . (859) 655-3200
Education: Cincinnati 2001 BA; Salmon P Chase 2004 JD
Assistant U.S. Attorney **Wade Napier** . . . . (859) 655-3200
E-mail: wade.napier@usdoj.gov
Assistant U.S. Attorney **Laura K. Voorhees** . . . . (859) 655-3200
E-mail: laura.voorhees@usdoj.gov
Legal Assistant **Amanda Johnson** . . . . (859) 652-7040
E-mail: amanda.johnson@usdoj.gov

London (KY) Office

601 Meyers Baker Road, Suite 200, London, KY 40741
Tel: (606) 864-5523 Fax: (606) 864-3590

Managing Assistant U.S. Attorney **Jason Parman** . . . . . . (606) 864-5523
E-mail: jason.parman@usdoj.gov

★ Presidential Appointment Requiring Senate Confirmation ☆ Presidential Appointment □ Schedule C Appointment ◇ Career Senior Foreign Service Appointment
● Career Senior Executive Service (SES) Appointment ○ Non-Career Senior Executive Service (SES) Appointment ■ Postal Career Executive Service

London (KY) Office *continued*

Assistant U.S. Attorney **Kathleen Coffey** . . . . (606) 864-5523
E-mail: kathleen.coffey@usdoj.gov
Assistant U.S. Attorney **Sam Dotson** . . . . (606) 864-5523
Assistant U.S. Attorney **Adam Reeves** . . . . (606) 864-5523
E-mail: adam.reeves@usdoj.gov

Kentucky - Western District

717 West Broadway, Louisville, KY 40202
Tel: (502) 582-5911 Fax: (502) 582-5097
Internet: www.usdoj.gov/usao/kyw

★ U.S. Attorney (Acting) **John E. Kuhn, Jr.** . . . . (502) 582-5911
E-mail: john.kuhn@usdoj.gov
Assistant to the U.S. Attorney **(Vacant)** . . . . (502) 625-7053
First Assistant U.S. Attorney **John E. Kuhn, Jr.** . . . . (502) 625-5902
E-mail: john.kuhn2@usdoj.gov
Administrative Officer **Charlene Hood** . . . . (502) 582-6989
E-mail: charlene.hood@usdoj.gov
Budget Analyst **Kimberly Campbell** . . . . (502) 582-5939
E-mail: kim.campbell@usdoj.gov
Human Resources Officer **Sandra "Sandy" Focken** . . . . . (502) 582-5998
Grand Jury Coordinator **Susan Cleffman-Huff** . . . . (502) 582-6326
E-mail: susan.huff@usdoj.gov
Law Enforcement Coordinator **MSG Brett Hightower** . . . (502) 582-6892
E-mail: brett.hightower@usdoj.gov
Affiliation: ARNG
Public Information Officer **Stephanie Collins** . . . . (502) 708-3200
E-mail: stephanie.collins@usdoj.gov Fax: (502) 582-5097
Victim-Witness Specialist **Helena Auberry** . . . . (502) 625-7040
E-mail: helena.auberry@usdoj.gov
Systems Manager **Robert Metzger** . . . . (502) 582-6420
E-mail: robert.metzger@usdoj.gov

Civil Division
717 West Broadway, Louisville, KY 40202
Fax: (502) 625-7110

Chief **Regina S. Edwards** . . . . (502) 625-7044
E-mail: regina.edwards@usdoj.gov
Assistant U.S. Attorney **William F. "Bill" Campbell** . . . . . (502) 582-6773
E-mail: bill.campbell@usdoj.gov
Assistant U.S. Attorney **Michael D. Ekman** . . . . (502) 625-7102
E-mail: michael.ekman@usdoj.gov
Assistant U.S. Attorney **Jay Gilbert** . . . . (502) 625-7103
E-mail: jay.gilbert@usdoj.gov
Assistant U.S. Attorney **W. Brady Miller** . . . . (502) 582-5166
E-mail: brady.miller@usdoj.gov
Assistant U.S. Attorney **Benjamin S. Schecter** . . . . (502) 582-6061
E-mail: Ben.Schecter@usdoj.gov
Assistant U.S. Attorney **Michael F. Spalding** . . . . (502) 625-7073
E-mail: mike.spalding@usdoj.gov
Assistant U.S. Attorney **(Vacant)** . . . . (502) 582-6942

Criminal Division
717 West Broadway, Louisville, KY 40202
Fax: (502) 582-5067

Chief **Michael A. Bennett** . . . . (502) 582-6023
E-mail: michael.bennett3@usdoj.gov
Deputy Chief **Bryan R. Calhoun** . . . . (502) 625-7064
E-mail: bryan.calhoun@usdoj.gov
Deputy Chief **Thomas W. Dyke** . . . . (502) 625-7042
E-mail: tom.dyke@usdoj.gov
Assistant U.S. Attorney **James H. Barr** . . . . (502) 625-7075
E-mail: jim.barr@usdoj.gov
Assistant U.S. Attorney **Randy Ream** . . . . (502) 582-6981
E-mail: randy.ream@usdoj.gov
Assistant U.S. Attorney **Robert Bonar** . . . . (502) 582-7062
E-mail: robert.bonar@usdoj.gov
Assistant U.S. Attorney **Terry M. Cushing** . . . . (502) 582-6936
E-mail: terry.cushing@usdoj.gov

Criminal Division *continued*

Assistant U.S. Attorney **J. Scott Davis** . . . . (502) 582-6988
E-mail: scott.davis@usdoj.gov
Assistant U.S. Attorney **Larry Fentress** . . . . (502) 582-6772
E-mail: larry.fentress@usdoj.gov
Assistant U.S. Attorney **Marisa J. Ford** . . . . (502) 582-5930
E-mail: marisa.ford@usdoj.gov
Assistant U.S. Attorney **Amanda Gregory** . . . . (502) 582-5016
E-mail: amanda.gregory@usdoj.gov
Assistant U.S. Attorney **Laura L. Hall** . . . . (502) 582-5901
E-mail: laura.hall@usdoj.gov
Assistant U.S. Attorney **Candace G. "Candy" Hill** . . . . . . (502) 625-7079
E-mail: candy.hill@usdoj.gov
Assistant U.S. Attorney **Lettricea Jefferson-Webb** . . . . . . (502) 582-6480
E-mail: lettricea.jefferson-webb@usdoj.gov
Assistant U.S. Attorney **Joshua Judd** . . . . (502) 625-7049
E-mail: joshua.judd@usdoj.gov
Education: Washington College of Law 2003 JD
Assistant U.S. Attorney **Daniel Kinnicutt** . . . . (502) 625-7408
E-mail: daniel.kinnicutt@usdoj.gov
Assistant U.S. Attorney **Jo Ellen Lawless** . . . . (502) 625-7065
E-mail: Jo.Lawless@usdoj.gov
Assistant U.S. Attorney **A. Spencer McKiness** . . . . (502) 582-6987
E-mail: spencer.mckiness@usdoj.gov
Assistant U.S. Attorney **Mac Shannon** . . . . (502) 582-6294
E-mail: mac.shannon@usdoj.gov
Assistant U.S. Attorney **Jason Snyder** . . . . (502) 582-6993
Education: Centre AB; Louisville JD
Assistant U.S. Attorney **Amy M. Sullivan** . . . . (502) 582-5449
E-mail: amy.sullivan@usdoj.gov
Assistant U.S. Attorney **Monica Wheatley** . . . . (502) 582-5938
E-mail: monica.wheatley@usdoj.gov
Assistant U.S. Attorney **Stephanie Dotson Zimdahl** . . . . (502) 582-6217
E-mail: stephanie.zimdahl@usdoj.gov
Education: Northwestern 2005 JD

Paducah (KY) Office

501 Broadway, Room 29, Paducah, KY 42001
Tel: (270) 442-7104 Fax: (270) 444-6794

Assistant U.S. Attorney **Nute Bonner** . . . . (270) 443-7104
E-mail: nute.bonner@usdoj.gov
Assistant U.S. Attorney **Seth Hancock** . . . . (270) 443-2899
E-mail: seth.hancock@usdoj.gov
Assistant U.S. Attorney **David Sparks** . . . . (270) 443-6188
E-mail: david.sparks@usdoj.gov

Louisiana - Eastern District

650 Poydras Street, Suite 1600, New Orleans, LA 70130
Tel: (504) 680-3000 Fax: (504) 589-4510
Internet: www.usdoj.gov/usao/lae/home.htm

★ U.S. Attorney **Kenneth Allen Polite, Jr.** . . . . (504) 680-3078
E-mail: kenneth.a.polite@usdoj.gov
Education: Harvard 1997 AB; Georgetown 2000 JD
Secretary to the U.S. Attorney **Anna Christman** . . . . (504) 680-3171
E-mail: anna.christman@usdoj.gov
First Assistant U.S. Attorney/Criminal Division Chief
Richard Westling . . . . (504) 680-3000
E-mail: richard.westling@usdoj.gov
Criminal Division Chief **Duane Evans** . . . . (504) 680-3000
E-mail: duane.evans@usdoj.gov
Criminal Division Deputy Chief
Maurice E. Landrieu, Jr. . . . . (504) 680-3000
E-mail: maurice.landrieu@usdoj.gov
Criminal Division Deputy Chief **(Vacant)** . . . . (504) 680-3000
Executive Assistant U.S. Attorney **Sharon Smith** . . . . (504) 680-3000
Appellate Division Chief and Assistant U.S. Attorney
Kevin G. Boitmann . . . . (504) 680-3000
E-mail: kevin.boitmann@usdoj.gov
Anti-Terrorism Unit Chief
Gregory M. "Gregg" Kennedy . . . . (504) 680-3103
E-mail: gregg.kennedy@usdoj.gov

(continued on next page)

REGIONAL OFFICES — US ATTORNEYS AND US MARSHALS SERVICE

★ Presidential Appointment Requiring Senate Confirmation ☆ Presidential Appointment □ Schedule C Appointment ◇ Career Senior Foreign Service Appointment
● Career Senior Executive Service (SES) Appointment ○ Non-Career Senior Executive Service (SES) Appointment ■ Postal Career Executive Service

Louisiana - Eastern District *continued*

Asset Forfeiture Unit Assistant U.S. Attorney **Michael Redmann** .... (504) 680-3000
E-mail: michael.redmann@usdoj.gov
Civil Division Chief **Peter Mansfield** .... (504) 680-3000
E-mail: peter.mansfield@usdoj.gov
Civil Division Deputy Chief **Sunni LeBeouf** .... (504) 680-3000
Cybercrimes Unit Chief **(Vacant)** .... (504) 680-3034
Fraud Unit Chief **Brian Klebba** .... (504) 680-3000
Organized Crime Drug Enforcement Task Force Unit Supervisor **Jay Quinlan** .... (504) 680-3000
E-mail: jay.quinlan@usdoj.gov
Public Integrity Unit Chief **Tracey Knight** .... (504) 680-3000
Violent Crimes Unit Supervisor **Mark Miller** .... (504) 680-3000
E-mail: mark.miller@usdoj.gov
Assistant U.S. Attorney **Rick Tickins** .... (504) 680-3012
Senior Litigation Counsel **Fred P. Harper, Jr.** .... (504) 680-3000
E-mail: fred.harper@usdoj.gov
Education: LSU 1976 JD
Senior Litigation Counsel **William "Bill" McSherry** .... (504) 680-3000
Victim-Witness Coordinator **Donna Duplantier** .... (504) 680-3000
E-mail: donna.duplantier@usdoj.gov
Systems Manager **Peter Bayer** .... (504) 680-3090
E-mail: peter.bayer@usdoj.gov

Louisiana - Middle District

Russell B. Long Federal Building, 777 Florida Street, Suite 208, Baton Rouge, LA 70801-1717
Tel: (225) 389-0443 Fax: (225) 389-0561
Internet: www.usdoj.gov/usao/lam

★ U.S. Attorney **James Walter Green** .... (225) 389-0443
Affiliation: USMCR
Education: LSU 1989 BA; Tulane 1993 JD
Secretary to the U.S. Attorney **Danette Willis** .... (225) 389-0443
First Assistant U.S. Attorney **Corey R. Amundson** .... (225) 389-0443
E-mail: corey.amundson@usdoj.gov
Administrative Officer **Miriam Fontaine** .... (225) 389-0443
E-mail: miriam.fontaine@usdoj.gov
Law Enforcement Committee Coordinator **Collins Harper** .... (225) 389-0443
Victim-Witness Coordinator **Holly Sheets** .... (225) 389-0443
Systems Manager **Daryl Blink** .... (225) 389-0443
E-mail: daryl.blink@usdoj.gov

Civil Division

Tel: (225) 389-0443 Fax: (225) 389-0685

Chief **Catherine M. Maraist** .... (225) 389-0443
E-mail: catherine.maraist@usdoj.gov
Assistant U.S. Attorney **Susan C. Amundson** .... (225) 389-0443
E-mail: susan.amundson@usdoj.gov
Assistant U.S. Attorney **John J. Gaupp** .... (225) 389-0443
E-mail: john.gaupp@usdoj.gov
Assistant U.S. Attorney **James P. Thompson** .... (225) 389-0443
Assistant U.S. Attorney **Jay Thompson** .... (225) 389-0443
E-mail: jay.thompson@usdoj.gov

Criminal Division

Tel: (225) 389-0443 Fax: (225) 389-0561

Chief **Corey R. Amundson** .... (225) 389-0443
E-mail: corey.amundson@usdoj.gov
Deputy Chief **Jennifer M. Kleinpeter** .... (225) 389-0443
E-mail: jennifer.kleinpeter@usdoj.gov
Senior Litigation Counsel **M. Patricia Jones** .... (225) 389-0443
Assistant U.S. Attorney **Brad Casey** .... (225) 389-0443
Assistant U.S. Attorney **Ryan Crosswell** .... (225) 389-0443
E-mail: ryan.crosswell@usdoj.gov
Assistant U.S. Attorney **Helina S. Dayries** .... (225) 389-0443
E-mail: helina.dayries@usdoj.gov
Assistant U.S. Attorney **J. Christopher Dippel** .... (225) 389-0443

Criminal Division *continued*

Assistant U.S. Attorney **Michael J. Jefferson** .... (225) 389-0443
Assistant U.S. Attorney **Cam T. Le** .... (225) 389-0443
Assistant U.S. Attorney **Frederick A. Menner, Jr.** .... (225) 389-0443
E-mail: fred.menner@usdoj.gov
Assistant U.S. Attorney **Robert Piedrahita** .... (225) 389-0443
E-mail: robert.piedrahita@usdoj.gov
Assistant U.S. Attorney **Adam Ptashkin** .... (225) 389-0443
Assistant U.S. Attorney **Paul Pugliese** .... (225) 389-0443
Assistant U.S. Attorney **Ryan Rezaei** .... (225) 389-0443
Assistant U.S. Attorney **René I. Salomon** .... (225) 389-0443
E-mail: rené.salomon@usdoj.gov
Assistant U.S. Attorney **Kevin Sanchez** .... (225) 389-0443
E-mail: kevin.sanchez@usdoj.gov
Assistant U.S. Attorney **Peter J. Smyczek** .... (225) 389-0443
Assistant U.S. Attorney **Alan Stevens** .... (225) 389-0443
E-mail: alan.stevens@usdoj.gov
Assistant U.S. Attorney **Lyman E. Thornton III** .... (225) 389-0443
E-mail: lyman.thornton@usdoj.gov
Education: LSU, JD
Assistant U.S. Attorney **Elizabeth White** .... (225) 389-0443

Maine District

East Tower, 100 Middle Street, 6th Floor, Portland, ME 04101
Tel: (207) 780-3257 TTY: (207) 780-3060 Fax: (207) 780-3304

★ U.S. Attorney **Thomas Edward Delahanty II** .... (207) 780-3257
E-mail: thomas.delahanty@usdoj.gov
Education: St Michael's 1967; Maine 1970 JD
Secretary to the U.S. Attorney **Laurie Janson** .... (207) 780-3257
E-mail: laurie.janson@usdoj.gov
Law Enforcement Coordinator **Heather Putnam** .... (207) 780-3257
E-mail: heather.putnam@usdoj.gov
Victim Witness Coordinator **Heather Putnam** .... (207) 780-3257
E-mail: heather.putnam@usdoj.gov
Administrative Officer **Sandra Dow** .... (207) 780-3257
E-mail: sandra.dow@usdoj.gov
IT Systems Manager **Karen Dube** .... (207) 780-3257
Intelligence Research Specialist **Mark Winter** .... (207) 780-3257 ext. 3242
E-mail: mark.winter@usdoj.gov

Appellate Section

Chief **Margaret D. McGaughey** .... (207) 780-3257
E-mail: margaret.mcgaughey@usdoj.gov
Assistant U.S. Attorney **Renee M. Bunker** .... (207) 780-3257
E-mail: renee.bunker@usdoj.gov

Civil Division

Chief **John G. Osborn** .... (207) 780-3257
Assistant U.S. Attorney **(Vacant)** .... (207) 780-3214

Criminal Division

Chief **Jonathan R. Chapman** .... (207) 780-3257
E-mail: jon.chapman@usdoj.gov
Anti-Terrorism Coordinator **Mark Winter** .... (207) 780-3257
Asset Forfeiture Unit Assistant U.S. Attorney **Donald E. Clark** .... (207) 780-3257
E-mail: donald.clark@usdoj.gov
Narcotics Section/Organized Crime Drug Enforcement Task Force Assistant U.S. Attorney **Daniel J. Perry** .... (207) 780-3257
First Assistant U.S. Attorney **Richard W. Murphy** .... (207) 780-3257 ext. 3250
Assistant U.S. Attorney **David B. Joyce** .... (207) 780-3257
E-mail: david.joyce@usdoj.gov
Education: Miami 2004 JD
Assistant U.S. Attorney **James W. Chapman** .... (207) 780-3257
E-mail: james.w.chapman@usdoj.gov
Assistant U.S. Attorney **Michael J. Conley** .... (207) 780-3257
E-mail: michael.conley@usdoj.gov
Assistant U.S. Attorney **Halsey Frank** .... (207) 780-3257
E-mail: halsey.frank@usdoj.gov

★ Presidential Appointment Requiring Senate Confirmation ☆ Presidential Appointment □ Schedule C Appointment ◇ Career Senior Foreign Service Appointment
● Career Senior Executive Service (SES) Appointment ○ Non-Career Senior Executive Service (SES) Appointment ■ Postal Career Executive Service

Criminal Division *continued*

Assistant U.S. Attorney **Darcie McElwee** .... (207) 780-3257
E-mail: darcie.mcelwee@usdoj.gov
Assistant U.S. Attorney **Craig M. Wolff** .... (207) 780-3257
E-mail: craig.wolff@usdoj.gov

Bangor (ME) Office

202 Harlow Street, Room 111, Bangor, ME 04401
Tel: (207) 945-0373 TTY: (207) 945-0307 Fax: (207) 945-0319

Branch Chief **Todd Lowell** .... (207) 945-0373
E-mail: todd.lowell@usdoj.gov
Assistant U.S. Attorney **Joel Casey** .... (207) 945-0373
E-mail: joel.casey@usdoj.gov
Assistant U.S. Attorney **Gail Fisk Malone** .... (207) 945-0373
E-mail: gail.f.malone@usdoj.gov
Assistant U.S. Attorney **James M. Moore** .... (207) 945-0373
E-mail: james.moore@usdoj.gov
Assistant U.S. Attorney **(Vacant)** .... (207) 945-0373
Deputy Administrative Officer **Wanda L. Smith** .... (207) 945-0373
E-mail: wanda.smith@usdoj.gov

Maryland District

36 South Charles Street, 4th Floor, Baltimore, MD 21201
Tel: (410) 209-4800 Fax: (410) 962-3124 Fax: (410) 962-0122
Internet: www.justice.gov/usao/md

★ U.S. Attorney **Rod J. Rosenstein** .... (410) 209-4800
E-mail: rod.rosenstein@usdoj.gov
Education: Wharton BS; Harvard JD
Secretary to the U.S. Attorney **Marcia Murphy** .... (410) 209-4800
E-mail: marcia.murphy@usdoj.gov
First Assistant U.S. Attorney **Stephen M. Schenning** .... (410) 209-4800
E-mail: stephen.schenning@usdoj.gov
Administrative Officer **Patrick Dunn** .... (410) 209-4800
E-mail: patrick.dunn@usdoj.gov
Law Enforcement Coordinator **Steven Hess** .... (410) 209-4800
E-mail: steven.hess@usdoj.gov
Assistant U.S. Attorney and Appellate Chief
Sujit Raman .... (301) 344-4433
Assistant U.S. Attorney (OCDETF/HIDTA
Coordinator) **Andrea L. Smith** .... (410) 209-4800
E-mail: andrea.smith@usdoj.gov

Civil Division

Chief, Civil Division **Allen F. Loucks** .... (410) 209-4800
E-mail: allen.loucks@usdoj.gov
Assistant Chief, Assistant U.S. Attorney (Health Care
Fraud Coordinator) **Thomas Corcoran** .... (410) 209-4800
E-mail: thomas.corcoran@usdoj.gov
Assistant U.S. Attorney **Jane Andersen** .... (410) 209-4800
E-mail: jane.andersen@usdoj.gov
Assistant U.S. Attorney **Thomas Barnard** .... (410) 209-4800
E-mail: thomas.barnard@usdoj.gov
Assistant U.S. Attorney **Tarra DeShields** .... (410) 209-4800
E-mail: tarra.deshields@usdoj.gov
Assistant U.S. Attorney **Molissa Farber** .... (410) 209-4800
E-mail: molissa.farber@usdoj.gov
Assistant U.S. Attorney **Alex Gordon** .... (301) 344-4433
E-mail: alex.gordon@usdoj.gov
Assistant U.S. Attorney **Jakarra Jones** .... (410) 209-4800
E-mail: jakarra.jones@usdoj.gov
Assistant U.S. Attorney **Rebecca Koch** .... (410) 209-4800
E-mail: rebecca.koch@usdoj.gov
Assistant U.S. Attorney **Sarah Marquardt** .... (410) 209-4800
E-mail: sarah.marquardt@usdoj.gov
Assistant U.S. Attorney **Roann Nichols** .... (410) 209-4800
E-mail: roann.nichols@usdoj.gov
Assistant U.S. Attorney **Matthew P. Phelps** .... (410) 209-4800
E-mail: matthew.phelps@usdoj.gov
Assistant U.S. Attorney **Neil White** .... (301) 344-4433
E-mail: neil.white@usdoj.gov

Civil Division *continued*

Assistant U.S. Attorney (Affirmative Civil
Enforcement) **(Vacant)** .... (410) 209-4800

Criminal Division

Chief **James A. Crowell** .... (410) 209-4800
E-mail: james.a.crowell@usdoj.gov
Asset Forfeiture and Money Laundering Section Chief
Evan Shea .... (410) 209-4800
Fraud and Corruption Section Chief
Kathleen O. Gavin .... (410) 209-4800
E-mail: kathleen.gavin@usdoj.gov
Fraud and Corruption Section Deputy Chief
Martin J. "Marty" Clarke .... (410) 209-4800
E-mail: marty.clarke@usdoj.gov
Major Crimes Section Chief **Sandra Wilkinson** .... (410) 209-4800
E-mail: sandra.wilkinson@usdoj.gov
Major Crimes Section Deputy Chief
Michael Cunningham .... (410) 209-4800
E-mail: michael.cunningham@usdoj.gov
National Security Section Chief **Harvey E. Eisenberg** .... (410) 209-4800
E-mail: harvey.eisenberg@usdoj.gov
Narcotics Section Chief **Robert Harding** .... (410) 209-4800
E-mail: robert.harding@usdoj.gov
Narcotics Section Deputy Chief **Christopher Romano** ... (410) 209-4800
E-mail: christopher.romano@usdoj.gov
Violent Crimes Section Chief **Michael Hanlon** .... (410) 209-4800
E-mail: michael.hanlon@usdoj.gov
Violent Crimes Section Deputy Chief **James Wallner** .... (410) 209-4800
E-mail: james.wallner@usdoj.gov
Assistant U.S. Attorney **Dana Brusca** .... (410) 209-4800
E-mail: dana.brusca@usdoj.gov
Education: Northwestern 2010 JD
Assistant U.S. Attorney **Paul Budlow** .... (410) 209-4800
E-mail: paul.budlow@usdoj.gov
Assistant U.S. Attorney **Kenneth Clark** .... (410) 209-4800
E-mail: kenneth.clark@usdoj.gov
Assistant U.S. Attorney **David Copperthite** .... (410) 209-4800
E-mail: david.copperthite@usdoj.gov
Assistant U.S. Attorney **Sean R. Delaney** .... (410) 209-4800
E-mail: sean.delaney@usdoj.gov
Assistant U.S. Attorney **Ayn Ducao** .... (410) 209-4800
E-mail: ayn.ducao@usdoj.gov
Education: Harvard 2001 JD
Assistant U.S. Attorney **Debra L. "Debbie" Dwyer** ...... (410) 209-4800
Note: On detail.
E-mail: debbie.dwyer@usdoj.gov
Assistant U.S. Attorney **Joshua Ferrentino** .... (410) 209-4800
E-mail: joshua.ferrentino@usdoj.gov
Assistant U.S. Attorney **Tamera Fine** .... (410) 209-4800
E-mail: tamera.fine@usdoj.gov
Assistant U.S. Attorney **Clinton J. Fuchs** .... (410) 209-4800
Note: On detail to the Senate Judiciary Committee.
E-mail: clinton.fuchs@usdoj.gov
Assistant U.S. Attorney **Jefferson M. Gray** .... (410) 209-4800
E-mail: jefferson.m.gray@usdoj.gov
Assistant U.S. Attorney **Bonnie S. Greenberg** .... (410) 209-4800
E-mail: bonnie.greenberg@usdoj.gov
Assistant U.S. Attorney **Harry Gruber** .... (410) 209-4800
E-mail: harry.gruber@usdoj.gov
Assistant U.S. Attorney **Richard C. Kay** .... (410) 209-4800
E-mail: richard.kay@usdoj.gov
Education: Maryland JD
Assistant U.S. Attorney **Matthew Maddox** .... (410) 209-4800
E-mail: matthew.maddox2@usdoj.gov
Assistant U.S. Attorney **Christine Manuelian** .... (410) 209-4800
E-mail: christine.manuelian@usdoj.gov
Assistant U.S. Attorney **Peter J. Martinez** .... (410) 209-4800
E-mail: peter.martinez@usdoj.gov
Assistant U.S. Attorney **Joyce K. McDonald** .... (410) 209-4800
E-mail: joyce.mcdonald@usdoj.gov

(continued on next page)

★ Presidential Appointment Requiring Senate Confirmation ☆ Presidential Appointment □ Schedule C Appointment ◇ Career Senior Foreign Service Appointment
● Career Senior Executive Service (SES) Appointment ○ Non-Career Senior Executive Service (SES) Appointment ■ Postal Career Executive Service

Criminal Division *continued*

Assistant U.S. Attorney **Patricia McLane** . . . . (410) 209-4800
E-mail: patricia.mclane@usdoj.gov
Assistant U.S. Attorney **Jason Medinger** . . . . (410) 209-4800
E-mail: jason.medinger@usdoj.gov
Assistant U.S. Attorney **Judson T. Mihok** . . . . (410) 209-4800
E-mail: judson.mihok@usdoj.gov
Assistant U.S. Attorney **Seema Mittal** . . . . (410) 209-4800
E-mail: seema.mittal@usdoj.gov
Education: George Washington 2008 JD
Assistant U.S. Attorney **Zachary A. Myers** . . . . (410) 209-4800
E-mail: zachary.myers@usdoj.gov
Assistant U.S. Attorney **John F. Purcell** . . . . (410) 209-4800
E-mail: john.purcell@usdoj.gov
Assistant U.S. Attorney **Philip Selden** . . . . (410) 209-4800
E-mail: philip.selden@usdoj.gov
Education: Columbia 2007 JD
Assistant U.S. Attorney **John Sippel** . . . . (410) 209-4800
E-mail: john.sippel@usdoj.gov
Assistant U.S. Attorney **Matthew C. Sullivan** . . . . (410) 209-4800
E-mail: matthew.sullivan@usdoj.gov
Education: Harvard 2006 AB, 2009 JD
Assistant U.S. Attorney **James G. Warwick** . . . . (410) 209-4800
E-mail: james.warwick@usdoj.gov
Assistant U.S. Attorney **Leo J. Wise** . . . . (410) 209-4800
E-mail: leo.wise@usdoj.gov
Education: Johns Hopkins; Harvard 2003 JD
Assistant U.S. Attorney **Rachel M. Yasser** . . . . (410) 209-4800
E-mail: rachel.yasser@usdoj.gov
Assistant U.S. Attorney **Aaron Zelinsky** . . . . (410) 209-4800
E-mail: aaron.zelinsky@usdoj.gov
Education: Yale 2010 JD
Assistant U.S. Attorney **(Vacant)** . . . . (410) 209-4800
Assistant U.S. Attorney **(Vacant)** . . . . (410) 209-4800

Greenbelt (MD) Office

6500 Cherrywood Lane, Room 400, Greenbelt, MD 20770
Tel: (301) 344-4433 Fax: (301) 344-4516

Southern Division Chief **Arun Rao** . . . . (301) 344-4433
E-mail: arun.rao@usdoj.gov
Education: NYU 2001 JD
Southern Division Deputy Chief **(Vacant)** . . . . (301) 344-4433
Senior Litigation Counsel **Deborah A. Johnston** . . . . (301) 344-4433
E-mail: deborah.johnston@usdoj.gov
Assistant U.S. Attorney **Adam Ake** . . . . (301) 344-4433
E-mail: adam.ake@usdoj.gov
Assistant U.S. Attorney **Joseph Baldwin** . . . . (301) 344-4433
Assistant U.S. Attorney **Leah Bressack** . . . . (301) 344-4433
E-mail: leah.bressack@usdoj.gov
Assistant U.S. Attorney **Bryan Foreman** . . . . (301) 344-4433
E-mail: bryan.foreman@usdoj.gov
Assistant U.S. Attorney **Daniel C. Gardner** . . . . (301) 344-4433
E-mail: daniel.gardner@usdoj.gov
Assistant U.S. Attorney **Mara Greenberg** . . . . (301) 344-4433
E-mail: mara.greenberg@usdoj.gov
Assistant U.S. Attorney **Kelly O. Hayes** . . . . (301) 344-4433
E-mail: kelly.hayes@usdoj.gov
Assistant U.S. Attorney **Lindsay E. Kaplan** . . . . (301) 344-4433
E-mail: lindsay.kaplan@usdoj.gov
Assistant U.S. Attorney **Ray McKenzie** . . . . (301) 344-4433
E-mail: ray.mckenzie@usdoj.gov
Assistant U.S. Attorney **Nicolas Mitchell** . . . . (301) 344-4433
E-mail: nicolas.mitchell@usdoj.gov
Assistant U.S. Attorney **William Moomau** . . . . (301) 344-4433
E-mail: william.moomau@usdoj.gov
Assistant U.S. Attorney **Jane F. Nathan** . . . . (301) 344-4433
E-mail: jane.nathan@usdoj.gov
Assistant U.S. Attorney **Kristi O'Malley** . . . . (301) 344-4433
Assistant U.S. Attorney **Michael Packard** . . . . (301) 344-4433
Assistant U.S. Attorney **David I. Salem** . . . . (301) 344-4433
E-mail: david.salem@usdoj.gov

Greenbelt (MD) Office *continued*

Assistant U.S. Attorney **Thomas Sullivan** . . . . (301) 344-4433
E-mail: thomas.sullivan@usdoj.gov
Assistant U.S. Attorney **Hollis R. Weisman** . . . . (301) 344-4433
E-mail: hollis.weisman@usdoj.gov
Assistant U.S. Attorney **Thomas P. Windom** . . . . (301) 344-4433
E-mail: thomas.windom@usdoj.gov
Education: Harvard 2000 AB; Virginia 2005 JD

Massachusetts District

John Joseph Moakley U.S. Courthouse, One Courthouse Way, Suite 9200, Boston, MA 02210
Tel: (617) 748-3100 Fax: (617) 748-3953
Internet: www.usdoj.gov/usao/ma

★ U.S. Attorney **Carmen Milagros Ortiz** . . . . (617) 748-3100
E-mail: carmen.ortiz@usdoj.gov
Education: Adelphi 1978 BBA; George Washington 1981 JD
Secretary to U.S. Attorney **Terry Caminiti** . . . . (617) 748-3100
E-mail: terry.caminiti@usdoj.gov
Public Affairs Specialist **Christina Dilorio-Sterling** . . . . . . (617) 748-3100
Executive Officer and Policy Advisor **Jill Reilly** . . . . (617) 748-3100
First Assistant U.S. Attorney **John McNeil** . . . . (617) 748-3100
Counsel to the U.S. Attorney **William Weinreb** . . . . (617) 748-3100
E-mail: william.weinreb@usdoj.gov
Victim - Witness Coordinator **Kathleen M. Griffin** . . . . . . (617) 748-3100
E-mail: kathleen.griffin@usdoj.gov
Administrative Officer **Paul W. Havey** . . . . (617) 748-3100
E-mail: paul.havey@usdoj.gov

Appeals Division

Chief **Dina M. Chaitowitz** . . . . (617) 748-3100
E-mail: dina.chaitowitz@usdoj.gov

Asset Forfeiture Unit

Fax: (617) 748-3967 Fax: (617) 748-3111

Chief **Christopher Donato** . . . . (617) 748-3100
E-mail: chris.donato@usdoj.gov

Civil Division

Fax: (617) 748-3969 Fax: (617) 748-3217

Chief **Rosemary Connolly** . . . . (617) 748-3100

Criminal Division

Chief **Cynthia Young** . . . . (617) 748-3100
Deputy Chief **James D. Herbert** . . . . (617) 748-3100
E-mail: james.herbert@usdoj.gov
Internet Crimes Unit Chief **Adam Bookbinder** . . . . (617) 748-3100
E-mail: adam.bookbinder@usdoj.gov

Economic Crimes Unit

Fax: (617) 740-3156

Chief **Sarah Walters** . . . . (617) 748-3100
E-mail: sarah.walters@usdoj.gov

Financial Litigation Unit

Fax: (617) 748-3248

Chief **Christopher Donato** . . . . (617) 748-3100
E-mail: chris.donato@usdoj.gov

Health Care Fraud Unit

Fax: (617) 748-3610

Chief **Nathaniel Yeager** . . . . (617) 748-3100
E-mail: nathaniel.yeager@usdoj.gov

Major Crimes Unit

Fax: (617) 748-3104 Fax: (617) 748-3234

Chief **Lori J. Holik** . . . . (617) 748-3100
E-mail: lori.holik@usdoj.gov

★ Presidential Appointment Requiring Senate Confirmation ☆ Presidential Appointment ☐ Schedule C Appointment ◇ Career Senior Foreign Service Appointment
● Career Senior Executive Service (SES) Appointment ○ Non-Career Senior Executive Service (SES) Appointment ■ Postal Career Executive Service

Major Crimes Unit *continued*

Assistant U.S. Attorney **B. Stephanie Siegmann** .... (617) 748-3100

Organized Crime Drug Enforcement Task Force Unit
Fax: (617) 748-3156 Fax: (617) 748-3164

Chief **Nathaniel Mendell** .... (617) 748-3100
E-mail: nathaniel.mendell@usdoj.gov

Public Corruption and Special Prosecutions Unit
Fax: (617) 748-3357 Fax: (617) 748-3357

Chief **Fred M. Wyshak, Jr.** .... (617) 748-3100
E-mail: fred.wyshak@usdoj.gov

Strike Force Unit
Fax: (617) 748-3214

Chief **Peter Levitt** .... (617) 748-3100
E-mail: peter.levitt@usdoj.gov

Springfield (MA) Office

United States Courthouse, 300 State Street,
Suite 230, Springfield, MA 01105-2926
Tel: (413) 785-0235 Fax: (413) 785-0394

Chief **Kevin O'Regan** .... (413) 785-0235

Worcester (MA) Office

Donohue Federal Building, 595 Main Street,
Suite 206, Worcester, MA 01608
Tel: (508) 368-0100 Fax: (508) 756-7120

Chief **Karin Bell** .... (508) 368-0100
E-mail: karin.bell@usdoj.gov
Education: Harvard 2002 JD

Michigan - Eastern District

211 West Fort Street, Suite 2001, Detroit, MI 48226-3211
Tel: (313) 226-9100 TTY: (313) 226-9560 Fax: (313) 226-4609
Internet: www.usdoj.gov/usao/mie/index.htm

★ U.S. Attorney **Barbara L. McQuade** .... (313) 226-9100
E-mail: barbara.mcquade@usdoj.gov
Education: Michigan 1987, 1991 JD
Secretary to the U.S. Attorney **Stacey Harris** .... (313) 226-9100
E-mail: stacey.harris@usdoj.gov
First Assistant U.S. Attorney **Jennifer M. Gorland** ...... (313) 226-9100
E-mail: jennifer.gorland@usdoj.gov
Executive Assistant U.S. Attorney
Stephanie Dawkins Davis .... (313) 226-9100
E-mail: stephanie.davis@usdoj.gov
Senior Counsel **(Vacant)** .... (313) 226-9100
Administrative Officer **Keri Miller** .... (313) 226-9100
E-mail: keri.miller@usdoj.gov
District Office Security Manager **Todd Paxton** .... (313) 226-9100
E-mail: todd.paxton@usdoj.gov
Immigration Coordinator **(Vacant)** .... (313) 226-9100
Law Enforcement Manager **Robert Poikey** .... (313) 226-9100
E-mail: robert.poikey@usdoj.gov
Librarian **Shannon Bass** .... (313) 226-9100
E-mail: shannon.bass@usdoj.gov
Public Affairs Officer **Gina Balaya** .... (313) 226-9758
Records Coordinator **(Vacant)** .... (313) 226-9100
Systems Manager **Danette Scagnetti** .... (313) 226-9100
E-mail: danette.scagnetti@usdoj.gov
Victim-Witness Coordinator **Sandy Palazzolo** .... (313) 226-9100
E-mail: sandy.palazzolo@usdoj.gov

Appellate Division
Chief **Patricia Gaedeke** .... (313) 226-9100
E-mail: patricia.gaedeke@usdoj.gov
Assistant U.S. Attorney **Kathleen Moro Nesi** .... (313) 226-9518
E-mail: kathleen.nesi@usdoj.gov

Civil Division
Chief **Elizabeth J. Larin** .... (313) 226-9100
E-mail: elizabeth.larin@usdoj.gov
Supervisory Assistant U.S. Attorney **(Vacant)** .... (313) 226-9786
Affirmative Litigation Chief **Peter A. Caplan** .... (313) 226-9100
E-mail: peter.caplan@usdoj.gov
Asset Forfeiture and Financial Litigation Chief
Julie Beck .... (313) 226-9100
E-mail: julie.beck@usdoj.gov
Civil Rights Chief **Susan DeClercq** .... (313) 226-9100
E-mail: susan.declercq@usdoj.gov
Defensive Litigation Chief **Vanessa Mays** .... (313) 226-9100
E-mail: vanessa.mays@usdoj.gov
Assistant U.S. Attorney **Julia A. Caroff Pidgeon** .... (313) 226-9100
Assistant U.S. Attorney **Rita Foley** .... (313) 226-9520
E-mail: rita.foley@usdoj.gov
Assistant U.S. Attorney **Jacqueline M. "Jackie" Hotz** ... (313) 226-9108
E-mail: jackie.hotz@usdoj.gov
Assistant U.S. Attorney **Derri T. Thomas** .... (313) 226-9153
E-mail: derri.thomas@usdoj.gov
Assistant U.S. Attorney **Leslie Matuja Wizner** .... (313) 226-9766
E-mail: leslie.wizner@usdoj.gov
Assistant U.S. Attorney **Tauras N. Ziedas** .... (313) 226-9573

Criminal Division
Chief **Daniel Lemisch** .... (313) 226-9100
E-mail: daniel.lemisch@usdoj.gov
Senior Litigation Counsel **Michael Leibson** .... (313) 226-9100
Supervisory Assistant U.S. Attorney **Robert P. Cares** ..... (313) 226-9736
E-mail: robert.cares@usdoj.gov
Supervisory Assistant U.S. Attorney **Lynn A. Helland** .... (313) 226-9730
E-mail: lynn.helland@usdoj.gov
Supervisory Assistant U.S. Attorney **Sheldon N. Light** ... (313) 226-9732
E-mail: sheldon.light@usdoj.gov
Complex Crimes Chief **Ross I. MacKenzie** .... (313) 226-0816
E-mail: ross.mackenzie@usdoj.gov
Drug Task Force Chief **Dawn Ison** .... (313) 226-9100
E-mail: dawn.ison@usdoj.gov
General Crimes Chief **Kevin M. Mulcahy** .... (313) 226-9100
E-mail: kevin.mulcahy@usdoj.gov
Health Care Fraud Chief **Wayne F. Pratt** .... (313) 226-9100
E-mail: wayne.pratt@usdoj.gov
National Security Chief **Jonathan Tukel** .... (313) 226-9100
E-mail: jonathan.tukel@usdoj.gov
Education: Michigan 1982 BA, 1988 JD
Public Corruption Chief **Mark D. Chutkow** .... (313) 226-9100
E-mail: mark.chutkow@usdoj.gov
Education: Yale 1987 BA
Violent and Organized Crime Chief **John N. O'Brien** .... (313) 226-9100
E-mail: john.obrien@usdoj.gov
White Collar Crime Chief **Cynthia Oberg** .... (313) 226-9100
E-mail: cynthia.oberg@usdoj.gov
Assistant U.S. Attorney **R. Michael Bullotta** .... (313) 226-9100
Assistant U.S. Attorney **Paul Burakoff** .... (313) 226-9100
E-mail: paul.burakoff@usdoj.gov
Assistant U.S. Attorney **Frances Carlson** .... (313) 226-9100
E-mail: frances.carlson@usdoj.gov
Assistant U.S. Attorney **Kenneth R. Chadwell** .... (313) 226-9689
E-mail: ken.chadwell@usdoj.gov
Assistant U.S. Attorney **Richard L. Delonis** .... (313) 226-9100
Assistant U.S. Attorney **John C. Engstrom** .... (313) 226-9571
Assistant U.S. Attorney **Gary M. Felder** .... (313) 226-9742
E-mail: gary.felder@usdoj.gov
Assistant U.S. Attorney **Susan E. Gillooly** .... (313) 226-9577
E-mail: susan.gillooly@usdoj.gov
Assistant U.S. Attorney **Carl Gilmer-Hill** .... (313) 226-9100
E-mail: carl.gilmer-hill@usdoj.gov
Assistant U.S. Attorney **Jerome F. Gorgon, Jr.** .... (313) 226-9676
E-mail: jerome.gorgon@usdoj.gov
Education: Michigan 2002 JD
Assistant U.S. Attorney **Terrence R. Haugabook** .... (313) 226-9157
E-mail: terrence.haugabook@usdoj.gov

(continued on next page)

REGIONAL OFFICES — US ATTORNEYS AND US MARSHALS SERVICE

★ Presidential Appointment Requiring Senate Confirmation ☆ Presidential Appointment ☐ Schedule C Appointment ◇ Career Senior Foreign Service Appointment
● Career Senior Executive Service (SES) Appointment ○ Non-Career Senior Executive Service (SES) Appointment ■ Postal Career Executive Service

Criminal Division *continued*

Assistant U.S. Attorney **Daniel R. Hurley** . . . . (313) 226-9100
E-mail: daniel.hurley@usdoj.gov
Assistant U.S. Attorney **Stanley J. "Lee" Janice** . . . . (313) 226-9740
E-mail: lee.janice@usdoj.gov
Assistant U.S. Attorney **Bruce C. Judge** . . . . (313) 226-9100
E-mail: bruce.judge@usdoj.gov
Assistant U.S. Attorney **Diane L. Marion** . . . . (313) 226-9703
E-mail: diane.marion@usdoj.gov
Assistant U.S. Attorney **David E. Morris** . . . . (313) 226-9646
E-mail: david.morris@usdoj.gov
Assistant U.S. Attorney **David J. Portelli** . . . . (313) 226-9711
Assistant U.S. Attorney **Sarah Resnick Cohen** . . . . (313) 226-9637
Assistant U.S. Attorney **Karen L. Reynolds** . . . . (313) 226-9672
E-mail: karen.reynolds@usdoj.gov
Assistant U.S. Attorney **Stephen T. Robinson** . . . . (313) 226-9100
Assistant U.S. Attorney **William J. Sauget** . . . . (313) 226-9575
E-mail: william.sauget@usdoj.gov
Assistant U.S. Attorney **Graham L. Teall** . . . . (313) 226-9118
E-mail: graham.teall@usdoj.gov
Assistant U.S. Attorney **Janice V. Terbush** . . . . (313) 226-9100
Assistant U.S. Attorney **Pamela J. Thompson** . . . . (313) 226-9770
E-mail: pamela.thompson@usdoj.gov
Assistant U.S. Attorney **Christopher Varner** . . . . (313) 226-9100
E-mail: christopher.varner@usdoj.gov
Assistant U.S. Attorney **Ronald W. Waterstreet** . . . . (313) 226-9593
E-mail: ronald.waterstreet@usdoj.gov
Assistant U.S. Attorney **Craig A. Weier** . . . . (313) 226-9678
E-mail: craig.weier@usdoj.gov
Assistant U.S. Attorney **James M. Wouczyna** . . . . (313) 226-9100
Assistant U.S. Attorney **(Vacant)** . . . . (313) 226-9692

Bay City (MI) Office

101 First Street, Suite 200, Bay City, MI 48708
Tel: (989) 895-5712 TTY: (989) 895-2501 Fax: (989) 895-5790

Supervisory Assistant U.S. Attorney **Craig Wininger** . . . . . (989) 891-5712
E-mail: craig.wininger@usdoj.gov
Assistant U.S. Attorney **Libby Kelly Dill** . . . . (989) 895-5712
E-mail: libby.dill@usdoj.gov
Assistant U.S. Attorney **Roy Kranz** . . . . (989) 895-5712
E-mail: roy.kranz@usdoj.gov
Assistant U.S. Attorney **Janet L. Parker** . . . . (989) 895-5712
E-mail: janet.parker2@usdoj.gov
Assistant U.S. Attorney **Anca I. Pop** . . . . (989) 895-5790
E-mail: anca.pop@usdoj.gov
Education: Michigan State 2006 JD

Flint (MI) Office

210 Federal Building, 600 Church Street,
Suite 200, Flint, MI 48502
Tel: (810) 766-5177 TTY: (810) 766-5100 Fax: (810) 766-5427

Supervisory Assistant U.S. Attorney **Craig Wininger** . . . . . (810) 766-5177
E-mail: craig.wininger@usdoj.gov
Assistant U.S. Attorney **Nancy A. Abraham** . . . . (810) 766-5020
E-mail: nancy.abraham@usdoj.gov
Assistant U.S. Attorney **Jules Deporre** . . . . (810) 766-5177
E-mail: jules.deporre@usdoj.gov
Assistant U.S. Attorney **Christopher Rawsthorne** . . . . (810) 766-5020
E-mail: christopher.rawsthorne@usdoj.gov
Assistant U.S. Attorney **Anthony Vance** . . . . (810) 766-5177
E-mail: anthony.vance@usdoj.gov

Michigan - Western District

330 Ionia NW, Suite 501, Grand Rapids, MI 49503
P.O. Box 208, Grand Rapids, MI 49501-0208
Tel: (616) 456-2404 Fax: (616) 456-2408
Internet: www.usdoj.gov/usao/miw/

★ U.S. Attorney **Patrick A. "Pat" Miles, Jr.** . . . . (616) 456-2404
Education: Aquinas Col 1988 BSBA; Harvard 1991 JD

Michigan - Western District *continued*

Administrative Assistant to the U.S. Attorney
Jettia Ramey . . . . (616) 456-2404
E-mail: jettia.ramey@usdoj.gov
First Assistant U.S. Attorney **Andrew Byerly Birge** . . . . . . (616) 456-2404
E-mail: andrew.birge@usdoj.gov
Administrative Officer **Sheryl A. Brugh** . . . . (616) 456-2404
E-mail: sheryl.brugh@usdoj.gov
Administrative Service Specialist **Kelly Johnson** . . . . (616) 456-2404
E-mail: kelly.johnson@usdoj.gov
Supervisory Administrative Services Specialist
Warren Olsen . . . . (616) 456-2404
E-mail: warren.olson@usdoj.gov
Law Enforcement Committee Coordinator
Kaye D. Hooker . . . . (616) 456-2404
Librarian **June VanWingen** . . . . (616) 456-2404
E-mail: june.vanwingen@usdoj.gov
Public Information Officer **Kaye D. Hooker** . . . . (616) 456-2404
E-mail: kaye.hooker@usdoj.gov
Systems Manager **Roger Hensley** . . . . (616) 456-2404
E-mail: roger.hensley@usdoj.gov
Assistant Systems Manager **Tom Keating** . . . . (616) 456-2404
E-mail: tom.keating@usdoj.gov
Victim-Witness Coordinator **Kathy Schuette** . . . . (616) 456-2404
E-mail: kathy.schuette@usdoj.gov
Victim-Witness Coordinator **Janet Strahan** . . . . (616) 456-2404
E-mail: janet.strahan@usdoj.gov

Civil Division

Chief **Ryan Cobb** . . . . (616) 456-2404
E-mail: ryan.cobb@usdoj.gov
Assistant U.S. Attorney **Carrie Almassian** . . . . (616) 456-2404
Assistant U.S. Attorney **W. Francesca Ferguson** . . . . (616) 456-2404
E-mail: francesca.ferguson@usdoj.gov
Assistant U.S. Attorney **Jeanne F. Long** . . . . (616) 456-2404
E-mail: jeanne.long@usdoj.gov
Education: Michigan 2007 JD
Assistant U.S. Attorney **Michael L. Shiparski** . . . . (616) 456-2404
E-mail: mike.shiparski@usdoj.gov
Assistant U.S. Attorney **Adam Townshend** . . . . (616) 456-2404
E-mail: adam.townshend@usdoj.gov

Criminal Division

Chief/Assistant U.S. Attorney **Nils Kessler** . . . . (616) 456-2404
E-mail: nils.kessler@usdoj.gov
Deputy Chief **Daniel Y. Mekaru** . . . . (616) 456-2404
E-mail: daniel.mekaru@usdoj.gov
Senior Litigative Counsel **(Vacant)** . . . . (616) 456-2404
Executive Counsel **Donald Daniels** . . . . (616) 456-2404
E-mail: donald.daniels@usdoj.gov
Anti-Terrorism Advisory Council Coordinator
Clay Matthew West . . . . (616) 456-2404
E-mail: clay.west@usdoj.gov
Education: Harvard 1997 AB; Cambridge (UK) 1998 MPhil;
Yale 2001 JD
Appellate Coordinator **Jennifer L. McManus** . . . . (616) 456-2404
E-mail: jennifer.mcmanus@usdoj.gov
Asset Forfeiture Coordinator **Joel Fauson** . . . . (616) 456-2404
E-mail: joel.fauson@usdoj.gov
Drug Unit Chief **Matthew G. Borgula** . . . . (616) 456-2404
E-mail: matthew.borgula@usdoj.gov
Tribal Liaison **Jeffrey J. Davis** . . . . (616) 456-2404
Assistant U.S. Attorney **Raymond E. Beckering III** . . . . . . (616) 456-2404
E-mail: ray.beckering@usdoj.gov
Assistant U.S. Attorney **Sally Berens** . . . . (616) 456-2404
E-mail: sally.berens@usdoj.gov
Education: Chicago 2001 JD
Assistant U.S. Attorney **Andrew Byerly Birge** . . . . (616) 456-2404
E-mail: andrew.birge@usdoj.gov
Assistant U.S. Attorney **John C. Bruha** . . . . (616) 456-2404
E-mail: john.bruha@usdoj.gov

★ Presidential Appointment Requiring Senate Confirmation ☆ Presidential Appointment ☐ Schedule C Appointment ◇ Career Senior Foreign Service Appointment
● Career Senior Executive Service (SES) Appointment ○ Non-Career Senior Executive Service (SES) Appointment ■ Postal Career Executive Service

Criminal Division *continued*

Assistant U.S. Attorney **Mark V. Courtade** . . . . (616) 456-2404
E-mail: mark.courtade@usdoj.gov
Assistant U.S. Attorney **Joel Fauson** . . . . (616) 456-2404
E-mail: joel.fauson@usdoj.gov
Assistant U.S. Attorney **Hagen W. Frank** . . . . (616) 456-2404
E-mail: hagen.frank@usdoj.gov
Assistant U.S. Attorney **Tessa Hessmiller** . . . . (616) 456-2404
E-mail: tessa.hessmiller@usdoj.gov
Assistant U.S. Attorney **Russell Kavalhuna** . . . . (616) 456-2404
E-mail: russell.kavalhuna@usdoj.gov
Assistant U.S. Attorney **Sean Lewis** . . . . (616) 456-2404
Assistant U.S. Attorney **Heath Lynch** . . . . (616) 456-2404
E-mail: heath.lynch@usdoj.gov
Assistant U.S. Attorney **Michael A. MacDonald** . . . . (616) 456-2404
E-mail: michael.macdonald@usdoj.gov
Assistant U.S. Attorney **Christopher O'Connor** . . . . (616) 456-2404
E-mail: christopher.oconnor@usdoj.gov
Assistant U.S. Attorney **B. Rene Shekmer** . . . . (616) 456-2404
E-mail: rene.shekmer@usdoj.gov
Assistant U.S. Attorney **Ronald M. Stella** . . . . (616) 456-2404
Assistant U.S. Attorney **Clay Stiffler** . . . . (616) 456-2404
E-mail: clay.stiffler@usdoj.gov
Assistant U.S. Attorney **Timothy P. VerHey** . . . . (616) 456-2404
E-mail: timothy.verhey@usdoj.gov
Assistant U.S. Attorney **Clay Matthew West** . . . . (616) 456-2404
E-mail: clay.west@usdoj.gov
Education: Harvard 1997 AB; Cambridge (UK) 1998 MPhil; Yale 2001 JD
Assistant U.S. Attorney **(Vacant)** . . . . (616) 456-2404

Lansing (MI) Office

315 West Allegan, Room 252, Lansing, MI 48933
Tel: (517) 377-1577 Fax: (517) 377-1698

Assistant U.S. Attorney **(Vacant)** . . . . (517) 377-1577

Marquette (MI) Office

First Merit Bank, 1930 U.S. 41 West, 2nd Floor, Marquette, MI 49855
Tel: (906) 226-2500 Fax: (906) 226-3700

Assistant U.S. Attorney **Paul D. Lochner** . . . . (906) 226-2500
E-mail: paul.lochner@usdoj.gov
Assistant U.S. Attorney **Hannah Bobee** . . . . (906) 226-2500
E-mail: hannah.bobee@usdoj.gov
Assistant U.S. Attorney **Maarten Vermaat** . . . . (906) 226-2500
E-mail: maarten.vermaat@usdoj.gov
Education: Yale 1999 JD

Minnesota District

600 U.S. Courthouse, 300 South Fourth Street, Minneapolis, MN 55415
Tel: (612) 664-5600 Tel: (651) 848-1950 (St. Paul, MN Office)
Fax: (612) 664-5787
Internet: www.usdoj.gov/usao/mn

★ U.S. Attorney **Andrew Mark "Andy" Luger** . . . . (612) 664-5600
E-mail: andrew.luger@usdoj.gov
Education: Amherst 1981 BA; Georgetown 1985 JD
Secretary to the U.S. Attorney **Tammie Cuddihy** . . . . . . (612) 664-5665
E-mail: tammie.cuddihy@usdoj.gov
First Assistant U.S. Attorney **Gregory G. Brooker** . . . . (612) 664-5600
E-mail: greg.brooker@usdoj.gov
Senior Litigation Counsel **Andrew S. Dunne** . . . . (612) 664-5600
E-mail: andrew.dunne@usdoj.gov
Senior Litigation Counsel **David MacLaughlin** . . . . (612) 664-5600
E-mail: david.maclaughlin@usdoj.gov
Administrative Officer **Keith Collier** . . . . (612) 664-5600
E-mail: keith.collier@usdoj.gov
Human Resources Officer **(Vacant)** . . . . (612) 664-5600
Systems Manager **Daniel "Dan" McConville** . . . . (612) 664-5600
E-mail: daniel.mcconville@usdoj.gov

Civil Division

Chief **Ana Voss** . . . . (612) 664-5600
E-mail: ana.voss@usdoj.gov
Deputy Chief **D. Gerald Wilhelm** . . . . (612) 664-5600
E-mail: gerald.wilhelm@usdoj.gov

Criminal Division

Chief **Tracy L. Perzel** . . . . (612) 664-5600
E-mail: tracy.perzel@usdoj.gov
Appellate Chief **James E. Lackner** . . . . (612) 848-1927
E-mail: james.lackner@usdoj.gov
Education: Macalester; Northwestern JD
Deputy Criminal Chief for Fraud and Public Corruption **Timothy G. Rank** . . . . (612) 664-5600
E-mail: timothy.rank@usdoj.gov
Deputy Criminal Chief for Major Crimes and Priority Prosecutions **Karen B. Schommer** . . . . (612) 664-5600
E-mail: karen.schommer@usdoj.gov
Deputy Criminal Chief for Organized Crime Drug Enforcement Task Force and Violent Crimes **Nate P. Petterson** . . . . (612) 664-5600
E-mail: nate.petterson@usdoj.gov

Saint Paul (MN) Office

404 United States Courthouse, 316 North Robert Street, St. Paul, MN 55101
Tel: (651) 848-1950 Fax: (651) 848-1943

Branch Chief **Steven L. Schleicher** . . . . (651) 848-1927

Mississippi - Northern District

900 Jefferson Avenue, Oxford, MS 38655-3608
Tel: (662) 234-3351 Fax: (662) 234-4818
E-mail: usa-msn-oxford@usdoj.gov

★ U.S. Attorney **Felicia C. Adams** . . . . (662) 234-3351
E-mail: felicia.adams@usdoj.gov
Education: Jackson State U 1981; Mississippi 1984 JD
Secretary to the U.S. Attorney **Anita S. McGehee** . . . . . (662) 234-3351
E-mail: anita.mcgehee@usdoj.gov
First Assistant U.S. Attorney **William C. Martin** . . . . (662) 234-3351
E-mail: william.martin@usdoj.gov
Administrative Officer **Jim T. Allen** . . . . (662) 234-3351
Law Enforcement Coordinator **Randall M. "Randy" Corban** . . . . (662) 234-3351
E-mail: randy.corban@usdoj.gov
Victim-Witness Coordinator **Jonathan D. Dozier** . . . . (662) 234-3351
E-mail: jonathan.dozier@usdoj.gov
Intelligence Specialist **James Paul Rowlett** . . . . (662) 234-3351
Public Affairs Officer **Chad Lamar** . . . . (662) 234-3351

Civil Division

Fax: (662) 234-3318

Chief **Ralph M. Dean III** . . . . (662) 234-3351
E-mail: ralph.dean@usdoj.gov
Assistant U.S. Attorney **John E. Gough, Jr.** . . . . (662) 234-3351
E-mail: john.gough@usdoj.gov
Assistant U.S. Attorney **Ava N. Jackson** . . . . (662) 234-3351
E-mail: ava.jackson@usdoj.gov
Assistant U.S. Attorney **Feleica T. Wilson** . . . . (662) 234-3351
E-mail: feleica.wilson@usdoj.gov
Assistant U.S. Attorney **Samuel D. Wright** . . . . (662) 234-3351
E-mail: samuel.wright@usdoj.gov
Paralegal Specialist **(Vacant)** . . . . (662) 234-3351

Criminal Division

Fax: (662) 234-0657

Chief **Chad Lamar** . . . . (662) 234-3351
E-mail: chad.lamar@usdoj.gov
Drug Task Force Lead Assistant U.S. Attorney **Scott F. Leary** . . . . (662) 234-3351
E-mail: scott.leary@usdoj.gov

(continued on next page)

★ Presidential Appointment Requiring Senate Confirmation ☆ Presidential Appointment □ Schedule C Appointment ◇ Career Senior Foreign Service Appointment
● Career Senior Executive Service (SES) Appointment ○ Non-Career Senior Executive Service (SES) Appointment ■ Postal Career Executive Service

Criminal Division *continued*

Assistant U.S. Attorney **Susan S. Bradley** .... (662) 234-3351
E-mail: susan.bradley@usdoj.gov
Assistant U.S. Attorney **Robert W. Coleman** .... (662) 234-3351
E-mail: robert.coleman@usdoj.gov
Assistant U.S. Attorney **Chad M. Doleac** .... (662) 234-3351
E-mail: chad.doleac@usdoj.gov
Assistant U.S. Attorney **James C. "Clay" Joyner** .... (662) 234-3351
E-mail: clay.joyner@usdoj.gov
Assistant U.S. Attorney **Robert H. Mims** .... (662) 234-3351
E-mail: robert.mims@usdoj.gov
Assistant U.S. Attorney **Robert H. Norman** .... (662) 234-3351
E-mail: robert.norman@usdoj.gov
Assistant U.S. Attorney **Paul D. Roberts** .... (662) 234-3351
E-mail: paul.roberts@usdoj.gov
Assistant U.S. Attorney **(Vacant)** .... (662) 234-3351

Mississippi - Southern District

501 East Court Street, Suite 4-430, Jackson, MS 39201
Tel: (601) 965-4480 Fax: (601) 965-4409
Internet: www.usdoj.gov/usao/mss

★ U.S. Attorney **Gregory Keith Davis** .... (601) 965-4480
Term Expires: 2016
E-mail: gregory.davis@usdoj.gov
Education: Mississippi State 1984; Tulane 1987 JD
Secretary to the U.S. Attorney **Sheila Wilbanks** .... (601) 973-2852
E-mail: sheila.wilbanks@usdoj.gov
First Assistant U.S. Attorney **Harold Brittain** .... (228) 563-1560
E-mail: harold.brittain@usdoj.gov
Administrative Officer **Denise Daniels** .... (601) 965-4480
E-mail: denise.daniels@usdoj.gov
Law Enforcement Committee Coordinator
Jesse Bingham .... (601) 965-4480
E-mail: jesse.bingham@usdoj.gov
Personnel Manager **Cindy Pittman** .... (601) 973-2861
Systems Manager **Donna McAlpin** .... (601) 973-2809
E-mail: donna.mcalpin@usdoj.gov
Webmaster **Gordon Huey** .... (601) 965-2807

Civil Division

Chief **Mitzi Dease Paige** .... (601) 965-4480
E-mail: mitzi.paige@usdoj.gov
Assistant U.S. Attorney **Pshon Barrett** .... (601) 965-4480
E-mail: pshon.barrett@usdoj.gov
Assistant U.S. Attorney **Dave Fulcher** .... (601) 965-4480
E-mail: dave.fulcher@usdoj.gov
Assistant U.S. Attorney **Angela Givens** .... (601) 965-4480
Assistant U.S. Attorney **Kristi Johnson** .... (601) 965-4480
E-mail: kristi.johnson2@usdoj.gov
Assistant U.S. Attorney **Lynn Murray** .... (601) 965-4480
E-mail: lynn.murray@usdoj.gov
Assistant U.S. Attorney **David Usry** .... (601) 965-4480
E-mail: david.usry@usdoj.gov
Assistant U.S. Attorney **(Vacant)** .... (601) 965-4480

Criminal Division

Chief **Carla Clark** .... (601) 965-4480
E-mail: carla.clark@usdoj.gov
Drug Task Force Lead Assistant U.S. Attorney
Erin O'Leary-Chalk .... (601) 965-4480
Assistant U.S. Attorney **John M. Dowdy** .... (601) 965-4480
Assistant U.S. Attorney **Scott Gilbert** .... (601) 965-4480
E-mail: scott.gilbert@usdoj.gov
Assistant U.S. Attorney **Glenda Haynes** .... (601) 965-4480
E-mail: glenda.haynes@usdoj.gov
Assistant U.S. Attorney **Greg Kennedy** .... (601) 965-4480
E-mail: greg.kennedy@usdoj.gov
Assistant U.S. Attorney **Darren LaMarca** .... (601) 965-4480
E-mail: darren.lamarca@usdoj.gov
Assistant U.S. Attorney **Pat Lemon** .... (601) 965-4480
E-mail: pat.lemon@usdoj.gov

Criminal Division *continued*

Assistant U.S. Attorney **Jerry Rushing** .... (601) 965-4480
E-mail: jerry.rushing@usdoj.gov
Assistant U.S. Attorney **Mary Helen Wall** .... (601) 965-4480
Assistant U.S. Attorney **Christopher Wansley** .... (601) 965-4480
E-mail: christopher.wansley@usdoj.gov
Assistant U.S. Attorney **(Vacant)** .... (601) 965-4480
Assistant U.S. Attorney **(Vacant)** .... (601) 965-4480
Assistant U.S. Attorney **(Vacant)** .... (601) 965-4480

Gulfport (MS) Office

1575 20th Avenue, Gulfport, MS 39501
Tel: (228) 563-1560 Fax: (228) 435-3303

Assistant U.S. Attorney **Stanley B. Harris** .... (228) 563-1560
Civil Division Assistant U.S. Attorney
Stephen R. Graben .... (228) 563-1560
E-mail: stephen.graben@usdoj.gov
Civil Division Assistant U.S. Attorney **(Vacant)** .... (228) 563-1560
Criminal Division Supervisory Assistant U.S. Attorney
Ruth R. Morgan .... (228) 563-1560
E-mail: ruth.morgan@usdoj.gov
Criminal Division Assistant U.S. Attorney
Gaines Cleveland .... (228) 563-1560
E-mail: gaines.cleveland@usdoj.gov
Criminal Division Assistant U.S. Attorney
Shundral Cole .... (228) 563-1560
E-mail: shundral.cole@usdoj.gov
Criminal Division Assistant U.S. Attorney
Andrea Cabell Jones .... (228) 563-1560
E-mail: andrea.jones@usdoj.gov
Education: Sophie Newcomb 1983 BA; Mississippi 1986 JD
Criminal Division Assistant U.S. Attorney
John Meynardie .... (228) 563-1560
E-mail: john.meynardie@usdoj.gov
Criminal Division Assistant U.S. Attorney **(Vacant)** ...... (228) 563-1560

Missouri - Eastern District

Thomas F. Eagleton U.S. Courthouse, 111 South 10th Street, Room 20.333, St. Louis, MO 63102
Tel: (314) 539-2200 Fax: (314) 539-2309
Internet: www.usdoj.gov/usao/moe

★ U.S. Attorney **Richard G. Callahan** .... (314) 539-2200
E-mail: richard.callahan@usdoj.gov
Education: Georgetown 1968 AB, 1972 JD
Secretary to the U.S. Attorney **Terri L. Dougherty** ..... (314) 539-2200
E-mail: terri.dougherty@usdoj.gov
First Assistant U.S. Attorney **(Vacant)** .... (314) 539-2200
Administrative Officer **Gary Livingston** .... (314) 539-2200
E-mail: gary.livingston@usdoj.gov
Public Affairs Officer **Jan W. Diltz** .... (314) 539-2200
E-mail: jan.diltz@usdoj.gov
Law Enforcement Committee Coordinator
Ronald J. Scaggs .... (314) 539-2200
E-mail: ron.scaggs@usdoj.gov
Victim Advocate **Kimberly Sanders** .... (314) 539-2200
E-mail: kimberly.sanders@usdoj.gov
Systems Manager **Dianne Michels** .... (314) 539-2200
E-mail: dianne.michels@usdoj.gov

Civil Division

Chief **Nicholas P. Llewellyn** .... (314) 539-3280
E-mail: nicholas.llewellyn@usdoj.gov
Financial Litigation Unit Supervisor **Karen Wilke** .... (314) 539-2200
E-mail: karen.wilke@usdoj.gov
Assistant U.S. Attorney **Josh Jones** .... (314) 539-3280
E-mail: josh.jones@usdoj.gov
Education: Georgia 2000 JD
Assistant U.S. Attorney **Roger Keller** .... (314) 539-3280
E-mail: roger.keller@usdoj.gov
Assistant U.S. Attorney **Andy Lay** .... (314) 539-3280

REGIONAL OFFICES — US ATTORNEYS AND US MARSHALS SERVICE

★ Presidential Appointment Requiring Senate Confirmation ☆ Presidential Appointment □ Schedule C Appointment ◇ Career Senior Foreign Service Appointment
● Career Senior Executive Service (SES) Appointment ○ Non-Career Senior Executive Service (SES) Appointment ■ Postal Career Executive Service

Civil Division *continued*

Assistant U.S. Attorney **Steven Luther** . . . . (314) 539-3280
E-mail: steven.luther@usdoj.gov
Assistant U.S. Attorney **Christina Moore** . . . . (314) 539-3280
E-mail: christina.moore@usdoj.gov
Assistant U.S. Attorney **Suzanne Moore** . . . . (314) 539-3280
E-mail: suzanne.moore@usdoj.gov
Assistant U.S. Attorney **A. Jane Rund** . . . . (314) 539-3280
Assistant U.S. Attorney **Karin Schute** . . . . (314) 539-3280
E-mail: karin.schute@usdoj.gov
Assistant U.S. Attorney **Jane Berman Shaw** . . . . (314) 539-3280
E-mail: jane.shaw@usdoj.gov

Criminal Division

Chief **James E. Crowe, Jr.** . . . . (314) 539-2200
E-mail: james.crowe@usdoj.gov
Deputy Chief **Antoinette Decker** . . . . (314) 539-2200
Regional Drug Task Force Coordinator
James C. Delworth . . . . (314) 539-2200
E-mail: james.delworth@usdoj.gov
Assistant U.S. Attorney **Thomas Albus** . . . . (314) 539-2200
Assistant U.S. Attorney **Tiffany Becker** . . . . (314) 539-2200
E-mail: tiffany.becker@usdoj.gov
Assistant U.S. Attorney **Allison Behrens** . . . . (314) 539-2200
Assistant U.S. Attorney **Tracy Berry** . . . . (314) 539-2220
E-mail: tracy.berry@usdoj.gov
Assistant U.S. Attorney **John Bird** . . . . (314) 539-2200
Assistant U.S. Attorney **Charles Birmingham** . . . . (314) 539-2200
E-mail: charles.birmingham@usdoj.gov
Assistant U.S. Attorney **Gwendolyn Carroll** . . . . (314) 539-2200
E-mail: gwen.carroll@usdoj.gov
Assistant U.S. Attorney **Stephen Casey** . . . . (314) 539-2200
Education: Regent U JD
Assistant U.S. Attorney **Dianna Collins** . . . . (314) 539-2200
Assistant U.S. Attorney **John T. Davis** . . . . (314) 539-2200
Assistant U.S. Attorney **Thomas E. Dittmeier** . . . . (314) 539-2200
E-mail: thomas.dittmeier@usdoj.gov
Assistant U.S. Attorney **Edward Dowd III** . . . . (314) 539-2200
E-mail; edward.dowd@usdoj.gov
Assistant U.S. Attorney **Matthew Drake** . . . . (314) 539-2200
Assistant U.S. Attorney **Richard Finneran** . . . . (314) 539-2200
Assistant U.S. Attorney **Sayler Anne Ault Fleming** . . . . . (314) 539-2200
Education: Mississippi State 2001 BACCY; Vanderbilt 2006 JD
Assistant U.S. Attorney **Anthony Franks** . . . . (314) 539-2200
Assistant U.S. Attorney **Erin Granger** . . . . (314) 539-2200
Assistant U.S. Attorney **Jeanette Graviss** . . . . (314) 539-2200
Assistant U.S. Attorney **Reginald Harris** . . . . (314) 539-2200
E-mail: reginald.harris@usdoj.gov
Assistant U.S. Attorney **Dean R. Hoag** . . . . (314) 539-2200
E-mail: dean.hoag@usdoj.gov
Assistant U.S. Attorney **Patrick Judge** . . . . (314) 539-2200
E-mail: patrick.judge@usdoj.gov
Assistant U.S. Attorney **Joseph M. Landolt** . . . . (314) 539-2200
E-mail: joseph.landolt@usdoj.gov
Assistant U.S. Attorney **Colleen Lang** . . . . (314) 539-2200
E-mail: colleen.lang@usdoj.gov
Assistant U.S. Attorney **Rob Livergood** . . . . (314) 539-2200
E-mail: rob.livergood@usdoj.gov
Assistant U.S. Attorney **John Mantovani** . . . . (314) 539-2200
E-mail: john.mantovani@usdoj.gov
Assistant U.S. Attorney **Howard J. Marcus** . . . . (314) 539-2200
E-mail: howard.marcus@usdoj.gov
Assistant U.S. Attorney **Dorothy L. McMurtry** . . . . (314) 539-2200
E-mail: dorothy.mcmurtry@usdoj.gov
Assistant U.S. Attorney **Thomas J. Mehan** . . . . (314) 539-2200
E-mail: thomas.mehan@usdoj.gov
Assistant U.S. Attorney **Steven A. Muchnick** . . . . (314) 539-2200
E-mail: steven.muchnick@usdoj.gov
Assistant U.S. Attorney **Thomas S. Rea** . . . . (314) 539-2200
E-mail: thomas.rea@usdoj.gov
Assistant U.S. Attorney **Michael Reilly** . . . . (314) 539-2200
E-mail: michael.reilly@usdoj.gov

Criminal Division *continued*

Assistant U.S. Attorney **Jennifer Roy** . . . . (314) 539-2200
Assistant U.S. Attorney **Cristian M. Stevens** . . . . (314) 539-2200
Assistant U.S. Attorney **Kenneth R. Tihen** . . . . (314) 539-2200
E-mail: kenneth.tihen@usdoj.gov
Assistant U.S. Attorney **John J. Ware** . . . . (314) 539-2200
E-mail: john.ware@usdoj.gov
Assistant U.S. Attorney **Amanda S. Wick** . . . . (314) 539-2200
E-mail: amanda.wick@usdoj.gov
Assistant U.S. Attorney **Jennifer Winfield** . . . . (314) 539-2200
Assistant U.S. Attorney **Sirena Wissler** . . . . (314) 539-2200
E-mail: sirena.wissler@usdoj.gov
Assistant U.S. Attorney **Julia M. Wright** . . . . (314) 539-2200
E-mail: julia.wright@usdoj.gov
Assistant U.S. Attorney **(Vacant)** . . . . (314) 539-2200
Assistant U.S. Attorney **(Vacant)** . . . . (314) 539-2200
Assistant U.S. Attorney **(Vacant)** . . . . (314) 539-2200
Assistant U.S. Attorney **(Vacant)** . . . . (314) 539-2200

Cape Girardeau (MO) Office

Rush H. Limbaugh, Sr. U.S. Courthouse,
555 Independence Street, Cape Girardeau, MO 63701
Tel: (573) 334-3736 Fax: (573) 335-2393

Special Assistant U.S. Attorney **Timothy Willis** . . . . (573) 334-3736
E-mail: timothy.willis@usdoj.gov
Assistant U.S. Attorney **Larry H. Ferrell** . . . . (573) 334-3736
E-mail: larry.ferrell@usdoj.gov
Assistant U.S. Attorney **Paul W. Hahn** . . . . (573) 334-3736
E-mail: paul.hahn@usdoj.gov
Assistant U.S. Attorney **Keith D. Sorrell** . . . . (573) 334-3736
Assistant U.S. Attorney **John "Jack" Koester** . . . . (573) 334-3736
E-mail: john.koester@usdoj.gov

Missouri - Western District

Charles Evans Whittaker Courthouse, 400 East Ninth Street,
Room 5510, Kansas City, MO 64106
Tel: (816) 426-3122 Fax: (816) 426-4210
Internet: www.usdoj.gov/usao/mow

★ U.S. Attorney **Angela Tammy Dickinson** . . . . (816) 426-3122
Education: Webster 1989 BA; Missouri (St Louis) 1998 JD
Executive Secretary **Emma Stump** . . . . (816) 426-4319
E-mail: emma.stump@usdoj.gov
First Assistant U.S. Attorney **David Ketchmark** . . . . (816) 426-3122
E-mail: david.ketchmark@usdoj.gov
Senior Litigation Counsel **Gregg Coonrod** . . . . (816) 426-4101
E-mail: gregg.coonrod@usdoj.gov
Administrative Officer **Christy Rodriguez** . . . . (816) 426-3122
E-mail: christy.rodriguez@usdoj.gov
Public Affairs Officer **Don Ledford** . . . . (816) 426-4220
Law Enforcement Coordinator **Les Kerr** . . . . (816) 426-3122
Victim-Witness Coordinator **Tina Sutter** . . . . (816) 426-3122
E-mail: tina.sutter@usdoj.gov
Systems Manager **Bill Waldram** . . . . (816) 426-3122
E-mail: william.waldram@usdoj.gov

Appellate Division

Chief **Lajuana Counts** . . . . (816) 426-3122
E-mail: lajuana.counts@usdoj.gov
Assistant U.S. Attorney **Phil Koppe** . . . . (816) 426-3122
E-mail: phil.koppe@usdoj.gov

Civil Division

Fax: (816) 426-3165

Deputy U.S. Attorney **Jeff Ray** . . . . (816) 426-3130
E-mail: jeffrey.ray@usdoj.gov
Monetary Penalties Unit Chief **Curt Bohling** . . . . (816) 426-4296
E-mail: curt.bohling@usdoj.gov
Assistant U.S. Attorney **Amy Blackburn** . . . . (816) 426-4269
E-mail: amy.blackburn@usdoj.gov

(continued on next page)

★ Presidential Appointment Requiring Senate Confirmation ☆ Presidential Appointment □ Schedule C Appointment ◇ Career Senior Foreign Service Appointment
● Career Senior Executive Service (SES) Appointment ○ Non-Career Senior Executive Service (SES) Appointment ■ Postal Career Executive Service

Civil Division *continued*

Assistant U.S. Attorney **Thomas M. Larson** (816) 426-3130
E-mail: tom.larson@usdoj.gov
Assistant U.S. Attorney **Stacey Perkins-Rock** (816) 426-3122
E-mail: stacey.perkins-rock@usdoj.gov
Assistant U.S. Attorney **Jerry Short** (816) 426-3130
E-mail: jerry.short@usdoj.gov
Assistant U.S. Attorney **Charles Thomas** (816) 426-3130
E-mail: charles.thomas@usdoj.gov
Assistant U.S. Attorney **Cari Walsh** (816) 426-3130
E-mail: cari.walsh@usdoj.gov
Assistant U.S. Attorney **Cindi Woolery** (816) 426-3130
E-mail: cindi.woolery@usdoj.gov

Criminal Division

Chief **Gene Porter** (816) 426-3122
E-mail: gene.porter@usdoj.gov
Computer Crimes and Child Exploitation Unit Chief **Teresa Moore** (816) 426-3122
E-mail: teresa.moore@usdoj.gov
Fraud and Corruption Unit Chief **Kathleen "Kate" Mahoney** (816) 426-3122
E-mail: kate.mahoney@usdoj.gov
Narcotics and Violent Crimes Unit Chief **Jeff Valenti** (816) 426-4262
E-mail: jeff.valenti@usdoj.gov
Narcotics and Violent Crimes Deputy Chief **Charles Ambrose** (816) 426-4278
E-mail: chuck.ambrose@usdoj.gov
Narcotics and Violent Crimes Deputy Chief **Jess Michaelsen** (816) 426-2605
E-mail: jess.michaelsen@usdoj.gov
Terrorism and National Security Unit Chief **Brian Casey** (816) 426-4138
E-mail: brian.casey@usdoj.gov
Assistant U.S. Attorney **David Barnes** (816) 426-2771
E-mail: david.barnes@usdoj.gov
Assistant U.S. Attorney **Paul S. Becker** (816) 426-2771
E-mail: paul.becker@usdoj.gov
Assistant U.S. Attorney **Jane Brown** (816) 426-2605
E-mail: jane.brown@usdoj.gov
Assistant U.S. Attorney **Bruce Clark** (816) 426-2771
E-mail: bruce.clark@usdoj.gov
Assistant U.S. Attorney **Catherine Connelly** (816) 426-4278
E-mail: catherine.connelly@usdoj.gov
Assistant U.S. Attorney **John Cowles** (816) 426-3122
E-mail: john.cowles@usdoj.gov
Assistant U.S. Attorney **Patrick Daly** (816) 426-4249
E-mail: patrick.daly@usdoj.gov
Assistant U.S. Attorney **Justin G. Davids** (816) 426-4189
E-mail: justin.davids@usdoj.gov
Education: Yale 2001 BA; Columbia 2005 JD
Assistant U.S. Attorney **Alison Dunning** (816) 426-3122
E-mail: alison.dunning@usdoj.gov
Assistant U.S. Attorney **Patrick Edwards** (816) 426-3122
E-mail: patrick.edwards@usdoj.gov
Assistant U.S. Attorney **Mike Green** (816) 426-2771
E-mail: mike.green@usdoj.gov
Assistant U.S. Attorney **Stefan Hughes** (816) 426-4314
E-mail: stefan.hughes@usdoj.gov
Assistant U.S. Attorney **David Luna** (816) 426-3122
E-mail: david.luna@usdoj.gov
Assistant U.S. Attorney **Joseph "Joe" Marquez** (816) 426-3122
E-mail: joseph.marquez@usdoj.gov
Assistant U.S. Attorney **Jeffrey McCarther** (816) 426-3122
E-mail: jeffrey.mccarther@usdoj.gov
Assistant U.S. Attorney **William Meiners** (816) 426-2605
E-mail: william.meiners@usdoj.gov
Assistant U.S. Attorney **Daniel M. Nelson** (816) 426-4125
E-mail: daniel.nelson@usdoj.gov
Assistant U.S. Attorney **Bruce Rhoades** (816) 426-4278
E-mail: bruce.rhoades@usdoj.gov
Assistant U.S. Attorney **Rudolph R. Rhodes IV** (816) 426-4278
E-mail: rudolph.rhodes@usdoj.gov

Criminal Division *continued*

Assistant U.S. Attorney **Christina Tabor** (816) 426-2771
E-mail: christina.tabor@usdoj.gov
Assistant U.S. Attorney **Brent Venneman** (816) 426-4255
E-mail: brent.venneman@usdoj.gov
Assistant U.S. Attorney **Matt Wolesky** (816) 426-3122
E-mail: matt.wolesky@usdoj.gov
Assistant U.S. Attorney **(Vacant)** (816) 426-2605

Jefferson City (MO) Office

80 Lafayette St, Ste. 2100, Jefferson City, MO 65101
Tel: (573) 634-8214 Fax: (573) 634-8723

Supervising Assistant U.S. Attorney **Mike Oliver** (573) 634-8214
E-mail: mike.oliver@usdoj.gov
Assistant U.S. Attorney **Anthony "Tony" Gonzalez** (573) 634-8214
E-mail: anthony.gonzalez@usdoj.gov
Assistant U.S. Attorney **Lauren Kummerer** (573) 634-8214
E-mail: lauren.kummerer@usdoj.gov
Assistant U.S. Attorney **Jim Lynn** (573) 634-8214
E-mail: jim.lynn@usdoj.gov
Assistant U.S. Attorney **Lawrence E. Miller** (573) 634-8214
E-mail: lawrence.miller@usdoj.gov

Springfield (MO) Office

901 St. Louis Street, Suite 500, Springfield, MO 65806-2511
Tel: (417) 831-4406 Fax: (417) 831-0078

Supervisory Assistant U.S. Attorney **Gary Milligan** (417) 831-4406
E-mail: gary.milligan@usdoj.gov
Assistant U.S. Attorney **Patrick A. N. Carney** (417) 831-4406
E-mail: patrick.carney@usdoj.gov
Assistant U.S. Attorney **Randy Eggert** (417) 831-4406
E-mail: randy.eggert@usdoj.gov
Assistant U.S. Attorney **Timothy "Tim" Garrison** (417) 831-4406
E-mail: timothy.garrison@usdoj.gov
Assistant U.S. Attorney **Cynthia Hyde** (417) 831-4406
E-mail: cynthia.hyde@usdoj.gov
Assistant U.S. Attorney **James "Jim" Kelleher** (417) 831-4406
E-mail: james.kelleher@usdoj.gov
Assistant U.S. Attorney **Abram "Abe" McGull** (417) 831-4406
E-mail: abram.mcgull@usdoj.gov
Assistant U.S. Attorney **Ami Miller** (417) 831-4406
E-mail: ami.miller@usdoj.gov
Assistant U.S. Attorney **Steven Mohlhenrich** (417) 831-4406
E-mail: steven.mohlhenrich@usdoj.gov
Assistant U.S. Attorney **(Vacant)** (417) 831-4406
Assistant U.S. Attorney **(Vacant)** (417) 831-4406

Montana District

2601 Second Ave North, Suite 3200, Billings, MT 59101
Tel: (406) 657-6101 Fax: (406) 657-6989
Internet: www.usdoj.gov/usao/mt

★ U.S. Attorney **Michael W. Cotter** (406) 457-5120
E-mail: michael.cotter@usdoj.gov
Education: Notre Dame 1971 BBA; Utah MBA; Notre Dame 1977 JD
Secretary to the U.S. Attorney **Cassandra "Cassie" Potter** (406) 457-5120
E-mail: cassie.potter@usdoj.gov
Appellate Division Chief **Leif M. Johnson** (406) 657-6101
E-mail: leif.johnson@usdoj.gov
Civil Division Chief **Victoria L. Francis** (406) 657-6101
E-mail: victoria.francis@usdoj.gov
Assistant U.S. Attorney **Zeno Benjamin Baucus** (406) 657-6101
E-mail: zeno.baucus@usdoj.gov
Education: Stanford 1999 BA; Georgetown 2004 JD
Assistant U.S. Attorney **Timothy J. Cavan** (406) 657-6101
Assistant U.S. Attorney **Brendan McCarthy** (406) 657-6101
E-mail: brendan.mccarthy@usdoj.gov
Assistant U.S. Attorney **Colin Rubich** (406) 657-6101
E-mail: colin.rubich@usdoj.gov

★ Presidential Appointment Requiring Senate Confirmation ☆ Presidential Appointment ☐ Schedule C Appointment ◇ Career Senior Foreign Service Appointment
● Career Senior Executive Service (SES) Appointment ○ Non-Career Senior Executive Service (SES) Appointment ■ Postal Career Executive Service

Montana District *continued*

Assistant U.S. Attorney **Mark S. Smith** . . . . (406) 657-6101
Victim-Witness Specialist **Rhonda Myron** . . . . (406) 657-6101
E-mail: rhonda.myron@usdoj.gov
Systems Manager **Jason Ferree** . . . . (406) 657-6101
E-mail: jason.ferree@usdoj.gov
Administrative Officer **Kora L. Connolly** . . . .(406) 657-6101
E-mail: kora.connolly@usdoj.gov

Indian Country Crime Unit

Deputy Chief and Assistant U.S. Attorney
Lori Harper Suek . . . .(406) 657-6101
E-mail: lori.suek@usdoj.gov
Assistant U.S. Attorney **Jessica A. Betley** . . . . (406) 761-7715
E-mail: jessica.betley@usdoj.gov
Assistant U.S. Attorney **Danna R. Jackson** . . . . (406) 457-5120
E-mail: danna.jackson@usdoj.gov
Education: Montana 1993 BA, 1996 JD
Assistant U.S. Attorney **John Sullivan** . . . . (406) 657-6101
Assistant U.S. Attorney **Ryan G. Weldon** . . . . (406) 761-7715
E-mail: ryan.weldon@usdoj.gov
Education: Montana 2009 JD
Assistant U.S. Attorney **(Vacant)** . . . . (406) 761-7715

Butte (MT) Office

Federal Building, 400 North Main, Suite 181, Butte, MT 59701
Tel: (406) 723-6611 Fax: (406) 723-5002

Assistant U.S. Attorney **(Vacant)** . . . . (406) 723-6611

Great Falls (MT) Office

119 First Avenue North, Number 300, Great Falls, MT 59401
P.O. Box 3447, Great Falls, MT 59403-3447
Tel: (406) 761-7715 Fax: (406) 453-9973

Managing Assistant U.S. Attorney
George F. Darragh, Jr. . . . . (406) 761-7715
E-mail: george.darragh@usdoj.gov
Executive Assistant U.S. Attorney **Carl E. Rostad** . . . . (406) 761-7715
Victim-Witness Specialist **Keri Brehm-Leggett** . . . . (406) 761-7715

Helena (MT) Office

100 North Park Avenue, Suite 100, Helena, MT 59601
Tel: (406) 457-5120 Fax: (406) 457-5130

Criminal Division Chief **Joseph E. Thaggard** . . . . (406) 457-5120
E-mail: joseph.thaggard@usdoj.gov
Assistant U.S. Attorney **Melissa Hornbein** . . . . (406) 457-5120
E-mail: melissa.hornbein@usdoj.gov
Assistant U.S. Attorney **Michael S. Lahr** . . . .(406) 457-5120
E-mail: michael.lahr@usdoj.gov
Assistant U.S. Attorney **Chad Spraker** . . . . (406) 657-6101
E-mail: chad.spraker@usdoj.gov
Assistant U.S. Attorney **Paulette Stewart** . . . .(406) 457-5120
E-mail: paulette.stewart@usdoj.gov
Assistant U.S. Attorney **Bryan Whitaker** . . . .(406) 457-5120
Intelligence Specialist **Michael Rankin** . . . . (406) 457-5120

Missoula (MT) Office

105 East Pine, 2nd Floor, Missoula, MT 59802
P.O. Box 8329, Missoula, MT 59807-8329
Tel: (406) 542-8851 Fax: (406) 542-1476

First Assistant U.S. Attorney **Kris A. McLean** . . . .(406) 542-8851
E-mail: kris.mclean@usdoj.gov
Deputy Criminal Division Chief and Assistant U.S.
Attorney **Timothy J. Racicot** . . . . (406) 542-8851
Education: Carroll Col (MT) 1996 BA; Notre Dame 2000 JD
Organized Crime Drug Enforcement Task Force
Assistant U.S. Attorney **Tara Elliott** . . . . (406) 542-8851
E-mail: tara.elliott@usdoj.gov
Education: Pennsylvania 2003 JD

Missoula (MT) Office *continued*

Assistant U.S. Attorney **Megan Dishong** . . . . (406) 542-8851
E-mail: megan.dishong@usdoj.gov
Education: Wooster 2000 BA; Montana 2007 JD
Assistant U.S. Attorney **Cyndee Peterson** . . . . (406) 542-8851
E-mail: cyndee.peterson@usdoj.gov

Nebraska District

1620 Dodge Street, Suite 1400, Omaha, NE 68102-1506
Tel: (800) 899-9124 Tel: (402) 661-3700 Fax: (402) 345-6958
Internet: www.usdoj.gov/usao/ne

★ U.S. Attorney **Deborah K. R. Gilg** . . . .(402) 661-3700
E-mail: deborah.gilg@usdoj.gov
Education: Nebraska, JD
Secretary to the U.S. Attorney **Colleen MacDonald** . . . . (402) 661-3700
E-mail: colleen.macdonald@usdoj.gov
First Assistant U.S. Attorney **Robert C Stuart** . . . . (402) 661-3700
E-mail: robert.stuart@usdoj.gov
Administrative Officer **Denise M. Smith** . . . . (402) 661-3700
E-mail: denise.smith@usdoj.gov
HIDTA Coordinator **Brenda Daley** . . . . (402) 661-3700
Law Enforcement Coordinator **Joseph P. Jeanette** . . . . . . (402) 661-3700
Victim-Witness Coordinator **Kimberly Roewert** . . . .(402) 661-3700
Computer Programmer Analyst **Jason D. Bray** . . . .(402) 661-3700
E-mail: jason.bray@usdoj.gov

Civil Division

Chief **Robert L. Homan** . . . . (402) 661-3700
E-mail: robert.homan@usdoj.gov
Assistant U.S. Attorney **Laurene M. Barrett** . . . .(402) 661-3700
Assistant U.S. Attorney **Timothy Hook** . . . .(402) 437-5241
E-mail: tim.hook@usdoj.gov
Assistant U.S. Attorney **Laurie Kelly** . . . . (402) 661-3700
E-mail: laurie.kelly@usdoj.gov
Assistant U.S. Attorney **Lynette Wagner** . . . . (402) 661-3700

Criminal Division

Chief **Jan W. Sharp** . . . .(402) 661-3700
E-mail: jan.sharp@usdoj.gov
Supervisory Assistant U.S. Attorney **John E. Higgins** . . . . (402) 661-3700
E-mail: john.higgins@usdoj.gov
Assistant U.S. Attorney **Kimberly C. Bunjer** . . . .(402) 661-3700
Assistant U.S. Attorney **Frederick Franklin** . . . .(402) 661-3700
Assistant U.S. Attorney **Bruce W. Gillan** . . . .(402) 437-5241
E-mail: bruce.gillan@usdoj.gov
Assistant U.S. Attorney **Susan Lehr** . . . . (402) 661-3700
Assistant U.S. Attorney **Russell X. Mayer** . . . . (402) 661-3700
Assistant U.S. Attorney **Matthew Molsen** . . . . (402) 661-3700
E-mail: matthew.molsen@usdoj.gov
Assistant U.S. Attorney **Michael P. Norris** . . . .(402) 661-3700
E-mail: michael.norris@usdoj.gov
Assistant U.S. Attorney **Douglas R. Semisch** . . . .(402) 661-3700
Assistant U.S. Attorney **Nancy A. Svoboda** . . . . (402) 661-3700
E-mail: nancy.svoboda@usdoj.gov
Assistant U.S. Attorney **Lecia Wright** . . . .(402) 661-3700
E-mail: lecia.wright@usdoj.gov

Lincoln (NE) Office

Federal Building, 100 Centennial Mall North,
Suite 487, Lincoln, NE 68508-3865
Tel: (800) 889-9123 Tel: (402) 437-5241 Fax: (402) 437-5390

Supervisory Assistant U.S. Attorney
Steven A. Russell . . . . (402) 437-5241
E-mail: steve.russell@usdoj.gov
Assistant U.S. Attorney **Alan L. Everett** . . . . (402) 437-5241
E-mail: alan.everett@usdoj.gov
Assistant U.S. Attorney **Sara E. Fullerton** . . . .(402) 437-5241
E-mail: sara.fullerton@usdoj.gov
Assistant U.S. Attorney **William W. Mickle** . . . . (402) 437-5241
E-mail: william.mickle@usdoj.gov

REGIONAL OFFICES — US ATTORNEYS AND US MARSHALS SERVICE

★ Presidential Appointment Requiring Senate Confirmation ☆ Presidential Appointment □ Schedule C Appointment ◇ Career Senior Foreign Service Appointment
● Career Senior Executive Service (SES) Appointment ○ Non-Career Senior Executive Service (SES) Appointment ■ Postal Career Executive Service

Nevada District
333 Las Vegas Boulevard South, Suite 5000, Las Vegas, NV 89101
Tel: (702) 388-6336 Fax: (702) 388-6296
Internet: www.usdoj.gov/usao/nv

★ U.S. Attorney **Daniel G. Bogden** .... (702) 388-6336
E-mail: daniel.bogden@usdoj.gov
Education: Ashland BS; Toledo JD
Secretary to the U.S. Attorney **Ashlin Brown** .... (702) 388-6336
E-mail: ashlin.brown@usdoj.gov
First Assistant U.S. Attorney **Steven W. Myhre** .... (702) 388-6336
E-mail: steven.myhre@usdoj.gov
Administrative Officer **Burton J. Carle** .... (702) 388-6336
E-mail: burton.carle@usdoj.gov
Human Resources Specialist **Darlene Beltran** .... (702) 388-6336
E-mail: darlene.beltran@usdoj.gov Fax: (702) 388-6735
Supervisory Information Technology Specialist
Angel Beltran .... (702) 388-6336
E-mail: angel.beltran@usdoj.gov Fax: (702) 388-6735
Public Affairs Officer **Natalie Collins** .... (702) 388-6336

Appellate Division
Tel: (702) 388-6336

Chief **Elizabeth White** .... (702) 388-6336
E-mail: elizabeth.white@usdoj.gov Fax: (702) 388-6418

Civil Division
Tel: (702) 388-6336 Fax: (702) 388-6787

Chief **Blaine T. Welsh** .... (702) 388-6336
E-mail: blaine.welsh@usdoj.gov
Health Care Fraud Assistant U.S. Attorney
Roger W. Wenthe .... (702) 388-6336
E-mail: roger.wenthe@usdoj.gov

Criminal Division
Tel: (702) 388-6336

Chief **Daniel R. Schiess** .... (702) 388-6336
E-mail: dan.schiess@usdoj.gov
Team 1 Deputy Chief **Cristina Silva** .... (702) 388-6336
E-mail: cristina.silva@usdoj.gov
Team 2 Deputy Chief **Crane Ponerentz** .... (702) 388-6336
Team 3 Deputy Chief **Pam Martin** .... (702) 388-6336
E-mail: pam.martin@usdoj.gov

Reno (NV) Office
100 West Liberty Street, Suite 600, Reno, NV 89501
Tel: (775) 784-5438 Fax: (775) 784-5181

Assistant U.S. Attorney-in-Charge **Sue Fahami** .... (775) 334-3342

Civil Division
Tel: (775) 784-5438 Fax: (775) 784-5181

Assistant U.S. Attorney **Gregory W. Addington** .... (775) 784-5438

Criminal Division
Tel: (775) 784-5438 Fax: (775) 784-5181

Narcotics and Violent Crimes Assistant U.S. Attorney
James E. Keller .... (775) 784-5438
White Collar and Economic Crimes Assistant U.S. Attorney **Brian L. Sullivan** .... (775) 784-5438
E-mail: brian.sullivan@usdoj.gov

New Hampshire District
James C. Cleveland Federal Building, 53 Pleasant Street, Concord, NH 03301-3904
Tel: (603) 225-1552 Fax: (603) 225-1470
Internet: www.usdoj.gov/usao/nh

★ U.S. Attorney (Acting) **Donald Feith** .... (603) 225-1552
E-mail: donald.feith@usdoj.gov

New Hampshire District *continued*

★ U.S. Attorney-Designate **Emily Gray Rice** .... (603) 225-1552
Education: Boston U 1977 BA; Northeastern 1984 JD
Secretary to U.S. Attorney **(Vacant)** .... (603) 225-1552
First Assistant U.S. Attorney **Donald Feith** .... (603) 225-1552
E-mail: donald.feith@usdoj.gov
Administrative Officer **Philip DeVincent** .... (603) 225-1552
E-mail: philip.devincent@usdoj.gov
Administrative Services Specialist **(Vacant)** .... (603) 225-1552
Budget Analyst **Thomas Kasyan** .... (603) 225-1552
E-mail: thomas.kasyan@usdoj.gov
Financial Technician **Janna Foote** .... (603) 225-1552
E-mail: janna.foote@usdoj.gov
Human Resources Specialist **(Vacant)** .... (603) 230-2544
Systems Manager **Jessica Magdziasz** .... (603) 225-1552
Intelligence Research Specialist **(Vacant)** .... (603) 225-1552
Law Enforcement Coordination Specialist **Mark Long** .... (603) 225-1552
Victim Witness Specialist **Jennifer Hunt** .... (603) 225-1552

Civil Division
Fax: (603) 225-1470

Chief **T. David Plourde** .... (603) 225-1552
E-mail: david.plourde@usdoj.gov
Assistant U.S. Attorney **Michael T. McCormack** .... (603) 225-1552
E-mail: michael.mccormack@usdoj.gov
Assistant U.S. Attorney **Robert Rabuck** .... (603) 225-1552

Criminal Division
Fax: (603) 225-1470

Chief **Robert J. Veiga** .... (603) 225-1552
E-mail: robert.viega@usdoj.gov
Deputy Chief **(Vacant)** .... (603) 225-1552
Senior Litigation Counsel **Robert Kinsella** .... (603) 225-1552
E-mail: robert.kinsella@usdoj.gov
Assistant U.S. Attorney **Nick Abramson** .... (603) 225-1552
E-mail: nick.abramson@usdoj.gov
Assistant U.S. Attorney **Seth Aframe** .... (603) 225-1552
E-mail: seth.aframe@usdoj.gov
Assistant U.S. Attorney **Jennifer C. Davis** .... (603) 225-1552
E-mail: jennifer.c.davis@usdoj.gov
Assistant U.S. Attorney **John J. Farley III** .... (603) 225-1552
E-mail: john.farley@usdoj.gov
Assistant U.S. Attorney **Helen White Fitzgibbon** .... (603) 225-1552
E-mail: helen.fitzgibbon@usdoj.gov
Assistant U.S. Attorney **Michael J. Gunnison** .... (603) 225-1552
E-mail: michael.gunnison@usdoj.gov
Assistant U.S. Attorney **Arnold H. Huftalen** .... (603) 225-1552
E-mail: arnold.huftalen@usdoj.gov
Assistant U.S. Attorney **William Morse** .... (603) 225-1552
E-mail: william.morse@usdoj.gov
Assistant U.S. Attorney **Terry Ollila** .... (603) 225-1552
E-mail: terry.ollila@usdoj.gov
Assistant U.S. Attorney **Alfred Rubega** .... (603) 225-1552
E-mail: alfred.rubega@usdoj.gov
Assistant U.S. Attorney **Debra M. Walsh** .... (603) 225-1552
E-mail: deb.walsh@usdoj.gov
Assistant U.S. Attorney **Mark Zuckerman** .... (603) 225-1552
E-mail: mark.zuckerman@usdoj.gov

New Jersey District
970 Broad Street, Suite 700, Newark, NJ 07102
Tel: (973) 645-2700 Fax: (973) 645-2702
Internet: www.usdoj.gov/usao/nj

★ U.S. Attorney **Paul Joseph Fishman** .... (973) 645-2700
E-mail: paul.fishman@usdoj.gov
Education: Princeton 1978; Harvard 1982 JD
Executive Assistant to the U.S. Attorney
Nancy Manteiga .... (973) 645-2700
E-mail: nancy.manteiga@usdoj.gov

★ Presidential Appointment Requiring Senate Confirmation ☆ Presidential Appointment □ Schedule C Appointment ◇ Career Senior Foreign Service Appointment
● Career Senior Executive Service (SES) Appointment ○ Non-Career Senior Executive Service (SES) Appointment ■ Postal Career Executive Service

New Jersey District *continued*

First Assistant U.S. Attorney **William E. Fitzpatrick** . . . . . (973) 645-2700
E-mail: william.fitzpatrick@usdoj.gov
Executive Assistant U.S. Attorney
Sabrina G. Comizzoli . . . . . (973) 645-2700
E-mail: sabrina.comizzoli@usdoj.gov
Deputy U.S. Attorney for the Southern Vicinages
William E. Fitzpatrick . . . . . (973) 645-2700
E-mail: william.fitzpatrick@usdoj.gov
Counsel to the United States Attorney
John M. Fietkiewicz . . . . . (973) 645-2700
E-mail: john.fietkiewicz@usdoj.gov
Counsel to the United States Attorney
Rachael A. Honig . . . . . (973) 645-2700
E-mail: rachael.honig@usdoj.gov
Administrative Officer (Acting) **Maryann Zekunde** . . . . . (973) 645-2700
E-mail: maryann.zekunde@usdoj.gov
Public Affairs Officer **Matthew Reilly** . . . . . (973) 645-2888
Victim-Witness Coordinator **Shirley Estreicher** . . . . . (973) 645-2700
E-mail: shirley.estreicher@usdoj.gov

Appellate Division
Tel: (973) 645-2755

Chief **Mark E. Coyne** . . . . . (973) 245-2700
E-mail: mark.coyne@usdoj.gov
Deputy Chief **Steven G. Sanders** . . . . . (973) 245-2700
E-mail: steven.sanders@usdoj.gov
Assistant U.S. Attorney **Bruce P. Keller** . . . . . (973) 245-2700
E-mail: bruce.keller@usdoj.gov
Education: Cornell 1976 BS; Boston U 1979 JD
Assistant U.S. Attorney **John F. Romano** . . . . . (973) 245-2700
E-mail: john.romano@usdoj.gov
Education: St John's U (NY) 2004 JD
Assistant U.S. Attorney **(Vacant)** . . . . . (973) 245-2700

Civil Division
Chief **Caroline A. Sadlowski** . . . . . (973) 645-2700
E-mail: caroline.sadlowski@usdoj.gov
Education: Harvard 1993 AB, 1996 MA; Michigan 2000 JD
Deputy Chief **David E. Dauenheimer** . . . . . (973) 645-2700
E-mail: david.dauenheimer@usdoj.gov
Deputy Chief **Leticia B. Vandehaar** . . . . . (973) 645-2700
E-mail: leticia.vandehaar@usdoj.gov
Deputy Chief **(Vacant)** . . . . . (973) 645-2700
Senior Litigation Counsel **Daniel J. Gibbons** . . . . . (973) 645-2700
E-mail: daniel.gibbons@usdoj.gov
Senior Litigation Counsel **Anthony J. LaBruna, Jr.** . . . . . (973) 645-2700
E-mail: anthony.labruna@usdoj.gov
Senior Litigation Counsel **(Vacant)** . . . . . (973) 645-2700
Assistant U.S. Attorney **Christopher D. Amore** . . . . . (973) 645-2700
E-mail: christopher.amore@usdoj.gov
Assistant U.S. Attorney **Jordan Anger** . . . . . (973) 645-2700
E-mail: jordan.anger@usdoj.gov
Assistant U.S. Attorney **Frances C. Bajada** . . . . . (973) 645-2700
E-mail: frances.bajada@usdoj.gov
Education: Baruch Col BA; New York Law JD
Assistant U.S. Attorney **Michael Campion** . . . . . (973) 645-2700
E-mail: michael.campion@usdoj.gov
Assistant U.S. Attorney **Eamonn O'Hagan** . . . . . (973) 645-2700
E-mail: eamonn.ohagan@usdoj.gov
Education: Boston Col 2004 JD
Assistant U.S. Attorney **Mark C. Orlowski** . . . . . (973) 645-2700
E-mail: mark.orlowski@usdoj.gov
Assistant U.S. Attorney **Valorie D. Smith** . . . . . (973) 645-2700
E-mail: valorie.d.smith@usdoj.gov
Assistant U.S. Attorney **Karen D. Stringer** . . . . . (973) 645-2700
E-mail: karen.stringer@usdoj.gov
Assistant U.S. Attorney **Thomas G. Strong** . . . . . (973) 645-2700
E-mail: thomas.strong@usdoj.gov
Assistant U.S. Attorney **Allan B. K. Urgent** . . . . . (973) 645-2700
E-mail: allan.urgent@usdoj.gov
Education: Fordham 1997 JD

Civil Division *continued*

Assistant U.S. Attorney **Kristin L. Vassallo** . . . . . (973) 645-2700
E-mail: kristin.vassallo@usdoj.gov
Assistant U.S. Attorney **(Vacant)** . . . . . (973) 645-2700

Criminal Division
Chief **Thomas J. Eicher** . . . . . (973) 645-2700
E-mail: thomas.eicher@usdoj.gov
Deputy Chief **Lisa M. Colone** . . . . . (973) 645-2700
E-mail: lisa.colone@usdoj.gov
Education: Virginia 2002 JD
Deputy Chief **John Gay** . . . . . (973) 645-2700
E-mail: john.gay@usdoj.gov
Asset Forfeiture and Money Laundering Unit Chief
Barbara A. Ward . . . . . (973) 645-2700
E-mail: barbara.ward@usdoj.gov
Economic Crimes Unit Chief **Gurbir S. Grewal** . . . . . (973) 645-2700
E-mail: gurbir.grewal@usdoj.gov
Education: Georgetown 1995 BSFS; William & Mary 1999 JD
General Crimes Unit Chief **Zach Intrater** . . . . . (973) 645-2700
E-mail: zach.intrater@usdoj.gov
Healthcare and Government Fraud Unit Chief
Jacob T. Elberg . . . . . (973) 645-2700
E-mail: jacob.elberg@usdoj.gov
Education: Harvard 2003 JD
Narcotics/OCDETF Unit Chief **Ronnell L. Wilson** . . . . . (973) 645-2700
E-mail: ronnell.wilson@usdoj.gov
National Security Unit Chief **Anthony C. Moscato** . . . . . (973) 645-2700
E-mail: anthony.moscato@usdoj.gov
Education: Columbia 1967 BA; George Washington 1970 JD
Organized Crime/Gangs Unit Chief
David E. Malagold . . . . . (973) 645-2700
E-mail: david.malagold@usdoj.gov
Education: NYU 2001 JD
Economic Crimes/Computer Hacking and IP Section
Unit Deputy Chief **Scott B. McBride** . . . . . (973) 645-2700
E-mail: scott.mcbride@usdoj.gov
Education: Georgetown 1997 BS, 2002 JD
General Crimes Unit Deputy Chief **Mary Toscano** . . . . . (973) 645-2700
E-mail: mary.toscano@usdoj.gov
Healthcare and Government Fraud Unit Deputy Chief
Joseph G. Mack . . . . . (973) 645-2700
E-mail: joseph.mack@usdoj.gov
Senior Litigation Counsel **Andrew Leven** . . . . . (973) 645-2700
E-mail: andrew.leven@usdoj.gov
Education: Ithaca 1982 BS; Syracuse 1986 JD
Senior Litigation Counsel **Margaret Ann Mahoney** . . . . . (973) 645-2700
E-mail: margaret.ann.mahoney@usdoj.gov
Senior Litigation Counsel **V. Grady O'Malley** . . . . . (973) 645-2700
Senior Litigation Counsel **Marion Percell** . . . . . (973) 645-2700
E-mail: marion.percell@usdoj.gov
Senior Litigation Counsel **(Vacant)** . . . . . (973) 645-2700
Assistant U.S. Attorney **Sharon E. Ashe** . . . . . (973) 645-2700
E-mail: sharon.ashe@usdoj.gov
Assistant U.S. Attorney **Osmar J. Benvenuto** . . . . . (973) 645-2700
E-mail: osmar.benvenuto@usdoj.gov
Assistant U.S. Attorney **Jamari Buxton** . . . . . (973) 645-2700
E-mail: jamari.buxton@usdoj.gov
Assistant U.S. Attorney **Dennis C. Carletta** . . . . . (973) 645-2700
E-mail: dennis.carletta@usdoj.gov
Assistant U.S. Attorney **Shana W. Chen** . . . . . (973) 645-2700
E-mail: shana.chen@usdoj.gov
Education: Georgetown 2001 JD
Assistant U.S. Attorney **Bernard J. Cooney** . . . . . (973) 645-2700
E-mail: bernard.cooney@usdoj.gov
Assistant U.S. Attorney **Danielle M. Corcione** . . . . . (973) 645-2700
E-mail: danielle.corcione@usdoj.gov
Assistant U.S. Attorney **James M. Donnelly** . . . . . (973) 645-2700
E-mail: james.donnelly@usdoj.gov
Assistant U.S. Attorney **Svetlana M. Eisenberg** . . . . . (973) 645-2700
E-mail: svetlana.eisenberg@usdoj.gov

(continued on next page)

★ Presidential Appointment Requiring Senate Confirmation ☆ Presidential Appointment ☐ Schedule C Appointment ◇ Career Senior Foreign Service Appointment
● Career Senior Executive Service (SES) Appointment ○ Non-Career Senior Executive Service (SES) Appointment ■ Postal Career Executive Service

Criminal Division *continued*

Assistant U.S. Attorney **David M. Eskew** . . . . (973) 645-2700
E-mail: david.eskew@usdoj.gov
Education: St John's U (NY) 2004 JD
Assistant U.S. Attorney **David W. Feder** . . . . (973) 645-2700
E-mail: david.feder@usdoj.gov
Education: Fordham 2007 JD
Assistant U.S. Attorney **Robert L. Frazer** . . . . (973) 645-2700
E-mail: robert.frazer@usdoj.gov
Assistant U.S. Attorney **Peter W. Gaeta** . . . . (973) 645-2700
E-mail: peter.gaeta@usdoj.gov
Assistant U.S. Attorney **Deborah J. Gannett** . . . . (973) 645-2700
E-mail: deborah.gannett@usdoj.gov
Assistant U.S. Attorney **Lorraine S. Gerson** . . . . (973) 645-2700
E-mail: lorraine.gerson@usdoj.gov
Assistant U.S. Attorney **Dara A. Govan** . . . . (973) 645-2700
E-mail: dara.govan@usdoj.gov
Education: Morgan State 1998 BS; Rutgers 2001 JD
Assistant U.S. Attorney **Charles Graybow** . . . . (973) 645-2700
E-mail: charles.graybow@usdoj.gov
Assistant U.S. Attorney **Nicholas P. Grippo** . . . . (973) 645-2700
E-mail: nicholas.grippo@usdoj.gov
Assistant U.S. Attorney **Joshua Hafetz** . . . . (973) 645-2700
E-mail: joshua.hafetz@usdoj.gov
Assistant U.S. Attorney **Elizabeth M. Harris** . . . . (973) 645-2700
E-mail: elizabeth.harris2@usdoj.gov
Assistant U.S. Attorney **Lakshmi Herman** . . . . (973) 645-2700
E-mail: lakshmi.herman@usdoj.gov
Assistant U.S. Attorney **Justin S. Herring** . . . . (973) 645-2700
E-mail: justin.herring@usdoj.gov
Assistant U.S. Attorney **Courtney Howard** . . . . (973) 645-2700
E-mail: courtney.howard@usdoj.gov
Assistant U.S. Attorney **Melissa Jampol** . . . . (973) 645-2700
E-mail: melissa.jampol@usdoj.gov
Assistant U.S. Attorney **Barry A. Kamar** . . . . (973) 645-2700
Assistant U.S. Attorney **Andrew D. Kogan** . . . . (973) 645-2700
E-mail: andrew.kogan@usdoj.gov
Assistant U.S. Attorney **Anthony J. Mahajan** . . . . (973) 645-2700
E-mail: anthony.mahajan@usdoj.gov
Assistant U.S. Attorney **Joyce M. Malliet** . . . . (973) 645-2700
E-mail: joyce.malliet@usdoj.gov
Assistant U.S. Attorney **Sara Merin** . . . . (973) 645-2700
E-mail: sara.merin@usdoj.gov
Assistant U.S. Attorney **Joseph N. Minish** . . . . (973) 645-2700
E-mail: joseph.minish@usdoj.gov
Assistant U.S. Attorney **Paul A. Murphy** . . . . (973) 645-2700
E-mail: paul.murphy@usdoj.gov
Assistant U.S. Attorney **Lucy E. Muzzy** . . . . (973) 645-2700
E-mail: lucy.muzzy@usdoj.gov
Assistant U.S. Attorney **Francisco J. Navarro** . . . . (973) 645-2700
E-mail: francisco.navarro@usdoj.gov
Assistant U.S. Attorney **Kathleen P. O'Leary** . . . . (973) 645-2700
Assistant U.S. Attorney **Courtney Oliva** . . . . (973) 645-2700
E-mail: courtney.oliva@usdoj.gov
Assistant U.S. Attorney **Andrew S. Pak** . . . . (973) 645-2700
E-mail: andrew.pak@usdoj.gov
Assistant U.S. Attorney **Michael H. Robertson** . . . . (973) 645-2700
E-mail: michael.robertson@usdoj.gov
Assistant U.S. Attorney **Jonathan W. Romankow** . . . . . . (973) 645-2700
E-mail: jonathan.romankow@usdoj.gov
Assistant U.S. Attorney **Daniel Shapiro** . . . . (973) 645-2700
E-mail: daniel.shapiro@usdoj.gov
Assistant U.S. Attorney **Mikie Sherrill** . . . . (973) 645-2700
E-mail: mikie.sherrill@usdoj.gov
Assistant U.S. Attorney **Joseph Bruce Shumofsky** . . . . . . (973) 645-2700
E-mail: joseph.shumofsky@usdoj.gov
Education: Cornell; Fordham 1998 JD
Assistant U.S. Attorney **Adam N. Subervi** . . . . (973) 645-2700
E-mail: adam.subervi@usdoj.gov
Education: Seton Hall 1997 BA; Rutgers (Newark) 2000 JD
Assistant U.S. Attorney **Brian L. Urbano** . . . . (973) 645-2700
E-mail: brian.urbano@usdoj.gov

Criminal Division *continued*

Assistant U.S. Attorney **Danielle A. Walsman** . . . . (973) 645-2700
E-mail: danielle.walsman@usdoj.gov
Assistant U.S. Attorney **Melissa M. Wangenheim** . . . . . . (973) 645-2700
E-mail: melissa.wangenheim@usdoj.gov
Assistant U.S. Attorney **L. Judson Welle** . . . . (973) 645-2700
Assistant U.S. Attorney **Meredith J. Williams** . . . . (973) 645-2700
E-mail: meredith.williams@usdoj.gov
Assistant U.S. Attorney **Jane H. Yoon** . . . . (973) 645-2700
E-mail: jane.yoon@usdoj.gov
Education: Yale; Michigan 2002 JD
Assistant U.S. Attorney **(Vacant)** . . . . (973) 645-2700
Assistant U.S. Attorney **(Vacant)** . . . . (973) 645-2700
Assistant U.S. Attorney **(Vacant)** . . . . (973) 645-2700
Assistant U.S. Attorney **(Vacant)** . . . . (973) 645-2700
Assistant U.S. Attorney **(Vacant)** . . . . (973) 645-2700

Special Prosecutions Division

Chief **James B. Nobile** . . . . (973) 645-2700
E-mail: james.nobile@usdoj.gov
Senior Litigation Counsel **J Fortier Imbert** . . . . (973) 645-2700
E-mail: j.imbert@usdoj.gov
Senior Litigation Counsel **Mark J. McCarren** . . . . (973) 645-2700
E-mail: mark.mccarren@usdoj.gov
Senior Litigation Counsel **Leslie F. Schwartz** . . . . (973) 645-2700
E-mail: leslie.schwartz@usdoj.gov
Assistant U.S. Attorney **Rahul Agarwal** . . . . (973) 645-2700
E-mail: rahul.agarwal@usdoj.gov
Education: Columbia 2006 JD
Assistant U.S. Attorney **Jose Almonte** . . . . (973) 645-2700
E-mail: jose.almonte@usdoj.gov
Assistant U.S. Attorney **Lee S. Cortes, Jr.** . . . . (973) 645-2700
E-mail: lee.cortes@usdoj.gov
Education: King's Col (UK) 2000 BA; Fordham 2003 JD
Assistant U.S. Attorney **Shirley U. Emehelu** . . . . (973) 645-2700
E-mail: shirley.emehelu@usdoj.gov
Assistant U.S. Attorney **Cari Fais** . . . . (973) 645-2700
E-mail: cari.fais@usdoj.gov
Assistant U.S. Attorney **David L. Foster** . . . . (973) 645-2700
E-mail: david.foster@usdoj.gov
Assistant U.S. Attorney **Mala Ahuja Harker** . . . . (973) 645-2700
E-mail: mala.harker@usdoj.gov
Education: Washington U (MO) 1996; Pennsylvania 1999 JD
Assistant U.S. Attorney **Vikas Khanna** . . . . (973) 645-2700
E-mail: vikas.khanna@usdoj.gov
Education: Harvard JD
Assistant U.S. Attorney **Barbara Llanes** . . . . (973) 645-2700
E-mail: barbara.llanes@usdoj.gov
Assistant U.S. Attorney **Jacques S. Pierre** . . . . (973) 645-2700
E-mail: jacques.pierre@usdoj.gov
Assistant U.S. Attorney **(Vacant)** . . . . (973) 645-2700

Camden (NJ) Office

Camden Federal Building and U.S. Courthouse, 401 Market Street, 4th Floor, Camden, NJ 08101
Tel: (856) 757-5026 Tel: (856) 757-5412 (Civil Division)
Fax: (856) 968-4917 Fax: (856) 757-5416 (Civil Division)

Assistant U.S. Attorney-in-Charge **R. Stephen Stigall** . . . . (856) 757-5026
E-mail: stephen.stigall@usdoj.gov
Deputy Assistant U.S. Attorney-in-Charge
Matthew Skahill . . . . (856) 757-5026
E-mail: matthew.skahill@usdoj.gov
Appellate Division Assistant U.S. Attorney
Norman J. Gross . . . . (856) 757-5026
E-mail: norman.gross@usdoj.gov
Appellate Division Assistant U.S. Attorney
Glenn J. Moramarco . . . . (856) 757-5026
E-mail: glenn.moramarco@usdoj.gov
Appellate Division Assistant U.S. Attorney
Deborah A. Prisinzano Mikkelsen . . . . (856) 757-5026
E-mail: deborah.mikkelsen@usdoj.gov
Education: Virginia 2001 JD

★ Presidential Appointment Requiring Senate Confirmation ☆ Presidential Appointment ☐ Schedule C Appointment ◇ Career Senior Foreign Service Appointment
● Career Senior Executive Service (SES) Appointment ○ Non-Career Senior Executive Service (SES) Appointment ■ Postal Career Executive Service

Camden (NJ) Office *continued*

Senior Litigation Counsel **Irene Dowdy** . . . . (856) 757-5412
E-mail: irene.dowdy@usdoj.gov
Senior Litigation Counsel **Jason M. Richardson** . . . . . . (856) 757-5026
Civil Division Assistant U.S. Attorney
Elizabeth A. Pascal . . . . (856) 757-5412
E-mail: elizabeth.pascal@usdoj.gov
Civil Division Assistant U.S. Attorney
Anne B. Taylor . . . . (856) 757-5412
E-mail: anne.taylor@usdoj.gov
Education: Georgetown 2007 JD
Criminal Division Assistant U.S. Attorney
Sara A. Aliabadi . . . . (856) 757-5026
Criminal Division Assistant U.S. Attorney
Patrick C. Askin . . . . (856) 757-5026
Criminal Division Assistant U.S. Attorney
Jacqueline M. Carle . . . . (856) 757-5026
Criminal Division Assistant U.S. Attorney
Diana V. Carrig . . . . (856) 757-5026
Criminal Division Assistant U.S. Attorney
Steven D'Aguanno . . . . (856) 757-5026
Criminal Division Assistant U.S. Attorney
Justin C. Danilewitz . . . . (856) 757-5026
Criminal Division Assistant U.S. Attorney
Matthew T. Smith . . . . (856) 757-5026
Education: Holy Cross Col 1995 BA; Emory 1998 MS; Rutgers (Camden) 2001 JD
Criminal Division Assistant U.S. Attorney
R. David Walk . . . . (856) 757-5026
Criminal Division Assistant U.S. Attorney
Howard J. Wiener . . . . (856) 757-5026
Criminal Division Assistant U.S. Attorney **(Vacant)** . . . . (856) 757-5026

Trenton (NJ) Office

402 East State Street, Suite 30, Trenton, NJ 08608
Tel: (609) 989-2190 Fax: (609) 989-2275
Fax: (609) 989-2360 (Civil Division)
Fax: (609) 989-0583 (Criminal Division)

Assistant U.S. Attorney-in-Charge **Eric W. Moran** . . . . (609) 989-2190
E-mail: eric.moran@usdoj.gov
Deputy Chief **J. Andrew Ruymann** . . . . (609) 989-2190
Civil Division Assistant U.S. Attorney **David Bober** . . . . . (609) 989-2190
E-mail: david.bober@usdoj.gov
Education: Seton Hall 2002 JD
Criminal Division Assistant U.S. Attorney
Brendan Day . . . . (609) 989-2190
E-mail: brendan.day@usdoj.gov
Criminal Division Assistant U.S. Attorney
R. Joseph Gribko . . . . (609) 989-2190
Criminal Division Assistant U.S. Attorney
Molly S. Lorber . . . . (609) 989-2190
E-mail: molly.lorber@usdoj.gov
Criminal Division Assistant U.S. Attorney
Fabiana Pierre-Louis . . . . (609) 989-2190
Education: Rutgers 2002 BA; Rutgers (Camden) 2006 JD
Criminal Division Assistant U.S. Attorney
Elisa T. Wiygul . . . . (609) 989-2190
E-mail: elisa.wiygul@usdoj.gov
Education: Yale JD
Criminal Division Assistant U.S. Attorney
Sarah M. Wolfe . . . . (609) 989-2190
Criminal Division Assistant U.S. Attorney **(Vacant)** . . . . . . (609) 989-2190

New Mexico District

201 Third Street, NW, Suite 900, Albuquerque, NM 87102
P.O. Box 607, Albuquerque, NM 87103-0607
Tel: (505) 346-7274 Fax: (505) 346-7296
E-mail: usanm.webmaster@usdoj.gov
Internet: www.usdoj.gov/usao/nm

★ U.S. Attorney **MAJ Damon Paul Martinez** . . . . (505) 346-7274
E-mail: damon.martinez@usdoj.gov
Affiliation: ARNG
Education: New Mexico 1989 BA, 1992 JD, 1993 MBA
Executive Assistant U.S. Attorney and Public Affairs Officer **Elizabeth Martinez** . . . . (505) 346-7274
E-mail: elizabeth.martinez@usdoj.gov
Secretary to the U.S. Attorney **Annamarie Maresca** . . . . (505) 346-7274
E-mail: annamarie.maresca@usdoj.gov
First Assistant U.S. Attorney **James "Jim" Tierney** . . . . . (505) 346-7274
E-mail: jim.tierney@usdoj.gov
Director of Administration **Ruth Cox** . . . . (505) 346-7274
E-mail: ruth.cox@usdoj.gov Fax: (505) 346-6890
Victim-Witness Coordinator **Anita Perry** . . . . (505) 346-7274
E-mail: anita.perry@usdoj.gov Fax: (505) 346-7208
District Office Security Manager **Glenn L.R. Wagner** . . . . (505) 346-7274
E-mail: glenn.wagner@usdoj.gov
Supervisory IT Manager **Edmund Lee** . . . . (505) 346-7274
E-mail: edmund.lee@usdoj.gov
Human Resources Officer **Audrey Sullivan** . . . . (505) 346-7274
E-mail: audrey.sullivan@usdoj.gov
Budget Officer **Margaret Rimbert** . . . . (505) 346-7274

Appeals Division

Tel: (505) 346-7274

Appeals Chief **(Vacant)** . . . . (505) 346-7274
Assistant U.S. Attorney **David N. Williams** . . . . (505) 346-7274
E-mail: david.williams@usdoj.gov
Assistant U.S. Attorney/Organized Crime Drug Enforcement Task Forces **James Braun** . . . . (505) 346-7274
E-mail: james.braun@usdoj.gov

Civil Division

Tel: (505) 346-7274 Fax: (505) 346-7205

Civil Division Chief **Michael Hoses** . . . . (505) 346-7274
E-mail: michael.hoses@usdoj.gov Fax: (505) 346-7205
Assistant U.S. Attorney **Ruth F. Keegan** . . . . (505) 346-7274
E-mail: ruth.f.keegan@usdoj.gov
Assistant U.S. Attorney **Erin Langenwalter** . . . . (505) 346-7274
E-mail: erin.langenwalter@usdoj.gov
Assistant U.S. Attorney **Manuel Lucero** . . . . (505) 346-7274
E-mail: manny.lucero@usdoj.gov
Assistant U.S. Attorney **Roberto Ortega** . . . . (505) 346-7274
E-mail: roberto.ortega@usdoj.gov
Assistant U.S. Attorney **Howard Thomas** . . . . (505) 346-7274
E-mail: howard.thomas@usdoj.gov
Assistant U.S. Attorney **Cynthia Weisman** . . . . (505) 346-7274
E-mail: cynthia.weisman@usdoj.gov

Criminal Division

Tel: (505) 346-7274 Fax: (505) 346-6887

Criminal Division Chief **Jack E. Burkhead** . . . . (505) 346-7274
Supervisory Assistant U.S. Attorney/Fraud and Public Corruption Section **Jonathon Gerson** . . . . (505) 346-7274
E-mail: jonathon.gerson@usdoj.gov
Supervisory Assistant U.S. Attorney/General Crimes Section **Kimberly Brawley** . . . . (505) 346-7274
E-mail: kimberly.brawley@usdoj.gov
Supervisory Assistant U.S. Attorney/Indian Country Section **Glynette R. Carson-McNabb** . . . . (505) 346-7274
Supervisory Assistant U.S. Attorney/National Security Section **Fred J. Federici** . . . . (505) 346-7274
E-mail: fred.federici@usdoj.gov

(continued on next page)

REGIONAL OFFICES – US ATTORNEYS AND US MARSHALS SERVICE

★ Presidential Appointment Requiring Senate Confirmation ☆ Presidential Appointment ☐ Schedule C Appointment ◇ Career Senior Foreign Service Appointment
● Career Senior Executive Service (SES) Appointment ○ Non-Career Senior Executive Service (SES) Appointment ■ Postal Career Executive Service

Criminal Division *continued*

Supervisory Assistant U.S. Attorney/Organized Crime Section **Joel R. Meyers** (505) 346-7274
E-mail: joel.meyers@usdoj.gov

Assistant U.S. Attorney **David Adams** (505) 346-7274
E-mail: david.adams3@usdoj.gov

Assistant U.S. Attorney **Rumaldo Armijo** (505) 346-7274
E-mail: rumaldo.armijo@usdoj.gov

Assistant U.S. Attorney **Norman Cairns** (505) 346-7274
E-mail: norman.cairns@usdoj.gov

Assistant U.S. Attorney **John Crews** (505) 346-7274
E-mail: john.crews@usdoj.gov

Assistant U.S. Attorney **Nicholas J. Ganjei** (505) 346-7274
E-mail: nicholas.j.ganjei@usdoj.gov
Education: Boalt Hall 2005 JD

Assistant U.S. Attorney **Shammara Henderson** (505) 346-7274
E-mail: shammara.h.henderson@usdoj.gov
Education: American U; New Mexico JD

Assistant U.S. Attorney **Kristopher N. Houghton** (505) 346-7274
E-mail: kristopher.houghton@usdoj.gov
Education: New Mexico 2008 JD

Assistant U.S. Attorney **Samuel A. Hurtado** (505) 346-7274
E-mail: samuel.a.hurtado@usdoj.gov

Assistant U.S. Attorney **Holland S. Kastrin** (505) 346-7274
E-mail: holland.s.kastrin@usdoj.gov

Assistant U.S. Attorney **Stephen R. Kotz** (505) 346-7224
E-mail: steve.kotz@usdoj.gov

Assistant U.S. Attorney **Shana B. Long** (505) 346-7274
E-mail: shana.b.long@usdoj.gov

Assistant U.S. Attorney **Sarah Mease** (505) 346-7274
E-mail: sarah.mease@usdoj.gov

Assistant U.S. Attorney **Paige Messec** (505) 346-7274
E-mail: paige.messec@usdoj.gov

Assistant U.S. Attorney **Linda J. Mott** (505) 346-7274
E-mail: linda.j.mott@usdoj.gov

Assistant U.S. Attorney **Paul Mysliwiec** (505) 346-7274
E-mail: paul.mysliwiec@usdoj.gov

Assistant U.S. Attorney **Kyle Nayback** (505) 346-7274
E-mail: kyle.nayback2@usdoj.gov

Assistant U.S. Attorney **Tara Neda** (505) 346-7274
E-mail: tara.neda@usdoj.gov

Assistant U.S. Attorney **Jeremy A. Pena** (505) 346-7274
E-mail: jeremy.pena@usdoj.gov

Assistant U.S. Attorney **William Pflugrath** (505) 346-7274
E-mail: william.pflugrath@usdoj.gov

Assistant U.S. Attorney **Elaine Ramirez** (505) 346-7274
E-mail: elaine.ramirez@usdoj.gov

Assistant U.S. Attorney **Jennifer M. Rozzoni** (505) 346-7274
E-mail: jennifer.m.rozzoni@usdoj.gov

Assistant U.S. Attorney **Raquel Ruiz-Velez** (505) 346-7274
E-mail: rruizvelez@usa.doj.gov

Assistant U.S. Attorney **Sasha Siemel** (505) 346-7274
E-mail: sasha.siemel@usdoj.gov

Assistant U.S. Attorney **Paul Spiers** (505) 346-7274
E-mail: paul.spiers@usdoj.gov

Assistant U.S. Attorney **Jon Stanford** (505) 346-7274
E-mail: jon.stanford@usdoj.gov

Assistant U.S. Attorney **Sean J. Sullivan** (505) 346-7274
E-mail: sean.j.sullivan@usdoj.gov

Assistant U.S. Attorney **Reeve Swainston** (505) 346-7274
E-mail: reeve.swainston@usdoj.gov

Assistant U.S. Attorney **Niki Tapia-Brito** (505) 346-7274
E-mail: Niki.Tapia-Brito@usdoj.gov

Assistant U.S. Attorney **Shaheen Torgoley** (505) 346-7274
E-mail: shaheen.torgoley@usdoj.gov

Assistant U.S. Attorney **Presiliano Torrez** (505) 346-7274
E-mail: presiliano.torrez@usdoj.gov
Education: Harvard 1999 AB; London School Econ (UK) 2001 MS; Stanford 2005 JD

Assistant U.S. Attorney **Dean Tuckman** (505) 346-7274
E-mail: dean.tuckman@usdoj.gov

Criminal Division *continued*

Assistant U.S. Attorney **Louis E. Valencia** (505) 346-7274
E-mail: louis.valencia@usdoj.gov

Assistant U.S. Attorney **Timothy Vasquez** (505) 346-7274
E-mail: timothy.vasquez@usdoj.gov

Assistant U.S. Attorney **David M. Walsh** (505) 346-7274
E-mail: david.m.walsh@usdoj.gov

Assistant U.S. Attorney **Lynn Wang** (505) 346-7274
E-mail: lynn.wang@usdoj.gov

Assistant U.S. Attorney **Novaline Wilson** (505) 346-7274
E-mail: novaline.wilson@usdoj.gov

Assistant U.S. Attorney **Jacob A. Wishard** (505) 346-7274
E-mail: jacob.a.wishard@usdoj.gov

Assistant U.S. Attorney **(Vacant)** (505) 346-7274

Assistant U.S. Attorney **(Vacant)** (505) 346-7274

Las Cruces (NM) Office

555 South Telshor, Suite 300, Las Cruces, NM 88011
Tel: (575) 522-2304 Fax: (575) 522-2391

Deputy Chief, Criminal Division **Renee Camacho** (575) 522-2304
E-mail: renee.camacho@usdoj.gov

Assistant U.S. Attorney/Trial Group Supervisor **Alfred Perez** (575) 522-2304
E-mail: alfred.perez@usdoj.gov

Assistant U.S. Attorney/Trial Group Supervisor **Richard C. Williams** (575) 522-2304
E-mail: richard.williams@usdoj.gov

Senior Litigation Counsel/OCDETF and Strike Force Coordinator **Terri Abernathy** (575) 522-2304
E-mail: terri.abernathy@usdoj.gov

Assistant U.S. Attorney **Maria Armijo** (505) 522-2304
E-mail: maria.armijo@usdoj.gov

Assistant U.S. Attorney **Randy Castellano** (575) 522-2304
E-mail: randy.castellano@usdoj.gov

Assistant U.S. Attorney **Sarah M. Davenport** (575) 522-2304
E-mail: sarah.m.davenport@usdoj.gov

Assistant U.S. Attorney **Amanda Gould** (575) 522-2304
E-mail: amanda.gould@usdoj.gov

Assistant U.S. Attorney **Aaron O. Jordan** (575) 522-2304
E-mail: aaron.o.jordan@usdoj.gov

Assistant U.S. Attorney **Marisa Lizarraga** (575) 522-2304
E-mail: marisa.lizarraga@usdoj.gov

Assistant U.S. Attorney **Luis A. Martinez** (575) 522-2304
E-mail: luis.martinez@usdoj.gov

Assistant U.S. Attorney **Mark Saltman** (575) 522-2304
E-mail: mark.saltman@usdoj.gov

Assistant U.S. Attorney **Alexander Shapiro** (575) 522-2304
E-mail: alexander.shapiro@usdoj.gov

Assistant U.S. Attorney **Brock Taylor** (575) 522-2304
E-mail: brock.taylor2@usdoj.gov

Assistant U.S. Attorney **Edwin Garreth Winstead** (575) 522-2304
E-mail: edwin.winstead3@usdoj.gov
Education: Colorado 2011 JD

Special Assistant U.S. Attorney **Selesia Winston** (575) 522-2304
E-mail: selesia.winston@usdoj.gov

Special Assistant U.S. Attorney **Anna Wright** (575) 522-2304
E-mail: anna.wright2@usdoj.gov

New York - Eastern District

271 Cadman Plaza East, Brooklyn, NY 11201
Tel: (718) 254-7000 Fax: (718) 254-6479
Internet: www.usdoj.gov/usao/nye

★ U.S. Attorney (Interim) **Robert L. Capers** (718) 254-7000
Note: On October 16, 2015 President Obama nominated Robert Capers to be U.S. Attorney. Mr. Capers is currently the Interim U.S. Attorney.
E-mail: robert.capers@usdoj.gov
Education: NYU 1992 BA; Albany Law 1996 JD

Secretary to the U.S. Attorney **Lisa Alper** (718) 254-7000
E-mail: lisa.alper@usdoj.gov

Chief Assistant U.S. Attorney **Kelly T. Currie** (718) 254-7000
E-mail: kelly.currie@usdoj.gov Fax: (718) 254-6300

★ Presidential Appointment Requiring Senate Confirmation ☆ Presidential Appointment □ Schedule C Appointment ◇ Career Senior Foreign Service Appointment
● Career Senior Executive Service (SES) Appointment ○ Non-Career Senior Executive Service (SES) Appointment ■ Postal Career Executive Service

New York - Eastern District *continued*

Secretary to the Chief Assistant U.S. Attorney
Lisa Alper .... (718) 254-7000
E-mail: lisa.alper@usdoj.gov

Executive Assistant U.S. Attorney **William J. Muller** ..... (718) 254-7000
E-mail: william.muller@usdoj.gov Fax: (718) 254-6329

Secretary to the Executive Assistant U.S. Attorney
Lynda Clarke .... (718) 254-7000
E-mail: lynda.clarke@usdoj.gov Fax: (718) 254-6329

Law Enforcement Coordinator **Richard Capobianco** ..... (718) 254-7000
E-mail: richard.capobianco@usdoj.gov

Public Information Officer **Zugiel Soto** .... (718) 254-7000
E-mail: zugiel.soto@usdoj.go

Victim - Witness Coordinator **Lisa Foster** .... (718) 254-7000
E-mail: lisa.foster@usdoj.gov

Webmaster **Richard Woo** .... (718) 254-7000

Administrative Division
271 Cadman Plaza East, Brooklyn, NY 11201

Administrative Officer **Peter M. Kurtin** .... (718) 254-7000
E-mail: peter.kurtin@usdoj.gov Fax: (718) 254-6587

Deputy Administrative Officer **Mary Breen** .... (718) 254-7000
E-mail: mary.breen@usdoj.gov

Systems Manager **Shafiul Khan** .... (718) 254-7000
E-mail: shafiul.khan@usdoj.gov

Support Services Supervisor **Marc Caffray** .... (718) 254-7000
E-mail: marc.caffray@usdoj.gov

Budget Officer **Jacquie Prince-Dempsey** .... (718) 254-7000
E-mail: jacquie.prince-dempsey@usdoj.gov Fax: (718) 254-6550

Budget Analyst **(Vacant)** .... (718) 254-7000

Security Officer **Richard Capobianco** .... (631) 715-7000
610 Federal Plaza, Central Islip, NY 11722
E-mail: richard.capobianco@usdoj.gov

Management Analyst **Kelly Thurston** .... (718) 254-7000

Librarian **John Malone** .... (718) 254-6306
E-mail: john.malone@usdoj.gov

Appeals Division
271 Cadman Plaza East, Brooklyn, NY 11201
Fax: (718) 254-6325

Appeals Division Chief/Ethics Advisor/Professional Responsibility Officer **Peter A. Norling** .... (718) 254-7000
E-mail: peter.norling@usdoj.gov

Deputy Chief **Emily Berger** .... (718) 254-7000
E-mail: emily.berger@usdoj.gov

Deputy Chief **David C. James** .... (718) 254-7000
E-mail: david.james@usdoj.gov

Assistant U.S. Attorney **Susan Corkery** .... (718) 254-7000
E-mail: susan.corkery@usdoj.gov

Assistant U.S. Attorney **Jo Ann Navickas** .... (718) 254-7000

Civil Division
One Pierrepont Plaza, Brooklyn, NY 11201
Tel: (718) 254-7000 Fax: (718) 254-8701

Chief **Susan L. Riley** .... (718) 254-7000
E-mail: susan.riley@usdoj.gov Fax: (718) 254-7483

Principal Deputy Chief **(Vacant)** .... (718) 254-7000

Deputy Chief **(Vacant)** .... (718) 254-7000

Affirmative Enforcement Chief **Richard K. Hayes** .... (718) 254-7000
E-mail: richard.hayes@usdoj.gov

Civil Appeals Chief **Varuni Nelson** .... (718) 254-7000
E-mail: varuni.nelson@usdoj.gov

Civil Rights Chief **Michael Goldberger** .... (718) 254-7000
E-mail: michael.goldberger@usdoj.gov

Chief of Environmental Litigation **Sandra Levy** .... (718) 254-7000
E-mail: sandra.levy@usdoj.gov

Chief of Trial Training **(Vacant)** .... (718) 254-7000

Employment Discrimination Chief
Catherine M. Mirabile .... (718) 254-7000
E-mail: catherine.m.mirabile@usdoj.gov

Civil Division *continued*

Financial Litigation Unit Chief **Beth P. Schwartz** .... (718) 254-7000
E-mail: beth.schwartz@usdoj.gov

Health Care Fraud Chief **Paul W. Kaufman** .... (718) 254-7000
E-mail: paul.kaufman@usdoj.gov

Senior Trial Counsel **Leslie Brodsky** .... (718) 254-7000

Senior Trial Counsel **Kevan Cleary** .... (718) 254-7000
E-mail: kevan.cleary@usdoj.gov

Assistant U.S. Attorney **Mary M. Dickman** .... (718) 254-7000
E-mail: mary.dickman@usdoj.gov

Assistant U.S. Attorney **Scott A. Dunn** .... (718) 254-7000
E-mail: scott.dunn@usdoj.gov

Assistant U.S. Attorney **Kelly Horan** .... (718) 254-7000
E-mail: kelly.horan@usdoj.gov

Assistant U.S. Attorney **Claire S. Kedeshian** .... (718) 254-7000
E-mail: claire.kedeshian@usdoj.gov

Assistant U.S. Attorney **Artemis Lekakis** .... (718) 254-7000
E-mail: artemis.lekakis@usdoj.gov

Assistant U.S. Attorney **Orelia Merchant** .... (718) 254-7000
E-mail: orelia.merchant@usdoj.gov

Assistant U.S. Attorney **Elliot Schachner** .... (718) 254-7000
E-mail: elliot.schachner@usdoj.gov

Assistant U.S. Attorney **(Vacant)** .... (718) 254-7000

Special Assistant U.S. Attorney **Dione Enea** .... (718) 254-7000

Special Assistant U.S. Attorney **(Vacant)** .... (718) 254-7000

Social Security Litigation Chief **Kathleen Mahoney** .... (718) 254-7000
E-mail: kathleen.mahoney@usdoj.gov

Criminal Division
271 Cadman Plaza East, Brooklyn, NY 11201
Tel: (718) 254-7614 (Business and Securities Fraud Hotline)
Tel: (718) 254-6582 (General Crimes Hotline)
Tel: (718) 254-6581 (Narcotics Hotline)
Tel: (718) 254-6584 (Public Integrity Hotline)
Tel: (718) 254-6583 (Organized Crime and Racketeering Hotline)
Tel: (718) 254-6580 (Violent Criminal Enterprises Hotline)
Fax: (718) 254-6324

Chief **James J. McGovern** .... (718) 254-7000

Deputy Chief **(Vacant)** .... (718) 254-7000

Chief of Appeals/Professional Responsibility Officer
Peter A. Norling .... (718) 254-7000
E-mail: peter.norling@usdoj.gov

Senior Litigation Counsel **(Vacant)** .... (718) 254-7000

Business/Securities Fraud Section Chief
James F. "Jay" McMahon .... (718) 254-7000
E-mail: james.mcmahon@usdoj.gov Fax: (718) 254-7499
Education: Fordham JD

Business/Security Fraud Deputy Chief **(Vacant)** .... (718) 254-7000

Business/Security Fraud Senior Trial Counsel
Walter Norkin .... (718) 254-7000
E-mail: walter.norkin@usdoj.gov
Education: NYU 2000 JD

Assistant U.S. Attorney **(Vacant)** .... (718) 254-7000

Assistant U.S. Attorney **Tanya Y. Hill** .... (718) 254-7000
E-mail: tanya.hill@usdoj.gov

Assistant U.S. Attorney **Shannon Jones** .... (718) 254-7000
E-mail: shannon.jones@usdoj.gov

Assistant U.S. Attorney **(Vacant)** .... (718) 254-7000

Assistant U.S. Attorney **(Vacant)** .... (718) 254-7000

Civil Rights Litigation Section Chief **Taryn A. Merkl** .... (718) 254-7000
E-mail: taryn.merkl@usdoj.gov
Education: Columbia 2000 JD

Senior Litigation Counsel **Robert L. Capers** .... (718) 254-7000
E-mail: robert.capers@usdoj.gov Fax: (718) 254-6076
Education: NYU 1992 BA; Albany Law 1996 JD

Assistant U.S. Attorney **Amy Busa** .... (718) 254-7000
One Pierrepont Plaza, Brooklyn, NY 11201
E-mail: amy.busa@usdoj.gov

Assistant U.S. Attorney **Carrie N. Capwell** .... (718) 254-7000
E-mail: carrie.capwell@usdoj.gov
Education: Georgetown 1998 JD

(continued on next page)

★ Presidential Appointment Requiring Senate Confirmation ☆ Presidential Appointment □ Schedule C Appointment ◇ Career Senior Foreign Service Appointment
● Career Senior Executive Service (SES) Appointment ○ Non-Career Senior Executive Service (SES) Appointment ■ Postal Career Executive Service

Criminal Division *continued*

Assistant U.S. Attorney **Charles S. Kleinberg** . . . . (718) 254-7000
E-mail: charles.kleinberg@usdoj.gov
Intake and Arraignments Section Chief
Judith A. "Judy" Philips . . . . (718) 254-7000
E-mail: judy.philips@usdoj.gov Fax: (718) 254-6482
Narcotics Chief **Steven L. Tiscione** . . . . (718) 254-7000
E-mail: steven.tiscione@usdoj.gov
Education: Yale 2002 JD
Narcotics Deputy Chief **Justin Lerer** . . . . (718) 254-7000
E-mail: justin.lerer@usdoj.gov
Education: Harvard 2002 JD
Assistant U.S. Attorney **(Vacant)** . . . . (718) 254-7000
Organized Crime and Racketeering Section Chief
Elizabeth Geddes . . . . (718) 254-7000
Fax: (718) 254-6480
Deputy Chief, Organized Crime **James D. Gatta** . . . . . . (718) 254-6339
E-mail: james.gatta@usdoj.gov
Education: Fordham 1998 BA, 2002 JD
General Crimes Chief **(Vacant)** . . . . (718) 254-7000
Deputy Chief, General Crimes **(Vacant)** . . . . (718) 254-7000
Assistant U.S. Attorney **James Loonam** . . . . (718) 254-7000
E-mail: james.loonam@usdoj.gov
Assistant U.S. Attorney **Patricia Notopoulos** . . . . (718) 254-7000
E-mail: patricia.notopoulos@usdoj.gov
Assistant U.S. Attorney **Daniel Spector** . . . . (718) 254-7000
E-mail: daniel.spector@usdoj.gov
Education: Virginia 1997 BA; Chicago 2001 JD
Assistant U.S. Attorney **Michael H. Warren** . . . . (718) 254-7000
E-mail: michael.warren@usdoj.gov
Assistant U.S. Attorney **(Vacant)** . . . . (718) 254-7000
Public Integrity Chief **(Vacant)** . . . . (718) 254-7000
Fax: (718) 254-6180
Deputy Chief, Public Integrity Section
Paul Tuchmann . . . . (718) 254-7000
E-mail: paul.tuchmann@usdoj.gov
Education: Harvard 2002 JD
Violent Crimes and Terrorism Section Chief
Zainab Ahmad . . . . (718) 254-7000
E-mail: zainab.ahmad@usdoj.gov Fax: (718) 254-6480
Deputy Chief, Violent Crimes **Celia Cohen** . . . . (718) 254-7000
E-mail: celia.cohen@usdoj.gov

Long Island Office

610 Federal Plaza, Central Islip, NY 11722-4454
Tel: (631) 715-7900 Fax: (631) 715-7922

Assistant U.S. Attorney-in-Charge **Nicole Boeckmann** . . . (631) 715-7900
E-mail: nicole.boeckmann@usdoj.gov
Office Manager **Jen Casto** . . . . (631) 715-7900

Civil Division
610 Federal Plaza, Central Islip, NY 11722-4454
Fax: (631) 715-7920

Chief **Thomas A. McFarland** . . . . (631) 715-7900
E-mail: thomas.mcfarland@usdoj.gov
Deputy Chief **Charles Kelly** . . . . (631) 715-7900
E-mail: charles.kelly@usdoj.gov
Assistant U.S. Attorney **James Knapp** . . . . (631) 715-7900
E-mail: james.knapp@usdoj.gov
Assistant U.S. Attorney **Vincent Lipari** . . . . (631) 715-7900
E-mail: vincent.lipari@usdoj.gov

Criminal Division
610 Federal Plaza, Central Islip, NY 11722-4454
Fax: (631) 715-7922

Chief **Nicole Boeckmann** . . . . (631) 715-7874
Deputy Chief **Demetri Jones** . . . . (718) 254-7000
E-mail: demetri.jones@usdoj.gov
Deputy Chief **James Miskiewicz** . . . . (631) 715-7900
E-mail: james.miskiewicz@usdoj.gov

Criminal Division *continued*

Criminal Investigator **Randy Cox** . . . . (631) 715-7900
E-mail: randy.cox@usdoj.gov
Narcotics Deputy Chief **Licha Nyiendo** . . . . (718) 254-7000
E-mail: licha.nyiendo@usdoj.gov
Education: Duke 2000 JD
Assistant U.S. Attorney **Carrie N. Capwell** . . . . (631) 715-7900
E-mail: carrie.capwell@usdoj.gov
Education: Georgetown 1998 JD
Assistant U.S. Attorney **John J. Durham** . . . . (718) 254-7000
Assistant U.S. Attorney **Lara Treinis Gatz** . . . . (631) 715-7900
E-mail: lara.gatz@usdoj.gov
Assistant U.S. Attorney **Demetri Jones** . . . . (631) 715-7900
E-mail: demetri.jones@usdoj.gov
Assistant U.S. Attorney **Burton T. Ryan** . . . . (631) 715-7900
E-mail: burton.ryan@usdoj.gov
Assistant U.S. Attorney **(Vacant)** . . . . (631) 715-7900
Assistant U.S. Attorney/Project Safe Childhood Task
Force **Allen L. Bode** . . . . (631) 715-7900
E-mail: allen.bode@usdoj.gov

New York - Northern District

James M. Hanley Federal Building, 100 South Clinton Street,
Room 900, Syracuse, NY 13261-7198
P.O. Box 7198, Syracuse, NY 13261-7198
Tel: (315) 448-0672 Fax: (315) 448-0689
Internet: www.usdoj.gov/usao/nyn

★ U.S. Attorney **Richard S. Hartunian** . . . . (518) 431-0247
E-mail: richard.hartunian@usdoj.gov
Education: Georgetown 1983; Albany Law 1986 JD
Paralegal to the U.S. Attorney **Linda Powers** . . . . (518) 431-0247
E-mail: linda.powers@usdoj.gov
First Assistant U.S. Attorney **Grant C. Jaquith** . . . . (518) 431-0247
E-mail: grant.jaquith@usdoj.gov
Education: Presbyterian Col 1979; Florida 1982 JD
Executive Assistant U.S. Attorney for Community and
Public Affairs **(Vacant)** . . . . (315) 448-0672
Administrative Officer **Martha J. Stratton** . . . . (315) 448-0672
E-mail: martha.stratton@usdoj.gov
Law Enforcement Committee Coordinator
Armond Scipione . . . . (315) 448-0672
Systems Manager **William Eckert** . . . . (315) 448-0672
E-mail: william.eckert@usdoj.gov
Syracuse Office Manager **Lisa M. Fletcher** . . . . (315) 448-0672
E-mail: lisa.fletcher@usdoj.gov

Appellate Division
Fax: (315) 448-0689

Appellate Chief **Steven D. Clymer** . . . . (315) 448-0672
E-mail: steven.clymer@usdoj.gov
Education: Cornell 1983, 1986 JD

Civil Division
Fax: (315) 448-0646

Chief **Thomas Spina, Jr.** . . . . (518) 431-0247
E-mail: thomas.spina@usdoj.gov
Education: Siena Col 1982; Albany Law 1995 JD
Assistant U.S. Attorney **Michael Cadarian** . . . . (315) 448-0672
Assistant U.S. Attorney **William F. Larkin** . . . . (315) 448-0672
E-mail: william.larkin@usdoj.gov
Assistant U.S. Attorney **Charles E. Roberts** . . . . (315) 448-0672
E-mail: charles.roberts@usdoj.gov

Criminal Division
Fax: (315) 448-0689

Chief **Elizabeth C. Coombe** . . . . (315) 448-0672
E-mail: elizabeth.coombe@usdoj.gov
Deputy Chief **(Vacant)** . . . . (518) 431-0247

Criminal Division *continued*

Assistant U.S. Attorney and National Security Coordinator **Stephen C. Green** . . . . (315) 448-0672
E-mail: stephen.green@usdoj.gov
Assistant U.S. Attorney and Senior Litigation Counsel **Edward R. Broton** . . . . (315) 448-0672
Education: Canisius 1975 BS; Albany Law 1979 JD
Assistant U.S. Attorney **Nicolas Commaudeur** . . . . (315) 448-0672
E-mail: nicolas.commaudeur@usdoj.gov
Assistant U.S. Attorney **Rajit Dosanjh** . . . . (315) 448-0672
E-mail: rajit.dosanjh@usdoj.gov
Assistant U.S. Attorney **Carl G. Eurenius** . . . . (315) 448-0672
E-mail: carl.eurenius@usdoj.gov
Assistant U.S. Attorney **Lisa M. Fletcher** . . . . (315) 448-0672
E-mail: lisa.fletcher@usdoj.gov
Assistant U.S. Attorney **Carla B. Freedman** . . . . (315) 448-0672
E-mail: carla.freedman@usdoj.gov
Assistant U.S. Attorney **Michael Perry** . . . . (315) 448-0672
E-mail: michael.perry@usdoj.gov
Education: Harvard 2009 JD
Assistant U.S. Attorney **Ransom P. Reynolds** . . . . (315) 448-0672
Assistant U.S. Attorney **Richard R. Southwick** . . . . (315) 448-0672
E-mail: richard.southwick@usdoj.gov
Assistant U.S. Attorney **Tamara Thompson** . . . . (315) 448-0672
E-mail: tamara.thompson@usdoj.gov

Organized Crime Drug Enforcement Task Force
Fax: (315) 448-0689

Chief **Daniel Hanlon** . . . . (518) 431-0247

Albany (NY) Office

James T. Foley Courthouse, 445 Broadway, Room 218, Albany, NY 12207
Tel: (518) 431-0247 Fax: (518) 431-0249

Office Chief **Thomas Spina, Jr.** . . . . (518) 431-0247
E-mail: thomas.spina@usdoj.gov
Education: Siena Col 1982; Albany Law 1995 JD

Asset Forfeiture Unit
Fax: (518) 431-0249

Assistant U.S. Attorney **Tamara Thompson** . . . . (315) 448-0672
E-mail: tamara.thompson@usdoj.gov

Civil Division
Fax: (518) 431-0249

Assistant U.S. Attorney **Cathleen Clark** . . . . (518) 431-0247
Assistant U.S. Attorney **Adam Katz** . . . . (518) 431-0247
E-mail: adam.katz@usdoj.gov
Assistant U.S. Attorney **Karen Lesperauce** . . . . (518) 431-0247

Criminal Division
Fax: (518) 431-0249

Assistant U.S. Attorney **Michael Barnett** . . . . (518) 431-0247
E-mail: michael.barnett@usdoj.gov
Assistant U.S. Attorney **Richard Belliss** . . . . (518) 431-0247
E-mail: richard.belliss@usdoj.gov
Assistant U.S. Attorney **Jeffrey Coffman** . . . . (518) 431-0247
Assistant U.S. Attorney **Emily Farber** . . . . (518) 431-0247
E-mail: emily.farber@usdoj.gov
Assistant U.S. Attorney **Edward P. Grogan** . . . . (518) 431-0247
E-mail: edward.grogan@usdoj.gov
Assistant U.S. Attorney **Wayne Meyers** . . . . (518) 431-0247
Assistant U.S. Attorney **Sean O'Dowd** . . . . (518) 431-0247
Assistant U.S. Attorney **Elizabeth Rabe** . . . . (518) 431-0247
E-mail: elizabeth.rabe@usdoj.gov
Assistant U.S. Attorney **Kofi Sansculotte** . . . . (518) 431-0247
E-mail: kofi.sansculotte@usdoj.gov
Assistant U.S. Attorney **Robert A. Sharpe** . . . . (518) 431-0247
E-mail: robert.sharpe@usdoj.gov

Criminal Division *continued*

Assistant U.S. Attorney **Solomon Shinerock** . . . . (518) 431-0247
E-mail: solomon.shinerock@usdoj.gov
Education: Washington College of Law 2009 JD
Assistant U.S. Attorney **Paul D. Silver** . . . . (518) 431-0247
E-mail: paul.silver@usdoj.gov
Special Assistant U.S. Attorney **Jason White** . . . . (518) 431-0247

Binghamton (NY) Office

Federal Building, 15 Henry Street, Room 304, Binghamton, NY 13901
Tel: (607) 773-2887 Fax: (607) 773-2901

Assistant U.S. Attorney **Miroslav "Miro" Lovric** . . . . (607) 773-2887
E-mail: miro.lovric@usdoj.gov
Assistant U.S. Attorney **(Vacant)** . . . . (607) 773-2887
Assistant U.S. Attorney **(Vacant)** . . . . (607) 773-2887

Plattsburgh (NY) Office

14 Durkee Street, Suite 340, Plattsburgh, NY 12910
Tel: (518) 314-7800 Fax: (518) 314-7811

Assistant U.S. Attorney **Douglas Collyer** . . . . (518) 314-7800
Assistant U.S. Attorney **Elizabeth Horsman** . . . . (518) 314-7800
Assistant U.S. Attorney **Katherine Kopita** . . . . (518) 314-7800
Assistant U.S. Attorney **Cyrus P.W. Rieck** . . . . (518) 314-7800
Education: Miami 2008 JD

New York - Southern District

One St. Andrew's Plaza, New York, NY 10007
Tel: (212) 637-2200
Internet: www.usdoj.gov/usao/nys

★ U.S. Attorney **Preetinder "Preet" Bharara** . . . . (212) 637-1025
Education: Harvard 1990 AB; Columbia 1993 JD
Administrative Assistant to the U.S. Attorney **Hilary Nabhan** . . . . (212) 637-2582
E-mail: hilary.nabhan@usdoj.gov
Chief Counsel **(Vacant)** . . . . (212) 637-2200
Chief of Staff **(Vacant)** . . . . (212) 637-2200
Deputy U.S. Attorney **Joon H. Kim** . . . . (212) 637-1087
E-mail: joon.kim@usdoj.gov
Education: Stanford 1993 BA; Harvard 1996 JD
Associate U.S. Attorney **John M. McEnany** . . . . (212) 637-2571
E-mail: john.mcenany@usdoj.gov
Executive Assistant U.S. Attorney **Neil M. Corwin** . . . . . . (212) 637-2707
E-mail: neil.corwin@usdoj.gov
Education: Amherst 1981 BS; NYU 1985 JD
Administrative Officer **Edward Tyrrell** . . . . (212) 637-2269
E-mail: edward.tyrrell@usdoj.gov
Deputy Administrative Officer **James Bullock** . . . . (212) 637-2584
Chief Public Information Officer **James M. "Jim" Margolin** . . . . (212) 637-2600
Senior Public Affairs Officer and Director of New Media **(Vacant)** . . . . (212) 637-2600

Civil Division
86 Chambers Street, New York, NY 10007

Chief **Sara L. Shudofsky** . . . . (212) 637-2695
E-mail: sara.shudofsky@usdoj.gov
Education: Pennsylvania 1983 BA; NYU 1986 JD
Deputy Chief **David S. Jones** . . . . (212) 637-2739
E-mail: david.jones@usdoj.gov
Deputy Chief **Sarah S. Normand** . . . . (212) 637-2709
E-mail: sarah.normand@usdoj.gov
Education: Georgetown 1991 JD
Deputy Chief **Jeffrey S. Oestericher** . . . . (212) 637-2698
E-mail: jeffrey.oestericher@usdoj.gov
Education: Yale 1990 JD
Chief Appellate Attorney **Benjamin Torrance** . . . . (212) 637-2706
E-mail: benjamin.torrance@usdoj.gov
Education: Columbia 2000 JD

(continued on next page)

★ Presidential Appointment Requiring Senate Confirmation ☆ Presidential Appointment ☐ Schedule C Appointment ◇ Career Senior Foreign Service Appointment
● Career Senior Executive Service (SES) Appointment ○ Non-Career Senior Executive Service (SES) Appointment ■ Postal Career Executive Service

Civil Division *continued*

Deputy Chief Appellate Attorney **(Vacant)** . . . . (212) 637-2777
Civil Frauds Co-Chief **Rebecca C. Martin** . . . . (212) 637-2714
E-mail: rebecca.martin@usdoj.gov
Education: Northwestern 1984; Rutgers 1993 JD
Civil Frauds Co-Chief **Pierre Armand** . . . . (212) 637-2724
E-mail: pierre.armand@usdoj.gov
Civil Rights Unit Chief **David Kennedy** . . . . (212) 637-2733
E-mail: david.kennedy2@usdoj.gov
Civil Rights Unit Deputy Chief **Laura Eshkenazi** . . . . . . (212) 637-2758
Environmental Protection Unit Chief **Robert Yalen** . . . . . . (212) 637-2734
E-mail: robert.yalen@usdoj.gov
Financial Litigation Unit Chief
Kathleen A. Zebrowski . . . . (212) 637-2710
E-mail: kathleen.zebrowski@usdoj.gov
Immigration Unit Chief **(Vacant)** . . . .(212) 637-2705
Tax and Bankruptcy Unit Chief **Jeannette A. Vargas** . . . . (212) 637-2739
E-mail: jeannette.vargas@usdoj.gov
Education: Harvard 1995 BA; Yale 2000 JD
Tax and Bankruptcy Unit Deputy Chief
Lawrence "Larry" Fogelman . . . . (212) 637-2739
E-mail: lawrence.fogelman@usdoj.gov
Budget and Fiscal Officer **Wanda Yu** . . . .(212) 637-2666
E-mail: wanda.yu@usdoj.gov
Personnel Officer **Ruby Hopkins** . . . . (212) 637-2659
E-mail: ruby.hopkins@usdoj.gov
Paralegal Mangager **Lisa Jones** . . . . (212) 637-2694
Office Manager **Carmen Sepulveda** . . . . (212) 637-2767
E-mail: carmen.sepulveda@usdoj.gov
Civil Clerk Office Chief **(Vacant)** . . . .(212) 637-1563

Criminal Division

Tel: (212) 637-2200

Chief **Daniel L. Stein** . . . . (212) 637-2508
E-mail: daniel.stein@usdoj.gov
Education: Yale 1999 JD
Deputy Chief **Andrew Dunber** . . . . (212) 637-2563
Deputy Chief **Diane Gujarati** . . . .(212) 637-2200
E-mail: diane.gujarati@usdoj.gov
Education: Barnard 1990 BA; Yale 1995 JD
Deputy Chief **Bonnie B. Jonas** . . . . (212) 637-2472
E-mail: bonnie.jonas@usdoj.gov
Education: Wharton 1991 BS; Columbia 1995 JD
Deputy Chief **Joan M. Loughnane** . . . .(212) 637-2265
E-mail: joan.loughnane@usdoj.gov
Education: Harvard 1992; Stanford 1998 JD
Chief Appellate Attorney **Michael A. "Mike" Levy** . . . . . .(212) 637-1044
E-mail: mike.levy@usdoj.gov
Deputy Chief Appellate Attorney **(Vacant)** . . . .(212) 637-2263
Deputy Chief Appellate Attorney **(Vacant)** . . . .(212) 637-2507
Deputy Chief Appellate Attorney **(Vacant)** . . . .(212) 637-2312
Complex Frauds Chief **(Vacant)** . . . .(212) 637-2330
Complex Frauds Deputy Chief **Nicole Fridander** . . . .(212) 637-2211
General Crimes Co-Chief **Nola Breglio Heller** . . . .(212) 637-2262
E-mail: nola.heller@usdoj.gov
Education: Yale 2004 JD
General Crimes Co-Chief **Telemachus Kasulis** . . . . (212) 637-1110
E-mail: telemachus.kasulis@usdoj.gov
Education: Cornell 2002 JD
Terrorism and International Narcotics Co-Chief
John Cronan . . . . (212) 637-2200
E-mail: john.cronan@usdoj.gov
Terrorism and International Narcotics Co-Chief
Brendan R. McGuire . . . .(212) 637-2407
E-mail: brendan.mcguire@usdoj.gov
Education: NYU 2002 JD
Narcotics Co-Chief **Paul Krieger** . . . .(212) 637-1084
E-mail: paul.krieger@usdoj.gov
Education: Harvard JD
Narcotics Co-Chief **Jessica Ortiz** . . . . (212) 637-2212
E-mail: jessica.ortiz@usdoj.gov

Criminal Division *continued*

Public Corruption Chief **Arlo Devlin-Brown** . . . . (212) 639-2407
E-mail: arlo.devlin-brown@usdoj.gov
Violent and Organized Crime Co-Chief
Laurie A. Korenbaum . . . .(212) 637-2266
E-mail: laurie.korenbaum@usdoj.gov
Education: NYU 1985; Brooklyn Law 1996 JD
Violent and Organized Crime Co-Chief **(Vacant)** . . . . (212) 637-2305
Senior Trial Counsel **Stanley Okula** . . . .(212) 637-1585
E-mail: stan.okula@usdoj.gov
Chief Asset Forfeiture Unit **(Vacant)** . . . .(212) 637-1060

White Plains (NY) Office

300 Quarropas Street, Third Floor, White Plains, NY 10601
Tel: (914) 993-1908 Fax: (914) 682-3392

Co-Chief **Perry A. Carbone** . . . .(914) 993-1908
E-mail: perry.carbone@usdoj.gov
Co-Chief **Miriam Rocah** . . . .(914) 993-1908
E-mail: miriam.rocah@usdoj.gov
Education: Harvard 1992; NYU 1997 JD
Deputy Chief **(Vacant)** . . . . (914) 993-1908
Senior Litigation Counsel **Elliott Jacobson** . . . . (914) 993-1940
E-mail: elliott.jacobson@usdoj.gov

New York - Western District

138 Delaware Avenue, Buffalo, NY 14202
Tel: (716) 843-5700 Fax: (716) 551-3052
Internet: www.usdoj.gov/usao/nyw

★ U.S. Attorney **William J. Hochul, Jr.** . . . . (716) 843-5700
E-mail: william.hochul@usdoj.gov
Education: Notre Dame 1981; SUNY (Buffalo) 1984 JD
Secretary to U.S. Attorney **(Vacant)** . . . .(716) 843-5836
First Assistant U.S. Attorney
James P. Kennedy, Jr. . . . . (716) 843-5700 ext. 892
E-mail: jp.kennedy@usdoj.gov
Senior Litigation Counsel **Anthony M. Bruce** . . . (716) 843-5700 ext. 886
E-mail: anthony.m.bruce@usdoj.gov
Administrative Officer **(Vacant)** . . . .(716) 843-5826
Health Care Investigator **Margaret McFarland** . . .(716) 843-5700 ext. 877
Human Resources Officer **Mary Pat Tyler** . . . .(716) 843-5878
Computer Technology Division Chief
Nicholas G. Baldauf . . . .(716) 843-5815
E-mail: nicholas.baldauf@usdoj.gov
Law Enforcement Coordinating Committee
Coordinator **Samuel M. Palmiere** . . . . (716) 843-5700 ext. 842
E-mail: samuel.palmiere@usdoj.gov
Public Affairs Officer **Barbara J. Burns** . . . .(716) 843-5700 ext. 817
Supervisory Legal Assistant **Karen Barone** . . . . . (716) 843-5700 ext. 865
Supervisory Legal Assistant **Karen A. Brown** . . . .(716) 716-5836
Supervisory Legal Assistant **Kea D. Rusch** . . . . . .(716) 716-5700 ext. 857
Victim Witness Coordinator
Sharon M. Knope . . . .(716) 843-5700 ext. 828
E-mail: sharon.knope2@usdoj.gov

Appeals Unit

Chief, Assistant U.S. Attorney
Joseph J. Karaszewski . . . .(716) 843-5700 ext. 837
E-mail: joseph.j.karaszewski@usdoj.gov
Assistant U.S. Attorney
Stephan J. Baczynski . . . . (716) 843-5700 ext. 893
E-mail: stephan.baczynski@usdoj.gov
Assistant U.S. Attorney **Monica J. Richards** . . . . (716) 843-5700 ext. 852
E-mail: monica.richards@usdoj.gov

Asset Forfeiture Financial Litigation Unit

Chief **Richard D. Kaufman** . . . .(716) 843-5700 ext. 871
E-mail: richard.kaufman@usdoj.gov
Deputy Chief **Kevin D. Robinson** . . . .(716) 843-5700 ext. 804
E-mail: kevin.d.robinson@usdoj.gov
Assistant U.S. Attorney **Grace M. Carducci** . . . . (585) 263-6760 ext. 2254

Asset Forfeiture Financial Litigation Unit *continued*

Assistant U.S. Attorney **Mary C. Kane** . . . . (716) 843-5700 ext. 809
E-mail: mary.kane@usdoj.gov
Assistant U.S. Attorney **Kathryn L. Smith** . . . . . (585) 263-6760 ext. 2261

Civil Division

Chief **Mary Pat Fleming** . . . . (716) 843-5700 ext. 867
E-mail: mary.pat.fleming@usdoj.gov
Senior Litigation Counsel
Mary K. "Molly" Roach . . . . (716) 843-5700 ext. 866
E-mail: mary.k.roach@usdoj.gov
District Office Security Manager
Michael Cerrone . . . . (716) 843-5700 ext. 851
E-mail: michael.cerrone@usdoj.gov
Assistant U.S. Attorney **Kathleen A. Lynch** . . . . (716) 843-5700 ext. 830
E-mail: kathleen.lynch@usdoj.gov
Assistant U.S. Attorney **Gail Y. Mitchell** . . . . (716) 843-5700 ext. 833
E-mail: gail.mitchell@usdoj.gov
Assistant U.S. Attorney **(Vacant)** . . . . (716) 843-5700 ext. 847

Criminal Division

Tel: (716) 843-5700

Criminal Chief **Joseph M. Guerra III** . . . . (716) 843-5700 ext. 824
E-mail: joseph.m.guerra@usdoj.gov

Fraud and Corruption Section

Chief, Fraud and Corruption **Trini E. Ross** . . . . . . (716) 843-5700 ext. 805
E-mail: trini.e.ross@usdoj.gov
Assistant U.S. Attorney
Elizabeth Russo-Moellering . . . . (716) 843-5700 ext. 872
E-mail: elizabeth.moellering@usdoj.gov

General Crimes Section

Chief **Michael "Mike" DiGiacomo** . . . . (716) 843-5700 ext. 885
E-mail: michael.digiacomo@usdoj.gov
Special Assistant U.S. Attorney
Carol Giarrizzo Bridge . . . . (716) 843-5831
E-mail: carol.bridge@usdoj.gov
Assistant U.S. Attorney **Scott S. Allen** . . . . (716) 843-5700 ext. 869
E-mail: scott.allen@usdoj.gov
Assistant U.S. Attorney **Paul J. Campana** . . . . . . (716) 843-5700 ext. 819
E-mail: paul.j.campana@usdoj.gov
Assistant U.S. Attorney **Marie P. Grisanti** . . . . (716) 843-5700 ext. 818
E-mail: marie.grisanti@usdoj.gov
Assistant U.S. Attorney **Mary Ellen Kresse** . . . . . (716) 843-5700 ext. 888
E-mail: maryellen.kresse@usdoj.gov
Assistant U.S. Attorney **Joel C. Moore** . . . . (716) 843-5700 ext. 860
E-mail: joel.moore@usdoj.gov
Assistant U.S. Attorney **Maura O'Donnell** . . . . . . (716) 843-5700 ext. 816
Assistant U.S. Attorney **Frank T. Pimentel** . . . . . . (716) 843-5700 ext. 868
Assistant U.S. Attorney **John E. Rogowski** . . . . . (716) 843-5700 ext. 873
E-mail: john.e.rogowski@usdoj.gov
Assistant U.S. Attorney **Gretchen L. Wylegala** . . . . (716) 843-5822
E-mail: gretchen.wylegala@usdoj.gov
Assistant U.S. Attorney **(Vacant)** . . . . (716) 843-5700 ext. 885

Narcotics and Organized Crime Section

Chief **Timothy C. Lynch** . . . . (716) 843-5846
E-mail: timothy.lynch@usdoj.gov
Deputy Chief **Joseph M. Tripi** . . . . (716) 843-5700 ext. 839
E-mail: joseph.tripi@usdoj.gov
Assistant U.S. Attorney **Scott S. Allen** . . . . (716) 843-5869
Assistant U.S. Attorney **Mary Catherine Baumgarten** . . . (716) 843-5864
E-mail: mary.catherine.baumgarten@usdoj.gov
Education: SUNY (Buffalo) 1989 JD
Assistant U.S. Attorney **George C. Burgasser** . . . . (716) 843-5811
E-mail: george.c.burgasser@usdoj.gov
Assistant U.S. Attorney **Thomas S. Duszkiewicz** . . . . (716) 843-5863
E-mail: thomas.s.duszkiewicz@usdoj.gov

Narcotics and Organized Crime Section *continued*

Assistant U.S. Attorney
Russell T. Ippolito, Jr. . . . . (716) 843-5700 ext. 843
E-mail: russell.ippolito@usdoj.gov
Assistant U.S. Attorney **Caleb Petzoldt** . . . . (716) 843-5821
Assistant U.S. Attorney **Joel L. Violanti** . . . . (716) 843-5700 ext. 854
E-mail: joel.l.violanti@usdoj.gov
Assistant U.S. Attorney
Edward "Ned" White . . . . (716) 843-5700 ext. 862
E-mail: edward.white@usdoj.gov
Assistant U.S. Attorney **Wei Xiang** . . . . (716) 843-5700 ext. 806
E-mail: wei.xiang@usdoj.gov

Rochester (NY) Office

620 Federal Building, 100 State Street, Rochester, NY 14614
Tel: (585) 263-6760 Fax: (585) 263-6226

Assistant U.S. Attorney-in-Charge
Richard A. Resnick . . . . (585) 263-6760 ext. 23949
E-mail: richard.resnick@usdoj.gov
Chief of General Crimes Section
Tiffany Lee . . . . (585) 263-6760 ext. 23951
E-mail: tiffany.lee@usdoj.gov
Chief of Narcotics and Organized Crime
Section **Brett A. Harvey** . . . . (585) 263-6760 ext. 23949
E-mail: brett.harvey@usdoj.gov
Assistant U.S. Attorney **Melissa M. Marangola** . . . . (585) 263-6760
E-mail: melissa.marangola@usdoj.gov
Civil Division Assistant U.S. Attorney
Katherine Smith . . . . (585) 263-6760 ext. 23961
Criminal Division Assistant U.S. Attorney
Grace M. Carducci . . . . (585) 263-6760 ext. 23954
Criminal Division Assistant U.S. Attorney
John Field . . . . (585) 263-6760 ext. 23933
E-mail: john.field@usdoj.gov
Criminal Division Assistant U.S. Attorney
Craig Gestring . . . . (585) 263-6760 ext. 23979
E-mail: craig.gestring@usdoj.gov
Criminal Division Assistant U.S. Attorney
Douglas Gregory . . . . (585) 263-6760 ext. 23938
E-mail: douglas.gregory@usdoj.gov
Criminal Division Assistant U.S. Attorney
Robert A. Marangola . . . . (585) 263-6760 ext. 23980
E-mail: robert.marangola@usdoj.gov
Criminal Division Assistant U.S. Attorney
Marisa J. Miller . . . . (585) 263-6760 ext. 23965
Criminal Division Assistant U.S. Attorney
Charles E. Moynihan . . . . (585) 263-6760 ext. 23971
E-mail: charles.moynihan@usdoj.gov
Criminal Division Assistant U.S. Attorney
Jennifer M. Noto . . . . (585) 263-6760 ext. 23966
E-mail: jennifer.noto@usdoj.gov
Criminal Division Assistant U.S. Attorney
Everardo "Andy" Rodriguez . . . . (585) 263-6760 ext. 23950
E-mail: everardo.rodriguez@usdoj.gov
Criminal Division Assistant U.S. Attorney
Franklin H. Sherman . . . . (585) 263-6760 ext. 23934
E-mail: frank.sherman@usdoj.gov
Criminal Division Assistant U.S. Attorney
Bradley E. Tyler . . . . (585) 263-6760 ext. 23931
E-mail: bradley.e.tyler@usdoj.gov
Criminal Division Assistant U.S. Attorney
(Vacant) . . . . (585) 263-6760 ext. 23951
Supervisory Paralegal Specialist
Lori Pietrzykowski . . . . (585) 263-6760 ext. 23928
Victim Witness Coordinator **Kim Pettit** . . . . (585) 263-6760 ext. 972
E-mail: kim.pettit@usdoj.gov

★ Presidential Appointment Requiring Senate Confirmation ☆ Presidential Appointment ☐ Schedule C Appointment ◇ Career Senior Foreign Service Appointment
● Career Senior Executive Service (SES) Appointment ○ Non-Career Senior Executive Service (SES) Appointment ■ Postal Career Executive Service

North Carolina - Eastern District

Terry Sanford Federal Building and U.S. Courthouse,
310 New Bern Avenue, Suite 800, Raleigh, NC 27601-1461
Tel: (919) 856-4530 Fax: (919) 856-4487
Internet: www.usdoj.gov/usao/nce

★ U.S. Attorney **Thomas Gray Walker** .... (919) 856-4530
E-mail: thomas.walker@usdoj.gov
Education: Baylor 1986 BA; Campbell 1990 JD
Secretary to the U.S. Attorney
Michelle Solomon-Brown .... (919) 856-4530
E-mail: michelle.solomon-brown@usdoj.gov
First Assistant U.S. Attorney **John Stuart Bruce** .... (919) 856-4850
E-mail: john.bruce@usdoj.gov
Education: North Carolina 1975, 1978 JD
Administrative Officer **Bret E. Lopes** .... (919) 856-4530
E-mail: bret.lopes@usdoj.gov
Personnel Officer **Sherry E. Bowden** .... (919) 856-4530
E-mail: sherry.bowden@usdoj.gov
Law Enforcement Committee Coordinator
Donald P. Connelly .... (919) 856-4530
E-mail: don.connelly@usdoj.gov
Victim-Witness Coordinator **Michelle D. Scott** .... (919) 856-4530
E-mail: michelle.scott@usdoj.gov
Librarian **Dakeisa Parker** .... (919) 856-4872
E-mail: dakeisa.parker@usdoj.gov
Systems Manager **Patrick Reynolds** .... (919) 856-4530
E-mail: patrick.reynolds@usdoj.gov
Administrative Services Specialist/Purchasing Officer
Vernon D. Hudgins .... (919) 856-4530
E-mail: vernon.hudgins@usdoj.gov
Information Technology Specialist **Sean Moody** .... (919) 856-4530
E-mail: sean.moody@usdoj.gov

Appellate Division

Appellate Division Chief and Assistant U.S. Attorney
Jennifer May-Parker .... (919) 856-4530
E-mail: jennifer.may-parker@usdoj.gov
Education: SUNY (Geneseo) 1988 BA; SUNY Col (Buffalo) 1991 JD
Assistant U.S. Attorney **Kristine L. Fritz** .... (919) 856-4530
E-mail: kristine.fritz@usdoj.gov
Education: Washington & Jefferson 2002 BA; Duquesne 2006 JD
Assistant U.S. Attorney **Joshua L. Rogers** .... (919) 856-4530
E-mail: joshua.rogers@usdoj.gov
Education: Mississippi 2004 JD; Southern Mississippi 2001 MS
Assistant U.S. Attorney **Shailika Shah** .... (919) 856-4530
E-mail: shailika.shah@usdoj.gov
Assistant U.S. Attorney
Yvonne V. Watford-McKinney .... (919) 856-4530
E-mail: yvonne.watford@usdoj.gov
Assistant U.S. Attorney **Seth Morgan Wood** .... (919) 856-4530
E-mail: seth.wood@usdoj.gov
Education: Virginia 2003 JD

Civil Division

Civil Division Chief and Assistant U.S. Attorney
Rudolf A. Renfer, Jr. .... (919) 856-4530
E-mail: rudy.renfer@usdoj.gov
Deputy Chief and Assistant U.S. Attorney
G. Norman Acker III .... (919) 856-4530
E-mail: norman.acker@usdoj.gov
Assistant U.S. Attorney **Matthew L. Fesak** .... (919) 856-4530
E-mail: matthew.fesak@usdoj.gov
Assistant U.S. Attorney **Neal I. Fowler** .... (919) 856-4530
E-mail: neal.fowler@usdoj.gov
Assistant U.S. Attorney **Michael G. James** .... (919) 856-4530
Assistant U.S. Attorney **Steve Matheny** .... (919) 856-4319
Assistant U.S. Attorney **Kimberly A. Moore** .... (919) 856-4530
Assistant U.S. Attorney **Joshua B. Royster** .... (919) 856-4530
E-mail: joshua.royster@usdoj.gov
Assistant U.S. Attorney **Denise Walker** .... (919) 856-4530
E-mail: denise.walker@usdoj.gov

Civil Division *continued*

Assistant U.S. Attorney **Stephen A. West** .... (919) 856-4530
E-mail: steve.west@usdoj.gov
Assistant U.S. Attorney **Sharon C. Wilson** .... (919) 856-4530
E-mail: sharon.wilson2@usdoj.gov

Criminal Division

Criminal Division Chief and Assistant U.S. Attorney
Dennis M. Duffy .... (919) 856-4530
E-mail: dennis.duffy@usdoj.gov
Organized Crime Drug Enforcement Task Force Chief
and Assistant U.S. Attorney **Leslie Cooley** .... (919) 856-4530
E-mail: leslie.cooley@usdoj.gov
Deputy Chief **Felice M. Corpening** .... (919) 856-4530
Assistant U.S. Attorney **J. Frank Bradsher** .... (919) 856-4530
E-mail: frank.bradsher@usdoj.gov
Assistant U.S. Attorney **David A. Bragdon** .... (919) 856-4808
Education: Virginia JD
Assistant U.S. Attorney **Katherine Burnette** .... (919) 856-4530
Assistant U.S. Attorney **William Gilmore** .... (919) 856-4530
E-mail: william.gilmore@usdoj.gov
Assistant U.S. Attorney **Eric D. Goulian** .... (919) 856-4530
Assistant U.S. Attorney **Edward D. Gray** .... (919) 856-4530
Assistant U.S. Attorney
Robert J. "Bobby" Higdon, Jr. .... (919) 856-4530
Assistant U.S. Attorney **Adam Hulbig** .... (919) 856-4530
Assistant U.S. Attorney **Jane J. Jackson** .... (919) 856-4530
Assistant U.S. Attorney **Jason Kellhofer** .... (919) 856-4530
E-mail: jason.kellhofer@usdoj.gov
Assistant U.S. Attorney **Sebastian Kielmanovich** .... (919) 856-4530
E-mail: sebastian.kielmanovich@usdoj.gov
Assistant U.S. Attorney **Barbara D. Kocher** .... (919) 856-4530
Assistant U.S. Attorney **James J. Kurosad** .... (919) 856-4530
Assistant U.S. Attorney **Toby Lathan** .... (919) 856-4530
Assistant U.S. Attorney **Susan Menzer** .... (919) 856-4530
E-mail: susan.menzer@usdoj.gov
Assistant U.S. Attorney **Brian Meyers** .... (919) 856-4530
Assistant U.S. Attorney **Thomas B. Murphy** .... (919) 856-4530
Assistant U.S. Attorney **Ethan A. Ontjes** .... (919) 856-4530
Assistant U.S. Attorney **Banumathi Rangarajan** .... (919) 856-4359
Assistant U.S. Attorney **Rudy E. Renfer** .... (919) 856-4530
Assistant U.S. Attorney **Evan Rikhye** .... (919) 856-4530
Education: Washington College of Law 2001 JD
Assistant U.S. Attorney **Jennifer Wells** .... (919) 856-4530
Assistant U.S. Attorney **(Vacant)** .... (252) 830-0335
Assistant U.S. Attorney **(Vacant)** .... (919) 856-4530
OCEDTF Special Assistant U.S. Attorney **(Vacant)** ...... (919) 856-4530
Special Assistant U.S. Attorney **Glenn Perry** .... (919) 856-4530
Special Assistant U.S. Attorney **Matthew Scott** .... (919) 856-4530
Special Assistant U.S. Attorney **Timothy Severo** .... (919) 856-4530
Special Assistant U.S. Attorney **(Vacant)** .... (919) 856-4530

North Carolina - Middle District

101 South Edgeworth Street, 4th Floor, Greensboro, NC 27401
Tel: (336) 333-5351 Fax: (336) 333-5438

★ U.S. Attorney **Ripley Eagles Rand** .... (336) 333-5351
E-mail: ripley.rand@usdoj.gov
Education: North Carolina 1990 BA, 1995 JD
First Assistant U.S. Attorney **Sandra Hairston** .... (336) 333-5351
E-mail: sandra.hairston@usdoj.gov
Civil Division Chief and Assistant U.S. Attorney
Lynne Klauer .... (336) 333-5351
E-mail: lynne.klauer@usdoj.gov Fax: (336) 333-5257
Criminal Division Chief and Assistant U.S. Attorney
Clifton T. Barrett .... (336) 333-5351
Fax: (336) 333-5381
Deputy Criminal Chief and Assistant U.S. Attorney
Stephen T. Inman .... (336) 333-5351
E-mail: stephen.inman@usdoj.gov

★ Presidential Appointment Requiring Senate Confirmation ☆ Presidential Appointment □ Schedule C Appointment ◇ Career Senior Foreign Service Appointment
● Career Senior Executive Service (SES) Appointment ○ Non-Career Senior Executive Service (SES) Appointment ■ Postal Career Executive Service

North Carolina - Middle District *continued*

Assistant U.S. Attorney **Lisa Boggs** .... (336) 333-5351
E-mail: lisa.boggs@usdoj.gov
Assistant U.S. Attorney **Frank J. Chut** .... (336) 333-5351
E-mail: frank.chut@usdoj.gov
Education: Duke, JD
Assistant U.S. Attorney **Michael A. DeFranco** .... (336) 333-5351
E-mail: michael.defranco@usdoj.gov
Assistant U.S. Attorney **Robert Hamilton** .... (336) 333-5351
E-mail: robert.hamilton@usdoj.gov
Assistant U.S. Attorney **Harry Hobgood** .... (336) 333-5351
E-mail: harry.hobgood@usdoj.gov
Assistant U.S. Attorney **Eric Iverson** .... (336) 333-5351
E-mail: eric.iverson@usdoj.gov
Assistant U.S. Attorney **Michael F. Joseph** .... (336) 333-5351
Assistant U.S. Attorney **Joanna McFadden** .... (336) 333-5351
Assistant U.S. Attorney **Angela H. Miller** .... (336) 333-5351
E-mail: angela.miller@usdoj.gov
Assistant U.S. Attorney **Kyle Pousson** .... (336) 333-5351
E-mail: kyle.pousson@usdoj.gov
Assistant U.S. Attorney **Anand P. Ramaswamy** .... (336) 333-5351
E-mail: anand.ramaswamy@usdoj.gov
Education: North Carolina Greensboro BA; North Carolina 1997 JD
Assistant U.S. Attorney **Cheryl Sloan** .... (336) 333-5351
E-mail: cheryl.sloan@usdoj.gov
Administrative Officer **Raquel Niles** .... (336) 333-5351
E-mail: raquel.niles@usdoj.gov
Victim-Witness Specialist **Marsha Thompson** .... (336) 333-5351
Systems Manager **Timothy Brooks** .... (336) 333-5351
E-mail: tim.brooks@usdoj.gov
Systems Manager **(Vacant)** .... (336) 333-5351
LEC Coordinator **Randy Tysinger** .... (336) 333-5351
E-mail: randy.tysinger@usdoj.gov

Winston-Salem (NC) Office

Federal Building, 251 North Main Street,
Room 505, Winston-Salem, NC 27101
Tel: (336) 631-5268 Fax: (336) 631-5308

Assistant U.S. Attorney **Joan Binkley** .... (336) 333-5268
E-mail: joan.binkley@usdoj.gov
Assistant U.S. Attorney **Randall Galyon** .... (336) 631-5268
E-mail: randall.galyon@usdoj.gov
Assistant U.S. Attorney **Graham T. Green** .... (336) 333-5268
E-mail: graham.green@usdoj.gov
Education: Appalachian State; Campbell JD
Assistant U.S. Attorney **Robert A. Lang** .... (336) 631-5268
E-mail: rob.lang@usdoj.gov
Assistant U.S. Attorney **Terry M. Meinecke** .... (336) 333-5268
E-mail: terry.meinecke@usdoj.gov
Education: North Carolina Greensboro BA; Nebraska JD

North Carolina - Western District

Carillon Building, 227 West Trade Street,
Suite 1650, Charlotte, NC 28202
Tel: (704) 344-6222 Fax: (704) 277-0259

★ U.S. Attorney (Acting) **Jill Westmoreland Rose** .... (704) 344-6222
E-mail: jill.rose@usdoj.gov
Special Assistant to the U.S. Attorney **Lia Bantavani** ... (704) 344-6222
Administrative Officer **Rhonda Ramsey** .... (704) 344-6222
E-mail: rhonda.ramsey@usdoj.gov
First Assistant U.S. Attorney **Jill Westmoreland Rose** ... (704) 344-6222
E-mail: jill.rose@usdoj.gov
Law Enforcement Committee Coordinator
Fred Hudson .... (704) 344-6222
Victim-Witness Coordinator **Shirley Rutledge** .... (704) 344-6222
E-mail: shirley.rutledge@usdoj.gov
Automated Litigation Support Specialist
Timothy Dunbar .... (704) 344-6222
Systems Manager **Terry Tate** .... (704) 344-6222
E-mail: terry.tate@usdoj.gov

Asset Forfeiture
Assistant U.S. Attorney **Benjamin Bain-Creed** .... (704) 344-6222
E-mail: benjamin.bain-creed@usdoj.gov
Assistant U.S. Attorney **Bill Brafford** .... (704) 344-6222

Civil Division
Chief Assistant U.S. Attorney (Acting)
James M. "Jim" Sullivan .... (828) 271-4661
Assistant U.S. Attorney **James M. "Jim" Sullivan** ...... (704) 344-6222
Assistant U.S. Attorney **(Vacant)** .... (704) 344-6222
Affirmative Civil Enforcement Assistant U.S. Attorney
Donald H. Caldwell, Jr. .... (704) 344-6222
E-mail: donald.h.caldwell@usdoj.gov

Criminal Division
Chief **Kurt W. Meyers** .... (704) 344-6222
E-mail: kurt.meyers@usdoj.gov
Education: Franklin & Marshall 1994 BA; Arizona 1998 MA; Harvard 2001 JD
Deputy Chief **Dana O. Washington** .... (704) 344-6222
E-mail: dana.washington@usdoj.gov
Deputy Chief **(Vacant)** .... (704) 344-6222
Assistant U.S. Attorney **Courtney Bumpers** .... (704) 344-6222
Assistant U.S. Attorney **Kimlani Murray-Ford** .... (704) 344-6222
Assistant U.S. Attorney **Tom O'Malley** .... (704) 344-6222
E-mail: tom.omalley@usdoj.gov
Assistant U.S. Attorney **Mark Odulio** .... (704) 344-6222
E-mail: mark.odulio@usdoj.gov
Assistant U.S. Attorney **Ann Claire Phillips** .... (704) 344-6222
Assistant U.S. Attorney **Kenneth Smith** .... (704) 344-6222
E-mail: kenneth.smith@usdoj.gov
Assistant U.S. Attorney **Maria Vento** .... (704) 344-6222

Drug Task Force
Assistant U.S. Attorney **Jennifer Dillon** .... (704) 344-6222
Assistant U.S. Attorney **Cortney Escarvage** .... (704) 344-6222
E-mail: cortney.escarvage@usdoj.gov
Assistant U.S. Attorney **Kelli Ferry** .... (704) 344-6222
Assistant U.S. Attorney **Robert "Bob" Gleason** .... (704) 344-6222
E-mail: robert.gleason@usdoj.gov
Assistant U.S. Attorney **Elizabeth Greene** .... (704) 344-6222
Assistant U.S. Attorney **George Guise** .... (704) 344-6222
Assistant U.S. Attorney **Steve Kaufman** .... (704) 344-6222
Assistant U.S. Attorney **Craig Randall** .... (704) 344-6222
E-mail: craig.randall@usdoj.gov
Assistant U.S. Attorney **Kevin H. Zolot** .... (704) 344-6222
E-mail: kevin.zolot@usdoj.gov

Asheville (NC) Office

U.S. Courthouse, 100 Otis Street, Room 207, Asheville, NC 28801-2611
Tel: (828) 271-4661 Fax: (828) 271-4670

Civil Division Chief **Paul Taylor** .... (828) 271-4661
E-mail: paul.taylor@usdoj.gov
Appellate Division Assistant U.S. Attorney
Amy E. Ray .... (828) 271-4661
E-mail: amy.ray@usdoj.gov
Education: Florida State 1995 JD
Asset Forfeiture Unit Assistant U.S. Attorney
Thomas R. Ascik .... (828) 271-4661
E-mail: thomas.ascik@usdoj.gov
Criminal Division Assistant U.S. Attorney
Richard Edwards .... (828) 271-4661
Criminal Division Assistant U.S. Attorney **Don Gast** ..... (828) 271-4661
E-mail: don.gast@usdoj.gov
Criminal Division Assistant U.S. Attorney
John Pritchard .... (828) 271-4661
E-mail: john.pritchard@usdoj.gov
Drug Task Force Assistant U.S. Attorney
Thomas Kent .... (828) 271-4661
E-mail: thomas.kent@usdoj.gov
Assistant U.S. Attorney **David Thorneloe** .... (828) 271-4661
E-mail: david.thorneloe@usdoj.gov

(continued on next page)

★ Presidential Appointment Requiring Senate Confirmation ☆ Presidential Appointment □ Schedule C Appointment ◇ Career Senior Foreign Service Appointment
● Career Senior Executive Service (SES) Appointment ○ Non-Career Senior Executive Service (SES) Appointment ■ Postal Career Executive Service

Asheville (NC) Office *continued*

Victim-Witness Coordinator **Lynne W. Crout** . . . . (828) 271-4661
E-mail: lynne.crout@usdoj.gov

North Dakota District

Quentin N. Burdick U.S. Courthouse, 655 First Avenue, North, Suite 250, Fargo, ND 58102-4932
Tel: (701) 297-7400 Fax: (701) 297-7405
Internet: www.usdoj.gov/usao/nd

★ U.S. Attorney (Acting) **Christopher C. Myers** . . . . (701) 297-7400
Education: Drake JD
First Assistant U.S. Attorney **Christopher C. Myers** . . . . . (701) 297-7400
Education: Drake JD
Administrative Officer **(Vacant)** . . . . (701) 297-7400
Civil Chief **Kent S. Rockstad** . . . . (701) 297-7400
P.O. Box 699, Bismarck, ND 58502
E-mail: kent.rockstad@usdoj.gov
Education: North Dakota JD
Assistant U.S. Attorney **Nicholas Whitney Chase** . . . . (701) 297-7400
Education: North Dakota JD
Assistant U.S. Attorney **Megan A. Healy** . . . . (701) 297-7400
Education: Concordia Col Moorhead MN 2002 BA; Minnesota 2007 JD
Assistant U.S. Attorney **Janice M. Morley** . . . . (701) 297-7400
E-mail: jan.morley@usdoj.gov
Education: North Dakota JD
Assistant U.S. Attorney **Jennifer Klemetsrud Puhl** . . . . . . (701) 297-7400
E-mail: jennifer.puhl@usdoj.gov
Education: North Dakota JD
Assistant U.S. Attorney **Keith W. Reisenauer** . . . . (701) 297-7400
E-mail: keith.reisenauer@usdoj.gov
Education: North Dakota JD
Assistant U.S. Attorney **Scott J. Schneider** . . . . (701) 297-7400
E-mail: scott.schneider@usdoj.gov
Education: North Dakota JD
Assistant U.S. Attorney **Brett M. Shasky** . . . . (701) 297-7400
E-mail: brett.shasky@usdoj.gov
Education: North Dakota JD
Financial Litigation Unit **Nicole Olson** . . . . (701) 297-7400
E-mail: nicole.olson@usdoj.gov
Librarian **Denise Fuchs** . . . . (701) 297-7400
E-mail: denise.fuchs@usdoj.gov
Systems Manager **Ray Bakke** . . . . (701) 297-7400
Intelligence Specialist/Law Enforcement Coordinator
Terry Van Horn . . . . (701) 297-7400
E-mail: terry.vanhorn@usdoj.gov
Victim - Witness Coordinator **Dimple Smith** . . . . (701) 297-7400
E-mail: dimple.smith@usdoj.gov

Bismarck (ND) Office

U.S. Post Office and Courthouse, 220 East Rosser Avenue, Room 372, Bismarck, ND 58501
P.O. Box 699, Bismarck, ND 58502-0699
Tel: (701) 530-2420 Fax: (701) 530-2421

Assistant U.S. Attorney/Criminal Chief
Clare R. Hochhalter . . . . (701) 530-2420
E-mail: clare.hochhalter@usdoj.gov
Education: North Dakota JD
Assistant U.S. Attorney **Gary L. Delorme** . . . . (701) 530-2420
E-mail: gary.delorme@usdoj.gov
Assistant U.S. Attorney **David D. Hagler** . . . . (701) 530-2420
E-mail: david.hagler@usdoj.gov
Education: North Dakota JD
Assistant U.S. Attorney **Cameron W. Hayden** . . . . (701) 530-2420
E-mail: cameron.hayden@usdoj.gov
Education: North Dakota JD
Assistant U.S. Attorney **Jennifer Holmes** . . . . (701) 530-2420
E-mail: jennifer.holmes@usdoj.gov
Assistant U.S. Attorney **Brandi Sasse Russell** . . . . (701) 530-2420
E-mail: brandi.russell@usdoj.gov

Bismarck (ND) Office *continued*

Assistant U.S. Attorney **James Thomas** . . . . (701) 530-2420
Assistant U.S. Attorney **Rick Lee Volk** . . . . (701) 530-2420
E-mail: rick.volk@usdoj.gov
Education: North Dakota JD
Victim - Witness Coordinator **Beth Lang** . . . . (701) 530-2420
E-mail: beth.lang@usdoj.gov

Ohio - Northern District

801 West Superior Avenue, Suite 400, Cleveland, OH 44113
Tel: (216) 622-3600 TTY: (216) 522-3086
Fax: (216) 522-3370 (Administrative Division)
Fax: (216) 522-7545 (Executive Division)
Fax: (216) 522-2806 (Law Enforcement Committee Coordinator)
Fax: (216) 522-7358 (Major Fraud and Corruption)
Fax: (216) 522-7499 (Organized Crime Drug Enforcement Task Force)
Internet: www.usdoj.gov/usao/ohn/

★ U.S. Attorney **Steven M. Dettelbach** . . . . (216) 622-3600
Education: Dartmouth 1988 AB; Harvard 1991 JD
Secretary to the U.S. Attorney **Roberta Sladick** . . . . (216) 622-3652
E-mail: roberta.sladick@usdoj.gov
First Assistant U.S. Attorney **Carole S. Rendon** . . . . (216) 622-3656
E-mail: carole.rendon@usdoj.gov
Administration Director **Renee G. Sykora** . . . . (216) 622-3613
E-mail: renee.sykora@usdoj.gov
Deputy Director **Nora Mauk** . . . . (216) 622-3611
E-mail: nora.mauk@usdoj.gov
Budget Officer **Heidi Lyons** . . . . (216) 622-3626
E-mail: heidi.lyons@usdoj.gov
Personnel Officer **(Vacant)** . . . . (216) 622-3615
Public Information Officer **Michael "Mike" Tobin** . . . . (216) 622-3651
E-mail: michael.tobin@usdoj.gov
Law Enforcement Manager **Craig A. Tame** . . . . (216) 622-3644
Systems Manager **Andrew Smith** . . . . (216) 622-3621
Victim-Witness Specialist **Darla R. Pendergrass** . . . . (216) 622-3725
E-mail: darla.pendergrass@usdoj.gov
Litigation Support Specialist **Michael Godshalk** . . . . (216) 622-3767
Litigation Support Specialist **Judith Spar** . . . . (216) 622-3981

Asset Forfeiture Unit

Tel: (216) 622-3743 Fax: (216) 522-7499

Assistant U.S. Attorney **James L. Morford** . . . . (216) 622-3743
E-mail: james.morford@usdoj.gov
Assistant U.S. Attorney **Phillip J. Tripi** . . . . (216) 622-3769
E-mail: phillip.tripi@usdoj.gov

Civil Division

Tel: (216) 622-3670 Fax: (216) 522-4982

Chief **Lynne H. Buck** . . . . (216) 622-3712
E-mail: lynne.buck@usdoj.gov
Deputy Chief **Kent W. Penhallurick** . . . . (216) 622-3682
E-mail: kent.penhallurick@usdoj.gov
Deputy Chief **Alex A. Rokakis** . . . . (216) 622-3673
E-mail: alex.rokakis@usdoj.gov
Assistant U.S. Attorney **Renee Bacchus** . . . . (216) 622-3707
E-mail: renee.bacchus@usdoj.gov
Assistant U.S. Attorney **James R. Bennett** . . . . (216) 622-3988
E-mail: james.bennett@usdoj.gov
Assistant U.S. Attorney **Erin E. Brizius** . . . . (216) 622-3670
E-mail: erin.e.brizius@usdoj.gov
Assistant U.S. Attorney **Lisa Hammond Johnson** . . . . (216) 622-3679
Assistant U.S. Attorney **Michelle Heyer** . . . . (216) 622-3686
E-mail: michelle.heyer@usdoj.gov
Assistant U.S. Attorney **Lori White Laisure** . . . . (216) 622-3911
E-mail: lori.w.laisure@usdoj.gov
Assistant U.S. Attorney **Steven J. Paffilas** . . . . (216) 622-3698
E-mail: steven.paffilas@usdoj.gov
Assistant U.S. Attorney **Marlon A. Primes** . . . . (216) 622-3684
E-mail: marlon.primes@usdoj.gov

★ Presidential Appointment Requiring Senate Confirmation ☆ Presidential Appointment □ Schedule C Appointment ◇ Career Senior Foreign Service Appointment
● Career Senior Executive Service (SES) Appointment ○ Non-Career Senior Executive Service (SES) Appointment ■ Postal Career Executive Service

Civil Division *continued*

Assistant U.S. Attorney **David Ruiz** . . . . . (216) 622-3718
E-mail: david.ruiz@usdoj.gov
Assistant U.S. Attorney **Heather Tonsing Volosin** . . . . . (216) 622-3797
E-mail: heather.tonsing.volosin@usdoj.gov
Auditor **(Vacant)** . . . . . (216) 622-3779

Criminal Division
Tel: (216) 622-3874 Fax: (216) 522-8354

Chief **David A. Sierleja** . . . . . (216) 622-3754
Chief, Major and Cyber Crimes Unit **Edward F. Feran** . . . (216) 622-3709
E-mail: edward.feran@usdoj.gov
Deputy Chief, Major and Cyber Crimes Unit **Carol M. Skutnik** . . . . . (216) 622-3785
E-mail: carol.skutnik@usdoj.gov
Chief, Major Fraud and Corruption Unit **Ann C. Rowland** . . . . . (216) 622-3847
E-mail: ann.rowland@usdoj.gov
Deputy Chief, Major Fraud and Corruption Unit **Michael Collyer** . . . . . (216) 622-3888
E-mail: michael.collyer@usdoj.gov
Chief, National Security, Human Rights and OC Unit **Thomas E. Getz** . . . . . (216) 622-3840
E-mail: thomas.getz@usdoj.gov
Deputy Chief, National Security, Human Rights and OC Unit **Matthew Shepherd** . . . . . (216) 622-3859
E-mail: matthew.shepherd@usdoj.gov
Chief, Organized Crime Drug Enforcement Task Force Unit **Joseph M. Pinjuh** . . . . . (216) 622-3771
E-mail: joseph.pinjuh@usdoj.gov
Deputy Chief, Organized Crime Drug Enforcement Task Force **Michelle Baeppler** . . . . . (216) 622-3995
E-mail: michelle.baeppler@usdoj.gov
Assistant U.S. Attorney **Antoinette Bacon** . . . . . (216) 622-3966
Assistant U.S. Attorney **Lauren Bell** . . . . . (216) 622-3873
Assistant U.S. Attorney **Mark Bennett** . . . . . (216) 622-3878
E-mail: mark.bennett@usdoj.gov
Assistant U.S. Attorney **Bridget M. Brennan** . . . . . (216) 622-3810
E-mail: bridget.brennan@usdoj.gov
Assistant U.S. Attorney **Duncan T. Brown** . . . . . (216) 622-3933
E-mail: duncan.brown@usdoj.gov
Assistant U.S. Attorney **Robert F. Corts** . . . . . (216) 622-3957
E-mail: robert.corts@usdoj.gov
Assistant U.S. Attorney **Matthew J. Cronin** . . . . . (216) 622-3995
E-mail: matthew.cronin@usdoj.gov
Assistant U.S. Attorney **Henry DeBaggis** . . . . . (216) 622-3929
E-mail: henry.debaggis@usdoj.gov
Assistant U.S. Attorney **Miranda E. Dugi** . . . . . (216) 622-3844
E-mail: miranda.dugi@usdoj.gov
Assistant U.S. Attorney **Laura M. Ford** . . . . . (216) 622-3817
E-mail: laura.ford@usdoj.gov
Assistant U.S. Attorney **Kelly L. Galvin** . . . . . (216) 622-3731
E-mail: kelly.l.galvin@usdoj.gov
Assistant U.S. Attorney **Christos N. Georgalis** . . . . . (216) 622-3971
E-mail: chris.georgalis@usdoj.gov
Assistant U.S. Attorney **Justin Gould** . . . . . (216) 622-3869
Assistant U.S. Attorney **Adam Hollingsworth** . . . . . (216) 622-3781
E-mail: adam.hollingsworth@usdoj.gov
Assistant U.S. Attorney **Om M. Kakani** . . . . . (216) 622-3756
E-mail: om.kakani@usdoj.gov
Assistant U.S. Attorney **Matthew Kall** . . . . . (216) 622-3915
Assistant U.S. Attorney **Vasile Katasaros** . . . . . (216) 622-3876
Assistant U.S. Attorney **Robert W. Kern** . . . . . (216) 622-3836
E-mail: robert.kern@usdoj.gov
Assistant U.S. Attorney **Kendra Klump** . . . . . (216) 622-3689
Assistant U.S. Attorney **James V. Moroney** . . . . . (216) 622-3827
Assistant U.S. Attorney **Robert J. Patton** . . . . . (216) 622-3856
Assistant U.S. Attorney **Dan R. Ranke** . . . . . (216) 622-3753
Assistant U.S. Attorney **Chelsea Rice** . . . . . (216) 622-3752
E-mail: chelsea.rice@usdoj.gov

Criminal Division *continued*

Assistant U.S. Attorney **Daniel J. Riedl** . . . . . (216) 622-3669
E-mail: daniel.riedl@usdoj.gov
Assistant U.S. Attorney **Justin J. Roberts** . . . . . (216) 622-3958
E-mail: justin.roberts@usdoj.gov
Education: Texas 1995 BA, 1998 JD
Assistant U.S. Attorney **Christian H. Stickan** . . . . . (216) 622-3818
E-mail: christian.stickan@usdoj.gov
Assistant U.S. Attorney **Michael A. Sullivan** . . . . . (216) 622-3977
Assistant U.S. Attorney **Margaret Sweeney** . . . . . (216) 622-3990
Assistant U.S. Attorney **(Vacant)** . . . . . (216) 622-3758
Auditor **Laurie Boyer** . . . . . (216) 622-3830
E-mail: laurie.boyer@usdoj.gov
Intelligence Research Specialist **Janeth Herman** . . . . . (216) 622-3730
E-mail: janeth.herman@usdoj.gov

Akron (OH) Office
Two South Main Street, Room 208, Akron, OH 44308
Tel: (330) 375-5716 Fax: (330) 375-5492

Branch Chief **Robert E. "Bob" Bulford** . . . . . (330) 761-0517
Civil Division Assistant U.S. Attorney **(Vacant)** . . . . . (330) 761-0523
Chief, Appellate Unit **Bernard A. Smith** . . . . . (330) 761-0524
Assistant U.S. Attorney **Teresa L. Dirksen** . . . . . (330) 761-0519
E-mail: teresa.dirksen@usdoj.gov
Education: Akron 2002 JD
Assistant U.S. Attorney **Rebecca C. Lutzko** . . . . . (330) 761-0530
E-mail: rebecca.lutzko@usdoj.gov
Criminal Division Assistant U.S. Attorney **Linda H. Barr** . . . . . (330) 761-0521
E-mail: linda.barr@usdoj.gov
Criminal Division Assistant U.S. Attorney **Samuel A. Yannucci** . . . . . (330) 761-0518

Toledo (OH) Office
Four Seagate, 3rd Floor, Toledo, OH 43604
Tel: (419) 259-6376 Fax: (419) 259-6360

Branch Chief **Ava Rotell-Dustin** . . . . . (419) 241-0767
E-mail: ava.rotell.dustin@usdoj.gov
Civil Division Assistant U.S. Attorney **Angelita Cruz Bridges** . . . . . (419) 241-0715
Civil Division Assistant U.S. Attorney **Guillermo Rojas** . . . . . (419) 241-0716
E-mail: guillermo.rojas@usdoj.gov
Civil Division Assistant U.S. Attorney **Holly Taft-Sydlow** . . . . . (419) 241-0718
E-mail: holly.sydlow@usdoj.gov
Criminal Division Assistant U.S. Attorney **Gene Crawford** . . . . . (419) 241-0726
E-mail: gene.crawford@usdoj.gov
Criminal Division Assistant U.S. Attorney **Michael J. Freeman** . . . . . (419) 241-0724
E-mail: michael.freeman2@usdoj.gov
Criminal Division Assistant U.S. Attorney **Noah P. Hood** . . . . . (419) 241-0725
E-mail: noah.hood@usdoj.gov
Criminal Division Assistant U.S. Attorney **Alissa Sterling** . . . . . (419) 241-0727
E-mail: alissa.sterling@usdoj.gov
Criminal Division Assistant U.S. Attorney **Thomas P. Weldon** . . . . . (419) 241-0721
E-mail: thomas.weldon@usdoj.gov
Paralegal Specialist **Gretchen Croniser** . . . . . (419) 241-0714
E-mail: gretchen.croniser@usdoj.gov
Paralegal Specialist **Jennifer Ramon** . . . . . (419) 241-0738
E-mail: jennifer.ramon@usdoj.gov

Youngstown (OH) Office
City Center One, 100 East Federal Plaza,
Suite 325, Youngstown, OH 44503
Tel: (330) 746-7974 Fax: (330) 746-0239

Criminal Division Assistant U.S. Attorney
Jason M. Katz .... (330) 746-7974
E-mail: jason.katz@usdoj.gov
Criminal Division Assistant U.S. Attorney
David M. "Dave" Toepfer .... (330) 746-6986
E-mail: david.toepfer@usdoj.gov

Ohio - Southern District
303 Marconi Boulevard, Suite 200, Columbus, OH 43215
Tel: (614) 469-5715 Fax: (614) 469-7769
Internet: www.usdoj.gov/usao/ohs

★ U.S. Attorney **Carter M. Stewart** .... (614) 469-5715
Education: Stanford 1991 BA; Columbia 1994 MA; Harvard 1997 JD
Executive Assistant **(Vacant)** .... (614) 469-5715
First Assistant U.S. Attorney **Mark T. D'Alessandro** ..... (614) 469-5715
E-mail: mark.dalessandro@usdoj.gov
Executive Assistant U.S. Attorney
Robert A. Behlen, Jr. .... (614) 469-5715
E-mail: robert.behlen@usdoj.gov

Criminal Division
Fax: (937) 225-2564

Assistant U.S. Attorney/Branch Chief
Laura I. Clemmens .... (614) 469-5715
Assistant U.S. Attorney **Kyle J. Healey** .... (937) 225-2910
E-mail: kyle.healey@usdoj.gov
Assistant U.S. Attorney **Andrew J. Hunt** .... (614) 469-5715
Assistant U.S. Attorney **Dwight K. Keller** .... (614) 469-5715
E-mail: dwight.keller@usdoj.gov
Assistant U.S. Attorney **Sheila G. Lafferty** .... (614) 469-5715
E-mail: sheila.lafferty@usdoj.gov
Assistant U.S. Attorney **Vipal J. Patel** .... (937) 225-2910
E-mail: vipal.patel@usdoj.gov
Assistant U.S. Attorney **Alexander Sistla** .... (937) 225-2910
E-mail: alex.sistla@usdoj.gov
Assistant U.S. Attorney **Pamela M. Stanek** .... (937) 225-2910
E-mail: pamela.stanek@usdoj.gov
Assistant U.S. Attorney **Brent G. Tabacchi** .... (614) 469-5715
Education: Illinois 2001 JD

Cincinnati (OH) Office
221 East Fourth Street, Suite 400, Cincinnati, OH 45202
Tel: (513) 684-3711 Fax: (513) 684-6710

Criminal Chief **Kenneth L. Parker** .... (614) 684-3711
E-mail: kenneth.parker@usdoj.gov
Assistant U.S. Attorney/Branch Chief
Anthony Springer .... (513) 684-3711
E-mail: anthony.springer@usdoj.gov
Victim-Witness Specialist **Krista Kent** .... (513) 684-3711
E-mail: krista.kent@usdoj.gov Fax: (513) 684-6385

Civil Division
Tel: (513) 684-3711 Fax: (513) 684-6972

Deputy Chief **Matthew Horwitz** .... (513) 684-3711
E-mail: matthew.horwitz@usdoj.gov
Senior Litigation Counsel **(Vacant)** .... (513) 684-3711
Assistant U.S. Attorney **Margaret Castro** .... (513) 684-3711
E-mail: margaret.castro@usdoj.gov
Assistant U.S. Attorney **Nicholas J. Pantel** .... (513) 684-3711
E-mail: nicholas.pantel@usdoj.gov

Criminal Division
Tel: (513) 684-3711 Fax: (513) 684-6385

Assistant U.S. Attorney/Organized Crime Drug
Enforcement Task Force Chief **(Vacant)** .... (513) 684-3711
Assistant U.S. Attorney/Appellate Chief
Benjamin Charles Glassman .... (513) 684-3711
E-mail: benjamin.glassman@usdoj.gov
Education: Harvard 2000 JD
Assistant U.S. Attorney **Robert A. Behlen, Jr.** .... (513) 684-3711
Assistant U.S. Attorney **Deborah Grimes** .... (513) 684-3711
E-mail: deborah.grimes@usdoj.gov
Assistant U.S. Attorney **Karl Kadon** .... (513) 684-3711
E-mail: karl.kadon@usdoj.gov
Assistant U.S. Attorney **Timothy Mangan** .... (513) 684-3711
E-mail: timothy.mangan@usdoj.gov
Assistant U.S. Attorney **Christy Muncy** .... (513) 684-3711
E-mail: christy.muncy@usdoj.gov
Assistant U.S. Attorney **Timothy D. Oakley** .... (513) 684-3711
E-mail: tim.oakley@usdoj.gov
Assistant U.S. Attorney **Anne L. Porter** .... (513) 684-3711
E-mail: anne.porter@usdoj.gov
Assistant U.S. Attorney **Alexis Zouhary** .... (513) 684-3711
E-mail: alexis.zouhary@usdoj.gov
Law Enforcement Coordination Specialist **Brian Capps** ... (513) 684-3711
E-mail: brian.capps@usdoj.gov

Columbus (OH) Office
303 Marconi Boulevard, Suite 200, Columbus, OH 43215
Tel: (614) 469-5715 Fax: (614) 469-2200

Assistant U.S. Attorney/Branch Chief **Gary L. Spartis** .... (513) 684-3711
E-mail: gary.spartis@usdoj.gov
Administrative Officer **Tina D. Kraus** .... (614) 469-5715
E-mail: tina.kraus@usdoj.gov Fax: (614) 469-7769
Victim-Witness Coordinator **Barbara E. Vanarsdall** ...... (614) 469-5715
E-mail: barbara.vanarsdall@usdoj.gov
Systems Manager **Lisa Tingley** .... (614) 469-5715
E-mail: lisa.tingley@usdoj.gov
IT Specialist **Kevin Baker** .... (614) 469-5715
E-mail: kevin.baker@usdoj.gov

Civil Division
Tel: (614) 469-5715 Fax: (614) 469-5240

Deputy Chief **(Vacant)** .... (614) 469-5715
Assistant U.S. Attorney **Bethany Hamilton** .... (614) 469-5715
Assistant U.S. Attorney **Andrew M. Malek** .... (614) 469-5715
E-mail: andrew.malek@usdoj.gov
Assistant U.S. Attorney **John J. Stark** .... (614) 469-5715
E-mail: john.stark@usdoj.gov
Assistant U.S. Attorney **Christopher R. Yates** .... (614) 469-5715
E-mail: christopher.yates@usdoj.gov
Assistant U.S. Attorney **(Vacant)** .... (614) 469-5715

Criminal Division
Tel: (614) 469-5715 Fax: (614) 469-5653

Deputy Chief **(Vacant)** .... (614) 469-5715
Assistant U.S. Attorney/Financial Crimes Chief
Brenda Shoemaker .... (614) 469-5715
E-mail: brenda.shoemaker@usdoj.gov
OCDETF Chief Assistant U.S. Attorney
Michael Hunter .... (614) 469-5715
Assistant U.S. Attorney **Kenneth F. Affeldt** .... (614) 469-5715
E-mail: ken.affedlt@usdoj.gov
Assistant U.S. Attorney **David J. Bosley** .... (614) 469-5715
Assistant U.S. Attorney **Daniel A. Brown** .... (614) 469-5715
E-mail: dan.brown@usdoj.gov
Assistant U.S. Attorney **David M. DeVillers** .... (614) 469-5715
Assistant U.S. Attorney **Salvador A. Dominguez** .... (614) 469-5715
E-mail: sal.dominguez@usdoj.gov
Assistant U.S. Attorney **Peter Glenn-Applegate** .... (614) 469-5715
E-mail: peter.glenn-applegate@usdoj.gov

★ Presidential Appointment Requiring Senate Confirmation ☆ Presidential Appointment ☐ Schedule C Appointment ◇ Career Senior Foreign Service Appointment
● Career Senior Executive Service (SES) Appointment ○ Non-Career Senior Executive Service (SES) Appointment ■ Postal Career Executive Service

Criminal Division *continued*

Assistant U.S. Attorney **Kevin W. Kelley** . . . . (614) 469-5715
E-mail: kevin.kelley@usdoj.gov
Assistant U.S. Attorney **Jessica Kim** . . . . (614) 469-5715
E-mail: jessica.kim@usdoj.gov
Assistant U.S. Attorney **J. Michael Marous** . . . . (614) 469-5715
E-mail: mike.marous@usdoj.gov
Assistant U.S. Attorney **Dana M. Peters** . . . . (614) 469-5715
E-mail: dana.peters@usdoj.gov
Assistant U.S. Attorney **Tim Prichard** . . . . (614) 469-5715
E-mail: tim.prichard@usdoj.gov
Assistant U.S. Attorney **Deborah A. Solove** . . . . (614) 469-5715
E-mail: deborah.solove@usdoj.gov
Assistant U.S. Attorney **Douglas W. Squires** . . . . (614) 469-5715
E-mail: douglas.squires@usdoj.gov
Assistant U.S. Attorney **Dale E. Williams, Jr.** . . . . (614) 469-5715
E-mail: dale.williams@usdoj.gov
Assistant U.S. Attorney **Mary Beth Young** . . . . (614) 469-5715
E-mail: mary.beth.young@usdoj.gov

Dayton Office

200 West Second Street, Suite 200, Dayton, OH 45402
Tel: (937) 225-2910

Civil Chief **(Vacant)** . . . . (614) 469-5715
Assistant U.S. Attorney **Gregory P. Dunsky** . . . . (614) 469-5715
E-mail: gregory.dunsky@usdoj.gov
Assistant U.S. Attorney **Brandi M. Stewart** . . . . (937) 225-2910
E-mail: brandi.stewart@usdoj.gov
Assistant U.S. Attorney **(Vacant)** . . . . (614) 469-5715
Victim-Witness Specialist **Aquanette Lindsay** . . . . (937) 225-2910

Oklahoma - Eastern District

1200 West Okmulgee Street, Muskogee, OK 74401
Tel: (918) 684-5100 Fax: (918) 684-5130
Internet: www.usdoj.gov/usao/oke

★ U.S. Attorney **Mark Frederick Green** . . . . (918) 684-5100
Education: Northeastern State 1972 (Attended); Oklahoma 1975, 1978 JD
Administrative Officer **Bonnie London** . . . . (918) 684-5131
First Assistant U.S. Attorney **Douglas A. Horn** . . . . (918) 684-5100
E-mail: doug.horn@usdoj.gov
Law Enforcement Committee Coordinator **(Vacant)** . . . . . . (918) 684-5100
Victim-Witness Specialist **Mary Jo Speaker** . . . . (918) 684-5100
E-mail: maryjo.speaker@usdoj.gov
Systems Manager/Webmaster **Dan Cott** . . . . (918) 684-5100
E-mail: dan.cott@usdoj.gov

Civil Division

Civil Division Chief and Assistant U.S. Attorney
Susan Brandon . . . . (918) 684-5100
E-mail: susan.brandon@usdoj.gov
Assistant U.S. Attorney **Michael Cooper** . . . . (918) 684-5100
E-mail: michael.cooper@usdoj.gov
Assistant U.S. Attorney **Robert Gay Guthrie** . . . . (918) 684-5100
Assistant U.S. Attorney **Cheryl R. Triplett** . . . . (918) 684-5100
E-mail: cheryl.triplett@usdoj.gov

Criminal Division

Assistant U.S. Attorney **Dean Burris** . . . . (918) 684-5100
E-mail: dean.burris@usdoj.gov
Assistant U.S. Attorney **Linda Epperley** . . . . (918) 684-5100
E-mail: linda.epperley@usdoj.gov
Assistant U.S. Attorney **Shannon L. Henson** . . . . (918) 684-5100
E-mail: shannon.henson@usdoj.gov
Assistant U.S. Attorney **Melody Noble Nelson** . . . . (918) 684-5100
Assistant U.S. Attorney **Edward "Ed" Snow** . . . . (918) 684-5100
E-mail: ed.snow@usdoj.gov
Assistant U.S. Attorney **Rob Wallace** . . . . (918) 684-5100
E-mail: rob.wallace@usdoj.gov
Education: Oklahoma 1985, 1988 JD

Criminal Division *continued*

Assistant U.S. Attorney **Chris Wilson** . . . . (918) 684-5100
E-mail: chris.wilson@usdoj.gov
Assistant U.S. Attorney **(Vacant)** . . . . (918) 684-5100

Oklahoma - Northern District

110 West Seventh Street, Suite 300, Tulsa, OK 74119
Tel: (918) 382-2700 Fax: (918) 560-7938
Internet: www.usdoj.gov/usao/okn

★ U.S. Attorney **Danny Chappelle Williams, Sr.** . . . . (918) 382-2700
E-mail: danny.c.williams@usdoj.gov
Education: Dillard 1988; Tulsa 1991 JD
Secretary to the U.S. Attorney **Anna Montgomery** . . . . (918) 382-2700
E-mail: anna.montgomery@usdoj.gov
First Assistant U.S. Attorney **Loretta F. Radford** . . . . (918) 382-2700
E-mail: loretta.radford@usdoj.gov
Senior Litigation Counsel **Janet S. "Jan" Reincke** . . . . . . (918) 382-2700
E-mail: jan.s.reincke@usdoj.gov
Administrative Officer **Carol L. de' Shaffon** . . . . (918) 382-2700
E-mail: carol.deshaffon@usdoj.gov
Law Enforcement Coordinator **Trisha Young** . . . . (918) 382-2700
E-mail: trisha.young@usdoj.gov
Victim-Witness Specialist **Gayla C. Stewart** . . . . (918) 382-2700
E-mail: gayla.stewart@usdoj.gov
Systems Manager **Hank Hampton** . . . . (918) 382-2700
E-mail: hank.hampton@usdoj.gov

Appellate Division

Assistant U.S. Attorney **Leena M. Alam** . . . . (918) 382-2700
E-mail: leena.alam@usdoj.gov

Civil Division

Chief **Cathryn "Cathy" McClanahan** . . . . (918) 382-2700
E-mail: cathy.mcclanahan@usdoj.gov
Assistant U.S. Attorney **Cheryl L. Baber** . . . . (918) 382-2700
E-mail: cheryl.baber@usdoj.gov
Education: Columbia 1993 JD
Assistant U.S. Attorney **Wyn Dee Ann Baker** . . . . (918) 382-2700
E-mail: wyndee.baker@usdoj.gov
Assistant U.S. Attorney **Marianne Hardcastle** . . . . (918) 382-2700
E-mail: marianne.hardcastle@usdoj.gov
Assistant U.S. Attorney **Thomas Scott Woodward** . . . . . (918) 382-2700
E-mail: scott.woodward@usdoj.gov
Education: Texas 1972; Oklahoma City 1981 JD

Criminal Division

Chief **Joseph F. "Joe" Wilson** . . . . (918) 382-2700
E-mail: joe.wilson@usdoj.gov
Deputy Chief **Timothy L. "Tim" Faerber** . . . . (918) 382-2700
E-mail: tim.faerber@usdoj.gov
Assistant U.S. Attorney **Clemon D. Ashley** . . . . (918) 382-2700
E-mail: clemon.ashley@usdoj.gov
Education: Loyola U (Chicago) 2007 JD
Assistant U.S. Attorney **Shannon Cozzoni** . . . . (918) 382-2700
E-mail: shannon.cozzoni@usdoj.gov
Assistant U.S. Attorney **Gary L. Davis** . . . . (918) 382-2700
E-mail: gary.l.davis@usdoj.gov
Assistant U.S. Attorney **Catherine J. Depew** . . . . (918) 382-2700
E-mail: catherine.depew@usdoj.gov
Assistant U.S. Attorney **Jeffrey A. Gallant** . . . . (918) 382-2700
E-mail: jeff.gallant@usdoj.gov
Assistant U.S. Attorney **Andrew "A.J." Hofland** . . . . (918) 382-2700
E-mail: andrew.hofland@usdoj.gov
Assistant U.S. Attorney **Neal C. Hong** . . . . (918) 382-2700
E-mail: neal.hong@usdoj.gov
Assistant U.S. Attorney **Clinton J. "Clint" Johnson** . . . . . (918) 382-2700
E-mail: clinton.j.johnson@usdoj.gov
Assistant U.S. Attorney **Eric Johnston** . . . . (918) 382-2700
E-mail: eric.johnston@usdoj.gov
Assistant U.S. Attorney **Kevin C. Leitch** . . . . (918) 382-2700
E-mail: kevin.leitch@usdoj.gov

(continued on next page)

★ Presidential Appointment Requiring Senate Confirmation ☆ Presidential Appointment ☐ Schedule C Appointment ◇ Career Senior Foreign Service Appointment
● Career Senior Executive Service (SES) Appointment ○ Non-Career Senior Executive Service (SES) Appointment ■ Postal Career Executive Service

Criminal Division *continued*

Assistant U.S. Attorney **Joel-lyn A. McCormick** . . . . (918) 382-2700
E-mail: joel-lyn.a.mccormick@usdoj.gov
Assistant U.S. Attorney **Charles M. McLoughlin** . . . . (918) 382-2700
E-mail: charles.mclaughlin@usdoj.gov
Assistant U.S. Attorney **R. Trent Shores** . . . . (918) 382-2700
E-mail: r.trent.shores@usdoj.gov
Organized Crime Drug Enforcement Task Force
Assistant U.S. Attorney **Allen J. Litchfield** . . . . (918) 382-2700
E-mail: allen.j.litchfield@usdoj.gov
Organized Crime Drug Enforcement Task Force
Assistant U.S. Attorney **Robert T. "Rob" Raley** . . . . (918) 382-2700
E-mail: rob.raley@usdoj.gov

Oklahoma - Western District

Oklahoma Tower, 210 Park Avenue, Suite 400,
Oklahoma City, OK 73102-5602
Tel: (405) 553-8700 Fax: (405) 553-8888

★ U.S. Attorney **Sanford C. Coats** . . . . (405) 553-8720
E-mail: sandy.coats@usdoj.gov
Education: Tulane 1994 BA; Oklahoma 1998 JD
Secretary to the U.S. Attorney **Nikki Winters** . . . . (405) 553-8731
E-mail: nikki.winters@usdoj.gov
Executive Assistant U.S. Attorney **Robert J. Troester** . . . . (405) 553-8809
E-mail: robert.troester@usdoj.gov
Administrative Officer **Lisa Engelke** . . . . (405) 553-8777
E-mail: lisa.engelke@usdoj.gov
Immigration Coordinator **(Vacant)** . . . . (405) 553-8700
Law Enforcement Committee Coordinator **(Vacant)** . . . . . . (405) 553-8926
Victim-Witness Specialist **Beverly LaRue** . . . . (405) 553-8872
E-mail: beverly.larue@usdoj.gov
Personnel Management Specialist **(Vacant)** . . . . (405) 553-8776
Systems Manager **Gary Murray** . . . . (405) 553-8780
E-mail: gary.murray@usdoj.gov

Appellate Division

Chief **Debra Paull** . . . . (405) 553-8741
E-mail: debra.paull@usdoj.gov
Education: Oklahoma 1978 JD
Assistant U.S. Attorney **Steven W. Creager** . . . . (405) 553-8726
E-mail: steven.w.creager@usdoj.gov

Civil Division

Chief **Kay Sewell** . . . . (405) 553-8805
E-mail: kay.sewell@usdoj.gov
Education: Oklahoma 1984 JD
Assistant U.S. Attorney **Matt Anderson** . . . . (405) 553-8788
E-mail: matthew.anderson2@usdoj.gov
Assistant U.S. Attorney **Robert Bradford** . . . . (405) 553-8805
E-mail: robert.bradford@usdoj.gov
Assistant U.S. Attorney **Rebecca Frazier** . . . . (405) 553-8831
E-mail: rebecca.frazier@usdoj.gov
Assistant U.S. Attorney **Ronald R. Gallegos** . . . . (405) 553-8844
E-mail: ron.gallegos@usdoj.gov
Assistant U.S. Attorney **Tom Majors** . . . . (405) 553-8814
E-mail: tom.majors@usdoj.gov
Assistant U.S. Attorney **Scott Maule** . . . . (405) 553-8832
E-mail: scott.maule@usdoj.gov
Assistant U.S. Attorney **H. Lee Schmidt** . . . . (405) 553-8745
E-mail: lee.schmidt@usdoj.gov
Education: Oklahoma 1977 JD

Criminal Division

Chief **Mark A. Yancey** . . . . (405) 553-8842
E-mail: mark.yancey@usdoj.gov
Deputy Chief **Leslie M. Maye** . . . . (405) 553-8846
E-mail: leslie.maye@usdoj.gov
Education: Oklahoma 1982 JD
Deputy Chief **Scott E. Williams** . . . . (405) 553-8752
E-mail: scott.e.williams@usdoj.gov

Criminal Division *continued*

Asset Recovery Unit Leader **Don Evans** . . . . (405) 553-8831
E-mail: don.evans@usdoj.gov
Drug Task Force Unit Leader **Leslie M. Maye** . . . . (405) 553-8846
E-mail: leslie.maye@usdoj.gov
Education: Oklahoma 1982 JD
Fraud/Corruption Unit Leader **Susan Cox** . . . . (405) 553-8740
E-mail: susan.cox@usdoj.gov
Education: Emory 1979 JD
Assistant U.S. Attorney **Julia Barry** . . . . (405) 553-8755
E-mail: julia.barry@usdoj.gov
Education: NYU JD
Assistant U.S. Attorney **Kerry Blackburn** . . . . (405) 553-8700
Assistant U.S. Attorney **Charles Brown** . . . . (405) 553-8871
E-mail: charles.brown4@usdoj.gov
Assistant U.S. Attorney **Robert Don Gifford III** . . . . (405) 553-8736
E-mail: robert.d.gifford@usdoj.gov
Education: Oklahoma 1996 JD
Assistant U.S. Attorney **Brandon Hale** . . . . (405) 553-8813
E-mail: brandon.hale@usdoj.gov
Assistant U.S. Attorney **Lori Hines** . . . . (405) 553-8853
E-mail: lori.hines@usdoj.gov
Assistant U.S. Attorney **Jessica Cárdenas Jarvis** . . . . (405) 553-8868
E-mail: jessica.jarvis@usdoj.gov
Assistant U.S. Attorney **Kerry A. Kelly** . . . . (405) 553-8700
Education: Oklahoma 1977 JD
Assistant U.S. Attorney **Ed Kumiega** . . . . (405) 553-8849
E-mail: ed.kumiega@usdoj.gov
Assistant U.S. Attorney **Amanda Maxfield-Green** . . . . (405) 553-8770
Assistant U.S. Attorney **David McCrary** . . . . (405) 553-8739
Assistant U.S. Attorney **Rozia McKinney-Foster** . . . . (405) 553-8806
E-mail: rozia.mckinney-foster@usdoj.gov
Education: Oklahoma City 1980 JD
Assistant U.S. Attorney **Arvo Mikkanen** . . . . (405) 553-8737
E-mail: arvo.mikkanen@usdoj.gov
Education: Dartmouth 1983 BA; Yale 1986 JD
Assistant U.S. Attorney **Tim Ogilvie** . . . . (405) 553-8851
E-mail: tim.ogilvie@usdoj.gov
Education: Oklahoma City 1987 JD
Assistant U.S. Attorney **Ashley Oltshuler** . . . . (405) 553-8700
Assistant U.S. Attorney **Jessica Perry** . . . . (405) 553-8754
E-mail: jessica.perry@usdoj.gov
Assistant U.S. Attorney **Dave Petermann** . . . . (405) 553-8855
E-mail: david.petermann@usdoj.gov
Assistant U.S. Attorney **Travis Smith** . . . . (405) 553-8772
Assistant U.S. Attorney **Chris Stephens** . . . . (405) 553-8783
E-mail: chris.stephens@usdoj.gov
Assistant U.S. Attorney **Scott E. Williams** . . . . (405) 553-8808

Oregon District

Mark O. Hatfield U.S. Courthouse, 1000 SW Third Avenue,
Suite 600, Portland, OR 97204-2902
Tel: (503) 727-1000 Fax: (503) 727-1117
Internet: www.usdoj.gov/usao/or/

★ U.S. Attorney (Acting) **Bill J. Williams** . . . . (503) 727-1000
Secretary to U.S. Attorney **V. Sue Marshall** . . . . (503) 727-1000
First Assistant U.S. Attorney (Acting) **Scott Asphaug** . . . (503) 727-1000
Assistant U.S. Attorney-in-Charge
Christopher Cardani . . . . (503) 727-1000
Immigration Coordinator **Ryan W. Bounds** . . . . (503) 727-1000
E-mail: ryan.bounds@usdoj.gov
Education: Stanford BA; Yale 1999 JD
Appellate Chief **Kelly Zusman** . . . . (503) 727-1000
E-mail: kelly.zusman@usdoj.gov
Education: Oregon 1989 JD
Asset Forfeiture Chief **Katherine Lorenz** . . . . (503) 727-1000
Civil Chief **Janice E. Hebert** . . . . (503) 727-1000
E-mail: janice.hebert@usdoj.gov
Criminal Chief **Pamela Holsinger** . . . . (503) 727-1000
Organized Crime Drug Enforcement Task Force Chief
Thomas "Tom" Edmonds . . . . (503) 727-1000

★ Presidential Appointment Requiring Senate Confirmation ☆ Presidential Appointment ☐ Schedule C Appointment ◇ Career Senior Foreign Service Appointment
● Career Senior Executive Service (SES) Appointment ○ Non-Career Senior Executive Service (SES) Appointment ■ Postal Career Executive Service

Oregon District *continued*

Administrative Officer **Angela Zerbe-Darnell** .... (503) 727-1000
Records Coordinator **Michelle Volker** .... (503) 727-1000
E-mail: michelle.volker@usdoj.gov

Eugene (OR) Office

701 High Street, Eugene, OR 97401
Tel: (541) 465-6771 Fax: (541) 465-6582

Assistant U.S. Attorney-in-Charge
Christopher Cardani .... (541) 465-6771
E-mail: chris.cardani@usdoj.gov Fax: (541) 465-6840

Medford (OR) Office

310 West Sixth Street, Medford, OR 97501
24 Mistletoe, Medford, OR 97501
Tel: (541) 776-3564 Fax: (541) 776-3583

Assistant U.S. Attorney-in-Charge
Christopher Cardani .... (541) 776-3564
E-mail: chris.cardani@usdoj.gov

Pennsylvania - Eastern District

615 Chestnut Street, Suite 1250, Philadelphia, PA 19106
Tel: (215) 861-8200 Fax: (215) 861-8618
Internet: www.usdoj.gov/usao/pae

★ U.S. Attorney **Zane David Memeger** .... (215) 861-8200
E-mail: zane.memeger@usdoj.gov
Education: James Madison 1996 BS; Virginia 1991 JD
Secretary to the U.S. Attorney **Nancy McElroy Dick** ... (215) 861-8553
E-mail: nancy.dick@usdoj.gov
First Assistant U.S. Attorney **Louis D. Lappen** .... (215) 861-8200
Secretary to the First Assistant U.S. Attorney
Pamela McCredy .... (215) 861-8657
E-mail: pamela.mccredy@usdoj.gov
Executive Assistant U.S. Attorney for Community
Outreach and Special Programs **Robert K. Reed** .... (215) 861-8422
E-mail: robert.reed2@usdoj.gov
Administrative Officer **Richard C. Rizzo** .... (215) 861-8403
E-mail: richard.rizzo@usdoj.gov
Media Contact **Patricia Hartman** .... (215) 861-8525
E-mail: patricia.hartman@usdoj.gov
Systems Manager **Michele Pashley** .... (215) 861-8651
E-mail: michele.pashley@usdoj.gov
Victim-Witness Coordinator **Marcia Thomas Bayne** ..... (215) 861-8905
E-mail: marcia.bayne@usdoj.gov

Civil Division

Fax: (215) 861-8618

Chief **Margaret L. Hutchinson** .... (215) 861-8282
E-mail: margaret.hutchinson@usdoj.gov
Legal Assistant **Desiree Wilkins** .... (215) 861-8375
E-mail: desiree.wilkins@usdoj.gov
Chief, Affirmative Litigation **Charlene K. Fullmer** .... (215) 861-8301
E-mail: charlene.fullmer@usdoj.gov
Deputy Chief, Defensive Litigation **Joan K. Garner** ..... (215) 861-8306
E-mail: joan.garner@usdoj.gov
Senior Litigation Counsel **Susan Dein Bricklin** .... (215) 861-8318
E-mail: susan.bricklin@usdoj.gov
Assistant U.S. Attorney **Judith A. Amorosa** .... (215) 861-8869
E-mail: judith.amorosa@usdoj.gov
Assistant U.S. Attorney **Susan R. Becker** .... (215) 861-8310
E-mail: susan.becker@usdoj.gov
Assistant U.S. Attorney **Richard M. Bernstein** .... (215) 861-8334
E-mail: richard.bernstein@usdoj.gov
Assistant U.S. Attorney **Colin M. Cherico** .... (215) 861-8788
E-mail: colin.cherico@usdoj.gov
Assistant U.S. Attorney **John T. Crutchlow** .... (215) 861-8622
E-mail: john.crutchlow@usdoj.gov
Assistant U.S. Attorney **Gregory B. David** .... (215) 861-8521
E-mail: gregory.david@usdoj.gov
Education: Virginia 2000 BA; Pennsylvania 2004 MA, 2004 JD

Civil Division *continued*

Assistant U.S. Attorney **David A. Degnan** .... (215) 861-8522
E-mail: david.degnan@usdoj.gov
Assistant U.S. Attorney **Veronica J. Finkelstein** .... (215) 861-8598
E-mail: veronica.finkelstein@usdoj.gov Fax: (215) 861-8618
Assistant U.S. Attorney **Eric D. Gill** .... (215) 861-8250
E-mail: eric.gill@usdoj.gov
Assistant U.S. Attorney **Thomas F. Johnson** .... (215) 861-8380
E-mail: thomas.johnson@usdoj.gov
Assistant U.S. Attorney **Landon Y. Jones** .... (215) 861-8323
E-mail: landon.jones@usdoj.gov
Education: Michigan 2004 JD
Assistant U.S. Attorney **Paul W. Kaufman** .... (215) 861-8579
E-mail: paul.kaufman2@usdoj.gov
Assistant U.S. Attorney **Michael S. Macko** .... (215) 861-8415
E-mail: michael.macko@usdoj.gov
Education: Pennsylvania 2006 JD
Assistant U.S. Attorney **Elizabeth S. Mattioni** .... (215) 861-8492
E-mail: elizabeth.mattioni@usdoj.gov
Assistant U.S. Attorney **Richard J. Mentzinger, Jr.** ...... (215) 861-8316
E-mail: rick.mentzinger@usdoj.gov
Assistant U.S. Attorney **Viveca D. Parker** .... (215) 861-8443
E-mail: viveca.parker@usdoj.gov
Assistant U.S. Attorney **Virginia R. Powel** .... (215) 861-8263
E-mail: virginia.powel@usdoj.gov
Assistant U.S. Attorney **Scott W. Reid** .... (215) 861-8358
E-mail: scott.reid@usdoj.gov
Education: West Chester 1996 BS; Widener 2002 JD
Assistant U.S. Attorney **Jacqueline C. Romero** .... (215) 861-8470
E-mail: jacqueline.romero@usdoj.gov
Assistant U.S. Attorney **Mark J. Sherer** .... (215) 861-8445
E-mail: mark.sherer@usdoj.gov
Assistant U.S. Attorney **Stacey L. B. Smith** .... (215) 861-8348
E-mail: stacey.smith@usdoj.gov
Assistant U.S. Attorney **Gerald B. Sullivan** .... (215) 861-8786
E-mail: gerald.sullivan@usdoj.gov
Assistant U.S. Attorney **Joel M. Sweet** .... (215) 861-8581
E-mail: joel.sweet@usdoj.gov

Criminal Division

Fax: (215) 861-8618

Chief **Peter F. Schenck** .... (215) 861-8570
E-mail: peter.schenck@usdoj.gov
Supervisory Legal Assistant **Kathie Smith** .... (215) 861-8421
E-mail: kathie.smith@usdoj.gov
Deputy Chief for White Collar Crime and Terrorism
M. Taylor Aspinwall .... (215) 861-8264
E-mail: taylor.aspinwall@usdoj.gov
Deputy Chief for Narcotics and Violent Crime
Christine E. Sykes .... (215) 861-8441
E-mail: christine.sykes@usdoj.gov
Crisis Management Coordinator (CMC) and District
Office Security Manager (DOSM) **Jose R. Arteaga** .... (215) 861-8711
E-mail: jose.arteaga@usdoj.gov
Appeals Chief **Robert A. "Bob" Zauzmer** .... (215) 861-8568
E-mail: bob.zauzmer@usdoj.gov
Asset Forfeiture, Victim Witness Program, and Trial
Advocacy Program Chief **J. Alvin Stout III** .... (215) 861-8461
E-mail: alvin.stout@usdoj.gov
Computer Crime, Child Exploitation and Intellectual
Property Crimes Chief **Michael L. Levy** .... (215) 861-8599
Education: Brown U 1966 BA; Pennsylvania 1969 LLB
Economic Crimes Chief and Crisis Managment
Coordinator **Richard W. Goldberg** .... (215) 861-8439
E-mail: richard.goldberg2@usdoj.gov
Economic Crimes Deputy Chief **Daniel A. Velez** .... (215) 861-8454
E-mail: daniel.velez@usdoj.gov
Health Care and Government Fraud and Environmental
Crime Chief **Mary E. Crawley** .... (215) 861-8519
E-mail: mary.crawley2@usdoj.gov

(continued on next page)

★ Presidential Appointment Requiring Senate Confirmation ☆ Presidential Appointment ☐ Schedule C Appointment ◇ Career Senior Foreign Service Appointment
● Career Senior Executive Service (SES) Appointment ○ Non-Career Senior Executive Service (SES) Appointment ■ Postal Career Executive Service

Criminal Division *continued*

Narcotics and Organized Crime Chief
Thomas R. Perricone . . . . . . (215) 861-8419
E-mail: thomas.perricone@usdoj.gov
Narcotics and Organized Crime Deputy Chief
Faithe Moore Taylor . . . . . . (215) 861-8515
E-mail: faithe.taylor@usdoj.gov
Official Corruption, Tax Fraud and Civil Rights Chief
Richard P. Barrett . . . . . . (215) 861-8420
E-mail: richard.barrett3@usdoj.gov
Violent Crimes and Firearms Chief **Kathy A. Stark** . . . . . . (215) 861-8438
E-mail: kathy.stark@usdoj.gov
Violent Crimes and Firearms Deputy Chief
Eric B. Henson . . . . . . (215) 861-8312
E-mail: eric.henson@usdoj.gov
Senior Litigation Counsel **Anthony J. Wzorek** . . . . . . (215) 861-8469
E-mail: anthony.wzorek@usdoj.gov
Assistant U.S. Attorney **Elizabeth F. Abrams** . . . . . . (215) 861-8670
E-mail: elizabeth.abrams@usdoj.gov
Assistant U.S. Attorney **Salvatore L. Astolfi** . . . . . . (215) 861-8431
E-mail: salvatore.astolfi@usdoj.gov
Assistant U.S. Attorney **Jennifer C. Barry** . . . . . . (215) 861-8388
E-mail: jennifer.barry@usdoj.gov
Assistant U.S. Attorney **Roberta Benjamin** . . . . . . (215) 861-8407
E-mail: roberta.benjamin@usdoj.gov
Assistant U.S. Attorney **Eric A. Boden** . . . . . . (215) 861-8327
E-mail: eric.boden@usdoj.gov
Assistant U.S. Attorney **Jason P. Bologna** . . . . . . (215) 861-8499
E-mail: jason.bologna@usdoj.gov
Assistant U.S. Attorney **Kevin R. Brenner** . . . . . . (215) 861-8274
E-mail: kevin.brenner@usdoj.gov
Assistant U.S. Attorney **Joan E. Burnes** . . . . . . (215) 861-8302
E-mail: joan.burnes@usdoj.gov
Assistant U.S. Attorney **Maria M. Carrillo** . . . . . . (215) 861-8401
E-mail: maria.carrillo@usdoj.gov
Assistant U.S. Attorney **Katayoun Copeland** . . . . . . (215) 861-8342
E-mail: katayoun.copeland@usdoj.gov
Assistant U.S. Attorney **Frank R. Costello, Jr.** . . . . . . (215) 861-8442
E-mail: frank.costello@usdoj.gov
Assistant U.S. Attorney **Mary Kay Costello** . . . . . . (215) 861-8923
E-mail: marykay.costello@usdoj.gov
Assistant U.S. Attorney **Marianne E. Cox** . . . . . . (215) 861-8391
E-mail: marianne.cox@usdoj.gov
Assistant U.S. Attorney **Priya T. DeSouza** . . . . . . (215) 861-8344
E-mail: priya.desouza@usdoj.gov
Assistant U.S. Attorney **Christopher Diviny** . . . . . . (215) 861-8205
E-mail: christopher.diviny@usdoj.gov
Assistant U.S. Attorney **Michael T. Donovan** . . . . . . (215) 861-8631
E-mail: michael.donovan@usdoj.gov
Assistant U.S. Attorney **Mark B. Dubnoff** . . . . . . (215) 861-8397
E-mail: mark.dubnoff@usdoj.gov
Assistant U.S. Attorney **Anita Eve** . . . . . . (215) 861-8577
E-mail: anita.eve@usdoj.gov
Assistant U.S. Attorney **Arlene D. Fisk** . . . . . . (215) 861-8356
E-mail: arlene.fisk@usdoj.gov
Assistant U.S. Attorney **Andrea G. Foulkes** . . . . . . (215) 861-8685
E-mail: andrea.foulkes@usdoj.gov
Assistant U.S. Attorney **Alicia M. Freind** . . . . . . (215) 861-8677
E-mail: alicia.freind@usdoj.gov
Assistant U.S. Attorney **John M. Gallagher** . . . . . . (215) 861-8636
E-mail: john.gallagher3@usdoj.gov
Assistant U.S. Attorney **Vineet Gauri** . . . . . . (215) 861-8644
E-mail: vineet.gauri@usdoj.gov
Assistant U.S. Attorney **Albert S. Glenn** . . . . . . (215) 861-8900
E-mail: albert.glenn@usdoj.gov
Assistant U.S. Attorney **Joel D. Goldstein** . . . . . . (215) 861-8429
E-mail: joel.goldstein@usdoj.gov
Assistant U.S. Attorney **Paul Gray** . . . . . . (215) 861-8257
E-mail: paul.gray@usdoj.gov
Assistant U.S. Attorney **Sarah L. Grieb** . . . . . . (215) 861-8261
E-mail: sarah.grieb@usdoj.gov
Assistant U.S. Attorney **Karen L. Grigsby** . . . . . . (215) 861-8572
E-mail: karen.gribsby@usdoj.gov

Criminal Division *continued*

Assistant U.S. Attorney **Randall P. Hsia** . . . . . . (215) 861-8204
E-mail: randall.hsia@usdoj.gov
Assistant U.S. Attorney **David J. Ignall** . . . . . . (215) 861-8687
E-mail: david.j.ignall@usdoj.gov
Assistant U.S. Attorney **Joseph J. Khan** . . . . . . (215) 861-8562
E-mail: joseph.khan@usdoj.gov
Assistant U.S. Attorney **Karen M. Klotz** . . . . . . (215) 861-8524
E-mail: karen.klotz@usdoj.gov
Education: Temple 2001 JD
Assistant U.S. Attorney **Joseph A. LaBar** . . . . . . (215) 861-8516
E-mail: joseph.labar@usdoj.gov
Assistant U.S. Attorney **Frank A. Labor III** . . . . . . (215) 861-8675
E-mail: frank.labor@usdoj.gov
Assistant U.S. Attorney **Joseph T. Labrum III** . . . . . . (215) 861-8412
E-mail: joseph.labrum@usdoj.gov
Assistant U.S. Attorney **M. Beth Leahy** . . . . . . (215) 861-8343
E-mail: mary.beth.leahy@usdoj.gov
Assistant U.S. Attorney **Jeanine M. Linehan** . . . . . . (215) 861-8303
E-mail: jeanine.linehan@usdoj.gov
Assistant U.S. Attorney **Robert J. Livermore** . . . . . . (215) 861-8464
E-mail: robert.livermore@usdoj.gov
Assistant U.S. Attorney **Michael S. "Mike" Lowe** . . . . . . (215) 861-8534
E-mail: mike.lowe@usdoj.gov
Assistant U.S. Attorney **Ashley K. Lunkenheimer** . . . . . . (215) 861-8432
E-mail: ashley.lunkenheimer@usdoj.gov
Assistant U.S. Attorney **Laurie Magid** . . . . . . (215) 861-8513
E-mail: laurie.magid@usdoj.gov
Education: Pennsylvania 1982 BS; Columbia 1985 JD
Assistant U.S. Attorney **Jerome Maiatico** . . . . . . (215) 861-8258
E-mail: jerome.maiatico@usdoj.gov
Assistant U.S. Attorney **Terri A. Marinari** . . . . . . (215) 861-8466
E-mail: terri.marinari@usdoj.gov
Assistant U.S. Attorney **Karen S. Marston** . . . . . . (215) 861-8291
Assistant U.S. Attorney **Maureen McCartney** . . . . . . (215) 861-8564
E-mail: maureen.mccartney@usdoj.gov
Assistant U.S. Attorney **Bernadette McKeon** . . . . . . (215) 861-8326
E-mail: bernadette.mckeon2@usdoj.gov
Assistant U.S. Attorney **Emily McKillip** . . . . . . (215) 861-8416
E-mail: emily.mckillip@usdoj.gov
Education: Bryn Mawr 1981 AB; Yale 1984 JD
Assistant U.S. Attorney **Floyd J. Miller** . . . . . . (215) 861-8265
E-mail: floyd.miller@usdoj.gov
Assistant U.S. Attorney **Mark S. Miller** . . . . . . (215) 861-8357
E-mail: mark.miller6@usdoj.gov
Assistant U.S. Attorney **Joseph F. Minni** . . . . . . (215) 861-8574
E-mail: joseph.minni@usdoj.gov
Assistant U.S. Attorney **Michelle L. Morgan** . . . . . . (215) 861-8458
E-mail: michelle.morgan2@usdoj.gov
Assistant U.S. Attorney **Patrick J. Murray** . . . . . . (215) 861-8456
E-mail: patrick.j.murray@usdoj.gov
Assistant U.S. Attorney **Kishan Nair** . . . . . . (215) 861-8411
E-mail: kishan.nair@usdoj.gov
Assistant U.S. Attorney **Jessica Natali** . . . . . . (215) 861-8505
E-mail: jessica.natali@usdoj.gov
Assistant U.S. Attorney **K. T. Newton** . . . . . . (215) 861-8329
E-mail: kt.newton@usdoj.gov
Assistant U.S. Attorney **Yvonne O. Osirim** . . . . . . (215) 861-8207
E-mail: yvonne.osirim@usdoj.gov
Assistant U.S. Attorney **Tomika S. Patterson** . . . . . . (215) 861-8328
E-mail: tomika.stevens.patterson@usdoj.gov
Assistant U.S. Attorney **James Pavlock** . . . . . . (215) 861-8339
E-mail: james.pavlock@usdoj.gov
Assistant U.S. Attorney **James Petkun** . . . . . . (215) 861-8658
E-mail: james.petkun@usdoj.gov
Education: Villanova 2007 JD
Assistant U.S. Attorney **Andrea Nicole Phillips** . . . . . . (215) 861-8447
E-mail: andrea.phillips@usdoj.gov
Assistant U.S. Attorney **Nancy E. Potts** . . . . . . (215) 861-8673
E-mail: nancy.potts@usdoj.gov
Assistant U.S. Attorney **Clare Pozos** . . . . . . (215) 861-8558
E-mail: clare.pozos@usdoj.gov
Education: Pennsylvania 2007 JD

Criminal Division *continued*

Assistant U.S. Attorney **Virginia Paige Pratter** . . . . (215) 861-8335
E-mail: virginia.pratter@usdoj.gov
Assistant U.S. Attorney **Michelle T. Rotella** . . . . (215) 861-8471
E-mail: michelle.rotella@usdoj.gov
Assistant U.S. Attorney **Nancy Rue** . . . . (215) 861-8683
E-mail: nancy.rue@usdoj.gov
Assistant U.S. Attorney **Andrew J. Schell** . . . . (215) 861-8646
E-mail: andrew.schell@usdoj.gov
Assistant U.S. Attorney **Paul G. Shapiro** . . . . (215) 861-8325
E-mail: paul.shapiro@usdoj.gov
Assistant U.S. Attorney **Judy Goldstein Smith** . . . . (215) 861-8511
Assistant U.S. Attorney **Mary Teresa Soltis** . . . . (215) 861-8445
E-mail: mary.soltis@usdoj.gov
Assistant U.S. Attorney **Sherri A. Stephan** . . . . (215) 861-8585
E-mail: sherri.stephan2@usdoj.gov
Assistant U.S. Attorney **Nelson S.T. Thayer, Jr.** . . . . (215) 861-8855
E-mail: nelson.thayer@usdoj.gov
Assistant U.S. Attorney **David E. Troyer** . . . . (215) 861-8475
E-mail: david.troyer@usdoj.gov
Assistant U.S. Attorney **Sozi P. Tulante** . . . . (215) 861-8567
E-mail: sozi.tulante@usdoj.gov
Education: Harvard 1997 AB, 2001 JD
Assistant U.S. Attorney **Virgil B. Walker** . . . . (215) 861-8446
E-mail: virgil.walker@usdoj.gov
Assistant U.S. Attorney **Jeffery W. Whitt** . . . . (215) 861-8404
E-mail: jeff.whitt@usdoj.gov
Assistant U.S. Attorney **Jennifer A. Williams** . . . . (215) 861-8474
E-mail: jennifer.a.williams@usdoj.gov
Education: Maine 2003 JD
Assistant U.S. Attorney **Melanie B. Wilmoth** . . . . (215) 861-8603
E-mail: melanie.babb.wilmoth@usdoj.gov
Assistant U.S. Attorney **Nancy B. Winter** . . . . (215) 861-8473
E-mail: nancy.winter@usdoj.gov
Assistant U.S. Attorney **Bea L. Witzleben** . . . . (215) 861-8680
E-mail: bea.witzleben@usdoj.gov
Assistant U.S. Attorney **Denise S. Wolf** . . . . (215) 861-8662
E-mail: denise.wolf@usdoj.gov
Assistant U.S. Attorney **Linwood C. Wright, Jr.** . . . . (215) 861-8512
E-mail: l.c.wright@usdoj.gov
Assistant U.S. Attorney **Thomas M. Zaleski** . . . . (215) 861-8460
E-mail: tom.zaleski@usdoj.gov
Assistant U.S. Attorney **Ewald Zittlau** . . . . (215) 861-8407
E-mail: ewald.zittlau@usdoj.gov

Pennsylvania - Middle District

Federal Building, 228 Walnut Street, Room 220,
Harrisburg, PA 17108-1754
Federal Building, P.O. Box 11754, Harrisburg, PA 17108-1754
Tel: (717) 221-4482 Fax: (717) 221-4582

★ U.S. Attorney **Peter J. Smith** . . . . (717) 221-4482
Term Expires: 2017
Education: King's Col (PA) 1962; Georgetown 1971 JD
First Assistant U.S. Attorney
Dennis C. Pfannenschmidt . . . . (717) 221-4482
E-mail: dennis.pfannenschmidt@usdoj.gov
Law Enforcement Committee Coordinator **(Vacant)** . . . . . . (717) 221-4482
Victim-Witness Coordinator **Laurie Reiley** . . . . (717) 221-4482
E-mail: laurie.reiley@usdoj.gov
Smart on Crime Coordinator **William S. Houser** . . . . (717) 221-4482
E-mail: william.houser@usdoj.gov
Smart on Crime Coordinator **Daryl Bloom** . . . . (717) 221-4482
E-mail: daryl.bloom@usdoj.gov

Civil Division
Fax: (717) 221-2246

Chief **Kate L. Mershimer** . . . . (717) 221-4482
E-mail: kate.l.mershimer@usdoj.gov
Assistant U.S. Attorney **Michael Butler** . . . . (717) 221-4482

Civil Division *continued*

Assistant U.S. Attorney **Anthony Scicchitano** . . . . (717) 221-4482
E-mail: anthony.scicchitano@usdoj.gov
Assistant U.S. Attorney **D. Brian Simpson** . . . . (717) 221-4482
E-mail: d.brian.simpson@usdoj.gov
Assistant U.S. Attorney **Melissa A. Swauger** . . . . (717) 221-4482
E-mail: melissa.swauger@usdoj.gov
Education: Hood 1992; Widener 1998 JD
Assistant U.S. Attorney **(Vacant)** . . . . (717) 221-4482
Senior Litigation Counsel **Mark E. Morrison** . . . . (717) 221-4482
E-mail: mark.e.morrison@usdoj.gov

Criminal Division
Chief **Bruce D. Brandler** . . . . (717) 221-4482
E-mail: bruce.brandler@usdoj.gov
Deputy Chief **Eric Pfisterer** . . . . (717) 221-4482
E-mail: eric.pfisterer@usdoj.gov
Assistant U.S. Attorney **William A. Behe** . . . . (717) 221-4482
E-mail: william.behe@usdoj.gov
Assistant U.S. Attorney **Daryl Bloom** . . . . (717) 221-4482
E-mail: daryl.bloom@usdoj.gov
Assistant U.S. Attorney **Stephen Cerutti** . . . . (717) 221-4482
Assistant U.S. Attorney **James Clancy** . . . . (717) 221-4482
E-mail: james.clancy@usdoj.gov
Assistant U.S. Attorney **Michael Consiglio** . . . . (717) 221-4482
E-mail: michael.consiglio@usdoj.gov
Assistant U.S. Attorney **Kim D. Daniel** . . . . (717) 221-4482
Assistant U.S. Attorney **Christy H. Fawcett** . . . . (717) 221-4482
E-mail: christy.fawcett@usdoj.gov
Assistant U.S. Attorney **Meredith Taylor** . . . . (717) 221-4482
E-mail: meredith.taylor@usdoj.gov
Assistant U.S. Attorney **Joseph J. Terz** . . . . (717) 221-4482
E-mail: joseph.terz@usdoj.gov
Senior Litigation Counsel **Gordon A. D. Zubrod** . . . . (717) 221-4482
E-mail: gordon.zubrod@usdoj.gov

Scranton (PA) Office

William J. Nealon Federal Building, 235 North Washington Avenue,
Suite 311, Scranton, PA 18501-0309
P.O. Box 309, Scranton, PA 18501-0309
Tel: (570) 348-2800 Fax: (570) 348-2037

Deputy Civil Division Chief and Assistant U.S.
Attorney **Michael "Mike" Thiel** . . . . (570) 348-2800
E-mail: mike.thiel@usdoj.gov
Civil Division Assistant U.S. Attorney
J. Justin Blewitt . . . . (570) 348-2800
E-mail: justin.blewitt@usdoj.gov
Civil Division Assistant U.S. Attorney **Timothy Judge** . . . (570) 348-2800
E-mail: timothy.judge@usdoj.gov
Criminal Division Chief **Bruce D. Brandler** . . . . (570) 348-2800
E-mail: bruce.brandler@usdoj.gov
Criminal Division Deputy Chief
John C. Gurganus, Jr. . . . . (570) 348-2800
E-mail: john.gurganus@usdoj.gov
Criminal Division Assistant U.S. Attorney
Todd Hinkley . . . . (570) 348-2800
E-mail: todd.hinkley@usdoj.gov
Criminal Division Assistant U.S. Attorney
Robert O'Hara . . . . (570) 348-2800
E-mail: robert.o'hara@usdoj.gov
Criminal Division Assistant U.S. Attorney
Michelle Olshefski . . . . (570) 348-2800
E-mail: michelle.olshefski@usdoj.gov
Criminal Division Assistant U.S. Attorney
Fran Sempa . . . . (570) 348-2800
E-mail: fran.sempa@usdoj.gov
Criminal Division Assistant U.S. Attorney **(Vacant)** . . . . . . (570) 348-2800
Criminal Division Assistant U.S. Attorney **(Vacant)** . . . . . . (570) 348-2800
Senior Litigation Counsel **William S. Houser** . . . . (717) 221-4482
E-mail: william.houser@usdoj.gov

(continued on next page)

Scranton (PA) Office *continued*

Administrative Officer **Linda L. Smith** .... (570) 348-2800
E-mail: linda.l.smith@usdoj.gov
Budget Officer **Cathy McGarry** .... (570) 348-2800
E-mail: cathy.mcgarry@usdoj.gov
Personnel Officer **Christine Osborne** .... (570) 348-2800
E-mail: christine.osborne@usdoj.gov
Purchasing Officer **Sharon Jones** .... (570) 348-2800
E-mail: sharon.jones2@usdoj.gov

Williamsport (PA) Office

Federal Building, 240 West Third Street,
Suite 316, Williamsport, PA 17701-6465
Tel: (570) 326-1935 Fax: (570) 326-7954

Branch Chief **George J. Rocktashel** .... (570) 326-1935
E-mail: george.rocktashel@usdoj.gov
Criminal Division Assistant U.S. Attorney
Jeffrey McArthur .... (570) 326-1935
Criminal Division Assistant U.S. Attorney
Wayne P. Samuelson .... (570) 326-1935
E-mail: wayne.samuelson@usdoj.gov

Pennsylvania - Western District

U.S. Post Office and Courthouse Building, 700 Grant Street,
Suite 4000, Pittsburgh, PA 15219
Tel: (412) 644-3500 Fax: (412) 644-4549
Internet: www.usdoj.gov/usao/paw

★ U.S. Attorney **David J. Hickton** .... (412) 894-7325
E-mail: david.hickton@usdoj.gov
Education: Penn State 1978 BA; Pittsburgh 1981 JD
Executive Assistant to the U.S. Attorney
Tamara Collier .... (412) 894-7333
E-mail: tamara.collier@usdoj.gov
Deputy U.S. Attorney **Leo M. Dillon** .... (412) 894-7329
E-mail: leo.dillon@usdoj.gov
First Assistant U.S. Attorney **Soo C. Song** .... (412) 894-7329
E-mail: soo.song@usdoj.gov
Education: Yale; George Washington JD
Secretary to the First Assistant U.S. Attorney
Anne E. Foley .... (412) 894-7360
E-mail: anne.foley@usdoj.gov
Counsel for Ethics **Lee J. Karl** .... (412) 894-7488
E-mail: lee.karl@usdoj.gov
Education: Pittsburgh 2001 JD
Counsel for Professional Responsibility
Marshall J. Piccinini .... (814) 452-0104
E-mail: marshall.piccinini@usdoj.gov
Counsel for Professional Responsibility
Christy Wiegand .... (412) 894-7452
E-mail: christy.wiegand@usdoj.gov
Appeals Chief **Rebecca Ross Haywood** .... (412) 894-7353
E-mail: rebecca.haywood@usdoj.gov
Education: Princeton; Michigan 1994 JD
Civil Division Chief **Michael A. Comber** .... (412) 894-7416
E-mail: michael.comber@usdoj.gov
Education: Purdue; Duquesne JD
Criminal Division Chief
Stephen R. "Steve" Kaufman .... (412) 894-7377
E-mail: steve.kaufman@usdoj.gov
Education: Allegheny; Harvard JD
Civil Rights, Exploitation and Corruption Section
Chief **Shaun E. Sweeney** .... (412) 644-3500
E-mail: shaun.sweeney@usdoj.gov
National Security, Cyber and Fraud Section Chief
Paul E. Hull .... (412) 644-3500
E-mail: paul.hull@usdoj.gov
Violent Crimes Section Chief **Troy Rivetti** .... (412) 644-3500
E-mail: troy.rivetti@usdoj.gov

Pennsylvania - Western District *continued*

Erie Division Chief/Assistant U.S. Attorney
Marshall J. Piccinini .... (814) 452-2906
United States Attorney's Office, Fax: (814) 455-6951
17 South Park Row,
Room A-330, Erie, PA 16501
E-mail: marshall.piccinini@usdoj.gov
Johnstown Division Chief/Assistant U.S. Attorney
John J. Valkovci, Jr. .... (814) 533-4547
United States Attorney's Office, Fax: (814) 533-4545
Penn Traffic Building, 319 Washington Street,
Suite 200, Johnstown, PA 15901
E-mail: john.valkovci@usdoj.gov
Administrative Officer **Barbara A. "Barb" Bacvinskas** ... (412) 894-7322
E-mail: barbara.bacvinskas@usdoj.gov
Budget Officer **(Vacant)** .... (412) 894-7394
Personnel Officer **Nicole L. Huff** .... (412) 894-7384
E-mail: nicole.huff@usdoj.gov
Public Affairs Officer **Margaret Philbin** .... (412) 894-7312
Supervisory IT Specialist **(Vacant)** .... (412) 894-7372
Victim-Witness Specialist **Gail M. McLaughlin** .... (412) 894-7400
E-mail: gail.mclaughlin@usdoj.gov

Puerto Rico District

350 Carlos Chardon Street, Torre Chardon,
Suite 1201, San Juan, PR 00918
Tel: (787) 766-5656 Fax: (787) 766-5632
Internet: www.justice.gov/usao/districts/pr.html

★ U.S. Attorney **Rosa Emilia Rodriguez-Velez** .... (787) 766-5656
Note: Rosa Rodriguez-Velez is serving under a court appointment.
E-mail: rosa.e.rodriguez@usdoj.gov
Education: Sacred Heart (PR) 1973; Inter American 1977 JD, ML
Secretary **Ivette Figueroa** .... (787) 766-5656
First Assistant U.S. Attorney **Timothy Henwood** .... (787) 766-5656
E-mail: timothy.henwood@usdoj.gov
Education: Indiana JD
Appellate Division Chief and Assistant U.S. Attorney
Nelson Perez .... (787) 766-5656
Civil Division Chief and Assistant U.S. Attorney
Hector Ramirez .... (787) 766-5656
E-mail: hector.ramirez@usdoj.gov
Criminal Division Chief and Assistant U.S. Attorney
Jose Ruiz .... (787) 766-5656
E-mail: jose.ruiz3@usdoj.gov
Criminal Division Deputy Chief and Assistant U.S.
Attorney **Myriam Y. Fernandez** .... (787) 766-5656
E-mail: myriam.y.fernandez@usdoj.gov
Criminal Division Deputy Chief and Assistant U.S.
Attorney **Jenifer Hernandez** .... (787) 766-5656
E-mail: jenifer.hernandez@usdoj.gov
Violent Crime Deputy Chief and Assistant U.S.
Attorney **Jose Capo** .... (787) 766-5656
E-mail: jose.capo2@usdoj.gov
Senior Litigation Counsel **Scott Anderson** .... (787) 766-5656
E-mail: scott.anderson@usdoj.gov
Administrative Officer **Lisa F. Western** .... (787) 766-5656
E-mail: lisa.f.western@usdoj.gov
Human Resources Officer **Carmen Pura Lopez** .... (787) 282-1873
E-mail: c.pura.lopez@usdoj.gov
Supervisory Information Technology Specialist
Marilyn Benitez .... (787) 766-5656
E-mail: marilyn.benitez@usdoj.gov Fax: (787) 766-5193

Rhode Island District

50 Kennedy Plaza, 8th Floor, Providence, RI 02903
Tel: (401) 709-5000 Fax: (401) 709-5001
Internet: www.usdoj.gov/usao/ri

★ U.S. Attorney **Peter F. Neronha** .... (401) 709-5000
E-mail: peter.neronha@usdoj.gov
Education: Boston Col 1985 BA, 1989 JD

★ Presidential Appointment Requiring Senate Confirmation ☆ Presidential Appointment □ Schedule C Appointment ◇ Career Senior Foreign Service Appointment
● Career Senior Executive Service (SES) Appointment ○ Non-Career Senior Executive Service (SES) Appointment ■ Postal Career Executive Service

Rhode Island District *continued*

Secretary to the U.S. Attorney
Karen E. Miszkiewicz .... (401) 709-5051
E-mail: karen.miszkiewicz@usdoj.gov

First Assistant U.S. Attorney **Stephen G. Dambruch** .... (401) 709-5000
E-mail: stephen.dambruch@usdoj.gov
Education: Providence 1982 BA; Boston Col 1985 JD

Administrative Officer **Robin S. Downey** .... (401) 709-5000
E-mail: robin.downey@usdoj.gov

Budget Officer **Vincent Onorato** .... (401) 709-5000
E-mail: vincent.onorato@usdoj.gov

Public Information Officer **Jim Martin** .... (401) 709-5357

Systems Manager **Troy Edwards** .... (401) 709-5000
E-mail: troy.edwards@usdoj.gov

Civil Division

Chief/Assistant U.S. Attorney **Richard B. Myrus** .... (401) 709-5000
E-mail: richard.myrus@usdoj.gov

Assistant U.S. Attorney **Zachary A. Cunha** .... (401) 709-5000
E-mail: zachary.cunha@usdoj.gov

Assistant U.S. Attorney **Leslie Kane** .... (401) 709-5000
E-mail: leslie.kane@usdoj.gov

Assistant U.S. Attorney **Mary E. Rogers** .... (401) 709-5000
E-mail: mary.rogers@usdoj.gov
Education: Marquette 1980 BA; Suffolk JD

Assistant U.S. Attorney **Bethany N. Wong** .... (401) 709-5000
E-mail: bethany.wong@usdoj.gov

Criminal Division

Chief/Assistant U.S. Attorney **Adi Goldstein** .... (401) 709-5000
E-mail: adi.goldstein@usdoj.gov

Appellate Section Assistant U.S. Attorney
Donald C. Lockhart .... (401) 709-5000

Organized Crime Chief and Assistant U.S. Attorney
William Ferland .... (401) 709-5000
E-mail: william.ferland@usdoj.gov

Organized Crime Drug Enforcement Task Force Chief and Assistant U.S. Attorney **Paul Daly, Jr.** .... (401) 709-5000
E-mail: paul.daly@usdoj.gov

Deputy Chief & Assistant U.S. Attorney **(Vacant)** .... (401) 709-5000

Assistant U.S. Attorney **Zechariah Chafee** .... (401) 709-5000
E-mail: zechariah.chafee@usdoj.gov

Assistant U.S. Attorney **Ly T. Chin** .... (401) 709-5000
E-mail: ly.chin@usdoj.gov
Education: William & Mary 1999 BA; Washington and Lee 2003 JD

Assistant U.S. Attorney **Pamela Chin** .... (401) 709-5000
E-mail: pamela.chin@usdoj.gov

Assistant U.S. Attorney **Terrence P. Donnelly** .... (401) 709-5000
E-mail: terrence.donnelly@usdoj.gov

Assistant U.S. Attorney **Dulce Donovan** .... (401) 709-5000
E-mail: dulce.donovan@usdoj.gov
Affiliation: Esq.
Education: Bates BA; Cornell 1993 JD

Assistant U.S. Attorney **John P. McAdams** .... (401) 709-5000
E-mail: john.mcadams@usdoj.gov

Assistant U.S. Attorney **Richard W. Rose** .... (401) 709-5000
E-mail: richard.rose@usdoj.gov
Education: Rhode Island Col; Northeastern JD

Assistant U.S. Attorney **Milind Shah** .... (401) 709-5000
E-mail: milind.shah@usdoj.gov

Assistant U.S. Attorney **Gerard B. Sullivan** .... (401) 709-5000
E-mail: gerard.sullivan@usdoj.gov

Assistant U.S. Attorney **Lee Vilker** .... (401) 709-5000
E-mail: lee.vilker@usdoj.gov
Education: Brandeis; NYU JD

South Carolina District

Wells Fargo Building, 1441 Main Street,
Suite 500, Columbia, SC 29201
Tel: (803) 929-3000 Fax: (803) 254-2912
Fax: (803) 254-2943 Fax: (803) 254-2889
Internet: www.usdoj.gov/usao/sc

★ U.S. Attorney **William N. "Bill" Nettles** .... (803) 929-3000
Education: Citadel 1983; Widener 1992 JD

Secretary to the U.S. Attorney **Ramona Geiger** .... (803) 929-3005
E-mail: ramona.geiger@usdoj.gov

First Assistant U.S. Attorney
Nancy E. "Beth" Caldwell Drake .... (803) 929-3000

Secretary to the First Assistant U.S. Attorney
(Vacant) .... (803) 929-3006

Administrative Officer **John Fonville** .... (803) 929-3074
E-mail: john.fonville@usdoj.gov

Personnel Officer **(Vacant)** .... (803) 929-3096

Law Enforcement Coordinator **Rebecca C. Plyler** .... (803) 929-3009

Victim-Witness Coordinator **Renee R. Mattox** .... (803) 929-3012
E-mail: renee.mattox@usdoj.gov

Appellate Division Chief **Robert "Bob" Daley** .... (803) 929-3000
E-mail: bob.daley@usdoj.gov

Civil Division Chief and Assistant U.S. Attorney
Barbara Bowens .... (803) 929-3054

Deputy Civil Division Chief and Assistant U.S. Attorney **Jennifer Aldrich** .... (803) 929-3052
E-mail: jennifer.aldrich@usdoj.gov

Criminal Division Chief and Assistant U.S. Attorney
Nancy Wicker .... (803) 929-3081
E-mail: nancy.wicker@usdoj.gov

General Crimes Section Chief and Assistant U.S. Attorney **Eric J. Klumb** .... (803) 929-3063
E-mail: eric.klumb@usdoj.gov

Narcotics Section Chief and Assistant U.S. Attorney
Jane Taylor .... (803) 929-3000
E-mail: jane.taylor@usdoj.gov

Violent Crimes Section Chief and Assistant U.S. Attorney **Jane Taylor** .... (803) 929-3000

Asset Forfeiture Unit Assistant U.S. Attorney
Carrie Sherrard .... (864) 282-2111

Financial Litigation Unit Assistant U.S. Attorney
Ann Young .... (803) 929-3055

Organized Crime Drug Enforcement Task Force Assistant U.S. Attorney **J.D. Rowell** .... (803) 929-3036

Systems Manager **(Vacant)** .... (803) 929-3099

Charleston (SC) Office

151 Meeting Street, Suite 200, Charleston, SC 29402
P.O. Box 978, Charleston, SC 29402
Tel: (843) 727-4381 Fax: (843) 727-4443

Assistant U.S. Attorney-in-Charge **Nathan Williams** ..... (843) 727-4381

Florence (SC) Office

John L. McMillan Federal Building, 401 West Evans Street,
Room 222, Florence, SC 29501
P.O. Box 1567, Florence, SC 29503-1567
Tel: (843) 665-6688 Fax: (843) 678-8809

Assistant U.S. Attorney-in-Charge **A. Bradley Parham** ... (843) 665-6688

Greenville (SC) Office

One Liberty Square Building, 55 Beattie Place,
Suite 700, Greenville, SC 29601
Tel: (864) 282-2100 Fax: (864) 233-3158

Assistant U.S. Attorney-in-Charge
William C. "Will" Lucius .... (864) 282-2100
E-mail: will.lucius@usdoj.gov

South Dakota District
325 South First Avenue, Suite 300, Sioux Falls, SD 57104
P.O. Box 2638, Sioux Falls, SD 57101-2638
Tel: (605) 330-4400 Fax: (605) 330-4410
Internet: www.usdoj.gov/usao/sd

★ U.S. Attorney (Acting) **Randolph J. "Randy" Seiler** .... (605) 330-4400
Note: On October 8, 2015 President Obama nominated Randolph Seiler to be U.S. Attorney. Mr. Seiler is currently acting in the position.
E-mail: randy.seiler@usdoj.gov
Education: Nebraska 1973 BA; South Dakota 1980 JD
Secretary to the U.S. Attorney **Heather Kostboth** ..... (605) 357-2304
E-mail: heather.kostboth@usdoj.gov
First Assistant U.S. Attorney
Randolph J. "Randy" Seiler .... (605) 224-5402
E-mail: randy.seiler@usdoj.gov
Education: Nebraska 1973 BA; South Dakota 1980 JD
Administrative Officer **Deborah K. Ford** .... (605) 357-2337
E-mail: deobrah.k.ford@usdoj.gov
Law Enforcement Coordinator **Daniel Mosteller** .... (605) 330-4400
E-mail: daniel.mosteller@usdoj.gov
Systems Manager **James Lichty** .... (605) 357-2370
E-mail: james.lichty@usdoj.gov
Victim-Witness Coordinator **Marlys Big Eagle** .... (605) 224-5402
E-mail: marlys.bigeagle@usdoj.gov

Civil Division
Civil Division Chief **Diana J. Ryan** .... (605) 357-2340
E-mail: diana.ryan@usdoj.gov
Assistant U.S. Attorney **Meghan Roche** .... (605) 357-2341
E-mail: meghan.roche@usdoj.gov
Assistant U.S. Attorney **Allison Ramsdell** .... (605) 357-2343
Assistant U.S. Attorney **Camela Theeler** .... (605) 357-2342
E-mail: camela.theeler@usdoj.gov

Criminal Division
Assistant U.S. Attorney and Criminal Chief
Dennis R. Holmes .... (605) 357-2350
E-mail: dennis.holmes@usdoj.gov
Appeals Chief **Kevin Koliner** .... (605) 330-4400
E-mail: kevin.koliner@usdoj.gov
Assistant U.S. Attorney **Jeff Clapper** .... (605) 357-2351
E-mail: jeff.clapper@usdoj.gov
Assistant U.S. Attorney **John Haak** .... (605) 357-2352
E-mail: john.haak@usdoj.gov
Assistant U.S. Attorney **Ann Hoffman** .... (605) 357-2363
E-mail: ann.hoffman@usdoj.gov
Assistant U.S. Attorney **Connie Larson** .... (605) 357-2362
E-mail: connie.larson@usdoj.gov
Assistant U.S. Attorney **Thomas J. Wright** .... (605) 357-2353

Pierre (SD) Office
337 Federal Building and U.S. Courthouse,
225 South Pierre Street, Pierre, SD 57501
P.O. Box 7249, Pierre, SD 57501-7240
Tel: (605) 224-5402 Fax: (605) 224-8305

Supervisory Assistant U.S. Attorney **Tim Maher** .... (605) 224-5402
E-mail: tim.maher@usdoj.gov
Civil Division Assistant U.S. Attorney **Cheryl DuPris** .... (605) 224-5402
E-mail: cheryl.dupris@usdoj.gov
Criminal Division Assistant U.S. Attorney
Meghan Dilges .... (605) 224-5402
E-mail: meghan.dilges@usdoj.gov
Criminal Division Assistant U.S. Attorney **Jay Miller** .... (605) 224-5402
E-mail: jay.miller@usdoj.gov
Criminal Division Assistant U.S. Attorney **Troy Morley** ... (605) 224-5402
E-mail: troy.morley@usdoj.gov
Criminal Division Assistant U.S. Attorney
Carrie Sanderson .... (605) 224-5402
Criminal Division Assistant U.S. Attorney **(Vacant)** ...... (605) 224-5402

Rapid City (SD) Office
515 Ninth Street, Room 201, Rapid City, SD 57701
Tel: (605) 342-7822 Fax: (605) 342-1108

Supervisory Assistant U.S. Attorney
Gregg S. Peterman .... (605) 342-7822
E-mail: gregg.peterman@usdoj.gov
Criminal Division Assistant U.S. Attorney
Sarah B. Collins .... (605) 342-7822
E-mail: sarah.b.collins@usdoj.gov
Criminal Division Assistant U.S. Attorney
Eric D. Kelderman .... (605) 342-7822
E-mail: eric.kelderman@usdoj.gov
Education: Creighton 2001 JD
Criminal Division Assistant U.S. Attorney
Ted McBride .... (605) 342-7822
E-mail: ted.mcbride@usdoj.gov
Criminal Division Assistant U.S. Attorney
Benjamin Patterson .... (605) 342-7822
E-mail: ben.patterson@usdoj.gov
Criminal Division Assistant U.S. Attorney
Megan Poppen .... (605) 342-7822
E-mail: megan.poppen@usdoj.gov
Criminal Division Assistant U.S. Attorney
Kathryn Rich .... (605) 342-7822
E-mail: kathryn.rich@usdoj.gov
Education: South Dakota 2009 JD
Victim-Witness Specialist **Aileen Crawford** .... (605) 342-7822
E-mail: aileen.crawford@usdoj.gov

Tennessee - Eastern District
800 Market Street, Suite 211, Knoxville, TN 37902
Tel: (865) 545-4167 Fax: (865) 545-4176
Internet: www.justice.gov/usao/tne

★ U.S. Attorney **William C. "Bill" Killian** .... (865) 545-4167
Education: Tennessee 1971, 1975 JD
First Assistant U.S. Attorney **Nancy S. Harr** .... (865) 545-4167
E-mail: nancy.harr@usdoj.gov
Administrative Officer **Connie Moody** .... (865) 545-4167
E-mail: connie.moody@usdoj.gov
Budget Officer **Sharon Sellers** .... (865) 545-4167
E-mail: sharon.sellers@usdoj.gov
Human Resource Officer **Cheryl Lykens** .... (865) 545-4167
E-mail: cheryl.lykens@usdoj.gov
Records Management Officer **Susan Leonard** .... (865) 545-4167
E-mail: susan.leonard@usdoj.gov
Systems Manager **Christopher English** .... (865) 545-4167
E-mail: chris.english@usdoj.gov
Law Enforcement Committee Coordinator
Sharry Dedman-Beard .... (865) 545-4167
Victim-Witness Coordinator **Susie DeLozier** .... (865) 545-4167
Intelligence Specialist **Paul Trask** .... (865) 545-4167
E-mail: paul.trask@usdoj.gov

Civil Division
Chief **Loretta Harber** .... (865) 545-4167
E-mail: loretta.harber@usdoj.gov
Social Security Assistant U.S. Attorney (Acting)
Loretta Harber .... (865) 545-4167
E-mail: loretta.harber@usdoj.gov
Assistant U.S. Attorney **Elizabeth Tonkin** .... (865) 545-4167
Assistant U.S. Attorney **Robert McConkey** .... (865) 545-4167
E-mail: robert.mcconkey@usdoj.gov
Assistant U.S. Attorney **(Vacant)** .... (865) 545-4167

Criminal Division
Chief **Steven H. Cook** .... (865) 545-4167
Supervisory Assistant U.S. Attorney **Charles Atchley** .... (865) 545-4167
E-mail: charles.atchley@usdoj.gov
Supervisory Assistant U.S. Attorney **Debra Breneman** ... (865) 545-4167
E-mail: debra.breneman@usdoj.gov

★ Presidential Appointment Requiring Senate Confirmation ☆ Presidential Appointment □ Schedule C Appointment ◇ Career Senior Foreign Service Appointment
● Career Senior Executive Service (SES) Appointment ○ Non-Career Senior Executive Service (SES) Appointment ■ Postal Career Executive Service

Criminal Division *continued*

Supervisory Assistant U.S. Attorney **David Jennings** .... (865) 545-4167
E-mail: david.jennings@usdoj.gov
Supervisory Assistant U.S. Attorney
Lisa Shepperd Zavogiannis .... (865) 545-4167
Note: Lisa Zavogiannis is the District Attorney General for the 31st Judicial District of Tennessee. She is currently working with the U.S. Attorney's office on federal cases regarding violent crimes, drugs, and human trafficking.
Assistant U.S. Attorney **Cynthia Davidson** .... (865) 545-4167
E-mail: cynthia.davidson@usdoj.gov
Assistant U.S. Attorney **F. M. "Trey" Hamilton** .... (865) 545-4167
E-mail: trey.hamilton@usdoj.gov
Assistant U.S. Attorney **David Lewen** .... (865) 545-4167
E-mail: david.lewen@usdoj.gov
Assistant U.S. Attorney **Kelly Norris** .... (865) 545-4167
E-mail: kelly.norris@usdoj.gov
Assistant U.S. Attorney **Tracy Stone** .... (865) 545-4167
E-mail: tracy.stone@usdoj.gov
Assistant U.S. Attorney **Jeffrey E. Theodore** .... (865) 545-4167
E-mail: jeffrey.theodore@usdoj.gov
Assistant U.S. Attorney **(Vacant)** .... (865) 545-4167
Assistant U.S. Attorney **(Vacant)** .... (865) 545-4167
Appellate Assistant U.S. Attorney **(Vacant)** .... (865) 545-4167
Asset Forfeiture Assistant U.S. Attorney **Frank Dale** ..... (865) 545-4167
E-mail: frank.dale@usdoj.gov
Organized Crime Drug Enforcement Task Force
Assistant U.S. Attorney **Caryn Hebets** .... (423) 282-1889
E-mail: caryn.hebets@usdoj.gov

Chattanooga (TN) Office

1110 Market Street, Suite 301, Chattanooga, TN 37402
Tel: (423) 752-5140 Fax: (423) 752-5150

Supervisory Assistant U.S. Attorney/Lead OCDETF
Assistant U.S. Attorney **Scott Winne** .... (423) 752-5140
E-mail: scott.winne@usdoj.gov
Civil Division Assistant U.S. Attorney
M. Kent Anderson .... (423) 752-5140
E-mail: kent.anderson@usdoj.gov
Civil Division Assistant U.S. Attorney **Tammy Combs** ... (423) 752-5140
E-mail: tammy.combs@usdoj.gov

Criminal Division

Supervisory Assistant U.S. Attorney **Scott Winne** .... (423) 752-5140
Assistant U.S. Attorney **Terra Bay** .... (423) 752-5140
Assistant U.S. Attorney **James Brooks** .... (423) 752-5140
E-mail: james.brooks@usdoj.gov
Assistant U.S. Attorney **Meredith Edwards** .... (423) 752-5140
E-mail: meredith.edwards@usdoj.gov
Assistant U.S. Attorney **Chris Poole** .... (423) 752-5140
E-mail: chris.poole@usdoj.gov
Assistant U.S. Attorney **Michael Porter** .... (423) 752-5140
E-mail: michael.porter2@usdoj.gov
Education: Case Western 2002 JD
Assistant U.S. Attorney **Gregg L. Sullivan** .... (423) 752-5140
E-mail: gregg.sullivan@usdoj.gov
Assistant U.S. Attorney **Jay Woods** .... (423) 752-5140

Greeneville (TN) Office

220 West Depot Street, Suite 423, Greeneville, TN 37743
Tel: (423) 639-6759 Fax: (423) 639-6451

Supervisory Assistant U.S. Attorney
Robert M. Reeves .... (423) 639-6759
E-mail: robert.reeves@usdoj.gov
Criminal Division Assistant U.S. Attorney
Greg Bowman .... (423) 639-6759
E-mail: greg.bowman@usdoj.gov
Criminal Division Assistant U.S. Attorney
J. Christian Lampe .... (423) 639-6759
E-mail: christian.lampe@usdoj.gov

Greeneville (TN) Office *continued*

Criminal Division Assistant U.S. Attorney
Nicholas Regalia .... (423) 639-6759
E-mail: nicholas.regalia@usdoj.gov
Criminal Division Assistant U.S. Attorney
Helen Smith .... (423) 639-6759
E-mail: helen.smith@usdoj.gov
Criminal Division Assistant U.S. Attorney
M. Neil Smith .... (423) 639-6759
E-mail: neil.smith@usdoj.gov
Criminal Division Assistant U.S. Attorney
D. Wayne Taylor .... (423) 282-1889
Criminal Division Assistant U.S. Attorney **(Vacant)** ...... (423) 639-6759
Criminal Division Assistant U.S. Attorney **(Vacant)** ...... (423) 639-6759

Tennessee - Middle District

110 Ninth Avenue South, Suite A-961, Nashville, TN 37203-3870
Tel: (615) 736-5151 Fax: (615) 736-5323
Internet: www.usdoj.gov/usao/tnm

★ U.S. Attorney **David Rivera** .... (615) 736-5151
E-mail: david.rivera@usdoj.gov
Education: Oral Roberts 1982 BS; Pace 1988 JD
Secretary to the U.S. Attorney **Darlene Danielson** ..... (615) 736-5151
E-mail: darlene.danielson@usdoj.gov
Victim-Witness Coordinator **John Hernandez** .... (615) 736-5151
E-mail: john.hernandez@usdoj.gov
First Assistant U.S. Attorney **John L. "Jack" Smith** ..... (615) 736-5151
E-mail: jack.smith2@usdoj.gov
Education: Harvard 1994 JD
Senior Litigation Counsel **Hilliard H. Hester III** .... (615) 736-5151
E-mail: hilliard.hester@usdoj.gov
Law Enforcement Committee Coordinator
David Boling .... (615) 736-5151
Human Resources Specialist **Dawn Woodside** .... (615) 736-5151
E-mail: dawn.woodside@usdoj.gov
Administrative Officer **Keith Preston** .... (615) 736-5151
E-mail: keith.preston@usdoj.gov

Civil Division

Chief **Mark Wildasin** .... (615) 736-5151
E-mail: mark.wildasin@usdoj.gov
Assistant U.S. Attorney **Ellen M. Bowden** .... (615) 736-5151
Assistant U.S. Attorney **Steve Jordan** .... (615) 736-5151
E-mail: steve.jordan@usdoj.gov
Assistant U.S. Attorney **Delk Kennedy** .... (615) 736-5151
E-mail: delk.kennedy@usdoj.gov
Assistant U.S. Attorney **Mercedes C. Maynor-Faulcon** ... (615) 736-5151
E-mail: mercedes.maynor-faulcon@usdoj.gov
Assistant U.S. Attorney **Debra T. Phillips** .... (615) 736-5151
E-mail: debra.phillips@usdoj.gov
Assistant U.S. Attorney **Michael L. Roden** .... (615) 736-5151
E-mail: michael.roden@usdoj.gov
Assistant U.S. Attorney **Christopher Sabis** .... (615) 736-5151
E-mail: christopher.sabis@usdoj.gov
Assistant U.S. Attorney **(Vacant)** .... (615) 736-5151
Assistant U.S. Attorney **(Vacant)** .... (615) 736-5151
Financial Litigation Unit Debt Collection Agent
Amanda Griggs .... (615) 736-5151
E-mail: amanda.griggs@usdoj.gov

Criminal Division

Chief **Jimmie Lynn Ramsaur** .... (615) 736-5151
Deputy Chief **Harold B. McDonough, Jr.** .... (615) 736-5151
Deputy Chief **John K. Webb** .... (615) 736-5151
Deputy Chief **Phil Wehby** .... (615) 736-5151
Assistant U.S. Attorney **William "Bill" Abely** .... (615) 736-5151
Assistant U.S. Attorney **Katherine Booth** .... (615) 736-5151
Assistant U.S. Attorney **Louis Chrisostomo** .... (615) 736-5151

(continued on next page)

Criminal Division *continued*

Assistant U.S. Attorney
S. Carran "Carrie" Daughtrey .... (615) 736-5151
E-mail: carrie.daughtrey@usdoj.gov
Education: Vanderbilt BS; Wisconsin; Vanderbilt 1994 JD
Assistant U.S. Attorney **Lee Deneke** .... (615) 736-5151
E-mail: lee.deneke@usdoj.gov
Assistant U.S. Attorney **Brent Hannafan** .... (615) 736-5151
E-mail: brent.hannafan@usdoj.gov
Assistant U.S. Attorney **Lynne Ingram** .... (615) 736-5151
E-mail: lynne.ingram@usdoj.gov
Assistant U.S. Attorney **Byron M. Jones** .... (615) 736-5151
E-mail: byron.jones@usdoj.gov
Assistant U.S. Attorney **Sunny Koshy** .... (615) 736-5151
E-mail: sunny.koshy@usdoj.gov
Assistant U.S. Attorney **Clay Lee** .... (615) 736-5151
Assistant U.S. Attorney **Joseph Montmimy** .... (615) 736-5151
Assistant U.S. Attorney **Sandra Moses** .... (615) 736-5151
E-mail: sandra.moses@usdoj.gov
Assistant U.S. Attorney **Stephanie Toussaint** .... (615) 736-5151
Assistant U.S. Attorney **Van Vincent** .... (615) 736-5151
E-mail: van.vincent@usdoj.gov
Assistant U.S. Attorney **(Vacant)** .... (615) 736-5151
Assistant U.S. Attorney **(Vacant)** .... (615) 736-5151
Assistant U.S. Attorney **(Vacant)** .... (615) 736-5151
Assistant U.S. Attorney **(Vacant)** .... (615) 736-5151
Intelligence Research Specialist **(Vacant)** .... (615) 736-5151
Administrative Officer **Keith Preston** .... (615) 736-4515
E-mail: keith.preston@usdoj.gov

Tennessee - Western District

Clifford Davis Federal Building, 167 North Main Street,
Suite 800, Memphis, TN 38103
Tel: (901) 544-4231 Fax: (901) 544-4230
Internet: www.usdoj.gov/usao/tnw

★ U.S. Attorney **Edward L. "Ed" Stanton III** .... (901) 544-4231
E-mail: edward.stanton@usdoj.gov
Education: U Memphis 1994, 1997 JD
Special Counsel **Kevin Ritz** .... (901) 544-4231
E-mail: kevin.ritz@usdoj.gov
Education: Virginia 2004 JD
Secretary to the U.S. Attorney **Terri L. Wiseman** .... (901) 544-4231
E-mail: terri.wiseman@usdoj.gov
First Assistant U.S. Attorney
Lawrence J. "Larry" Laurenzi .... (901) 544-4231
E-mail: larry.laurenzi@usdoj.gov
Executive Assistant United States Attorney
C. David Biggers .... (901) 544-4231
E-mail: david.biggers@usdoj.gov
Administrative Officer **Demetrice Rufus** .... (901) 544-4231
Budget Officer **Denise Johnson** .... (901) 544-4231
E-mail: denise.johnson@usdoj.gov
Personnel Officer **Donald Stinson** .... (901) 544-4231
E-mail: donald.stinson@usdoj.gov
Law Enforcement Committee Coordinator **(Vacant)** .... (901) 544-4231
Victim-Witness Specialist **LaRita Bearden** .... (901) 544-4231
Information Technology Manager **(Vacant)** .... (901) 544-4231

Civil Division

Chief and Senior Litigation Counsel **Bill Siler** .... (901) 544-4231
E-mail: bill.siler@usdoj.gov
Bankruptcy/Collections Assistant U.S. Attorney
Barbara Zoccola .... (901) 544-4010
E-mail: barbara.zoccola@usdoj.gov
Assistant U.S. Attorney **David Brackstone** .... (901) 544-4231
Assistant U.S. Attorney **S. Keenan Carter** .... (901) 544-4231
E-mail: keenan.carter@usdoj.gov
Assistant U.S. Attorney **Monica Simmons** .... (901) 544-4231
E-mail: monica.simmons@usdoj.gov
Assistant U.S. Attorney **Gary Vanasek** .... (901) 544-4231
E-mail: gary.vanasek@usdoj.gov

Civil Division *continued*

Health Care Fraud Assistant U.S. Attorney
Stuart Canale .... (901) 544-4231
E-mail: stuart.canale@usdoj.gov

Criminal Division

Chief **Joseph Murphy, Jr.** .... (901) 544-4231
Deputy Chief **Fred Godwin** .... (901) 544-4231
Senior Litigation Counsel **Tony Arvin** .... (901) 544-4231
Assistant U.S. Attorney **Carroll Andre III** .... (901) 544-4231
Assistant U.S. Attorney **Christopher Cotten** .... (901) 544-4231
Assistant U.S. Attorney **Lorraine Craig** .... (901) 544-4231
E-mail: lorraine.craig@usdoj.gov
Assistant U.S. Attorney **Mark Erskine** .... (901) 544-4231
Assistant U.S. Attorney **John D. Fabian** .... (901) 544-4231
E-mail: john.fabian@usdoj.gov
Assistant U.S. Attorney **Damon Griffin** .... (901) 544-4231
Assistant U.S. Attorney **Stephen Hall** .... (901) 544-4231
Assistant U.S. Attorney **Deb Ireland** .... (901) 544-4231
E-mail: deb.ireland@usdoj.gov
Assistant U.S. Attorney **David Pritchard** .... (901) 544-4231
E-mail: david.pritchard@usdoj.gov
Assistant U.S. Attorney **Reagan Taylor** .... (901) 544-4231
E-mail: reagan.taylor2@usdoj.gov
Assistant U.S. Attorney **Kasey Weiland** .... (901) 544-4231
E-mail: kasey.weiland@usdoj.gov
Special Assistant U.S. Attorney **Samuel Stringfellow** .... (901) 544-4231
E-mail: samuel.stringfellow@usdoj.gov
Community Outreach Specialist **Louis Goggans** .... (901) 544-4231
E-mail: louis.goggans@usdoj.gov

Drug Task Force

Assistant U.S. Attorney **Daniel French** .... (901) 544-4231
E-mail: daniel.french@usdoj.gov

Jackson (TN) Office

109 South Highland, Suite 300, Jackson, TN 38301
Tel: (731) 422-6220 Fax: (731) 422-6668

Branch Chief **Victor "Vic" Ivy** .... (731) 422-6220
E-mail: vic.ivy@usdoj.gov
Deputy Chief **James Powell** .... (731) 422-6220
E-mail: james.powell@usdoj.gov
Assistant U.S. Attorney **Beth Boswell** .... (731) 422-6220
E-mail: beth.hall@usdoj.gov
Assistant U.S. Attorney **Matthew Wilson** .... (731) 422-6220
E-mail: matthew.wilson@usdoj.gov
Assistant U.S. Attorney **(Vacant)** .... (731) 422-6220

Texas - Eastern District

Federal Building, 350 Magnolia Avenue,
Suite 150, Beaumont, TX 77701
Tel: (409) 839-2538 Fax: (409) 839-2550
Internet: www.usdoj.gov/usao/txe

★ U.S. Attorney **John Malcolm Bales** .... (409) 839-2538
Education: Texas 1977, 1980 JD
Secretary to the U.S. Attorney **Sharon Beckum** .... (409) 839-2538
First Assistant U.S. Attorney **Mark McBride** .... (972) 509-1201
E-mail: mark.mcbride@usdoj.gov
Attorney in Charge **Matt Quinn** .... (409) 839-2538
E-mail: matt.quinn@usdoj.gov
Administrative Officer **Gretchen Randall** .... (409) 839-2538
E-mail: gretchen.randall@usdoj.gov
Personnel Officer **Princess Franklin** .... (409) 839-2538
Paralegal Specialist/Librarian **Glenda Martin** .... (409) 839-2538
E-mail: glenda.martin@usdoj.gov
Public Affairs Specialist/Law Enforcement Coordinator
Davilyn Walston .... (409) 839-2538
E-mail: davilyn.walston@usdoj.gov
Systems Manager **Fredrick Schultz** .... (409) 839-2538

★ Presidential Appointment Requiring Senate Confirmation ☆ Presidential Appointment ☐ Schedule C Appointment ◇ Career Senior Foreign Service Appointment
● Career Senior Executive Service (SES) Appointment ○ Non-Career Senior Executive Service (SES) Appointment ■ Postal Career Executive Service

Texas - Eastern District *continued*

Systems Manager/Webmaster
Joseph "Butch" Henderson .... (409) 839-2538
E-mail: joseph.henderson@usdoj.gov

Civil Division

Assistant U.S. Attorney **Michael Lockhart** .... (409) 839-2538
E-mail: michael.lockhart@usdoj.gov
Assistant U.S. Attorney **Andrea Parker** .... (409) 839-2538
E-mail: andrea.parker@usdoj.gov

Criminal Division

Chief **Alan R. Jackson** .... (936) 590-1400
E-mail: alan.jackson@usdoj.gov
Assistant U.S. Attorney **Lesley Bartow** .... (409) 839-2538
Assistant U.S. Attorney **Joseph R. "Joe" Batte** .... (409) 839-2538
E-mail: joe.batte@usdoj.gov
Assistant U.S. Attorney **John Craft** .... (409) 839-2538
Assistant U.S. Attorney **Michelle Englade** .... (409) 839-2538
E-mail: michelle.englade@usdoj.gov
Assistant U.S. Attorney **Randall L. Fluke** .... (409) 839-2538
E-mail: randall.fluke@usdoj.gov
Assistant U.S. Attorney **Robert L. Rawls** .... (409) 839-2538
Assistant U.S. Attorney **John Ross** .... (409) 839-2538
E-mail: john.ross@usdoj.gov
Assistant U.S. Attorney **Baylor Wortham** .... (409) 839-2538
E-mail: baylor.wortham@usdoj.gov
Education: Baylor 2005 JD

Lufkin (TX) Office

Bank of America Building, 415 South First Street,
Suite 201, Lufkin, TX 75901
Tel: (936) 639-4003 Fax: (936) 639-4033

Assistant U.S. Attorney **Lauren Gaston** .... (936) 639-4003
Assistant U.S. Attorney **Paul Hable** .... (936) 639-4003

Plano (TX) Office

101 East Park Boulevard, Suite 500, Plano, TX 75074-6749
Tel: (972) 509-1201 Fax: (972) 509-1209

Attorney-in-Charge **Kevin McClendon** .... (972) 509-1201
E-mail: kevin.mcclendon@usdoj.gov
Assistant U.S. Attorney **Tracey Batson** .... (972) 509-1201
E-mail: tracey.batson@usdoj.gov
Assistant U.S. Attorney **Jay Combs** .... (972) 509-1201
E-mail: jay.combs@usdoj.gov
Assistant U.S. Attorney **Chris Eason** .... (972) 509-1201
E-mail: chris.eason@usdoj.gov
Assistant U.S. Attorney **Ernest Gonzalez** .... (972) 509-1201
E-mail: ernest.gonzalez@usdoj.gov
Assistant U.S. Attorney **Terri L. Hagan** .... (972) 509-1201
E-mail: terri.hagan@usdoj.gov
Assistant U.S. Attorney **Glenn Rogue Jackson** .... (972) 509-1201
Assistant U.S. Attorney **Camelia Lopez** .... (972) 509-1201
E-mail: camelia.lopez@usdoj.gov
Assistant U.S. Attorney **Marisa Miller** .... (972) 509-1201
Assistant U.S. Attorney **Heather Rattan** .... (972) 509-1201
E-mail: heather.rattan@usdoj.gov
Assistant U.S. Attorney **Milton Andrew Stover** .... (972) 509-1201
E-mail: andrew.stover@usdoj.gov
Assistant U.S. Attorney **Bradley Visosky** .... (972) 509-1201
E-mail: bradley.visosky@usdoj.gov
Education: Texas 2001 JD
Assistant U.S. Attorney **James Andrew Williams** .... (972) 509-1201
E-mail: james.williams@usdoj.gov
Assistant U.S. Attorney **(Vacant)** .... (972) 509-1201
Systems Manager **Frank Peters** .... (972) 509-1201
E-mail: frank.peters@usdoj.gov

Sherman (TX) Office

1800 Teague Drive, Suite 500, Sherman, TX 75090
Tel: (903) 868-9454 Fax: (903) 892-2792

Attorney in Charge **Maureen Clancey Smith** .... (903) 868-9454
E-mail: maureen.smith@usdoj.gov
Assistant U.S. Attorney **Lesley Brooks** .... (903) 868-9454
Assistant U.S. Attorney **Steve Buys** .... (903) 868-9454
Assistant U.S. Attorney **William "Will" Tatum** .... (409) 839-2538
E-mail: william.tatum@usdoj.gov
Assistant U.S. Attorney **(Vacant)** .... (903) 868-9454

Texarkana (TX) Office

U.S. Courthouse, 500 State Line Avenue North,
Room 402, Texarkana, TX 75501
Tel: (903) 794-9481 Fax: (903) 792-5164

Assistant U.S. Attorney **Ryan Locker** .... (903) 794-9481

Tyler (TX) Office

110 North College, Suite 700, Tyler, TX 75702
Tel: (903) 590-1400 Fax: (903) 590-1436

Victim-Witness Specialist **Susan Johnson** .... (903) 590-1400
E-mail: susan.johnson@usdoj.gov
Systems Manager **Terrance Williams** .... (903) 590-1400

Civil Division

Civil Division Chief and Assistant U.S. Attorney
Randi D. Russell .... (903) 590-1400
E-mail: randi.russell@usdoj.gov
Assistant U.S. Attorney **James Gillingham** .... (903) 590-1400
E-mail: james.gillingham@usdoj.gov
Assistant U.S. Attorney **Robert Wells** .... (903) 590-1400
Assistant U.S. Attorney **Ruth H. Yeager** .... (903) 590-1400
E-mail: ruth.yeager@usdoj.gov

Criminal Division

Criminal Division Chief **Alan R. Jackson** .... (903) 590-1400
E-mail: alan.jackson@usdoj.gov
Attorney in Charge **Robert J. Middleton** .... (903) 590-1400
E-mail: robert.middleton@usdoj.gov
Assistant U.S. Attorney Appellate Chief
Traci L. Kenner .... (903) 590-1400
E-mail: traci.kenner@usdoj.gov
Assistant U.S. Attorney **Bill Baldwin** .... (903) 590-1400
E-mail: bill.baldwin@usdoj.gov
Assistant U.S. Attorney **Frank Coan** .... (903) 590-1400
Assistant U.S. Attorney **Mary Ann Cozby** .... (903) 590-1400
Assistant U.S. Attorney **Tom Gibson** .... (903) 590-1400
E-mail: tom.gibson@usdoj.gov
Assistant U.S. Attorney **Allen H. Hurst** .... (903) 590-1400
E-mail: allen.hurst@usdoj.gov
Assistant U.S. Attorney **Nathaniel Kummerfeld** .... (903) 590-1400
Assistant U.S. Attorney **Richard W. Moore** .... (903) 590-1400
E-mail: richard.moore@usdoj.gov
Education: Spring Hill BS; Cumberland JD
Assistant U.S. Attorney **Jim Noble** .... (903) 590-1400
Special Assistant U.S. Attorney **Kenneth McGurk** .... (903) 590-1400
E-mail: kenneth.mcgurk@usdoj.gov

Texas - Northern District

Earle Cabell Federal Building, 1100 Commerce Street,
3rd Floor, Dallas, TX 75242-1699
Tel: (214) 659-8600 Fax: (214) 659-8806
Internet: www.usdoj.gov/usao/txn

★ U.S. Attorney (Acting) **John R. Parker** .... (214) 659-8600
E-mail: john.parker@usdoj.gov
Secretary to the U.S. Attorney **Susan Parker** .... (214) 659-8600
E-mail: susan.parker@usdoj.gov
First Assistant U.S. Attorney **John R. Parker** .... (214) 659-8600
E-mail: john.parker@usdoj.gov

(continued on next page)

★ Presidential Appointment Requiring Senate Confirmation ☆ Presidential Appointment ☐ Schedule C Appointment ◇ Career Senior Foreign Service Appointment
● Career Senior Executive Service (SES) Appointment ○ Non-Career Senior Executive Service (SES) Appointment ■ Postal Career Executive Service

Texas - Northern District *continued*

Executive Assistant U.S. Attorney **Jennifer Tourje** . . . .(214) 659-8600
E-mail: jennifer.tourje@usdoj.gov
Administrative Officer **Brian Barr** . . . .(214) 659-8600
E-mail: brian.barr@usdoj.gov
Public Affairs Officer **Kathy Colvin** . . . .(214) 659-8600
E-mail: kathy.colvin@usdoj.gov
Law Enforcement Coordinator **Dow Croyle** . . . . (214) 659-8600
E-mail: dow.croyle@usdoj.gov
Civil Division Chief **Steve P. Fahey** . . . . (214) 659-8600
E-mail: steve.p.fahey@usdoj.gov
Civil Division Deputy Chief **Scott Hogan** . . . .(214) 659-8600
E-mail: scott.hogan@usdoj.gov
Criminal Chief **Chad Meacham** . . . . (214) 659-8600
E-mail: chad.meacham@usdoj.gov
Criminal Deputy Chief **Rick Calvert** . . . .(214) 659-8600
E-mail: rick.calvert@usdoj.gov
Criminal Deputy Chief **Melissa Childs** . . . . (214) 659-8600
E-mail: melissa.childs@usdoj.gov
Criminal Deputy Chief **Katherine Miller** . . . . (214) 659-8600
E-mail: katherine.miller@usdoj.gov
Criminal Deputy Chief **Lisa Miller** . . . . (214) 659-8600
E-mail: lisa.miller@usdoj.gov
Criminal Deputy Chief **Gary Tromblay** . . . . (214) 659-8600
E-mail: gary.tromblay@usdoj.gov
Organized Crime Drug Enforcement Task Force Lead
Assistant U.S. Attorney **Suzanna Etessam** . . . . (214) 659-8600
E-mail: suzanna.etessam@usdoj.gov

Abilene (TX) Office

341 Pine Street, Suite 2101, Abilene, TX 79601
Tel: (325) 672-8160 Fax: (325) 673-3139

Criminal Deputy Chief **(Vacant)** . . . .(325) 672-8160

Amarillo (TX) Office

Amarillo National Plaza Two, 500 South Taylor Street,
Suite 300, Amarillo, TX 79101-2442
Tel: (806) 324-2356 Fax: (806) 324-2399

Criminal Division Deputy Chief **Denise Williams** . . . . (806) 472-7351
E-mail: denise.williams@usdoj.gov

Fort Worth (TX) Office

Burnett Plaza, 801 Cherry Street, Unit #4,
Suite 1700, Fort Worth, TX 76102-6882
Tel: (817) 252-5200 Fax: (817) 252-5455

Civil Division Deputy Chief **Tami Parker** . . . . (817) 252-5200
E-mail: tami.parker@usdoj.gov
Criminal Deputy Chief **Alex Lewis** . . . . (817) 252-5232
E-mail: alex.lewis@usdoj.gov

Lubbock (TX) Office

U.S. Federal Building, 1205 Texas Avenue,
Suite 700, Lubbock, TX 79401-4002
Tel: (806) 472-7351 Fax: (806) 472-7394

Criminal Division Deputy Chief **Denise Williams** . . . . (806) 472-7351
E-mail: denise.williams@usdoj.gov

Texas - Southern District

1000 Louisiana Street, Suite 2300, Houston, TX 77002
P.O. Box 61129, Houston, TX 77208-1129
Tel: (713) 567-9000 Fax: (713) 718-3300
E-mail: usatty.txs@usdoj.gov
Internet: www.usdoj.gov/usao/txs

★ U.S. Attorney **Kenneth Magidson** . . . . (713) 567-9300
E-mail: ken.magidson@usdoj.gov
Secretary **Maria Lerma** . . . . (713) 567-9310
E-mail: maria.lerma@usdoj.gov

Texas - Southern District *continued*

First Assistant U.S. Attorney **Abe Martinez** . . . .(713) 567-9000
E-mail: abe.martinez@usdoj.gov
Executive Assistant U.S. Attorney - Litigation Support
Vernon Lewis . . . .(713) 567-9000
E-mail: vernon.lewis@usdoj.gov
Administrative Officer **Rodney Mattix** . . . . (713) 567-9317
E-mail: rodney.mattix@usdoj.gov Fax: (713) 718-3306
Law Enforcement Committee Coordinator **(Vacant)** . . . . . . (713) 567-9336
Victim-Witness Coordinator **Kesha Handy** . . . . (713) 567-9335
Public Affairs Specialist **Angela C. Dodge** . . . . (713) 567-9388
Librarian **(Vacant)** . . . .(713) 567-9337

Appellate Division

Fax: (713) 718-3302

Chief **Renata Gowie** . . . .(713) 567-9000
E-mail: renata.gowie@usdoj.gov

Asset Forfeiture Division

Fax: (713) 718-3304

Chief **Susan "Sue" Kempner** . . . .(713) 567-9565

Civil Division

Fax: (713) 718-3309

Chief **Keith Wyatt** . . . .(713) 567-9713
E-mail: keith.wyatt@usdoj.gov

Criminal Division

Fax: (713) 718-3361

Division Chief **Michael Wright** . . . . (713) 567-9584
E-mail: michael.wright@usdoj.gov

Brownsville (TX) Office

600 East Harrison, Suite 201, Brownsville, TX 78520-5106
Tel: (956) 548-2554 Fax: (956) 548-2549

Assistant U.S. Attorney-in-Charge
Richard "Rick" Lara . . . . (956) 983-6001
E-mail: rick.lara@usdoj.gov

Corpus Christi (TX) Office

Wilson Plaza, 800 North Shoreline Boulevard,
Suite 500, Corpus Christi, TX 78401
Tel: (361) 888-3111 Fax: (361) 888-3200

Assistant U.S. Attorney-in-Charge **Kenneth A. Cusick** . . . (361) 903-7921
E-mail: kenneth.cusick@usdoj.gov

Laredo (TX) Office

1100 Matamoros Street, Suite 200, Laredo, TX 78040-4912
P.O. Box 1179, Laredo, TX 78042-1179
Tel: (956) 723-5523 Fax: (956) 726-2266

Assistant U.S. Attorney-in-Charge **Jose A. Flores** . . . . (956) 721-4958
E-mail: jose.flores@usdoj.gov

McAllen (TX) Office

Bentsen Tower, 1701 West Highway 83,
Suite 600, McAllen, TX 78501-5160
Tel: (956) 630-3173 Fax: (956) 618-8016

Assistant U.S. Attorney-in-Charge **James Sturgis** . . . . (956) 992-9359
E-mail: james.sturgis@usdoj.gov

Victoria (TX) Office

312 South Main, 3rd Floor, Victoria, TX 77901
P.O. Box 2685, Victoria, TX 77902-2685
Tel: (361) 576-9988 Fax: (361) 579-6820

Note: Currently being served by the Corpus Christi Office.

★ Presidential Appointment Requiring Senate Confirmation ☆ Presidential Appointment ☐ Schedule C Appointment ◇ Career Senior Foreign Service Appointment
● Career Senior Executive Service (SES) Appointment ○ Non-Career Senior Executive Service (SES) Appointment ■ Postal Career Executive Service

Victoria (TX) Office *continued*

Assistant U.S. Attorney-in-Charge **Patti Booth** .... (361) 576-9988
E-mail: patti.booth@usdoj.gov

Texas - Western District

601 NW Loop 410, Suite 600, San Antonio, TX 78216
Tel: (210) 384-7100 Fax: (210) 384-7106
Internet: www.usdoj.gov/usao/txw

★ U.S. Attorney (Acting) **Richard L. Durbin, Jr.** .... (210) 384-7400
Secretary to the U.S. Attorney **Addie Cote** .... (512) 916-5858
E-mail: addie.cote@usdoj.gov Fax: (512) 916-5855
Counselor to the U.S. Attorney **Mickey Tapken** .... (210) 384-7100
First Assistant U.S. Attorney **Richard L. Durbin, Jr.** .... (210) 384-7400
Secretary to the First Assistant U.S. Attorney **Addie Cote** .... (210) 384-7400
E-mail: addie.cote@usdoj.gov Fax: (210) 384-7460
Executive Assistant U.S. Attorney **Sharon Pierce** .... (210) 384-7100
Law Enforcement Coordinating Committee **(Vacant)** .... (210) 384-7100
Victim-Witness Coordinator (Austin) **Kathi West** .... (512) 916-5858
816 Congress Avenue, Austin, TX 78701
E-mail: kathi.west@usdoj.gov
Victim-Witness Coordinator (El Paso) **Thelma Luna** .... (915) 534-6884
Federal Building, 700 East San Antonio, Suite 200, El Paso, TX 79901
E-mail: thelma.luna@usdoj.gov
Victim-Witness Coordinator (San Antonio) **Danielle Deisch** .... (210) 384-7100
E-mail: danielle.deisch@usdoj.gov
Administrative Officer **Dianne Dziuk** .... (210) 384-7200
E-mail: dianne.dziuk@usdoj.gov
Budget Officer **Ed Cimmino** .... (210) 384-7100
Deputy Administrative Officer **Steven Garza** .... (210) 384-7200
E-mail: steven.garza@usdoj.gov
Human Resources Officer **Linda A. Dickson** .... (210) 384-7200
E-mail: linda.dickson@usdoj.gov
Public Affairs Officer **Daryl Fields** .... (210) 384-7100
E-mail: daryl.fields@usdoj.gov
LIONS Systems Manager **Robin Sandin** .... (210) 384-7200
Systems Manager **Robert Mercer** .... (210) 384-7200
E-mail: robert.mercer@usdoj.gov
Litigation Support Specialist **Lora Makowski** .... (210) 384-7100
E-mail: lora.makowski@usdoj.gov

Civil Division

Chief **John Paniszczyn** .... (210) 384-7300
E-mail: john.paniszczyn@usdoj.gov
Deputy Chief **Joe Rodriguez** .... (210) 384-7300
E-mail: joe.rodriguez@usdoj.gov
Affirmative Civil Enforcement Chief **John LoCurto** .... (210) 384-7300
E-mail: john.locurto@usdoj.gov
Assets Forfeiture Fund and Field Offices Chief **Robert Shaw-Meadow** .... (210) 384-7300
E-mail: rob.shaw-meadow@usdoj.gov
Financial Litigation Unit Chief **Kristy Callahan** .... (210) 384-7250
E-mail: kristy.callahan@usdoj.gov
Assistant U.S. Attorney **Gary Anderson** .... (210) 384-7300
E-mail: gary.anderson@usdoj.gov
Assistant U.S. Attorney **Clayton Diedrichs** .... (210) 384-7300
E-mail: clayton.diedirchs@usdoj.gov
Assistant U.S. Attorney **James F. "Jim" Gilligan, Jr.** .... (210) 384-7300
E-mail: jim.gilligan@usdoj.gov
Assistant U.S. Attorney **Susan Strawn** .... (210) 384-7300
Assistant U.S. Attorney **(Vacant)** .... (210) 384-7300
Assistant U.S. Attorney **(Vacant)** .... (210) 384-7300
Assistant U.S. Attorney **(Vacant)** .... (210) 384-7300
Assistant U.S. Attorney **(Vacant)** .... (210) 384-7300

Criminal Division

Chief **Margaret F. Leachman** .... (210) 384-7100
Chief (San Antonio) **Erica Giese** .... (210) 384-7131
E-mail: erica.giese@usdoj.gov

Criminal Division *continued*

Appellate Section Chief **Joe Gay** .... (210) 384-7090
Asset Forfeiture Section Chief **Diana Cruz-Zapata** .... (210) 384-7040
E-mail: diana.cruz-zapata@usdoj.gov
Major Crimes Section Chief **Jose Contreras** .... (210) 384-7150
OCDETF Section Chief **Russell Leachman** .... (210) 384-7100
E-mail: russell.leachman@usdoj.gov
White Collar Crime Chief **Mark Roomberg** .... (210) 384-7179
E-mail: mark.roomberg@usdoj.gov
Senior Litigation Counsel **(Vacant)** .... (210) 384-7400
Special Assistant U.S. Attorney **Kimberly Johnson** .... (210) 384-7150
E-mail: kimberly.johnson@usdoj.gov
Assistant U.S. Attorney **James K. "Jim" Blankinship** .... (210) 384-7100
E-mail: jim.blakinship@usdoj.gov
Assistant U.S. Attorney **Margaret Embry** .... (210) 384-7090
E-mail: margaret.embry@usdoj.gov
Assistant U.S. Attorney **Priscilla Garcia** .... (210) 384-7025
E-mail: priscilla.garcia@usdoj.gov
Assistant U.S. Attorney **Mike Hardy** .... (210) 384-7150
E-mail: mike.hardy@usdoj.gov
Assistant U.S. Attorney **Bill Harris** .... (210) 384-7150
E-mail: bill.harris@usdoj.gov
Assistant U.S. Attorney **Charles Jenkins** .... (210) 384-7100
E-mail: charles.jenkins@usdoj.gov
Assistant U.S. Attorney **Diane Kirstein** .... (210) 384-7150
E-mail: diane.kirstein@usdoj.gov
Assistant U.S. Attorney **Matthew Lathrop** .... (210) 384-7150
E-mail: matthew.lathrop@usdoj.gov
Assistant U.S. Attorney **Ellen Lockwood** .... (210) 384-7100
E-mail: ellen.lockwood@usdoj.gov
Assistant U.S. Attorney **Thomas P. "Tom" Moore** .... (210) 384-7150
E-mail: tom.moore@usdoj.gov
Assistant U.S. Attorney **Karen Norris** .... (210) 384-7025
E-mail: karen.norris@usdoj.gov
Assistant U.S. Attorney **Judith Patton** .... (210) 384-7100
E-mail: judith.patton@usdoj.gov
Assistant U.S. Attorney **Walter L. "Bud" Paulissen** .... (210) 384-7150
E-mail: bud.paulissen@usdoj.gov
Assistant U.S. Attorney **Christina Playton** .... (210) 384-7150
E-mail: christina.playton@usdoj.gov
Assistant U.S. Attorney **Sam Ponder** .... (210) 384-7025
E-mail: sam.ponder@usdoj.gov
Assistant U.S. Attorney **Angela S. "Angie" Raba** .... (210) 384-7090
E-mail: angie.raba@usdoj.gov
Assistant U.S. Attorney **Bettina Richardson** .... (210) 384-7150
E-mail: bettina.richardson@usdoj.gov
Assistant U.S. Attorney **David Shearer** .... (210) 384-7150
E-mail: david.shearer@usdoj.gov
Assistant U.S. Attorney **Charlie Strauss** .... (210) 384-7025
E-mail: charlie.strauss@usdoj.gov
Assistant U.S. Attorney **Gregory J. Surovic** .... (210) 384-7020
E-mail: greg.surovic@usdoj.gov
Assistant U.S. Attorney **Tracy Thompson** .... (210) 384-7150
E-mail: tracy.thompson@usdoj.gov
Assistant U.S. Attorney **Mary Nelda Valadez** .... (210) 384-7100
Assistant U.S. Attorney **Sarah Wannarka** .... (210) 384-7150
E-mail: sarah.wannarka@usdoj.gov
Assistant U.S. Attorney **(Vacant)** .... (210) 384-7100
Assistant U.S. Attorney **(Vacant)** .... (210) 384-7150
Assistant U.S. Attorney **(Vacant)** .... (210) 384-7090
Special Assistant U.S. Attorney **(Vacant)** .... (210) 384-7150

Alpine - Pecos (TX) Office

2500 North Highway 118, Alpine, TX 79830
Tel: (432) 837-7332 Fax: (432) 837-7485

Chief **James J. "Jay" Miller, Jr.** .... (432) 837-7332
Criminal Division Assistant U.S. Attorney **Sandra L. "Sandy" Stewart** .... (432) 837-7332
E-mail: sandy.stewart@usdoj.gov
Assistant U.S. Attorney **Layton Duer** .... (432) 837-7332
E-mail: layton.duer@usdoj.gov

(continued on next page)

REGIONAL OFFICES — US ATTORNEYS AND US MARSHALS SERVICE

★ Presidential Appointment Requiring Senate Confirmation ☆ Presidential Appointment ☐ Schedule C Appointment ◇ Career Senior Foreign Service Appointment
● Career Senior Executive Service (SES) Appointment ○ Non-Career Senior Executive Service (SES) Appointment ■ Postal Career Executive Service

Alpine - Pecos (TX) Office *continued*

Assistant U.S. Attorney **Monty Kimball** . . . . (432) 837-7332
E-mail: monty.kimball@usdoj.gov

Austin (TX) Office

816 Congress Avenue, Suite 1000, Austin, TX 78701
Tel: (512) 916-5858 Fax: (512) 916-5854

Chief **Ashley Hoff** . . . . (512) 916-5858
E-mail: ashley.hoff@usdoj.gov
Deputy Chief **Michelle Fernald** . . . . (512) 916-5858
E-mail: michelle.fernald@usdoj.gov
Victim-Witness Coordinator **Kathi West** . . . . (512) 916-5858
E-mail: kathi.west@usdoj.gov

Civil Division

Assistant U.S. Attorney **Steven Bass** . . . . (512) 916-5858
E-mail: steven.bass@usdoj.gov
Assistant U.S. Attorney **Marco "Mark" Guerrero** . . . . (512) 916-5858
E-mail: mark.guerrero@usdoj.gov
Assistant U.S. Attorney **Zachary Richter** . . . . (512) 916-5858

Criminal Division

Assistant U.S. Attorney **Anthony W. "Tony" Brown** . . . . (512) 916-5858
E-mail: tony.brown@usdoj.gov
Assistant U.S. Attorney **Alan M. Buie** . . . . (512) 916-5858
E-mail: alan.buie@usdoj.gov
Assistant U.S. Attorney **Matthew Harding** . . . . (512) 916-5858
E-mail: matt.harding@usdoj.gov
Education: Texas 2010 JD
Assistant U.S. Attorney **Matthew Devlin** . . . . (512) 916-5858
E-mail: matt.devlin@usdoj.gov
Assistant U.S. Attorney **(Vacant)** . . . . (512) 916-5858

Del Rio (TX) Office

U.S. Courthouse, 111 East Broadway, Room 300, Del Rio, TX 78840
Tel: (830) 703-2025 Fax: (830) 703-3741

Chief **Patrick Burke** . . . . (830) 703-2025
E-mail: patrick.burke@usdoj.gov
Deputy Chief **Meghan McCalla** . . . . (830) 703-2025
E-mail: meghan.mccalla@usdoj.gov
Assistant U.S. Attorney **Daniel Castillo** . . . . (830) 703-2025
E-mail: daniel.castillo@usdoj.gov
Assistant U.S. Attorney **Elizabeth Cunningham** . . . . (830) 703-2025
Assistant U.S. Attorney **Matthew Devlin** . . . . (830) 703-2025
E-mail: matt.devlin@usdoj.gov
Assistant U.S. Attorney **Michelle Fernald** . . . . (830) 703-2025
E-mail: michelle.fernald@usdoj.gov
Assistant U.S. Attorney **Jennifer Freel** . . . . (830) 703-2025
E-mail: jennifer.freel@usdoj.gov
Assistant U.S. Attorney **Douglas Gardner** . . . . (830) 703-2025
E-mail: douglas.gardner@usdoj.gov
Assistant U.S. Attorney **Dan Guess** . . . . (830) 703-2025
E-mail: dan.guess@usdoj.gov
Assistant U.S. Attorney **Jay Hulings** . . . . (830) 703-2025
E-mail: jay.hulings@usdoj.gov
Assistant U.S. Attorney **Mark Marshall** . . . . (830) 703-2025
E-mail: mark.marshall@usdoj.gov
Assistant U.S. Attorney **Sharon Pierce** . . . . (830) 703-2025
E-mail: sharon.pierce@usdoj.gov
Assistant U.S. Attorney **Gregg N. Sofer** . . . . (830) 703-2025
E-mail: gregg.sofer@usdoj.gov
Assistant U.S. Attorney **Grant Sparks** . . . . (830) 703-2025
E-mail: grant.sparks@usdoj.gov
Assistant U.S. Attorney **Mark Stelmach** . . . . (830) 703-2025
E-mail: mark.stelmach@usdoj.gov
Assistant U.S. Attorney **(Vacant)** . . . . (830) 703-2025

El Paso (TX) Office

Federal Building, 700 East San Antonio,
Suite 200, El Paso, TX 79901
Tel: (915) 534-6884 Fax: (915) 534-6024

Chief **Jose Luis Gonzalez** . . . . (915) 534-6884
Senior Litigation Counsel **Debra Kanof** . . . . (915) 534-6884
E-mail: debra.kanof@usdoj.gov
Complex Fraud and Public Corruption Chief
Donna Miller . . . . (915) 534-6884
E-mail: donna.miller@usdoj.gov
General Crimes Chief **Laura Franco-Gregory** . . . . (915) 534-6884
General Crimes Deputy Chief **Steven R. Spitzer** . . . . (915) 534-6884
E-mail: steven.r.spitzer@usdoj.gov
OCDETF Chief Assistant U.S. Attorney
Anthony "Tony" Franco . . . . (915) 534-6884
OCDETF Deputy Chief Assistant U.S. Attorney
John M. Gibson . . . . (915) 534-6884
E-mail: john.m.gibson@usdoj.gov

Asset Forfeiture Division

Assistant U.S. Attorney **Anna Arreola** . . . . (915) 534-6884
E-mail: anna.arreola@usdoj.gov
Education: Stanford 2002 JD

Civil Division

Assistant U.S. Attorney **Eduardo "Eddie" Castillo** . . . . . . (915) 534-6884
E-mail: eddie.castillo@usdoj.gov
Assistant U.S. Attorney
Magdalena G. "Maggie" Jara . . . . (915) 534-6884
Assistant U.S. Attorney **Lisa Leontiev** . . . . (915) 534-6884
E-mail: lisa.leontiev@usdoj.gov
Assistant U.S. Attorney **Angelica Saenz** . . . . (915) 534-6884

Criminal Division

Assistant U.S. Attorney **Jose Luis Acosta** . . . . (915) 534-6884
E-mail: jose.acosta@usdoj.gov
Assistant U.S. Attorney **Patricia Acosta** . . . . (915) 534-6884
E-mail: patricia.acosta@usdoj.gov
Assistant U.S. Attorney **Patricia Aguayo** . . . . (915) 534-6884
E-mail: patricia.aguayo@usdoj.gov
Assistant U.S. Attorney **Robert Almonte II** . . . . (915) 534-6884
Assistant U.S. Attorney **Joseph E. Blackwell** . . . . (915) 534-6884
E-mail: joseph.blackwell@usdoj.gov
Assistant U.S. Attorney **Mara Blatt** . . . . (915) 534-6884
E-mail: mara.blatt@usdoj.gov
Assistant U.S. Attorney **Janet M. Bonner** . . . . (915) 534-6884
E-mail: janet.bonner@usdoj.gov
Assistant U.S. Attorney **Daniel Crumby** . . . . (915) 534-6884
E-mail: daniel.crumby@usdoj.gov
Assistant U.S. Attorney **Juanita Fielden** . . . . (915) 534-6884
E-mail: juanita.fielden@usdoj.gov
Assistant U.S. Attorney **Stephen G. "Steve" Garcia** . . . . (915) 534-6884
E-mail: stephen.garcia@usdoj.gov
Assistant U.S. Attorney **J. Brandy Gardes** . . . . (915) 534-6884
Assistant U.S. Attorney **Yvonne Gonzalez** . . . . (915) 534-6884
E-mail: yvonne.gonzalez@usdoj.gov
Assistant U.S. Attorney **Ian Hanna** . . . . (915) 534-6884
E-mail: ian.hanna@usdoj.gov
Assistant U.S. Attorney **Carlos Hermosillo** . . . . (915) 534-6884
E-mail: carlos.hermosillo@usdoj.gov
Assistant U.S. Attorney **John Johnston** . . . . (915) 534-6884
E-mail: john.johnston@usdoj.gov
Assistant U.S. Attorney **Stephen Jurecky** . . . . (915) 534-6884
Assistant U.S. Attorney **Ken Kaplan** . . . . (915) 534-6884
E-mail: ken.kaplan@usdoj.gov
Assistant U.S. Attorney **Gregory E. McDonald** . . . . (915) 534-6884
E-mail: gregory.mcdonald@usdoj.gov
Assistant U.S. Attorney **Daphne Newaz** . . . . (915) 534-6884
E-mail: daphne.newaz@usdoj.gov
Assistant U.S. Attorney **Rifian Newaz** . . . . (915) 534-6884
E-mail: rifian.newaz@usdoj.gov

Criminal Division *continued*

Assistant U.S. Attorney **Andres Ortega** . . . . (915) 534-6884
E-mail: andres.ortega@usdoj.gov
Assistant U.S. Attorney **Stanley M. Serwatka, Jr.** . . . . . . (915) 534-6884
E-mail: stanley.serwatka@usdoj.gov
Assistant U.S. Attorney
James Christopher "Chris" Skillern . . . . (915) 534-6884
E-mail: chris.skillern@usdoj.gov
Assistant U.S. Attorney **Kristal Wade** . . . . (915) 534-6884
E-mail: kristal.wade@usdoj.gov
Assistant U.S. Attorney **Michael Waits** . . . . (915) 534-6884
E-mail: michael.waits@usdoj.gov
Assistant U.S. Attorney **Richard Watts** . . . . (915) 534-6884
E-mail: richard.watts@usdoj.gov
Assistant U.S. Attorney **Michael Whyte** . . . . (915) 534-6884
E-mail: michael.whyte@usdoj.gov
Assistant U.S. Attorney **(Vacant)** . . . . (915) 534-6884
Assistant U.S. Attorney **(Vacant)** . . . . (915) 534-6884
Assistant U.S. Attorney **(Vacant)** . . . . (915) 534-6884

Midland (TX) Office

400 West Illinois Street, Suite 1200, Midland, TX 79702
Tel: (432) 686-4110 Fax: (432) 686-4131

Chief **William F. "Bill" Lewis** . . . . (432) 686-4110
Assistant U.S. Attorney **Austin M. Berry** . . . . (432) 686-4110
E-mail: austin.berry@usdoj.gov
Education: Baylor 1999 BA; Seton Hall 2006 JD
Assistant U.S. Attorney **Glenn Harwood** . . . . (432) 686-4110
E-mail: glenn.harwood@usdoj.gov
Assistant U.S. Attorney **Latawn Warsaw** . . . . (432) 686-4110
E-mail: latawn.warsaw@usdoj.gov
Assistant U.S. Attorney **Brandi Young** . . . . (432) 686-4110
E-mail: brandi.young@usdoj.gov

Waco (TX) Office

800 Franklin Avenue, Suite 280, Waco, TX 76701
Tel: (254) 750-1580 Fax: (254) 750-1599

Chief **Mark Frazier** . . . . (254) 750-1580
E-mail: mark.frazier@usdoj.gov
Assistant U.S. Attorney **Gregory S. Gloff** . . . . (254) 750-1580
E-mail: greg.gloff@usdoj.gov
Assistant U.S. Attorney **Mary Kucera** . . . . (254) 750-1580
E-mail: mary.kucera@usdoj.gov
Assistant U.S. Attorney **Stephanie Smith-Burris** . . . . (254) 750-1580
E-mail: stephanie.smith-burris@usdoj.gov
Assistant U.S. Attorney **(Vacant)** . . . . (254) 750-1580

Utah District

185 South State Street, Suite 300, Salt Lake City, UT 84111-1506
Tel: (801) 524-5682 Fax: (801) 524-6924
Internet: www.usdoj.gov/usao/ut

★ U.S. Attorney **John W. Huber** . . . . (801) 325-3224
E-mail: john.huber@usdoj.gov
First Assistant U.S. Attorney **Diana Hagen** . . . . (801) 325-3322
E-mail: diana.hagen@usdoj.gov
Education: Utah 1998 JD
Executive Assistant U.S. Attorney **Andrew Choate** . . . . . . (801) 325-1423
E-mail: andrew.choate@usdoj.gov
Administrative Officer **Linda J. McFarlane** . . . . (801) 325-3208
E-mail: linda.mcfarlane@usdoj.gov
Budget Officer **Kelli L. Divino** . . . . (801) 325-3207
E-mail: kelli.divino@usdoj.gov
Personnel Officer **Danna M. Reichert** . . . . (801) 325-3242
E-mail: danna.reichert@usdoj.gov
Systems Administrator **Barbara Atencio** . . . . (801) 325-3330
E-mail: barbara.atencio@usdoj.gov
Law Enforcement Committee Coordinator/Press Officer
Melodie Rydalch . . . . (801) 325-3206
E-mail: melodie.rydalch@usdoj.gov

Utah District *continued*

Victim-Witness Coordinator
Candelaria "Candy" Bennett . . . . (801) 325-3256
E-mail: candelaria.bennett@usdoj.gov
Librarian **Allison Turner** . . . . (801) 325-3304
E-mail: allison.turner@usdoj.gov
Contracting Officer **Kristy Begay** . . . . (801) 325-1416
E-mail: kristy.begay@usdoj.gov

Civil Division

Chief **Jared C. Bennett** . . . . (801) 325-3259
E-mail: jared.bennett@usdoj.gov
Education: Utah 2001 JD
Deputy Chief **Daniel D. Price** . . . . (801) 325-3234
E-mail: daniel.price@usdoj.gov
Assistant U.S. Attorney **John Mangum** . . . . (801) 325-3216
E-mail: john.mangum@usdoj.gov
Education: Chicago 1980 JD
Assistant U.S. Attorney **Allison J. Moon** . . . . (801) 325-3319
E-mail: allison.moon@usdoj.gov
Education: UC Santa Barbara 2005 BA; Boston U 2009 JD
Assistant U.S. Attorney **Jeffrey E. Nelson** . . . . (801) 325-3250
E-mail: jeffrey.nelson@usdoj.gov
Education: UCLA 1979 JD
Assistant U.S. Attorney **Anna Pugsley** . . . . (801) 325-3236
E-mail: anna.pugsley@usdoj.gov
Assistant U.S. Attorney **Stephen J. Sorenson** . . . . (801) 325-1425
E-mail: stephen.sorenson@usdoj.gov
Education: Utah 1977 JD
Assistant U.S. Attorney **Sandra Steinvoort** . . . . (801) 325-3233
E-mail: sandra.steinvoort@usdoj.gov

Criminal Division

Chief **Robert C. Lunnen** . . . . (801) 325-3251
E-mail: robert.lunnen@usdoj.gov
Deputy Chief **David F. Backman** . . . . (801) 325-3315
E-mail: david.backman@usdoj.gov
Civil Rights and Public Corruption Section Chief
Alicia Cook . . . . (801) 325-3350
E-mail: alicia.cook@usdoj.gov
Narcotics Section Chief **Vernon Stejskal** . . . . (801) 325-1404
E-mail: vernon.stejskal@usdoj.gov
Violent Crime Section Chief **Karin Fojtik** . . . . (801) 325-3229
E-mail: karin.fojtik@usdoj.gov
Violent Crime Section Deputy Chief **Drew Yeates** . . . . (801) 325-3252
E-mail: drew.yeates@usdoj.gov
White Collar Chief **Robert A. "Rob" Lund** . . . . (801) 325-3314
E-mail: robert.lund@usdoj.gov
Senior Litigation Counsel **Barbara Bearnson** . . . . (801) 325-3267
E-mail: barbara.bearnson@usdoj.gov
Senior Litigation Counsel **Stewart C. Walz** . . . . (801) 325-3238
E-mail: stewart.walz@usdoj.gov
Education: Vanderbilt 1976 JD
Assistant U.S. Attorney **Matthew Bell** . . . . (435) 229-3684
Note: Operates out of a branch office.
E-mail: matthew.bell@usdoj.gov
Assistant U.S. Attorney **Amanda A. Berndt** . . . . (801) 325-3267
E-mail: amanda.berndt@usdoj.gov
Assistant U.S. Attorney **Jason Burt** . . . . (801) 325-1439
E-mail: jason.burt@usdoj.gov
Assistant U.S. Attorney **Cy Castle** . . . . (801) 325-3214
E-mail: cy.castle@usdoj.gov
Assistant U.S. Attorney **Carlie Christensen** . . . . (801) 325-3235
E-mail: carlie.christensen@usdoj.gov
Assistant U.S. Attorney **Aaron Clark** . . . . (801) 325-1405
E-mail: aaron.clark@usdoj.gov
Assistant U.S. Attorney **Carol Dain** . . . . (801) 325-3353
E-mail: carol.dain@usdoj.gov
Assistant U.S. Attorney **Richard W. Daynes** . . . . (801) 325-3361
E-mail: richard.daynes@usdoj.gov
Assistant U.S. Attorney **Lake Dishman** . . . . (801) 325-1409
E-mail: lake.dishman@usdoj.gov

(continued on next page)

Criminal Division *continued*

Assistant U.S. Attorney **Adam S. Elggren** . . . . (801) 325-3316
E-mail: adam.elggren@usdoj.gov
Assistant U.S. Attorney **Carlos A. Esqueda** . . . . (801) 325-3352
E-mail: carlos.esqueda@usdoj.gov
Assistant U.S. Attorney **Trina A. Higgins** . . . . (801) 325-3356
E-mail: trina.higgins@usdoj.gov
Assistant U.S. Attorney **Mark Y. Hirata** . . . . (801) 325-3239
E-mail: mark.hirata@usdoj.gov
Assistant U.S. Attorney **Michael P. Kennedy** . . . . (801) 325-3300
E-mail: michael.kennedy@usdoj.gov
Education: George Mason 1993 JD
Assistant U.S. Attorney **Paul Kohler** . . . . (435) 680-4421
Note: Operates out of a branch office.
E-mail: paul.kohler@usdoj.gov
Assistant U.S. Attorney **Lynda R. Krause** . . . . (801) 325-3354
E-mail: lynda.krause@usdoj.gov
Assistant U.S. Attorney **Andrea Martinez** . . . . (801) 325-1406
E-mail: andrea.martinez@usdoj.gov
Assistant U.S. Attorney **Holly Shick** . . . . (801) 325-1403
E-mail: holly.shick@usdoj.gov
Assistant U.S. Attorney **Elizabethanne C. Stevens** . . . . . . (801) 325-3257
E-mail: elizabethanne.stevens@usdoj.gov
Assistant U.S. Attorney **Jacob Strain** . . . . (801) 325-3285
E-mail: jacob.strain@usdoj.gov
Assistant U.S. Attorney **Kevin L. Sundwall** . . . . (801) 325-3303
E-mail: kevin.sundwall@usdoj.gov
Assistant U.S. Attorney **Jeannette F. Swent** . . . . (801) 325-3220
E-mail: jeannette.swent@usdoj.gov
Education: Yale 1982 MPhil, 1984 PhD; Stanford 1991 JD
Assistant U.S. Attorney **Scott J. Thorley** . . . . (801) 325-3266
E-mail: scott.thorley@usdoj.gov
Assistant U.S. Attorney **Veda M. Travis** . . . . (801) 325-3295
E-mail: veda.travis@usdoj.gov
Assistant U.S. Attorney **Mark K. Vincent** . . . . (801) 325-3249
E-mail: mark.vincent@usdoj.gov
Education: Pepperdine 1987 JD
Assistant U.S. Attorney **Felice J. Viti** . . . . (801) 325-3230
E-mail: felice.viti@usdoj.gov
Education: Fordham 1983 JD
Assistant U.S. Attorney **Drew Yeates** . . . . (801) 325-3252
E-mail: drew.yeates@usdoj.gov
Assistant U.S. Attorney **Stewart Young** . . . . (801) 325-3213
E-mail: stewart.young@usdoj.gov
Assistant U.S. Attorney **(Vacant)** . . . . (801) 325-3373
Assistant U.S. Attorney **(Vacant)** . . . . (801) 325-3229
DOJ Trial Attorney **Brent D. Ward** . . . . (801) 325-1407
E-mail: brent.ward@usdoj.gov

Vermont District

U.S. Federal Building, 11 Elmwood Avenue,
3rd Floor, Burlington, VT 05401
P.O. Box 570, Burlington, VT 05402
Tel: (802) 951-6725 Fax: (802) 951-6540
Internet: www.usdoj.gov/usao/vt

★ U.S. Attorney **Eric Steven Miller** . . . . (802) 951-6725
E-mail: eric.miller@usdoj.gov
Secretary to the U.S. Attorney **Laura Harvey** . . . . (802) 951-6725
E-mail: laura.harvey@usdoj.gov
First Assistant U.S. Attorney **Eugenia A.P. Cowles** . . . . . . (802) 951-6725
E-mail: eugenia.cowles@usdoj.gov
Administrative Officer **Lisa J. Graves** . . . . (802) 951-6725
E-mail: lisa.j.graves@usdoj.gov
Law Enforcement Coordinator **James Leene** . . . . (802) 951-6725
E-mail: james.leene@usdoj.gov
Victim/Witness Coordinator **Aimee Stearns** . . . . (802) 951-6725
E-mail: aimee.stearns@usdoj.gov
Systems Manager **Charlene Tallman** . . . . (802) 951-6725
E-mail: charlene.tallman@usdoj.gov
Records Coordinator **Charlene Tallman** . . . . (802) 951-6725
E-mail: charlene.tallman@usdoj.gov

Civil Division
Tel: (802) 951-6725

Civil Chief **Nikolas Kerest** . . . . (802) 951-6725
E-mail: nikolas.kerest@usdoj.gov
Assistant U.S. Attorney **James J. Gelber** . . . . (802) 951-6725
E-mail: james.gelber@usdoj.gov
Assistant U.S. Attorney **Melissa A. D. Ranaldo** . . . . (802) 951-6725
E-mail: melissa.ranaldo@usdoj.gov
Assistant U.S. Attorney **(Vacant)** . . . . (802) 951-6725

Criminal Division
Tel: (802) 951-6725

Chief **Paul Van de Graaf** . . . . (802) 951-6725
E-mail: paul.van.de.graaf@usdoj.gov
Assistant U.S. Attorney **William B. Darrow** . . . . (802) 951-6725
E-mail: bill.darrow@usdoj.gov
Assistant U.S. Attorney **Timothy C. Doherty** . . . . (802) 951-6725
E-mail: timothy.c.doherty@usdoj.gov
Education: Yale 2003 JD
Assistant U.S. Attorney **Kevin J. Doyle** . . . . (802) 951-6725
E-mail: kevin.doyle@usdoj.gov
Assistant U.S. Attorney **Michael P. Drescher** . . . . (802) 951-6725
E-mail: michael.drescher@usdoj.gov
Assistant U.S. Attorney **Wendy L. Fuller** . . . . (802) 951-6725
E-mail: wendy.fuller@usdoj.gov
Assistant U.S. Attorney **Barbara A. Masterson** . . . . (802) 951-6725
E-mail: barbara.masterson@usdoj.gov
Assistant U.S. Attorney **Jonathan Ophardt** . . . . (802) 951-6725
E-mail: jonathan.ophardt@usdoj.gov
Education: Duke 2010 JD
Assistant U.S. Attorney **Joseph R. Perella** . . . . (802) 951-6725
E-mail: joseph.perella@usdoj.gov
Assistant U.S. Attorney **Heather E. Ross** . . . . (802) 951-6725
E-mail: heather.ross@usdoj.gov
Assistant U.S. Attorney **Gregory Waples** . . . . (802) 951-6725
E-mail: gregory.waples@usdoj.gov
Education: Yale 1971 BA
Assistant U.S. Attorney **(Vacant)** . . . . (802) 951-6725

Rutland (VT) Office

151 West Street, Room 304, Rutland, VT 05701
P.O. Box 10, Rutland, VT 05701
Tel: (802) 773-0231 Fax: (802) 773-0214

Assistant U.S. Attorney **(Vacant)** . . . . (802) 951-6725

Virgin Islands District

Ron DeLugo Federal Building and U.S. Courthouse, 5500 Veterans Drive,
Room 260, St. Thomas, VI 00802-6424
Tel: (340) 774-5757 Fax: (340) 776-3474
Internet: www.usdoj.gov/usao/vi

★ U.S. Attorney **Ronald W. Sharpe** . . . . (340) 773-3920
E-mail: ronald.sharpe@usdoj.gov
Education: Tulane 1987 BS; Stanford 1991 JD
Secretary to the U.S. Attorney **(Vacant)** . . . . (340) 773-3920
Administrative Officer **Steve Maged** . . . . (340) 774-5757
E-mail: steve.maged@usdoj.gov
First Assistant U.S. Attorney **(Vacant)** . . . . (340) 774-5757
Special Litigation Counsel **Kim L. Chisholm** . . . . (340) 774-5757
E-mail: kim.chisholm@usdoj.gov
Budget Officer **(Vacant)** . . . . (340) 774-5757
Law Enforcement Coordinator Specialist
James Latham . . . . (340) 774-5757
E-mail: james.latham@usdoj.gov
Victim-Witness Specialist **Antoinette M. James** . . . . (340) 773-3920
E-mail: antoinette.james@usdoj.gov

Civil Division

Civil Chief **Joycelyn Hewlett** . . . . (340) 774-5757
E-mail: joycelyn.hewlett@usdoj.gov

★ Presidential Appointment Requiring Senate Confirmation ☆ Presidential Appointment ☐ Schedule C Appointment ◇ Career Senior Foreign Service Appointment
● Career Senior Executive Service (SES) Appointment ○ Non-Career Senior Executive Service (SES) Appointment ■ Postal Career Executive Service

Civil Division *continued*

Assistant U.S. Attorney **Jason Cohen** . . . . (340) 774-5757
E-mail: jason.cohen@usdoj.gov
Assistant U.S. Attorney **Noah Sacks** . . . . (340) 774-5757
Education: Pennsylvania 2001 BA; San Diego 2007 JD

Criminal Division

Chief **Christian Fisanick** . . . . (340) 774-5757
Organized Crime Drug Enforcement Task Force
Assistant U.S. Attorney **(Vacant)** . . . . (340) 774-5757
Assistant U.S. Attorney **Kim L. Chisholm** . . . . (340) 774-5757
E-mail: kim.chisholm@usdoj.gov
Assistant U.S. Attorney **Nelson L. Jones** . . . . (340) 774-5757
E-mail: nelson.jones@usdoj.gov
Assistant U.S. Attorney **Everard Potter** . . . . (340) 774-5757
E-mail: everard.potter@usdoj.gov
Assistant U.S. Attorney **Sigrid M. Tejo-Sprottle** . . . . (340) 774-5757
Assistant U.S. Attorney **David White** . . . . (340) 774-5757

Saint Croix (VI) Office

1108 King Street, Suite 201, Christiansted, VI 00820-4951
Tel: (340) 773-3920 Fax: (340) 773-1407

Senior Litigation Counsel **Kim L. Chisholm** . . . . (340) 773-3920
Branch Administrative Officer **Ingrid Richardson** . . . . (340) 773-3920
E-mail: ingrid.richardson@usdoj.gov

Civil Division

Assistant U.S. Attorney **Romi Badaway** . . . . (340) 773-3920
E-mail: romi.badaway@usdoj.gov
Assistant U.S. Attorney **Christian Stringer** . . . . (340) 773-3920
E-mail: christian.stringer@usdoj.gov
Assistant U.S. Attorney **Angela Tyson-Floyd** . . . . (340) 773-3920

Criminal Division

Deputy Chief **Alphonso Andrews, Jr.** . . . . (340) 773-3920
E-mail: alphonso.andrews@usdoj.gov
Assistant U.S. Attorney **Rhonda Williams-Henry** . . . . (340) 773-3920

Virginia - Eastern District

2100 Jamieson Avenue, Alexandria, VA 22314-5794
Tel: (703) 299-3700 Fax: (703) 299-3983
Internet: www.usdoj.gov/usao/vae

★ U.S. Attorney (Acting) **Dana James Boente** . . . . (703) 299-3700
Note: On October 8, 2015 President Obama nominted Dana Boente to be U.S. Attorney. Mr. Boente is currently acting in the position.
E-mail: dana.boente@usdoj.gov
Education: Saint Louis U JD
Secretary to the U.S. Attorney **Fay Brundage** . . . . (703) 299-3700
E-mail: fay.brundage@usdoj.gov
First Assistant U.S. Attorney **Dana James Boente** . . . . (703) 299-3700
E-mail: dana.boente@usdoj.gov
Education: Saint Louis U JD
Administrative Officer **Arline Gause** . . . . (703) 299-3700
E-mail: arline.gause@usdoj.gov
Public Information Officer
Zachary "Zach" Terwilliger . . . . (703) 842-4050
Note: On detail to the Senate Judiciary Committee.
E-mail: zachary.terwilliger@usdoj.gov
Systems Manager **Katy Law** . . . . (703) 299-3700
E-mail: katy.law@usdoj.gov
Victim-Witness Coordinator **Karen M. Spinks** . . . . (703) 299-3700

Civil Division

Chief **Lauren A. Wetzler** . . . . (703) 299-3700
E-mail: lauren.wetzler@usdoj.gov
Education: Harvard 2000 BA; Yale 2004 JD
Deputy Chief **R. Joseph Sher** . . . . (703) 299-3700
Education: NYU BA, MA; Michigan State JD

Criminal Division

Chief **Robert W. "Bob" Wiechering** . . . . (804) 819-5400
Education: Ohio State JD
Deputy Chief and Assistant U.S. Attorney **Michael Dry** . . . (804) 819-5400
Education: William & Mary JD; Nebraska MBA
Chief, Appellate Division **(Vacant)** . . . . (703) 299-3700
Chief, Financial Crime and Public Corruption **(Vacant)** . . . (703) 299-3700
Chief, Major Crimes **Morris Parker** . . . . (703) 299-3700
E-mail: morris.parker@usdoj.gov
Chief, Major Frauds **(Vacant)** . . . . (703) 299-3700
Chief, Narcotics Unit **Morris Parker** . . . . (703) 299-3700
E-mail: morris.parker@usdoj.gov
Chief, National Security **Daniel "Danny" Grooms** . . . . . . (703) 299-3700
E-mail: daniel.grooms@usdoj.gov
Education: Harvard 2002 JD
Chief, Organized Crime and Drug Enforcement Task Force **(Vacant)** . . . . (757) 591-4000
Chief, Terrorism Unit **Daniel "Danny" Grooms** . . . . (703) 299-3700
E-mail: daniel.grooms@usdoj.gov
Education: Harvard 2002 JD

Newport News (VA) Office

Newport News (VA) Office, 721 Lakefront Commons, Suite 300, Newport News, VA 23606
Tel: (757) 591-4000 Fax: (757) 591-0866

Managing Assistant United States Attorney
Howard Zlotnick . . . . (757) 591-4000
E-mail: howard.zlotnick@usdoj.gov

Norfolk (VA) Office

101 West Main Street, Suite 8000, Norfolk, VA 23510
Tel: (757) 441-6331 Fax: (757) 441-6689

Managing Assistant U.S. Attorney
Robert J. Seidel, Jr. . . . . (757) 441-6331

Richmond (VA) Office

600 East Main Street, Suite 1800, Richmond, VA 23219
Tel: (804) 819-5400 Fax: (804) 771-2316

Managing Assistant U.S. Attorney **Stephen W. Miller** . . . (804) 819-5400
E-mail: stephen.miller@usdoj.gov

Virginia - Western District

BB&T Building, 310 First Street, SW, Room 906, Roanoke, VA 24011
P.O. Box 1709, Roanoke, VA 24008-1709
Tel: (540) 857-2250 Fax: (540) 857-2614
Internet: www.usdoj.gov/usao/vaw

★ U.S. Attorney (Acting) **Anthony P. Giorno** . . . . (540) 857-2878
E-mail: anthony.giorno@usdoj.gov
★ U.S. Attorney-Designate **John P. Fishwick, Jr.** . . . . (540) 857-2250
Education: Harvard 1979 BA; Washington and Lee 1983 JD
Secretary to the U.S. Attorney **Jo Brooks** . . . . (540) 857-2977
E-mail: jo.brooks@usdoj.gov Fax: (540) 857-2179
First Assistant U.S. Attorney (Acting)
Stephen "Steve" Pfleger . . . . (540) 857-2250
E-mail: stephen.pfleger@usdoj.gov
Education: Princeton 1983; Cornell 1986 JD
Administrative Officer **Jason Austin** . . . . (540) 857-2929
E-mail: jason.austin@usdoj.gov
Community Outreach Coordinator **Erin Kulpa** . . . . (434) 293-4283
255 West Main Street, Charlottesville, VA 22901
E-mail: erin.kulpa@usdoj.gov
Law Enforcement Committee Coordinator
Isaac "Zac" Van Patten . . . . (540) 857-2959
E-mail: isaac.vanpatten@usdoj.gov
Victim-Witness Coordinator **Al Smith** . . . . (540) 857-2957
E-mail: albert.smith@usdoj.gov
Webmaster **Deborah J. "Debbie" Wood** . . . . (540) 857-2760
E-mail: debbie.wood@usdoj.gov

(continued on next page)

Virginia - Western District *continued*

Personnel Specialist **Jason Austin** .... (540) 857-2929
E-mail: jason.austin@usdoj.gov Fax: (540) 857-2179

Asset Forfeiture Unit
Tel: (540) 857-2250

Assistant U.S. Attorney **Kartic Padmanabhan** .... (540) 857-2250
E-mail: kartic.padmanabhan@usdoj.gov

Civil Division
Tel: (540) 857-2250 Fax: (540) 857-2283

Chief **Rick A. Mountcastle** .... (540) 857-2254
E-mail: rick.mountcastle@usdoj.gov
Education: Marquette 1977 BS; George Washington 1980 JD

Assistant U.S. Attorney **Thomas L. Eckert** .... (540) 857-2761
E-mail: thomas.eckert@usdoj.gov
Education: Pennsylvania 1972 JD

Assistant U.S. Attorney **Joseph W. H. Mott** .... (540) 857-2256
E-mail: joseph.mott@usdoj.gov
Education: George Mason 1974 BSBA; Richmond 1982 JD

Assistant U.S. Attorney **Sara B. Winn** .... (540) 857-2984
E-mail: sara.winn@usdoj.gov
Education: Minnesota 1988 BS; Hamline 1993 JD

Criminal Division
Tel: (540) 857-2250

Chief **Stephen "Steve" Pfleger** .... (540) 857-2250
E-mail: stephen.pfleger@usdoj.gov
Education: Princeton 1983; Cornell 1986 JD

Deputy Chief **Craig J. Jacobsen** .... (540) 857-2252
Education: UC Berkeley 1984 BA; Santa Clara U 1988 JD

Senior Litigation Counsel **Donald R. Wolthuis** .... (540) 857-2762
E-mail: donald.wolthuis@usdoj.gov
Education: Mary Washington Col 1977 BA; William & Mary 1980 JD

Assistant U.S. Attorney **R. Andrew Bassford** .... (540) 857-2799
E-mail: andrew.bassford@usdoj.gov
Education: Georgetown 1986 BSFS; Virginia 1998 JD

Assistant U.S. Attorney **Daniel "Dan" Bubar** .... (540) 857-2880
E-mail: daniel.bubar@usdoj.gov

Assistant U.S. Attorney **Charlene Day** .... (540) 278-1485
E-mail: charlene.day@usdoj.gov Fax: (540) 857-2179
Education: Virginia BA; Indiana JD

Assistant U.S. Attorney **C. Patrick Hogeboom III** .... (540) 857-2217
E-mail: pat.hogeboom@usdoj.gov Fax: (540) 857-2179
Education: New Mexico State 1971 BS; Gonzaga 1986 JD

Assistant U.S. Attorney **Ashley Neese** .... (540) 857-2938
Education: Emory & Henry 2004 BA; Ohio Northern 2007 JD

Assistant U.S. Attorney **Laura Rottenborn** .... (540) 857-2250
E-mail: laura.rottenborn@usdoj.gov

Assistant U.S. Attorney **Jennie L. M. Waering** .... (540) 857-2257
E-mail: jennie.waering@usdoj.gov
Education: Lynchburg 1976; Richmond 1981 JD

Abingdon (VA) Office

310 Cummings Street, Suite A, Abingdon, VA 24210
Tel: (276) 628-4161 Fax: (276) 628-7399

Managing Assistant U. S. Attorney
S. Randall "Randy" Ramseyer .... (276) 628-4161
E-mail: randy.ramseyer@usdoj.gov
Education: Wilmington Col (OH) 1986 BA; Vanderbilt 1990 JD

Assistant U.S. Attorney **Jennifer Bockhorst** .... (276) 628-4161
E-mail: jennifer.bockhorst@usdoj.gov
Education: Delaware 1993 BA; New Mexico 1996 MA; Stanford 2001 JD

Assistant U.S. Attorney **Zachary T. Lee** .... (276) 628-4161
E-mail: zachary.lee@usdoj.gov
Education: Washington and Lee 1998 BA; Wyoming 2001 JD

Charlottesville (VA) Office

255 West Main Street, Room 130, Charlottesville, VA 22902
Tel: (434) 293-4283 Fax: (434) 293-4910

Managing Assistant U.S. Attorney
Ronald "Ron" Huber .... (434) 293-4283
E-mail: ron.huber@usdoj.gov
Education: Michigan State 1984 BA; George Mason 1989 JD

Assistant U.S. Attorney **Nancy S. Healey** .... (434) 293-4283
E-mail: nancy.healey@usdoj.gov
Education: Northwestern BA; George Washington 1986 JD

Assistant U.S. Attorney **Jean B. Hudson** .... (434) 293-4283
E-mail: jean.hudson@usdoj.gov
Education: North Carolina Greensboro 1978 BM; Washington and Lee 1985 JD

Assistant U.S. Attorney **Christopher Kavanaugh** .... (434) 293-4283
E-mail: christopher.kavanaugh@usdoj.gov

Assistant U.S. Attorney **Erin Kulpa** .... (434) 293-4283
E-mail: erin.kulpa@usdoj.gov

Harrisonburg (VA) Office

116 North Main Street, Room 130, Harrisonburg, VA 22802
Tel: (540) 432-6636 Fax: (540) 433-9296

Assistant U.S. Attorney **Grayson Hoffman** .... (540) 432-6636
E-mail: grayson.hoffman@usdoj.gov

Assistant U.S. Attorney **Drew Smith** .... (540) 432-6636

Assistant U.S. Attorney **Elizabeth Wright** .... (540) 432-6636
E-mail: elizabeth.wright@usdoj.gov

Louisiana - Western District

300 Fannin Street, Suite 3201, Shreveport, LA 71101-3068
Tel: (318) 676-3600 TTY: (318) 676-3680
Fax: (318) 676-3641 Fax: (318) 676-3654
Internet: www.usdoj.gov/usao/law

★ U.S. Attorney **Stephanie A. Finley** .... (337) 262-6618
E-mail: stephanie.finley@usdoj.gov Fax: (337) 262-6680
Education: Grambling State 1988; Southern U Law 1991 JD

Counsel to the U.S. Attorney **(Vacant)** .... (318) 676-3600

Legal Assistant to the U.S. Attorney
Mona Hardwick .... (337) 262-6600

First Assistant U.S. Attorney **Alexander C. Van Hook** ... (318) 676-3600

Legal Assistant **Lisa Langley** .... (318) 676-3600
E-mail: lisa.langley@usdoj.gov

Administrative Division

Administrative Officer **C. Vincent Mangum** .... (318) 676-3600

Budget Officer **Samuel Glass** .... (318) 676-3600

Management Analyst **(Vacant)** .... (318) 676-3600

Systems Manager **Victor Sheppard** .... (318) 676-3600

Administrative Specialist **Dee A. Breedlove** .... (318) 676-3600
E-mail: dee.breedlove@usdoj.gov

Human Resources Specialist **Vicky Willmon** .... (318) 676-3600

Litigation Support Specialist **Karen B. Levo** .... (318) 676-3600

Civil Division

Chief **Katherine W. Vincent** .... (337) 262-6618
E-mail: katherine.vincent@usdoj.gov

Assistant U.S. Attorney **Monique Hudson** .... (318) 676-3600
E-mail: monique.hudson@usdoj.gov

Assistant U.S. Attorney **Joseph Landreneau** .... (318) 676-3600
E-mail: joseph.landreneau@usdoj.gov

Assistant U.S. Attorney **Cristina Walker** .... (318) 676-3600

Criminal Division

Chief **Mary J. Mudrick** .... (318) 676-3600
E-mail: mary.mudrick@usdoj.gov

Deputy Chief **(Vacant)** .... (318) 676-3600

Lead OCDETF Attorney
James G. "Jim" Cowles, Jr. .... (318) 676-3600
E-mail: james.cowles@usdoj.gov

Criminal Division *continued*

Assistant U.S. Attorney OCDETF **Allison Bushnell** . . . . . . (318) 676-3600
E-mail: allison.bushnell@usdoj.gov
Assistant U.S. Attorney **Brandon B. Brown** . . . . (318) 676-3600
E-mail: brandon.brown2@usdoj.gov
Assistant U.S. Attorney **Earl M. Campbell** . . . . (318) 676-3600
E-mail: earl.campbell@usdoj.gov
Assistant U.S. Attorney **William J. Flanagan** . . . . (318) 676-3600
E-mail: william.flanagan@usdoj.gov
Assistant U.S. Attorney **C. Mignonne Griffing** . . . . (318) 676-3600
Assistant U.S. Attorney **Cynthia Jernigan** . . . . (318) 676-3600
Assistant U.S. Attorney **Mlchael O'Mara** . . . . (318) 676-3600
E-mail: michael.omara@usdoj.gov
Assistant U.S. Attorney **Seth Reeg** . . . . (318) 676-3600
E-mail: seth.reeg@usdoj.gov
Assistant U.S. Attorney **(Vacant)** . . . . (318) 676-3600
Senior Litigation Counsel **Joseph G. Jarzabek** . . . . (318) 676-3600
E-mail: joseph.jarzabek@usdoj.gov
Victim-Witness Coordinator **Vicki T. Chance** . . . . (318) 676-3600
E-mail: vicki.chance@usdoj.gov

Lafayette (LA) Office

800 Lafayette Street, Suite 2200, Lafayette, LA 70501
Tel: (337) 262-6618 TTY: (337) 262-6650
Fax: (337) 262-6682 Fax: (337) 262-6680 (Criminal)
Internet: www.usdoj.gov/usao/law

Administrative Services Specialist
Melanie Hutchinson . . . . (337) 262-6618
E-mail: melanie.hutchinson@usdoj.gov

Civil Division

Civil Chief **Katherine W. Vincent** . . . . (337) 262-6618
E-mail: katherine.vincent@usdoj.gov
Assistant U.S. Attorney **Jennifer B. Frederick** . . . . (337) 262-6618
Assistant U.S. Attorney **Karen J. King** . . . . (337) 262-6618
E-mail: karen.king@usdoj.gov
Assistant U.S. Attorney **Desiree Williams** . . . . (337) 262-6618
E-mail: desiree.williams@usdoj.gov
Assistant U.S. Attorney **(Vacant)** . . . . (337) 262-6618

Criminal Division

Chief **Richard A. Willis** . . . . (337) 262-6618
E-mail: richard.willis@usdoj.gov
Assistant U.S. Attorney **Robert Abendroth** . . . . (337) 262-6618
E-mail: robert.abendroth@usdoj.gov
Assistant U.S. Attorney **Jim Illa Bynog** . . . . (337) 262-6618
Assistant U.S. Attorney **Camille A. Domingue** . . . . (337) 262-6618
E-mail: camille.domingue@usdoj.gov
Assistant U.S. Attorney **David C. Joseph** . . . . (337) 262-6618
E-mail: david.c.joseph@usdoj.gov
Education: LSU 2003 JD
Assistant U.S. Attorney **Daniel McCoy** . . . . (337) 262-6618
Assistant U.S. Attorney **Joseph T. Mickel** . . . . (337) 262-6618
E-mail: joseph.mickel@usdoj.gov
Assistant U.S. Attorney **Robert Moore** . . . . (337) 262-6618
E-mail: robert.moore@usdoj.gov
Assistant U.S. Attorney **Namie Myers** . . . . (337) 262-6618
Assistant U.S. Attorney **Howard C. Parker** . . . . (337) 262-6618
E-mail: howard.parker@usdoj.gov
Assistant U.S. Attorney **Dominic Rossetti** . . . . (337) 262-6618
E-mail: dominic.rossetti@usdoj.gov
Assistant U.S. Attorney **Kelly P. Uebinger** . . . . (337) 262-6618
E-mail: kelly.uebinger@usdoj.gov
Assistant U.S. Attorney **John Luke Walker** . . . . (337) 262-6618
E-mail: john.walker@usdoj.gov

Washington - Eastern District

Federal Courthouse, 920 West Riverside Avenue,
Room 340, Spokane, WA 99201
P.O. Box 1494, Spokane, WA 99210-1494
Tel: (509) 353-2767 Fax: (509) 353-2766

★ U.S. Attorney **Michael C. "Mike" Ormsby** . . . . (509) 353-2767
Education: Gonzaga 1979 BA, 1981 JD
First Assistant U.S. Attorney **Joseph H. Harrington** . . . . . (509) 353-2767
E-mail: joseph.harrington@usdoj.gov
Administrative Officer **Heidi J. Krummel** . . . . (509) 353-2767
E-mail: heidi.krummel@usdoj.gov
Intelligence Research Specialist **(Vacant)** . . . . (509) 353-2767
Law Enforcement Coordinator **Steven R. Tomson** . . . . (509) 353-2767
E-mail: steven.tomson@usdoj.gov
Systems Manager **(Vacant)** . . . . (509) 353-2767
Victim-Witness Coordinator **Amy L. Mayther** . . . . (509) 353-2767
E-mail: amy.mayther@usdoj.gov
Investigator **Kathy S. Fagyas** . . . . (509) 353-2767
Investigator **(Vacant)** . . . . (509) 353-2767

Civil Division

Fax: (509) 353-2766

Chief **Pamela J. DeRusha** . . . . (509) 353-2767
E-mail: pamela.derusha@usdoj.gov
Financial Litigation Unit Assistant U.S. Attorney
(Vacant) . . . . (509) 353-2767
Assistant U.S. Attorney **Timothy M. Durkin** . . . . (509) 353-2767
Assistant U.S. Attorney **(Vacant)** . . . . (509) 353-2767
Assistant U.S. Attorney **(Vacant)** . . . . (509) 353-2767

Criminal Division

Chief **Aine Ahmed** . . . . (509) 353-2767
E-mail: aine.ahmed@usdoj.gov
Supervisory Assistant U.S. Attorney **Russell E. Smoot** . . . (509) 353-2767
Assistant U.S. Attorney **K. Jill Bolton** . . . . (509) 353-2767
Assistant U.S. Attorney **Pamela J. Byerly** . . . . (509) 353-2767
E-mail: pamela.byerly@usdoj.gov
Assistant U.S. Attorney **Matthew Duggan** . . . . (509) 353-2767
Assistant U.S. Attorney **James "Jim" Goeke** . . . . (509) 353-2767
E-mail: james.goeke@usdoj.gov
Assistant U.S. Attorney **Earl A. Hicks** . . . . (509) 353-2767
E-mail: earl.hicks@usdoj.gov
Assistant U.S. Attorney **George J.C. Jacobs** . . . . (509) 353-2767
Assistant U.S. Attorney **Jared C. Kimball** . . . . (509) 353-2767
Assistant U.S. Attorney **Stephanie J. Lister** . . . . (509) 353-2767
E-mail: stephanie.lister@usdoj.gov
Assistant U.S. Attorney **Timothy J. Ohms** . . . . (509) 353-2767
E-mail: timothy.ohms@usdoj.gov
Assistant U.S. Attorney **Tyler H.L. Tornabene** . . . . (509) 353-2767
Assistant U.S. Attorney **Stephanie A. Van Marter** . . . . . . (509) 353-2767
E-mail: stephanie.vanmarter@usdoj.gov
Assistant U.S. Attorney **Rudy J. Verschoor** . . . . (509) 353-2767
Assistant U.S. Attorney **(Vacant)** . . . . (509) 353-2767

Yakima (WA) Office

402 East Yakima Avenue, Suite 210, Box 4065, Yakima, WA 98901-2760
Tel: (509) 454-4425 Fax: (509) 454-4435

Supervisory Assistant U.S. Attorney
Shawn N. Anderson . . . . (509) 454-4425
E-mail: shawn.anderson@usdoj.gov
Assistant U.S. Attorney **Mary Dimke** . . . . (509) 454-4425
Assistant U.S. Attorney **Ian Garriques** . . . . (509) 454-4425
Assistant U.S. Attorney **Alison L. Gregoire** . . . . (509) 454-4425
Assistant U.S. Attorney **Thomas J. Hanlon** . . . . (509) 454-4425
Assistant U.S. Attorney **Ben Seal** . . . . (509) 454-4425
Assistant U.S. Attorney **(Vacant)** . . . . (509) 454-4425
Victim-Witness Specialist **Adela Garza** . . . . (509) 454-4425

★ Presidential Appointment Requiring Senate Confirmation ☆ Presidential Appointment ☐ Schedule C Appointment ◇ Career Senior Foreign Service Appointment
● Career Senior Executive Service (SES) Appointment ○ Non-Career Senior Executive Service (SES) Appointment ■ Postal Career Executive Service

Washington - Western District

700 Stewart Street, Suite 5220, Seattle, WA 98101
Tel: (206) 553-7970 Fax: (206) 553-0882
Internet: www.usdoj.gov/usao/waw

★ U.S. Attorney (Interim) **Annette L. Hayes** ....(206) 553-7970
Executive Specialist to the U.S. Attorney
Colleen O'Reilly Bernier ....(206) 553-7970
E-mail: colleen.bernier@usdoj.gov
First Assistant U.S. Attorney
Helen J. "Micki" Brunner ....(206) 553-7970
E-mail: micki.brunner@usdoj.gov
Executive Assistant U.S. Attorney **(Vacant)** ....(206) 553-7970
Law Enforcement Coordinator **Sean Tepfer** ....(206) 553-7970
Victim-Witness Coordinator **Deborah "Debbie" Lee** .....(206) 553-7970
Administrative Officer **Michael Marzano** ....(206) 553-7970
Human Resources Officer **Gerri Cerna** ....(206) 553-7970
E-mail: gerri.cerna@usdoj.gov
Systems Manager **Frank Ohira** ....(206) 553-7970
E-mail: frank.ohira@usdoj.gov

Civil Division

Chief **Kerry Keefe** ....(206) 553-7970
E-mail: kerry.keefe@usdoj.gov
Deputy Chief **Harold Malkin** ....(206) 553-7970
E-mail: harold.malkin@usdoj.gov
Assistant U.S. Attorney **Jessica Andrade** ....(206) 553-7970
Assistant U.S. Attorney **Lisca Borichewski** ....(206) 553-7970
E-mail: lisca.borichewski@usdoj.gov
Assistant U.S. Attorney **Priscilla Chan** ....(206) 553-7970
E-mail: priscilla.chan@usdoj.gov
Assistant U.S. Attorney **Mike Diaz** ....(206) 553-7970
E-mail: mike.diaz@usdoj.gov
Assistant U.S. Attorney **David East** ....(206) 553-7970
E-mail: david.east@usdoj.gov
Assistant U.S. Attorney **Christina Fogg** ....(206) 553-7970
Assistant U.S. Attorney **Kyle A. Forsyth** ....(206) 553-7970
Education: Whitworth 1999 BA; Notre Dame 2003 JD
Assistant U.S. Attorney **Kristin Johnson** ....(206) 553-7970
Assistant U.S. Attorney **Brian C. Kipnis** ....(206) 553-7970
E-mail: brian.kipnis@usdoj.gov
Assistant U.S. Attorney **Jamie Mittet** ....(206) 553-7970
E-mail: jamie.mittet@usdoj.gov
Assistant U.S. Attorney **Sarah Morehead** ....(206) 553-7970
Education: Hamilton 1995 BA; Georgetown 1999 JD
Assistant U.S. Attorney **Kayla Stahman** ....(206) 553-7970
E-mail: kayla.stahman@usdoj.gov
Assistant U.S. Attorney **Jamal Whitehead** ....(206) 553-7970

Criminal Division

Chief **Tessa Gorman** ....(206) 553-7970
E-mail: tessa.gorman@usdoj.gov
Education: Yale 1993 BA

Appeals Section

Supervisor **Helen J. "Micki" Brunner** ....(206) 553-7970
Assistant U.S. Attorney **Teal Miller** ....(206) 553-7970
Assistant U.S. Attorney **Michael Morgan** ....(206) 553-7970

Asset Forfeiture Section

Assistant U.S. Attorney **Richard E. "Rich" Cohen** ....(206) 553-7970
Assistant U.S. Attorney **Matthew H. Thomas** ....(206) 553-7970
Assistant U.S. Attorney **(Vacant)** ....(206) 553-7970

Complex Crimes Section

Supervisor **Andrew C. Friedman** ....(206) 553-7970
E-mail: andrew.friedman@usdoj.gov
Education: Yale 1986 BA
Assistant U.S. Attorney **Norman Barbosa** ....(206) 553-7970
E-mail: norman.barbosa@usdoj.gov
Assistant U.S. Attorney **Matthew "Matt" Diggs** ....(206) 553-7970
E-mail: matthew.diggs@usdoj.gov

Complex Crimes Section *continued*

Assistant U.S. Attorney **Katheryn Kim Frierson** ....(206) 553-7970
Assistant U.S. Attorney **Mike Lang** ....(206) 553-7970
E-mail: mike.lang@usdoj.gov
Assistant U.S. Attorney **Seth Wilkinson** ....(206) 553-7970
E-mail: seth.wilkinson@usdoj.gov
Education: Michigan 2001 JD
Assistant U.S. Attorney **(Vacant)** ....(206) 553-7970
Assistant U.S. Attorney **(Vacant)** ....(206) 553-7970
Assistant U.S. Attorney **(Vacant)** ....(206) 553-7970

Criminal Enterprises Section

Supervisor **Sarah Vogel** ....(206) 553-7970
E-mail: sarah.vogel@usdoj.gov
Assistant U.S. Attorney **Jeffrey Backhus** ....(206) 553-7970
Assistant U.S. Attorney **Matt Hampton** ....(206) 553-7970
Education: Washington U (MO) JD
Assistant U.S. Attorney **Karyn Johnson** ....(206) 553-7970
Assistant U.S. Attorney **Vincent Lombardi** ....(206) 553-7970
E-mail: vince.lombardi@usdoj.gov
Assistant U.S. Attorney **Mark Parrent** ....(206) 553-7970
Assistant U.S. Attorney **(Vacant)** ....(206) 553-7970
Special Assistant U.S. Attorney **Steven Hobbs** ....(206) 553-7970

General Crimes I

Supervisor **Mike Dion** ....(206) 553-7970
Assistant U.S. Attorney **Justin W. Arnold** ....(206) 553-7970
E-mail: justin.arnold@usdoj.gov
Assistant U.S. Attorney **Becca Cohen** ....(206) 553-7970
Assistant U.S. Attorney **Steven Masada** ....(206) 553-7970
E-mail: steven.masada@usdoj.gov
Assistant U.S. Attorney **Donald M. "Don" Reno, Jr.** .....(206) 553-7970
E-mail: don.reno@usdoj.gov
Assistant U.S. Attorney **Barbara J. "Barb" Sievers** .....(206) 553-7970
E-mail: barbara.sievers@usdoj.gov
Assistant U.S. Attorney **Kate S. Vaughan** ....(206) 553-7970
E-mail: kate.vaughan@usdoj.gov
Education: U Washington 2004 JD
Assistant U.S. Attorney **(Vacant)** ....(206) 553-7970
Assistant U.S. Attorney **(Vacant)** ....(206) 553-7970

General Crimes II

Supervisor **Jim Oesterle** ....(206) 553-7970
E-mail: jim.oesterle@usdoj.gov
Assistant U.S. Attorney **Erin Becker** ....(206) 553-7970
Assistant U.S. Attorney **Francis Franze-Nakamura** ......(206) 553-7970
Assistant U.S. Attorney **Nicholas Manheim** ....(206) 553-7970
Assistant U.S. Attorney **Jerrod Patterson** ....(206) 553-7970
Assistant U.S. Attorney **(Vacant)** ....(206) 553-7970

Terrorism and Violent Crimes Section

Supervisor **Todd Greenberg** ....(206) 553-7970
Deputy Supervisor **Bruce Miyake** ....(206) 553-7970
E-mail: bruce.miyake@usdoj.gov
Assistant U.S. Attorney **Kate Crisham** ....(206) 553-7970
Assistant U.S. Attorney **Susan Roe** ....(206) 553-7970
E-mail: susan.roe@usdoj.gov
Assistant U.S. Attorney **J. Tate London** ....(206) 553-7970
E-mail: tate.london@usdoj.gov
Assistant U.S. Attorney **Ye Ting Woo** ....(206) 553-7970
Assistant U.S. Attorney **Tom Woods** ....(206) 553-7970

Tacoma (WA) Office

Tacoma Financial Center, 1201 Pacific Avenue,
Suite 700, Tacoma, WA 98402
Tel: (253) 428-3810

Supervisor **David Reese Jennings** ....(253) 428-3810
E-mail: david.r.jennings@usdoj.gov

★ Presidential Appointment Requiring Senate Confirmation ☆ Presidential Appointment ☐ Schedule C Appointment ◇ Career Senior Foreign Service Appointment
● Career Senior Executive Service (SES) Appointment ○ Non-Career Senior Executive Service (SES) Appointment ■ Postal Career Executive Service

Tacoma (WA) Office *continued*

Civil Division Assistant U.S. Attorney [District Election Official] **Arlen R. Storm** .... (253) 428-3800
E-mail: arlen.storm@usdoj.gov
Special Criminal Division Assistant U.S. Attorney **(Vacant)** .... (206) 553-7970
Criminal Division Assistant U.S. Attorney **Gregory A. Gruber** .... (253) 428-3800
Criminal Division Assistant U.S. Attorney **Patricia D. Gugin** .... (253) 428-3800
Criminal Division Assistant U.S. Attorney **Matthew H. Thomas** .... (253) 428-3800
Criminal Division Assistant U.S. Attorney **Brian Werner** .... (206) 553-7970
E-mail: brian.werner@usdoj.gov
Criminal Division Assistant U.S. Attorney **Amy Jaquette** .... (206) 553-7970
Assistant U.S. Attorney **Marci Ellsworth** .... (206) 553-7970
Assistant U.S. Attorney **Grady Leupold** .... (206) 553-7970

West Virginia - Northern District

Federal Building, 1125 Chapline Street,
Suite 3000, Wheeling, WV 26003
Tel: (304) 234-0100 Fax: (304) 234-0110 (Main)
Fax: (304) 234-0112 (Civil) Fax: (304) 234-0111 (Criminal)

★ U.S. Attorney **William J. Ihlenfeld II** .... (304) 234-0100
Education: Ohio 1994 BSJ; West Virginia 1997 JD
Counsel to the U.S. Attorney **John C. Parr** .... (304) 234-0100
E-mail: john.parr@usdoj.gov
Executive Assistant to the U.S. Attorney **(Vacant)** ...... (304) 234-0100
First Assistant U.S. Attorney **Betsy Steinfeld Jividen** ... (304) 234-0100
Administrative Officer **Fawn E. Thomas** .... (304) 234-7709
E-mail: fawn.thomas@usdoj.gov
Budget Officer **M. Catherine Northcraft** .... (304) 234-0100
E-mail: cathy.northcraft@usdoj.gov
Public Affairs Specialist **Tara Tighe** .... (304) 234-0100
E-mail: tara.tighe@usdoj.gov
Systems Manager **Michael G. Malek** .... (304) 234-0100
E-mail: michael.malek@usdoj.gov
Support Services Specialist **Sybil D. Ott** .... (304) 234-0100
E-mail: sybil.ott@usdoj.gov
Administrative Technician/Receptionist **Greta W. Anderson-Williams** .... (304) 234-0100
E-mail: greta.anderson@usdoj.gov
Law Enforcement Coordinator **Gary M. Gaus** .... (304) 234-0100
E-mail: gary.gaus@usdoj.gov
FSA Records Manager **(Vacant)** .... (304) 234-0100
FSA Data Analyst **Sharon K. Perry** .... (304) 234-0100
E-mail: sharon.perry2@usdoj.gov

Civil Division
Tel: (304) 234-0100 Fax: (304) 234-0112

Chief **Helen Campbell Altmeyer** .... (304) 234-0100
E-mail: helen.altmeyer@usdoj.gov
Assistant U.S. Attorney **Alan G. McGonigal** .... (304) 234-0100
E-mail: alan.mcgonigal@usdoj.gov
Assistant U.S. Attorney **Jarod J. Douglas** .... (304) 234-0100
E-mail: jarod.j.douglas@usdoj.gov
Paralegal Specialist **Susan M. Collins** .... (304) 234-0100
E-mail: susan.collins@usdoj.gov
Lead Legal Assistant **Janet K. Evick** .... (304) 234-0100
E-mail: janet.evick@usdoj.gov
Legal Assistant **Stephanie H. Roten** .... (304) 234-0100
E-mail: stephanie.roten@usdoj.gov
Health Care Fraud Auditor **Donald W. Shelek** .... (304) 234-0100
E-mail: donald.shelek@usdoj.gov
FSA Legal Clerk **Janet L. Corey** .... (304) 234-0100
E-mail: janet.corey@usdoj.gov
FSA Paralegal IV **Joy L. Sarris** .... (304) 234-0100
E-mail: joy.sarris@usdoj.gov

Criminal Division
Tel: (304) 234-0100 Fax: (304) 234-0111

Chief **Randolph John "Randy" Bernard** .... (304) 234-0100
E-mail: randy.bernard@usdoj.gov
Deputy Chief **Paul T. Camilletti** .... (304) 234-0100
E-mail: paul.camilletti@usdoj.gov
Financial Crimes Unit Coordinatorl **John C. Parr** .... (304) 234-0100
E-mail: john.parr@usdoj.gov
Assistant U.S. Attorney **Robert H. McWilliams, Jr.** ...... (304) 234-0100
E-mail: rob.mcwilliams@usdoj.gov
Assistant U.S. Attorney **David J. Perri** .... (304) 234-0100
E-mail: david.perri@usdoj.gov
Assistant U.S. Attorney **Michael D. Stein** .... (304) 234-0100
E-mail: michael.stein@usdoj.gov
Assistant U.S. Attorney **Stephen L. Vogrin** .... (304) 234-0100
E-mail: stephen.vogrin@usdoj.gov
Victim Witness Coordinator **Christina J. Frizzell** .... (304) 234-0100
E-mail: chris.frizzell@usdoj.gov
Supervisory Paralegal Specialist **(Vacant)** .... (304) 234-0100
Legal Assistant **Rebecca R. Moore** .... (304) 234-0100
E-mail: becky.moore@usdoj.gov
Legal Assistant **(Vacant)** .... (304) 234-0100
FSA Senior Law Clerk **L. Danae DeMasi** .... (304) 234-0100
E-mail: danae.demasi@usdoj.gov
FSA Clerk **Lori A. Farmer** .... (304) 234-0100
E-mail: lori.farmer@usdoj.gov
FSA Data Analyst **Joyce A. Sizemore** .... (304) 234-0100
E-mail: joyce.sizemore@usdoj.gov

Clarksburg (WV) Office

Federal Center, 320 West Pike Street,
Suite 300, Clarksburg, WV 26301-2710
Tel: (304) 623-7030 Fax: (304) 623-7031

Assistant U.S. Attorney-in-Charge **Shawn Angus Morgan** .... (304) 623-7030
E-mail: shawn.morgan@usdoj.gov
Assistant U.S. Attorney **Andrew R. Cogar** .... (304) 623-7030
E-mail: andy.cogar@usdoj.gov
Assistant U.S. Attorney **Sarah Montoro** .... (304) 623-7030
E-mail: sarah.montoro@usdoj.gov
Assistant U.S. Attorney **Zelda E. Wesley** .... (304) 623-7030
E-mail: zelda.wesley@usdoj.gov
Assistant U.S. Attorney **(Vacant)** .... (304) 623-7030
Intelligence Specialist **Glenn M. Borrelli** .... (304) 623-7030
E-mail: glenn.borrelli@usdoj.gov
Legal Assistant **Laurel K. Jones** .... (304) 623-7030
E-mail: laurel.k.jones@usdoj.gov
Legal Assistant **Lisa Bishop** .... (304) 623-7030
Legal Assistant **Michelle E. Longerbeam** .... (304) 623-7030

Elkins (WV) Office

Federal Building, 300 Third Street, Suite 300, Elkins, WV 26241
P.O. Box 190, Elkins, WV 26241-0190
Tel: (304) 636-1739 Fax: (304) 636-1967

Assistant U.S. Attorney **Stephen D. Warner** .... (304) 636-1739
Financial Litigation Paralegal Specialist **Cheryl J. Given** .... (304) 636-1739
E-mail: cheryl.given@usdoj.gov
Financial Litigation Paralegal Specialist **(Vacant)** .... (304) 636-1739

Martinsburg (WV) Office

217 West King Street, Suite 400, Martinsburg, WV 25401
Tel: (304) 262-0590 Fax: (304) 262-0591

Assistant U.S. Attorney-in-Charge (Acting) **Paul T. Camilletti** .... (304) 262-0590
E-mail: paul.camilletti@usdoj.gov
Assistant U.S. Attorney **Shawn Adkins** .... (304) 262-0590
E-mail: shawn.adkins@usdoj.gov

(continued on next page)

★ Presidential Appointment Requiring Senate Confirmation ☆ Presidential Appointment ☐ Schedule C Appointment ◇ Career Senior Foreign Service Appointment
● Career Senior Executive Service (SES) Appointment ○ Non-Career Senior Executive Service (SES) Appointment ■ Postal Career Executive Service

Martinsburg (WV) Office *continued*

Assistant U.S. Attorney **Erin Reisenweber** .... (304) 262-0590
E-mail: erin.reisenweber@usdoj.gov
Education: Boston Col BA; Pittsburgh MLS; West Virginia 2003 JD
Legal Assistant **Leanna B. Murray** .... (304) 262-0590
E-mail: leanna.murray@usdoj.gov
Paralegal Specialist **Tracie L. Weaver** .... (304) 262-0590
E-mail: tracie.weaver@usdoj.gov

West Virginia - Southern District

300 Virginia Street East, Room 4000, Charleston, WV 25301
P.O. Box 1713, Charleston, WV 25326
Tel: (304) 345-2200 Fax: (304) 347-5104

★ U.S. Attorney **Robert Booth Goodwin II** .... (304) 345-2200
E-mail: booth.goodwin@usdoj.gov
Education: West Virginia 1993 BSE; Washington and Lee 1996 JD
Secretary to the U.S. Attorney **Robin Y. Justice** .... (304) 345-2200
E-mail: robin.justice@usdoj.gov
Administrative Officer **(Vacant)** .... (304) 345-2200
Systems Manager **Wayne Vaughn** .... (304) 345-2200
E-mail: wayne.vaughn@usdoj.gov

Civil Division

Civil Division Chief and Assistant U.S. Attorney
Stephen M. Horn .... (304) 345-2200
E-mail: steve.horn@usdoj.gov
Asset Forfeiture Unit Assistant U.S. Attorney **(Vacant)** ... (304) 345-2200
Assistant U.S. Attorney **Gary L. Call** .... (304) 345-2200
E-mail: gary.call@usdoj.gov
Assistant U.S. Attorney **John F. Gianola** .... (304) 345-2200
E-mail: john.gianola@usdoj.gov
Assistant U.S. Attorney **Jennifer M. Mankins** .... (304) 345-2200
E-mail: jennifer.mankins@usdoj.gov
Assistant U.S. Attorney **Fred B. Westfall, Jr.** .... (304) 345-2200
E-mail: fred.westfall@usdoj.gov

Criminal Division

First Assistant U.S. Attorney **Carol A. Casto** .... (304) 345-2200
E-mail: carol.casto@usdoj.gov
Special Crimes and Appellate Chief and Assistant U.S.
Attorney **Philip H. Wright** .... (304) 345-2200
E-mail: philip.wright@usdoj.gov
Violent Crime and Narcotics Chief and Assistant U.S.
Attorney **Steven I. Loew** .... (304) 345-2200
E-mail: steven.loew2@usdoj.gov
Assistant U.S. Attorney **Eric P. Bacaj** .... (304) 345-2200
E-mail: eric.bacaj@usdoj.gov
Assistant U.S. Attorney **Timothy D. Boggess** .... (304) 345-2200
E-mail: timothy.boggess@usdoj.gov
Assistant U.S. Attorney **C. Haley Bunn** .... (304) 345-2200
E-mail: haley.bunn@usdoj.gov
Assistant U.S. Attorney **W. Clinton Carte** .... (304) 345-2200
E-mail: clint.carte@usdoj.gov
Assistant U.S. Attorney **Eumi L. Choi** .... (304) 345-2200
E-mail: eumi.choi@usdoj.gov
Assistant U.S. Attorney **Monica D. Coleman** .... (304) 345-2200
E-mail: monica.coleman@usdoj.gov
Assistant U.S. Attorney **John J. Frail** .... (304) 345-2200
E-mail: john.frail@usdoj.gov
Assistant U.S. Attorney **Erik S. Goes** .... (304) 345-2200
E-mail: erik.goes@usdoj.gov
Assistant U.S. Attorney **Joshua C. "Josh" Hanks** .... (304) 345-2200
E-mail: josh.hanks@usdoj.gov
Assistant U.S. Attorney **Jennifer R. Herrald** .... (304) 345-2200
E-mail: jennifer.herrald@usdoj.gov
Assistant U.S. Attorney **Lisa G. Johnston** .... (304) 345-2200
E-mail: lisa.johnston@usdoj.gov
Assistant U.S. Attorney **Blaire L. Malkin** .... (304) 345-2200
E-mail: blaire.malkin@usdoj.gov
Assistant U.S. Attorney **Meredith G. Thomas** .... (304) 345-2200
E-mail: meredith.thomas@usdoj.gov

Criminal Division *continued*

Assistant U.S. Attorney **Gabriele Wohl** .... (304) 345-2200
E-mail: gabriele.wohl@usdoj.gov
Education: West Virginia 2009 JD
Counsel to United States Attorney and Assistant U.S.
Attorney **Steven R. Ruby** .... (304) 345-2200
E-mail: steven.ruby@usdoj.gov
Education: Duke 2000 BA; Washington and Lee 2006 JD
Senior Litigation Counsel **Larry R. Ellis** .... (304) 345-2200
E-mail: larry.ellis@usdoj.gov

Beckley (WV) Office

U.S. Courthouse and IRS Complex, 110 North Heber Street,
Room 257, Beckley, WV 25801
Tel: (304) 253-6722 Fax: (304) 253-9206

Assistant U.S. Attorney **Miller A. Bushong III** .... (304) 253-6722
E-mail: miller.bushong@usdoj.gov
Assistant U.S. Attorney **John L. File** .... (304) 253-6722
E-mail: john.file@usdoj.gov

Huntington (WV) Office

Sydney L. Christie Federal Building, 845 Fifth Avenue,
Room 209, Huntington, WV 25701
Tel: (304) 529-5799 Fax: (304) 529-5545

Assistant U.S. Attorney **Joseph F. Adams** .... (304) 529-5799
E-mail: joe.adams@usdoj.gov
Assistant U.S. Attorney **R. Gregory McVey** .... (304) 529-5799
E-mail: greg.mcvey@usdoj.gov

Wisconsin - Eastern District

Federal Courthouse, 517 East Wisconsin Avenue,
Room 530, Milwaukee, WI 53202
Tel: (414) 297-1700 Fax: (414) 297-1738
Internet: www.usdoj.gov/usao/wie

★ U.S. Attorney (Acting) **Gregory J. "Greg" Haanstad** ... (414) 297-1700
E-mail: greg.haanstad@usdoj.gov
Secretary to the U.S. Attorney **Nancy Zepnick** .... (414) 297-1700
E-mail: nancy.zepnick@usdoj.gov
First Assistant U.S. Attorney
Gregory J. "Greg" Haanstad .... (414) 297-1700
Secretary to the First Assistant U.S. Attorney
Nancy Zepnick .... (414) 297-1700
E-mail: nancy.zepnick@usdoj.gov
Administrative Officer **Robert Sperry** .... (414) 297-1700
Budget Officer **LaQuisha Schroeder** .... (414) 297-1700
Law Enforcement Committee Coordinator
Dean Puschnig .... (414) 297-1700
Victim-Witness Coordinator **Faith Coburn** .... (414) 297-1700
E-mail: faith.coburn@usdoj.gov
Personnel Officer **Denise M. Mondry** .... (414) 297-1700
Systems Manager **Christine Pinkowsky** .... (414) 297-1700

Civil Division

Chief **Susan M. Knepel** .... (414) 297-1700
E-mail: susan.knepel@usdoj.gov
Deputy Chief **Stacy Gerber Ward** .... (414) 297-1700
Assistant U.S. Attorney **Michael A. Carter** .... (414) 297-1700
E-mail: michael.a.carter@usdoj.gov
Assistant U.S. Attorney **Charles A. Guadagnino** .... (414) 297-1700
E-mail: charles.guadagnino@usdoj.gov
Assistant U.S. Attorney **Matthew D. Krueger** .... (414) 297-1700
Assistant U.S. Attorney **Christian R. Larsen** .... (414) 297-1700
Assistant U.S. Attorney **Brian Pawlak** .... (414) 297-1700
E-mail: brian.pawlak@usdoj.gov
Assistant U.S. Attorney **Lisa T. Warwick** .... (414) 297-1700
E-mail: lisa.warwick@usdoj.gov
Assistant U.S. Attorney **Lisa Yun** .... (414) 297-1700
E-mail: lisa.yun@usdoj.gov

★ Presidential Appointment Requiring Senate Confirmation ☆ Presidential Appointment ☐ Schedule C Appointment ◇ Career Senior Foreign Service Appointment
● Career Senior Executive Service (SES) Appointment ○ Non-Career Senior Executive Service (SES) Appointment ■ Postal Career Executive Service

Criminal Division

Chief **Richard Glen "Rick" Frohling** . . . . . . (414) 297-1700
E-mail: richard.frohling@usdoj.gov
Education: Yale 1993 BA

Deputy Chief/Financial Fraud **Kelly Watzka** . . . . . . (414) 297-1700

Deputy Chief/Lead Attorney, OCDETF **Erica O'Neil** . . . . . (414) 297-1700
E-mail: erica.oneil@usdoj.gov

Deputy Chief/National Security **(Vacant)** . . . . . . (414) 297-1700

Assistant U.S. Attorney/Senior Litigation Counsel **Mel S. Johnson** . . . . . . (414) 297-1700

Assistant U.S. Attorney/Senior Litigation Counsel **William J. Lipscomb** . . . . . . (414) 297-1700
E-mail: william.lipscomb@usdoj.gov

Assistant U.S. Attorney **Keith S. Alexander** . . . . . . (414) 297-1700
E-mail: keith.alexander@usdoj.gov
Education: Notre Dame 2003 JD

Assistant U.S. Attorney **Scott Campbell** . . . . . . (414) 297-1700
E-mail: scott.campbell@usdoj.gov

Assistant U.S. Attorney **Michael J. Chmelar** . . . . . . (414) 297-1700
E-mail: michael.chmelar@usdoj.gov

Assistant U.S. Attorney **Penelope L. Coblentz** . . . . . . (414) 297-1700
E-mail: penelope.coblentz@usdoj.gov

Assistant U.S. Attorney **Bridget Domaszek** . . . . . . (414) 297-1700

Assistant U.S. Attorney **Gordon P. Giampietro** . . . . . . (414) 297-1700

Assistant U.S. Attorney **Mario Gonzales** . . . . . . (414) 297-1700

Assistant U.S. Attorney **Gail J. Hoffman** . . . . . . (414) 297-1700
E-mail: gail.hoffman@usdoj.gov

Assistant U.S. Attorney **Margaret B. Honrath** . . . . . . (414) 297-1700

Assistant U.S. Attorney **Daniel R. Humble** . . . . . . (414) 297-1700

Assistant U.S. Attorney **Stephen A. Ingraham** . . . . . . (414) 297-1700
E-mail: stephen.ingraham@usdoj.gov

Assistant U.S. Attorney **Matthew L. Jacobs** . . . . . . (414) 297-1700

Assistant U.S. Attorney **Tracy Johnson** . . . . . . (414) 297-1700
E-mail: tracy.johnson@usdoj.gov

Assistant U.S. Attorney **Paul L. Kanter** . . . . . . (414) 297-1700
E-mail: paul.kanter@usdoj.gov

Assistant U.S. Attorney **Jonathan H. Koenig** . . . . . . (414) 297-1700
Education: Georgetown 1987 AB; William & Mary 1995 JD

Assistant U.S. Attorney **Carol Kraft** . . . . . . (414) 297-1700
E-mail: carol.kraft@usdoj.gov

Assistant U.S. Attorney **Laura Kwaterski** . . . . . . (414) 297-1700

Assistant U.S. Attorney **Elizabeth Monfils** . . . . . . (414) 297-1700
E-mail: elizabeth.monfils@usdoj.gov

Assistant U.S. Attorney **Karine Moreno-Taxman** . . . . . . (414) 297-1700
E-mail: karine.moreno-taxman@usdoj.gov

Assistant U.S. Attorney **Benjamin W. Proctor** . . . . . . (414) 297-1700
E-mail: benjamin.proctor@usdoj.gov

Assistant U.S. Attorney **William Roach** . . . . . . (414) 297-1700

Assistant U.S. Attorney **Joseph R. Wall** . . . . . . (414) 297-1700
E-mail: joseph.wall@usdoj.gov

Assistant U.S. Attorney **Melvin K. Washington** . . . . . . (414) 297-1700
E-mail: melvin.washington@usdoj.gov

Assistant U.S. Attorney **Lisa Wesley** . . . . . . (414) 297-1700
E-mail: lisa.wesley@usdoj.gov

Assistant U.S. Attorney **Benjamin Whittemore** . . . . . . (414) 297-1700

Wisconsin - Western District

222 West Washington Avenue, Suite 700, Madison, WI 53703
Tel: (608) 264-5158 TTY: (608) 264-5006 Fax: (608) 264-5172

★ U.S. Attorney **John W. Vaudreuil** . . . . . . (608) 264-5158
Education: Wisconsin 1976, 1979 JD
Secretary to the U.S. Attorney **Loni Broefeh** . . . . . . (608) 264-5158

First Assistant U.S. Attorney **Stephen P. "Steve" Sinnott** . . . . . . (608) 264-5158
E-mail: steve.sinnott@usdoj.gov

Administrative Officer **Brian M. McCarthy** . . . . . . (608) 264-5158
E-mail: brian.mccarthy@usdoj.gov

Law Enforcement Committee Coordinator **Myra J. Longfield** . . . . . . (608) 264-5158

Victim-Witness Coordinator **Barbara E. Williams** . . . . . . (608) 264-5158

Wisconsin - Western District *continued*

Senior Systems Manager **Michelle Almanza** . . . . . . (608) 264-5158
E-mail: michelle.almanza@usdoj.gov

ALS Manager **David Taylor** . . . . . . (608) 264-5158
E-mail: david.taylor@usdoj.gov

Civil Division

Civil Division Chief and Assistant U.S. Attorney **Leslie K. Herje** . . . . . . (608) 264-5158
E-mail: leslie.herje@usdoj.gov

Assistant U.S. Attorney **David Conway** . . . . . . (608) 264-5158
E-mail: david.conway@usdoj.gov

Assistant U.S. Attorney **Daniel Fructer** . . . . . . (608) 264-5158
E-mail: daniel.fructer@usdoj.gov

Assistant U.S. Attorney **Richard Humphrey** . . . . . . (608) 264-5158
E-mail: richard.humphrey@usdoj.gov

Assistant U.S. Attorney **Heidi L. Luehring** . . . . . . (608) 264-5158
E-mail: heidi.luehring@usdoj.gov

Assistant U.S. Attorney **Barbara Oswald** . . . . . . (608) 264-5158

Criminal Division

Criminal Division Chief and Assistant U.S. Attorney **Laura Przybylinksi Finn** . . . . . . (608) 264-5158

Senior Litigation Counsel and Assistant U.S. Attorney **Timothy M. O'Shea** . . . . . . (608) 264-5158
E-mail: tim.oshea@usdoj.gov

Organized Crime Drug Enforcement Task Force Unit Chief and Assistant U.S. Attorney **Jeffrey M. Anderson** . . . . . . (608) 264-5158
E-mail: jeff.anderson@usdoj.gov

Asset Forfeiture Unit Assistant U.S. Attorney **Elizabeth Altman** . . . . . . (608) 264-5158
E-mail: elizabeth.altman@usdoj.gov

Assistant U.S. Attorney **Meredith Duchemin** . . . . . . (608) 264-5158
E-mail: meredith.duchemin@usdoj.gov

Assistant U.S. Attorney **Daniel Graber** . . . . . . (608) 264-5158
E-mail: dan.graber@usdoj.gov

Assistant U.S. Attorney **Alice H. Green** . . . . . . (608) 264-5158
E-mail: alice.green@usdoj.gov

Assistant U.S. Attorney **Peter M. Jarosz** . . . . . . (608) 264-5158
E-mail: peter.jarosz2@usdoj.gov

Assistant U.S. Attorney **Grant C. Johnson** . . . . . . (608) 264-5158
E-mail: grant.johnson@usdoj.gov

Assistant U.S. Attorney **David Reinhard** . . . . . . (608) 264-5158
E-mail: david.reinhard@usdoj.gov

Assistant U.S. Attorney **Rita M. Rumbelow** . . . . . . (608) 264-5158
E-mail: rita.rumbelow@usdoj.gov

Assistant U.S. Attorney **Antonio "Tony" Trillo** . . . . . . (608) 264-5158

Assistant U.S. Attorney **(Vacant)** . . . . . . (608) 264-5158

Assistant U.S. Attorney **(Vacant)** . . . . . . (608) 264-5158

Wyoming District

J.C. O'Mahoney Federal Building, 2120 Capitol Avenue, Room 4002, Cheyenne, WY 82001
P.O. Box 668, Cheyenne, WY 82003-0668
Tel: (307) 772-2124 Fax: (307) 772-2123

★ U.S. Attorney **Christopher A. "Kip" Crofts** . . . . . . (307) 772-2124
Education: Wyoming 1965, 1974 JD

First Assistant U.S. Attorney **John R. Green** . . . . . . (307) 772-2124
E-mail: john.green@usdoj.gov

Administrative Officer **John R. Powell** . . . . . . (307) 772-2124
E-mail: john.powell@usdoj.gov
Budget Officer **Patsy Wrede** . . . . . . (307) 772-2124
E-mail: patsy.wrede@usdoj.gov

Intelligence Officer **John R. Powell** . . . . . . (307) 772-2124
E-mail: john.powell@usdoj.gov

Law Enforcement Coordination Specialist and Press Officer **John R. Powell** . . . . . . (307) 772-2124
E-mail: john.powell@usdoj.gov

Victim-Witness Specialist **Vicki Powell** . . . . . . (307) 772-2124
E-mail: vpowell@usa.doj.gov

(continued on next page)

★ Presidential Appointment Requiring Senate Confirmation ☆ Presidential Appointment □ Schedule C Appointment ◇ Career Senior Foreign Service Appointment
● Career Senior Executive Service (SES) Appointment ○ Non-Career Senior Executive Service (SES) Appointment ■ Postal Career Executive Service

Wyoming District *continued*

Systems Manager **Richard Peterson** . . . . (307) 772-2124

Civil Division

Supervisory Assistant U.S. Attorney/Civil Division Chief/Executive Assistant **Nick Vassallo** . . . . (307) 772-2124
E-mail: nick.vassallo@usdoj.gov

Assistant U.S. Attorney **Mark A. Klaassen** . . . . (307) 772-2124
E-mail: mark.klaassen@usdoj.gov

Assistant U.S. Attorney **C. Levi Martin** . . . . (307) 772-2124

Assistant U.S. Attorney **(Vacant)** . . . . (307) 772-2124

Criminal Division

Chief **Robert Murray** . . . . (307) 772-2124

Assistant U.S. Attorney **James Anderson** . . . . (307) 772-2124
E-mail: james.anderson@usdoj.gov

Assistant U.S. Attorney **Lisa E. Leschuck** . . . . (307) 772-2124
E-mail: lisa.leschuck@usdoj.gov

Assistant U.S. Attorney **Timothy J. Sorwood** . . . . (307) 772-2124

Assistant U.S. Attorney **Thomas A. Szott** . . . . (307) 772-2124
E-mail: tszott@usa.doj.gov

Casper (WY) Office

Dick Cheney Federal Building, 100 East B Street,
Suite 2211, Casper, WY 82601
Tel: (307) 261-5434 Fax: (307) 261-5471

Supervisory Assistant U.S. Attorney/Branch Office Chief **Stephanie Sprecher** . . . . (307) 261-5434
E-mail: stephanie.sprecher@usdoj.gov

Senior Litigation Counsel **David Kubichek** . . . . (307) 261-5434
E-mail: david.kubichek@usdoj.gov

Criminal Division Assistant U.S. Attorney **Todd I. Shugart** . . . . (307) 261-5434
E-mail: todd.shugart@usdoj.gov

Criminal Division Assistant U.S. Attorney **(Vacant)** . . . . . . (307) 261-5434

Lander (WY) Branch Office

331 Main Street, Suite A, Lander, WY 82520
PO Box 449, Lander, WY 82520
Tel: (307) 332-8195 Fax: (307) 332-7104

Supervisory Assistant U.S. Attorney/Branch Office Chief **Kerry Jacobson** . . . . (307) 332-8195
E-mail: kerry.jacobson@usdoj.gov

Criminal Division Assistant U.S. Attorney **Jason M. Conder** . . . . (307) 332-8195
E-mail: jason.conder@usdoj.gov

Yellowstone (WY) Branch Office

P.O. Box 703, Yellowstone National Park, WY 82190-0703
Tel: (307) 690-7394

Assistant U.S. Attorney **Francis Leland Pico** . . . . (307) 690-7394

United States Marshals Service [USMS]

United States Marshals Headquarters, 2604 Jefferson Davis Highway, Alexandria, VA 22301
Tel: (202) 307-9100 (Communications Center)
Tel: (202) 336-0162 (Public Affairs After hours)
E-mail: us.marshals@usdoj.gov
Internet: www.usmarshals.gov

The United States Marshals Service is the oldest federal law enforcement agency, and is the enforcement arm of the federal courts, protecting federal courts and ensuring the effective operation of the judicial system. It also operates the Witness Security Program, transports federal prisoners and seizes property acquired by criminals through illegal activity. The Service includes 94 Presidentially appointed U.S. Marshals, each representing a federal judicial district.

OFFICE OF THE DIRECTOR

United States Marshals Headquarters, 2604 Jefferson Davis Highway, Alexandria, VA 22301
Fax: (703) 603-7021

Office of the Deputy Director

Directorate of Operations

Justice Prisoner and Alien Transportation System [JPATS]

1251 Northwest Briar Cliff Parkway, Suite 300, Kansas City, MO 64116
Tel: (816) 467-1900 Tel: (405) 680-3400 (Prisoner Transportation)
Fax: (816) 467-1980
Internet: www.usdoj.gov/marshals/jpats

The Justice Prisoner and Alien Transportation System (JPATS) transports sentenced prisoners who are in the custody of the Federal Bureau of Prisons as well as Immigration and Customs Enforcement criminal/administrative aliens to hearings, court appearances and detention facilities. The Justice Prisoner and Alien Transportation System also provides regular international flights for the removal of deportable aliens. Military and civilian law enforcement agencies use the Justice Prisoner and Alien Transportation System to shuttle their prisoners between different jurisdictions at a fraction of what commercial sources would charge.

● Assistant Director **Shannon Brown** . . . . (816) 467-1900

Tactical Operations Division

● Assistant Director **Neil DeSousa** . . . . (202) 307-3437
E-mail: neil.desousa@usdoj.gov
Education: John Jay Col

Deputy Assistant Director (Acting) **Marti Stanley** . . . . (800) 336-0102
E-mail: marti.stanley@usdoj.gov

Special Operations Tactical Center Commander **Eric Kessel** . . . . (318) 640-4560
E-mail: eric.kessel@usdoj.gov

District Offices

Alabama - Northern District

1729 Fifth Avenue North, Room 240, Birmingham, AL 35203
Tel: (205) 307-7335 Fax: (205) 776-6220

★ U.S. Marshal **Chester Martin Keely** . . . . (205) 307-7335
E-mail: martin.keely@usdoj.gov
Education: Samford BGS; Birmingham JD

Chief Deputy U.S. Marshal **Cliff Labarge** . . . . (205) 776-6210
E-mail: cliff.labarge@usdoj.gov

Supervisory Deputy U.S. Marshal (Operations) **Don Snider** . . . . (205) 776-6215
Fax: (205) 776-6206

Administrative Officer **Jill Ellis** . . . . (205) 776-6224
E-mail: jill.ellis3@usdoj.gov

★ Presidential Appointment Requiring Senate Confirmation ☆ Presidential Appointment □ Schedule C Appointment ◇ Career Senior Foreign Service Appointment
● Career Senior Executive Service (SES) Appointment ○ Non-Career Senior Executive Service (SES) Appointment ■ Postal Career Executive Service

Alabama - Northern District *continued*

Administrative Support Specialist **Natalie Harrison** ...... (205) 776-6223
E-mail: natalie.harrison@usdoj.gov
Criminal Program Specialist **(Vacant)** .... (205) 731-0100 ext. 235
Criminal Program Specialist **(Vacant)** .... (205) 776-6221
Investigative Research Analyst
Gaytan Glover .... (205) 731-0100 ext. 221
Budget Analyst **Sandrieka Moore** .... (205) 776-6232
E-mail: sandrieka.moore@usdoj.gov

Huntsville (AL) Office

101 Holmes Avenue, NE, Room 210, Huntsville, AL 35801
Tel: (256) 534-4520 Fax: (256) 539-8574

Deputy U.S. Marshal **Mark Mobley** .... (256) 534-4529 ext. 2
Deputy U.S. Marshal **Ron Whelpley** .... (256) 534-4529 ext. 1
E-mail: ron.whelpley@usdoj.gov
Deputy U.S. Marshal **Curtis Yates** .... (256) 534-4520 ext. 4
E-mail: curtis.yates@usdoj.gov

Alabama - Middle District

One Church Street, Suite A-100, Montgomery, AL 36104
Tel: (334) 223-7401 Fax: (334) 223-7726

★ U.S. Marshal **(Vacant)** .... (334) 954-3717
Chief Deputy U.S. Marshal **Thomas Hession** .... (334) 223-3090
E-mail: thomas.bession@usdoj.gov
Supervisory Deputy U.S. Marshal **Ashley Hefelfinger** .... (334) 223-3095
E-mail: ashley.hefelfinger@usdoj.gov
Administrative Officer **June Rylant** .... (334) 223-3100
E-mail: june.rylant@usdoj.gov

Alabama - Southern District

113 St. Joseph Street, Room 413, Mobile, AL 36602
Tel: (251) 690-2841 Fax: (251) 694-4285

★ U.S. Marshal **Charles Edward Andrews** .... (251) 690-2900
E-mail: charles.andrews@usdoj.gov
Education: Alabama 1977 BSCrimJ
Chief Deputy U.S. Marshal **Vernon Johnson** .... (251) 690-2931
Supervisory Deputy U.S. Marshal (Operations)
(Vacant) .... (251) 690-2939
Supervisory Deputy U.S. Marshal (Enforcement)
Sean Carney .... (251) 690-2841
E-mail: sean.carney@usdoj.gov
Deputy U.S. Marshal **Delvin Brown** .... (251) 690-2841
E-mail: delvin.brown4@usdoj.gov
Deputy U.S. Marshal **Michael Clemmons** .... (251) 690-2841
E-mail: michael.clemmons@usdoj.gov
Deputy U.S. Marshal **Joshua Devine** .... (251) 690-2841
E-mail: joshua.devine@usdoj.gov
Deputy U.S. Marshal **Nolan Dice** .... (251) 690-2011
E-mail: nolan.dice@usdoj.gov
Deputy U.S. Marshal **Jordan Futo** .... (251) 690-2841
E-mail: jordan.futo@usdoj.gov
Deputy U.S. Marshal **Timothy Garrett** .... (251) 690-2841
E-mail: timothy.garrett2@usdoj.gov
Deputy U.S. Marshal **James "Jim" Glisson** .... (251) 690-2841
E-mail: jim.glisson@usdoj.gov
Deputy U.S. Marshal **Lawanda Hewitt** .... (251) 690-2841
Deputy U.S. Marshal **William McAdam** .... (251) 690-2841
Deputy U.S. Marshal **Oscar Torres** .... (251) 690-2841
Sex Offender Investigative Coordinator
Edward Eversman .... (251) 690-2769
E-mail: edward.eversman@usdoj.gov
Judicial Security Inspector **Scott R. Page** .... (251) 690-2770
E-mail: scott.page@usdoj.gov
Administrative Officer **Angela D. Garriz** .... (251) 690-2841
E-mail: angela.garriz@usdoj.gov
Administrative Support Assistant **(Vacant)** .... (251) 690-2841
Criminal Program Specialist **Jamie Lybrand** .... (251) 690-2841
E-mail: jamie.lybrand@usdoj.gov

Alabama - Southern District *continued*

Budget Analyst **Philomenia Klopner** .... (251) 690-2841
E-mail: philomenia.y.klopner@usdoj.gov

Alaska District

Federal Building and U.S. Courthouse, 222 West Seventh Avenue #28, Room 170, Anchorage, AK 99513
Tel: (907) 271-5154 Fax: (907) 271-3674

★ U.S. Marshal **Robert William "Rob" Heun** .... (907) 271-5154
E-mail: rob.heun@usdoj.gov
Education: West Point 1977 BS
Chief Deputy U.S. Marshal **David Long** .... (907) 271-3543
Supervisory Deputy U.S. Marshal **John Olson** .... (907) 271-1229
E-mail: john.olson@usdoj.gov
Deputy U.S. Marshal **Bryson Barnes** .... (907) 271-5154
E-mail: bryson.barnes@usdoj.gov
Deputy U.S. Marshal **Mick Bunn** .... (907) 271-5154
E-mail: mick.bunn@usdoj.gov
Deputy U.S. Marshal **Kevin S. Guinn** .... (907) 271-5154
E-mail: kevin.guinn@usdoj.gov
Deputy U.S. Marshal **Rochelle L. Liedike** .... (907) 271-5154
E-mail: rochelle.liedike@usdoj.gov
Deputy U.S. Marshal **Gilbert Morales** .... (907) 271-5154
E-mail: gilbert.morales@usdoj.gov
Deputy U.S. Marshal **Katie Willson** .... (907) 271-3501
Deputy U.S. Marshal **(Vacant)** .... (907) 271-5154
Deputy U.S. Marshal and District Pilot
James "Sonny" Caudill .... (907) 271-5154
E-mail: james.caudill@usdoj.gov
Court Security Inspector **James "Jimmy" Johnson** ..... (907) 271-1229
E-mail: jimmy.johnson@usdoj.gov
Administrative Officer **Tanya Lauseher** .... (907) 271-5159
Asset Forfeiture Analyst **Rivkah Stansfield** .... (907) 271-5154
E-mail: rivkah.stansfield@usdoj.gov
Budget Analyst **(Vacant)** .... (907) 271-4375
Criminal Program Specialist **(Vacant)** .... (907) 271-4374
Senior Inspector Sex Offender Investigations
Lisa Norbert .... (907) 271-5154
E-mail: lisa.norbert@usdoj.gov
Task Force Supervisor **Randy Coyne** .... (907) 271-5154
E-mail: randy.coyne@usdoj.gov
Warrant Supervisor **Randy Coyne** .... (907) 271-5154
E-mail: randy.coyne@usdoj.gov

Fairbanks (AK) Office

U.S. Courthouse and Federal Building, 101 - 12th Avenue, #6, Room 336, Fairbanks, AK 99701
Tel: (907) 456-0246 Fax: (907) 456-0383

Supervisory Deputy U.S. Marshal
Andrew "Andy" Mazerik .... (907) 456-0246
E-mail: andy.mazerik@usdoj.gov
Deputy U.S. Marshal **Scott Ireton** .... (907) 456-0246
E-mail: scott.ireton@usdoj.gov
Deputy U.S. Marshal **(Vacant)** .... (907) 456-0380

Arizona District

Sandra Day O'Connor U.S. Courthouse, 401 West Washington Street, Suite 270, SPC 64, Phoenix, AZ 85003-2159
Tel: (602) 382-8767 Fax: (602) 258-1857
Internet: http://www.usmarshals.gov/district/az/

★ U.S. Marshal **David P. Gonzales** .... (602) 382-8767
Education: Arizona 1997 BS
Secretary **(Vacant)** .... (602) 382-8767
Chief Deputy U.S. Marshal **Fidencio Rivera** .... (602) 761-2002
Assistant Chief Deputy U.S. Marshal
Matthew Hershey .... (602) 382-2010
Supervisory Deputy of Operations
Jerome Fairweather .... (602) 382-8781
E-mail: jerome.fairweather@usdoj.gov

(continued on next page)

REGIONAL OFFICES – US ATTORNEYS AND US MARSHALS SERVICE

★ Presidential Appointment Requiring Senate Confirmation ☆ Presidential Appointment ☐ Schedule C Appointment ◇ Career Senior Foreign Service Appointment
● Career Senior Executive Service (SES) Appointment ○ Non-Career Senior Executive Service (SES) Appointment ■ Postal Career Executive Service

Arizona District *continued*

Supervisory Deputy for Civil **Charles Roland** .... (602) 761-2641
Fax: (602) 382-8760
Criminal Desk **Joann Sandoval-Tirado** .... (602) 761-2653
E-mail: joann.sandoval@usdoj.gov
Investigations Desk **April Rowley** .... (602) 761-2632
Operations Support Specialist **(Vacant)** .... (928) 213-0045
Supervisory Deputy U.S. Marshal - Warrants
Sterling Carter .... (602) 761-2631
E-mail: sterling.carter@usdoj.gov
Judicial Security Inspector Deputy U.S. Marshal
Jennifer Harkins .... (602) 761-2411
E-mail: jennifer.harkins@usdoj.gov
Deputy U.S. Marshal **Ronald Krause** .... (602) 382-8757
Deputy U.S. Marshal **Jeff Parris** .... (602) 382-8764
E-mail: jeff.parris@usdoj.gov
Deputy U.S. Marshal **Albert Reble** .... (602) 382-8773
Deputy U.S. Marshal **Pat Willhite** .... (602) 382-8755
E-mail: pat.willhite@usdoj.gov
Deputy U.S. Marshal **(Vacant)** .... (602) 382-8766
Deputy U.S. Marshal **(Vacant)** .... (602) 382-8775
Deputy U.S. Marshal **(Vacant)** .... (602) 382-8777
Program Analyst **(Vacant)** .... (602) 382-8767
Detention Enforcement Officer **Troy Hookom** .... (602) 382-8785
E-mail: troy.hookom@usdoj.gov
Detention Enforcement Officer **William Nelson, Jr.** ...... (602) 382-8785
Asset Forfeiture Supervisor **(Vacant)** .... (602) 382-8722
Computer Specialist **James Dugger** .... (602) 382-8768
E-mail: james.dugger@usdoj.gov
Budget Analyst **(Vacant)** .... (602) 382-8713
Program Analyst **Cynthia Abril** .... (602) 382-8716
E-mail: cynthia.abril@usdoj.gov
Purchasing Officer **(Vacant)** .... (602) 382-8711

Flagstaff (AZ) Office

123 North San Francisco Street, Room 101, Flagstaff, AZ 86001
Tel: (928) 213-0045 Fax: (928) 213-0152

Supervisory Deputy U.S. Marshal (Acting) **Bill Noble** .... (928) 213-0453
Senior Deputy U.S. Marshal **Bill Noble** .... (928) 213-0045

Prescott (AZ) Office

101 West Goodwin Street, Room 207, Prescott, AZ 86301
Tel: (928) 778-0710 Fax: (928) 445-0157

Note: The Prescott (AZ) Office is staffed by U.S. Marshals from the Arizona District only when court is in session.

Tucson (AZ) Office

Evo A. DeConcini Courthouse, 405 West Congress Street,
Suite 2300, Tucson, AZ 85701
Tel: (520) 879-6900 Fax: (520) 879-6920

Assistant Chief Deputy U.S. Marshal **Tom Henmen** ..... (520) 209-0900
Supervisory Deputy U.S. Marshal (District Court
Operations) **Rick L. Lovelace** .... (520) 879-6951
E-mail: rick.lovelace@usdoj.gov
Supervisory Deputy U.S. Marshal (Enforcement)
Michael Lavin .... (520) 879-6941
Supervisory Deputy U.S. Marshal (Enforcement)
Ron Schlagel .... (520) 879-6931
E-mail: ron.schlagel@usdoj.gov
Supervisory Deputy U.S. Marshal (Magistrate Court
Operations) **Jose Valenzuela, Jr.** .... (520) 879-6972
E-mail: jose.valenzuela@usdoj.gov
Supervisory Deputy U.S. Marshal (Prisoner Operations)
(Vacant) .... (520) 879-6921
Deputy U.S. Marshal **Audra Bidegain** .... (520) 879-6936
Deputy U.S. Marshal **Ricardo Camacho** .... (520) 879-6968
Deputy U.S. Marshal **Mike Coronado** .... (520) 879-6997
Deputy U.S. Marshal **Matthew Crossman** .... (520) 879-6913

Tucson (AZ) Office *continued*

Deputy U.S. Marshal **Hector Dominguez** .... (520) 879-6963
E-mail: hector.dominguez@usdoj.gov
Deputy U.S. Marshal **Frederick Freeman** .... (520) 879-6971
E-mail: frederick.freeman@usdoj.gov
Deputy U.S. Marshal **Daniel Hernandez** .... (520) 879-6915
E-mail: daniel.hernandez@usdoj.gov
Deputy U.S. Marshal **Eugene Honce** .... (520) 879-6965
E-mail: eugene.honce@usdoj.gov
Deputy U.S. Marshal **Pete Little** .... (520) 879-6947
Deputy U.S. Marshal **Carlos Najera** .... (520) 879-6912
E-mail: carlos.najera@usdoj.gov
Deputy U.S. Marshal **Art Olivas** .... (520) 879-6978
E-mail: arthur.olivas@usdoj.gov
Deputy U.S. Marshal **Brian Teston** .... (520) 879-6987
E-mail: brian.teston@usdoj.gov
Deputy U.S. Marshal **James Thursby** .... (520) 879-6917
E-mail: james.thursby@usdoj.gov
Deputy U.S. Marshal **Michael Villegas** .... (520) 879-6923
E-mail: michael.villegas@usdoj.gov
Criminal Investigator **Jeffrey Baptista** .... (520) 879-6983
Criminal Investigator **James Bennett** .... (520) 879-6995
E-mail: james.bennett2@usdoj.gov
Criminal Investigator **Bryan Bia** .... (520) 879-6986
E-mail: bryan.bia@usdoj.gov
Criminal Investigator **David Bland** .... (520) 879-6976
E-mail: david.bland@usdoj.gov
Criminal Investigator **Cary Bunker** .... (520) 879-6956
Criminal Investigator **Patrick Conover** .... (520) 879-6958
E-mail: patrick.conover@usdoj.gov
Criminal Investigator **Cesar Cordova** .... (520) 879-6900
E-mail: cesar.cordova@usdoj.gov
Criminal Investigator **Allan Magno** .... (520) 879-6926
E-mail: allan.magno@usdoj.gov
Criminal Investigator **George Martinez** .... (520) 879-6967
E-mail: george.martinez@usdoj.gov
Criminal Investigator **Patrick Muldowney** .... (520) 879-6969
Criminal Investigator **Oscar Pintor** .... (520) 879-6989
Criminal Investigator **Jennifer Rippey** .... (520) 879-6908
E-mail: jennifer.rippey@usdoj.gov
Criminal Investigator **Tresa Rodriguez** .... (520) 879-6984
E-mail: tresa.rodriguez@usdoj.gov
Lead Detention Enforcement Officer **Beatriz Gonzalez** ... (520) 879-6997
E-mail: beatriz.gonzalez@usdoj.gov
Detention Enforcement Officer **Rafael Gonzalez** .... (520) 879-6997
E-mail: rafael.gonzalez1@usdoj.gov
Detention Enforcement Officer **Frank Rubalcava** .... (520) 879-6964
Judicial Security Inspector **Rich Tracy** .... (520) 209-0956
E-mail: rich.tracy@usdoj.gov
Contract Oversight Specialist **(Vacant)** .... (520) 879-6925
Criminal Program Specialist **Adria Fernandez** .... (520) 879-6952
E-mail: adria.fernandez@usdoj.gov
Criminal Program Specialist **Olga Ravago** .... (520) 879-6955
E-mail: olga.ravago@usdoj.gov
Investigative Research Analyst **Sylvia Stoddard** .... (520) 879-6934
E-mail: sylvia.stoddard@usdoj.gov
Investigative Research Specialist **(Vacant)** .... (520) 879-6933
Investigative Research Specialist **(Vacant)** .... (520) 879-6933
Records Examiner and Analyst **Jeff Braddock** .... (520) 879-6932
Lead Administrative Support Assistant **(Vacant)** .... (520) 209-0952
Administrative Support Specialist **Myriam Estrada** ..... (520) 209-0921
E-mail: myriam.estrada@usdoj.gov
Administrative Support Assistant **(Vacant)** .... (520) 209-0959

Yuma (AZ) Office

John M. Roll United States Courthouse,
98 West First Street, Yuma, AZ 85364
Tel: (928) 783-6337 Fax: (928) 783-6356

Supervisory Deputy U.S. Marshal **Tom Smith** .... (928) 373-6582
Supervisory Deputy U.S. Marshal **Jennifer Wells** .... (928) 783-6337
E-mail: jennifer.wells@usdoj.gov

★ Presidential Appointment Requiring Senate Confirmation ☆ Presidential Appointment ☐ Schedule C Appointment ◇ Career Senior Foreign Service Appointment
● Career Senior Executive Service (SES) Appointment ○ Non-Career Senior Executive Service (SES) Appointment ■ Postal Career Executive Service

REGIONAL OFFICES – US ATTORNEYS AND US MARSHALS SERVICE

Yuma (AZ) Office *continued*

Deputy U.S. Marshal **Tony Adame** .... (928) 373-6584
Deputy U.S. Marshal **Omar Ballesteros** .... (928) 783-6337
Deputy U.S. Marshal **Jesus Cordova** .... (928) 783-6337
E-mail: jesus.cordova@usdoj.gov
Deputy U.S. Marshal **Joshua Finniss** .... (928) 783-6337
Deputy U.S. Marshal **Ricky Gonzales** .... (928) 783-6337
Deputy U.S. Marshal **Steven Lipscomb** .... (928) 783-6337
Deputy U.S. Marshal **William McAvoy** .... (928) 783-6337
Deputy U.S. Marshal **Efrain Velazquez** .... (928) 373-6584
Deputy U.S. Marshal **Vinnie Viola** .... (928) 373-6584
Deputy U.S. Marshal **Matthew B. Waring** .... (928) 373-6584
Deputy U.S. Marshal **(Vacant)** .... (928) 783-6337
Deputy U.S. Marshal **(Vacant)** .... (928) 783-6337
Deputy U.S. Marshal **(Vacant)** .... (928) 783-6337
Detention Enforcement Officer **Max Esparza** .... (928) 783-6337 ext. 224
Detention Enforcement Officer
Carlos Garabito .... (928) 783-6337 ext. 224
Detention Enforcement Officer **(Vacant)** .... (928) 783-6337 ext. 224
Administrative Support Specialist
Javier Hernandez .... (928) 783-6337 ext. 277
Operational Support Specialist **Joan Demott** .... (928) 783-6337 ext. 228
Operational Support Specialist **Kira Shurtleff** .... (928) 783-6337 ext. 228

Arkansas - Eastern District

U.S. Courthouse, 600 West Capitol Avenue,
Room 445, Little Rock, AR 72201
Tel: (501) 324-6256 Fax: (501) 324-6252

★ U.S. Marshal **Clifton Timothy Massanelli** .... (501) 324-6256
Education: Arkansas (Little Rock) 1980 BA
Chief Deputy U.S. Marshal **David Rahbany** .... (501) 324-6256
E-mail: david.rahbany@usdoj.gov
Supervisory Deputy U.S. Marshal **Robert Lashley** .... (501) 324-6256
Deputy U.S. Marshal **Kevin Sanders** .... (501) 324-6256
E-mail: kevin.sanders@usdoj.gov
Deputy U.S. Marshal **Reagan Stephens** .... (501) 324-6256
E-mail: reagan.stephens@usdoj.gov
Deputy U.S. Marshal **Jay L. Tuck** .... (501) 324-6256
E-mail: jay.tuck@usdoj.gov
Deputy U.S. Marshal **Charles "Chuck" Uchtman** .... (501) 324-6256
E-mail: charles.uchtman@usdoj.gov
Deputy U.S. Marshal **(Vacant)** .... (501) 324-6256
Deputy U.S. Marshal **(Vacant)** .... (501) 324-6256
Deputy U.S. Marshal **(Vacant)** .... (501) 324-6256
Court Security Inspector **(Vacant)** .... (501) 324-6256
Asset Forfeiture Investigator **Lynn Ollar** .... (501) 324-6256
E-mail: lynn.ollar@usdoj.gov
Administrative Officer **Beverly Kaplon** .... (501) 324-6256
E-mail: beverly.kaplon@usdoj.gov
Administrative Staff **Diane Darbonne** .... (501) 324-6256
E-mail: diane.darbonne@usdoj.gov
Administrative Staff **Michelle Haskins** .... (501) 324-6256
E-mail: michelle.haskins@usdoj.gov
Administrative Staff **Laura Yancey** .... (501) 324-6256
E-mail: laura.yancey@usdoj.gov

Jonesboro (AR) Office

311 Federal Building, 615 South Main Street, Jonesboro, AR 72403
Tel: (870) 972-4611

Deputy U.S. Marshal **Bob Clark** .... (870) 972-4611
E-mail: bob.clark@usdoj.gov

Pine Bluff (AR) Office

100 East Eighth Street, Room 316, Pine Bluff, AR 71601
Tel: (870) 536-0098 Fax: (870) 536-0079

Deputy U.S. Marshal **Mike Koberlein** .... (870) 536-0098

Arkansas - Western District

Judge Isaac C. Parker Federal Building, 30 South Sixth Street,
Room 243, Fort Smith, AR 72901-2410
Tel: (479) 783-5215 Fax: (479) 782-4204

★ U.S. Marshal **Harold Michael "Mike" Oglesby** .... (479) 783-5215
Chief Deputy U.S. Marshal **Dewaine Allen** .... (479) 783-5215
E-mail: dewaine.allen@usdoj.gov
Supervisory Deputy U.S. Marshal **Tony L. Overstreet** .... (479) 783-5215
E-mail: tony.l.overstreet@usdoj.gov
Deputy U.S. Marshal **Jeffrey D. Landers** .... (479) 783-5215
E-mail: jeff.landers@usdoj.gov
Deputy U.S. Marshal **Cory Thomas** .... (479) 783-5215
E-mail: cory.thomas@usdoj.gov
Deputy U.S. Marshal **Randy Moon** .... (479) 783-5215
Administrative Officer **Steve Moody** .... (479) 783-5215
E-mail: steve.moody@usdoj.gov

El Dorado (AR) Office

101 South Jackson Street, Room 202, El Dorado, AR 71730
Tel: (870) 863-4734 Fax: (870) 863-7726

Deputy U.S. Marshal **Lance Hancock** .... (870) 863-4734 ext. 222
Deputy U.S. Marshal **Thomas Malone** .... (870) 863-4734 ext. 221

Fayetteville (AR) Office

35 East Mountain Street, Room 516, Fayetteville, AR 72701
Tel: (479) 442-6141 Fax: (479) 443-1674

Deputy U.S. Marshal **Dustin Chastin** .... (479) 442-6141
Deputy U.S. Marshal **Randy Moon** .... (479) 442-6141
Deputy U.S. Marshal **Tyler Winkle** .... (479) 442-6141

Hot Springs (AR) Office

100 Reserve Street, Room 352, Hot Springs, AR 71901
Tel: (501) 623-9547 Fax: (501) 321-9613

Deputy U.S. Marshal **(Vacant)** .... (501) 623-9547 ext. 222
Deputy U.S. Marshal **(Vacant)** .... (501) 623-9547 ext. 223

Texarkana (AR) Office

500 Stateline Road, Texarkana, AR 75501
Tel: (870) 774-9922

Deputy U.S. Marshal **Matthew Bremer** .... (870) 774-9922 ext. 221
E-mail: matthew.bremer@usdoj.gov

California - Central District

U.S. Federal Courthouse, 312 North Spring Street,
Room G23, Los Angeles, CA 90012-4798
Tel: (213) 894-2485 Fax: (213) 894-2078
Internet: www.usmarshals.gov

★ U.S. Marshal **David Mark Singer** .... (213) 894-2485
Education: Cal State (Long Beach) BSCrimJ, MPA
Executive Assistant **Tyree Rios** .... (213) 894-2724
E-mail: tyree.rios@usdoj.gov
Chief Deputy U.S. Marshal **Kurt Ellingson** .... (213) 894-2485
Assistant Chief Deputy U.S. Marshal **Larry O'Connor** .... (213) 894-2485
Assistant Chief Deputy U.S. Marshal **Michael Peerson** ... (213) 894-2485
Systems Administrator **Patrick Tsai** .... (213) 894-2485
E-mail: patrick.tsai@usdoj.gov

Riverside (CA) Office

3470 12th Street, Room G-122, Riverside, CA 92501
Tel: (951) 276-6120 Fax: (951) 276-6101

Supervisory Deputy U.S. Marshal **Joe Lewis** .... (951) 276-6120

★ Presidential Appointment Requiring Senate Confirmation ☆ Presidential Appointment □ Schedule C Appointment ◇ Career Senior Foreign Service Appointment
● Career Senior Executive Service (SES) Appointment ○ Non-Career Senior Executive Service (SES) Appointment ■ Postal Career Executive Service

Santa Ana (CA) Office

411 West Fourth Street, Santa Ana, CA 92701-4516
Tel: (714) 338-4610 Fax: (714) 338-4601

Supervisory Deputy U.S. Marshal **Tyrone Kilpatrick** ..... (714) 338-4610

California - Eastern District

5-600 U.S. Courthouse, 501 I Street, Sacramento, CA 95814
Tel: (916) 930-2030 Fax: (916) 930-2050

★ U.S. Marshal **Albert Nájera** .... (916) 930-2030
Education: Sacramento; Cal State (Sacramento) BA; Cal Poly (Pomona) MM
Chief Deputy U.S. Marshal **Richard Hunter** .... (916) 930-2032
E-mail: richard.hunter@usdoj.gov
Supervisory Deputy U.S. Marshal **Anne Gaskins** .... (916) 930-2034
E-mail: anne.gaskins@usdoj.gov
Supervisory Deputy U.S. Marshal **Marco Rodriguez** ..... (916) 930-2047
Deputy U.S. Marshal **Jared Belcher** .... (916) 930-2044
E-mail: jared.belcher@usdoj.gov
Deputy U.S. Marshal **G. Kevin Biernat** .... (916) 930-2037
E-mail: kevin.biernat@usdoj.gov
Deputy U.S. Marshal **Jason Garcia** .... (916) 930-2030
Deputy U.S. Marshal **Richard King** .... (916) 930-2048
E-mail: richard.king@usdoj.gov
Deputy U.S. Marshal **Philip "Joe" McKeough** .... (916) 930-2041
E-mail: philip.mckeough@usdoj.gov
Deputy U.S. Marshal **Brandon McMullen** .... (916) 930-2030
E-mail: brandon.mcmullen@usdoj.gov
Deputy U.S. Marshal **Robert Murphy** .... (916) 930-2030
E-mail: robert.murphy@usdoj.gov
Deputy U.S. Marshal **Frank Newsom** .... (916) 930-2047
E-mail: frank.newsom@usdoj.gov
Deputy U.S. Marshal **Kelly Pope** .... (916) 930-2214
E-mail: kelly.pope@usdoj.gov
Deputy U.S. Marshal **Jason Serak** .... (916) 930-2036
E-mail: jason.serak@usdoj.gov
Deputy U.S. Marshal **Sarah Sloan** .... (916) 930-2049
Deputy U.S. Marshal **Michael Smith** .... (916) 930-2057
E-mail: michael.smith@usdoj.gov
Deputy U.S. Marshal **(Vacant)** .... (916) 930-2052
Deputy U.S. Marshal **(Vacant)** .... (916) 930-2046
Administrative Officer **Victoria Humphrey** .... (916) 930-2033
E-mail: victoria.humphrey@usdoj.gov

Fresno (CA) Office

U.S. Courthouse, 2500 Tulare Street, Suite 3501, Fresno, CA 93721
Tel: (559) 487-5600 Fax: (559) 487-5616

Supervisory Deputy U.S. Marshal **Gilbert Rodriguez** .... (559) 487-5551
E-mail: gilbert.rodriguez@usdoj.gov
Assistant Chief Deputy U.S. Marshal **Russell Yorke** ...... (559) 487-5550
E-mail: russell.yorke@usdoj.gov
Deputy U.S. Marshal **Joseph "Joe" Faranda** .... (559) 487-5600
E-mail: joseph.faranda@usdoj.gov
Deputy U.S. Marshal **Anne Gaskins** .... (559) 487-5600
E-mail: anne.gaskins@usdoj.gov
Deputy U.S. Marshal **John Arosteguy** .... (559) 487-5600
Deputy U.S. Marshal **Edward Zucker** .... (559) 487-5600
E-mail: edward.zucker@usdoj.gov
Deputy U.S. Marshal **Shawn Mimura** .... (559) 487-5600
E-mail: shawn.mimura@usdoj.gov
Deputy U.S. Marshal **Stephen Drayton** .... (559) 487-5600
Detention Officer **Mark Yang** .... (559) 487-5600

California - Northern District

U.S. Courthouse, 450 Golden Gate Avenue, Room 20-6888, San Francisco, CA 94102
Tel: (415) 436-7677 Fax: (415) 436-7622

★ U.S. Marshal **Donald Martin O'Keefe** .... (415) 436-7688
Education: Notre Dame de Namur 1995 BS; U San Francisco 1999 MPA

California - Northern District *continued*

Chief Deputy U.S. Marshal **Christopher Johannsen** ..... (415) 436-7689
Assistant Chief Deputy U.S. Marshal **Jay Bieber** .... (415) 436-7689
E-mail: jay.bieber@usdoj.gov
Supervisory Deputy U.S. Marshal **Frank Conroy** .... (415) 436-7674
Supervisory Deputy U.S. Marshal **Jason Ferrell** .... (415) 436-7658
Supervisory Deputy U.S. Marshal **Chris Hanson** .... (415) 436-7680
Administrative Officer **Judith Tejada** .... (415) 436-7632
E-mail: judith.tejada@usdoj.gov

Oakland (CA) Office

1301 Clay Street, Room 150C, Oakland, CA 94612-5217
Tel: (510) 637-3650

Supervisory Deputy U.S. Marshal **Mike Dyke** .... (510) 637-3650

San Jose (CA) Office

280 South First Street, Room 2100, San Jose, CA 95113
Tel: (408) 535-5484

Supervisory Deputy U.S. Marshal **Marc Harwell** .... (408) 808-3950

California - Southern District

U.S. Courthouse Annex, 333 West Broadway, Suite 100, San Diego, CA 92101-8930
Tel: (619) 557-6620 Fax: (619) 557-5215

★ U.S. Marshal **Steven Clayton Stafford** .... (619) 557-6620
Education: Northeastern BSCrimJ
Chief Deputy U.S. Marshal **Thomas Carruthers** .... (619) 557-6620
Assistant Chief Deputy U.S. Marshal **Keith Johnson** .... (619) 557-6620
Assistant Chief Deputy U.S. Marshal **(Vacant)** .... (619) 557-6620
Supervisory Deputy U.S. Marshal **Paul Beal** .... (619) 557-6620
Supervisory Deputy U.S. Marshal **Greg Doss** .... (619) 557-6620
E-mail: greg.doss@usdoj.gov
Supervisory Deputy U.S. Marshal **Steve Jurman** .... (619) 557-6620
Supervisory Deputy U.S. Marshal **Kenneth Lavigna** ..... (619) 557-6620
Supervisory Deputy U.S. Marshal (Acting) **Thomas Maranda** .... (619) 557-6620
Supervisory Deputy U.S. Marshal **Michael Oliver** .... (619) 557-6620
E-mail: michael.oliver@usdoj.gov
Supervisory Deputy U.S. Marshal **Matthew Peters** ...... (619) 557-6620
Supervisory Deputy U.S. Marshal **Jaime Schimmel** ..... (619) 557-6620
E-mail: jaime.schimmel@usdoj.gov
Supervisory Deputy U.S. Marshal **Dexter Vilain** .... (619) 557-6620
E-mail: dexter.vilain@usdoj.gov
Supervisory Deputy U.S. Marshal **(Vacant)** .... (619) 557-6620
Supervisory Deputy U.S. Marshal **(Vacant)** .... (619) 557-6620

El Centro (CA) Office

2003 West Adams Avenue, Suite 210, El Centro, CA 92243
Tel: (760) 353-9790 Fax: (760) 370-3945

Supervisory Deputy U.S. Marshal **Jeryl Isaac** .... (760) 353-9790
E-mail: jeryl.isaac@usdoj.gov

Colorado District

U.S. Courthouse, 901 19th Street, Suite 300, Denver, CO 80294
Tel: (303) 335-3400 Fax: (303) 335-3366

★ U.S. Marshal (Acting) **Ken Deal** .... (303) 335-3400
E-mail: ken.deal@usdoj.gov
Chief Deputy U.S. Marshal **Ken Deal** .... (303) 335-3400
E-mail: ken.deal@usdoj.gov
Assistant Chief Deputy U.S. Marshal **Rodney Robinson** .... (303) 335-3400
E-mail: rodney.robinson@usdoj.gov
Supervisory Deputy U.S. Marshal **Steve Wallisch** .... (303) 335-3400
E-mail: steve.wallisch@usdoj.gov
Supervisory Deputy U.S. Marshal **(Vacant)** .... (303) 335-3400
Administrative Officer **Shae Haley** .... (303) 335-3400
E-mail: shae.haley@usdoj.gov

★ Presidential Appointment Requiring Senate Confirmation ☆ Presidential Appointment ☐ Schedule C Appointment ◇ Career Senior Foreign Service Appointment
● Career Senior Executive Service (SES) Appointment ○ Non-Career Senior Executive Service (SES) Appointment ■ Postal Career Executive Service

Connecticut District

U.S. Courthouse, 141 Church Street - Mezzanine,
New Haven, CT 06510-2030
Tel: (203) 773-2107 Fax: (203) 773-2419

★ U.S. Marshal **Joseph Patrick Faughnan, Sr.** .... (203) 773-2107 ext. 3001
E-mail: joseph.faughnan@usdoj.gov
Chief Deputy U.S. Marshal **Brian Taylor** .... (203) 773-2107
E-mail: brian.taylor@usdoj.gov
Supervisory Deputy U.S. Marshal **Caitlin Dunkin** .... (203) 773-2107
Deputy U.S. Marshal **John Iverson** .... (203) 773-2107
E-mail: john.iverson@usdoj.gov
Deputy U.S. Marshal **Michael Curra** .... (203) 773-2107
E-mail: michael.curra@usdoj.gov
Deputy U.S. Marshal **Mark Benjamin** .... (203) 773-2107
E-mail: mark.benjamin@usdoj.gov
Deputy U.S. Marshal **Matthew Moore** .... (203) 773-2107
E-mail: matthew.moore@usdoj.gov
Asset Forfeiture Program Coordinator
Yeugenya Bendersky .... (203) 773-2107
E-mail: yeugenya.bendersky@usdoj.gov
Inspector, Court Security **Tim Smith** .... (203) 773-2107
Warrant Coordinator **Michael Novak** .... (203) 773-2107
E-mail: michael.novak@usdoj.gov
Administrative Officer **Roland Albert** .... (203) 773-2107 ext. 3007
Administrative Support Assistant **Lorraine Dean** .... (203) 773-2107
E-mail: lorraine.dean@usdoj.gov
Criminal Clerk **James Hilaire** .... (203) 773-2107
E-mail: james.hilaire@usdoj.gov

Bridgeport (CT) Office

Federal Building and U.S. Courthouse, 915 Lafayette Boulevard,
Room 211, Bridgeport, CT 06604
Tel: (203) 579-5897 Fax: (203) 579-5612

Supervisory Deputy U.S. Marshal **Lawrence Bobnick** .... (203) 579-5899
E-mail: lawrence.bobnick@usdoj.gov
Deputy U.S. Marshal **Sarah Calgreen** .... (203) 579-5892
E-mail: sarah.calgreen@usdoj.gov
Deputy U.S. Marshal **Adam Mackey** .... (203) 579-5897
E-mail: adam.mackey@usdoj.gov
Deputy U.S. Marshal **Michael J. Moore** .... (203) 579-5532
E-mail: michael.moore@usdoj.gov
Deputy U.S. Marshal **(Vacant)** .... (203) 579-5589
Senior Inspector **James Masterson** .... (203) 579-5589
E-mail: james.masterson@usdoj.gov

Hartford (CT) Office

Federal Building and U.S. Courthouse, 450 Main Street,
Suite 317, Hartford, CT 06103
Tel: (860) 240-3245 Fax: (860) 240-3248

Supervisory Deputy U.S. Marshal **Andrew Tingley** ...... (860) 240-3228
E-mail: andrew.tingley@usdoj.gov
Deputy U.S. Marshal **Gregory Chester** .... (860) 240-3245
E-mail: greg.chester@usdoj.gov
Deputy U.S. Marshal **Fred Gengler** .... (860) 240-3216
E-mail: fred.gengler@usdoj.gov
Deputy U.S. Marshal **Kevin Perreault** .... (860) 240-3246
E-mail: kevin.perreault@usdoj.gov
Deputy U.S. Marshal **Frank Roche** .... (860) 240-3245
E-mail: frank.roche@usdoj.gov
Deputy U.S. Marshal **John Stevens** .... (860) 240-3048
E-mail: john.stevens@usdoj.gov

Delaware District

1100 U.S. Courthouse, 844 King Street, Wilmington, DE 19801-3519
Tel: (302) 573-6176 Fax: (302) 573-6218

★ U.S. Marshal (Acting) **Glen A. Paul** .... (302) 573-6176
E-mail: glen.paul@usdoj.gov

Delaware District *continued*

★ U.S. Marshal **Michael C. "Mike" McGowan** .... (302) 573-6176
Note: On September 17, 2015 the U.S. Senate confirmed Michael McGowan to be U.S. Marshal for Delaware.
Education: Delaware; Wilmington U MPA
Chief Deputy U.S. Marshal **Glen A. Paul** .... (302) 573-6176
E-mail: glen.paul@usdoj.gov
Supervisory Deputy U.S. Marshal **William G. David** ..... (302) 573-6176
E-mail: william.david@usdoj.gov
Deputy U.S. Marshal **Toby Conrad** .... (302) 573-6176
E-mail: toby.conrad@usdoj.gov
Deputy U.S. Marshal **Robert E. Henderson** .... (302) 573-6176
E-mail: robert.henderson@usdoj.gov
Deputy U.S. Marshal **Brian Park** .... (302) 573-6176
E-mail: brian.park@usdoj.gov
Deputy U.S. Marshal **Brian Powers** .... (302) 573-6176
E-mail: brian.powers@usdoj.gov
Deputy U.S. Marshal **Jeffrey Zimmer** .... (302) 573-6176
E-mail: jeffrey.zimmer@usdoj.gov
Judicial Security Inspector **Barbara Fahey** .... (302) 573-6176
E-mail: barbara.fahey@usdoj.gov
Administrative Officer **Leslie S. Jamison** .... (302) 573-6176
E-mail: leslie.jamison@usdoj.gov
Budget Analyst **Mindy Coverdale-Moss** .... (302) 573-6176
E-mail: mindy.coverdale-moss@usdoj.gov
Criminal Program Specialist **Rene Rivera** .... (302) 573-6176
E-mail: rene.rivera@usdoj.gov

District of Columbia District

U.S. Courthouse, 333 Constitution Avenue, NW,
Room 1500, Washington, DC 20001
Tel: (202) 353-0600 Fax: (202) 273-5036

★ U.S. Marshal (Acting) **David L. Baldwin** .... (202) 353-0600
E-mail: david.baldwin@usdoj.gov
Chief Deputy U.S. Marshal (Acting)
Robert Byron Robeson .... (202) 353-0600
E-mail: robert.robeson@usdoj.gov
Assistant Chief Deputy U.S. Marshal **(Vacant)** .... (202) 353-0600
Supervisory Deputy U.S. Marshal (Criminal Investigations) **Linwood "Chuck" Battle** .... (202) 353-0600
E-mail: linwood.battle@usdoj.gov
Supervisory Deputy U.S. Marshal (General Operations)
Gina Chambliss .... (202) 353-0600
E-mail: gina.chambliss@usdoj.gov
Supervisory Deputy U.S. Marshal (Prisoner Logistics and Services) **Henry D. Alvarado** .... (202) 353-0600
E-mail: henry.alvarado@usdoj.gov
Supervisory Deputy U.S. Marshal **Michelle Drinkard** .... (202) 353-0600
E-mail: michelle.drinkard@usdoj.gov

District of Columbia Superior Court

500 Indiana Avenue, NW, Room C-250, Washington, DC 20001
Tel: (202) 616-8600 Fax: (202) 616-8666

★ U.S. Marshal **Michael A. Hughes** .... (202) 616-8604
E-mail: michael.hughes@usdoj.gov
Education: Montclair State U 1990; American U 2007 MPA
Chief Deputy U.S. Marshal **Charlotta Allen-Brown** ..... (202) 616-8600
E-mail: charlotta.allen@usdoj.gov
Assistant Chief Deputy U.S. Marshal **Corina Zamora** .... (202) 307-9269
E-mail: corina.zamora@usdoj.gov
Assistant Chief Deputy U.S. Marshal **Jacob Green** ...... (202) 616-8600
E-mail: jacob.green@usdoj.gov
Supervisory Deputy U.S. Marshal **Damon Adams** .... (202) 616-8600
E-mail: damon.adams@usdoj.gov
Supervisory Deputy U.S. Marshal **Ronnie Bolls** .... (202) 616-8555
E-mail: ronald.bolls@usdoj.gov
Supervisory Deputy U.S. Marshal **Bobby Brooks** .... (202) 616-8600
E-mail: bobby.brooks@usdoj.gov
Supervisory Deputy U.S. Marshal **Randy Foster** .... (202) 616-1962

(continued on next page)

District of Columbia Superior Court *continued*

Supervisory Deputy U.S. Marshal **Pablo Irizarry** . . . . (202) 616-8600
E-mail: pablo.irizarry@usdoj.gov
Supervisory Deputy U.S. Marshal **Rafael Ortega** . . . . (202) 616-8600
E-mail: rafael.ortega@usdoj.gov
Supervisory Deputy U.S. Marshal **Michael Parks** . . . . (202) 616-8556
E-mail: michael.parks@usdoj.gov
Supervisory Deputy U.S. Marshal **Fayette Reid** . . . . (202) 616-8600
E-mail: fayette.reid@usdoj.gov
Supervisory Deputy U.S. Marshal
Christopher Schwartz . . . . (202) 616-8600
Supervisory Deputy U.S. Marshal **Todd Singleton** . . . . (202) 616-8600
E-mail: todd.singleton@usdoj.gov
Supervisory Deputy U.S. Marshal **John Waters** . . . . (202) 616-8600
E-mail: john.waters@usdoj.gov
Supervisory Deputy U.S. Marshal **Floriano Whietwell** . . . (202) 616-8550
Supervisory Deputy U.S. Marshal **Torrance Wilson** . . . . . . (202) 616-8550
E-mail: torrance.wilson@usdoj.gov
Supervisory Deputy U.S. Marshal **Tam M. Wyatt** . . . . (202) 616-8600
Supervisory Deputy U.S. Marshal **(Vacant)** . . . . (202) 616-2294

Florida - Middle District

U.S. Courthouse, 801 North Florida Avenue,
4th Floor, Tampa, FL 33602
Tel: (813) 483-4200 Fax: (813) 274-6487

★ U.S. Marshal **William Berger, Sr.** . . . . (813) 483-4201
E-mail: william.berger@usdoj.gov
Education: St Thomas U BA, MA; Nova Southeastern 2003 JD
Chief Deputy U.S. Marshal **Thomas Figmik** . . . . (813) 483-4200
E-mail: thomas.figmik@usdoj.gov
Assistant Chief Deputy U.S. Marshal **Pete Cajigal** . . . . (813) 483-4200
E-mail: pete.cajigal@usdoj.gov
Supervisory Deputy U.S. Marshal **Chris Kipp** . . . . (813) 483-4222
E-mail: christopher.kipp@usdoj.gov
Supervisory Deputy U.S. Marshal **Dexter Sylvester** . . . . . (813) 483-4245
E-mail: dexter.sylvester@usdoj.gov
Administrative Officer **Amy Warner** . . . . (813) 483-4218
E-mail: amy.warner@usdoj.gov

Fort Myers (FL) Office

2110 First Street, Room 1-116, Fort Myers, FL 33901
Tel: (239) 337-0002 Fax: (239) 337-7849

Supervisory Deputy U.S. Marshal **Ryan Barry** . . . . (239) 337-0002
E-mail: ryan.barry@usdoj.gov

Jacksonville (FL) Office

300 North Hogan Street, Suite 2-450, Jacksonville, FL 32202
Tel: (904) 301-6687

Supervisory Deputy U.S. Marshal **Penelope Knox** . . . . (904) 301-6670
E-mail: penelope.knox@usdoj.gov

Orlando (FL) Office

401 N. Central Boulevard, Suite 2300, Orlando, FL 32801-0230
Tel: (407) 316-5500 Fax: (407) 316-5510

Supervisory Deputy U.S. Marshal (Interim)
Silvestre Del Rosario . . . . (407) 316-5500

Florida - Northern District

U.S. Courthouse, 111 North Adams Street,
Room 277, Tallahassee, FL 32301
Tel: (850) 942-8400 Fax: (850) 942-8388

★ U.S. Marshal **Edward M. Spooner** . . . . (850) 942-8400
E-mail: ed.spooner@usdoj.gov
Chief Deputy U.S. Marshal **Brian Nerney** . . . . (850) 942-8400
E-mail: brian.nerney@usdoj.gov
Supervisory Deputy U.S. Marshal **Paul J. Joanos** . . . . (850) 942-8400
E-mail: paul.joanos2@usdoj.gov

Florida - Northern District *continued*

Assistant Chief Deputy U.S. Marshal (Enforcement)
Scott Wilson . . . . (850) 942-8400
Deputy U.S. Marshal **Heather Gloetzner** . . . . (850) 942-8400
E-mail: heather.gloetzner@usdoj.gov
Deputy U.S. Marshal **Kerry Phillips** . . . . (850) 942-8400
E-mail: kerry.phillips@usdoj.gov
Deputy U.S. Marshal **Marty West** . . . . (850) 942-8400
E-mail: marty.west@usdoj.gov
Deputy U.S. Marshal **(Vacant)** . . . . (850) 942-8400
Deputy U.S. Marshal **(Vacant)** . . . . (850) 942-8400
District Judicial Security Inspector **(Vacant)** . . . . (850) 942-8400
Investigative Research Specialist **Robyn Dixon** . . . . (850) 942-8400
E-mail: robyn.dixon@usdoj.gov
Seizure/Forfeiture Specialist **Julie White** . . . . (850) 942-8400
Administrative Officer **Jan Bell** . . . . (850) 942-8400
E-mail: jan.bell@usdoj.gov
Budget Analyst **Kathy Sparman** . . . . (850) 942-8400
Criminal Program Specialist **(Vacant)** . . . . (850) 942-8394

Gainesville (FL) Office

401 SE First Avenue, Room 255, Gainesville, FL 32601
Tel: (352) 378-2082 Fax: (352) 372-1421

Supervisory Deputy U.S. Marshal **John Hallman** . . . . (352) 378-2082
E-mail: john.hallman@usdoj.gov
Deputy U.S. Marshal **Don McAfee** . . . . (352) 378-2082
E-mail: don.mcafee@usdoj.gov
Deputy U.S. Marshal **Adam Myers** . . . . (352) 240-0430
E-mail: adam.myers@usdoj.gov
Deputy U.S. Marshal **(Vacant)** . . . . (352) 378-2082
Administrative Assistant **Jennifer Tallarico** . . . . (352) 378-2082
E-mail: jennifer.tallarico@usdoj.gov

Panama City (FL) Office

30 West Government Street, Panama City, FL 34201
Tel: (850) 763-0771 Fax: (850) 763-0643

Deputy U.S. Marshal **John Farrish** . . . . (850) 763-6449
E-mail: john.farrish@usdoj.gov
Deputy U.S. Marshal **Christopher "Chris" Mask** . . . . (850) 763-0771
E-mail: christopher.mask@usdoj.gov
Deputy U.S. Marshal **Stephen Thaggard** . . . . (850) 763-0771
E-mail: stephen.thaggard@usdoj.gov
Deputy U.S. Marshal **(Vacant)** . . . . (850) 763-0771
Administrative Assistant **David Byrd** . . . . (850) 763-0771
E-mail: david.byrd@usdoj.gov

Pensacola (FL) Office

U.S. Courthouse, One North Palafox Street, Pensacola, FL 32595
Tel: (850) 469-8270 Fax: (850) 432-2741

Supervisory Deputy U.S. Marshal **Tom Miller** . . . . (850) 469-8270
E-mail: thomas.miller@usdoj.gov
Deputy U.S. Marshal **Nicole Dugan** . . . . (850) 469-8270
Deputy U.S. Marshal **Dominic Guadagnoli** . . . . (850) 469-8270
Deputy U.S. Marshal **Chris Leachman** . . . . (850) 469-8270
E-mail: chris.leachman@usdoj.gov
Deputy U.S. Marshal **Tom Little** . . . . (850) 469-8270
E-mail: tom.little@usdoj.gov
Deputy U.S. Marshal **Carl LoPresti** . . . . (850) 469-8276
E-mail: carl.lopresti@usdoj.gov
Deputy U.S. Marshal **Pam McKissick-Hardy** . . . . (850) 469-8270
Deputy U.S. Marshal **(Vacant)** . . . . (850) 469-8270
Deputy U.S. Marshal **(Vacant)** . . . . (850) 469-8270
Investigative Research Specialist **Donna Cato** . . . . (850) 469-8270

Florida - Southern District

400 North Miami Avenue, 6th Floor, Miami, FL 33128
Tel: (786) 433-6340 Fax: (305) 536-5907

★ U.S. Marshal **Amos Rojas, Jr.** . . . . (786) 433-6342
E-mail: amos.rojas@usdoj.gov
Education: Alabama Huntsville 1983
Chief Deputy U.S. Marshal **Keith Kluttz** . . . . (786) 433-6342
E-mail: keith.kluttz@usdoj.gov
Assistant Chief Deputy U.S. Marshal **Manny Puri** . . . . (786) 433-6500
51 SW First Avenue, Room 900, Miami, FL 33130
E-mail: manny.puri2@usdoj.gov
Assistant Chief Deputy Northern Division **Glen Wilner** . . . (954) 356-7256
E-mail: glen.wilner@usdoj.gov
Deputy-in-Charge **John Karlovitch** . . . . (561) 467-2347
500 Orange Avenue, Fort Pierce, FL 34950
E-mail: john.karlovitch@usdoj.gov
Supervisor **Wayne Pickering** . . . . (561) 832-7195
701 Clematis Street, Room 215, West Palm Beach, FL 33042
E-mail: wayne.pickering@usdoj.gov
Supervisor **Sabrina Livingston** . . . . (954) 356-7578
299 East Broward Boulevard, Room 312, Fort Lauderdale, FL 33301
Asset Seizure Supervisor **Jacqueline Vazquez** . . . . (786) 433-6391
51 SW First Avenue, Room 900, Miami, FL 33130
E-mail: jacqueline.vazquez@usdoj.gov
Court Security Supervisor **Bill Berry** . . . . (786) 433-6635
E-mail: william.berry@usdoj.gov
Prisoner/Fugitive Operations Supervisor **(Vacant)** . . . . (786) 433-6603
Administrative Officer **Madeleine Rivera** . . . . (786) 433-6610
E-mail: madeleine.rivera@usdoj.gov

Georgia - Middle District

U.S. Courthouse, 475 Mulberry Street,
4th Floor, Macon, GA 31201
P.O. Box 7, Macon, GA 31202
Tel: (478) 752-8280 Fax: (478) 752-8214

★ U.S. Marshal **Willie Lee Richardson, Jr.** . . . . (478) 752-8280
E-mail: willie.richardson@usdoj.gov
Education: Air U (USAF) 1984 AAB
Chief Deputy U.S. Marshal **Tricia Ashford** . . . . (478) 752-8280
E-mail: tricia.ashford@usdoj.gov
Supervisory Deputy U.S. Marshal **Will Hawkins** . . . . (478) 752-8280
E-mail: will.hawkins@usdoj.gov
Senior Deputy U.S. Marshal/Criminal Investigator/Judicial Security Inspector
Marc Howard . . . . (478) 752-8280
E-mail: marc.howard@usdoj.gov
Senior Deputy U.S. Marshal/Criminal Investigator
Tom Patton . . . . (478) 752-8280
E-mail: tom.patton@usdoj.gov
Deputy U.S. Marshal/Criminal Investigator
Thad Binford . . . . (478) 752-8280
E-mail: thad.binford@usdoj.gov
Deputy U.S. Marshal/Criminal Investigator **Ken Britt** . . . . . (478) 752-8280
E-mail: ken.britt@usdoj.gov
Deputy U.S. Marshal/Criminal Investigator
John Devenney . . . . (478) 752-8280
E-mail: john.devenney@usdoj.gov
Deputy U.S. Marshal/Criminal Investigator **Don Haney** . . . (478) 752-8280
E-mail: don.haney@usdoj.gov
Deputy U.S. Marshal/Criminal Investigator
Stephenie Usher . . . . (478) 752-8280
E-mail: stephenie.usher@usdoj.gov
Deputy U.S. Marshal/Criminal Investigator
Lemuel Watkins . . . . (478) 752-8280
E-mail: lemuel.watkins@usdoj.gov
Deputy U.S. Marshal/Criminal Investigator **Brad Wood** . . . (478) 752-8280
E-mail: brad.wood@usdoj.gov
Deputy U.S. Marshal/Criminal Investigator
Chris Wright . . . . (478) 752-8280
E-mail: christopher.wright@usdoj.gov
Seizure and Forfeiture Specialist **Janet Wallace** . . . . (478) 752-8280

Georgia - Middle District *continued*

Investigative Research Specialist **Theresa Christian** . . . . . (478) 752-8280
Administrative Officer **Melody Young** . . . . (478) 752-8280
E-mail: melody.young@usdoj.gov
Budget Analyst **Gena Goodwin** . . . . (478) 752-8280
E-mail: gena.goodwin@usdoj.gov
Criminal Program Specialist **Tomeko Bryant** . . . . (478) 752-8280

Albany (GA) Office

U.S. Post Office and Courthouse, 201 West Broad Avenue,
Room 133, Albany, GA 31701
Tel: (229) 430-8436

Senior Deputy U.S. Marshal-in-Charge **Steve Sparks** . . . . (229) 430-8436
Senior Deputy U.S. Marshal/Criminal Investigator
Elorm Blake . . . . (229) 430-8436
E-mail: elorm.blake@usdoj.gov
Senior Deputy U.S. Marshal/Criminal Investigator
Rodger Hormell . . . . (229) 430-8436
E-mail: rodger.hormell@usdoj.gov
Senior Deputy U.S. Marshal/Criminal Investigator
(Vacant) . . . . (229) 430-8436
Operational Support Specialist **Kimberley Kvistad** . . . . . . (229) 430-8436

Columbus (GA) Office

U.S. Courthouse, 120 12th Street, Columbus, GA 31901
Tel: (706) 649-7822

Deputy U.S. Marshal **Byron Pelote** . . . . (706) 649-7822
E-mail: byron.pelote@usdoj.gov
Supervisory Deputy U.S. Marshal **Lamont Ruffin** . . . . (706) 649-7822
E-mail: lamont.ruffin@usdoj.gov
Senior Deputy in Charge/Criminal Investigator
Laura Irby . . . . (706) 649-7822
E-mail: laura.irby@usdoj.gov
Deputy U.S. Marshal/Criminal Investigator
Lataria Cheatham . . . . (706) 649-7822
E-mail: lataria.cheatham@usdoj.gov
Deputy U.S. Marshal/Criminal Investigator
Robert Greene . . . . (706) 649-7822
E-mail: robert.greene@usdoj.gov

Georgia - Northern District

Richard B. Russell Federal Building, 75 Ted Turner Drive S.W.,
Suite 1600, Atlanta, GA 30303
Tel: (404) 331-6833 Fax: (404) 331-3139

★ U.S. Marshal **Beverly Joyce Harvard** . . . . (404) 331-6833
E-mail: beverly.harvard@usdoj.gov
Education: Morris Brown 1972 BA; Georgia State 1980 MS
Chief Deputy U.S. Marshal **Dawn Anderson** . . . . (404) 331-6833
E-mail: dawn.anderson@usdoj.gov
Assistant Chief Deputy U.S. Marshal **Daniel Hall** . . . . (404) 331-6833
E-mail: daniel.hall@usdoj.gov
Supervisory Deputy U.S. Marshal **(Vacant)** . . . . (404) 331-6833
Administrative Officer **Terri Hawkins-Smith** . . . . (404) 730-9245
E-mail: terri.hawkins@usdoj.gov
Budget Analyst **(Vacant)** . . . . (404) 730-9204

Georgia - Southern District

U.S. Courthouse, 125 Bull Street, Room 333, Savannah, GA 31401
Tel: (912) 652-4212 Fax: (912) 652-4064

★ U.S. Marshal **Stephen James Smith** . . . . (912) 652-4212
E-mail: ssmith5@usms.doj.gov
Education: Armstrong Atlantic State 1975 BS, 1987 MSc
Chief Deputy U.S. Marshal
James T. "Tom" Morefield . . . . (912) 652-4212
E-mail: tom.morefield@usdoj.gov
Supervisory Deputy U.S. Marshal **Keith Sampsell** . . . . (912) 652-4212
Supervisory Deputy U.S. Marshal **Ramiro Suarez** . . . . (912) 652-4212
E-mail: ramiro.suarez@usdoj.gov

★ Presidential Appointment Requiring Senate Confirmation ☆ Presidential Appointment □ Schedule C Appointment ◇ Career Senior Foreign Service Appointment
● Career Senior Executive Service (SES) Appointment ○ Non-Career Senior Executive Service (SES) Appointment ■ Postal Career Executive Service

Augusta (GA) Office
600 James Brown Boulevard, Augusta, GA 30901
Tel: (706) 724-5040 Fax: (706) 724-5041

Criminal Investigator **Mike Brant** .... (706) 724-5040
Criminal Investigator **Brandon Williams** .... (706) 724-5040
Education: Arizona 2001 JD
Criminal Investigator **Chance Hutto** .... (706) 724-5040
Criminal Investigator **Tim Keen** .... (706) 724-5040

Brunswick (GA) Office
801 Gloucester Street, Room 213, Brunswick, GA 31520
Tel: (912) 264-8429 Fax: (912) 264-8434

Criminal Investigator **Jay Chambrone** .... (912) 264-8429
Criminal Investigator **Marty Fitzjurles** .... (912) 264-8429
Criminal Investigator **Craig Murray** .... (912) 264-8429
E-mail: craig.murray@usdoj.gov

Statesboro (GA) Office
P.O. Box 81, Statesboro, GA 30459
Tel: (912) 489-4735 Fax: (912) 489-4862

Criminal Investigator **(Vacant)** .... (912) 489-4735

Guam and Northern Mariana Islands District
520 West Soledad Avenue, Room 344, Hagatna, GU 96910
Tel: (671) 477-7827 Fax: (671) 473-9195

★ U.S. Marshal **Frank G. Leon Guerrero** .... (671) 473-9101
E-mail: frank.leonguerrero@usdoj.gov
Education: U Guam 1997 BA
Chief Deputy U.S. Marshal **Chuck Ellis** .... (671) 473-9122
E-mail: chuck.ellis@usdoj.gov
Sex Offender Investigation Coordinator
John C. Untalan, Jr. .... (671) 473-9157
E-mail: john.untalan2@usdoj.gov
Judicial Security Inspector **Tanya Muna** .... (671) 473-9104
E-mail: tanya.muna@usdoj.gov
Deputy U.S. Marshal **Alfred A. "Jake" Celes II** .... (671) 473-9105
E-mail: Alfred.Celes@usdoj.gov
Deputy U.S. Marshal **Carlos D. Griffith** .... (671) 473-9106
E-mail: carlos.griffith@usdoj.gov
Deputy U.S. Marshal **Marciano Patricio** .... (671) 473-9103
E-mail: marciano.patricio@usdoj.gov
Deputy U.S. Marshal **David Punzalan** .... (671) 473-9153
E-mail: david.punzalan@usdoj.gov
Deputy U.S. Marshal **(Vacant)** .... (671) 473-9104
Administrative Officer **Elaine J. Gogue** .... (671) 473-9166
E-mail: elaine.gogue@usdoj.gov
Education: U Guam BS
Administrative Support Assistant **Therese Quinata** .... (671) 473-9174
E-mail: therese.quinata@usdoj.gov
Budget Analyst **Roger L. Ranson** .... (671) 473-9176
E-mail: roger.ranson@usdoj.gov
FSA Property Custodian **Tina B. Diras** .... (671) 473-9169
E-mail: tina.diras@usdoj.gov

Northern Mariana Islands Office
Horiguchi Building, Garapan Village Beach Road,
1st Floor, Saipan, MP 96950-0570
P.O. Box 500570, Saipan, MP 96950-0570
Tel: (670) 236-2954 Fax: (670) 236-2956

Supervisory Deputy U.S. Marshal **Don Hall** .... (670) 236-2954
E-mail: don.hall@usdoj.gov
Deputy U.S. Marshal **John Vega** .... (670) 236-2953
E-mail: john.vega@usdoj.gov
Education: U Guam 2010 BSCrimJ
Deputy U.S. Marshal **(Vacant)** .... (670) 236-2955

Hawaii District
Prince Jonah Kuhio Kalanianaole Federal Building,
300 Ala Moana Boulevard, Room 2800, Honolulu, HI 96850
Tel: (808) 541-3000 Tel: (800) 336-0102 (National Command Center)
Fax: (808) 541-3056 (Administration)
Fax: (808) 541-3015 (General Operations)

★ U.S. Marshal **Gervin K. Miyamoto** .... (808) 541-3030
E-mail: gervin.miyamoto@usdoj.gov
Education: Chaminade 1980 BS; U Phoenix 1999 MA
Chief Deputy U.S. Marshal **Gary H. Yandell** .... (808) 541-3000
E-mail: gary.yandell@usdoj.gov
Supervisory Deputy U.S. Marshal **Russ Jacobs** .... (808) 541-3000
E-mail: russell.jacobs@usdoj.gov
Supervisory Deputy U.S. Marshal **Justin Leong** .... (808) 541-3000
E-mail: justin.leong@usdoj.gov
Deputy U.S. Marshal **Jeremy Alford** .... (808) 436-9019
E-mail: jeremy.alford@usdoj.gov
Deputy U.S. Marshal **Brad Bolen** .... (808) 541-3000
E-mail: bradley.bolen@usdoj.gov
Deputy U.S. Marshal **Annabelle Bolter** .... (808) 541-3000
E-mail: annabelle.bolter@usdoj.gov
Deputy U.S. Marshal **Erica Harrington** .... (808) 541-3000
E-mail: erica.harrington@usdoj.gov
Deputy U.S. Marshal **Cindy Chu** .... (808) 541-3000
E-mail: cindy.chu@usdoj.gov
Deputy U.S. Marshal **Thomas Decker** .... (808) 541-3000
E-mail: thomas.decker@usdoj.gov
Deputy U.S. Marshal **Harvey Scott Fuata** .... (808) 541-3000
E-mail: harvey.fuata@usdoj.gov
Deputy U.S. Marshal **Dexter Gapusan** .... (808) 541-3000
E-mail: dexter.gapusan@usdoj.gov
Deputy U.S. Marshal **John Gilman** .... (808) 541-3000
E-mail: john.gilman@usdoj.gov
Deputy U.S. Marshal **Anton "Tony" Hopkins** .... (808) 292-4956
E-mail: anton.hopkins@usdoj.gov
Deputy U.S. Marshal **Eric Kalima** .... (808) 541-3000
E-mail: eric.kalima@usdoj.gov
Deputy U.S. Marshal **Kerry Lasso** .... (808) 541-3000
E-mail: kerry.lasso@usdoj.gov
Deputy U.S. Marshal **Gabriel Ganibe** .... (808) 541-3000
E-mail: gabriel.ganibe@usdoj.gov
Deputy U.S. Marshal **Stanley Sales** .... (808) 541-3000
E-mail: stanley.sales@usdoj.gov
Deputy U.S. Marshal **Nolan Sasaki** .... (808) 541-3000
E-mail: nolan.sasaki@usdoj.gov
Administrative Officer **Channing T. Iwamuro** .... (808) 541-3000
E-mail: channing.iwamuro@usdoj.gov
Budget Analyst **(Vacant)** .... (808) 541-3000
Criminal Program Specialist **Sharon Kanakaole** .... (808) 541-3000
DAFC Coordinator **Channing T. Iwamuro** .... (808) 541-3000
E-mail: channing.iwamuro@usdoj.gov
Judicial Security Inspector **Fred Edwards** .... (808) 541-3000
E-mail: fred.edwards@usdoj.gov

Idaho District
Federal Building and U.S. Courthouse,
550 West Fort Street, Boise, ID 83724
Tel: (208) 334-1298 Fax: (208) 334-9383

★ U.S. Marshal **Brian Todd Underwood** .... (208) 334-1298
E-mail: brian.underwood@usdoj.gov
Education: Idaho State 1998 BS
Chief Deputy U.S. Marshal **Kevin M. Platts** .... (208) 334-1298
E-mail: kevin.platts@usdoj.gov
Education: South Florida BA; Louisville MS
Supervisory Deputy U.S. Marshal
Peter "Pete" Thompson .... (208) 334-1298
E-mail: peter.thompson@usdoj.gov
Deputy U.S. Marshal **Vance Kosir** .... (208) 334-1298
E-mail: vance.kosir@usdoj.gov
Court Security **George Matthews** .... (208) 334-9679

REGIONAL OFFICES – US ATTORNEYS AND US MARSHALS SERVICE

★ Presidential Appointment Requiring Senate Confirmation ☆ Presidential Appointment □ Schedule C Appointment ◇ Career Senior Foreign Service Appointment
● Career Senior Executive Service (SES) Appointment ○ Non-Career Senior Executive Service (SES) Appointment ■ Postal Career Executive Service

Idaho District *continued*

Administrative Officer **Heidi Moore** .... (208) 334-9495
E-mail: heidi.moore@usdoj.gov

Coeur d'Alene (ID) Office

Federal Building and U.S. Court House,
205 North Fourth Street, Coeur d'Alene, ID 83814
Tel: (208) 667-6840

Deputy U.S. Marshal **Alex Claunts** .... (208) 667-6840 ext. 210
E-mail: alex.claunts@usdoj.gov
Deputy U.S. Marshal **Glenn Morgan** .... (208) 667-6840 ext. 211
E-mail: glenn.morgan@usdoj.gov

Pocatello (ID) Office

U.S. Court House, 801 East Sherman, Pocatello, ID 83201
Tel: (208) 478-4186

Supervisory Deputy U.S. Marshal **Darrin Lambert** .... (208) 478-4191
E-mail: darrin.lambert@usdoj.gov

Illinois - Central District

Paul Finley Building and U.S. Courthouse, 600 East Monroe Street,
Room 333, Springfield, IL 62701
Tel: (217) 492-4430 Fax: (217) 492-5053 (Administration)
Fax: (217) 492-4428 (Operations)
Fax: (217) 492-4840 (Seized Assets, Warrants)

★ U.S. Marshal **Kenneth F. Bohac** .... (217) 492-4466
Chief Deputy U.S. Marshal **Brent L. Broshow** .... (217) 492-4467
E-mail: brent.broshow@usdoj.gov
Supervisory Deputy U.S. Marshal **Kevin P. Jackson** ..... (309) 208-6384
Areas Covered: Warrants
E-mail: kevin.jackson@usdoj.gov
Supervisory Deputy U.S. Marshal **Brett Jackson** .... (217) 492-4227
Areas Covered: Operations
E-mail: brett.jackson@usdoj.gov
Deputy U.S. Marshal **Karl Hein** .... (217) 492-4229
E-mail: karl.hein@usdoj.gov
Deputy U.S. Marshal **Craig Kmett** .... (217) 492-5008
E-mail: craig.kmett@usdoj.gov
Deputy U.S. Marshal **Mark Fowell** .... (217) 492-4435
E-mail: mark.fowell@usdoj.gov
Administrative Officer **(Vacant)** .... (217) 492-5052
Fax: (217) 492-4534
Administrative Support Assistant/Criminal Program Specialist **Rory Nihsen** .... (217) 492-5000
E-mail: rory.nihsen@usdoj.gov
Financial Specialist **Kevin Weber** .... (217) 492-4535
E-mail: kevin.weber@usdoj.gov
Seizure and Forfeiture Specialist **Crystal Y. Gregory** ..... (217) 492-5001
Senior Systems Administrator **Michael Jagels** .... (217) 492-4835
E-mail: michael.jagels@usdoj.gov
Judicial Security Inspector **J. Glen Williams** .... (217) 492-5006
E-mail: glen.williams@usdoj.gov

Danville (IL) Office

Federal Building, 201 North Vermilion Street,
Room 013, Danville, IL 61832
Tel: (217) 442-4068 (CSO Post) Fax: (217) 442-1187

Note: This office is staffed only when bankruptcy court is in session.

Deputy U.S. Marshal **(Vacant)** .... (217) 442-0875

Peoria (IL) Office

Federal Building, 100 NE Monroe Street,
Room 42, Peoria, IL 61602
Tel: (309) 671-7053 Fax: (309) 671-7845

Supervisory Deputy U.S. Marshal **Doug Sparks** .... (309) 671-7156
E-mail: douglas.sparks@usdoj.gov

Peoria (IL) Office *continued*

Deputy U.S. Marshal **Brent Cranford** .... (309) 671-7185
E-mail: brent.cranford@usdoj.gov
Deputy U.S. Marshal **Jeff Dale** .... (309) 671-7184
E-mail: jeff.dale@usdoj.gov
Deputy U.S. Marshal **Shawn Langley** .... (309) 671-7042
E-mail: shawn.langley@usdoj.gov
Deputy U.S. Marshal **J. Glen Williams** .... (309) 671-7158
Deputy U.S. Marshal **(Vacant)** .... (309) 671-7244
Administrative Support Assistant **(Vacant)** .... (309) 671-7157

Rock Island (IL) Office

211 - 19th Street, Room G18, Rock Island, IL 61201
Tel: (309) 793-5796 Fax: (309) 793-5808

Deputy U.S. Marshal-in-Charge **Scott Shepherd** .... (309) 793-5794
E-mail: scott.shepherd@usdoj.gov
Deputy U.S. Marshal **Greg Sims** .... (309) 793-5795

Urbana (IL) Office

201 South Vine Street, Room 15, Urbana, IL 61801
Tel: (217) 344-9935 Fax: (217) 344-9972

Supervisory Deputy U.S. Marshal **Brett Jackson** .... (217) 344-9945
E-mail: brett.jackson@usdoj.gov
Deputy U.S. Marshal **Mark Aughenbaugh** .... (217) 344-9963
E-mail: mark.aughenbaugh@usdoj.gov
Deputy U.S. Marshal **Justin Moreau** .... (217) 344-9951
E-mail: justin.moreau@usdoj.gov
Deputy U.S. Marshal **Tom Greiner** .... (217) 344-9968
E-mail: thomas.greiner@usdoj.gov
Deputy U.S. Marshal **Danielle J. Sapp** .... (217) 344-9958

Illinois - Northern District

Dirksen Federal Building, 219 South Dearborn Street,
Room 2444, Chicago, IL 60604
Tel: (312) 353-5290 Fax: (312) 353-4132

★ U.S. Marshal (Acting) **Roberto Robinson** .... (312) 353-5043
★ U.S. Marshal **Edward L. Gilmore** .... (312) 353-5043
Note: On October 29, 2015 the U.S. Senate confirmed Edward Gilmore to be U.S. Marshal.
Chief Deputy U.S. Marshal **Thomas J. Smith** .... (312) 353-4979
Supervisory Deputy U.S. Marshal **Matthew Block** ...... (312) 353-5291
E-mail: matthew.block@usdoj.gov
Supervisory Deputy U.S. Marshal (Asset Seizure) **Cynthia Villarruel** .... (312) 353-5291
E-mail: cynthia.villarruel@usdoj.gov
Supervisory Deputy U.S. Marshal (Lock-Up) **Christopher Shaw** .... (312) 353-5290
E-mail: christopher.shaw@usdoj.gov
Supervisory Deputy U.S. Marshal (Warrants) **Belkis Sandoval** .... (312) 353-6363
E-mail: belkis.sandoval@usdoj.gov
Assistant Chief Deputy U.S. Marshal (Acting) **Ken Robinson** .... (312) 353-7192
E-mail: ken.robinson@usdoj.gov
Senior Judicial Security Inspector **Richard Walenda** ..... (312) 353-5290
E-mail: richard.walenda@usdoj.gov
Judicial Security Inspector **Paul Banos** .... (312) 353-5290
E-mail: paul.banos@usdoj.gov
Administrative Officer **David Shereyk** .... (312) 353-7034
E-mail: david.shereyk@usdoj.gov

Illinois - Southern District

U.S. Courthouse, 750 Missouri Avenue, East St. Louis, IL 62201
Tel: (618) 482-9336 Fax: (618) 482-9235

★ U.S. Marshal **Donald Slazinik** .... (618) 482-9339
E-mail: don.slazinik@usdoj.gov
Education: Southeast Missouri State BA; Webster MA

(continued on next page)

★ Presidential Appointment Requiring Senate Confirmation ☆ Presidential Appointment □ Schedule C Appointment ◇ Career Senior Foreign Service Appointment
● Career Senior Executive Service (SES) Appointment ○ Non-Career Senior Executive Service (SES) Appointment ■ Postal Career Executive Service

Illinois - Southern District *continued*

Chief Deputy U.S. Marshal **Karen Simons** . . . . (618) 482-9421
E-mail: karen.simons@usdoj.gov
Supervisory Deputy U.S. Marshal **Dave Davis** . . . . (618) 439-7701
Supervisory Deputy U.S. Marshal **Thomas Woods** . . . . . . (618) 482-9236
E-mail: thomas.woods@usdoj.gov
Supervisory Deputy U.S. Marshal **Christopher Boyce** . . . . (618) 482-9321
Deputy U.S. Marshal **Donald Berry** . . . . (618) 482-9137
E-mail: donald.berry@usdoj.gov
Deputy U.S. Marshal **James Brigham** . . . . (618) 482-9159
E-mail: james.brigham@usdoj.gov
Deputy U.S. Marshal **James Jackson III** . . . . (618) 482-9087
E-mail: james.jackson@usdoj.gov
Deputy U.S. Marshal **Roderick Johnson** . . . . (618) 482-9239
E-mail: roderick.johnson@usdoj.gov
Deputy U.S. Marshal **Brenda Larson** . . . . (618) 482-9086
E-mail: brenda.larson@usdoj.gov
Deputy U.S. Marshal **James Milner** . . . . (618) 482-9089
Deputy U.S. Marshal **Kyle Shirley** . . . . (618) 482-9238
Deputy U.S. Marshal **Chad Uhl** . . . . (618) 482-9085
E-mail: chad.uhl@usdoj.gov
Deputy U.S. Marshal **Clay Weier** . . . . (618) 482-9487
Purchasing Agent **Phyllis Gonzalez** . . . . (618) 482-9336
E-mail: phyllis.gonzalez@usdoj.gov
Criminal Program Specialist **Angel Jones** . . . . (618) 482-9490
E-mail: angel.jones@usdoj.gov
Administrative Officer **Wendy Winston** . . . . (618) 482-9065
E-mail: wendy.winston@usdoj.gov
Accounting Technician **(Vacant)** . . . . (618) 482-9337
Court Security Inspector **Jeffrey Larson** . . . . (618) 482-9048
E-mail: jeff.larson@usdoj.gov
Investigative Research Specialist **(Vacant)** . . . . (618) 482-9065
Detention Enforcement Officer **(Vacant)** . . . . (618) 482-9492

Benton (IL) Office

301 West Main Street, Benton, IL 62812
Tel: (618) 439-6442 Fax: (618) 439-4482

Supervisory Deputy U.S. Marshal **Pete Kell** . . . . (618) 439-7701
Deputy U.S. Marshal **Kevin Castleman** . . . . (618) 439-7703
E-mail: kevin.castleman@usdoj.gov
Deputy U.S. Marshal **Clark Meadows** . . . . (618) 439-7704
E-mail: clark.meadows@usdoj.gov
Deputy U.S. Marshal **Jim Robertson** . . . . (618) 439-7704
E-mail: jim.robertson@usdoj.gov
Operations Support Specialist **Lynn Steh** . . . . (618) 439-7700
E-mail: lynn.steh@usdoj.gov

Indiana - Northern District

5400 Federal Plaza, Suite 1200, Hammond, IN 46320
Tel: (219) 852-6776 Fax: (219) 852-6771

★ U.S. Marshal **Myron Martin Sutton** . . . . (219) 852-6776
E-mail: myron.sutton@usdoj.gov
Education: Northwestern (Attended)
Chief Deputy U.S. Marshal **Todd L. Nukes** . . . . (219) 852-6776
E-mail: todd.nukes@usdoj.gov
Supervisory Deputy U.S. Marshal **Melanie Thompson** . . . (219) 852-6776
E-mail: melanie.thompson@usdoj.gov
Deputy U.S. Marshal **Timothy Craigin** . . . . (219) 852-6776
E-mail: timothy.craigin@usdoj.gov
Deputy U.S. Marshal **Lauren Holly** . . . . (219) 852-6776
E-mail: lauren.holly@usdoj.gov
Deputy U.S. Marshal **John Kaznowski IV** . . . . (219) 852-6776
E-mail: john.kaznowski@usdoj.gov
Deputy U.S. Marshal **Dennis Nation** . . . . (219) 852-6776
E-mail: dennis.nation@usdoj.gov
Deputy U.S. Marshal **Edward Payne** . . . . (219) 852-6776
E-mail: ed.payne@usdoj.gov
Deputy U.S. Marshal **Derek Rubarts** . . . . (219) 852-6776
E-mail: derek.rubarts@usdoj.gov

Indiana - Northern District *continued*

Deputy U.S. Marshal **Gregory Thiel** . . . . (219) 852-6776
E-mail: greg.thiel@usdoj.gov
Detention Enforcement Officer **Chris Knudsen** . . . . (219) 852-6776
Administrative Officer **Rita Anthony** . . . . (219) 852-6776
E-mail: rita.anthony@usdoj.gov
Administrative Assistant **Colette Kapost** . . . . (219) 852-6776
E-mail: colette.kapost@usdoj.gov
Budget Analyst **Lorraine Ward** . . . . (219) 852-6776
Operational Support Specialist **Tamar DeCosta** . . . . (219) 852-6776
E-mail: tamar.decosta@usdoj.gov

Fort Wayne (IN) Office

1300 South Harrison Street, Room 1147, Fort Wayne, IN 46802
Tel: (260) 423-4667 Fax: (260) 424-8753

Deputy U.S. Marshal **Eric Anderson** . . . . (260) 423-4667
E-mail: eric.anderson@usdoj.gov
Deputy U.S. Marshal **John Simpson** . . . . (260) 423-4667
E-mail: john.simpson@usdoj.gov
Deputy U.S. Marshal **David Veasey** . . . . (260) 423-4667
E-mail: david.veasey@usdoj.gov
Deputy U.S. Marshal **(Vacant)** . . . . (260) 423-4667
Investigative Research Specialist **Joan Reed** . . . . (260) 423-4667

South Bend (IN) Office

204 South Main Street, Room 233, South Bend, IN 46601
Tel: (574) 236-8291 Fax: (574) 236-8815

Supervisory Deputy U.S. Marshal
Pamela D. Mozdzierz . . . . (574) 236-8291
E-mail: pamela.mozdzierz@usdoj.gov
Deputy U.S. Marshal **William Boothe** . . . . (574) 236-8291
E-mail: william.boothe@usdoj.gov
Deputy U.S. Marshal **Alex Lubarsky** . . . . (574) 236-8291
Deputy U.S. Marshal **James Ratobylski** . . . . (574) 236-8291
E-mail: james.ratobylski@usdoj.gov
Deputy U.S. Marshal **Rodney Shields** . . . . (574) 236-8291
E-mail: rodney.shields@usdoj.gov
Senior Inspector **Laura McKesson** . . . . (574) 236-8291
E-mail: laura.mckesson@usdoj.gov

Indiana - Southern District

179 Birch Bayh Federal Building and U.S. Courthouse,
46 East Ohio Street, Room 179, Indianapolis, IN 46204
Tel: (317) 226-6566 Fax: (317) 226-7695

★ U.S. Marshal **Kerry Joseph Forestal** . . . . (317) 226-6566
E-mail: kerry.forestal@usdoj.gov
Chief Deputy U.S. Marshal **William "Buz" Brown** . . . . . . (317) 226-6566
E-mail: buz.brown@usdoj.gov
Administrative Officer **Lisa R. Black** . . . . (317) 226-5411
E-mail: lisa.black@usdoj.gov
Operational Supervisor **Andrew "Drew" Arnold** . . . . (317) 226-0253
E-mail: andrew.arnold@usdoj.gov
Warrants Supervisor **John Beeman** . . . . (317) 226-6059
E-mail: john.beeman@usdoj.gov
Senior Deputy U.S. Marshal **John Pappas** . . . . (317) 614-0006
E-mail: john.pappas@usdoj.gov
Deputy U.S. Marshal - SOIC **(Vacant)** . . . . (317) 226-6570
Deputy U.S. Marshal **(Vacant)** . . . . (317) 226-7789
Judicial Security Inspector **Robert Jackson** . . . . (317) 226-6570
E-mail: rob.jackson@usdoj.gov
Criminal Clerk **Sherita Byrdsong** . . . . (317) 614-0011
E-mail: sherita.byrdsong@usdoj.gov
Financial Specialist **Diana Dickerson** . . . . (317) 226-6569
E-mail: diana.dickerson@usdoj.gov
District Asset Forfeiture Coordinator **Nneka Greene** . . . . . (317) 226-6123
E-mail: nneka.greene@usdoj.gov
Investigative Research Specialist (Warrants)
Jarmila "Joi" Howard . . . . (317) 226-0254
E-mail: joi.howard@usdoj.gov

★ Presidential Appointment Requiring Senate Confirmation ☆ Presidential Appointment □ Schedule C Appointment ◇ Career Senior Foreign Service Appointment
● Career Senior Executive Service (SES) Appointment ○ Non-Career Senior Executive Service (SES) Appointment ■ Postal Career Executive Service

Evansville (IN) Office
101 NW Martin Luther King Boulevard,
Room 332, Evansville, IN 47708
Tel: (812) 465-6437 Fax: (812) 465-6473

Deputy U.S. Marshal **John Albright** .... (812) 465-6437
Deputy U.S. Marshal **David Lewis** .... (812) 465-6437
Operations Supervisory Deputy U.S. Marshal
Ryan Filson .... (812) 465-6437

New Albany (IN) Office
121 West Spring Street, Room 229, New Albany, IN 47150
Tel: (812) 948-5235 Fax: (812) 948-5207

Deputy U.S. Marshal **Kevin Ferran** .... (812) 948-5235
E-mail: kevin.ferran@usdoj.gov

Terre Haute (IN) Office
30 North Seventh Street, Room 218, Terre Haute, IN 47807
Tel: (812) 232-5058 Fax: (812) 232-3561

Deputy U.S. Marshal **Greg Snyder** .... (812) 232-5058

Iowa - Northern District
111 Seventh Avenue SE, Box 7, Cedar Rapids, IA 52401
Tel: (319) 362-4411 Fax: (319) 362-7098

★ U.S. Marshal **Kenneth James Runde** .... (319) 362-4411
E-mail: kenneth.runde@usdoj.gov
Education: Pepperdine 1975 AA; Wisconsin 1982 BA
Chief Deputy U.S. Marshal **Myron McDaniel** .... (319) 362-4411
E-mail: myron.mcdaniel@usdoj.gov
Deputy U.S. Marshal **Michael Glockner** .... (319) 362-4411
E-mail: michael.glockner@usdoj.gov
Deputy U.S. Marshal **Pedro "Pete" Lozano** .... (319) 362-4411
E-mail: pedro.lozano@usdoj.gov
Deputy U.S. Marshal **Tyrus Lester** .... (319) 362-4411
E-mail: tyrus.lester@usdoj.gov
Deputy U.S. Marshal **Jeffrey "Jeff" Lour** .... (319) 362-4411
E-mail: jeff.lour@usdoj.gov
Deputy U.S. Marshal **Richard Manning** .... (319) 362-4411
E-mail: richard.manning@usdoj.gov
Deputy U.S. Marshal **Earl Plattner** .... (319) 362-4411
E-mail: earl.plattner@usdoj.gov
Administrative Officer **Mellissa Brockes** .... (319) 362-4411
E-mail: mellissa.brockes@usdoj.gov
Management and Program Analyst **Gail Arndt** .... (319) 362-4411
Criminal Program Specialist **Lance Akery** .... (319) 362-4411
E-mail: lance.akery@usdoj.gov
Administrative Support Assistant **Joshua Hammitt** ...... (319) 362-4411
E-mail: joshua.hammitt@usdoj.gov

Sioux City (IA) Office
320 Sixth Street, Room 308, Sioux City, IA 51101
Tel: (712) 252-3077 Fax: (712) 252-3300

Supervisory Deputy U.S. Marshal **(Vacant)** .... (712) 252-3077
Deputy U.S. Marshal **Jamey Dickson** .... (712) 252-3077
E-mail: jamey.dickson@usdoj.gov
Deputy U.S. Marshal **Michael A. Fuller** .... (712) 252-3077
E-mail: michael.fuller@usdoj.gov
Deputy U.S. Marshal **David Hubbell** .... (712) 252-3077
E-mail: david.hubbell@usdoj.gov
Deputy U.S. Marshal **Brandon Johnson** .... (712) 252-3077
E-mail: brandon.johnson@usdoj.gov
Deputy U.S. Marshal **Christopher Kegley** .... (712) 252-3077
E-mail: christopher.kegley@usdoj.gov
Deputy U.S. Marshal **Charles McCormick** .... (712) 252-3077
E-mail: charles.mccormick@usdoj.gov
Deputy U.S. Marshal **Peter Zellmer** .... (712) 252-3077
E-mail: peter.zellmer@usdoj.gov
Deputy U.S. Marshal **(Vacant)** .... (712) 252-3077

Sioux City (IA) Office *continued*

Operations Support Specialist **Lanae Minten** .... (712) 252-3077
E-mail: lanae.minten@usdoj.gov

Iowa - Southern District
U.S. Courthouse, 123 East Walnut Street,
Room 343A, Des Moines, IA 50309
Tel: (515) 284-6240 Fax: (515) 284-6204
Fax: (515) 323-2800 (Criminal Division)

★ U.S. Marshal **Michael R. Bladel** .... (515) 284-6240
E-mail: michael.bladel@usdoj.gov
Education: St Ambrose 1991 BA
Chief Deputy U.S. Marshal **Robert Otto** .... (515) 284-6423
E-mail: robert.otto@usdoj.gov
Supervisory Deputy U.S. Marshal **Michael Powell** .... (515) 323-2854
E-mail: michael.powell@usdoj.gov
Deputy U.S. Marshal **Justin Barlow** .... (515) 284-6240
E-mail: justin.barlow@usdoj.gov
Deputy U.S. Marshal **Justin Buell** .... (515) 284-6240
E-mail: justin.buell@usdoj.gov
Deputy U.S. Marshal **Scott Cannon** .... (515) 284-6240
E-mail: scott.cannon@usdoj.gov
Deputy U.S. Marshal **Nick Gries** .... (515) 323-2883
E-mail: nicholas.gries@usdoj.gov
Deputy U.S. Marshal **Luke Peters** .... (515) 323-2880
E-mail: luke.peters@usdoj.gov
Deputy U.S. Marshal **Robert Schulte** .... (515) 323-2887
E-mail: robert.schulte@usdoj.gov
Deputy U.S. Marshal **Mark A. Shepard** .... (515) 323-2893
E-mail: mark.shepard@usdoj.gov
Deputy U.S. Marshal **Jonathan M. Stewart** .... (515) 323-2889
E-mail: jonathan.stewart@usdoj.gov
Deputy U.S. Marshal **David Zimmer** .... (515) 323-2899
E-mail: david.zimmer@usdoj.gov
Administrative Officer **Rita Mason** .... (515) 323-2884
E-mail: rita.mason@usdoj.gov
Criminal Program Specialist **Jeanne O'Keefe** .... (515) 323-2944
E-mail: jeanne.okeefe@usdoj.gov
Computer Specialist **Christopher Newcomb** .... (515) 323-2882
E-mail: chris.newcomb@usdoj.gov
Judicial Security Inspector **James Batey** .... (515) 323-6166
E-mail: james.batey@usdoj.gov
Information and Resources Specialist **Steve Svendsen** ... (515) 284-6240
E-mail: steve.svendsen@usdoj.gov

Council Bluffs (IA) Office
8 South Sixth Street, Room 344, Council Bluffs, IA 51501
Tel: (712) 322-2034 Fax: (712) 322-2024

Deputy U.S. Marshal **Corey Sherven** .... (712) 322-2034
E-mail: corey.sherven@usdoj.gov

Davenport (IA) Office
131 East Fourth Street, Room 300, Davenport, IA 52801
Tel: (563) 884-7667 Fax: (563) 884-7660

Supervisory Deputy U.S. Marshal **Sean O'Neal** .... (563) 884-7659
Deputy U.S. Marshal **Terry Bumann** .... (563) 884-7663
E-mail: terry.bumann@usdoj.gov
Deputy U.S. Marshal **Joe McCaffry** .... (563) 884-7667
E-mail: joe.mccaffry@usdoj.gov
Deputy U.S. Marshal **William Weier** .... (563) 884-7661
E-mail: william.weier@usdoj.gov
Deputy U.S. Marshal **(Vacant)** .... (563) 884-7667
Operations Support **Jennifer Buntemeyer** .... (563) 884-7667

Kansas District

Robert Dole Courthouse, 500 State Avenue,
Suite 380, Kansas City, KS 66101
Tel: (913) 551-6727 Fax: (913) 551-6535

★ U.S. Marshal **Ronald Lee Miller** . . . . . (913) 551-6727
Education: Central Missouri 1972 BA; Wichita State 1975 MA
Chief Deputy U.S. Marshal **Craig Beam** . . . . . (913) 551-6727
Supervisory Deputy U.S. Marshal **Michael Thibault** . . . . . (913) 551-6727
E-mail: michael.thibault@usdoj.gov
Inspector **Matthew Cahill** . . . . . (913) 551-6727
E-mail: matthew.cahill@usdoj.gov
Inspector **Sean Franklin** . . . . . (913) 551-6727
E-mail: sean.franklin@usdoj.gov
Deputy U.S. Marshal **Jovan Archuleta** . . . . . (913) 551-6727
E-mail: jovan.archuleta@usdoj.gov
Deputy U.S. Marshal **David Dane** . . . . . (913) 551-6727
E-mail: david.dane@usdoj.gov
Deputy U.S. Marshal **Brady Flannigan** . . . . . (913) 551-6727
E-mail: brady.flannigan@usdoj.gov
Deputy U.S. Marshal **R. Brett Hoffer** . . . . . (913) 551-6727
Deputy U.S. Marshal **Zachary Howard** . . . . . (913) 551-6727
E-mail: zachary.howard@usdoj.gov
Deputy U.S. Marshal **Christopher Johnson** . . . . . (913) 551-6727
E-mail: christopher.johnson@usdoj.gov
Deputy U.S. Marshal **William Lynn** . . . . . (913) 551-6727
E-mail: william.lynn@usdoj.gov
Deputy U.S. Marshal **Brad Owens** . . . . . (913) 551-6727
Deputy U.S. Marshal **John Volk** . . . . . (913) 551-6727
E-mail: john.volk@usdoj.gov
Deputy U.S. Marshal **Christopher Wallace** . . . . . (913) 551-6727
E-mail: christopher.wallace@usdoj.gov

Topeka (KS) Office

Federal Building, 444 SE Quincy Street,
Suite 456, Topeka, KS 66683
Tel: (785) 295-2775 Fax: (785) 295-2548

Supervisory Deputy U.S. Marshal **Troy Schuster** . . . . . (785) 295-2775
E-mail: troy.schuster@usdoj.gov
Deputy U.S. Marshal **Jeffrey Andrew** . . . . . (785) 295-2775
E-mail: jeffrey.andrew@usdoj.gov
Deputy U.S. Marshal **Travis Edwards** . . . . . (785) 295-2775
E-mail: travis.edwards@usdoj.gov
Deputy U.S. Marshal **Angel Espinal** . . . . . (785) 295-2775
E-mail: angel.espinal@usdoj.gov
Deputy U.S. Marshal **Romel Sinclair** . . . . . (785) 295-2775
E-mail: romel.sinclair@usdoj.gov
Deputy U.S. Marshal **Jerry Viera** . . . . . (785) 295-2775
E-mail: jerry.viera@usdoj.gov

Wichita (KS) Office

Federal Courthouse, 401 North Market Street,
Suite 207, Wichita, KS 67202
Tel: (316) 269-6479 Fax: (316) 269-6480

Supervisory Deputy U.S. Marshal **Troy Oberly** . . . . . (316) 269-6479
E-mail: troy.oberly@usdoj.gov
Deputy U.S. Marshal **Michael Caraway** . . . . . (316) 269-6479
E-mail: michael.caraway@usdoj.gov
Deputy U.S. Marshal **Jacob Hilton** . . . . . (316) 269-6479
E-mail: jacob.hilton@usdoj.gov
Deputy U.S. Marshal **Lesley Kal** . . . . . (316) 269-6479
E-mail: lesley.kal@usdoj.gov
Deputy U.S. Marshal **Logan Kline** . . . . . (316) 269-6479
E-mail: logan.kline@usdoj.gov
Deputy U.S. Marshal **Keith Lane** . . . . . (316) 269-6479
E-mail: keith.lane@usdoj.gov
Deputy U.S. Marshal **Blake Lemer** . . . . . (316) 269-6479
E-mail: blake.lemer@usdoj.gov
Deputy U.S. Marshal **Josh Moff** . . . . . (316) 269-6479
E-mail: joshua.moff@usdoj.gov

Wichita (KS) Office *continued*

Deputy U.S. Marshal **Quentin Terrel** . . . . . (316) 269-6479
E-mail: quentin.terrel@usdoj.gov
Inspector **David Stevens** . . . . . (316) 269-6479
E-mail: david.stevens@usdoj.gov

Kentucky - Eastern District

Federal Building, 101 Barr Street, Room 162, Lexington, KY 40507
Tel: (859) 233-2513 Fax: (859) 233-2517

★ U.S. Marshal (Acting) **Timothy Stec** . . . . . (859) 233-2629
E-mail: tim.stec@usdoj.gov
Chief Deputy U.S. Marshal (Acting)
Gordon Hotchkiss . . . . . (859) 233-8022
E-mail: gordon.hotchkiss2@usdoj.gov
Supervisory Deputy U.S. Marshal (Enforcement)
(Acting) **Roger Daniel** . . . . . (859) 410-8034
E-mail: roger.daniel@usdoj.gov
Supervisory Deputy U.S. Marshal (Operational)
Robert Kostenbader . . . . . (859) 233-2600
E-mail: robert.kostenbader@usdoj.gov
Deputy U.S. Marshal **Tyronne Bartley** . . . . . (859) 410-8025
E-mail: tyronne.bartley@usdoj.gov
Deputy U.S. Marshal **Jonathan Baus** . . . . . (859) 233-2513 ext. 234
E-mail: jonathan.baus@usdoj.gov
Deputy U.S. Marshal **Roger Daniel** . . . . . (859) 410-8024
E-mail: roger.daniel@usdoj.gov
Deputy U.S. Marshal **Jeffrey Kelly** . . . . . (859) 233-2513 ext. 241
E-mail: jeffrey.kelly@usdoj.gov
Deputy U.S. Marshal **David Lee** . . . . . (859) 233-2513 ext. 231
Deputy U.S. Marshal **Kenneth "Kenny" Vanover** . . . . . (859) 410-8021
E-mail: kenneth.vanover@usdoj.gov
Deputy U.S. Marshal **Wade Yonts** . . . . . (859) 233-2513 ext. 237
Deputy U.S. Marshal **(Vacant)** . . . . . (859) 233-2513 ext. 226
Court Security Inspector **Rick Kelley** . . . . . (859) 233-2513 ext. 227
E-mail: rick.kelley@usdoj.gov
Administrative Officer **Sandra K. King** . . . . . (859) 410-8029
E-mail: sandy.king@usdoj.gov
Criminal Administrative Support Assistant
Tammi Bissen . . . . . (859) 233-2513 ext. 244
E-mail: tammi.bissen@usdoj.gov
DAFC **Missy Berryhill** . . . . . (859) 410-8028
E-mail: missy.berryhill2@usdoj.gov
Data Analyst **Lydia Fuller** . . . . . (859) 410-8028
E-mail: lydia.fuller@usdoj.gov
Data Analyst **Jennifer Reynolds** . . . . . (859) 410-8030
E-mail: jennifer.reynolds@usdoj.gov
Management Program Analyst **Melissa Smith** . . . . . (859) 410-8035
E-mail: melissa.smith6@usdoj.gov
Purchasing Agent **Susan Moore** . . . . . (859) 410-8026
E-mail: susan.moore@usdoj.gov
AFI **Eric Marcotte** . . . . . (859) 685-4844
E-mail: eric.marcotte@usdoj.gov
Investigative Research Specialist
Tammi Bissen . . . . . (859) 233-2513 ext. 244
E-mail: tammi.bisson@usdoj.gov

Ashland (KY) Office

1405 Greenup Avenue, Ashland, KY 41101
Tel: (606) 329-2587 Fax: (606) 329-2559

Deputy U.S. Marshal **Michael Blackburn** . . . . . (606) 329-2587
E-mail: michael.blackburn@usdoj.gov

Covington (KY) Office

U.S. Courthouse, 35 West Fifth Street, Covington, KY 41012
Tel: (859) 392-7918 Fax: (859) 392-7924

Deputy U.S. Marshal **Paul Fetchik** . . . . . (859) 392-7918
E-mail: paul.fetchik@usdoj.gov
Deputy U.S. Marshal **Donnie Ray** . . . . . (859) 392-7918
E-mail: donnie.ray@usdoj.gov

★ Presidential Appointment Requiring Senate Confirmation ☆ Presidential Appointment □ Schedule C Appointment ◇ Career Senior Foreign Service Appointment
● Career Senior Executive Service (SES) Appointment ○ Non-Career Senior Executive Service (SES) Appointment ■ Postal Career Executive Service

Covington (KY) Office *continued*

Deputy U.S. Marshal **Allan Shaw** .... (859) 392-7918
E-mail: allan.shaw@usdoj.gov
Deputy U.S. Marshal **Zachary Thompson** .... (859) 392-7918
E-mail: zachary.thompson@usdoj.gov

Frankfort (KY) Office

330 West Broadway, Room 326, Frankfort, KY 40602
Tel: (502) 223-5608 Fax: (502) 223-2745

Note: This office is staffed as needed.

Deputy U.S. Marshal **Gary Heiden** .... (502) 223-5608
E-mail: gary.heiden@usdoj.gov

London (KY) Office

Federal Building, Third and Main, London, KY 40741
Tel: (606) 864-6993 Fax: (606) 878-9310

Deputy U.S. Marshal **Eric Delahoussaye** .... (606) 864-6993
E-mail: eric.delahoussaye@usdoj.gov
Deputy U.S. Marshal **David Elmadolar** .... (606) 864-6993
E-mail: david.elmadolar@usdoj.gov
Deputy U.S. Marshal **Daniel Garland** .... (606) 864-6993
E-mail: daniel.garland@usdoj.gov
Deputy U.S. Marshal **Todd Hansford** .... (606) 864-6993
E-mail: todd.hansford@usdoj.gov
Deputy U.S. Marshal **(Vacant)** .... (606) 864-6993

Pikeville (KY) Office

Federal Building, 110 Main Street, Pikeville, KY 41502
Tel: (606) 437-6537 Fax: (606) 432-8457

Deputy U.S. Marshal **Rick Newsome** .... (606) 437-6537

Kentucky - Western District

114 U.S. Courthouse, 601 West Broadway Street,
Louisville, KY 40202-2278
Tel: (502) 588-8000 Fax: (502) 588-8005

★ U.S. Marshal **James Edward "Jim" Clark** .... (502) 588-8010
E-mail: jim.clark2@usdoj.gov
Chief Deputy U.S. Marshal **Brian A. Parrish** .... (502) 588-8020
E-mail: brian.parrish@usdoj.gov
Supervisory Deputy U.S. Marshal **Jennifer Fitzgerald** ... (502) 588-8040
E-mail: jennifer.fitzgerald@usdoj.gov
Supervisory Deputy U.S. Marshal **David Hale** .... (502) 588-8080
E-mail: david.hale@usdoj.gov

Louisiana - Eastern District

500 Camp Street, Room 724, New Orleans, LA 70130
Tel: (504) 589-6079 Fax: (504) 589-4028

★ U.S. Marshal **Genevieve Lynn "Genny" May** .... (504) 589-3683
E-mail: genny.may@usdoj.gov
Education: Southeastern Louisiana BS; LSU MPA; Southern U A&M MS
Chief Deputy U.S. Marshal **(Vacant)** .... (504) 589-3627

Louisiana - Middle District

Russell B. Long Federal Building and U.S. Courthouse, 777 Florida Street,
Room G48, Baton Rouge, LA 70801
Tel: (225) 389-0364 Fax: (225) 389-0370

★ U.S. Marshal **Kevin Charles Harrison** .... (225) 389-0364
E-mail: kevin.harrison@usdoj.gov
Education: Nicholls State 1976 BA
Chief Deputy U.S. Marshal **Wayne Plylar** .... (225) 382-2168
E-mail: wayne.plylar@usdoj.gov
Supervisory Deputy U.S. Marshal
Randall "Randy" Breckwoldt .... (225) 382-2156
E-mail: randall.breckwoldt@usdoj.gov
Deputy U.S. Marshal **(Vacant)** .... (225) 382-2003

Louisiana - Middle District *continued*

Deputy U.S. Marshal **(Vacant)** .... (225) 382-2023
Criminal Investigator **Brian Benton** .... (225) 382-2022
E-mail: brian.benton@usdoj.gov
Criminal Investigator **Jeff Bowie** .... (225) 382-2026
E-mail: jeff.bowie@usdoj.gov
Criminal Investigator **Bobby Bradstreet** .... (225) 389-0364
E-mail: robert.bradstreet@usdoj.gov
Criminal Investigator **Bernie Deschamp** .... (225) 382-0364
E-mail: bernie.deschamp@usdoj.gov
Criminal Investigator **Clayton McDonough** .... (225) 382-0280
E-mail: clayton.mcdonough@usdoj.gov
Criminal Investigator **Josh Reich** .... (225) 382-2023
E-mail: joshua.reich@usdoj.gov
Investigative Research Specialist **Barbara Junius** .... (225) 382-2034
E-mail: barbara.junius@usdoj.gov
Warrant Supervisor **Brian Lucio** .... (225) 382-2010
E-mail: brian.lucio@usdoj.gov
Judicial Security Inspector **Mike Attaway** .... (225) 389-0359
E-mail: mike.attaway@usdoj.gov
Administrative Officer **Alison Alsept** .... (225) 382-2169
E-mail: alison.alsept@usdoj.gov
Criminal Program Specialist **Danielle Lacy** .... (225) 382-0304
Budget Analyst **Jenevia Johnson** .... (225) 382-2031
E-mail: jjohnson12@usms.doj.gov

Louisiana - Western District

U.S. Courthouse, 300 Fannin Street, Suite 1202,
Shreveport, LA 71101-6304
Tel: (318) 934-4300 Fax: (318) 676-4295

★ U.S. Marshal **Henry Lee Whitehorn, Sr.** .... (318) 934-4300
E-mail: henry.whitehorn@usdoj.gov
Education: LSU (Shreveport) 1986 BA; Grambling State 1989 MS
Chief Deputy U.S. Marshal
Quintella Downs-Bradshaw .... (318) 934-4300
E-mail: quintella.downs@usdoj.gov
Supervisory Deputy U.S. Marshal
Christopher "Chris" Turner .... (318) 934-4304
E-mail: christopher.turner@usdoj.gov
Administrative Officer (Acting) **Maurine Crenshaw** ..... (318) 934-4300
E-mail: maurine.crenshaw@usdoj.gov
Senior Systems Analyst **Dennis K. Austin** .... (318) 676-4296
E-mail: dennis.austin@usdoj.gov

Lafayette (LA) Office

800 Lafayette, Suite 1100, Lafayette, LA 70501
Tel: (337) 262-6666 Fax: (337) 262-6846

Supervisory Deputy U.S. Marshal (Acting)
Alonda Guilbeau .... (337) 262-6666
Senior Inspector/Court Security **Alonda Guilbeau** .... (337) 262-6666
E-mail: alonda.guilbeau@usdoj.gov

Maine District

156 Federal Street, Suite 180, Portland, ME 04101
Tel: (207) 780-3365 Fax: (207) 780-3230

★ U.S. Marshal **Noel C. March** .... (207) 780-3355
E-mail: noel.march@usdoj.gov
Education: U New England 1998 BS
Chief Deputy U.S. Marshal **Sean Willitts** .... (207) 780-3355
E-mail: sean.willitts@usdoj.gov
Supervisory Deputy U.S. Marshal **Dean Knightly** .... (207) 780-3355
E-mail: dean.knightly@usdoj.gov
Deputy U.S. Marshal **Jesse Belanger** .... (207) 780-3355
E-mail: jesse.belanger@usdoj.gov
Deputy U.S. Marshal **Spencer Christie** .... (207) 780-3355
E-mail: spencer.christie@usdoj.gov
Deputy U.S. Marshal **Sean Joyce** .... (207) 780-3355
E-mail: sean.joyce@usdoj.gov

(continued on next page)

★ Presidential Appointment Requiring Senate Confirmation ☆ Presidential Appointment ☐ Schedule C Appointment ◇ Career Senior Foreign Service Appointment
● Career Senior Executive Service (SES) Appointment ○ Non-Career Senior Executive Service (SES) Appointment ■ Postal Career Executive Service

Maine District *continued*

Deputy U.S. Marshal **Andrew LeConte** . . . . (207) 780-3355
E-mail: andrew.leconte@usdoj.gov
Deputy U.S. Marshal **Elyse Reagan** . . . . (207) 780-3355
Deputy U.S. Marshal **Mike Tenuta** . . . . (207) 780-3355
E-mail: michael.tenuta@usdoj.gov
Deputy U.S. Marshal **(Vacant)** . . . . (207) 780-3355
Purchasing Agent **Tina M. Moore** . . . . (207) 780-3355
E-mail: tina.moore@usdoj.gov
Administrative Officer **Lisa Caron** . . . . (207) 780-3355
E-mail: lisa.caron@usdoj.gov
Criminal Program Specialist **Kathy Perron** . . . . (207) 780-3355
Forfeiture Specialist **Katie Downey** . . . . (207) 780-3355

Bangor (ME) Office

Federal Building, 202 Harlow Street, Room 322, Bangor, ME 04401
Tel: (207) 945-0416 Fax: (207) 945-0419

Supervisory Deputy U.S. Marshal **Alexander Patnode** . . . (207) 945-0416
E-mail: alexander.patnode@usdoj.gov
Senior Deputy U.S. Marshal **Tom Britt** . . . . (207) 945-0416
E-mail: tom.britt@usdoj.gov
Administrative Support Clerk **Lorie Wing** . . . . (207) 945-0416
E-mail: lorie.wing@usdoj.gov

Maryland District

Garmatz Federal Courthouse Building, 101 West Lombard Street, Suite 6115, Baltimore, MD 21201
Tel: (410) 962-2220 Fax: (410) 962-3780

★ U.S. Marshal **Johnny Lewis Hughes** . . . . (410) 962-2519
E-mail: johnny.hughes@usdoj.gov
Chief Deputy U.S. Marshal **Pat J. Monardo** . . . . (410) 962-2256
E-mail: pat.monardo@usdoj.gov
Assistant Chief Deputy U.S. Marshal **Steven D. Akers** . . . (410) 962-7562
E-mail: steve.akers@usdoj.gov
Greenbelt (MD) Office Supervisory Deputy U.S. Marshal **Paul Rivers** . . . . (301) 344-8406
U.S. Courthouse, 6500 Cherrywood Lane, Suite 170, Greenbelt, MD 20770
E-mail: paul.rivers@usdoj.gov
Prisoner Operations Supervisory Deputy U.S. Marshal **Sterling Johnson** . . . . (410) 962-3533
E-mail: sterling.johnson@usdoj.gov
Warrants Supervisory Deputy U.S. Marshal **Kurt Vogan** . . . . (410) 779-7331
E-mail: kurt.vogan@usdoj.gov
Administrative Officer **Annabelle Perez** . . . . (410) 779-7345
E-mail: annabelle.perez@usdoj.gov
Management and Program Analyst **Mary M. Goldsmith** . . . . (410) 962-7564
E-mail: mary.goldsmith@usdoj.gov

Massachusetts District

John Joseph Moakley U.S. Courthouse, One Courthouse Way, Suite 500, Boston, MA 02210
Tel: (617) 748-2500 Fax: (617) 748-2539

★ U.S. Marshal **John Gibbons** . . . . (617) 748-2500
E-mail: john.gibbons2@usdoj.gov
Education: American International 1978 BA, 1979
Chief Deputy U.S. Marshal **Jonathan Murray** . . . . (617) 748-2500
E-mail: jon.murray@usdoj.gov
Assistant Chief Deputy U.S. Marshal **Jeffrey Bohn** . . . . . . (617) 748-2500
E-mail: jeff.bohn@usdoj.gov
Supervisory Deputy U.S. Marshal **Donald Freeman** . . . . . (617) 748-2500
E-mail: donald.freeman@usdoj.gov
Supervisory Deputy U.S. Marshal **Alison Hodgkins** . . . . . (617) 748-2500
Supervisory Deputy U.S. Marshal **Kevin Neal** . . . . (617) 748-2500
E-mail: kevin.neal@usdoj.gov
Administrative Officer **George Farren** . . . . (617) 748-2516
E-mail: george.farren@usdoj.gov

Springfield (MA) Office

Federal Building and Courthouse, 300 State Street, Springfield, MA 01105-2926
Tel: (413) 504-1051

Supervisory Deputy U.S. Marshal **Daniel Spellacy** . . . . . . (413) 504-1051
E-mail: daniel.spellacy@usdoj.gov

Worcester (MA) Office

Donahue Federal Building, 595 Main Street, Worcester, MA 01608
Tel: (508) 368-7300

Supervisory Deputy U.S. Marshal **John Wickham** . . . . (508) 368-7300
E-mail: john.wickham@usdoj.gov

Michigan - Eastern District

Federal Building and U.S. Courthouse, 231 West Lafayette Boulevard, 3rd Floor, Detroit, MI 48226
Tel: (313) 234-5600 Fax: (313) 234-5632

★ U.S. Marshal **Robert M. Grubbs** . . . . (313) 234-5600
E-mail: robert.grubbs@usdoj.gov
Chief Deputy U.S. Marshal **Mark Jankowski** . . . . (313) 234-5600
E-mail: mark.jankowski2@usdoj.gov
Assistant Chief Deputy U.S. Marshal **(Vacant)** . . . . (313) 234-5600

Michigan - Western District

110 Michigan Street, NW, Room 744, Grand Rapids, MI 49503
Tel: (616) 456-2438 Fax: (616) 456-2446

★ U.S. Marshal **Peter Christopher Munoz** . . . . (616) 456-2438
E-mail: peter.munoz@usdoj.gov
Education: Detroit 1978 BS
Chief Deputy **Bruce A. Nordin** . . . . (616) 456-2438
E-mail: bruce.nordin@usdoj.gov
Supervisory Deputy U.S. Marshal **Mark Hill** . . . . (616) 456-2438
E-mail: mark.hill@usdoj.gov

Kalamazoo (MI) Office

410 West Michigan Avenue, Room 154, Kalamazoo, MI 49006
Tel: (269) 349-8700 Tel: (269) 349-9867 Fax: (269) 349-0906

Deputy U.S. Marshal **Ken Groneveld** . . . . (269) 349-1869
Deputy U.S. Marshal **Mark Holloway** . . . . (269) 349-3053

Lansing (MI) Office

315 West Allegan Street, Room 154, Lansing, MI 48933
Tel: (517) 377-1571 Fax: (517) 377-1575

Deputy U.S. Marshal **Scott Masteller** . . . . (517) 377-1571
E-mail: scott.masteller@usdoj.gov
Deputy U.S. Marshal **(Vacant)** . . . . (517) 377-1571

Marquette (MI) Office

Federal Building, 202 West Washington Street, Room 233, Marquette, MI 49855
P.O. Box 698, Marquette, MI 49855
Tel: (906) 226-8812 Fax: (906) 226-7733

Deputy U.S. Marshal **Joshua Ramey** . . . . (906) 226-8812
E-mail: joshua.ramey@usdoj.gov
Deputy U.S. Marshal **(Vacant)** . . . . (906) 226-8812

Minnesota District

300 South Fourth Street, Room 402, Minneapolis, MN 55415
Tel: (612) 664-5900 Fax: (612) 664-5955

★ U.S. Marshal **Sharon Jeanette Lubinski** . . . . (612) 664-5905
E-mail: sharon.lubinski@usdoj.gov
Education: Wisconsin BA; Hamline MPA
Chief Deputy U.S. Marshal **Chris Kawaters** . . . . (612) 664-5906
E-mail: chris.kawaters@usdoj.gov
Assistant Chief Deputy U.S. Marshal **Daniel Elbers** . . . . . (612) 664-5970

★ Presidential Appointment Requiring Senate Confirmation ☆ Presidential Appointment □ Schedule C Appointment ◇ Career Senior Foreign Service Appointment
● Career Senior Executive Service (SES) Appointment ○ Non-Career Senior Executive Service (SES) Appointment ■ Postal Career Executive Service

Minnesota District *continued*

Supervisory Deputy U.S. Marshal **Chris Connolly** . . . . (612) 664-5900
E-mail: chris.connolly@usdoj.gov
Deputy U.S. Marshal **(Vacant)** . . . . (612) 664-5960
Deputy U.S. Marshal **(Vacant)** . . . . (612) 664-5921
Supervisory Deputy U.S. Marshal **Rich Pederson** . . . . (612) 644-5931
E-mail: richard.pederson@usdoj.gov
Administrative Officer **Sharon Eliason** . . . . (612) 664-5909
E-mail: sharon.eliason@usdoj.gov
Judicial Security Division Inspector **Tom Knutson** . . . . (612) 664-5910
E-mail: tom.knutson@usdoj.gov
Prisoner Operations Supervisor **(Vacant)** . . . . (612) 664-5970

Saint Paul (MN) Office

316 North Robert Street, Room 670, St. Paul, MN 55101
Tel: (651) 848-1435 Fax: (651) 848-1440

Supervisory Deputy U.S. Marshal **Chris Connolly** . . . . (651) 848-1435
E-mail: chris.connolly@usdoj.gov
Deputy U.S. Marshal **(Vacant)** . . . . (651) 848-1435

Mississippi - Northern District

911 Jackson Avenue, Room 348, Oxford, MS 38655
Tel: (662) 234-6661 Fax: (662) 234-0219

★ U.S. Marshal **Dennis J. Erby** . . . . (662) 234-6661
Term Expires: 2016
E-mail: dennis.erby@usdoj.gov
Education: Mississippi State
Chief Deputy U.S. Marshal **Jeff Woodfin** . . . . (662) 234-6661
E-mail: jeff.woodfin@usdoj.gov
Supervisory Deputy U.S. Marshal **Michael Quarles** . . . . . . (662) 234-6661
E-mail: michael.quarles@usdoj.gov
Deputy U.S. Marshal **Charles Force** . . . . (662) 332-6661
E-mail: charles.force@usdoj.gov
Deputy U.S. Marshal **James E. "Bo" Rambo** . . . . (662) 234-6661
E-mail: james.rambo@usdoj.gov
Deputy U.S. Marshal **Victor Theobald** . . . . (662) 234-6661
Deputy U.S. Marshal **(Vacant)** . . . . (662) 234-6661
Deputy U.S. Marshal **(Vacant)** . . . . (662) 234-6661
Deputy U.S. Marshal **(Vacant)** . . . . (662) 234-6661
Asset Forfeiture Unit Deputy U.S. Marshal **Jill Strauss** . . . (662) 234-6661
E-mail: jill.strauss@usdoj.gov
Sex Offender Unit Deputy U.S. Marshal
Richard UpChurch . . . . (662) 234-6661
E-mail: charles.upchurch@usdoj.gov
Administrative Officer **Katherine Brock** . . . . (662) 234-2323
E-mail: katherine.brock@usdoj.gov
Purchasing Agent **(Vacant)** . . . . (662) 234-6661
Budget Analyst **(Vacant)** . . . . (662) 234-6661
Investigative Research Specialist **Carole Arnold** . . . . (662) 234-6661
Judicial Security Inspector **Gregory Loftin** . . . . (662) 234-6661
E-mail: gregory.loftin@usdoj.gov

Aberdeen (MS) Office

Federal Building, 301 West Commerce Street,
Room 360, Aberdeen, MS 39730
Tel: (662) 369-4892 Fax: (662) 369-6936

Deputy U.S. Marshal **Joseph Stephens** . . . . (662) 369-4892
E-mail: joseph.stephens@usdoj.gov
Deputy U.S. Marshal **(Vacant)** . . . . (662) 369-4892

Greenville (MS) Office

Federal Building, Main and Poplar Streets,
Room 343, Greenville, MS 38701
Tel: (662) 332-5680 Fax: (662) 335-4703

Deputy U.S. Marshal **William Donald** . . . . (662) 332-5680
E-mail: william.donald@usdoj.gov
Deputy U.S. Marshal **(Vacant)** . . . . (662) 332-5680

Mississippi - Southern District

501 East Court Street, Suite 1.150, Jackson, MS 39201
Tel: (601) 608-6800 Fax: (601) 965-4245

★ U.S. Marshal **George White** . . . . (601) 608-6800
E-mail: george.white@usdoj.gov Fax: (601) 965-4245
Education: Alcorn State 2009 BS
Chief Deputy U.S. Marshal **(Vacant)** . . . . (601) 608-6800
Supervisory Deputy U.S. Marshal **James McIntosh** . . . . . (601) 608-6804
E-mail: james.mcintosh@usdoj.gov
Deputy U.S. Marshal **Chris Baker** . . . . (601) 608-6822
Deputy U.S. Marshal **Shelly Boone** . . . . (601) 608-6810
Deputy U.S. Marshal **Miranda Holloway** . . . . (601) 608-6810
Deputy U.S. Marshal **Howard Sanford** . . . . (601) 608-6807
E-mail: howard.sanford@usdoj.gov
Deputy U.S. Marshal **Jeremy Stilwell** . . . . (601) 608-6800
Deputy U.S. Marshal **Shermaine Sullivan** . . . . (601) 608-6817
Deputy U.S. Marshal **(Vacant)** . . . . (601) 608-6812
Deputy U.S. Marshal **(Vacant)** . . . . (601) 608-6821
Judicial Security Division Inspector
Brandon Pritchard . . . . (601) 965-4444
Administrative Officer **Linda M. Shepherd** . . . . (601) 608-6850
E-mail: linda.shepherd@usdoj.gov

Gulfport (MS) Office

Federal Building, 2012 15th Street, Room 302, Gulfport, MS 39501
Tel: (228) 563-1505 Fax: (228) 563-1511

Supervisory Deputy U.S. Marshal **Melanie Rube** . . . . (228) 563-1505
E-mail: melanie.rube@usdoj.gov
Deputy U.S. Marshal **Steven Davis** . . . . (228) 563-1505
E-mail: steven.davis@usdoj.gov
Deputy U.S. Marshal **Brian Dial** . . . . (228) 563-1505
Deputy U.S. Marshal **Ivy Jenkins** . . . . (228) 563-1505
Deputy U.S. Marshal **Raymond Stewart** . . . . (228) 563-1505
E-mail: raymond.stewart@usdoj.gov

Hattiesburg (MS) Office

Federal Building, 701 North Main Street,
Room 331, Hattiesburg, MS 39401
Tel: (601) 582-8464

Deputy U.S. Marshal **Stephen Newell** . . . . (601) 582-8464
E-mail: stephen.newell@usdoj.gov
Deputy U.S. Marshal **Billy Valentine** . . . . (601) 582-8464
E-mail: william.valentine@usdoj.gov
Deputy U.S. Marshal **Marcus Bass** . . . . (601) 582-8464
E-mail: marcus.bass@usdoj.gov

Missouri - Eastern District

Thomas Eagleton Courthouse, 111 South 10th Street,
Room 2-319, St. Louis, MO 63102-1125
Tel: (314) 539-2212 Fax: (314) 539-2225

★ U.S. Marshal **William Claud Sibert** . . . . (314) 539-2212
E-mail: william.sibert@usdoj.gov
Education: Western Illinois 1983 BA
Chief Deputy U.S. Marshal **Virgil Rickey** . . . . (314) 539-2212
Assistant Chief Deputy U.S. Marshal
Robert O'Connor . . . . (314) 539-2212
E-mail: robert.oconnor@usdoj.gov
Supervisory Deputy U.S. Marshal **(Vacant)** . . . . (314) 539-2212
Administrative Officer **Geraldine Webb** . . . . (314) 539-2212

Cape Girardeau (MO) Office

555 Independence Street, Suite 2100, Cape Girardeau, MO 63701
Tel: (573) 986-4747 Fax: (573) 986-4770

Supervisory Deputy U.S. Marshal **Charlie Doerge** . . . . (573) 986-4750
Fax: (573) 986-4752

★ Presidential Appointment Requiring Senate Confirmation ☆ Presidential Appointment □ Schedule C Appointment ◇ Career Senior Foreign Service Appointment
● Career Senior Executive Service (SES) Appointment ○ Non-Career Senior Executive Service (SES) Appointment ■ Postal Career Executive Service

Missouri - Western District

400 East Ninth Street, Suite 3740, Kansas City, MO 64106
Tel: (816) 512-2000 Fax: (816) 512-2005

★ U.S. Marshal **Alfred Cooper Lomax** . . . . (816) 512-2000
E-mail: alomax@usms.doj.gov
Education: Missouri (Kansas City); Central Missouri

Chief Deputy U.S. Marshal **Scott Seeling** . . . . (816) 512-2000
E-mail: scott.seeling@usdoj.gov

Supervisory Deputy U.S. Marshal **Shane VanMeter** . . . . . (816) 512-2000
E-mail: shane.vanmeter@usdoj.gov

Administrative Officer (Acting) **Beverly Cunningham** . . . (816) 512-2000
E-mail: beverly.cunningham@usdoj.gov

Montana District

James F. Battin United States Courthouse, 2601 2nd Avenue North, Suite 2300, Billings, MT 59101
Tel: (406) 247-7030 Fax: (406) 247-7035

★ U.S. Marshal **Darrell James Bell** . . . . (406) 247-7030
E-mail: darrell.bell@usdoj.gov
Education: Montana State (Billings)

Chief Deputy U.S. Marshal **Rodney Ostermiller** . . . . (406) 247-7030
E-mail: rod.ostermiller@usdoj.gov

Supervisory Deputy U.S. Marshal **Tim Hornung** . . . . (406) 247-7030
E-mail: timothy.hornung@usdoj.gov

Administrative Officer **Carol L. Rash** . . . . (406) 247-7030
E-mail: carol.rash@usdoj.gov

Nebraska District

Roman L. Hruska U.S. Courthouse, 111 South 18th Plaza, Suite B06, Omaha, NE 68102
Tel: (402) 221-4782 Fax: (402) 221-3006

★ U.S. Marshal **Mark Anthony Martinez** . . . . (402) 221-4782
E-mail: mark.martinez@usdoj.gov
Education: Nebraska (Omaha) 1982 BS, 1993 MS

Chief Deputy U.S. Marshal **Jaime Galindo** . . . . (402) 221-4782
E-mail: jaime.galindo@usdoj.gov

Administrative Officer **Jane A. Loeck** . . . . (402) 221-4782
E-mail: jane.loeck@usdoj.gov

Administrative Support Assistant **(Vacant)** . . . . (402) 221-4782

Asset Forfeiture Coordinator **Chris A. Newton** . . . . (402) 221-4782
E-mail: chris.newton@usdoj.gov

Criminal Program Specialist **Kamela Skinner** . . . . (402) 221-4782
E-mail: kamela.skinner@usdoj.gov

Management and Program Analyst **Kellie A. Strain** . . . . (402) 221-4782
E-mail: kellie.strain@usdoj.gov

Purchasing Agent **(Vacant)** . . . . (402) 221-4782

Supervisory Deputy U.S. Marshal **Bill D. Bitting** . . . . (402) 221-4782
E-mail: bill.bitting@usdoj.gov

Supervisory Deputy U.S. Marshal **(Vacant)** . . . . (402) 221-4782

Deputy U.S. Marshal **Thadd W. Baird** . . . . (402) 221-4782
E-mail: thadd.baird@usdoj.gov

Deputy U.S. Marshal **Shane Knopp** . . . . (402) 221-4782
E-mail: shane.knopp@usdoj.gov

Deputy U.S. Marshal **Rovance Lewis** . . . . (402) 224-4782
E-mail: rovance.lewis@usdoj.gov

Deputy U.S. Marshal **Eric C. Mayo** . . . . (402) 221-4782
E-mail: eric.mayo@usdoj.gov

Deputy U.S. Marshal **Chad Reynoldson** . . . . (402) 221-4782
E-mail: chad.reynoldson@usdoj.gov

Deputy U.S. Marshal **Jack Sides** . . . . (402) 221-4782
E-mail: jack.sides@usdoj.gov

Deputy U.S. Marshal **Steven Walter** . . . . (402) 221-4782

Deputy U.S. Marshal/Criminal Investigator
Mark C. Anderson . . . . (402) 221-4782
E-mail: mark.anderson@usdoj.gov

Deputy U.S. Marshal/Criminal Investigator
Kenneth C. Bessey . . . . (402) 221-4782
E-mail: kenneth.bessey@usdoj.gov

Nebraska District *continued*

Deputy U.S. Marshal/Criminal Investigator
John M. Huggins . . . . (402) 221-4782
E-mail: john.huggins@usdoj.gov

Deputy U.S. Marshal/Criminal Investigator
Daniel Potter . . . . (402) 221-4782
E-mail: dan.potter@usdoj.gov

Deputy U.S. Marshal/Criminal Investigator
Brandon D. VanBuskirk . . . . (402) 221-4782
E-mail: brandon.vanbuskirk@usdoj.gov

Deputy U.S. Marshal/Criminal Investigator
Chris L. White . . . . (402) 221-4782
E-mail: chris.white@usdoj.gov

Deputy U.S. Marshal/Criminal Investigator/Court Security Inspector **W. Chris West** . . . . (402) 221-4677
E-mail: chris.west@usdoj.gov

Lincoln (NE) Office

Federal Building, 100 Centennial Mall North, Room 552, Lincoln, NE 68508
Tel: (402) 742-7021 Fax: (402) 742-7077

Supervisory Deputy U.S. Marshal **William Iverson** . . . . . . (402) 742-7021
E-mail: william.iverson@usdoj.gov

Administrative Operations Assistant **Mark Long** . . . . (402) 742-7021
E-mail: mark.long3@usdoj.gov

Deputy U.S. Marshal/Criminal Investigator
Allen E. Jewitt, Jr. . . . . (402) 742-7021
E-mail: allen.jewitt@usdoj.gov

Deputy U.S. Marshal **Aaron Crooks** . . . . (402) 742-7021
E-mail: aaron.crooks@usdoj.gov

Deputy U.S. Marshal **Kevin Garrard** . . . . (402) 742-7021

Deputy U.S. Marshal **Jay Mason** . . . . (402) 742-7021
E-mail: jay.mason@usdoj.gov

Nevada District

Lloyd D. George Federal Building & U.S. Courthouse, 333 Las Vegas Boulevard, South, Suite 2058, Las Vegas, NV 89101
Tel: (702) 388-6355 Fax: (702) 388-6703

★ U.S. Marshal **Christopher Tobias Hoye** . . . . (702) 388-6355
E-mail: christopher.hoye@usdoj.gov
Education: Arizona State 1985 BS; U Phoenix 2007

Chief Deputy U.S. Marshal **Doyle Decker** . . . . (702) 388-6356
E-mail: doyle.decker@usdoj.gov

Supervisory Deputy U.S. Marshal **Michael Banez** . . . . (702) 388-6356
E-mail: michael.banez@usdoj.gov

Supervisory Deputy U.S. Marshal **Melinda Kormos** . . . . . (702) 388-6355
E-mail: melinda.kormos@usdoj.gov

Supervisory Deputy U.S. Marshal **Nathan Powell** . . . . (702) 388-6356
E-mail: nathan.powell@usdoj.gov

Deputy U.S. Marshal **John Kozisek** . . . . (702) 388-6356
E-mail: john.kozisek@usdoj.gov

Deputy U.S. Marshal **Rudy Lara** . . . . (702) 388-6356
E-mail: rudy.lara@usdoj.gov

Deputy U.S. Marshal **(Vacant)** . . . . (702) 388-6356

Court Security Inspector **Reuben Bugtong** . . . . (702) 388-6356
E-mail: reuben.bugtong@usdoj.gov

Task Force Supervisor **(Vacant)** . . . . (702) 388-6356

Reno (NV) Office

Bruce R. Thompson Federal Building, 400 South Virginia Street, Room 201, Reno, NV 89501
Tel: (775) 686-5780 Fax: (775) 686-5794

Supervisory Deputy U.S. Marshal **Robert Alexander** . . . . (775) 686-5780
E-mail: robert.alexander@usdoj.gov

Deputy U.S. Marshal **Rhonda Adams** . . . . (775) 686-5780
E-mail: rhonda.adams@usdoj.gov

Deputy U.S. Marshal **Eric Beyersdorf** . . . . (775) 686-5780
E-mail: eric.beyersdorf@usdoj.gov

Deputy U.S. Marshal **Ryan Burrows** . . . . (775) 686-5780
E-mail: ryan.burrows@usdoj.gov

★ Presidential Appointment Requiring Senate Confirmation ☆ Presidential Appointment □ Schedule C Appointment ◇ Career Senior Foreign Service Appointment
● Career Senior Executive Service (SES) Appointment ○ Non-Career Senior Executive Service (SES) Appointment ■ Postal Career Executive Service

Reno (NV) Office *continued*

Deputy U.S. Marshal **Don Harvey** . . . . (775) 686-5780
E-mail: don.harvey@usdoj.gov
Deputy U.S. Marshal **Daryl Hollenbach** . . . . (775) 686-5780
Deputy U.S. Marshal **Quinn Pardo** . . . . (775) 686-5780
E-mail: quinn.pardo@usdoj.gov

New Hampshire District

Warren Rudman Courthouse, 55 Pleasant Street,
Suite 207, Concord, NH 03301
Tel: (603) 225-1632 Fax: (603) 225-1633

★ U.S. Marshal **David Lyle Cargill, Jr.** . . . . (603) 225-1632
E-mail: david.cargill@usdoj.gov
Education: Granite State 2007 BSc
Chief Deputy U.S. Marshal **Brenda Mikelson** . . . . (603) 225-1632
Supervisory Deputy U.S. Marshal **Eugene Robinson** . . . . (603) 225-1635
Deputy U.S. Marshal **Jamie Berry** . . . . (603) 226-7341
E-mail: jamie.berry@usdoj.gov
Deputy U.S. Marshal **Chris Deaton** . . . . (603) 226-7757
E-mail: chris.deaton@usdoj.gov
Deputy U.S. Marshal **Daniel Dempsey** . . . . (603) 225-7379
E-mail: daniel.dempsey@usdoj.gov
Deputy U.S. Marshal **Mark Lewis** . . . . (603) 226-7372
E-mail: mark.lewis@usdoj.gov
Deputy U.S. Marshal **Gregory Murano** . . . . (603) 225-1595
E-mail: gregory.murano@usdoj.gov
Deputy U.S. Marshal **Joseph Vetanze** . . . . (603) 226-7765
E-mail: joseph.vetanze@usdoj.gov
Deputy U.S. Marshal **Jeffrey White, Jr.** . . . . (603) 226-7376
E-mail: jeffrey.white@usdoj.gov
Deputy U.S. Marshal **(Vacant)** . . . . (603) 226-7302
Judicial Security Inspector **Douglas Bartlett** . . . . (603) 225-1636
E-mail: douglas.bartlett@usdoj.gov
Administrative Officer **Barbara Gatti** . . . . (603) 225-1443
E-mail: barbara.gatti@usdoj.gov
Administrative Assistant **Wanda Dechaine** . . . . (603) 225-1630
E-mail: wanda.dechaine@usdoj.gov
Budget Analyst **(Vacant)** . . . . (603) 225-1651
Financial Specialist **Kimberly Dow** . . . . (603) 225-1646
E-mail: kimberly.dow@usdoj.gov
District Asset Forefeiture Specialist **Kathleen Renaud** . . . (603) 226-7375
E-mail: kathleen.renaud@usdoj.gov

New Jersey District

Martin Luther King, Jr. Courthouse, 50 Walnut Street,
Room 2009, Newark, NJ 07102
Tel: (973) 645-2404 Fax: (973) 693-4142

★ U.S. Marshal **Juan Mattos, Jr.** . . . . (973) 645-2404
E-mail: juan.mattos@usdoj.gov
Education: Jersey City State; Monmouth U MA
Chief Deputy U.S. Marshal **John M. Svinos** . . . . (973) 645-2404 ext. 250
E-mail: john.svinos@usdoj.gov
Administrative Officer **Yariel Brown** . . . . (973) 645-2626
E-mail: yariel.brown@usdoj.gov
Administrative Support Assistant
Elizabeth Baskerville . . . . (973) 645-2404 ext. 247
E-mail: elizabeth.baskerville@usdoj.gov

Camden (NJ) Office

P.O. Box 288, Camden, NJ 08101
Tel: (856) 757-5024 Fax: (856) 757-5161

Supervisor **Terrance Merrigan** . . . . (856) 757-5024

Trenton (NJ) Office

402 East State Street, Trenton, NJ 08608
Tel: (609) 989-2069 Fax: (609) 989-2145

Supervisor **Lourdes Temperman** . . . . (609) 989-2069

New Mexico District

U.S. Courthouse, 333 Lomas, NW, Suite 180, Albuquerque, NM 87102
Tel: (505) 346-6400 Fax: (505) 346-6417

★ U.S. Marshal **Conrad Ernest Candelaria** . . . . (505) 346-6400
E-mail: conrad.candelaria@usdoj.gov
Education: New Mexico BA, MPA, AA
Chief Deputy U.S. Marshal **Alejandro "Alex" Ramos** . . . . (505) 346-6400
E-mail: alex.ramos@usdoj.gov
Supervisory Deputy U.S. Marshal **Lasha Boyden** . . . . (505) 462-2306
E-mail: lasha.boyden@usdoj.gov
Supervisory Deputy U.S. Marshal **Vincent Gambone** . . . . (505) 462-2368
E-mail: vincent.gambone@usdoj.gov
Asset Forfeiture Criminal Investigator **Mitch Varley** . . . . . . (505) 346-6400
Administrative Officer **Randy Rettinger** . . . . (505) 462-2302
E-mail: randy.rettinger@usdoj.gov

New York - Eastern District

225 Cadman Plaza East, Room G-20, Brooklyn, NY 11201
Tel: (718) 260-0400 Fax: (718) 260-0436 Fax: (718) 260-0431

★ U.S. Marshal **Charles Gillen Dunne** . . . . (718) 260-0401
E-mail: charles.dunne@usdoj.gov
Education: Fairfield 1989 BA; John Jay Col 1997 MA;
St John's U (NY) 2002 JD
Chief Deputy U.S. Marshal **Bryan Mullee** . . . . (718) 260-0402
E-mail: bryan.mullee@usdoj.gov
Assistant Chief Deputy U.S. Marshal **James Elcik** . . . . . . (718) 260-0403
E-mail: james.elcik@usdoj.gov
Assistant Chief Deputy U.S. Marshal **Juan Tavarez** . . . . . . (718) 260-0407
E-mail: juan.tavarez@usdoj.gov
System Administrator **Raymond Ng** . . . . (718) 260-0433
E-mail: raymond.ng@usdoj.gov

New York - Northern District

Federal Building, 100 South Clinton Street,
10th Floor, Syracuse, NY 13261
Tel: (315) 473-7601 Fax: (315) 473-7600

★ U.S. Marshal **David L. McNulty** . . . . (315) 473-7601
E-mail: david.mcnulty@usdoj.gov
Chief Deputy U.S. Marshal **Theodore Gloo** . . . . (315) 473-7612
E-mail: theodore.gloo@usdoj.gov
Supervisory Deputy U.S. Marshal **(Vacant)** . . . . (315) 473-7613
Deputy U.S. Marshal **Christopher Amoia** . . . . (315) 473-7630
E-mail: christopher.amoia@usdoj.gov
Deputy U.S. Marshal **Dan Driscoll** . . . . (315) 473-7627
E-mail: daniel.driscoll@usdoj.gov
Deputy U.S. Marshal **Gerald Gordon** . . . . (315) 473-7614
E-mail: gerald.gordon@usdoj.gov
Deputy U.S. Marshal **Julie Gossin** . . . . (315) 473-7629
E-mail: julie.gossin@usdoj.gov
Deputy U.S. Marshal **Mark Jenkusky** . . . . (315) 473-7621
E-mail: mark.jenkusky@usdoj.gov
Deputy U.S. Marshal **Greg Morawiec** . . . . (315) 473-7618
E-mail: gregory.morawiec@usdoj.gov
Deputy U.S. Marshal **Jim Nichols** . . . . (315) 473-7617
E-mail: james.nichols@usdoj.gov
Deputy U.S. Marshal **Robert V. Rosato** . . . . (315) 473-7601
Deputy U.S. Marshal **Robert Sweeney** . . . . (315) 473-7623
Deputy U.S. Marshal **(Vacant)** . . . . (315) 473-7620
Administrative Officer **Barbara D. Wright** . . . . (315) 473-7603
E-mail: barbara.wright@usdoj.gov
Fiscal Officer **Steven Seaman** . . . . (315) 473-7670
E-mail: steven.seaman@usdoj.gov
Investigative Research Specialist **(Vacant)** . . . . (315) 473-7608
Property Manager **Yolanda Brzostowski** . . . . (315) 473-7605
Criminal Clerk **(Vacant)** . . . . (315) 473-7670
Civil Clerk **Jacqueline Cleary** . . . . (315) 473-7669
E-mail: jacqueline.cleary@usdoj.gov

Albany (NY) Office

James T. Foley Courthouse, 445 Broadway, Albany, NY 12207
Tel: (518) 472-5401 Tel: (315) 473-7601 (24 Hours)
Fax: (518) 472-5400

Supervisory Deputy U.S. Marshal **Brandon LaMora** ..... (518) 472-5413
E-mail: brandon.lamora@usdoj.gov
Deputy U.S. Marshal **Alex Baker** ..... (518) 472-5401
E-mail: alexander.baker@usdoj.gov
Deputy U.S. Marshal **Joseph Graziane** ..... (518) 472-5401
E-mail: joseph.graziane@usdoj.gov
Deputy U.S. Marshal **Anthony Loquidice** ..... (518) 472-5401
Deputy U.S. Marshal **Ken Mead** ..... (518) 472-5416
E-mail: kenneth.mead@usdoj.gov
Deputy U.S. Marshal **Stuart Smith** ..... (518) 472-5426
Deputy U.S. Marshal **Jeff Susi** ..... (518) 472-5421
Deputy U.S. Marshal **Michael Tracey** ..... (518) 472-5420
E-mail: michael.tracey@usdoj.gov
Deputy U.S. Marshal **William C. O'Toole** ..... (518) 472-5430
E-mail: william.otoole@usdoj.gov
Deputy U.S. Marshal **Mark Voellm** ..... (518) 472-5425
E-mail: mark.voellm@usdoj.gov
Deputy U.S. Marshal **Michael Woerner** ..... (518) 472-5427
Administrative Assistant **Marlene Lyons** ..... (518) 472-5408
E-mail: marlene.lyons@usdoj.gov
Detention Officer **(Vacant)** ..... (518) 472-5417

Binghamton (NY) Office

U.S. Courthouse and Federal Building, 15 Henry Street,
Room 228, Binghamton, NY 13902
Tel: (607) 773-2723 Tel: (315) 732-2123 (24 Hours)
Fax: (607) 773-2726

Deputy U.S. Marshal **Andre J. Kolut** ..... (607) 773-2723

Utica (NY) Office

Federal Building, 10 Broad Street, Room 213, Utica, NY 13501
Tel: (315) 793-8109 Tel: (315) 732-2123 (24 Hours)
Fax: (315) 793-8196

Deputy U.S. Marshal **Jamie Farrington** ..... (315) 793-8109
E-mail: jamie.farrington@usdoj.gov

New York - Southern District

500 Pearl Street, 4th Floor, New York, NY 10007
Tel: (212) 331-7200 Fax: (212) 637-6130

★ U.S. Marshal **Michael Greco** ..... (212) 331-7100
E-mail: michael.greco@usdoj.gov
Education: Excelsior 2012 AA
Chief Deputy U.S. Marshal
Eric B. Timberman ..... (212) 331-7200 ext. 7102
E-mail: eric.timberman@usdoj.gov

New York - Western District

Robert H. Jackson United States Courthouse,
2 Niagara Square, Buffalo, NY 14202
Tel: (716) 348-5300 Fax: (716) 551-5505

★ U.S. Marshal **Charles F. Salina** ..... (716) 348-5300
E-mail: charles.salina@usdoj.gov
Education: SUNY (Oswego)
Chief Deputy U.S. Marshal **(Vacant)** ..... (716) 348-5300
Supervisory Deputy U.S. Marshal **Daniel Larish** ..... (716) 348-5300
Supervisory Deputy U.S. Marshal **Madonna Pursell** ..... (716) 348-5300
E-mail: madonna.pursell@usdoj.gov
Deputy U.S. Marshal **Scott Baryza** ..... (716) 348-5300
E-mail: scott.baryza@usdoj.gov
Deputy U.S. Marshal **Lee Eckenrode** ..... (716) 348-5300
E-mail: lee.eckenrode@usdoj.gov
Deputy U.S. Marshal **Mark Fialkiewicz** ..... (716) 348-5300
E-mail: mark.fialkiewicz@usdoj.gov

New York - Western District *continued*

Deputy U.S. Marshal **Kenneth Gordon** ..... (716) 348-5300
E-mail: kenneth.gordon@usdoj.gov
Deputy U.S. Marshal **Mark Gomez** ..... (716) 348-5300
E-mail: mark.gomez@usdoj.gov
Deputy U.S. Marshal **Michael Malcolm** ..... (716) 348-5300
E-mail: michael.malcolm@usdoj.gov
Deputy U.S. Marshal **Brent Novak** ..... (716) 348-5300
E-mail: brent.novak@usdoj.gov
Deputy U.S. Marshal **Kenneth Pirone** ..... (716) 348-5300
E-mail: ken.pirone@usdoj.gov
Deputy U.S. Marshal **Richard Rooney** ..... (716) 348-5300
E-mail: richard.rooney@usdoj.gov
Deputy U.S. Marshal **Doug Wilson** ..... (716) 348-5300
E-mail: doug.wilson@usdoj.gov
Deputy U.S. Marshal **(Vacant)** ..... (716) 348-5300
Deputy U.S. Marshal **(Vacant)** ..... (716) 348-5300
Administrative Officer **Jennifer Pearson** ..... (716) 348-5300
68 Court Street, Room 129, Buffalo, NY 14202
E-mail: jennifer.pearson@usdoj.gov
Criminal Program Specialist **Diane Dobbin** ..... (716) 348-5300
Criminal Program Specialist **Sandra Olden** ..... (716) 348-5300
68 Court Street, Room 129, Buffalo, NY 14202
Property Management Specialist **Mary Lidkea** ..... (716) 348-5300
68 Court Street, Room 129, Buffalo, NY 14202
Administrative Support Specialist **Brenda Huppe** ..... (716) 348-5300
E-mail: brenda.huppe@usdoj.gov
DAFC **Beata Hosking** ..... (716) 348-5300
E-mail: beata.hosking@usdoj.gov
Management and Program Analyst **Jennifer Pearson** ..... (716) 348-5300

Rochester (NY) Office

U.S. Courthouse, 100 State Street, Room 2240, Rochester, NY 14614
Tel: (585) 263-5787 Fax: (585) 263-6741

Supervisory Deputy U.S. Marshal **(Vacant)** ..... (585) 263-5850
Deputy U.S. Marshal **Abhay Dave** ..... (585) 263-5787
Deputy U.S. Marshal **Khari Davis** ..... (585) 263-5787 ext. 226
E-mail: khari.davis@usdoj.gov
Deputy U.S. Marshal **Christopher Lamp** ..... (585) 263-5787 ext. 224
E-mail: christopher.lamp@usdoj.gov
Deputy U.S. Marshal **Mark Leveque** ..... (585) 263-5787
E-mail: mark.leveque@usdoj.gov
Deputy U.S. Marshal **Shane Marshall** ..... (585) 263-5787
Deputy U.S. Marshal **Chris Pfohl** ..... (585) 263-6765
Deputy U.S. Marshal **Carlton Smith** ..... (585) 263-5787
Deputy U.S. Marshal **Rebecca Smith** ..... (585) 263-5787
E-mail: rebecca.smith@usdoj.gov
Deputy U.S. Marshal **(Vacant)** ..... (585) 263-5787 ext. 229
Operational Support Specialist
Steven Pascuzzi ..... (585) 263-5787 ext. 221
E-mail: steven.pascuzzi@usdoj.gov

North Carolina - Eastern District

550 Federal Building, 310 New Bern Avenue, Raleigh, NC 27601
Tel: (919) 856-4153 Fax: (919) 856-4812

★ U.S. Marshal **Scott Jerome Parker** ..... (919) 856-4153
Chief Deputy U.S. Marshal **Robert Pettit** ..... (919) 856-4153 ext. 6151
E-mail: robert.pettit@usdoj.gov
Supervisory Deputy U.S. Marshal **Paul Sugrue** ..... (919) 856-4153
E-mail: paul.sugrue@usdoj.gov
Administrative Officer **Lisa Vajdl** ..... (919) 856-4153
E-mail: lisa.vajdl@usdoj.gov

Elizabeth City (NC) Office

306 East Main Street, Elizabeth City, NC 27909
P.O. Box 787, Elizabeth City, NC 27909
Tel: (252) 338-1439 Fax: (252) 338-5770

Deputy U.S. Marshal **James K. "Kelly" Jones** ..... (252) 338-1422

★ Presidential Appointment Requiring Senate Confirmation ☆ Presidential Appointment ☐ Schedule C Appointment ◇ Career Senior Foreign Service Appointment
● Career Senior Executive Service (SES) Appointment ○ Non-Career Senior Executive Service (SES) Appointment ■ Postal Career Executive Service

Fayetteville (NC) Office
301 Federal Building, 301 Green Street, Fayetteville, NC 28302
Tel: (910) 483-0550 Fax: (910) 483-2628

Deputy U.S. Marshal **Daniel Tubman** . . . . (910) 483-0550
E-mail: daniel.tubman@usdoj.gov

Greenville (NC) Office
Federal Building, 201 South Evans Street, Greenville, NC 27858
Tel: (252) 752-0901 Fax: (252) 752-7030

Supervisory Deputy U.S. Marshal **Howard Turner** . . . . (252) 752-1054
E-mail: howard.turner@usdoj.gov

New Bern (NC) Office
413 Middle Street, New Bern, NC 28560
Tel: (252) 638-2705 Fax: (252) 638-1073

Deputy U.S. Marshal **John Payne** . . . . (252) 638-2705

Wilmington (NC) Office
Two Princess Street, Room 223, Wilmington, NC 28401
Tel: (910) 815-4707 Fax: (910) 815-4706

Deputy U.S. Marshal **Mark Mansell** . . . . (910) 815-4707
E-mail: mark.mansell@usdoj.gov

North Carolina - Middle District
U.S. Courthouse, 324 West Market Street,
Room 234, Greensboro, NC 27401
Tel: (336) 332-8700 Fax: (336) 332-8750

★ U.S. Marshal **Willie Ransome "Bill" Stafford III** . . . . (336) 332-8700
E-mail: bill.stafford@usdoj.gov
Education: North Carolina 1975 BA, 1988 MPA
Chief Deputy U.S. Marshal **Chris Atwater** . . . . (336) 332-8700
E-mail: chris.atwater@usdoj.gov
Supervisory Deputy U.S. Marshal **Michael Potter** . . . . (336) 332-8700
E-mail: michael.potter@usdoj.gov
Supervisory Deputy U.S. Marshal **(Vacant)** . . . . (336) 332-8700
Deputy U.S. Marshal **Michael Browning** . . . . (336) 332-8700
E-mail: michael.browning@usdoj.gov
Deputy U.S. Marshal **Charles "Chuck" Peeler** . . . . (336) 332-8700
E-mail: charles.peeler@usdoj.gov
Deputy U.S. Marshal **Michael Penland** . . . . (336) 332-8700
E-mail: michael.penland@usdoj.gov
Deputy U.S. Marshal **Jason Robertson** . . . . (336) 332-8700
E-mail: jason.robertson@usdoj.gov
Deputy U.S. Marshal **Joshua Shuba** . . . . (336) 332-8700
E-mail: joshua.shuba@usdoj.gov
Deputy U.S. Marshal **Michael Sprague** . . . . (336) 332-8700
E-mail: michael.sprague@usdoj.gov
Deputy U.S. Marshal **Steve Underwood** . . . . (336) 332-8700
E-mail: steve.underwood2@usdoj.gov
Detention Enforcement Officer **Ingra R. Smith** . . . . (336) 332-8700
E-mail: ingra.smith@usdoj.gov
Judicial Security Inspector **Albert R. Moore, Jr.** . . . . (336) 332-8700
E-mail: albert.moore@usdoj.gov
Administrative Officer **Brantley Williams** . . . . (336) 332-8700
E-mail: brantley.williams@usdoj.gov
Administrative Support Assistant **(Vacant)** . . . . (336) 332-8700
Budget Analyst **Angela C. Wilson** . . . . (336) 332-8700
E-mail: angela.wilson@usdoj.gov
Criminal Program Specialist **Jessica Williams** . . . . (336) 332-8700
Purchasing Agent **Teresa Brookshire** . . . . (336) 332-8700
E-mail: teresa.brookshire@usdoj.gov

Durham (NC) Office
U.S. Courthouse, 323 East Chapel Hill Street, Durham, NC 27702
Tel: (919) 541-5452

Deputy U.S. Marshal **Donald Johnson** . . . . (919) 541-5452
E-mail: donald.johnson@usdoj.gov

Winston-Salem (NC) Office
Federal Building, 251 North Main Street,
Room 304, Winston-Salem, NC 27101
Tel: (336) 631-5166

Deputy U.S. Marshal **Arthur Gandy** . . . . (336) 631-5101
E-mail: arthur.gandy@usdoj.gov
Deputy U.S. Marshal **Joel McCready** . . . . (336) 631-5101
E-mail: joel.mccready@usdoj.gov
Deputy U.S. Marshal **Jason Morton** . . . . (336) 631-5101
E-mail: jason.morton@usdoj.gov

North Carolina - Western District
Charles R. Jonas Federal Building, 401 West Trade Street,
Charlotte, NC 28202
U.S. Courthouse, 100 Otis Street, Asheville, NC 28802 (Asheville Office)
Tel: (704) 350-8000 Tel: (828) 771-7400 (Asheville Office)
Fax: (704) 344-6523 Fax: (828) 271-4578 (Asheville Office)

★ U.S. Marshal **Kelly McDade Nesbit** . . . . (704) 350-8000
E-mail: kelly.nesbit@usdoj.gov
Education: North Carolina Charlotte 1982 BS
Chief Deputy U.S. Marshal **Kevin Stone** . . . . (704) 350-8000
E-mail: kevin.stone@usdoj.gov

North Dakota District
Quentin Burdick U.S. Courthouse, 655 First Avenue North,
Suite 110, Fargo, ND 58102-4932
Tel: (701) 297-7300 Fax: (701) 297-7305

★ U.S. Marshal **Paul Ward** . . . . (701) 297-7301
E-mail: paul.ward@usdoj.gov
Education: Minot State 1983 BS
Chief Deputy U.S. Marshal **Dan Orr** . . . . (701) 297-7302
E-mail: dan.orr@usdoj.gov
Administrative Officer **Cindy Fontaine** . . . . (701) 297-7307
E-mail: cindy.fontaine@usdoj.gov

Ohio - Northern District
U.S. Courthouse, 801 West Superior Avenue,
Suite 12-100, Cleveland, OH 44113-1853
Tel: (216) 522-2150 Fax: (216) 522-7908

★ U.S. Marshal **Peter J. Elliott** . . . . (216) 522-2150
E-mail: peter.elliott@usdoj.gov
Education: Capital U BA
Chief Deputy U.S. Marshal **Roberto Robinson** . . . . (216) 522-2150
E-mail: roberto.robinson@usdoj.gov
Assistant Chief Deputy U.S. Marshal **Andrew Deserto** . . . (216) 522-2150
E-mail: andrew.deserto@usdoj.gov
Administrative Officer **Denise Bortnick** . . . . (216) 522-2150
E-mail: denise.bortnick@usdoj.gov

Ohio - Southern District
U.S. Courthouse, 85 Marconi Boulevard,
Room 460, Columbus, OH 43215
Tel: (614) 469-5540 Fax: (614) 469-2298

★ U.S. Marshal **Peter C. "Pete" Tobin** . . . . (614) 469-5540
E-mail: peter.tobin@usdoj.gov
Chief Deputy U.S. Marshal **Patrick J. Sedoti** . . . . (614) 469-5540
E-mail: pat.sedoti@usdoj.gov

Oklahoma - Eastern District
Fifth and Okmulgee Streets, Muskogee, OK 74401
P.O. Box 738, Muskogee, OK 74402
Tel: (918) 687-2523 Fax: (918) 687-2526

★ U.S. Marshal **Patrick J. Wilkerson** . . . . (918) 687-2523
E-mail: patrick.wilkerson@usdoj.gov
Chief Deputy U.S. Marshal **Donald Abdallah** . . . . (918) 687-2523
Supervisory Deputy U.S. Marshal **Matthew Hyde** . . . . . . (918) 687-2523

(continued on next page)

REGIONAL OFFICES — US ATTORNEYS AND US MARSHALS SERVICE

★ Presidential Appointment Requiring Senate Confirmation ☆ Presidential Appointment □ Schedule C Appointment ◇ Career Senior Foreign Service Appointment
● Career Senior Executive Service (SES) Appointment ○ Non-Career Senior Executive Service (SES) Appointment ■ Postal Career Executive Service

Oklahoma - Eastern District *continued*

Judicial Security Inspector U.S. Marshal **(Vacant)** .... (918) 687-2523
Criminal Investigator Deputy U.S. Marshal
Jeffrey Lundy .... (918) 687-2523
E-mail: jeffrey.lundy@usdoj.gov
Criminal Investigator Deputy U.S. Marshal
Jim Morrissey .... (918) 687-2523
E-mail: james.morrissey@usdoj.gov
Criminal Investigator Deputy U.S. Marshal
Tom Wayerski .... (918) 687-2523
E-mail: thomas.wayerski@usdoj.gov
Deputy U.S. Marshal **Billy Banks** .... (918) 687-2523
E-mail: billy.banks@usdoj.gov
Deputy U.S. Marshal **James Edge** .... (918) 687-2523
E-mail: james.edge@usdoj.gov
Deputy U.S. Marshal **Nic Nigraham** .... (918) 687-2523
Deputy U.S. Marshal **Dustin Ramsey** .... (918) 687-2523
E-mail: dustin.ramsey@usdoj.gov
Deputy U.S. Marshal **Misty Stewart** .... (918) 687-2523
E-mail: misty.stewart@usdoj.gov
Administrative Officer **Rita Burris** .... (918) 687-2523
Asset Forfeiture Contracts **Cathy Cott** .... (918) 687-2523
E-mail: cathy.cott@usdoj.gov
Criminal Program Specialist **Aimee Karnes** .... (918) 687-2523
E-mail: aimee.karnes@usdoj.gov

Oklahoma - Northern District

333 West Fourth Street, Room 2050, Tulsa, OK 74103
P.O. Box 1097, Tulsa, OK 74101-1097
Tel: (918) 581-7738 Fax: (918) 581-7735

★ U.S. Marshal **Clayton D. Johnson** .... (918) 581-7738
E-mail: clayton.johnson@usdoj.gov
Chief Deputy U.S. Marshal **Carroll Allbery** .... (918) 581-7738
Supervisory Deputy U.S. Marshal **Lyle Brown** .... (918) 581-7738
E-mail: lyle.brown@usdoj.gov
Deputy U.S. Marshal **(Vacant)** .... (918) 581-7738
Deputy U.S. Marshal **(Vacant)** .... (918) 581-7738
Deputy U.S. Marshal **(Vacant)** .... (918) 581-7738
Deputy U.S. Marshal **(Vacant)** .... (918) 581-7738
Fugitive Task Force Coordinator **John Gage** .... (918) 581-7738
E-mail: john.gage@usdoj.gov
Judicial Security Division Inspector **Jerry D. Pierce** ..... (918) 581-7738
E-mail: jerry.pierce@usdoj.gov
Criminal Program Specialist **Mary J. Layfield** .... (918) 581-7738
Security Officer in Charge **(Vacant)** .... (918) 581-7738
Warrants Coordinator **John Gage** .... (918) 581-7738
Seizure and Forfeiture Specialist
Pamela B. Johnson .... (918) 581-7858
E-mail: pamela.johnson@usdoj.gov
Budget Analyst **Angela Liter** .... (918) 581-7738
E-mail: angela.liter@usdoj.gov
Administrative Officer **Michelle McLaughlin** .... (918) 581-7738
E-mail: michelle.mclaughlin@usdoj.gov

Oklahoma - Western District

200 NW Fourth Street, 2nd Floor, Oklahoma City, OK 73102
Tel: (405) 231-4206 Fax: (405) 231-5597

★ U.S. Marshal **Charles Thomas Weeks II** .... (405) 231-4206 ext. 101
E-mail: charles.weeks@usdoj.gov
Education: Southwestern Oklahoma St 1982 BA
Chief Deputy U.S. Marshal **Craig Hines** .... (405) 231-4206 ext. 102
E-mail: craig.hines@usdoj.gov
Administrative Officer **Karen Reihing** .... (405) 231-4209 ext. 110
E-mail: karen.reihing@usdoj.gov

Oregon District

401 U.S. Courthouse, 1000 SW Third Avenue, Portland, OR 97204-2902
Tel: (503) 326-2209 Fax: (503) 326-3145

★ U.S. Marshal **Russel Edwin Burger** .... (503) 326-2209
E-mail: russel.burger@usdoj.gov
Education: Oregon State BABA
Chief Deputy U.S. Marshal **William C. Knaust** .... (503) 326-2209
E-mail: william.knaust@usdoj.gov
Supervisory Deputy U.S. Marshal (Warrants)
Buddy Delay .... (503) 326-5777
E-mail: bud.delay@usdoj.gov
Assistant Chief Deputy U.S. Marshal
John Shoemaker .... (503) 326-2209
E-mail: john.shoemaker@usdoj.gov
Inspector - Judicial Security **Karl Knobbs** .... (503) 326-5007
Operations Supervisor **(Vacant)** .... (503) 326-7806
VOTF Supervisor **Eric Wahlstrom** .... (503) 326-3695
E-mail: eric.wahlstrom@usdoj.gov
Deputy U.S. Marshal **Barbara Alfano** .... (503) 326-5709
E-mail: barbara.alfano@usdoj.gov
Deputy U.S. Marshal **Vincent Byford** .... (503) 326-7112
E-mail: vincent.byford@usdoj.gov
Deputy U.S. Marshal **Troy Gangwisch** .... (503) 326-4177
E-mail: troy.gangwisch@usdoj.gov
Deputy U.S. Marshal **Don Holdon** .... (503) 326-7048
Deputy U.S. Marshal **Brian Kelly** .... (503) 326-3157
E-mail: brian.kelly@usdoj.gov
Deputy U.S. Marshal **Jonathan Lobell** .... (503) 326-5472
E-mail: jonathan.lobell@usdoj.gov
Deputy U.S. Marshal **Pat McGarrah** .... (503) 326-5473
E-mail: pat.mcgarrah@usdoj.gov
Deputy U.S. Marshal **John Moody** .... (503) 326-3491
E-mail: john.moody@usdoj.gov
Deputy U.S. Marshal **Brian Petty** .... (503) 326-5176
E-mail: brian.petty@usdoj.gov
Deputy U.S. Marshal **James Stratton** .... (503) 326-7808
E-mail: james.stratton@usdoj.gov
Deputy U.S. Marshal **(Vacant)** .... (503) 326-5276
Deputy U.S. Marshal **(Vacant)** .... (503) 326-7842
Deputy U.S. Marshal **(Vacant)** .... (503) 326-5176
Deputy U.S. Marshal **(Vacant)** .... (503) 326-3903
Detention Officer **Jesse Lindgren** .... (503) 326-3462
E-mail: jesse.lindgren@usdoj.gov
Warrant Administration **Sheila Meyer** .... (503) 326-3939
E-mail: sheila.meyer@usdoj.gov
Senior Inspector - Asset Forfeiture Division
Larry Gloth .... (503) 727-1058
E-mail: larry.gloth@usdoj.gov
Seizure and Forfeiture Specialist **Janice Harrison** .... (503) 326-4194
E-mail: janice.harrison@usdoj.gov
Administrative Officer **Brett Caillier** .... (503) 326-4184
E-mail: brett.caillier@usdoj.gov
System Administrator **Roger O'Connor** .... (503) 326-5178
E-mail: roger.oconnor@usdoj.gov
Management and Program Analyst **Rebecca Cook** .... (503) 326-3126
E-mail: rebecca.cook@usdoj.gov
Budget Analyst **(Vacant)** .... (503) 326-7807
Criminal Clerk **Erin Bennett-Howard** .... (503) 326-5177
E-mail: erin.bennett-howard@usdoj.gov
Criminal Clerk **Rufus Black** .... (503) 326-2318
E-mail: rufus.black@usdoj.gov
Purchasing Agent **Lisa Nickel** .... (503) 326-3531
E-mail: lisa.nickel@usdoj.gov

Eugene (OR) Office

405 East Eighth Avenue, Suite 1200, Eugene, OR 97401
Tel: (541) 465-6701

Supervisory Deputy U.S. Marshal **Bryon Carroll** .... (541) 465-6701
Deputy U.S. Marshal **Michael Bryant** .... (541) 465-6965
E-mail: michael.bryant2@usdoj.gov

★ Presidential Appointment Requiring Senate Confirmation ☆ Presidential Appointment ☐ Schedule C Appointment ◇ Career Senior Foreign Service Appointment
● Career Senior Executive Service (SES) Appointment ○ Non-Career Senior Executive Service (SES) Appointment ■ Postal Career Executive Service

Eugene (OR) Office *continued*

Deputy U.S. Marshal **Bryce Collins** . . . . (541) 465-6568
E-mail: bryce.collins@usdoj.gov
Deputy U.S. Marshal **Eric Kinney** . . . . (541) 465-6701
E-mail: eric.kinney@usdoj.gov
Deputy U.S. Marshal **Kara Kinney** . . . . (541) 465-6766
E-mail: kara.kinney@usdoj.gov
Deputy U.S. Marshal **Andrew Simpson** . . . . (541) 465-6851
E-mail: andrew.simpson@usdoj.gov
Administrative Support **Sandra Mitten** . . . . (541) 465-6701
E-mail: sandra.mitten@usdoj.gov

Medford (OR) Office

Federal Building and U.S. Courthouse, 310 West Sixth Street, Room 131, Medford, OR 97501
Tel: (541) 776-4277

Supervisory Deputy U.S. Marshal
Timothy Sundheim . . . . (541) 776-4277 ext. 1000
E-mail: timothy.sundheim@usdoj.gov
Deputy U.S. Marshal **Omar Ampie** . . . . (541) 776-4277 ext. 1006
E-mail: omar.ampie@usdoj.gov
Deputy U.S. Marshal **Rodney Lowe** . . . . (541) 776-4277 ext. 1007
E-mail: rodney.lowe@usdoj.gov
Deputy U.S. Marshal **Brad Sholer** . . . . (541) 776-4277 ext. 1001
E-mail: brad.sholer@usdoj.gov

Pennsylvania - Eastern District

U.S. Courthouse, 601 Market Street, Room 2110, Philadelphia, PA 19106
Tel: (215) 597-7272 Fax: (215) 597-1688

★ U.S. Marshal **David Blake Webb** . . . . (215) 597-1852
E-mail: david.webb@usdoj.gov
Secretary **Maryann Shelinsky** . . . . (215) 597-1687
E-mail: maryann.shelinsky@usdoj.gov
Chief Deputy U.S. Marshal **John Patrignani** . . . . (215) 597-9688
E-mail: john.patrignani@usdoj.gov
Assistant Chief Deputy U.S. Marshal **(Vacant)** . . . . (215) 597-0753
Supervisory Deputy U.S. Marshal (JSI)
Michael P. Green . . . . (267) 232-4100
E-mail: michael.green@usdoj.gov
Supervisory Deputy U.S. Marshal (Criminal Squad)
Gary Hipple . . . . (267) 232-4159
E-mail: gary.hipple@usdoj.gov
Supervisory Deputy U.S. Marshal **Gary Hippele** . . . . (610) 433-4307
1700 U.S. Courthouse, 504 Hamilton Street West, Allentown, PA 18101
E-mail: gary.hippele@usdoj.gov
Supervisory Deputy U.S. Marshal **David Sprague** . . . . (267) 232-4162
E-mail: david.sprague@usdoj.gov
Deputy U.S. Marshal **Chris Alegado** . . . . (267) 232-4125
E-mail: christopher.alegado@usdoj.gov
Deputy U.S. Marshal **David Austin** . . . . (267) 232-4117
E-mail: david.austin@usdoj.gov
Deputy U.S. Marshal **Christopher Berdos** . . . . (267) 232-4112
E-mail: christopher.berdos@usdoj.gov
Deputy U.S. Marshal **Michael Burke** . . . . (215) 861-8490
E-mail: michael.burke@usdoj.gov
Deputy U.S. Marshal **Dawn M. Cardinal** . . . . (267) 232-4121
E-mail: dawn.cardinal@usdoj.gov
Deputy U.S. Marshal **Richard Castle** . . . . (267) 232-4131
E-mail: richard.castle@usdoj.gov
Deputy U.S. Marshal **Brian DeRosa** . . . . (267) 232-4160
E-mail: brian.derosa@usdoj.gov
Deputy U.S. Marshal **Steve Eckman** . . . . (267) 232-4161
E-mail: steven.eckman@usdoj.gov
Deputy U.S. Marshal **Joseph Franchi** . . . . (267) 232-4097
E-mail: joseph.franchi@usdoj.gov
Deputy U.S. Marshal **Thomas Gabriel** . . . . (267) 232-4124
E-mail: thomas.gabriel@usdoj.gov
Deputy U.S. Marshal **Edwin George** . . . . (267) 232-4129
E-mail: edwin.george@usdoj.gov
Deputy U.S. Marshal **Joseph Gibboni** . . . . (267) 232-4130

Pennsylvania - Eastern District *continued*

Deputy U.S. Marshal **Niklaus "Nik" Hannevig** . . . . (610) 433-2176
E-mail: niklaus.hannevig@usdoj.gov
Deputy U.S. Marshal **Megan Hartman** . . . . (267) 232-4122
Deputy U.S. Marshal **Brian D. Hicks** . . . . (610) 320-5157
The Madison Building, 400 Washington Street, Reading, PA 19601
E-mail: brian.hicks@usdoj.gov
Deputy U.S. Marshal **Enrico L. Ilagan** . . . . (267) 232-4124
E-mail: enrico.ilagan@usdoj.gov
Deputy U.S. Marshal **Johannes Jarkowsky** . . . . (267) 232-4127
E-mail: johannes.jarkowsky@usdoj.gov
Deputy U.S. Marshal **Kenny King** . . . . (215) 597-7272
E-mail: kenneth.king@usdoj.gov
Deputy U.S. Marshal **Michael Longo** . . . . (267) 232-4120
E-mail: michael.longo@usdoj.gov
Deputy U.S. Marshal **Gregory Marks** . . . . (267) 232-4119
E-mail: gregory.marks@usdoj.gov
Deputy U.S. Marshal **Rob Miller** . . . . (267) 232-4156
E-mail: robert.miller@usdoj.gov
Deputy U.S. Marshal **William O'Shaughnessy** . . . . (267) 232-4118
E-mail: william.oshaughnessy@usdoj.gov
Deputy U.S. Marshal **Jeffery Sharp** . . . . (267) 232-4118
E-mail: jeffery.sharp@usdoj.gov
Deputy U.S. Marshal **Kanti Somani** . . . . (215) 560-1663
E-mail: kanti.somani@usdoj.gov
Deputy U.S. Marshal **Alan Stifler** . . . . (610) 320-5157
Deputy U.S. Marshal **James Toland** . . . . (267) 232-4128
Deputy U.S. Marshal **Christopher Wuyts** . . . . (215) 232-4121
E-mail: christopher.wuyts@usdoj.gov
Deputy U.S. Marshal **Victor Yepez** . . . . (267) 232-4155
E-mail: victor.yepez@usdoj.gov
Deputy U.S. Marshal **(Vacant)** . . . . (267) 232-4094
Deputy U.S. Marshal **(Vacant)** . . . . (267) 232-4158
Deputy U.S. Marshal (Warrants) **Roger Bomenblit** . . . . . . (215) 597-4234
E-mail: roger.bomenblit@usdoj.gov
Deputy U.S. Marshal (Warrants) **Daniel Donnelly** . . . . (215) 597-4253
E-mail: daniel.donnelly@usdoj.gov
Deputy U.S. Marshal (Warrants) **Shawn Eck** . . . . (610) 433-3973
E-mail: shawn.eck@usdoj.gov
Deputy U.S. Marshal (Warrants) **Chad W. Grant** . . . . (215) 597-4241
E-mail: chad.grant@usdoj.gov
Deputy U.S. Marshal (JSI) **Richard Craig** . . . . (267) 232-4099
Deputy U.S. Marshal and Threat Coordinator
Mark D. Dunaway . . . . (267) 232-4095
E-mail: mark.dunaway@usdoj.gov
Deputy U.S. Marshal (PII) **Michael "Mickey" Pease** . . . . (267) 232-4093
E-mail: michael.pease@usdoj.gov
Detention Enforcement Officer **Gabriel Rodriguez** . . . . . . (215) 597-9468
Detention Enforcement Officer **Stanley Sawyer** . . . . (215) 597-9468
E-mail: stanley.sawyer@usdoj.gov
Administrative Officer **Daniel A. Orr** . . . . (215) 597-1685
E-mail: danny.orr@usdoj.gov
Budget Analyst **Irene Foster** . . . . (267) 232-4149
E-mail: irene.foster@usdoj.gov
Civil, National Asset Seizure and Forfeiture (NASAF)
Supervisor **Patrick Ennis** . . . . (215) 597-1683
E-mail: patrick.ennis@usdoj.gov
Civil, NASAF Deputy **Charles Harvey** . . . . (215) 597-0024
Civil Administrative **Nicole Lee** . . . . (267) 232-4146
E-mail: nicole.lee@usdoj.gov
NASAF Administrative **Cheryl Lee** . . . . (267) 232-4153
E-mail: cheryl.lee@usdoj.gov
Criminal Squad Administrative **Miriam Burnstein** . . . . . (215) 597-9443
Criminal Squad Administrative **Denise Vought** . . . . (215) 597-8562
E-mail: denise.vought@usdoj.gov
Forfeiture Support Associates Administrative
Marie Gohn . . . . (267) 232-4147
E-mail: marie.gohn@usdoj.gov
Prison Operations Supervisor **Frank Norris** . . . . (215) 597-3507
E-mail: frank.norris@usdoj.gov
Warrant Squad Supervisor **James Burke** . . . . (215) 597-4203
E-mail: james.burke@usdoj.gov

(continued on next page)

★ Presidential Appointment Requiring Senate Confirmation ☆ Presidential Appointment ☐ Schedule C Appointment ◇ Career Senior Foreign Service Appointment
● Career Senior Executive Service (SES) Appointment ○ Non-Career Senior Executive Service (SES) Appointment ■ Postal Career Executive Service

Pennsylvania - Eastern District *continued*

Warrant Squad Deputy **Robert Clark** .... (215) 597-4236
E-mail: robert.clark@usdoj.gov
Warrant Squad Deputy **Christian Tumolo** .... (215) 597-4235
E-mail: christian.tumolo@usdoj.gov
Warrant Squad Administrative **Sandra Becker** .... (215) 597-4204
E-mail: sandy.becker@usdoj.gov

Pennsylvania - Middle District

Federal Building, 235 North Washington Avenue,
Room 215, Scranton, PA 18501
Tel: (570) 346-7277 Fax: (570) 346-7342

★ U.S. Marshal **Martin John Pane** .... (570) 346-7277
Education: Mansfield 1987 BA
Chief Deputy U.S. Marshal **James Cunfer** .... (570) 346-7277
E-mail: james.cunfer@usdoj.gov
Assistant Chief Deputy U.S. Marshal **James Nelson** ..... (570) 346-7277
E-mail: james.nelson@usdoj.gov
Supervisory Deputy U.S. Marshal **Christopher Kane** ..... (570) 346-7277
E-mail: chris.kane@usdoj.gov
Administrative Officer **Donna M. Addley** .... (570) 346-7277
E-mail: donna.addley@usdoj.gov

Harrisburg (PA) Office

Federal Building, 228 Walnut Street, Room 1004, Harrisburg, PA 17108
P.O. Box 11668, Harrisburg, PA 17108
Tel: (717) 221-2212 Fax: (717) 221-4412

Supervisory Deputy U.S. Marshal **Brad Reiff** .... (717) 221-2212

Williamsport (PA) Office

240 West Third Street, Williamsport, PA 17701
Tel: (570) 323-7245 Fax: (570) 323-7268

Supervisory Deputy U.S. Marshal **Edward Holst** .... (570) 323-7245
E-mail: edward.holst@usdoj.gov

Pennsylvania - Western District

U.S. Courthouse Building, 700 Grant Street,
Room 2360, Pittsburgh, PA 15219
Tel: (412) 644-3351 Fax: (412) 644-4769

★ U.S. Marshal **Steven R. Frank** .... (412) 355-2456
E-mail: steven.r.frank@usdoj.gov
Chief Deputy U.S. Marshal **Michael D. Baughman** ...... (412) 644-6747
Administrative Officer **James Bailey** .... (412) 644-4531
E-mail: james.bailey2@usdoj.gov

Puerto Rico District

200 Federal Building, 150 Carlos Chardon Avenue,
San Juan, PR 00918-1740
Tel: (787) 766-6000 Fax: (787) 766-6211

★ U.S. Marshal **(Vacant)** .... (787) 754-4018
Program Management Specialist **Yartiza Diaz** .... (787) 754-4245
E-mail: yarita.diaz-ponce@usdoj.gov
Chief Deputy U.S. Marshal **Antonio Torres** .... (787) 754-4023
E-mail: antonio.torres@usdoj.gov
Assistant Chief Deputy U.S. Marshal
Arnaldo H. Rodriguez .... (787) 754-4048
E-mail: arnaldo.rodriguez@usdoj.gov
Supervisory Deputy U.S. Marshal **Noel Camacho** .... (787) 754-6000
E-mail: noel.camacho@usdoj.gov
Supervisory Deputy U.S. Marshal **Daniel Cruz** .... (787) 754-4450
E-mail: daniel.cruz@usdoj.gov
Supervisory Deputy U.S. Marshal **(Vacant)** .... (787) 754-6000
Supervisory Deputy U.S. Marshal **(Vacant)** .... (787) 754-4387
Deputy U.S. Marshal **John Coleman** .... (787) 766-6000
Deputy U.S. Marshal **Pedro Fortier** .... (787) 766-6000
E-mail: pedro.fortier@usdoj.gov

Puerto Rico District *continued*

Deputy U.S. Marshal **Carlos Fuentes** .... (787) 766-6000
E-mail: carlos.fuentes@usdoj.gov
Deputy U.S. Marshal **Roberto Gonzalez** .... (787) 766-6000
Deputy U.S. Marshal **Anthony Lopez** .... (787) 766-6000
Deputy U.S. Marshal **Luis Mendez** .... (787) 766-6000
E-mail: luis.mendez@usdoj.gov
Deputy U.S. Marshal **Luis Ramirez** .... (787) 766-6000
Deputy U.S. Marshal **George Rodriguez** .... (787) 766-6000
E-mail: george.rodriguez@usdoj.gov
Deputy U.S. Marshal **Gustavo Rodriguez** .... (787) 766-6000
E-mail: gustavo.rodriguez@usdoj.gov
Deputy U.S. Marshal **Jose Rodriques-Diaz** .... (787) 766-6000
Deputy U.S. Marshal **Shelia San Miguel** .... (787) 766-6000
Deputy U.S. Marshal **Javier Villanueva** .... (787) 766-6000
E-mail: javier.villanueva@usdoj.gov
Deputy U.S. Marshal **(Vacant)** .... (787) 766-6000
Criminal Investigator/Deputy U.S. Marshal/Supervisor
Edwin Maldonado .... (787) 754-4285
E-mail: edwin.maldonado@usdoj.gov
Criminal Investigator/Deputy U.S. Marshal
Christian Cepeda .... (787) 754-4167
Criminal Investigator/Deputy U.S. Marshal
John Massa .... (787) 754-4261
Criminal Investigator/Deputy U.S. Marshal
Luis B. Perez .... (787) 754-4120
E-mail: luis.perez2@usdoj.gov
Criminal Investigator/Deputy U.S. Marshal
Jose Román .... (787) 754-4233
E-mail: jose.román@usdoj.gov
Criminal Investigator **Marlon Blandon** .... (787) 766-6000
E-mail: marlon.blandon@usdoj.gov
Criminal Investigator **Jose Carreras** .... (787) 766-6000
E-mail: jose.carreras@usdoj.gov
Criminal Investigator **Felix Carrion** .... (787) 766-6000
Criminal Investigator **Benjamin Fountain** .... (787) 766-6000
Criminal Investigator **Andrés E. Jimenez** .... (787) 766-6000
E-mail: andres.jimenez@usdoj.gov
Criminal Investigator **(Vacant)** .... (787) 766-6000
Criminal Investigator **(Vacant)** .... (787) 766-6000
Administrative Officer **Robert Gonzalez-Arturet** .... (787) 754-4028
E-mail: robert.gonzalez2@usdoj.gov
Detention Manager Inspector **Griselle Mirabal** .... (787) 766-6000
E-mail: griselle.mirabal@usdoj.gov
Detention Officer **Eduardo Burgos** .... (787) 754-4243
E-mail: eduardo.burgos@usdoj.gov
Detention Officer **(Vacant)** .... (787) 754-4243
Detention Officer **(Vacant)** .... (787) 754-4243
Judicial Security Inspector **Alexis Powell** .... (787) 754-4109
E-mail: alex.powell@usdoj.gov
Judicial Security Inspector **Manuel Varela** .... (787) 754-4312
E-mail: manuel.varela@usdoj.gov
Criminal Clerk **Waldemar Lorenzo** .... (787) 754-4205
E-mail: waldemar.lorenzo@usdoj.gov
District Asset Forfeiture Coordinator **Lizette Delpin** ..... (787) 766-6000
Seizure and Forfeiture Specialist **(Vacant)** .... (787) 754-4113
Budget Analyst **Gilberto Serrano** .... (787) 754-4046
E-mail: g.serrano@usdoj.gov
Contract Specialist **Roberto Schmidt** .... (787) 754-4047
E-mail: roberto.schmidt@usdoj.gov
Investigative Research Specialist
William Meadows-Marquiz .... (787) 754-4254
Property Manager **(Vacant)** .... (787) 754-4067
Administrative Assistant
Maylene Vazquez De Jesus .... (787) 766-6000
Prisoner Support/Administrative Specialist
Anais Velez-Perez .... (787) 754-4415

★ Presidential Appointment Requiring Senate Confirmation ☆ Presidential Appointment ☐ Schedule C Appointment ◇ Career Senior Foreign Service Appointment
● Career Senior Executive Service (SES) Appointment ○ Non-Career Senior Executive Service (SES) Appointment ■ Postal Career Executive Service

Rhode Island District

John O. Pastore Federal Building, Two Exchange Terrace, Providence, RI 02903
P.O. Box 1524, Providence, RI 02901-1524
Tel: (401) 528-5300 Fax: (401) 528-5307

★ U.S. Marshal **Jamie A. Hainsworth** . . . . . (401) 528-5300
E-mail: jamie.hainsworth@usdoj.gov
Education: Roger Williams
Chief Deputy U.S. Marshal **David G. Remington** . . . . . (401) 528-5303
E-mail: david.remington@usdoj.gov
Supervisory Deputy U.S. Marshal **Robert J. Charette** . . . . (401) 528-5305
E-mail: robert.charette@usdoj.gov
Deputy U.S. Marshal **Justin Carvalho** . . . . . (401) 528-5320
E-mail: justin.carvalho@usdoj.gov
Deputy U.S. Marshal **Elden DaSilva** . . . . . (401) 528-5326
E-mail: elden.dasilva@usdoj.gov
Deputy U.S. Marshal **John Edson** . . . . . (401) 528-5306
E-mail: john.edson@usdoj.gov
Deputy U.S. Marshal **Justin Engen** . . . . . (401) 528-5476
E-mail: justin.engen@usdoj.gov
Deputy U.S. Marshal **Brian McDonald** . . . . . (401) 528-5323
Deputy U.S. Marshal **Brenton Moore** . . . . . (401) 528-5324
E-mail: brenton.moore@usdoj.gov
Deputy U.S. Marshal **Joseph Murphy** . . . . . (401) 528-5326
E-mail: joseph.murphy@usdoj.gov
Deputy U.S. Marshal **(Vacant)** . . . . . (401) 528-5323
Administrative Officer **Karen W. Green** . . . . . (401) 528-5308
E-mail: karen.green@usdoj.gov
Administrative Support Specialist **Anne Browning** . . . . . (401) 528-5298
E-mail: anne.browning@usdoj.gov
Budget Analyst **Linda Ramos** . . . . . (401) 528-5304
E-mail: linda.ramos@usdoj.gov
Criminal Investigator **Justin Carvalho** . . . . . (401) 528-5324
Detention Enforcement Officer **John Cinquegrana** . . . . . (401) 528-5473
Investigative Research Specialist **Karen A. Lundgren** . . . . (401) 528-5327
E-mail: karen.lundgren@usdoj.gov
Judicial Security Inspector **William T. Francis** . . . . . (401) 528-4196
E-mail: william.francis@usdoj.gov
Property Custodian **Dianna Prete** . . . . . (401) 528-5470
E-mail: dianna.prete@usdoj.gov

South Carolina District

U.S. Courthouse, 901 Richland Street, Suite 1300, Columbia, SC 29201
Tel: (803) 765-5821 Fax: (803) 765-5824

★ U.S. Marshal **Kelvin Corneilius Washington** . . . . . (803) 765-5866
Education: American InterContinental 2006 BS; Troy U 2008 MS
Chief Deputy U.S. Marshal **Richard T. "Rick" Long, Jr.** . . . . . (803) 765-5825
E-mail: rick.long@usdoj.gov
Assistant Chief Deputy U.S. Marshal **Patricia Miller** . . . . . (803) 253-3575
E-mail: patricia.miller@usdoj.gov
Supervisory Deputy U.S. Marshal (Operations) **Johnny Goodwin** . . . . . (803) 765-5821
E-mail: johnny.goodwin@usdoj.gov
Supervisory Deputy U.S. Marshal (Warrants) **Rodney Duckett** . . . . . (803) 253-3298
E-mail: rodney.duckett@usdoj.gov
Deputy U.S. Marshal **John Alexander** . . . . . (803) 765-5821
E-mail: jonathan.lorenzen@usdoj.gov
Deputy U.S. Marshal **James "Jim" Brewton** . . . . . (803) 765-5821
E-mail: james.brewton@usdoj.gov
Deputy U.S. Marshal **Brent Daniels** . . . . . (803) 765-5821
Deputy U.S. Marshal **Gerald Hotchkiss** . . . . . (803) 765-5821
E-mail: gerald.hotchkiss@usdoj.gov
Deputy U.S. Marshal **Jonathan Lorenzen** . . . . . (803) 765-5821
Deputy U.S. Marshal **Amanda Lyons** . . . . . (803) 765-5821
E-mail: amanda.lyons@usdoj.gov
Deputy U.S. Marshal **Rohn Morales** . . . . . (803) 765-5821
E-mail: rohn.morales@usdoj.gov
Deputy U.S. Marshal **John Radney** . . . . . (803) 765-5921
E-mail: john.radney@usdoj.gov

South Carolina District *continued*

Deputy U.S. Marshal **Christopher Taylor** . . . . . (803) 765-5821
E-mail: christopher.taylor@usdoj.gov
Deputy U.S. Marshal **(Vacant)** . . . . . (803) 765-5821
Deputy U.S. Marshal **(Vacant)** . . . . . (803) 765-5821
Deputy U.S. Marshal and Sexual Offender Investigation Coordinator **Derek Miller** . . . . . (803) 253-3963
E-mail: derek.miller@usdoj.gov
Administrative Assistant **Brenda Strickland** . . . . . (803) 253-3308
E-mail: brenda.strickland@usdoj.gov
Budget Analyst **Mary Harper** . . . . . (803) 765-5610
E-mail: mary.harper@usdoj.gov
Criminal Program Specialist **Pam Schwartz** . . . . . (803) 765-5823
E-mail: pamela.schwartz@usdoj.gov
District Asset Forfeiture Coordinator **Sonya Adams** . . . . . (803) 765-5868
Accounting Technician **Sheron Bauldrick** . . . . . (803) 765-5338
E-mail: sheron.bauldrick@usdoj.gov
Criminal Program Specialist **Cheryll Stetar** . . . . . (803) 765-3965
E-mail: cheryll.stetar@usdoj.gov
Criminal/Civil Administrative Support Assistant **Jacqui Moses** . . . . . (803) 253-3855
Criminal/Civil Administrative Support Assistant **Judy Williams** . . . . . (803) 765-5822
E-mail: judy.williams@usdoj.gov
Fugitive Task Force Investigative Research Analyst **(Vacant)** . . . . . (803) 253-3966
Judicial Security Inspector **Jose Cuevas Soto** . . . . . (803) 253-3569
E-mail: jose.soto@usdoj.gov

Anderson (SC) Office

315 South McDuffie Street, Anderson, SC 29622
Tel: (864) 224-0927 Fax: (864) 224-2129

Deputy U.S. Marshal-in-Charge **(Vacant)** . . . . . (864) 224-0927

Charleston (SC) Office

Hollings Judicial Center, 81 Broad Street, Charleston, SC 29403
Tel: (843) 727-4255 Fax: (843) 727-4423
Fax: (803) 727-4103 (Warrants)

Supervisory Deputy U.S. Marshal **Gregg Lee** . . . . . (843) 727-4255
E-mail: gregg.lee@usdoj.gov
Deputy U.S. Marshal **Russell H. Channell** . . . . . (843) 727-4255
E-mail: russell.channell@usdoj.gov
Deputy U.S. Marshal **Ellen DePatie** . . . . . (843) 727-4255
E-mail: ellen.depatie@usdoj.gov
Deputy U.S. Marshal **Jimmy Dyches** . . . . . (843) 727-4255
E-mail: jimmy.dyches@usdoj.gov
Deputy U.S. Marshal **Kaitlyn Kent** . . . . . (843) 727-4255
Deputy U.S. Marshal **Rob Roe** . . . . . (843) 727-4255
E-mail: robert.roe@usdoj.gov
Deputy U.S. Marshal **Dennis Suszko** . . . . . (843) 727-4255
E-mail: dennis.suszko@usdoj.gov
Deputy U.S. Marshal **Tim Zayac** . . . . . (843) 727-4255
E-mail: tim.zayac@usdoj.gov
Deputy U.S. Marshal **(Vacant)** . . . . . (843) 727-4255
Operational Support Assistant **Kathy Roberts** . . . . . (843) 727-4255

Florence (SC) Office

McMillan Federal Building, 401 West Evans Street, Room 341, Florence, SC 29503
Tel: (843) 662-0750 Fax: (843) 662-0794

Supervisory Deputy U.S. Marshal **Joseph Rick "Joe" Tessari** . . . . . (843) 662-0750
E-mail: joseph.tessari@usdoj.gov
Deputy U.S. Marshal **Roberto Carrillo** . . . . . (843) 662-0750
E-mail: roberto.carrillo@usdoj.gov
Deputy U.S. Marshal **Bradley Dorn** . . . . . (843) 662-0750
E-mail: brad.dorn@usdoj.gov
Deputy U.S. Marshal **Brian A. Jordan** . . . . . (843) 662-0750
E-mail: brian.jordan@usdoj.gov

(continued on next page)

REGIONAL OFFICES — US ATTORNEYS AND US MARSHALS SERVICE

★ Presidential Appointment Requiring Senate Confirmation ☆ Presidential Appointment ☐ Schedule C Appointment ◇ Career Senior Foreign Service Appointment
● Career Senior Executive Service (SES) Appointment ○ Non-Career Senior Executive Service (SES) Appointment ■ Postal Career Executive Service

Florence (SC) Office *continued*

Deputy U.S. Marshal **Tony Jordan** .... (843) 662-0750
Deputy U.S. Marshal **William "Trey" Laffin** .... (843) 662-0750
E-mail: william.laffin@usdoj.gov
Deputy U.S. Marshal **Lori McKelvey** .... (843) 662-0750
Deputy U.S. Marshal **Stephen Perry** .... (843) 662-0750
Deputy U.S. Marshal **Janet Ward** .... (843) 662-0750
E-mail: janet.ward@usdoj.gov
Administrative Assistant **(Vacant)** .... (843) 662-0750

Greenville (SC) Office

Federal Building, 300 East Washington Street,
Room 232, Greenville, SC 29603
Tel: (864) 232-1566 Fax: (864) 370-9752

Supervisory Deputy U.S. Marshal **Johnson Bond** .... (864) 232-1566
E-mail: johnson.bond@usdoj.gov Fax: (864) 370-3276
Deputy U.S. Marshal **Bo Barrett** .... (864) 232-1566
Deputy U.S. Marshal **Patrick Campbell** .... (864) 232-1566
Deputy U.S. Marshal **William Cook** .... (864) 232-1566
E-mail: william.cook@usdoj.gov
Deputy U.S. Marshal **David Cranford** .... (864) 232-1566
Deputy U.S. Marshal **Doug Leslie** .... (864) 232-1566
Deputy U.S. Marshal **Anne McPoland** .... (864) 232-1566
Deputy U.S. Marshal **Leon Pernell** .... (864) 232-1566
Deputy U.S. Marshal **Patrick Pruitt** .... (864) 232-1566
E-mail: patrick.pruitt@usdoj.gov
Deputy U.S. Marshal **Douglas Skutka** .... (864) 232-1566
Deputy U.S. Marshal **Joseph Rick "Joe" Tessari** .... (864) 232-1566
Administrative Support Assistant **(Vacant)** .... (864) 232-1566

South Dakota District

216 Federal Building, 400 South Phillips Avenue, Sioux Falls, SD 57104
Tel: (605) 330-4351 Fax: (605) 330-4586

★ U.S. Marshal **Paul Charles Thielen** .... (605) 330-4351
E-mail: paul.thielen@usdoj.gov
Education: South Dakota 2003 BA
Chief Deputy U.S. Marshal **Scott Rolstad** .... (605) 330-4351
E-mail: scott.rolstad@usdoj.gov

Aberdeen (SD) Office

102 SE Fourth Avenue, Room 409, Aberdeen, SD 57401
Tel: (605) 226-7300 Fax: (605) 226-7329

Supervisory Deputy U.S. Marshal **(Vacant)** .... (605) 226-7300
Note: Occupied only during term of court

Pierre (SD) Office

459 U.S. Courthouse, 225 South Pierre Street, Pierre, SD 57501
P.O. Box 397, Pierre, SD 57501
Tel: (605) 224-8396 Fax: (605) 224-0214

Supervisory Deputy U.S. Marshal
Stephen Houghtaling .... (605) 224-8396

Rapid City (SD) Office

323 U.S. Courthouse, 515 Ninth Street, Rapid City, SD 57701
Tel: (605) 342-6331 Fax: (605) 342-7161

Supervisory Deputy U.S. Marshal **Jane A. Koball** .... (605) 342-6331
E-mail: jane.koball@usdoj.gov

Tennessee - Eastern District

Howard Baker Courthouse, 800 Market Street,
Suite 320, Knoxville, TN 37902
Tel: (865) 545-4182 Fax: (865) 545-4187

★ U.S. Marshal **James Thomas "Jim" Fowler** .... (865) 545-4182
E-mail: jim.fowler@usdoj.gov
Education: Columbia Southern

Tennessee - Eastern District *continued*

Chief Deputy U.S. Marshal **Frank Castiglia** .... (865) 545-4182
E-mail: frank.castiglia@usdoj.gov
Supervisory Deputy U.S. Marshal **Kent C. Miller** .... (865) 545-4182
E-mail: kent.c.miller@usdoj.gov
Deputy U.S. Marshal **Dustin Anderson** .... (865) 545-4182
E-mail: dustin.anderson@usdoj.gov
Deputy U.S. Marshal **Gregory "Greg" Dahl** .... (865) 545-4182
E-mail: gregory.dahl@usdoj.gov
Deputy U.S. Marshal **Becky Gambill** .... (865) 545-4182
E-mail: becky.gambill@usdoj.gov
Deputy U.S. Marshal **Brett Hall** .... (865) 545-4182
E-mail: brett.hall@usdoj.gov
Deputy U.S. Marshal **Brad Redmond** .... (865) 545-4182
E-mail: bradley.redmond@usdoj.gov
Deputy U.S. Marshal **John Sanchez** .... (865) 545-4182
E-mail: john.sanchez@usdoj.gov
Deputy U.S. Marshal **Amanda Shields** .... (865) 545-4182
E-mail: amanda.shields@usdoj.gov
Deputy U.S. Marshal **David Suggs** .... (865) 545-4182
E-mail: david.suggs@usdoj.gov
Deputy U.S. Marshal **Jason Tarwater** .... (865) 545-4182
E-mail: jason.tarwater@usdoj.gov
Deputy U.S. Marshal **(Vacant)** .... (865) 545-4182
District Asset Forfeiture Coordinator
Heather Harrington .... (865) 545-4182
E-mail: heather.harrington@usdoj.gov
Forfeiture Support Associate **Barbara "Sue" Norris** .... (865) 545-4182
E-mail: bnorris1@usms.doj.gov
Judicial Security Inspector **Richie Bradley** .... (865) 545-4182
E-mail: richie.bradley@usdoj.gov
Sex Offender Investigation Coordinator
Derrick Swenson .... (865) 545-4182
E-mail: derrick.swenson@usdoj.gov
Senior Systems Administrator **(Vacant)** .... (865) 545-4182
Administrative Officer **Doug Brooks** .... (865) 545-4182
E-mail: doug.brooks@usdoj.gov
Financial Specialist **Kim Seals** .... (865) 545-4182
E-mail: kim.seals@usdoj.gov
Criminal Program Specialist **Ronald Coots** .... (865) 545-4182
E-mail: ronald.coots@usdoj.gov
Management/Program Manager **Eileen Darden** .... (865) 545-4182
E-mail: eileen.darden@usdoj.gov

Chattanooga (TN) Office

U.S. Courthouse, 900 Georgia Avenue,
Room 340, Chattanooga, TN 37401
Tel: (423) 752-5115 Fax: (423) 752-5119

Supervisory Deputy U.S. Marshal **John Bieber** .... (423) 752-5115
E-mail: john.bieber@usdoj.gov
Deputy U.S. Marshal **Michael Fugate** .... (423) 752-5115
E-mail: michael.fugate@usdoj.gov
Deputy U.S. Marshal **Edward "Ted" Gregory** .... (423) 752-5115
E-mail: edward.gregory@usdoj.gov
Deputy U.S. Marshal **Jason Ladd** .... (423) 752-5115
E-mail: jason.ladd@usdoj.gov
Deputy U.S. Marshal **James Miller III** .... (423) 752-5115
E-mail: james.miller4@usdoj.gov
Deputy U.S. Marshal **James Robinson** .... (423) 752-5115
E-mail: james.robinson4@usdoj.gov
Deputy U.S. Marshal **Terese Robinson** .... (423) 752-5115
E-mail: terese.robinson@usdoj.gov
Deputy U.S. Marshal **Paul Salayko** .... (423) 752-5115
E-mail: paul.salayko@usdoj.gov
Deputy U.S. Marshal **Joshua Scarborough** .... (423) 752-5115
E-mail: joshua.scarborough@usdoj.gov
Deputy U.S. Marshal **Bronco Sullivan** .... (423) 752-5115
E-mail: bronco.sullivan@usdoj.gov
Administrative **Brandy Hanson** .... (423) 752-5115
E-mail: brandy.hanson@usdoj.gov

★ Presidential Appointment Requiring Senate Confirmation ☆ Presidential Appointment ☐ Schedule C Appointment ◇ Career Senior Foreign Service Appointment
● Career Senior Executive Service (SES) Appointment ○ Non-Career Senior Executive Service (SES) Appointment ■ Postal Career Executive Service

Greeneville (TN) Office

220 West Depot, Suite 100, Greeneville, TN 37744
Tel: (423) 638-3391 Fax: (423) 638-4971

Supervisory Deputy U.S. Marshal **Karen Burke** . . . . (423) 638-3391
E-mail: karen.burke@usdoj.gov
Deputy U.S. Marshal **Claude "Matt" Byrum** . . . . (423) 638-3391
E-mail: claude.byrum@usdoj.gov
Deputy U.S. Marshal **Paul Glassmyer** . . . . (423) 638-3391
E-mail: paul.glassmyer@usdoj.gov
Deputy U.S. Marshal **Michael "Mike" McCoy** . . . . (423) 638-3391
E-mail: michael.mccoy3@usdoj.gov
Deputy U.S. Marshal **(Vacant)** . . . . (423) 638-3391
Administrative **Sharon Maxey** . . . . (423) 328-3391
E-mail: sharon.maxey@usdoj.gov

Tennessee - Middle District

110 Ninth Avenue South, Room A750, Nashville, TN 37203
Tel: (615) 736-5417 Fax: (615) 736-5134

★ U.S. Marshal **Louise W. Kelton** . . . . (615) 736-5417
E-mail: louise.kelton@usdoj.gov
Education: Tennessee State; Cumberland U MPSA
Chief Deputy U.S. Marshal **John Shell** . . . . (615) 736-5417
E-mail: john.shell@usdoj.gov
Supervisory Deputy U.S. Marshal **Jeffrey Dill** . . . . (615) 736-5417
E-mail: jeff.dill@usdoj.gov
Deputy U.S. Marshal **Christopher Burtt** . . . . (615) 736-5417
E-mail: christopher.burtt@usdoj.gov
Deputy U.S. Marshal **Cordell Frazier** . . . . (615) 736-5417
E-mail: cordell.frazier@usdoj.gov
Deputy U.S. Marshal **Victor Gribben** . . . . (615) 736-5417
E-mail: victor.gribben@usdoj.gov
Deputy U.S. Marshal **John Hargis** . . . . (615) 736-5417
E-mail: john.hargis@usdoj.gov
Deputy U.S. Marshal **Kevin Koback** . . . . (615) 736-5417
E-mail: kevin.koback@usdoj.gov
Deputy U.S. Marshal **Bryon Osborne** . . . . (615) 736-5417
E-mail: bryon.osborne@usdoj.gov
Deputy U.S. Marshal **Patrick Pruter** . . . . (615) 736-5417
E-mail: pat.pruter@usdoj.gov
Deputy U.S. Marshal **Adrian Romaniuk** . . . . (615) 736-5417
E-mail: adrian.romaniuk@usdoj.gov
Deputy U.S. Marshal **Robin Romaniuk** . . . . (615) 736-5417
Deputy U.S. Marshal **Daniel Shelton** . . . . (615) 736-5417
E-mail: daniel.shelton@usdoj.gov
District Asset Forfeiture Coordinator
Brian E. Biermann . . . . (615) 736-5417
District Asset Forfeiture Coordinator **Harold Higgins** . . . . (615) 736-5417
E-mail: harold.higgins2@usdoj.gov
Judicial Security Inspector **Thomas L. Wehby** . . . . (615) 736-5417
E-mail: thomas.wehby@usdoj.gov
Administrative Officer **Marnie Lehew** . . . . (615) 736-5417
E-mail: marnie.lehew@usdoj.gov
Data Analyst **Katrina Burch** . . . . (615) 736-5417
Data Analyst **(Vacant)** . . . . (615) 736-5417
Records Examiner **Jennifer Justice** . . . . (615) 736-5417
E-mail: jennifer.justice2@usdoj.gov
Task Force Coordinator **(Vacant)** . . . . (615) 736-5417

Tennessee - Western District

Clifford Davis Federal Building, 167 North Main Street,
Room 1072, Memphis, TN 38103
Tel: (901) 544-3304 Fax: (901) 544-4111

★ U.S. Marshal **Jeffrey T. Holt** . . . . (901) 544-3304
E-mail: jeffrey.holt@usdoj.gov
Education: Tennessee (Martin) 1977 BSCrimJ
Chief Deputy U.S. Marshal **William E. "Ed" Laster** . . . . . (901) 544-3304
Operations Supervisory Deputy U.S. Marshal
Owen R. Woods . . . . (901) 544-3304
E-mail: owen.woods@usdoj.gov

Tennessee - Western District *continued*

Warrant Supervisory Deputy U.S. Marshal **Huey Pugh** . . . (901) 544-3304
E-mail: huey.pugh@usdoj.gov
Deputy U.S. Marshal **Thomas A. Ballard** . . . . (901) 544-3304
E-mail: thomas.ballard@usdoj.gov
Deputy U.S. Marshal **Joseph Beidl** . . . . (901) 544-3304
E-mail: joseph.beidl@usdoj.gov
Deputy U.S. Marshal **James Bradbury** . . . . (901) 544-3304
E-mail: james.bradbury@usdoj.gov
Deputy U.S. Marshal **Seth Bruce** . . . . (901) 544-3304
E-mail: seth.bruce@usdoj.gov
Deputy U.S. Marshal **Jessica DeBoer** . . . . (901) 544-3304
E-mail: jessica.deboer@usdoj.gov
Deputy U.S. Marshal **David Gaines** . . . . (901) 544-3304
E-mail: david.gaines@usdoj.gov
Deputy U.S. Marshal **Dustin Ivie** . . . . (901) 544-3304
Deputy U.S. Marshal **Bobby James** . . . . (901) 544-3304
E-mail: bobby.james@usdoj.gov
Deputy U.S. Marshal **George Mavromatis** . . . . (901) 544-3304
E-mail: george.mavromatis@usdoj.gov
Deputy U.S. Marshal **Michael McCord** . . . . (901) 544-3304
E-mail: michael.mccord@usdoj.gov
Deputy U.S. Marshal **Trayon Murray** . . . . (901) 544-3304
E-mail: trayon.murray@usdoj.gov
Deputy U.S. Marshal **Michael Patton** . . . . (901) 544-3304
E-mail: michael.patton@usdoj.gov
Deputy U.S. Marshal **Brian Sanders** . . . . (901) 544-3304
E-mail: brian.sanders@usdoj.gov
Deputy U.S. Marshal **Kyle Singletary** . . . . (901) 544-3304
Deputy U.S. Marshal **James Smith** . . . . (901) 544-3304
E-mail: james.smith@usdoj.gov
Deputy U.S. Marshal **(Vacant)** . . . . (901) 544-3304
Deputy U.S. Marshal for Sexual Offender
Investigations **Don Hankinson, Jr.** . . . . (901) 544-3304
E-mail: don.hankinson@usdoj.gov
Judicial Security Inspector **(Vacant)** . . . . (901) 544-3304
Administrative Officer **Toxis St. Clair** . . . . (901) 544-4287
E-mail: toxis.st.clair@usdoj.gov

Jackson (TN) Office

111 South Highland Avenue, Room 214, Jackson, TN 38301
Tel: (731) 427-4661 Fax: (731) 427-8934

Deputy U.S. Marshal **Shane Brown** . . . . (731) 427-4661
Deputy U.S. Marshal **Russell Kinard** . . . . (731) 427-4661
E-mail: russell.kinard@usdoj.gov
Deputy U.S. Marshal **William Love** . . . . (731) 427-4661
Deputy U.S. Marshal **Paul Melson** . . . . (731) 427-4661

Texas - Eastern District

U.S. Courthouse, 211 West Ferguson Street,
Room 307, Tyler, TX 75702
Tel: (903) 590-1370 Fax: (903) 590-1379

★ U.S. Marshal **Robert L. Hobbs** . . . . (903) 590-1370
E-mail: robert.hobbs@usdoj.gov
Education: Lamar 1987 BS; South Texas 1996 JD
Chief Deputy U.S. Marshal **Steve Tiller** . . . . (903) 590-1370
E-mail: steve.tiller@usdoj.gov
Assistant Chief Deputy U.S. Marshal
Reggie Bradshaw . . . . (903) 590-1370
E-mail: reggie.bradshaw@usdoj.gov
Supervisory Deputy U.S. Marshal **Christopher Hicks** . . . . (903) 590-1370
E-mail: christopher.hicks@usdoj.gov
Deputy U.S. Marshal **Victor Paul Barry** . . . . (903) 590-1370
E-mail: victor.barry@usdoj.gov
Deputy U.S. Marshal **Matt Bunnell** . . . . (903) 590-1370
E-mail: matt.bunnell@usdoj.gov
Deputy U.S. Marshal **Brian Leach** . . . . (903) 590-1370
E-mail: brian.leach@usdoj.gov
Deputy U.S. Marshal **Michael Rogillio** . . . . (903) 590-1370
E-mail: michael.rogillio@usdoj.gov

(continued on next page)

REGIONAL OFFICES – US ATTORNEYS AND US MARSHALS SERVICE

★ Presidential Appointment Requiring Senate Confirmation ☆ Presidential Appointment ☐ Schedule C Appointment ◇ Career Senior Foreign Service Appointment
● Career Senior Executive Service (SES) Appointment ○ Non-Career Senior Executive Service (SES) Appointment ■ Postal Career Executive Service

Texas - Eastern District *continued*

Deputy U.S. Marshal **(Vacant)** . . . . . (903) 590-1370
Deputy U.S. Marshal **(Vacant)** . . . . . (903) 590-1370
Judicial Security Inspector Deputy U.S. Marshal
John M. Garrison . . . . . (903) 590-1370
E-mail: john.garrison@usdoj.gov
Senior Inspector U.S. Marshal **Shirley Saathoff** . . . . . (903) 590-1370
Administrative Officer **Melinda Holcomb** . . . . . (903) 590-1370
E-mail: melinda.holcomb@usdoj.gov
Administrative (Criminal) **(Vacant)** . . . . . (903) 590-1370
DAFC **Denise Reynolds** . . . . . (903) 590-1370
E-mail: denise.reynolds@usdoj.gov
Asset Forfeiture Contractor **Melissa Sullivan** . . . . . (903) 590-1370
Budget Analyst **Karen Clopton** . . . . . (903) 590-1370
E-mail: karen.clopton@usdoj.gov

Beaumont (TX) Office

Federal Building, 300 Willow Street, Room 116, Beaumont, TX 77701
Tel: (409) 839-2581 Fax: (409) 839-2585

Supervisory Deputy U.S. Marshal **Rhonda Sowell** . . . . . (409) 839-2581
E-mail: rhonda.sowell@usdoj.gov
Deputy U.S. Marshal **Christopher Christian** . . . . . (409) 839-2581
E-mail: christopher.christian@usdoj.gov
Deputy U.S. Marshal **Vincent Doan** . . . . . (409) 839-2581
E-mail: vince.doan@usdoj.gov
Deputy U.S. Marshal **James Fulcher** . . . . . (409) 839-2581
E-mail: james.fulcher@usdoj.gov
Deputy U.S. Marshal **James McNeely** . . . . . (409) 839-2581
E-mail: james.mcneely@usdoj.gov
Deputy U.S. Marshal **Eugene Rachal** . . . . . (409) 839-2581
Deputy U.S. Marshal **Hunter Sykes** . . . . . (409) 839-2581
E-mail: hunter.sykes@usdoj.gov
Deputy U.S. Marshal **(Vacant)** . . . . . (409) 839-2581
Administrative **Stacey Plummer** . . . . . (409) 839-2581
Administrative **Shannon Woods** . . . . . (409) 839-2581

Lufkin (TX) Office

104 North Third Street, Lufkin, TX 75901
Tel: (936) 634-9733 Fax: (936) 634-9741

Note: This office is staffed only when court is in session by marshals from the Beaumont office.

Marshall (TX) Office

U.S. Courthouse, 100 East Houston Street, Marshall, TX 75672
Tel: (903) 935-5737 Fax: (903) 938-9033

Deputy U.S. Marshal **Justin Pierce** . . . . . (903) 935-5737
E-mail: justin.pierce@usdoj.gov

Plano (TX) Office

7940 Preston Road, Room 107, Plano, TX 75024
Tel: (214) 705-9850 Fax: (214) 705-1380

Deputy in Charge **Jake Herrington** . . . . . (214) 705-9850
E-mail: jake.herrington@usdoj.gov
Deputy U.S. Marshal **Paul Denton** . . . . . (214) 705-9850
E-mail: paul.denton@usdoj.gov
Deputy U.S. Marshal **Mark Freeman** . . . . . (214) 705-9850
E-mail: mark.freeman@usdoj.gov
Deputy U.S. Marshal **Osvaldo Ortiz** . . . . . (214) 705-9850
E-mail: osvaldo.ortiz2@usdoj.gov
Deputy U.S. Marshal **David Ramirez** . . . . . (214) 705-9850
E-mail: david.ramirez@usdoj.gov
Administrative Officer **Kathleen Goldynia** . . . . . (214) 705-9850
E-mail: kathleen.goldynia@usdoj.gov

Sherman (TX) Office

U.S. Courthouse, 101 East Pecan Street,
Room 302, Sherman, TX 75090
Tel: (903) 868-2379 Fax: (903) 868-9398

Supervisory Deputy U.S. Marshal **Melinda Robinson** . . . . (903) 868-2379
E-mail: melinda.robinson2@usdoj.gov
Deputy U.S. Marshal **Kenny Abel** . . . . . (903) 868-2379
E-mail: kenny.abel@usdoj.gov
Deputy U.S. Marshal **Jack Bass** . . . . . (903) 868-2379
E-mail: jack.bass@usdoj.gov
Deputy U.S. Marshal **Matt Charske** . . . . . (903) 868-2379
E-mail: matt.charske@usdoj.gov
Deputy U.S. Marshal **Michael Patterson** . . . . . (903) 868-2379
E-mail: michael.patterson@usdoj.gov
Asset Forfeiture Financial Investigator
Dustin Williams . . . . . (903) 868-2379
E-mail: dustin.williams@usdoj.gov
Administrative **(Vacant)** . . . . . (903) 868-2379

Texarkana (TX) Office

U.S. Courthouse, Fifth and State Line, Room 209, Texarkana, TX 75504
Tel: (903) 793-8782 Fax: (903) 792-2286

Deputy U.S. Marshal **Andrew Leach** . . . . . (903) 793-8782 ext. 22
E-mail: andrew.leach@usdoj.gov
Deputy U.S. Marshal **Darrell Williams** . . . . . (903) 793-8782 ext. 23
E-mail: darrell.williams@usdoj.gov
Administrative Officer **(Vacant)** . . . . . (903) 793-8782 ext. 24

Texas - Northern District

Earle Cabell Federal Building, 1100 Commerce Street,
Room 1657, Dallas, TX 75242-1698
Tel: (214) 767-0836 Fax: (214) 767-4974

★ U.S. Marshal (Acting) **Fidencio Rivera** . . . . . (214) 767-0836
E-mail: fidencio.rivera@usdoj.gov
Chief Deputy U.S. Marshal **Richard "Rick" Taylor** . . . . . (214) 767-0836
E-mail: rick.taylor@usdoj.gov
Assistant Chief Deputy U.S. Marshal
Trent Touchstone . . . . . (214) 767-0836
E-mail: trent.touchstone@usdoj.gov
Administrative Officer **John Aragon** . . . . . (214) 767-0836
E-mail: john.aragon@usdoj.gov

Texas - Southern District

U.S. Courthouse, 515 Rusk Avenue, 10th Floor, Room 10002,
Houston, TX 77002
Tel: (713) 718-4800 Fax: (713) 718-4849

★ U.S. Marshal **Gary Blankinship** . . . . . (713) 718-4800
E-mail: gary.blankinship@usdoj.gov
Chief Deputy U.S. Marshal **(Vacant)** . . . . . (956) 618-4800
Assistant Chief Deputy (Warrants) **Marco Villarreal** . . . . . (713) 718-4800
E-mail: marco.villarreal@usdoj.gov
Prisoner Movement/Civil Supervisor **Isaac Karam** . . . . . (713) 718-4800
E-mail: isaac.karam@usdoj.gov
Warrant Supervisor **Julio Villegas** . . . . . (713) 718-4259
E-mail: julio.villegas@usdoj.gov
Warrant Supervisor/Commander **Arthur Fernandez** . . . . . (713) 718-4259
E-mail: arthur.fernandez@usdoj.gov
Administrative Officer **Ann Adams** . . . . . (713) 718-4800
E-mail: anna.adams@usdoj.gov
Public Affairs Officer **Alfredo Perez** . . . . . (713) 718-4259
Purchasing Agent **Noel Bautista** . . . . . (713) 718-4800
E-mail: noel.bautista@usdoj.gov

Brownsville (TX) Office

600 East Harrison, Room 104, Brownsville, TX 78520
Tel: (956) 548-2519 Fax: (956) 548-2534

Supervisory Deputy **Doug Atkinson** . . . . . (956) 548-2519

Brownsville (TX) Office *continued*

Supervisory Deputy (Enforcement) **George Ramirez** ..... (956) 548-2519
E-mail: george.ramirez@usdoj.gov

Corpus Christi (TX) Office

1133 North Shoreline Boulevard, Suite 109,
Corpus Christi, TX 78401-2349
Tel: (361) 888-3154 Fax: (361) 888-3174

Supervisory Deputy **Carlos Alvarado** .... (361) 888-3154
E-mail: carlos.alvarado@usdoj.gov
Supervisory Deputy **Russell O'Riley** .... (361) 888-3154
E-mail: russell.oriley@usdoj.gov

Galveston (TX) Office

601 Rosenberg, Room 502, Galveston, TX 77550
Tel: (409) 684-9421 Fax: (409) 766-3707

Supervisory Deputy U.S. Marshal **George Hephner** ..... (409) 684-9421
E-mail: george.hephner@usdoj.gov

Laredo (TX) Office

1300 Victoria Street, Suite 1197, Laredo, TX 78040
Tel: (956) 794-1060 Fax: (956) 726-2335

Supervisory Deputy **William Grunez** .... (956) 794-1060
Supervisory Deputy **Kevin Labrador** .... (956) 794-1060
E-mail: kevin.labrador@usdoj.gov
Supervisory Deputy **Carlos Palos** .... (956) 794-1060
E-mail: carlos.palos@usdoj.gov
Supervisory Deputy (Warrant Division) **Robert Julien** ... (956) 794-1060
E-mail: robert.julien@usdoj.gov

McAllen (TX) Office

1701 West Business Highway 83, Suite 1125, McAllen, TX 78501
Tel: (956) 618-8025 Fax: (956) 618-8029

Supervisory Deputy (Enforcement) **John Allen** .... (956) 618-8025
E-mail: john.allen@usdoj.gov
Supervisory Deputy (Enforcement) **(Vacant)** .... (956) 618-8025
Supervisory Deputy (Operations) **Dagoberto Lopez** ..... (956) 618-8025
E-mail: dagoberto.lopez@usdoj.gov
Supervisory Deputy (Operations) **Baldo Montano** .... (956) 618-8025
E-mail: baldo.montano@usdoj.gov

Victoria (TX) Office

312 South Main Street, Room 326, Victoria, TX 77902
Tel: (361) 578-4932 Fax: (361) 576-0065

Supervisory Deputy (Enforcement) **Carlos Alvarado** ..... (361) 578-4932
E-mail: carlos.alvarado@usdoj.gov
Supervisory Deputy (Operations) **Russell O'Riley** .... (361) 578-4932
E-mail: russell.oriley@usdoj.gov

Texas - Western District

John H. Wood Federal Courthouse, 655 East Durango Boulevard,
Room 235, San Antonio, TX 78206
Tel: (210) 472-6540 Fax: (210) 472-4134

★ U.S. Marshal **Robert R. Almonte** .... (210) 472-6540
E-mail: robert.almonte@usdoj.gov
Education: Park U 2002 BS
Administrative Support Specialist
Elaine Anaya-Ortiz .... (210) 472-6540
E-mail: elaine.anaya-ortiz@usdoj.gov
Education: Texas (San Antonio) BA
Chief Deputy U.S. Marshal **Melesio Hernandez** .... (210) 472-6540
Assistant Chief Deputy U.S. Marshal **Lucy Schott** .... (210) 472-6540
E-mail: lucy.schott@usdoj.gov
Assistant Chief Deputy U.S. Marshal **(Vacant)** .... (210) 472-6540
Supervisory Deputy U.S. Marshal **Preston Browning** .... (210) 472-6540
E-mail: preston.browning2@usdoj.gov

Texas - Western District *continued*

Supervisory Deputy U.S. Marshal **Mark McPherson** ..... (210) 472-6540
E-mail: mark.mcpherson@usdoj.gov
Deputy U.S. Marshal **Vincent "Vinnie" Bellino** .... (210) 472-6540
E-mail: vincent.bellino@usdoj.gov
Deputy U.S. Marshal **Christopher Bozeman** .... (210) 472-6540
E-mail: christopher.bozeman@usdoj.gov
Deputy U.S. Marshal **Dennis Collins** .... (210) 472-6540
Deputy U.S. Marshal **Lee De La Fuente** .... (210) 472-6540
Deputy U.S. Marshal **John Gonzales** .... (210) 472-6540
E-mail: john.gonzalez@usdoj.gov
Deputy U.S. Marshal **Edward Hernandez** .... (210) 472-6540
E-mail: edward.hernandez@usdoj.gov
Deputy U.S. Marshal **Bobby J. Hogeland** .... (210) 472-6540
E-mail: bobby.hogeland@usdoj.gov
Deputy U.S. Marshal **Michael "Mike" Parsley** .... (210) 472-6540
E-mail: michael.parsley@usdoj.gov
Deputy U.S. Marshal **Matthew Rector** .... (210) 472-6540
E-mail: matthew.rector@usdoj.gov
Deputy U.S. Marshal **Nicholas Rose** .... (210) 472-6540
E-mail: nicholas.rose@usdoj.gov
Deputy U.S. Marshal **Edgar Santana** .... (210) 472-6540
E-mail: edgar.santana@usdoj.gov
Deputy U.S. Marshal **Alan Schrecongost** .... (210) 472-6540
E-mail: alan.schrecongost@usdoj.gov
Deputy U.S. Marshal **Kristopher Waterman** .... (210) 472-6540
E-mail: kristopher.waterman@usdoj.gov
Deputy U.S. Marshal **(Vacant)** .... (210) 472-6540
Detention Enforcement Officer **Mark Gonzalez** .... (210) 472-6540
E-mail: mark.gonzalez@usdoj.gov
Judicial Security Inspector **(Vacant)** .... (210) 472-6540
Protective Intelligence Investigator **Luke Chastain** .... (210) 472-6540
Senior Inspector **(Vacant)** .... (210) 472-5633
Administrative Officer **Sherry Poligala** .... (210) 271-2529
E-mail: sherry.poligala@usdoj.gov
Accounting Technician **Ana Santana** .... (210) 472-6540
E-mail: ana.santana@usdoj.gov
Budget Analyst **Joanna Zuniga** .... (210) 472-6540
E-mail: joanna.zuniga@usdoj.gov
Criminal Program Specialist **Charla Mora** .... (210) 472-6540
Investigative Research Specialist **Shirley Hodges** .... (210) 271-2555
Management and Program Analyst **Julissa Falconi** ...... (210) 472-6540
Program Analyst **(Vacant)** .... (210) 472-6540
Purchasing Agent **Anna Marmolejo** .... (210) 472-5636
E-mail: anna.marmolejo@usdoj.gov
Seizure and Forfeiture Specialist **Nancy Crandall** .... (210) 472-6540
Senior Computer Specialist **James Cobarruvias** .... (210) 472-6540
E-mail: james.cobarruvias@usdoj.gov
Supervisory Property Management Specialist
Diane Young .... (210) 472-6685
E-mail: diane.young@usdoj.gov
Property Management Specialist **Heidi Schroeder** ..... (210) 472-6540
E-mail: heidi.schroeder@usdoj.gov

Alpine (TX) Office

803 North Second Street, Alpine, TX 79830
Tel: (432) 837-7295 Fax: (432) 837-1629

Deputy U.S. Marshal **(Vacant)** .... (432) 837-7295

Austin (TX) Office

316 U.S. Courthouse, 200 West Eighth Street,
Suite 316, Austin, TX 78701
Tel: (512) 916-5393 Fax: (512) 916-5405

Supervisory Deputy U.S. Marshal **Hector Gomez** .... (512) 916-5393
E-mail: hector.gomez@usdoj.gov
Supervisory Deputy U.S. Marshal **Darren Sartin** .... (512) 916-5393
E-mail: darren.sartin@usdoj.gov
Deputy U.S. Marshal **Carlos Camacho** .... (512) 916-5393
E-mail: carlos.camacho@usdoj.gov

(continued on next page)

Austin (TX) Office *continued*

Deputy U.S. Marshal **Adam Campbell** . . . . (512) 916-5393
E-mail: adam.campbell@usdoj.gov
Deputy U.S. Marshal **John Clifton** . . . . (512) 916-5393
Deputy U.S. Marshal **Marvin Conley** . . . . (512) 916-5393
E-mail: marvin.conley@usdoj.gov
Deputy U.S. Marshal **Aaron Greenwood** . . . . (512) 916-5393
E-mail: aaron.greenwood@usdoj.gov
Deputy U.S. Marshal **James Johnson** . . . . (512) 916-5393
E-mail: james.johnson@usdoj.gov
Deputy U.S. Marshal **Yolanda Pesina** . . . . (512) 916-5393
E-mail: yolanda.pesina@usdoj.gov
Deputy U.S. Marshal **Brian Sheely** . . . . (512) 916-5393
E-mail: brian.sheely@usdoj.gov
Operations Support Specialist **Sasha Guerra** . . . . (512) 916-5393
E-mail: sasha.guerra@usdoj.gov
Operations Support Specialist **Gabariel Rodriguez** . . . . . . (512) 916-5393

Del Rio (TX) Office

A106 U.S. Courthouse, 111 East Broadway, Del Rio, TX 78840
Tel: (830) 703-2075 Fax: (830) 703-2084

Supervisory Deputy U.S. Marshal **Christian Casson** . . . . . (830) 703-2075
E-mail: christian.casson@usdoj.gov
Supervisory Deputy U.S. Marshal
Mario Delayo . . . . (830) 703-2075 ext. 200
Supervisory Deputy U.S. Marshal **Kevin Scott** . . . . (830) 703-2075
E-mail: kevin.scott@usdoj.gov
Criminal Investigator **Michael Caro** . . . . (830) 703-2075
E-mail: michael.caro@usdoj.gov
Deputy U.S. Marshal **Steven Fernandez** . . . . (830) 703-2075
E-mail: steven.fernandez@usdoj.gov
Deputy U.S. Marshal **Keith Lawson** . . . . (830) 703-2075
E-mail: keith.lawson@usdoj.gov
Deputy U.S. Marshal **Adrian Pena** . . . . (830) 703-2075
E-mail: adrian.pena@usdoj.gov
Deputy U.S. Marshal **Korey Reichert** . . . . (830) 703-2075
E-mail: korey.reichert@usdoj.gov
Deputy U.S. Marshal **Vicente Rodriguez** . . . . (830) 703-2075
E-mail: vicente.rodriguez@usdoj.gov
Investigative Research Specialist **Lilian Galindo** . . . . (830) 703-2075
Administrative Support Assistant **Sylvia Cuevas** . . . . (830) 703-2075
E-mail: sylvia.cuevas@usdoj.gov
Administrative Support Assistant **Pamela Geis** . . . . (830) 703-2075
E-mail: pamela.geis@usdoj.gov
Administrative Support Assistant **Samuel Lopez** . . . . . . (830) 703-2075
E-mail: sam.lopez@usdoj.gov
Criminal Program Specialist **Rosie Perez** . . . . (830) 703-2075
E-mail: rose.perez@usdoj.gov

El Paso (TX) Office

305 U.S. Courthouse, 511 East San Antonio, El Paso, TX 79901
Tel: (915) 534-6779 Tel: (915) 534-6018 (Warrants)
Fax: (915) 534-6777 Fax: (915) 534-6262 (Warrants)

Assistant Chief Deputy U.S. Marshal **Patrick Hayes** . . . . . (915) 534-6779
Supervisory Deputy U.S. Marshal **Adrian Aranda** . . . . (915) 534-6779
E-mail: adrian.aranda@usdoj.gov
Supervisory Deputy U.S. Marshal **Sylvia Rodriguez** . . . . . (915) 534-6779
Supervisory Deputy U.S. Marshal **Jesus Solorzano** . . . . . (915) 534-6779
E-mail: jesus.solorzano@usdoj.gov
Supervisory Deputy U.S. Marshal **Javier Velasco** . . . . (915) 534-6779
E-mail: javier.velasco@usdoj.gov
Deputy U.S. Marshal **Karla Almazan** . . . . (915) 534-6779
E-mail: karla.almazan@usdoj.gov
Deputy U.S. Marshal **Miguel Alvarado** . . . . (915) 534-6779
Deputy U.S. Marshal **Emiliano Baca** . . . . (915) 534-6779
E-mail: emiliano.baca@usdoj.gov
Deputy U.S. Marshal **John Botello, Jr.** . . . . (915) 534-6779
Deputy U.S. Marshal **Yvette Castro** . . . . (915) 534-6779
E-mail: yvette.castro@usdoj.gov

El Paso (TX) Office *continued*

Deputy U.S. Marshal **Mayra Contreras** . . . . (915) 534-6779
E-mail: mayra.contreras@usdoj.gov
Deputy U.S. Marshal **Steve Douglas** . . . . (915) 534-6779
E-mail: steven.douglas@usdoj.gov
Deputy U.S. Marshal **Iva Esquiral** . . . . (915) 534-6779
Deputy U.S. Marshal **Damian Fernandez** . . . . (915) 534-6779
E-mail: damian.fernandez@usdoj.gov
Deputy U.S. Marshal **Albert Flores** . . . . (915) 534-6779
Deputy U.S. Marshal **Jesse Flores** . . . . (915) 534-6779
Deputy U.S. Marshal **Greg Haley** . . . . (915) 534-6779
E-mail: greg.haley@usdoj.gov
Deputy U.S. Marshal **Patrick Hayes** . . . . (915) 534-6779
Deputy U.S. Marshal **Salvador Martinez** . . . . (915) 534-6779
E-mail: salvador.martinez@usdoj.gov
Deputy U.S. Marshal **Sam Neverz** . . . . (915) 534-6779
Deputy U.S. Marshal **David Ogaz** . . . . (915) 534-6779
E-mail: david.ogaz@usdoj.gov
Deputy U.S. Marshal **Josh Paulson** . . . . (915) 534-6779
E-mail: joshua.paulson@usdoj.gov
Deputy U.S. Marshal **Greg Pean** . . . . (915) 534-6779
Deputy U.S. Marshal **Emir Perez** . . . . (915) 534-6779
E-mail: emir.perez@usdoj.gov
Deputy U.S. Marshal **Lee Rosas** . . . . (915) 534-6779
E-mail: lee.rosas@usdoj.gov
Deputy U.S. Marshal **Anthony Rossi** . . . . (915) 534-6779
E-mail: anthony.rossi@usdoj.gov
Deputy U.S. Marshal **Edward Sanchez** . . . . (915) 534-6779
Deputy U.S. Marshal **Kenneth Schmidt** . . . . (915) 534-6779
E-mail: kenneth.schmidt@usdoj.gov
Deputy U.S. Marshal **Jesus Soto** . . . . (915) 534-6779
E-mail: jesus.soto@usdoj.gov
Deputy U.S. Marshal **Alex Trejo** . . . . (915) 534-6779
Deputy U.S. Marshal **Juan Trujillo** . . . . (915) 534-6779
E-mail: juan.trujillo@usdoj.gov
Deputy U.S. Marshal **Mike Uehara** . . . . (915) 534-6779
E-mail: michael.uehara@usdoj.gov
Deputy U.S. Marshal **Salvador Vazquez, Jr.** . . . . (915) 534-6779
E-mail: salvador.vazquez@usdoj.gov
Deputy U.S. Marshal **Scott William** . . . . (915) 534-6779
Deputy U.S. Marshal **(Vacant)** . . . . (915) 534-6779
Deputy U.S. Marshal **(Vacant)** . . . . (915) 534-6779
Detention Enforcement Officer **Jose Perez-Rivera** . . . . (915) 534-6779
Criminal Investigator **Daniel Galvan** . . . . (915) 534-6779
E-mail: daniel.galvan@usdoj.gov
Criminal Investigator **David Ochoa** . . . . (915) 534-6779
E-mail: david.ochoa@usdoj.gov
Criminal Investigator **Michael Sharboneau** . . . . (915) 534-6779
E-mail: michael.sharboneau@usdoj.gov
Administrative Support Assistant **Inez Cage** . . . . (915) 534-6779
E-mail: inez.cage@usdoj.gov
Administrative Support Assistant **Minerva Mercado** . . . . . (915) 534-6779
E-mail: minerva.mercado@usdoj.gov
Administrative Support Assistant **Sam Quijas** . . . . (915) 534-6779
Administrative Support Assistant **(Vacant)** . . . . (915) 534-6779
Administrative Support Assistant **(Vacant)** . . . . (915) 534-6779
Investigative Research Specialist **Betty Cabrera** . . . . (915) 534-6779
E-mail: betty.cabrera@usdoj.gov
Investigative Research Specialist **Darlene Medina** . . . . (915) 534-6779
E-mail: darlene.medina@usdoj.gov
Prisoner Support Specialist **Maria Fuentez** . . . . (915) 534-6779
E-mail: maria.fuentez@usdoj.gov
Property Management Specialist **Rejane Hinkle** . . . . (915) 534-6779
E-mail: rejane.hinkle@usdoj.gov
Purchasing Agent **Sal Bretado** . . . . (915) 534-6779
E-mail: sal.bretado@usdoj.gov
Seizure and Forfeiture Specialist
Esther Gonzales-Flores . . . . (915) 534-6779
E-mail: esther.gonzales-flores@usdoj.gov

Midland (TX) Office

George H.W. Bush and George W. Bush U.S. Courthouse, 200 East Wall, Room 213, Midland, TX 79701
P.O. Box 593, Midland, TX 79701
Tel: (432) 686-4100 Fax: (432) 686-4105

Supervisory Deputy U.S. Marshal
Jason Schwaninger . . . . . (432) 686-4100
E-mail: jason.schwaninger@usdoj.gov
Deputy U.S. Marshal **Monica Almengor** . . . . . (432) 686-4100
Deputy U.S. Marshal **George Butcher** . . . . . (432) 686-4100
E-mail: george.butcher@usdoj.gov
Deputy U.S. Marshal **Steve Clark** . . . . . (432) 686-4100
Deputy U.S. Marshal **Jay Easley** . . . . . (432) 686-4100
Deputy U.S. Marshal **Cynthia Myers** . . . . . (432) 686-4100
E-mail: cynthia.myers@usdoj.gov
Deputy U.S. Marshal **John Pennington** . . . . . (432) 686-4100
E-mail: john.pennington@usdoj.gov
Deputy U.S. Marshal **Thomas Reese** . . . . . (432) 686-4100
E-mail: thomas.reese@usdoj.gov
Deputy U.S. Marshal **Brent Sheets** . . . . . (432) 686-4100
E-mail: brent.sheets@usdoj.gov
Deputy U.S. Marshal **(Vacant)** . . . . . (432) 686-4100
Operations Support Specialist **Ana De Los Rios** . . . . . (432) 686-4100
Criminal Program Specialist **Mandy Hinojos** . . . . . (432) 686-4100

Pecos (TX) Office

Post Office Building, 410 South Cedar, Room 204, Pecos, TX 79772
Tel: (432) 445-5495 Fax: (432) 445-4308

Supervisory Deputy U.S. Marshal **Kenneth Roberts** . . . . . (432) 445-5495
Deputy U.S. Marshal **Adrian Bolanos** . . . . . (432) 445-5495
Deputy U.S. Marshal **Chad Hasz** . . . . . (432) 445-5495
E-mail: chad.hasz@usdoj.gov
Deputy U.S. Marshal **Robert Heier** . . . . . (432) 445-5495
Deputy U.S. Marshal **Joe Sorge** . . . . . (432) 445-5495
Administrative Support Specialist **Hilda Woods** . . . . . (432) 445-5495

Waco (TX) Office

800 Franklin Avenue, Suite 200, Waco, TX 76701
Tel: (254) 750-1570 Fax: (254) 750-1575

Supervisory Deputy U.S. Marshal **Arthur Thomas** . . . . . (254) 750-1570
E-mail: arthur.thomas@usdoj.gov
Deputy U.S. Marshal **Chad Brown** . . . . . (915) 534-6779
Deputy U.S. Marshal **Anton Slavich** . . . . . (254) 750-1570
E-mail: anton.slavich@usdoj.gov
Deputy U.S. Marshal **Alan Stephens** . . . . . (254) 750-1570
E-mail: alan.stephens@usdoj.gov
Deputy U.S. Marshal **(Vacant)** . . . . . (254) 750-1570

Utah District

351 South West Temple, Suite 4.200, Salt Lake City, UT 84101
Tel: (801) 524-5693 Fax: (801) 524-4359

★ U.S. Marshal **James Alfred Thompson** . . . . . (801) 524-5693
E-mail: james.thompson@usdoj.gov
Education: Tennessee (Memphis) BAE
Chief Deputy U.S. Marshal **David Carnahan** . . . . . (801) 524-5693
E-mail: david.carnahan@usdoj.gov
Supervisory Deputy U.S. Marshal
David "Dave" Gelement . . . . . (801) 524-5693
E-mail: david.gelement@usdoj.gov
Supervisory Deputy U.S. Marshal
Michael "Mike" Wingert . . . . . (801) 524-5693
E-mail: mike.wingert@usdoj.gov
Deputy U.S. Marshal **Robert Barnes** . . . . . (801) 524-5693
E-mail: robert.barnes@usdoj.gov
Deputy U.S. Marshal **Brett Glissmeyer** . . . . . (801) 524-5693
E-mail: brett.glissmeyer@usdoj.gov

Vermont District

U.S. Federal Building, 11 Elmwood Avenue, Room 601, Burlington, VT 05401
P.O. Box 946, Burlington, VT 05402-0946
Tel: (802) 951-6271 Fax: (802) 951-6378

★ U.S. Marshal **David Edward Demag** . . . . . (802) 951-6271
E-mail: david.demag@usdoj.gov
Education: Trinity Col (VT)
Chief Deputy U.S. Marshal **(Vacant)** . . . . . (802) 951-6271
Supervisory Deputy U.S. Marshal **Insup Shin** . . . . . (802) 951-6202
E-mail: insup.shin@usdoj.gov
Criminal Investigator **John P. Curtis** . . . . . (802) 951-6271
E-mail: john.curtis@usdoj.gov
Criminal Investigator **Max Galusha** . . . . . (802) 951-6271
E-mail: max.galusha@usdoj.gov
Deputy U.S. Marshal **Michael Barron** . . . . . (802) 951-6271
E-mail: michael.barron@usdoj.gov
Deputy U.S. Marshal **Christopher Kopac** . . . . . (802) 951-6271
E-mail: christopher.kopac@usdoj.gov
Deputy U.S. Marshal **Brandon Wilson** . . . . . (802) 951-6271
E-mail: brandon.wilson@usdoj.gov
Deputy U.S. Marshal **(Vacant)** . . . . . (802) 951-6271
Inspector **Joseph Gaines** . . . . . (802) 951-6271
E-mail: joe.gaines@usdoj.gov
Inspector **(Vacant)** . . . . . (802) 951-6204
Administrative Officer **Kim Merker** . . . . . (802) 951-9202

Brattleboro (VT) Office

P.O. Box 37, Brattleboro, VT 05301
Tel: (802) 257-1464

Deputy U.S. Marshal **(Vacant)** . . . . . (802) 257-1464

Virgin Islands District

Ron DeLugo Federal Building and U.S. Courthouse, Veterans Drive, Charlotte Amalie, Room 115, St. Thomas, VI 00802
P.O. Box 9018, Charlotte Amalie, St. Thomas, VI 00801
Tel: (340) 774-2743 Fax: (340) 776-1105

★ U.S. Marshal **(Vacant)** . . . . . (340) 774-2743 ext. 234
Administrative Officer **Joyce Ann Carter** . . . . . (340) 774-2743 ext. 227
Chief Deputy U.S. Marshal **(Vacant)** . . . . . (340) 774-2743 ext. 225

Virginia - Eastern District

Albert V. Bryan, Sr., U.S. Courthouse, 401 Courthouse Square, Alexandria, VA 22314-5795
Tel: (703) 837-5500 Fax: (703) 837-5546

★ U.S. Marshal **Robert W. "Bobby" Mathieson** . . . . . (703) 837-5500
E-mail: robert.mathieson@usdoj.gov
Education: St Leo U 1988
Chief Deputy U.S. Marshal **John Bolen** . . . . . (703) 837-5524
E-mail: john.bolen@usdoj.gov
Assistant Chief/Deputy U.S. Marshal **Brian Thomas** . . . . . (804) 545-8542
E-mail: brian.thomas@usdoj.gov
Supervisory Deputy U.S. Marshal **(Vacant)** . . . . . (703) 837-5500
Deputy U.S. Marshal **Charles Bradley** . . . . . (703) 837-5500
E-mail: charles.bradley@usdoj.gov
Deputy U.S. Marshal **Keith Burgos** . . . . . (703) 837-5500
E-mail: keith.burgos@usdoj.gov
Deputy U.S. Marshal **(Vacant)** . . . . . (703) 451-2001
Deputy U.S. Marshal **James Knapp** . . . . . (703) 837-5500
E-mail: james.knapp2@usdoj.gov
Deputy U.S. Marshal **John Noel** . . . . . (703) 837-5500
E-mail: john.noel@usdoj.gov
Deputy U.S. Marshal **Amanda Shields** . . . . . (703) 837-5500
E-mail: amanda.shields@usdoj.gov
Deputy U.S. Marshal **Gregory Soklewics** . . . . . (703) 837-5500
Deputy U.S. Marshal **Carl Staley** . . . . . (703) 837-5500
E-mail: carl.staley@usdoj.gov

(continued on next page)

Virginia - Eastern District *continued*

Deputy U.S. Marshal **James Turner** (703) 837-5500
E-mail: james.turner@usdoj.gov
Criminal Program Specialist **Jewel Hodges** (703) 837-5538
Investigative Research Specialist **Jennie Helms** (703) 837-5500
Program Analyst **Ronda Patterson** (703) 837-5525
E-mail: ronda.patterson@usdoj.gov
Property Management Specialist **Andrew Russell** (703) 837-5500
E-mail: andrew.russell@usdoj.gov
Purchasing Specialist **Karen Norton** (703) 837-5517
E-mail: karen.norton@usdoj.gov
Administrative Officer **Wendy Putnam** (703) 837-5518
E-mail: wendy.putnam@usdoj.gov
Budget Analyst **Yolanda Sylvia** (703) 837-5500
Detention Officer **(Vacant)** (703) 837-5500
Administrative Support Assistant **Maiya Morales** (703) 837-5512
E-mail: maiya.morales@usdoj.gov

Norfolk (VA) Office

U.S. Courthouse, 600 Granby Street, Norfolk, VA 23510
Tel: (757) 963-5963

Chief Deputy U.S. Marshal **(Vacant)** (703) 837-5500
Supervisory Deputy U.S. Marshal **(Vacant)** (757) 963-5963
Supervisory Deputy U.S. Marshal **(Vacant)** (757) 963-5963
Deputy U.S. Marshal **Timothy Alley** (757) 963-5963
E-mail: timothy.alley@usdoj.gov
Deputy U.S. Marshal **Sherri Annan** (757) 963-5963
E-mail: sherri.annan@usdoj.gov
Deputy U.S. Marshal **Eldin Da Silva** (757) 963-5963
Deputy U.S. Marshal **Carter Davis** (757) 963-5963
E-mail: carter.davis@usdoj.gov
Deputy U.S. Marshal **Lemuel Powers** (757) 963-5963
E-mail: lemuel.powers@usdoj.gov
Deputy U.S. Marshal **Nick Profitt** (757) 963-5963
Deputy U.S. Marshal **Jerold Rozier** (757) 963-5963
E-mail: jerold.rozier@usdoj.gov
Deputy U.S. Marshal **Jason Silvia** (757) 963-5963
E-mail: jason.silvia@usdoj.gov
Deputy U.S. Marshal **Douglas Toliver** (757) 963-5963
Deputy U.S. Marshal **Robert Wilhite** (757) 963-5963
E-mail: robert.wilhite@usdoj.gov
Deputy U.S. Marshal **Patrick Yetzer** (757) 963-5963
E-mail: patrick.yetzer@usdoj.gov
Administrative Clerk **James Wilkins** (757) 963-5963
E-mail: james.wilkins@usdoj.gov
Civil Processing Clerk **Lori Harrell** (757) 963-5963
E-mail: lori.harrell@usdoj.gov
Detention Officer **(Vacant)** (757) 963-5963

Richmond (VA) Office

74 Broad Street, Suite 2800, Richmond, VA 23219
Tel: (804) 545-8501

Supervisory Deputy U.S. Marshal **Daniel Simms** (804) 545-8501
Deputy U.S. Marshal **Lisa Berger** (804) 545-8501
E-mail: lisa.berger@usdoj.gov
Deputy U.S. Marshal **James Gurley** (804) 545-8501
E-mail: james.gurley@usdoj.gov
Deputy U.S. Marshal **Adam Hundley** (804) 545-8501
E-mail: adam.hundley@usdoj.gov
Deputy U.S. Marshal **Phillip Patterson** (804) 545-8501
E-mail: phillip.patterson@usdoj.gov
Deputy U.S. Marshal **William Stanton** (804) 545-8501
E-mail: william.stanton@usdoj.gov
Deputy U.S. Marshal **Kevin R. Trevillian** (804) 545-8501
E-mail: kevin.trevillian@usdoj.gov
Deputy U.S. Marshal **(Vacant)** (804) 545-8501
Civil Clerk **(Vacant)** (804) 545-8501
Criminal Clerk **Sonya Moseley** (804) 545-8501
E-mail: sonya.moseley@usdoj.gov

Virginia - Western District

Federal Office Building, 210 Franklin Road, SW,
Room 247, Roanoke, VA 24011
P.O. Box 2280, Roanoke, VA 24009
Tel: (540) 857-2230 Fax: (540) 857-2032

★ U.S. Marshal **Gerald Sidney Holt** (540) 857-2230
E-mail: gerald.holt@usdoj.gov
Education: Radford 1995 BGS
Chief Deputy U.S. Marshal **Richard B. Sellers** (434) 293-2230
255 West Main Street, Charlottesville, VA 22901
Supervisory Deputy U.S. Marshal **Wade Hepburn** (540) 857-2230
E-mail: wade.hepburn@usdoj.gov
Deputy U.S. Marshal **(Vacant)** (540) 857-2230
Administrative Officer **Sean Verlik** (540) 857-2320
E-mail: sean.verlik@usdoj.gov
Criminal Program Specialist
Christine "Chrissy" Dinnerville (540) 857-2231
E-mail: christine.dinnerville@usdoj.gov
Accounting Technician/Purchasing Agent
Laura Nieberlein (540) 857-2230
E-mail: laura.nieberlein@usdoj.gov

Abingdon (VA) Sub-Office

180 West Main Street, Abingdon, VA 24210
Tel: (276) 628-9402 Fax: (276) 628-8650

Supervisory Deputy U.S. Marshal
Matthew Davis (276) 628-1398 ext. 501
E-mail: matthew.davis@usdoj.gov
Deputy U.S. Marshal **Woodrow McGlothlin** (276) 628-9402 ext. 506
Deputy U.S. Marshal **Jim Satterwhite** (276) 628-9402 ext. 502
E-mail: jim.satterwhite@usdoj.gov
Deputy U.S. Marshal **Byron Schiesz** (276) 628-9402
E-mail: byron.schiesz@usdoj.gov

Charlottesville (VA) Sub-Office

255 West Main Street, Charlottesville, VA 22901
Tel: (434) 293-6612 Fax: (434) 293-3299

Supervisory Deputy U.S. Marshal **Steve Carter** (434) 293-6612
E-mail: steve.carter@usdoj.gov
Deputy U.S. Marshal **Ann Calbi-Alley** (434) 293-6612

Washington - Eastern District

Thomas S. Foley U.S. Courthouse, 920 West Riverside Avenue,
Room 200, Spokane, WA 99201
P.O. Box 1463, Spokane, WA 99210-1463
Tel: (509) 368-3600 Fax: (509) 353-2766

★ U.S. Marshal **Craig Ellis Thayer** (509) 368-3600
E-mail: craig.thayer@usdoj.gov
Education: Gonzaga BS, JD
Chief Deputy U.S. Marshal **Kevin Kilgore** (509) 368-3600
E-mail: kevin.kilgore@usdoj.gov
Deputy U.S. Marshal/ Asset Forfeiture Financial
Investigator **Jerome Brown** (509) 353-0533
E-mail: jerome.brown@usdoj.gov
Deputy U.S. Marshal **David Breese** (509) 353-2781
E-mail: david.breese@usdoj.gov
Deputy U.S. Marshal **David Brod** (509) 353-2781
E-mail: david.brod@usdoj.gov
Deputy U.S. Marshal **Scott Hershey** (509) 353-2788
E-mail: scott.hershey@usdoj.gov
Deputy U.S. Marshal **Martin J. Kridler** (509) 353-0615
E-mail: martin.kridler@usdoj.gov
Deputy U.S. Marshal **(Vacant)** (509) 353-2781
Deputy U.S. Marshal (K9) **Hank Shafer** (509) 353-0624
E-mail: hank.shafer@usdoj.gov
Supervisory Criminal Investigator **Robert L. Doty** (509) 368-3600
Supervisory Officer In Charge **(Vacant)** (509) 368-3600
Supervisory Criminal Investigator **(Vacant)** (509) 353-0617

★ Presidential Appointment Requiring Senate Confirmation ☆ Presidential Appointment ☐ Schedule C Appointment ◇ Career Senior Foreign Service Appointment
● Career Senior Executive Service (SES) Appointment ◎ Non-Career Senior Executive Service (SES) Appointment ■ Postal Career Executive Service

Washington - Eastern District *continued*

Judicial Security Inspector **Ben Haraseth** . . . . (509) 353-7011
E-mail: benjamin.haraseth@usdoj.gov
Administrative Officer **Jacqueline P. Gabert** . . . . (509) 368-3600
E-mail: jacqueline.gabert@usdoj.gov
Criminal Program Specialist **Debbie Anderson** . . . . (509) 353-0623
Investigative Research Specialist **Reagan Havey** . . . . (509) 353-0706
Management and Program Analyst **(Vacant)** . . . . (509) 353-0534
Administrative Support Specialist **Mary McGoldrick** . . . . . (509) 368-3600
E-mail: mary.mcgoldrick@usdoj.gov
Administrative Support Specialist **Vicky Lynn Peters** . . . . (509) 368-3610
E-mail: victoria.peters@usdoj.gov

Richland (WA) Office

Federal Building, 825 Jadwyn Avenue,
Room G-69, Richland, WA 99352-3586
P.O. Box 1026, Richland, WA 99352-1026
Tel: (509) 946-9423 Fax: (509) 946-8893

Deputy U.S. Marshal **Julio Hernandez** . . . . (509) 946-9423
Deputy U.S. Marshal **Ryan Johnsen** . . . . (509) 946-9423
E-mail: ryan.johnsen@usdoj.gov
Deputy U.S. Marshal **Darrick Swick** . . . . (509) 946-9423
Deputy U.S. Marshal **(Vacant)** . . . . (509) 946-9423
Administrative Support Specialist **Tricia Moore** . . . . (509) 368-3600
E-mail: tricia.moore@usdoj.gov

Yakima (WA) Office

402 East Yakima Avenue, Suite 210, Yakima, WA 98901
Tel: (509) 575-5917 Fax: (509) 575-5812

Supervisory Deputy U.S. Marshal **Jeffrey Marty** . . . . (509) 575-5917
E-mail: jeff.marty@usdoj.gov
Deputy U.S. Marshal **Arik Coleman** . . . . (509) 575-5917
E-mail: arik.coleman@usdoj.gov
Deputy U.S. Marshal **Bradley LeCompte** . . . . (509) 575-5917
Deputy U.S. Marshal **Christopher Smith** . . . . (509) 575-5917
Deputy U.S. Marshal **Roy Thompson** . . . . (509) 575-5917
Operations Support Specialist **Nancy Martinez** . . . . (509) 575-5917

Washington - Western District

700 Stewart Street, Suite 9000, Seattle, WA 98101-1271
Tel: (206) 370-8600 Fax: (206) 370-8670

★ U.S. Marshal (Acting) **David Miller** . . . . (206) 370-8601
E-mail: david.miller@usdoj.gov
Chief Deputy U.S. Marshal (Acting) **John Williams** . . . . . (206) 370-8602
E-mail: john.williams@usdoj.gov
Supervisory Deputy U.S. Marshal **(Vacant)** . . . . (206) 370-8606
Administrative Officer **Stephen E. Blue** . . . . (206) 370-8650
E-mail: stephen.blue@usdoj.gov

Tacoma (WA) Office

1170 U.S. Courthouse, 1717 Pacific Avenue, Tacoma, WA 98402
Tel: (253) 302-8680 Fax: (253) 302-8668

Supervisory Deputy U.S. Marshal **Ed Muldowney** . . . . (206) 370-8607
E-mail: ed.muldowney@usdoj.gov

West Virginia - Northern District

U.S. Post Office, 500 W. Pike Street, Clarksburg, WV 26301
P.O. Box 2807, Clarksburg, WV 26302
Tel: (304) 623-0486 Fax: (304) 623-5708

★ U.S. Marshal **Gary M. Gaskins** . . . . (304) 623-0486
E-mail: gary.gaskins@usdoj.gov
Education: Fairmont State Col 1994 BS
Chief Deputy U.S. Marshal **Alex P. Neville** . . . . (304) 623-0486
E-mail: alex.neville@usdoj.gov
Supervisory Deputy U.S. Marshal **Terry Moore** . . . . (304) 623-0486
E-mail: terry.moore@usdoj.gov

West Virginia - Northern District *continued*

Deputy U.S. Marshal **Wesley Frederick** . . . . (304) 623-0486
E-mail: wesley.frederick@usdoj.gov
Deputy U.S. Marshal **John D. Hare** . . . . (304) 623-0486
E-mail: john.hare@usdoj.gov
Deputy U.S. Marshal **Paul Hickman** . . . . (304) 623-0486
E-mail: paul.hickman@usdoj.gov
Deputy U.S. Marshal **Dustin Hotsinpiller** . . . . (304) 623-0486
E-mail: dustin.hotsinpiller@usdoj.gov
Deputy U.S. Marshal **Joseph "Joe" McCarty** . . . . (304) 636-0332
E-mail: joseph.mccarty@usdoj.gov
Deputy U.S. Marshal **Joseph "Joe" Nichols** . . . . (304) 623-0486
E-mail: joseph.nichols@usdoj.gov
Deputy U.S. Marshal **Derek Patrick** . . . . (304) 623-0486
E-mail: derek.patrick@usdoj.gov
Deputy U.S. Marshal **(Vacant)** . . . . (304) 623-0486
Deputy U.S. Marshal **(Vacant)** . . . . (304) 623-0486
Criminal Investigative Specialist **Kenneth Stillwell** . . . . . . (304) 623-0486
Seizure and Forfeiture Specialist **Kimberly Landes** . . . . . . (304) 623-0486
E-mail: kimberly.landes@usdoj.gov
Administrative Officer **Rhonda Kirby** . . . . (304) 623-0486
E-mail: rhonda.kirby@usdoj.gov

Elkins (WV) Office

Jennings Randolph Federal Center, 300 Third Street,
Room 317, Elkins, WV 26241
P.O. Box 1454, Elkins, WV 26241
Tel: (304) 636-0332 Fax: (304) 636-6712

Deputy U.S. Marshal **Joseph "Joe" McCarty** . . . . (304) 636-0332
E-mail: joseph.mccarty@usdoj.gov

Martinsburg (WV) Office

217 W. King St., Martinsburg, WV 25401
Tel: (304) 267-7179 Fax: (304) 267-9369

Supervisory Deputy U.S. Marshal **Mark A. Tracy** . . . . (304) 267-7179
E-mail: mark.tracy@usdoj.gov
Deputy U.S. Marshal **Jon LaLiberte** . . . . (304) 267-7179
E-mail: jon.laliberte@usdoj.gov
Deputy U.S. Marshal **Michael Ulrich** . . . . (304) 267-7179
E-mail: michael.ulrich@usdoj.gov
Deputy U.S. Marshal **Alphonso Wideman** . . . . (304) 267-7179
E-mail: alphonso.wideman@usdoj.gov

Wheeling (WV) Office

Federal Building, 1125-1141 Chapline Street,
Room 407, Wheeling, WV 26003
P.O. Box 726, Wheeling, WV 26003
Tel: (304) 232-2980 Fax: (304) 232-0410

Deputy U.S. Marshal **Sara Ahrens** . . . . (304) 232-2980
E-mail: sara.ahrens@usdoj.gov
Deputy U.S. Marshal **Jason Dias** . . . . (304) 232-2980
E-mail: jason.dias@usdoj.gov
Deputy U.S. Marshal **Chad Simpson** . . . . (304) 232-2980
E-mail: chad.simpson@usdoj.gov
Deputy U.S. Marshal **Don Walker** . . . . (304) 232-2980
E-mail: don.walker@usdoj.gov
Deputy U.S. Marshal **Matt Wilson** . . . . (304) 267-7179
E-mail: matt.wilson@usdoj.gov
Judicial Security Inspector **Ryan Morris** . . . . (304) 232-2980
E-mail: ryan.morris@usdoj.gov

West Virginia - Southern District

Robert C. Byrd U.S. Courthouse, 300 Virginia Street East,
Room 3602, Charleston, WV 25301
Tel: (304) 347-5136 Fax: (304) 347-5394

★ U.S. Marshal **John D. Foster** . . . . (304) 347-5140
E-mail: john.foster@usdoj.gov
Education: Marshall 1986 AA; Comm Col Air Force 1989 AS;
Glenville State 1991 BA

(continued on next page)

West Virginia - Southern District *continued*

Chief Deputy U.S. Marshal **Timothy Goode** .... (304) 347-5136
E-mail: timothy.goode@usdoj.gov
Supervisory Deputy U.S. Marshal **Madonna Bursell** ..... (304) 347-5652
Supervisory Deputy U.S. Marshal **Jeremy Honaker** ..... (304) 347-5651
E-mail: jeremy.honaker@usdoj.gov
Deputy U.S. Marshal **Patrick Hernandez** .... (304) 347-5136
E-mail: patrick.hernandez@usdoj.gov
Deputy U.S. Marshal **Scott Hill** .... (304) 347-5662
E-mail: scott.hill@usdoj.gov
Deputy U.S. Marshal **James Ingram** .... (304) 347-5136
E-mail: james.ingram@usdoj.gov
Deputy U.S. Marshal **William L. Seckman** .... (304) 347-5136
E-mail: william.seckman@usdoj.gov
Deputy U.S. Marshal **Joshua Usrey** .... (304) 347-5136
E-mail: joshua.usrey@usdoj.gov
Budget Analyst **Melinda K. Brown** .... (304) 347-5582
E-mail: melinda.brown@usdoj.gov
Administrative Officer **Christopher C. Thompson** ...... (304) 347-5135
E-mail: christopher.thompson@usdoj.gov
Civil Program Assistant **Jody M. Wills** .... (304) 347-5553
Court Security Inspector **Christopher T. Lair** .... (304) 347-5136
E-mail: christopher.lair@usdoj.gov
Seized Assets Specialist **Shonda M. Treadway** .... (304) 347-5582
E-mail: shonda.treadway@usdoj.gov

Beckley (WV) Office

Robert C. Byrd U.S. Courthouse, 110 Heber Street,
Suite G-56, Beckley, WV 25801-4501
Tel: (304) 253-1519 Fax: (304) 253-1382

Deputy U.S. Marshal **Shane Osgood** .... (304) 253-1519
E-mail: shane.osgood@usdoj.gov
Deputy U.S. Marshal **Frederick Lamey** .... (304) 253-1519
E-mail: frederick.lamey@usdoj.gov
Deputy U.S. Marshal **Chris Dockter** .... (304) 253-1519
E-mail: christopher.dockter@usdoj.gov

Bluefield (WV) Office

2114 Federal Building, 601 Federal Street, Bluefield, WV 24701
Tel: (304) 327-6000 Fax: (304) 325-9778

Deputy U.S. Marshal **Karen A. Long** .... (304) 347-5136
E-mail: karen.long@usdoj.gov

Huntington (WV) Office

201 U.S. Courthouse and Federal Building,
845 Fifth Avenue, Huntington, WV 25701
Tel: (304) 529-5560 Fax: (304) 529-5130

Deputy U.S. Marshal **John LaJeunesse** .... (304) 529-5560
E-mail: john.lajeunesse@usdoj.gov
Deputy U.S. Marshal **James Mounts** .... (304) 529-5560
E-mail: james.mounts@usdoj.gov
Deputy U.S. Marshal **Justin Mounts** .... (304) 529-5560
E-mail: justin.mounts@usdoj.gov

Wisconsin - Eastern District

Federal Courthouse, 517 East Wisconsin Avenue,
Suite 711, Milwaukee, WI 53202
Tel: (414) 297-3707 Fax: (414) 297-1825

★ U.S. Marshal **Kevin Anthony Carr** .... (414) 297-3707
E-mail: kevin.carr@usdoj.gov
Education: Concordia U (WI) 1997 BA
Chief Deputy U.S. Marshal **Thomas P. Conlon** .... (414) 297-3707
E-mail: thomas.conlon@usdoj.gov
Supervisory Deputy U.S. Marshal **Douglas L. Bachert** ... (414) 297-3707
E-mail: douglas.bachert@usdoj.gov
Supervisory Deputy U.S. Marshal **Gary Enos** .... (414) 297-3707
E-mail: gary.enos@usdoj.gov

Wisconsin - Eastern District *continued*

Criminal Investigator **Joshua Bissey** .... (414) 297-3707
E-mail: joshua.bissey@usdoj.gov
Criminal Investigator **Rodney Clauss** .... (414) 297-3707
E-mail: rodney.clauss@usdoj.gov
Criminal Investigator **Kasey Doty** .... (414) 297-3707
E-mail: kasey.doty@usdoj.gov
Criminal Investigator **Wayne Ellinghausen II** .... (414) 297-3707
E-mail: wayne.ellinghausen@usdoj.gov
Criminal Investigator **Kristina Haven** .... (414) 297-3707
Criminal Investigator **Zachary Kadish** .... (414) 297-3707
Criminal Investigator **Scott Keller** .... (414) 297-3707
E-mail: scott.keller@usdoj.gov
Criminal Investigator **Jeremy Loesch** .... (414) 297-3707
E-mail: jeremy.loesch@usdoj.gov
Criminal Investigator **Trevor McPolin** .... (414) 297-3707
Criminal Investigator **Brian Nodes** .... (414) 297-3707
E-mail: brian.nodes@usdoj.gov
Criminal Investigator **Rasheda StHill** .... (414) 297-3707
E-mail: rasheda.sthill@usdoj.gov
Court Security Inspector **Michael Schulte** .... (414) 297-3707
E-mail: michael.schulte@usdoj.gov
Administrative Officer **Tony Herald** .... (414) 297-3707
E-mail: tony.herald@usdoj.gov
Administrative Support Assistant **(Vacant)** .... (414) 297-3707
Budget Analyst **Pamela Wenzel** .... (414) 297-3707
E-mail: pamela.wenzel@usdoj.gov
Seizure and Forfeiture Specialist **Vicki L. Gove** .... (414) 297-3707
Seizure and Forfeiture Specialist **Dion Hill** .... (414) 297-3707
Investigative Research Specialist **Patricia A. Jacomet** .... (414) 297-3707
E-mail: patricia.jacomet@usdoj.gov
Purchasing Agent **(Vacant)** .... (414) 297-3707

Wisconsin - Western District

Federal Courthouse, 120 North Henry Street,
Room 440, Madison, WI 53703
Tel: (608) 661-8300 Fax: (608) 661-8304

★ U.S. Marshal **Dallas S. Neville** .... (608) 661-8300
E-mail: dallas.neville@usdoj.gov
Chief Deputy U.S. Marshal **Kirk R. Papenthien** .... (608) 661-8300
E-mail: kirk.papenthien@usdoj.gov
Supervisory Deputy U.S. Marshal **Jeff Michaelis** .... (608) 661-8300
E-mail: jeff.michaelis@usdoj.gov
Deputy U.S. Marshal **Lucas Balde** .... (608) 661-8300
E-mail: lucas.balde@usdoj.gov
Deputy U.S. Marshal **Kent Halverson** .... (608) 661-8300
E-mail: kent.halverson@usdoj.gov
Deputy U.S. Marshal **Emily Krueger** .... (608) 661-8300
E-mail: emily.krueger@usdoj.gov
Deputy U.S. Marshal **Brad Meng** .... (608) 661-8300
E-mail: brad.meng@usdoj.gov
Deputy U.S. Marshal **Michael Pritchard** .... (608) 661-8300
E-mail: michael.pritchard@usdoj.gov
Deputy U.S. Marshal **Loretta Sanchez** .... (608) 661-8300
E-mail: loretta.sanchez@usdoj.gov
Deputy U.S. Marshal (SOIC) **Patrick Kirchenwitz** .... (608) 661-8300
E-mail: patrick.kirchenwitz@usdoj.gov
Judicial Security Inspector **Dale Emmerton** .... (608) 661-8300
E-mail: dale.emmerton2@usdoj.gov
Senior Systems Administrator **Roland Perez** .... (608) 661-8300
E-mail: roland.perez@usdoj.gov
Administrative Officer **Dionne Smith** .... (608) 661-8300
E-mail: dionne.smith@usdoj.gov
Budget Analyst **Diana Forsberg** .... (608) 661-8300
Criminal Program Specialist **Mary Nowik** .... (608) 661-8300
E-mail: mary.nowik@usdoj.gov

★ Presidential Appointment Requiring Senate Confirmation ☆ Presidential Appointment □ Schedule C Appointment ◇ Career Senior Foreign Service Appointment
● Career Senior Executive Service (SES) Appointment ○ Non-Career Senior Executive Service (SES) Appointment ■ Postal Career Executive Service

Wyoming District

J.C. O'Mahoney Federal Building, 2120 Capitol Avenue, Room 1100, Cheyenne, WY 82001
Tel: (307) 772-2196 Fax: (307) 772-2735

★ U.S. Marshal (Acting) **Mark Wood** . . . . (307) 772-2196
E-mail: mark.wood@usdoj.gov
Chief Deputy U.S. Marshal (Acting) **Dennis Conmay** . . . . (307) 772-2952
E-mail: dennis.conmay@usdoj.gov
Supervisory Deputy U.S. Marshal **Jason Griess** . . . . (307) 772-2265
E-mail: jason.griess@usdoj.gov
Deputy U.S. Marshal **Justin Cline** . . . . (307) 772-2198
E-mail: justin.cline@usdoj.gov
Deputy U.S. Marshal **Phillip Feezer** . . . . (307) 772-2198
E-mail: phillip.feezer@usdoj.gov
Deputy U.S. Marshal **Jon Goodman** . . . . (307) 772-2198
E-mail: jon.goodman@usdoj.gov
Deputy U.S. Marshal **Robert MacMaster** . . . . (307) 772-2198
E-mail: robert.macmaster@usdoj.gov
Deputy U.S. Marshal **Ross P. Mueske** . . . . (307) 772-2198
E-mail: ross.mueske@usdoj.gov
Deputy U.S. Marshal **Justin Stephenson** . . . . (307) 772-2198
E-mail: justin.stephenson@usdoj.gov
Sex Offender Investigations Coordinatior/Deputy U.S. Marshal **Dennis Conmay** . . . . (307) 772-2198
E-mail: dennis.conmay@usdoj.gov
Administrative Officer **Christine E. Butterfield** . . . . (307) 772-2926
E-mail: chris.butterfield@usdoj.gov Fax: (307) 772-2271
Budget Analyst **Tim Liddle** . . . . (307) 772-2510
E-mail: timothy.liddle@usdoj.gov
Investigative Research Specialist **Peggy P. Stumpf** . . . . . . (307) 772-2257
E-mail: peggy.stumpf@usdoj.gov
Judicial Security Inspector **Douglas Lineen** . . . . (307) 772-2927
E-mail: douglas.lineen@usdoj.gov
Administrative Support Assistant **Amanda Neubeck** . . . . . (307) 772-2668
E-mail: amanda.neubeck@usdoj.gov

Casper (WY) Office

111 South Wolcott Street, Room 128, Casper, WY 82601
Tel: (307) 261-5411 Fax: (307) 261-5410

Supervisory Deputy U.S. Marshal **Jason Griess** . . . . (307) 261-5417
E-mail: jason.griess@usdoj.gov
Deputy U.S. Marshal **Matthew Berg** . . . . (307) 262-5400
E-mail: matthew.berg@usdoj.gov
Deputy U.S. Marshal **Zachary Cantrell** . . . . (307) 262-5418
E-mail: zachary.cantrell@usdoj.gov
Deputy U.S. Marshal **Brian Hoose** . . . . (307) 261-5405
E-mail: brian.hoose@usdoj.gov
Deputy U.S. Marshal **Del Ramsey** . . . . (307) 262-5412
E-mail: del.ramsey@usdoj.gov

Jackson (WY) Office

145 East Simpson, Jackson, WY 83001
P.O. Box 1660, Jackson, WY 83001
Tel: (307) 733-1066 Fax: (307) 733-1179

Note: Occupied only during term of court.

Lander (WY) Office

125 Sunflower, Lander, WY 82520
Tel: (307) 332-8696 Fax: (307) 332-8646

Supervisory Deputy U.S. Marshal **Carl Von Rein** . . . . (307) 332-8696
E-mail: carl.vonrein@usdoj.gov
Deputy U.S. Marshal **Dylan Schauer** . . . . (307) 332-1384
E-mail: dylan.schauer@usdoj.gov
Deputy U.S. Marshal **Troy Medeiros** . . . . (307) 332-8696
E-mail: troy.medeiros@usdoj.gov

Yellowstone National Park (WY) Office

Yellowstone National Park (WY) Office, Building 13-A UpperMammoth, P.O. Box 588, Yellowstone National Park, WY 82190
Tel: (307) 344-6517 Fax: (307) 344-6515

Deputy U.S. Marshal **Travis Mangum** . . . . (307) 344-7775

★ Presidential Appointment Requiring Senate Confirmation ☆ Presidential Appointment ☐ Schedule C Appointment ◇ Career Senior Foreign Service Appointment
● Career Senior Executive Service (SES) Appointment ○ Non-Career Senior Executive Service (SES) Appointment ■ Postal Career Executive Service

Indexes

Law School Index

This index lists all judges and law clerks by the law school they attended and the year of graduation. Law schools appear in alphabetical order by the full name of the law school. Below each law school, we list its abbreviated version (in italics), which is the format used in the directory listings.

Albany Law School of Union University
[Albany Law]

1964 McAvoy, Thomas J., 352
1968 Rose, Robert S., 722
1970 Lahtinen, John A., 722
1974 Eaton, Richard K., 13
1975 Gabel, Patricia, 806
1976 Littlefield, Robert E., Jr., 355
1976 Siragusa, Charles J., 373
1978 Mayberger, Robert D., 721
1979 Cangilos-Ruiz, Margaret, 354
1980 Egan, John C., Jr., 722
1981 Stein, Leslie E., 716
1983 Andrews, Alison, 170
1988 McCarthy, William E., 722
1989 Platt, Cynthia A., 355
1990 Garry, Elizabeth A., 722
1991 Davis, Diane, 355
1994 Bergevin, Brian J., 168
1997 Gioia, Allison P., 374
2001 Morton, Sean M., 721
2010 Loefke, Benjamin, 352
Dalrymple, Jill N., 355
Denefrio, Carey Ann, 374
Foederer, Adrienne A., 354

American University
[American U]

2014 Gupta, Rishi R., 12
2015 Sgambato, Sydney, 328
Richardson, Monte C., 187

The American University in London (UK)
[American U (London)]

Loughry, Allen H., II, 820

Antioch School of Law
[Antioch Law]

1976 Lenard, Joan A., 194
1979 Cannon, George W., Jr., 520
1981 Kilbride, Thomas L., 613

Appalachian School of Law
[Appalachian Law]

2007 Parish, Erica, 812

Arizona State University
[Arizona State]

1970 Hawkins, Michael Daly, 87

Arizona State University
continued

1971 Silver, Roslyn O., 119
1976 Howard, Joseph W., 546
1976 Silverman, Barry G., 78
1977 Campbell, Tena, 477
1977 Norris, Patricia K., 544
1978 Rayes, Douglas L., 117
1985 Timmer, Ann Scott, 542
1986 Jones, Kenton D., 545
1988 Howe, Randall M., 545
1989 McKinney, Denise K., 78
1990 Martin, Brenda K., 122
1992 Navarro, Gloria M., 321
1993 Humetewa, Diane J., 117
1994 Tuchi, John Joseph, 117
1996 Miles, Kim, 543
1997 Giroux, Elicia, 119
1998 Schultz, Mark W., 543
Bade, Bridget S., 120

Baylor University
[Baylor]

1966 Smith, Walter S., Jr., 469
1970 Cummings, Sam R., 457
1974 Davis, Rex D., 799
1974 Kinkeade, Ed, 456
1976 Fitzwater, Sidney A., 455
1977 Owen, Priscilla R., 56
1978 Hanen, Andrew S., 461
1979 Scoggins, Al, 799
1979 Stacy, Frances H., 466
1980 Hussey, Margaret L., 799, 800
1981 Baker, Carol, 790
1981 Francis, Molly, 794
1981 Gilstrap, James Rodney, 451
1983 Steger, Christopher H., 443
1984 Hooks, Tammy, 469
1985 Gray, Tom, 798
1988 Greggs, Morris, 787
1990 Mazzant, Amos L., III, 451
1990 Mitchell, Karen, 454
1992 Schenck, David J., 795
1993 Cureton, Jeffrey L., 458
1993 Stevens, Pauline, 799
1994 Hoyle, Brian, 800
1996 Parham, Patrick, 647
1997 Skotnik, Michael, 796
2000 Sowards, Michael, 148
2002 Stander, Margot, 790
2005 Golden, Leah, 128
Cimics, Donald, 787
Myers, Lana, 795

Benjamin N. Cardozo School of Law, Yeshiva University
[Cardozo]

1979 Feuerstein, Sandra J., 347
1981 Shulman, Martin, 725
1984 Schumacher, Eric B., 716
1987 Renwick, Dianne T., 718
1994 Shalit, Melissa, 559
2004 Bogen, Timothy, 333
2009 Daulton, Elizabeth, 625
2011 Pelaez, Jenny, 342

Boalt Hall Law School, University of California, Berkeley
[Boalt Hall]

1950 Pregerson, Harry, 77
1955 Blease, Coleman A., 565
1955 Wallace, J. Clifford, 84
1960 Kay, Alan C., 216
1960 Russell, David E., 152
1961 George, Lloyd D., 322
1961 McDonald, Alex C., 568
1962 Donovan, Thomas B., 142
1962 Henderson, Thelton E., 156
1963 Gilbert, Arthur, 562
1963 Shubb, William B., 147
1964 Singleton, James K., Jr., 114
1966 Breyer, Charles R., 26, 157, 529
1967 Chesney, Maxine M., 157
1968 Montali, Dennis, 160
1969 McConnell, Judith, 566
1971 Bedsworth, William W., 570
1971 Sinclair, Kent, 809
1972 Paez, Richard A., 80
1973 Berzon, Marsha S., 80
1973 Bruiniers, Terence L., 558
1973 Ishii, Anthony W., 148
1974 Manibusan, Joaquin V. E., Jr., 515
1975 Fairbank, Valerie Baker, 136
1975 Wilken, Claudia A., 157, 525
1976 Wallach, Evan Jonathan, 29
1977 Appel, Brent R., 633
1978 Daniels, George B., 356
1978 Mark, Robert A., 202
1979 Chen, Edward Milton, 154
1981 Gonzalez, Gloria Maria, 557
1981 Streeter, Jon B., 557
1982 Phillips, Virginia A., 131
1982 Smith, Erithe A., 142
1983 Faris, Robert J., 88, 218
1985 Fitzgerald, Michael Walter, 134
1985 Foley, Maurice B., 20
1985 Ross, Matthew, 571

Boalt Hall Law School, University of California, Berkeley
continued

1987 Andrews, Richard G., 178
1987 Rabkin, Hannah, 556
1988 Talwani, Indira, 282
1989 Olguin, Fernando M., 130
1989 Tigar, Jon S., 155
1990 Werdegar, Kathryn Mickle, 552
1991 Bielak, A. Margaret, 557
1991 González, Steven C., 814
1993 Claire, Allison, 150
1994 Du, Miranda, 321
1994 Hersler, Ronnie, 152
1994 Thapar, Amul R., 255
1995 Dawson, Melissa, 158
1996 Márquez, Miguel A., 574
1996 Pearce, John A., 805
1998 Chhabria, Vince Girdhari, 155
2003 Chapman, Matthew P.S., 607
2003 Howitt, Luke W., 138
2003 Stevens, Victoria E., 496
2005 Eng, Elizabeth, 157
Abrams, Paul L., 138
Berggren, Lydia, 93
Dondero, Robert L., 554
Falk, Susan M., 538
Glass, Rebecca "Rebe", 157
Rushing, Conrad L., 573
Ryu, Donna M., 159
Thompson, Todd Elliott, 554

Boston College
[Boston Col]

1954 Redden, James A., Jr., 406
1962 Clifford, Robert W., 659
1963 Pellegrino, Joseph H., 584
1968 Dooley, John A., 806
1971 Spina, Francis X., 666
1972 Fecteau, Francis R., 669
1973 Deasy, J. Michael, 34, 327
1975 Huvelle, Ellen Segal, 26, 513
1976 Palmer, William D., 599
1977 Kishel, Gregory F., 300
1977 Messano, Carmen, 710
1979 Dein, Judith Gail, 284
1979 Orrick, William Horsley, III, 155
1980 Barbadoro, Paul James, 326, 523
1980 Scola, Robert N., Jr., 196
1983 Kobayashi, Leslie E., 216
1983 Wong, Lena M., 667
1985 Lambert, Kelly B., 172
1987 Wholly, James R. "Jim", 272

Detroit College of Law at Michigan State University
[Detroit Law]

1963 Suhrheinrich, Richard F., 65
1968 Friedman, Bernard A., 289
1969 Pesce, Michael L., 726
1972 Battani, Marianne O., 291
1975 O'Connell, Peter D., 675
1978 Greer, Larry A., 241
1982 Servitto, Deborah A., 676
1985 Hylenski, Linda S., 286
1989 Hood, Karen Fort, 676
1989 Malayang-Daley, Ann E. Y., 286
1989 Nolan, Jahel, 295
1994 Valuk, Gail M., 771
1997 York, Tamara, 671
1998 Dubuque, Rebecca, 676
Borrello, Stephen L., 676

The Dickinson School of Law of The Pennsylvania State University
[Dickinson Law]

1951 Caldwell, William W., 424
1951 Kosik, Edwin M., 424
1962 Rambo, Sylvia H., 424
1965 Surrick, R. Barclay, 418
1972 Stevens, Correale F., 762
1972 Thomas, John J., 426
1975 Eakin, J. Michael, 762
1975 Gibson, Kim R., 427
1976 Simpson, Robert E., Jr., 767
1976 Smith, D. Brooks, 43
1978 Brown, Kristen W., 766
1978 Leavitt, Mary Hannah, 768
1978 Vanaskie, Thomas I., 45
1979 Fehling, Richard E., 421
1980 Grant, Robert E., 241
1980 Jones, John E., III, 422
1980 Kristoff, Carol, 424
1980 Rueter, Thomas J., 418
1981 DiGirolamo, Thomas M., 277
1982 Conner, Christopher C., 422
1984 Morano, John A., 423
1986 Smith, Edward G., 413
1986 Waldron, Marcia M., 42
1988 Sanger, Gail N., 763
1988 Svirsko, Dawn, 43
1989 Foley, Arnold A., 413
1990 Brann, Matthew W., 423
1992 Vohs, William C., 762
1993 Sayres, Melissa E., 425
1993 Stoltenberg, Rachel M., 769
1995 Bainbridge, Sherry, 768
1995 Fink, Vance A., Jr., 768
1996 Whitehead, Louis, 425
1996 Woffington, Kristie, 429
1998 Bacon, Jennifer, 768
2000 Fisher, Jill Radomsky, 413
2001 Slone, Kelly Jo, 423
2002 Zito, Alicia, 413
2004 Miller, Alexandra, 422
2010 Sweigart, Chad, 425

Drake University
[Drake]

1969 McLaren, Robert D., 619
1975 Bennett, Mark W., 246
1976 Doyle, Richard H., 634
1976 Wiggins, David S., 632

Drake University *continued*

1978 Cady, Mark S., 632
1979 Gritzner, James E., 248
1980 Reade, Linda R., 245
1980 Zager, Bruce, 633
1981 Jarvey, John A., 247
1982 Mullins, Michael R., 635
1983 Vogel, Gayle Nelson, 634
1987 Bower, Thomas N., 635
1988 Margolies, Susan, 439
1992 Hamborg, Carla J., 248
1999 Meyer, Ann, 634
2001 Murad, Cheryl M., 248
Shodeen, Anita L., 76, 249

Duke University
[Duke]

1957 Tjoflat, Gerald Bard, 95
1964 Wilson, Thomas G., 185
1965 Edgar, R. Allan, 294
1969 Mullen, Graham C., 382
1970 Glenn, Paul M., 188
1971 Durham, Christine M., 804
1974 Collier, Curtis L., 442
1974 St. Amant, Joseph L. S., 53
1975 Duncan, Allyson Kay, 51
1976 Wiggins, Charles K., 814
1977 Meredith, Timothy E., 663
1977 Pauley, William H., III, 356
1977 Peck, Andrew J., 368
1977 Williams, Mary Ellen Coster, 8
1978 Adler, Jan M., 166
1978 Kehoe, Christopher B., 664
1979 Gergel, Richard Mark, 434
1979 Stormes, Nita L., 165
1980 Smith, Lisa Margaret, 368
1981 Corrigan, Timothy J., 180
1981 Gustafson, David D., 20
1981 Ruskell, Jean M., 601, 603
1982 Logue, Thomas "Tom", 596
1982 Thornton, Michael B., 20
1982 Toomey, Joel B., 187
1983 Langer, Mark J., 99
1983 Taylor, Laura S., 89, 167
1986 Kennedy, Lisa, 30
1987 Dever, James C., III, 376
1988 Wakefield, Michael, 604
1989 Rosenberg, Robin L., 197
1990 Shogan, Jacqueline O., 765
1991 Coulson, J. Mark, 277
1991 Nazarian, Douglas R.M., 664
1992 Davis, Thomas P., 728
1992 Hughes, Todd M., 29
1992 Simms, Wayne, 535
1992 Willett, Don R., 786
1993 Blackwood, Ray, 802
1994 Porter, Hazel Landwehr, 168
1995 Terry, Anita, 298
1997 Stone, Elizabeth Chandler, 602
1998 Reed, Heather, 495
2004 Milton, Tia C., 601
2011 Lenning, Nicholas F., 513
2012 Eichenberger, Sarah, 510
2012 Gorkin, Russell T., 356
2013 Cronogue, Graham, 513

Duquesne University
[Duquesne]

1956 Diamond, Gustave, 428

Duquesne University *continued*

1968 McVerry, Terrence F., 429
1970 Ambrose, Donetta W., 429
1970 Pellegrini, Dan, 766
1972 Perkin, Henry S., 419
1973 Conti, Joy Flowers, 427
1975 Baer, Max, 762
1976 Bender, John T., 763
1977 Cercone, David Stewart, 427
1977 Lydon, Michael J., 430
1978 Elliott, Kate Ford, 764
1979 Bohm, Carlota, 431
1980 Donohue, Christine L., 763, 764
1980 Flick, Virginia "Ginny", 182
1982 Olson, Judith Ference "Judy", The Honorable, 765
1984 Crouch, Margaret M., 34, 285
1987 Kelly, Maureen P., 430
1989 Fogl, Frank C., III, 429
1991 Shelly, Catherine L., 762
1992 Barowich, Cynthia A., 764
1992 DeLisio, Daniel, 762
1992 Tomb, Heather, 767
1993 Fisfis Marzina, Barbara, 428
1993 Robinson, Gary P., 429
1995 Collins, Kimberly A., 762
1997 Dickson, Ann R., 430
2000 Payne, Michael, 764
2005 Carver, Brenda L., 767
2007 Kravetz, Brian, 428
2008 Salemme, Andrew, 764
2013 Wilk, Ryan, 429
Deller, Jeffery A., 430

Emory University
[Emory]

1948 Hill, James C., 98
1953 Musgrave, R. Kenton, 13
1953 O'Kelley, William C., 19, 209
1954 Hunt, Willis B., Jr., 209
1964 Lawson, Hugh, 205
1967 Cooper, Clarence, 210
1968 Evans, Orinda D., 209
1968 Hines, P. Harris, 601
1968 Whaley, Robert H., 490
1973 Hull, Frank M., 96
1973 Schaikewitz, Steve, 601
1973 Wells, Thomas B., 25
1975 Brill, Gerrilyn G., 210
1977 Gordon, Leo M., 11
1978 Robinson, Deborah A., 514
1979 Cohen, Mark Howard, 208
1979 Ross, John A., 309
1980 McGhee-Glisson, Martha, 604
1981 Baverman, Alan J., 211
1981 Olack, Neil P., 303, 307
1982 Williams, Alana, 380
1986 Haynes, Catharina, 56
1986 Kilpatrick, Pamela, 604
1987 Smith, John P., 682
1988 Hutchinson, Robin M., 603
1988 Miller, M. Yvette, 604
1989 DuBose, Kristi K., 111
1990 Whittenburg, Nicholas W. "Nick", 444
1993 Brown, Alicia S., 205
1995 Harrill, Beth Anne, 212
1997 McBride, Valeri, 604

Emory University *continued*

1999 Brown, Ada, 795
2001 Patel, Sona, 237
2007 Placey, Caroline, 211
2009 Spielman, Brian, 302
Branch, Elizabeth L. "Lisa", 604

Faulkner University
[Faulkner]

1999 Windom, Mary Becker, 536
2007 Butler, Mary-Coleman Mayberry, 536
2009 Frisby, Stephen, 537
2009 Womack, Beau, 537

Florida Coastal School of Law
[Florida Coastal]

1999 Rivera, Radhika K., 185
1999 Shaddock, Eric K., 183
1999 Weisman, Susanne R., 181
2008 Wood, Kara, 187

Florida State University
[Florida State]

1971 Antoon, John, II, 184
1976 Wells, Linda Ann, 595
1977 Collier, Lacey A., 191
1977 Lewis, Joseph, Jr., 590
1978 Northcutt, Stevan T., 592
1978 Stevenson, W. Matthew, 597
1981 Ciklin, Cory, 596
1983 Torpy, Vincent G., Jr., 598
1985 Nertney, Lorrie, 593
1986 Polston, Ricky L., 589
1987 Lawson, C. Alan, 598
1987 Peacock, Carol, 590
1987 Scriven, Mary Stenson, 181
1989 Faenza, Heidi M., 601
1991 Roberts, L. Clayton, 589
1992 Johnson, Dalana W., 588
1995 Wetherell, T. Kent, II, 590
1995 Williams Ray, Stephanie, 591
1997 Rowe, Lori Sellers, 591
1998 Derry, Kasandra, 536
1998 Van Whittle, Lyyli M., 588
1999 Mackland, Dawn, 590
2002 Huber, Susan, 590
2007 Poarch, Jessica, 590

Fordham University
[Fordham]

1954 Keenan, John F., 362
1958 Duffy, Kevin Thomas, 363
1966 Hurley, Denis R., 344
1967 Kelly, Paul J., 90
1969 Horn, Marian Blank, 7
1973 Preska, Loretta A., 355
1974 Sweeny, John W., Jr., 717
1975 Bernstein, Stuart M., 371
1976 Eagan, Claire V., 399
1976 Millman, Laura D., 7
1976 Moore, K. Michael, 193
1978 Chin, Denny, 38
1978 Pitman, Henry B., 367
1980 Briccetti, Vincent L., 358

LAW SCHOOL INDEX

Fordham University *continued*

1980 Wolfe, Catherine O'Hagan, 35
1984 Agostino, Aprilanne, 719
1984 Dillon, Mark C., 719
1984 Papalia, Vincent F., 336
1984 Weiner, Jay L., 720
1985 Hennessey, David H., 284
1985 Seibel, Cathy, 358
1987 Kaplan, Michael B., 335
1989 Cecchi, Claire C., 330
1992 DiSalvo, Rosemary, 371
2007 Somekh, Sogol, 367
2010 Calabrese, Corey, 349
2010 Kress, Stephen J. "Steve", 358
2013 Duane, Jane Mackenzie, 193
2013 Fiur, Seth, 46
2013 Fresco, Michael, 358
2015 Lash, Devon, 90

Franklin Pierce College
[Franklin Pierce Col]

1986 Hall, Laura L., 326
1999 Moeller, Andrew W., 373
1999 Potter, Parker B., Jr., 326

Franklin Pierce Law Center
[Pierce Law]

1976 Huff, Glen, 811
1978 Conboy, Carol Ann, 705

George Mason University
[George Mason]

1977 O'Grady, Liam, 482
1980 Lynch, James M., 285
1980 Young, Richard L., 242
1991 McDermott, Patricia M., 27
2004 Gray, Carrie L., 52

The George Washington University
[George Washington]

1949 Dawson, Howard A., Jr., 23
1956 Merow, James F., 9
1959 Kay, Alan, 514
1960 Cacheris, James C., 18, 484
1961 Hamilton, Clyde H., 53
1962 Quist, Gordon J., 294
1962 Werdegar, Kathryn Mickle, 552
1964 Lucero, Carlos F., 90
1968 Hurley, Daniel T. K., 198
1970 Hunt, Roger L., 322
1970 Swift, Stephen J., 24
1970 Wallach, Frederick E., 21
1972 Chronister, Allen, 696
1972 Cornell, Dennis A., 572
1972 Ripple, Kenneth F., 70
1972 Sessions, William K., III, 480
1973 Pariente, Barbara J., 588
1973 Phillips, Thomas W., 442
1973 Wilson, Stephen V., 130
1974 Keenan, Barbara Milano, 52
1974 Potterfield, Amanda, 634
1975 Currie, Cameron McGowan, 436

The George Washington University *continued*

1978 Anderson, David A., 14
1978 Orme, Gregory K., 805
1979 Rosen, Gerald E., 286
1979 Snyder, Paul B., 497
1981 Thompson, Phyllis D., 829
1982 Murray, William J., Jr., 566
1982 Swanson, Ronald V., 591
1983 Bush, Ronald E., 218
1983 Hagel, Lawrence B., 16
1983 Parker, Linda Vivienne, 289
1983 Stucky, Scott W., 14
1984 Mims, William C. "Bill", 810
1984 Prost, Sharon, 27, 524
1984 Seabright, J. Michael, 216
1985 Brandon-Arnold, Cynthia, 16
1985 DeCicco, William A. "Bill", 14
1985 Silverstein, Laurie Selber, 179
1986 Anderson, David A., 14
1986 Ludaway, Natalie O., 831
1986 Secrest, Perry, 244
1988 Cozzette, Catherine, 351
1988 Mulligan, Deborah, 514
1988 Witherow, John A., Jr., 761
1991 Alonso, Jorge Luis, 228
1991 Seijas, Martha, 63
1992 Kemp, Natonne E., 276
1992 Tao, Jerome T., 703
1993 Gayles, Darrin P., 197
1993 Schoelen, Mary J., 17
1994 Wehrkamp, Beth A., 492
1995 Rogers, Dawn L., 255
1996 Clay, Candace W., 254
1996 Mitchell, Suzanne, 403
1997 Kaplan, Jeffrey H., 619
2002 Watson, Monica, 176
2003 Kammerer, John, 51
2006 Fried, Zachary, 25
2010 Albanese, Matt, 18
2013 Davis, Charles Andrew, 100
2013 Salgado, Suzanne, 510
Espinosa, Carmen Elisa, 581

Georgetown University
[Georgetown]

1956 Belson, James A., 831
1958 Mannes, Paul, 278
1959 Pryor, William C., 829
1959 Timlin, Robert James, 136
1960 Terry, John A., 831
1961 Mannes, Paul, 278
1962 Belson, James A., 831
1962 Garbis, Marvin Joseph, 275
1962 Kornmann, Charles B., 439
1962 Schroeder, H. Kenneth, Jr., 374
1964 Chabot, Herbert L., 23
1964 Goodman, Jerry L., 755
1964 Siler, Eugene E., Jr., 65
1964 Timlin, Robert James, 136
1965 Flynn, Joseph P., 583
1965 Jacobs, Julian I., 23
1966 Hogan, Thomas F., 512
1966 Titus, Roger W., 276
1968 Anello, Michael M., 163
1969 Chiechi, Carolyn P., 24
1969 Fisher, D. Michael, 43
1969 Linn, Richard, 30
1970 Shea, Edward F., 491

Georgetown University *continued*

1970 Whalen, Laurence J., 24
1971 Chiechi, Carolyn P., 24
1971 Colvin, John O., 20
1971 Sullivan, Eugene R., 15
1971 Whalen, Laurence J., 24
1972 Clevert, Charles N., Jr., 504
1972 Murtha, J. Garvan, 480
1972 Niedermeier, Jerome J., 285
1972 Roman, Sheri S., 721
1973 Armen, Robert N., Jr., 25
1973 Edmondson, James E., 752
1973 McAuliffe, Steven James, 326
1973 Robart, James L., 494
1973 Seitz, Patricia A., 198
1973 Wheeler, Thomas Craig, 9
1974 Hollander, Ellen Lipton, 274
1974 Miller, Robert J., 721
1974 Sebelius, K. Gary, 252
1975 Ambro, Thomas L., 43
1975 DeGostin, Lucille, 124
1975 McKeown, M. Margaret, 79
1975 Ruiz, Vanessa, 830
1975 Woodlock, Douglas P., 283
1976 Bush, Lynn J., 10
1976 Vaughn, James T., Jr., 585
1976 Vigil, Michael Edward, 714
1976 Williamson, Michael G., 189
1977 Noel, Franklin L., 299
1978 Chatigny, Robert N., 173
1978 Colvin, John O., 20
1978 Davis, Robert N., 17
1978 Stith, Laura Denvir, 689
1979 Besosa, Francisco Augusto, 517
1979 Connelly, William G., 276
1979 Herrera, Judith C., 337
1979 Kaplan, Elaine D., 9
1979 Sayenga, Jill C., 526
1979 Stanceu, Timothy C., 11, 524
1980 Constantine, Katherine A., 301
1980 Hernandez Covington, Virginia M., 181
1980 Shedd, Dennis W., 51
1981 Duff, James C. "Jim", 522, 526
1981 Gates, James E., 377
1981 Howard, Jeffrey R., 31, 524
1981 Kistler, Rives, 757
1981 Sklar, Cary P., 16
1982 Bredar, James K., 273
1982 Mathy, Pamela Ann, 473
1982 Mauskopf, Roslynn Renee, 342
1983 Gesner, Beth P., 277
1984 Connolly, Francis J., 681
1984 Daley, Janet, 263
1984 Jordan, Kent A., 44
1985 Catliota, Thomas J., 278
1986 Berg, Terrence G., 288
1986 Chen, Pamela Ki Mai, 342
1986 Gildea, Lorie Skjerven, 678
1986 Hessman-Talbot, Elizabeth, 16
1986 Mims, William C. "Bill", 810
1987 Schuele, Therese M., 253
1987 Smith, William E., 431
1987 Sullivan, Timothy J., 277
1988 Foley, Maurice B., 20
1988 Holmes, Jerome A., 91
1988 Kosobucki, Lynne C., 45

Georgetown University *continued*

1989 Hovland, Marie, 440
1990 Guerin Zipps, Jennifer C., 117
1990 Hardiman, Thomas Michael, 44
1990 Heller, Laura, 420
1990 Laplante, Joseph N., Jr., 325
1990 Mariani, Patricia, 14
1990 Whisnant, Julianne Swilley, 604
1993 Byrne, Linda M., 716
1993 Griggsby, Lydia Kay, 9
1994 Moore, Kimberly Ann, 28
1997 Huerta, Rebecca, 119
1997 Seckinger, John, 571
1997 Stoll, Kara Farnandez, 29
1999 Hazel, George Jarrod, 275
2000 Jackson, Brian A., 265
2001 Lehr, Jonathan H., 312
2002 Figeroux, Davina, 344
2004 Shoffner, Stan, 81
2009 Danauy, Caroline, 513
2009 Duncombe, Thomas "Tom", 17
2013 Gong, LiJia, 342
2013 Pennekamp, Aaron D., 5
Daniels, Charles W., 712
Kasold, Bruce E., 17
Manke, Dana, 497
Matsumoto, Kiyo A., 342
Sullivan, Lee G., 556

Georgia State University
[Georgia State]

1989 Hines, Mary H., 603
1995 Story, Laura, 96

Golden Gate University
[Golden Gate]

1976 Snyder, Sandra M., 148
1977 Jaroslovsky, Alan, 160
1986 Christen, Morgan B., 83
1998 Hanan, Jennifer I., 624

Gonzaga University
[Gonzaga]

1957 Quackenbush, Justin L., 491
1974 Kurtz, Frank L., 89, 492
1975 McGrath, Mike, 696
1976 Hutton, James P., 492
1976 Kellison, Craig M., 149
1977 Dietzen, Christopher J., 678
1977 Madsen, Barbara A., 813
1978 Rodgers, John T., 492
1984 Fairhurst, Mary E., 814
1986 Karau, Fred, 492
1986 Rice, Thomas O., 490
1988 Wanslee, Madeleine C., 122
1992 McCrorey, Dennyl, 491
1996 Hendrix, Jill, 543
1997 Zorich, Carolyn, 818
1998 Johnston, Michael E., 813
Flynn, Meagan A., 760

Hamline University
[Hamline]

1977 Frank, Donovan W., 297
1981 Rodenberg, John R., 682

Hofstra University *continued*

1996 Adell, April, 347
2001 Midwood, Laura M., 367
2002 Minerva, Deanna, 344
2007 Jasinski, Melanie, 16
2011 Barth, Lauren, 630
Scarcella, Louis A., 351

Howard University
[Howard U]

1949 Keith, Damon Jerome, 64
1961 Marshall, Consuelo B., 135
1964 Thompson, Anne E., 331
1968 Hall, L. Priscilla, 720
1969 Adams, Henry Lee, Jr., 183
1969 Skretny, William M., 373, 523
1970 Swan, Ive Arlington, 808
1971 Daniel, Wiley Y., 170
1971 Sullivan, Emmet G., 509, 831
1974 Joyner, J. Curtis, 417
1977 Miles-LaGrange, Vicki, 401
1978 Cabret, Maria M., 808
1978 Wright, Carolyn, 794
1979 Biggs, Loretta Copeland, 379
1979 Hotten, Michele D., 664
1981 Draper, George W., III, 689
1984 Pratt, Tanya Walton, 243
1986 Clark, Darcel D., 719
1987 Blackburne-Rigsby, Anna, 828
1995 Nutall, Tracy B., 828
Davis, Ivan D., 486
Newton, Thomas H., 694
White, Patrick A., 200

Indiana University at Indianapolis
[Indiana (Indianapolis)]

1989 LaRue, Denise K., 244
2004 Bentley, Cassandra, 243
2010 Ballard-Barnett, Jessica, 629

Indiana University Bloomington
[Indiana]

1956 Abrahamson, Shirley S., 821
1963 Moody, James T., 240
1966 Lozano, Rudy, 240
1968 Kanne, Michael S., 68
1969 McKinney, Larry J., 243
1969 Van Bokkelen, Joseph S., 239
1971 Baker, John G., 627
1973 Manion, Daniel A., 70
1974 Dees, Harry C., Jr., 241
1974 Kirsch, James S., 628
1974 Lorch, Basil H., III, 245
1974 Riley, Patricia A., 629
1975 Carr, James M., 245
1975 Miller, Robert L., Jr., 238
1976 Curiel, Gonzalo P., 164
1978 Robb, Margret G., 630
1979 Curiel, Gonzalo P., 164
1979 Delano, Caryl E., 189
1979 DePrez, Mary L., 625
1979 Mathias, Paul D., 628
1982 Brown, Elaine B., 630
1982 David, Steven H., 626

Indiana University Bloomington *continued*

1983 Rush, Loretta Hogan, 626
1983 Wise, Tracey N., 257
1984 May, Melissa, 629
1984 Perkins, Thomas L., 222
1986 Bradford, Cale J., 628
1986 Drew, Robert, 630
1987 Newby, Tom, 629
1987 Simon, Philip P., 238
1989 Massa, Mark S., 626
1990 Thomas, Rosemary, 165
1991 Morris, Larry L., 627
1991 Wilson, Steve, 445
1992 Thielmeyer, Lisa Hamilton, 243
1994 Egloff, Cynthia S., 628
1995 Cooper, Tina, 630
1995 Sullivan, Kathryn A., 242
1996 Smith, Kevin S., 625, 627, 630
1997 Arvin, Christina D., 629
1997 Euzen, Eileen, 629
1997 Remondini, David, 625
1999 Johnson, Glenn R., 629
1999 Peters, Maggie B., 310
1999 Sarafoglu, Heather L., 197
2000 Ballard, Jonathan, 628
2000 Lantzer, Erin Heuer, 628
2000 Pyle, Rudolph, III, 629
2000 Warriner, Jennifer D., 629
2002 Yoon, Angela M., 628
2003 Porter, Inge, 629
2005 Maness, Julia I., 617
2006 Barr, Kellie, 243
2006 Chanin, Brandee A., 630
2007 Dame, Sarah W., 243
Gallo, Allison, 628
Lynch, Debra McVicker, 244
Murphy, Kristy, 630
Nuzum, W. Milt, III, 736
Priluck, Noah, 30
Wentworth, Martha Blood, 630

Indiana University-Purdue University Indianapolis
[IU-Purdue U Indianapolis]

1972 Maguire, James, 625
1973 Lawrence, William T., 242
1983 Magnus-Stinson, Jane E., 243
1992 Brauneller, Scott B., 628
1995 Hauck, Angela J., 627

Inter American University of Puerto Rico
[Inter American]

1989 Mulet, Joan, 518

J. Reuben Clark Law School, Brigham Young University
[J Reuben Clark Law]

1976 Benson, Dee V., 477
1976 Warner, Paul Michael, 478
1977 Smith, Norman Randy, 82
1978 Nuffer, David, 476
1978 Voros, J. Frederic "Fred", Jr., 804
1980 Bybee, Jay S., 81

J. Reuben Clark Law School, Brigham Young University *continued*

1984 Ormsby, Peter E., 467
1986 Healey, Troy, 322
1987 Collins, Mitzi, 477
1987 Snow, G. Murray, 116
1988 Stout, Shauna, 477
2009 Petersen, Jessame, 805
Mosman, Michael W., 405
Roth, Stephen L., 805

John Marshall Law School
[John Marshall]

1962 Freeman, Charles E., 613
1966 Harris, Sheldon A., 615
1969 Norgle, Charles Ronald, Sr., 223
1971 Hoffman, Thomas E., 618
1975 D'Alesio, Joseph D., 580
1975 Smith, James Fitzgerald, 617
1976 Jones, Charmaine Tellefsen, 618
1978 Mangan, Robert J., 619
1979 Perrone, Charles P., 767
1980 Spence, Robert B., 620
1981 Birkett, Joseph E. "Joe", 620
1981 Block, Lawrence J., 7
1982 Cunningham, Joy Virginia, 615
1983 Johnson, Cheryl, 787
1983 Shadid, James E., 220
1984 Kravitt, Sandra F., 619
1985 Delort, Mathias W., 615
1985 Walsh, Patrick J., 138
1987 Kaplan, Cheryl A., 203
1988 Laderta, Marie C., 607
1989 Krawczyk, Kimberly L., 234
1989 Markov, Frank J., Jr., 619
1997 Givhan-Edwards, Darvionne J., 617
1997 Jack, Nancy B., 614
2000 Gonnella, Maria, 617
2000 Hoffman, Maya, 615
2002 Rutter, David, 225
2004 Barry, Mary Wilson, 233
2004 Butler, Matthew G., 621
2006 Clayton, Meaghan, 227
Hudson, Donald C., 620
Morris, Cecelia G., 370

Judge Advocate General's School
[Judge Advocate Gen]

1989 Anderson, David A., 14

Lewis and Clark College
[Lewis & Clark]

1953 Jones, Robert E., 406
1976 Hubel, Dennis J., 407
1978 Chang, Kevin S. C., 217
1980 Brown, Anna J., 405
1980 Landau, Jack L., 758
1981 Shetterly, Francine S., 758
1982 Dickerson, Nancy B., 121
1985 Herzfeld, Marc, 406
1988 Russo, Jolie, 404
1989 Dixon, Sandra J., 405
1989 Kent, Amy, 405
1992 Canfield, Cindy, 407

Lewis and Clark College *continued*

1995 Keenan, Lora, 758
1995 Wells, Margaret, 405
1999 Nin, Norma B., 200
2000 Plumlee, Rachel, 539
2004 Phelps, Janie, 94, 401
2009 Raher, Stephen, 409
Melnick, Rich, 817

London School of Economics (UK)
[London School Econ (UK)]

1979 Morgenstern-Clarren, Patricia E., 389

Louisiana State University and Agricultural and Mechanical College
[LSU]

1956 Trimble, James T., Jr., 269
1962 Dennis, James L., 55
1964 Walter, Donald E., 268
1966 Brown, Henry N., Jr., 650
1966 Duval, Stanwood R., Jr., 263
1968 Saunders, John D., 652
1969 Brady, James J., 266
1969 Johnson, Bernette Joshua, 646
1969 Joseph, Cheney C., Jr., 646
1970 Ezell, Billy H., 653
1970 Peters, Jimmie C., 652
1971 Drew, Harmon, Jr., 651
1971 Drew, Jean Talley, 651
1971 James, Robert G., 267
1972 Pettigrew, John T., 648
1975 Kirk, James D., 269
1975 Zainey, Jay C., 262
1976 Cooks, Sylvia R., 652
1976 Hill, C. Michael, 269
1976 McDonald, J. Michael, 648
1976 Moore, D. Milton, III, 651
1977 Berrigan, Helen Ginger, 260
1977 Hays, Sarah, 315
1977 Hicks, S. Maurice, Jr., 268
1977 Payne, Roy S., 453
1977 Riedlinger, Stephen C., 266
1978 Hibler, Barbara Beck, 468
1979 Johnson, Marsha, 266
1979 Langhetee, Leslie M., 646
1980 Caraway, J. Jay, 650
1980 Morgan, Susie, 263
1980 Weimer, John L., 647
1981 Crow, Christine L., 648
1981 Doherty, Rebecca F., 267
1981 Kammler, Kim, 649
1982 Hale, Harlin DeWayne "Cooter", 459
1982 Wise, Gail N., 647
1983 Landry, Janet C., 653
1983 Lindanger, Susan Jiles, 651
1983 Odom, Hal, 651
1984 Davis, Ellen E., 651
1984 Yager, Barry L., 264
1985 Engelhardt, Kurt D., 262
1985 Guidry, Greg Gerard, 646
1986 Segner, Jennifer L., 650
1986 Vujnovich, Sandra, 646
1987 Zerangue, Clare, 266
1988 Dick, Shelly Deckert, 265
1988 Hornsby, Mark L., 269

Louisiana State University and Agricultural and Mechanical College *continued*

1989 Guillot, Gaynel, 647
1989 Lowe, Sylvia S., 654
1990 Slatten, Christopher, 270
1990 Strickland, Gary F., 651
1990 Williams, Janet McVea, 789
1991 Gayle, Priscilla P., 653
1991 Hays, Frances, 269
1991 Vincent, Darla, 652
1991 Williams, Donald, 652
1992 Barkley, Bill, 270
1992 Brown, Jennifer, 650
1992 Triche Milazzo, Jane Margaret, 263
1994 LaBruyere, Joana O., 653
1995 Edwards, Rebecca Armand, 650
1995 Good, Terri, 453
1995 Gremillion, Shannon J., 653
1995 Tullis, David P., 651
1996 Hanchey, Lisa D., 269
1997 Gleeson, Jennifer, 657
1997 Naquin, Rodd, 648
1997 Rogers, Jennifer, 262
1998 Strickland, Cynthia J., 650
1998 Sues, Jennifer, 270
1999 Petrofes, Toni, 269
2000 Couvillion, Matthew, 653
2001 Kelty, Joseph B., 653
2002 Randall, Elizabeth, 267, 269
2002 Tebbe, Lauren, 265
2003 Szczurek, Deelee, 266
Hughes, Jefferson D., III, 647

Louisiana State University at Alexandria
[LSU (Alexandria)]

1978 Knowles, Daniel E., III, 264

Louisiana State University Paul M. Hebert Law Center
[LSU Hebert Law]

1974 deGravelles, John W., 266
1978 Foote, Elizabeth Erny, 268
1981 Richie, Lillian Evans, 649
1985 Clark, Marcus R., 647
1986 Byron, Paul G., 182
1990 Zietz, Marité Cruz, 648

Loyola Law School Los Angeles
[Loyola Law]

1964 Rylaarsdam, William F., 570
1977 Woehrle, Carla M., 137
1978 Chavez, Victoria M., 559
1978 White-Redmond, Marilyn, 563
1984 Codrington, Carol D., 570
1992 Chow, Josephine M., 570
2006 Yates, Angella, 145
Curtis, Donna Marie, 143

Loyola Marymount University
[Loyola Marymount]

1950 Enright, William B., 164

Loyola Marymount University *continued*

1967 Klausner, R. Gary, 132
1969 Walter, John F., 135
1974 Kitching, Patti S., 560
1974 Nelson, Lauren, 562
1974 Ramirez, Manuel A., 569
1975 Gibbons, Mark, 702
1975 Munson, Alex R., 516
1977 Bamattre-Manoukian, Patricia, 574
1977 Mund, Geraldine, 145
1978 Hollows, Gregory G., 148
1979 Hollis, Pamela S., 234
1980 McFarlane, Amy, 115
1982 Calkins, Jeffrey "Jeff", 570
1996 Troyan, Michele, 571
2003 Chang, Deborah, 141
Chaney, Victoria Gerrard, 558
Kriegler, Sandy R., 562
Willhite, Thomas L., Jr., 560

Loyola University (Chicago)
[Loyola U (Chicago)]

1951 Hart, William T., 229
1969 Darrah, John W., 225
1970 Adler, Louise DeCarl, 167
1974 Gilbert, J. Phil, 237
1976 Howse, Nathaniel R., Jr., 617
1981 Thomas, Robert R., 614
1982 Doyle, Carol A., 234
1982 Wright, Vicki R., 622
1989 Healy, Peggy, 68
1991 Kim, Young B., 232
1994 Ellis, Sara Lee, 227
1996 Wietbrock, Shawn A., 619
1997 Rosenthal, Deborah, 563
2000 Cameron, Cecilia, 306
2001 O'Meara, Maura, 232
2003 McGinley, Erin, 69
2005 Haines, Mark, 618
2006 Sroka, Glenn, 615
2006 Vaccaro, Emily, 616

Loyola University (New Orleans)
[Loyola U (New Orleans)]

1951 Real, Manuel L., 129
1964 Lemmon, Mary Ann Vial, 263
1969 Knoll, Jeannette Theriot, 647
1970 Barbier, Carl J., 261
1974 Genovese, James T., 653
1974 Lemelle, Ivan L.R., 263
1974 McKay, James F., III, 654
1974 Stewart, Carl Edmund, 54, 523
1975 Haik, Richard T., Sr., 269
1976 Casanueva, Darryl C., 593
1976 Lynch, Frank J., Jr., 199
1977 Pizzo, Mark A., The Honorable, 186
1979 Olivier, John Tarlton, 646
1980 Stewart, James E., Sr., 650
1985 Chehardy, Susan M., 656
1985 Landrieu, Cheryl Q., 656
1985 Tart, Susan, 655
1987 Killory, Victor, 650
1987 Rosato, Paige Freeman, 655

Loyola University (New Orleans) *continued*

1988 Lobrano, Joy Cossich, 655
1988 Theriot, Mitchell R. "Mitch", 649
1991 Butler, Dana, 648
1992 Barbier, Kelly, 646
1992 Maiorana, Kristi, 648
1993 Bucaro, Inez M., 654
1993 Hernandez-Weimer, Janet F., 269
1994 Cusimano, Patrice D., 655
1995 Jones, Robin, 651
1995 Tynes, Dianne, 652
1996 Blanke, Stacey, 268
1996 Bouzon, Nicholas S., 654
1997 Broussard, Troy, 657
1999 Starns, Pam, 262
2001 Johnson, Ryan, 500
2003 Danos, Julie Hebert, 647
2005 Eidson, Lisa R., 654
Lolley, John Larry, 651

Loyola University of Los Angeles
[Loyola U (Los Angeles)]

1992 Klein, Sandra R., 144
2009 Tran, Lily, 145
Stuart, Allison, 559

Marquette University
[Marquette]

1967 Stadtmueller, J. P., 503
1968 Kessler, Joan F., 823
1973 Callahan, William E., Jr., 504
1973 Curley, Patricia S., 823
1974 Sickel, James R., 505
1977 Gorence, Patricia J., 504
1977 Schneider, Michael E., 53
1979 Griesbach, William C., 503
1979 Wynn, James Andrew, Jr., 52
1984 Sykes, Diane S., 69
1989 Ziegler, Annette Kingsland, 822
1994 Trapp, Kristine, 505
1995 Deitrich, Jonathan I., 504
1997 Szymborski, Kimberly A., 504
2001 Schanen, Christine M., 435
2002 Hruz, Thomas M., 824
2004 Couture, Joseph Edward, 621
2006 Olszewski, Daryl J., 504
2009 Monsils, Elizabeth, 504
2011 Chapman, Carol Ann, 824
Cothroll, Hillary M., 823

Marshall University
[Marshall]

1993 Herbert, Anne, 614
Hopper, Lelia B., 809

McGeorge School of Law, University of the Pacific
[McGeorge]

1972 Gomes, Gene M., 572
1972 Yegan, Kenneth, 562
1975 Callahan, Consuelo Maria, 81

McGeorge School of Law, University of the Pacific *continued*

1976 Hagel, Lawrence B., 16
1976 King, Jeffrey, 569
1977 Levy, Herbert I., 572
1978 Beesley, Bruce T., 325
1979 Mills, Carol Diane, 572
1979 Rawlinson, Johnnie B., 81
1980 Foley, George W., Jr., 323
1981 Gerrard, John M., 319
1981 Lorge, Cynthia McMahon, 119
1983 England, Morrison C., Jr., 146
1984 Hoch, Andrea Lynn, 566
1985 Forbath, Elizabeth Cowles, 570
1985 Sabraw, Dana M., 162
1989 Werth, Robert, 572
1994 Lawrence, Steven T., 542
1995 Boone, Stanley A., 150
2000 Loumber, Valery P., 151
2004 Clar, Jeremy, 150
2006 Miceli, Antonia, 309
2007 Moebius, Breann, 147
2008 Alley, Amanda, 146
Hardesty, James W., 702

Memphis State University
[Memphis State]

1972 Todd, James Dale, 448
1976 Wedemeyer, Robert W., 783
1979 Donald, Bernice B., 63
1980 Vescovo, Diane K., 447
1984 Smith, Rhoda, 449
1986 Latta, Jennie D., 449
1993 King, Nancy, 446
Bomar, Rayna, 448
Claxton, Charmiane G., 448

Mercer University
[Mercer]

1956 Drake, Walter Homer, Jr., 212
1957 Mills, Richard, 221
1966 Laney, John T., III, 206
1969 Thompson, Hugh P., 601
1974 Sands, W. Louis, 205
1977 Graham, James E., 214
1979 Chandler, Joe, 603
1980 Miller, M. Yvette, 604
1981 Barnes, Therese S. "Tee", 601
1981 Craig, John W. L., II, 489
1981 Treadwell, Marc Thomas, 204
1981 Withers, John, 602
1983 Turner, Cindy L., 188
1984 Kelley, Ann, 605
1986 Clanton, Cynthia Hinrichs, 601
1987 Brown, J. Alvin, 206
1990 Boggs, Michael P., 604
1994 Wright, Laura F., 105
1998 Johnson, Lynn, 604
2000 O'Neill, James, 221
2002 Dwyer, Erin David, 214
2011 Wiegele, Jordan, 202
Doyle, Sara L., 603

Michigan State University
[Michigan State]
2001 Nowak, Cheryl, 672
2004 Fellows, Stephan M., 677
2008 Hoogerhyde, Robin, 577
Buch, Ronald Lee, 22

Mississippi College
[Mississippi Col]
1973 Lee, L. Joseph, 685
1980 Aycock, Sharion, 301
1980 Featherston, D. Elizabeth "Beth", 303
1988 Kimble, Denise, 306
1990 Shelton, Wendy, 306
1993 Domangue, Julie S., 648
1994 Jicka, Yvonne W., 306
1996 Dillard, Stephen Louis A., 604
1996 Luke, Dianne, 306
2003 Howell, Elizabeth Q., 304
2006 Russell, Kathy, 686
Gabbert, Rex, 695
James, Ceola, 686

Nashville School of Law
[Nashville]
1979 Clement, Frank G., Jr., 781

National University of Singapore
[National U Singapore]
Tookey, Douglas L. "Doug", 759

New England School of Law
[New England]
1977 Crawford, Susan Jean, 15
1981 Alonso, Beth M., 753
1990 Crossen, Judith P., 285
1992 Blake, Amy Lyn, 670
1994 Stanton, Joseph F., 667
2001 Nasello Graves, Jill, 648
2003 Lawrence, Emily, 705
2007 Winkelhake, David, 745

New Mexico State University
[New Mexico State]
Vigil, Barbara J., 712

New York Law School
[New York Law]
1951 Tsoucalas, Nicholas, 12
1969 Goldberg, Martin R., 370
1975 Friedman, David, 717
1977 Falk, Mark, 333
1977 Mastro, William F., 719
1979 Azrack, Joan Marie, 343
1980 Friedkin, Neil, 717
1989 Lee, James M., 715
1991 O'Boyle, Una, 370
1997 O'Neill, James, 356
2001 Nace, Christopher, 764
2011 Shepard, William, 725

New York University
[NYU]
1950 Wexler, Leonard D., 344
1958 Bowman, Pasco M., II, 74
1958 Newman, Pauline, 27
1960 Norris, Alan E., 64
1964 Hittner, David, 464
1966 Haines, Harry Allen, 23
1967 Berman, Richard M., 366
1968 Lippman, Jonathan, 715
1968 Schiller, Berle M., 417
1969 Wechsler, James J., 713
1970 Laro, David, 24
1970 Slomsky, Joel H., 412
1971 Korman, Edward R., 345
1971 Vitaliano, Eric Nicholas, 341
1972 Oliver, Solomon, Jr., 385
1972 Peters, Karen K., 722
1972 Saxe, David B., 717
1972 Wherry, Robert A., Jr., 25
1973 Guzman, Ronald A., 225
1973 Hall, Janet C., 173
1973 Jacobs, Dennis, 35
1974 Atlas, Nancy Friedman, 465
1975 Ellis, Ronald L., 369
1975 Halpern, James S., 21
1975 Levy, Robert M., 348
1975 Lindsay, Arlene Rosario, 347
1976 Maas, Frank, 367
1976 Roman, Sheri S., 721
1978 Agee, G. Steven, 51
1978 Preska, Loretta A., 355
1978 Vasquez, Juan F., 22
1978 Wells, Thomas B., 25
1979 Riblet, Robin L., 141
1980 Seltzer, Barry S., 199
1981 Schofield, Lorna G., 360
1982 Barros, Betsy, 721
1983 Jones, Gary R., 192
1983 McAliley, Chris M., 201
1983 McNulty, Kevin, 330
1984 Seltzer, Barry S., 199
1985 Carlson, Thomas E., 160
1985 Leung, Tony N., 300
1985 McLeese, Roy W., III, 829
1985 Nakamoto, Lynn R., 759
1986 Freeman, Debra, 369
1986 Goodman, Lois H., 334
1986 Orenstein, James, 349
1987 Lipman, Sheryl H. "Sheri", 447
1988 Diaz, Albert, 52
1988 Gur-Arie, Mira, 528
1988 Zinkin, Anne, 705
1990 Forrest, Katherine B., 359
1990 Meyers, John M., 53
1991 Lane, Sean H., 371
1991 Lohier, Raymond Joseph, Jr., 38
1991 Rubin, Leslie, 348
1993 Jason, Karen, 368
1993 Reyes, Ramon E., Jr., 349
1994 Chen, Raymond T. "Ray", 29
1996 Harris, Elizabeth, 579
1998 Hillman, Noel Lawrence, 329
1999 Lyons, Jennifer P., 272
1999 Proujansky, Josh, 347
2001 Piriz, Marielena, 333
2005 Gaynor, Amanda, 422
2005 Terranova, Robert, 343
2005 Windrow, Hayden, 12
2008 Reger, Stephanie, 328

New York University *continued*
2010 Weingold, Brett D., 495, 513
2011 Marshak, Amy, 5
2011 Nowlin, Lisa, 512
2011 Shahabian, Matthew R., 6
2011 Stone-Tharp, Alexander, 368
2014 Frenkel, Amelia, 102
2015 Reyneri, Rafael, 342
McCormack, Bridget, 672
Mead, Andrew M., 658
Rivera, Jenny, 715
Spearman, Michael S., 815

North Carolina Central University
[North Carolina Central]
1982 Alston, Rossie D., Jr., 811
1982 Bryant, Wanda G., 730
1982 Elmore, Richard A. "Rick", 731
1985 Wright Allen, Arenda L., 483
2013 Wright, Brandon R., 514

Northeastern University
[Northeastern]
1973 Botsford, Margot, 667
1976 Fabe, Dana, 538
1976 Roberts, Victoria A., 287
1977 Arterton, Janet Bond, 175
1979 Ridgway, Delissa A., 11
1981 Sullivan, Mary T., 670
1984 Newcomb, Martha, 771
1985 Maldonado, Diana L., 670
1987 Burgess, Timothy Mark, 113
1991 Cabell, Donald L., 285
1995 Reed, Pierce, 736
2007 Jusczyk, Michael "Mike", 32

Northern Illinois University
[Northern Illinois]
1985 Klock, Diane R., 221
1994 Collender, Cary, 620
1996 Drinkwine, Christopher J., 226
1996 Mandell, Stacey, 620
1997 Angus, Julie, 621
2000 Murdoch, Jeffrey, 620
2001 Johnson, Heather K., 621
2001 McCabe, Catherine, 622
2001 Rouleau, Heather, 220

Northwestern University
[Northwestern]
1958 Aspen, Marvin E., 229
1963 Flaum, Joel M., 67
1963 King, Garr M., 407
1964 Flaum, Joel M., 67
1967 Jones, Jim, 610
1968 Gettleman, Robert W., 229
1968 Lytton, Tom M., 621
1971 Lefkow, Joan Humphrey, 231
1972 Bucklo, Elaine E., 228
1972 Skretny, William M., 373, 523
1977 Hyman, Michael B., 616
1978 Tallman, Richard C., 80
1979 Caldwell, Charles M., 396

Northwestern University *continued*
1979 Castillo, Ruben, 223
1979 Marbley, Algenon L., 392
1979 Schenkier, Sidney I., 231
1980 Gilbert, Jeffrey T., 233
1980 Spaulding, Karla Rae, 186
1982 Goldgar, A. Benjamin, 234
1983 Cooke, Valerie P., 323
1983 Crocker, Stephen L., 506
1983 Jubelirer, Renée Cohn, 767
1983 Reifurth, Lawrence M., 609
1984 Payson, Marian W., 374
1988 Boyce, William J., 802
1988 Lange, Roberto A., 439
1988 McShane, Michael J., 405
1990 Gould, Andrew W., 544
1990 Tharp, John J. "Jay", Jr., 227
1992 Michelson, Laurie J., 289
1993 Lipman, Margaret, 233
1994 Chang, Edmond E-Min, 227
1995 Freitag, Jason, 614
1995 Klein, Kimberly P., 220
1997 Rice, Anne E., 477
1998 Huebl, John C., 16
2002 Christensen, Mariah, 68
2002 McLaughlin, Dorothy R., 139
2006 Hagedorn, Brian K., 824
2006 Lindstrom, Richard S., 352
2007 Davenport, Maria-Teresa, 114
2011 Dawson, Elana Nightingale, 4
2013 Joshi, Sopan, 4
2013 Siller, Margaret Marie, 365
2015 Cuevas, Jesse, 52
2015 Lonky, Hannah, 327
Allendorf, Thea, 747
Bernstein, Richard H., 672

Nova Southeastern University
[Nova Southeastern]
1981 Cholodofsky, Debra, 200
1987 Chappell, Sheri Polster, 182
2011 Ott, London, 201

Nova University
[Nova]
1981 May, Melanie, The Honorable, 596
1987 Faerber, Susan, 595

Ohio Northern University
[Ohio Northern]
1972 Rogers, Richard M., 740
1974 Frost, Gregory L., 392
1975 Shaw, Stephen R., 740
1975 Thynge, Mary Pat, 178
1977 Cherry, Paul R., 240
1977 Welbaum, Jeffrey M., 739
1979 Pietrykowski, Mark L., 742
1979 Wise, John W., 742
1989 Byers, Brad R., 748
1992 Wehrkamp, Beth A., 492
1997 Price Smith, Jessica E., 390
2002 Kidd, Theresa, 758
2006 Castle, Joshua Michael, 643
2011 Nuss, Ryan, 740

Saint Louis University *continued*

2002 Lappas, Catherine, 691
2003 Sengheiser, Jason, 691
2003 Westermann, Amy S., 691
2005 Anderson, Lisa, 691
Baker, Nannette A., 311
Sullivan, Sherri B., 691
Van Amburg, Lisa, 690

St. Mary's University (Texas)
[St Mary's U (TX)]

1965 Heartfield, Thad, 452
1972 Ezra, David Alan, 217
1976 Mummert, Thomas C., III, 310
1976 Primomo, John W., 473
1977 Dowd, Robert G., Jr., 690
1977 Green, Paul W., 785
1978 Carroll, Peter H., 140
1979 Angelini, Karen, 793
1979 Cardone, Kathleen, 471
1979 Hervey, Barbara P., 788
1980 Marion, Sandee Bryan, 793
1986 Manske, Jeffrey C., 474
1989 Deml, Gail, 470
1989 Martinez, Wendy, 793
1990 Christmas, Gloria, 469
1990 Sullivan, Joani, 469
1991 Townsend, Gregory, 336
1992 Barnard, Marialyn Price, 793
1992 Gonzales, Richard A., 795
1996 Marmolejo, Marina Garcia, 463
1998 Najera, Valerie, 793
2013 Marion, Natalee, 473
Goodwin, Melissa, 792

Salmon P. Chase College of Law, Northern Kentucky University
[Salmon P Chase]

1970 Ruwe, Robert P., 23
1975 Hendon, Sylvia Sieve, 738
1981 Reeves, Danny C., 254
1981 Stout, Alan C., 260
1983 Black, Timothy S., 393
1987 Givens, Samuel, Jr., 643
1990 Keller, Michelle M., 642
1991 Christian, Vicki, 256
1992 Smith, Candace J., 256
1995 Denton, Heather, 645
1996 Kramer, Joy A., 644
2011 Ingalsbe, Gregory, 194
Lambert, James H., Sr., 644

Sam Houston State University
[Sam Houston State]

1997 Holmes, Heather, 786

San Francisco Law School
[San Francisco Law]

1979 Needham, Henry E., Jr., 558

San Joaquin College of Law
[San Joaquin Law]

1976 Austin, Gary S., 149
1976 Owdom, Deborah, 150
1995 Bertalotto, Tim, 149
Lee, W. Richard, 151

Santa Barbara College of Law
[Santa Barbara Law]

1994 Graham, Katy, 562

Santa Clara University
[Santa Clara U]

1962 Premo, Eugene M., 573
1975 Elia, Franklin D., 574
1976 Hamilton, Phyllis J., 153
1983 Efremsky, Roger L., 159
1984 Gold, Melanie, 567
1990 Grover, Adrienne M., 574
1999 Pack, Christine A., 574
2000 Corp, Richard, 148
2002 Meyere, Marina, 573
Poochigian, Charles S. "Chuck", 573

Seattle University
[Seattle]

1976 Alley, Frank R., III, 409
1983 Haas, Joseph A., 438
1986 Boyd, Lauri, 492
1990 Rein, Randy, 165
1999 Chase, Michelle E., 817
2004 Burnside, William, 494
2015 Herd, Rachel, 90
Klein, Colleen, 495
Selby, Carrie, 497

Seton Hall University
[Seton Hall]

1967 Mautone, Anthony R., 335
1975 Hayden, Katharine S., 332
1975 St. John, Jerome M., 709
1977 Sheridan, Peter G., 329
1985 Hillman, Noel Lawrence, 329
1987 Chagares, Michael A., 44
1994 Dunican, Tara A., 334
1994 Shipp, Michael A., 330
2003 Corneal, Devon A., 329
2007 Racanelli, Margherita, 726
2013 Pavlick, Phillip, 332
2014 Silagi, Alex, 331
Block, Gregory O., COL, 16
Bongiovanni, Tonianne J., 333
Campbell, Daniel R., 11
Fang, Wayne, 328
Fasciale, Douglas M., 711

South Dakota State University
[South Dakota State]

1985 Hodson, Kay Cee, 440

South Texas College of Law
[South Texas]

1980 Worthen, James T., 800
1981 Jack, Janis Graham, 465
1982 Valenti, Donna K., 593
1984 McKeithen, Steve, 798
1989 Guzman, Eva M., 786
1989 O'Connor, Reed Charles, 457
1990 Baffes, Kathryn, 471
1990 Frobese, Douglas, 795
1990 McCally, Sharon, 802
1992 Indelicato, Nina Reilly, 801
1993 Fox, Maria Teresa "Terry", 579
1994 Etheridge, Anna L., 802
2000 Tobor, Robert, 789
2002 Allen, Christy, 128
2008 Laine, Marianne, 451
Kreger, Charles, 798

Southern Illinois University Carbondale
[Southern Illinois]

1976 Stewart, Bruce D., 624
1977 Herndon, David R., 236
1980 Frazier, Philip M., 236
1980 Myerscough, Sue E., 220
1982 Chambers, Cathleen, 222
1982 Stallman, Karen, 236
1982 Wilgenbusch, Shirley, 622
1983 Noffke, Kim G., 614
1986 Fiore, Melissa G., 536
1987 Greathouse, Michael, 623
1987 Grosboll, Carolyn Taft, 613
1987 Hunsicker, Sheila O'Malley, 236
1987 Keltner, Joan, 624
1992 Brown, Rebecca S., 237
1993 Rosenstengel, Nancy J., 236
1995 Atterberry, Mark, 622
1996 Quivey, Lara L., 220
2002 Mills, Lisa M., 189
2008 Jeralds, Amber, 237
Dixon, Donna L., 645
Holdridge, William E., 621

Southern Methodist University
[Southern Methodist]

1972 Rainey, John D., 465
1973 Biery, Fred, 469
1974 Averitte, Clinton E., 457
1974 Hecht, Nathan L., 785
1974 Means, Terry R., 457
1975 Buettner, Kenneth L., 754
1975 Schell, Richard A., 452
1976 Bush, Don D., 452
1976 Limbaugh, Stephen N., Jr., 308
1976 Lynn, Barbara M. G., 456
1978 Dauphinot, Lee Ann, 791
1978 Houser, Barbara J., 459
1978 Keller, Sharon, 787
1981 Boyle, Jane J., 456
1985 Johnson, Susanna, 455
1986 Bush, Don D., 452
1987 Brister, Peggy E., 160
1990 Raper, Cheryl, 457
1991 Ramirez, Irma Carrillo, 458
1994 Colwell, Robert, 459

Southern Methodist University *continued*

1996 Chadwick, Lauren, 791
1996 Daley, Cynthia, 457
1998 Helms, Jennifer, 454
1998 Rutherford, Rebecca Tustin, 456
2000 Willie, Abigail B., 312
2004 Harden, Alicia, 256
2010 Capehart, John, 102

Southern University and A & M College at Baton Rouge
[Southern U A&M]

1980 Williams, Felicia Toney, 650
1987 Guidry, John Michael, 648
1999 Collins, Kacy Renea, 648
2000 Richard, Alyce C., 653

Southern University at New Orleans
[Southern U (New Orleans)]

1976 McClarty, John, 780
1985 Jackson, Brian A., 265
1996 White-Bazile, Angela, 646
2007 Jefferson, Erica Nicole, 650

Southern University Law Center
[Southern U Law]

1984 Jenkins, Sandra Cabrina, 656

Southwestern School of Law
[Southwestern Law]

1971 Lew, Ronald S. W., 136
1979 Bardwil, Robert S., 151

Southwestern University
[Southwestern]

1975 O'Leary, Kathleen E., 570
1980 Smith, Richard D., 135
1980 Wright, Otis D., II, 133
1989 Reichman, Kenneth, 135
1989 Silver, Abbi, 704
1994 Irwin, Douglas S., 563
1999 Sarenas, Lovee, 143
Margulies, Sandra L., 554

St. Thomas University
[St Thomas U]

2006 Brackins, Patrick, 187

Stanford University
[Stanford]

1948 Conti, Samuel, 156
1958 Bea, Carlos T., 82
1958 Griesa, Thomas P., 363
1958 Hug, Procter, Jr., 84
1963 McIntyre, James A., 568
1966 Fisher, Raymond C., 88
1968 Lettow, Charles F., 8
1970 Selna, James V., 132
1972 Brett, Dean, 496

Stanford University *continued*

1972 Snyder, Christina A., 130
1973 Gottschall, Joan B., 231
1973 Illston, Susan Yvonne, 157
1974 Chasanow, Deborah K., 276
1975 Dunn, Randall L., 88, 409
1975 Mann, Roanne L., 348
1976 Otero, S. James, 132
1979 Leman, Valerie, 567
1980 Grimes, Elizabeth A., 564
1981 Whipple, Mary Ann, 390
1982 Dodd, Douglas D., 266
1982 Johnsen, Diane M., 545
1986 Dupont, Mark, 68
1986 Eckerstrom, Peter J., 545
1987 Kivel, Maria, 554
1988 Delaney, Carolyn K., 150
1988 Donato, James, 155
1989 Bernal, Jesus G., 131
1991 Feinerman, Gary, 226
1993 Cooper, Christopher Reid "Casey", 511
1993 Krause, Cheryl Ann, 46
1995 Mueller, Kimberly J., 147
1995 Srinivasan, Srikanth "Sri", 102
1996 Owens, John B., 84
1997 Aubrejuan, Alison, 157
1998 Ozerden, Halil Suleyman, 304
2000 Friedland, Michelle T., 84
2000 Wu, Shao-Bai, 154
2002 Sepulveda, Sandra, 130
2003 Fellers, James P., 133
2004 Kunz, Maria D., 194
2004 Walker, Elizabeth, 84
2008 Stewart, Scott G., 4
2012 Rhodes, C. Harker, 4
2012 Smith Grieco, Barbara, 6
2014 Friedman, David, 58
2014 Fu, Thomas K., 6
2015 Barmore, Cynthia, 101
2015 George, Jason, 86
Ching, Kristine, 158
Duarte, Elena J., 566
Heideman, James Lawrence, 555
Rice, Jordan, 52

State University College at Buffalo
[SUNY Col (Buffalo)]

1980 Gische, Judith J., 718

State University of New York at Albany
[SUNY (Albany)]

1975 Ahart, Alan M., 141

State University of New York at Buffalo
[SUNY (Buffalo)]

1949 Curtin, John T., 372
1955 Telesca, Michael A., 19, 373
1961 Schroeder, H. Kenneth, Jr., 374
1965 Foschio, Leslie G., 375
1968 Friedman, Paul L., 513
1970 White, Jeffrey S., 153
1973 Pigott, Eugene F., Jr., 715
1973 Sconiers, Rose H., 724

State University of New York at Buffalo *continued*

1975 Eaglin, James B., 528
1975 Fuentes, Julio M., 43
1977 Rufe, Cynthia M., 410
1982 Pedersen, Mark W., 373
1982 Reed, Christopher K., 375
1983 Brown, Colleen A., 480
1984 Cohen, Wendy, 719
1984 Fahey, Eugene M., 716
1984 Gillmeister, William J., 374
1984 Peradotto, Erin M., 724
1985 Bloom, Lois, 349
1986 Benedict, Mary Hope, 723
1986 McMahon, Karen, 373
1987 Schoellkopf, William C., 373
1994 Hopkins, Thérèse A., 375
1997 Farrell, Colleen, 724
1997 Richardson, Karen E., 374
2000 Barovick, Robin, 520
2000 Bertino-Beaser, Lisa, 375
2006 Fox-Solomon, Elizabeth, 724
2010 Scaramuzzino, Chelsea L., 352

Stetson University
[Stetson]

1961 Kovachevich, Elizabeth A., 180
1973 Brown, Stephen M., 818
1976 Hunstein, Carol W., 601
1977 Bucklew, Susan Cawthon, 184
1977 Marra, Kenneth A., 195
1977 McCoun, Thomas B., III, 186
1977 Sawaya, Thomas D., 599
1977 Villanti, Craig C., 592
1977 Whittemore, James D., 180
1984 Bedell, Cynthia A., 184
1984 Burton, Nancy Noble, 592
1990 Eshleman, Bonnie E., 593
1992 Jank, Rick, 191
1992 Wallis, F. Rand, 600
1993 Bates, Douglas M., Jr., 184
1993 Kuenzel, Mary Elizabeth, 592
1994 Kanfer, Dana, 186
1994 Tomsich, Racquel, 183
1996 Arzt, Mishannock, 597
1996 Castleberry, Carol, 593
1996 Phillips, Michelle, 622
1997 Leduc, Tracy E., 592
1997 Meisner, Julie C., 180
1999 Meyers, Adrienne, 300
2002 Kemp, Douglas, 182
2003 Caracciolo, Angel, 17
2003 Keller Landkammer, Kelley A., 181
Bodiford, Larry A., 192
Marstiller, Simone, 591
Preston, C. Kathryn, 66, 397
Tozier, Debbie, 592

Suffolk University
[Suffolk]

1969 Panuthos, Peter J., 25
1970 Tutalo, Ronald, 771
1973 Hillman, Timothy S., 282
1974 Carhart, Judd J., 670
1974 Dalianis, Linda S., 705
1974 Leon, Richard J., 510

Suffolk University *continued*

1974 Reiber, Paul L., 806
1975 Agnes, Peter W., Jr., 670
1975 Flaherty, Francis X., 772
1975 Zarella, Peter T., 580
1976 Bowler, Marianne B., 284
1976 Suttell, Paul A., 771
1977 Goodnow, Donald D., 705
1978 Feeney, Joan N., 34, 285
1978 Goldberg, Maureen McKenna, 771
1980 Bailey, Frank J., 34, 285
1983 Skomal, Bernard G., 166
1984 Curtin, David, 771
1986 Cypher, Elspeth B., 668
1987 Thurston, Susan M., 432
1987 Zierk, Marsha K., 281
1989 Bourcier-Fargnoli, Carol, 771
1989 Pline, Richard A., 668
1990 Quinn, Thomas F., Jr., 284
1991 Gelpí, Gustavo Antonio, Jr., 517
1991 Sharon, Mary P., 33
1992 Mittman, Susan, 568
1995 Burpee, Robert L., 736
1996 Kruse-Weller, Erika, 771
2004 Mosca, Carrie E., 432
Trainor, Joseph A., 669

Swarthmore College
[Swarthmore]

2008 Work, Alyssa, 365

Syracuse University
[Syracuse]

1963 Hurd, David N., 352
1964 Scullin, Frederick J., Jr., 353
1971 Mordue, Norman A., 353
1971 Schoenfeld, Martin, 725
1973 Paul, Letitia Z., 468
1975 DeJoseph, Brian F., 725
1975 McKee, Theodore A., 42, 523
1975 Peebles, David E., 353
1976 Mariani, Robert David, 423
1976 Townes, Sandra L., 346
1977 Dailey, John Daniel, 577
1977 McCullough, Annelle, 353
1980 D'Agostino, Mae A., 352
1980 Graves, James E., Jr., 57
1981 Feldman, Jonathan W., 374
1982 Gensini, Gioia A., 354
1983 Hayes, William Q., 163
1985 Suddaby, Glenn T., 351
1988 Lawrence, Susan G., 93
1989 Castanzo, Erin Butler, 421
1991 Moore, Debbie, 353
1995 Iacobucci, Jennifer Powers, 723
1999 Pfohl, Lillian Abbott, 36
2001 Kamps, Laura, 617
Goerdt, John A., 632
Yannotti, Joseph L., 711

Temple University
[Temple]

1956 Stafford, William H., Jr., 191
1959 Padova, John R., 416
1960 Kelly, Robert F., 415

Temple University *continued*

1963 Munley, James M., 425
1967 Van Antwerpen, Franklin S., 48
1968 Stafford, William H., Jr., 191
1970 Lourie, Alan D., 28
1971 Angell, M. Faith, 420
1971 Savage, Timothy J., 410
1975 Moran, J. Denis, 821
1976 Tucker, Petrese B., 410
1977 Lisi, Mary M., 432
1978 Linares, Jose L., 328
1978 Nakazato, Arthur, 137
1981 Ott, Paula Francisco, 765
1983 Baxter, Susan Paradise, 429
1983 Rogers, Richard P., 426
1984 Heffley, Marilyn, 420
1984 Lee, Seung Jai, 767
1987 Deasy, Susan, 418
1987 McGrath, Timothy B., 420
1987 Walsh, Noreen, 421
1989 Lunn, Deborah, 446
1990 Kiesel, Judith J., 420
1992 Ferrandez, Camilo, 418
1992 Plum, Anna Marie, 419
1992 Reichman, Evelyn W., 763
1992 Soltys, P. Mark, 42
1993 Halfhill, Sherry, 429
1993 Speranza, Denise M., 418
2000 Devlin, Michael, 47
2000 Reichert, Maren, 419
2001 Clements, William, 764
2005 Kohler, Benjamin D., 764
2014 Linsey, Katherine S., 332
2014 Yim, Kevin, 349
Kossler, Douglas H., 540

Texas Southern University
[Texas Southern]

1972 Hoyt, Kenneth M., 465
1973 King, Leslie D., 684
1979 Valdez, Rogelio, 800
1980 García, Victor Roberto, 474
1981 Rodriguez, Nelda V., 801
1992 Berles, James "Jim", 239
1994 Wimes, Brian C., 309, 313
2001 Sherer, Kronsky, 465

Texas Tech University
[Texas Tech]

1971 Wright, Jim R., 799
1974 Hancock, Mackey K., 797
1975 Johnson, Phil, 786
1976 Junell, Robert A., 473
1977 Pirtle, Patrick A., 797
1978 Nelms, Russell F., 459
1981 Quinn, Brian, 796
1982 Jones, Robert L., 459
1982 Koenig, Nancy M., 458
1983 Frost, Kem Thompson, 801
1983 Puryear, David, 792
1984 Bridges, David L., 794
1986 Walker, Sue, 791
1986 Waters, Kay, 797
1987 Kotara, Stephen W, 799
1988 Freas, Charles A., 455
1988 McIlhany, Tom, 797
1991 Blount, Elyse D., 796
1993 Durrett, Aileen, 452
1993 Mayfield, Amanda, 457

Texas Tech University *continued*

1998 Redding, Jeffrey W., 210
1999 Eckols, Linda S., 466
2001 Howey, Ann, 458
2002 Simpson, Carrie, 797
2003 Clark, Boyd L., 457
2015 Schmucker, Catherine, 90
Gabriel, Lee, 791
Palmer, Stephen, 797
Stoddart, Craig, 795

Texas Wesleyan University
[Texas Wesleyan U]

1994 Humpa, Gayle, 794
2005 Kent, Casey, 799
2007 Walker, Johannes, 791
Wesson, Cliffie, 794

Thomas Goode Jones School of Law, Faulkner University
[Jones Law]

1977 Cassady, William E., 112
1983 Bryan, Tommy Elias, 534
1988 Webb, Linda S., 534
1990 Williams, Dwight H., Jr., 107
1994 Wise, Alisa Kelli, 534

Thomas Jefferson University
[Thomas Jefferson]

1998 Bostwick, Laura, 163

Thomas M. Cooley Law School
[Thomas M Cooley]

1981 Harsha, William H., 740
1981 Markey, Jane E., 674
1988 Smith, Carma L., 624
1998 Geiger, Kathleen, 294
2006 Baumann, Joseph J., 671
2010 Worden, I. Marie, 275
2011 Regal, Jonathon M., 672
Royster, Larry, 671

Tulane University
[Tulane]

1957 Duhé, John M., Jr., 58
1957 Feldman, Martin L. C., 261
1959 Brown, Jerry A., 265
1960 Davis, W. Eugene, 54
1961 Wiener, Jacques L., Jr., 58
1962 Fallon, Eldon E., 261
1969 Schall, Alvin Anthony, 30
1971 Drell, Dee D., 267
1971 O'Keefe, Michael, 264
1971 Tobias, Max N., Jr., 655
1972 Clement, Edith Brown, 55
1974 Drake, Ernest G. "Ernie", 649
1975 Richie, Michael S., 751, 753, 755
1975 Thibodeaux, Ulysses Gene, 652
1976 Kane, Yvette, 422
1976 Ray, J. Thomas, 125

Tulane University *continued*

1977 Wicker, Fredericka Homberg, 656
1978 Vance, Sarah S., 26, 260
1979 Shaffer, Craig B., 171
1980 Fulton, Thomas H., 259
1980 Mulet, Joan, 518
1980 Pohorelsky, Viktor V., 348
1980 Wilkinson, Joseph C., Jr., 264
1981 Bagneris, Dennis R., Sr., 654
1981 McClendon, Page, 649
1981 Otts, Anne M., 655
1982 Cagney, Nanette, 268
1982 Zanchelli, Mark J., 48
1983 Minaldi, Patricia Head, 268
1983 Sirera, Julie L., 655
1984 Durette, Deborah G., 657
1984 Michel, Carol L., 260
1984 Pickett, Elizabeth A., 653
1985 Franklin, Betsy W., 430
1985 Gates, Eugenia, 98
1986 Love, Terri F., 654
1986 Restrepo, Luis Felipe, 413
1987 Pryor, William Holcombe "Bill", Jr., 96, 529
1987 Roby, Karen Wells, 264
1988 Jolivette-Brown, Nannette, 262
1989 Grotta, Patty, 756
1989 Haikala, Madeline H., 108
1989 Lackey, Kevin, 683
1989 Manchester, Kathy, 264
1989 Schneider, Karen, 692
1992 Campbell-Smith, Patricia E., 7
1995 Killory, Victor, 650
1998 Jolivette-Brown, Nannette, 262
2001 Mehalchick, Karoline, 425
2003 Miller, Andrea "Annie", 261
2004 Arnold, Erin K., 265
2006 Dupuy, Megan, 263
2007 Escandon, Joseph H., 262
2012 Fulton, Duncan T., 261
2014 Perrone, Samuel, 58
Belsome, Roland L., 655
Windhorst, Stephen J. "Steve", 657

UC Berkeley School of Law, University of California, Berkeley
[Berkeley Law]

2013 Ly, Jessica, 39
2014 Anand, Easha, 6
2014 Sivaram, Anuradha, 77
2015 Hawkins, Salah, 81
2015 Tevah, Shira, 67

UC Hastings College of the Law
[Hastings]

1966 Reardon, Timothy A., 556
1967 Nicholson, George, 565
1971 Hollenhorst, Thomas E., 569
1971 McKinster, Art W., 569
1972 Cooney, Peter, 562
1973 Swisher, Peter N., 811
1974 Douglas, Michael L., 703
1974 Ikola, Raymond J., 571
1975 Corrigan, Carol A., 553

UC Hastings College of the Law *continued*

1975 DeBose, Lorene, 156
1975 Mihara, Nathan D., 574
1975 Siggins, Peter, 556
1976 Kane, Stephen J., 572
1976 Leighton, Ronald B., 493
1978 Franson, Donald R., Jr., 573
1979 Davila, Edward J., 154
1979 O'Neill, Lawrence J., 146
1982 Cauchon, Helene, 567
1983 Gutierrez, Sergio A., 612
1983 Hill, Brad R., 572
1983 Novack, Charles Daniel, 160
1985 Foodim, Lauren, 717
1985 Lafferty, William J., 161
1986 Bashant, Cynthia Ann, 164
1988 Amsbary, Bill, 571
1989 Hughes, Karen S., 164
1990 Nunley, Troy L., 147
1992 Delaney, Christian, 153
1994 Cogliati, Syda, 574
1998 Converse, Lisa, 297
2001 Nathan, Christopher D., 158
2003 Rogers, Adrienne, 557
Johnson, Stephen L., 160
Nakayama, Paula A., 608
Petrich, Alexandra, 153
Pollack, Richard W., 608
Schafler, Rebecca, 136
Vadas, Nandor J., 158
Wind, Amy, 99

The University of Akron
[Akron]

1971 Batchelder, Alice M., 60
1974 Arbuckle, William I., III, 426
1976 Gwin, W. Scott, 741
1976 Hoffman, William B., 742
1978 Cook, Deborah L., 62
1978 Donofrio, Gene, 743
1979 Gwin, James S., 385
1982 Whitmore, Beth, 746
1983 Adams, John R., 386
1990 Burton, Diane, 741
1990 Dingwell, Ruthanne, 742
1993 Sander, Cynthia, 429
1993 Witner, Kristine Scott, 742
1996 Burns, Susan A., 388
1998 Dossi, Jacqueline Marks, 742
1999 Hively, Aaron, 743
2000 Hendrickson, Jeffrey E., 744
2001 Czopur-Gaffney, Melanie, 743
2001 Dobbs, Shaunna Lincoln, 742
2002 Krocker, Michelle L., 745
2004 Andrews, Carol, 741
2004 Little, Jonathan, 386
2004 Staley, Cara, 386
2006 Keating, Tara T., 748
2010 Beadle, Julie, 749
2011 Peterson, Caryn, 517
Carr, Donna J., 747
Curtin, Christopher, 60
Dahler, F. William, 742

University of Alabama
[Alabama]

1957 Hancock, James Hughes, 109
1959 Cox, Emmett Ripley, 99
1960 Albritton, W. Harold, III, 105
1961 Higginbotham, Patrick E., 57
1966 Butler, Charles R., Jr., 112
1971 Milling, Bert W., Jr., 112
1971 Smith, C. Lynwood, Jr., 109
1975 Bruggink, Eric G., 9
1975 Coody, Charles S., 106
1975 Shulman, William S., 113
1976 Hatten, James N., 206
1976 Watkins, W. Keith, 105
1976 Welch, Samuel Henry, COL, 536
1979 Putnam, Terry Michael, 109
1980 Steele, William H., 111
1980 Stuart, Lyn, 533
1983 Peeler, David R., 111
1983 Watson, Ann Morris, 108
1984 Coogler, L. Scott, 108
1984 Kellum, J. Elizabeth "Beth", 536
1985 Fisher, Marilyn, 112
1985 Gladden, Lesley, 110
1985 Pearson, Anne McVay, 537
1987 Smith, Michael A., 112
1987 Youngpeter, Laura L., 112
1988 Bivins, Sonja Faye, 112
1988 Corbett, James Thomas, 110
1989 Williamson, Ruth, 99
1990 Powers, Susan, 113
1992 Cornelius, Staci G., 110
1993 Hivner, James M., 779
1993 Moore, Terry A., 535
1994 Burke, Liles C., 537
1994 Higdon, James R. "Jim", 260
1995 Nickson, Christine Brannon, 535
1996 Harden, Lisa, 106
1996 Michael, Renée, 533
1997 Coughlin, Tammy, 534
2001 Butler, Barney A., 534
2001 Nuckolls, Sonya Sheth, 211
2002 Kirk, Kelly, 536
2003 Illman, Robert, 106
2005 Hatley, Julia, 536
Granger, Trey, 105
Main, James Allen, 534
Moore, Roy S., 533
Surratt, Carol, 536
Veal, Jeremy, 534

University of Arizona
[Arizona]

1960 Baldock, Bobby R., 93
1963 Rosenblatt, Paul G., 118
1966 Teilborg, James A., 119
1967 Bury, David C., 118
1969 McNamee, Stephen M., 118
1973 Pyle, Charles R., 120
1973 Zapata, Frank R., 118
1974 Velasco, Bernardo P., 119
1975 Collins, Raner C., 115
1976 Corson, Richard, 118
1976 Gemmill, John C., 543
1976 Pelander, A. John, 541
1977 Jorgenson, Cindy K., 116
1981 Hollowell, Eileen W., 122

University of Arizona *continued*

1982 Brutinel, Robert M., 542
1983 Espinosa, Philip G., 546
1984 Vasquez, Garye L., 545
1985 Marsh, Sandra Gooding, 106
1986 Rateau, Jacqueline J., 120
1987 Duncan, David K., 119
1989 Orozco, Patricia A., 544
1990 Hartshorne, Marcia, 163
1990 Reyna, Cindy, 118
1991 Jarecki, Elizabeth J., 116
1992 Barkley, Greer, 118
1992 Clark, Melissa, 628
1992 Coates, Cynthia, 542
1993 Márquez, Rosemary, 117
1996 Kraft, Gary, 120
1997 Welles, Talbot A., 175
2004 Howell, Lisa, 545
2006 Gust, Emily, 322
2007 Buechel, David, 545

University of Arkansas at Little Rock
[Arkansas (Little Rock)]

1977 Caviness, Keith, 547
1979 Vaught, Larry D., 549
1981 Gay, Donna, 547
1986 Deere, Beth, 125
1987 Baker, Karen R., 548
1987 Carlson, Melanie, 548
1988 Jones, Michael, 128
1989 Grimes, Ann, 550
1989 Harris, Patricia, 125
1990 Pectol, Stacey, 547, 549
1991 Hickman-Tanner, Connie, 547
1991 Warner, Allison, 550
1992 Hathaway, Pam, 550
1993 Ervin, Edie, 124
1994 Raycher, Shay, 549
1994 Setser, Erin, 128
1995 Volpe, Joe, 125
1996 Sopel, Timothy D., 548
1996 Wood, Paul, 125
1999 Lee, Tina Bowers, 548
1999 Padilla, Shannon, 550
2000 Miller-Rice, Rebecca, 548
2001 Mensik, Carrie B., 550
2001 Rucker, Gwendolyn, 125
2001 Singleton, Spencer, 73
2004 Ligon, Leslie J., 127
2005 Brown, Tiffany, 72
2007 Umeda, Courtney, 547
2008 Albritton, Allison, 126, 128
2008 Lafferty, Amanda, 128

University of Arkansas, Fayetteville
[Arkansas]

1964 Barnes, Harry F., 127
1965 Dawson, Robert T., 127
1969 Glover, David M. "Mac", 549
1971 Hart, Josephine Linker, 548
1975 Danielson, Paul E., 548
1975 Wright, Susan Webber, 124
1976 Shepherd, Bobby E., 73
1978 Holmes, Paul Kinloch, III, 126
1980 Gingerich, James D., 547
1980 Hickey, Susan Owens, 127
1980 Taylor, Richard D., 126, 128

University of Arkansas, Fayetteville *continued*

1981 Gladwin, Robert J., 549
1982 Holmes, Leon, 123
1983 Whitworth, Matt J., 315
1984 Parker, Bill, 454
1985 Virden, Bart, 551
1986 Johnson, Leanne, 798
1987 Kays, David Gregory, 312
1987 Rahmeyer, Nancy Steffen, 693
1987 Smith, Lavenski R., 72
1988 Ward, Barry, 124
1989 Brooks, Timothy L., 127
1989 Moody, James Maxwell, Jr., 124
1990 Craven, Caroline M., 452
1993 Pitcock, Kathleen, 549
1994 Dean, Kala, 549
1995 Longino, Jim, 126, 129
1996 Baker, Kristine Gerhard, 123
1996 Hatfield, Stacy, 124
1998 Baldwin, Jo-Jo, 124
1998 Goodson, Courtney Hudson, 548
1999 Taylor, Jennifer Jones, 547
2000 Merrill, Michelle L., 127
2001 Bolden, Lakesha, 550
2007 Nosari-Wall, Courtney, 549
2007 Stolzer, Erika, 126, 129
2010 Smith, Jaletta, 548
Gruber, Rita Williamson, 550
Kinard, M. Michael "Mike", 550

University of Baltimore
[Baltimore]

1972 Schneider, James F., 278
1980 Rice, David E., 279
1990 Stoker, Kimberly, 278
2001 Buettner, Kathryn, 663
2003 Smalkin, Roxanne, 663

University of Buffalo
[Buffalo]

1983 Desmond, James C., 214
1986 Chapus, David P., 373
1989 Lindley, Stephen K., 724
2001 Hammond-Benz, Rayne, 373
2004 Pastrick, Michael, 716

University of California, Berkeley
[UC Berkeley]

2012 Sandberg, Cara, 157
2015 Mukerjee, Purba, 829
Major, Barbara L., 166

University of California, Davis
[UC Davis]

1973 Restani, Jane A., 12
1976 Pregerson, Dean D., 130
1977 Crozier, Steven, 493
1977 Pickering, Kristina "Kris", 702
1978 Carbullido, F. Phillip, 606
1980 Nakagawa, Mike K., 324

University of California, Davis *continued*

1981 Butz, M. Kathleen, 565
1981 Kaplan, Madeleine, 574
1982 Burton, Walter M., 813
1982 Zurzolo, Vincent P., 144
1983 Gleason, Sharon L., 113
1984 Cantil-Sakauye, Tani G., 552
1985 Stowers, Craig F., 538
1987 Mauro, Louis, 566
1990 Fong, Keith K., 156
1992 Rogers, Derek, 559
1995 Wood, Mele R., 88
1997 Chen, Laurent, 161
2003 Na, Belle S., 409
Rimel, Whitney, 152

University of California, Los Angeles
[UCLA]

1953 Nelson, Dorothy Wright, 85
1958 Epstein, Norman L., 560
1960 Keller, William D., 136
1963 Aldrich, Richard D., 560
1966 Russell, Barry, 140
1967 Miller, Jeffrey T., 164
1967 Perren, Steven Z., 563
1971 Fybel, Richard D., 571
1971 Rubin, Laurence D., 564
1972 Carter, David O., 131
1972 Turner, Paul, 561
1973 Boren, Roger Wayne, 559
1975 Anderson, Percy, 132
1975 Guilford, Andrew J., 133
1975 Jones, Robert C., 321
1975 Kozinski, Alex, 77
1976 Jury, Meredith A., 88, 142
1977 Brown, Janice Rogers, 101
1977 Collins, Audrey B., 561
1978 Albert, Theodor C., 143
1978 McManus, Michael S., 151
1979 Metcalf, David L., 218
1979 Wardlaw, Kim McLane, 79
1980 Drozd, Dale A., 147
1980 Joplin, Stephen, 568
1980 Peña, Rosendo, Jr., 573
1981 de Kelaita, Meri A., 561
1981 Winfree, Daniel E., 539
1983 Madsen, Greg, 146
1983 Thompson, David A., 571
1984 Gee, Dolly M., 134
1984 Gutierrez, Philip S., 133
1984 Riegelhaupt, Barbara, 33
1985 Bluebond, Sheri, 140
1988 Ikuta, Sandra Segal, 82
1990 Bancroft, Julianne, 571
1991 Nguyen, Jacqueline H., 83
1991 Roth, Sandy, 84
1992 Barak, Randee, 563
1992 Gleb, Gary, 561
1993 Posner, Judith, 558
1994 Pym, Sheri, 139
1994 Watford, Paul J., 83
1994 Wentz, T. J., 138
1995 Tongsuthi, Janet, 560
1996 Center, Vivian K., 132
1997 Mendoza, Salvador, Jr., 490
2002 Chaudhary, Amna Riaz, 143
2010 Montes De-Oca, Hilda, 142
2014 Fallon, Ethan P., 340
2015 Muzzio, Franco, 78
Gandhi, Vijay C. "Jay", 139

University of California, Los Angeles *continued*

Hoffman, Jamie, 77
Peralta, Adriane, 85

University of Cambridge (UK)
[Cambridge (UK)]

1981 Wallach, Evan Jonathan, 29
1997 Barnes, Donna M., 686

University of Chicago
[Chicago]

1949 Shadur, Milton I., 229
1960 Hatter, Terry J., Jr., 135
1960 McKay, Monroe G., 92
1962 Lee, William C., 239
1962 Leinenweber, Harry D., 230
1965 Rossmeissl, John A., 492
1965 Schroeder, Mary M., 85
1965 Weinberg, John L., 497
1966 Messitte, Peter J., 275
1966 Tatel, David S., 100
1967 Alexander, Donald G., 658
1968 Boggs, Danny J., 60
1969 Martin, Robert D., 507
1969 Smith, Milan D., Jr., 82
1970 Simons, Mark B., 557
1973 Abbott, Larry A., 806
1973 Easterbrook, Frank H., 68
1973 Ginsburg, Douglas H., 102
1975 Brown, Geraldine Soat, 231
1975 Stewart, Janice M., 407
1975 Wu, George H., 134
1976 Cassling, Donald R., 235
1976 Klein, Christopher M., 151
1976 Wistrich, Andrew J., 137
1977 Balmer, Thomas A. "Tom", 757
1977 Rosenthal, Lee H., 463
1978 Pollak, Cheryl L., 348
1979 Pallmeyer, Rebecca R., 224
1980 Martinez, William J., 169
1983 van Dyke Holmes, Mark, 21
1984 Edwalds, Michael, 616
1985 Kafker, Scott L., 667
1986 Ayvazian, Kim E., 586
1986 Finnegan, Sheila M., 232
1986 Recktenwald, Mark E., 607
1987 Neubauer, Lisa S., 824
1989 Himonas, Constandinos "Deno", 804
1989 Robinson, Beth, 807
1991 Eid, Allison H., 576
1991 Halfenger, G. Michael "Mike", 505
1991 Lee, Thomas Rex "Tom", 804
1996 Grewal, Paul S., 159
1997 Stasell, Wendy, 223
1998 Shah, Manish S., 228
2000 Garrett, Chris, 760
2000 Karsh-Fogel, Tamar, 231
2003 Longnecker, Lars, 533
2004 Debush, Angela Bradley "Anna", 232
2008 Tucker, Ross W., 82
2011 Maleck, Marisa C., 4
2014 Janove, Raphael, 412
2014 Kylstra, James, 226
2015 Harper, Nick, 102
Brittan, Jillisa, 66

LAW SCHOOL INDEX

University of Chicago *continued*

Jones, Warren E., 611
Morrison, Richard T., 21

University of Cincinnati
[Cincinnati]

1961 Bertelsman, William O., 255
1968 Beckwith, Sandra S., 394
1970 Ringland, Robert P., 749
1973 Rose, Thomas M., 392
1974 Markman, Stephen J., 671
1977 Barrett, Michael R., 393
1977 Vecchiarelli, Nancy A., 388
1978 Johnson, Nancy K., 466
1984 Litkovitz, Karen, 395
1985 Buffington, Carolyn, 396
1986 Walter, Lawrence S., 396
1987 Cunningham, Penelope R., 738
1988 Leonard, Margaret M. "Molly", 738
1991 Langlois, Thomas W., 738
1991 Sauter, Keith, 738
1993 Murray, Kate, 738
1994 Finn-Deluca, Valerie, 739
1994 Stier, Mary, 738
1995 Minnillo, Mary, 738
1996 Stainforth, Jennifer, 385
1997 Peters, Lora, 737
1999 Durben, Annette M., 390
1999 Schaen, Susan, 738
2001 Singletary, Jennifer D., 819
2004 Royalty, Elizabeth, 34, 286
2009 Serfozo, M. Scott, 390

University of Colorado at Boulder
[Colorado]

1968 Hicks, Larry R., 323
1969 Wherry, Robert A., Jr., 25
1974 Blackburn, Robert E., 168
1977 Coats, Nathan B., 575
1977 Kapsner, Carol Ronning, 734
1978 Bernard, Steven L., 578
1979 Banke, Kathleen M., 554
1979 Krieger, Marcia S., 168
1979 Thompson, Jon W., 543
1982 Tymkovich, Timothy M., 89, 524
1985 Aycrigg, Charlotte, 171
1985 Kelson, Jeffrey P., 168
1986 Brown, Elizabeth E., 172
1988 Harris, Thomas M., Jr., 623
1989 Tighe, David, 89
1990 Seely, Tiff, 493
1992 Whitsitt, Karla, 304
2005 Miller, Richard C., 516
2009 Gaddy, Stephanie, 171
2009 Gervey, Garen, 169
2014 Judkins, Sarah, 90
Berger, Michael H., 579

The University of Connecticut
[Connecticut]

1959 Foti, Paul M., 583
1960 Covello, Alfred Vincent, 175
1962 Mihalakos, Socrates H., 583
1968 Murtha, J. Garvan, 480
1969 West, Thomas G., 583

The University of Connecticut *continued*

1972 Eveleigh, Dennis G., 581
1974 McHargh, Kenneth S., 389
1975 Lynn, Robert J., 705
1975 Vertefeuille, Christine S., 581
1977 Lavine, Douglas S., 582
1977 Palmer, Richard N., 580
1978 Bryant, Vanessa Lynne, 174
1978 Margolis, Joan G., 176
1978 Martinez, Donna F., 176
1979 DiPentima, Alexandra D., 582
1979 Droney, Christopher F., 39
1982 Alvord, Bethany J., 582
1984 Cole, Sara B., 284
1984 Gruendel, F. Herbert, 582
1988 Almond, Lincoln D., 432
1990 Lane, Sharron B., 446
1991 Farley, Melissa A., 580, 581
1991 McDonald, Andrew J., 581
1997 Constantine, Amy, 176
1998 Adams, Patricia, 177
Keller, Christine E., 582

University of Dayton
[Dayton]

1977 Donovan, Mary E., 739
1977 Geraci, Frank Paul, Jr., 372
1979 Hall, Michael T., 739
1979 McSherry, Shauna, 739
1981 Ovington, Sharon L., 394
1981 Piper, Robin N., 749
1981 Powell, Stephen W., 750
1982 Warren, Paul R., 375
1989 McShea, Michael B., 394
1990 Shively, David A., 744
1996 Militello, Colleen R., 396
1997 Buchanan, Beth A., 396
1997 Konya-Grabill, Janice R., 395
1998 Lindsay, Karen, 739
2002 Berg, Mary, 739
2002 Winquist, Stephanie L., 395
2003 Worsham, Jacob, 739
McClanahan, Elizabeth A., 810

University of Delaware
[Delaware]

1975 Ott, Paula Francisco, 765
1981 Sweeney, Margaret Mary, 9

University of Denver
[Denver]

1959 Porfilio, John C., 92
1960 Kane, John Lawrence, 170
1968 Babcock, Lewis Thornton, 170
1971 Brooks, Sidney B., 172
1975 Tallman, Howard R., 172
1977 Collyer, Rosemary M., 510
1977 Fowlkes, John T., Jr., 447
1980 Johns, Frank G., 381
1983 Ashby, Karen M., 579
1985 Shickich, R. Michael, 508
1988 Lichtenstein, Nancy Jean, 578
1988 Shahidi, Sharon, 170
1989 Furman, David M., 578

University of Denver *continued*

1993 Cooper, Melinda S., 741
1993 Paris, Elizabeth Crewson, 21
1997 Langton, Tanya R., 320
2007 Carman, Jenny, 578
2007 Carrington, Laura, 249
2007 Hodges, Jamie L., 171
Dunn, Stephanie, 579

University of Detroit
[Detroit]

1971 Talbot, Michael J., 673
1973 Steele, John E., 185
1975 Maloney, Paul Lewis, 294, 523
1976 Majzoub, Mona K., 291
1977 Jansen, Kathleen, 674
1981 Kelly, Kirsten Frank, 676
1982 Cavanagh, Mark J., 673
1983 Cox, Sean F., 287
1987 Jacobs, Karen L., 614
1987 Zahra, Brian K., 672
1988 Kelly, Michael J., 677
1990 Murray, Christopher M., 673
2004 Humphreys, Amy, 291

University of Detroit Mercy
[Detroit Mercy]

1998 Harbus, Kimberly, 673
2006 Balow, Brian, 672
2011 Blair, Amanda, 16
2011 Wenner, Adam M., 290
Riordan, Michael J. "Mike", 677

University of Florida
[Florida]

1949 Castagna, William J., 183
1953 King, James Lawrence, 197
1956 Fay, Peter T., 98
1957 Gonzalez, Jose A., Jr., 197
1958 Hodges, William Terrell, 183
1958 Plager, S. Jay, 29
1960 Paul, Maurice M., 191
1965 Huck, Paul C., 198
1966 Presnell, Gregory A., 184
1967 Black, Susan Harrell, 99
1967 Hodges, William Terrell, 183
1970 Benton, Robert Tyrie, II, 590
1970 Lazzara, Richard Alan, 184
1971 Ray, Raymond B., 203
1972 Middlebrooks, Donald M., 194
1972 Moody, James S., Jr., 185
1972 Smoak, John Richard, Jr., 190
1973 Fawsett, Patricia C., 184
1973 Swanson, Ronald V., 591
1974 Warner, Martha C., 597
1975 Conway, Anne C., 185
1975 Crenshaw, Marva L., 593
1975 Dimitrouleas, William P., 194
1975 Merryday, Steven D., 180
1975 Ungaro, Ursula, 194
1976 Dalton, Roy Bale, Jr., 182
1976 Jenkins, Elizabeth A., 185
1976 Millican, Melissa, 185
1976 Orfinger, Richard B., 598

University of Florida *continued*

1977 Kahn, Charles J., Jr., 192
1977 Lanahan, Barbara P., 98
1977 Smith, Thomas B., 187
1978 Cohen, Jay P., 599
1978 Lanahan, Barbara P., 98
1979 Labarga, Jorge, 587
1980 Davis, Brian J., 182
1980 Evander, Kerry I., 599
1981 Honeywell, Charlene Edwards, 181
1981 Khouzam, Nelly N., 593
1982 Kennedy, Sharon, 98
1982 Silberman, Morris, 592
1982 Thomas, Bradford L., 590
1984 Jackson, Cynthia C. "Cyndi", 189
1984 Lester, Jane, 181
1984 Simmons, Joanne P., 598
1985 Klingensmith, Mark W., 598
1985 Teagle, Blan, 587
1986 Kelly, Patricia J., 593
1986 Toomey, Frances H., 592
1986 Waters, Craig, 587
1987 Makar, Scott D., 591
1990 Howard, Marcia Morales, 181
1990 Lefton, Shari, 201
1991 Martinson, Gregory, 591
1991 Mullins, Rima, 201
1991 Scales, Edwin Ayres, III, 596
1992 Dekle, Lynn, 111
1992 Walker, Mark E., 190
1993 Bilbrey, Ross L., 591
1994 Barr, David M., 598
1995 Veilleux, April, 595
1996 Barksdale, Patricia, 188
1996 Coffey, Channon, 199
1998 McCausland, Jessica W., 188
1999 Dentel, Eric, 184
1999 Hollingsworth, Jodie, 189
2000 Deeb, Jennifer M., 184
2001 Leedekerken, Kristyn, 188
2001 Weissblum, Lonn, 596
2002 Reed, Amanda, 187
2004 Williams, Jake, 597
2007 Faggion, Jennifer M., 187
2007 Freeman, Brenda, 594
2007 Lawton, Lindsey, 591
2011 Flack, Joseph, 152
2012 Raiford, Anitra, 182
Bilodeau, Christine, 185
Branyon, Steve, 185
Conner, Burton, 598
Dupee, Michael, 191
Hoffman, Leslie, 183
Kasold, Bruce E., 17
Lucas, Matthew C. "Matt", 594
Newton, Sherrill, 180

The University of Georgia
[Georgia]

1948 Shoob, Marvin H., 209
1949 Murphy, Harold L., 207
1964 Moore, William T., Jr., 213
1965 Bowen, Dudley H., Jr., 214
1970 Benham, Robert, 602
1970 Pannell, Charles A., Jr., 210
1971 Andrews, Gary Blaylock, 603
1971 Edmondson, J. L., 99

The University of Georgia *continued*

1973 Davis, Lamar W., Jr., 215
1974 Royal, C. Ashley, 204
1975 Bonapfel, Paul W., 212
1975 Carnes, Julie E., 97
1975 Harrison, Marian F., 66, 446
1977 Dalis, John S., 215
1978 Story, Richard W., 207
1978 Sullivan, Patricia, 408
1979 Caproni, Valerie E., 361
1980 King, Janet F., 210
1981 Martin, Beverly Baldwin, 97
1981 Montgomery, Pamela G., 529
1982 Hall, James Randal, 214
1982 Robinson, Michael, 209
1982 Rucker, Shelley D., 443
1983 Barnes, Anne Elizabeth, 603
1983 Cooley Smith, Christina, 603
1984 Batten, Timothy C., Sr., 208
1985 Ellington, John J., 603
1985 Johnson, Walter E., 211
1985 Land, Clay D., 204
1985 Robison, Laura, 605
1987 Jones, Steven CarMichael, 208
1988 Long, Corrie, 106
1988 Pike, Seunhee, 19, 209
1989 Walker, Linda T., 210
1990 Wood, Lisa Godbey, 213
1991 Melton, Harold D., 602
1995 Minor, Marti, 210
1997 Kirby, Mary S., 207
1998 Butler, Susan, 186
1998 May, Leigh Martin, 208
1999 Blackwell, Keith R., 602
2001 Anderson, Robert, 178
2001 Hatcher, Sally Sanders, 204
2004 Baker, R. Stan, 214
2004 Mills, Emily M., 18
2004 Varin, Julie, 218
2005 Rutledge, Vita Salvemini, 211
2006 Barnes, Francis L., III, 737
2010 Snedeker, Alice, 208
2013 Johnson, Crystal M., 361
McMillian, Carla, 605

University of Hawaii Manoa
[Hawaii]

1977 Kurren, Barry M., 217
1978 Maile, Rodney A., 607
1982 McKenna, Sabrina, 608
1991 Leonard, Katherine G., 609
1995 May, Kenneth C., 215
1997 Hattori, Judith P., 515
1999 Odani, Donna, 216
2002 Park-Hoapili, Shellie K., 607
2005 Suarez, Adrienne Iwamoto, 608
2006 Kane, Kanoelani, 217
Fujise, Alexa D.M., 609
Ginoza, Lisa M., 609

University of Houston
[Houston]

1971 Schneider, Michael H., 451
1972 Benavides, Fortunato P., 58
1973 Brown, Karen Kennedy, 468
1977 Vasquez, Juan F., 22

University of Houston *continued*

1978 Cain Crone, Marcia Ann, 450
1978 Miller, Gray Hampton, 462
1979 McClure, Ann Crawford, 797
1981 Gilmore, Vanessa D., 461
1983 Thomas, Kris, 468
1985 Ramos, Dorina, 466
1987 Benjamin, Nancy, 462
1987 Keyes, Evelyn, 789
1987 Lane, Mark, 474
1987 Sherman, JoAnne, 409
1989 Durbin, Jill A., 798
1989 Higley, Laura Carter, 789
1990 Contreras Garza, Dori, 801
1991 Jewell, Pamela, 793
1991 Kamen, Greg, 468
1992 Schwab, Karen M., 466
1999 Jones, Bryce, 323
2000 Nassar, Susan, 455
2002 McNicholas, Alexandra, 452
2006 Archer, Anna, 462
2006 Rea, Laurie, 459
2010 Miller, Ben K., 467
2013 Breaux, Natasha, 58
Benavides, Gina M., 801
Brown, Jeffrey V. "Jeff", 787
Isgur, Marvin, 468
Jennings, Terry, 789
Moseley, Bailey C., 796
Radack, Sherry, 789
Wise, Ken, 802

University of Idaho
[Idaho]

1961 Arnold, J. Kelley, 497
1961 Lodge, Edward J., 219
1968 Suko, Lonny R., 492
1969 Williams, Mikel H., 218
1970 Carpenter, Ronald R., 813
1972 Boyle, Larry M., 219
1974 Burdick, Roger S., 610
1976 Eismann, Daniel T., 610
1977 Pappas, Jim D., 88, 219
1977 Trout, Linda Copple, 610
1980 Myers, Terry L., 219
1981 Melanson, John M., 611
1985 Horton, Joel D., 611
1991 Baskin, Nancy, 219
2001 Hickok, Suzanne J., 219
2002 Hartliep, Erika, 491
2002 Vowels, Anna, 492
Gibbons, Michael P., 703
Gratton, David W., 612
Thompson, Lauri, 219

University of Illinois at Chicago
[Illinois (Chicago)]

1996 Beveridge, Charles, 233

University of Illinois at Urbana-Champaign
[Illinois]

1954 Marovich, George M., 231
1956 Baker, Harold Albert, 19, 221
1963 Altenberger, William V., 223, 238

University of Illinois at Urbana-Champaign *continued*

1964 Karmeier, Lloyd A., 614
1964 Reinhard, Philip G., 230
1967 Laro, David, 24
1968 Steigmann, Robert J., 622
1971 Black, Bruce W., 233
1972 Hull, Harry E., Jr., 565
1974 Carter, Robert L., 621
1976 Bernthal, David G., 222
1976 Kapala, Frederick J., 226
1981 Edmon, Lee Smalley, 559
1982 Doherty, J. Mark, 230
1983 Black, Anthony K., 594
1984 McDade, Mary W., 621
1989 Bruce, Colin Stirling, 220
1993 White, Lisa Holder, 623
1998 Ambrose, Russell, 295
1998 Dennor, Jill, 228
1998 Shearer, Kendra, 240
2000 Anders, Stephanie, 623
2000 Shumaker, Robert, 623
2001 Abrams, Susan, 221
2001 LaFratta, Angela K., 619
2001 Martell, Troy, 503
2004 Maurer, Paul, 226
2005 Dimitrijevic, Sonja, 617
2005 Kuenster, Christine S., 619
2007 Martinez, Antonio, 623
Bader, Douglas, 690
Dempsey, Kevin P., 245
Lynch, William P., 338

University of Indianapolis
[Indianapolis]

1968 Dickson, Brent E., 626
1975 Judson, Lilia G., 625
1979 Carusillo, Thomas, 625
1982 Bailey, L. Mark, 627
1999 Niemeyer, Cathy, 241

The University of Iowa
[Iowa]

1942 McManus, Edward J., 246
1958 Vietor, Harold D., 247
1961 Wolle, Charles R., 247
1965 Longstaff, Ronald E., 248
1966 Coughenour, John C., 496
1968 Garman, Rita B., 613
1974 Melloy, Michael J., 74
1975 Bolton, Susan R., 116
1977 Bremer, Celeste F., 248
1977 Walters, Ross A., 249
1978 Bolger, Joel H., 539
1979 Scoles, Jon S., 246
1984 Cook, Kimberly, 633
1984 Vaitheswaran, Anuradha, 634
1984 Waterman, Thomas D., 633
1986 Rush, David P., 315
1987 Johnson, Robert, 246
1988 Thumma, Samuel A., 542
1989 Williams, Annette O., 190
1990 Strand, Leonard Terry "Len", 246
1991 Mastalir, Roger, 246
1991 Tabor, Mary E., 635
1992 Fossen, Lori, 440
1992 Mastalir, Roger, 246
1993 Marvin, Daniel R., 634
1996 Rose, Stephanie M., 247
1998 Stilwell, Douglas, 74

The University of Iowa *continued*

2000 Reid, Lynn, 310
2001 Clark, Benjamin T., 314
2001 McDonald, Christopher, 635
Beneke, Ann, 247
Mayberry, Christine A., 632
Ross, Kevin G., 680

University of Kansas
[Kansas]

1958 Rushfelt, Gerald L., 252
1968 Bostwick, Donald W., 253
1970 Lungstrum, John Watson, 251
1971 Pierron, G. Joseph, Jr., 638
1973 Briscoe, Mary Beck, 89
1973 Meyers, Lawrence E., 787
1975 Green, Henry W., Jr., 638
1975 Vratil, Kathryn Hoefer, 252
1977 Buser, Michael B., 639
1977 Click, Kingsley W., 757
1977 Fillmore, Robert M., 795
1979 Dixon, Nancy Maydew, 636
1980 Karlin, Janice Miller, 94, 254
1980 Nugent, Robert E., 94, 253
1981 Arnold-Burger, Karen, 639
1981 Atcheson, G. Gordon, 639
1981 Crabtree, Daniel D., 251
1981 Robinson, Julie A., 250
1982 Leben, Steve, 639
1982 Murguia, Carlos, 250
1982 Nuss, Lawton R., 636
1983 Trump, Melanie, 94, 399
1984 Heider, Susan, 310
1984 James, Teresa J., 253
1985 Beier, Carol A., 637
1985 Lyle, Rachel, 249
1985 Murguia, Mary Helen, 83
1986 Wood, Brian P., 250
1988 Venters, Tracy, 89
1990 Ketchmark, Roseann A., 313
1994 Rempel, David J., 251
1995 Fisher, Dwight, 253
1995 Martucci, Kelly A., 251
1996 Seang, Samantha H., 94
1997 Castle, Amii, 250
1998 Andra, John, 639
1999 Locke, Lori, 316
1999 Quinlan, Allen, 251
1999 Stras, David R., 679
2000 Stegall, Caleb, 637
2002 Paretsky, Jonathan, 637
2003 O'Hara, Skyler, 249
2003 Seymour, Amy Miller, 251
2011 Clement, Gloria, 252
Gerstenlauer, James P., COL, 95

University of Kentucky
[Kentucky]

1960 Wilhoit, Henry Rupert, Jr., 256
1969 Cunningham, Bill, 642
1969 Wehrman, J. Gregory, 257
1970 Russell, Thomas B., 258
1971 Truitt, Jerry D., 257
1972 Hood, Joseph M., 256
1972 Thompson, Kelly, 644
1975 Goeke, Joseph Robert, 20
1975 Venters, Daniel J., 642

LAW SCHOOL INDEX

University of North Carolina at Chapel Hill *continued*

1968 Sentelle, David Bryan, 103
1968 Voorhees, Richard Lesley, 381
1969 Henderson, Karen LeCraft, 100
1972 Cleland, Robert Hardy, 291
1973 Hunter, Robert Neal "Bob", Jr., 731
1973 McGee, Linda M., 730
1974 Beaty, James A., Jr., 379
1974 Taylor, Carole Y., 597
1975 Africk, Lance M., 262
1975 Edmunds, Robert H., Jr., 729
1975 Owens, Susan, 814
1976 Hudson, Robin E., 729
1979 Cameron Roeder, Christie Speir, 728
1979 Stephens, Linda, 731
1983 Geer, Martha A., 731
1984 Reidinger, Martin Karl, 381
1985 Connell, John H., 730
1987 Osteen, William Lindsay, Jr., 378
1987 Whitney, Frank D., 381
1988 Martin, Mark D., 728
1990 Jackson, Barbara, 729
1990 Moyer, John R., 766
1990 Spraul, Susan M., 88
1991 Coble, Debbie Q., 382
1991 Grigg, David L., Jr., 382
1992 Davis, Tracy, 378
1993 Wilcox, Reid, 380
1998 Beyer, Laura Turner, 383
1998 James, Lena M., 380
2001 Erickson, Ian, 376
2002 Anderson, Bryan, 730
2003 Hockaday, Alyssa, 377
2003 Wiggins, Stacey, 377
2007 Nayer, Tracy, 730
2010 Maxwell, Lauren T., 438
Hammond, M. Elaine, 161
Harris, John, 100
Humrickhouse, Stephani, 378
Newby, Paul M., 729

University of North Dakota
[North Dakota]

1958 VandeWalle, Gerald W., 733
1962 Bye, Kermit Edward, 74
1966 Gierke, H. F. "Sparky", 15
1975 Sandstrom, Dale V., 733
1976 Miller, Charles S., Jr., 384
1979 Hovland, Daniel L., 384
1982 Crothers, Daniel J., 734
1984 Erickson, Ralph R., 383
1985 Miller, Penny, 733
1986 Smith, Ted, 733
1986 Vik, LaDonne R., 383
1987 Bruggman, Colette M., 564
1990 Nicolai, James E., 75
1991 Peterson, Rosanna Malouf, 490
1995 Hagburg, Michael, 733
1997 McEvers, Lisa K. Fair, 734
2000 Gumeringer, Brian, 384
2000 Hegstad, MaryBeth, 384
2008 Strankowski, Amy, 384

University of North Dakota *continued*

Hastings, Shon Kaelberer, 384
Hettich, Susan, 383

The University of Notre Dame
[Notre Dame]

1953 Leavy, Edward, 86
1966 Niemeyer, Paul V., 49
1969 Larimer, David G., 373
1972 Martone, Frederick J., 119
1973 Barnes, Michael P., 629
1973 Zive, Gregg W., 325
1974 Baughman, William H., Jr., 388
1974 Zloch, William J., 193
1975 Sammartino, Janis L., 163
1975 Williams, Ann Claire, 69
1976 Fischer, Nora Barry, 428
1977 Cotter, Patricia, 696
1977 Crone, Terry A., 628
1978 Gaughan, Patricia A., 385
1978 LaVille, Daniel M., 295
1979 Guaderrama, David Campos, 472
1979 Vázquez, Martha A., 336, 525
1979 Wilson, Charles Reginald, 96
1980 Parchem, David F., 744
1980 Springmann, Theresa L., 239
1981 Klatt, William A., 747
1984 Schroeder, Thomas David, Judge, 379
1985 Opfel, Greg, 240
1986 Gornik, Maureen Watz, 71
1986 Schmitt, Glenn R., 529
1988 Pappert, Gerald J. "Jerry", 414
1989 D'Eramo, Kimberly, 520
1990 Baker, John J., 460
1990 Kerrigan, Kathleen M. "Kathy", 21
1992 Blakey, John Robert, 228
1992 Cleveland, Margot, 70
1992 Wolford, Elizabeth A., 372
1993 Gallagher, Kari A., 70
1998 Brossart, Joseph A., 392
2000 O'Neill, Darren, 429
2002 Whitman, Lisa, 449
2005 Numbers, Robert T., II, 378
2011 Wold, Theodore, 101
2012 Gallucci, Alexander "Alex", 672
2015 Bond, Andrew, 414
Griffith, Beverly Peyton, 274
Kennedy, David, 694
Krause, Amy Ronayne, 677
Meter, Patrick Murphy, 675
Ryan, Margaret A., 15

University of Oklahoma
[Oklahoma]

1949 Panner, Owen M., 406
1956 West, Lee R., 402
1962 Dalton, A. T., 754
1963 Seay, Frank H., 398
1965 Leonard, Tim, 402
1965 Russell, David L., 402
1966 Payne, James Hardy, 397, 399

University of Oklahoma *continued*

1968 Cornish, Tom R., 94, 399
1969 Kern, Terence C. "Terry", 400
1970 Raye, Vance W., 564
1971 Joplin, Larry E., 753
1972 Friot, Stephen P., 403
1974 Lumpkin, Gary L., 756
1974 Taylor, Steven W., 752
1976 Heaton, Joe, 401
1976 Marroney, Gerald A. "Jerry", 575
1977 Cauthron, Robin J., 403
1979 Mitchell, E. Bay, III, 754
1980 Askins, Jari P., 751
1982 Colbert, Tom, 751
1982 Thompson, Judy J., 402
1982 White, Paul, 752
1983 Lewis, David B., 756
1983 Ruggiers, Christopher M., 753
1984 Buthod, Therese, 398
1984 Yeary, Janice, 403
1985 Emerson-Mitchell, Caroline, 756
1985 Willis, Lu, 755
1986 Erwin, Shon T., 403
1986 White, Ronald A., 398
1987 Anderson, Kurt, 398
1987 Rupert, Marcia, 402
1988 DeGiusti, Timothy D., 402
1988 Howard, M. Elaine, 753
1989 Lynn, Donald B., 754
1989 Seward, Gail Jacobs, 397, 399
1989 Williams, Sheila, 402
1990 Fent, Tomme J., 407
1990 Stone, Jacqueline, 402
1991 Blosser, Lendell S., 756
1991 Dupler, Bryan, 756
1991 Jones, Selden, 751
1992 Logan, Steven Paul, 117
1994 Beaty, Susan R., 754
1994 Shifflett, Kyle, 752
1996 van Egmond, Jill, 752
1997 Fagan, Lori, 401
2002 Jayne, Jodi F., 400
Hudson, Robert, 756
Johnson, Arlene, 756

University of Oregon
[Oregon]

1951 Goodwin, Alfred T., 84
1954 Marsh, Malcolm F., 406
1971 Marsh, Malcolm F., 406
1976 Sercombe, Timothy J., 759
1977 Armstrong, Rex, 759
1977 Brewer, David V., 758
1979 Aiken, Ann L., 404
1979 Dodds, Kathy, 86
1982 Acosta, John V., 408
1982 Overstreet, Karen A., 497
1982 Shinn, Carmelita Reeder, 401
1983 Clarke, Mark D., 408
1984 Newman, Howard J., 409
1990 Anderson, Mary Anne, 407
1990 Gibson, Paul, 407
1992 Brice, Lee, 409
1995 Bloomer, Danette, 404
1995 Houle, Marie, 140
1998 Smith, Julie E., 758

University of Oregon *continued*

2010 Page, Christopher, 759
2011 Webber, Tanner, 407
DeVore, Joel S., 760
Tsuchida, Brian, 496

University of Papua New Guinea
[U Papua New Guinea]

1979 Castro, Alexandro C., 735

University of Pennsylvania
[Pennsylvania]

1943 Kravitch, Phyllis A., 98
1948 Ditter, J. William, Jr., 414
1951 Shapiro, Norma L., 415
1953 O'Neill, Thomas N., Jr., 415
1956 Sloviter, Dolores K., 46
1963 Caputo, A. Richard, 425
1964 Baylson, Michael M., 418
1964 Platt, William H., 766
1965 Bartle, Harvey, III, 416
1967 Hart, Jacob P., 420
1969 Dalzell, Stewart, 416
1969 Randolph, A. Raymond, 104
1972 Fain, Mike, 739
1972 Halpern, James S., 21
1972 Holland, Randy J., 585
1972 Krauser, Peter B., 662
1975 Noble, John W., 586
1975 Pratter, Gene E. K., 411
1976 Frank, Eric L., 420
1976 McLaughlin, Mary A., 418
1976 Simandle, Jerome B., 327
1977 Diamond, Paul S., 411
1978 Robinson, Sue L., 178
1978 White, Helene Nita, 63
1979 Ahart, Alan M., 141
1979 McHugh, Gerald Austin, Jr., 413
1980 Carlson, Martin C., 425
1981 Sánchez, Juan R., 412
1983 Pesto, Keith A., 430
1985 Moore Wells, Carol Sandra, 418
1986 Cormier, Elizabeth, 42
1986 Shwartz, Patty, 45
1987 Chutkan, Tanya S., 512
1987 Gabriel, Richard Lance, 576
1988 Burroughs, Allison Dale, 282
1988 Strine, Leo E., Jr., 585
1989 Cross, Iris, 726
1989 Duncan, Thomasenia P. "Tommie", 26
1990 Herman, Nicole L., 410
1991 Brodie, Margo Kitsy, 342
1991 Contreras, Rudolph "Rudy", 511
1991 Gupta, Angela, 252
1991 Kregenow, LB, 493
1991 Wilner, Michael R., 139
1992 Johnson, Wayne, 144
1993 Beetlestone, Wendy, 414
1993 Harvey, G. Michael, 514
1993 Kallon, Abdul K., 108
1994 Gordon, Brett, 252
1998 Schupansky, Susan, 429
2001 Hoang, Hieu T., 561
2003 Bacchus, Michael, 368
2007 Sosnov, Maya, 417

University of Pennsylvania *continued*

2010 Salicrup, Alejandro, 32
2013 Bonelli, Alison, 356
2013 Morales, Francisco, 77
2015 Arrow, Sara, 412

University of Pittsburgh
[Pittsburgh]

1956 Cohill, Maurice B., Jr., 428
1958 Bloch, Alan N., 429
1967 Mitchell, Robert C., 430
1970 McGinley, Bernard L., 767
1971 Leadbetter, Bonnie Brigance, 767
1972 Friedman, Rochelle S., 768
1978 Harvey, Maureen Dunn, 764
1978 Nelson, Susan Richard, 297
1979 Bowes, Mary Jane, 764
1980 Stengel, Lawrence F., 411
1981 Hornak, Mark R., 428
1981 McCullough, Patricia A., 768
1981 Taylor, Wendy, 764
1982 Sasinoski, Lisa, 762
1982 Todd, Debra, 762
1983 Lenihan, Lisa Pupo, The Honorable, 430
1986 Vaskov, John, 761
1989 Davis, Diane L., 768
1992 Reyes, Lisa, 7
1992 Roberts, James, 767
1992 Williams, Richard T., 428
1996 Donehue, David C., 428
1996 Winters, Sean M., 762
1998 Chilcote, Damon S., 764
1998 Salzman Kurzweg, Anne, 429
1999 Moschetta, Nicole, 427
2008 Campbell, Yvonne, 423
2008 Thomas, Maribeth, 431
2009 Yuhaniak, Emily J., 763
Allen, Cheryl Lynn, 765

University of Puerto Rico
[Puerto Rico]

1960 Casellas, Salvador E., 518
1964 De Morán, Frances Ríos, 516
1966 Cerezo, Carmen Consuelo, 517
1968 Fusté, José Antonio, 516
1968 Pérez-Giménez, Juan M., 518
1970 Domínguez, Daniel R., 518
1972 García-Gregory, Jay A., 517
1975 Quiñones Alejandro, Nitza I., 413
1976 Lamoutte, Enrique S., 34, 519
1979 Delgado Hernández, Pedro A., 518
1989 Santiago-Velez, Ramon F., 517
2000 Garcia-Wirshing, Eileen, 516
Martinez Torres, Rafael L., 770
Mas, Madeline, 34, 519
Matta Hon, Liana Fiol, 770
Rodriguez Rodriguez, Anabelle, 770
Velez-Rive, Camille L., 518

University of Puget Sound
[U Puget Sound]

1974 Beistline, Ralph R., 113
1975 Snyder, Paul B., 497
1976 Johnson, Charles W., 813
1982 Neel, Mary S., 815
1984 Swanson, Mark, 815
1985 Breitenbach, Carole, 816
1985 Lehman, Frank, 815
1985 Schmidt, Eric, 816
1990 Bruggeman, Clair J., 817

University of Richmond
[Richmond]

1959 Stamp, Frederick P., Jr., 499
1965 Koontz, Lawrence L., Jr., 810
1965 Schlesinger, Harvey E., 183
1981 Warren, Gail, 809
1983 Harrington, Patricia L., 809
1985 Black, Paul M., 490
1985 Tucker, John T., III, 811
1986 Macon, Edward M., 809
2002 Berry, Heather, 487
2002 Hoppe, Joel, 489
2009 Jones, Scott, 489
Vu, Tu-Quynh N., 598

University of San Diego
[San Diego]

1965 Whelan, Thomas J., 165
1967 Nares, Gilbert, 567
1972 Ruvolo, Ignazio J., 556
1974 Benke, Patricia D., 567
1975 Aronson, Richard M., 571
1975 Riblet, Robin L., 141
1979 Burns, Larry Alan, 162
1979 Leen, Peggy A., 323
1979 Ludington, Thomas L., 288
1982 Stevenson, James, 724
1985 Bothamley, William M., 567
1985 Parraguirre, Ronald, 703
1985 Schwartz, Mark, 166
1989 McAuliffe, Barbara A., 149
1993 Kunkel, Daniel James, 608
1994 Six, Marjeta D., 162
1995 Rein, Randy, 165
1999 Cotner, Christine, 166
2003 Sullivan, Monica, 161
2005 Amin, Marsha, 568
2012 Lou, Jihong, 28
Horie, Dustin H., 608

University of San Francisco
[U San Francisco]

1964 Ross, Herbert A., 115
1965 Richman, James A., 555
1967 Chin, Ming W., 553
1972 McGuiness, William R., 555
1973 Theis, Mary Jane, 614
1974 Foley, Daniel R., 609
1974 Jones, Barbara J. R., 557
1975 DeCicco, William A. "Bill", 14
1977 Armstrong, Saundra Brown, 156
1978 James, Maria-Elena, 158
1980 Jenkins, Martin J., 556

University of San Francisco *continued*

1996 Wallace, Kirsten, 218
1999 McClelland, Danika, 149
Rivera, Maria P., 557

University of South Carolina
[South Carolina]

1946 Blatt, Sol, Jr., 435
1954 Anderson, G. Ross, Jr., 435
1956 Houck, C. Weston, 435
1967 Cox, Walter T., III, 15
1968 Duffy, Patrick Michael, 435
1968 Pleicones, Costa M., 773
1968 Toal, Jean Hoefer, 773
1970 Herlong, Henry M., Jr., 434
1970 McCullough, J. Douglas, 732
1971 Short, Paul E., Jr., 775
1973 Floyd, Henry F., 52
1973 Traxler, William B., Jr., 49, 522
1975 Huff, Thomas E., 774
1975 Norton, David C., 433
1976 Buchanan, Robert L., Jr., 437
1977 Duffey, William S., Jr., 207
1977 Hearn, Kaye G., 774
1978 Shedd, Dennis W., 51
1979 Beatty, Donald W., 774
1979 Shearouse, Daniel E., 773
1980 Ferguson, Aline, 775
1980 Marchant, Bristow, 436
1980 Wooten, Terry L., 433
1982 Harwell, Robert Bryan, 433
1982 Kittredge, John W., 774
1982 Williams, H. Bruce, 775
1983 Wells, Mary, 433
1983 Widener, Susan, 774
1984 Lewis, Mary Geiger, 434
1986 Cain, Timothy M., 434
1986 Geathers, John D., 775
1986 Leaman, Lucia Hoefer, 774
1986 Secreast-Doll, Rita, 436
1986 Thomas, Paula H., 775
1988 Emanuel, Tony, 51
1988 Few, John C., 774
1988 Vroegop, Virginia, 436
1989 Hendrix, Amy C., 49
1990 Dunn, Leslie S., 625
1990 Hendricks, Bruce H., 434
1990 Lawson, Lisa A., 437
1990 McDonald, Kevin F., 437
1991 Childs, J. Michelle, 433
1991 Morgan, Deborah P., 436
1992 Alexander, Melissa Jones, 436
1992 Davis, Dodd M., 49
1992 Frierson, Rosalyn Woodson, 773
1992 Loggins, Thorne B., 49
1992 Rogers, Thomas E., III, 437
1994 Barber, Jeanette F., 775
1994 Tidwell, Robin Reid, 53
1995 Fitzer, Matthew, 49
1996 Madsen, Jennifer Bush, 774
1999 Douglas, Vincent, 434
1999 Nye, Stephanie A., 773
2000 West, Kaymani, 437
2001 Wedge, Douglas E., 110
2005 Harrill, Emily Deck, 436
2008 Arnold, Tyler, 696
2008 Harper, John P., III, 214

University of South Carolina *continued*

2010 deHoll, Andrew R., 435
Anderson, Joseph F., Jr., 436
Brewer, Joe, 434
Konduros, Aphrodite K., 775
Sargent, Pamela Meade, 489

University of South Dakota
[South Dakota]

1953 Jones, John B., 439
1962 Wollman, Roger L., 72
1965 Piersol, Lawrence L., 439
1975 Gilbertson, David, 777
1975 Severson, Glen A., 777
1975 Zinter, Steven L., 777
1977 Hecht, Daryl L., 633
1977 Viken, Jeffrey L., 438
1977 Wilbur, Lori S., 778
1981 Stickney, Paul, 458

University of Southern California
[USC]

1956 Nelson, Dorothy Wright, 85
1962 Fernandez, Ferdinand Francis, 86
1962 Neiter, Richard M., 143
1965 Huffman, Richard D., 567
1967 Cohen, Mary Ann, 25
1967 Whyte, Ronald M., 156
1971 Cooke, John S., 528
1972 Miller, Robert, 562
1974 King, George H., 129
1975 Manella, Nora, 561
1981 Mann, Margaret M., 167
1983 Michael, Terrence L., 94, 401
1984 Doherty, Sue, 141
1985 Bauer, Catherine E., 143
1985 Brand, Julia W., 145
1985 Oberto, Sheila K., 150
1987 Huffman, Julie, 563
1989 Quinn, Jean Ann, 758
1995 Hall, Bruce, 137
2001 Stevenson, Sarah, 88
2002 Lippsmith, Mary Beth, 85

University of Tennessee at Knoxville
[Tennessee]

1960 Jordan, Robert Leon, 442
1963 Susano, Charles D., Jr., 780
1969 Scudder, Henry J., 723
1973 Witt, James Curwood, Jr., 782
1975 Breen, J. Daniel, 447
1976 Reaves, Richard D. "Rich", 601
1977 Shirley, C. Clifford, Jr., 442
1977 Smith, John Marshall, 442
1977 Thomas, D. Kelly, Jr., 782
1978 Lee, Sharon Gail, 779
1978 Swiney, D. Michael, 780
1979 Knowles, E. Clifton, 445
1979 Reeves, Pamela L., 441
1980 Greer, J. Ronnie, 441
1980 Parsons, Marcia Phillips, 443
1980 Sullivan, Carol, 441
1980 Tate, Deborah Taylor, 779

University of Tennessee at Knoxville *continued*

1981 Mattice, Harry S., Jr., 441
1982 Campbell, Todd J., 444
1983 Frierson, Thomas R. "Skip", 780
1986 Proctor, R. David, 26, 108
1987 Campbell, Marvin L., 443
1990 Bass, Teresa B., 696
1991 Beasley, Cheri, 729
1992 Rippy, Lisa A., 779
1995 Gensheimer, Michelle, 442, 443
1995 Gerdeman, Matthew "Matt", 780
1996 McMullen, Camille R., 784
1997 Ferrell, Pat, 441
1998 May, Kayla D., 267
1998 Watson, Jason, 446
1999 Ritter, Lori, 381
2000 Easley, Brian R., 442
2000 Long, Carol Anne, 782
2000 Paul, Amy, 782
2001 Calhoun, Paula L., 782
2001 Dral, Christy H., 291
2001 Graves, Christy, 783
2001 Hammond, Renee, 782
2008 McClanahan, Leah, 442, 443
2010 Woods, William "Will", 445
Cruze, Lois, 448
Inman, Dennis H., 442
McMillian, Robin, 780
Ogle, Norma McGee, 782

University of Texas at Austin
[Texas]

1950 Robinson, Mary Lou, 455
1956 McBryde, John H., 455
1958 Hudspeth, Harry Lee, 472
1961 Kazen, George P., 464
1961 Werlein, Ewing, Jr., 464
1962 Parker, James A., 338
1963 Nowlin, James Robertson, 472
1963 Sparks, Sam, 469
1966 Gardner, Anne, 791
1966 Hughes, Lynn Nettleton, 462
1966 Meier, William C. "Bill", 791
1967 Keasler, Michael, 788
1967 Lamberth, Royce C., 513
1968 Head, Hayden, 464
1969 Lacy, Elizabeth B., 810
1969 Lake, Sim, 462
1969 Yeakel, Lee, 471
1971 Briones, David, 472
1972 Harmon, Melinda, 462
1972 Prado, Edward Charles, 55
1972 Watt, Joseph M., 752
1973 Bryson, William C., 31
1974 Jones, Edith Hollan, 54
1975 Granade, Callie V. S. "Ginny", 111
1975 Morriss, Josh R., III, 796
1975 Southwick, Leslie H., 56
1975 Wood, Diane Pamela, 67, 523
1976 Solis, Jorge A., 454
1977 Jamison, Martha Hill, 802
1977 King, Ronald B., 475
1977 Lindsay, Sam A., 455
1978 Eick, Charles F., 137

University of Texas at Austin *continued*

1978 Garcia, Orlando L., 470
1979 Clark, Ron, 450
1980 Horton, Hollis, 798
1980 Livingston, Terrie, 790
1981 Brown, Harvey G., 790
1981 Christopher, Tracy, 802
1982 Booras, Laurie A., 579
1982 Lehrmann, Debra H., 786
1982 Saia, Leslie A., 798
1984 Crabb, Elizabeth A. "Beth", 793
1984 McLaughlin, Minerva, 797
1985 Austin, Andrew W., 473
1985 Caldwell, Brian D., 254
1986 Moses, Alia, 470
1987 Alvarez, Patricia O'Connell, 793
1987 Crane, Randy, 461
1987 McHaney, Sarah, 475
1987 Rodriguez, Xavier, 470
1988 Pitman, Robert Lee, 472
1988 Solis, Aries, 797
1989 Alcala, Elsa, 788
1989 Alvarez, Micaela, 460
1989 Jernigan, Stacey G. C., 460
1989 Olvera, Jose Rolando, Jr., 464
1989 Snyder, Ellen C., 338
1990 Gsanger, Cecile Foy, 800
1990 Kring, Linda, 467
1990 Wille, Leslie, 473
1991 Bennett, Alfred H., 463
1991 Gonzales Ramos, Nelva, 463
1991 Rogers, Yvonne Gonzalez, 154
1993 Carmona, Katie, 471
1994 Polinard, Cindy, 801
1995 Durst, Desiree, 473
1995 Marroquin, Terri L., 473
1996 Laux, Lauren, 471
1996 Strubel Wiele, Sandy, 474
1997 Saldaña, Diana, 463
1999 Huddle, Rebeca, 790
1999 Orgeron, Jennifer, 452
2000 Dart, Jessica, 467
2002 Dankof, Elizabeth, 148
2003 Gilman, Tyler, 316, 318
2003 Holmes, Heather, 786
2004 Rollans, Ryan, 792
2007 Secco, Marisa, 785
2008 Yunes, Yamil Farid, 463
2014 Quinn, Julia, 514
2015 Foster, Michael, 58
Bland, Jane, 789
Costa, Gregg Jeffrey, 57
Hughes, Steve, 798
Massengale, Michael C., 790
Tagle, Hilda G., 465

University of the Pacific
[U Pacific]

2007 Pitcher, Jinnifer D., 82

The University of Toledo
[Toledo]

1973 Lance, Alan G., Sr., 17
1976 Singer, Arlene, 743
1976 Zouhary, Jack, 386
1980 Aemmer, David W., 89
1980 Kennedy, Roderick T., 713

The University of Toledo *continued*

1980 Preston, Vernon L., 740
1980 Schmehl, Jeffrey L., 413
1981 Osowik, Thomas J., 743
1982 Mullins, C. Ray, 212
1985 Burns, Michelle H., 120
1988 Henderson, Philip G., 295
1988 Kelly, Gregory J., 187
1988 Miller, Joann K., 743
1989 Garcia-Feehan, Catherine, 387
1989 Sullivan, Mary Anne, 743
1990 Coombs, Marie, 290
1990 Roehrig, Molly Jo, 291
1992 Knepp, James R., II, 389
1993 Hensal, Jennifer L., 746
1995 Berman, Neil, 397
1995 Waymire, Douglas, 739
1996 Bell, Tamara, 740
1996 Jones, Richard B., 396
1997 Smith, Patrick F., 394
1998 Kuchmay, Lori, 239
2001 Coriden, Ann C., 629
2001 Fellhauer, Amy, 489
Delaney, Patricia A., 742
Dinsmore, Mark J., 244
Kirby, JoAnne, 743
Lanzinger, Judith Ann, 737
Yarbrough, Stephen A., 743

University of Tulsa
[Tulsa]

1968 Rapp, Keith, 754
1973 Wiseman, Jane P., 753
1977 McCarthy, F. H., 400
1977 Reif, John F., 751
1980 Cullem, Catherine, 753
1980 Smith, Clancy, 755
1981 Cleary, Paul J., 400
1981 Dowdell, John E., 400
1982 Harlton, Hilda, 751
1985 Cunningham, Robert M., 755
1985 Keaney, Patrick, 397
1986 Schneider, Ann Makela, 400
1987 Paris, Elizabeth Crewson, 21
1988 Jarvis, Sandra, 754
1988 Smith, Allen, 755
1990 Eden, Barbara J., 401
1992 Bell, Robert Dick, 754
1995 Goodell, Tammie, 753
2005 Haugen, Nicholas, 399
Goree, Brian, 755

University of Utah
[Utah]

1952 Jenkins, Bruce S., 476
1960 Anderson, Stephen H., 92
1960 Sam, David, 477
1967 Kimball, Dale A., 477
1971 Dawson, Kent J., 323
1974 Thurman, William T., 94, 479
1975 Rice, Nancy E., 575
1975 Stewart, Ted, 478
1976 Braithwaite, Robert T., 478
1977 Wells, Brooke C., 478
1979 Campbell, David G., 116
1979 Siddoway, Laurel H., 817
1980 Mosier, R. Kimball, 479

University of Utah *continued*

1982 McHugh, Carolyn B., 92
1982 Thompson, Karen S., 804
1983 Straley, M. John, 479
1988 Mattsson, Michele, 804
1992 Mills, Carol Keating, 219
1993 Morgan, Anne, 477
1993 Ross, Del J., 93
1994 Adams, Alison Johnson, 477
1995 Christiansen, Michele M., 805
1995 Inskeep Hindley, Susie, 477
1998 Westby, Mary E., 804
2002 Roberts, Jennifer, 791
2005 Copeland, Thomas, 478
2011 Lauter, Cindy, 477
Hayman, Bret, 804
Waddoups, Clark, 476

The University of Vermont
[Vermont]

1980 Smith, Nancy E., 723
1996 Basso, Andrea, 373
2004 Taylor, Andrew D., III, 382

University of Virginia
[Virginia]

1953 Doumar, Robert George, 484
1954 Shapero, Walter, 293
1955 Stanton, Louis L., 364
1960 Shiff, Alan H. W., 177
1961 Straub, Chester J., 41
1963 Lovegreen, Robert W., 432
1963 Sharp, George Kendall, 183
1963 Siler, Eugene E., Jr., 65
1965 Jones, James P., 488
1965 Wiese, John P., 10
1967 Motz, J. Frederick, 276
1968 Motz, Diana Gribbon, 50
1968 Ripple, Kenneth F., 70
1969 Welsh, James G., 489
1970 Teel, S. Martin, Jr., 515
1971 Amon, Carol Bagley, 340
1972 Schwab, Arthur J., 427
1972 Wilkinson, J. Harvie, III, 49
1973 Jackson, Raymond A., 481
1973 Jones, Thomas Rawles, Jr., 486
1974 Trenga, Anthony John, 483
1975 Gibbons, Julia Smith, 61
1975 Mayer, Robert G., 487
1976 Baker, David A., 186
1976 Gibney, John A., Jr., 483
1976 Lemons, Donald W., 809
1976 Salter, Vance E., 595
1977 Agee, G. Steven, 51
1977 Cooke, John S., 528
1977 Hopkins, Virginia Emerson, 108
1977 Kemp, Terence P., 394
1977 Smith, Stephen Wm., 467
1977 St. John, Stephen C., 487
1980 Gale, Joseph H., 20
1980 Gleeson, John, 340
1981 Browning, James O., 337
1981 Connor, Patricia S., 48
1981 Guyton, H. Bruce, 443
1981 Murdock, Glenn, 534
1981 Urbanski, Michael F., 488
1982 Cornish, Tom R., 94, 399

University of Virginia *continued*

1982 Mills, Richard, 221
1982 Powell, Cleo Elaine, 810
1982 Surrick, R. Barclay, 418
1983 Conrad, Robert J., Jr., 381, 525
1983 Reavley, Thomas M., 57
1984 Black, Susan Harrell, 99
1984 Dennis, James L., 55
1984 Stapleton, Walter K., 46
1984 Torruella, Juan R., 31
1985 Griffith, Thomas B., 101
1985 Ohlson, Kevin A., 15
1986 Beales, Randolph A., 811
1986 Bowman, Pasco M., II, 74
1986 Goodwyn, S. Bernard, 809
1986 Holloman, Deborah, 486
1986 Norris, Alan E., 64
1987 Keesler, David C., 382
1988 Babcock, Lewis Thornton, 170
1988 Batchelder, Alice M., 60
1988 DalleMura, Steven L., 809
1988 Doumar, Robert George, 484
1988 Flanagan, Louise W., 376
1988 Moon, Norman K., 489
1988 Reid, Michael, 483
1988 Rogers, Judith W., 100
1989 Reeves, Carlton W., 305
1989 Robertson, Karen, 170
1990 Benham, Robert, 602
1990 Briscoe, Mary Beck, 89
1990 Edmondson, J. L., 99
1990 Hunt, Willis B., Jr., 209
1990 Lipez, Kermit V., 33
1991 Wolski, Victor J., 8
1992 Grossman, Alison E., 513
1992 Hughes, Lynn Nettleton, 462
1992 Keenan, Barbara Milano, 52
1992 Lacy, Elizabeth B., 810
1992 O'Scannlain, Diarmuid F., 78
1993 Harris, Scott S., 3
1993 Jenkins, Cheryl, 211
1993 Jordan, Daniel Porter, III, 304
1994 Pugh, Cary Douglas, 22
1995 Baker, John G., 627
1995 Benton, Duane, 73
1995 Hollenhorst, Thomas E., 569
1995 Morse, Julia, 87
1995 Shaw, Stephen R., 740
1995 Siler, Eugene E., Jr., 65
1995 Valentine, Jeanette D., 307, 308
1995 Warner, Martha C., 597
1995 Wynn, James Andrew, Jr., 52
1996 Knoll, Jeannette Theriot, 647
1996 Saltzman, Deborah J., 143
1996 Weigle, Charles H., 205
1997 Mehta, Amit Priyavadan, 512
1998 Altenbernd, Chris W., 592
1998 Clifford, Robert W., 659
1998 Cone, Charles Tyler, 345
1998 Cooks, Sylvia R., 652
1998 Evans, Orinda D., 209
1998 Faber, David A., 502
1998 Hawkins, Michael Daly, 87
1998 Hearn, Kaye G., 774
1998 Holland, Randy J., 585
1998 Kinkeade, Ed, 456
1998 Martin, Mark D., 728

University of Virginia *continued*

1998 Morgan, Henry Coke, Jr., 484
1998 Pelander, A. John, 541
1998 Rylaarsdam, William F., 570
1998 Shelby, Robert J., 476
2000 Reddy, Kenya J., 181
2001 Amy, Marc T., 653
2001 Antoon, John, II, 184
2001 Casanueva, Darryl C., 593
2001 McDonald, Alex C., 568
2001 Mills, Michael P., 302
2001 Moore, William T., Jr., 213
2001 Wolf, James R., 590
2001 Yeakel, Lee, 471
2002 Trueblood, Amy, 308
2004 Aronson, Richard M., 571
2004 Barnes, Anne Elizabeth, 603
2004 Beier, Carol A., 637
2004 Callahan, Consuelo Maria, 81
2004 Edmunds, Robert H., Jr., 729
2004 Hecht, Daryl L., 633
2004 Kern, Terence C. "Terry", 400
2004 Love, Terri F., 654
2004 Middlebrooks, Donald M., 194
2004 Miller, M. Yvette, 604
2004 Moore, Eileen C., 571
2004 Ruvolo, Ignazio J., 556
2004 Saylor, Thomas G., 761
2004 Shaw, Greg, 534
2004 Todd, Debra, 762
2004 Tyson, John Marsh, 732
2004 Worthen, James T., 800
2005 Johnson, Kristin, 488
2005 McKinley, James, 489
2008 Welti, Tyler, 82
2010 Phillips, Cathleen, 241
2010 Schoen, Chris B., 434
2012 Rowen, Zach, 414
2013 Bascom, Galen B., 5
2013 Urick, Jonathan D., 4
2014 Kilberg, Andrew, 4
2014 Tyson, Joseph B. "Ben", III, 3
2015 Baasch, Ryan, 100
Bassett, James P. "Jim", 706
Beach, Robert E., Jr., 582
Chandler, David A., 684
Easterly, Catharine Friend "Kate", 829
Hood, William W., III, 576
Laster, J. Travis, 586
Rucker, Robert D., 626
Schneider, Michael H., 451
Smith, Anna, 186
Wagner, Jessica, 55

University of Washington
[U Washington]

1950 McGovern, Walter T., 494
1953 Dimmick, Carolyn R., 495
1958 Bryan, Robert J., 495
1958 Farris, Jerome, 85
1962 Nielsen, Wm. Fremming, 491
1968 Van Sickle, Fred L., 491
1972 Brandt, Philip H., 152, 498
1973 Cox, Ronald E., 816
1975 Jones, Richard A., 494
1976 Leach, J. Robert, 815

University of Washington *continued*

1977 Schindler, Ann, 815
1978 Lasnik, Robert S., 493
1979 Appelwick, Marlin J., 816
1980 Martinez, Ricardo S., 494
1982 Becker, Mary Kay, 816
1982 Dwyer, Stephen J., 815
1982 Korsmo, Kevin M., 818
1983 Barreca, Marc, 498
1983 Bastian, Stanley Allen, 490
1986 Hernandez, Marco A., 405
1987 Dore, Timothy W., 498
1987 Holt, Kerry, 498
1991 Salway, Garon Dee, 322
1992 Kim, Kathryn, 495
1994 Marlow, Elena, 200
1995 Miyashiro, Carol M., 215
2006 Foe, Heather, 491
2008 Lennon, Erin L., 814
2014 Watts, Lauren, 83
Beeler, Laurel, 158
Worswick, Lisa, 817

University of Wisconsin-Madison
[Wisconsin]

1962 Crabb, Barbara B., 506
1966 Randa, Rudolph T., 503
1967 Goodstein, Aaron E., 505
1968 Prosser, David T., 822
1971 Hines, Geraldine S., 667
1973 Sherman, Gary E., 825
1975 Papak, Paul J., 408
1976 Bradley, Ann Walsh, 822
1978 Mathy, Pamela Ann, 473
1978 Strombom, Karen L., 496
1980 Furay, Catherine J., 507
1980 Roggensack, Patience Drake, 821
1982 Gegios, Sandra R., 503
1982 Stark, Lisa Kay, 824
1983 Lundsten, Paul, 825
1983 Sannes, Brenda K., 352
1983 Sobel, Sylvan A., 528
1984 Conley, William M., 506
1985 Higginbotham, Paul B., 825
1986 Williams, Sandra B., 598
1987 Reilly, Paul F., 824
1988 Kloppenburg, JoAnne F., 825
1988 Quentel, Patty, 435
1989 Ryan, Clare T., 824
1991 Watson, Marisa J. G., 42
1992 O'Driscoll, Kelly Kinzel, 506
1994 Gundrum, Mark, 824
1994 Harms, Joan, 504
1995 Nelson, Ingrid Anna, 821
1995 Plum, Christina, 823
1998 Peterson, James D., 506
1999 Quinata, Jeanne G., 515
2000 Lucchesi, Anthony J., 825
2001 Monks, Jeffrey, 506
2002 Waranka, Emily, 823
2003 Ashton, Michael, 503
2003 Kinnunen, Erik, 824
2008 Marsch, Jennifer, 823
2011 Holt, Cora, 27
Beckering, Jane M., 676
Brennan, Kitty, 823

University of Wyoming
[Wyoming]

1964 Johnson, Alan B., 507
1972 Murphy, Michael R., 93
1972 O'Brien, Terrence L., 94
1974 Hill, William U., 827
1977 Burke, E. James, 827
1978 Kautz, Keith G., 827
1980 Freudenthal, Nancy D., 507
1984 Harris, Edward W., 827
1984 Veal, Sherrill, 507
1987 Phillips, Gregory Alan, 92
1988 Bach, Jack, 685
1988 Heller, Niki, 89
1992 Golden, Jennifer, 827
1992 Skavdahl, Scott W., 507
1993 Anderson, Kelley, 508
Davis, Michael K., 827
Fox, Catherine M. "Kate", 827

Valparaiso University
[Valparaiso]

1963 Lindquist, Kent, 242
1973 Hoekstra, Joel P., 674
1973 Rodovich, Andrew P., 241
1973 Sawyer, David H., 673
1975 Hussmann, William G., Jr., 244
1976 Nuechterlein, Christopher A., 240
1976 Rucker, Robert D., 626
1980 Vaidik, Nancy H., 630
1981 DeGuilio, Jon E., 239
1982 Genakos, Anthony, 444
1982 Sawyer, William R., 107
1983 Marshall, Patricia, 245
1983 Potts, Sheri, 238
1988 Campbell, Ingrid A., 249
1989 Baker, Tim A., 244
1989 Reed, Wanda F., 239
1993 Aker, Erica E., 631
1994 Freitag, Jason, 614
1996 Buitendorp, Rita, 294
1998 Doden, Maci, 239
1998 Shead, Suzanne "Sue", 238
2002 Ortiz, Jennifer, 240
2003 Goffette, Erin, 240
2005 Berta, Chanda J., 239
Graham, Jeffrey J., 245

Vanderbilt University
[Vanderbilt]

1960 Merritt, Gilbert S., 64
1960 Nixon, John T., 445
1965 Brown, Joe B., 445
1965 Wilson, Billy Roy, 124
1966 Musmanno, John L., 766
1968 Carter, William B. Mitchell, 354
1968 Daughtrey, Martha Craig, 65
1968 Glenn, Alan E., 783
1969 Phillips, Thomas W., 442
1971 Vinson, Roger, 191
1973 Bryant, John S., 446
1973 Haynes, William J., Jr., 445
1973 Mahan, James C., 321
1973 Woodward, Patrick L., 663
1974 Campbell, James T., 797
1974 McCalla, Jon P., 448
1976 Lundin, Keith M., 446
1976 Smith, Mary Mann, 176

LAW SCHOOL INDEX

Vanderbilt University *continued*

1976 Trauger, Aleta Arthur, 444
1977 Dinkins, Richard H., 781
1978 Stranch, Jane Branstetter, 63
1981 Varlan, Thomas A., 441
1986 Bivins, Jeffrey S., 779
1987 Yandle, Staci Michelle, 236
1988 Finn, Robert J., 326
1991 Wooten, McKinley, Jr., 728
1993 Sharp, Kevin Hunter, 444
1995 Hartzell, Page, 225
1995 Miller, Brian Stacy, 123
2002 Holt, Shannon, 109
2002 Miranda, Mary Ann, 256
2003 Taaffe, Laura, 108, 109
2006 Small, Allison M., 455
2010 Giani, Jamie, 127
Ashford, Tamara W., 22
Clark, Cornelia A., 779
Parker, Tom, 533
Rose, Jeff L., 792

Ventura College
[Ventura]

1974 Harrell, David, 563

Vermont Law School
[Vermont Law]

1987 Young, Shari, 806
1993 Kehoe, J. Michael, 373
1998 Killigrew, Patricia A., 177
2001 Mortier, Tiffany, 577

Villanova University
[Villanova]

1965 Arcara, Richard J., 374
1971 Colins, James Gardner, 768
1971 Strawbridge, David R., 419
1972 Cooper, Mary L., 332
1973 Rendell, Marjorie O., 26, 48
1974 Carluzzo, Lewis R., 25
1977 Gantman, Susan Peikes, 763
1979 Carey, Kevin J., 179
1983 Seitz, Collins J. "C.J.", 585
1984 Kohler, Pauline Felice, 421
1986 Hopkins, Susan, 599
1986 Novak, David J., 485
1987 Kearney, Mark A., 414
1988 Marchant, Jeffrey, 421
1992 Sheehan, Timothy J., 411
1996 Bensley, Beth Cannon, 418
1998 Pettit, Lisa N., 768
2003 Keeler, Paul, 423
2004 Henderson, Kimberly N., 418
2014 Lagreca, Megan, 332
Fitzgerald, James J., III, 766
McNabb, Kathleen, 415

Wake Forest University
[Wake Forest]

1958 Britt, W. Earl, 377
1969 Tilley, Norwood Carlton "Woody", Jr., 379
1970 Howard, Malcolm J., 377
1980 Aron, Catharine R., 380
1983 Hoke, David F., 728
1984 Whitley, J. Craig, 383
1986 Dillon, Elizabeth K., 488

Wake Forest University *continued*

1988 Spivey, Gregory O., 380
1992 White, Mimi, 643
1999 Henson, Amy M., 252
2002 Dietz, Richard, 732
2003 Stark, Jeanette M., 380
2003 Willis, Jennifer, 488
2005 Carr, Matthew, 482
2006 Bennett, Allison L., 380
2010 Dildine, Laura, 379
2011 Byrne, Cynthia, 487

Washburn University of Topeka
[Washburn]

1952 Crow, Sam A., 251
1974 Ross, Richard D., 636, 637
1975 Hill, Stephen D., 638
1976 Marten, J. Thomas "Tom", 250
1978 Biles, William Daniel, 637
1978 Dow, Dennis R., 316
1979 Malone, Thomas E., 638
1980 Gale, Kenneth G., 252
1980 Johnson, Lee Alan, 637
1980 Luckert, Marla J., 636
1980 Roberts, Keith L., 14
1982 Schroeder, Kim R., 640
1984 Abbott, Jana D., 253
1984 Bruns, David E., 640
1984 Rosen, Eric S., 637
1985 Lowry, Lauren M., 251
1985 Melgren, Eric F., 251
1985 Moritz, Nancy L., 92
1991 Matthews, Mary, 252
1992 Birzer, Gwynne E., 253
1993 Oldham, Jason P., 636
1994 Shima, Douglas, 638
1996 Verna, Kristi N., 458
1998 Powell, Charisse M., 639
2005 McDowell, Anna, 338
2008 Hesler, Brooke, 252
Cocking, Jennifer Marie, 636
Gannon, James M., 639
Kean, Nicole, 94
Powell, Anthony, 640

Washington and Lee University
[Washington and Lee]

1952 Kiser, Jackson L., 488
1960 Morgan, Henry Coke, Jr., 484
1966 Bumgardner, Rudolph, III, 812
1967 Bacigal, Ronald J. "Ron", 811
1967 Payne, Robert E., 485
1978 Kayuha, Bruce A., 819
1981 Brown, Trish M., 409
1984 Nelson, Cynthia, 820
1985 Johnson, William P., 337
1988 Davis, Mark S., 482
1990 Connolly, Walter A., III, 259
1993 Przirembel, Dawn A., 774
2007 Clifton, Abby, 279
2007 McCook, Jill E., 441
2008 Seliber, Megan, 168
2013 Nunes, Steven, 161
2014 Wagner, Christopher D., 242

Washington and Lee University *continued*

Connelly, Rebecca B., 489
Lord, K. Lorraine "Lori", 809

Washington College of Law of the American University
[Washington College of Law]

1956 Nebeker, Frank Q., 830
1966 Hilton, Claude M., 483
1967 King, Warren R., 829
1969 Barker, Sarah Evans, 243
1970 Boyle, Terrence W., 376
1973 Farrell, Michael W., 831
1974 Hudson, Henry E., 482
1974 Walton, Reggie B., 509
1975 Jones, C. Darnell, II, 412
1976 Lee, Gerald Bruce, 482
1977 Seymour, Margaret B., 436
1978 Annunziata, Rosemarie, 812
1979 Prost, Sharon, 27, 524
1980 Weinberger, Robin, 71
1985 Snyderman, Lynn, 762
1989 Newman, Michael J., 395
1993 Bartley, Margaret "Meg", 18
1994 Schroeder, Robert William, III, 451
1995 Kimble, Tina Potuto, 11
1998 Maerten-Moore, Sharon, 741
2000 Pfeiffer, G. Cameron, 112
2006 Leviton, Matthew, 13
2010 Diluccia, Daniel "Dan", 18
2014 Kestle, Sydney R., 28

Washington University
[Washington U (MO)]

1969 Cherry, Michael A., 702
1971 Ellis, Joseph M., 694
1971 Hamilton, Jean C., 310
1973 Schermer, Barry S., 75, 311
1973 Teitelman, Richard B., 689
1977 Gans, Michael E., 71, 75
1980 Fleissig, Audrey Goldstein, 309
1980 Perry, Catherine D., 26, 307
1981 Day, Bonnie M., 310
1981 Harwood, Bruce A., 35, 327
1981 Marty, Karen, 508
1981 Sippel, Rodney W., 308
1983 Hurwitz, Diane M., 624
1983 Schmidt, Daniel L., 621
1984 Coleman, Sharon Johnson, 226
1985 Bacharach, Robert E., 91
1987 Gruender, Raymond W., III, 73
1991 Surratt-States, Kathy A., 311
1993 Brookman, Matthew P. "Matt", 244
1993 Snidman, Elizabeth, 310
1994 Stuart, Susan Q., 120
1996 Engel, Allison M., 232
1999 Peterson, Eric, 689
2000 Cohen, Emily K., 75, 312
2001 Carpenter, Lisa, 308
2001 Stone, Holly, 315
2003 Vehik, Liisa, 17
2006 Ricks, Cynthia, 92
2014 Uelk, Bryan, 75

Washington University *continued*

Armstrong, Michael, 236
Brady, Larry, 547

Wayne State University
[Wayne State U]

1956 Keith, Damon Jerome, 64
1965 Tarnow, Arthur J., 290
1969 Bell, Robert Holmes, 294
1970 Murphy, William B., 673
1970 Neff, Janet T., 294
1974 Saad, Henry William, 674
1976 Edmunds, Nancy G., 290
1976 Lawson, David M., 287
1976 Whalen, R. Steven, 291
1977 Cooke, Marcia G., 196
1980 Greeley, Timothy P., 295
1982 Capel, Wallace, Jr., 106
1983 Hillard, Martin J., 673
1985 Montalvo, Frank, 471
1986 Saitta, Nancy M., 703
1987 Dighe, Kristin, 510
1987 Kenny, Patricia, 64
1988 Bailey, Barbara A., 292
1989 Kurzawa, Rodney B., 295
1995 Altman, Kimberly G., 290
2000 Staub, Katrina, 288
2003 Tykoski, Amber O., 676
2004 Krieger, Nicholas C. "Nick", 674
Crowley, Dale, 674
Gleicher, Elizabeth L., 676
Koenig, Toby, 676
Shefferly, Phillip J., 292

West Virginia University
[West Virginia]

1950 Copenhaver, John T., Jr., 501
1967 Ketchum, Menis E., II, 820
1968 King, Robert B., 50
1969 Seibert, James E., 499
1970 Goodwin, Joseph Robert, 500
1974 Workman, Margaret L., 819
1976 Bailey, John Preston, 498
1978 Chambers, Robert C., 500
1979 Berger, Irene Cornelia, 501
1979 Levy, Jon David, 271
1980 Keeley, Irene M., 499
1982 Davis, Robin Jean, 820
1984 Robinson, Richard A., 581
1989 Groh, Gina Marie, 498
1990 Thacker, Stephanie Dawn, 53
1992 Johnston, Thomas E., 501
1992 Palmer, Louis J., 820
1992 Slack, Sandra Mickle, 500
1992 Volk, Frank W., 502
1993 Chambers, Peter, 820
1994 Bowman, Cynthia, 820
1994 Fife, Kate, 501
1994 Perry, Rory L., II, 819
1995 Takarsh, Toni Harvey, 820
1996 Lipscomb, Bobby F., 820
1997 Mendoza, Carlos Eduardo, 182
2000 Glover, Rochelle Lantz, 50
2002 Loughney, Matthew T., 446
2002 Niday, Mary Beth, 502
2006 Parsons, Jeff, 499
2010 Voithofer, James, 500

Name Index

This index lists all individuals in the directory alphabetically by last name.

B

C

NAME INDEX

D

G

H

L

NAME INDEX

M

N

O

P

NAME INDEX

Q

R

S

NAME INDEX

T

U

V

W

Organization Index

This index lists all organizations in the directory alphabetically.

A

B

ORGANIZATION INDEX

C

D

E

F

ORGANIZATION INDEX

G

H

I

J

K

ORGANIZATION INDEX

L

M

N

O

P

Q

R

S

ORGANIZATION INDEX

T

U

V

ORGANIZATION INDEX

Y

Z

